PSYCHOLOGY

NINTH EDITION

Douglas A. Bernstein

University of South Florida

Louis A. Penner

Wayne State University
University of Michigan

Alison Clarke-Stewart

University of California, Irvine

Edward J. Roy

University of Illinois at Urbana-Champaign

WADSWORTH
CENGAGE Learning™

Australia • Brazil • Japan • Korea • Mexico • Singapore • Spain • United Kingdom • United States

Psychology, **Ninth Edition**
Douglas A. Bernstein, Louis A. Penner, Alison Clarke-Stewart, and Edward J. Roy

Executive Editor: Jon-David Hague

Developmental Editor: Tangelique Williams

Consulting Editor: William S. Altman

Assistant Editor: Alicia McLaughlin

Editorial Assistant: Sheli DeNola

Media Editor: Mary Noel

Marketing Manager: Jessica Egbert

Marketing Assistant: Anna Andersen

Marketing Communications Manager: Talia Wise

Content Project Manager: Charlene Carpentier

Design Director: Rob Hugel

Art Director: Vernon Boes

Print Buyer: Linda Hsu

Rights Acquisitions Specialist: Roberta Broyer

Production Service: Dovetail Publishing Services

Text Designer: Gary Hespenheide

Photo Researcher: Stephen Forsling

Text Researcher: Sarah D'Stair

Copy Editor: Bruce Emmer

Cover Designer: Gary Hespenheide

Cover Image: Ralph Mercer Photography

Compositor: Integra

For product information and technology assistance, contact us at
Cengage Learning Customer & Sales Support, 1-800-354-9706.

For permission to use material from this text or product, submit all requests online at www.cengage.com/permissions. Further permissions questions can be e-mailed to **permissionrequest@cengage.com.**

Library of Congress Control Number: 2010935619

Student Edition:
ISBN-13: 978-1-111-30155-2
ISBN-10: 1-111-30155-7

Loose-leaf Edition:
ISBN-13: 978-1-111-30270-2
ISBN-10: 1-111-30270-7

Wadsworth
20 Davis Drive
Belmont, CA 94002-3098
USA

Cengage Learning is a leading provider of customized learning solutions with office locations around the globe, including Singapore, the United Kingdom, Australia, Mexico, Brazil, and Japan. Locate your local office at **www.cengage.com/global.**

Cengage Learning products are represented in Canada by Nelson Education, Ltd.

To learn more about Wadsworth, visit **www.cengage.com/ wadsworth**

Purchase any of our products at your local college store or at our preferred online store **www.cengagebrain.com.**

Printed in Canada
1 2 3 4 5 6 7 14 13 12 11 10

Applications of Psychology In the Real World *(continued)*

▶ **Patients can begin to combat their phobias using virtual reality systems,** rather than immediately confronting their fears in real situations. (page 661)

▶ **Flooding is a relatively quick, effective treatment for specific phobias.** (page 664)

▶ **Special pretreatment orientation programs may be offered to clients** who are unfamiliar with the rules and procedures of psychotherapy. These programs provide a preview of what psychotherapy is, how it can help, and what the client is expected to do to make it more effective. (page 679)

▶ **Professional and nonprofessional staff members of community mental health centers provide traditional therapy and mental health education,** along with walk-in facilities and hotlines for people who are suicidal or in crises because of rape or domestic violence. They also offer day treatment to former mental patients, many of whom are homeless. (page 691)

Chapter 17

▶ **Many charities and educational groups use photographs of people in need** to evoke the emotions of potential donors. (page 709)

▶ **Cooperative contact between people of different ethnic groups can promote mutual respect and reduce ethnic prejudice.** (page 717)

▶ **Advertisers and others who wish to persuade people to make certain decisions can use the mere-exposure effect to sway people to their point of view.** (page 710)

▶ **One way to strengthen a relationship is to strengthen the patterns of communication between partners.** (page 724)

Chapter 18

▶ **Hotels can make guests more likely to re-use their towels and recycle their newspapers by using descriptive norms.** They give specific information about how other people actually behave in a given situation. There is evidence, for example, that how much college students use tobacco and alcohol is influenced both by how much they think other students drink and smoke. (page 730)

▶ **Supporters of various causes know that people who comply with a small request,** such as signing a petition, are the best ones to contact later with requests to do more. Complying with larger requests is made more likely because it is consistent with the signer's initial commitment to the cause. (page 736)

▶ **The door-in-the-face technique is sometimes used successfully by teenagers to influence parents to comply with many kinds of requests.** After asking to stay out overnight, a youngster whose curfew is normally 11 p.m. might be allowed to stay out until 1 a.m.—a "compromise" that was actually the original goal. (page 737)

▶ **Salespeople often use the low-ball technique to get people to buy things at a higher price than the customers originally intended.** First, the salesperson obtains a person's oral commitment to purchase the item at a certain price. Once this commitment is made, the cost of fulfilling increases, perhaps due to an "error" in calculating the price. (page 737)

▶ **The military and other organizations use the proximity principle to enhance obedience to authority.** Consistent with Milgram's research on obedience, they ensure that no one is ever far away from the authority of a higher-ranking person. (page 740)

▶ **Psychologists working with architects to design prisons that minimize the sense of crowding may help prevent some of the violence that endangers staff and prisoners.** (page 750)

▶ **You can get a more intense reaction from your romantic partner, or a more aggressive reaction from someone you bump into, if they've been exercising right before you see them,** because physiological arousal from one experience may carry over to an independent situation, producing what is called *excitation transfer.* (page 749)

▶ **Evidence from computer simulation studies shows that societies whose members use cooperative strategis with one another are more likely to survive and prosper than are societies whose members act competitively.** (page 759)

▶ **Communication is key to reducing conflict and increasing cooperation.** (page 760)

▶ **Researchers have worked on developing techniques to help organizations avoid groupthink.** One way is to teach group members to imagine all the negative outcomes of each course of action they are considering. Another is to designate someone to take the unpopular role of "devil's advocate"—to constantly challenge the group's emerging consensus and offer additional alternatives. (page 764)

Chapter 19

▶ **Industrial and organizational psychologists helped the U.S. government create its Uniform Guidelines on Employee Selection Procedures,** a document that outlines the steps organizations must take to assure fairness in hiring and promotion. (page 780)

▶ **Employee training programs help workers who portray cartoon characters at theme parks understand why it is important to remain in character at all times.** They emphasize the general principle that the organization's goal is to create a fantasy world for customers. (page 781)

▶ **To help working couples deal with both job demands and family obligations, many organizations have adopted family-friendly programs and policies,** including workplace day-care services and the availability of flexible work schedules (flextime). These programs and policies have been associated with higher levels of job satisfaction and less absenteeism among employees with children. (page 787)

▶ **I/O and engineering psychologists help to develop improved wrist support for keyboard users to prevent repetitive strain injuries.** These would otherwise result from performing the same movements on the job hour after hour and day after day. (page 793)

▶ **I/O psychologists' research on the negative impact of extended work shifts has led to organizational and U.S. government rules requiring rest breaks at fixed intervals for commercial airline pilots, long-haul bus and truck drivers, and others whose jobs require constant attention to complex tasks and systems.** These rules also limit the total number of hours these employees can work in any twenty-four-hour period. (page 794)

Chapter 20

▶ **By giving many different tests, the clinical neuropsychologist can get a glimpse into many different aspects of a person's psychological functioning and also measure each area separately.** Analyzing the overall pattern of results may help to pinpoint where the difficulties in the brain may lie. (page 805)

▶ **New medications can stop or slow the progression of certain dementias.** Drugs such as dimebolin (Dimebon), galantamine (Reminyl), and rivastignime (Exelon) were shown to be somewhat effective at slowing the progress of Alzheimer's disease. Certain antidepressant medications may have similar benefits, and antipsychotic drugs such as risperidone have shown potential for treating some of the behavioral and psychological symptoms of Alzheimer's disease. (page 828)

To the researchers, past and present,
whose work embodies psychology today,
and to the students who will follow in their footsteps
to shape the psychology of tomorrow.

BRIEF CONTENTS

Entries that appear in light blue refer to the optional Industrial and Organizational Psychology or Neuropsychology chapters.

CONTENTS

Entries that appear in light blue refer to the optional Industrial and Organizational Psychology or Neuropsychology chapters.

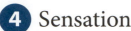

7 Memory   240

8 Cognition and Language   284

9 Consciousness

10 Cognitive Abilities

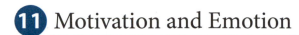

11 Motivation and Emotion 412

12 Human Development 464

16   Treatment of Psychological Disorders   650

17   Social Cognition   696

FEATURES

All titles in blue refer to features in the optional Industrial and Organizational Psychology or Neuropsychology chapters that can be packaged with the text upon request. See your sales representative for further details.

LINKAGES

▸ Psychological Research Methods and Behavioral Genetics

▸ Human Development and the Changing Brain

▸ Sensation and Biological Aspects of Psychology

▸ Perception and Human Development

▸ Neural Networks and Learning

▸ Memory, Perception, and Eyewitness Testimony

▸ Group Processes in Problem Solving and Decision Making

▸ Meditation, Health, and Stress

▸ Emotionality and the Measurement of Cognitive Abilities

▸ Conflicting Motives and Stress

▸ Development and Memory

▸ Stress and Psychological Disorders

▸ Personality, Culture, and Human Development

▸ Anxiety Disorders and Learning

▸ Biological Aspects of Psychology and the Treatment of Psychological Disorders

▸ Biological and Social Psychology

▸ Motivation and the Presence of Others

▸ Aggression in the Workplace

▸ Language Disorders and the Brain

FOCUS ON RESEARCH METHODS

▸ Manipulating Genes in Animal Models of Human Disease

▸ The Case of the Mysterious Spells

▸ An Experiment in "Mind Reading"

▸ Measuring Explicit Versus Implicit Memory

▸ Locating Analogical Thinking

▸ Subliminal Messages in Popular Music

▸ Tracking Cognitive Abilities over the Life Span

▸ A Survey of Human Sexual Behavior

▸ Exploring Developing Minds

▸ Personality and Health

▸ Longitudinal Studies of Temperament and Personality

▸ Exploring Links Between Child Abuse and Antisocial Personality Disorder

▸ Which Therapies Work Best for Which Problems?

▸ Self-Esteem and the Ultimate Terror

▸ Does Family Matter?

▸ Can People Learn to Be Charismatic Leaders?

▸ Studying Hemineglect

THINKING CRITICALLY

▸ What Can fMRI Tell Us About Behavior and Mental Processes?

▸ Does Acupuncture Relieve Pain?

▸ Can Subliminal Stimuli Influence Your Behavior?

▸ Does Watching Violence on Television Make People More Violent?

▸ Can Traumatic Memories Be Repressed and Then Recovered?

▸ Can Nonhumans Use Language?

▸ Is Marijuana Dangerous?

▸ Are Intelligence Tests Unfairly Biased Against Certain Groups?

▸ What Shapes Sexual Orientation?

▸ Does Day Care Harm the Emotional Development of Infants?

▸ Does Hostility Increase the Risk of Heart Disease?

▸ Are Personality Traits Inherited?

▸ Is Psychological Diagnosis Biased?

▸ Are All Forms of Therapy Equally Effective?

▸ Is Ethnic Prejudice Too Ingrained Ever to Be Eliminated?

▸ Do Violent Video Games Make People More Aggressive?

▸ Is Job Satisfaction Genetic?

▸ Can Someone Be Partially Paralyzed and Not Know It?

PREFACE

In revising *Psychology,* we have rededicated ourselves to the goals we pursued in the first eight editions:

- To explore the full range of psychology, from cell to society, in a manner as free as possible of theoretical bias.
- To balance our need to explain the content of psychology with an emphasis on the doing of psychology, through a blend of conceptual discussion and description of research studies.
- To foster scientific attitudes and to help students learn to think critically by examining the ways that psychologists have solved, or failed to solve, fascinating puzzles of behavior and mental processes.
- To produce a text that, without oversimplifying psychology, is clear, accessible, and enjoyable to read.
- To demonstrate that in spite of its breadth and diversity, psychology is an integrated discipline in which each subfield is linked to other subfields by common interests and overarching research questions. The productive cross-fertilization among social, clinical, and biological psychologists in researching health and illness is just one example of how psychologists from different subfields benefit from and build on one another's work.

Preparing the Ninth Edition provided us with new ways to do justice to our goals. We sought to respond to the needs of instructors who wanted us to reduce or expand coverage of various topics. For example, many instructors asked us to increase the amount of material on applied psychology without losing the book's emphasis on basic research in psychology. As a result, we have added material relating to applied areas such as industrial and organizational psychology, neuropsychology, and forensic psychology throughout the book, wherever appropriate. As always, we sought to strike an ideal balance between classic and current research. The important historic findings of psychological research are here, but so is coverage of much recent work. Approximately 20 percent of the research citations are new to the Ninth Edition, and these reflect the addition of new information in every chapter.

Chapter 1

- Latest figures on employment settings for psychologists
- Latest figures on graduate degrees in psychology earned by men, women, and members of ethnic minority groups

Chapter 2

- Latest research methods used to evaluate claims for the effectiveness of eye movement desensitization and reprocessing

- Introduction of the law of parsimony in evaluating scientific theories
- Epigenetic influences in understanding the interacting roles of heredity and environment

Chapter 3

- Updated research on stem cells and their use in repairing brain damage
- Latest techniques for studying the brain, including transcranial magnetic stimulation

Chapter 4

- New information on the effect of brain damage on color vision
- New information on the use of fMRI to identify brain activity associated with hearing different kinds of sounds (e.g. familiar versus unfamiliar voices)
- New information on development of an "electronic nose" to help detect explosives in security screening
- New information on loss of olfaction as an early sign of neurological disorder
- New material on research designed to assess the presence of human pheromones
- Expanded coverage of research on the value of acupuncture in pain control
- New examples of the interaction of senses in synesthesia

Chapter 5

- Addition of perceptual grouping principles such as synchrony and connectedness
- New examples of the role of motivation and perceptual set causing errors in judgment and decision making
- New example from the field of aviation on how overly focused attention can lead to pilot errors
- New applications of depth cue research to prevent speeding on suburban streets
- Latest research on the impact of cell phone use while driving

Chapter 6

- Latest research on the impact of corporal punishment on children
- Latest research on the impact of violent television programs and video games on aggression and violence
- Applying active learning principles in the classroom

Chapter 7

- Latest research on the biological bases of memory
- New research on brain damage that not only causes amnesia for the past but also impairs the ability to think about the future

Chapter 8

- New research on the role of prototypes in affecting the chances that smokers will be able to quit their habit
- New example of the role of mental models in affecting the success of Internet searches
- Locating brain areas involved in analogical thinking

Chapter 9

- New information on the possible value of sleep deprivation following trauma to reduce the intensity of traumatic memories
- New research on the role of waking experience in affecting dream content
- Latest information on the controversy over using marijuana for medical purposes

Chapter 10

- New research on the impact of stereotype threat on performance on high-stakes standardized tests
- Updated evaluation of Gardner's theory of multiple intelligences

Chapter 11

- New material on the role of the small intestine in regulating eating
- Discussion of obesity as unhealthy eating but not as an eating disorder, as defined in DSM-IV
- Latest figures on the growth of the obesity problem worldwide
- New material on efforts to prevent and treat obesity
- New research on sexual activity in the elderly
- New research on the impact of previous pregnancies on the sexual orientation of later-born children
- New coverage of the conceptual act model of emotion
- New research on the impact of situational context on the interpretation of facial expressions

Chapter 12

- Updated information on the combined effects of alcohol and other environmental toxins on infant development
- New material on the "prone to play" campaign, advising parents to put babies face-down when awake to promote learning and play
- New information on the possible causes of infantile amnesia

- Updated information on poverty as a developmental danger
- New information about online access for children and their enhanced development in reading and problem solving
- New information about infants' attentiveness to adults' negative emotions
- New information about infants' use of gestures in communicating with their caregivers
- New information about infants' temperaments being affected by mothers' stress levels during pregnancy, nursing, and thereafter
- New information on the effect of mothers' attentiveness on the security of infants' attachments
- Inclusion of the "uninvolved" (rejecting-neglecting) style as the fourth category in Baumrind's parenting model
- New Focus on Research Methods feature highlighting Renee Baillargeon's work on infants' theory of mind
- Updated information on children and gender-appropriate interests
- Updated information on the challenges of early adolescence with regard to the differential development of specific parts of the brain
- Updated statistics about adolescents, sex, and teenage pregnancy
- Updated information about emotional development and stability during emerging adulthood
- New information about older adults' emotional memories and emotional reactions to conflict
- New information about the role of video games in promoting physical fitness

Chapter 13

- New statistics on worldwide deaths due to health-damaging behaviors
- Updated information on hospitals' procedures for lowering patients' stress and giving patients control of their own pain medications
- Updated information on the association between strong social networks and happiness
- New information about the stress associated with suppression of emotion
- New information on the correlation between worries about terrorism and the development of coronary heart disease
- New information on the relationship among socioeconomic status, lack of control, and premature death in lower socioeconomic groups

Chapter 14

- New information on researchers' attempts to conduct empirical investigations of psychodynamic theory
- New information on modern approaches to Allport's trait theory
- New research on Gray's reinforcement sensitivity theory
- Updated information about relationships between attachment style in childhood and stress reactions,

helping behavior, relationship quality, and anxiety and emotional difficulties in adulthood
- New discussion of other possible universal personality factors (honesty and humility) in addition to the Big Five
- Updated information about the behavior of children and college students with internal versus external locus of control
- New information about impact of positive psychology and added empirically based research on humanistic psychology

Chapter 15

- Updated information on the incidence of psychological disorders
- Inclusion of dysfunction as a criterion for abnormality, thus providing "3 D's" as a mnemonic device (deviance, distress, and dysfunction)
- Updated explanation of possible causes of psychological disorders, how concepts of causality are driven by our attitudes, and how those attitudes affect views about treatment options
- Updated information on culture-specific disorders
- New information about the expected features of the forthcoming DSM-V
- Updated information on evaluating DSM-IV
- Updated information on Szasz's views of the concept of mental illness
- Updated research on bias in psychological diagnosis
- Inclusion of *cyberchondria* as a new term, similar to medical students' syndrome
- Updated statistics on the incidence of anxiety disorders in general and about agoraphobia, specific phobias, and OCD in particular
- New and updated information about the possible causes of anxiety disorders
- New and updated information about hypochondriasis
- Additional information about body dysmorphic disorder
- New information on the possible role of serotonin in hypochondriasis, conversion disorder, and body dysmorphic disorder
- Updated statistics about the incidence of and current trends in major depression
- Updated statistics about the incidence of suicide
- Updated information on biological factors in affective disorders, including the role of epigenetics
- New information about integrating biological and social-cognitive causes of affective disorders
- Updated information about hallucinations in schizophrenia
- New discussion of the schizophrenia spectrum
- New and updated information about the possible causes of schizophrenia
- Updated statistics about the incidence of antisocial personality disorders, with accompanying crime statistics

- Updated statistics and information about the causes of conduct disorders
- Updated information about possible bias in the diagnosis of hyperactivity in children
- Updated statistics about the incidence of autism
- New information about functions of mirror neurons in the brain with regard to autism
- New statistics about psychoactive substance abuse in the United States and its attendant problems

Chapter 16

- New information on the most common treatment targets among children
- New information comparing the characteristics of inpatients and outpatients
- New and updated information about evidence based practice and empirically supported therapies
- Updated information about cultural diversity training for graduate students in clinical and counseling psychology
- New information on deep brain stimulation as a therapeutic technique
- Updated information about antidepressant drugs' effectiveness, side effects, costs, and benefits
- Updated information on the availability of treatment for psychological disorders and other mental health needs in developed and developing countries
- Updated information about the effectiveness of psychoactive medications for mental disorders and their value in combination with psychotherapy

Chapter 17

- Updated information about schema-consistent versus schema-inconsistent information and memory
- Updated information about the speed and accuracy of first impressions
- Updated information about unrealistic optimism and health risks
- Updated information on the mere-exposure effect and reducing prejudice
- Updated information on terror management theory and social cognitive neuroscience

Chapter 18

- New information on Sternberg's duplex theory of love
- New information on the disappearance of some cultural differences with regard to love and marriage
- Updated information on obedience and people's responses to authority

The Ninth Edition also contains substantial material on culture and human diversity. Throughout the text, students will encounter recent research on multicultural phenomena occurring in North America and around the world. We introduce this multicultural emphasis in Chapter 1, and we follow up on it in other chapters regarding topics such as the following:

- Selecting human participants for research (Chapter 2)
- Culture, experience, and perception (Chapter 5)
- Classrooms across cultures (Chapter 6)
- Culture, language, and thought (Chapter 8)
- Ethnic differences in IQ (Chapter 10)
- Flavor, cultural learning, and food selection (Chapter 11)
- Social and cultural factors in sexuality (Chapter 11)
- Cultural and gender differences in achievement motivation (Chapter 11)
- Cultural aspects of emotional expression (Chapter 11)
- Culture and cognitive development (Chapter 12)
- Sociocultural factors in adult development (Chapter 12)
- Cultural background and heart disease (Chapter 13)
- Personality, culture, and human development (Chapter 14)
- Ethnic bias in psychodiagnosis (Chapter 15)
- Sociocultural factors in psychological disorders (Chapter 15)
- Gender and cultural differences in depression and suicide (Chapter 15)
- Cultural factors in psychotherapy (Chapter 16)
- Ethnic differences in responses to drug treatment (Chapter 16)
- Cultural differences in attribution (Chapter 17)
- The roots of ethnic stereotyping and prejudice (Chapter 17)
- Cultural factors and love (Chapter 17)
- Cultural factors in social norms (Chapter 18)
- Culture and conformity (Chapter 18)
- Culture and social loafing (Chapter 18)
- Cultural factors in aggression (Chapter 18)

We also have updated our coverage of behavioral genetics and evolutionary psychology. These topics are introduced in Chapters 1 and 2 and in the online behavioral genetics appendix. They are also explored wherever appropriate—for example, when we discuss the following topics:

- Gene manipulation research on the causes of Alzheimer's disease (Chapter 3)
- Biopreparedness for learning (Chapter 6)
- Genetic components of intelligence (Chapter 10)
- Genetic components of sexual orientation (Chapter 11)
- Evolutionary explanations of mate selection (Chapter 11)
- Innate expressions of emotion (Chapter 11)
- The genetics of prenatal development (Chapter 12)
- The heritability of personality (Chapter 14)
- Genetic factors in psychological disorders (Chapter 15)
- Evolutionary and genetic explanations for aggression, helping, and altruism (Chapter 18)

We have also emphasized in the Ninth Edition the significant new developments and research occurring in the field of *positive psychology.* This emphasis appears in the introductory chapter, where we describe positive psychology, as well as in coverage of positive psychology perspectives on and research in topics such as high achievement (Chapter 6),

character strengths (Chapter 14), rounded approaches to diagnosing mental disorders (Chapter 15), exploiting strengths and promoting positive emotion in psychotherapy (Chapter 16), and teaching skills that enhance well-being and resilience in the face of stress (Chapter 16).

Chapter Organization

We have designed each chapter to be a freestanding unit so that you may assign chapters in any order you wish. For example, many instructors prefer to teach the material on human development relatively late in the course, which is why it appears as Chapter 12 in the Ninth Edition. But that chapter can be comfortably assigned earlier in the course as well.

An optional nineteenth chapter, *Industrial and Organizational Psychology,* is available. It was contributed by Paul Spector, University of South Florida, and edited by Douglas A. Bernstein. We also offer an optional twentieth chapter, *Neuropsychology,* written by Douglas A. Bernstein and Joel Shenker, a diplomate of the American Board of Neurology and Psychiatry who specializes in memory loss, dementia, and neurocognitive behavioral impairments. Either chapter (or both) may be included in the textbook upon request, and most ancillaries contain supporting material for these chapters. Note that references to content in these chapters in the Contents and Features in the frontmatter, and in the References and Indices are printed in blue.

Special Features

Psychology contains a number of special features designed to promote efficient learning and student mastery of the material.

Linkages

In our experience, most students enter the introductory course thinking that psychology concerns itself mainly with personality, psychological testing, mental disorders, psychotherapy, and other aspects of clinical psychology. They have little or no idea of how broad and multifaceted psychology is. Many students are surprised, therefore, when we ask them to read about neuroanatomy, neural communication, the endocrine system, sensory and perceptual processes and principles, prenatal risk factors, and many other topics that they tend to associate with disciplines other than psychology.

We have found that students are better able to appreciate the scope of psychology when they see it not as a laundry list of separate topics but as an interrelated set of subfields, each of which contributes to and benefits from the work going on in all the others. To help students see these relationships, we have built into the book an integrating tool called "Linkages." There are four elements in the Linkages program:

1. Beginning with Chapter 2, a Linkages diagram presents a set of questions that illustrate three of the ways in which material in the chapter is related to other chapters in the book. For example, the Linkages diagram in Chapter 3, "Biological Aspects of Psychology," contains questions about how biological psychology is related to consciousness ("Does the brain shut down when we sleep?"), human development ("How do our brains change over a lifetime?"), and treatment of psychological disorders ("How do drugs help people diagnosed with schizophrenia?").

2. The Linkages diagrams are placed at the end of each chapter so that students will be more familiar with the material to which each linkage refers when they encounter this feature. To help students notice the Linkages diagrams and appreciate their purpose, we provide an explanatory caption with each.

3. The page number following each question in the Linkages diagram directs the student to the section of the chapter that carries further discussion of that question. The relevant material is marked by a Linkages logo in the margin next to the discussion.

4. One of the questions in each chapter's Linkages diagram is treated more fully in a special section within the chapter, titled—appropriately enough—"Linkages." A full list of topics appears on page xiv.

The Linkages elements combine with the text narrative to highlight the network of relationships among psychology's subfields. This Linkages program is designed to help students see the "big picture" that is psychology, no matter how many chapters their instructor assigns or in what sequence.

Thinking Critically

We try throughout the book to describe research on psychological phenomena in a way that reveals the logic of the scientific enterprise, identifies possible flaws in design or interpretation, and leaves room for more questions and further research. In other words, we try to display critical thinking processes. The "Thinking Critically" sections in each chapter are designed to make these processes more explicit and accessible by providing a framework for analyzing evidence before drawing conclusions. The framework is built around five questions that the reader should find useful in analyzing not only studies in psychology but other forms of communication as well. The questions, first posed when we discuss the importance of critical thinking in Chapter 2, are these:

1. What am I being asked to believe or accept?
2. What evidence is available to support the assertion?
3. Are there alternative ways of interpreting the evidence?
4. What additional evidence would help evaluate the alternatives?
5. What conclusions are most reasonable?

All the Thinking Critically sections retained from the Eighth Edition have been revised and updated. A full list of topics appears on page xiv.

Focus on Research Methods

This feature, appearing in Chapters 3 through 20, examines the ways in which the research methods described in Chapter 2, "Research in Psychology," have been applied to help advance our understanding of some aspect of behavior and mental processes. To make this feature more accessible, it is organized around the following five questions:

1. What was the researcher's question?
2. How did the researcher answer the question?
3. What did the researcher find?
4. What do the results mean?
5. What do we still need to know?

Examples of these Focus on Research Methods sections include the use of experiments to study attention (Chapter 5), learned helplessness (Chapter 6), the use of neuroimaging technology to locate areas of the brain involved in analogical thinking (Chapter 8), the development of a "theory of mind" (Chapter 12), and self-esteem (Chapter 17). Other sections illustrate the use of survey, longitudinal, and laboratory analogue designs. All of the Focus on Research Methods sections retained from the Eighth Edition were revised and updated. A full list of topics appears on page xiv.

An Emphasis on Active Learning

To help students become active learners rather than just passive readers, we have created an Active Learning online booklet (available at Psychology CourseMate), filled with activities that allow students hands-on experience with the key concepts covered in the text. An annotated instructor version of the booklet provides instructors with tips for assigning the activities and for ensuring that students derive the full benefit from these activities.

We have retained for the Ninth Edition a number of the "Try This" features from the Eighth Edition and have added several more in each chapter. These features encourage students to become more deeply involved with the material.

Dozens of figure and photo captions help students understand and remember a psychological principle or phenomenon by suggesting ways in which they can demonstrate it for themselves. In Chapter 7, "Memory," for example, a photo caption suggests that students show the photo to a friend and then ask the friend questions about it to illustrate the operation of constructive memory. These captions are all identified with a **TRY THIS** symbol.

TRY THIS symbols also appear in page margins at the many places throughout the book where active learning opportunities are encouraged in the narrative. At these points, we ask students to stop reading and actually do something to illustrate or highlight the psychological principle or phenomenon under discussion. For example, in Chapter 5, "Perception," we ask the student to focus attention on various targets as a way of appreciating the difference between overt and covert shifts in attention.

Online Behavioral Genetics Appendix

This feature is designed to amplify the coverage of behavioral genetics methodology that is introduced in Chapter 2, "Research in Psychology." The appendix includes a discussion of the impact of the Human Genome Project, a section on the basic principles of genetics and heredity, a brief history of genetic research in psychology, a discussion of what it means to say that genes influence behavior, and an analysis of what behavioral genetics research can and cannot tell us about the origins of such human attributes as intelligence, personality, and mental disorders. This appendix is available online through Psychology CourseMate. Note that the end-of-book materials for this appendix (as well as the online Statistics in Psychological Research appendix)—such as References, Name index, and the combined Subject Index and Glossary—are printed in blue.

"In Review" Charts

"In Review" charts summarize information in a convenient tabular format. We have placed two or three such charts strategically in each chapter to help students synthesize and assimilate large chunks of information—for example, on drug effects, key elements of personality theories, and stress responses and mediators. For the Ninth Edition, each In Review chart incorporates three fill-in-the-blanks quiz items to help students test their knowledge of the material reviewed in the chart.

Key Terms

As in the Eighth Edition, key terms and their definitions appear in the margin of the Ninth Edition where the terms are first used and in the subject index and glossary at the end of the book. New to the Ninth Edition is a thorough revision of all key terms to match the American Psychological Association's *Thesaurus of Psychological Index Terms* (11th Edition) and the *APA Dictionary of Psychology*. We believe that using key terms from these sources will help students do their own research by making it easier for them to engage in key term searches in the field's most popular databases (PsycINFO & PsycARTICLES). Using these key terms will also improve students' abilities to transfer terms learned in introductory courses to advanced courses. (For the Ninth Edition, we have revised many of our phonetic guides to make it even easier for students to correctly pronounce unfamiliar key terms as well as other terms whose pronunciation is not immediately obvious.)

Linkages to Further Learning and Talking Points

In the Ninth Edition, each chapter now ends with an invitation to learn more about the chapter's topics by consulting a list of readings and accessing Psychology CourseMate.

In addition, we remind students to be aware that when they mention that they are taking a psychology course, family and friends tend to want to know what they are learning. Because it can be difficult to give a short answer to that question, we now offer at the end of each chapter a few "talking points" that can help students summarize the chapter in a straightforward way, without technical jargon and without giving a lecture.

Teaching and Learning Support Package

Many useful materials have been developed to support *Psychology*, emphasizing its role as an integrated teaching and learning experience for instructors, teaching assistants, and students alike. These materials are well integrated with the text and include some of the latest technologies. Several components are new to this edition.

Instructor's Resource Manual

The *Instructor's Resource Manual*, by Travis Sola (Parkland College) and Doug Bernstein, contains for each chapter a complete set of learning objectives, detailed chapter outlines, suggested readings, and numerous specific teaching aids—including ideas for discussion, class activities, focus on research sections, and the accompanying handouts. It also contains sections on pedagogical strategies, as well as material geared toward teachers of large introductory courses, including a section on classroom management and another on the administration of multisection courses. Please note that the Ninth Edition *Instructor's Resource Manual* now includes supporting material for the two optional chapters—Chapter 19, "Industrial and Organizational Psychology," and Chapter 20, "Neuropsychology." As noted earlier, either or both of these chapters can be included in your text upon request—see your Cengage sales representative for details.

Test Bank

The *Test Bank*, by Chris Armstrong (University of Illinois) and Doug Bernstein, contains multiple-choice items plus several essay questions per chapter. All multiple-choice items are keyed to the learning objectives that appear in the *Instructor's Resource Manual* and *Study Guide*. Each question is identified by whether it tests simple factual recall or deeper conceptual understanding. Most items have been class-tested with between 500 and 2,500 students, and a statistical performance analysis is provided for those items. An additional 100 multiple-choice test questions and essay questions have been added to the Ninth Edition for each of the two optional chapters (Chapter 19, "Industrial and Organizational Psychology," and Chapter 20, "Neuropsychology") that may be bundled with the text.

PowerLecture with JoinIn and ExamView

This one-stop lecture and class preparation tool, created by William S. Altman (Broome Community College), makes it easy for you to assemble, edit, publish, and present custom lectures for your course using Microsoft PowerPoint. The PowerLecture lets you bring together ready-to-use, text-specfic lecture outlines and art from the Ninth Edition, along with video and animations from the Web or your own materials, culminating in a powerful, personalized, media-enhanced presentation. The CD-ROM also includes ExamView, a computerized test bank that allows you to create, deliver, and customize tests, and JoinIn, for in-class polls or on-the-spot quizzes. It also includes a full instructor's manual, test bank, and other instructor resources.

Psychology CourseMate

Cengage Learning's Psychology CourseMate brings course concepts to life with interactive learning, study, and exam preparation tools that support the printed textbook. To access an integrated eBook and chapter-specific learning tools including flash cards, quizzes, videos, and more, log in at www.CengageBrain.com.

Psychology CourseMate also features several exclusive resources:

Active Learning online booklet. Hands-on activities help students apply key concepts to their own experiences. Exercises range from visiting libraries and toy stores to observe and record differential gender roles to popping balloons in front of a friend to create a classically conditioned response. This exclusive resource was written by Sandra Goss Lucas, William S. Altman, and Doug Bernstein.

Critical Thinking online booklet. Activities, written by William S. Altman and Doug Bernstein, include assessing the impact of legislation, evaluating the utility of multitasking, analyzing the nature of dreams, and deciding if computers are beneficial in the classroom give students the chance to explore key text topics while developing their own critical thinking skills.

The annotated instructor versions of both online booklets contain additional tips for helping students fully benefit from the activities and include suggested answers to questions raised by some of the activities.

Psychology: Concept Maps. Comprehensive outlines of key text concepts, created by William S. Altman, are an ideal reinforcement tool for students to utilize as they study for exams and quizzes.

CengageNOW with eBook and Psychology Resource Center

CengageNOW is an online teaching and learning resource that gives instructors more control in less time and delivers better outcomes—NOW. It includes a Cengage Learning eBook and easy-to-use online resources that help students study in less time to get the grade they want. Go to www.CengageBrain.com.

WebTutor on BlackBoard or WebCT

Jump-start your course with customizable, rich, text-specific content within your Course Management System. Whether you want to Web-enable your class or put an entire course online, WebTutor delivers. WebTutor offers a wide array of resources, including quizzes and videos. Visit www.cengage.com/coursecare/cartridge to learn more.

Industrial and Organizational Psychology and Neuropsychology Chapters

The optional chapters on industrial and organizational psychology and neuropsychology are available for inclusion in the main text via the custom group. Supporting material for these chapters is available in all of the print supplements and in the computerized testing program. Please consult your sales representative for details.

Study Guide

The *Study Guide,* written by Kelly Bouas Henry (Missouri Western State College) and Douglas A. Bernstein, employs numerous techniques that help you learn. Each chapter—including the optional industrial and organizational psychology and neuropsychology chapters—contains a detailed outline, a key terms section that presents fresh examples and aids to remembering, a fill-in-the-blank test, and a set of learning objectives (shared by the instructor's *Test Bank* and *Instructor's Resource Manual*). Also included is a concepts and exercises section that shows you how to apply your knowledge of psychology to everyday issues and concerns, a critical thinking exercise, and personal learning activities. In addition, each chapter concludes with a two-part self-quiz consisting of forty multiple-choice questions. An answer key tells you not only which response is correct but also why each of the other choices is wrong, and quiz analysis tables enable you to track patterns to your wrong answers, either by topic or by type of question—definition, comprehension, or application.

Our Commitment to You

We are committed to the highest standards of customer support and service. Please contact us with any questions or comments you may have.

Acknowledgments

Many people provided us with the help, criticism, and encouragement we needed to create the Ninth Edition.

Once again we must thank Katie Steele, who got the project off the ground in 1983 by encouraging us to stop talking about this book and start writing it.

We are indebted to a number of our colleagues for their expert help and advice on the revisions of a number of chapters for the Ninth Edition. These colleagues include, for Chapters 4, 9, and the optional Chapter 20, Joel Shenker (University of Missouri School of Medicine); for Chapter 5, Larry Gottlob (University of Kentucky); for Chapter 6, Doug Williams (University of Winnipeg); for Chapter 7, Kathleen McDermott (Washington University); for Chapter 8, Paul Whitney (Washington State University); for Chapter 10, Rose Mary Webb (Appalachian State University); for Chapter 11, Christopher Trentacosta (Wayne State University); for Chapter 13, Catherine Stoney (National Institutes of Health); for Chapter 15, David Sue (Western Washington University); for Chapter 16, Vicky Phares (University of South Florida); and for the optional Chapter 19, Kim Schneider (Illinois State University).

We are particularly grateful to William S. Altman of Broome Community College, who worked closely with us on the revision of every chapter of this new edition. His extensive teaching experience, wisdom, and sense of humor were appreciated every step of the way. We also want to thank David Daniel of James Madison University for his ongoing support of our book and for his valuable suggestions for improving the teaching technology that accompanies it.

We owe a lot to the colleagues who provided prerevision evaluations or reviewed the manuscript for the Ninth Edition as it was being developed:

Christina D. Aldrich, *Folsom Lake College, El Dorado Center*

Anastasia Dimitropoulos, *Case Western Reserve University*

Kimberley Duff, *Cerritos College*

Carmela V. Gottesman, *University of South Carolina, Salkehatchie*

George Handley, *Ohio State University*

Susan Kennedy, *Denison University*

Suzanne Morin, *Shippensburg University*

Their advice and suggestions for improvement are responsible for many of the good qualities you will find in the book. If you have any criticisms, they probably involve areas these people warned us about.

We want to acknowledge as well the colleagues listed next for their valuable contributions to the text over the life of many editions:

Gregory F. Ball, *Johns Hopkins University*

David R. Barkmeier, *Northeastern University*

James L. Becker, *Pulaski Technical College*

Edward Bernat, *University of Minnesota*

Ramesh Bhatt, *University of Kentucky*

Joseph Bilotta, *Western Kentucky University*

Brian Burke, *Fort Lewis College*

James F. Calhoun, *University of Georgia*

Nancy Dess, *Occidental College*

Douglas Detterman, *Case Western Reserve University*

Julie Feldman, *University of Arizona*

Oney D. Fitzpatrick, *Lamar University*

Anastasia Houndoumadi, *Deree College, Athens*

Geoffrey Kramer, *West Shore Community College*

Robert Krueger, *University of Minnesota*

David Lohman, *University of Iowa*

Kathleen McDermott, *Washington University*

Elizabeth Marsh, *Duke University*

Connie Meinholdt, *Ferris State University*

J. Bruce Overmier, *University of Minnesota*

Frank Penedo, *University of Miami*

Christopher Peterson, *University of Michigan*

Brett Roark, *Oklahoma Baptist University*

Doug Rohrer, *University of South Florida*

Wendy M. Scinta, *Medical Weight Loss of New York*

Jana S. Spain, *High Point University*

Paul Spector, *University of South Florida*

Eric Stephens, *University of the Cumberlands*

Matt Traxler, *University of California, Davis*

Eric Vanman, *Georgia State University*

Paul Whitney, *Washington State University*

Jun Zhang, *University of Michigan*

A special word of thanks to our very creative and dedicated ancillary team members, past and present, who have worked with us on creating various aspects of the supplements program: William S. Altman, Chris Armstrong, David B. Daniel, Missa Murry Eaton, Jamie Goldenberg, Lora Harpster, Kelly Bouas Henry, Suzanne E. Juraska, Kent Korek, Mark Laumakis, Linda Lebie, Sandra Goss Lucas, Billa Reiss, Jill Shultz, Travis Sola, Chris Thomas, and Valeri Werpetinski.

The process of creating the Ninth Edition was greatly facilitated by the work of many dedicated people at Cengage Learning. From the sales representatives and sales managers who told us of faculty members' suggestions for improvement to the marketing staff who developed innovative ways of telling our colleagues about the changes we have made, it seems that everyone had a hand in shaping and improving the Ninth Edition. Several people deserve special thanks, however. Executive Editor for Psychology Jon-David Hague gave us especially valuable advice about structural, pedagogical, and content changes for the new edition. Media Editor Mary Noel was instrumental in implementing the integrated technology plan for this edition. Developmental Editor Tangelique Williams applied her editorial expertise and disciplined approach to helping us create this manuscript. Jonathan Peck, with Dovetail Publishing Services, again contributed his awe-inspiring organizational skills and dedication to excellence that were matched by a wonderfully helpful and cooperative demeanor. Charlene Carpentier, Production Project Manager, and Editorial Assistant Alicia McLaughlin lent capable hands to various important aspects of the project. Kelly Miller, Assistant Editor, helped enormously by coordinating a wide range of tasks including those related to the *Test Bank, Study Guide,* and *Instructor's Manual.* Special thanks to Marketing Manager Elisabeth Rhoden and Marketing Coordinator Anna Anderson for their continued stellar efforts in marketing this text. We also thank Stephen Forsling for diligently selecting and tracking down outstanding new photos. A big thank-you goes to Bruce Emmer for his dedication and expertise in copyediting the manuscript. Thanks also to Pete Shanks, who checked page proofs to ensure their typographical accuracy, and to Leoni McVey, who tackled the monumental task of creating the indexes. Without these people, and those who worked with them, this revision simply could not have happened.

Finally, we want to express our deepest appreciation to our families and friends. Once again, their love saw us through an exhilarating but demanding period of our lives. They endured our hours at the computer, missed meals, postponed vacations, and occasional irritability during the creation of the First Edition of this book, and they had to suffer all over again during the lengthy process of revising it once more. Their faith in us is more important than they realize, and we will cherish it forever.

D. A. B.

L. A. P.

A. C.-S.

E. J. R.

1

Introducing Psychology

In this opening chapter, we give you an overview of psychology as a whole and of the many specialized areas in which psychologists work. We describe the linkages that tie these areas to one another and to other subjects, such as economics and medicine, and how research in psychology is being applied in everyday life every day. We then tell the story of how psychology came to be and the various ways in which psychologists approach their work.

Here are some people who have truly interesting jobs. What do you think they studied to qualify for those jobs? See if you can fill in the blank next to each job description with one of the fields of study listed in Table 1.1.

- Kristen Beyer works for the Federal Bureau of Investigation, where she develops questionnaires and conducts interviews aimed at identifying common features in the backgrounds of serial killers. _____
- Jason Kring, a professor at Embry-Riddle Aeronautical University, conducts research on how the gender composition of a team affects performance under the stress of space flight and military combat. _____
- Anne Marie Apanovitch is employed by a drug company to study which of the company's marketing strategies are most effective in promoting sales. _____
- Rebecca Snyder studies the giant pandas at Zoo Atlanta in an effort to promote captive breeding and ultimately increase the wild population of this endangered species. _____
- Michael Moon's job at a software company is to find new ways to make Internet Web sites more informative and easier to navigate. _____
- Elizabeth Kolmstetter works at the Transportation Security Administration, where, following the September 11 terrorist attacks, she took charge of a program to establish higher standards for hiring and training security screeners at U.S. airports. _____
- Marissa Reddy, codirector of the U.S. Secret Service's Safe Schools initiative, tries to prevent school shootings by identifying risk factors for violent behavior in high school students. _____
- Sharon Lundgren, founder of Lundgren Trial Consulting, Inc., helps prepare witnesses to testify in court, conducts mock trials in which attorneys rehearse their questioning strategies, and teaches attorneys how to present themselves and their evidence in the most convincing way. _____
- Evan Byrne works at the National Transportation Safety Board, where he investigates the role of memory lapses, disorientation, errors in using equipment, and other human factors in causing airplane crashes. _____
- Karen Orts, a captain in the U.S. Air Force, is chief of mental health services at an air base, where, among other things, she provides psychotherapy to military personnel suffering combat-related stress disorders and teaches leadership courses to commissioned and noncommissioned officers. _____

Because Captain Orts offers psychotherapy, you probably guessed that she is a psychologist, but what academic field did you associate with Rebecca Snyder, who studies giant pandas? It would have been perfectly reasonable to assume that she is a zoologist, but she, too, is a psychologist. So is Evan Byrne, whose work on Web site design might suggest that he was a computer science major. And although Sharon Lundgren spends her time working with witnesses and conducting mock trials, she is a psychologist, not a lawyer. The fact is that *all* these people are psychologists! They may not all fit your image of what psychologists do, but as you will see in this chapter and throughout this book, psychology is much broader and more diverse than you may have expected.

Many different kinds of psychologists are doing all sorts of fascinating work in one or more of psychology's many specialty areas, or *subfields*. Most of these people took their first psychology course without realizing how many of these subfields there are or how many different kinds of jobs are open to psychologists. But like the people we have just described, they found something in psychology—perhaps something unexpected—that captured their interest, and they were hooked. And who knows? By the time you have finished this book and this course, you may have found some aspect of psychology so compelling that you will want to make it your life's work too. Or not. At the very least, we hope you enjoy learning about psychology, about the work of psychologists, and about how that work benefits people everywhere.

The World of Psychology: An Overview

Psychology is the science that seeks to understand behavior and mental processes and to apply that understanding in the service of human welfare. It is a science that covers a lot of territory, as illustrated by the vastly different jobs that occupy the ten psychologists we described. They are all psychologists because they are all involved in studying, predicting, improving, or explaining some aspect of behavior and mental processes.

TRY THIS

To begin to appreciate all the things that are included under the umbrella of *behavior* and *mental processes*, take a moment to think about how you would answer this question: Who are you? Would you describe your personality, your 20/20 vision, your interests and goals, your skills and accomplishments, your IQ, your cultural background, or perhaps a physical or emotional problem that bothers you? You could have listed these and dozens of other things about yourself, and every one of them would reflect some aspect of what psychologists mean by behavior and mental processes. It is no wonder, then, that this book's table of contents features so many different topics, including some—such as vision and hearing—that you may not have expected to see in a book about psychology. The topics have to be diverse in order to capture the full range of behaviors and mental processes that make you who you are and that come together in other ways in people of every culture around the world.

Some of the world's half-million psychologists focus on what can go wrong in behavior and mental processes—psychological disorders, problems in childhood development, stress-related illnesses, and the like—while others study what goes right. They explore, for example, the factors that lead people to be happy and satisfied with their lives, to achieve at a high level, to be creative, to help others, and to develop their full potential as human beings. This focus on what goes right, on the things that make life most worth living, has become known as **positive psychology** (e.g., Peterson, 2006a; Snyder & Lopez, 2009; Uchida & Kitayama, 2009), and you will see many examples of it in the research described throughout this book.

psychology The science of behavior and mental processes.

positive psychology A field of research that focuses on people's positive experiences and characteristics, such as happiness, optimism, and resilience.

biological psychologists Psychologists who analyze the biological factors influencing behavior and mental processes. Also called *physiological psychologists*.

cognitive psychologists Psychologists who study the mental processes underlying judgment, decision making, problem solving, imagining, and other aspects of human thought or cognition. Also called *experimental psychologists*.

engineering psychology A field in which psychologists study human factors in the use of equipment and help designers create better versions of that equipment.

TABLE 1.1 What's My Line?		
TRY THIS Try matching educational backgrounds with the people described at the beginning of the chapter by writing the letter for the correct field of study next to each person's job description.	A. Engineering	F. Advertising
	B. Criminal justice	G. Biology
	C. Computer science	H. Education
	D. Law	I. Zoology
	E. Psychology	J. Business administration

FIGURE 1.1
Visualizing Brain Activity
Magnetic resonance imaging (MRI) techniques allow biological psychologists to study the brain activity accompanying various mental processes. In the study illustrated here, males (left) and females (right) showed different patterns of brain activity (indicated by the brightly colored areas) while reading (Shaywitz et al., 1995).

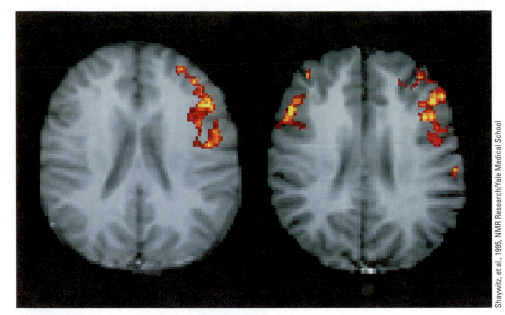

Shaywitz, et al., 1995, NMR Research/Yale Medical School

FIGURE 1.2
Husband and Father-in-Law
TRY THIS This figure is called "Husband and Father-in-Law" (Botwinick, 1961) because you can see an old man or a young man, depending on how you mentally organize its features. The elderly father-in-law faces to your right and is turned slightly toward you. He has a large nose, and the dark areas represent his coat pulled up to his protruding chin. However, the tip of his nose can also be seen as the tip of a younger man's chin; the younger man is in profile, also looking to your right, but away from you. The old man's mouth is the young man's neckband. Both men are wearing a broad-brimmed hat.

From Botwinick, J., "Husband and father-in-law: A reversible figure," American Journal of Psychology, 74, 312–313. Copyright © 1961 by the Board of Trustees of the University of Illinois. Used with permission of the University of Illinois Press.

Subfields of Psychology

When psychologists choose to focus their attention on certain aspects of behavior and mental processes, they enter one of psychology's subfields. Let's take a quick look at the typical interests and activities of psychologists in each subfield. We will describe their work in more detail in later chapters.

Biological Psychology   **Biological psychologists**, also called *physiological psychologists*, use high-tech scanning devices and other methods to study how biological processes in the brain affect, and are affected by, behavior and mental processes (see Figure 1.1). Have you ever had the odd feeling that a new experience, such as entering an unfamiliar house, has actually happened to you before? Biological psychologists studying this illusion of *déjà vu* (French for "already seen") suggest that it may be due to a temporary malfunction in the brain's ability to combine incoming information from the senses, creating the impression of two "copies" of a single event (Brown, 2004). In the chapter on biological aspects of psychology, we describe biological psychologists' research on many other topics, such as how your brain controls your movements and speech and what organs help you cope with stress and fight disease.

Cognitive Psychology   **TRY THIS**   Stop reading for a moment and look left and right. Your ability to follow this suggestion, to recognize whatever you saw, and to understand the words you are reading right now are the result of mental, or *cognitive*, abilities. Those abilities allow you to receive information from the outside world, understand it, and act on it. **Cognitive psychologists** (some of whom prefer to be called *experimental psychologists*) study mental abilities such as sensation and perception, learning and memory, thinking, consciousness, intelligence, and creativity. Cognitive psychologists have found, for example, that we don't just receive incoming information—we mentally manipulate it. Notice that the drawing in Figure 1.2 stays physically the same, but two different versions emerge, depending on which of its features *you* emphasize.

Applications of cognitive psychologists' research are all around you. The work of those whose special interest is **engineering psychology**—also known as *human factors*—has helped designers create computer keyboards, mobile phones, MP3 players, Internet Web sites, aircraft instrument panels, automobile navigation systems, nuclear power plant controls, and even TV remotes that are more logical, easier to use, and less

A Bad Design

Consultation with human factors psychologists would surely have improved the design of this self-service gasoline pump. The pump will not operate until you press the red "start" button under the yellow "push to" label (see enlargement at the upper right). The button is difficult to locate among all the other signs and stickers. Such user-unfriendly designs are all too common these days (e.g., Cooper, 2004; visit www. baddesigns.com for some amazing examples).

Photograph courtesy of www.baddesigns.com

likely to cause errors. You will read more about human factors research and many other aspects of cognitive psychology in several chapters of this book.

Developmental Psychology   **Developmental psychologists** describe the changes in behavior and mental processes that occur from birth through old age and try to understand the causes and effects of those changes (see Figure 1.3). Their research on the development of memory and other mental abilities, for example, is used by judges and attorneys in deciding how old a child has to be in order to serve as a reliable witness in court or to responsibly choose which divorcing parent to live with. The chapter on human development describes other research by developmental psychologists and how it is being applied in areas such as parenting, evaluating day care, and preserving mental capacity in elderly people.

Personality Psychology   **Personality psychologists** study individuality—the unique features that characterize each of us. Using personality tests, some of these psychologists seek to describe how your own combination of personality traits, like your fingerprints, differs from everyone else's in terms of traits such as openness to experience, emotionality, reliability, agreeableness, and sociability. Others study the combinations of personality traits that are associated with the appearance of ethnic prejudice, depression, or vulnerability to stress-related health problems. And personality psychologists interested in positive psychology are trying to identify and understand the human strengths that help people to remain optimistic, even in the face of stress or tragedy, and to find happiness in their lives (Snyder & Lopez, 2009).

Clinical, Counseling, Community, and Health Psychology   Clinical psychologists and **counseling psychologists** conduct research on the causes and treatment of mental disorders and offer services to help troubled people overcome those disorders. Their research is improving our understanding of the genetic and environmental forces that shape disorders ranging from anxiety and depression to schizophrenia and

developmental psychologists
Psychologists who seek to understand, describe, and explore how behavior and mental processes change over a lifetime.

personality psychologists
Psychologists who study the characteristics that make individuals similar to or different from one another.

clinical and counseling psychologists   Psychologists who seek to assess, understand, and change abnormal behavior.

FIGURE 1.3
Where Would You Put a Third Eye?
In a study of how thinking develops, children were asked to show where they would place a third eye if they could have one. Nine-year-old children, who were still in an early stage of mental development, drew the extra eye between their existing eyes, "as a spare." Having developed more advanced thinking abilities, eleven-year-olds drew the third eye in more creative places, such as the palm of their hand "so I can see around corners."

From Shaffer, Developmental Psychology: Theory, Research and Applications. Copyright © 1985 Wadsworth, a part of Cengage Learning Inc. Reproduced by permission.www.cengage.com/ permissions

Drawing by a nine-year-old   Drawing by an eleven-year-old

autism, and it is providing guidance to therapists about which treatment methods are likely to be most effective with each category of disorder.

Community psychologists work to ensure that psychological services reach the homeless and others who need help but tend not to seek it. They also try to prevent psychological disorders by promoting people's resilience and other personal strengths and by working with community leaders and neighborhood organizations to improve local schools and reduce the crime, poverty, and other stressful conditions that often lead to psychological disorders.

Health psychologists study the relationship between risky behaviors such as smoking or lack of exercise and the likelihood of suffering heart disease, stroke, cancer, or other health problems. They also explore the impact that illnesses such as diabetes, cancer, or multiple sclerosis can have on people's behavior, thinking, emotions, and family relationships. Their research is applied in programs that help people to cope effectively with illness, as well as to reduce the risk of cancer, heart disease, and stroke by changing the behaviors that put them at risk.

Generally, clinical psychologists have Ph.D. degrees in psychology; counseling, community, and health psychologists have either a Ph.D. or a master's degree in psychology. All of these psychologists differ from *psychiatrists*, who are medical doctors specializing in abnormal behavior (psychiatry). You can read more about the work of clinical, counseling, community, and health psychologists in the chapters on health, stress, and coping; psychological disorders; and treatment of psychological disorders.

Educational and School Psychology **Educational psychologists** conduct research and develop theories about teaching and learning. The results of their work are applied in programs designed to improve teacher training, refine school curricula, reduce dropout rates, and help students learn more efficiently and remember what they learn. For example, they have supported the use of the "jigsaw" technique, a type of classroom activity, described in the social cognition chapter, in which children from various ethnic groups must work together to complete a task or solve a problem. These cooperative experiences appear to promote learning, generate mutual respect, and reduce intergroup prejudice (Aronson, 2004).

School psychologists once specialized in IQ testing, diagnosing learning disabilities and other academic problems, and setting up programs to improve students' achievement and satisfaction in school. Today, however, they are also involved in activities such as early detection of students' mental health problems and crisis intervention following school violence.

community psychologists
Psychologists who work to obtain psychological services for people in need of help and to prevent psychological disorders by working for changes in social systems.

health psychologists Psychologists who study the effects of behavior and mental processes on health and illness and vice versa.

educational psychologists Psychologists who study methods by which instructors teach and students learn and who apply their results to improving those methods.

school psychologists Psychologists who test IQs, diagnose students' academic problems, and set up programs to improve students' achievement.

Getting Ready for Surgery

Health psychologists have learned that when patients are mentally prepared for a surgical procedure, they are less stressed by it and recover more rapidly. Their research is now routinely applied in hospitals through programs in which children and adults are given more information about what to expect before, during, and after their operations.

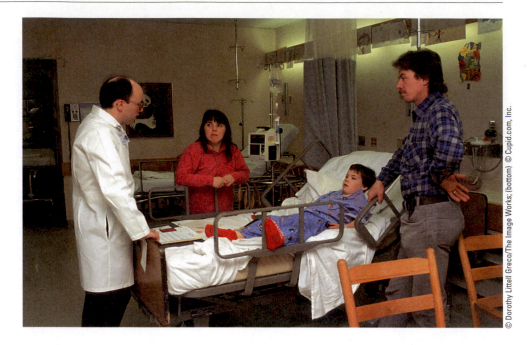

© Dorothy Littell Greco/The Image Works; (bottom) © Cupid.com, Inc.

Social Psychology   **Social psychologists** study the ways that people think about themselves and others and how people influence one another. Their research on persuasion has been applied to the creation of safe-sex advertising campaigns designed to stop the spread of AIDS. Social psychologists also explore how peer pressure affects us, what determines whom we like (or even love), and why and how prejudice forms. They have found, for example, that although we may pride ourselves on not being prejudiced, we may actually hold unconscious negative beliefs about certain groups that affect the way we relate to people in those groups. The chapters on social cognition and social influence describe these and many other examples of research in social psychology.

Got a Match?

Some commercial matchmaking services apply social psychologists' research on interpersonal attraction in an effort to pair up people whose characteristics are most likely to be compatible.

social psychologists Psychologists who study how people influence one another's behavior and mental processes, individually and in groups.

Industrial and Organizational Psychology   Industrial and organizational psychologists conduct research on leadership, stress, competition, pay scales, and other factors that affect the efficiency, productivity, and satisfaction of people in the workplace. They also explore topics such as worker motivation, work team cooperation, conflict resolution procedures, and employee selection methods. Learning more about how businesses and industrial organizations work—or fail to work—allows industrial and organizational psychologists to make evidence-based recommendations for helping them work better. Today, companies all over the world are applying research from industrial and organizational psychology to promote the development of *positive organizational behavior*. The results include more effective employee training programs, ambitious but realistic goal-setting procedures, fair and reasonable evaluation tools, and incentive systems that motivate and reward outstanding performance.

Quantitative Psychology   Quantitative psychologists develop and use statistical tools to analyze vast amounts of data collected by their colleagues in all of psychology's subfields. These tools are of help in evaluating the quality of psychological tests, tracing the relationships between childhood experiences and adult behaviors, and even estimating the relative contributions of heredity and environment in shaping intelligence. To what extent are people born smart—or not so smart—and to what extent are their mental abilities created by their environments? This is one of the hottest topics in psychology today, and quantitative psychologists are right in the middle of it.

Other Subfields   Our list of psychology's subfields is still not complete. There are **sport psychologists**, who use visualization and relaxation training programs, for example, to help athletes reduce excessive anxiety, focus attention, and make other changes that let them perform at their best. **Forensic psychologists** assist in jury selection, evaluate defendants' mental competence to stand trial, and deal with other issues involving psychology and the law. And **environmental psychologists** study the effects of the environment on people's behavior and mental processes. The results of their

industrial and organizational psychologists Psychologists who study ways to improve efficiency, productivity, and satisfaction among workers and the organizations that employ them.

quantitative psychologists Psychologists who develop and use statistical tools to analyze research data.

sport psychologists Psychologists who explore the relationships between athletic performance and such psychological variables as motivation and emotion.

forensic psychologists Psychologists who assist in jury selection, evaluate defendants' mental competence to stand trial, and deal with other issues involving psychology and the law.

environmental psychologists Psychologists who study the effects of the physical environment on behavior and mental processes.

Forensic Psychology

Forensic psychologists may assist police and other agencies in profiling criminals, evaluating the mental competence of defendants, participating in jury selection, and performing many other tasks related to psychology and the law. Actor B. D. Wong's performance as forensic psychiatrist Dr. George Huang on *Law and Order: SVU* is so accurate that the Media Psychology division of the American Psychological Association gave the show its 2004 Golden Psi award for excellence in the fictional portrayal of mental health professionals.

research are applied by architects and interior designers as they plan or remodel residence halls, shopping malls, auditoriums, hospitals, prisons, offices, and other spaces to make them more comfortable and functional for the people who will occupy them. There are also neuropsychologists, military psychologists, consumer psychologists, rehabilitation psychologists, and more.

Further information about the subfields we have mentioned—and some that we haven't—is available on the Web sites of the American Psychological Association (www.apa.org) and the Association for Psychological Science (www.psychologicalscience .org).

Where do the psychologists in all these subfields work? Table 1.2 contains a summary of where the approximately 160,000 psychologists....in the United States find employment, as well as the kinds of things they typically do in each setting.

Linkages Within Psychology and Beyond

We have listed psychology's subfields as though they were separate, but they often overlap, and so do the activities of the psychologists working in them. When developmental psychologists study the changes that take place in children's thinking skills, for example, their research is linked to the research of cognitive psychologists. Similarly, biological psychologists have one foot in clinical psychology when they look at how chemicals in the brain affect the symptoms of depression. And when social psychologists apply their research on cooperation to promote group learning activities in the classroom, they are linking up with educational psychology. Even when psychologists work mainly in one subfield, they are still likely to draw on, and contribute to, knowledge in other subfields.

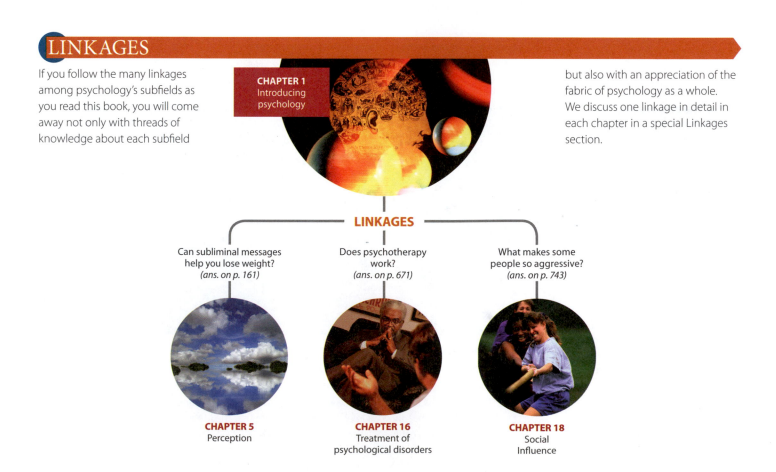

LINKAGES

If you follow the many linkages among psychology's subfields as you read this book, you will come away not only with threads of knowledge about each subfield

CHAPTER 1
Introducing psychology

but also with an appreciation of the fabric of psychology as a whole. We discuss one linkage in detail in each chapter in a special Linkages section.

LINKAGES

Can subliminal messages help you lose weight?
(ans. on p. 161)

Does psychotherapy work?
(ans. on p. 671)

What makes some people so aggressive?
(ans. on p. 743)

CHAPTER 5
Perception

CHAPTER 16
Treatment of psychological disorders

CHAPTER 18
Social Influence

TABLE 1.2 Typical Activities and Work Settings for Psychologists

The fact that psychologists can work in such a wide variety of settings and do so many interesting—and often well-paying—jobs helps account for the popularity of psychology as an undergraduate major (Goldstein, 2010, Dillow, & Hoffman, 2008). Psychology courses also provide excellent background for students planning to enter medicine, law, business, and many other fields.

Work Setting	Typical Activities
Colleges, universities, and professional schools	Teaching, research, and writing, often in collaboration with colleagues from other disciplines
Mental health facilities (e.g., hospitals, clinics, counseling centers)	Testing and treatment of children and adults
Private practice (alone or in a group of psychologists)	Testing and treatment of children and adults; consultation to business and other organizations
Business, government, and organizations	Testing potential employees; assessing employee satisfaction; identifying and resolving conflicts; improving leadership skills; offering stress management and other employee assistance programs; improving equipment design to maximize productivity and prevent accidents
Schools (including those for intellectually disabled and emotionally disturbed children)	Testing mental abilities and other characteristics; identifying problem children; consulting with parents; designing and implementing programs to improve academic performance
Other	Teaching prison inmates; research in private institutes; advising legislators on educational, research, or public policy; administering research funds; research on effectiveness of military personnel; etc.

So if you want to understand psychology as a whole, you have to understand the linkages among its subfields. To help you recognize these linkages, we highlight three of them in a Linkages diagram at the end of each chapter—similar to the one shown here. Each linkage is represented by a question that connects two subfields, and the page numbers in parentheses tell you where you can read more about each question (look for "Linkages" symbols on those pages). We pay particular attention to one of the questions in each diagram by discussing it in a special Linkages section. If you follow the linkages in these diagrams, the relationships among psychology's many subfields will become much clearer. We hope that you find this kind of detective work to be interesting and that it will lead you to look for the many other linkages that we did not mention. Tracing linkages might even improve your grade in the course, because it is often easier to remember material in one chapter by relating it to linked material in other chapters.

Links to Other Fields Just as psychology's subfields are linked to one another, psychology itself is linked to many other fields. Some of these linkages are based on interests that psychologists share with researchers from other disciplines. For example, psychologists are working with computer scientists to create artificial intelligence systems that can recognize voices, solve problems, and make decisions in ways that will equal or exceed human capabilities (Haynes, Cohen, & Ritter, 2009; Wang, 2007). Psychologists are also collaborating with specialists in neuroanatomy, neurophysiology, neurochemistry, genetics, and other disciplines in the field known as **neuroscience**. The goal of this multidisciplinary research enterprise is to examine the structure and function of the nervous system in animals and humans at levels ranging from the individual cell to overt behavior.

Many of the links between psychology and other disciplines appear when research conducted in one field is applied in the other. For example, biological psychologists are learning about the brain with scanning devices developed by computer scientists, physicists, and engineers. Physicians and economists are using research by psychologists to better understand the thought processes that influence (good and bad) decisions about caring for patients and choosing investments. In fact, the psychologist Daniel Kahneman recently won a Nobel Prize in economics for his work in this area. Other psychologists' research on memory has influenced how lineups and "mug shot" photos are displayed to eyewitnesses attempting to identify criminals, how attorneys

neuroscience The scientific study of all levels of the nervous system, including neuroanatomy, neurochemistry, neurology, neurophysiology, and neuropharmacology.

Linking Psychology and Law

Cognitive psychologists' research on the quirks of human memory has led to revised guidelines for police and prosecutors when dealing with crime witnesses (U.S. Department of Justice, 1999). These guidelines warn that asking witnesses leading questions (e.g., "Do you remember seeing a gun?") can distort their memories and that false accusations are less likely if witnesses are told that the real criminal might not be in a lineup or in a group of photos (Doyle, 2005).

© Fat Chance Productions/Corbis

question eyewitnesses in court, and how lawyers and judges question witnesses and instruct juries. And psychological studies of the effect of aging and brain disorders on people's vision, hearing, and mental abilities is shaping doctors' recommendations about whether and when elderly patients should stop driving cars. This book is filled with examples of other ways in which psychological theories and research have been applied to health care, law, business, engineering, architecture, aviation, and sports, to name just a few.

Research: The Foundation of Psychology

The knowledge that psychologists share across subfields and with other disciplines stems from the research they conduct on many aspects of behavior and mental processes. For example, rather than just speculating about why some people eat too much or too little, psychologists look for answers by using the methods of science. This means that they perform experiments and other scientific procedures to systematically gather and analyze information about behavior and mental processes and then base their conclusions—and their next questions—on the results of those procedures.

To follow up on the topic of eating, consider what would happen if you had just finished a big lunch at your favorite restaurant and a waiter got mixed up and brought you a plate of the same food that was meant for someone else. You would probably send it away, but why? Decisions to start eating or stop eating are affected by many biological factors, including signals from your blood that tell your brain how much "fuel" you have available. But the psychologist Paul Rozin was interested in how these decisions are affected by psychological factors, such as being aware that you have already eaten (Rozin et al., 1998). What if you didn't remember that you just had lunch? Would you have started eating that second plate of food?

To explore this question, Rozin conducted a series of tests with R. H. and B. R., two men who had suffered a kind of brain damage that left them unable to remember anything for more than a few minutes. (You can read more about this condition, called *anterograde amnesia*, in the memory chapter.) The men were tested individually, on three different days, in a private room where they sat with a researcher at lunchtime and were served a tray of their favorite food. Before and after eating, they were asked to rate their hunger on a scale from 1 (extremely full) to 9 (extremely hungry). Once lunch was over, the tray was removed, and the researcher continued chatting, making sure that each man drank enough water to clear his mouth of food residue. After ten to thirty minutes, a hospital attendant arrived with an identical meal tray and announced, "Here's lunch." These men had no memory of having eaten lunch already, but would signals from their stomachs or their blood be enough to keep them from eating another one?

Apparently not. Table 1.3 shows that in every test session, R. H. and B. R. ate all or part of the second meal and in all but one session ate at least part of a third lunch that was offered to them ten to thirty minutes after the second one. Rozin conducted similar tests with J. C. and T. A., a woman and a man who had also suffered brain damage but whose memories had not been affected. In each of two test sessions, these people finished their lunch but refused the opportunity to eat a second one. These results suggest that the memory of when we last ate can indeed be a factor in guiding decisions about when to eat again. They also support a conclusion described in the motivation and emotion chapter, namely, that eating is controlled by a complex combination of biological, social, cultural, and psychological factors. As a result, we may eat when we *think* it is time to eat, regardless of what our bodies tell us about our physical need to eat.

Rozin's study illustrates the fact that although psychologists often begin with speculation about behavior and mental processes, they take additional steps toward understanding those processes. Using scientific methods to test their ideas, they reach informed conclusions and generate new questions. Even psychologists who don't conduct research still benefit from it. They are constantly applying the results of their colleagues' studies to improve the quality, accuracy, and effectiveness of their teaching, writing, or service to clients and organizations. In the developing field of *performance psychology*, for example, practicing clinical psychologists are combining their psychotherapy skills with research from cognitive, industrial and organizational, and sport psychology to help business executives, performing artists, and athletes excel (Hays, 2009).

TABLE 1.3   The Role of Memory in Deciding When to Eat

Here are the results of a study in which brain-damaged people were offered a meal shortly after having eaten an identical meal. Their hunger ratings (1–9, where 9 = extremely hungry) before and after eating are shown in parentheses. B. R. and R. H. had a kind of brain damage that left them unable to remember recent events (anterograde amnesia); J. C. and T. A. had normal memory. These results suggest that the decision to start eating is determined partly by knowing when we last ate. Notice that hunger ratings, too, were more consistently affected by eating for the people who remembered having eaten.

Session	B. R. (Amnesia)	R. H. (Amnesia)	J. C.	T. A.
One				
Meal 1	Finished (7/8)	Partially eaten (7/6)	Finished (5/2)	Finished (5/4)
Meal 2	Finished (2/5)	Partially eaten (7/7)	Rejected (0)	Rejected (3)
Meal 3	Rejected (3)	Partially eaten (7/7)	—	—
Two				
Meal 1	Finished (6/5)	Partially eaten (7/6)	Finished (7/2)	Finished (7/3)
Meal 2	Finished (5/3)	Partially eaten (7/6)	Rejected (1)	Rejected (3)
Meal 3	Partially eaten (5)[a]	Partially eaten (7/6)	—	—
Three				
Meal 1	Finished (7/3)	Partially eaten (7/6)	—	—
Meal 2	Finished (2/3)	Partially eaten (7/6.5)	—	—
Meal 3	Partially eaten (5/3)	Partially eaten (7.5)	—	—

[a]B. R. began eating his third meal but was stopped by the researcher, presumably to avoid illness.

From P. Rozin, S. Dow, M. Moscovitch, and S. Rajaram, "The Role of Memory for Recent Eating Experiences in Onset and Cessation of Meals. Evidence from the Amnesic Syndrome," Psychological Science, 9, 1998, pp. 392–396. Reprinted by permission of Sage Publications, Inc.

The rules and methods of science that guide psychologists in their research are summarized in the chapter on research in psychology. We have placed that chapter early in the book to highlight the fact that without scientific research methods and the foundation of evidence they provide, psychologists' statements and recommendations about behavior and mental processes would carry no more weight than those of astrologers, psychics, or tabloid journalists. Accordingly, we will be relying on the results of psychologists' scientific research when we tell you what they have discovered so far about behavior and mental processes and also when we evaluate their efforts to apply that knowledge to improve the quality of human life.

A Brief History of Psychology

How did scientific research in psychology get started? Psychology is a relatively new discipline, but its roots can be traced through centuries, especially in the history of philosophy. Since at least the time of Socrates, Plato, and Aristotle in ancient Greece, philosophers had been debating psychological topics, such as "What is the nature of the mind and the soul?" "What is the relationship between the mind and the body?" and "Are we born with a certain amount of knowledge, or do we have to learn everything for ourselves?" They even debated whether it is possible to study such things scientifically.

A philosophical view known as *empiricism* was particularly important to the development of scientific psychology. Beginning in the 1600s, proponents of empiricism—especially the British philosophers John Locke, George Berkeley, and David Hume—challenged the long-accepted claim that some knowledge is innate. Empiricists argued instead that what we know about the world comes to us through experience and observation, not through imagination or intuition. This view suggests that at birth, our minds are like a blank slate (*tabula rasa* in Latin) on which our experiences write a lifelong story. For well over a century now, empiricism has guided psychologists in seeking knowledge about behavior and mental processes through observations governed by the rules of science.

Wundt and the Structuralism of Titchener

The "official" birth date of modern psychology is usually given as 1879, the year that a physiologist named Wilhelm Wundt (pronounced "voont") established the first formal psychology research laboratory at the University of Leipzig in Germany (Benjamin, 2000). At around this time, a number of other German physiologists, including Hermann von Helmholtz and Gustav Fechner (pronounced "FECK-ner"), had been studying vision and other sensory and perceptual processes that empiricism identified as the channels through which human knowledge flows. Fechner's work was especially valuable because he realized that one could study these mental processes by observing people's reactions to changes in sensory stimuli. By exploring, for example, how much brighter a light must become before we see it as twice as bright, Fechner discovered complex but predictable relationships between changes in the *physical* characteristics of stimuli and changes in our *psychological experience* of them. Fechner's approach, which he called *psychophysics*, paved the way for much of the research described in the chapter on perception.

Wundt, too, used the methods of laboratory science to study sensory-perceptual systems, but the focus of his work was **consciousness**, the mental experiences created by these systems. Wundt wanted to describe the basic elements of consciousness, how they are organized, and how they relate to one another (Schultz & Schultz, 2004). He developed ingenious laboratory methods to study the speed of decision making and other mental events, and in an attempt to observe conscious experience, Wundt used the technique of *introspection*, which means "looking inward." After training research participants in this method, he repeatedly showed a light or made a sound and asked them to describe the sensations and feelings these stimuli created. Wundt concluded that "quality" (e.g., cold or blue) and "intensity" (e.g., brightness or loudness) are the two essential elements of any sensation and that feelings can be described

consciousness The awareness of external stimuli and our own mental activity.

Wilhelm Wundt (1832–1920)

In an early experiment on the speed of mental processes, Wundt (third from left) first measured how quickly people could respond to a light by releasing a button they had been holding down. He then measured how much longer the response took when they held down one button with each hand and had to decide, based on the color of the light, which one to release. Wundt reasoned that the additional response time reflected how long it took to perceive the color and decide which hand to move. As noted in the chapter on cognition and language, the logic behind this experiment remains a part of research on cognitive processes today.

Archives of the History of American Psychology/The University of Akron

in terms of pleasure or displeasure, tension or relaxation, and excitement or depression (Schultz & Schultz, 2004). In conducting this kind of research, Wundt began psychology's transformation from the *philosophy* of mental processes to the *science* of mental processes.

Edward Titchener, an Englishman who had been a student of Wundt's, used introspection in his own laboratory at Cornell University. He studied Wundt's basic elements of consciousness, as well as images and other aspects of conscious experience that are harder to quantify (see Figure 1.4). One result was that Titchener added "clearness" as an element of sensation (Schultz & Schultz, 2004). Titchener called his approach *structuralism* because he was trying to define the structure of consciousness.

Wundt was not alone in the scientific study of mental processes, nor was his work universally accepted. Some of his fellow German scientists, including Hermann Ebbinghaus, believed that analyzing consciousness through introspection was not as important as exploring the capacities and limitations of mental processes such as learning and memory. Ebbinghaus's own laboratory experiments—in which he served as the only participant—formed the basis for some of what we know about memory today. Around 1912, other German colleagues, including Max Wertheimer, Kurt Koffka, and Wolfgang Köhler, argued against Wundt's efforts to break down human experience or consciousness into its component parts. They were called *Gestalt psychologists* because they pointed out that the whole shape (*Gestalt* in German) of conscious experience is not the same as the sum of its parts. Wertheimer pointed out, for example, that if a pair of lights goes on and off in just the right sequence, we don't experience two separate flashing lights but a single light that appears to "jump" back and forth. You have probably seen this *phi phenomenon* in action on advertising signs that create the impression of a series of lights racing around a display. Movies provide another example. It would be incredibly boring to look one at a time at the thousands of still images printed on a reel of film. Yet when those same images are projected onto a screen at a particular rate, they combine to create a rich and seemingly seamless emotional experience. To understand consciousness, then, said the Gestaltists, we have to study the whole "movie," not just its component parts.

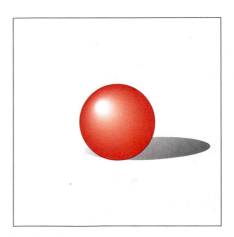

FIGURE 1.4
A Stimulus for Introspection

TRY THIS Look at this object, and try to ignore what it is. Instead, try to describe only your conscious experience, such as redness, brightness, and roundness, and how intense and clear the sensations and images are. If you can do this, you would have been an excellent research assistant in Titchener's laboratory.

Freud and Psychoanalysis   While Wundt and his colleagues in Leipzig were conducting scientific research on consciousness, Sigmund Freud was in Vienna, Austria, beginning to explore the unconscious. As a physician, Freud had presumed that all behavior and mental processes have *physical* causes somewhere in the nervous system. He began to question that assumption in the late 1800s, however, after encountering several patients who displayed a variety of physical ailments that had no apparent physical cause. After interviewing these patients using hypnosis and other methods, Freud became convinced that the causes of these people's physical problems were not physical. The real causes, he said, were deep-seated problems that the patients had pushed out of consciousness (Friedman & Schustack, 2003). He eventually came to believe that all behavior—from everyday slips of the tongue to severe forms of mental disorder—is motivated by *psychological* processes, especially by mental conflicts that occur without our awareness, at an unconscious level. For nearly fifty years, Freud developed his ideas into a body of work known as *psychoanalysis*, which included a theory of personality and mental disorder, as well as a set of treatment methods. Freud's ideas are by no means universally accepted, partly because they were based on a small number of medical cases, not on extensive laboratory experiments. Still, he was a groundbreaker whose theories have had a significant influence on psychology and many other fields.

William James and Functionalism   Scientific research in psychology began in North America not long after Wundt started his work in Germany. William James founded a psychology laboratory at Harvard University in the late 1870s, though it was used mainly to conduct demonstrations for his students (Schultz & Schultz, 2004). It was not until 1883 that G. Stanley Hall at Johns Hopkins University established the first psychology research laboratory in the United States. The first Canadian psychology research laboratory was established in 1889 at the University of Toronto by James Mark Baldwin, Canada's first modern psychologist and a pioneer in research on child development.

William James's Lab

William James (1842–1910) established this psychology demonstration laboratory at Harvard University in the late 1870s. Like the Gestalt psychologists, James saw the approach used by Wundt and Titchener as a scientific dead end; he said that trying to understand consciousness by studying its components is like trying to understand a house by looking at individual bricks (James, 1884). He preferred instead to study the ways in which consciousness functions to help people adapt to their environments.

Like the Gestalt psychologists, William James rejected both Wundt's approach and Titchener's structuralism. He saw no point in breaking consciousness into component parts that never operate on their own. Instead, in accordance with Charles Darwin's theory of evolution, James wanted to understand how images, sensations, memories, and the other mental events that make up our flowing "stream of consciousness" *function* to help us adapt to our environment (James, 1890, 1892). This idea was consistent with an approach to psychology called *functionalism*, which focused on the role of consciousness in guiding people's ability to make decisions, solve problems, and the like.

James's emphasis on the functions of mental processes encouraged North American psychologists to look not only at how those processes work to our advantage but also at how they differ from one person to the next. Some of these psychologists began to measure individual differences in learning, memory, and other mental processes associated with intelligence, made recommendations for improving educational practices in the schools, and even worked with teachers on programs tailored to children in need of special help (Kramer, Bernstein, & Phares, 2009).

John B. Watson and Behaviorism   Besides fueling James's interest in the functions of consciousness, Darwin's theory of evolution led other psychologists—especially those in North America after 1900—to study animals as well as humans. These researchers reasoned that if all species evolved in similar ways, perhaps the behavior and mental processes of all species followed the same or similar laws and we can learn something about people by studying animals. They could not expect cats or rats or pigeons to introspect, so they watched what animals did when confronted with laboratory tasks such as finding the correct path through a maze. From these observations, psychologists made *inferences* about the animals' conscious experience and about the general laws of learning, memory, problem solving, and other mental processes that might apply to people as well.

John B. Watson, a psychology professor at Johns Hopkins University, agreed that the observable behavior of animals and humans is the most important source of scientific information for psychology. However, he thought it was utterly unscientific to use behavior as the basis for making inferences about consciousness, as structuralists and functionalists did—let alone about the unconscious, as Freudians did. In 1913, Watson published an article titled "Psychology As the Behaviorist Views It." In it, he argued that psychologists should ignore mental events and base psychology only on what they can actually see in overt behavior and in responses to various stimuli (Watson, 1913, 1919).

Watson's view, called *behaviorism*, recognized the existence of consciousness but did not consider it worth studying because it would always be private and therefore not observable by scientific methods. In fact, said Watson, preoccupation with consciousness would prevent psychology from ever being a true science. He believed that the most important determinant of behavior is *learning* and that it is through learning that animals and humans are able to adapt to their environments. Watson was famous for claiming that with enough control over the environment, he could create learning experiences that would turn any infant into a doctor, a lawyer, or even a criminal.

The American psychologist B. F. Skinner was another early champion of behaviorism. From the 1930s until his death in 1990, Skinner worked on mapping out the details of how rewards and punishments shape, maintain, and change behavior through what he termed "operant conditioning." By conducting a *functional analysis of behavior*, he would explain, for example, how parents and teachers can unknowingly encourage children's tantrums by rewarding them with attention and how a virtual addiction to gambling can result from the occasional and unpredictable rewards it brings.

Many psychologists were drawn to Watson's and Skinner's vision of psychology as the learning-based science of observable behavior. In fact, behaviorism dominated psychological research from the 1920s through the 1960s, while the study of consciousness received less attention, especially in the United States. ("In Review: The Development of Psychology" summarizes behaviorism and the other schools of thought that have influenced psychologists in the past century.)

Psychology Today   Psychologists continue to study all kinds of overt behavior in humans and in animals. By the end of the 1960s, however, many had become dissatisfied with the limitations imposed by behaviorism (some, especially in Europe, had never accepted it in the first place). They grew uncomfortable about ignoring mental processes that might be important in more fully understanding behavior (e.g., Ericsson & Simon, 1994). The dawn of the computer age influenced these psychologists to think about mental activity in a new way—as information processing. Computers and rapid progress in computer-based biotechnology began to offer psychologists exciting new ways to study mental processes and the biological activity that underlies them. As shown in Figure 1.1 on page 5, for example, it is now possible to literally see what is going on in the brain when a person reads or thinks or makes decisions.

Armed with ever more sophisticated research tools, psychologists today are striving to do what Watson thought was impossible: to study mental processes with precision and scientific objectivity. In fact, there are probably now as many psychologists who study cognitive and biological processes as there are who study observable behaviors. So mainstream psychology has come full circle, once again accepting consciousness—in the form of cognitive processes—as a legitimate topic for scientific research and justifying the definition of psychology as the science of behavior and mental processes.

IN REVIEW The Development of Psychology			
School of Thought	**Early Advocates**	**Goals**	**Methods**
Structuralism	Edward Titchener, trained by Wilhelm Wundt	To study conscious experience and its structure	Experiments; introspection
Gestalt psychology	Max Wertheimer	To describe the organization of mental processes: "The whole is different from the sum of its parts."	Observation of sensory-perceptual phenomena
Psychoanalysis	Sigmund Freud	To explain personality and behavior; to develop techniques for treating mental disorders	Study of individual cases
Functionalism	William James	To study how the mind works in allowing an organism to adapt to the environment	Naturalistic observation of animal and human behavior
Behaviorism	John B. Watson, B. F. Skinner	To study only observable behavior and explain behavior through learning principles	Observation of the relationship between environmental stimuli and behavioral responses

1. Darwin's theory of evolution had an especially strong influence on _____ ism and _____ ism.
2. Which school of psychological thought was founded by a European medical doctor? _____
3. In the history of psychology, _____ was the first school of thought to appear.

Approaches to the Science of Psychology

Suppose you wanted to know why some people stop to help an injured stranger lying on the sidewalk and others just keep walking. Where would you start? You could look for answers in these people's personality traits, in what they have learned from family, friends, and cultural traditions, or even in their genes and brain cells and hormones.

The Biology of Emotion

Robert Levenson, a psychologist at the University of California at Berkeley, takes a biological approach to the study of social interactions. He measures heart rate, muscle tension, and other physical reactions as couples discuss problems in their relationships. He then looks for patterns of physiological activity in each of the partners (such as overreactions to criticism) that might be related to success or failure in resolving their problems.

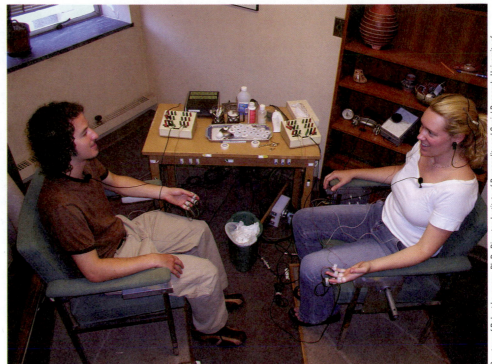

Courtesy of Robert Levenson, Ph.D., Director, Institute of Personality and Social Research, University of California

With so many research directions available, you'd have to decide which sources of information are most likely to help you explain and predict people's behavior in this situation.

Psychologists have to make the same kinds of decisions, not only about where to focus their research but also about what treatment methods to use or what services to provide to schools, businesses, government agencies, or other clients. Their decisions are guided mainly by their overall *approach* to psychology—that is, by the assumptions, questions, and methods they believe will be most useful in their work. The approaches we described earlier as structuralism and functionalism have faded into history now, but the *psychodynamic* and *behavioral* approaches remain, along with others known as *biological, evolutionary, cognitive,* and *humanistic* approaches. Some psychologists adopt just one of these approaches, but most psychologists are *eclectic.* This means that they blend assumptions and methods from two or more approaches in an effort to more fully understand behavior and mental processes. Some approaches to psychology are more influential than others these days, but we will review the main features of all of them to help you understand how they differ and how they have affected psychologists' work over the years.

The Biological Approach

As its name implies, the **biological approach** to psychology assumes that behavior and mental processes are largely shaped by biological processes. Psychologists who take this approach study the psychological effects of hormones, genes, and the activity of the nervous system, especially the brain. So if they are studying memory, they might try to identify the changes taking place in the brain as information is stored there (Figure 7.16, in the chapter on memory, shows an example of these changes). If they are studying thinking, they might look for patterns of brain activity associated with, say, making quick decisions or reading a foreign language.

Research discussed in nearly every chapter of this book reflects the enormous influence of the biological approach on psychology today. To help you better understand the terms and concepts used in that research, we have provided an appendix on the principles of genetics and a chapter on biological aspects of psychology.

biological approach An approach to psychology in which behavior and behavior disorders are seen as the result of physical processes, especially those relating to the brain and to hormones and other chemicals.

FIGURE 1.5
What Do You See?

TRY THIS Take a moment to jot down what you see in these clouds.

According to the psychodynamic approach to psychology, what we see in cloud formations and other vague patterns reflects unconscious wishes, impulses, fears, and other mental processes. In the personality chapter, we discuss the value of personality tests based on this assumption.

The Evolutionary Approach

Biological processes also figure prominently in an approach to psychology based on Charles Darwin's 1859 book *On the Origin of Species*. Darwin argued that the forms of life we see today are the result of *evolution*—of changes in life forms that occur over many generations. He said that evolution occurs through **natural selection**, which promotes the survival of the fittest individuals. Those whose behavior and appearance allow them to withstand the elements, avoid predators, and mate are able to survive and produce offspring with similar characteristics. Those less able to adjust (or *adapt*) to changing conditions are less likely to survive and reproduce. Most evolutionists today see natural selection operating at the level of genes, but the process is the same. Genes that result in characteristics and behaviors that are adaptive and useful in a certain environment will enable the creatures that inherit them to survive and reproduce, thereby passing those genes on to the next generation. According to evolutionary theory, many (but not all) of the genes that animals and humans possess today are the result of natural selection.

The **evolutionary approach** to psychology assumes that the *behavior and mental processes* of animals and humans today are also the result of evolution through natural selection. Psychologists who take this approach see cooperation as an adaptive survival strategy, aggression as a form of territory protection, and gender differences in mate selection preferences as reflecting different ways through which genes survive in future generations (Griskevicius et al., 2009). The evolutionary approach has generated a growing body of research (e.g., Buss, 2009; Confer et al., 2010); in later chapters, you will see how it is applied in relation to topics such as helping and altruism, mental disorders, temperament, and interpersonal attraction.

The Psychodynamic Approach

The **psychodynamic approach** to psychology offers a different slant on the role of inherited instincts and other biological forces in human behavior. Rooted in Freud's psychoanalysis, this approach assumes that our behavior and mental processes reflect constant and mostly unconscious psychological struggles within us (see Figure 1.5). Usually, these struggles involve conflict between the impulse to satisfy instincts (such as

natural selection The evolutionary mechanism through which Darwin said the fittest individuals survive to reproduce.

evolutionary approach An approach to psychology that emphasizes the inherited, adaptive aspects of behavior and mental processes.

psychodynamic approach A view developed by Freud that emphasizes the interplay of unconscious mental processes in determining human thought, feelings, and behavior.

for food, sex, or aggression) and the need to follow the rules of civilized society. So psychologists taking the psychodynamic approach might see aggression, for example, as a case of primitive urges overcoming a person's defenses against expressing those urges. They would see anxiety, depression, or other disorders as overt signs of inner turmoil.

Freud's original theories are not as influential today as they once were (Mischel, 2004a), but you will encounter modern versions of the psychodynamic approach in other chapters when we discuss theories of personality, psychological disorders, and psychotherapy.

The Behavioral Approach

The assumptions of the **behavioral approach** to psychology contrast sharply with those of the psychodynamic, biological, and evolutionary approaches. The behavioral approach is rooted in the behaviorism of Watson and Skinner, which, as already mentioned, focused entirely on observable behavior and on how that behavior is *learned*. Accordingly, psychologists who take a strict behavioral approach concentrate on understanding how past experiences with rewards and punishments act on the "raw materials" provided by genes and evolution to shape observable behavior into what it is today. So whether they are trying to understand a person's aggressiveness, fear of spiders, parenting methods, or drug abuse, behaviorists look mainly at that person's learning history. And because they believe that behavior problems develop through learning, behaviorists seek to eliminate those problems by helping people replace maladaptive habits with new and more appropriate ones.

Recall, though, that the peak of behaviorism's popularity passed precisely because it ignored everything but observable behavior. That criticism has had an impact on

© Mary Kate Denny/PhotoEdit

Why Is He So Aggressive?

Psychologists who take a cognitive-behavioral approach suggest that behavior is not shaped by rewards and punishments alone. They say that children's aggressiveness, for example, is learned partly by being rewarded (or at least not punished) for aggression but also partly by seeing family and friends acting aggressively. Further, attitudes and beliefs about the value and acceptability of aggressiveness can be learned as children hear others talk about aggression as the only way to deal with threats, disagreements, and other conflict situations (e.g., Cooper, Gomez, & Buck, 2008; Wilkowski & Robinson, 2008).

behavioral approach An approach to psychology emphasizing that human behavior is determined mainly by what a person has learned, especially from rewards and punishments.

the many behaviorists who now apply their learning-based approach in an effort to understand thoughts, or cognitions, as well as observable behavior. Those who take this *cognitive-behavioral*, or *social-cognitive*, approach explore how learning affects the development of thoughts, attitudes, and beliefs and, in turn, how these learned cognitive patterns affect overt behavior.

The Cognitive Approach

The growth of the cognitive-behavioral perspective reflects the influence of a broader cognitive view of psychology. This **cognitive approach** focuses on how we take in, mentally represent, and store information; how we perceive and process that information; and how all these cognitive processes affect our behavior. Psychologists who take the cognitive approach study the rapid series of mental events—including those outside of awareness—that accompany observable behavior. So in analyzing, say, an aggressive incident in a movie theater line, these psychologists would describe the following series of information processing events: First, the aggressive person (1) *perceived* that someone has cut into the ticket line, then (2) *recalled* information stored in memory about appropriate social behavior, (3) *decided* that the other person's action was inappropriate, (4) *labeled* the person as rude and inconsiderate, (5) *considered* possible responses and their likely consequences, (6) *decided* that shoving the person is the best response, and (7) *executed* that response.

Psychologists who take a cognitive approach focus on these and other mental processes to understand many kinds of individual and social behaviors, from decision making and problem solving to interpersonal attraction and intelligence, to name but a few. In the situation just described, for example, the person's aggression would be seen as the result of poor problem solving, because there were probably several better ways to deal with the problem of line-cutting. The cognitive approach is especially important in the field of *cognitive science*, in which researchers from psychology, computer science, biology, engineering, linguistics, and philosophy study intelligent systems in humans and computers. Together, they are trying to discover the building blocks of cognition and to determine how these components produce complex behaviors such as remembering a fact, naming an object, writing a word, or making a decision.

The Humanistic Approach

Mental events play a different role in the **humanistic approach** to psychology (also known as the *phenomenological approach*). Psychologists who favor the humanistic perspective see behavior as determined primarily by each person's capacity to choose how to think and act. They don't see these choices as driven by instincts, biological processes, or rewards and punishments but rather by each individual's unique perceptions of the world. So if you see the world as a friendly place, you are likely to be optimistic and secure. If you perceive it as full of hostile, threatening people, you will probably be defensive and fearful.

Like their cognitively oriented colleagues, psychologists who choose the humanistic approach would see aggression in a theater line as stemming from a perception that aggression is justified. But where the cognitive approach leads psychologists to search for laws governing *all* people's thoughts and actions, humanistic psychologists try to understand how each individual's unique experiences guide *that* person's thoughts and actions. In fact, many who prefer the humanistic approach claim that because no two people are exactly alike, the only way to understand behavior and mental processes is to focus on how they operate in each individual. Humanistic psychologists also believe that people are essentially good, that they are in control of themselves, and that they have an innate tendency to grow toward their highest potential.

cognitive approach A way of looking at human behavior that emphasizes research on how the brain takes in information, creates perceptions, forms and retrieves memories, processes information, and generates integrated patterns of action.

humanistic approach An approach to psychology that views behavior as controlled by the decisions that people make about their lives based on their perceptions of the world.

Cognitive Science at Work

Psychologists and other cognitive scientists are working on a "computational theory of the mind" in which they create computer programs and robotic devices that simulate how humans process information. In the chapter on cognition and language, we discuss their progress in creating "artificial intelligence" in computers that can help make medical diagnoses and perform other complex cognitive tasks, including the Internet searches you do using Google and other sophisticated Web search engines.

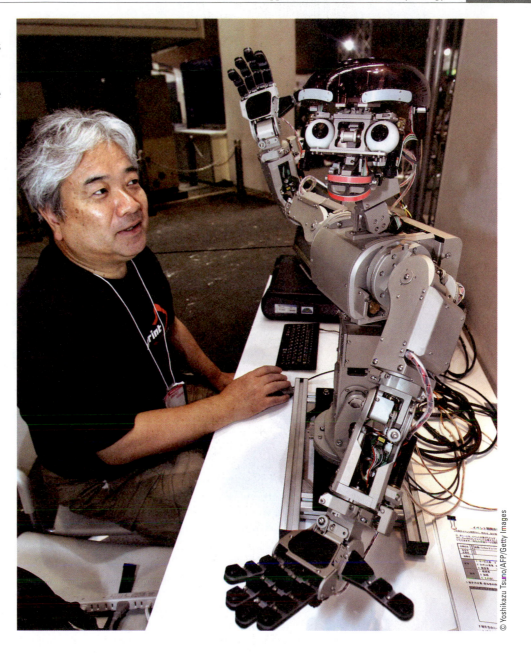

© Yoshikazu Tsuno/AFP/Getty Images

The humanistic approach began to attract attention in North America in the 1940s through the writings of Carl Rogers, a psychologist who had been trained in, but later rejected, the psychodynamic approach. We describe his views on personality and his psychotherapy methods in the chapters on personality and the treatment of psychological disorders. Another influential figure of the same era was Abraham Maslow, a psychologist who shaped and promoted the humanistic approach through his famous hierarchy-of-needs theory of motivation, which we describe in the chapters on motivation and emotion and personality. Today, the impact of the humanistic approach to psychology is limited, mainly because many psychologists find humanistic concepts and predictions too vague to be expressed and tested scientifically. It has, however, helped inspire the theories and research in positive psychology that are now becoming so popular (Snyder & Lopez, 2009). (For a summary of all the approaches we have discussed, see "In Review: Approaches to the Science of Psychology.")

IN REVIEW Approaches to the Science of Psychology	
Approach	**Characteristics**
Biological	Emphasizes activity of the nervous system, especially of the brain; the action of hormones and other chemicals; and genetics
Evolutionary	Emphasizes the ways in which behavior and mental processes are adaptive for survival
Psychodynamic	Emphasizes internal conflicts, mostly unconscious, which usually pit sexual or aggressive instincts against environmental obstacles to their expression
Behavioral	Emphasizes learning, especially each person's experience with rewards and punishments; the *cognitive-behavioral approach* adds emphasis on learning by observation and the learning of certain ways of thinking
Cognitive	Emphasizes mechanisms through which people receive, store, retrieve, and otherwise process information
Humanistic	Emphasizes individual potential for growth and the role of unique perceptions in guiding behavior and mental processes

1. Teaching people to be less afraid of heights reflects the _____ approach.
2. Charles Darwin was not a psychologist, but his work influenced the _____ approach to psychology.
3. Assuming that people inherit mental disorders suggests a _____ approach.

Human Diversity and Psychology

Today, the diversity seen in psychologists' approaches to their work is matched by the diversity in their own backgrounds. This was not always the case. As in other academic disciplines in the early twentieth century, most psychologists were white, middle-class men (Walker, 1991). Almost from the beginning, however, women and people of color were also part of the field (Schultz & Schultz, 2004). Throughout this book, you will find discussions of the work of their modern counterparts, whose contributions to research, service, and teaching have all increased in tandem with their growing representation in psychology. In the United States, women now constitute almost 60 percent of all psychologists holding doctoral degrees (American Psychological Association, 2009a). Women are also earning 60 percent of the new master's degrees and 49 percent of the new doctoral degrees awarded in psychology each year (American Psychological Association, 2009b). Moreover, about 25 percent of new doctoral degrees in psychology are being earned by members of ethnic minority groups (American Psychological Association, 2009a; National Science Foundation, 2009). These numbers reflect continuing efforts by psychological organizations and governmental bodies, especially in the United States and Canada, to promote the recruitment, graduation, and employment of women and ethnic minorities in psychology.

The Impact of Sociocultural Diversity on Psychology

Another aspect of diversity in psychology lies in the wide range of people psychologists study and serve. This change is significant because most psychologists once assumed that all people are very much alike and that whatever principles emerged from research or treatment efforts with one group would apply to everyone, everywhere. They were partly right, because people around the world *are* alike in many ways. They tend to live in groups, have religious beliefs, and create rules, music, dances, and games. The principles of nerve cell activity or reactions to heat or a sour taste are the same in men and women everywhere, as is their recognition of a smile. But are all people's moral values, achievement motivation, or communication styles the same too? Would the results of research on white male college students in the midwestern United States apply to

Mary Whiton Calkins (1863–1930)

Mary Whiton Calkins studied psychology at Harvard University, where William James described her as "brilliant." Because she was a woman, though, Harvard refused to grant her a doctoral degree unless she received it through Radcliffe, which was then an affiliated school for women. She refused but went on to do research on memory and in 1905 became the first woman president of the American Psychological Association (APA). Margaret Washburn (1871–1939) encountered similar sex discrimination at Columbia University, so she transferred to Cornell and became the first woman to earn a doctorate in psychology. In 1921, she became the second woman president of the APA.

Courtesy of Wilberforce University, Archives and Special Collections

Gilbert Haven Jones (1883–1966)

When Gilbert Haven Jones graduated from the University of Jena in Germany in 1909, he became one of the first African Americans to earn a doctorate in psychology. Many others were to follow, including J. Henry Alston, who was the first African American to publish research in a major U.S. psychology journal (Alston, 1920).

sociocultural factors Social identity and other background factors, such as gender, ethnicity, social class, and culture.

culture The accumulation of values, rules of behavior, forms of expression, religious beliefs, occupational choices, and the like for a group of people who share a common language and environment.

African American women or to people in Greece, Korea, Argentina, or Egypt? Not always. These and many other aspects of behavior and mental processes are affected by **sociocultural factors**, including people's gender, ethnicity, social class, and the culture in which they grow up. These variables create many significant differences in behavior and mental processes, especially from one culture to another (e.g., Shiraev & Levy, 2010).

Culture has been defined as the accumulation of values, rules of behavior, forms of expression, religious beliefs, occupational choices, and the like for a group of people who share a common language and environment (Fiske et al., 1998). Culture is an organizing and stabilizing influence. It encourages or discourages particular behaviors and thoughts; it also allows people to understand and know what to expect from others in that culture. It is a kind of group adaptation, passed along by tradition and example rather than by genes from one generation to the next (Castro & Toro, 2004). Culture determines, for example, whether children's education will focus on skill at hunting or reading, how close people stand during a conversation, and whether or not they form lines in public places. Psychologists and anthropologists have found that cultures can differ in many ways (Cohen, 2009). They may have strict or loose rules governing social behavior. They might place great value on achievement or on self-awareness. Some seek dominance over nature; others seek harmony with it. Time is of great importance in some cultures but not in others. Psychologists have tended to focus on the differences between cultures that can best be described as individualist or collectivist (Triandis & Trafimow, 2001). As shown in Table 1.4, many people in *individualist* cultures, such as those typical of North America and western Europe, tend to value personal rather than group goals and achievement. Competitiveness to distinguish oneself from others is common in these cultures, as is a sense of isolation. By contrast, many people in *collectivist* cultures, such as Japan, tend to think of themselves mainly as part of their families or work groups. Cooperative effort aimed at advancing the welfare of these social units is highly valued, and although loneliness is seldom a problem, fear of rejection by the family or other group is common. Many aspects of U.S. culture—from self-reliant cowboy heroes and bonuses for "top" employees to the invitation to "help yourself" at a buffet table—reflect its tendency toward an individualist orientation (see Table 1.5).

TABLE 1.4   Some Characteristics of Behavior and Mental Processes Typical of Individualist vs. Collectivist Cultures

Psychologists and anthropologists have noticed that cultures can create certain general tendencies in behavior and mental processes among the people living in them (Bhagat et al., 2002). As shown here, individualist cultures tend to support the idea of placing one's personal goals before the goals of the extended family or work group, whereas collectivist cultures tend to encourage putting the goals of those groups ahead of personal goals. Remember, however, that these labels represent very rough categories. Cultures cannot be pigeonholed as being either entirely individualist or entirely collectivist, and not everyone raised in a particular culture always thinks or acts in exactly the same way (Na et al., 2010).

Variable	Individualist	Collectivist
Personal identity	Separate from others	Connected to others
Major goals	Self-defined; be unique; realize your personal potential; compete with others	Defined by others; belong; occupy your proper place; meet your obligations to others; be like others
Criteria for self-esteem	Ability to express unique aspects of the self; self-assurance	Ability to restrain the self and be part of a social unit; modesty
Sources of success and failure	Success comes from personal effort; failure is caused by external factors	Success is due to help from others; failure is due to personal faults
Major frame of reference	Personal attitudes, traits, and goals	Family, work group

TABLE 1.5 Cultural Values in Advertising

TRY THIS The statements listed here appeared in advertisements in Korea and the United States. Those from Korea reflect collectivist values, whereas those from the United States emphasize a more individualist orientation (Han & Shavitt, 1994). See if you can tell which are which; then check the bottom of page 28 for the answers. To follow up on this exercise, try identifying cultural values in ads you see in newspapers and magazines, as well as on billboards and television. By surfing the Internet or scanning international newspapers online, you can compare the values conveyed by ads in your culture with those in ads from other cultures.

1. "She's got a style all her own."
2. "You, only better."
3. "A more exhilarating way to provide for your family."
4. "We have a way of bringing people closer together."
5. "Celebrating a half-century of partnership."
6. "How to protect the most personal part of the environment: Your skin."
7. "Our family agrees with this selection of home furnishings."
8. "A leader among leaders."
9. "Make your way through the crowd."
10. "Your business success: Harmonizing with [company name]."

Source: Brehm, Kassin, & Fein (2005).

A culture is often associated with a particular country, but most countries are actually *multicultural;* in other words, they host many *subcultures* within their borders. Often these subcultures are formed by people of various ethnic origins. The population of the United States, for instance, includes African Americans, Hispanic Americans, Asian Americans, and American Indians, as well as European Americans whose families came from Italy, France, Germany, Britain, Poland, Brazil, and many other places. In each of these groups, the individuals who identify with their cultural heritage tend to share behaviors, values, and beliefs based on their culture of origin, thus forming a *subculture.*

Like fish unaware of the water in which they are immersed, people often fail to notice how their culture or subculture has shaped their thinking and behavior until they come in contact with people whose culture or subculture has shaped different patterns. Consider hand gestures, for example. The "thumbs up" sign means that "everything is OK" to people in North America and Europe but is considered a rude gesture in Australia, Nigeria, and Bangladesh. And although in North America, making eye contact during social introductions is usually seen as a sign of interest or sincerity, it is likely to be considered rude in Japan. Even some of the misunderstandings that occur between men and women in the same culture can be traced to slight

The Impact of Culture

Culture helps shape almost every aspect of our behavior and mental processes, from how we dress to how we think to what we believe is important. Because we grow up immersed in our culture, we may be unaware of its influence on our own thoughts and actions until—like these young women who emigrated from Africa to Denmark—we encounter people whose culture has shaped them in different ways.

© Francis Dean/The Image Works

culturally influenced differences in their communication styles (Tannen, 2001). In the United States, for example, women's efforts to connect with others by talking are perceived by some men as "pointless" unless the discussion is aimed at solving a specific problem. As a result, women may feel frustrated and misunderstood by men who offer well-intentioned but unwanted advice instead of conversation.

For decades, the impact of culture on behavior and mental processes was of concern mainly to a relatively small group of researchers working in *cross-cultural psychology*. In the chapters to come, however, you will see that psychologists in almost every subfield are now looking at how ethnicity, gender, age, and many other sociocultural variables can influence behavior and mental processes. In short, psychology is striving to be the science of *all* behavior and mental processes, not just of those in the cultures where it began.

SUMMARY

Psychology is the science that seeks to understand behavior and mental processes and to apply that understanding in the service of human welfare.

The World of Psychology: An Overview

The concept of "behavior and mental processes" is a broad one, encompassing virtually all aspects of what it means to be a human being. Some psychologists study and seek to alleviate the problems that can plague human life, while those working in *positive psychology* focus their attention on understanding happiness, optimism, human strengths, and the like.

Subfields of Psychology

Because the subject matter of psychology is so diverse, most psychologists work in particular subfields within the discipline. For example, *biological psychologists*, also called physiological psychologists, study topics such as the role played by the brain in regulating normal and disordered behavior. *Cognitive psychologists*, some of whom prefer to be called experimental psychologists, focus on basic psychological processes such as learning, memory, and perception; they also study judgment, decision making, and problem solving. *Engineering psychology*, the study of human factors in the use of equipment, helps designers create better versions of that equipment. *Developmental psychologists* specialize in trying to understand the development of behavior and mental

processes over a lifetime. *Personality psychologists* focus on characteristics that set people apart from one another and by which they can be compared. *Clinical psychologists* and *counseling psychologists* provide direct service to troubled people and conduct research on abnormal behavior. *Community psychologists* work to prevent mental disorders and to extend mental health services to those who need them. *Health psychologists* study the relationship between behavior and health and help promote healthy lifestyles. *Educational psychologists* conduct and apply research on teaching and learning, whereas *school psychologists* specialize in assessing and alleviating children's academic problems. *Social psychologists* examine questions regarding how people influence one another. *Industrial and organizational psychologists* study ways to increase efficiency and productivity in the workplace. *Quantitative psychologists* develop ways to analyze research data from all subfields. *Sport psychologists*, *forensic psychologists*, and environmental psychologists exemplify some of psychology's many other subfields.

Linkages Within Psychology and Beyond

Psychologists often work in more than one subfield and usually share knowledge with colleagues in many subfields. Psychologists also draw on and contribute to knowledge in other disciplines, such as computer science, economics, and law.

Research: The Foundation of Psychology

Psychologists use the methods of science to conduct research. This means that they perform experiments and use other scientific procedures to systematically gather and analyze information about psychological phenomena.

A Brief History of Psychology

The founding of modern psychology is usually marked as 1879, when Wilhelm Wundt established the first psychology research laboratory. Wundt studied consciousness in a manner that was expanded by Edward Titchener into an approach he called *structuralism*. It was in the late 1800s, too, that Sigmund Freud, in Vienna, began his study of the unconscious, while in the United States, William James took the functionalist approach, suggesting that psychologists should study how consciousness helps us adapt to our environments. In 1913, John B. Watson founded *behaviorism*, arguing that to be scientific, psychologists should study only the behavior they can see, not private mental events. Behaviorism dominated psychology for decades, but psychologists are once again studying consciousness in the form of cognitive processes.

Approaches to the Science of Psychology

Psychologists differ in their approaches to psychology—that is, in their assumptions, questions, and research methods. Some adopt just one approach; most combine features of two or more approaches. Those adopting a *biological approach* focus on how physiological processes shape behavior and mental processes. Psychologists who prefer the *evolutionary approach* emphasize the inherited, adaptive aspects of behavior and mental processes. In the *psychodynamic approach*, behavior and mental processes are seen as reflecting struggles to resolve conflicts between raw impulses and the social rules that limit the expression of those impulses. Psychologists who take the *behavioral approach* view behavior as determined primarily by learning based on experiences with

rewards and punishments. The *cognitive approach* assumes that behavior can be understood through analysis of the basic mental processes that underlie it. To those adopting the *humanistic approach*, behavior is controlled by the decisions that people make about their lives based on their perceptions of the world.

Human Diversity and Psychology

Psychologists are diverse in their backgrounds and in their activities. Most of the prominent figures in psychology's early history were white males,

but women and people of color made important contributions from the start and continue to do so.

The Impact of Sociocultural Diversity on Psychology

Psychologists are increasingly taking into account the influence of culture and other sociocultural variables such as gender and ethnicity in shaping human behavior and mental processes.

LINKAGES TO FURTHER LEARNING

Now that you have finished reading this chapter, how about exploring some of the topics and information that you found most interesting? Here are some places to start.

Books

Ludy T. Benjamin and D. B. Baker, *From Seance to Science: A History of the Profession of Psychology in America* (Wadsworth, 2004). The development of clinical, counseling, school, and industrial and organizational psychology.

Alan M. Goldstein (Ed.), *Forensic Psychology* (Wiley, 2006). An overview of the role of psychological science in the legal system.
Paul Bell, *Environmental Psychology* (Wadsworth, 2001). Applications of psychology to solving problems in natural and artificial environments, including college campuses.

On the Internet

 Access an integrated eBook and chapter-specific learning tools including flashcards, quizzes, videos, and more. Go to CengageBrain.com.

Want to maximize the value of your online study time? Take this easy-to-use study system's diagnostic pre-test, and it will create a personalized study plan for you. By helping you identify the topics that you need to understand better and then directing you to valuable online resources, it can speed up your chapter review. CengageNOW even provides a post-test so you can confirm that you are ready for an exam. Go to CengageBrain.com.

TALKING POINTS

When they discover that you are taking a psychology course, family and friends tend to want to know what you are learning about (and they might worry that you will "analyze" them!). It can be tough to give a short answer, so here are a few talking points to help you summarize this chapter without giving a lecture (we'll offer others for each chapter to come).

1. Psychology is the science that explores behavior and mental processes.

2. Psychologists' research is widely applied in the service of human welfare.
3. Clinical psychology is the most famous subfield, but psychology also includes a wide range of other subfields.
4. Psychologists have Ph.D. or master's degrees in psychology; psychiatrists have medical degrees.
5. Some psychologists study human problems; others focus on learning about human strengths.

6. Scientific psychology began in the late 1800s in a psychological research laboratory in Germany.
7. Sigmund Freud was a medical doctor, not a psychologist.
8. Some kinds of behavior and thinking are the same for everyone, everywhere; others are influenced by people's gender, ethnicity, and cultural background.

Answer key for Table 1.5: U.S. ads are numbers 1, 2, 6, 8, and 9.

2

Research in Psychology

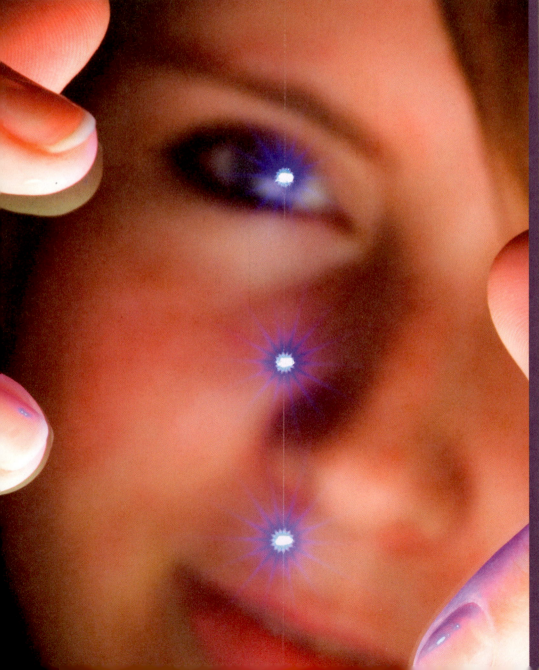

Our goal in this chapter is to describe the research methods psychologists use to help answer their questions about behavior and mental processes. *We will also describe the critical thinking processes that help psychologists form those questions and make sense of research results.*

Francine Shapiro, a clinical psychologist in California, had an odd experience one day back in 1987. She was taking a walk and thinking about some distressing events when she noticed that her emotional reaction to them was fading away (Shapiro, 1989b). In trying to figure out why this should be, she realized that she had been moving her eyes from side to side. Could these eye movements have caused the change in her emotions? To test this possibility, she made more deliberate eye movements and found that the emotion-reducing effect was even stronger. Would the same thing happen to others? Curious, she first tested the effects of side-to-side eye movements with friends and colleagues and then with clients who had suffered traumatic experiences such as sexual abuse, military combat, or rape. She asked these people to think about unpleasant experiences in their lives while keeping their eyes on her finger as she moved it rapidly back and forth in front of them. Like her, they found that during and after these eye movement sessions, their reactions to unpleasant thoughts faded away. They also reported that their emotional flashbacks, nightmares, fears, and other trauma-related problems decreased dramatically, often after only one session (Shapiro, 1989b).

Based on the success of these cases, Shapiro developed a treatment method she calls *eye movement desensitization and reprocessing*, or EMDR (Leeds, 2009; Shapiro, 1991, 2001; Shapiro & Forrest, 2004). She and her associates have trained more than 30,000 therapists in fifty-two countries to use EMDR in the treatment of an ever-widening range of anxiety-related problems in adults and children, from phobias and posttraumatic stress disorder to marital conflicts and skin rashes (e.g., Adúriz, Bluthgen, & Knopfler, 2009; Bloomgarden & Calogero, 2008; Cvetek, 2008; Gauvreau & Bouchard, 2008; Hase, Schallmayer, & Sack, 2008; Konuk et al., 2006; Lawson, 2004; Manfield & Shapiro, 2004; Marcus, 2008; Phillips et al., 2009; Rodenburg et al., 2009; Russell et al., 2007; Shapiro, 2005).

Suppose you had an anxiety-related problem. Would the growth of EMDR be enough to convince you to try this treatment? If not, what would you want to know about EMDR before deciding? As a cautious person, you would probably ask some of the same questions that have occurred to many scientists in psychology: Are the effects of EMDR caused by the treatment itself or by the faith that clients might have in any new and impressive treatment? And are EMDR's effects faster, stronger, and longer lasting than those of other treatments?

Raising tough questions about cause and effect, quality, and value is part of the process of *critical thinking*. Whether you are choosing a therapy method or an Internet provider, a college or a computer, a political candidate or a cell phone plan, critical thinking can guide you to ask the kinds of questions that lead to informed decisions. But asking good questions is not enough; you also have to try answering them. Critical thinking helps here, too, by prompting you to do some research on each of your options. For most people, this means asking the advice of friends or relatives, reading *Consumer Reports*, surfing the Internet, studying a candidate's background, or the like. For psychologists, research means using scientific methods to gather information about behavior and mental processes.

In this chapter, we summarize five questions that emerge when thinking critically about behavior and mental processes. Then we describe the scientific methods psychologists use in their research and show how some of those methods have been applied in evaluating EMDR.

Thinking Critically About Psychology (or Anything Else)

TRY THIS   Ask several friends and relatives if mental patients become more agitated when the moon is full, if psychics help the police solve crimes, and if people have suddenly burst into flames for no apparent reason. They will probably agree with at least one of these statements, even though not one of them is true (see Table 2.1). Perhaps you already knew that all the statements are myths, but don't feel too smug. At one time or another, we all accept things we are told simply because the information seems to come from a reliable source or because "everyone knows" it is true (Losh et al., 2003). If this were not the case, advertisers, politicians, salespeople, social activists, and others who seek our money, our votes, or our loyalty would not be as successful

TABLE 2.1   Some Popular Myths

Many people believe in the statements listed here, but critical thinkers who take the time to investigate them will discover that they are not true.

Myth	Fact
Many children are injured each year in the United States when razor blades, needles, or poison is put in Halloween candy.	Reported cases are rare, most turn out to be hoaxes, and in the only documented case of a child dying from poisoned candy, the culprit was the child's own parent (Brunvald, 1989).
If your roommate commits suicide during the school term, you automatically get A's in all your classes for that term.	No college or university anywhere has ever had such a rule.
People have been known to burst into flames and die from fire erupting within their own bodies.	In rare cases, humans have been consumed by fires that caused little or no damage to the surrounding area, but every alleged case of "spontaneous human combustion" has been traced to an external source of ignition (Benecke, 1999; Nienhuys, 2001; Weir, 2003).
Most big-city police departments rely on the advice of psychics to help them solve murders, kidnappings, and missing persons cases.	Only about 35 percent of urban police departments ever seek psychics' advice, and that advice is virtually never more helpful than other means of investigation (Nickell, 1997; Radford, 2006; Wiseman, West, & Stemman, 1996).
Murders, suicides, animal bites, and episodes of mental disorder are more likely to occur when the moon is full.	Records of crimes, dog bites, and mental hospital admissions do not support this common belief (Bickis, Kelly, & Byrnes, 1995; Biermann et al., 2009; Chapman & Morrell, 2000).
You can't fool a lie detector.	Lie detectors can be helpful in solving crimes, but they are not perfect; their results can free a guilty person or send an innocent person to jail (see the chapter on motivation and emotion).
Viewers never see David Letterman walking to his desk after the opening monologue because his contract prohibits him from showing his backside on TV.	When questioned about this story on the air, Letterman denied it and, to prove his point, lifted his jacket and turned a full circle in front of the cameras and studio audience (Brunvald, 1989).
Psychics have special abilities to see into the future.	An Internet search will show you that even the most famous psychics are almost always wrong, as in these predictions for 2009: "Five major hurricanes will make landfall in the United States"; "The New York Giants will win the Super Bowl"; "The Golden Gate Bridge will collapse"; "Oprah Winfrey will become an ordained minister." No psychic's 2001 predictions included the September 11 terrorist attacks. When psychics do appear to be correct, it is usually because their forecasts are either vague ("Something tragic will happen in the United States"; "The stock market will go up and down") or easy to predict without special powers ("Terrorism will continue to threaten American soil"; "The Middle East will remain unstable").
If you are stopped for drunken driving, sucking on a penny will cause a police Breathalyzer test to show you are sober.	This is not true, nor can Breathalyzers be fooled by sucking on a nickel or a mint or by eating garlic, peanuts, curry powder, or vitamin C tablets (D. Emery, 2004).

Uncritically accepting claims for the value of astrologers' predictions, get-rich-quick investment schemes, new therapies, or proposed government policies can be embarrassing, expensive, and dangerous. Critical thinkers carefully evaluate evidence for and against such claims before drawing a final conclusion.

DOONESBURY

"Doonesbury" © 1997 G. B. Trudeau. Reprinted with permission of Universal Uclick. All rights reserved.

as they are. These people want you to believe their promises or claims without careful thought. In other words, they don't want you to think critically.

They often get their wish. Millions of people around the world waste untold amounts of money every year on worthless predictions by online and telephone "psychics"; on bogus cures for cancer, heart disease, and arthritis; on phony degrees offered by nonexistent Internet "universities"; and on "miracle" defrosting trays, eat-all-you-want weight loss pills, "effortless" exercise gadgets, and other consumer products that simply don't work. Millions more lose money to investment scams and fraudulent charity appeals (Cassel & Bernstein, 2007).

Critical thinking is the process of assessing claims and making judgments on the basis of well-supported evidence (Wade, 1988). One way to apply critical thinking to EMDR—or to any other topic—is by asking these five questions:

1. *What am I being asked to believe or accept?* In this case, the assertion to be examined is that EMDR reduces or eliminates anxiety-related problems.

2. *What evidence is available to support the assertion?* Francine Shapiro experienced a reduction in her own emotional distress following certain kinds of eye movements. Later, she found the same effect in others.

3. *Are there alternative ways of interpreting the evidence?* The dramatic effects reported by Shapiro might not have been due to EMDR but to people's desire to overcome their problems or perhaps their desire to prove her right. And who knows? They might eventually have improved without any treatment. Even the most remarkable evidence can't automatically be accepted as proof of an assertion until other plausible alternatives have been ruled out. The ruling-out process leads to the next step in critical thinking: conducting scientific research.

4. *What additional evidence would help evaluate the alternatives?* An ideal method for collecting further evidence about the value of EMDR would be to identify three groups of people who not only suffered anxiety-related problems of the same kind and intensity but also were alike in every other way except for the anxiety treatment they received. One group would receive EMDR, a second group would get an equally impressive but useless treatment, and a third group would get no treatment at all. Now suppose that the people in the EMDR group improved much more than those who got no treatment or the impressive but useless treatment. Results such as these would make it harder to explain away the improvements following EMDR as due to client motivation or the mere passage of time.

5. *What conclusions are most reasonable?* The research evidence collected so far has not yet ruled out alternative explanations for the effects of EMDR (e.g., Goldstein et al., 2000; Hertlein & Ricci, 2004; Hughes, 2006; Lohr et al., 2003). And although those effects are often greater than the effects of no treatment at all, they appear to be no stronger than those of several other kinds

critical thinking The process of assessing claims and making judgments on the basis of well-supported evidence.

Taking Your Life in Your Hands?

Does exposure to microwave radiation from cell phone antennas cause brain tumors? Do the dangers of hormone replacement therapy (HRT) for postmenopausal women outweigh its benefits? And what about the value of herbal remedies, dietary supplements, and other controversial treatments for cancer, AIDS, and depression? These questions generate intense speculation, strong opinions, and a lot of wishful thinking, but the answers ultimately depend on scientific research based on critical thinking. So even though there is no conclusive evidence that cell phones cause tumors (Christensen et al., 2005; Hepworth et al., 2006; Schoemaker et al., 2005)—and some scientists say that the physics of cell phone emissions make this impossible (Lakshmikumar, 2009)—others have offered evidence to suggest that there may be danger in long-term exposure (Cardis et al., 2009; Manti et al., 2008; Sadetzki et al., 2008; Vijayalaxmi, 2008), and research continues. Evidence that HRT may be related to breast cancer and heart disease led to the cancellation of a large clinical trial in the United States (Kolata, 2003) and a decrease in the use of certain kinds of HRT (Chlebowski et al., 2009; Heiss et al., 2008).

© Jack Hollingsworth/Getty Images

of treatment (e.g., Bériault & Larivée, 2005; Bradley et al., 2005; Cvetek, 2008; Lilienfeld & Arkowitz, 2007; Wanders, Serra, & de Jongh, 2008). So the only reasonable conclusions to be drawn at this point are that EMDR remains a controversial treatment, it seems to benefit some clients, and further research is needed in order to understand it.

Do these conclusions sound inconclusive? Critical thinking sometimes does seem to be indecisive thinking. Like the rest of us, scientists in psychology would love to find quick, clear, and final answers to their questions, but to have scientific value, the conclusions they reach must be supported by evidence. So if the evidence about EMDR is limited in some way, conclusions about whether and why the treatment works have to be limited too. In the long run, though, critical thinking opens the way to understanding. To help you sharpen your own critical thinking skills, we include in each chapter to come a section called "Thinking Critically" in which we examine a particularly interesting issue in psychology by asking the same five questions we raised here about EMDR.

Critical Thinking and Scientific Research

Scientific research often begins with questions born of curiosity, such as "Can eye movements reduce anxiety?" Like many seemingly simple questions, this one is more complex than it first appears. How rapid are the eye movements? How long do they continue in each session, and how many sessions should there be? What kind of anxiety is to be treated, and how will we measure improvement? In other words, scientists have to ask *specific* questions in order to get meaningful answers.

Psychologists and other scientists clarify their questions about behavior and mental processes by phrasing them in terms of a **hypothesis**—a specific, testable proposition about something they want to study. Hypotheses are precise, clearly worded statements that describe what researchers think may be true and how they will know if it is not. A hypothesis about EMDR might be "EMDR treatment causes significant reduction in anxiety." To make it easier to understand and evaluate their hypotheses, scientists employ **operational definitions**, which are descriptions of the exact operations or methods they will use in their research. In relation to our EMDR hypothesis, for example, "EMDR treatment" might be operationally defined as creating

hypothesis In scientific research, a specific, testable proposition about a phenomenon.

operational definition A statement that defines the exact operations or methods used in research.

I Love It!

When we want something—or someone—to be perfect, we may ignore all evidence to the contrary. This is one reason why people end up in faulty used cars—or in bad relationships. Psychologists and other scientists use special procedures, such as the double-blind methods described later in this chapter, to help keep confirmation bias from distorting the conclusions they draw from research evidence.

© Mason Morfit/Taxi/Getty Images

a certain number of side-to-side eye movements per second for a particular period of time. And "significant reduction in anxiety" might be operationally defined as a decline of at least 10 points on a test that measures anxiety. The kind of treatment a client is given (say, EMDR versus no treatment) and the results of that treatment (the amount of anxiety reduction observed) are examples of research **variables**, the specific factors or characteristics that are manipulated and measured in research.

To determine whether a study's results provide support for a hypothesis, researchers look at the numbers or scores that represent client improvement or whatever other variables are of interest. This kind of evidence is called **data** (the plural of *datum*), or a *data set*. The data themselves are objective, and scientists try to be objective when interpreting them. But like all human beings, scientists may sometimes pay a little more attention to numbers or scores that confirm their hypotheses, especially if they expect or hope that those hypotheses are true. (We describe this *confirmation bias* in the chapter on cognition and language.) Scientists have a special responsibility to combat confirmation bias by looking for evidence that contradicts their hypotheses, not just for evidence that supports them.

Scientists must also consider the value of the evidence they collect. They usually do this by evaluating its statistical reliability and validity. **Statistical reliability** (usually just called **reliability**) is the degree to which the data are stable and consistent. The **statistical validity** (usually just called **validity**) of data is the degree to which they accurately represent the topic being studied. For example, the first evidence for EMDR was based on Francine Shapiro's own experience with eye movements. If she had not been able to consistently repeat, or *replicate*, those initial effects in other people, she would have had to question the reliability of her data. And if her clients' reports of reduced anxiety were not supported by, say, their overt behavior or the reports of their close relatives, she would have had to doubt the validity of her data.

The Role of Theories

After examining research evidence, scientists may begin to favor certain explanations as to why particular results occurred. Sometimes they organize their explanations into a **theory**, which is a set of statements designed to account for, predict, and even

variable A factor or characteristic that is manipulated or measured in research.

data Numbers that represent research findings and provide the basis for research conclusions.

statistical reliability (reliability) The degree to which test results or other research evidence occurs repeatedly.

statistical validity (validity) The degree to which evidence from a test or other research method measures what it is supposed to measure.

theory An integrated set of propositions that can be used to account for, predict, and even suggest ways of controlling certain phenomena.

© Keith Brofsky/Getty Images

Theories of Prejudice

It is all too easy these days to spot evidence of prejudice against almost any identifiable group, including Muslims, Jews, Protestants, Catholics, blacks, Hispanics, Asians, gays and lesbians, and even teenagers and the elderly. But why does prejudice occur? The chapter on social cognition describes several theories that researchers have proposed to explain the causes of prejudice and how to prevent it. The testing of these theories is an example of how theory and research go hand in hand. Without research results, there would be nothing to explain; without explanatory theories, the results might never be organized in a useful way. The knowledge generated by psychologists over the past century and a half has been based on this constant interaction of theory and research.

suggest ways of controlling certain phenomena. Shapiro's theory about the effects of EMDR suggests that eye movements activate parts of the brain in which information about trauma or other unpleasant experiences has been stored but never fully processed. EMDR, she says, promotes the "adaptive information processing" required for the elimination of certain anxiety-related emotional and behavioral problems (Leeds, 2009; Shapiro & Forrest, 2004). Others (e.g., Lee, Taylor, & Drummond, 2006) suggest that EMDR may help troubled people think about stressful material in a more detached, less emotional way, perhaps as in a dream (Elofsson et al., 2008). In the chapter on introducing psychology, we review broader and more famous examples of explanatory theories, including Charles Darwin's theory of evolution and Sigmund Freud's theory of psychoanalysis.

Because they are only tentative explanations, theories must be subjected to scientific examination based on critical thinking. So although theories may be based on research results, they also generate hypotheses to be tested in further research. The predictions of one psychologist's theory will be evaluated by many other psychologists. If research does not support a theory, that theory will be revised or abandoned.

The process of creating, evaluating, and revising psychological theories does not always lead to a single "winner." You will discover in later chapters that there are several competing explanations for color vision, memory, sleep, aggression, eating disorders, and many other behaviors and mental processes. As research on these topics continues, explanations become more complete, and sometimes they change. So the conclusions we offer are always based on what is known so far, and we always cite the need for additional research. We do this because research usually raises at least as many questions as it answers. The results of one study might not apply to every situation or to all people. A treatment might be effective for mild depression in women, but it would have to be tested in more severe cases and with both sexes before drawing final conclusions about the full extent of its value. Keep this point in mind the next time you hear a talk show guest confidently offering simple solutions to complex problems such as obesity or anxiety or presenting easy formulas for a happy marriage and perfect children. These self-proclaimed experts—called "pop" (for *popular*) psychologists by the scientific community—tend to oversimplify issues, to cite evidence for their views without concern for its reliability or validity, and to ignore good evidence that contradicts their pet theories.

Psychological scientists have to be more cautious, often delaying final judgments about behavior and mental processes until they have collected better evidence. In evaluating theories and deciding among conclusions, they are guided not only by the research methods described in the next section but also by the *law of parsimony* (also known as *simplicity*), sometimes referred to by nonscientists as KISS ("Keep it simple, stupid"). The principle of parsimony is based on experience in the long history of science. It suggests that when several alternative conclusions or several competing theories offer nearly equally convincing explanations of something, the correct explanation tends to be the simplest. Throughout this book, you will see examples of how the parsimony principle has helped psychological scientists sift and refine explanatory theories in search of the ones that offer the simplest yet fullest understanding of behavior and mental processes.

You will also see that research in psychology has created an enormous body of knowledge that is being put to good use in many ways. Let's now look at the scientific methods that psychologists use in their research and at some of the pitfalls that lie in their path.

Research Methods in Psychology

Like other scientists, psychologists strive to achieve four main goals in their research: to *describe* behavior and mental processes, to make accurate *predictions* about them, to demonstrate some *control* over them, and ultimately to *explain* how and why behavior and mental processes occur. Consider depression, for example.

Researchers in clinical psychology and other subfields have been involved in *describing* the nature, intensity, and duration of depressive symptoms, as well as the various kinds of depressive disorders that commonly appear in various cultures around the world. They are also studying the genetic characteristics, personality traits, life situations, and other factors that allow better *predictions* about those who are at the greatest risk for developing depressive disorders. In addition, clinical researchers have developed and tested a whole range of treatments designed to *control* depressive symptoms and even to prevent them. Finally, they have proposed a number of theories to *explain* depression, including why and how it occurs, why it is more common in women than in men, and why particular treatment methods are (or are not) likely to be effective.

Certain research methods are especially useful for reaching certain of these goals. Psychologists tend to use *naturalistic observation*, *case studies*, *surveys*, and *correlational studies* to describe and predict behavior and mental processes. They use *experiments* to control and explain behavior and mental processes. For example, Francine Shapiro initially used naturalistic observation to describe the effects of eye movements on her emotional state. She then conducted case studies to test her prediction that if the change in her emotions had something to do with eye movements, the same effects should occur in other people. Later we discuss an experiment in which she tried to more systematically control people's emotional reactions and to evaluate various explanations for EMDR's apparent effects. Let's take a closer look at how psychologists use these and other scientific research methods as they seek to describe, predict, control, and explain many kinds of behavior and mental processes.

Observational Methods: Watching Behavior

Sometimes the best way to describe behavior is through **observational methods** such as **naturalistic observation**, which is the process of watching without interfering as behavior occurs in the natural environment (Hoyle, Harris, & Judd, 2002). This method is especially valuable when more intrusive methods might alter the behavior you want to study or create false impressions about it. Suppose you wanted to know about people's exercise habits. You could ask them to keep track of how often they work out, but your request might prompt them to exercise more than usual, thus creating an inaccurate picture of their typical behavior.

With proper permission, psychologists can observe people in many kinds of situations. For example, much of what we know about gender differences in how children play and communicate with each other has come from observations in classrooms and playgrounds. Live or videotaped observations of adults as they work on together on a task, talk about current events, or discuss problems in their relationships have provided valuable insights into friendships, couple communication patterns, and even responses to terrorism (e.g., Mehl & Pennebaker, 2003). And to understand the problems people encounter in doing their jobs, human factors psychologists often find it helpful to observe employees as they work.

Although naturalistic observation can provide large amounts of useful research evidence, it is not problem free. For one thing, if people know they are being observed (and research ethics usually require that they do know), they tend to act differently than they otherwise would. Researchers usually combat this problem by observing long enough for participants to get used to the situation and begin behaving more naturally. Observational data can also be distorted if the observers expect to see certain behaviors. Suppose you were hired to watch videos of people who had just participated in a study of EMDR. Your job is to rate how anxious they appear to be, but if you knew which participants had received EMDR and which had not, you might tend to see the treated participants as less anxious, no matter how they actually behave. To get the most out of naturalistic observation, psychologists have to counteract problems such as these. So when conducting observational evaluations of treatment, for example, they don't tell the observers which participants have received treatment.

observational methods Procedures for systematically watching behavior in order to summarize it for scientific analysis.

naturalistic observation The process of watching without interfering as a phenomenon occurs in the natural environment.

Little Reminders

If you asked this person what she needs to use various computer programs efficiently, she might not think to mention the notes on her monitor that list all her log-in names and passwords. Accordingly, researchers in human factors and industrial and organizational psychology usually arrange to watch employees at work rather than just ask them what they do, how they do it, and how they interact with machines and fellow employees. Other researchers are studying the shape of social networks by getting permission to examine cell phone records to see whom people call and text and how often (Eagle, Pentland, & Lazer, 2009).

© Ausloeser/Corbis

Case Studies: Taking a Closer Look

Observations are often an important part of **case studies**, which are intensive examinations of behavior or mental processes in a particular individual, group, or situation. Case studies can also include tests, interviews, and the analysis of letters, school transcripts, or other written records. Case studies are especially useful when studying something that is new, complex, or relatively rare. Shapiro's EMDR treatment, for example, first attracted psychologists' attention through case studies of its apparently remarkable effects on her clients.

In fact, case studies have a long tradition in clinical work. Freud's theory of psychoanalysis was largely developed from case studies of people whose paralysis or other physical symptoms disappeared when they were hypnotized or asleep. Case studies have

Translating Naturalistic Observation into Data

TRY THIS It is easy to observe people in natural situations, but it is not so easy to translate observations into a form that accurately captures what happened. Untrained observers might use different words to describe the same behaviors, or they might be biased by the age, gender, or ethnicity of those whom they are observing (Harvey et al., 2009). To make the translation process easier and more consistent, psychologists use coding systems that help observers decide how to categorize the various kinds of behavior that they might see. Imagine that you are studying these children at play. Try creating your own coding system by making a list of the exact behaviors that you would count as "aggressive," "shy," "fearful," "cooperative," and "competitive."

© David Young-Wolff/PhotoEdit

Learning from Rare Cases

Dustin Hoffman's character in *Rain Man* was based on the case of "Joseph," a man with autistic disorder who can, for example, mentally multiply or divide six-digit numbers. Other case studies have described autistic *savants* who can correctly identify the day of the week for any date in the past or the future or tell at a glance that, say, exactly 125 paper clips are scattered on the floor. By carefully studying such rare cases, cognitive psychologists are learning more about human mental capacities and how they might be maximized in everyone (Biever, 2009; Geddes, 2008).

Everett Collection

also played a special role in **neuropsychology**, the study of the relationships among brain activity, thinking, and behavior. Consider the case of Dr. P., a patient described by the neurologist Oliver Sacks (1985). A distinguished musician with superior intelligence, Dr. P. began to display odd symptoms, such as the inability to recognize familiar people or to distinguish between people and objects. During a visit to Sacks's office, Dr. P. mistook his foot for his shoe. When he rose to leave, he tried to lift off his wife's head and put it on his own as if it were a hat. He could not name common objects when he looked at them, although he could describe them. When handed a glove, for example, he said, "A continuous surface, infolded on itself. It appears to have . . . five outpouchings, if this is the word. . . . A container of some sort." Only later, when he put it on his hand, did he exclaim, "My God, it's a glove!" (Sacks, 1985, p. 13). Case studies such as this one have helped pioneers in neuropsychology describe the difficulties suffered by people with particular kinds of brain damage or disease. Eventually, neuropsychologists were able to tie specific disorders to certain types of injuries, tumors, poisons, and other causes (Banich, 2004). (Dr. P.'s symptoms may have been caused by a large brain tumor.)

Case studies are also used by industrial and organizational (I/O) psychologists. For example, an I/O psychologist might review documents, make observations, and conduct interviews with an employee team in order to understand how its members handled a production problem, an interpersonal conflict, or a change in company policy (May, 2006). Such case studies would then help guide the psychologist's recommendations for how company executives might increase productivity, reduce stress, or improve communication with employees.

Case studies do have their limitations, however. They may contain only the evidence that a particular researcher considered important (Loftus & Guyer, 2002), and, of course, they are unlikely to be representative of people in general. Nonetheless, case studies can provide valuable raw material for further research. They can also be vital sources of information about particular people, and they serve as the testing ground for new treatments, training programs, and other applications of research.

Surveys: Looking at the Big Picture

In contrast to the individual close-ups provided by case studies, surveys provide wide-angle views of large groups. In **surveys**, researchers use interviews or questionnaires to ask people about their behavior, attitudes, beliefs, opinions, or intentions.

case study A research method involving the intensive examination of some phenomenon in a particular individual, group, or situation.

neuropsychology The study of the relationships among brain activity, thinking, and behavior.

survey A research method that involves giving people questionnaires or special interviews designed to obtain descriptions of their attitudes, beliefs, opinions, and intentions.

Designing Survey Research

How do people feel about whether gay men and lesbians should have the right to legally marry? To appreciate the difficulties of survey research, try writing a question about this issue that you think is clear enough and neutral enough to generate valid data. Then ask some friends whether or not they agree it would be a good survey question and why.

Just as politicians and advertisers rely on opinion polls to test the popularity of policies or products, psychologists use surveys—conducted in person, through the mail, or online—to gather descriptive data on just about anything related to behavior and mental processes, from parenting practices to sexual behavior.

The validity of survey data depends partly on whether the wording is clear and how questions are phrased (Bhopal et al., 2004). For example, a recent survey in New Zealand asked registered voters what they thought about a law in that country that prohibits parents from spanking their children (the term for it there is "smacking"). Responses indicated that 87.6 percent of the respondents favored eliminating the law; only 11.8 favored keeping it; the rest were undecided (Associated Press, 2009). However, the survey question was written by opponents of the antispanking law and read as follows: "Should a smack as part of good parental correction be a criminal offense in New Zealand?" Supporters of the law argued that the overwhelming number of "no" votes was influenced by the wording of the survey question, which included a justification for spanking and implied that parents could be jailed for doing it. Indeed, the results might have differed if the question had read "Do you think the current law against smacking children should be repealed?"

A survey's validity also depends on who is included in it. If the particular people surveyed do not represent the views of the population you are interested in, it is easy to be misled by survey results (Gosling et al., 2004). If you were interested in Americans' views on the prevalence of religious prejudice, you would come to the wrong conclusion if you surveyed only Christians or only Muslims. To get a complete picture, you would have to survey people from all religious groups so that each group's opinions could be fairly represented.

A Severely Flawed Survey

Using survey methods like this, you could probably get whatever results you want! Psychologists work hard to write questions and use methods that maximize the validity of their surveys' results.

Other limitations of the survey method are more difficult to avoid. For one thing, even if they can't be personally identified, people may be reluctant to admit undesirable or embarrassing things about themselves. Or they might say what they think they *should* say about a survey question (Uziel, 2010). The American Society for Microbiology (ASM) found that 95 percent of the U.S. adults it surveyed said that they wash their hands after using the toilet. However, naturalistic observations of thousands of people in public restrooms across the United States revealed that the figure is closer to 77 percent (Harris Interactive, 2007). So surveys that ask people to say whether they cheat on exams, use illegal drugs, drive while drunk, or engage in other forms of socially disapproved or dangerous behaviors will probably underestimate the frequency of these behaviors. Further, suppose you send out a questionnaire about raising local taxes. If those who are opposed to the tax increase are more likely to return their questionnaire, you will probably get an inaccurate view of public opinion. These response biases and data collection problems have the potential to distort survey results and the conclusions that are drawn from them (Hoyle, Harris, & Judd, 2002). Still, surveys provide an efficient way to gather large amounts of data about people's attitudes, beliefs, or other characteristics.

Correlational Studies: Looking for Relationships

The data collected from naturalistic observations, case studies, and surveys provide valuable descriptions of behavior and mental processes, but they can do more than that. These data can also be examined to see what they reveal about the relationships, or correlations, between one research variable and another. For example, fear surveys show that most people have fears, but correlational analysis of those surveys also shows that the number of fears is related to age. Specifically, adults have fewer fears than children (e.g., Kleinknecht, 1991). **Correlational studies** examine relationships between variables in order to describe research data more fully, test predictions, evaluate theories, and suggest new hypotheses about why people think and act as they do.

Consider the question of how aggression develops. One theory suggests that people learn to be aggressive by seeing aggressiveness in others. Psychologists have tested this theory through correlational studies that focus on the relationship between children's aggressiveness and the amount of aggression they see on television. Just as the theory predicts, those who watch a lot of televised violence do tend to be more aggressive than other children. Another theory asserts that sexual aggressiveness in adults can be triggered by viewing pornography. And in fact, correlational analyses of case studies and surveys show that sex criminals often view pornographic material just prior to committing their offenses. And correlational studies of observational data indicate that children in day care for more than thirty hours a week are more aggressive than those who stay at home with their mothers.

Do violent television, pornography, and separation from parents actually *cause* the various forms of aggressiveness with which they have been associated? They might, but psychologists must be careful about jumping to such conclusions. The most obvious explanation for the relationship found in a correlational study may not always be the correct one (see Table 2.2). Perhaps the correlation between aggression and violent television appears because children who were the most aggressive in the first place are also the ones who choose to watch the most violent television. Perhaps sex offenders exaggerate the role of pornography in their crimes because they hope to avoid taking responsibility for those crimes. And perhaps the aggressiveness seen among some children in day care might have something to do with the children themselves or with what happens to them in day care, not just with separation from their parents.

One way psychologists evaluate hypotheses such as these is to conduct further correlational studies in which they look for trends in observational, case study, and survey data that support or conflict with those hypotheses (Rutter, 2007; West, 2009). Further analysis of day care research, for example, shows that the aggressiveness seen in preschoolers who spend a lot of time in day care is the exception, not the rule.

correlational study A research method that examines relationships between variables in order to analyze trends in data, test predictions, evaluate theories, and suggest new hypotheses.

TABLE 2.2	Correlation and Causation

TRY THIS Look at the relationships described in the left-hand column, and then ask yourself why the two variables in each case are correlated. Could one variable be causing an effect on the other? If so, which variable is the cause, and how might it exert its effect? Could the relationship between the two variables be caused by a third one? If so, what might that third variable be? We suggest some possible explanations in the right-hand column. Can you think of others?

Correlation	Possible Explanation
A survey found that the more sexual content that U.S. teenagers reported watching on television, the more likely they were to begin having sex themselves during the following year (Collins et al., 2004).	It might have been some teens' greater interest in sex that led them to watch more sexually oriented shows and also to become sexually active.
The number of drownings in the United States rises and falls along with the amount of ice cream sold each month.	This relationship probably reflects a third variable—time of year—that affects both ice cream consumption and the likelihood of swimming and boating.
In places where beer prices are raised, the number of new cases of sexually transmitted disease falls among young people living in those places.	If price increases cause less beer consumption, people might stay sober enough to remember to use condoms during sexual encounters. The relationship could also reflect coincidence, because prices do not always affect alcohol use. More research is required to understand this correlation.
A study found that the more antibiotics a woman has taken and the longer she has taken them, the greater is her risk of breast cancer (Velicer et al., 2004).	Long-term antibiotic use might have impaired the women's immune systems, but the cancer risk might also have been increased by the diseases that were being treated with antibiotic drugs, not the drugs themselves. Obviously, much more research would be required before condemning the use of antibiotics.
Individuals and teams wearing red are more likely to win fights and other athletic contests than those wearing other colors (Hill & Barton, 2005).	Does red convey a signal of dominance that intimidates opponents? Possibly, but other research has found color-related outcome patterns when *neither* contestant wears red (Rowe, Harris, & Roberts, 2005), so other factors, including coincidence, might be at work.
The U.S. stock market rises during years in which a team from the National Football Conference wins the Super Bowl and falls during years in which an American Conference team wins.	The so-called Super Bowl effect has occurred thirty times in thirty-seven years; striking as this might seem, coincidence seems to be the most likely explanation.

Most children don't show any behavior problems, no matter how much time they have spent in day care. This more general trend suggests that whatever effects separation has, it may be different for different children in different settings, causing some to express aggressiveness, others to display fear, and still others to find enjoyment. As described in the chapter on human development, psychologists are exploring this possibility by examining correlations between children's personality traits, qualities of different day care programs, and reactions to day care (Belsky et al., 2007). Throughout this book, you will see many more examples of how correlational studies help shed light on a wide range of topics in psychology.

Experiments: Exploring Cause and Effect

The surest way to test hypotheses and confirm cause-and-effect relationships between variables is to exert some control over those variables (Falk & Heckman, 2009). This kind of research usually takes the form of an experiment. In an **experiment**, the researcher manipulates one variable and then observes the effect of that manipulation on another variable, while holding all other variables constant.

Consider the experiment Francine Shapiro conducted in an attempt to understand the effects of EMDR. As illustrated in Figure 2.1, she first identified twenty-two people who were suffering the ill effects of traumas such as rape or military combat. These were her research participants. She then assigned each of the participants to one of two groups. Members of the first group received a single fifty-minute session of EMDR treatment. Members of the second group received no EMDR treatment; instead, they focused on their unpleasant memories for eight minutes, without moving their eyes back and forth (Shapiro, 1989a).

The group that receives an experimental treatment such as EMDR is called, naturally enough, the **experimental group**. The group that receives no treatment or some

experiment A situation in which the researcher manipulates one variable and then observes the effect of that manipulation on another variable, while holding all other variables constant.

experimental group In an experiment, the group that receives the experimental treatment.

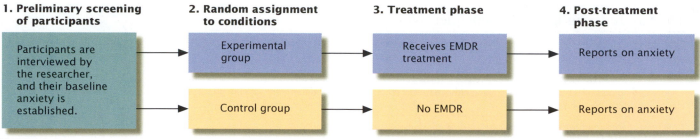

1. Preliminary screening of participants	2. Random assignment to conditions	3. Treatment phase	4. Post-treatment phase
Participants are interviewed by the researcher, and their baseline anxiety is established.	Experimental group	Receives EMDR treatment	Reports on anxiety
	Control group	No EMDR	Reports on anxiety

FIGURE 2.1

A Simple Two-Group Experiment

Ideally, the only difference between the experimental and control groups in experiments such as this one is whether the participants receive the treatment the experimenter wishes to evaluate. Under these ideal circumstances, at the end of the experiment, any difference in the two groups' reported levels of anxiety would be due only to whether or not they received treatment.

other treatment is called the **control group**. Control groups provide baselines against which to compare the performance of other groups. In Shapiro's experiment, having a control group allowed her to measure how much change in anxiety could be expected from exposure to bad memories without EMDR treatment. If everything about the two groups were exactly the same before the experiment, any difference in anxiety between the groups afterward would have something to do with the EMDR treatment rather than with mere exposure to unpleasant memories.

Notice that Shapiro controlled one variable: whether or not her participants received EMDR. In an experiment, the variable controlled by the experimenter is called the **independent variable**. It is called *independent* because the experimenter is free to adjust it at will, offering one, two, or three kinds of treatment, for example, or perhaps setting the length of treatment at one, five, or ten sessions. Notice, too, that Shapiro looked for the effects of treatment by measuring a different variable, her clients' anxiety level. This second variable is called the **dependent variable** because it is affected by or depends on the independent variable. So in Shapiro's experiment, the presence or absence of treatment was the independent variable, because she manipulated it. Her participants' anxiety level was the dependent variable, because she measured it to see how it was affected by treatment. (Table 2.3 describes the independent and dependent variables in other experiments.)

The results of Shapiro's experiment showed that participants who received EMDR treatment experienced a complete and nearly immediate reduction in anxiety related to their traumatic memories, whereas those in the control group showed no change (Shapiro, 1989a). This difference suggests that EMDR caused the improvement. But look again at the structure, or design, of the experiment. The EMDR group's session lasted about fifty minutes, but members of the control group focused on their memories for only eight minutes. Would the people in the control group have improved, too, if they had spent fifty minutes focusing on their memories? We don't know, because the experiment did not compare methods of equal duration.

Anyone who conducts or relies on research must be on guard for such flaws in experimental design. So before drawing conclusions from research, experimenters must consider factors that might confound, or confuse, the interpretation of results. Any factor, such as differences in the length of treatment, that might have affected the dependent variable along with or instead of the independent variable can become a **confound**. When confounds are present, the experimenter cannot know whether the independent variable or the confound produced the results. Let's examine three kinds of confounds: random variables, participants' expectations, and experimenter bias.

Random Variables   In an ideal research world, everything about the experimental and control groups would be the same except for their exposure to the independent variable (such as whether or not they received treatment). In the real world, however,

control group In an experiment, the group that receives no treatment or provides some other baseline against which to compare the performance or response of the experimental group.

independent variable The variable manipulated by the researcher in an experiment.

dependent variable In an experiment, the factor affected by the independent variable.

confound In an experiment, any factor that affects the dependent variable, along with or instead of the independent variable.

TABLE 2.3 Independent and Dependent Variables	
TRY THIS Fill in the names of the independent and dependent variables in each of these experiments (the answers are listed at the bottom of page 46). Remember that the independent variable is manipulated by	the experimenter. The dependent variable is measured to determine the effect of the independent variable. How did you do on this task?
1. Children's reading skill is measured after taking either a special reading class or a standard reading class.	The independent variable is _____. The dependent variable is _____.
2. College students' memory for German vocabulary words is tested after a normal night's sleep or a night of no sleep.	The independent variable is _____. The dependent variable is _____.
3. Experiment title: "The effect of a daily walking program on elderly people's lung capacity."	The independent variable is _____. The dependent variable is _____.
4. People's ability to avoid "accidents" in a driving simulator is tested before, during, and after talking on a cell phone.	The independent variable is _____. The dependent variable is _____.

there are always other differences between the groups that reflect random variables (West, 2009). **Random variables** are uncontrolled, sometimes uncontrollable, factors such as the time of year when research takes place and differences in the participants' cultural backgrounds, personalities, life experiences, and sensitivity to stress, for example.

In fact, there are so many ways in which participants might vary from one another that it is usually impossible to form groups that are matched in all respects. Instead, experimenters simply flip a coin or use some other random process to assign each research participant to the experimental or control group. These procedures—called *random assignment* or **randomizing**—are presumed to distribute the impact of uncontrolled variables randomly (and probably about equally) across groups, thus minimizing the chance that these variables will distort the results of the experiment (Shadish, Cook, & Campbell, 2002).

Participants' Expectations: The Placebo Effect   After eight minutes of focusing on unpleasant memories, participants in the control group in Shapiro's experiment were instructed to begin moving their eyes from side to side. At that point they, too, said they began to experience a reduction in anxiety. Was this improvement caused by the eye movements themselves, or could it be that the instructions made the participants feel more confident that they were now getting "real" treatment? This question illustrates a second kind of confound: differences in what people *think* about the experimental situation. If participants who receive an impressive treatment expect that it will help them, they may try harder to improve than those in a control group who receive no treatment or a less impressive treatment. When improvement occurs as a result of a participant's knowledge and expectations, it is called the *placebo effect*. A **placebo** (pronounced "pluh-SEE-boh") is a treatment that contains nothing known to be helpful but that still produces benefits because the person receiving the treatment believes it will be beneficial.

How can researchers measure the extent to which a result is caused by the independent variable or by the placebo effect? Usually, they include a special control group that receives *only* a placebo treatment. Then they compare results for the experimental group, the placebo group, and a no-treatment group. In one quit-smoking study, for example, participants in a placebo group took sugar pills described by the experimenter as "fast-acting tranquilizers" that would help them learn to endure the stress of giving up cigarettes (Bernstein, 1970). These people did far better at quitting than those who got no treatment; in fact, they did as well as participants in the experimental group, who received extensive treatment. These results suggested that the success of the experimental group may have been due largely to the participants' expectations, not to the treatment methods.

Some studies suggest the same conclusion about the effects of EMDR, because significant anxiety reduction has been observed in clients who got a version of the

random variable   In an experiment, a confound in which uncontrolled or uncontrollable factors affect the dependent variable, along with or instead of the independent variable.

randomizing   Assigning participants in an experiment to various groups through a random process to ensure that random variables are evenly distributed among the groups.

placebo   A physical or psychological treatment that contains no active ingredient but produces an effect because the person receiving it believes it will.

© AP Photo/Jason E. Miczek

Ever Since I Started Wearing Titanium . . .

Placebo-controlled experiments are vital for establishing cause-and-effect relationships between treatments and outcomes with human participants. For example, many people swear that titanium bracelets and necklaces relieve the pain of sports injuries and even arthritis (Atkinson, 2006; Galdeira, 2006; Marchman, 2008; Siber, 2005). The Web site of Phiten, the leading manufacturer and marketer of titanium accessories, presents many glowing testimonials and a scientific-sounding explanation of the technology behind titanium's alleged effects, but it offers no evidence from placebo-controlled experiments to support the company's claims (Boyles, 2008; Wagg, 2008). So something other than the jewelry—wishful thinking, perhaps—could be causing the reported benefits.

experimenter bias A confound that occurs when an experimenter unintentionally encourages participants to respond in a way that supports the experimenter's hypothesis.

double-blind design A research design in which neither the experimenter nor the participants know who is in the experimental group and who is in the control group.

sampling The process of selecting participants who are members of the population that the researcher wishes to study.

treatment that did not involve eye movements or even focusing on traumatic memories (Cahill, Carrigan, & Frueh, 1999; Cusack & Spates, 1999; Rosen, 1999; Seidler & Wagner, 2006; Servan-Schreiber et al., 2006). Other experiments have shown that EMDR can outperform placebo treatments, but the fact that its effects are not significantly better than those of other more established treatments has led many researchers to conclude that EMDR should not be a first-choice treatment for anxiety-related disorders (Bisson, 2007; Davidson & Parker, 2001; Goldstein et al., 2000; Lilienfeld & Arkowitz, 2007; Lohr et al., 2003; Taylor, 2004).

Experimenter Bias   Another potential confound is **experimenter bias**, the unintentional effect that researchers may exert on their results. Robert Rosenthal (1966) was among the first to demonstrate a kind of experimenter bias called *experimenter expectancies*. His research participants were laboratory assistants whose job was to place rats in a maze. Rosenthal told some of the assistants that their rats were "maze-bright"; he told the others that their rats were "maze-dull." In fact, both groups of rats were randomly drawn from the same population and had about equal maze-learning capabilities. But the "maze-bright" animals learned the maze significantly faster than the "maze-dull" rats. Why? Rosenthal concluded that the results had nothing to do with the rats and everything to do with the experimenters. He suggested that the assistants' expectations about their rats' supposedly superior or inferior capabilities caused them to slightly alter their training and handling techniques. These slight differences may have speeded or slowed the animals' learning. Similarly, when therapists are asked to give different kinds of treatment to different groups of clients in a therapy evaluation experiment, the therapists may do a slightly better job with the treatment that they expect to have the best results. This slight unintentional difference could improve the effects of that treatment compared with the others.

To prevent experimenter bias from influencing results, experimenters often use a **double-blind design**. In this arrangement, both the research participants and those giving the treatments are unaware of ("blind" to) who is receiving a placebo, and they do not know what results are expected from various treatments. Only researchers who have no direct contact with participants have this information, and they do not reveal it until the experiment is over. The fact that double-blind studies of EMDR have not yet been conducted is another reason for caution in drawing conclusions about this treatment.

To sum up, experiments are vital tools for examining cause-and-effect relationships between variables, but like the other methods we have described (see "In Review: Methods of Psychological Research"), they are vulnerable to error. To maximize the value of their experiments, psychologists try to eliminate as many confounds as possible. Then they replicate their work to ensure consistent results and temper their interpretation of those results to take into account the limitations or problems that remain.

Selecting Human Participants for Research

Visitors from outer space would be wildly mistaken if they tried to describe the typical earthling after meeting only, say, Arnold Schwarzenegger, Lady Gaga, Kanye West, and a trained seal. Likewise, the conclusions that psychologists draw from their observations, case studies, surveys, correlational studies, and experiments will be distorted if the participants they study are not typical of the people or animals they are interested in. Accordingly, the process of selecting participants for research, called **sampling**, is an extremely important step.

Suppose that you want to conduct a survey of television viewing habits. Your research budget is small, so you restrict your survey to the residents of your apartment building, all of whom, by some strange coincidence, turn out to be male Asian American concert violinists. The responses you get from these people might be perfectly accurate, but their favorite shows might differ significantly from those of the general population. So sampling procedures can not only affect research results but also limit

Keeping Experimenters "Blind"

TRY THIS Suppose that you are a sport psychologist conducting an experiment to evaluate two methods for reducing performance anxiety: standard coaching and a new relaxation-based technique. How might you create a double-blind design for this experiment? If you cannot, how might you try to keep coaches in the dark about which method is expected to produce better results?

© Christopher Bissell/Stone/Getty Images

their meaning. In this case, your results would probably apply, or *generalize*, mainly to other male Asian American musicians. If that were the only group you want to draw conclusions about, your limited sample might not be too problematic—assuming that the men in your building were typical of other Asian American musicians. If they were all also ex-convicts, your results would be even more limited!

The main point is that if psychologists want to make scientific statements about the behavior and mental processes of any large group, they must conduct a **representative sampling** of participants whose characteristics fairly reflect the characteristics of other people in that group. This point is important, because psychologists often study behavior or mental processes that are affected by age, gender, ethnicity, cultural background, socioeconomic status, sexual orientation, disability, or other participant characteristics.

In theory, psychologists could draw representative samples of people in general, of Canadians, of Florida college students, or of any other group by choosing them at random from the entire population of interest. To do this, though, they would first have to find and put into a computer the names of all the hundreds of thousands, perhaps millions, of people in that population. Then they would have to run a program to randomly select participants from this enormous group, track those people down, and invite them to take part in the research. This method would constitute truly **random sampling**, because every member of the population to be studied would have an equal chance of being chosen. Any selection procedure that does not offer this equal chance is said to be **biased sampling**. Unfortunately, not even truly random sampling will create a perfectly representative sample of Canadians, Florida college students, or the like. For one thing, the people who happen to be selected may be slightly different from the people who are not selected. In other words, the luck of the draw gives rise to what psychologists call *sampling error*. Further, not everyone who is randomly selected for a research project will agree to participate, creating a problem called *nonresponse error*. These two kinds of errors help explain why the results of random surveys are not always accurate. Still, a group of individuals selected at random from a larger population will usually provide a reasonably representative sample of that population. The big problem, though, is that random sampling is often too expensive and time-consuming to be practical.

representative sampling A process for selecting research participants whose characteristics fairly reflect the characteristics of the population from which they were drawn.

random sampling The process of selecting a group of research participants from a population whose members all had an equal chance of being chosen.

biased sampling The process of selecting a group of research participants from a population whose members did not have an equal chance of being chosen.

Answers to Table 2.3

1. Independent variable: type of reading class; dependent variable: reading skill. **2.** Independent variable: amount of sleep; dependent variable: score on a memory test. **3.** Independent variable: amount of exercise; dependent variable: lung capacity **4.** Independent variable: using or not using a cell phone; dependent variable: performance on a simulated driving task.

So in the real world of research, psychologists often draw their participants from the populations that are conveniently available. The populations from which these *convenience samples* are drawn depend to some extent on the size of the researcher's budget. They might include, for example, the students enrolled in a particular course, the students on a local campus, the students who are willing to sign up for a study, or visitors to particular Internet Web sites or chat rooms (e.g., Stone & Pennebaker, 2002). Ideally, this selection process will yield a sample that fairly represents the population from which it was drawn, but researchers must confirm this by recording the age, gender, ethnicity, and other characteristics of the participants. Further, they must limit the conclusions they draw in light of any limitations in the samples they drew (Kraut et al., 2004). The more representative the samples, the broader the conclusions that can legitimately be drawn from research on them. Even so, concerns about sampling often lead psychologists to conduct additional studies to determine the extent to which their initial conclusions apply to people who differ in important ways from their original sample.

IN REVIEW Methods of Psychological Research

Method	Features	Strengths	Pitfalls
Observational methods (e.g., naturalistic observation)	Observation of human or animal behavior in the environment in which it typically occurs	Provides descriptive data about behavior presumably uncontaminated by outside influences	Observer bias and participant self-consciousness can distort results
Case studies	Intensive examination of the behavior and mental processes associated with a specific person or situation	Provide detailed descriptive analyses of new, complex, or rare phenomena	May not provide a representative picture of phenomena
Surveys	Standard sets of questions asked of a large number of participants	Gather large amounts of descriptive data relatively quickly and inexpensively	Sampling errors, poorly phrased questions, and response biases can distort results
Correlational studies	Examine relationships between research variables	Can test predictions, evaluate theories, and suggest new hypotheses	Cannot confirm causal relationships between variables
Experiments	Manipulation of an independent variable and measurement of its effect on a dependent variable	Can establish a cause-and-effect relationship between independent and dependent variables	Confounds may prevent valid conclusions

1. The _____ method is most likely to use a double-blind design.

2. Research on a new treatment method is most likely to begin with _____.

3. Studying language by listening to people in public places is an example of _____ research.

LINKAGES

Psychological Research Methods and Behavioral Genetics

One of the most fascinating and difficult challenges in psychology is to find research methods that can help us understand the ways in which people's genetic inheritance (their biological *nature*) intertwines with environmental events and conditions before and after birth (often called *nurture*) to shape their behavior and mental processes (Moffitt, Caspi, & Rutter, 2005). Consider Mark and John, identical twins who were both adopted at birth because their biological parents were too poor to care for them. John grew up with a married couple who made him feel secure and loved. Mark

Selecting Research Participants

TRY THIS Imagine that as a social psychologist, you want to study people's willingness to help each other. You have developed a method for testing helpfulness, but now you want a random sample of people to test. Take a minute to think about the steps necessary to select a truly random sample; then ask yourself how you might obtain a representative sample instead. Remember that although the names are similar, *random sampling* is not the same as *randomizing*. Random sampling is used in many kinds of research to ensure that the people studied are representative of some larger group. Randomizing is used in experiments to distribute participant characteristics as evenly as possible across various groups.

© Lee Christensen/Flickr/Getty Images

LINKAGES How much of our behavior is due to genetics and how much to our environment? (a link to Biological Aspects of Psychology, p. 63)

went from orphanage to foster home to hospital and, finally, back to his biological father's second wife. In other words, these genetically identical people had encountered quite different environments. Still, when they met for the first time at the age of 24, they discovered similarities that went far beyond physical appearance. They used the same aftershave lotion, smoked the same brand of cigarettes, used the same imported brand of toothpaste, and liked the same sports. They had joined the military within eight days of each other, and their IQ scores were nearly identical. How had genetic influences operated in two different environments to shape such similarities?

Exploring questions such as these has taken psychologists into the field of **behavioral genetics**, the study of how genes and environments work together to shape behavior. They have discovered that most behavioral tendencies are likely to be influenced by interactions between the environment and many different genes. Accordingly, research in behavioral genetics is designed to explore the relative roles of genetic and environmental factors in producing differences among people in personality, mental ability, mental disorders, and other phenomena. It also seeks to identify specific genes that contribute to hereditary influences.

Some behavioral genetics research takes the form of experiments, mainly on the selective breeding of animals (Suomi, 2004). For example, Stephen Suomi (1999) identified monkeys whose genes predisposed them to show strong or weak reactions to stress. He then mated strong reactors with other strong reactors and mated weak reactors with other weak reactors. Within a few generations, descendants of the strong-reactor pairs reacted much more strongly to stressors than did the descendants of the weak-reactor pairs. Selective-breeding experiments must be interpreted with caution, though, because animals do not inherit specific behaviors. Instead, they inherit differing sets of physical structures and capacities that make certain behaviors more likely or less likely. But these behavioral tendencies can be altered by the environment (Grigorenko, 2002; Parker et al., 2006). For example, when Suomi (1999) placed young, highly stress-reactive monkeys with unrelated "foster mothers," he discovered that the foster mothers' own stress reactivity amplified or dampened the youngsters' genetically influenced behavioral tendencies. If stress-reactive monkeys were placed with stress-reactive foster mothers, they tended to be fearful of exploring their environments and had strong reactions to stressors. But if equally stress-reactive young monkeys had calm, supportive foster mothers, they appeared eager to explore

behavioral genetics The study of how genes and environment work together to shape behavior.

their environments and were much less upset by stressors than their peers with stress-reactive foster mothers.

Research on behavioral genetics in humans must be interpreted with even greater care. Legal, moral, and ethical considerations obviously prohibit experiments on the selective breeding of people, so research in human behavioral genetics depends on correlational studies. These usually take the form of family studies, twin studies, and adoption studies (Plomin et al., 2008). Let's consider the logic of these behavioral genetics research methods. (The behavioral genetics appendix offers more on the basic principles of genetics and heredity that underlie these methods.)

In *family studies*, researchers look at whether close relatives are more likely than distant ones to show similar behavior and mental processes. If increasing similarity is associated with closer family ties, the similarities might be inherited. For example, family studies suggest a genetic basis for schizophrenia because this severe mental disorder appears much more often in the closest relatives of schizophrenics than in other people (see Figure 2.2). But remember that a correlation between variables does not guarantee that one is causing the other. The appearance of similar disorders in close relatives might be due to environmental factors instead of or in addition to genetic ones. After all, close relatives tend to share environments as well as genes. So family studies alone cannot establish the role of genetic factors in mental disorders or other characteristics.

Twin studies explore the heredity-environment mix by comparing the similarities seen in identical twins with those of nonidentical pairs (Johnson et al., 2009). Twins usually share the same family environment as they grow up, and they may also be treated very much the same by parents and others. So if identical twins (whose genes are exactly the same) are more alike on some characteristic than nonidentical twins (whose genes are no more similar than those of other siblings), that characteristic

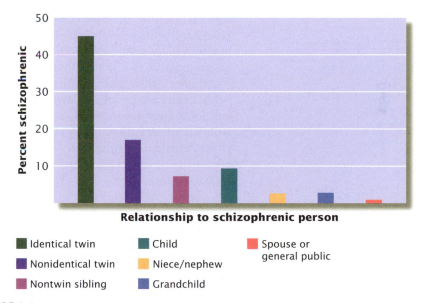

FIGURE 2.2

Family and Twin Studies of Schizophrenia

The risk of developing schizophrenia, a severe mental disorder, is highest for the siblings and children of schizophrenia patients and lowest for those who are not genetically related to anyone with schizophrenia. Does this mean that schizophrenia is inherited? These results are consistent with that interpretation, but the question cannot be answered through family studies alone. Studies comparing identical and nonidentical twins also suggest genetic influence, but even twin studies cannot eliminate the role of environmental influences. Environmental factors, such as stressors that close relatives share, could also play an important role and may even contribute to *genomic imprinting*, as suggested by the epigenetic perspective discussed later in this section (Crespi, 2008; Ivleva, Thaker, & Tamminga, 2008; Singh & O'Reilly, 2009; Tandon, Keshavan, & Nasrallah, 2008).

Twins and Behavioral Genetics

Like other identical twins, each member of this pair has identical genes. Twin studies and adoption studies help reveal the interaction of genetic and environmental influences in human behavior and mental processes. Cases in which identical twins who had been separated at birth are found to have similar interests, personality traits, and mental abilities suggest that these characteristics are significantly influenced by genetic factors.

© George Shelley/Corbis

may have a significant genetic component. As described in later chapters, this pattern of results holds for a number of characteristics, including some measures of intelligence and some mental disorders. As shown in Figure 2.2, for example, if one member of an identical twin pair develops schizophrenia, the chances are about 45 percent that the other twin will too. Those chances drop to about 17 percent if the twins are nonidentical.

Adoption studies take scientific advantage of cases in which babies are adopted very early in life. The logic of these studies is that if adopted children's characteristics are more like those of their biological parents than of their adoptive parents, genetics probably plays a clear role in those characteristics. In fact, as described in the chapter on personality, the traits of young adults who were adopted at birth tend to be more like those of their biological parents than those of their adoptive parents. Adoption studies can be especially valuable when they focus on identical twins who, like Mark and John, were separated at or near birth. If identical twins show similar characteristics after years of living in very different environments, the role of heredity in those characteristics is highlighted. Adoption studies of intelligence tend to support the role of genetics in variations in mental ability, but they show the impact of environmental influences too.

Family, twin, and adoption studies have played an important role in behavioral genetics research, but when you read in other chapters about the role of genes in personality, intelligence, mental disorders, and other characteristics, remember this important point: Research on human behavioral genetics can tell us about the relative roles of heredity and environment in creating differences *among* individuals, but it cannot determine the degree to which a *particular* person's behavior is due to heredity or environment. The two factors are too closely entwined in an individual to be separated that way. In the future, though, behavioral genetics will also be shaped by research methods made possible by the Human Genome Project, which has now unlocked the genetic code contained in the DNA that makes each human being unique (International Human Genome Sequencing Consortium, 2001; see the behavioral genetics appendix). This achievement has allowed behavioral geneticists and other scientists to begin pinpointing some of the many genes that contribute to individual differences in disorders such as autism, learning disabilities, hyperactivity, and Alzheimer's disease, as well as to the normal variations in personality and cognitive abilities that we see all around us (Plomin et al., 2008). Finding the DNA differences responsible for certain personal attributes and behaviors will eventually make it possible to understand exactly how heredity interacts with the environment as development unfolds. Analysis of DNA—collected by rubbing a cotton swab inside an individual's cheek—may someday be used not only in behavioral genetics research but also in clinics, where it will help psychologists more precisely diagnose clients' problems and choose the most appropriate treatments (Plomin et al., 2008).

But DNA does not tell the whole story of behavioral genetics. Biological and psychological scientists have also begun to study the complex interactions between people's genetic inheritance (DNA) and the environments in which their genes operate (Champagne, 2009; Champagne & Mashoodh, 2009). This field of study, called **epigenetics**, describes the ways that events within cells can alter the *functions* of genes, even though the genetic code itself—the sequence of chemicals in the DNA—remains unchanged (Gräff & Mansuy, 2008; Keverne & Curley, 2008; Lickliter, 2008). Research in epigenetics suggests that the cellular environment can not only affect the expression of an individual's genetic characteristics but may also create structural changes in genes (called *imprinted genes*) that can be passed on to future generations (Keverne & Curley, 2008; Lamm & Jablonka, 2008; Lickliter, 2008). Epigenetic effects—which can be triggered by many environmental influences, including diseases and stress—have been linked to individual differences in learning, memory, and brain development (Gräff & Mansuy, 2008; Keverne & Curley, 2008; Lickliter, 2008), and they may also play a role in the appearance of cognitive disorders such as Alzheimer's disease, mental disorders such as schizophrenia and depression, illnesses such as cancer, and health problems such as obesity (Gräff & Mansuy, 2008; Keverne & Curley, 2008).

Statistical Analysis of Research Results

Observational methods, case studies, surveys, correlational studies, and experiments generate mountains of numbers that represent research findings and provide the basis for conclusions about them. These data might represent scores on intelligence tests, levels of stress hormones in blood samples, tiny differences in the time required to detect visual signals, ratings of people's personality traits, or whatever else a psychologist might be studying.

Like other scientists, psychologists use descriptive and inferential *statistics* to summarize and analyze their data and interpret what those data mean. As the name suggests, **descriptive statistics** describe data. **Inferential statistics** are mathematical procedures that help psychologists make inferences about what the data mean. Let's consider a few of the statistical terms that you will encounter in later chapters; you can find more information about these terms in the statistics appendix.

Descriptive Statistics

The three most important descriptive statistics are *measures of central tendency*, which describe the typical score in a set of data; *measures of variability*, which describe the spread, or dispersion, among the scores in a set of data; and *correlation coefficients*, which describe relationships between variables.

Measures of Central Tendency
Suppose you wanted to test the effects of EMDR treatment on fear of the dark. You find participants by giving volunteers an anxiety test and end up collecting the eleven self-ratings of anxiety listed on the left side of Table 2.4. What is the typical score, the *central tendency*, that best represents the anxiety level of this group of people? There are three measures designed to capture this typical score: the mode, the median, and the mean.

The **mode** is the value or score that occurs most frequently in a data set. You can find it by simply counting how many times each score appears. On the left side of Table 2.4, the mode is 50, because the score of 50 occurs more often than any other. Notice, however, that in this data set the mode is actually an extremely high score. Sometimes

epigenetics The study of potentially inheritable changes in gene expression that are caused by environmental factors that do not alter a cell's DNA.

descriptive statistics Numbers that summarize a set of research data.

inferential statistics A set of mathematical procedures that help psychologists make inferences about what their research data mean.

mode A measure of central tendency that is the value or score that occurs most frequently in a data set.

TABLE 2.4   A Set of Pretreatment Anxiety Ratings

Here are scores representing people's self-ratings, on a 1–100 scale, of their fear of the dark.

Data from 11 Participants		Data from 12 Participants	
Participant Number	**Anxiety Rating**	**Participant Number**	**Anxiety Rating**
1	20	1	20
2	22	2	22
3	28	3	28
4	35	4	35
5	40	5	40
6	45 (Median)	6	45 (Median = 46[a])
7	47	7	47
8	49	8	49
9	50	9	50
10	50	10	50
11	50	11	50
		12	100
Measures of central tendency Mode = 50 Median = 45 Mean = 436/11 = 39.6		**Measures of central tendency** Mode = 50 Median = 46 Mean = 536/12 = 44.7	
Measures of variability Range = 30 Standard deviation = 11.064		**Measures of variability** Range = 80 Standard deviation = 19.763	

[a]When there is an even number of scores, the exact middle of the list lies between two numbers. The median is the value halfway between those numbers.

the mode acts like a microphone for a small but vocal minority that, though speaking loudest or most frequently, does not represent the views of the majority.

Unlike the mode, the median takes all of the scores into account. The **median** is the halfway point in a set of data. When scores are arranged from lowest to highest, half the scores fall above the median, and half fall below it. For the scores on the left side of Table 2.4, the halfway point—the median—is 45.

The third measure of central tendency is the **mean**, which is the *arithmetic average* of a set of scores. When people talk about the "average" in everyday conversation, they are usually referring to the mean. To find the mean, add the scores and divide by the number of scores. For the data on the left side of Table 2.4, the mean is 436/11 = 39.6.

Like the median (and unlike the mode), the mean reflects all the data to some degree, not just the most frequent data. Notice, however, that the mean reflects the actual values of all the scores, whereas the median gives each score equal weight, whatever its value. This distinction can have a big effect on how well the mean and median represent the scores in a particular set of data. Suppose that you add to your sample a twelfth participant, whose anxiety rating is 100. When you reanalyze the anxiety data (see the right side of Table 2.4), the median hardly changes, because the new participant counts as just one more score. However, when you compute the new mean, the actual *amount* of the new participant's rating is added to everyone else's ratings; as a result, the mean jumps 5 points. As this example shows, the median is sometimes a better measure of central tendency than the mean because the median is less sensitive to extremely high or extremely low scores. But because the mean is more representative of the values of all the data, it is often the preferred measure of central tendency.

median A measure of central tendency that is the halfway point in a set of data: Half the scores fall above the median, and half fall below it.

mean A measure of central tendency that is the arithmetic average of the scores in a set of data.

Descriptive statistics are valuable for summarizing research results, but we must evaluate them carefully before drawing conclusions about what they mean. Given this executive's reputation for uncritical thinking, you can bet that Dogbert's impressive-sounding restatement of the definition of *median* will win him an extension of his pricey consulting contract.

Measures of Variability   The variability (also known as *spread* or *dispersion*) in a set of data is described by statistics known as the *range* and the *standard deviation*. The **range** is simply the difference between the highest and the lowest scores in a data set (it would be 30 for the data on the left side of Table 2.4 and 80 for the data on the right side). In contrast, the **standard deviation (SD)** measures the average difference between each score and the mean of the data set. So the standard deviation tells us how much the scores in a data set vary, or differ from one another. The more variable the data are, the higher the standard deviation will be. For example, the SD for the eleven participants on the left side of Table 2.4 is 11.064, but it rises to 19.763 once that very different twelfth score is added on the right side. We show how to calculate the standard deviation in the statistics appendix.

Correlation and Correlation Coefficients   When we described correlational studies of the relationship between media violence and aggression, we left out one important question: How do psychologists describe, in terms of numbers, the correlation between these variables or between any other pair of variables?

The Effect of Variability

TRY THIS   Suppose that on your first day as a substitute teacher at a new school, you are offered either of two classes. The mean IQ score in both classes is 100, but the standard deviation (SD) of scores is 16 in one class and 32 in the other. Before you read the next sentence, ask yourself which class you would choose if you wanted an easy day's work or if you wanted a tough challenge. (A higher standard deviation means more variability, so students in the class with the SD of 32 will vary more in ability, thus creating a greater challenge for the teacher.)

range   A measure of variability that is the difference between the highest and the lowest scores in a data set.

standard deviation (SD)   A measure of variability that is the average difference between each score and the mean of the data set.

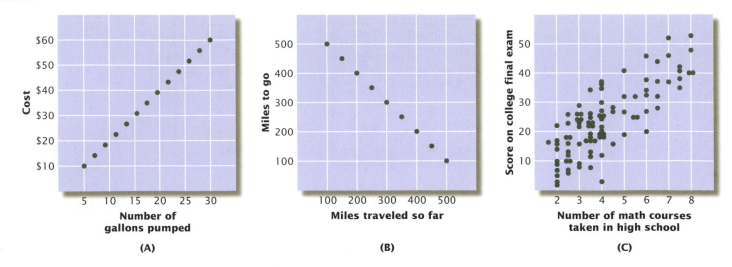

FIGURE 2.3
Three Correlations

The strength and direction of the correlation between any two variables can be seen in a graph called a *scatterplot*. Here are three examples. In part A, we have plotted the cost of a gasoline purchase against the number of gallons pumped. The number of gallons is positively and perfectly correlated with their cost, so the scatterplot appears as a straight line, and you can predict the value of either variable from a knowledge of the other. Part B shows a perfect negative correlation between the number of miles you have traveled toward a destination and the distance remaining. Again, one variable can be exactly predicted from the other. Part C illustrates a correlation of +.81 between the number of math courses students had in high school and their scores on a college math exam; each dot represents one student (Hays, 1981). As correlations decrease, they are represented by less and less organization in the pattern of dots. A correlation of .00 would appear as a shapeless cloud.

Correlation means just what it says, "co-relation," and it refers both to how strongly one variable is related to another and to the direction of the relationship. A *positive correlation* means that two variables increase together or decrease together. A *negative correlation* means that the variables move in opposite directions: When one increases, the other decreases. For example, James Schaefer observed 4,500 customers in sixty-five bars and found that the tempo of the music being played was negatively correlated with the rate at which the customers drank alcohol; the slower the tempo, the faster the drinking (Schaefer et al., 1988).

Does this mean that Schaefer could have worn a blindfold and predicted exactly how fast people were drinking by timing the music? Or could he have plugged his ears and determined the musical tempo by watching how fast people drink? No and no, because the accuracy of predictions about one variable from knowledge of another depends on the strength of the correlation. Only a perfect correlation between two variables would allow you to predict the exact value of one from a knowledge of the other. The weaker the correlation, the less one variable can tell you about the other.

Psychologists describe correlations using a statistic called the **correlation coefficient** (the statistics appendix shows how to calculate it). The correlation coefficient is given the symbol *r*, and it can vary from +1.00 to –1.00. The actual size of the correlation, such as .20 or .80, tells us how strong the correlation is. The higher the number, the stronger the correlation. The plus or minus sign tells the direction of the correlation. A plus sign says the correlation is positive; a minus sign says the correlation is negative.

So an *r* of +.80 between people's height and weight would tell us that the correlation between these two variables is strong and positive: The taller people are, the more they tend to weigh. A correlation of +.01 between their shoe size and the age of their cars would indicate that there is almost no relationship between these two variables. An *r* of –1.00 describes a perfectly predictable but negative relationship between two variables (see part B of Figure 2.3). The variables that psychologists study are seldom perfectly correlated. Most of the correlational studies described in this book yield correlation coefficients in the .20 to .50 range, though some are as high as .90.

correlation In research, the degree to which one variable is related to another.

correlation coefficient A statistic, *r*, that summarizes the strength and direction of a relationship between two variables.

Remember, too, that even a strong correlation between two variables doesn't guarantee that one is *causing* an effect on the other. And even if one *does* affect the other, a correlation coefficient can't tell us which variable is influencing which. As mentioned earlier, correlations can reveal and describe relationships, but correlations alone cannot explain them.

Inferential Statistics

To help interpret the meaning of correlations and the other descriptive statistics that flow from research results, psychologists rely on *inferential statistics*. For example, it was on the basis of analyses using inferential statistics that many researchers concluded that the benefits of EMDR are not great enough when compared with other treatment options to recommend it as a first choice in cases of anxiety.

Inferential statistics use certain rules to evaluate whether a correlation or a difference between group means is a significant finding or might have occurred just by chance. Suppose that a group of people treated with EMDR showed a mean decrease of 10 points on a posttreatment anxiety test, whereas the scores of a no-treatment control group decreased by a mean of 7 points. Does this 3-point difference between the groups' means reflect the impact of EMDR, or could it have been caused by random factors that made EMDR appear more powerful than it actually is? Traditionally, psychologists have answered questions such as this by using statistical tests to estimate how likely it is that an observed difference was due to chance alone (Krueger, 2001). When those tests show that a correlation coefficient or the difference between two means is larger than would be expected by chance alone, that correlation or difference is said to have reached **statistical significance**. In the statistics appendix, we describe some of these tests and discuss the factors that affect their results.

Positive outcomes on tests of statistical significance are important, but they do not necessarily prove that a difference is "real" or that a particular treatment is effective or ineffective. Accordingly, psychologists who specialize in quantitative methods recommend that research findings be evaluated using other statistical analysis methods too (e.g., Kileen, 2005; Kline, 2004; Krueger, 2001). Whatever the methods, though, psychological scientists are more confident in, and pay the most attention to, correlations or other research findings that statistical analyses suggest are robust and not flukes. (For a review of the statistical measures discussed in this section, see "In Review: Descriptive and Inferential Statistics.")

Statistics and Research Methods as Tools in Critical Thinking

As you think critically about evidence for or against any hypothesis, remember that part of the process is to ask some tough questions. Does the evidence come from a study whose design is free of major confounds and other flaws? Have the results been subjected to careful statistical analysis? Have the results been replicated? Using your critical thinking skills to evaluate research designs and statistical methods becomes especially important when you encounter results that are dramatic or unexpected.

This point was well illustrated when Douglas Biklen (1990) began promoting a procedure called "facilitated communication" (FC) to help people with severe autistic disorder use language for the first time (autistic disorder is described in the chapter on psychological disorders). Biklen claimed that these people have language skills and coherent thoughts but no way to express them. He reported case studies in which autistic people were apparently able to answer questions and speak intelligently using a special keyboard, but only when assisted by a "facilitator" who physically supported their unsteady hands. Controlled experiments have repeatedly shown this claim to be groundless, however (Jacobson, Mulick, & Schwartz, 1995; Mostert, 2001; Randi, 2009; Wegner, Fuller, & Sparrow, 2003). The alleged communication abilities of these autistic people disappeared under conditions in which the facilitator (1) did not

statistical significance Referring to a correlation, or a difference between two groups, that is larger than would be expected by chance.

The Social Impact of Research

The impact of research in psychology depends partly on the quality of the results and partly on how people feel about those results. Despite negative results of controlled experiments on facilitated communication, the Facilitated Communication Institute's Web site continues to announce training for the many professionals and relatives of people with autistic disorder who still believe in its value. The fact that some people ignore or even attack research results that challenge cherished beliefs reminds us that scientific research has always affected and been affected by the social and political values of the society in which it takes place (Lynn et al., 2003; Tavris, 2002).

© Robin Nelson/PhotoEdit

IN REVIEW	Descriptive and Inferential Statistics	
Statistic	**Characteristics**	**Information Provided**
Mode	Describes the central tendency in a set of scores	The score that occurs most frequently in a data set
Median	Describes the central tendency in a set of scores	The halfway point in a data set; half the scores fall above this score, half below
Mean	Describes the central tendency in a set of scores	The arithmetic average of the scores in a data set
Range	Describes the variability in a set of scores	The difference between the highest and lowest scores in a data set
Standard deviation	Describes the variability in a set of scores	The average difference between each score and the mean of a data set
Correlation coefficient	Describes the relationship between two variables	How strongly the two variables are related and whether the relationship is positive (variables move in same direction) or negative (variables move in opposite directions)
Tests of significance	Help make inferences about the relationships between descriptive statistics	How likely it is that the difference between measures of central tendency or the size of a correlation coefficient is due to chance alone

1. The measure of central tendency that is most affected by extremely high or extremely low scores is the _____.

2. A set of data with a high standard deviation contains scores that are _____ variable than a set of data with a low standard deviation.

3. True or false: Correlation coefficients of +.50 and −.50 indicate relationships that are of different strengths. _____

know the question being asked of the participant or (2) could not see the keyboard (Delmolino & Romanczyk, 1995). The discovery that facilitators were—perhaps inadvertently (Spitz, 1997)—guiding participants' hand movements has allowed those who work with autistic disorder to see FC in a different light. So when a doctor in Belgium recently claimed that a man who had been in a coma for twenty-three years was suddenly able to communicate via a computer keyboard, skeptics were quick to point out that the person "supporting" his arm was clearly also guiding it (Black, 2009). The claim was soon withdrawn (BBC News, 2010).

The role of experiments and other scientific research methods in understanding behavior and mental processes is so important that in each chapter to come we include a special feature called "Focus on Research Methods." These features describe in detail the specific procedures used in one particularly interesting research project. Our hope is that by reading these sections, you will see how the research methods discussed in this chapter are applied in every subfield of psychology.

Ethical Guidelines for Psychologists

The obligation to analyze and report research fairly and accurately is one of the many ethical requirements that guide psychologists in their work. Preserving the welfare and dignity of research participants, both animal and human, is another. So although researchers *could* measure severe anxiety by putting a loaded gun to people's heads or study marital conflicts by telling one partner that the other has been unfaithful, those methods might cause harm and are therefore unethical. Whatever their research topic, psychologists' first priority is to investigate it in accordance with the highest ethical standards. They must find ways to protect their participants from harm while still gathering data that will have potential benefits for everyone. So to measure anxiety, a researcher might ask people to enter a situation that is anxiety-provoking but not traumatic (e.g., approaching a feared animal or sitting in a dark room). And research on marital conflict usually involves videotaping couples as they discuss problems in their relationship.

Psychologists take very seriously the obligation to minimize any immediate discomfort or risk for research participants, as well as the need to protect those participants from long-term harm. They are careful to inform prospective participants about every aspect of the study that might influence the decision to participate, and they ensure that each person's involvement is voluntary. But what if the purpose of the study is to measure people's emotional reactions to being insulted? Participants might not react naturally if they know ahead of time that an "insult" will be part of the experiment. When deception is necessary to create certain experimental conditions, ethical standards require the researcher to "debrief" participants as soon as the study is over by revealing all relevant information about the research and correcting any misconceptions it created.

Laws in the United States, Canada, and many other countries require that any research involving human participants must be approved by an *institutional review board* (IRB) whose members have no connection to the research. If a proposed study is likely to create risks or discomfort for participants, the IRB members weigh its potential benefits in terms of knowledge and human welfare against its potential for harm. Standards set by organizations such as the Association for the Accreditation of Human Research Protection Programs also help psychologists think through the ethical implications of any research that might have the slightest risk of harm to human participants.

The obligation to protect participants' welfare also extends to animals, which are used in 7 to 8 percent of psychological research studies (American Psychological Association Committee on Animal Research and Ethics, 2009). Psychologists study

© Holger Winkler/zefa/Corbis

Caring for Animals in Research

Psychologists are careful to protect the welfare of animal participants in research. They do not wish to see animals suffer, and undue stress on animals can provoke reactions that can act as confounds. For example, in a study of how learning is affected by food rewards, the researcher could starve animals to make them hungry enough to want rewards. But this would introduce discomfort, making it impossible to separate the effects of the rewards from the effects of starvation.

animals—mainly rats, mice, and pigeons—partly because their behavior is interesting and partly because research with animals can provide information that would be impossible or unethical to collect from humans. For example, researchers can randomly assign animals to live alone or with others and then look at how these conditions affect later social interactions. The same thing could not ethically be done with people, but animal studies such as this can provide clues about how social isolation might affect humans (see the chapter on motivation and emotion).

Contrary to the claims of some animal rights activists, animals used in psychological research are not routinely subjected to extreme pain, starvation, or other inhumane conditions. Even in the small proportion of studies that require the use of electric shock, the discomfort created is mild, brief, and not harmful. High standards for the care and treatment of animal participants are outlined in the Animal Welfare Act, the National Institutes of Health's *Guide for the Care and Use of Laboratory Animals*, the National Institute of Mental Health's *Methods and Welfare Considerations in Behavioral Research with Animals*, the American Psychological Association's *Principles on Animal Use*, and other laws and regulations (APA Committee on Animal Research and Ethics, 2009). In those relatively rare studies that require animals to undergo short-lived pain or other forms of moderate stress, legal and ethical standards require that funding agencies—as well as local committees charged with monitoring animal research—first determine that the discomfort is justified by the expected benefits to human welfare.

The responsibility for conducting research in the most humane fashion is just one aspect of the "Ethical Principles of Psychologists and Code of Conduct" developed by the American Psychological Association (2002b). This document not only emphasizes the importance of ethical behavior but also describes specific ways in which psychologists can protect and promote the welfare of society in general and of the particular people with whom they work in any capacity. So as teachers, psychologists should give students complete, accurate, and up-to-date coverage of each topic, not a narrow, biased point of view. Psychologists should perform only those services and use only those techniques for which they are adequately trained; a psychologist untrained in clinical methods, for example, should not try to offer psychotherapy. Except in the most unusual circumstances (discussed in the chapter on treatment of psychological disorders), psychologists should not reveal information obtained from clients or students. They should also avoid situations in which a conflict of interest might impair their judgment or harm someone else. They should not, for example, have sexual relations with their clients, their students, or their employees.

Despite these guidelines, doubt and controversy arise in some cases about whether a proposed experiment or a particular practice, such as deceiving participants, is ethical. The American Psychological Association has published a casebook to help psychologists resolve such issues (Nagy, 1999). The ethical principles themselves must continually be updated to deal with complex new questions—such as how to protect the confidentiality of e-mail and other online communications—that psychologists face in their ever-expanding range of work (APA, 2002b; Hays, 2006; Pipes, Holstein, & Aguirre, 2005; Warmerdam et al., 2010).

LINKAGES

As noted in the chapter on introducing psychology, all of psychology's subfields are related to one another. Our discussion of behavioral genetics illustrates just one way in which the topic of this chapter, research in psychology, is linked to the subfield of biological psychology (see the chapter on biological aspects of

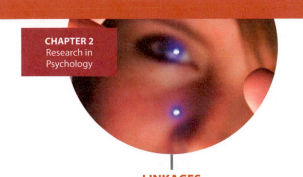

CHAPTER 2
Research in Psychology

psychology). The Linkages diagram shows ties to two other subfields as well, and there are many more ties throughout the book. Looking for linkages among subfields will help you see how they all fit together and help you better appreciate the big picture that is psychology.

LINKAGES

How much of our behavior is due to genetics and how much to our environment?
(ans. on p. 48)

Is it possible to do experiments on psychotherapy?
(ans. on p. 676)

Is it ethical to deceive people in order to learn about their social behavior?
(ans. on p. 741)

CHAPTER 3
Biological Aspects of Psychology

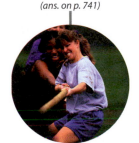

CHAPTER 16
Treatment of Psychological Disorders

CHAPTER 18
Social Influence

SUMMARY

Thinking Critically About Psychology (or Anything Else)

Critical thinking is the process of assessing claims and making judgments on the basis of well-supported evidence.

Critical Thinking and Scientific Research

Often questions about behavior and mental processes are phrased in terms of *hypotheses* about *variables* that have been specified by *operational definitions*. Tests of hypotheses are based on objective, quantifiable evidence, or *data*, representing the variables of interest. If data are to be useful, they must be evaluated for *reliability* and *validity*.

The Role of Theories

Explanations of phenomena often take the form of a *theory*, which is a set of statements that can be used to account for, predict, and even suggest ways of controlling certain phenomena. Theories must be subjected to careful evaluation.

Research Methods in Psychology

Research in psychology, as in other sciences, focuses on four main goals: description, prediction, control, and explanation.

Observational Methods: Watching Behavior

Observational methods such as *naturalistic observation* entail watching

without interfering as behavior occurs in the natural environment. These methods can be revealing, but care must be taken to ensure that observers are unbiased and do not alter the behavior being observed.

Case Studies: Taking a Closer Look

Case studies are intensive examinations of a particular individual, group, or situation. They are useful for studying new or rare phenomena and for evaluating new treatments or training programs.

Surveys: Looking at the Big Picture

Surveys ask questions, through interviews or questionnaires, about behavior, attitudes, beliefs, opinions, and intentions. They provide an efficient way to gather large amounts of data from many people at a relatively low cost, but their results can be distorted if questions are poorly phrased, if answers are not given honestly, or if respondents do not constitute a representative sample of the population whose views are of interest.

Correlational Studies: Looking for Relationships

Correlational studies examine relationships between variables in order to describe research data, test predictions, evaluate theories, and suggest hypotheses. Correlational studies are an important part of psychological research. However, the reasons behind the relationships they reveal cannot be established by correlational studies alone.

Experiments: Exploring Cause and Effect

In *experiments*, researchers manipulate an *independent variable* and observe the effect of that manipulation on a *dependent variable*. Participants receiving experimental treatment are called the *experimental group*; those in comparison conditions are called *control groups*. Experiments can reveal cause-and-effect relationships between variables, but only if researchers use *randomizing* procedures, *placebo* conditions, *double-blind designs*, and other strategies to avoid being misled

by *random variables*, participants' expectations, *experimenter bias*, and other *confounds*.

Selecting Human Participants for Research

Psychologists' research can be limited if their *sampling* procedures do not give them a fair cross section of the population they want to study and about which they want to draw conclusions. Anything other than *random sampling* is said to be *biased sampling* of participants. In most cases, psychologists try to conduct *representative sampling* of the populations that are available to them.

Statistical Analysis of Research Results

Psychologists use *descriptive statistics* and *inferential statistics* to summarize and analyze data.

Descriptive Statistics

Descriptive statistics include measures of central tendency (such as the *mode, median,* and *mean*), measures of variability (such as the *range* and *standard deviation*), and *correlation coefficients.* Although valuable for describing relationships, *correlations* alone cannot establish that two variables are causally related, nor can they

determine which variable might affect which or why.

Inferential Statistics

Psychologists employ inferential statistics to guide conclusions about data and especially to determine if correlations or differences between means have reached *statistical significance*—that is, are larger than would be expected by chance alone.

Statistics and Research Methods as Tools in Critical Thinking

Scientific evaluation of research requires the use of critical thinking to carefully assess the design and statistical analysis of even the most dramatic or desirable results.

Ethical Guidelines for Psychologists

Ethical guidelines promote the protection of humans and animals in psychological research. They also set the highest standards for behavior in all other aspects of psychologists' scientific and professional lives.

LINKAGES TO FURTHER LEARNING

Now that you have finished reading this chapter, how about exploring some of the topics and information that you found most interesting? Here are some places to start.

Books

F. Barbara Orlans, Tom Beauchamp, Rebecca Dresser, and John Gluck (Eds.), *The Human Use of Animals: Case Studies in Ethical Choice* (Oxford University Press, 1998). Case studies related to animal research.

Roger Hock, *Forty Studies That Changed Psychology* (Prentice Hall, 1995). Reports of famous psychological studies.

Joel Best, *Damned Lies and Statistics: Untangling Numbers from the Media, Politicians, and Activists* (University of California Press, 2001). Examples of why we need to think critically about statistics.

On the Internet

CourseMate Access an integrated eBook and chapter-specific learning tools including flashcards, quizzes, videos, and more. Go to CengageBrain.com.

 Want to maximize the value of your online study time? Take this easy-to-use study system's diagnostic pre-test, and it will create a personalized study plan for you. By helping you identify the topics that you need to understand better and then directing you to valuable online resources, it can speed up your chapter review. CengageNOW even provides a post-test so you can confirm that you are ready for an exam. Go to CengageBrain.com.

TALKING POINTS

Here are a few talking points to help you summarize this chapter for family and friends without giving a lecture.

1. Psychologists draw scientific conclusions about behavior and mental processes by using research methods based on critical thinking.

2. Critical thinking about a claim requires asking five main questions: What am I being asked to believe? What is the evidence for it? Is there more than one way to interpret that evidence? What additional evidence would help me choose the best interpretation? What conclusions are most reasonable?

3. To be valid, surveys must ask clear, unbiased questions of a large, representative sample of people.

4. The fact that two things are correlated does not guarantee that one is causing the other.

5. The value of an experiment depends on the quality of its design and sampling methods.

6. Behavior and mental processes are shaped by a mixture of genetic inheritance and environmental influences.

7. There are few, if any, "final answers" in scientific research in psychology; even statistically significant results lead to further questions and more research.

8. Psychologists sometimes use deception in their research, but the strict ethical standards they follow protect the welfare of the people they study.

3

Biological Aspects of Psychology

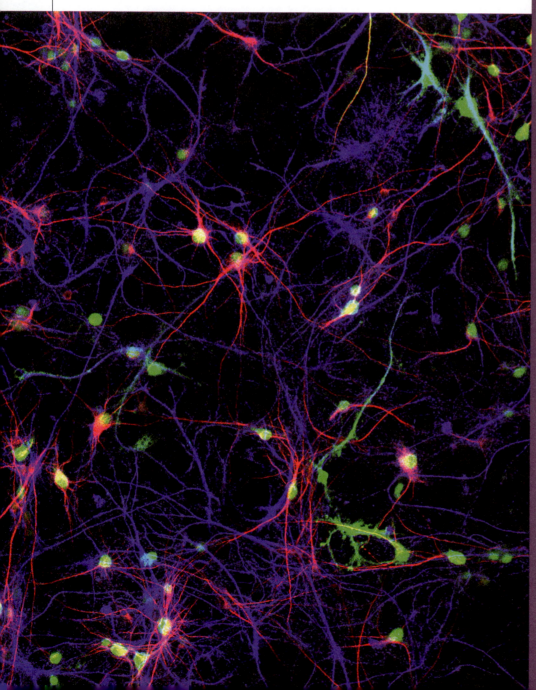

Before you read the next sentence, close your eyes and touch your nose. This task is easy, but it is not simple. To get the job done, your brain used specific nerves to tell your eyelids to close. It used other nerves to tell your hand to extend a finger and then sent a series of messages that moved your arm in just the right direction until it received a message that your finger and your nose were in contact. This example illustrates that everything you do—including how you feel and think—is based on some kind of biological activity in your body, especially in your brain. This chapter tells the story of that activity, beginning with the neuron, one of the body's most basic biological units. We describe how neurons form systems capable of receiving and processing information and translate it into behavior, thoughts, and biochemical changes.

Do you drink coffee, cola, or other caffeinated drinks? Do you consume alcoholic beverages? Have you been unable to quit smoking? If so, you know that caffeine, alcohol, and nicotine can change the way you feel. The effects of these substances are based largely on their ability to change the chemistry of your brain. There are many other examples of how our mental experiences, and our identity as individuals, are rooted in biological processes. Each year, millions of people who have been diagnosed with anxiety, depression, and other psychological disorders take prescription drugs that alter brain chemistry in ways that relieve their distress. Millions of others have the resilience to bounce back, without drugs, from even the worst experiences life can throw at them and find meaning and fulfillment in their lives. To what extent are these negative and positive reactions rooted in biological differences among people?

The importance and impact of biological processes stem from the fact that brain cells, hormones, genes, and other biological factors are related to everything you think and feel and do, from the fleeting memory you had a minute ago to the anxiety or excitement or fatigue you felt last night to the movements of your eyes as you read right now. In this chapter, we describe these biological factors in more detail. Reading it will take you into the realm of **biological psychology**, which is the study of the cells and organs of the body and the physical and chemical changes involved in behavior and mental processes. It is here that we begin to consider the relationship between your body and your mind, your brain and your behavior.

It is a complex relationship. Scientific psychologists are no doubt correct when they say that every thought, every feeling, and every action are represented somehow in the nervous system and that none of these events could occur without it. However, we must be careful not to oversimplify or overemphasize biological explanations in psychology. Many people assume, for example, that if a behavior or mental process has a strong biological basis, it is beyond our control—that "biology is destiny." Accordingly, many smokers don't even try to quit because they are sure that their biological addiction to nicotine will doom them to failure. This is not necessarily true, as millions of ex-smokers can confirm. The fact that all behavior and mental processes are *based on* biological processes does not mean that they can be fully understood through the study of biological processes alone.

In fact, reducing all of psychology to the analysis of brain chemicals would seriously underestimate the complexity of the interactions between our biological selves and our psychological experiences, between our genes and our environments. Just as all behaviors and mental processes are influenced by biology, all biological processes are influenced by the environment. We will see later that the experiences we have can change our brain chemistry and even our brain anatomy—often by affecting whether certain aspects of our genetic makeup are expressed. Examples of

biological psychology The psychological specialty focused on the physical and chemical changes that cause, and occur in response to, behavior and mental processes.

FIGURE 3.1
Three Functions of the Nervous System

The nervous system's three main functions are to receive information (input), integrate that information with past experiences (processing), and guide actions (output). When the alarm clock goes off, this person's nervous system, like yours, gets the message, recognizes what it means, decides what to do, and then takes action—by getting out of bed or perhaps hitting the snooze button.

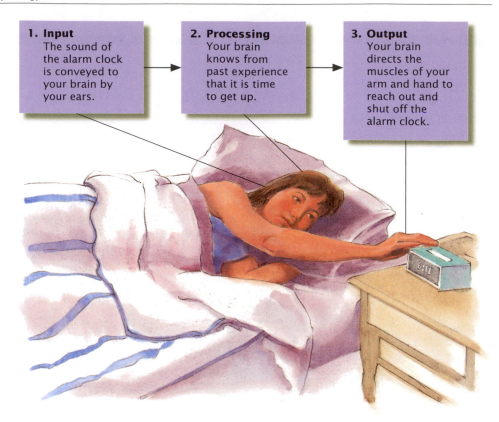

1. Input The sound of the alarm clock is conveyed to your brain by your ears.

2. Processing Your brain knows from past experience that it is time to get up.

3. Output Your brain directs the muscles of your arm and hand to reach out and shut off the alarm clock.

experience-dependent gene expression are discussed in the appendix on behavioral genetics, but for now, just consider height. Your height is strongly influenced by genetics, but how tall you actually become depends heavily on nutrition and other environmental factors (Tanner, 1992). Hereditary and environmental influences also combine to determine intelligence, personality, mental disorders, and all our other characteristics.

In short, understanding behavior and mental processes requires that we combine information from many sources, ranging from the activity of cells and organ systems to the activity of individuals and groups in social contexts. This chapter focuses on the biological level, not because it reveals the whole story of psychology but because it tells an important part of that story.

We begin by considering the **nervous system**, the billions of cells that make up your brain, your spinal cord, and other nerve fibers. The combined activity of these cells tells you what is going on inside and outside your body and allows you to make appropriate responses. For example, if you are jabbed with a pin, your nervous system gets the message and immediately causes you to flinch. But your nervous system can do far more than detect information and execute responses. When information about the world reaches your brain, that information is *processed*—meaning that it is combined with information about past experiences and current wants and needs—so that you can make a decision about how to respond. The chosen action is then taken (see Figure 3.1). In other words, your nervous system displays the characteristics of an information-processing system: It has input, processing, and output capabilities.

The processing capabilities of the nervous system are especially important, not only because the brain interprets information, makes decisions, and guides action but also because the brain can actually adjust the impact of incoming information. This phenomenon helps explain why you can't tickle yourself. In one study, simply telling ticklish people that they were about to be touched on the bottom of their feet caused activation in the brain region that receives sensory information from the foot (Carlsson et al., 2000). The anticipation of being touched made these people all the more sensitive to that touch. However, when they were asked to touch the bottoms

nervous system A complex combination of cells whose primary function is to allow an organism to gain information about what is going on inside and outside the body and to respond appropriately.

of their own feet, there was far less advance activation of this brain region, and they did not overreact to their touch. Why? The explanation is that when the brain plans a movement, it also predicts which of its own touch-detecting regions will be affected by that movement. So predictable, self-controlled touches, even in a normally "ticklish" spot, reduce activation of the sensory regions associated with that spot (Blakemore, Wolpert, & Frith, 2000).

The nervous system is able to do what it does partly because it is made up of cells that communicate with each other. Like all cells in the body—indeed, like all living cells—those in the nervous system can respond to various kinds of signals. Many of the signals that cells respond to come in the form of chemicals released by other cells. So even as various cells specialize during prenatal development to become skin, bone, hair, and other tissues, they still "stay in touch" through chemical signals. Bone cells, for example, add or lose calcium in response to hormones secreted in another part of the body. Cells in the bloodstream respond to viruses and other invaders by destroying them. Let's focus first on the cells of the nervous system, because their ability to communicate is the most efficient and complex.

The Nervous System

We begin our exploration of the nervous system by describing the individual cells and molecules that compose it. Then we consider how these cells are organized to form the structures of the human nervous system.

Cells of the Nervous System

When viewed through a microscope, brain tissue appears to be a hopelessly complex web of interconnecting fibers, but about a hundred years ago, the great Spanish anatomist Santiago Ramón y Cajal (pronounced "rah-MOHN ee kah-HAHL) argued that the nervous system is made up of separate cells, called *neurons*. When the invention of the electron microscope allowed scientists to see individual neurons, and the gaps between them, Ramón y Cajal's idea was confirmed. **Neurons** are cells that are specialized to rapidly respond to signals and to quickly send signals of their own. For many years, communication in the nervous system was thought to take place only between neurons, but this *neuron doctrine* has turned out to be incorrect (Bullock et al., 2005). Nonneuronal cells perform important communication functions too. These cells are called *glial cells* because *glia* in Greek means "glue," and scientists had long believed that they did no more than hold neurons together. However, we now know that **glial cells** also help neurons communicate by directing their growth, keeping their chemical environment stable, providing energy, and secreting chemicals to help restore damage (Rouach et al., 2008). So without glial cells, neurons could not function. Further, glial cells are capable of the signature functions of neurons, including releasing chemicals that influence neurons, responding to chemicals from neurons, and changing in response to experience (Barres, 2008). So the nervous system is actually made of two major types of cells—neurons and glial cells—that together allow the system to carry out its complex signaling tasks so efficiently.

Common Features of Neurons

Common Features of Neurons   Figure 3.2 shows three features that neurons share with almost every other kind of cell in the body. First, neurons have an *outer membrane* that acts like a fine screen, letting some substances pass in and out while blocking others. Second, nervous system cells have a *cell body,* which contains a *nucleus* (only red blood cells have no nucleus). The nucleus carries the genetic information that determines how a cell will function. Third, nervous system cells contain *mitochondria* (pronounced "my-toh-KAHN-dree-uh"), which are structures that turn oxygen and glucose into energy. This process is especially vital to brain cells. Although the brain accounts for only 2 percent of the body's weight, it consumes more than 20 percent of

neurons Fundamental units of the nervous system; nerve cells.

glial cells Cells in the nervous system that hold neurons together and help them communicate with one another.

FIGURE 3.2

The Neuron

Part A shows fibers extending outward from the cell body of a neuron, which is a nervous system cell. These fibers, called *axons* and *dendrites,* are among the features that make neurons unique. Part B shows an enlarged drawing of the neuron's cell body. The cell body of a neuron includes an outer membrane, a nucleus, and mitochondria.

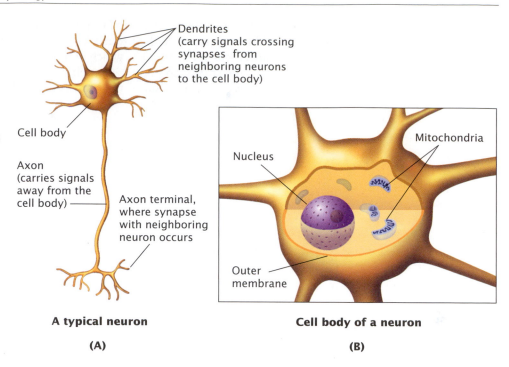

A typical neuron

(A)

Cell body of a neuron

(B)

the body's oxygen (Sokoloff, 1981). All of this energy is required because brain cells transmit signals among themselves to an even greater extent than cells in the rest of the body.

Special Features of Neurons   Neurons have three special features that enable them to communicate signals efficiently. The first is their structure. Although neurons come in many shapes and sizes, they all have long, thin fibers that extend outward from the cell body (see part A of Figure 3.2). When these fibers get close to other neurons, communication between the cells can occur. The intermixing of all these fibers with fibers from other neurons allows each neuron to be close to thousands or even hundreds of thousands of other neurons.

Two types of fibers extend from a neuron's cell body: axons and dendrites. **Axons** are the fibers that carry signals away from the cell body, out to where communication occurs with other neurons. Each neuron generally has only one axon leaving the cell body, but that one axon may have many branches. Axons can be very short or, like the axon that sends signals from your spinal cord to your big toe, several feet long. **Dendrites** are the fibers that receive signals from the axons of other neurons and carry those signals to the cell body. A neuron can have many dendrites. Dendrites, too, usually have many branches. Remember that *axons* carry signals *away* from the cell body, whereas *dendrites detect* signals from other cells.

The neuron's ability to communicate efficiently also depends on two other features: the "excitable" surface membrane of some of its fibers and the tiny spaces between neurons, called *synaptic gaps,* or **synapses**. Let's consider how these features allow a signal to be sent rapidly from one end of a neuron to the other and from one neuron to another.

Action Potentials

To understand how signals are sent in the nervous system, you first need to know something about nerve cell membranes and the chemicals that are found inside and outside these cells. The neuron's cell membrane is a *semipermeable* barrier, meaning that, as already mentioned, it lets some chemical ions pass through but blocks others. These ions are atoms that carry a positive or negative electrical charge. Normally, the

axons   Fibers that carry signals from the body of a neuron out to where communication occurs with other neurons.

dendrites   Neuron fibers that receive signals from the axons of other neurons and carry those signals to the cell body.

synapses   The tiny gaps between neurons across which they communicate.

FIGURE 3.3
The Beginning of an Action Potential

This greatly simplified view of a polarized nerve cell shows the normally closed gates in the cell membrane. An electrochemical potential across the membrane is created because there are more positively charged ions outside the membrane than inside. There are also more negatively charged ions on the inside than on the outside. If stimulation causes depolarization near a particular gate, that gate may swing open, allowing positively charged ions to rush in. This, in turn, depolarizes the neighboring region of membrane and stimulates the next gate to open, and so on down the axon. This wave of depolarization is called an *action potential*. Membrane gates allow action potentials to spread along dendrites in a similar fashion.

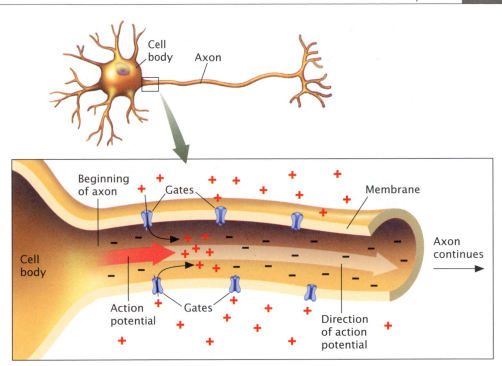

cell pumps positively charged ions out through its membrane, making the inside of the cell slightly more negative than the outside. In this state, the cell membrane is said to be *polarized*. Ions with a positive charge are attracted to those with a negative charge. This attraction creates a force called an *electrochemical potential*, which drives the positively charged ions toward the inside of the cell.

The cell membrane keeps out many of these positively charged ions, but some are able to enter by passing through special openings, called *channels*. These membrane channels are distributed along the axon and dendrites and act as "gates" that can be opened or closed (see Figure 3.3). Normally the channels along the axon are closed, but changes in the environment around the cell can *depolarize* part of its membrane, causing the gates in that area to swing open and allowing positively charged ions to rush in. When this happens, the next area of the axon becomes depolarized, causing the neighboring gate to open. This sequence continues, creating a wave of changes in electrochemical potential that spreads rapidly all the way down the axon.

This sudden wave of electrochemical changes in the axon is called an **action potential**. When an action potential shoots down an axon, the neuron is said to have "fired." This term is appropriate because action potentials in axons follow the *all-or-none law*. Like a gunshot, the cell either fires at full strength or it does not fire at all. For many years, scientists believed that only axons are capable of generating action potentials. However, later research revealed that action potentials also occur in dendrites (Magee & Johnston, 1997). In many neurons, action potentials beginning in the axon go in both directions—down the axon and also "backward" through the cell body and into the dendrites.

The speed of the action potential as it moves down an axon is constant for a particular cell, but in different cells that speed can range from 0.2 meters per second to 120 meters per second (about 260 miles per hour). The speed depends on the diameter of the axon—larger ones are faster—and on whether myelin is present. **Myelin** (pronounced "MY-uh-lin") is a fatty substance that wraps around some axons like a stocking and speeds action potentials. Larger myelinated cells are usually found in parts of the nervous system that carry the most urgently needed information. For example, the neurons that receive information from the environment about hot irons, oncoming cars, and other dangers are fast-acting myelinated cells. Multiple sclerosis

action potential An abrupt wave of electrochemical changes traveling down an axon when a neuron becomes depolarized.

myelin A fatty substance that wraps around some axons and increases the speed of action potentials.

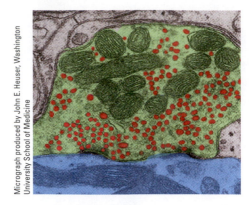

FIGURE 3.4
A Synapse
This photograph taken with an electron microscope shows part of a synaptic gap between two neurons, magnified 50,000 times. The ending of the first cell's axon is shaded green; the green ovals are mitochondria. The red spots are vesicles, which contain neurotransmitters. The synapse itself appears as the narrow gap between the first cell's green-shaded axon and the blue-shaded dendrite of the cell below.

refractory period A short rest period between action potentials.

neurotransmitters Chemicals that assist in the transfer of signals from one neuron to another.

neural receptors (receptors) Sites on the surface of a cell that allow only one type of neurotransmitter to fit into them, triggering a chemical response that may lead to an action potential.

postsynaptic potential The change in the membrane potential of a neuron that has received stimulation from another neuron.

excitatory postsynaptic potential A postsynaptic potential that depolarizes the neuronal membrane, making the cell more likely to fire an action potential.

(MS), a severe brain disorder that destroys myelin, may occur because some viruses and bacteria are very similar to components of myelin (Greene et al., 2008). When the MS patient's immune system attacks those pathogens, it destroys vital myelin as well, resulting in disruption of vision, speech, balance, and other important functions.

Neurons can fire over and over again because their membrane gates open only briefly and then close. Between firings there is a very short rest, called a **refractory period**, during which the neuron cannot fire. As the positively charged ions are pumped back outside the membrane, the cell returns to its original polarized state. When this *repolarization* process is complete, the neuron can fire again. The rate of firing can vary from just a few action potentials per second to as many as 1,000 per second. Patterns of neuron firing amount to coded messages that, for example, ions us about the intensity of light or sound. We describe some of the codes used by the nervous system in the chapter on sensation.

Synapses and Communication Between Neurons

How does an action potential fired by one neuron affect the activity of other neurons? For communication to occur between cells, a signal must be transmitted across the synapse, or gap, between neurons. Usually, the axon of one cell delivers its signals across a synapse to the dendrites of a second cell. Those dendrites, in turn, transmit the signal to their cell body, which may relay the signal down its axon to a third cell, and so on. But there can be other communication patterns too. Axons can signal to other axons or even directly to the cell body of another neuron. And dendrites of one cell can send signals to the dendrites of other cells. These and other communication patterns allow the brain to conduct extremely complex information-processing tasks (Bullock et al., 2005).

Neurotransmitters Communication between neurons across the synapse relies first on chemical messengers called **neurotransmitters**. These chemicals are usually stored in numerous little "bags," called *vesicles,* at the tips of axons (see Figure 3.4). When an action potential reaches the end of an axon, a neurotransmitter is released into the synapse, where it spreads to reach the next, or *postsynaptic,* cell (see Figure 3.5). (In the less common case of dendrite-to-dendrite communication, neurotransmitters are released by unknown mechanisms; Pape, Munsch, & Budde, 2004).

When they reach the membrane of the postsynaptic cell, neurotransmitters attach to proteins called **neural receptors**, or simply **receptors**. Like a puzzle piece fitting into its proper place, a neurotransmitter snugly fits, or "binds" to, its own receptors but not to receptors for other neurotransmitters (again, see Figure 3.5). Although each receptor "recognizes" only one type of neurotransmitter, each neurotransmitter type can bind to several different receptor types. As a result, the same neurotransmitter can have different effects depending on the type of receptor to which it binds.

When a neurotransmitter binds to a receptor, it stimulates channels in the membrane of the postsynaptic cell to open, allowing chemical ions to flow in or out. The flow of these ions into and out of the postsynaptic cell produces a change in its membrane potential. So the *chemical* signal that crosses the synapse creates an *electrochemical* signal in the postsynaptic cell.

Excitatory and Inhibitory Signals The change that takes place in the membrane potential of the postsynaptic cell is called the **postsynaptic potential**. The change can make the cell either more likely or less likely to fire. For example, if positively charged ions of chemicals such as sodium or calcium flow *into* the neuron, it becomes slightly less polarized. Because this *depolarization* of the membrane can lead the neuron to fire an action potential, a depolarizing postsynaptic potential is called an **excitatory postsynaptic potential**, or EPSP. However, if positively

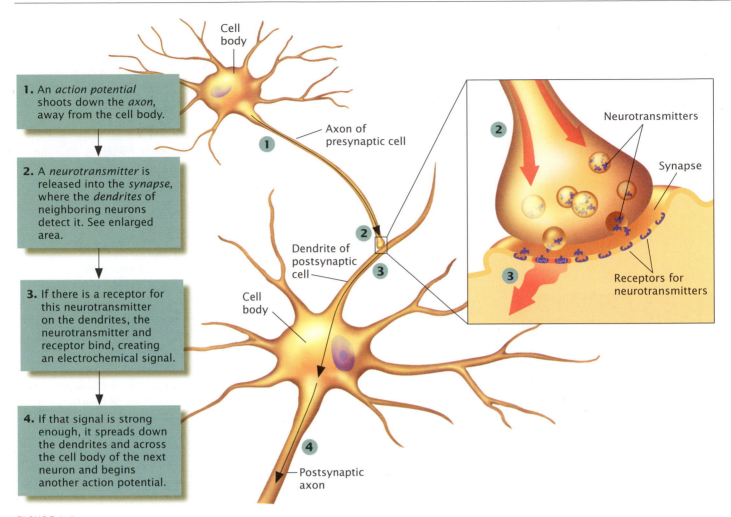

1. An *action potential* shoots down the *axon*, away from the cell body.

2. A *neurotransmitter* is released into the *synapse*, where the *dendrites* of neighboring neurons detect it. See enlarged area.

3. If there is a receptor for this neurotransmitter on the dendrites, the neurotransmitter and receptor bind, creating an electrochemical signal.

4. If that signal is strong enough, it spreads down the dendrites and across the cell body of the next neuron and begins another action potential.

Cell body

Axon of presynaptic cell

Dendrite of postsynaptic cell

Cell body

Postsynaptic axon

Neurotransmitters

Synapse

Receptors for neurotransmitters

FIGURE 3.5

Communication Between Neurons
When a neuron fires, an action potential shoots to the end of its axon, triggering the release of a neurotransmitter into the synapse. Neurotransmitters influence neighboring cells by stimulating special receptors on the surface of those cells' membranes. Each type of receptor receives only one type of neurotransmitter; the two fit together like puzzle pieces or like a lock and its key. As shown here, when stimulated by their neurotransmitter, a cell's receptors can help generate a wave of depolarization in that cell's dendrites, making it more likely to fire. A cell's receptors can also receive signals that have the opposite effect, making the cell less likely to fire.

inhibitory postsynaptic potential A postsynaptic potential that hyperpolarizes the neuronal membrane, making a cell less likely to fire an action potential.

charged ions (such as potassium) flow *out* of the neuron, or if negatively charged ions flow in, the neuron becomes slightly *more* polarized. This *hyperpolarization* makes it less likely that the neuron will fire an action potential. For this reason, a hyperpolarizing postsynaptic potential is called an **inhibitory postsynaptic potential**, or IPSP.

The postsynaptic potential spreads along the membrane of the postsynaptic cell. But unlike the action potential in an axon, which remains at a constant strength, the postsynaptic potential fades as it goes along. Usually, it is not strong enough to pass all the way along the dendrite and through the cell body to the axon, so a single EPSP will not cause a neuron to fire. However, each neuron is constantly receiving EPSPs and IPSPs. The combined effect of rapidly repeated potentials—or of potentials coming from many locations—can create a signal strong enough to reach the junction of the axon and cell body, a specialized region in which new action potentials are generated.

Whether or not the postsynaptic cell fires and how rapidly it fires depend on whether, at a given moment, there are more excitatory ("fire") or more inhibitory ("don't fire") signals from other neurons at this junction (see Figure 3.6). So as neurotransmitters transfer information across many neurons, each neuron constantly integrates or processes this information.

Neurotransmitters are involved in every aspect of behavior and mental processes, as you will see later in this chapter and in other chapters. In the chapter on sensation, for example, we describe some of the neurotransmitters used in pathways that convey pain messages throughout the brain and spinal cord. In the consciousness chapter, we describe how neurotransmitters are affected by alcohol and illegal drugs.

FIGURE 3.6

Integration of Neural Signals

Most of the signals that a neuron receives arrive at its dendrites or at its cell body. These signals typically come from many neighboring cells and can contain conflicting messages. Excitatory signals make the cell more likely to fire. Inhibitory signals make the cell less likely to fire. Whether or not the cell actually fires at any given moment depends on whether excitatory or inhibitory messages predominate at the junction of the cell body and the axon.

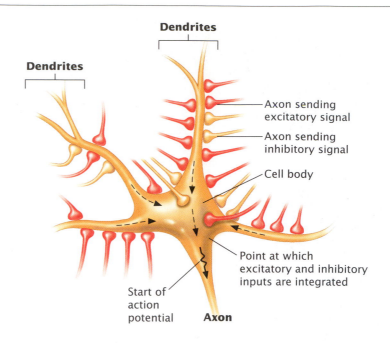

Dendrites

Dendrites

Axon sending excitatory signal

Axon sending inhibitory signal

Cell body

Point at which excitatory and inhibitory inputs are integrated

Start of action potential

Axon

© Ariel Skelley/Corbis

A Damaged Nervous System

If axons, dendrites, or other components of the nervous system are damaged or disordered, serious problems can result. The spinal cord injury that this woman suffered in a car accident cut the neural communication lines that had allowed her to feel and move the lower part of her body.

neural networks Neurons that operate together to perform complex functions.

central nervous system (CNS) The parts of the nervous system encased in bone; specifically, the brain and the spinal cord.

peripheral nervous system (PNS) The parts of the nervous system not housed in bone.

In the chapter on psychological disorders, we discuss the role that neurotransmitters play in schizophrenia and depression, and in the chapter on the treatment of psychological disorders, we consider how prescription drugs act on neurotransmitters to reduce the symptoms of those disorders. Neurotransmitters are affected by many other chemicals, too, from the nerve agents used in biological weapons to the Botox used in antiwrinkle treatments.

Organization and Functions of the Nervous System

Impressive as individual neurons are (see "In Review: Neurons, Neurotransmitters, and Receptors"), we can best understand their functions by looking at how they operate in groups. In the brain and spinal cord, neurons are organized into groups called **neural networks**. Many neurons in a network are closely connected, sending axons to the dendrites of many other neurons in the network. Signals from one network also go to other networks, and small networks are organized into bigger collections. By studying these networks, neuroscientists have begun to see that the nervous system conveys information not by the activity of single neurons sending single messages with a particular meaning but rather through the activity of groups of neurons firing together in varying combinations (Kilavik et al., 2009). So the same neurons may be involved in producing different patterns of behavior, depending on which combinations of them are active.

The groups of neurons in the nervous system that provide information about the environment are known as *sensory systems,* or the *senses.* These senses—hearing, vision, taste, smell, and touch—are described in the chapter on sensation. Integration and processing of information occur mainly in the brain. Output flows through *motor systems,* which are the parts of the nervous system that the brain uses to influence muscles and other organs to respond to the environment.

The nervous system has two major divisions, which work together: the peripheral nervous system and the central nervous system (see Figure 3.7). The **central nervous system (CNS)** consists of the brain and spinal cord, which are encased in bone for protection. Like the chief executive officer in a company, the CNS receives information, processes it, and determines what actions should result (Banich, 2009). The **peripheral nervous system (PNS)** extends throughout the body and, like an e-mail or instant messaging service, relays information to and from the brain. Let's take a closer look at these divisions of the nervous system.

IN REVIEW Neurons, Neurotransmitters, and Receptors

Part	Function	Type of Signal Carried
Axon	Carries signals away from the cell body	The action potential, an all-or-nothing electrochemical signal that shoots down the axon to vesicles at the tip of the axon, releasing neurotransmitters
Dendrite	Detects and carries signals to the cell body	The postsynaptic potential, an electrochemical signal moving toward the cell body
Synapse	Provides an area for the transfer of signals between neurons, usually between the axon of one cell and the dendrite of another	Chemicals that cross the synapse and reach receptors on another cell
Neurotransmitter	A chemical released by one cell that binds to the receptors on another cell	A chemical message telling the next cell to fire or not to fire its own action potential
Receptor	Protein on the cell membrane that receives chemical signals	Recognizes certain neurotransmitters, thus allowing it to begin a postsynaptic potential in the dendrite

1. For one neuron to communicate with another, a _____ has to cross the _____ between them.
2. The nervous system's main functions are to _____ , _____ , and _____ information.
3. The two main types of cells in the nervous system are _____ and _____ .

The Peripheral Nervous System: Keeping in Touch with the World

As shown in Figure 3.7, the peripheral nervous system has two components, each of which performs both sensory and motor functions.

The Somatic Nervous System

The first of these components is the **somatic nervous system**, which transmits information from the senses to the CNS and carries signals from the CNS to the muscles that move the skeleton. **Sensory neurons** bring information into the brain. **Motor neurons** carry information from the brain to direct motion. For example, imagine that you are at the beach. You feel the warmth of the sun and smell the ocean because

somatic nervous system The subsystem of the peripheral nervous system that transmits information from the senses to the central nervous system and carries signals from the central nervous system to the muscles.

sensory neurons Cells in the nervous system that provide information to the brain about the environment.

motor neurons Cells in the nervous system that the brain uses to influence muscles and other organs to respond to the environment in some way.

FIGURE 3.7
Organization of the Nervous System
The brain and spinal cord make up the bone-encased central nervous system (CNS), the body's central information processor, decision maker, and director of actions. The peripheral nervous system, which is not housed in bone, functions mainly to carry messages. The somatic subsystem of the peripheral nervous system transmits information to the CNS from the outside world and conveys instructions from the CNS to the muscles. The autonomic subsystem conveys messages from the CNS that alter the activity of organs and glands, and it sends information about that activity back to the brain.

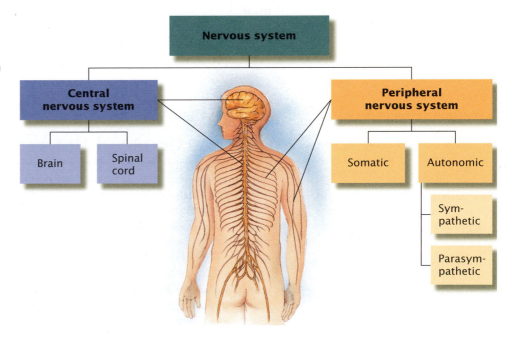

sensory neurons in your somatic nervous system take in these pieces of sensory information and send them to the central nervous system for processing. And when you decide it is time to turn over, sit up, or put on more sunscreen, your brain sends movement instructions through motor neurons in the somatic nervous system. These motor neurons extend from your spinal cord to your muscles, where the release of a neurotransmitter onto them causes the muscles to contract.

The Autonomic Nervous System

The second component of the peripheral nervous system, the **autonomic nervous system**, carries messages back and forth between the CNS and the heart, lungs, and other organs and glands. These messages increase or decrease the activity of the organs and glands to meet varying demands placed on the body. For example, neural connections from your liver to your brain influence how much fat you burn and how much you store (Friedman, 2007). And as you lie on the beach, it is your autonomic nervous system that makes your heart beat a little faster when an attractive stranger walks by and smiles at you.

The name *autonomic* means "autonomous" and suggests independent operation. This term is appropriate because even though the autonomic nervous system is influenced by the brain, it controls activities that are normally outside of conscious control, such as digestion and perspiration (sweating). The autonomic nervous system exercises this control through its two divisions: the sympathetic and parasympathetic branches. Generally, the **sympathetic nervous system** mobilizes the body for action in the face of stress. The responses that result from intense activity of the sympathetic system are collectively referred to as the *fight-or-flight syndrome* or *fight-flight reaction*. The **parasympathetic nervous system** regulates the body's energy-conserving functions. The two branches of the autonomic nervous system often create opposite effects. For example, the sympathetic nervous system can make your heart beat faster, whereas the parasympathetic nervous system can slow it down.

The functions of the autonomic nervous system may not get star billing, but you would miss them if they were gone. Just as a race-car driver is nothing without a good pit crew, the somatic nervous system depends on the autonomic nervous system to get its job done. For example, when you want to move your muscles, you create a demand for energy. The autonomic nervous system fills the bill by increasing sugar fuels in the bloodstream. If you decide to stand up, you need increased blood pressure so that your blood does not flow out of your brain and settle in your legs. Again, the autonomic nervous system makes the adjustment. Disorders of the autonomic nervous system can make people sweat uncontrollably or faint whenever they stand up; they can also lead to other problems, such as an inability to have sex. We examine the autonomic nervous system in more detail in the chapter on motivation and emotion.

autonomic nervous system A subsystem of the peripheral nervous system that carries messages between the central nervous system and the heart, lungs, and other organs and glands.

sympathetic nervous system The subsystem of the autonomic nervous system that readies the body for vigorous activity.

parasympathetic nervous system The subsystem of the autonomic nervous system that typically influences activity related to the protection, nourishment, and growth of the body.

The Central Nervous System: Making Sense of the World

The amazing speed and efficiency of the neural networks that make up the central nervous system—the brain and spinal cord—have prompted many people to compare it to the central processor in a computer. In fact, to better understand how human and other brains work and how they relate to sensory and motor systems, computational neuroscientists have created *neural network models* on computers. The brain activity described by these models is called *parallel distributed processing* because information is processed by a number of brain regions at the same time. The chapters on sensation, perception, learning, and memory present examples of how parallel distributed processing models have been applied to improve our understanding of some of the brain's most complex functions.

Neural network models are neatly laid out like computer circuits or the carefully planned streets of a new suburb, but the flesh-and-blood central nervous system is far more difficult to follow. In fact, the CNS looks more like Boston or Paris, with distinct neighborhoods, winding back streets, and multilaned highways. Its "neighborhoods" are collections of neuronal cell bodies called *nuclei* (pronounced "NEW-klee-eye"; the plural of *nucleus*). The "highways" of the central nervous system are made up of axons that travel together in bundles called *fiber tracts* or *pathways*. Like a freeway ramp, the axon from a given cell may merge with and leave fiber tracts, and it may send branches into other tracts. The pathways travel from one nucleus to other nuclei, and scientists have learned much about how the brain works by tracing the connections among nuclei. To begin our description of some of these nuclei and anatomical connections, let's consider a practical example of nervous system functioning.

At 6:00 A.M., your alarm goes off. The day begins innocently enough with what appears to be a simple case of information processing. Input in the form of sound from the alarm clock is received by your ears, which convert the sound into neural signals that reach your brain. Your brain compares these signals with previous experiences stored in memory and correctly associates the sound with "alarm clock." However, your output is somewhat impaired because your brain's activity has not yet reached the waking state. It directs your muscles poorly: You get out of bed and shuffle into the kitchen, where, in your drowsy condition, you touch a hot burner as you reach for the coffeepot. Now things get livelier. Heat energy activates sensory neurons in your fingers, and action potentials flash along fiber tracts going into the spinal cord.

The Spinal Cord

The **spinal cord** receives signals from the senses, including pain and touch from the fingertips, and relays those signals to the brain through fibers within the cord. Neurons in the spinal cord also carry signals downward, from the brain to the muscles. In addition, cells of the spinal cord can direct some simple behaviors without instructions from the brain. These behaviors are called **reflexes** because the response to an incoming signal is directly "reflected" back out (see Figure 3.8).

For example, when you touched that hot burner, impulses from sensory neurons in your fingers reflexively activated motor neurons, which caused muscles in your arm to contract and quickly withdraw your hand. Because spinal reflexes like this one include few time-consuming synaptic links, they are very fast. And because spinal reflexes occur without instructions from the brain, they are considered involuntary. Still, they do send action potentials along fiber tracts going to the brain. So you officially "know" you have been burned a fraction of a second after your reflex got you out of trouble.

The story does not end there, however. When a simple reflex set off by touching something hot causes one set of arm muscles to contract, an opposing set of muscles relaxes. If this did not happen, the arm would go rigid. Furthermore, muscles have receptors that send impulses to the spinal cord to let it know how extended they are, so that a reflex pathway can adjust the muscle contraction to allow smooth movement. This is an example of a *feedback system,* a series of processes in which information about the consequences of an action goes back to the source of the action so that adjustments can be made.

In the spinal cord, sensory neurons are called *afferent* neurons and motor neurons are called *efferent* neurons, because *afferent* means "coming toward" and *efferent* means "going away." To remember these terms, notice that *afferent* and *approach* both begin with *a*; *efferent* and *exit* both begin with *e*.

The Brain

When pain messages from that hot burner reach your brain, you don't become aware just of being burned. You might also realize that you have burned yourself twice before in the past week and get annoyed at your own carelessness. The brain is the most complex element in the central nervous system, and it is your brain's astonishing

spinal cord The part of the central nervous system within the spinal column that relays signals from peripheral senses to the brain and conveys messages from the brain to the rest of the body.

reflexes Involuntary, unlearned reactions in the form of swift, automatic, and finely coordinated movements in response to external stimuli.

FIGURE 3.8
A Reflex Pathway

TRY THIS Sit on a chair, cross one leg over the other, and then use the handle of a butter knife or some other solid object to gently tap your top knee, just below the kneecap, until you get a "knee jerk" reaction. Tapping your knee at just the right spot sets off an almost instantaneous sequence of events that begins with stimulation of sensory neurons that respond to stretch. When those neurons fire, their axons, which end within the spinal cord, cause spinal neurons to fire. This firing stimulates the firing of motor neurons with axons ending in your thigh muscles. As a result those muscles contract, causing a kicking motion of the lower leg and foot. Information about the knee tap and about what the leg has done also goes to your cerebral cortex, but the reflex is completed without waiting for guidance from the brain.

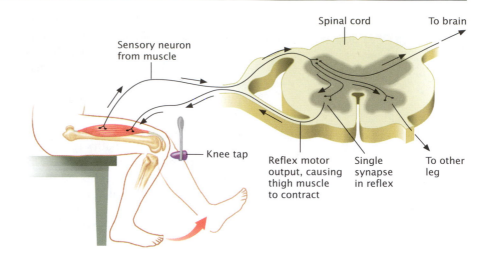

capacity for information processing that allows you to have these thoughts and feelings. A variety of modern brain-scanning techniques, combined with some older ones, have allowed neuroscientists to learn more than ever before about the workings of the human brain (see Table 3.1).

TABLE 3.1	Techniques for Studying Human Brain Function and Structure	
Technique	**What It Shows**	**Advantages (+) and Disadvantages (−)**
EEG (electroencephalography) Multiple electrodes are pasted to the outside of the head	Lines that chart the summed electrical fields resulting from the activity of billions of neurons	+ Detects very rapid changes in electrical activity, allowing analysis of stages of cognitive processing − Provides poor spatial resolution of the source of electrical activity; EEG is sometimes combined with magnetoencephalography (MEG), which localizes electrical activity by measuring magnetic fields associated with it
PET (positron emission tomography) and SPECT (single-photon emission computed tomography) Positrons and photons are emissions from radioactive substances	An image of the amount and localization of any molecule that can be injected in radioactive form, such as neurotransmitters, drugs, or tracers for blood flow or glucose use (which indicates specific changes in neuronal activity)	+ Allows functional and biochemical studies + Provides visual image corresponding to anatomy − Requires exposure to low levels of radioactivity − Provides spatial resolution better than that of EEG but poorer than that of MRI − Cannot follow rapid changes (those faster than 30 seconds)
MRI (magnetic resonance imaging) Exposes the brain to a magnetic field and measures radio frequency waves	Traditional MRI provides high-resolution image of brain anatomy. Functional MRI (fMRI) provides images of changes in blood flow (which indicate specific changes in neural activity). A new variant, diffusion tensor imaging (DTI), shows water flow in neural fibers, thus revealing the "wiring diagram" of neural connections in the brain.	+ Requires no exposure to radioactivity + Provides high spatial resolution of anatomical details (smaller than 1 mm) + Provides high temporal resolution (less than one-tenth of a second)
TMS (transcranial magnetic stimulation) Temporarily disrupts electrical activity of a small region of brain by exposing it to an intense magnetic field	Normal function of a particular brain region can be studied by observing changes after TMS is applied to a specific location.	+ Shows which brain regions are necessary for given tasks − Long-term safety not well established

FIGURE 3.9
Combining a PET Scan and Magnetic Resonance Imaging

Researchers have superimposed images from PET scans and MRI to construct a three-dimensional view of the living brain. Here you can see the brain of a young girl with epilepsy. The picture of the outer surface of the brain is from the MRI. The pink area is from the PET scan and shows the source of epileptic activity. The images at the right are the MRI and PET images at one plane, or "slice," through the brain (indicated by the line on the brain at the left).

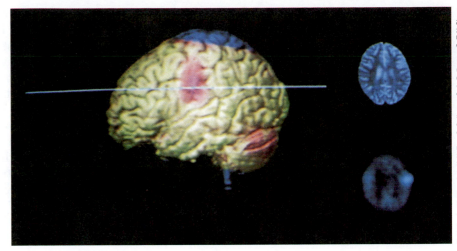

D. N. Levin, H. Xiaoping, K. K. Tan, S. Galhotra, C. A. Palizzare, G. Y. Chen, R. N. Beck, C. T. Chen, M. D. Cooper, J. F. Mullan, J. Hekmatpanah, & J. P. Spire (1989). "The Brain: Integrated three-dimensional display of MR and PET images," *Radiology*, 172: 783–789

Each technique can indirectly measure the activity of neurons firing, and each has advantages and disadvantages. One of the earliest of these techniques, called the *electroencephalograph (EEG)*, measures general electrical activity of the brain. Electrodes are pasted on the scalp to detect the electrical fields resulting from the activity of billions of neurons. This tool can associate rapidly changing electrical activity with changes in the activity of the brain, but it cannot tell us exactly where the active cells are.

A newer technique, called the *PET scan*, can locate cell activity by recording where substances such as glucose or other cellular fuels become concentrated after being made radioactive and injected into the bloodstream. *PET* stands for *positron emission tomography*. It records images from the brain that indicate the location of the radioactivity as the brain performs various tasks. For instance, PET studies have revealed that specific brain regions are activated when we look at fearful facial expressions or hear fearful voices (Pourtois et al., 2005) and which neurotransmitter receptors are stimulated when a smoker inhales on a cigarette (McClernon, 2009). PET scans can tell us a lot about where certain chemical changes in the brain occur, but they reveal only crude information about the details of the brain's physical structure.

A detailed structural picture of the brain can be seen, however, using *magnetic resonance imaging*, or *MRI*. MRI exposes the brain to a magnetic field and measures the resulting radio frequency waves to get amazingly clear pictures of the brain's anatomical details (see Figure 3.9). *Functional MRI*, or *fMRI* (see Figure 3.10), combines the advantages of PET and MRI and is capable of detecting changes in blood flow that reflect

FIGURE 3.10
Linking Eastern Medicine and Western Neuroscience Through Functional MRI

Scientists are using functional magnetic resonance imaging (fMRI) to investigate the role of the brain in the effects of acupuncture (Zhang et al., 2009), an ancient Asian medical practice in which physical disorders are treated by stimulating specific skin locations with needles. Most acupuncture points are far from the organ being treated. For example, vision problems are treated by inserting needles at "acupoints" in the foot. This may sound far-fetched, but MRI shows that both visual information entering the eyes and needle stimulation of certain acupoints in the foot do activate similar areas of the brain. The MRI image on the left was produced by visual stimuli; the one on the right shows activation of the same brain area in response to acupuncture at a certain spot in the foot. Acupoints in the foot are located near nerves, but the pathways to specific parts of the brain have not been charted. (Acupuncture is discussed further in the sensation chapter.)

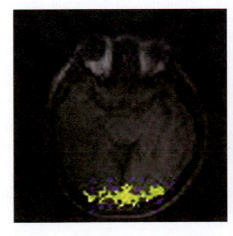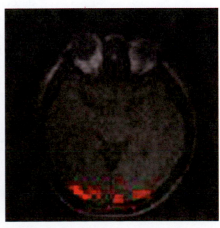

From "New findings of the correlation between acupoints and corresponding brain cortices using functional MRI," by Cho et al, *Proceedings of the National Academy of Sciences*, vol. 95, pp. 2670–2673, March 1998. © 1998 National Academy of Sciences, USA

ongoing changes in the activity of neurons—providing a sort of "moving picture" of the brain. The newest techniques offer even deeper insight into brain activity, structure, and functioning. One of these techniques is a variant on fMRI called *diffusion tensor imaging (DTI)*, which traces activity along axon pathways. Another, called *transcranial magnetic stimulation (TMS)*, uses strong magnetic fields to temporarily stimulate or disrupt the activity of neurons in a particular region of the brain (Lagopoulos & Malhi, 2008; López-Ibor, López-Ibor, & Pastrana, 2008). So if one region is stimulated by TMS and fMRI shows changes occurring in another region, this indicates that the functions occurring in the two regions are connected (Bestmann et al., 2008). Similarly, if the ability to perform a certain behavior is affected when TMS disrupts activity in a certain brain region, this suggests that the behavior is somehow controlled or influenced by that brain region (Muggleton, 2010). TMS may also have unexpected value in the treatment of depression and migraine headaches (O'Reardon et al., 2007).

THINKING CRITICALLY

What Can fMRI Tell Us About Behavior and Mental Processes?

A picture may be worth a thousand words, but the pictures of brain activity offered by fMRI are generating millions of them. As of 2009, more than seventeen thousand scientific articles have discussed the results of fMRI scans taken while people engaged in various kinds of thinking or experienced various emotions. Neuroscientists who use brain imaging techniques are now to be found in psychology departments around the world, and as described in other chapters, their work is changing the research landscape in cognitive, social, and abnormal psychology. Excitement over fMRI is not confined to scientists. Popular and scientific magazines routinely carry fMRI pictures that appear to "show" people's thoughts and feelings as they happen. Readers see these articles as more believable than those offering the same data in less dramatic tables or graphs (McCabe & Castel, 2008), which may be one reason why so many companies these days are making money by offering brain imaging services that can supposedly improve the quality of employee selection, lie detection, political campaign strategies, product design, and diagnosis of mental disorders. The editor of one scientific journal summed up this trend by saying that "a picture is worth a thousand dollars" (Farah, 2009).

What am I being asked to believe or accept?

In the early 1800s, similar excitement surrounded phrenology, a technique that involved feeling bumps and depressions on the skull. It was claimed that these contours reflect the size of twenty-seven structures on the brain's surface that determine personality traits, mental abilities, talents, and other characteristics. Although wildly popular with the public (Benjamin & Baker, 2004), phrenology did not survive the critical thinking of nineteenth-century scientists, and the technique has long been discredited. Today, some scientists wonder whether fMRI is a twenty-first-century version of phrenology, at least in the sense that their colleagues might be accepting its value too readily. These scientists point out that although fMRI images can indicate where brain activity occurs as people think and experience emotion, there is no guarantee that this activity is actually causing the associated thoughts and feelings (Aldridge, 2005). Questions are also being raised about the assumption that particular thought processes or emotions occur in a particular brain structure or set of structures. It is easy to talk about "thinking" or "attention," but these psychological terms might not correspond to specific biological processes that can be isolated and located by any technology.

Is there evidence available to support the claim?

When the participant in an fMRI experiment thinks or feels something, you can actually see the colors in the brain scan change, much like the color changes you see on weather radar as a rainstorm intensifies or weakens. Looking at an fMRI scan, you get a clear impression that the brain areas that "light up" when a person experiences an emotion or performs a mental task are the ones involved in that emotion or task (see Figure 1.1 in the chapter on introducing psychology).

These scans are not as precise as they seem, though, because fMRI doesn't directly measure brain cell activity. The colors seen in an fMRI scan reflect instead the flow of blood in the brain and the amount of oxygen the blood is carrying. Changes in blood flow and blood oxygen are *related* to changes in the firing rates of neurons, but the relationship is complex and not yet fully understood (Maandag et al., 2007; Perthen et al., 2008). Further, when brain cells process information, their firing rate may either increase or decrease (Gonsalves et al., 2005). If the increases and decreases in a particular brain region happen to cancel each other out, an fMRI scan will miss the neuronal activity taking place in that region. In fact, compared to the direct measurement of brain cell activity that can be done in research with animals, fMRI technology is still rather crude. It takes coordinated changes in millions of neurons to produce a detectible change in the fMRI signal.

Critics also argue that the results of fMRI research can depend too much on how experimenters choose to interpret them. In a typical fMRI experiment, participants are shown some kind of display, such as pairs of photos, and asked to perform various tasks. One task might be to press a button if the photos are exactly the same. A second task might be to press the button if objects in the photos are arranged in the same way. In this second task, a participant should press the button if one photo shows, say, a short man standing to the left of a tall woman, and the other photo shows a small dog standing to the left of a giraffe. Both versions of the task require the participant to compare two images, but only the second of them requires considering whether things that look different are actually similar in some way. The fMRI scans taken during these tasks might show certain brain areas "lighting up" only during the second task. If so, the researcher would suggest that those areas are involved in recognizing *analogies,* or the similarities between apparently different things (Wharton et al., 2000). The researcher would base this conclusion on a computer program that first compares fMRI scans taken during two tasks, subtracts all the "lighted" areas that are the same in both scans, and keeps only those that are different. But what the computer classifies as "different" depends on a rule that is set by the experimenter. If the experimenter programs the computer to display only big differences between the scans, not many "lit up" areas will remain after the comparison process. But if even tiny differences are allowed to count as "different," many more "lighted" areas will remain after the subtraction process. In our example, then, there could be large or small areas apparently associated with recognizing analogies, all depending on a rule set by the researcher.

These problems aside, critics wonder what it really means when fMRI research shows that certain brain areas appear activated during certain kinds of tasks or experiences. Their concern focuses on studies such as one from the new field of *neuroeconomics* that suggests that excessive activity in a particular brain area leads to bad investment decisions (Kuhnen & Knutson, 2005). Other fMRI studies have claimed to show the "neural foundations of religious belief" (Kapogiannis et al., 2009) or the "neural basis of romantic love." In the latter study, investigators scanned people's brains as they looked at pictures of their romantic partner and compared these scans to those taken while the same people viewed a nonromantic friend (Bartels & Zeki, 2000). According to the "difference" rule established by the experimenters, four brain areas were more active when viewing a romantic loved one than when viewing a friend. But does this result tell us anything about how or why these areas became active or what results this activity might have? In other words, do we now know more about love? Critics of fMRI would say no.

Exploring Brain Functions with fMRI

As a research participant performs a mental task, a functional magnetic resonance imaging scanner records blood flow and blood oxygen levels in her brain. The resulting computer analysis shows as "lit up" areas the parts of the brain that appear to be activated during the task, but critics doubt that fMRI scanning is as clear or accurate as its proponents suggest.

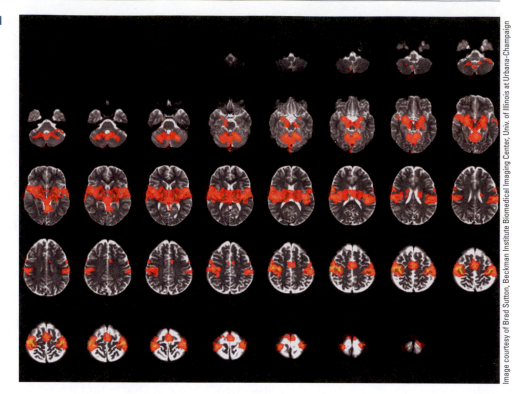

Image courtesy of Brad Sutton, Beckman Institute Biomedical Imaging Center, Univ. of Illinois at Urbana-Champaign

Can that evidence be interpreted another way?

Supporters of fMRI disagree. They believe that the colorful areas seen on fMRI scans can provide vital new information that will eventually allow scientists to answer important questions about behavior and mental processes. They would point, for example, to fMRI research on brain mechanisms that help us appreciate what other people are feeling—that is, help us experience empathy—and learn by watching others.

These *mirror neuron mechanisms* were discovered accidentally by scientists who had been using surgical techniques to directly record the activity of neurons in monkeys' brains (Caggiano et al., 2009; Rizzolatti et al., 1996). They found that neurons in an area called F5 are activated not only when a monkey plans to reach for an object, such as a peanut, but also if the monkey sees *an experimenter* reach for a peanut! After fMRI scanning became available, researchers could begin looking for mirror mechanisms in the human brain (e.g., Kilner et al., 2009). And in fact, some of the mirror systems they found in humans correspond to the F5 region in monkeys (Rizzolatti & Arbib, 1998). One of them is called *Broca's area* and, as described later, is an important component of our ability to speak. It makes sense that Broca's area contains a mirror mechanism because language is a skill that we learn partly by imitation. The fMRI findings suggest that Broca's area may also be important for many other skills that involve imitation. One study found that this area "lights up" when a guitar student learns chords by watching a professional guitarist (Buccino et al., 2004). Other fMRI research has found that mirror systems in other parts of the brain become active when a person sees someone experiencing emotion. For example, the brain area that is activated when you experience disgust (from the smell of rotten eggs, for example) is also activated if you see a video in which someone else reacts to a smell with disgust (Wicker et al., 2003).

So fMRI can be uniquely useful, say its defenders. Without it, research on mirror neurons in humans could not have taken place. And because of it, we have evidence that the experience of empathy comes about because seeing the actions and emotions of others activates the same brain regions that would be active if we were doing or feeling the same things ourselves. Some fMRI studies have also found that malfunctioning mirror mechanisms are associated with the impairments in language development, imitative skills, and empathy seen in children diagnosed with autistic disorder (Dapretto et al., 2006; Oberman & Ramachandran, 2007; see the chapter on psychological disorders).

It may also be that fMRI can help answer centuries-old but still unanswered questions about the location of our consciousness and self-awareness. Studies using fMRI have suggested that these functions may be located in a region called the anterior insular cortex because this region appears to be involved in all kinds of subjective feelings and is activated by a wide range of experiences, including everything from pressure in the bowels to orgasm, from cigarette craving to maternal love and from decision making to sudden insight (Craig, 2009).

What evidence would help evaluate the alternatives?

As technology continues to be refined, the quality of fMRI scans will continue to improve, giving us ever better images of where brain activity is taking place. But the value of this scanning technology will depend on a better understanding of what it can and cannot tell us about how brain activity is related to behavior and mental processes. We also need more evidence about correlation and causation in fMRI research. For example, one study conducted fMRI scans on compulsive gamblers as they played a simple guessing game (Reuter et al., 2005). When they won the game, these people showed an unusually small amount of activity in a brain area that is normally activated by the experience of rewards or pleasure. Noting the correlation between compulsive gambling and lower-than-normal activity in the reward area, the researchers suggested that an abnormality in the brain's reward mechanisms might be responsible for gambling addiction. But case studies have also found that compulsive gambling appears when people with movement disorders (such as Parkinson's disease or restless leg syndrome) take a prescription drug that *increases* activity in reward areas—and that the gambling stops when the drug is discontinued (Abler et al., 2009; Cilia et al., 2008; Dodd et al., 2005; Ferrara & Stacy, 2008; Tippmann-Piekert et al., 2007).

As noted in the chapter on introducing psychology, correlation does not guarantee causation. Is the brain activity reflected in fMRI scans causing the thoughts and feelings taking place during the scanning process? Possibly, but those thoughts and feelings may themselves be caused *by* activity elsewhere in the brain that affects the areas being scanned. The transcranial magnetic stimulation (TMS) procedures mentioned earlier may help identify causal versus correlational relationships in the brain. TMS is capable of temporarily disrupting neural activity in brain regions identified by fMRI as related to a particular kind of thought or feeling, so perhaps scientists can determine if those thoughts or feelings are temporarily disrupted when TMS occurs. Though TMS appears to be safe (López-Ibor, López-Ibor, & Pastrana, 2008), we don't yet know about its possible long-term negative side effects, so neuroscientists will have to proceed carefully in their use of this technique to explore basic questions about the mind and the brain.

A full understanding of fMRI will require continuing debate and dialogue between those who dismiss the technique and those who sing its praises. To make this interaction easier, a group of government agencies and private foundations funded an fMRI Data Center (www.fmridc.org/f/fmridc). This facility has stored information from fMRI experiments and makes it available to both critics and supporters of fMRI, who can review the research data, conduct their own analyses, and offer their own interpretations. Having access to this database will no doubt help scientists get the most out of fMRI technology while also helping each other avoid either overstating or underestimating the meaning of fMRI research.

What conclusions are most reasonable?

When the EEG was invented nearly a century ago, scientists had their first glimpse of brain cell activity, as reflected in the "brain waves" traced on a long sheet of paper rolling from the EEG machine (see Figure 9.4 in the chapter on consciousness). To many of these scientists, EEG must have seemed a golden gateway to an understanding of the brain and its relationship to behavior and mental processes. EEG has, in fact, helped advance knowledge of the brain, but it certainly didn't solve all its many mysteries. The same will probably be true of fMRI. It is an exciting new tool, and it offers previously undreamed-of images of the structure and functioning of the brain, but it is unlikely on its own to explain just how the brain creates our behavior and mental processes. It seems reasonable to conclude, then, that those who question the use of fMRI to study psychological processes are right in calling for a careful analysis of the value of this important high-tech tool.

Although the meaning of fMRI data will remain a subject for debate, there is no doubt that brain-scanning techniques in general have opened new frontiers for biological psychology, neuroscience, and medicine. Much of our growing understanding of how and why behavior and mental processes occur is coming from research with these techniques (Poldrack, Halchenko, & Hanson, 2009). Let's explore some of the structures they have highlighted, starting with the brain's three major subdivisions: the hindbrain, the midbrain, and the forebrain.

The Hindbrain   As you can see in Figure 3.11, the **hindbrain** lies just inside the skull and is actually a continuation of the spinal cord. So signals coming from the spinal cord reach the hindbrain first. Blood pressure, heart rate, breathing, and many other vital autonomic functions are controlled by nuclei in the hindbrain, particularly in an area called the **medulla oblongata** (pronounced "muh-DOO-luh ah-blon-GAH-da"). Reflexes and feedback systems are important to the functioning of the hindbrain, just as they are in the spinal cord. If you stand up very quickly, your blood pressure can drop so suddenly that it produces lightheadedness until the hindbrain reflex "catches up." If the hindbrain does not activate autonomic nervous system mechanisms to increase blood pressure, you will faint.

Threading throughout the hindbrain and into the midbrain is a collection of cells that are not arranged in any well-defined nucleus. Because the collection resembles a net, it is called the **reticular formation** (*reticular* means "netlike"). This network is important in altering the activity of the rest of the brain. It is involved, for example, in arousal and attention. If the fibers from the reticular system are disconnected from the rest of the brain, a person would enter a permanent coma. Some of the fibers carrying pain signals from the spinal cord make connections in the reticular formation, which immediately arouses the rest of the brain from sleep. Within seconds, the hindbrain causes heart rate and blood pressure to increase.

Activity of the reticular formation also leads to activity in a small nucleus within it called the **locus coeruleus** (pronounced "LOH-kuss seh-ROO-lee-uss"), which means "blue spot" (see Figure 3.11). There are relatively few cells in the locus coeruleus—only about 30,000 of the 100 billion or so in the human brain (Foote, Bloom, & Aston-Jones, 1983)—but each sends out an axon that branches extensively, making contact with as many as 100,000 other cells. Brain-imaging studies suggest that the locus coeruleus is involved in directing our attention toward particularly important stimuli in the environment (Minzenberg et al., 2008). Abnormalities in the locus coeruleus have been linked to depression, attention deficit hyperactivity disorder, sleep disorders, and posttraumatic stress disorder (Aston-Jones, 2005).

The hindbrain also includes the **cerebellum** (pronounced "sayr-uh-BEL-um"). One of its primary functions is the coordination of movements, such as those involved in threading a needle (Aso et al., 2010). However, it may also be the storehouse for well-rehearsed movements, such as those associated with dancing, playing a musical instrument, and athletics (McCormick & Thompson, 1984). Brain-imaging studies have led neuroscientists to believe that the cerebellum is involved, too, in many activities that are not directly related to physical movement, such as memory, impulse control, pain, emotion, language, and other higher-order cognitive processes (e.g., Strick, Dum, & Fiez, 2009). For example, the cerebellum is important in timing, including our ability to estimate how much time has passed

hindbrain An extension of the spinal cord contained inside the skull where nuclei control blood pressure, heart rate, breathing, and other vital functions.

medulla oblongata An area in the hindbrain that controls blood pressure, heart rate, breathing, and other vital functions.

reticular formation A network of cells and fibers threaded throughout the hindbrain and midbrain that alters the activity of the rest of the brain.

locus coeruleus A small nucleus in the reticular formation that is involved in directing attention.

cerebellum The part of the hindbrain whose main functions include controlling finely coordinated movements and storing memories about movement but which may also be involved in impulse control, emotion, and language.

FIGURE 3.11
Major Structures of the Brain (with Hindbrain Highlighted)

This side view of a section cut down the middle of the human brain reveals the forebrain, midbrain, hindbrain, and spinal cord. Many of these subdivisions do not have clear-cut borders because they are all interconnected by fiber tracts. The anatomy of the mammalian brain reflects its evolution over millions of years. Newer structures (such as the cerebral cortex, which is the outer surface of the forebrain) that handle higher mental functions were built on older structures (such as the medulla oblongata) that coordinate heart rate, breathing, and other more basic functions.

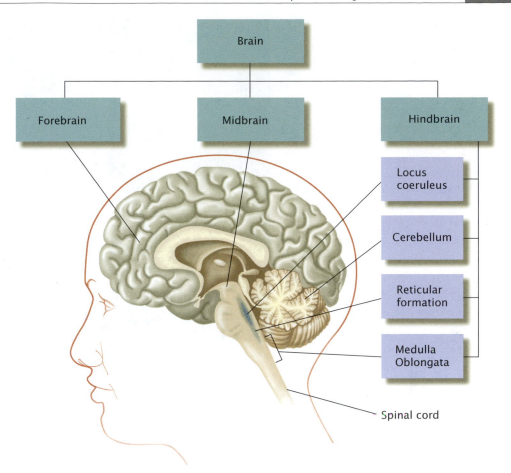

(Manto, 2008). Timing, in turn, plays a vital role in normal speech, integrating moment-to-moment feedback about vocal sounds with a sequence of precise movements of the lips and tongue (Leiner, Leiner, & Dow, 1993). When this process of integration and sequencing is disrupted, stuttering can result (Lu et al., 2009). Even nonstutterers who hear their own speech with a slight delay begin to stutter. (This is why radio talk show hosts ask callers to turn off their radios. A momentary gap occurs before the shows are actually broadcast, and listening to the delayed sound of their own voice on the radio can cause callers to stutter.) Surgery that affects the cerebellum sometimes results in a syndrome called *cerebellar mutism,* in which patients become unable to speak for periods ranging from a few days to several years (De Smet et al., 2009). In short, the cerebellum seems to be involved in both physical and cognitive agility.

The Midbrain   Above the hindbrain is the **midbrain.** In humans, it is a small structure, but it serves some important functions. Certain types of automatic behaviors that integrate simple movements with sensory input are controlled there. If you focus your eyes on another person and then move your head, midbrain circuits allow you to move your eyes smoothly in the direction opposite from your head movement so that you never lose focus. When you swing a bat, swat a mosquito, or jump a rope, part of the midbrain and its connections to the forebrain allow you to produce those movements smoothly. And when a sudden loud noise causes you to turn your head reflexively and look in the direction of the sound, your midbrain circuits are at work.

One particularly important nucleus in the midbrain is the **substantia nigra** (pronounced "sub-stan-shuh NY-gruh"), meaning "black substance." This small area and its connections to the **striatum** (pronounced "stry-AY-tum" and named for its

midbrain   A small structure between the hindbrain and forebrain that relays information from the eyes, ears, and skin and that controls certain types of automatic behaviors.

substantia nigra   An area of the midbrain involved in the smooth beginning of movement.

striatum   A structure within the forebrain that is involved in the smooth beginning of movement.

A Field Sobriety Test

The cerebellum is involved in the balance and coordination required for walking. When the cerebellum's activity is impaired by alcohol, these skills are disrupted, which is why the police ask suspected drunk drivers to walk a straight line. The cerebellum's importance is suggested by the fact that its size is second only to the cerebral cortex. And compared with other species, the human cerebellum has grown more than any other part of the brain, tripling in size during the last million years.

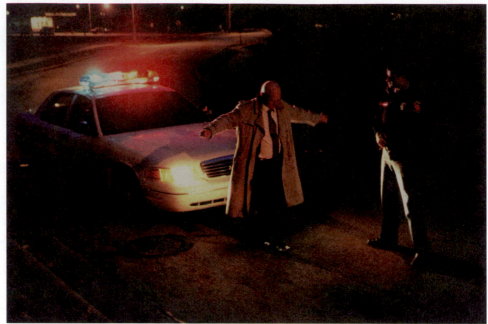

© Jonathan Kirn

"striped" appearance) in the forebrain are necessary in order to smoothly begin movements. Without them, you would find it difficult, if not impossible, to get up out of a chair, lift your hand to swat a fly, move your mouth to form words, or reach for that coffeepot at 6:00 A.M. Together, the midbrain and parts of the hindbrain other than the cerebellum are called the *brain stem*.

The Forebrain Like the cerebellum, the human **forebrain** has grown out of proportion to the rest of the brain, so much so that it folds back over and completely covers the other parts. It is responsible for the most complex aspects of behavior and mental life. As Figure 3.12 shows, the forebrain includes a variety of structures.

Two of these structures lie deep within the brain. The first is the **thalamus,** which relays pain signals from the spinal cord, as well as signals from the eyes and most other sense organs, to upper levels in the brain. It also plays an important role in processing and making sense out of this information. The other is the **hypothalamus,** which lies under the thalamus (*hypo-* means "under") and is involved in regulating hunger, thirst, and sex drive. It has many connections to and from the autonomic nervous system, as well as to other parts of the brain. Destruction of one section of the hypothalamus results in an overwhelming urge to eat (see the chapter on motivation and emotion). Damage to another area of a male's hypothalamus causes his sex organs to degenerate and his sex drive to decrease drastically. There is also a fascinating part of the hypothalamus that contains the brain's own timepiece: the **suprachiasmatic nuclei.** The suprachiasmatic (pronounced "soo-pruh-ky-az-MAT-ik") nuclei keep an approximately twenty-four-hour clock that establishes your biological rhythms such as waking and sleeping, as well as cycles of body temperature. Studies of the suprachiasmatic nuclei in animals suggest that having different energy levels at different times of day is biological and stable throughout a lifetime (Cofer et al., 1992). In humans, such differences may make some of us "morning people" and others "night people." We discuss these biological rhythms in the chapter on consciousness.

Two other forebrain structures, the **amygdala** (pronounced "uh-MIG-duh-luh") and the **hippocampus,** are part of the **limbic system.** The interconnected structures of this system, which also includes the hypothalamus and the septum, play important roles in regulating memory and emotion. For example, the amygdala associates features of stimuli from two different senses, as when we link the shape and feel of objects in memory (Murray & Mishkin, 1985). It is also involved in fear and other

forebrain The most highly developed part of the brain; it is responsible for the most complex aspects of behavior and mental life.

thalamus A forebrain structure that relays signals from most sense organs to higher levels in the brain and plays an important role in processing and making sense out of this information.

hypothalamus A structure in the forebrain that regulates hunger, thirst, and sex drive.

suprachiasmatic nuclei Nuclei in the hypothalamus that generate biological rhythms.

amygdala A structure in the forebrain that, among other things, associates features of stimuli from two sensory modalities.

hippocampus A structure in the forebrain associated with the formation of new memories.

limbic system A set of brain structures that play important roles in regulating emotion and memory.

FIGURE 3.12

Major Structures of the Forebrain

The structures of the forebrain are covered by an outer "bark" known as the *cerebral cortex*. This diagram shows some of the structures that lie within the forebrain. The amygdala, the hippocampus, the hypothalamus, the septum, and portions of the cerebral cortex are all part of the limbic system.

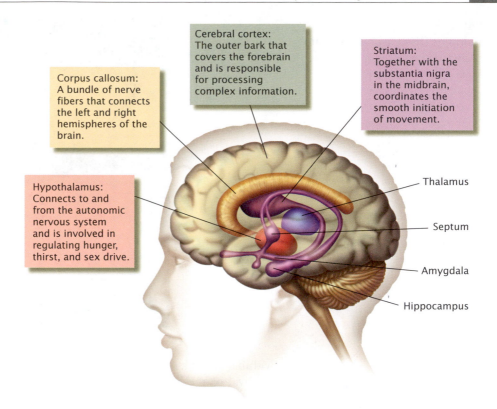

Corpus callosum: A bundle of nerve fibers that connects the left and right hemispheres of the brain.

Cerebral cortex: The outer bark that covers the forebrain and is responsible for processing complex information.

Striatum: Together with the substantia nigra in the midbrain, coordinates the smooth initiation of movement.

Hypothalamus: Connects to and from the autonomic nervous system and is involved in regulating hunger, thirst, and sex drive.

Thalamus

Septum

Amygdala

Hippocampus

emotions (Rodrigues, LeDoux, & Sapolsky, 2009). People with posttraumatic stress disorder show unusual activity in the amygdala (Liberzon & Sripada, 2008; see the chapter on health, stress, and coping). The amygdala may also influence our sensitivity to other people and the strength of our reactions to their facial expressions (Corden et al., 2006; Furmark et al., 2009).

The hippocampus is important in the formation of memories, as becomes evident in certain cases of brain damage. People with damage to the hippocampus may lose the ability to remember new events, a condition called *anterograde amnesia*. In one case, a patient known as R. B. had a stroke (an interruption of blood flow in the brain) that damaged only his hippocampus. Although tests indicated that his intelligence was above average and that he could still recall old memories, he was almost totally unable to build new ones (Squire, 1986). In the memory chapter, we describe H. M., a man who, after developing a similar condition following brain surgery at the age of 27, became the single most studied patient in all of neuropsychology (Corkin, 2002; Preilowski, 2009). The role of the hippocampus in memory is further supported by MRI studies of normal elderly people. These studies have found that memory ability is correlated with the size and activity of the hippocampus (Golomb et al., 1996; Zimmerman et al., 2008). In fact, having a small hippocampus predicts the development of severe memory problems in the elderly (Devanand et al., 2007). Other studies suggest that some people's inborn response to stress includes a loss of neurons in the hippocampus (Caspi, Sugden, et al., 2003; Frodl et al., 2004). This effect was demonstrated in a study of people who were in the New York City area on 9/11. Compared to those more distant from the World Trade Center, people who were exposed to the trauma at close range showed greater reductions in hippocampus volume, even three years after the event (Ganzel et al., 2008). The loss of neurons in this region may help explain the memory problems that appear in some people affected by depression or posttraumatic stress disorder (Bremner et al., 2003, 2004; Z. Wang et al., 2010).

Although the hippocampus is vital in the creation of new memories, it doesn't hold on to them for long. Animal studies have shown that damage to the hippocampus

FIGURE 3.13
Alzheimer's Disease and the Brain
Compared to a normal brain (bottom), the brain of a person with Alzheimer's disease shows considerable degeneration in the cerebral cortex. The limbic system deteriorates, too (Callen et al., 2001). For example, the hippocampus of Alzheimer's patients is about 40 percent smaller than normal.

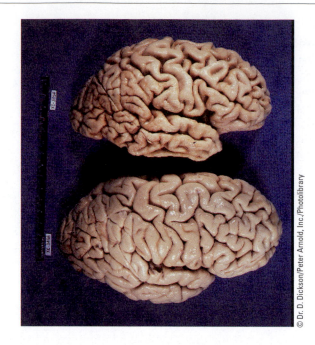

© Dr. D. Dickson/Peter Arnold, Inc./Photolibrary

within a day of a mildly painful experience erases memories of the experience but that removal of the hippocampus several days after the experience has no effect on the memory. So the memories must have been transferred elsewhere. As described in the chapter on memory, maintaining your storehouse of memories—and having the ability to recall them—depends on the coordinated activities of many parts of the brain.

One of the greatest threats to the brain's memory capacities comes from Alzheimer's disease. Alzheimer's is a major cause of *dementia*, the deterioration of cognitive capabilities often associated with aging. The symptoms of Alzheimer's disease stem from severe degeneration of neurons in specific regions of the hippocampus and other limbic and cortical structures (Small et al., 2002; see Figure 3.13).

About 13 percent of people over the age of 65, and more than 47 percent of people over 85, have this disorder Alzheimer's Disease Association, 2009; (Kukull et al., 2002; U.S. Department of Health and Human Services, 2001a). The number of cases worldwide is expected to quadruple by 2050 (Ziegler-Graham et al., 2008). The financial cost of Alzheimer's disease is more than $148 billion a year in the United States alone (Alzheimer's Association, 2007), and the worldwide cost in human suffering is incalculable. It is no wonder that scientists are searching so diligently for the causes of Alzheimer's and for ways of preventing and possibly curing this devastating illness.

FOCUS ON **RESEARCH METHODS**

Manipulating Genes in Animal Models of Human Disease

Alzheimer's disease is named for Alois Alzheimer, a German neurologist. Almost a century ago, Alzheimer examined the brain of a woman who had died after years of progressive mental deterioration and dementia. In looking for what caused her disorder, he found that cells in her cerebral cortex and hippocampus were bunched up like a knotted rope and that cellular debris had collected around the affected nerves. These features came to be known as tangles and plaques. *Tangles* are twisted fibers within neurons; their main protein component is called *tau*. *Plaques* are deposits of protein and parts of dead cells found between neurons. The major component of plaques was found to be a small protein called *beta-amyloid*, which is made from a larger protein called *amyloid precursor protein*. Accumulation of beta-amyloid plaques can now be visualized in living people through the use of PET scans (Klunk et al., 2005; see Figure 3.14).

FIGURE 3.14

Diagnosing Alzheimer's Disease

Researchers have developed a molecule that binds with beta-amyloid plaques and can be seen on a PET scan. As shown in the brightly colored areas of these scans, when the molecule was injected into Alzheimer's patients (bottom row), it became concentrated in the hippocampus and other regions where amyloid usually accumulates in Alzheimer's disease (Klunk et al., 2004, 2005). As shown by the darker colors in the upper row, the molecule does not build up in the brains of older people who do not have the disease. This procedure holds great promise as a tool for diagnosing Alzheimer's disease long before its symptoms appear, allowing treatment efforts to begin as early as possible.

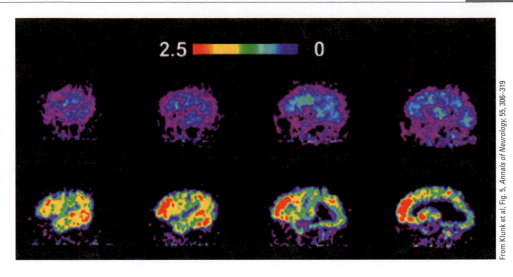

From Klunk et al, Fig. 5, *Annals of Neurology*, 55, 306–319

What was the researchers' question?

Ever since Alzheimer described plaques and tangles, researchers have been trying to learn about the role they play. One specific question that researchers have addressed is whether the proteins found in plaques and tangles actually *cause* Alzheimer's disease. They are certainly correlated with Alzheimer's, but as emphasized in the chapter on research in psychology, we can't confirm a causal relationship from a correlation alone. To discover if beta-amyloid and tau cause the death of neurons seen in Alzheimer's disease, researchers knew that controlled experiments would be necessary. This means manipulating an independent variable and measuring its effect on a dependent variable. In the case of Alzheimer's, the experiment would involve creating amyloid plaques and tangles (the independent variable) and looking for their effects on memory (the dependent variable). Such experiments cannot ethically be conducted on humans, so scientists began looking for Alzheimer's-like conditions in another species. Progress in finding the causes of Alzheimer's disease depended on their finding an "animal model" of the disease.

How did the researchers answer the question?

Previous studies of the genes of people with Alzheimer's disease had revealed that in some cases it is associated with a mutation, or error, in the beta-amyloid precursor protein. However, the mutations seen in many Alzheimer's patients appeared not in this protein but in other ones. Researchers called these other proteins *presenilins* because they are associated with senility. To determine whether these mutated proteins could actually cause the brain damage and memory impairment associated with Alzheimer's disease, they had to find a way to insert the proteins into the cells of animals. New genetic engineering tools allowed them to do just that. Genes can now be modified, eliminated, or added to cells, and if those cells give rise to sperm or eggs, the animals that result will have these altered genes in all their cells. Such animals are called "transgenic."

In their first attempts to create an animal model of Alzheimer's disease, researchers inserted a gene for a mutant form of beta-amyloid precursor protein into a group of mice. If Alzheimer's disease is indeed caused by faulty beta-amyloid precursor protein, inserting the gene for this faulty protein should cause deposits of beta-amyloid and the loss of neurons in the same brain structures that are affected in human Alzheimer's patients. No such changes should be observed in a control group of untreated animals.

What did the researchers find?

For more than a decade, scientists have been creating dozens of different transgenic mice with differing abnormalities in the proteins associated with tangles and plaques. As a result of this work, most researchers believe that amyloid and tau are somehow involved in causing Alzheimer's disease. When multiple abnormalities in amyloid are introduced into mice, the animals show memory impairments, and they develop plaques in the brain. However, they do not develop tangles. So it appears that the development of tangles and the loss of neurons are indirect effects of amyloid accumulation, interacting with other factors (Denk & Wade-Martins, 2009; McGowan, Eriksen, & Hutton, 2006). In other words, scientists are getting closer to a good animal model of Alzheimer's disease, but they still have a way to go (McGeer & McGeer, 2010).

Nevertheless, transgenic mice have paved the way for an exciting new possibility in the treatment of Alzheimer's disease: a vaccine against beta-amyloid. Mice given this vaccine have shown not only improved memory but also a reversal of beta-amyloid deposits in their brains (Morgan et al., 2000; Younkin, 2001). Early clinical trials of beta-amyloid vaccines in humans showed encouraging results, but a small percentage of patients developed fatal reactions, so the trials were stopped for a while (Broytman & Malter, 2004). Scientists believe that they now understand what caused these reactions, and new clinical trials of more specific vaccines have begun (Lemere et al., 2006; Morrissette et al., 2008).

What do the results mean?

Scientists will continue to use transgenic mice to evaluate the roles of mutations in beta-amyloid precursor protein, presenilins, tau, and other proteins in causing Alzheimer's disease (e.g., Crouch et al., 2009). This research is important not only because it might eventually solve the mystery of this terrible disorder but also because it illustrates the power of experimental modification of animal genes for testing all kinds of hypotheses about biological factors influencing behavior.

Besides inserting new or modified genes into brain cells, scientists can also manipulate an independent variable by "knocking out" or disrupting specific genes and then looking at the effect on dependent variables. One research team has shown, for example, that knocking out a gene for a particular type of neurotransmitter receptor causes mice to become obese and to overeat even when given appetite-suppressing drugs (Tecott et al., 1995). Another has shown the role of taste receptors in explaining why fat-containing foods taste so good (Gaillard, Passilly-Degrace, & Besnard, 2008). Still another team using protein-disrupting technology has found important clues to the neural basis of cocaine's addictive power (Chen et al., 2006).

What do we still need to know?

The scarcity of animal models of obesity, drug addiction, and other problems has slowed progress in finding biological treatments for them. As animal models for these conditions become more available through genetic engineering techniques, they will open the door to new types of animal studies that are directly relevant to human problems. The next challenge will be to use these animal models to develop and test treatments that can effectively be applied to humans.

The Cerebral Cortex

cerebral hemispheres The left and right halves of the rounded, outermost part of the brain.

cerebral cortex The outer surface of the brain.

sensory cortex (sensory area) The parts of the cerebral cortex that receive stimulus information from the senses.

motor cortex The part of the cerebral cortex whose neurons control voluntary movements in specific parts of the body.

So far, we have described some key structures *within* the forebrain; now we turn to a discussion of the structures on its surface. The outermost part of the brain appears rather round and has a long groove down the middle, creating right and left halves that are similar in appearance. These halves are called the **cerebral hemispheres.** The outer part of the cerebral hemispheres, the **cerebral cortex,** has a surface area of 1 to 2 square feet—an area that is larger than it looks because of the folds that allow the cortex to fit inside the skull. The cerebral cortex is much larger in humans than in most other animals (dolphins are an exception). It is associated with the analysis of information from all the senses, control of voluntary movements, higher-order thought, and other complex aspects of our behavior and mental processes.

The left side of Figure 3.15 shows the *anatomical* or physical features of the cerebral cortex. The folds of the cortex give the surface of the human brain its wrinkled

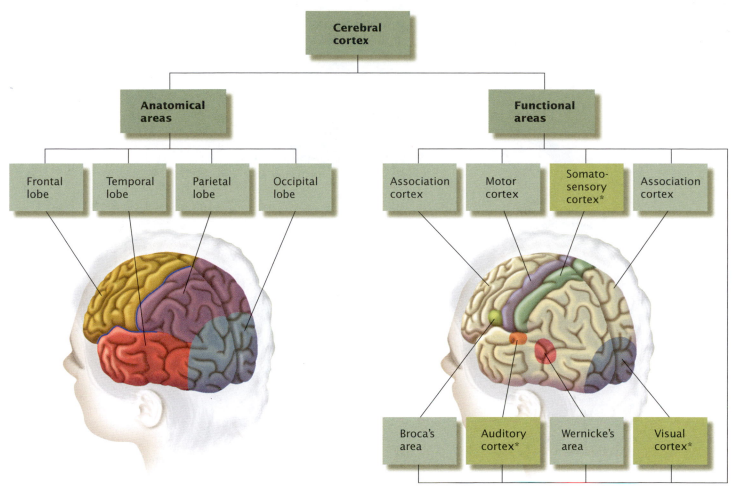

*Somatosensory cortex, auditory cortex, and visual cortex make up the sensory cortex.

FIGURE 3.15
The Cerebral Cortex (viewed from the left side)

The brain's ridges (gyri) and valleys (sulci) are landmarks that divide the cortex into four lobes: the frontal, parietal, occipital, and temporal. These terms describe where the regions are (the lobes are named for the skull bones that cover them), but the cortex is also divided in terms of function. These functional areas include the motor cortex (which controls movement), sensory cortex (including somatosensory, auditory, and visual areas that receive information from the senses), and association cortex (which integrates information). Also labeled are Wernicke's area and Broca's area, two regions that are found only on the left side of the cortex and that are vital to the interpretation and production of speech.

appearance—its ridges and valleys. The ridges are called *gyri* (pronounced "JY-ry"), and the valleys are called *sulci* (pronounced "SUL-sy") or *fissures*. As you can see in the figure, several deep sulci divide the cortex into four areas: the *frontal, parietal, occipital,* and *temporal* lobes. The right side of Figure 3.15 depicts the areas of the cerebral cortex in which various *functions* or activities occur. The functional areas do not exactly match the anatomical areas because some functions occur in more than one area. Let's consider three of these functional areas—the sensory cortex, the motor cortex, and the association cortex.

Sensory Cortex The brain's **sensory cortex,** or **sensory area,** lies in the parietal, occipital, and temporal lobes and is the part of the cerebral cortex that receives information from our senses. Different regions of the sensory cortex receive information from different senses. Visual information is received by the *visual cortex,* made up of cells in the occipital lobe; auditory information is received by the *auditory cortex,* made up of cells in the temporal lobe; and information from the skin about touch, pain, and temperature is received in the *somatosensory cortex,* made up of cells in the parietal lobe (*soma* is Greek for "body").

Information about skin sensations from neighboring parts of the body comes to neighboring parts of the somatosensory cortex. As Figure 3.16 illustrates, the places on the cortex where information from each area of skin arrives can be represented by the figure of a tiny person stretched out along the cortex. This figure is called the sensory *homunculus,* which is Latin for "little man." The links between skin locations and locations in somatosensory cortex have been demonstrated during brain surgery. If a

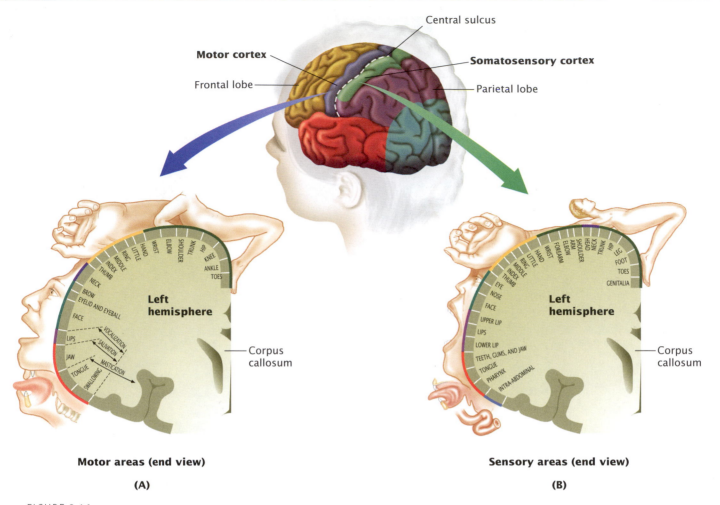

FIGURE 3.16

Motor and Somatosensory Cortex

The areas of the cortex that move parts of the body (motor cortex) and receive sensory input from body parts (somatosensory cortex) appear in both hemispheres of the brain. Here we show cross sections of only those on the left side, looking from the back of the brain toward the front. Areas receiving input from neighboring body parts, such as the lips and tongue, are near one another in the sensory cortex. Areas controlling movement of neighboring parts of the body, such as the foot and leg, occupy neighboring parts of the motor cortex. Notice that the size of these areas is uneven; the larger the area devoted to each body part, the larger that body part appears on the "homunculus."

Note: Did you notice the error in this classic drawing? The figure of the homunculus shows the right side of its body but its left hand and the left side of its face.

Source: From Penfield/Rasmussen. *The Cerebral Cortex of Man.* Copyright © 1950 Gale, a part of Cengage Learning, Inc. Reproduced by permission. www.cengage.com/permissions

surgeon stimulates a particular spot on the somatosensory cortex, the patient experiences a touch sensation at the place on the skin that normally sends information to that spot on the cortex. It was long assumed that the organization of the homunculus remains the same throughout life, but research has shown that the amount of sensory cortex that responds to particular sensory inputs can be changed by experience (Pascual-Leone et al., 2005). For example, practicing the violin can increase the number of neurons in the somatosensory cortex that respond to finger touches (Candia et al., 2005; Hyde et al., 2009). And if a person loses an arm, the areas of the somatosensory cortex that had been stimulated by that arm will eventually be stimulated by the mouth or some other region of skin. Temporary reassignment of sensory cortex has even been produced in the laboratory. In one study, volunteers had an artificial third arm and hand attached to their bodies. After mirrors were used to create the illusion that the third limb was theirs, some of these people experienced "feeling" it, and their brains appeared to begin the process of assigning neurons in the sensory cortex to represent it (Schaefer, Heinze, & Rotte, 2008). These changes appear to be coordinated partly by brain areas outside the cerebral cortex, which reassign more neurons to process particular sensory inputs.

Motor Cortex   Neurons in specific areas of the **motor cortex,** which is in the frontal lobe, create voluntary movements in specific parts of the body. Some control movement of the hand; others stimulate movement of the foot, the knee, the head, and so on. As you can see in Figure 3.16, the motor homunculus mirrors the somatosensory homunculus. That is, the parts of the motor cortex that control the hands, for instance, are near parts of the somatosensory cortex that receive sensory information from the hands. The specific muscles activated by these regions are linked not to specific neurons but, as mentioned earlier, to the patterned activity of many neurons. For example, some of the same neurons are active in moving more than one finger. In other words, different parts of the homunculus in the motor cortex overlap somewhat (Indovina & Sanes, 2001).

Controlling the movement of your body seems simple: You have a map of body parts in the motor cortex, and you activate cells in the hand region if you want to move your hand. But the process is actually much more complex. Recall again your sleepy reach for the coffeepot. The motor cortex must first translate the coffeepot's location in space into a location relative to your body. For example, your hand might have to be moved forward and a certain number of degrees to the right or to the left of your body. Next, the motor cortex must determine which muscles must be contracted to produce those movements. Populations of neurons work together to produce just the right combinations of direction and force in the particular muscle groups necessary to create the desired effects. Making these determinations involves many interconnected areas of the cortex, and the specific neurons involved can change over time (Gallivan, Cavina-Pratesi, & Culham, 2009; W. Wang et al., 2010). Computer models of neural networks are showing how these complex problem-solving processes might occur (Graziano, Taylor, & Moore, 2002; Krauzlis, 2002).

Association Cortex   The parts of the cerebral cortex not directly involved with either receiving specific sensory information or creating movement are referred to as **association cortex.** These are the areas that perform complex cognitive tasks, such as associating words with images. The term *association* is appropriate because these areas either receive information from more than one sense or combine sensory and motor information. Damage to association areas can create severe losses, or deficits, in all kinds of mental abilities.

One of the most devastating deficits, called *aphasia* (pronounced "uh-FAY-zhuh"), causes difficulty in understanding or producing speech and can involve all

association cortex The parts of the cerebral cortex that receive information from more than one sense or that combine sensory and motor information to perform complex cognitive tasks.

Movement and the Brain

Scientists are trying to understand exactly how smooth movements are coordinated by neural activity in the brain and the spinal cord. The complexity of the processes involved presents a challenge to researchers working on devices to restore movement in paralyzed individuals. As shown here, delivering computer-controlled electrical stimulation to leg muscles allows walking movements to occur, though they are jerkier than the movements the brain normally produces. It has also been possible to implant a device that records activity from the motor cortex of a completely paralyzed man. When data from the device was fed into a computer that controlled an artificial hand, the man was able to open and close the hand by imagining these movements (Hochberg et al., 2006).

Cleveland FES Center, Cleveland VA Medical Center, Case Western Reserve University, Cleveland, Ohio

the functions of the cerebral cortex. Language information comes from the auditory cortex (for spoken language) or from the visual cortex (for written language). Areas of the motor cortex produce speech (Geschwind, 1979). But language also involves activity in association cortex.

LINKAGES Where are the brain's language centers? (a link to Cognition and Language, p. 321)

Scientists have long known that two areas of association cortex are involved in different aspects of language. In 1861, the French surgeon Paul Broca described the difficulties that result from damage to the association cortex in the frontal lobe near motor areas that control facial muscles, an area now called *Broca's area* (see Figure 3.15). The hand and arm gestures that accompany speech are also controlled by neurons in this area (Gentilucci & Dalla Volta, 2008; Xu et al., 2009). When Broca's area is damaged, the mental organization of speech suffers, a condition called *Broca's aphasia*. People with damage in this region have great difficulty speaking, and what they say is often grammatically incorrect. Each word comes slowly.

A different set of language problems results from damage to a portion of association cortex first described in the 1870s by Carl Wernicke (pronounced "VAYR-nih-kuh") and hence called *Wernicke's area*. As Figure 3.15 shows, it is located in the temporal lobe, near an area of the cortex that receives information from the ears and eyes. Wernicke's area is involved in the interpretation of both speech and written words. Damage to this area can leave a person able to speak, but it disrupts the ability to understand the meaning of words or to speak understandably.

Case studies illustrate the differing effects of damage to Broca's area versus Wernicke's area (Lapointe, 1990). In response to the request "Tell me what you do with a cigarette," a person with Broca's aphasia replied, "Uh ... uh ... cigarette (*pause*) smoke it." Though halting and ungrammatical, this speech was meaningful. In response to the same request, a person with Wernicke's aphasia replied, "This is a segment of a pegment. Soap a cigarette." Here the speech is fluent but without meaning. A fascinating aspect of Broca's aphasia is that when a person with the disorder sings, the words come fluently and correctly. Indeed, PET scans show that words set to music are handled by a different part of the brain than spoken words (Jeffries, Fritz, & Braun, 2003). Capitalizing on this observation, "melodic intonation therapy" helps Broca's aphasia patients gain fluency in speaking by teaching them to speak in a "singsong" manner (Lapointe, 1990).

It appears that the particular areas of association cortex that are activated depend on whether language is spoken or written and whether particular grammatical and conceptual categories are involved (Shapiro, Moo, & Caramazza, 2006). For example, consider the cases of two women—H. W. and S. J. D.—who had strokes that damaged different language-related parts of their association cortex (Caramazza & Hillis, 1991). Afterward, neither woman had difficulty speaking or writing nouns, but both have difficulty with verbs. H. W. can write verbs but cannot speak them: She has difficulty pronouncing *watch* when it is used as a verb in the sentence "I watch TV," but she speaks the same word easily when it appears as a noun in "My watch is slow." S. J. D. can speak verbs but has difficulty writing them. Another odd language abnormality following brain damage, known as "foreign accent syndrome," was illustrated by a 32-year-old stroke patient whose native language was English. His speech was slurred immediately after the stroke, but as it improved, he began to speak with a Scandinavian accent, adding syllables to some words ("How are you today-ah?") and pronouncing *hill* as "heel." His normal accent did not fully return for four months (Takayama et al., 1993). Case studies of "foreign accent syndrome" suggest that specific regions of the brain are involved in the sound of language, whereas others are involved in various aspects of its meaning.

Other association areas in the front of the brain, called the *prefrontal cortex,* are involved in the complex processes necessary for the conscious control of thoughts and actions and for understanding the world (Fincham & Anderson, 2006; Koechlin & Hyafil, 2007). For example, these areas of association cortex allow us to understand sarcasm or irony—that is, when someone says one thing but means the opposite. In one study, people with prefrontal cortex damage listened to sarcastic stories such as this: "Joe came to work, and instead of beginning to work, he sat down to rest.

Language Areas of the Brain

TRY THIS Have you ever tried to write notes while you were talking to someone? Like this teacher, you can probably write and talk at the same time because each of these language functions uses different association cortex areas. However, stop reading for a moment and try writing one word with your left hand and a different word with your right hand. If you had trouble, it is partly because you asked the same language area of your brain to do two things at once.

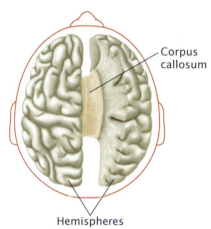

Corpus callosum

Hemispheres

FIGURE 3.17

The Brain's Left and Right Hemispheres

The brain's two hemispheres are joined by a core bundle of nerve fibers known as the *corpus callosum*. In this figure, the hemispheres are separated to reveal the corpus callosum. The two cerebral hemispheres look nearly the same but perform somewhat different tasks. For one thing, the left hemisphere receives sensory input from and controls movement on the right side of the body. The right hemisphere senses and controls the left side of the body.

lateral dominance (lateralization) The tendency for one cerebral hemisphere to excel at a particular function or skill compared with the other hemisphere.

corpus callosum A massive bundle of fibers that connects the right and left cerebral hemispheres and allows them to communicate with each other.

His boss noticed his behavior and said, 'Joe, don't work too hard.'" Normal people immediately understood what the boss really meant, but people with prefrontal damage had difficulty understanding that she was being sarcastic (Shamay-Tsoory & Tomer, 2005).

The Divided Brain in a Unified Self

A striking idea emerged from observations of people with damage to the language areas of the brain. Researchers noticed that when damage was limited to areas of the left hemisphere, there were impairments in the ability to use or understand language. Damage to corresponding parts of the right hemisphere usually did not have these effects. Perhaps, they reasoned, the right and left halves of the brain serve different functions.

This concept was not entirely new. It had long been understood, for example, that most sensory and motor pathways cross over as they enter or leave the brain. As a result, the left hemisphere receives information from and controls movements of the right side of the body, and the right hemisphere receives input from and controls the left side of the body. However, both sides of the brain perform these functions. The fact that language centers, such as Broca's area and Wernicke's area, are found almost exclusively on the left side of the brain suggested that each hemisphere might show **lateral dominance**, also known as **lateralization**. That is, each might be specialized to perform some functions more efficiently than, and almost independently of, the other hemisphere (Stephan et al., 2003).

Split-Brain Studies As far back as the late 1800s, scientists had wanted to test the hypothesis that the cerebral hemispheres might be specialized, but they had no techniques for doing so. Then, during the 1960s, Roger Sperry, Michael Gazzaniga, and their colleagues began to study *split-brain* patients—people who had undergone a surgical procedure in an attempt to control severe epilepsy. Before the surgery, their seizures began in one hemisphere and then spread to engulf the whole brain. As a last resort, surgeons isolated the two hemispheres from each other by severing the **corpus callosum,** a massive bundle of more than a million fibers that connects the two hemispheres (see Figure 3.17).

FIGURE 3.18
**Apparatus for Studying
Split-Brain Patients**
When the person stares at a dot in the center of the screen, images briefly presented on one side of the screen go to only one side of the brain. For example, a picture of a spoon presented on the left side of the screen goes to the right side of the brain. The right side of the brain can find the spoon and direct the left hand to touch it. However, because the language areas on the left side of the brain did not see the spoon, the person is unable to say what it is.

Source: From Hubel, D., *Eye, Brain, and Vision,* Scientific American Library, 1988, pp. 138–139.

After the surgery, researchers used a special apparatus to present visual images to only one side of these patients' split brains (see Figure 3.18). They found that severing the tie between the hemispheres had dramatically affected the way these people thought about and dealt with the world. For example, when the image of a spoon was presented to the left, language-oriented side of one patient's split brain, she could say what the spoon was; but when the spoon was presented to the right side of her brain, she could not describe the spoon in words. She still knew what it was, however. Using her left hand (controlled by the right hemisphere), she could pick out the spoon from a group of other objects by its shape. But when asked what she had just grasped, she replied, "A pencil." The right hemisphere recognized the object, but the patient could not describe it because the left (language) half of her brain did not see or feel it (Sperry, 1968).

Although the right hemisphere has no control over spoken language in split-brain patients, it does have important capabilities, including some related to nonspoken language. For example, a split-brain patient's right hemisphere can guide the left hand in spelling out words with Scrabble tiles (Gazzaniga & LeDoux, 1978). Thanks to this ability, researchers discovered that the right hemisphere of split-brain patients has self-awareness and normal learning abilities. In addition, it is superior to the left hemisphere on tasks dealing with spatial relations (especially drawing three-dimensional shapes) and at recognizing human faces.

Lateralization of Normal Brains   Sperry (1974) concluded from his studies that each hemisphere in the split-brain patient has its own "private sensations, perceptions, thoughts, and ideas all of which are cut off from the corresponding experiences in the opposite hemisphere . . . . In many respects each disconnected hemisphere appears to have a separate 'mind of its own'" (p. 7). But what about people whose hemispheres are connected normally? Are certain of their functions, such as mathematical reasoning or language skills, lateralized?

To find out, researchers presented images to just one hemisphere of people with normal brains and then measured how fast they could analyze information. If information is presented to one side of the brain, and if that side is specialized to analyze that type of information, a person's responses will be faster than if the information must first be transferred to the other hemisphere for analysis. These studies have confirmed that the left hemisphere has better logical and language abilities than the

FIGURE 3.19
Lateralization of the Cerebral Hemispheres

These PET scans show overhead views of a section of a person's brain while the person was receiving different kinds of stimulation. At the upper left, the person was resting, with eyes open and ears plugged. Note that the greatest brain activity (as indicated by the red color) was in the visual cortex, which was receiving input from the eyes. As shown at the lower left, when the person listened to spoken language, the auditory cortex in the left temporal lobe became more active, but the right temporal lobe did not. When the person listened to music (lower right), there was intense activity in the right temporal lobe but little in the left. When the person heard both words and music, the temporal cortex on both sides of the brain became activated. Here is visual evidence of the involvement of each side of the brain in processing different kinds of information (Phelps & Mazziotta, 1985).

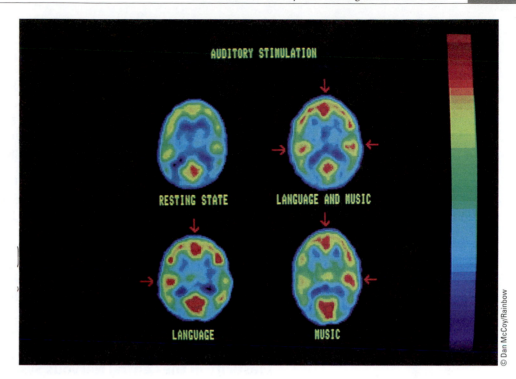

© Dan McCoy/Rainbow

right, whereas the right hemisphere has better spatial, artistic, and musical abilities (Springer & Deutsch, 1989). Positron emission tomography (PET) scans of normal people receiving varying kinds of auditory stimulation also demonstrate these differences (see Figure 3.19). We know that the language abilities of the left hemisphere are not specifically related to auditory information, though, because people who are deaf also use the left hemisphere, Broca's area specifically, more than the right for sign language (Horwitz et al., 2003).

The precise nature and degree of lateralization vary quite a bit among individuals. Functional MRI studies show, for example, that one person in ten shows activation of both hemispheres during language tasks, and the brains of another 10 percent of people appear to coordinate language in the right hemisphere (Fitzgerald, Brown, & Daskalakis, 2002). Both of these patterns are seen mostly in left-handed people (Knecht et al., 2002). Evidence of sex differences in lateralization comes from EEG studies and from research on the cognitive abilities of normal men and women, on the effects of brain damage on cognitive function, and on sex differences in brain anatomy before birth (Kivilevitch, Achiron, & Zalel, 2010; Koles, Lind, & Flor-Henry, 2009). Among normal individuals, there are sex differences in the ability to perform tasks that are known to be lateralized in the brain. For example, women tend to do better than men at perceptual fluency tasks, such as rapidly identifying matching items, and at arithmetic calculations. Men tend to be better at imagining the rotation of an object in space and tasks involving target-directed motor skills, such as guiding projectiles or intercepting them, in real or virtual-reality situations (Halperin, 1992; Waller, 2000). However, these sex differences tend to be quite small (Boles, 2005; Frost et al., 1999; Haut & Barch, 2006).

Damage to just one side of the brain is more disabling to men than to women. In particular, men show larger deficits in language ability than women when the left side is damaged (McGlone, 1980). This difference may reflect a wider distribution of language abilities in the brains of women compared with those of men. When participants in one study performed language tasks, such as thinking about whether particular words rhyme, MRI scans showed increased activity on the left side of the brain for men but on both sides for women (Shaywitz et al., 1995; see Figure 1.1 in the chapter on introducing psychology). Women appear to have proportionately more of their association cortex devoted to language tasks (Harasty et al., 1997).

Although humans and animals show definite sex differences in brain anatomy (Allen, Hines, et al., 1989; Gur et al., 1995; Juraska, 1998), no particular anatomical feature has been identified as underlying sex differences in lateralization. One study reported that the corpus callosum is larger in women than in men (de Lacoste-Utamsing & Holloway, 1982), but more than fifty attempts to replicate this finding have failed (Kivilevitch, Achiron, & Zalel, 2010; Morton & Rafto, 2006; Olivares, Michalland, & Aboitz, 2000; Wallentin, 2009). Despite the overwhelming evidence against it, the original report of a sex difference in the corpus callosum continues to be cited, suggesting that scientists are sometimes not entirely unbiased.

Having two somewhat specialized hemispheres allows the brain to more efficiently perform some tasks, particularly difficult ones, but the differences between the hemispheres should not be exaggerated. The corpus callosum usually integrates the functions of the "two brains," a role that is particularly important in tasks that require sustained attention (Rueckert et al., 1999). As a result, the hemispheres work so closely together, and each makes up so well for whatever lack of ability the other may have, that people are normally unaware that their brains are made up of two partly independent, somewhat specialized halves (Banich, 2009; Staudt et al., 2001).

Plasticity in the Central Nervous System

We mentioned earlier that the amount of somatosensory cortex devoted to finger touch changes as people practice a musical instrument. Such changes are possible because of **neural plasticity,** the remarkable ability of the central nervous system to strengthen neural connections at synapses, as well as to establish new connections (Herdener et al., 2010; Tailby et al., 2005). Plasticity depends partly on neurons and partly on glial cells (Lee & Silva, 2009), and it provides the basis for the learning and memory processes described in other chapters (Roberts et al., 2010). The connections between brain cells are highly dynamic, changing from week to week (Stettler et al., 2006), and the strength of the synaptic connections between brain cells can change in a fraction of a second (Bikbaev & Manahan-Vaughan, 2008). Plasticity occurs throughout the central nervous system. Even the simplest reflex in the spinal cord can be modified by experience (Wolpaw & Chen, 2006).

Brain-scanning technology allows researchers to directly observe the effects of neural plasticity. They have seen that as blind people learn to read Braille, the amount of sensory cortex devoted to the "reading" fingertip increases dramatically (Pascual-Leone & Torres, 1993). They have seen, too, that as blind people read Braille, there is activity in the occipital lobe, a brain area that normally receives visual information (Chen, Cohen, & Hallett, 2002). MRI studies of individuals who were learning to juggle found an increase in the density of cortical regions associated with processing visual information about moving objects (Draganski et al., 2004). Motor cortex is "plastic," too. Musicians have a larger portion of cortex devoted to the movements of their hands than nonmusicians, and nonmusicians who practice making rhythmic finger movements increase the amount of cortex devoted to this task as they become better at it (Munte, Altenmuller, & Jancke, 2002). Even more amazing is the finding that merely *imagining* practicing these movements causes changes in the motor cortex (Pascual-Leone, 2001). Athletes have long engaged in exercises in which they visualize skilled sports movements; brain imaging research reveals that this "mental practice" can change the brain. However, the athlete must already be skilled at a task in order to visualize it properly. When skilled high jumpers visualize high jumping, fMRI reveals that their motor cortex is activated, but when beginners visualize high jumping, their visual cortex is activated, as if they are seeing the movements from the outside rather than experiencing it themselves (Olsson et al., 2008).

neural plasticity The ability to create new synapses and to change the strength of synapses.

Repairing Brain Damage   Unfortunately, the power of neural plasticity is limited, especially when it comes to repairing damage to the brain and spinal cord. Unlike the skin or the liver, the adult central nervous system does not automatically replace damaged cells. Still, it does display a certain amount of self-healing. Undamaged neurons may take over for damaged ones, partly by changing their own function and partly by sprouting axons whose connections help neighboring regions take on new functions (Bareyre et al., 2004). These changes rarely result in complete restoration of lost functions, though, so most people who have a severe stroke, Alzheimer's disease, a spinal cord injury, or some other central nervous system disorder are permanently disabled in some way.

Scientists are searching for ways to help a damaged central nervous system heal some of its own wounds. One approach has been to transplant, or graft, tissue from a still-developing fetal brain into the brain of an adult animal. If the receiving animal does not reject it, the graft sends axons out into the brain and makes some functional connections. This treatment has reversed animals' learning difficulties, movement disorders, and other results of brain damage (Noble, 2000). The technique has also been used to treat a small number of people with Parkinson's disease—a disorder characterized by tremors, rigidity of the arms and legs, difficulty in beginning movements, and poor balance (Lindvall & Hagell, 2001). The initial results were encouraging (Mendez et al., 2005, 2008). Some patients showed improvement for several years, though improvement faded for others, and some patients developed serious side effects (Freed et al., 2001).

The brain tissue transplant procedure is promising, but because its use with humans requires tissue from aborted fetuses, it has generated considerable controversy. As an alternative, some scientists have tried transplanting neural tissue from another species, such as the pig, into humans (Savitz et al., 2005). The difficulty with this approach is that the immune system rejects foreign tissue, even in the brain.

The most promising source for new neurons now appears to be an individual's own body, whose cells would not be rejected. This is a revolutionary idea, because it was long believed that once humans reached adulthood, the cells of the central nervous system stopped dividing, leaving each of us with a fixed set of neurons (Rakic, 2002). However, research has shown that cell division *does* take place in the adult central nervous systems of humans, nonhuman primates, and other animals (Altman & Das, 1965; Eriksson et al., 1998; Gould et al., 1999; Steindler & Pincus, 2002). These new cells have been found in areas such as the hippocampus, which is critical to the formation of new memories and is vulnerable to degeneration through Alzheimer's disease. The factors that influence how much cell division occurs in the brain are being investigated in rats and mice, with surprising findings. For example, exercise increases the rate of neuronal cell division in mice (van Praag et al., 1999), as does exposure to a complex environment, even in old mice (Kempermann, Gast, & Gage, 2002). Stress hormones and antidepressant drugs also influence the rate of neuronal cell division (Cameron, Tanapat, & Gould, 1998; Malberg et al., 2000). Finding newly divided neurons in the brain led to the discovery that there are **neural stem cells** in the adult brain. These are special glial cells that are capable of dividing to form new tissue, including new neurons (Cheng, Tavazoie, & Doetsch, 2005; Sanai et al., 2004). The process of creating new neurons is called *neurogenesis*.

This discovery has generated a great deal of excitement and controversy. There is excitement because stem cells raise the hope that damaged tissue may someday be replaced by cells created from a person's own body. There is controversy, though, because stem cells are linked in many people's minds with the cloning of whole individuals and because it was at first believed that these cells could come only from human embryos, which must be destroyed in the process of harvesting the cells. The ethical storm raging around embryonic stem cell research is abating, however, since researchers have demonstrated that stem cells can be harvested from other sources,

neural stem cells Special cells in the nervous system that are capable of dividing to form new tissue, including new neurons.

© AP Photo/Ron Edmonds

He Was a Super Man

After suffering a spinal cord injury in 1995, *Superman* actor Christopher Reeve was told he would never again be able to move or feel his body. He refused to accept this gloomy prediction, and after years of devoted adherence to an exercise-oriented rehabilitation program, he regained some movement, and by the time of his death in 2004, he was able to feel sensations from most of his body (Blakeslee, 2002). Physicians and physical therapists hope to make such therapy programs even more effective in the future (e.g., Dunlop, 2008; Raineteau, 2008).

LINKAGES

LINKAGES How do our brains change over a lifetime? (a link to Human Development, p.472)

such as bone marrow, the lining of the nose, skin cells, or other relatively accessible sites (Vierbuchen et al., 2010) and made to grow into brain cells. The benefits in treating brain disorders would be substantial. Patients with spinal cord injuries, as well as those with Parkinson's disease or Alzheimer's disease, might someday be cured by treatments that replace damaged or dying neurons with new ones grown from the patients' own stem cells (Chen, Magavi, & Macklis, 2004; Cowan et al., 2005; Horner & Gage, 2002; Koshizuka et al., 2004; Mezey et al., 2003; Redmond et al., 2007; Takahashi & Yamanaka, 2006; Teng et al., 2002; Wernig et al., 2008; Zhao et al., 2003).

There is still a long way to go before these strategies can be routinely used in the clinic (Lindvall & Kokaia, 2010), and in any case, generating new neurons is only half the battle. The new cells' axons and dendrites still have to reestablish all the synaptic connections that had been lost to damage or disease. In the peripheral nervous system, glial cells form "tunnels" that guide the regrowth of axons. But in the central nervous system, reestablishing communication links is much more difficult because glial cells actively suppress connections between newly sprouted axons and other neurons (Olson, 1997). Scientists have also found several related proteins that prevent newly sprouted axons from making connections with other neurons in the central nervous system. The first protein they discovered was aptly named *Nogo*.

Despite these challenges, researchers are reporting exciting results in their efforts to promote healing in damaged brains and spinal cords. They have found, for example, that blocking the receptor for the Nogo proteins in rats allowed surviving neurons to make new axonal connections and actually repair spinal cord damage (Harvey et al., 2009; Kastin & Pan, 2005). Other research with animals has shown that both spontaneous recovery and the effectiveness of brain tissue transplants can be greatly enhanced by adding naturally occurring proteins called *growth factors,* or *neurotrophic factors,* which promote the survival of neurons (Wu et al., 2009). One of these proteins is called *nerve growth factor.* Another, called *glial cell line–derived neurotrophic factor,* or *GDNF,* actually causes neurons to produce the neurotransmitter needed to reverse the effects of Parkinson's disease (Kordower et al., 2000; Theofilopoulos et al., 2001).

While scientists continue to try to make such therapies a reality, there are things that patients themselves can do to promote the neural plasticity needed to restore lost central nervous system functions. Special mental and physical exercise programs appear useful in "rewiring" the brains of stroke and spinal cord injury patients, thus reversing some forms of paralysis and improving some sensory and cognitive abilities (Blakeslee, 2001; Kao et al., 2009; Liepert et al., 2000; Taub, 2004).

Human Development and the Changing Brain

Fortunately, most of the changes that take place in the brain throughout life are not the kind associated with damage and disease. Let's consider these changes and how they are linked to the growth of sensory and motor capabilities, mental abilities, and other characteristics described in the chapter on human development.

By conducting anatomical studies, PET scans, and functional MRIs, researchers have found that association areas of the cerebral cortex develop later than sensory and motor cortex (Casey, Galvan, & Hare, 2005). And they have uncovered some interesting correlations between changes in neural activity and the behavior of human newborns and young infants. Among newborns, activity is relatively high in the thalamus but low in the striatum. This pattern may be related to the way newborns move: They make nonpurposeful, sweeping movements of the arms and legs, much like adults who have a hyperactive thalamus and a degenerated striatum (Chugani & Phelps, 1986). During the second and third months after birth, activity increases in many regions of the cortex, a change that is correlated with the loss of reflexes such as the grasping reflex. When infants are around 8 or 9 months old, activity in the frontal cortex increases, a development that correlates well with the apparent beginnings of cognitive activity in infants (Chugani & Phelps, 1986). The brain continues to mature even through adolescence, showing evidence of ever more efficient neural communication in its major fiber tracts (Gogtay et al., 2004; Thompson et al., 2000). Diffusion tensor imaging reveals, though, that the connections from the prefrontal cortex to the striatum that are involved in judgment and decision making are not yet fully developed (Asato et al., 2010). Some researchers suggest that these underdeveloped connections may be related to the difficulty that many teenagers have in resisting dangerous peer influences and foreseeing the negative consequences of certain actions (Grosbras et al., 2007).

The changes we have described mainly reflect changes in neural connections, not the appearance of new cells. After birth, the number of dendrites and synapses increases. In one area of the cortex, the number of synapses increases tenfold from birth to 12 months of age (Huttenlocher, 1990). By the time children are 6 or 7 years old, their brains have more dendrites and use twice as much metabolic fuel as those of adults (Chugani & Phelps, 1986). Then, in early adolescence, the number of dendrites and neural connections begins to drop, so that the adult level is reached by about the age of 14 (see Figure 3.20). MRI scans show an actual loss of gray-matter volume in the cortex throughout the adolescent years as adult cognitive abilities develop (Sowell et al., 2003). In other words, as we reach adulthood, we develop more brainpower with less brain.

FIGURE 3.20
Developmental Changes in the Cerebral Cortex

During childhood, the brain overproduces neural connections, establishes the usefulness of certain connections, and then "prunes" the extra ones. Overproduction of synapses, especially in the frontal cortex, may be essential for children to develop certain intellectual abilities. One research team used repeated MRI scans to track the thickness of the cerebral cortex in children of average and exceptionally high intelligence as they grew from age 6 to 19. There were no differences between groups at the beginning of the study or at the end, but cortical thickness had reached a higher preadolescent peak in the bright youngsters. So adult cognitive ability was correlated not with the final thickness of cortex but with how thick it had once been (Shaw, Greenstein, et al., 2006). As described in the chapter on cognitive abilities, the relationship between intelligence and brain development is not a simple one.

Source: From Jesse LeRoy Conel. *The Postnatal Development Of The Human Cerebral Cortex, Vol. I–VIII,* Copyright © 1939, 1975 by the President and Fellows of Harvard College. Reprinted with permission.

At birth

Six years old

Fourteen years old

Throughout the life span, the brain retains its neural plasticity, rewiring itself to form new connections and to eliminate connections too (Hua & Smith, 2004; Kozorovitskiy et al., 2005). Our genes apparently determine the basic pattern of growth and the major lines of connections—the "highways" of the brain and its general architecture. (For a summary of this architecture, see "In Review: Organization of the Brain.") But the details of the connections depend on experience, including the amount of complexity and stimulation in the environment. For example, researchers have compared the brains of rats raised alone with only a boring view of the side of their cages to the brains of rats raised with interesting toys and stimulating playmates. The cerebral cortex of those from the enriched environment had more and longer dendrites, as well as more synapses and neurotrophic factors, than the cortex of animals from barren, individual housing (Klintsova & Greenough, 1999). Furthermore, the number of cortical synapses increased when isolated animals were moved to an enriched environment. To the extent that these ideas and research findings apply to humans, they hold obvious implications for how people raise children and treat the elderly.

In any event, this line of research highlights the interaction of environmental and genetic factors. Some overproduced synapses may reflect genetically directed preparation for certain types of experiences. Generation of these synapses is an "experience-expectant" process, and it accounts for sensitive periods during development when certain things can be most easily learned (Hensch, 2005). But overproduction of synapses also occurs in response to totally new experiences; this process is "experience-dependent" (Greenough, Black, & Wallace, 1987). Within constraints set by genetics, interactions with the world mold the brain itself (e.g., Chang & Merzenich, 2003; Holtmaat et al., 2006).

IN REVIEW   Organization of the Brain

Major Division	Some Important Structures	Some Major Functions
Hindbrain	Medulla oblongata	Regulates breathing, heart rate, and blood pressure
	Reticular formation (also extends into midbrain)	Regulates arousal and attention
	Cerebellum	Controls fine movements and coordinates certain cognitive processes
Midbrain	Various nuclei	Relays sensory signals to forebrain; creates automatic responses to certain stimuli
	Substantia nigra	Initiates smooth movements
Forebrain	Hypothalamus	Regulates hunger, thirst, and sex drives
	Thalamus	Interprets and relays sensory information
	Hippocampus	Forms new memories
	Amygdala	Connects sensations and emotions
	Cerebral cortex	Analyzes sensory information; controls voluntary movements, abstract thinking, and other complex cognitive activity
	Corpus callosum	Transfers information between the two cerebral hemispheres

1. The oldest part of the brain is the _____.

2. Cells that operate as the body's twenty-four-hour "time clock" are found in the _____.

3. Memory problems seen in Alzheimer's disease are related to shrinkage of the _____.

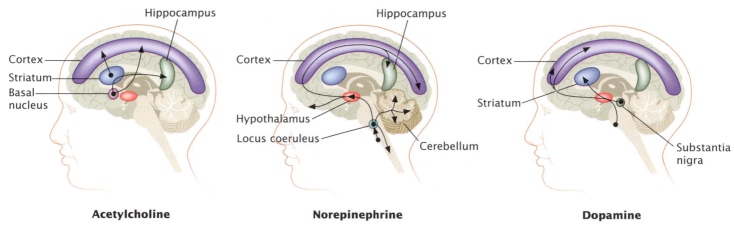

Acetylcholine   **Norepinephrine**   **Dopamine**

FIGURE 3.21
Some Neurotransmitter Pathways
Neurons that use a certain neurotransmitter may be concentrated in one particular region (indicated by dots) and send fibers into other regions with which they communicate (arrows). Here are examples for three major neurotransmitters. Psychoactive drugs affect behavior and mental processes by altering these systems. In the consciousness chapter, we discuss how drugs of abuse, such as cocaine, affect neurotransmitters. The neurotransmitter effects of therapeutic drugs are described in the chapter on the treatment of psychological disorders.

acetylcholine A neurotransmitter used by neurons in the peripheral and central nervous systems in the control of functions ranging from muscle contraction and heart rate to digestion and memory.

norepinephrine A neurotransmitter involved in arousal, as well as in learning and mood regulation.

The Chemistry of Psychology

We have described how the cells of the nervous system communicate by releasing neurotransmitters at their synapses, and we have outlined some of the basic structures of the nervous system and their functions. Let's now pull these topics together by considering which neurotransmitters occur in which structures and how neurotransmitters affect behavior. As we mentioned earlier, different sets of neurons use different neurotransmitters; a group of neurons that communicates using the same neurotransmitter is called a *neurotransmitter system*. Certain neurotransmitter systems play a dominant role in particular functions, such as emotion or memory, and in particular problems, such as Alzheimer's disease. Chemical neurotransmission was first demonstrated, in frogs, by Otto Loewi (pronounced "LOH-ee") in 1921. Since then more than a hundred different neurotransmitters have been identified.

Three Classes of Neurotransmitters

The neurotransmitters used in the nervous system fall into three main categories, based on their chemical structure: *small molecules, peptides,* and *gases*. Let's consider some examples in each category.

Small Molecules The *small-molecule* neurotransmitters were discovered first, partly because they occur in both the central nervous system and the peripheral nervous system. For example, **acetylcholine** (pronounced "uh-see-tuhl-KOH-leen") is used by neurons of the parasympathetic nervous system to slow the heartbeat and activate the digestive system and by neurons that make muscles contract. In the brain, neurons that use acetylcholine (called *cholinergic* neurons) are especially plentiful in the midbrain and striatum, where they occur in circuits that are important for movement (see Figure 3.21). Axons of cholinergic neurons also make up major pathways in the limbic system, including the hippocampus, and in other areas of the forebrain that are involved in memory. Drugs that interfere with acetylcholine prevent the formation of new memories. In Alzheimer's disease, there is a nearly complete loss of cholinergic neurons in a nucleus in the forebrain that sends fibers to the cerebral cortex and hippocampus—a nucleus that normally enhances neural plasticity in these regions (Ramanathan, Tuszynski, & Conner, 2009).

Three other small-molecule neurotransmitters are known as *catecholamines* (pronounced "kat-uh-KOHL-uh-meenz"). They include *norepinephrine, serotonin,* and *dopamine*. **Norepinephrine** (pronounced "nor-ep-uh-NEF-rin"), also called *noradrenaline,* occurs in both the central and peripheral nervous systems. In both places, it contributes to arousal. Norepinephrine (and its close relative, *epinephrine,* or *adrenaline*) are the neurotransmitters used by the sympathetic nervous system to activate you and prepare you for action. Approximately half of the norepinephrine in the entire brain is contained in cells of the locus coeruleus, which is near the reticular formation in the hindbrain (see Figure 3.21). Because norepinephrine systems cover a lot of territory, it is logical that norepinephrine would affect several broad categories of behavior. Indeed, norepinephrine is involved in the appearance of wakefulness and sleep, in learning, and in the regulation of mood.

Serotonin is similar to norepinephrine in several ways. First, most of the cells that use it as a neurotransmitter occur in an area along the midline of the hindbrain. Second, axons from neurons that use serotonin send branches throughout the forebrain, including the hypothalamus, the hippocampus, and the cerebral cortex. Third, serotonin affects sleep and mood. Serotonin differs from norepinephrine, however, in that the brain can get one of the substances from which it is made, *tryptophan,* directly from food. So what you eat can affect the amount of serotonin in your brain. Carbohydrates increase the amount of tryptophan reaching the brain and, in combination with proteins eaten in the same meal, affect how much serotonin is made (Choi et al., 2009). A meal high in carbohydrates produces increased levels of serotonin, which normally causes a reduction in the desire for carbohydrates. Some researchers suspect that malfunctions in the serotonin feedback system are responsible for the disturbances of mood and appetite seen in certain types of obesity, premenstrual tension, and depression (Lira et al., 2003; Wurtman & Wurtman, 1995). Serotonin has also been implicated in aggression and impulse control. One of the most consistently observed relationships between a particular neurotransmitter system and a particular behavior is the low level of serotonin metabolites in the brains of people who have committed suicide; these people tend to show a combination of depressed mood, self-directed aggression, and impulsivity (Bach-Mizrachi et al., 2006; McCloskey et al., 2009; Oquendo & Mann, 2000). Antidepressant medications such as Prozac, Zoloft, and Paxil appear to relieve some of the symptoms of depression by acting on serotonin systems to maintain proper levels of this neurotransmitter.

Dopamine is the neurotransmitter used in the substantia nigra and striatum, which are important for movement. Malfunctioning of the dopamine-using (or *dopaminergic*) system in these regions contributes to movement disorders, including Parkinson's disease (Sasaki et al., 2006). As dopamine cells in the substantia nigra degenerate, people with Parkinson's disease experience severe shakiness and difficulty in beginning movements. Parkinson's disease is most common in elderly people, and it may result in part from sensitivity to environmental toxins. For example, certain agricultural pesticides may damage dopaminergic neurons (Jenner, 2001). At least two studies have found dramatically higher rates of Parkinson's disease among people who have been exposed to these pesticides as compared to those who were not exposed (Ascherio et al., 2006; Dhillon et al., 2008). Parkinson's disease has been treated, with partial success, using drugs that enable neurons to make more dopamine (Chase, 1998). Permanently implanting an electrode that stimulates neurons in the brain's dopamine-influenced motor system offers an even more effective treatment but also carries a risk of surgical complications (Weaver et al., 2009).

Malfunctioning of a separate group of dopaminergic neurons whose axons go to the cerebral cortex may be partly responsible for schizophrenia, a severe disorder in which perception, emotional expression, and thought are severely distorted (Marenco & Weinberger, 2000). Other dopaminergic systems that send axons from the midbrain to the forebrain are important in the experiencing of reward or pleasure (Wise & Rompre, 1989). Animals will work hard to receive a direct infusion of dopamine into their forebrains. These dopamine systems play a role in the rewarding properties of many drugs, including cocaine. In fact, current theories of addiction suggest that the normal mechanisms of reward-based learning are exploited by these drugs and

serotonin A neurotransmitter used by cells in parts of the brain involved in the regulation of sleep, mood, and eating.

dopamine A neurotransmitter used in the parts of the brain involved in regulating movement and experiencing pleasure.

that dopaminergic systems play an important role in the process (Hyman, Malenka, & Nestler, 2006).

Two other small-molecule neurotransmitters—*GABA* and *glutamate*—are amino acids. Neurons in widespread regions of the brain use **gamma-amino butyric acid (GABA).** GABA reduces the likelihood that postsynaptic neurons will fire an action potential. In fact, it is the major inhibitory neurotransmitter in the central nervous system. When you fall asleep, neurons that use GABA deserve part of the credit. Drugs that cause reduced neural activity often do so by amplifying the "braking" action of GABA. In the case of alcohol, for example, the result is an impairment of thinking, judgment, and motor skills.

Malfunctioning of GABA systems contribute to a variety of disorders, including severe anxiety and *Huntington's disease,* an inherited and incurable disorder whose symptoms include uncontrollable jerky movement of the arms and legs, along with dementia. Huntington's disease results in the loss of many GABA-containing neurons in the striatum. Normally these GABA systems inhibit dopamine systems, so when they are lost through Huntington's disease, the dopamine systems may run wild, impairing many motor and cognitive functions. Because drugs that block GABA receptors produce intense repetitive electrical discharges, known as *seizures,* researchers suspect that malfunctioning GABA systems probably contribute to *epilepsy*, a brain disorder associated with seizures and convulsive movements. Repeated or sustained seizures can result in permanent brain damage. Drug treatments can reduce the frequency and severity of seizures but do not eliminate them and may cause undesirable side effects. An alternative treatment approach may someday come from *optogenetics,* a newly developing field of neuroscience in which the genes of light-sensitive plant proteins are inserted into animal neurons (Airan et al., 2009). This procedure allows the firing of these neurons to be increased or decreased by shining a particular kind of light on them, and there is already some evidence that this procedure is capable of stopping seizure activity in animal brain cells (Tonneson et al., 2009). If this strategy can be adapted for use in humans, it would provide welcome relief for millions of people with epilepsy.

Glutamate is the major excitatory neurotransmitter in the central nervous system. It is used by more neurons than any other neurotransmitter, and its synapses are especially plentiful in the cerebral cortex and the hippocampus. Glutamate is particularly important because it plays a major role in the ability of the brain to strengthen its synaptic connections, allowing messages to cross the synapse more easily. This strengthening process is necessary for normal development and may be at the root of learning and memory (Newpher & Ehlers, 2008). At the same time, overactivity of glutamate synapses can cause neurons to die. In fact, this overactivity is the main cause of the brain damage that occurs when oxygen is cut off from neurons during a stroke. Glutamate can "excite neurons to death," so blocking glutamate receptors immediately after a brain trauma can prevent permanent brain damage (Colak et al., 2003). Studies have revealed that glutamate helps glial cells provide energy for neurons (Rouach et al., 2008).

Peptides   Hundreds of chemicals called *peptides* have been found to act as neurotransmitters. The first of these was discovered in the 1970s, when scientists were investigating *opiates,* such as heroin and morphine. Opiates can relieve pain, produce feelings of elation, and in high doses, bring on sleep. After marking morphine with a radioactive substance, researchers traced where it became concentrated in the brain. They found that opiates bind to receptors that were not associated with any known neurotransmitter. Because it was unlikely that the brain had developed opiate receptors just in case a person might want to use morphine or heroin, researchers reasoned that the body must already contain a substance similar to opiates. This hypothesis led to the search for a naturally occurring, or endogenous, morphine, which was called *endorphin* (short for *endogenous morphine*). As it turned out, there are many natural opiate-like compounds. So the term **endorphins** refers to all neurotransmitters that

gamma-amino butyric acid (GABA) A neurotransmitter that inhibits the firing of neurons.

glutamate An excitatory neurotransmitter that helps strengthen synaptic connections between neurons.

endorphins A class of neurotransmitters that bind to opiate receptors and moderate pain.

can bind to the same receptors stimulated by opiates. Neurons in several parts of the brain use endorphins, including neuronal pathways that modify pain signals to the brain.

Gases The concept of what neurotransmitters can be was radically altered following the discovery that *nitric oxide* and *carbon monoxide*—two toxic gases that contribute to air pollution—can act as neurotransmitters (Boehning & Snyder, 2003). When nitric oxide or carbon monoxide is released by a neuron, it spreads to nearby neurons, sending a signal that affects chemical reactions inside those neurons rather than binding to receptors on their surface. Nitric oxide is not stored in vesicles, as most other neurotransmitters are; it can be released from any part of the neuron. Nitric oxide appears to be one of the neurotransmitters responsible for such diverse functions as penile erection and the formation of memories—not at the same site, obviously. (For a summary of the main neurotransmitters and the consequences of malfunctioning neurotransmitter systems, see "In Review: Classes of Neurotransmitters.")

IN REVIEW Classes of Neurotransmitters		
Neurotransmitter Class	**Normal Function**	**Disorder Associated with Malfunction**
Small Molecules		
Acetylcholine	Memory, movement	Alzheimer's disease
Norepinephrine	Mood, sleep, learning	Depression
Serotonin	Mood, appetite, impulsivity	Depression
Dopamine	Movement, reward	Parkinson's disease, schizophrenia
GABA	Sleep, movement	Anxiety, Huntington's disease, epilepsy
Glutamate	Memory	Damage after stroke
Peptides		
Endorphins	Pain control	No established disorder
Gases		
Nitric oxide	Memory	No established disorder

1. The main neurotransmitter for slowing, or inhibiting, brain activity is _____.
2. A group of neurons that use the same neurotransmitter is called a _____.
3. Which neurotransmitter's activity causes brain damage during a stroke?

The Endocrine System: Coordinating the Internal World

endocrine system Cells that form organs called glands and that communicate with one another by secreting chemicals called hormones.

glands Organs that secrete hormones into the bloodstream.

hormones Chemicals secreted by a gland into the bloodstream, which carries them throughout the body.

As we mentioned earlier, neurons are not the only cells that can use chemicals to communicate with one another in ways that affect behavior and mental processes. Another class of cells with this ability resides in the **endocrine system** (pronounced "EN-doh-krin"), which regulates functions ranging from stress responses to physical growth. The cells of endocrine organs, or **glands,** communicate by secreting chemicals, much as neurons do. In the case of endocrine organs, the chemicals are called **hormones.** Figure 3.22 shows the location and functions of some of the major endocrine glands.

FIGURE 3.22
Some Major Glands of the Endocrine System
Each of the glands shown releases its hormones into the bloodstream. Even the hypothalamus, a part of the brain, regulates the nearby pituitary gland by secreting hormones.

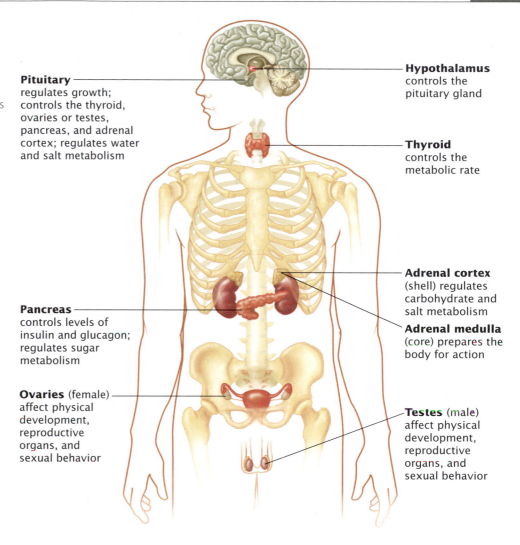

Pituitary
regulates growth; controls the thyroid, ovaries or testes, pancreas, and adrenal cortex; regulates water and salt metabolism

Hypothalamus
controls the pituitary gland

Thyroid
controls the metabolic rate

Adrenal cortex
(shell) regulates carbohydrate and salt metabolism

Adrenal medulla
(core) prepares the body for action

Pancreas
controls levels of insulin and glucagon; regulates sugar metabolism

Ovaries (female)
affect physical development, reproductive organs, and sexual behavior

Testes (male)
affect physical development, reproductive organs, and sexual behavior

Hormones secreted from the endocrine organs are similar to neurotransmitters. In fact, many of these chemicals, including norepinephrine and the endorphins, act both as hormones and as neurotransmitters. However, whereas neurons release neurotransmitters into synapses, endocrine organs release their chemicals into the bloodstream, which carries them throughout the body. In this way, endocrine glands can stimulate cells with which they have no direct connection. But not all cells receive the hormonal message. Hormones, like neurotransmitters, can influence only cells with receptors capable of receiving them. Organs whose cells have receptors for a hormone are called *target organs*.

Each hormone acts on many target organs, producing coordinated effects throughout the body. For example, when the sex hormone *estrogen* is secreted by a woman's ovaries, it activates her reproductive system. It causes the uterus to grow in preparation for nurturing an embryo; it enlarges the breasts to prepare them for nursing; it stimulates the brain to enhance interest in sexual activity; and it stimulates the pituitary gland to release another hormone that causes a mature egg to be released by the ovary for fertilization. Male sex organs, called the *testes,* secrete *androgens,* which are sex hormones such as *testosterone.* Androgens stimulate the maturation of sperm, increase a male's motivation for sexual activity, and increase his aggressiveness (Romeo, Richardson, & Sisk, 2002).

Can differences between hormones in men and women account for some of the differences between the sexes? During development and in adulthood, sex differences in hormones are relative rather than absolute. In other words, both men and women have androgens and estrogens, but men have relatively higher concentrations of androgens and women have relatively higher concentrations of estrogens. There is plenty of evidence from animal studies that the presence of higher concentrations of androgens in males during development, at around the time of birth, and at puberty leads to both structural sex differences in the brain and sex differences in adult behaviors (Gooren & Kruijver, 2002). Other animal studies suggest that estrogens may contribute to the development of the female brain (Bakker et al., 2003). It is likely that humans, too, are affected by hormones early in development. For example, studies of girls who were exposed to high levels of androgens before birth found that they were later more aggressive than their sisters who had not had such exposure (Berenbaum & Resnick, 1997). Even the artwork of such girls is affected by exposure to androgens; they are more likely than nonexposed girls to draw pictures of cars, boats, and airplanes, for example (Iijima et al., 2001). And as shown in Figure 1.1, MRI studies have revealed specific brain regions that function differently in men and women. However, such sex differences may not be simple, inevitable, or caused by the actions of hormones alone. Most likely, the sex differences we see in behavior depend not only on hormones but also on complex interactions of biological and social forces, as described in the chapter on motivation and emotion.

The brain has ultimate control over the secretion of hormones. Through the hypothalamus, it controls the pituitary gland, which in turn controls endocrine organs in the body. The brain is also one of the target organs for most endocrine secretions. In fact, the brain creates some of the same hormones that are secreted in the endocrine system and uses them for neural communication (Compagnone & Mellon, 2000). In summary, the endocrine system typically involves four elements: the brain, the pituitary gland, an endocrine organ, and the target organs, which include the brain. Each element in the system uses hormones to signal to the next element, and the secretion of each hormone is stimulated or suppressed by other hormones (Dubrovsky, 2005).

In stress hormone systems, for example, the brain controls the pituitary gland by signaling the hypothalamus to release hormones that stimulate receptors of the pituitary gland, which secretes another hormone, which stimulates another endocrine gland to secrete its hormones. More specifically, when the brain interprets a situation as threatening, the pituitary releases *adrenocorticotropic hormone (ACTH),* which causes the adrenal glands to release the hormone *cortisol* into the bloodstream. These hormones, in turn, act on cells throughout the body, including the brain. One effect of cortisol, for example, is to activate the emotion-related limbic system, making it more likely that you will remember stressful or traumatic events (Cahill & McGaugh, 1998). The combined effects of the adrenal hormones and the activation of the sympathetic system result in a set of responses called the **fight-or-flight syndrome** (also known as the **fight-flight reaction**), which, as mentioned earlier, prepares us for action in response to danger or other stress. With these hormones at high levels, the heart beats faster, the liver releases glucose into the bloodstream, fuels are mobilized from fat stores, and we usually enter a state of high arousal.

The hormones provide feedback to the brain, as well as to the pituitary gland. Just as a thermostat and furnace regulate heat, this feedback system regulates hormone secretion so as to keep it within a certain range. If a hormone rises above a certain level, feedback about this situation signals the brain and pituitary to stop stimulating that hormone's secretion. So after the immediate threat is over, feedback about cortisol's action in the brain and in the pituitary stops the secretion of ACTH and, in turn, cortisol. Because the feedback suppresses further action, this arrangement is called a *negative feedback system.*

Feedback systems are just one illustration of how the nervous system and the endocrine system—both systems of communication between and among cells—are integrated to form the biological basis for a smoothly functioning self. Together,

fight-or-flight syndrome (fight-flight reaction) A physical reaction triggered by the sympathetic nervous system that prepares the body to fight or to run from a threatening situation.

they allow interaction of our thoughts and emotions and provide us with the ability to respond to life's challenges and opportunities with purposeful and adaptive behavior.

LINKAGES

As noted in the chapter on introducing psychology, all of psychology's subfields are related to one another. Our discussion of developmental changes illustrates just one way in which the topic of this chapter, the biological aspects of psychology, is linked to the subfield of developmental psychology, which is

CHAPTER 3
Biological Aspects of Psychology

described in the chapter on human development. The Linkages diagram shows ties to two other subfields as well, and there are many more ties throughout the book. Looking for linkages among subfields will help you see how they all fit together and help you better appreciate the big picture that is psychology.

LINKAGES

Does the brain shut down when we sleep? *(ans. on p. 340)*

How do our brains change over a lifetime? *(ans. on p. 96)*

How do drugs help people diagnosed with schizophrenia? *(ans. on p. 690)*

CHAPTER 9
Consciousness

CHAPTER 12
Human Development

CHAPTER 16
Treatment of Psychological Disorders

SUMMARY

Biological psychology focuses on the biological aspects of our being, including the nervous system, which provide the physical basis for behavior and mental processes. The *nervous system* is a system of cells that allows an organism to gain information about what is going on inside and outside the body and to respond appropriately.

The Nervous System

Much of our understanding of the biological aspects of psychology has stemmed from research on animal and human nervous systems at levels ranging from single cells to complex organizations of cells.

Cells of the Nervous System

The main units of the nervous system are cells called *neurons* and *glial cells*. Neurons are especially good at receiving signals from and transmitting signals to other neurons. Neurons have cell bodies and two types of fibers, called *axons* and *dendrites*. Axons usually carry signals away from the cell body, and dendrites usually carry signals to the cell body. Neurons can transmit signals because of the structure of these fibers, the excitable surface of some of the fibers, and the *synapses*, or gaps, between cells.

Action Potentials

The membranes of neurons normally keep the distribution of electrically charged ions uneven between the inside of cells and the outside, creating an electrochemical force, or potential. The membrane surface of the axon can transmit a disturbance in this potential, called an *action potential*, from one end of the axon to the other. The speed of the action potential is fastest in neurons sheathed in *myelin*. Between firings there is a very brief rest, called a *refractory period*.

Synapses and Communication Between Neurons

When an action potential reaches the end of an axon, the axon releases a chemical called a *neurotransmitter*. This chemical crosses the synapse and interacts with the postsynaptic cell at special sites called *neural receptors*. This interaction creates a *postsynaptic potential*—either an *excitatory postsynaptic potential (EPSP)* or an *inhibitory postsynaptic potential (IPSP)*—that makes the postsynaptic cell more likely or less likely to fire an action potential of its own. So whereas communication within a neuron is electrochemical, communication between neurons is chemical. Because the fibers of neurons have many branches, each neuron can interact with thousands of other neurons. Each neuron constantly integrates signals received at its many synapses; the result of this integration determines how often the neuron fires an action potential.

Organization and Functions of the Nervous System

Neurons are organized in *neural networks* of closely connected cells. Sensory systems receive information from the environment, and motor systems influence the actions of muscles and other organs. The two major divisions of the nervous system are the *central nervous system (CNS)*, which includes the brain and spinal cord, and the *peripheral nervous system (PNS)*.

The Peripheral Nervous System: Keeping in Touch with the World

The peripheral nervous system has two components: the somatic nervous system and the autonomic nervous system.

The Somatic Nervous System

The first component of the peripheral nervous system is the *somatic nervous system*, which transmits information from the senses to the CNS via *sensory neurons* and carries signals from the CNS via *motor neurons* to the muscles that move the skeleton.

The Autonomic Nervous System

The second component of the peripheral nervous system is the *autonomic nervous system*, whose two subsystems, the *sympathetic nervous system* and the *parasympathetic nervous system*, carry messages back and forth between the CNS and the heart, lungs, and other organs and glands.

The Central Nervous System: Making Sense of the World

The CNS is laid out in interconnected groups of neuronal cell bodies, called nuclei, whose collections of axons travel together in fiber tracts, or pathways.

The Spinal Cord

The *spinal cord* receives information from the peripheral senses and sends it to the brain; it also relays messages from the brain to the periphery. In addition, cells of the spinal cord can direct simple behaviors, called *reflexes*, without instructions from the brain.

The Brain

The brain's major subdivisions are the *hindbrain*, *midbrain*, and *forebrain*. The hindbrain includes the *medulla oblongata*, the *locus coeruleus*, and the *cerebellum*. The midbrain includes the *substantia nigra*. The *reticular formation* is found in both the hindbrain and the midbrain. The forebrain is the largest and most highly developed part of the brain; it includes many structures, including the *hypothalamus* and *thalamus*. A part of the hypothalamus called the *suprachiasmatic nuclei* maintains a clock that determines biological rhythms. Other forebrain structures include the *striatum*, *hippocampus*, and *amygdala*. Several of these structures form the *limbic system*, which plays an important role in regulating emotion and memory.

The Cerebral Cortex

The outer surface of the *cerebral hemispheres* is called the *cerebral cortex*; it is responsible for many of the higher functions of the brain, including speech and reasoning. The functional areas of the cortex include the *sensory cortex*, *motor cortex*, and *association cortex*.

The Divided Brain in a Unified Self

The functions of the right and left hemispheres of the cerebral cortex show a certain degree of *lateral dominance*, or *lateralization*, which means they are somewhat specialized. In most people, the left hemisphere is more active in language and logical tasks and the right hemisphere is more active in spatial, musical, and artistic tasks. The hemispheres are connected through the *corpus callosum*, allowing them to operate in a coordinated fashion.

Plasticity in the Central Nervous System

Neural plasticity in the central nervous system, the ability to strengthen neural connections at its synapses as well as to establish new synapses, forms the basis for learning and memory. Scientists are searching for ways to increase neural plasticity following brain damage, including through the use of *neural stem cells*.

The Chemistry of Psychology

Neurons that use the same neurotransmitter form a neurotransmitter system.

Three Classes of Neurotransmitters

There are three classes of neurotransmitters: small molecules, peptides, and gases. *Acetylcholine* systems in the brain influence memory processes and movement. *Norepinephrine* is released by neurons whose axons spread widely throughout the brain; it is involved in arousal, mood, and learning. *Serotonin*, another widespread neurotransmitter, is active in systems regulating mood and appetite. *Dopamine* systems are involved in movement, motivation, and higher cognitive activities. Both Parkinson's disease and schizophrenia involve a disturbance of dopamine systems. *Gamma-amino butyric acid (GABA)* is an inhibitory neurotransmitter involved in anxiety and epilepsy. *Glutamate* is the most common excitatory neurotransmitter. It is involved in learning and memory and, in excess, may cause neuronal death. *Endorphins* are peptide neurotransmitters that affect pain pathways. Nitric oxide and carbon monoxide are gases that function as neurotransmitters.

The Endocrine System: Coordinating the Internal World

Like nervous system cells, those of the *endocrine system* communicate by releasing a chemical that signals to other cells. However, the chemicals released by endocrine organs, or *glands*, are called *hormones* and are carried by the bloodstream to remote target organs. The target organs often produce a coordinated response to hormonal stimulation. One of these responses is the *fight-or-flight syndrome*, which is triggered by adrenal hormones that prepare for action in times of stress. Hormones also affect brain development, contributing to sex differences in the brain and behavior. Negative feedback systems are involved in the control of most endocrine functions. The brain is the main controller. Through the hypothalamus, it controls the pituitary gland, which in turn controls endocrine organs in the body. The brain is also a target organ for most endocrine secretions.

LINKS TO FURTHER LEARNING

Now that you have finished reading this chapter, how about exploring some of the topics and information that you found most interesting? Here are some places to start.

Books

David Bainbridge, *Beyond the Zonules of Zinn: A Fantastic Journey Through Your Brain* (Harvard University Press, 2008). The title says it all.

William Calvin, *The Throwing Madonna: Essays on the Brain* (Bantam, 1991). Brain and behavior.

Steven Pinker, *How the Mind Works* (Norton, 1997). Brain and behavior.

V. S. Ramachandran, *Phantoms in the Brain: Probing the Mysteries of the Human Mind* (Quill, 1999). A doctor explores neurological disorders.

Bonnie Sherr Klein, *Slow Dance: A Story of Stroke, Love, and Disability* (PageMill Press, 1998). A personal account of recovery from a series of strokes.

Maryanne Wolf, *Proust and the Squid: The Story and Science of the Reading Brain* (HarperCollins, 2007). The story of all the systems in the brain that allow us to read.

Katrina Firlik, *Another Day in the Frontal Lobe: A Brain Surgeon Exposes Life on the Inside* (Random House, 2007). A neurosurgeon talks about her work and life.

On the Internet

 Access an integrated eBook and chapter-specific learning tools including flashcards, quizzes, videos, and more. Go to CengageBrain.com.

CENGAGENOW Want to maximize the value of your online study time? Take this easy-to-use study system's diagnostic pre-test, and it will create a personalized study plan for you. By helping you identify the topics that you need to understand better and then directing you to valuable online resources, it can speed up your chapter review. CengageNOW even provides a post-test so you can confirm that you are ready for an exam. Go to CengageBrain.com.

TALKING POINTS

Here are a few talking points to help you summarize this chapter for family and friends without giving a lecture.

1. Everything we think and feel and do is based on the operation of our body's biological processes.

2. Biological processes shape us, but they don't enslave us; addiction may have a biological basis, but people with addictions can overcome their habits.

3. Our ability to see and hear, to think and decide, to learn and remember, and to walk, run, or dance all depend on the fact that the billions of cells in our nervous systems are able to communicate with one another.

4. If any part of the nervous system is damaged, the ability normally handled by that part will be impaired or destroyed.

5. There are reflexes in the nervous system that allow us to react so quickly to a sudden pain that we can escape the danger even before our brains know about it.

6. The most complex aspects of thinking occur in cells located in the cerebral cortex, which is on the outer surface of the brain.

7. Brain-scanning techniques such as functional magnetic resonance imaging provide clear pictures of the brain and its activity but are not necessarily able to pinpoint the exact location of particular thoughts or feelings.

8. Each side of the brain is somewhat better than the other at some tasks, but both sides can do most things well; people are not "right-brained" or "left-brained" the way they are right-handed or left-handed.

9. The brain can change in response to damage or experience; piano lessons can increase the number of brain cells devoted to touch, for example.

10. The sudden changes in heart rate, muscle tension, and breathing that you feel in the face of danger are coordinated by the glands and hormones of your endocrine system.

4

Sensation

How do you know where you are

right now? Your brain tells you, of course, but it must get its information from your eyes and ears and your other senses.

In this chapter, we draw your attention to the amazing processes through which your senses work and to some of the problems that occur when they don't.

Years ago, Fred Aryee lost his right arm below the elbow in a boating accident, yet he still "feels" his missing arm and hand (Shreeve, 1993). Like Fred, many people who have lost an arm or a leg continue to feel itching and other sensations from a "phantom limb" (Glummarra et al., 2007; Ramachandran, 2008). When asked to "move" it, they can feel it move, and some people feel intense pain when their missing hand suddenly seems to tighten into a fist, digging nonexistent fingernails into a phantom palm. Worse, they may not be able to "open" this hand to relieve the pain. To try to help these people, scientists have seated them in front of a mirror and then angled the mirror to create the illusion that the amputated arm and hand have been restored. When these patients move their real hands while looking in the mirror, they not only "feel" movement in their phantom hands but can also "unclench" their phantom fists and stop their intense pain (Mervier & Sirigu, 2009). This clever strategy arose from research on how vision interacts with the sense of touch. To experience this kind of interaction yourself, sit across a table from someone and ask that person to stroke the tabletop while stroking your knee under the table in exactly the same way, in exactly the same direction. If you watch the person's hand as it strokes the table, you will soon experience the touch sensations coming from the table, not your knee! If the person's two hands do not move in sync, however, the illusion will not occur (Tsakiris & Haggard, 2005).

TRY THIS

This illusion illustrates several points about our senses. It shows, first, that the streams of information coming from different senses interact. Second, it reveals that our minds can change the sensations we receive. Third, and most important, the illusion suggests that "reality" differs from person to person. This last point sounds silly if you assume that there is an objective reality that is the same for everyone. After all, the seat you sit on and the book you are reading are solid objects. You can see and feel them with your senses, so they must look and feel the same to you as they would to anyone else. But research in sensory psychology tells us that reality is not that simple—the reality captured by our senses is not like the objective snapshot that appears when a camera captures an image. Instead, as in the case of a person who feels a hand that is not actually there, each individual's senses actively shape information about the outside world to create a *personal reality*. The sensory experiences of different species—and individual humans—vary. You do not see the same world a fly sees, people from California may not hear music quite the same way as people from Singapore do, and different people experience color differently.

To understand how your own sensory systems create your own personal reality, you have to understand something about the senses themselves. A **sense** is a system that translates information from outside the nervous system into neural activity. For example, vision is the system through which the eyes convert light into nerve cell activity. This activity tells the brain something about the source of the light (that it is bright or dim, for example) or about objects from which the light is reflected (say, that the object is round and red). These messages from the senses, called **sensations**, provide a map of the world outside the brain. This map is vital because what we see, hear, smell, taste, and touch shapes many aspects of our behavior and mental processes and helps us adapt and survive in our environment.

sense A system that translates information from outside the nervous system into neural activity.

sensations Messages from the senses that make up the raw information that affects many kinds of behavior and mental processes.

109

Traditionally, psychologists have distinguished between *sensation*—the initial message from the senses—and *perception,* the process through which messages from the senses are given meaning. They point out, for example, that you do not actually sense a cat lying on the sofa; you sense shapes and colors—visual sensations. You then use your knowledge of the world to interpret, or perceive, these sensations as a cat. However, it is impossible to draw a clear line between sensation and perception, partly because the process of interpreting sensations begins in the sense organs themselves. For example, a frog's eye immediately interprets any small black object as "fly!"—thus enabling the frog to attack the fly with its tongue without waiting for its brain to process the sensory information (Lettvin et al., 1959).

This chapter focuses on the first steps of the sensation-perception process; the chapter on perception deals with the later ones. Together, these two chapters illustrate how we human beings, with our sense organs and brains, create our own realities. Let's start by exploring how sensations are produced, received, and acted on. We will first consider what sensations are and how they inform us about the world. Then we'll examine the physical and psychological mechanisms involved in the auditory, visual, and chemical senses. And finally, we'll discuss the somatic senses, which allow us to feel things, to experience temperature and pain, and to know where our body parts are in relation to one another.

Sensory Systems

Each sense gives us information about the world by responding to a specific kind of energy, such as sound, light, heat, or physical pressure. The eyes respond to light energy, the ears respond to the energy of sound, and the skin responds to the energy of heat and pressure. Humans are especially dependent on vision, hearing, and the skin senses to get information about the world; we depend less than other animals on smell and taste. To your brain, "the world" also includes the rest of your body, and there are sensory systems that provide information about its movement and position.

All of these senses respond to incoming stimulus energy, encode it in the form of nerve cell activity, and send this coded information to the brain. Figure 4.1 illustrates the basic steps in sensation. At each step, sensory information is "processed" in some way. So the information that arrives at one point in the system is not quite the same as the information that goes to the next step.

In some sensory systems, the first step in sensation involves **accessory structures**, which reshape the light or sound or other energy that comes to us from the environment (Step 1 in Figure 4.1). For example, the outer part of the ear is an accessory structure that helps to collect and redirect sound. The lens of the eye is an accessory structure, too; it changes incoming light by focusing it.

The second step in sensation is **transduction**, which is the process of converting incoming energy into nerve cell activity (Step 2 in Figure 4.1). Just as your cell phone receives electromagnetic energy and transduces it into sounds, your ears receive sound energy and transduce it into the nerve cell activity that you recognize as voices, music, noise, and other auditory experiences. Transduction takes place in **neural receptors**, which are specialized cells that respond to certain forms of energy. Neural receptors are somewhat like the neurons that we describe in the chapter on biological aspects of psychology. Like neurons, they respond to incoming energy by firing an action potential that causes the release of neurotransmitters, which are chemical messengers that carry signals to neighboring nerve cells. (Some neural receptors differ from neurons, though, in that they may not have the axons and dendrites seen in neurons.) Neural receptors respond best to changes in energy (Graziano et al., 2002). A constant level of stimulation usually produces **sensory adaptation**, a condition in which responsiveness to an unchanging stimulus decreases over time. So shortly after you have put on your glasses or wristwatch, you no longer notice any touch sensations coming from them. Sensory adaptation also occurs when you have been in a foul-smelling room for

accessory structures Structures, such as the lens of the eye, that modify a stimulus.

transduction The process of converting incoming energy into neural activity.

neural receptors Specialized cells that detect certain forms of energy and transduce them into nerve cell activity.

sensory adaptation The process through which responsiveness to an unchanging stimulus decreases over time.

encoding Translating the physical properties of a stimulus into a pattern of nerve cell activity that specifically identifies those properties.

specific energy doctrine The discovery that stimulation of a particular sensory nerve provides codes for that sense, no matter how the stimulation takes place.

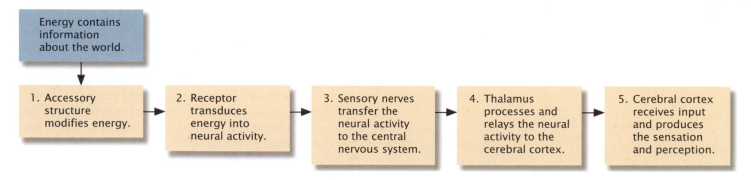

Energy contains information about the world.

| 1. Accessory structure modifies energy. | 2. Receptor transduces energy into neural activity. | 3. Sensory nerves transfer the neural activity to the central nervous system. | 4. Thalamus processes and relays the neural activity to the cerebral cortex. | 5. Cerebral cortex receives input and produces the sensation and perception. |

FIGURE 4.1

Elements of a Sensory System

In each sensory system, energy from the world is focused by accessory structures and detected by sensory receptors, which convert the energy into nerve cell activity. The pattern of activity in nerve cells acts as a signal that is relayed to and through the brain, which processes it into perceptual experience.

© Ed Bock/Corbis

What Is It?

In the split second before you recognized this stimulus as a hot-fudge sundae, sensory neurons in your visual system detected the light reflected off this page and transduced it into a neural code that your brain could interpret. The encoding and decoding process occurs so quickly and efficiently in all our senses that we are seldom aware of it. Later in this chapter, we describe how this remarkable feat is accomplished.

a while: for you, the odor will have almost disappeared, but for someone arriving from outside, the change in stimulation will hit like a ton of bricks.

Next, sensory nerves carry the output from receptors to the central nervous system—the spinal cord and the brain (Step 3 in Figure 4.1). For all the senses except smell, sensory information entering the brain goes to the thalamus (Step 4). The thalamus does some preliminary processing of each kind of information (Sherman, 2007) and then relays it to the appropriate sensory area of the cerebral cortex (Step 5). It is in the sensory cortex that the most complex processing occurs.

The Problem of Encoding

As neural receptors transduce incoming energy into patterns of nerve cell activity, they create a coded message that describes the properties of whatever stimulus—such as a light or a sound—produced that energy. The brain decodes this coded neural activity, allowing you to make sense of the stimulus—to decide, for example, whether you are looking at a cat, a dog, or a person. In other words, each psychological dimension of a sensation, such as the brightness or color of light, is based on a corresponding physical dimension, as encoded by neural receptors.

To better appreciate the problem of encoding physical stimuli into neural activity, imagine that for your birthday you receive a Pet Brain. You are told that your Pet Brain is alive, but it does not respond when you open the box and talk to it. You remove it from the box and show it a hot-fudge sundae; no response. You show it pictures of other attractive brains; still no response. You are about to toss your Pet Brain in the trash when you suddenly realize that the two of you are not speaking the same language. As described in the chapter on biological aspects of psychology, the brain usually receives information from sensory neurons and responds by activating motor neurons. So if you want to communicate with your Pet Brain, you will have to send it messages by stimulating its sensory nerves. To read its responses, you will have to record signals from its motor nerves.

After having this insight and setting up an electric stimulator and a recording device, you are faced with an awesome problem. How do you describe a hot-fudge sundae to sensory nerves so that they will pass on the correct information to the brain? This is the problem of **encoding**, the translation of the physical properties of a stimulus into a pattern of nerve cell activity that specifically identifies those properties.

If you want the brain to see the sundae, you should stimulate its optic nerve (the nerve from the eye to the brain) rather than its auditory nerve (the nerve from the ear to the brain). This idea is based on the **specific energy doctrine**, which says that stimulation of a particular sensory nerve provides codes for that one sense, no matter how the stimulation takes place. To experience this phenomenon, apply some gentle pressure to your closed eye; doing so will produce activity in the optic nerve so you will sense little spots of light.

Having chosen the optic nerve to send visual information, you must now develop a code for all the specific features of the sundae: the soft white curves of the vanilla ice cream, the dark richness of the chocolate, the bright red roundness of the cherry on top. These dimensions must be coded in the language of nerve cell activity—that is, in the firing of action potentials.

Some attributes of a stimulus can be encoded relatively simply. For example, certain neurons in the visual system fire faster in response to a bright light than to a dim light. This is called a *temporal code* because it reflects changes in the *timing* pattern of nerve firing. Other temporal codes can be more complex. For example, a burst of firing followed by a slower firing rate means something different than a steady rate of firing does. Information about a stimulus can also take the form of a *spatial code,* which reflects the *location* of neurons that are firing and those that are not. For example, different sensory neurons will fire depending on whether someone touches your hand or your foot. Sensory information can also be recoded at several relay points as it makes its way to and through the brain.

In summary, the problem of encoding is solved by means of sensory systems, which allow the brain to receive detailed, accurate, and useful information about stimuli in its environment. If you succeed in creating the right coding system, your Pet Brain will finally know what a hot-fudge sundae looks like.

LINKAGES

LINKAGES How is information from the senses organized in the brain? (a link to Biological Aspects of Psychology, p. 87)

Sensation and Biological Aspects of Psychology

As sensory systems transfer information to the brain, they also organize that information. This organized information is called a *representation*. If you have read the chapter on biological aspects of psychology, you are already familiar with some characteristics of sensory representations. In humans, representations of vision, hearing, and the skin senses in the cerebral cortex share the following features:

1. The information from each of these senses reaches the cortex through connections in the thalamus. (Figure 3.12 shows where this area of the brain is.)

2. Each side of the cerebral cortex builds a sensory representation of the opposite, or *contralateral,* side of the world. So the left side of the visual cortex "sees" the right side of the world, and the right side of that cortex "sees" the left side of the world. Similarly, the contralateral representation of skin senses occurs because most sensory nerve fibers from each side of the body cross over to the opposite side of the thalamus and go from there to the cerebral cortex.

3. The cortex contains neural maps, or *topographical representations,* of each sense. These maps are organized so that features that are near each other in the world eventually stimulate neurons that are near each other in the brain. For example, two notes that are similar in pitch activate neighboring neurons in the auditory cortex, and the neurons that respond to sensations in the elbow and in the forearm are relatively close to one another in the somatosensory cortex. There are multiple maps representing each sense, but the area that receives information directly from the thalamus is called the *primary cortex* for that sense.

4. The density of nerve fibers in various parts of a sensory system determines how extensively those parts are represented in the cortex. The skin on your fingertip, for example, has more touch receptors per square inch than the skin on your back does. So the area of cortex that represents your fingertip is larger than the area that represents your back.

5. Each region of primary sensory cortex is organized as columns of cells, each of which has a somewhat specialized role in sensory processing. For example, some columns of cells in the visual cortex respond most strongly to diagonal lines, whereas other columns respond most strongly to horizontal lines.

6. For each of the senses, regions of cortex other than the primary areas do additional processing of sensory information. As described in the chapter on biological aspects of psychology, these areas of *association cortex* may contain representations of more than one sense, thus setting the stage for the combining of sensory information that we described at the beginning of this chapter.

In summary, sensory systems convert various forms of physical energy into nerve cell activity. (As described in Figure 4.1, the energy may first be modified by accessory structures.) The resulting pattern of nerve cell activity encodes the physical properties of the energy. The codes are modified as the information is transferred to the brain and processed further. Let's now consider how these processes take place in hearing, vision, and other sensory systems.

Hearing

In 1969, when Neil Armstrong became the first human to step onto the moon, millions of people back on the earth heard his radio transmission: "That's one small step for a man, one giant leap for mankind." But if Armstrong had taken off his space helmet and shouted, "Whoo-ee! I can moonwalk!" another astronaut a foot away would not have heard him. Why? Because Armstrong would have been speaking into airless, empty space. **Sound** is a repeated fluctuation, a rising and falling, in the pressure of air, water, or some other substance called a *medium*. On the moon, which has almost no atmospheric medium, sound cannot exist.

Sound

Vibrating objects create the fluctuations in pressure that we experience as sound. Each time an object moves outward, it increases the pressure in the surrounding medium. As the object moves back, the pressure drops. When you speak, for example, your vocal cords vibrate, producing fluctuations in air pressure that spread as waves. A *wave* is a repeated, rhythmic variation in pressure that spreads out in all directions. The wave can move great distances, but the air itself barely moves. Imagine a jam-packed line of people waiting to get into a movie. If someone at the rear of the line shoves the next person, a wave of people jostling against people may spread all the way to the front of the line, but the impatient person who shoved first is still no closer to getting into the theater.

Physical Characteristics of Sound   Sound is represented graphically by waveforms like those in Figure 4.2. A *waveform* represents a wave in two dimensions, but remember that waves actually move through the air in all directions. This is the reason that when people talk to each other in a movie theater or a lecture, others all around them are distracted by the conversation.

To understand the nature of sound, it is important to know about three characteristics of sound waveforms. First, the difference in air pressure from the baseline to the peak of the wave is the **amplitude** of the sound, or its intensity. Second, the distance from one wave peak to the next is called the **wavelength**. Third, a sound's **frequency** is the number of complete waveforms, or cycles, that pass by a given point in one second. Frequency is described in a unit called *hertz*, abbreviated *Hz* (named for Heinrich Hertz, a nineteenth-century physicist). One cycle per second is 1 Hz. Because the speed of sound is constant in a given medium, wavelength and frequency are related: The longer the wavelength, the lower the frequency; the shorter the wavelength, the higher the frequency. Most sounds are mixtures of many different frequencies and amplitudes. In contrast, a pure tone is made up of only one frequency and can be represented by what is known as a *sine wave* (Figure 4.2 shows such sine waves).

Psychological Dimensions of Sound   The physical characteristics of sound waves—their amplitude and frequency—determine the psychological dimensions of sound that we know as *loudness, pitch,* and *timbre.*

Loudness is determined by the amplitude of the sound wave; waves with greater amplitude create sensations of louder sounds. Loudness is described in units called *decibels,* abbreviated *dB*. By definition, 0 dB is the minimum detectable sound for

© Bonnie Kamin/PhotoEdit

Noise Eliminators

Complex sound, including noise, can be analyzed into the simple sine waves it is composed of by means of a mathematical process called *Fourier analysis*. Noise-eliminating headphones perform this waveform analysis and then use a sound synthesizer to produce exactly opposite waveforms. The opposing waves cancel each other out, and the amazing result is near-silence. Similar devices are being developed to treat chronic tinnitus, or "ringing in the ear."

sound A repetitive fluctuation in the pressure of a medium, such as air.

amplitude The difference between the peak and the baseline of a waveform.

wavelength The distance from one peak to the next in a waveform.

frequency The number of complete waveforms, or cycles, that pass a given point in space every second.

loudness A psychological dimension of sound determined by the amplitude of a sound wave.

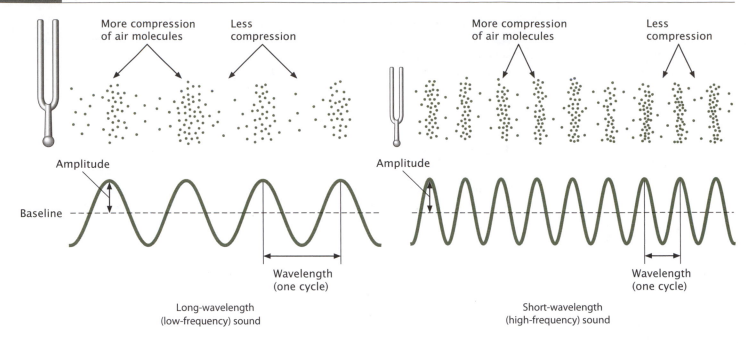

More compression of air molecules   Less compression

More compression of air molecules   Less compression

Amplitude

Amplitude

Baseline

Wavelength (one cycle)

Wavelength (one cycle)

Long-wavelength (low-frequency) sound

Short-wavelength (high-frequency) sound

FIGURE 4.2

Sound Waves and Waveforms
Sound is created when objects, such as a tuning fork, vibrate. The vibrations create alternating regions of greater and lesser compression of air molecules, which can be represented as a waveform. The point of greatest compression is the peak of the graph. The lowest point, or trough, is where compression is least.

normal hearing. Table 4.1 gives examples of the loudness, or intensity, of a wide range of sounds.

Pitch, or how high or low a tone sounds, depends on the frequency of sound waves. High-frequency waves are sensed as sounds of high pitch. The highest note on a piano has a frequency of about 4,000 Hz; the lowest note has a frequency of about 50 Hz. Humans can hear sounds ranging from about 20 Hz to about 20,000 Hz.

Almost everyone hears relative pitch; that is, people can tell whether one note is higher than, lower than, or equal to another note. However, some people have **absolute pitch**, more commonly known as *perfect pitch*, which means they can identify specific frequencies and the notes they represent. They can say, for example, that a 262-Hz tone is middle C. Though perfect pitch appears to be an inborn trait, it may also be possible

pitch How high or low a tone sounds.

absolute pitch The ability to identify the musical notes associated with specific sound frequencies.

TABLE 4.1 Intensity of Sound Sources	
Sound intensity varies across an extremely wide range. A barely audible sound is, by definition, 0 decibels (dB). Every increase of 20 dB reflects a tenfold increase in the amplitude of sound waves.	So the 40-dB sounds of an office are actually 10 times as intense as a 20-dB whisper, and traffic noise of 100 dB is 10,000 times as intense as that whisper.

Source	Sound Level (dB)
Spacecraft launch (45 meters away)	180
Loudest rock band on record	160
Pain threshold (approximate)	140
Large jet motor (22 meters away)	120
Loudest human shout on record	111
Heavy auto traffic	100
Conversation (about 1 meter away)	60
Quiet office	40
Soft whisper	20
Threshold of hearing	0

Source: M. W. Levine and J. M. Shefner, *Fundamentals of Sensation and Perception*. Copyright © 2000. Reprinted by permission of Oxford University Press.

to develop it through learning (Bella & Peretz, 2003; Gore & Marks, 2005). Some children can improve their skill at pitch identification if given special training before about the age of 6 (Takeuchi & Hulse, 1993). About 4 percent of people appear to be "tone deaf," which means they are not good at discriminating among musical tones, even though they can discriminate the pitches of nonmusical sounds (Hyde & Peretz, 2004; Hyde et al., 2006).

Timbre (pronounced "TAM-bur") is the quality of sound. It is determined by complex wave patterns that are added onto the lowest, or *fundamental*, frequency of a sound. The extra waves allow you to tell, for example, the difference between a note played on a flute and the same note played on a clarinet. Experiencing this dimension of sound appears to depend on specialized neurons in the auditory system; there are cases of brain injury in which timbre is no longer sensed even though all other aspects of hearing remain intact (Kohlmetz et al., 2003).

The Ear

The human ear converts sound energy into nerve cell activity through a series of accessory structures and transduction mechanisms.

Auditory Accessory Structures   Sound waves are collected in the outer ear, beginning with the *pinna,* the crumpled part of the ear visible on the side of the head. The pinna funnels sound down through the ear canal (see Figure 4.3). (People straining to hear a faint sound may cup a hand to their ear and bend the pinna forward, thus enlarging the sound-collection area. Try this yourself, and you will notice that everything sounds a little louder.) At the end of the ear canal, the sound waves reach the middle ear, where they strike a tightly stretched membrane known as the *eardrum,* or **tympanic membrane**. The sound waves cause matching vibrations in the tympanic membrane.

The vibrations of the tympanic membrane then pass through a chain of three tiny bones: the *malleus,* or *hammer;* the *incus,* or *anvil;* and the *stapes,* or *stirrup.* These bones (whose names are pronounced "MAL-ee-uss," "INK-uss," and "STAY-peez") amplify the vibrations coming from the tympanic membrane by focusing them onto a smaller membrane called the *oval window* (all these structures are shown in Figure 4.3).

Auditory Transduction   When sound vibrations pass through the oval window, they enter the inner ear, reaching the **cochlea** (pronounced "KOH-klee-uh"), the structure in which transduction occurs. The cochlea is wrapped into a coiled spiral. (*Cochlea* comes from the Greek word for "snail.") If you unwrapped the spiral, you would see a fluid-filled tube along its length. The **basilar membrane** forms the floor of this long tube (see Figure 4.3). Whenever a sound wave passes through the fluid in the tube, it causes the basilar membrane to move up and down, and this movement bends *hair cells* of the *organ of Corti,* a group of cells resting on the membrane. These hair cells connect with fibers from the **acoustic nerve**, also known as the *auditory nerve,* a bundle of axons that goes into the brain. When the hair cells bend, they stimulate neurons in the acoustic nerve to fire, and the pattern of firing creates a coded message that tells the brain about the amplitude and frequency of the incoming sound waves (Griesinger, Richards, & Ashmore, 2005). You experience this information as loudness and pitch.

Deafness   The middle and inner ear are among the most delicate structures in the body. If they deteriorate or are damaged, deafness can result. One form of deafness is caused by problems with the bones of the middle ear. Over time they can fuse together, thus preventing accurate conduction of vibrations from one bone to the next. This condition, called *conduction deafness,* can be treated by surgery to break the bones apart or to replace the natural bones with plastic ones (Ayache et al., 2003). Hearing aids that amplify incoming sounds can also help (Palmer, 2009).

A more common problem, called *nerve deafness,* results when the acoustic nerve or, more commonly, the hair cells are damaged (Shepherd & McCreery, 2006). Hair cell

TRY THIS

© Ed Roy

An Accessory Structure

Some animals, like Annie here, have large pinnae that can be rotated to help detect sounds and locate their source.

timbre The mixture of frequencies and amplitudes that make up the quality of sound.

tympanic membrane A membrane in the middle ear that generates vibrations that match the sound waves striking it.

cochlea A fluid-filled spiral structure in the ear in which auditory transduction occurs.

basilar membrane The floor of the fluid-filled duct that runs through the cochlea.

acoustic nerve The bundle of axons that carries stimuli from the hair cells of the cochlea to the brain.

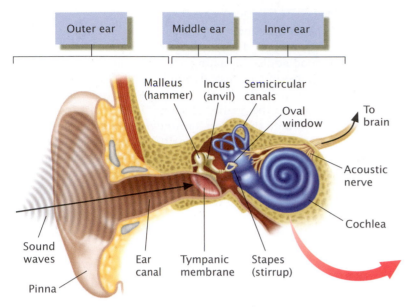

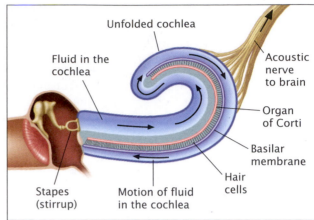

FIGURE 4.3
Structures of the Ear

The outer ear (pinna and ear canal) channels sounds into the middle ear, where the vibrations of the tympanic membrane are amplified by three delicate bones, creating vibrations in the fluid inside the cochlea in the inner ear. The coils of the cochlea are unfolded in this illustration to show the path of the fluid waves along the basilar membrane. Movements of the basilar membrane stimulate the hair cells of the organ of Corti, which transduce the vibrations into changes in neural firing patterns, which are sent along the acoustic nerve to the brain.

damage occurs gradually with age, but it can also be caused more quickly by extended exposure to the noise of jet engines, industrial equipment, gunfire, loud music, and other intense sounds (Goldstein, 2002; see Figure 4.4).

For example, Stephen Stills, Pete Townshend, and other 1970s rock musicians have become partially deaf after many years of performing extremely loud music (Ackerman, 1995). Listening to music at high volume through the earpieces of iPods and other portable devices can also cause hearing loss (Petrescu, 2008; Vogel et al., 2009). In the United States and other industrialized countries, people born after World War II are experiencing hearing loss at a younger age than those in earlier generations, possibly because "noise pollution" has increased during the past sixty years (Levine, 1999).

Hair cells can regrow in chickens and other birds (who seldom listen to rock music), and a certain kind of inner-ear hair cell has been regenerated in some mammals (Malgrange et al., 1999), fueling optimism about the possibility of regenerating human auditory hair cells. This feat might be accomplished by implanting stem cells or by treating damaged areas with growth factors similar to those used to repair damaged brain cells (Beisel et al., 2008; Shepherd et al., 2005; see the chapter on biological aspects of psychology). Gene therapy offers another promising approach. In one study, researchers inserted into the inner ears of deaf guinea pigs the gene that normally guides prenatal development of hair cells in these animals. As a result,

FIGURE 4.4
Effects of Loud Sounds

High-intensity sounds can actually tear off the hair cells of the inner ear. Part A shows the organ of Corti of a normal guinea pig. Part B shows the damage caused by exposure to twenty-four hours of 2,000-Hz sound at 120 dB. Generally, any sound loud enough to produce tinnitus (ringing in the ears) causes some damage. In humans, small amounts of damage can accumulate over time to produce a significant hearing loss by middle age—as many veteran rock musicians can attest.

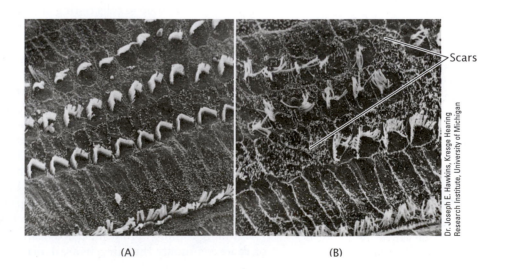

(A)   (B)

Dr. Joseph E. Hawkins, Kresge Hearing Research Institute, University of Michigan

Shaping the Brain

The auditory cortex is larger in trained musicians than in people whose jobs are less focused on fine gradations of sound. How much larger this area becomes is correlated with how long the musicians have studied their art. This finding reminds us that, as described in the chapter on biological aspects of psychology, the brain can literally be shaped by experience and other environmental factors.

© Jupiterimages

hair cells regrew in the cochlea, and the animals' hearing was restored (Izumikawa et al., 2005). Gene therapy has had similar effects on some hearing-impaired humans (Husseman & Raphael, 2009). Hair cell regeneration could revolutionize the treatment of nerve deafness, which cannot be overcome by conventional hearing aids. As work on this front continues, other scientists have developed electronic devices that can be implanted in the inner ear to serve as an artificial cochlea. These *cochlear implants* can't eliminate deafness, but they provide enough coded stimulation of the acoustic nerve to restore a useful degree of hearing in many people (Basura, Eapen, & Buchman, 2009; Niparko et al., 2010).

Auditory Pathways, Representations, and Experiences

Before you can hear sounds, the information encoded in the activity of the many axons that make up the acoustic nerve must be sent to the brain for further processing. The acoustic nerve connects to structures in the brain stem, and from there the information is sent to the thalamus. After preliminary processing in the thalamus, the sound information goes to the **auditory cortex**. As described in the chapter on biological aspects of psychology, this area is in the brain's temporal lobe, close to the areas involved in language perception and production (see Figure 3.15). It is in the auditory cortex and in these nearby areas that information about sound is subjected to the most intense and complex analysis (Ciocca, 2008). The auditory cortex is also activated by imagined sounds, such as those occurring when people mentally rehearse a phone number, replay a song in their heads, or experience auditory hallucinations (Ford et al., 2009; Voisin et al., 2006).

Different parts of the brain's auditory system process different aspects of sound. For example, information about the frequency of a sound and about where it is coming from are processed in separate regions of the auditory cortex (Nelken, 2008). Further, cells in the auditory cortex have similar *preferred frequencies,* meaning that they respond most vigorously to sounds of a particular frequency. The cells are arranged so as to create a frequency "map" in which cells with similar preferred frequencies are closer to each other than those with very different preferred frequencies. Each axon in the acoustic nerve, too, comes from a neuron that is particularly responsive to a certain frequency, though each also responds to some extent to a range of frequencies (Schnee et al., 2005). The auditory cortex examines the pattern of activity of a number of neurons in order to determine the frequency of a sound.

auditory cortex The area in the brain's temporal lobe that is first to receive information about sounds from the thalamus.

Processing Language

As this student and teacher communicate using American Sign Language, the visual information they receive from each other's hand movements is processed by the same areas of their brains that allow hearing people to understand spoken language (Neville et al., 1998).

Certain parts of the auditory cortex process certain types of sounds. One part, for example, specializes in responding to information coming from human voices (Belin, Zatorre, & Ahad, 2002); others are particularly responsive to sounds made by animals, sounds made by tools, or the sounds of musical instruments (Lewis et al., 2005; Zatorre, 2003). This specialization in the auditory cortex can be seen in fMRI brain scans. Observing which brain areas become activated by which kind of sound has allowed researchers to detect whether a person is listening to words spoken by a familiar or unfamiliar voice and even to identify some details about what is being said (Formisano et al., 2008).

The auditory cortex receives information from other senses as well. It is activated, for example, when you watch someone say words (but not when the person makes other facial movements). This activity forms part of the biological basis for the lip reading that helps you to hear what people say (Campbell & Capek, 2008).

Sensing Pitch   The frequency of a sound determines the pitch that you experience, but sensing pitch is not as simple as you might expect. The reason is that most sounds are made up of mixtures of frequencies. The mixtures in musical chords and voices, for example, can produce sounds whose pitch is ambiguous, or open to interpretation. As a result, different people may experience the "same" sound as different pitches (Patel & Balaban, 2001). In fact, the same sequence of chords can sound like an upward progression to one person and a downward progression to another. As mentioned earlier, pitch recognition abilities are influenced by genetics (Drayna et al., 2001), but cultural factors can have an effect too (Morrison & Demorest, 2009). For instance, people in the United States tend to hear ambiguous musical scales as progressing in a direction that is opposite to the way they are heard by people from Canada and England (Dawe, Platt, & Welsh, 1998). This cross-cultural difference appears to be a reliable one, though no one yet knows exactly why it occurs.

Locating Sounds   Your brain analyzes the location of sound sources based partly on the very slight difference in the time at which a sound arrives at each of your ears (it reaches the closer ear slightly sooner). The brain also uses information about the difference in sound intensity at each ear (sounds from sources that are closer to one ear are slightly louder in that ear). As a result, you can be reasonably sure where a voice or other sound is coming from even when you can't see its source. To perform this feat, the brain analyzes the activities of groups of neurons that, individually, signal only a rough approximation of the location. It is the combined firing frequencies of these many neurons in the auditory cortex that creates a sort of "Morse code" that describes where a sound is coming from (Wright & Fitzgerald, 2001). Other codes tell the brain about the intensity and frequency of sounds. Let's consider those coding systems next.

Coding Intensity and Frequency

People can hear an incredibly wide range of sound intensities. The faintest sound that can be heard moves the inner ear's hair cells less than the diameter of a single hydrogen atom (Hudspeth, 1997). Sounds more than a trillion times more intense can also be heard. Between these extremes, the auditory system codes intensity in a straightforward way: The more intense the sound, the more rapid the firing of a given neuron.

Dogs and some other animals can hear a wider range of sound frequencies than humans can, but people are much better than most other mammals at hearing slight differences between frequencies (Shera, Guinan, & Oxenham, 2002). How do we discriminate these differences? Frequency appears to be coded in two ways, which are described by place theory and frequency-matching theory.

Place Theory   Georg von Bekesy's pioneering experiments in the 1930s and 1940s were built on Hermann von Helmholtz's earlier research on how frequency is coded (Evans, 2003; von Bekesy, 1960). Studying human cadavers, von Bekesy made an opening in the cochlea in order to see the basilar membrane within. He then presented sounds of differing frequencies by vibrating a rubber membrane that was installed in place of the oval window. Using special optical instruments, von Bekesy could see ripples of waves moving down the basilar membrane. He saw that these waves grew, reached a peak, and then quickly tapered off, much as ocean waves crest and then dissolve.

As shown in Figure 4.5, the critical feature of waves in the inner ear is that the place on the basilar membrane where they peak depends on the frequency of the sound that produces them. High-frequency sounds produce a wave that peaks soon after it starts down the basilar membrane. Lower-frequency sounds produce a wave that peaks farther along the basilar membrane, farther from the oval window.

How does the location of the peak affect the coding of frequency? Helmholtz suggested an explanation. According to his **place theory**, later called the *traveling wave theory* by von Bekesy, the greatest response by hair cells occurs at the peak of the wave. Because the location of the peak varies with the frequency of the sound, it follows that hair cells at a particular place on the basilar membrane respond most to a particular frequency of sound, called a *characteristic frequency*. In other words, place theory describes a spatial, or place-related, code for frequency. When hair cells at a particular location respond to a sound, we hear a pitch that is at the characteristic frequency of those cells. One important result of this arrangement is that extended exposure to a very loud sound of a particular frequency can destroy hair cells at one spot on the basilar membrane, making it impossible to hear sounds of that frequency.

place theory A theory that hair cells at a particular place on the basilar membrane respond most to a particular frequency of sound.

FIGURE 4.5
Movements of the Basilar Membrane
As waves of fluid in the cochlea spread along the basilar membrane, the membrane is bent and then recovers. As shown in these three examples, the point at which the bending of the basilar membrane reaches its peak is different for each sound frequency. According to place theory, these peaks are the locations at which the hair cells receive the greatest stimulation.

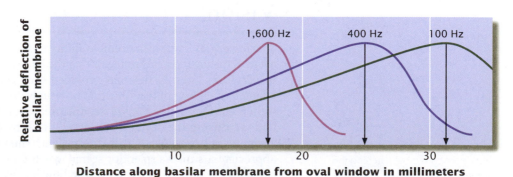

Frequency-Matching Theory Place theory accounts for much of what we know about hearing, but it cannot explain the coding of very low frequencies, such as that of a deep bass note. That is because humans can hear frequencies as low as 20 Hz even though no auditory nerve fibers respond to very low characteristic frequencies. These low frequencies must be coded in some other way. The answer appears to be *frequency matching,* a process in which certain neurons in the acoustic nerve fire each time a sound wave passes. So a sound wave whose frequency is, say, 25 cycles per second would cause those neurons to fire 25 times per second.

Frequency matching by individual neurons could apply up to about 1,000 Hz, but no neuron can fire faster than 1,000 times per second. A frequency-matching code can be created for frequencies somewhat above 1,000 Hz, though, through the combined activity of a group of neurons. For example, some neurons in the group might fire at every other wave peak, others at every fifth peak, and so on, producing a *volley* of firing at a combined frequency that is higher than any of these neurons could manage alone. Accordingly, frequency matching is sometimes referred to as the **volley theory** of frequency coding.

In summary, the nervous system uses more than one way to code the range of frequencies you can hear. The lowest sound frequencies are coded by frequency matching, whereby the frequency is matched by the firing rate of auditory nerve fibers. Low to moderate frequencies are coded by both frequency matching and the place on the basilar membrane at which the wave peaks. High frequencies are coded only by the place at which the wave peaks. (For a review of how changes in air pressure become signals in the brain that are experienced as sounds, see "In Review: Hearing.")

IN REVIEW Hearing

Aspect of Sensory System	Elements	Key Characteristics
Energy	Sound: pressure fluctuations of air produced by vibrations	The amplitude, frequency, and complexity of sound waves determine the loudness, pitch, and timbre of sounds.
Accessory structures	Ear: pinna, tympanic membrane, malleus, incus, stapes, oval window, basilar membrane	Changes in pressure produced by the original wave are amplified.
Transduction mechanism	Hair cells of the organ of Corti	Frequencies are coded by the location of the hair cells receiving the greatest stimulation (place theory) and by the firing rate of neurons (frequency-matching, or volley, theory).
Pathways and representations	Acoustic nerve to thalamus to auditory cortex	Auditory cortex decodes patterns of information from the acoustic nerve, creating sensations of loudness, pitch, and timbre.

1. Sound energy is converted to nerve cell activity in an inner-ear structure called the _____.
2. Hearing loss due to damage to hair cells or the acoustic nerve is called _____.
3. How high or low a sound sounds is called _____ and is determined by the _____ of a sound wave.

Vision

Soaring eagles have the incredible ability to see a mouse move in the grass from a mile away. Cats have special "reflectors" at the back of their eyes that help them to see even in very dim light. Nature has provided each species with a visual system uniquely adapted to its way of life. The human visual system is also adapted to do many things well: It combines great sensitivity and great sharpness, enabling us to see objects near and far, during the day and at night. Our night vision is not as good as that of some animals, but our color vision is excellent. This is not a bad trade-off; being able to appreciate a sunset's splendor seems worth an occasional stumble in the dark. Let's consider the human visual sense and how it responds to light.

volley theory The view that some sounds are coded by matching the frequency of neural firing.

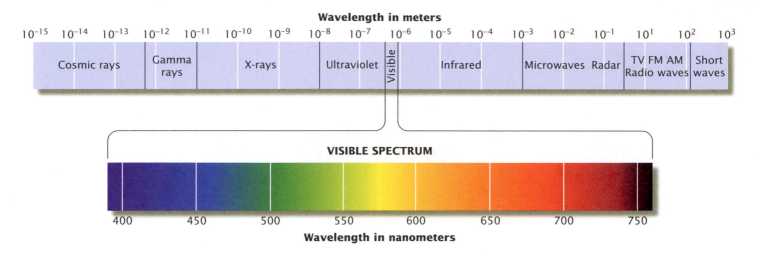

Wavelength in meters

| 10^{-15} | 10^{-14} | 10^{-13} | 10^{-12} | 10^{-11} | 10^{-10} | 10^{-9} | 10^{-8} | 10^{-7} | 10^{-6} | 10^{-5} | 10^{-4} | 10^{-3} | 10^{-2} | 10^{-1} | 10^{1} | 10^{2} | 10^{3} |

Cosmic rays | Gamma rays | X-rays | Ultraviolet | Visible | Infrared | Microwaves | Radar | TV FM AM Radio waves | Short waves

VISIBLE SPECTRUM

400 450 500 550 600 650 700 750

Wavelength in nanometers

FIGURE 4.6

The Spectrum of Electromagnetic Energy

The range of wavelengths that the human eye can see as visible light is limited to a narrow band within the much wider spectrum of electromagnetic energy. To detect energy outside this range, we must rely on electronic instruments such as radios, TV sets, mobile phones, radar, and infrared night-vision scopes that can "see" this energy, just as the eye sees visible light.

visible light Electromagnetic radiation that has a wavelength of approximately 400 to 750 nm.

light intensity A physical dimension of light waves that refers to how much energy the light contains; it determines the brightness of light.

light wavelength The distance between peaks in light waves.

cornea The curved, transparent, protective layer through which light rays enter the eye.

pupil An opening in the eye, just behind the cornea, through which light passes.

iris The colorful part of the eye, which constricts or relaxes to adjust the amount of light entering the eye.

lens The part of the eye behind the pupil that bends light rays, focusing them on the retina.

retina The surface at the back of the eye onto which the lens focuses light rays.

Light

Light is a form of energy known as *electromagnetic radiation*. Most electromagnetic radiation—including X-rays, radio waves, television signals, and radar—is invisible to the human eye. In fact, as shown in Figure 4.6, the range, or spectrum, of **visible light** is just the tiny slice of electromagnetic radiation whose wavelength is from just under 400 nanometers (nm) to about 750 nanometers (a *nanometer* is one-billionth of a meter). Unlike sound, light can travel without a medium such as air or water. So even on the airless moon, astronauts can see one another, even if they can't hear one another without radios. Light waves are like particles that pass through space, but they vibrate with a certain wavelength. In other words, light has some properties of waves and some properties of particles, and it is correct to refer to light as either *light waves* or *light rays*.

Sensations of light depend on two physical dimensions of light waves: intensity and wavelength. **Light intensity** refers to how much energy the light contains; it determines the brightness of light, much as the amplitude of sound waves determines the loudness of sound. What color you sense depends mainly on **light wavelength**. At a given intensity, different wavelengths produce sensations of different colors, much as different sound frequencies produce sensations of different pitch. For instance, 440-nm light appears violet blue, and 700-nm light appears orangish red.

Focusing Light

Just as sound energy is converted to nerve cell activity in the ear, light energy is transduced into nerve cell activity in the eye. Before this transduction process occurs, accessory structures in the human eye modify incoming light rays. The light rays enter the eye by passing through a transparent, protective layer called the **cornea** (see Figure 4.7). Then the light passes through the **pupil**, the opening just behind the cornea. The **iris**, which gives the eye its color, adjusts the amount of light allowed into the eye by constricting to reduce the size of the pupil or relaxing to enlarge it. Directly behind the pupil is the **lens**. The cornea and the lens of the human eye are both curved so that, like the lens of a camera, they bend light rays. The light rays are focused into an image on the surface at the back of the eye; this surface is called the **retina**. Light rays from the top of an object are focused at the bottom of the image on the retinal surface. Light rays from the right side of the object end up on the left side of the retinal image (see Figure 4.8). The brain rearranges this upside-down and reversed image so that we can see the object as it is.

The lens of the human eye bends light rays entering the eye from various angles so that they meet on the retina (see Figure 4.8). If the rays meet either in front of the retina or behind it, the image will be out of focus. The muscles that hold the lens adjust its shape

FIGURE 4.7

Major Structures of the Eye

As shown in this top view of the eye, light rays bent by the combined actions of the cornea and the lens are focused on the retina, where the light energy is transduced into nerve cell activity. Nerve fibers known collectively as the *optic nerve* exit at the back of the eye and continue to the brain.

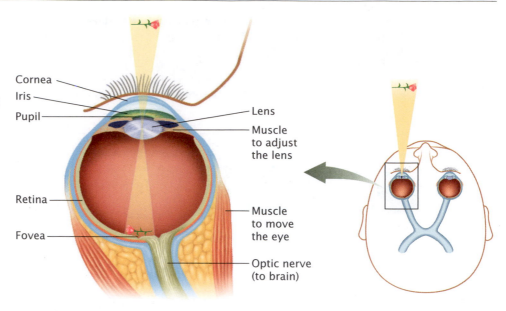

Cornea
Iris
Pupil
Lens
Muscle to adjust the lens
Retina
Fovea
Muscle to move the eye
Optic nerve (to brain)

TRY THIS

so that images of either near or far objects can be focused on the retina. To illustrate this for yourself, try reading the next sentence while holding the book as close to your face as possible. To maintain a focused image at close range, your muscles have to tighten your lenses, making them more curved. This ability to change the shape of the lens to bend light rays is called **ocular accommodation**. Over time, the lens loses some of its flexibility, making accommodation more difficult. This is why most older people become "farsighted," seeing distant objects clearly but having trouble with reading or close work. A more common problem in younger people is *myopia,* or nearsightedness, in which close objects are in focus but distant ones are blurry. This condition is partly genetic, but as shown in the accompanying photo, it can also be influenced by environmental factors such as reading habits (Zadnik, 2001). For example, in the United States in 1971, 25 percent of people in the 12-to-54 age range were nearsighted; by 2005, that figure had grown to 45 percent (Vitale, Sperduto, & Ferris, 2009), possibly because people are spending so much more time these days looking at close-up images on the screens of computers and cell phones (Seppa, 2009). These vision problems can usually be corrected with glasses or contact lenses that assist in the light-bending process. Another option is laser-assisted in situ keratomileusis (LASIK) surgery, which reshapes and stretches the cornea (Vuori, Tervo, & Holopainen, 2009). LASIK increases the degree to which the cornea bends light rays, thus requiring the lens to do less accommodation and eliminating the need for glasses or contacts.

FIGURE 4.8

The Lens and the Retinal Image

You see objects as they are because your brain rearranges the upside-down and reversed images that the lens focuses on the retina. If light rays are out of focus when they reach the retina, glasses or contact lenses can usually correct the problem. In some older people, vision is impaired by cataracts, a condition in which a "cloudy" lens severely reduces incoming light. Cataracts can be cleared up with laser surgery or by replacing the natural lens with an artificial one (Snellingen et al., 2002).

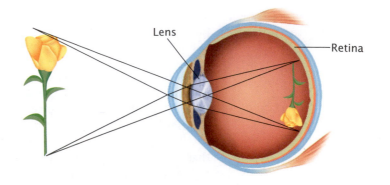

Lens
Retina

Dr. Frank Schaeffel

Reading and Nearsightedness

Visual experience can modify the eye. When chicks are raised with light-diffusing goggles that allow only a blank image to enter the eye, their eyeballs become elongated, and they become nearsighted (Wallman et al., 1987). Humans may be vulnerable to the same elongation because reading presents areas around the fovea with a constant, relatively featureless image.

ocular accommodation The ability of the lens to change its shape and bend light rays so that objects are in focus.

photoreceptors Specialized cells in the retina that code light energy into nerve cell activity.

photopigments Chemicals in photoreceptors that respond to light and assist in converting light into nerve cell activity.

dark adaptation The increasing ability to see in the dark as time in the dark increases.

rods Highly light-sensitive but color-insensitive photoreceptors in the retina that allow vision even in dim light.

cones Photoreceptors in the retina that help us distinguish colors.

fovea A region in the center of the retina where cones are highly concentrated.

Converting Light into Images

Visual transduction, the conversion of light energy into nerve cell activity, occurs in the retina. The word *retina* is Latin for "net"; the retina is an intricate network of cells.

Photoreceptors Photoreceptors are specialized cells in the retina that convert light energy into nerve cell activity. Photoreceptors contain **photopigments**, which are chemicals that respond to light. When light strikes a photopigment, the photopigment breaks apart, changing the membrane potential of the photoreceptor cell. This change in membrane potential generates a signal that can be transferred to the brain.

After a photopigment has broken down in response to light, new photopigment molecules are created. This process takes a little time, however. So when you first come from bright sunshine into, say, a dark theater, you cannot see because your photoreceptors do not yet have enough photopigment. In the dark, as your photoreceptors create more photopigments, your ability to see gradually increases. In fact, you become about 10,000 times more sensitive to light after about half an hour in a darkened room. This increasing ability to see in the dark as time passes is called **dark adaptation**.

The retina has two main types of photoreceptors: **rods** and **cones**. As their names suggest, these cells differ in shape, but they also differ in their response to light. The photopigment in rods includes a substance called *rhodopsin* (pronounced "roh-DAHP-sin"), whereas the photopigment in cones includes one of three kinds of *iodopsin*. As we explain later, each kind of iodopsin responds most strongly to a particular range of light wavelengths, thus providing the basis for color vision. Rods have only one pigment, so they respond about equally to all wavelengths. As a result, rods can't help us discriminate colors, but they are more sensitive to light than cones are. So when there is very little light, as on a moonlit night, your rods allow you to see, but mainly in black and white. Your color-sensitive cones become most active only in brighter light. These characteristics of rods and cones explain why you may put on what you thought was a matched pair of socks in a darkened bedroom only to go outside and discover that one is dark blue and the other is dark green.

Rods and cones also differ in their location in the eye. Cones are concentrated in the center of the retina, a region called the **fovea**, where the eye focuses the light

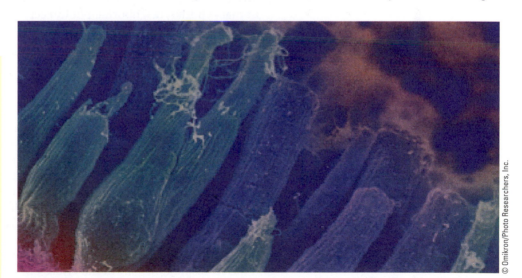

© Omikron/Photo Researchers, Inc.

Rods and Cones

TRY THIS This electron microscope view of rods (blue) and cones (aqua) shows what your light receptors look like. Rods are more light-sensitive, but they do not detect color. Cones can detect color, but they require more light in order to be activated. To experience the difference in how these cells work, look at an unfamiliar color photograph in a room where there is barely enough light to see. Even this dim light will activate your rods and allow you to make out images in the picture. But because there is not enough light to activate your cones, you will not be able to see colors in the photo.

coming from objects you look at. The high density of cones in the fovea accounts for the fact that our **visual acuity**, or ability to see details, is greatest in the fovea. The fact that some people's visual acuity is better than others is probably related to individual differences in cone density (Beirne, Zlatkova, & Anderson, 2005). There are no rods in the human fovea. With increasing distance from the fovea, though, the number of cones gradually decreases and the proportion of rods gradually increases. So the next time you are trying to detect a weak light, such as that from a faint star, notice that it is better to look slightly away from where you expect to see it. This focuses the light on the rods outside the fovea, which are the most light-sensitive. Because cones do not work well in low light, looking directly at the star will make it seem to disappear.

TRY THIS

Interactions in the Retina   If the eye simply transferred to the brain the stimuli that reach the retina, we would experience images that look like a blurry TV picture. Instead, the eye first sharpens visual images. How? The answer lies in the interactions among cells of the retina.

As illustrated in Figure 4.9, incoming light rays must actually pass through several layers of cells in the retina to reach photoreceptor cells. Notice in the figure that the most direct connections from the photoreceptor cells to the brain go first to *bipolar cells* and then to *ganglion cells*. The axons of the ganglion cells extend out of the eye and into the brain in a bundle known as the **optic nerve**.

However, this direct pathway is modified by interactions with other cells that change the information reaching the brain. These interactions enhance the sensation of contrast between areas of light and dark. Here's how it works: Most of the time, the amount of light reaching any two photoreceptors differs slightly, because the edges and other specific features of objects create differing patterns of incoming light. When this happens, the receptor that is receiving more light inhibits, or reduces, the activity of the nearby photoreceptor that is receiving less light. As a result, the brain gets the impression that there is even less light at that nearby cell's location than there really is. How can one photoreceptor suppress the output of its neighbor? The process is called *lateral inhibition,* and it is made possible by *interneurons,* which are cells that make sideways, or lateral, connections between photoreceptors (see Figure 4.9). In other words, the brain is always receiving information about *differences* in the amount of light that is hitting neighboring photoreceptors. Lateral inhibition serves to exaggerate those differences, and this exaggeration helps us see more clearly. The image of the buttons on your cell phone, for example, consists of lighter areas next to darker ones. Lateral inhibition in the retina amplifies these differences, creating greater contrast that sharpens the edges of the buttons and makes them more noticeable.

Ganglion Cells and Their Receptive Fields   Photoreceptors (rods and cones) and bipolar cells communicate by releasing neurotransmitters. But as discussed in the chapter on biological aspects of psychology, neurotransmitters cause only small, graded changes in the membrane potential of the next cell, which are not strong enough to travel the distance from the eye to the brain. It is the **ganglion cells** in the retina that generate action potentials that are capable of traveling that distance along axons that extend out of the retina and into the brain.

As illustrated in Figure 4.9, each ganglion cell receives information from a certain group of photoreceptors. Accordingly, each ganglion cell can tell the brain about what is going on only in its own particular **visual receptive field**, which is the part of the retina and the corresponding part of the visual world to which the cell responds (Sekuler & Blake, 1994). Some ganglion cells respond to light in, say, the upper right-hand side of the visual field, whereas others respond to light in the lower left-hand side, and so on. The visual receptive fields of most ganglion cells are shaped a bit like a doughnut, with a center and a surround. These *center-surround receptive fields* allow ganglion cells to compare the amount of light stimulating photoreceptors in the center of their visual receptive fields with the amount of light stimulating photoreceptors in the area around the center. Some ganglion cells are called *center-on cells* because they are activated by light in the center of their visual receptive fields and inhibited by light in the regions

visual acuity Visual clarity, which is greatest in the fovea because of its large concentration of cones.

optic nerve A bundle of fibers composed of axons of ganglion cells that carries visual information to the brain.

ganglion cells Cells in the retina that generate action potentials.

visual receptive field The portion of the retina, and the visual world, that affects a given ganglion cell.

FIGURE 4.9

Cells in the Retina

Light rays have to pass through several layers of retinal cells before striking photoreceptors, which are called rods and cones. Signals generated by the rods and cones then go back toward the surface of the retina, passing through bipolar cells and ganglion cells and on to the brain via the optic nerve. Interconnections among interneurons, bipolar cells, and ganglion cells allow the eye to begin analyzing visual information and sharpening images even before the information leaves the retina.

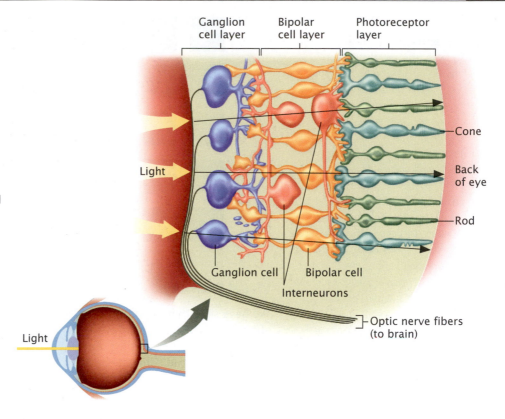

around the center (see Figure 4.10). *Center-off* ganglion cells work in just the opposite way. They are inhibited by light in the center of their visual receptive fields and activated by light in the surrounding areas.

The center-surround visual receptive fields of ganglion cells make it easier for you to see edges and, as illustrated in Figure 4.11, also make the contrast between darker and lighter areas appear sharper than it actually is. By enhancing the sensation of important features, the retina gives your brain an "improved" version of the visual world. As described next, the brain then performs even more elaborate processing of visual information than the retina does.

Uniform lighting produces moderate activity because the excitatory and inhibitory receptors cancel each other's effects.

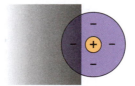

Higher activity when a region of light borders a darker region, because some inhibitory surround receptors are not activated.

Low activity because light is only stimulating receptors in the inhibitory surround.

FIGURE 4.10

Center-Surround Receptive Fields of Ganglion Cells

Having center-surround visual receptive fields allows ganglion cells to act as edge detectors. As shown at the left, if an edge is outside the visual receptive field of a center-on ganglion cell, there will be a uniform amount of light on both the excitatory center and the inhibitory surround, creating some baseline level of activity. If, as shown in the middle drawing, the dark side of an edge covers part of the inhibitory surround but leaves light on the excitatory center, the output of the cell will increase, signaling an edge in its visual receptive field. If, as shown at right, a dark area covers both the center and the surround, the cell's activity will decrease, because neither segment of its visual receptive field is receiving much stimulation.

FIGURE 4.11
The Hermann Grid

The shadows at the intersections of this *Hermann grid* disappear when you look directly at them. To understand why, look at the smaller grid at right. The circles on that grid represent the visual receptive fields of two center-on ganglion cells in your retina. The cell whose visual receptive field includes the grid intersection has more whiteness shining on its inhibitory surround than the cell whose visual receptive field is just to the right of the intersection. So the output of the "intersection" cell will be lower than that of the one on the right, creating the impression of darkness at the intersection. Looking directly at an intersection projects its image onto your fovea, the area of the retina where ganglion cells have the smallest visual receptive fields. Now the whiteness of the intersection is stimulating the excitatory centers of several ganglion cells, creating a greater sensation of whiteness and making the shadow disappear.

Visual Pathways

We have seen that visual information is sent to the brain through the axons of ganglion cells, which leave the eye as the optic nerve (see Figures 4.7 and 4.9). There can be no photoreceptors at the point where the optic nerve exits the eyeball, so you have a **blind spot** at that point, as Figure 4.12 shows.

After leaving the retina, about half the fibers of each eye's optic nerve cross over to the opposite side of the brain, creating a crisscross structure called the **optic chiasm**. (*Chiasm* means "cross" and is pronounced "KY-az-um.") Fibers from the inside half of each eye, nearest to the nose, cross over; fibers from the outside half of each eye do not (see Figure 4.13). As a result of this arrangement, no matter where you look, information from the right half of your visual field goes to the left side of your brain and information from the left half of your visual field goes to the right side.

The optic chiasm lies on the bottom surface of the brain. Beyond the chiasm, optic fibers ascend into the brain itself. As shown in Figure 4.13, the axons from most of the retina's ganglion cells send their messages to a region of the thalamus called the *lateral geniculate nucleus (LGN)*. Neurons in the LGN then send this visual information to the **visual cortex**, which lies in the occipital lobe at the back of the brain. The visual cortex itself sends the information to many other areas of cortex for further processing. Studies of monkeys have identified thirty-two separate visual areas interconnected by more than three hundred pathways (Van Essen, Anderson, & Felleman, 1992).

The retina is organized into a map of the visual world, such that neighboring points on the retina receive information from neighboring points in the visual world. "Copies" of this map are also to be found in the LGN, in the visual cortex, and in each of the many other visual areas of the brain. Through this spatial coding system, neighboring points in the retina are represented in neighboring cells in the brain. Larger areas of cortex are devoted to the areas of the retina that have larger numbers of photoreceptors. For example, the fovea, which is densely packed with photoreceptors, is represented in an especially large segment of cortex (Schira et al., 2009).

Visual Representations

By now you can see that your seemingly effortless experience of vision is based on a very complex system in which visual information is transmitted from the retina through the thalamus and on to various cortical regions. You can further appreciate the complexities of this system by considering two more of its remarkable characteristics: *parallel processing of visual properties* and *hierarchical processing of visual information*.

Parallel Processing of Visual Properties   Like ganglion cells, neurons of the LGN in the thalamus have center-surround visual receptive fields. However, the LGN is organized in several layers, and each layer contains a complete map of the retina. Further, neurons in

blind spot   The light-insensitive point at which axons from all of the ganglion cells converge and exit the eyeball.

optic chiasm   Part of the bottom surface of the brain where half of each optic nerve's fibers cross over to the opposite side of the brain.

visual cortex   An area at the back of the brain to which neurons in the lateral geniculate nucleus relay visual input.

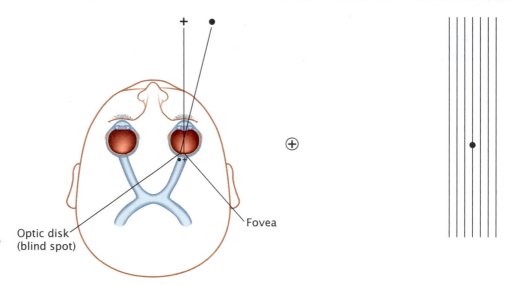

FIGURE 4.12
Finding Your Blind Spot

TRY THIS There is a blind spot where axons from the ganglion cells leave the eye. To "see" your blind spot, cover your left eye and stare at the cross inside the circle. Move the page closer and then farther away, and at some point the dot to the right should disappear. However, the vertical lines around the dot will probably look continuous, because the brain tends to fill in visual information at the blind spot (Spillmann et al., 2006). We are normally unaware of this "hole" in our vision because the blind spot of one eye is in the normal visual field of the other eye.

Optic disk (blind spot)

Fovea

different layers respond to particular aspects of visual stimuli. For example, the *form* of an object and its *color* are handled by one set of neurons (called the "what" system), whereas the *movement* of an object and *cues to its distance* are handled by another set (called the "where" system; Milner & Goodale, 2008). These are called *parallel processing systems* because they allow the brain to conduct separate kinds of analysis on the same information at the same time (Livingstone & Hubel, 1987).

These parallel streams of visual information are sent to the cerebral cortex, but the question of how they are assembled into a unified conscious experience is still being debated (Seymour et al., 2009; Tsotsos et al., 2008). Some researchers argue that the separate streams of processing never actually converge in a single brain region (Engel et al., 1992). Instead, they say, cortical regions that process separate aspects of visual sensation are connected, or perhaps just activated at the same time, allowing integration of their activity into a distributed, but unified, experience of vision (Dong et al., 2008; Gilbert, 1992).

Positron emission tomography (PET) scans provide evidence for the existence of separate processing channels in the brain. They show, for example, that one area of visual cortex is activated when a person views a colorful painting; a different area

FIGURE 4.13
Pathways from the Ganglion Cells into the Brain

Light rays from the right side of the visual field (the right side of what you are looking at) end up on the left half of each retina (shown in red). Light rays from the left visual field end up on the right half of each retina (shown in blue). From the right eye, axons from the nasal side of the retina (the side nearer the nose, which receives information from the right visual field) cross over the midline and travel to the left side of the brain with those fibers from the left eye that also receive input from the right side of the visual world. A similar arrangement unites left-visual-field information from both eyes in the right side of the brain.

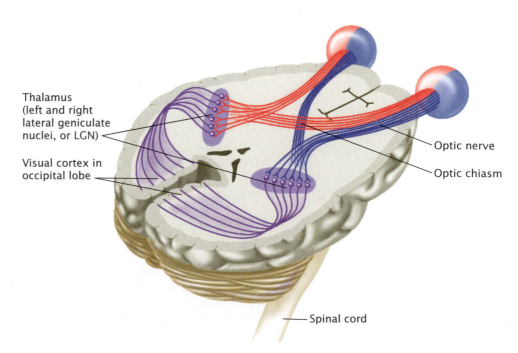

Thalamus (left and right lateral geniculate nuclei, or LGN)

Visual cortex in occipital lobe

Optic nerve

Optic chiasm

Spinal cord

FIGURE 4.14

Construction of a Feature Detector

This figure shows several center-on ganglion cells connecting to several cells in the lateral geniculate nucleus (LGN) that connect to one cell in the visual cortex. This "wiring" arrangement means that the cortical cell will respond most vigorously when it receives stimulation from all the LGN cells that feed into it. That combined LGN cell stimulation will occur when light falls on the center of the visual receptive fields of their ganglion cells. In this case, those visual receptive fields lie in a row, so it will take a bar-shaped feature at that same angle to stimulate all their centers. This cortical cell is called a feature detector because it responds best when a bar-shaped feature appears at a particular angle in its visual receptive field. If the bar were rotated to a different angle, this particular cortical cell would stop responding.

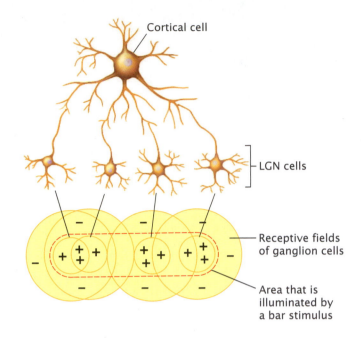

is activated by viewing black-and-white moving images (Zeki, 1992). Cases of brain damage have also helped reveal these separate channels (Heilman & Valenstein, 2003). Damage in one area can leave a person unable to see colors or even remember them but still able to see and recognize objects. Damage in another area can leave a person able to see only stationary objects; as soon as an object moves, it disappears. People with brain damage in still other regions can see moving objects but not stationary ones (Zeki, 1992). The same kinds of separate processing channels apparently operate even when we just imagine visual information. Some patients with brain damage can recall parts of a visual image but not their correct relationship in space. So they may be able to "see" a mental image of a bull's horns and ears but be unable to assemble them mentally to form a bull's head (Kosslyn, 1988).

Hierarchical Processing of Visual Information   Figure 4.14 shows that individual cells in the visual cortex receive input from several LGN neurons in the thalamus. The visual receptive fields of these cortical cells are more complex than the center-surround visual receptive fields of LGN cells. For example, a cell in the cortex might respond only to vertical edges that appear in its visual receptive field. One class of cells responds only to moving objects; a third class responds only to objects with corners; and so on. Because cortical cells respond to specific features of objects in the visual field, they have been described as **feature detectors** (Hubel & Wiesel, 1979; Jia et al., 2010).

Complex feature detectors can be built from more and more elaborate connections among simpler feature detectors (Hubel & Wiesel, 1979). For example, several center-surround cells might feed into one cortical cell to make a line detector, and several line detectors might feed into another cortical cell to make a cell that responds to a certain orientation in space, such as vertical. With further connections, a more complex "box detector" might be built from simpler line and corner detectors. Feature detectors illustrate that some of the cortical processing of visual information occurs in a *hierarchical,* or stepwise, fashion.

Cells that respond to similar kinds of stimulation are stacked into columns that descend into the cerebral cortex. For example, if you locate a cortical cell that responds to diagonal lines at a particular spot in the visual field, most of the cells above and below that cell will also respond to diagonal lines. Other properties, too, are represented by columns of cells. For example, there are columns in which all of the cells are most sensitive to a particular color. Research has also revealed that individual

feature detectors   Cells in the cortex that respond to a specific feature of an object.

neurons in the cortex perform several different tasks, allowing complex visual processing (Grossberg, 2007).

Seeing Color

Like beauty, color is in the eye of the beholder. Many animals see only shades of gray, even when they look at a rainbow, but for humans, color is a major feature of vision. A marketer might tell you about the impact of color on buying preferences, and a poet might tell you about the emotional power of color, but we will tell you about how you see colors—a process that is itself a thing of beauty and elegance.

Wavelengths and Color Sensations   We mentioned earlier that at a given intensity, each wavelength of light is seen as a certain color (look again at Figure 4.6). However, the eye is seldom, if ever, exposed to pure light of a single wavelength. Sunlight, for example, is a mixture of all wavelengths of light. When sunlight passes through a droplet of water, each wavelength of light within it bends to a different extent, separating into a colorful rainbow. The spectrum of color found in the rainbow illustrates an important concept: The sensation produced by a mixture of different wavelengths of light is not the same as the sensations produced by separate wavelengths. So just as most sounds are a mixture of sound waves of different frequencies, most colors are a mixture of light of different wavelengths.

Three characteristics of this wavelength mixture determine our sensation of color: hue, saturation, and brightness. These are *psychological* dimensions that correspond roughly to the physical properties of light. **Hue** is the essential "color," determined by the dominant wavelength in the mixture of the light that enters the eye. For example, the wavelength of yellow is about 570 nm and that of red is about 700 nm. Black, white, and gray are not considered hues because no wavelength predominates in them. **Color saturation** is related to how pure a color is. A color is more saturated (more pure) if just one wavelength is relatively more intense (contains more energy) than other wavelengths. If many wavelengths are added to a pure hue, the color is said to be *desaturated*. For example, pastels are colors that have been desaturated by adding whiteness. **Brightness** refers to the overall intensity of all of the wavelengths in the incoming light.

The color circle shown in Figure 4.15 arranges hues according to their perceived similarities. If lights of two different wavelengths but of equal intensity are mixed, the color you sense is at the midpoint of a line drawn between the two original colors on the color circle. This process is called *additive color mixing* because the effects of the wavelengths from each light are added together. If you keep adding different colored lights, you eventually get white when all wavelengths are combined.

You are probably more familiar with a different form of color mixing, called *subtractive color mixing,* which occurs when paints are combined. Like other physical objects, paints reflect certain wavelengths and absorb all others. For example, grass is green because it absorbs all wavelengths except the ones that we sense as green. White objects are white because they reflect all wavelengths. Light reflected from paints or other colored objects is seldom a pure wavelength, so predicting the color resulting from mixing paint is not as easy as combining pure wavelengths of light. But if you keep combining different colored paints, all of the wavelengths will eventually be subtracted, resulting in black. (The discussion that follows refers to *additive color mixing,* the mixing of light.)

By mixing lights of just a few wavelengths, we can produce different color sensations. How many wavelengths are needed to create any possible color? Figure 4.16 illustrates an experiment that addresses this question. The results of such experiments helped lead scientists to an important theory of how people sense color—the trichromatic theory of color vision.

The Trichromatic Theory of Color Vision   Early in the 1800s, Thomas Young and, later, Hermann von Helmholtz demonstrated that any color could be matched by mixing pure lights of only three wavelengths. For example, by mixing blue light

hue The essential "color," determined by the dominant wavelength of light.

color saturation The purity of a color.

brightness The overall intensity of all of the wavelengths that make up light.

FIGURE 4.15

The Color Circle

Arranging colors according to their psychological similarities creates a color circle that predicts the result of additive mixing of two colored lights. The resulting color will be on a line between the two starting colors, the exact location on the line depending on the relative proportions of the two colors. For example, mixing equal amounts of pure green and pure red light will produce yellow, the color that lies at the midpoint of the line connecting red and green. (*Nm* stands for *nanometers,* the unit in which wavelengths of light are measured.)

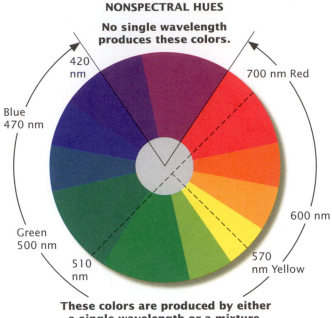

NONSPECTRAL HUES

No single wavelength produces these colors.

420 nm
Blue 470 nm
Green 500 nm
510 nm
700 nm Red
600 nm
570 nm Yellow

These colors are produced by either a single wavelength or a mixture.

SPECTRAL HUES

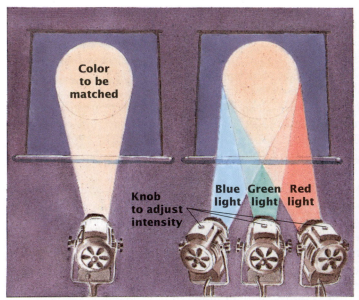

Color to be matched

Knob to adjust intensity

Blue light Green light Red light

Mixture of many wavelengths

Each projector produces one pure-wavelength color

FIGURE 4.16

Matching a Color by Mixing Lights of Pure Wavelengths

In this experiment, colored light is aimed at white paper, which reflects all wavelengths and therefore appears to be the color of the light shining on it. A target color is projected on the left-hand paper. The research participant's task is to adjust the intensity of different pure-wavelength lights until the resulting mixture looks exactly like the target color. It turns out that a large number of colors can be matched by mixing two pure-wavelength lights, but *any* color can be matched by mixing three pure-wavelength lights. Experiments such as this provided information that led to the trichromatic theory of color vision.

FIGURE 4.17
Relative Responses of Three Cone Types to Different Wavelengths of Light

Each type of cone responds to a range of light wavelengths but responds more to some wavelengths than to others. Any combination of wavelengths that creates a particular pattern of cone activity will create a particular color sensation. For example, a pure light of 570 nm (arrow A) stimulates long-wavelength cones at 1.0 relative units and medium-wavelength cones at about 0.7 relative units. This ratio of cone activity (1/0.7 = 1.4) gives the sensation of yellow. But any combination of wavelengths at the proper intensity that generates this same ratio of activity in these cone types will also produce the sensation of yellow.

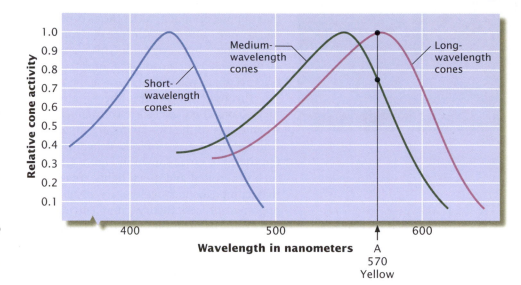

(about 440 nm), green light (about 510 nm), and red light (about 700 nm) in different ratios, they could produce any other color. This finding led Young and Helmholtz to conclude that there must be three types of visual elements in the eye, each of which is most sensitive to different wavelengths, and that it is the combined responses of these three elements that produce the sensation of color. This Young-Helmholtz theory is better known as the **trichromatic theory** of color vision.

Support for the trichromatic theory has come from research on photoreceptor responses to particular wavelengths of light and on the activity of cones in the human eye (Schnapf, Kraft, & Baylor, 1987). This research revealed that there are three types of cones. Each type responds to a broad range of wavelengths, but each is most sensitive to a different range of wavelengths. *Short-wavelength* cones respond most to light in the blue range. *Medium-wavelength* cones are most sensitive to light in the green range. *Long-wavelength* cones respond best to light in the reddish-yellow range (these have traditionally been called "red cones").

No single type of cone can signal the color of a light. It is the *ratio* of responses by the three types of cones that determines the color you see. In other words, color vision is encoded by the *pattern of activity* of the different cone types. For example, a light looks yellow if it has a pure wavelength of about 570 nm; this light stimulates both medium- and long-wavelength cones, as illustrated by arrow A in Figure 4.17. But you will also see yellow whenever any mixture of other lights stimulates the same pattern of activity in these two types of cones. The trichromatic theory was applied in the invention of color television screens, which contain thousands of tiny red, green, and blue dots, called *pixels*. A television broadcast excites these dots to varying degrees, mixing their colors to produce many other colors. You see color mixtures on the screen—not patterns of red, green, and blue dots—because the dots are too small and close together to be seen individually (with a magnifying glass, you may be able to see similar pixels in the color photos in your local newspaper).

TRY THIS

trichromatic theory A theory of color vision identifying three types of visual elements, each of which is most sensitive to different wavelengths of light.

opponent-process theory A theory of color vision stating that color-sensitive visual elements are grouped into red-green, blue-yellow, and black-white elements.

The Opponent-Process Theory of Color Vision   Brilliant as it is, the trichromatic theory alone cannot explain all aspects of color vision. For example, it cannot account for the fact that if you stare at the flag in Figure 4.18 for thirty seconds and then look at the dot in the blank white space below it, you will see a color afterimage. What was yellow in the original image will be blue in the afterimage, what was green before will appear red, and what was black will now appear white.

This type of phenomenon led Ewald Hering to propose the **opponent-process theory** as an alternative to the trichromatic theory of color vision. According to this theory, the color-sensitive elements in the eye are grouped into three pairs, and the members of each

FIGURE 4.18
Afterimages Produced by the Opponent-Process Nature of Color Vision

TRY THIS Stare at the black dot in the center of the flag for at least thirty seconds; then focus on the dot in the white space below it.

pair oppose, or inhibit, each other. There are *red-green elements, blue-yellow elements* and *black-white elements*. Each type of element signals one color or the other—red or green, for example—but never both. This theory explains color afterimages. When one part of an opponent pair is no longer stimulated, the other is activated. So as in Figure 4.18, if the original image you look at is green, the afterimage will be red.

The opponent-process theory also explains the phenomenon of complementary colors. Two colors are *complementary* if a neutral color, such as gray, appears when lights of the two colors are mixed. (The neutral color can appear as anything from white to gray to black, depending on the intensity of the lights being mixed.) On the color circle shown in Figure 4.15, complementary colors are roughly opposite each other. Red and green lights are complementary, as are yellow and blue. Notice that complementary colors are *opponent* colors in Hering's theory. According to opponent-process theory, complementary colors stimulate the same visual element (e.g., red-green) in opposite directions, canceling each other out. This theory helps explain why mixing lights of complementary colors produces gray.

A Synthesis and an Update   The trichromatic and opponent-process theories seem quite different, but both are correct to some extent, and together they can explain most of what is known about color vision. Further research on the activities of the different types of cells in the retina has paved the way for a synthesis, or blending, of the two theories (Gegenfurtner & Kiper, 2003).

At the level of the photoreceptors, a slightly revised version of the trichromatic theory is correct. As a rule, there *are* three types of cones that have three different photopigments. However, molecular biologists who isolated the genes for cone pigments have found variations in the genes for the cones that are sensitive to middle-wavelength and long-wavelength light. These variants have slightly different sensitivities to different wavelengths. So a person can have two, three, or even four genes for long-wavelength pigments (Deeb, 2005). Individual differences in people's long-wavelength pigments become apparent in color-matching tasks. When asked to mix a red light and a green light to match a yellow light, a person with one kind of long-wavelength pigment will choose a different red-to-green ratio than someone with a different kind of long-wavelength pigment. Women are more likely than men to have four distinct photopigments, and anyone who has them also has a richer experience of color. These people can detect more shades of color than people with the more common three photopigments, but their experience of color pales in comparison to that of certain tropical shrimp. These shrimp live on colorful coral reefs and have twelve different photopigments, which allows them to see colors even in the ultraviolet range, which no human—male or female—can sense (Marshall & Oberwinkler, 1999).

Color vision works a little differently at the level of ganglion cells. As we mentioned earlier, information about light from many photoreceptors feeds into each ganglion cell, and the output from each ganglion cell goes to the brain. We also said that the visual receptive fields of most ganglion cells are arranged in center-surround patterns. It turns out that the center and the surround are color-coded, as illustrated in Figure 4.19. The center responds best to one color, and the surround responds best to a different color. This color coding arises because varying proportions of the three cone types feed into the center and the surround of the ganglion cell.

When either the center or the surround of a ganglion cell's visual receptive field is stimulated, the other area is inhibited. In other words, the center and the surround of a given ganglion cell's receptive field are most responsive to opponent colors. Electrical recordings taken from many ganglion cells show that three particularly common pairs of opponent colors are the ones predicted by Hering's opponent-process theory: red-green, blue-yellow, and black-white. Stimulating both the center and the surround of these cells' receptive fields cancels the effects of either light, producing gray. Black-white cells receive input from all types of cones, so it does not matter what color stimulates them.

Color vision also depends on what happens in the brain—especially in the thalamus and in specific regions of the visual cortex. There, encoded color information

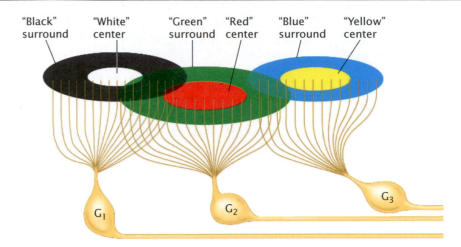

FIGURE 4.19
Color Coding and the Ganglion Cells
The center-surround visual receptive fields of ganglion cells form the basis for opponent colors. Some ganglion cells, like G_2, have a center whose photoreceptors respond best to red wavelengths and a surround whose photoreceptors respond best to green wavelengths. Other ganglion cells pair blue and yellow, whereas still others receive input from all types of photoreceptors.

from the retinas is assembled and processed by cells that respond in opponent pairs that are sensitive to the red-green and blue-yellow input coming from ganglion cells (Conway, 2009; Gegenfurtner & Kiper, 2003; Heywood & Kentridge, 2003). Damage to these brain regions can weaken or destroy color vision, even though all the cones in the retina are working normally (Bouvier & Engel, 2006).

In summary, color vision is possible because three types of cones have different sensitivities to different wavelengths, as the trichromatic theory suggests. The sensation of different colors results from stimulating the three cone types in different ratios. Because there are three types of cones, any color can be produced by mixing three different wavelengths of light. But the story does not end there. The output from cones is fed into ganglion cells whose receptive fields have centers and surrounds that respond to opponent colors and inhibit each other. This arrangement provides the basis for color afterimages. So the trichromatic theory describes the properties of the photoreceptors, whereas the opponent-process theory describes the properties of the ganglion cells. Both theories are needed to account for the complexity of visual sensations of color (Jacobs, 2008).

Colorblindness   People who are born with cones containing only two of the three possible color-sensitive pigments are described as having **colorblindness** (Carroll et al., 2004; see Figure 4.20), but they are not actually blind to all color: They simply discriminate fewer colors than other people. Two centuries ago, a colorblind chemist named John Dalton carefully described the colors he sensed—to him, a red ribbon appeared the same color as mud—and concluded that the fluid in his eyeball must be tinted blue. He instructed his doctor to examine the fluid after he died, but it turned out to be clear. His preserved retinas were examined recently by molecular biologists. The scientists were not surprised to find that, just as most colorblind people today lack the genes that code one or more of the pigments, Dalton had no gene for medium-wavelength pigments (Deeb & Kohl, 2003; Hunt et al., 1995). ("In Review: Seeing" summarizes how the nervous system gathers and processes the information that allows us to see—and to see in color.)

Interaction of the Senses: Synesthesia

At the beginning of this chapter, we described the interaction of two senses, vision and touch, but there are many other kinds of interactions. For example, vision interacts with hearing. If a brief sound occurs just as lights are flashed, it can create the impression of more lights than there actually are (Shams, Kamitani, & Shimojo, 2000), and hearing a sound as objects collide can affect your perception of their motion (Watanabe & Shimojo, 2001). Sound can also improve your ability to see an object at the sound's source, which can help you avoid or respond to danger (McDonald, Teder-Salejarvi, & Hillyard, 2000). Hearing sounds can alter sensitivity to touch (Hötting & Röder, 2004),

colorblindness A condition in which lack of certain photopigments leave a person unable to sense certain colors.

IN REVIEW   Seeing

Aspect of Sensory System	Elements	Key Characteristics
Energy	Light: electromagnetic radiation from about 400 nm to about 750 nm	The intensity and wavelength of light waves determine the brightness and color of visual sensations.
Accessory structures	Eye: cornea, pupil, iris, lens	Light rays are bent to focus on the retina.
Transduction mechanism	Photoreceptors (rods and cones) in the retina	Rods are more sensitive to light than cones, but cones discriminate among colors. Sensations of color depend first on the cones, which respond differently to different light wavelengths. Interactions among cells of the retina exaggerate differences in the light stimuli reaching the photoreceptors, enhancing the sensation of contrast.
Pathways and representations	Optic nerve to optic chiasm to LGN of thalamus to visual cortex	Neighboring points in the visual world are represented at neighboring points in the LGN and visual cortex. Neurons there respond to particular aspects of the visual stimulus—such as color, movement, distance, or form.
Color vision	Short-, medium-, and long-wavelength cones in the retina; ganglion cells in the retina and cells in the thalamus and visual cortex with color-sensitive center-surround visual receptive fields	The combined activity of three cone types create color sensations (trichromatic theory); output from ganglion cells signals opponent colors (opponent process theory).

1. The ability to see in very dim light depends on photoreceptors called _____.
2. Nearsightedness and farsightedness occur when images are not focused on the eye's _____.
3. Colorblindness results when _____ cells in the retina lack one of three kinds of color-sensitive photopigments.

and there is even evidence that smells are more readily detected when accompanied by images related to them (Gottfried & Dolan, 2003). Such interactions occur in everyone, but some people also report **synesthesia** (pronounced "sin-ess-THEE-zhuh"), a more unusual and stronger mixing of senses or of dimensions within senses (Hochel & Milán, 2008). Some of these people say that they "feel" colors or sounds as touches or that they "taste" shapes or "smell" sounds; others say that they see certain colors, such as red, when they hear certain sounds, such as a trumpet or spoken words (Bargary et al., 2009). One study of such people found that they experienced a different color sensation

FIGURE 4.20

Are You Colorblind?

TRY THIS At the upper left is a photo as it appears to people who have all three cone photopigments. The other photos simulate how colors appear to people who are missing photopigments for short wavelengths (lower left), long wavelengths (upper right), or medium wavelengths (lower right). If any of these photos look to you just like the one at the upper left, you may have a form of colorblindness.

Dr. Françoise Vienot

synesthesia A blending of sensory experience that causes some people to "see" sounds or "taste" colors, for example.

FIGURE 4.21
Synesthesia

In this experiment on synesthesia, a triangular pattern of Hs was embedded in a background of other letters, as shown at left. Most people find it difficult to detect the triangle, but J. C., a person with synesthesia, picked it out immediately because, as simulated at right, he saw the Hs as green, the Fs as yellow, and the Ps as red.

Source: Ramachandran, V.S. & Hubbard, E.M. "Psychophysical Investigations into the Neural Basis of Synaesthesia." Proceedings Of The Royal Society of London B: Biological Sciences, 268, 979–983. Copyright © 2001 The Royal Society. Reprinted by permission.

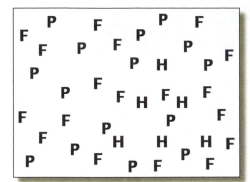
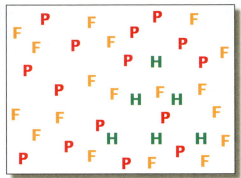

in response to different emotions in an opera singer's voice (Takayanagi, 2008). Still others report feeling certain textures, such as smoothness, when looking at certain objects, such as a piece of shiny marble (Eagleman & Goodale, 2009), and there are those for whom certain tastes, numbers, or letters are experienced as vivid visual patterns or as particular colors. These synesthetic experiences are so continuous and automatic that they are difficult to suppress or ignore (Ward & Mattingley, 2006). In some cases, visual sensations triggered by touch or hearing persist even after the person has lost his or her eyesight (Steven, Hansen, & Blakemore, 2006).

Though once dismissed as poetic delusions, many claims of synesthesia have been supported by scientific investigation (e.g., Hochel & Milán, 2008; see Figure 4.21). In one case, a man reported that he always sees numbers in distinct colors, even when they are printed in black ink. To him, he said, the 2s look orange and the 5s look green. And in fact, when he was asked to pick out a 2 that was embedded in an array of 5s, he could do so much more rapidly than other people. To him, orange 2s seemed to "pop out" of the array (Palmeri et al., 2002).

Some researchers suggest that synesthesia occurs partly because brain areas that process one aspect of sensation (such as color) are near areas that process other aspects (such as the features of letters and numbers). Perhaps the connections between these neighboring areas are more extensive in people who experience synesthesia (Bargary & Mitchell, 2008; Wesson & Wilson, 2010). Synesthesia experiences are also associated with unusually wide-ranging activity in brain regions that process different kinds of sensory information (Hubbard & Ramachandran, 2005). Studies of people who experience color sensations when they hear words, for example, show that hearing words activates both auditory cortex in the temporal lobes and visual cortex in the occipital lobe (Aleman et al., 2001; Nunn et al., 2002). Similar but less extensive connections in nonsynesthetic people may be partly responsible for their use of intersensory descriptions in which a shirt is "loud," a cheese is "sharp," or a wine has "a light straw color with greenish hues" (Martino & Marks, 2001).

Growing scientific interest in synesthesia is indicated by the fact that there are now standardized procedures for identifying people who experience these fascinating sensory phenomena (Eagleman et al., 2007) and that research is under way to determine if synesthesia can be stimulated, through hypnosis and other means, in people who do not normally experience it (Ito et al., 2009; Kadosh et al., 2009).

The Chemical Senses: Smell and Taste

There are animals without vision, and there are animals without hearing, but there are no animals without some form of chemical sense. Chemical senses arise from the interaction of chemicals and receptors. **Olfactory perception** (our sense of smell) detects chemicals that are airborne, or volatile. **Taste perception**, also known as *gustatory perception* or our sense of taste, detects chemicals in solution that come into contact with receptors inside the mouth.

olfactory perception The sense of smell.

taste perception The sense of taste.

FIGURE 4.22
The Olfactory System
Airborne chemicals reach the olfactory area through the nostrils and through the back of the mouth. Fibers pass directly from the olfactory area to the olfactory bulb in the brain, and from there signals pass to areas such as the hypothalamus and amygdala, which are involved in emotion.

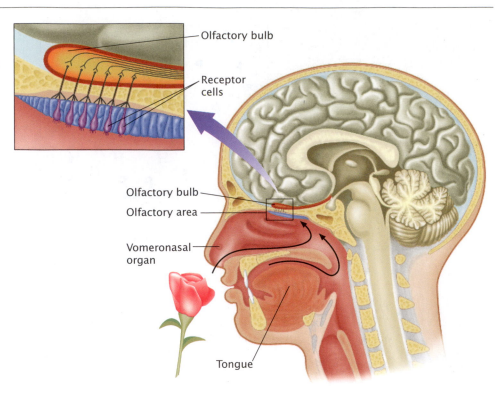

Olfaction

As in other senses, accessory structures in the olfactory system shape sensations. In humans, these accessory structures include the nose, the mouth, and the upper part of the throat, all of which help funnel odor molecules to receptors. So just as you can bend your ear's pinna forward to help collect sound waves, if you tape a nasal dilator strip over the bridge of your nose, you should notice intensified food odors (Raudenbush & Meyer, 2002). Even the lungs serve as an accessory structure for olfaction because when you sniff at something, the lungs help move odor molecules into the mouth and nose. Odor molecules can reach olfactory receptors in the nose either through the nostrils or through an opening in the palate at the back of the mouth. This second route allows us to smell odors from food as we eat it (see Figure 4.22). The olfactory receptors themselves are located on the dendrites of specialized neurons that extend into the *mucous membrane,* the moist inner lining of the nose. Odor molecules bind to these receptors, causing depolarization of the dendrites' membranes, which in turn leads to changes in the firing rates of the neurons. A single molecule of an odorous substance can cause a change in the membrane potential of an olfactory neuron, but detection of the odor by a human normally requires about fifty molecules (Reed, 2004). (A hot pizza generates lots more than that.) The number of molecules needed to trigger an olfactory sensation can vary, however. For example, women are more sensitive to odors during certain phases of their menstrual cycles (Navarrete-Palacios et al., 2003).

Olfactory neurons are repeatedly replaced with new ones, as each lives only about two months (Ruitenberg & Vukovic, 2008). Scientists are especially interested in this process because, as noted in the chapter on biological aspects of psychology, most neurons cannot divide to create new ones. An understanding of how new olfactory neurons are generated—and re-create appropriate connections in the brain—may someday be helpful in treating brain and spinal cord damage.

In contrast to vision, which uses only four basic receptor types (rods and three kinds of cones), the olfactory system employs about a thousand different types of receptors. In fact, up to 2 percent of the human genetic code may be devoted to these olfactory receptors, perhaps because a good sense of smell helped the earliest humans adapt and survive (Firestein, 2001). A given odor stimulates various olfactory receptors to varying degrees, and the particular patterns of stimulation create codes for particular odor sensations (Kajiya et al., 2001). So many stimulation patterns are possible that humans can discriminate tens of thousands of different odors (Su, Menuz, & Carlson, 2009). We know that substances with similar chemical structures tend to have similar odors, but exactly how olfactory receptors discriminate various smells and send coded messages about them to the brain is still being determined (Ma, 2007).

The question of how smells are coded has been of growing interest to government and industry. Particularly since the September 11, 2001, terrorist attacks in the United States, researchers have hastened their work on "electronic noses" capable of detecting odorants associated with firearms and explosives (Thaler, Kennedy, & Hanson, 2001). Versions of these devices are already in use at some airports. An "electronic nose" has also been developed that can detect diseases such as lung cancer that might not be evident to an examining doctor (D'Amico et al., 2009), and other artificial olfactory devices are being used to examine the condition and composition of food products and the air we breathe (Marin et al., 2007). There are even efforts under way to use specially trained insects to "sniff out" specific chemicals of interest (Rains et al., 2008).

Olfaction is the only sensory system that does not connect to the brain through the thalamus. Instead, axons from neurons in the nose extend through a bony plate directly into the brain, reaching a structure called the **olfactory bulb**, where processing of olfactory information continues (Kay & Sherman, 2007). Pathways from the olfactory bulb send the information on for further processing in several brain regions, including the frontal lobe and the amygdala, which is involved in learning, memory, and emotional experience (Su, Menuz, & Carlson, 2009).

These features of the olfactory system may account for the fact that losing the sense of smell can sometimes be an early sign of brain diseases that disrupt memory and emotion (Doty, 2009; Wattendorf et al., 2009). These same features may also help explain the strong relationship between olfaction, memory, and emotion (Yeshurun & Sobel, 2010). For example, associations between particular odors and particular experiences, especially emotional ones, may not weaken with time or later experiences (Lawless & Engen, 1977). So catching a whiff of the scent once worn by a lost loved one can reactivate intense feelings associated with that person. Smells can also bring back accurate memories of significant experiences linked with them, especially positive experiences (Mohr, Rohrenbach, et al., 2001).

The mechanisms of olfaction are remarkably similar in species ranging from humans to worms. And all mammals, including humans, have brain systems for detecting the source of odors by comparing the strength of sensory inputs reaching the left and right nostrils (Porter et al., 2005). Different species vary considerably, however, in their sensitivity to smell and in the degree to which they depend on it for survival. For example, humans have about 9 million olfactory neurons, whereas there are about 225 million in dogs, a species that is far more dependent on smell to identify food, territory, and receptive mates. In addition, dogs and many other species depend on an accessory olfactory system to detect pheromones. **Pheromones** (pronounced "FAYR-oh-mohnz") are chemicals that are released by an animal that when detected by another animal of the same species can shape the second animal's behavior or physiology (Swaney & Keverne, 2009). For example, when male snakes detect a chemical exuded on the skin of female snakes, they are stimulated to "court" the female.

In mammals, pheromones can be nonvolatile chemicals that, when licked, are passed into a portion of the olfactory system called the **vomeronasal system**, or *vomeronasal organ* (Witt & Wozniak, 2006). In female mice, for example, the vomeronasal system detects chemicals in the male's urine (Kang et al., 2009). By this means, a male can cause a female to ovulate and become sexually receptive, and an unfamiliar male can cause a pregnant female to abort her pregnancy (Bruce, 1969).

The role of pheromones in humans is much less clear (Wyatt, 2009). Perfume advertisers want us to believe that their products contain sexual attractants that act as pheromones capable of subconsciously influencing the behavior of desirable partners. Skeptics argue against this view and note that in humans, the vomeronasal organ is

olfactory bulb A brain structure that receives messages regarding smell.

pheromones Chemicals released by one animal and detected by another that shape the second animal's behavior or physiology.

vomeronasal system A portion of the mammalian olfactory system that is sensitive to pheromones.

an utterly nonfunctional vestige, like the appendix. In fact, most of us may not even have one. A vomeronasal organ was identified in only 32 to 38 percent of adults in one study (Besli et al., 2004). But the vomeronasal organ may not be the only pheromone-responsive component of the human olfactory system. It has been suggested that the main olfactory epithelium in the uppermost reaches of the human nose might also be capable of responding to pheromones (Wang, Aguilar-Gaxiola, et al., 2007).

Current evidence suggests cautious conclusions about the role of pheromones in humans. For individuals who have one, the vomeronasal organ does appear able to respond to certain hormonal substances and can influence certain hormonal secretions (Miller & Maner, 2010; Zhou & Chen, 2009). Whatever the anatomical basis, humans probably do have some sort of pheromone-like system (Berglund, Lindström, & Savic, 2006; Bhutta, 2007; Savic, Berglund, & Lindström, 2005). For example, odorants that are not consciously detectable can influence people's moods (Jacob & McClintock, 2000). Odorants can also alter activity in brain areas that are not directly involved in olfaction (Jacob et al., 2001). In one study, specific areas of the hypothalamus were activated in men and women when they were exposed to an odorless substance similar to the hormones—either estrogen or testosterone—that are associated with the opposite sex (Savic et al., 2001). A possible human gene for pheromone receptors has been found (Rodriguez et al., 2000), and pheromones have been shown to cause reproduction-related physiological changes in humans (Grammer, Fink, & Neave, 2005). Specifically, pheromonal signals secreted in the perspiration of a woman can shorten or prolong the menstrual cycle of other women nearby (Stern & McClintock, 1998). In such cases, pheromones are responsible for *menstrual synchrony,* the tendency of women living together to menstruate at the same time.

Despite the steamy perfume ads, though, there is still no solid evidence that humans, or even nonhuman primates, give off or can detect pheromones that act as sexual attractants (Mast & Samuelsen, 2009). In one study, for example, exotic dancers reported that their income from customer tips increased during the ovulation phase of their menstrual cycles (Miller, Tybur, & Jordan, 2007), but the difference was probably not due to pheromones. During ovulation, females tend to speak in a more sexually attractive manner (Pipitone & Gallup, 2008), to be more interested in erotic stimuli (Mass et al., 2008), and to be more receptive to courtship (Gueguen, 2008; Rosen & López, 2009). So it could well be that differences in their behavior, and not pheromones, were responsible for their higher tip income during ovulation (Miller, Tybur, & Jordan, 2007).

If a certain scent does enhance a person's readiness for sex, it is probably because the person has learned to associate that scent with previous sexual experiences. There are many other examples of people using olfactory information in social situations. For example, after just a few hours of contact, mothers can usually identify their newborn babies by the infants' smell (Porter, Cernich, & McLaughlin, 1983). And if infants are breast-fed, they can discriminate their own mothers' odor from that of other breast-feeding women, and they appear to be comforted by it (Porter, 1991). In fact, individual mammals, including humans, have a distinct "odortype," which is determined by their immune cells and other inherited physiological factors (Beauchamp et al., 1995). During pregnancy, a woman's own odortype combines with the odortype of her fetus to form a third odortype. Each of these three odors is distinguishable, suggesting that recognition of odortypes may help establish the mother-infant bonds discussed in the chapter on human development.

Gustation

The chemical sense system in the mouth is gustation, or taste. The receptors for taste are in the *taste buds,* which are grouped together in structures called **papillae** (pronounced "pah-PIL-ee"). Normally, there are about 10,000 taste buds in a person's mouth, mostly on the tongue but also on the roof of the mouth and on the back of the throat (Cheng & Robinson, 1991; Miller, 1986).

papillae Structures on the tongue containing groups of taste receptors, or taste buds.

Taste Receptors

Taste buds are grouped into structures called *papillae*. Two kinds of papillae are visible in this greatly enlarged photo of the surface of the human tongue.

© Omikron/Photo Researchers, Inc.

In contrast to the olfactory system, which can discriminate thousands of different odors, the human taste system generates only a few elementary sensations (Chandrashekar et al., 2006). The most familiar of these are sweet, sour, bitter, and salty. Each taste bud responds best to one or two of these categories, but it also responds weakly to others (Zhang, Hoon, et al., 2003). The taste of a particular substance appears to come from the responses of taste buds that are mainly sensitive to a specific category. Behavioral studies and electrical recordings from taste neurons have identified two additional taste sensations. One, called *umami* (which means "delicious" in Japanese), enhances other tastes. It is produced by certain proteins and also by monosodium glutamate (MSG; Beauchamp, 2009). The other, called *astringent,* is the taste produced by tannins, which are found in tea and some wines, for example.

Different tastes are transduced into neural activity by different types of taste receptors and in different ways (Chandrashekar et al., 2006). For example, sweet and bitter are signaled when chemicals fit into specific receptor sites (Montmayeur et al., 2001), but sour and salty act by altering ion channels in the membranes of taste cells. Understanding the chemistry of sweetness has helped scientists design new chemicals that fit into sweetness receptors and taste thousands of times sweeter than sugar. As a result, weight-conscious people have more ways to enjoy low-calorie candy, hot-fudge sundaes, and other treats. Knowing how to create pleasant tastes and avoid unpleasant ones has also allowed drug companies to offer medications that patients are more likely to take as directed (Gupta et al, 2010).

A taste component in its own right, saltiness also enhances the taste of food by suppressing bitterness (Breslin & Beauchamp, 1997). In animals, taste responses to salt are determined early, before and just after birth. Research with animals has shown that if mothers are put on a low-salt diet, their offspring are less likely to prefer salty tastes (Hill & Przekop, 1988). In humans, experiences with salty foods over the first four years of life may alter the sensory systems that detect salt and contribute to enduring preferences for salty foods (Hill & Mistretta, 1990).

Individual differences in how people taste things is partly determined by genetics. Because of genetic variations in sweet receptors, some people detect sweetness more easily than others (Mainland & Matsunami, 2009). And about 25 percent of humans are "supertasters" who have an especially large number of papillae on their tongues (Bartoshuk, 2000)—thousands of taste buds, whereas "nontasters" have just a few hundred (see Figure 4.23). Most people fall between these extremes. Supertasters are

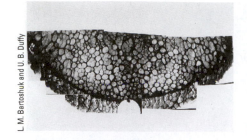

L. M. Bartoshuk and U. B. Duffy

FIGURE 4.23
Are You a Supertaster?

TRY THIS This photo shows the large number of papillae on the tongue of a "supertaster." If you don't mind a temporary stain on your mouth and teeth, you can look at your own papillae by painting the front of your tongue with a cotton swab soaked in blue food coloring. Distribute the dye by moving your tongue around and swallowing; then look into a magnifying mirror as you shine a flashlight on your tongue. The pink circles you see against the blue background are papillae, each of which has about six taste buds buried in its surface. Get several friends to do this test, and you will see that genes create wide individual differences in taste bud density.

TRY THIS

more sensitive than other people to bitterness, as revealed in their reaction to things such as beer, broccoli, soy products, and grapefruit. Having different numbers of taste buds may help account for differences in people's food intake, as well as weight problems. For example, Linda Bartoshuk has found that compared with overweight people, thin people have many more taste buds (Duffy et al., 1999). Perhaps they do not have to eat as much to experience the good tastes of food.

Smell, Taste, and Flavor

People with *anosmia* (pronounced "uh-NAHZ-mee-uh") are unable to distinguish different smells. Some are born this way, but anosmia can also result from damage to the brain or to nerve cells high inside the nose (Doty, 2009; Hawkes, 2003; Leopold, 2002). Anosmic individuals also have trouble distinguishing different tastes, even though there is nothing wrong with their taste system. Why? For the same reason that when you have a stuffy nose, everything may seem to taste the same—usually like cardboard. Smell and taste act as two components of a single system, known as *flavor* (Rozin, 1982). Most of the properties that make food taste good are actually odors detected by the olfactory system, not activities of the taste system. The olfactory and gustatory pathways converge in the *orbitofrontal cortex* (Rolls, 2006), where neurons also respond to the sight and texture of food. The responses of neurons in this "flavor cortex" are also influenced by conditions of hunger and satiety ("fullness").

Both tastes and odors prompt strong emotional responses. For tastes, the emotional reaction to bitterness or sweetness appears to be inborn (Mueller et al., 2005), but for most mammals, including humans, there are few other innate flavor preferences. Most of what we like to eat, and what we avoid, is based on the experiences we have had with various foods (Myers & Sclafani, 2006). Our emotional reactions to odors, too, are shaped by learning (Bartoshuk, 1991). In one study, people smelled a variety of odors while experiencing either pleasant or unpleasant tastes. Later, odors they had once rated as neutral were rated as pleasant if they had been paired with pleasant tastes (Barkat et al., 2008). Emotional reactions to smells can also be affected by expectations. Consider a study in which people sniffed an air sample that was described as coming from either cheddar cheese or body odor. Those who thought they were smelling body odor rated the air sample as more unpleasant than those who thought they were smelling cheese (de Araujo et al., 2005).

Variations in a person's nutritional state can affect the taste, flavor, and pleasure of eating food, as well as the motivation to eat certain foods (Yeomans & Mobini, 2006). For example, hunger or salt deficiency makes sweet or salty things taste better and more likely to be eaten. Influences on protein and fat intake are less direct. Protein and fat molecules have no particular taste or smell. So preferring or avoiding foods that contain these nutrients is based on associations between scent cues from other volatile substances in food and on the nutritional results of eating the foods (Bartoshuk, 1991; Schiffman et al., 1999).

Flavor includes other characteristics of food, too—including how it feels in your mouth and, especially, its temperature. Temperature does not alter saltiness, but warm foods tend to taste sweeter. In fact, simply warming the taste receptors creates a sensation of sweetness (Cruz & Green, 2000; you can experience this sensation simply by holding some warm water in your mouth for a few seconds). Aromas released from warm food rise from the mouth into the nose and create more flavor sensations. This is probably why some people find hot pizza delicious and cold pizza disgusting. Spicy foods actually stimulate pain fibers in the mouth because they contain a substance called *capsaicin* (pronounced "kap-SAY-uh-sin"), which opens ion channels in pain neurons that are also opened by heat. As a result, these foods seem "hot" (Caterina et al., 1997). Why do people eat spicy foods even though they cause pain? The practice may have started because many "hot" spices have antibacterial properties. In fact, researchers have found a strong correlation between frequent use of antibacterial spices and living in climates that promote bacterial contamination (Billing & Sherman, 1998). Capsaicin also tends to create a sense of fullness (Westerterp-Plantenga, Smeets, & Lejeune, 2005), so perhaps eating spicy foods originally helped people curb hunger during times of famine.

In short, experiencing the flavor of the foods we eat is not just a process of sensing chemical signals coming from the tongue and the nose. It also involves temperature and texture, and it can be affected too by what we have learned (Verhagen, 2006). ("In Review: Smell and Taste" summarizes our discussion of these senses.)

IN REVIEW Smell and Taste		
Aspect of Sensory System	**Elements**	**Key Characteristics**
Energy	Smell: volatile chemicals Taste: chemicals in solution	The amount, intensity, and location of the chemicals determine taste and smell sensations.
Structures of taste and smell	Smell: chemical receptors in the mucous membrane of the nose Taste: taste buds grouped in papillae in the mouth	Odor and taste molecules stimulate chemical receptors.
Pathways to the brain	Smell: olfactory bulb Taste: taste buds	Axons from the nose bypass the thalamus and extend directly to the olfactory bulb.

1. The flavor of food arises from a combination of _____ and _____.
2. Emotion and memory are linked especially closely to our sense of _____.
3. Perfume ads suggest that humans are affected by _____ that increase sexual attraction.

Cutaneous Senses and the Vestibular System

Some senses are not located in a specific organ, such as the eye or the ear. These are the **cutaneous senses**, also known as the *somatic senses* or *somatosensory systems,* which are spread throughout the body. The cutaneous senses include the skin senses of touch, temperature, and pain, as well as *proprioception,* the sense that tells the brain about body position and movements. Closely related to proprioception is the *vestibular system,* or *sense of equilibrium,* which tells the brain about the position and movements of the head. Although not strictly a cutaneous sense, the sense of equilibrium will also be considered in this section.

Touch and Temperature

Touch is crucial. People can function and prosper without vision, hearing, or smell, but without a sense of touch, you would have difficulty surviving. You could not even swallow food, because you could not tell where it was in your mouth and throat.

Stimulus and Receptors for Touch   The energy detected by the sense of touch is physical pressure on tissue, usually the skin, or hairs on the skin. The skin covers nearly 2 square yards of surface and weighs more than 20 pounds. The receptors that transduce pressure into neural activity are in, or just below, the skin (Lumpkin & Caterina, 2007).

Many nerve endings in the skin act as touch receptors. Some neurons come from the spinal cord, enter the skin, and simply end; these are called *free nerve endings.* Many other neurons end in a variety of elaborate specialized structures. However,

cutaneous senses Senses of touch, temperature, pain, and kinesthesia.

there is generally little relationship between the type of nerve ending and the type of sensory information carried by the neuron. Many types of nerve endings respond to mechanical stimuli, but the exact process by which they transduce mechanical energy is still unclear. These somatosensory neurons are unusual in that they have no dendrites. Their cell bodies are outside the spinal cord, and their axon splits and extends both to the skin and to the spinal cord. Action potentials travel from the nerve endings in the skin to the spinal cord and onward from there into the brain. Information from the touch system tells us what is happening to our bodies, but we do more than just passively respond. For humans, touch is also an active sense that is used for getting specific information. In much the same way that you can look as well as just see, you can also touch as well as feel. When people are involved in active sensing, they usually use the part of the sensory apparatus that has the greatest sensitivity. For vision, this is the eye's fovea; for touch, the fingertips. (The area of primary somatosensory cortex devoted to the fingertips is especially large.) Fingertip touch is the principal way people sense the textures of surfaces, but these touch sensations depend not just on stimulation of skin receptors but also on the timing of that stimulation. You can experience this for yourself by noticing how difficult it is to sense the roughness of sandpaper, for example, by just placing your fingers on it. A clear sensation of roughness will not appear until you slide your fingers over the surface (Hollins & Bensamaia, 2007). As you do so, the ridges that form your fingerprints vibrate in succession, activating special skin receptors in each ridge. Encoded messages about the timing of this sequence of activation tells the brain about the characteristics of the surface you are touching (Scheibert et al., 2009). Fingertip touch can be extremely sensitive, as evidenced by blind people who can read Braille as rapidly as two hundred words per minute (Foulke, 1991) or by the ease with which sighted but blindfolded people can identify objects and learn to recognize faces by touching them (Kilgour & Lederman, 2002).

Stimulation of the touch sense can also have psychological and physiological effects. For example, premature infants gain weight 47 percent faster when they are given massages. (They do not eat more; rather, they process their food more efficiently; Diego, Field, & Hernandez-Reif, 2005). Massage is also associated with reduced pain and lowered stress hormones in arthritic children (Field et al., 1997) and with reduced anxiety, increased alertness, and improved math performance in adults (Field et al., 1996; Simmons et al., 2004).

Adaptation of Touch Receptors Constant input from all your touch neurons would provide a lot of unnecessary information. Once you get dressed, for example, you do not need to be constantly reminded that you are wearing clothes. Thanks in part to the process of adaptation mentioned earlier, you do not continue to feel your clothes against your skin.

The most important sensory information involves *changes* in touch—as when your belt or shoe suddenly loosens. The touch sense emphasizes these changes and filters out the excess information. How? Typically, a touch neuron responds with a burst of firing when a stimulus is applied and then quickly returns to its baseline firing rate, even though the stimulus may still be in contact with the skin. If the touch pressure increases, the neuron again responds with an increase in firing rate but then slows down. Some neurons in the somatosensory cortex also stop firing if a tactile stimulus remains constant (Graziano et al., 2002). A few touch neurons adapt more slowly, continuing to fire at an elevated rate as long as pressure is applied to the skin. By attending to this input, you can sense a constant stimulus (try doing this by focusing on sensations from your glasses or shoes).

Encoding and Representation of Touch Information Your sense of touch encodes information about the weight and location of any object that comes in contact with your skin. The *intensity* of the stimulus—how heavy it is—is encoded by both the firing rate of individual neurons and the number of neurons stimulated. A heavy object produces a higher rate of firing and stimulates more neurons than a light object. The *location* of touch is coded much as it is for vision: by the location of the neurons that are responding to the touch.

Touch information is organized so that signals from neighboring points on the skin stay next to one another as they travel from the skin through the spinal cord to the thalamus and on to the somatosensory cortex. So just as there is a map of the visual field in the brain, the area of cortex that receives touch information resembles a map of the surface of the body (see Figure 3.16). As with the other senses, these representations are contralateral; that is, input from the left side of the body goes to the right side of the brain, and vice versa. In nonhuman primates, however, touch information from each hand is sent to both sides of the brain. This arrangement amplifies information from manual exploration of objects and improves feedback from hand movements (Iwamura, Iriki, & Tanaka, 1994).

Temperature   When you dig your toes into a sandy summer beach, the pleasant experience you get comes partly from the sensation of warmth. Touch and temperature seem to be separate senses, and to some extent they are, but the difference between the two senses is not always clear.

Some of the skin's sensory neurons respond to a change in temperature but not to simple contact. There are "warm fibers," which are nerve fibers that increase their firing rates when the temperature changes in the range of about 95° to 115°F (35° to 47°C). Temperatures above this range are painful and stimulate different fibers. Other nerve fibers are "cold fibers"; they respond to a broad range of cool temperatures. However, many of the fibers that respond to temperature also respond to touch, so sensations of touch and temperature sometimes interact. For example, warm and cold objects can feel up to 250 percent heavier than body-temperature objects (Stevens & Hooper, 1982). Also, if you touch an object made up of alternating warm and cool metal bars, you will have the sensation of intense heat (Thunberg, 1896).

Pain

Stimulation of the skin senses can give a great deal of pleasure, but if you increase the intensity of the same kind of stimulation, you have a much different sensation: pain. Pain provides you with information about the impact of the world on your body. It can tell you, for example, that "a hammer just crushed your left thumb." Pain also has a distinctly negative emotional component. Researchers have focused on the information-carrying aspects of pain, its emotional components, and the various ways that the brain can adjust the amount of pain that reaches consciousness.

Pain as an Information Sense   The information-carrying aspect of pain is very similar to that of touch and temperature. The receptors for pain are free nerve endings. As mentioned earlier, for example, capsaicin, the active ingredient in chili peppers, creates pain in the mouth by stimulating these pain nerve endings. Painful stimuli cause the release of chemicals that fit into specialized receptors in pain neurons, causing them to fire. The axons of pain-sensing neurons release neurotransmitters not only near the spinal cord, sending information to the brain, but also near the skin, causing local inflammation.

Two types of nerve fibers carry pain signals from the skin to the spinal cord. *A-delta fibers* carry sharp, pricking pain sensations. Their axons are coated with myelin, which speeds the transmission of these sharp pain messages. *C fibers* carry long-lasting, dull aches and burning sensations. So when you stub your toe, the immediate wave of sharp, intense pain is signaled by messages from A-delta fibers. That slightly delayed wave of gnawing, dull pain is signaled by messages from C fibers.

Both kinds of pain come from the same place, but the sensations follow separate pain fibers all the way to the brain, where they activate different brain regions (Ploner et al., 2002). Pain fibers enter the spinal cord, where they form synapses with neurons that carry pain signals to the thalamus and other parts of the brain (see Figure 4.24).

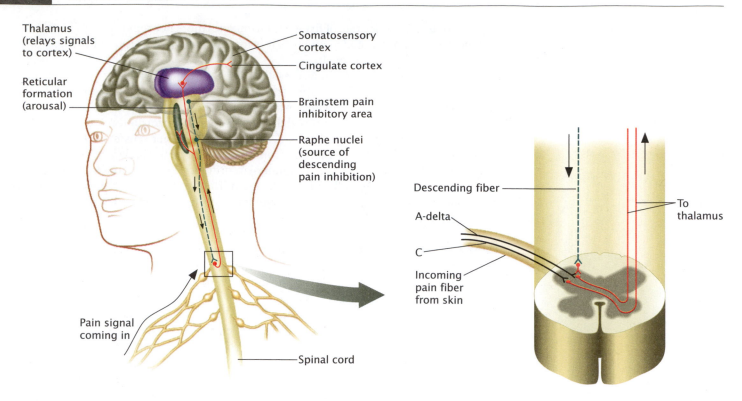

FIGURE 4.24
Pain Pathways
Pain messages are carried to the brain by way of the spinal cord. Myelinated *A-delta fibers* carry information about sharp pain. Unmyelinated *C fibers* carry several types of pain, including chronic, dull aches. Pain fibers make synapses in the reticular formation, causing arousal. They also go to the thalamus and from there to the cortex. Pain sensations can be intensified when activity in pain-carrying neurons stimulates activity in glial cells in the spinal cord (Watkins & Maier, 2003; see the chapter on biological aspects of psychology).

gate control theory of pain A theory suggesting that a functional "gate" in the spinal cord can either let pain impulses travel upward to the brain or block their progress.

Different pain neurons are activated by different degrees of painful stimulation. Numerous types of neurotransmitters are used by different pain neurons, a phenomenon that has allowed the development of a variety of new drugs for pain management.

Scientists once believed that the cerebral cortex played little or no role in the experience of pain, but they now know otherwise. Key cortical areas are involved in pain processing, including the *somatosensory strip* in the parietal lobe; the *insular cortex,* a region wedged deep between the frontal and parietal lobes; and the *anterior cingulate cortex,* which is involved in emotion (Xie, Huo, & Tang, 2009). Some of the evidence for the role of these areas in pain comes from research revealing that people whose insular cortex has been damaged show reduced responsiveness to pain stimuli (Velhuijzen et al., 2009). Other studies show that when pain-producing heat—but not other kinds of stimulation—is applied to the skin of normal individuals, the neurotransmitter GABA is released in an area of the cingulate cortex (Kupers et al., 2009). Functional magnetic resonance imaging (fMRI) studies of healthy volunteers have documented activation of the somatosensory cortex and anterior cingulate cortex during pain experiences (Mohr, Binkofski, et al., 2005; Tracey, 2005). Further, when hypnosis is used to increase or decrease the unpleasantness of pain, fMRI scans show corresponding changes in the anterior cingulate cortex (Schulz-Stubner et al., 2004). Reductions in anterior cingulate cortex activity also occur in response to pain-reducing drugs and even to pain-reducing placebos (Petrovic et al., 2002).

Emotional Aspects of Pain   All senses can have emotional components, most of which are learned responses. For example, the smell of baking cookies can make you feel good if it has been associated with happy childhood times. The emotional response to pain is more direct. Specific pathways carry an emotional component of the painful stimulus to areas of the hindbrain and reticular formation (see Figure 4.24), as well as to the cingulate cortex via the thalamus (Johansen, Fields, & Manning, 2001).

Nevertheless, the overall emotional response to pain depends greatly on cognitive factors, that is, on how we think about it (Chen, 2009). In one study, some participants were told about the kind of painful stimulus they were to receive and

A Life with No Pain

Ashlyn Blocker, shown here at age 5 being checked for injuries, was born with a rare genetic disorder that prevented the development of pain receptors. As a result, she feels no pain if she is cut or bruised, if she bites her tongue while eating, or even if she is burned by hot soup or a hot stove. She only knows she has been injured if she sees herself bleeding, so she will have to find ways to protect herself from danger without the vital information provided by the pain system. Now 10 years old, Ashlyn is beginning to understand the seriousness of her condition, and her worried mother has said, "I would give anything for her to feel pain" (Associated Press, 2004).

© AP Photo/Stephen Morton

© Alain Evrard/Photo Researchers, Inc.;

The Complex Nature of Pain

If pain were based only on the nature of incoming stimuli, this participant in a purification ceremony in Singapore would be hurting. However, as described in the chapter on consciousness, the experience of pain is a complex phenomenon affected by psychological and biological variables that can make it more or, as in this case, less intense.

when to expect it. Others were not informed. Those who knew what to expect objected less to the pain, even though the sensation was reported to be equally noticeable in both groups (Mayer & Price, 1982). Cognitive strategies such as focusing on pleasant music or pictures (including pictures of loved ones) or on distracting thoughts can also reduce the unpleasantness of pain to some extent (Edwards et al., 2009; Master et al., 2009; Roy et al., 2009), especially when people expect these strategies to succeed (Bantick et al., 2002). In one study, distraction created by a cognitively demanding task reduced both the unpleasantness of painful heat stimuli and activity in brain regions involved in processing pain sensations (Bantick et al., 2002). Scientists are also developing special biofeedback systems that may someday allow patients to relieve chronic pain by reducing activity in the brain regions involved in pain perception (de Charms et al., 2005).

The Gate Control Theory of Pain   Pain is extremely useful because in the long run it protects you from harm. However, there are times when enough is enough. Fortunately, the nervous system has several mechanisms for controlling the experience of pain.

One explanation of how the nervous system controls the amount of pain that reaches the brain is the **gate control theory of pain** (Melzack & Wall, 1965). It proposes that there is a "gate" in the spinal cord that either lets pain impulses travel upward to the brain or blocks their progress. Many details of the original gate control theory turned out to be incorrect, but later work supported the idea that natural mechanisms can block some aspects of pain sensations at the level of the spinal cord, so it remains the most comprehensive account of pain modulation (De Leo, 2006). According to the gate control theory, input from other skin senses can come into the spinal cord at the same time the pain gets there and "take over" the pathways that the pain impulses would have used. This theory may explain why rubbing the skin around a wound temporarily reduces pain from the wound and why electrical stimulation of the skin around a painful spot relieves that pain (Henderson, 2008; Slavin, 2008). If the spinal "gate" malfunctions, as it seems to do in some chronic pain patients, pain pathways are not only open but "sensitized" and thus more likely to send signals to the brain (D'Mello & Dickenson, 2008).

Itchy and Scratchy

The gate control theory of pain may partly explain why scratching relieves itching, because itch sensations involve activity in fibers located close to pain fibers (Andrew & Craig, 2001). Scratching itchy skin also activates brain regions related to reward (Vierow et al., 2009) and creates the temporary pleasure you get from doing so. Itch was once thought to result from low-level activity in pain neurons, but recent research has identified sensory pathways from the skin to the brain that are specifically dedicated to itch (Sun et al., 2009). Scientists are working on ways to block the spinal cord's response to itch signals from the skin. If they succeed, their methods may someday be applied in reducing the suffering of thousands of people afflicted with chronic itchiness (Gawande, 2008).

© AJPhoto/Photo Researchers, Inc.

The brain itself can close the gate to pain impulses by sending signals down the spinal cord. These messages from the brain block incoming pain signals at spinal cord synapses. The result is **analgesia**, the absence of pain sensations in the presence of a normally painful stimulus.

Natural Analgesics   At least three substances play a role in the brain's ability to block pain signals: (1) the neurotransmitter *serotonin*, (2) natural opiates called *endorphins*, and (3) *endocannabinoids*, all of which are chemicals released by the body during stress (Hohmann et al., 2005). As described in the chapter on biological aspects of psychology, endorphins are natural painkillers that act as neurotransmitters at many levels of the pain pathway, including the spinal cord, where they block the synapses of pain-carrying fibers. Endorphins may also relieve pain when released into the bloodstream as hormones by the adrenal and pituitary glands. The more endorphin receptors a person has inherited, the more pain tolerance that person has (Benjamin, Wilson, & Mogil, 1999).

Several conditions are known to cause the body to ease its own pain. For example, endorphins are released by immune cells that arrive at sites of inflammation (Cabot, 2001). And during the late stages of pregnancy, an endorphin system is activated that reduces the mother's labor pains (Dawson-Basoa & Gintzler, 1997). An endorphin system is also activated when people believe they are receiving a painkiller even though they are not (Zubieta et al., 2005). This phenomenon may be one of the mechanisms underlying the placebo effect, which is discussed in the chapter on research in psychology (Stewart-Williams, 2004). Remarkably, the resulting pain inhibition is experienced in the part of the body where relief was expected to

analgesia   The absence of pain sensations in the presence of a normally painful stimulus.

Natural Analgesia

The stress of athletic exertion causes the release of endorphins, natural painkillers that have been associated with pleasant feelings known as "runner's high" (Benedetti, 2007).

© Alexander Hassenstein/Bongarts/Getty Images

occur but not elsewhere (Benedetti, Arduino, & Amanzio, 1999). Physical or psychological stress, too, can activate natural analgesic systems. Stress-induced release of natural analgesics may account for cases in which injured soldiers and athletes continue to perform in the heat of battle or competition with no apparent pain (Colloca & Benedetti, 2005).

There are also mechanisms for reactivating pain sensitivity once a crisis is past. Studies with animals show that they can learn that certain situations signal "safety" and that these safety signals trigger the release of a neurotransmitter that counteracts endorphins' analgesic effects (Wiertelak, Maier, & Watkins, 1992). Blocking these "safety signals" increases the painkilling effects brought on by a placebo (Benedetti & Amanzio, 1997).

THINKING **CRITICALLY**

Does Acupuncture Relieve Pain?

Acupuncture is a widely used three-thousand-year-old Asian medical treatment that is alleged to work many wonders, including curing epilepsy, speeding stroke recovery, helping people quit smoking, reducing nausea from chemotherapy, and aiding weight loss efforts (Cho et al., 2009; Li, Jack, & Yang, 2006; Shouzhuang & Chao, 2006; Wang, Tian, & Han, 2008; Yongxia, 2006). Most notably, though, acupuncture is said to be capable of relieving pain (Lin & Chen, 2008). The treatment is based on the idea that body energy, called *qi*, flows along channels that link particular internal organs to particular places on the skin (see Figure 4.25). It is said that there are fourteen main channels and that a person's health depends on the balance of energy flowing in them. Inserting fine needles into the skin and twirling them is meant to stimulate these channels and restore

FIGURE 4.25
Linking Internal Organs to the Skin's Surface

These diagrams illustrate the skin locations which are said by acupuncturists to be linked to the large intestine (LI4), the lung (Lu 5), the gallbladder (GB34), and the stomach (ST36).

Source: Wang, S. M., Kain, Z. N. and White, P. (2008) "Acupuncture Analgesia: I. The Scientific Basis." *Anesthesia and Analgesia*, 106(2), 602–610. Reprinted by permission of Lippincott, Williams & Wilkins.

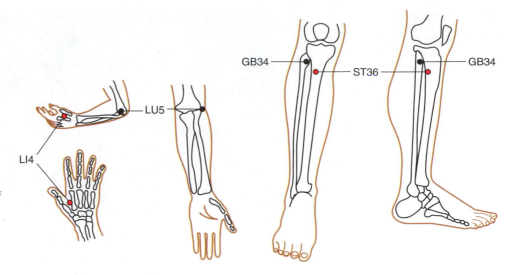

a balanced flow of energy. The needles produce an aching and tingling sensation called *teh-ch'i* at the site of stimulation, but they are said to relieve pain at distant, seemingly unrelated parts of the body (Liu & Akira, 1994; Yan et al., 1992).

What am I being asked to believe or accept?

Acupuncturists assert that twirling a needle in the skin can relieve pain caused by everything from tooth extraction to cancer.

What evidence is available to support the assertion?

There is no scientific evidence for the existence of the energy channels proposed in the theory behind acupuncture (Wang, Kain, & White, 2008). However, as described in the chapter on biological aspects of psychology, some acupuncture stimulation sites are near peripheral nerves, and evidence from functional MRI scans suggests that stimulating these sites changes activity in brain regions related to the targets of treatment (Zhang, Qin, et al., 2009).

What about the more specific assertions that acupuncture relieves pain and that it does so through direct physical mechanisms? Several studies have shown positive results in 50 to 80 percent of patients treated with acupuncture for various kinds of pain (Brinkhaus et al., 2006; Manheimer et al., 2005; Witt et al., 2005). One summary of eleven such studies found greater overall reductions in headache pain among patients who had been randomly assigned to receive acupuncture when compared to those randomly assigned to receive standard drug therapies (Linde et al., 2009). Adding acupuncture to a program of drugs and exercise was followed by a greater reduction in the pain of fibromyalgia, and the difference remained apparent three months after treatment (Targino et al., 2008). Another study found that acupuncture before surgery reduced postoperative pain and nausea, decreased the need for pain-relieving drugs, and reduced patients' stress responses (Kotani et al., 2001). Yet another found electrical-stimulation acupuncture to be more effective than either drugs or fake stimulation at reducing nausea following major breast surgery; the acupuncture group also reported the least postoperative pain (Gan et al., 2004).

Such well-controlled studies are rare, however, and their results can be contradictory. Some studies of patients with back or neck pain, for example, have found acupuncture to be no better than a placebo or massage therapy (Assefi et al., 2005; Cherkin et al., 2009; Foster et al., 2007; Linde et al., 2009); others have found that acupuncture benefits only certain patients (Yuan et al., 2008).

There is evidence that acupuncture activates the endorphin system. It is associated with the release of endorphins in the brain, and drugs that slow the breakdown of opiates also prolong the analgesia produced by acupuncture (He, 1987). Furthermore, the pain-reducing effects of acupuncture during electrical stimulation of a tooth can be reversed by naloxone, a substance that blocks the painkilling effects of endorphins and

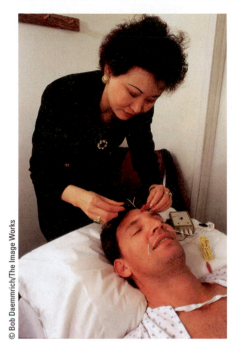

© Bob Daemmrich/The Image Works

How Does Acupuncture Work?

This acupuncturist is inserting fine needles in her patient's face in hopes of treating poor blood circulation in his hands and feet. Acupuncture treatments appear to alleviate a wide range of problems, including many kinds of pain, but the mechanisms through which it works are not yet determined.

other opiate drugs. This finding suggests that acupuncture somehow activates the body's natural painkilling system. If acupuncture does activate endorphins, is the activation brought about only through the placebo effect? Probably not entirely, because acupuncture produces naloxone-reversible analgesia in monkeys and rats, who could not have developed positive expectancies by reading about acupuncture (Kishioka et al., 1994).

Are there alternative ways of interpreting the evidence?

Yes. Evidence about acupuncture might be interpreted as simply confirming that the body's painkilling system can be stimulated by external means. Acupuncture may merely provide one activating method (Pariente et al., 2005); there may be other, even more efficient ways (Petrovic et al., 2005; Ulett, 2003). We already know, for example, that successful placebo treatments for human pain appear to operate by activating the endorphin system.

What additional evidence would help evaluate the alternatives?

More placebo-controlled studies of acupuncture are needed, but it is difficult to control for the placebo effect in acupuncture treatment, especially in double-blind fashion (Derry et al., 2006; Kaptchuk et al., 2006). How could a study be set up so that therapists would not know whether the treatment they are giving is acupuncture or not? What placebo treatment could look and feel like having a needle inserted and twirled in the skin? Some researchers have created single-blind placebo acupuncture using sham techniques in which the needles do not actually break the skin or are inserted but not twirled or are inserted in locations that should not, according to acupuncturists, have any effect on pain. In one study of sham techniques, research participants were indeed unable to tell whether or not they were getting genuine acupuncture (Enblom et al., 2008). So far, only a few studies have used sophisticated sham methods (Madsen, Gøtzsche, & Hróbjartsson, 2009), and some have found acupuncture to be no more effective than placebo methods (e.g., Haake et al., 2007; Linde et al., 2009). Future controlled experiments should eventually reveal the degree to which placebo effects play a role in the results of acupuncture treatment.

Researchers must also go beyond focusing on the effects of acupuncture to consider the general relationship between internal painkilling systems and external methods for stimulating them. Regarding acupuncture itself, scientists do not yet know what factors govern its ability to activate the endorphin system. Other important unknowns include the types of pain for which acupuncture is most effective, the types of patients who respond best, and the precise procedures that are most effective.

What conclusions are most reasonable?

Although acupuncture is not a cure-all, there seems little doubt that in some circumstances, it does relieve pain and reduce nausea (British Medical Association, 2000; National Institutes of Health Consensus Conference, 1998). What we still don't know is exactly why this may be and through what mechanism any genuine effects might operate. So acupuncture remains a fascinating phenomenon, a treatment used on millions of people all over the world, and a continuing source of controversy. Some critics argue that further expenditures for acupuncture research are not warranted, but it seems likely that studies will continue. The quality of these studies' methodology and the nature of their results will determine whether acupuncture finds a more prominent place in Western medicine.

Proprioception: Sensing Body Position

Most sensory systems receive information from the external world, such as the light reflected from a flower or the feeling of cool water. But as far as the brain is concerned, the rest of the body is "out there" too. You know about the position of your body and what each of its parts is doing only because sensory systems provide this information to the brain. These sensory systems are called **proprioceptive senses** (*proprioceptive* means "received from the self" and is pronounced "proh-pree-oh-SEP-tiv").

proprioceptive senses The sensory systems that allow us to know about body position and what each part of our body is doing.

© Alain Evrard/Photo Researchers, Inc.

Balancing Act

The smooth coordination of all physical movement, from scratching your nose to complex feats of balance, depends on proprioception, the senses that provide information about the position of the head and body, their movements, and where each body part is in relation to all the others.

sense of equilibrium (vestibular sense) The proprioceptive sense that provides information about the position of the head (and hence the body) in space and about its movements.

vestibular sacs Organs in the inner ear that connect the semicircular canals and the cochlea and contribute to the body's sense of balance.

otoliths Small crystals in the fluid-filled vestibular sacs of the inner ear that, when shifted by gravity, stimulate nerve cells that inform the brain of the position of the head.

semicircular canals Tubes in the inner ear whose fluid, when shifted by head movements, stimulates nerve cells that tell the brain about those movements.

kinesthetic perception The proprioceptive sense that tells you where the parts of your body are with respect to one another.

proprioceptors Receptors in muscles and joints that provide information to the brain about movement and body position.

Sense of Equilibrium   The **sense of equilibrium**, also called the **vestibular sense** (pronounced "vess-TIB-yuh-lur"), tells the brain about the position of the head (and to some degree, the rest of the body) in space and about its general movements. It is a primary component of what people think of as the *sense of balance*. People usually become aware of their sense of equilibrium only when it is overstimulated and they become dizzy or motion-sick.

The organs for the sense of equilibrium are two vestibular sacs and three semicircular canals in your inner ears. (You can see the semicircular canals in Figure 4.3; the vestibular sacs connect these canals and the cochlea.) The **vestibular sacs** are filled with a thick, oily fluid and contain small crystals called **otoliths** ("ear stones") that rest on hair endings. The **semicircular canals** are fluid-filled, arc-shaped tubes, with tiny hairs extending into the fluid. When your head moves, the otoliths shift in the vestibular sacs and the fluid moves in the semicircular canals, stimulating hair endings. These changes activate neurons that travel with the acoustic nerve, informing the brain about the amount and direction of head movement (Angelaki & Cullen, 2008).

Nerve cells from the vestibular system connect to several brain regions, including the cerebellum, the part of the autonomic nervous system (ANS) that affects the digestive system, and areas that move the eyes. The connections to the cerebellum help coordinate accurate body movements. The connections to the ANS are partly responsible for the nausea that sometimes follows intense stimulation of the vestibular system—on amusement park rides, for example. Finally, the connections to the eye muscles create *vestibular-ocular reflexes*. For instance, when your head moves in one direction, your eyes reflexively move in the opposite direction. This reflex allows your eyes to focus on a fixed point in space even if your head is moving—as when you track a ball in flight while running to catch it. **TRY THIS** You can experience this reflex by having a friend spin you around on a stool for fifteen to thirty seconds. When you stop spinning, try to fix your gaze on one point in the room. You will be temporarily unable to do so, because the excitation of the vestibular system will cause your eyes to move repeatedly in the direction opposite to the spinning. Because vestibular reflexes adapt to the lack of gravity in outer space, astronauts returning to earth have postural and movement difficulties until their vestibular systems readjust to the effects of gravity (Paloski, 1998).

Kinesthetic Perception   Your sense of balance depends partly on **kinesthetic perception** (pronounced "kin-ess-THET-ik"), which tells you where the parts of your body are with respect to one another. You probably do not think much about kinesthetic information, but you definitely use it, and you can demonstrate it for yourself. **TRY THIS** Close your eyes, hold your arms out in front of you, and try to touch your two index fingertips together. You probably did this easily because your kinesthetic sense told you where each finger was with respect to your body. You also depend on kinesthetic information to guide all your movements. Otherwise, it would be impossible to develop or improve any motor skill, from walking to complex athletic movements. These movement patterns become simple and fluid because with practice, the brain uses kinesthetic information automatically.

Kinesthetic information comes from special receptors, called **proprioceptors**, in joints and muscles. Proprioceptors in muscle fibers send information to the brain about the stretching of muscles (Proske, 2006). When the position of your bones changes, as when you move your arms and legs, proprioceptors in the joints transduce this mechanical energy into nerve cell activity, providing information about both the rate of change and the angle of the bones. This encoded information goes to the spinal cord and is sent from there to the thalamus, along with sensory information from the skin. Eventually the information goes to the cerebellum and to the somatosensory cortex (see Figures 3.11 and 3.15), where it is used in the smooth coordination of movements.

Proprioception is a critical sense for success in physical therapy and rehabilitative medicine, especially for people who have to relearn how to move their muscles after strokes or other problems. Research in a branch of physics called *nonlinear dynam- ics* has been applied to problems in proprioception. For example, using the discovery that the right amount of random background noise can improve the detection of sig- nals, rehabilitation neurologists have added a small amount of vibration (or "noise") to muscle and joint sensations. This procedure dramatically increases patients' ability to detect joint movements and position (Glanz, 1997). (See "In Review: Body Senses" for a summary of our discussion of touch, temperature, pain, and kinesthetic perception.)

IN REVIEW   Body Senses

Sense	Energy	Conversion of Physical Energy to Nerve Activity	Pathways and Characteristics
Touch	Mechanical deformation of skin	Skin receptors (may be stimulated by hair on the skin)	Nerve endings respond to changes in weight (intensity) and location of touch.
Temperature	Heat	Sensory neurons in the skin	Changes in temperature are detected by warm-sensing and cool-sensing fibers. Temperature interacts with touch.
Pain	Increases with intensity of touch or temperature	Free nerve endings in or near the skin surface	Changes in intensity cause the release of chemicals detected by receptors in pain neurons. Some fibers convey sharp pain; others convey dull aches and burning sensations.
Sense of equilibrium	Mechanical energy of head movements	Neural receptors in the inner ear	Information about fluid moving in the semicircular canals is sent to the brain along the acoustic nerve.
Kinesthetic perception	Mechanical energy of joint and muscle movement	Neural receptors (proprioceptors) in joints and muscle fibers	Information from joints and muscle fibers is sent to the spinal cord, thalamus, cerebellum, and cortex.

1. The gate control theory offers an explanation of why we sometimes do not feel _____.

2. Professional dancers look at the same spot as long as possible during repeated spins. They are trying to avoid the dizziness caused when the sense of _____ is overstimulated.

3. Without your sense of _____, you would not be able to swallow food without choking.

FOCUS ON **RESEARCH METHODS**

The Case of the Mysterious Spells

Early in this chapter, we discussed the specific energy doctrine, which says that each sensory system can send information to the brain only about its own sense, regardless of how the stimulation occurs. So gently pressing on your closed eye will send touch sensations from the skin on your eyelid and visual sensations from your eye. This doctrine applies even when stimulation of sensory systems arises from within the brain itself. For example, *tinnitus,* a continuous "ringing in the ears," occurs as a result of spontaneous activation of nerve cells in auditory areas of the brain, not from any external sound source. The following case study illustrates a far less common example in which spontaneous brain activity resulted in erotic sensations.

What was the researcher's question?

A 31-year-old woman we'll call "Linda" reported that for many years, she had been experiencing recurring "spells" that began with what seemed like sexual sensations (Janszky et al., 2002). These "orgasm-like euphoric erotic sensations" were followed by a staring, unresponsive state in which she lost consciousness. The spells, which occurred without warning and in response to no obvious trigger, interfered severely with her ability to function normally in everyday life. Linda was examined by József Janszky, a neurologist, who suspected that she might be suffering from epilepsy, a seizure disorder in which nerve cells in the brain suddenly start firing uncontrollably. The symptoms of an epileptic seizure depend on which brain areas are activated. Seizures that activate the motor area of the cerebral cortex will cause uncontrollable movements, seizures that activate visual cortex will create the sensation of images, and so on. Could there be a specific brain region that, when activated by a seizure, cause the sensations of orgasm that are normally brought on by external stimulation?

How did the researcher answer the question?

It is not easy to study the neurological basis of sexual sensations because most people are understandably reluctant to allow researchers to monitor their sexual activity. In the process of diagnosing Linda's problem, Janszky had a unique opportunity to learn something about the origin of orgasmic sensations without intruding on his patient's privacy. His approach exemplifies the *case study* method of research. As described in the chapter on research in psychology, case studies focus intensively on a particular individual, group, or situation. Sometimes they lead to important insights about clinical problems or other phenomena that occur so rarely that they cannot be studied through surveys or controlled experiments. In this case, Janszky decided to study Linda's brain activity while she was actually having a spell. He reasoned that if the spells were caused by seizures in a specific brain region, it might be possible to eliminate the problem through surgery.

What did the researcher find?

Linda's brain activity was recorded during five of her spells, using electroencephalography (EEG), a method described in more detail in the chapter on biological aspects of psychology. During each spell, the EEG showed that she was having seizures in the right temporal lobe of her brain. A subsequent MRI of her brain revealed a small area of abnormal tissue in the same area of the right temporal lobe. The organization of nerve cells in abnormal brain tissue can make it easier for seizures to occur, so Linda was advised to have some tissue surgically removed from the problem area. After the surgery, her seizures stopped.

What do the results mean?

Janszky concluded that Linda had been having "localization-related epilepsy," meaning that her spells were seizures coming from a specific brain location. This conclusion was supported by the fact that she had right temporal lobe seizures on the EEG each time she had a spell. Her MRI showed an abnormality in the same region that commonly gives rise to seizures, and her spells disappeared after the abnormality was removed. Linda's case also led Janszky to suggest that the right temporal lobe may play a special role in creating the sensory experience of orgasm.

What do we still need to know?

Janszky's suggestion might be correct, meaning that activation of the right temporal cortex may be sufficient for the sensory experience of orgasm. But at least one important question remains: How specific is the linkage between activity in this brain region and the sensory experiences of orgasm? Could seizures in other brain regions cause similar experiences? Is right temporal cortex activity one of many ways to generate orgasm-like experiences, or is it necessary for these experiences? Answering this question would be easier if we knew whether Linda continued to experience orgasms during sexual activity. If she did, the implication would be that the area of right temporal lobe tissue that was removed was not necessary for the experience of orgasm. Unfortunately, Janszky's report is silent on this point, but future cases and further research will no doubt shed additional light on this fascinating sensory puzzle.

LINKAGES

As noted in the chapter on introducing psychology, all of psychology's many subfields are related to one another. Our discussion of the representation of sensory systems in the brain illustrates just one way in which the topic of this chapter, sensation, is linked to the subfield of biological psychology, which is the

CHAPTER 4
SENSATION

focus of the chapter on biological aspects of psychology. The Linkages diagram shows ties to two other subfields as well, and there are many more ties throughout the book. Looking for linkages among subfields will help you see how they all fit together and help you appreciate the big picture that is psychology.

LINKAGES

How is information from the senses organized in the brain?
(ans. on p. 112)

Can information from one sense override information from another?
(ans. on p. 170)

Can people see and hear without being aware of it?
(ans. on p. 334)

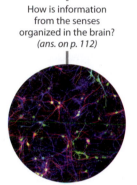

CHAPTER 3
Biological Aspects of Psychology

CHAPTER 5
Perception

CHAPTER 9
Consciousness

SUMMARY

A *sense* is a system that translates information from outside the nervous system into nerve cell activity. Messages from the senses are called *sensations*.

Sensory Systems

The first step in sensation involves *accessory structures*, which collect and modify sensory stimuli. The second step is *transduction*, the process of converting incoming energy into nerve cell activity; it is accomplished by *neural receptors*, cells specialized to detect energy of some type. *Sensory adaptation* takes place when receptors receive unchanging stimulation. Nerve cell activity is transferred through the thalamus (except in the case of olfaction) and on to the cortex.

The Problem of Encoding

Encoding is the translation of physical properties of a stimulus into a pattern of nerve cell activity that specifically

identifies those physical properties. It is the language the brain uses to describe sensations. Encoding is characterized by the *specific energy doctrine*: Stimulation of a particular sensory nerve provides codes for that one sense, no matter how the stimulation takes place. There are two basic types of sensory codes: temporal codes and spatial codes.

Hearing

Sound is a repetitive fluctuation in the pressure of a medium such as air. It travels in waves.

Sound

The *amplitude* and *frequency* (which is related to *wavelength*) of sound waves produce the psychological dimensions of *loudness* and *pitch*, respectively. (People with *absolute pitch* can identify specific frequencies as specific musical notes.) *Timbre*, the quality of sound, depends on

complex wave patterns added to the lowest frequency of the sound.

The Ear

The energy from sound waves is collected and transmitted to the *cochlea* through a series of accessory structures, including the *tympanic membrane*. Transduction occurs when sound energy stimulates hair cells of the organ of Corti on the *basilar membrane* of the cochlea, which in turn stimulate the *acoustic nerve*.

Auditory Pathways, Representations, and Experiences

Auditory information is relayed through the thalamus to the *auditory cortex*. Sounds of similar frequency activate neighboring cells in the cortex, but loudness is coded temporally.

Coding Intensity and Frequency

The intensity of a sound stimulus is encoded by the firing rate of auditory neurons. *Place theory* describes the encoding of higher frequencies: They are encoded by the place on the basilar membrane where the wave envelope peaks. Each neuron in the auditory nerve is most sensitive to a specific frequency (its characteristic frequency). Very low frequencies are encoded by frequency matching, which refers to the fact that the firing rate of a neuron matches the frequency of a sound wave. According to frequency-matching theory, or *volley theory,* some frequencies may be matched by the firing rate of a group of neurons. Low to moderate frequencies are encoded through a combination of these methods.

Vision

Light
Visible light is electromagnetic radiation with wavelengths ranging from about 400 nm to about 750 nm. *Light intensity,* or the amount of energy in light, determines its brightness. Differing *light wavelengths* are sensed as different colors.

Focusing Light
Accessory structures of the eye include the *cornea, pupil, iris,* and *lens.* Through *ocular accommodation* and other means, these structures focus light rays on the *retina,* the netlike structure of cells at the back of the eye.

Converting Light into Images
Photoreceptors in the retina—*rods* and *cones*—have *photopigments* and can transduce light into neural activity. Rods and cones differ in their shape, their sensitivity to light, their ability to discriminate colors, and their distribution across the retina. The *fovea,* the area of highest *visual acuity,* has only cones, which are color-sensitive. Rods are more sensitive to light but do not discriminate colors; they are distributed in areas around the fovea. Both types of photoreceptors contribute to *dark adaptation.* From the photoreceptors, energy transduced from light is transferred to bipolar cells and then to *ganglion cells,* aided by lateral connections between photoreceptors, bipolar cells, and ganglion cells.

Through lateral inhibition, the retina enhances the contrast between dark and light areas. Most ganglion cells, in effect, compare the amount of light falling on the center of their *visual receptive fields* with that falling on the surrounding area.

Visual Pathways
The ganglion cells send action potentials out of the eye, at a point where a *blind spot* is created. Axons of ganglion cells leave the eye as a bundle of fibers called the *optic nerve;* half of these fibers cross over (creating the *optic chiasm*) and terminate in the lateral geniculate nucleus (LGN) of the thalamus. Neurons in the LGN send visual information on to the *visual cortex.*

Visual Representations
Visual form, color, movement, and distance are processed by parallel systems. Complex *feature detectors* in the visual cortex are built in hierarchical fashion out of simpler units that detect and respond to features such as lines, edges, and orientations.

Seeing Color
The color of an object depends on which of the wavelengths striking it are absorbed and which are reflected. The sensation of color has three psychological dimensions: *hue, color saturation,* and *brightness.* According to the *trichromatic* (or Young-Helmholtz) *theory,* color vision results from the fact that the eye has three types of cones, each of which is most sensitive to short, medium, or long wavelengths of light. Information from these three cone types combines to produce the sensation of color. Individuals vary in the number and sensitivity of their cone pigments. According to the *opponent-process theory,* there are red-green, blue-yellow, and black-white visual elements in the eye. Members of each pair inhibit each other so that only one member of a pair may produce a signal at a time. This theory explains color afterimages, as well as the fact that lights of complementary colors cancel each other out and produce gray when mixed together. *Colorblindness* occurs in people born with cones that are missing a color-sensitive photopigment.

Interaction of the Senses: Synesthesia
Various dimensions of vision interact, and vision can also interact with hearing and other senses in a process known as *synesthesia.* For example, some people experience certain colors when stimulated by certain letters, numbers, or sounds.

The Chemical Senses: Smell and Taste

The chemical senses include olfaction (smell) and gustation (taste).

Olfaction
Olfactory perception detects volatile chemicals that come into contact with olfactory receptors in the nose. Olfactory signals are sent to the *olfactory bulb* in the brain without passing through the thalamus. *Pheromones* are odors from an animal that change the physiology or behavior of another animal; in mammals, pheromones act through the *vomeronasal system.*

Gustation
Taste perception, or gustatory perception, detects chemicals that come into contact with taste receptors in *papillae* on the tongue. Elementary taste sensations are limited to sweet, sour, bitter, salty, umami, and astringent. The combined responses of many taste buds determine a taste sensation.

Smell, Taste, and Flavor
The senses of smell and taste interact to produce flavor.

Cutaneous Senses and the Vestibular System
The *cutaneous senses* (also called somatic senses or somatosensory systems) include the skin senses and kinesthetic perception, which tells the brain about body position. The skin senses include touch, temperature, and pain.

Touch and Temperature
Nerve endings in the skin generate touch sensations when they are stimulated. Some nerve endings are sensitive to temperature, and some respond to both temperature and touch. Signals from neighboring points on the skin stay next to one another all the way to the cortex.

Pain

Pain provides information about damaging stimuli. Sharp pain and dull, chronic pain are carried by different fibers—A-delta and C fibers, respectively. The emotional response to pain depends on how the painful stimulus is interpreted. According to the *gate control theory of pain,* incoming pain signals can be blocked by a "gate" in the spinal cord. Messages sent down the spinal cord from the brain can also block pain signals, producing *analgesia.* Endorphins and other chemicals act at several levels of the pain systems to reduce sensations of pain.

Proprioception: Sensing Body Position

Proprioceptive senses provide information about the body. The *sense of equilibrium,* or *vestibular sense,* provides information about the position of the head in space through the *otoliths* in *vestibular sacs* and the *semicircular canals,* and *kinesthetic perception* provides information through *proprioceptors* about the positions of body parts with respect to one another.

LINKAGES TO FURTHER LEARNING

Now that you have finished reading this chapter, how about exploring some of the topics and information that you found most interesting? Here are some places to start.

Books

Chandler Burr, *The Emperor of Scent* (Random House, 2003). About the perfume industry and a scientist who is testing a new theory of smell.

Richard Cytowic, *The Man Who Tasted Shapes* (MIT Press, 2003). About synesthesia, a condition in which senses are mixed.

Henry Grunwald, *Twilight: Losing Sight, Gaining Insight* (Knopf, 1999). Former editor-in-chief of *Time* magazine writes about going blind.

Michael Posner and Marcus Raichle, *Images of Mind* (Freeman, 1997). Brain imaging.

Richard L. Gregory and J. Harris (Eds.), *The Artful Eye* (Oxford University Press, 1995). Visual perception.

Richard L. Gregory and Andrew M. Colman (Eds.), *Sensation and Perception* (Longman, 1995). The senses and psychophysics.

Oliver Sacks, *The Island of the Colorblind* (Knopf, 1997). About a Pacific island where colorblindness is common.

Oliver Sacks, *The Man Who Mistook His Wife for a Hat* (Touchstone Books, 1998). Descriptions of patients with sensory and perceptual disorders.

Oliver Sacks, *Seeing Voices: A Journey into the World of the Deaf* (Vintage, 2000). How deaf people experience the world.

Roger Shepard, *Mind Sights* (Freeman, 1990). Visual illusions, ambiguous figures.

J. Richard Block and Harold Yuker, *Can You Believe Your Eyes?* (Gardner Press, 1989). More illusions and visual oddities.

On the Internet

 CourseMate Access an integrated eBook and chapter-specific learning tools including flashcards, quizzes, videos, and more. Go to CengageBrain.com.

CENGAGENOW Want to maximize the value of your online study time? Take this easy-to-use study system's diagnostic pre-test, and it will create a personalized study plan for you. By helping you identify the topics that you need to understand better and then directing you to valuable online resources, it can speed up your chapter review. CengageNOW even provides a post-test so you can confirm that you are ready for an exam. Go to CengageBrain.com.

TALKING POINTS

Here are a few talking points to help you summarize this chapter for family and friends without giving a lecture.

1. Our five senses give us a personal version of reality, so everyone experiences the world a little bit differently.
2. Our ability to see, hear, touch, taste, and smell depend on our brains' ability to decode messages about the world coming from nerve cells in our eyes, ears, and other sense organs.
3. Listening to sounds that are too loud for too long can cause partial deafness.
4. Our eyes see the world as being upside-down, but our brains flip these images so that we can see the world right-side up.
5. Nearsightedness can be worsened by excessive amounts of reading or focusing for too long on computer or cell phone screens.
6. Sense information can combine, sometimes so dramatically that people experience sounds as colors or colors as touch sensations.
7. As in other animals, chemicals called pheromones can affect humans, but they don't serve as strong sexual attractants, no matter what perfume makers suggest.
8. Everything tastes bland when you have a stuffy nose because the flavor of food is actually a combination of how it tastes and how it smells.
9. The intensity of the pain we experience depends on what is causing it but also on how we think about it.

5

Perception

© Mark Hamilton/Corbis

You are using perception right now in order to understand this sentence. Perception allows you to translate the shapes and patterns of the letters you see here and turn them into meaningful words and sentences. Without perception, you could still see the letters, but they would make no more sense than if they were written in an unfamiliar language. In this chapter, we tell you more about the amazing perceptual systems that allow you to understand what you see and hear.

At a traffic circle in Scotland, fourteen fatal accidents occurred in a single year, partly because drivers failed to slow down as they approached the circle. When warning signs failed to solve the problem, Gordon Denton, a British psychologist, proposed an ingenious solution. White lines were painted across the road leading to the circle, spaced to form a pattern that looked something like this:

/   /   /   /   /   / / /////

If drivers crossed these progressively more closely spaced lines at a constant speed, they got the impression that they were speeding up, so their automatic response was to slow down (Denton, 1980). During the fourteen months after Denton's idea was put to use, there were only two fatalities at the traffic circle. The same striping is now being used to slow drivers on roads approaching intersections and small towns in many countries, including the United States. Denton's solution to this problem relied heavily on his knowledge of the principles of human perception.

Perception is the process through which sensations are interpreted, using knowledge and understanding of the world, so that they become meaningful experiences. Perception is not a passive process of simply absorbing and decoding incoming sensations. If it were, our experience of the environment would be a constantly changing, utterly confusing mishmash of light and color. Instead, our brains take sensations and create a coherent world, often by filling in missing information and using past experience to give meaning to what we see, hear, or touch. For example, the raw sensations coming to your eyes from Figure 5.1 convey only the information that there is a series of intersecting lines. But your perceptual system automatically interprets this image as a rectangle (or window frame) on its side.

Let's first consider these perceptual processes and the various approaches that psychologists have taken in trying to understand them. We will then explore how people detect incoming sensory stimuli, organize these sensations into stable patterns, and recognize those patterns. We'll also examine the role of attention in guiding the perceptual system to analyze some parts of the world more closely than others. Finally, we provide some examples of how research on perception has been applied to some practical problems.

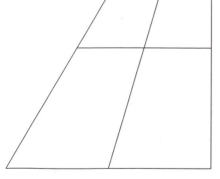

FIGURE 5.1
What Do You See?

The Perception Paradox

As in the case of drivers who find themselves slowing down in response to lines on the pavement, perception often takes place automatically, without conscious awareness. This quick and seemingly effortless aspect of perceptual processing suggests that perception is a rather simple affair. But perception contains a basic contradiction, or paradox: What is so easy for the perceiver to do has proved difficult for psychologists to understand and explain. The difficulty lies in the fact that to function so effectively and efficiently, our perceptual systems must be exceedingly complex.

FIGURE 5.2
Misperceiving Reality
Which line is longer: *AB* or *AC?* They are
exactly the same length, but you probably
perceived *AC* as longer. Understanding
why our perceptual systems make this
kind of error has helped psychologists
understand the basic principles of
perception.

To illustrate the workings of these complex systems, psychologists draw attention
to *perceptual failures,* cases in which our perceptual experience of a stimulus differs
from the actual characteristics of that stimulus. You can experience a perceptual failure
for yourself by looking at Figure 5.2. Perceptual failures provide clues to the problems
that our perception systems must solve and to the solutions they reach. Consider, for
example, why the two lines in Figure 5.2 appear to differ in length. Part of the answer
is that your visual system always tries to interpret stimuli as three-dimensional, even
when they are not. A three-dimensional interpretation of the drawing would lead you
to see the two lines as defining the edges of two parallel paths, one of which ends closer
to you than the other. Because your eyes tell you that the two paths start at about the
same point (the castle entrance), you solved the perceptual problem by assuming that
the closer line must be the longer of the two. You can remove the three-dimensional
cues by tracing the two intersecting lines onto a sheet of clear plastic and placing it
on a white surface. In this more clearly two-dimensional display, the impression of
unequal length will disappear.

TRY THIS

Three Approaches to Perception

Psychologists have taken three main approaches in their efforts to understand human
perception. The most recent of these is based on a **computational model,** which tries
to determine the calculations that a computer would have to perform to solve perceptual problems. Psychologists taking this computational approach believe that
understanding these calculations will help them explain how complex computations
within the nervous systems of humans and animals might turn raw sensory stimulation into a representation of the world. Computational theorists also hope that it
might eventually be possible to build computerized robots capable of near-human levels of perceptual skill at jobs such as bomb detection and product inspection (Thaler,
Kennedy, & Hanson, 2001). The computational model owes much to two earlier but
still influential views of perception: the constructivist approach and the ecological
approach.

Psychologists who take the **constructivist approach** argue that our perceptual
systems construct a representation of reality from fragments of sensory information.

computational model An approach
to perception that focuses on how
computations by the nervous system
translate raw sensory stimulation into an
experience of reality.

constructivist approach An approach
to perception taken by those who
argue that the perceptual system uses
fragments of sensory information to
construct an image of reality.

Is Anything Missing?

Because you know what animals look like, you perceive a whole cat in this picture even though its midsection is hidden. The constructivist approach to perception emphasizes our ability to use knowledge and expectations to fill in the gaps in incomplete objects and to perceive them as unified wholes, not disjointed parts.

© Stephen Swinburne/Stock, Boston

These psychologists are particularly interested in situations in which the same stimulus creates different perceptions in different people. As described later, for example, the optical illusion you experienced in Figure 5.2 may not be experienced by people from cultures where there is little or no experience with the objects or linear perspectives shown in the drawing (Leibowitz et al., 1969). Constructivists emphasize that our perception is strongly influenced by what we have learned from our experiences and by the expectations and inferences that those experiences create (Rock, 1983). For example, a desk might prevent you from seeing the lower half of a person seated behind it, but you still "see" the person as a complete human being. Experience tells you to expect that people remain intact even when parts of them are obscured.

Researchers influenced by the **ecological approach** to perception claim that most of our perceptual experience comes directly from the wealth of information contained in the stimuli coming to us from the environment rather than from our interpretations, inferences, and expectations. J. J. Gibson (1979), founder of the ecological approach, argued that the primary goal of perception is to support actions, such as walking, grasping, or driving, by "tuning in" to the part of the environment that is most important for performing those actions. So these researchers are less interested in our inferences about the person behind the desk than in how we would use visual information from that person, from the desk, and from other objects in the room to guide us as we walk toward a chair and sit down (Nakayama, 1994).

In summary: To explain perception, the *computational* approach focuses on the nervous system's manipulations of incoming signals, the *constructivist* approach emphasizes the inferences that people make about the environment, and the *ecological* approach emphasizes the information provided by the environment. Later, we discuss evidence in support of each of these approaches.

Psychophysics

How can psychologists measure perceptions when there is no way to get inside people's heads to experience what they are experiencing? One solution to this problem is to present people with lights, sounds, and other stimuli and ask them to report their perception of the stimuli. This method of studying perception, called **psychophysics**, describes the relationship between *physical energy* in the environment and our *psychological experience* of that energy (e.g., Purves et al., 2004).

ecological approach An approach to perception maintaining that humans and other species are so well adapted to their natural environment that many aspects of the world are perceived without requiring higher-level analysis and inferences.

psychophysics An area of research focusing on the relationship between the physical characteristics of environmental stimuli and the psychological experiences those stimuli produce.

Absolute Thresholds: Is Something Out There?

How strong must a stimulus be in order to trigger a conscious perceptual experience? Not very strong. Normal human vision can detect the light equivalent to a candle flame burning in the dark 30 miles away. The smallest amount of light, sound, pressure, or other physical energy we can detect is called the *absolute threshold* (see Table 5.1). Stimulation that is below this threshold—that is too weak or too brief for us to notice—is traditionally referred to as **subliminal stimulation**. Stimulation that is above the absolute threshold and thus consistently perceived is referred to as **supraliminal stimulation**.

If you were participating in a typical experiment to measure the absolute threshold for vision, you would sit in a darkened laboratory. After your eyes adapted to the darkness, you would be presented with a long series of brief flashes of light that varied in brightness. After each one, you would be asked if you saw a stimulus. If your absolute threshold were truly "absolute," your detection accuracy should jump from 0 to 100 percent at the exact level of brightness where your threshold is. This ideal absolute threshold is illustrated by the point at which the green line in Figure 5.3 suddenly rises. But research shows that the average of your responses over many trials would actually form a curve much like the purple line in that figure. In other words, the "absolute" threshold is not really an all-or-nothing phenomenon. Notice in Figure 5.3 that a flash

TABLE 5.1	Some Absolute Thresholds

TRY THIS Absolute thresholds can be amazingly low. Here are examples of stimulus equivalents at the absolute threshold for the five primary senses in humans. Set up the conditions for testing the absolute threshold for sound, and see if you can detect this minimal amount of auditory stimulation. If you can't hear it, the signal detection theory we discuss later in this chapter may help explain why.

Human Sense	Absolute Threshold Equivalent
Vision	A candle flame seen at 30 miles on a clear night
Hearing	The tick of a watch from 20 feet away
Taste	One teaspoon of sugar in 2 gallons of water
Smell	One drop of perfume diffused into the entire volume of air in a six-room apartment
Touch	The wing of a fly falling on your cheek from a distance of 1 centimeter

Source: Galanter (1962).

subliminal stimulation Stimulation that is too weak or brief to be perceived.

supraliminal stimulation Stimulation that is strong enough to be consistently perceived.

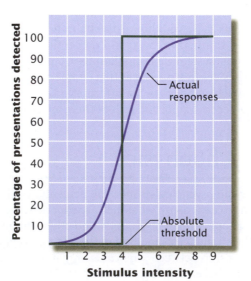

FIGURE 5.3

The Absolute Threshold

The curved line shows the relationship between the intensity of a signal and the chance that it will be detected. If the absolute threshold were truly absolute, signals at or above a particular intensity would always be detected, and signals below that intensity would never be detected (as shown by the green line). But this response pattern almost never occurs, so the "absolute" threshold is defined as the intensity at which the signal is detected 50 percent of the time.

whose brightness (intensity) is 3 is detected 20 percent of the time and missed 80 percent of the time. Is that stimulus *subliminal* or *supraliminal*? Psychologists have dealt with questions of this sort by redefining the **absolute threshold** as the smallest amount of stimulus energy that can be detected 50 percent of the time.

THINKING **CRITICALLY**

LINKAGES Can subliminal messages help you lose weight? (a link to Introducing Psychology, p. 10)

Can Subliminal Stimuli Influence Your Behavior?

In 1957, an adman named James Vicary claimed that a New Jersey theater flashed messages such as "buy popcorn" and "drink Coke" on a movie screen, too briefly to be noticed, while customers watched the movie *Picnic*. He said that these subliminal messages caused a 15 percent rise in sales of Coca-Cola and a 58 percent increase in popcorn sales. Can such "mind control" really work? Many people seem to think so: They spend millions of dollars each year on CDs and videos that promise subliminal help to lose weight, boost self-esteem, quit smoking, make more money, or achieve other goals.

What am I being asked to believe or accept?

Two types of claims have been made about subliminal stimuli. The more general claim is that subliminal stimuli can influence our behavior. The second, more specific assertion is that subliminal stimuli provide an effective means of changing people's buying habits, political opinions, self-confidence, and other complex attitudes and behaviors, with or without their awareness or consent.

What evidence is available to support the assertion?

Most evidence for the first claim—that subliminal stimuli can influence behavior in a general way—comes from research on visual perception. For example, using a method called *subliminal priming*, participants are shown clearly visible (supraliminal) stimuli, such as pictures of people, and then asked to make some sort of judgment about them. What they don't know is that each of the visible pictures is preceded by other pictures or words flashed so briefly that the participants are unaware of them. The critical question is whether the information in the subliminal stimuli influences participants' responses to the visible stimuli that follow them.

In one subliminal priming study, visible pictures of individuals were preceded by subliminal pictures that were either "positive" (e.g., happy children) or "negative" (e.g., a monster). The participants in this study judged the people in the visible pictures as more likable, polite, friendly, successful, and reputable when their pictures had been preceded by a subliminal picture that was positive rather than negative (Krosnick et al., 1992). Researchers have also found that subliminally presented words can influence decisions about the meaning of words. For example, after being exposed to subliminal presentations of a man's name (e.g., "Tom"), participants were able to decide more rapidly whether a visible stimulus (e.g., "John") was a man's or woman's name. However, the impact of the subliminally presented name lasted for only about one-tenth of a second (Greenwald, Draine, & Abrams, 1996).

Other research shows that subliminal stimuli can lead to a change in people's physiological responses. In one study, participants were exposed to subliminal photos of snakes, spiders, flowers, and mushrooms while researchers recorded their *galvanic skin resistance (GSR)*, a measure of physiological arousal. Although the slides were flashed too quickly to be perceived consciously, participants who were afraid of snakes or spiders showed increased GSR measurements (and reported fear) in response to snake and spider photos (Öhman & Soares, 1994).

The results of studies such as these support the claim that subliminal information can have at least a temporary impact on judgment and emotion, but they say little or nothing about the effects of subliminal advertising or the value of subliminal self-help programs. In fact, there is no laboratory evidence to support the alleged effectiveness of such programs. Their promoters offer only testimonials from satisfied customers.

absolute threshold The minimum amount of stimulus energy that can be detected 50 percent of the time.

Are there alternative ways of interpreting the evidence?

Many claims for subliminal advertising—including those reported in the New Jersey theater case—have turned out to be publicity stunts using phony data (Haberstroh, 1995; Pratkanis, 1992). And testimonials from satisfied customers could be biased by what these people want to believe about the subliminal recordings they bought. In one study designed to test this possibility, half the participants were told that they would be hearing tapes containing subliminal messages that would improve their memory skills. The other half were told that the subliminal messages would improve their self-esteem. However, half the participants who expected self-esteem tapes actually received memory-improvement tapes, and half the participants who expected memory-improvement tapes actually received self-esteem tapes. Regardless of which tapes they actually heard, participants who thought they had heard memory-enhancement messages reported improved memory; those who thought they had heard self-esteem messages said that their self-esteem had improved (Pratkanis, Eskenazi, & Greenwald, 1994). In other words, the effects of the tapes were determined by the listeners' expectations, not by the tapes' subliminal content. These results suggest that customers' reports about the value of subliminal self-help recordings may reflect placebo effects based on optimistic expectations rather than the effects of subliminal messages.

What additional evidence would help evaluate the alternatives?

The effectiveness of self-help tapes and other subliminal products must be evaluated through further experiments—like the one just mentioned—that carefully control for expectations. Those who advocate subliminal influence methods are responsible for conducting those experiments, but as long as customers are willing to buy subliminal products on the basis of testimonials alone, any scientific evaluation efforts will probably come only from those interested in protecting consumers from fraud.

What conclusions are most reasonable?

Scientific evidence suggests that subliminal perception does occur but that it has no potential for "mind control" (Greenwald, Klinger, & Schuh, 1995; Strahan, Spencer, & Zanna, 2005). Subliminal effects are usually small and short-lived, and they mainly affect simple judgments and general measures of overall arousal. Most researchers agree that subliminal messages have no special power to create major changes in people's needs, goals, skills, or actions (Pratkanis & Aronson, 2001; Randolph-Seng & Mather, 2009; Strahan, Spencer, & Zanna, 2005). In fact, advertisements, political speeches, and other messages that people *can* perceive consciously have far stronger persuasive effects.

Signal Detection Theory

Look again at Figure 5.3. It shows that stimuli just above and just below the absolute threshold are sometimes detected and sometimes missed. For example, a stimulus at intensity level 3 appears to be subliminal, even though you will perceive it 20 percent of the time; a stimulus at level 5 is above threshold, but it will be missed 20 percent of the time. Why should the "absolute" threshold vary this way? The two most important reasons have to do with sensitivity and our response criterion.

Sensitivity refers to our ability to pick out a particular stimulus, or *signal*. Sensitivity is influenced by the intensity of the signal (stronger ones are easier to detect), the power of our sensory systems (good vision or hearing makes us more sensitive), and the amount of background stimulation, or *noise,* arriving at the same time. Some noise comes from outside the person, as when electrical equipment hums or overhead lights flicker. There is also noise coming from the spontaneous, random firing of cells in our own nervous systems. A varying amount of this *internal noise* is always occurring, whether or not we are stimulated by physical energy. You might think of it as a little like the "snow" on an unused television channel or static between radio stations.

sensitivity The ability to detect a stimulus.

Detecting Vital Signals

According to signal detection theory, the likelihood that airport security screeners will detect the outline of a bomb or other weapon in body scans or on X-rays of a passenger's luggage depends partly on the sensitivity of their visual systems and partly on their response criterion. That criterion is affected by their expectations that weapons might appear and by how motivated they are to look carefully for them. Airport security officials occasionally attempt to smuggle a simulated weapon through a checkpoint. This procedure serves to evaluate the inspectors' performance but also to improve it by keeping their response criterion low enough to avoid missing real weapons (Fleck & Mitroff, 2007; McCarley et al., 2004; Wolfe et al., 2007).

© John Tlumacki/Boston Globe/Landov

The second source of variation in absolute threshold comes from the **response criterion**, which reflects our willingness to say that a particular stimulus is a signal rather than noise. Motivation—our wants and needs—as well as expectancies affect the response criterion. Suppose that you work at an airport security checkpoint, where you spend hours looking at passenger body scans or X-ray images of their handbags, briefcases, and luggage. The signal to be detected in this situation is a weapon or bomb, whereas the "noise" consists of all the harmless objects appearing on the viewing screen. If there has been a recent terrorist attack or if the threat level has just been elevated, your airport will be on special alert. Accordingly, your response criterion will be lower, meaning that a questionable object that you might previously have allowed to pass will now lead you to investigate further. In other words, expecting a signal makes it more likely that you will detect it than if it is unexpected.

Once researchers understood that detecting a signal depends on a combination of each person's sensitivity and response criterion, they realized that the measurement of absolute thresholds could never be more precise than the 50 percent rule mentioned earlier. So they abandoned the notion of absolute thresholds and focused instead on **signal detection theory**, a mathematical model of how each person's sensitivity and response criterion combine to determine decisions about whether or not a near-threshold stimulus has occurred (Green & Swets, 1966).

As in a threshold experiment, a psychologist using signal detection theory would analyze your responses to a series of trials on which lights (or sounds) may or may not be presented. The lights would be so faint that you would find it hard to tell whether a signal occurred or whether there was only background "noise." Your response on each trial would be placed into one of four categories: a false alarm, a miss, a hit, or a correct rejection. A *false alarm* is an error that occurs when external or internal noise is high enough to make you report a signal when no signal was presented. If a signal occurs but is so faint that it does not produce enough stimulation for you to detect it, you will have made an error known as a *miss*. A person with a more sensitive sensory system might have correctly detected that same stimulus when it occurred—which is called a *hit*. If no signal occurs and you don't report one, you will have made a *correct rejection*.

By analyzing the pattern of hits, misses, false alarms, and correct rejections, research based on signal detection theory allows precise measurement of people's sensitivity to stimuli of any kind. It also provides a way to understand and predict people's responses in a wide range of situations (MacMillan & Creelman, 2004; Swets, 1996).

Consider tornado warnings. Signal detection theory can help us understand why, even with the latest Doppler radar systems, weather forecasters sometimes fail to warn of a tornado that local residents can clearly see. The forecasters' task is not easy, because their radar systems are so sensitive that they don't just detect a tornado's spinning funnel but also harmless patterns created by swirling dust and swarming insects. So even a tornado's telltale radar "signature" will appear against a potentially confusing background of visual "noise." Whether or not that signature will be picked

response criterion The internal rule a person uses to decide whether or not to report a stimulus.

signal detection theory A mathematical model of what determines a person's report that a near-threshold stimulus has or has not occurred.

FIGURE 5.4
Signal Detection

Part A shows the possible outcomes of examining a weather radar display: a *hit* (correctly detecting a tornado), a *miss* (failing to detect a tornado), a *correct rejection* (seeing no tornado when there is none), or a *false alarm* (reporting a tornado when none existed). The rest of the figure illustrates the impact of two different response criteria: Part B represents outcomes of a high response criterion, which would be set under conditions when tornadoes are expected only half the time; part C represents outcomes of a low response criterion, which would be set under conditions when tornadoes are very likely to appear.

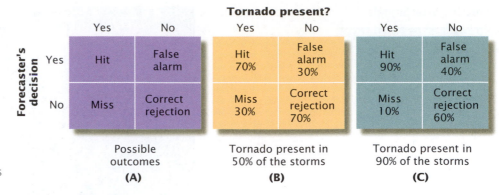

out and reported depends both on the forecaster's sensitivity to the signal and on the response criterion being used. In establishing the criterion for sounding a warning, the forecaster must consider the consequences. If the response criterion is too low and warnings are issued at the slightest hint of a tornado, there would surely be false alarms that would unnecessarily disrupt people's lives, activate costly emergency plans, and even lead people to ignore future warnings. But setting the criterion too high, so that warnings occur only when the forecaster is certain of a tornado, could allow a dangerous storm to go unreported. Such a miss could cost many lives if it left a populated area with no warning of danger (see Figure 5.4). In other words, there is a trade-off. To minimize false alarms, the forecaster could set a very high response criterion, but doing so would also make misses more likely.

Let's examine how various kinds of expectations or assumptions can change the response criterion and how those changes might affect the accuracy of a forecaster's decisions. If a forecaster knows it's a time of year when tornadoes occur in only about 50 percent of the storm systems seen on radar, a rather high response criterion would be appropriate. That is, it will take relatively strong evidence to trigger a tornado warning. The hypothetical data in part B of Figure 5.4 show that under these conditions, the forecaster correctly detected 70 percent of actual tornadoes but missed 30 percent of them. Also, 30 percent of the tornado reports were false alarms. Now suppose that the forecaster learns that a different kind of storm system is on the way and that about 90 percent of such systems spawn tornadoes. This information is likely to increase the forecaster's expectation that a tornado signature will appear, thus lowering the response criterion. The forecaster will now require less evidence of a tornado before reporting one. Under these conditions, as shown in part C of Figure 5.4, the hit rate might rise from 70 percent to, say, 90 percent, but the false-alarm rate might also increase from 30 percent to 40 percent.

The hit rate and false-alarm rate will also be affected by the forecaster's sensitivity to tornado signals. Forecasters with greater sensitivity to these signals will have high hit rates and low false-alarm rates. Those with less sensitivity are still likely to have high hit rates, but their false-alarm rates will be higher, too.

Psychologists' research on signal detection theory helps us understand why people sometimes make mistakes at spotting tornadoes, inspecting luggage, diagnosing medical conditions, searching for oil, or looking for clues at a crime scene. That research is also being applied to improve people's performance on these kinds of signal detection tasks. For example, psychologists recommend that manufacturers occasionally place flawed items among a batch of objects to be inspected. This strategy increases inspectors' expectations of seeing flaws, thus lowering their response criterion and raising their hit rate.

Judging Differences: Has Anything Changed?

Sometimes our perceptual task is not to detect a faint stimulus but rather to notice small differences as a stimulus changes or to judge whether there are differences between two stimuli. For example, when tuning up, musicians must focus on whether the notes played by two instruments are the same or different. When evaluating a

Perfect!

This chef's ability to taste the difference in his culinary creation before and after he has adjusted the seasonings depends on the same psychophysical laws that apply to judging differences in sights, sounds, and other sensory stimuli.

body shop's repair work, you must judge whether the color of the newly painted section matches the rest of your car. And you have to decide if your soup tastes any spicier after you have added some pepper.

Your ability to judge differences between stimuli depends partly on the strength of the stimuli you are dealing with. The weaker the stimuli are, the easier it is to detect small differences between them. For example, if you are comparing the weight of two envelopes, you will be able to detect a difference of as little as a fraction of an ounce. But if you are comparing two boxes weighing around 50 pounds each, you may not notice a difference unless it is a pound or more.

The smallest difference between stimuli that we can detect is called the *difference threshold* or **just-noticeable difference (JND)**. How small is that difference? The size of a JND is described by one of the oldest laws in psychology. Named after the nineteenth-century German physiologist Ernst Weber (pronounced "VAY-bur"), **Weber's law** states that the smallest detectable difference in stimulus energy is a constant fraction of the intensity of the stimulus. This fraction, often called *Weber's constant* or Weber's fraction, is given the symbol K. As shown in Table 5.2, K is different for each of the senses. The smaller K is, the more sensitive a sense is to stimulus differences.

Specifically, Weber's law says that $JND = KI$, where K is the Weber's constant for a particular sense and I is the amount, or intensity, of the stimulus. To compute the JND for a particular stimulus, we must know its intensity and what sense it is stimulating. For example, as shown in Table 5.2, the value of K for weight is .02. If an object weighs 25 pounds (I), the JND is only half a pound (.02 × 25 pounds). So while carrying a 25-pound bag of groceries, you would have to add or remove half a pound before you would be able to detect a change in its weight. But candy snatchers beware: It takes a change of only two-thirds of an ounce to determine that someone has been into a 2-pound box of chocolates!

Weber's constants vary somewhat among individuals, and as we get older, we tend to become less sensitive to stimulus differences. There are exceptions to this rule, however. If you like candy, you will be happy to know that Weber's fraction for sweetness stays fairly constant throughout life (Gilmore & Murphy, 1989). Weber's law does not hold when stimuli are very intense or very weak, but it does apply to complex, as well as simple, stimuli. We all tend to have our own personal Weber's fractions that describe how much prices can increase before we notice or worry about the change. For example, if your Weber's fraction for cost is .10, then you would surely notice, and perhaps protest, a 50-cent increase in a $1 bus fare. But the same 50-cent increase in monthly rent would be less than a JND and thus unlikely to cause much notice or concern.

Magnitude Estimation: How Intense Is That?

How much would you have to turn up the volume on your stereo to make it sound twice as loud as your neighbor's? How much would you have to turn it down to make it sound only half as loud as it was before your neighbor complained? These are

just-noticeable difference (JND) The smallest detectable difference in stimulus energy.

Weber's law A law stating that the smallest detectable difference in stimulus energy is a constant fraction of the intensity of the stimulus.

TABLE 5.2	Weber's Fraction *(K)* for Different Stimuli	
The value of Weber's fraction, *K*, differs from one sense to another. Differences in *K* demonstrate the adaptive nature of perception. Humans, who depend more heavily on vision than on taste for survival, are more sensitive to vision than to taste.	**Stimulus**	**K**
	Pitch	.003
	Brightness	.017
	Weight	.02
	Odor	.05
	Loudness	.10
	Pressure on skin	.14
	Saltiness of taste	.20

questions about *magnitude estimation*—about how our perception of stimulus intensity is related to the actual strength of the stimulus. In 1860, Gustav Fechner used Weber's law to study the relationship between the physical magnitude of a stimulus and its *perceived* magnitude. He reasoned that if just-noticeable differences get progressively larger as stimulus magnitude increases, then the amount of change in the stimulus required to double or triple its perceived intensity must get larger too. He was right. For example, it takes only a small increase in volume to make a soft sound seem twice as loud, but imagine how much additional volume it would take to make a rock band seem twice as loud. To put it another way, constant increases in physical energy will produce progressively smaller increases in perceived magnitude. This observation, when expressed as a mathematical equation relating actual stimulus intensity to perceived intensity, became known as *Fechner's law.*

Fechner's law applies to most, but not all, stimuli. For example, it takes larger and larger increases in light or sound to create the same amount of change in perceived magnitude, but this is not the case for stimuli such as electric shock. It takes a relatively large increase in shock intensity to make a weak shock seem twice as intense, but if the shock is already painful, it takes only a small increase in intensity before you would perceive it as twice as strong. Stanley Smith Stevens offered a formula (known as *Stevens's power law*) for magnitude estimation that works for a wider array of stimuli, including electric shock, temperature, and sound and light intensity. Stevens's law is still used today by psychologists who want to determine how much larger, louder, longer, or more intense a stimulus must be for people to perceive a specific difference or amount of change.

Overall, people do well at estimating differences between stimuli. For example, we are very good at estimating how much longer one line is than another. Yet as shown in Figure 5.2, this perceptual comparison process can be disrupted when the lines are embedded in more complex figures (Figure 5.5 offers some additional examples). The perceptual laws that we have discussed, and the exceptions to these laws, all emphasize a fundamental principle: Perception is a relative process. Our experience of one stimulus depends on its relationship to others. In the next section, on perceptual

FIGURE 5.5
Length Illusions
People can usually estimate the relative length of lines very accurately, but this ability can be impaired under certain conditions. The pairs of lines marked *A* and *B* are the same length in each drawing, but most people report that line *A* appears longer than line *B*. These optical illusions, like the one in Figure 5.2, occur partly because of our tendency to see two-dimensional figures as three-dimensional. With the exception of the top hat, all or part of line *A* in each drawing can easily be interpreted as being farther away than line *B*. When two equal-size objects appear to be at different distances, the visual system tends to infer that the more distant object must be larger.

Source: From J.P. Frisby, *Seeing: Illusion, Brain, and Mind,* 1979, p. 14. Reprinted by permission of Oxford University Press.

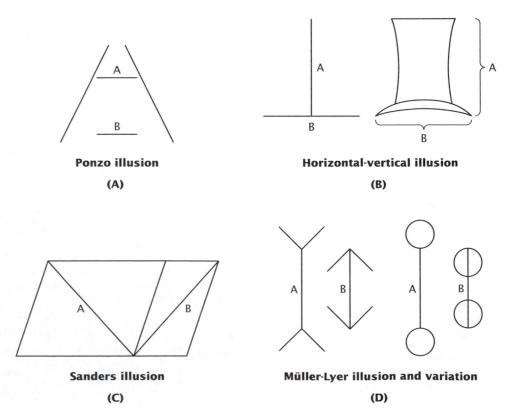

Ponzo illusion
(A)

Horizontal-vertical illusion
(B)

Sanders illusion
(C)

Müller-Lyer illusion and variation
(D)

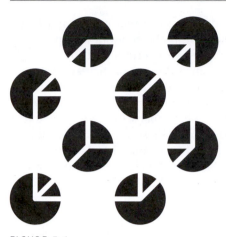

FIGURE 5.6
Organize This!

TRY THIS Psychologists have employed the principles of figure-ground organization and grouping to help explain how your visual system allows you to perceive these disconnected lines as a cube, to see it from above or below, and to see it as being either on the page or "behind" it.

perceptual organization The task of determining what edges and other stimuli go together to form an object.

figure ground discrimination The ability to organize a visual scene so that it contains meaningful figures set against a less relevant ground.

organization, we discuss what researchers have learned about the way in which our perceptual system relates one stimulus to another.

Organizing the Perceptual World

To further appreciate the wonder of the complicated perceptual work you do every day, imagine yourself driving on a busy road searching for Barney's Diner, an unfamiliar restaurant where you are supposed to meet a friend. The roadside is crammed with signs of all shapes and colors, some flashing and some rotating. If you are ever to recognize the sign that says "Barney's Diner," you must impose some sort of organization on this overwhelming mixture of visual information. How do you do this? How do you know where one sign ends and another begins? And how do you know that an apparently tiny sign is not really tiny but just far away?

Perceptual organization is the task performed by the perceptual system to determine what edges and other stimuli go together to form an object (Peterson & Rhodes, 2003). In this case, the object would be the sign for Barney's Diner. It is perceptual organization, too, that makes it possible for you to separate the sign from its background of lights, colors, letters, and other competing stimuli. Figure 5.6 shows some of the ways in which your perceptual system can organize stimuli. The figure appears as a hollow cube, but notice that you can see it from two angles: either looking down at the top of the cube or looking up toward the bottom of the cube. Notice, too, that the "cube" is not really a cube at all but rather a series of unconnected arrows and *Y*'s. Your perceptual system organizes these elements into a cube by creating imaginary connecting lines called *subjective contours*. That system can also change the apparent location of the cube. You probably first saw it as "floating" in front of a background of large black dots, but those dots can also become "holes" through which you see the cube against a solid black background "behind" the page. It may take a little time to see this second perceptual organization, but when you do, notice that the subjective contours you saw earlier are gone. They disappear because your perceptual system adjusts for the fact that when an object is partially obscured, we should not be able to see all of it.

Basic Processes in Perceptual Organization

To explain phenomena such as these and to understand the way our perceptual systems organize more naturalistic scenes, psychologists have focused on two basic processes: *figure ground discrimination* and *grouping*.

Figure Ground Discrimination When you look at a complex scene or listen to a noisy environment, your perceptual apparatus automatically emphasizes certain features, objects, or sounds; all other stimuli in that environment become the background. So as you drive toward an intersection, a stop sign stands out clearly against the background of trees, houses, and cars. This is an example of **figure ground discrimination**. A *figure,* as the part of the visual field that has meaning, stands in front of the rest and always seems to include the contours or edges that separate it from the less relevant *ground,* or background. As described in the chapter on sensation, edges are one of the most basic features detected by our visual system; they combine to form figures.

To experience how your perceptual system creates figure and ground, look at the drawings in Figure 5.7. These drawings are called *reversible figures* because you can repeatedly reverse your perceptual organization of what is figure and what is ground. Your ability to do this shows that perception is not only an active process but also a categorical one. People usually organize sensory stimulation into one perceptual category or another, but rarely into both or into something in between. In Figure 5.7, for instance, you cannot easily see both faces and a vase or the words *figure* and *ground* at the same time.

GROUND

(A)

(B)

FIGURE 5.7
Reversible Images

TRY THIS *Reversible images* can be organized by your perceptual system in two ways. If you perceive part A as the word *figure,* the space around the letters becomes meaningless background. Now emphasize the word *ground,* and what had stood out a moment ago now becomes background. In part B, when you emphasize the white vase, the two black profiles become background; if you organize the faces as the figure, what had been a vase now becomes background.

FIGURE 5.8
Gestalt Principles of Perceptual Grouping

We tend to perceive part A as two groups of two circles plus two single circles, rather than as, say, six single circles. In part B, we tend to see two columns of X's and two columns of O's, not four rows of XOXO. We see the X in part C as made out of two continuous lines, not a combination of the odd forms shown. We perceive the disconnected segments of part D as a triangle and a circle. In part E, we tend to pair up dots in the same oval even though they are far apart. Part F shows that connected objects are grouped together.

Grouping To distinguish figure from ground, our perceptual system must first identify stimulus elements in the environment, such as the edges of a stop sign or billboard, that belong together as figures. But why is it that certain parts of the world become figure and others become ground, even when nothing in particular stands out in the pattern of light that falls on the retina? The answer is that certain properties of stimuli lead us to group them together more or less automatically. In the early 1900s, several German psychologists began to study how this happens. They concluded that people perceive sights and sounds as organized wholes. These wholes, they said, are different from the sum of individual sensations, much as a house is something other than just a pile of bricks and wood and glass. Because the German word meaning (roughly) "whole figure" is *Gestalt* (pronounced "guh-SHTAHLT"), these researchers became known as *Gestalt psychologists.* They proposed a number of principles, or "Gestalt laws," that describe how perceptual systems group stimuli into a world of shapes and objects (Kimchi, 2003). Some of the most enduring of these principles are the following:

1. *Proximity.* The closer objects or events are to one another, the more likely we are to perceive them as belonging together, as part A of Figure 5.8 illustrates.

2. *Similarity.* We tend to perceive similar elements as part of a group, as in part B of Figure 5.8.

3. *Continuity.* When sensations appear to create a continuous form, we tend to perceive them as belonging together, as in part C of Figure 5.8.

4. *Closure.* We tend to fill in missing contours to form a complete object, as in part D of Figure 5.8. The gaps are easy to see, but as illustrated in Figure 5.6, the tendency to fill in missing contours can be so strong that you may see faint connections that are not really there (Lleras & Moore, 2006).

5. *Texture.* When basic features of stimuli have the same texture (such as the angle of several elements), we tend to group those stimuli together. So we group standing trees together and perceive them as separate from their fallen neighbors.

6. *Simplicity.* We tend to group features of a stimulus in a way that provides the simplest interpretation of the world. You can see the simplicity principle in action in Figure 5.6, where it is simpler to see a single cube than an assortment of separate and unrelated arrows and Y's.

7. *Common fate.* When objects are moving in the same direction at the same speed, we tend to perceived them as being together. So even though individual birds in a flock are separated from each other in space, they will be perceived as a group as they fly south. Choreographers use the principle of common fate when they arrange for groups or subgroups of dancers to move in unison, creating the illusion of waves of motion or of a single object moving across the stage.

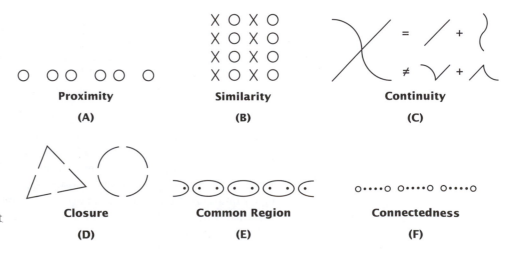

Proximity	Similarity	Continuity
(A)	**(B)**	**(C)**
Closure	Common Region	Connectedness
(D)	**(E)**	**(F)**

Common Fate

When a set of objects move together, we see them as a group or even as a single large object. Marching band directors put this perceptual grouping process to good use. By arranging for musicians to move together, they make it appear as though huge letters and other large "objects" are in motion on the field during half-time shows at college football games.

© John Summers II/Reuters/Landov

Stephen Palmer (1999) has introduced three additional grouping principles:

1. *Synchrony.* When different stimuli occur at the same time, we are likely to perceive them as belonging together. For example, if you see a car up ahead stop violently at the same instant you hear a crash, you will probably perceive these visual and auditory stimuli as part of the same event.

2. *Common region.* When stimulus elements are located within some boundary, we tend to perceive them as being together. The boundary can be created by an enclosing perimeter, as in part E of Figure 5.8; a region of color; or other factors.

3. *Connectedness.* When stimulus elements are connected by other elements, we tend to group them together. Part F of Figure 5.8 demonstrates how important this law is. The circles connected by dotted lines seem to go together even though they are farther apart than some pairs of unconnected circles. In this situation, the principle of connectedness appears more important than the principle of proximity.

Why do we organize the world according to these grouping principles? One answer is that they reflect the way stimuli are likely to be organized in the natural world. Nearby elements are in fact more likely than separated elements to be part of the same object. Stimulus elements moving in the same direction at the same rate are also likely to be part of the same object. Your initial impression of the cube in Figure 5.6 reflects this *likelihood principle* in action. At first glance, you probably saw the cube as being below you rather than above you. This tendency makes adaptive sense, because boxes and other cube-shaped objects are more likely to be on the ground than hanging in midair.

The likelihood principle is consistent with both the ecological and constructivist approaches to perception. From the ecological perspective, the likelihood principle evolved because it worked, giving our ancestors reliable information about how the world is likely to be organized and thus increasing their chances of survival. Constructivists point out, however, that our personal experiences in the world also help determine the likelihood of interpreting a stimulus in one way over another. The likelihood principle operates automatically and accurately most of the time. As shown in Figure 5.9, however, when we try using it to organize very *unlikely* stimuli, it can lead to frustrating misperceptions.

Perception of Location and Distance

One of the most important perceptual tasks we face is to determine where objects and sound sources are located. This task involves knowing both their two-dimensional position (left or right, up or down) and their distance from us.

FIGURE 5.9
Impossible Objects

TRY THIS These objects can exist as two-dimensional drawings, but could they exist in three-dimensional space? When you try to use the likelihood principle to organize them as the three-dimensional objects you expect them to be, you'll discover that they are "impossible."

LINKAGES Can information from one sense override information from another? (a link to Sensation, p. 153)

© AP Photo

A Case of Depth Misperception

The runner in this photo is actually farther away than the man on the pitcher's mound. But because he is lower, not higher, in the visual field—and because it is easy to misperceive his leg as being in front of, not behind, the pitcher's leg—the runner appears smaller than normal rather than farther away (Vecera, Vogel, & Woodman, 2002).

depth perception The ability to perceive distance.

interposition A depth cue whereby closer objects block one's view of things farther away.

Two-Dimensional Location   Determining whether an object is to your right or your left appears to be simple. All the perceptual system has to do, it seems, is determine where the object's image falls on the retina. If the image falls on the center of the retina, then the object must be straight ahead. But when an object is, say, far to your right, and you focus its image on the center of your retina by turning your head and eyes toward it, you do not assume it is straight ahead. According to the computational approach, your brain calculates an estimate of the object's location by combining information about where an image strikes the retina with information about the movement of your eyes and head.

As mentioned in the chapter on sensation, localization of sounds depends on cues about differences in the information received by each of your ears. Sound waves coming toward the right side of your head will reach the right ear before reaching the left ear. Similarly, a sound coming toward the right side of your head will seem a little bit louder to the right ear than to the left ear, because your head blocks some of the sound to the left ear. The brain uses these slight differences in the timing and the intensity of a sound as cues to locate its source. Visual cues are often integrated with auditory cues to determine the exact identity and location of the sound source. Most often, information from the eyes and the ears converges on the same likely sound source. However, there are times when the two senses produce conflicting impressions; in such cases, we tend to believe our eyes rather than our ears. This bias toward using visual information is known as *visual dominance*. The phenomenon is illustrated by our impression that the sound of a television program is coming from the screen rather than the speaker. **TRY THIS** Next time you hear someone talking on television, close your eyes. If your TV set has a single speaker below or to the side of the screen, you will notice that the sound no longer seems to be coming from the screen but rather from the speaker itself. As soon as you open your eyes, the false impression resumes; words once again seem to come from the obvious visual source of the sound—the person on the screen.

Depth Perception   One of the oldest puzzles in psychology relates to **depth perception**, our ability to perceive distance. How are we able to experience the world in three-dimensional depth even though the visual information we receive from it is projected onto two-dimensional retinas? The answer lies in the many *depth cues* provided by the environment and by certain properties of our visual system (B. L. Anderson, 2004).

To some extent, people perceive depth through the same cues that artists use to create the impression of depth and distance on a two-dimensional canvas. Figure 5.10 illustrates several of these cues:

- One of the most important depth cues is **interposition**, or *occlusion:* Closer objects block the view of things farther away. This cue is illustrated in Figure 5.10 by the couple walking away from the camera. Because their bodies block out part of the buildings, we perceive them as being closer to us than the buildings are.

- You can see the principle of *relative size* operating in Figure 5.10 by measuring the image of that same couple and comparing it to the size of the man in the foreground. If two objects are assumed to be about the same size, the object producing a larger image on the retina is perceived as closer than the one producing a smaller image.

- Another cue comes from *height in the visual field:* On the ground, more distant objects are usually higher in the visual field than those nearby. Because the building in the center of Figure 5.10 is higher than the people in the restaurant, the building appears to be farther away from you. This is one reason why objects higher in the visual field are more likely to be interpreted as the background for objects that are lower in a scene (Vecera, Vogel, & Woodman, 2002).

- The tiny figures near the center of Figure 5.10 are seen as very far away because they are near a point where the buildings on each edge of the plaza, like all parallel lines that recede into the distance, appear to converge toward a single point. This

FIGURE 5.10
Stimulus Cues for Depth Perception

TRY THIS See if you can identify the cues of relative size, interposition, linear perspective, height in the visual field, gradient of texture, and shadows that combine to create a sense of three-dimensional depth in this photograph. Notice, too, that sidewalk artist Kurt Wenner has used some of these same cues to create a dramatic illusion of depth in his drawing. (You can see more of Wenner's amazing work at www.kurtwenner.com/street.)

Dies Irae, Copyright © Kurt Wenner, 1988

apparent convergence provides a cue called **linear perspective**. The closer together two converging lines are, the greater the perceived distance. So objects that are nearer the point of convergence are seen as farther away.

- Notice that the street in Figure 5.10 fades into a hazy background. Increased distance usually produces less clarity, and this *reduced clarity* is interpreted as a cue for greater distance. (Hazy, distant objects also tend to take on a bluish tone, which is why art students are taught to add a little blue when mixing paint for deep background features.)

- *Light and shadow* also contribute to the perception of three dimensions (Kingdom, 2003; Ramachandran, 1988). The buildings in Figure 5.10 are seen as three-dimensional, not flat, because of the shadows on some of their surfaces. Figure 5.11 shows a more dramatic example.

- An additional depth cue comes from continuous changes across the visual field, called *gradients*. For example, a **gradient of texture** is a graduated change in the texture, or "grain," of the visual field, as you can see in the plaza and the street in Figure 5.10. Texture appears finer and less detailed as distance increases. So as the texture of a surface changes across the retinal image, you perceive a change in distance.

An important visual depth cue that cannot be demonstrated in Figure 5.10, or in any other still image, comes from motion. You may have noticed, for example, that when you look out the side window of a moving car, objects nearer to you seem to speed across your visual field, whereas objects in the distance seem to move slowly, if at all. This difference in the apparent rate of movement is called **motion parallax**, and it provides cues to differences in the distance of various objects.

Several additional depth cues result from the way human eyes are built and positioned. As mentioned in the chapter on sensation, for example, the eye's lens changes shape, or *accommodates*, bending light rays and focusing images on the retina. To accomplish this task, muscles surrounding the lens either tighten, to make the lens more curved for focusing on close objects, or relax, to flatten the lens for focusing on

linear perspective A depth cue whereby objects closer to the point at which two lines appear to converge are perceived as being at a greater distance.

gradient of texture A graduated change in the texture, or grain, of the visual field, whereby objects with finer, less detailed textures are perceived as more distant.

motion parallax A depth cue whereby a difference in the apparent rate of movement of different objects provides information about the relative distance of those objects.

FIGURE 5.11
Light, Shadow, and Depth Perception

TRY THIS The shadows cast by these protruding rivets and deep dents make it easy to see them in three dimensions. But if you turn the book upside down, the rivets now look like dents and the dents look like bumps. This reversal in depth perception occurs partly because we normally assume that illumination comes from above and interpret the pattern of light and shadow accordingly (Adams, Graf, & Ernst, 2004). With the picture upside down, light coming from the top would produce the observed pattern of shadows only if the circles were dents, not rivets.

TRY THIS

ocular accommodation The ability of the lens of the eye to change its shape and bend light rays so that objects are in focus.

eye convergence A depth cue involving the rotation of the eyes to project the image of an object on each retina.

retinal disparity A depth cue based on the difference between two retinal images of the world.

A Gradient of Texture

The details of a scene fade gradually as distance increases. This gradient of texture helps us perceive the less detailed birds in this photo as being farther away.

more distant objects. Information about this muscle activity is relayed to the brain, providing an **ocular accommodation** cue that helps create the perception of an object's distance.

The relative location of our two eyes produces two other depth cues. The first is called **eye convergence**. Because the eyes are located a short distance apart, they must converge, or rotate inward, to project an object's image on each retina. The brain receives information about this movement from the eye muscles and uses it to help calculate an object's distance. The closer the object, the more the eyes must converge, which sends more intense stimulation to the brain. Focusing on more distant objects requires less convergence and creates less feedback from the eye muscles. To experience feedback from your eye muscles, hold up a finger at arm's length and try to keep it in focus as you move it toward your nose.

Second, because of their differing locations, each eye receives a slightly different view of the world. The difference between the two retinal images of an object is called **retinal disparity**, or *binocular disparity*. For any particular object, this difference gets smaller as distance increases. To see for yourself how retinal disparity changes with distance, hold a pencil vertically about 6 inches in front of your nose; then close one

© Rod Planck/NHPA/Photoshot

TRY THIS eye and notice where the pencil is in relation to the background. Now open that eye, close the other one, and notice how much the pencil "shifts." These are the two different views your eyes have of the pencil. Repeat the procedure while holding the pencil at arm's length. There is now less disparity or "shift," because there is now less difference in the angles from which your two eyes see the pencil. The brain not only combines the two images of an object but also takes into account how much they differ. This information helps generate the impression of a single object that has depth as well as height and width and is located at a particular distance. Three-dimensional movies and some virtual reality systems use these binocular cues to create the appearance of depth in a two-dimensional stimulus. They show each eye an image of a scene as viewed from a slightly different angle.

The wealth of depth cues available to us is consistent with the ecological approach to perception. However, researchers taking the constructivist and computational approaches argue that even when temporarily deprived of these depth cues, we can still move about and locate objects in an environment. In one study, for example, participants viewed an object from a particular place in a room. Then, with their eyes closed, they were guided to a point well to the side of the object and asked to walk toward it from this new position. The participants were amazingly accurate at this task, leading the researchers to suggest that seeing an object at a particular point in space creates a spatial model in our minds—a model that remains intact even when immediate depth cues are removed.

Perception of Motion

Sometimes the most important thing about an object is not its size or shape or distance but its motion—how fast it is going and where it is heading. For example, a car in front of you may change speed or direction, requiring that you change your own speed or direction, often in a split second.

As with the detection of location and depth, your brain "tunes in" to a host of cues to perceive changes in motion. Many of these cues come from *optical flow,* or the changes in retinal images across the entire visual field. One particularly meaningful pattern of optical flow is known as **looming**, the rapid expansion in the size of an image so that it fills the retina. When an image looms, you tend to interpret it as an approaching stimulus. Your perceptual system quickly assesses whether the expansion on the retina is about equal in all directions or greater to one side than to the other. If there is more expansion to the right, for example, it means that the approaching stimulus will pass to your right. If the retinal expansion is approximately equal in all directions, though, it means that the object is coming straight for your eyes. In other words, you had better duck!

Two questions have been of particular interest to psychologists who study motion perception. First, how do we know whether the flow of images across the retina is due to the movement of objects in the environment or to our own movements? If changes in retinal images were the only factor contributing to motion perception, then moving your eyes would create the perception that everything in the visual field was moving. This is not the case, though, because, as noted earlier, the brain also receives and **TRY THIS** processes information about the motion of your eyes and head. If you look around right now, tables, chairs, and other stationary objects will not appear to move. That's because your brain determines that all the movement of images on your retinas is due to your eye and head movements (Goltz et al., 2003). But now close one eye and wiggle your open eyeball by gently pushing your lower eyelid. Because your brain receives no signals that your eye is being moved by its own muscles, everything around you will appear to move.

A second question about motion perception relates to the fact that there is a delay of about one-twentieth of a second between the moment when an image is registered on your retina and the moment when information about that image reaches your brain. In theory, each moment's perception of, say, a dog running toward you

looming A motion cue involving a rapid expansion in the size of an image so that it fills the retina.

is actually a perception of where the dog was about one-twentieth of a second earlier. How does the perceptual system deal with this time lag so as to accurately interpret information about an object's motion and location? Psychologists have found that when a stimulus is moving along a relatively constant path, the brain corrects for the image delay by predicting where the stimulus should be one-twentieth of a second in the future (Nijhawan, 1997).

Motion perception is of special interest to sport psychologists. They try to understand, for example, why some individuals are so good at perceiving motion. One team of British psychologists discovered a number of cues and computations apparently used by "expert catchers." In catching a ball, these individuals seem to be especially sensitive to the angle between their "straight ahead" gaze and the gaze used when looking up at a moving ball. Their task is to move the body continuously, and often quickly, to make sure that this "gaze angle" never becomes too small (such that the ball falls in front of them) or too large (such that the ball sails overhead). In other words, these catchers appear to unconsciously use a specific mathematical rule: "Keep the tangent of the angle of gaze elevation to zero" (McLeod, Reed, & Dienes, 2003).

LINKAGES Can the senses be fooled? (a link to Sensation, p. 153)

Sometimes we perceive motion when there is none. Psychologists are interested in these motion illusions because they can tell us something about how the brain processes various kinds of movement-related information. When you accelerate in a car, for example, the experience of motion doesn't come just from the flow of visual information across your retinas. It also comes from touch information as you are pressed against the seat and from vestibular information as your head tilts backward. If a visual flow suggests that you are moving but you don't receive appropriate sensations from other parts of your body, particularly the vestibular senses, you may experience a nauseating movement illusion. This explains why you might feel queasy while in a motion simulator or playing certain video games, especially those with virtual reality technology. The images suggest that you are moving through space when there is no real motion.

Other illusions of motion are more enjoyable. The most important of these occurs when still images appear, one at a time, in rapid succession, as they do on films, videos, and DVDs. Because each image differs slightly from the preceding one, the brain sees the people and objects in each image appearing in one place for only a fraction of a second before they disappear and then immediately reappear in a slightly different location. The entertaining result is the **stroboscopic illusion**; when objects appear, disappear, and then quickly reappear nearby, you perceive them as moving smoothly from the first location to the next. The same illusion occurs when flashing lights on a theater or casino sign seem to move around the sign. Stroboscopic motion is based on the organizing principles of likelihood and simplicity. Objects in the world do not usually disappear, only to be immediately replaced by a similar object nearby. Accordingly, your brain makes the simpler and more likely assumption that a disappearing and reappearing object has moved.

Perceptual Constancy

TRY THIS

Suppose that one sunny day you are watching someone walking toward you along a tree-lined sidewalk. The visual sensations produced by this person are actually rather strange. For one thing, the size of the image on your retinas keeps getting larger as the person gets closer. To see this for yourself, hold your hand out at arm's length and look at someone far away. The retinal image of that person will be so small that your hand can easily cover it. If you do the same when the person is 3 feet away, the retinal image will be much larger than your hand, but you will perceive the person as being closer now, not bigger. Similarly, if you watch people pass from bright sunshine through the shadows of trees, your retinas receive images that are darker, then lighter, then darker again. Still, you perceive individuals whose coloring remains the same.

These examples illustrate **perceptual constancy**, the perception of objects as constant in size, shape, color, and other properties despite changes in their retinal image.

stroboscopic illusion An illusion of motion that is created when we see slightly different images or slightly displaced lights flashed in rapid succession.

perceptual constancy The perception of objects as constant in size, shape, color, and other properties despite changes in their retinal image.

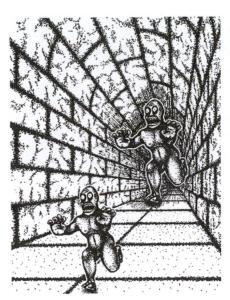

FIGURE 5.12
A Size Illusion

TRY THIS The monster that is higher in the drawing probably appears larger than the other one, but they are actually the same size. Why does this illusion occur? The converging lines of the tunnel provide strong depth cues telling us that the higher monster is farther away, but because that monster casts an image on our retinas that is just as big as the "nearer" one, we assume that the more distant monster must be bigger. (To confirm that they are the same size, measure them with a ruler; look again at part A of Figure 5.5 for another example of this illusion.)

TRY THIS

TRY THIS

Without perceptual constancy, the world would be an *Alice in Wonderland* kind of place in which objects continuously changed their properties.

Size Constancy   Why do objects appear to remain about the same size, no matter what changes occur in the size of their retinal image? One explanation emphasizes the computational aspects of perception. It suggests that as objects move closer or farther away, our brains perceive the change in distance and automatically adjust our perception. This calculation can be expressed as a formula: The perceived size of an object is equal to the size of the retinal image multiplied by the perceived distance (Holway & Boring, 1941). As an object moves closer, its retinal image increases, but the perceived distance decreases at the same rate, so the perceived size remains constant. If, instead, a balloon is inflated in front of your eyes, perceived distance remains constant, and the perceived size (correctly) increases as the retinal image size increases.

The computational perspective is reasonably good at explaining most aspects of size constancy, but it cannot fully account for the fact that people are better at judging the true size (and distance) of familiar rather than unfamiliar objects. This phenomenon suggests that in line with the constructivists' view, there is an additional, knowledge-based mechanism for size constancy: Our knowledge and experience tell us that most objects (aside from balloons) do not suddenly change size.

The perceptual system usually produces size constancy correctly and automatically, but it can sometimes fail, resulting in size illusions such as the one illustrated in Figure 5.12. Because this figure contains strong linear perspective cues (lines converging in the "distance") and because objects nearer the point of convergence are interpreted as farther away, we perceive the monster near the top of the figure as the larger one, even though both are exactly the same size. Size illusions can have serious consequences when the objects involved are, say, moving automobiles. A small car produces a smaller retinal image than a large one at the same distance. As a result, the driver of a following vehicle can easily overestimate the distance to the small car (especially in dim light) and therefore fail to brake in time to avoid a collision. Size illusions may help explain why, in countries in which cars vary greatly in size, small cars have higher accident rates than large ones (Eberts & MacMillan, 1985). Size misjudgments illustrate the *inferential* nature of perception emphasized by constructivists: People make logical inferences or hypotheses about the world based on the available cues. Unfortunately, if the cues are misleading or the inferences are wrong, perceptual errors may occur.

Shape Constancy   The principles behind shape constancy are closely related to those of size constancy. To see shape constancy at work, remember what page you are on, close this book, and tilt it toward and away from you several times. The book will continue to look rectangular, even though the shape of its retinal image changes dramatically as you move it. The brain automatically integrates information about retinal images and distance as movement occurs. In this case, the distance information involves the difference in distance between the near and far edges of the book.

As with size constancy, much of the ability to judge shape constancy depends on automatic computational mechanisms in the nervous system, but expectations about the shape of objects also play a role. For example, in Western cultures, most corners are at right angles. Knowledge of this fact helps make "rectangle" the most likely interpretation of the retinal image shown in Figure 5.1. Sometimes, shape constancy mechanisms are so good at creating perceptions of a stable world that they can keep us from seeing changes when they occur. In one study, for example, participants looking at a computer image of a person's head failed to notice that as the head turned, it morphed gradually into the head of a different person (Wallis & Bülthoff, 2001).

Brightness Constancy   Even with dramatic changes in the amount of light striking an object, the object's perceived brightness remains relatively constant (MacEvoy & Paradiso, 2001). To see this for yourself, place a piece of charcoal in sunlight and a piece of white paper in nearby shade. The charcoal will look dark and the paper will look bright, even though a light meter would reveal much more light reflected from the

A Failure of Shape Constancy

When certain stimuli are viewed from an extreme angle, the brain's ability to maintain shape constancy can break down. Traffic engineers take this phenomenon into account in the design of road markings, as shown in these photos from a London airport. The arrow in the top photo appears to be about the same height as the lettering below it, but it isn't. The arrow had to be greatly elongated, as shown in the side view, so that approaching drivers would see its shape clearly. If the arrow had been painted to match the height of the accompanying letters, it would appear "squashed" and only half as tall as the lettering.

Phillip Kent/www.anamorphosis.com

sun-bathed coal than from the shaded paper. One reason the charcoal continues to look dark, no matter what the illumination, is that you *know* that charcoal is nearly black, illustrating once again the knowledge-based nature of perception. Another reason is that the charcoal is still the darkest object relative to its background in the sunlight, and the paper is the brightest object relative to its background in the shade. As shown in Figure 5.13, the brightness of an object is perceived in relation to its background.

For a summary of this discussion, see "In Review: Principles of Perceptual Organization and Constancy."

IN REVIEW	Principles of Perceptual Organization and Constancy	
Principle	**Description**	**Example**
Figure ground discrimination	Certain objects or sounds are automatically identified as figures, whereas others become meaningless background.	You see a person standing against a building, not a building with a person-shaped hole in it.
Grouping	Properties of stimuli lead us to automatically group them together. These include proximity, similarity, continuity, closure, texture, simplicity, common fate, synchrony, common region, and connectedness.	People who are sitting together or who are dressed similarly are perceived as a group.
Perception of location and depth	Knowing an object's two-dimensional position (left and right, up and down) and distance enables us to locate it. The image on the retina and the orientation of the head provide information about the two-dimensional position of visual stimuli; auditory localization relies on differences in the information received by the ears. Depth or distance perception uses stimulus cues such as interposition, relative size, height in the visual field, gradient of texture, linear perspective, clarity, color, and shadow.	A person who looks tiny and appears high in the visual field is perceived as being of normal size but at a great distance.
Perceptual constancy	Objects are perceived as constant in size, shape, brightness, color, and other properties, despite changes in their retinal images.	A train coming toward you is perceived as getting closer, not larger; a restaurant sign is perceived as rotating, not changing shape.

1. The movement we see in movies, videos, and DVDs is due to a perceptual illusion called _____.
2. People who have lost an eye also lose the depth cue called _____.
3. The grouping principle of _____ allows you to identify objects seen through a picket fence.

Recognizing the Perceptual World

In discussing how people organize the perceptual world, we have set the stage for addressing one of the most vital questions that perception researchers must answer: How do people recognize what objects are? If you are driving in search of Barney's Diner, exactly what happens when your eyes finally locate the pattern of light that spells out its name?

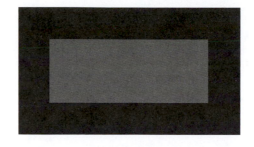

FIGURE 5.13
Brightness Contrast

`TRY THIS` At first glance, the inner rectangle on the left probably looks brighter than the inner rectangle on the right. But carefully examine the inner rectangles alone by covering their surroundings. You will see that they are equally bright. The brighter border in the right-hand figure leads you to perceive its inner rectangle as relatively darker.

To know that you have finally found what you have been looking for, your brain must analyze incoming patterns of information and compare them with information stored in memory. If your brain finds a match, recognition takes place, and the stimulus is classified into a *perceptual category*. Once recognition occurs, your perception of a stimulus may never be the same again. Look at Figure 5.14. Do you see anything familiar? If not, look ahead to Figure 5.16, then look at Figure 5.14 again. You should now see it in an entirely new light. The difference between your "before" and "after" experiences of Figure 5.14 is the difference between the sensory world before and after a perceptual match occurs and recognition takes place.

Exactly how does such matching occur? Some aspects of recognition begin at the "top," guided by knowledge, expectations, and other psychological factors. This phenomenon is called **top-down processing** because it involves higher-level, knowledge-based information. Other aspects of recognition begin at the "bottom," relying on specific, detailed information elements from the sensory receptors that are integrated and assembled into a whole. This phenomenon is called **bottom-up processing** because it begins with basic information units that serve as a foundation for recognition. Let's consider the contributions of bottom-up and top-down processing to recognition, as well as the use of neural network models to understand both.

Bottom-Up Processing

Research on the visual system is providing a detailed picture of how bottom-up processing works. As described in the chapter on sensation, all along the path from the eye to the brain, certain cells respond to certain features of a stimulus. So the stimulus

FIGURE 5.14
Categorizing Perceptions

`TRY THIS` What do you see here? If you can't recognize this pattern of information as falling into any perceptual category, turn to Figure 5.16 for some help in doing so.

Source: Stanley Coren, Lawrence M. Ward, and James T. Enns. *Sensation and Perception,* Fourth Edition. Copyright © 1994. Reprinted with permission of John Wiley & Sons, Inc.

top-down processing Aspects of recognition that are guided by higher-level cognitive processes and psychological factors such as expectations.

bottom-up processing Aspects of recognition that depend first on the information about the stimulus that comes to the brain from the sensory receptors.

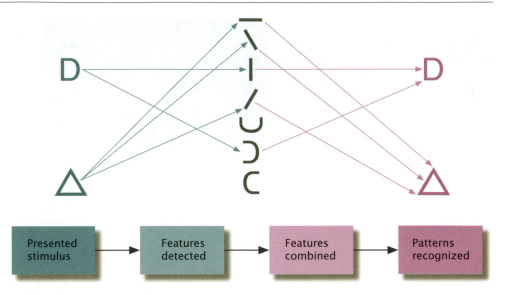

FIGURE 5.15
Feature Analysis
Feature detectors operating at lower levels of the visual system analyze incoming stimuli, such as the letter *D* or a triangle, into the corners and angles shown in the center of this figure. Later in the perceptual sequence, bottom-up processing recombines these features to aid in pattern recognition, as shown on the right.

is first analyzed into basic features before those features are recombined to create a perceptual experience.

What are these features? As also noted in the sensation chapter, certain cells specialize in responding to stimuli that have certain orientations in space (Hubel & Wiesel, 1979). For example, one cell in the cerebral cortex might fire only in response to a diagonal line, so it acts as a *feature detector* for diagonal lines. Figure 5.15 illustrates how the analysis by such feature detectors, early in the information-processing sequence, may contribute to recognition of letters or judgments of shape. Color, motion, and even corners are other sensory features that appear to be analyzed separately in different parts of the brain prior to full perceptual recognition (Beatty, 1995; Treisman, 1999).

How do psychologists know that feature analysis is actually involved in pattern recognition? Recordings of brain activity indicate that the sensory features we have listed here cause particular sets of neurons to fire. In fact, scientists have shown that it may be possible to determine what category of object a person is looking at (e.g., a face vs. a house) based on the pattern of activity occurring in visual processing areas of the person's brain (Haxby et al., 2001). Further, as described in the chapter on sensation,

FIGURE 5.16
Another Version of Figure 5.14
Now that you can identify a dog in this figure, it should be much easier to recognize when you look back at the original version.

Source: Stanley Coren, Lawrence M. Ward, and James T. Enns. *Sensation and Perception,* Fourth Edition. Copyright © 1994. Reprinted with permission of John Wiley & Sons, Inc.

The Eye of the Beholder

Top-down processing can affect our perception of people as well as objects. As noted in the chapter on social cognition, for example, if you expect everyone in a certain ethnic or social group to behave in a certain way, you may perceive a particular group member's behavior in line with this prejudice. And have you ever noticed that someone's physical attractiveness seemed to increase or decrease as you got to know the person better? This change in perception occurs largely because new information alters your interpretation of the raw sensations you get from the individual.

people with certain kinds of brain damage show selective impairment in the ability to perceive certain sets of sensory features, such as an object's color or movement.

Top-Down Processing

Bottom-up feature analysis can explain why you recognize the letters in a sign for Barney's Diner. But why is it that you can recognize the sign more easily if it appears where you were told to expect it rather than a block earlier? And why can you recognize it even if a few letters are missing from the sign? The answers are provided by top-down processing. Fo- ex-mp-e, y-u c-n r-ad -hi- se-te-ce -it- ev-ry -hi-d l-tt-r m-ss-ng. In top-down processing, people use their knowledge in making inferences or "educated guesses" to recognize objects, words, or melodies, especially when sensory information is vague or ambiguous. Once you knew that there was a dog in Figure 5.14, it became much easier for you to perceive it. Similarly, police officers find it easy to identify familiar people on blurry security camera videos, but it is much more difficult for them to identify strangers (Burton et al., 1999).

In hearing, too, top-down processing can compensate for ambiguous stimuli. In one experiment, participants heard strings of five words in meaningless order, such as "wet brought who socks some." There was so much background noise, however, that only about 75 percent of the words could be recognized (Miller, Heise, & Lichten, 1951). The words were then read to a second group of participants in a meaningful order (e.g., "who brought some wet socks"). The second group was able to recognize almost all of the words, even under the same noisy conditions. In fact, it took twice as much noise to reduce their performance to the level of the first group. Why? When the words were in meaningless order, only bottom-up processing was available. Recognizing one word was no help in identifying the next. Meaningful phrases, however, provided a more familiar context and allowed for some top-down processing. Hearing one word helped the listener make a reasonable guess (based on knowledge and experience) about the others.

Top-down processing is also involved in a phenomenon called *pareidolia* (pronounced "payr-uh-DOHL-ee-uh"), the perception of a specific image in an ambiguous stimulus array. For example, look at Figure 5.17, which shows the World Trade Center under attack. Some people see an image of the devil in the smoke. This interpretation requires some knowledge of paintings and other representations of the devil. Expectancy plays a role too. Many people who have not heard about the image do not see a demonic face in this photo.

FIGURE 5.17
What Does it Look Like to You?

TRY THIS Many people reported seeing a demonic face in the smoke pouring from New York's World Trade Center after terrorists attacked it on September 11, 2001. This perceptual categorization results from a combination of bottom-up and top-down recognition processes. Feature detectors automatically register the edges and colors of images, whereas knowledge and beliefs about the evil of the attack can create expectations that give meaning to these features. A person who does not expect to see a face in the smoke—or whose cultural background does not include the concept of "the devil"—might not see one until that interpretation is suggested. To check that possibility, show this photo to people from various religions and cultures who have not seen it before (don't tell them what to look for), and make a note of which individuals require prompting in order to identify a demonic face.

These examples illustrate that top-down processing can have a strong influence on pattern recognition. Our experiences create **schemas**, which are mental representations of what we know and have come to expect about the world. Schemas can bias our perception toward one recognition or another by creating a *perceptual set,* a readiness or predisposition to perceive a stimulus in a certain way. Perceptual sets help us deal with the world more efficiently. In one study, for example, people who were reminded that pilots have excellent vision showed better visual acuity while "piloting" a flight simulator (Langer et al., 2010). But perceptual sets can sometimes lead to errors. A tragic example occurred on the evening of November 13, 2007, when New York City police officers shot to death a highly agitated man after a 911 operator told them that the man had a gun. The man approached the officers holding a black object, and when he ignored their orders to stop, they fired. The object in his hand turned out to be a hairbrush, but in the dark they interpreted the object in accordance with their expectations about a gun and assumed that the man was about to fire at them.

Perceptual predispositions can be shaped by the context in which a stimulus occurs. For example, we expect to see people, not gorillas, on a city street, so when a large gorilla escaped from Boston's Franklin Park zoo a few years ago, a woman who saw him at a bus stop later said, "I thought it was a guy with a big black jacket and a snorkel on" (MacQuarrie & Belkin, 2003). Context has biasing effects for sounds too. People who hear gunshots on a downtown street tend to perceive the sound as firecrackers or a car backfiring. The same sounds heard at a shooting range would immediately be interpreted as gunfire.

Motivation is another aspect of top-down processing that can affect perception (Balcetis & Dunning, 2006). For example, people tend to perceive desirable objects as being closer to them than less desirable ones (Balcetis & Dunning, 2010), and if you are extremely hungry, you might misperceive a sign for "Burger's Body Shop" as indicating a place to eat. Similarly, if you have ever watched sports, you can probably remember a time when an obviously incompetent referee incorrectly called a penalty on your favorite team. You knew the call was wrong because you clearly saw the other team's player at fault. But suppose you had been cheering for that other team. The chances are good that you would have seen the referee's call as the right one.

Motivation and other aspects of top-down processing can even affect elements of the brain's bottom-up processing. For example, cells in the visual cortex that fire in response to specific features of an object show higher levels of activity if that object is of particular importance at the moment (Li, Piëch, & Gilbert, 2004). So corner-detecting cells will show more intense firing in response to the corners of the Barney's Diner sign you are looking for than to the corners of other signs.

Network Processing

Researchers taking a computational approach to perception have attempted to explain various aspects of object recognition in terms of both top-down and bottom-up processing. In one study, participants were asked to say whether a particular feature, like the dot and angled line on the left side of Figure 5.18, appeared within a pattern that was briefly flashed on a computer screen. The participants detected this feature faster when it was embedded in a pattern resembling a three-dimensional object than when it appeared within a random pattern of lines (Purcell & Stewart, 1991). This result is called the *object superiority effect.* There is also a *word superiority effect:* When strings of letters are briefly flashed on a screen, people's ability to detect target letters is better if the string forms a word than if it is a nonword (Prinzmetal, 1992).

Neural network models have been used to explain findings such as these. As described in the chapter on biological aspects of psychology, each element in these networks is connected to every other element, and each connection has a specific strength. Applying network processing models to pattern recognition involves focusing on the

schemas Mental representations about what we know and expect about the world.

interactions among the various feature analyzers we have discussed. More specifically, some researchers explain recognition using **parallel distributed processing (PDP)** models (Rumelhart & McClelland, 1986). According to PDP models, the units in a network operate in parallel—simultaneously. Connections between units either excite or inhibit other units. If the connection is excitatory, activating one unit spreads the activation to connected units. Using a connection may strengthen it.

How does this process apply to recognition? According to PDP models, recognition occurs as a result of the simultaneous operation of connected units. Units are activated when matched by features in a stimulus. To the extent that features, such as the letters in a word or the angles in a box, have occurred together in the past, the links between them will be stronger, and detection of any of them will be made more likely by the presence of all the others. This appears to be what happens in the word and object superiority effects, and the same phenomenon is illustrated in Figure 5.19. PDP models, sometimes called *connectionist models,* clearly represent the computational approach to perception. Researchers have achieved many advances in theories of pattern recognition by programming computers to carry out the kinds of complex computations that neural networks are assumed to perform in the human perceptual system. These computers have "learned" to read, recognize faces, and process color in a manner that may turn out to be similar to the way humans learn and perform the same perceptual tasks (e.g., Behnke, 2003). (For a summary of our discussion of recognition processes, see "In Review: Mechanisms of Pattern Recognition.")

Culture, Experience, and Perception

So far we have talked as if all aspects of perception work or fail in the same way for everyone, everywhere. The truth is, though, that perception can vary if people's experiences have created differing expectations and other knowledge-based, top-down processes (Chua, Boland, & Nisbett, 2005; Kitayama et al., 2003). For example, researchers have compared responses to depth cues by people from cultures that do and do not use pictures and paintings to represent reality. The results suggest that people in cultures that provide little experience with pictorial representations, such

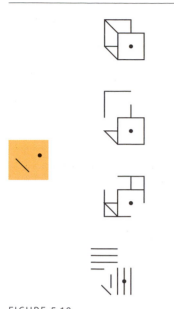

FIGURE 5.18

The Object Superiority Effect

When people are asked to say whether the feature at left appears in patterns briefly flashed on a computer screen, the feature is more likely to be detected when it appears in patterns like those at the top right, which most resemble three-dimensional objects. This "object superiority effect" supports the importance of network processing in perception (Sayim, Westheimer, & Herzog, 2010).

Source: Weisstein & Harris. "Visual Detection of Line Segments: An Object Superiority Effect," *Science,* 1974, 186, 725–755. Copyright © 1974 AAAS. Reprinted by permission.

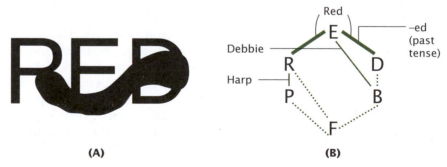

(A)   (B)

FIGURE 5.19

Recognizing a Word

You probably recognized the pattern shown in part A as the word *red,* even though the first letter of the word shown could be *R* or *P,* the second *E* or *F,* and the third *D* or *B.* According to PDP models, your recognition occurred because together the letters excite each other's correct interpretation. This mutual excitation process is illustrated in part B by a set of letter "nodes" (corresponding to activity sites in the brain) and some of the words they might activate. These nodes will be activated if the feature they detect appears in the stimulus array. They will also be activated if nodes to which they are linked become active. All six letters shown in part B will initially be excited when the stimulus in part A is presented, but mutual excitement along the strongest links leads to perception of the word *red.*

Source: Romelhart, D.E., and McClelland, J.L. (1986) *Parallel Distributing Processing, Volume 1: Foundations.* Cambridge, MA: MIT Press. Copyright © 1986 by the Massachusetts Institute of Technology. Reprinted by permission.

parallel distributed processing (PDP) A theoretical model of object recognition in which various elements of the object are thought to be simultaneously analyzed by several widely distributed but connected neural units in the brain.

IN REVIEW   Mechanisms of Pattern Recognition

Mechanism	Description	Example
Bottom-up processing	Raw sensations from the eye or the ear are analyzed into basic features, such as form, color, or movement; these features are then recombined at higher brain centers, where they are compared with stored information about objects or sounds.	You recognize a dog as a dog because its features—four legs, barking, panting—match your perceptual category for "dog."
Top-down processing	Knowledge of the world and experience in perceiving allow people to make inferences about the identity of stimuli, even when the quality of raw sensory information is low.	On a dark night, what you see as a small, vague blob pulling on the end of a leash is recognized as a dog because the stimulus occurs at a location where you would expect a dog to be.
Network, or PDP, processing	Recognition depends on communication among feature analysis systems operating simultaneously and enlightened by past experience.	A dog standing behind a picket fence will be recognized as a dog even though each disjointed "slice" of the stimulus may not look like a dog.

1. Your ability to read a battered old sign that has some letters missing is a result of _____ processing.
2. When stimulus features match the stimuli we are looking for, _____ takes place.
3. Schemas can create a _____ that makes us more likely to perceive stimuli in a particular way.

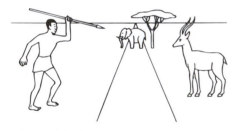

FIGURE 5.20
Culture and Depth Cues
People in various cultures were shown drawings like these and asked to judge which animal is closer to the hunter. Those in cultures that provide lots of experience with pictured depth cues choose the antelope, which is at the same distance from the viewer as the hunter. Those in cultures less familiar with such cues may choose the elephant, which, though closer on the page, is more distant when depth cues are considered (Hudson, 1960).

as the Nuba in Africa, have a more difficult time judging distances shown in pictures (see Figure 5.20). These individuals also tend to have a harder time sorting pictures of three-dimensional objects into categories, even though they can easily sort the objects themselves (Derogowski, 1989).

Experience even teaches us when to ignore certain stimulus cues. To fully experience the depth portrayed in a painting, for example, you have to ignore ridges, scratches, dust, or other texture cues from the canvas that would remind you of its flatness. **TRY THIS** And the next time you are watching TV, notice the reflections of objects in the room that appear on the screen. You have learned to ignore these reflections, so it will take a little effort to perceive them and a lot of effort to focus on them for long.

What if you hadn't had a chance to learn or practice these perceptual skills? One way to explore this question is through case studies of people who had been blind for decades and then had surgery that restored their sight. It turns out that these people can immediately recognize simple objects and perceive movement, but they usually have problems with other aspects of perception (Gregory, 2005; Ostrovsky et al., 2009). For example, M. M. had been blind from early childhood. When his vision was restored in his forties, he adjusted well overall, but he still has difficulty with depth perception and object recognition (Fine et al., 2003). As people move toward or away from him, they may appear to shrink or inflate. Identifying common objects can be difficult for him, and faces pose a particular challenge. To recognize individuals, he depends on features such as hair length or eyebrow shape. M. M. has trouble, too, distinguishing male faces from female ones and great difficulty recognizing the meaning of facial expressions. And like people from cultures that provide little or no experience with straight lines, he is unable to experience many of the perceptual illusions shown in this chapter.

LINKAGES >

Perception and Human Development

Knowledge and experience play an important role in recognition, but are they also required for more basic aspects of perception? Which perceptual abilities are babies born with, and which do they develop by seeing, hearing, smelling, touching, and tasting things? How do their perceptions compare with those of adults? To learn about infants' perception, psychologists have studied two inborn patterns called *habituation* and *dishabituation*. For example, infants stop looking when they repeatedly see stimuli that are perceived to be the same. This is habituation. If a stimulus appears that is perceived to be different, infants resume looking. This is dishabituation. Researchers have used the habituation and dishabituation phenomena, along with measurements of brain activity, to study color perception in infants. They have found that newborns can perceive differences among stimuli showing different amounts of black-and-white contrast but that they are unable to distinguish differences between colors (Burr, Morrone, & Fiorentini, 1996). By 3 months of age, though, infants can discriminate among blue, green, yellow, and red (Adams, Courage, & Mercer, 1991). Other researchers have found that newborns can perceive differences in the angles of lines (Slater et al., 1991). These studies and others suggest that we are born with some of the basic components of feature detection.

Are we also born with the ability to combine features into perceptions of whole objects? This question generates lively debate among specialists in infant perception. Some research indicates that at 1 month of age, infants concentrate their gaze on one part of an object, such as the corner of a triangle (Goldstein, 2002). By 2 months, though, the eyes systematically scan all the edges of the object, suggesting that only then has the infant begun to perceive the pattern of the object, or its shape, rather than just its component features. However, other researchers have found that once newborns have become habituated to specific combinations of features, they show dishabituation (that is, they pay attention) when those features are combined in a new way. The implication is that even newborns notice, and keep track of, the way some features are put together (Slater et al., 1991).

There is evidence that infants may be innately tuned to perceive at least one important complex pattern—the human face. In one study of newborns, some less than an hour old, patterns such as those in Figure 5.21 were moved slowly past the infants' faces (Johnson et al., 1991). The infants moved their heads and eyes to follow these patterns, but they tracked the facelike pattern shown on the left side of Figure 5.21 significantly farther than any of the nonfaces. The difference in tracking indicates that the infants could discriminate between faces and nonfaces and were more interested in the faces, or at least in facelike patterns (Simion et al., 2003).

Infants also notice differences among faces. At first, this ability to discriminate applies to both human and nonhuman faces. So at the age of 6 months, infants are actually better than adults at discriminating among the faces of monkeys (Pascalis, de Haan, & Nelson, 2002). By about the age of 9 months, however, face discrimination ability has become focused on human faces, the kind most babies see most often. Researchers who take an evolutionary approach suggest that interest in faces, especially human faces, is adaptive because it helps newborns focus on their only source of food and care.

Other research on perceptual development suggests that our ability to use certain distance cues develops more slowly than our recognition of object shapes (see Figure 5.22). For example, infants' ability to use retinal disparity and relative motion cues to judge depth appears to develop some time after about 3 months of age (Yonas, Arterberry, & Granrud, 1987). Infants do not use texture gradients and linear perspective as cues about depth until they are 3 to 7 months old (Arterberry, Craton, & Yonas, 1993; Bhatt & Bertin, 2001).

In summary, there is little doubt that many of the basic building blocks of perception are present within the first few days after birth. The basics include organ-based

LINKAGES What does the world look like to infants? (a link to Human Development, p. 470)

FIGURE 5.21
Infants' Perceptions of Human Faces

Newborns show significantly greater interest in the facelike pattern at the far left than in any of the other patterns. Evidently, some aspects of face perception are innate.

Source: Johnson, M.A., Dziurawiec, S., Ellis, H., and Morton, J. "Newborns' Preferential Tracking of Face-Like Stimuli and Its Subsequent Decline." *Cognition,* 4, 1–19. Reprinted by permission of Elsevier.

FIGURE 5.22
The Visual Cliff
The *visual cliff* is a glass-topped table that creates the impression of a sudden drop-off. A 10-month-old placed at what looks like the edge will calmly crawl across the shallow side to reach a parent but will hesitate and cry rather than crawl over the "cliff" (Gibson & Walk, 1960). Changes in heart rate show that infants too young to crawl also perceive the depth but are not frightened by it. Here again, nature and nurture interact adaptively: Depth perception appears shortly after birth, but fear and avoidance of dangerous depth do not develop until an infant is old enough to crawl into trouble.

cues to depth, such as accommodation and convergence. Maturation of the visual system adds to these basics as time goes by. For example, over the first few months after birth, the eye's fovea gradually develops the number of cone cells necessary for high visual acuity and perception of small differences in color (Goldstein, 2002). However, visual experience may also be necessary if the infant is to recognize some patterns and objects in frequently encountered stimuli, to interpret depth and distance cues, and to use these cues in moving safely through the world (Johnson, 2004; Quinn & Bhatt, 2005). In other words, like so many aspects of human psychology, perception is the result of a blending of heredity and environment. From infancy onward, the perceptual system creates a personal reality based in part on the experience that shapes each individual's feature analysis networks and knowledge-based expectancies.

Attention

Believe it or not, you still haven't found Barney's Diner! By now, you understand *how* you will recognize the right sign when you perceive it, but how can you be sure you *will* perceive it? As you drive, the diner's sign will appear as just one small piece in a sensory puzzle that also includes road signs, traffic lights, sirens, talk radio, and dozens of other stimuli. You can't perceive all of them at once, so to find Barney's you are going to have to be sure that the information you select for perceptual processing includes the stimuli that will help you reach your goal. In other words, you are going to have to pay attention.

Attention is the process of directing and focusing certain psychological resources to enhance perception, performance, and mental experience. We use attention to *direct* our sensory and perceptual systems toward certain stimuli, to *select* specific information for further processing, to *ignore* or screen out unwanted stimuli, to *allocate* the mental energy required to process selected stimuli, and to *regulate* the flow of resources necessary for performing a task or coordinating several tasks at once (Wickens & Carswell, 2006).

Psychologists have discovered three important characteristics of attention. First, it *improves mental processing;* you often have to concentrate attention on a task to do your best at it. If your attentional system temporarily malfunctions, you might drive

attention The process of directing and focusing psychological resources to enhance perception, performance, and mental experience.

right past Barney's Diner. Second, attention takes *effort*. Prolonged concentration of attention can leave you feeling drained (McNay, McCarty, & Gold, 2001). And when you are already tired, focusing attention on anything becomes more difficult. Third, attentional resources are *limited*. If your attention is focused on reading this book, for example, you'll have less attention left over to listen to a conversation in the next

TRY THIS

room. To experience attention as a process, try "moving it around" a bit. When you finish reading this sentence, look at something behind you, then face forward and notice the next sound you hear, then visualize your best friend, and then focus on how your tongue feels. You just used attention to direct your perceptual systems toward different aspects of your external and internal environments. Sometimes, as when you looked behind you, shifting attention involves *overt orienting*—pointing sensory systems at a particular stimulus. But you were able to shift attention to an image of your friend's face without having to move a muscle. This is called *covert orienting*. (We've heard a rumor that students sometimes use covert orienting to shift their attention from their lecturer to thoughts that have nothing to do with the lecture.)

FOCUS ON RESEARCH METHODS

An Experiment in "Mind Reading"

Everyone knows what it is like to covertly shift attention, but how can we tell when someone else is doing it? The study of covert attention requires the sort of "mind reading" that has been made possible by innovative experimental research methods. These techniques are helping psychologists measure where a person's attention is focused.

What was the researchers' question?

Michael Posner and his colleagues were interested in finding out what changes in perceptual processing occur when people covertly shift their attention to a specific location in space (Posner, Nissen, & Ogden, 1978). Specifically, the researchers addressed the question of whether these attentional shifts lead to more sensitive processing of stimuli in the location to which attention is focused.

How did the researchers answer the question?

Posner and his colleagues took advantage of an important property of mental events: They take time. Moreover, the time taken by mental events can vary considerably, thus providing important clues about internal processes such as covert attention.

The researchers designed a study in which participants were asked to focus their eyes on a fixation point that appeared at the center of a computer screen. One second later, a tiny square appeared at either the right or left edge of the screen. The participants were then asked to indicate, by pressing a key as quickly as possible, when they detected the square. Because their vision was focused on the fixation point, they could detect the square only out of the corners of their eyes.

On any given trial, a participant could never be sure where the square would appear. However, the researchers provided a cue, or "hint," at the start of some of the trials, in the form of an arrow at the fixation point. Sometimes the arrow pointed to the right edge of the screen (→). This cue gave correct information 80 percent of the time. On other trials, the arrow pointed to the left edge of the screen (←). This cue was also correct 80 percent of the time. On still other trials, participants saw a plus sign (+) at the fixation point, which indicated that the square was equally likely to appear on the left or the right.

The researchers reasoned that when the plus sign appeared, the best strategy for quickly detecting the square would be to keep attention focused on the center of the screen and to shift it only after the square appeared. When one of the arrow cues appeared, though, the best strategy would be to covertly shift attention in the direction indicated by the arrow before the square appeared. If the participants were covertly shifting their attention in this way, they should be able to detect the square

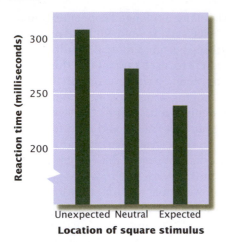

FIGURE 5.23
Measuring Covert Shifts in Attention

It took people less time (measured in thousandths of a second) to detect a square appearing at an expected location than at an unexpected one. This result suggests that even though their eyes did not move, these research participants covertly shifted their attention to the expected location before the stimulus was presented.

fastest when the cue provided accurate information about where the square would appear—even though they were not actually moving their eyes.

The dependent variable in this study was the speed of target detection, measured in milliseconds. The independent variable was the type of cue given: correct, incorrect, or neutral. Correct cues were arrows that accurately predicted the target location; incorrect ones were arrows that pointed the wrong way. Neutral cues gave no guidance.

What did the researchers find?

As shown in Figure 5.23, the target square was detected significantly faster when the cue gave correct information about where the square would appear. Incorrect cues resulted in a distinct drop in target detection speed: When participants were led to covertly shift their attention in the wrong direction, it took them longer to detect the square.

What do the results mean?

The data provide evidence that the participants used cues to shift their attention to the expected location. This shift readied their perceptual systems to detect information at that location. When a cue led them to shift their attention to the wrong location, they were less ready to detect information at the correct location, and their detection speed was slower. In short, attention can enhance the processing of information at one location, but it does so at the expense of processing information elsewhere.

What do we still need to know?

More recent research on the costs and benefits associated with perceptual expectancies has been generally consistent with the findings of Posner's pioneering team (e.g., Ball & Sekuler, 1992; Carrasco & McElree, 2001). However, there are still many unanswered questions about how covert attention actually operates. How quickly can we shift attention from one location to another? Estimates range from about a quarter of a second to as fast as a tenth of a second (Theeuwes, Godijn, & Pratt, 2004; Wolfe, 1998). And how quickly can we shift attention between sensory modalities—from watching to listening, for example? It will be difficult to find the methods necessary to address these questions, but they are fundamental to understanding our ability to deal with the potentially overwhelming load of stimuli that reaches our sensory receptors. Experiments designed to answer such questions not only expand our understanding of attention but also illustrate the possibility of measuring hidden mental events through observation of overt behavior (Wolfe, Alvarez, & Horowitz, 2000).

Directing Attention

As shown in Posner's experiment on "mind reading," attending to some stimuli leaves us less able to attend to others. In other words, attention is *selective;* it is like a spotlight that can illuminate only a part of the external or internal environment at any particular moment. How do you control, or allocate, your attention?

Control over attention can be voluntary or involuntary (Yantis, 1993). *Voluntary,* or goal-directed, control occurs when you purposely focus your attention in order to perform a task, such as listening for your name to be called in a noisy restaurant or watching for a friend in a crowd. Voluntary control reflects top-down processing because attention is guided by intentions, beliefs, expectations, motivation, or other knowledge-based factors. As people learn certain skills, they voluntarily direct their attention to information they once ignored. For example, experienced drivers notice events taking place farther down the road than new drivers do. If you are watching a sports event, learning where to allocate your attention is important if you are to understand what is going on. And if you are a competing in a sport, the proper allocation of attention is absolutely essential for success.

When, in spite of these top-down factors, some aspect of the environment—such as a loud noise—diverts your attention, control is said to be *involuntary.* In such cases, attentional control is a bottom-up, or stimulus-driven, process. Stimulus characteristics that tend to capture attention include sudden changes in lighting or color (such as flashing signs), movement, and the appearance of unusual shapes. Research by human factors psychologists, also known as engineering psychologists, on the stimuli most likely to attract—and distract—attention has been used in the design of everything from Internet Web sites to operator warning devices for airliners, nuclear power plants, and other complex systems (Clay, 2000; Laughery, 1999). Other psychologists use the results of attention research to help design advertisements, logos, and product packaging that "grab" potential customers' attention.

Ignoring Information

When the spotlight of your attention is voluntarily or involuntarily focused on one part of the environment, you may ignore, or be "blind" to, stimuli occurring in other parts. This phenomenon, called *inattentional blindness* (Mack, 2003; Mack & Rock, 1998), can be helpful when it allows us to ignore construction noise while we are taking an exam. But it can also endanger us if we ignore information—such as a stop sign—that we should be attending to. Inattentional blindness can cause us to miss some rather dramatic changes in our environment.

In one study, a researcher asked college students for directions to a campus building (Simons & Ambinder, 2005). During each conversation, two other researchers dressed as workmen passed between the first researcher and the student, carrying a large door. As the door hid the researcher from the student's view, one of the "workmen" took his place. This new person then resumed the conversation with the student as though nothing had happened. Amazing as it seems, only half of the students noticed that they were suddenly talking to a new person! The rest had apparently been paying so much attention to the researcher's question or to the map he was showing that they did not notice what he looked like. In other studies, the majority of participants were so focused on their cell phone conversations or on their assigned task of counting the passes made during a videotaped basketball game that they failed to notice a clown riding by on a unicycle or a woman in a gorilla suit walking across the court (Hyman et al., 2010; Simons & Chabris, 1999). And perhaps you recall the October 2009 incident in which two commercial airline pilots became so involved in conversation and use of their laptops that they allowed their aircraft to fly on autopilot 150 miles past its destination; their distraction was so complete that for seventy-seven minutes, they failed to hear radioed warnings from air traffic controllers (Pasztor, 2009). Magicians take advantage of inattentional blindness when they use sudden movements or other attention-grabbing stimuli to draw our attention away from the actions that lie behind their tricks. To experience a type of inattentional blindness known as "change blindness," take a look at the photos in Figure 5.24.

Divided Attention

People can sometimes divide their attention in ways that allow them to do more than one thing at a time, a skill sometimes called *multitasking*. You can drive a car, listen to the radio, sing along, and keep a beat by drumming on the steering wheel, all at the same time. In fact, as Figure 5.25 illustrates, it is sometimes difficult to stop dividing our attention and to stay focused on just one thing. However, your attention can't be divided beyond a certain point without a loss in performance and mental processing ability. For example, it is virtually impossible to read and talk at the same time. The reason is that attention is a limited resource. If you try to spread it over too many targets or between certain kinds of tasks, you "run out" of attention.

Why is it sometimes so easy and at other times so difficult to do two things at once? When one task is so *automatic* that it requires little or no attention, it is usually easy to do something else at the same time, even if the other task takes some attention (Schneider, 1985). When two tasks both require attention, it may still be

FIGURE 5.24
Change Blindness

TRY THIS These two photos are almost, but not exactly, the same. If you can't see the difference, or if it took you a while to see it, you may have been focusing your attention on the similarity of main features, resulting in blindness to one small but obvious difference. (See page 190 for the answer).

Courtesy Dr. Ronald Rensink

possible to perform them simultaneously, as long as each taps into different kinds of attentional resources (Wickens, 2002). For example, some attentional resources are devoted to perceiving incoming stimuli, whereas others handle making responses. This specialization of attention allows a skilled pianist to read musical notes and press keys simultaneously, even the first time through a piece. Apparently, the human brain has more than one type of attentional resource and more than one spotlight of attention (Wickens, 1989). This notion of different types of attention also helps explain why a driver can listen to a news story on the radio while steering safely and why voice control can be an effective way of performing a second task in an aircraft while the pilot's hands are busy with the controls. If two tasks require the same kind of attention, however, performance on both tasks will suffer (Just et al., 2001).

BLUE   GREEN

GREEN   ORANGE

PURPLE ORANGE

GREEN   BLUE

RED   RED

GRAY   GRAY

RED   BLUE

BLUE   PURPLE

FIGURE 5.25

The Stroop Task

TRY THIS Look at these words and, as rapidly as possible, call out the *color of the ink* in which each word is printed. This Stroop Color Word Test (Stroop, 1935) is not easy because your brain automatically processes the *meaning* of each word, which then competes for attention with the response you are supposed to give. To do well, you must focus on the ink color and not allow your attention to be divided between color and meaning. Children just learning to read have less trouble with this task because they do not yet process word meanings as automatically as experienced readers do.

Attention and Automatic Processing

Your search for Barney's Diner will be helped by your ability to voluntarily allocate attention to a certain part of the environment, but it would be even easier if you knew that Barney's had the only bright red sign on that stretch of road. Your search would not take much effort in this case because you could simply set your attention to filter out all signs except red ones.

Our ability to search for targets rapidly and automatically is called *parallel processing*. It is as if you can examine all nearby locations at once (in parallel) and rapidly detect the target no matter where it appears. So if the sign you are looking for is bright red and twice as large as any other one on the road, you could conduct a parallel search, and the sign would quickly stand out. The automatic parallel processing that allows detection of color or size suggests that these features are analyzed before the point at which attention is required. However, if the target you seek shares many features with others nearby, you must conduct a slower serial search, examining each item in turn (Treisman, 1988).

Attention and the Brain

If directing attention to a task causes extra mental work to be done, there should be evidence of that work in brain activity. Such evidence has been provided by positron emission tomography (PET) and magnetic resonance imaging (MRI) scans, which reveal increased blood flow and greater nerve cell activity in regions of the brain associated with the mental processing necessary for the task. In one study, for example, people were asked either to focus attention on reporting only the color of a stimulus or to divide attention in order to report its color, speed of motion, and shape (Corbetta et al., 1991). When attention was focused on color alone, increased blood flow appeared only in the part of the brain where that stimulus feature was analyzed; when attention was divided, the added supply of blood was shared between two locations. Similarly, increased nerve cell activity occurs in two different areas of the brain when participants perform two different tasks, such as deciding whether sentences are true while also deciding whether a pair of three-dimensional objects are the same or different (Just et al., 2001).

Because attention appears to be a linked set of resources that improve information processing at several levels and locations in the brain, it is not surprising that no single brain region has been identified as an "attention center" (Posner & Peterson, 1990; Sasaki et al., 2001). However, scientists have found regions in the brain that are involved in momentary lapses in attention and in the *switching* of visual attention from one stimulus element or location to another (Posner & Raichle, 1994; Weissman et al., 2006).

Applications of Research on Perception

Throughout this chapter, we have mentioned ways in which perceptual systems shape people's ability to handle tasks ranging from recognizing restaurant signs to detecting tornadoes. We have also shown how research on perception explains the principles behind movies and videos and affects the design of advertisements. In this section, we examine three other areas in which perception research has been applied: aviation, human-computer interaction, and traffic safety.

Aviation Psychology

To land an aircraft, pilots must make accurate judgments of how far they are from the ground, as well as how fast and from what angle they are approaching the runway. In this situation, the visual environment provides many overlapping bottom-up

Avoiding Perceptual Overload

APPLYING PSYCHOLOGY The pilot of a modern commercial jetliner is faced with a potentially overwhelming array of visual and auditory signals that must be correctly perceived and interpreted to ensure a safe flight. Engineering psychologists contribute to the design of new instrument displays, warning systems, and communication links that make the pilot's task easier and make errors less likely.

perceptual cues (Gibson, 1979). Pilots can also use their experience-based expectations about the approaching ground surface, thus adding top-down processing to produce an accurate perception of reality. But suppose that there are few depth cues because the landing occurs at night, and suppose that the lay of the land differs from what the pilot normally experiences. With both bottom-up and top-down processing impaired, the pilot's interpretation of reality may be disastrously incorrect. If, for example, the runway is much smaller than a pilot expects, it might be perceived as farther away than it actually is—especially at night—and thus may be approached too fast. (This illusion is similar to the one mentioned earlier in which drivers overestimate their distance from small cars.) Or if a pilot expects the runway to be perfectly flat but it actually slopes upward, the pilot might falsely perceive that the aircraft is too high. Misguided attempts to "correct" a plane's altitude under these circumstances have caused pilots to fly in too low, an error that resulted in a series of major nighttime crashes in the 1960s (Kraft, 1978).

Research on the perceptual processes—and possible perceptual failures—that occur while flying an airplane has made major contributions to aviation safety. For example, psychologists' analysis of the tragedies just described led to successful prevention of similar accidents. They recommended that airline pilot training programs emphasize the dangers of visual illusions and the importance of relying on their flight instruments during landings, especially at night.

Psychologists have also addressed problems related to the information those instruments provide. In a traditional aircraft cockpit, that information bears little resemblance to the perceptual world. Especially when visibility is poor, a pilot depending on flight instruments must do a lot of time-consuming and effortful serial processing to perceive and piece together the information necessary to understand the aircraft's position and movement. To ease this cognitive and attentional burden, engineering psychologists have helped develop instrument displays that present a realistic three-dimensional image of the flight environment—similar in some ways to a video game screen. This image more accurately captures the many cues for depth perception that the pilot needs.

Research on auditory perception has also contributed to aviation safety, both in the creation of warning signals that are most likely to catch the pilot's attention and in efforts to minimize communication errors. Air traffic control communications use a special vocabulary and standardized phrases designed to avoid misunderstandings. But as a result, these communications are usually short, with little of the built-in redundancy that in normal conversation allows people to understand a sentence even if some words are missing. For example, if a pilot eager to depart on time perceives an expected message as "clear for takeoff" when the actual message is "hold for takeoff," the results can be catastrophic. Problems like these have been addressed "bottom up," through noise-canceling microphones and visual message displays, as well as through the use of slightly longer messages that aid top-down processing by providing more contextual cues.

Human-Computer Interaction

The principles of perception are also being applied by engineering (human factors) psychologists serving on design teams at computer hardware and software companies. For example, in line with the ecological approach to perception, they have duplicated in the world of computer displays many of the depth cues that help people navigate in the physical world. The next time you visit a Web site or use a word-processing or spreadsheet program, you might notice that shading cues make the "buttons" on the screen seem to protrude from their background, as real buttons would. Similarly, when you open several documents or spreadsheets in a cascade format, interposition cues make them appear to be lying on top of one another.

The difference between the photos in Figure 5.24 is that in the top picture, a clump of trees appears just to the left of the statue.

The results of research on attention have even been applied to your cursor. It blinks to attract your attention, making it possible to do a quick parallel search rather than a slow serial search when you are looking for it amid all the other stimuli on the screen. Perceptual principles have also guided creation of the pictorial images, or icons, that are used to represent objects, processes, and commands in your computer programs. These icons speed your use of the computer if their features are easy to detect, recognize, and interpret (McDougall, de Bruijn, & Curry, 2000; Niemela & Saarinen, 2000). This is the reason a little trash can icon is used in some programs to show you where to click when you want to delete a file. A tiny eraser or paper shredder might have worked, too, but its features might be harder to recognize. These are just a few of the ways in which psychologists are applying perception research to make computers easier to use.

Traffic Safety

Research on perception is being applied in many ways to enhance traffic safety. For example, human factors psychologists are identifying features of automobile controls, instrument displays, road signs, and traffic signals that are likely to reduce older drivers' involvement in car accidents (Vance et al., 2006). Others are studying ways of increasing drivers' perception of danger in various situations, including night driving (Pradhan et al. 2005; Wood, Tyrrell, & Carberry, 2005). Psychologists are also involved in the design of night vision displays that make it easier for drivers to see low-visibility targets, such as pedestrians wearing dark clothing; they have also helped design pavement paintings that look so much like real speed bumps that—like the striping described at the beginning of this chapter—they cause speeding drivers to slow down (Associated Press, 2008).

Further, research on divided attention is informing the debate over the use of cell phones while driving. The demands of traffic safety groups and the examples set by many countries around the world have already led California, Connecticut, New York, New Jersey, Oregon, Washington, the District of Columbia, and the U.S. Virgin Islands to outlaw drivers' use of handheld cell phones. Nineteen states and the District of Columbia have also made it illegal for drivers to text while driving (Governors' Highway Traffic Safety Association, 2010). Most other U.S. states are considering similar laws; some of these laws would ban even hands-free phone conversations while driving. Cell phone manufacturers and network providers agree that using a phone while driving can be dangerous, but only because looking at the handset, pushing its buttons, and holding it in place during the call can distract the driver from steering and watching the road. These companies, and most of their customers, claim that hands-free phones and voice-controlled dialing eliminate any dangers associated with drivers' use of cell phones (White et al., 2010).

That argument is contradicted by research showing that drivers' ability to attend to visual cues is impaired simply by holding a phone to their ears, even if the phone is off (Oommen & Stahl, 2005). Other research shows that driving performance is impaired and the risk of accidents is increased while talking on *any* cell phone, whether handheld or hands-free (Beede & Kass, 2006; Dingus et al., 2006; McEvoy et al., 2005; Spence & Read, 2003; Strayer & Drews, 2007; Strayer, Drews, & Johnston, 2003; Törnros & Bolling, 2005, 2006). This research suggests that the dangers of driving while using a phone do not stem simply from listening to someone speak or even from talking. The driving performance of research participants was not impaired by listening to books on tape or by repeating words that they heard. Performance *did* decline, though, when participants were asked to do more elaborate processing of auditory information, such as rephrasing what they heard. (You may have experienced similar effects if you have ever missed a turn or had a near-accident while deeply engaged in conversation with a passenger.) One study of people's performance on a driving simulator found that the accident avoidance skills of sober drivers talking on cell phones were impaired more than those of drivers who were legally drunk but not using phones (Strayer, Drews, & Crouch, 2003).

Driven to Distraction?

Recent research shows that at any given moment, about 11 percent of drivers in the United States are talking on a cell phone, and about 6 percent, or nearly one million of them, are driving while using a handheld model (Glassbrenner, 2005; U.S. Department of Transportation, 2010). Some cell phone manufacturers claim that hands-free models can eliminate any dangers associated with using a phone while driving, but perception research indicates that using any kind of phone can create inattentional blindness and distractions that impair driving performance and may contribute to accidents (e.g., Beede & Kass, 2006; Hyman et al., 2010; Strayer & Drews, 2007).

© Radius Images/Alamy

These results suggest that using a cell phone—let alone texting or reading texts—while driving is dangerous not only because it can take your eyes off the road and a hand off the wheel but also because the phone conversation—or texting or reading process—competes for the attentional and other cognitive resources you need to drive safely. Perception researchers suggest that this competition can actually create a form of inattentional blindness that is unlikely to be reduced by hands-free cell phones (Hyman et al., 2010; Strayer & Drews, 2006; Strayer, Drews, & Johnston, 2003; Strayer et al., 2004).

LINKAGES

As noted in the chapter on introducing psychology, all of psychology's subfields are related to one another. Our discussion of how perceptual processes develop in infants illustrates just one way in which the topic of this chapter, perception, is linked to the subfield of developmental psychology (which is the topic of the chapter on human development). The Linkages diagram shows ties to two other subfields as well, and there are many more ties throughout the book. Looking for linkages among subfields will help you see how they all fit together and better appreciate the big picture that is psychology.

CHAPTER 5
Perception

LINKAGES

Can the senses be fooled?
(ans. on p. 174)

What does the world look like to infants?
(ans. on p. 183)

Can subliminal stimuli influence our judgments about people?
(ans. on p. 718)

CHAPTER 4
Sensation

CHAPTER 12
Human Development

CHAPTER 17
Social Cognition

SUMMARY

Perception is the process through which people actively use knowledge and understanding of the world to interpret sensations as meaningful experiences.

The Perception Paradox

Because perception often seems so rapid and effortless, it appears to be a rather simple operation; however, this is not the case. An enormous amount of processing is required to transform energy received by receptors into perceptual experience. The complexity of perception is revealed by various perceptual errors (e.g., illusions).

Three Approaches to Perception

The *computational model* of perception emphasizes the computations performed by the nervous system. The *constructivist approach* suggests that the perceptual system constructs the experience of reality, making inferences and applying knowledge in order to interpret sensations. The *ecological approach* holds that the environment itself provides the cues that people use to form perceptions.

Psychophysics

Psychophysics is the study of the relationship between stimulus energy and the psychological experience of that energy.

Absolute Thresholds: Is Something Out There?

Psychophysics has traditionally been concerned with matters such as determining absolute thresholds for the detection of stimuli. Research shows that this threshold is not, in fact, absolute. The *absolute threshold* has been redefined as the minimum amount of stimulus energy that can be detected 50 percent of the time. *Supraliminal stimulation* falls above this threshold; *subliminal stimulation* falls below it.

Signal Detection Theory

Signal detection theory describes how people respond to faint or ambiguous stimuli. Detection of a signal is affected by external and internal noise,

sensitivity, and the *response criterion.* Signal detection theory has been applied to understanding decision making and performance in areas such as the detection of tornadoes on radar.

Judging Differences: Has Anything Changed?

Weber's law states that the minimum detectable amount of change in a stimulus—the difference threshold, or *just-noticeable difference (JND)*—increases in proportion to the initial amount of the stimulus. The less the initial stimulation, the smaller the change that will be detected.

Magnitude Estimation: How Intense Is That?

Fechner's law and *Stevens's power law* describe the relationship between the magnitude of a stimulus and its perceived intensity.

Organizing the Perceptual World

Basic Processes in Perceptual Organization

Perceptual organization is the process whereby order is imposed on the information received by your senses. The perceptual system automatically engages in *figure ground discrimination,* and it groups stimuli into patterns. Gestalt psychologists and others identified laws or principles that guide such grouping: proximity, similarity, continuity, closure, texture, simplicity, common fate, synchrony, common region, and connectedness. These laws appear to ensure that perceptual organization creates interpretations of incoming information that are simple and most likely to be correct.

Perception of Location and Distance

Visual localization requires information about the position of the body and eyes, as well as information about where a stimulus falls on the retinas. Auditory localization depends on detecting differences in the information that reaches the two ears, including differences in timing and intensity. Perception of distance,

or *depth perception,* depends partly on stimulus cues and partly on the physical structure of the visual system. Some of the stimulus cues for depth perception are *interposition,* relative size, height in the visual field, *gradient of texture, linear perspective,* and *motion parallax.* Cues based on the structure of the visual system include *ocular accommodation* (the change in the shape of the lenses as objects are brought into focus), *eye convergence* (the fact that the eyes must move to focus on the same object), and *retinal disparity* (the fact that the eyes are set slightly apart).

Perception of Motion

The perception of motion results in part from the movement of stimuli across the retinas. Expanding or *looming* stimulation is perceived as an approaching object. Movement of the retinal image is interpreted along with information about movement of the head, eyes, and other parts of the body so that one's own movement can be discriminated from the movement of external objects. The *stroboscopic illusion* accounts for our ability to see smooth motion in films, videos, and DVDs.

Perceptual Constancy

Because of *perceptual constancy,* the brightness, size, and shape of objects are seen to remain the same, even though the sensations received from those objects may change. Size constancy and shape constancy depend on the relationship between the retinal image of an object and the knowledge-based perception of its distance. Brightness constancy depends on the perceived relationship between the brightness of an object and its background.

Recognizing the Perceptual World

Both *bottom-up processing* and *top-down processing* contribute to recognition of the world. The ability to recognize objects is based on finding a match between the pattern of sensations organized by the perceptual system and a pattern that is stored in memory.

Bottom-Up Processing

Bottom-up processing is accomplished by the analysis of stimulus features or combinations of features, such as form, color, and motion.

Top-Down Processing

Top-down processing is influenced by expectancy and motivation. *Schemas* based on past experience can create a perceptual set, the readiness or predisposition to perceive stimuli in certain ways. Expectancies can also be created by the context in which a stimulus appears.

Network Processing

Research on pattern recognition has focused attention on network models, or *parallel distributed processing (PDP)* models, of perception. These emphasize the simultaneous activation and interaction of feature analysis systems and the role of experience.

Culture, Experience, and Perception

To the extent that the visual environments of people in different cultures differ, their perceptual experiences—as evidenced by their responses to perceptual illusions—may differ as well.

Attention

Attention is the process of focusing psychological resources to enhance perception, performance, and mental experience. We can shift attention overtly—by moving the eyes, for example—or covertly, without any movement of sensory systems.

Directing Attention

Attention is selective; it is like a spotlight that illuminates different parts of the external environment or various mental processes. Control over attention can be voluntary and knowledge-based or involuntary and driven by environmental stimuli.

Ignoring Information

Sometimes attention can be so focused that it results in inattentional blindness, a failure to detect or identify normally noticeable stimuli.

Divided Attention

Although there are limits to how well people can divide attention, they can sometimes attend to two tasks at once. For example, tasks that have become automatic can often be performed along with more demanding tasks, and tasks that require very different types of processing, such as gardening and talking, can be performed together because each task depends on a different supply of mental resources.

Attention and Automatic Processing

Some information can be processed automatically, in parallel, whereas other situations demand focused attention and a serial search.

Attention and the Brain

Although the brain plays a critical role in attention, no single brain region has been identified as the main attention center.

Applications of Research on Perception

Research on human perception has numerous practical applications.

Aviation Psychology

Accurate size and distance judgments, top-down processing, and attention are all important to safety in aviation.

Human-Computer Interaction

Perceptual principles relating to recognition, depth cues, and attention are being applied by psychologists who work with designers of computers and computer programs.

Traffic Safety

Research on divided attention is being applied to help understand the potential dangers of driving while texting or using cell phones.

LINKAGES TO FURTHER LEARNING

Now that you have finished reading this chapter, how about exploring some of the topics and information that you found most interesting? Here are some places to start.

Books

Richard L. Gregory and J. Harris (Eds.), *The Artful Eye* (Oxford University Press, 1995). Visual perception.

Richard L. Gregory and Andrew M. Colman (Eds.), *Sensation and Perception* (Longman, 1995). The senses and psychophysics.

Oliver Sacks, *The Man Who Mistook His Wife for a Hat* (Touchstone Books, 1998). Descriptions of patients with sensory and perceptual disorders.

Roger Shepard, *Mind Sights* (Freeman, 1990). Visual illusions, ambiguous figures.

J. Richard Block and Harold Yuker, *Can You Believe Your Eyes?* (Gardner Press, 1989). More illusions and visual oddities.

On the Internet

 Access an integrated eBook and chapter-specific learning tools including flashcards, quizzes, videos, and more. Go to CengageBrain.com.

CENGAGENOW Want to maximize the value of your online study time? Take this easy-to-use study system's diagnostic pre-test, and it will create a personalized study plan for you. By helping you identify the topics that you need to understand better and then directing you to valuable online resources, it can speed up your chapter review. CengageNOW even provides a post-test so you can confirm that you are ready for an exam. Go to CengageBrain.com.

TALKING POINTS

Here are a few talking points to help you summarize this chapter for family and friends without giving a lecture.

1. The amazing process of perception occurs quickly and automatically, but scientists still don't understand everything about it.

2. Unlike a video camera that dispassionately records events, our perceptions of the world are not fixed and objective; they are affected by our past experience, our wants and needs, our expectations, and the situations in which we find ourselves.

3. Information that we do not consciously perceive can affect some limited aspects of our thinking and behavior, but subliminal messages do not have the power to control us or to help us lose weight or quit smoking.

4. Because perception depends to some extent on experience, people from different cultures may differ in their sensitivity to certain optical illusions.

5. The most basic elements of perceptual ability are present at birth, but it takes many months, and sometimes years, for all aspects of perception to develop.

6. When we are concentrating on one thing, we may become blind to other important information. Limits on our ability to divide attention between tasks make it dangerous to text or talk on a cell phone while driving.

7. Research on perception has helped in the design of automotive, aviation, and computer systems that reduce the likelihood of errors and accidents.

6

Learning

Live and learn. This simple phrase captures the idea that learning is a lifelong process that affects our behavior every day. Understanding how learning takes place is an important part of understanding ourselves, and in this chapter, we explore the learning process and the factors that affect it.

Can you recall how you felt on your first day of kindergarten? Like many young children, you may have been bewildered, even frightened, as the comforting familiarity of home or day care was suddenly replaced by an environment filled with new names and faces, rules and events. But like most youngsters, you probably adjusted to this new situation within a few days, much as you did again when you started middle school, high school, and college.

Your adjustment, or *adaptation,* to these new environments occurred in many ways. Ringing bells, lunch lines, midterm grades, and other once-strange new school events not only became part of your expectations about the world but also began to serve as signals. You soon realized that if a note was delivered to your teacher during class, someone would be called to the main office. If your teacher arrived with a box of papers, you knew that the tests had been graded. Adapting to school also meant developing new knowledge about what behavior was appropriate and inappropriate in the new settings you encountered. Although your parents may have encouraged you to talk whenever you wanted to at home, perhaps you found that at school, you had to raise your hand first. And the messy finger painting that got you in trouble at home may have earned you praise in art class. You found, too, that there were things you could do—such as paying attention in class and getting to school on time—to reap rewards and avoid punishment. Finally, of course, you adapted to school by absorbing facts about the world and developing skills ranging from kickball and reading to writing and debating.

The entire process of development, from birth to death, involves a biological adaptation to increasingly complex, ever-changing environments using continuously updated knowledge gained through experience. Although perhaps most highly developed in humans, the ability to adapt to changing environments appears to varying degrees in all species. According to the evolutionary approach to psychology, it is individual differences in the capacity to adapt that shapes the evolution of appearance and behavior in animals and humans. Individuals who don't adapt may not survive to reproduce.

Many forms of animal and human adaptation follow the principles of learning. **Learning** is the adaptive process through which experience modifies preexisting behavior and understanding. The preexisting behavior and understanding may have been present at birth, acquired automatically as we mature, or learned earlier. Learning plays a central role in the development of most aspects of human behavior. It allows us to build the motor skills we need to walk or tie a shoe, the language skills we use to communicate, and the object categories—such as "food," "vehicle," or "animal"—that help us organize our perceptions and think logically about the world. Sayings such as "Once burned, twice shy" and "Fool me once, shame on you; fool me twice, shame on me" reflect this vital learning process. If you want to know who you are and how you became the person you are today, examining what and how you have learned is a good place to start.

Humans and other animals learn primarily by experiencing events, observing relationships between those events, and noticing consistencies in the world around them. For example, when two events repeatedly take place together, we can predict the occurrence of one from knowledge of the other. We learn that a clear blue sky means

learning The modification through experience of preexisting behavior and understanding.

dry weather, that too little sleep makes us irritable, and that we can communicate with someone by clicking on a certain e-mail address. Some learning takes place consciously, as when we study for an exam, but as you will see, we can also learn things without being aware we are doing so (Watanabe, Náñez, & Sasaki, 2001).

In this chapter, we first consider the simplest forms of learning—learning about sights, sounds, and other *stimuli* (the plural of *stimulus*). Then we examine the two major kinds of learning that involve *associations* between events—classical conditioning and operant conditioning. Next we consider the role of thinking, or cognition, in learning, and we conclude by discussing how research on learning might help people learn better.

Learning About Stimuli

In a changing world, our senses are constantly bombarded by massive amounts of information. If we tried to pay attention to every sight and sound, our information-processing systems would be overloaded, and we would be unable to concentrate on anything. People appear to be genetically tuned to attend to certain kinds of events, such as loud sounds, special tastes, or pain. *Novel* stimuli—things we have not experienced before—also tend to attract our attention.

By contrast, our response to *unchanging* stimuli decreases over time. This aspect of adaptation is a simple form of learning called **habituation,** and it can occur in relation to sights, sounds, smells, tastes, or touches. As described in the chapter on sensation, it is through habituation that you eventually lose awareness of your glasses or your watch and that after being in a room for a while, you no longer smell its odor or hear its ticking clock. Habituation is especially important for adapting to initially startling but harmless events such as the repeated popping of balloons, but it occurs in some degree to all kinds of stimuli and in all kinds of animals, from simple sea snails to humans (Gottfried, O'Doherty, & Dolan, 2003; Pinel, 1993). After our response to a stimulus has habituated, it may quickly return if the stimulus changes. So if that ticking

Learning to Live with It

People who move from a small town to a big city may at first be distracted by the din of traffic, low-flying aircraft, and other urban sounds, but after a while, the process of habituation makes all this noise far less noticeable.

habituation The process of adapting to stimuli that do not change.

clock suddenly stops, you may become aware of it again because now, something in your environment has changed. The reappearance of your original response when a stimulus changes is called *dishabituation*. In the perception chapter, we describe how habituation and dishabituation processes have helped psychologists determine what babies notice, and fail to notice, as perceptual skills develop.

A second simple form of learning, called *sensitization,* appears as an increase in responsiveness to a stimulus. Sensitization occurs, for example, when people and animals show exaggerated responses to unexpected, potentially threatening sights or sounds, especially during periods of emotional arousal. So while breathlessly exploring a dark, spooky house, you might scream, run, or violently throw something in response to the unexpected creaking of a door.

Habituation and sensitization provide organisms with a useful way to adapt to their environments, but notice that these kinds of learning result from exposure to a single stimulus. Neither kind requires the association of one stimulus with another, as when we learn that, say, dark clouds signal rain. For this reason, habituation and sensitization are referred to as *nonassociative learning* (Chance, 2009).

Psychologists have been especially interested in how habituation occurs. According to Richard Solomon's (1980) *opponent process theory,* new stimulus events—especially those that arouse strong positive or negative emotions—disrupt the individual's physiological state of equilibrium, or *homeostasis.* This disruption triggers an opposite, or opponent, process that counteracts the disruption and eventually restores equilibrium. If the arousing event occurs repeatedly, this opponent process gets stronger and occurs more rapidly. It eventually becomes so quick and strong that it actually suppresses the initial response to the stimulus, creating habituation.

As described in the motivation and emotion chapter, the opponent process theory of habituation may help explain why some people skydive and engage in other highly arousing activities. It may also help explain some of the dangers associated with certain drugs. Consider, for example, what happens as someone continues to use a drug such as heroin. The "high," or pleasurable reaction that follows a particular dose of the drug, begins to decrease, or habituate, with repeated doses. Habituation occurs, Solomon says, because the initial, pleasurable reaction to the drug is followed by an unpleasant, increasingly rapid opposing reaction that counteracts the drug's primary effects. As drug users become habituated, they must take progressively larger doses to get the same high. According to Solomon and other researchers, these opponent

Sensitization

TRY THIS The documentary filmmakers portrayed in *The Blair Witch Project* demonstrated the simple learning process called *sensitization* as their behavioral reactions to sudden stimuli became more and more extreme. The next time you are watching a tense or "scary" film, look for similar examples of sensitization in the reactions of the audience—and perhaps in yourself, too!

Photofest

processes form the basis of the drug tolerance and addiction that are described in the chapter on consciousness.

Could similar opponent processes be partly responsible for some accidental drug overdoses? Some researchers think so. Suppose that the unpleasant reaction that counteracts a drug's initial effects becomes associated with a particular room, person, or other stimulus that is normally present when the drug is taken. This stimulus may eventually come to trigger the counteracting process, allowing the user to tolerate larger drug doses. Now suppose that a person takes this larger drug dose in an environment in which this stimulus is not present. The strength of the drug's primary effect will remain the same, but without the familiar environmental stimulus, the counteracting process may be weaker. The net result may be a stronger-than-usual drug reaction, possibly leading to an overdose (Melchior, 1990; Siegel, 2005; Siegel et al., 1982).

Notice that opponent process explanations of drug abuse and overdose are based not just on simple habituation and sensitization but also on a *learned association* between certain environmental stimuli and certain opponent responses. Indeed, the nonassociative processes of habituation and sensitization cannot, by themselves, explain many of the behaviors and mental processes that are the focus of psychology. To better understand how learning affects our thoughts and behaviors, we have to consider forms of learning that involve the building of associations between various stimuli, as well as between stimuli and responses. One major type of associative learning is called *classical conditioning*.

Classical Conditioning: Learning Signals and Associations

An athlete's heart may start pounding at the first notes of the national anthem; those sounds signal that the game is about to begin. A flashing red light on the instrument panel may raise your heart rate too, because it means that something is wrong with your car. We are not born with these reactions. We learn them by observing relationships or *associations* between events in the world. The experimental study of this kind of learning was begun, almost by accident, by Ivan Petrovich Pavlov.

Pavlov's Discovery

Pavlov is one of the best-known figures in psychology, but he was not a psychologist. A Russian physiologist, Pavlov won a Nobel Prize in 1904 for his research on the digestive processes of dogs. In the course of this work, Pavlov noticed a strange phenomenon: The first stage of the digestive process—salivation, or drooling—sometimes occurred when no food was present. His dogs salivated, for example, when they saw the assistant who normally brought their food, even if the assistant was empty-handed.

Pavlov devised a simple experiment to determine why salivation occurred without an obvious physical cause. First he performed a simple operation to divert a dog's saliva into a container so that the amount of salivation could be measured precisely. He then placed the dog in an apparatus similar to the one shown in Figure 6.1. The experiment had three phases.

In the first phase of the experiment, Pavlov and his associates confirmed that when meat powder was placed on the dog's tongue, the dog salivated, but it did not salivate in response to a neutral stimulus—a musical tone, for example. Thus the researchers had established the two basic components for Pavlov's experiment: (1) a *reflex,* which is a quick, automatic response to a stimulus, and (2) a *neutral stimulus* that does not trigger that reflex.

It was the second and third phases of the experiment that showed how one type of associative learning can occur. In the second phase, the tone sounded, and then a

FIGURE 6.1
Apparatus for Measuring Conditioned Responses
In this more elaborate version of Pavlov's original apparatus, the amount of saliva flowing from a dog's cheek is measured and then recorded on a slowly revolving drum of paper.

Pen recording on cylinder

classical conditioning A procedure in which a neutral stimulus is repeatedly paired with a stimulus that elicits a reflex or other response until the neutral stimulus alone comes to elicit a similar response.

unconditioned stimulus (UCS) A stimulus that elicits a response without conditioning.

few seconds later, meat powder was placed in the dog's mouth. The dog salivated. This *pairing*—the tone followed immediately by meat powder—was repeated several times. The tone predicted that the meat powder was coming, but the question remained: Would the animal learn that the tone signals the meat powder? The answer was yes. In the third phase of the experiment, the tone was sounded, and even though no meat powder was presented, the dog again salivated. In other words, the tone by itself now elicited salivation. You may have seen a similar process if you regularly open pet food with an electric can opener. The sound of the opener probably brings your pet running (and salivating) because that sound means that food is on its way.

Pavlov's experiment was the first laboratory demonstration of a basic form of associative learning. Today, it is called **classical conditioning**—a procedure in which a neutral stimulus is repeatedly paired with a stimulus that already triggers a reflexive response. As a result of this pairing, the previously neutral stimulus itself comes to trigger a response that is similar to that reflex. Figure 6.2 shows the basic elements of classical conditioning. The stimulus that elicits a response without conditioning, such as the meat powder in Pavlov's experiment, is called the **unconditioned stimulus (UCS)**.

FIGURE 6.2
Classical Conditioning
Before classical conditioning has occurred, meat powder on a dog's tongue produces salivation, but the sound of a tone—a neutral stimulus—produces nothing more than orienting responses, such as turning toward the sound. During the process of conditioning, the tone is repeatedly paired with the meat powder. After classical conditioning has taken place, the sound of the tone alone acts as a conditioned stimulus, triggering salivation.

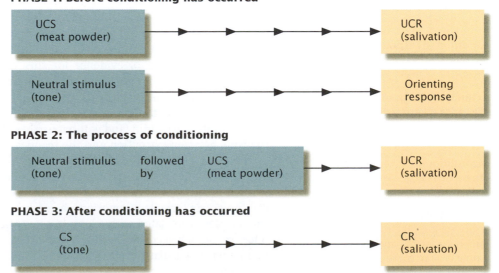

PHASE 1: Before conditioning has occurred

| UCS (meat powder) | → → → → | UCR (salivation) |
| Neutral stimulus (tone) | → → → | Orienting response |

PHASE 2: The process of conditioning

| Neutral stimulus (tone) followed by UCS (meat powder) | → → | UCR (salivation) |

PHASE 3: After conditioning has occurred

| CS (tone) | → → → | CR (salivation) |

FIGURE 6.3

Changes over Time in the Strength of a Conditioned Response (CR)
As the conditioned stimulus (CS) and the unconditioned stimulus (UCS) are repeatedly paired during initial conditioning, the strength of the conditioned response (CR) increases. If the CS is repeatedly presented without the UCS, the CR weakens—and eventually disappears—through a process called *extinction*. However, if a significant amount of time has passed since the CS was last presented and then it is presented again, the CR will generally reappear. This phenomenon is called *spontaneous recovery*.

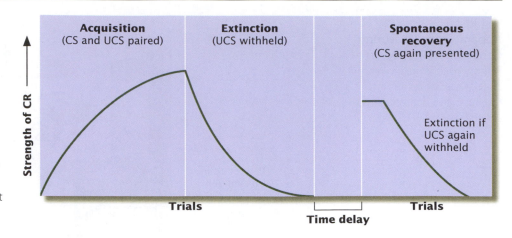

The automatic reaction to this stimulus is called the **unconditioned response (UCR).** As the neutral stimulus is repeatedly paired with the unconditioned stimulus, it becomes a **conditioned stimulus (CS),** and the response it comes to elicit is called the **conditioned response (CR).**

Conditioned Responses over Time: Extinction and Spontaneous Recovery

Continued pairings of a conditioned stimulus with an unconditioned stimulus strengthen conditioned responses. The curve on the left side of Figure 6.3 shows an example: Repeated associations of a tone (CS) with meat powder (UCS) caused Pavlov's dogs to increase their salivation (CR) to the tone alone.

What if the meat powder is no longer given? In general, if the conditioned stimulus continues to occur without being followed at least occasionally by the unconditioned stimulus, the conditioned response will gradually disappear. This fading process is known as **extinction** (see the center section of Figure 6.3). The term *extinction* is not entirely accurate, though, because it suggests that like the dinosaurs, the conditioned response has been wiped out, never to return. The fact is, though, that the conditioned response is simply *suppressed* by a counteracting tendency not to respond.

Two kinds of evidence support the conclusion that extinction suppresses but does not destroy a conditioned response. The first comes from research showing that if a conditioned stimulus (tone) and an unconditioned stimulus (meat powder) are again paired after the conditioned response has been extinguished, that conditioned response will return to its original strength after as few as one or two trials. This **reconditioning** process occurs much faster than the original conditioning did, suggesting that extinction did not entirely erase the association between the conditioned stimulus and the conditioned response (Bouton, 1993, 2002; Myers & Davis, 2007).

The second kind of evidence for this view is illustrated on the right side of Figure 6.3 which shows that even after a conditioned response has been extinguished, it will temporarily reappear if the conditioned stimulus occurs again. This phenomenon is called **spontaneous recovery,** the temporary reappearance of a conditioned response after extinction (and without further CS-UCS pairings). In general, the longer the time between extinction and the reappearance of the CS, the stronger the recovered conditioned response (Devenport, 1998; Rescorla, 2005). Unless the UCS is again paired with the CS, extinction will reoccur and will further suppress the conditioned response (Leung & Westbrook, 2008). Still, even after many years, spontaneous recovery can create a ripple of emotion—a conditioned response—when we hear a song or catch a scent associated with a long-lost lover or a departed relative. This *renewal* of a once-extinguished conditioned response is especially likely when extinction occurred in only one particular situation (Bouton, 2002). Renewal is seen all too often, for example, following residential treatment for drug or alcohol abuse. Conditioned craving for

unconditioned response (UCR) The automatic or unlearned reaction to a stimulus.

conditioned stimulus (CS) The originally neutral stimulus that, through pairing with the unconditioned stimulus, comes to elicit a conditioned response.

conditioned response (CR) The response that the conditioned stimulus elicits.

extinction The gradual disappearance of a conditioned response when a conditioned stimulus is no longer followed by an unconditioned stimulus.

reconditioning The quick relearning of a conditioned response following extinction.

spontaneous recovery The reappearance of the conditioned response after extinction and without further pairings of the conditioned and unconditioned stimuli.

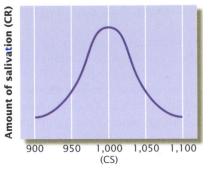

Sound of buzzer (hertz)

FIGURE 6.4
Stimulus Generalization
The strength of a conditioned response (CR) is greatest when the original conditioned stimulus (CS) occurs but the CR also appears following stimuli that closely resemble the CS. Here, the CS is the sound of a buzzer at a frequency of 1,000 hertz (Hz), and the CR is salivation. Notice that the CR generalizes well to stimuli at 990 or 1,010 Hz but becomes weaker and weaker in response to stimuli that are less and less similar to the CS.

these substances may eventually disappear while an abuser is in a treatment center, but once back in an environment full of conditioned stimuli for substance abuse, the old craving may immediately return to threaten long-term recovery (Goldstein et al., 2009).

Stimulus Generalization and Discrimination

After a conditioned response is learned, stimuli that are similar but not identical to the conditioned stimulus also elicit the response—but to a lesser degree. This phenomenon is called **stimulus generalization.** Usually, the greater the similarity between a new stimulus and the conditioned stimulus, the stronger the conditioned response will be. So a person who was bitten by a small, curly-haired dog is likely to be most afraid of dogs that closely resemble it. Figure 6.4 shows another example involving sounds.

Stimulus generalization has obvious adaptive advantages. For example, it is important for survival that if you get sick after drinking sour-smelling milk, you now avoid dairy products that have a similar odor. Generalization would be a problem, though, if it had no limits. Like most people, you would probably be frightened if you found a lion in your home, but imagine the disruption if your fear response generalized so widely that you were panicked by a picture of a lion or even by reading the word *lion*.

Stimulus generalization does not run wild because it is balanced by a complementary process called **stimulus discrimination.** Through stimulus discrimination, people and animals learn to differentiate among similar stimuli. Many parents find that the sound of their own baby whimpering during the night may become a conditioned stimulus that triggers a conditioned response that wakes them up. That conditioned response might not occur if a visiting friend's baby whimpers.

The Signaling of Significant Events

You have seen that after a tone has been repeatedly associated with the appearance of an unconditioned stimulus (UCS) such as food, the once-neutral tone becomes a conditioned stimulus (CS) that leads a dog to salivate. Pavlov showed that this classical conditioning process takes place gradually as a result of continued experience, but he believed that there is more to the story. Through repeated association, he said, the conditioned stimulus (tone) becomes a *signal* that tells the dog the unconditioned stimulus (food) is coming, and the dog's conditioned response (salivation) occurs in preparation for the food. In this case, the conditioned response looks just like the unconditioned response (both involve salivation), but this is not always so. For example, a rat's natural, *unconditioned,* reflexive responses to a mild shock (UCS) are to flinch and jump. But after classical conditioning in which a tone (CS) always precedes shock, the rat's *conditioned* response will be to freeze—much as it would if threatened by a predator (Domjan, 2005). In other words, classical conditioning involves more than the appearance of reflexive, robotlike responses.

Like Pavlov, most psychologists today believe that conditioned responses develop when one event reliably predicts, or *signals,* the appearance of another. They also believe that instead of giving rise to simple reflexes, classical conditioning leads to responses based on the *information* provided by conditioned stimuli. As a result, animals and people develop *mental representations* of the relationships between important events in their environment and expectancies about when such events will occur (Rescorla, 1988; Shanks, 1995). These representations and expectancies aid adaptation and survival.

What determines whether and how a conditioned response is learned? Important factors include the timing, predictability, and strength of signals; the amount of attention they receive; and how easily the signals can be associated with other stimuli.

stimulus generalization A phenomenon in which a conditioned response is elicited by stimuli that are similar but not identical to the conditioned stimulus.

stimulus discrimination A process through which individuals learn to differentiate among similar stimuli and respond appropriately to each one.

Timing If your instructor always ends class at 9:59 and a bell rings at 10:00, the bell comes too late to act as a signal for the end of the session. For the same reason, classical conditioning works best when the conditioned stimulus precedes the unconditioned

Safety Signals

Pavlov discovered that associating a conditioned stimulus tone with the appearance of food led dogs to salivate in response to the tone alone. Babkin, one of Pavlov's students, later found that if a different conditioned stimulus (a whistle) is associated with the *absence* of food, the dogs would learn to inhibit (suppress) their salivation. The effect of this *inhibitory conditioning* can be seen in the adjustments sometimes made by people who suffer with agoraphobia and panic disorder (see the chapter on psychological disorders). These people are normally intensely afraid of leaving home, but some of them find that the presence of a trusted friend acts as a safety signal that inhibits their conditioned fear responses enough to let them venture out into the world (Schmidt et al., 2006).

stimulus. In this arrangement, known as *forward conditioning,* the conditioned stimulus signals that the unconditioned stimulus is coming.

There is also an arrangement, called *backward conditioning,* in which the conditioned stimulus (e.g., a tone) is presented just *after* the unconditioned stimulus (food). When this happens, however, a conditioned response develops very slowly, if at all. Part of the explanation is that the CS in backward conditioning comes too late to signal the approach of the UCS. In fact, as described later, the CS signals the *absence* of the UCS and eventually triggers a response that is opposite to the conditioned response, thus inhibiting its development.

Research shows that conditioning usually works best when there is an interval between the conditioned stimulus and the unconditioned stimulus. This interval can range from a fraction of a second to a few seconds to more than a minute, depending on the particular CS, UCS, and UCR involved (Longo, Klempay, & Bitterman, 1964; Ross & Ross, 1971). Classical conditioning will always be weaker if the interval between the CS and the UCS is longer than what is ideal for the stimuli and responses in a given situation. This makes adaptive sense. Normally, the appearance of food, predators, or other significant events is most reliably predicted by smells, growls, or other stimuli that occur at varying intervals before those events. So it is logical that organisms are "wired" to form associations most easily between things that occur in a relatively tight time sequence.

Predictability   For classical conditioning to occur, though, it is not enough that the conditioned stimulus precede the unconditioned stimulus and that the two events occur close together in time. Suppose you have two dogs, Moxie and Fang, each with different personalities. When Moxie growls, she sometimes bites, but sometimes she doesn't. Other times, she bites without growling first. Fang, however, growls *only* before biting. Your conditioned fear response to Moxie's growl will probably occur slowly, if at all, because her growl is a stimulus that does not reliably signal the danger of a bite. But you are likely to quickly develop a classically conditioned fear response to Fang's growl, because classical conditioning proceeds most rapidly when the conditioned stimulus *always* signals the unconditioned stimulus and *only* the unconditioned stimulus. So even if both dogs provide the same number of pairings of the conditioned stimulus (growl) and the unconditioned stimulus (bite), it is only in Fang's case that the conditioned stimulus *reliably* predicts the unconditioned stimulus (Rescorla, 1968).

Signal Strength   A conditioned response will be greater if the unconditioned stimulus is stronger. So a predictive signal associated with a strong UCS, such as an intense shock, will come to evoke more fear than one associated with a weak shock. As with timing and predictability, the effect of signal strength on classical conditioning makes adaptive sense. It is more important to be prepared for major events than for minor ones.

How quickly a conditioned response is learned also depends on the strength of the conditioned stimulus. As described in the chapter on perception, louder tones, brighter lights, or other, more intense stimuli tend to get attention, so they are most rapidly associated with an unconditioned stimulus—as long as they remain reliable predictive signals.

Attention   In the classical conditioning laboratory, a single neutral stimulus is presented, followed shortly by an unconditioned stimulus. In the natural environment, however, several stimuli may be present just before an unconditioned stimulus occurs. Suppose that you are at the beach, sipping lemonade, reading a magazine, listening to a Beyoncé CD, and inhaling the scent of sunscreen when you are stung by a wasp. Where your attention was focused at that moment can influence which potential conditioned stimulus—the taste of lemonade, the sight of the magazine, the sound of Beyoncé, or the smell of sunscreen—becomes associated with that painful unconditioned stimulus. The stimulus you were attending to most closely—and thus most fully perceiving—is the one likely to be more strongly associated with pain than any of the others (Hall, 1991).

Biopreparedness   After Pavlov's initial experiments, many psychologists believed that the associations formed through classical conditioning were like Velcro. Just as Velcro pieces of any size or shape can be easily attached, some believed that any conditioned stimulus has an equal potential for becoming associated with any unconditioned stimulus, as long as the two stimuli occur in the right time sequence. This view, called *equipotentiality,* was later challenged by experiments showing that certain signals or events are especially likely to form associations with other events (Logue, 1985). This apparent natural tendency for certain events to become linked suggests that humans and animals are "biologically prepared" or "genetically tuned" to develop certain conditioned associations.

The most dramatic example of this *biopreparedness* is seen in conditioned taste aversions. Consider the results of a study in which rats were either shocked or made nauseous in the presence of a bright light, a loud buzzer, and water flavored with an artificial sweetener. Only certain conditioned associations were formed. Specifically, the animals that had been shocked developed a conditioned fear response to the light and the buzzer but not to the flavored water. Those that had been made nauseous developed a conditioned aversion to the flavored water but showed no particular response to the light or buzzer (Garcia & Koelling, 1966). Notice that these associations are useful and adaptive: Nausea is more likely to be produced by something we eat or drink than by a noise or some other external stimulus. So nausea is more likely to become a conditioned response to an internal stimulus, such as a flavor, than to an external stimulus, such as a light or buzzer. In contrast, the sudden pain of a shock is likely to have been caused by an external stimulus, so it makes evolutionary sense that organisms should be "tuned" to associate pain with external stimuli such as sights or sounds.

Conditioned taste aversion shows that for certain kinds of stimuli, classical conditioning can occur even when there is a long delay between the CS (taste) and the UCS (sickness). For example, the illness caused by poisons or other nauseating substances is usually delayed by minutes or hours, which is far longer than the intervals that normally produce conditioning. But for people who have experienced food poisoning or stomach flu after eating a certain kind of food, just the smell of it can make them queasy, and they may never eat that food again. Taste aversion makes sense in evolutionary terms because organisms that are biologically prepared to link taste signals with illness, even if it occurs after a considerable delay, are more likely to survive than organisms not so prepared.

Evidence from several sources suggests other ways in which animals and people are innately prepared to learn aversions to certain stimuli. For example, experiments with animals suggest that they are prone to learn the types of associations that are most common in or most relevant to their environments (Wilcoxon, Dragoin, & Kral, 1971). Birds are strongly dependent on their vision in searching for food and may develop taste aversions on the basis of visual stimuli. Coyotes and rats, more dependent on their sense of smell, tend to develop aversions related to odor. In humans, preparedness results in far more cases of conditioned fear of harmless dogs or snakes than of potentially more dangerous objects, such as electrical outlets or knives (Öhman & Mineka, 2001, 2003). We are also particularly likely to learn fear responses to people who are "different," such as members of other ethnic groups (Olsson et al., 2005).

Higher-Order Conditioning   Once we learn that a conditioned stimulus (CS) signals the arrival of an unconditioned stimulus (UCS), the CS may operate as if it actually were that UCS. For instance, suppose that a child endures a painful medical procedure (UCS) at the doctor's office, and the pain becomes associated with the doctor's white coat. The white coat might then become a conditioned stimulus (CS) that can trigger a conditioned fear response. Once the white coat is able to set off a conditioned

Taste Aversions

Humans can develop classically conditioned taste aversions, even to preferred foods. Ilene Bernstein (1978) gave one group of cancer patients Mapletoff ice cream an hour before they received nausea-provoking chemotherapy. A second group ate the same kind of ice cream on a day they did not receive chemotherapy. A third group got no ice cream. Five months later, the patients were asked to taste several ice cream flavors. Those who had never tasted Mapletoff and those who had not eaten it in association with chemotherapy chose it as their favorite. Those who had eaten Mapletoff before receiving chemotherapy found it very distasteful.

The Power of Higher-Order Conditioning

Cancer patients may feel queasy when they enter a chemotherapy room because they have associated the room with treatment that causes nausea. Through higher-order conditioning, almost anything associated with that *room* can also become a conditioned stimulus for nausea. One cancer patient, flying out of town on a business trip, became nauseated just by seeing her hospital from the air.

LINKAGES Can people learn their way out of a disorder? (a link to Treatment of Psychological Disorders, p. 661)

higher-order conditioning A phenomenon in which a conditioned stimulus acts as an unconditioned stimulus, creating conditioned stimuli out of events associated with it.

fear response, the coat may take on some properties of an unconditioned stimulus. So if the child later sees a white-coated pharmacist at the drugstore, that once-neutral store can become a conditioned stimulus for fear because it signals the appearance of a white coat, which in turn signals pain. When a conditioned stimulus (the white coat) acts as an unconditioned stimulus, creating conditioned stimuli (the drugstore) out of events associated with it, the process is called **higher-order conditioning.**

Conditioned fear and higher-order conditioning illustrate one of the most important adaptive characteristics of classical conditioning. They allow a person or an animal to prepare for threatening events—unconditioned stimuli—that are reliably signaled by a conditioned stimulus. Unfortunately, higher-order conditioning can also cause problems. For example, the high blood pressure seen in medical patients known as *white-coat hypertensives* (Ugajin et al., 2005) is not caused by a physical disorder. It occurs simply because the mere sight of a doctor or nurse has become a conditioned stimulus for fear. Medical staff must be alert to such cases in order not to prescribe blood pressure medication to patients who don't need it.

Some Applications of Classical Conditioning

"In Review: Basic Phenomena in Classical Conditioning" summarizes the principles of classical conditioning. These principles have been applied in many areas, including in overcoming fears, controlling predators, and detecting explosives.

Phobias   Classical conditioning can play a role in the development of mild fears (such as a child's fear of a doctor's white coat), and it may also lead to phobias (Bouton, Mineka, & Barlow, 2001; Waters, Henry, & Neumann, 2009). *Phobias* are extreme fears of objects or situations that either are not objectively dangerous—public speaking, for example—or are less dangerous than the phobic person's reaction suggests. In some instances, phobias can seriously disrupt a person's life. A child who is frightened by a large dog may learn a fear of that dog that is so intense and generalized that it creates a phobia of all dogs and avoidance of all situations in which dogs might be encountered. Classically conditioned fears can be very long-lasting, especially when they are based on experiences with strong unconditioned stimuli. Combat veterans and victims of violent crime, terrorism, or other traumatic events may show intense fear responses to trauma-related stimuli for many years afterward. As described in the chapter on health, stress, and coping, these symptoms, combined with others such as distressing dreams about the troubling events, characterize posttraumatic stress disorder (PTSD).

Classical conditioning procedures can be employed to treat phobias and even PTSD. Joseph Wolpe (1958) pioneered the development of this methodology. Using techniques first developed with laboratory animals, Wolpe showed that irrational fears could be relieved through *systematic desensitization,* a procedure that associates a new response, such as relaxation, with a feared stimulus. To treat a thunderstorm phobia, for instance, a therapist might first teach the client to relax deeply and then associate that relaxation with increasingly intense sights and sounds of thunderstorms presented on a video (Öst, 1978). Because, as Wolpe noted, a person cannot be relaxed and afraid at the same time, the new conditioned response (relaxation) to thunderstorms replaces the old one (fear). Desensitization is discussed in more detail in the chapter on the treatment of psychological disorders.

Predator Control   The power of classically conditioned taste aversion has been put to work to help ranchers who are plagued by wolves and coyotes that kill and eat their sheep. To alleviate this problem without killing the predators, some ranchers have set out lithium-laced mutton for wolves and coyotes to eat. The dizziness and nausea caused by the lithium become associated with the smell and taste of mutton, thus making sheep an undesirable meal for these predators and protecting the ranchers' livelihood (Garcia, Rusiniak, & Brett, 1977).

Detecting Explosives   Researchers are using classical conditioning to teach insects to detect explosive material. In one project with wasps, the taste of sugar water is

© Gerard Lacz/Peter Arnold, Inc./Photolibrary

Using Classical Conditioning to Save People and Tigers

A program supported by the government of India has greatly reduced human deaths from tiger attacks, as well as the need to kill marauding tigers. Stuffed dummies—connected by hidden wires to a shock generator—are placed in areas in which tigers have attacked people. When the animals approach, they receive a shock (unconditioned stimulus), which they learn to associate with the human form. Humans thus become a conditioned stimulus for fear, and the tigers learn to be wary of them (conditioned response). Other classical conditioning methods have helped ranchers in the western United States to prevent grazing horses and cattle from eating poisonous plants (Pfister et al., 2003).

repeatedly paired with the smell of a chemical used in certain explosives. The wasps quickly develop a conditioned response to the smell alone. When several of these trained insects are placed in a plastic tube and brought near the target chemical, they display an immediate attraction to it (Rains, Utley, & Lewis, 2006). Researchers hope that it may someday be possible to use these so-called wasp hounds and other similar devices to detect explosives or drugs concealed in airline passengers' luggage (Tomberlin, Rains, & Sanford, 2008)

IN REVIEW	Basic Phenomena in Classical Conditioning	
Process	**Description**	**Example**
Acquisition	A neutral stimulus and an unconditioned stimulus are paired. The neutral stimulus becomes a conditioned stimulus, eliciting a conditioned response.	A child learns to fear (conditioned response) the doctor's office (conditioned stimulus) by associating it with the reflexive emotional reaction (unconditioned response) to a painful injection (unconditioned stimulus).
Stimulus generalization	A conditioned response is elicited not only by the conditioned stimulus but also by stimuli similar to the conditioned stimulus.	A child fears most doctors' offices and places that smell like them.
Stimulus discrimination	Generalization is limited so that some stimuli similar to the conditioned stimulus do not elicit the conditioned response.	A child learns that his mother's doctor's office is not associated with the unconditioned stimulus.
Extinction	The conditioned stimulus is presented alone, without the unconditioned stimulus. Eventually, the conditioned stimulus no longer elicits the conditioned response.	A child visits the doctor's office several times for a checkup but does not receive an injection. Fear may eventually cease.

1. If a man's conditioned fear of spiders is triggered by the sight of other creatures that look somewhat like spiders, he is demonstrating stimulus _____.
2. Because of _____, we are more likely to learn a fear of snakes than a fear of cars.
3. Feeling sad upon hearing a song associated with a long-lost relationship illustrates _____.

Operant Conditioning: Learning the Consequences of Behavior

Classical conditioning is an important kind of learning, but it can't explain most of what people learn on a daily basis. In classical conditioning, neutral and unconditioned stimuli are predictably paired, and the result is an association between the two. The association is shown by the conditioned response that occurs when the conditioned stimulus appears. Notice that both stimuli occur *before* or *along with* the conditioned response. But people also learn associations between their actions and the stimuli that *follow* them—in other words, between behavior and its consequences. A child learns to say "please" to get a piece of candy; a headache sufferer learns to take a pill to escape pain; a dog learns to "shake hands" to get a treat.

From the Puzzle Box to the Skinner Box

Much of the groundwork for research on the consequences of behavior was done by Edward L. Thorndike, an American psychologist. While Pavlov was exploring classical conditioning in animals, Thorndike was studying animals' intelligence and ability

FIGURE 6.5
Thorndike's Puzzle Box
This drawing illustrates the kind of "puzzle box" used in Thorndike's research. His cats learned to open the door and reach food by stepping on the pedal, but the learning occurred gradually. Some cats actually took longer to get out of the box on a later trial than on a previous trial.

to solve problems. He would place an animal, usually a hungry cat, in a *puzzle box,* where it had to learn some response—say, stepping on a pedal—in order to unlock the door and get to some food (see Figure 6.5). The animal would solve the puzzle, but very slowly. It did not appear to understand, or suddenly gain insight into, the problem (Thorndike, 1898).

So what were Thorndike's cats learning? Thorndike argued that any response (such as pressing the pedal) that produces a satisfying effect (such as access to food) gradually becomes stronger, whereas any response (such as pacing or meowing) that does not produce a satisfying effect gradually becomes weaker. The cats' learning, said Thorndike, is governed by the **law of effect.** According to this law, if a response to a particular stimulus is followed by satisfaction (such as a reward), that response is more likely to be made the next time the stimulus is encountered. Responses that produce discomfort are less likely to be performed again. Thorndike described this kind of learning as *instrumental conditioning* because responses are strengthened when they are instrumental in producing rewards (Thorndike, 1905).

About forty years after Thorndike published his work, B. F. Skinner extended and formalized many of Thorndike's ideas. Skinner (1938) emphasized that during instrumental conditioning, an organism learns a response by *operating on* the environment, so he called the process of learning these responses **operant conditioning.** His primary aim was to analyze how behavior is changed by its consequences. To study operant conditioning, Skinner devised a chamber that, despite his objections, became known as the *Skinner box.* This chamber differed from Thorndike's puzzle box in an important way: The puzzle box measured learning in terms of whether an animal successfully completed a trial (i.e., got out of the box) and how long it took to do so. The Skinner box measures learning in terms of how often an animal responds during a specified period of time.

Basic Components of Operant Conditioning

The tools Skinner devised allowed him and other researchers to precisely arrange relationships between a response and its consequences and then to analyze how those consequences affected behavior over time. They found that the basic phenomena seen in classical conditioning—such as stimulus generalization, stimulus discrimination, extinction, and spontaneous recovery—also occur in operant conditioning. However, operant conditioning involves additional concepts and processes as well. Let's consider these now.

Operants and Reinforcers   Skinner introduced the term *operant* or *operant response* to distinguish the responses in operant conditioning from those in classical conditioning. Recall that in classical conditioning, the conditioned response doesn't

law of effect   A law stating that if a response made in the presence of a particular stimulus is followed by satisfaction, that response is more likely the next time the stimulus is encountered.

operant conditioning   A process through which an organism learns to respond to the environment in a way that produces positive consequences and avoids negative ones.

Edward L. Thorndike (1874–1949) and B. F. Skinner (1904–1990)

Edward Thorndike (left) and B. F. Skinner (shown at right with a "Skinner box") studied instrumental and operant conditioning, respectively. Though similar in most respects, instrumental and operant conditioning differ in one way. In instrumental conditioning, the experimenter defines each opportunity for the organism to respond, and conditioning is usually measured by how long it takes for the response to appear. In operant conditioning, the organism can make responses at any time; conditioning is measured by the *rate* of responding. In this chapter, the term *operant conditioning* refers to both kinds of conditioning.

Archives of the History of American Psychology/The University of Akron

© Nina Leen/Time & Life Pictures/Getty Images

affect whether or when a stimulus occurs. Dogs salivated when a tone sounded, but the salivation had no effect on the tone or on whether food was presented. In contrast, an **operant** is a response that has some effect on the world; it is a response that *operates on* the environment. For example, when a child says, "Momma, I'm hungry," and is then fed, the child has made an operant response that influences when food will appear.

A **reinforcer** increases the probability that an operant behavior will occur again. There are two main types of reinforcers: positive and negative. **Positive reinforcers** strengthen a response if they are experienced after that response occurs. They are roughly equivalent to rewards. The food given to a hungry pigeon after it pecks at a switch is a positive reinforcer; it increases the pigeon's switch pecking. For people, positive reinforcers can include food, smiles, money, and other desirable outcomes. The process of presenting a positive reinforcer after some response is called *positive reinforcement*. **Negative reinforcers** are unpleasant stimuli such as pain, noise, threats, or a disapproving frown that strengthen a response if that response removes them. For example, the disappearance of headache pain after you take an aspirin is a negative reinforcer that makes you more likely to take that pain reliever in the future. When a response is strengthened by the removal of an unpleasant stimulus, the process is called *negative reinforcement*. Notice that **reinforcement** can be presenting something pleasant or removing something unpleasant, but in either case it always *increases* the strength of the behavior that precedes it (see Figure 6.6).

Escape and Avoidance Conditioning
The effects of negative reinforcement can be seen in escape conditioning and avoidance conditioning. **Escape conditioning** occurs as a person or animal learns responses that put an end to an aversive stimulus. The left-hand panel of Figure 6.7 shows a laboratory example in which dogs learn to jump over the barrier in a shuttle box to get away from a shock. In humans, escape conditioning appears not only when we learn to take pills to stop pain but also when parents learn to stop a child's annoying demands for a toy by agreeing to buy it. And television viewers learn to use the mute button to shut off obnoxious commercials.

When an animal or a person responds to a signal in a way that avoids an aversive stimulus that has not yet arrived, **avoidance conditioning** has occurred. Look at the

---

operant A response that has some effect on the world.

reinforcer A stimulus event that increases the probability that the response that immediately preceded it will occur again.

positive reinforcers Stimuli that strengthen a response if they follow that response.

negative reinforcers Unpleasant stimuli, such as pain, that strengthen a response if they are removed following that response.

reinforcement The process through which a particular response is made more likely to recur.

escape conditioning A type of learning in which an organism learns to make a particular response in order to terminate an aversive stimulus.

avoidance conditioning A type of learning in which an organism responds to a signal in a way that prevents exposure to an aversive stimulus.

FIGURE 6.6
Positive and Negative Reinforcement

TRY THIS Remember that behavior is strengthened through *positive reinforcement* when something good follows the behavior. Behavior is strengthened through *negative reinforcement* when something bad is removed following the behavior. To see how these principles apply in your own life, list two examples of situations in which your behavior was affected by positive reinforcement and two in which you were affected by negative reinforcement.

POSITIVE REINFORCEMENT

| **Behavior** You put coins into a vending machine. | **Presentation of a pleasant or positive stimulus** You receive a cold can of soda. | **Frequency of behavior increases** You put coins in vending machines in the future. |

NEGATIVE REINFORCEMENT

| **Behavior** In the middle of a boring date, you say you have a headache. | **Termination of an unpleasant stimulus** The date ends early. | **Frequency of behavior increases** You use the same tactic on future boring dates. |

FIGURE 6.7
A Shuttle Box

A shuttle box has two sections, and its floor is an electric grid. The left-hand panel shows escape conditioning, in which an animal learns to get away from a mild shock by jumping over the barrier when the electricity is turned on. The next two panels show avoidance conditioning. Here the animal has learned to avoid shock by jumping over the barrier when it hears a warning buzzer just before shock occurs. Remember that in escape conditioning, the learned response *stops* an aversive stimulus; in avoidance conditioning, the learned response *prevents* the aversive stimulus from occurring in the first place.

Source: Douglas Hintzman, *The Psychology Of Learning And Memory.* Copyright © 1978. Adapted with permission of the author.

right-hand sections of Figure 6.7 and imagine that a buzzer sounds a few seconds before one side of the shuttle box is electrified. The animal will soon learn to jump over the barrier when the warning buzzer sounds, thus avoiding the shock. Along with positive reinforcement, avoidance conditioning is one of the most important influences on everyday behavior. We go to work or school even when we would rather stay in bed, we stop at red lights even when we are in a hurry, and we apologize for our mistakes even before they are discovered. Each of these behaviors helps us avoid a negative consequence, such as lost pay, bad grades, a traffic ticket, or a scolding.

Notice that avoidance conditioning involves a marriage of classical and operant conditioning. In the shuttle box, for example, the buzzer signals that an unconditioned stimulus (shock) is about to occur. Through classical conditioning, this signal becomes a conditioned stimulus that triggers fear as a conditioned response. Like the shock itself, fear is unpleasant. Once the animal learns to jump over the barrier to avoid shock, this operant response is reinforced by its consequences—the reduction of fear. In short, avoidance conditioning takes place in two steps. The first step involves classical conditioning—a signal is repeatedly paired with shock. The second step involves operant conditioning—learning to make a response that reduces fear.

Once learned, avoidance is a difficult habit to break, because avoidance responses continue to be reinforced by fear reduction (Solomon, Kamin, & Wynne, 1953). So even

Escape conditioning

Avoidance conditioning

if the shock is turned off in a shuttle box, animals may keep jumping when the buzzer sounds because they never discover that avoidance is no longer necessary. The same is often true of people. Those who fear and avoid, say, escalators never get a chance to find out that they are safe. And those with limited social skills may avoid potentially embarrassing social situations, but doing so also prevents them from learning how to be successful in those situations.

The study of avoidance conditioning has not only expanded our understanding of negative reinforcement but has also led psychologists to consider more complex cognitive processes in learning. They suggest, for example, that in order for people to learn to avoid an unpleasant event (such as getting fired or paying a fine), they must have established an expectancy or other mental representation of that event. The role of these mental representations is emphasized later in this chapter in our discussion of the cognitive factors involved in learning.

Discriminative Conditioned Stimuli and Stimulus Control The consequences of behavior can be different in different situations, so success in life often depends on the ability to identify and quickly adjust to changing environments. For example, if pigeons are reinforced with food for pecking at a switch when a red light is on but are not reinforced for pecking when a green light is on, they will soon learn to peck only when they see a red light. Their behavior demonstrates the effect of **discriminative conditioned stimuli,** which are stimuli that signal whether a reinforcer is available if a certain response is made. Most people, too, are sensitive to discriminative conditioned stimuli. They know that a flirtatious comment about someone's appearance may be welcomed on a date but not at the office. And even if you have been repeatedly rewarded for telling jokes, you are not likely to do so at a funeral.

When an organism learns to make a particular response in the presence of one stimulus but not another, *stimulus discrimination* has occurred (see Figure 6.8). Another way to say this is that the response is now under *stimulus control*. In general, stimulus discrimination allows people and animals to learn what is appropriate (reinforced) and inappropriate (not reinforced) in particular situations.

Stimulus generalization also occurs in operant conditioning. For example, a pigeon might peck when it sees an amber light because that light is similar to the red one that had previously signaled the availability of food. And as in classical conditioning, the more similar the new stimulus is to the old one, the more likely it is that the response will be performed. So if you had a wonderful dinner at Captain Jack's, a restaurant

discriminative conditioned stimuli Stimuli that signal whether reinforcement is available if a certain response is made.

Although the artist may not have intended it, this cartoon nicely illustrates one way in which discriminative conditioned stimuli can affect behavior.

"Oh, not bad. The light comes on, I press the bar, they write me a check. How about you?"

FIGURE 6.8
Stimulus Discrimination
In this experiment, the rat could jump from a stand through any of three doors, but it was reinforced with food only if it jumped through the door with the vertical stripes. The vertically striped door appeared in a different location on each trial, but the rat soon learned to discriminate the vertical from the horizontal stripes and to choose the correct door.

© Frank Lotz Miller/Black Star

that was decorated to look like the inside of a sailing ship, you might later choose to eat at places with similar names or interiors.

As in classical conditioning, stimulus discrimination and stimulus generalization often complement each other in operant conditioning. In one study, for example, pigeons received food for pecking at a switch, but only when they saw certain works of art (Watanabe, Sakamoto, & Wakita, 1995). As a result, these birds learned to discriminate the works of the impressionist painter Claude Monet from those of the cubist painter Pablo Picasso. Later, when the birds were shown new paintings by other impressionist and cubist artists, they were able to generalize from the original artists to other artists who painted in the same style. It was as if they had learned the conceptual categories of "impressionism" and "cubism." We humans learn to place people and things into even more finely detailed categories, such as "honest," "dangerous," or "tax-deductible." We discriminate one stimulus from another and then, through generalization, respond similarly to all stimuli we perceive to be in a particular category. This ability to respond in a similar way to all members of a category can save us considerable time and effort, but as described in the chapter on social cognition, it can also lead to the development of unwarranted prejudice against certain groups of people.

Forming and Strengthening Operant Behavior

Daily life is full of examples of operant conditioning. People go to movies, parties, classes, and jobs primarily because doing so brings reinforcers. Let's consider how operant behavior develops and how the type and timing of reinforcers affect the operant conditioning process.

Shaping   Imagine that you want to train your dog, Henry, to sit and to "shake hands." The basic method using positive reinforcement is obvious: Every time Henry sits and shakes hands, you give him a treat. But the problem is also obvious: Smart as Henry is, he may never make the desired response on his own, so you will never be able to give the reinforcer. Instead of your teaching and Henry's learning, the two of you will just stare at each other (and he'll probably wag his tail).

The way around this problem is to *shape* Henry's behavior. **Shaping** is accomplished by reinforcing *successive approximations*—that is, responses that come successively closer to the desired response. So you might first give Henry a treat whenever he sits down. Then you might reinforce him only when he sits and partially lifts

shaping The process of reinforcing responses that come successively closer to the desired response.

Getting the Hang of It

Learning to eat with a spoon is, as you can see, a hit-and-miss process at first. However, this child will learn to hit the target more and more often as the food reward gradually shapes a more efficient, and far less messy, pattern of behavior.

Secondary Reinforcers

Words of praise or thanks, gold stars, check marks, and "two thumbs up" gestures are just a few of the stimuli that can serve as secondary reinforcers for humans. Parents and teachers have used these reinforcers for generations to shape the behavior of children in accordance with their cultural values.

primary reinforcers Reinforcers that meet an organism's basic needs, such as food and water.

secondary reinforcer A reward that people or animals learn to like.

a paw. Next, you might reinforce more complete paw lifting. Eventually, you would require that Henry perform the entire sit-lift-shake sequence before giving the treat. Shaping is an extremely powerful, widely used tool. Animal trainers use it to teach chimpanzees to roller-skate, dolphins to jump through hoops, and pigeons to play Ping-Pong (Coren, 1999).

Secondary Reinforcement   Operant conditioning often begins with the use of **primary reinforcers,** events or stimuli—such as food or water—that are innately rewarding. But Henry's training will be slowed if he has to stop and eat every time he makes a correct response. Also, once he is full, food will no longer act as an effective reinforcer. To avoid these problems, animal trainers and others in the teaching business rely on the principle of secondary reinforcement.

A **secondary reinforcer** is a previously neutral stimulus that takes on reinforcing properties when paired with a stimulus that is already reinforcing. In other words, secondary reinforcers are rewards that people or animals learn to like (Seo & Lee, 2009). For example, if you say, "Good boy!" a moment before you give Henry each food reward, these words will become associated with the food and can then be used alone to reinforce Henry's behavior (as long as the words are again paired with food now and then). Does this remind you of classical conditioning? It should, because the primary reinforcer (food) is an unconditioned stimulus. If the sound of "Good boy!" predictably precedes, and thus signals, food, it becomes a conditioned stimulus. For this reason, secondary reinforcers are sometimes called *conditioned reinforcers.*

The power of operant conditioning can be greatly increased by using secondary reinforcers. Consider the secondary reinforcer we call money. Some people will do almost anything for it despite the fact that it tastes terrible and won't quench your thirst. Its reinforcing power lies in its association with the many rewards it can buy. Other forms of social approval (such as the words "Great work!") are also important secondary reinforcers for human beings. However, secondary reinforcers can vary a great deal from person to person and culture to culture. For example, tickets to a rock concert are an effective secondary reinforcer for some people but not everyone. And a ceremony honoring outstanding job performance might be highly reinforcing to most employees in individualist cultures but embarrassing for some employees from cultures in which group cooperation is valued more than personal distinction (Miller, 2001). Still, when chosen carefully, secondary reinforcers can build or maintain behavior even when primary reinforcement is absent for long periods.

Delay and Size of Reinforcement   Much of our behavior is learned and maintained because it is regularly reinforced. But many people overeat, smoke, drink too much, or procrastinate, even though they know these behaviors are bad for them. They may want to change, but they seem to lack self-control. If behavior is controlled by its consequences, why do people do things that are ultimately harmful?

Part of the answer lies in the *timing* of reinforcers. In general, the effect of a reinforcer is stronger when it comes soon after a response occurs (Rachlin, 2000). The good feelings (positive reinforcers) that follow, say, drinking too much are immediate and strong. The hangovers and other negative consequences are usually delayed, so their effects on future drinking are weakened. Similarly, a dieter's efforts to eat less will eventually lead to weight loss, but because that reinforcer is delayed, it may have less impact than the immediate pleasure of eating a jelly donut. In fact, under some conditions, delaying a positive reinforcer for even a few seconds can decrease the effectiveness of positive reinforcement. (An advantage of using praise or other secondary reinforcers is that they can easily be delivered immediately after a desired response occurs.)

The *size* of a reinforcer is also important. In general, operant conditioning occurs more quickly when the reinforcer is large than when it is small. For example, a strong electrical shock will cause a faster escape or avoidance response than a weak one.

© Bruce Forster/Stone/Getty Images

Reinforcement Schedules on the Job

TRY THIS Make a list of all the jobs you have ever held, along with the reinforcement schedule on which each employer paid you. Which of the four types of schedules (FR, FI, VR, VI) was most common, and which did you find most satisfying?

continuous reinforcement A pattern in which a reinforcer is delivered every time a particular response occurs.

partial reinforcement A pattern in which a reinforcer is administered only some of the time after a particular response occurs.

fixed-ratio (FR) reinforcement A partial reinforcement schedule that provides reinforcement following a fixed number of responses.

variable-ratio (VR) reinforcement A partial reinforcement schedule that provides reinforcement after a varying number of responses.

fixed-interval (FI) reinforcement A partial reinforcement schedule that provides reinforcement for the first response that occurs after some fixed time has passed since the last reward.

variable-interval (VI) reinforcement A partial reinforcement schedule that provides reinforcement for the first response after varying periods of time.

reinforcement schedules In operant conditioning, rules that determine how and when certain responses will be reinforced.

Schedules of Reinforcement   We flip a light switch, and the light comes on. We put money in a vending machine, and the item we want comes out. When a reinforcer is delivered every time a particular response occurs, the arrangement is called **continuous reinforcement,** or a *continuous reinforcement schedule*. This schedule can be helpful when teaching someone a new skill, but it can be impractical in the long run. Imagine how inefficient it would be, for example, if an employer had to deliver praise or pay following every little task employees performed all day long. So quite often reinforcement is administered only some of the time, an arrangement called **partial reinforcement,** also called a *partial*, or *intermittent, reinforcement schedule*.

Most partial reinforcement schedules can be described in terms of when and how reinforcers are given. "When" refers to the number of responses that have to occur, or the amount of time that must pass, before a reinforcer will occur. "How" refers to whether the reinforcer will be delivered in a predictable or unpredictable way. Accordingly, there are four basic types of intermittent reinforcement schedules:

1. **Fixed-ratio (FR) reinforcement** provides a reinforcer following a fixed number of responses. So rats might receive food after every tenth time they press the lever in a Skinner box (FR 10) or after every twentieth time (FR 20). Computer help desk technicians might be allowed to take a break after every fifth call they handle or every tenth.

2. **Variable-ratio (VR) reinforcement** also provides a reinforcer after a given number of responses, but that number can vary. On these schedules, it is impossible to predict which particular response will bring reinforcement. A rat on a VR 30 schedule might sometimes be reinforced after ten lever presses, sometimes after fifty, and sometimes after five, but the *average* number of responses required to get a reinforcer would be thirty. Gambling offers humans a similar variable-ratio schedule. A slot machine, for example, pays off only after a frustratingly unpredictable number of trials averaging perhaps one in twenty.

3. **Fixed-interval (FI) reinforcement** provides a reinforcer for the first response that occurs after some fixed time has passed since the last reward, no matter how many responses have been made during that interval. For example, on an FI 60 schedule, the first response after sixty seconds have passed will be rewarded. Some radio stations create fixed-interval schedules by telling listeners who just won a prize that they are not eligible to win again for thirty days. Under these circumstances, there is no point in competing until that time has elapsed.

4. **Variable-interval (VI) reinforcement** gives a reinforcer for the first response after some period of time, but the amount of time varies. On a VI 60 schedule, for example, the first response to occur after an average of sixty seconds is reinforced, but the actual time between reinforcements might vary from, say, one second to 120 seconds. Kindergarten teachers use VI schedules to help keep order in class by giving rewards to children who are in their seats when a chime sounds—at unpredictably varying intervals.

Figure 6.9 shows that different **reinforcement schedules** produce different patterns of behavior (Skinner, 1961). The figure illustrates two important points. First, both fixed-ratio and variable-ratio schedules produce high rates of behavior overall. The reason in both cases is that the frequency of the reward depends directly on the rate of responding. Industrial and organizational psychologists have applied this principle to help companies increase worker productivity and reduce absenteeism. Workers who are paid on the basis of the number of items they produce or the number of days they show up for work usually produce more items and miss fewer workdays (Muchinsky, 2003). Similarly, gamblers reinforced on a variable-ratio schedule for pushing a slot machine button, rolling dice, or playing other games of chance tend to maintain a high rate of responding—some people are virtually unable to stop.

The second important aspect of Figure 6.9 relates to the curves, or "scallops," shown in the fixed-interval schedule. Under this schedule, it does not matter how

FIGURE 6.9
Schedules of Reinforcement

These curves illustrate the patterns of behavior typically seen under different reinforcement schedules. The steeper the curve, the faster the response rate. The thin diagonal lines crossing the curves show when reinforcement was given. In general, the rate of responding is higher under ratio schedules than under interval schedules.

Source: Data from "Teaching Machines," by B.F. Skinner. *Scientific American*, 1961, 205(11), 90–102.

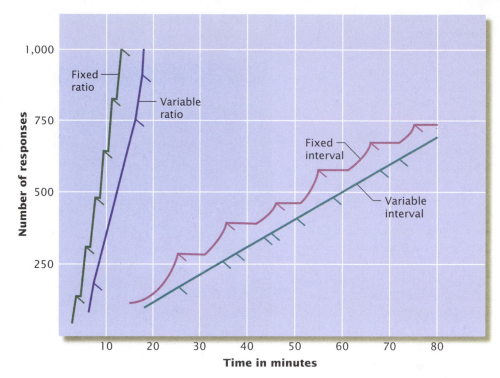

many responses are made during the time between rewards. As a result, the rate of responding typically drops dramatically immediately after a reinforcer occurs and then increases as the time for another reward approaches. When teachers schedule all their quizzes in advance, for example, some students study just before each quiz and then virtually stop studying in that course until just before the next quiz. Behavior rewarded on variable-interval schedules looks quite different. The unpredictable timing of rewards typically generates slow, steady responding. So students whose teacher might give a pop quiz at any class session are more likely to study for that course almost every day (Kouyoumdjian, 2004).

Schedules and Extinction   In the section on classical conditioning, you saw that if a conditioned stimulus no longer predicts the appearance of an unconditioned stimulus, the conditioned response to that conditioned stimulus will weaken through the process called extinction. Similarly, if an operant response is no longer followed by a reinforcer, the response will occur less and less often and eventually may disappear, or *extinguish*. If lever pressing no longer brings food, a rat stops pressing; if repeated text messages to a friend are not answered, you eventually stop sending them. As in classical conditioning, **extinction** in operant conditioning does not totally erase previously learned relationships (Delamater, 2004). If a discriminative conditioned stimulus reappears at some time after an operant response has been extinguished, that response may recur (spontaneously recover), and if it is again reinforced, it will quickly return to its former level, as though extinction had never happened.

In general, behaviors learned under a partial reinforcement schedule are far more difficult to extinguish than those learned on a continuous reinforcement schedule. This phenomenon—called the **partial reinforcement effect**—is easy to understand if you imagine yourself in a gambling casino, standing near a broken slot machine and a broken candy machine. You might put money in the broken candy machine once, but this behavior will probably stop (extinguish) very quickly. The candy machine should deliver its goodies on a continuous reinforcement schedule, so you can easily tell that it is not going to provide a reinforcer. But slot machines offer rewards on an unpredictable intermittent schedule, so you might put in coin after coin, unsure of whether the machine is broken or is simply not paying off at that particular moment.

extinction The gradual disappearance of operant behavior due to elimination of rewards for that behavior.

partial reinforcement effect A phenomenon in which behaviors learned under a partial reinforcement schedule are more difficult to extinguish than behaviors learned on a continuous reinforcement schedule.

Superstition and Partial Reinforcement

Partial reinforcement helps sustain superstitious athletic rituals—such as a fixed sequence of actions prior to hitting a golf ball or shooting a free throw in a basketball game. If the ritual has preceded success often enough, failure to execute it may upset the player and disrupt performance. Former Oakland Athletics infielder Nomar Garciaparra used to loosen, tug, and retighten each batting glove after every pitch. Those who watch sports have their superstitious rituals too. One Pittsburgh Steelers football fan we know insists on wearing the same outfit while watching every game and eats a particular brand of lime-flavored corn chips to be sure his team will score.

© AP Photo/Ben Margot

Partial reinforcement also helps explain why superstitious behavior is so resistant to extinction (Vyse, 2000). Suppose that you had been out for a run just before hearing that you passed an important exam. The run did nothing to cause this outcome; the reward followed it through sheer coincidence. Still, for some people, this *accidental reinforcement* can strengthen actions that preceded, and thus appeared to "cause," good news or other rewards or events (Mellon, 2009; Pronin et al., 2006). Those people might then run "for luck" after every exam or take exams only with their "lucky pen" or while wearing their "lucky shirt" (Hendrick, 2003). Of course, the laws of chance dictate that doing such things is bound to be followed by something good every now and then, thus further strengthening the superstitious behavior on a sparse partial schedule (Vyse, 2000).

Why Reinforcers Work

What makes reinforcers reinforcing? For primary reinforcers, at least, the reason could be that they satisfy hunger, thirst, and other needs that are basic to survival. This explanation is incomplete. For example, artificial sweeteners, which have no nutritional value, can have as much reinforcing power as sugar, which is nutritious.

Some psychologists have argued that reinforcement is based not on a stimulus itself but on the opportunity to engage in an activity that involves the stimulus. According to David Premack (1965), at any moment, each person maintains a list of behavioral preferences, ranked from most desirable to least desirable, like a kind of psychological "Top Ten." The higher on the list an activity is, the greater is its power as a reinforcer. This means that a preferred activity can serve as a reinforcer for any other activity that is less preferred at the moment. So when parents allow their teenage daughter to use the car in return for mowing the lawn, they are using something high on her preference list (driving) to reinforce an activity that is lower on the list (lawn mowing). This idea is known as *Premack's principle.*

Taking Premack's principle a step further, some psychologists have suggested that virtually any activity can become a reinforcer if a person or animal has not been allowed to perform that activity for a while (Timberlake & Farmer-Dougan, 1991). To understand how this *response deprivation hypothesis* works, suppose that you would rather study than work out at the gym. Now suppose that the gym has been closed for several weeks. According to the response deprivation hypothesis, because your opportunity to exercise has been held below its normal level, its value as a reinforcer has been raised. In fact, it might have become so preferred that it could be used to reinforce studying! In short, under certain circumstances, even activities that are normally not strongly preferred can become reinforcers for normally more preferred activities. The response deprivation hypothesis helps explain why money is such a powerful secondary reinforcer: It can be exchanged for whatever a person finds reinforcing at the moment. In fact, some researchers believe that the response deprivation hypothesis may provide a better overall explanation of why reinforcers work than Premack's principle does (Hergenhahn & Olson, 1997).

Research by biological psychologists suggests that the stimuli and activities we know as reinforcers may work by exerting particular effects within the brain. This possibility was raised decades ago when James Olds and Peter Milner (1954) discovered that mild electrical stimulation of certain areas of the hypothalamus can be such a powerful reinforcer that a hungry rat will ignore food in a Skinner box, preferring to spend hours pressing a lever that stimulates these "pleasure centers" in its brain (Olds, 1973). It is not yet clear whether physiological mechanisms underlie the power of all reinforcers, but evidence available so far suggests that these mechanisms are important components of the process (Waelti, Dickinson, & Schultz, 2001). For example, as mentioned in the chapter on biological aspects of psychology, activation of dopamine systems is associated with the pleasure of many stimuli, including food, music, sex, the uncertainty involved in gambling, and some addictive drugs, such as cocaine (Blood & Zatorre, 2001; Ciccocioppo, Sanna, & Weiss, 2001; Hewig et al., 2010; Reuter et al., 2005; Tobler, Fiorillo, & Schultz, 2005). Indeed, it appears that complex and widespread patterns of brain activity are involved in our response to reinforcers, allowing us to enjoy them, to learn to want them, and to learn how to get them (Dreher et al., 2010; Montague, Hyman, & Cohen, 2004; Pessiglione et al., 2006; Robinson et al., 2005).

Punishment

So far we have discussed positive and negative reinforcement, both of which *increase* the frequency of a response, either by presenting something pleasurable or by removing something unpleasant. In contrast, **punishment** *reduces* the frequency of an operant behavior by presenting an unpleasant stimulus or removing a pleasant one. Shouting "No!" and swatting your cat when she begins chewing on your plants illustrates the kind of punishment that presents an unpleasant stimulus following a response. Taking away a child's TV privileges because of rude behavior is a second kind of punishment—sometimes called *penalty*—that removes a positive stimulus (see Figure 6.10).

Punishment is often confused with negative reinforcement, but they are actually quite different. Reinforcement of any sort always *strengthens* behavior; punishment weakens it. If shock is *turned off* when a rat presses a lever, that is negative reinforcement. It increases the chances that the rat will press the lever when shock occurs again. But if shock is *turned on* when the rat presses the lever, that is punishment. The rat will be less likely to press the lever again.

Punishment can certainly alter behavior, but it has several potential drawbacks (Gershoff & Bitensky, 2007). First, it does not "erase" an undesirable habit; it merely suppresses it. This suppression usually occurs in the presence of stimuli (such as a parent or teacher) that were around at the time of punishment. In other words, people may repeat previously punished acts when they think they can avoid detection. This tendency is summed up in the adage "When the cat's away, the mice will play." Second,

punishment Presentation of an aversive stimulus or the removal of a pleasant stimulus.

FIGURE 6.10
Two Kinds of Punishment

In one form of punishment, a behavior is followed by an aversive or unpleasant stimulus. In a second form of punishment, sometimes called *penalty,* a pleasant stimulus is removed following a behavior. In either case, punishment reduces the chances that the behavior will occur in the future. When a toddler reaches toward an electric outlet and her father says, *"No!"* and gently taps her hand, is that punishment or negative reinforcement? (If you said "punishment," you are right, because it will *reduce* the likelihood of touching outlets in the future.)

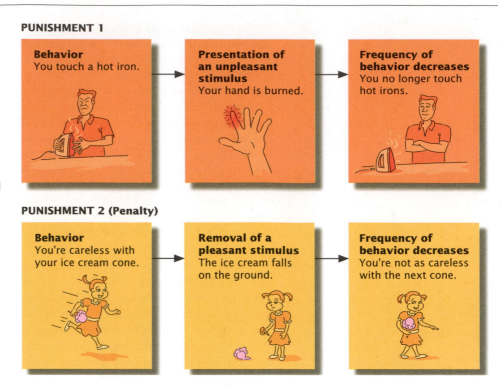

PUNISHMENT 1

Behavior
You touch a hot iron.
→
Presentation of an unpleasant stimulus
Your hand is burned.
→
Frequency of behavior decreases
You no longer touch hot irons.

PUNISHMENT 2 (Penalty)

Behavior
You're careless with your ice cream cone.
→
Removal of a pleasant stimulus
The ice cream falls on the ground.
→
Frequency of behavior decreases
You're not as careless with the next cone.

punishment sometimes produces unwanted side effects. For example, if you severely punish a child, the child may associate punishment with the punisher and end up fearing you. Third, punishment is often ineffective unless it is given immediately after the response and each time the response is made. This is especially true in relation to animals or young children. If a child gets into a cookie jar and enjoys a few cookies before being discovered and punished, the effect of the punishment will be greatly reduced. Similarly, if a child confesses to misbehavior and is then punished, the punishment may discourage honesty rather than eliminate undesirable behavior. Fourth, physical punishment can become aggression and even abuse if administered in anger or with an object other than a hand (Zolotor et al., 2008). Fifth, because children tend to imitate what they see, children who are frequently punished may be more likely to behave aggressively themselves (Gilbert, 1997). Finally, although punishment signals that inappropriate behavior occurred, it does not specify what should be done instead. An F on a term paper says the assignment was poorly done, but that punishing grade alone tells the student nothing about how to improve.

In the 1970s and 1980s, concerns over these drawbacks led many professionals to discourage parents from using spanking and other forms of punishment with their children (Rosellini, 1998). More recent studies suggesting that occasional mild spanking can be an effective way to control the behavior of children who are between 3 and 13 years of age (e.g., Larzelere, 2000) have served to reopen the debate about this issue (Benjet & Kazdin, 2003; Berlin et al., 2009; Kazdin & Benjet, 2003; Slade & Wissow, 2004; Straus, 2005). These studies found that occasional spanking does not harm children's development, if used in combination with other disciplinary practices. These other practices include requiring that the children pay some penalty for their misdeeds, having them provide some sort of restitution to the victims of their actions, and making them aware of what they did wrong (Gunnoe & Mariner, 1997; Larzelere, 1996).

When used *properly,* then, punishment can be a valuable tool (Baumrind, Larzelere, & Cowan, 2002). Occasionally, it may be the only alternative. For example, some children with developmental disabilities hit or mutilate themselves or display other potentially life-threatening behaviors. As shown in Figure 6.11, punishing these behaviors has sometimes proved to be the only effective treatment (e.g., Flavell et al.,

FIGURE 6.11

Lifesaving Punishment

This child suffered from chronic ruminative disorder, a condition in which he vomited everything he ate. At left, the boy was approximately 1 year old and had been vomiting for four months. At right is the same child thirteen days after punishment with electric shock had eliminated the vomiting behavior. His weight had increased 26 percent. He was physically and psychologically healthy when tested six months, one year, and two years later.

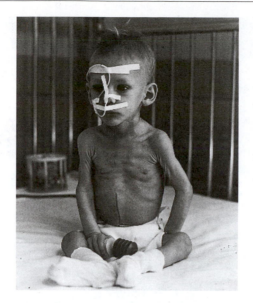
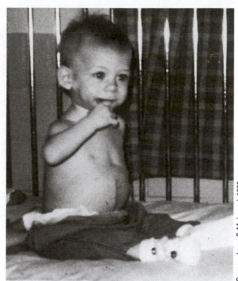

Source: Lang & Melamed, 1969

1982). Whatever the case, punishment is most effective when it is administered in accordance with several guidelines. First, the person giving punishment should specify why it is being given and that its purpose is to change the person's behavior, not to harm or demean the person. This step helps prevent a general fear of the punisher. Second, without being abusive, punishment should be immediate and noticeable enough to eliminate the undesirable behavior. A halfhearted "Quit it" may actually reinforce a child's misbehavior, because almost any attention is reinforcing to some children. Moreover, if children become habituated to very mild punishment, the parent may end up using substantially more severe punishment to stop inappropriate behavior than would have been necessary if a stern but moderate punishment had been used in the first place. (You may have witnessed this *escalation effect* in grocery stores or restaurants, where parents are often not initially firm enough in dealing with their children's misbehavior.) Finally, because punishment alone is usually not enough to change behavior in the long run, it is important also to identify what the person should do instead of the punished act and then to reinforce the appropriate behavior when it occurs. As the frequency of appropriate behavior increases through reinforcement, the frequency of undesirable responses (and the need for further punishment) should decline.

When these guidelines are not followed, the potentially beneficial effects of punishment may disappear or be only temporary. As illustrated in many countries' justice systems, punishment for criminal acts is typically administered long after the acts have occurred, and initial punishments are often relatively mild—as when offenders are repeatedly given probation. Even being sent to prison rarely leads to rehabilitation, because this punishment is usually not supplemented by efforts to teach and reinforce noncriminal lifestyles (Cassel & Bernstein, 2007). It is no wonder, then, that about two-thirds of U.S. prison inmates are rearrested for felonies or serious misdemeanors within three years of completing their sentences and that about 50 percent of them will return to prison (Cassel & Bernstein, 2007).

Some Applications of Operant Conditioning

The principles of operant conditioning were originally developed with animals in the laboratory, but they are valuable for understanding human behavior in an endless variety of everyday situations. ("In Review: Reinforcement and Punishment" summarizes some key principles of operant conditioning.) The unscientific but effective use of rewards and punishments by parents, teachers, and peers is vital to helping

Speak Up!

Students are often reluctant to make comments or to ask or answer questions, especially in large classrooms. Some professors have used operant conditioning principles to help overcome this problem. In one introductory psychology course, classroom participation was reinforced with coinlike tokens that students could exchange for extra credit (Boniecki & Moore, 2003). The students responded faster to the professor's questions and offered many more comments and questions when this "token economy" was introduced. The frequency of student questions and comments dropped again when tokens were no longer given, but students continued their quick responses to the professor's questions. By that time, apparently, the professor's social reinforcement was enough to encourage this aspect of classroom participation.

children learn what is and is not appropriate behavior at the dinner table, in the classroom, or at a birthday party. People learn how to be "civilized" in their own cultures partly through positive ("Good!") and negative ("Stop that!") responses from others. As described in the chapter on human development, differing patterns of rewards and punishments for boys and girls also underlie the development of behaviors that fit culturally approved *gender roles*.

The scientific study of operant conditioning has led to numerous treatment programs for modifying problematic behavior. These programs combine rewards for appropriate behaviors with extinction methods or carefully administered punishment for inappropriate behaviors. They have helped countless mental patients, people with intellectual disability or traumatic brain injuries, children with severe forms of autistic disorder, and preschoolers with emotional and behavioral disorders develop the behaviors they need to live happier and more productive lives (e.g., Alberto, Troutman, & Feagin, 2002; Dickerson, Tenhula, & Green-Paden, 2005; Pear & Martin, 2002). These same methods have been used successfully to help people lose weight, give up addictive drugs, and reduce alcohol-related memory problems (Hochhalter et al., 2001; Silverman et al., 2001; Volpp et al., 2008). Many self-help books also incorporate principles of positive reinforcement, recommending self-reward following each small victory in efforts to lose weight, stop smoking, avoid procrastination, or reach other goals (e.g., Grant & Kim, 2002; Rachlin, 2000).

When people can't do anything about the consequences of a behavior, discriminative conditioned stimuli may hold the key to changing the behavior. For example, a compulsive gambler might fight the urge to gamble by staying away from casinos (Tremblay, Boutin, & Ladouceur, 2008), and people trying to quit smoking often find it easier to do so if they avoid bars and other places where there are discriminative conditioned stimuli for smoking. Stimulus control can also be applied in the treatment of insomnia. Many insomniacs use their beds for working, watching television, texting, reading, eating, talking on the phone, and worrying. Soon the bedroom becomes a discriminative conditioned stimulus for so many activities that relaxation and sleep become less and less likely. *Stimulus control therapy* encourages insomniacs to use their beds only for sleeping, and perhaps sex, making it more likely that they will sleep better when in bed (Edinger et al., 2001).

IN REVIEW	Reinforcement and Punishment	
Concept	**Description**	**Example or Comment**
Positive reinforcement	Increasing the frequency of a behavior by following it with the presentation of a positive reinforcer—a pleasant, positive stimulus or experience	You say, "Good job!" after someone works hard to perform a task.
Negative reinforcement	Increasing the frequency of a behavior by following it with the removal of an unpleasant stimulus or experience	You learn to use the "mute" button on the TV remote control to remove the sound of an obnoxious commercial.
Escape conditioning	Learning to make a response that removes an unpleasant stimulus	A little boy learns that crying will cut short the time that he must stay in his room.
Avoidance conditioning	Learning to make a response that avoids an unpleasant stimulus	You slow your car to the speed limit when you spot a police car, thus avoiding being stopped and reducing the fear of a fine; very resistant to extinction.
Punishment	Decreasing the frequency of a behavior by either presenting an unpleasant stimulus or removing a pleasant one (penalty)	You swat the dog after it steals food from the table, or you take a favorite toy away from a child who misbehaves. A number of cautions should be kept in mind before using punishment.

1. Taking an aspirin can relieve headache pain, so people learn to do so through the process of _____ reinforcement.

2. The "walk" sign that tells people it is safe to cross the street is an example of a _____ stimulus.

3. Response rates tend to be higher under _____ schedules of reinforcement than under _____ schedules.

LINKAGES How are learned associations stored in memory? (a link to Memory, p. 246)

LINKAGES

Neural Networks and Learning

You have seen that associations between conditioned stimuli and reflexes or between responses and their consequences play an important role in learning. How are these associations actually stored in the brain? No one yet knows for sure, but neural network models provide a good way of thinking about the process. As suggested in the chapters on perception and memory, networks of neural connections in the brain are believed to play a critical role not only in recognizing objects but also in storing and organizing information. These associative networks can be very complex. Consider the word *dog*. As shown in Figure 6.12, each person's experience creates many associations with this word, and the strength of each association will reflect the frequency with which *dog* has been mentally linked to the other objects, events, and ideas in that person's life.

Using what they know about the laws of learning and about the way neurons communicate and alter their synaptic connections, psychologists have been developing models of how these associations are established (Messinger et al., 2001). We discuss some of their efforts in the chapters on perception and memory in terms of *neural networks* and *parallel distributed processing* models. An important feature of these models is the idea of distributed memory or distributed knowledge. They suggest, for example, that the knowledge of "dog" does not lie in a single location, or node, in your brain. Instead, knowledge is distributed throughout the network of associations that connect the letters *D*, *O*, and *G*, along with other dog-related experiences. In

FIGURE 6.12
An Associative Network
Here is an example of a network of associations with the word *dog*. Network theorists suggest that the connections shown here represent patterns of neural connections in the brain.

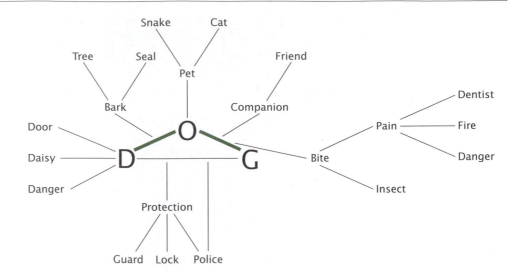

addition, as shown in Figure 6.12, each of the interconnected nodes that make up your knowledge of "dog" is connected to many other nodes as well. So the letter *D* will be connected to "daisy," "danger," and a host of other concepts. Networks of connections also appear to be the key to explaining how people come to understand the words and sentences they read (Wolman, van den Broek, & Lorch, 1997).

Neural network models of learning focus on how these connections are developed through experience (Hanson & Burr, 1990). For example, suppose that you are learning a new word in a foreign language. Each time you read the word and associate it with its English equivalent, you strengthen the neural connections between the sight of the letters forming that word and all of the nodes activated when its English equivalent is brought to mind. Neural network, or *connectionist,* models of learning predict how much the strength of each linkage grows (in terms of the likelihood of neural communication between the two connected nodes) each time the two words are experienced together. The details of various theories about how these connections grow are very complex, but a theme common to many of them is that the weaker the connection between two items, the greater the increase in connection strength when they are experienced together. So in a simple classical conditioning experiment, the connections between the nodes characterizing the conditioned stimulus and those characterizing the unconditioned stimulus will show the greatest increase in strength during the first few learning trials. Notice that this prediction nicely matches the typical learning curve shown in Figure 6.3 (Rescorla & Wagner, 1972).

Neural network models have yet to fully explain the learning of complex tasks, nor can they easily account for how people adapt when the "rules of the game" are suddenly changed and old habits must be unlearned and replaced. Nevertheless, a better understanding of what we mean by *associations* may very well lie in future research on neural network models (Boden, 2006; Houghton, 2005).

Cognitive Processes in Learning

During the first half of the twentieth century, psychologists in North America tended to look at classical and operant conditioning through the lens of behaviorism, the theoretical approach that was dominant in psychology at the time. As described in the chapter on introducing psychology, behaviorists tried to identify the stimuli, responses, and consequences that build and alter overt behavior. They paid almost no attention to the role of conscious mental activity that might accompany the learning process.

This strictly behavioral view of classical and operant conditioning is challenged by the cognitive approach, which has become increasingly influential in recent decades. Cognitive psychologists see a common thread in these apparently different forms of learning (Blaisdell, Sawa, & Leising, 2006). To them, both classical and operant conditioning help animals and people detect causality—to understand what causes what. They view conditioning as the product of complex mental and neural processes, including how people represent, store, and use information. It is these processes, they say, that underlie our ability to adapt to and understand the world around us (Dickinson, 2001).

Cognitive psychologists have found, for example, that a classically conditioned response (such as fear) is more likely to develop if an unconditioned stimulus (such as electric shock) comes as a surprise than if it is expected (Kamin, 1969). Even the brain's reaction to a given stimulus can differ depending on whether that stimulus was expected or unexpected (Waelti, Dickinson, & Schultz, 2001). In other words, according to the cognitive view, learning is affected not only by the nature of the stimuli we experience but also by our expectations about them. Expectations also allow us to calculate the likely consequences of various courses of actions (Lohrenz et al., 2007; Tanaka, Balleine, & O'Doherty, 2008). Further, just as our perceptions depend on the meaning we attach to sensations (see the chapter on perception), what we learn can depend on the meaning we attach to events. So a good evaluation by a boss we respect may serve as a stronger reinforcer than the same good evaluation from a boss we hate.

Evidence for the role of these cognitive processes in learning comes from research on learned helplessness, latent learning, cognitive maps, insight, and observational learning.

Learned Helplessness

Babies learn that crying attracts attention, children learn which button turns on the TV, and adults learn what behaviors are rewarded or punished in the workplace. On the basis of this learning, we come to expect that certain actions on our part cause certain consequences. But sometimes events are beyond our control. What happens when behavior has no effects on events, especially when escape or avoidance behaviors fail? If such ineffectiveness is prolonged, one result may be **learned helplessness,** a tendency to give up any effort to control the environment (Overmier, 2002; Seligman, 1975).

Learned helplessness was first demonstrated in animals. As described earlier, dogs placed in a shuttle box (see Figure 6.7) will normally learn to jump over a barrier to escape a shock. However, if these dogs first receive shocks that they cannot escape, they later do not even try to escape when a shock is turned on in the box (Overmier & Seligman, 1967). It is as if the animals had learned that "shock happens, and there is nothing I can do to control it."

FOCUS ON RESEARCH METHODS ▶

An Experiment on Human Helplessness

The results of animal studies on learned helplessness led psychologists to wonder whether learned helplessness might also play a role in human psychological problems. But they first had to deal with a more basic question: Does lack of control over the environment lead to helplessness in humans, as it does in other species?

What was the researcher's question?

Donald Hiroto (1974) conducted an experiment to test the hypothesis that people would develop learned helplessness after either experiencing lack of control or simply being told that their control was limited.

How did the researcher answer the question?

Hiroto assigned research participants to one of three groups. One group heard a series of thirty random bursts of loud, obnoxious noise, and like dogs receiving inescapable shock, they had no way to stop it. A second group could control the noise by pressing a button to turn it off. The third group heard no noise at all. After this preliminary phase, all three groups were exposed to eighteen additional bursts of noise, each preceded by a red warning light. During this second phase, *all* participants could stop the noise by pushing a lever. However, they didn't know

learned helplessness Learning that responses do not affect consequences, resulting in failure to try to exert control over the environment.

whether to push the lever to the left or the right on any given trial. Still, they could prevent the noise if they acted quickly enough.

Before these new trials began, the experimenter led half the participants in each group to expect that avoiding or escaping the noise depended on their skill. The other half were led to expect that their success would be a matter of chance. So in this experiment, the dependent variable—the participants' efforts to control noise—could be affected by either or both of two independent variables: prior experience with noise (control, lack of control, or no noise) and expectation (skill or chance) about the ability to influence the noise.

What did the researcher find?

On average, participants who had previously experienced lack of control now failed to control noise on almost four times as many trials (50 percent vs. 13 percent) as participants who had earlier been in control. *Expectation* of control also had an effect on behavior. Regardless of whether participants had experienced control before, those who expected noise control to depend on their skill exerted control on significantly more trials than did those who expected chance to govern the outcome.

What do the results mean?

These results supported Hiroto's hypothesis that people, like other animals, tend to make less effort to control their environment when prior experience leads them to expect that their efforts will be in vain. Unlike other animals, though, people can develop expectations of helplessness either by personally experiencing lack of control or by being *told* that they are powerless. Hiroto's (1974) results appear to reflect a general phenomenon: When people's prior experience leads them to *believe* that nothing they do can change their lives or control their destiny, they generally stop trying (Faulkner, 2001; LoLordo, 2001; Peterson, Maier, & Seligman, 1993). Instead, they tend to passively endure distressing situations.

What do we still need to know?

Further research is needed on when and how learned helplessness affects people's thoughts, feelings, and actions. For example, could learned helplessness explain why some battered women remain with abusive partners? We do know that learned-helplessness experiences are associated with the development of a generally pessimistic way of thinking that can produce depression and other disorders (Peterson & Seligman, 1984). People with this *pessimistic explanatory style* see the good things that happen to them as temporary and due to chance and the bad things as permanent and due to internal factors (e.g., lack of ability). This explanatory style has in fact been associated with poor grades, inadequate sales performance, health problems, and other negative outcomes (Bennett & Elliott, 2002; Seligman & Schulman, 1986; Taylor, 2002). The exact mechanisms responsible for this connection are still unknown, but understanding how pessimistic (or optimistic) explanatory styles can lead to negative (or positive) consequences remains an important focus of research (e.g., Brennan & Charnetski, 2000).

Does repeated success at controlling events create a sense of "learned mastery" or "learned resourcefulness" that supports efforts to exert control in new situations? Animal experiments suggest that this is the case (Volpicelli et al., 1983). Further, people with a history of successful control appear more likely than others to develop the *optimistic cognitive style,* hopefulness, and resilience that lead to even more success and healthier lives (Gillham, 2000; Zimmerman, 1990). (We discuss this cognitive style in the chapter on health, stress, and coping.) Accordingly, research is focusing on how best to minimize learned helplessness and maximize learned optimism in areas such as education, parenting, and psychotherapy (e.g., Jackson, Sellers, & Peterson, 2002). One option is the use of "resiliency training" for children and adults at risk for depression or other problems (Bradshaw et al., 2007; Cardemil, Reivich, & Seligman, 2002; Waite & Richardson, 2004). Time will tell if such training leads to beneficial outcomes.

Latent Learning and Cognitive Maps

The study of cognitive processes in learning goes back at least to the 1920s and Edward Tolman's research on maze learning in rats. The rats' task was to find the goal box of the maze, where food awaited them. The animals typically took lots of wrong turns, but over the course of many trials, they made fewer and fewer mistakes. The strict behavioral interpretation of these results was that the rats learned a long chain of turning responses that were ultimately reinforced by the food. To Tolman, this behavioral interpretation was incomplete, and he offered evidence that the animals' behavior was also influenced by cognitive processes.

In one study, for example, Tolman allowed rats to explore a maze once a day for several consecutive days (Tolman & Honzik, 1930). For rats in Group A, food was placed in the goal box on each trial. As shown in Figure 6.13, these rats gradually improved their performance so that by the end of the experiment, they made only one or two mistakes as they ran through the maze. For rats in Group B, there was never any food in their goal box. These animals continued to make many errors throughout the experiment. Neither of these results is surprising, and each is consistent with a behavioral view of learning as driven strictly by associating behavior with reward.

A third group of rats, Group C, was the critical one. For the first ten days, there was no food in their goal box, and like Group B, they continued to make many mistakes. But on the eleventh day, food was placed in their goal box for the first time. Figure 6.13 shows the surprising result: On day 12, the day after receiving their first positive reinforcement, these rats made almost no mistakes. In fact, their performance was as good as that of the rats that had been reinforced every day. In other words, for Group C, the single reinforcement trial on day 11 produced a dramatic change in behavior the next day.

Tolman argued that these results supported two conclusions. First, the reinforcement on day 11 could not have significantly affected the rats' *learning* of the maze; it simply changed their *performance*. They must have learned the maze earlier as they wandered around making mistakes on their way to the end of the maze. These rats demonstrated **latent learning**—learning that is not evident when it first occurs. (Latent learning occurs in humans too; after years of experience in your neighborhood, you could probably tell a visitor that the corner drugstore is closed on Sundays, even if you had never tried to go there on a Sunday yourself.)

Second, the rats' improved performance immediately after the first reinforcement trial could have occurred only if the rats had already developed a **cognitive map**—that

FIGURE 6.13
Latent Learning

Notice that when rats in Group C did not receive food reinforcement, they continued to make many errors in locating the goal box of a maze (Tolman & Honzik, 1930). The day after first finding food there, however, they took almost no wrong turns! The reinforcement, argued Tolman, affected only the rats' performance; they must have learned the maze earlier, without reinforcement.

latent learning Learning that is not demonstrated at the time it occurs.

cognitive map A mental representation of the environment.

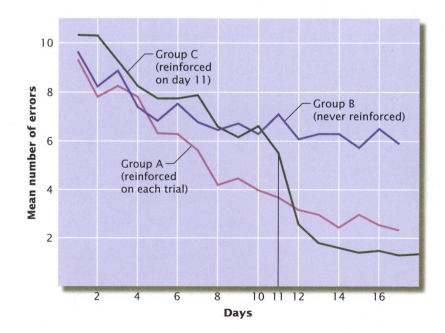

is, a mental representation of how the maze was arranged. Tolman concluded that cognitive maps develop naturally, and without the need for reinforcement, as people and animals gain experience with the world. Research on learning in the natural environment has supported this view. For example, we develop mental maps of shopping malls and city streets, even when we receive no direct reward for doing so (Tversky & Kahneman, 1991). Having such a map allows you to tell that visitor to your neighborhood exactly how to get to the corner drugstore from where you are standing.

Insight and Learning

Wolfgang Köhler was a psychologist whose work on the cognitive aspects of learning came about almost by accident. He was visiting the island of Tenerife when World War I broke out in 1914. As a German in an area controlled by Germany's enemy, Britain, he was confined to the island for the duration of the war, and he devoted his time to studying problem solving by chimpanzees housed there (Köhler, 1924, 1976). For example, Köhler would put a chimpanzee in a cage and place a piece of fruit so that it was visible but out of the animal's reach. He sometimes hung the fruit from a string too high to reach or laid it on the ground too far outside the cage to be retrieved. Many of the chimps overcame these obstacles easily. If the fruit was out of reach on the ground outside the cage, some chimps looked around the cage and, finding a long stick, used it to rake in the fruit. Surprised that the chimpanzees could solve these problems, Köhler tried more difficult tasks. Again, the chimps proved very skilled, as Figure 6.14 illustrates.

From *The Mentality of Apes* by W. Köhler, 1976, published by Routledge and Kegan Paul

FIGURE 6.14
Insight
Here are three impressive examples of problem solving by chimpanzees. At left, the animal fixed a 15-foot pole in the ground, climbed to the top, and dropped down after grabbing fruit that had been out of reach. In the center photo, the chimp stacked two boxes from different areas of the compound, climbed to the top, and used a pole to knock down the fruit. The chimp at right stacked three boxes and climbed them to reach the fruit.

Three aspects of Köhler's observations convinced him that animals' problem solving does not have to depend solely on trial and error and the gradual association of responses with consequences. First, once a chimpanzee solved a particular problem, it would immediately do the same thing in a similar situation. In other words, it acted as if it understood the problem. Second, the chimpanzees rarely tried a solution that didn't work. Apparently, the solution was not discovered randomly but "thought out" ahead of time and then successfully executed. Third, the animals often reached a solution suddenly. When confronted with a piece of fruit hanging from a string, for example, a chimp might jump for it several times. Then it would stop jumping, look up, and pace back and forth. Finally, it would run over to a wooden crate, place it directly under the fruit, and climb on top of it to reach the fruit. Once, when there were no other objects available, a chimp went over to Köhler, dragged him by the arm until he stood beneath the fruit, and then started climbing up his back!

Köhler believed that the only explanation for these results was that the chimpanzees had sudden **insight,** an understanding of the problem as a whole. However, demonstrating that a particular performance is the product of sudden insight requires experiments that are more sophisticated than those conducted by Köhler. Some cases of "insight" in his chimps might actually have been the result of a process known as *learning to learn,* in which previous experiences in problem solving are applied to new ones in a way that makes their solution seem to be instantaneous (Birch, 1945; Harlow, 1949). After all, chimpanzees have lots of experience at jumping on things and playing with sticks and other objects that can be used to solve the problems that Köhler posed for them (Epstein et al., 1984; Kounios et al., 2006; Wynne, 2004). True insight seems to result from a "mental trial-and-error process" in which people (and perhaps certain other animals) envision a course of action, mentally simulate its results, compare it with the imagined outcome of other alternatives, and settle on the course of action most likely to aid complex problem solving and decision making (Klein, 1993). So although Köhler's work helped establish the importance of cognitive processes in learning, questions remain about whether it demonstrated true insight.

Observational Learning: Learning by Imitation

Research on the role of cognitive processes in learning has been further stimulated by the finding that learning can occur not only by doing but also by observing what others do and what happens to them as a result. Learning by watching others—called **observational learning** or **social learning**—is efficient and adaptive. For example, young chimpanzees learn how to use a stone to crack open nuts by watching their mothers do so (Inoue-Nakamura & Matsuzawa, 1997). And we don't have to find out for ourselves that a door is locked or an iron is hot if we have just seen someone else try the door or suffer a burn.

The biological basis for observational learning may lie partly in the operation of *mirror neurons* in the brain (Fogassi et al., 2005). As described in the chapter on biological aspects of psychology, mirror neurons fire not only when we do something or experience something but also when we see someone do or experience the same thing. This mirrored pattern of activity in our own brains makes it almost as though we are actually performing the observed action or having the observed experience. Mirror neurons are active, for example, when we feel disgust upon seeing someone react to the taste of sour milk. They probably are firing too when we are trying to imitate the correct pronunciation of foreign words or to use an unfamiliar tool.

Children are particularly influenced by the adults and peers who act as models for appropriate behavior in various situations. In one classic experiment, Albert Bandura showed nursery school children a film featuring an adult and a large, inflatable, bottom-heavy "Bobo" doll (Bandura, 1965). The adult in the film punched the Bobo doll in the nose, kicked it, threw things at it, and hit its head with a hammer while saying things like "Sockeroo!" There were different endings to the film. Some children saw an ending in which the aggressive adult was called a "champion" by a second adult and

IN THE BLEACHERS By Steve Moore

OK, MAYBE WE COULD PLAY ONE QUICK GAME. THEY PROBABLY WON'T EVEN KNOW WE'RE HERE.

Despite of the power of observational learning, some people just have to learn things the hard way.

insight A sudden understanding about what is required to solve a problem.

observational learning (social learning) Learning how to perform new behaviors by watching others.

Learning by Imitation

TRY THIS Much of our behavior is learned by imitating others, especially those who serve as role models. To appreciate the impact of social learning in your life, list five examples of how your own actions, speech, mannerisms, or appearance have come to match those of a parent, a sibling, a friend, a teacher, or even a celebrity.

© Paul Chesley/Stone/Getty Images

rewarded with candy and soft drinks. Some saw the aggressor scolded and called a "bad person." Some saw a neutral ending in which there was neither reward nor punishment. After the film, each child was allowed to play alone with a Bobo doll. How the children played in this and similar studies led to some important conclusions about learning and about the role of cognitive factors in it.

Bandura found that children who saw the adult rewarded for aggression showed the most aggressive acts in play (see Figure 6.15). Their observational learning had

FIGURE 6.15
Observational Learning

Albert Bandura found that after observing an aggressive model, many children imitate the model's acts precisely, especially if the model's aggression was rewarded.

Source: Bandura, Ross, & Ross (1963).

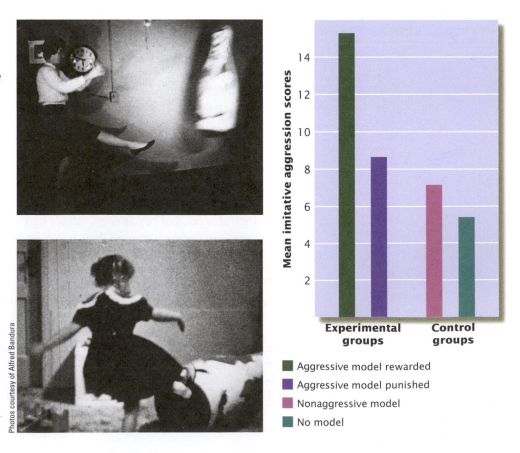

Photos courtesy of Alfred Bandura

Mean imitative aggression scores

Experimental groups   Control groups

- Aggressive model rewarded
- Aggressive model punished
- Nonaggressive model
- No model

come about through a secondhand or **vicarious experience** in which a person is influenced by seeing or hearing about the consequences of other people's behavior, especially people whom they perceive as being similar to themselves in some way (Mobbs et al., 2009). The children who had seen the adult punished for aggressive acts showed less aggression, but they still learned something. When later offered rewards for all the aggressive acts they could perform, these children displayed just as many as the children who had watched the rewarded adult. Observational learning can occur even when there are no vicarious consequences; many children in the neutral condition also imitated the model's aggression.

Observational learning is one of the most powerful sources of the *socialization* process through which children learn about which behaviors are—and are not—appropriate in their cultures (Bandura, 1999; Caldwell & Millen, 2009). Experiments show, for example, that children are more willing to help and share after seeing a demonstration of helping by a friendly, impressive model—even after some months have elapsed (Schroeder et al., 1995). Indeed, watching or even just hearing about the selfless or heroic acts of others can inspire us to seek higher goals ourselves (Haidt, 2003). Fears, too, can be learned partly by the sight of fearfulness in others (Askew & Field, 2008), and seeing other people behave dishonestly may lead observers to do the same (Gino, Ayal, & Ariely, 2009).

THINKING **CRITICALLY**

Does Watching Violence on Television Make People More Violent?

If observational learning is important, then surely television—and televised violence—must teach children a great deal. It is estimated that the average child in the United States spends about three hours each day watching television, either at home or in day care (Annenberg Public Policy Center, 2000; Christakis & Garrison, 2009). Much of what children see is violent. In addition to the real-life violence portrayed on the news (van der Molen, 2004), prime-time entertainment programs in the United States present an average of five acts of simulated violence per hour. Some Saturday morning cartoons include more than twenty per hour (American Psychological Association, 1993; Gerbner, Morgan, & Signorielli, 1994). As a result, the average child will have witnessed at least eight thousand murders and more than one hundred thousand other acts of televised violence before finishing elementary school and twice that number by age 18 (Annenberg Public Policy Center, 1999; Parents Television Council, 2006).

Psychologists have long speculated that watching so much violence might be emotionally arousing, making viewers more likely to react violently to frustration (Huston & Wright, 1989). In fact, there is evidence that exposure to media violence can trigger or amplify viewers' aggressive thoughts and feelings, thus increasing the likelihood that they will act aggressively (Anderson & Dill, 2000; Bushman, 1998). Televised violence may also provide models that viewers imitate, particularly if the violence is carried out by attractive, impressive models—the "good guys," for example (Huesmann et al., 2003). Finally, prolonged viewing of violent TV programs may "desensitize" viewers, making them less distressed when they see others suffer and less disturbed about inflicting pain on others (Aronson, 1999; Donnerstein, Slaby, & Eron, 1995). Concern over the influence of violence on television led to the development of a violence-blocking "V chip" for new television sets in the United States.

What am I being asked to believe or accept?

Many theorists have argued that through one or more of the mechanisms just listed, watching violence on television causes violent behavior in viewers (Anderson et al., 2003; Anderson & Bushman, 2002b; Bushman & Huesmann, 2000; Eron et al., 1996; Huesmann, 1998). A 1993 report by the National Academy of Sciences concluded that "overall, the vast majority of studies, whatever their methodology, showed that exposure to television violence resulted in increased aggressive behavior, both contemporaneously

vicarious experience Conditions that allow us to learn by watching what happens to others.

and over time" (Reiss & Roth, 1993, p. 371). The American Psychological Association Commission on Violence and Youth (1993) reached the same conclusion.

What evidence is available to support the assertion?

Three types of evidence support the claim that watching violent television programs increases violent behavior. First, there is evidence from anecdotes and case studies. Children have poked one another in the eye after watching the Three Stooges appear to do so on television, and adults have claimed that watching TV shows prompted them to commit murders or other violent acts matching those seen on the shows (Werner, 2003).

Second, many correlational studies have found a relationship between watching violent television programs and later acts of aggression and violence (Johnson, Cohen, et al., 2002). One such study tracked people from the time they were 6 or 7 (in 1977) until they reached their early twenties (in 1992). Those who had watched more violent television as children were significantly more aggressive as adults (Huesmann et al., 1997; Huesmann et al., 2003) and more likely to engage in criminal activity (Huesmann, 1995). They were also more likely to use physical punishment on their own children, who themselves tended to be much more aggressive than average. These latter results have been found not only in the United States but also in Israel, Australia, Poland, the Netherlands, and even Finland, where the number of violent TV shows is very small (Centerwall, 1990; Huesmann & Eron, 1986).

Finally, the results of numerous experiments also support the view that TV violence increases aggression among viewers (American Psychological Association, 1993; Paik & Comstock, 1994; Reiss & Roth, 1993). In one study, groups of boys watched violent or nonviolent programs in a controlled setting and then played floor hockey (Josephson, 1987). Boys who had watched the violent shows were more likely than those who had watched nonviolent programs to behave aggressively on the hockey floor. This effect was greatest for those boys who had the most aggressive tendencies to begin with. More extensive experiments, in which children are exposed for long periods to carefully controlled types of television programs, also suggest that exposure to large amounts of violent activity on television results in aggressive behavior (Eron et al., 1972).

Are there alternative ways of interpreting the evidence?

To some observers, this evidence leaves no doubt that media violence causes increases in aggressive and violent behavior, especially in children (Anderson et al., 2003). Others suggest that the evidence is not conclusive and is open to some qualifications and alternative interpretations (e.g., Browne & Hamilton-Giachritsis, 2005; Freedman, 2002; Thakkar, Garrison, & Christakis, 2006). Anecdotal reports and case studies are particularly suspect. When people face imprisonment or execution for their violent acts, how much confidence can we place in their claims that these acts were triggered by television programs? And how many other people might say that the same programs made them *less* likely to be violent? Anecdotes alone do not provide a good basis for drawing solid scientific conclusions.

What about the correlational evidence from studies that followed children over time? As discussed in the chapter on research in psychology, a *correlation* between two variables does not necessarily mean that one is *causing* an effect on the other. Both might be affected by a third factor. Why, for example, are certain people watching so much violent television in the first place? This question suggests a possible third factor that might account for the observed relationship between watching TV violence and acting aggressively: People who tend to be aggressive may prefer to watch more violent TV programs *and* may behave aggressively toward others. In other words, personality may partly account for the observed correlations (e.g., Aluja-Fabregat & Torrubia-Beltri, 1998).

The results of controlled experiments on the effects of televised violence have been criticized as well (Freedman, 2002; Geen, 1998). The major objection is that both the

"I have HAD it with you two and your viotent video games!"

The violence that may affect children's aggressive behavior may not be limited to what they see on television and in video games.

independent and dependent variables in these experiments are artificial, so they may not apply beyond the laboratory or last very long (Browne & Hamilton-Giachristsis, 2005; Freedman, 2002). For example, the kinds of violent shows viewed by the participants during some of these experiments, as well as the ways in which their aggression has been measured, may not reflect what goes on in the real-world situations we most want to know about.

What additional evidence would help evaluate the alternatives?

By their very nature, correlational studies of the role of TV violence in violent behavior can never be conclusive. As we've pointed out, a third, unidentified causal variable could always be responsible for the results. So it would be useful to have evidence from controlled experiments in which equivalent groups of people were exposed for years to differing "doses" of the violence actually portrayed on TV and in which the effects on their subsequent behavior were observed in real-world situations. Such experiments could also explore the circumstances under which different people (e.g., children vs. adults) were affected by various forms of violence. However, studies like these would create an ethical dilemma. If watching violent television programs really does cause violent behavior, are psychologists justified in creating conditions that might lead some people to be more violent? If such violence occurred, would the researchers be partly responsible to the victims and to society? Difficulty in answering questions such as these is partly responsible for the use of short-term experiments and correlational designs in this research area, as well as for some of the remaining uncertainty about the effects of television violence.

One approach to this problem might be to conduct experiments in which children watch television shows that portray cooperative rather than violent behavior. If exposure to such *prosocial* programming were followed by significant increases in viewers' own prosocial behavior, it would strengthen—though still not prove— the argument that what children see on television can have a causal impact on their actions. A recent series of experiments has already shown that children who played prosocial video games were later more helpful than those who had played neutral games (Greitemeyer & Osswald, 2010).

What conclusions are most reasonable?

The evidence collected so far makes it reasonable to conclude that watching TV violence may be one cause of violent behavior, especially in some children and especially in boys (Anderson & Bushman, 2002b; Bushman & Anderson, 2001; Browne & Hamilton-Giachritsis, 2005; Huesmann et al., 1997; Robinson et al., 2001; Smith & Donnerstein, 1998). Playing violent video games may be another (C. A. Anderson, 2004; Anderson & Bushman, 2001; Anderson et al., 2008, 2010). But a cause-and-effect relationship between watching TV violence (or playing violent video games) and acting violently is not inevitable and may not be strong or long-lasting (Browne & Hamilton-Giachritsis, 2005; Ferguson & Kilburn, 2009, 2010; Ferguson et al., 2010; Savage, 2004; Savage & Yancey, 2008). Further, there are many circumstances in which the effect does not occur (Charleton, Gunter, & Coles, 1998; Ferguson, 2009; Freedman, 1992, 2002). Parents, peers, and other environmental influences, along with personality factors, may dampen or amplify the effect of watching televised violence. Indeed, not every viewer interprets violence in the same way, and not every viewer is equally vulnerable (Ferguson, 2002, 2009; Feshbach & Tangney, 2008; Wood, Wong, & Chachere, 1991). The most vulnerable may be young boys, and especially those who are most aggressive or violence-prone in the first place, a trait that could well have been acquired by observing the behavior of parents or peers (Ferguson et al., 2010).

Still, the possibility that violence on television *can* have a causal impact on violent behavior is reason for serious concern and continues to influence public debate about what should and should not be aired on television.

Using Research on Learning to Help People Learn

Teaching and training—explicit efforts to assist learners in mastering a specific skill or body of material—are major aspects of socialization in virtually every culture. So the study of how people learn has important implications for improved teaching in our schools (Bjork & Linn, 2006; Halpern & Hakel, 2003; Li, 2005; Newcombe et al., 2009) and for helping people develop skills ranging from typing to tennis.

Classrooms Across Cultures

Many people are concerned that schools in the United States are not doing a very good job. The average performance of U.S. students on tests of reading, math, and other basic academic skills has tended to fall short of that of youngsters in other countries, especially some Asian countries (International Association for the Evaluation of Education Achievement, 1999; National Center for Education Statistics, 2002; Program for International Student Assessment, 2005). In one early comparison study, Harold Stevenson (1992) followed a sample of pupils in Taiwan, Japan, and the United States from first grade, in 1980, to eleventh grade, in 1991. In first grade, the Asian students scored no higher than their U.S. peers on tests of mathematical aptitude and skills, nor did they enjoy math more. However, by fifth grade, the U.S. students had fallen far behind. Corresponding differences were seen in reading skills, and more recent studies have found similar results (Mullis et al., 2004, 2007).

Some possible causes of these differences have been found in various countries' educational policies and in the classroom itself (Rindermann & Ceci, 2009). In a typical U.S. classroom session, teachers talked to students as a group. The students then worked at their desks independently. Reinforcement or other feedback about performance on their work was usually delayed until the next day or often not provided at all. In contrast, the typical Japanese classroom placed greater emphasis on cooperative work among students (Kristof, 1997). Teachers provided more immediate feedback on a one-to-one basis. And there was an emphasis on creating teams of students with varying abilities, an arrangement in which faster learners help teach slower ones. However, before concluding that the differences in performance are the result of social factors alone, we must consider another important distinction: The Japanese children practiced more. They spent more days in school during the year and on average spent more hours doing homework.

Although the significance of these cultural differences in learning and teaching is not yet clear, the educational community in the United States is paying attention to them (e.g., Felder & Brent, 2001). Psychologists and educators are also considering how other principles of learning can be applied to improve education. Anecdotal and experimental evidence suggests that some of the most successful educational techniques are those that apply basic principles of operant conditioning, offering frequent testing, positive reinforcement for correct performance, and immediate corrective feedback following mistakes (Kass, 1999; Oppel, 2000; Roediger, McDaniel, & McDermott, 2006).

Further, research in cognitive psychology (e.g., Cepeda et al., 2008; Pashler, Rohrer, & Cepeda, 2006) also suggests that students are more likely to retain what they learn if they engage in numerous study sessions rather than in a single "cramming" session on the night before a quiz or exam. To encourage this more beneficial "distributed practice" pattern, researchers say, teachers should give enough exams and quizzes (some unannounced, perhaps) that students will be reading and studying more or less continuously. And because learning is aided by repeated opportunities to use new information, these exams and quizzes should cover material from throughout the term, not just from recent classes. Such recommendations are not necessarily popular with students, but there is evidence that they promote long-term retention of course material (e.g., Bjork, 2001; Bjork & Linn, 2006).

Reciprocal Teaching

Ann Brown and her colleagues (1992) demonstrated the success of reciprocal teaching, in which children take turns teaching each other. This technique, which is similar to the cooperative arrangements seen in Japanese education, has become increasingly popular in North American schools (Palincsar, 2003).

Active Learning

The importance of cognitive processes in learning is apparent in instructional methods that emphasize *active learning* (Bonwell & Eison, 1991). These methods take many forms, such as small-group problem-solving tasks, discussion of "one-minute essays" written in class, use of student response devices ("clickers") or just "thumbs up" or "thumbs down" gestures to indicate agreement or disagreement with the instructor's lecture, and multiple-choice questions that give students feedback about their understanding of the previous fifteen minutes of lecture (Goss Lucas & Bernstein, 2005). There is little doubt that for many students, the inclusion of active learning experiences makes classes more interesting and enjoyable (Bruff, 2009; Moran, 2000; Murray, 2000). Active learning methods also provide immediate reinforcement and help students go beyond memorizing isolated facts by encouraging them to think more deeply about new information, consider how it relates to what they already know, and apply it in new situations. The more elaborate mental processing associated with active learning makes new information not only more personally meaningful but also easier to remember. (The many Try This opportunities sprinkled throughout this book are designed to promote active learning and better retention.)

Studies of students in elementary schools, high schools, community colleges, and universities have found that compared to more passive instructional techniques, active learning approaches result in better test performance and greater class participation (e.g., Altman, 2007; Hake, 1998; Kellum, Carr, & Dozier, 2001; Meyers & Jones, 1993; Saville et al., 2006). In one study, a fifth-grade teacher spent some days calling only on students whose hands were raised. On other days, all students were required to answer every question by holding up a card with their response written on it. Scores on next-day quizzes and biweekly tests showed that students remembered more of the material that had been covered on the active learning days than on the "passive" days (Gardner, Heward, & Grossi, 1994). In another study of two consecutive medical school classes taught by the same instructor, scores on the final exam were significantly higher when students learned mainly through small-group discussions and case studies than when they were taught mainly through lectures (Chu, 1994). Similarly, among adults being taught to use a new computer program, active learning with hands-on practice was more effective than passively watching a

Virtual Surgery

Using a virtual reality system, this medical student can actively learn and practice eye surgery skills before working with real patients. Computer-based human body simulators are also giving new doctors active learning experience in emergency room diagnosis and treatment; in heart, lung, and abdominal surgery; and other medical skills (Aggarwal, Cheshire, & Darzi, 2008; Heinrichs et al., 2008; Kanno et al., 2008; Larsen et al., 2009; Prabhudesai et al., 2008; Seymour, 2008; Tsang et al., 2008).

© Marshall Ikonography/Alamy

demonstration video (Kerr & Payne, 1994). Finally, high school and college students who passively listened to a physics lecture received significantly lower scores on a test of lecture content than students who participated in a virtual reality lab that allowed them to interact with the physical forces covered in the lecture (Brelsford, 1993).

Results like these have fueled the development of other science education programs that place students in virtual laboratory environments where they can actively manipulate materials and test hypotheses (e.g., Horwitz & Christie, 2000). Despite the enthusiasm generated by active learning methods, rigorous experimental research is still needed to compare their short- and long-term effects with those of more traditional methods in teaching various kinds of course content (Moran, 2006; Saber & Johnson, 2008).

Skill Learning

The complex action sequences, or *skills,* that people learn to perform in everyday life—tying a shoe, opening a door, operating a computer, shooting a basketball, driving a car—develop through direct and vicarious learning processes involving imitation, instruction, reinforcement, and, of course, lots of practice. Some skills, such as those of a basketball player or violinist, demand exceptional perceptual-motor coordination. Others, such as those involved in scientific thinking, have a large cognitive component, requiring rapid understanding. In either case, the learning of skills usually involves practice and feedback (Ackerman, 2007).

Practice—the repeated performance of a skill—is the most critical component of skill learning (Howe, Davidson, & Sloboda, 1998). For perceptual-motor skills, both physical and mental practice are beneficial (Druckman & Bjork, 1994). To be most effective, practice should continue past the point of correct performance until the skill can be performed automatically, with little or no need for attention. As mentioned earlier, in learning many cognitive skills, what counts most seems to be practice in retrieving relevant information from memory. Trying to recall and write down facts that you have read, for example, is a more effective learning tool than simply reading the facts a second time.

Feedback about the correctness of responses is also necessary. As with any learning process, the feedback should come soon enough to be effective but not so quickly that it interferes with the learner's efforts to learn independently. Large amounts of guidance may produce very good performance during practice, but too much guidance may impair later performance (Kluger & DeNisi, 1998; Wickens, 1992). Coaching

Try It This Way

Good coaches provide enough guidance and performance feedback to help budding athletes develop their skills to the fullest, but not so much that the guidance interferes with the learning process. Striking this delicate balance is one of the greatest challenges faced by coaches and by teachers in general.

© Jim Cummins/Photographer's Choice/Getty Images

students about correct responses in math, for example, may impair their ability later to retrieve the correct response from memory on their own. And in coaching athletes, if feedback is given too soon after an action occurs or while it is still taking place, it may divert the learner's attention from understanding how that action was achieved and what it felt like to perform it (Schmidt & Bjork, 1992). Independent practice at retrieving previously learned responses or information requires more effort, but it is critical for skill development (Ericsson & Charness, 1994).

How do some people reach high levels of achievement in physical or cognitive skills? A number of researchers in the field of positive psychology are studying such people (e.g., Murray, 2003; Simonton, 2000). They have found that stellar accomplishments in the arts and sciences and athletics, for example, are associated with having worked very hard for a very long time, with having a helpful coach or mentor, with being optimistic about success, and also with being in the right place at the right time. This research suggests that to reach your own highest potential, you should first identify your interests and skills, choose a field in which these are likely to fit well, then find a good mentor, put in lots of time and effort, stay optimistic even in the face of setbacks, and take advantage of every opportunity that presents itself (Peterson, 2006b). There appears to be little or no evidence to support "sleep learning" or other schemes designed to make learning effortless (Druckman & Bjork, 1994; Phelps & Exum, 1992). In short, "no pain, no gain."

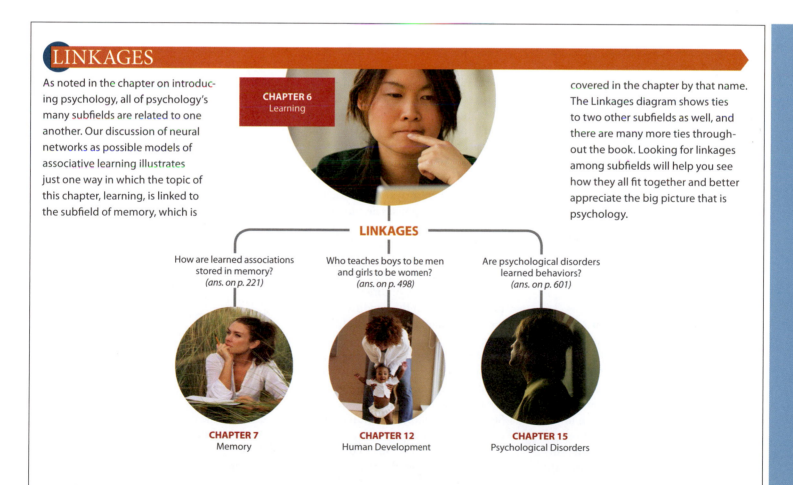

LINKAGES

As noted in the chapter on introducing psychology, all of psychology's many subfields are related to one another. Our discussion of neural networks as possible models of associative learning illustrates just one way in which the topic of this chapter, learning, is linked to the subfield of memory, which is

CHAPTER 6
Learning

covered in the chapter by that name. The Linkages diagram shows ties to two other subfields as well, and there are many more ties throughout the book. Looking for linkages among subfields will help you see how they all fit together and better appreciate the big picture that is psychology.

LINKAGES

How are learned associations stored in memory?
(ans. on p. 221)

CHAPTER 7
Memory

Who teaches boys to be men and girls to be women?
(ans. on p. 498)

CHAPTER 12
Human Development

Are psychological disorders learned behaviors?
(ans. on p. 601)

CHAPTER 15
Psychological Disorders

SUMMARY

Individuals adapt to changes in the environment through the process of *learning,* which is the modification through experience of preexisting behavior and understanding.

Learning About Stimuli

One kind of learning is *habituation,* which is reduced responsiveness to a repeated stimulus. According to Richard Solomon's opponent process theory, habituation results as two processes balance each other. The first process is a relatively automatic response to some stimulus. The second, or opponent, process follows and counteracts the first. This theory may help explain drug tolerance and some overdose cases.

Classical Conditioning: Learning Signals and Associations

Pavlov's Discovery

One form of associative learning is *classical conditioning.* It occurs when a neutral stimulus (such as a tone) is repeatedly paired with an *unconditioned stimulus,* or *UCS* (such as food), which naturally brings about an *unconditioned response,* or *UCR* (such as salivation). Through its association with the UCS, the neutral stimulus eventually becomes a *conditioned stimulus,* or *CS,* that will elicit a response, known as the *conditioned response,* or *CR,* even when the unconditioned stimulus is not presented.

Conditioned Responses over Time: Extinction and Spontaneous Recovery

In general, the strength of a conditioned response grows as CS-UCS pairings continue. If the conditioned stimulus is repeatedly presented without being paired with the unconditioned stimulus, the conditioned response eventually disappears; this is *extinction.* Following extinction, the conditioned response often reappears if the conditioned stimulus is presented after some time; this is *spontaneous recovery.* In addition, if the conditioned and unconditioned stimuli are paired once or twice after extinction, *reconditioning* occurs: The conditioned response regains its original strength.

Stimulus Generalization and Discrimination

Because of *stimulus generalization,* conditioned responses are elicited by stimuli that are similar, but not identical, to conditioned stimuli. Generalization is limited by *stimulus discrimination,* which reduces conditioned responses to stimuli that are substantially different from the conditioned stimulus.

The Signaling of Significant Events

Classical conditioning involves learning that the conditioned stimulus is an event that predicts the occurrence of another event, the unconditioned stimulus. This form of learning creates associations between a CS and a UCS, as well as a means through which animals and people develop mental models of the relationships between events. Classical conditioning works best when the conditioned stimulus precedes the unconditioned stimulus, an arrangement known as forward conditioning. Conditioned responses develop best when the conditioned stimulus precedes the unconditioned stimulus by intervals ranging from less than a second to a minute or more, depending on the stimuli involved. Conditioning is also more likely when the conditioned stimulus reliably signals the unconditioned stimulus.

In general, the strength of a conditioned response and the speed of conditioning increase as the intensity of the unconditioned stimulus increases. Stronger conditioned stimuli also speed conditioning. The particular conditioned stimulus likely to be linked to a subsequent unconditioned stimulus depends in part on which stimulus was being attended to when the unconditioned stimulus occurred. Some stimuli are easier to associate than others; organisms seem to be biologically prepared to learn certain associations, as exemplified by taste aversions. *Higher-order conditioning* occurs when a conditioned stimulus becomes powerful enough to function as an unconditioned stimulus for another stimulus associated with it.

Some Applications of Classical Conditioning

Classical conditioning principles are being applied in understanding the development and treatment of phobias, in the humane control of predators in the wild, and in the detection of explosives.

Operant Conditioning: Learning the Consequences of Behavior

Learning occurs not only through associating stimuli but also through associating behavior with its consequences.

From the Puzzle Box to the Skinner Box

Edward L. Thorndike's *law of effect* holds that any response that produces satisfaction becomes more likely to occur again when the same stimulus is encountered, and any response that produces discomfort becomes less likely to occur again. Thorndike called this type of learning *instrumental conditioning.* B. F. Skinner called the same basic process *operant conditioning.* In operant conditioning, the organism is free to respond at any time, and conditioning is measured by the rate of responding.

Basic Components of Operant Conditioning

An *operant* is a response that has some effect on the world. A *reinforcer* increases the probability that the operant preceding it will occur again. In other words, *reinforcement* strengthens behavior.

There are two types of reinforcers: *positive reinforcers,* which are pleasant stimuli that strengthen a response if they are presented after that response occurs, and *negative reinforcers,* which are unpleasant stimuli that strengthen a response if they are removed following that response. Both kinds of reinforcers strengthen the behaviors that precede them. *Escape conditioning* results when behavior terminates an aversive event. *Avoidance conditioning* results when behavior prevents or avoids an aversive stimulus; it reflects both classical and operant conditioning. Behaviors learned through avoidance conditioning are highly resistant to extinction. *Discriminative conditioned stimuli* indicate whether reinforcement is available for a particular behavior.

Forming and Strengthening Operant Behavior

Complex responses can be learned through *shaping,* which involves reinforcing successive approximations of the desired response. *Primary reinforcers* are innately rewarding; *secondary reinforcers* are rewards that people or animals learn to like because of their association with primary reinforcers. In general, operant conditioning proceeds more quickly when the delay in receiving reinforcement is short rather than long and when the reinforcer is large rather than small. Reinforcement may be delivered through *continuous reinforcement* or one of four types of *partial reinforcement* (also called partial or intermittent reinforcement schedules): *fixed-ratio (FR)reinforcement, variable-ratio (VR) reinforcement, fixed-interval (FI) reinforcement,* and *variable-interval (VI) reinforcement.* Ratio schedules lead to a rapid rate of responding. Behavior learned through partial reinforcement, particularly through variable schedules, is very resistant to extinction; this phenomenon is called the *partial reinforcement effect.* Partial reinforcement is involved in superstitious behavior, which results when a response is coincidentally followed by a reinforcer.

Why Reinforcers Work

Research suggests that reinforcers are rewarding because they provide an organism with the opportunity to engage in desirable activities, which may change from one situation to the next. Another possibility is that activity in the brain's pleasure centers plays a role in reinforcement.

Punishment

The frequency of a behavior can be decreased through *punishment,* in which the behavior is followed by either an unpleasant stimulus or the removal of a pleasant stimulus. Punishment modifies behavior but has several drawbacks. It suppresses behavior without erasing it; fear of punishment may generalize to the person doing the punishing; it is ineffective when delayed; it can be physically harmful and may teach aggressiveness; and it teaches only what not to do, not what should be done to obtain reinforcement.

Some Applications of Operant Conditioning

The principles of operant conditioning have been used in many areas of life, including the teaching of everyday social skills, the treatment of sleep disorders, the development of self-control, and the improvement of classroom education.

Cognitive Processes in Learning

Cognitive processes—how people represent, store, and use information—play an important role in learning.

Learned Helplessness

Learned helplessness appears to result when people believe that their behavior has no effect on the world.

Latent Learning and Cognitive Maps

Humans and other animals display *latent learning,* learning that is not obvious at the time it occurs. They also form *cognitive maps* of their environments, even in the absence of any reinforcement for doing so.

Insight and Learning

Experiments on *insight* also support the idea that cognitive processes and learned strategies play an important role in learning, perhaps even by animals.

Observational Learning: Learning by Imitation

The process of learning by watching others is called *observational learning* or *social learning.* Some observational learning occurs through *vicarious experience,* in which an individual is influenced by seeing or hearing about the consequences of others' behavior. Observational learning is more likely to occur when the person observed is rewarded for the observed behavior. Observational learning is a powerful source of socialization.

Using Research on Learning to Help People Learn

Research on how people learn has implications for improved teaching and for the development of a wide range of skills.

Classrooms Across Cultures

The degree to which immediate reinforcement and extended practice are used in teaching varies considerably from culture to culture, but research suggests that the application of these and other basic learning principles is important to promoting effective teaching and learning.

Active Learning

The importance of cognitive processes in learning is seen in active learning methods designed to encourage people to think deeply about and apply new information instead of just memorizing isolated facts.

Skill Learning

Observational learning, practice, and corrective feedback play important roles in the learning of skills.

LINKAGES TO FURTHER LEARNING

Now that you have finished reading this chapter, how about exploring some of the topics and information that you found most interesting? Here are some places to start.

Books

Kieran Egan, *The Educated Mind: How Cognitive Tools Shape Our Understanding* (University of Chicago Press, 1997). How children learn.

James Garbarino, *Lost Boys: Why Our Sons Turn Violent and How We Can Save Them* (Free Press, 1999). Development of violence examined from several perspectives, including learning theories.

Laurence Steinberg, *The Ten Basic Principles of Good Parenting* (Simon & Schuster, 2004). Learning-based parenting skills.

Martin Seligman, *What You Can Change and What You Can't: The Complete Guide to Successful Self-Improvement* (Fawcett Books, 1995). Using learning principles for self-improvement.

Martin Seligman, with Karen Reivich, Lisa Jaycox, and Jane Gillham, *The Optimistic Child* (Harper Perennial, 1996). The role of cognitive processes in learning and behavior.

On the Internet

CourseMate Access an integrated eBook and chapter-specific learning tools including flashcards, quizzes, videos, and more. Go to CengageBrain.com.

CENGAGENOW Want to maximize the value of your online study time? Take this easy-to-use study system's diagnostic pre-test, and it will create a personalized study plan for you. By helping you identify the topics that you need to understand better and then directing you to valuable online resources, it can speed up your chapter review. CengageNOW even provides a post-test so you can confirm that you are ready for an exam. Go to CengageBrain.com.

TALKING POINTS

Here are a few talking points to help you summarize this chapter for family and friends without giving a lecture.

1. If we could not learn from experience, we would have a hard time surviving life's dangers or taking advantage of its opportunities.
2. Some learning involves associating events, as when a bell signals that class is over.
3. Some associations, such as between illness and tastes, form especially easily, and this "biopreparedness" is responsible for many food aversions.
4. Some learning is based on the rewards or punishments that follow our actions.
5. Some things, like food or shock, are innately rewarding or punishing, but the power of others, such as money or criticism, must be learned through experience.
6. Positive reinforcement occurs when a behavior is strengthened by some positive event, such as a reward.
7. Punishment and negative reinforcement are different. Negative reinforcement strengthens behavior; punishment weakens it.
8. We can learn from our own experiences and also by watching what happens to other people.
9. One reason that gambling or superstitious rituals are so difficult to give up is that they are rewarded on a random and unpredictable schedule.
10. Watching violent television or playing violent video games has been associated with aggressive behavior, but further research is needed to confirm that this correlation represents a cause-and-effect relationship.

7

Memory

© Tim Hall/Cultura/Aurora Photos

Have you ever forgotten someone's name five seconds after you were introduced? What happened to that memory and why you lost it are just two of the many questions that memory researchers study.

In this chapter, we'll review what they have discovered about memory so far, and we'll suggest some ideas for improving your own memory.

Several years ago, an air traffic controller at Los Angeles International Airport cleared a US Airways flight to land on runway 24L. A couple of minutes later, the US Airways pilot radioed the control tower that he was on approach for runway 24L, but the controller did not reply because she was conversing with another pilot. After finishing that conversation, the controller told a Sky West commuter pilot to taxi onto runway 24L for takeoff, completely forgetting about the US Airways plane that was about to land on the same runway. The US Airways jet hit the commuter plane, killing thirty-four people. The controller's forgetting was so complete that she assumed the fireball from the crash was an exploding bomb. How could her memory have failed her at such a crucial time?

Memory is full of contradictions. You can probably remember the name of your first-grade teacher but not the phone number you called five minutes ago. Like perception, memory is selective. So although we retain a great deal of information, we also lose a great deal (Wixted, 2004). Consider Tatiana Cooley. She was the U.S. National Memory Champion for three years in a row, but she confesses that she is so absent-minded that she relies on Post-it Notes to remember everyday errands (Schacter, 2001). In other words, memory is made up of many abilities, some of which may be better than others from person to person and from time to time.

Memory plays a critical role in your life. Without it, you would not know how to shut off your alarm clock, take a shower, get dressed, or recognize objects. You would be unable to communicate with other people because you would not remember what words mean or even what you had just said. You would be unaware of your own likes and dislikes. You would have no idea of who you are. In this chapter, we describe what is known about both memory and forgetting. First, we discuss what memory is—the different kinds of memory and the different ways we remember things. Then we examine how new memories are formed and later recalled and why they are sometimes forgotten. We continue with a discussion of the biological bases of memory, and we conclude with some practical advice for improving your memory and study skills.

The Nature of Memory

The mathematician John Griffith estimated that in an average lifetime, each of us will have stored roughly five hundred times as much information as can be found in all the volumes of the *Encyclopaedia Britannica* (Hunt, 1982). The impressive capacity of human memory depends on the operation of a complex mental system (Schacter, 2002).

Basic Memory Processes

In February 2002, prison warden James Smith lost his set of master keys to the Westville Correctional Facility. As a result, 2,559 inmates were kept under partial lockdown for eight days while the Indiana Department of Correction spent $53,000 to

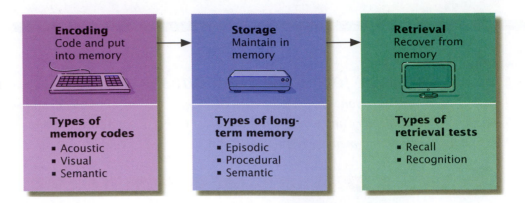

FIGURE 7.1

Basic Memory Processes

Remembering something requires, first, that the item be encoded—put in a form that can be placed in memory. It must then be stored and, finally, retrieved, or brought into awareness. If any of these processes fails, forgetting will occur.

change locks in the affected areas. As it turned out, the warden had put the keys in his pocket when he went home, forgot he had done so, and reported the keys "missing" when they were not in their usual place in his office the next day ("Odds and Ends," 2002). What went wrong? There are several possibilities. Memory depends on three basic processes: encoding, storage, and retrieval (see Figure 7.1). The absent-minded warden might have had problems with any one of these processes.

First, information must be put into memory, a step that requires **encoding**. Just as incoming sensory information must be coded so that it can be communicated to the brain, information to be remembered must be put in a form that the memory system can accept and use. We use various *memory codes* to translate information from the senses into mental representations of that information. Codes for **acoustic memory** (also known as **auditory memory**) represent information as sequences of sounds, such as a tune or a rhyme. Codes for **visual memory** represent information as pictures, such as the image of your best friend's face. Codes for *semantic memory* represent the general meaning of an experience. So if you see a billboard that reads "Huey's Going-Out-of-Business Sale," you might encode the sound of the words as if they had been spoken (*acoustic encoding*), the image of the letters as they were arranged on the sign (*visual encoding*), or the fact that you recently saw an ad for Huey's (*semantic encoding*). The type of encoding we use can influence what we remember. For example, semantic encoding might allow you to remember that a car was parked in your neighbors' driveway just before their house was robbed. If there was little or no other encoding, however, you might not be able to remember the make, model, or color of the car.

The second basic memory process is **storage**, which refers to keeping information in memory over time—often over a very long time. When you find that you can still use a pogo stick that you haven't played with since you were a child or that you can recall a vacation from many years ago, you are depending on the storage capacity of your memory.

The third memory process, **retrieval**, occurs when you locate information stored in memory and bring it into consciousness. Retrieving stored information such as your address or telephone number is usually so fast and effortless that it seems automatic. The search-and-retrieval process becomes more noticeable, however, when you read a quiz question but cannot quite recall the answer. Retrieval involves both recall and recognition. To *recall* information, you have to retrieve it from memory without much help. This is what is required when you answer an essay test question or play *Jeopardy!* In *recognition*, retrieval is aided by clues, such as the response alternatives given on multiple-choice tests and the questions on *Who Wants to Be a Millionaire*. Accordingly, recognition tends to be easier than recall.

Types of Memory

When was the last time you saw a movie? Who was the first president of the United States? How do you keep your balance on a bike? Answering each of these questions involves different aspects of memory. To answer the first question, you must remember

encoding The process of acquiring information and entering it into memory.

auditory (acoustic) memory Mental representations of information as a sequence of sounds.

visual memory The mental representation of information as images.

storage The process of maintaining information in memory over time.

retrieval The process of recalling information stored in memory.

© Rick Gomez/Corbis

How Does She Do That?

TRY THIS As she practices, this youngster is developing procedural memories of how to ride a bike that may be difficult to put into words. To appreciate the special nature of procedural memory, try writing a step-by-step description of *exactly* how you tie a shoe.

a particular event in your life. To answer the second one, you must recall general knowledge that is unlikely to be tied to a specific event. And the answer to the third is easier to demonstrate than to describe. So how many types of memory are there? No one is sure, but most research suggests that there are at least three. Each type of memory is named for the kind of information it handles: episodic, semantic, and procedural (Rajaram & Barber, 2008).

Any memory of a specific event that happened while you were present—that is, during an "episode" in your life—is called **episodic memory** (Tulving, 2005). Remembering what you had for dinner yesterday, what you did last summer, or where you were last Friday night all require episodic memory. **Semantic memory** contains generalized knowledge of the world that does not involve memory of a specific event. So if you were asked, "Are wrenches pets or tools?" you could answer correctly using your semantic memory; you don't have to remember a specific episode in which you learned that wrenches are tools. As a general rule, people report episodic memories by saying, "I remember when . . . ," whereas they convey semantic memories by saying, "I know that . . ." (Tulving, 2000). Memory of how to do things, such as riding a bike or tying a shoelace, is called **procedural memory**, or **procedural knowledge** (Cohen & Squire, 1980). Procedural knowledge often consists of a sequence of movements that are difficult or impossible to put into words. For example, a gymnast might not be able to describe the exact motions in a particular routine. Accordingly, teachers of gymnastics, music, dance, cooking, woodworking, and other skills usually prefer to first show their students what to do rather than describe how to do it.

Many activities require all three types of memory. Consider the game of tennis. Knowing the official rules or how to score a match involves semantic memory. Remembering which side served last requires episodic memory. Knowing how to hit the ball involves procedural memory.

Explicit and Implicit Memory

Recalling these three kinds of memories can be either intentional or unintentional, that is, explicit or implicit. You are using **explicit memory** when you consciously and intentionally try to remember something, such as where you went on your last vacation or the correct answer to an exam question (Masson & MacLeod, 1992). In contrast, **implicit memory** involves the unintentional recollection and influence of prior experiences (McDermott, 2002). For example, if you were to read this chapter a second time, implicit memories from your first reading would help you read it more quickly the second time. For the same reason, you can solve a puzzle faster if you have solved it in the past. This improvement in performance—often called *priming*—is automatic, and it occurs without conscious effort. Have you ever found yourself disliking someone you just met, but you didn't know why? One explanation is that implicit memory may have been at work. Specifically, you may have reacted as you did because the person bore a resemblance to someone from your past who treated you badly. In such cases, we are usually unaware of any connection between the two individuals (Lewicki, 1992). Episodic, semantic, and procedural memories can be explicit or implicit, but procedural memory usually operates implicitly—once you have learned to do something well, you can just do it. This is the reason that, for example, you can skillfully ride a bike even though you cannot explicitly remember all the procedures necessary to do so. In fact, trying to perform a skill slowly enough to demonstrate each step can disrupt your performance!

It is not surprising that experience affects how people behave. The surprising thing is that they are often unaware that their actions have been influenced by previous events (see the chapter on consciousness). Because some influential events cannot be recalled even when people try to do so, implicit memory has been said to involve "retention without remembering" (Roediger, Guynn, & Jones, 1995).

episodic memory Memory of an event that happened while one was present.

semantic memory A type of memory containing generalized knowledge of the world.

procedural knowledge (procedural memory) A type of memory containing information about how to do things.

explicit memory The process of intentionally trying to remember something.

implicit memory The unintentional influence of prior experiences.

Making Implicit Memories

By the time they reach adulthood, these boys may have no explicit memories of the interactions they had in early childhood with friends from differing ethnic groups. Research suggests, however, that their implicit memories of such experiences could have an unconscious effect on their attitudes toward and judgments about members of those groups.

© Jeff Greenberg/The Image Works

FOCUS ON RESEARCH METHODS

Measuring Explicit Versus Implicit Memory

In Canada, Endel Tulving and his colleagues undertook a series of experiments to map the differences between explicit and implicit memory (Tulving, Schacter, & Stark, 1982).

What was the researcher's question?

Tulving knew he could measure explicit memory by giving a recognition test. On such a test, participants are given a set of words and asked to say whether they remember seeing each of the words on a previous list. The question was, How would it be possible to measure implicit memory?

How did the researcher answer the question?

First, Tulving asked the participants in his experiment to study a long list of words—the "study list." An hour later, they took a recognition test involving explicit memory—saying which words on a new list had been on the original study list. Then, to test their implicit memory, Tulving asked them to perform a "fragment completion" task. In this task, participants were shown a "test list" of word fragments, such as $d\_li\_\_u\_$ and were asked to complete the word (in this case, *delirium*). On the basis of priming studies such as those described in the chapter on consciousness, Tulving assumed that memory from a previous exposure to the correct word would improve the participants' ability to complete the fragment, even if they were unable to consciously recall having seen the word before. A week later, all participants took a second test of their explicit memory (recognition) and implicit memory (fragment completion) of the study list. Some of the words on this second test list had been on the original study list, but none had been used in the first set of memory tests. The independent variable in this experiment, then, was the amount of time that had elapsed since the participants read the study list (one hour versus one week), and the dependent variable was performance on each of the two types of memory tests, explicit and implicit.

What did the researcher find?

As shown in Figure 7.2, explicit memory for the study list decreased dramatically over time, but implicit memory (or priming) was virtually unchanged. Results from several other experiments also show that the passage of time affects explicit memory

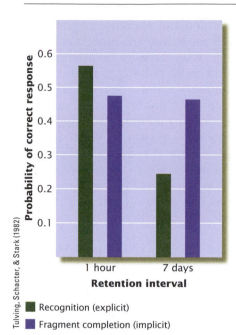

Tulving, Schacter, & Stark (1982)

FIGURE 7.2
Measures of Explicit and Implicit Memory

This experiment showed that the passage of time greatly affected people's recognition (explicit memory) of a word list but left fragment completion (implicit memory) essentially intact. Results such as these suggest that explicit and implicit memory may be different memory systems.

more than implicit memory (Komatsu & Naito, 1992; Mitchell, 1991). For example, it appears that the aging process has fewer negative effects on implicit memory than on explicit memory (Light, 1991).

What do the results mean?

The work of Tulving and others supports the idea of a dissociation, or independence, between explicit and implicit memory, suggesting that the two may operate on different principles (Gabrieli et al., 1995). In fact, some researchers believe that explicit and implicit memory may involve the activity of distinct neural systems in the brain (Squire, 1987; Tulving & Schacter, 1990). Others argue that the two types of memory are best described as requiring different cognitive processes (Nelson, McKinney, & Bennett, 1999; Roediger & McDermott, 1992).

What do we still need to know?

Psychologists have studied the role of implicit memory (and dissociations between explicit and implicit memory) in such important psychological phenomena as amnesia (Schacter, Church, & Treadwell, 1994; Tulving, 1993), depression (Elliott & Greene, 1992), posttraumatic stress disorder (McNally & Amir, 1996), problem solving (Jacoby, Marriott, & Collins, 1990), prejudice and stereotyping (Payne, Jacoby, & Lambert, 2004), the development of self-concept in childhood (Nelson, 1993), and even the power of ads to associate brand names with good feelings (Duke & Carlson, 1994). The results of these studies are shedding new light on implicit memory and how it operates in the real world.

For example, some social psychologists are trying to determine whether consciously held attitudes are independent of *implicit social cognitions*—past experiences that unconsciously influence a person's judgments about a group of people (Greenwald et al., 2009). A case in point would be a person whose explicit thoughts about members of a particular ethnic group are positive but whose implicit thoughts are negative. Some research in social neuroscience (Stanley, Phelps, & Banaji, 2008) has found that implicit and explicit forms of racial bias activate different parts of the brain, suggesting that the two processes may be independent. It is also the case, though, that people can learn to control implicit prejudice and its effects on their behavior, especially if they are motivated to avoid expressing their prejudice (Monteith, 2011; Stewart & Payne, 2008). The question of whether explicit and implicit forms of racial bias are separate processes is still a matter of debate and continuing research (Banaji & Heiphetz, 2010; Dovidio & Gaertner, 2010; see the Linkages section of the chapter on social cognition).

Further research is needed to determine what mechanisms are responsible for implicit versus explicit memory and how these two kinds of memory are related (Lustig & Hasher, 2001; Nelson et al., 1998). Functional neuroimaging techniques will facilitate that research. As described later, these techniques allow scientists to observe brain activity during various memory tasks and to determine which areas are associated with the explicit and implicit cognitive processes involved in these tasks (Buckner & Wheeler, 2001; McDermott, 2002; Schacter, Dobbins, & Schnyer, 2004).

Models of Memory

We remember some information far better than other information. For example, suppose that your friends throw a surprise party for you. When you enter the room, you might barely notice the flash of a camera, and later you might not recall it. And you might forget in a few seconds the name of a person you met at the party. But if you live to be 100, you will never forget where the party took place or how surprised and pleased you were. Why do some stimuli leave no more than a fleeting impression and others remain in memory forever? Each of five *models* of memory provides a somewhat different explanation. Let's see how the levels-of-processing, transfer-appropriate processing, parallel distributed processing, multiple memory systems, and information-processing models describe and explain memory.

Levels of Processing

The **levels-of-processing model of memory** suggests that what you remember depends on the extent to which you encode and process information when you first encounter it (Craik & Lockhart, 1972). Consider, for example, the task of remembering a phone number you just heard on the radio. If you were unable to write it down, you would probably repeat the number over and over to yourself until you could find a pen or get to your phone. This repetition process is called **maintenance rehearsal**. It can be an effective way of remembering information temporarily, but what if you need to remember something for hours, months, or years? In that case, you are better off using **elaborative rehearsal**, a process in which you relate new material to information you have already stored in memory. For example, instead of trying to remember a new person's name by simply repeating it to yourself, you could try thinking about how the name is related to something you know well. So if you are introduced to a man named Jim Crews, for example, you might think, "He is as tall as my uncle Jim, who always wears a crew cut."

Study after study has shown that memory is improved when people use elaborative rehearsal rather than maintenance rehearsal (Jahnke & Nowaczyk, 1998). According to the levels-of-processing model, elaborative rehearsal improves memory because information is mentally processed to a greater degree or "depth" (Roediger, Gallo, & Geraci, 2002). The more you think about new information, organize it, and relate it to existing knowledge, the "deeper" the processing and the better your memory of it becomes. Teachers use this idea when they ask their students not only to define a new word but also to use it in a sentence. Figuring out how to use the new word takes deeper processing than merely defining it does. (The next time you come across an unfamiliar word in this book, don't just read its definition. Try using the word in a sentence by coming up with an example of the concept that relates to your knowledge and experience.)

TRY THIS

Transfer-Appropriate Processing

Level of processing is not the only factor affecting what we remember (Baddeley, 1992). The **transfer-appropriate processing model of memory** suggests another critical factor, namely, the match between how we try to retrieve information and how we originally encoded it. In one study, for example, half the students in a class were told that their next exam would contain multiple-choice questions. The rest of the students were told to expect essay questions. Only half the students actually got the type of exam they expected, however. These students did much better on the exam than those who took an unexpected type of exam. Apparently, in studying for the exam, the two groups used encoding strategies that were more appropriate to the type of exam they expected. Those who tried to retrieve the information in a way that did not match their encoding method had a harder time (d'Ydewalle & Rosselle, 1978). Results such as these illustrate that the harmony between encoding and retrieval processes can be as important as depth of processing in memory.

Parallel Distributed Processing

A third way of thinking about memory is based on **parallel distributed processing (PDP) models of memory** (Rumelhart & McClelland, 1986). These models suggest that new experiences do more than provide specific facts that are stored and later retrieved one at a time. Those facts are also combined with what you already know so that each new experience changes your overall understanding of the world and how it operates. For example, when you first arrived on campus, you learned many specific facts, such as where classes are held, what time the library closes, and where to get the best pizza. Over time, these and many other facts about student life form a network of information that creates a more general understanding of how the whole college system works. The development of this network makes experienced students not only more knowledgeable than new students but also more sophisticated. It allows them to, say, allocate their study time so as to do well in their most important courses and to plan a schedule that does not cause conflict with work commitments and maybe even avoids early morning classes—and certain professors.

levels-of-processing model of memory The view that how well something is remembered depends on the degree to which incoming information is mentally processed.

maintenance rehearsal Repeating information over and over to keep it active in short-term memory.

elaborative rehearsal A memorization method that involves thinking about how new information relates to information already stored in long-term memory.

transfer-appropriate processing model of memory A model that suggests that a critical determinant of memory is how well the retrieval process matches the original encoding process.

parallel distributed processing (PDP) models of memory Memory models in which new experiences change one's overall knowledge base.

PDP models of memory reflect this notion of knowledge networks. PDP memory theorists begin by considering how *neural networks* might provide the framework for a functional memory system (Anderson, 2000). As described in the chapters on perception, learning, and biological aspects of psychology, the structure of neural networks allows each part to be linked to every other part. When this network model is applied to memory, each unit of knowledge is seen as connected to every other unit, and the connections between units are seen as getting stronger the more often the units are experienced together. From this perspective, then, "knowledge" is distributed across a dense network of associations. When this network is activated, *parallel processing* occurs. That is, different portions of the network operate simultaneously, allowing people to quickly and efficiently draw inferences and make generalizations. Just seeing the word *sofa,* for example, allows us immediately to gain access to knowledge about what a sofa looks like, what it is used for, where it tends to be located, who might buy one, and so on. PDP models of memory explain this process very effectively.

Multiple Memory Systems   The *multiple memory systems model* suggests that the brain contains several relatively separate memory systems, each of which resides in a different area and each of which serves somewhat different purposes (Schacter & Tulving, 1994; Schacter, Wagner, & Buckner, 2000). As mentioned in the Focus on Research Methods section, for example, the fact that explicit and implicit memory appear to operate on different principles suggests that they are separate systems, each of which is supported by activity in different regions of the brain. Additional evidence for the multiple memory systems approach comes from case studies in which damage to the brain's hippocampus impairs performance on tests of explicit memory but not on implicit memory tests (e.g., Warrington & Weiskrantz, 1970). Other research shows that inactivating the hippocampus with drugs causes massive disruption of explicit but not implicit memory processes (Frank, O'Reilly, & Curran, 2006).

Information Processing   The **information-processing model of memory** is the earliest and probably the most influential and comprehensive model of memory (Roediger, 1990). It suggests that for information to become firmly implanted in memory, it must pass through three stages of mental processing: sensory memory, short-term memory, and long-term memory (Atkinson & Shiffrin, 1968; see Figure 7.3).

In *sensory memory,* information from the senses—sights or sounds, for example—is held very briefly, often for less than a second, before being lost. But if information in sensory memory is attended to, analyzed, and encoded as a meaningful pattern, we say that it has been *perceived* (see the chapters on sensation and perception). Information in sensory memory that has been perceived can now enter short-term memory. If nothing further is done with it, the information will disappear in less than twenty seconds. However, if information in short-term memory is processed further, it may be encoded into *long-term memory,* where it may remain indefinitely.

The act of reading illustrates all three stages of memory processing. As you read any sentence in this book, light energy reflected from the page reaches your eyes, where it is converted to neural activity and registered in your sensory memory. If

information-processing model of memory   A memory model in which information is seen as passing through sensory memory, short-term memory, and long-term memory.

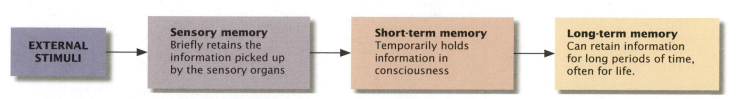

FIGURE 7.3
Three Stages of Memory
The traditional information-processing model describes three stages in the memory system.

Sensory Memory at Work

TRY THIS In a darkened room, ask a friend to switch on a small flashlight and move it slowly in a circle. You will see a moving point of light. If it appears to have a "tail," like a comet, that is your sensory memory of the light before it fades away. Now ask your friend to speed up the movement. You should now see a complete circle of light, because as the light moves, its impression on your sensory memory does not have time to fade before the circle is completed. A similar process allows us to see "sparkler circles."

© Nick Daly/Photodisc/Getty Images

you pay attention to these visual stimuli, your perception of the patterns of light can be held in short-term memory. This stage of memory holds the early parts of the sentence so that they can be integrated and understood as you read the rest of the sentence. As you read, you are constantly recognizing words by matching your perceptions of them with the patterns and meanings you have stored in long-term memory. In other words, all three stages of memory are necessary for you to understand a sentence.

The information-processing model emphasizes these constant interactions among sensory, short-term, and long-term memory. For example, sensory memory can be thought of as the part of your knowledge base (or long-term memory) that is momentarily activated by information sent to the brain via the sensory nerves. And short-term memory can be thought of as the part of your knowledge base that is the focus of attention at any given moment (Cowan, 2008; Wagner, 1999). Like perception, memory is an active process, and what is already in long-term memory influences how new information is encoded (Cowan, 1988). To understand this interaction better, try the exercise in Figure 7.4.

"In Review: Models of Memory" summarizes the five memory models we have discussed. Each of these models provides an explanation of why we remember some things and forget others. Which one offers the best explanation? The answer is that more than one model may be required to understand memory. Just as it is helpful for physicists to characterize light in terms of both waves and particles, psychologists find it useful to think of memory as both a sequence of cognitive processes as suggested by the information-processing, levels-of-processing, and transfer-appropriate processing approaches, and in terms of underlying brain activity, as suggested by the parallel distributed processing and multiple memory systems approaches.

FIGURE 7.4

The Role of Memory in Comprehension

TRY THIS Read the paragraph shown here; then turn away and try to recall as much of it as possible. Next, read the footnote on page 250 and reread the paragraph. The second reading probably made a lot more sense and was much easier to remember because knowing the title of the paragraph allowed you to retrieve from long-term memory your knowledge about the topic (Bransford & Johnson, 1972).

The procedure is actually quite simple. First, you arrange items into different groups. Of course, one pile may be sufficient, depending on how much there is to do. If you have to go somewhere else due to lack of facilities that is the next step; otherwise, you are pretty well set. It is important not to overdo things. That is, it is better to do too few things at once than too many. In the short run, this may not seem important, but complications can easily arise. A mistake can be expensive as well. At first, the whole procedure will seem complicated. Soon, however, it will become just another facet of life. It is difficult to foresee any end to the necessity for this task in the immediate future, but then, one never can tell. After the procedure is completed, one arranges the materials into different groups again. Then they can be put into their appropriate places. Eventually they will be used once more, and the whole cycle will then have to be repeated. However, that is part of life.

IN REVIEW	Models of Memory
Model	**Assumptions**
Levels of processing	The more deeply material is processed, the better the memory of it.
Transfer-appropriate processing	Retrieval is improved when we try to recall material in a way that matches how the material was encoded.
Parallel distributed processing (PDP)	New experiences add to and alter our overall knowledge base; they are not separate, unconnected facts. PDP networks allow us to draw inferences and make generalizations about the world.
Multiple memory systems	There are several separate memory systems, each in a different brain area and each serving different purposes.
Information processing	Information is processed in three stages: sensory, short-term, and long-term memory.

1. **The value of elaborative rehearsal over maintenance rehearsal has been cited as evidence for the _____ model of memory.**

2. **Deliberately trying to remember something means using your _____ memory.**

3. **Playing the piano uses _____ memory.**

Storing New Memories

We can't retrieve information if we haven't stored it. According to the information-processing model, sensory, short-term, and long-term memory each provide a different type of storage system. Let's take a closer look at these three memory systems in order to better understand how they work—and sometimes fail.

Sensory Memory

As described in the perception chapter, our ability to recognize that we are looking at a car, for example, depends on the brain's ability to analyze, compare, and match the features of that car with information about cars that is already stored in long-term memory. This process is very quick, but it still takes time. The major function of **sensory memory** is to hold information long enough for it to be processed further (Nairne, 2003). This maintenance is the job of the **sensory registers**, which act as temporary storage bins. There is a separate register for each of the five senses, and each register can store a nearly complete representation of sensory stimuli. Although sensory memories are stored only briefly, often for less than one second, this is long enough for stimulus identification to begin (Eysenck & Keane, 2005).

Sensory memory helps us experience a constant flow of information, even if that flow is interrupted. To see this for yourself, turn your head and eyes slowly from left to right. It may seem as though your eyes are moving smoothly, like a movie camera scanning a scene, but that's not what is happening. Instead, your eyes fixate at one point for about one-fourth of a second and then rapidly jump to a new position. You perceive smooth motion through the visual field because you hold each scene in your visual sensory register (also known as your **iconic memory**) until your eyes fixate again. Similarly, when you listen to someone speak, your auditory sensory register allows you to experience a smooth flow of information, even though there are actually short silences between or within words. Information remains in each of the five sensory registers for varying amounts of time. For example, information in the auditory sensory register lasts longer than information in the visual sensory register.

The fact that sensory memories quickly fade if they are not processed further is actually an adaptive characteristic of the memory system. You simply could not deal with all of the sights, sounds, odors, tastes, and touch sensations that reach your sense organs

TRY THIS

sensory memory A type of memory that holds large amounts of incoming information very briefly, but long enough to connect one impression to the next.

sensory registers Memory systems that hold incoming information long enough for it to be processed further.

iconic memory The sensory register for visual information.

at any given moment. As mentioned in the chapter on perception, **selective attention** focuses your mental resources on only some of the stimuli around you, thus controlling what information is processed further. Your perceptual systems capture the fleeting impressions of sensory memory and transfer them to short-term memory.

Short-Term Memory and Working Memory

The sensory registers allow your memory system to develop a representation of a stimulus. However, they can't perform the more thorough analysis needed if the information is going to be used in some way. That function is accomplished by short-term memory and working memory.

Short-term memory (STM) is the part of your memory system that stores limited amounts of information for up to about eighteen seconds. When you check the building directory to see which floor your new dentist's office is on and then keep that number in mind as you press the correct elevator button, you are using short-term memory. **Working memory** is the part of the memory system that allows us to mentally work with, or manipulate, the information being held in short-term memory. When you mentally calculate what time you have to leave home in order to have lunch on campus, return a library book, and still get to class on time, you are using working memory.

Short-term memory is actually a component of working memory, and together these memory systems allow us to do many kinds of mental work (Baddeley, 2003). Suppose that you are buying something for 83 cents. You go through your change and pick out two quarters, two dimes, two nickels, and three pennies. To do this, you use both short-term and working memory to remember the price, retrieve the rules of addition from long-term memory, and keep a running count of how much change you have so far. Now

TRY THIS

try to recall how many windows there are on the front of the house or apartment where you grew up. In answering this question, you probably formed a mental image of the building. You used one kind of working-memory process to form that image, and then you maintained the image in short-term memory while you "worked" on it by counting the windows. So working memory has at least two components: *maintenance* (holding information in short-term memory) and *manipulation* (working on that information).

Encoding in Short-Term Memory   Encoding information in short-term memory is much more elaborative and varied than it is in the sensory registers (Brandimonte, Hitch, & Bishop, 1992). *Acoustic encoding* (by sound) seems to dominate. This conclusion comes from research on the mistakes people make when encoding information in short-term memory. These mistakes tend to involve the substitution of similar sounds. For example, Robert Conrad (1964) showed people strings of letters and asked them to repeat the letters immediately. Among their most common mistakes was the replacement of the correct letter with one whose name sounded like it. So if the correct letter was *C,* it was often replaced with a *D, P,* or *T.* The research participants made these mistakes even though the letters were presented visually, without any sound. Evidence for acoustic encoding in short-term memory also comes from studies showing that items are more difficult to remember if their spoken sounds are similar. For example, native English speakers do less well when asked to remember a string of letters such as *ECVTGB* (in which all the letter names rhyme) than when asked to remember one like *KRLDQS* (in which all the letter names sound different).

Encoding in short-term memory is not *always* acoustic, however. Visual codes are also used, but information encoded visually tends to fade much more quickly from short-term memory than information that is encoded acoustically (Cornoldi, DeBeni, & Baldi, 1989). There is also evidence for kinesthetic encoding, which involves physical movements (Best, 1999). In one study, deaf people were shown a list of words and then asked to immediately write down as many as they could remember (Shand, 1982). When these people made errors, they wrote words that are expressed through

---

selective attention The focusing of mental resources on only part of the stimulus field.

short-term memory (STM) The maintenance component of working memory, which holds unrehearsed information for a limited time.

working memory The part of the memory system that allows us to mentally work with, or manipulate, information being held in short-term memory.

The title of the paragraph in Figure 7.4 is "Washing Clothes."

FIGURE 7.5

Capacity of Short-Term Memory

TRY THIS Here is a test of your immediate memory span. Ask someone to read to you the numbers in the top row at the rate of about one per second. Then try to repeat them in the same order. Do the same test on the next row and then the one after that and so on until you make a mistake. Your immediate memory span is the maximum number of items you can repeat perfectly. Similar tests can be performed using the rows of letters and words.

```
9 2 5                          G M N
8 6 4 2                        S L R R
3 7 6 5 4                      V O E P G
6 2 7 4 1 8                    X W D X Q O
0 4 0 1 4 7 3                  E P H H J A E
1 9 2 2 3 5 3 0                Z D O F W D S V
4 8 6 8 5 4 3 3 2              D T Y N R H E H Q
2 5 3 1 9 7 1 7 6 8            K H W D A G R O F Z
8 5 1 2 9 6 1 9 4 5 0          U D F F W H D Q D G E
9 1 8 5 4 6 9 4 2 9 3 7        Q M R H X Z D P R R E H
```

CAT BOAT RUG
RUN BEACH PLANT LIGHT
SUIT WATCH CUT STAIRS CAR
JUNK LONE GAME CALL WOOD HEART
FRAME PATCH CROSS DRUG DESK HORSE LAW
CLOTHES CHOOSE GIFT DRIVE BOOK TREE HAIR THIS
DRESS CLERK FILM BASE SPEND SERVE BOOK LOW TIME
STONE ALL NAIL DOOR HOPE EARL FEEL BUY COPE GRAPE
AGE SOFT FALL STORE PUT TRUE SMALL FREE CHECK MAIL LEAF
LOG DAY TIME CHESS LAKE CUT BIRD SHEET YOUR SEE STREET WHEEL

similar *hand movements* in American Sign Language, rather than words that sounded similar to the correct words. Apparently, these individuals had encoded the words on the basis of the movements they would use when making the signs for them.

Storage Capacity of Short-Term Memory How much information can you hold in short-term memory? The simple experiment presented in Figure 7.5 will help you determine your **immediate memory span**, which is the largest number of items you can recall perfectly after one presentation. If your memory span is like most people's, you can repeat six or seven items from the test in this figure. And you will probably come up with about the same result whether you test your immediate memory span with digits, letters, words, or anything else. George Miller (1956) noticed that many studies using a variety of tasks showed the same limit on the ability to process information. This "magic number," which is seven (plus or minus two), appears to be the typical immediate memory span or capacity of short-term memory, at least in laboratory settings. In addition, the "magic number" refers not only to discrete elements, such as words or digits, but also to *chunks,* which are meaningful groupings of information that are produced by a cognitive process called **chunking**.

TRY THIS To see the difference between discrete elements and chunks, read the following letters to a friend, pausing at each dash: *FB–IAO–LM–TVI–BMB–MW.* The chances are very good that your friend will not be able to repeat this string of letters perfectly. Why? There are fifteen letters, which exceeds most people's immediate memory span. Now give your friend the test again, but group the letters like this: *FBI–AOL–MTV–IBM–BMW.* Your friend will probably repeat that string easily. Although the same fifteen letters are involved, they will be processed as only five meaningful chunks of information.

The Power of Chunking Chunks of information can be quite complex. If you heard someone say, "The boy in the red shirt kicked his mother in the shin," you could probably repeat the sentence perfectly. Yet it contains twelve words and forty-three letters. How can you repeat the sentence so effortlessly? The answer is that you can build bigger and bigger chunks of information (Ericsson & Staszewski, 1989). In this case, you might represent "the boy in the red shirt" as one chunk of information rather than as six words or nineteen letters. Similarly, you might represent all the letters in "kicked his mother" and "in the shin" as just two chunks of information.

immediate memory span The maximum number of items a person can recall perfectly after one presentation of the items.

chunking Organizing individual stimuli so that they will be perceived as larger units of meaningful information.

Chunking in Action

The people who provide instantaneous translation of speeches—such as this one at the United Nations—must store long, often complicated segments of speech in short-term memory while searching long-term memory for the equivalent second-language expressions. The task is made easier by chunking the speaker's words into phrases and sentences.

© Monika Graff/The Image Works

Learning to use bigger and bigger chunks of information can enhance short-term memory. In fact, children's memories improve partly because they gradually become able to hold as many as seven chunks in memory and also because they get better at grouping information into chunks (Servan-Schreiber & Anderson, 1990). Adults, too, can greatly increase the capacity of their short-term memory by more appropriate chunking. For example, after extensive training, one college student increased his immediate memory span from seven digits to eighty digits (Ericsson, Chase, & Faloon, 1980), and experienced waiters often use chunking techniques to help them remember the details of numerous dinner orders without taking notes (Bekinschtein, Cardozo, & Manes, 2008). In short, although the capacity of short-term memory is more or less constant—five to nine chunks of meaningful information—the size of those chunks can vary tremendously.

Duration of Short-Term Memory   Imagine how hard it would be to mentally calculate your waitress's tip if your short-term memory was cluttered with every other bill you had ever paid, every phone number you had ever called, and every conversation you had ever heard. There are rare cases of people whose inability to forget interferes with their ability to concentrate (Parker, Cahill, & McGaugh, 2006), but normally—unless you continue repeating information to yourself (maintenance rehearsal) or use elaborative rehearsal to transfer it to long-term memory—information in short-term memory is usually forgotten quickly. This feature of short-term memory is adaptive because it gets rid of a lot of useless information, but it can also be inconvenient. You may have discovered this if you have ever looked up a phone number, got distracted before you could call it, and then forgot the number.

How long does information remain in short-term memory if you don't keep rehearsing it? John Brown (1958) and Lloyd and Margaret Peterson (1959) devised the **Brown-Peterson distractor technique** to measure the duration of short-term memory when no rehearsal is allowed. In this procedure, participants are presented with a group of three letters, such as *GRB*. They then count backward by threes from some number until they get a signal. Counting serves as a distraction that prevents the participants from rehearsing the letters. At the signal, they stop counting and try to recall the letters. By varying the number of seconds spent counting backward, the experimenter can determine how much forgetting takes place over time. As you can see in Figure 7.6, information in short-term memory is forgotten rapidly: After eighteen seconds, participants can remember almost nothing.

Brown-Peterson distractor technique A method for determining how long unrehearsed information remains in short-term memory.

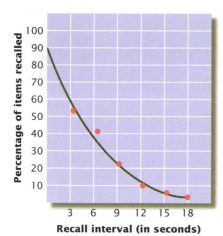

FIGURE 7.6
Forgetting in Short-Term Memory
This graph shows the percentage of items recalled after various intervals during which rehearsal was prevented. Notice that virtually complete forgetting occurred after a delay of eighteen seconds.

Source: Data from Peterson & Peterson (1959).

TRY THIS

long-term memory (LTM) A relatively long-lasting stage of memory whose capacity to store new information is believed to be unlimited.

Evidence from other such experiments also suggests that unrehearsed information can be held in short-term memory for no more than about eighteen seconds. However, if the information is rehearsed or processed further, it may be encoded into long-term memory.

Long-Term Memory

When people talk about memory, they are usually talking about **long-term memory (LTM)**, the part of the memory system that encodes and stores memories that can last a lifetime.

Encoding in Long-Term Memory   Some information is encoded into long-term memory even if we make no conscious effort to memorize it (Ellis, 1991). However, putting information into long-term memory is often the result of more conscious processing that usually involves *semantic encoding*. As we mentioned earlier, semantic encoding often leaves out details in favor of the more general meaning of the information.

In a classic study, Jacqueline Sachs (1967) demonstrated the dominance of semantic encoding in long-term memory. Her participants first listened to tape recordings of people speaking. She then showed them sets of similar sentences and asked them to choose which one contained the exact wording heard on the tape. The participants did well at this task when tested immediately, using mainly short-term memory. However, after twenty-seven seconds, they could not be sure which of two similar sentences they had heard. For example, they could not determine whether they had heard "He sent a letter about it to Galileo, the great Italian scientist" or "A letter about it was sent to Galileo, the great Italian scientist." They didn't do as well after the delay because by then they had to recall the information from long-term memory, where they had encoded the general meaning of what they had heard but not the exact wording.

Perhaps you are thinking, "So what?" After all, the two sentences mean the same thing. Unfortunately, when people encode the general meaning of information they hear or read, they can make mistakes about the details (Brewer, 1977). For example, after listening to a list of words such as *hot, snow, warm, winter, ice, wet, frigid, chilly, heat, weather, freeze, air, shiver, Arctic,* and *frost,* people often remember having heard the related word *cold* even though it was not presented (Gallo, 2006; Roediger & McDermott, 1995). You can replicate this research by reading this list to five friends and then asking them to recall as many of its words as they can. Chances are that, like participants in laboratory experiments, several of them will be so certain that *cold* was on the list that they may not believe you when you tell them it wasn't! This kind of false memory can be a problem when recalling exact words is important—as in the courtroom, during business negotiations, and in discussions between students and teachers about previous agreements. Later in this chapter, we show that such mistakes occur partly because people encode into long-term memory not only the general meaning of information but also what they think and assume about that information (McDermott & Chan, 2006). Those expectations and assumptions—like the one that a list containing so many "winter-related" words must have included *cold*—may alter what is recalled.

Counterfeiters depend on the fact that people encode the general meaning of visual stimuli rather than specific details. For example, look at Figure 7.7, and identify the correct drawing of the U.S. penny (Nickerson & Adams, 1979). Research shows that most people from the United States are unsuccessful at this task; people from other countries do just as poorly at recognizing their nation's coins (Jones, 1990). The same problem occurs in relation to paper money, which has prompted the U.S. Treasury to begin using more distinctive drawings on its currency.

Although long-term memory normally involves semantic encoding, people can also use visual encoding to process images into long-term memory. In one study, people viewed 2,500 pictures. It took sixteen hours just to present the stimuli, but the participants later recognized more than 90 percent of the pictures on which they were tested (Standing, Conezio, & Haber, 1970). *Dual coding theory* suggests that pictures tend to be remembered better than words because pictures are represented in two

(A)   **(B)**   **(C)**   **(D)**   **(E)**

FIGURE 7.7

Encoding into Long-Term Memory

TRY THIS Which is the correct image of a U.S. penny? (See the footnote on page 256 for the answer.) It is often difficult for people to explicitly remember the specific details of information stored in long-term memory, but priming studies suggest that they do retain some implicit memory of them (e.g., Srinivas, 1993).

Source: Nickerson & Adams (1979).

codes—visual and verbal—rather than in only one (Paivio, 1986). This suggestion is supported by brain-imaging studies showing that when people are asked to memorize pictures, they tend to create a verbal label for the picture (e.g., "frog"), as well as to look at the drawing's visual features (Kelley et al., 1998).

Storage Capacity of Long-Term Memory   The capacity of long-term memory is extremely large. In fact, many psychologists believe that it is unlimited (Matlin, 1998). There is no way to prove this, but we do know that people store vast quantities of information in long-term memory that can be remembered remarkably well after long periods of time. For example, people are amazingly accurate at recognizing the faces of high school classmates they have not seen for over twenty-five years (Bruck, Cavanagh, & Ceci, 1991). They also do surprisingly well on tests of a foreign language or high school algebra fifty years after having formally studied these subjects (Bahrick & Hall, 1991; Bahrick et al., 1994; Bowers, Mattys, & Gage, 2009).

However, long-term memories are also subject to distortion. In one study that illustrates this point, college students were asked to recall their high school grades. Even though the students were motivated to be accurate, they correctly remembered 89 percent of their A grades but only 29 percent of their D grades. And you might not be surprised to learn that when they recalled grades incorrectly, they usually erred by remembering grades as being higher than they actually were (Bahrick, Hall, & Berger, 1996). What about *flashbulb memories*—those vivid recollections of personally significant events that, like a snapshot, seem to preserve all the details of the moment (Brown & Kulik, 1997)? They, too, can be distorted (Sharot et al., 2006). For example, one group of students was asked to describe where they were and what they were doing when they heard about the not-guilty verdict in the 1995 O. J. Simpson murder trial (Schmolck, Buffalo, & Squire, 2000). The students first reported their recollections three days after the verdict and then again after either fifteen months or thirty-two months. Only half the recollections reported at fifteen months were accurate, and 11 percent contained major errors or distortions. Among those reporting after thirty-two months, 71 percent of their recollections were inaccurate, and just over 40 percent contained major errors or distortions. For example, three days after the verdict, one student said he heard about it while in a campus lounge with other students. Thirty-two months later, this same person recalled hearing the news in the living room of his home with his father and sister. Do you remember where were you were and what you were doing when you heard about the 9/11 terrorist attacks on the United States? You may be quite sure that you do, but if you are like the students tested in one study, your flashbulb memories of 9/11 may not be entirely correct (Talarico & Rubin, 2003). Most of the students whose flashbulb memories had been substantially distorted over time were unaware that this distortion had occurred. In fact, they were very confident that their reports were accurate. Later, we will see that such overconfidence can also appear in courtroom testimony by eyewitnesses to crime.

Magnani's painting

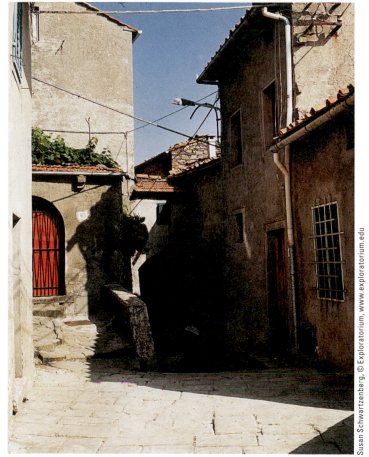

Photo of the same scene

Remarkable Memory

TRY THIS Using only his long-term memory, Franco Magnani created amazingly accurate paintings of his hometown in Italy even though he had not seen it for more than thirty years (Sacks, 1992). People like Magnani display *eidetic imagery,* commonly called *photographic memory.* It is not actually photographic, but it does create automatic, detailed, and vivid images of virtually everything they have ever seen. About 5 percent of school-age children have eidetic imagery, but it is extremely rare in adults (Haber, 1979). You can test yourself for eidetic imagery by drawing a detailed picture or map of a place that you know well but have not seen recently and then comparing your version with a photo or map of the same place. How did you do?

Distinguishing Between Short-Term and Long-Term Memory

Some psychologists say that short-term memory and long-term memory have different features and obey different laws (Cowan, 1988; Talmi et al., 2005). ("In Review: Storing New Memories" summarizes the characteristics of these two memory systems.) Let's consider some evidence from experiments on recall that suggest that information is transferred from short-term memory to a distinct storage system.

TRY THIS **Experiments on Recall** You can conduct your own recall experiment by reading aloud a list of words at a slow pace (about one word every two seconds). After reading the list just once, look away and write down as many of the words as you can, in any order. Here is a list you can use: *desk, frame, carburetor, flag, grill, book, urn, candle, briefcase, screen, tree, soup, ocean, castle, monster, bridge.* Did you notice anything about which words you remembered and which ones you forgot? If you are like most people, your recall depended partly on where each word appeared on the list—that

IN REVIEW   Storing New Memories

Storage System	Function	Capacity	Duration
Sensory memory	Briefly holds representations of stimuli from each sense for further processing	Large: absorbs all sensory input from a particular stimulus	Less than 1 second
Short-term and working memory	Hold information in awareness and manipulate it to accomplish mental work	Five to nine distinct items or chunks of information	About 18 seconds
Long-term memory	Stores new information indefinitely	Unlimited	Unlimited

1. If you looked up a phone number but forgot it before you could call it, the information was probably lost from _____ memory.
2. The capacity of short-term memory is about _____ to _____ items.
3. Encoding is usually _____ in short-term memory and _____ in long-term memory.

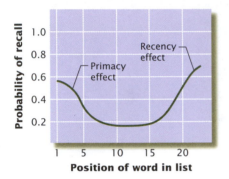

FIGURE 7.8
A Serial-Position Curve
This curve shows the probability of recalling items that appear at various serial positions in a list. Generally, the first several items and the last several items are the most likely to be recalled.

is, on its serial position. As shown in the serial-position curve in Figure 7.8, memory researchers have found that recall tends to be very good for the first two or three words in a list. This result is called the **primacy effect**. The probability of recall decreases for words in the middle of the list and then rises dramatically for the last few words. The ease of recalling words near the end of a list is called the **recency effect**. The primacy effect may reflect the rehearsal that puts early words into long-term memory. The recency effect may occur because the last few words are still in short-term memory when you try to recall the list (Glanzer & Cunitz, 1966; Koppenaal & Glanzer, 1990).

Retrieving Memories

Have you ever been unable to recall the name of an old television show or movie star, only to think of it the next day? Remembering something requires not only the encoding and storing of information but also the ability to bring it into consciousness. In other words, you have to be able to *retrieve* it.

Retrieval Cues and Encoding Specificity

Retrieval cues are stimuli that help you retrieve information from long-term memory. They allow you to recall things that were once forgotten and help you recognize information stored in memory. As mentioned earlier, retrieval cues are what make recognition tasks (such as multiple-choice tests) easier than recall tasks (such as essay exams).

The effectiveness of retrieval cues depends on the extent to which they tap into information that was encoded at the time of learning (Tulving, 1983). This rule is known as the **encoding specificity principle**, and it is consistent with the transfer-appropriate processing model of memory. Because long-term memories are often encoded semantically, in terms of their general meaning, cues that trigger the *meaning* of the stored information tend to work best. Imagine that you have learned a long list of sentences. One of them was either (1) "The man lifted the piano" or (2) "The man tuned the piano." Now suppose that on a later recall test, you were given the retrieval cue "something heavy." This cue would probably help you remember the first sentence (because you probably encoded something about the weight of a piano), but the cue would probably not help you recall the second sentence (because that sentence has nothing to do with weight). Similarly, the cue "makes nice sounds" would probably help you recall the second sentence but not the first (Barclay et al., 1974).

primacy effect A characteristic of memory in which recall of the first two or three items in a list is particularly good.

recency effect A characteristic of memory in which recall of the last few items in a list is particularly good.

retrieval cue A stimulus that aids the recall or recognition of information stored in memory.

encoding specificity principle A principle stating that the ability of a cue to aid retrieval depends on the degree to which it taps into information that was encoded at the time of the original learning.

Answer for Figure 7.7: Drawing A shows the correct penny image.

Context-Dependent Memories

Many people attending a reunion at their old high school find that being in the building again provides context cues that help bring back memories of their school days. Visit your elementary school or high school and see if it helps you remember things you'd forgotten. Be sure to look into specific rooms where you had classes or assemblies, and check out the restroom and your old locker too.

Context and State Dependence

Have you ever revisited a place that you hadn't been to in a long time and suddenly found yourself remembering events that happened there? In general, people remember more of what they learned when they are in the place where they learned it (Smith & Vela, 2001). Why? Because if they have encoded features of the environment in which the learning occurred, those features may later act as retrieval cues (Richardson-Klavehn & Bjork, 1988). In one experiment, people studied a series of photos while in the presence of a particular odor. Later, they reviewed a larger set of photos and tried to recognize the ones they had seen earlier. Half of the people were tested in the presence of the original odor while taking the recognition test. The rest were tested in the presence of a different odor. Those who smelled the same odor during learning and testing did significantly better on the recognition task than those who were tested in the presence of a different odor. The matching odor served as a powerful retrieval cue (Cann & Ross, 1989).

Context-specific memory, also known as **context-specific learning**, refers to memories that are helped or hindered by similarities or differences in environmental context. Police and prosecutors sometimes take advantage of context-specific memory by asking eyewitnesses to revisit the scene of the crime they saw, either in person or by mentally reconstructing it during an interview. The goal is to reinstate retrieval cues that can improve the accuracy of eyewitness testimony (e.g., Campos & Alonso-Quecuty, 2006), but as we will see later, these techniques may not result in perfect retrieval.

Sometimes we encode information about how we were feeling during a learning experience, and this information can also act as a retrieval cue. When our internal state influences retrieval, we have a **state-dependent memory**, also known as **state-dependent learning**. For example, if people learn new material while under the influence of marijuana, they tend to recall it better if they are tested under the influence of marijuana (Eich et al., 1975). Similar effects have been found with alcohol (Overton, 1984) and other psychoactive drugs (Eich, 1989). But don't get the wrong idea: Memory works best overall when people are not using any drugs during encoding and retrieval. Mood states, too, can affect memory (Eich & Macaulay, 2000). People tend to remember more pleasant events when they are feeling good at the time of recall and more negative events when they are in a sad or angry mood (Eich & Macaulay, 2007; Lewinsohn & Rosenbaum, 1987). These *mood congruency effects* are strongest when people try to recall personally meaningful episodes (Eich & Metcalfe, 1989) because those episodes were most likely to be colored by their moods.

context-specific memory (context-specific learning) Memory that can be helped or hindered by similarities or differences between the context in which it is learned and the context in which it is recalled.

state-dependent memory (state-dependent learning) Memory that is aided or impeded by a person's internal state.

IN REVIEW	Factors Affecting Retrieval from Long-Term Memory
Process	**Effect on Memory**
Encoding specificity	Retrieval cues are effective only to the extent that they tap into information that was originally encoded.
Context-specific memory	Retrieval is most successful when it occurs in the same environment in which the information was originally learned.
State-dependent memory	Retrieval is most successful when people are in the same physiological or psychological state as when they originally learned the information.

1. Stimuli called _____ help you recall information stored in long-term memory.
2. If it is easier to remember something in the place where you learned it, you have _____ learning.
3. The tendency to remember the first few items in a list is called the _____ effect.

Retrieval from Semantic Memory

The retrieval situations we have discussed so far are all relevant to episodic memory—our memory for events. ("In Review: Factors Affecting Retrieval from Long-Term Memory" summarizes this material.) But how do we retrieve information from semantic memory, where we store our general knowledge about the world? Researchers studying this process typically ask participants general-knowledge questions, such as (1) "Are fish minerals?" (2) "Is a beagle a dog?" (3) "Do birds fly?" and (4) "Does a car have legs?" As you might imagine, most people answer such questions correctly. But by measuring how long it takes to answer them, psychologists have found important clues about how semantic memory is organized and how we retrieve information from it.

Semantic Networks   One view of semantic memory suggests that virtually everything we know about, including concepts such as "bird" or "animal," is represented in a dense network of associations (Churchland, 1989). Figure 7.9 presents just a tiny part of what such a *semantic memory network* might look like. In general, semantic network theories suggest that information is retrieved from memory through **spreading activation** (Medin, Ross, & Markman, 2001). In other words, when you think about some concept, it becomes activated in the network, and this activation—in the form of neural energy—begins to spread along all the paths that are related to it. So if you are asked if a robin is a bird, the concepts of both "robin" and "bird" will become activated, and the spreading activation from each will meet somewhere along the path between them. When they do, you know what answer to give.

Some associations within the network are stronger than others, as illustrated by the thicker lines between some concepts in Figure 7.9. For example, you probably have a stronger association between "bat" and "wings" than between "bat" and "mammal." Spreading activation travels faster along stronger paths than along weaker ones. As a result, you'd probably respond more quickly to "Can a bat fly?" than to "Is a bat a mammal?"

Because of the tight organization of semantic networks and the speed at which activation spreads through them, we can gain access to an enormous body of knowledge about the world quickly and effortlessly. We can retrieve not only facts we have learned from others but also the knowledge that allows us to draw our own conclusions and inferences (Matlin, 1998). For example, imagine answering these two questions: "Is a robin a bird?" and "Is a robin a living thing?" You can probably answer the first question "directly" because at some point in your life you probably learned that robins are birds. However, you may never have consciously thought about the second question, so answering it requires you to make an inference. Figure 7.9 illustrates the path to that inference. Because you know that a robin is a bird, a bird is an animal, and animals are living things, you can infer that a robin must be a living thing. As you might expect, however, it takes slightly longer to answer the second question than the first.

spreading activation A principle that explains how information is retrieved in semantic network theories of memory.

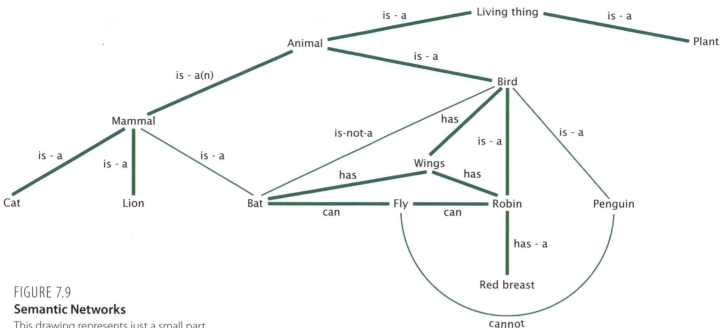

FIGURE 7.9
Semantic Networks

This drawing represents just a small part of a network of semantic associations. Semantic network theories of memory suggest that networks like these allow us to retrieve specific pieces of previously learned information, draw conclusions about how concepts are related, and make new inferences about the world.

Retrieving Incomplete Knowledge Figure 7.9 also shows that concepts such as "bird" or "living thing" are represented in semantic memory as unique sets of features or attributes. As a result, there may be times when you can retrieve some features of a concept from your semantic network but not enough of them to identify the concept. For example, you might know that there is an animal that has wings and can fly and yet be unable to retrieve its name. When this happens, you are retrieving *incomplete knowledge*. (The animal in question is a bat.)

You have probably experienced a particular example of incomplete knowledge called the *tip-of-the-tongue phenomenon*. In a typical experiment on this phenomenon, people listen to dictionary definitions and are asked to name the word being defined (Brown & McNeill, 1966). If they can't recall the correct word, they are asked if they can recall any feature of it, such as its first letter or how many syllables it has. People are surprisingly good at this task, indicating that they are able to retrieve at least some knowledge of the word (Brennen et al., 1990). Being almost—but not quite—able to recall the precise word or name we are looking for is a common experience. Most people experience the tip-of-the-tongue phenomenon about once a week, and older people experience it more often than younger people (Brown & Nix, 1996).

Another example of retrieving incomplete knowledge is the *feeling-of-knowing experience*, which some researchers study by asking trivia questions (Reder & Ritter, 1992). When research participants cannot answer a question, they are asked to say how likely it is that they could recognize the correct answer among several options. Again, people are remarkably good at this task. Even though they cannot recall the answer, they can retrieve enough knowledge to determine whether the answer is actually stored in their memory (Costermans, Lories, & Ansay, 1992).

Constructing Memories

Our memories are affected by what we experience but also by what we already know about the world (Schacter, Norman, & Koutstaal, 1998). We use that knowledge to organize new information as we encounter it, and we fill in gaps in the information as we encode and retrieve it (Sherman & Bessenoff, 1999). These processes are called *constructive memory*.

In one study of constructive memory, undergraduates were asked to wait for several minutes in the office of a graduate student (Brewer & Treyens, 1981). Later,

Constructive Memory

TRY THIS Here is a photo of the office used in the Brewer & Treyens (1981) study. Ask a friend to examine this photo for a minute or so (cover the caption). Then close the book and ask whether each of the following items appeared in the photo: chair, wastebasket, bottle, typewriter, coffeepot, book. If your friend reports having seen a wastebasket or book, you will have demonstrated constructive memory.

Courtesy Professor William F. Brewer. From Brewer, W. F., & Treyens, J.C. (1981). Role of schemata in memory of places. *Cognitive Psychology, 13,* 207–230

they were asked to recall everything that was in the office. Most of the students mistakenly "remembered" seeing books, even though there were none. Apparently, the general knowledge that graduate students read many books influenced the participants' memory of what was in the room (Roediger, Meade, & Bergman, 2001). In another study, participants read one of two versions of a story about a man and woman at a ski lodge. One version ended with the man proposing marriage to the woman. The second version was identical until the end, when instead of proposing, the man sexually assaulted the woman. A few days after reading the story, all the participants were asked what they remembered from it. Those who had read the "proposal" version recalled nice things about the man, such as that he wanted the woman to meet his parents. Those who read the "assault" version recalled negative things, such as that the man liked to drink a lot. However, neither kind of information had actually been part of the original story. The participants had "recalled" memories of the man that they had constructed in accordance with their overall impression of him (Carli, 1999).

Relating Semantic and Episodic Memory: PDP Models   How is semantic and episodic information integrated in constructive memories? Parallel distributed processing models offer one explanation. As mentioned earlier, PDP models suggest that newly learned facts alter our general knowledge of the world. In these network models, learned associations between specific facts come together. Let's say, for example, that your own network "knows" that your friend Joe is a male European American business major. It also "knows" that Claudia is a female African American student, but it has never learned her major. Now suppose that every other student you know is a business major. In this case, the connection between "students you know" and "business majors" would be so strong that you would conclude that Claudia is a business major, too. You would be so confident in this belief that it would take overwhelming evidence for you to change your mind (Rumelhart & McClelland, 1986). In other words, you would have constructed a memory about Claudia.

PDP networks also produce *spontaneous generalizations.* So if your friend tells you that she just bought a new car, you would know without asking that like other

FIGURE 7.10

The Effect of Schemas on Recall

In a classic experiment, participants were shown figures like those in the left column along with labels designed to activate certain schemas (Carmichael, Hogan, & Walter, 1932). For example, when showing the top figure, the experimenter said either "This resembles eyeglasses" or "This resembles a dumbbell." When the participants were later asked to draw these figures from memory, their drawings tended to resemble the items mentioned by the experimenter. In other words, the labels activated their schemas, and the schemas altered their memories.

Figure shown to participants	Group 1		Group 2	
	Label given	Figure drawn by participants	Label given	Figure drawn by participants
○—○	Eyeglasses	○○	Dumbbell	○—○
✕	Hourglass	✕	Table	✕
٦	Seven	7	Four	4
⊐—	Gun	(rifle drawing)	Broom	(broom drawing)

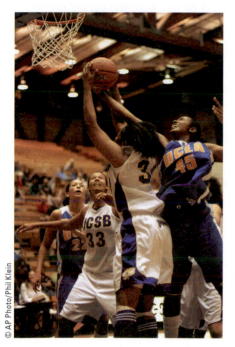

PDP Models and Constructive Memory

If you hear that "our basketball team won last night," your schema about basketball might cause you to encode, and later retrieve, the fact that the players were men. Such spontaneous, though sometimes incorrect, generalizations associated with PDP models of memory help account for constructive memory.

cars you have seen, it has four wheels. This is a spontaneous generalization from your knowledge base. Spontaneous generalizations are obviously helpful, but they can also create significant errors if the network is based on limited or biased experience with a class of objects (there are, in fact, three-wheeled cars).

If it occurs to you that ethnic prejudice can result from spontaneous generalization errors, you are right (Greenwald & Banaji, 1995). Researchers are actually encouraged by this aspect of PDP networks, though, because it accurately reflects human thought and memory. Virtually all of us make spontaneous generalizations about males, females, European Americans, African Americans, the young, the old, and many other categories (Rudman et al., 1999). Is prejudice, then, a process that we have no choice in or control over? Not necessarily. Relatively unprejudiced people tend to recognize that they are making generalizations and consciously try to ignore or suppress them (Amodio et al., 2004).

Schemas   PDP models also help us understand constructive memory by explaining the operation of the schemas that guide it. As described in the chapters on social cognition and on cognition and language, **schemas** are mental representations of categories of objects, events, and people. For example, most North Americans have a schema for *baseball game,* so simply hearing these words is likely to activate whole clusters of information in long-term memory, including the rules of the game, images of players, bats, balls, a green field, summer days, and perhaps hot dogs and stadiums. The generalized knowledge contained in schemas provides a basis for making inferences about incoming information during the encoding stage. So if you hear that a baseball player was injured, your schema about baseball might lead you to encode the incident as game-related, even though the cause was not mentioned. Later, you are likely to recall the injury as having occurred during a game. Similarly, if your experience has created a schema that most world news comes through television, your flashbulb memory of how you heard about 9/11 might be that you were watching TV, even if you weren't (Neisser & Harsch, 1992; Wright, 1993; see Figure 7.10 for another example).

LINKAGES

Memory, Perception, and Eyewitness Testimony

There are few situations in which accurate retrieval of memories is more important—and constructive memory is more dangerous—than when an eyewitness testifies in court about a crime. Eyewitnesses provide the most compelling evidence in many trials, but they can sometimes be mistaken (Wells, Memon, & Penrod, 2006;

schemas Mental representations of categories of objects, events, and people.

© AP Photo/Phil Klein

Wells, Olson, & Charman, 2002; Wright et al., 2009). Let's consider the accuracy of eyewitness memory and how it can be distorted.

In 1984, a North Carolina college student, Jennifer Thompson, confidently identified Ronald Cotton as the man who had raped her at knifepoint. Mainly on the basis of Thompson's testimony, Cotton was convicted of rape and sentenced to life in prison. He was released eleven years later when DNA evidence revealed that he was innocent (and identified another man as the rapist). The eyewitness-victim's certainty had convinced a jury, but her memory had been faulty (O'Neill, 2000).

Witnesses are asked to report exactly what they saw or heard; but no matter how hard they try to be accurate, there are limits to how valid their reports can be (Kassin, Rigby, & Castillo, 1991). For one thing, the semantic encoding typical of long-term memory may preserve general information but not all the important details (Fahsing, Ask, & Granhag, 2004). Further, hearing new information about a crime, including information contained in discussions with other witnesses and in the form of questions asked by police or lawyers, can alter a witness's memory (Belli & Loftus, 1996; Wells & Quinlivan, 2009; Wright et al., 2009). Experiments show that when witnesses are asked, "How fast were the cars going when they *smashed into* each other?" they are likely to recall a higher speed than when they were asked, "How fast were the cars going when they *hit* each other?" (Loftus & Palmer, 1974; see Figure 7.11). There is also evidence that an object mentioned or merely suggested by an interviewer's gestures during questioning about an incident is often mistakenly remembered as having been there during the incident (Broaders & Goldin-Meadow, 2010; Roediger, Meade, & Bergman, 2001). So if a lawyer says that a screwdriver was lying on the ground (when it was not), witnesses may recall with great certainty having seen it (Ryan & Geiselman, 1991). A version of this *misinformation effect* operated in 2002 when, over a three-week period, a sniper shot more than a dozen people in Maryland, Virginia, and Washington, D.C. After early media reports suggested that the sniper might be driving a white van, eyewitnesses to later shootings recalled seeing a white van nearby. In truth, though, the sniper was driving a blue car. The misinformation effect can occur in several ways (Loftus & Hoffman, 1989). In some cases, hearing new information can make it harder to retrieve the original memory (Tversky & Tuchin, 1989). In others, the new information may be integrated into the old memory, making it impossible to distinguish the new information from what was originally seen (Loftus, 1992). In still others, an eyewitness report might be influenced by the person's assumption that if a lawyer or police officer says an object was there or that something happened, it must be true (Chan, Thomas, & Bulevich, 2009).

Jurors' belief in a witness's testimony often depends as much (or even more) on *how* the witness presents evidence as on the content or relevance of that evidence

LINKAGES How accurate is eyewitness testimony? (a link to Perception, p. 177)

FIGURE 7.11

The Impact of Questioning on Eyewitness Memory

After seeing a filmed traffic accident, people were asked, "About how fast were the cars going when they (*smashed into, hit, or contacted*) each other?" As shown here, the witnesses' responses were influenced by the verb used in the question; *smashed* was associated with the highest average speed estimates. A week later, people who heard the "smashed" question remembered the accident as being more violent than people in the other two groups did (Loftus & Palmer, 1974).

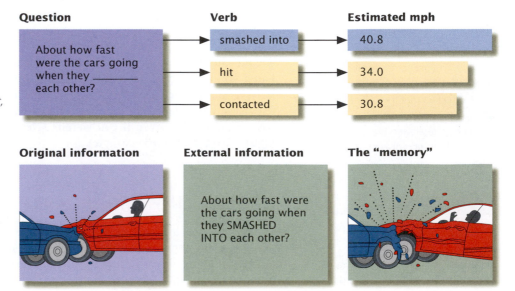

(Leippe, Manion, & Romanczyk, 1992). For example, many jurors are impressed by witnesses who give lots of details about what they saw or heard. Extremely detailed testimony from prosecution witnesses is especially likely to lead to guilty verdicts, even when the details reported are irrelevant (Bell & Loftus, 1989). Apparently, when a witness reports details, such as the exact time of the crime or the color of the criminal's shoes, jurors assume that the witness had paid especially close attention or has a particularly good memory. This assumption seems reasonable, but as discussed in the chapter on perception, there are limits on how much information people can pay attention to at the same time. A witness whose attention was drawn to details such as shoe color might not have had time to focus attention on the criminal's facial features—particularly if the witness was emotionally aroused and the crime happened quickly (Backman & Nilsson, 1991). So the fact that an eyewitnesses reports many details doesn't guarantee that all of them were remembered correctly.

Juries also tend to believe witnesses who are confident about their testimony (Leippe, Manion, & Romanczyk, 1992). Unfortunately, research shows that witnesses' confidence in their testimony is frequently much higher than the accuracy of their reports (Devilly et al., 2007; Wells, Olson, & Charman, 2002). In some cases, repeated exposure to misinformation and the repeated recall of that misinformation can lead witnesses to feel certain about their testimony even when, as in the Jennifer Thompson case, it may not be correct (Lamb, 1998; Mitchell & Zaragoza, 1996; Roediger, Jacoby, & McDermott, 1996).

The weaknesses inherent in eyewitness memory can be amplified by the use of police lineups and certain other criminal identification procedures (Haw & Fisher, 2004; Wells, Memon, & Penrod, 2006; Wells & Olson, 2003). In one study, for example, participants watched a videotaped crime and then tried to identify the criminal from a set of photographs (Wells & Bradfield, 1999). None of the photos showed the person who had committed the crime, but some participants nevertheless identified one of them as the criminal they saw on tape. When these mistaken participants were led to believe that they had correctly identified the criminal, they became even more confident in the accuracy of their false identification (Semmler, Brewer, & Wells, 2004; Wells, Olson, & Charman, 2003). These incorrect but confident witnesses became more likely than other participants to claim that it had been easy for them to identify

This is exactly the sort of biased police lineup that *Eyewitness Evidence: A Guide for Law Enforcement* (U.S. Department of Justice, 1999) is designed to avoid. Based on research in memory and perception, the guide recommends that no one in a lineup should stand out from the others, that police should not suggest that the real criminal is in the lineup, and that witnesses should not be encouraged to guess when making an identification (Zarkadi, Wade, & Stewart, 2009).

"Thank you, gentlemen—you may all leave except for No. 3."

the criminal from the photos because they had had a good view of him and had paid careful attention to him.

Since 1973, at least 138 people, including Ronald Cotton, have been released from U.S. prisons after DNA tests or other evidence revealed that they had been falsely convicted—mostly on the basis of faulty eyewitness testimony (Death Penalty Information Center, 2010). DNA evidence freed Charles Fain, who had been convicted of murder and spent almost eighteen years on death row in Idaho (Bonner, 2001). Maryland officials approved $900,000 in compensation for Bernard Webster, who served twenty years in prison for rape before DNA revealed that he was innocent ("Man to Get $900,000," 2003). And in April 2010, after eighteen years behind bars, Frank Sterling was released when DNA testing confirmed that he was innocent of murder. Research on memory and perception helps explain how these miscarriages of justice can occur, and it is also guiding efforts to prevent such errors in the future. The U.S. Department of Justice has acknowledged the potential for errors in eyewitness evidence, as well as the dangers of asking witnesses to identify suspects from lineups and photo arrays. One result is *Eyewitness Evidence: A Guide for Law Enforcement* (U.S. Department of Justice, 1999), the first-ever guide for police and prosecutors involved in obtaining eyewitness evidence. The guide warns that asking leading questions about what witnesses saw can distort their memories. It also suggests that witnesses should examine photos of possible suspects one at a time and points out that false identifications are less likely if witnesses viewing suspects in a lineup are told that the real criminal may or may not be included (Beresford & Blades, 2006; Wells & Olson, 2003; Wells et al., 2000).

Forgetting

The frustrations of forgetting—where you left your keys, the information needed to answer a test question, an anniversary—are apparent to most people nearly every day (Neisser, 2000b). Let's look more closely at the nature of forgetting and what causes it.

How Do We Forget?

Hermann Ebbinghaus, a German psychologist, began the systematic study of memory and forgetting in the late 1800s, using only his own memory as his laboratory. His aim was to study memory in its "pure" form, uncontaminated by emotional reactions and other preexisting associations between new material and what was already in memory. To eliminate any such associations, Ebbinghaus created the *nonsense syllable,* a meaningless set of two consonants and a vowel, such as *pof, xem,* and *qal.* He read a list of nonsense syllables aloud at a constant rate and then tried to recall the syllables.

Ebbinghaus devised a special **relearning method** to measure how much he forgot over time. This method involved comparing the number of trials (repetitions) it took him to learn a list of items and the number of trials he needed to relearn that same list later. Any reduction in the number of trials required for relearning represented the *savings* from one learning to the next. If it took Ebbinghaus ten trials to learn a list and another ten trials to relearn it, there would be no savings. Forgetting would have been complete. If it took him ten trials to learn the list and only five trials to relearn it, there would be a savings of 50 percent.

Ebbinghaus's research produced two lasting discoveries. One is the shape of the forgetting curve, shown in Figure 7.12. Even when psychologists substitute words, sentences, and even stories for nonsense syllables, the forgetting curve shows the same strong initial drop in memory, followed by a more moderate decrease over time (Wixted, 2004). Of course, we remember sensible stories better than nonsense syllables, but the shape of the curve is the same no matter what type of material is involved (Davis & Moore, 1935). Even the forgetting of events from daily life tends to follow Ebbinghaus's forgetting curve (Thomson, 1982).

© Hola Images/Getty Images

It's All Coming Back to Me

This grandfather hasn't fed an infant for decades, but his memory of how to do it is not entirely gone. He showed some "savings"; it took him less time to relearn the skill than it took him to learn it initially.

relearning method A way to measure forgetting by comparing the number of repetitions needed to learn and, after a delay, relearn the same material.

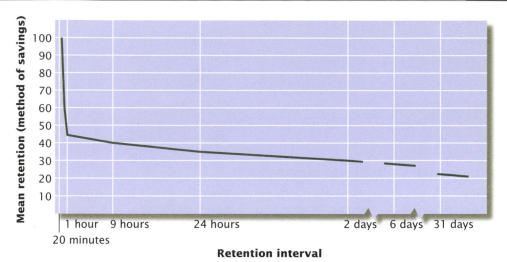

FIGURE 7.12
Ebbinghaus's Curve of Forgetting

TRY THIS Make a list of thirty words, chosen at random from a dictionary, and spend a few minutes memorizing them. After an hour has passed, write down as many of these words as you can remember, but don't look at the original list again. Test yourself again eight hours later, a day later, and two days later. Then look at the original list and see how well you did on each recall test. Ebbinghaus found that most forgetting occurs during the first nine hours after learning, especially during the first hour. If this was not the case for you, why do you think your results were different?

Ebbinghaus also discovered just how long-lasting "savings" in long-term memory can be. Psychologists now know from Ebbinghaus's relearning method that information about everything from algebra to bike riding is often retained for decades (Matlin, 1998). You may forget something you have learned if you do not use the information, but it is easy to relearn the material if the need arises, indicating that the forgetting was not complete (Hall & Bahrick, 1998).

Why Do We Forget? The Roles of Decay and Interference

We have seen *how* forgetting occurs, but *why* does it happen? In principle, either of two processes can be responsible. One process is described by **decay theory**, which suggests that information gradually disappears from memory, much as the inscription engraved on a ring or bracelet wears away and fades over time. Forgetting may also occur because of **interference**, a process through which the storage or retrieval of information is impaired by the presence of other information. Interference may occur because one piece of information actually *displaces* other information, pushing it out of memory. It may also occur because one piece of information makes storing or recalling other information more difficult.

In short-term memory, if an item is not rehearsed or elaborated, memory of it decreases consistently over the course of about eighteen seconds. So decay appears to play the main role in forgetting information in short-term memory. But interference through displacement can also be operating. Like the top of a desk, short-term memory can hold only so much. Once it is full, adding more items tends to make others "fall off" and become unavailable (Haberlandt, 1999). Displacement is one reason why the phone number you just looked up is likely to drop out of short-term memory if you read another number immediately afterward. Rehearsal prevents displacement by continually reentering the same information into short-term memory.

In long-term memory, forgetting seems to be more directly tied to interference. Sometimes, the interference is due to **retroactive inhibition**, in which learning of new

decay theory A description of forgetting as the gradual disappearance of information from memory.

interference The process through which either the storage or the retrieval of information is impaired by the presence of other information.

retroactive inhibition A cause of forgetting in which new information placed in memory interferes with the ability to recall information already in memory.

PROACTIVE INTERFERENCE EXPERIMENT

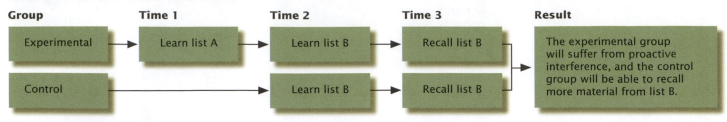

Group	Time 1	Time 2	Time 3	Result
Experimental	Learn list A	Learn list B	Recall list B	The experimental group will suffer from proactive interference, and the control group will be able to recall more material from list B.
Control		Learn list B	Recall list B	

RETROACTIVE INTERFERENCE EXPERIMENT

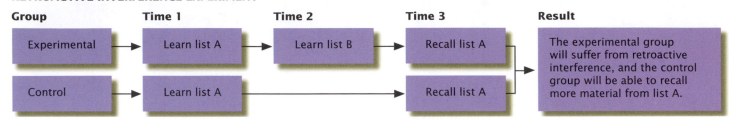

Group	Time 1	Time 2	Time 3	Result
Experimental	Learn list A	Learn list B	Recall list A	The experimental group will suffer from retroactive interference, and the control group will be able to recall more material from list A.
Control	Learn list A		Recall list A	

FIGURE 7.13
Procedures for Studying Interference
To remember the two types of interference processes, keep in mind that the prefixes *pro-* and *retro-* indicate directions in time. *Pro-* means "forward," and *retro-* means "backward." In *proactive* inhibition, previously learned material "comes forward" to interfere with new learning. *Retroactive* inhibition occurs when new information "goes back" to interfere with the recall of past learning.

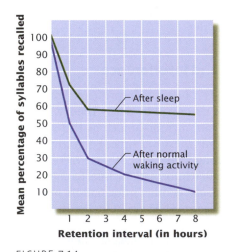

FIGURE 7.14
Interference and Forgetting
In this study, college students forgot more of what they had learned, and forgot it faster, if they engaged in normal activity after learning than if they spent the time asleep. These results suggest that interference is more important than decay in forgetting information in long-term memory.

information interferes with our ability to recall older information (Wixted, 2005). Interference can also occur because of **proactive inhibition**, a process by which old information interferes with our ability to learn or remember new information. Retroactive inhibition would help explain why studying French vocabulary this term might make it more difficult to remember the Spanish words you learned last term. And because of proactive inhibition, the French words you are learning now might make it harder to learn German next term. Figure 7.13 outlines the types of experiments that are used to study the influence of each form of interference in long-term memory.

We know that if you learn something and are then tested on it after various intervals, you will remember less and less as time passes. But is your forgetting due to decay or to interference? It is not easy to tell, because the passage of time produces both more decay and more retroactive inhibition from the new information you encounter after the original learning. To separate the effects of decay from those of interference, Karl Dallenbach created situations in which time passed but there was little or no accompanying interference. Evidence of forgetting in such situations would suggest that decay, not interference, was operating.

In one of Dallenbach's studies, college students learned a list of nonsense syllables and then either continued with their usual routine or were sheltered from interference by going to sleep (Jenkins & Dallenbach, 1924). Although the delay (and thus the potential for decay) was held constant for both groups, the greater interference associated with being awake produced much more forgetting (see Figure 7.14).

Results such as these suggest that although decay sometimes occurs, interference is the major cause of forgetting from long-term memory. But does interference actually push the forgotten information out of memory, or does it just make it harder to retrieve the information? To find out, Endel Tulving and Joseph Psotka (1971)

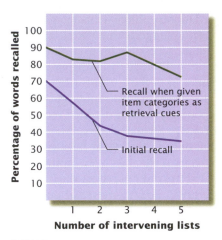

FIGURE 7.15

Retrieval Failures and Forgetting

Tulving and Psotka found that people's ability to recall a list of items was strongly affected by the number of other lists they learned before being tested on the first one. When retrieval cues were provided on a second test, however, interference from the additional lists almost disappeared.

Source: Tulving & Psotka (1971).

THINKING CRITICALLY

LINKAGES Do forgotten memories remain in the subconscious? (a link to Consciousness, p. 334)

proactive inhibition A cause of forgetting in which information already in long-term memory interferes with the ability to remember new information.

repressed memory A painful memory that is said to be kept out of consciousness by psychological processes.

presented people with lists of words that represented particular categories. For example, there was a "buildings" list (containing words such as *hut, cottage, tent,* and *hotel*) and a "geographical features" list (containing words such as *cliff, river, hill,* and *volcano*). Some people learned a list and then recalled as many of the words as possible. Other groups learned one list and then learned up to five additional lists before trying to recall the first one.

The results were dramatic. As the number of additional lists increased, the number of words that people could recall from the original list decreased. This finding reflected strong retroactive inhibition; the new lists were interfering with recall of the first one. Then the researchers gave a second test, but this time they provided a retrieval cue by telling the category of the words (such as "buildings") to be recalled. Now the number of additional lists had almost no effect on the number of words recalled from the original list, as Figure 7.15 shows. These results indicate that the words from the first list were still in long-term memory. They had not been pushed out, but the participants could not remember them without appropriate retrieval cues. In other words, faulty retrieval, not decay, had caused the original forgetting. Putting more and more information in long-term memory may be like putting more and more CDs into a storage cabinet. None of the CDs disappear, but it becomes increasingly difficult to find the one you are looking for.

Does this mean that everything in long-term memory remains there for life, even if you cannot always or ever recall it? No one knows for sure yet, but as described in the next section, this question lies at the heart of some controversial court cases.

Can Traumatic Memories Be Repressed and Then Recovered?

In 1989, Eileen Franklin-Lipsker told California police that when she looked into her young daughter's eyes one day, she suddenly remembered seeing her father kill her childhood friend more than twenty years earlier. On the basis of her testimony about this memory, her father, George Franklin Sr., was sent to prison for murder (Loftus & Ketcham, 1994).

What am I being asked to believe or accept?

The prosecution in the Franklin case successfully argued that Eileen had recovered a long-buried memory of a murder. Similar arguments in a number of other court cases in the early 1990s resulted in the imprisonment of other parents whose now-adult children claimed to have recovered childhood memories of being physically or sexually abused by them. The juries in these trials accepted the assertion that all memory of shocking events can be *repressed,* or pushed into an inaccessible corner of the mind where subconscious processes keep it out of awareness yet potentially subject to accurate recall decades later (Hyman, 2000). Jurors are not the only ones who believe in this **repressed memory** phenomenon. Some years ago, a large American news organization reported that the United States had illegally used nerve gas during the war in Vietnam. The story was based in part on a Vietnam veteran's account of recovered memories of having been subjected to a nerve gas attack.

What evidence is available to support the assertion?

Proponents of the recovered-memory argument point to several lines of evidence to support their claims. First, as discussed in the chapter on consciousness, a substantial amount of mental activity occurs outside of conscious awareness. Second, research on implicit memory shows that our behavior can be influenced by information that we are not aware of (Betch et al., 2003; Kouider & Dupoux, 2005; Schacter, Chiu, & Ochsner, 1993). Third, research on *motivated forgetting* suggests that people are able to willfully suppress information so that it is no longer accessible on a later memory test (Anderson & Green, 2001; Anderson & Levy, 2009). Even suppressing emotional reactions to events can interfere with a person's memories of those events (Richards & Gross, 2000). And people appear more likely to forget unpleasant events than pleasant ones (Erdelyi, 1985). In one study, a psychologist kept a detailed record of his daily life over a six-year period. When he later tried to recall those experiences, he remembered more than half of the positive ones but only a third of the negative ones (Waagenaar, 1986). In another study, 38 percent of women who had been brought to a hospital when they were children because of sexual abuse did not report the incident when they were interviewed as adults (Williams, 1994). Fourth, retrieval cues can help people recall memories that had previously been inaccessible to conscious awareness (Andrews et al., 2000; Landsdale & Laming, 1995). Such cues have helped soldiers remember for the first time the circumstances under which they had been wounded many years before (Karon & Widener, 1997). Finally, there is the confidence with which people report recovered memories; they say they are just too vivid to be anything but real.

Are there alternative ways of interpreting the evidence?

Psychologists who are skeptical about repressed memories know that subconscious memory and retrieval processes exist (Kihlstrom, 1999). They also recognize that, sadly, child abuse and other traumas are all too common. But to these psychologists, the available evidence is not strong enough to support the conclusion that traumatic memories can be repressed and then accurately recalled. Any given "recovered" memory, they say, might actually be a distorted or constructed memory (Clancy et al., 2000; Hyman, 2000; Loftus, 1998). As already mentioned, our recall of past events is affected by what happened at the time, what we knew beforehand, and everything we have experienced since. The people in the study mentioned earlier who "remembered" nonexistent books in an office inadvertently used their prior knowledge of what is usually in graduate students' offices to construct a memory of seeing books. Similarly, that Vietnam veteran's "recovered memory" of a nerve gas attack appears to have no basis in fact; the news organization that published the story later retracted it.

Research shows that *false memories*—distortions of actual events and the recall of events that didn't actually happen—can be at least as vivid as real, accurate memories and that people can feel just as confident in them (Brainerd & Reyna, 2005; Brainerd et al., 2003; Loftus, 2004; Nourkova, Bernstein, & Loftus, 2004; Roediger & McDermott, 2000). Most of us have experienced everyday versions of false memories. It is not unusual to "remember" turning off the coffeepot or mailing the rent check, only to discover later that we didn't. Researchers have demonstrated that false memories can occur in relation to more emotional events too. In one case study, a teenager named Chris was given descriptions of four incidents from his childhood and asked to write about each of them every day for five days (Loftus, 1997a). One of those incidents—being lost in a shopping mall at age 5—never really happened. Yet Chris eventually "remembered" this event and even added many details about the mall and the stranger whose hand he was supposedly found holding. He also rated this (false) memory as being more vivid than two of the other three (real) incidents he wrote about. Similar results occurred in about half of seventy-seven child participants in other case studies (Porter, Yuille, & Lehman, 1999).

The same pattern of results has appeared in formal experiments about planting emotion-laden false memories (Hyman & Pentland, 1996; Loftus & Pickrell, 1995). Researchers have been able to create vivid and striking (but completely false) memories of events that people thought they experienced the day after they were born (DuBreuil, Garry, & Loftus, 1998). In other experiments, children who were repeatedly asked about a nonexistent trauma (getting a hand caught in a mousetrap) eventually developed a clear and unshakable false memory of experiencing it (Ceci et al., 1994). Some

Exploring Memory Processes

Elizabeth Loftus (at the far right) is shown here with her students and the actor Alan Alda, who hosted a documentary about her research. Loftus and other cognitive psychologists have demonstrated mechanisms through which false memories can be created. They have found, for example, that false memories appear even in research participants who are told about them and are asked to avoid them (McDermott & Roediger, 1998). Their work has helped focus scientific scrutiny on reports of recovered memories, especially those arising from contact with therapists who assume that most people have repressed memories of abuse.

Courtesy of Dr. Elizabeth Loftus, University of California, Irvine

people will even begin to avoid a certain food after researchers create in them a false memory of having been ill after eating that food as a child (Bernstein & Loftus, 2009a; Geraerts, Bernstein, et al., 2008).

In other words, people sometimes have a difficult time distinguishing between what has happened to them and what they have only imagined or have come to believe has happened (Garry & Polaschek, 2000; Henkel, 2004; Johnson & Raye, 1998; Mazzoni & Memon, 2003; Zaragoza et al., 2001). Some studies have found that people with certain brain characteristics and those who are prone to fantasy, who easily confuse real and imagined stimuli, and who tend to have lapses in attention and memory are more likely than others to develop false memories and possibly more likely to report the recovery of repressed memories (Fuentemilla et al., 2009; McNally, 2003; McNally et al., 2000a, 2000b, 2005; Porter et al., 2000; Wilson & French, 2006). Two other studies have found that women who have suffered physical or sexual abuse are more likely to falsely remember words on a laboratory recall test (Bremner, Shobe, & Kihlstrom, 2000; Zoellner et al., 2000). This tendency appears strongest among abused women who show signs of posttraumatic stress disorder (Bremner, Shobe, & Kihlstrom, 2000). Another study found that the tendency to have false memories during a word recall task was greater in women who reported recovered memories of sexual abuse than in nonabused women or in those who had always remembered the abuse they suffered (Clancy et al., 2000).

Why would anyone "remember" a traumatic event that did not actually occur? Elizabeth Loftus (1997b) suggests that for one thing, popular books such as *The Courage to Heal* (Bass & Davis, 1994), *Secret Survivors* (Blume, 1998), and *Surviving Babylon* (Garson, 2006) may lead people to believe that anyone who experiences guilt, depression, low self-esteem, overemotionality, or any of a long list of other problems is harboring repressed memories of abuse. This message, says Loftus, is reinforced and elaborated by some psychotherapists, particularly those who specialize in using guided imagination, hypnosis, and other methods to "help" clients recover repressed memories (Lindsay et al., 2004; McHugh, 2009; Pendergrast, 1996). In doing so, these therapists may influence people to construct false memories by encouraging them to imagine experiencing events that may never have actually occurred or that occurred only in a dream (Mazzoni & Loftus, 1996; Olio, 1994). As one client described her therapy, "I was rapidly losing the ability to differentiate between my imagination and my real memory" (Loftus & Ketcham, 1994, p. 25). To such therapists, a client's failure to recover memories of abuse or refusal to accept their existence is evidence of denial of the truth (Loftus, 1997a; Tavris, 2003).

The possibility that recovered memories may actually be false memories has led to dismissed charges or not-guilty verdicts for defendants in some repressed-memory cases. In other cases, previously convicted defendants have been released. (George Franklin's conviction was overturned, but only after he spent five years in prison.) Concern over the potential damage resulting from false memories prompted the establishment in 1992 of the False Memory Syndrome Foundation, an organization of families affected by abuse accusations stemming from allegedly repressed memories. More than a hundred of these families (including Franklin's family) have filed lawsuits against hospitals and therapists. In 1994, California winery executive Gary Ramona received $500,000 in damages from two therapists who had "helped" his daughter recall his alleged sexual abuse of her. A more recent suit led to a $2 million judgment against a Minnesota therapist whose client discovered that her "recovered" memories of childhood abuse were false. A similar case in Wisconsin brought a $5 million judgment against two therapists. And an Illinois case resulted in a $10.6 million settlement and the suspension of the license of the psychiatrist who had "found" his patient's "lost" memories (Loftus, 1998).

What additional evidence would help evaluate the alternatives?

Evaluating reports of recovered memories would be easier if we had more information about whether it is possible for people to repress traumatic events. If it *is* possible, we also need to know how common it is and how accurate recovered memories might be. So far, we know that some people apparently do forget intense emotional experiences but that most people's memories of them are vivid and long-lasting, like the flashbulb memories discussed earlier (Alexander et al., 2005; Goodman et al., 2003; Henckens et al., 2009; McGaugh, 2003; Porter & Peace, 2007). In fact, many people who live through trauma are *unable* to forget it, though they wish they could (Henig, 2004). In the sexual abuse study mentioned earlier, for example (Williams, 1994), 62 percent of the abuse victims recalled as adults the trauma that had been documented in their childhoods. A similar study of a different group of adults found that about 92 percent of them recalled their documented childhood abuse (Alexander et al., 2005; Goodman et al., 2003). The true recall figures may actually be even higher in such studies because some people who remember abuse may not wish to talk about it. In any case, additional studies like these—studies that track the fate of memories in known abuse cases—would not only help us estimate the prevalence of this kind of forgetting but might also offer clues as to the kinds of people and events most likely to be associated with it.

It would also be valuable to know more about the processes through which repression might occur and how they are related to empirically established theories of human memory. Is there a mechanism that specifically pushes traumatic memories out of awareness and then keeps them at a subconscious level for long periods? Despite some suggestive results (Anderson & Levy, 2009; Anderson et al., 2004; DePrince & Freyd, 2004), cognitive psychologists have so far not found reliable evidence for such a mechanism (Bulevich et al., 2006; Geraerts et al., 2006; Loftus, 1997a; McNally, 2003; McNally, Clancy, & Schacter, 2001; McNally et al., 2000a; Pope et al., 1998).

What conclusions are most reasonable?

An objective reading of the available research evidence suggests that recovery of traumatic memories is at least possible but that the implantation of false memories is also possible—and has been demonstrated repeatedly in controlled experiments. With this in mind, it is not easy to decide whether any particular case is an instance of recovered memory or false memory, especially when there is no objective corroborating evidence to guide the decision.

The intense conflict between those who uncritically accept claims of recovered memories and those who are more wary about the accuracy of such claims reflects a fundamental disagreement about evidence (Tavris, 2003). To many therapists who deal daily with victims of sexual abuse and other traumas, clients' reports constitute stronger proof of recovered memories than the results of laboratory experiments do. Client reports are viewed with considerably more skepticism by psychologists who engage in or rely on empirical research on the processes of memory and forgetting. They would like to have additional sources of evidence, including from research on brain activity "signatures" that might someday distinguish true memories from false ones (e.g., Bernstein & Loftus, 2009b; Cabeza et al., 2001; Rissman, Greely, & Wagner, 2010; Sederberg et al., 2007; Slotnick & Schacter, 2004).

So people's responses to claims of recovered memory may be determined by the relative weight they assign to reports of personal experiences versus evidence from controlled experiments. Still, the apparent ease with which false memories can be created should lead judges, juries, and the general public to exercise great caution before accepting unverified memories of traumatic events as the truth. At the same time, we should not automatically reject the claims of people who appear to have recovered memories (Geraerts et al., 2007; McNally & Geraerts, 2009). Perhaps the wisest course is to use all the scientific and circumstantial evidence available to carefully and critically examine claims of recovered memories while keeping in mind that constructive memory processes *may* have influenced those memories (Alison, Kebbell, & Lewis, 2006; Geraerts et al., 2007). This careful, scientific approach is vital if we are to protect the rights and welfare of those who report recovered memories, as well as of those who face accusations arising from them (Geraerts, Lindsay, et al., 2008).

Biological Bases of Memory

Many psychologists who study memory focus on explicit and implicit mental processes (e.g., Schott et al., 2005). Others explore the physical, electrical, and chemical changes that occur in the brain when people encode, store, and retrieve information (Abraham, 2006; Fields, 2005; Touzani, Puthanveettil, & Kandel, 2007). The story of the scientific search for the biological bases of memory begins with the work of Karl Lashley and Donald Hebb, who spent many years studying how memory is related to brain structures and processes. Lashley (1950) taught rats new behaviors and then observed how damage to various parts of the rats' brains changed their ability to perform the tasks they had learned. Lashley hoped that his work would identify the brain area that contained the "engram"—the physical manifestation of memory in the brain. However, after many experiments, he concluded that memories are not localized in one specific region but instead are distributed throughout large areas of brain tissue.

Hebb, who was a student of Lashley's, proposed another biological theory of memory. Hebb believed that each memory is represented by a group of interconnected neurons in the brain. These neurons, which he called a *cell assembly,* form a network in the cortex. The connections among these neurons are strengthened, he said, when the neurons are simultaneously stimulated through sensory experiences (Hebb, 1949). Though not correct in all its details, Hebb's theory stimulated research and contributed to an understanding of the physical basis of memory. His theory is also consistent, in many respects, with contemporary parallel distributed processing models of memory and with the results of neuroimaging research on networks of brain activity (Fair et al., 2008).

Let's consider more recent research on the biochemical mechanisms and brain structures that are most directly involved in memory processes.

The Biochemistry of Memory

As described in the chapter on biological aspects of psychology, communication among brain cells takes place at the synapses between axons and dendrites using chemicals called *neurotransmitters* that are released at the synapses. The formation and storage of new memories are associated with at least two kinds of changes in synapses.

FIGURE 7.16

Building Memories

These models of synapses are based on electron microscope images of synapses in the brain. The model on the left shows that before signals were repeatedly sent across the synapse, just one spine (shown in white) appears on this part of the dendrite. Afterward, as shown in the other model, there are two spines, which helps improve communication across the synapse. The creation and changing of many individual synapses in the brain appears to underlie the formation and storage of new memories.

Source: Toni et al. (1999).

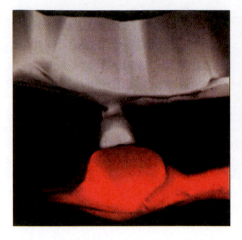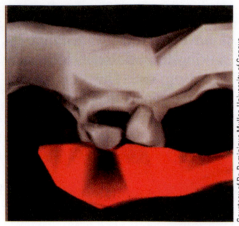

Courtesy of Dr. Dominique Muller, University of Geneva

The first kind of change occurs when stimulation from the environment promotes the formation of *new* synapses, thus increasing the complexity of the communication networks through which neurons receive information. Scientists can now actually see this process occur. As shown in Figure 7.16, repeatedly sending signals across a particular synapse increases the number of special little branches, called *spines,* that appear on the receiving cell's dendrites (Hofer et al., 2009; Lang et al., 2004; Nägerl et al., 2008).

The second kind of change occurs as new experiences change the operation of *existing* synapses. For example, when two neurons fire at the same time and together stimulate a third neuron, that third neuron will later be more responsive than before to stimulation by either neuron alone (Sejnowski, Chattarji, & Stanton, 1990). This process of "sensitizing" synapses is called *long-term potentiation* (Li, Cullen, et al., 2003; Mozzachiodi et al., 2008; Rioult-Pedotti, Friedman, & Donoghue, 2000). Other patterns of electrical stimulation can weaken synaptic connections, a process called *long-term depression* (Malenka, 1995). Changes in sensitivity could account for the development of conditioned responses and other types of learning and for the operation of working memory (Olson et al., 2006; Mongillo, Barak, & Tsodyks, 2008; Whitlock et al., 2006).

In the hippocampus (see Figure 7.17), these changes appear to occur at synapses that use the neurotransmitter glutamate (Malenka & Nicoll, 1999). Other neurotransmitters, such as *acetylcholine,* also play important roles in memory formation (e.g., Furey, Pietrini, & Haxby, 2000; Li, Cullen, et al., 2003). The memory problems seen in people with Alzheimer's disease are related to a lack of neurons that use acetylcholine and send fibers to the hippocampus and the cortex (Muir, 1997). Drugs that interfere with the action of acetylcholine impair memory, and drugs that increase the amount of acetylcholine in synapses can improve memory somewhat in aging animals and humans (Pettit, Shao, & Yakel, 2001; Sirvio, 1999).

In summary, research has shown that the formation of memories is associated with changes in many individual synapses that together strengthen and improve the communication in networks of neurons. These findings provide some support for the ideas formulated by Hebb many years ago.

Brain Structures and Memory

LINKAGES   Where are memories stored? (a link to Biological Aspects of Psychology, p. 83)

Are the biochemical processes involved in memory concentrated in certain brain regions, or are they distributed throughout the brain? The latest research suggests that memory involves both specialized regions for various types of memory formation and widespread areas for storage (Takashima et al., 2006). Several of the brain regions shown in Figure 7.17, including the hippocampus and nearby parts of the cortex and the thalamus, are vital to the formation of new memories. Evidence for the memory-related functions of these regions comes from two main sources. First, there are case

FIGURE 7.17

Some Brain Structures Involved in Memory

Combined nerve cell activity in many parts of the brain allows us to encode, store, and retrieve memories. The complexity of the biological bases of these processes is underscored by research showing that different aspects of a memory—such as the sights and sounds associated with some event—are stored in different parts of the cerebral cortex.

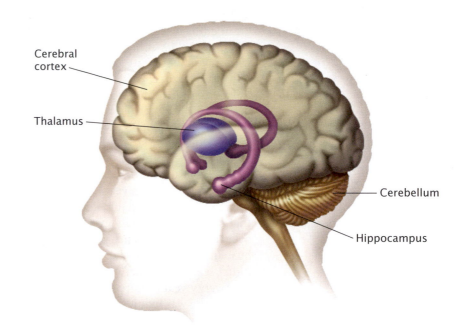

Cerebral cortex

Thalamus

Cerebellum

Hippocampus

studies of patients with brain injuries that allow neuropsychologists to determine how damage to specific brain areas is related to specific kinds of memory problems. Second, studies using PET scans, functional MRI, and other neuroimaging methods (described in the chapter on biological aspects of psychology) have allowed neuroscientists to observe where brain activity is concentrated as normal people perform various memory tasks. Data from these two sources are leading to an ever-growing understanding of how the brain encodes and retrieves memories.

The Impact of Brain Damage Research has confirmed that the hippocampus, which is part of the limbic system, is among the brain regions involved in the formation of new memories. Damage to the hippocampus, nearby parts of the cerebral cortex, and the thalamus often results in **anterograde amnesia**, a loss of memory for any event occurring after the injury. People who suffer this kind of damage are unable to form new memories.

The case of H. M. provides a striking example of anterograde amnesia (Milner, 1966). When H. M. was 27 years old, part of his hippocampus was removed in order to stop his severe epileptic seizures. After the operation, his long-term and short-term memory appeared normal, but something was wrong. Two years later, he still believed that he was 27. When his family moved into a new house, H. M. couldn't remember the new address or how to get there. When his uncle died, he grieved in a normal way, but soon afterward he began to ask why his uncle had not visited him. He had to be repeatedly reminded of the death and, each time, H.M., began the mourning process all over again. The surgery had apparently destroyed the mechanism that transfers information from short-term to long-term memory. Until his death in 2008 at the age of 82, H. M. lived in a nursing home, where his only long-term memories were from fifty years earlier, before the operation. He was still unable to recall events and facts he had experienced since then—not even the names of people he saw every day (Corkin, 2002; Hathaway, 2002; Squire, 2009).

Although patients with damage to the hippocampus cannot form new episodic memories following hippocampal damage, they may still be able to form implicit memories. For example, H. M.'s performance on a complicated puzzle improved steadily over several days of practice, just as it does with normal people, and eventually it became virtually perfect. But each time he tried the puzzle, he insisted that he

anterograde amnesia A loss of memory for any event that occurs after a brain injury.

had never seen it before (Cohen & Corkin, 1981). A musician with a similar kind of brain damage was able to use his implicit memory to continue leading choral groups (Vattano, 2000). Other researchers, too, have found intact implicit memory in patients who have anterograde amnesia for new episodic material (Squire & McKee, 1992; Tulving, Hayman, & Macdonald, 1991). These patients are also able to keep information temporarily in working memory, which depends on the activity of dopamine neurons in the prefrontal cortex (Williams & Goldman-Rakic, 1995). So it appears that the hippocampus is crucial in the formation of new episodic memories but that implicit memory, procedural memory, and working memory are governed by other regions of the brain (Schott et al., 2005; Touzani, Puthanveettil, & Kandel, 2007).

Retrograde amnesia involves a loss of memory for events that took place in the days, months, or even years before an injury (Kapur, 1999). In 1994, head injuries from a car crash left 36-year-old Perlene Griffith-Barwell with retrograde amnesia so severe that she forgot virtually everything she had learned about everything and everyone over the previous twenty years. She thought she was still 16 and did not recognize her husband, Malcolm, or her four children. She said, "The children were sweet, but they didn't seem like mine," and she "didn't feel anything" for Malcolm. Her memories of the twenty years before the accident never fully returned. She is divorced, but at last report, she was living with her children, working in a bank, and planning to remarry (Echo News, 2000; Weinstein, 1999).

Unlike Perlene, most victims of retrograde amnesia gradually recover their memories (Riccio, Millin, & Gisquet-Verrier, 2003). The most distant events are recalled first, and the person gradually regains memory for events leading up to the injury. Recovery is seldom complete, however, and the person may never remember the last few seconds before the injury. One man received a severe blow to the head after being thrown from his motorcycle. Upon regaining consciousness, he claimed that he was 11 years old. Over the next three months, he slowly recalled more and more of his life. He remembered when he was 12, 13, and so on—right up until the time he was riding his motorcycle the day of the accident. But he was never able to remember what happened just before the accident (Baddeley, 1982). Those final events were probably encoded into short-term memory but were never transferred into long-term memory (Dudai, 2004).

The appearance of retrograde amnesia following a blow to the head has led researchers to suggest that as memories are transferred from short-term memory to long-term memory, they are initially unstable and therefore vulnerable to disruption (Dudai, 2004). It may take minutes, hours, or days before these memories are fully solidified, or *consolidated* (Donegan & Thompson, 1991).

A Famous Case of Retrograde Amnesia

After Ralf Schumacher slammed his race car into a wall during the United States Grand Prix in June of 2004, he sustained a severe concussion that left him with no memory of the crash. Retrograde amnesia is relatively common following concussions, so if you ride a motorcycle, wear that helmet!

© Paul Gilham/Getty Images

retrograde amnesia A loss of memory for events prior to a brain injury.

This consolidation process appears to depend on movement of electrochemical impulses within clusters of neurons in the brain (Taubenfeld et al., 2001). Accordingly, conditions that suppress nerve cell activity in the brain may also disrupt the transfer of information from short-term to long-term memory. These conditions include anesthetic drugs, poisoning by carbon monoxide or other toxins, and strong electrical impulses such as those in the electroconvulsive therapy that is sometimes used to treat cases of severe depression (see the chapter on treatment of psychological disorders).

An additional clue to the role of specific brain areas in memory comes from research on people with *Korsakoff's psychosis* (also known as *Korsakoff's syndrome*), a disorder that is usually seen in people with chronic alcoholism. These individuals' brains become unable to use glucose as fuel, resulting in severe and widespread brain damage. Damage to the mediodorsal nucleus of the thalamus is particularly implicated in the memory problems typical of these patients, which can include both anterograde and retrograde amnesia (Squire, Amara, & Press, 1992). Moreover, like patients with hippocampal damage, Korsakoff's patients show impairments in the ability to form new episodic memories but retain some implicit memory abilities. Research has demonstrated that damage to the prefrontal cortex (also common in Korsakoff's patients) is related to disruptions in remembering the order in which events occur (Squire, 1992). Other studies have found that regions within the prefrontal cortex are involved in working memory in both animals and humans (D'Esposito et al., 1995; Smith, 2000; Touzani, Puthanveettil, & Kandel, 2007).

Multiple Storage Areas   Obviously, the hippocampus does not permanently store long-term memories (Bayley, Hopkins, & Squire, 2003; Rosenbaum et al., 2000). (If it did, H. M. would not have retained memories from the years before part of his hippocampus was removed.) However, the hippocampus and the thalamus send nerve impulses to the cerebral cortex, and it is in and around the cortex that memories are probably stored—but not all in one place (Levy, Bayley, & Squire, 2004; Maviel et al., 2004; Miceli et al., 2001).

As described in the chapters on biological aspects of psychology and on sensation, different regions of the cortex receive messages from different senses. Information about specific aspects of an experience is probably stored in or near these regions. For example, damage to the auditory association cortex disrupts memory for sounds (Colombo et al., 1990). A memory, however, involves more than one sensory system. Even in the simple case of a rat remembering a maze, the experience of the maze includes vision, smell, movements, and emotions, and memories of each of them may be stored in different regions of the brain (Gallagher & Chiba, 1996). So memories are both localized and distributed. Certain brain areas store specific aspects of each remembered event, but many brain regions are involved in experiencing a whole event (Brewer et al., 1998; Kensinger & Corkin, 2004). For example, the cerebellum (see Figure 7.17) is involved in the storage of procedural knowledge, such as dance steps and other movements.

What happens in the brain as we retrieve memories? Brain-imaging studies show that the hippocampus and various regions of the cerebral cortex are active during memory retrieval (Buckner & Wheeler, 2001; Cabeza et al., 2001; Davachi, Mitchell, & Wagner, 2003; McDermott & Buckner, 2002; McDermott, Szpunar, & Christ, 2009). There is also evidence to suggest that retrieving memories of certain experiences, such as a conversation or a tennis game, reactivates the sensory and motor regions of the brain that had been involved during the event itself (Danker & Anderson, 2010; Nyberg et al., 2001). Research shows, too, that when animals recall an emotional (fear-related) memory, that memory may have to be stored again. During this biological restorage process, the memory may be distorted (Eisenberg et al., 2003; Lee, Everitt, & Thomas, 2004; Nader, Schafe, & Le Doux, 2000). Researchers are exploring the question of whether this *reconsolidation* process occurs in humans too (Dudai, 2004; Schiller et al., 2010; Walker et al., 2003). Cognitive neuroscientists are also trying to determine whether different patterns of brain activity are associated with the storage and retrieval of accurate versus inaccurate memories (Bernstein & Loftus, 2009b; Cabeza et al., 2001; Gonsalves & Paller, 2000; Slotnick & Schacter, 2004; Urbach, et al., 2005). These lines of research will have obvious applications in areas such as lie detection, the understanding of false memory processes, and the evaluation of claims of recovered memories.

Another line of research on the biological aspects of memory concerns the ability to think about the future (Atance & O'Neill, 2001; Szpunar, 2010). Scientists have found, for example, that patients with amnesia due to damage to the medial temporal lobe are not only unable to recollect the past but also cannot vividly envision future events, such as their next birthday party (Hassabis et al., 2007). It appears from neuroimaging studies that the same brain regions involved in remembering are important for envisioning too (Addis, Wong, & Schacter, 2007; Szpunar, Chan, & McDermott, 2009; Szpunar, Watson, & McDermott, 2007).

Applications of Memory Research

Some questions remain about what memory is and how it works, but the results of memory research offer many valuable guidelines to help people improve their memories and function more effectively (Neisser, 2000a).

Improving Your Memory

The most valuable memory enhancement strategies are based on the elaboration of incoming information and especially on linking new information to what you already know.

Mnemonic Strategies   One way to improve your memory is to use *mnemonic* (pronounced "nee-MAHN-ik") *strategies.* Named for Mnemosyne, the Greek goddess of memory, **mnemonic strategies** are methods for placing information into an organized framework in order to remember it more easily. To remember the names of the Great Lakes, for example, you could use the acronym HOMES (for *Huron, Ontario, Michigan, Erie,* and *Superior*). Verbal organization is the basis for many mnemonic strategies. You can link items by weaving them into a story, a sentence, or a rhyme. To help customers remember where they have parked their cars, some large garages have replaced section designations such as "A1" or "G8" with the names of colors, months, or animals. Customers can then tie the location of their cars to information already in long-term memory—for example, "I parked in the month of my mother's birthday."

One simple but powerful mnemonic strategy is called the *method of loci* (pronounced "LOH-sy"), or the "method of places." To use this method, first think about a set of familiar locations. Use your home, for example. You might imagine walking through the front door, around all four corners of the living room, and through each of the other rooms. Next, imagine that each item you want to remember is in one of these locations. Creating vivid or unusual images of how the items appear in each location seems to be particularly effective (Kline & Groninger, 1991). For example, tomatoes smashed against the front door or bananas hanging from the bedroom ceiling might be helpful in recalling these items on a grocery list. Whenever you want to remember a new list, you can create new images using the same locations in the same order.

TRY THIS

Guidelines for More Effective Studying   The success of mnemonic strategies demonstrates again the importance of relating new information to knowledge already stored in memory. All mnemonic systems require that you have a well-learned body of knowledge (such as locations) that can be used to provide a framework, or context, for organizing incoming information (Hilton, 1986).

When you want to remember complex material, such as a textbook chapter, the same principles apply (Palmisano & Herrmann, 1991). You can improve your memory

mnemonic strategies Methods for placing information in an organized context in order to remember it.

for text material by first creating an outline or some other overall context for learning, rather than just reading and rereading (Glover et al., 1990). Repetition may *seem* effective because it keeps material in short-term memory; but for retaining information over long periods, repetition alone tends to be ineffective, no matter how much time you spend on it (Bjork, 1999; Bjorklund & Green, 1992). In short, "work smarter, not harder."

In addition, spend your time wisely. **Distributed practice** is much more effective than **massed practice** for learning new information. If you are going to spend ten hours studying for a test, you will be much better off studying for ten 1-hour blocks separated by periods of sleep and other activity. "Cramming" for one 10-hour block will not be as effective (Rohrer & Pashler, 2007). By scheduling more study sessions, you will stay fresh and tend to think about the material from a new perspective at each session. This method will help you elaborate on the material, as in elaborative rehearsal, and thus remember it better (Cepeda et al., 2009).

You should also practice retrieving what you have learned by repeatedly testing yourself. For example, instead of simply rereading a section to help you remember it, close the book and try to jot down the section's main points from memory. You can test yourself on important vocabulary terms by creating a deck of flash cards, each of which has a key term on one side and its definition on the other. Then browse through the cards, trying to recall the definition of each term before turning the card over to give yourself feedback on your performance. To take advantage of the benefits of distributed practice, don't wait until the day before the test to write your flash cards. Create new ones after each study session and each lecture, and carry them around with you. That way, you can review them whenever you have a spare moment. Laboratory studies have found that students' later exam performance is significantly better after self-testing than after merely reading and rereading the material they are trying to learn (Karpicke, 2009; Roediger & Karpicke, 2006).

Reading a Textbook   More specific advice for remembering textbook material comes from a study that examined how successful and unsuccessful college students approached their reading (Whimbey, 1976). Unsuccessful students tended to read the material straight through. They did not slow down when they reached a difficult section, and they kept going even when they didn't understand what they were reading. In contrast, successful college students monitored their understanding, reread difficult sections, and stopped now and then to review what they had learned. (This book's "In Review" features are designed to help you do that.) In other words, effective learners engage in a deep level of processing. They are active learners. They think of each new fact in relation to other material, and they develop a context in which many new facts can be organized effectively.

Research on memory suggests two specific guidelines for reading a textbook. First, make sure you understand what you are reading before moving on (Herrmann & Searleman, 1992). Second, use the *PQ4R method* (Thomas & Robinson, 1972). PQ4R stands for six activities to engage in when you read a chapter: *preview, question, read, reflect, recite,* and *review.* These activities are designed to increase the depth to which you process the information you read and should be done as follows:

1. *Preview.* First, take a few minutes to skim the chapter. Look at the section headings and any boldfaced or italicized terms. Get a general idea of what material will be discussed, the way it is organized, and how its topics relate to one another and to what you already know. Some students find it useful to survey the entire chapter once and then survey each major section a little more carefully before reading it.

2. *Question.* Before reading each section, ask yourself what content will be covered and what information you should be getting from it.

3. *Read.* Now read the text, but *think about* the material as you read. Are you understanding the material? Are the questions you raised earlier being answered?

4. *Reflect.* As you read, think of your own examples—and create visual images—of the concepts and phenomena you encounter. Ask yourself what the material

distributed practice The spacing of study sessions over days or weeks.

massed practice A long period of concentrated study ("cramming").

Understand and Remember

Research on memory suggests that students who simply read their textbooks will not remember as much as those who, like these women, read for understanding using the PQ4R method. Further, memory for the material is likely to be better if you read and study it over a number of weeks rather than in one marathon session the night before a test.

© David Fischer/Photodisc/Getty Images

means, and consider how each section relates to other sections in the chapter and to other chapters in the book (this book's "Linkages" features are designed to promote this kind of reflection).

5. *Recite.* At the end of each section, recite the major points. Resist the temptation to be passive and say, "Oh, I'll remember that." Be active. Put the ideas into your own words by reciting them aloud to yourself or by summarizing the material in a minilecture to a friend or study partner. Recitation is another form of the important self-testing process mentioned earlier.

6. *Review.* Finally, at the end of the chapter, review all the material. You should see connections not only within each section but also among sections. The objective is to see how the material is organized. Once you grasp the organization, the individual facts will be far easier to remember.

By following these procedures, you will learn and remember the material better, and you will also save yourself considerable time.

Lecture Notes   Students and employees often have to learn and remember material from lectures or other presentations. Taking notes will help, but effective notetaking is a learned skill that improves with practice (Pauk & Owens, 2010). Research on memory suggests some simple strategies for taking and using notes effectively.

Recognize first that in notetaking, more is not necessarily better. Taking detailed notes of everything you hear requires that you pay close attention to both important and unimportant content, leaving little time for thinking about the material. Notetakers who concentrate on expressing the major ideas in relatively few words remember more than those who try to catch every detail (Pauk & Owens, 2010). So the best way to take notes is to think about what is being said. Draw connections with other material in the presentation, and then summarize the major points clearly and concisely (Kiewra, 1989).

Once you have a set of lecture notes, review them as soon as possible after the lecture so that you can fill in missing details and create flash cards for key terms. (Remember that most forgetting from long-term memory occurs within the first hour after learning.) When the time comes for serious study, use your notes as if they were a chapter in a textbook. Write a detailed outline. Think about how various points are related. Once you have organized the material, the details will make more sense and will be much easier to remember. ("In Review: Improving Your Memory" summarizes tips for studying.)

Design for Memory

The scientific study of memory has influenced the design of the electronic and mechanical devices that play an increasingly important role in our lives. Designers of computers, MP3 and DVD players, digital cameras, and even microwave ovens face a choice: Either place the operating instructions on the devices themselves or else assume that users will remember how to operate them. Understanding the limits of both working memory and long-term memory has helped designers distinguish between information that is likely to be stored in and easily retrieved from the user's memory and information that should be presented in the form of labels, instructions, or other cues that reduce memory demands (Norman, 2009). Placing unfamiliar or hard-to-recall information in plain view makes it easier to use the device as intended and with less chance of errors (Segal & Suri, 1999).

Psychologists have influenced advertisers and designers to create many other "user-friendly" systems (Wickens et al., 2004). As a result, toll-free numbers are designed to

IN REVIEW Improving Your Memory	
Goal	**Helpful Techniques**
Remembering lists of items	Use mnemonic strategies.
	Look for meaningful acronyms.
	Try the method of loci.
Remembering textbook material	Follow the PQ4R system.
	Allocate your time to allow for distributed practice.
	Read actively, not passively.
	Test yourself as you read.
Taking lecture notes	Take notes, but record only the main points.
	Think about the overall organization of the material.
	Review your notes as soon after the lecture as possible in order to fill in missing points.
Studying for exams	Write a detailed outline of your lecture notes rather than passively reading them.
	Do further self-testing; review key term flash cards.

1. Using mnemonic strategies and the PQ4R system to remember course material are examples of the value of _____ rehearsal.

2. "Cramming" illustrates _____ practice that usually leads to _____ long-term retention than _____ practice.

3. To minimize forgetting, you should review lecture notes _____ after a lecture ends.

take advantage of chunking, which, as mentioned earlier, provides an efficient way to maintain information in working memory. Which do you think would be easier to remember: 1-800-438-4357 or 1-800-GET-HELP? Obviously, the more meaningful "get help" number is more memorable (there are Web sites that can help you translate any phone number into words or a phrase). In the automotive arena, designers ensure that navigation systems provide audible reminders about where to turn and that turn signals emit an audible cue when activated. Features such as these help reduce your memory load while driving and leave you with enough working memory capacity to keep in mind that there is a car in your "blind spot."

As ever more complex devices appear in the marketplace, it will be increasingly important that instructions about how to operate them be presented clearly and memorably. With guidance from research on memory, it should be possible for almost anyone to operate these devices efficiently.

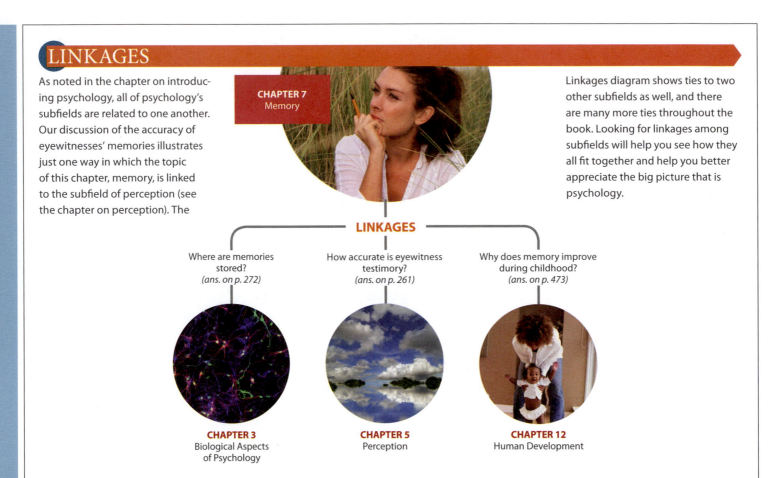

LINKAGES

As noted in the chapter on introducing psychology, all of psychology's subfields are related to one another. Our discussion of the accuracy of eyewitnesses' memories illustrates just one way in which the topic of this chapter, memory, is linked to the subfield of perception (see the chapter on perception). The

CHAPTER 7
Memory

Linkages diagram shows ties to two other subfields as well, and there are many more ties throughout the book. Looking for linkages among subfields will help you see how they all fit together and help you better appreciate the big picture that is psychology.

LINKAGES

Where are memories stored?
(ans. on p. 272)

How accurate is eyewitness testimory?
(ans. on p. 261)

Why does memory improve during childhood?
(ans. on p. 473)

CHAPTER 3
Biological Aspects of Psychology

CHAPTER 5
Perception

CHAPTER 12
Human Development

SUMMARY

The Nature of Memory

Human memory depends on a complex mental system.

Basic Memory Processes

There are three basic memory processes. *Encoding* transforms information into some type of mental representation. Codes for *auditory* (or *acoustic*) *memory* represent information as sounds, codes for *visual memory* represent information as images, and codes for semantic memory represent information as general meanings. *Storage* maintains information in the memory system over time. *Retrieval* is the process of gaining access to previously stored information.

Types of Memory

Most psychologists agree that there are at least three types of memory. *Episodic memory* contains information about specific events in a person's life. *Semantic memory* contains generalized knowledge about the world. *Procedural knowledge (procedural memory)* contains information about how to do things.

Explicit and Implicit Memory

Some research on memory concerns *explicit memory,* the processes through which people intentionally try to remember something. Psychologists also examine *implicit memory,* which refers to the unintentional influence of prior experiences.

Models of Memory

Five theoretical models of memory have guided most research. According to the *levels-of-processing model of memory,* the most important determinant of memory is how extensively information is encoded or processed when it is first received. In general, *elaborative rehearsal* is more effective than *maintenance rehearsal* in learning new information because it represents a deeper level of processing. According to the *transfer-appropriate processing model of memory,* the critical determinant of memory is not how deeply information is encoded but whether processes used during retrieval match those used during encoding. *Parallel distributed processing (PDP) models of memory* suggest that new experiences not only provide specific information but also become part of, and alter, a whole network of associations. The multiple memory systems approach emphasizes the role of different brain areas in different aspects of memory encoding and retrieval. The *information-processing model of memory* suggests that in order for information to become firmly embedded in memory, it must pass through three stages of processing: sensory memory, short-term memory, and long-term memory.

Storing New Memories

Sensory Memory

Sensory memory maintains incoming information in the *sensory registers,* such as in *iconic memory,* for a very brief time. *Selective attention,* which focuses mental resources on only part of the stimulus field, controls what information in the sensory registers is actually perceived

and transferred to short-term and working memory.

Short-Term Memory and Working Memory

Working memory is a system that allows us to store, organize, and manipulate information in order to think, solve problems, and make decisions. The storage, or maintenance, component of working memory is referred to as *short-term memory.* Remembering a phone number long enough to call it involves simple maintenance of the information in short-term memory.

Various memory codes can be used in short-term memory, but acoustic codes seem to dominate in most verbal tasks. Studies of the *immediate memory span* indicate that the storage capacity of short-term memory is approximately seven meaningful groupings of information, created by *chunking.* Studies using the *Brown-Peterson distractor technique* show that information in short-term memory is usually forgotten within about eighteen seconds if it is not rehearsed.

Long-Term Memory

Long-term memory normally involves semantic encoding, which means that people tend to encode the general meaning of information, not specific details, in long-term memory. The capacity of long-term memory to store new information is extremely large, perhaps even unlimited.

Distinguishing Between Short-Term and Long-Term Memory

According to some psychologists, there is no need to distinguish between short-term and long-term memory. Still, some evidence suggests that these systems are distinct. For example, the *primacy* and *recency effects* that occur when people try to recall a list of words may indicate the presence of two different systems.

Retrieving Memories

Retrieval Cues and Encoding Specificity

Retrieval cues help people remember things that they would otherwise not be able to recall. The effectiveness of retrieval cues follows the *encoding*

specificity principle: Cues help retrieval only if they match some feature of the information that was originally encoded.

Context and State Dependence

All else being equal, memory may be better when one attempts to retrieve information in the same environment in which it was learned; this is called *context-specific memory,* or *context-specific learning.* When a person's physiological or mood state can aid or impede retrieval, the person is said to have *state-dependent memory,* or *state-dependent learning.*

Retrieval from Semantic Memory

Researchers usually study retrieval from semantic memory by examining how long it takes people to answer general-knowledge questions. It appears that ideas are represented as associations in a dense semantic memory network and that the retrieval of information occurs by a process of *spreading activation.* Each concept in the network is represented as a collection of features or attributes. The tip-of-the-tongue phenomenon and the feeling-of-knowing experience represent the retrieval of incomplete knowledge.

Constructing Memories

In the process of constructive memory, people use their existing knowledge to fill in gaps in the information they encode and retrieve. Parallel distributed processing models provide one explanation of how people make spontaneous generalizations about the world. They also explain the *schemas* that shape the memories people construct.

Forgetting

How Do We Forget?

In his research on long-term memory and forgetting, Hermann Ebbinghaus introduced the *relearning method.* He found that most forgetting from long-term memory occurs during the first several hours after learning and that "savings" can be extremely long-lasting.

Why Do We Forget? The Roles of Decay and Interference

Decay theory and *interference* describe two mechanisms of forgetting. Although there is evidence of both decay and interference in short-term memory, it appears that most forgetting from long-term memory is due to interference caused by either *retroactive inhibition* or *proactive inhibition*. There is considerable controversy over the possibility of *repressed memory* of traumatic events, especially about whether recovered memories of such events are more likely to be true recollections or false, constructed ones.

Biological Bases of Memory

The Biochemistry of Memory

Research has shown that memory can result as new synapses are formed in the brain and as communication at existing synapses is improved. Several neurotransmitters appear to be involved in the strengthening that occurs at synapses.

Brain Structures and Memory

Neuroimaging studies of normal people, as well as research with patients with *anterograde amnesia, retrograde amnesia,* Korsakoff's syndrome, and other memory problems, provide valuable information about the brain structures involved in memory. The hippocampus and thalamus are known to play a role in the formation of memories. These structures send nerve fibers to the cerebral cortex, in which memories are probably stored and which is activated during memory retrieval. Memories appear to be both localized and distributed throughout the brain.

Applications of Memory Research

Improving Your Memory

Among the many applications of memory research are *mnemonic strategies,* devices that are used to remember things better. One of the simplest but most powerful mnemonics is the method of loci. It is useful because it provides a context for organizing material more effectively. Guidelines for effective studying have also been derived from memory research. For example, the key to remembering textbook material is to read actively rather than passively. One of the most effective ways to do this is to follow the PQ4R method: preview, question, read, reflect, recite, and review. To take good lecture notes and to study them effectively, organize the points into a meaningful framework and think about how each main point relates to the others. When preparing for an exam, don't cram. Space your study sessions over time, and be sure to test yourself repeatedly.

Design for Memory

Research on the limits of memory has helped product designers create more user-friendly electronic and mechanical systems and devices.

LINKAGES TO FURTHER LEARNING

Now that you have finished reading this chapter, how about exploring some of the topics and information that you found most interesting? Here are some places to start.

Books

Daniel L. Schacter, *The Seven Sins of Memory: How the Mind Forgets and Remembers* (Mariner Books, 2002). An overview of memory and memory research.

Eric R. Kandell, *In Search of Memory: The Emergence of a New Science of Mind* (Norton, 2007). The biology of memory.

Elizabeth Loftus and Katherine Ketcham, *The Myth of Repressed Memory* (St. Martin's Press, 1996). Describes research casting doubt on the validity of some recovered memories.

Paul McHugh, *Try to Remember* (Dana Press. 2009). An account of the role of psychotherapy and psychotherapists in reports of repressed and recovered memories of abuse.

E. Sue Blume, *Secret Survivors: Uncovering Incest and Its Aftereffects in Women* (Ballantine, 1998). Presents the position of some therapists who believe in the validity of all reports of recovered memories.

Elizabeth Loftus, *Eyewitness Testimony* (Harvard University Press, 1996). Summarizes research on the limitations of eyewitness testimony.

Lawrence Wright, *Remembering Satan: A Tragic Case of Recovered Memory* (Vintage, 1994). How false memories led to a man's conviction for sexual abuse.

Kathryn Lyon, *Witch Hunt* (Avon, 1998). Documents how hysteria in Washington State in the 1990s led to dozens of false convictions for sexual abuse.

Moira Johnson, *Spectral Evidence* (Westview, 1997). Traces the Gary Ramona case, in which a therapist was found liable for inducing false memories of sexual abuse.

Susan Clancy, *Abducted: How People Come to Believe They Were Kidnapped by Aliens* (Harvard University Press, 2006). A fascinating summary of research on this topic.

Walter Pauk and Ross Owens, *How to Study in College* (Wadsworth, 2010). Effective study methods based on the results of memory research.

On the Internet

 Access an integrated eBook and chapter-specific learning tools including flashcards, quizzes, videos, and more. Go to CengageBrain.com.

Want to maximize the value of your online study time? Take this easy-to-use study system's diagnostic pre-test, and it will create a personalized study plan for you. By helping you identify the topics that you need to understand better and then directing you to valuable online resources, it can speed up your chapter review. CengageNOW even provides a post-test so you can confirm that you are ready for an exam. Go to CengageBrain.com.

TALKING POINTS

Here are a few talking points to help you summarize this chapter for family and friends without giving a lecture.

1. Sometimes memories influence our thoughts and behavior without our being aware of it.
2. Most adults can hold about seven items in short-term memory, but only for about eighteen seconds unless we keep repeating the information to ourselves.
3. Long-term memory has a virtually unlimited capacity, but this does not necessarily mean that we can remember everything that we have ever experienced.
4. The things that occur after an event can change our memory of it, which is one reason why eyewitness testimony may not be as accurate as people think it is.
5. There is controversy over the question of whether recovered memories of childhood abuse are real or imagined.
6. We can be fooled by counterfeit money because we tend to remember the overall appearance of our currency but not all of its precise details.
7. You are more likely to do well on a test if you study in many relatively short sessions distributed over time than if you put in one long session just before the test.

8

Cognition and Language

What are you thinking right now?
This can actually be a hard question, because thoughts don't come to us in clear, complete sentences. We have to construct those sentences—using the language we've learned—from the words, images, ideas, and other mental materials in our minds. In this chapter, we explore what thoughts are, what language is, and how we translate one into the other as we reason, make decisions, and solve problems.

Humans are animals, but we are different from other species in some very important ways. Most scientists agree that what sets us apart is our ability to reason logically, to solve complex problems, and to use language. We tend to take these abilities for granted, but the truth is that they are precious and fragile; they can be disrupted or even lost if our brains are damaged by injury or disease.

Consider "Elliot," an intelligent and successful young businessman who had a cancerous tumor removed from the frontal area of his brain. After the surgery, his normally sharp reasoning and decision-making abilities failed. On a simulated gambling task, for example, he made bets without regard for the risks of losing, and with real money he made a series of reckless, impulsive business moves that forced him into bankruptcy (Damasio, 1994). D. J., a bilingual physician, experienced very different problems when, in his early sixties, he suffered a stroke on the left side of his brain (Kohnert, 2004). Unlike Elliot, D. J. could think and reason as well as ever and could still understand what people said in English or Spanish, but his ability to speak either language was severely impaired. It took great effort for him to produce even two- or three-word sentences, and he was unable to name most of the common objects he saw every day. Obviously, his ability to practice medicine was affected.

These cases illustrate that our success in life depends largely on the proper operation of both thinking and language skills and that these skills involve different areas of the brain. When either cognitive or language functions are impaired, we become vulnerable to all sorts of failures and errors. What pitfalls threaten the effectiveness of human cognition? What factors influence our success? How are our thoughts transformed into language? Many of the answers to these questions come from **cognitive psychology**, the study of the mental processes by which the information humans receive from their environment is modified, made meaningful, stored, retrieved, used, and communicated to others (Reed, 2004). Many cognitive psychologists are working with biological psychologists and other neuroscientists to study the brain activity involved in these mental processes. Their collaboration in the field of *cognitive neuroscience* (e.g., Fellows et al., 2005; Purves et al., 2008) is leading to a better understanding of the relationship between mind and brain.

In this chapter, we first consider what thought is and what functions it serves. Then we examine the basic ingredients of thought and the cognitive processes people use as they interact with their environments. These cognitive processes include reasoning, problem solving, and decision making. Next, we discuss language and how it is acquired and used. We cover cognition and language in the same chapter because they often involve the same mental processes. Learning about thought helps us understand language, and learning about language helps us understand thought.

cognitive psychology The study of the mental processes by which information from the environment is modified, made meaningful, stored, retrieved, used, and communicated to others.

Basic Functions of Thought

Let's begin our exploration of human cognition by considering the five core functions of thought: to *describe, elaborate, decide, plan,* and *guide action*. These functions can be envisioned as forming a *circle of thought* (see Figure 8.1).

FIGURE 8.1
The Circle of Thought
The circle of thought begins as our sensory systems take in information from the world. Our perceptual system describes and elaborates this information, which is represented in the brain in ways that allow us to make decisions, formulate plans, and guide our actions. As those actions change our world, we receive new information—and the circle of thought begins again.

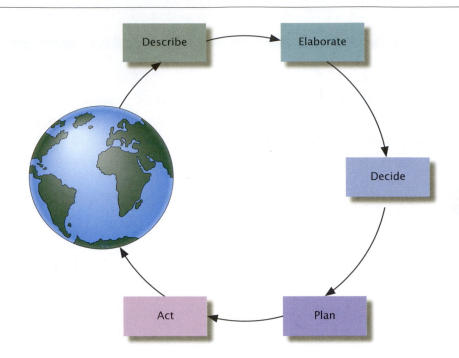

The Circle of Thought

Here is an example of what happens when these functions work as they should: Dr. Joyce Wallace, a New York City internist, was trying to diagnose a 43-year-old patient's problem. "Laura McBride" reported pains in her stomach and abdomen, aching muscles, irritability, dizzy spells, and fatigue (Rouéché, 1986). The doctor's first hypothesis was that Laura had iron deficiency anemia, a condition in which there is too little oxygen-carrying hemoglobin in the blood. There was some evidence to support that hypothesis. Blood tests showed low hemoglobin and high production of red blood cells, suggesting that Laura's body was attempting to compensate for the loss of hemoglobin. However, other tests revealed normal iron levels. Perhaps she was losing blood through internal bleeding, but an additional test ruled that out. Had Laura been vomiting blood? She said no. Blood in the urine? No. Abnormally heavy menstrual flow? No. During the next week, Laura reported more intense pain, cramps, shortness of breath, and severe loss of energy. Her blood was becoming less and less capable of sustaining her, but if it was not being lost, what was happening to it? When the doctor looked at a smear of Laura's blood under the microscope, she saw that some kind of poison was destroying the red blood cells. What could it be? Laura spent most of her time at home, but her teenage daughters, who lived with her, were healthy. Dr. Wallace asked herself, "What does Laura do that the girls don't?" She repairs and restores paintings. Paint. Lead! She might be suffering from lead poisoning! When a blood test showed a lead level seven times higher than normal, Dr. Wallace knew she had solved this medical mystery at last.

Notice how the circle of thought operated in Dr. Wallace. It began when she received the information about Laura's symptoms that allowed her to *describe* the problem. Next, she *elaborated* on this information by using her knowledge and experience to consider what disorders might cause such symptoms. Then she made a *decision* to investigate a possible cause, such as anemia. To implement this decision, she made a *plan*—to order a blood test—and then *acted* on that plan. But the circle of thought did not stop there. Information from the blood test provided new descriptive information, which Dr. Wallace elaborated further to reach another decision, create a new plan, and guide her next action. Each stage in the circle of thought was also influenced by her *intention*—in this case, to find and cure her patient's problem.

"Automatic" Thinking

The sensory, perceptual, decision-making, and response-planning components that make up the circle of thought can occur so rapidly that—as when playing a fast-paced video game—we may be unaware of anything other than incoming information and our quick response to it. In such cases, our thinking processes become so well practiced that they are virtually automatic.

© AP Photo/Shiho Fukada

Scientific analysis of the circle of thought is difficult because its processes are so complex and usually occur so quickly. Some psychologists approach the problem by studying thought processes as if they were part of a computer-like information-processing system. An **information-processing system** receives information, represents the information with symbols, and then manipulates those representations (Anderson, Bothell, et al., 2004). In this information-processing model, then, **thinking** is defined as the manipulation of mental representations. Figure 8.2 shows how an information-processing model might describe the sequence of events that occur during one spin around the circle of thought. Notice that according to this model, information from the world is transformed somewhat as it passes through each stage of processing.

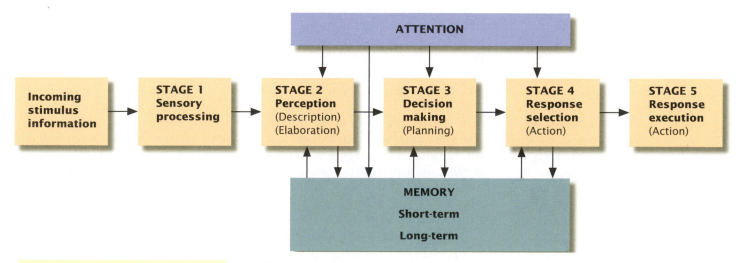

information-processing system Mechanisms for receiving information, representing it with symbols, and manipulating it.

thinking The manipulation of mental representations.

FIGURE 8.2

An Information-Processing Model

According to the information-processing model, each stage in the circle of thought takes a certain amount of time. Some stages depend heavily on both short-term and long-term memory and require some attention—that limited supply of mental energy required for information processing to be carried out efficiently.

In the first stage, information about the world reaches the brain by way of the sensory receptors described in the chapter on sensation. This stage does not require attention. In the second stage, the information must be perceived and recognized, using the attentional and perceptual processes described in the chapter on perception. It is also during this stage that the information is consciously elaborated, using short-term and working-memory processes that allow us to think about it in relation to knowledge stored in long-term memory. Once the information has been elaborated in this way, we must decide what to do with it. This third stage—decision making—also demands attention. The decision may be simply to store the information in memory. If, however, a decision is made to take some action, a response must be planned in the third stage and then carried out through a coordinated pattern of responses—the action itself—in the fourth and fifth stages. As suggested in Figure 8.1, this action usually affects the environment, providing new information that is "fed back" to the system for processing in the ongoing circle of thought.

Measuring Information Processing

The brain damage that Elliot suffered appeared to have mainly affected the decision-making and response selection stages of information processing. Analyzing the effects of brain damage is just one of several methods that scientists use to study the details of how the entire information-processing sequence normally works and what can interfere with it.

Mental Chronometry   Drivers and video game players know that there is always a slight delay between seeing a red light or a "bad guy" and hitting the brakes or firing the laser gun. The delay occurs because each of the processes described in Figure 8.2 takes some time. Psychologists began the laboratory study of thinking by exploring *mental chronometry*, the timing of mental events (Posner, 1978). Specifically, they examined **reaction time**, the time elapsing between the presentation of a stimulus and the appearance of an overt response to it. Reaction time, they reasoned, should give us an idea of how long it takes for all the processes shown in Figure 8.2 to occur. In a typical reaction time experiment, a person is asked to say a word or to push a button as rapidly as possible after a stimulus appears. Even in such simple situations, several factors influence reaction times (Wickens, Gordon-Becker, & Liu, 2004).

One important factor in reaction time is the *complexity* of the decision. The more options we have in responding to a set of stimuli, the longer the reaction time. The tennis player who knows that her opponent usually serves to a particular spot on the court will have a simple decision to make when the serve is completed and will react rapidly. But if she faces an opponent whose serve is less predictable, her reaction will be slower, because a more complex decision about which way to move is now required.

Expectancy, too, affects reaction time. People respond faster to stimuli that they are expecting and more slowly to stimuli that surprise them. So your reaction time will be shorter when braking for a traffic light that you knew might turn red than when dodging a ball thrown at you unexpectedly. Expectancy appears to operate partly by activating in advance the neural circuits we will need for the particular response we are expecting to make (Sinclair & Hammond, 2008). So if you expect that traffic light to turn red, the motor neurons you will need in order to move your foot from the gas pedal to the brake will become more active even before the light changes.

Reaction time is also influenced by *stimulus-response compatibility*. If the relationship between a set of stimuli and possible responses is a natural or compatible one, reaction time will be fast. If not, reaction time will be slower. Figure 8.3 illustrates compatible and incompatible relationships. Incompatible stimulus-response relationships are major culprits in causing errors in the use of all kinds of equipment, especially if it is unfamiliar or if the operator is under stress (Segal & Suri, 1999).

Finally, in any reaction time task, there is a *speed-accuracy trade-off.* If you attempt to respond quickly, errors increase. If you try for an error-free performance, reaction

Courtesy of BadDesigns.com

FIGURE 8.3
Stimulus-Response Compatibility

TRY THIS Imagine standing in front of an unfamiliar stove when a pot starts to boil over. Your reaction time in turning down the heat will depend in part on the stove's design. The response you make will be quicker on the stove shown in the top photo, because each knob is positioned to indicate the burner it controls. There is compatibility between the source of the stimulus and the location of the response. The stove in the bottom photo shows far less compatibility. Here, which knob you should turn is not as obvious, so your reaction time will be slower. Are there devices in your own house or apartment that lack stimulus-response compatibility? If so, how would you redesign them?

reaction time The time between the presentation of a stimulus and an overt response to it.

On Your Mark . . .

The runner who reacts quickest to the starting gun will have an advantage over other competitors, but too much eagerness can cause an athlete to literally jump the gun and lose the race before it starts. Yet trying too hard to avoid a false start can slow reaction time and cost precious time in getting off the mark. This is the speed-accuracy trade-off in action.

© moodboard RF/Photolibrary

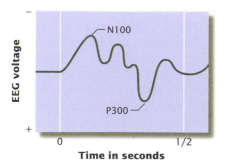

FIGURE 8.4
Evoked Potentials

Here is the average EEG, or brain wave, tracing produced from several trials on which a research participant's name was presented. Evoked potentials are averaged in this way so as to eliminate random variations in the tracings. The result is the appearance of a *negative* peak (N100) followed by a large *positive* peak (P300). Traditionally, positive peaks are shown as decreases on such tracings, whereas negative ones are shown as increases.

evoked potential A small, temporary change in EEG voltage in the brain that is caused by some stimulus.

time increases (Wickens & Carswell, 2006). At a track meet, for example, contestants who try too hard to anticipate the starting gun may have especially quick starts but may also have especially frequent false starts that disqualify them.

Research on reaction time has helped establish the time required for information processing to occur. It has also revealed how the entire sequence can be made faster or slower. But reaction times alone cannot provide a detailed picture of what goes on between the presentation of a stimulus and the execution of a response. They do not tell us, for example, how long the perception stage lasts. Nor do they tell us whether we respond more quickly to an expected stimulus because we perceive it faster or because we make a decision about it faster. Reaction time measures have been used in many ingenious efforts to make inferences about such things; but to analyze mental events more directly, psychologists have turned to other methods, such as the analysis of evoked brain potentials.

Evoked Potentials   The **evoked potential** is a small, temporary change in voltage on an *electroencephalogram* (EEG) that occurs as the brain responds to specific events. Figure 8.4 shows an example. Each peak on the EEG reflects the firing of large groups of neurons in different regions of the brain at different times during the information-processing sequence. The pattern of the peaks provides information that is more precise than overall reaction time. For example, a large positive peak, called the P300, occurs 300 to 500 milliseconds (thousandths of a second) after a stimulus is presented. The exact delay before a P300 occurs is a sensitive measure of how long it takes to complete the first two stages of information processing shown in Figure 8.2. Further, the size of the P300 reflects the operation of attention in the second of those stages. For example, P300s are normally larger in response to unusual or surprising stimuli than to unchanging or predictable ones. If this is not the case, there may be a problem, as was revealed in a study of college students who had suffered concussions. Although these students showed no obvious symptoms of brain damage, their P300s to surprising stimuli were abnormally small, which suggested some lingering disruption in their brains' information-processing capacity (Lavoie et al., 2004). More recent research shows that these disruptions can persist for thirty years or more (De Beaumont et al., 2009).

Neuroimaging   Using positron emission tomography (PET), functional magnetic resonance imaging (fMRI), and other neuroimaging techniques described in the chapter on biological aspects of psychology, cognitive neuroscientists can watch what happens in the brain during information processing (e.g., Amaro & Barker,

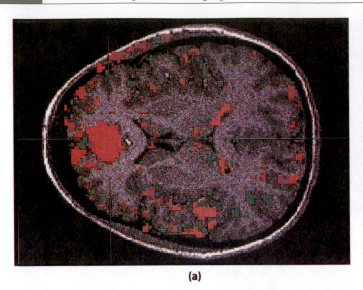 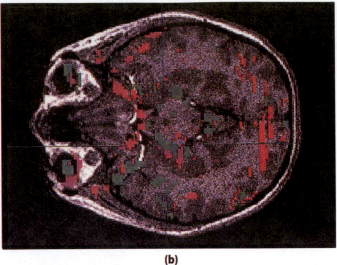

(a) **(b)**

From Cognitive Psychology and Its Implications by John R. Anderson © 2000, 1995, 1985, 1980, by Worth Publishers and W. H. Freeman and Company.

FIGURE 8.5
Watching People Think

Cognitive psychologists and other cognitive neuroscientists have found ways to watch brain activity as information processing takes place. These fMRI pictures show activity in two "slices" of the brain of a research participant who was practicing a complex problem-solving task. The areas shown in red were activated early in the learning process. As skill developed, the areas shown in green became activated.

Source: Anderson (2000).

2006; Badre & Wagner, 2006). In one study, for example, participants performed a task that required complex problem-solving skills. The frontal lobe of the brain was especially active when this task was still relatively new and difficult, as shown by the red-shaded areas in Figure 8.5. As the participants learned the skills, however, frontal lobe involvement decreased. When the task was well learned, the hippocampus became especially active (see the green-shaded areas in the bottom panel of Figure 8.5). Activation in the hippocampus suggests that the participants were no longer struggling with a problem-solving task but instead were performing it from memory.

A number of other studies of brain activity during the performance of cognitive tasks have also found that the frontal lobes are especially important for making decisions and solving problems (Wallis, Anderson, & Miller, 2001; Yarkoni et al., 2005; this chapter's Focus on Research Methods describes another example). These tasks involve coordinated activity in many other brain areas too (Andrés, 2003), but it is certainly no wonder that damage to Elliot's frontal area disrupted his decision-making and impulse-control abilities. Neuroimaging research has shown that even in people without brain damage, abnormal information processing in the frontal lobes is associated with behaviors such as excessive gambling (Clark, 2010).

Mental Representations: The Ingredients of Thought

Just as measuring, stirring, and baking are only part of the story of cookie making, describing the processes involved in thinking tells only part of the story behind the circle of thought. To understand thinking more fully, we also need to know what it is that these processes manipulate. Most psychologists describe the ingredients of thought as *information.* But this is like saying that you make cookies with "ingredients." What specific forms does information take in our minds? In other words, how do we mentally represent information? Researchers in cognitive psychology have found that information can be mentally represented in many ways, including as *concepts, propositions, schemas, scripts, mental models, images,* and *cognitive maps.* Let's consider each of these ingredients of thought and how we manipulate them as we think.

Concepts

When you think about anything—dogs, happiness, sex, movies, pizza—you are manipulating a basic ingredient of thought called *concepts.* **Concepts** are categories of objects, events, or ideas with common properties. To "have a concept" is to recognize the properties, or *features,* that tend to be shared by the members of the category. For example, the concept "bird" includes such properties as having feathers, laying eggs, and being able to fly. The concept "scissors" includes such properties as having two blades, a connecting hinge, and a pair of finger holes. Concepts allow you to relate each object, event, or idea you encounter to a category you already know. Using concepts, you can say, "No, that's not a dog," or "Yes, that's a car." Concepts also make it possible to think logically. If you have the concepts "whale" and "bird," you can decide whether a whale is bigger than a bird without having either creature in the room with you.

Types of Concepts Some concepts—called *formal concepts*—can be clearly defined by a set of rules or properties such that members of the concept have all of the defining properties and nonmembers don't. For example, the concept "square" can be defined as "a shape with four equal sides and four right-angle corners." Any object that does not have all of these features simply is not a square, and any object with all these features is a square. To study concept learning in the laboratory, psychologists often use formal concepts because the members of the concept can be neatly defined.

There are many other concepts, though, that can't be defined by a fixed set of necessary features. For example, take a moment to list a small set of features that precisely defines the concept "home." Your list might differ from other people's because "home" can be defined as the place where you were born, the house in which you grew up, where you live now, your country of origin, the place where you are most comfortable, and so on. "Home" is an example of a **natural concept** (also known as a **natural category**), a concept that has no fixed set of defining features but instead has a set of typical or characteristic features. So just as members of the same family might resemble each other in some ways but not in every way, members of a natural concept need not have all of its characteristic features. One characteristic feature of the natural concept "bird," for example, is the ability to fly—but an ostrich is a bird even though it cannot fly. It's a bird because it possesses enough of the other characteristic features of the concept "bird" (feathers, wings, and the like). Having just one bird property is not enough. A snake lays eggs and a bat flies, but neither one is a bird. It is usually a combination of properties that defines a concept. Outside the laboratory, most of the concepts that people use in thinking are natural rather than formal concepts. Natural concepts include relatively concrete object categories, such as "bird" or "house"; abstract idea categories, such as "honesty" or "justice"; and temporary goal-related categories that help people make plans, such as "things I need to pack for my trip" (Barsalou, 1993).

The boundaries of a natural concept are fuzzy, and some members of it are better examples of the concept than others because they share more of its characteristic features (Rosch, 1975). A robin, a chicken, an ostrich, and a penguin are all birds. But a robin is the best example, because a robin can fly and is closer to the size and shape of what most people have learned to think of as a typical bird. A member of a natural concept that possesses all or most of its characteristic features is called a **prototype** (Smith, 1998). A robin, then, is a *prototypical* bird. The more prototypical a member of a concept is, the more quickly people can decide if it is an example of the concept.

TRY THIS

concept A category of objects, events, or ideas that have common properties.

natural concept (natural category) A concept that has no fixed set of defining features but has a set of characteristic features.

prototype A member of a natural concept that possesses all or most of its characteristic features.

A Natural Concept

A space shuttle and a hot-air balloon are two examples of the natural concept "aircraft," but most people think of the space shuttle, with its wings, as the better example. A prototype of the concept is probably an airplane. Members of natural concepts share a kind of "family resemblance" that helps us recognize items that belong in the same category, even if they are not identical.

As a result, it takes slightly less time for people to answer when asked "Is a robin a bird?" than when asked "Is a penguin a bird?" Because prototypes are fundamental to the way we perceive and understand the world, understanding the nature of people's prototypes can have great practical value. For example, smokers—particularly young male smokers—are at greater risk for long-term cigarette use if their prototype for "smoker" includes traits such as "smart and independent" (Piko, Bak, & Gibbons, 2007). This is why health psychologists' antismoking programs often include efforts to create in smokers' minds a more negative prototype of the "typical smoker."

Propositions

We often combine concepts in units known as propositions. A **proposition** is a mental representation that expresses a relationship between concepts. Propositions can be true or false. Suppose you hear that your friend Heather broke up with her boyfriend, Jason. Your mental representation of this event will include a proposition that links your concepts of "Heather" and "Jason" in a particular way. This proposition could be diagrammed (using unscientific terms) as follows: Heather→dumped→Jason.

The diagram looks like a sentence, but it isn't one. Propositions can be expressed as sentences, but they are actually general ideas that can be conveyed in any number of specific ways. In this case, "Jason was dumped by Heather" and "Heather is not dating Jason anymore" would both express the same proposition. If you later discover that it was Jason who initiated the breakup, your proposition about the event would change to reflect this new information: Heather←dumped←Jason. Propositions are part of the network of associations that many psychologists regard as the basis for our knowledge of the world (see Figure 7.9 in the chapter on memory). So hearing the name *Heather*, for example, will activate lots of associated information about her, including the proposition about her relationship to Jason.

Schemas, Scripts, and Mental Models

Sets of propositions are often so closely associated that they form more complex mental representations called *schemas*. As described in the chapters on perception, memory, and human development, **schemas** are generalizations that we develop about categories of objects, places, events, and people. Our schemas help us make sense of

proposition A mental representation of the relationship between concepts.

schemas Generalizations about categories of objects, places, events, and people.

You Can't Judge a Book by Its Cover

Does this person look like a millionaire to you? Our schemas tell us what to expect about objects, events, and people, but those expectations can sometimes be wrong. This was dramatically illustrated when Gordon Elwood, a Medford, Oregon, man who dressed in rags and collected cans, died and left over $9 million to charity (McMahon, 2000).

the world. If you borrow a friend's car, your "car" schema will give you a good idea of where to put the ignition key, where the accelerator and brake are, and how to raise and lower the windows. Schemas also create expectations about objects, places, events, and people—telling us that stereo systems have speakers, that picnics occur in the summer, that rock concerts are loud, and so on.

Scripts   One particularly useful type of schema is called a script (Anderson, 2000). **Scripts** are schemas about familiar activities, such as going to a restaurant, visiting a doctor's office, or attending a lecture. Your "restaurant" script, for example, represents the sequence of events you can expect when you go out to eat (see Figure 8.6). That

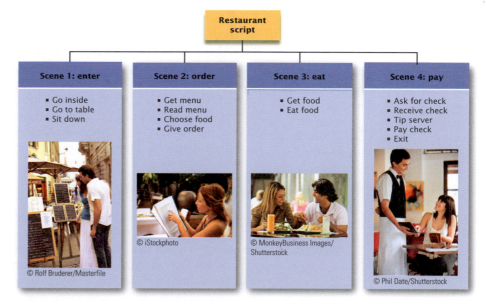

FIGURE 8.6
Following a Script: Eating at a Restaurant

Schemas about what happens in restaurants and how to behave in them take the form of a *script,* represented here in four "scenes." Scripts guide our actions in all sorts of familiar situations and also help us understand descriptions of events occurring in those situations (e.g., "Our service was really slow").

script A mental representation of a familiar sequence of activity.

script tells you what to do when you are in a restaurant and helps you understand stories involving restaurants (Whitney, 2001). Scripts also shape your interpretation of events. For example, on your first day at college, you no doubt assumed that the person standing at the front of the class was a teacher, not a security guard or a janitor.

If our scripts are violated, however, it is easy to misinterpret events. In London, a person having a heart attack lay unattended in the hallway of an apartment building for nine hours after an ambulance crew smelled alcohol on his breath and assumed he was "sleeping it off." The crew's script for what happens in the poorer sections of big cities told them that someone slumped in a hallway is drunk, not sick. Because script-violating events are unexpected, our reactions to them tend to be slower and less effective than our reactions to expected events. Your "grocery shopping" script, for example, probably includes pushing a cart, putting items in it, going to the checkout stand, and paying for your purchases. But suppose you are at the back of the store when a robber near the entrance fires a gun and shouts at the manager to open the safe. People sometimes ignore these script-violating events, interpreting gunshots as a car backfiring and shouted orders as "someone fooling around" (Raisig et al., 2010). Others simply "freeze," unsure of what to do and failing to realize that they could call the police on their cell phones.

Mental Models   Related concepts can be organized not only as schemas and scripts but also as **mental models**, which are representations of particular situations or arrangements of objects (Johnson-Laird, 1983). For example, suppose someone tells you, "My living room has blue walls, a white ceiling, and an oval window across from the door." You will mentally represent this information as propositions about how the concepts "wall," "blue," "ceiling," "white," "door," "oval," and "window" are related. However, you will also combine these propositions to create in your mind a three-dimensional model of the room. The more information we receive from existing memories or from new information, the more complete our mental models become.

Accurate mental models are excellent guides for thinking about and interacting with many of the things we encounter (Ashcraft, 2006). If a mental model is incorrect or incomplete, however, we are likely to make mistakes (see Figure 8.7). For example, college students conduct more effective Internet searches if their mental models of search engines recognize that computers require precise search terms. Students who think that human operators read and interpret the meaning of the search terms they enter are less likely to use precise terms and so tend to get less useful results (Zang, 2008). Similarly, people who hold an incorrect mental model of how physical illness is cured might stop taking their antibiotic medication when their symptoms begin to disappear, well before the bacteria causing those symptoms have been eliminated (Medin, Ross, & Markman, 2001). Others overdose on medication because their faulty mental model tells them, "If taking three pills a day is good, taking six would be even better."

Images and Cognitive Maps

Some mental models stem from sets of propositions that describe a situation, but these models are more often based on images in the "mind's eye." For example, take a moment to think about how your best friend would look in a clown suit. The mental picture you just created illustrates that thinking often involves the manipulation of **images**—mental representations of visual information. Cognitive psychologists refer to mental images as *analogical representations* because we mentally manipulate these images in a way that is similar, or *analogous,* to manipulating the actual objects (Reed, 2004). This similarity was demonstrated in a classic study by Roger Shepard and Jacqueline Metzler (1971). They measured how long it took people to decide whether pairs of objects such as those in Figure 8.8 were the same or different. They found that the amount of decision time depended on how far one object had to be "mentally rotated" to compare it with the other. The more rotation required, the longer the decision took. In other words, rotating the mental image of an object was like rotating the

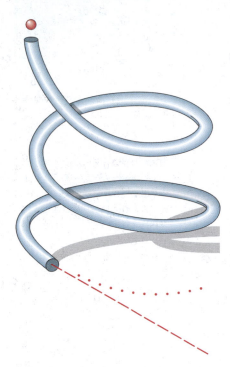

FIGURE 8.7
Applying a Mental Model
TRY THIS   Try to imagine the path that the marble will follow when it leaves the curved tube. In one study, most people drew the incorrect (curved) path indicated by the dotted line, rather than the correct (straight) path indicated by the dashed line (McCloskey, 1983). Their errors were based on a faulty mental model of the behavior of physical objects.

TRY THIS

mental model   A representation of particular situations or arrangements of objects that guides our interaction with them.

image   A mental representation of visual information.

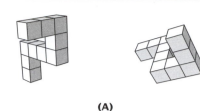

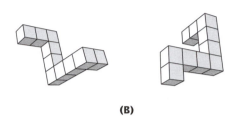

FIGURE 8.8
Manipulating Images

TRY THIS Are the two objects in (A) the same? How about the two in (B)? To decide, you will have to rotate one member of each pair. Because manipulating mental images, like manipulating actual objects, takes some time, the speed of your decision will depend on how far you have to mentally rotate one object to line it up with the other for comparison. (The answer can be found at the bottom of page 296.)

From R. Shepard et al. "Mental Rotation of Three-Dimensional Objects," *Science,* volume 171, no. 3972, pp. 701–703, 19 February 1971. Copyright © 1971 AAAS. Reprinted with permission.

real object. More recent studies using neuroimaging have confirmed that manipulating mental images activates some of the same areas of the brain that are active during comparable tasks with real objects (Farah, 2000). The relationship between imagined and actual movement has been employed by physical therapists, who help stroke victims restore at least partial movement in paralyzed limbs by asking them to imagine moving those limbs (Page et al., 2009).

Our ability to think using images extends beyond the mental manipulation of stimuli such as those in Figure 8.8. We also create images that serve as mental models of written or spoken descriptions of scenes. In fact, brain areas involved in vision are activated as we construct mental images of those scenes (Mazoyer et al., 2002). You probably created a mental image a minute ago when you read about that blue-walled room, and you would do the same thing when someone gives you directions to a new pizza place in town. In the latter case, you would scan your **cognitive map**—a mental model of familiar parts of your world—to find the location. In doing so, you would use a mental process similar to the visual process of scanning a paper map (Anderson, 2000; Taylor & Tversky, 1992). Scanning images on a different cognitive map would help you if a power failure left your home pitch dark. Even though you couldn't see a thing, you could still find a flashlight or candle because your cognitive map would show the floor plan, furniture placement, door locations, and other physical features of your home. You would not have this mental map for an unfamiliar house. There, you would have to walk slowly, arms outstretched, to avoid wrong turns and painful collisions. In the chapter on learning we describe how experience shapes the cognitive maps that help animals navigate mazes and people navigate shopping malls.

Thinking Strategies

We have seen that our thinking capacity is based largely on our ability to manipulate mental representations—the ingredients of thought—much as a baker manipulates the ingredients of cookies (see "In Review: Ingredients of Thought" for a summary of these representations). But whereas the baker's food-processing system combines and transforms flour, sugar, milk, eggs, and chocolate into a delicious treat, our information-processing system combines, transforms, and elaborates mental representations in ways that allow us to engage in reasoning, problem solving, and decision making. Let's begin our discussion of these thinking strategies by considering **reasoning**, the process through which we generate and evaluate arguments, as well as reach conclusions about them.

Formal Reasoning

Astronomers tell us that the temperature at the core of the sun is about 27 million degrees Fahrenheit. They can't put a temperature probe inside the sun, so how can they be so confident about this assertion? Their estimate is based on *inferences* from other things that they know about the sun and about physical objects in general. Telescopic observations of the sun's volume and mass allowed astronomers to calculate its density, using the formula *density = mass ÷ volume*. These observations also enabled them to measure the energy coming from one small region of the sun and—using what geometry told them about the surface area of spheres—to estimate the energy output from the sun as a whole. Further calculations told them how hot a body would have to be to generate that much energy.

In other words, the astronomers' estimate of the sun's core temperature was based on **formal reasoning** (also called *logical reasoning*), the process of following a set of rigorous procedures to reach valid, or correct, conclusions. Some of these procedures included the application of specific mathematical formulas to existing data in order to generate new data. Such formulas are examples of **algorithms**, systematic methods that always produce a correct solution to a problem if a solution exists (Jahnke & Nowaczyk, 1998). The astronomers also followed the rules of **logic**, which are sets of statements

cognitive map A mental model of familiar parts of the environment.

reasoning The process by which people generate and evaluate arguments and reach conclusions about them.

formal reasoning The process of following a set of rigorous procedures for reaching valid conclusions.

algorithm A systematic procedure that cannot fail to produce a correct solution to a problem if a solution exists.

logic A system of formulas for drawing valid conclusions.

IN REVIEW	Ingredients of Thought	
Ingredient	**Description**	**Examples**
Concepts	Categories of objects, events, or ideas with common properties; basic building blocks of thought	"Square" (a formal concept); "game" (a natural concept).
Propositions	Mental representations that express relationships between concepts; can be true or false	Assertions such as "The cow jumped over the moon."
Schemas	Sets of propositions that create generalizations and expectations about categories of objects, places, events, and people	A schema might suggest that all grandmothers are elderly, have gray hair, and bake a lot of cookies.
Scripts	Schemas about familiar activities and situations; guide behavior in those situations	You pay before eating in fast-food restaurants and after eating in fancier restaurants.
Mental models	Sets of propositions about how things relate to each other in the real world; can be correct or incorrect	Mistakenly assuming that airflow around a convertible with its top down will carry thrown objects upward, a driver tosses a lighted cigarette butt overhead, causing it to land in the back seat.
Images	Mental representations of visual information	Hearing a description of your blind date creates a mental picture of the person.
Cognitive maps	Mental representations of familiar parts of the world	You can get to class by an alternate route even if your usual route is blocked by construction.

1. Thinking is the manipulation of _____ .
2. Arguments over what is "fair" occur because "fairness" is a _____ concept.
3. Your _____ of "hotel room" would lead you to expect yours to include a bathroom.

© Paul Howell/Getty Images

Pitfalls in Formal Reasoning

"Elderly people cannot be astronauts; this is an elderly man; therefore, he cannot be an astronaut." The logic of this syllogism is correct, but the first premise is wrong. In 1962, John Glenn became the first American astronaut to orbit the earth. Here he is in 1998, at the age of 77, just before he returned to space as a crew member on the space shuttle *Discovery*. Most of us try to use formal reasoning to reach correct conclusions, but even perfect logic can lead to incorrect conclusions if we start with false assumptions.

that provide a formula for drawing valid conclusions about the world. For example, each step in the astronomers' thinking took the form of "if-then" statements: If we know how much energy comes from one part of the sun's surface and if we know how big the whole surface is, then we can calculate the total energy output. You use the same formal reasoning processes when you conclude, for example, that if your friend José is two years older than you are, then his twin brother, Juan, will be two years older too. This kind of formal reasoning is called *deductive* reasoning because it takes a general rule (e.g., twins are the same age) and applies it to draw, or deduce, conclusions about specific cases (e.g., José and Juan).

The rules of logic provide a system for drawing correct conclusions from a set of statements known as *premises*. Consider, for example, what conclusion can be drawn from the following premises:

Premise 1: People who study hard do well in this course.

Premise 2: You have studied hard.

According to the rules of logic, you would be correct to conclude that you will do well in this course. Logical arguments that contain two or more premises and a conclusion are known as **syllogisms** (pronounced "SIL-uh-jiz-umz"). Notice that the conclusion in a syllogism goes beyond what the premises actually say. The conclusion is an inference based on the premises and on the rules of logic. The logical rule in this particular syllogism was this: If something is true of all members of a category, and if A is in that category, then that something will also be true of A.

Your ability to make everyday decisions and solve everyday problems depends heavily on your ability to draw correct inferences about facts. For example, if a course you want to take is open only to seniors and you are a sophomore, you'll infer that it would be a waste of time to try to get in. This would be the syllogism:

Premise 1: This class is open only to seniors.

Premise 2: I am not a senior.

Conclusion: I can't take this class.

syllogism An argument made up of two propositions, called premises, and a conclusion based on those premises.

Answer to Figure 8.8: The objects in part A are the same; the objects in part B are different.

Logical reasoning skills can be so well learned that they seem to come naturally, but there are some tendencies toward errors in reasoning that seem to come naturally too. These common pitfalls can lead us astray in our problem solving and decision making. Two of the most important of these pitfalls are *belief bias* and *limits on memory*.

Belief Bias Sometimes what we already know and believe biases our reasoning processes (e.g., Roberts & Sykes, 2003). For example, consider this syllogism:

Premise 1: Some professors wear ties.

Premise 2: Some men wear ties.

Conclusion: Some professors are men.

The conclusion happens to be true, but it doesn't actually follow logically from these premises. Conclusions such as this one *look* logical and valid, but only because they conform to what our experience has taught us to believe about the world. To see how belief bias affected your view of this syllogism, substitute the word *scarecrows* for *men* in premise 2. The syllogism now reads: *Some professors wear ties. Some scarecrows wear ties. Therefore, some professors are scarecrows.* No matter what you think of your professors, you would probably not accept this new conclusion as valid.

Belief bias is related to a more general problem in human reasoning, called **confirmation bias**—a tendency to seek evidence and reach conclusions that are consistent with our existing beliefs. Confirmation bias can affect thinking in many situations. When people first fall in love, they often focus only on their loved one's best qualities and ignore evidence of less desirable ones. In the courtroom, jurors may pay little attention to evidence of a defendant's guilt if that defendant is, say, a beloved celebrity or a harmless-looking senior citizen. In such cases, prosecutors' logical arguments based on true premises may not lead to a conviction because the logical conclusion ("guilty") does not match jurors' beliefs about celebrities, the elderly, or some other favored group. Similarly, if jurors believe that the defendant represents a category of people who tend to commit crimes, they may not be swayed much by evidence suggesting innocence. In other words, the conclusions that people reach are often based on both logical thinking and biased thinking (Evans et al., 1999; O'Brien, 2009).

Limits on Working Memory *Some A's are B. All B's are C. Therefore, some A's are C.* Do you agree? This syllogism is correct, but evaluating it requires you to hold a lot of information in short-term, or working, memory while mentally manipulating it. This task is particularly difficult if elements in a syllogism involve negatives, as in *No dogs are nonanimals.* There is also the related problem of trying to keep in mind several possible versions of the same premise (see Figure 8.9). If the amount of material to be mentally manipulated exceeds the capacity of a person's short-term memory, logical errors can easily result.

Psychologists have discovered that both kinds of pitfalls we just described can lead people to make errors in logical reasoning. This finding is one reason that misleading advertisements or speeches can still attract sales and votes (Cialdini, 2007).

Informal Reasoning

Using the rules of formal logic to deduce answers about specific cases is an important kind of reasoning, but it is not the only kind. A second kind, **informal reasoning**, comes into play when we are trying to assess the *believability* of a conclusion based on the evidence available to support it. Informal reasoning is also known as *inductive reasoning* because its goal is to induce a general conclusion to appear on the basis of specific facts or examples. Psychologists use this kind of reasoning when they design experiments and other research methods whose results will provide evidence for or against a theory. Jurors use informal reasoning when weighing evidence for the guilt or innocence of a defendant. Air crash investigators use it when they consider all the possible causes of an accident and then try to eliminate the incorrect ones.

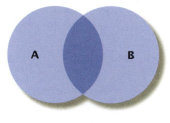

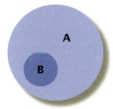

FIGURE 8.9

Two Versions of the Same Premise

As these drawings show, the same premise—*Some A's are B*—can be represented in more than one way. Keeping in mind two or more versions of a premise, or of two premises, can tax short-term memory. As a result, people tend to work with only one version of each premise. If they don't choose the right one, it may be difficult or impossible to reach a valid conclusion.

From Whitney, The Psychology of Language, Fig. 3.4. Copyright © 1998 Wadsworth, a part of Cengage Learning, Inc. Reproduced by permission. www. cengage.com/permissions

confirmation bias The tendency to pay more attention to evidence in support of one's hypothesis than to evidence that refutes that hypothesis.

informal reasoning The process of evaluating a conclusion, theory, or course of action on the basis of the believability of evidence.

Formal reasoning follows the rules of logic, but there are no foolproof rules for informal reasoning, as this fool demonstrates.

Formal reasoning is guided by algorithms and the rules of logic, but there are no foolproof methods for informal reasoning. Consider, for example, how many white swans you would have to see before concluding that all swans are white. Fifty? A hundred? A million? A strictly formal, algorithmic approach would require that you observe every swan in existence to be sure they are all white. A more practical approach is to base your conclusion on the number of observations that you believe to be "enough." In other words, you would take a mental "shortcut" to reach a conclusion that is probably, but not necessarily, correct (there are, in fact, black swans). Such mental shortcuts are called **heuristics** (pronounced "hyoo-RIST-iks").

Suppose that you are about to leave home but can't find your watch. Applying an algorithm would mean searching in every possible location, room by room, until you find the watch. But you can reach the same outcome more quickly by using a heuristic—that is, by searching only where your experience suggests you might have left the watch. In short, heuristics are often valuable in guiding judgments about which events are probable or which hypotheses are likely to be true. These "rules of thumb" are easy to use and frequently work well.

However, heuristics can also bias our thinking and result in errors. Suppose that your rule of thumb is to vote for all the candidates in a particular political party instead of researching the views of each candidate. You might help elect someone with whom you strongly disagree on some issues. The extent to which heuristics are responsible for important errors in judgment and decision making is a matter of continuing research and debate by cognitive psychologists (Hilton, 2002), but awareness of their potentially biasing influences has caused reexamination of decision-making processes in many fields, including medicine and economics (e.g., Handgraaf & Van Raaij, 2005; Kahneman & Shane, 2005; Slovic et al., 2005).

Indeed, psychological research on how these biases affect people's purchasing patterns and other financial decisions has proved so important that Daniel Kahneman, a psychologist, received the 2002 Nobel Prize in economics for his work in this area. Kahneman and his colleague, Amos Tversky (Tversky & Kahneman 1974, 1993), described three potentially problematic heuristics that people seem to use intuitively in making judgments: the *anchoring heuristic,* the *representativeness heuristic,* and the *availability heuristic.*

The Anchoring Heuristic   What are the chances that you will be mugged while visiting a big city? If you estimate the probability at, say, 50 percent and then learn that the actual figure is closer to 1 percent, you would probably revise your estimate downward, but perhaps only to about 40 percent. Why would your estimate remain so inaccurate? The reason is that people tend to use the **anchoring heuristic** (also known as **anchoring bias**), which means that they estimate the probability of an event not by starting from scratch but by adjusting an earlier estimate (Rottenstreich & Tversky, 1997). This strategy sounds reasonable, but even when new information suggests that their first estimate is way off, people may not adjust that estimate enough. It is as if they have dropped a "mental anchor" that keeps them from moving very far from their original judgment. The anchoring heuristic presents a challenge for defense attorneys in U.S. courtrooms because once a jury has been affected by the

heuristic   A time-saving mental shortcut used in reasoning.

anchoring heuristic (anchoring bias)   A mental shortcut that involves basing judgments on existing information.

prosecution's evidence (which is presented first), it may be difficult to alter jurors' belief in a criminal defendant's guilt or in the amount of money the defendant in a civil case should have to pay (Greene & Loftus, 1998; Hogarth & Einhorn, 1992). In much the same way, our first impressions of people are not easily shifted by later evidence (see the chapter on social cognition).

The Representativeness Heuristic

Using the **representativeness heuristic**, people decide whether an example belongs in a certain class on the basis of how similar it is to other items in that class. This can be a sensible way to make decisions, but people sometimes use this heuristic even when there is better information available. Suppose that you were shown a folder containing thirty personality sketches and were told that twenty-five of them described humanities majors and five described computer science majors. Your task is to draw one at random and guess that person's major. Here's the one you choose (read it and then make your guess):

> Tom W. is of high intelligence, although lacking in true creativity. He has a need for order and clarity and for neat and tidy systems in which every detail finds its appropriate place. His writing is rather dull and mechanical, occasionally enlivened by somewhat corny puns and flashes of imagination of the sci-fi type. He has a strong drive for competence. He seems to have little feel and little sympathy for other people and does not enjoy interacting with others. Self-centered, he nonetheless has a deep moral sense.

Knowing that there are five times as many humanities sketches as computer science sketches should guide your guess about Tom's major. After all, if you had been told that there were twenty-five red and five blue jelly beans in a jar, you would probably use that information to guess that the one you drew at random would be red. Research shows, however, that most people ignore the odds in the personality sketch situation. They guess that Tom is a computer science major simply because he seems more representative of that category than of the other one (Tversky & Kahneman, 1974). The odds are against them though, so they will probably be wrong.

The impact of the representativeness heuristic can be seen in many real-life judgments and decisions. For example, when jurors hear technical or scientific evidence presented by an expert witness, they are supposed to consider only the validity of the evidence itself, not the characteristics of the person presenting it. However, they are more likely to be persuaded by the evidence if the witness looks and acts in ways that are representative of the "expert" category (McAuliff, Kovera, & Nuñez, 2008). (See the chapter on social influence for more on the role of communicator characteristics in persuasion.)

The Availability Heuristic

A third source of biased thinking is the **availability heuristic**, which involves judging the likelihood of an event or the correctness of a hypothesis on the basis of how easily the hypothesis or event comes to mind (Tversky & Kahneman, 1974). In other words, people tend to choose the hypothesis or predict the event that is most mentally "available" to them, much as they might select the box of cereal that happens to be at the front of the supermarket shelf.

Like other heuristics, this shortcut often works well. After all, frequent events or likely hypotheses are easy to remember. However, the availability heuristic can lead to biased judgments, especially when the mental availability of events does not reflect their true frequency (Morewedge, Gilbert, & Wilson, 2005). For example, news reports about shark attacks and plane crashes lead many people to overestimate how often these memorable but relatively rare events actually occur (Ungemach, Chater, & Stewart, 2009). As a result, these people may suffer undue anxiety over swimming in the ocean or traveling by air (Bellaby, 2003). Similarly, many students stick with their first responses on multiple-choice test questions because it is especially easy to recall those galling occasions when they changed a right answer to a wrong one. Research shows, though, that an answer changed after further reflection is more likely to be correct than incorrect (Kruger, Wirtz, & Miller, 2005).

Anchoring to a Price

The anchoring heuristic operates in many bargaining situations. The asking price of this house, for example, has probably anchored the sellers' perception of its value. As a result, they may be reluctant to accept a lower price, even if their sales agent suggests that in a sluggish real estate market, they should. The buyers' judgment of the house's value will also be anchored to some extent by the seller's asking price. Even if the buyers discover that the house needs some repairs, they are more likely to offer 90 percent of the price rather than 50 percent.

representativeness heuristic A mental shortcut that involves judging whether something belongs in a given class on the basis of its similarity to other members of that class.

availability heuristic A mental shortcut in which judgments are based on information that is most easily brought to mind.

A Memorable Outcome

The availability heuristic can have a strong impact on people's judgments about the chances of winning a lottery. Splashy media coverage makes it far easier to recall the few people who have won big prizes than the millions whose tickets turned out to be worthless.

The heuristics we have discussed represent only three of the many mental short-cuts that people use more or less automatically in making everyday judgments, and they touch on only some of the biases and limitations that affect human reasoning. Indeed, research on human thinking has confirmed the ancient idea that we sometimes depend on careful deliberation and sometimes on intuition. Psychologists have formalized this idea in *dual process theories* (Kahneman & Shane, 2005; Reyna & Farley, 2006; Stanovich & West, 2002), which suggest that the quicker, easier intuitive system tends to take over in complex situations or when background knowledge suggests what the right conclusion should be. The effort required for careful, rational thinking is worthwhile, though, because intuition has its limits, especially when it is based on potentially biasing heuristics that can lead us astray (Kahneman & Klein, 2009; Myers, 2004). We'll encounter other biases and limitations as we consider two important goals of thinking: problem solving and decision making.

Problem Solving

Suppose that you're lost, you don't have a map or a navigation system, and there's nobody around to ask for directions. You have a *problem*. As suggested by the circle of thought, the most efficient approach to problem solving would be first to diagnose the problem in the elaboration stage, then to come up with a plan for solving it, then to execute the plan, and finally to evaluate the results to determine whether the problem remains (Bransford & Stein, 1993). But people's problem-solving efforts are not always so systematic, which is one reason that medical tests are sometimes given unnecessarily, diseases are sometimes misdiagnosed, and auto parts are sometimes replaced when there is nothing wrong with them.

Strategies for Problem Solving

When you are trying to get from one place to another, the best path may not necessarily be a straight line. In fact, obstacles may force you to go in the opposite direction temporarily. So it is with problem solving. Sometimes the best strategy is not to take mental steps aimed straight at your goal. For example, when a problem is especially difficult, it can sometimes be helpful to allow it to "incubate" by setting it aside for a

Simply knowing about problem-solving strategies, such as means-end analysis, is not enough. As described in the chapter on motivation and emotion, people must see that the benefits of solving the problem are worth the effort required.

Calvin and Hobbes   by Bill Watterson

while. A solution that once seemed out of reach may suddenly appear after you think about other things for a while. The benefit of incubation probably arises from forgetting incorrect ideas that may have been blocking the path to a correct solution (Anderson, 2000). Incubation alone may not be enough to solve life's problems, though, so people often use other more direct problem-solving strategies, such as means-ends analysis, working backward, and finding analogies.

Means-End Analysis   To use *means-end analysis,* you continually check on where you are in relation to your final goal and then decide on the means by which you can get one step closer to it (Newell & Simon, 1972). In other words, rather than trying to solve the problem all at once, you identify a subgoal that will take you toward a solution (this process is referred to as *decomposition*). After reaching that subgoal, you identify another one that will get you even closer to the solution, and you continue this step-by-step process until the problem is solved. Some students apply this approach to the problem of writing a major term paper. The task may seem overwhelming at first, but their first subgoal is simply to write an outline of what they think the paper should cover. When the outline is complete, they decide whether a paper based on it will satisfy the assignment. If so, the next subgoal might be to search the library and the Internet for information about each section. If they decide that this information is adequate, the next subgoal would be to write a rough draft of the introduction, and so on.

Working Backward   A second strategy in problem solving, called *working backward*, is based on the notion that many problems are like a tree: The trunk is the information you are given, and the solution is a twig on one of the limbs. If you work forward by taking the givens of the problem and try to find the solution, it is easy to branch off in the wrong direction. A more efficient approach might be to start at the twig end and work backward toward your goal (Galotti, 1999). Consider, for example, the problem of deciding when to leave home in order to meet someone at the airport at 6:00 P.M. on a day when you also have to return a book to the library and visit a friend in the hospital. The best strategy is to figure out, first, how long it will take to get to the meeting point from the airport parking lot. Next, you have to decide how long it will take to find a parking place in the lot, then how long it will take to get to the airport from the hospital, how long you will be at the hospital, how long it will take to get to the hospital from the library, the time required to return the book, and how long it will take to get from home to the library. If the total of these time estimates is, say, three hours, you know you should leave home no later than 3:00 P.M. It is easy to overlook the working-backward strategy because it runs counter to the way most of us have learned to think. It is hard to imagine that the first step in solving a problem could be to assume that you have already solved it.

Working Backward to Forge Ahead

Whether you are organizing a family vacation or, as 16-year-old Jessica Watson did in 2010, sailing around the world alone and unassisted, working backward from the final goal through all the steps necessary to reach that goal is a helpful approach to solving complex problems.

Using Analogies   A third problem-solving strategy is trying to find *analogies,* or similarities between a problem you are facing today and others you have encountered before. An office manager may find, for example, that a seemingly hopeless conflict between employees can be resolved using the same compromise that worked during a recent family squabble. To take advantage of analogies, we must first recognize the similarities between current and previous problems and then recall the solution that worked before. Most people are surprisingly poor at recognizing such similarities (Anderson, 2000). They tend to concentrate on the surface features that make problems appear different.

FOCUS ON **RESEARCH METHODS**

Locating Analogical Thinking

The value of using analogies in problem solving was beautifully illustrated after the Hubble Space Telescope was placed in orbit around the earth in 1990. It was designed to take detailed photographs of distant galaxies, but because its main mirror was not focusing light properly, the pictures were blurry. Then NASA engineer James Crocker happened to notice the way a hotel bathroom's showerhead pivoted, and it gave him the idea for a system of movable mirrors to correct for the flaw in the Hubble's mirror. When shuttle astronauts installed these mirrors in 1993, the problem was solved (Stein, 1993).

What was the researchers' question?

Charles Wharton and his colleagues (2000) wanted to know what goes on in the brain when people do this kind of *analogical mapping*—recognizing similarities between things that appear to be different and even unrelated.

How did the researchers answer the question?

The researchers knew that PET scan technology could show brain activity while participants performed an analogy task, but how could the activity associated with analogical mapping be separated from everything else going on in the brain at the same time? The answer was to use a *subtraction technique*. They asked people to perform two tasks—one after the other—that involved making comparisons between pairs of stimulus patterns. Both tasks placed similar demands on the brain, but only one of them required the participants to *make analogies* between the patterns (see Figure 8.10). The researchers then compared the resulting PET scans, looking for areas of the brain that were active in the analogy task but not in the other one. What their computers did, in essence, was to take all the brain activity that occurred during the analogy task and "subtract" from it all the activity that occurred during the other task. The activity remaining was presumed to reflect analogical mapping.

What did the researchers find?

As you can see in Figure 8.11, the brain areas activated only during the analogy task were in the left hemisphere, particularly in the frontal and parietal areas. Other neuroimaging studies have shown activation of similar areas during abstract problem solving, reasoning, and making simple ethical judgments (e.g., Heekeren et al., 2003; Osherson et al., 1998).

What do the results mean?

These results show that it is possible to locate specific brain activities associated with a specific kind of cognitive activity. They also fit well into what we already know about where certain brain functions are localized. As mentioned earlier, the frontal areas of the brain are involved in complex processing tasks, including those requiring coordination of information in working memory with information coming from the senses. There is also evidence that parietal areas are involved in our ability to perceive the arrangements of objects and relationships among them. Both of these regions were activated during the analogy task in this experiment, suggesting that this task required both kinds of abilities.

What do we still need to know?

There is no doubt that Wharton and his colleagues devised a clever way to examine the analogical-mapping process as it occurs in the human brain, but are the brain areas identified the only ones involved in analogies? Would the same results appear

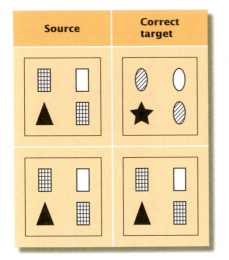

FIGURE 8.10
Comparing Stimulus Patterns
The top row shows an example of the stimulus patterns that were compared in an analogy task. Participants had to say whether the pattern on the right is similar, or *analogous,* to the one on the left. (In this case it is, because even though the specific shapes used in one pattern differ from those in the other pattern, their shading and physical arrangement are similar.) The bottom row shows an example of the patterns that were compared in a "same-different" task. Here participants were asked only to decide whether the two patterns are *exactly the same* (Wharton et al., 2000).

From C.M. Wharton et al. "Toward Neuroanatomical Models of Analogy: A Positron Emission Tomography Study of Analogical Mapping" *Cognitive Psychology Journal*, Vol. 40, pg. 179. Copyright © 2000. Reprinted by permission of Elsevier.

FIGURE 8.11
Brain Activity During Analogical Mapping

Comparing PET scans of brain activity during an analogy task and a task not requiring analogical thinking revealed that making analogies appears to involve areas of the left frontal and parietal lobes, as seen here from below and highlighted in red.

Source: Wharton et al. (2000).

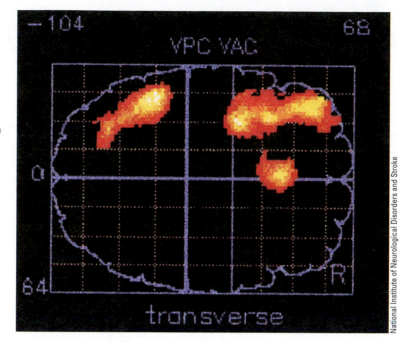

National Institute of Neurological Disorders and Stroke

if the analogy task had been verbal instead of visual, requiring participants to make analogies such as "Dark is to light as cold is to ___"? A more recent study suggests that the answer is yes (Bunge et al., 2005), though more research will be needed to confirm this.

Consider also that even though the analogy task used in Wharton's study involved processing visual-spatial information (shape, shading, and location) rather than verbal information (words), the PET scans showed activation only on the left side of the brain. This is surprising because, as mentioned in the chapter on biological aspects of psychology, visual-spatial processing is usually handled mainly in the brain's right hemisphere. These results remind us that, as also mentioned in that chapter, the left hemisphere may predominate in verbal tasks and the right in spatial tasks, but both hemispheres are involved to some extent in virtually all complex cognitive activity.

Remember, too, that we have to be careful when interpreting the brain activity detected in neuroimaging studies. Increased activity in a particular brain region doesn't always mean that the region is performing the processing we are trying to locate. As discussed in the Thinking Critically section of the biological aspects of behavior chapter, the study of brain activity during higher-level thinking is still quite new, so it will take some time, and a lot more research, to learn how to interpret the data coming from neuroimaging techniques (Buxton et al., 2004; Gonsalves et al., 2005).

Obstacles to Problem Solving

Failing to use analogies is just one example of the obstacles that problem solvers encounter every day. Difficulties frequently occur at the beginning, during the diagnosis stage, when a person forms and then tests hypotheses about a problem.

As a case in point, consider this true story: John Gatiss was in the kitchen of his rented house in Cheltenham, England, when he heard a faint meowing sound. He couldn't find the source of the sound, but he assumed that a kitten was trapped in the walls or under the flooring, so he called for the fire brigade to rescue the animal. The sound seemed to be coming from the electric stove, so the rescuers dismantled it, disconnecting the power cord in the process. The sound stopped, but everyone assumed that wherever the kitten was, it had become too frightened to meow. The search was reluctantly abandoned, and the stove was reconnected. Four days later, the meowing began again. This time, Gatiss and his landlord called the

Royal Society for the Prevention of Cruelty to Animals (RSPCA), whose inspectors heard the kitten in distress and asked the fire brigade to return. They spent the next three days searching for the cat. First, they tore down parts of the kitchen walls and ripped up the floorboards. Next, they called in plumbing and drainage specialists, who used cables tipped with fiber-optic cameras to search remote cavities where a kitten might hide. Rescuers then brought in members of a disaster search team, who tried to find the kitten using acoustic and ultrasonic equipment designed to locate victims trapped in the debris of earthquakes and explosions. Not a sound could be heard. Increasingly concerned about how much longer the kitten could survive, the fire brigade tried to coax it from hiding with the finest-quality fish, to no avail. Suddenly, there was a burst of "purring," which to everyone's surprise (and the landlord's dismay), the ultrasonic equipment traced to the clock in the control panel of the electric stove! Later, the landlord commented that everyone had assumed that Gatiss's hypothesis was correct—that the meowing sound came from a cat trapped somewhere in the kitchen. "I just let them carry on. If there is an animal in there, you have to do what it takes. The funniest thing was that it seemed to reply when we called out to it" ("'Cat,'" 1998).

How could fifteen fire rescue workers, three RSPCA inspectors, four drainage workers, and two acoustics experts waste eight days and cause nearly $2,000 in damage to a house in pursuit of a nonexistent kitten? The answer lies in the fact that they, like the rest of us, are prone to four main obstacles to efficient problem solving, described in the following sections.

Multiple Hypotheses   Often people begin to solve a problem with only a vague notion of which hypotheses to test. Suppose that you heard a strange sound in your kitchen. It could be caused by several things, but which hypotheses should you test, and in what order?

People have a difficult time considering more than two or three hypotheses at a time. The limited capacity of short-term memory may be part of the reason (Halford et al., 2005). As discussed in the chapter on memory, we can hold only about seven chunks of information in short-term memory at the same time. A single hypothesis, let alone two or three, might include many more than seven chunks, so it might be difficult or impossible to keep them all in mind at once. Further, the availability and representativeness heuristics may lead people to choose the hypothesis that comes most easily to mind and seems most likely to fit the circumstances (Tversky & Kahneman, 1974). That hypothesis may be wrong, though, meaning that the correct hypothesis might never be considered (Bilalić, McLeod, & Gobet, 2010). Mr. Gatiss diagnosed the noise he heard as distressed meowing because it sounded more like a kitten than a clock and because it was easier to imagine an animal trapped behind the stove than a suddenly faulty clock mechanism.

Mental Sets   Sometimes people are so blinded by one hypothesis or strategy that they continue to apply it even when better alternatives should be obvious (a clear case of the anchoring heuristic at work). Once Gatiss reported hearing a "trapped kitten," his description created an assumption that everyone else accepted and no one challenged. A laboratory example of this phenomenon devised by Abraham Luchins (1942) is shown in Figure 8.12. In each problem shown in the figure, the task is to use three jars of varying sizes to end up with a certain amount of water. For example, in the first problem, you are to obtain 21 quarts by using three jars that can hold 8, 35, and 3 quarts, respectively. Before reading any further, try to solve this problem and all the others listed in Figure 8.12.

TRY THIS

How did you do? You probably figured out that the solution to the first problem is to fill jar B to its capacity, 35 quarts, and then use its contents to fill jar A to its capacity of 8 quarts, leaving 27 quarts in jar B. Then pour liquid from jar B to fill jar C to its capacity twice, leaving 21 quarts in jar B [$27 - (2 \times 3) = 21$]. You probably also found that a general solution formula ($B - A - 2C$), worked for every problem. But did you notice anything unusual about Problem 7? By the time you reached that one, you had

FIGURE 8.12
The Luchins Jar Problem

TRY THIS In this problem-solving task, you are trying to end up with the number of quarts of water shown in the first column by filling jars with the capacities shown in the next three columns. Each row represents a different problem, and you have an unlimited supply of water. Try to solve all seven problems without looking at the answers in the text. In dealing with such problems, people often fall prey to mental sets that prevent them from using the most efficient solution. After solving all the problems shown here, read on to see if your performance, too, was affected by a mental set.

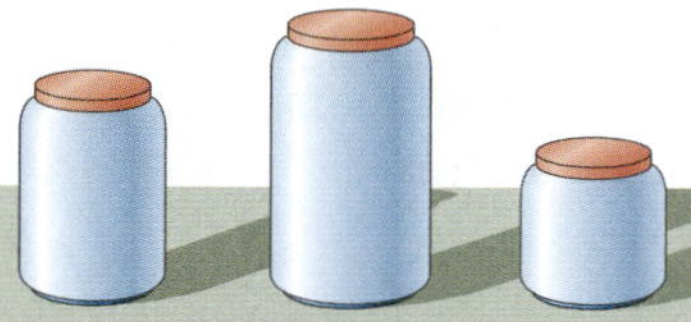

Quantity	Jar A	Jar B	Jar C
1. 21 quarts	8	35	3
2. 10 quarts	6	18	1
3. 19 quarts	5	32	4
4. 21 quarts	20	57	8
5. 18 quarts	8	40	7
6. 6 quarts	7	17	2
7. 15 quarts	12	33	3

probably developed a **mental set**, a tendency for old patterns of problem solving to persist (Sweller & Gee, 1978). That mental set may have caused you to use the general solution formula ($B - A - 2C$) for problem 7 even though a simpler one ($A + C$) would have worked just as well. Figures 8.13 and 8.15 show that a mental set can also restrict your perception of the problem itself.

A related restriction on problem solving may come from our experience with objects. Once people are accustomed to using an object for one purpose, they may be blinded to its other possible functions. Experience may produce **functional fixedness**, a tendency to use familiar objects in familiar rather than creative ways (German & Barrett, 2005). Figure 8.14 illustrates an example. An incubation strategy often helps break mental sets.

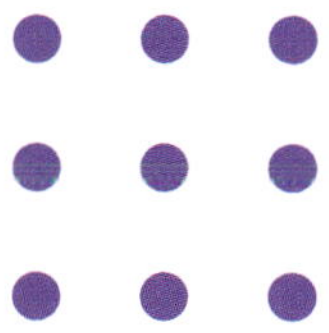

Ignoring Negative Evidence   On September 26, 1983, Lieutenant Colonel Stanislav Petrov was in command of a secret facility that analyzed information from Russian early-warning satellites. Suddenly, alarms went off as computers found evidence of five U.S. missiles being launched toward Russia. Tension between the two countries was high at the time, so the availability heuristic led Petrov to hypothesize that a nuclear attack was under way. He was about to alert his superiors to launch a counterattack on the United States when it occurred to him that if this were a real nuclear attack, it would involve many more than five missiles. Fortunately for everyone, he realized that the "attack" was a false alarm (Hoffman, 1999). As this near-disaster shows, signs, symptoms, or events that do *not* appear can provide important evidence for or against a hypothesis. Compared with evidence that is present, however, the absence of evidence is less likely to be noticed (Hunt & Rouse, 1981). As a result, people have a hard time using missing evidence to help eliminate hypotheses from consideration (Hyman, 2002). If there had really been a kitten trapped in John Gatiss's kitchen, its "meowing" should have been almost continuous, but when the sounds were suddenly absent, rescuers assumed that the animal had been frightened into silence. They ignored the possibility that their cat hypothesis was incorrect in the first place.

Confirmation Bias   Anyone who has had a series of medical tests knows that diagnosis is not a one-shot decision. Instead, physicians choose their first hypothesis on the basis of observed symptoms and then order tests or evaluate additional symptoms to confirm or reject that hypothesis (Trillin, 2001). This process can be distorted by the *confirmation bias* mentioned earlier: Humans have a strong bias to confirm rather than to reject the hypothesis they have chosen, even in the face of strong evidence against it (Aronson, Wilson, & Akert, 2010; Groopman, 2007). Confirmation bias can be seen as a form of the anchoring heuristic, in that it involves "anchoring" to an initial hypothesis and being unwilling to abandon it. The would-be rescuers of the "trapped

FIGURE 8.13
The Nine-Dot Problem

TRY THIS The problem is to draw no more than four straight lines that run through all nine dots on the page without lifting your pen from the paper. Can you figure out how to do it? Compare your solution to Figure 8.15, which shows two ways of going beyond mental sets to solve this problem.

mental set The tendency for old patterns of problem solving to persist, even when they might not be the best ones available.

functional fixedness A tendency to think about familiar objects in familiar ways that may prevent using them in other ways.

FIGURE 8.14

An Example of Functional Fixedness

TRY THIS Before reading the next sentence, look at this drawing and see if you can figure out how to tie together two strings that are hanging from the ceiling but are out of reach of each other. Several tools are available, yet most people do not think of attaching, say, the pliers to one string and swinging it like a pendulum until it can be reached while holding the other string. This solution is not obvious because we tend to fixate on the function of pliers as a tool rather than as a weight. People are more likely to solve this problem if the tools are scattered around the room. When the pliers are in a tool box, their function as a tool is emphasized, and functional fixedness becomes nearly impossible to break.

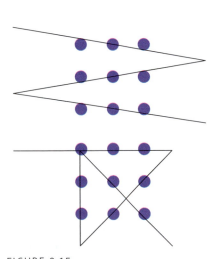

FIGURE 8.15

Two Creative Solutions to the Nine-Dot Problem

Many people find puzzles such as this difficult because their mental sets create artificial limits on the range of possible solutions. In this case, the mental sets involve the tendency to draw within the frame of the dots and to draw through the middle of each dot. As shown here, however, there are other possibilities.

kitten" were so intent on their efforts to locate it that they never stopped to question its existence. Similarly, as described in the chapter on social cognition, when evaluating other people's behavior or abilities, we tend to look for and pay extra attention to information that is consistent with any prior beliefs we have about them. This tendency can create positive or negative bias in, say, a teacher's impressions of a child's mental abilities or an interviewer's impressions of a job candidate's skills. Confirmation bias can also serve to perpetuate and intensify differences of opinion. People tend to get their news from media outlets that support their own political views, and during discussions with individuals who hold differing views, they pay more attention to areas of discord than to areas of agreement (Wojcieszak & Price, 2010). With this phenomenon in mind, some psychologists have developed programs designed to reduce the confirmation bias that can impair communication on "hot button" issues (Lilienfeld, Ammirati, & Landfield, 2009).

Building Problem-Solving Skills

How do experts in any field avoid some of the obstacles that normally limit problem solving? What do they bring to a situation that a beginner does not? Knowledge based on experience is particularly important (Mayer, 1992). Using that knowledge, experts frequently proceed by looking for similarities or analogies between current and past problems. Their experience makes experts better than beginners at identifying the common principles that underlie seemingly different problems. Experts' superior ability to link information about a new problem to what they already know (Anderson, 1995) also allows them to organize information about a problem into manageable and memorable units called *chunks,* a process described in the chapter on memory. By chunking many elements of a problem into a smaller number of units, experts are better than beginners at visualizing problems clearly and efficiently (Reingold et al., 2001).

It is no wonder, then, that experts are often better problem solvers than beginners, but their expertise also carries a danger: Extensive experience may create mental sets. Top-down, knowledge-driven processes can bias experts toward seeing what they expect or want to see and prevent them from seeing a problem in new ways (Groopman, 2007). As in the case of the "trapped kitten," confirmation bias sometimes prevents experts from appreciating that a proposed solution is incorrect. Several

TABLE 8.1   Some Expert Opinions

Experts typically have a large store of knowledge about their area of expertise, but even confidently stated opinions based on this knowledge can turn out to be wrong. In 1768, one expert critic called William Shakespeare's now-revered play *Hamlet* "the work of a drunken savage" (Henderson & Bernard, 1998). Here are some equally incorrect expert pronouncements from *The Experts Speak* (Cerf & Navasky, 1998).

On the possibility of painless surgery through anesthesia:

"'Knife' and 'pain' are two words in surgery that must forever be associated. . . . To this compulsory combination we shall have to adjust ourselves." (Dr. Alfred Velpeau, professor of surgery, Paris Faculty of Medicine, 1839)

On the hazards of cigarette smoking:

"If excessive smoking actually plays a role in the production of lung cancer, it seems to be a minor one." (Dr. W. C. Heuper, National Cancer Institute, 1954)

On the stock market (one week before the disastrous 1929 crash that wiped out over $50 billion in investments):

"Stocks have reached what looks like a permanently high plateau." (Irving Fisher, professor of economics, Yale University, 1929)

On the prospects of war with Japan (three years before the December 1941 Japanese attack on Pearl Harbor):

"A Japanese attack on Pearl Harbor is a strategic impossibility." (Major George F. Eliot, military science writer, 1938)

On the value of personal computers:

"There is no reason for any individual to have a computer in their home." (Ken Olson, president, Digital Equipment Corporation, 1977)

On the concept of the airplane:

"Heavier-than-air flying machines are impossible." (Lord Kelvin, mathematician, physicist, and president of the British Royal Society, 1895)

studies have shown that although experts may be more confident in their solutions (Payne, Bettman, & Johnson, 1992), they are not always more accurate than others in such areas as medical diagnosis, accounting, pilot judgment, and predicting political events (Tetlock, 2006; Wickens et al., 1992).

In other words, there is a fine line between using past experience and being trapped by it. Experience alone does not ensure excellence at problem solving, and practice may not make perfect (see Table 8.1). (For a summary of our discussion of human problem solving, see "In Review: Solving Problems.")

IN REVIEW   Solving Problems

Steps	Pitfalls	Remedies
Define the problem	Inexperience: the tendency to see each problem as unique.	Gain experience and practice in seeing the similarity between present problems and previous ones.
Form hypotheses about solutions	Availability heuristic: the tendency to recall the hypothesis or solution that is most available to memory.	Force yourself to entertain different hypotheses.
	Anchoring heuristic or mental set: the tendency to anchor on the first solution or hypothesis that comes to mind and not adjust your beliefs in light of new evidence or failures of the current approach.	Break the mental set, stop, and try a fresh approach.
Test hypotheses	The tendency to ignore negative evidence.	Ask how well each hypothesis can explain what is happening and also what is *not* happening.
	Confirmation bias: the tendency to seek only evidence that confirms your hypothesis.	Look for disconfirming evidence that, if found, would show your hypothesis to be false.

1. People stranded without water could use their shoes to collect rain, but they might not do so because of an obstacle to problem solving called _____.

2. Because of the _____ heuristic, once sellers set a value on their house, they may refuse to take much less for it.

3. If you tackle a massive problem one small step at a time, you are using an approach called _____.

Artificial Intelligence

Chess master Garry Kasparov had his hands full when he was challenged by Deep Blue, a chess-playing computer that was programmed so well that it has won games against the world's best competitors, including Kasparov. Still, even the most sophisticated computers cannot perceive and think about the world in general anywhere near as well as humans can. Some observers believe that this situation will eventually change as progress in computer technology—and a deepening understanding of human cognitive processes—leads to dramatic breakthroughs in artificial intelligence.

© Barbara L. Johnston/Reuters

Problem Solving by Computer

Medical and scientific researchers have created artificial limbs, retinas, cochleas, and even hearts to help people with disabilities move, see, hear, and live more normally. They are developing artificial brains, too, in the form of computer systems that not only see, hear, and manipulate objects but also reason and solve problems. These systems are the product of research in **artificial intelligence (AI)**, a field focused on creating computers that imitate the processes of human perception and thought (O'Reilly, 2006). For problems such as those involved in making complex business decisions and medical diagnoses, for example, computerized *expert systems* can already perform as well as humans and sometimes even better (e.g., Khan et al., 2001; Workman, 2005).

Symbolic Reasoning and Computer Logic   An IBM computer known as Deep Blue has won chess games against the world's best chess masters. This result is not surprising, because chess is a clearly defined, logical game at which computers can perform effectively. However, it is precisely their reliance on logic and formulas that accounts for the shortcomings of today's artificial intelligence systems. For one thing, expert systems are successful only in narrowly defined fields. And even within a specific domain, computers show limited ability. It has so far been impossible to put into computer code all aspects of expert human reasoning, partly because the experts themselves cannot always describe their reasoning in words. Sometimes they can only say, "I know it when I see it." Second, the vital ability to draw analogies and make other connections among seemingly unrelated knowledge domains is still beyond the grasp of expert systems, mainly because the system designers seldom know ahead of time which knowledge domains the computer might need to reach a solution. In other words, humans can't always tell computers where to look for new ideas or how to use them. Finally, logic-based AI systems depend on "if-then" rules, and it is often difficult to tell a computer how to recognize the "if" condition in the real world (Dreyfus & Dreyfus, 1988). Consider just one example: *If it's a clock, then set it.* Humans can recognize all kinds of clocks because they have the natural concept of "clock," but computers perform this task very poorly. As discussed earlier, forming natural concepts requires putting into the same category many examples that may have very different physical features—from a bedside digital alarm clock to London's Big Ben. The fact that computers cannot yet do this allows online businesses to protect themselves from potentially dangerous computer programs that pose as human customers. So when ordering something online, you may be shown a set of distorted, odd-looking letters

artificial intelligence (AI)   The field that studies how to program computers to imitate the products of human perception, understanding, and thought.

and numbers and then asked to type them into a box. By doing so, you are proving that you are a human being and not a computer.

Neural Network Models   Teaching computers to form natural concepts has proved so difficult that many researchers in AI have shifted to the *connectionist,* or *neural network,* approach discussed in other chapters. This approach simulates the information processing taking place at many different but interconnected locations in the brain. It is very effective for modeling many aspects of perceptual recognition. It has contributed to the development of computers that are able to perform many complex tasks such as recognizing voices, understanding speech, reading printed material, and guiding missiles (Ashcraft, 2006). Other connectionist programs have been shown superior to human decision making in areas ranging from judging meat quality and running credit checks to detecting credit card fraud and predicting the recurrence of cancer (McNelis, 2004; Rabunal & Dorado, 2006). Google and other "intelligent" Internet search engines are also based on neural network models.

The capacities of neural-network–based computer systems still fall well short of those of the human perceptual system, however. For example, computers are slow to learn how to classify visual patterns, which has impaired the development of computerized face recognition systems capable of identifying terrorists and criminals in public places. Computers may also fail to show sudden insight when a key common feature is identified. But even though neural networks are still far from perfect "thinking machines," progress in artificial intelligence is accelerating and is sure to play an important role in psychologists' efforts to build ever more intelligent systems and to better understand the principles of human problem solving (Schapiro & McClelland, 2009).

Computer-Assisted Problem Solving   One approach to maximizing the quality of problem solving and decision making by both computers and humans is to have them work together in ways that create a better outcome than either could achieve alone (e.g., Khan et al., 2001; Workman, 2005). In medical diagnosis, for example, the human's role is to establish the presence and nature of a patient's symptoms. The computer then combines this information in a completely unbiased way to identify the most likely diagnosis (Roy et al., 2009; Swets, Dawes, & Monahan, 2000). Similarly, laboratory technologists who examine blood samples for the causes of disease are assisted by computer programs that serve to reduce errors and memory lapses by keeping track of the findings from previous tests, listing possible tests that remain to be tried, and indicating either that certain tests have been left undone or that a new sequence of tests should be done. This kind of human-machine teamwork can also help in the assessment of psychological problems (Kramer, Bernstein, & Phares, 2009).

Decision Making

"Laura McBride," the medical patient described at the beginning of this chapter, faced a simple decision: risk death by doing nothing or take steps to protect herself from lead poisoning. Most decisions are not so easy. Patients must decide whether to undergo a dangerous operation; a college graduate must choose a career; a corporate executive must decide whether to shut down a factory. Unlike the high-speed decisions discussed earlier, these decisions require considerable time, planning, and mental effort.

Even carefully considered decisions sometimes lead to undesirable outcomes, however, because the world is an uncertain place. Decisions made when the outcome is uncertain are called *risky decisions* or *decisions under uncertainty.* Let's consider what psychologists have discovered about why human decisions sometimes lead to unsatisfactory outcomes.

Evaluating Options

Suppose that you have to choose between an academic major you love but that is unlikely to lead to a good job and a boring major that virtually guarantees a high-paying job. The fact that each option has positive and negative features, or *attributes,* greatly complicates decision making. Deciding which car to buy, which college to attend, or even how to spend the evening are all examples of *multiattribute decision making* (Edwards, 1977). Often these decisions are further complicated by difficulties in comparing the attributes and in estimating the probabilities of various outcomes.

Comparing Attributes

Part of the difficulty in making multiattribute decisions lies in the limited capacity of short-term memory. Sometimes we simply can't keep in mind all of the attributes of all of our options long enough to compare them. Instead, we tend to focus on the one attribute that is most important to us. If, for instance, finishing a degree quickly is most important to you, you might choose courses based mainly on graduation requirements, without giving much consideration to professors' reputations. (Listing the pros and cons of each option offers a helpful way of keeping them all in mind as you think about decisions.)

Furthermore, when making most important decisions, it may be impossible to compare the attributes of our options in terms of money or other objective criteria. In other words, we are often forced to compare "apples and oranges." Psychologists use the term **utility** to describe the subjective value that each attribute holds for each of us. In deciding on a major, for example, you have to think about the positive and negative utilities of each attribute—such as the job prospects and interest level—of each major. Then you must somehow weigh and combine these utilities. Will the positive utility of enjoying your courses be higher than the negative utility of risking unemployment?

Estimating Probabilities   Uncertainty further complicates the decision-making process: To make a good decision, you should take into account not only the attributes of each option but also the probabilities and risks of their possible outcomes. For example, the economy could change by the time you graduate, closing many of today's job opportunities in one of the majors you are considering and perhaps opening opportunities in another.

In studying risky decision making, psychologists begin by assuming that the best decision is the one that maximizes **expected value**, or the average benefit you could expect if the decision were repeated on several occasions. Suppose that some-one asks you to buy a charity raffle ticket. You know that it costs $2 to enter and that the probability of winning the $100 prize is one in ten (.10). Assuming that you are more interested in the prize money than in donating to the charity, should you enter the contest? The expected value of entering is determined by multiplying the probability of gain (.10) by the size of the gain ($100). The result is the average benefit you would receive if you entered the raffle many times. Next, from this product you subtract the probability of loss, which is 1.0 (the entry fee is a certain loss), multiplied by the amount of the loss ($2). That is, (.10 × $100) − (1.0 × $2) = $8. Because this $8 expected value is greater than the expected value of not entering (which is zero), you should enter. However, if the odds of winning the raffle were one in a hundred (.01), the expected value of entering would be (.01 × $100) − (1.0 × $2) = −$1. In this case, the expected value is negative, so you should not enter the raffle.

Biases and Flaws in Decision Making

Most people think of themselves as logical and rational, but in making decisions about everything from giving up smoking to investing in the stock market, they do not always act in ways that maximize expected value (Farmer, Patelli, & Zovko, 2005; Shiller, 2001). Why not?

utility   A subjective measure of value.

expected value   The total benefit to be expected if a decision were to be repeated several times.

Analyzing your choices and the possible outcomes of each takes some time and effort, but the results are usually worthwhile. Like Dilbert's boss, many people prefer to make decisions more impulsively, and although their decisions sometimes turn out well, they often don't (Gladwell, 2005; Myers, 2004).

Gains, Losses, and Probabilities   For one thing, positive utilities are not mirror images of negative utilities. Our pain over losing a certain amount is usually greater than the pleasure we feel after gaining the same amount (Kermer et al., 2006). This phenomenon is known as *loss aversion* (Dawes, 1998; Tversky & Kahneman, 1991). Because of loss aversion, you might go to more trouble to collect a $100 debt, for example, than to try to win a $100 prize.

It also appears that the utility of a specific gain depends not on how large the gain actually is but on what the starting point was. Suppose that you won a $10 gift certificate from a restaurant but you have to drive 10 miles to pick it up. This gain has the same monetary value as having an extra $10 added to your paycheck. However, most people tend to behave as if the difference in utility between $0 and $10 is much greater than the difference between, say, $300 and $310. So the person who turns down the chance to do an after-work errand across town for an extra $10 on payday might gladly make the same trip to pick up a $10 gift certificate. This tendency conforms to Weber's law of psychophysics, discussed in the chapter on perception. The subjective value of a certain amount of gain depends on how much you already have (Dawes, 1998); the more you have, the less that gain means.

People are also biased in how they perceive probability, and this bias may lead to less-than-optimal decisions. One kind of probability bias comes into play when making decisions about extremely likely or extremely unlikely events. In such cases, we tend to overestimate the probability of the unlikely events and to underestimate the probability of the likely ones (Kahneman & Tversky, 1984). This bias helps explain why people gamble and enter lotteries, even though the odds are against them and the

Bias in Perceiving Risk

Just after 9/11, the risks of flying seemed so high that many more people than usual traveled by car instead. But automobile travel is more dangerous overall than flying, so the decision to drive actually increased these people's risk of death. With more cars on the road, traffic fatalities in the last three months of 2001 were about 350 higher than usual (Gigerenzer, 2004). Similar bias in risk perception leads many people to buy big, heavy sport utility vehicles that make them feel safer, even though the risk of serious injury is actually greater in an SUV than it is in a minivan or family sedan (Gladwell, 2004). Their heightened sense of safety may even lead some SUV owners to drive less carefully (Thomas & Walton, 2007), which further increases the injury risk.

decision to do so has a negative expected value. According to the formula for expected value, buying a $1 lottery ticket when the probability of winning $4 million is 1 in 10 million yields an expected value of minus 60 cents. But because people overestimate the probability of winning, they believe there is a positive expected value. In one study, not even a course that highlighted gambling's mathematical disadvantages could change university students' gambling behavior (Williams & Connolly, 2006). The tendency to overestimate the likelihood of unlikely events is amplified by the availability heuristic: Vivid memories of rare gambling successes and the publicity given to lottery winners help people recall gains rather than losses when deciding about future gambles. Sometimes our bias in estimating probability costs more than money. For example, many people underestimate the risk of infection by HIV/AIDS and continue to engage in unprotected sex (Specter, 2005).

Another bias relating to probability is called the *gambler's fallacy:* People believe that future events in a random process will be affected by past events. This belief is false. For example, if you flip a coin and it comes up heads ten times in a row, the chance that it will come up heads on the eleventh try is still 50 percent. Some gamblers, however, will continue feeding a slot machine that hasn't paid off much for hours, assuming that it is "due." This assumption may be partly responsible for the persistence of gambling and other behaviors that are rewarded only now and then. We discuss this phenomenon, called the partial reinforcement effect, in the chapter on learning.

Poor decision making can also stem from people's tendency to be unrealistically confident in the accuracy of their predictions. Baruch Fischoff and Donald MacGregor (1982) found a clever way to study this bias. They asked research participants to make a prediction about an event—for example, whether a certain sports team would win— and to say how confident they were about the prediction. After the events took place, the accuracy of the forecasts was compared with the confidence people had expressed in those forecasts. Sure enough, the participants' confidence in their predictions was consistently greater than their accuracy. The moral of the story is to be wary when people express confidence that a forecast or decision is correct. They will be wrong more often than they think.

How Biased Are We?   Almost all of us make decisions we later regret, but these outcomes may not be due entirely to biased thinking about gains, losses, and probabilities. Some decisions are not intended to maximize expected value but rather to satisfy other criteria, such as minimizing expected loss, producing a quick and easy resolution, or preserving a moral principle (Galotti, 2007; McCaffery & Baron, 2006). For example, decisions may depend not just on how likely we are to gain or lose a certain amount of something but also on what that something is. So a decision that could cost or save a human life might be made differently than one that could cost or save a few dollars, even though the probabilities of each outcome are exactly the same in both cases.

Even the "goodness" or "badness" of decisions can be difficult to measure. Many of them depend on personal values (utilities), which can vary from person to person and from culture to culture. People in individualist cultures, for example, may tend to assign high utilities to attributes that promote personal goals, whereas people in collectivist cultures might place greater value on attributes that bring group harmony and the approval of family and friends (Markus, Kitayama, & Heiman, 1996).

LINKAGES

LINKAGES Do groups solve problems more effectively than individuals? (a link to Social Influence, p. 764)

Group Processes in Problem Solving and Decision Making

Problem solving and decision making often take place in groups. The processes that influence an individual's problem solving and decision making continue to operate when the individual is in a group, but group interactions also shape the outcome.

When groups are trying to make a decision, they usually begin by considering the preferences or opinions stated by various members. Not all of these views have equal influence, though. Views that are shared by the greatest number of group members will have the greatest impact on the group's final decision (Tindale & Kameda, 2000). This means that extreme proposals or opinions will usually have less effect on group decisions than those that are more representative of the majority's views.

Nevertheless, group discussions sometimes result in decisions that are more extreme than the group members would make individually. This tendency toward extreme decisions by groups is called *group polarization* (Baron, Branscombe, & Byrne, 2008), and it appears to result from two mechanisms. First, most arguments presented during the discussion favor the majority view. Most criticisms are directed at the minority view, and influenced by confirmation bias, group members tend to seek additional information that supports the majority position (Schulz-Hardt et al., 2000). In this atmosphere, it seems rational to those favoring the majority view to adopt an even stronger version of it (Kassin, Fein, & Markus, 2010). Second, once some group members begin to agree that a particular decision is desirable, other members may try to associate themselves with that decision, perhaps by suggesting an even more extreme version (Kassin, Fein, & Markus, 2010).

Are people better at problem solving and decision making when working in groups than on their own? This is one of the questions about human thought studied by social psychologists. In a typical experiment, a group of people is asked to solve a problem such as the one in Figure 8.13 or to make a decision about the guilt or innocence of a defendant in a fictional court case. Each person is asked to work alone and then to join with the others to try to agree on a decision. These studies have found that when problems have solutions that can be demonstrated easily to all members, groups will usually outperform individuals at solving them (Laughlin, 1999). When problems have less obvious solutions, groups may be somewhat better at solving them than their average member but usually no better than their most talented member (Hackman, 1998). And because of the phenomena of *social loafing* and *groupthink* (discussed in the chapter on social influence), people working in a group are often less productive than people working alone (Williams & Sommer, 1997).

Other research (e.g., Stasser, Stewart, & Wittenbaum, 1995) suggests that a critical element in successful group problem solving is the sharing of individual members' unique information and expertise. For example, when asked to diagnose an illness,

Groups Working at a Distance

Research on group problem solving and decision making now includes "electronic groups," whose members use teleconferencing and computer-mediated communication to work together from a distance. Research indicates that groups that meet via teleconferencing perform about as well as those meeting face-to-face and that over time, the levels of trust and patterns of communication that develop are about the same in both formats. However, other kinds of electronic communication, such as chat rooms, can impair group performance (Wilson, Straus, & McEvily, 2006).

© Jon Feingersh/zefa/Corbis

One disadvantage of brainstorming sessions is that running comments and bizarre ideas from some group members can interfere with the creative process in others (Nijstad, Stroebe, & Lodewijkx, 2003).

groups of physicians were much more accurate when they pooled their knowledge (Larson et al., 1998). However, *brainstorming,* a popular strategy that supposedly encourages group members to generate innovative solutions to a problem, may actually produce fewer ideas than are generated by individuals working alone (Baumeister & Bushman, 2008). This result may occur because the lively and freewheeling discussion associated with brainstorming can disrupt each member's ability to think clearly and productively (Nijstad, Stroebe, & Lodewijkx, 2003). Further, some participants in a brainstorming session may be reluctant to offer an idea, even a good one, for fear it will be rejected or ridiculed by the group (Kerr & Tindale, 2004). To prevent these problems, brainstorming groups today may be instructed to disagree with one another and to debate the quality of individual ideas. Others meet electronically, using a form of e-mail to present and comment on ideas. Participants in these meetings can offer their suggestions anonymously and without being interrupted yet still have access to the ideas of all the other members. Because this arrangement allows people to think more clearly and express even "oddball" ideas without fear, electronic brainstorming groups may actually outperform groups that meet face-to-face (Nijstad, Stroebe, & Lodewijkx, 2003).

As they work to solve a problem, the members of a group manipulate their own concepts, propositions, images, and other mental representations. How does each person share these private events to help the group perform its task? The answer lies in the use of language, which not only aids group decision making but is also a fundamental part of many other human activities. Let's consider what language is and how it develops.

Language

Many pet owners swear that their animals "talk" to them. Maybe Harry barks in a particular way when he wants to go outside, or Cleo meows to be fed. But are Harry's barks and Cleo's meows really language? Probably not. These pets are communicating something to their owners, but the noises they make lack many of the components of human language (Slocombe & Zuberbühler, 2005). So although Harry may let out three high-pitched yelps when he wants to go outside, he may bark in exactly the same way when asked whether he agrees with the local leash laws. For this reason, we wouldn't call his barking "language." Humans, however, can use language to express everything from simple requests to abstract principles. We can create stories that pass on cultural information and traditions from one generation to the next. Our language abilities are usually well integrated with our memory, thinking, and other cognitive abilities. As a result, we can speak about our thoughts and memories and think about what people tell us. It is only when strokes or other forms of damage interfere with the brain's language areas that we are reminded that language is a very special kind of cognitive ability (Kohnert, 2004).

The Elements of Language

A **language** has two basic elements: *symbols,* such as words, and *rules,* called **grammar,** for combining those symbols. With our knowledge of approximately 50,000 to 100,000 words (Miller, 1991), we humans can create and understand an infinite number of sentences. All of the sentences ever spoken are built from just a few dozen categories of sounds. The power of language comes from the way these rather unimpressive raw materials are organized according to certain rules. This organization occurs at several levels.

From Sounds to Sentences   Organization occurs first at the level of sounds. A **phoneme** is the smallest unit of sound that affects the meaning of speech. Changing a phoneme changes the meaning of a spoken word, much as changing a letter in a printed word changes its meaning. *Tea* has a meaning different from *sea,* and *sight* is different from *sigh.*

The number of phonemes in the world's languages varies from a low of thirteen (Hawaiian) to a high of over sixty (Hindi). Most languages have between thirty and fifty phonemes; English uses about forty. With forty basic sounds and an alphabet of only twenty-six letters, you can see that the same letters must sometimes signal different sounds. For example, the letter *a* stands for different phonemes in the words *cat* and *cake.*

Although changing a phoneme affects the meaning of speech, phonemes themselves are not meaningful. We combine them to form a higher level of organization: morphemes. A **morpheme** is the smallest unit of language that has meaning. For example, because they have meaning, *dog* and *run* are morphemes; but so are prefixes such as *un-* and suffixes such as *-ed* because they, too, have meaning, even though they cannot stand alone.

Words are made up of one or more morphemes. Words, in turn, are combined to form phrases and sentences according to a set of grammatical rules called **syntax.** According to English syntax, a subject and a verb must be combined to form a sentence, adjectives typically appear before the nouns that they modify, and so on. Compare the following sentences:

> Fatal accidents deter careful drivers.
>
> Snows sudden floods melting cause.

The first sentence makes sense, but the second sentence violates English syntax. If the words were reordered, however, they would produce the perfectly acceptable sentence "Melting snows cause sudden floods."

Even if you use English phonemes combined in proper ways to form morphemes strung together according to the laws of English syntax, you may still not end up with an acceptable sentence. Consider the sentence "Rapid bouquets deter sudden neighbors." It somehow sounds right, but it is nonsense. Why? It has syntax, but it ignores the set of rules, called **semantics,** that govern the meaning of words and sentences. For example, because of its meaning, the noun *bouquets* cannot be modified by the word *rapid.*

Surface Structure and Deep Structure   So far we have discussed elements of language that are apparent in the sentences people produce. These elements were the focus of study by linguists for many decades. Then, in 1965, Noam Chomsky started a revolution in the study of language. He argued that if linguists looked only at the sentences people produce, they would never uncover the principles that underlie language. Without looking deeper into language, he said, they could not explain, for example, why the sentence "This is my old friend" can have more than one meaning. Nor could they account for the similar meaning conveyed by such seemingly different sentences as "Don't give up just because things look bad" and "It ain't over till it's over."

language Symbols and a set of rules for combining them that provide a vehicle for communication.

grammar A set of rules for combining the words used in a given language.

phoneme The smallest unit of sound that affects the meaning of speech.

morpheme The smallest unit of language that has meaning.

syntax The set of rules that govern the formation of phrases and sentences in a language.

semantics Rules governing the meaning of words and sentences.

Making sure that the surface structures we create accurately convey the deep structures we intend is one of the greatest challenges people face when communicating through language.

To take these aspects of language into account, Chomsky proposed a more abstract level of analysis. He said that behind the strings of words people produce, called **surface structures**, there is a **deep structure**, an abstract representation of the relationships expressed in a sentence. For example, the surface structure "The shooting of the psychologist was terrible" can represent either of two deep structures: (1) that the psychologist had terrible aim or (2) that it was terrible that someone shot the psychologist. Chomsky's analysis of deep and surface structures was important because it encouraged psychologists to analyze not just verbal behavior and grammatical rules but also mental representations.

Understanding Speech

When someone speaks to you in your own language, your sensory, perceptual, and other cognitive systems reconstruct the sounds of speech in a way that allows you to detect, recognize, and understand what the person is saying. The process may seem effortless, but it involves amazingly complex feats of information processing. Scientists trying to develop neural-network–based speech recognition software systems have discovered just how complex the process is. What makes understanding speech so complicated?

One factor is that the physical features of a particular speech sound are not always the same. This phenomenon is illustrated in Figure 8.16, which shows how the sounds of particular letters differ, depending on the sounds that follow them. A second factor complicating our understanding of speech is that each of us creates slightly different speech sounds, even when saying the same words. Third, as we speak, our words are not usually separated by silence. So if the speech spectrograms in Figure 8.16 showed whole sentences, you would not be able to tell where one word ended and the next began.

Perceiving Words and Sentences   Despite these challenges, humans can instantly recognize and understand the words and sentences produced by almost anyone speaking a familiar language. In contrast, even the best voice recognition software must learn to recognize words spoken by a new voice, and even then it may make many

surface structure The order in which words are arranged in sentences.

deep structure An abstract representation of the underlying meaning of a given sentence.

FIGURE 8.16

Speech Spectrograms

These speech spectrograms show what the sound frequencies of speech look like as people say various words. Notice that even when words begin with the same consonant (such as *b* or *d*), the first part of the speech signal differs, depending on what sounds are used in the rest of the word (Jusczyk, Smith, & Murphy, 1981).

Source: Jusczyk, Smith, & Murphy (1981).

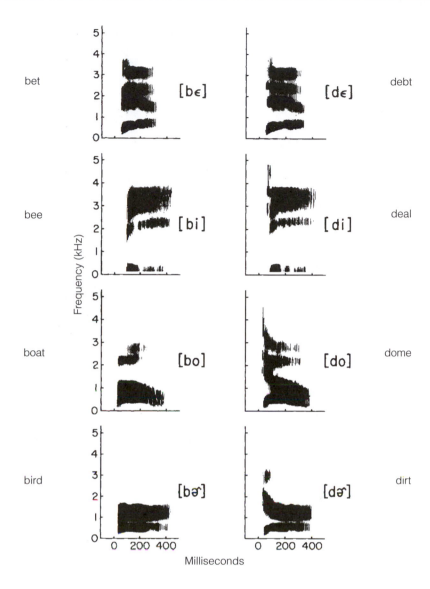

mistakes. (A man we know recently requested the toll-free number for the Maglite Corporation, and the voice recognition software in a directory assistance computer gave him the number for MetLife insurance.)

Scientists have yet to discover all the details about how people overcome the challenges of understanding speech, but some general answers are emerging. Just as we recognize objects by analyzing their visual features (as discussed in the chapter on perception), it appears that humans identify and recognize the specific—and changing—features of the sounds created when someone speaks. And as in visual perception, this *bottom-up processing* of stimulus features combines with *top-down processing* guided by knowledge-based factors, such as context and expectation, to aid understanding (Samuel, 2001). For example, knowing the general topic of conversation helps you to recognize individual words that might otherwise be hard to understand (Cole & Jakimik, 1978). This ability to use context is especially helpful for people with hearing impairments or when trying to understand what someone is saying at a loud party or in other noisy environments (Davis, Johnsrude, et al., 2005).

Understanding speech can also be guided by nonverbal cues. The frown, the enthusiastic nod, or the bored yawn that accompanies a person's words all carry information that helps you to get the full meaning of the message. So if someone says, "Wow, are you smart!" but really means "I think you're a jerk," you will detect the

Understanding Spoken Language

The top-down perceptual processes described in the perception chapter help explain why people speaking an unfamiliar language seem to produce a continuous stream of abnormally rapid speech. The problem is that you don't know where each word starts and stops. Without any perceived gaps, the sounds of speech run together, creating the impression of rapid-fire "chatter." People unfamiliar with your language think you are speaking extremely fast, too!

© Frans Lemmens/The Image Bank/Getty Images

truth based on the context, facial expression, and tone of voice. Without these extra cues, we can easily miss some elements of people's intended deep structure, which is why misunderstandings are more likely when people converse by telephone, texting, or e-mail rather than face-to-face (Kato et al., 2007).

The Development of Language

LINKAGES How do we learn to speak? (a link to Human Development, p. 474)

Children the world over develop language with impressive speed. The average 6-year-old already has a vocabulary of about 13,000 words (Pinker, 1994). But acquiring a language involves more than just learning vocabulary. We also have to learn how words are combined and how to produce and understand sentences. Psychologists who study the development of language have found that the process begins in the earliest days of a child's life and follows some predictable steps (Saffran, Senghas, & Trueswell, 2001).

The First Year Within the first few months after they are born, babies can tell the difference between the sounds of their native language and those of other languages (Gerken, 1994; Peña, Pittaluga, & Mehler, 2010), and by 10 months of age, they pay closer attention to speech in their native language (Werker et al., 1996). In the first year, then, infants become more and more attuned to the sounds that will be important in acquiring their native language. In fact, this early experience with language appears to be vital. Without it, language acquisition can be impaired (Mayberry & Lock, 2003).

The first year is also the time when babies begin to produce particular kinds of **infant vocalizations**, called **babblings**, which are patterns of meaningless sounds that begin to resemble speech. These alternating consonant and vowel sounds (such as "bababa," "dadada," and "mamimamima") appear at about 4 months of age, once the infant has developed the necessary coordination of the tongue and mouth. Though

infant vocalizations (babblings) The first sounds infants make that resemble speech.

Getting Ready to Talk

Long before they utter their first words, babies are getting ready to talk. Experiments in Patricia Kuhl's laboratory show that even 6-month-olds tend to look longer at faces whose lip movements match the sounds of spoken words. This tendency reflects babies' abilities to focus on, recognize, and discriminate the sounds of speech, especially in their native language. These abilities are crucial to the development of language (Mayberry, Lock, & Kazmi, 2002). Their language skills will blossom during the years from 2 to 4, and the richness of the vocabulary they eventually develop will be influenced by the richness of the language that they hear and the encouragement they receive for their earliest efforts to communicate using both words and gestures (Goldstein & Schwade, 2008; Rowe & Goldin-Meadow, 2009).

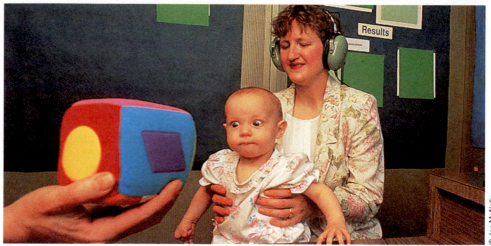

meaningless to the baby, babblings are a delight to parents. Infants everywhere begin with the same set of babbling sounds, but at about 9 months of age, they begin to produce only the sounds that occur in the language they hear the most. At about the same time, babbling becomes more complex and begins to sound like "sentences" in the babies' native language (Goldstein, King, & West, 2003). Babies who hear English, for example, begin to shorten some of their vocalizations to "da," "duh," and "ma." These sounds seem very much like language, and babies use them in specific contexts and with obvious purpose (Blake & de Boysson-Bardies, 1992). Accompanied by appropriate gestures, they may be used to express joy ("oohwow") or anger ("uh-uh-uh"), to get something that is out of reach ("engh-engh"), or to point out something interesting ("dah!").

By 10 to 12 months of age, babies can understand several words—certainly more words than they can say (Fenson et al., 1994). Proper names and object labels are among the earliest words they understand. Often the first word they understand is a pet's name. Proper names and object words—such as *mama, daddy, cookie, doggy,* and *car*—are also among the first words children are likely to say when, at around 12 months of age, they begin to talk (some do this a little earlier and some a little later). Nouns for simple object categories (*dog, flower*) are acquired before more general nouns (*animal, plant*) or more specific names (*collie, rose;* Rosch et al., 1976).

Of course, these early words do not sound exactly like adult language. English-speaking babies usually reduce them to a shorter, easier form, such as "duh" for *duck* or "mih" for *milk.* Children make themselves understood, however, by using gestures, tone of voice, facial expressions, and endless repetitions. Once they have a word for an object, they may "overextend" it to cover more ground. So they might use *doggy* to refer to cats, bears, and horses (Clark, 1993). Children make these "errors" because their vocabularies are limited, not because they fail to notice the difference between dogs and cats and bears (Fremgen & Fay, 1980; Rescorla, 1981).

Until they can say the correct words for objects, children overextend the words they have, use all-purpose sounds (such as "dat" or "dis"), and coin new words (such as *pepping* for "shaking the pepper shaker"; Becker, 1994). Being around people who don't understand these overextensions encourages children to learn and use more precise words (Markman, 1994). During this period, children build up their vocabularies one word at a time. They also use their limited vocabulary one word at a time; they cannot yet put words together into sentences.

one-word stage A stage of language development during which children tend to use one word at a time.

The Second Year   The **one-word stage** of speech lasts for about six months. Then, sometime around 18 months of age, children's vocabularies expand dramatically (Gleitman & Landau, 1994). They may learn several new words each day, and by the age of 2, most youngsters can use fifty to well over one hundred words. They also start using two-word combinations to form efficient little sentences. These two-word sentences are called *telegraphic* because, like telegrams or text messages, they are brief and to the point, leaving out anything that is not absolutely essential. So if she wants her mother to give her a book, a 20-month-old might first say, "Give book," then "Mommy give," and if that does not work, "Mommy book." The child also uses rising tones to indicate a question ("Go out?") and puts stress on certain words to indicate location ("Play *park*") or new information ("*Big* car").

Three-word sentences come next in the development of language. They are still telegraphic but more nearly complete: "Mommy give book." The child can now speak in sentences that have the usual subject-verb-object form of adult sentences in English. Other words and word endings begin appearing, too, such as the suffix *-ing*, the prepositions *in* and *on*, the plural *-s*, and irregular past tenses ("It broke," "I ate"; Brown, 1973). Children learn to use the suffix *-ed* for the past tense ("I walked"), but then they often overapply this rule to irregular verbs that they previously used correctly. They'll say, for example, "It breaked," "It broked," or "I eated" (Marcus, 1996). Children also expand their sentences with adjectives, although at first they make some mistakes. For instance, they are likely to use both *less* and *more* to mean "more" or both *tall* and *short* to mean "tall" (Smith & Sera, 1992).

The Third Year and Beyond   By age 3 or so, children begin to use auxiliary verbs ("Adam is going") and to ask questions using *wh-* words, such as *what, where, who,* and *why*. They begin to put together clauses to form complex sentences ("Here's the ball I was looking for"). By age 5, children have acquired most of the grammatical rules of their native language.

How Is Language Acquired?

Despite all that has been discovered about the steps children follow in acquiring language, mystery and debate still surround the question of just how they do it. We know that children pick up the specific content of language from the speech they hear around them: English children learn English, and Italian children learn Italian. As parents and children share meals, playtime, and conversations, children learn that words refer to objects and actions and what the labels for them are. But how do children learn syntax, the rules of grammar?

Conditioning, Imitation, and Rules   Our discussion of conditioning in the chapter on learning would suggest that children learn syntax because their parents reward them for using it. This idea sounds reasonable, but observational studies show that positive reinforcement is not the main character in the story of language acquisition. Parents are usually more concerned about what is said than about its grammatical form (Hirsch-Pasek, Treiman, & Schneiderman, 1984). So when the little boy with chocolate crumbs on his face says, "I not eat cookie," his mother is more likely to say, "Yes, you did" than to ask the child to say, "I did not eat the cookie," and then praise him for his grammatical correctness.

Learning through modeling, or imitation, appears to be more influential. Children learn grammar most rapidly when adults demonstrate the correct syntax in the course of a conversation (Zimmerman et al., 2009), as in the following example:

Child:	Mommy fix.
Mother:	OK, Mommy will fix the truck.
Child:	It breaked.
Mother:	Yes, it broke.
Child:	Truck broke.
Mother:	Let's see if we can fix it.

But if children learn syntax by imitation, why would they overgeneralize rules, such as the rule for making the past tense? Why, for example, do children who at one time said "I went" later say "I goed"? Adults don't use this form of speech, so neither reward nor imitation can account for its sudden appearance. It seems more likely that children analyze for themselves the underlying patterns in the language they hear around them and then learn the rules governing those patterns (Bloom, 1995).

Biological Bases for Language Acquisition   The ease with which children everywhere discover these underlying patterns and learn language has led some experts to argue that language acquisition is at least partly innate. For example, Chomsky (1986) believes that we have a built-in *universal grammar,* a mechanism that allows us to identify the basic dimensions of language (see also Baker, 2002; Nowak, Komarova, & Niyogi, 2001). One of these dimensions is how important word order is in the syntax of a particular language. In English, for example, word order tells us who is doing what to whom (the sentences "Heather dumped Jason" and "Jason dumped Heather" contain the same words, but they have different meanings). In languages such as Russian, however, word order is less important than the modifiers, also called *inflections,* attached to words. According to Chomsky, a child's universal grammar might initially be "set" to assume that word order is important to syntax, but it would change if the child hears language in which word order is not so important. In Chomsky's system, then, we don't entirely learn language—we develop it as genetic predispositions interact with experience (Senghas & Coppola, 2001).

Evidence that supports claims of a genetic predisposition for language comes from studies of *specific language impairment (SLI).* Children displaying SLI have trouble acquiring language despite having otherwise normal mental abilities, normal hearing, and adequate early exposure to language sounds (Gopnik & Crago, 1991). Because SLI runs in families, several investigators have proposed that it reflects a defect in the genes that normally provide us with our universal grammar (e.g., Pinker, 1994; Van der Lely, 1994; White, 2006). This is a controversial idea, though, partly because of evidence that people with SLI have specific deficiencies in auditory processing that might account for their difficulty in acquiring grammar (e.g., Stevens, Sanders, & Neville, 2006).

Indeed, the development of language probably reflects the development of more general sensory, motor, and cognitive skills, not just innate, language-specific mechanisms (Bates, 1993). In other words, we probably don't inherit a single, specific "grammar gene" (White, 2006). Still, the existence of SLI and other gene-linked speech and language disorders (Barry, Yasin, & Bishop, 2007) reminds us that, as is true for all other aspects of human behavior and mental processes, our language abilities are based partly on biological factors. For example, the unique speech-generating properties of the human mouth and throat, the existence of language-related brain regions such as Broca's area and Wernicke's area (see Figure 3.15 in the chapter on biological aspects of psychology), and genetic research all suggest that humans are innately "prewired," or biologically programmed, for language (Buxhoeveden et al., 2001; Fisher, 2005; Lai et al., 2001). In addition, there appears to be a *critical period* in childhood during which we can learn language more easily than at any other time (Ridley, 2000). Evidence for the existence of this critical period comes from research on the difficulties adults have in learning a second language (e.g., Patkowski, 1994) and also by cases in which unfortunate children spent their early years in isolation from human contact and the sound of adult language. Even after years of therapy and language training, these individuals are not able to combine ideas into sentences (Rymer, 1993). These cases suggest that, as mentioned earlier, acquiring the complex features of language depends on being exposed to speech before a certain age.

Bilingualism   Does trying to learn two languages at once, even before the critical period is over, impair the learning of either? Research suggests just the opposite. Although their earliest language utterances may be confused or delayed, and though

Learning a Second Language

As these international students are discovering, people who learn a second language as adults do so more slowly and less easily than younger people (Johnson & Newport, 1989) and virtually never learn to speak it without an accent (Lenneberg, 1967). Still, the window of opportunity for learning a second language remains open long after the end of the critical period in childhood during which first-language acquisition must occur (Hakuta, Bialystok, & Wiley, 2003).

© Michael Grecco/Stock, Boston

they may have somewhat smaller vocabularies, children who are raised in a bilingual environment before the end of the critical period seem to show enhanced performance in each language (Bialystok & Craik, 2010; De Houwer, 1995). There is also some evidence that *balanced bilinguals*—those who developed roughly equal mastery of two languages in childhood—are superior to other children in cognitive flexibility, concept formation, and creativity. It is as if each language offers a slightly different perspective on thinking, and this dual perspective makes the brain more flexible (Bialystok & Craik, 2010; Kovács & Mehler, 2009). Indeed, bilinguals also have an easier time than other people do in learning yet another language later in life, even if the grammar of the new language is very different from the languages they already know (Kaushanskaya, 2009).

THINKING CRITICALLY

Can Nonhumans Use Language?

We have said that it is our ability to acquire and use language that helps set humans apart from all other creatures. Yet those creatures, too, use symbols to communicate. Bees perform a dance that tells other bees where they found sources of nectar, killer whales signal one another as they hunt in groups, and the grunts and gestures of chimpanzees signify varying desires and emotions. These forms of communication do not necessarily have the grammatical characteristics of language, however (Fitch & Hauser, 2004; Povinelli & Bering, 2002; Rendall et al., 2000; Zuberbühler, 2005). Are any animals other than humans capable of learning language?

What am I being asked to believe or accept?

Over the past forty years, several researchers have claimed that nonhumans can master language. Chimpanzees and gorillas have been the most popular targets of study because at maturity they are estimated to have the intelligence of 2- or 3-year-old human children, who are usually well on their way to learning language. Dolphins have also been studied because they have a complex communication system and exceptionally large brains relative to their body size (Janik, 2000; Pack & Herman, 2007; Reiss & Marino, 2001). It would seem that if these animals were unable to learn language, their general intelligence could not be blamed. Instead, failure would be attributed to the absence of a genetic makeup that permits language learning.

What evidence is available to support the assertion?

The question of whether nonhuman mammals can learn to use language is not a simple one, for at least two reasons. First, language is more than just communication, but defining just when animals are exhibiting that "something more" is a source of debate. What seems to set human language apart from the gestures, grunts, chirps, whistles, or cries of other animals is grammar—a formal set of rules for combining words. Also, because of their anatomical structures, nonhuman mammals will never be able to "speak" in the same way that humans do (Lieberman, 1991; Nishimura et al., 2003). To test these animals' ability to learn language, investigators therefore must devise novel ways for them to communicate.

David and Ann Premack taught their chimp, Sarah, to communicate by placing differently shaped chips, each symbolizing a word, on a magnetic board (Premack, 1971). Lana, a chimpanzee studied by Duane Rumbaugh (1977), learned to communicate by pressing keys on a specially designed computer. A simplified version of American Sign Language (ASL) has been used by Beatrice and Allen Gardner with the chimp Washoe, by Herbert Terrace with Nim Chimpsky (a chimp named after Noam Chomsky), and by Penny Patterson with a gorilla named Koko. Kanzi, a bonobo, or pygmy chimpanzee, studied by Sue Savage-Rumbaugh (1990; Savage-Rumbaugh et al., 1993), learned to recognize spoken words and to communicate by both gesturing and pressing word symbol keys on a computer that would "speak" them. Kanzi was a special case: He learned to communicate by listening and watching as his mother, Matata, was being taught and then used what he had learned to interact with her trainers.

Studies of these animals suggested that they could use combinations of words to refer to things that were not present. Washoe, Lana, Sarah, Nim, and Kanzi all mastered between 130 and 500 words. Their vocabulary included names for concrete objects, such as *apple* or *me*; verbs, such as *tickle* and *eat*; adjectives, such as *happy* and *big*; and adverbs, such as *again*. The animals combined the words to express wishes such as "You tickle me" or "If Sarah good, then apple." Sometimes their expressions referred to things in the past. When an investigator called attention to a wound that Kanzi had received, the animal responded with "Matata hurt," referring to a disciplinary bite his mother had recently given him (Savage-Rumbaugh, 1990). Finally, all these animals seemed to enjoy their communication tools and used them spontaneously to interact with their caretakers and with other animals.

Most of the investigators mentioned here have argued that their animals mastered a crude grammar (Premack & Premack, 1983; Savage-Rumbaugh, Shanker, & Taylor, 2001).

Animal Language?

Here is Nim Chimpsky, learning the sign for "drink" by imitating one of his teachers. Nim died in 2000 at the age of 26, but Koko, the gorilla trained by Penny Patterson, is still with us. In 1998, Patterson made Koko available for an Internet chat session. She relayed online questions to Koko in American Sign Language, and a typist sent back Koko's signed responses. This procedure left some questioners wondering whether they were talking to Koko or to her trainer. (You can decide for yourself by reading the transcript of the session at www.koko.org/world/talk_aol.html.)

© Susan Kuklin/Photo Researchers, Inc.

For example, if Washoe wanted to be tickled, she would gesture, "You tickle Washoe." But if she wanted to do the tickling, she would gesture, "Washoe tickle you." The correct placement of object and subject in these sentences suggested that Washoe was following a set of rules for word combination—in other words, a grammar (Gardner & Gardner, 1978). Louis Herman and his colleagues documented similar grammatical sensitivity in dolphins, who rarely confused subject-verb order in following instructions given by human hand signals (Herman, Richards, & Wolz, 1984). Furthermore, Savage-Rumbaugh observed several hundred instances in which Kanzi understood sentences he had never heard before. Once, for example, while his back was turned to the speaker, Kanzi heard the sentence "Jeanie hid the pine needles in her shirt." He turned around, approached Jeanie, and searched her shirt to find the pine needles. His actions would seem to indicate that he understood this new sentence the first time he heard it.

Are there alternative ways of interpreting the evidence?

Many of the early conclusions about primate language learning were challenged by Herbert Terrace and his colleagues (1979) in their investigation of Nim and by other critics' responses to other cases. For example, Terrace noticed many characteristics of Nim's communications that seemed quite different from a child's use of language.

First, he said, Nim's sentences were always very short. For example, Nim could combine two or three gestures but never used strings that conveyed more sophisticated messages. The ape was never able to say anything equivalent to a 3-year-old child's "I want to go to Wendy's for a hamburger, OK?" Others have noted that even the most intelligent of primates are unable to master the full grammatical possibilities of either ASL or specially developed artificial languages (Fitch & Hauser, 2004). Further, apes don't point at things, as humans do from a young age as they develop language and use it in joint communication (e.g., Tomasello, 2006). Second, Terrace questioned whether the animals' use of language demonstrated the spontaneity, creativity, and expanding complexity characteristic of children's language. Many of the animals' sentences were requests for food, tickling, baths, pets, and other pleasurable objects and experiences. Is such behavior really any different from the kind of behavior shown by the family dog who learns to sit up and beg for table scraps? Other researchers also pointed out that chimps are not naturally predisposed to associate seen objects with heard words, as human infants are (Savage-Rumbaugh et al., 1983). Finally, Terrace questioned whether experimenter bias influenced the reports of the chimps' communications. Consciously or not, experimenters who want to conclude that chimps learn language might tend to ignore strings of symbols that violate grammatical order or to reinterpret ambiguous strings so that they make grammatical sense. If Nim sees someone holding a banana and signs, "Nim banana," the experimenter might assume that the word order is correct and means "Nim wants the banana" rather than, for example, "That banana belongs to Nim," in which case the word order would be wrong.

Critics also point out that the results presented in support of animal language capabilities are usually only samples of an animal's behavior. They say that the unedited sequences of an animal's signing or other behavior presents a picture that is far more repetitive, chaotic, and random than one might expect on the basis of the selected samples (Aitchison, 2008).

What additional evidence would help evaluate the alternatives?

Studies of animals' ability to learn language are expensive and take many years. As a result, the amount of evidence in the area is small—just a handful of studies, each based on a few animals. Obviously, more data are needed from more studies that use a common methodology.

It is important, too, to study the extent to which limits on the length of primates' spontaneous sentences result from limits on short-term and working memory (Savage-Rumbaugh & Brakke, 1996). If memory is in fact the main limiting factor, then the failure to produce progressively longer sentences does not necessarily reflect an inability to master language.

Research on how primates might spontaneously acquire language by listening and imitating, as Kanzi did, as well as naturalistic observations of communications among primates in their natural habitat, would also help scientists better understand primates' capacity to communicate (Savage-Rumbaugh, Shanker, & Taylor, 2001; Sevcik & Savage-Rumbaugh, 1994).

What conclusions are most reasonable?

Psychologists are still not in full agreement about whether our sophisticated mammalian cousins can learn language. Two things are clear, however. First, whatever the chimp, gorilla, and dolphin have learned is a much more primitive and limited form of communication than that learned by children. Second, their level of communication does not do justice to their overall intelligence; these animals are smarter than their "language" production suggests. In short, the evidence to date favors the view that humans have language abilities that are unique (Buxhoeveden et al., 2001), but that under the right circumstances and with the right tools, other animals can communicate using abstract symbols.

Culture, Language, and Thought

When ideas from one language are translated into another, the intended meaning can easily be distorted, as shown in Table 8.2. But differences in language and culture may have more serious and more important implications as well. The language that people speak forms part of their knowledge of the world, and that knowledge, as noted in the chapter on perception, guides perceptions. This relationship raises the question of whether differences among languages create differences in the ways that people perceive and think about the world.

Benjamin Whorf (1956) claimed that language actually determines how we can think, a process he called *linguistic determinism*. He noted, for example, that the Inuit (Eskimos) have several different words for "snow" and proposed that this feature of their language should lead to a greater perceptual ability to discriminate among varieties of snow.

Whorf's description of Inuit language and words for snow turned out not to be very accurate, but was he also wrong in claiming that language determines how we think? Eleanor Rosch (1975) conducted an interesting test of linguistic determinism by comparing North Americans' color perception with that of people in the Dani tribe of New Guinea. In the language of the Dani, there are only two color names—one for dark, "cold" colors and one for lighter, "warm" ones. In contrast, English speakers have names for a vast number of hues. Of these, it is possible to identify eleven focal colors; these are prototypes, the particular wavelengths of light that are the best examples of the eleven major categories (red, yellow, green, blue, black, gray, white, purple, orange, pink, and brown). Fire engine red is the focal color for red. Rosch reasoned

TABLE 8.2 Lost in Translation	
Sometimes a lack of familiarity with the formal and informal aspects of other languages gets American advertisers in trouble. Here are three examples.	When the Clairol Company introduced its "Mist Stick" curling iron in Germany, it was unaware that *Mist* is the German word for "manure." Not many people wanted to buy a manure stick.
	In Chinese, the Kentucky Fried Chicken slogan "Finger lickin' good" came out as "Eat your fingers off."
	In Chinese, a slogan for Pepsi, "Come alive with the Pepsi Generation," became "Pepsi brings your ancestors back from the grave."

that if Whorf's views were correct, then English speakers, who have verbal labels for focal colors, should recognize them better than nonfocal colors. For the Dani, the focal-nonfocal distinction should make no difference. In fact, however, Rosch found that both the Dani and the English-speaking North Americans perceived focal colors more efficiently than nonfocal ones (Heider, 1972). More recent studies have found similar results (e.g., Lindsey & Brown, 2006; Regier, Kay, & Cook, 2005).

Rosch's study was long seen as providing conclusive evidence against Whorf's linguistic determinism hypothesis. Recently, though, some psychologists have suggested that language may have some effects on our thinking and that we shouldn't discount some weaker versions of Whorf's hypothesis (e.g., Gilbert et al., 2006; Gordon, 2004; Kay & Regier, 2006; Özgen, 2004; Özgen & Davies, 2002). For example, having words for particular concepts can make it easy to remember things based on verbal labels for those concepts. This verbal labeling can affect color memory, if not color perception (Lau, Lee, & Chiu, 2004; Winawer et al., 2007).

Another example of the influence of language on thinking comes from a study of children's understanding of mathematics (Miura et al., 1993). The study found that compared with children who speak Japanese or Korean, children who speak English or French have more trouble understanding the concept of "place value"—such as that the number *eleven* means "one 10 and one 1." As described in the chapter on human development, one important reason for this difference is that some languages make place values more obvious than others. The Korean word for *eleven*, which is *shib-il*, means "ten-one." English speakers have to remember what *eleven* refers to every time they hear it.

TRY THIS Even within a culture, language can affect reasoning, problem solving, and decision making. For example, consider whether you would choose A or B in each of the following situations:

> The government is preparing for the outbreak of an unusual disease, which you know will kill six hundred people if nothing is done. Two programs are proposed. If program A is adopted, two hundred people will be saved. If program B is adopted, there is a one-third chance that all six hundred people will be saved and a two-thirds chance that no one will be saved.

> A ship hits a mine in the middle of the ocean, and six hundred passengers onboard will die if action is not taken immediately. There are two options. If option A is adopted, four hundred passengers will die. If option B is adopted, there is a one-third chance that no one will die and a two-thirds chance that no one will be saved.

The logic of each situation is the same (program A and option A will both save two hundred lives), so people who choose program A in one case should choose option A in the other. But this is not what happens. In one study, 72 percent of participants chose program A in the disease situation but 78 percent chose option B in the ship situation (Kahneman & Tversky, 1984). Their choices were not logically consistent because people's thinking tends to be influenced by the words used to describe situations. Here program A was framed in terms of lives saved; option B was framed in terms of lives lost. Advertisers are well aware of how this *framing effect* alters decisions; as a result, your grocer stocks ground beef labeled as "75 percent lean," not "25 percent fat." Advocates of various political views, too, seek to attract support by framing their positions in the most positive ways possible, using labels such as "pro-choice" or "pro-life" rather than, say, "proabortion" or "antichoice." So although it appears that Whorf was wrong in claiming that language determines *what* we think, it may still influence *how* we think (Hardisty, Johnson, & Weber, 2010).

LINKAGES

As noted in the chapter on introducing psychology, all of psychology's subfields are related to one another. Our discussion of group processes in problem solving illustrates just one way in which the topic of this chapter, cognition and language, is linked to the subfield of social psychology (especially to the chapter

CHAPTER 8
Cognition and Language

on social influence). The Linkages diagram shows ties to two other subfields as well, and there are many more ties throughout the book. Looking for linkages among subfields will help you see how they all fit together and help you better appreciate the big picture that is psychology.

LINKAGES

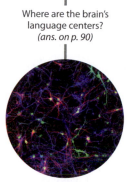

Where are the brain's language centers?
(ans. on p. 90)

CHAPTER 3
Biological Aspects of Psychology

How do schizophrenic individuals think?
(ans. on p. 628)

CHAPTER 15
Psychological Disorders

Do people solve problems better alone or in a group?
(ans. on p. 312)

CHAPTER 18
Social Influence

SUMMARY

Cognitive psychology is the study of the mental processes by which the information we receive from the environment is modified, made meaningful, stored, retrieved, used, and communicated to others.

Basic Functions of Thought

The five core functions of thought are to describe, elaborate, decide, plan, and guide action.

The Circle of Thought

Many psychologists think of the components of the circle of thought as constituting an *information-processing system* that receives, represents, transforms, and acts on incoming stimuli. *Thinking,* then, is defined as the manipulation of mental representations by this system.

Measuring Information Processing

The time elapsing between the presentation of a stimulus and an overt response to it is the *reaction time*. Among the factors affecting reaction times are the complexity of the choice of a response,

stimulus-response compatibility, expectancy, and the trade-off between speed and accuracy. Using methods such as the EEG and neuroimaging techniques, psychologists can also measure mental events as reflected in *evoked potentials* and other brain activity.

Mental Representations: The Ingredients of Thought

Mental representations take the form of concepts, propositions, schemas, scripts, mental models, images, and cognitive maps.

Concepts

Concepts are categories of objects, events, or ideas with common properties. They may be formal or natural. Formal concepts are precisely defined by the presence or absence of certain features. *Natural concepts (natural categories)* are fuzzy; no fixed set of defining properties determines membership in a natural

concept. A member of a natural concept that displays all or most of its characteristic features is called a *prototype*.

Propositions

Propositions are assertions that state how concepts are related. Propositions can be true or false.

Schemas, Scripts, and Mental Models

Schemas are sets of propositions that serve as generalized mental representations of concepts and also generate expectations about them. *Scripts* are schemas of familiar activities that help people think about those activities and interpret new events. *Mental models* are representations of particular situations or arrangements of objects that guide our thinking about them. Mental models may be accurate or inaccurate.

Images and Cognitive Maps

Information can be represented as *images* and can be mentally rotated, inspected, and otherwise manipulated. *Cognitive maps* are mental models of the spatial arrangements in familiar parts of the world.

Thinking Strategies

By combining and transforming mental representations, our information-processing system makes it possible for us to reason, solve problems, and make decisions. *Reasoning* is the process through which people generate and evaluate arguments, as well as reach conclusions about them.

Formal Reasoning

Formal reasoning seeks valid conclusions through the application of rigorous procedures. These procedures include formulas, or *algorithms,* which are guaranteed to produce correct solutions if they exist, and the rules of *logic,* which are useful in evaluating sets of premises and conclusions called *syllogisms.* To reach a sound conclusion, we must consider both the truth or falsity of the premises and the logic of the argument itself. People are prone to logical errors; their belief in a conclusion is often affected by the extent to which the conclusion is consistent with their attitudes, as well as by other factors, including *confirmation bias* and limits on working memory.

Informal Reasoning

People use *informal reasoning* to assess the believability of a conclusion based on the evidence for it. Errors in informal reasoning often stem from the misuse of *heuristics,* or mental shortcuts. Three important heuristics are the *anchoring heuristic* or *anchoring bias* (estimating the probability of an event by adjusting a starting value), the *representativeness heuristic* (categorizing an event by how representative it is of a category), and the *availability heuristic* (estimating probability by how available an event is in memory).

Problem Solving

Steps in problem solving include diagnosing the problem and then planning, executing, and evaluating a solution.

Strategies for Problem Solving

Especially when solutions are not obvious, problem solving can be aided by the use of strategies such as incubation, means-end analysis, working backward, and using analogies.

Obstacles to Problem Solving

Many of the difficulties that people experience in solving problems arise when they are dealing with hypotheses. People do not easily entertain multiple hypotheses. Because of *mental sets,* people may stick to a particular hypothesis even when it is unsuccessful and, through *functional fixedness,* may tend to miss opportunities to use familiar objects in unusual ways. Confirmation bias may lead people to be reluctant to revise or abandon hypotheses, especially cherished ones, on the basis of new evidence, and they may fail to use the absence of information as evidence in solving problems.

Building Problem-Solving Skills

Experts are usually superior to beginners in problem solving because of their knowledge and experience. They can draw on knowledge of similar problems, visualize related components of a problem as a single chunk, and perceive relations among problems in terms of underlying principles rather than surface features. Extensive knowledge is the main component of expertise, yet expertise itself can prevent experts from seeing problems in new ways.

Problem Solving by Computer

Some specific problems can be solved by computer programs known as expert systems. These systems are one application of *artificial intelligence (AI).* One approach to AI focuses on programming computers to imitate the logical manipulation of symbols that occurs in human thought. Another approach—involving connectionist, or neural network, models—attempts to imitate the connections among neurons in the human brain. Current problem-solving computer systems deal most successfully with specific domains. Often the best outcomes occur when humans and computers work together.

Decision Making

Cognitive abilities play an important role in making decisions.

Evaluating Options

Decisions are sometimes difficult because there are too many alternatives and too many attributes of each alternative to consider at the same time. Furthermore, decisions often involve comparisons of subjective *utility,* not objective value. Decision making is also complicated by the fact that the world is unpredictable, which makes decisions risky. In risky decision making, the best decision is one that maximizes *expected value.*

Biases and Flaws in Decision Making

People often fail to maximize expected value in their decisions for two reasons. First, losses are perceived differently from gains of equal size. Second, people tend to overestimate the probability of unlikely events, to underestimate the probability of likely events, and to feel overconfident in the accuracy of their forecasts. The gambler's fallacy leads people to believe that future events in a random process are affected by previous events. People sometimes make decisions aimed at goals other than maximizing expected value. These goals may be determined by personal and cultural factors.

Language

People's ability to communicate their thoughts depends on their ability to learn and use language.

The Elements of Language

Language consists of symbols such as words and rules for their combination—a *grammar.* Spoken words are made up of *phonemes,* which are combined to make *morphemes.* Combinations of words must have both *syntax* (grammar) and *semantics* (meaning). Behind the word strings, or *surface structures,* is an underlying representation, or *deep structure,* that expresses the relationship among the ideas in a sentence. Ambiguous sentences occur when one surface structure reflects two or more deep structures.

Understanding Speech

When people listen to speech in a familiar language, their perceptual system allows them to perceive gaps between words, even when those gaps are not physically present. To understand language generally and conversations in particular, people use their knowledge of the context and of the world. In addition, understanding is guided by nonverbal cues.

The Development of Language

Children develop grammar according to an orderly pattern. *Infant vocalizations* called *babblings* and the *one-word stage* of speech come first; telegraphic two-word sentences follow. Next come three-word sentences and certain grammatical forms that appear in a somewhat predictable order. Once children learn certain regular verb forms and plural endings, they may overgeneralize rules. Children acquire most of the syntax of their native language by the time they are 5 years old.

How Is Language Acquired?

Conditioning and imitation both play a role in a child's acquisition of language, but neither can provide a complete explanation of how children acquire syntax. Humans may be biologically programmed to learn language. In any event, it appears that language must be learned during a certain critical period if normal language is to result. The critical-period notion is supported by research on second-language acquisition.

Culture, Language, and Thought

Research across cultures and within North American culture suggests that although language does not determine what we can think, it does influence how we think.

LINKAGES TO FURTHER LEARNING

Now that you have finished reading this chapter, how about exploring some of the topics and information that you found most interesting? Here are some places to start.

Books

Gerd Gigerenzer, Peter M. Todd, and ABC Research Group, *Simple Heuristics That Make Us Smart* (Oxford University Press, 2000). Research on and ideas for using mental shortcuts.

Peter Bernstein, *Against the Gods: The Remarkable Story of Risk* (Wiley, 1998). A history of efforts to understand risk and probability in decision making.

James Surowiecki, *The Wisdom of Crowds: Why the Many Are Smarter Than the Few and How Collective Wisdom Shapes Business, Economies, Societies, and Nations* (Doubleday, 2004). Presents theories and evidence for the value of group rather than individual decisions.

Philip Tetlock, *Expert Political Judgment: How Good Is It? How Can We Know?* (Princeton University Press, 2006). Presents evidence that the judgment of even revered political experts is subject to the same flaws and pitfalls that plague the rest of us.

On the Internet

 Access an integrated eBook and chapter-specific learning tools including flashcards, quizzes, videos, and more. Go to CengageBrain.com.

CENGAGENOW Want to maximize the value of your online study time? Take this easy-to-use study system's diagnostic pre-test, and it will create a personalized study plan for you. By helping you identify the topics that you need to understand better and then directing you to valuable online resources, it can speed up your chapter review. CengageNOW even provides a post-test so you can confirm that you are ready for an exam. Go to CengageBrain.com.

TALKING POINTS

Here are a few talking points to help you summarize this chapter for family and friends without giving a lecture.

1. Our ability to respond "automatically," as when playing a video game or suddenly slamming on the brakes, depends on a lightning-fast sequence of cognitive processes that includes sensation, perception, decision making, and response selection.

2. We all carry in our heads cognitive maps of familiar places that allow us to get around in them, even in the dark.

3. Faulty mental models of how things work can lead to serious mistakes, as in the case of a driver who tried to take a nap on an expressway because he thought his cruise control would also steer his car.

4. Even when armed with strong evidence, prosecutors may have trouble convincing jurors of a defendant's guilt if the defendant is a harmless-looking senior citizen whose appearance and demeanor violates the jurors' schemas of what a "criminal" looks like.

5. In a slumping real estate market, even desperate sellers may refuse to accept a buyer's offer because the anchoring heuristic leaves them convinced that their house is still worth what it was when the market was at its peak.

6. Sometimes the best way to solve a complex problem is to break it into smaller parts and approach the solution one step at a time.

7. People sometimes misunderstand each other, especially when e-mailing or texting, because the surface structure of what they say (e.g., "Yeah, I'm really going to do that") can be interpreted as having more than one underlying meaning (deep structure).

9

Consciousness

© Dex Image/Getty Images

In this chapter, we delve into the topic of consciousness and describe research on altered states of consciousness. We'll examine sleep and dreams, *hypnosis, and meditation and how they differ from normal waking consciousness. We'll also look at how consciousness is affected by psychoactive drugs.*

I n an old *Sesame Street* episode, Ernie is trying to find out whether Bert is asleep or awake. Ernie notices that Bert's eyes are closed, and he comments that Bert usually closes his eyes when he is asleep. Ernie also knows that when Bert is asleep, he does not respond to pokes, so naturally, he delivers a few pokes. At first, Bert does not respond. After a few more pokes, though, he awakes, very annoyed, and yells at Ernie for waking him. Ernie then tells Bert that he just wanted to let him know it was time for his nap.

Doctors face a similar situation in dealing with the millions of people each year who receive general anesthesia during surgery. These patients certainly appear asleep, but it is hard to know for sure if they are truly unconscious. It turns out that a very small number of patients—0.2 to 0.4 percent of adults and up to 1.1 percent of children—have some degree of consciousness during the surgical procedure (Andrade, Deeprose, & Barker, 2008; Xu, Wu, & Yue, 2009). In rare cases, patients have conscious awareness of surgical pain and remember it later. Although their surgical incisions heal, these people may be psychologically scarred by the experience and may even show symptoms of posttraumatic stress disorder (Schwender et al., 1995). To reduce the possibility of performing surgery on someone who may not be unconscious, some physicians suggest that patients' brain activity should be monitored during every operation (Jameson & Sloan, 2006), but even these efforts are not entirely successful (Avidan et al., 2008).

The fact that even under the influence of powerful anesthetic drugs, people can be conscious while appearing to be asleep shows how difficult it can be to define consciousness (Sarà & Pistoia, 2009). In fact, after decades of discussion and research by philosophers, psychologists, and even physicists, some believe that consciousness is still not yet understood well enough to allow a precise definition. Given the ethical and legal concerns raised by the need to ensure that patients are not subjected to pain during surgery, medical doctors tend to define *consciousness* as awareness that is demonstrated by either explicit or implicit recall (Schwender et al., 1995). In psychology, the usual definition is somewhat broader: **Consciousness** is generally defined as awareness of your thoughts, actions, feelings, sensations, perceptions, and other mental processes (Metzinger, 2000; Zeman, 2001).

This definition suggests that consciousness is not itself a mental process but rather an aspect of many mental processes. For example, memories can be conscious, but consciousness is not just memory. Perceptions can be conscious, but consciousness is not just perception. The definition also allows for the possibility that humans are not the only creatures to experience consciousness. It appears that some animals whose brains are similar to ours have some capacity for self-awareness, even though they do not have the language abilities to tell us about it (Edelman & Seth, 2009). One way to assess this awareness is to determine if a creature recognizes itself in a mirror. Children can do so at about 2 years of age. Monkeys never display this ability, but chimpanzees do, and so do dolphins and elephants (Plotnik, de Waal, & Reiss, 2006; Reiss & Marino, 2001; Suddendorf & Collier-Baker, 2009).

In this chapter, we consider the nature of consciousness and the ways in which it affects our mental activity and behavior. Then we examine what happens when

© David Welling/Animals, Animals

Keeping an Eye Out

Humans are not the only creatures capable of processing information while apparently unconscious. While ducks sleep, one hemisphere of their brains can process visual information from an eye that remains open. Birds positioned where they are most vulnerable to predators, such as at the end of a row, may spend twice as much time in this "alert" sleep than birds in more protected positions (Rattenborg, Lima, & Amlaner, 1999).

consciousness Awareness of external stimuli and one's own mental activity.

331

consciousness is altered by sleep, hypnosis, and meditation. Finally, we explore the changes in consciousness that occur when people use certain drugs.

Analyzing Consciousness

Psychologists have been fascinated by the study of consciousness for more than a century, but only in the past few decades has consciousness reemerged as an active and vital research area in psychology. As described in the chapter on introducing psychology, behaviorism dominated psychological research in the United States from the 1920s through the 1960s. During that period, the emphasis was on overt behavior, so relatively little research was conducted on mental processes, including the structure and functions of consciousness. But when advanced brain-imaging techniques began to appear in the latter part of the twentieth century, psychologists had the tools necessary to explore the relationship between conscious experience and brain activity. They can see what is happening in the brain during mental activity that is conscious and during activity that occurs outside of awareness (Faulkner & Foster, 2002). Some scientists who study consciousness today describe their work as *cognitive science* or *cognitive neuroscience* because their research is closely tied to the subfields of biological psychology, sensation, perception, memory, and human cognition (Koch, 2003). In fact, most cognitive psychologists who study memory, reasoning, problem solving, and decision making can be described as studying various aspects of consciousness.

Other psychologists study consciousness more directly by addressing three central questions about it. First, like the philosophers who preceded them, psychologists have grappled with the *mind-body problem:* What is the relationship between the conscious mind and the physical brain? One approach, known as *dualism*, sees the mind and brain as different. This idea was championed in the 1600s by the French philosopher René Descartes. Descartes claimed that a person's soul, or consciousness, is separate from the brain but can "view" and interact with brain events through a small brain structure called the pineal gland. Once a popular point of view, dualism has virtually disappeared from psychology.

Another mind-body perspective, known as *materialism*, suggests that mind and brain are one and the same. Materialists argue that complex interactions among the brain's nerve cells create consciousness, much as hardware and software interact to create the image that appears on a computer screen. A good deal of support for the materialist view comes from case studies in which damage to the brain causes disruptions in consciousness.

A second question about consciousness focuses on whether it is a unified phenomenon or several different ones. Does consciousness occur as a single "point" in mental processing or as several parallel mental operations that occur independently? According to the *theater* view, consciousness is a single phenomenon, a kind of "stage" on which all the various aspects of awareness converge to "perform" before the "audience" of your mind. Those adopting the theater view see support for it in the fact that, as described in the perception chapter, the same psychophysical laws govern our subjective experience of the intensity of light, sound, weight, and other stimuli. It is as if each sensory system passes its information to a single "monitor" that coordinates the experience of stimulus magnitude (Teghtsoonian, 1992).

In contrast, the *parallel distributed processing (PDP) models* discussed in the perception chapter describe the mind as processing many parallel streams of information, whose interactions create the unitary experience we call consciousness (John, 2004; Leisman & Koch, 2009; Lou et al., 2004). PDP models became influential when research on sensation, perception, memory, cognition, and language suggested that components of these processes are analyzed in separate brain regions. For example, our ability to perceive a visual scene requires the combined activity of many separate brain regions, some of which analyze what each object is while others determine where it is (Aymoz & Viviani, 2004; Ishai, Ungerleider, & Haxby, 2000). Scientists still do not know whether these parallel streams of information ever unite in a common brain region.

A third question about consciousness focuses on how conscious and unconscious mental activities are related. More than a century ago, Sigmund Freud argued that some mental processes occur without our awareness and that these processes can affect us in many ways. Most aspects of Freud's theory are not supported by modern research, but there is evidence that many important mental activities do occur outside of awareness. Let's examine some of these activities and consider the functions they serve.

The Functions of Consciousness

Francis Crick and Christof Koch (2003) have suggested that one function of consciousness is to provide the best current interpretation of sensory information in light of past experience and to make this interpretation available to the parts of the brain that can act on it. Their idea is that having a *single* conscious representation, rather than multiple ones, allows us to be more decisive in taking action. From this perspective, the conscious brain experiences a representation of the world that is the result of many complex computations. It has access to the results of these computational processes but not to the processes themselves. Some of these processes occur so quickly that our conscious experience can't keep up with them. For example, people who are skilled at playing tennis or computer games can respond to a fast serve or a threatening alien even before they consciously "see" these stimuli. Conscious processing is not always the fastest that your brain is capable of, but it is extremely helpful when dealing with life's most complex problems. Consciousness helps you engage in the most adaptive and efficient blending of your brain's sensory input, motor responses, and knowledge resources (Baars, 2002; Guterman, 2010).

As described in the chapter on memory, the contents of consciousness at any given moment are limited by the capacity of short-term memory, but the overall process of consciousness allows access to a vast store of information. In one study, for example, participants paid brief conscious attention to ten thousand different pictures over several days. A week later, they were able to recognize more than 90 percent of the photographs. Evidently, mere consciousness of an event helps store a recognizable memory that can later be brought into consciousness (Kosslyn, 1994).

Over a century ago, the psychologist William James compared consciousness to a stream, describing it as ever-changing, multilayered, and varying in both quantity and quality. Variations in quantity—that is, in the degree to which one is aware of mental events—result in different *levels of consciousness*. Variations in quality—in the nature of the mental processing available to awareness—are referred to as different *consciousness states* (Tassi & Muzet, 2001). Appreciating the difference between levels of consciousness and states of consciousness takes a little thought. When you are alert and aware of your mental activity and of incoming sensations, you are fully conscious. At the same time, however, there is other mental activity taking place in your brain at varying "distances" from your conscious awareness. These activities are occurring at other *levels* of consciousness (Morin, 2006). It is when your experience of yourself varies in focus and clarity—as when you sleep or are under the influence of a mind-altering drug—that there are variations in your *state* of consciousness. Let's first consider various levels of consciousness.

Levels of Consciousness

At any moment, the mental events that you are aware of are said to exist at the **conscious level**. For example, look at the Necker cube in Figure 9.1. If you are like most people, you can see the cube in one orientation for only a few seconds before the other orientation "pops out" at you. The orientation that you experience at any moment is at your conscious level of awareness for that moment.

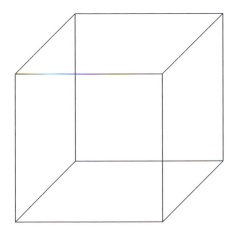

FIGURE 9.1
The Necker Cube

TRY THIS Each of the two squares in the Necker cube can be perceived as either the front or rear surface the cube. Try to make the cube switch of back and forth between these two orientations. Now try to hold only one orientation. You probably cannot maintain the whole cube in consciousness for longer than about three seconds before it "flips" from one orientation to the other.

conscious level The level at which mental activities that people are normally aware of occur.

TRY THIS

Some mental events, however, cannot be experienced consciously. For example, you are not directly aware of your brain regulating your blood pressure. That kind of mental processing occurs at the **nonconscious level**, which is entirely outside of conscious awareness. Although we cannot experience nonconscious processes, some people can learn to control them through *biofeedback training*. This training allows you to receive information about your biological processes and try to change them. Usually, special equipment is required, but you can approximate a biofeedback session by having a friend take your pulse at one-minute intervals while you sit quietly. First, establish a baseline pulse; then imagine a peaceful scene or think about lowering your pulse rate. Then ask your friend to softly say whether your pulse is higher or lower compared with the baseline. After four or five minutes of having this information "fed back" to you, you will probably be able to keep your pulse below the original baseline. Yet the pulse-regulating processes themselves remain out of consciousness.

Other mental events are not normally conscious, but they can either become conscious or influence our conscious experience. These mental events make up the *cognitive unconscious* (Reber, 1992), which includes the preconscious and unconscious (or subconscious). Mental events at the **preconscious level** are outside of awareness but can easily be brought into awareness. For example, what did you have for dinner last night? The information you needed to answer this question was probably not at a conscious level, but it was at a preconscious level and ready to be brought into awareness. When playing a trivia game, you draw on your storehouse of preconscious memories to come up with obscure facts.

There are still other mental activities that can alter thoughts, feelings, and actions but are more difficult to bring into awareness (Ratner, 1994). As described in the chapter on personality, Freud suggested that mental events at the **unconscious level**—especially those involving unacceptable sexual and aggressive urges—are actively kept out of consciousness. Many psychologists do not accept Freud's view but still use the term *unconscious* or *subconscious* to describe the level of mental activity that influences consciousness but is not conscious (Dijksterhuis & Nordgren, 2006).

LINKAGES Can subliminal messages help you lose weight? (a link to Perception, p. 161)

Mental Processing Without Awareness

A fascinating demonstration of mental processing without awareness comes from an experiment with patients who had surgery under general anesthesia. While they were still unconscious in the recovery room, a recording of fifteen word pairs was played over and over. After regaining consciousness, these patients could not say what words had been played—or even whether anything had been played at all. Yet when given one word from each of the word pairs on the recording and asked to say the first word that came to mind, the patients were able to produce the other member of the word pair (Cork, Kihlstrom, & Hameroff, 1992).

Even conscious and alert people process information without awareness (Adams et al., 2010; Gaillard et al., 2006). Research participants in one study watched a computer screen as an X flashed in one of four locations. The participants' task was to indicate where the X appeared by rapidly pushing one of four buttons. The X's location seemed to vary randomly, but the movement sequence actually followed a set of complex rules, such as "If the X moves horizontally twice in a row, then it will move vertically next." The participants' responses became progressively faster and more accurate. But when the rules were suddenly abandoned and the X appeared in truly random locations, the participants' speed and accuracy immediately worsened. They had learned a complex rule-bound strategy that improved their performance but were apparently unaware of it. Even when offered a monetary reward if they could state the rules that had guided the movement sequence, they were unable to do so; in fact, they doubted that any such rules existed (Lewicki, 1992).

Visual processing without awareness may also occur in cases of people who have been blinded by brain damage that is limited to the primary visual cortex. In such cases, fibers from the eyes are still connected to other brain areas that process visual

nonconscious level A level of mental activity that is inaccessible to conscious awareness.

preconscious level A level of mental activity that is not currently conscious but of which we can easily become conscious.

unconscious level A level of mental activity that influences consciousness but is not conscious.

Evidence for the operation of subconscious mental processing includes research showing that surgery patients may be able to hear and later comply with instructions or suggestions given while they are under anesthesia and of which they have no memory (Bennett, Giannini, & Davis, 1985). Another study found that people have physiological responses to emotionally charged words even when they are not paying attention to them (Von Wright, Anderson, & Stenman, 1975). These and other similar studies provide evidence for the operation of subconscious mental processing (Deeprose & Andrade, 2006).

BLOOM COUNTY by Berke Breathed

FIGURE 9.2
Possible or Impossible?

TRY THIS Look at these figures, and decide, as quickly as you can, whether each can actually exist. Priming studies show that this task would be easier for figures you have seen in the past, even if you don't recall seeing them. How did you do? (The correct answers appear at the bottom of page 336.)

Source: D.L. Schacter, L.A. Cooper, S.M. Delaney, M.A. Peterson, and M. Tharan. "Implicit Memory for Possible and Impossible Objects: Constraints on the Construction of Structural Descriptions". *Journal Of Experimental Psychology.* Copyright © American Psychological Association. Reprinted by permission.

information. Some of these surviving pathways may permit visual processing without visual awareness—a condition known as *blindsight* (Binsted et al., 2007; Galpin, Underwood, & Chapman, 2008). Even though they report seeing nothing, if forced to guess, these people can still locate visual targets, identify where images are moving, reach for objects, name the color of lights, and even discriminate happy from fearful faces (Morris et al., 2001; Striemer, Chapman, & Goodale, 2009). Blindsight has been created in visually normal volunteers using transcranial magnetic brain stimulation to temporarily disable the primary visual cortex (Ro & Rafal, 2006).

Another example of mental processing without awareness comes from research on *priming.* In a typical priming study, certain stimuli are presented so briefly that participants are not consciously aware of seeing them (Breuer et al., 2009). Later, people tend to respond faster or more accurately to previously seen stimuli, even though they cannot consciously recall them (Abrams & Greenwald, 2000; Kouider & Dupoux, 2005). In one set of studies, research participants looked at a set of drawings such as those in Figure 9.2 and had to decide which could actually exist as three-dimensional objects and which could not. The participants were better at correctly classifying drawings that they had seen before, even though they could not remember having seen them (Cooper et al., 1992; Schacter et al., 1991).

Priming can alter other kinds of behavior too. For example, experimenters asked research participants to unscramble scrambled sentences (e.g., "Finds he it instantly"). For one group of participants, the scrambled sentences all contained words associated with rudeness (e.g., *rude, bother, annoying*). A second group read sentences whose scrambled words were associated with politeness (e.g., *respect, honor, polite*). The scrambled words read by a third group were neutral (e.g., *normally, sends, rapidly*). After completing the unscrambling task, each participant was asked to go to another room to get further instructions from the experimenter. But by design, the experimenter was always found talking to a research assistant. The dependent variable in this experiment was the percentage of participants who interrupted the experimenter.

1

2

3

4

5

6

7

8

9

10

11

12

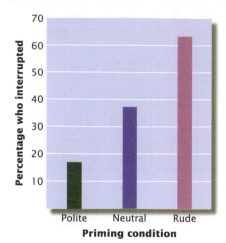

FIGURE 9.3

Priming Behavior Without Awareness

Participants in this study were primed with rude, polite, or neutral words before being confronted with the problem of interrupting a conversation. Though not consciously aware of the priming process, participants who had been exposed to rude words were most likely to interrupt, whereas those previously exposed to polite words were least likely to do so.

Source: John A Bargh, Mark Chen, and Lara Burrows. "Automaticity of Social Behavior: Direct Effects of Trait Construction and Stereotype Activation on Action". *Journal Of Personality And Social Psychology*, vol. 71, No. 2, p. 235, figure 1. Copyright © 1996 by The American Psychological Association. Reprinted by permission.

As shown in Figure 9.3, participants in the "rude priming" condition were most likely to interrupt, whereas those in the "polite priming" condition were least likely to do so. Those in the "neutral" condition fell in between the other two groups (Bargh, Chen, & Burrows, 1996).

The results of priming studies not only confirm the extent to which mental processing occurs outside of awareness but also challenge some of the traditional Freudian views about the functions of the unconscious. Freud argued that unconscious processes act mainly to protect us from painful or frightening thoughts, feelings, and memories by keeping them out of awareness (Pervin, 2003). However, research on priming, blindsight, and other unconscious processes leads many psychologists to believe that a primary function of these processes is to help us more effectively carry out mundane, day-to-day mental activities (Dijksterhuis et al., 2006, 2009; Myers, 2004). For example, the "hunch," or "gut feeling," or intuition that guided your "lucky" choice of the fastest-moving supermarket checkout line may actually have been based on previous visits that gave you useful information about the speed and efficiency of the various clerks—information that you didn't know you had (Adolphs et al., 2005). In a laboratory study that supports this notion, people watched videotaped television commercials while the changing stock prices of fictional companies "crawled" across the bottom of the screen. Later, these people were asked to choose which of these companies they liked best. They couldn't recall anything they had seen about the companies' stock, so they had to make their choice on the basis of their "gut reaction" to the company names. Nevertheless, their choices were not random; they more often chose companies whose stock prices had been rising rather than those whose stock had been falling (Betch et al., 2003).

Many questions remain about the relationship between conscious and unconscious processes. One of the most significant questions is whether conscious and unconscious thoughts are independent of each other. Priming studies seem to suggest that they are independent, but other research suggests that that may not always be so. For example, one study found a correlation between unconscious indicators of age prejudice—as seen in implicit memory for negative stereotypes about the elderly—and consciously held attitudes toward the elderly (Hense, Penner, & Nelson, 1995). Another study found similarity between unconscious and conscious forms of ethnic prejudice (Lepore & Brown, 1997). Overall, however, if there is a relationship between explicit and implicit cognitions, it appears to be weak and not yet clearly understood (Dovidio, Kawakami, & Beach, 2001). We consider this question further in the chapter on social cognition.

FOCUS ON RESEARCH METHODS

Subliminal Messages in Popular Music

According to Wikipedia and various other Internet Web sites and blogs, Satanic or drug-related messages have been embedded in the recorded music of Marilyn Manson, Eminem, Led Zeppelin, the Beatles, the Rolling Stones, and nearly a hundred other performers. The story goes that because these alleged messages were recorded backward, they are *subliminal* (that is, not consciously perceived), but they have supposedly influenced listeners to commit suicide or murder. For this claim to be true, however, the subliminal backward message would have to be perceived at some level of consciousness.

What was the researchers' question?

If you have ever searched the Internet for backward music clips, you were probably able to hear the messages you are supposed to be listening for. That's because, as discussed in the perception chapter, your expectations about what you were supposed to hear led you to organize meaningless noise into a pattern that resembles words. But suppose for a moment that meaningful messages were actually inserted, backward, into popular music. Could those messages be perceived and understood, and could they have any effect on behavior? These were the crucial questions posed by John R. Vokey and J. Don Read.

Answers for Figure 9.2: Figures 1, 4, 5, 7, 10, and 12 can exist in three-dimensional space.

Subliminal Messages in Popular Music?

These demonstrators are protesting outside a Marilyn Manson concert. Some people believe that Manson's music, as well as that of other musicians, contains subliminal messages advocating drug use, violence, and Satanism.

© AP Photo/Florida Times-Union, Stuart Tannehill

How did the researchers answer the question?

Vokey and Read (1985) conducted a classic series of multiple case studies on people's ability to understand backward-recorded messages. First, they recorded readings of portions of the Bible's Twenty-Third Psalm and Lewis Carroll's poem "Jabberwocky." They then asked college students to listen to these recordings being played backward. In other words, the researchers created a recording that actually does contain a backward message. If it is possible to understand backward messages, the students should have been able to hear something meaningful—the words of the psalm or the poem—in the recordings. Failing that, they should have at least been able say whether or not the recordings would have been meaningful if played in a normal direction.

What did the researchers find?

As it turned out, the students were unable to perceive anything meaningful when the biblical or poetic messages were played backward. They could not tell the difference between declarative sentences and questions, let alone identify the original content of the recordings. In short, the students could not consciously make sense of the Bible passage or the poem when they were played backward. But perhaps the students perceived some meaning subconsciously, without being aware of it. To find out, the researchers asked the participants to sort the backward statements they had heard into one of five categories: nursery rhyme, Christian, Satanic, pornographic, or advertising. They reasoned that if some sort of meaning could be subconsciously understood, the participants would be able to sort the statements in some logical way. However, the participants did no better at this task than random chance would predict. Taken together, these results suggest that even if someone were to purposely insert messages backward into popular music, they could not be perceived.

Can even *unperceived* backward messages unconsciously shape behavior? To answer this question, Vokey and Read presented a backward version of a message whose sentences contained homophones (words that sound alike but have two spellings and two different meanings, such as *feat* and *feet*). When heard in the normal forward direction, such messages affect people's spelling of ambiguous words that are read aloud to them at a later time. (For example, people tend to spell out *f-e-a-t* rather than *f-e-e-t* if they previously heard the sentence "It was a great feat of strength.") This example of priming occurs even if people do not recall having heard the message. After hearing a backward version of the message, however, the participants in this study did not show the expected spelling bias.

What do the results mean?

Obviously, it wasn't possible for the participants to subconsciously understand meaning in the backward messages. Backward messages are evidently not consciously or unconsciously understood, nor do they influence behavior (Vokey, 2002).

What do we still need to know?

Researchers would like to know why the incorrect idea persists that backward messages can influence behavior. Its staying power appears to be an example of the fact that strongly held beliefs and suspicions do not simply disappear in the face of contrary scientific evidence (Vyse, 2000; Winer et al., 2002). Indeed, it seems likely that some people so deeply want to believe in the existence and power of backward messages in music that their beliefs will forever hold the status of folk myths in Western culture.

The Neuropsychology of Consciousness

Studies of brain damage have proved valuable in deepening our understanding of various levels of consciousness and how various brain regions are involved in each of them. Some forms of brain damage cause a condition known as *prosopagnosia* (pronounced "proh-soh-pag-NOH-zhuh"). People with prosopagnosia cannot consciously recognize faces—not even their own reflection—yet they can see and recognize many other objects and can recognize people by their voices (Barton, 2003; Stone & Valentine, 2003). This condition may be part of a more general inability to recognize familiar objects, but in most cases the problem is relatively specific for faces. One farmer with prosopagnosia could recognize and name his sheep but could not recognize humans (McNeil & Warrington, 1993). Still, when such people see faces that they should know—but do not consciously recognize—they show eye movement patterns, changes in brain activity, and autonomic nervous system responses that do not occur when viewing unfamiliar faces (Schweinberger & Burton, 2003). These covert responses are especially strong when the face shows an emotional expression (de Gelder et al., 2003). So some vestige of face recognition can be preserved in prosopagnosia, but it is unavailable to conscious experience.

Brain damage can also impair conscious access to other mental abilities. Consider *anterograde amnesia,* the inability to form new memories, which can be caused by damage to the hippocampus. Anterograde amnesics seem unable to remember any new information, even about the passage of time. One man who developed this condition in 1957 still needed to be reminded more than thirty years later that it was no longer 1957 (Smith, 1988). Yet anterograde amnesics can learn new skills, even though they may not consciously recall the practice sessions (Milner, 1965). Their brain activity, too, shows different reactions to words they have recently studied than to other words, even though they have no memory of studying them (Düzel et al., 2001).

Consciousness States

Mental activity is always changing. The features of consciousness at any instant—what reaches your awareness, the decisions you are making, and so on—make up your **consciousness state** at that moment (Tassi & Muzet, 2001). States of consciousness can range from deep sleep to alert wakefulness; they can also be affected by drugs and other influences. Consider, for example, the range of consciousness states among the people aboard an airplane en route from New York to Los Angeles. In the cockpit, the pilot calmly scans instrument displays while talking to an air traffic controller. In seat 9B, a lawyer has just finished her second cocktail while planning a courtroom strategy. Nearby, a young father gazes out a window, daydreaming, while his small daughter sleeps in his lap, dreaming dreams of her own.

All these people are experiencing different states of consciousness. Some states are active, and some are passive. The daydreaming father is letting his mind wander, passively noting images, memories, and other mental events that come unbidden to mind. The lawyer is actively directing her mental activity, evaluating various options and considering their likely outcomes.

Most people spend most of their time in a waking state of consciousness. Mental processing in this state varies with changes in attention or arousal (J. G. Taylor, 2002).

consciousness state The characteristics of consciousness at any particular moment.

Altered States and Cultural Values

Cultures define which altered states of consciousness are approved and which are not. Here we see members of a Brazilian spirit possession cult in various stages of trance (left) and, in Peru (right), a Moche *curandero,* or healer, attempting to cure a patient by using fumes from a potion—and a drug from the San Pedro cactus—to put himself in an altered state of consciousness.

While reading, for example, you may temporarily ignore sounds around you. Similarly, if you are upset or bored or talking on a cell phone, you may miss important environmental cues, making it dangerous to drive a car.

When changes in mental processes are great enough to produce noticeable differences in how you function, you have entered an **altered state of consciousness.** In an altered state, mental processing shows distinct changes unique to that state. Cognitive processes or perceptions of yourself or the world may change, and normal inhibitions or self-control may weaken (Vaitl et al., 2005).

The phrase *altered states of consciousness* recognizes waking consciousness as the most common state, a baseline against which "altered" states are compared. However, this is not to say that waking consciousness is universally considered more normal, proper, or valued than other states. In fact, value judgments about different states of consciousness vary considerably across cultures (Ward, 1994).

Consider, for instance, *hallucinations,* which are perceptual experiences (such as hearing voices) that occur in the absence of sensory stimuli. In the United States, hallucinations are considered so undesirable that even normal people who develop visual hallucinations due to an eye disorder may be reluctant to seek the medical help they need to resolve the problem (Menon et al., 2003). Among mental patients, those who hallucinate often feel stress and self-blame and may choose not to report their hallucinations (Karidi et al., 2010). Patients who do report them tend to be considered more disturbed and may receive more drastic treatments than those who keep their hallucinations to themselves (Wilson et al., 1996). Among the Moche of Peru, however, hallucinations have a culturally approved place. When someone is beset by illness or misfortune, a healer conducts an elaborate ritual to find causes and treatments. During the ceremony, the healer ingests mescaline, a drug that causes hallucinations. These hallucinations are thought to give the healer spiritual insight into the patient's problems (de Rios, 1992). In the context of many other tribal cultures, too, purposeful hallucinations are revered, not demeaned (Grob & Dobkin-de Rios, 1992).

In other words, consciousness states differ not only in their basic characteristics but also in their value to members of particular cultures. In the sections to follow, we describe some of the most interesting altered states of consciousness, beginning with the most common one, sleep.

altered state of consciousness A condition in which changes in mental processes are extensive enough that a person or others notice significant differences in psychological and behavioral functioning.

Sleeping and Dreaming

According to ancient myths, sleepers lose control of their minds, flirting with death as their souls wander freely. Early researchers thought sleep was a time of mental inactivity. In fact, however, sleep is an active, complex state (Hobson, 2005).

A Sleep Lab

The electroencephalograph (EEG) allows scientists to record brain activity through electrodes attached to the scalp. The development of this technology in the 1950s opened the door to the scientific study of sleep.

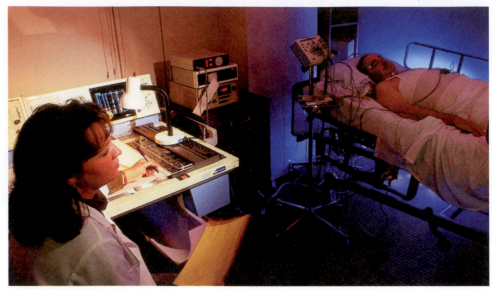

© Will & Deni McIntyre/Photo Researchers, Inc.

LINKAGES Does the brain shut down when we sleep? (a link to Biological Aspects of Psychology, p. 74)

Stages of Sleep

Sleep researchers monitor the brain's electrical activity during sleep by attaching tiny disks called electrodes to a person's scalp and connecting them to an *electroencephalograph,* or *EEG.* The resulting EEG recordings, often called *brain waves,* show changes in height (amplitude) and speed (frequency) as behavior or mental processes change. The brain waves of an awake, alert person have high frequency and low amplitude. They appear as small, closely spaced, irregular EEG waves. A person who is awake but relaxing with closed eyes shows *alpha waves,* which are regular rhythmic brain waves occurring at speeds of 8 to 12 cycles per second. During a normal night's sleep, your brain waves show distinctive and systematic changes in amplitude and frequency as you pass through various stages of sleep (Durka et al., 2005).

Non-REM Sleep Imagine that you are participating in a sleep study. You are hooked up to an EEG and various monitors, and a video camera watches as you sleep through the night. If you were to review the results, here's what you'd see: At first, you are relaxed, with your eyes closed, but you are awake. At this point, your muscle tone and eye movements are normal, and your EEG shows the slow brain waves associated with relaxation. As you drift into sleep, your breathing deepens, your heartbeat slows, and your blood pressure falls. Over the next half hour, you descend through four stages of sleep characterized by even slower brain waves with even higher amplitude (see Figure 9.4). The deepest of these, stages 3 and 4, are known as *slow-wave sleep.* When you reach stage 4, it is quite difficult to wake up. If you were roused from this stage of deep sleep, you would be groggy and confused. Together, these four stages are called **non-REM (NREM) sleep** because they do not include the rapid eye movements (REM) described in the next section.

REM Sleep After thirty to forty-five minutes in stage 4, you quickly return to stage 2 and then enter a special stage in which your eyes move rapidly beneath their eyelids. This is called **rapid eye movement (REM) sleep**, or *paradoxical sleep.* It is called *paradoxical* because its characteristics present a paradox, or contradiction. In REM sleep, your EEG resembles that of an awake, alert person, and your physiological arousal—heart rate, breathing, and blood pressure—is also similar to when you are awake. However, your muscles are nearly paralyzed. Sudden, twitchy spasms appear, especially in your face and hands, but your brain actively suppresses other movements (Blumberg & Lucas, 1994).

In other words, there are two distinctly different types of sleep, REM sleep and NREM sleep (Lu et al., 2006).

non-REM (NREM) sleep Sleep stages 1, 2, 3, and 4; they are accompanied by gradually slower and deeper breathing, a calm and regular heartbeat, reduced blood pressure, and slower brain waves. (Stages 3 and 4 are called *slow-wave sleep.*)

Rapid eye movement (REM) sleep A stage of sleep in which brain activity and other functions resemble the waking state but that is accompanied by rapid eye movements and virtual muscle paralysis.

FIGURE 9.4

EEG During Sleep

EEG recordings of brain wave activity show four relatively distinct stages of sleep. Notice the regular patterns of alpha waves that occur just before a person goes to sleep, followed by the slowing of brain waves as sleep becomes deeper (stages 1 through 4). In REM (rapid eye movement) sleep, the frequency of brain waves increases dramatically and in some ways resembles patterns seen in people who are awake.

Source: James Horne. *Why We Sleep: The Functions of Sleep in Humans and Other Mammals.* Copyright © 1989. Reprinted by permission of Oxford University Press. For more information, go to www.oup.com

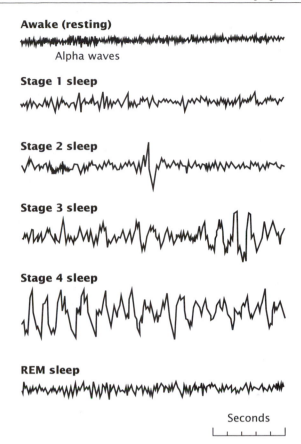

A Night's Sleep   Most people pass through the cycle of sleep stages four to six times each night. Each cycle lasts about ninety minutes, but with a somewhat changing pattern of stages and stage duration. Early in the night, most of the time is spent in NREM sleep, with only a few minutes in REM sleep (see Figure 9.5). As sleep continues, though, it is dominated by stage 2 and REM sleep, from which sleepers finally awaken.

Sleep patterns change with time; overall, people sleep less as they age (Floyd, 2002), though that pattern varies to some degree across cultures and countries (Ohayon,

FIGURE 9.5

A Night's Sleep

During a typical night, a sleeper goes through this sequence of EEG stages. Notice that sleep is deepest during the first part of the night and more shallow later on, when REM sleep becomes more prominent.

Adapted from Cartwright, A Primer of Sleep and Dreaming. Copyright © 1978 Addison-Wesley. Reprinted by permission of Pearson Education, Inc.

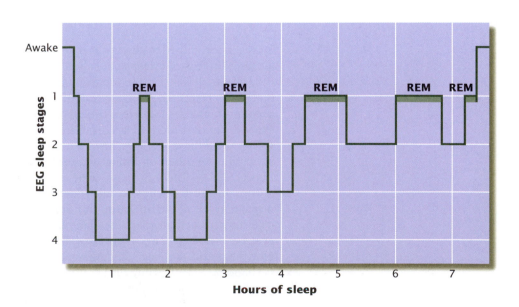

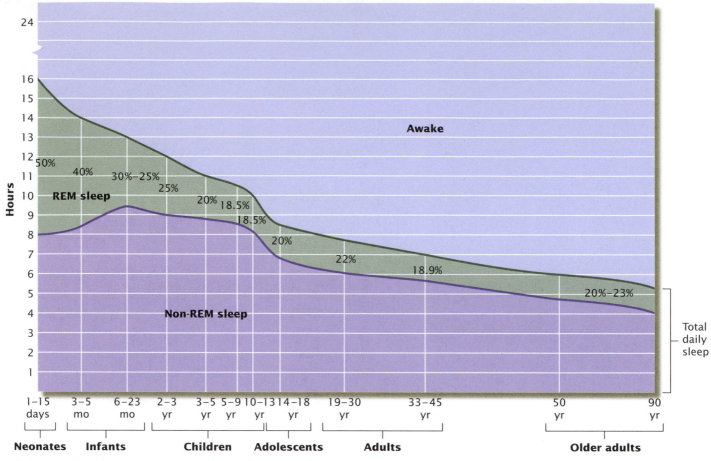

Note: Percentages indicate portion of total sleep time in REM sleep.

FIGURE 9.6

Sleep and Dreaming over the Life Span

People tend to sleep less as they get older. There is also a sharp reduction in the percentage of REM sleep, from about eight hours per day in infancy to about an hour per day by age seventy. Non-REM sleep time also decreases but, compared with the drop in REM, remains relatively stable. After age 20, however, non-REM sleep contains less and less of the deepest, or stage 4, sleep.

Roffwarg et al. "Ontogenetic Development of the Human Sleep Dream Cycle". Science, vol. 152, p. 606, 29 April 1966 (revised 1969). © Copyright 1966 AAAS. Reprinted with permission.

2004). In the United States, the average infant sleeps about sixteen hours a day and the average 70-year-old sleeps only about six hours (Roffwarg, Muzio, & Dement, 1966). Elderly people also tend to wake up more often during the night than younger people do (Floyd, 2002). The composition of sleep changes, too (see Figure 9.6). REM sleep accounts for half of total sleep time at birth but less than 25 percent in young adults and even less in the elderly (Darchia, Campbell, & Feinberg, 2003). Individuals may vary widely from these averages, however. Some people feel well rested after four hours of sleep, whereas others of similar age require ten hours to feel satisfied (Clausen, Sersen, & Lidsky, 1974). There are also wide variations among cultural and socioeconomic groups in the tendency to take daytime naps. Contrary to stereotypes about the popularity of siestas in Latin and South American countries, urban Mexican college students actually nap less than many other college populations (Valencia-Flores et al., 1998). Sleep patterns are also partly a matter of choice or necessity. For example, North American college students get less sleep than other people their age (Hicks, Fernandez, & Pellegrini, 2001). This trend has grown over the past thirty years as students deal with academic and job responsibilities, along with family obligations

The Cost of Jet Lag

Twice a year, thousands of exhibitors freshly arrived from around the world groggily set up dazzling displays at Asia's largest jewelry show. Then they try to wait on customers while keeping track of their treasures. Taking advantage of these jet-lagged travelers' inattentiveness, thieves steal millions of dollars' worth of merchandise at every show (Fowler, 2004). The effects of jet lag can also be seen in the results of Major League Baseball games. In 24,121 games played over a ten-year period, the usual home field advantage appeared; visiting teams won only 46.3 percent of the time. But when the visitors played after traveling across three time zones the previous day, they won only 39.4 percent of the time (Winter et al., 2009).

© Jodi Cobb/National Geographic Image Collection/Getty Images

and a variety of recreational activities—including late-night sessions of playing computer games or surfing the Internet. You have probably noticed the results of sleep deprivation as your classmates (or you?) struggle to stay awake during lectures.

Why Do People Sleep?

In trying to understand why we sleep, psychologists have studied both the functions that sleep serves and the ways in which brain mechanisms shape its characteristics.

Sleep as a Circadian Rhythm   The sleep-wake cycle is one example of the rhythmic nature of life. In almost all animals, including humans, certain cycles of behavior and physiology repeat about every twenty-four hours (Markov & Goldman, 2006). These cyclical patterns are called **circadian rhythms** (from the Latin *circa dies*, meaning "about a day"), or **human biological rhythms**. Circadian (pronounced "sur-KAY-dee-in") rhythms are linked, or *entrained*, to signals such as the light and dark of day and night, but most of them continue even when no such cues are available. Volunteers living for months without external time cues maintain approximately twenty-four-hour rhythms in sleeping and waking, hormone release, eating, urination, and other physiological functions (Czeisler et al., 1999).

Changing the sleep-wake cycle can create problems. For example, air travel across several time zones often causes **jet lag,** a pattern of fatigue, irritability, inattention, and sleeping problems that can last several days (Akerstedt, 2007). The traveler's body feels ready to sleep at the wrong time for the new locale. Because it tends to be easier to stay awake longer than usual than to go to sleep earlier than usual, sleep-wake rhythms readjust to altered light-dark cycles more easily when sleep is shifted to a later, rather than an earlier, time (Lemmer et al., 2002). As a result, people usually have more intense symptoms of jet lag after eastward travel (when time is lost) than after westward travel (when time is gained; Doane et al., 2010). Symptoms resembling jet lag also affect workers who repeatedly change between day and night shifts (Arendt, 2010). The same is true for people who have trouble getting to sleep at their normal bedtime on a Sunday night after a weekend of later-than-usual bedtimes (Czeisler et al., 2005; Di Milia, 2006). Their Monday morning "blues" may actually be symptoms of a disrupted sleep-wake cycle. This problem is especially noticeable

circadian rhythm (human biological rhythm) A cycle, such as waking and sleeping, that repeats about once a day.

jet lag A syndrome of fatigue, irritability, inattention, and sleeping problems caused by air travel across several time zones.

FIGURE 9.7

Sleep, Dreaming, and the Brain
Here are some of the brain structures thought to be involved in sleep, dreaming, and other altered states of consciousness discussed later in the chapter. Scientists have discovered two specialized areas in the hypothalamus that appear to coordinate sleep and wakefulness. The preoptic nucleus appears to promote sleep. People with damage in this hypothalamic region find it difficult to ever go to sleep. The posterior lateral hypothalamus appears to promote wakefulness. Damage here causes continuous sleeping from which the person can be awakened only briefly

Source: Salin-Pascual et al., 2001; Saper, Chou, & Scammell, 2001.

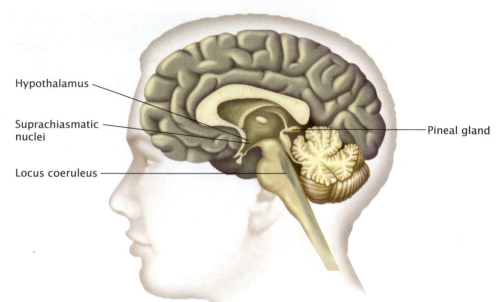

on the Monday after the weekend when the start of daylight savings time has cost us yet another hour of sleep (Barnes & Wagner, 2009). Collective grogginess may be partly responsible for the unusually high number of traffic accidents on that Monday (Varughese & Allen, 2001).

The length of circadian rhythms varies from person to person. Some people have a natural tendency to stay up later at night ("owls") or to wake up earlier in the morning ("larks"). And there are those who suffer because their circadian rhythms are never quite in sync with the local light-dark cycle (Ando, Kripke, & Ancoli-Israel, 2002). Because our circadian rhythms continue without external cues about light and dark, the brain must contain a "biological clock" that keeps track of time. This clock is in the *suprachiasmatic nuclei (SCN)* of the hypothalamus (see Figure 9.7; Kalsbeek et al., 2006). The SCN receives information about light and darkness from a special set of photoreceptors in the eye and then sends signals to areas in the hindbrain that promote sleep or wakefulness (Albus et al., 2005; Lee, Nelms, et al., 2003; Saper, Scammell, & Lu, 2005).

SCN neurons show a rhythm of activity that repeats itself every twenty-four to twenty-five hours, even if the neurons are removed from the brain and put in a laboratory dish (Yamaguchi et al., 2003). When animals with SCN damage receive transplanted SCN cells from another animal, their new circadian rhythms are similar to those of the donor animal (Menaker & Vogelbaum, 1993). SCN neurons also regulate the release of the hormone *melatonin* from the pineal gland. Melatonin, in turn, appears to be important in maintaining circadian rhythms (Beaumont et al., 2004; Cardinali et al., 2002). In fact, many of the symptoms associated with jet lag and other disruptions in sleep-wake cycles can be prevented or treated by taking melatonin (Lack & Wright, 2007; Revell & Eastman, 2005), although regular use, such as by commercial airline crew members, is not recommended (Simons & Valk, 2009). There is some evidence, too, that sildenafil—a drug normally prescribed for erectile dysfunction—can speed recovery from jet lag after eastbound but not westbound travel (Stephenson, 2007). Exercise and exposure to natural lighting conditions upon daytime arrival or exposure to dim light upon nighttime arrival may also reduce jet lag (Armstrong, 2006; Edwards, Reilly, & Waterhouse, 2009; Evans, Elliott, & Gorman, 2009).

The Value of Sleep   One way to explore the benefits of sleep is to study what happens when people are prevented from sleeping. People who go without sleep for as long as a week usually do not suffer serious long-term effects, but prolonged sleeplessness does lead to fatigue, irritability, and inattention (Drummond et al., 2000; Turner et al., 2007). The effects of short-term sleep deprivation—which is a common condition in busy adolescents and adults—can also take their toll (Calamaro, Mason, & Ratcliffe, 2009; Lim & Dinges, 2010; Steptoe, Peacey, & Wardle, 2006). Mistakes in patient care may be more likely among medical interns and residents who work sleep-disrupting extended hospital shifts (Ayas et al., 2006; Landrigan et al., 2004; West et al., 2009). Most of the fatal auto accidents in the United States occur during the "fatigue hazard" hours of midnight to 6:00 A.M. (Coleman, 1992), and sleepiness resulting from long work shifts or other causes is a major factor in up to 25 percent of all auto accidents (Barger et al., 2005; Garbarino et al., 2001; Philip et al., 2001). Fatigue also plays a role in many injuries suffered by sleepy young children at play or in day care (Valent, Brusaferro, & Barbone, 2001). Learning and performance on IQ tests are impaired after sleep deprivation (Gruber et al., 2010; Yoo et al., 2007), and it can reduce the ability of the body's immune system to fight off colds (Cohen et al., 2009). Exposure to light can reduce the effects of drowsiness (Shirani & Saint Louis, 2009), and so may getting extra sleep before a period of sleep deprivation (Rupp et al., 2009). Drug companies are looking for medications to combat the effects of sleep deprivation (Porrino et al., 2005), but there appears to be no substitute for sleep itself.

Some researchers suggest that sleep helps restore the body and the brain for future activity and helps consolidate memories of newly learned facts (Gais et al., 2007; Korman et al., 2007; Racsmány, Conway, & Demeter, 2010; Rasch & Born, 2008; Walker & Stickgold, 2006). Restorative functions are especially associated with non-REM sleep, which would help explain why most people get their non-REM sleep in the first part of the night (see Figure 9.5).

There is also an apparent need for REM sleep. Sleep-deprived people do not make up lost sleep hour for hour. Instead, they sleep about 50 percent more than usual and awake feeling rested. But if people are deprived only of REM sleep, they later compensate more directly. In a classic study, participants were awakened whenever their EEG tracings showed REM sleep. When allowed to sleep uninterrupted the next night, the participants "rebounded," nearly doubling the percentage of time spent in REM sleep (Dement, 1960). Even after total sleep deprivation, the next night of uninterrupted sleep includes an unusually high percentage of REM sleep (Feinberg & Campbell, 1993).

The Effects of Sleep Deprivation

Here scientists at Loughborough University, England, test the effects of sleep deprivation on motor coordination. Driving while sleep-deprived can be so dangerous that at least one U.S. state (New Jersey) has expanded the definition of reckless driving to include "driving while fatigued." This condition is presumed to be present when someone has had no sleep in the previous twenty-four hours, but research is under way to identify more reliable biological indicators of when a person is dangerously fatigued (Seugnet et al., 2006).

© Patrick Ward/Stock, Boston

This research suggests that REM has its own special functions. What these special functions might be is still unclear, but there are several interesting possibilities.

First, REM sleep may improve the functioning of neurons that use norepinephrine (Siegel & Rogawski, 1988). Norepinephrine is a neurotransmitter released by cells in the *locus coeruleus* (pronounced "LOH-kuss seh-ROO-lee-uss"; see Figure 9.7). During waking hours, norepinephrine affects alertness and mood. But the brain's neurons lose sensitivity to norepinephrine if it is released continuously for too long. Because the locus coeruleus is almost completely inactive during REM sleep, researchers suggest that REM helps restore sensitivity to norepinephrine and thus its ability to keep us alert (Steriade & McCarley, 1990). Animals deprived of REM sleep show unusually high norepinephrine levels and decreased daytime alertness (Brock et al., 1994).

REM sleep may also help strengthen new connections between nerve cells in the brain (Graves, Pack, & Abel, 2001; Maquet, 2001; Peigneux et al., 2001). If so, it would explain why children and infants, whose brains are still developing, spend so much time in REM sleep (see Figure 9.6). Evidence favoring this possibility comes from research showing that REM sleep enhances the creation of neural connections in response to altered visual experience during the development of the visual cortex (Frank et al., 2001). REM sleep may also help solidify and absorb the day's experiences, including newly learned skills (Diekelman & Born, 2010). In one study, people who were REM-deprived showed poorer retention of a skill learned the day before than people who were either deprived of non-REM sleep or allowed to sleep normally (Karni et al., 1994). Other studies have found that information, including emotional information, is remembered better and longer when followed immediately by sleep, especially REM sleep (Djonlagic et al., 2009; Gais, Lucas, & Born, 2006; Gomez, Bootzin, & Nadel, 2006; Hu, Stylos-Allan, & Walker, 2006). Accordingly, some researchers have suggested that sleep deprivation in the aftermath of a traumatic event might reduce or even prevent the appearance of posttraumatic stress disorder (Wagner et al., 2006). Even sixty- to ninety-minute naps in which REM sleep appears can be enough to solidify the learning of visual information (Mednick, Nakayama, & Stickgold, 2003). There is also some evidence that REM sleep may improve daytime creativity (Cai et al., 2009).

Sleep Disorders

Most people experience sleep-related problems at some point in their lives (Krahn, 2003). These can range from occasional nights of tossing and turning to the more serious and long-term *sleep disorders* that affect as many as 70 million people in the United States alone (Institute of Medicine, 2006; Morin et al., 2009). The most common sleeping problem is **insomnia,** persistent difficulty falling asleep or staying asleep at night, resulting in fatigue the following day (Neubauer & Flaherty, 2009). About a third of American adults suffer from insomnia in any given year (LeBlanc et al., 2009). If you have trouble getting to sleep or staying asleep and the problem persists for more than a month at a time, you may be suffering from insomnia. Insomnia is tied to mental distress, a reduced sense of well-being, and impaired daily functioning (Hamilton et al., 2007). Fatigue-related loss of productivity in workers has been estimated to cost an average of $1,967 a year per employee (Rosekind et al., 2010). Insomnia is also associated with mental disorders, especially depressive and anxiety disorders (Baglioni et al., 2010); overall, insomniacs are three times as likely to suffer a mental disorder as those without sleep complaints (Ohayon & Roth, 2003). It is unclear from such correlations, however, whether insomnia causes mental disorders, mental disorders cause insomnia, or some other factor causes both.

Most prescription sleeping pills can relieve insomnia, but they may interact dangerously with alcohol, disturb REM sleep, and eventually lead to *increased* sleeplessness (Curry, Eisenstein, & Walsh, 2006). Some people become dependent on these drugs. One novel medication, called ramelteon, mimics the action of melatonin, a hormone that is involved in the onset of normal sleep. Ramelteon is unusual because it appears to work better the longer one takes it (Pandi-Peerumal et al., 2009).

insomnia A sleep disorder involving difficulty falling asleep or staying asleep at night.

Stimulus Control Therapy

Insomnia can often be reduced through a combination of cognitive behavior therapy (see the chapter on treatment of psychological disorders), relaxation techniques, and *stimulus control therapy,* in which the person goes to bed only when sleepy and gets out of bed if sleep does not come within fifteen to twenty minutes. The goal is for the bed to become a stimulus associated with sleeping, and perhaps sex, but not with reading, eating, watching television, worrying, or anything else that is incompatible with sleep (Edinger et al., 2001; Ong, Cvengros, & Wyatt, 2008; Whitworth, Crownover, & Nichols, 2007).

© Colin Young-Wolff/PhotoEdit

Even more helpful ways to treat insomnia may lie in learning-based methods, including cognitive behavior therapy (described in the chapter on treatment of psychological disorders) and the progressive relaxation training techniques mentioned in the chapter on health, stress, and coping (Vincent & Lewycky, 2009; Yang, Spielman, & Glovinsky, 2006). Both have been shown to promote better sleeping by reducing anxiety, tension, and other reactions to stress (Bernstein, Borkovec, & Hazlett-Stevens, 2000; Jacobs et al., 2004). Short daytime naps and moderate evening exercise can also help some people get to sleep more easily, sleep better, and experience better mood and performance the next day (Tanaka et al., 2001).

Narcolepsy is a disturbing daytime sleep disorder that usually begins between the ages of 15 and 25 (Dyken & Yamada, 2005; Zeman et al., 2004). People with narcolepsy shift abruptly from an active, often emotional waking state into a few minutes of REM sleep. Because of the loss of muscle tone in REM, narcoleptics may experience *cataplexy,* which means that they collapse and remain briefly immobile even after awakening. These attacks are associated with decreased activity in the hypothalamus (Dauvilliers et al., 2009). The most common cause of narcolepsy appears to be a lack or deficiency of a neurotransmitter called *orexin,* also known as *hypocretin;* this neurotransmitter problem may stem from a genetic defect (Caylak, 2009; Miyagawa et al., 2008). Regularly scheduled daily naps can be a helpful treatment, as can combinations of certain drugs (Robinson & Keating, 2007; Schwartz, 2005). One of these, modafinil, appears to be effective not only for narcolepsy but also for counteracting the effects of sleep deprivation (Schwartz, 2009).

People with **sleep apnea** briefly stop breathing hundreds of times every night, waking up each time long enough to resume breathing (Dempsey et al., 2010). In the morning, they do not recall the awakenings, but they feel tired and tend to show reduced attention and learning ability (Naëgelé et al., 2006). In one tragic case, two members of a train crew—both of whom had apnea—fell asleep on the job, resulting in a collision that killed two people (Pickler, 2002). Sleep apnea has many causes, including genetic predisposition, obesity, failure of brain mechanisms controlling breathing, and compression of the windpipe (Pashayan, 2005). Effective treatments include weight loss and use of a continuous positive airway pressure (CPAP) mask that keeps breathing passages open by providing a steady stream of air all night (Foster et al., 2009; Lam et al., 2006). It may be necessary in some cases to surgically widen the air passageway in the upper throat (Friedman et al., 2003; Patel et al., 2003).

narcolepsy A daytime sleep disorder in which a person shifts abruptly from an active, often emotional, waking state into several minutes of REM sleep.

sleep apnea A sleep disorder in which people briefly but repeatedly stop breathing during the night.

© David Young-Wolff/PhotoEdit

Preventing Sudden Infant Death Syndrome (SIDS)

In SIDS cases, seemingly healthy infants stop breathing while asleep in their cribs. All the causes of SIDS are not known, but health authorities now urge parents to ensure that infants sleep on their backs, as this baby demonstrates, to avoid accidental suffocation.

sudden infant death syndrome (SIDS) A disorder in which a sleeping baby stops breathing and suffocates.

nightmare A frightening dream that takes place during REM sleep.

sleep terror disorder (night terrors) The occurrence of horrific dream images during stage 4 sleep, followed by rapid awakening in a state of intense fear.

sleepwalking A phenomenon primarily occurring in non-REM sleep in which people walk while asleep.

REM behavior disorder A sleep disorder in which a person does not lose muscle tone during REM sleep, allowing the person to act out dreams.

In cases of **sudden infant death syndrome (SIDS),** sleeping infants stop breathing and die. SIDS is the most common cause of unexpected infant death in Western countries (Hunt & Hauck, 2006). In the United States, for example, SIDS strikes about two of every thousand infants, especially very low birthweight babies, usually when they are 2 to 4 months old (Smith & White, 2006; Vernacchio et al., 2003). Some SIDS cases may stem from problems with brain systems regulating breathing, from exposure to cigarette smoke or other forms of air pollution, and possibly from genetic causes (Anderson, Johnson, & Batal, 2005; Audero et al., 2008; Creery & Mikrogianakis, 2004; Duncan et al., 2010; Ostfeld et al., 2010). SIDS rates appear to be lower in some countries where infants and parents sleep in the same bed (Gessner, Ives, & Perham-Hester, 2001; Li, Petitti, et al., 2003) but higher in others, including the United States and Ireland (McGarvey et al., 2006; Ostfeld et al., 2006). The differing risks may have to do with the kinds of bedding used or with sleeping position. As many as half of apparent SIDS cases may actually be accidental suffocations caused when infants sleep face-down on a soft surface (Corwin et al., 2003; Dwyer & Ponsonby, 2009; Shields et al., 2005). Observational evidence indicates that the face-down position poses the gravest danger to babies who do not usually sleep in that position or who do not sleep with a pacifier in their mouths (Li et al., 2006; Vennemann et al., 2009a, 2009b). Since 1994, when doctors began advising parents to place their babies in a face-up sleeping position, the number of SIDS deaths in the United States and the United Kingdom has dropped by 50 percent (Blair et al., 2006; Daley, 2004; Moon, Calabrese, & Aird, 2008; Rasinski et al., 2003). Babies who sleep face-up may also be less likely to inhale potentially toxic bacteria that grow in some foam mattresses (Jenkins & Sherbum, 2005; Weber et al., 2008).

Nightmares are distressing REM sleep dreams that occur in 4 to 8 percent of the general population. They occur in a much higher percentage of people who suffer from posttraumatic stress disorder following military combat, torture, or rape (Hinton et al., 2009; Kryger, Roth, & Dement, 2000). Drugs have proved helpful in reducing the frequency of nightmares (Raskind et al., 2006), and so has imagery therapy, in which people repeatedly imagine new and less frightening outcomes to their nightmares (Forbes, Phelps, & McHugh, 2001; Krakow et al., 2001). Whereas nightmares occur during REM sleep, **sleep terror disorder** (also known as **night terrors)** involves horrific dream images that occur during stage 4 sleep. Sleepers often awake from a night terror with a bloodcurdling scream and remain intensely frightened for up to thirty minutes, yet they may not recall the episode in the morning. Sleep terror disorder is especially common in boys, but adults can suffer milder versions. The condition is sometimes treatable with drugs.

Like sleep terror disorder, **sleepwalking** occurs during non-REM sleep, usually in childhood (Guilleminault et al., 2003). By morning, most sleepwalkers have forgotten their wanderings and their sometimes bizarre activities. One sleepwalking man had no recollection of tying his 4-month-old daughter to a clothesline in his attic (Pillmann, 2009). There are no consistently effective medical treatments for sleepwalking (Harris & Grunstein, 2009), although sleepwalkers who also have sleep apnea often find relief for both conditions by wearing a CPAP mask at night (Guilleminault et al., 2005). Most children simply outgrow the problem. Incidentally, waking a sleepwalker is not harmful. In fact, one man's sleepwalking was cured after his wife blew a whistle whenever he began a nocturnal stroll (Meyer, 1975).

In **REM behavior disorder,** the near paralysis that normally accompanies REM sleep does not occur, so sleepers move as if acting out their dreams, which may include eating, drinking, defecating, or even having sex (Oudiette et al., 2009; Schenck, 2005). The disorder can be dangerous to the dreamer or people nearby (Schenck et al., 2009). In January 2001, a 9-year-old boy in New York City was seriously injured when he jumped from a third-floor window while dreaming that his parents were being murdered. In another case, a man shot his wife to death while dreaming that their home was being invaded by burglars (de Bruxelles, 2009). He was acquitted of murder charges, but most defendants who offer a REM behavior disorder or sleepwalking defense—especially those who also attempt to conceal evidence—are not successful (Lyon, 2009). REM behavior disorder sometimes occurs along with daytime narcolepsy (Billiard, 2009; Schenck & Mahowald, 1992) and in one case was found to be caused by a brain tumor (Zambelis, Paparrigopoulos, & Soldatos, 2002). REM behavior disorder is also common in patients with Parkinson's disease and is often the first sign of a degenerative brain condition (Gagnon, Postuma, & Montplaisir, 2006; Postuma et al., 2009). Fortunately, prescription drugs are usually effective in treating REM behavior disorder (Gagnon et al., 2006; Takeuchi et al., 2001).

Dreams and Dreaming

We have seen that the brain is active in all sleep stages (for a summary of our discussion, see "In Review: Sleep and Sleep Disorders"). Some of this brain activity during sleep is experienced as the storylike sensations and perceptions known as **dreaming.** Dreams can last from seconds to minutes and may be organized or chaotic, realistic or fantastic, peaceful or exciting (Hobson & Stickgold, 1994).

Some dreaming occurs during non-REM sleep, but most dreams—and the most bizarre and vivid dreams—occur during REM sleep (Dement & Kleitman, 1957; Eiser, 2005). Even when dreams seem to make no sense, they may contain a certain amount of logic. In one study, for example, when segments from dream descriptions were scrambled, readers could correctly say which reports had been rearranged and which were intact (Stickgold, Rittenhouse, & Hobson, 1994). And although dreams often involve one person becoming another person or one object turning into another object, it is rare that objects become people or vice versa (Cicogna et al., 2006).

Daytime activities and experiences may influence the content of dreams to some degree (Valli et al., 2006; Wegner, Wenzlaff, & Kozak, 2004). In one study, people who had just attended an animal rights conference reported an unusually high number of animal characters in their dreams (Lewis, 2008). In another, people with more health problems reported more dreams that included illness or injury (King & DiCicco, 2007), and several studies have found that dream images of violence, terrorism, and disaster became more common in the days and weeks following the 9/11 terrorist attacks in the United States (e.g., Bulkeley & Kahan, 2008). It is also sometimes possible to intentionally direct dream content, especially during **lucid dreaming,** in which the sleeper is aware of dreaming while a dream is happening (Stickgold et al., 2000).

Research leaves little doubt that everyone dreams during every night of normal sleep. Whether you remember a dream depends on how you sleep and wake up. You'll remember more if you awaken abruptly and lie quietly while writing or recording your recollections.

Why Do We Dream? Theories about why we dream abound (Antrobus, 2001; Domhoff, 2001; Eiser, 2005; Revonsuo, 2001). Some researchers see dreaming as a process through which all mammals analyze and consolidate information that has personal significance or survival value (Payne & Nadel, 2004; Porte & Hobson, 1996; Zadra, Desjardins, & Marcotte, 2006). This view is supported by the fact that dreaming appears to occur in most mammals, as indicated by the appearance of REM sleep. For example, after researchers disabled the neurons that cause REM sleep paralysis, sleeping cats ran around and attacked, or seemed alarmed by, unseen objects, presumably the images from dreams (Winson, 1990).

According to Freud (1900), dreams are a disguised form of *wish fulfillment,* a way to satisfy unconscious urges or resolve unconscious conflicts that are too upsetting to deal with consciously. So sexual desires might appear in a dream as the rhythmic motions of a horseback ride. Conflicting feelings about a parent might appear as a dream about a fight. Seeing patients' dreams as a "royal road to a knowledge of the unconscious," Freud interpreted their meaning as part of his psychoanalytic therapy (see the chapter on treatment of psychological disorders).

dreaming The experience of storylike sequences of images, sensations, and perceptions occurring mainly during REM sleep.

lucid dreaming Awareness that a dream is a dream while it is happening.

In contrast, the *activation-synthesis theory* describes dreams as the meaningless by-products of REM sleep (Eiser, 2005; Hobson, 1997). According to this theory, hindbrain arousal during REM sleep creates random messages that *activate* the brain, especially the cerebral cortex. Dreams result as the cortex combines, or *synthesizes,* these random messages as best it can, using stored memories and current feelings to impose a coherent perceptual organization on confusingly random inputs. From this perspective, dreams arise as the brain attempts to make sense of meaningless stimulation during sleep, much as it does during waking hours when trying to find meaningful shapes in cloud formations (Bernstein & Roberts, 1995; Tierney, 2009).

Even if dreams stem from our effort to organize random physiological activity, the way we do so can still have psychological significance (Bulkeley & Kahan, 2008; Horton, Moulin, & Conway, 2009). Some psychologists believe that dreams give people a chance to review and address some of the problems they face during the day (Cartwright, 1993). This view is supported by evidence that people's current concerns can affect both the content of their dreams and the ways in which dreams are organized and recalled (Domhoff, 1996, 1999; Domhoff & Schneider, 2008; Stevens, 1996).

IN REVIEW   Sleep and Sleep Disorders

Types of Sleep	Characteristics	Possible Functions
NREM (non–rapid eye movement) sleep; stages 3 and 4 are called *slow-wave sleep*	The deepest stages of sleep, characterized by slowed heart rate and breathing, reduced blood pressure, and low-frequency, high-amplitude brain waves	Refreshing of body and brain; memory consolidation
REM (rapid eye movement) sleep	Characterized by eye movements and waking levels of heart rate, breathing, blood pressure, and brain waves but near paralysis in muscles; most dreaming occurs during REM	Restoring sensitivity to norepinephrine, thus improving waking alertness; creating and solidifying nerve cell connections; consolidating memories and new skills

Sleep Disorders	Characteristics	Possible Causes
Insomnia	Persistent difficulty in falling asleep or staying asleep	Worry, anxiety
Narcolepsy	A sudden shift from a waking state to REM sleep	Lack or deficiency of *orexin* (*hypocretin*)
Sleep apnea	Frequent episodes of interrupted breathing while asleep	Genetic predisposition, obesity, faulty breathing-related brain mechanisms, windpipe compression
Sudden infant death syndrome (SIDS)	Interruption of an infant's breathing, resulting in death	Genetic predisposition, faulty breathing-related brain mechanisms, exposure to cigarette smoke
Nightmares	Frightening dreams during REM sleep	Stressful or traumatic events or experiences
Sleep terror disorder (night terrors)	Frightening dream images during non-REM sleep	Stressful or traumatic events or experiences
REM behavior disorder	Lack of paralysis during REM sleep that allows dreams to be enacted, sometimes with harmful consequences	Malfunction of brain mechanism normally creating REM paralysis

1. Jet lag occurs because of a disruption in a traveler's _____.

2. The importance of non-REM sleep is suggested by its appearance _____ in the night.

3. The safest sleeping position for babies is _____.

However, neuroimaging studies show that while we are asleep, brain areas involved in emotion tend to be overactive, whereas areas controlling logical thought tend to be suppressed (Braun, Balkin, & Wesensten, 1998; Hobson et al., 1998). In fact, as we reach deeper sleep stages and then enter REM sleep, thinking subsides and hallucinations increase (Fosse, Stickgold, & Hobson, 2001). This is probably why dreams rarely provide realistic, logical solutions to our problems (Blagrove, 1996).

Hypnosis

The word *hypnosis* comes from the Greek word *hypnos,* meaning "sleep," but hypnotized people are not sleeping. People who have been hypnotized say that their bodies felt "asleep," but their minds were active and alert. **Hypnosis** has traditionally been defined as an altered state of consciousness brought on by special techniques and producing responsiveness to suggestions for changes in experience and behavior (Kirsch, 1994b). Most hypnotized people do not feel forced to follow the hypnotist's instructions; they simply see no reason to refuse (Hilgard, 1965). In fact, the more that people want to cooperate with the hypnotist, the more likely it is they will experience hypnosis (Lynn et al., 2002). People cannot be hypnotized against their will.

Experiencing Hypnosis

Usually, hypnosis begins with suggestions that the participant feels relaxed and sleepy. The hypnotist then gradually focuses the participant's attention on a particular, often monotonous set of stimuli while suggesting that the participant should ignore everything else and imagine certain feelings.

There are special tests to measure **hypnotic susceptibility,** the degree to which people respond to hypnotic suggestions (Kumar & Farley, 2009). Different tests can yield somewhat different results (Barnes, Lynn, & Pekala, 2009), but in general, they show that about 10 percent of adults are difficult or impossible to hypnotize (Hilgard, 1982). At the other extreme are highly susceptible individuals who report vivid hypnotic experiences. In one study, for example, such individuals were unable to tell the difference between images that a hypnotist told them to imagine and images that were actually projected on a screen (Bryant & Mallard, 2003). Hypnotically susceptible people typically differ from others in several ways, including differences in certain brain structures (Horton et al., 2004), greater ability to focus attention and ignore distraction (Iani et al., 2006), more active imaginations (Spanos, Burnley, & Cross, 1993), a tendency to fantasize (Lynn & Rhue, 1986), a capacity for processing information quickly and easily (Dixon, Brunet, & Laurence, 1990), a tendency to be suggestible (Kirsch & Braffman, 2001), and more positive attitudes and expectations about hypnosis (Benham et al., 2006; Spanos, Burnley, & Cross, 1993). As suggested earlier, the willingness to be hypnotized is the most important factor of all.

The results of hypnosis can be fascinating. People told that their eyes cannot open may struggle unsuccessfully to open them. They may appear deaf or blind or insensitive to pain. They may be unable to say their own names. Some appear to remember forgotten things. Others show *age regression,* apparently recalling or reenacting their childhoods (see Figure 9.8). Hypnotic effects can last for hours or days through *posthypnotic suggestions*—instructions about behavior that is to take place after hypnosis has ended (such as smiling whenever someone says "Paris"). Some people show *posthypnotic amnesia,* an inability to recall what happened while they were hypnotized, even after being told what happened (Sutcher, 2008; Wark, 2008).

Ernest Hilgard (1965, 1992) described the main changes that people display during hypnosis. First, hypnotized people show *reduced planfulness.* They tend not to begin actions on their own, waiting instead for the hypnotist's instructions. One participant said, "I was trying to decide if my legs were crossed, but I couldn't tell, and

Inducing Hypnosis

In the late 1700s, an Austrian physician named Franz Anton Mesmer became famous for his treatment of physical disorders using *mesmerism,* a forerunner of hypnosis. His procedures included elaborate trance induction rituals, but despite what you might see in movies and on TV, hypnosis can be induced far more easily, often simply by asking a person to stare at an object, as this woman did (Barrett, 2006).

hypnosis A phenomenon brought on by special induction techniques and characterized by varying degrees of responsiveness to suggestions for changes in experience and behavior.

hypnotic susceptibility The degree to which a person responds to hypnotic suggestions.

FIGURE 9.8

Hypnotic Age Regression

TRY THIS Here are the signatures of two adults before hypnotically induced age regression (top of each pair) and while age regressed (bottom of each pair). The lower signatures in each pair look less mature, but was the change due to hypnosis? To find out, ask a friend to write his or her name on a blank sheet of paper, first as usual and then as if he or she were 5 years old. If the two signatures look significantly different, what does this say about the cause of certain age regression effects?

Source: Ernest R. Hilgard, *Hypnotic Age Susceptibility.* Copyright © 1965. Reprinted by permission of the Estate of Ernest R. Hilgard.

didn't quite have the initiative to move to find out" (Hilgard, 1965, p. 6). Second, they tend to ignore all but the hypnotist's voice and whatever it points out; their *attention is redistributed.* Third, hypnosis enhances the *ability to fantasize,* so participants more vividly imagine a scene or relive a memory. Fourth, hypnotized people display *increased role taking;* they more easily act like a person of a different age or a member of the opposite sex, for example. Fifth, hypnotic participants show *reduced reality testing,* tending not to question if statements are true and more willingly accepting apparent distortions of reality. A hypnotized person might shiver in a warm room if a hypnotist says it is snowing.

Explaining Hypnosis

Hypnotized people and nonhypnotized people act differently and may look different, too (Hilgard, 1965). Do these differences reflect an altered state of consciousness?

Advocates of **state theories of hypnosis** say that they do. They point to the notable changes in brain activity that occur during hypnosis (Egner, Jamieson, & Gruzelier, 2005; Mohr, Binkofski, et al., 2005; Raij et al., 2005) and to the dramatic effects that hypnosis can produce, including insensitivity to pain and the disappearance of warts (Noll, 1994). They also note slight differences in the way hypnotized and nonhypnotized people carry out suggestions. In one study, hypnotized people and those who had been asked to simulate hypnosis were told to run their hands through their hair whenever they heard the word *experiment* (Orne, Sheehan, & Evans, 1968). Simulators did so only when the hypnotist said the cue word. Hypnotized participants complied no matter who said it. Another study found that hypnotized people complied more often than simulators with a posthypnotic suggestion to mail postcards to the experimenter (Barnier & McConkey, 1998).

There are also several **nonstate theories of hypnosis.** Advocates of *role theory,* for example, argue that hypnosis is *not* a special state of consciousness. They point out that some of the changes in brain activity associated with hypnosis can also be created without hypnosis (Mohr, Binkofski, et al., 2005). They suggest that hypnotized people are merely complying with social demands and acting in accordance with the special social role of "hypnotic subject" (Kirsch, 1994a). From this perspective, then, hypnosis simply provides a socially acceptable reason to follow certain suggestions, much as during a physical examination, your role as "medical patient" provides you with a socially acceptable reason to follow a request to take off your clothes.

Support for role theory comes from several sources. First, nonhypnotized people sometimes display behaviors that are usually associated with hypnosis. For example, contestants on television game shows and reality shows do lots of odd, silly, disgusting, or even dangerous things without first being hypnotized. Second, laboratory experiments show that motivated but nonhypnotized volunteers can duplicate many aspects of hypnotic behavior, from arm rigidity and visual hallucinations to age regression (Dasgupta et al., 1995; Mazzoni et al., 2009; Orne & Evans, 1965). Other studies have found that people rendered blind or deaf by hypnosis can still see or hear, even though their actions and beliefs suggest that they cannot (Bryant & McConkey, 1989; Pattie, 1935; see Figure 9.9).

Hilgard's *dissociation theory* of hypnosis blends role and state theories. He suggested that hypnosis is not a specific state but a general condition in which our normal control of thoughts and actions is temporarily reorganized or broken down (Hilgard, 1992). Hypnosis, he said, activates a process called *dissociation,* meaning a split in consciousness (Hilgard, 1979). As a result, body movements normally under voluntary control can occur on their own, and normally involuntary processes (such as reactions to pain) can be controlled voluntarily. Hilgard argued that this relaxation of central control occurs as part of a *social agreement* to share control with the hypnotist. In other words, people usually decide for themselves how to act or what to attend to, perceive, or remember, but during hypnosis, the hypnotist is allowed to control some of these experiences and actions. So Hilgard regarded hypnosis as a socially agreed display of

state theories of hypnosis Theories proposing that hypnosis is an altered state of consciousness.

nonstate theories of hypnosis Theories, such as role theory, proposing that hypnosis does not create an altered state of consciousness.

FIGURE 9.9

Can Hypnosis Produce Blindness?

The top row looks like gibberish, but if you closed one eye while wearing special glasses, you could detect within it the numbers and letters shown in the lower row. Yet when hypnotized people wore such glasses and were told that they were blind in one eye, they were unable to read the display. This result indicated that despite the hypnotic suggestion, both their eyes were working normally (Pattie, 1935).

Source: Pattie, F.A. (1935). "A Report at Attempts to Produce Unoicular Blindness by Hypnotic Suggestion." *British Journal of Clinical Psychology,* vol. 15, pp. 230–241. Copyright © The British Psychological Society. Reprinted by permission.

Surgery Under Hypnosis

Bernadine Coady, of Wimblington, England, has a condition that makes it dangerous for her to have general anesthesia. In April 1999, when a hypnotherapist failed to show up to help her through a painful foot operation, she used self-hypnosis as her only anesthetic. She imagined the pain as "waves lashing against a sea wall… [and] going away, like the tide." Coady's report that the operation was painless is believable because in December 2000, she underwent the same operation on her other foot, again using only self-hypnosis for pain control (Morris, 2000).

dissociated mental functions. Compliance with a social role may account for part of the story, he said, but hypnosis also leads to significant changes in mental processes.

Support for Hilgard's theory comes from brain imaging studies showing that the ability to dissociate certain mental processes is greater in people who are more hypnotically susceptible (Bob, 2008; Egner, Jamieson, & Gruzelier, 2005). Dissociation was also demonstrated behaviorally by asking hypnotized participants to immerse one hand in ice water (Hilgard, Morgan, & MacDonald, 1975). They were told they would feel no pain, but they were asked to press a button with their other hand if "any part of them" felt pain. These participants said they felt almost no pain, but their button pressing told a different story. Hilgard concluded that a "hidden observer" was reporting on pain that was reaching the person but had been separated, or dissociated, from conscious awareness (Hilgard, 1977).

Much remains to be learned about the nature of hypnosis. Contemporary research continues to test the validity of various explanatory theories of hypnosis, but traditional distinctions between state and nonstate theories have become less important as researchers focus on larger questions, such as why people are susceptible to hypnosis and what roles biological, social, and cognitive factors may play in it (e.g., Lynn & Kirsch, 2006; Raz, Fan, & Posner, 2005).

Applications of Hypnosis

Whatever hypnosis is, it has proved useful, especially in relation to pain (Patterson, 2010). Magnetic resonance imaging (MRI) studies of hypnotized pain patients show altered activity in the anterior cingulate cortex, a brain region associated with the emotional component of pain (Faymonville et al., 2000; Mohr, Binkofski et al., 2005). For some people, hypnosis is the only anesthetic needed to block the pain of dental work, childbirth, burns, and surgery (Morris, 2000; Van Sickel, 1992). For others, hypnosis relieves chronic pain from arthritis, nerve damage, migraine headaches, and cancer (Stewart, 2005). Hypnotic suggestion can also help eliminate diarrhea (Tan, Hammond, & Joseph, 2005), reduce nausea and vomiting due to chemotherapy (Richardson et al., 2007), limit surgical bleeding (Gerschman, Reade, & Burrows, 1980), and speed postoperative recovery (Astin, 2004). It has even been used in the treatment of stress-related hair loss (Willemsen & Vanderlinden, 2008).

Other applications of hypnosis are more controversial, especially the use of hypnosis to aid memory (Loftus & Davis, 2006). For example, hypnotic age regression is sometimes attempted in an effort to help people recover lost memories. However, the memories of past events reported by age-regressed individuals are not as accurate as those of nonhypnotized individuals (Lynn, Myers, & Malinoski, 1997). It is doubtful, then, that hypnosis can improve the ability of witnesses to recall details of a crime. In fact, their positive expectations about the value of hypnosis may lead them to unintentionally distort or reconstruct memories of what they saw and heard (Garry & Loftus, 1994; Wells & Olson, 2003). So although hypnosis may not enhance people's memory for information, it may make them more confident about their reports, even if they are inaccurate. As discussed in the memory chapter, confident witnesses tend to be especially impressive to juries.

LINKAGES Does meditation relieve stress? (a link to Health, Stress, and Coping, p. 551)

LINKAGES | # Meditation, Health, and Stress

Meditation is intended to create an altered state of consciousness characterized by inner peace and tranquillity (Chiesa & Serretti, 2009; Walsh & Shapiro, 2006). Some people claim that meditation has increased their awareness and understanding of themselves and their environment, improved their health, helped them quit smoking, eased drug withdrawal symptoms, reduced the symptoms of menopause, and enhanced their performance in everything from work to tennis (Dakwar & Levin, 2009; Davidson et al., 2003; Lee et al., 2009; MacLean et al., 2010; Mahesh Yogi, 1994; Oman, Hedberg, & Thoreson, 2006; Paul-Labrador et al., 2006; Vidrine et al., 2009; Zeidan et al., 2010). Meditators also report significant reductions in stress-related problems such as depression, generalized anxiety, high blood pressure, headache, back pain, and insomnia (Astin et al., 2003; Beauchamp-Turner & Levinson, 1992; Nidich et al., 2009). Meditators' scores on personality tests indicate increases in overall mental health, self-esteem, and social openness (Janowiak & Hackman, 1994; Sakairi, 1992).

The techniques used to achieve a meditative state differ, depending on belief and philosophy (for example, Eastern meditation, Sufism, yoga, or prayer). However, in the most common meditation methods, attention is focused on just one thing—a word, sound, or object—until the meditator stops thinking about anything and experiences nothing but "pure awareness" (Benson, 1975; Perlman et al., 2010). In this way, the individual becomes more fully aware of the present moment rather than being caught up in the past or the future.

What a meditator focuses on is less important than adopting a passive attitude. To organize attention, meditators might inwardly name every sound or thought that reaches consciousness, focus on the sound of their own breathing, or slowly repeat a *mantra,* which is a soothing word or phrase. During a typical meditation session, breathing, heart rate, muscle tension, blood pressure, and oxygen consumption decrease (Wallace & Benson, 1972). Most forms of meditation induce alpha-wave EEG activity, the brain wave pattern commonly found in a relaxed, eyes-closed, waking state (see Figure 9.4). Meditation is also associated with increases in the brain's level of dopamine, a neurotransmitter thought to be involved in the experience of reward or pleasure, and fMRI scans show that during meditation, activity increases

"Are you not thinking what I'm not thinking?"

in brain areas involved in concentrated attention (Brefczynski-Lewis et al., 2007; Kjaer et al., 2002).

Exactly how meditation works is unclear, though its effects on dopamine activity may tell one part of the story. Meditation may also create lasting changes in the brain. For example, certain areas of the cerebral cortex become thicker in individuals who practice long-term meditation, and nerves in certain areas of the brainstem become more densely packed (Grant et al., 2010; Lazar et al, 2005; Vestergaard-Poulson et al., 2009). These changes in neurotransmitter activity and brain structure may affect the brain's responses to the environment, even when meditation is not occurring. In one functional MRI study, people who meditated regularly and those who had never meditated were subjected to a painful stimulus. The meditators reported less pain than the nonmeditators did, and their brains showed less activation in areas that normally process pain signals. When the nonmeditators were retested after having learned and practiced meditation, they, too, experienced less pain and reduced activity in pain-processing areas of their brains (Orme-Johnson et al., 2006).

The changes meditation evokes, though, are probably not unique to meditation. Further, the benefits associated with meditation have also been associated with techniques such as biofeedback, hypnosis, tai chi, and just relaxing (Bernstein, Borkovec, & Hazlett-Stevens, 2000; Wang, Collet, & Lau, 2004).

Psychoactive Drugs

Every day, most people in the world use drugs that alter brain activity and consciousness. For example, 80 to 90 percent of people in North America use caffeine, the stimulant found in coffee (Gilbert, 1984). A drug is a chemical that is not usually needed for physiological activity but can affect the body upon entering it. You may say that you "need" a cup of coffee in the morning, but you will still wake up without it; accordingly, the caffeine in coffee is defined as a drug. (Some people use the word *drug* to mean therapeutic medicines but refer to nonmedicinal drugs as *substances,* as in *substance abuse.*) Drugs that affect the brain, changing consciousness and other psychological processes, are called **psychoactive drugs**. The study of psychoactive drugs is called **psychopharmacology**.

Psychopharmacology

Most psychoactive drugs affect the brain by altering the interactions between neurotransmitters and receptors, as described in the chapter on biological aspects of psychology. To have their effects, these drugs must first reach the brain by crossing the **blood-brain barrier**, a feature of blood vessels in the brain that block some substances from entering brain tissue (Urquhart, & Kim, 2009). Once past this barrier, a psychoactive drug's effects depend on several factors: With which neurotransmitter systems does the drug interact? How does the drug affect these neurotransmitters or their receptors? What psychological functions are normally performed by the brain systems that use these neurotransmitters?

Drugs can affect neurotransmitters or their receptors through several mechanisms. As shown in Figure 9.10, neurotransmitters fit into their own receptors. However, some drugs are similar enough to a particular neurotransmitter to fool its receptors. These drugs, called **agonists**, bind to the receptor and mimic the effects of the normal neurotransmitter. Other drugs are similar enough to a neurotransmitter to occupy its receptors but cannot mimic its effects. So they bind to a receptor and prevent the normal neurotransmitter from binding. These drugs are called **antagonists**. Still other drugs work by increasing or decreasing the release of a specific neurotransmitter. Finally, some drugs work by speeding or slowing the *removal* of a neurotransmitter from synapses.

psychoactive drug A substance that acts on the brain to cause some psychological effect.

psychopharmacology The study of psychoactive drugs and their effects.

blood-brain barrier A feature of blood vessels supplying the brain that allows only certain substances to leave the blood and interact with brain tissue.

agonist A drug that mimics the effects of the neurotransmitter that normally binds to a neural receptor.

antagonist A drug that binds to a receptor and prevents the normal neurotransmitter from binding.

Agonists and Antagonists
In part A, a molecule of neurotransmitter interacts with a receptor on a neuron's dendrites by fitting into and stimulating it. Part B shows a drug molecule acting as an *agonist*, affecting the receptor in the same way a neurotransmitter would. Part C depicts an *antagonist* drug molecule blocking a natural neurotransmitter from reaching and acting on the receptor.

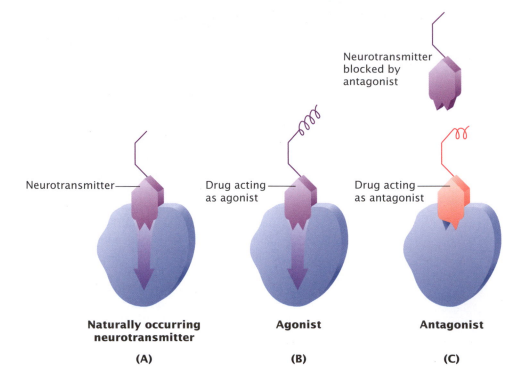

Neurotransmitter blocked by antagonist

Neurotransmitter

Drug acting as agonist

Drug acting as antagonist

Naturally occurring neurotransmitter

(A)

Agonist

(B)

Antagonist

(C)

Predicting a psychoactive drug's effects on behavior is complicated by the fact that most psychoactive drugs interact with many neurotransmitter systems. Also, the nervous system may compensate for a drug's effects. For example, repeated exposure to a drug that blocks receptors for a certain neurotransmitter often leads to an increase in the number of receptors available to accept that neurotransmitter.

The Varying Effects of Drugs

Unfortunately, the chemical properties that give drugs their medically desirable *main effects,* such as pain relief, often cause undesirable *side effects* as well.

Drug Abuse One side effect may be the potential for abuse. **Drug abuse** (also referred to as *substance abuse*) is a pattern of use that causes the user to have significant impairment or distress and serious social, legal, or interpersonal problems (American Psychiatric Association, 2000). Drug abuse may lead to psychological or physical dependence. *Psychological dependence* is a condition in which a person continues to use the drug despite its adverse effects, needs the drug for a sense of well-being, and becomes preoccupied with obtaining the drug. However, the person can still function without the drug. Psychological dependence can occur with or without *physical dependence,* or **addiction**, which is a physiological state in which continued drug use becomes necessary in order to prevent the unpleasant symptoms of **drug withdrawal** (sometimes called a *withdrawal syndrome*). Withdrawal symptoms vary, depending on the drug, but they often include an intense craving for the drug and physical effects generally opposite those of the drug itself. Eventually, users may develop **drug tolerance**, a condition in which increasingly larger drug doses are needed to produce the same effect (Sokolowska, Siegel, & Kim, 2002). With the development of tolerance, many addicts need the drug just to prevent the negative effects of not taking it. However, most researchers believe that a craving for the positive effects of drugs is what keeps addicts coming back to drug use (Ciccocioppo, Martin-Fardon, & Weiss, 2004; Everitt & Robbins, 2005). This view is supported by functional MRI studies of addicts who are exposed to drug-related words or asked to imagine cocaine or alcohol use. The resulting craving activated regions of the brain related to the rewards, positive

drug abuse The self-administration of psychoactive drugs in ways that deviate from cultural norms and cause serious problems for the user.

addiction Development of a physical need for a psychoactive drug.

drug withdrawal Symptoms associated with discontinuing the use of a habit-forming substance.

drug tolerance A condition in which increasingly larger drug doses are needed to produce a given effect.

emotions, and other pleasures they had learned to associate with using the drug (George et al., 2001; Goldstein et al., 2009; Kilts et al., 2001). Further, stimulating these regions in the brains of rats that had once been physically dependent on cocaine causes them to seek out the drug again (Vorel et al., 2001).

It is tempting to think that drug addiction can only happen to other people, but we should never underestimate how easily drug dependence can develop in anyone, including ourselves. Physical dependence can develop gradually, without a person's awareness. In fact, scientists believe that the changes in the brain that underlie addiction may be similar to those that occur during learning (Koob & Kreek, 2007; Nestler, 2001; Ross & Peselow, 2009). All addictive drugs stimulate the brain's "pleasure centers," regions that are sensitive to the neurotransmitter dopamine (Koob & Volkow, 2010). Neuronal activity in these areas creates intensely pleasurable feelings, including the pleasant feelings of a good meal, a "runner's high," or sex (Haber & Knutson, 2010; Reuter et al., 2005). Neuroscientists once believed that these feelings stem directly from the action of dopamine itself, but activity in dopamine systems may actually be more involved in responding to the novelty associated with pleasurable events than in actually creating the experience of pleasure (Bevins, 2001; Garris et al., 1999). In any case, by affecting the regulation of dopamine and other neurotransmitters in the brain's "pleasure centers," addictive drugs have the capacity to produce tremendously rewarding effects in most people (Boyd, 2006; Cannon, 2005; Maldonado, Valverde, & Berrendero, 2006). The changes in the brain caused by drug addiction can remain long after drug use ends (Diana, Spiqa, & Acquas, 2006), which may be one reason that people who succeed in giving up addictive drugs remain in danger of relapse months or even years later.

Expectations and Drug Effects   Drug effects are not determined by biochemistry alone (Crombag & Robinson, 2004). Learned expectations also play a role (Pollo & Benedetti, 2009; Siegel, 2005). Merely *expecting* to drink alcohol can create activity in the same brain areas that are affected by actually drinking it (Gundersen et al., 2008). Further, several studies have shown that people who consume alcohol-free drinks that they *think* contain alcohol are likely to behave in line with their expectations about alcohol's effects. So they tend to feel drunk and to become more aggressive, more interested in violent and sexual material, and more easily sexually aroused (Darkes & Goldman, 1993; George & Marlatt, 1986; Lang et al., 1975). And because they know that alcohol impairs memory, these people are more vulnerable to developing false memories about a crime they witnessed on videotape (Assefi & Garry, 2003).

Expectations about drug effects develop, in part, as people watch other people react to drugs (Sher et al., 1996). Because what they see can differ from one individual and culture to the next, drug effects vary considerably throughout the world (Lin, Smith, & Ortiz, 2001; MacAndrew & Edgerton, 1969). In the United States, for example, loss of inhibition, increased anger and violence, and sexual promiscuity are often associated with drinking alcohol. These effects are not seen in all cultures, however. In Bolivia's Camba culture, people engage in extended bouts of drinking a brew that is 89 percent alcohol (178 proof). During these binges, the Camba repeatedly pass out, wake up, and start drinking again—all the while maintaining peaceful social relations. The learned nature of responses to alcohol is also demonstrated by cases in which people are exposed to new ideas about the drug's effects. When Europeans brought alcohol to Tahiti in the 1700s, the Tahitians who drank it just became relaxed and disoriented, much as when consuming *kava,* their traditional nonalcoholic tranquilizing drink. But after years of watching European sailors' drunken violence, Tahitian alcohol drinkers became violent themselves. Fortunately, subsequent learning experiences moderated their response to alcohol (MacAndrew & Edgerton, 1969). Learned expectations also contribute to the effects of heroin, cocaine, and marijuana (Robbins & Everitt, 1999; Schafer & Brown, 1991; Smith et al., 1992).

As these examples show, the effects of psychoactive drugs are complex and variable. In the chapter on treatment of psychological disorders, we discuss some of the psychoactive drugs being used to help troubled people. Here we consider several categories of psychoactive drugs that are used to alter consciousness. They include depressant drugs, stimulating drugs, opiates, and hallucinogenic drugs.

CNS Depressant Drugs

Drugs such as alcohol and barbiturates are called **CNS depressant drugs** because they reduce, or depress, activity in the central nervous system (CNS), mainly in the brain. They do so partly by affecting the neurotransmitter GABA. As described in the chapter on biological aspects of psychology, GABA reduces, or inhibits, neuron activity. Depressants increase the availability of GABA, which in turn reduces the activity of many neural circuits. So the results of using depressants include relaxation, drowsiness, and sometimes depression (Hanson & Venturelli, 1995).

Alcohol   In the United States, more than 100 million people drink *alcohol*. It is equally popular worldwide (Leigh & Stacy, 2004). Alcohol affects several neurotransmitters, including dopamine, endorphins, endocannabinoids, glutamate, serotonin, and most notably, GABA (Daglish & Nutt, 2003; Enoch, 2003; Vinod et al., 2006). Drugs that interact with GABA receptors can block some of alcohol's effects, as shown in Figure 9.11 (Suzdak et al., 1986). Alcohol also enhances the effect of endorphins (the body's natural painkillers, described in the chapter on sensation). This action may underlie the "high" that people feel when drinking alcohol and may explain why *naltrexone* and *naloxone*, which block endorphins, are better than placebos at reducing alcohol craving and relapse rates in recovering alcoholics (Garbutt et al., 2005; Soyka & Rösner, 2008). Alcohol also interacts with dopamine systems, a component of the brain's pleasure and reward mechanisms (Tupala & Tiihonen, 2004). Prolonged alcohol use can have lasting effects on the brain's ability to regulate dopamine levels (Tiihonen et al., 1995). Dopamine antagonists reduce alcohol craving and withdrawal effects (Vergne & Anton, 2009).

Alcohol affects specific brain regions. For example, it reduces activity in the locus coeruleus, an area that helps activate the cerebral cortex (Koob & Bloom, 1988). This reduced activity may in turn cause cognitive changes and a release of culturally prescribed inhibitions (Casbon et al., 2003). Some drinkers begin talking loudly, acting silly, or telling others what they think of them. Emotional reactions range from giddy happiness to deep despair. Normally shy people may become impulsive or violent. Alcohol's effects on the hippocampus causes memory problems, including difficulty in forming new memories (Matsumoto & Matsumoto, 2008). The effects on

CNS depressant drugs Psychoactive drugs that inhibit the functioning of the central nervous system.

FIGURE 9.11
GABA Receptors and Alcohol
These rats each received the same amount of alcohol, enough to incapacitate them with drunkenness. The rat on the right then received a drug that reverses alcohol's intoxicating effects by blocking the ability of alcohol to stimulate GABA receptors. Within two minutes, the animal was acting utterly sober. There is a serious problem with the drug, though: It did not reverse the effects of alcohol on the brain's breathing centers. So a person who took the drug could consume a fatal overdose of alcohol without ever feeling drunk. Needless to say, the drug's manufacturer discontinued its development.

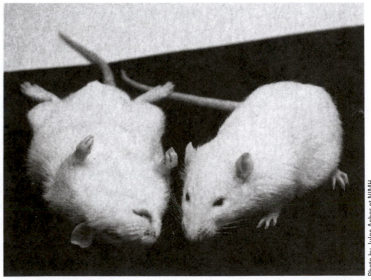

Photo by Jules Asher at NIMH

Drinking and Driving Don't Mix

Although practice makes it seem easy, driving a car is a complex information-processing task. As described in the chapter on cognition and language, such tasks require constant vigilance, quick decisions, and skillful execution of responses. Alcohol can impair all these processes, as well as the ability to judge the degree of impairment—thus making drinking and driving a deadly combination that results in 275,000 injuries and almost 13,000 deaths each year in the United States alone (National Highway Traffic Safety Administration, 2008).

© Code Red/Getty Images

the hippocampus may be permanent; brain imaging studies have shown that the hippocampus is smaller in heavy drinkers than in nondrinkers (Beresford et al., 2006). Alcohol's suppression of the cerebellum causes poor motor coordination, and its ability to depress hindbrain mechanisms that control breathing and heartbeat can make overdoses fatal.

As mentioned earlier, some effects of alcohol—such as anger and aggressiveness—depend on both biochemical factors and learned expectations (Goldman, Darkes, & Del Boca, 1999; Kushner et al., 2000). But other effects—especially disruptions in motor coordination, speech, and thought—result from biochemical factors alone. These biological effects depend on the amount of alcohol the blood carries to the brain. It takes the body about an hour to break down an ounce of alcohol (the amount in an average drink), so alcohol has milder effects if consumed slowly (Zakhari, 2006). Effects increase with faster drinking or with drinking on an empty stomach, thereby speeding the absorption of alcohol into the blood. Even after allowing for differences in average male and female body weight, researchers have found metabolic differences that allow males to tolerate somewhat larger amounts of alcohol. As a result, equal doses of alcohol may have greater effects in women than in men (York & Welte, 1994). Overindulgence by either sex results in unpleasant physical hangover effects that cannot be prevented or relieved by aspirin, bananas, vitamins, coffee, eggs, exercise, fresh air, honey, pizza, herbal remedies, more alcohol, or any of the dozens of other "surefire" hangover cures you may have heard about (Pittler, Verster, & Ernst, 2005).

Genetics seems to play a role in determining alcohol's biochemical effects on the body (Edenberg, 2007; Scholz, Franz, & Heberlein, 2005). Some people appear to have a genetic predisposition toward alcohol dependence (Stacy, Clarke, & Schumann, 2009), although all the specific genes involved have not yet been identified. Others, such as people of Japanese descent, may have inherited metabolic characteristics that increase the adverse effects of alcohol, thus possibly inhibiting the development of alcohol abuse (Iwahashi et al., 1995).

Barbiturates Sometimes called "downers" or "sleeping pills," *barbiturates* work by stimulating GABA receptors (Czapinski, Blaszczyk, & Czuczwar, 2005) and are extremely addictive. Small doses cause relaxation, feelings of well-being, loss of muscle coordination, and reduced attention. Higher doses cause deep sleep, but continued use can distort sleep patterns (Zammit, 2007). So long-term use of barbiturates as sleeping pills is unwise. Overdoses can be fatal. Withdrawal symptoms are among the most severe for any drug and can include intense agitation, violent outbursts, seizures, hallucinations, and even sudden death.

GHB *Gamma hydroxybutyrate,* or *GHB,* is a naturally occurring substance similar to the neurotransmitter GABA (Drasbek, Christensen, & Jensen, 2006). Introduced many years ago as a nutritional supplement, a laboratory-manufactured version of GHB (also known as "G") has become a popular recreational drug that is often used at nightclubs. This "club drug" is known for inducing relaxation, elation, loss of inhibition, suggestibility, and increased sex drive (Wood, Nicolaou, & Dargan, 2009). GHB can also cause nausea and vomiting, headaches, dizziness, loss of muscle control or paralysis, breathing problems, and even death—especially when taken with alcohol or other drugs (Miotto et al., 2001; Stillwell, 2002). Nearly half of people who use GHB report episodes of memory loss, and two-thirds report losing consciousness (Miotto et al., 2001). Because these effects can facilitate sexual assault, GHB is one of several compounds known as "date rape" drugs (Lee & Levounis, 2008). As with most CNS depressant drugs, long-term use of GHB can lead to dependence, and suddenly stopping the drug can cause a withdrawal syndrome that may include seizures, hallucinations, agitation, coma, or death (Van Noorden et al., 2009).

CNS Stimulating Drugs

Whereas depressants slow down central nervous system activity, **CNS stimulating drugs** speed it up. Amphetamines, cocaine, caffeine, and nicotine are all examples of CNS stimulating drugs.

Amphetamines Also called "uppers" or "speed," *amphetamines* (such as Benzedrine) increase the release and decrease the removal of norepinephrine and dopamine at synapses, causing increased activity at these neurotransmitters' receptors (Bonci et al., 2003). This increased activity results in alertness, arousal, and appetite suppression. These effects are further enhanced by the fact that amphetamines also reduce activity of the inhibitory neurotransmitter GABA (Centonze et al., 2002). A particularly fast-acting, intense, and addictive form of amphetamine, called *methamphetamine,* is nicknamed "crystal meth" because of its crystallized form (Hser et al., 2008; Kish, 2008). The feelings of pleasure induced by these drugs are probably due in part to their activation of dopamine reward systems, because taking dopamine antagonists reduces amphetamine use (Holman, 1994).

Amphetamines stimulate both the brain and the sympathetic branch of the autonomic nervous system, raising heart rate and blood pressure, constricting blood vessels, shrinking mucous membranes (relieving stuffy noses), and reducing appetite (Cruickshank & Dyer, 2009). Amphetamines also increase response speed, especially in tasks requiring prolonged attention (Koelega, 1993), and they may improve memory for verbal material (Whiting et al., 2007).

Abuse of amphetamines usually begins as an effort to lose weight, stay awake, or experience a "high." Continued use leads to anxiety, insomnia, heart problems, brain damage, abnormal movements, confusion, paranoia, nonstop talking, and psychological and physical dependence (Cadet & Krasnova, 2009; Thompson et al., 2004). In some cases, the symptoms of amphetamine abuse are virtually identical to those of paranoid schizophrenia, a serious mental disorder associated with malfunctioning dopamine systems.

CNS stimulating drugs Psychoactive drugs that have the ability to increase behavioral and mental activity.

Cocaine Like amphetamines, *cocaine* increases norepinephrine and dopamine activity and decreases GABA activity, so it produces many amphetamine-like effects (Kolb et al., 2003). Cocaine's extremely fast and powerful effect on dopamine activity

Deadly Drug Use

Billy Mays, the famous loud-talking TV pitchman, died of a cocaine-related heart attack in 2009. He joined a long list of celebrities (including the actor Chris Farley, Righteous Brother Bobby Hatfield, and Who bass player John Entwistle) and an even longer list of ordinary people whose lives have been destroyed by the abuse of cocaine or other drugs. In fact, cocaine intoxication is the most common cause of drug-related death in the United States (Phillips et al., 2009).

© AP Photo/Chris O'Meara

may account for its remarkably addictive nature (Bonci et al., 2003; Ciccocioppo, Martin-Fardon, & Weiss, 2004; Ungless et al., 2001). Drugs with rapid onset and short duration are generally more addictive than others (Kato, Wakasa, & Yamagita, 1987), which may explain why *crack*—a purified, fast-acting, highly potent, smokable form of cocaine—is especially addictive (Falck, Wang, & Carlson, 2007). In the United States, about 5.3 million people over the age of 12 have used cocaine and about 1.1 million have used crack at least once in the last year (Substance Abuse and Mental Health Services Administration, 2009).

Cocaine stimulates self-confidence, a sense of well-being, and optimism. But continued use brings nausea, overactivity, insomnia, paranoia, a sudden depressive "crash," hallucinations, sexual dysfunction, and seizures (Lacayo, 1995). Overdoses, especially of crack cocaine, can be deadly, and even small doses can cause a fatal heart attack or stroke (Klausner & Lewandowski, 2002; Phillips et al., 2009). Using cocaine during pregnancy harms the fetus (Hurt et al., 1995; Konkol et al., 1994; Snodgrass, 1994) and is associated with lasting cognitive and behavioral problems for the child (Salisbury et al., 2009). Some of the problems seen in "cocaine babies" stem from poverty and neglect after birth, but the mother's cocaine use beforehand is also partly to blame (Ackerman, Riggins, & Black, 2010). Early intervention can reduce the effects of both cocaine and the hostile environment that confronts most cocaine babies (Mayes et al., 2003; Singer et al., 2004).

It is difficult to end a cocaine addiction (Penberthy et al., 2010). One reasonably successful treatment combines counseling and *buprenorphine,* an opiate antagonist that suppresses cocaine self-administration in addicted monkeys (Marsden et al., 2009). Another approach is to use *baclofen,* a drug that reduces the stimulating effects of cocaine by enhancing the inhibitory neurotransmitter GABA (Dobrovitsky et al., 2002). Baclofen has been shown to help reduce cocaine use in addicted people (Shoptaw et al., 2003). So has a somewhat more radical treatment in which electrodes are implanted in the brain to counteract reward system activation (Rouaud et al., 2010). The results of other methods have been mixed; fewer than 25 percent of cocaine addicts who have undergone even long-term pharmacological and psychological treatments are drug-free five years later ("New Treatments," 2001).

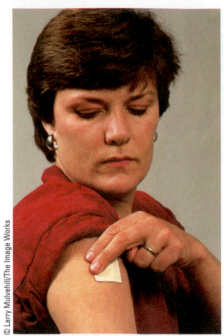

© Larry Mulvehill/The Image Works

Giving Up Smoking

The chemical effects of nicotine, combined with strongly learned associations between smoking and relaxation, stimulation, mealtimes, alcohol, and a wide variety of pleasant social interactions, make it extremely difficult for most smokers to give up their dangerous habit. The more promising treatment programs available today offer some combination of nicotine replacement (via a patch such as the one this woman is wearing), antismoking drugs such as Chantix or Zyban, and behavioral training in how to resist cravings and cope with the stress of not smoking, especially in situations usually associated with smoking (Moore et al., 2009; Schnoll et al., 2010).

Caffeine   *Caffeine* is the world's most popular drug. It is found in chocolate, many soft drinks, tea, and coffee. A typical cup of coffee has 58 to 259 milligrams of caffeine, and even "decaffeinated" coffee may still contain as much as 16 mg (McCusker, Goldberger, & Cone, 2006; McCusker et al., 2003). Caffeine reduces drowsiness, enhances mood, and promotes vigilance (Brunyé et al., 2010; Childs & de Wit, 2006). It improves problem solving, boosts the capacity for physical work, and increases urine production (Warburton, 1995); it has also been associated with a decreased risk of developing Alzheimer's disease (Eskelinen & Kivipelto, 2010; Santos et al., 2010). At high doses, caffeine causes tremors and anxiety, and long-term use can result in tolerance, as well as physical dependence (Strain et al., 1994). Withdrawal symptoms—including headaches, fatigue, anxiety, shakiness, and craving—appear on the first day of abstinence and last about a week (Juliano & Griffiths, 2004). Caffeine may make it harder for women to become pregnant and may increase the risk of miscarriage or stillbirth (Kuczkowski, 2009). Taking caffeine in coffee or tea temporarily raises blood pressure but does not necessarily increase the risk of chronic high blood pressure (Geleijnse, 2008). Indeed, caffeine appears to have few, if any, negative effects overall (Lopez-Garcia et al., 2008; Winkelmayer et al., 2005).

Nicotine   A powerful stimulant of the autonomic nervous system (ANS), nicotine is a potent psychoactive ingredient in tobacco. Nicotine's best-known effect is to enhance the action of acetylcholine (Penton & Lester, 2009), but it does much more. It also increases the release of glutamate, the brain's primary excitatory neurotransmitter (McGehee et al., 1995), activates the brain's dopamine-related pleasure system (Balfour, 2002), and stimulates endogenous cannabinoid and opioid systems (Berrendero at al., 2010; Maldonado & Berrendero, 2009). It is no wonder, then, that nicotine has many psychoactive effects, including autonomic nervous system arousal, elevated mood, and improved memory and attention (Domino, 2003; Ernst et al., 2001; Pomerleau & Pomerleau, 1992). Like heroin and cocaine, nicotine is physically addictive (White, 1998), but some people are more vulnerable to nicotine addiction than others (Hiroi & Scott, 2009).

Nicotine does not create the "rush" characteristic of many drugs of abuse, but stopping nicotine use often provokes a withdrawal syndrome that includes craving, irritability, anxiety, reduced heart rate, and reduced activity in the brain's reward pathways (Epping-Jordan et al., 1998; Hughes, Higgins, & Bickel, 1994). The tendency to become physically dependent on nicotine appears to be at least partly inherited (Bierut et al., 2008; Li, 2006), so some smokers appear to develop only a psychological dependence (Robinson & Pritchard, 1995). But whatever the blend of physical and psychological dependence, there is no doubt that smoking is a difficult habit to break (Breteler et al., 2004; Shiffman et al., 1997). As discussed in the chapter on health, stress, and coping, it is also clearly recognized as a major risk factor for cancer, heart disease, and respiratory disorders (U.S. Department of Health and Human Services, 2001b).

MDMA   "Ecstasy," or *MDMA* (short for 3,4-methylenedioxymethamphetamine), is a popular drug in nightclubs and on college campuses in the United States. MDMA increases the activity of dopamine-releasing neurons, so it leads to some of the same effects as cocaine and amphetamines (Steele, McCann, & Ricaurte, 1994). These include a sense of well-being, increased sex drive, and a sense of greater closeness to others. But MDMA may also cause dry mouth, hyperactivity, jaw muscle spasms that may result in "lockjaw," elevated blood pressure, fever, abnormal heart rhythms, and visual hallucinations (Baylen & Rosenberg, 2006). The hallucinations may appear because MDMA stimulates serotonin receptors and increases serotonin release (Green, Cross, & Goodwin, 1995). The day after using MDMA—also known as "XTC," "clarity," "essence," "E," and "Adam"—people often report muscle aches, fatigue, depression, and poor concentration. With continued use, MDMA's positive effects decrease, but its negative effects persist.

Although it does not appear to be physically addictive, MDMA can be a dangerous, potentially deadly drug, especially when taken by women (Liechti, Gamma, & Vollenweider, 2001; National Institute on Drug Abuse, 2000). It causes permanent brain injury in humans and other animals (Capela et al., 2009), and when given to pregnant animals, MDMA produces permanent behavioral changes in offspring (Thompson et al., 2009). Both animal studies and human studies indicate that MDMA impairs memory, judgment, and other psychological functions, even after its use is discontinued (Kalechstein et al., 2007; Smith, Tivarus, et al., 2006).

Opiates The **opiates** (opium, morphine, heroin, and codeine) are unique in their capacity to induce sleep and relieve pain (Julien, 2008). *Opium,* derived from the poppy plant, relieves pain and causes feelings of well-being and dreamy relaxation (Cowan et al., 2001). One of its most active ingredients, *morphine,* was first isolated in the early 1800s and is used worldwide for pain relief. Oxycodone, hydrocodone, and propoxyphene are common morphinelike drugs. *Heroin* is derived from morphine but is three times more powerful, causing intensely pleasurable reactions when first taken.

Opiates have complex effects on consciousness (Gruber, Silveri, & Yurgelun-Todd, 2007). Drowsy, cloudy feelings occur, perhaps because opiates depress activity in wide areas of the cerebral cortex. But many people also experience euphoria or elation (Bozarth & Wise, 1984). One way that opiates may exert their effects is by acting as agonists for endorphins. When opiates activate endorphin receptors, they are "tricking" the brain into an exaggerated activation of its painkilling and mood-altering systems (Julien, 2008). Like marijuana, which we discuss later, opiates also appear to stimulate the endocannabinoid system, perhaps explaining their euphoric effects (Vigano, Rubino, & Parolaro, 2005).

Opiates are highly addictive, partly because they stimulate a type of glutamate receptor on brain neurons that can physically change the neurons' structure. This change may alter neurons so that they come to require the drug to function properly (Bajo et al., 2006; Martin, Guadano-Ferraz, et al., 2004). Supporting this idea are data showing that glutamate antagonists appear to prevent morphine dependence yet leave the drug's painkilling effects intact (Trujillo & Akil, 1991). Beyond the hazard of addiction itself, heroin addicts risk death through overdoses, contaminated drugs, or AIDS contracted through sharing needles (Hser et al., 2001).

Hallucinogenic Drugs

Hallucinogenic drugs, also called *psychedelics,* produce a loss of contact with reality and alter other aspects of emotion, perception, and thought. They can cause distortions in body image (the user may feel gigantic or tiny), loss of identity (confusion about who one actually is), dreamlike fantasies, and hallucinations. Because these effects resemble many severe forms of mental disorder, hallucinogenic drugs are also called *psychotomimetics* (mimicking psychosis).

LSD One of the most powerful hallucinogenic drugs is *lysergic acid diethylamide,* or *LSD,* first made from a rye fungus by a Swiss chemist, Albert Hofmann. In 1938, after Hofmann accidentally ingested a tiny amount of the drug, he discovered its strange effects in the world's first LSD "trip" (Julien, 2008). LSD hallucinations can be bizarre. Time may seem distorted, sounds may cause visual sensations, and users may feel as if they have left their bodies. LSD's hallucinatory effects have been attributed partly to its ability to stimulate a specific type of serotonin receptors in the forebrain (Carlson, 1998). Supporting this assertion is evidence that serotonin antagonists greatly reduce LSD's hallucinatory effects (Leonard, 1992). LSD also stimulates a subtype of dopamine receptors whose activation leads to hallucinations and delusions (Minuzzi et al., 2005).

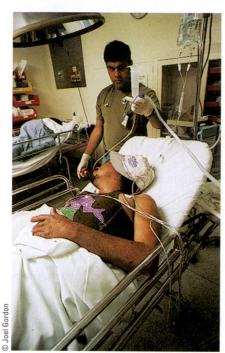

© Joel Gordon

Another Drug Danger

Oxycodone, a morphinelike drug prescribed by doctors under the label OxyContin, has become popular among recreational substance abusers. It was designed as a timed-release painkiller, but when people crush OxyContin tablets and then inject or inhale the drug, they get a much stronger and potentially lethal dose, especially when they are also using other drugs such as alcohol or cocaine (Cone et al., 2004). Deaths from OxyContin abuse have been on the rise in the United States in recent years.

opiates Psychoactive drugs, such as opium, morphine, and heroin, that produce sleep-inducing and pain-relieving effects.

hallucinogenic drugs Psychoactive drugs that alter consciousness by producing a temporary loss of contact with reality and changes in emotion, perception, and thought.

The precise effects of LSD on a particular individual are unpredictable. Unpleasant hallucinations and delusions can occur during a person's first—or two hundredth—LSD experience. Although LSD is not addictive, tolerance to its effects does develop. Some users suffer lasting adverse effects, including severe short-term memory loss, paranoia, violent outbursts, nightmares, and panic attacks (Gold, 1994). Distortions in visual sensations can remain for years after heavy use has ended (Dyck, 2005). Sometimes flashbacks occur, in which a person suddenly returns to an LSD-like state of consciousness weeks or even years after using the drug.

Ketamine   *Ketamine* is an anesthetic widely used by veterinarians to ease pain in animals and by physicians for sedating critically ill patients or suppressing dangerous seizure activity (Hirota, 2006; Robakis & Hirsch, 2006). But because it also has hallucinogenic effects, ketamine is being stolen and sold as a recreational drug known as "Special K." Its effects include dissociative feelings that create what some users describe as an "out-of-body" or "near death" experience. Ketamine can also cause amnesia and other lasting memory problems (Curran & Monaghan, 2001; Smith, Larive, & Romananelli, 2002), probably because it damages memory-related brain structures such as the hippocampus (Jevtovic-Todorovic et al., 2001).

Marijuana   A mixture of crushed leaves, flowers, and stems from the hemp plant (*Cannabis sativa*) makes up *marijuana*. The active ingredient is *tetrahydrocannabinol*, or THC (Fisar, 2009). When inhaled, THC is absorbed in minutes by many organs, including the brain. It alters blood flow to many brain regions (Martin-Santos et al., 2010) and continues to affect consciousness for several hours. Low doses of marijuana may initially create restlessness and hilarity, followed by a dreamy, carefree relaxation, an expanded sense of space and time, more vivid sensations, food cravings, and subtle changes in thinking (Kelly et al., 1990).

THC tends to collect in fatty deposits of the brain and reproductive organs, where it can remain for weeks. The brain contains several receptors for THC. The first to be discovered was named *ananda* (from a Sanskrit word meaning "bliss") and is normally activated by a naturally occurring brain substance called anandamide (Fride & Mechoulam, 1993). Later research established that the body produces a number of its own "endogenous cannabinoids" whose receptors in the brain also respond to THC (Wegener & Koch, 2009). This *endocannabinoid* system interacts with the pleasure-producing actions of the endorphin and dopamine systems, and it is involved in generating the psychoactive effects of several of the other drugs discussed earlier in this chapter (Maldonado, Valverde, & Berrendero, 2006). Scientists hope that it may someday be possible to safely stimulate the endocannabinoid system without producing harmful side effects (Thakur et al., 2009) and to block the system so as to help addicted people discontinue their drug use (Huestis et al., 2001).

For a summary of the effects of marijuana and other psychoactive drugs, see "In Review: Major Classes of Psychoactive Drugs."

THINKING CRITICALLY ▶ ## Is Marijuana Dangerous?

Marijuana is the most commonly used illegal drug in the world (Copeland & Swift, 2009). Surveys in the United States suggest that about 14.6 million people over the age of 12 use it at least once a month and that about 3.1 million do so daily or almost daily (National Institute on Drug Abuse, 2004). U.S. government officials have condemned marijuana use as "dangerous, illegal, and wrong," and concern about the drug has also been voiced in many other countries. At the same time, individuals and organizations in the United States and around the world argue for decriminalizing marijuana use, and the medical community is in serious discussions about whether marijuana should be used for medicinal purposes (Cohen, 2009a, 2009b).

Those who support legalization of marijuana cite its medical benefits, which were first described by Chinese physicians around 2700 B.C., and for which

IN REVIEW Major Classes of Psychoactive Drugs

Drug	Trade Name or Street Name	Main Effects	Potential for Physical/ Psychological Dependence
CNS Depressant Drugs			
Alcohol	"booze"	Relaxation, anxiety reduction, sleep	High/high
Barbiturates	Seconal, Tuinal, Nembutal ("downers")	Relaxation, anxiety reduction, sleep	High/high
GHB	"G," "Jib," "Scoop," "GH Buddy"	Relaxation, euphoria	High/high
CNS Stimulating Drugs			
Amphetamines	Benzedrine, Dexedrine, Methadrine ("speed," "uppers," "ice")	Alertness, euphoria	Moderate/high
Cocaine	"coke," "crack"	Alertness, euphoria	Moderate to high/high
Caffeine	—	Alertness	Moderate/moderate
Nicotine	"smokes," "coffin nails"	Alertness	High (?)/high
MDMA	"ecstasy," "clarity"	Hallucinations	Low/(?)
Opiates			
Opium		Euphoria	High/high
Morphine	Percodan, Demerol	Euphoria, pain control	High/high
Heroin	"junk," "smack"	Euphoria, pain control	High/high
Hallucinogenic Drugs			
LSD/ketamine	"acid"/"Special K"	Altered perceptions, hallucinations	Low/low
Marijuana (cannabis)	"pot," "dope," "reefer"	Euphoria, relaxation	Low/moderate

1. Physical dependence on a drug is a condition more commonly known as _____.
2. Drugs that act as antagonists _____ the interaction of neurotransmitters and receptors.
3. Drug effects are determined partly by what we learn to _____ the effects to be.

marijuana was used in the United States until the drug was declared illegal in the 1930s (Aggarwal et al., 2009). Some claim to have successfully used marijuana in the treatment of problems such as asthma, glaucoma, epilepsy, chronic pain, and nausea from cancer chemotherapy (Abrams et al., 2007; Di Marzo & Petrocellis, 2006; Gorter et al., 2005; Rog et al., 2005; Tramer et al., 2001). There is also evidence that marijuana can affect the immune system in ways that help fight some types of cancer (Parolaro et al., 2002). But others argue that medical legalization of marijuana is premature because its medicinal value has not been clearly established and because it may add unnecessary treatment risks. They point out, too, that even though patients may prefer marijuana-based drugs, other medications may be equally effective and less dangerous (e.g., Campbell, Tramer, et al., 2001; Fox, Bain, et al., 2004) Hall & Degenhardt, 2003).

What am I being asked to believe or accept?

Those who see marijuana as dangerous usually assert four beliefs: (1) that marijuana is addictive; (2) that it leads to the use of other drugs, such as heroin; (3) that marijuana intoxication endangers the user and other individuals; and (4) that long-term marijuana use leads to undesirable behavioral changes, disruption of brain functions, and other adverse effects on health.

What evidence is available to support the assertion?

Without a doubt, some people do use marijuana to such an extent that it disrupts their lives. According to the criteria normally used to define alcohol abuse, these people are dependent on marijuana—at least psychologically (Stephens, Roffman, & Simpson, 1994). The question of physical dependence (addiction) is less clear, inasmuch as withdrawal from chronic marijuana use was long thought not to produce any severe physical symptoms. Several studies now make it clear, though, that a withdrawal syndrome does exist when chronic marijuana users suddenly stop (Budney & Hughes, 2006; Preuss et al., 2010); the symptoms include cravings, irritability, restlessness, anxiety, and depression (Cornelius et al., 2008). Other research has found that marijuana interacts with the same dopamine and opiate receptors as heroin, implying that marijuana use could be a "gateway" to the use of more dangerous drugs (Lopez-Moreno et al., 2008; Lynskey et al., 2003; Spano et al., 2007).

The question of addiction aside, it is clear that smoking marijuana can have a number of other undesirable effects, including respiratory, cardiovascular, and immune system problems (Hall & Degenhardt, 2009; Jayanthi et al., 2010; McHale & Hunt, 2008; Pope et al., 2001). Marijuana also affects muscle coordination, making it dangerous to drive while under its influence (Hall & Degenhardt, 2009). Compounding the danger is the fact that impaired coordination continues long after the obvious effects of the drug have worn off. In one study, pilots continued to have difficulty landing a simulated aircraft even a full day after smoking one marijuana cigarette (Yesavage et al., 1985). Marijuana easily reaches a developing fetus and therefore should not be used by pregnant women (Fried, Watkinson, & Gray, 1992; Spano et al., 2007). As for marijuana's effects on intellectual and cognitive functioning, long-term use can lead to lasting impairments in reasoning, memory, and judgment that can hinder performance on complex tasks (Bolla et al., 2002; McHale & Hunt, 2008; Pope et al., 2001; Solowij et al., 2002). One study found that adults who frequently used marijuana scored lower on a twelfth-grade academic achievement test than nonusers with the same IQs (Block & Ghoneim, 1993). Among long-term users, impairments in memory and attention can persist for years after their drug use has stopped (Solowij et al., 2002). And despite the fact that people may feel more creative while using marijuana, the drug appears to actually reduce creativity (Bourassa & Vaugeois, 2001). Heavy use of marijuana in teenagers has also been associated with smaller than normal volume in brain areas involved in emotion and memory as well with the later appearance of

The Cannabis Controversy

Marijuana is illegal in North America and in many other places, but the question of whether it should remain so is a matter of hot debate between those who see the drug as a dangerous gateway to using more dangerous addictive substances and those who view it as a harmless source of pleasure that may also have important medical benefits.

© Frances M. Roberts/UPPA/Photoshot

anxiety, depression, and other mental disorders as severe as schizophrenia (McGrath et al., 2010; Moore et al., 2007; Yücel et al., 2008; Zammit et al., 2002).

Are there alternative ways of interpreting the evidence?

There are indeed other points of view (Hall & Lynskey, 2009). Those who see marijuana as a harmless or even beneficial substance criticize studies such as those just mentioned as providing an inaccurate or incomplete picture of marijuana's effects. They argue, for example, that the same dopamine receptors activated by marijuana and heroin are also activated by sex and chocolate—and that few people would call for the criminalization of those pleasures (Grinspoon et al., 1997). The correlation between early marijuana use and later use of other drugs could be due more to the people with whom marijuana users become involved than to any property of the drug itself (Fergusson & Horwood, 1997).

Questions about marijuana's long-term effects on memory and reasoning are also difficult to resolve, partly because studies of academic achievement scores and marijuana use tend to be correlational in nature. As noted in the chapter on research in psychology, cause and effect cannot easily be determined in such studies. Does marijuana use lead to poor academic performance, does poor academic performance lead to increased marijuana use, or might some other factor such as stress account for both? Each of these possibilities is credible. The same can be said of the correlation between marijuana and mental disorder. Heavy use of marijuana could be a reaction to or an early symptom of mental disorder, not necessarily its cause.

What additional evidence would help evaluate the alternatives?

We obviously need more definitive evidence about marijuana's short- and long-term effects, and that evidence should be based on well-controlled experiments with large and representative samples of participants. Still, evaluating the meaning of even the best possible evidence will be difficult. The issues in the marijuana debate involve questions of degree and relative risk. For example, is the risk of marijuana dependence greater than that of alcohol dependence? And what about individual differences? Some people are at much greater risk than others for negative consequences from marijuana use. So far, however, we have not determined what personal characteristics account for these differences. Nor do we know why some people use marijuana only occasionally, whereas others use it so often and in such quantities that it seriously disrupts their ability to function. The physical and psychological factors underlying these differences have yet to be identified.

What conclusions are most reasonable?

Those who would decriminalize the use of marijuana argue that when marijuana was outlawed in the United States, there was no evidence that it was any more harmful than alcohol or tobacco. Scientific evidence supports that claim, but more by illuminating the dangers of alcohol and tobacco than by declaring marijuana safe. In fact, although marijuana is less dangerous than, say, cocaine or heroin, it is by no means harmless. Further, because possession of marijuana is still a crime almost everywhere in the United States, as well as in many other countries throughout the world, it would be foolish to flout existing laws without regard for the legal consequences.

Nevertheless, in Canada , it is legal to grow and use marijuana for medicinal purposes, and the same is true in thirteen U.S. states, despite federal laws to the contrary and the continued threat of federal intervention to enforce those laws. Although the American Medical Association has rejected the idea of medical uses for marijuana, scientists are intent on objectively studying its potential value in the treatment of certain diseases, as well as its possible dangers. Their work is being encouraged by some scientific groups, and drug companies are working to develop new cannabis-based medicines (Altman, 2000; Tuller, 2004). The United Nations, too, has recommended that governments worldwide sponsor additional work on the medical uses of marijuana. The most reasonable conclusions about marijuana use must await the outcome of this research.

LINKAGES

As noted in the chapter on introducing psychology, all of psychology's subfields are related to one another. Our discussion of meditation, health, and stress illustrates just one way in which the topic of this chapter, consciousness, is linked to the subfield of health psychology (which is a focus of the chapter

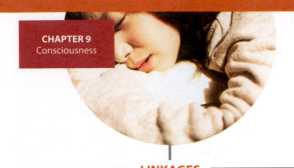

CHAPTER 9
Consciousness

on health, stress, and coping). The Linkages diagram shows ties to two other subfields as well, and there are many more ties throughout the book. Looking for linkages among subfields will help you see how they all fit together and help you better appreciate the big picture that is psychology.

LINKAGES

Do forgotten memories remain in the subconscious?
(ans. on p. 267)

Does meditation relieve stress?
(ans. on p. 354)

Can subconscious processes alter our reactions to people?
(ans. on p. 718)

CHAPTER 7
Memory

CHAPTER 13
Health, Stress, and Coping

CHAPTER 17
Social Cognition

SUMMARY

Consciousness can be defined as awareness of the outside world and of one's own thoughts, feelings, perceptions, and other mental processes.

Analyzing Consciousness

Current research on consciousness focuses on three main questions. First, what is the relationship between the mind and the brain? Second, does consciousness occur as a single "point" in mental processing or as several parallel and independent mental operations? Third, what mental processes are outside awareness, and how do they affect conscious processes?

The Functions of Consciousness

Consciousness produces the best current interpretation of sensory information in light of past experience and makes this interpretation available to the parts of the brain that plan voluntary actions and speech.

Levels of Consciousness

Variations in how much awareness you have for a mental function are described by different levels of consciousness. The *preconscious* level includes mental activities that are outside of awareness but can easily be brought to the *conscious* level. At the *unconscious* (or *subconscious*) level are thoughts, memories, and processes that are more difficult to bring to awareness. Mental processes that cannot be brought into awareness are said to occur at the *nonconscious* level.

Mental Processing Without Awareness

Awareness is not always required for mental operations. Priming studies show that our responses to some stimuli can be speeded, improved, or modified, even when we are not consciously aware of the priming stimuli.

The Neuropsychology of Consciousness

The thalamus and the cerebral cortex are among the brain structures involved in the experience of consciousness. Brain

injuries can impair consciousness and reveal ways in which mental processing can occur without conscious awareness.

Consciousness States

A person's *consciousness state* is constantly changing. When the changes are particularly noticeable, they are called *altered states of consciousness*. Examples include sleep, hypnosis, meditation, and some drug-induced conditions. Cultures vary considerably in the value they place on different consciousness states.

Sleeping and Dreaming

Sleep is an active and complex state.

Stages of Sleep

Different stages of sleep are defined on the basis of changes in brain activity (as recorded by an electroencephalograph, or EEG) and physiological arousal. Sleep normally begins with stage 1 sleep and progresses gradually to stage 4 sleep. Sleep stages 3 and 4 constitute slow-wave sleep, which is part of *non-REM (NREM) sleep.* After passing back to stage 2, people enter *rapid eye movement (REM)* sleep, or paradoxical sleep. The sleeper passes through these stages several times each night, gradually spending more time in stage 2 and REM sleep later in the night.

Why Do People Sleep?

The cycle of waking and sleeping is a natural *circadian rhythm,* or *human biological rhythm,* controlled by the suprachiasmatic nuclei in the brain. *Jet lag* can be one result of disrupting the normal sleep-wake cycle. The purpose of sleep is still being debated. Non-REM sleep may aid bodily rest and repair. REM sleep may help maintain activity in brain areas that provide daytime alertness, and it may allow the brain to solidify and absorb the day's experiences.

Sleep Disorders

Sleep disorders can disrupt the natural rhythm of sleep. Among the most common is *insomnia,* in which persistent difficulty in falling asleep or staying asleep at night results in feelings of fatigue during the day. *Narcolepsy* produces sudden daytime sleeping episodes. In *sleep apnea,* people briefly, but repeatedly, stop breathing during sleep. *Sudden infant death syndrome* (SIDS) may be due to brain abnormalities or accidental suffocation. *Nightmares* and *sleep terror disorder* (*night terrors*) are different kinds of frightening dreams. *Sleepwalking* occurs most frequently during childhood. *REM behavior disorder* is potentially dangerous because it allows people to act out REM dreams.

Dreams and Dreaming

Dreaming is the experience of storylike sequences of images, sensations, and perceptions that occur during sleep, most commonly during REM sleep. Evidence from research on *lucid dreaming* suggests that people may sometimes be able to control the content of their dreams. According to activation-synthesis theory, dreams are the meaningless by-products of brain activity, but they may still have psychological significance.

Hypnosis

Hypnosis is a well-known but still poorly understood phenomenon.

Experiencing Hypnosis

Tests of *hypnotic susceptibility* suggest that some people cannot be hypnotized. Hypnotized people tend to focus attention on the hypnotist and passively follow instructions. Their ability to fantasize and take roles shows improvement, and they may exhibit apparent age regression, experience posthypnotic amnesia, and obey posthypnotic suggestions.

Explaining Hypnosis

According to *state theories of hypnosis,* hypnosis is a special state of consciousness. *Nonstate theories of hypnosis,* such as role theory, suggest that hypnosis creates a special social role that gives people permission to act in unusual ways. *Dissociation theory* combines aspects of role and state theories, suggesting that hypnotic participants enter into a social contract with the hypnotist to allow normally integrated mental processes to become dissociated and to share control over these processes.

Applications of Hypnosis

Hypnosis is useful in the control of pain and the reduction of nausea associated with cancer chemotherapy. Its use as a memory aid is open to serious question.

Psychoactive Drugs

Psychoactive drugs affect the brain, changing consciousness and other psychological processes. *Psychopharmacology* is the field that studies drug effects and their mechanisms.

Psychopharmacology

Psychoactive drugs exert their effects primarily by influencing specific neurotransmitter systems and hence certain brain activities. To reach brain tissue, drugs must cross the *blood-brain barrier.* Drugs that mimic the receptor effects of a neurotransmitter are called *agonists,* and drugs that block the receptor effects of a neurotransmitter are called *antagonists.* Some drugs alter the release or removal of specific neurotransmitters, thus affecting the amount of neurotransmitter available for receptor effects.

The Varying Effects of Drugs

The use of some psychoactive drugs can lead to *drug abuse.* Abuse can in turn be accompanied by psychological dependence, physical dependence (*addiction*), *drug tolerance,* and symptoms of *drug withdrawal.* Drugs that produce dependence share the property of directly stimulating certain areas of the brain known as pleasure centers. The consequences of using a psychoactive drug depend both on how the drug affects neurotransmitters and on the user's expectations.

CNS Depressant Drugs

Alcohol and barbiturates are examples of *CNS depressant drugs.* They reduce activity in the central nervous system, often by enhancing the action of inhibitory neurotransmitters. They have considerable potential for producing both psychological and physical dependence.

CNS Stimulating Drugs

CNS stimulating drugs such as amphetamines and cocaine increase behavioral and mental activity mainly by increasing the action of dopamine and norepinephrine and decreasing GABA activity. These drugs can produce both psychological and physical dependence. Caffeine, one of the world's most popular stimulants, may also create dependence. Nicotine is a potent stimulant. MDMA is one of several psychoactive drugs that may permanently damage brain tissue.

Opiates

Opiates such as opium, morphine, and heroin are highly addictive drugs that induce sleep and relieve pain.

Hallucinogenic Drugs

LSD, ketamine, and marijuana are examples of *hallucinogenic drugs,* or psychedelics. Hallucinogenic drugs alter consciousness by producing a temporary loss of contact with reality and changes in emotion, perception, and thought.

LINKAGES TO FURTHER LEARNING

Now that you have finished reading this chapter, how about exploring some of the topics and information that you found most interesting? Here are some places to start.

Books

Susan Cheever, *Note Found in a Bottle: My Life as a Drinker* (Washington Square Press, 2000). Memoirs of an alcoholic.

Nicholas Humphrey, *A History of the Mind: Evolution and the Birth of Consciousness* (Copernicus, 1999). Description of how consciousness has arisen from brain activity.

Ernest Keen, *Chemicals for the Mind: Pharmacology and Human Consciousness* (Praeger, 2000). Theories of consciousness and drugs' effects on it.

Robert M. Julien, *A Primer of Drug Action: A Concise, Nontechnical Guide to the Actions, Uses, and Side Effects of Psychoactive Drugs* (11th ed.; Worth, 2008). The title says it all.

Daniel Goleman, *The Meditative Mind: Varieties of Meditative Experience* (Tarcher, 1996). Meditation and its effects.

Steven J. Lynn and Irving Kirsch, *Essentials of Clinical Hypnosis: An Evidence-Based Approach* (American Psychological Association, 2005). Summary of hypnotic techniques, evidence for the clinical use of hypnosis, and theories of hypnosis.

Stanley Coren, *Sleep Thieves: An Eye-Opening Exploration into the Science and Mysteries of Sleep* (Free Press, 1996). An introduction to sleep research.

Edward F. Pace-Schott, Mark Solms, Mark Blagrove, and Stevan Harnad (Eds.), *Sleep and Dreaming: Scientific Advances and Reconsiderations* (Cambridge University Press, 2003). A comprehensive set of research articles.

On the Internet

Access an integrated eBook and chapter-specific learning tools including flashcards, quizzes, videos, and more. Go to CengageBrain.com.

Want to maximize the value of your online study time? Take this easy-to-use study system's diagnostic pre-test, and it will create a personalized study plan for you. By helping you identify the topics that you need to understand better and then directing you to valuable online resources, it can speed up your chapter review. CengageNOW even provides a post-test so you can confirm that you are ready for an exam. Go to CengageBrain.com.

TALKING POINTS

Here are a few talking points to help you summarize this chapter for family and friends without giving a lecture.

1. Our minds operate at several levels of consciousness, some of which are outside of our awareness.
2. Our thoughts, emotions, and actions can be influenced by information that we are not aware of, but this does not mean that we can be controlled by subliminal messages or other attempts at "mind control."
3. It is not dangerous to awaken a sleepwalker.
4. Dreams are probably the result of our efforts to make sense of random brain activity, but how we organize that activity can be affected by events of the day, our current concerns, or other psychological factors.
5. You cannot be hypnotized against your will.
6. Psychoactive drugs operate by altering the amount or availability of neurotransmitters in the brain.
7. Though marijuana may have medicinal properties, it also has a number of harmful and potentially dangerous effects.

10

Cognitive Abilities

Intelligence tests are used to guide decisions about which children need special education, which job applicants should be hired, which students will be admitted to college, which individuals should be classified as gifted or intellectually disabled, and whether mental functioning has been impaired by head injury or disease. Intelligence tests have even been used to determine who is eligible for the death penalty. With so many important decisions being based on the results of intelligence tests, it is no wonder that there is controversy about them. In theory, these tests measure intelligence, but what does that mean? What, exactly, is "intelligence," where does it come from, and how good are the tests that are designed to measure it? These are some of the questions that we explore in this chapter on cognitive abilities.

Consider the following sketches of four college seniors and their varying abilities and interests. Do any of these descriptions remind you of anyone you know? Do any of them sound like you?

Jack's big-city "street smarts" were not reflected in his high school grades. After testing revealed a learning disability, Jack worked to compensate for it, graduating with a grade-point average (GPA) of 3.78; but when he took the SAT, his score was only 860 out of a then-possible 1600. He attended a local college, where he was given extra time to complete exams because of his learning disability. He held a half-time job throughout all four years, and his GPA was 2.95. When he completes his undergraduate degree, Jack will apply to master's degree programs in special education.

Deneace earned straight A's in public grade school. She attended a private high school, where she placed in the top fifth of her class and played the violin. Her SAT score was 1340, but because her school did not give letter grades, she had no grade-point average to include in college applications. Instead, she submitted teachers' evaluations and a portfolio containing papers and class projects. Deneace was accepted at several prestigious small colleges but not at major research universities. She is enrolled in a premed program, and with a GPA of 3.60, Deneace is hoping to be accepted by a medical school.

Ruthie has a wide range of interests and many friends, loves physical activities, and can talk to anybody about almost anything. Her high school grades, however, were only fair, averaging 2.60; but she played four sports, was captain of the state champion volleyball team, and was vice president of her senior class. She scored rather poorly on the SAT but received an athletic scholarship at a large university. She majored in sociology and minored in sport psychology. Focusing on just one sport helped her achieve a 3.25 GPA. She has applied to graduate schools but has also looked into a job as a city recreation director.

George showed an early interest in computers. In high school, he earned straight A's in math, art, and shop, but his overall GPA was only 2.55, and he didn't get along with other students. Everyone was surprised when he scored 1320 on the SAT and went on to major in math and computer science at a large public university. His grades suffered at first as he began to spend time with people who shared his interests, but his GPA is now 3.33. He writes computer animation software and has applied to graduate programs in fields relating to artificial intelligence and human factors engineering.

TRY THIS Before reading further, rank these four people on **cognitive ability**—the capacity to reason, remember, understand, solve problems, and make decisions. Who came out on top? Now ask a friend to do the same, and see if your rankings match. They may not, because each of the four students is outstanding in different ways.

Deneace might score highest on general intelligence tests, which emphasize remembering, reasoning, and verbal and mathematical abilities. But would these tests

cognitive ability The capacity to reason, remember, understand, solve problems, and make decisions.

measure Ruthie's social skills, Jack's street smarts, or George's computer skills and artistic abilities? If you were hiring an employee or evaluating a student, what characteristics would you want a test to measure? Can test scores be compared without considering the social and academic background of the people who took the tests? The answers to these questions are important because, as our examples illustrate, measures of cognitive abilities often determine the educational and employment opportunities people have or don't have.

There are many kinds of cognitive abilities, but in this chapter we will focus mainly on the abilities that have come to be known as *intelligence*. We can't use X-rays or brain scans to see intelligence, so we have to draw conclusions about people's intelligence from what can be observed and measured (Borkenau et al., 2004). This usually means looking at scores on tests designed to measure intelligence.

Testing for Intelligence

What, exactly is *intelligence*? There is no single, universally accepted definition, but the vast majority of psychologists agree that **intelligence** includes three main characteristics: (1) abstract thinking or reasoning abilities, (2) problem-solving abilities, and (3) the capacity to acquire knowledge (Gottfredson, 1997; Snyderman & Rothman, 1987). Standard tests of intelligence measure some of these characteristics, but they don't address all of them. Accordingly, some psychologists argue that these tests fail to provide a complete picture of someone's intelligence in its broadest sense. Others say that broadening the definition of intelligence will make it meaningless. Still others suggest dropping the term altogether in favor of the more descriptive and less emotionally charged concept of *cognitive ability*. To better understand the controversy, let's look at how standard intelligence tests were created, what they are designed to measure, and how well they do their job. Later, we will consider some alternative intelligence tests that have been proposed by those who find fault with traditional ones.

A Brief History of Intelligence Tests

The story of modern intelligence tests begins in France in 1904, when the French government appointed a psychologist named Alfred Binet (pronounced "bee-NAY") to a committee whose job was to identify, study, and provide special educational programs for children who were not doing well in school. As part of his work, Binet developed a set of test items that provided the model for today's intelligence tests. Binet assumed that reasoning, thinking, and problem solving all depend on intelligence, so he looked for tasks that would highlight differences in children's ability to do these things (Binet & Simon, 1905). His test included tasks such as unwrapping a piece of candy, repeating numbers or sentences from memory, and identifying familiar objects (Rogers, 1995).

Binet also assumed that children's abilities increase with age. With this in mind, he tried out his test items on children of various ages and, in later versions of his test, categorized each item according to the age at which the typical child could respond correctly. For example, a "6-year-old item" was one that half of 6-year-olds could answer. In other words, Binet's test contained a set of *age-graded* items. It measured a child's "mental level"—later called **mental age**—by determining the age level of the most-advanced items a child could consistently answer correctly. Children whose mental age equaled their actual age, or *chronological age,* were considered to be of "regular" intelligence (Schultz & Schultz, 2000).

In 1910, Henry Goddard brought Binet's test to the United States, translated it into English, and began using it at the Vineland (New Jersey) Training School to identify children who were "mentally retarded" (Zenderland, 1998). Another English-language version of Binet's test was published by Lewis Terman at Stanford University.

intelligence Personal attributes that center around skill at information processing, problem solving, and adapting to new or changing environments.

mental age A score corresponding to the age level of the most-advanced items a child could answer correctly on Alfred Binet's first intelligence test.

It became known as the **Stanford-Binet Intelligence Scale** (Terman, 1916). Table 10.1 gives examples of the kinds of items included on the Stanford-Binet test. Terman added items to measure the intelligence of adults and, following a formula devised by William Stern (1912), revised the scoring procedure. Mental age was divided by chronological age, and the result, multiplied by 100, was called the *intelligence quotient,* or *IQ.* So a child whose mental age and chronological age were equal would have an IQ of 100, which is considered "average" intelligence. A 10-year-old who scored at the mental age of a 12-year-old would have an IQ of $12/10 \times 100 = 120$. In the ensuing years, the term *IQ test* has come to be applied to any test designed to measure intelligence on an objective, standardized scale.

This scoring method allowed testers to rank people on IQ, which was seen as an important advantage by Terman and others who promoted the test in the United States. Unlike Binet—who believed that intelligence improved with education and training—they saw intelligence as a fixed and inherited entity, and they believed that IQ tests could pinpoint who did and who did not have a suitable amount of intelligence. These beliefs were controversial because they were not supported by empirical evidence and in some instances served to reinforce prejudices against certain people. In other words, enthusiasm for testing outpaced understanding of what was being tested.

In 1917, as the United States moved closer to entering World War I, the government asked a team of psychologists to develop the first group-administered intelligence tests to assess the cognitive abilities of military recruits. One of these tests, called the Army Alpha, presented arithmetic problems, verbal analogies (e.g., hot is to cold as high is to ___), and general knowledge questions to all recruits who could read English. The Army Beta test was developed for recruits who could not read or speak English; it presented nonverbal tasks, such as visualizing three-dimensional objects and solving mazes. Unfortunately, the verbal tests contained items that were unfamiliar to many recruits. Further, the tests were often given under stressful conditions in

Stanford-Binet Intelligence Scale A test for determining a person's intelligence quotient, or IQ.

TABLE 10.1	The Stanford-Binet Intelligence Scale

Here are samples of the types of items included on Lewis Terman's original Stanford-Binet Intelligence Scale. As in Alfred Binet's test, an age level was assigned to each item.

Age	Task
2	Place geometric shapes into corresponding openings; identify body parts; stack blocks; identify common objects.
4	Name objects from memory; complete analogies (e.g., fire is hot; ice is _____); identify objects of similar shape; answer simple questions (e.g., "Why do we have schools?").
6	Define simple words; explain differences (e.g., between a fish and a horse); identify missing parts of a picture; count out objects.
8	Answer questions about a simple story; identify absurdities (e.g., in statements such as "John had to walk on crutches because he hurt his arm"); explain similarities and differences among objects; tell how to handle certain situations (e.g., finding a stray puppy).
10	Define more difficult words; give explanations (e.g., about why people should wait their turn to be served in a store list as many words as possible; repeat six-digit numbers.
12	Identify more difficult verbal and pictured absurdities; repeat five-digit numbers in reverse order; define abstract words (e.g., *sorrow*); fill in a missing word in a sentence.
14	Solve reasoning problems; identify relationships among points of the compass; find similarities in apparently opposite concepts (e.g., "high" and "low"); predict the number of holes that will appear when folded paper is cut and then opened.
Adult	Supply several missing words for incomplete sentences; repeat six-digit numbers in reverse order; create a sentence using several unrelated words (e.g., *forest, businesslike,* and *dismayed*); describe similarities between concepts (e.g., "teaching" and "business").

Source: Nietzel & Bernstein (1987).

Coming to America

Early in the twentieth century, immigrants to the United States, including these new arrivals at Ellis Island in New York harbor, were tested for both physical and mental weaknesses. Especially for those who could not read, speak, or understand English, the intelligence tests they took tended to greatly underestimate their intellectual capacity. Today, psychologists recognize that cognitive abilities are developed partly through education and experience (Cronbach, 1975; Lohmann, 2004; Martinez, 2000), and they take much greater care in administering and interpreting intelligence tests.

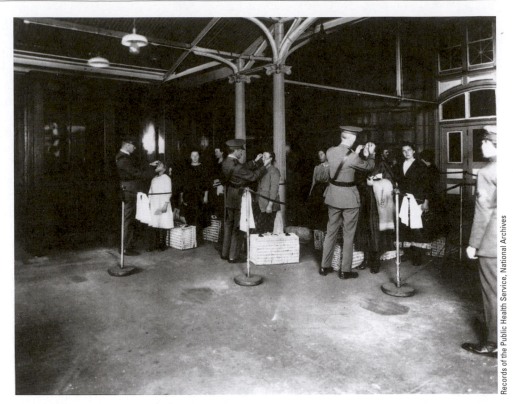

Records of the Public Health Service, National Archives

crowded rooms where instructions were not always audible or (for those who did not speak English) understandable. Nevertheless, when 47 percent of the recruits scored at a mental age of 13 years or lower (Yerkes, 1921), some psychologists incorrectly concluded that all of these recruits—even those who did not speak English—lacked normal intelligence (Brigham, 1923).

In the late 1930s, David Wechsler (1939, 1949) developed new tests designed to improve on the earlier ones in three important ways. First, the new tests included both verbal and nonverbal subtests. Second, success on these tests depended less on having formal schooling. Third, each subtest was scored separately, resulting in a profile that described an individual's performance on all the subtests. Special versions of these tests were developed for adults (the Wechsler Adult Intelligence Scale, or WAIS) and for children (the Wechsler Intelligence Scale for Children, or WISC).

Intelligence Tests Today

Today's editions of the Wechsler tests and the Stanford-Binet Intelligence Scale are the most widely used individually administered intelligence tests. The Wechsler Adult Intelligence Scale (WAIS IV; Wechsler, 2008) contains fifteen subtests. Seven of them require verbal skills and make up the *verbal scale* of the test. These subtests include such items as remembering a series of digits, solving arithmetic problems, defining vocabulary words, and understanding and answering general-knowledge questions. The other eight subtests have little or no verbal content and make up the *performance scale*. They include tasks that require understanding the relationships between objects and manipulation of various materials—tasks such as assembling blocks, solving visual puzzles, and completing unfinished pictures. The WAIS-IV allows the calculation of a verbal IQ, a performance IQ, and an overall IQ, as well as scores that reflect a person's mental processing speed, memory ability, perceptual skills, and understanding of verbal information. The latest edition of the Wechsler Intelligence Scale for Children (WISC-IV; Wechsler, 2003) yields four similar index scores, along with an overall IQ (see Figure 10.1).

FIGURE 10.1

Performance Items Similar to Those on the Wechsler Intelligence Scale for Children (WISC-IV)

The WISC-IV is made up of ten standard and five supplemental subtests, grouped into four clusters. The *perceptual reasoning* cluster includes tasks, such as those shown here, that involve assembling blocks, solving mazes, and reasoning about pictures. Tests in the *verbal comprehension* cluster require defining words, explaining the meaning of sentences, and identifying similarities between words. Tests in the *working memory* cluster ask children to recall a series of numbers, put a random sequence of numbers into logical order, and the like. The *processing speed* cluster tests children's ability to search for symbols on a page and to decode simple coded messages.

Source: Simulated Items Similar to Those Used in the Wechsler Intelligence Scale For Children, Fourth Edition (WISC-IV). Copyright © 2003 NCS Pearson, Inc. Reproduced with permission. All rights reserved. "Wechsler Intelligence Scale for Children" and "WISC" are trademarks, in the US and/or other countries, of Pearson Education, Inc. or its affiliate(s)

"Wechsler" is a trademark of Harcourt Assessment, Inc. registered in the United States of America and/or other jurisdictions.

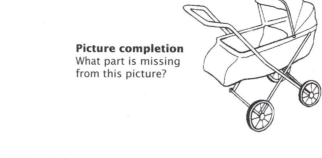

Picture completion
What part is missing from this picture?

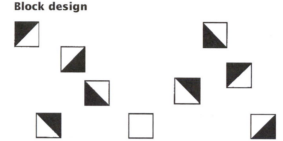

Block design

Put the blocks together to make this picture.

Like the WISC-IV, the fifth edition of the Stanford-Binet (SB5; Roid, 2003) also consists of ten main subtests. However, the SB5 subtests are designed to measure five different abilities: *fluid reasoning* (e.g., completing verbal analogies), *knowledge* (e.g., defining words, detecting absurdities in pictures), *quantitative reasoning* (e.g., solving math problems), *visual-spatial processing* (e.g., assembling a puzzle), and *working memory* (e.g., repeating a sentence). Each of these five abilities is measured by one verbal and one nonverbal subtest, so it is possible to calculate a score for each of the five abilities, a total score on all the verbal tests, a total score on all the nonverbal tests, and an overall score for all ten tests combined.

IQs are no longer calculated by dividing mental age by chronological age. If you take an IQ test today, the points you earn for each correct answer are added up. That total score is then compared with the scores earned by other people. The average score obtained by people at each age level is assigned the IQ value of 100. Other

Taking a New Intelligence Test

New intelligence tests are always being developed to measure newly identified aspects of cognitive abilities. This child is taking the Woodcock-Johnson Psychoeducational Battery, developed in 1997 and currently in its third edition (WJ-III; Woodcock, McGrew, & Mather, 2001). The WJ-III measures eight abilities that are somewhat more specific than the ones assessed by the Stanford-Binet and Wechsler tests. These eight abilities are fluid reasoning, verbal comprehension and knowledge, quantitative ability, visual-spatial thinking, short-term memory, retrieval from long-term memory, processing of auditory information, and mental processing speed. Testing results in an overall ability score, as well as a profile of scores on these eight abilities.

FIGURE 10.2
The Normal Distribution of IQ Scores in a Population
When IQs in the general population are plotted on a graph, a bell-shaped curve appears. The average IQ of any given age group is 100. Half are higher than 100, and half are lower than 100. Approximately 68 percent of the IQs of any age group fall between 84 and 116; about 16 percent fall below 84, and about 16 percent fall above 116.

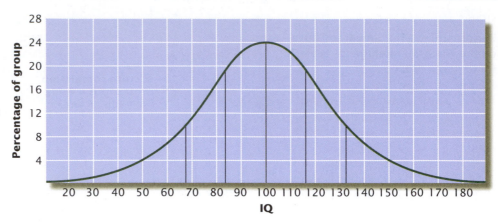

scores are given IQ values that reflect how far each score deviates from that average. If you do better on the test than the average person in your age group, you will receive an IQ above 100; how far above depends on how much better than average you do. Similarly, a person scoring below the age-group average will have an IQ below 100. This procedure is based on a well-documented aspect of many characteristics: Most people's scores fall in the middle of the range of possible scores, creating a bell-shaped curve that approximates the normal distribution shown in Figure 10.2. (The statistics appendix provides a fuller explanation of the normal distribution and how IQ tests are scored.) As a result of this scoring method, your **intelligence quotient, or IQ**, reflects your relative standing within a population of your age.

Aptitude and Achievement Measures

Closely related to intelligence tests are measures of aptitude and achievement. **Aptitude measures** are designed to assess a person's readiness to learn certain things or perform certain tasks (Corno et al., 2002). Although such tests may contain questions about what you already know, their ultimate goal is to assess your *potential* to learn or to perform well in some future situation. High performance in college or graduate school, for example, requires well-developed reading and mathematics skills, among other things. The SAT (originally called the Scholastic Aptitude Test), the American College Testing Assessment (ACT), and the verbal and quantitative components of the Graduate Record Examination (GRE) are the aptitude measures most commonly used by colleges and universities in the United States to help guide decisions about which applicants to admit (e.g., Kuncel & Hezlett, 2007; Sackett, Borneman, & Connelly, 2008). Corporations also use measures of aptitude as part of their employee selection processes. These tests usually involve brief assessments of cognitive abilities; examples include the Otis-Lennon Mental Abilities Test and the Wonderlic Personnel Test (Aiken, 1994). Corporations may also use the General Aptitude Test Battery (GATB) to assess both general and specific skills ranging from learning ability and verbal aptitude to motor coordination and finger dexterity at computer or clerical tasks.

Schools also commonly administer **achievement measures**, which test what a person has accomplished or learned in a particular area. For example, schoolchildren are tested on what they have learned about language, mathematics, and reading (Linn & Gronlund, 2000). Their performance on these tests is then compared with that of other students in the same grade to evaluate their educational progress. Similarly, college students' scores on the Subject Tests of the Graduate Record Examination assess how much they have learned about the field in which they wish to pursue graduate work.

Intelligence tests and measures of aptitude and achievement all assess related cognitive abilities, so as you might expect, their results are likely to be related too. One study found a positive correlation between SAT scores and scores on various IQ tests that was almost as high as the correlation among the IQ tests themselves

intelligence quotient (IQ) An index of intelligence that reflects the degree to which a person's score on an intelligence test deviates from the average score of others in the same age group.

aptitude measures Tests designed to measure a person's capacity to learn certain things or perform certain tasks.

achievement measures Tests designed to measure what a person has accomplished or learned in a particular area.

(Frey & Detterman, 2004). Another study found that scores on IQ tests were excellent predictors of British students' scores on national achievement measures (Deary et al., 2007).

Measuring the Quality of Tests

LINKAGES How do you know if a personality test (or any other kind of test) is any good? (a link to Personality, p. 585)

What does your IQ or SAT score say about you? Can it predict your performance in school or on the job? Is it a fair summary of your cognitive abilities? To answer questions like these scientifically, we have to measure the quality of the tests that yield these scores, using the same criteria that apply to tests of personality, language skills, driving, or anything else. Let's review these criteria and then see how they are used to evaluate IQ tests.

A **test** is a systematic procedure for observing behavior in a standard situation and describing it with the help of a numerical scale or a system of categories (Cronbach, 1990). Tests have two major advantages over interviews and other means of evaluating people. First, they are *standardized;* that is, conditions surrounding a test are as similar as possible for everyone who takes it. Standardization helps ensure, for example, that test results will not be significantly affected by who gives and scores the test. Because the biases of the individuals giving or scoring the test are minimized, a standardized test is said to be *objective.* Second, tests summarize the test taker's performance with a specific number, known as a *score.* Scores, in turn, allow the calculation of **norms,** which describe the frequency of particular scores. Norms tell us, for example, what percentage of high school students obtained each possible score on a college entrance exam. They also allow us to say whether a person's overall test performance was above or below average and whether that person is particularly strong or weak in certain skill areas, such as verbal reasoning or mathematics.

All tests, including IQ tests, should fairly and accurately measure a person's performance. The two most important things to know about when determining the value of a test are its statistical reliability and its statistical validity.

Statistical Reliability

If you stepped on a scale, checked your weight, stepped off, stepped back on, and found that your weight had increased by 20 pounds, you would know it was time to buy a new scale. A good scale, like a good test, must have **statistical reliability**; in other words, the results must be repeatable or stable. Suppose that you received a very high score on a reasoning test the first time you took it but a very low score when the test was repeated the next day. Your reasoning ability probably didn't change much overnight, so the test is probably unreliable. The higher the statistical reliability of a test, the less likely it is that its scores will be affected by temperature, hunger, or other irrelevant changes in the environment or the test taker.

To estimate the statistical reliability of a test, researchers usually get two sets of scores on the same test and then compute a *correlation coefficient* between the two (see the chapter on research in psychology and the statistics appendix). If the correlation is high and positive (usually above +.80 or so), the test is considered statistically reliable. The two sets of scores can be obtained in several ways. To measure statistical reliability across time, the same group of people takes the same test twice. This method assesses *test-retest reliability;* it is based on the assumption that whatever is being measured should not change much between the two testing sessions, so the correlation between the first and second testing should be high. Of course, if you practiced on your keyboard before taking a second test of typing skill, your second score would be higher than the first, so researchers sometimes use a different version of the test at the second session to reduce this practice effect. This *alternative form* method provides a measure of consistency across forms, but great care must be taken to ensure that the tasks or items on the second test are equivalent to, but not exactly the same as, those on the first. The most common method of assessing statistical reliability is to measure the

test A systematic procedure for observing behavior in a standard situation and describing it with the help of a numerical scale or a category system.

norms Descriptions of the frequency at which particular scores occur, allowing scores to be compared statistically.

statistical reliability The degree to which a test can be repeated with the same results.

internal consistency of the test's items. One way to do this, called the *split-half* method, is to calculate a correlation coefficient between each person's scores on two comparable halves of the test (Thorndike & Dinnel, 2001). If the test's items are internally consistent, this correlation should be high. To be on the safe side, some researchers employ more than one of these methods to check the statistical reliability of their tests.

Statistical Validity

Most scales reliably measure your weight, giving you about the same reading day after day. But what if you use these readings as a measure of your height? This far-fetched example illustrates that a reliable scale reading can be incorrect, or *invalid,* if it is misinterpreted. The same is true of tests. Even the most reliable test will not provide a correct, or valid, measure of intelligence, anxiety, typing skill, or anything else if those are not the things the test really measures. In other words, we can't say that a test itself is "valid" or "invalid." Instead, **statistical validity** refers to the degree to which test scores are interpreted appropriately and used properly (American Educational Research Association [AERA], American Psychological Association [APA], & National Council on Measurement in Education [NCME], 1999; Messick, 1989). As in our scale example, a test can be valid for one purpose but invalid for another.

To further illustrate this point, suppose you are teaching English to native Spanish speakers who are studying for their U.S. citizenship test. On the first day of class, you give your students a test of their ability to understand a magazine article written in English and find that their scores are quite low. Was the test valid? The answer depends on how you interpret its results. The scores are probably a valid measure of your students' ability to understand written English but probably not a valid measure of their verbal intelligence. If you had given the test using an article written in Spanish, the resulting scores would have been a valid indicator of verbal intelligence but not a valid measure of English comprehension.

Evidence about the validity of test scores can be gathered in several ways. For example, we can look at *content validity,* the degree to which the content of a test is a fair and representative sample of what the test is supposed to measure. If an instructor spends only five minutes out of forty lectures discussing the mating behavior of the tree frog and then devotes half of the final exam to this topic, that exam would be low on content validity. It would not allow us to draw accurate conclusions about what students learned in the course as a whole. Similarly, a test that measures only math skills would not have acceptable content validity as an intelligence test. A content-valid test includes items relating to the entire area of interest, not just a narrow slice of it (Linn & Gronlund, 2000).

Another way to evaluate validity is to determine how well test scores correlate with an independent measure of whatever the test is supposed to assess. This independent measure is called a *criterion.* For example, a test of eye-hand coordination would have high *criterion validity* for hiring diamond cutters if scores on the test correlated highly with a test of actual skill at diamond cutting. Why give a test if there is an independent criterion we can measure? The reasons often relate to convenience and cost. It would be silly to hire everyone who wants to work as a diamond cutter and then fire all the clumsy ones if a twenty-minute performance test could identify the best candidates. Criterion validity is called *predictive validity* when test scores are correlated with a criterion that cannot be measured until some time in the future—such as success in a pilot training program or grade-point average at graduation.

We can also look at *construct validity* (pronounced "KAHN-strukt"), the extent to which scores suggest that a test is actually measuring the theoretical construct, such as anxiety, that it claims to measure (Messick, 1989). Suppose that you are developing a test of anxiety and you know that various theories predict that anxiety occurs when people are uncertain about the future. With these theories in mind, you would expect that people waiting for the results of a job interview or a brain scan should score higher on your anxiety test than those who already have a good job or know

statistical validity The degree to which test scores are interpreted correctly and used appropriately.

that they are healthy. If this is not the case, then scores on your test would have low construct validity, at least with regard to most theories of anxiety.

Evaluating Intelligence Tests

Criteria for assessing the reliability and validity of tests have been incorporated into the testing standards established by the American Psychological Association and other organizations (AERA, APA, & NCME, 1999). These standards are designed to maintain quality in educational and psychological testing by providing guidelines for the administration, interpretation, and application of tests in such areas as therapy, education, employment, certification or licensing, and program evaluation (Turner et al., 2001). The standards tell us that in evaluating intelligence tests, we must take into account not only the statistical reliability and validity of test scores but also a number of sociocultural factors that might influence those scores.

The Statistical Reliability and Validity of Intelligence Tests

Intelligence tests are generally evaluated on the basis of the stability or consistency of their results (statistical reliability) and on their accuracy in guiding statements and predictions about people's cognitive abilities (statistical validity).

How Reliable Are Intelligence Tests?

IQs obtained before the age of 7 typically correlate only moderately (+.30 to +.60) with scores on intelligence tests given later (Fagan & Detterman, 1992; Fagan, Holland, & Wheeler, 2007; Rose & Feldman; 1995). There are two key reasons that this should be so. First, test items used with very young children are different from those used with older children. Second, in the early years, cognitive abilities change rapidly and at different rates for different children (see the chapter on human development). During the school years, however, IQ tends to remain more stable (Mayer & Sutton, 1996). For teenagers and adults, the stability of IQ is high, generally between +.85 and +.95. In one long-term study (Deary et al., 2000, 2004), the same people took the same intelligence test at age 11 and again at age 77; the correlation between the two sets of scores was +.73.

Of course, a person's score may vary from one time to another if testing conditions, motivation or anxiety, health status, or other factors change. Scores will also vary across different intelligence tests because each presents a somewhat different collection of items. So a child's scores on the WISC-IV and the SB5 would probably differ somewhat. Accordingly, testers do not usually make decisions about a person's abilities on the basis of a single IQ test. Overall, though, modern intelligence tests usually provide exceptionally consistent results—especially compared with most other kinds of mental tests.

How Valid Are Intelligence Tests?

If everyone agreed on exactly what intelligence is (having a good memory, for example), we could evaluate the statistical validity of IQ tests simply by correlating people's IQs with their performance on various tasks (in this case, memory tasks). IQ tests whose scores correlated most highly with scores on memory tests would be the most valid measures of intelligence. But because psychologists do not fully agree on a single definition of intelligence, they don't have a single standard against which to compare intelligence tests. Therefore, they cannot say whether these tests are valid measures of intelligence. Because intelligence is always displayed on specific tasks and in specific social situations, psychologists can only assess the validity of intelligence tests for specific purposes.

Intelligence test scores appear to be most statistically valid for assessing aspects of intelligence that are related to schoolwork, such as abstract reasoning and verbal comprehension. The validity of individually administered tests—as measured by correlating IQ with high school grades—is reasonably good, about +.50 (Brody &

If only measuring intelligence were this easy!

Ehrlichman, 1998). Scores on the Cognitive Abilities Test (Lohman & Hagen, 2001a) and other group-administered tests that focus more specifically on reasoning skills show even higher correlations with school performance (Kuncel, Hezlett, & Ones, 2004). And correlations between intelligence test scores and the level of education that people achieve range from +.60 to +.80 (e.g., Colom & Flores-Mendoza, 2007; Judge, Ilies, & Dimotakis, 2010; Lynn & Mikk, 2007).

There is also evidence that employees who score high on tests of verbal and mathematical reasoning tend to perform better on the job (and are paid more) than those who earned lower scores (Borman, Hanson, & Hedge, 1997; Johnson & Neal, 1998). Later, we describe a study that kept track of people for sixty years and found that children with high IQs tended to be well above average in terms of academic and financial success in adulthood (Cronbach, 1996; Oden, 1968; Terman & Oden, 1947). IQ also appears to be highly correlated with performance on "real-life" tasks such as reading medicine labels and using the telephone book (Gottfredson, 1997, 2004). So by the standard measures for judging psychological tests, scores on intelligence tests have good reliability and reasonably good validity for predicting success in school and in many life situations and occupations (Sackett, Borneman, & Connelly, 2008; Schmidt & Hunter, 2004). Indeed, few psychological tests of any kind show better reliability or validity.

How Fair Are IQ Tests?   As noted earlier, though, IQ is not a perfect measure of how "smart" a person is. Because intelligence tests do not measure the full array of cognitive abilities, a particular test score tells only part of the story, and even that part may be distorted. Individuals who administer intelligence tests must remember that many factors other than cognitive ability—including how the test taker responds to the tester—can influence test performance on a particular day. Children may not do as well if they are suspicious of strangers, for example (Jones & Appelbaum, 1989). And if older adults worry about making mistakes in unfamiliar situations, they may fail to even try to answer some questions, thus artificially lowering their IQ (Fagan, 2000).

Test scores can also be affected by anxiety, physical disabilities, and language differences and other cultural barriers (Fagan, 2000; Steele, 1997). As already mentioned, early efforts at intelligence testing in the United States probably underestimated the abilities of people who were unfamiliar with English or with the vocabulary and experiences associated mainly with middle-class culture at the time. For example, consider this multiple-choice question: Which is most similar to a xylophone? (violin, tuba, drum, marimba, piano). No matter how intelligent children are, if they have never seen an orchestra or learned about these instruments, they may miss this question. Accordingly, test designers have developed sophisticated procedures to detect and eliminate obviously biased questions (AERA, APA, & NCME, 1999; Serpell, 2000).

IQ and Job Performance

IQ is a reasonably good predictor of the ability to learn job-relevant information and to deal with unpredictable, changing aspects of the work environment—characteristics that are needed for success in complex jobs such as this one.

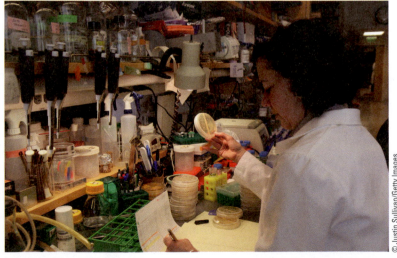

Furthermore, because intelligence tests now include more than one scale, areas that are most influenced by culture, such as vocabulary, can be assessed separately from areas that are less influenced by cultural factors.

The solutions to many of the technical problems in intelligence tests, however, have not resolved the controversy over the fairness of intelligence *testing*. The debate continues partly because the results of intelligence tests can have important consequences. Some students who score well above average on these tests may receive advanced educational opportunities that set them on the road to further high achievement. Those whose relatively low test scores identify them as having special educational needs may find themselves in separate classes that isolate them from other students and carry negative social labels. Obviously, the social consequences of testing can be evaluated separately from the quality of the tests themselves; but those consequences cannot be ignored, especially if they tend to affect some groups more than others.

LINKEAGES

Emotionality and the Measurement of Cognitive Abilities

LINKEAGES How does excessive emotional arousal affect scores on tests of cognitive ability? (a link to Motivation and Emotion, p. 418)

What noncognitive factors can potentially influence scores on cognitive ability tests? One of the most important is emotional arousal. As described in the chapter on motivation and emotion, people tend to perform best when their arousal level is moderate. Too little arousal tends to result in decreased performance, and so does too much. People whose overarousal impairs their ability to do well in testing situations are said to suffer from *test anxiety*.

These people fear that they will do poorly on the test and that others will think they are "stupid." In a testing situation, they may experience physical symptoms such as heart palpitations and sweating, as well as negative thoughts such as "I am going to blow this exam" (Chapell et al., 2005). In the most severe cases of test anxiety, individuals may be so distressed that they are unable to complete the test.

Test anxiety may affect up to 40 percent of elementary school students and about the same percentage of college students. It is seen about equally often in males and females (Turner et al., 1993). High test anxiety is correlated with lower IQ, but even among people with high IQ, those who experience severe test anxiety tend to do poorly on tests such as the SAT. Test-anxious elementary school students are likely to receive low grades and to perform poorly on evaluated tasks and on those that require new learning (Campbell, 1986). Some children with test anxiety refuse to attend school or "play sick" on test days, creating a vicious circle that further harms their performance on standardized achievement tests.

Anxiety, frustration, and other emotions may also be at work in a testing phenomenon that Claude Steele and his colleagues have identified as *stereotype threat* (Steele & Aronson, 2000). In one study, bright African American students read test instructions designed to make them more sensitive to negative stereotypes about the intelligence of their ethnic group. These students performed less well on a standardized test than equally bright African American students whose sensitivity to the stereotypes had not been increased (Steele & Aronson, 2000). In another study, women with good math skills were randomly assigned to one of two groups. The first group was given information intended to create concern over the stereotype that women aren't as good as men at math. In fact, they were told that men usually do better than women on the difficult math test they were about to take. The second group was not given this information. As shown in Figure 10.3, the women in the second group performed much better on the test than those in the first. In fact, their performance was equal to that of men who took the same test (Spencer, Steele, & Quinn, 1997).

According to Steele, concern over negative stereotypes about the cognitive abilities of the group to which they belong can impair the performance of some women—and some members of ethnic minorities—such that the test scores they earn, in laboratory settings at least, underestimate their cognitive abilities (Blascovich et al., 2001; Cadinu

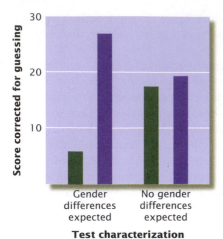

FIGURE 10.3

The Stereotype Threat Effect

In this experiment, male and female college students took a difficult math test. Beforehand, some of the students were told that men usually outscore women on such tests. Women who heard this gender stereotype information scored lower than those who did not hear it; they also scored lower than the men, even though their mathematical ability was equal to that of the men. Men's scores were not significantly affected by gender stereotype information (Spencer, Steele, & Quinn, 1997). The stereotype threat effect has been found to be especially strong when women are told that gender differences in math ability are based on genetic causes (Dar-Nimrod & Heine, 2006).

Source: Steele, C.M., "A Threat in the Air: How Stereotypes Shape Intellectual Identity and Performance". *American Psychologist,* June 1997, vol. 652, no. 6, p. 620. Copyright © 1997 by the American Psychological Association. Reprinted with permission.

et al., 2005; Inzlicht & Ben-Zeev, 2000; Murphy, Steele, & Gross, 2007; Schmader, 2010; Schmader, Johns, & Forbes, 2008). However, research on the performance of females and minority group members on high-stakes tests such as the SAT has yielded mixed results. Some studies suggest that scores on these tests can be artificially lowered by stereotype threat (Davis, Aronson, & Salinas, 2006; Lesko & Corpus, 2006; Walton & Spenser, 2009), while others find no effects or only a weak effect (Cullen, Hardison, & Sackett, 2004; Cullen, Waters, & Sackett, 2006; Fischer & Massey, 2007; Sackett, Hardison, & Cullen, 2004; Stricker & Ward, 2004). So the extent to which stereotype threat impairs performance on cognitive abilities tests in real-world settings remains uncertain.

Test anxiety is associated with lower performance on cognitive ability tests, but it does not appear to decrease the accuracy of predictions made on the basis of the tests' scores (Reeve & Bonaccio, 2008; Wicherts & Scholten, 2010). In other words, if people's performance is hampered by anxiety in a testing situation, it may be hampered in other stressful situations as well. The good news for people who suffer from test anxiety is that the counseling centers at most colleges and universities have effective programs for dealing with it. Test anxiety can be remedied through some of the same procedures used to treat other anxiety disorders (see the chapter on treatment of psychological disorders). There is also reason to be cautiously optimistic about reducing the impact of the stereotype threat phenomenon on the academic performance of African Americans and other minority groups (Schmader, 2010). A program at the University of Michigan that directly addresses this phenomenon has produced substantial improvements in the grades of minority students in their first year of study (Cohen & Steele, 2002; Steele, 1997).

These and other research findings indicate that the relationship between anxiety and test performance is complex, but one generalization seems to hold true: People who are severely test-anxious do not perform to the best of their ability on intelligence tests (Lang & Lang, 2010).

Innate and Environmental Influences on IQ

Concern over the fairness of intelligence tests is based partly on what many people assume to be true about these tests. A good intelligence test, they believe, should be able to see through the surface ripples created by an individual's cultural background, experience, and motivation to discover the innate cognitive abilities that lie beneath. But many researchers who study human intelligence argue that this is an impossible task for any test (Cronbach, 1990; Lohman, 1989). Years of research have led them to conclude that intelligence is *developed ability,* influenced partly by genetics but also by educational, cultural, and other life experiences that shape the very knowledge, reasoning, and other skills that intelligence tests measure (Atran, Medin, & Ross, 2005; Garlick, 2003; Plomin & Spinath, 2004; Taylor et al., 2010). For example, when brighter, more curious children ask more questions of their parents and teachers, they are generating a more enriching environment for themselves. Their innate abilities are allowing these children to take better advantage of their environment (Scarr, 1997; Scarr & Carter-Saltzman, 1982). The parents of these children are likely to be bright too. If so, their own biologically influenced intelligence probably helped them acquire resources that enrich their children's environment. That enriched environment helps develop the children's intelligence, so these children are favored by both heredity and environment.

Psychologists have explored the influence of genetics on individual differences in intelligence by comparing the correlation between the IQs of people who have differing degrees of similarity in their genetic makeup and environment. For example, they have examined the IQs of identical twins—pairs with exactly the same genes—who were separated when very young and raised in different environments. They have also examined the IQs of identical twins raised together. (You may want to review the Linkages section of the chapter on research in psychology, as well as the behavioral genetics appendix, for more on the research designs typically used to analyze hereditary and environmental influences.)

These studies find, first, that hereditary factors are strongly related to IQ. When identical twins who were separated at birth and adopted by different families are tested many years later, the correlation between their scores is usually at least +.60 (e.g., Bouchard, 1999). That is, if one twin scores high on an IQ test, the other probably will too; if one twin's IQ is low, the other's is likely to be low as well. However, studies of IQ correlations also highlight the importance of the environment (Scarr, 1998). Consider any two people—twins, siblings, or unrelated children—brought up together in a foster home. No matter what the degree of genetic similarity in these pairs, the correlation between their IQs is higher if they share the same home than if they are raised in different environments, as Figure 10.4 shows (Scarr & Carter-Saltzman, 1982).

The role of environmental influences is also seen in the results of studies that compare children's IQs before and after environmental changes such as adoption (van IJzendoorn & Juffer, 2005). Generally, when children from relatively impoverished backgrounds were adopted into homes offering a more enriching intellectual environment—including interesting materials and experiences, as well as a supportive, responsive adult—they showed modest increases in their IQs (Weinberg, Scarr, & Waldman, 1992).

A study of French children who were adopted soon after birth demonstrates the importance of both genetic and environmental influences. These children were tested after years of living in their adopted homes. Children whose biological parents were from upper socioeconomic groups (in which higher IQs are more common) had higher IQs than children whose biological parents came from lower socioeconomic groups, regardless of the socioeconomic status of the adoptive homes (Capron & Duyme, 1989, 1996). These findings were supported by data from the Colorado Adoption Project (Cardon & Fulker, 1993; Cardon et al., 1992), and they suggest that a genetic component of children's cognitive abilities continues to exert an influence even in their adoptive environment. At the same time, when children from low socioeconomic backgrounds were adopted by parents who provided academically enriched environments, their IQs rose by 12 to 15 points (Capron & Duyme, 1989). As described later, exposure to early intervention programs that improve school readiness and academic ability also tends to improve children's scores on tests of intelligence (Neisser et al., 1996; Ripple et al., 1999). Negative effects on cognitive abilities have been associated with factors such as poverty, poor nutrition, exposure to lead or alcohol, low birth weight, and complications during birth (Matte et al., 2001; Strathearn et al., 2001).

FIGURE 10.4
Correlations of IQ Scores

The correlation in IQ between pairs increases with increasing similarity in heredity or environment.

Source: T. Bouchard et al. "Familial Studies of Intelligence: A Review". *Science,* vol. 212, no. 4498, pp. 1055-9, 29. May 1981. Copyright © 1981 AAAS. Reprinted with permission.

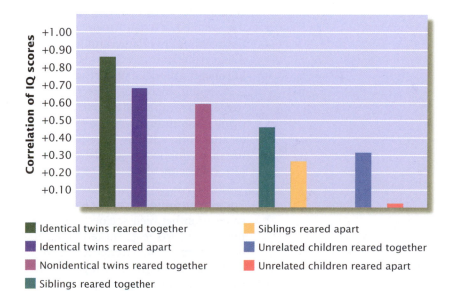

Research on genetic and environmental influences can help us understand the differences we see *among* people in terms of cognitive abilities and other characteristics, but it cannot tell us how strong each influence is in any *particular* person, including in this person.

Indeed, it has been suggested that living in an impoverished environment does more to impair the development of cognitive skills than living in an enriched environment does to enhance that development (Turkheimer et al., 2003).

Some researchers have concluded that the influence of heredity and environment on differences in cognitive abilities appears to be about equal. Others see a somewhat larger role for heredity (Herrnstein & Murray, 1994; Loehlin, 1989; Petrill et al., 1998; Plomin, 1994), and they are working to identify specific groups of genes that might be associated with variations in cognitive abilities (Posthuma & de Geus, 2006). It is important to understand, though, that estimates of the relative contributions of heredity and environment apply only to groups, not to individuals. It would be inaccurate to say that 50 percent of your IQ is inherited and 50 percent learned. It is far more accurate to say that about half of the *variability* in the IQs of a group of people can be attributed to hereditary influences. The other half can be attributed to environmental influences and measurement error.

Intelligence provides yet another example of nature and nurture working together to shape human behavior and mental processes. It also illustrates how the relative contributions of genetic and environmental influences can change over time. Environmental influences, for example, seem to be greater at younger ages (Davis, Haworth, & Plomin, 2009; Plomin & Spinath, 2004) and tend to diminish over the years. So IQ differences in a group of children will probably be affected more by parental help with preschool reading than by, say, the courses they take in junior high school ten years later.

Group Differences in IQ

Much of the controversy over the roles played by genes and the environment in intelligence has been sparked by efforts to explain differences in the average IQs seen in particular groups of people. For example, the average IQ of Asian Americans is typically the highest among the various ethnic groups in the United States, followed, in order, by European Americans, Hispanic Americans, and African Americans (e.g., Fagan, 2000; Herrnstein & Murray, 1994; Lynn, 2006; Taylor & Richards, 1991). Similar patterns appear on a number of other tests of cognitive ability and achievement (e.g., Bobko, Roth, & Potosky, 1999; Jencks & Phillips, 1998; Koretz, Lynch, & Lynch, 2000; Sackett et al., 2001). Further, the average IQ of people from high-income areas in the United States and elsewhere is consistently higher than that of people from low-income communities with the same ethnic makeup (Jordan, Huttenlocher, & Levine, 1992; McLoyd, 1998; Rowe, Jacobson, & Van den Oord, 1999).

To understand these differences and where they come from, we must remember two things. First, group scores are just that; they do not describe individuals. Although the mean IQ of Asian Americans is higher than the mean IQ of European Americans, there will still be large numbers of European Americans who score well above the Asian American mean and large numbers of Asian Americans who score below the European American mean (see Figure 10.5).

Second, increases in average IQ in recent decades, and other similar findings, suggest that inherited characteristics are not necessarily fixed. A favorable environment can improve a child's performance somewhat, even if the inherited influences on that child's IQ are negative (Humphreys, 1984). There is also evidence that living in an impoverished environment can impair the development of cognitive skills (Turkheimer et al., 2003).

Socioeconomic Differences   We have already mentioned that there is a positive correlation between socioeconomic status (SES) and scores on IQ and other cognitive ability tests (e.g., Sackett et al., 2009). Why should this be? Four factors seem to be involved. First, parents' jobs and status depend on characteristics related to their own intelligence. This intelligence is partly determined by a genetic component that in turn contributes to their children's IQ. Second, parents' income affects their children's

FIGURE 10.5

A Representation of Ethnic Group Differences in IQ Scores

The average IQ of Asian Americans is about 4 to 6 points higher than the average IQ of European Americans, who average 12 to 15 points higher than African Americans and Hispanic Americans. Notice, though, that there is much more variation *within* these groups than there is among their average scores.

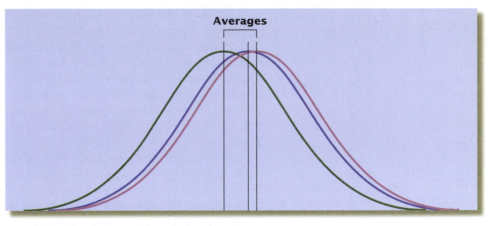

— African Americans and Hispanic Americans
— European Americans
— Asian Americans

environment in ways that can increase or decrease IQ (Bacharach & Baumeister, 1998; Suzuki & Valencia, 1997). Third, motivational differences may play a role. Parents in upper- and middle-income families tend to provide more financial and psychological support for their children's motivation to succeed and excel in academic endeavors (Erikson et al., 2005; Nelson-LeGall & Resnick, 1998). As a result, children from middle- and upper-income families may exert more effort in testing situations and therefore obtain higher scores (Bradley-Johnson, Graham, & Johnson, 1986; Robbins et al., 2004; Zigler & Seitz, 1982). Fourth, because colleges, universities, and businesses usually select people who score high on various cognitive ability tests, those with higher IQs—who tend to do better on such tests—may have greater opportunities to earn more money (Sackett et al., 2001).

Ethnic Differences   Some experts have argued that the average differences in IQ among ethnic groups in the United States are due at least partly to heredity (Rowe, 2005; Rushton & Jensen, 2005). Remember, though, that the existence of hereditary differences among individuals *within* groups does not indicate whether differences *between* groups result from similar genetic causes (Lewontin, 1976). As shown in Figure 10.5, variation within ethnic groups is much greater than variation among the mean scores of those groups (Zuckerman, 1990).

We must also take into account the significantly different environments in which average children in various ethnic groups grow up. To take only the most blatant evidence, recent Census Bureau figures show 24.5 percent of African American families and 21.8 percent of Hispanic American families living below the poverty level, compared with 10.2 percent of Asian American families and 8.2 percent of European American families (U.S. Census Bureau, 2008). Compared with European Americans, African Americans are more likely to have parents with less extensive educational backgrounds and to have less access to good nutrition, health care, and schools (Evans, 2004; W. J. Wilson, 1997). All of these conditions are likely to pull down scores on IQ tests (Brooks-Gunn, Klebanov, & Duncan, 1996).

The influence of environmental factors on the average black-white difference in IQ is supported by data from adoption studies. One such study involved African American children from disadvantaged homes who were adopted by middle- to upper-class European American families in the first years of their lives (Scarr & Weinberg, 1976). When measured a few years later, the mean IQ of these children was 110. A comparison of this mean score with that of nonadopted children from similar backgrounds suggests that the new environment raised the children's IQs at least 10 points. A ten-year follow-up study of these youngsters showed that their average IQ was still higher than the average of African American children raised in disadvantaged homes (Weinberg, Scarr, & Waldman, 1992).

As discussed in the chapter on human development, cultural factors may also contribute to differences among the mean scores of various ethnic groups. For example, those means may partly reflect differences in the value that is placed on academic achievement. In one study of fifteen thousand African American, Asian American, Hispanic American, and European American high school students, parental and peer influences related to achievement tended to vary by ethnic group (Steinberg, Dornbusch, & Brown, 1992). The Asian American students received strong support for academic pursuits from both their parents and their peers. European American students whose parents expected high academic achievement tended to associate with peers who also encouraged achievement, and they tended to do better academically than African American and Hispanic American students. The parents of the African American students in the study supported academic achievement, but because these students' peers often did not, the students may have been less motivated, and their performance may have suffered. The performance of the Hispanic American students may have suffered because, in this study at least, they were more likely than the others to have authoritarian parents whose emphasis on obedience (see the chapter on human development) may have created conflicts with the schools' emphasis on independent learning.

In short, it appears that some important nongenetic factors decrease the mean scores of African American and Hispanic American children. Whatever heredity might contribute to children's performance, under the right conditions it may be possible for them to improve.

Conditions That Can Raise IQ

Environmental conditions can help or deter cognitive development (see the chapter on human development). For example, lack of caring attention or of normal intellectual stimulation can inhibit a child's mental growth. Low test scores have been linked to poverty, chaos, and noise in the home; poor schools; and inadequate nutrition and health care (Alaimo, Olson, & Frongillo, 2001; Kwate, 2001; Weinberg, 1989). Can the effects of bad environments be reversed? Not always, but efforts to intervene

Helping with Homework

There are differences in the average IQs of European Americans and African Americans, but these differences are due in large measure to various environmental, social, and other nongenetic factors.

© Andy Sacks/Stone/Getty Images

in the lives of children and enrich their environments have had some limited success. Conditions for improving children's performance include rewards for progress, encouragement of effort, and creation of expectations for success.

In the United States, the best-known attempt to enrich children's environments is Project Head Start, a set of programs established by the federal government in the 1960s to help preschoolers from lower-income backgrounds. In some of these programs, teachers visit the home and work with the child and parents on cognitive skills. In others, the children attend classes in nursery schools. Some programs emphasize health and nutrition and family mental health and social skills as well. Head Start has brought measurable benefits to children's health (Abbot-Shim, Lambert, & McCarty, 2003; Spernak et al., 2006), as well as improvements in their academic, intellectual, and language skills (Barnett, 1998; Bierman, Domitrovich, et al., 2008; Bierman, Nix, et al., 2008; Hammer, Lawrence, & Miccio, 2007).

Do the gains achieved by preschool enrichment programs last? Although program developers sometimes claim long-term benefits (Schweinhart & Weikart, 1991), these claims are disputed (Caputo, 2004; Spitz, 1991). Various findings from more than a thousand such programs are often contradictory, but the effect on IQ typically diminishes after a year or two (Woodhead, 1988). A study evaluating two of the better preschool programs concluded that their effects are at best only temporary (Locurto, 1991). These fading effects reflect the fact that IQ describes a person's performance compared with others of the same age. To keep the same IQ, a child must keep improving at the same rate as other children in the same age group (Kanaya, Scullin, & Ceci, 2003). So IQ will drop from year to year in children whose rate of cognitive growth falls behind that of their age-mates. This slowing in the cognitive growth rate is often seen when children leave special preschool programs and enter the substandard schools that often serve the poor (Finn-Stevenson & Zigler, 1999; Zigler & Muenchow, 1992; Zigler & Seitz, 1982).

Fading effects have also been seen in programs such as the Abecedarian Project (Ramey, 1992). Children at risk for intellectual disabilities were identified while they were still in the womb. They then received five years of intense interventions to improve their chances of academic success. When they started school, children in this enrichment program had IQs that were 7 points higher than those of at-risk children who were not in the program. At age 12, they still scored higher on IQ tests, but the size of the difference at that time was just 5 points. This difference was still evident nearly a decade later, when the participants were assessed at the age of 21 (Campbell et al., 2001).

Project Head Start

This teacher is working in Project Head Start, a U.S. government program designed to enrich the academic environments of preschoolers from lower-income backgrounds and improve their chances of succeeding in grade school.

© Mark Richards/PhotoEdit

The primary benefit of early-enrichment programs probably lies in improving children's attitudes toward school (Woodhead, 1988). This can be an important benefit because, especially in borderline cases, children with favorable attitudes toward school may be less likely to be held back or placed in special education classes. Avoiding these experiences may in turn help children retain positive attitudes about school and enter a cycle in which gains due to early enrichment are maintained and amplified on a long-term basis.

IQ in the Classroom

IQ does not provide a crystal ball that can predict a person's destiny, nor does it reflect some fixed amount of cognitive ability. But might IQ affect how people are treated and how they behave? Decades ago, Robert Rosenthal and Lenore Jacobson (1968) argued that labels placed on students create teacher expectancies that can become self-fulfilling prophecies. They made this claim on the basis of a study in which they gave grade school teachers the names of students who were about to enter a "blooming" period of rapid academic growth. These students had supposedly scored high on a special test, but the researchers had actually selected the "bloomers" at random. Nevertheless, the IQs of two-thirds of the bloomers dramatically increased during the following year. Only one-quarter of the other children showed the same increase. Apparently, the teachers' expectancies about certain children influenced those children in ways that showed up on IQ tests.

Several attempts to replicate these findings have failed, and researchers who reanalyzed the data concluded that they did not support Rosenthal and Jacobson's claims (Elashoff, 1979; Fielder, Cohen, & Feeney, 1971; Thorndike, 1968). Others have found that the effect of teacher expectancies may be statistically significant but that it is relatively small (Jussim, 1989; Snow, 1995). Still, there is little doubt that IQ-based teacher expectancies can have an effect on teachers' interactions with students (Rosenthal, 1994). To find out how, Alan Chaiken and his colleagues (Chaiken, Sigler, & Derlega, 1974) videotaped teacher-child interactions in a classroom in which teachers had been informed (falsely) that certain pupils were particularly bright. They found that the teachers tended to favor the supposedly brighter students—smiling at them more often than at other students, making more eye contact, and reacting more positively to their comments. Children receiving this extra social reinforcement not only get more intense teaching but are also more likely to enjoy school, to have their mistakes corrected, and to continue trying to improve. Later research found that teachers provide a wider range of classroom activities for students for whom they have higher expectations, suggesting another way in which expectancies may influence students' academic achievement and, indirectly, their IQ (Blatchford et al., 1989).

These results suggest that the "rich get richer." Individuals perceived to be blessed with better cognitive abilities are given better opportunities to improve those abilities. There may also be a "poor get poorer" effect. Some studies have found that teachers tend to be less patient, less encouraging, and less likely to try teaching as much material to students whom they do not consider bright (Cooper, 1979; Trujillo, 1986). Other studies indicate that teachers simply favor students who are most like themselves. Teachers who themselves had difficulty in math, for example, may favor students who have similar difficulties. Further, differential expectations among teachers—and even parents—about the academic potential of boys versus girls may contribute to gender differences in academic performance (e.g., Beilock et al., 2010; Else-Quest, Hyde, & Linn, 2010; Nosek et al., 2009). In summary, the operation of teacher expectancies is probably far more complex than Rosenthal and Jacobson originally thought (Snow, 1995).

IQ tests have been criticized for being biased and for labeling people on the basis of scores or profiles. ("In Review: Influences on IQ" lists the factors that can shape IQ.) "Summarizing" a person with a score on an IQ test does indeed run the risk of oversimplifying reality and making errors. But intelligence tests can also *prevent* errors. Specifically, they can reduce the chances that inaccurate stereotypes, false preconceptions, and faulty generalizations will influence important educational and employment decisions. For example, boredom or lack of motivation at school might make a child appear mentally slow or perhaps even intellectually disabled. But a test of cognitive abilities conducted under the right conditions is likely to reveal the child's potential. The test can prevent the mistake of moving a child of average intelligence to a class for children with intellectual disabilities. And as Alfred Binet had hoped, intelligence tests have been enormously helpful in identifying children who need special educational attention. So despite their limitations and potential for bias, IQ tests can minimize the likelihood of assigning children to remedial work they do not need or to advanced work they cannot yet handle.

IN REVIEW Influences on IQ		
Source of Effect	**Description**	**Examples of Evidence for Effect**
Genetics	Genes appear to play a significant role in differences among people on intelligence test performance.	The IQs of siblings who share no common environment are positively correlated. There is a greater correlation between scores of identical twins than between those of nonidentical twins.
Environment	Environmental conditions interact with genetic inheritance. Nutrition, medical care, sensory and intellectual stimulation, educational experiences, interpersonal relations, and influences on motivation are all significant features of the environment.	IQs have risen among children who are adopted into homes that offer a stimulating, enriching environment. Correlations between IQs of identical twins reared together are higher than for those reared apart.

1. Intelligence is influenced by both _____ and _____.

2. Children living in poverty tend to have _____ IQs than those in middle-income families.

3. IQs of children whose parents encourage learning tend to be _____ than those of children whose parents do not.

THINKING **CRITICALLY**

Are Intelligence Tests Unfairly Biased Against Certain Groups?

We have seen that intelligence tests can have great value but also that IQ can be negatively affected by poverty, inferior educational opportunities, and other environmental factors. So there is concern that members of ethnic minorities and other disadvantaged groups have not had an equal chance to develop the knowledge and skills that are required to achieve high scores on IQ tests.

What am I being asked to believe or accept?

Some critics claim that standard intelligence tests are not fair. They argue that a disproportionately large number of people in some ethnic minority groups receive low scores on intelligence tests for reasons that are unrelated to cognitive ability, job potential, or other criteria that the tests are supposed to predict (Helms, 1992, 1997; Kwate, 2001; Neisser et al., 1996). They say that using ability and aptitude measures to make decisions about people—such as assigning them to particular jobs or special classes—may unfairly deprive members of some ethnic minority groups of equal employment or educational opportunities.

What evidence is available to support the assertion?

Research reveals several possible sources of bias in tests of cognitive abilities. First, as noted earlier, noncognitive factors such as anxiety, lack of motivation, or distrust can impair test performance and may put certain individuals at a disadvantage. For example, children from some minority groups may be less motivated to perform well on standardized tests and less likely to trust the adult tester (Steele, 1997). So differences in test scores may partly reflect motivational or emotional differences among various groups, not intellectual ones.

Second, many intelligence test items still reflect the vocabulary and experiences of the dominant middle-class culture in the United States. Individuals who are less familiar with the knowledge and skills valued by that culture will not score as well as those who are more familiar with them. Not all cultures value the same things, however (Sternberg & Grigorenko, 2004b). A study of Cree Indians in northern Canada revealed that words and phrases associated with *competence* included "good sense of direction"; at the *incompetent* end of the scale was the phrase "lives like a white person" (Berry & Bennett, 1992). A European American might not perform well on a Cree intelligence test based on these criteria. In fact, as illustrated in Table 10.2, poor performance on a culture-specific test is probably due more to unfamiliarity with culture-based concepts than to lack of cognitive ability. Compared with more traditional measures, "culture-fair" tests—such as the Universal Nonverbal Intelligence Test—that reduce dependence on oral skills do produce smaller differences between native English speakers and English-language learners (Bracken & McCallum, 1998).

Third, some tests may reward individuals who interpret questions as expected by the test designer. Conventional intelligence tests have clearly defined "right" and "wrong" answers. Yet a person may interpret test questions in a manner that is "intelligent" or "correct" but that produces a "wrong" answer. For example, when one child was asked, "In what way are an apple and a banana alike?" he replied, "They both give me diarrhea." And when Liberian rice farmers were asked to sort objects, they tended to put a knife in the same group as vegetables. This was the clever way to do it, they said, because the knife is used to cut vegetables. When asked to sort the objects as a "stupid" person would, the farmers grouped the cutting tools together, the vegetables together, and so on, as most North Americans would (Segall et al., 1990). In other words, the fact that people don't give the answer that the test designer was looking for does not mean that they *can't* (which is why well-trained test administrators would ask for another answer before moving on).

Are there alternative ways of interpreting the evidence?

This same evidence might be interpreted as showing that although intelligence tests do not provide a pure measure of innate cognitive ability, they do provide a fair picture of whether a person has developed the skills necessary to succeed in school or in certain jobs. When some people have had more opportunity than others to develop their abilities, the difference will be reflected in their IQs. From this point of view, intelligence tests are fair measures of the cognitive abilities developed by people living in a society that, unfortunately, contains some unfair elements. In other words, the tests may be accurately detecting knowledge and skills that are not represented equally in all groups, but this doesn't mean that the tests discriminate *unfairly* among those groups.

TABLE 10.2   An Intelligence Test?
TRY THIS How did you do on this "intelligence test"? If, like most people, you are unfamiliar with the material being tested by these rather obscure questions, your score was probably low. Would it be fair to say, then, that you are not very intelligent?
Take a minute to answer each of these questions; then check your answers against the key at the bottom of page 394.
1. What fictional detective was created by Leslie Charteris?
2. What dwarf planet travels around the sun every 248 years?
3. What vegetable yields the most pounds of produce per acre?
4. What was the infamous pseudonym of broadcaster Iva Toguri d'Aquino?
5. What kind of animal is Dr. Dolittle's pushmi-pullyu?

To some observers, concern over cultural bias in intelligence tests stems from a tendency to think of IQ as a measure of innate ability. These psychologists suggest instead that intelligence tests are measuring ability that is developed and expressed in a cultural context—much as athletes develop the physical skills needed to play certain sports (Lohman, 2004). Eliminating language and other cultural elements from intelligence tests, they say, would eliminate a vital part of what the term *intelligence* means in any culture (Sternberg, 2004). This may be why "culture-fair" tests do not predict academic achievement as well as conventional intelligence tests do (Aiken, 1994; Lohman, 2005). Perhaps familiarity with the culture reflected in intelligence tests is just as important for success at school or work in that culture as it is for success on the tests themselves. After all, the ranking among groups on measures of academic achievement is similar to the ranking for average IQs (Sue & Okazaki, 1990).

What additional evidence would help evaluate the alternatives?

If the problem of test bias is really a reflection of differences between various groups' opportunities to develop their cognitive skills, it will be important to conduct research on interventions that can reduce those differences. Making "unfair" cultures fairer by enhancing the skill development opportunities of traditionally disadvantaged groups should lead to smaller differences between groups on tests of cognitive ability (Martinez, 2000). It will also be important to find better ways to encourage members of disadvantaged groups to take advantage of those opportunities (Sowell, 2005).

At the same time, alternative tests of cognitive ability must also be explored, particularly those that include assessment of problem-solving skills and other abilities not measured by most intelligence tests (e.g., Sternberg & Kaufman, 1998). If new tests show smaller between-group differences than traditional tests but have equal or better predictive validity, many of the issues discussed in this section will have been resolved. So far, efforts in this direction have not been successful.

What conclusions are most reasonable?

The effort to reduce unfair cultural biases in tests is well founded, but "culture-fair" tests will be of little benefit if they fail to predict academic or occupational success as well as traditional tests do (Anastasi & Urbina, 1997; Sternberg, 1985). Whether one considers this situation good or bad, fair or unfair, the fact remains that it is important for people to have the information and skills that are valued by the culture in which they live and work. So it seems reasonable to continue using conventional cognitive ability tests as long as they accurately measure the skills and knowledge that people need for success in their culture.

In other words, there is probably no value-free, experience-free, or culture-free way to measure the construct known as intelligence when that construct is defined by the behaviors that a culture values and that are developed through experience in that culture (Sternberg, 1985, 2004). This conclusion has led some researchers to worry less about how cultural influences might "contaminate" tests of innate cognitive abilities and to focus instead on how to help people develop the abilities that are required for success in school and society. As mentioned earlier, if more attention were focused on combating poverty, poor schools, inadequate nutrition, lack of health care, and other conditions that result in lower average IQs and reduced economic opportunities for certain groups of people, many of the reasons for concern about test bias might be eliminated. ◀━━

Understanding Intelligence

People who are skilled at using and understanding language, at learning and remembering, and at thinking, problem-solving, and other information-processing tasks are likely to do well on standard intelligence tests such as the Stanford-Binet and the Wechsler. But these standard tests do not measure all the abilities highlighted by other approaches to the concept of "intelligence" (Berry & Bennett, 1992; Carroll, 1993; Eysenck, 1986; Gardner, 1999; Hunt, 1983; Kanazawa, 2004; Meyer & Salovey, 1997; Sternberg, 1996; Sternberg, Lautrey, & Lubart, 2003). Let's consider these approaches and a few of the nontraditional intelligence tests that have emerged from some of them.

The Psychometric Approach

Standard intelligence tests are associated with **psychometrics,** the scientific study and measurement of knowledge, abilities, attitudes, personality, and other psychological characteristics. The **psychometric approach** to intelligence focuses on the *products* of intelligence, including scores on IQ tests. Researchers taking this approach ask whether intelligence is one general trait or a bundle of more specific abilities. The answer matters, because if intelligence is a single trait, then an employer might assume that someone with a low IQ could not do any tasks well. But if intelligence is composed of many abilities that are somewhat independent of one another, then a poor showing in one area—say, imagining the rotation of objects in space—would not rule out good performance in others, such as understanding information or solving mathematical word problems.

Early in the twentieth century, the statistician Charles Spearman made a suggestion that began the modern debate about the nature of intelligence. Spearman noticed that scores on almost all tests of cognitive abilities were positively correlated (Spearman, 1904, 1927). That is, people who did well on one test also tended to do well on all of the others. Spearman concluded that these correlations were created by general cognitive ability, which he called **g**, for *general intelligence,* and a group of special intelligences, which he collectively referred to as **s**. The *s* factors, he said, are the specific information and skills needed for particular tasks.

Spearman argued that people's scores on a particular test depend on both *g* and *s*. Further examination of test scores, however, revealed correlations that could not be explained by either *g* or *s;* these were called *group factors*. Although Spearman modified his theory to accommodate these group factors, he continued to claim that *g* represented a measure of mental force, or intellectual power.

In 1938, the psychologist Louis L. Thurstone published a paper criticizing Spearman's mathematical methods. Using the statistical technique of *factor analysis,* Thurstone examined the correlations among intelligence tests to identify the underlying factors, or abilities, being measured by those tests. His analyses did not reveal a single, dominating *g* factor. Instead, he found seven relatively independent *primary mental abilities:* numerical ability, reasoning, verbal fluency, spatial visualization, perceptual ability, memory, and verbal comprehension. Thurstone did not deny that *g* exists, but he argued that it was not as important as these primary mental abilities in describing a particular person. Similarly, Spearman did not deny the existence of special abilities, but he maintained that *g* tells us most of what we need to know about a person's cognitive ability.

Raymond B. Cattell (1963) agreed with Spearman, but his own factor analyses suggested that there are two kinds of *g*, consisting of *fluid abilities* and *crystallized abilities*. **Fluid intelligence,** he said, is the basic power of reasoning and problem solving. **Crystallized intelligence,** in contrast, involves specific knowledge gained as a result of applying fluid intelligence. It produces, for example, a good vocabulary and familiarity with the multiplication tables.

Who is right? After decades of research and debate, most psychologists today agree that there is a positive correlation among various tests of cognitive ability, a correlation that is due to a factor known as *g* (e.g., Carroll, 1993; Frey & Detterman, 2004). Further, it appears that the *g* factor can be measured by many different groups of cognitive tests, even if the tests in each group are entirely different (Johnson et al., 2004).

However, the brain probably does not contain some unified "thing" corresponding to what people call intelligence. Instead, cognitive abilities appear to be organized in "layers," beginning with as many as fifty or sixty narrow and specific skills that can

psychometrics The scientific study and measurement of knowledge, abilities, attitudes, personality, and other psychological characteristics.

psychometric approach A way of studying intelligence that emphasizes analysis of the products of intelligence, especially scores on intelligence tests.

g A general intelligence factor that Charles Spearman postulated as accounting for positive correlations between people's scores on all sorts of cognitive ability tests.

s A group of special abilities that Charles Spearman saw as accompanying general intelligence (*g*).

fluid intelligence The basic power of reasoning and problem solving.

crystallized intelligence The specific knowledge gained as a result of applying fluid intelligence.

Answers to Table 10.2: (1) Simon Templar; (2) Pluto; (3) cabbage; (4) Tokyo Rose; (5) a two-headed llama

be grouped into seven or eight more general ability factors, all of which combine into *g*, the broadest and most general of all (Carroll, 1993; Gustafsson & Undheim, 1996; Lubinski, 2004). Understanding *g* and how it arises is a major goal of research in cognitive psychology (Colom, Jung, & Haier, 2006; Detterman, 1982, 1987, 1994; Garlick, 2002; Gläscher et al., 2010; van der Maas et al., 2006).

The Information-Processing Model

As described in the chapter on cognition and language, many cognitive psychologists see the brain as an information-processing system that receives and works on information in ways that allow us to think, remember, and engage in other cognitive activities. When applied to the concept of intelligence, this **information-processing model** focuses on identifying the mental *processes* involved in intelligent behavior, not the abilities that result in test scores and other *products* of intelligence (Das, 2002; Jensen, 2006; Lohman, 2000; Sternberg, 2000). Researchers taking this information-processing approach ask, What mental operations are necessary to perform intellectual tasks? What aspects depend on past learning, and what aspects depend on attention, working memory, and processing speed? Are there individual differences in these processes that correlate with measures of intelligence? More specifically, are measures of intelligence related to differences in the amount of attention people have available for basic mental processes or in the speed of those processes?

The notion that intelligence may be related to attention builds on the results of research by Earl Hunt and others (Ackerman, 1994; Ackerman, Beier, & Boyle, 2002; Eysenck, 1987; Hunt, 1980). As discussed in the chapter on perception, attention represents a pool of resources or mental energy. When people perform difficult tasks or perform more than one task at a time, they must call on greater amounts of these resources. Does intelligent behavior depend on the amount of attention that can be mobilized? Early research by Hunt (1980) suggests that it does—that people with greater intellectual ability have more attentional resources available. There is also evidence of a positive correlation between IQ and performance on tasks requiring attention, such as silently counting the number of words in the "animal" category while reading a list of varied terms aloud (Stankov, 1989).

Another possible link between differences in information processing and differences in intelligence relates to processing speed. Perhaps more intelligent people have "faster brains"—perhaps they carry out basic mental processes more quickly. When a task is complex, having a "fast brain" might reduce the chance that information will fade from memory before it can be used (Jensen, 1993; Larson & Saccuzzo, 1989). A fast brain might also allow people to do a better job of mastering material in everyday life and therefore to build up a good knowledge base (Miller & Vernon, 1992). Hans Eysenck (1986) even proposed that intelligence can be defined as the error-free transmission of information through the brain. Following his lead, some researchers have attempted to measure various aspects of intelligence by looking at activity in particular parts of the brain (Colom, Jung, & Haier, 2006; Deary & Caryl, 1993; Eysenck, 1994; Garlick, 2002; Gläscher et al., 2010; Haier, White, & Alkire, 2003; Koten et al., 2009). Others have focused more specifically on the role of working-memory resources in intelligence (e.g., Gray, Chabris, & Braver, 2003; Kyllonen & Christal, 1990; Süss et al., 2002). In fact, some of these researchers suggest that *g* is nothing more than working memory (Jensen, 1998), whereas others believe that *g* is more than memory alone (Ackerman, Beier, & Boyle, 2002; Mackintosh & Bennett, 2003).

Evidence that better performance on intellectual tasks is related to more efficient information processing (Koten et al., 2009; Neubauer & Fink, 2009; Rypma & Prabhakaran, 2009) highlights the role of brain processes in intelligence, but it probably doesn't tell the whole story. Other research suggests that only a portion of the variation seen in people's performance on cognitive abilities tests can be accounted for by differences in their speed of access to long-term memory, the capacity of short-term and working memory, or other information-processing abilities (Baker, Vernon, & Ho, 1991; Friedman et al., 2006; Miller & Vernon, 1992).

information-processing model An approach to the study of intelligence that focuses on mental operations, such as attention and memory, that underlie intelligent behavior.

Brainpower and Intelligence

The information-processing model of intelligence suggests that people with the most rapid information processors—the "fastest" brains—should do best on cognitive ability tests, including intelligence tests and college entrance exams. Research suggests that there is more to intelligent behavior than sheer processing speed, though.

© Stephen Collins/Photo Researchers, Inc.

The Triarchic Theory of Intelligence

Robert Sternberg's **triarchic theory of intelligence** (1988b, 1999) says that there are three different types of intelligence: analytic, creative, and practical. *Analytic intelligence,* the kind that is measured by traditional intelligence tests, would help you solve a physics problem; *creative intelligence* is what you would use to compose music; and you would draw on *practical intelligence* to figure out what to do if you were stranded on a lonely road during a blizzard.

Sternberg recognizes that analytic intelligence is important for success at school and in other areas, but he argues that universities and employers should not select people solely on the basis of tests of this kind of intelligence (Sternberg, 1996; Sternberg & Williams, 1997). Why? Because the tasks posed by tests of analytic intelligence are often of little interest to the people taking them and typically have little relationship to their daily experience. For one thing, each task is usually clearly defined and comes with all the information needed to find the one right answer (Neisser et al., 1996), a situation that seldom occurs in the real world. The practical problems people face every day are generally of personal interest and are related to more common life experiences. That is, they are ill-defined and do not contain all the information necessary to solve them, they typically have more than one correct solution, and there may be several paths to a solution (Sternberg et al., 1995).

It is no wonder, then, that some children who do poorly in school may nevertheless show high degrees of practical intelligence, including—as in the case of Brazilian street children—the ability to live by their wits in hostile environments (Carraher, Carraher, & Schliemann, 1985). Some racetrack bettors whose IQs are as low as 82 are experts at predicting race odds at post time by combining many different kinds of complex information about horses, jockeys, and track conditions (Ceci & Liker, 1986). In these particular cases, practical intelligence appears almost unrelated to the analytic intelligence measured by traditional cognitive tests, but research with larger populations shows that there is actually a significant correlation between the two (Gottfredson, 2003).

Sternberg's theory is important because it extends the concept of intelligence into areas that most psychologists have traditionally not examined and because it emphasizes what intelligence means in everyday life. The theory is so broad, however, that many parts of it are difficult to test. For example, methods for measuring practical "street smarts" have been proposed (Sternberg, 2001; Sternberg et al., 1995), but they remain controversial (Brody, 2003; Gottfredson, 2003). Sternberg and his colleagues have also developed new intelligence tests designed to assess analytic, practical, and creative intelligence (see Figure 10.6), and they offer evidence

triarchic theory of intelligence
Robert Sternberg's theory that describes intelligence as having analytic, creative, and practical dimensions.

FIGURE 10.6

Testing for Practical and Creative Intelligence

TRY THIS Robert Sternberg argues that traditional tests measure mainly analytic intelligence. Here are sample items from tests he developed to test both practical and creative intelligence. Try answering them before you check the answers at the bottom of the figure. How did you do?

Source: Sternberg (1996).

PRACTICAL

1. Think of a problem that you are currently experiencing in real life. Briefly describe the problem, including how long it has been present and who else is involved (if anyone). Then describe three different practical things you could do to try to solve the problem. *(Students are given up to 15 minutes and up to 2 pages.)*

2. Choose the answer that provides the **best** solution, given the specific situation and desired outcome.

   John's family moved to Iowa from Arizona during his junior year in high school. He enrolled as a new student in the local high school two months ago but still has not made friends and feels bored and lonely. One of his favorite activities is writing stories. What is likely to be the most effective solution to this problem?

   A. Volunteer to work on the school newspaper staff.

   B. Spend more time at home writing columns for the school newsletter.

   C. Try to convince his parents to move back to Arizona.

   D. Invite a friend from Arizona to visit during Christmas break.

3. Each question asks you to use information about everyday things. Read each question carefully and choose the best answer.

   Mike wants to buy two seats together and is told there are pairs of seats available only in Rows 8, 12, 49, and 95–100. Which of the following is not one of his choices for the total price of the two tickets?

   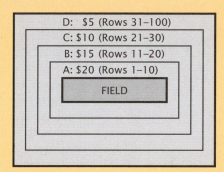

   A. $10.   **B.** $20.   **C.** $30.   **D.** $40.

CREATIVE

1. Suppose you are the student representative to a committee that has the power and the money to reform your school system. Describe your ideal school system, including buildings, teachers, curriculum, and any other aspects you feel are important. *(Students are given up to 15 minutes and up to 2 pages.)*

2. Each question has a "Pretend" statement. You must suppose that this statement is true. Decide which word goes with the third underlined word in the same way that the first two underlined words go together.

   Colors are audible.

   flavor is to *tongue* as *shade* is to

   A. ear.   **B.** light.   **C.** sound.   **D.** hue.

3. First, read how the operation is defined. Then, decide what is the correct answer to the question.

   *There is a new mathematical operation called **flix**. It is defined as follows:*

   A flix B = A + B, if A > B

   but   A flix B = A x B, if A < B

   and   A flix B = A / B, if A = B

   How much is 4 flix 7?

   A. 28.   **B.** 11.   **C.** 3.   **D.** −11.

ANSWERS. Practical: (2) A, (3) B. Creative: (2) A, (3) A.

that scores on these tests can predict success in college and at some jobs at least as well as standard intelligence tests (Leonhardt, 2000; Sternberg & Kaufman, 1998; Sternberg et al., 1995; Sternberg & Rainbow Project, 2006). Other researchers have questioned this interpretation (Brody, 2003). The value of these newer tests, they say, may be due in part to the correlation between practical and analytic intelligence. To some extent, the newer tests may be measuring the same thing as the older ones (Gottfredson, 2003).

Multiple Intelligences

Some people whose IQs are only average, or even below average, may have exceptional ability in certain specific areas. One child whose IQ was just 50 could correctly state the day of the week for any date between 1880 and 1950 (Scheerer, Rothmann, & Goldstein, 1945). He could also play melodies on the piano by ear and sing Italian operatic pieces he had heard. In addition, he could spell—forward or backward—any word spoken to him and could memorize long speeches, although he had no understanding of what he was doing.

Cases such as this are part of the evidence cited by Howard Gardner in support of his theory of **multiple intelligences** (Gardner, 1993, 2002). To study intelligence, Gardner focuses on how people learn and use symbol systems such as language, mathematics, and music. He asks, Do these systems all require the same abilities and processes, the same "intelligence"? According to Gardner, the answer is no. All people, he says, possess a number of intellectual potentials, or intelligences, each of which involves a somewhat different set of skills. Biology provides raw capacities; cultures provide symbolic systems—such as language—to use those raw capacities. Although the intelligences normally interact, they can function with some independence, and individuals may develop certain intelligences further than others. ("In Review: Analyzing Cognitive Abilities" summarizes Gardner's theory, along with the other views of intelligence we have discussed.)

The specific intelligences that Gardner (1999) proposes are (1) *linguistic* intelligence (reflected in good vocabulary and reading comprehension), (2) *logical-mathematical* intelligence (as indicated by skill at arithmetic and certain kinds of reasoning), (3) *spatial* intelligence (seen in the ability to visualize relationships among objects in the environment), (4) *musical* intelligence (as in abilities involving rhythm, tempo, and sound identification), (5) *body-kinesthetic* intelligence (reflected in skill at dancing, athletics, and eye-hand coordination), (6) *intrapersonal* intelligence (displayed by self-understanding), (7) *interpersonal* intelligence (seen in the

A Musical Prodigy?

According to Gardner's theory of multiple intelligences, skilled artists, athletes, and musicians—such as the young flutist shown here—display forms of intelligence not assessed by standard intelligence tests.

multiple intelligences Eight semi-independent kinds of intelligence postulated by Howard Gardner.

© Comstock Images/Alamy

ability to understand and interact with others), and (8) *naturalistic* intelligence (the ability to see patterns in nature). Other researchers have suggested that people also possess *emotional* intelligence, which involves the capacity to perceive, use, understand, and manage their emotions (Meyer & Salovey, 1997; Salovey & Grewal, 2005). Gardner says that traditional intelligence tests sample only the first three of these intelligences, mainly because these are the forms of intelligence most valued in school. To measure intelligences not tapped by standard tests, Gardner suggests collecting samples of children's writing, assessing their ability to appreciate or produce music, and obtaining teacher reports of their strengths and weaknesses in athletic and social skills (Gardner, 1991).

Gardner's view of intelligence is appealing, partly because it allows virtually everyone to be highly intelligent in at least one way. However, his critics argue that including athletic or musical skill dilutes the validity and usefulness of the intelligence concept, especially as it is applied in school and in many kinds of jobs. They suggest that intrapersonal, interpersonal, body-kinesthetic, and naturalistic abilities are best described as collections of specific skills. Therefore, it makes more sense to speak of, say, "interpersonal skills" rather than "interpersonal intelligence." At the moment, Gardner's theory lacks the empirical evidence necessary to challenge other, more established theories of intelligence (Klein, 1997; Waterhouse, 2006a, 2006b). This is true in part because there are still no dependable measures of the various intelligences he proposes (Lubinski & Benbow, 1995; Visser, Ashton, & Vernon, 2006). Until and unless such measures are developed, say Gardner's critics, his theory will be of little scientific value.

IN REVIEW Analyzing Cognitive Abilities		
Approach	**Method**	**Key Findings or Propositions**
Psychometric	Define the structure of intelligence by examining factor analyses of the correlations between scores on tests of cognitive abilities.	Performance on many tests of cognitive abilities is highly correlated, but this correlation, represented by *g*, reflects a bundle of abilities, not just one trait.
Information-processing	Understand intelligence by examining the mental operations involved in intelligent behavior.	The speed of basic cognitive processes and the amount of attentional resources available make significant contributions to performance on intelligence tests.
Sternberg's triarchic theory	Understand intelligence by examining the information-processing involved in thinking, changes with experience, and effects in different environments.	There are three distinct kinds of intelligence: analytic, creative, and practical. Intelligence tests measure only analytic intelligence, but creative intelligence (which involves dealing with new problems) and practical intelligence (which involves adapting to one's environment) may also be important to success in school and at work.
Gardner's theory of multiple intelligences	Understand intelligence by examining test scores, information-processing, biological and developmental research, the skills valued by different cultures, and exceptional people.	Biology provides the capacity for eight distinct "intelligences": linguistic, logical-mathematical, spatial, musical, body-kinesthetic, intrapersonal, interpersonal, and naturalistic.

1. The concepts of fluid and crystallized intelligence developed from research on the _____ approach to intelligence

2. Using fMRI scanning to relate memory skills to intelligence reflects which approach to intelligence?

3. Which theory of intelligence highlights the fact that some people with low IQs can still succeed at complex tasks of daily living?

FOCUS ON RESEARCH METHODS ▶

LINKAGES Which research designs are best for studying changes in cognitive abilities as people age? (a link to Research in Psychology, p. 42)

Tracking Cognitive Abilities over the Life Span

As described in the chapter on human development, significant changes in cognitive abilities occur from infancy through adolescence, but development does not stop there. One major study has focused specifically on the changes in cognitive abilities that occur during adulthood.

What was the researchers' question?

The researchers began by asking what appears to be a relatively simple question: How do adults' cognitive abilities change over time?

How did the researchers answer the question?

Answering this question is extremely difficult because findings about age-related changes in cognitive abilities depend to some extent on the methods that are used to observe those changes. None of the methods includes true experiments, because psychologists cannot randomly assign people to be a certain age and then give them mental tests. So changes in cognitive abilities must be explored through a number of other research designs.

One of these, the *cross-sectional study,* compares data collected at the same point in time from people of different ages. However, cross-sectional studies contain a major confounding variable: Because people are born at different times, they may have had very different educational, cultural, nutritional, and medical experiences. This confounding variable is referred to as a *cohort effect.* Suppose that two cohorts, or age groups, are tested on their ability to imagine the rotation of an object in space. The cohort born around 1940 might not do as well as the one born around 1980, but does the difference reflect declining spatial ability in the older people? It might, but it might also be due in part to the younger group's greater experience with video games and other spatial tasks. In other words, differences in experience, and not just age, could account for differences in ability between older and younger people in a cross-sectional study.

Changes associated with age can also be examined through *longitudinal studies,* in which people are repeatedly tested as they grow older. But longitudinal designs, too, have some built-in problems. For one thing, fewer and fewer members of an age cohort can be tested over time as death, physical disability, relocation, and lack of interest reduce the sample size. Researchers call this problem the *mortality effect.* Further, the remaining members are likely to be the healthiest in the group and may also have retained better mental powers than the dropouts. As a result, longitudinal studies may underestimate the degree to which abilities decline with age. Another confounding factor can come from the *history effect.* Here, some event—such as a reduction in health care benefits for senior citizens—might have an effect on cognitive ability scores that is mistakenly attributed to age. Finally, longitudinal studies may be confounded by *testing effects,* meaning that participants may improve over time because of what they learn during repeated testing procedures. People who become "test wise" in this way might even remember answers from one testing session to the next.

As part of the Seattle Longitudinal Study of cognitive aging, K. Warner Schaie (1993) developed a research design that measures the impact of the confounding variables we have discussed and allows corrections to be made for them. In 1956, Schaie identified a random sample of five thousand members of a health maintenance organization (HMO) and invited some of them to volunteer for his study. The volunteers, who ranged in age from 20 to 80, were given a set of intelligence tests designed to measure Thurstone's primary mental abilities (PMA). The cross-sectional comparisons allowed by this first step were, of course, confounded by cohort effects. To control for those effects, the researchers retested the same participants seven years later, in 1963. By doing so, the study combined cross-sectional with longitudinal methods in what is called a *cross-sequential with resampling design.* This design allowed the researchers to compare the size of the *difference* in PMA scores between, say, the 20-year-olds and 27-year-olds tested in 1956 with the size of the *change* in PMA scores for these same people as they aged from 20 to 27 and from 27 to 34. Schaie reasoned that if the size of the longitudinal change was about the same as the size of the cross-sectional difference, the cross-sectional difference could probably be attributed to aging, not to the era in which the participants were born.

What about the effect of confounding variables on the longitudinal changes themselves? To measure the impact of testing effects, the researchers randomly drew a new set of participants from their original pool of five thousand. These people were of the same age range as the first sample, but they had not yet been tested. If people from the first sample did better on their second PMA testing than the people of the same age who now took the PMA for the first time, a testing effect would be suggested. (In this case, the size of the difference would indicate the size of the testing effect.) To control for history effects, the researchers examined the scores of people who were the same age in different years. For example, they compared people who were 30 in 1956 with those who were 30 in 1963, people who were 40 in 1956 with those who were 40 in 1963, and so on. If PMA scores were the same for people of the same age no matter what year they were tested, it is unlikely that events that happened in any particular year would have influenced test results. The researchers tested participants six times between 1956 and 1991. On each occasion, they retested some previous participants and tested others for the first time.

What did the researchers find?

The results of the Seattle Longitudinal Study and other, more limited longitudinal studies suggest a reasonably consistent conclusion: Unless people are impaired by Alzheimer's disease or other brain disorders, most of their cognitive abilities usually decline very slightly between early adulthood and old age. Some aspects of *crystallized intelligence,* which depends on retrieving information and facts about the world from long-term memory, may remain robust well into old age. Other components of intelligence, however, may have failed quite noticeably by the time people reach 65 or 70. *Fluid intelligence,* which involves rapid and flexible manipulations of ideas and symbols, is the most likely to decline (Bugg et al., 2006; Gilmore, Spinks, & Thomas, 2006; Schaie, 1996; see Figure 12.7 in the chapter on human development). The decline shows up in the following areas:

1. *Working memory.* The ability to hold and organize material in working memory declines beyond age 50 or 60, particularly when attention must be redirected (Parkin & Walter, 1991).

The Voice of Experience

Even in old age, people's crystallized intelligence may remain intact. Their extensive storehouse of knowledge, experience, and wisdom makes older people a valuable resource for the young.

© Konstantin Sutyagin/Shutterstock

2. *Processing speed.* There is a general slowing of all mental processes (Salthouse, 1996, 2000). Research has not yet isolated whether this slowing is due to reduced storage capacity, impaired processing efficiency, problems in coordinating simultaneous activities, or some combination of these factors (Babcock & Salthouse, 1990; Li et al., 2004; Salthouse, 1990). For many tasks, this slowing does not create obstacles. But if a problem requires manipulating material in working memory, quick processing of information is critical. To multiply two 2-digit numbers mentally, for example, you must combine the subsums before you forget them. In some cases, internal distractions may interfere with older people's processing efficiency (Li et al., 2004).

3. *Organization.* Older people seem to be less likely to solve problems by adopting specific strategies, or mental shortcuts (Charness, 2000). For example, to locate a wiring problem, you might perform a test that narrows down the regions where the problem might be. The tests carried out by older people tend to be more random and haphazard (Young, 1971). This result may occur partly because many older people are out of practice at solving such problems.

4. *Flexibility.* Older people tend to be less flexible than younger people in problem solving. They are less likely to consider alternative solutions (Salthouse & Prill, 1987), and they require more information before making a tentative decision (Ackerman, Beier, & Boyle, 2002; Rabbitt, 1977). Laboratory studies suggest that older people are also more likely than younger ones to choose conservative, risk-free options (Botwinick, 1966).

5. *Control of attention.* The ability to direct or control attention declines with age (Kramer et al., 1999). When required to switch their attention from one task to another, older participants typically perform less well than younger ones. Older adults also tend to be overwhelmed by distracting information, which may help account for many of the cognitive problems accompanying aging (Gazzaley et al., 2005).

What do the results mean?

This study indicates that different kinds of cognitive abilities change in different ways throughout our lifetimes. In general, there is a gradual, continual accumulation of knowledge about the world, some systematic changes in the limits of cognitive processes, and changes in the way those processes are carried out. This finding suggests that a general decline in cognitive abilities during adulthood is neither inevitable nor universal (Richards et al., 2004).

What do we still need to know?

There is an important question that the Schaie (1993) study doesn't answer: Why do age-related changes in cognitive abilities occur? Some researchers suggest that these changes are largely due to a decline in the speed and accuracy with which older people process information (Li et al., 2004; Salthouse, 2000). If this interpretation is correct, it would explain why some older people are less successful than younger ones at tasks that require rapidly integrating several pieces of information in working memory prior to making a choice or a decision.

It is also vital to learn why some people do *not* show declines in cognitive abilities, even when they reach their eighties. By understanding the biological and psychological factors responsible for these exceptions to the general rule, we might be able to reverse or delay some of the intellectual consequences of growing old.

Diversity in Cognitive Abilities

Although psychologists still don't agree on the details of what intelligence is, the study of intelligence tests and intelligent behavior has yielded many insights into human cognitive abilities. It has also highlighted the diversity of those abilities. In this section, we briefly examine some of that diversity.

Creativity

If you watch *The Simpsons* on television, you have probably noticed that Bart writes a different "punishment" sentence on the blackboard at the beginning of every episode. To maintain this tradition, the show's writers have had to create a unique—and funny—sentence for each of the hundreds of shows that have aired since 1989. In every area of human endeavor, there are people who demonstrate **creativity,** the ability to produce new, high-quality ideas or products (Simonton, 1999, 2004; Sternberg & Grigorenko, 2004a). Whether a corporate executive or a homemaker, a scientist or an artist, everyone is creative to some degree (Klahr & Simon, 1999). Yet like the concept of intelligence, the concept of creativity is difficult to define. Does creativity include innovation based on previous ideas, or must it be utterly new? And must it be new to the world, as in Pablo Picasso's paintings, or only new to the creator, as when a child "makes up" the word *waterbird* without having heard it before? As with intelligence, psychologists have not defined *creativity* as a "thing" that people have or don't have. They have defined it instead as a process or cognitive activity that can be inferred from performance on creativity tests, as well as from the writing and computer programs, artwork, and other products that result from the creative process (Sternberg & Dess, 2001).

To measure creativity, some psychologists have devised tests of **divergent thinking,** the ability to think along many paths to generate many solutions to a problem (Diakidoy & Spanoudis, 2002). The Consequences Test is an example. It contains items such as "Imagine all of the things that might possibly happen if all national and local laws were suddenly abolished" (Guilford, 1959). Divergent-thinking tests are scored by counting the number of reasonable responses that a person can list for each

TRY THIS item and how many of those responses differ from other people's responses. Try this yourself and see how you do. Unfortunately, these tests may underestimate creativity, because even creative people may find it difficult to create on demand in the same way they could, say, spell words or do multiplication problems when asked. Further, there is no guarantee that having the ability to come up with different answers or different ways of looking at a situation will lead to creative results. Creative behavior requires divergent thinking that is appropriate for a given situation or problem. To be productive rather than just weird, a creative person must be firmly anchored to reality; understand society's expectations, values, and needs; and learn from the experience and knowledge of others (Sternberg & Lubart, 1992). Teresa Amabile has identified three kinds of cognitive and personality characteristics necessary for creativity (Amabile, 1996; Amabile, Hennessey, & Grossman, 1986):

1. *Expertise* in the field of endeavor, which is directly tied to what a person has learned. For example, a painter or composer must know the paints, techniques, or instruments available.

2. A set of *creative skills,* including willingness to work hard, persistence at problem solving, capacity for divergent thinking, ability to break out of old problem-solving habits, and willingness to take risks. Amabile believes that training can influence many of these skills (some of which are closely linked to the strategies for problem solving discussed in the chapter on cognition and language).

3. The *motivation* to pursue creative production for internal reasons, such as satisfaction, rather than for external reasons, such as money. In fact, Amabile and her colleagues found that external rewards can deter creativity (e.g., Amabile, Hennessey, & Grossman, 1986). In one study, they asked groups of children or adults to create artistic products such as paintings or stories. Some were simply asked to work on the project. Others were told that their project would be judged for its creativity and excellence and that rewards would be given or winners announced. Experts—who did not know which products were created by which group—judged the work of the "reward" group to be significantly less creative. Similar effects have been found in other studies (Deci, Koestner, & Ryan, 1999, 2001), though research by Robert Eisenberger suggests that there may also be circumstances in which rewarding people's creativity can strengthen it—in

creativity The ability to produce new, high-quality ideas or products.

divergent thinking The ability to think along many alternative paths to generate many different solutions to a problem.

much the same way that positive reinforcement strengthens any other behavior (Eisenberger & Rhoades, 2001; Eisenberger & Shanock, 2003).

Is creativity inherited? To some extent, perhaps it is (Kéri, 2009; Lykken, 1998b), but there is evidence that a person's environment—including the social, economic, and political forces within it—can influence creative behavior at least as much as it influences intelligence (Amabile, 2001; Nakamura & Csikszentmihalyi, 2001). For example, the correlation between the creativity scores of identical twins reared apart is lower than that between their IQs (Nichols, 1978). Environmental factors, such as growing up around musicians or scientists, may focus one's creativity in a particular area, such as writing music or doing research. There are some notable exceptions, but most people who are creative in one domain are not especially creative in others.

Do you have to be smart to be creative? Creativity does appear to require a certain degree of intelligence (Sternberg, 2001). For example, longitudinal studies have shown that individuals identified as particularly smart in adolescence were up to eight times more likely than other people to show creativity as adults by patenting inventions or producing scientific publications (Park, Lubinski, & Benbow, 2008; Wai, Lubinski, & Benbow, 2005). But you don't have to be a genius to be creative (Simonton, 1984, 2002; Sternberg, 2001). In fact, although correlations between scores on creativity tests and intelligence tests are almost always positive, they are relatively modest (Simonton, 1999). This finding is not surprising, because creativity as psychologists measure it requires broad, divergent thinking, whereas high scores on traditional intelligence tests require **convergent thinking**—the ability to apply logic and knowledge in order to narrow down the number of possible solutions to a problem. Research on creativity and its relationship to intelligence has intensified in recent years (Sternberg & Dess, 2001). One result of that research has been to define the combination of intelligence and creativity in the same person as *wisdom* (Baltes & Smith, 2008; Sternberg, 2001; Sternberg & O'Hara, 1999).

Unusual Cognitive Ability

Our understanding of cognitive abilities has been advanced by research on people whose cognitive abilities are unusual—people who are gifted, intellectually disabled, or have learning disabilities (Robinson, Zigler, & Gallagher, 2000).

Giftedness   People who show remarkably high levels of accomplishment in particular domains or who show promise for such accomplishment are often referred to as **gifted.** Giftedness is typically measured by school success and other evidence of unusually high achievement, such as outstanding science projects, written products, and the like. The potential for this kind of accomplishment is usually assessed with intelligence tests or measures of scholastic aptitude. Researchers caution, though, against predicting academic potential from a single measure, such as the score on an IQ test (Hagen, 1980; Lohman & Hagen, 2001b; Thorndike & Hagen, 1996).

For one thing, people with unusually high IQs do not necessarily become famous and successful in their chosen fields, although they are more likely than others to do so. One of the best-known studies of the intellectually gifted was conducted by Louis Terman and his colleagues (Oden, 1968; Sears, 1977; Terman & Oden, 1947, 1959). This study began in 1921 with the identification of more than fifteen hundred children whose IQs were very high—most higher than 135 by age 10. Interviews and tests conducted over the next sixty years revealed that few, if any, became truly creative geniuses—such as world-famous inventors, authors, artists, or composers—but that only eleven failed to graduate from high school and that more than two-thirds graduated from college. Ninety-seven earned doctorates; ninety-two, law degrees; and fifty-seven, medical degrees. In 1955, their median family income was well above the national average (Terman & Oden, 1959). In general, they were physically and mentally healthier than nongifted people and appear to have led happier lives (Cronbach, 1996). These results are consistent with more recent studies showing that people with

convergent thinking The ability to apply logic and knowledge to narrow down the number of possible solutions to a problem or perform some other complex cognitive task.

gifted A term referring to people who show remarkably high levels of accomplishment or promise for such accomplishment in particular cognitive domains.

higher IQs have lower rates of heart or lung disease, high blood pressure, diabetes, arthritis, and depression or other mental disorders (Der, Batty, & Deary, 2009; Koenen et al., 2009). The gifted also tend to live longer (Deary et al., 2004; Gottfredson, 2004; Leon et al., 2009; Weiss et al., 2009), perhaps because they have the reasoning and problem-solving skills that lead them to take better care of themselves and to avoid danger (Breslau, Lucia, & Alvarado, 2006; Deary & Der, 2005; Gottfredson & Deary, 2004; Hall et al., 2009; see the Focus on Research Methods section of the chapter on health, stress, and coping).

Although higher IQs tend to predict longer, more successful lives (Judge, Hurst, & Simon, 2009; Lubinski et al., 2006; Simonton & Song, 2009; Wai, Lubinski, & Benbow, 2005), an extremely high IQ does not guarantee special distinction. Some research suggests that gifted children are not fundamentally different from other children; they just have "more" of the same basic cognitive abilities seen in all children (Dark & Benbow, 1993; Singh & O'Boyle, 2004). Other work suggests that the gifted have an unusually intense motivation to master certain tasks or areas of intellectual endeavor (Lubinski et al., 2001; Winner, 2000).

Intellectual Disability   People whose IQs are less than about 70 *and* who fail to display the skill at daily living, communication, and other tasks expected of those their age were once described as *mentally retarded* (American Psychiatric Association, 1994). They now are referred to as *intellectually disabled, developmentally disabled, cognitively disabled,* or *mentally challenged* (Schalock et al., 2009). People in this very broad category differ greatly in their cognitive abilities, as well as in their ability to function independently in daily life. Table 10.3 shows a classification that divides the range of low IQ into categories that reflect these differences.

Some cases of intellectual disability have a clearly identifiable cause. The best known example is *Down syndrome,* which affects about eleven of every ten thousand newborns and occurs when an abnormality during conception results in an extra twenty-first chromosome (Hattori et al., 2000; Shin et al., 2009). Children with Down syndrome typically have IQs in the range of 40 to 55, though some may score higher than that. There are also several inherited causes of intellectual disability. The most

The Eagle Has Landed

In February 2000, Richard Keebler, 27, became an Eagle Scout, the highest rank in the Boy Scouts of America. His achievement is notable not only because only 4 percent of all Scouts reach this pinnacle but also because Keebler has Down syndrome. As we come to better understand the potential, not just the limitations, of people with intellectual disabilities, their opportunities and their role in society will continue to expand.

Level of Intellectual Disability	IQ Range	Characteristics
TABLE 10.3 Categories of Intellectual Disability		
These categories are approximate. Especially at the upper end of the scale, many intellectually disabled people can be taught to handle tasks well beyond what their IQ might suggest. Furthermore, IQ is not the only diagnostic criterion for intellectual disability. Many people with IQs lower than 70 can function adequately in their communities and so would not be classified as intellectually disabled.		
Mild	50–70	A majority of all intellectually disabled people. Usually show no physical symptoms of abnormality. Individuals with higher IQs can marry, maintain a family, and work in unskilled jobs. Abstract reasoning is difficult for those with the lower IQs of this category. Capable of some academic learning to a sixth-grade level.
Moderate	35–49	Often lack physical coordination. Can be trained to take care of themselves and to acquire some reading and writing skills. Abilities of a 4- to 7-year-old. Capable of living outside an institution with their families.
Severe	20–34	Only a few can benefit from any schooling. Can communicate vocally after extensive training. Most require constant supervision.
Profound	Below 20	Mental age less than 3. Very limited communication. Require constant supervision. Can learn to walk, utter a few simple phrases, and feed themselves.

© Fraser Hale/St. Petersburg Times

An Inventive Genius

Thomas Edison invented the electric light bulb and the phonograph, among many other things, but as a child, he did so poorly in school that his teacher sent him home to be educated by his mother. When students' academic performance falls short of what intelligence tests say they are capable of, a learning disability may be present. However, poor study skills, lack of motivation, and even the need for eyeglasses are among the many factors other than learning disabilities that can create a discrepancy between IQ and academic achievement. Accordingly, accurately diagnosing learning disabilities is not an easy task.

LINKAGES   Is intellectual disability mainly a matter of poor memory? (a link to Memory, p. 256)

cultural familial intellectual disability   Cases of mild cognitive disability for which there is no obvious genetic or environmental cause.

learning disabilities   Conditions that may account for a significant discrepancy between a person's measured intelligence and academic performance.

common of these is *fragile X syndrome,* caused by a defect on chromosome 23 (known as the *X chromosome*). More rarely, intellectual disability is caused by inheriting *Williams syndrome* (a defect on chromosome 7) or by inheriting a gene for *phenylketonuria,* or PKU (which causes the body to create toxins out of milk and other foods). Intellectual disability can also result from environmental causes, such as exposure to German measles (rubella) or alcohol or other toxins before birth; oxygen deprivation during birth; and head injuries, brain tumors, and infectious diseases (such as meningitis or encephalitis) in childhood (U.S. Surgeon General, 1999).

Cultural familial intellectual disability refers to the 30 to 40 percent of (usually mild) cases in which there is no obvious genetic or environmental cause (American Psychiatric Association, 1994). In these cases, intellectual disability appears to result from a complex and as yet unknown interaction between heredity and environment that researchers are continuing to explore (Croen, Grether, & Selvin, 2001; Spinath, Harlaar, et al., 2004).

People who display mild intellectual disability differ from other people in three important ways, all of which appear to reflect limitations in working memory and mental processing speed (Campione, Brown, & Ferrara, 1982):

1. They perform certain mental operations more slowly, such as retrieving information from long-term memory. When asked to repeat something they have learned, they are not as quick as a person of normal intelligence.

2. They simply know fewer facts about the world. It is likely that this deficiency is caused by the third problem.

3. They are not very good at remembering to use mental strategies that may be important in learning and problem solving. For example, they do not remember to rehearse material that must be held in short-term memory, even though they know how to do so.

Despite such difficulties, the cognitive skills of intellectually disabled people can be improved to some extent. One program emphasizing positive parent-child communications began when the children were as young as 30 months old. It ultimately helped children with Down syndrome master reading skills at a second-grade level, providing the foundation for further achievement (Rynders & Horrobin, 1980; Turkington, 1987). However, designing effective programs for intellectually disabled children is complicated because the way people learn depends not just on cognitive skills but also on social and emotional factors, including *where* they learn. Much debate has focused on *inclusion* (once known as *mainstreaming*), the policy of teaching children with disabilities, including those with intellectual disabilities, in regular classrooms with children who do not have disabilities. Is inclusion good for children with intellectual disabilities? A number of studies of the cognitive and social skills of students who were included in regular classes and those who were separated show few significant differences overall, although it appears that students at higher ability levels may gain more from being included than their less cognitively able peers (Cole et al., 1991; Mills et al., 1998).

Learning Disabilities   People who show a significant discrepancy between their measured intelligence and their academic performance may have **learning disabilities** (National Information Center for Children and Youth with Disabilities, 2000). These disabilities are often seen in people with average or above-average IQs. For example, the problems with reading, writing, and math that Leonardo da Vinci and Thomas Edison had as children may have been due to such a disability; the problems certainly did not reflect a lack of cognitive ability!

There are several kinds of learning disabilities (Myers & Hammill, 1990; Wadsworth et al., 2000). People with *dyslexia* find it difficult to understand the meaning of what they read; they may also have difficulty in sounding out and identifying written words. *Dysphasia* is difficulty with understanding spoken words or with recalling the words needed for effective speech. *Dysgraphia*—problems with writing—appears as an inability to form letters or as the omission or reordering of words and parts of words in one's writing. The least common learning disability, *dyscalculia,* is a difficulty with arithmetic that reflects not poor mathematical ability but rather an impairment in the understanding of quantity and/or in the comprehension of basic arithmetic principles and operations, such as addition and subtraction.

The National Joint Committee on Learning Disabilities (1994) has suggested that these disorders are caused by dysfunctions in the brain. However, although evidence from brain imaging and other studies are helping locate areas of dysfunction (e.g., Pugh et al., 2000; Richards et al., 2000; Wright & Zecker, 2004), specific neurological causes have not yet been found. Accordingly, most researchers describe learning disabilities in terms of dysfunctional information processing (Kujala et al., 2001; Shaw et al., 1995). Diagnosis of a learning disability includes several steps. First, it is important to look for significant weaknesses in a person's listening, speaking, reading, writing, reasoning, or arithmetic skills (Brinckerhoff, Shaw, & McGuire, 1993). The person's actual ability is compared with that predicted by the person's IQ. Tests for brain damage are also given. To help rule out alternative explanations of poor academic performance, the person's hearing, vision, and other sensory systems are tested, and factors such as poverty, family conflicts, and inadequate instruction are reviewed. Finally, alternative diagnoses such as attention deficit hyperactivity disorder (see the chapter on psychological disorders) must be eliminated.

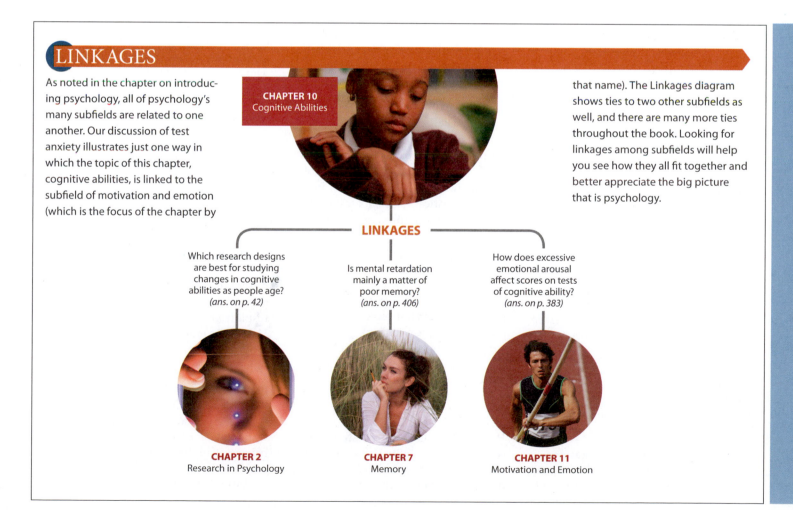

LINKAGES

As noted in the chapter on introducing psychology, all of psychology's many subfields are related to one another. Our discussion of test anxiety illustrates just one way in which the topic of this chapter, cognitive abilities, is linked to the subfield of motivation and emotion (which is the focus of the chapter by

CHAPTER 10
Cognitive Abilities

that name). The Linkages diagram shows ties to two other subfields as well, and there are many more ties throughout the book. Looking for linkages among subfields will help you see how they all fit together and better appreciate the big picture that is psychology.

LINKAGES

Which research designs are best for studying changes in cognitive abilities as people age?
(ans. on p. 42)

Is mental retardation mainly a matter of poor memory?
(ans. on p. 406)

How does excessive emotional arousal affect scores on tests of cognitive ability?
(ans. on p. 383)

CHAPTER 2
Research in Psychology

CHAPTER 7
Memory

CHAPTER 11
Motivation and Emotion

SUMMARY

Cognitive ability refers to the capacity to perform higher mental processes, such as reasoning, remembering, understanding, problem solving, and decision making.

Testing for Intelligence

Psychologists have not reached a consensus on how best to define intelligence. A working definition describes *intelligence* in terms of reasoning, problem solving, and dealing with changing environments.

A Brief History of Intelligence Tests

Alfred Binet's pioneering test of intelligence included questions that required reasoning and problem solving of varying levels of difficulty, graded by age and resulting in a *mental age* score. Lewis Terman developed a revision of Binet's test that became known as the *Stanford-Binet Intelligence Scale;* it included items designed to assess the intelligence of adults as well as children and became the model for IQ tests. David Wechsler's tests remedied some of the deficiencies of the earlier IQ tests. Made up of subtests, some of which have little verbal content, these tests allowed testers to generate scores for different aspects of cognitive ability.

Intelligence Tests Today

The Stanford-Binet and Wechsler tests are the most popular individually administered intelligence tests. Both include subtests and provide scores for parts of the test, as well as an overall score. For example, in addition to a full-scale IQ, the Wechsler tests yield scores for verbal comprehension, perceptual reasoning, working memory, and processing speed. Currently, a person's *intelligence quotient,* or *IQ,* reflects how far that person's performance on the test deviates from the average performance of people in the same age group. An average performance is assigned an IQ of 100.

Aptitude and Achievement Measures

Aptitude measures are intended to assess a person's potential to learn new skills; *achievement measures* are intended to assess what a person has already learned. Both kinds of measures are used by schools for the placement or admission of students and by companies for the selection of new employees.

Measuring the Quality of Tests

Tests have two key advantages over other techniques of evaluation. First, they are standardized, which means that the conditions surrounding a test are as similar as possible for everyone who takes it. Second, they produce scores that can be compared with *norms,* thus allowing people's strengths or weaknesses in various areas to be compared with those of other people.

Statistical Reliability

A good test must be *statistically reliable,* which means that the results for each person are consistent, or stable. Statistical reliability can be measured by various methods, including the test-retest, alternate-form, and split-half methods.

Statistical Validity

Statistical validity refers to the degree to which test scores are interpreted appropriately and used properly. We cannot say whether a test itself is valid or invalid, but the statistical validity of test scores for a particular purpose can be evaluated in several ways. These include measurement of content validity (the degree to which test items include a fair sample of what the test is supposed to measure), criterion and predictive validity (the correlation between test scores and some present or future criterion), and construct validity (the extent to which the test measures the theoretical construct it was designed to measure).

Evaluating Intelligence Tests

In evaluating intelligence tests, we must consider the reliability and validity of test scores as well as sociocultural factors that might influence those scores.

The Statistical Reliability and Validity of Intelligence Tests

Intelligence tests are reasonably reliable, and they do a good job of predicting academic success. However, these tests assess only some of the abilities that might be considered aspects of intelligence, and they tend to favor people most familiar with middle-class culture. Nonetheless, this familiarity is important for academic and occupational success.

Innate and Environmental Influences on IQ

Both heredity and the environment influence IQ, and their effects interact. The influence of heredity is shown by the high correlation between the IQs of identical twins raised in separate households and by the similarity in the IQs of children adopted at birth and their biological parents. The influence of the environment is revealed by the higher correlation of IQs among siblings who share the same environment than among siblings who do not, as well as by the effects of environmental changes such as adoption.

Group Differences in IQ

Average IQs differ across socioeconomic and ethnic groups. These differences appear to be due to numerous factors, including differences in educational opportunity, motivation to achieve, family support for cognitive development, and other environmental conditions.

Conditions That Can Raise IQ

An enriched environment sometimes raises preschool children's IQs. Initial gains in cognitive performance that result from interventions such as Project Head Start may decline over time, but the programs may improve children's attitudes toward school.

IQ in the Classroom

Like any label, IQ can generate expectations that affect both how other people respond to a person and how that person behaves. Children labeled with low IQ may be offered fewer or lower-quality educational opportunities. However, scores on an IQ test can help educators identify a student's strengths and weaknesses and offer the curriculum that will best serve that student.

Understanding Intelligence

Researchers have taken several approaches to understanding the concept of intelligence.

The Psychometric Approach

Based on the field of *psychometrics,* the *psychometric approach* to intelligence attempts to analyze the structure of intelligence by examining correlations between tests of cognitive ability. Because scores on almost all tests of cognitive ability are positively correlated, Charles Spearman concluded that such tests measure a general factor of mental ability, called *g,* as well as more specific factors, called *s.* As a result of factor analysis, other researchers have concluded that intelligence is not a single general ability but a collection of abilities and subskills needed to succeed on any test of intelligence. Raymond B. Cattell distinguished between *fluid intelligence,* the basic power of reasoning and problem solving, and *crystallized intelligence,* the specific knowledge gained as a result of applying fluid intelligence. Modern psychometric theories of intelligence describe it as a hierarchy that is based on a host of specific abilities that fit into about eight groups that themselves combine into a single, general category of cognitive ability.

The Information-Processing Model

The *information-processing model* of intelligence focuses on the processes underlying intelligent behavior. Varying degrees of correlation have been found between IQ and measures of the flexibility and capacity of attention and between IQ and measures of the speed of information processing. This model has helped deepen our understanding of the processes that create individual differences in intelligence.

The Triarchic Theory of Intelligence

According to Robert Sternberg's *triarchic theory of intelligence,* there are three different types of intelligence: analytic, creative, and practical. Intelligence tests typically focus on analytic intelligence, but recent research has suggested ways to assess practical and creative intelligence too.

Multiple Intelligences

Howard Gardner's approach to intelligence suggests that biology equips us with the capacities for *multiple intelligences* that can function with some independence—specifically, linguistic, logical-mathematical, spatial, musical, body-kinesthetic, intrapersonal, interpersonal, and naturalistic intelligences.

Diversity in Cognitive Abilities

Research on human cognitive abilities has served to highlight the diversity of those abilities.

Creativity

Tests of *divergent thinking* are used to measure differences in *creativity.* In contrast, intelligence tests typically require *convergent thinking.* Although creativity and IQ are not highly correlated, creative behavior requires a certain amount of intelligence, along with expertise in a creative field, skills at problem solving and divergent thinking, and motivation to pursue a creative endeavor for its own sake.

Unusual Cognitive Ability

Knowledge about cognitive abilities has been expanded by research on giftedness, intellectual disabilities, and learning disabilities. *Gifted* people, those with very high IQs, tend to be healthier and more successful, but they are not necessarily geniuses. People are considered intellectually disabled if their IQs are below about 70 and if their communication and daily living skills are less than expected of people their age. Some cases of intellectual disability have a known cause; in *cultural familial intellectual disability,* the mix of genetic and environmental causes is unknown. Compared with people of normal intelligence, intellectually disabled people process information more slowly, know fewer facts, and are deficient at knowing and using mental strategies. Despite such difficulties, the cognitive skills of some intellectually disabled people can be improved to some extent. People who show a significant discrepancy between their measured intelligence and their academic performance may have *learning disabilities.* These can take several forms and must be carefully diagnosed.

LINKAGES TO FURTHER LEARNING

Now that you have finished reading this chapter, how about exploring some of the topics and information that you found most interesting? Here are some places to start.

Books

Howard Gardner, *Multiple Intelligences: New Horizons in Theory and Practice* (Basic Books, 2006). Theory of multiple intelligences.

Nicholas Lemann, *The Big Test: The Secret History of American Meritocracy* (Farrar, Straus & Giroux, 1999). History of testing in the United States.

Hans Eysenck, with Darrin Evans, *Test Your IQ* (Penguin, 1995). Self-testing.

Richard Herrnstein and Charles Murray, *The Bell Curve* (Free Press, 1994). Controversial book about group differences in intelligence.

Steven Fraser (Ed.), *The Bell Curve Wars* (Basic Books, 1995). Essays critical of *The Bell Curve.*

Daniel Seligman, *A Question of Intelligence: The IQ Debate in America* (Citadel Press, 1994). Nature, nurture, and IQ.

Richard Nisbett, *Intelligence and How to Get It: Why Schools and Cultures Count* (Norton, 2010). Making the case for the role of environment in shaping intelligence.

On the Internet

 Access an integrated eBook and chapter-specific learning tools including flashcards, quizzes, videos, and more. Go to CengageBrain.com.

Want to maximize the value of your online study time? Take this easy-to-use study system's diagnostic pre-test, and it will create a personalized study plan for you. By helping you identify the topics that you need to understand better and then directing you to valuable online resources, it can speed up your chapter review. CengageNOW even provides a post-test so you can confirm that you are ready for an exam. Go to CengageBrain.com.

TALKING POINTS

Here are a few talking points to help you summarize this chapter for family and friends without giving a lecture.

1. We all have an idea of what intelligence is, but there is no universally accepted definition.
2. Most psychologists agree that intelligence includes the ability to think, reason, learn, and solve problems.
3. The average IQ in the general population is 100.
4. IQ used to be calculated by a formula comparing your mental age with your actual age, but it is now expressed as the degree to which your score on an intelligence test differs from the average scores of people in your age group.
5. Overall, intelligence test scores tend to be quite consistent (reliable), and they are valid for predicting people's later performance in various academic and work situations.
6. There are some differences among the average IQs of various ethnic groups, but these differences tend to be small and are probably related more to environmental than to genetic factors.
7. Intelligence and creativity are somewhat related, but because they involve different kinds of thinking, you can be creative without being extremely smart, and vice versa.
8. The diagnosis of intellectual disability is not based on IQ alone; people with relatively low IQs who have the skill to live and work as others do are not considered disabled.

11

Motivation and Emotion

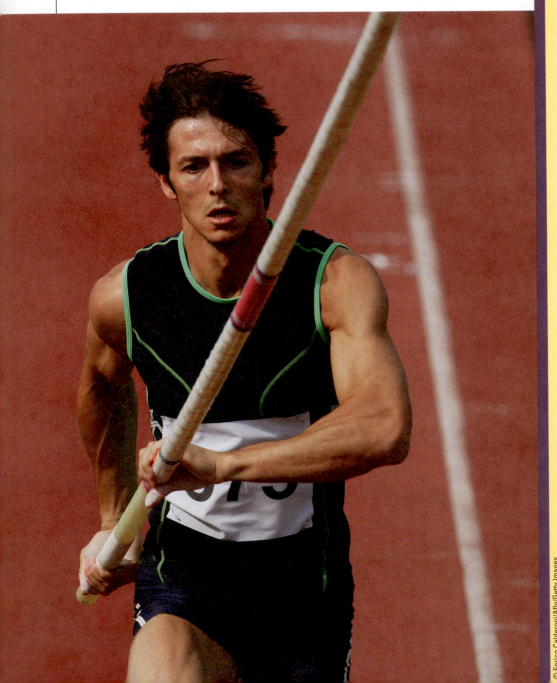

© Enrico Calderoni/Aflo/Getty Images

When your clock goes off in the morning, do you jump out of bed, eager to face the day, or do you bury your head in the blankets? Once you're at your job or on campus, do you always do your best, or do you work just hard enough to get by? Are you generally happy? *Do you sometimes worry or feel sad? In this chapter, we explore the physical, mental, and social factors that motivate behavior in areas ranging from eating to sexuality to achievement. We also examine what emotions are and how they are expressed.*

One January day, despite temperatures of 30 degrees below zero, Brian Carr caught 155 fish, beating out thirty-six other competitors to win the annual ice-fishing contest at upstate New York's Lake Como Fish and Game Club. He also netted the grand prize of $8 (Shepherd, 1994). Why would thirty-seven people endure such harsh conditions in pursuit of such a small reward?

This is a question about **motivation,** the factors that influence the initiation, direction, intensity, and persistence of behavior (Reeve, 1996). Like the study of *how* people and other animals behave and think, the puzzle of *why* they do so has intrigued psychologists for many decades. Why do we help others or ignore them, eat what we want or stick to a diet, visit art museums or hang out in sleazy bars, attend college or drop out of high school? Why, for that matter, do any of us do whatever it is that we do? Psychologists who study motivation have noticed that behavior is based partly on the desire to feel certain emotions, such as the joy that comes with winning a contest or climbing a mountain or becoming a parent. They've also found that motivation affects emotion, as when hunger makes you irritable. In short, motivation and emotion are closely intertwined.

Let's consider what psychologists have learned so far about motivation and emotion.

Concepts and Theories of Motivation

Suppose that a man works two jobs, refuses party invitations, wears old clothes, drives a beat-up car, eats food others leave behind at lunch, never gives to charity, and keeps his house at 60 degrees in the dead of winter. To explain why he does what he does, you could propose a separate reason for each of his behaviors, or you could suggest a **motive,** a reason or purpose that provides a single explanation for this man's diverse and apparently unrelated behaviors. That unifying motive might be his desire to save as much money as possible.

This example illustrates the fact that motivation cannot be observed directly. We have to infer, or presume, that motivation is present from what we *can* observe. So psychologists think of motivation, whether it be hunger or thirst or love or greed, as an *intervening variable*—something that is used to explain the relationships between environmental stimuli and behavioral responses. The three different responses shown in Figure 11.1, for example, can be understood as guided by a single unifying motive: thirst. In order to be considered a motive, an intervening variable must have the power to change behavior in some way. For example, suppose that we arrange for some party guests to eat only salted peanuts and other guests to eat only unsalted peanuts. The people who ate salted peanuts would probably drink more than those who ate the unsalted nuts. In this situation, we can use the motive known as thirst to explain the observed differences in drinking.

motivation The influences that account for the initiation, direction, intensity, and persistence of behavior.

motive A reason or purpose for behavior.

413

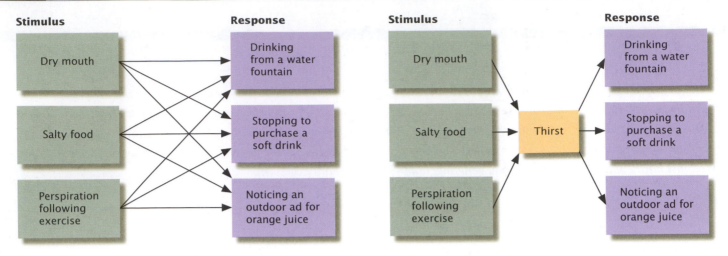

Stimulus

Dry mouth

Salty food

Perspiration following exercise

Response

Drinking from a water fountain

Stopping to purchase a soft drink

Noticing an outdoor ad for orange juice

Stimulus

Dry mouth

Salty food

Perspiration following exercise

Thirst

Response

Drinking from a water fountain

Stopping to purchase a soft drink

Noticing an outdoor ad for orange juice

FIGURE 11.1

Motives as Intervening Variables

Motives can explain the links between stimuli and responses that in some cases might seem unrelated. In this example, inferring the motive of *thirst* provides an organizing explanation for why each stimulus triggers the responses shown.

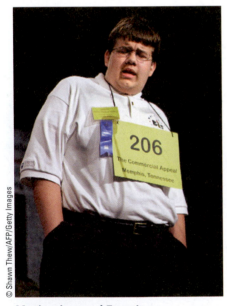

Motivation and Emotion

The link between motivation and emotion is obvious in many everyday situations. For example, being motivated to win the U.S. National Spelling Bee creates strong emotions in this contestant as he struggles with a tough word. And the link works both ways. Often emotions create motivation, as when anger leads a parent to become aggressive toward a child or when love leads the parent to provide for that child.

Figure 11.1 shows that motives can help explain why different stimuli can lead to the same response and why the same stimulus can elicit different responses. Motivation also helps explain why behavior varies over time. For example, many people cannot manage to lose weight, quit smoking, or exercise until they have a heart attack or symptoms of other serious health problems. At that point, these people may suddenly start to eat a healthier diet, work out regularly, and give up tobacco (Keenan, 2009; West & Sohal, 2006). In other words, because of changes in motivation, particular stimuli—such as ice cream, cigarettes, and health clubs—trigger different responses at different times.

Sources of Motivation

The number of possible motives for human behavior seems endless, but psychologists have found it useful to organize them into four somewhat overlapping categories. First, human behavior is motivated by basic *physiological factors,* such as the need for food and water. *Emotional factors* are a second source of motivation. Panic, fear, anger, love, and hatred can influence behavior ranging from selfless giving to brutal murder. Third, *cognitive factors* can motivate behavior. People behave in certain ways—becoming arrogant or timid, for example—partly because of these cognitive factors, which include their perceptions of the world, their beliefs about what they can or cannot do, and their expectations about how others will respond to them. Cognitive factors help explain why it is that some of the least musical contestants who try out for *American Idol* and other talent shows seem utterly confident in their ability to sing. Fourth, motivation may stem from *social factors,* including the influence of parents, teachers, siblings, friends, television, and other sociocultural forces. Have you ever bought a jacket or tried a particular hairstyle not because you liked it but because it was in fashion? This is just one example of how social factors can affect almost all human behavior.

Various combinations of all four of these motivational sources appear in four prominent theories of human motivation. None of these theories can fully explain all aspects of why we behave as we do, but each of them—the instinct doctrine, drive reduction theory, arousal theory, and incentive theory—helps tell part of the story.

The Instinct Doctrine and Its Descendants

In the early 1900s, many psychologists explained motivation in terms of the **instinct doctrine,** which highlights the instinctive nature of behavior. **Instinctive behaviors** are automatic, involuntary behavior patterns that are consistently triggered, or "released," by particular stimuli (Tinbergen, 1989). Such behaviors, originally called *fixed-action patterns,* are unlearned, species-typical responses to specific "releaser" stimuli. For example, releaser stimuli such as a male bird's colored plumage and behavior can cause a female bird of the same species to join him in a complex mating dance.

In 1908, William McDougall listed eighteen human instinctive behaviors, including self-assertion, reproduction, pugnacity (aggressiveness), and gregariousness (sociability). Within a few years, McDougall and others had named more than ten thousand more, prompting one critic to suggest that his colleagues had "an instinct to produce instincts" (Bernard, 1924). The problem was that instincts had become labels that do little more than describe behavior. Saying that someone gambles because of a gambling instinct or works hard because of a work instinct explains nothing about how these behaviors develop or why they appear in some people and not others. Applying the instinct doctrine to human motivation also seemed problematic because people display few, if any, instinctive fixed-action patterns.

Today, psychologists continue to investigate the role of inborn tendencies in human motivation. Their work has been inspired partly by findings that a number of human behaviors are present at birth. Among these are sucking and other reflexes, certain facial expressions such as grimacing at bitter tastes (Steiner et al., 2001), and as described in the chapter on learning, a tendency toward learning to fear snakes and other potential dangers (Öhman & Mineka, 2003). But psychologists' thinking about instinctive behaviors is more sophisticated now than it was a century ago. For one thing, they recognize that inborn tendencies are more flexible than early versions of the instinct doctrine suggested. It turns out that so-called fixed-action patterns—even the simple ones shown by baby chicks as they peck at seeds—actually vary quite a bit among individuals and can be modified by experience (Deich, Tankoos, & Balsam, 1995). Accordingly, these tendencies are now often referred to as *modal action patterns.* Psychologists recognize, too, that even though certain behaviors reflect inborn motivational tendencies, those behaviors may or may not actually appear, depending on each individual's experience. So although we might be biologically *prepared* to learn to fear snakes, that fear won't develop if we never see a snake. In other words, inherited tendencies can influence motivation, but that doesn't mean that all motivated behavior is genetically determined. It can still be shaped, amplified, or even suppressed by experience and other factors operating in particular individuals.

instinct doctrine A view that explains human behavior as motivated by automatic, involuntary, and unlearned responses.

instinctive behaviors Innate, automatic dispositions toward responding in a particular way when confronted with a specific stimulus.

Fixed-Action Patterns

The male three-spined stickleback fish attacks aggressively when it sees the red underbelly of another male. This automatic response is called a *fixed-action pattern* because it can be triggered by almost any red stimulus. These fish have been known to fly into an aggressive frenzy in response to a wooden fish model sporting a red spot or even to a red truck driving past a window near their tank.

Psychologists who take an evolutionary approach to behavior suggest that a wide range of behavioral tendencies have evolved partly because over the centuries, those tendencies were adaptive for promoting individual survival in particular circumstances. The individuals who possessed these behavioral tendencies and expressed them at the right times and places were the ones who were more likely than others to survive to produce offspring. We are the descendants of those ancestral human survivors, so to the extent that our ancestors' behavioral tendencies were transmitted genetically, we should have inherited similar tendencies. Evolutionary psychologists also argue that many aspects of human social behavior, such as helping and aggression, are motivated by inborn factors—especially by the desire to maximize our genetic contribution to the next generation (Buss, 2004a). We may not be aware of this specific desire, they say, but we nevertheless behave in ways that promote it (Geary, 2000). So you are more likely to hear someone say, "I can't wait to have children," than to say, "I want to pass on my genes."

The Instinct Doctrine and Mate Selection   The evolutionary approach suggests, for example, that people's choice of a marriage partner or sexual mate is influenced by the consequences of the choices made by their ancestors over countless generations. For instance, research across generations in many different cultures shows that both men and women express a strong preference for a partner who is dependable, emotionally stable, and intelligent—all characteristics associated with creating a good environment for having and raising children (Buss et al., 1990). Evolutionary psychologists also point to sex differences in mating preferences and strategies. They argue that because women can produce relatively few children in their lifetimes, they are more psychologically invested than men in the survival and development of those children. This greater investment is said to motivate women to be choosier than men when selecting mates. So although women tend to prefer athletic men with symmetrical ("handsome") faces and deep voices, this preference is strongest at the point in the menstrual cycle when fertility peaks and mating with these "genetically fit" men would most likely result in pregnancy (Barber, 1995; Gangestad et al., 2007; Garver-Apgar, Gangestad, & Thornhill, 2008; Puts, 2005). More generally, say evolutionary psychologists, women are drawn to men whose intelligence, maturity, ambition, and earning power demonstrate the ability to amass resources and mark them as "good providers" who will help raise children and ensure their survival.

It takes some time to assess these resource-related characteristics (he drives an expensive car, but can he afford it?), which is why, according to the evolutionary view, women are more likely than men to prefer a period of courtship prior to mating. Men tend to be less selective and to want to begin a sexual relationship sooner than women (Buss, 2004b; Buss & Schmitt, 1993) because compared to their female partners, they have little to lose from doing so. On the contrary, their eagerness to engage in sex early in a relationship is seen as reflecting their evolutionary ancestors' tendency toward opportunistic sex as a means of maximizing their genetic contribution to the next generation. Evolutionary psychologists suggest that the desire to produce as many children as possible motivates males' attraction to women whose fertility and good health are signaled by factors generally associated with physical beauty, such as clear skin and a low waist-to-hip ratio (Buss, 2009).

These ideas have received some support. For instance, preference ratings from several thousand people in more than three dozen cultures reveal that males generally prefer physical attractiveness and good health in prospective mates and that females generally prefer mates with higher levels of social status and financial resources (Shackelford, Schmitt, & Buss, 2005). This sex difference is reflected, too, in the fact that men are far more likely than women to specify body type preferences in Internet personals ads (Glasser et al., 2009).

Critics argue that such preferences stem from cultural traditions, not genetic predispositions. Among the Zulu of South Africa, where women are expected to build houses, carry water, and perform other physically demanding tasks, men tend to value maturity and ambition in a mate more than women do (Buss, 1989). The fact that

© Rune Hellestad/UPI/Landov

Evolution at Work?

The marriage of Rod Stewart and Penny Lancaster, a former model who is twenty-six years his junior, illustrates the worldwide tendency for older men to prefer younger women and for younger women to prefer older men. This tendency has been interpreted as evidence supporting an evolutionary explanation of mate selection, but skeptics see social and economic forces at work in establishing these preference patterns.

women have been systematically denied economic and political power in many cultures may account for their tendency to rely on the security and economic power provided by men (Eagly, Wood, & Johannesen-Schmidt, 2004; Silverstein, 1996). Indeed, an analysis of data from thirty-seven cultures showed that women valued potential mates' access to resources far more in cultures that sharply limited women's reproductive freedom and educational opportunities (Kasser & Sharma, 1999). Evolutionary theorists acknowledge the role of cultural forces and traditions in shaping behavior, but they ask whether evolutionary factors might contribute to the appearance of these forces and traditions, including the relative ease with which certain gender roles and mate preferences emerge (Geher, Camargo, & O'Rourke, 2008; Hrdy, 1997, 2003; Swami & Furnham, 2008).

By emphasizing the evolutionary roots of human behavior, contemporary versions of the instinct doctrine focus on the ultimate, long-term reasons behind what we do and the circumstances in which evolved predispositions are or are not expressed. The theories of motivation discussed next highlight influences that serve as more immediate causes of behavior (Alcock, 2009).

Drive Reduction Theory

homeostasis The tendency for organisms to keep their physiological systems at a stable, steady level by constantly adjusting themselves in response to change.

drive reduction theory A theory of motivation stating that motivation arises from imbalances in homeostasis.

needs Biological requirements for well-being that are created by an imbalance in homeostasis.

drive A psychological state of arousal created by an imbalance in homeostasis that prompts an organism to take action to restore the balance and reduce the drive.

Like the instinct doctrine, drive reduction theory emphasizes internal factors, but it is based on the concept of homeostasis. **Homeostasis** (pronounced "hoh-mee-oh-STAY-siss") is the tendency to keep physiological systems at a steady level, or *equilibrium*, by constantly making adjustments in response to change—much as a thermostat functions to maintain a constant temperature in a house. We describe a version of this concept in the chapter on biological aspects of psychology, in relation to feedback loops that keep hormones at desirable levels.

According to **drive reduction theory,** any imbalances in homeostasis create **needs,** which are biological requirements for well-being. The brain responds to needs by creating a psychological state called a **drive**—a feeling of arousal that prompts an organism to take action, restore the balance, and as a result, reduce the drive (Hull, 1943). For example, if you have had no water for some time, the chemical balance of your body fluids is disturbed, creating a biological need for water. One consequence of this need is a drive—thirst—that motivates you to find and drink water. After you drink, the need for water is met, so the drive to drink is reduced. In other words, drives push people to satisfy needs, thereby reducing the drives and the arousal they create (see Figure 11.2).

FIGURE 11.2
Drive Reduction Theory and Homeostasis

The mechanisms of homeostasis, such as the regulation of body temperature or food and water intake, are often compared to thermostats. If the temperature in a house drops below the thermostat setting, the furnace comes on and brings the temperature up to that preset level, achieving homeostasis. When the temperature reaches the preset point, the furnace shuts off.

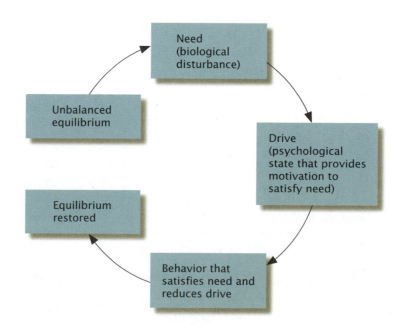

© Andrew Shennan/Getty Images

Arousal and Personality

According to arousal theory, boldness, shyness, and other personality traits and behavioral tendencies reflect individual differences in the level of arousal that people find ideal for them. As described in the personality chapter, differences in arousal arise largely from inherited differences in the nervous system (Eysenck, 1990a).

primary drives Drives that arise from basic biological needs.

secondary drives Drives that arise through learning and can be as motivating as primary drives.

physiological arousal A general level of activation that is reflected in several physiological systems.

arousal theory A theory of motivation stating that people are motivated to behave in ways that maintain what is for them an optimal level of arousal.

incentive theory A theory of motivation stating that behavior is directed toward attaining desirable stimuli and avoiding unwanted stimuli.

Early drive reduction theorists made a distinction between two types of drives. The first kind, called **primary drives,** stem from inborn physiological needs, such as for food or water, that people do not have to learn (Hull, 1951). The second kind, known as **secondary drives,** are learned through experience. They motivate us to act as if we have unmet basic needs. For example, as people learn to associate money with the ability to buy things to satisfy primary drives for food, shelter, and so on, having money becomes a secondary drive. Having too little money then motivates many behaviors—from hard work to stealing—to obtain more funds.

Arousal Theory

Drive reduction theory can account for a wide range of motivated behaviors. But humans and other animals are also motivated to do things that don't appear to reduce drives. Consider curiosity. People, rats, monkeys, dogs, and many other creatures explore and manipulate their surroundings, even though these activities do not lead to drive reduction (Bergman & Kitchen, 2009; Hughes, 2007; Kaulfuss & Mills, 2008). They will also exert considerable effort simply to enter a new environment, especially if it is complex and full of new or unusual objects (Loewenstein, 1994). We go to the new mall, watch builders work, surf the Internet, and travel the world just to see what there is to see. Some of us also go out of our way to ride roller coasters, skydive, drive race-cars, and do countless other things that, like curiosity-motivated behaviors, do not reduce any known drive. In fact, these behaviors cause an *increase* in **physiological arousal,** a general level of activation that is reflected in the state of several physiological systems, including the brain, heart, lungs, and muscles (Plutchik & Conte, 1997).

The realization that we sometimes act in ways that increase arousal and sometimes act in ways that decrease it has led some psychologists to argue that people are motivated to *regulate arousal* so that it stays at roughly the same level most of the time. Specifically, according to **arousal theory,** we are motivated to behave in ways that maintain or restore an ideal, or *optimal,* level of arousal (Hebb, 1955). In other words, we try to increase arousal when it is too low and decrease it when it is too high. So after a day of dull chores, you may want to see an exciting movie, but if your day was spent playing baseball, debating a political issue, and helping a friend move, an evening of quiet relaxation may seem ideal.

Where is the optimal level of arousal? In general, people perform best, and may feel best, when arousal is moderate (Teigen, 1994; see Figure 11.3). Too much arousal can hurt performance, as when test anxiety interferes with some students' ability to recall what they have studied or when some athletes "choke" so badly that they miss an easy catch or a simple shot (Smith et al., 2000; Wright et al., 1995). Underarousal, too, can cause problems, as you probably know if you have ever tried to work, drive, or study when you are sleepy. So the optimal level of arousal lies somewhere between these extremes, but exactly where that level is can vary from person to person. People whose optimal arousal is relatively high try to keep it there, so they are more likely than other people to smoke, drink alcohol, engage in frequent sexual activity, listen to loud music, eat spicy foods, and do things that are novel and risky (Farley, 1986; Zuckerman, 1979, 1996). The resulting increase in arousal activates brain regions associated with reward (Joseph et al., 2009). Those with relatively low optimal arousal try to keep it low, so they tend to take fewer risks and behave in ways that are not overly stimulating. Most of these differences in optimal arousal have a strong biological basis and, as discussed in the personality chapter, may help shape other characteristics, such as whether we tend to be introverted or extraverted (Eysenck, 1990a).

Incentive Theory

Instinct, drive reduction, and arousal theories of motivation all focus on internal processes that prompt people to behave in certain ways. By contrast, **incentive theory** emphasizes the role of external stimuli that can motivate behavior by pulling us toward

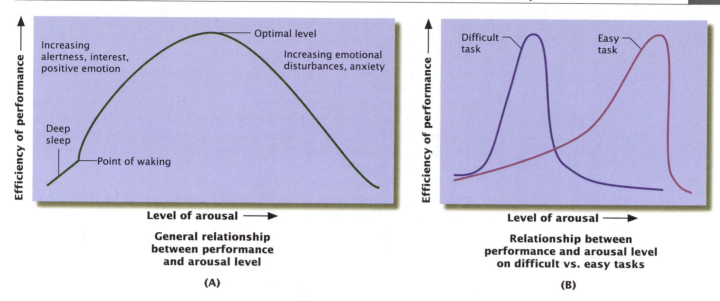

FIGURE 11.3

The Arousal-Performance Relationship

Notice in part A that performance is poorest when arousal is very low or very high and best when arousal is at a moderate level. When you are either sleepy or overly excited, for example, it may be difficult to think clearly or to be physically coordinated. In general, optimal performance comes at a lower level of arousal on difficult or complex tasks and at a higher level of arousal on easy tasks, as shown in part B. Even a relatively small amount of overarousal can cause students to perform far below their potential on difficult tests (Sarason, 1984). Because animal research early in this century by Robert Yerkes and his colleagues provided supportive evidence, this arousal-performance relationship is sometimes referred to as the *Yerkes-Dodson law*, even though Yerkes never actually discussed performance as a function of arousal (Teigen, 1994).

them or pushing us away from them. More specifically, people are said to behave in order to get positive incentives and avoid negative incentives. According to incentive theory, then, differences in behavior from one person to another, or in the same person from one situation to another, can be traced to the incentives available and the value a person places on them at the time. If you expect a behavior (such as buying a lottery ticket) to lead to a valued outcome (winning lots of money), you will want to engage in that behavior. The value of an incentive is influenced by physiological as well as cognitive and social factors—or as drive reduction theorists might put it, by both primary and secondary drives. For example, food is a more motivating incentive when you are hungry than when you are full (Balleine & Dickinson, 1994). As for cognitive and social influences, notice that the value of some things we eat and drink—such as communion wafers or protein shakes—isn't determined by hunger but by what we have learned in our culture about spirituality, health, or attractiveness.

It may seem obvious that people are motivated to approach things they like and to avoid things they don't like, but the story of incentive theory is not quite that simple. Psychologists have found that people sometimes work hard for some incentives only to find that they don't enjoy having them nearly as much as they thought they would (Gilbert, 2006; Wilson & Gilbert, 2005). Further, motivation theorists have highlighted the distinction between wanting and liking. *Wanting* is the process of being attracted to incentives, whereas *liking* is the immediate evaluation of how pleasurable a stimulus is (Berridge & Kringelbach, 2008). Studies with laboratory animals have shown that these two systems involve activity in different parts of the brain, and they involve different neurotransmitters (Peciña, 2008). For example, the wanting system appears to be activated by dopamine, a neurotransmitter associated with experiencing the pleasure of sex, drugs, and gambling. Some evidence for this idea comes from a study that found an unusual increase in compulsive gambling among people who had begun taking dopamine-enhancing drugs for Parkinson's disease (Dodd et al., 2005). It appears, too, that the wanting system can compel behavior to a far greater extent than the liking system does. For instance, the drug-seeking efforts made by addicted people are often far more intense than the actual pleasure of drug use (Robinson & Berridge, 2003). Further, the operation of the wanting system, in particular, varies according to whether an individual has been deprived (Nader, Bechara, & Van der Kooy, 1997). So although you might like pizza, your motivation to eat some would be affected by different brain regions, depending on whether the pizza is served as an appetizer (when you are hungry) or at the end of a big meal (when you are full; Jiang et al., 2008).

The theories of motivation we have outlined (see "In Review: Theories of Motivation") complement one another. Each emphasizes different sources of motivation, and each has helped guide research into motivated behaviors, including eating, sex, and achievement-related activities, which are the topics of the next three sections.

IN REVIEW Theories of Motivation	
Theory	**Main Points**
Instinct doctrine	Innate biology produces instinctive behavior.
Drive reduction theory	Behavior is guided by biological needs and learned ways of reducing drives arising from those needs.
Arousal theory	People seek to maintain an optimal level of physiological arousal, which differs from person to person. Maximum performance occurs at optimal arousal levels.
Incentive theory	Behavior is guided by the lure of positive incentives and the avoidance of negative incentives. Cognitive factors influence expectations of the value of various rewards and the likelihood of attaining them.

1. The fact that some people like roller coasters and other scary amusement park rides has been cited as evidence for the _____ theory of motivation.
2. Evolutionary theories of motivation are modern outgrowths of theories based on _____.
3. The value of incentives can be affected by _____, _____, and _____ factors.

Hunger and Eating

At first glance, hunger and eating seem to be a simple example of drive reduction. You get hungry when you haven't eaten for a while. Much as a car needs gas, you need fuel from food. But what bodily mechanism acts as a "gas gauge" to signal your need for fuel? What determines which foods you eat, and how do you know when to stop? The answers to these questions involve interactions between the brain and the rest of the body, but they also involve learning, social, and environmental factors (Hill & Peters, 1998; Pinel, Lehman, & Assand, 2002).

Biological Signals for Hunger and Satiation

hunger The general state of wanting to eat.

satiation The satisfaction of a need such as hunger.

satiety The condition of no longer wanting to eat.

A variety of mechanisms underlie **hunger,** the general state of wanting to eat, and **satiation** (pronounced "say-shee-AY-shun"), the satisfaction of a need such as hunger. Satiation leads to **satiety** (pronounced "suh-TY-uh-tee"), the state in which we no longer want to eat. In order to maintain body weight, we must have ways to regulate food intake over the short term (a question of how often we eat and when we stop eating a given meal) and to regulate the body's stored energy reserves (fat) over the long term.

Signals from the Gut   The stomach would seem to be a logical source of signals for hunger and satiety. After all, people say they feel "hunger pangs" from an "empty" stomach, and they complain of a "full stomach" after overeating. It is true that the stomach does contract during hunger pangs and that increased pressure in the stomach can reduce appetite (Cannon & Washburn, 1912; Houpt, 1994). But people who have lost their stomachs due to illness still get hungry when they don't eat, and they still eat normal amounts of food (Janowitz, 1967). So stomach cues affect eating, but they do not play a major role in the normal control of eating. These cues appear to operate mainly when you are very hungry or very full. The small intestine, too, is involved in the regulation of eating (Maljaars et al., 2008). It is lined with cells that detect the presence of nutrients and send neural signals to the brain about the need to eat (Capasso & Izzo, 2008).

LINKAGES How does your brain know when you are hungry? (a link to Biological Aspects of Psychology, p. 103)

Signals from the Blood   The most important signals about the body's fuel level and nutrient needs are sent to the brain from the blood. The brain's ability to "read" bloodborne signals about the body's nutritional needs was shown years ago when researchers deprived rats of food and then injected them with blood from rats that had just eaten. When offered food, the injected rats ate little or nothing (Davis et al., 1969); something in the injected blood of the well-fed animals apparently signaled the hungry rats' brains that there was no need to eat. What sent that satiety signal? More recent research has shown that the brain constantly monitors both the level of food *nutrients* absorbed into the bloodstream from the stomach and the level of *hormones* released into the blood in response to those nutrients and from stored fat (Korner & Leibel, 2003).

Some bloodborne signals affect short-term intake—telling us when to start and stop eating a meal—whereas others reflect and regulate the body's long-term supply of fat. The short-term signals are called *satiety factors.* One such signal comes from *cholecystokinin* (pronounced "koh-luh-siss-tuh-KY-nin" and abbreviated CCK), a neuropeptide that regulates meal size (Woods et al., 1998). During a meal, CCK affects the levels of hormones in the gut and neurotransmitters in the brain (Crawley & Corwin, 1994). The activity of CCK in the brain signals animals to stop eating (Parrott, 1994), and even a well-fed animal will start to eat if receptors in the brain for CCK are blocked (Brenner & Ritter, 1995). Moderate doses of CCK given to humans cause them to eat less of a given meal, whereas high doses can cause nausea—thus possibly explaining why we sometimes feel sick after overeating. However, research with animals suggests that increasing production of CCK doesn't necessarily result in weight loss, because the animals made up for smaller meals by eating more often. This phenomenon reflects the fact that the brain monitors the long-term storage of fat as well as the short-term status of nutrients.

The nutrients that the brain monitors include *glucose,* the main form of sugar used by body cells. Researchers have long been aware that when the level of blood glucose drops, eating increases sharply (e.g., Chaput & Tremblay, 2009). More recent work has shown that glucose acts indirectly by affecting certain chemical messengers. For example, when glucose levels rise, the pancreas releases *insulin,* a hormone that most body cells need in order to use the glucose they receive. Insulin may amplify the brain's satiety response to CCK. In one study, animals receiving CCK after insulin infusions into the brain ate less food and gained less weight than animals getting either CCK or insulin alone (Riedy et al., 1995). Insulin itself may also provide a satiety signal by acting directly on brain cells (Brüning et al., 2000; Schwartz et al., 2000).

The long-term regulation of fat stores involves a hormone called *leptin* (from the Greek word *leptos,* meaning "thin"). The process works like this: Cells that store fat have genes that produce leptin in response to increases in fat supplies. The leptin is released into the bloodstream, and when it reaches special receptors for it in the hypothalamus, it provides information to the brain about the increasing fat supplies (Tamashiro & Bello, 2008). When leptin levels are high, hunger decreases, which helps reduce food intake. When leptin levels are low, hunger increases, as illustrated in animals that are obese because of defects in leptin-producing genes (Bouret, Draper, & Simerly, 2004; Zhang et al., 1994). Researchers have found that injections of leptin cause these animals to lose weight and body fat rapidly, with no effect on muscle or other body tissue (Forbes et al., 2001). Leptin injections, or leptin intake during the suckling period of infancy, can also protect normal animals from *obesity,* or severe weight gain (Fox & Olster, 2000; Priego et al., 2010). Some cases of obesity in humans, too, have been linked to problems in leptin regulation (Considine et al., 1996; Müller et al., 2009). At first, these results raised hope that leptin might be a "magic bullet" for treating obesity in humans, but this is not the case. It can help those rare individuals who are obese because their cells make no leptin (Baicy et al., 2007; Kelesidis et al., 2010), but leptin injections are far less effective for people whose obesity results from excessive eating or a high-fat diet (Gura, 1999; Heymsfield et al., 1999). In these far more common cases of obesity, the brain appears to become less sensitive to leptin's signals (Lin et al., 2000; Lustig et al., 2004).

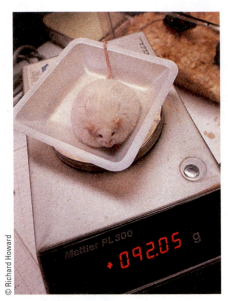

© Richard Howard

One Fat Mouse

After surgical destruction of its ventromedial nucleus, this mouse ate enough to triple its body weight. Such animals become picky eaters, choosing only foods that taste good and ignoring all others.

Hunger and the Brain

Many parts of the brain contribute to the control of hunger and eating, but research has focused on several regions of the hypothalamus that may play primary roles in detecting and reacting to the blood's signals about the need to eat. Some regions of the hypothalamus detect leptin and insulin; these regions generate signals that either increase hunger and reduce energy expenditure or else reduce hunger and increase energy expenditure. At least twenty neurotransmitters and *neuromodulators*—substances that modify the action of neurotransmitters—convey these signals to networks in other parts of the hypothalamus and in the rest of the brain (Cota et al., 2006; Woods et al., 1998, 2000).

Activity in a part of the network that passes through the *ventromedial nucleus* of the hypothalamus tells an animal that there is no need to eat. So if a rat's ventromedial nucleus is electrically or chemically stimulated, the animal will stop eating (Kent et al., 1994). However, if the ventromedial nucleus is destroyed, the animal will eat continuously, increasing its weight up to threefold.

The *lateral hypothalamus* contains networks that stimulate eating. When the lateral hypothalamus is electrically or chemically stimulated, rats eat huge quantities, even if they just had a large meal (Stanley et al., 1993). When the lateral hypothalamus is destroyed, however, rats stop eating almost entirely.

Decades ago, these findings suggested that activity in the ventromedial and lateral areas of the hypothalamus interact to maintain some homeostatic level, or *set point*, based on food intake, body weight, or other eating-related signals (Powley & Keesey, 1970). According to this application of drive reduction theory, normal animals eat until their set point is reached, then stop eating until desirable intake falls below the set point and hunger appears again (Cabanac & Morrissette, 1992).

This theory turned out to be too simplistic. More recent research shows that the brain's control of eating involves more than just the interaction of a pair of "stop-eating" and "start-eating" areas in the brain (Winn, 1995). For example, the *paraventricular nucleus* in the hypothalamus also plays an important role. As with the ventromedial nucleus, stimulating the paraventricular nucleus results in reduced food intake. Damaging it causes animals to become obese (Leibowitz, 1992). In addition, hunger—and the eating of particular types of food—is related to the effects of various neurotransmitters on certain neurons in the brain. One of these neurotransmitters, called *neuropeptide Y,* stimulates increased eating of carbohydrates (Kishi & Elmquist, 2005; Kuo et al., 2007). Another one, *serotonin,* suppresses carbohydrate intake. *Galanin* motivates the eating of high-fat food (Krykouli et al., 1990), whereas *enteristatin* reduces it (Lin et al., 1998). *Endocannabinoids* stimulate eating in general, especially the eating of tasty foods (DiPatrizio & Simansky, 2008; Mahler, Smith, & Berridge, 2007). They affect the same hypothalamic receptors as the active ingredient in marijuana, which may account for the "munchies," a sudden hunger that marijuana use often creates (Cota et al., 2003; Di Marzo et al., 2001). *Peptide YY3-36* causes a feeling of fullness and reduces food intake (Batterham et al., 2002, 2003).

In other words, several brain regions and many chemicals help regulate hunger and food selection. These internal regulatory processes are not set in stone, however. They are themselves shaped, and sometimes overridden, by social, cultural, and other factors.

Flavor, Sociocultural Experience, and Food Selection

One factor that can override a set point is the *flavor* of food—the combination of its taste and smell. In one experiment, some animals were offered just a single type of food, whereas others were offered foods of several different flavors. The group getting the varied menu ate nearly four times more than the one-food group. As each new food appeared, the animals began to eat voraciously, regardless of how much they had already eaten (Peck, 1978). Humans behave in similar ways. All things being equal, people eat more food during a multicourse meal than when only one food is served (Remick, Polivy, & Pliner, 2009). Apparently, the flavor of any particular food becomes less enjoyable as more of it is eaten (Swithers & Hall, 1994). In one study, for example, people rated how much they liked four kinds of food. Then they ate one of the foods and rated all four again. The food they had just eaten now got a lower rating, whereas liking increased for all the rest (Johnson & Vickers, 1993).

Another factor that can override bloodborne signals about satiety is *appetite,* the motivation to seek food's pleasures (Zheng et al., 2009). For example, the appearance and aroma of certain foods create conditioned physiological responses—such as secretion of saliva, gastric juices, and insulin—in anticipation of eating those foods. (The process is based on the principles of classical conditioning described in the chapter on learning.) These responses then increase appetite. So merely seeing a pizza on television may prompt you to order one—even if you hadn't been feeling hungry—and if you see a delicious-looking cookie, you do not have to be hungry to start eating it. In fact, as described in the chapter on introducing psychology, brain-damaged patients who can't remember anything for more than a minute will eat a full meal ten to thirty minutes after finishing one just like it. They may even start a third meal ten to thirty minutes later, simply because the food looks good (Rozin et al., 1998). In other words, people eat not only to satisfy nutritional needs but also to experience enjoyment (Lundy, 2008; Stroebe, Papies, & Aarts, 2008).

Eating can also be influenced by *specific hungers,* or desires for particular foods at particular times. These hungers appear to reflect the biological need for the nutrients contained in certain foods. In one study, for example, rats were given three bowls of tasty, protein-free food and one bowl of food that tasted bad but was rich in protein. The rats learned to eat enough of the bad-tasting food to get a proper supply of dietary protein (Galef & Wright, 1995).

These results are remarkable in part because protein and many other nutrients such as vitamins and minerals have no taste or odor. So how can these nutrients guide food choices? As with appetite, learning is probably involved. The taste and odor of food appears to become associated with the food's nutritional value. Evidence for this kind of learning comes from experiments in which rats received infusions of liquid directly into their stomachs. Some of these infusions consisted of plain water; others included nutritious oil or carbohydrate. Each kind of infusion was paired with a different flavor in the animals' normal supply of drinking water. Later, water of both flavors was made available. When the animals got hungry, they drank more of the water whose flavor had been associated with the nutritious infusions (Yiin, Ackroff, & Sclafani, 2004). Related research shows that children come to prefer flavors that have been associated with high-fat ingredients (Johnson, McPhee, & Birch, 1991).

The role of learning is also seen when we start to eat in response to sights, sounds, and places that have been associated with eating in the past (Epstein et al., 2009). If you usually eat when reading or watching television, for example, you may find yourself wanting a snack as soon as you sit down with a book or your favorite show. The same phenomenon has been demonstrated in a laboratory study in which for several days in a row, hungry rats heard a buzzer just before they were fed. The buzzer eventually became so strongly associated with eating that the rats would start eating when it sounded, even if they had just eaten their fill (Weingarten, 1983). Similarly, even after finishing a big meal, children have been found to resume eating if they enter a room where they have previously had snacks (Birch et al., 1989). Such food-related cues tend to have an especially strong effect on people who are concerned about their weight (Coelho et al., 2009). The food industry has applied research on learning to increase demand for its products. For example, the flavorings that fast-food chains routinely add to french fries and hamburger buns have little or no nutritional value, but after becoming associated with those items, these flavorings can trigger strong and distracting cravings for them (Kemps, Tiggemann, & Grigg, 2008; Schlosser, 2001).

People also learn social rules and cultural traditions that influence eating. Munching popcorn at movies and hot dogs at baseball games are examples from North American culture of how certain social situations can stimulate appetite for particular food items. Similarly, how much you eat may depend on what others do. Courtesy or custom may lead you to eat foods you would otherwise avoid. The mere presence of other people, even strangers, tends to increase our food consumption (Redd & de Castro, 1992). Most people consume 60 to 75 percent more food when they are with others than when eating alone (Clendenen, Herman, & Polivy, 1995); the same effect has been observed in other species, from monkeys to chickens (Galloway et al., 2005; Keeling & Hurink, 1996). And if others stop eating, we may do the same even if we are still hungry—especially if we want to impress them with our self-control (Herman, Roth, & Polivy, 2003).

Eating and food selection are central to the way people function within their cultures. Celebrations, holidays, vacations, and even daily family interactions often revolve around food and what has been called a *food culture* (Rozin, 2007). As any world traveler knows, there are wide cultural variations in foods and food selection. For example, chewing coca leaves is popular in the Bolivian highlands but illegal in the United States (Burchard, 1992). In China, people in urban areas eat a high-cholesterol diet rich in animal meat, whereas those in rural areas eat so little meat as to be cholesterol-deficient (Tian et al., 1995). Insects known as palm weevils are a popular food for people in Papua New Guinea (Paoletti, 1995) but are regarded as disgusting by many westerners (Springer & Belk, 1994). And the beef those same westerners enjoy is morally repugnant to devout Hindus in India. Even within the same culture, different groups may have sharply contrasting food traditions. Squirrel brains won't be found on most dinner tables in the United States, but some people in the rural South consider them a tasty treat.

Culture also plays a role in the amount of food we eat. For example, portion sizes in restaurants, grocery stores, and even cookbook recipes tend to be smaller in France, Britain, and other European countries than in the United States (Rozin et al., 2003). Europeans also tend to eat more slowly, which allows satiety signals to reach their brains before they have overindulged. Some of these differences between "slow-food" and "fast-food" cultures might account for why residents of some countries eat less than those in other countries but feel equally satisfied (Geier, Rozin, & Doros, 2006; Slow Food Movement, 2001).

In summary, eating serves functions that go well beyond nutrition—functions that remind us of who we are and with whom we identify.

Unhealthy Eating

Problems in the processes regulating hunger and eating may cause *eating disorders* such as anorexia nervosa or bulimia nervosa or in a level of food intake that leads to obesity.

© Peter Menzel/Stock, Boston

Bon Appétit!

TRY THIS The definition of "delicacy" differs from culture to culture. At this elegant restaurant in Mexico, diners pay to feast on baby alligators, insects, and other dishes that some people from other cultures would not eat even if the restaurant paid *them*. To appreciate your own food culture, make a list of foods that are traditionally valued by your family or cultural group but that people from other groups do not eat or might even be unwilling to taste.

Obesity   The World Health Organization (WHO) defines **obesity** as a condition in which a person's body mass index, or BMI, is greater than 30. BMI is determined by taking a person's weight in pounds, multiplying it by 703, and dividing that number by the square of the person's height in inches. So someone who is 5 feet 2 inches tall and weighs 165 pounds would be classified as obese, as would someone 5 feet 10 inches tall who weighs 210 pounds. BMI calculators appear on Web sites such as www.nhlbisupport.com/bmi. People whose BMI is 25.0 to 29.9 are considered overweight. (Keep in mind, though, that a given volume of muscle weighs more than the same volume of fat, so very muscular individuals may have an elevated BMI without being overweight.)

Using the BMI criterion, about 34 percent of adults in the United States are obese, as are about 16 percent of children and adolescents (Broyles et al., 2010; Flegal et al., 2010; Ogden et al., 2007). These percentages are even higher among the poor and members of some ethnic minority groups (Kumanyika, 2008; Skelton et al., 2009). Obesity has become so common that commercial jets now have to burn excess fuel to carry heavier loads, parents of obese young children have trouble finding car safety seats to fit them, and the funeral industry has to offer larger-than-normal coffins and buy wider hearses (Dannenberg, Burton, & Jackson, 2004; Saint John, 2003; Trifiletti et al., 2006). The problems of overweight and obesity are especially severe in the United States, but they are also growing worldwide. An analysis of data from 106 countries in Asia, Europe, South America, and Africa—comprising about 88 percent of the world's population—found that 23.2 percent of adults are overweight and another 10 percent are obese. Projections based on present trends suggest that by 2030, there will be over one billion obese people living in these countries (Kelly et al., 2008).

Obesity is associated with disability and with health problems such as Type 2 diabetes, high blood pressure, certain cancers, liver and gallbladder disease, osteoarthritis, and increased risk of heart attack and stroke (Baker, Olsen, & Sørensen, 2007; Bibbins-Domingo et al., 2007; Centers for Disease Control and Prevention, 2009b; Franks et al., 2010; Owen et al., 2009; Reeves et al., 2007). In the United States alone, obesity is blamed for about three hundred thousand deaths each year and for a predicted shortening of life expectancy in the twenty-first century (Adams et al., 2006; Flegal et al., 2005; Olshansky et al., 2005; Shimazu et al., 2009). Especially in adolescence, obesity is associated with the development of anxiety and depression (Anderson et al., 2007; Baumeister & Härter, 2007; BeLue, Francis, & Colaco, 2009; Gariepy, Nitka, & Schmitz, 2010; Kasen et al., 2008; Zhao et al., 2009), although it is not yet clear whether the relationship is causal and, if it is, which condition might be causing which problem (Atlantis & Baker, 2008; Kivimäki et al., 2009; Scott et al., 2008). A recent review of numerous longitudinal studies suggests that the relationship may be bidirectional: that is, obesity can lead to depression, and depression can lead to obesity (Luppino et al., 2010).

The precise reasons for this obesity epidemic are unknown, but possible causes include big portion sizes at fast-food outlets, greater prevalence of high-fat foods, and less physical activity associated with both work and recreation (e.g., Adachi-Mejia et al., 2007; Slentz et al., 2004). These are important factors, because the body maintains a given weight through a combination of food intake and energy output (Keesey & Powley, 1986). Obese people get more energy from food than their body *metabolizes,* or "burns up"; the excess energy, measured in *calories,* is stored as fat. Metabolism declines during sleep and rises with physical activity. Because women tend to have a lower metabolic rate than men, even when equally active, they tend to gain weight more easily than men with similar diets (Ferraro et al., 1992). Most obese people have normal resting metabolic rates, but they tend to eat too much high-calorie, tasty foods and too little low-calorie, less tasty foods (Kauffman, Herman, & Polivy, 1995). Further, some obese people are less active than lean people, a pattern that often begins in childhood (Jago et al., 2005; Marshall et al., 2004; Strauss & Pollack, 2001). Spending long hours watching television or playing computer games is a major cause of the inactivity seen in overweight children (Adachi-Mejia et al., 2007; Cleland et al., 2008; Eisenmann et al., 2008).

obesity   A condition in which a person is severely overweight, as measured by a body mass index greater than 30.

In short, inadequate physical activity, combined with overeating—especially of the high-fat foods so prevalent in most Western cultures—has a lot to do with obesity (Arsenault et al., 2010). But not everyone who is inactive and eats a high-fat diet becomes obese, and some obese people are as active as lean people, so other factors must also be involved (Blundell & Cooling, 2000; Parsons, Power, & Manor, 2005). Some people have a genetic predisposition toward obesity (Bochukova et al., 2010; Bouchard et al., 2007; Frayling et al., 2007; Loos et al., 2006; Su, Korstanje, et al., 2008). For example, although most obese people have the genes to make leptin, they may not be sensitive to its weight-suppressing effects—perhaps because of genetic codes in leptin receptors in the hypothalamus. Brain-imaging studies also suggest that obese people's brains may be slower to "read" satiety signals coming from their blood, thus causing them to continue eating when leaner people would have stopped (Morton et al., 2006; Thorens, 2008). These genetic factors, along with the presence in the body of viruses associated with the common cold and other infectious diseases (Dhurandhar et al., 2000; Vasilakopoulou & LeRoux, 2007), may help explain obese people's tendency to eat more, to accumulate fat, and to feel more hunger than lean people.

Other explanations for obesity focus on factors such as learning from the examples set by parents who overeat, too little parental control over what and how much children eat, and maladaptive reactions to stress (Birch et al., 2001; Hood et al., 2000). Many people do tend to eat more when under stress, a reaction that may be especially extreme among those who are obese (Dallman et al., 2003).

For most people, and especially for people who are obese, it is a lot easier to gain weight than to lose it and keep it off. The problem arises partly because our evolutionary ancestors—like nonhuman animals in the wild today—could not always be sure that food would be available. Those who survived lean times were the ones whose genes created tendencies to build and maintain fat reserves (e.g., Hara et al., 2000; Wells, 2009). These "thrifty genes" are adaptive in famine-plagued environments, but they can be harmful and even deadly in affluent societies in which overeating is unnecessary and in which doughnut shops and fast-food restaurants are on every corner (DiLeone, 2009). Further, if people starve themselves to lose weight, their bodies may burn calories more slowly. This drop in metabolism saves energy and fat reserves and slows weight loss (Leibel, Rosenbaum, & Hirsch, 1995). And because restricted eating enhances activation of the brain's "pleasure centers" when a hungry person merely looks at energy-rich foods (Siep et al., 2009), restraint becomes even more difficult. That is why health and nutrition experts warn that obese people (and others) should not try to lose a great deal of weight quickly by dramatically cutting food intake (Carels et al., 2008).

Given the complexity of factors leading to obesity and the seriousness of its health consequences, it is not surprising that many treatment approaches have been developed. The most radical of these is *bariatric surgery* (Hamad, 2004), which restructures the stomach and intestines so that less food energy is absorbed and stored (Vetter et al., 2009). Despite its costs and risks—postoperative mortality rates are between 0.1 and 2 percent (Longitudinal Assessment of Bariatric Surgery Consortium, 2009; Morino et al., 2007)—bariatric surgery is performed on more than one hundred thousand people in the United States each year (Santry, Gillen, & Lauderdale, 2005). Millions of other people are taking medications designed either to suppress appetite or to increase the "burning" of fat (Fernstrom & Choi, 2008; Kolonin et al., 2004; Neovius & Narbro, 2008).

Though they may seem to offer relatively quick and easy options, neither medication nor surgery alone is likely to solve the problem of obesity. In fact, no single antiobesity treatment is likely to be a safe, effective solution that works for everyone. To achieve the kind of gradual weight loss that is most likely to last, obese people are advised to make lifestyle changes instead of, or in addition to, seeking medical solutions. The weight loss programs that are most effective in the long term include components designed to reduce food intake, change eating habits and attitudes toward food, and increase energy expenditure through regular exercise (Bray & Tartaglia,

A Radical Approach to Obesity

The popularity of bariatric surgery has been fueled to a certain extent by the examples of television personality Al Roker and other celebrities whose surgical procedures resulted in dramatic weight loss. The surgery is not risk-free, though, and so is recommended mainly for extreme and life-threatening cases of obesity.

2000; Stice & Shaw, 2004; Wadden et al., 2001). Aerobic exercise and weight training are particularly important because they burn calories while increasing metabolism (Binzen, Swan & Manore, 2001; Curioni & Lourenço, 2005; Wadden et al., 2005). Some people pursue these programs individually, others work in groups, and still others enroll in medical weight loss treatments carried out under the close and constant supervision of specialists known as bariatric physicians (Wadden et al., 2001, 2009).

Of course, the ultimate remedy for the obesity epidemic is prevention. To accomplish that goal, parents and other caregivers must begin to promote exercise and healthy eating habits in their children from an early age (Swinburn, 2009). We have a long way to go. A recent report from the Feeding Infants and Toddlers Study (Fox, Pac, et al., 2004) found that the top vegetable choice of U.S. toddlers is french fries, that one in five babies eats candy every day, and that 44 percent of babies consume sugary drinks. Further, their preference for high-fat fast food is so well learned that when children in one experiment were given identical foods wrapped either in plain paper or in paper bearing the logo of a popular fast-food restaurant, they rated the restaurant-branded food as tasting better (Robinson et al., 2009). Changing these habits and preferences will not be easy, but the need to do so is obvious and urgent.

Anorexia Nervosa   In stark contrast to the problem of obesity is the eating disorder called **anorexia nervosa** (pronounced "an-uh-REK-see-uh nur-VOH-suh"). It is characterized by a combination of self-starvation, self-induced vomiting, excessive exercise, and laxative use that results in a body weight that is below 85 percent of normal (Kaye et al., 2000). Anorexia affects about 0.5 to 1 percent of young people in the United States and is a significant problem in many other industrialized nations as well (Currin et al., 2005; Hoek, 2006; Hudson et al., 2007). About 95 percent of people with anorexia are young females. These individuals often feel hungry, and many are obsessed with food and its preparation, yet they refuse to eat. Anorexic self-starvation causes serious and often irreversible physical damage, including a reduction in bone density that enhances the risk of fractures (Grinspoon et al., 2000). The health dangers may be especially high in dancers, gymnasts, and other female athletes with anorexia because the combination of self-starvation and excessive exercise increases their risk for stress fractures and heart problems (Davis & Kapstein, 2006; Sherman & Thompson, 2004). It has been estimated that from 4 to 30 percent of those who suffer severe anorexia eventually die of starvation, biochemical imbalances, or suicide. Their death rate is twelve times higher than that of other young women (Crow et al., 2009; Millar et al., 2005; National Association of Anorexia Nervosa and Associated Disorders, 2002).

The causes of anorexia are not entirely clear, but they probably involve a combination of factors, including genetic predispositions, hormonal and other biochemical imbalances, social influences, and psychological characteristics (Bulik et al., 2006; Jacobi et al., 2004; Klump et al., 2009; Procopio & Marriott, 2007; Ribases et al., 2005; Terracciano et al., 2009; Treat & Viken, 2010; Vink et al., 2001). Psychological factors that may contribute to the problem include a self-punishing, perfectionistic personality and a culturally reinforced obsession with thinness and attractiveness (APA Task Force on the Sexualization of Girls, 2007; Cooley et al., 2008; Dittmar, Halliwell, & Ive, 2006; Dohnt & Tiggemann, 2006; Grabe, Ward, & Hyde, 2008; Wilksch & Wade, 2010). Individuals with anorexia appear to develop a fear of being fat, which they take to dangerous extremes; many continue to view themselves as fat or misshapen even as they are wasting away.

Drugs, hospitalization, and psychotherapy are all used to treat anorexia. In many cases, treatment brings recovery and maintenance of normal weight (National Institutes of Health, 2001; Pike et al., 2003), but more effective treatment methods and early intervention methods are still needed. Prevention programs now being tested with college women at high risk for developing anorexia are showing promising results (e.g., Barr Taylor et al., 2006b; Black Becker, et al., 2008).

© John Shearer Archive/WireImage/Getty Images

Thin Is In

In Western cultures today, thinness is a much-sought-after ideal, especially among young women who are dissatisfied with their appearance. That ideal is seen in fashion models and some celebrities, as well as in Miss America pageant winners, whose body mass index has decreased from the "normal" range of 20 to 25 in the 1920s to an "undernourished" 18.5 more recently (Rubinstein & Caballero, 2000; Voracek & Fisher, 2002). In the United States, 35 percent of normal-weight girls—and 12 percent of underweight girls!—begin dieting when they are as young as 9 or 10. Correlational studies suggest that many of these children's efforts to lose weight may have come in response to criticism from family members (Barr Taylor et al., 2006a); for some, the result is anorexia nervosa. To help combat the problem, some fashion shows have now established a certain minimum BMI for all models.

anorexia nervosa An eating disorder characterized by self-starvation and dramatic weight loss.

Bulimia　Like anorexia, bulimia (pronounced "boo-LEE-mee-uh") involves intense fear of being fat, but the person may be thin, normal in weight, or even overweight. **Bulimia** (also referred to as *bulimia nervosa*) involves eating huge amounts of food (say, several boxes of cookies, a half-gallon of ice cream, and a bucket of fried chicken) and then getting rid of the food through self-induced vomiting or strong laxatives. These "binge-purge" episodes may occur as often as twice a day (Weltzin et al., 1995).

Bulimia shares many features with anorexia (Fairburn et al., 2008). For instance, most people with bulimia are female, and like anorexia, bulimia usually begins with a desire to be slender. However, bulimia and anorexia are quite different disorders (Eddy et al., 2008). For one thing, most people with bulimia see their eating habits as problematic, whereas most individuals with anorexia do not. In addition, bulimia nervosa is usually not life-threatening (Thompson, 1996). There are health consequences, however, including dehydration, nutritional problems, and intestinal damage. Many people with bulimia develop dental problems from the acids associated with vomiting. Frequent vomiting and the insertion of objects to trigger it can also cause damage to the throat.

Estimates of the frequency of bulimia in adolescent and college-age women range from 1 to 3 percent (National Institutes of Health, 2001; U.S. Surgeon General, 1999), a figure that has remained relatively stable since the early 1990s (Crowther et al., 2008). The combination of factors that contribute to bulimia include perfectionism, low self-esteem, stress, a culturally encouraged preoccupation with being thin, and depression and other emotional problems. Problems in the brain's satiety mechanisms may also be involved (Crowther et al., 2001; Smith, Simmons, et al., 2007; Stice & Fairburn, 2003; Zalta & Keel, 2006). Treatment for bulimia typically includes individual or group therapy and sometimes antidepressant drugs. These treatments help about 72 percent of people with bulimia eat more normally; more refined approaches are still needed to help those who do not improve (Herzog et al., 1999; Le Grange et al., 2007; Steinhausen & Weber, 2009).

For a summary of the processes involved in hunger and eating, see "In Review: Major Factors Controlling Hunger and Eating."

IN REVIEW　Major Factors Controlling Hunger and Eating		
	Stimulate Eating	**Inhibit Eating**
Biological factors	Glucose and insulin in the blood provide signals that stimulate eating; neurotransmitters affecting neurons in the hypothalamus also stimulate eating and influence hungers for specific kinds of foods. Stomach contractions are associated with subjective feelings of hunger but don't play a major role in the stimulation of eating.	Hormones released into the bloodstream produce signals that inhibit eating; hormones such as leptin, CCK, and insulin act as neurotransmitters or neuromodulators and affect neurons in the hypothalamus and inhibit eating. The ventromedial nucleus of the hypothalamus may be a "satiety center" that monitors these hormones.
Nonbiological factors	Sights and smells of particular foods elicit eating because of prior associations; family customs and social occasions include norms for eating in particular ways; stress is often associated with eating more.	Values in contemporary U.S. society encourage thinness and thus can inhibit eating.

1. People may continue eating when they are full, suggesting that eating is not controlled by _____ alone.
2. People with an eating disorder called _____ know that they have a problem; those with an eating disorder called _____ tend not to.
3. The best strategy for lasting weight loss includes regular _____ as well as improved eating habits.

Sexual Behavior

Unlike food, sex is not necessary for an individual's survival, but it is obviously vital for improving the chances that an individual's genes will be represented in the next generation. The various factors shaping sexual motivation and behavior differ in strength across species, but they often include a combination of the individual's physiology, learned behavior, and the physical and social environment. For example, one species of desert bird requires adequate sex hormones, a suitable mate, and a particular environment before it

bulimia　An eating disorder that involves eating massive amounts of food and then eliminating the food by self-induced vomiting or the use of strong laxatives.

begins sexual behavior. During the dry season, it shows no interest in sex, but within ten minutes after the first rain shower, the birds vigorously court and then copulate.

Rainfall is obviously much less influential as a sexual trigger for humans. People show an amazing diversity of *sexual scripts,* or patterns of behavior that lead to sex. Surveys of college-age men and women identified 122 specific acts and 34 different tactics used for promoting sexual encounters (Greer & Buss, 1994; Meston & Buss, 2007). What actually happens during sex? The matter is difficult to address scientifically because most people are reluctant to respond to specific questions about their sexual practices, let alone to allow researchers to observe their sexual behavior. Yet having valid information about the nature of human sexual behavior is a vital first step for psychologists and other scientists who study such topics as individual differences in sexuality, gender differences in sexual motivation and behavior, sources of sexual orientation, types of sexual dysfunctions, and the pathways through which HIV and other sexually transmitted infections reach new victims. This information can also help people think about their own sexual behavior in relation to trends in the general population.

FOCUS ON **RESEARCH METHODS**

A Survey of Human Sexual Behavior

The first extensive studies of sexual behavior in the United States were done by Alfred Kinsey during the late 1940s and early 1950s (Kinsey, Pomeroy, & Martin, 1948; Kinsey et al., 1953). These were followed in the 1960s by the work of William Masters and Virginia Johnson (1966). Kinsey conducted surveys of people's sex lives; Masters and Johnson actually recorded volunteers' **sexual arousal,** their physiological responses to erotic stimuli that arose during natural or artificial stimulation in a laboratory. Together, these studies broke new ground in the exploration of human sexuality, but the people who volunteered for them were probably not a representative sample of the adult population. Accordingly, the results—and any conclusions drawn from them—may not apply to people in general. Further, the data are now so old that they may not reflect sexual practices today. Unfortunately, the results of more recent surveys, such as reader polls in *Cosmopolitan* and other magazines, are also flawed by the use of unrepresentative samples (e.g., Davis & Smith, 1990).

What was the researchers' question?

Is it possible to gather data on sexual behavior that are more representative and therefore more revealing about people in general? Researchers at the University of Chicago believe it is, so they undertook the National Health and Social Life Survey, the first extensive survey of sexual behavior in the United States since the Kinsey studies (Laumann et al., 1994).

How did the researchers answer the question?

This survey included important design features that had been neglected in most other surveys of sexual behavior. First, the study did not depend on self-selected volunteers. The researchers sought out a carefully constructed sample of 3,432 people, ranging in age from 18 to 59. Second, the sample reflected the sociocultural diversity of the U.S. population in terms of gender, ethnicity, socioeconomic status, geographical location, and the like. Third, unlike previous mail-in surveys, the Chicago study was based on face-to-face interviews. This approach made it easier to ensure that the participants understood each question and had the opportunity to explain their responses. To encourage honesty, the researchers allowed participants to answer some questions anonymously by placing written responses in a sealed envelope.

What did the researchers find?

The researchers found that people in the United States have sex less often and with fewer people than had been assumed. For most, sex occurs about once a week and only between partners in a stable relationship. About a third of the participants reported having sex only a few times, or not at all, in the past year. And in contrast to certain

sexual arousal Physiological responses that arise from sexual contact or erotic thoughts.

celebrities' splashy tales of dozens or even hundreds of sexual partners per year, the average male survey participant had only six sexual partners in his entire life. The average female respondent reported a lifetime total of two. Further, the survey data suggested that people in committed, one-partner relationships had the most frequent and the most satisfying sex. And although a wide variety of specific sexual practices were reported, the overwhelming majority of heterosexual couples said they tend to engage mainly in penis-vagina intercourse. Many of these findings are consistent with the results of more recent surveys conducted by other researchers (e.g., National Center for Health Statistics, 2007).

What do the results mean?

The Chicago survey challenges some of the cultural and media images of sexuality in the United States. In particular, it suggests that people in the United States may be more sexually conservative than one might think on the basis of magazine reader polls and discussions on daytime talk shows.

What do we still need to know?

Many questions remain. The Chicago survey did not ask about some of the more controversial aspects of human sexuality, such as the effects of pornography, the prevalence of pedophilia (sexual attraction to children), and the role in sexual activity of sexual fetishes such as shoes or other clothing. Had the researchers asked about such topics, their results might have painted a less conservative picture. Further, because the original Chicago survey focused on people in the United States, it told us little or nothing about the sexual practices, traditions, and values of people in the rest of the world.

The Chicago team has continued to conduct interviews, and the results are beginning to fill in the picture about sexual behavior in the United States and around the world (Youm & Laumann, 2002). They have found, for example, that nearly one-quarter of U.S. women prefer to achieve sexual satisfaction without partners of either sex. And although people in the United States tend to engage in a wider variety of sexual behaviors than those in Britain, there is less tolerance in the United States of disapproved sexual practices (Laumann & Michael, 2000; Michael et al., 1998). They have found, too, that although sexual activity declines with advancing age, it by no means disappears. About 26 percent of people in the 75-to-85 age group—especially men—reported that they were still sexually active (Lindau & Gavrilova, 2010; Lindau et al., 2007).

Other researchers have found a number of consistent gender differences in sexuality. For example, men tend to have a stronger interest in and desire for sex than women, whereas women are more likely than men to associate sexual activity with love and to be affected by cultural and situational influences on sexual attitudes and behavior (Baumeister & Stillman, 2006; Diamond, 2008; Peplau, 2003; Petersen & Hyde, 2010).

The results of even the best survey methods—like the results of all research methods—usually raise as many questions as they answer. When do people become interested in sex, and why? How do they choose to express these desires, and why? What determines their sexual likes and dislikes? How do learning and sociocultural factors modify the biological forces that seem to provide the raw material of human sexual motivation? These are some of the questions about human sexual behavior that a survey cannot easily or accurately explore (Benson, 2003b).

The Biology of Sex

Observations in Masters and Johnson's laboratory led to important findings about the **sexual response cycle**—the pattern of physiological arousal during and after sexual activity (see Figure 11.4).

People's motivation to engage in sexual activity has biological roots in **sex hormones**. The female sex hormones include **estrogens** and **progestational hormones** (also called *progestins;* the main ones are *estradiol* and *progesterone*). The male hormones are **androgens**; the main one is *testosterone*. Each sex hormone flows in the

---

sexual response cycle The pattern of physiological arousal during and after sexual activity.

sex hormones Chemicals in the blood of males and females that have both organizational and activational effects on sexual behavior.

estrogens Sex hormones that circulate in the bloodstream of both men and women; more estrogens circulate in women than in men.

progestational hormones Sex hormones that circulate in the bloodstream of both men and women, also known as *progestins;* more progestins circulate in women than in men.

androgens Sex hormones that circulate in the bloodstream in both sexes; more androgens circulate in men than in women.

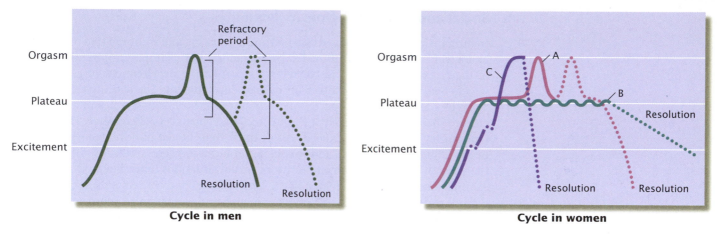

FIGURE 11.4

The Sexual Response Cycle

As shown in the left-hand graph, Masters and Johnson (1966) found that men display one main pattern of sexual response. Women display at least three different patterns from time to time; these are labeled A, B, and C in the right-hand graph. For both men and women, the *excitement* phase begins with sexual stimulation from the environment or one's own thoughts. Continued stimulation leads to intensified excitement in the *plateau* phase, and if stimulation continues, to the intensely pleasurable release of tension in the *orgasmic* stage. During the *resolution* phase, both men and women experience a state of relaxation. Following resolution, men enter a *refractory* phase, during which they are unresponsive to sexual stimulation. Women are capable of immediately repeating the cycle.

Source: Adapted from W.H. Masters and V.E. Johnson. *Human Sexual Response*, p. 5 (Boston: Little, Brown and Company, 1966).

blood of both sexes, but the average man has more male than female hormones, and the average woman has more female than male hormones.

Sex hormones have both organizational and activational effects on the brain. The *organizational* effects are permanent changes that alter the brain's response to hormones. The *activational* effects are temporary behavioral changes that last only as long as a hormone level remains elevated, such as during puberty or in the ovulation phase of the monthly menstrual cycle. In mammals, including humans, the organizational effects of hormones occur around the time of birth, when certain brain areas are sculpted into a "malelike" or "femalelike" pattern. These areas are described as *sexually dimorphic*. In rodents, for example, a sexually dimorphic area of the hypothalamus appears to underlie specific sexual behaviors. When these areas are destroyed in male gerbils, the animals can no longer copulate; yet damage to other nearby brain regions does not affect sexual behavior (Yahr & Jacobsen, 1994). Sexually dimorphic areas also exist in the human hypothalamus and elsewhere in the brain (Breedlove, 1994; Kimura, 1999). For example, an area of the hypothalamus called the *bed nucleus of the stria terminalis* (*BnST*) is generally smaller in women than in men. Its possible role in some aspects of human sexuality was suggested by a study of transsexual men—genetic males who feel like women and who may request surgery and hormone treatments in order to appear more female. The BnST in these men was smaller than in other men; in fact, it was about the size usually seen in women (Zhou et al., 1995).

Rising levels of sex hormones during puberty have activational effects, resulting in increased sexual desire and interest in sexual behavior. Generally, estrogens and androgens stimulate females' sexual interest (Burleson, Gregory, & Trevarthen, 1995; Sherwin & Gelfand, 1987). Androgens raise males' sexual interest (Davidson, Camargo, & Smith, 1979). The activational effects of hormones are also seen in reduced sexual motivation and behavior among people whose hormone-secreting ovaries or testes have been removed for medical reasons. Injections of hormones help restore these people's sexual interest and activity.

Social and Cultural Factors in Sexuality

In humans, sexuality is shaped by a lifetime of learning and thinking that modifies the biological "raw materials" provided by hormones. For example, children learn some of their sexual attitudes and behaviors as part of the development of *gender roles,* which we discuss in the chapter on human development. The specific attitudes and behaviors learned depend partly on the nature of those gender roles in a particular culture (Baumeister, 2000; Hyde & Durik, 2000; Peplau, 2003; Petersen & Hyde, 2010). One survey of the sexual experiences of more than fifteen hundred college students in the United States, Japan, and Russia found numerous cross-cultural differences in the ways that men and women behave in sexual situations (Sprecher et al., 1994). For example, more women than men in the United States had consented to sex when they did not really want it. In Russia and Japan, men and women were about equally likely to have had this experience.

There are gender differences, too, in what people find sexually appealing. For example, in many cultures, men are far more interested in and responsive to pornographic films and other erotic stimuli than women are (Herz & Cahill, 1997; Petersen & Hyde, 2010; Symons, 1979). The difference in responsiveness was demonstrated in an MRI study that scanned the brain activity of males and females while they looked at erotic photographs (Hamann et al., 2004). As expected, the males showed greater activity in the amygdala and hypothalamus than the females. But even though there were gender differences in brain activity, the male and female participants rated the photos as equally appealing and arousing. In another study, when men reported sexual arousal in response to erotic films, they also showed signs of physiological arousal. For women, self-reports of arousal were not strongly correlated with signs of physiological arousal (Chivers et al., 2004). Further, though men and women both show more sexual arousal to more intensely erotic films, the level of women's arousal may not depend as much as men's does on whether the actors are males or females (Chivers, Seto, & Blanchard, 2007).

These are just a few examples of the fact that sexuality is a product of a complex mixture of factors. Each person's learning history, cultural background, and perceptions of the world interact so deeply with such a wide range of physiological processes that—as in many other aspects of human behavior and mental processes—it is impossible to separate their influence on sexuality. Nowhere is this point clearer than in the case of sexual orientation.

Social Influences on Sexual Behavior

Sexual behavior is shaped by many sociocultural forces. For example, concern over teenage pregnancy and sexually transmitted diseases, including HIV/AIDS, has prompted school-based educational programs in the United States to encourage premarital sexual abstinence or "safe sex" using condoms. These efforts have helped change young people's sexual attitudes and practices (e.g., Jemmott, Jemmott, & Fong, 2010).

Sexual Orientation

Sexual orientation refers to the nature of a person's enduring emotional, romantic, or sexual attraction to others (American Psychological Association, 2002a; Ellis & Mitchell, 2000). The most common sexual orientation is **heterosexuality,** in which the attraction is to members of the other sex. When attraction focuses on members of one's own sex, the orientation is called **homosexuality;** male homosexuals are referred to as *gay men* and female homosexuals as *lesbians.* **Bisexuality** refers to people who are attracted to members of both sexes. Sexual orientation involves feelings that may or may not be translated into corresponding patterns of sexual behavior (Diamond, 2008; Pathela et al., 2006). For example, some people whose orientation is gay, lesbian, or bisexual may have sex only with opposite-sex partners. Similarly, people whose orientation is heterosexual may have had one or more same-sex encounters.

In many cultures, heterosexuality has long been regarded as a moral norm, and homosexuality has been cast as a disease, a mental disorder, or even a crime (Hooker, 1993). Yet attempts to alter the sexual orientation of gay men and lesbians—using psychotherapy, brain surgery, or electric shock—have usually been ineffective (American Psychiatric Association, 1999; Smith, Bartlett, & King, 2004). In 1973, the American Psychiatric Association dropped homosexuality from the *Diagnostic and Statistical Manual of Mental Disorders,* thus ending its official status as a form of psychopathology. The same change was made by the World Health Organization in its *International Classification of Diseases* in 1993, by Japan's psychiatric organization in 1995, and by the Chinese Psychiatric Association in 2001.

Nevertheless, some people still disapprove of homosexuality. Because gays, lesbians, and bisexuals are often the victims of discrimination and even hate crimes, many are reluctant to let their sexual orientation be known (Bernat et al., 2001; Meyer, 2003). It is difficult, therefore, to paint an accurate picture of the mix of heterosexual, homosexual, and bisexual orientations in a population. In the Chicago sex survey mentioned earlier, 1.4 percent of women and 2.8 percent of men identified themselves as exclusively homosexual (Laumann et al., 1994), figures much lower than the 10 percent found in Kinsey's studies. However, the Chicago survey's face-to-face interviews did not allow respondents to give anonymous answers to questions about sexual orientation. Some researchers suggest that if anonymous responses to those questions had been permitted, the prevalence figures for gay, lesbian, and bisexual orientations would have been higher (Bullough, 1995). In fact, studies that have allowed anonymous responding estimate that gay, lesbian, and bisexual people may make up anywhere from 2 to 21 percent of the population in the United States, Canada, and Western Europe (Aaron et al., 2003; Bagley & Tremblay, 1998; Binson et al., 1995; Savin-Williams, 2006; Sell, Wells, & Wypij, 1995).

THINKING CRITICALLY

What Shapes Sexual Orientation?

The question of where sexual orientation comes from is a topic of intense debate in scientific circles, on talk shows, on the Internet, and in everyday conversations.

What am I being asked to believe or accept?

Some people believe that genes exert a major influence on our sexual orientation. According to this view, we do not learn a sexual orientation but rather are born with a strong predisposition to develop a particular orientation.

What evidence is available to support the assertion?

In 1995, a report by a respected research group suggested that one kind of sexual orientation—namely, that of gay men—is associated with a particular gene on the X chromosome (Hu et al., 1995). This finding was not supported by later studies (Rice et al., 1999), but a growing body of evidence from research in behavioral genetics suggests that genes may indeed influence sexual orientation (Kendler et al., 2000; Pillard & Bailey, 1998). One study examined pairs of monozygotic male twins (whose genes are identical), nonidentical twin pairs (whose genes are no more alike than those

sexual orientation The nature of a person's enduring emotional, romantic, or sexual attraction to others.

heterosexuality Sexual motivation that is focused on members of the other sex.

homosexuality Sexual motivation that is focused on members of one's own sex.

bisexuality Sexual motivation that is focused on members of both sexes.

of any brothers), and pairs of adopted brothers (who are genetically unrelated). To participate in this study, at least one brother in each pair had to be gay. As it turned out, the other brother was also gay or bisexual in 52 percent of the identical-twin pairs. This was the case in only 22 percent of the nonidentical twin pairs and in just 11 percent of the pairs of adopted brothers (Bailey & Pillard, 1991). Similar findings have been reported for male identical twins raised apart, whose shared sexual orientation cannot be attributed to the effects of a shared environment (Whitam, Diamond, & Martin, 1993). The few available studies of female sexual orientation have yielded similar results (Bailey & Benishay, 1993; Bailey, Dunne, & Martin, 2000).

Other evidence for the role of biological factors in sexual orientation comes from research on the impact of sex hormones. In adults, differences in the levels of these hormones are not generally associated with differences in sexual orientation. However, hormonal differences during prenatal development may be involved in the shaping of sexual orientation (Lalumière, Blanchard, & Zucker, 2000; Lippa, 2003; Williams et al., 2000), and the influences may differ for men and women (Mustanski, Chivers, & Bailey, 2002). For example, one study found that women—but not men—who had been exposed to high levels of androgens during their fetal development were much more likely to report bisexual or homosexual behaviors or fantasies than relatives of the same sex who had not been exposed (Hines, Brook, & Conway, 2004; Meyer-Bahlburg et al., 2008).

Another line of research focuses on the possibility that previous pregnancies may permanently affect a woman's hormones in ways that influence the sexual orientation of her next child (Blanchard, 2001). Some evidence for this hypothesis comes from a study showing that the more older biological brothers a man has, the higher the probability that he will have a homosexual orientation (Blanchard & Lippa, 2007; Bogaert, Blanchard, & Crosthwait, 2007). These results appear to reflect mainly hormonal rather than mainly environmental influences because the number of *nonbiological* (adopted) brothers that the men had was not predictive of their sexual orientation. Further, because sexual orientation in women was not predicted by the number and gender of their older biological siblings, it was thought that the hormonal consequences of carrying male fetuses might influence only males' sexual orientation. The picture is not that simple, though. Other researchers have found that women's sexual orientation, too, is related to the number of older biological brothers they have (McConaghy et al., 2006), and still others have reported a relationship between men's sexual orientation and the number of older biological sisters they have (Francis, 2008; Vasey & VanderLaan, 2007). We don't yet know exactly how prenatal hormonal influences might operate to affect sexual orientation, but studies of nonhuman animals have found that such influences alter the structure of the hypothalamus, a brain region known to underlie some aspects of sexual functioning (Swaab & Hofman, 1995).

Finally, a biological basis for sexual orientation is suggested by the fact that sexual orientation is not predicted by environmental factors. Several studies have shown, for example, that the sexual orientation of children's caregivers has little or no effect on those children's own sexual orientation. Several studies have shown that children adopted by gay or lesbian parents are no more or less likely to have a homosexual orientation than children raised by heterosexual parents (Anderssen, Amlie, & Ytteroy, 2002; Bailey et al., 1995; Stacey & Biblarz, 2001; Tasker & Golombok, 1995).

Are there alternative ways of interpreting the evidence?

Like all correlational data, correlations between genetics and sexual orientation are open to alternative interpretations. As discussed in the chapter on research in psychology, a correlation describes the strength and direction of a relationship between variables, but it does not guarantee that one variable is actually influencing the other. Consider again the data showing that brothers who shared the most genes (identical twins) were also most likely to share a gay sexual orientation. It is possible that what the brothers shared was not a "gay gene" but rather a set of genes that influenced the boys' activity levels, emotionality, aggressiveness, and the like. One example is

A Committed Relationship, with Children

Like heterosexual relationships, gay and lesbian relationships can be brief and stormy or stable and permanent (Kurdek, 2005). These gay men are committed to each other for the long haul, as can be seen in their decision to adopt two children together. The strong role of biological factors in sexual orientation is supported by research showing that their children's orientation will not be influenced much, if at all, by that of their adoptive parents (e.g., Anderssen, Amlie, & Ytteroy, 2002; Patterson, 2004; Stacey & Biblarz, 2001).

gender conformity or nonconformity in childhood, the tendency for children to either conform or not conform to the behaviors, interests, and appearance that are typical for their gender in their culture (Bailey, Dunn, & Martin, 2000; Knafo, Iervolino, & Plomin, 2005). These general aspects of their temperaments or personalities in childhood—and other people's reactions to them—could influence the likelihood of a particular sexual orientation (Bem, 2000). In other words, sexual orientation could arise as a reaction to the way people respond to a genetically determined but nonsexual aspect of personality. Prenatal hormone levels, too, could influence sexual orientation by shaping aggressiveness or other nonsexual aspects of behavior.

It is also important to look at behavioral genetics evidence for what it can tell us about the role of *environmental factors* in sexual orientation. When we read that both members of identical twin pairs have a gay sexual orientation 52 percent of the time, it is easy to ignore the fact that the orientation of the twin pair members was *different* in 48 percent of the cases. Viewed in this way, the results suggest that genes do not tell the entire story of sexual orientation. Indeed, evidence that sexual orientation has its roots in biology does not mean that it is determined by unlearned genetic forces alone. As described in the chapter on biological aspects of psychology, the brains and bodies we inherit are quite responsive to environmental influences. The behaviors we engage in and the environmental experiences we have often result in physical changes in the brain and elsewhere (Wang et al., 1995). Every time we form a new memory, for example, changes occur in the brain's synapses. So differences in the brains of people with differing sexual orientations could be the effect, not the cause, of their behavior or experiences.

What additional evidence would help evaluate the alternatives?

Much more evidence is needed about the role of genes in shaping sexual orientation. We also have much to learn about the extent to which genes and hormones shape physical and psychological characteristics that lead to various sexual orientations. In studying these topics, researchers will want to know more not only about the genetic characteristics of people with different sexual orientations but also about their mental and behavioral styles. Are there personality characteristics associated with different sexual orientations? If so, do those characteristics have a strong genetic component? To what extent are gay men, lesbians, bisexuals, and heterosexuals similar—and different—in terms of cognitive styles, biases, coping skills, developmental histories, and the like? And are there any differences in how sexual orientation is shaped in males versus females (Bailey, Dunn & Martin, 2000)?

The more we learn about sexual orientation in general, the easier it will be to interpret data relating to its origins. But even defining sexual orientation is not simple because people do not always fall into discrete categories (American Psychological Association, 2002a; Diamond, 2008; Savin-Williams, 2006; Thompson & Morgan, 2008; Worthington et al., 2008). Should a man who identifies himself as gay be considered bisexual because he occasionally has heterosexual daydreams? What sexual orientation label would be appropriate for a 40-year-old woman who experienced a few lesbian encounters in her teens but has engaged in exclusively heterosexual sex since then? Progress in understanding the origins of sexual orientation would be enhanced by a generally accepted system for describing and defining exactly what is meant by the term *sexual orientation*.

What conclusions are most reasonable?

The evidence available so far suggests that genetic factors, probably operating through prenatal hormones, create differences in the brains of people with different sexual orientations. However, the manner in which a person expresses a genetically influenced sexual orientation will be profoundly shaped by what that person learns through social and cultural experiences (Bancroft, 1994). In short, as is true of so many other psychological phenomena, sexual orientation most likely results from the complex interplay of both genetic and nongenetic mechanisms—both nature and nurture.

Achievement Motivation

This sentence was written at 6:00 A.M. on a beautiful Sunday in June. Why would someone get up that early to work on a weekend? Why do people take their work seriously and try to do the best that they can? People work hard partly due to *extrinsic motivation,* a desire for external rewards such as money. But work and other human behaviors also reflect *intrinsic motivation,* a desire to attain internal satisfaction (Deci, Koestner, & Ryan, 2001), including the kind that has been described by some psychologists as *flow* (Hektner, Schmidt, & Csikszentmihalyi, 2007). If you have ever lost track of time while utterly absorbed in some intensely engaging work or recreation or athletics or creative activity, you have experienced flow, or what some people call being "in the zone."

The next time you visit someone's home or office, look at the mementos displayed there. You may see framed diplomas and awards, trophies and ribbons, and photos of children and grandchildren. These badges of achievement affirm that a person has accomplished tasks that merit approval or establish worth. Much of our behavior is motivated by a desire for approval, admiration, and achievement—in short, for *esteem*—from others and from ourselves. In this section, we examine two of the most common avenues to esteem: achievement in general and a job in particular.

Need for Achievement

Many athletes who already hold world records still train intensely; many people who built multimillion-dollar businesses still work fourteen-hour days. What motivates these people?

Some psychologists suggest that the answer is a desire for *mastery* or *effectance* (Kusyszyn, 1990; Surtees et al., 2006; White, 1959), the motivation to behave competently. These terms are similar to an earlier concept described by Henry Murray (1938) as *need achievement.* People with a high **achievement motivation** seek to master tasks—be they sports, business ventures, intellectual puzzles, or artistic creations— and obtain intense satisfaction from doing so. They strive for excellence, enjoy themselves in the process, and take great pride in achieving at a high level.

Individual Differences   How do people with strong achievement motivation differ from others? To find out, researchers gave children a test to measure their need for achievement (Figure 11.5 shows a test used with adults) and then asked them to play a ring-toss game. Children scoring low on the need achievement test usually stood either so close to the ring-toss target that they couldn't fail or so far away that they couldn't succeed. In contrast, children scoring high on the need achievement test stood at a moderate distance from the target, making the game challenging but not impossible (McClelland, 1958). These and other experiments suggest that people with high achievement motivation tend to set challenging but realistic goals for themselves. They are interested in their work, actively seek success, take risks when necessary, and are intensely satisfied when they succeed (Eisenberger et al., 2005). And if they feel they have tried their best, people with high achievement motivation are not too upset by failure. Those with low achievement motivation also like to succeed, but instead of joy, success tends to bring them relief at having avoided failure (Winter, 1996). There is some evidence that the differing emotions—such as anticipation versus worry—that accompany the efforts of people with high and low achievement motivation can affect how successful those efforts will be (Pekrun, Elliot, & Maier, 2009).

Differences in achievement motivation also appear in the kinds of goals people seek in achievement-related situations (Molden & Dweck, 2000). Some people tend to adopt *learning goals.* When they play golf, take piano lessons, work at puzzles and problems, go to school, and get involved in other achievement-oriented activities, they do so mainly to get better at those activities. Realizing that they may not yet have the

achievement motivation   The degree to which a person establishes specific goals, cares about meeting those goals, and experiences feelings of satisfaction by doing so.

FIGURE 11.5
Assessing Achievement Motivation
This picture is similar to those included in the Thematic Apperception Test, or TAT (Morgan & Murray, 1935). The strength of people's achievement motivation is inferred from the stories they tell about TAT pictures. A response such as "The young woman is hoping to make her grandmother proud of her" would be seen as reflecting high achievement motivation.

Reprinted by permission of the publishers from THEMATIC APPERCEPTION TEST by Henry A. Murray, Card 12F, Cambridge, Mass.: Harvard University Press, Copyright © 1943 by the President and Fellows of Harvard College, Copyright © 1971 by Henry A. Murray.

skills necessary to achieve at a high level, they tend to learn by watching others and to struggle with problems on their own rather than asking for help (Mayer & Sutton, 1996). When they do seek help, people with learning goals are likely to ask for explanations, hints, and other forms of task-related information, not for quick, easy answers that remove the challenge from the situation. In contrast, people who adopt *performance goals* are usually more concerned with demonstrating the skill they believe they already possess. They tend to seek information about how well they have performed compared with others rather than about how to improve their performance (Butler, 1998). When they seek help, it is usually to ask for the right answer rather than for tips on how to find that answer themselves. Because their primary goal is to demonstrate their competence, people with performance goals tend to avoid new challenges if they are not confident that they will be successful, and they tend to quit in response to failure (Grant & Dweck, 2003). Those with learning goals tend to be more persistent and less upset when they don't immediately perform well (Niiya, Crocker, & Bartmess, 2004); having learning goals also predicts better adjustment among students who are going to school in an unfamiliar culture (Gong & Fan, 2006).

Development of Achievement Motivation   Achievement motivation develops in early childhood, under the influence of both genetic and environmental forces. As described in the personality chapter, children inherit general behavioral tendencies, such as impulsiveness and emotionality, and these tendencies may support or undermine the development of achievement motivation. The motivation to achieve is also shaped by what children learn from watching and listening to others, especially their parents. Evidence for the influence of parental teachings about achievement comes from a study in which young boys were given a difficult task at which they were sure to fail. Fathers whose sons scored low on achievement motivation tests often became annoyed as they watched their boys struggle. They discouraged them from continuing, interfered, or even completed the task themselves (Rosen & D'Andrade, 1959). A different pattern of behavior appeared among parents of children who scored high on tests of achievement motivation. Those parents tended to encourage the child to try difficult tasks, especially new ones; give praise and other rewards for success; encourage the child to find ways to succeed rather than merely complaining about failure; and prompt the child to go on to the next, more difficult challenge (McClelland, 1985). Research with adults shows that even the slightest cues that bring a parent to mind can boost people's efforts to achieve a goal (Shah, 2003) and that college students—especially those who have learning goals—feel closer to their parents while taking exams (Moller, Elliot, & Friedman, 2008).

More general cultural influences also affect the development of achievement motivation. For example, subtle messages about a culture's view of how achievement occurs often appear in the books children read and the stories they hear. Does the story's main character work hard and overcome obstacles, thus creating expectations of a payoff for persistence? Or does a lazy main character drift aimlessly and then win the lottery, suggesting that rewards come randomly, regardless of effort? If the main character succeeds, is it the result of personal initiative, as is typical of stories in individualist cultures? Or is success based on ties to a cooperative and supportive group, as is typical of stories in collectivist cultures? These themes appear to act as blueprints for reaching culturally approved goals. It should not be surprising, then, that ideas about how people achieve differ from culture to culture. In one study, individuals from Saudi Arabia and from the United States were asked to comment on short stories describing people who succeeded at various tasks. Saudis tended to see the people in the stories as having succeeded because of the help they got from others, whereas Americans tended to attribute success to the personal traits of each story's main character (Zahrani & Kaplowitz, 1993). Achievement motivation is also influenced by how much a particular culture values and rewards achievement. For example, the motivation to excel is likely to be especially strong in cultures in which demanding standards lead students to fear rejection if they fail to attain high grades (Eaton & Dembo, 1997).

Helping Them Do Their Best

Learning-oriented goals are especially appropriate in classrooms, where students typically have little knowledge of the subject matter. This is why most teachers tolerate errors and reward gradual improvement. They do not usually encourage performance goals, which emphasize doing better than others and demonstrating immediate competence (Reeve, 1996). Still, to help students do their best in the long run, teachers sometimes promote performance goals too. The proper combination of both kinds of goals may be more motivating than either kind alone (Barron & Harackiewicz, 2001).

© Monkey Business Images/Shutterstock

In short, achievement motivation is strongly influenced by social and cultural learning experiences, as well as by the beliefs about oneself that these experiences help create. People who come to believe in their ability to achieve are more likely to do so than those who expect to fail (Dweck, 1998; Greven et al., 2009; Tuckman, 2003; Wigfield & Eccles, 2000).

Goal Setting and Achievement Motivation

Why are you reading this chapter instead of watching television or hanging out with your friends? Your motivation to study is probably based on your goal of doing well in a psychology course, which relates to broader goals, such as earning a degree, having a career, and the like. Psychologists have found that we set goals when we recognize a discrepancy between our current situation and how we want that situation to be (Oettingen, Pak, & Schnetter, 2001). Establishing a goal motivates us to engage in behaviors designed to reduce the discrepancy we have identified. The kinds of goals we set can influence the amount of effort, persistence, attention, and planning we devote to a task (Morisano et al., 2010).

In general, the more difficult the goal, the harder people will try to reach it. This rule assumes, of course, that the goal is seen as realistic. Goals that are impossibly difficult may not motivate us to exert maximum effort. The rule also assumes that we value the goal. If a difficult goal is set by someone else—as when a parent assigns a teenager to keep a large lawn and garden trimmed and weeded—people may not accept it as their own and may not work very hard to attain it. Setting goals that are clear and specific tends to increase people's motivation to persist at a task (Locke & Latham, 2002). For example, you are more likely to keep reading this chapter if your goal is to "read the motivation section of the motivation and emotion chapter today" than if it is to "do some studying." Clarifying your goal makes it easier to know when you have reached it and when it is time to stop. Without clear goals, a person can be more easily distracted by fatigue, boredom, or frustration and more likely to give up before completing a task. Clear goals also tend to focus people's attention on creating plans for pursuing them, on the activities they believe will lead to goal attainment, and on evaluating their progress. In short, the process of goal setting is more than just wishful thinking. It is an important first step in motivating all kinds of behavior.

Children raised in environments that support the development of strong achievement motivation tend not to give up on difficult tasks—even if all the king's horses and all the king's men do!

"Maybe they didn't try hard enough."

Achievement and Success in the Workplace

In the workplace, there is usually less concern with employees' general level of achievement motivation than with their motivation to work hard during business hours. In fact, employers tend to set up jobs in accordance with their ideas about how intrinsic motivation and extrinsic motivation combine to shape their employees' performance (Riggio, 1989). Employers who see workers as lazy, dishonest, and lacking in ambition tend to offer highly structured, heavily supervised jobs that give employees little say in deciding what to do or how to do it. These employers assume that workers are motivated mainly by extrinsic rewards—money in particular. So they tend to be surprised when, despite good pay and benefits, employees sometimes express dissatisfaction with their jobs and show little motivation to work hard (Diener & Seligman, 2004; Igalens & Roussel, 1999).

If good pay and benefits alone don't bring job satisfaction and the desire to excel on the job, what does? In Western cultures, low worker motivation comes largely from the feeling of having little or no control over the work environment (Rosen, 1991). Compared with those in rigidly structured jobs, workers tend to be more satisfied and productive if they are encouraged to participate in decisions about how work should be done; given problems to solve, without being told how to solve them; taught more than one skill; given individual responsibility; and given public recognition, not just money, for good performance (Fisher, 2000).

Allowing people to set and achieve clear goals is one way to increase both job performance and job satisfaction (Maynard, Joseph & Maynard, 2006). As suggested by our earlier discussion, some goals are especially effective at maintaining work motivation (Katzell & Thompson, 1990). First, effective goals are personally meaningful. When a form letter from a remote administrator tells employees that they should increase production, the employees tend to feel manipulated and not particularly motivated to meet the goal. Before assigning difficult goals, good managers try to ensure that employees accept those goals (Klein et al., 1999). They include employees in the goal-setting process, make sure that the employees have the skills and resources to reach the goal, and emphasize the benefits to be gained from success—perhaps including financial incentives (Locke & Latham, 1990). Second, effective goals are specific and concrete (Locke & Latham, 2002). The goal of "doing better" is usually not a strong motivator because it provides no direction about how to proceed and fails to specify when the goal has been met. A specific target, such as increasing sales

Teamwork Pays Off

Many U.S. companies have followed Japanese examples by redesigning jobs to increase workers' responsibility and flexibility. The goal is to increase productivity and job satisfaction by creating teams in which employees are responsible for solving production problems and making decisions about how best to do their jobs. Team members are publicly recognized for outstanding work, and part of their pay depends on the quality (not just the number) of their products and on the profitability of the company as a whole.

© Jupiterimages/Getty Images

by 10 percent, is a far more motivating goal. It can be measured objectively, allowing feedback on progress, and it tells workers whether the goal has been reached. Finally, goals are most effective if management supports the workers' own goal setting, offers special rewards for reaching goals, and gives encouragement for renewed efforts after failure (Kluger & DeNisi, 1998).

In summary, motivating jobs offer personal challenges, independence, and both intrinsic and extrinsic rewards. They provide enough satisfaction for people to feel excitement and pleasure in working hard (Burke & Fiksenbaum, 2009). For employers, the rewards are more productivity, less absenteeism, and greater employee loyalty (Ilgen & Pulakos, 1999).

Achievement and Well-Being

Some people believe that the more they achieve at work and elsewhere and the more money and other material goods they amass as a result, the happier they will be. Are they right? Researchers in the field of *positive psychology* have become increasingly interested in the systematic study of what it actually takes to achieve happiness, or more formally, well-being (Seligman et al., 2005; Sheldon & King, 2001). **Well-being** (also known as *subjective well-being*) is a combination of a cognitive judgment of satisfaction with life, the frequent experiencing of positive moods and emotions, and the relatively infrequent experiencing of unpleasant moods and emotions (Diener & Biswas-Diener, 2002; Eid & Larsen, 2008; Fredrickson & Losada, 2005; Urry et al., 2004).

Research on well-being indicates that, as you might expect, people living in extreme poverty or in war-torn or politically chaotic countries are not as happy as people in better circumstances (Diener et al., 2010). And people everywhere react to good or bad events with corresponding changes in mood. As described in the chapter on health, stress, and coping, for example, severe or long-lasting stressors—such as the death of a loved one—can lead to psychological and physical problems. But although events do have an impact, the depressing or elevating effects of major changes, such as being promoted or fired or even being imprisoned, seriously injured, or disabled, tend not to last as long as we might think they would (Abrantes-Pais et al., 2007; Gilbert et al., 2004). In other words, how happy you are may have less to do with what happens to you than you might expect (Bonanno, 2004; Gilbert & Wilson, 1998; Kahneman et al., 2006; Lyubomirsky, 2001; Riis et al., 2005).

well-being   A combination of a cognitive judgment of satisfaction with life, the frequent experiencing of positive moods and emotions, and the relatively infrequent experiencing of unpleasant moods and emotions; also known as *subjective well-being*.

Most event-related changes in mood subside within days or weeks, and most people then return to their previous level of happiness (Suh, Diener, & Fujita, 1996). Even when events create permanent changes in circumstances, most people adapt by changing their expectancies and goals, not by radically and permanently changing their baseline level of happiness (e.g., Smith et al., 2009). For example, people may be thrilled after getting a big salary increase, but as they get used to having it, the thrill fades, and they may eventually feel just as underpaid as before. In fact, although there are exceptions (Fujita & Diener, 2005; Lucas, 2007), most people's level of subjective well-being tends to be remarkably stable throughout their lives. This baseline level may be related to temperament or personality, and it has been likened to a set point for body weight (Lykken, 1999). Like many other aspects of temperament, our baseline level of happiness may be influenced by genetics. Twin studies have shown, for example, that individual differences in happiness are more strongly associated with inherited personality characteristics than with environmental factors such as money, popularity, or physical attractiveness (Lykken, 1999; Tellegen et al., 1988).

Beyond inherited tendencies, the things that appear to matter most in generating happiness are close social ties (including friends and a satisfying marriage or partnership), religious faith, and having the resources necessary to allow progress toward one's goals (Diener, 2000; Mehl et al., 2010; Myers, 2000). So you don't have to be a rich, physically attractive high achiever to be happy, and it turns out that most people in Western cultures are relatively happy (Diener & Diener, 1995; Gow et al., 2005; Stone et al., 2010).

These results are consistent with the views expressed over many centuries by philosophers, psychologists, and wise people in all cultures (Ekman et al., 2005). As discussed in the personality chapter, for example, Abraham Maslow (1970) noted that when people in Western cultures experience unhappiness and psychological problems, those problems can often be traced to a *deficiency orientation*. He said that these people seek happiness by trying to acquire the goods and reach the status they don't currently have—but think they need—rather than by appreciating life itself and the material and nonmaterial riches they already have. Others have amplified this point, suggesting that efforts to get more of the things we think will bring happiness may actually contribute to unhappiness if what we get is never "enough" (Diener & Seligman, 2004; Luthar & Latendresse, 2005; Nickerson et al., 2003; Quoidbach et al., 2010). Indeed, the old saying that "life is a journey, not a destination" suggests that we are more likely to find happiness by experiencing full engagement in what we are doing rather than by focusing on what we are or are not *getting*.

Relations and Conflicts Among Motives

Maslow's ideas about deficiency motivation were part of his more general view of human behavior as reflecting a hierarchy of needs, or motives (see Figure 11.6). Needs at the lowest level of the hierarchy, he said, must be at least partially satisfied before people can be motivated by higher-level goals. From the bottom to the top of Maslow's hierarchy, these five needs are as follows:

1. *Physiological,* such as the need for food, water, oxygen, and sleep.
2. *Safety,* such as the need to be cared for as a child and have a secure income as an adult.
3. *Belongingness and love,* such as the need to be part of groups and to participate in affectionate sexual and nonsexual relationships.
4. *Esteem,* such as the need to be respected as a useful, honorable individual.
5. *Self-actualization,* which means reaching one's fullest potential. People motivated by this need explore and enhance relationships with others; follow interests for intrinsic pleasure rather than for money, status, or esteem; and are concerned with issues affecting all people, not just themselves.

FIGURE 11.6
Maslow's Hierarchy of Needs

TRY THIS Abraham Maslow (1970) saw human needs or motives as organized in a hierarchy in which those at lower levels take precedence over those at higher levels. According to this view, self-actualization is the essence of mental health, but Maslow recognized that only rare individuals, such as Mother Teresa or Martin Luther King Jr., approach full self-actualization. Take a moment to consider which level of Maslow's hierarchy you are focused on at this point in your life. Which level do you ultimately hope to reach?

Source: Adapted from Maslow (1943).

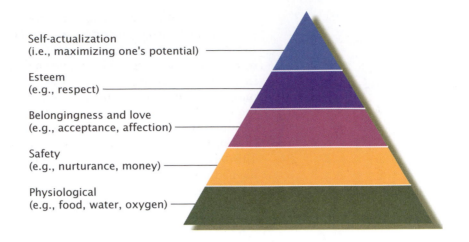

Self-actualization
(i.e., maximizing one's potential)

Esteem
(e.g., respect)

Belongingness and love
(e.g., acceptance, affection)

Safety
(e.g., nurturance, money)

Physiological
(e.g., food, water, oxygen)

Maslow's hierarchy has been very influential over the years, partly because the needs associated with basic survival and security do generally take precedence over those related to self-enhancement or personal growth (Baumeister & Leary, 1995). But critics see the hierarchy as far too simplistic (Hall, Lindzey, & Campbell, 1998; Neher, 1991). It does not predict or explain, for example, the motivation of people who starve themselves to death to draw attention to political or moral causes. Further, people may not have to satisfy one kind of need before addressing others; we can seek several needs at once. Finally, the ordering of needs within the survival and security category and the enhancement and growth category differs from culture to culture, suggesting that there may not be a single, universal hierarchy of needs.

To address some of the problems in Maslow's theory, Clayton Alderfer (1969) proposed *existence, relatedness, and growth theory* (*ERG theory*), which places human needs into just three categories: *existence needs* (such as for food and water), *relatedness needs* (e.g., for social interactions and attachments), and *growth needs* (such as for developing one's capabilities). Unlike Maslow, Alderfer doesn't assume that these needs must be satisfied in a particular order. Instead, he sees needs in each category as rising and falling from time to time and from situation to situation. When a need in one area is fulfilled, or even if it is frustrated, a person will be motivated to pursue some other

Choices based on Maslow's proposed hierarchy of needs are not usually this clear, nor are they always dictated strictly by that hierarchy.

© Jack Ziegler/The New Yorker Collection/www.cartoonbank.com

needs. For example, if a breakup frustrates relatedness needs, a person might focus on existence or growth needs by eating more or volunteering to work late.

More recently, Douglas Kenrick and his colleagues (2010) have proposed that Maslow's original hierarchy should be expanded and adjusted rather than discarded. They offer a revised hierarchy based on evolutionary theory in which the need for self-actualization is replaced by three others: the need to find a mate, the need to keep a mate, and the need to become a parent.

LINKAGES

LINKAGES Can motivational conflicts cause stress? (a link to Health, Stress, and Coping, p. 526)

Conflicting Motives and Stress

As in the case of hunger strikes, in which the desire to promote a cause is pitted against the desire to eat, human motives can sometimes conflict. The usual result is some degree of discomfort. For example, imagine that you are alone and bored on a Saturday night, and you think about going to the store to buy some snacks. What are your motives? Hunger might prompt you to go out, as might the prospect of increased arousal that a change of scene will provide. Even sexual motivation might be involved as you fantasize about meeting someone exciting in the snack food aisle. But safety-related motives may also kick in—is your neighborhood safe enough for you to go out alone at night? An esteem motive might come into play, too, making you hesitate to be seen on your own on a weekend night.

These are just a few motives that may shape a trivial decision. When the decision is more important, the number and strength of motivational pushes and pulls are often greater, creating far more internal conflict. Four basic types of motivational conflict have been identified (Elliot, 2008; Miller, 1959):

1. *Approach-approach conflicts.* When a person must choose only one of two desirable activities—say, going with friends to a movie or to a party—an *approach-approach conflict* exists.

2. *Avoidance-avoidance conflicts.* An *avoidance-avoidance conflict* arises when a person must pick one of two undesirable alternatives. Someone forced either to sell the family home or to declare bankruptcy faces an avoidance-avoidance conflict.

3. *Approach-avoidance conflicts.* If someone you dislike had tickets to your favorite group's sold-out concert and invited you to come along, what would you do? When a single event or activity has both attractive and unattractive features, an *approach-avoidance conflict* is created.

4. *Multiple approach-avoidance conflicts.* Suppose that you must choose between two jobs. One offers a good salary with a well-known company, but it requires long hours and relocation to a miserable climate. The other boasts advancement opportunities, fringe benefits, and a better climate but also lower pay and an unpredictable work schedule. This is an example of a *multiple approach-avoidance conflict*, in which two or more alternatives each have both positive and negative features. Such conflicts are difficult to resolve partly because it may be hard to compare the features of each option. For example, how much more money per year does it take to compensate you for living in a climate you hate?

A Stressful Conflict

TRY THIS Think back to the time when you were deciding about which college to attend or whether you could or should go to college at all. Was the decision easy and obvious, or did it create a motivational conflict? If there was a conflict, was it an approach-approach, approach-avoidance, avoidance-avoidance, or multiple approach-avoidance conflict? What factors were most important in deciding how to resolve the conflict, and what emotions and signs of stress did you experience during and after the decision-making process?

In fact, all of these conflicts can be difficult to resolve and can create significant emotional arousal and other signs of stress, a topic described in the chapter on health, stress, and coping. Most people in the midst of motivational conflicts are tense, irritable, and more vulnerable than usual to physical and psychological problems. These reactions are especially likely when none of the choices available is obviously "right," when conflicting motives have approximately equal strength, and when the final choice can have serious consequences (as in decisions about marrying, splitting up, or placing an elderly parent in a nursing home). People may take a long time to resolve these conflicts, or they may act impulsively and thoughtlessly, if only to end the discomfort of uncertainty. And even after resolving a conflict on the basis of careful thought, people may continue to experience stress responses such as worrying about whether they made the right decision or blaming themselves for bad choices. These and other consequences of conflicting motives can even lead to depression or other serious disorders.

Opponent Processes, Motivation, and Emotion

Resolving approach-avoidance conflicts is often complicated by the fact that some behaviors have more than one emotional effect, and those effects may be opposite to one another. People who ride roller coasters or skydive, for example, often say that the experience is scary but also thrilling. How do they decide whether or not to repeat these behaviors? One answer lies in the changing value of incentives and the regulation of arousal described in Richard Solomon's *opponent-process theory,* which is discussed in the chapter on learning. Opponent-process theory is based on two assumptions. The first is that any reaction to a stimulus is followed by an opposite reaction, called the *opponent process.* For example, being startled by a sudden sound is typically followed by relaxation and relief. Second, after repeated exposure to the same stimulus, the initial reaction weakens, and the opponent process becomes quicker and stronger.

Research on opponent-process theory has revealed a predictable pattern of emotional changes that helps explain some people's motivation to repeatedly engage in arousing but fearsome activities, such as skydiving. Before each of their first several jumps, people usually experience stark terror, followed by intense relief when they reach the ground. With more experience, however, the terror becomes mild anxiety, and what had been relief grows to a sense of elation that may start to appear *during* the activity (Solomon, 1980). As a result, said Solomon, some people's motivation to pursue skydiving and other "extreme sports" can become a virtual addiction. Opponent-process theory has also been used to improve our understanding of the effects of pain-relieving drugs (Leknes et al., 2008; Vargas-Perez et al., 2007).

The emotions associated with motivational conflicts and with the operation of opponent processes provide just two examples of the close ties between motivation and emotion. Motivation can intensify emotion, as when a normally calm but extremely hungry person makes an angry phone call about a late pizza delivery. But emotions can also create motivation (Brehm, Miron, & Miller, 2009). For example, most people want to feel happiness, to savor pleasant experiences, and to have other positive emotions, so they engage in whatever behaviors—studying, creating art, investing, beachcombing—they think will lead to those emotions. Similarly, as an emotion that most people want to avoid, anxiety prompts many behaviors, from leaving the scene of an accident to avoiding poisonous snakes. But sometimes, as when facing a stressful job interview or agreeing to a painful medical procedure, people are motivated to endure anxiety or other unpleasant emotions because they believe that doing so will eventually lead to a desired goal (Tamir, 2009). Let's take a closer look at emotions.

The Nature of Emotion

Everyone seems to agree that joy, sorrow, anger, fear, love, and hate are emotions, but it is hard to identify exactly what it is that makes these experiences emotions rather than, say, thoughts or impulses. In fact, some cultures see emotion and thought as the same thing. The Chewong of Malaysia, for example, consider the liver the seat of both what we call thoughts and feelings (Russell, 1991).

Defining Characteristics

Most psychologists in Western cultures see emotions as organized psychological and physiological reactions to changes in our relationship to the world. These reactions are partly private, or *subjective,* experiences and partly *objective,* measurable patterns of behavior and physiological arousal. The subjective experience of emotion has several characteristics:

1. Emotion is *usually temporary;* it tends to have a relatively clear beginning and end, as well as a relatively short duration. Moods, by contrast, tend to last longer.

2. Emotional experience can be *positive,* as in joy, or *negative,* as in sadness. It can also be a mixture of both, as in the bittersweet feelings parents experience when watching their child leave for the first day of kindergarten.

3. Emotional experience *alters thought processes,* often by directing attention toward some things and away from others. Negative emotions, such as fear, tend to narrow attention. So anxiety about terrorism, for example, might lead you to focus your attention on potential threats in airports and other public places (Nobata, Hakoda, & Ninose, 2010; Yovel & Mineka, 2005). Positive emotions tend to widen our attention, which makes it easier to take in a broader range of visual information and perhaps to think more broadly too (Fredrickson et al., 2008).

4. Emotional experience triggers an *action tendency,* the motivation to behave in certain ways. Positive emotions, such as joy, contentment, and pride, often lead to playfulness, creativity, and exploration of the environment (Cacioppo, Gardner, & Berntson, 1999; Fredrickson, 2001). These behaviors, in turn, can generate further positive emotions by creating stronger social ties, greater skill at problem solving, and the like. The result may be an "upward spiral" of positivity (Burns et al., 2008). Negative emotions, such as sadness and fear, often promote withdrawal from threatening situations, whereas anger might lead to actions aimed at revenge or constructive change. Grieving parents' anger, for example, might motivate them to harm their child's killer. But for John Walsh, whose son was kidnapped and murdered, grief led him to help prevent such crimes by creating *America's Most Wanted,* a TV show dedicated to bringing criminals to justice.

5. Emotional experiences are *passions* that you feel, usually whether you want to or not. You can exert at least some control over emotions in the sense that they depend partly on how you interpret situations (Gross, 2001). For example, your emotional reaction might be less extreme after a car accident if you remind yourself that no one was hurt and that you are insured. Still, such control is limited. You cannot *decide* to experience joy or sorrow; instead, you "fall in love" or "explode in anger" or are "overcome by grief."

In other words, the subjective aspects of emotions are both *triggered* by the thinking self and felt as *happening* to the self. They reveal each of us as both agent and object, both I and me, both the controller of thoughts and the recipient of passions. The extent to which we are "victims" of our passions versus rational designers of our

Winners and Losers

Emotional experiences depend in part on our interpretation of situations and how those situations relate to our goals. A single event—the announcement of the results of this wrestling match—triggered drastically different emotional reactions in the contestants, depending on whether it made them the winner or the loser. Similarly, an exam score of 75 percent may thrill you if your best previous score had been 50 percent, but it may upset you if you had never before scored below 90 percent.

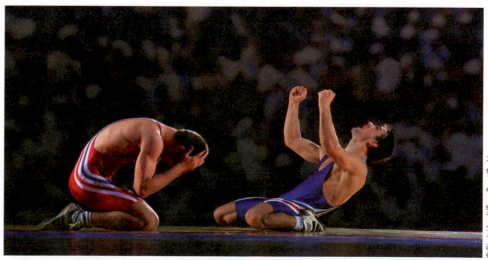

© Dimitri Iundt/TempSport/Corbis

emotions is a central dilemma of human existence, as much a subject of philosophy and literature as of psychology.

The *objective* aspects of emotion include learned and innate *expressive displays* and *physiological responses*. Expressive displays—such as a smile or a frown—communicate feelings to others. Physiological responses—such as changes in heart rate—are the biological adjustments needed to perform the action tendencies generated by emotional experience. If you throw a temper tantrum or jump for joy, your heart must deliver additional oxygen and fuel to your muscles.

In summary, **emotions** are temporary experiences with either positive, negative, or mixed qualities. People experience emotion with varying intensity, as happening to them, as generated in part by a mental assessment of situations, and accompanied by both learned and innate physical responses. Through emotion, whether they mean to or not, people communicate their internal states and intentions to others. Emotion often disrupts thinking and behavior, but it also triggers and guides thinking and organizes, motivates, and sustains behavior and social relations (Izard, 2007).

The Biology of Emotion

The role of biology in emotion can be seen in mechanisms of the central nervous system and the autonomic nervous system. In the *central nervous system,* several brain areas are involved in the generation of emotions, as well as in our experience of those emotions (Barrett & Wager, 2006). The *autonomic nervous system* gives rise to many of the physiological changes associated with emotional arousal.

Brain Mechanisms   Although many questions remain, researchers have described three main aspects of how emotion is processed in the brain. First, it appears that activity in the *limbic system,* especially in the amygdala, is central to emotion (Kensinger &

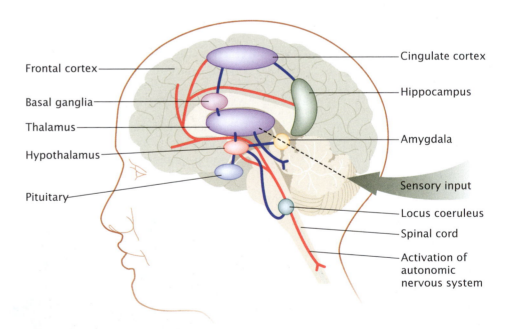

FIGURE 11.7
Brain Regions Involved in Emotions
Incoming sensory information alerts the brain to an emotion-evoking situation. Most of the information goes through the thalamus. The cingulate cortex and hippocampus are involved in the interpretation of this sensory input. Output from these areas goes to the amygdala and hypothalamus, which control the autonomic nervous system via brainstem connections. There are also connections from the thalamus directly to the amygdala. The locus coeruleus is an area of the brainstem that causes both widespread arousal of cortical areas and changes in autonomic activity.

emotions Transitory positive or negative experiences that are felt as happening to the self, are generated in part by cognitive appraisal of a situation, and are accompanied by both learned and innate physical responses.

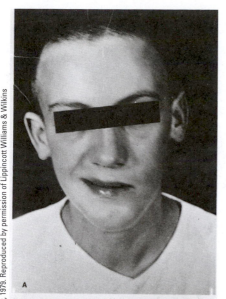

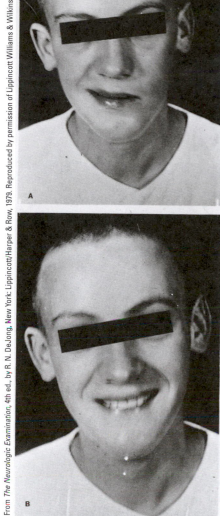

FIGURE 11.8
Control of Voluntary and Emotional Facial Movements

This man has a tumor in his motor cortex that prevents him from voluntarily moving the muscles on the left side of his face. In the photograph at the top, he is trying to smile in response to instructions from the examiner. He cannot smile on command, but as shown in the photo at the bottom, he can smile with happiness, because involuntary movements associated with genuine emotion are controlled by the extrapyramidal motor system.

Corkin, 2004; Phelps & LeDoux, 2005; see Figure 11.7). Normal functioning in the amygdala appears critical to learning emotional associations, recognizing emotional expressions, and perceiving emotionally charged words (e.g., Anderson & Phelps, 2001; Suslow et al., 2006). In one brain-imaging study, when researchers paired an uncomfortably loud noise with pictures of faces, the participants' brains showed activation of the amygdala while the noise-picture association was being learned (LaBar et al., 1998). In another study, victims of a disease that destroys only the amygdala were found to be unable to judge other people's emotional states by looking at their faces (Adolphs et al., 1994). Faces that normal people rated as expressing strong negative emotions were rated by the amygdala-damaged individuals as approachable and trustworthy (Adolphs, Tranel, & Damasio, 1998).

A second aspect of the brain's involvement in emotion is its control over emotional and nonemotional facial expressions. **TRY THIS** Take a moment to look in a mirror and put on your best fake smile. The voluntary facial movements you just made, like all voluntary movements, are controlled by the *pyramidal motor system,* a brain system that includes the motor cortex (see Figures 3.15 and 3.16 in the chapter on biological aspects of psychology). However, a smile that expresses genuine happiness is involuntary. That kind of smile, like the other facial movements associated with emotions, is governed by the *extrapyramidal motor system,* which depends on areas beneath the cortex. Brain damage can disrupt either system (see Figure 11.8). People with pyramidal motor system damage show normal facial expressions during genuine emotion, but they cannot fake a smile. In contrast, people with damage to the extrapyramidal system can pose facial expressions at will, but they remain expressionless even when feeling joy or sadness (Hopf, Muller, & Hopf, 1992).

A third aspect of the brain's role in emotion is revealed by research on the cerebral cortex and particularly on differences in the activity of its two hemispheres in relation to emotional experience. For example, after suffering damage to the right but not the left hemisphere, people no longer laugh at jokes, even though they can still understand the jokes' words, their logic (or illogic), and their punch lines (Critchley, 1991). Brain-imaging studies of sports fans watching their favorite team in action have revealed greater activation in the left hemisphere when their team is ahead and more activation in the right hemisphere when their team is behind (Park et al., 2009). And there is evidence that the experience of anger and depression is associated with greater brain activity on the right side than on the left (Carver & Harmon-Jones, 2009; Herrington et al., 2010).

So the brain's two hemispheres appear to make somewhat different contributions to the perception, experience, and expression of emotion (Davidson, 2000; Davidson, Shackman, & Maxwell, 2004). Further, different brain areas can be involved in displaying and experiencing positive and negative emotions (Harmon-Jones, 2004; Harmon-Jones & Sigelman, 2001; Heller, 1993). As a result, it is extremely challenging for neuroscientists to map the brain's role in emotion (Bourne, 2010; Root, Wong, & Kinsbourne, 2006; Vingerhoets, Berckmoes, & Stroobant, 2003).

Mechanisms of the Autonomic Nervous System The autonomic nervous system (ANS) is involved in many of the physiological changes that accompany emotions (see Figure 11.9). If your hands get cold and clammy when you are nervous, it is because the ANS has increased perspiration and decreased the blood flow in your hands.

As described in the chapter on biological aspects of psychology, the ANS carries information between the brain and most organs of the body—the heart and blood vessels, the digestive system, and so on. Each of these organs has its own ongoing activity, but ANS input increases or decreases this activity. By doing so, the ANS coordinates the functioning of these organs to meet the body's general needs and to prepare it for change. If you are aroused to take action—to run to catch a bus, say—you need more glucose to fuel your muscles. The ANS frees needed energy by stimulating secretion of glucose-generating hormones and promoting blood flow to the muscles.

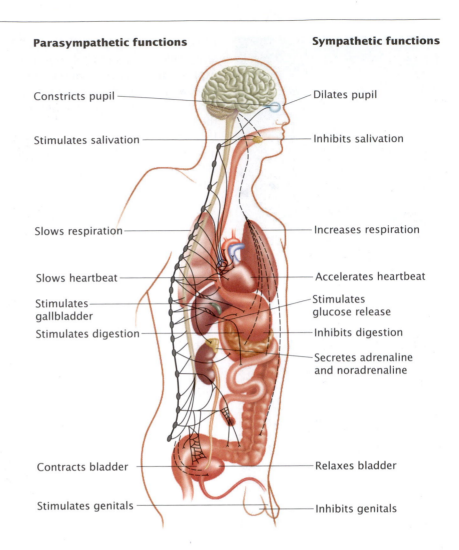

Parasympathetic functions | Sympathetic functions

Constricts pupil — Dilates pupil
Stimulates salivation — Inhibits salivation
Slows respiration — Increases respiration
Slows heartbeat — Accelerates heartbeat
Stimulates gallbladder — Stimulates glucose release
Stimulates digestion — Inhibits digestion
— Secretes adrenaline and noradrenaline
Contracts bladder — Relaxes bladder
Stimulates genitals — Inhibits genitals

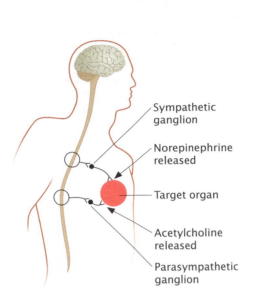

Sympathetic ganglion

Norepinephrine released

Target organ

Acetylcholine released

Parasympathetic ganglion

FIGURE 11.9
The Autonomic Nervous System

TRY THIS Emotional responses involve activation of the autonomic nervous system, which includes sympathetic and parasympathetic subsystems. Look at the bodily responses depicted here, and make a list of the ones that you associate with emotional experiences.

---

sympathetic nervous system The subsystem of the autonomic nervous system that usually prepares the organism for vigorous activity.

parasympathetic nervous system The subsystem of the autonomic nervous system that typically influences activity related to the protection, nourishment, and growth of the body.

fight-flight reaction (fight-or-flight syndrome) The physical reaction initiated by the sympathetic nervous system that prepares the body to fight or to run from a threatening situation.

As shown in Figure 11.9, the autonomic nervous system is organized into two divisions: the **sympathetic nervous system** and the **parasympathetic nervous system.** Emotions can activate either of these divisions, both of which send axon fibers to each organ in the body. Generally, the sympathetic and parasympathetic fibers have opposite effects on these *target organs.* Axons from the parasympathetic system release *acetylcholine* onto target organs, leading to activity related to the protection, nourishment, and growth of the body. For example, parasympathetic activity increases digestion by stimulating movement of the intestinal system so that more nutrients are taken from food. Axons from the sympathetic system release a different neurotransmitter, *norepinephrine,* onto target organs, helping prepare the body for vigorous activity. When one part of the sympathetic system is stimulated, other parts are activated "in sympathy" with it. For example, input from sympathetic neurons to the adrenal medulla causes that gland to release norepinephrine and epinephrine into the bloodstream, thereby activating all sympathetic target organs (see Figure 13.3 in the health, stress, and coping chapter). The result is the **fight-flight reaction** (also called the **fight-or-flight syndrome**), a pattern of increased heart rate and blood pressure, rapid or irregular breathing, dilated pupils, perspiration, dry mouth, increased blood sugar, piloerection ("goose bumps"), and other changes that help prepare the body to combat or run from a threat.

The ANS is not directly connected to brain areas involved in consciousness, so sensations about organ activity reach the brain at a nonconscious level. You may hear your stomach grumble, but you can't actually feel it secrete acids. Similarly, you can't consciously experience the brain mechanisms that alter the activity of your autonomic nervous system. This is why most people don't have direct, conscious control over blood pressure or other aspects of ANS activity. However, there are things you can do to indirectly affect the ANS. For example, to create autonomic stimulation of your sex organs, you might imagine an erotic situation. To raise your blood pressure, you might hold your breath or strain your muscles; to lower it, you can lie down, relax, and think calming thoughts or engage in various forms of meditation (Greeson, 2009; see the chapter on consciousness).

Theories of Emotion

How does activity in the brain and the autonomic nervous system relate to the emotions we experience? Are autonomic responses to events enough to *create* the experience of emotion, or are those responses the *result* of emotional experiences that begin in the brain? And how are emotional reactions affected by the way we think about events? For over a century, psychologists have searched for the answers to these questions. In the process, they have developed a number of theories that explain emotion primarily in terms of biological or cognitive factors. The main biological theories are those of William James and Walter Cannon. The most prominent cognitive theories are those of Stanley Schachter and Richard Lazarus. In this section, we review these theories, along with some research designed to evaluate them.

James's Peripheral Theory

Suppose that you are camping in the woods when a huge bear approaches your tent. You would probably be afraid and run away. But would you run because you are afraid, or would you be afraid because you ran? The example and the question come from William James, who in the late 1800s offered one of the first formal accounts of how physiological responses relate to emotional experience. James argued that you are afraid because you run. Your running and the physiological responses associated with it, he said, follow directly from your perception of the bear. Without these physiological responses, you would feel no fear, because, said James, recognition of physiological responses *is* fear. Because James saw activity in the peripheral nervous system as the cause of emotional experience, his theory is known as a *peripheral theory* of emotion.

At first, James's theory might seem ridiculous; it doesn't make sense to run from something unless you already fear it. James (1890) concluded otherwise after examining his own mental processes. He decided that once you strip away all physiological responses, nothing remains of the experience of an emotion. Emotion, he reasoned, must therefore be the result of experiencing a particular set of physiological responses. A similar argument was offered by Carl Lange (pronounced "LAHN-guh"), a Danish physician, so James's view is sometimes called the *James-Lange theory* of emotion.

Observing Peripheral Responses   Figure 11.10 outlines the components of emotional experience, including those emphasized by James. First, a perception affects the cerebral cortex, said James; "then quick as a flash, reflex currents pass down through their pre-ordained channels, alter the condition of muscle, skin, and viscus; and these alterations, perceived, like the original object, in as many portions of the cortex, combine with it in consciousness and transform it from an object-simply-apprehended into an object-emotionally-felt" (James, 1890, p. 759). In other words, the brain interprets a situation and automatically directs a particular set of peripheral physiological changes—a racing heart, sinking stomach, facial grimace, perspiration, and certain patterns of blood flow. We are not conscious of the process, said James, until we become aware of these bodily changes; at that point, we experience an emotion. One implication of this view is that each particular emotion is created by a particular pattern of physiological responses. For example, fear would follow from one pattern of bodily responses, and anger would follow from a different pattern.

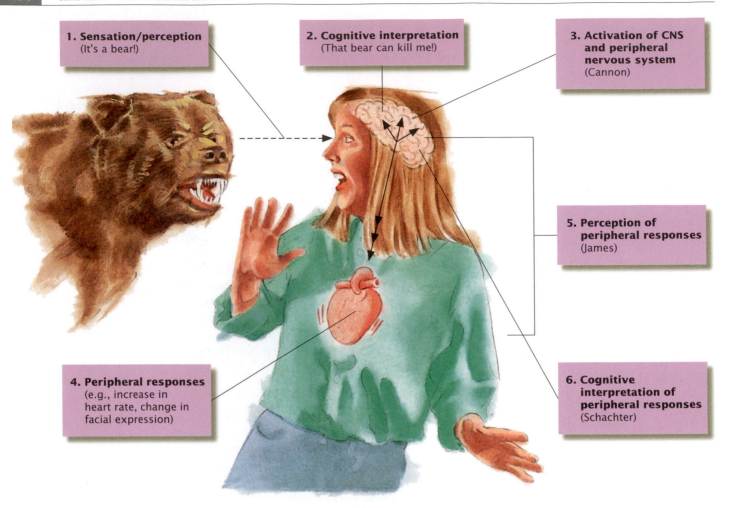

1. **Sensation/perception**
(It's a bear!)

2. **Cognitive interpretation**
(That bear can kill me!)

3. **Activation of CNS and peripheral nervous system**
(Cannon)

5. **Perception of peripheral responses**
(James)

4. **Peripheral responses**
(e.g., increase in heart rate, change in facial expression)

6. **Cognitive interpretation of peripheral responses**
(Schachter)

FIGURE 11.10

Components of Emotion

Emotion is associated with activity in the central nervous system (the brain and spinal cord), as well as with responses elsewhere in the body (called *peripheral* responses), and with cognitive interpretations of events. Emotion theorists have differed about which of these components is essential for emotion. William James focused on the perception of peripheral responses, such as changes in heart rate. Walter Cannon said that emotion could occur entirely within the brain. Stanley Schachter emphasized cognitive factors, including how we interpret events and how we label our peripheral responses to them.

Notice that according to James's view, emotional experience is not generated by activity in the brain alone. There is no special "emotion center" in the brain where the firing of neurons creates a direct experience of emotion. If this theory is accurate, it might account for the difficulty we sometimes have in knowing our true feelings: We must figure out what emotions we feel by perceiving slight differences in specific physiological response patterns (Katkin, Wiens, & Öhman, 2001).

Evaluating James's Theory The English language includes more than five hundred labels for emotions (Averill, 1980). Does a different pattern of physiological activity precede each of these specific emotions? Probably not, but research shows that certain emotional states are indeed associated with certain patterns of autonomic activity (Christie & Friedman, 2004; Craig, 2002; Damasio et al., 2000). For example, blood flow to the hands and feet increases in association with anger and declines in association with fear (Levenson, Ekman, & Friesen, 1990). So fear involves "cold feet"; anger does not. A pattern of activity associated with disgust includes increased muscle activity but no change in heart rate. Even when people mentally relive different kinds of emotional experiences, they show patterns of autonomic activity associated with those emotions (Ekman, Levenson, & Friesen, 1983). These emotion-specific patterns of physiological activity have been found in widely different cultures (Levenson et al., 1992). Further, people who are keenly aware of physiological changes in their bodies are likely to experience emotions more intensely than those who are less aware of such changes (Wiens, Mezzacappa, & Katkin, 2000). It has even been suggested that the "gut feelings" that cause us to approach or avoid certain situations might be the result of physiological changes that are perceived without conscious awareness

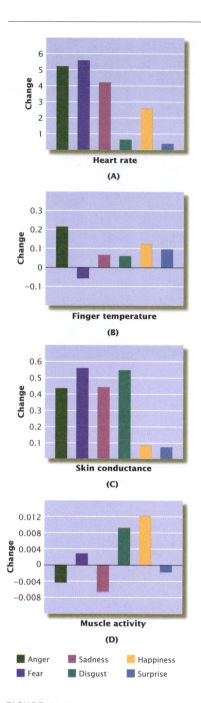

FIGURE 11.11
Physiological Changes Associated with Different Emotions

In this experiment, facial movements characteristic of different emotions produced different patterns of change in (A) heart rate; (B) peripheral blood flow, as measured by finger temperature; (C) skin conductance; and (D) muscle activity (Levenson, Ekman, & Friesen, 1990). For example, making an angry face caused heart rate and finger temperature to rise, whereas making a fearful face raised heart rate but lowered finger temperature.

Source: Levenson, Ekman, & Friesen (1990).

(Bechara et al., 1997; Damasio, 1994; Katkin, Wiens, & Öhman, 2001; Winkielman & Berridge, 2004).

Different patterns of autonomic activity are closely tied to specific emotional facial expressions. In one study, when participants were asked to make certain facial movements, autonomic changes occurred that resembled those normally accompanying emotion (Ekman, Levenson, & Friesen, 1983; see Figure 11.11). Almost all these participants also reported *feeling the emotion*—such as fear, anger, disgust, sadness, or happiness—associated with the expression they had created, even though they could not see their own expressions and did not realize that they had portrayed a specific emotion. Other studies have confirmed that people feel emotions such as anger or sadness when simply making an "angry" or "sad" face (Schnall & Laird, 2003) and that they can ease these feelings just by relaxing their faces (Duclos & Laird, 2001).

TRY THIS To get an idea of how facial expressions can alter, as well as express, emotion, look at a photograph of someone whose face is expressing a strong emotion and try your best to imitate it. Did this create in you the same feelings that the other person appears to be experiencing? The emotional effects of this kind of "face making" appear strongest in people who are the most sensitive to internal bodily cues. When such people pose facial expressions, the emotions created can be significant enough to affect their social judgments. Research participants who were asked to smile, for example, tended to form more positive impressions of other people than did those who received no special instructions (Ohira & Kurono, 1993).

James's theory implies that the experience of emotion would be blocked if a person were unable to detect physiological changes occurring in the body's periphery. So spinal cord injuries that reduce feedback from peripheral responses should reduce the intensity of emotional experiences. Indeed, some people with such injuries have reported reductions in the intensity of their emotions, especially if the injuries are at higher points in the spinal cord, which cuts off feedback from more areas of the body (Hohmann, 1966). Brain-imaging studies, too, show differences in the processing of emotional stimuli by people with spinal cord injuries (Nicotra et al., 2006). However, most studies show that when people with spinal injuries continue to pursue their life goals, they experience a full range of emotions, including as much happiness as noninjured people (e.g., Bermond et al., 1991; Cobos et al., 2004). These people report that their emotional experiences are just as intense as before their injuries, even though they notice less intense physiological changes associated with their emotions.

Such reports seem to contradict James's theory. But spinal cord injuries do not usually affect facial expressions, which James included among the bodily responses that are experienced as emotions. A variant of James's theory, the *facial feedback hypothesis,* suggests that involuntary facial movements provide enough peripheral information to create emotional experience (Ekman & Davidson, 1993). This hypothesis helps explain why posed facial expressions generate the emotions normally associated with them. So the next time you want to cheer yourself up, it might help to smile—even though you don't feel like it (Fleeson, Malanos, & Achille, 2002)!

Lie Detection James's view that different patterns of physiological activity are associated with different emotions forms the basis for the lie detection industry. If people experience anxiety or guilt when they lie, specific patterns of physiological activity accompanying these emotions should be detectable on instruments, called *polygraphs,* that record heart rate, breathing, perspiration, and other autonomic responses (Granhag & Stromwall, 2004; Iacono & Patrick, 2006).

To examine a criminal suspect using the *control question test,* a polygraph operator would ask questions specific to the crime, such as "Did you stab anyone on November 6, 2010?" Responses to such *relevant questions* are then compared with responses to *control questions,* such as "Have you ever lied to get out of trouble?" Innocent people may have lied at some time in the past and might feel guilty when asked about it, but they should have no reason to feel guilty about what they did on

Searching for the Truth

On the TV show *Lie to Me,* Dr. Cal Lightman is portrayed as a virtually infallible human lie detector (Conkle, 2009). His abilities to detect and correctly interpret facial "microexpressions" are exaggerated, though, and polygraph tests are not foolproof either. Polygraphs may nevertheless intimidate people who believe in their power. In one small town where the police department could not afford a polygraph, a suspect confessed his crime when a "lie detector" consisting of a kitchen colander was placed on his head and attached by wires to a copy machine (Shepherd, Kohut, & Sweet, 1989).

© David Strick/Redux

November 6, 2010. So an innocent person should have a stronger emotional response to control questions than to relevant questions (Rosenfeld, 1995). Another approach, called the *directed lie test,* compares a person's physiological reactions when asked to lie about something and when telling what is known to be the truth. Finally, the *guilty knowledge test* seeks to determine if a person reacts in a notable way to information about a crime that only the criminal would know (Ben-Shakhar, Bar-Hillel, & Kremnitzer, 2002).

Most people do have emotional responses when they lie, but statistics about the accuracy of polygraphs are difficult to obtain. Estimates vary widely, from those suggesting that polygraphs detect 90 percent of guilty, lying individuals (Gamer et al., 2006; Honts & Quick, 1995; Kircher, Horowitz, & Raskin, 1988; Raskin, 1986) to those suggesting that polygraphs mislabel as many as 40 percent of truthful, innocent people as guilty liars (Ben-Shakhar & Furedy, 1990; Saxe & Ben-Shakhar, 1999). Obviously, the results of a polygraph test are not determined entirely by whether a person is telling the truth. What people think about the act of lying and about the value of the test can also influence the accuracy of its results. For example, people who consider lying acceptable—and who do not believe in the power of polygraphs—are unlikely to display emotion-related physiological responses while lying during the test. However, an innocent person who believes in such tests and who thinks that "everything always goes wrong" might show a large fear response when asked about a crime, thus wrongly suggesting guilt (Lykken, 1998b).

Polygraphs can catch some liars, but most researchers agree that a guilty person can "fool" a polygraph and that some innocent people can be mislabeled as guilty (Ruscio, 2005). After reviewing the relevant research literature, a panel of distinguished psychologists and other scientists in the United States expressed serious reservations about the value of polygraph tests in detecting deception and argued against their use as evidence in court or in employee screening and selection (Committee to Review the Scientific Evidence on the Polygraph, 2003). Scientists are now working on other lie-detecting techniques that focus on brain activity, brief facial "microexpressions," and other measures that do not depend on a link between deception and autonomic nervous system responses (Bhatt et al., 2009; Ekman, 2001, 2009; Gronau, Ben-Shakhar, & Cohen, 2005; Kozel, Padgett, & George, 2004; Langleben et al., 2005; Lee et al., 2009).

Cannon's Central Theory

James said the experience of emotion depends on feedback from physiological responses occurring outside the brain, but Walter Cannon disagreed. According to Cannon (1927), you feel fear at the sight of a wild bear even before you start to run. He said that emotional experience starts in the central nervous system—specifically, in the thalamus, the brain structure that relays information from most sense organs to the cortex.

According to Cannon's *central theory* (also known as the *Cannon-Bard theory*, in recognition of Philip Bard's contribution), when the thalamus receives sensory information about emotional events and situations, it sends signals to the autonomic nervous system and—at the same time—to the cerebral cortex, where the emotion becomes conscious. So when you see a bear, the brain receives sensory information about it, perceives it as a bear, and *directly* creates the experience of fear while at the same time sending messages to the heart, lungs, and muscles to do what it takes to run away. In other words, Cannon said that the experience of emotion appears directly in the brain, with or without feedback from peripheral responses (see Figure 11.10).

Updating Cannon's Theory   Research conducted since Cannon proposed his theory indicates that the thalamus is actually not the "seat" of emotion but that through its connections to the amygdala (see Figure 11.7), the thalamus does participate in some aspects of emotional processing (Lang, 1995). For example, studies in laboratory animals and humans show that the emotion of fear is generated by connections from the thalamus to the amygdala (Anderson & Phelps, 2000; LeDoux, 1995). The implication is that strong emotions can sometimes bypass the cortex without requiring conscious thought to activate them (Feinstein, Duff, & Tranel, 2010). One study showed, for example, that people presented with stimuli such as angry faces display physiological signs of arousal even if they are not conscious of seeing those stimuli (Morris et al., 1998). The same processes might explain why people find it so difficult to overcome an intense fear, or phobia, even though they may consciously know the fear is irrational.

An updated version of Cannon's theory suggests that in humans and other animals, activity in specific brain areas is experienced as either enjoyable or aversive and produces the feelings of pleasure or discomfort associated with emotion. In humans, these areas have extensive connections throughout the brain (Fossati et al., 2003). As a result, the representation of emotions in the brain probably involves activity in widely distributed neural circuits, not just in a narrowly localized emotion "center" (Derryberry & Tucker, 1992). Still, there is evidence to support the main thrust of Cannon's theory: that emotion occurs through the activation of specific circuits in the central nervous system. What Cannon did not foresee is that different parts of the central nervous system may be activated for different emotions and for different aspects of the total emotional experience.

Cognitive Theories of Emotion

Suppose that you are about to be interviewed for your first job or go out on a blind date or take your first ride in a hot-air balloon. In situations such as these, it is not always easy to know exactly what you are feeling. Is it fear, excitement, anticipation, worry, happiness, dread, or what? Stanley Schachter suggested that the emotions we experience every day are shaped partly by how we interpret the arousal we feel. His cognitive theory of emotion, known as the *Schachter-Singer theory* in recognition of the contributions of Jerome Singer, took shape in the early 1960s, when many psychologists were raising questions about the validity of James's theory of emotion. Schachter argued that the theory was essentially correct—but required a few modifications (Cornelius, 1996).

In Schachter's view, feedback about physiological changes may not vary enough to create the many shades of emotion that people can experience. He argued instead that emotions emerge from a combination of feedback from peripheral responses and our *cognitive interpretation* of the nature and cause of those responses (Schachter & Singer, 1962). Cognitive interpretation first comes into play, said Schachter, when you perceive the stimulus that leads to bodily responses ("It's a bear!"). Interpretation occurs again when you identify feedback from those responses as a particular emotion (see Figure 11.10). The same physiological responses might be given many different labels, depending on how you interpret those responses. So, according to Schachter, when that bear approaches your campsite, the emotion you experience might be fear, excitement, astonishment, or surprise, depending on how you label your bodily reactions.

Schachter also said that the labeling of arousal depends on **attribution,** the process of identifying the cause of an event. Physiological arousal might be attributed to one of several emotions, depending on the information available about the situation. If you are watching the final seconds of a close basketball game, you might attribute your racing heart, rapid breathing, and perspiration to excitement. You might attribute the same physiological reactions to anxiety if you are waiting for a big exam to begin. Schachter predicted that our emotional experiences will be less intense if we attribute arousal to a nonemotional cause. So if you notice your heart pounding before an exam but say to yourself, "Sure my heart's racing—I just drank five cups of coffee!" then you should feel "wired" from caffeine rather than afraid or worried. This prediction has received some support (Mezzacappa, Katkin, & Palmer, 1999; Sinclair et al., 1994), but other aspects of Schachter's theory have not.

The Schachter-Singer theory stimulated an enormous amount of valuable research, including studies of **excitation transfer theory.** This theory focuses on a phenomenon in which physiological arousal from one experience carries over to affect emotion in an independent situation (Reisenzein, 1983; Zillmann, 1998). For example, people who have been aroused by physical exercise become more angry when provoked or experience more intense sexual feelings when in the company of an attractive person than people who have been less physically active (Allen, Kenrick, et al., 1989). Arousal from fear, like arousal from exercise, can also enhance emotions, including sexual feelings. One study of this transfer took place in Canada, near a deep river gorge. The gorge could be crossed either by a shaky swinging bridge or by a more stable wooden one. A female researcher asked men who had just crossed each bridge to respond to a questionnaire that included pictures from the TAT, the projective test described in Figure 11.5. The amount of sexual content in the stories these men wrote about the pictures was much higher among those who met the woman after crossing the more dangerous bridge than among those who had crossed the stable bridge. Furthermore, they were more likely to rate the researcher as attractive and to attempt to contact her afterward (Dutton & Aron, 1974).When the person giving out the questionnaire was a male, however, the type of bridge crossed had no effect on sexual imagery. To test the possibility that the men who crossed the dangerous bridge were simply more adventurous in both bridge crossing and heterosexual encounters, the researcher repeated the study, but with one change. This time, the woman approached the men farther down the trail, long after arousal from the bridge crossing had subsided. Now the apparently adventurous men were no more likely than others to rate the woman as attractive. So it was probably excitation transfer, not just differing amounts of adventurousness, that produced the original result.

Schachter focused on the cognitive interpretation of our bodily responses to events, but other theorists have argued that it is our cognitive interpretation of *events themselves* that are most important in shaping emotional experiences. For example, as we mentioned earlier, a person's emotional reaction to receiving exam results can depend partly whether the score is seen as a sign of improvement or a grade worthy of shame. According to Richard Lazarus's *cognitive appraisal theory* of emotion, these differing reactions can be best explained by how we think exam scores, job interviews, blind dates, bear sightings, and other events will affect our personal well-being. According to Lazarus (1966, 1991), the process of cognitive appraisal, or evaluation, begins when we decide whether or not an event is relevant to our well-being. That is, do we even care about it? If we don't, as might be the case if an exam doesn't count toward our grade, we are unlikely to have an emotional experience when we get the

attribution The process of explaining the causes of an event.

excitation transfer theory The theory that physiological arousal stemming from one situation is carried over to and enhances emotional experience in an independent situation.

Labeling Arousal

Schachter's cognitive theory of emotion predicts that these people will attribute their physiological arousal to the game they are watching and will label their emotion "excitement." Further, as described in the chapter on health, stress, and coping, the emotions they experience will also depend partly on their cognitive interpretation of the outcome (Lazarus & Folkman, 1984). If their team loses, those who see the defeat as a disaster will experience more negative emotions than those who think of it as a challenge to improve.

© Hans Lippert/UPPA/Photoshot

results. If the event is relevant to our well-being, we will experience an emotional reaction to it. That reaction will be positive or negative, said Lazarus, depending on whether we see the event as advancing our personal goals or obstructing them. The specific emotion we experience depends on our individual goals, needs, standards, expectations, and past experiences. As a result, a particular exam score can create contentment in one person, elation in another, mild disappointment in a third person, and despair in someone else. Individual differences in goals and standards are at work, too, when a second-place finisher in a marathon experiences bitter disappointment at having "lost," while someone at the back of the pack may be thrilled just to have completed the race (Larsen et al., 2004).

More recently, researchers have developed cognitive theories of emotion that depart from Schachter's in some new directions. In the *conceptual act model* of emotion, for instance, core affect—pleasant or unpleasant feelings—is distinguished from emotion. According to this model, emotion results when we attach to our feelings a category label—such as guilt, shame, anger, or resentment—that our cultural and language training has taught us to use (Barrett et al., 2007). Models like this one are valuable because they incorporate research on language and culture into efforts to better understand the labeling processes involved in human emotional experience.

"In Review: Theories of Emotion" summarizes key elements of the theories we have discussed. Research on these theories suggests that both peripheral autonomic responses (including facial responses) and the cognitive interpretation of those responses add to emotional experience. So does cognitive appraisal of events themselves. In addition, the brain can apparently generate emotional experience on its own, independent of physiological arousal. In short, emotion is probably both in the heart and in the head (including the face). The most basic emotions probably occur directly within the brain, whereas the many shades of emotions probably arise from attributions, categorization, and other cognitive interpretations of physiological responses and environmental events (Barrett et al., 2007). No theory has completely resolved the issue of which component of emotion, if any, is primary. However, the theories we have discussed have helped psychologists better understand how these components interact to produce emotional experience. Cognitive appraisal theories, in particular, have been especially useful in studying and treating stress-related emotional problems (see the chapters on health, stress, and coping; psychological disorders; and treatment of psychological disorders).

IN REVIEW Theories of Emotion		
Theory	**Source of Emotions**	**Example**
James-Lange	Emotions are created by awareness of specific patterns of peripheral (autonomic) responses.	Anger is associated with increased blood flow in the hands and feet; fear is associated with decreased blood flow in these areas.
Cannon-Bard	The brain generates direct experiences of emotion.	Stimulation of certain brain areas can create pleasant or unpleasant emotions.
Cognitive (Schachter-Singer; Lazarus)	Cognitive interpretation of events and of physiological reactions to them shapes emotional experiences.	Autonomic arousal can be experienced as anxiety or excitement, depending on how it is labeled. A single event can lead to different emotions, depending on whether it is perceived as threatening or challenging.

1. Research showing that there are pleasure centers in the brain has been cited in support of the _____ theory of emotions.
2. The use of polygraphs in lie detection is based on the _____ theory of emotions.
3. The process of attribution is most important to _____ theories of emotions.

Communicating Emotion

So far, we have described emotion from the inside, as people experience their own emotions. Let's now consider how people communicate emotions to one another. One way they do this is through words. Some people describe their feelings relatively simply, mainly in terms of pleasantness or unpleasantness. Others include information about the intensity of their emotions (Barrett, 1995; Barrett et al., 2001). In general, women are more likely than men to talk about their emotions and the complexity of their feelings (Barrett et al., 2000; Kring & Gordon, 1998). Humans also communicate emotion through the movement and posture of their bodies (de Gelder et al., 2004; Hadjikhani & de Gelder, 2003), through their tone of voice (Simon-Thomas et al., 2009), and especially through their facial movements and expressions.

Imagine a woman watching television. You can see her face but not what she sees on the screen. She might be engaged in complex thought, perhaps comparing her investments with those of the experts on a business channel. Or she might be thinking of nothing at all as she loses herself in a rerun of *The Beverly Hillbillies*. In other words, you won't be able to tell much about what the woman is thinking. But if the TV program creates an emotional experience, you will be able to make a reasonably accurate guess about what she is feeling simply by looking at the expression on her face. The human face can create thousands of different expressions, and people—especially females—are good at detecting them (McClure, 2000; Zajonc, 1998). Observers can notice even tiny facial movements—a twitch of the mouth or eyebrow can carry a lot of information (Ambadar, Schooler, & Cohn, 2005; Ekman, 2009). Are emotional facial expressions innate, or are they learned? And how are they used in communicating emotion?

Innate Expressions of Emotion

Charles Darwin (1872) observed that some facial expressions seem to be universal. He proposed that these expressions are genetically determined, passed on biologically from one generation to the next. The facial expressions seen today, said Darwin, are those that have been most effective at telling others something about how a person is feeling. If someone is scowling with teeth clenched, for example, you will probably assume that he or she is angry, and you will be unlikely to choose that particular moment to ask for a loan (Marsh, Ambady, & Kleck, 2005).

Infants provide one source of evidence that some facial expressions are innate. Newborns do not need to be taught to grimace in pain or to smile in pleasure or to blink when startled (Balaban, 1995). Even blind infants, who cannot imitate adults' expressions, show the same emotional expressions as sighted infants (Goodenough, 1932).

A second line of evidence for innate facial expressions comes from studies showing that for the most basic emotions, people in all cultures show similar facial responses to similar emotional stimuli (Hejmadi, Davidson, & Rozin, 2000; Matsumoto & Willingham, 2006; Zajonc, 1998). Participants in these studies look at photographs of people's faces and then try to name the emotion each person is feeling. Though there may be some subtle differences from culture to culture (Marsh, Elfenbein, & Ambady, 2003), the overall pattern of facial movements we call a smile, for example, is universally related to positive emotions. Sadness is almost always accompanied by slackened muscle tone and a "long" face. Likewise, in almost all cultures, people contort their faces in a similar way when shown something they find disgusting. A furrowed brow is frequently associated with frustration, and pride is often associated with a slight smile accompanied by a slight backward tilt of the head (Ekman, 1994; Tracy & Robins, 2008). Anger is also linked with a facial expression recognized by almost all cultures.

Social and Cultural Influences on Emotional Expression

Not all emotional expressions are innate or universal, however (Ekman, 1993). Some are learned through contact with a particular culture, and all of them, even innate expressions, are flexible enough to change as necessary in the social situations in which they occur (Fernández-Dols & Ruiz-Belda, 1995). For example, facial expressions become more intense and change more frequently while people are imagining social scenes as opposed to solitary scenes (Fridlund et al., 1990). Similarly, facial expressions in response to odors tend to be more intense when others are watching than when people are alone (Jancke & Kaufmann, 1994).

Further, although some basic emotional facial expressions are recognized by all cultures (Hejmadi, Davidson, & Rozin, 2000), even these can be interpreted differently, depending on body language and environmental cues. For example, research participants interpreted a particular expression as disgust when it appeared on the

What Are They Feeling?

TRY THIS People's emotions are usually "written on their faces." Jot down the emotions you think these people are feeling, and then look at the footnote on page 458 to see how well you "read" their emotions.

© AP Photo

The Universal Smile

The idea that some emotional expressions are innate is supported by the fact that the facial movement pattern we call a smile is related to happiness, pleasure, and other positive emotions in cultures throughout the world.

face of a person who was holding a dirty diaper, but that same expression was seen as anger when it was digitally superimposed on a person in a fighting stance (Aviezer et al., 2008). There is even a certain degree of cultural variation when it comes to recognizing some emotions (Russell, 1995). In one study, for example, Japanese and North American people agreed about which facial expressions signaled happiness, surprise, and sadness, but they frequently disagreed about which faces showed anger, disgust, and fear (Matsumoto & Ekman, 1989). Members of preliterate cultures, such as the Fore of New Guinea, agree even less with people in Western cultures on the labeling of facial expressions (Russell, 1994). In addition, there are variations in how people in different cultures interpret emotions expressed by tone of voice (Mesquita & Frijda, 1992). For instance, Taiwanese participants were best at recognizing a sad tone of voice, whereas Dutch participants were best at recognizing happy tones (Van Bezooijen, Otto, & Heenan, 1983).

People learn how to express certain emotions in particular ways, as specified by cultural rules. Suppose you say, "I just bought a new car," and all your friends stick their tongues out at you. In North America, this would mean that they are envious or resentful. But in some regions of China, such a display expresses surprise.

Even smiles can vary as people learn to use them to communicate certain feelings. Paul Ekman and his colleagues categorized seventeen types of smiles, including "false smiles," which fake enjoyment, and "masking smiles," which hide unhappiness. They called the smile that occurs with real happiness the Duchenne smile (pronounced "doo-SHEN"), after the French researcher who first noticed a difference between spontaneous, happy smiles and posed smiles. A genuine Duchenne smile includes contractions of the muscles around the eyes (creating a distinctive wrinkling of the skin in these areas), as well as of the muscles that raise the lips and cheeks. Most people are not able to contract the muscles around the eyes during a posed smile, so this feature can be used to distinguish "lying smiles" from genuine ones (Frank, Ekman, & Friesen, 1993).

Learning About Emotions   The effects of learning are seen in a child's growing range of emotional expressions. Although infants begin with an innate set of emotional responses, they soon learn to imitate facial expressions and use them

---

The picture on page 457 shows the wife and daughter of a U.S. Marine helicopter pilot waving goodbye as he departs for deployment in a war zone. Their emotions at that moment probably included sadness, anxiety, worry, dread, uncertainty, hope, and perhaps anger.

for more and more emotions. In time, these expressions become more precise and personalized, so that a particular expression conveys a clear emotional message to anyone who knows that person well.

If facial expressions become *too* personalized, however, no one will know what the expressions mean. Operant shaping (described in the chapter on learning) probably helps keep emotional expressions within certain limits. If you could not see other people's facial expressions or observe their responses to yours, you might show fewer, or less intense, facial signs of emotion. And in fact, there is some evidence that among people blind from birth, those who are older tend to show less animated facial expressions than those who are younger (Izard, 1977; Matsumoto & Willingham, 2009).

As children grow, they learn an *emotion culture*—rules that govern what emotions are appropriate in what circumstances and what emotional expressions are allowed. These rules can vary between genders and from culture to culture (LaFrance, Hecht, & Paluck, 2003; Tsai, Levenson, & McCoy, 2006). For example, TV news cameras show that men in the U.S. military leaving for duty in a war zone tend to keep their emotions in check as they say goodbye to wives, girlfriends, and parents. However, in Italy—where mother-son ties are particularly strong—many male soldiers wail with dismay and weep openly as they leave. In a laboratory study, when viewing a distressing movie with a group of peers, Japanese students exhibited much more control over their facial expressions than North American students did. When they watched the film while alone, however, the Japanese students' faces showed the same emotional expressions as those of the North American students (Ekman, Friesen, & Ellsworth, 1972).

Emotion cultures shape how people describe and categorize feelings, resulting in both similarities and differences across cultures (Russell, 1991). At least five of the seven basic emotions listed in an ancient Chinese book called the *Li Chi*—joy, anger, sadness, fear, love, liking, and dislike—are considered primary emotions by most Western theorists. Yet even though English has more than five hundred emotion-related words, some emotion words in other languages have no English equivalent.

Similarly, other cultures have no equivalent for some English emotion words. Many cultures do not see anger and sadness as different, for example. The Ilongot tribe in the Philippines have only one word, *liget,* for both anger and grief (Russell, 1991). Tahitians have words for forty-six different types of anger but no word for sadness and, apparently, no concept of it.

Social Referencing   Facial expressions, tone of voice, body postures, and gestures can do more than communicate emotion. They can also influence others' behavior, especially the behavior of people who are not sure what to do. An inexperienced chess player, for instance, might reach out to move the queen, catch sight of a spectator's grimace, and infer that another move would be better. The process of letting another person's emotional state guide our own behavior is called *social referencing* (Campos, 1980).

The visual-cliff studies described in the chapter on perception have been used to create an uncertain situation for infants. To reach its mother, an infant in these experiments must cross the visual cliff (see Figure 5.22). If the apparent drop-off is very small or very large, there is no question about what to do: A 1-year-old knows to crawl across in the first case and to stay put in the second case. However, if the apparent drop-off is just large enough (say, 2 feet) to create uncertainty, the infant relies on its mother's facial expression to decide what to do. In one study, mothers were asked to make either a fearful or a happy face. When the mothers made a fearful face, no infant crossed the glass floor. But when they posed a happy face, most infants crossed (Sorce et al., 1981). Here is yet another example of the adaptive value of sending and receiving emotional communications.

LINKAGES

As noted in the chapter on introducing psychology, all of psychology's many subfields are related to one another. Our discussion of conflicting motives and stress illustrates just one way in which the topic of this chapter, motivation and emotion, is linked to the subfield of health psychology (which is discussed in

CHAPTER 11
Motivation and Emotion

the chapter on health, stress, and coping). The Linkages diagram shows ties to two other subfields as well, and there are many more ties throughout the book. Looking for linkages among subfields will help you see how they all fit together and better appreciate the big picture that is psychology.

LINKAGES

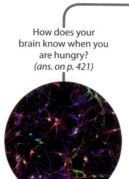

How does your brain know when you are hungry?
(ans. on p. 421)

CHAPTER 3
Biological Aspects of Psychology

Can motivational conflicts cause stress?
(ans. on p. 443)

CHAPTER 13
Health, Stress, and Coping

What role does arousal play in aggression?
(ans. on p. 748)

CHAPTER 18
Social Influence

SUMMARY

Motivation refers to factors that influence the initiation, direction, intensity, and persistence of behavior. Emotion and motivation are often linked: Motivation can influence emotion, and people are often motivated to seek certain emotions.

Concepts and Theories of Motivation

Focusing on a *motive* often reveals a single theme within apparently diverse behaviors. Motivation is said to be an intervening variable, a way of linking various stimuli to the behaviors that follow them.

Sources of Motivation
The many sources of motivation fall into four categories: biological factors, emotional factors, cognitive factors, and social factors.

The Instinct Doctrine and Its Descendants
An early argument held that motivation follows from *instinctive behaviors*,

which are automatic, involuntary, and unlearned action patterns consistently "released" by particular stimuli. Modern versions of the *instinct doctrine* are seen in evolutionary accounts of helping, aggression, mate selection, and other aspects of social behavior.

Drive Reduction Theory
Drive reduction theory is based on *homeostasis*, a tendency to maintain equilibrium in a physical or behavioral process. When disruptions of equilibrium create *needs* of some kind, people are motivated to reduce the resulting *drives* by behaving in a way that satisfies the needs and restores balance. *Primary drives* are unlearned; *secondary drives* are learned.

Arousal Theory
According to *arousal theory*, people are motivated to behave in ways that maintain a level of *physiological arousal* that is optimal for their functioning.

Incentive Theory
Incentive theory highlights behaviors that are motivated by attaining desired stimuli (positive incentives) and avoiding undesirable ones (negative incentives).

Hunger and Eating

Eating is controlled by a complex mixture of learning, culture, and biology.

Biological Signals for Hunger and Satiation
The desire to eat (*hunger*) and the satisfaction (*satiation*) of that desire (*satiety*) that leads us to stop eating depends primarily on signals from bloodborne substances such as cholecystokinin (CCK), glucose, insulin, and leptin.

Hunger and the Brain
Activity in the ventromedial nucleus of the hypothalamus results in satiety, whereas activity in the lateral hypothalamus results in hunger. These brain

regions act together to maintain a set point of body weight, but control of eating is more complex than that. For example, a variety of neurotransmitters in various regions of the hypothalamus can create hunger for specific types of foods.

Flavor, Sociocultural Experience, and Food Selection
Eating may also be influenced by the flavor of food and by appetite for the pleasure of food. Food selection is influenced by biological needs (specific hungers) for certain nutrients, as well as by food cravings, social contexts, and cultural traditions.

Unhealthy Eating
Obesity has been linked to overconsumption of certain kinds of foods, to low energy metabolism, and to genetic factors. People with *anorexia nervosa* starve themselves. Those with *bulimia* engage in binge eating, followed by purging through self-induced vomiting or laxatives.

Sexual Behavior

Sexual motivation and behavior result from a rich interplay of biology and culture.

The Biology of Sex
Sexual stimulation generally produces *sexual arousal*, which appears in a stereotyped *sexual response cycle* of physiological arousal during and after sexual activity. *Sex hormones*, which include *androgens*, *estrogens*, and *progestational hormones*, occur in different relative amounts in both sexes. They can have organizational effects, such as physical differences in the brain, and activational effects, such as increased desire for sex.

Social and Cultural Factors in Sexuality
Gender-role learning and educational experiences are examples of cultural factors that can bring about variations in sexual attitudes and behaviors.

Sexual Orientation
Sexual orientation—heterosexuality, homosexuality, or *bisexuality*—is increasingly viewed as a sociocultural variable that affects many other aspects of behavior and mental processes. Though undoubtedly shaped by a lifetime of learning, sexual orientation appears to have strong biological roots.

Achievement Motivation

People gain esteem from achievement in many areas, including the workplace.

Need for Achievement
The motive to succeed has been called mastery, effectance, and need for achievement. Individuals with high *achievement motivation* strive for excellence, persist despite failures, and set challenging but realistic goals.

Goal Setting and Achievement Motivation
Goals influence motivation, especially the amount of effort, persistence, attention, and planning we devote to a task.

Achievement and Success in the Workplace
Workers are most satisfied when they are working toward their own goals and are getting concrete feedback. Jobs that offer clear and specific goals, a variety of tasks, individual responsibility, and other intrinsic rewards are the most motivating.

Achievement and Well-Being
People tend to have a characteristic level of happiness, or *well-being*, that is not necessarily related to the attainment of money, status, or other material goals.

Relations and Conflicts Among Motives

Human behavior reflects many motives, some of which may be in conflict. Abraham Maslow proposed a hierarchy of five classes of human motives or needs, from meeting basic biological requirements to attaining a state of self-actualization. Needs at the lowest levels, according to Maslow, must be at least partly satisfied before people can be motivated by higher-level goals.

Opponent Processes, Motivation, and Emotion
Motivated behavior sometimes gives rise to opponent emotional processes, such as the fear and excitement associated with a roller coaster ride. Opponent-process theory illustrates the close link between motivation and emotion.

The Nature of Emotion

Defining Characteristics
Emotions are temporary experiences with positive or negative qualities that are felt with some intensity as happening to the self, are generated in part by a cognitive appraisal of a situation, and are accompanied by both learned and innate physical responses.

The Biology of Emotion
Several brain mechanisms are involved in emotion. The amygdala, in the limbic system, is deeply involved in various aspects of emotion. The expression of emotion through involuntary facial movement is controlled by the extrapyramidal motor system. Voluntary facial movements are controlled by the pyramidal motor system. The brain's right and left hemispheres play somewhat different roles in emotion. In addition to specific brain mechanisms, both branches of the autonomic nervous system, the *sympathetic nervous system* and the *parasympathetic nervous system*, are involved in physiological changes that accompany emotional activation. The *fight-flight reaction*, for example, follows from activation of the sympathetic system.

Theories of Emotion

James's Peripheral Theory
William James's theory of emotion holds that peripheral physiological responses are the primary source of emotion and that awareness of these responses constitutes emotional experience. James's theory is supported by evidence that at least for several basic emotions, physiological responses are distinguishable enough for emotions to be generated in this way. Distinct facial expressions are linked to particular patterns of physiological change.

Cannon's Central Theory
Walter Cannon's theory of emotion proposes that emotional experience occurs independent of peripheral physiological responses and that there is a direct experience of emotion based on activity of the

central nervous system. Updated versions of this theory suggest that various parts of the central nervous system may be involved in different emotions and different aspects of emotional experience. Some pathways in the brain, such as that from the thalamus to the amygdala, allow strong emotions to occur before conscious thought can take place. And specific parts of the brain appear to be responsible for the feelings of pleasure or pain in emotion.

Cognitive Theories of Emotion

Stanley Schachter's modification of James's theory proposes that physiological responses are primary sources of emotion but that the cognitive labeling of those responses—a process that depends partly on *attribution*—strongly influences the emotions we experience. Schachter's theory stimulated research on *excitation transfer theory*. Other cognitive theories, such as that of Richard Lazarus, emphasize that emotional experience depends heavily on how we think about the situations and events we encounter.

Communicating Emotion

Humans communicate emotions mainly through facial movement and expressions but also through voice tones and bodily movements.

Innate Expressions of Emotion

Charles Darwin suggested that certain facial expressions of emotion are innate and universal and that these expressions evolved because they effectively communicate one creature's emotional condition to other creatures. Some facial expressions of basic emotions, such as happiness, do appear to be innate.

Social and Cultural Influences on Emotional Expression

Many emotional expressions are learned, and even innate expressions are modified by learning and social contexts. As children grow, they learn an emotion culture, the rules of emotional expression appropriate to their culture. Accordingly, the same emotion may be communicated by different facial expressions in different cultures. Especially in ambiguous situations, other people's emotional expressions may serve as a guide about what to do or what not to do, a phenomenon called social referencing.

LINKAGES TO FURTHER LEARNING

Now that you have finished reading this chapter, how about exploring some of the topics and information that you found most interesting? Here are some places to start.

Books

Gelsey Kirkland, *Dancing on My Grave* (Doubleday, 1987). Eating disorders.

Steven Pinker, *The Blank Slate: The Modern Denial of Human Nature* (Viking Press, 2002). Wide-ranging description of evolutionary and genetic explanations of motivation.

David Goldstein (Ed.), *The Management of Eating Disorders and Obesity* (Humana Press, 2005). A summary of research on and treatment of eating disorders.

Aldert Vrij, *Detecting Lies and Deceit: The Psychology of Lying and Implications for Professional Practice* (Wiley, 2000). A summary of various approaches.

David Lykken, *Happiness: The Nature and Nurture of Joy and Contentment* (Griffin, 2000). A summary of research on the "happiness set point" and other aspects of well-being.

Antonio R. Damasio, *Descartes' Error: Emotion, Reason, and the Human Brain* (Penguin, 2005). An exploration of the biology of emotion and reason and how they're intertwined in the brain.

Dalai Lama and Paul Ekman, *Emotional Awareness: Overcoming the Obstacles to Psychological Balance and Compassion* (Times Books, 2008). Conversations between Paul Ekman and the Dalai Lama about the experiences and meanings of emotions and human interaction.

On the Internet

 CourseMate Access an integrated eBook and chapter-specific learning tools including flashcards, quizzes, videos, and more. Go to CengageBrain.com.

CENGAGENOW Want to maximize the value of your online study time? Take this easy-to-use study system's diagnostic pre-test, and it will create a personalized study plan for you. By helping you identify the topics that you need to understand better and then directing you to valuable online resources, it can speed up your chapter review. CengageNOW even provides a post-test so you can confirm that you are ready for an exam. Go to CengageBrain.com.

TALKING POINTS

Here are a few talking points to help you summarize this chapter for family and friends without giving a lecture.

1. You can't actually see motives such as love or hatred or greed, but you can use them to help understand the reasons for people's behavior.

2. Motivation and emotion are linked. Hunger can make you irritable, and being in love can motivate you to do almost anything for a loved one.

3. The arousal theory of motivation has been used to help explain why some people are introverts and others are extroverts.

4. Crash diets are not the best way to lose weight and keep it off. The key is to increase fat-burning through regular exercise while also reducing food intake.

5. Sexual orientation is shaped by biological factors as well as social influences.

6. Achieving success in school, at work, and elsewhere is more likely if we have a sense of control and a set of clear and challenging but not impossible goals.

7. The emotions we experience in a particular situation depend partly on how we think about that situation; adjusting our view of an event can change our emotional reaction to it.

Infancy, childhood, adolescence, adulthood, and old age. These words can be read in seconds, but the stages they represent take a lifetime to play out. The story of development is different for each of us, but there are some common threads, too, and developmental psychologists are exploring them. In this chapter, we describe what they have discovered so far about how people change and grow over the course of their lives.

© Najlah Feanny/Corbis Saba

A Deadly Child

Andrew Golden was barely out of diapers when he was given camouflage clothing and taught to fire a hunting rifle. In March 1998, at the age of 11, he and a 13-year-old friend, Mitchell Johnson, used their rifles to kill four classmates and a teacher at their elementary school in Jonesboro, Arkansas. Many youngsters learn to hunt; what led these two to commit murder? Researchers in developmental psychology study the genetic and environmental factors that underlie violent aggression and many other patterns of behavior and mental processes.

Jeff Weise, Dylan Klebold, Eric Harris, Kip Kinkel, Asa Coon, and Tim Kretschmer are just a few of the teenage boys whose deadly shooting sprees in recent years have shocked people in North America and around the world. As mass murder plots by disgruntled students continue to make news, everyone wants to know what's behind it all. Had these young people been rejected by their peers? Had they watched too much violence on television or played too many violent video games? Were their actions the fault of a "gun culture" that allows children access to firearms? Had they been victims of abuse and neglect? Were their parents too strict—or not strict enough? Did they come from "broken homes," or had they witnessed violence within their own families? Did they behave violently because they were going through a difficult "stage," because they had not been taught right from wrong, because they wanted to impress their peers, because males are more aggressive in general, or because their brains were "defective"? Were they just "bad kids"?

These are the kinds of questions that developmental psychologists try to answer. They investigate when certain behaviors first appear and how behaviors change with age. They explore how development in one area, such as thinking about moral issues, relates to development in other areas, such as aggressive behavior. They look at whether most people develop at the same rate and, if not, whether slow starters ever catch up to early bloomers. They ask why some children become well-adjusted and caring individuals, whereas others become murderers; why some adolescents go on to win honors in college while others drop out of high school. They seek to explain how development throughout the life span is affected by both genetics and the environment, analyzing the extent to which development is a product of what we arrive with at birth (our inherited, biological *nature*) and the extent to which it is a product of what the world provides (the *nurture* of the environment). In short, **developmental psychology** is concerned with the course and causes of the developmental changes that take place over a person's entire lifetime (Heckhausen, Wrosch, & Schulz, 2010).

In this chapter, we examine many such changes. We begin by describing the physical and biological changes that occur from the moment of conception to the moment of birth. Then we discuss cognitive, social, and emotional development during infancy and childhood. Next, we examine the changes and challenges that occur during adolescence. We conclude by considering the significant physical, intellectual, and social changes that take place as people move through early, middle, and late adulthood.

Exploring Human Development

The question of whether development is the result of nature or nurture was the subject of philosophical debate centuries before psychologists began studying it scientifically. In essays published in the 1690s, the British philosopher John Locke argued for nurture. He believed that experiences provided by the environment during childhood have a profound and permanent effect. As mentioned in the chapter on introducing psychology, Locke thought of the newborn as a blank slate, or *tabula rasa*. Adults

465

write on that slate, he said, as they teach children about the world and how to behave. Seventy years later, the French philosopher Jean-Jacques Rousseau (pronounced "roo-SOH") made the opposite argument. He claimed that children are capable of discovering how the world operates and how they should behave without instruction from adults. According to Rousseau, children should be allowed to grow as their natures dictate, with little guidance or pressure from parents.

The first psychologist to systematically investigate the role of nature in behavior was Arnold Gesell. In the early 1900s, Gesell (pronounced "guh-ZEL") observed many children of all ages. He found that their motor skills, such as those involved in standing and walking, picking up a cube, and throwing a ball, developed in a fixed sequence of stages, as Figure 12.1 illustrates. The order of the stages and the age at which they develop, he suggested, are determined by nature and relatively unaffected by nurture. Only under extreme conditions, such as famine, war, or poverty, he claimed, are children thrown off their biologically programmed timetable. Gesell used the term **maturation** to refer to this type of natural growth or change, which unfolds in a fixed sequence relatively independent of the environment. The broader term *development* encompasses not only maturation but also changes that are due to learning.

John B. Watson, founder of the behaviorist approach to psychology, disagreed with Gesell. He claimed that the environment, not nature, molds and shapes development. His experiments with children left him convinced that we learn *everything,*

FIGURE 12.1

Motor Development

When did you start walking? The left end of each bar indicates the age at which 25 percent of the infants tested were able to perform a particular behavior; 50 percent of the babies were performing the behavior at the age indicated by the vertical line in the bars. The right end of each bar indicates the age at which 90 percent could do so (Frankenberg & Dodds, 1967). Although different infants, especially in different cultures, achieve milestones of motor development at slightly different ages, all infants—regardless of their ethnicity, social class, or temperament—achieve them in the same order.

Source: Frankenberg & Dodds, 1967.

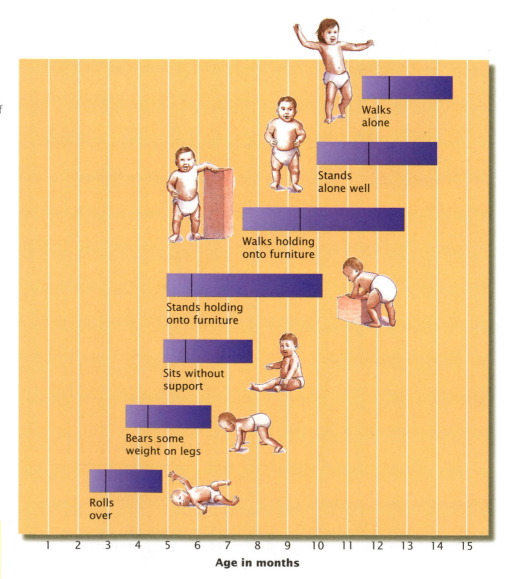

maturation Natural growth or change that unfolds in a fixed sequence relatively independent of the environment.

from skills to fears. In his words, "there is no such thing as an inheritance of capacity, talent, temperament, mental constitution and characteristics. These things … depend on training that goes on mainly in the cradle" (Watson, 1925, pp. 74–75).

It was the Swiss psychologist Jean Piaget (pronounced "pyah-ZHAY") who first suggested that nature and nurture work together and that their influences are inseparable and interactive. Piaget had a lifelong interest in human intellectual and cognitive development. His ideas, presented in numerous books and articles published from the 1920s until his death in 1980, influenced the field of developmental psychology more than those of any other person before or since.

Guided by research in *behavioral genetics* (described in the chapter on research in psychology), most developmental psychologists now accept the idea that nature and nurture contribute jointly to development—in two ways. First, they operate together to make all people similar in some respects. For example, we all achieve milestones of physical development in the same order and at roughly the same rate. This pattern is a result of the nature of biological maturation supported by the nurture of basic care, nutrition, and exercise. Second, nature and nurture also both operate to make each person unique. The nature of inherited genes and the nurture of widely different family and cultural environments produce differences among individuals in such dimensions as athletic abilities, intelligence, language skills, and personality (Brendgen et al., 2008; Ducci & Goldman, 2008; Gregory et al., 2009; Haddad et al., 2008; Malouff, Rooke, & Schutte, 2008; South & Krueger, 2008). Heredity creates *predispositions* that interact with environmental influences, including family and teachers, books and computers, and friends and random events (Caspi et al., 2002). It is this interaction that produces the developmental outcomes we see in individuals. So Michael Jordan, Michael Phelps, Michael Douglas, and Michael Moore differ from one another and from other men because of both their genes and their experiences.

Just how much nature and nurture contribute varies from one characteristic to another. Nature shapes some characteristics, such as physical size and appearance, so strongly that only extreme environmental conditions can affect them. Variation in height, for example, has been estimated to be 80 to 95 percent genetic. This means that 80 to 95 percent of the differences in height that we see among people are due to their genes. Less than 20 percent of the differences are due to prenatal or postnatal diet or to early illness or other growth-stunting environmental factors. Nature's influence on other characteristics, such as intelligence or personality, is not as strong. Complex traits such as these are influenced not only by genes but by many environmental factors as well.

Nature and Nurture Entwined

The combined effects of nature and nurture are illustrated in this family photo of Peyton and Eli Manning and their father, Archie Manning. The effect of nature on their athleticism could be seen in the fact that both boys weighed over 12 pounds at birth and were built like athletes, even as toddlers. The influence of nurture on their success—Peyton is the quarterback of the Indianapolis Colts and Eli is quarterback of the New York Giants—came about partly through the fact that their father was quarterback of the New Orleans Saints. Their family life revolved around sports; they were tossing a football at the age of 3—and honing their skills with help from their father's coaching.

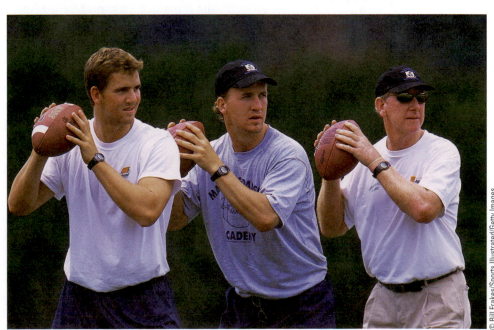

© Bill Frakes/Sports Illustrated/Getty Images

It is impossible for researchers to separate the influences that nature and nurture exert on such complex traits, partly because heredity and environment are *correlated*. For instance, highly intelligent biological parents give their children genes related to high intelligence, and typically provide a stimulating environment too. Heredity and environment also influence each other. The environment promotes or hampers the expression of an individual's abilities, and those inherited abilities affect the individual's environment. For example, a stimulating environment full of toys, books, and lessons encourages children's mental development and increases the chances that their full inherited intelligence will emerge. At the same time, more intelligent children seek out environments that are more stimulating, ask more questions, draw more attention from adults, and ultimately learn more from these experiences.

Beginnings

Nowhere are the intertwined effects of nature and nurture clearer than in the womb, as a single fertilized egg becomes a functioning infant.

Prenatal Development

The process of development begins when sperm from the father-to-be penetrates, or fertilizes, the ovum of the mother-to-be, and a brand-new cell, called a **zygote**, is formed. This new cell carries a genetic heritage from both mother and father (see the behavioral genetics appendix).

Stages of Prenatal Development   In the first stage of prenatal development, called the *germinal stage,* the zygote divides into many more cells, which by the end of the second week have formed an **embryo** (pronounced "EM-bree-oh"). What follows is the *embryonic stage* of development, during which the embryo develops a heart, nervous system, stomach, esophagus, and ovaries or testes. By two months after conception, when the embryonic stage ends, the inch-long embryo has developed eyes, ears, a nose, a jaw, a mouth, and lips. The tiny arms have elbows, hands, and stubby fingers; the legs have knees, ankles, and toes.

During the remaining seven-month period until birth, called the *fetal stage* of prenatal development, the organs grow and start to function. By the end of the third month, the **fetus** can kick, make a fist, turn its head, open its mouth, swallow, and frown. In the sixth month, the eyelids, which have been sealed, open. The fetus now has taste buds and a well-developed grasp and, if born prematurely, can breathe regularly for as long as twenty-four hours at a time. By the end of the seventh month, the organ systems, though immature, are all functional. In the eighth and ninth months, fetuses respond to light and touch, and they can hear sounds. They can remember a particular sound that they had heard a month earlier (Dirix et al., 2009), and when they hear an unpleasant sound, they may respond with movements that are just like those a crying newborn would make (Gingras, Mitchell, & Grattan, 2005). They can also learn. When they hear their mother's familiar voice, their heart beats a little faster, but it slows if they hear a stranger (Kisilevsky et al., 2003).

Prenatal Risks   Nature determines the timing and stages of prenatal development, but that development is also affected by the nurture provided in the womb. During prenatal development, a spongy organ called the *placenta* forms from the outside layer of the zygote and attaches itself to the mother's uterus through an *umbilical cord*. (The cord is detached at birth, but you can see where yours was by looking at your navel.) The placenta sends nutrients from the mother to the fetus and carries away wastes. It also screens out many potentially harmful substances, including most bacteria. This screening is imperfect, however: Gases and viruses, as well as nicotine, alcohol, and other drugs, can pass through. Severe damage can occur if the baby's mother takes

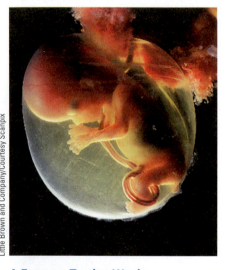

A Fetus at Twelve Weeks

At this point in prenatal development, the fetus can kick its legs, curl its toes, make a fist, turn its head, squint, open its mouth, swallow, and take a few "breaths" of amniotic fluid.

zygote A new cell, formed from a father's sperm and a mother's ovum.

embryo The developing individual from the fourteenth day after fertilization until the end of the second month after conception.

fetus The developing individual from the third month after conception until birth.

certain drugs, is exposed to toxic substances, or has certain illnesses while organs are forming in the embryonic stage (Koger, Schettler, & Weiss, 2005).

Harmful external substances that invade the womb and result in birth defects are called **teratogens** (pronounced "tuh-RAT-uh-jinz"). Teratogens are especially damaging during the embryonic stage, because it is a **critical period** in prenatal development, a time when certain kinds of growth must occur if the infant's development is to proceed normally. If the heart, eyes, ears, hands, and feet do not appear during this period, they cannot form later on. If they form incorrectly, the defects are permanent. So even before a mother knows she is pregnant, she may accidentally damage her infant by exposing it to teratogens. For example, a baby whose mother has rubella (German measles) during the third or fourth week after conception has a 50 percent chance of being blind, deaf, or intellectually disabled or of having a malformed heart. If the mother has rubella later in the pregnancy, after the infant's eyes, ears, brain, and heart have formed, the likelihood that the baby will have one of these defects is much lower. Later, during the fetal stage, teratogens affect the baby's size, behavior, intelligence, and health, rather than the formation of organs and limbs.

Of special concern today are the effects of drugs on infants' development (e.g., Eroglu et al., 2008; Forcelli, & Heinrichs, 2008; Jones, 2006; Weiss, Saint Jonn-Seed, & Harris-Muchell, 2007). Pregnant women who use substances such as cocaine create a substantial risk for their fetuses, which do not yet have the enzymes necessary to break down the drugs. "Cocaine babies" or "crack babies" may be born premature, underweight, tense, fussy, and less likely than other infants to interact smoothly with their mothers (Tronick et al., 2005). They may also suffer delayed physical growth and motor development (Richardson, Goldschmidt, & Larkby, 2007) and are more likely to have behavioral and learning problems (Bada et al., 2007; Singer et al., 2001; Singer et al., 2002; Tan-Laxa et al., 2004). They may display slower than normal cognitive processing too (Mayes et al., 2005), but other aspects of their cognitive abilities are not necessarily different from those of any baby born into an impoverished environment (Behnke et al., 2006; Frank et al., 2001; Jones, 2006). How well these children ultimately do in school depends on how supportive that environment turns out to be (Ackerman, Riggins, & Black, 2010; Bennett, Bendersky, & Lewis, 2008; Messinger et al., 2004; Singer et al., 2004).

Alcohol is another dangerous teratogen because it interferes with infants' brain development (Sayal et al., 2009). Almost half the children born to expectant mothers who abuse alcohol will develop **fetal alcohol syndrome**, a pattern of defects that includes intellectual disability and malformations of the face (Jenkins & Culbertson, 1996). Pregnant women who drink as little as a glass or two of wine a day can harm their infants' intellectual functioning (Willford, Leech, & Day, 2006). Those who engage in bouts of heavy drinking triple the odds that their child will develop alcohol-related problems by the age of 21 (Baer, Sampson, et al., 2003; Landgren et al., 2010). The effects of prenatal exposure to alcohol can be even more severe when combined with the effects of other environmental toxins, such as air pollution (Mancinelli, Binetti, & Ceccanti, 2007).

Smoking, too, can affect the developing fetus. Smokers' babies often suffer from respiratory problems, irritability, and social and attention problems, and they are at greater risk for nicotine addiction in adolescence and adulthood (Buka, Shenassa, & Niaura, 2003; Linnet et al., 2005; Stroud et al., 2009; Stéphan-Blanchard et al., 2010; Wakschlag et al., 2006). Worse, they may be born prematurely, and they are usually underweight. Babies who are premature or underweight—for whatever reason—are likely to have cognitive and behavioral problems that continue throughout their lives (Bhutta et al., 2002; Ginzel et al., 2007; Jefferis, Power, & Hertzman, 2002).

Defects caused by teratogens are most likely when a genetically susceptible infant receives a strong dose of a damaging substance during a critical period of prenatal development. The risk of behavioral and psychological difficulties in later life is also increased for children whose mothers were under significant stress (Huizink, Mulder, & Buitelaar, 2004; Khashan et al., 2008; O'Connor et al., 2005; Van den Bergh &

teratogens Harmful substances that can cause birth defects.

critical period An interval during which certain kinds of growth must occur if development is to proceed normally.

fetal alcohol syndrome A pattern of physical and mental defects found in babies born to women who abused alcohol during pregnancy.

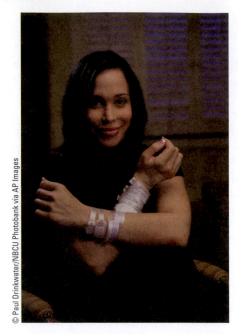

A Rare Multiple Birth

When Nadya Suleman delivered eight babies on January 26, 2009, it was only the second time that octuplets have been known to survive for more than a few hours. The infants remained at severe risk for a considerable time, though, because they were premature and underweight (the heaviest weighed 3 pounds, 4 ounces, and the lightest, only 1 pound, 8 ounces).

Marcoen, 2004), were depressed (Diego, Field, & Hernandez-Reif, 2005), or got the flu during the first six months of pregnancy (Brown et al., 2005). However, milder degrees of maternal anxiety or depression during pregnancy may actually advance maturation of the fetus (DiPietro et al., 2006). Fortunately, mental or physical problems resulting from all harmful prenatal factors affect fewer than 10 percent of the babies born in Western nations. Mechanisms built into the human organism maintain normal development under all but the most adverse conditions. The vast majority of fetuses arrive at the end of their nine-month gestation averaging a healthy 7 pounds and ready to continue a normal course of development in the world.

The Newborn

Determining what newborns are able to see, hear, and do is one of the most fascinating—and frustrating—research challenges in developmental psychology. Young infants are very difficult to study. About 70 percent of the time, they are asleep. When they aren't sleeping, they may be drowsy, crying, or restlessly moving about. It is only when they are in a state of quiet alertness, which occurs infrequently and only for a few minutes at a time, that researchers can assess infants' abilities.

During these brief periods, psychologists present sounds or show objects or pictures and watch where infants look and for how long. They film the infants' eye movements and record changes in their heart rates, sucking rates, brain waves, body movements, and skin conductance (a measure of perspiration associated with emotion) to learn what infants can see and hear (Kellman & Arterberry, 2006).

Vision and Other Senses   Infants can see at birth, but their vision is blurry. Researchers estimate that newborns have 20/300 eyesight. In other words, an object 20 feet away looks as clear as it would if viewed from 300 feet by an adult with normal vision. The reason infants' vision is so limited is that their eyes and brains still need time to grow and develop. Newborns' eyes are smaller than those of adults, and the cells in their foveas—the area of each retina on which images are focused—are fewer and far less sensitive. Their eye movements are slow and jerky. Pathways connecting the eyes to the brain are still inefficient, as is the processing of visual information within the brain.

Although infants cannot see small objects on the other side of the room, they are able to see large objects close up. They stare longest at objects that have large visible elements, movement, clear contours, and a lot of contrast between lighter and darker areas—all qualities that exist in the human face (Farroni et al., 2005). In fact, from the time they are born, infants will shift their gaze to track a moving face, and they stare at a human face longer than at other figures (Johnson, Dziurawiec, et al., 1991; Valenza et al., 1996). They are particularly interested in the eyes, as shown by their preference for faces that are looking directly at them (Farroni et al., 2002). They also experience a certain degree of *size constancy*. This means that objects appear to be the same size despite changes in the size of their image on the eye's retina (see the perception chapter). So a baby perceives the mother's face as remaining about the same size, whether she is looking over the edge of the crib or coming close enough to kiss the baby's cheek. By the time they are 4 months old, infants can categorize objects according to their shape (Farran & Brown, 2006), but they do not experience *depth perception* until some time later. It takes about seven months before they begin to use the pictorial cues about depth described in the chapter on perception.

The course of development for hearing is similar to that of vision. Infants at birth are not deaf, but they hear poorly; their hearing is not as sharp as that of adults until well into childhood. However, even at 2 or 3 days of age, they can hear soft voices and notice the difference between tones about one note apart on the musical scale; they also turn their heads toward sounds (Clifton, 1992). Their hearing is particularly attuned to the sounds of speech. When they hear voices, babies open their eyes wider and look for the speaker. By 4 months of age, they can discriminate differences among

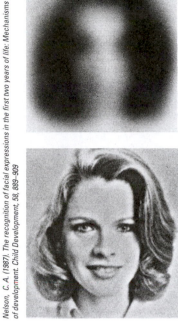

Nelson, C. A. (1987). The recognition of facial expressions in the first two years of life: Mechanisms of development. Child Development, 58, 889–909

A Baby's-Eye View of the World

The top photograph simulates what the mother in the bottom photograph looks like to her newborn infant. Although their vision is blurry, infants particularly seem to enjoy looking at faces. As mentioned in the perception chapter, their eyes will follow a moving facelike image, and they will stare at a human face longer than at other figures.

reflexes Simple, involuntary, unlearned behaviors directed by the spinal cord without instructions from the brain.

almost all of the phonetic contrasts in adult languages (Hespos & Spelke, 2004). Infants also prefer certain kinds of speech. They like rising tones spoken by women or children, and they like speech that is high-pitched, exaggerated, and expressive. In other words, they like to hear the "baby talk" used by most adults when they talk to babies. They even seem to learn language faster when they hear "baby talk" (Thiessen, Hill, & Saffran, 2005).

Newborns' sense of smell is similar to that of adults, but again, less well developed. Certain smells and tastes appeal to them more than others. For instance, they like the smell of flowers and the taste of sweet drinks (Ganchrow, Steiner, & Daher, 1983) but dislike the smell of ammonia (in wet diapers). They like the odor of their own mother's breast and breast milk—when they smell these odors, they cry less, open their eyes, and try to suck (Doucet et al., 2007). They also develop preferences for the food flavors consumed by their mothers (Mennella & Beauchamp, 1996).

Although limited, these sensory abilities are important for survival and development because they focus the infant's attention on the caregiver and draw the caregiver into interaction with the infant. Newborns' attraction to the sweet smell and taste of mother's milk helps them locate appropriate food and identify their caregiver. Their sensitivity to speech allows them to focus on language and encourages the caregiver to talk to them. Because infants' vision is limited to the distance at which most interaction with a caregiver takes place and is attuned to the special qualities of faces, the caregiver's face is especially noticeable to them. Accordingly, infants are exposed to emotional expressions and come to recognize the caregiver by sight, further encouraging the caregiver to interact.

Reflexes and Motor Skills   In the first few weeks and months after birth, babies demonstrate involuntary, unlearned motor behaviors called **reflexes.** These are swift, automatic movements that occur in response to external stimuli. Figure 12.2 illustrates the *grasping reflex,* one of more than twenty reflexes that have been observed in newborn infants. Another is the *rooting reflex,* which causes the infant to turn its mouth toward a nipple (or anything else) that touches its cheek. The *sucking reflex* causes the newborn to suck on anything that touches its lips. Many of these reflexes evolved because, like seeing and hearing, they were important for infants' survival. But infants' behavior doesn't remain under the control of these reflexes for long. Most reflexes disappear after the first three or four months, when infants' brain development allows them to control their muscles voluntarily. At that point, infants can develop motor skills, so they are soon able to roll over, sit up, crawl, stand, and by about the end of the year, walk (see Figure 12.1).

Until a few years ago, most developmental psychologists accepted Gesell's view that barring extreme environmental conditions, these motor abilities occur spontaneously as the central nervous system and muscles mature. It turns out, though, that maturation does not tell the whole story, even in normal environments (Thelen, 1995). Experience matters too. Consider the fact that many babies today aren't learning to crawl on time—or at all. Why? One reason has to do with the "back to sleep" campaign launched in 1995 in an effort to prevent sudden infant death syndrome (see the chapter on consciousness). This public health campaign urged parents to put babies to sleep on their backs rather than face-down. The campaign was successful, but researchers discovered that many babies who were never placed on their tummies went directly from sitting to toddling, skipping the crawling stage but reaching all other motor milestones on schedule (Kolata & Markel, 2001). A related result followed the "prone to play" campaign. Beginning in 2001, parents were advised to place their babies in a prone (face-down) position when awake to encourage play and learning. Babies of parents who followed this advice showed earlier than expected skill at rolling, crawling on their abdomens, and crawling on all fours (Kuo et al., 2008).

Further, skills such as crawling don't just suddenly appear. It takes the development of enough muscle strength to support the abdomen—and some active experimentation—to get the job done. Six infants in one observational study first tried

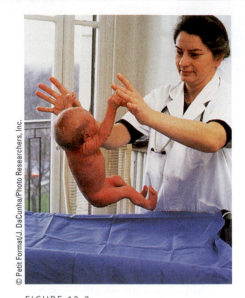

FIGURE 12.2
Reflexes in the Newborn
When a finger is pressed into a newborn's palm, the *grasping reflex* causes the infant to hold on tightly enough to suspend its entire weight. And when a newborn is held upright over a flat surface, the *stepping reflex* leads to walking movements.

various crawling techniques—moving backward, moving one limb at a time, using the arms only, and so on (Freedland & Bertenthal, 1994). It was only after a week or two of trial and error that all six arrived at the same method: moving diagonal limbs (right arm and left leg, left arm and right leg) together. This pattern turned out to be the most efficient way of getting around quickly without tipping over. Such observations suggest that as maturation increases infants' strength, they try out motor patterns and select the ones that work best (C. A. Nelson, 1999).

In short, motor development results from a combination of maturation and experience. It is not the result of an entirely automatic sequence genetically etched in the brain. Yet again, we see that nature and nurture influence each other. The brain controls developing behavior, but its own development is affected by experience, including efforts to build motor skills.

Infancy and Childhood: Cognitive Development

In just ten years or so, the tiny infant becomes a competent child who can read a book, write a poem, and argue for a new computer. Researchers who study *cognitive development* explore the dramatic shifts in thinking, knowing, and remembering that occur between early infancy and later childhood.

Changes in the Brain

One factor that underlies the cognitive leaps of infancy and childhood is the continued growth and development of the brain. When infants are born, they already have a full quota of brain cells, but the neural networks connecting the cells are immature. With time, the connections grow increasingly complex and then, with pruning, more efficient. Studies reveal how, as different regions of the brain develop more complex and efficient neural networks, new cognitive abilities appear (Nelson, Thomas, & de Haan, 2006).

In the first few months of infancy, the cerebellum is the most mature area of the brain. Its early maturation allows infants to display simple associative abilities, such as sucking more when they see their mother's face or hear her voice. Between 6 and 12 months of age, neurological development in the medial temporal lobe of the cerebral cortex makes it possible for infants to remember and imitate an action they have seen earlier or to recognize a picture of an object they have never seen but have held in their hands. Neurological development in the frontal cortex, which occurs later in childhood, allows for the development of higher cognitive functions such as reasoning. In other words, brain structures provide the "hardware" for cognitive development. How does the "software" of thinking develop, and how does it modify the "wiring" of the brain's "hardware"? These questions have been pursued by many developmental psychologists, beginning with Piaget.

The Development of Knowledge: Piaget's Theory

Piaget dedicated his life to a search for the origins of intelligence in infancy and the factors that lead to changes in knowledge over the life span. He was the first to chart the fascinating journey from the simple reflexes of the newborn to the complex understandings of the adolescent. Piaget's theory was not correct in every respect—later we discuss some of its weaknesses—but his ideas about cognitive development were extremely influential.

Piaget proposed that cognitive development proceeds through a series of distinct *periods* or *stages* (see Table 12.1). He believed that all children's thinking goes through the same stages, in the same order, without skipping—building on previous stages and

TABLE 12.1   Piaget's Periods of Cognitive Development

According to Piaget, a predictable set of features characterizes each period of a child's cognitive development. The ages associated with the stages are approximate; Piaget realized that some children move through the stages slightly faster or slower than others.

Period	Activities and Achievements
Sensorimotor	
Birth–2 years	Infants discover aspects of the world through their sensory impressions, motor activities, and coordination of the two. They learn to differentiate themselves from the external world. They learn that objects exist even when they are not visible and that objects are independent of the infant's own actions. They gain some appreciation of cause and effect.
Preoperational	
2–4 years	Children cannot yet manipulate and transform information in logical ways, but they now can think in images and symbols.
4–7 years	They become able to represent something with something else, acquire language, and play games that involve pretending. Intelligence at this stage is said to be intuitive because children cannot make general, logical statements.
Concrete operational	
7–11 years	Children can understand logical principles that apply to concrete external objects. They can appreciate that certain properties of an object remain the same despite changes in appearance, and they can sort objects into categories. They can appreciate the perspective of another viewer. They can think about two concepts, such as "longer" and "wider," at the same time.
Formal Operational	
Over 11 years	Only adolescents and adults can think logically about abstractions, can speculate, and can consider what might be or what ought to be. They can work in probabilities and possibilities. They can imagine other worlds, especially ideal ones. They can reason about purely verbal or logical statements. They can relate any element or statement to any other, manipulate variables in a scientific experiment, and deal with proportions and analogies. They reflect on their own activity of thinking.

then moving to higher ones. According to Piaget, the thinking of infants is different from the thinking of children, and the thinking of children is different from that of adolescents. He concluded that children are not just miniature adults and that they are not less intelligent than adults. They just think differently. Entering each stage involves a *qualitative* change from the previous stage, much as a caterpillar is transformed into a butterfly. What drives children to higher stages is their constant struggle to make sense of their experiences. They are active thinkers who are always trying to construct more advanced understandings of the world.

Building Blocks of Development   To explain how infants and children move to ever-higher stages of understanding and knowledge, Piaget used the concept of *schemas*. As noted in the chapters on perception, memory, and cognition, **schemas** are the generalizations that form as people experience the world. Schemas organize past experiences and provide a framework for understanding future experiences. Piaget saw schemas as organized patterns of action or thought that children construct as they adapt to the environment; they are the basic units of knowledge, the building blocks of intellectual development. Schemas, he said, can involve behaviors (such as sucking on a finger or tying a shoelace), mental symbols (including words and images), or mental activities (e.g., doing arithmetic "in our head" or imagining actions).

At first, infants form simple schemas. For example, a "sucking schema" consolidates their experiences of sucking into images of what objects can be sucked on

schemas Generalizations based on experience that form the basic units of knowledge.

© George S. Zimbel 2010

FIGURE 12.3
Accommodation

Because the bars of the playpen are in the way, this child discovers that her schema for grasping and pulling objects toward her will not work. She then adjusts, or accommodates, her schema in order to achieve her goal.

assimilation The process of trying out existing schemas on objects that fit those schemas.

accommodation The process of modifying schemas when familiar schemas do not work.

(bottles, fingers, pacifiers) and what kinds of sucking can be done (soft and slow, speedy and vigorous). Later, children form more complex schemas, such as a schema for tying a knot or making a bed. Still later, adolescents form schemas about what it is to be in love.

Two related processes guide the development of schemas: assimilation and accommodation. In the process of **assimilation**, infants and children take in information about new objects by using existing schemas that will fit the new objects. So when an infant boy is given a new toy, he will suck on it, assimilating it into the sucking schema he has developed with his bottle and pacifier. In the same way, a toddler who sees a butterfly for the first time may assimilate it into her "birdie" schema because, like a bird, it's colorful and it flies. When an older child encounters a large dog, she will assimilate this new experience in a way that depends on her existing schema of dogs. If she has had positive experiences with a friendly family pet, she will expect the dog to behave the same, and she will greet it happily. If she has been frightened by dogs in the past, she may have a negative schema and react to this new dog with fear. In other words, past experiences affect what and how children think about new ones.

Like Cinderella's stepsisters trying to squeeze their oversized feet into the glass slipper, children sometimes distort information about a new object to make it fit their existing schema. When squeezing won't work, though, they are forced to change, or accommodate, their schema to the new object. In **accommodation**, children find that a familiar schema cannot be made to fit a new object, and so they change the schema (see Figure 12.3). So when that infant boy discovers that his new toy squeaks when it is squeezed, he accommodates his sucking schema and starts biting on the toy. When the toddler realizes that butterflies are not birds because they don't have beaks and feathers, she accommodates her "birdie" schema to include two kinds of "small flying creatures"—birds and butterflies. And if the child with the positive "doggie" schema meets a snarling stray, she discovers that her original schema does not extend to all dogs, and she refines it to distinguish between friendly dogs and aggressive ones. Through assimilation and accommodation, said Piaget, we build our knowledge of the world, block by block.

Sensorimotor Development   Piaget called the first stage of cognitive development the **sensorimotor stage** because, he claimed, the infant's mental activity and schemas are confined to sensory functions, such as seeing and hearing, and motor skills, such as grasping and sucking. According to Piaget, during this stage, infants can form schemas only of objects and actions that are present—things they can see, hear, or touch. They cannot think about absent objects because they cannot act on them. For infants, then, thinking is doing. They do not lie in the crib thinking about their mother or their teddy bear because they are not yet able to form schemas that are *mental representations* of objects and actions.

The sensorimotor period ends when infants *can* form mental representations. Now they can think about objects and actions even while the objects are not visible or the actions are not occurring. This is a remarkable milestone, according to Piaget; it frees the child from the here-and-now of the sensory environment and allows for the development of thought. One sign that children have reached this milestone is their ability to find a hidden object. This behavior was of particular interest to Piaget because for him it reflected infants' knowledge that they don't have to look at, touch, or suck an object to know that it exists. They know it exists even when it's out of sight. Piaget called this knowledge **object permanence**.

Before they acquire knowledge of object permanence, infants do not search for objects that are placed out of their sight. They act as if out of sight is literally out of mind. The first evidence of developing object permanence appears when infants are 4 to 8 months old. At this age, for the first time, they recognize a familiar object even if part of it is hidden. They know it's their bottle even if they can see only the nipple peeking out from under the blanket. In Piaget's view, infants now have some primitive mental representation of objects. If an object is completely hidden, however, they will not search for it.

Several months later, infants will search briefly for a hidden object, but their search is random and ineffective. Not until they are 18 to 24 months old, Piaget found, did infants look for an object in places other than where they saw it last, sometimes in a completely new place. According to Piaget, infants' concept of the object as permanent is now fully developed. They have a mental representation of the object that is completely separate from their immediate perception of it, and they are able to picture and follow events in their minds.

Preoperational Development   According to Piaget, the sensorimotor stage of development is followed by the **preoperational stage**. During the first half of this stage, from about ages 2 to 4, children begin to understand, create, and use *symbols* (words, images, and objects) to represent things that are not present. This ability opens up a new world for them. As described in the chapter on cognition and language, these youngsters now begin to use words to stand for objects: *Mommy, cup, me*. They are able to play "pretend." They make their fingers "walk" or "shoot" and use a spoon to make a bridge. By the age of 3 or 4, children can symbolize complex roles and events as they play "house," "doctor," or "superhero." They can also use drawing in a symbolic way: Pointing to their scribble, they might say, "This is Mommy and Daddy and me going for a walk."

During the second half of the preoperational stage, 4- to 7-year-olds begin to make intuitive guesses about the world as they try to figure out how things work. Piaget observed, though, that they cannot at first tell the difference between imagination and reality. For example, they might claim that dreams are real and take place outside of themselves as "pictures on the window" or "a circus in my room." They believe that inanimate objects are alive and have intentions, feelings, and consciousness, a belief called *animism*: "Clouds go slowly because they have no legs" and "Empty cars feel lonely." They are also highly *egocentric*, meaning that they appear to believe that the way things look to them is also how they look to everyone else. (This helps explain why they may stand between you and the TV screen and assume you can still see it, or ask, "What's this?" as they look at a picture book in the back seat of the car you're driving.)

Children's thinking is so dominated by what they can see and touch for themselves, Piaget said, that they do not realize that something is the same if its appearance changes. In one study, for example, preoperational children thought that a cat wearing a dog mask was actually a dog—because that's what it looked like (DeVries, 1969).

sensorimotor stage The first of Piaget's stages of cognitive development, when the infant's mental activity is confined to sensory perception and motor skills.

object permanence The knowledge that objects exist even when they are not in view.

preoperational stage According to Piaget, the second stage of cognitive development, during which children begin to use symbols to represent things that are not present.

During the second half of the preoperational stage, according to Piaget, children believe that inanimate objects are alive and have feelings, intentions, and consciousness.

THE FAMILY CIRCUS®   **By Bil Keane**

FAMILY CIRCUS © 1993 Bil Keane, Inc.
King Features Syndicate

"I think the moon likes us. It keeps on followin' us."

© Ellen B. Senisi

Testing for Conservation

TRY THIS If you know a child who is between the ages of 4 and 7, get parental permission to test the child for what Piaget called *conservation*. Show the child two identical lumps of clay and ask which lump is bigger. The child will probably say they are the same. Now roll one lump into a long "rope" and again ask which lump is bigger. If the child says that they are still the same, this is evidence of conservation. If the longer one is seen as bigger, conservation has not yet developed—at least not for this task. The older the child, the more likely it is that conservation will appear, but some children display conservation much earlier than Piaget thought was possible.

---

conservation The ability to recognize that the important properties of a substance remain constant despite changes in shape, length, or position.

concrete operations According to Piaget, the third stage of cognitive development, during which children's thinking is no longer dominated by visual appearances.

formal operational stage According to Piaget, the fourth stage in cognitive development, usually beginning around age 11, when abstract thinking first appears.

These children do not yet have what Piaget called **conservation**, the ability to recognize that important properties of a substance or object—including its volume, weight, and species—remain constant despite changes in its shape.

In a test of conservation, Piaget first showed children equal amounts of water in two identical containers. He then poured water from one of the containers into a tall, thin glass and the other into a short, wide glass and asked whether one glass contained more water than the other. Children at the preoperational stage of development said that one glass (usually the taller one) contained more. Their conclusion was dominated by the evidence of their eyes. If the glass looked bigger, they thought it contained more. In other words, they did not understand the logical concepts of *reversibility* (you just poured the water from one container to another, so you can pour it back, and it will still be the same amount) or *complementarity* (one glass is taller but also narrower; the other is shorter but also wider). Piaget named this stage *preoperational* because children at this stage do not yet understand logical mental operations such as these.

Concrete and Formal Operational Thought Sometime around the age of 6 or 7, Piaget observed, children develop the ability to conserve number and amount. When this happens, they enter what Piaget called the stage of **concrete operations**. Now, he said, they can count, measure, add, and subtract. Their thinking is no longer dominated by the appearance of things. They can use simple logic and perform simple mental manipulations and mental operations on things. They can also sort objects into classes (such as tools, fruit, and vehicles) or series (such as largest to smallest). Still, concrete operational children can perform their logical operations only on real, concrete objects—sticks and glasses, tools and fruit—not on abstract concepts such as justice and freedom. They can reason about what *is* but not yet about what is *possible*. The ability to think logically about abstract ideas, according to Piaget, comes in the next stage of cognitive development as children enter adolescence.

This new period is called the **formal operational stage**, and it is marked by the ability to engage in hypothetical thinking, including the imagining of logical consequences. For example, adolescents who have reached this level can consider various strategies for finding a part-time job and recognize that some methods are more likely to succeed than others. They can form general concepts and understand the impact of the past on the present and the present on the future. They can question social institutions; think about the world as it might be and ought to be; and consider the consequences and complexities of love, work, politics, and religion. They can think logically and systematically about symbols and propositions.

Piaget explored adolescents' formal operational abilities by asking them to perform science experiments that involved forming and investigating hypotheses. Research indicates that only about half the people in Western cultures ever reach the formal operational level necessary to succeed in Piaget's experiments (Kuhn & Franklin, 2006). People who have not studied science and math at a high school level are less likely to do well in those experiments (Keating, 1990). In adulthood, people are more likely to use formal operations for problems based on their own occupations; this is one reason that people who think logically at work may still become victims of a home repair or investment scam (Cialdini, 2001).

Modifying Piaget's Theory

Piaget was right in pointing out that there are significant shifts with age in children's thinking and that thinking becomes more systematic, consistent, and integrated as children get older. His idea that children are active explorers and constructors of knowledge has been absorbed into contemporary ways of thinking about childhood, and his work has inspired many other psychologists to test his findings and theory with experiments of their own. The results of these experiments suggest that Piaget's theory needs some modification.

Thinking About the Future

Once they have reached the formal operational stage, many young people become involved in politics because for the first time they can think about the consequences of differing approaches to government and which approach might support their emerging ideals.

New Views of Infants' Cognitive Development   In the years since Piaget's death, psychologists have found new ways to measure what is going on in infants' minds. They use infrared photography to record infants' eye movements, time-lapse photography to detect slight hand movements, special equipment to measure infants' sucking rates, and computer technology to track and analyze it all. Their research shows that infants know a lot more, and know it sooner, than Piaget thought they did (Onishi & Baillargeon, 2005).

It turns out that infants are not just sensing and moving during the sensorimotor period; they are already thinking as well (Saxe, Tzelnic, & Carey, 2007; Sobel & Kirkham, 2006). They are not merely experiencing isolated sights and sounds but are combining these experiences (Vouloumanos et al., 2009). This ability has been demonstrated by studies in which infants were shown two different videos at the same time but heard the soundtrack for only one of them coming from a speaker placed between the two video screens. The infants tended to look at the video that went with the soundtrack—at a toy bouncing in time with a tapping sound, at father's face when his voice was on the audio, or at an angry face when an angry voice was heard (Soken & Pick, 1992; Walker-Andrews et al., 1991). Infants can remember, too. Babies as young as 2 to 3 months of age can recall a particular mobile that was hung over their cribs a few days before (Rovee-Collier, 1999; see Figure 12.4). When they are a year old, infants can also solve simple problems, such as how to use a little "bridge" to leave a raised platform in a laboratory (Berger & Adolph, 2003). The infants thought ahead and worked out a plan of attack. When the bridge was wide, they strode across. When it was narrow, they lingered on the platform, explored the bridge with their hands or feet, clung to the handrail with both hands, and took lots of tiny steps or sidled along. Infants even seem to have a primitive understanding of some principles of physics, including gravity. For example, Renee Baillargeon (1994, 2002) found that 3-month-olds expected a box to fall if it was pushed off a platform, and they acted surprised if it didn't. Six-month-olds knew that a box could balance on a platform if most of it was on the platform.

Young babies even seem to have a sense of object permanence. Piaget had required infants to demonstrate object permanence by making effortful movements, such as removing a cover that had been placed over a hidden object. Researchers now recognize that finding a hidden object under a cover requires several abilities: mentally representing the hidden object, figuring out where it might be, and pulling off the cover. Piaget's tests did not allow for the possibility that infants know a hidden object still exists but do not have adequate strategies for finding it or memory skills for remembering it while they search. When researchers create situations in which infants merely have to stare to indicate that they know where an object is hidden, even infants under the age of 1 year have demonstrated this cognitive ability, especially

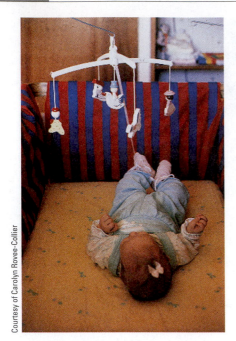

FIGURE 12.4

Infant Memory

This 3-month-old infant learned to move a mobile by kicking her left foot, which is tied to the mobile with a ribbon. Even a month later, the baby will show recognition of this particular mobile by kicking more vigorously when she sees it than when she sees another one.

when the object is a familiar one (Baillargeon, 2008; Bertenthal, Longo, & Kenny, 2007; Hespos & Baillargeon, 2001; Keen & Berthier, 2004; Shinskey & Munakata, 2005). In fact, when experimenters simply turn off the lights, infants as young as 5 months of age will reach for now-unseen objects in the dark (Clifton et al., 1991). So developmental psychologists now generally agree that infants develop some mental representations earlier than Piaget suggested.

New Views of Developmental Stages   Researchers have also shown that changes from one stage to the next are less consistent and global than Piaget thought. For example, 3-year-olds can sometimes make the distinction between physical and mental phenomena; they know the characteristics of real dogs versus pretend dogs (Woolley, 1997). Moreover, they are not always egocentric. In one study, children of this age knew that a white card, which looked pink to them when they were wearing rose-colored glasses, still looked white to someone who was not wearing the glasses (Liben, 1978). Preoperational children can even do conservation tasks if they are allowed to count the number of objects or have been trained to focus on relevant dimensions such as number, height, and width (Gelman & Baillargeon, 1983). Children succeed on conservation tasks at younger ages if their culture values a particular conservation ability (Gardiner & Kosmitzki, 2005). For example, children in cultures where pottery-making is important develop conservation of mass at younger ages than children in North American culture.

Taken together, these studies suggest that children's knowledge and mental strategies develop at different ages in different areas and in "pockets" rather than at global levels of understanding (Sternberg, 1989). Knowledge in particular areas is demonstrated sooner in children who are given specific experience in those areas or who are presented with very simple questions and tasks. Children's reasoning depends not only on their general level of development but also on how easy the task is, how familiar they are with the objects involved, how well they understand the language being used, and what experiences they have had in similar situations (Siegal, 1997). Research has also shown that the level of a child's thinking varies from day to day and may even shift when the child solves the same problem twice in the same day (Siegler, 1994).

In summary, psychologists today tend to think of cognitive development in terms of rising and falling "waves," not fixed stages (Siegler, 2006). Psychologists now suggest that children systematically try out many different solutions to problems and gradually come to select the best of them.

Information Processing During Childhood

An alternative to Piaget's theory of cognitive development is based on **information processing**, an approach discussed in the chapters on memory and on cognition and language. This approach describes cognitive activities in terms of how people take in information, use it, and remember it. Developmental psychologists taking this approach focus on gradual increases in children's mental capacities rather than on dramatic changes in their stages of development.

Their research demonstrates that as children get older, their information-processing skills gradually get better, and the children can perform more complex tasks faster and more easily (Munakata, 2006). Older children have longer attention spans and are better at filtering out irrelevant information. These skills help them overcome distractions and concentrate intently on a variety of tasks, from hobbies to homework. Older children also take in information faster and can shift their attention from one task to another more quickly. (This is how they manage to do their homework while watching TV and reading text messages.) And older children can process the information they take in more rapidly and efficiently. Compared with younger children, they code information into fewer dimensions and divide tasks into steps that can be dealt with one after another. This helps them organize and complete their homework

information processing The process of taking in, remembering or forgetting, and using information.

Courtesy of Carolyn Rovee-Collier

assignments. Older children are also better at choosing problem-solving strategies that fit the tasks they are facing (Schwenck, Bjorklund, & Schneider, 2009; Siegler, 2006).

Children's memory improves with age, too (Gathercole et al., 2004; Riggs et al., 2006). Whereas preschoolers can keep only two or three pieces of information in their short-term memory at the same time, older children can hold four or five pieces of information. Older children can also put more information into their long-term memory storage, so they remember things longer than younger children. After about age 7, children can remember information that is more complex and abstract, such as the gist of what several people have said during a conversation. Their memories are more accurate, extensive, and well organized. Because they have accumulated more knowledge during their years of learning about the world, older children can integrate new information into a more complete network of facts. This makes it easier for them to understand and remember new information. (See "In Review: Milestones of Cognitive Development in Infancy and Childhood.")

LINKAGES Why does memory improve during childhood (a link to Memory, p. 252)

What accounts for these increases in children's attention, information processing, and memory capacities? It should not be surprising that it's nature plus nurture. As mentioned earlier, maturation of the brain contributes to better and faster information processing as children grow older (Bell & Wolfe, 2007; Luciana et al., 2005; Richmond & Nelson, 2007). Experience contributes too. The importance of experience has been demonstrated by researchers who have tested children's cognitive abilities using familiar versus unfamiliar materials. In one study, for example, Mayan children in Mexico lagged behind their age-mates in the United States on standard memory tests, but this may have been because the items to be remembered were unfamiliar to them. The Mexican children did much better when researchers gave them a more familiar task,

IN REVIEW	Milestones of Cognitive Development in Infancy and Childhood	
Age*	**Achievement**	**Description**
3–4 months	Maturation of senses	Immaturities that limit the newborn's vision and hearing are overcome.
	Voluntary movement	Reflexes disappear, and infants begin to gain voluntary control over their movements.
12–18 months	Mental representation	Infants can form images of objects and actions in their minds.
	Object permanence	Infants understand that objects exist even when out of sight.
18–24 months	Symbolic thought	Young children use symbols to represent things that are not present in their pretend play, drawing, and talk.
4 years	Intuitive thought	Children reason about events, real and imagined, by guessing rather than by engaging in logical analysis.
6–7 years	Concrete operations; conservation	Children can apply simple logical operations to real objects. For example, they recognize that important properties of a substance, such as number or amount, remain constant despite changes in shape or position.
7–8 years	Information processing	Children can remember more information; they begin to learn strategies for memorization.

*These ages are approximate; the sequence, however, indicates the order in which children reach each of these milestones of cognitive development.

1. **Research in cognitive development suggests that children form mental representations _____ than Piaget thought they did.**

2. **Recognizing that changing the shape of clay doesn't change the amount of clay is evidence of a cognitive ability called _____.**

3. **The appearance of object permanence signals the end of the _____ period.**

such as recalling the objects they saw in a model of a Mayan village (Rogoff & Waddell, 1982). The children's memory for these familiar objects was better, presumably because they could process information about them more easily and quickly.

Knowing how to memorize things also improves children's memories. To a great extent, children acquire memorization strategies in school. They learn to repeat information over and over to help fix it in memory, to place information into categories, and to use memory aids such as "*i* before *e* except after *c*" to help them remember. They also learn what situations call for deliberate memorization and what factors, such as the length of a list, affect memory.

LINKAGES

LINKAGES What happens to our memories of infancy? (a link to Memory, p. 241)

Development and Memory

The ability to remember facts, figures, pictures, and objects improves as we get older and more expert at processing information. **TRY THIS** But take a minute right now and try to recall anything that happened to you when you were, say, 1 year old. Most people can accurately recall a few memories from age 5 or 6 but remember virtually nothing from before the age of 3 or 4 (Bauer, 2006; Bruce, Dolan, & Phillips-Grant, 2000; Davis, Gross, & Hayne, 2008).

Psychologists have not yet found a fully satisfactory explanation for this "infantile amnesia." Some have suggested that young children lack the memory encoding and storage processes described in the chapter on memory. Yet children 2 or 3 years old can clearly recall experiences that happened weeks or even months earlier (Bauer, 2006; Cleveland & Reese, 2008). Others suggest that infantile amnesia occurs because very young children lack a sense of self. They don't recognize themselves in a mirror, so they may not have a framework for organizing memories about what happens to them (Howe, 2003). However, this explanation cannot apply to the entire period up to 3 years of age, because children do recognize themselves in the mirror by the time they are 2. In fact, research suggests that infants even younger than 2 can recognize their own faces, as well as their voices on tape (Legerstee, Anderson, & Schaffer, 1998).

Another possibility is that early memories, though "present," are implicit rather than explicit. As described in the chapter on memory, *implicit memories* form automatically and can affect our emotions and behavior even when we do not consciously recall them. Young children's implicit memories were demonstrated in a study in which 2½-year-olds apparently remembered a dark room where they had participated in an experiment two years earlier (Perris, Myers, & Clifton, 1990). Unlike children who had never been in the room, these children were unafraid and reached for noise-making objects in the dark, just as they had learned to do at the previous session. However, children's implicit memories of their early years, like their explicit memories, are quite limited. In one study, researchers showed photographs of young children to a group of 10-year-olds (Newcombe & Fox, 1994). Some of the photos were of preschool classmates whom the children had not seen since they were 5. They explicitly recalled 21 percent of their former classmates, and their skin conductance (an index of emotion) indicated that they had implicit memories of an additional 5 percent. Yet these children had no memory of 74 percent of their preschool pals, in contrast to adults in another study, who correctly identified 90 percent of the photographs of high school classmates they had not seen in thirty years (Bahrick, Bahrick, & Wittlinger, 1975).

Other psychologists have proposed that our early memories are lost because in those years we did not yet have the language skills to talk about, and thus solidify, our memories (Simcock & Hayne, 2002). Still others say that early memories were stored, but because the schemas we used in early childhood to mentally represent them changed in later years, we no longer have the retrieval cues necessary to recall them. Another possibility is that early experiences tend to be merged into generalized event representations, such as "going to Grandma's" or "playing at the beach," so it becomes difficult to remember any specific event. It is also possible that adults have difficulty accessing early memories because when they were very young children, they lacked the emotional knowledge necessary for interpreting, representing, organizing, and retrieving information about the events they experience (Wang, 2008). Some researchers have suggested, too, that infantile amnesia is due partly to the ways that people are asked about their early memories and that specialized questioning techniques might allow retrieval of early memories that are normally unavailable (Jack & Hayne, 2007).

Research on hypotheses such as these may someday unravel the mystery of infantile amnesia (Nelson & Fivush, 2004; Newcombe et al., 2000; Wang, 2006).

Culture and Cognitive Development

To explain cognitive development, Piaget focused on the physical world of objects. The Russian psychologist Lev Vygotsky (pronounced "vuh-GAHT-skee") focused on the social world of people. He viewed cognitive abilities as the product of cultural history. The child's mind, said Vygotsky, grows through interaction with other minds. Support for this idea comes from dramatic cases such as the "Wild Boy of Aveyron," a French child who, in the late 1700s, was apparently lost or abandoned by his parents at an early age and grew up with animals. At about 11 years of age, he was captured by hunters and sent to Paris, where scientists observed him. What the scientists saw was a dirty, frightened creature who trotted like a wild animal and spent most of his time silently rocking. Although the scientists worked with the boy for more than ten years, he was never able to live unguarded among other people, and he never learned to speak.

Consistent with Vygotsky's ideas, this tragic case suggests that without society, children's minds would not develop much beyond those of animals—that children acquire their ideas through interaction with parents, teachers, and other members of their culture. Vygotsky's followers have studied the effects of the social world on children's cognitive development, especially how participation in social routines affects children's developing knowledge of the world (Gauvain, 2001). In Western societies, those routines include shopping, eating at McDonald's, going to birthday parties, and attending religious services. In other cultures, they might include making pottery, going hunting, and weaving baskets. Quite early, children develop mental representations, called *scripts,* for these activities (see the chapter on cognition and language). By the time they are 3, children can accurately describe the scripts for their routine activities (Nelson, 1986). Scripts, in turn, affect children's knowledge and understanding of cognitive tasks. As mentioned earlier, in cultures in which pottery making is important, children display conservation about the mass of objects sooner than children do in other cultures. Similarly, middle-class, suburban children can understand conservation problems earlier than poor inner-city children if the problems are presented, as Piaget's were, like miniature science experiments. But the performance of inner-city children is improved when the task is presented through a more familiar script, such as one involving what a "con artist" would do to fool someone (White & Glick, 1978).

Children's cognitive abilities are also influenced by the language of their culture. Consider, for instance, the way people think about relations between objects in space. Children who learn a language that has no words for spatial concepts—such as *in, on, in front of, behind, to the left,* and *to the right*—will acquire cognitive categories that are different from those of people in North America. These individuals do, in fact, have difficulty distinguishing between the left and right sides of objects, and they tend not to use the symbolic associations with left and right hands that North Americans do (Bowerman, 1996; Levinson, 1996).

As a cultural tool, language can also affect academic achievement. For example, Korean and Chinese children show exceptional ability at adding and subtracting large numbers (Miller et al., 1995). As third-graders, they can do in their heads three-digit problems (such as 702 – 125) that would stump most North American children. The difference seems due in part to the clear way that Asian languages label the numbers from 11 to 19. In English, the meaning of the words *eleven* and *twelve,* for instance, is not as clear as the Asian *ten-one* and *ten-two.* In addition, Asians use the metric system of measurement and a manual computing device called the *abacus,* both of which are structured around the number 10. Korean math textbooks emphasize this tens

Babies at Risk

The cognitive development of infants raised in this understaffed Russian orphanage will be permanently impaired if they are not given far more stimulation in the orphanage or, better yet, adopted into a loving family before they're 6 months of age (Beckett et al., 2006; Kreppner et al., 2007). It's likely that they'll suffer from reduced brain metabolism and reduced activity in regions associated with higher cognitive functions, memory, and emotion (Nelson, 2007). Their IQs at the end of childhood are likely to be lower than other children's by an average of 15 points.

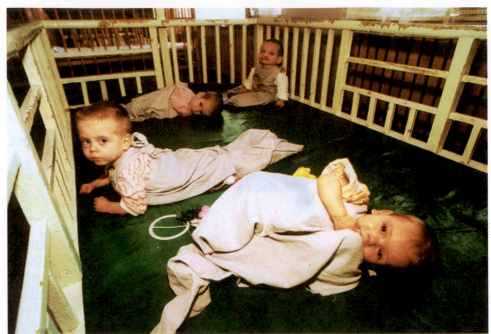

© Josef Polleross/The Image Works

structure by presenting the ones digits in red, the tens in blue, and the hundreds in green. Above all, in Asian cultures, educational achievement, especially in mathematics, is encouraged at home and strongly supported in school (Naito & Miura, 2001). In short, children's cognitive development is affected in ways large and small by the culture in which they live (Cole, 2006).

Improving or Endangering Cognitive Development

Even within a single culture, some children are mentally advanced while others lag behind their peers. Cognitive development is seriously delayed if children are raised in environments that deprive them of the everyday sights, sounds, and feelings provided by conversation and loving interaction with family members, by pictures and books, and by toys, television, and the Internet. Children subjected to this kind of severe deprivation show marked impairment in intellectual development by the time they are 2 or 3 years old. They may never fully recover, even if they are given special attention later on. "Genie" was one such child. When rescued at age 14, she weighed only 59 pounds. The only things she could say were "stop it" and "no more." Investigators discovered that she had spent her life confined to a small bedroom, harnessed to a potty chair during the day and caged in a crib at night. She had not been permitted to hear or make many sounds. Although scientists and therapists worked intensively with Genie in the years after her rescue, she never learned to speak in complete sentences, and she remains in an adult care facility.

Children's inherited potential for cognitive development can also be impaired by less extreme conditions of deprivation, including the neglect, malnourishment, noise, and chaos that occur in many poor households (Berger, Paxson, & Waldfogel, 2009; Turkheimer et al., 2003). The physical conditions in poor homes are more likely to be inadequate, and mothers are more likely to be stressed, depressed, harsh, and unresponsive (Berger, Paxson, & Waldfogel, 2009). One study found that by the time they were 5 years old, children growing up in poverty scored 9 points lower on intelligence tests than children in families whose incomes were twice the poverty level (Duncan, Brooks-Gunn, & Klebanov, 1994). These differences continue as poor children enter school. Children who remain in poverty have lower IQs and poorer school achievement (McLoyd, 1998; Siegler, 2003; Stipek & Ryan, 1997); they have more learning disabilities

When Does Stimulation Become Overstimulation?

A child's cognitive development is enhanced by a stimulating environment, but can there be too much stimulation? In the face of an avalanche of electronic media aimed specifically at babies and toddlers, some people are beginning to wonder. These stimulating media include computer "lapware," such as this baby is enjoying, videos and DVDs for even the tiniest infants, and of course, the *Teletubbies*. Many babies in Western countries are immersed in electronic media for hours each day. In the United States, 20 to 25 percent of children under the age of 2 have a TV set in their rooms, and one-third of them have videos in the "Baby Einstein" series (Lewin, 2003; Vandewater et al., 2007). We don't yet know how all this well-intentioned electronic stimulation is affecting young children, but in 2009, the Disney corporation offered refunds to customers who had purchased Baby Einstein DVDs because despite earlier claims, the company could provide no evidence that these videos promote babies' cognitive development (Lewin, 2009).

© Jim Craigmyle/Corbis

(Bigelow, 2006), they are less engaged in school (Teachman, 2008), and they do worse on neurocognitive tests (Farah et al., 2006). They are twice as likely to be held back a grade and 3½ times as likely to drop out of high school (Children's Defense Fund, 2004). One study of more than ten thousand children found that the economic status of a child's family is a much better predictor of the child's later cognitive development than physical risk factors such as low birth weight (Jefferis, Power, & Hertzman, 2002). The effects of poverty come from a buildup of problems that often begins with prenatal complications and continues through childhood with lack of cognitive stimulation and, perhaps most important, harsh and inconsistent parenting (NICHD Early Child Care Research Network, 2005b). It is no wonder, then, that lower average IQs are seen in countries where higher numbers of children are living in poverty (Weiss, 2007).

In families above the poverty line, too, children's cognitive development is related to their surroundings, their experiences, and their parents' behavior. For example, 2-year-old children whose mothers gave them lots of hints, suggestions, and other cognitive guidance during a problem-solving task had higher IQ scores when they were 5 years old than children whose mothers had simply told them what they needed to do to complete the task (Fagot & Gauvain, 1997). Reading to children at a very early age is also related to enhanced development of language and other cognitive skills (Raikes et al., 2006). Higher cognitive test scores are seen in preschoolers whose parents have the income to provide a more stimulating learning environment (Yeung, Linver, & Brooks-Gunn, 2002), one that is not crowded and chaotic and where, as a result, parents can be more responsive (Evans et al., 2010). Some aspects of that environment are more beneficial than others, though. One study found, for example, that early access to a computer at home has a positive influence on young children's cognitive development (Fish et al., 2008). In another study, third-graders whose parents had bought them a TV for their bedrooms but not a computer scored 10 to 20 points lower on tests of math, reading, and language than children who had a computer but no TV in the bedroom (Borzekowski & Robinson, 2005).

To improve the cognitive skills of children who do not get the optimum stimulation and guidance at home, developmental psychologists have provided extra lessons, materials, and educational contact with sensitive adults. In a variety of such programs, ranging from weekly home visits to daily preschools, children's cognitive abilities have been enhanced (Love et al., 2005; Ramey, Ramey, & Lanzi, 2006), and some effects have lasted into adulthood (Campbell, Pungello, et al., 2001). Music lessons also promote children's cognitive development, especially verbal memory (Ho, Cheung, & Chan, 2003; Schellenberg, 2004). Access to the Internet has been related to improved reading scores and school grades among poor children (Jackson et al., 2006), and even electronic games, although no substitute for adult attention, can provide opportunities for school-age children to hone spatial skills that can improve their performance in math and science (Blumberg, Rosenthal, & Randall, 2008; Canada & Goering, 2008; de Freitas & Griffiths, 2007; Green & Bavelier, 2003; Subrahmanyam et al., 2001).

Infancy and Childhood: Social and Emotional Development

Life for a child is more than learning about objects, doing math problems, and getting good grades. It is also about social relationships and emotional reactions. From the first months onward, infants are sensitive to the people around them (Mumme & Fernald, 2003), and they are both attracted by and attractive to other people—especially parents and other caregivers.

During the first hour or so after birth, mothers gaze into their infants' eyes and give them gentle touches (Klaus & Kennell, 1976). This is the first opportunity for the mother to display her *bond* to her infant—an emotional tie that begins even before the baby is born (Feldman et al., 2007). Psychologists once believed that this immediate contact was critical—that the mother-infant bond would never be strong if the opportunity for early interaction was missed. Research has revealed, however, that such interaction in the first few hours is not a requirement for a close relationship (Myers, 1987). With or without early contact, mothers and fathers, whether biological or adoptive, come to form close attachments to their infants by interacting with them day after day.

As the mother gazes at her baby, the baby gazes back. By the time infants are 2 days old, they recognize—and like—their mother's face. When allowed to control a videotape player by sucking, they will suck more vigorously to see a video of her face than to see that of a stranger (Walton, Bower, & Bower, 1992). Soon they begin to respond to the mother's facial expressions as well. By the time they are a year old, children use their mothers' emotional expressions to guide their own behavior in uncertain situations (Saarni et al., 2006). Research on infants' brain activity suggests that they pay particular attention to fear and other negative emotions (Carver & Vaccaro, 2007). So if the mother looks frightened when a stranger approaches, for example, the child is more likely to avoid the stranger. As mentioned in the chapter on motivation and emotion, this phenomenon is called *social referencing*. Children can pick up emotion cues from many sources, including television. In one study, after seeing a video in which an adult showed fear of an object, infants later avoided that object (Mumme & Fernald, 2003). As described in the chapter on learning, observation of other people's reactions can sometimes lead to the development of fears and even phobias.

Infants communicate feelings as well as recognize them. They do so by crying and screaming but also by more subtle behavior. When they want to interact, they look and smile; when they do not want to interact, they turn away and suck their thumbs (Tronick, 1989). And even before they can speak a word, infants use gestures to show their caregivers that they are feeling happy, mad, sad, scared, sleepy, or cold (Vallotton, 2008).

Individual Temperament

From the moment they are born, infants differ from one another in the emotions they express most often. Some infants are happy, active, and vigorous; they splash, thrash, and wriggle. Others are usually quiet. Some infants approach new objects with enthusiasm; others turn away or fuss. Some infants whimper; others kick, scream, and wail. Characteristics such as these make up the infant's **temperament**—the infant's individual style and frequency of expressing needs and emotions. Although temperament mainly reflects nature's contribution to the beginning of an individual's personality, it can also be affected by the prenatal environment, including—as noted earlier—the mother's stress level, smoking, and drug use during pregnancy. The stress experienced by the mother after her baby's birth also affects the baby's temperament. Research indicates that breast-fed infants who ingest more of the stress-related hormone cortisol tend to have more fearful temperaments (Glynn et al., 2007). And if mothers of babies with negative temperaments continue to experience stress, the babies tend to express even more negative emotion during the next five years (Pesonen et al., 2008).

In some of the earliest research on infant temperament, Alexander Thomas and Stella Chess (1977) found that most babies fall into one of three general temperament patterns. *Easy babies* are the most common kind. They get hungry and sleepy at predictable times, react to new situations cheerfully, and seldom fuss. In contrast, *difficult babies* are irregular and irritable. *Slow-to-warm-up babies* react warily to new situations but eventually come to enjoy them. Later research has shown that traces of these early temperament patterns weave their way throughout childhood (Komsi et al., 2008; Rothbart & Bates, 2006). Easy infants usually stay easy (Zhou et al., 2004) and tend not to develop conduct problems (Lahey et al., 2008); difficult infants often remain difficult, sometimes developing attention and aggression problems in childhood (Else-Quest et al., 2006; Miner & Clarke-Stewart, 2008). Timid or slow-to-warm-up toddlers tend to be shy as preschoolers, restrained and inhibited as 8-year-olds, and somewhat anxious as teenagers (Roberts, Caspi, & Moffitt, 2001). The differences even seem to extend into adulthood. In one study, the brains of adults who were timid toddlers reacted especially strongly to novel stimuli (Schwartz et al., 2003).

However, these tendencies are not set in stone. In temperament, as in cognitive development, nature interacts with nurture (Jaffari-Bimmel et al., 2006). Many events take place between infancy and adulthood that can shift an individual's development in one direction or another. One source of influence suggested by Thomas and Chess (1977) is the degree to which an infant's temperament matches the parents' personal styles and what they want and expect from their baby. When the match is a good one, parents tend to support and encourage the infant's behavior, thus increasing the chances that temperamental qualities will be stable. Consider, for example, the temperament patterns of Chinese American and European American children. At birth, Chinese American infants are calmer, less likely to become upset, and more easily consoled than is typical of European American infants (Kagan et al., 1994). The possibility of an inherited predisposition toward self-control among the Chinese is supported by the fact that only about 2 percent of children in China have a genetic pattern associated with impulse control problems, compared with about 48 percent of children in the United States (Chang et al., 1996). This tendency toward self-control is powerfully reinforced by the Chinese culture. Compared with European American parents, Chinese parents are less likely to reward and stimulate their infants' babbling and smiling and more likely to maintain close control. The children, in turn, are less vocal, noisy, and active than European American children (Smith & Freedman, 1983), and as preschoolers, they show far more impulse control, including the ability to wait their turn (Sabbagh et al., 2006).

These temperamental differences between children in different ethnic groups illustrate the combined contributions of nature and nurture. There are many other illustrations as well. Mayan infants, for example, are relatively inactive from birth. The Zinacantecos, a Mayan group in southern Mexico, reinforce this innate predisposition toward restrained motor activity by swaddling their infants and by nursing them at the slightest sign of movement (Greenfield & Childs, 1991). This combination of genetic predisposition and cultural reinforcement is culturally adaptive. Quiet Mayan infants do not kick off their covers at night, which is important in the cold highlands where they

temperament An individual's basic disposition, which is evident from infancy.

live. Inactive infants are able to spend long periods on their mothers' backs as the mothers work. Infants who do not begin to walk until they can understand some language do not wander into the open fire at the center of the house. This adaptive interplay of innate and cultural factors in the development of temperament operates in all cultures.

Nature and nurture combine to influence individual differences within cultures too. A variety of studies show that children are more likely to display aggressiveness, anxiety, depression, or academic and social problems if they have suffered the "double whammy" of starting life with a difficult temperament and then being raised in a harsh, insensitive, unsupportive, or anxiety-provoking family environment (Miner & Clarke-Stewart, 2008; Paulussen-Hoogeboom et al., 2008; Stright, Gallagher, & Kelley, 2008). For example, children who had both timid temperaments and mothers who were unsupportive, negative, or depressed were more likely to remain fearful, to be socially withdrawn, to have more negative moods, and to have difficulty controlling their negative emotions (Feng et al., 2008; Gilissen et al., 2008; Hane et al., 2008). However, if a difficult or shy baby is lucky enough to have patient parents who allow their baby to respond to new situations and changes in daily routines at a more relaxed pace, the baby is likely to become less difficult or shy over time.

Attachment

During the first year of life, as infants and caregivers watch and respond to one another, the infants begin to form an **attachment** to their caregivers—a deep, affectionate, close, and enduring relationship. **Attachment theory** was first developed by John Bowlby, a British psychoanalyst who drew attention to the importance of attachment after he observed children who had been orphaned in World War II. These children's depression and other emotional scars led Bowlby to develop a theory about the importance of developing and maintaining a strong attachment to a primary caregiver, a tie that normally keeps infants close to their caregivers and therefore safe (Bowlby, 1951, 1973). Soon after Bowlby presented his theory, researchers in the United States began to investigate how such attachments are formed and what happens when they are not formed or when they are broken by loss or separation. Some of the most dramatic of these studies were conducted by Harry Harlow.

Motherless Monkeys—and Children Harlow (1959) explored two hypotheses about what leads infants to develop attachments to their mothers. The first hypothesis was that attachment occurs because mothers feed their babies. Perhaps food, along with the experience of being fed, creates an emotional bond with the mother. Harlow's second hypothesis was that attachment is based on the warm, comforting contact the baby gets from the mother.

To evaluate these hypotheses, Harlow separated newborn monkeys from their mothers and raised them in cages containing two artificial mothers. One "mother" was made of wire, but it had a rubber nipple from which the infant could get milk (see Figure 12.5). In other words, it provided food but no physical comfort. The other artificial mother had no nipple but was made of soft, comfortable terrycloth. Harlow found that the infants preferred the terrycloth mother, spending most of their time with it, especially when frightened. The terrycloth mother provided feelings of softness and cuddling, which were things the infants needed when they sensed danger.

Harlow also investigated what happens when attachments do not form. He isolated some newborn monkeys from all social contact. After a year of this isolation, the monkeys showed dramatic disturbances. When visited by normally active, playful monkeys, they withdrew to a corner, huddling or rocking for hours. As adults, they were unable to have normal sexual relations. When some of the females did have babies through artificial insemination, they tended to ignore them. When their infants became distressed, the mothers physically abused and sometimes even killed them.

Humans who spend their first few years without a consistent caregiver react in a tragically similar manner. At Romanian and Russian orphanages where children

attachment A deep and enduring relationship with a caregiver or other person with whom a baby has shared many early experiences.

attachment theory The idea that children form a close attachment to their earliest caregivers and that this attachment pattern can affect aspects of the children's later life.

FIGURE 12.5
Wire and Terrycloth "Mothers"
These are the two types of artificial mothers used in Harlow's research. Although baby monkeys received milk from the wire mother, they spent most of their time with the terrycloth version, and they clung to it when frightened.

were neglected by institutional caregivers, visitors discovered that the children, like Harlow's deprived monkeys, had not developed attachments to their caregivers; they were withdrawn and engaged in constant rocking (Holden, 1996; Zeanah et al., 2005, 2009). Emotional problems continued even after the children were adopted. In one study, researchers observed 4-year-old children who had been in a Romanian orphanage for at least eight months before being adopted. The behavior of these children was compared with the behavior of children matched for age and gender who had been adopted before the age of 4 months (Chisholm, 1997). The late-adopted children were found to have many more serious problems. Depressed or withdrawn, they stared blankly, demanded attention, and could not control their temper (Holden, 1996). They interacted poorly with their adoptive mothers but were inappropriately friendly with all strangers, trying to cuddle and kiss them. At age 6, a third of late-adopted children still showed no preference for their parents or any tendency to look to them when stressed (Rutter, O'Connor, & ERA Study Team, 2004). Neuroscientists suggest that the dramatic problems observed in isolated monkeys and humans are the result of developmental brain dysfunction or damage brought on by a lack of touch and body movement in infancy and by the absence of early play, conversation, and other normal childhood experiences (Prescott, 1996; Rutter, O'Connor, & ERA Study Team, 2004; Wismer Fries, Shirtcliff, & Pollak, 2008).

Forming an Attachment   Fortunately, most infants do have a consistent caregiver, usually the mother, to whom they can form an attachment. They learn to recognize her and are able to distinguish her from a stranger at an early age. Some infants vocalize more to their mothers than to a stranger when they are only 3 months old. These babies are the smart ones; years later, they do better on tests, get higher grades, complete more education, and in their twenties are more likely to be in stable romantic relationships (Roe, 2001). By the age of 6 or 7 months, almost all infants show signs of preferring their mothers to anyone else—watching her closely, crawling after her, clambering up into her lap, protesting when she leaves, and brightening when she returns (Ainsworth, 1973). After an attachment has been formed, separation from the mother for even thirty minutes can be a stressful experience (Larson, Gunnar, & Hertsgaard, 1991). Soon after, infants develop attachments to their fathers as well (Lamb, 1997). However, interactions with fathers are typically less frequent and of a somewhat different nature than with mothers (Parke, 2002). Mothers tend to feed, bathe, dress, cuddle, and talk to their infants, whereas fathers are more likely to play with, jiggle, and toss them, especially sons.

Variations in Attachment   The amount of closeness and contact infants seek with either the mother or the father depends to some extent on the infant. Those who are ill, tired, or slow to warm up may require more closeness. Closeness also depends to some extent on the parents. An infant whose parent has been absent, aloof, or unresponsive is likely to need more closeness than one whose parent is consistently accessible and responsive.

Researchers have studied the differences in infants' **attachment behavior** in a special situation that simulates the natural comings and goings of parents and children—the so-called *Strange Situation* (Ainsworth et al., 1978). This assessment occurs in an unfamiliar playroom where the infant interacts with the mother and an unfamiliar woman in brief episodes: The infant plays with the mother and the stranger, the mother leaves the baby with the stranger for a few minutes, the mother and the stranger leave the baby alone in the room briefly, and the mother returns to the room.

Videos of these sessions show that most infants display a *secure attachment* to the mother in the Strange Situation (Thompson, 2006). In the unfamiliar room, they use the mother as a home base, leaving her side to explore and play but returning to her periodically for comfort or contact. When the mother returns after the brief separation, the infant is happy to see her and receptive when she initiates contact. Some infants, however, display an *insecure attachment*. Their relationship with their

attachment behavior Actions such as crying, smiling, vocalizing, and gesturing that help bring an infant into closer proximity to its caregiver.

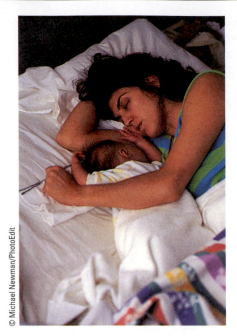

Cultural Differences in Parent-Child Relations

Variations in the intimacy of family interactions, including whether infants sleep in their parents' bed, may contribute to cross-cultural differences in attachment patterns.

mother may be (1) *avoidant*—they avoid or ignore their mother when she returns after the brief separation; (2) *ambivalent*—they are upset when the mother leaves, but when she returns, they vacillate between clinging to her and angrily rejecting her efforts at contact; or (3) *disorganized*—their behavior is inconsistent, disturbed, and disturbing; they may begin to cry after their mother has returned and comforted them, or they may reach out for their mother while looking away from her (Moss et al., 2004).

Patterns of attachment vary widely in different parts of the world and are related to how parents treat their children. In northern Germany, for example, where parents promote children's independence with strict discipline, the number of infants who display avoidant attachments is quite high (Spangler, Fremmer-Bombik, & Grossman, 1996). In Japan, where mothers are completely devoted to their young children and are seldom apart from them, including at night, children develop an attachment relationship that emphasizes harmony and union; these children cannot bear it when their mothers try to leave the room in the Strange Situation (Rothbaum et al., 2000). Both of these attachment patterns differ from the secure one that is most common in North America, where, with their parents' encouragement, children balance closeness and proximity with exploration and autonomy.

In all countries, the likelihood that children will develop a secure attachment depends on the mother's attentiveness; if the mother is generally sensitive and responsive to the baby's needs and signals, a secure attachment is likely; if she is rejecting or neglectful, the child's attachment is more likely to be insecure (Bakermans-Kranenburg, van IJzendoorn, & Juffer, 2008; Nievar & Becker, 2008).

Consequences of Attachment Patterns A secure attachment to the mother is reflected in the child's relationships with other people too. For example, compared to other children, those with secure attachments tend to have better relations with their peers in childhood and adolescence (Thompson, 2006), and they are especially likely to have good relationships with close friends (Lucas-Thompson & Clarke-Stewart, 2007; McElwain et al., 2008). Securely attached children also require less contact, guidance, and discipline from their teachers and are less likely to seek excessive attention, to act impulsively or aggressively, to express frustration, or to display helplessness (see the chapter on learning; Carlson, Sroufe, & Egeland, 2004; NICHD Early Child Care Research Network, 2006; Sroufe et al., 2005). Their teachers like them better, expect more of them, and rate them as more competent (Diener et al., 2008).

Why should this be? According to Bowlby, securely attached children develop positive relationships with other people because they develop mental representations, or *internal working models,* of the social world that lead them to expect that, like their mothers, everyone else will respond to them in a positive way. But secure attachment at the age of one doesn't guarantee a life of social competence and emotional well-being. If the mother or other primary caregiver later becomes neglectful or rejecting as the result of marital strife, divorce, or depression, for example, the secure attachment is likely to disintegrate, and the child may begin to have problems (Thompson, 2006). So although a secure attachment alone does not predict long-term sociability and well-being, in concert with continuing supportive care, it sets the stage for positive psychological growth.

THINKING CRITICALLY

Does Day Care Harm the Emotional Development of Infants?

With about 60 percent of mothers in North America working outside the home, concern has been expressed about how daily separations from their children might affect the children, especially infants (Clarke-Stewart & Allhusen, 2005). Some have argued that leaving infants with a babysitter or putting them in a day care center

© Lawrence Migdale/Stone/Getty Images

The Effects of Day Care

Parents are understandably concerned that leaving their infants in a day care center all day might interfere with the mother-infant attachment or with other aspects of the children's development. Research shows that most infants in day care do form attachments to their parents but that if children spend many hours in day care between infancy and kindergarten, they are more likely to have behavior problems in school, such as talking back to the teacher or getting into fights with other children (Belsky et al., 2007). Some employers try to help parents build attachments with their infants by providing on-site day care or allowing employees to keep their babies in their offices while working (Armour, 2008). While this may help parents and their children stay in contact throughout the day, what problems might it cause in the workplace?

damages the quality of the mother-infant relationship and increases the babies' risk for psychological problems later on.

What am I being asked to believe or accept?

The claim to be evaluated is that daily separations brought about by a mother's wish or need to work undermine the infant's ability to form a secure attachment and harm the infant's emotional development.

What evidence is available to support the assertion?

There is clear evidence that separation from the mother is painful for young children. Furthermore, if separation lasts a week or more, young children may become apathetic and mournful and eventually lose interest in the missing mother (Robertson & Robertson, 1971). But day care does not involve such lasting separations, and research has shown that infants in day care do form and maintain attachments to their mothers (Lamb & Ahnert, 2006).

Are these attachments as secure as the attachments formed by infants whose mothers do not work outside the home? Researchers first examined this question by comparing infants' behavior in the Strange Situation. A review of their data showed that on average, infants in full-time day care were somewhat more likely to be classified as insecurely attached. Specifically, 36 percent of the infants in full-time care received this classification, compared with 29 percent of the infants not in full-time care (Clarke-Stewart, 1989). These results appear to support the suggestion that day care hinders the development of infants' attachments to their mothers.

Are there alternative ways of interpreting the evidence?

Perhaps factors other than day care could explain this difference between infants in day care and those at home with their mothers. One such factor could be the method used to assess attachment—the Strange Situation. Infants in these studies were judged insecure if they did not run to their mothers after a brief separation. But maybe infants who experience daily separations from their mothers are less disturbed by the separations in the Strange Situation and therefore seek out less closeness with their mothers. A second factor could be differences between the infants' mothers: Perhaps mothers who value independence in themselves and in their children are more likely to be working and to place their children in care, whereas mothers who emphasize closeness with their children are more likely to stay home.

What additional evidence would help evaluate the alternatives?

Finding insecure attachment to be more common among the infants of working mothers does not, by itself, prove that day care is harmful. To judge the effects of care, we must use other measures of emotional adjustment. If infants in care show consistent signs of troubled emotional relations in other situations (at home, say) and with other caregivers (such as the father), this evidence would support the argument that day care harms children's emotional development. Another useful method would be to statistically control for differences in the attitudes and behaviors of parents who do and do not use day care and then examine the differences in their children.

In fact, this research design has already been employed. The U.S. government funded a study of infant day care in ten sites around the country. The psychological and physical development of more than thirteen hundred randomly selected infants was tracked from birth through age 3. The results showed that when factors such as parents' education, income, and attitudes were statistically controlled, infants in day care were no more likely to have emotional problems or to be insecurely attached to their mothers than infants not in day care. However, when infants were placed in poor-quality day care—where the caregivers were insensitive and unresponsive—and the infants' mothers were insensitive to their needs at home, the children were less likely to develop a secure attachment to their mothers (Belsky et al., 2007; NICHD Early Childhood Research Network, 2005a, 2006).

What conclusions are most reasonable?

Based on available evidence, the most reasonable conclusion appears to be that day care by itself does not lead to insecure attachment or cause emotional harm to infants. But if the care is of poor quality, it can worsen a risky situation at home and increase the likelihood that infants will have problems forming a secure attachment to their mothers. The U.S. government study is still under way, and the children's progress is being followed into adolescence.

Relationships with Parents

Like Bowlby, Erik Erikson (1968) saw the first year of life as the time when infants develop a feeling of basic trust (or mistrust) about the world. According to his theory, an infant's first year represents the first of eight stages of lifelong psychosocial development (see Table 12.2). Each stage focuses on an issue or "crisis" that is especially

TABLE 12.2 Erikson's Stages of Psychosocial Development

In each of Erikson's stages of development, a different psychological issue presents a new crisis for the person to resolve. The person focuses attention on that issue and by the end of the period has worked through the crisis and resolved it either positively, in the direction of healthy development, or negatively, hindering further psychological development.

Age	Central Psychological Issue or Crisis
First year	**Trust versus mistrust** Infants learn to trust that their needs will be met by the world, especially by the mother—or they learn to mistrust the world.
Second year	**Autonomy versus shame and doubt** Children learn to exercise their will, to make choices, and to control themselves—or they become uncertain and doubt that they can do things by themselves.
Third to fifth year	**Initiative versus guilt** Children learn to initiate activities and enjoy their accomplishments, acquiring direction and purpose. But if they are not allowed initiative, they feel guilty about their attempts at independence.
Sixth year through puberty	**Industry versus inferiority** Children develop a sense of industry and curiosity and are eager to learn—or they feel inferior and lose interest in the tasks before them.
Adolescence	**Identity versus role confusion** Adolescents come to see themselves as unique and integrated persons with an ideology—or they become confused about what they want out of life.
Early adulthood	**Intimacy versus isolation** Young people become able to commit themselves to another person—or they develop a sense of isolation and feel they have no one in the world but themselves.
Middle age	**Generativity versus stagnation** Adults are willing to have and care for children and to devote themselves to their work and the common good—or they become self-centered and inactive.
Old age	**Integrity versus despair** Older people enter a period of reflection, becoming assured that their lives have been meaningful and ready to face death with acceptance and dignity. Or they are in despair for their unaccomplished goals, failures, and ill-spent lives.

important at that time of life. If the crisis is not resolved positively, the person will be psychologically troubled and cope less effectively with later crises. After children have formed emotional attachments to their parents, their next psychological task is to begin to develop a more independent, or autonomous, relationship with them. This task is part of Erikson's second stage, when children begin to exercise their will, develop some independence from their parents, and begin activities on their own. According to Erikson, children who are not allowed to exercise their will or begin their own activities will feel uncertain about doing things for themselves and guilty about seeking independence. The extent to which parents allow or encourage their children's autonomy depends largely on their parenting style.

Parenting Styles   Most parents try to channel their children's impulses into socially accepted outlets and to teach them the skills and rules needed to function in their society. As they engage in this **socialization** process, European American parents tend to employ one of four distinct **parenting styles** (Baumrind, 1971; Maccoby & Martin, 1983). **Authoritarian parents** are relatively strict, punitive, and unsympathetic. They value obedience and try to shape their children's behavior to meet a set standard and to curb the children's will. They do not encourage independence. They are detached and seldom praise their youngsters. **Permissive parents** are more affectionate with their children and give them lax discipline and a great deal of freedom. **Authoritative parents** fall between these two extremes. They reason with their children, encouraging give-and-take and setting limits but also encouraging independence. They are firm but understanding; their demands are reasonable and consistent. As their children get older and better at making decisions, authoritative parents give their children more responsibility. **Uninvolved parents** (also known as **rejecting-neglecting parents**) are indifferent to their children. They do whatever is necessary to minimize the costs of having children by investing as little time, money, and effort as possible. They focus on their own needs before their children's. These parents often fail to monitor their children's activities, particularly when the children are old enough to be out of the house alone.

Research shows some clear relationships between parenting styles and children's social and emotional development (Eisenberg, Fabes, & Spinrad, 2006; Parke & Buriel, 2006; Paulussen-Hoogeboom et al., 2008; Thompson, 2006). The children of authoritarian parents tend to be unfriendly, distrustful, and withdrawn. They are less likely than other children to be empathic and more likely to be aggressive. They are also more likely to cheat, and after doing something wrong, they are less likely to feel guilty or accept blame. Children of permissive parents are relatively immature, dependent, and unhappy; they often have tantrums or ask for help when they encounter even slight difficulties. Children raised by authoritative parents tend to be friendly, cooperative, self-reliant, and socially responsible (Ginsburg et al., 2009). They do better in school and are more popular than children with other kinds of parents. Children of uninvolved parents are less likely than other children to form secure attachments and more likely to have problems with impulsivity, aggression, noncompliance, moodiness, and low self-esteem.

The results of research on parenting styles are interesting and important, but they are limited in several ways. First, they are based on correlations, which, as discussed in the chapter on research in psychology, do not prove causation. Finding consistent correlations between parenting styles and children's behavior does not establish that the parents' behavior is *causing* the differences seen in their children. Socialization is a two-way street: Parents' behavior is shaped by their children as well as the reverse. Children's temperament, size, appearance, and behavior all influence the way parents treat them (Bugental & Grusec, 2006). Some psychologists have even suggested that it is not the parents' behavior itself that influences children but rather how the children perceive the discipline they receive—as stricter or more lenient than what an older sibling receives, for example (Reiss et al., 2000). A second limitation of these studies is that the correlations between parenting styles and children's behavior, though statistically significant, are not terribly large and therefore do not apply to every child in every family. In fact, the effects of parents' socialization may depend partly on a

socialization The process by which parents, teachers, and others teach children the skills and social norms necessary to be well-functioning members of society.

parenting styles The varying patterns of behavior that parents display as they interact with and discipline their children.

authoritarian parents Firm, punitive, and unsympathetic parents who value obedience from the child and authority for themselves.

permissive parents Parents who give their child great freedom and lax discipline.

authoritative parents Parents who reason with the child, encourage give-and-take, and are firm but understanding.

uninvolved (rejecting-neglecting) parents Parents who are indifferent to their children.

Parent-Training Programs

Research on how parenting styles affect children's behavior has helped shape parent-training programs based on the learning principles described in the chapter on learning and on the social-cognitive and humanistic approaches described in the chapter on personality. These programs are designed to teach parents authoritative methods that can avoid scenes like this.

© David Young-Wolff/PhotoEdit

child's temperament. The gentle parental guidance that has a noticeable effect on a child with a fearful temperament might have far less impact on a child whose temperament is less fearful (Kochanska, Aksan, & Joy, 2007). Similarly, harsh authoritarian parenting seems to disrupt emotion regulation and the development of conscience in children who are temperamentally fearful (Feng et al., 2008; Schwartz & Bugental, 2004; Kochanska, 1997).

Parenting Styles and Culture   Yet another limitation of parenting studies is that most of them were conducted with European American families. Is the impact of various parenting styles different in other ethnic groups and other cultures? Possibly. Parents in Latino cultures in Mexico, Puerto Rico, and Central America and in Asian cultures in China and India, for example, tend to be influenced by a collectivist tradition in which family and community interests are emphasized over individual goals. Children in these cultures are expected to respect and obey their elders and to do less of the questioning, negotiating, and arguing that is encouraged—or at least allowed—in many middle-class European and European American families (Greenfield, Suzuki, & Rothstein-Fisch, 2006; Parke & Buriel, 2006). In short, their parents' style tends to be relatively authoritarian. When parents from these cultures immigrate to the United States, they bring their authoritarian parenting style with them. There is evidence, though, that the authoritarian discipline often seen in Asian American, Hispanic American, and African American families does not have the same negative consequences for young children's behavior as it does in European American families (Chao & Tseng, 2002; Slade & Wissow, 2004). The difference is likely due to the fact that different disciplinary styles have different meanings in different cultures and subcultures (Ho, Bluestein, & Jenkins, 2008). Chinese American parents, for example, use authoritarian discipline to "govern" (*guan*) and provide "training" (*chiao shun*) for their children so that they will know what is expected of them (Chao, 2001). By contrast, European American parents are more likely to use authoritarian discipline to keep children in line and break their will. In countries such as India and Kenya, where physical punishment tends to be an accepted form of discipline, punishment is associated with less aggression and anxiety than in Thailand and China, where it is rarely used (Lansford et al., 2005). These findings remind us that it is important to evaluate parenting styles in their cultural context. There is no single, universally "best" style of parenting (Parke & Buriel, 2006).

Peer Friendships and Popularity

Social development over the years of childhood occurs in a world that broadens to include brothers, sisters, playmates, and classmates. Relationships with other children start early (Rubin, Bukowski, & Parker, 2006). By 2 months of age, infants engage in mutual gazing. By 6 months, they vocalize and smile at each other. By 8 months, they prefer to look at another child rather than at an adult (Bigelow et al., 1990). In other words, even infants are interested in other people, but it's a long journey from interest to intimacy.

Observations of 2-year-olds show that the most they can do with their peers is to look at them, imitate them, and exchange—or grab—toys. By age 4, they begin to play "pretend" together, agreeing about roles and themes. This kind of play is important because it provides a new context for communicating desires and feelings and offers an opportunity to form first "friendships" (Dunn & Hughes, 2001; Rubin, Bukowski, & Parker, 2006). In the school years, peer interaction becomes more frequent, complex, and structured. Children play games with rules, join teams, tutor each other, and cooperate—or compete—in achieving goals. Friends become more important and friendships longer lasting as school-age children find that friends are a source of companionship, stimulation, support, and affection (Hartup & Stevens, 1997). In fact, companionship and fun are the most important aspects of friendship for children at this age. Psychological intimacy does not enter the picture until adolescence (Parker et al., 2001).

Friends help children establish their sense of self-worth (Harter, 2006). Through friendships, children can compare their own strengths and weaknesses with those of others in a supportive and accepting atmosphere. Some children have more friends than others. When children are asked to nominate the classmates they like the best and the least, those who get the most votes—the *popular children*—tend to be the ones

Children's Friendships

Though relationships with peers may not always be this friendly, they are often among the closest and most positive in a child's life. Friends are more interactive than nonfriends; they smile and laugh together more, pay closer attention to equality in their conversation, and talk about mutual goals, not just personal ones. Having at least one close friend in childhood predicts good psychological functioning later on (Laursen et al., 2007; Reis & Gable, 2003).

© David Grossman/Photo Researchers, Inc.

who are friendly, assertive, and good at communication; they help set the rules for their group, and they engage in positive social behavior, such as helping others. Especially in early adolescence, children who are athletic, arrogant, or aggressive may also be popular, as long as their aggressiveness is not too extreme (Rubin, Bukowski, & Parker, 2006). Unfortunately, about 10 percent of schoolchildren do not have friends. Some, known as *rejected children,* are actively disliked, either because they are too aggressive and lacking in self-control or because they are anxious and socially unskilled. Others, called *neglected children,* are seldom even mentioned in peer nominations; they are isolated, quiet, and withdrawn but not necessarily disliked. Friendless children tend to do poorly in school and usually experience psychological and behavior problems in later life (Asher & Hopmeyer, 2001; Ladd & Troop-Gordon, 2003). It appears that having even one close, stable friend can protect schoolchildren from loneliness and other problems (Laursen et al., 2007; Parker et al., 2001). It also appears that the single most important factor in determining children's popularity is the *social skills* that they learn over the years of childhood and adolescence (Rubin, Bukowski, & Parker, 2006).

Social Skills and Understanding

LINKAGES Do children perceive others as adults do? (a link to Social Cognition, p. 720)

One of the most basic of these social skills is the ability to engage in sustained, responsive interactions with peers. These interactions require cooperation, sharing, and taking turns—behaviors that first appear in the preschool years. A second social skill that children learn is the ability to detect and correctly interpret other people's emotional signals. Much as children's school performance depends on processing academic information, their social performance depends on processing information about other people (Slomkowski & Dunn, 1996). A related set of social skills involves the ability to feel what another person is feeling, or something close to it (*empathy*), and to respond with comfort or help if the person is in distress. Children who understand another person's perspective, who appreciate how that person might be feeling, and who behave accordingly tend to be the most popular members of their peer group (Izard et al., 2001; Rubin, Bukowski, & Parker, 2006). Children who do not have these skills are rejected or neglected; they may become bullies or the victims of bullies.

Parents can help their children develop social skills by engaging them in lots of "pretend" play and other prosocial activities and by encouraging them to express their emotions constructively (Eisenberg et al., 2006; Ladd, 2005). Affectionate mothers who discuss emotions openly and who provide clear messages about the consequences of their child's hurtful behavior effectively encourage the child to be empathic (Eisenberg, 1997). In contrast, children who have been abused by their parents tend to lack important interaction skills and are thus more likely to be victimized by their peers (Bolger & Patterson, 2001). Older siblings can help children develop social skills by acting out social roles during play and by talking about their feelings (Ruffman et al., 1998). Teachers' ratings suggest that children with siblings tend to have better social skills than those without sibs (Downey & Condron, 2004). And those who have closer relationships with siblings also tend to develop better relationships with peers (Kim et al., 2007).

The ability to control one's emotions and behavior—an ability known as **self-regulation**—is another social skill that develops in childhood (Rothbart & Bates, 2006; Thompson, Lewis, & Calkins, 2008). In the first few years of life, children learn to calm or console themselves by sucking their thumbs or cuddling their favorite blanket (Posner & Rothbart, 2000). Later they learn more sophisticated strategies of self-regulation. These include waiting for something they want rather than crying or grabbing for it (Eisenberg et al., 2004), counting to ten in order to control anger, planning ahead to avoid a problem (e.g., getting on the first bus if the school bully usually takes the second one), and recruiting social support (e.g., casually joining a group of big kids to walk past the bully on the playground). Children who cannot regulate their emotions tend to experience anxiety and distress and have trouble recovering from stressful events. They become emotionally overaroused when they see someone in

self-regulation The ability to control one's emotions and behavior.

distress and are often unsympathetic and unhelpful (Eisenberg et al., 2006). Further, boys whose emotions are easily aroused and have difficulty regulating this arousal become less and less popular with their peers and may develop problems with aggressiveness (Eisenberg et al., 2004, 2009; Fabes et al., 1997; Spinrad et al., 2007).

FOCUS ON RESEARCH METHODS

Exploring Developing Minds

Children's ability to develop social skills depends partly on their ability to understand other people's behavior and the thinking that might be behind it. Critical to this understanding is the recognition that other people's thinking might differ from our own and that the other person's actions might be based on incorrect information. For more than two decades, researchers have argued that children under 4 years of age cannot understand other people's mental states because they do not yet have a "theory of mind."

This argument was based on studies that asked children questions about other people's beliefs (e.g., Baron-Cohen, Leslie, & Frith, 1985). In one study, children were brought to a laboratory one at a time and shown a simple little drama starring two dolls, "Sally" and "Anne." First, Sally puts a marble in her basket and then leaves the stage. While Sally is away, Anne takes the marble out of Sally's basket and puts it into her own box. Then Sally returns to get her marble, and each child is asked where Sally will look for her marble. To correctly predict that Sally will look in the basket where she last saw the marble, the children would have to recognize that Sally has a false belief about its location. Even though they know where the marble really is, they will have to be able to "read Sally's mind," realize what she must be thinking, and say, "Sally will look in her basket." However, most children under the age of 4 ignore the fact that Sally thinks the marble is still in her basket and say that she will look in Anne's box.

What was the researcher's question?
Renee Baillargeon (pronounced "by-ahr-ZHON") wondered, though, whether the inability of these young children to recognize what others are thinking reflected a true lack of a "theory of mind" or was the result of using research methods that were not sensitive enough to detect its existence. So her research question was whether more specialized research methods might reveal that even children under 4 can understand that the behavior they see in others is affected by the other people's mental states, including false beliefs and false perceptions.

How did the researcher answer the question?
Instead of requiring children to answer questions about other people's behavior, Baillargeon used a potentially more sensitive method to probe young children's knowledge. Specifically, she showed infants various events and then carefully measured the amount of time they spent looking at them. She reasoned that infants' tendency to look longer at certain events indicates that those events violate their expectations about the world.

Baillargeon used this method to measure the ability of 15-month-old infants to predict where a woman would look for a toy, depending on whether she had a true or a false belief about the toy's location (Onishi & Baillargeon, 2005). Each infant first watched the woman play with a toy watermelon slice for a few seconds and then hide it inside a green box. Next, the woman watched the toy being moved from the green box to a yellow box. Then she left the scene, and while she was gone, the toy was put back into the green box. When she came back, she looked for the toy by reaching into either the green box or the yellow box.

Baillargeon reasoned that if the infants expected the woman to search for the toy on the basis of her false belief that it was still in the yellow box, they would look longer at her if she violated their expectation by searching in the green box instead. This longer looking would convey the message "Hey, how could she know the toy had been moved? I expected her to look where she last saw it!" But if, as earlier studies had found, the infants really had no "theory of mind," they would ignore the woman's false belief and expect her to look in the green box, where they knew the toy now lay. If she met this expectation, they would not pay any special attention to her action.

What did the researcher find?

The results of this study showed that contrary to what would be expected from previous research, the infants looked reliably longer when the woman searched for the toy in the green box.

What do the results mean?

These results support the view that despite lots of earlier research evidence to the contrary, infants under the age of 4 do have a "theory of mind." When evaluated using the right kinds of research methods, these children demonstrate an ability to recognize that other people have beliefs and perceptions that can be false, that those beliefs and perceptions can differ from the child's own, and that these mental states affect the other person's behavior.

What do we still need to know?

Among other things, it would be good to know more about the extent of infants' understanding of mental states. Does it appear in other situations? Baillargeon has conducted a series of studies to begin to explore this question (Song & Baillargeon, 2008). In one of these, infants viewed a scene in which a woman looked for a doll with blue pigtails. She could look either in a plain box or in a box that had a blue tuft of hair sticking out from under its lid. The infants knew that the doll was in the plain box, but they stared longer when the woman looked in that box first; this meant that they expected her to be misled by the blue tuft of hair and to falsely perceive it as belonging to the doll. In another study, Baillargeon investigated whether infants know that new information can correct an adult's false belief (Song et al., 2008). In this case, infants saw an adult hide a ball in a box while another adult watched. After the first adult left the scene, the second adult moved the ball from the box to a cup. When the first adult returned, the second adult told her, "The ball is in the cup!" Infants stared longer if despite this corrective information, the adult searched for the ball in the box. Those who saw her reach for the cup did not pay special attention, suggesting that the infants expected her to do so once her false belief had been corrected. What mental states besides beliefs and perceptions can infants understand? Do they also realize that other people's behavior can be influenced by goals, intentions, emotions, and even the fairness or unfairness of a situation? How soon after birth does a "theory of mind" develop? These are among the dozens of additional questions that remain for future research in this fascinating area of developmental psychology (Woodward, 2009).

Gender Roles

LINKAGES Who teaches boys to be men and girls to be women? (a link to Learning, p. 220)

Another important aspect of understanding other people and being socially skilled is knowing about social roles, including **gender roles**, also known as **sex roles**, which are the general patterns of appearance and behavior associated with being a male or a female. Gender roles appear in every culture, but they are more pronounced in some cultures than in others. One analysis revealed, for example, that where there are smaller male-female differences in social status, gender role differences are smaller too (Wood & Eagly, 2002). Research by Deborah Best (1992; Williams & Best, 1990) suggests that children show gender role expectations earliest in Muslim countries (where the differences in roles are perhaps most extreme), but children in all twenty-five countries she studied eventually developed them. In North America, some aspects of traditional gender roles are weakening. For example, men today are less likely than they were in the 1970s to describe themselves as "tough" and "aggressive" (Spence & Buckner, 2000). And one sample of students in counseling psychology defined a mentally healthy woman as independent and ready for a challenge—traditionally

gender roles (sex roles) Patterns of work, appearance, and behavior that a society associates with being male or female.

masculine traits—as well as nice and nurturing, which are traditionally feminine characteristics (Seem & Clark, 2006). When it comes to occupations, though, most traditional gender stereotypes remain (Liben & Bigler, 2002). Both children and adults still think of doctors, dentists, mechanics, pilots, plumbers, truck drivers, firefighters, electricians, architects, police officers, and engineers as male and think of librarians, nurses, teachers, secretaries, dancers, hairdressers, and decorators as female (Kee et al., 2005; Oakhill, Garnham, & Reynolds, 2005).

Gender roles exist because they are deeply rooted in both nature and nurture. Small physical and behavioral differences between the sexes are evident early on (Eagly, 1996). Girls tend to speak and write earlier and to be better at grammar and spelling than boys (Halpern, 1997). Girls are more attracted than boys are to baby faces (Maestripieri, 2004), and by 4 months of age, the average duration of mutual gazing between girls and women is four times longer than that between boys and women (Leeb & Rejskind, 2004). Girls are able to read emotional signals at younger ages than boys can, and by school age, they are likely to be more sensitive, kind, considerate, and empathic (Rose & Rudolph, 2006). They are more emotionally responsive to others and more likely to ask for help as well as to offer it (Benenson & Koulnazarian, 2008; Bornstein et al., 2008). They can also control their emotions better than boys can (Else-Quest et al., 2006). Girls engage in more social conversation and self-disclosure with their friends, and they care more about their friendships than boys do (Rose & Rudolph, 2006).

Boys, in contrast, tend to be more skilled than girls at manipulating objects, constructing three-dimensional forms, and mentally manipulating complex figures and pictures (Choi & Silverman, 2003; Newhouse, Newhouse, & Astur, 2007). They are also more physically active. They play in larger groups and spaces and enjoy noisier, more strenuous physical games (Fabes, Martin, & Hanish, 2003; Rose & Rudolph, 2006). From the age of 2, boys engage in riskier behaviors and are injured at a rate that is two to four times that of girls (Morrongiello & Hogg, 2004). On the playground, boys are the overtly aggressive ones; they push and punch each other more than girls do (Baillargeon et al., 2007; Card et al., 2008; Ostrov, 2006). They are more competitive and more concerned with dominance than with friendship (Rose & Rudolph, 2006). Girls are more likely to use "relational" or "social" aggression than physical aggression; they hurt with gossip and threats to withdraw friendship rather than with sticks and stones (Crick et al., 2004).

Biological Factors in Gender Roles

A biological contribution to these male-female differences is suggested by several lines of evidence. First, studies show sex differences in anatomy, hormones, and brain organization and functioning that are related to sex-typed patterns of behavior (Auyeung et al., 2009; Geary, 1999; Ruble, Martin, & Berenbaum, 2006). Second, cross-cultural research reveals consistent gender patterns at an early age, even in the face of differing socialization practices (Baillargeon et al., 2007; Simpson & Kenrick, 1997). Third, research with nonhuman primates finds sex differences that parallel those seen in human children. Young female animals prefer playing with dolls, and young males prefer playing with a toy car, for example (Alexander & Hines, 2002; Williams & Pleil, 2008). Fourth, research in behavioral genetics shows that genes exert a moderate influence on the appearance of gender-typed behaviors (Iervolino et al., 2005).

Socialization of Gender Roles

There is no doubt, though, that gender roles are also influenced by socialization, partly by exaggerating whatever biological gender differences may already exist (Hyde, 2005, 2007). From the moment they are born, boys and girls are treated differently. Adults usually play more gently and talk more to infants they believe to be girls than to infants they believe to be boys. They shower girls with dolls and doll clothes, boys with trucks and tools. They encourage boys to achieve, compete, explore, control their feelings, be independent, and assume personal responsibility. They encourage girls to be reflective, dependent, domestic, obedient,

Learning Gender Roles

In every culture, socialization by adults and peers typically encourages interests, activities, and other characteristics traditionally associated with a child's own gender.

© Superstudio/The Image Bank/Getty Images

and unselfish (Ruble, Martin, & Berenbaum, 2006). They speak with more feeling to girls and in more supportive ways (Kitamura & Burnham, 2003; Leaper, Anderson, & Sanders, 1998) and are harsher with boys (McKee et al., 2007). When asked to imagine that their child has been injured, parents are more concerned about even minor injuries to daughters than to sons (Morrongiello & Hogg, 2004). They are also more likely to stop a fight between their children when a daughter is involved (Martin & Ross, 2005). In these and many other ways, adults, including television role models, pass on their ideas about "appropriate" behaviors for boys and girls (Else-Quest et al., 2010; Parke & Buriel, 2006; Ruble, Martin, & Berenbaum, 2006). They also convey information about gender-appropriate interests. For example, sixth-grade girls and boys express equal interest in science and earn the same grades. However, parents tend to underestimate their daughters' interest, believe that science is difficult for them, and are less likely to give them scientific explanations when working on a physics task (Tenenbaum & Leaper, 2003).

Children also pick up notions of what is gender-appropriate behavior from their peers. By the time they are in preschool, boys and girls are more likely to play with children of the same sex (Martin & Ruble, 2009). These same-sex peers model and enforce gender role standards and provide the strongest influence on children's gender-typed behavior (Leaper & Friedman, 2007; Rose & Rudolph, 2006).

Cognitive Factors in Gender Roles   Because most children want to be accepted, especially by their peers, they become "gender detectives," searching for clues about who should do what, who can play with whom, and in what ways girls and boys are different (Martin & Ruble, 2004). In the process, they develop **gender schemas**, which are generalizations about the toys and activities that are "appropriate" for boys and for girls and the jobs that are "meant" for men or for women (Fagot, 1995). Once they have developed these gender schemas and know that they themselves are male or female, children tend to choose the activities, toys, and behaviors deemed appropriate for their own gender (Ruble, Martin, & Berenbaum, 2006; Zosuls et al., 2009). They

gender schemas The generalizations children develop about what toys, activities, and occupations are "appropriate" for males and for females.

become "sexist self-socializers" as they work at developing the masculine or feminine attributes they view as consistent with their self-image as a male or a female. By the age of 8 or 9, they may have become a little more flexible about what's acceptable for members of each sex to do—but most still say they wouldn't be friends with a boy who wore lipstick or a girl who played football (Levy, Taylor, & Gelman, 1995). Later in elementary school, when most girls outperform boys in language arts, math, science, and social studies, girls think of themselves as good only in language arts, because that's what they are "supposed" to be good at (Pomerantz, Altermatt, & Saxon, 2002).

In summary, social training by both adults and peers, along with the child's own cognitions about the world, tends to bolster and amplify any biological predispositions that distinguish boys and girls. This process in turn creates gender roles that are the joint and inextricably linked products of nature and nurture. This and other elements of early development are summarized in "In Review: Social and Emotional Development During Infancy and Childhood."

The efforts of some parents to deemphasize gender roles in their children's upbringing may help reduce the magnitude of gender differences in areas such as verbal and quantitative skills, occupational ambitions, and preferences for particular toys. However, the evolutionary approach to psychology suggests that other gender differences—such as males' greater ability to visualize the rotation of objects in space and females' greater ability to read facial expressions—are unlikely to change much (Quinn & Liben, 2008). Evolutionary psychologists see these differences as deeply rooted in the distant past, when males' major activity was hunting and females' was child rearing (Buss, 2004a). Other psychologists have suggested that prenatal exposure to male or female hormones influences the organization of male and female brains in different ways (Halpern, 1997; Vuoksimaa et al., 2010). Still others see such differences as reflecting social inequality, not just biological destiny (Wood & Eagly, 2002). Whatever the source of gender differences, it is important to remember that most of them are quite small (Hyde, 2005). So even though a popular book suggests that "men are from Mars and women are from Venus," a more accurate metaphor might be to say that men are from one state and women are from another (Hyde, 2005).

IN REVIEW	Social and Emotional Development During Infancy and Childhood		
Age	**Relationships with Parents**	**Relationships with Other Children**	**Social Understanding**
Birth–2 years	Infants form an attachment to the primary caregiver.	Play focuses on toys, not on other children.	Infants respond to emotional expressions of others.
2–4 years	Children become more autonomous and no longer need their parents' constant attention.	Toys are a way of eliciting responses from other children.	Young children can recognize emotions of others.
4–10 years	Parents actively socialize their children.	Children begin to cooperate, compete, play games, and form friendships with peers.	Children learn social rules, such as politeness, and roles, such as being male or female; they learn to control their emotions.

1. As part of their social development, children learn _____, which tell them what patterns of appearance and behavior are associated with being male or female.

2. Teaching children to talk quietly in a restaurant is part of the process called _____.

3. Strict rules and the threat of punishment are typical of _____ parenting.

Risk and Resilience

Family instability, child abuse, homelessness, parental unemployment, poverty, substance abuse, and domestic violence put many children at risk for various difficulties in social and emotional development (Ackerman, Brown, & Izard, 2004; Karevold et al., 2009). When parents divorce, for example, their children may develop serious problems (Clarke-Stewart & Brentano, 2006; Lansford, 2009). By two or three years after the divorce, the intense psychological stress is over, and most children are functioning competently, but there can be long-lasting effects. Adults whose parents had divorced when they were children may not live as long as those from intact families, and a high proportion of people who were young adolescents when their parents divorced are unable to form committed relationships even years later. Children are also at risk if their parents have violent fights. Nearly half the children exposed to marital violence exhibit various forms of psychological disorder—a rate six times higher than that in the general population (Garber, 1992).

Children vary in how well they ultimately adjust to all these stressors. Even when the odds are against them, some children are left virtually unscathed by even the most dangerous risk factors. These children are said to be resilient. **Resilience** is a characteristic that permits successful development in the face of significant challenge. It has been studied throughout the world in a variety of adverse situations, including war, natural disaster, family violence, child maltreatment, and poverty. This research has consistently identified certain qualities in children and their environments that are associated with resilience. Specifically, resilient children tend to be intelligent and to have easy temperaments, high self-esteem, talent, and faith (Masten & Coatsworth, 1998). They are cheerful, focused, and persistent in completing a task (Wills et al., 2001). They also typically have significant relationships with a warm and authoritative parent, with someone in their extended family, or with other caring adults outside the family, at school, or in clubs or religious organizations (Rutter, 2006). In addition, they have genes that direct optimal regulation of serotonin, a neurotransmitter that, as described in the chapter on biological aspects of psychology, plays a role in mood and stress-related responses (Kim-Cohen & Gold, 2009).

Adolescence

The years of middle childhood usually pass smoothly, but adolescence changes things drastically. All adolescents undergo significant changes in size, shape, and physical capacities. Many also experience big changes in their social lives, reasoning abilities, and views of themselves.

Changes in Body, Brain, and Thinking

A sudden spurt in physical growth is the most visible sign that adolescence has begun. This growth spurt peaks at about age 12 for girls and age 14 for boys (Tanner, 1978; see Figure 12.6). Suddenly, adolescents find themselves in new bodies. At the end of the growth spurt, females begin to menstruate, and males produce live sperm. This state of being able for the first time to reproduce is called **puberty**.

These dramatic changes in teenagers' bodies are accompanied by significant changes in their brains, especially in parts of the frontal lobes known as the prefrontal cortex (Kuhn, 2006; Spear, 2000; see Figure 3.15 in the chapter on biological aspects of psychology). These areas are vital to the ability to think flexibly, to act appropriately in challenging situations, and to juggle multiple pieces of information. They are also involved in skills such as planning and organization, controlling impulses, and allocating attention.

As described in the Linkages section of the chapter on biological aspects of psychology, the brain overproduces neuronal connections during childhood, but during

resilience A quality allowing children to develop normally in spite of severe environmental risk factors.

puberty The condition of being able, for the first time, to reproduce.

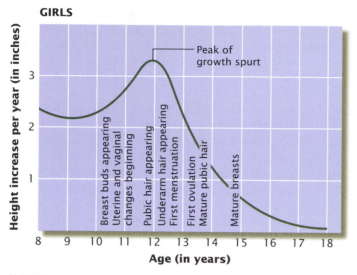

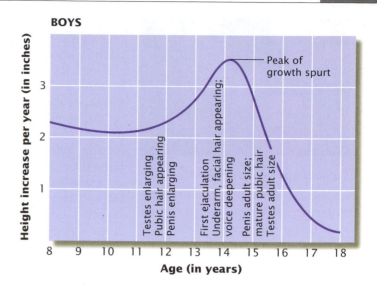

FIGURE 12.6

Physical Changes in Adolescence

At about 10½ years of age, girls begin their growth spurt, and by age 12, they are taller than their male peers. Boys begin their growth spurt at about 12½ years of age and usually grow faster and for a longer period of time than girls. Adolescents may grow in height as much as 5 inches a year. Increases in sex hormones (e.g., estrogen and testosterone) lead to the development of sexual characteristics such as pubic hair. The ages at which these changes occur vary considerably across individuals, but their sequence is the same.

puberty, the connections that are not being used much are eliminated, or "pruned." At the same time, many neurons acquire a sheath of myelin, which speeds their communication with one another. So by the end of adolescence, teenagers' brains have fewer neural connections, but those that remain are more selective, stronger, and more efficient. At the same time, dopamine, a neurotransmitter associated with the experience of pleasure, becomes more prominent.

Changes in the brain are reflected in changes in the ways that adolescents think. As mentioned earlier, Piaget described this new stage of thinking as the *formal operational stage.* He said it is marked by the ability to engage in abstract, hypothetical thinking, but researchers now suggest that cognitive changes in adolescence also include a whole range of executive functions controlled by the prefrontal cortex (Keil, 2006; Kuhn, 2006). By late adolescence, young people are able to reason better, plan for the future, and foresee consequences. When they investigate a topic, they are able to consider and control several factors at once and analyze the impact of what they discover. This ability to engage in strategic, self-organized thinking also allows them to perform more than one mental task at the same time (Luciana et al., 2005). Moreover, they increasingly take charge of their mental life, choosing what to think about, when and where to do so, and how to allocate their mental effort.

Adolescent Feelings and Behavior

In Western cultures, the changes occurring during *early adolescence,* from ages 11 to 14 or so, can be disorienting. Adolescents—especially early-maturing girls—may experience bouts of depression, insomnia, and other psychological problems (Johnson et al., 2006; Mendle, Turkheimer, & Emery, 2007; Ohring, Graber, & Brooks-Gunn, 2002). This is also the time when eating disorders are likely to first appear (Wilson et al., 1996) and when the incidence of attempted and completed suicides begins to rise (Centers for Disease Control and Prevention, 2007).

As sex hormones and pleasure-related brain systems become more active, sexual interest stirs, and the prospect of smoking, drinking alcohol, and taking other drugs becomes more appealing (Patton et al., 2004; Reyna & Farley, 2006). Opportunities to do these things increase too because adolescents spend more time with their peers and take more risks than younger children do (Gardner & Steinberg, 2005; Steinberg, 2007, 2008). Much of this risk-taking seems to be due to the different rates at which parts of the adolescent brain develop. The impulse control areas in the prefrontal cortex complete their development long after the emotional and reward-related areas of the limbic system do (Casey, Getz, & Galvan, 2008; Steinberg, 2007, 2008). Of course, a certain amount of adolescent risk-taking and sensation-seeking is normal. In fact,

© Charles Gulling/zefa/Corbis

Contacting Friends—Instantly

Adolescents spend more time online and more often use instant messaging (texting) and other electronic communication technologies than either adults or children. Most often they use the Internet to communicate with their existing network of friends and find that this enhances both their friendships and their sense of well-being (Valkenburg & Peter, 2007a, 2007b). About a third believe that online communication is more effective than in-person chat for disclosing intimate personal information. Some early studies created concern that intense Internet use might have negative long-term effects on adolescent texters' ability to plan, think flexibly and abstractly, learn rules, inhibit inappropriate actions, and focus on relevant information. More recent research suggests that these concerns may be exaggerated (Valkenburg & Peter, 2009). There is no doubt, though, that the Internet carries risks, including exposure to degrading or obscene material and attempted contact by sexual predators.

adolescents who engage in moderate risk-taking tend to be more socially competent than those who either take no risks or take extreme risks (Spear, 2000). Extreme risk-taking is often maladaptive, leading to excessive use of drugs and alcohol or to reckless and even life-threatening activities. So for some people, early adolescence marks the beginning of a downward spiral that ends up in academic failure, delinquency, and substance abuse.

Many of the problems of adolescence are associated with challenges to young people's *self-esteem,* their sense of being worthy, capable, and deserving of respect (Harter, 2006). Adolescents are especially vulnerable if many stressors occur at the same time (Kling et al., 1999). The switch from elementary school to middle school or junior high is particularly challenging (Eccles, Lord, & Buchanan, 1996). The new teachers may have less time to nurture students and may exert more control, impose higher standards, and evaluate students' work in a more public way. Under these circumstances, grades may drop, especially for students who were already having trouble in school or who don't have confidence in their own abilities (Rudolph et al., 2001). But grades don't affect self-esteem in all teens. Some base their self-esteem more on athletic success and on their peers' opinions of them than on their academic achievement (Crocker & Wolfe, 2001). In fact, adolescents' academic performance is strongly affected by the peers with whom they spend their time. For example, adolescents whose grades and motivation decline from the end of elementary school to the end of their first year in middle school tend to be those who affiliated themselves with other academic underachievers (Ryan, 2001).

The changes and pressures of adolescence are often played out at home as adolescents try to have a greater say in a parent-child relationship once ruled by the parents. Serious conflicts may lead adolescents—especially those who do not feel close to their parents—to serious problems, including running away, getting pregnant, stealing, taking drugs, or even attempting suicide (Blum, Beuhring, & Rinehart, 2000; Goldstein, Davis-Kean, & Eccles, 2005). Fortunately, although the bond with parents deteriorates during the transition from early to mid adolescence, most adolescents maintain a reasonably good relationship with their parents (McGue et al., 2005; Moore, 2005; van Wel, ter Bogt, & Raaijmakers, 2002). Children who report positive relationships with their parents tend not to associate with risk-taking peers in middle school or develop problem behaviors in high school (Eisenberg et al., 2005; Goldstein, Davis-Kean, & Eccles, 2005; Soenens et al., 2006).

Teens are most likely to share confidences with parents who keep tabs on their youngsters' activities and expect them to discuss those activities (Smetana et al., 2006; Soenens et al., 2006), but how much involvement and control is enough and how much is too much? It is not easy for parents to know. In one study, seventh-graders who felt they had a lot of autonomy at home—such as deciding how late to stay out at night—did more unsupervised socializing with peers in eighth grade and were at greater risk for problem behavior in eleventh grade (Goldstein, Davis-Kean, & Eccles, 2005). At the same time, seventh-graders who thought their parents were too intrusive also ran into problems. They hung out more with deviant peers in eighth grade and by eleventh grade showed elevated rates of behavior problems.

Love and Sex in Adolescence   On top of everything else, adolescence is usually the time when romance first takes center stage (Collins & Steinberg, 2006). Nearly half of 15-year-olds and 70 percent of 18-year-olds in the United States have romantic relationships; 60 percent of these relationships last a year or more (Carver, Joyner, & Udry, 2003). Being in a romantic relationship is linked with feelings of self-worth, competence, and belonging to a peer group (Collins & Roisman, 2006; Harter, 2006). Dating a popular, socially skilled partner is even better because this can increase a previously isolated or poorly adjusted teen's popularity while reducing victimization and feelings of sadness (Simon, Aikins, & Prinstein, 2008).

Surveys suggest that almost half of teens in the United States have had sexual intercourse by age 16 (Kaiser Family Foundation, 2005). Teens who have sex differ from those who do not in a number of ways. They hold less conventional attitudes and values, and they are more likely to smoke, drink alcohol, and use other drugs (National Center on Addiction and Substance Abuse, 2004), to be aggressive, and to have attention problems in school (Schofield et al., 2008). They are also likely to have more unsupervised time after school (Cohen et al., 2002), to be in peer groups whose norms support risk-taking (diNoia & Schinke, 2008), and to have a sexually active best friend (Jaccard, Blanton, & Dodge, 2005). Their parents tend to be less educated, to have less control over them, and not to talk openly with them. They are more likely to have spent their childhood without their father (Ellis et al., 2003; Mendle et al., 2009). The typical pairing of heterosexually active teens is a "macho" male and a "girly" female (Udry & Chantala, 2003). Adolescents who displayed poorer self-regulatory skills as children are the ones most likely to take greater sexual risks, such as having multiple partners or not using condoms (Atkins, 2008; Raffaelli & Crockett, 2003).

All too often, sexual activity leads to declining school achievement, sexually transmitted diseases, and unplanned and unwanted pregnancies. Teenage girls have higher rates of gonorrhea, chlamydia, pelvic inflammatory disease, and other sexually transmitted diseases than any other age group in the United States (Forhan et al., 2009; Malhotra, 2008; Ross, 2002). Nearly 18 percent of them become pregnant (Perper & Manlove, 2009). Although the rates of teen pregnancy and birth in the United States declined between 1991 and 2005, they are once again on the rise (Moore, 2009). The teens most likely to become pregnant are those with low confidence in themselves and their educational futures, along with those whose parents are unmarried and have a low level of education (Chandra et al., 2008; Young et al., 2004).

Giving birth in adolescence can create problems for the mother, the baby, and others in the family. For one thing, the younger sisters of teenage mothers may have to take time away from schoolwork to help care for the child, and they are at increased risk for drug and alcohol use and for becoming pregnant themselves (East & Jacobson, 2001). Worse still is the fact that the babies of teenage mothers are less likely than babies of older mothers to survive their first year (Phipps, Blume, & DeMonner, 2002). This situation occurs partly because compared with older parents, teenage parents are less positive and stimulating with their children and more likely to abuse them (Brooks-Gunn & Chase-Lansdale, 2002). The children of teenage parents are more likely to develop behavior problems and to do poorly in school than children with more

Mothers Too Soon?

More than half of the U.S. adolescents who become pregnant elect to keep their babies and become single mothers. These young women and their children are likely to face special academic, social, and other problems. Accordingly, support programs for teenage mothers have been developed, and some of them have reported success in alleviating symptoms of depression, increasing the young mothers' parenting capabilities, and helping them achieve their educational goals (Cox et al., 2008; Sadler et al., 2007).

© bilderlounge/Getty Images

mature parents (Furstenberg, Brooks-Gunn, & Chase-Lansdale, 1989; Moffitt, 2002). They do better if they have a strong attachment to their father and if their mother was prepared for maternal responsibilities and was knowledgeable about children and parenting before the baby was born (Miller et al., 1996; Whitman et al., 2001).

Violent Adolescents As described at the beginning of this chapter, some individuals respond to the challenges of adolescence with violence. The roots of teenage violence run deep and lie partly in genetic factors (Brendgen et al., 2005). From childhood to adolescence, aggression is just as stable as intelligence (Dodge, Coie, & Lynam, 2006). Among the childhood characteristics that increase the risk of violent behavior in adolescence are fearlessness, low intelligence, lack of empathy, lack of emotional self-regulation, aggressiveness, and moral disengagement (Eisenberg et al., 2004; Hay et al., 2003; Pepler et al., 2008; Rutter, 2003). Gender is another important factor (Ostrov & Godleski, 2010): It is no coincidence that teenage killers are almost always boys. In cultures around the world, homicides committed by males outnumber those committed by females by more than thirty to one (Cassel & Bernstein, 2007).

Several environmental factors are also associated with an increased risk of youth violence (Duke et al., 2010). These factors include maternal depression and rejection and involvement with delinquent gangs or antisocial peers (Burt, McGue, & Iacono, 2009; Rutter, 2003), as well as poverty (Strohschein, 2005), malnutrition (Liu et al., 2004), and exposure to violent television and video games (Comstock & Scharrer, 2006; Nicoll & Kieffer, 2005). Peers are especially influential. In one study, adolescents were more likely to say they would engage in aggressive behaviors if they believed they were in a chat room with popular adolescents who favored aggressive behaviors (Cohen & Prinstein, 2006). Another contributor to violence is the growing use and abuse of anabolic steroids (Grimes, Ricci, & Melloni, 2006). Adolescent violence is also more likely among youngsters who grow up witnessing family violence, clashing with siblings, or experiencing physical abuse (Ehrensaft et al., 2003; Noland et al., 2004). The risk is raised, too, among children who live in neighborhoods plagued by violence and crime (Herrenkohl et al., 2004; Pearce et al., 2003). Young people who are exposed to even a single incident of firearm violence are twice as likely as other children to later engage in violent behavior (Bingenheimer, Brennan, & Earls, 2005).

The cascade of environmental conditions leading to violent behavior in adolescence was described in a study of children as they grew from ages 5 through 18 (Dodge et al., 2008). These children spent their early years in a socially and economically disadvantaged family situation where harsh, inconsistent parenting impaired the children's social and cognitive development. This impaired development made these children prone to learning and conduct problems that led to social and academic failure in elementary school. As their increasingly unmanageable behavior caused their parents to stop supervising and monitoring them, these children were more likely to associate with antisocial peers (sometimes including gangs). The final result, in adolescence, was that these youngsters became more likely to carry a weapon, to threaten others with that weapon, to be involved in gang fights, and to attack anyone whom they perceive as a threat to their safety.

Despite all the potential dangers and problems of adolescence, most teens in Western cultures are not violent and do not experience major personal turmoil or family conflicts. So although most parents and teachers seem to believe that adolescence is a time of "storm and stress" (Hines & Paulson, 2007), research suggests that more than half of today's teens find adolescence relatively trouble-free (Arnett, 1999, 2007b; Chung, Flook, & Fuligni, 2009). Only about 15 percent of the adolescents studied experience serious distress (Steinberg, 1990). The vast majority of adolescents cope well with the changes puberty brings and soon find themselves in the midst of perhaps the biggest challenge of their young lives: preparing themselves for the transition to young adulthood.

Identity and Development of the Self

In many less developed countries today, as in the United States in the nineteenth century, the end of early adolescence, around the age of 15, marks the beginning of adulthood: of work, parenting, and grown-up responsibilities. In modern North America, though, the transition from childhood to adulthood often lasts well into the twenties. This lengthened adolescence has created special problems, including the matter of finding or forming an identity.

Most adolescents have not previously thought deeply about who they are. At the age of 3 or 4, if asked to describe themselves, they would probably have mentioned their physical features ("I have blue eyes"), preferences ("I like pizza"), and possessions ("I have a kitty"). At ages 5 to 7, they would have described their competencies ("I'm a good runner, and I get good grades at school"). Around the age of 8, they would have used labels that focus on more complex and general abilities ("I'm smart") and interpersonal attributes ("I'm popular") and would have used this knowledge about themselves to actively evaluate and reflect on their thoughts and behavior (Davis-Kean, Jager, & Collins, 2009). It is in early adolescence, around age 11, that they would have begun to describe themselves in terms of social relationships, personality traits, and other general, stable psychological characteristics; by the end of adolescence, their self-descriptions emphasize their personal beliefs, values, and moral standards (Harter, 1999, 2006). Adolescents come to recognize that they are somewhat different people in different social contexts (such as with friends versus at a family party), and they can think about the possible selves they might be in the future. They can also integrate their seemingly opposite traits, such as "cheerful" and "depressed," into a broader characteristic, such as "moody."

These changes in the way adolescents describe themselves suggest changes in the way they think about themselves too. As they become more self-conscious, they gradually develop a personal identity as unique individuals. That personal identity may be affected by their **ethnic identity**—the part of a person's identity that reflects the racial, religious, or cultural group to which the person belongs (Quintana, 2010). Adolescents who achieve a clear, positive ethnic identity exhibit higher self-esteem, greater optimism, and more social competence, as well as more positive feelings toward their own ethnic group (Chavous et al., 2003; Spencer, 2006; Wong, Eccles, & Sameroff, 2003; Yip & Fuligni, 2002). This pattern is seen especially among adolescents who do not experience much ethnic discrimination (Greene, Way, & Pahl, 2006). Adolescents with a strong ethnic identity are also more positive about education, more likely to

Ethnic Identity

TRY THIS Ethnic identity is that part of our personal identity that reflects the racial, religious, or cultural group to which we belong. Ethnic identity often leads people to interact mainly with others who share that identity. To what extent is this true of you? You can get a rough idea by jotting down the ethnicity of all the people you chose to spend time with over the past week or so.

ethnic identity The part of a person's identity associated with the racial, religious, or cultural group to which the person belongs.

© Spencer Grant/PhotoEdit

do better academically, and less likely to become delinquents (Adelabu, 2008; Bruce & Waelde, 2008; Fuligni, Witkow, & Garcia, 2005).

As described in the chapter on social cognition, the same processes that create a strong ethnic identity can also sow the seeds of ethnic prejudice. For example, thinking favorably about your own ethnic group can lead to thinking of other groups as inferior. Fortunately, prejudice is not inevitable. Adolescents who regularly interact with members of other ethnic groups usually develop more mature ethnic identities and express more favorable attitudes toward people of other ethnicities (Phinney, Ferguson, & Tate, 1997; Phinney, Jacoby, & Silva, 2007).

Moral Development

Adolescents are able to develop a personal and ethnic identity partly because, according to Piaget's theory, they have entered the formal operational stage, which allows them to think logically and reason about abstract concepts. Adolescents often find themselves applying these advanced cognitive skills to questions of morality.

Kohlberg's Stages of Moral Reasoning

To examine how people think about morality, Lawrence Kohlberg asked them to resolve moral dilemmas. Perhaps the most famous of his dilemmas was the "Heinz dilemma," which requires people to decide whether a man named Heinz should steal a rare and unaffordable drug in order to save his wife's life. Kohlberg found that the reasons people give for their moral choices change systematically with age (Kohlberg & Gilligan, 1971). He proposed that moral reasoning develops in six stages, which are summarized in Table 12.3. These stages are not tightly linked to a person's age. There is a range of ages for reaching each stage, and not everyone reaches the highest level.

Stage 1 and Stage 2 moral judgments are most typical of children under the age of 9 and tend to be selfish. Kohlberg called this level **preconventional reasoning** because it is not yet based on the conventions or rules that guide social interactions in society. At this level of **moral development**, people are concerned with avoiding punishment or following rules when it is to their own advantage. At the **conventional reasoning** level, Stages 3 and 4, people are concerned about other people; they believe that morality consists of following rules and conventions such as duty to the family, to marriage vows, and to the country. Conventional thinkers would never think it was proper to burn their country's flag in protest, for example. The moral reasoning of children and adolescents from ages 9 to 19 is most often at this level. Stages 5 and 6 represent what Kohlberg called **postconventional reasoning** because it occurs after conventional reasoning. Moral judgments at this level are based on personal standards or universal principles of justice, equality, and respect for human life rather than on the demands of authority figures or society. People whose moral reasoning is at this level view rules and laws as arbitrary but respect them because they protect human welfare. They believe that individual rights can sometimes justify violating these laws if the laws become destructive. People do not usually reach this level until sometime in young adulthood—if at all. Stage 6 is seen only rarely in extraordinary individuals.

Limitations of Kohlberg's Stages

Studies of Kohlberg's stages have generally supported the sequence he proposed (e.g., Turiel, 2006). Evidence for Kohlberg's first four stages has been found in twenty-seven cultures from Alaska to Zambia. Stages 5 and 6, however, have not always appeared (Gibbs et al., 2007; Snarey & Hooker, 2006; Turiel, 2006; Wainryb, 2006). Further, moral judgments made in some cultures do not always fit neatly into Kohlberg's stages. Some people in collectivist cultures—Papua New Guinea, Taiwan, and Israeli kibbutzim, for example—explained their answers to moral dilemmas by pointing to the importance of the community rather than to personal standards. People in India included in their moral reasoning the importance of acting in accordance with one's gender and caste and with maintaining personal purity. As in other areas of cognitive development, culture plays a significant role in shaping moral judgments.

Gender may also play a role. Carol Gilligan (1982, 1993) suggested that for females, the moral ideal is not the abstract, impersonal concept of justice that Kohlberg found

preconventional reasoning Moral reasoning that is not yet based on the conventions or rules that guide social interactions in society.

moral development The growth of an individual's understanding of the concepts of right and wrong.

conventional reasoning Moral reasoning that reflects the belief that morality consists of following rules and conventions.

postconventional reasoning Moral reasoning in which judgments are based on personal standards or universal principles of justice, equality, and respect for human life.

TABLE 12.3 Kohlberg's Stages of Moral Development

Kohlberg's stages of moral reasoning describe differences in how people think about moral issues. Here are examples of the answers that people at different stages of development might give to the "Heinz dilemma" described in the text. This dilemma is more realistic than you might think. In 1994, a man was arrested for robbing a bank after being turned down for a loan to pay for his wife's cancer treatments; a similar case occurred in 2004.

Stage	What Is Right?	Should Heinz Steal the Drug?
Preconventional		
1	Obeying, and avoiding punishment from, a superior authority	"Heinz should not steal the drug because he will be jailed."
2	Making a fair exchange, a good deal	"Heinz should steal the drug because his wife will repay him later."
Conventional		
3	Pleasing others and getting their approval	"Heinz should steal the drug because he loves his wife and because she and the rest of the family will approve."
4	Doing your duty, following rules and social order	"Heinz should steal the drug for his wife because he has a duty to care for her" or "He should not steal the drug because stealing is illegal."
Postconventional		
5	Respecting rules and laws but recognizing that they may have limits	"Heinz should steal the drug because life is more important than property."
6	Following universal ethical principles, such as justice, reciprocity, equality, and respect for human life and rights	"Heinz should steal the drug because of the principle of preserving and respecting life."

in males but rather the need to protect enduring relationships and fulfill human needs. When Gilligan asked her research participants about moral conflicts, the majority of men focused on justice, but only half of the women did. The other half focused on caring. Although this difference between men and women has not always been found, there does seem to be a tendency for females to focus on caring more than males do and for males to focus on justice more than females do when they are talking about real-life moral issues they have personally experienced (Jaffe & Hyde, 2000). However, when they are asked about hypothetical moral dilemmas, there is no substantial difference in how males and females reason (Jaffe & Hyde, 2000; Raaijmakers, Engels, & Van Hoof, 2005; Walker, 2006).

Taken together, the results of research in many countries and with both genders suggest that moral ideals are not absolute and universal. Moral development is an adaptation to the world in which one lives, a world that differs from place to place and time to time (Turiel, 2006; Wainryb & Psaupathi, 2008).

Moral Reasoning and Moral Action Moral reasoning is related to moral behavior. In one study, adolescents who committed crimes ranging from burglary to murder tended to see obedience to laws mainly as a way of avoiding jail—a Stage 1 belief. Their nondelinquent peers, who showed Stage 4 reasoning, believed that one should obey laws because they prevent chaos in society (Gregg, Gibbs, & Basinger, 1994). But having advanced moral reasoning ability is no guarantee that a person will always act morally; other factors, such as the likelihood of being caught in an immoral act, also affect behavior. For example, people have been shown to behave in less moral ways when dim lighting or the use of e-mail creates a sense of anonymity or distance (Naquin, Kurtzberg, & Belkin, 2010; Zhong, Bohns, & Gino, 2010) and to behave more honestly when they feel they are being watched. In one study, even people alone in a coffee lounge were nearly three times as likely to pay for their coffee when a poster on the wall portrayed human eyes looking at them rather than an image of flowers (Bateson, Nettle, & Roberts, 2006).

In summary, learning to behave in moral ways requires three things: (1) consistent modeling of moral reasoning and behavior by parents and peers, (2) real-life experience with moral issues, and (3) situational factors that support moral actions (Aquino et al., 2009).

Emerging Adulthood

In Western cultures, adolescence is typically followed by a period of "emerging adulthood" that lasts from about 18 to about 25. During this period, young people explore life's possibilities through education, dating, and travel before settling into stable adult roles and responsibilities (Arnett, 2000, 2007a; Roisman et al., 2004). One of the tasks of particular importance for emerging adults is resolving their "identity crisis."

Facing the Identity Crisis   According to Erikson (1968), events of late adolescence, such as graduating from high school, going to college, and building new relationships, challenge one's self-concept and precipitate an **identity crisis** (see Table 12.2). In this crisis, the person must develop an integrated self-image as a unique individual by pulling together self-knowledge acquired during childhood. If infancy and childhood brought trust, autonomy, and initiative, according to Erikson, individuals will resolve the identity crisis positively, feeling self-confident and competent. If infancy and childhood resulted in feelings of mistrust, shame, guilt, and inferiority, individuals will be confused about their identity and goals.

In Western cultures, there is some limited empirical support for Erikson's ideas about the identity crisis. In the period of emerging adulthood, young people do become more open to new experiences and consider alternative identities (Roberts, Walton, & Viechtbauer, 2006). They "try out" being rebellious, studious, or detached as they attempt to resolve questions about sexuality, self-worth, industriousness, and independence. Some college students, for example, make a commitment to an identity and then reevaluate that commitment; these students are more likely to repeat their freshman year or change their major (Luyckx, Goossens, & Soenens, 2006). Recreational identities may be especially important; not all college students are successful academically, so they may try out alternative identities associated with extracurricular activities (Eccles & Gootman, 2002). People of college age may also try out identities through online message boards and multiplayer Internet games (Whitlock, Powers, & Eckenrode, 2006).

As young people learn to cope with challenges, handle their emotions, and settle on their identity during emerging adulthood, their psychological well-being tends to improve. The prevalence of serious depression, which tends to be quite high at the end of adolescence, especially for girls, declines (Galambos, Barker, & Krahn, 2006). By the time they are 21, about half of the people studied have resolved the identity crisis in a way that is consistent with their self-image and the historical era in which they are living. They are ready to enter adulthood with greater self-confidence, more mature attitudes and behavior, more consistent goals and values, and a clearer idea of who they are (Savin-Williams & Demo, 1984). Many have become more aware of their obligations to their families (Fuligni & Pedersen, 2002). Those who explore matters of identity more extensively tend to have had opportunities to express and develop their own points of view in a supportive environment at home, at school, and in the community (Dumas et al., 2009; Grotevant, 1998). For those who fail to resolve identity issues—either because they avoided an identity crisis by accepting whatever identity their parents set for them or because they postponed dealing with the crisis and remain uncommitted and lacking in direction—problems often lie ahead (Lange & Byrd, 2002).

identity crisis A phase during which an adolescent attempts to develop an integrated self-image.

Adulthood

As emerging adults enter adulthood itself, the process of development continues. The changes and transitions in adulthood can be divided roughly into three periods: early adulthood (from 20 to about 39), middle adulthood (from 40 to 65), and late adulthood (beyond 65).

Physical Changes

In *early adulthood,* physical growth continues. Shoulder width, height, and chest size increase. People continue to develop their athletic abilities. For most people, the years of early adulthood are the prime of life.

In *middle adulthood,* one of the most common physical changes is the loss of sensory sharpness. By this time, nearly everyone shows some hearing impairment. People in their early forties become less sensitive to light, and their vision deteriorates somewhat. Increased farsightedness is an inevitable change that usually results in a need for reading glasses. Inside the body, bone mass is dwindling, the risk of heart disease is increasing, and fertility declines. In their late forties or early fifties, women generally experience the shutdown of reproductive capability, a process known as **menopause.** Estrogen and progesterone levels drop, and the menstrual cycle eventually ceases.

In *late adulthood,* men shrink about an inch and women about 2 inches as their posture changes and cartilage disks between the spinal vertebrae become thinner. Hardening of the arteries and a buildup of fat deposits on the artery walls may lead to heart disease. The digestive system slows down and becomes less efficient. In addition, the brain shrinks, and the flow of blood to the brain slows. The few reflexes that remained after infancy (such as the knee-jerk reflex) weaken or disappear. Bedtime comes earlier, and naps are more frequent (Park et al., 2002). But as in earlier years, declines in physical functioning can be delayed or diminished by a healthy diet and exercise (Brach et al., 2003; Larson et al., 2006; Sun et al., 2010).

Cognitive Changes

Adulthood is marked by both increases and decreases in cognitive abilities. Reaction times become slower and more variable (Deary & Der, 2005), and abilities that involve intensive information processing begin to decline, even in early adulthood. However, abilities that depend on accumulated knowledge and experience increase and don't begin to decline until old age, if at all. In fact, older adults may function as well as or even better than younger adults in situations that tap their long-term memories and well-learned skills (Campbell, Hasher, & Thomas, 2010).

Cognitive Advances in Early, Middle, and Late Adulthood
In early and middle adulthood, until age 60 at least, important cognitive abilities improve. During this period, adults do better on tests of vocabulary, comprehension, and general knowledge, especially if they use these abilities in their daily lives (Park, 2001). Young and middle-aged adults learn new information and new skills; they remember old information and hone old skills. It is in their forties through their early sixties that people tend to put in the best performance of their lives on complex mental tasks such as reasoning, verbal memory, and vocabulary (Willis & Schaie, 1999).

The nature of thought may also change during adulthood. Adult thought is often more complex and adaptive than adolescent thought (Labouvie-Vief, 1992). Adults can understand, as adolescents cannot, the contradictions inherent in thinking. They see both the possibilities and the problems in every course of action—in deciding whether to start a new business, back a political candidate, move to a new community, or change jobs, for example. Middle-aged adults are more adept than adolescents or young adults at making rational decisions and at relating logic and abstractions to

menopause The process whereby a woman's reproductive capacity ceases.

actions, emotions, social issues, and personal relationships (Tversky & Kahneman, 1981). Their thought becomes more global, more concerned with broad moral and practical concerns (Labouvie-Vief, 1982). It has been suggested that this new kind of thinking reflects a stage of cognitive development that goes beyond Piaget's formal operational period. In this advanced stage, people's thinking becomes *dialectical*, which means they understand that knowledge is relative, not absolute—such that what is seen as wise today may have been thought foolish in times past (Lutz & Sternberg, 1999). They see life's contradictions as an inevitable part of reality, and they tend to weigh various solutions to problems rather than just accepting the first one that springs to mind (Grossmann et al., 2010).

Declining Cognitive Abilities in Late Adulthood   It is not until late adulthood—after age 65 or so—that some intellectual abilities decline noticeably (Craik & Salthouse, 2008). Generally, the abilities most severely affected are those that require rapid and flexible manipulation of ideas and symbols, active thinking and reasoning, and sheer mental effort (Baltes, 1994; Finkel et al., 2003; Gilmore, Spinks, & Thomas, 2006; see Figure 12.7). Older adults do just as well as younger ones at tasks they know well, such as naming familiar objects (Radvansky, 1999). It is when they are asked to perform an unfamiliar task or to solve a complex problem they have not seen before that older adults are generally slower and less effective than younger ones (Craik & Rabinowitz, 1984). When facing complex problems, older people apparently suffer from having too much information to sift through (Gazzaley et al., 2005). They have trouble considering, choosing, and executing solutions (Peters et al., 2007). As people age, they grow less efficient at organizing the elements of a problem and at holding and manipulating more than one idea at a time. They have difficulty doing tasks that require them to divide their attention between two activities (Smith et al., 2001) and are slower at shifting their attention back and forth between those activities (Wecker et al., 2005). If older adults have enough time, though, and can separate the two activities, they can perform just as well as younger adults (Hawkins, Kramer, & Capaldi, 1993).

Usually, the loss of intellectual abilities in older adults is slow and need not cause major problems (Bashore & Ridderinkhoff, 2002). A study of Swedish adults (Nilsson, 1996) found that memory problems among older adults appear mainly when retrieving events from *episodic memory* (such as what they ate for lunch yesterday) rather than in retrieving general knowledge from *semantic memory* (such as the name of the capital of Spain). In short, everyday competencies that involve verbal processes are likely to remain

FIGURE 12.7
Mental Abilities over the Life Span
Mental abilities collectively known as "fluid" intelligence—speed and accuracy of information processing, for example— begin to decline quite early in adult life. Changes in these biologically based aspects of thinking are usually not marked until late adulthood, however. "Crystallized" abilities learned over a lifetime—such as reading, writing, comprehension of language, and professional skills—decline too, but later and at a slower pace (Finkel et al., 2007; Li et al., 2004).

Source: Adapted from Baltes (1994).

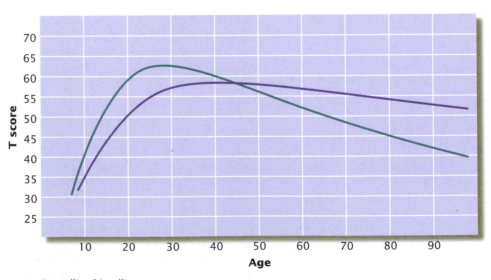

intact into advanced old age (Freedman, Aykan, & Martin, 2001; Willis & Schaie, 1999). Unfortunately, however, there is one way in which older adults' declining memories can have negative effects: They may be more likely than younger adults to recall false information as being true (Jacoby & Rhodes, 2006; Park, 2001), making some of them prone to victimization by scam artists. For example, the more warnings they hear about a false medical claim—such as that shark cartilage supposedly cures arthritis—the more familiar it becomes, and the more likely they are to believe it. As described in the chapter on memory, younger people are also vulnerable to memory distortions, but they are more likely to remember that false information is false, even when it is familiar.

The decline in cognitive abilities in old age, as well as the rate of that decline, is partly a matter of genetics (Finkel et al., 2009; Reynolds et al., 2005), but other factors are important too. For example, long term use of tobacco or alcohol is associated with reductions in the speed and accuracy of thinking among the elderly and with reductions in IQ (Glass et al., 2006). The risk of cognitive decline is much lower for people who are healthy and psychologically flexible; who eat a healthy diet; who have a high level of education and income and have a satisfying occupation; who live in an intellectually stimulating environment with mentally able spouses or companions; and who had high IQs and were physically active in adolescence (Fritsch et al., 2005; Morris et al., 2006; Yaffe et al., 2009). Scientists speculate that devoting years to obtaining an education and working at a complex job multiplies connections among brain regions and creates "cognitive reserves" that can be drawn on in old age (Hall et al., 2009; Milgram et al., 2006; Springer et al., 2005; Tucker-Drob, Johnson, & Jones, 2009).

Mental exercise—such as doing puzzles, painting, and talking to intelligent friends—also helps older adults continue to think and remember effectively and creatively (Hall et al., 2009; Schooler, 2007). Practice at memory and other information-processing tasks may even lead to some improvement in skills impaired by old age and disuse (Erickson et al., 2007; Kramer & Willis, 2002; Rapp, Brenes, & Marsh, 2002; Tranter & Koutstaal, 2008). Continued physical exercise helps too. A lifetime of fitness through dancing or other forms of aerobic exercise has been associated with better maintenance of skills on a variety of mental tasks, including reaction time, reasoning, and divided attention (Abbott et al., 2004; Baker et al., 2010; McAuley, Kramer, & Colcombe, 2004; Smith et al., 2010; Weuve et al., 2004).

In short, an "engaged lifestyle" filled with volunteer work, travel, and other organized activities that provide opportunities to interact with a variety of individuals—not just family members—seems to provide the best environment for preventing decline in cognitive abilities (Hertzog et al., 2009; Keller-Cohen et al., 2004). Having an optimistic, emotionally stable, extroverted, open, and conscientious personality can help too (Martin et al., 2009). People who believe that they can keep their memories sharp are more likely to use the memory strategies (described in the memory chapter) that help them do just that (Lachman & Andreoletti, 2006). The effect of positive expectations has been demonstrated in the laboratory, where memory performance was better among older adults who were tested after first being exposed to positive words such as *accomplished, alert, knowledgeable,* and *successful* rather than to negative words such as *confused, feeble, forgot,* and *senile* (Hess, Hinson, & Statham, 2004).

The greatest threat to cognitive abilities in late adulthood is *Alzheimer's disease,* which strikes about 10 percent of people over the age of 65 and more than 47 percent of those over 85. As the disease runs its course, parts of these individuals' brains begin to deteriorate (Dauwels et al., 2010; Pengas et al., 2010) and they become emotionally flat, disoriented, and eventually mentally vacant. They usually die prematurely. The average duration of the disease, from onset to death, is seven years. But the age of onset and rate of deterioration depend on a number of factors, such as intelligence (Fritsch et al., 2005; Rentz et al., 2004), gender (Molsa, Marttila, & Rinne, 1995), and education (Mortimer, Snowdon, & Markesbery, 2003). Highly intelligent people show clinical signs of Alzheimer's later than the general population. Women and well-educated people of either gender tend to deteriorate more slowly (Wilson, Scherr, et al., 2007).

Social Changes

In adulthood, people develop new relationships and take on new roles. These changes do not come in neat, predictable stages but instead follow various paths, depending on each individual's experiences. Transitions—such as divorcing, getting fired from a job, going back to school, remarrying, losing a spouse to death, being hospitalized, getting arrested, or retiring—are turning points that can redirect a person's life path and lead to changes in personality (Caspi & Shiner, 2006; Roberts, Helson, & Klohnen, 2002).

Early Adulthood: Work, Marriage, Parenthood   Men and women in industrialized cultures typically enter the adult world in their mid to late twenties. At the beginning of this period, about 20 percent of young people are still really emerging adults who live with their parents, and just under half are still financially dependent (Cohen, Kasen, et al., 2003). Gradually, they become more organized, disciplined, and able to plan as they decide on an occupation or at least take a job and become preoccupied with their careers (Srivastava et al., 2003). They also become more agreeable—warmer, more generous and helpful, more controlled and confident; more socially dominant, conscientious, and emotionally stable; and less angry and alienated (Roberts, Caspi, & Moffitt, 2001; Roberts & Mroczek, 2008; Roberts, Walton, & Viechtbauer, 2006; Srivastava et al., 2003).

Young adults become concerned with matters of romantic love. Having reached the sixth of Erikson's stages of psychosocial development noted in Table 12.2 (intimacy versus isolation), they begin to focus on forming mature, committed relationships based on sexual intimacy, friendship, or mutual intellectual stimulation. Those who remain without partners report the lowest levels of happiness, self-esteem, and life satisfaction (Kamp Dush & Amato, 2005). The happiest young adults tend to be those who get married rather than merely live together, go steady, or date casually. Just how willing and able people are to make romantic commitments is predictable in part from the nature of their earlier relations with parents, including the attachment pattern that developed in infancy (Birnbaum et al., 2006; Holland & Roisman, 2010; Treboux, Crowell, & Waters, 2004). Young adults whose view of relationships reflects a secure attachment tend to feel valued and worthy of support and affection. They develop closeness easily and have relationships characterized by joy, trust, and commitment. If their view reflects an insecure attachment, however, they tend to be preoccupied with relationships and may feel misunderstood, underappreciated, and worried about being abandoned. Their relationships are often negative, obsessive, jealous, or promiscuous. Those who develop warm and supportive romantic relationships in early adulthood are likely to have had parents who were accepting and supportive (Conger et al., 2000; Overbeek et al., 2007).

For many young adults, the experience of becoming a parent represents entry into a major new developmental phase that is accompanied by personal, social, and occupational changes (Palkovitz, Copes, & Woolfolk, 2001). This milestone is usually reached earlier for young adults from lower-income backgrounds, who are more likely to be in full-time employment and less likely to be living at home (Cohen, Kasen, et al., 2003). Satisfaction with the marriage or partnership often declines once a baby is born (Doss et al., 2009; Twenge, Campbell, & Foster, 2003). Young mothers may experience particular dissatisfaction, especially if they see their career as important, if parenthood fails to meet their expectations, if they resent the constraints the infant brings, if the infant is temperamentally difficult, if the partnership is not strong, and if their partner is not supportive (Cowan & Cowan, 2000, 2009; Harwood, McLean, & Durkin, 2007; Hogan & Msall, 2002; Jokela, 2010; Shapiro, Gottman, & Carrere, 2000). When the father does not do his share of child care, both mothers and fathers are dissatisfied (Levy-Shiff, 1994). The ability of young parents to provide adequate care for their babies is related to their own childhood histories. New mothers whose attachments to their own mothers were secure tend to be more responsive to their infants, and the infants, in turn, are more likely to develop secure attachments to them (Adam, Gunnar, & Tanaka, 2004; Behrens,

The Transition to Parenthood

Becoming a parent can be a joy, but it may be accompanied by dissatisfaction if it fails to meet a couple's expectations, severely restricts their lives, or uncovers weaknesses in their relationship.

© Blend Images/Photoshot

Hesse, & Main, 2007; van IJzendoorn, 1995). Parents who experienced harsh treatment as children are likely to be harsh with their own children; those who had more positive parenting in childhood tend to be kinder to their children (Bailey et al., 2009; Conger, Belsky, & Capaldi, 2009).

The challenges of young adulthood are complicated by the nature of family life today. Forty years ago, about half of North American households consisted of married couples in their twenties and thirties—a breadwinner husband and a homemaker wife—raising at least two children together. This picture now describes only about 23.5 percent of households (Frey, 2003). Today, parents are older because they marry later and wait longer to have children. Many are having children without marrying. About 75 percent of African American women become single mothers, and 11 percent of European American college-educated women in their thirties are also choosing single motherhood, a dramatic increase over past decades (Weinraub, Horvath, & Gringlas, 2002). Most of these women become pregnant "the old-fashioned way," but some are taking advantage of technological advances that allow them to conceive through *in vitro fertilization* (Hahn & DiPietro, 2001).

Many gay men and lesbians are becoming parents too. Some estimates suggest that at least four million families in the United States are headed by openly gay or lesbian adults who became parents by retaining custody of children born in a previous heterosexual marriage, adopting children, or having children through artificial insemination or surrogacy (Patterson, 2002). They face special challenges in making the transition to parenthood. Many of them confront discrimination by health care organizations and employer policies that do not recognize their parental role. They may also experience pervasive hostility, even from members of their own extended families.

Whether homosexual or heterosexual, the 60 percent of mothers who hold full-time jobs outside the home often find the demands of children and career pulling them in opposite directions. Devotion to their jobs leaves many of these mothers feeling guilty about spending too little time with their children (Booth et al., 2002), but placing too much emphasis on home life may reduce their productivity at work and threaten their advancement. This stressful balancing act can lead to anxiety, frustration, and conflicts at home and on the job. It affects fathers too. The husbands of employed women are more involved in child care (Pleck, 2004), and they can be effective caregivers (Parke, 2002), but mothers still do most of the child care and housework (Coltrane & Adams, 2008).

Research indicates that gay and lesbian parents share duties more equally—and are more satisfied with the division of labor—than is typically the case in heterosexual families (Patterson, 2002; Solomon, Rothbaum, & Balsam, 2004).

Nearly half of all marriages in the United States end in divorce, creating yet another set of challenges for adults (Clarke-Stewart & Brentano, 2006). Although it frees people from bad relationships, divorce can leave them feeling anxious, guilty, incompetent, depressed, and lonely. Divorce is correlated with health problems and ultimately with earlier mortality. Often divorce creates new stressors, including money problems, changes in living circumstances and working hours, and for custodial parents, a dramatic increase in housework and child care tasks. One study found that two years after divorcing, most women were happier than they were during the final year of their marriage but more stressed than mothers in two-parent families (Hetherington & Stanley-Hagan, 2002). How effectively divorced people deal with these stressors depends on many factors, including the support they receive from friends and family, their general psychological stability and coping skills, their ability to form new relationships, and the degree to which they remain in conflict with their ex-spouses.

In short, the changes seen in families and family life over the past several decades have made it more challenging than ever to successfully navigate the years of early adulthood.

Middle Adulthood: Reappraising Priorities   At around age 40, people go through a *midlife transition* during which they may reappraise and modify their lives and relationships. Many feel invigorated and liberated; some feel upset and have a "midlife crisis." Women who chose a career over a family now hear the biological clock ticking out their last childbearing years. Those who have had children become more independent and oriented toward achievement and events outside the family (Helson & Moane, 1987). For both men and women, the emerging sexuality of their teenage children, the emptiness of the nest as their children leave home, or the declining health of a parent may precipitate a crisis.

Following the midlife transition, the middle years of adulthood are often a time of satisfaction, happiness, and other positive emotions as people enjoy a wide variety of leisure activities, including just spending time with the family (Mroczek & Spiro, 2005; Taylor, 2001). Many people become concerned with producing something that will outlast them—usually through parenthood or job achievements. Erikson called

The "Sandwich" Generation

During their midlife transition, many people feel "sandwiched" between generations—pressured by the social, emotional, and financial needs of their children on one side and of their aging parents on the other (Keene & Prokos, 2007; Wujcik, 2008).

© Michael Newman/PhotoEdit

this concern the crisis of **generativity** because people begin to focus on activities that will produce or generate something that might benefit future generations. If they do not resolve this crisis by striking a good balance between generativity and self-centeredness, he suggested, people stagnate. Research shows that after the age of 40, people are indeed more likely to strive for generativity goals (Sheldon & Kasser, 2001; Zucker, Ostrove, & Stewart, 2002). These might include writing a book, helping people in need, developing closer relationships with children, being a good role model for them, acting as a coach or mentor, and trying in other ways to make a lasting contribution to society.

In their fifties, most people become grandparents (Smith & Drew, 2002). This new status often amazes them. For example, a survey of professionals in their fifties found that they could not quite believe they were no longer young (Karp, 1991). Most described themselves as healthy but acknowledged that their bodies were slowing down. At this age, spending time caring for young grandchildren can be stressful. One study found that grandmothers who spent more time providing care for their grandchildren were at increased risk of coronary heart disease (Lee, Colditz, et al., 2003). Overall, the degree of happiness and healthiness people experience during middle adulthood depends on how much control they feel they have over their work, finances, marriage, children, and sex life, as well as on the nature of their personality, how many years of education they completed, and what kind of job they have (Azar, 1996; Griffin, Mroczek, & Spiro, 2006).

Late Adulthood: Retirement and Restriction   Even when they are 65 to 75, most people think of themselves as about thirteen years younger than they are and consider themselves middle-aged, not old (Kleinspehn-Ammerlahn, Kotter-Grühn, & Smith, 2008). They are active and influential politically and socially; they are often physically vigorous. Ratings of life satisfaction, well-being, and self-esteem are, on average, as high as they were during earlier adulthood (Ben-Zur, 2002; Hamarat et al., 2002; Sheldon & Kasser, 2001; Stone et al., 2010). Those most likely to enjoy good physical and mental health in late adulthood are the ones who had lots of parental support during childhood (Shaw et al., 2004); who can accept their feelings, memories, and ways of thinking (Butler & Ciarrochi, 2007); and who can adjust to age-related declines as they come (Cheng, Fung, & Chan, 2009).

Late adulthood is the time when men and women usually retire from their jobs, but many people underestimate older people's ability and willingness to work. This misperception was once translated into laws that forced workers to retire at age 65 regardless of their abilities. Thanks to changes in those laws in the United States and some other countries, most people can now continue working as long as they wish. Being forced to retire can result in psychological and physical problems. In one study of cardiovascular disease, men who retired involuntarily were found to be more depressed, less healthy, and less well adjusted than those who retired voluntarily (Clay, 1996). Such problems may also occur when husbands retire before their wives do (Rubin, 1998). Men tend to view retirement as a time to wind down, whereas women see it as a time to try new things and to reinvent themselves (Helgesen, 1998). In general, it seems, voluntary retirees are more likely to be satisfied with their lives than people who continue, by choice or financial necessity, to work through their sixties and seventies (Moen et al., 2000). Satisfaction is especially likely among those who had made careful financial plans long before retirement (Noone, Stephens, & Alpass, 2009).

More people than ever are reaching old age. In fact, people over 75 make up the fastest-growing segment of the population. This group is twenty-five times larger today than it was a hundred years ago. Today, about one hundred thousand people in the United States are older than 100, and the Census Bureau has predicted that this number will rise to 834,000 by 2050 (Volz, 2000). Old age is not necessarily a time of loneliness and desolation, but it is a time when people generally become more inward-looking, cautious, and conforming (Reedy, 1983). It is a time when people develop coping strategies that increasingly take into account the limits of their control—accepting chronic health

"When I was your age, I was an adult."

Most people in their sixties want their children to be independent, so they may have mixed feelings toward children who continue to need financial support during an extended period of emerging adulthood (Pillemer & Suitor, 2002).

generativity Adult concerns about producing something that may be of benefit to others in the future.

Able at Eighty

At the age of 80, actor and Academy Award–winning director Clint Eastwood is a famous example of the many people whose late adulthood is healthy and vigorous. And he is not slowing down. His acting remains as riveting as ever, and the films he directs just seem to get better and better.

problems and other things they cannot change (Brandtstadter & Renner, 1990). One such coping strategy is to direct attention to positive thoughts, activities, and memories (Charles, Mather, & Carstensen, 2003; Mather et al., 2004). In fact, when older adults are asked to look at pictures of faces portraying various emotions, they spend more time looking at happy faces; people of college-age look longer at fearful faces (Isaacowitz et al., 2006). According to socioemotional selectivity theory (Charles & Carstensen, 2007), this difference occurs because in old age, people become more aware than ever that their time on earth is limited. Accordingly, they regulate their emotions so as to focus more on positive than on negative information. So when experimenters deliberately induce negative emotions in a laboratory situation, older adults are better than younger ones at quickly recovering their previous mood (Kliegel, Jager, & Phillips, 2007).

In old age, people interact with others less frequently, but they enjoy their interactions more (Carstensen, 1997). They find relationships more satisfying, supportive, and fulfilling than they did earlier in life. During the last twenty years of their lives, people gradually restrict their social network to loved ones. As long as there are at least three close friends or relatives in their network, they tend to be content, especially if these relationships are good ones (Litwin & Shiovitz-Ezra, 2006).

The many changes associated with adolescence and adulthood are summarized in "In Review: Milestones of Adolescence and Adulthood."

Death and Dying

In old age, people become increasingly aware that death is approaching. They watch as their friends disappear. They feel their health deteriorating, their strength waning, and their intellectual capabilities declining. A few years or a few months before death, some people experience a sharp decline in mental functioning known as **terminal drop** (Wilson, Beck, et al., 2007).

The awareness of impending death brings about the last psychological crisis, according to Erikson's theory, in which people evaluate their lives and accomplishments and affirm them as meaningful (leading to a feeling of integrity) or meaningless

IN REVIEW	Milestones of Adolescence and Adulthood		
Age	**Physical Changes**	**Cognitive Changes**	**Social Events and Psychological Changes**
Early adolescence (ages 11–15)	Puberty brings reproductive capacity and marked bodily changes.	Formal operations and principled moral reasoning become possible for the first time.	Social and emotional changes result from growing sexual awareness; adolescents experience mood swings, physical changes, and conflicts with parents.
Late adolescence (ages 16–19)	Physical growth continues.	Formal operations and principled moral reasoning become more likely.	An identity crisis accompanies graduation from high school.
Early adulthood (ages 20–39)	Physical growth continues.	Increases continue in knowledge, problem-solving ability, and moral reasoning.	People choose a job and often a mate; they may become parents.
Middle adulthood (ages 40–65)	Size and muscle mass decrease; fat increases; eyesight declines; reproductive capacity in women ends.	Thought becomes more complex, adaptive, and global.	Midlife transition may lead to change; for most, the middle years are satisfying.
Late adulthood (beyond age 65)	Size decreases; organs become less efficient.	Reasoning, mathematical ability, comprehension, novel problem solving, and memory may decline.	Retirement requires adjustments; people look inward; awareness of death precipitates life review.

1. The greatest threat to cognitive abilities in late adulthood is _____ disease.

2. Adolescents' _____ identity may be more defining than their national citizenship.

3. Not stealing because "I might get caught" reflects the _____ stage of moral reasoning.

(leading to a feeling of despair). People at this stage tend to become more philosophical and reflective. They attempt to put their lives into perspective. They reminisce, resolve past conflicts, and integrate past events. They may also become more interested in the religious and spiritual side of life. This "life review" may trigger anxiety, regret, guilt, and despair, or it may allow people to face their own deaths and the deaths of friends and relatives with a feeling of peace and acceptance (Steinhauser et al., 2008; Torges, Stewart, & Nolen-Hoeksema, 2008).

Even the actual confrontation with death does not have to bring despair and depression. People generally want to be told if they are dying (Hinton, 1967). When death finally is imminent, old people strive for a death with dignity, love, affection, physical contact, and no pain. As they think about death, they are likely to be comforted by their religious faith, their achievements, and the love of their friends and family.

Developmental Trajectories

The life span development we have described is a bit like the flight of an airplane, beginning with a takeoff, cruising along for a while, and eventually entering its final descent. Like aircraft bound for differing destinations, the flight path, or trajectory, of our lives can be long or short, reach high or low altitudes, and be bumpy or smooth. There may be midcourse corrections during flight, of course, but researchers who have tracked developmental trajectories find a remarkable degree of stability from childhood through adulthood on many dimensions. For example, people who are intelligent and have good memories, who are good with numbers or poor at languages, tend to retain these advantages or disadvantages throughout their lifetimes (e.g., Anstey, Hofer, & Luszcz, 2003; Chodosh et al., 2002). Personality and social development also remain consistent (Roberts, Caspi, & Moffitt, 2001; Roberts, Helson, & Klohnen, 2002; Shiner, Masten, & Roberts, 2003). Children who are creative, persistent, enthusiastic about their activities, and motivated to achieve are likely to become adults who take pleasure in their pursuits, enjoy challenges, work hard to succeed, and become effective leaders who handle stress well. Children who take their schoolwork seriously and finish their homework promptly are likely to become adults who are traditional in their views, who plan well, and who are not apt to take risks. Children and adolescents who do well in school and have friends and social skills tend to have good romantic relationships, strong friendships, and occupational success as adults (Roisman et al., 2004; Shiner, Masten, & Roberts, 2003). And those who are psychologically healthy in early adolescence tend to remain so into late adulthood (Jones & Peskin, 2010). In contrast, highly aggressive children are likely to develop academic problems in adolescence and to become anxious and depressed young adults and ultimately antisocial adults as each kind of problem cascades into the next (Masten et al., 2005; Schaeffer et al., 2003). In other words, people tend to stay on relatively consistent developmental paths throughout their lives.

Longevity: The Length of Life

terminal drop A sharp decline in mental functioning that tends to occur in late adulthood, a few years or months before death.

The length of life's trajectory depends on a number of factors. Researchers have discovered, for example, that longevity is greater in women and in people without histories of heavy drinking, smoking, or heart problems (Poon, 2008). It is also related to personality characteristics such as conscientiousness as a child (Friedman et al., 1995a) and curiosity and purpose in life as an adult (Boyle et al., 2009; Swan & Carmelli, 1996). Men tend to live longer if their mother was in the "right" age range (between 20 and 34) when they were born and if they had a higher IQ and higher levels of income and education. Women tend to live longer if they had fewer children and had them at a later point in the "right" age range. Men and women alike tend to live longer if they are religious and, perhaps most important from a genetic standpoint, if members of their extended family were long-lived (Deary & Der, 2005; Smith et al., 2009). In fact, the secret of extreme longevity—one hundred years or more—may lie in a group of genes seen in some people that can slow the aging process (Puca et al., 2001; Willcox et al., 2006, 2009).

Longer life is also more often seen in people who experienced more happiness, enthusiasm, contentment, and other forms of *positive affect* during adulthood (Cohen & Pressman, 2006; Pressman & Cohen, 2007). Adults who had more positive self-perceptions when they were in their fifties and sixties lived an average of seven and a half years longer than those with less positive self-perceptions. This factor was more predictive of longevity than health problems such as high blood pressure, high cholesterol, smoking, lack of exercise, or being overweight (Levy et al., 2002). A network of good friends, even more than close family ties, is also related to longer life (Giles et al., 2005; Poon, 2008).

Older adults can be made to feel better physically and psychologically if they continue to be socially active and useful. For example, old people who are given parties, plants, or pets are happier and more alert than those who receive less attention, and they do not die as soon (Clark et al., 2001). People who restrict their caloric intake, engage in regular physical and mental exercise, and have a sense of control over important aspects of their lives are also likely to live longer (Manini et al., 2006; Sun et al., 2010; Yaffe et al., 2001). So eat your veggies, stay physically fit, and continue to think actively—not just to live longer later but to live better now.

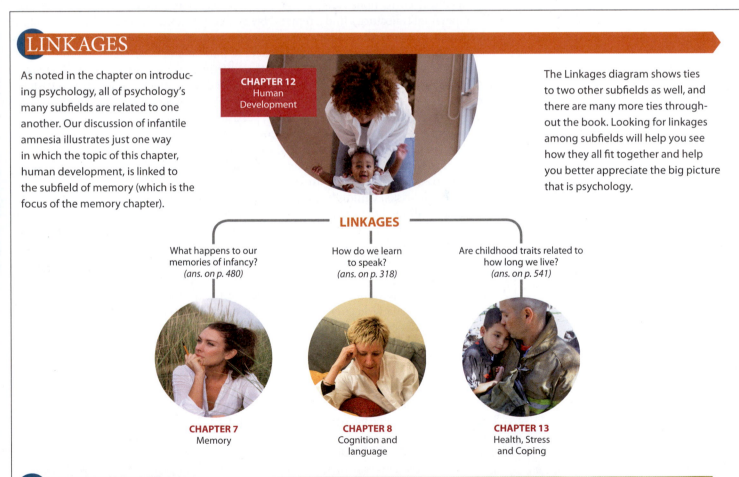

LINKAGES

As noted in the chapter on introducing psychology, all of psychology's many subfields are related to one another. Our discussion of infantile amnesia illustrates just one way in which the topic of this chapter, human development, is linked to the subfield of memory (which is the focus of the memory chapter).

CHAPTER 12
Human Development

The Linkages diagram shows ties to two other subfields as well, and there are many more ties throughout the book. Looking for linkages among subfields will help you see how they all fit together and help you better appreciate the big picture that is psychology.

LINKAGES

What happens to our memories of infancy?
(ans. on p. 480)

How do we learn to speak?
(ans. on p. 318)

Are childhood traits related to how long we live?
(ans. on p. 541)

CHAPTER 7
Memory

CHAPTER 8
Cognition and language

CHAPTER 13
Health, Stress and Coping

SUMMARY

Developmental psychology is the study of the course and causes of age-related changes in mental abilities, social relationships, emotions, and moral understanding over the life span.

Exploring Human Development

A central question in developmental psychology concerns the relative influences of nature and nurture, a theme that has

its origins in the philosophies of John Locke and Jean-Jacques Rousseau. In the twentieth century, Arnold Gesell stressed nature in his theory of development, proposing that development is *maturation*—the natural unfolding of abilities with age. John B. Watson took the opposite view, claiming that development is learning—shaped by the external environment. In his theory of cognitive development, Jean Piaget described how nature and nurture work together. Today we accept the notion that both nature and nurture affect development and ask how and to what extent each contributes.

Beginnings

Prenatal Development

Development begins with the union of an ovum and a sperm to form a *zygote,* which becomes an *embryo.* The embryonic stage is a *critical period* for development, a time when certain organs must develop properly or they never will. Development of organs at this stage is irrevocably affected by harmful *teratogens,* such as drugs and alcohol. After the embryo develops into a *fetus,* adverse conditions during the fetal stage may harm the infant's size, behavior, intelligence, or health. Babies born to women who drink heavily have a strong chance of suffering from *fetal alcohol syndrome.*

The Newborn

Newborns have limited but effective senses of vision, hearing, taste, and smell. They exhibit many reflexes, which are swift, automatic responses to external stimuli. Motor development proceeds as the nervous system matures, muscles grow, and the infant experiments with and selects the most efficient movement patterns.

Infancy and Childhood: Cognitive Development

Cognitive development includes the development of thinking, knowing, and remembering.

Changes in the Brain

The development of increasingly complex and efficient neural networks in various regions of the brain provides the "hardware" for the increasingly complex cognitive abilities that arise during infancy and childhood.

The Development of Knowledge: Piaget's Theory

According to Piaget, cognitive development occurs in a fixed sequence of stages, as *schemas* are modified through the complementary processes of *assimilation* (fitting new objects or events into existing schemas) and *accommodation* (changing schemas when new objects will not fit existing ones). During the *sensorimotor stage,* infants progress from using only simple senses and reflexes to forming mental representations of objects and actions. Thus the child becomes capable of thinking about objects that are not present. The ability to recognize that objects continue to exist even when they are hidden from view is what Piaget called *object permanence.* During the *preoperational stage,* children can use symbols, but they do not have the ability to think logically and rationally. Their understanding of the world is intuitive and egocentric. They do not understand the logical operations of reversibility or complementarity. When children develop the ability to think logically about concrete objects, they enter the stage of *concrete operations.* At this time, they can solve simple problems. They also have an understanding of *conservation,* recognizing that, for example, the amount of a substance is not altered even when its shape changes. The *formal operational stage* begins in adolescence and allows a wide range of complex executive functions, including planning, imagining consequences, and thinking logically about abstract ideas.

Modifying Piaget's Theory

Research reveals that Piaget underestimated infants' mental abilities. Developmental psychologists now also believe that new levels of cognition are reached not in sharply marked stages of global understanding but more gradually and in specific areas. Children's reasoning is affected by factors such as task difficulty and degree of familiarity with the objects and language involved.

Information Processing During Childhood

Psychologists who explain cognitive development in terms of information processing have documented age-related improvements in children's attention, their abilities to explore and focus on features of the environment, and their memories.

Culture and Cognitive Development

The specific content of cognitive development, including the development of scripts, depends on the cultural context in which children live.

Improving or Endangering Cognitive Development

How fast children develop cognitive abilities depends to a certain extent on how stimulating and supportive their environments are. Children growing up in poverty are likely to have delayed or impaired cognitive abilities.

Infancy and Childhood: Social and Emotional Development

Infants and their caregivers, from the early months, respond to each other's emotional expressions. When an infant's behavior in an ambiguous situation is affected by the caregiver's emotional expression, social referencing is said to have occurred.

Individual Temperament

Most infants can be classified as having an easy, difficult, or slow-to-warm-up *temperament.* Whether they retain their initial temperamental style depends to some extent on their parents' expectations and demands.

Attachment

According to *attachment theory,* over the first year of life, infants form a deep and abiding emotional *attachment* to their mothers or other primary caregivers. Their attachment behavior may be secure or insecure.

Relationships with Parents

The process of *socialization* begins as parents teach their children the skills and rules needed in their culture using various parenting styles. They can be described as *authoritarian, permissive, authoritative,* or *uninvolved (rejecting-neglecting) parents.* Among European and European American parents, those with an authoritative style tend to have more competent and cooperative children. However, parenting styles and their impact depend to some extent on the culture and conditions in which parents find themselves.

Peer Friendships and Popularity
Over the childhood years, interactions with peers evolve into cooperative and competitive encounters, and friendships become more important.

Social Skills and Understanding
Children become increasingly able to interpret and understand social situations and emotional signals. They begin to express empathy and sympathy and to engage in the *self-regulation* of their emotions and behaviors. They also learn social rules and roles.

Gender Roles
Children develop *gender roles,* also known as *sex roles,* that are based both on biological differences between the sexes and on implicit and explicit socialization by parents, teachers, peers, and the media. Children are also influenced by *gender schemas,* which affect their choices of activities and toys.

Risk and Resilience
Children who lead successful lives despite such adversities as family instability, child abuse, homelessness, poverty, or war are described as having *resilience.* Factors associated with this characteristic include good intellectual functioning and strong relationships with caring adults.

Adolescence

Adolescents undergo significant changes not only in size, shape, and physical capacity but also in their social lives, reasoning abilities, and views of themselves.

Changes in Body, Brain, and Thinking
Puberty brings about physical changes that lead to psychological changes. Changes in the brain alter the ways adolescents think. Specifically, they develop the capacity for formal operational thought and the ability to control their own thinking.

Adolescent Feelings and Behavior
Early adolescence is a period of shaky self-esteem. It is also a time when conflict with parents, as well as closeness with and conformity to friends, is likely to rise. A particularly difficult challenge for adolescents is the transition from elementary school to junior high or middle school.

Identity and Development of the Self
Late adolescence focuses on finding an answer to the question "Who am I?" Adolescents begin to develop an integrated self-image as a unique person, an image that often includes *ethnic identity.*

Moral Development
Principled moral judgment—shaped by gender and culture—becomes possible for the first time in adolescence. The development of moral reasoning may progress through *preconventional, conventional,* and *postconventional reasoning* stages. A person's moral development may be reflected in moral action.

Emerging Adulthood
Going to college challenges the emerging adult's self-concept, precipitating an *identity crisis.* Resolving this identity crisis and choosing a career direction are two major tasks in this stage of life.

Adulthood

Physical, cognitive, and social changes occur throughout adulthood.

Physical Changes
Middle adulthood sees changes that include decreased acuity of the senses, increased risk of heart disease, and the end of fertility (*menopause*). Nevertheless, major health problems may not appear until late adulthood.

Cognitive Changes
The cognitive changes that occur in early and middle adulthood are generally positive, including improvements in reasoning and problem-solving ability. In late adulthood, some intellectual abilities decline—especially those involved in tasks that are unfamiliar, complex,

or difficult. Other abilities, such as recalling facts or making wise decisions, tend not to decline. Individuals with Alzheimer's disease become disoriented and mentally vacant, and they die prematurely.

Social Changes
In their twenties, young adults make occupational choices and form intimate commitments. In middle adulthood, they become concerned with *generativity*—with producing something that will outlast them. Sometime around age 40, adults experience a *midlife transition,* which may or may not be a crisis. The forties and fifties are often a time of satisfaction. In their sixties, people contend with retirement. They generally become more inward-looking, cautious, and conforming. Adults' progress through these ages is influenced by the unique personal events that befall them.

Death and Dying
In their seventies and eighties, people confront their own mortality. They may become more philosophical and reflective as they review their lives. A few years or months before death, some individuals experience a sharp decline in mental functioning known as *terminal drop.* They strive for a death with dignity, love, and no pain.

Developmental Trajectories
Researchers who have tracked developmental trajectories have found stability from childhood through adulthood in terms of cognitive abilities, personality characteristics, and social skills.

Longevity: The Length of Life
Death is inevitable, but certain factors—including healthy diets, exercise, personality traits such as conscientiousness and curiosity, a sense of control over one's life, and genetics—are associated with living longer and happier lives. Older adults feel better and live longer if they receive attention from other people, maintain an open attitude toward new experiences, and keep their minds active.

LINKAGES TO FURTHER LEARNING

Now that you have finished reading this chapter, how about exploring some of the topics and information that you found most interesting? Here are some places to start.

Books

Deborah Blum, *Love at Goon Park: Harry Harlow and the Science of Affection* (Perseus, 2002). About Harlow's famous research.

Thomas Hine, *The Rise and Fall of the American Teenager* (Avon, 1999). Social and cultural history of adolescence.

Alison Gopnik, Andrew N. Meltzoff, and Patricia K. Kuhl, *The Scientist in the Crib: Minds, Brains, and How Children Learn* (Morrow, 1999).

Readable summary of research in cognitive development.

Rachel Simmons, *Odd Girl Out: The Hidden Culture of Aggression in Girls* (Harcourt, 2002). Study of girls' relational aggression.

Robin Karr-Morse and Meredith S. Wiley, *Ghosts from the Nursery: Tracing the Roots of Violence* (Grove/Atlantic, 1999). How biological predispositions may lead to violence.

On the Internet

CourseMate Access an integrated eBook and chapter-specific learning tools including flashcards, quizzes, videos, and more. Go to CengageBrain.com.

 Want to maximize the value of your online study time? Take this easy-to-use study system's diagnostic pre-test, and it will create a personalized study plan for you. By helping you identify the topics that you need to understand better and then directing you to valuable online resources, it can speed up your chapter review. CengageNOW even provides a post-test so you can confirm that you are ready for an exam. Go to CengageBrain.com.

TALKING POINTS

Here are a few talking points to help you summarize this chapter for family and friends without giving a lecture.

1. The way we come to think and behave, from childhood to old age, is shaped by a combination of what we inherit at birth and what we experience afterward.

2. We have almost no memories of the time before we were 3 years old, and no one is yet sure why this "infantile amnesia" occurs.

3. Normal social and emotional development requires lots of human contact in the earliest years, which is why the development of orphans who have been neglected is so often impaired.

4. Our temperament at birth can vary from easy to difficult and forms the basis for the development of our personality.

5. Fair but firm parenting tends to be associated with the best outcomes

for child development, but there is no single "best" way to raise children.

6. Many people think of adolescence as a time of storm and stress, but most teens navigate this period without suffering major problems.

7. The ability to process information rapidly often begins to decline in late middle age, but most adults retain most of their mental capacities well into old age.

13

Health, Stress, and Coping

How long will you live? To some extent, the answer lies in your genes, but it is also affected by how you behave, how you think, and what stressors you face. In this chapter, you will learn about several kinds of stressors, how people respond to them, and the relationship between stress reactions and illness. You'll also discover what you can do to protect your own health.

I n Bangor, Maine, where snow and ice have paralyzed the community, Angie's headache gets worse as her 4-year-old daughter and 6-year-old son start bickering again. The day care center and elementary school are closed, so Angie must stay home from her job at the grocery store. She probably couldn't have gotten there anyway, because the buses have stopped running. During the latest storm, the power went out and the house is now almost unbearably cold; the can of spaghetti Angie opens is nearly frozen. Worry begins to creep into her head: "If I can't work, how will I pay for rent and day care?" Her parents have money problems, too, so they can't offer financial help, and her ex-husband rarely makes his child support payments. On top of everything else, Angie is coming down with the flu.

How do people manage such adversity, and what are its consequences for the individual? Psychologists who study questions such as these have established a specialty known as **health psychology** (also called **health care psychology**), "a field within psychology devoted to understanding psychological influence on how people stay healthy, why they become ill, and how they respond when they do get ill" (Taylor, 1999, p. 4).

Health psychologists use knowledge from many subfields of psychology to enhance understanding of the psychological and behavioral processes associated with health and illness (Smith & Suls, 2004). Their work is part of the broader field of *behavioral medicine*, in which psychologists pursue their health-related goals in cooperation with physicians, nurses, public health workers, and other biomedical specialists. In this chapter, we describe some of what has been discovered so far about psychological, social, and behavioral influences on health and how research in health psychology and behavioral medicine is being applied to prevent illness and promote better health. We begin by examining the nature of stressors and people's physical, psychological, and behavioral responses to stress. Then we consider factors that might alter the impact of stressful life events on a person. Next, we consider the psychological factors responsible for specific physical disorders and some behaviors that endanger people's health. We conclude by discussing health psychologists' recommendations for coping with stress and promoting health and some of their programs for doing so.

Health Psychology

Although the field of health psychology is relatively new, the themes underlying it date back to ancient times. For thousands of years, in many cultures around the world, people have believed that their mental state, their behavior, and their health are linked.

Today, there is scientific evidence to support this belief (Schneiderman, 2004; Antoni & Lutgendorf, 2007). We now know that the stresses of life influence health through their impact on psychological and physiological processes. For example, the

health psychology (health care psychology) A field in which psychologists conduct and apply research aimed at promoting human health and preventing illness.

appearance of physical illness has been associated with anger, hostility, pessimism, depression, social isolation, and hopelessness. Poor health has also been linked to behavioral factors such as lack of exercise, inadequate diet, smoking, and abuse of alcohol and other drugs (Freedman et al., 2006; Mente et al., 2009; van Dam et al., 2008; Vollset, Tverdal, & Gjessing, 2006). Good health, on the other hand, is associated with being optimistic, experiencing positive emotions, and behaviors such as adequate exercise and following medical advice.

Health psychology has become an increasingly important area of research and practice in North America, in part because of changing patterns of illness. Until the middle of the twentieth century, the major causes of illness and death in the United States and Canada were acute infectious diseases, such as influenza, tuberculosis, and pneumonia. With these afflictions now tamed, chronic illnesses—such as coronary heart disease, cancer, and diabetes—have joined stroke, accidents, and injuries as the leading causes of disability and death (Heron, 2007). Compared with acute diseases, these chronic diseases develop more slowly and are more strongly associated with people's psychological makeup, lifestyle, and environment (Centers for Disease Control and Prevention, 2008). For example, whether or not a person smokes affects the risk of the five leading causes of death for men and women in the United States (see Table 13.1). The psychological and behavioral factors that contribute to these illnesses can be changed by intervention programs such as those that promote nonsmoking, physical activity, and healthy eating (e.g., Bazzano et al., 2003; Kraus et al., 2002). In fact, about half the deaths in the United States are due to potentially preventable health risk behaviors (Greenland et al., 2003; Khot et al., 2003; Mokdad et al., 2004). Yet as few as 3 percent of people in the United States follow a lifestyle that includes maintaining a healthy weight, getting regular exercise, eating a proper diet, and not smoking (Reeves & Rafferty, 2005).

One goal of health psychology is to help people understand the role they can play in controlling their own health and life expectancy (Nash et al., 2003; Nicassio, Meyerowitz, & Kerns, 2004). For example, health care psychologists develop programs to educate people about the warning signs of cancer, heart disease, and other serious illnesses; encourage them to engage in self-examinations; and emphasize the importance of seeking medical attention while lifesaving treatment is still possible. Health psychologists also study and help people understand the role played by stress in physical health and illness. And clinical health care psychologists help individuals cope as effectively as possible with cancer, diabetes, heart disease, and many other kinds of serious illness.

Running for Your Life

APPLYING PSYCHOLOGY Health psychologists have developed programs to help people increase exercise, stop smoking, eat healthier diets, and make other lifestyle changes that can lower their risk of illness and death. They have even helped bolster community blood supplies by finding ways to make blood donation less stressful (Bonk, France, & Taylor, 2001).

TABLE 13.1	Lifestyle Behaviors That Affect the Leading Causes of Death in the United States

This table shows five of the leading causes of death in the United States today, along with behavioral factors that contribute to their development (Centers for Disease Control and Prevention, 2008; Jemal et al., 2005). Worldwide, the number of deaths caused by health-damaging behaviors is expected to continue its upward climb (World Health Organization, 2008).

	Contributing Behavioral Factor				
Cause of Death	*Excessive Alcohol Consumption*	*Tobacco Smoking*	*Unhealthy Diet*	*Inadequate Exercise*	*Inadequate Sleep*
Heart disease	×	×	×	×	×
Cancer	×	×	×		
Stroke	×	×	×	?	×
Lung disease		×			×
Accidents and injury	×	×			×

Source: Data from the Centers for Disease Control and Prevention (2008).

Understanding Stress and Stressors

You have probably heard that death and taxes are the only two things you can be sure of in life. If there is a third, it must be stress. Health psychologists define **stress** as the internal processes that occur as people try to adjust to events and situations. Stress is woven into the fabric of life. No matter how wealthy, powerful, attractive, or happy you might be, stress happens. The events and situations that create stress are called **stressors**, and they come in many forms: a big exam, an automobile accident, waiting in a long line, reading about frightening world events, or just having a day when everything goes wrong. What all stressors have in common is that they disrupt, or threaten to disrupt, daily functioning and cause people to make adjustments. Stressors can be mild and temporary or severe and long-lasting. Some, such as getting married, having a baby, or landing a better job, can be stimulating, motivating, and desirable. However, when people feel that their stressors exceed their ability to cope, the result can be physical, psychological, and behavioral problems. Stress in the workplace, for example, costs U.S. businesses more than $150 billion each year as a result of employee absenteeism, reduced productivity, and health care costs (Chandola, Brunner, & Marmot, 2006; Schwartz, 2004).

Stress reactions are the physical, psychological, and behavioral responses that occur in the face of stressors (Taylor, 2002). In other words, stress involves a *transaction* between people and their physical and psychological environments. Figure 13.1 lists the main types of stressors and illustrates that when confronted by stressors, people may respond physically (with nausea or fatigue, for example) and psychologically (with anxiety, lack of concentration, or changes in eating habits).

As also shown in Figure 13.1, the transactions between people and their environments can be influenced by *stress mediators*. These mediators include such variables as the extent to which people can predict and control their stressors, how they interpret the threat involved, the amount of social support they perceive as available from family and friends, and their stress-coping skills. (We discuss these mediators in greater detail later.) Mediating factors can either minimize or magnify a stressor's impact. In other words, stress is not a specific event but an ever-changing *process* in which the nature and intensity of our responses depend not only on what stressors occur but also on how we think about them and how much confidence we have in our coping skills and stress-coping resources at any particular time.

Many of our stressors have both physical and psychological components. For example, students are challenged by psychological demands to do well in their courses, as well as by the physical fatigue that can result from a heavy load of classes, combined perhaps with a job and family responsibilities. Similarly, for people with arthritis, AIDS, and other chronic illnesses, pain and fatigue are accompanied by worry and other forms of psychological distress. In the next section, we focus on psychological stressors, which can stimulate some of the same physiological responses as physical stressors (Cacioppo et al., 1995).

stress The internal processes that occur as people try to adjust to events and situations, especially those that they perceive to be beyond their coping capacity.

stressors Events or situations to which people must adjust.

stress reactions The physical, psychological, and behavioral responses that occur in the face of a stressor.

FIGURE 13.1
The Process of Stress
Stressful events, stress reactions, and stress mediators are all important components of the stress process. Notice that the process involves many two-way relationships. For example, if a person has effective coping skills, stress responses will be less severe. Having milder stress responses can act as a "reward" that strengthens those skills. Further, as coping skills (such as refusing unreasonable demands) improve, certain stressors (such as a boss's unreasonable demands) may become less frequent.

Stressors	Stress mediators	Stress responses
▪ Life changes and strains ▪ Catastrophic events ▪ Acute stressors ▪ Daily hassles ▪ Chronic stressors	▪ Cognitive appraisal ▪ Predictability ▪ Control ▪ Coping resources and methods ▪ Social support	Physical Psychological ▪ Emotional ▪ Cognitive ▪ Behavioral

Psychological Stressors

Any event that forces people to adjust or change can be a psychological stressor. A promotion, for example, can bring higher pay and status, but the increased responsibilities can be a stressor, especially for those who are not sure they can handle the increased pressure (Schaubroeck, Jones, & Xie, 2001). The most adverse psychological stressors are events and situations that are perceived as unpleasant and threatening (Kiecolt-Glaser et al., 2005). These include catastrophic events, life changes and strains, chronic problems, and daily hassles.

Catastrophic events are sudden, unexpected, potentially life-threatening experiences or traumas, such as physical or sexual assault, military combat, natural disasters, terrorist attacks, and accidents. *Life changes* and *strains* include divorce, illness in the family, difficulties at work, and other circumstances that create demands to which people must adjust (see Table 13.2). *Chronic problems*—those that continue over a long period of time—include circumstances such as living in a high-crime neighborhood or under the threat of terrorism, having a serious illness, being unable to earn a decent living, being the victim of discrimination, and even enduring years of academic pressure. *Daily hassles* are irritations, pressures, and annoyances that may not be significant stressors by themselves but whose cumulative effects can be significant (Almeida, 2005; Evans & Wener, 2006).

Measuring Stressors

Which stressors are most harmful? To study stress more precisely, psychologists have tried to measure the impact of particular stressors. In 1967, Thomas Holmes and Richard Rahe (pronounced "ray") made a pioneering effort to find a standard way of measuring the stress in a person's life. Working on the assumption that all change, positive or negative, is stressful, they asked a large number of people to rate—in terms of *life change units* (LCUs)—the amount of change and demand for adjustment associated with events such as divorcing, being fired, retiring, losing a loved one, or becoming pregnant. (Getting married, the event against which raters were told to compare all other stressors, came in as slightly more stressful than losing one's job.) On the basis of these ratings, Holmes and Rahe created the Social Readjustment Rating Scale, or

Coping with Catastrophe

Catastrophic events such as earthquakes, explosions, hurricanes, plane crashes, school shootings, and other traumas are stressors that can be psychologically devastating for victims, their families, and rescue workers. Health psychologists and other professionals provide on-the-spot counseling and follow-up sessions to help people deal with the consequences of trauma.

© Reuters/Marco Dormino/Minustah/Landov

TABLE 13.2   The Undergraduate Stress Questionnaire

TRY THIS Here are some sample items from the Undergraduate Stress Questionnaire, which asks students to indicate whether various stressors have occurred during the previous week (Crandall, Preisler, & Aussprung, 1992). Check off the items that apply to you, and then make a list of other stressful events you have encountered recently that are not on this list. Keep these stressors in mind as you read the rest of this chapter, and consider whether any of them have led you to experience any of the physical and psychological stress responses described later.

____   Assignments in several classes due the same day

____   Roommate conflict

____   Lack of money

____   Trying to decide on a major

____   Difficulty understanding a professor

____   Staying up late writing a paper

____   Sitting through a boring class

____   Going into a test unprepared

____   Parents getting divorced

____   Problems at the registrar's office

A Daily Hassle

Relatively minor daily hassles can combine to create significant physical and psychological stress responses. The frustrations of daily commuting in heavy traffic, for example, can become so intense for some drivers that they may display a pattern of anger and aggression called "road rage." Between 1990 and 1996, more than ten thousand road rage incidents in the United States alone resulted in 218 deaths and 12,610 injuries (Rathbone & Huckabee, 1999), and the problem continues today.

SRRS. People taking the SRRS receive a stress score equal to the sum of the LCUs for the events they have recently experienced (Holmes & Rahe, 1967).

Numerous studies show that people scoring high on the SRRS and other life change scales are more likely to suffer physical or mental disorders than those with lower scores (e.g., Monroe, Thase, & Simons, 1992). Other researchers questioned, though, whether life changes alone can tell the whole story about the effects of stressors because those changes are only one aspect of the total stress process. Some of those researchers developed scales, such as the Life Experiences Survey, or LES (Sarason, Johnson, & Siegel, 1978), that go beyond the SRRS to measure not just life events but also people's perceptions, or cognitive appraisals, of how positive or negative the events were, how controllable they were, and how well they were able to cope. This information is particularly important for understanding the impact of life experiences that may have different meanings to different individuals. For example, a woman eager to have a child is likely to see pregnancy as a blessing, but for someone who doesn't want a baby or can't afford the costs, a positive pregnancy test can be a significant stressor.

The LES also gives respondents the opportunity to write in and rate any stressors they have experienced that are not on the printed list. This personalized approach is particularly valuable for capturing the differing impact and meaning that experiences may have for men compared with women and for individuals from various cultural or subcultural groups. Divorce, for example, may have very different meanings to people of different religious or cultural backgrounds. Similarly, members of certain ethnic groups are likely to experience stressors—such as prejudice and discrimination—that are not felt by other groups (Flores et al., 2010; Lewis et al., 2006; Matthews et al., 2005; Merritt et al., 2006; Yip, Gee, & Takeuchi, 2008).

Stress Responses

Physical and psychological responses to stress often occur together, especially as stressors become more intense. Furthermore, one type of stress response can set off other types. For example, a physical stress response—such as mild chest pain—may lead to the psychological stress response of worrying about having a heart attack. Still, it is useful to consider each category of stress responses one at a time.

FIGURE 13.2
The General Adaptation Syndrome

Hans Selye found that physical reactions to stressors include an initial alarm reaction, followed by resistance and then exhaustion. During the alarm reaction, the body's resistance to stress temporarily drops below normal as it absorbs a stressor's initial impact. Resistance increases and then levels off in the resistance stage, but it ultimately declines if the exhaustion stage is reached.

Source: Hans Selye, M.D. "The General Adaptation Syndrome" from *Stress Without Distress.* Copyright © 1974 by Hans Selye, M.D. Reprinted by permission of HarperCollins Publishers Inc.

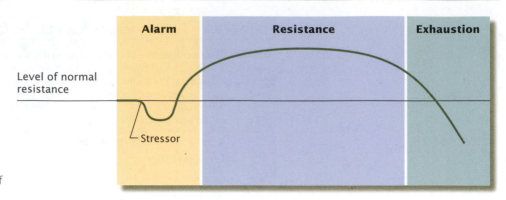

Physical Responses

If you have ever experienced a near accident or some other sudden, frightening event, you know that the immediate physical responses to stressors include rapid breathing, increased heartbeat, sweating, and, a little later, shakiness. These reactions are part of a general pattern known as the *fight-flight reaction* or the *fight-or-flight syndrome.* As described in the chapters on biological aspects of psychology and on motivation and emotion, this syndrome prepares the body to face or flee from an immediate threat. When the danger has passed, the fight-flight reaction subsides (Gump et al., 2005). However, when stressors are long-lasting or when recovery from them is slow, these initial responses are only the beginning of a longer sequence of physical and psychological reactions.

The General Adaptation Syndrome   Careful observation of humans and other animals led Hans Selye (pronounced "SEL-yay") to suggest that physical responses to stress occur in a consistent pattern and are triggered by the effort to adapt to any stressor. Selye (1976) called this sequence the **general adaptation syndrome,** or **GAS.** The GAS has three stages, as shown in Figure 13.2.

The first stage is the *alarm reaction,* which involves some version of the fight-or-flight syndrome. In the face of a mild stressor such as an overheated room, the reaction may simply involve changes in heart rate, respiration, and perspiration that help the body regulate its temperature. More severe stressors prompt more dramatic alarm reactions, rapidly mobilizing the body's adaptive energy, much as a burglar alarm alerts the police to take action (Kiecolt-Glaser et al., 1998).

Alarm reactions are controlled by the sympathetic branch of the autonomic nervous system (ANS) through organs and glands that make up the *sympatho-adreno-medullary* (*SAM*) system. As shown on the right side of Figure 13.3, environmental demands (stressors) trigger a process in the brain in which the hypothalamus activates the sympathetic branch of the ANS, which stimulates the medulla (inner part) of the adrenal gland. The adrenal gland, in turn, secretes *catecholamines* (pronounced "kat-uh-KOH-luh-meenz")—especially adrenaline and noradrenaline—which circulate in the bloodstream, activating various organs, including the liver, kidneys, heart, and lungs. The results are increased blood pressure, enhanced muscle tension, increased blood sugar, and other physical changes that provide the energy needed to cope with acute stressors. Even brief exposure to a mild stressor can produce major changes in these coordinated physiological mechanisms (Stoney et al., 2002).

As shown on the left side of Figure 13.3, stressors also activate the *hypothalamic-pituitary-adrenocortical* (*HPA*) *system,* in which the hypothalamus stimulates the

general adaptation syndrome (GAS) A three-stage pattern of responses triggered by the effort to adapt to any stressor.

pituitary gland in the brain. The pituitary, in turn, secretes hormones such as adrenocorticotropic hormone (ACTH). Among other things, ACTH stimulates the cortex (outer surface) of the adrenal glands to secrete *corticosteroids;* these hormones release the body's energy supplies and fight inflammation. The pituitary gland also triggers the release of endorphins, the body's natural painkillers.

The overall effect of these stress systems is to generate emergency energy. The more stressors there are and the longer they last, the more resources the body must expend in response.

If stressors persist, the *resistance stage* of the GAS begins. Here, obvious signs of the initial alarm reaction fade as the body settles in to resist the stressor on a long-term basis. The drain on adaptive energy is slower during the resistance stage than it was during the alarm reaction, but the body is still working hard, physiologically, to cope.

This continued campaign of biochemical resistance is costly. It slowly but surely uses up the body's reserves of adaptive energy. The body then enters the third GAS stage, known as *exhaustion*. In extreme cases, such as prolonged exposure to freezing temperatures, the result is death. More commonly, the exhaustion stage brings signs of physical wear and tear, especially in organ systems that were weak to begin with or that were heavily involved in the resistance process. For example, if adrenaline and cortisol, which help fight stressors during the resistance stage, remain at high levels for an extended time, they can damage the heart and blood vessels. They also suppress the functioning of the body's disease-fighting immune system, leaving people vulnerable

FIGURE 13.3

Organ Systems Involved in the General Adaptation Syndrome

Stressors produce a variety of physiological responses that begin in the brain and spread to organs throughout the body. In the sympatho-adreno-medullary system (SAM; green arrows), for example, the hypothalamus stimulates the release of catecholamines, which mobilize the body for action. Some of these substances may interact with sex hormones to create different physical stress responses and coping methods in men and women (Taylor, Klein, et al., 2000; Taylor et al., 2006). Through the hypothalamic-pituitary-adrenocortical system (HPA; purple arrows), the hypothalamus causes the pituitary gland to trigger the release of endorphins, the body's natural painkillers. The HPA also stimulates the release of corticosteroids, which help resist stress but also tend to suppress the immune system.

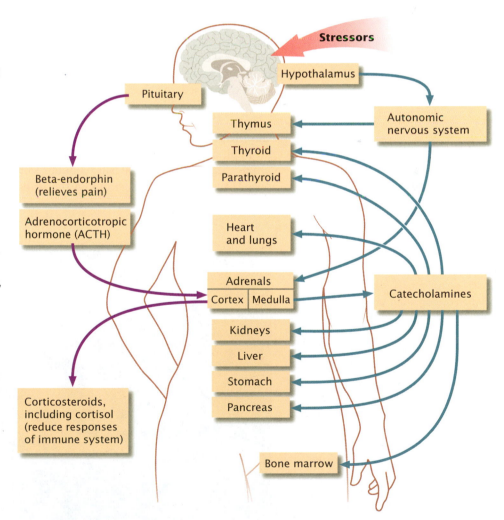

to illnesses such as heart disease, high blood pressure, arthritis, colds, and flu (Robles, Glaser, & Kiecolt-Glaser, 2005). Selye referred to illnesses that are caused or worsened by stressors as **diseases of adaptation**.

Psychological Responses

Selye's model has been very influential, but it has also been criticized for underestimating the role of psychological factors in stress, such as a person's emotional state or the way a person thinks about stressors. These criticisms led to the development of *psychobiological models,* which emphasize the importance of psychological as well as biological variables in regulating and producing stress responses (Ganzel, Morris, & Wethington, 2010; Lazarus & Folkman, 1984; Suls & Rothman, 2004). Psychological responses to stress can appear as changes in emotions and thoughts (cognitions), along with changes in behavior.

Emotional Changes   The physical stress responses we have described are usually accompanied by emotional stress responses. If someone pulls out a gun and demands your money, you will no doubt experience physiological changes, such as a spike in heart rate, but you will also feel some strong emotion—probably fear, maybe anger. When people describe stress, they are more likely to say, "I was angry and frustrated!" than "My heart rate increased and my blood pressure went up." In other words, they are likely to mention changes in the emotions they are experiencing.

In most cases, emotional stress responses subside soon after the stressors are gone. However, if stressors continue for a long time or occur in a tight sequence, emotional stress reactions may persist. When people do not have a chance to recover their emotional equilibrium, they commonly report feeling tense, irritable, sad, or anxious more and more of the time. In some cases, these reactions can become severe enough to be diagnosed as generalized anxiety disorder, major depressive disorder, or other stress-related problems described in the chapter on psychological disorders.

Cognitive Changes   In 1995, in the busy, noisy intensive care unit of a London hospital, a doctor misplaced a decimal point while calculating the amount of morphine a day-old premature baby should receive, and the child died of a massive overdose (Davies, 1999). Reductions in the ability to concentrate, to think clearly, or to

Another Funeral

Even severe emotional stress responses usually ease eventually, but people plagued by numerous stressful events in quick succession—such as those living in strife-torn areas of the world where violent death is all too frequent—may experience increasingly intense feelings of fear, sadness, and helplessness. These reactions can become severe enough to be diagnosed as generalized anxiety disorder, major depression or other depressive disorder, or other stress-related problems described in the chapter on psychological disorders.

diseases of adaptation Illnesses that are caused or worsened by stressors.

AP Photo/Ali Haider

remember accurately are typical cognitive stress reactions (Cavenett & Nixon, 2006; Liston, McEwan, & Casey, 2009; Morgan et al., 2006). Sometimes these problems appear because of *ruminative thinking,* the repeated intrusion of thoughts about stressful events (Lyubomirsky & Nolen-Hoeksema, 1995). Ruminative thoughts about problems in a romantic relationship, for example, can seriously interfere with studying for a test. A related phenomenon is *catastrophizing,* dwelling on and overemphasizing the potential consequences of negative events. During examinations, test-anxious college students are likely to say to themselves, "I'm falling behind," or, "Everyone else is doing better than I am." As catastrophizing or ruminative thinking impairs cognitive functioning, a person may experience anxiety and other emotional arousal that adds to the total stress response and further hampers performance at school or at work (Beilock et al., 2004).

Overarousal created by stressors can also lead to a narrowing of attention, making it harder to scan the full range of possible solutions to complex problems. In fact, stress-narrowed attention may increase the problem-solving errors described in the chapter on cognition and language. People under stress are more likely to cling to *mental sets*, which are well learned but not always efficient approaches to problems. Stress can also intensify *functional fixedness*, the tendency to use objects for only one purpose. Victims of hotel fires, for example, sometimes die trapped in their rooms because in the stress of the moment, it did not occur to them to use the telephone or a piece of furniture to break a window (Renner & Beversdorf, 2010).

Stressors may also impair judgment and decision making (Blanchette & Richards, 2010). People who normally consider all aspects of a situation before making a decision

"Stress for $500, Alex"

The negative effects of stress on memory, thinking, decision making, and other cognitive functions are often displayed by players on quiz shows such as *Jeopardy!* and *Who Wants to Be a Millionaire.* Under the intense pressure of time, competition, and the scrutiny of millions of viewers, contestants may miss questions that seem ridiculously easy to those calmly recalling the correct answers at home.

may, under stress, act impulsively and sometimes foolishly. High-pressure salespeople try to take advantage of this phenomenon by setting a time limit on a special deal, claiming that "supplies are limited" (some TV shopping channels even show a "countdown clock" or an "items remaining" counter) or telling customers that others are waiting to buy the item they are considering (Cialdini, 2001).

Behavioral Responses Clues about people's physical and emotional stress responses come from changes in how they look, act, or talk. Strained facial expressions, a shaky voice, tremors or spasms, and jumpiness are common behavioral stress responses. Posture can also convey information about stress, a fact well known to skilled interviewers.

Even more obvious behavioral stress responses appear as people attempt to escape or avoid stressors. They turn to alcohol, overeat (especially high-fat "comfort" foods), and either sleep too much or skimp on sleep in favor of late-night socializing. These tactics may provide some temporary relief, but they can also have negative health consequences (Cohen et al., 2009; Frone, 2008; Hamer, Molloy, & Stamatakis, 2008; King et al., 2008). In the face of severe or long-lasting stress, some people quit their jobs, drop out of school, or even attempt suicide. In the month after Hurricane Katrina struck the U.S. Gulf Coast in 2005, for example, more than double the normal number of calls were placed from the affected area to the National Suicide Prevention Hotline, and stress-related mental health problems remained long after the storm's immediate effects abated (Breed, 2006; Kessler, Galea, et al., 2008; Roberts et al., 2010). Unfortunately, as discussed in the chapter on learning, escape and avoidance tactics deprive people of the opportunity to learn more adaptive ways of coping with stressful environments, including college. Aggression is another common behavioral response to stressors. All too often, this response is directed at members of one's own family (Hellmuth & McNulty, 2008; Polusny & Follette, 1995). So areas devastated by hurricanes and other natural disasters are likely to see not only suicides but also dramatic increases in reports of domestic violence (Curtis, Miller, & Berry, 2000).

LINKAGES

LINKAGES When do stress responses become mental disorders? (a link to Psychological Disorders, p. 602)

Stress and Psychological Disorders

Physical, psychological, and behavioral stress responses sometimes appear together in patterns known as *burnout* and *posttraumatic stress disorder*. **Burnout** is an increasingly intense pattern of physical and psychological dysfunction in response to a continuous flow of stressors or to chronic stress situations (Maslach, 2003). As burnout approaches, previously reliable workers or once-attentive spouses may become indifferent, disengaged, impulsive, or accident-prone. They may miss work frequently, oversleep, perform their jobs poorly, abuse alcohol or other drugs, and become irritable, suspicious, withdrawn, depressed, and unwilling to talk about stress or anything else (Fahrenkopf et al., 2008; Taylor, 2002). Burnout is particularly common among individuals who do "people work," such as teachers and nurses, and those who perceive themselves as being treated unjustly by employers (Elovainio, Kivimäki, & Vahtera, 2002; Hoobler & Brass, 2006). Research suggests a direct and causal relationship between burnout and increased risk for mental and physical health problems (Melamed et al., 2006; Shirom, 2003). Each year, it accounts for a significant percentage of occupational disease claims by U.S. workers (Schwartz, 2004).

A different pattern of severe stress reactions is illustrated by the case of "Mary," a 33-year-old nurse who was raped at knifepoint by an intruder in her apartment (Spitzer et al., 1983). In the weeks following the attack, she became afraid of being alone and was preoccupied with the attack and with the fear that it might happen again. She had additional locks installed on her doors and windows but experienced difficulty concentrating and could not immediately return to work. The thought of sex repelled her.

burnout A gradually intensifying pattern of physical, psychological, and behavioral dysfunction in response to a continuous flow of stressors.

Mary suffered from **posttraumatic stress disorder (PTSD)**, a pattern of adverse reactions following a traumatic and threatening event. Among the characteristic reactions are anxiety, irritability, jumpiness, inability to concentrate or work productively, sexual dysfunction, and difficulty in getting along with others. People suffering from PTSD may also experience sleep disturbances, intense startle responses to noise or other sudden stimuli, long-term suppression of their immune systems, and elevated risk of coronary heart disease (Goenjian et al., 2001; Guthrie & Bryant, 2005; Johnson, Westermeyer, et al., 2002; Kawamura, Kim, & Asukai, 2001; Kubzansky et al., 2009). High-tech scanning techniques reveal that PTSD symptoms are accompanied by noticeable changes in brain functioning and even in brain structure (Kitayama et al., 2005).The most common feature of PTSD is reexperiencing the trauma through nightmares or vivid memories. In rare cases, *flashbacks* occur in which the person behaves for minutes, hours, or days as if the trauma were occurring again.

Posttraumatic stress disorder is usually associated with being in military combat or experiencing other traumatic events such as terrorist attacks, assault, rape, or abuse in childhood (e.g., Dohrenwend et al., 2006; Galea et al., 2002; Shalev & Freedman, 2005; Shalev et al., 2006). Researchers now believe, though, that some PTSD symptoms can be triggered—especially in anxiety-sensitive people—by any major stressor, including car accidents, being diagnosed with a life-threatening disease, being stalked, or living in a community threatened by terrorism or a serial killer (Diamond et al., 2010; Kangas, Henry, & Bryant, 2005; Marshall, Miles, & Stewart, 2010; Schulden et al., 2006).

© Reuters New Media Inc./Corbis

Life Hanging in the Balance

Symptoms of burnout often plague firefighters, police officers, emergency medical personnel, and others who are repeatedly exposed to time pressure, trauma, danger, and other stressors (Fullerton, Ursano, & Wang, 2004; Perrin et al., 2007). Posttraumatic stress disorder can be another result of these conditions, but it can also occur following a single catastrophic event. Surveys taken in the weeks and months following the 9/11 terrorist attacks on the World Trade Center revealed that 7.5 percent of adults and 10.6 percent of children who lived near the devastated area experienced symptoms of PTSD; in many cases, these symptoms persisted for years (DeLisi et al., 2003; Farfel et al., 2008; Galea et al., 2002; Hoven et al., 2005; Simeon et al., 2003). Even higher rates of PTSD symptoms were widely reported by adult survivors of the massive tidal waves that devastated South and Southeast Asia in 2004 (van Griensven et al., 2006).

posttraumatic stress disorder (PTSD) A pattern of adverse and disruptive reactions following a traumatic event.

Posttraumatic stress disorder may appear immediately following a trauma, but the full expression of its symptoms may not appear until weeks later (Andrews et al., 2007; Gilboa-Schechtman & Foa, 2001; Port, Engdahl, & Frazier, 2001). Many people who develop PTSD require professional help, although some seem to recover without it (Bradley et al., 2005; Perkonigg et al., 2005). For most, improvement takes time; for nearly all, the support of family and friends is vital to recovery (Foa et al., 2005). For some people, though, PTSD never appears, even after severe trauma (Breslau et al., 2005). In fact, some people report enhanced psychological growth after surviving a trauma (Zoellner & Maercker, 2006). Researchers are working to discover what protective factors are operating in these individuals and whether those factors can be strengthened through PTSD treatment programs (Bonanno & Mancini, 2008; Haskett et al., 2006; Kolassa et al., 2010). Stress is also thought to play a role in the development of a number of other psychological disorders, including depression and schizophrenia (Cutrona et al., 2005; see the chapter on psychological disorders). The *diathesis-stress model* suggests that certain people are predisposed to these disorders but that whether or not individuals actually display them depends on the frequency, nature, and intensity of the stressors they encounter. If untreated, stress-related mental health problems can threaten physical health, too. For example, depression or anxiety may leave people unmotivated or forgetful when it comes to taking prescribed medication for high blood pressure or other medical conditions they may have. Similarly, some schizophrenia patients develop delusions that doctors, and the medicines they prescribe, will hurt them and thus begin to avoid both. As a result, all these people are likely to be at increased risk for worsening health.

Stress Mediators

Particular people may react to particular stressors in different ways. The stress of combat, for example, is partly responsible for the errors in judgment and decision making that lead to "friendly fire" deaths and injuries in almost every military operation (Adler, 1993). But the stress in these situations disrupts the performance of some people more than others. Why? And why does one individual survive, and even thrive, under the same circumstances that lead another to break down, give up, and burn out? A number of the mediating factors listed in Figure 13.1 help determine how much impact a given stressor will have (Bonanno, 2005; Kemeny, 2003).

How Stressors Are Perceived

As discussed in the chapter on perception, our view of the world depends on which stimuli we attend to and how we interpret, or appraise, them. Any potential stressor, whether it is a crowded elevator or a deskful of work, usually has a more negative impact on those who perceive it as a threat than on those who see it as a challenge (Lazarus, 1999; Maddi & Khoshaba, 2005).

Evidence for the effects of cognitive factors on stress responses comes from both laboratory experiments and surveys (e.g., Abelson et al., 2005). Figure 13.4 shows the results of a classic experiment that demonstrated these effects. In this case, the intensity of physiological arousal during a film depended on how the viewers were instructed to think about the film (Lazarus et al., 1965). In a more recent study, students who were first trained to see the threatening aspects of information showed more emotional arousal to a stressful video than those who had been trained to see information as nonthreatening (Wilson et al., 2006). Similarly, physical and psychological symptoms associated with the stress of airport noise, of being diagnosed with a serious illness, of learning about toxins in local soil, or of living with terrorism threats are more common in people who engage in catastrophic thinking about these problems (Bryant & Guthrie, 2005; Lerner et al., 2003; Matthies, Hoeger, & Guski, 2000; Speckhard, 2002). Those who hold a more

FIGURE 13.4
Cognitive Influences on Stress Responses

Richard Lazarus and his colleagues found that students' physiological stress reactions to a film showing bloody industrial accidents were affected by the way they thought about the film. Those who had been instructed to remain detached from the film (the "intellectualizers") or to think of it as unreal (the "denial" group) were less upset—as measured by sweat-gland activity—than those in an "unprepared" group. These results were among the first to show that people's cognitive appraisal of stressors can affect their responses to those stressors.

Source: Lazarus, Opton, Nornikos, and Rankin. "The Principle of Short-Circuiting of Threat: Further Evidence". *Journal Of Personality*, 33.4. Copyright © John Wiley & Sons. Reprinted with permission.

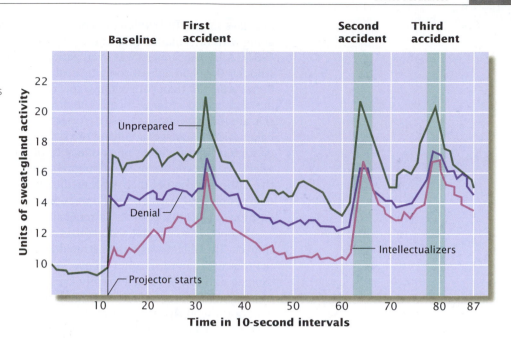

optimistic outlook tend to show milder stress responses, better health outcomes, and longer life spans (de Moor et al., 2006; Taylor , Lerner, et al., 2003; Xu & Roberts, 2010).

The influence of cognitive factors weakens somewhat as stressors become more extreme. For example, chronic-pain patients who feel a sense of control over the pain tend to be more physically active, but this effect does not hold for those whose pain is severe (Jensen & Karoly, 1991). Still, even the impact of natural disasters or major stressors such as divorce may be less intense among those who think of them as challenges to be overcome. In other words, many stressful events are not inherently stressful. Their impact depends partly on how people perceive them. An important aspect of this appraisal is the degree to which the stressors are perceived to be predictable or controllable.

Predictability and Control

Why is the threat of terrorism so terrorizing? For one thing, knowing that a particular stressor might occur but being uncertain about whether or when it will occur tends to increase the stressor's impact (Lerner et al., 2003; Sorrentino & Roney, 2000). In other words, *unpredictable* stressors tend to have more impact than those that are predictable (Lazarus & Folkman, 1984; Pham, Taylor, & Seeman, 2001), especially when the stressors are intense and relatively brief. For example, people whose spouses have died suddenly tend to display more immediate disbelief, anxiety, and depression than those who had weeks or months to prepare for the loss (Schulz et al., 2001; Swarte et al., 2003). This is not to say that predictability provides total protection against stressors. Research with animals shows that predictable stressors, even if relatively mild, can be more damaging than unpredictable ones if they occur over long periods of time (Abbott, Schoen, & Badia, 1984).

The *perception of control* can also mediate the effects of stressors. If people can exert some control over them, stressors usually have less impact on health (e.g., Christensen, Stephens, & Townsend, 1998; Krause & Shaw, 2000). Studies of several thousand employees in the United States, Sweden, and the United Kingdom have found that workers who had little or no control over their work environments were more likely to suffer heart disease and other health problems than workers with a high degree of control over those environments (Bosma et al., 1997; Cheng et al., 2000; Spector, 2002). In another study, researchers randomly selected a group of patients awaiting surgery and gave them a full explanation of the procedures that they could expect to undergo, along with information that would help them manage postsurgical pain (Egbert et al., 1964). After the surgery was over, patients who had been given this information and who felt they had at least some control over the pain they experienced not only were better adjusted than patients in a control group who received no special preparation but also healed faster and could be discharged from the hospital sooner. So impressive are findings such as these that it is now standard procedure in many hospitals to help patients manage or control the stress of emergency treatment or the side effects of surgery by providing preparatory information about what to expect during and after a medical procedure, teaching relaxation skills, and allowing patients to control the administration of their pain medication. These strategies have all been shown to help people heal faster and go home sooner (Broadbent et al., 2003; Chamberlin, 2000; Gordon et al., 2005; Kiecolt-Glaser et al., 1998; Ludwig-Rosenthal & Neufeld, 1988).

Simply *believing* that a stressor is controllable, even if it isn't, can also reduce its impact. This effect was demonstrated in a study in which people with panic disorder (discussed in the chapter on psychological disorders) inhaled a mixture of carbon dioxide and oxygen that typically causes them to experience fear and other symptoms of a panic attack (Sanderson, Rapee, & Barlow, 1989). Half the clients were led to believe (falsely) that they could control the concentration of the mixture. Compared with those who believed they had no control, significantly fewer of the "in control" clients experienced full-blown panic attacks during the session, and their panic symptoms were fewer and less severe.

People who feel they have no control over negative events appear especially prone to physical and psychological problems. They often experience feelings of helplessness and hopelessness that may in turn leave them more vulnerable to heart disease and other serious illnesses as well as to mental disorders such as depression (Sarin, Abela, & Auerbach, 2005; Whang et al., 2009). It has even been suggested that a perceived lack of control partly explains why people in lower socioeconomic groups are at somewhat elevated risk for early death (Stringhini et al., 2010; Trumbetta et al., 2010).

Coping Resources and Coping Methods

People usually suffer fewer ill effects from a stressor if they have adequate coping resources and effective coping methods. *Coping resources* include, for example, the money and time to deal with stressful events. So the physical and psychological responses you experience if your car breaks down are likely to be more negative if you are low on cash and pressed for time than if you have money for repairs and the freedom to take a day off from work.

The impact of stressors can also be reduced by the use of effective *coping methods* (Coté & Pepler, 2002). Most of these methods can be classified as either problem-focused or emotion-focused. *Problem-focused* coping involves efforts to alter or eliminate a source of stress, whereas *emotion-focused* techniques are aimed at regulating the negative emotional consequences of the stressor (Folkman et al., 1986). Some people use both kinds of coping. For example, you might deal with the problem of noise from a nearby airport by forming a community action group to push for tougher noise regulations and, at the same time, calm your anger when noise occurs by mentally focusing on the group's efforts to improve the situation (e.g., Hatfield et al., 2002). As mentioned earlier, coping efforts may not always be so adaptive. In the face of a financial crisis or impending exams, for example, some people rely on emotion-focused methods such as using alcohol or other drugs to ease anxiety but take no problem-focused steps to get out of debt or learn difficult material. These emotion-focused strategies may reduce distress in the short run, but the long-term result may be a financial or academic situation that is worse than it was before. Susan Folkman and Richard Lazarus (1988) have devised a widely used questionnaire to assess the specific ways in which people cope with stressors; Table 13.3 shows some examples of responses to their questionnaire.

TABLE 13.3   Ways of Coping

TRY THIS Coping is defined as the cognitive and behavioral efforts to manage specific demands that people perceive as taxing their resources (Folkman et al., 1986). This table illustrates two major approaches to coping measured by the Ways of Coping questionnaire: problem-focused and emotion-focused coping. Ask yourself which approach you usually take when faced with stressors. Now rank the coping skills listed under each major approach in terms of how often you tend to use each of them. Do you rely on just one or two, or do you adjust your coping strategies to fit different kinds of stressors?

Coping Skills	Example
Problem-focused coping	
Confronting	"I stood my ground and fought for what I wanted."
Seeking social support	"I talked to someone to find out more about the situation."
Planful problem solving	"I made a plan of action, and I followed it."
Emotion-focused coping	
Self-controlling	"I tried to keep my feelings to myself."
Distancing	"I didn't let it get to me; I tried not to think about it too much."
Positive reappraisal	"I changed my mind about myself."
Accepting responsibility	"I realized I brought the problem on myself."
Escape/avoidance (wishful thinking)	"I wished that the situation would go away or somehow be over with."

Sources: Folkman et al. (1986); Taylor (2002).

Particularly when a stressor is difficult to control, it is sometimes helpful to express fully and think about the emotions you are experiencing in relation to the stressful event (Langens & Schüler, 2007; Niederhoffer & Pennebaker, 2002). The benefits of this cognitive strategy have been observed among many individuals whose religious beliefs allow them to bring meaning to the death of a loved one or the devastation of a natural disaster, events that might otherwise seem to be senseless tragedies (Heppner et al., 2006; Powell, Shahabi, & Thoresen, 2003; Tallman, Altmaier, & Garcia, 2007). And when cancer patients are encouraged to express their feelings about their diagnosis and to search for positive aspects of their illness (such as bringing their family closer together), they experience fewer symptoms, need fewer medical visits, and adjust better to their disease (Antoni et al., 2001; Low, Stanton, & Danoff-Burg, 2006). Humor may also play a role. Some individuals who use humor to help them cope show better adjustment and milder physiological reactivity to stressful events (Martin, 2001; Moran, 2002).

Social Support

Has a good friend ever given you comfort and reassurance during troubled times? If so, you have experienced the value of *social support* in easing the impact of stressful events. **Social support** consists of emotional, tangible, or informational resources provided by other people. These people might help eliminate a stressor (by, say, helping you fix your car), suggest how to deal with the stressor (by recommending a good mechanic), or reduce a stressor's impact by providing companionship and reassurance that you are cared about and valued and that everything will be all right (Sarason, Sarason, & Gurung, 1997). The people you can depend on for support make up your network of social support (Burleson, Albrecht, & Sarason, 1994).

The stress-reducing effects of social support have been documented for a wide range of stressors, including cancer, stroke, military combat, loss of loved ones, natural

social support The network of friends and social contacts on whom one can depend for help in dealing with stressors.

You've Got a Friend

Even when social support cannot eliminate stressors, it can help people, such as these cancer survivors, feel less anxious, more optimistic, more capable of control, and more willing to try new ways of dealing with stressors (Trunzo & Pinto, 2003). Those who provide social support may feel better too (Brown et al., 2003).

© Manchan/Photographer's Choice RF/Getty Images

disasters, arthritis, AIDS, and even ethnic discrimination (e.g., Antoni & Lutgendorf, 2007; Boden-Albala et al., 2005; Foster, 2000; Jason, Witter, & Torres-Harding, 2003; Penner, Dovidio, & Albrecht, 2001; Savelkoul et al., 2000; Weihs, Enright, & Simmens, 2008). Social support can have health benefits too. For example, students who get emotional support from friends show better immune system functioning than those with less adequate social support (Cohen & Herbert, 1996). This may be why people in strong social support networks are less vulnerable to colds and flu during exams and other periods of high academic stress (Kop et al., 2005; Pressman et al., 2005; Taylor, Dickerson, & Klein, 2002). Having strong social support is also associated with faster recovery from surgery or illness, possibly because helpful friends and family members encourage patients to follow medical advice (Brummett et al., 2005; Krohne & Slangen, 2005; Taylor, 2002). People in stronger social networks—especially those filled with happy people—tend to be happier than those in weaker networks and may even enjoy better mental functioning in old age (Barnes et al., 2004; Fowler & Christakis, 2008). According to some researchers, having inadequate social support can be as dangerous as smoking, obesity, or lack of exercise in that it nearly doubles a person's risk of dying from disease, suicide, or other causes (House, Landis, & Umberson, 1988; Kiecolt-Glaser & Newton, 2001; Rutledge et al., 2004).

Exactly how social support brings about its positive effects is not entirely clear. James Pennebaker (1995, 2000) has suggested that social support may help prevent illness by providing the person under stress with an opportunity to express pent-up thoughts and emotions. In fact, keeping important things to yourself can itself be a stressor (e.g., Dalgleish, Hauer, & Kuyken, 2008; Srivastava et al., 2009). One laboratory experiment found that participants who were asked to deceive an experimenter showed elevated physiological arousal (Pennebaker & Chew, 1985). Other studies suggest that if the spouses of people who die as the result of an accident or suicide do not or cannot confide their feelings to others, they are especially likely to develop physical illness during the year following the spouse's death (Pennebaker & O'Heeron, 1984). Disclosing (even anonymously) the stresses and traumas one has experienced is associated with enhanced immune functioning, reduced physical symptoms, and decreased use of health services (Broderick, Junghaenel, & Schwartz, 2005; Campbell & Pennebaker, 2003; Epstein, Sloan, & Marx, 2005; Pachankis & Goldfried, 2010). This

Fighting a Deadly Disease

The impact of psychological factors on immune system functioning can be seen in the progression of HIV/AIDS. Sustained depression, concealment of gay identity, negative expectancies, and reliance on passive, emotion-focused coping methods such as denial have all been related to faster disease progression. Openly expressing emotions, collaborating closely with doctors, having optimistic expectations, remaining involved in normal activities, finding meaning in the situation, and other active, problem-focused coping strategies have all been associated with slower disease progression (Balbin, Ironson, & Solomon, 1999).

© Bruce Ayres/Stone/Getty Images

may explain why support groups for a wide range of problems such as bereavement, overeating, and alcohol and drug abuse tend to promote participants' physical health (Taylor et al., 2002).

Research in this area is made more challenging by the fact that the relationship between social support and the impact of stressors is not a simple one. For one thing, the quality of social support may influence people's ability to cope with stress, but the reverse may also be true: Your ability to cope may determine the quality of social support you receive (McLeod, Kessler, & Landis, 1992). People who complain endlessly about stressors but never try to do anything about them may discourage social support, whereas those with an optimistic, action-oriented approach may attract support.

Second, *social support* refers not only to relationships with others but also to the recognition that others care and can be depended on to help (Demaray & Malecki, 2002). If some relationships in a seemingly strong social support network are actually stormy and fragile, they can create interpersonal conflicts that undermine confidence in the dependability of support. The resulting uncertainly can have an adverse effect on health (Ben-Ari & Gil, 2002; Malarkey et al., 1994).

Third, having too much support or the wrong kind of support can be as bad as not having enough (Reynolds & Perrin, 2004). Dangerous behaviors such as smoking or overeating, for example, can be harder to give up if one's social support consists largely or entirely of smokers or overeaters (Christakis & Fowler, 2007). People whose friends and family overprotect them from stressors may actually put less energy into coping efforts or have less opportunity to learn effective coping strategies. In one study of people with physical disabilities, nearly 40 percent of them were found to have experienced emotional distress in response to the well-intentioned help they received from their spouses. This distress, in turn, was a predictor of depression nearly a year later (Newsome & Schulz, 1998). Similarly, people living in crowded conditions may at first perceive the situation as providing lots of social support, but these conditions may eventually become an added source of stress (Lepore, Evans, & Schneider, 1991).

Finally, the value of social support may depend on the kind of stressor being encountered. So although having a friend present might reduce the impact of some stressors, it might amplify the impact of others. Researchers have found, for example, that individuals preparing to speak in public or endure other social stress situations experienced stronger physical and psychological stress responses when a friend or a supportive audience was watching than when they were alone (Stoney & Finney, 2000; Taylor et al., 2010). In short, the efforts or presence of members of a social support network can sometimes become annoying, disruptive, or interfering, thereby increasing stress and intensifying psychological problems (Newsome, 1999; Ruiz et al., 2006). It has even been suggested that among people under intense stress, the benefits of having a large social support network may be offset by the dangers of catching a cold or the flu from people in that network (Hamrick, Cohen, & Rodriguez, 2002).

Stress, Personality, and Gender

The impact of stress on health appears to depend not only on how people think about particular stressors but also to some extent on how they think about and react to the world in general. For instance, stress-related health problems tend to be especially common among people whose "disease-prone" personalities lead them to try to ignore stressors when possible; perceive stressors as long-term, catastrophic threats that they brought on themselves; and be pessimistic about their ability to overcome stressors (e.g., Penninx et al., 2001; Roy et al., 2010; Segerstrom et al., 1998; Suinn, 2001).

Other cognitive styles, such as those characteristic of "disease-resistant" personalities, help insulate people from the ill effects of stress. These people tend to think of stressors as temporary challenges to be overcome, not catastrophic threats, and they do not constantly blame themselves for bringing them about. One particularly important component of the disease-resistant personality is *dispositional optimism,* the belief or expectation that things will work out positively (Folkman & Moskowitz, 2000; Rosenkranz et al., 2003; Taylor, Kemeny, et al., 2000). Optimistic people tend to live longer (Giltay et al., 2004, 2006), to experience fewer health consequences following major stressors, and to have more resistance than pessimists to colds and other infectious diseases (Cohen et al., 2003a, 2003b; Kivimäki et al., 2005; Pressman & Cohen, 2005; Segerstrom & Sephton, 2010). These data help explain why optimistic students experience fewer physical symptoms at the end of the academic term (Aspinwall & Taylor, 1992; Ebert, Tucker, & Roth, 2002). Optimistic coronary bypass surgery patients tend to heal faster and stay healthier than pessimists (Scheier et al., 1989) and to experience a higher quality of life following their surgery than those with less optimistic outlooks (Fitzgerald et al., 1993). And among HIV-positive men, dispositional optimism has been associated with less psychological distress, fewer worries, and lower perceived risk of developing full-blown AIDS (Johnson & Endler, 2002; Taylor et al., 1992). These effects appear due in part to optimists' tendency to use challenge-oriented, problem-focused coping strategies that attack stressors directly, in contrast to pessimists' tendency to use emotion-focused coping, such as denial and avoidance (Bosompra et al., 2001; Brenes et al., 2002; Moskowitz et al., 2009). They also tend to be happier than pessimists, a tendency associated not only with less intense and less dangerous physiological responses to stressors but also with greater success in life (e.g., Lyubomirsky, King, & Diener, 2005; Steptoe, Wardle, & Marmot, 2005).

Indeed, like optimism, happiness and other positive emotions, such as hope and curiosity, have been associated with better health and longer life (Cohen et al., 2003a; Ong et al., 2006; Ostir et al., 2006; Richman et al., 2005; Xu & Roberts, 2010). For example, a long-term study of Catholic nuns found that those who wrote with the most positive emotional style when they were young lived longer than those whose writing contained less positive emotions (Danner, Snowden, & Friesen, 2001). Studies like these represent a new line of research in health psychology that focuses on investigating and promoting the positive emotions, behaviors, and cognitive styles associated with better health (Kashdan & Rottenberg, 2010; Seligman, Steen, et al., 2005).

Gender may also play a role in responses to stress (Goldstein et al., 2010). In a review of two hundred studies of stress responses and coping methods, Shelley Taylor and her colleagues found that males under stress tended to get angry, avoid stressors, or both, whereas females were more likely to help others and to make use of their social support networks (Taylor, Klein, et al., 2000; Taylor et al., 2002). Further, in the face of equally intense stressors, men's physiological responses, including changes in heart rate and blood pressure, tend to be more intense than women's (Stoney et al., 1988). This is not true in every case, of course (Smith et al., 2008), but why should a significant difference show up at all? Though the gender role learning discussed in the chapter on human development surely plays a part (Eagly & Wood, 1999), Taylor proposes that women's "tend-and-befriend" style differs from the "fight-or-flight" pattern so often seen in men because of gender differences in how hormones combine under stress. Consider oxytocin (pronounced "ahk-see-TOH-sin"), a hormone released in both sexes as part of the general adaptation syndrome (Taylor et al., 2006; Uvnas-Moberg, Arn, & Magnusson, 2005). Taylor suggests that oxytocin may interact differently with male and female sex hormones: It amplifies physical responses to stressors in men but reduces those responses in women (Light et al., 2005). This gender difference could lead to the more intense emotional and behavioral stress responses typical of men, and it may be partly responsible for men's greater vulnerability to heart disease and other stress-related illnesses (Kajantie & Phillips, 2006). If that is the case, gender differences in stress responses may help explain why women in industrialized societies live an average of five to ten years longer than men (Hoyert, Kung, & Smith, 2005; Kajantie, 2008). The role of gender-related hormones in responding to stress is supported by the fact that there are few, if any, gender differences in children's stress responses. Those differences begin to appear only around adolescence, when the influences of sex hormones become pronounced (Allen & Matthews, 1997).

FOCUS ON RESEARCH METHODS

LINKAGES Are childhood traits related to how long we live? (a link to Human Development, p. 517)

Personality and Health

The way people think and act in the face of stressors, the ease with which they attract social support, and their tendency to be optimists or pessimists are but a few aspects of their *personalities*.

What was the researchers' question?

Are there other personality characteristics that protect or threaten people's health? This was the research question asked by Howard Friedman and his associates (Friedman, 2000; Friedman et al., 1995a, 1995b). In particular, they attempted to identify aspects of personality that increase the likelihood of premature death from heart disease, high blood pressure, or other chronic diseases.

How did the researchers answer the question?

Friedman suspected that an answer might lie in the Terman Life Cycle Study of Intelligence, which was named after Louis Terman, author of the Stanford-Binet intelligence test. As described in the chapter on cognitive abilities, the study was originally designed to document the long-term development of 1,528 gifted California children (856 boys and 672 girls)—nicknamed the "Termites" (Terman & Oden, 1947).

Starting in 1921 and every five to ten years thereafter, Terman's research team gathered information about the Termites' personality traits, social relationships, stressors, health habits, and many other variables. The data were collected through questionnaires and interviews with the Termites themselves, as well as with their teachers, parents, and other family members. When, by the early 1990s, about half of the Termites had died, Friedman realized that the Terman Life Cycle Study could serve as a longitudinal study in health psychology. As in most such studies, the independent variable (in this case, personality characteristics) was not actually manipulated (the Termites had obviously not been randomly assigned different personalities by the researchers), but the various personality traits identified in these people could still be related to a dependent variable (namely, how long they lived). So Friedman and his colleagues gathered the death certificates of the Termites, noted the dates and causes of death, and then looked for associations between personality and longevity.

What did the researchers find?

One of the most important predictors of long life turned out to be a personality dimension known as *conscientiousness,* or social dependability (described in the chapter on personality). Termites who in childhood had been regarded as truthful, prudent, reliable, hardworking, and free from vanity tended to live longer than those whose parents and teachers had identified them as impulsive and lacking in self-control.

Friedman and his colleagues also examined the Terman Life Cycle Study data to investigate the relationship between social support and health. They compared the life spans of Termites whose parents had divorced or who had been in unstable marriages themselves with those who grew up in stable homes and who had stable marriages. The researchers found that people who had experienced parental divorce during childhood or who themselves had unstable marriages died an average of four years earlier than those whose close social relationships had been less stressful.

What do the results mean?

Did these differences in personality traits and social support actually cause some Termites to live longer than others? Friedman's research was based mainly on the analysis of correlations, so it is difficult to draw conclusions about what caused the relationships he observed. Still, Friedman and his colleagues searched the Terman data for clues to mechanisms through which personality and other factors might have exerted a causal influence on how long the Termites lived (Peterson et al., 1998). For example, they evaluated the hypothesis that conscientious, dependable Termites who lived socially stable lives may have followed healthier lifestyles than their impulsive and socially stressed age-mates. They found that people in the latter group did indeed tend to eat less healthy diets and were more likely to smoke, drink to excess, or use drugs. However, these behaviors alone did not fully account for their shorter average life spans. Another possible explanation is that conscientiousness and stability in social relationships create a general attitude of caution that goes beyond eating right and avoiding substance abuse. Friedman found some support for this idea in the Terman data. Termites who were impulsive or low on conscientiousness were somewhat more likely to die from accidents or violence than those who were less impulsive. (A similar finding is reported in the Focus on Research Methods section of the personality chapter.)

What do we still need to know?

The Terman Life Cycle Study cannot provide definite answers about the relationship between personality and health. However, it has generated some important clues and a number of intriguing hypotheses to be evaluated in future research with more representative samples of people. Some of that research has already taken place and tends to confirm Friedman's findings about conscientiousness (Hampson et al., 2006; Kern & Friedman, 2008; Roberts et al., 2009; Terracciano et al., 2008). Further, Friedman's decision to reanalyze a set of data on psychosocial development as a way of exploring issues in health psychology stands as a fine example of how a creative researcher can pursue answers to complex questions that are difficult or impossible to study via controlled experiments.

Our discussion of personality and other factors that can alter the impact of stressors should make it obvious that what is stressful for a particular individual is not determined simply by predispositions, coping styles, or situations. (See "In Review: Stress Responses and Stress Mediators.") Even more important are interactions between the person and the situation, the mixture of each individual's coping resources with the specific characteristics of the situations encountered.

IN REVIEW	Stress Responses and Stress Mediators
Category	**Examples**
Responses	
Physical	Fight-flight reaction involves increased heart rate, respiration, and muscle tension as well as sweating and dilated pupils. Activation of SAM and HPA systems releases catecholamines and corticosteroids. Organ systems involved in prolonged resistance to stressors eventually break down.
Psychological	*Emotional:* anger, anxiety, depression, and other emotional states. *Cognitive:* inability to concentrate or think logically, ruminative thinking, catastrophizing. *Behavioral:* aggression and escape/avoidance tactics (including suicide attempts) and health risk behaviors.
Mediators	
Appraisal	Thinking of a difficult new job as a challenge will create less discomfort than focusing on the threat of failure.
Predictability	A tornado that strikes without warning may have a more devastating emotional impact than a long-predicted hurricane.
Control	Repairing a disabled spacecraft may be less stressful for the astronauts doing the work than for their loved ones on earth, who can do nothing to help.
Coping resources and methods	Having no effective way to relax after a hard day may prolong tension and other stress responses.
Social support	Having no one to talk to about a rape or other trauma may amplify the negative impact of the experience.

1. The friends and family we can depend on to help us deal with stressors are called our _____ network.

2. Fantasizing about winning money is a(n) _____ focused way of coping with financial stress.

3. Sudden, extreme stressors may cause psychological and behavioral problems known as _____.

The Physiology and Psychology of Health and Illness

A large body of research in health psychology has focused on the relationship between stress and illness. In the following sections, we focus on some of the ways in which stress can lead, directly or indirectly, to physical illnesses by affecting the *immune system* and the *cardiovascular system*.

Stress, Illness, and the Immune System

The role of physiological stress responses in altering the body's ability to fight disease was demonstrated well over a century ago. On March 19, 1878, at a seminar before the Académie de Médecine de Paris, Louis Pasteur showed his distinguished audience three chickens. One was a healthy bird that had been raised normally. A second bird had been intentionally infected with bacteria but given no other treatment; it was also healthy. The third chicken Pasteur presented was dead. It had been infected with the same bacteria as the second bird, but it had also been stressed by being exposed to cold temperatures. As a result, the bacteria had killed it (Kelley, 1985).

The First Line of Defense

A patrolling immune system cell sends out an extension known as a *pseudopod* (pronounced "SOO-doh-pahd") to engulf and destroy a bacterial cell before alerting more defenders. Psychological stressors can alter immune system functions through a number of mechanisms. For example, they can activate neural connections between the sympathetic nervous system and organs of the immune system through response systems that have direct suppressant effects on immune function. These suppressant effects are due largely to the release of cortisol and other corticosteroid hormones from the adrenal cortex (see Figure 13.3).

psychoneuroimmunology A field of research on the interaction of psychological, social, behavioral, neural, hormonal, and immune system processes that affect the body's defenses against disease.

immune system The body's first line of defense against invading substances and microorganisms.

Research conducted since Pasteur's time has greatly expanded knowledge about how stressors affect the body's reaction to disease. **Psychoneuroimmunology** is the field that examines the interaction of psychological, social, behavioral, neural, hormonal, and immune system processes that affect the body's ability to defend itself against disease (Ader, 2001).

The Immune System and Illness   The **immune system** is the body's first line of defense against invading substances and microorganisms. It is perhaps as complex as the nervous system and contains as many cells as the brain (Guyton, 1991). Some of these cells are in organs such as the thymus and spleen, while others circulate in the bloodstream, entering tissues throughout the body. Components of the immune system kill or deactivate viruses, bacteria, and other foreign or harmful agents in the body (Simpson, Hurtly, & Marx, 2000). If our immune system is impaired—by stressors, for example—we are left more vulnerable to colds, mononucleosis, and many other infectious diseases (Potter & Zautra, 1997). It is by disabling the immune system that HIV infection leads to AIDS and leaves the HIV-infected person defenseless against other infections or cancers. The immune system can also become overactive, with devastating results. Many chronic, progressive diseases—including arthritis, diabetes, and lupus erythematosus—are now recognized as *autoimmune disorders*. In these cases, cells of the immune system begin to attack and destroy normal body cells (Oldenberg et al., 2000).

An important aspect of the human immune system is the action of the white blood cells, called *leukocytes* (pronounced "LOO-koh-sytss"). These cells are formed in the bone marrow and serve as the body's mobile defense units. Leukocytes are called into action when foreign substances are detected. Among the varied types of leukocytes are *B-cells,* which mature in the bone marrow, and *T-cells,* which mature in the thymus. Generally, T-cells kill other cells and B-cells produce *antibodies,* which are circulating proteins that bind to specific toxins and other foreign cells and begin to deactivate them. *Natural killer cells,* another type of leukocyte, destroy a wide variety of foreign organisms, but they have particularly important antiviral and antitumor functions. Yet another type of immune system cell is the *macrophage* (pronounced "MAK-roh-fayj). Macrophages engulf foreign cells and digest them in a process called *phagocytosis* (pronounced "fag-uh-sy-TOH-siss"), or "eating cells." These scavengers are able to squeeze out of the bloodstream and enter organs, where they destroy foreign cells.

The activity of immune system cells can be either strengthened or weakened by a number of systems, including the endocrine system and the central and autonomic nervous systems. It is through these connections that stress-related psychological and emotional factors can affect the functioning of the immune system. The exact mechanisms by which the nervous system affects the immune system are not yet fully understood, but they appear to involve both indirect and direct connections (Rosenkranz et al., 2003). The brain can influence the activity of the immune system indirectly by altering the secretion of hormones (including cortisol secretion by the adrenal gland) that stimulate receptors in circulating T-cells and B-cells. More direct influences occur as nerves affect immune organs, such as the thymus, where T-cells and B-cells are stored (Felten et al., 1991; Maier & Watkins, 2000).

The Immune System and Stress   Researchers have found that people under stress are more likely than less stressed people to develop infectious diseases and to experience flare-ups of latent viruses responsible for oral herpes (cold sores) or genital herpes. For example, Sheldon Cohen and his colleagues in the United Kingdom (1995) exposed 394 healthy adult volunteers either to one of five respiratory viruses or to a placebo. The participants were then isolated and asked about the number and severity of life stresses they had experienced in the previous year. After controlling for factors such as prior history of colds, exposure to other viruses, and health practices, the researchers found that the more stress the participants had experienced, the greater the likelihood that their exposure to a virus would result in colds and respiratory infections.

These findings are supported by other research showing that a variety of stressors lead to suppression of the immune system. The effects are especially strong in the elderly (Penedo & Dahn, 2004), but they occur in everyone (Kiecolt-Glaser et al., 2002). For example, one study found that as first-year law students participated in classes, took exams, and experienced other stressful aspects of law school, they showed a decline in several measures of immune functioning (Segerstrom et al., 1998). Similarly, reduction in natural killer cell activity has been observed in both men and women following the death of a spouse (Irwin et al., 1987), and a variety of immune system impairments have been found in people suffering the effects of prolonged marital conflict, divorce, unemployment, lack of social support, and loneliness (Cohen et al., 2007; Kiecolt-Glaser & Glaser, 1992). Providing care for an elderly relative who is mentally or physically incapacitated is a particularly stressful circumstance that has been reliably shown to diminish immune function (Kiecolt-Glaser et al., 2003, 2005; Vitaliano, Zhang, & Scanlan, 2003).

The relationship between stress and the immune system is especially important in people who are HIV-positive but do not yet have AIDS. Because their immune systems are already seriously compromised, further stress-related impairments could be life-threatening. Research indicates that psychological stressors are associated with the progression of HIV-related illnesses (e.g., Gore-Felton & Koopman, 2008; Heckman et al., 2004). Unfortunately, people with HIV (and AIDS) face a particularly heavy load of immune-suppressing psychological stressors, including bereavement, unemployment, uncertainty about the future, and daily reminders of serious illness. A lack of perceived control and resulting depression can further amplify their stress responses (Sewell et al., 2000).

Stress, Illness, and the Cardiovascular System

Earlier we discussed the role of the sympatho-adreno-medullary (SAM) system in mobilizing the body's defenses during times of threat. Because the SAM system is linked to the cardiovascular system, its repeated activation in response to stressors, especially chronic ones, has been associated with the development of coronary heart disease (CHD), high blood pressure (hypertension), and stroke (Chida & Steptoe, 2009; Krantz & McCeney, 2002). For example, adults in a nationwide sample who reported the strongest and longest-lasting worry about terrorism after 9/11 were three times more likely than less worried people to develop heart problems over the next three years. Even those who reported the most intense temporary distress right after 9/11 were at elevated risk of developing heart problems over those same three years (Holman et al., 2008).

The link between CHD and physical stress responses appears especially strong in people who show intense physiological reactivity to stressors (Ming et al., 2004; Treiber et al., 2001). For example, among healthy young adult research participants, those whose blood pressure rose most dramatically in response to a mild stressor or a series of stressors were the ones most likely to develop hypertension later in life (Light et al., 1999; Matthews et al., 2004).

As also mentioned earlier, these physiological reactions to stressors—and the chances of suffering stress-related health problems—depend partly on personality, especially on how people tend to think about stressors and about life in general. For example, the trait of *hostility*—particularly when accompanied by irritability and impatience—has been associated with the appearance of coronary heart disease (Bunde & Suls, 2006; Day & Jreige, 2002; Krantz & McCeney, 2002; Smith, Uchino, et al., 2007).

THINKING CRITICALLY   ▶

Does Hostility Increase the Risk of Heart Disease?

Hostility is characterized by suspiciousness, resentment, frequent anger, antagonism, and distrust of others (Krantz & McCeney, 2002; Williams, 2001). The identification of hostility as a risk factor for coronary heart disease and *myocardial infarction,* or *MI* (commonly known as heart attack), could be an important breakthrough in understanding the chief cause of death in the United States and most other Western nations. But is hostility as dangerous as health psychologists suspect?

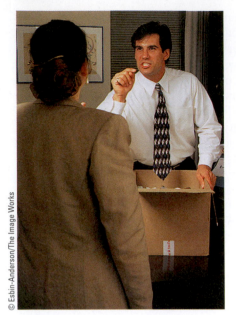

"You Can't Fire Me—I Quit!"

For a time, researchers believed that anyone who displayed the pattern of aggressiveness, competitiveness, and nonstop work known as "Type A" behavior was at elevated risk for heart disease (Friedman & Rosenman, 1974). More recent research shows, however, that the danger lies not in these characteristics alone but in hostility, a pattern seen in some, but not all, Type A people.

What am I being asked to believe or accept?

Many researchers claim that individuals displaying hostility are at increased risk for coronary heart disease and heart attack (e.g., Bleil et al., 2004; Boyle et al., 2004). This risk, they say, is independent of other risk factors such as heredity, diet, smoking, and drinking.

What evidence is available to support the assertion?

There is evidence that hostility and heart disease are related, but scientists are still not sure what explains that relationship. Some suggest that the risk of CHD and MI may be elevated in hostile people because these people tend to have an unusually strong reaction to stressors, especially when challenged. During interpersonal conflicts, for example, people predisposed to hostile behavior display not only overt hostility but also unusually large increases in blood pressure, heart rate, and other aspects of SAM reactivity (Brondolo et al., 2003; Suls & Wan, 1993). In addition, it takes hostile individuals longer than normal to get back to their resting levels of SAM functioning (Gerin et al., 2006). Like a driver who damages a car by pressing the accelerator and brake pedals at the same time, these "hot reactors" may create excessive wear and tear on the arteries of the heart as their increased heart rate forces blood through tightened vessels (Johnston, Tuomisto, & Patching, 2008). Increased sympathetic nervous system activation not only puts a strain on the coronary arteries but also leads to surges of stress-related hormones from the adrenal glands, including the catecholamines (adrenaline and noradrenaline). High levels of these hormones are associated with increases in cholesterol and other fatty substances that are deposited in arteries and contribute to coronary heart disease (Bierhaus et al., 2003; Stoney & Hughes, 1999). Cholesterol levels do appear to be elevated in hostile people, even when they are not under stress (Dujovne & Houston, 1991; Engebretson & Stoney, 1995).

Hostility might also affect heart disease risk less directly, through its impact on social support. Some evidence suggests that hostile people get fewer benefits from social support than other people do (Lepore, 1995). Failing to use this support, and possibly offending potential supporters in the process, may intensify the impact of stressful events on hostile people. The result may be increased anger, antagonism, and ultimately, additional stress on the cardiovascular system.

Are there alternative ways of interpreting the evidence?

Studies suggesting that hostility causes CHD or MI are not true experiments. Researchers cannot manipulate the independent variable, hostility, by creating it in randomly selected people, nor can they create experimental conditions in which individuals who differ only in terms of hostility are compared on heart disease, the dependent variable. So although the available evidence suggests an association between hostility and heart disease, it cannot confirm that hostility is causing heart disease. Accordingly, we have to consider other possible explanations of the hostility–heart disease relationship.

For example, some researchers suggest that higher rates of heart problems among hostile people are due not to the impact of hostility on autonomic reactivity and hormone surges but rather to a third variable that accounts for the other two. Specifically, genetically determined autonomic reactivity might increase the likelihood of both hostility and heart disease (Krantz et al., 1988). Supporting this alternative interpretation is evidence that people with an inherited predisposition toward strong physiological responses to the stressors of everyday life not only have a higher risk for CHD but also tend to be more hostile (Cacioppo et al., 1998). It is at least plausible, then, that some individuals are biologically predisposed to exaggerated autonomic reactivity and to hostility, each of which is independent of the other.

It has also been suggested that hostility may be only one of many traits linked to heart disease. Depression, hopelessness, pessimism, and anxiety may also be involved (Frasure-Smith & Lespérance, 2005; Kubzansky, Davidson, & Rozanski, 2005; Nicholson, Fuhrer, & Marmot, 2005; Roy et al., 2010; Suls & Bunde, 2005).

What additional evidence would help evaluate the alternatives?

One way to test whether hostile people's higher rates of heart disease are related to their hostility or to a more general tendency toward intense physiological arousal is to examine how hostile individuals react to stressors when they are not angry. Some researchers have done this by observing the physiological reactions of hostile people during the stress of surgery. One study found that even under general anesthesia, hostile people show unusually strong autonomic reactivity (Krantz & Durel, 1983). Because these patients were not conscious, it appears that oversensitivity to stressors, not hostile thinking, caused their exaggerated stress responses. This possibility is supported by research showing that compared with other people, individuals who have strong blood pressure responses to stressors also show different patterns of brain activity during stress (Gianaros et al., 2005).

What conclusions are most reasonable?

Most studies continue to find that among generally healthy people, those who are hostile—especially men—are at greater risk for heart disease and heart attacks than other people (Chida & Steptoe, 2009; Haukkala et al., 2010; Krantz & McCeney, 2002; Stansfeld & Marmot, 2002). However, the picture is probably more complex than researchers first thought; it appears that many interacting factors affect the relationship between hostility and CHD (Sloan et al., 2010).

A more elaborate psychobiological model may be required—one that takes into account that some individuals may be biologically predisposed to react to stress and challenge with hostility and increased cardiovascular activity, each of which can contribute to heart disease; that hostile people may help create and maintain stressors through aggressive thoughts and actions, which can provoke others to be aggressive; and that hostile people are more likely than others to smoke, drink alcohol to excess, overeat, fail to exercise, and engage in other heart-damaging behaviors (Kiecolt-Glaser, 2010).

We must also keep in mind that the relationship between heart problems and hostility may not be universal. Although this relationship appears to hold for women as well as for men and for individuals in various ethnic groups (e.g., Nakano & Kitamura, 2001; Olson et al., 2005; Stoney & Engebretson, 1994; Yoshimasu et al., 2002), final conclusions must await further research that examines the link between hostility and heart disease in other cultures (Finney, Stoney, & Engebretson, 2002).

Promoting Healthy Behavior

Health psychologists are deeply involved in the development of smoking cessation programs, in campaigns to prevent young people from taking up smoking, in alcohol education and obesity prevention efforts, in the prevention of skin cancer through education about sun safety, and in the fight against the spread of HIV infection and AIDS (Albarracín et al., 2008; Buller, Buller, & Kane, 2005; Durantini et al., 2006; Lombard et al., 2010; Morisky et al., 2006; Stice, Shaw, & Nathan, 2006). They have also helped promote early detection of disease. Encouraging women to perform breast self-examinations and men to do testicular self-examinations are just two examples of health psychology programs that can save thousands of lives each year (Taylor, 2002). Health psychologists have also explored the reasons behind some people's failure to follow treatment regimens that are vital to the control of diseases such as diabetes, heart disease, HIV/AIDS, and high blood pressure (Bartlett, 2002; Gonzalez et al., 2004). Understanding these reasons and devising procedures that encourage greater adherence to medical advice could speed recovery, prevent unnecessary suffering, decrease costs, and save many lives (Barclay et al., 2007; Simpson et al., 2006).

Efforts to reduce, eliminate, or prevent behaviors that pose health risks and to increase healthy behavior patterns are known as **health promotion** (Smith, Orleans, & Jenkins, 2004). For example, health psychologists have developed programs that teach children as young as 9 to engage in health-enhancing behaviors and avoid health-risk

health promotion The process of altering or eliminating behaviors that pose risks to health, as well as encouraging healthy behavior patterns.

Doctor's Orders

Despite their physicians' instructions, many patients fail to take their blood pressure medication and continue to eat unhealthy diets. Noncompliance with medical advice is especially common when cultural values and beliefs conflict with that advice. Aware of this problem, health psychologists have developed culture-sensitive approaches to health promotion and disease prevention (Kazarian & Evans, 2001).

© Gustavo Gilabert/Corbis

behaviors. School systems now offer a variety of these programs, including those that give children and adolescents the skills necessary to refuse cigarettes, drugs, and unprotected sex. To meet the more difficult challenge of modifying existing health-threatening behaviors, health psychologists go into workplaces and communities with the goal of helping people adopt healthier lifestyles by altering diet, smoking, and exercise patterns. They also teach stress management techniques (Langenberg et al., 2000; Tuomilehto et al., 2001). These programs can reduce the need for future medical treatment (Blumenthal et al., 2002; Schneiderman et al., 2001) and lead to better health for participants (Lisspers et al., 2005; Orth-Gomér et al., 2009).

Health Beliefs and Health Behaviors

Health psychologists are also trying to understand the thought processes that lead people to engage in health-endangering behaviors and that can interfere with efforts to adopt healthier lifestyles. Their research has led to intervention programs that seek to change these patterns of thinking or at least take them into account. In one study, for example, women who avoid thinking about the risks of breast cancer were more likely to get a mammogram screening after receiving health information that was tailored to their cognitive styles (Williams-Piehota et al., 2005).

© Steve Kelley/Copley News Service.

As described in the chapter on cognition and language, humans tend to underestimate the likelihood of common outcomes and to overestimate the likelihood of rare events. When this tendency causes people to ignore the dangers of smoking and other health-risk behaviors, the results can be disastrous.

This cognitive approach to health psychology is embodied in various *health belief models.* One of the most influential of these models was developed by Irwin Rosenstock (1974). This model is based on the assumption that people's decisions about health-related behaviors (such as smoking) are guided by four main factors:

1. Perceiving a *personal threat* of, or susceptibility to, developing a specific health problem. (Do you believe that *you* will get lung cancer from smoking?)

2. Perceiving the seriousness of the illness and the consequences of having it. (How serious do *you* think lung cancer is, and what will happen if *you* get it?)

3. Believing that changing a particular behavior will reduce the threat. (Will giving up smoking prevent *you* from getting lung cancer?)

4. A comparison of the *perceived costs* of enacting a health-related behavior change and the *benefits expected* from that change. (Will the reduced chance of getting cancer in the future be worth the discomfort and loss of pleasure associated with not smoking now?)

According to this health belief model, the people most likely to quit smoking would be those who believe that they are at risk for getting cancer from smoking, that cancer is serious and life-threatening, that quitting will reduce their chances of getting cancer, and that the benefits of preventing cancer clearly outweigh the difficulties associated with quitting (McCaul et al., 2006).

Other cognitive factors are emphasized in other health belief models. For example, people generally do not try to quit smoking unless they believe they can succeed. So *self-efficacy,* the belief that one is able to perform some behavior, is an additional consideration in decisions about health behaviors (Armitage, 2005; Bandura, 1992). A related factor is the person's *intention* to engage in a behavior designed to improve health or protect against illness (Albarracín et al., 2001; Schwarzer, 2001; Webb & Sheeran, 2006).

Health belief models have been useful in predicting a variety of health behaviors, including exercise (McAuley, 1992), safe-sex practices (Fisher, Fisher, & Rye, 1995), adherence to doctors' orders (Bond, Aiken, & Somerville, 1992), and having routine vaccinations and mammograms (Brewer et al., 2007; Champion & Huster, 1995).

Changing Health Behaviors: Stages of Readiness

Changing health-related behaviors depends not only on a person's health beliefs but also on that person's readiness to change. According to James Prochaska and his colleagues, the process of successful change occurs in five stages (Prochaska, DiClemente, & Norcross, 1992; Schumann et al., 2005):

1. *Precontemplation.* The person does not perceive a health-related problem and has no intention of changing in the foreseeable future.

2. *Contemplation.* The person is aware of a health-related behavior that should be changed and is seriously thinking about changing it.

3. *Preparation.* The person has a strong intention to change and has made specific plans to do so.

4. *Action.* The person is engaging successfully in behavior change.

5. *Maintenance.* The healthy behavior has continued for at least six months, and the person is using newly learned skills to prevent relapse, or "backsliding."

These stages may actually overlap somewhat; for example, some "precontemplators" may actually be starting to contemplate change (Herzog & Blagg, 2007). In any case, the path from precontemplation through maintenance can be a bumpy one. Usually, people relapse and go through the stages repeatedly before finally achieving stability in the healthy behavior they desire (Polivy & Herman, 2002). Smokers, for example, typically require three to four cycles through the stages over several years before they finally reach the maintenance stage (Piasecki, 2006).

Programs for Coping with Stress and Promoting Health

Improving people's stress-coping skills is an important part of health psychologists' health promotion work (e.g., Keogh, Bond, & Flaxman, 2006). Let's consider a few specific procedures and programs associated with this effort.

Planning to Cope   Just as people with money in the bank have a better chance of weathering a financial crisis, those with effective coping skills may escape some of the more harmful effects of intense stress. Like family money, the ability to handle stress appears to come naturally—perhaps even genetically—to some people (Caspi et al., 2010), but coping can also be learned.

The first step in learning to cope with stress is to make a systematic assessment of the degree to which stress is disrupting your life. This assessment involves (1) identifying the specific events and situations, such as conflicts or life changes, that are operating as stressors, and (2) noting the effects of these stressors, such as headaches, lack of concentration, or excessive drinking. Table 13.4 lists the other steps in a program to cope with stress. Notice that the second step is to select an appropriate goal. Should you try to eliminate stressors or try to change your response to them? Knowing the difference between changeable and unchangeable stressors is important. Stress-related problems are especially common among people who either exhaust themselves trying to change unchangeable stressors or miss opportunities to change stressors that can be changed (Folkman, 1984).

Bear in mind, though, that no single method of coping with stressors is right for every person or every stressor. As mentioned earlier, for example, denying the existence of an uncontrollable stressor may be fine in the short run but may eventually lead to problems if no other coping method is used. Similarly, people who rely exclusively on an active problem-solving approach may handle controllable stressors well but find themselves nearly helpless in the face of uncontrollable ones (Murray & Terry, 1999). The most successful stress managers may be those who can adjust their coping methods to the demands of changing situations and differing stressors (Kashdan & Rottenberg, 2010; Taylor, 2002).

LINKAGES   How can people manage stress? (a link to Treatment of Psychological Disorders, p. 653)

Developing Coping Strategies   Like stress responses, strategies for coping with stress can be cognitive, emotional, behavioral, or physical. *Cognitive coping strategies* involve changing how we think about stressors. These changes include thinking more calmly, rationally, and constructively in the face of stressors and may lead to a more hopeful emotional outlook. For example, students with heavy

---

TABLE 13.4   Stages in Coping with Stress

Many successful programs for systematically coping with stress guide people through several stages and are aimed at removing stressors that can be changed and at reducing responses to stressors that cannot be changed (Taylor, 2002).

Stage	Task
1. Assessment	Identify the sources and effects of stress.
2. Goal setting	List the stressors and stress responses to be addressed. Designate which stressors are and are not changeable.
3. Planning	List the specific steps to be taken to cope with stress.
4. Action	Implement coping plans.
5. Evaluation	Determine the changes in stressors and stress responses that have occurred as a result of coping methods.
6. Adjustment	Alter coping methods to improve results, if necessary.

course loads may experience anxiety, confusion, discouragement, lack of motivation, and the desire to run away from it all. Frightening, catastrophizing thoughts about their tasks (for example, "What if I fail?") magnify these stress responses. Cognitive coping strategies replace catastrophic thinking with thoughts in which stressors are viewed as challenges rather than threats (Ellis & Bernard, 1985). This substitution process is called *cognitive restructuring* (Lazarus, 1971; Meichenbaum, 1977). It involves first identifying upsetting thoughts (such as "I'll never figure this out!") and then developing and practicing more constructive thoughts to use when under stress (such as "All I can do is the best I can"). Cognitive coping does not eliminate stressors, but it can help people perceive them as less threatening and thus make them less disruptive (Antoni et al., 2001; Chesney et al., 2003).

Finding social support is an effective *emotional coping strategy.* As mentioned earlier, feeling that you are cared about and valued by others can be a buffer against the ill effects of stressors (Taylor, 2002; Taylor, Klein, et al., 2000). Research suggests that having enhanced social support is associated with improved immune function (Kiecolt-Glaser & Newton, 2001) and more rapid recovery from illness (Taylor, 2002).

Behavioral coping strategies involve changing behavior in ways that minimize the impact of stressors. Time management is one example. If it seems that you are always pressed for time, consider developing a time management plan. The first step is to use a calendar or day planner to record how you spend each hour of each day in a typical week. Next, analyze the information to locate when and how you might be wasting time and how you might use your time more efficiently. Then set out a schedule for the coming week and stick to it. Make adjustments in subsequent weeks as you learn more realistic ways to manage your time. Time management can't create more time, but it can help control catastrophizing thoughts by providing reassurance that there is enough time for everything and a plan for handling all that you have to do.

Physical coping strategies can be used to alter the undesirable physiological responses that occur before, during, or after the appearance of stressors. The most common physical coping strategy is some form of drug use. Prescription medications are sometimes an appropriate coping aid, especially when stressors are severe and acute, such as the sudden death of one's child. However, people who rely on prescribed or nonprescription drugs, including alcohol, to help them face stressors may come to believe that their ability to cope is due to the drug, not to their own skill. This belief can make people more and more psychologically dependent on the drug. Furthermore, the drug effects that blunt stress responses may also interfere with the ability to apply other coping strategies. The resulting loss of perceived control over stressors may make those stressors even more threatening and disruptive.

Nonchemical methods of reducing physical stress reactions and improving health and functioning include progressive muscle relaxation training (Bernstein, Borkovec, & Hazlett-Stevens, 2000; Scheufele, 2000), physical exercise (Anshel, 1996), biofeedback (Nestoriuc, Rief, & Martin, 2008), yoga (Kiecolt-Glaser et al., 2010), meditation, and tai chi (Carlson et al., 2003; Li et al., 2001).

Progressive muscle relaxation training is one of the most popular physical methods for coping with stress. It was developed by Edmund Jacobson (1938) and involves tensing a group of muscles (such as the hand and arm) for a few seconds and then releasing the tension and focusing on the resulting feelings of relaxation. This procedure is repeated for each of sixteen muscle groups throughout the body (Bernstein, Borkovec, & Hazlett-Stevens, 2000). Once people develop some skill at relaxation, they can use it to calm themselves down anywhere and anytime, often without lying down. ("In Review: Methods for Coping with Stress" summarizes our discussion of stress-coping methods.)

TRY THIS

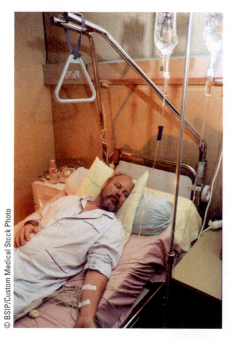

© BSIP/Custom Medical Stock Photo

Dealing with Chemotherapy

Progressive muscle relaxation training can be used to ease a variety of health-related problems. For example, one study found that this training resulted in significant reductions in anxiety, physiological arousal, and nausea following cancer chemotherapy (Burish & Jenkins, 1992).

progressive muscle relaxation training A procedure for learning to relax that involves tensing muscles and then releasing the tension in those muscles.

IN REVIEW   Methods for Coping with Stress

Type of Coping Method	Examples
Cognitive	Thinking of stressors as challenges rather than as threats; avoiding perfectionism
Emotional	Seeking social support; getting advice
Behavioral	Implementing a time management plan; where possible, making life changes to eliminate stressors
Physical	Progressive relaxation training; exercise; meditation

1. Catastrophizing thoughts are best overcome through _____ coping strategies.
2. The first step in coping with stress is to _____ the sources and effects of your stressors.
3. True or false: It is best to rely on one basic coping strategy. _____

LINKAGES

As noted in the chapter on introducing psychology, all of psychology's many subfields are related to one another. Our discussion of posttraumatic stress disorder illustrates just one way in which the topic of this chapter, health, stress, and coping, is linked to the subfield of psychological disorders (which is the focus

CHAPTER 13
HEALTH, STRESS, AND COPING

of the chapter by that name). The Linkages diagram shows ties to two other subfields as well, and there are many more ties throughout the book. Looking for linkages among subfields will help you see how they all fit together and help you better appreciate the big picture that is psychology.

LINKAGES

Can stress give you the flu?
(ans. on p. 544)

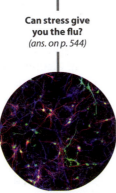

CHAPTER 3
Biological aspects of psychology

When do stress responses become mental disorders?
(ans. on p. 532)

CHAPTER 15
Psychological disorders

How does stress affect group decision making?
(ans. on p. 764)

CHAPTER 18
Social influence

SUMMARY

Health Psychology

The development of *health psychology* (also called *health care psychology*) was prompted by recognition of the link between stress and illness, as well as the role of behaviors such as smoking, in elevating the risk of illness. Researchers in this field explore how psychological factors are related to physical disease and vice versa. Health psychologists also help people behave in ways that prevent or minimize disease and promote health.

Understanding Stress and Stressors

The term *stress* refers in part to *stressors*, which are events and situations to which people must adjust. More generally, stress is viewed as an ongoing, interactive process that takes place as people adjust to and cope with their environment. Stressors may be physical or psychological.

Psychological Stressors

Psychological stressors include life changes and strains, catastrophic events, chronic problems, and daily hassles.

Measuring Stressors

Stressors can be measured by tests such as the Social Readjustment Rating Scale (SRRS) and the Life Experiences Survey (LES), as well as by surveys of daily hassles, but scores on such tests provide only a partial picture of the stress in an individual's life.

Stress Responses

Responses to stressors can be physical or psychological. They can occur alone or in combination, and the appearance of one response can stimulate others.

Physical Responses

Physical stress responses include sympatho-adreno-medullary (SAM) activation, such as increases in heart rate, respiration, and many other processes, as well as hypothalamic-pituitary-adrenocortical (HPA) activation, including the release of corticosteroids. These responses are part of a pattern known as the *general adaptation syndrome*, or *GAS*. The GAS has three stages: alarm, resistance, and exhaustion. The GAS helps people resist stress, but if present too long, it can lead to depletion of physiological resources, as well as to physical illnesses, which Hans Selye called *diseases of adaptation*.

Psychological Responses

Psychological stress responses can be emotional, cognitive, and behavioral. Cognitive stress reactions include ruminative thinking, catastrophizing, and disruptions in the ability to think clearly, remember accurately, and solve problems efficiently. Behavioral stress responses include irritability, aggression, absenteeism, and even suicide attempts. Extreme or chronic stressors can lead to *burnout* or *posttraumatic stress disorder* (PTSD).

Stress Mediators

The fact that different individuals react to the same stressors in different ways can be explained in part by stress mediators, such as the extent to which individuals can predict and control their stressors, how they interpret the threat involved, the social support they get, and their stress-coping skills.

How Stressors Are Perceived

Many stressors are not inherently stressful; their impact depends partly on how people perceive them. In particular, stressors appraised as threats are likely to have greater impact than those appraised as challenges.

Predictability and Control

Knowing that a particular stressor might occur but being uncertain whether it will occur tends to increase the stressor's impact, as does lack of control over stressors.

Coping Resources and Coping Methods

The people most likely to react strongly to a stressor are those whose coping resources and coping methods are inadequate.

Social Support

Social support, which consists of resources provided by other people, can lessen the impact of stressors. The friends and social contacts on whom a person can depend for support constitute that person's network of social support.

Stress, Personality, and Gender

Certain personality characteristics help insulate people from the ill effects of stress. One such characteristic appears to be dispositional optimism, the belief or expectation that things will work out positively. Gender can also play a role in stress responses.

The Physiology and Psychology of Health and Illness

Stress, Illness, and the Immune System

Psychoneuroimmunology is the field that examines the interaction of psychological and physiological processes that affect the body's ability to defend itself against disease. When a person is under stress, some of the hormones released

from the adrenal gland, such as cortisol, reduce the effectiveness of the cells of the *immune system* (for example, T-cells, B-cells, natural killer cells, and macrophages) in combating foreign invaders such as viruses.

Stress, Illness, and the Cardiovascular System

Heart disease is a major cause of death in most Western countries, including the United States. People who are hostile appear to be at greater risk for heart disease than other people, possibly because their heightened reactivity to stressors can damage their cardiovascular system.

Promoting Healthy Behavior

The process of altering or eliminating health-risk behaviors and fostering healthy behavior patterns is known as *health promotion*.

Health Beliefs and Health Behaviors

People's health-related behaviors are partly guided by their beliefs about health risks and what they can do about them.

Changing Health Behaviors: Stages of Readiness

The process of changing health-related behaviors may involve several stages, including precontemplation, contemplation, preparation, action, and maintenance. Understanding which stages people are in and helping them move through these stages are important tasks in health psychology.

Programs for Coping with Stress and Promoting Health

To cope with stress, people must recognize the stressors affecting them, note the effects of those stressors, and develop ways of handling them. Important coping skills include cognitive restructuring and using emotional and behavioral means to minimize the intensity and impact of stressors. *Progressive muscle relaxation training* and other physical coping strategies can reduce physical stress reactions. These coping procedures are often part of health psychologists' disease prevention and health promotion efforts.

LINKAGES TO FURTHER LEARNING

Now that you have finished reading this chapter, how about exploring some of the topics and information that you found most interesting? Here are some places to start.

Books

David J. Mahoney, *The Longevity Strategy: How to Live to 100 Using the Brain-Body Connection* (Wiley, 1998). The origins of longevity.

Lance Armstrong and Sally Jenkins, *It's Not About the Bike: My Journey Back to Life* (Berkley Books, 2001). Armstrong focuses on the origins of his surviving a deadly form of cancer.

Lewis B. Puller, *Fortunate Son* (Bantam, 1996). Son of a famous Marine deals with posttraumatic stress and multiple amputations after the Vietnam War.

Tony Cassidy, *Stress, Cognition, and Health* (Routledge, 1999). Summarizes research on the effects of stress on thinking and physical well-being.

Jerrold Greenberg, *Comprehensive Stress Management* (McGraw-Hill, 1999). Ideas for stress management.

Robert M. Sapolsky, *Why Zebras Don't Get Ulcers* (Owl Books, 2004). Describes the stress process, stress-related diseases, and coping skills.

James W. Pennebaker, *Opening Up: The Healing Power of Expressing Emotions* (Guilford Press, 1997). Describes research on the benefits of self-disclosure.

On the Internet

CourseMate Access an integrated eBook and chapter-specific learning tools including flashcards, quizzes, videos, and more. Go to CengageBrain.com.

 Want to maximize the value of your online study time? Take this easy-to-use study system's diagnostic pre-test, and it will create a personalized study plan for you. By helping you identify the topics that you need to understand better and then directing you to valuable online resources, it can speed up your chapter review. CengageNOW even provides a post-test so you can confirm that you are ready for an exam. Go to CengageBrain.com.

TALKING POINTS

Here are a few talking points to help you summarize this chapter for family and friends without giving a lecture.

1. Our lifestyle, especially as it relates to diet, smoking, alcohol use, and exercise, has a lot to do with how healthy we are and how long we will live.

2. In general, predictable stressors have less impact on us than sudden, unpredictable ones.

3. Daily hassles may not be intense stressors by themselves, but they can combine to create significant negative effects.

4. Over time, the effects of stressors can hurt our disease-fighting immune system and leave us vulnerable to many kinds of illness.

5. The impact of stressors on a particular person depends on a combination of what those stressors are, how long they last, and how stress-prone or disease-prone the person is.

6. Some stressors cannot be eliminated or avoided, but we can reduce their impact by thinking of them as challenges rather than as threats.

7. Having a flexible stress-coping plan is a key factor in minimizing the psychological and physical dangers of stress.

14

Personality

© John Beebe/Aurora Photos

If you've ever been stuck in a traffic jam, *you've probably noticed that some people are tolerant and calm. Others become so fearful and cautious that they worsen the congestion. Still others get so impatient and angry that they may trigger a shouting match or cause an* accident. *How people handle frustration is just one aspect of their personalities. In this chapter, we examine the concept of personality, review some of the tests that psychologists have developed to measure it, and look at how personality theories and research are being applied in everyday life.*

Businesses all over the world lose more than $15 billion each year as a result of employee theft (Bamfield, 2008). Millions more are spent on security and surveillance designed to curb these losses, but it would be far better if companies could simply avoid hiring dishonest employees in the first place. Some firms have tried to screen out potential thieves by requiring prospective employees to take polygraph ("lie detector") tests. As described in the chapter on motivation and emotion, however, these tests may not be reliable or valid. In fact, the federal government of the United States has banned their use in most kinds of employee selection.

Thousands of companies have turned instead to paper-and-pencil "integrity" tests designed to identify job applicants who are likely to steal or behave in other dishonest or irresponsible ways (Berry, Sackett, & Wiemann, 2007). Some of these tests simply ask applicants if they have stolen from previous employers and if they might steal in the future. Such questions can screen out people who are honest about their stealing, but most people who steal would probably also lie to conceal previous crimes or criminal intentions. Accordingly, some companies now use tests to assess applicants' general psychological characteristics and compare their scores with those of current or past employees. Applicants whose characteristics are most like the company's honest employees are hired; those who appear similar to dishonest employees are not.

Can undesirable employee behaviors be predicted on the basis of such tests? To some extent, they can. For example, scores on the Reliability Scale—which includes questions about impulsivity and disruptive behavior during school years—are significantly correlated with a broad range of undesirable activities in the workplace (Hogan, 2006). But psychological tests are far from perfect predictors of those activities (Berry, Sackett, & Wiemann, 2007). Although considerably better than polygraph tests, psychological tests still fail to detect dishonesty in some people, and worse, they may falsely identify some honest people as potential thieves. The best that companies can hope for is to find tests that will help reduce the overall likelihood of hiring dishonest people.

The use of psychological tests to help select honest employees is a more formal version of the process that most of us use when we meet someone new. We observe the person's behavior, form impressions, and draw conclusions—often within just a few seconds (Borkenau & Mauer, 2006)—about how that person will act at other times or under other circumstances. Like the employer, we are looking for clues to *personality.* Although there is no universally accepted definition, psychologists generally view **personality** as the unique pattern of enduring thoughts, feelings, and actions that characterize a person. Personality research, in turn, focuses on understanding the origins or causes of the similarities and differences among people in their patterns of thinking, emotion, and behavior (Carver & Connor-Smith, 2010).

With such a large agenda, personality researchers must incorporate information from many other areas of psychology. In fact, personality psychology lies at the

personality The pattern of psychological and behavioral characteristics by which each person can be compared with and contrasted with others.

crossroads of all psychological research (Funder, 2007). It is the merging, in a particular individual, of all the psychological, behavioral, and biological processes discussed in this book. To gain a full understanding of anyone's personality, for example, you must know something about that person's developmental experiences (including cultural influences), genetic and other biological characteristics, perceptual and other information-processing habits and biases, typical patterns of emotional expression, and social skills. Psychologists also want to know about personality in general, including how it develops and changes across the life span, why some people are usually optimistic whereas others are usually pessimistic, and how consistent or inconsistent people's behavior tends to be from one situation to the next.

In this chapter, we describe four approaches to the study of personality and some of the ways in which personality theory and research are being applied. We begin by presenting the *psychodynamic approach,* which was developed by Sigmund Freud and later modified by a number of people he influenced. Next, we describe the *trait approach,* which focuses on the consistent patterns of thoughts, feelings, and actions that form individual personalities. Then we present the *social-cognitive approach,* which explores the ways in which learning—and learned ways of thinking—shape human behavior. Finally, we consider the *humanistic approach,* with its emphasis on personality as a reflection of personal growth and the search for meaning in life. After reviewing these approaches, we describe how psychologists measure and compare people's personalities. We also give some examples of how psychological tests are being used in personality research and in other ways as well.

Founder of the Psychodynamic Approach

Here is Sigmund Freud with his daughter, Anna, who became a psychoanalyst herself and eventually developed a revised version of her father's theories.

The Psychodynamic Approach

Some people think they can understand personality by simply watching people. Someone with an "outgoing personality," for example, shows it by acting friendly and sociable. But is that all there is to personality? Not according to Sigmund Freud. Trained as a medical doctor in the late 1800s, Freud spent most of his life in Vienna, Austria, where he treated patients who displayed "neurotic" disorders, such as blindness or paralysis, for which there was no physical cause. Freud's experience with these patients, as well as his reading of the works of Charles Darwin and other scientists of his day, led him to believe that our personalities and behavior, including disordered behavior, are determined mainly by basic drives and past psychological events (Allen, 2006). He agreed, too, with Sir Francis Galton and other nineteenth-century writers when he proposed that people may not know why they feel, think, or act the way they do because these activities are partly controlled by the unconscious part of the personality—the part of which we are not normally aware (Friedman & Schustack, 2009). From these ideas Freud created the **psychodynamic approach** to personality, which assumes that our thoughts, feelings, and behavior are determined by the interaction of various unconscious psychological processes (Schultz & Schultz, 2009).

The Structure and Development of Personality

Freud believed that people have certain basic impulses or urges, related not only to food and water but also to sex and aggression. Freud described these impulses and urges with a German word that translates as "instinct," but he did not believe that they are all inborn and unchangeable, as the word *instinct* might imply (Schultz & Schultz, 2009). He did believe, though, that our desires for love, knowledge, security, and the like arise from these more basic impulses. He said that each of us faces the task of figuring out how to satisfy basic urges. Our personality develops, he claimed, as we struggle with that task, and it is reflected in the ways we go about satisfying a range of urges.

psychodynamic approach Freud's view that personality is based on the interplay of unconscious mental processes.

FIGURE 14.1
Freud's Model of Personality
According to Freud, some parts of the personality are conscious, while others are unconscious. Between these levels is the *preconscious,* which Freud regarded as the location of memories and other material that is not usually in awareness but that can be brought into consciousness with minimal effort.

Source: From Leibert/Springer. *Personality: Strategies and Issues, 6E.* Copyright © 1990 Wadsworth, a part of Cengage Learning, Inc. Reproduced by permission. www.cengage.com/permissions.

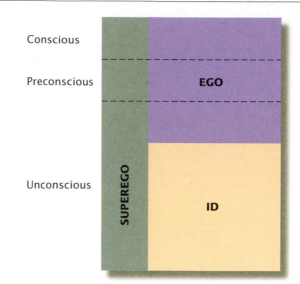

id The unconscious portion of personality that contains basic impulses and urges.

libido The psychic energy contained in the id.

pleasure principle The id's operating principle, which guides people toward whatever feels good.

ego The part of the personality that mediates conflicts between and among the demands of the id, the superego, and the real world.

reality principle The operating principle of the ego that creates compromises between the id's demands and those of the real world.

superego The component of personality that tells people what they should and should not do.

defense mechanisms Psychological responses that help protect a person from anxiety and guilt.

Id, Ego, and Superego   As shown in Figure 14.1, Freud described the structure of personality as having three major components: the id, the ego, and the superego (Carver & Scheier, 2008).

He regarded the **id** as the unconscious portion of personality, in which two kinds of "instincts" reside. There are life instincts, which he called *Eros.* They promote positive, constructive behavior and reflect a source of energy (sometimes called *psychic energy*) known as **libido**. There are also death instincts, or *Thanatos,* which Freud perceived as responsible for aggression and destructiveness (Hergenhahn & Olson, 2007). The id operates on the **pleasure principle**, seeking immediate satisfaction of both kinds of instincts, regardless of society's rules or the rights or feelings of others. The hungry person who pushes to the front of the line at Burger King would be satisfying an id-driven impulse.

Children's expression of their id impulses are soon increasingly restricted by parents, teachers, and others. In the face of these restrictions, a second part of the personality—the **ego**—develops from the id. The ego tries to find ways to get what a person wants in the real world, as opposed to the fantasy world of the id. Operating on the **reality principle**, the ego makes compromises between the id's unreasoning demands for immediate satisfaction and the practical limits imposed by the social world. The ego would lead that hungry person at Burger King to wait in line and think about what to order rather than risk punishment by pushing ahead.

As children learn about the rules and values of society, they tend to adopt them. This process of *internalizing* parental and cultural values produces the third component of personality. It is called the **superego**, and it tells us what we should and should not do. The superego becomes our moral guide, and it is just as relentless and unreasonable as the id in its demand to be obeyed. It would make the hungry person at Burger King feel guilty for even thinking about violating society's rules.

Conflicts and Defenses   Freud described the inner clashes among the three personality components as *intrapsychic* or *psychodynamic conflicts*. He believed that each person's personality is shaped by the number, nature, and outcome of these conflicts. Freud said that the ego's primary function is to prevent the anxiety or guilt we would feel if we became aware of our socially unacceptable id impulses or if we thought about violating the superego's rules (Westen et al., 2008). Sometimes the ego motivates sensible actions, as when a parent asks for help in dealing with impulses to abuse a child. However, the ego may also use **defense mechanisms**, which are unconscious tactics that protect against anxiety and guilt by either

---

TABLE 14.1   Ego Defense Mechanisms

TRY THIS According to Freud, defense mechanisms prevent or deflect anxiety or guilt in the short run, but they sap energy. Further, using them to avoid dealing with the source of problems can make those problems worse in the long run. Try listing some incidents in which you or someone you know may have used each of the defenses described here. What questions would a critical thinker ask to determine whether these behaviors were unconscious defense mechanisms or actions motivated by conscious intentions?

Defense Mechanism	Description	Example
Repression	Unconsciously pushing threatening memories, urges, or ideas from conscious awareness	A person may experience loss of memory for unpleasant events.
Rationalization	Attempting to make actions or mistakes seem reasonable	The reasons or excuses given for behavior (e.g., "I spank my children because it is good for them") sound rational, but they may not be the real reasons.
Projection	Unconsciously attributing one's own unacceptable thoughts or impulses to another person	Instead of recognizing that "I hate him," a person may feel that "he hates me."
Reaction formation	Defending against unacceptable impulses by acting opposite to them	Sexual interest in a married coworker might appear as strong dislike instead.
Sublimation	Converting unacceptable impulses into socially acceptable actions and perhaps expressing them symbolically	Sexual or aggressive desires may appear as artistic creativity or devotion to athletic excellence.
Displacement	Deflecting an impulse from its original target to a less threatening one	Anger at one's boss may be expressed through hostility toward a clerk, a family member, or even a pet.
Denial	Simply discounting the existence of threatening impulses	A person may vehemently deny ever having had even the slightest degree of physical attraction to a person of the same sex.
Compensation	Striving to make up for unconscious impulses or fears	A business executive's extreme competitiveness might be aimed at compensating for unconscious feelings of inferiority.

Big Cheese Photo RF/Jupiterimages

The Oral Stage

According to Freud, personality evolves in several stages of psychosexual development. At each stage, a different part of the body becomes the primary focus of pleasure. This baby would appear to be in the oral stage.

preventing threatening material from surfacing or disguising it when it does appear (Cramer, 2009) (see Table 14.1).

Stages in Personality Development Freud proposed that personality evolves during childhood in several stages of **psychosexual development**. Failure to resolve the problems and conflicts that appear at a given stage can leave a person *fixated*—that is, unconsciously preoccupied with the area of pleasure associated with that stage. Freud believed that the stage at which a person became fixated in childhood can be seen in adult personality characteristics.

In Freud's theory, a child's first year or so is called the **oral stage** because the mouth—which infants use to eat and to explore everything from toys to their own hands and feet—is the center of pleasure during this period. Freud said fixation at the oral stage can stem from weaning that is too early or too late and may result in adult characteristics ranging from overeating or childlike dependence (late weaning) to the use of "biting" sarcasm (early weaning).

The **anal stage** occurs during the second year, when the child's ego develops to cope with parental demands for socially appropriate behavior. For example, in most Western cultures, toilet training clashes with the child's freedom to have bowel movements at will. Freud said that if toilet training is too harsh or begins too early, it can produce an anal fixation that leads, in adulthood, to stinginess or excessive neatness (symbolically withholding feces). If toilet training is too late or too lax, however, the result could be a kind of anal fixation that is reflected in adults who are disorganized or impulsive (symbolically expelling feces).

TRY THIS Which of Freud's ego defense mechanisms is operating here? (Check the answer at the bottom of page 562.)

DILBERT: © Scott Adams/Dist. by United Feature Syndicate, Inc.

psychosexual development Periods of personality development in which, according to Freud, conflicts focus on particular issues.

oral stage The first of Freud's psychosexual stages of personality development, in which the mouth is the center of pleasure and conflict.

anal stage The second of Freud's psychosexual stages of personality development, in which the focus of pleasure and conflict shifts from the mouth to the anus.

phallic stage The third of Freud's psychosexual stages of personality development, in which the focus of pleasure and conflict shifts to the genital area.

Oedipal complex A pattern described by Freud in which a boy has sexual desire for his mother and wants to eliminate his father's competition for her attention.

Electra complex A pattern described by Freud in which a young girl develops an attachment to her father and competes with her mother for his attention.

latency period The fourth of Freud's psychosexual stages of personality development, in which sexual impulses lie dormant.

genital stage The last of Freud's psychosexual stages of personality development, which begins during adolescence, when sexual impulses appear at the conscious level.

According to Freud, between the ages of 3 and 5, the child's focus of pleasure shifts to the genital area. Because he emphasized male psychosexual development, Freud called this period the **phallic stage** (*phallus* is another word for *penis*). He believed that during this stage, a boy experiences sexual desire for his mother and a desire to eliminate, or even kill, his father, with whom the boy competes for the mother's affection. (Freud named this pattern of impulses the **Oedipal complex** because it reminded him of the plot of *Oedipus Rex*, the classical Greek play in which Oedipus, upon returning to his homeland, unknowingly slays his father and marries his mother.) The boy's fantasies make him fear that his powerful "rival" (his father) will castrate him. To reduce this fear, the boy's ego represses his incestuous desires and leads him to "identify" with his father and try to be like him. It is during this stage that the male's superego begins to develop.

According to Freud, a girl begins the phallic stage with a strong attachment to her mother. When she realizes that boys have penises and girls don't, though, she supposedly develops *penis envy* and transfers her love to her father. This pattern has become known as the **Electra complex** because it parallels the plot of another classical Greek play, but Freud himself never used this term. To avoid her mother's disapproval, the girl identifies with and imitates her, thus forming the basis for her own superego.

Freud believed that unresolved conflicts from the phallic stage can lead to many problems in adulthood, including difficulties in dealing with authority figures and an inability to maintain a stable love relationship.

As the phallic stage draws to a close and its conflicts are dealt with by the ego, an interval of psychological peace occurs. During this **latency period**, which lasts through childhood, sexual impulses stay in the background as the youngster focuses on education, same-sex peer play, and the development of social skills. In adolescence, when sexual impulses reappear at a conscious level, the genitals again become the focus of pleasure. Thus begins what Freud called the **genital stage**, which he saw as lasting for the rest of a person's life. The quality of relationships and the degree of fulfillment experienced during this final stage, he claimed, are influenced by how intrapsychic conflicts were resolved during the earlier stages.

Variations on Freud's Personality Theory

Freud's ideas—especially those involving the Oedipus and Electra complexes and the role of infantile sexuality—were, and still are, controversial. Even many of Freud's followers did not entirely agree with him. Some of them have been called *neo-Freudians* because they maintained many of the basic ideas in Freud's theory but developed their own approaches. Others are known as *ego psychologists* because their ideas focused more on the ego than on the id (Larsen & Buss, 2010).

Jung's Analytic Psychology Carl Jung (pronounced "yoong") was the most prominent of Freud's early followers to chart his own theoretical course. Jung (1916) emphasized that libido is not just sexual instinct but rather a more general life force that includes an innate drive for creativity, for growth-oriented resolution of conflicts, and for the productive adjustment of basic impulses in light of real-world demands. Jung did not identify specific stages in personality development. He suggested instead that people gradually develop differing degrees of *introversion* (a tendency to reflect on one's own experiences) or *extraversion* (a tendency to focus on the social world), along with differing tendencies to rely on specific psychological functions, such as thinking versus feeling. Combinations of these differing tendencies, said Jung (1933), create personalities that display distinctive and predictable patterns of behavior.

Jung also claimed there is a *collective unconscious*, which contains the memories we have inherited from our human and nonhuman ancestors (Freidman & Schustack, 2009). According to Jung, we are not consciously aware of these memories, but they are responsible for our innate tendencies to react in particular ways to certain things. For example, Jung believed that our collective memory of mothers influences how each of us perceives our own mother. Although the notion of a collective unconscious is widely accepted by Jung's followers, there is no empirical evidence that it exists. In fact, Jung himself acknowledged that to objectively demonstrate the existence of a collective unconscious would be impossible (Feist & Feist, 2009).

Other Neo-Freudian Theorists Jung was not the first theorist to challenge Freud. Alfred Adler, once a loyal follower of psychoanalysis, came to believe that the power behind the development of personality comes not from id impulses but from an innate desire to overcome infantile feelings of helplessness and to gain some control over the environment. Adler (1927/1963) referred to this process as *striving for superiority*, by which he meant a drive for fulfillment as a person, not just a desire to do better than others. Other prominent neo-Freudians, including Erik Erikson, Erich Fromm, and Harry Stack Sullivan, focused on how people's personalities are shaped by those around them. They argued that once our biological needs are met, the attempt to meet social needs (to feel protected, secure, and accepted, for example) is the primary influence on personality. And according to these theorists, the strategies people use to meet these social needs, such as by dominating others or being dependent on them, become central features of their personalities.

The first feminist personality theorist, Karen Horney (pronounced "HORN-eye"), disputed Freud's view that women's lack of a penis causes them to envy men and feel inferior to them. Horney (1937) argued that, in fact, it is men who envy women: Realizing that they cannot bear children and that they often play only a small role in raising them, males see their lives as having less meaning or substance than women's. Horney believed that it is this *womb envy* that leads men to belittle and disrespect women. She argued further that when women feel inferior, it is because of the personal and political restrictions that men have placed on them, not because of penis envy. Horney's position on this issue reflected her strong belief that cultural factors, rather than instincts, play a major role in personality development (Hergenhahn & Olson, 2007). This greater emphasis on cultural influences is one of the major theoretical differences between Freud and the neo-Freudians.

Contemporary Psychodynamic Theories

Some of the most influential psychodynamic approaches to personality now focus on *object relations*—that is, on how people's perceptions of themselves and others influence their view of, and reactions to, the world (Westen et al., 2008). Early object relations theorists including Melanie Klein (1991), Otto Kernberg

© Bettmann/Corbis

An Early Feminist

After completing medical school at the University of Berlin in 1913, Karen Horney (1885–1952) trained as a Freudian psychoanalyst. She accepted some aspects of Freud's views, including the idea of unconscious motivation, but she eventually developed her own neo-Freudian theory. She saw the need for security as more important than biological instincts in motivating infants' behavior. She also rejected Freud's notion that the psychological development of females is influenced by penis envy.

The defense mechanism illustrated in the cartoon on page 561 is displacement.

(1984), Heinz Kohut (1984), and Margaret Mahler (1968) regarded the first relationships between infants and their love objects—usually the mother and other primary caregivers—as vitally important in the development of personality (Klein, 1975; Kohut, 1984; Sohlberg & Jansson, 2002). In their view, these relationships shape a person's thoughts and feelings about social relationships later in life (Westen et al., 2008).

A close cousin of object relations theory is called *attachment theory* because it focuses specifically on the early attachment process. As described in the chapter on human development, the ideal attachment pattern occurs when infants form a secure early bond to their mothers or other caregivers, tolerate gradual separation from this "attachment object," and eventually develop the ability to relate to others as independent, secure individuals (Ainsworth & Bowlby, 1991). Some infants do not develop this *secure attachment,* though. Instead, they may display various kinds of *insecure attachments.* Attachment theorists have found evidence that the nature of people's early attachments is associated with differences in their self-image, identity, security, and social relationships in adolescence, adulthood, and even old age (Mattanah, Hancock, & Brand, 2004; Mikulincer & Shaver, in press; Simpson et al., 2007; Simpson, Rholes, & Winterheld, 2010). In one study, women who had been securely attached in childhood were more likely to have happy marriages than women whose childhood attachments had been insecure (Klohnen & Bera, 1998). In another study, people with insecure attachments were less likely than those with secure attachments to be helpful when they encountered a person in distress (Mikulincer & Shaver, 2005). Further evidence along these lines comes from a long-term study of children diagnosed with severe heart disease. The children whose mothers had not been securely attached to their own mothers tended to show greater evidence of anxiety and other emotional difficulties in the years following the diagnosis than those whose mothers had been more securely attached (Berant, Mikulincer, & Shaver, 2008). In short, attachment theorists suggest that people who miss the opportunity to become securely attached to their mothers or other adults may suffer significant disturbances in their later relationships (Aizawa, 2002), including those with their own children.

Evaluating the Psychodynamic Approach

Freud's personality theory is probably the most comprehensive and influential psychological theory ever proposed, and it has influenced modern Western thinking about medicine, literature, religion, sociology, and anthropology. It has also shaped a wide range of psychotherapy techniques and stimulated the development of several personality assessments, including the projective tests described later in this chapter. Some of Freud's ideas have received support from research on cognitive processes. For example, psychologists have found that people do employ several of the defense mechanisms Freud described (Cramer, 2007), although it is unclear whether these always operate at an unconscious level. As mentioned in the chapter on consciousness, there is also evidence that people's thoughts and actions can be influenced by unrecalled events and experiences (Bargh & Morsella, 2008; Dijksterhuis et al., 2008; Kihlstrom, 2008) and perhaps by emotions that are not consciously felt (Williams et al., 2009). Some researchers believe that unconscious processes may affect people's health (Goldenberg et al., 2008).

However, Freud's psychodynamic theories have several weaknesses. For one thing, they are based almost entirely on case studies of a few individuals. As discussed in the chapter on research in psychology, conclusions drawn from case studies may not apply to people in general. Nor was Freud's sample representative of people in general. Most of his patients were upper-class Viennese women who not only had psychological problems but also were raised in a culture in which discussion of sex was considered to be uncivilized. Moreover, Freud's thinking about personality reflected western European and North American values, which may or may not be helpful in understanding people in other cultures (Schultz & Schultz, 2009). For example, the concepts of ego and self that are so central to Freud's personality theory (and those of his followers) are based on the self-oriented values of individualist cultures. These values may be less central to personality development in the more collectivist cultures of, say, Asia and South America (Morling & Kitayama, 2008).

Freud's conclusions may have been distorted by other biases as well. Freudian scholars suggest, for example, that Freud may have modified reports of what happened during therapy so as to better fit his theory (Esterson, 2001; Schultz & Schultz, 2009). He may also have asked leading questions that influenced patients to "recall" events from childhood that never really happened (Esterson, 2001). Today, as noted in the chapter on memory, there are similar concerns that some patients who recover allegedly repressed memories about childhood sexual abuse by parents may actually be reporting false memories implanted by their therapists (Loftus, Garry & Hayne, 2008).

Freud's focus on male psychosexual development and his notion that females envy male anatomy have also caused feminists of both sexes to reject some or all of his ideas. In the tradition of Horney, some contemporary female neo-Freudians have proposed theories that focus specifically on the psychosexual development of women (Sayers, 1991).

Finally, judged by today's standards, Freud's theory is not very scientific. His definitions of id, ego, unconscious conflict, and other concepts lack the precision required for scientific measurement and testing (Carver & Scheier, 2008). His belief that human beings are driven mainly by unconscious desires ignores evidence that much human behavior goes beyond impulse gratification. The conscious drive to reach personal, social, and spiritual goals is also an important determinant of behavior, as is learning from others.

Some of the weaknesses in Freudian theory have been addressed by theorists who have altered some of Freud's concepts and devoted more attention to social influences on personality. Attempts have also been made to increase precision and objectivity in the measurement of psychodynamic concepts (e.g., Barber, Crits-Christoph, & Paul, 1993). Research on concepts from psychodynamic theory is, in fact, becoming more sophisticated and increasingly reflects interest in subjecting psychodynamic principles to empirical tests (e.g., Betan & Westen, 2009; Roffman & Gerber, 2008; Wegner, Wenzlaff, & Kozak, 2004). Still, the psychodynamic approach is better known for generating hypotheses about personality than for scientifically testing them. Accordingly, this approach to personality is now much less influential in mainstream psychology than it was in the past (Feist & Feist, 2009; Friedman & Schustack, 2009).

The Trait Approach

You could probably describe the personality of someone you know well with just a few statements. For example, you might say, "He is a caring person and a true extravert. He is generous with his time and conscientious about everything he does. Yet sometimes he is not very assertive or confident. He always gives in to other people's demands because he wants to be accepted by them."

In other words, most people describe others by referring to the kinds of people they are ("extravert," "conscientious"); to the thoughts, feelings, and actions that are most typical of them ("caring," "not very assertive," "generous"); or to their needs ("wants to be accepted"). Together these statements describe personality *traits*—the inclinations or tendencies that direct how a person usually thinks and behaves (Pervin, Cervone, & John, 2005).

The **trait approach** to personality makes three basic assumptions:

1. Personality traits are relatively stable and therefore predictable over time. So a gentle person tends to stay that way day after day, year after year (Cervone & Pervin, 2008).

2. Personality traits are relatively stable across situations, and they can explain why people act in predictable ways in many different situations. A person who is competitive at work will probably also be competitive in sports or at a party (Roberts, Woods, & Caspi, 2008).

3. People differ in how much of a particular personality trait they possess; no two people are exactly alike on all traits. The result is an endless variety of unique human personalities.

Traits Versus Types   Theories about enduring differences in people's personality characteristics go back at least as far as Hippocrates, a physician of ancient Greece. He suggested that a certain temperament, or basic behavioral tendency, is associated with each of four bodily fluids, or humors: blood, phlegm, black bile, and yellow bile. Personality, said Hippocrates, depends on how much of each humor a person has. His terms for the four humor-based personalities—*sanguine* (optimistic), *phlegmatic* (slow, lethargic), *melancholic* (sad, depressive), and *choleric* (angry, irritable)—still survive today.

Notice that Hippocrates was describing personality *types,* not traits. Traits involve *quantitative* differences among people—such as how much of a certain characteristic they have. Types involve *qualitative* differences, such as whether someone possesses a certain characteristic at all. When people are "typed," they are said to belong to one class or another—such as male or female. Modern type theories of personality try to do the same by placing people in one category or another (Funder, 2007). For example, some researchers claim to have identified three qualitatively different basic personality types (Caspi, 1998; Hart, Atkins, & Fegley, 2003; van Leeuwen, de Fruyt, & Mervielde, 2004): the *well-adjusted,* or *resilient, person,* who is flexible, resourceful, and successful with other people; the *maladjusted overcontrolling person,* who is too self-controlled to enjoy life and is difficult for others to deal with; and the *maladjusted undercontrolling person,* whose excessive impulsiveness can be dangerous both for the

Selecting a Jury

APPLYING PSYCHOLOGY   Some psychologists employ type and trait theories of personality as they advise prosecution or defense attorneys about which potential jurors are most likely to be sympathetic to their side in a court case.

trait approach   The view that personality is a combination of characteristics that people display over time and across situations.

© John Neubauer/PhotoEdit

person and for others. (This chapter's Focus on Research Methods section contains more information on these and other types.)

Type theories have recently gained acceptance among some personality researchers, but the majority of researchers doubt that it's possible to compress the dazzling range of human characteristics into a just few discrete types (McRae & Costa, 2006). Accordingly, the trait approach to personality remains much more influential. Trait theorists are interested in measuring the relative strength of the many personality characteristics that they believe are present in everyone (see Figure 14.2). Most of today's trait theories of personality have their origins in the work of Gordon Allport, Raymond Cattell, and Hans Eysenck.

Allport's Trait Theory

Gordon Allport spent thirty years searching for the traits that combine to form personality. He found nearly eighteen thousand dictionary terms that can be used to describe human behavior (Allport & Odbert, 1936; John, Naumann, & Soto, 2008), but he noticed that many of these terms referred to the same thing (e.g., *hostile, nasty,* and *mean* all convey a similar meaning). So if you were to jot down the personality traits that describe a close friend or relative, you would probably be able to capture that individual's personality using only about seven trait labels. Allport believed that the set of labels chosen to describe a particular person reflects that person's *central traits*—characteristics that are usually obvious to others and that organize and control behavior in many different situations. Central traits are roughly equivalent to the descriptive terms used in letters of recommendation (*reliable* or *distractible,* for example) that are meant to convey what can be expected from a person most of the time (Schultz & Schultz, 2009). Allport also believed that people possess *secondary traits*—characteristics that are more specific to certain situations and control far less behavior. "Dislikes crowds" is an example of a secondary trait.

FIGURE 14.2
Two Personality Profiles

TRY THIS Trait theory describes personality in terms of the strength of particular dimensions, or traits. Here are trait profiles for Rodney, a social worker, and James, a sales clerk. Compared with James, Rodney is about equally industrious, more generous, and less nervous, extraverted, and aggressive. Just for fun, mark this figure to indicate how strong you think you are on each of the listed traits. Trait theorists suggest that this should be easy for you to do because, they say, virtually everyone displays a certain amount of almost any personality characteristic.

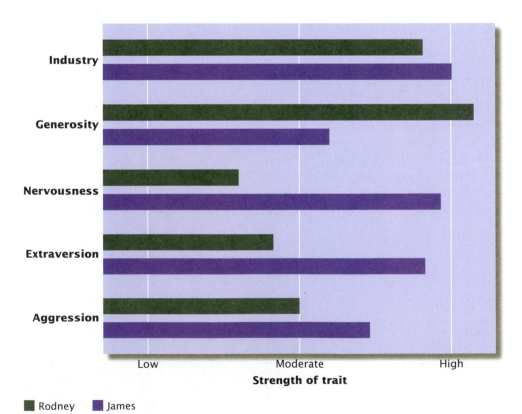

Allport's research helped lay the foundation for modern research on personality traits. And though his emphasis on the uniqueness of each individual personality made it difficult to draw conclusions about the structure of human personality in general (Barenbaum & Winter, 2008), some researchers today continue to employ a modern version of Allport's approach (e.g., Caldwell, Cervone, & Rubin, 2008).

The Five-Factor Personality Model

In recent years, trait approaches have continued to focus on identifying and describing a core structure of personality that appears in everyone. This work owes much to Allport and also to a British psychologist named Raymond Cattell (pronounced "kuh-TEL"). Cattell asked people to rate themselves and others on many of the trait-descriptive terms that Allport had identified. He then used a mathematical technique called *factor analysis* to study which of these terms were related to one another. Factor analysis can reveal, for example, whether someone who is moody is also likely to be anxious, rigid, and unsociable. Cattell believed that the sets of traits clustering together in this analysis would reflect a set of basic personality *factors* or dimensions. His analyses eventually identified sixteen such factors, including shy versus bold, trusting versus suspicious, and relaxed versus tense. Cattell believed that these factors can be found in everyone, and he measured their strength using a test called the Sixteen Personality Factor Questionnaire, or 16PF (Cattell, Eber, & Tatsuoka, 1970).

More recent factor analyses by researchers such as Paul Costa and Robert McCrae (2008) have led many trait theorists to believe that personality is organized around only five basic factors. The components of this **five-factor personality model** (also known as the **Big Five model**) are *openness to experience, conscientiousness, extraversion, agreeableness,* and *neuroticism* (see Table 14.2). The importance of the five-factor model is suggested by the fact that different investigators find these factors (or a set very similar to them) when they factor-analyze data from personality inventories, peer ratings of personality characteristics, checklists of descriptive adjectives, and many other sources (John, Naumann, & Soto, 2008; McCrae & Costa, 2008). The fact that some version of the Big Five factors reliably appears in many countries and cultures—including Canada, China, the Czech Republic, Germany, Greece, Finland, India, Japan, Korea, the Philippines, Poland, Turkey, and Zimbabwe (Ashton et al., 2004; Heine & Buchtel, 2009; McCrae & Costa, 2006; Yamagata et al., 2006)—provides further evidence that these few dimensions may represent the most important components of human personality (McCrae, Terracciano, & Personality Profiles of Cultures Project, 2005).

Five-factor personality model (Big Five model) A view based on factor-analytic studies suggesting the existence of five basic components of human personality: openness, conscientiousness, extraversion, agreeableness, and neuroticism.

TABLE 14.2 Dimensions of the Five-Factor Personality Model

Here is a list of the adjectives that define the Big Five personality factors. It will be easier to remember these factors if you notice that the first letters of their names spell the word *ocean*.

Dimension	Defining Descriptors
Openness to experience	Artistic, curious, imaginative, insightful, original; having wide interests, unusual thought processes, intellectual interests
Conscientiousness	Efficient, organized, planful, reliable, thorough, dependable, ethical, productive
Extraversion	Active, assertive, energetic, outgoing, talkative, gesturally expressive, gregarious
Agreeableness	Appreciative, forgiving, generous, kind, trusting, noncritical, warm, compassionate, considerate, straightforward
Neuroticism	Anxious, self-pitying, tense, emotionally unstable, impulsive, vulnerable, touchy, worrying

Source: Adapted from McCrae & John (1992).

Animal Personalities

The idea that personality can be described in terms of five main dimensions seems to hold for some animals as well as humans. The five animal dimensions vary from human traits but are related to them. For example, hyenas differ from one another in terms of dominance, excitability, agreeableness (toward people), sociability (toward each other), and curiosity. Some of these same traits have been observed in a wide variety of other species, including sheep, langurs, orangutans, chipmunks, chimpanzees, and even fish (Bell & Sih, 2007; Gosling, 2001; King, Weiss, & Farmer, 2005; Konecná et al., 2008; Martin & Réale, 2008; Michelana et al., 2009; Weiss, King, & Perkins, 2006). Dog and cat lovers often report such traits in their pets, too (Gosling, Kwan, & John, 2003; Lee, Ryan, & Kreiner, 2007; Ley, Bennett, & Coleman, 2009).

© Robert Caputo/Aurora Photos

Many trait theorists believe that the five-factor model represents a major breakthrough in examining the personalities of people who come from different backgrounds, differ in age, and live in different parts of the world (John, Naumann, & Soto, 2008). It has certainly enabled psychologists to provide a comprehensive description of the basic similarities and differences in people's personalities and to explore how these factors are related to everything from attachment styles, social skills, and personality disorders to happiness, academic performance, physical well-being, and even future weight gain (e.g., Brummett et al., 2006; Cuperman & Ickes, 2009; Diener, 2000; Lynam & Widiger, 2001; Noftle & Shaver, 2006; Poropat, 2009; Roberts et al., 2009).

Biological Trait Theories

Some personality theorists are interested not only in what traits form the core of human personality but also in why people differ on these traits. Their research suggests that trait differences reflect the operation of some important biological factors (DeYoung et al., 2010; Terracciano et al., 2010).

Eysenck's Biological Trait Theory   Like Cattell, the British psychologist Hans Eysenck (pronounced "EYE-sink") used factor analysis to study the structure of personality and thus helped lay the groundwork for the five-factor personality model. Eysenck suggested that most people's traits could be described using two main dimensions—*introversion-extraversion* and *emotionality-stability* (Eysenck 1990a, 1990b; see Figure 14.3):

1. *Introversion–extraversion.* Extraverts are sociable and outgoing, enjoy parties and other group activities, take risks, and love excitement and change. Introverts tend to be quiet, thoughtful, and reserved, enjoying solitary pursuits and avoiding excitement and social involvement.

2. *Emotionality–stability.* At one extreme of the emotionality–stability dimension are people who display such characteristics as moodiness, restlessness, worry, anxiety, and other negative emotions. Those at the opposite extreme are calm, even-tempered, relaxed, and emotionally stable. (This dimension is also often called *neuroticism.*)

FIGURE 14.3
Eysenck's Main Personality Dimensions

TRY THIS According to Eysenck, varying degrees of emotionality–stability and introversion–extraversion combine to produce predictable trait patterns. Notice that an introverted but stable person is likely to be controlled and reliable, whereas an introverted emotional person is likely to be rigid and anxious. (The traits appearing in the quadrants created by crossing these two personality dimensions correspond roughly to Hippocrates' four temperaments.) Which section of the figure do you think best describes your personality traits? How about those of a friend or a relative? Did you find it any easier to place other people's personalities in a particular section than it was to place your own personality? If so, why do you think that might be?

Source: Eysenck, H.J., Rachman, S. *The Causes and Cures of Neurosis: An Introduction to Modern Behavior Therapy Based on Learning Theory and the Principle of Conditioning.* Copyright © 1965. Edits. Reprinted with permission.

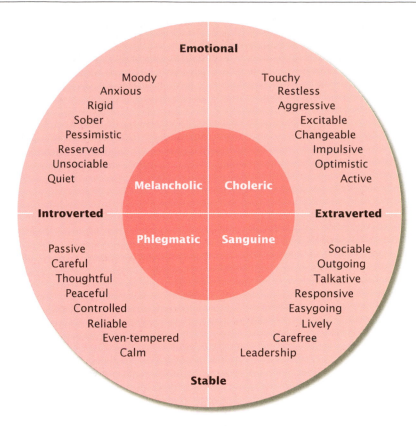

Eysenck argued that the variations in personality characteristics that we see among individuals can be traced to inherited differences in their nervous systems, especially in their brains. These biological differences, he said, create variations in people's typical levels of physiological arousal and in their sensitivity to stress and other environmental stimulation. For example, as mentioned in the motivation and emotion chapter, people who inherit a nervous system that normally operates below their optimum arousal level will always be on the lookout for excitement, change, and social contact in order to increase their arousal. As a result, these people will be *extraverted*. In contrast, people whose nervous system is normally "overaroused" will tend to avoid excitement, change, and social contact in order to reduce arousal to their optimum level. In short, they will be *introverted*. What about the emotionality–stability dimension? Eysenck said that people who score toward the stability side have nervous systems that are relatively insensitive to stress; those who are more emotional have nervous systems that react more strongly to stress.

Gray's Reinforcement Sensitivity Theory Jeffrey Gray, another British psychologist, agrees with Eysenck about the two basic dimensions of personality, but he offers a different explanation of the biological factors underlying them (Corr, 2002; DeYoung et al., 2010; Gray & McNaughton, 2000). According to Gray's *reinforcement sensitivity theory*, differences among people in introversion–extraversion and emotionality–stability originate in brain regions containing systems that influence how sensitive people are to different kinds of events: the behavioral approach system and the flight or freeze system (Pickering & Gray, 1999). The *behavioral approach system*, or *BAS*, affects people's sensitivity to rewards and their motivation to seek those rewards. The BAS has been called a "go" system because it is responsible for how impulsive or uninhibited a person is. The *flight or freeze system*, or *FSS*, affects how sensitive people are to potential punishment and the motivation to avoid being punished (Smillie, Pickering, & Jackson, 2006). The FSS is a "stop" system that is responsible for how fearful or inhibited a person is (Bijttebier et al., 2009).

In explaining Eysenck's personality dimensions, Gray sees extraverts as having a sensitive reward system (BAS) and an insensitive punishment system (FSS). Introverts are just the opposite—they are relatively insensitive to rewards but highly sensitive to punishment. Similarly, emotionally unstable people are much more sensitive to both rewards and punishments than those who are emotionally stable.

Gray's theory has its critics (e.g., Jackson, 2003; Matthews, 2008), but it is now more widely accepted than Eysenck's theory—primarily because it is being supported by other research (e.g., Revelle, 2008) and because it is more consistent with what neuroscientists know about brain structures, neurotransmitters, and how they operate (Buckholtz et al., 2008; Joseph et al., 2009; Read et al., 2010; Reuter et al., 2006).

THINKING CRITICALLY

Are Personality Traits Inherited?

Gray's reinforcement sensitivity theory is one of several new biologically oriented explanations of the origins of personality traits (e.g., Depue, 2007). A related approach involves investigating the genetics of these traits (e.g., Joyce et al., 2009; Terracciano et al., 2010). Consider the case of identical twins who were separated at 5 weeks of age and did not meet again for thirty-nine years. Both men drove Chevrolets, chain-smoked the same brand of cigarettes, had been divorced from women named Linda, had remarried women named Betty, had sons named James Allan, had dogs named Toy, enjoyed similar hobbies, and had served as sheriff's deputies (Tellegen et al., 1988).

What am I being asked to believe or accept?

Case studies like these have helped focus the attention of behavioral geneticists on the possibility that some core aspects of personality may be partly, or even largely, inherited (Johnson et al., 2009; Kreuger & Johnson, 2008; Yamagata et al. 2006).

What evidence is available to support the assertion?

The evidence and the arguments regarding this assertion are much like those presented in the chapter on cognitive abilities, in which we discuss the origins of differences in intelligence. Stories about children who seem to have their parents' or grandparents' bad temper, generosity, or shyness are often presented in support of the heritability of personality. And in fact, family resemblances in personality do provide an important source of evidence. Several studies have found moderate but significant correlations between children's personality test scores and those of their parents and siblings (Davis, Luce, & Kraus, 1994; DeYoung, Quilty, & Peterson, 2007; Loehlin et al., 1998).

Even stronger evidence comes from studies conducted around the world comparing identical twins raised together, identical twins raised apart, nonidentical twins raised together, and nonidentical twins raised apart (Larsen & Buss, 2010). Whether they are raised apart or together, identical twins (who have exactly the same genes) tend to be more alike in personality than nonidentical twins (whose genes are no more similar than those of other siblings). This research also shows that identical twins are more alike than nonidentical twins in general temperament, such as how active, sociable, anxious, and emotional they are, their positive attributes, and where they fall on the Big Five personality dimensions (e.g., Borkenau et al., 2006; Johnson et al., 2009). On the basis of such twin studies, behavioral geneticists have concluded that about 50 percent of the differences among people in terms of personality traits are due to genetic factors (Kreuger et al., 2008).

Are there alternative ways of interpreting the evidence?

Family resemblances in personality could reflect genetic or social influence. So an obvious alternative interpretation of this evidence might be that family similarities come not from common genes but from a common environment, especially from the examples set by parents and siblings. Children learn many rules, skills, and actions by

Family Resemblance

Do children inherit personality traits in the same direct way as they inherit facial features, coloration, and other physical characteristics? Research in behavioral genetics suggests that personality is the joint product of genetically influenced behavioral tendencies and the environmental conditions each child encounters.

© Rosanne Olson/Taxi/Getty Images

watching the people around them; perhaps children learn their personalities as well (Funder, 2007). The fact that siblings who aren't twins are less alike than twins may well result from what are called *nonshared environments* (Plomin, 2004). A child's place in the family birth order, differences in the way parents treat each of their children, and accidents and illnesses that alter a particular child's life or health are examples of nonshared factors that can have a differential impact on each individual (Loehlin, Neiderhiser, & Reiss, 2003). Nontwins are more likely than twins, especially identical twins, to be affected by nonshared environmental factors.

What additional evidence would help evaluate the alternatives?

One way to evaluate the idea that personality is inherited would be to locate genes that are associated with certain personality characteristics (Ebstein, 2006). Genetic differences have already been tentatively associated with certain behavior disorders, but most behavioral genetics researchers doubt that there are direct links between specific genes and particular personality traits (Kreuger & Johnson, 2008; Caspi, Roberts, & Shiner, 2005).

Another way to evaluate the role of genes in personality is to study people in infancy, before the environment has had a chance to exert its influence. If the environment were entirely responsible for personality, all newborns should be essentially alike. However, as discussed in the chapter on human development, they show immediate differences in *temperament*—varying markedly in activity, sensitivity to the environment, tendency to cry, and interest in new stimuli (Rothbart & Derryberry, 2002). These differences suggest biological and perhaps genetic influences.

To evaluate the relative contributions of nature and nurture beyond infancy, psychologists have examined the characteristics of adopted children. If adopted children are more like their biological parents than their adoptive parents, this suggests the influence of heredity in personality. If they are more like their adoptive families, a strong role for environmental factors in personality would be suggested. In actuality, adopted children's personalities tend to resemble the personalities of their biological parents and siblings more than those of the families in which they are raised (Kreuger & Johnson, 2008).

Further research is needed to determine more clearly what aspects of the environment are most important in shaping personality. So far, the evidence suggests that elements in the shared environment that affect all children in the family to varying degrees (socioeconomic status, for example) are probably not the main reason that identical twins show similar personalities. As mentioned earlier, however, nonshared environmental influences may be very important in personality development (Kendler & Neale, 2009). In fact, some researchers believe that nonshared influences must be considered even when trying to explain the greater similarities between identical twins reared apart than among nontwin siblings reared together. Additional research on the role of nonshared factors in personality development and the ways in which these factors might differentially affect twin and nontwin siblings' development is obviously vital. It will also be important to investigate the ways in which the personalities of individual children may affect the nature of the environment in which they are raised (Krueger, Markon, & Bouchard, 2003; see also the behavioral genetics appendix).

What conclusions are most reasonable?

Even researchers who support genetic theories of personality caution that we should not replace "simpleminded environmentalism" with the equally incorrect view that personality is almost completely biologically determined (Plomin & Crabbe, 2000). As with cognitive abilities, it is pointless to talk about heredity *versus* environment as causes of personality because nature and nurture always intertwine to exert joint and simultaneous influences. For example, we know that genetic factors affect the environment in which people live (e.g., their families) and how they react to their environment, but research in *epigenetics* has shown that environmental factors can influence which of a person's genes are activated (or "expressed") and how much those genes affect the person's behavior (see the chapter on research in psychology; Champagne & Mashoodh, 2009; Kreuger & Johnson, 2008).

With these findings in mind, it is best to draw rather tentative conclusions about the sources of differences in people's personalities. The evidence available so far suggests that genetic influences do appear to contribute significantly to personality differences. However, it is important to understand the implications of this statement. There is still no evidence that there is any single gene for any specific personality trait (Kreuger & Johnson, 2008). The genetic contribution to personality most likely comes through the influence of *sets* of genes that shape people's nervous systems and thus influence their general predispositions toward certain temperaments (Arbelle et al., 2003; Ebstein, 2006; Grigorenko, 2002). Temperamental factors—such as how active, emotional, and sociable a person is—then combine with environmental factors, such as a person's interactions with other people, to produce specific features of personality (Caspi, Roberts, & Shiner, 2005). For example, children who inherit a tendency toward emotionality might play less with other children, withdraw from social interactions, and thereby fail to learn important social skills (Spinrad et al, 2006). These experiences and tendencies, in turn, might lead to the self-consciousness and shyness seen in introverted personalities. Genes also appear to influence people's emotional responses to specific events, such as having a child or being socially rejected (Dornbos et al., 2009; Way, Taylor, & Eisenberger, 2009).

Notice, though, that genetic predispositions toward particular personality characteristics may or may not appear in behavior, depending on whether the environment supports or suppresses them. Changes in genetically influenced traits are not only possible but may actually be quite common as children grow (Cacioppo et al., 2000). So even though there is a strong genetic basis for shyness, many children learn to overcome this tendency and become rather outgoing (Leary, 2001). In summary, it appears that rather than inheriting specific traits, people inherit the raw materials out of which personality is shaped by the world.

Evaluating the Trait Approach

The trait approach, especially the five-factor personality model, has gained such wide acceptance that it tends to dominate contemporary research into personality. Yet there are several problems and weaknesses associated with this approach.

For one thing, trait theories seem better at describing people than at understanding them. It is easy to say, for example, that Marilyn is nasty to others because she has a strong hostility trait; but other factors, such as the way people treat her, could also be responsible. Indeed, trait theories have typically focused more on *how* people behave than on *why* they act as they do (Mischel, 2004a, 2004b). Nor do trait theories say much about how traits are related to the thoughts and feelings that precede, accompany, and follow behavior. Do introverts and extraverts decide to act as they do, can they behave otherwise, and how do they feel about their actions and experiences? Some personality psychologists are now linking their research to that of cognitive psychologists in an effort to better understand how thoughts and emotions influence, and are influenced by, personality traits (e.g., Shoda & LeeTiernan, 2002). And as suggested in the Thinking Critically discussion, other psychologists have become interested in the role of genes, brain structures, and neurotransmitters as causes of the individual differences we see among people's personality traits (e.g., Canli, 2008; Netter, 2006).

Still, the trait approach has been faulted for offering a short list of traits that provides, at best, a fixed and superficial description of personality that fails to capture how traits combine to form a complex and dynamic individual (Block, 2001; Funder, 2007). Also, some people have questioned whether there are exactly five core dimensions of personality. Some research suggests, for example, that there might be a sixth dimension, involving honesty and humility (Lee, Ogunfowora, & Ashton, 2005). Others have questioned whether the factors are exactly the same in all cultures (De Raad et al., 2010; Heine & Buchtel, 2009). But even if the five-factor model is correct and universal, its factors are not all-powerful because situations also affect behavior. For example, people high in extraversion are not always sociable. Whether they behave sociably depends in part on where they are and who else is present.

In fairness, early trait theorists such as Allport did implicitly acknowledge the importance of situations in influencing behavior, but it is only recently that consideration of person-situation interactions has become an explicit part of trait-based approaches to personality. This change is largely the result of research conducted by psychologists who have taken a social-cognitive approach to personality, which we describe next.

The Social-Cognitive Approach

The **social-cognitive approach** to personality differs from the psychodynamic and trait approaches in two important ways. First, social-cognitive theorists look to *conscious* thoughts and emotions for clues to how people differ from one another and what guides their behavior (Mischel & Shoda, 2008). Second, the social-cognitive approach did not grow out of clinical cases or other descriptions of people's personalities. It was based instead on the principles of animal and human learning described in the chapter on learning. In fact, the founders of the social-cognitive approach were originally known as *social-learning theorists* because of their view that what we call "personality" consists mainly of the thoughts and actions we learn through observing and interacting with family and others in social situations (Bandura & Walters, 1963; Cervone & Pervin, 2008).

Roots of the Social-Cognitive Approach

social-cognitive approach The view that personality reflects learned patterns of thinking and behavior.

functional analysis Analyzing behavior by studying what responses occur under what conditions of operant reward and punishment.

Elements of the social-cognitive approach can be traced back to the behaviorism of John B. Watson. As described in the chapter on introducing psychology, Watson (1925) used research on classical conditioning to support his claim that all human behavior is determined by learning. B. F. Skinner broadened the behavioral approach by emphasizing the importance of operant conditioning in learning. Through what he called **functional analysis**, Skinner tried to understand behavior in terms of the function it serves in obtaining rewards or avoiding punishment. For example, if observations show that a schoolboy's aggressive behavior occurs mainly when a certain teacher is present, it may be that aggression is tolerated by that teacher and may even be rewarded with special attention. Rather than describing personality traits, then, functional analysis summarizes what people find rewarding, what they are capable of doing, and what skills they lack.

The principles of classical and operant conditioning launched social-learning explanations of personality, but because they were focused on observable behavior, they were of limited usefulness to researchers who wanted to explore the role of thoughts in guiding behavior. As the social-learning approach evolved into the social-cognitive approach, it incorporated learning principles but also went beyond them.

Today, proponents of this very popular approach to personality seek to assess and understand how learned patterns of thoughts and feelings contribute to behavior and how behavior and its consequences alter cognitive activity, as well as future actions. In dealing with that aggressive schoolboy, for example, social-cognitive theorists would want to know not only what he has learned to do in certain situations (and how he learned it) but also what he thinks about himself, his teachers, and his behavior—and his expectations about each (Shoda & Mischel, 2006).

Prominent Social-Cognitive Theories

Julian Rotter, Albert Bandura, and Walter Mischel have presented the most influential social-cognitive personality theories.

Rotter's Expectancy Theory   Julian Rotter (1982) argued that learning creates cognitions, known as *expectancies,* that guide behavior. Specifically, he said that a person's decision to engage in a behavior is determined by what the person expects to happen following the behavior and the value the person places on the outcome. For example, people spend lots of money on new clothes to be worn at job interviews, first because they have learned to expect that doing so will help get them the job and also because they place a high value on having the job. To Rotter, then, behavior is determined not only by the kinds of consequences that Skinner called *positive reinforcers* but also by the expectation that a particular behavior will result in those consequences (Mischel, 2004b).

Rotter himself focused mainly on how expectations shape particular behaviors in particular situations, but several of the researchers he influenced also examined people's more general expectations about what controls life's rewards and punishments. Those researchers noticed that some people (whom they called *internals*) are inclined to expect events to be controlled by their own efforts. These individuals assume that what they achieve and the reinforcements they receive are due to efforts they make themselves. Others (*externals*) are more inclined to expect events to be determined by external forces over which they have no control. When externals succeed, they are likely to believe that their success was due to chance or luck.

Research on differences in generalized expectancies does show that they are correlated with differences in behavior. For example, when threatened by a hurricane or other natural disaster, internals—in accordance with their belief that they can control what happens to them—are more likely than externals to buy bottled water and make other preparations (Sattler, Kaiser, & Hittner, 2000). When confronted with a personal problem, internals are more likely than externals to work to solve this problem. Externals are more likely to regard it as unsolvable (Gianakos, 2002). Internals also tend to work harder than externals at staying physically healthy and as a result may be healthier than externals (Stürmer, Hasselbach, & Amelang, 2006). We know, for example, that children with an internal control orientation are less likely than externals to become obese in later life (Gale, Batty, & Deary, 2008). Internals also tend to be more careful with money (Lim, Teo, & Loo, 2003). As college students, internals tend to be better informed about the courses they take, including what they need to do to

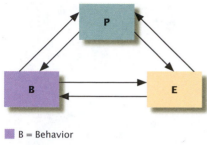

■ B = Behavior

■ E = The external environment

■ P = Personal factors, such as thoughts, feelings, and biological events

FIGURE 14.4
Reciprocal Determinism

Albert Bandura's notion of reciprocal determinism suggests that personal factors (such as cognitions, or thoughts), behavior, and the environment are constantly affecting one another. For example, a person's hostile thoughts may lead to hostile behavior, which gives rise to even more hostile thoughts. At the same time, the hostile behavior offends other people, which creates a threatening environment that causes the person to think and act in even more negative ways. As increasingly negative thoughts alter the person's perceptions of the environment, that environment seems to be more threatening than ever (Bushman et al., 2005).

Source: A. Bandura, "The Assessment And Predictive Generality Of Self-Percepts Of Efficacy". *Journal of Behavior Therapy and Experimental Psychiatry,* vol. 13, pp. 195–199. Copyright © 1982. Reprinted with permission from Elsevier.

self-efficacy According to Albert Bandura, learned expectations about the probability of success in given situations.

get a high grade. Perhaps as a result, internals tend to get better grades and to graduate sooner than externals (Dollinger, 2000; Hall, Smith, & Chia, 2008).

Bandura and Reciprocal Determinism   In his social-cognitive theory, Albert Bandura (1999, 2006) sees personality as shaped by the ways in which thoughts, behavior, and the environment influence one another. He points out that regardless of whether people learn through direct experience with rewards and punishments or through the observational learning processes described in the chapter on learning, their behavior causes changes in their environment. Observing these changes in turn affects how they think, which then affects their behavior, and so on in a constant web of mutual influence that Bandura calls *reciprocal determinism* (see Figure 14.4).

According to Bandura, an especially important cognitive element in this web of influence is perceived **self-efficacy**—the learned expectation of success. Bandura says that what we do, and what we try to do, is largely controlled by our perceptions or beliefs about our chances of success at a particular task or problem. The higher our perceived self-efficacy in relation to a particular situation or task, the greater our actual accomplishments in that situation or task (Greven et al., 2009; Zimmerman & Schunk, 2003). So going into a job interview with the belief that you have the skills necessary to be hired may lead to behaviors that help you get the job.

Expectancies about succeeding at a specific task can interact with expectancies about the consequences of behavior in general, thus helping shape the person's psychological well-being (Maddux & Gosselin, 2003). For example, if a person has low perceived self-efficacy about getting a better job and also expects that nothing anyone does has much effect on the world, the result may be apathy. But if a person with low perceived self-efficacy about a new job also believes that other people are enjoying the benefits of their efforts, the result may be self-criticism and depression.

Mischel's Cognitive-Affective Theory   Social-cognitive theorists argue that learned beliefs, feelings, and expectancies characterize each individual and make that individual different from other people. Walter Mischel calls these characteristics *cognitive person variables,* and he believes that they outline the dimensions along which individuals differ (Mischel, 2009).

According to Mischel, the most important cognitive person variables are *encodings* (beliefs about the world and other people), *expectancies* (including self-efficacy and what can be expected following various actions), *affects* (feelings and emotions), *goals and values* (what a person believes in and wants to achieve), and *competencies and self-regulatory plans* (the things a person can do and the ability to thoughtfully plan and control goal-directed behavior) (Shoda & Mischel, 2006).

To predict a person's behavior in a particular situation, says Mischel, we need to know about these cognitive person variables, as well as about the features of the situation the person will face. In short, the person and the situation interact to produce behavior. Mischel's view has been called an "if-then" theory because he proposes that *if* people encounter a particular situation, *then* they will engage in the characteristic behaviors (called *behavioral signatures*) they have learned to display in that situation (Kammrath, Mendoza-Denton, & Mischel, 2005).

Mischel was once highly critical of trait theories of personality but now regards his own theory as generally consistent with that approach. In fact, the concept of behavioral signatures is quite similar to the concept of traits. However, Mischel still argues that trait theorists underestimate the power of situations to alter behavior and do not pay enough attention to the cognitive and emotional processes that underlie people's overt actions. Despite their remaining differences, most advocates of the trait and social-cognitive approaches are now focusing on the similarities between their views (Cervone, 2005; Funder, 2008). This trend toward reconciliation has clarified somewhat the relationship between personal and situational variables and how they

The Impact of Situations

Arnold Schwarzenegger's behavior as an actor in the *Terminator* movies differed greatly from his behavior as the governor of California. Mischel's theory of personality emphasizes that person-situation interactions are vitally important in determining the behavior of everyone in a given environment.

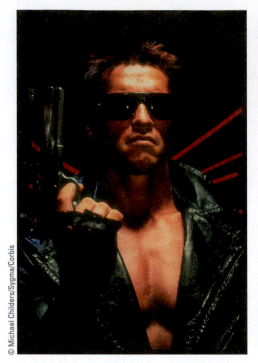

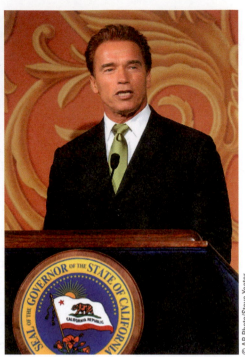

affect behavior under various conditions. Many of the conclusions that have emerged are consistent with Bandura's concept of reciprocal determinism:

1. Personal dispositions (which include traits and cognitive person variables) influence behavior only in relevant situations. The trait of anxiousness, for example, may predict anxiety, but only in situations in which an anxious person feels threatened.

2. Personal dispositions can lead to behaviors that alter situations, and those altered situations in turn promote other behaviors. For example, a hostile child can trigger aggression in others and thus start a fight.

3. People choose to be in situations that are in tune with their personal dispositions. Introverts, for instance, are likely to choose quiet environments, whereas extraverts tend to seek out livelier, more social ones (Beck & Clark, 2009).

4. Personal dispositions are more important in some situations than in others. Under circumstances in which many different behaviors would all be appropriate—a company picnic, for example—what people do may be predicted from their dispositions (extraverts will probably play games and socialize while introverts watch). However, in situations such as a funeral, in which fewer options are socially acceptable, personal dispositions will not differentiate one person from another; everyone is likely to be quiet and somber.

Today, social-cognitive theorists devote much of their research to examining how cognitive person variables develop, how they are related to stress and health, and how they interact with situational variables to affect behavior.

Evaluating the Social-Cognitive Approach

The original behavioral view of personality appealed to many people. It offered an objective, experimentally oriented approach that operationally defined its concepts, relied on empirical data for its basic principles, and based its applications on the results of empirical research (Pervin, Cervone, & John, 2005). However, its successor, the social-cognitive approach, has gained even wider acceptance because it blends theories from behavioral and cognitive psychology and applies them to such socially important areas as aggression, the effects of mass media on children, and the development of self-regulatory processes that enhance personal control over behavior. The popularity of this approach also stems from the ease with which its principles can be translated into treatment procedures for many types of psychological disorders (O'Donohue, Fisher, & Hayes, 2003; see the chapter on treatment of psychological disorders).

Still, the social-cognitive approach has not escaped criticism. Psychodynamic theorists point out that social-cognitive theories leave no role for unconscious thoughts and feelings in determining behaviors (e.g., Westen et al., 2008). Some advocates of trait theory complain that social-cognitive theorists have focused more on explaining why traits are unimportant than on why situations are important and that they have failed to identify what it is about specific situations that brings out certain behaviors (Funder, 2008). The social-cognitive approach has also been faulted for failing to present a general theory of personality, offering instead a set of more limited theories that share certain common assumptions about the nature of personality (Feist & Feist, 2009). Most generally, the social-cognitive approach is considered incapable of capturing the complexity, richness, and uniqueness that some critics see as inherent in human personality (Carver & Scheier, 2008). According to these critics, a far more attractive alternative is provided by the humanistic psychology approach to personality.

The Humanistic Psychology Approach

Unlike theories that emphasize the instincts and learning processes that humans seem to share with other animals, the **humanistic psychology approach** to personality focuses on mental capabilities that set humans apart: self-awareness, creativity, planning, decision making, and responsibility. Theorists who adopt the humanistic approach see human behavior as motivated mainly by an innate drive toward growth that prompts people to fulfill their unique potential. And like the planted seed whose natural potential is to become a flower, people are seen as naturally inclined toward goodness, creativity, love, and joy. Humanistic psychologists also believe that to explain people's actions in any particular situation, it is more important to understand their view of the world than their instincts, traits, or learning experiences. To humanists,

humanistic psychology approach The view that personality develops through an actualizing tendency that unfolds in accordance with each person's unique perceptions of the world.

What Is Reality?

Each of these people has a different perception of what happened during the play that started this argument—and each is sure he is right! Disagreement about the "same" event illustrates *phenomenology*, each person's unique perceptions of the world. The humanistic psychology approach holds that these perceptions shape personality and guide behavior. As described in the perception chapter, our perceptions are often influenced by top-down processing. In this case, expectations and motivation stemming from differing loyalties are likely to influence reality—and reactions—for each team's players, coaches, and fans.

that worldview is a bit different for each of us, and it is this unique *phenomenology* (pronounced "fuh-nahm-uh-NAHL-uh-jee"), or way of perceiving and interpreting the world, that shapes personality and guides behavior (Kelly, 1980). From this perspective, then, no one can understand another person without somehow perceiving the world through that person's eyes. All behavior, even seemingly weird behavior, is presumed to be meaningful to the person displaying it. Because it emphasizes the importance of looking at people's perceptions, this approach is sometimes called the *phenomenological approach*.

The humanistic psychology approach to personality has many roots. The idea that each person perceives a different reality reflects the views of existential philosophers such as Søren Kierkegaard and Jean-Paul Sartre. The idea that people actively shape their own reality stems in part from the Gestalt psychologists, whose work is described in the chapter on perception, and from George Kelly, a psychologist who also influenced social-cognitive theorists. We can also hear echoes of Alfred Adler, Erich Fromm, and other psychodynamic theorists who emphasized the positive aspects of human nature and the importance of the ego in personality development. Humanistic theories of personality have themselves helped fuel research in positive psychology, which focuses on character strengths such as wisdom, courage, and humanity, as well as on happiness, thriving, and other aspects of human experience associated with maximum personal development and functioning (Peterson, 2006a; Fredrickson & Cohn, 2008; Seligman, 2002).

Prominent Humanistic Theories

By far the most prominent humanistic theories of personality are those of Carl Rogers and Abraham Maslow.

Rogers's Self Theory   In his extensive writings, Carl Rogers (e.g., 1961, 1970, 1980) emphasized the **actualizing tendency**, which he described as an innate inclination toward growth and fulfillment that motivates all human behavior and is expressed in a unique way by each individual (Raskin & Rogers, 2001). Rogers considered personality the expression of that actualizing tendency as it unfolds in each individual's uniquely perceived reality (Feist & Feist, 2009). The centerpiece of Rogers's theory is the *self*, the part of experience that a person identifies as "I" or "me." According to Rogers, those who accurately experience the self—with all its preferences, abilities, fantasies, shortcomings, and desires—are on the road to what Kurt Goldstein (1939) had called *self-actualization*. For people whose experiences of the self become distorted, however, progress toward self-actualization is likely to be slowed or stopped.

Rogers saw personality development beginning early, as children learn to need other people's approval, or as he called it, *positive regard*. Evaluations by parents, teachers, and others soon begin to affect children's self-evaluations. When these evaluations are in agreement with a child's own self-evaluations, the child reacts in a way that matches, or is *congruent* with, self-experience. The child not only experiences positive regard but also evaluates the self as "good" for having earned approval. This positive self-experience becomes part of the **self-concept**, which is the way one thinks of oneself. But what if a positive self-experience is evaluated negatively by others, as when a little boy is teased by his father for having fun playing with dolls? In this case, the child must either do without a parent's positive regard or, more likely, reevaluate the self-experience—deciding perhaps that "I don't like dolls" or "Feeling good is bad."

In other words, said Rogers, personality is shaped partly by the actualizing tendency and partly by evaluations made by others. In this way, people come to like what they are "supposed" to like and to behave as they are "supposed" to behave. This socialization process is adaptive, because it helps people function in society, but it often requires that they suppress their self-actualizing tendency and distort their experience. Rogers argued that psychological discomfort, anxiety, or even mental disorder can result when the feelings people experience or express are *incongruent*, or at odds, with their true feelings.

actualizing tendency   According to Carl Rogers, an innate inclination toward growth that motivates all people.

self-concept   The way one thinks of oneself.

Parents are not usually this obvious about creating conditions of worth, but according to Carl Rogers, the message gets through in many more subtle ways.

"Just remember, son, it doesn't matter whether you win or lose—unless you want Daddy's love."

Incongruence is likely, said Rogers, when parents and teachers act in ways that lead children to believe that their worth as people depends on displaying the "right" attitudes, behaviors, and values. These **conditions of worth** are created whenever *people* are evaluated instead of their behavior. For example, parents who find their toddler smearing fingerpaint on the dog are unlikely to say, "I love you, but I don't approve of this particular behavior." They are more likely to shout, "Bad boy!" or "Bad girl!" This reaction sends a message that the child is lovable and worthwhile only when well behaved. As a result, the child's self-experience is not "I like painting Fang, but Mom and Dad don't approve," but instead, "Playing with paint is bad, and I am bad if I like it, so I don't like it," or "I like it, so I must be bad." The child may eventually display overly neat and tidy behaviors that do not reflect the real self but rather are part of the ideal self that is dictated by the parents.

As with Freud's concept of superego, conditions of worth are first set up by external pressure but eventually become part of the person's belief system. So Rogers considered rewards and punishments important in personality development not just because they shape overt behavior but also because they can so easily lead to distorted self-perceptions and incongruence (Roth et al., 2009).

Maslow's Growth Theory   Like Rogers, Abraham Maslow (1954, 1971) regarded personality as the expression of a basic human tendency toward growth and self-actualization. In fact, Maslow believed that self-actualization is not just a human capacity but a human need. As described in the motivation and emotion chapter, he placed self-actualization as the highest in a hierarchy of motives, or needs. Yet, said Maslow, people are often distracted from seeking self-actualization because they focus on needs that are lower on the hierarchy.

Maslow believed that most people are controlled by **deficiency motivation**, the preoccupation with perceived needs for material things, especially things they do not have. Ultimately, he said, deficiency-motivated people come to see life as a meaningless exercise in disappointment and boredom, and they may begin to behave in problematic ways. For example, in an attempt to satisfy the need for love and belongingness, people may focus on what love can give them (security) and not on what they can give

conditions of worth According to Carl Rogers, the feelings an individual experiences when an evaluation is applied to the person rather than to the person's behavior.

deficiency motivation According to Abraham Maslow, a preoccupation with perceived needs for things a person does not have.

The Joys of Growth Motivation

According to Abraham Maslow's theory of personality, the key to personal growth and fulfillment lies in focusing on what we have, not on what we don't have or on what we have lost. Rachel Barton Pine could have let the accident that took her leg destroy her career as a concert violinist and with it her joy in life—but she didn't. You can find out more about her life in music at http://www.rachelbartonpine.com. Researchers in the field of positive psychology are studying the development of resilience, as well as other character strengths, as part of an effort to understand and promote all the things that can go right in human life (Peterson, 2006a).

to another person. This deficiency orientation may lead a person to be jealous and to focus on what is missing in relationships. As a result, the person will never truly experience either love or security.

In contrast, people with **growth motivation** do not focus on what is missing but draw satisfaction from what they have, what they are, and what they can do. This orientation opens the door to what Maslow called *peak experiences,* in which people feel joy, even ecstasy, in the mere fact of being alive, being human, and knowing that they are realizing their fullest potential.

Evaluating the Humanistic Psychology Approach

The humanistic psychology approach to personality is consistent with the way many people view themselves. It gives a central role to each person's immediate experiences and emphasizes the uniqueness of each individual. The humanistic approach and its phenomenological perspective inspired the person-centered therapy of Rogers and other forms of psychotherapy (see the chapter on treatment of psychological disorders). This approach also underlies various short-term personal growth experiences—such as sensitivity training and encounter groups designed to help people become more aware of themselves and the way they relate to others (e.g., Cain & Seeman, 2002). It has led to programs designed to teach parents how to avoid creating conditions of worth while maximizing their children's potential. And as already mentioned, the humanistic approach has helped promote research in positive psychology, which studies what and how things go right in human development (Diener, Oishi, & Lucas, 2009; Peterson, 2006a, 2006b; Snyder & Lopez, 2006).

Yet to some observers, the humanistic view is naive, romantic, and unrealistic. Are people all as inherently good and growth-oriented as this approach suggests? Critics wonder about that, and they also fault humanistic personality theories for paying too little attention to the importance of inherited characteristics, learning, situational influences, and unconscious motivation in shaping personality. The idea that everyone is directed only by an innate growth potential is viewed by these critics as an oversimplification. So, too, is the assumption that all human problems stem from blocked actualization. Like the trait approach, humanistic theories seem to do a better job of describing personality than explaining it. And like many of the concepts in psychodynamic theories, humanistic concepts seem too vague to be tested empirically. Accordingly, the humanistic approach has not been very popular among psychologists who rely on empirical research to learn about personality (Feist & Feist, 2009). This may be changing, though, as the explosion of research in positive psychology leads

growth motivation According to Abraham Maslow, a tendency to draw satisfaction from what is available in life, rather than to focus on what is missing.

to new humanistically oriented theories that lend themselves to empirical evaluation (e.g., Burton et al., 2006; Cohn et al., 2009; Waugh, Fredrickson, & Taylor, 2008).

Even so, humanists' tendency to define ideal personality development in terms of personal growth, independence, and self-actualization has been criticized for emphasizing culture-specific ideas about mental health that may not apply outside North America and other Western cultures (Heine & Buchtel, 2009). As described in the next section, the individualist foundations of humanistic personality theories may be in direct conflict with the values of non-Western, collectivist cultures.

"In Review: Major Approaches to Personality" summarizes key features of the humanistic psychology approach, along with those of the other approaches we have described. Which approach is most accurate? There is no simple answer to that question, partly because each approach emphasizes different aspects of personality. Accordingly, it has been suggested that a full understanding of the origins and development of personality will come only by recognizing the roles of all the factors that various approaches have shown to be important (Mayer, 2005; McAdams & Pals, 2006).

IN REVIEW Major Approaches to Personality		
Approach	**Basic Assumptions About Behavior**	**Typical Research Methods**
Psychodynamic	Determined by largely unconscious intrapsychic conflicts	Case studies
Trait	Determined by traits or needs	Analysis of tests for basic personality dimensions
Social-cognitive	Determined by learning, cognitive factors, and specific situations	Analysis of interactions between people and situations
Humanistic	Determined by innate growth tendency and individual perception of reality	Studies of relationships between perceptions and behavior

1. Tests that measure the five-factor personality model's dimensions are based on the _____ approach to personality.

2. The role of learning is most prominent in the _____ approach to personality.

3. Object relations and attachment theories are modern variants on _____ personality theories.

LINKAGES

LINKAGES Does culture determine personality? (a link to Human Development, p. 508)

Personality, Culture, and Human Development

In many Western cultures, it is common to hear people encourage others to "stand up for yourself" or to "blow your own horn" in order to "get what you have coming to you." In middle-class North America, for example, the values of achievement and personal distinction are taught to children, particularly male children, very early in life (Kitayama, Duffy, & Uchida, 2007). North American children are encouraged to feel special, to want self-esteem, and to feel good about themselves, partly because these characteristics are associated with happiness, popularity, and superior performance in school. Whether self-esteem is the cause or the result of these good outcomes (Baumeister et al., 2003), children who learn and display these values nevertheless tend to receive praise and encouragement for doing so.

As a result of this cultural training, many people in North America and Europe develop personalities that are largely based on a sense of high self-worth. In a study by Hazel Markus and Shinobu Kitayama (1997), for example, 70 percent of a sample of U.S. students believed they were superior to their peers, and 60 percent believed they were in the top 10 percent on a wide variety of personal attributes! This tendency toward self-enhancement is evident as early as age 4.

Many Western personality theorists regard a sense of independence, uniqueness, and self-esteem as fundamental to mental health. As noted in the chapter on human development, for example, Erik Erikson included the appearance of personal identity and self-esteem as part of normal psychosocial development. Middle-class Americans who fail to value and strive for independence, self-promotion, and unique personal achievement may be thought to have a personality disorder, some form of depression, or other psychological problems.

Are these ideas based on universal truths about personality development, or do they reflect the values of the cultures that generated them? It is certainly clear that people in many non-Western cultures develop personal orientations that are different from those of North Americans and Europeans (Heine & Buchtel, 2009; Lehman, Chiu, & Schaller, 2004). In China and Japan, for example, an independent, unique self is not emphasized (Ho & Chiu, 1998). Children there are encouraged to develop and maintain harmonious relations with others and not to stand out from the crowd because doing so might make others seem inferior by comparison. So whereas children in the United States hear that "the squeaky wheel gets the grease" (meaning that you don't get what you want unless you ask for it), Japanese children are warned that "the nail that stands out gets pounded down" (meaning that it is not a good idea to draw attention to yourself). From a very young age, Japanese children are taught to be modest, to play down the value of personal contributions, and to appreciate the joy and value of group work (Kitayama & Uchida, 2003).

In contrast to the *independent* self-system prevalent in individualist cultures such as the United States, the United Kingdom, and Switzerland, countries characterized by a more collectivist orientation (e.g., Japan, China, Brazil, and Nigeria) promote an *interdependent* self-system in which people perceive themselves as a small fraction of a social whole. Each person has little or no meaningful definition without reference to the group. These differences in self-systems may produce differences in what gives people a sense of well-being and satisfaction (Tsai, Knutson, & Fung, 2006). In the United States, a sense of personal well-being is typically associated with the feeling of *having positive attributes,* such as intelligence, creativity, competitiveness, and persistence. In Japan and other Asian countries, it is more likely to be associated with the feeling of *having no negative attributes* (Eliot et al., 2001). Similarly, the results of studies conducted with thousands of people around the world indicate that in collectivist

The goal of esteem building is clear these days in many children's activities at school and in some team sports, too, which are designed either to eliminate competition or, as in this case, ensure that everyone feels like a winner. The same goal is reflected in day care centers, summer camps, and other children's programs with names such as Starkids, Little Wonders, Superkids, and Precious Jewels.

"We lost!"

Culture and Personality

TRY THIS In individualist cultures, most children learn early that personal distinction is valued by parents, teachers, and peers. In cultures that emphasize collectivist values, a strong sense of personal self-worth tends to be regarded as less important. In other words, the features of "normal" personality development vary from culture to culture. Make a list of the core values you have learned. Which of them are typical of individualist cultures, which are typical of collectivist cultures, and which reflect a combination of both?

cultures, life satisfaction is associated with social approval and harmonious relations with others, whereas in individualist cultures, life satisfaction is associated with high self-esteem and feeling good about one's own life (Uchida et al., 2001).

Because cultural factors shape notions about ideal personality development, it is important to evaluate various approaches to personality in terms of how well they apply to cultures other than the one in which they were developed (Church, 2001; Cross & Markus, 1999). Their applicability to males and females must also be considered. Even within North American cultures, for example, there are gender differences in the development of self-esteem. Females tend to display an interdependent self-system, achieving their sense of self and self-esteem from attachments to others. By contrast, males' self-esteem tends to develop in relation to personal achievement, in a manner more in keeping with an independent self-system (Cross & Madson, 1997). Cross-gender and cross-cultural differences in the nature and determinants of a sense of self underscore the pervasive effects of gender and culture on the development of many aspects of personality (Acerbi, Engquist, & Ghirlanda, 2009; Matsumoto, Yoo, & Nakagawa, 2008; Zakriski, Wright, & Underwood, 2005).

FOCUS ON RESEARCH METHODS

Longitudinal Studies of Temperament and Personality

Studying the development of personality over the life span requires longitudinal research, in which the same people are followed from infancy to adulthood so that their characteristics can be assessed at different points in their lives. A number of studies have used longitudinal methods to explore a variety of questions about changes in personality over time.

What was the researchers' question?

The specific question addressed by Avshalom Caspi and his colleagues was whether the temperament children display at birth and in their early years predicts their personality and behavior as adults (Caspi, 2000; Caspi, Harrington, et al., 2003; Caspi & Silva, 1995; Caspi et al., 1995, 1997). As discussed in the chapter on human development, it is generally agreed that differences in temperament are influenced more by heredity than by the environment (Clark & Watson, 2008).

How did the researchers answer the question?

Caspi's research team studied all the children born in Dunedin, New Zealand, between April 1972 and March 1973—a total of about a thousand individuals. When the children were 3 years old, an examiner gave each of them a test of their cognitive abilities and motor skills and, using a 3-point scale, rated their reactions to the testing situation. Some of the children displayed uncontrolled behaviors; some interacted easily; some were withdrawn and unresponsive. (To avoid bias while making their ratings, the examiners were told nothing about the children's typical behavior outside of the testing room.) These observations were used to place each child into one of five temperament categories: *undercontrolled* (irritable, impatient, emotional), *inhibited* (shy, fearful, easily distracted), *confident* (eager to perform, responsive to questions), *reserved* (withdrawn, uncomfortable), and *well adjusted* (friendly, well controlled). The children were observed and categorized again when they were 5, 7, and 9 years old. On each occasion, a different person did the ratings, thus ensuring that the observers' ratings would not be biased by earlier impressions. Almost all correlations among the independent ratings made at various ages were positive and statistically significant, indicating that the temperament classifications were stable across time.

When the participants were 18 years old, they completed a standard personality test, and at 21, they were interviewed about the degree to which they engaged in risky and unhealthy behaviors such as excessive drinking, violent crime, unprotected sexual activity, and unsafe driving habits. To avoid bias, the interviewers were given no information about the participants' temperament when they were children or about their scores on the personality test. Finally, at the age of 26, the participants again took a standard personality test and were also rated by their friends on the Big Five personality dimensions.

What did the researchers find?

Several significant differences were found among the average personality scores for the five original temperament categories. For example, the average test scores of 26-year-olds who had been classified as "undercontrolled" in childhood showed that they were more alienated, uninhibited, and stressed than any other temperament group. Further, people who had been classified as "confident" or "well adjusted" as children tended to be better adjusted and more extraverted at 26 than people who had been classified as "inhibited" or "reserved" when they were children. Young adults who as children had been classified as "well adjusted" tended to be effective individuals who were likely to assume leadership roles. These findings held true for males and females alike.

There were also small but significant correlations between early temperament and health-risk and criminal behaviors (Caspi, Harrington, et al., 2003). For example, people classified as "overcontrolled" were more likely to avoid dangerous and exciting activities at the age of 21 than those who had been classified as "undercontrolled." In fact, participants classified as "undercontrolled" were significantly more likely than any of the other groups to engage in risky behaviors and to have criminal records. The relationship between temperament in childhood and health-risk behaviors in young adulthood was not a direct one, though. Statistical analyses revealed that temperament at age 3 affected personality at age 18, which in turn affected later behavior patterns.

What do the results mean?

The results of Caspi's studies provide persuasive empirical support for a hypothesis long endorsed by personality psychologists, namely, that we can make relatively accurate predictions about adult personality and behavior if we know about childhood temperament (e.g., Glenn et al., 2007). But as critical thinkers, we must be careful not to overstate the strength of these results. Although the correlations between temperament and personality and between temperament and various problematic behaviors were statistically significant, they were also relatively small. For example, not all the participants classified as "undercontrolled" at age 3 turned out to be aggressive or violent at age 21. The implication is that personality is influenced and shaped by temperament but not completely determined by it (Clark & Watson, 2008; Roberts, Walton, & Viechtbauer, 2006).

The results of these studies also confirm a point made in the chapter on health, stress, and coping—that personality plays a significant role in health. Specifically, personality characteristics predispose people to engage in behaviors that can affect their mental and physical health.

What do we still need to know?

Caspi's research has revealed some consistency between temperament in childhood and personality in adulthood, but it also leaves some unanswered questions (Roberts & Delvecchio, 2000). For example, what factors underlie this consistency? The fact that there are individual differences in adult behavior within temperament groups shows that a child is not simply biologically programmed to display certain personality traits later (Hampson, 2008). One explanation offered by Caspi and his colleagues draws heavily on social-cognitive theories, particularly on Bandura's notion of reciprocal determinism. These researchers believe that long-term consistencies in behavior result from the mutual influence that temperament and environmental events have on one another. They propose, for example, that people tend to put themselves in situations that reinforce their temperament. So "undercontrolled" people might choose to spend time with people who accept and even encourage rude or impolite behavior. And when such behavior brings negative reactions, the world seems that much more hostile, and they become even more aggressive and negative. Caspi and his colleagues (2003) regard the results of their studies as evidence that this process of mutual influence between personality and situations can continue over a lifetime.

Assessing Personality

We all want to know something about our own personality and other people's, too, so it is no wonder that various kinds of personality assessments are widely available in newspapers and magazines and on the Internet. For example, there is a Web site called TweetPsych that offers personality profiles of frequent Twitter users based on the content of their tweets. Information available on Facebook and MySpace has also been used to assess various personality dimensions (Back et al., 2010), but psychologists usually describe people's personalities using information from four main sources: *life outcomes* (such as level of education, income, or marital status), *situational tests* (laboratory measurements of behavioral, emotional, and physiological reactions to conflict, frustration, and the like), *observer ratings* (judgments about a person made by family or friends), and *self-reports* (responses to interviews and personality tests). The data gathered through these methods are used for many purposes, including diagnosing psychological disorders, predicting dangerousness, selecting new employees, and even choosing astronaut candidates best suited to space travel (Kramer, Bernstein, & Phares, 2009; Meyer et al., 2001).

Life outcomes, observer ratings, and situational tests allow direct assessment of many aspects of behavior, including how often, how effectively, and how consistently various actions occur. *Interviews* provide a way to gather information about personality from the person's own point of view. Some interviews are *open-ended,* meaning that questions are tailored to the intellectual level, emotional state, and special needs of the person being interviewed. Others are *structured,* meaning that the interviewer asks a fixed set of questions about specific topics in a particular order. Structured interviews are routinely used in personality research because they are sure to cover matters of special interest to the researcher.

Personality tests offer a way of gathering self-report information that is more standardized and economical than interviews. To be useful, however, a personality test must be reliable and valid. As described in the chapter on cognitive abilities, reliability refers to how stable or consistent the results of a test are; validity reflects the degree to which test scores are interpreted appropriately and used properly in making inferences about people. The many personality tests available today are traditionally classified as either *projective* or *nonprojective* measures of personality.

• FIGURE 14.5

A Draw-a-Person Test

These drawings were done by an 18-year-old male who had been caught stealing a television set. A psychologist interpreted the muscular figure as the young man's attempt to boast of masculine prowess but saw the muscles' "puffy softness" as suggesting feelings of inadequacy. The drawing of the babylike figure was seen to reveal vulnerability, dependency, and a need for affection. Appealing as these interpretations may be, research does not generally support the value of projective tests in personality assessment (Lilienfeld, Wood, & Garb, 2000).

Source: Emmanuel F. Hammer, PhD. "Projective Drawings," in Rabin (ed.) *Projective Techniques in Personality Assessment.* pp. 375–376. Copyright © 1968 by Springer Publishing Company, Inc., New York. Used by permission.

projective personality measures Personality assessments made up of ambiguous stimuli that can be perceived and responded to in many different ways.

nonprojective personality measures Paper-and-pencil tests containing direct, unambiguous items relating to the personality of the individual being assessed.

Projective Personality Measures

Projective personality measures contain items or tasks that are ambiguous, meaning that they can be perceived in many different ways. People taking projective tests might be asked to draw a house, a person, a family, or a tree (see Figure 14.5); to fill in the missing parts of incomplete pictures or sentences; to say what they associate with particular words; or to report what they see in a drawing or picture. Projective techniques are sometimes used in personality research, but they are far more popular among psychodynamically oriented clinical psychologists, who use them to assess psychological disorders (Garb et al., 2005). These psychologists believe that people's responses to projective tests are guided by unconscious needs, motives, fantasies, conflicts, thoughts, and other hidden aspects of personality.

One prominent projective test, developed by Henry Murray and Christina Morgan, is called the Thematic Apperception Test, or TAT. As described in the chapter on motivation and emotion, the TAT is used to measure need for achievement (see Figure 11.5 in that chapter). It is also used to assess other needs (e.g., for power or affiliation) that Murray and Morgan considered the basis for personality. Another widely used projective test, the Rorschach Inkblot Test, asks people to say what they see in a series of inkblots similar to the one in Figure 14.6.

Psychologists who support the use of projective tests claim that ambiguous test items make it difficult for respondents to detect what is being measured and what the "best" answers would be. They argue, therefore, that these tests can measure aggressive and sexual impulses and other personality features that people might otherwise be able to hide. However, in comparison with the results of nonprojective tests, responses to projective tests are much more difficult to translate into numerical scores for scientific analysis. In an effort to reduce the subjectivity involved in projective-test interpretation, some psychologists have developed more structured—and thus potentially more reliable—scoring systems for instruments such as the Rorschach (Erdberg, 1990; Exner, 2003). And there are in fact specific instances—as in studies assessing implicit social motives with the TAT—in which projective tests show acceptable reliability and validity (Meyer, Mihura, & Smith, 2005; Schultheiss, 2008; Schultheiss & Rohde, 2002). Overall, though, projective personality tests are substantially less reliable and valid than nonprojective tests (Garb et al., 2005; Hunsley, Lee, & Wood, 2003; Lilienfeld, Wood, & Garb, 2000). In fact, because of their generally poor ability to predict behavior, projective tests may add little information about people that goes beyond what might be inferred from interviews and nonprojective personality measures (Hunsley, Lee, & Wood, 2003).

Nonprojective Personality Measures

Nonprojective personality measures, also known as *objective personality measures,* contain clearly stated items that relate to a person's thoughts, feelings, or behavior (such as "Do you like parties?"). Responses to these items are used to guide conclusions about the individual's personality. The most common kind of objective personality test is similar in format to the multiple-choice or true-false examinations used in many classrooms. Like those exams, self-report personality tests can be administered to many people at the same time. They can also be machine-scored. However, whereas there is only one correct answer for each item on a classroom exam, the "correct" answers to an objective personality test depend on who is taking it. Each person is asked to respond in a way that best describes him or her.

The person's responses to an objective test's items are combined into a score. That score can be used to draw conclusions about the individual's personality, but only after it has been compared with the responses of thousands of other people who have taken the same test. For example, before interpreting your score on a self-report test of extraversion, a psychologist would compare that score with *norms,* or average scores from other individuals of your age and gender. Only if you were well above these averages would you be considered unusually extraverted.

FIGURE 14.6
The Rorschach Inkblot Test

TRY THIS The Rorschach test consists of ten patterns similar to this one, some in color, some in black and white. People taking the test are asked to say what each pattern might be and to explain why. Jot down what you see in this inkblot and why, and then compare your responses to those of some friends. Most scoring methods focus on (1) what part of the blot the person responds to; (2) what details, colors, or other features appear to determine each response; (3) the content of responses (such as seeing animals, maps, or body parts); and (4) the popularity or commonness of the responses.

© Charlotte Miller

Some nonprojective personality measures focus on one particular trait, such as optimism (Carver & Scheier, 2002). Others measure a set of related traits, such as empathy and social responsibility (Penner & Orom, 2009). Still others measure the strength of a wider variety of traits to reveal general psychological functioning. For example, the Neuroticism-Extraversion-Openness Personality Inventory, Revised, or NEO-PI-R (Costa & McCrae, 1992), is designed to measure the Big Five personality factors described earlier. Table 14.3 shows how the test's results are presented. One innovative feature of the NEO-PI-R is its "private" and "public" versions. The first version asks for the respondent's self-assessment. The second version asks a person who knows the respondent to rate him or her on various dimensions. Personality descriptions based

TABLE 14.3 Sample Summary of Results from the NEO-PI-R

The NEO-PI-R assesses the Big Five personality dimensions. In this example of the results a respondent might receive, the five factors scored are, from the top row to the bottom row, neuroticism, extraversion, openness, agreeableness, and conscientiousness. Because people with different NEO profiles tend to have different psychological problems, this test has been used to aid in the diagnosis of personality disorders (Trull & Sher, 1994).

Compared with the responses of other people, your responses suggest that you can be described as:

☐ Sensitive, emotional, and prone to experience feelings that are upsetting.	☒ Generally calm and able to deal with stress, but you sometimes experience feelings of guilt, anger, or sadness.	☐ Secure, hardy, and generally relaxed even under stressful conditions.
☐ Extraverted, outgoing, active, and high-spirited. You prefer to be around people most of the time.	☐ Moderate in activity and enthusiasm. You enjoy the company of others, but you also value privacy.	☒ Introverted, reserved, and serious. You prefer to be alone or with a few close friends.
☐ Open to new experiences. You have broad interests and are very imaginative.	☐ Practical but willing to consider new ways of doing things. You seek a balance between the old and the new.	☒ Down-to-earth, practical, traditional, and pretty much set in your ways.
☐ Compassionate, good-natured, and eager to cooperate and avoid conflict.	☒ Generally warm, trusting, and agreeable, but you can sometimes be stubborn and competitive.	☐ Hardheaded, skeptical, proud, and competitive. You tend to express your anger directly.
☒ Conscientious and well organized. You have high standards and always strive to achieve your goals.	☐ Dependable and moderately well organized. You generally have clear goals but are able to set your work aside.	☐ Easygoing, not very well organized, and sometimes careless. You prefer not to make plans.

on the two versions are often quite similar, but discrepancies may indicate problems. For example, if a person's self-ratings are substantially different from those of a spouse, marital problems may be indicated. The nature of the discrepancies could suggest a focus for marital therapy.

The NEO-PI-R is quite reliable (Costa & McCrae, 2008), and people's scores on its various dimensions have been successfully used to predict social status (Anderson et al., 2001), as well as a number of behaviors, including success in business, performance in specific jobs (Conte & Gintoft, 2005; Zhao & Seibert, 2006), and the likelihood of engaging in criminal activities and risky sexual behaviors (Miller et al., 2004).

LINKAGES Can personality tests be used to diagnose mental disorders? (a link to Psychological Disorders, p. 603)

When the goal of personality testing is to diagnose psychological disorders, the most commonly used objective test is the Minnesota Multiphasic Personality Inventory, or MMPI (Butcher, 2006). The original 566-item true-false test was developed during the 1930s at the University of Minnesota by Starke Hathaway and J. C. McKinley. It has now been revised and updated to become the MMPI-2 RF (restructured form; Ben-Porath & Tellegen, 2008). The MMPI's items are organized into ten *clinical scales*. These are groups of items that in earlier research had drawn a characteristic pattern of responses only from people who displayed particular psychological disorders or personality characteristics. The MMPI-2 RF also contains several validity scales. Responses to these scales detect whether respondents are distorting their answers, misunderstanding the items, or being uncooperative. For example, someone who responds "true" to items such as "I never get angry" may not be giving honest answers to the test as a whole.

Interpreting the MMPI is largely a matter of using computer programs to compare test profiles—such as those shown in Figure 14.7—to the profiles of people already known to display certain personality characteristics. It is presumed that people share characteristics with the group whose profile most closely resembles their own. But although a very high score on one scale, such as depression, might indicate a problem in the dimension measured by that scale, MMPI interpretation usually focuses on the overall pattern in the clinical scales—particularly on the combination of two or three scales on which a person has unusually high scores.

There is considerable evidence for the reliability and validity of MMPI clinical scales (Forbey & Ben-Porath, 2008), but even the latest editions of the test are far from perfect measurement tools (Carr, Moretti, & Cue, 2005; Munley, 2002; Rouse, 2007). The validity of MMPI interpretations may be particularly suspect when, because of cultural factors, the perceptions, values, and experiences of a respondent are notably different from those of the test developers and the people to whom the respondent's results are compared. A profile that looks typical of people with a certain disorder might actually reflect the culture-specific way the respondent interpreted the test items rather than a mental problem (Butcher, 2004; Groth-Marnat, 1997). Even though the MMPI-2 RF uses comparison norms that represent a more culturally diverse population than the original MMPI did, psychologists must always use caution when interpreting profiles of people who are members of minority subcultures (Butcher, 2004).

("In Review: Personality Tests" summarizes the characteristics of projective and nonprojective measures, along with some of their advantages and disadvantages.)

Personality Tests and Employee Selection

How good are personality tests at selecting people for jobs? Most industrial and organizational psychologists believe that these tests are valuable tools in the selection of good employees. The MMPI (and even some projective tests) are occasionally employed for such purposes (e.g., Matyas, 2004), but the majority of personality tests used by large organizations are those that measure the Big Five personality dimensions or related characteristics (Borman, Hanson, & Hedge, 1997; Costa, 2001). Several researchers have found significant relationships between scores on these characteristics and

FIGURE 14.7
MMPI Clinical Scales and Sample Profiles

A score of 50 on the clinical scales of the MMPI is average. Scores at or above 65 mean that the person's responses on that scale are more extreme than at least 95 percent of the normal population. The red line represents the profile of Kenneth Bianchi, the "Hillside Strangler," who murdered thirteen women in the late 1970s. His profile is characteristic of a shallow person with poor self-control and little personal insight who is sexually preoccupied and unable to reveal himself to others. The profile in green comes from a more normal man, but it is characteristic of someone who is self-centered, passive, unwilling to accept personal responsibility for his behavior, and, when under stress, complains of numerous vague physical symptoms. The clinical scales abbreviated in the figure are as follows:

1. Hypochondriasis (Hs; concern with bodily functions and symptoms)
2. Depression (D; pessimism, hopelessness, slowed thinking)
3. Hysteria (Hy; use of physical or mental symptoms to avoid problems)
4. Psychopathic deviate (Pd; disregard for social customs, emotional shallowness)
5. Masculinity/femininity (Mf; interests associated with a particular gender)
6. Paranoia (Pa; delusions, suspiciousness)
7. Psychasthenia (Pt; worry, guilt, anxiety)
8. Schizophrenia (Sc; bizarre thoughts and perceptions)
9. Hypomania (Ma; overactivity, excitement, impulsiveness)
10. Social introversion (Si; shy, insecure)

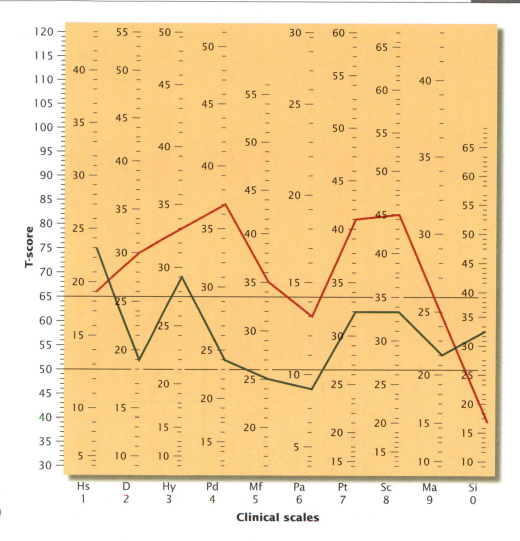

measures of overall job performance and effective leadership (Hirschfeld et al., 2008; Kieffer, Schinka, & Curtiss, 2004; Lim & Ployhart, 2004; Motowidlo, Brownlee, & Schmit, 2008; Silverthorne, 2001). A more general review of studies involving thousands of people has shown that nonprojective personality tests are of value in helping businesses reduce thefts and other disruptive employee behaviors (Berry, Sackett, & Wiemann, 2007; Hogan, 2006; Ones & Viswesvaran, 2001; Ones, Viswesvaran, & Schmidt, 2003).

Still, personality tests are not perfect, and as noted earlier, they sometimes lead to incorrect predictions about behavior. Many tests measure traits that may be too general to predict specific aspects of job performance (Berry, Sackett, & Wiemann, 2007; Furnham, 2001). In fact, features of the work situation are often better predictors of employee behavior than personality tests are (Mumford et al., 2001). Further, some employees consider personality tests an invasion of their privacy. They worry also that test results in their personnel files might later be misinterpreted and hurt their chances for promotion or for employment by other companies. Lawsuits have resulted in a ban on the use of personality tests in the selection of U.S. federal employees. Concerns about privacy and other issues surrounding personality testing have also led the American Psychological Association and other organizations to publish joint ethical standards relating to procedures for the development, dissemination, and use of all psychological tests (American Educational Research Association, American

Psychological Association, and National Council on Measurement in Education, 1999; American Psychological Association, 2002b). The goal is not only to improve the reliability and validity of tests but also to ensure that their results are properly used and do not infringe on individuals' rights (Turner et al., 2001).

IN REVIEW	Personality Tests		
Type of Test	**Characteristics**	**Advantages**	**Disadvantages**
Projective	Ambiguous stimuli allow maximum freedom of response; scoring is subjective, though some objective methods exist	"Correct" answers not obvious; designed to tap unconscious impulses; flexible use	Reliability and validity lower than those of nonprojective tests
Nonprojective	Direct questions presented in paper-and-pencil format; quantitatively scored	Efficiency, standardization	Subject to deliberate distortion

1. Projective personality measures are based on the _____ approach to personality.

2. The NEO-PI-R and the MMPI-2 RF are examples of _____ tests.

3. Most personality researchers use _____ tests in their work.

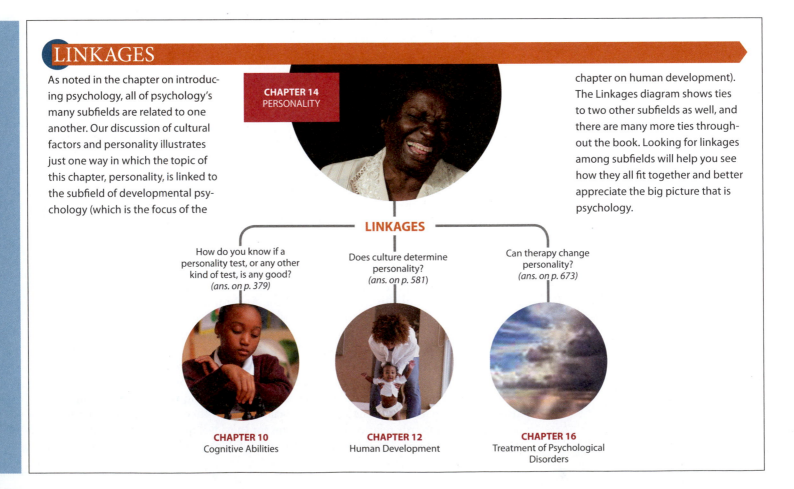

LINKAGES

As noted in the chapter on introducing psychology, all of psychology's many subfields are related to one another. Our discussion of cultural factors and personality illustrates just one way in which the topic of this chapter, personality, is linked to the subfield of developmental psychology (which is the focus of the

CHAPTER 14 PERSONALITY

chapter on human development). The Linkages diagram shows ties to two other subfields as well, and there are many more ties throughout the book. Looking for linkages among subfields will help you see how they all fit together and better appreciate the big picture that is psychology.

LINKAGES

How do you know if a personality test, or any other kind of test, is any good?
(ans. on p. 379)

Does culture determine personality?
(ans. on p. 581)

Can therapy change personality?
(ans. on p. 673)

CHAPTER 10
Cognitive Abilities

CHAPTER 12
Human Development

CHAPTER 16
Treatment of Psychological Disorders

SUMMARY

Personality refers to the unique pattern of psychological and behavioral characteristics by which each person can be compared and contrasted with other people. The four main theoretical approaches to personality are psychodynamic, trait, social-cognitive, and humanistic.

The Psychodynamic Approach

The *psychodynamic approach*, first proposed by Sigmund Freud, assumes that personality arises out of the interplay of various unconscious psychological processes.

The Structure and Development of Personality

Freud believed that personality has three components—the *id*, which has a reservoir of *libido* and operates according to the *pleasure principle*; the ego, which operates according to the *reality principle*; and the *superego*, which internalizes society's rules and values. The ego uses *defense mechanisms* to prevent unconscious conflicts among these components from becoming conscious and causing anxiety or guilt. Freud proposed that the focus of conflict changes as the child passes through five stages of *psychosexual development*: the *oral stage*, the *anal stage*, the *phallic stage* (during which the *Oedipal complex* or the *Electra complex* arises), the *latency period*, and the *genital stage*.

Variations on Freud's Personality Theory

Many of Freud's early followers developed new theories that differed from his. Among these theorists were Carl Jung, Alfred Adler, and Karen Horney. These and other theorists tended to downplay the role of instincts and the unconscious, emphasizing instead the importance of conscious processes, ego functions, and social and cultural factors. Horney also challenged the male-oriented nature of Freud's original theory.

Contemporary Psychodynamic Theories

Current psychodynamic theories are derived from the neo-Freudians' emphasis on family and social relationships. According to object relations and attachment theorists, personality development depends mainly on the nature of early interactions between individuals and their caregivers.

Evaluating the Psychodynamic Approach

Despite evidence in support of some psychodynamic concepts and recent attempts to test psychodynamic theories more precisely and objectively, critics still fault the approach for its lack of a scientific base and for its view of human behavior as driven by unmeasurable forces.

The Trait Approach

The *trait approach* to personality assumes that personality is made up of stable internal characteristics that appear at varying strengths in different people and guide their thoughts, feelings, and behavior.

Allport's Trait Theory

Gordon Allport believed that personality is created by a small set of central traits and a larger number of secondary traits in each individual. He analyzed language to try to identify those traits, thus laying the foundation for modern research on personality traits.

The Five-Factor Model of Personality

Building on the work of Allport and Raymond Cattell, contemporary researchers have used factor analysis to identify five basic dimensions of personality, collectively referred to as the *five-factor* (or *Big Five*) *personality model*. These dimensions—openness to experience, conscientiousness, extraversion, agreeableness, and neuroticism—have been found in many different cultures.

Biological Trait Theories

Hans Eysenck believed that differences in nervous system arousal are responsible for differences in core dimensions of personality, especially introversion–extraversion and emotionality–stability. Newer biological theories such as Jeffrey Gray's reinforcement sensitivity theory, have largely replaced Eysenck's theory, and they suggest instead that these differences are due to biological differences in the sensitivity of brain systems involved with responsiveness to rewards and to punishments.

Evaluating the Trait Approach

The trait approach has been criticized for being better at describing personality than at explaining it, for failing to consider mechanisms that motivate behavior, and for underemphasizing the role of situational factors. Nevertheless, the trait approach—particularly the five-factor model—currently dominates the field of personality.

The Social-Cognitive Approach

The *social-cognitive approach* to personality focuses on the thoughts and feelings that influence people's behavior and assumes that personality is a label that summarizes the unique patterns of thinking and behavior that a person learns in the social world.

Roots of the Social-Cognitive Approach

With roots in research on classical and operant conditioning (including Skinner's *functional analysis* of behavior), the social-cognitive approach has expanded on traditional behavioral approaches by emphasizing the role of cognitive factors, such as observational learning, in personality development.

Prominent Social-Cognitive Theories

Julian Rotter's theory focuses on cognitive expectancies that guide behavior, and it generated interest in assessing general beliefs about whether rewards occur because of personal efforts (internal control) or chance (external control). Albert Bandura believes that personality develops largely through cognitively mediated learning, including observational learning. He regards personality as reciprocally determined by interactions among cognition, environmental stimuli, and behavior. Perceived *self-efficacy*—the belief in one's ability to accomplish a specific task—is an important determinant of behavior. Walter Mischel emphasizes the importance of cognitive person variables and their interactions with the characteristics of particular situations in determining behavior. According to Mischel, we must look at both cognitive person variables and situational variables in order to understand human consistencies and inconsistencies.

Evaluating the Social-Cognitive Approach

The social-cognitive approach has gained wide acceptance because it has merged theories from behavioral and cognitive psychology and used them to explain a wide range of important social behaviors. However, the approach has been criticized for failing both to provide one coherent theory of personality and to capture the complexity, richness, and uniqueness of human personalities.

The Humanistic Psychology Approach

The *humanistic psychology approach* to personality is based on the assumption that people are primarily motivated by a desire to fulfill their natural potential in a uniquely perceived version of reality. So to understand a person, you have to understand the person's view of the world, which serves as the basis for personality and guides behavior.

Prominent Humanistic Theories

Carl Rogers believed that personality development is driven by an innate *actualizing tendency* but also that one's *self-concept* is shaped by social evaluations. He proposed that when people are free from the effects of *conditions of worth*, they are more likely to be psychologically healthy and to achieve self-actualization. Abraham Maslow considered self-actualization as the highest in a hierarchy of needs. Personality development is healthiest, he said, when people have *growth motivation* rather than *deficiency motivation*.

Evaluating the Humanistic Psychology Approach

Although it has an intuitive appeal, the humanistic psychology approach has been faulted for being too idealistic, for failing to explain personality development, for being vague and unscientific, and for underplaying cultural differences in "ideal" personalities.

Assessing Personality

The information used in personality assessment comes from four main sources: life outcomes, situational tests, observer ratings, and self-reports. To be useful, personality assessments must be both reliable and valid.

Projective Personality Measures

Based on psychodynamic theories, *projective personality measures* present ambiguous stimuli in an attempt to tap unconscious personality characteristics. Two popular projective tests are the TAT and the Rorschach Inkblot Test. In general, projective personality measures are less reliable and valid than nonprojective personality measures.

Nonprojective Personality Measures

Nonprojective personality measures contain clearly worded items relating to the individual being assessed; their scores can be compared with group norms. The MMPI and the NEO-PI-R are examples of nonprojective measures.

Personality Tests and Employee Selection

Nonprojective personality measures are often used to identify the people best suited for certain occupations. Although such measures can be helpful in this regard, the people who use them must be aware of the tests' limitations and take care not to violate the rights of test respondents.

LINKAGES TO FURTHER LEARNING

Now that you have finished reading this chapter, how about exploring some of the topics and information that you found most interesting? Here are some places to start.

Books

David C. Funder, Ross D. Parke, Carol Tomlinson-Keasey, and Keith Widaman (Eds.), *Studying Lives Through Time* (American Psychological Association, 1996). Famous studies in personality and development.

Harry Stack Sullivan, *The Interpersonal Theory of Psychiatry* (Norton, 1968). Sullivan's neo-Freudian theory.

Duane P. Schultz and Sydney E. Schultz, *Theories of Personality* (Brooks-Cole, 2009). Summary of personality theories.

Stella Chess and M. D. Alexander, *Temperament: Theory and Practice* (Brunner/Mazel, 1996). Differences in temperament.

Edward Chang and Lawrence Sanna, *Virtue, Vice, and Personality: The Complexity of Behavior* (American Psychological Association, 2003). Readable chapters on how cultural factors alter evaluation of personality traits.

On the Internet

CourseMate   Access an integrated eBook and chapter-specific learning tools including flashcards, quizzes, videos, and more. Go to CengageBrain.com.

CENGAGENOW   Want to maximize the value of your online study time? Take this easy-to-use study system's diagnostic pre-test, and it will create a personalized study plan for you. By helping you identify the topics that you need to understand better and then directing you to valuable online resources, it can speed up your chapter review. CengageNOW even provides a post-test so you can confirm that you are ready for an exam. Go to CengageBrain.com.

TALKING POINTS

Here are a few talking points to help you summarize this chapter for family and friends without giving a lecture.

1. We all know someone who seems to have "no personality," but the truth is that everybody has a personality; it is a matter of *what* personality characteristics they have.

2. According to modern versions of Freud's psychodynamic personality theory, our personality characteristics are influenced by the quality of our attachment to caregivers when we were infants.

3. Research in trait theory suggests that everyone's personality can be described in terms of just five main dimensions: openness, conscientiousness, extraversion, agreeableness, and neuroticism.

4. We don't inherit particular personality traits, but we do inherit general temperament, and temperament in childhood provides a reasonably good predictor of adult personality.

5. Humanistic psychology theories of personality suggest that everyone is basically good.

6. According to social-cognitive theories, it is through experiences with other people that we learn the thoughts and actions that become our personality.

7. Personality tests can be useful, but even the best ones cannot provide completely accurate descriptions of individuals or their future behavior.

15

Psychological Disorders

Many people pursue what other people consider odd hobbies, such as collecting string, but when does oddness become abnormality? In this chapter, we discuss how society answers that question. We also describe the main types of psychological disorders, their possible causes, their legal status, and how they have been explained over the centuries.

During his first year at college, Mark began to worry about news stories describing the deadly diseases resulting from HIV, the virus that causes AIDS. He took a blood test for HIV and was relieved when it showed no infection. But then he wondered if he might have contracted HIV after he took the test. Internet research revealed that HIV antibodies may not appear until six months after infection. Mark took another blood test, also negative, but he still worried when he learned that the AIDS virus can live outside of the human body for anywhere from ten minutes to several hours or even days.

Given this uncertainty, Mark concluded that HIV can live indefinitely outside of the body and could therefore be anywhere and everywhere. He decided that the only safe course was not just sexual abstinence but absolute cleanliness. Mark began to scrub himself whenever he touched doorknobs, money, walls, floors—anything. People with HIV, he thought, could have touched these things, or they might have bled on the street and he might have tracked their infected blood into his car and house and bathroom. Eventually he felt the need to scrub everything around him up to forty times in each direction; it took him several exhausting hours just to shower and dress. He washed the shower knobs before touching them and, once in the shower, felt that he had to wash his body in cycles of thirteen strokes. If his feet touched the bare floor, he had to wash them again before putting on his underwear to ensure that his feet would not contaminate the fabric. He was sure that his hands, rubbed raw from constant washing, were especially susceptible to infection, so he wore gloves at all times except in the summer, when he wrapped his fingers in bandages. The process of protecting himself from infection was wearing him out and severely restricting his activities; he could not go anywhere without first considering the risk of infection.

Mark suffers from a psychological disorder, also called a *mental disorder* or *psychopathology*. **Psychopathology** is generally defined as patterns of thought, emotion, and behavior that result in personal distress or a significant impairment in a person's social or occupational functioning. Surveys reveal that in any given year in the United States alone, about 26 percent of adults—about 60 million people—display some form of mental disorder and that about half of all Americans can expect to experience a disorder by age 75 (Kessler & Wang, 2008; National Institute of Mental Health [NIMH], 2006; see Figure 15.1). These overall rates of mental disorder are found, with only minor variations, in all segments of U.S. society, including males and females in all ethnic groups and in the young and old. Many of these disorders appear quite early in life. In any given year, about 13 percent of U.S. children display significant mental disorders (Merikangas et al., 2010), and about three-quarters of adult disorders first appear by age 24; half begin as early as 14 (Egan & Asher, 2005; Kessler & Wang, 2008; Twenge et al., 2010).

Bear in mind, though, that the prevalence of psychological disorders may be even higher than the percentages just cited. For one thing, major survey studies have examined fewer than half of all known psychological disorders. Further, these studies count each case only once, even though about 45 percent of people

psychopathology Patterns of thinking, feeling, and behaving that are maladaptive, disruptive, or uncomfortable for those who are affected or for those with whom they come in contact.

FIGURE 15.1
Incidence of Specific Psychological Disorders

Several large-scale surveys of adults in the United States revealed that about 26 percent of them experience some form of mental disorder in any given year and that almost half of them have displayed a disorder at some time in life (Kessler & Wang, 2008; National Institute of Mental Health, 2006). Indeed, one survey suggested that only about 20 percent of adults in the U.S. are both free of any form of mental disorder and flourishing (Keyes, 2007). The data shown here summarize the lifetime findings by category of disorder. The same general patterns appear among the more than 400 million people worldwide who suffer from some form of psychological disorder (Kessler & Üstün, 2008; World Health Organization Mental Health Survey Consortium, 2004).

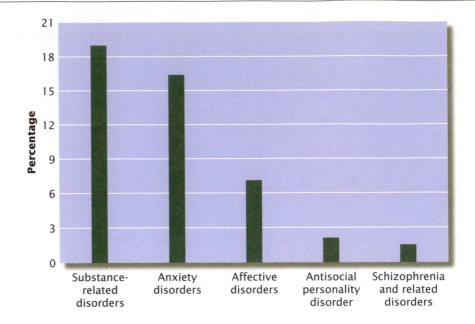

who are diagnosed with one disorder actually display *comorbidity*, meaning that they are diagnosed as having two or even three disorders (Kessler & Wang, 2008; NIMH, 2006).

Psychological disorders are enormously costly in terms of human suffering, wasted potential, and lost resources (e.g., Adler et al., 2006; Insel, 2008; Kessler, Chui, et al., 2008). They are the leading cause of disability in the United States and Canada for people aged 15 to 44 (NIMH, 2006), and a similar pattern appears around the world. Studies have found that psychological disorders ranked second (after cardiovascular disease) in producing disability and shortened life expectancy in industrialized economies (Kessler & Üstün, 2008; World Health Organization Mental Health Survey Consortium, 2004). The impact of these disorders is even greater in less developed countries where treatment is less available (Gureje et al., 2006; Kawakami et al., 2005; Medina-Mora et al., 2005; Miller, 2006; Stewart et al., 2003).

Beyond causing personal suffering and disability, psychological disorders also impose a huge financial burden on families, communities, and society. Expenditures for the diagnosis and treatment of mental disorders increased from $35.2 billion in 1996 to $57.5 billion in 2006—a sharper rise in spending than for heart conditions and cancer (Soni, 2009). Let's consider how these disorders are defined and classified.

Defining Psychological Disorders

A California woman's husband dies, and in her grief, she stays in bed all day, weeping, refusing to eat, at times holding "conversations" with him. In India, a Hindu holy man on a pilgrimage rolls along the ground across 1,000 miles of deserts and mountains, pelted by monsoon rains, until he reaches the sacred place he seeks. In the Middle East, a young man straps explosives to his body and detonates them in a crowded market, killing himself and dozens of others. In London, a British artist randomly scratches parked cars as part of his "creative process." A survey of Swiss adults finds that 18 percent reported having thoughts "that are not my own" (Rössler et al., 2007), and hundreds of people around the world claim to have been abducted by space aliens (Clancy, 2005). These examples and countless others raise the question of where to draw the line between normality and abnormality, between eccentricity, criminality, and mental disorder.

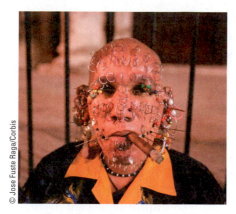

Is This Person Abnormal?

Whether unusual individuals are labeled "abnormal" and perhaps given treatment for psychological disorder depends on a number of factors, including how *abnormality* is defined by the culture in which they live, who is most directly affected by their behavior, and how much distress they suffer or cause.

What Is Abnormal?

The criteria for judging whether people's thinking, emotions, or behaviors are abnormal have been called the "three D's": deviance, distress, and dysfunction. Each criterion has value but also some flaws.

Deviance If we define as *normal* the things most people think and do, an obvious criterion for abnormality is *statistical infrequency*—what is unusual or rare would be considered deviant. By this criterion, the few people who believe that space aliens are stealing their thoughts would be judged abnormal, and the many people who worry about crime or terrorism would not. But statistical infrequency alone is a poor criterion for abnormality because it would define as abnormal any rare quality, including creative genius or world-class athletic ability. Further, the infrequency criterion implies that to be normal, one must conform to all aspects of the majority's standards. Equating nonconformity with abnormality can result in the oppression of those who express unusual or unpopular views or ideas. Finally, just how rare must a behavior be to warrant the designation "abnormal"? The dividing line is not easy to locate.

A related criterion for abnormality is the violation of social norms—the cultural rules that tell us how we should and should not behave in various situations, especially in relation to others (see the chapter on social influence). According to this *norm violation* criterion, people can be described as abnormal if they behave in ways that are unusual or disturbing enough to violate social norms. Like infrequency, though, norm violation alone is an inadequate measure of abnormality. For one thing, some norm violations are better characterized as eccentric or illegal than as abnormal. People who seldom bathe or who stand too close during conversation violate social norms, but are they abnormal or merely annoying? Further, whose norms are we talking about? Social norms vary across cultures, subcultures, and historical eras, so actions that qualify as abnormal in one part of the world might be perfectly acceptable elsewhere.

Distress Another criterion for abnormality is distress, or *personal suffering*. In fact, experiencing distress is the criterion that people often use to decide that their psychological problems are severe enough to require treatment. But personal suffering alone is not an adequate criterion for abnormality. It does not take into account the fact that people are sometimes distressed about characteristics (such as being gay or lesbian) that are not mental disorders. Further, people can display psychological disorders without

Situational Factors in Defining Abnormality

TRY THIS When men in Delhi, India, need a restroom, they can take advantage of outdoor urinals like this one. In some countries, it is even acceptable for men to urinate against buildings on city streets. In the United States and many other places, though, males who urinate anywhere other than the relative privacy of a men's room are considered deviant and might even be arrested for indecent exposure. In other words, situational factors can determine whether a particular behavior is labeled "normal" or "abnormal." Make a list of the reasons you would give for or against calling these men "abnormal." Which criteria for abnormality did you use?

experiencing distress if the disorders have impaired their ability to recognize how maladaptive their behavior is. Those who sexually abuse children, for example, create far more distress in victims and their families than they suffer themselves.

Dysfunction   A final criterion for abnormality is *impaired functioning*, which means having difficulty in fulfilling appropriate and expected roles in family, social, and work-related situations (Üstün & Kennedy, 2009). For example, it is normal for people to experience sadness at one time or another, but if their sadness becomes so intense or long-lasting that it interferes with their ability to hold a job or care for their children, it is likely to be considered abnormal. But it isn't quite fair to call someone abnormal just because the person is dysfunctional. The dysfunction might be caused by physical illness, by an overwhelming but temporary family problem, or by a variety of things other than a psychological disorder. Further, some people who display significant psychological disorders are still able to function reasonably well at school, at work, or at home.

Behavior in Context: A Practical Approach

Because no single criterion is entirely adequate for identifying abnormality, mental health practitioners and researchers tend to adopt a *practical approach* that combines aspects of all the criteria we have discussed. They consider the *content* of behavior (what the person does), the sociocultural *context* of the person's behavior, and the *consequences* of the behavior for that person and others.

LINKAGES   How do societies define what is abnormal? (a link to Social Influence, p. 730)

Mental health professionals also recognize that the definition of "appropriate," "expected," and "functional" behavior depends to some extent on age, gender, and culture, as well as on the particular situation and the historical era in which people live. For example, a short attention span and unemployment are considered normal in a 2-year-old but inappropriate and problematic in an adult. There are gender-specific norms as well. In some countries, for example, it is more appropriate for women than for men to display emotion. Kisses, tears of happiness, and long embraces are common when women greet each other after a long absence. Men tend to simply shake hands or, at most, hug briefly. Because of cultural differences, hearing a dead relative's voice calling from the afterlife would be more acceptable in certain American Indian tribes than among, say, the families of suburban Toronto. Situational factors are important too. Falling to the floor and speaking an unintelligible language is considered appropriate, even desirable, during the worship services of certain religious groups, but the same behavior would be seen as inappropriate, and a sign of disorder, in a college classroom. Finally, judgments about behavior are shaped by changes in social trends and cultural values. For example, the American Psychiatric Association (APA) once listed homosexuality as a mental disorder but in 1973 dropped this category from its *Diagnostic and Statistical Manual of Mental Disorders*. In taking this step, it was responding to changing views of homosexuality that were prompted in part by the political and educational efforts of gay and lesbian rights groups.

In summary, it is difficult, and probably impossible, to define a specific set of behaviors that everyone, everywhere, will agree constitutes abnormality. The practical approach defines abnormality as patterns of thought, behavior, and emotional reaction that significantly impair people's functioning within their culture (Wakefield, 1992).

Explaining Psychological Disorders

Since the dawn of civilization, people throughout the world have tried to understand the causes of psychological disorder. The earliest explanations of abnormal behavior focused on possession by gods or demons. Disordered people were seen either as innocent victims of spirits or as social or moral deviants suffering supernatural punishment. In Europe during the late Middle Ages, for example, people who displayed threatening or unusual behavior were thought to be controlled by the devil or other evil beings. Supernatural explanations of psychological disorders are still invoked

An Exorcism

The exorcism being performed by this Buddhist monk in Thailand is designed to cast out the evil forces believed to be causing this child's disorder. Supernatural explanations of mental disorders remain influential among religious groups in many cultures and subcultures around the world (Fountain, 2000). Awareness of this influence in the United States and Europe has increased recently following cases in which people have died during exorcism rituals (e.g., Christopher, 2003; Radford, 2005).

© J. L. Dugast/Peter Arnold, Inc./Photolibrary

today in many cultures around the world—including certain ethnic and religious subcultures in North America (Glazer et al., 2004; Legare & Gelman, 2008). Other explanations have focused on mental incompetence, weak character, personal choices, illness or other physical problems, faulty learning, and difficult social conditions.

Different explanations generate differing attitudes and responses toward people who display mental disorders (Fontaine, 2009). In societies where disorder is seen as a sign that a person is evil, that person may be the target of anger and punishment, but where the cause of disorder is thought to be demonic possession, the person may be the object of sympathy and might be offered an exorcism ceremony. If abnormality is viewed as a personal decision to behave in odd ways, those who do so are likely to be avoided, isolated, and ignored, but if psychological problems are assumed to be caused by illness or learned habits, troubled people are likely to be given drugs or offered programs designed to teach less troublesome behaviors.

The Biopsychosocial Approach

Today, most mental health researchers in Western cultures attribute psychopathology to three main causes: biological factors, psychological processes, and sociocultural contexts. For many decades, there was controversy over which of these three causes is most important, but it is now widely agreed that they can all be important. Accordingly, researchers have adopted a **biopsychosocial approach** in which mental disorders are regarded as resulting from the combination and interaction of biological, psychological, and sociocultural factors, each of which contributes in varying degrees to particular problems in particular people (Andrews, 2008; Krueger & Markon, 2006).

biopsychosocial approach A view of mental disorders as caused by a combination of interacting biological, psychological, and sociocultural factors.

medical model (neurobiological model) A view in which psychological disorders are seen as reflecting disturbances in the anatomy and chemistry of the brain and in other biological processes.

Biological Factors   The biological factors thought to be involved in causing mental disorders include physical illnesses, disruptions or imbalances in bodily processes, and genetic influences. This **medical model** of psychopathology has a long history. For example, the ancient Greek physician Hippocrates said that psychological disorders resulted from imbalances among four *humors,* or bodily fluids (blood, phlegm, black bile, and yellow bile). In ancient Chinese cultures, psychological disorders were thought to result from an imbalance of *yin* and *yang,* the dual forces of the universe flowing in the physical body.

As the medical model gained prominence in Western cultures after the Middle Ages, special hospitals for the insane were established throughout Europe. Treatment

Visiting Bedlam

As shown here in William Hogarth's portrayal of *Bedlam* (slang for London's Saint Mary Bethlehem Hospital), most asylums of the 1700s were little more than prisons. Notice the well-dressed visitors; in those days, people could buy tickets to tour the cells and gawk at the patients.

"The Interior of Bedlam," from *A Rake's Progress* by William Hogarth, 1763

in these early asylums consisted mainly of physical restraints, laxative purges, bleeding of "excess" blood, and induced vomiting. Cold baths, fasts, spinning chairs, and other physical discomforts were also used in efforts to "shock" patients back to normality.

The medical model gave rise to the idea that abnormality is *mental illness,* and in fact, most people in Western cultures today still tend to seek medical doctors and hospitals for the diagnosis and treatment of psychological disorders (Wang et al., 2006). The medical model is now more properly called the **neurobiological model** because it explains psychological disorders in terms of particular disturbances in the anatomy and chemistry of the brain and in other biological processes, including genetic influences (e.g., Kendler, 2005; Plomin & McGuffin, 2003; Williams, 2008). Neuroscientists and others who adopt a neurobiological model study the causes and treatment of these disorders as they would study any physical illness, assuming that problematic symptoms stem primarily from an underlying illness that can be diagnosed, treated, and cured.

Psychological Processes If biological factors are the "hardware" of mental disorders, the "software" is psychological factors, such as our wants, needs, and emotions; our learning experiences; our attachment history; and our way of looking at the world. The roots of this **psychological model** of mental disorders can be seen in ancient Greek literature and drama dealing with the *psyche,* or mind—especially with the mind's struggles to resolve inner conflicts or to overcome the effects of stressful events. These ideas took center stage in the late 1800s when Sigmund Freud challenged the assumption that psychological disorders had only physical causes. As described in the personality chapter, Freud's explanations of mental disorders were part of his *psychodynamic approach.* He believed that those disorders are the result of unresolved, mostly unconscious conflicts that begin in childhood. These conflicts pit people's inborn impulses against the limits placed on those impulses by society.

Other psychological processes can contribute to the development of mental disorders. As described in the personality chapter, *social-cognitive* theorists, also known as *social learning* theorists, see most psychological disorders as resulting from the interaction of past learning and current situations. Just as people learn to avoid hot grills after being burned, say these theorists, bad experiences in school or a dental

psychological model A view in which mental disorder is seen as arising from psychological processes.

LINKAGES Are psychological disorders learned behaviors? (a link to Learning, p. 206)

office can "teach" people to fear such places. Social-cognitive theorists also emphasize that learned expectations, schemas, and other mental processes discussed in the chapter on cognition and language can influence the development of disorders (e.g., Johnson-Laird, Mancini, & Gangemi, 2006). Depression, for example, is seen as stemming from negative events, such as losing a job, but also from the irrational or maladaptive thoughts that people have learned in relation to these events—thoughts such as "I never do anything right."

The *humanistic* approach to personality suggests that behavior disorders appear when a person's natural tendency toward healthy growth is blocked, usually by a failure to be aware of and to express true feelings. When this happens, the person's perceptions of reality become distorted. The greater the distortion, the more serious the psychological disorder.

Sociocultural Context Together, neurobiological and psychological factors go a long way toward explaining many forms of mental disorder. Still, these factors relate mainly to causes residing within the individual. The **sociocultural perspective** suggests that we cannot fully explain all forms of psychopathology without also looking outside the individual—especially at the social and cultural factors that form the background of abnormal behavior. To find causes of disorders in this *sociocultural context,* we must pay attention to **sociocultural factors** such as gender, age, and marital status; the physical, social, and economic situations in which people live; and the cultural values, traditions, and expectations in which they are immersed (Appignanesi, 2009; Lim, 2006; Sue & Sue, 2008). Sociocultural context influences not only what is and is not labeled "abnormal" but also who displays what kind of disorder and how likely people are to receive treatment for it.

Consider gender, for instance. The higher rates of depression among women compared to men may appear partly because many cultures are more tolerant of emotional distress among women than among men (Hightower, 2005; Wupperman & Neumann, 2006). Similarly, the view held in many cultures that excessive alcohol consumption is less appropriate for women than for men is a sociocultural factor that may help explain higher rates of alcohol abuse among men in those cultures (Helzer et al., 1990; Timko, Finney, & Moos, 2005).

Sociocultural factors can influence the overall prevalence of disorders too. For instance, anxiety disorders and depression tend to be less common in China and Japan than in Western countries, including the United States (Lee et al., 2007; Kawakami et al., 2005). And many kinds of psychological disorders increase in frequency among people living in countries ravaged by wars or other stressful conditions (Alhasnawi et al., 2009; Karam et al., 2006).

Sociocultural factors also influence the form that abnormality takes. For example, depression is a *culture-general* disorder, appearing virtually everywhere in the world, but the symptoms that sufferers report tend to differ, depending on cultural background (Falicov, 2003; Hopper & Wanderling, 2000; Whaley & Hall, 2009). In Western cultures, emotional and physical components of disorders are generally viewed separately, so symptoms of depression tend to revolve around despair and other signs of emotional distress. But in China, Japan, and certain other Asian cultures, emotional and physical experiences tend to be viewed as one, so a depressed person is as likely to report stomach or back pain as to complain of sadness (Nakao & Yano, 2006; Weiss et al., 2009).

There are also culture-specific forms of disorder. For instance, Puerto Rican, Guatemalan, Mexican, and Dominican Hispanic women sometimes experience *ataques de nervios* ("attacks of nerves"), a unique way of reacting to stress that includes heart palpitations, shaking, shouting, nervousness, depression, and, on occasion, fainting or seizurelike episodes (Baer, Weller, et al., 2003; Lizardi, Oquendo, & Graver, 2009). In Asia, Khmer refugees sometimes suffer from panic-related fainting spells known as *kyol goeu* (Hinton, Um, & Ba, 2001). And genital retraction syndromes are occasionally observed in a number of places around the world. In Southeast Asia,

sociocultural perspective A way of looking at mental disorders in relation to gender, age, ethnicity, and other social and cultural factors.

sociocultural factors Characteristics or conditions that can influence the appearance and form of maladaptive behavior.

southern China, and Malaysia, men suffering from *koro* fear that their penis will shrivel, retract into the body, and cause death (in females, the fear relates to shriveling of the breasts).

In short, sociocultural factors create differing stressors, social roles, opportunities, experiences, and avenues of expression for different groups of people. They also help shape the disorders and symptoms to which certain categories of people are prone, and they even affect responses to treatment. For example, among people diagnosed with schizophrenia, those living in a developing country such as India are much more likely to improve than those living in a more developed country, such as the United States (Hopper & Wanderling, 2000). We don't yet know for certain what is responsible for this difference, but it may have something to do with the ways in which schizophrenia is understood in different cultures. In the West, schizophrenia is considered a chronic, debilitating, potentially dangerous, long-term illness. As a result, many people diagnosed with schizophrenia find themselves left on the fringes of society. In some non-Western societies, the disorder is seen as less severe and less resistant to treatment. Perhaps this more optimistic view encourages more intense efforts at socialization and, as a result, better outcomes (Mathews, Basily, & Mathews, 2006). Whatever the explanation, these data highlight the fact that any attempt to fully explain psychological disorders must take sociocultural factors into account.

Diathesis-Stress as an Integrative Explanation

The biopsychosocial model is currently the most comprehensive and influential approach to explaining psychological disorders. It is prominent partly because it encompasses so many important causal factors: biological imbalances, genetically inherited characteristics, brain damage, enduring psychological traits, socioculturally influenced learning experiences, stressful life events, and many more.

But how do all these factors interact to actually create disorder? Most researchers believe that inherited characteristics, biological processes, and early learning experiences combine to create a predisposition, or *diathesis* (pronounced "dy-ATH-uh-siss"), for a psychological disorder. Whether or not a person actually develops symptoms of a disorder depends on the nature and amount of stress the person encounters (Elwood et al., 2009; Turner & Lloyd, 2004). For example, a person may have inherited a biological tendency toward depression or may have learned depressing patterns of thinking, but these predispositions may not be expressed as a depressive disorder unless the person is faced with a financial crisis or suffers the loss of a loved one. If such major stressors don't occur, or if the person has adequate skills for coping with them, depressive symptoms may never appear or may be relatively mild (Canli et al., 2006).

This way of thinking about mental disorder is known as the **diathesis-stress model**. It assumes that biological, psychological, and sociocultural factors can predispose us toward a disorder but that it takes a certain amount of stress to actually trigger that disorder. People with a strong diathesis are more vulnerable, so even relatively mild stress may be enough to create a problem. People whose diathesis is weaker may not show signs of a disorder until stress becomes extreme or prolonged. Another way to think about the notion of diathesis-stress is in terms of *risk:* The more risk factors for a disorder a person has—whether in the form of genetic tendencies, personality traits, cultural traditions, or stressful life events—the more likely it is that the person will display a form of psychological disorder associated with those risk factors.

Table 15.1 provides an example of how a particular case of psychopathology might be explained by various biopsychosocial factors and how the case might be summarized in terms of the diathesis-stress model. Later, you'll see how these same factors, and the diathesis-stress model, have been applied to help explain the causes of several other psychological disorders.

diathesis-stress model The notion that psychological disorders arise when a predisposition for a disorder combines with sufficient amounts of stress to trigger symptoms.

TABLE 15.1 The Biopsychosocial Model of Psychopathology

Here are the factors that would be considered by the biopsychosocial approach and combined in the diathesis-stress model to explain the case of José, a 55-year-old electronics technician. A healthy and vigorous father of two adult children, he was forced to take medical leave because of a series of sudden panic attacks in which he experienced dizziness, heart palpitations, sweating, and a sense of impending death. The attacks also kept him from his favorite pastime, scuba diving, but he has been able to maintain a part-time computer business out of his home. (Panic disorder is discussed in more detail later in this chapter; the outcome of this case is described in the chapter on treatment of psychological disorders.)

Explanatory Domain	Possible Contributing Factors
Medical (neurobiological)	José may have organic disorders (e.g., genetic tendency toward anxiety; brain tumor, endocrine dysfunction; neurotransmitter imbalance).
Psychological: psychodynamic	José has unconscious conflicts and desires. Instinctual impulses are breaking through ego defenses into consciousness, causing panic.
Psychological: social-cognitive	José interprets physical stress symptoms as signs of serious illness or impending death. Panic is rewarded by reduction in work stress when he stays home.
Psychological: humanistic	José fails to recognize his genuine feelings about work and his place in life, and he fears expressing himself.
Sociocultural	A culturally based belief that "a man should not show weakness" amplifies the intensity of stress reactions.
Diathesis-stress	José has a biological (possibly genetic) predisposition to be overly responsive to stressors. The stress of work and extra activity exceeds his capacity to cope and triggers panic as a stress response.

Classifying Psychological Disorders

Although definitions of abnormality differ somewhat within and across cultures, there is a set of culture-general and culture-specific behavior patterns that characterize what most mental health professionals consider to be psychopathology. Most of these behavior patterns qualify as disorders because they result in impaired functioning, a main criterion of the practical approach to defining abnormality. It has long been the goal of those who study abnormal behavior to organize these patterns into a system of diagnostic categories.

The main purpose of diagnosing psychological disorders is to determine the nature of people's problems. Once the characteristics of the problems are understood, the most appropriate method of treatment can be chosen. Diagnoses are also important for research on the causes of mental disorders. If researchers can accurately and reliably classify people into particular disorder categories, they will have a better chance of spotting genetic flaws, biological abnormalities, cognitive processes, and environmental experiences that people in the same category might share. Finding that people in a certain diagnostic category share a set of features that differ from those seen in other categories could provide clues about which features are related to the development of each disorder. In short, proper classification can lead to the discovery of causes.

The official North American diagnostic classification system, the *Diagnostic and Statistical Manual of Mental Disorders* (*DSM*), was first published by the American Psychiatric Association in 1952. It contained 168 pages and included sixty-six disorders. Each new edition of the *DSM* has added more categories of disorders. The latest editions, *DSM-IV* and *DSM-IV-TR* (which contains some text revisions), exceed 800 pages and include more than three hundred specific diagnostic labels (American Psychiatric Association, 1994, 2000). Each of these editions was designed to improve the quality of the diagnostic system by taking into account the results of the most recent research on psychopathology.

Outside North America, mental health professionals diagnose mental disorders using the classification systems that appear in the tenth edition of the World Health Organization's *International Classification of Diseases* (*ICD-10*) and its companion volume, the second edition of the *International Classification of Impairments, Disabilities and Handicaps* (*ICIDH-2*). To facilitate international communication and cross-cultural research with respect to psychopathology, *DSM-IV* was designed to be compatible with these manuals, and efforts are under way to remove inconsistencies existing between the systems (Cottler & Grant, 2007; Löwe et al., 2008; Widiger et al., 2006).

A Classification System: *DSM-IV-TR*

DSM-IV-TR describes the abnormal patterns of thinking, emotion, and behavior that define various mental disorders. For each disorder, *DSM* provides specific criteria outlining the conditions that must be present before a person can be given that diagnostic label. Diagnosticians using *DSM-IV-TR* can evaluate troubled people on as many as five dimensions, or *axes* (plural of *axis*). In keeping with the biopsychosocial approach, evaluations on all relevant dimensions are combined to create a broad outline of the person's biological and psychological problems, as well as of any sociocultural factors that might contribute to them. As shown in Table 15.2, major mental disorders, such as schizophrenia or major depressive disorder, are recorded on Axis I. Personality disorders, intellectual disability (previously known as mental retardation), and other lifelong conditions that tend not to change much over time are noted on Axis II. Any medical conditions that might be important in understanding the person's cognitive, emotional, or behavioral problems are listed on Axis III. On Axis IV, the diagnostician notes any psychosocial and environmental factors that are important for understanding the person's psychological problems. These factors include the loss of a loved one, physical or sexual abuse, discrimination, unemployment, poverty, homelessness, inadequate health care, and conflict with religious or cultural traditions. Finally, a rating (from 100 down to 1) of the person's current level of psychological, social, and occupational functioning appears on Axis V. Here is a sample *DSM-IV-TR* diagnosis for a person who received labels on all five axes:

Axis I:	Major depressive disorder, single episode; alcohol abuse.
Axis II:	Dependent personality disorder.
Axis III:	Alcoholic cirrhosis of the liver.
Axis IV:	Problems with primary support group (death of spouse).
Axis V:	Global assessment of functioning: 50.

Notice that the terms *neurosis* and *psychosis* are not included as they once were in *DSM*. They were dropped because they are too vague, but some mental health professionals still sometimes use them as shorthand descriptions. *Neurosis* refers to conditions in which some form of anxiety is the major characteristic. *Psychosis* refers to conditions involving severe thought disorders that leave people "out of touch with reality" or unable to function on a daily basis. The disorders once gathered under these headings now appear in various Axis I categories in *DSM-IV-TR*.

Further changes will appear in a new edition of *DSM*, *DSM-V*, currently in the final stages of development and slated for publication in 2013. For example, because it is common for certain kinds of disorders, such as anxiety and depression, to appear together, *DSM-V* diagnoses may include some labels that designate "mixed" disorders (Das-Munshi et al., 2008). A variety of other suggestions have been made, such as a new category for disorders characterized primarily by obsessive-compulsive symptoms (Hollander, Braum, & Simeon, 2008; Huprich, 2009). Another proposal is to organize *DSM-V* around symptom clusters or symptom dimensions rather than around specific diagnostic categories (Widiger & Lowe, 2008). The idea behind this *dimensional approach* would be to create a set of symptom "building blocks" that could be combined in many different ways so as to better describe the precise contours of each person's problems. Ratings of the severity of symptoms in each dimension would paint an even more detailed and meaningful picture of the problems a person is experiencing, a picture that would be of more use to clinicians (Krueger & Markon, 2006; Samuel & Widiger, 2006). There are also proposals for *DSM-V* that would label as addictions things such as preoccupation with sex and excessive amounts of eating, shopping, video game playing, texting, e-mailing, and other kinds of Internet use (Young, 2009).

TABLE 15.2   Axes I and II of the American Psychiatric Association's *Diagnostic and Statistical Manual of Mental Disorders*

Axis I of the fourth edition (*DSM-IV-TR*) lists the major categories of mental disorders. Personality disorders and intellectual disability (mental retardation) are listed on Axis II.

Axis I (Clinical Syndromes)

1. ***Disorders usually first diagnosed in infancy, childhood, or adolescence.*** Problems such as hyperactivity, childhood fears, conduct disorders, frequent bed-wetting or soiling, and other problems in normal social and behavioral development. Autistic disorder (severe impairment in social, behavioral, and language development), as well as learning disorders.

2. ***Delirium, dementia, and amnestic and other cognitive disorders.*** Problems caused by physical deterioration of the brain due to aging, disease, drugs or other chemicals, or other possible unknown causes. These problems can appear as an inability to "think straight" (delirium) or as loss of memory and other intellectual functions (dementia).

3. ***Substance-related disorders.*** Psychological, behavioral, physical, social, or legal problems caused by dependence on or abuse of a variety of chemical substances, including alcohol, heroin, cocaine, amphetamines, painkillers, hallucinogenic drugs, marijuana, and tobacco.

4. ***Schizophrenia and other psychotic disorders.*** Severe conditions characterized by abnormalities in thinking, perception, emotion, movement, and motivation that greatly interfere with daily functioning. Problems involving false beliefs (delusions).

5. ***Affective disorders*** (also called ***mood disorders***). Severe disturbances of mood, especially depression, overexcitement (mania), or alternating episodes of each extreme (as in bipolar disorder).

6. ***Anxiety disorders.*** Specific fears (phobias); panic attacks; generalized feelings of dread; rituals of thought and action (obsessive-compulsive disorder) aimed at controlling anxiety; and problems caused by traumatic events, such as rape or military combat (see the chapter on health, stress, and coping for more on posttraumatic stress disorder.)

7. ***Somatoform disorders.*** Physical symptoms, such as paralysis and blindness, that have no physical cause. Unusual preoccupation with physical health or with nonexistent physical problems (hypochondriasis, somatization disorder, pain disorder).

8. ***Factitious disorders.*** False mental disorders, which are intentionally produced to satisfy some psychological need.

9. ***Dissociative disorders.*** Psychologically caused problems of consciousness and self-identification—e.g., loss of memory (amnesia) or the development of more than one identity (dissociative identity disorder, or multiple personality).

10. ***Sexual and gender identity disorders.*** Problems of (a) finding sexual arousal through unusual objects (such as shoes) or situations (such as exposing one's genitals in public), (b) unsatisfactory sexual activity (sexual dysfunction), or (c) identifying with the opposite gender.

11. ***Eating disorders.*** Problems associated with eating too little (anorexia nervosa) or binge eating followed by self-induced vomiting (bulimia). (See the chapter on motivation and emotion.)

12. ***Sleep disorders.*** Severe problems involving the sleep-wake cycle, especially an inability to sleep well at night or to stay awake during the day. (See the chapter on consciousness.)

13. ***Impulse control disorders.*** Compulsive gambling, stealing, or fire setting.

14. ***Adjustment disorders.*** Failure to adjust to or deal well with such stressors as divorce, financial problems, family discord, or other unhappy life events.

Axis II (Personality Disorders and Intellectual Disability)

1. ***Personality disorders.*** Diagnostic labels given to individuals who may or may not receive an Axis I diagnosis but who show lifelong behavior patterns that are unsatisfactory to them or that disturb other people. These patterns may involve unusual suspiciousness, unusual ways of thinking, self-centeredness, shyness, overdependency, excessive concern with neatness and detail, or overemotionality, among others.

2. ***Intellectual disability (mental retardation).*** As described in the chapter on cognitive abilities, the label of intellectual disability (previously called mental retardation) is applied to individuals whose measured IQ is less than about 70 *and* who fail to display the skills of daily living, communication, and other tasks expected of people their age.

Not everyone is happy with these proposed changes. Critics, including those involved in the development of *DSM-III, DSM-IV,* and *DSM-IV-TR,* are concerned that some of the proposals being considered for *DSM-V* will have unintended negative consequences (Frances, 2009, 2010; Spitzer, 2009). They worry, for example, that giving ratings on many symptom dimensions might make it too easy for people with mild depression or anxiety to be labeled as having an affective or anxiety disorder. Similarly, rating the severity of "symptoms" such as shopping or Internet use—behaviors that are quite common in the general population—could greatly expand the concept of addiction and increase the number of individuals who qualify for a psychiatric diagnosis. These changes, say the skeptics, could create "false epidemics" of mental disorder and

Anxiety and Depression

People who experience anxiety disorders—particularly panic disorder, generalized anxiety disorder, or posttraumatic stress disorder—are likely to display some other mental disorder as well, most often depression (Byers et al., 2010; Kaufman & Charney, 2000; Roy-Byrne et al., 2000). Accordingly, the next edition of the *DSM* may include a new category, called *mixed anxiety-depression disorder,* to identify people whose symptoms of anxiety and depression combine to impair their daily functioning.

result in the "medicalization of normality." The American Psychiatric Association and its *DSM-V* task force defend the changes planned for *DSM-V* as reflecting the best and most current research available in the field of psychopathology (Schatzberg et al., 2009). The final outcome of the debate will not be known for some time.

In the meantime, some researchers have suggested that the diagnosis of behavior disorders should consider not just people's weaknesses and problems but also their character strengths, virtues, prosocial values, and other psychological resources on which they can potentially build during treatment. For example, each problem-oriented *DSM* diagnosis could be supplemented by a list of the strengths (such as resilience, courage, kindness, and tolerance) that contribute to the level of functioning rating that is noted on Axis V. Some researchers have even offered comprehensive lists of human strengths and values from which diagnosticians can choose (Baumgardner & Crothers, 2009; Park, Peterson, & Seligman, 2004; Peterson, 2006b). From the perspective of *positive psychology,* then, diagnosis via the *DSM* alone is regarded as valuable but incomplete. Not only does it tend to ignore people's strengths and values, but it also fails to recognize that people who *lack* certain character strengths and prosocial values can experience or cause a significant amount of discomfort and social impairment, even if they don't meet the "official" criteria for mental disorder.

Evaluating the Diagnostic System

Many changes are on the horizon, but how good is the current diagnostic system? One way to evaluate *DSM-IV-TR* is to consider *interrater reliability,* the degree to which different mental health professionals give the same person the same diagnostic label. Reviews of research show that the reliability of *DSM-IV-TR* is acceptable or high for some disorders but not others. For example, interrater agreement is strong on Axis I categories such as anxiety disorders, affective disorders, some childhood disorders, and schizophrenia (e.g., Brown et al., 2001; Jakobsen et al., 2005; Keenan et al., 2007; Simpson et al., 2002). It is much lower, though, for other categories such as somatoform disorders and Axis II personality disorders (Mayou et al., 2005; Shedler & Westen, 2004; Westen, Shedler, & Bradley, 2006; Wollert, 2007). Overall, interrater agreement appears highest overall when diagnosis is based on structured or semistructured interviews that systematically address each area of functioning and provide uniform guidelines for interpreting people's responses (Brown et al., 2001; Rogers, 2003; Widiger & Sanderson, 1995).

Do diagnostic labels carry enough information to accurately describe the people who receive those labels? This *validity* question is difficult to answer because accuracy can be judged in different ways. A diagnosis could be evaluated, for example, on how well it predicts a person's future behavior or perhaps on whether the person is helped by treatment that has helped others in the same diagnostic category. There is certainly evidence for the validity of most *DSM-IV-TR* criteria (Deep-Soboslay et al., 2006; Keenan & Wakschlag, 2004; Kim-Cohen et al., 2005; Langenbucher & Nathan, 2006; Simon & von Korff, 2006; Vieta & Phillips, 2007), but as with reliability, validity is stronger for some diagnoses (e.g., schizophrenia, depression) than for others (e.g., ADHD, somatoform disorders).

In short, the diagnostic system is far from perfect (Beutler & Malik, 2002; Kendell & Jablensky, 2003; Krueger & Markon, 2006; Nestadt et al., 2005; Widiger & Sankis, 2000). First, as already mentioned, people's problems often do not fit neatly into a single category; mixed (or "comorbid") disorders are common. Second, the same symptom (such as sleeplessness) may appear as part of more than one disorder. Third, *DSM-IV-TR* specifies that to be given a particular diagnosis, a person must display a certain number of symptoms at a certain level of severity for a certain period of time. If these criteria are met, a person is said to "have" a certain disorder. But in setting these criteria, the authors of *DSM-IV-TR* had to identify some rather arbitrary boundaries between "having" a disorder and "not having" it. These sharp boundaries fail to capture the varying levels of distress that different people experience. Further,

© John Birdsall/The Image Works

diagnostic criteria often specify that there be "clinically significant impairment," but they provide few, if any, guidelines for what that phrase means. When mental health professionals must decide for themselves whether a particular person's symptoms are severe enough to warrant a particular diagnosis, personal bias can creep into the system (Kim & Ahn, 2002; Widiger & Clark, 2000). All of these factors can lead to misdiagnosis in some cases. Concern over this possibility is especially relevant as the nations of North America and Western Europe become increasingly multicultural. The current *DSM* disorder categories sometimes fail to take into account the ways that different cultures influence the experience and expression of distress. Diagnosticians in these countries are encountering more and more people whose cultural backgrounds they may not fully understand and whose behavior they may misunderstand.

Some people whose behavior differs enough from cultural norms to cause annoyance feel that society should tolerate their "neurodiversity" instead of giving them a diagnostic label (Harmon, 2004). In the same vein, Thomas Szasz (pronounced "sahz") and other critics of the medical model (e.g., Caplan, 1995; Kutchins & Kirk, 1997; Peterson, 2003; Snyder & Lopez, 2006; Szasz, 2003; Wampold, Ahn, & Coleman, 2001) argue that labeling people instead of describing them is dehumanizing because it ignores features that make each person unique. Calling people "schizophrenics" or "alcoholics," Szasz says, may actually encourage the behaviors associated with these labels and undermine the confidence of clients (and therapists) about the chances of improvement.

Obviously, the current system for diagnosing psychological disorders has not satisfied everyone, and it is unlikely that any system ever will. No shorthand diagnostic label can fully describe a person's problems or predict exactly how that person will behave. All that can be reasonably expected of a diagnostic system is that it be based on the latest research on psychopathology and that it provide informative, general descriptions of the types of problems displayed by people who have been placed in various categories.

THINKING CRITICALLY

Is Psychological Diagnosis Biased?

Some researchers and clinicians worry that problems with the reliability and validity of the diagnostic system are due partly to bias in its construction and use. They point out, for example, that if the diagnostic criteria for various disorders are based on research that focused on one culture, one gender, one ethnic group, or one age group, those criteria might not apply to other groups. Moreover, because diagnosticians, like other people, hold expectations and make assumptions about males versus females and about individuals from differing cultures or ethnic groups, those cognitive biases could color their judgments. This "prejudging" process could lead to the application of diagnostic criteria in ways that are slightly but significantly different from one case to the next.

What am I being asked to believe or accept?

Here we focus on ethnicity as a possible source of bias in diagnosing psychopathology. It is of special interest because there is evidence that like social class and gender, ethnicity is an important sociocultural factor in the development of mental disorder. So the assertion to be considered is that clinicians in the United States base their diagnoses partly on clients' ethnic background and, more specifically, that there is bias in diagnosing African Americans.

What evidence is available to support the assertion?

Several facts suggest the possibility of ethnic bias in psychological diagnosis. For one thing, African Americans receive the diagnosis of schizophrenia more frequently than European Americans do (American Psychiatric Association, 2000; Barnes, 2004; Kilbourne et al., 2004; Minsky et al., 2003). In fact, certain kinds of odd symptoms tend to be diagnosed as an affective disorder in European Americans but as schizophrenia in African Americans (Neighbors et al., 2003; Schwartz & Feisthamel, 2009). Further, relative to their presence in the general population, African Americans are overrepresented in public mental hospitals, where the most serious forms of disorder are seen, and underrepresented in private hospitals and outpatient clinics, where less severe problems are treated (Barnes, 2004; Snowden & Cheung, 1990; U.S. Surgeon General, 1999). African Americans are also more likely than European Americans to be discharged from mental hospitals without a definitive diagnosis, suggesting that clinicians have more difficulty diagnosing their disorders (Sohler & Bromet, 2003). Other research suggests that emergency room physicians are less likely to recognize psychiatric disorders in African American patients than in patients from other groups (Kunen et al., 2005).

There is also evidence that African Americans and members of other ethnic minority groups are underrepresented in research on mental disorders. One review found that minority participants were included in less than 30 percent of the research published in five leading clinical psychology journals over a seventeen-year period (Iwamasa, Sorocco, & Koonce, 2002). If such underrepresentation leaves clinicians less sensitive to the operation of sociocultural factors in certain groups, the quality of their diagnoses could be affected. For example, a European American diagnostician might interpret an African American patient's suspiciousness as evidence of paranoid thinking when it might actually reflect the patient's history of unpleasant experiences with white authority figures (Whaley, 2001).

Are there alternative ways of interpreting the evidence?

Differences among ethnic groups in diagnosis or treatment do not automatically indicate bias based on ethnicity. Perhaps there are real differences in psychological functioning across different ethnic groups. If, relative to other groups, African Americans are exposed to more risk factors for disorder, such as poverty, violence, or other major stressors, they could be more vulnerable to more serious forms of mental disorder (Plant & Sachs-Ericsson, 2004; Turner & Lloyd, 2004). And poverty, not diagnostic bias, could be responsible for the fact that African Americans more often seek help at less expensive public hospitals than at more expensive private ones. Indeed, African Americans are more likely than European Americans to bring mental health problems to hospital emergency rooms rather than to family physicians or other mental health service providers. So perhaps African Americans are less likely to come to the attention of mental health professionals until their disorders have become more severe (Nelson, 2006).

What additional evidence would help evaluate the alternatives?

So do African Americans actually display more signs of schizophrenia, or do diagnosticians just perceive them as more disordered? One way of approaching this question is to conduct experiments in which diagnosticians assign labels to clients on the basis of case histories, test scores, and the like. In some studies, the cases are selected so that pairs of clients show about the same degree of disorder but one member of the pair is identified as European American and the other as African American. In other studies, the same case materials, identified as representing either African American or European American patients, are presented to different diagnosticians. Bias in diagnosis would be suggested if, for example, patients identified as African American were labeled as more seriously disordered than others.

The results of such studies are mixed. Most have found little or no ethnic bias (e.g., Angold et al., 2002; Garb, 1997; Kales et al., 2005a, 2005b; Littlewood, 1992), but because the diagnosticians could have been aware of the purpose of the research, they might have gone out of their way to be unbiased (Abreu, 1999). Some evidence of diagnostic bias against African Americans *has* been found when clinicians were unaware of the purpose of the research (e.g., Baskin, Bluestone, & Nelson, 1981; Jones, 1982). But bias can result in underdiagnosis as well as overdiagnosis. One review of research found that African American children exhibited more signs of hyperactivity disorder than

European American children did but were given that diagnosis less often (Miller, Nigg, & Miller, 2009). In another study, socially disruptive African American youngsters were less likely than disruptive European American adolescents to be diagnosed with conduct disorder (Pottick et al., 2007). These results suggest that some diagnosticians may believe that a certain amount of overactivity, inattention, and misbehavior is to be expected of African Americans and that this behavior is therefore "normal" for them.

Bias has also appeared in studies aimed at identifying the factors influencing clinicians' diagnostic judgments following extensive interviews with patients. One study conducted in a hospital setting found that in arriving at a diagnosis, psychiatrists were more likely to see hallucinations and paranoid thinking in African American patients than in patients who were not African American. Symptoms of affective disorders were more likely to be seen in those who were not African American (Trierweiler et al., 2000). As noted earlier, these differences could reflect differences in the rate of disorder in different populations, but when people were interviewed in their own homes as part of large-scale mental health surveys, the diagnosis of schizophrenia was given only slightly more often to African Americans than to European Americans (Robins & Regier, 1991; Snowden & Cheung, 1990). In other words, ethnic bias is suggested, at least for some diagnoses, for patients who are evaluated in mental hospitals (Trierweiler et al., 2000, 2005).

What conclusions are most reasonable?

Just as *DSM-IV-TR* is imperfect, so are the people who use it. As described in the chapters on cognition and language and on social cognition, biases and stereotypes affect human thinking to some extent in virtually every social situation. It should not be surprising, then, that they operate in diagnosis as well. But diagnostic bias does not necessarily reflect deliberate discrimination. Like the processes of prejudice discussed in the chapter on social cognition, diagnostic bias based on ethnicity can operate unconsciously, without the diagnostician's awareness (Abreu, 1999; Boysen, 2009). So no matter how precisely researchers specify the criteria for assigning diagnostic labels, conscious or unconscious cognitive biases and stereotypes are likely to threaten the objectivity of the diagnostic process (Poland & Caplan, 2004; Trierweiler et al., 2000). Still, it would be incorrect to conclude that the entire diagnostic system is biased against African Americans because there is evidence that given the same symptom information, clinicians are just as likely to assign certain diagnoses, such as depression, to African Americans as to European Americans (Kales et al., 2005a, 2005b).

To minimize the bias that does operate, it has been suggested that diagnosticians should focus more intently than ever on the fact that their concepts of "normality" and "abnormality" are affected by sociocultural values that they may not share with a given client (Kales et al., 2006; Landrine, 1991; Whaley & Hall, 2009). They must also become more aware that the cognitive shortcuts and biases that affect everyone else's thinking and decision making can impair their own clinical judgments (Lopez, 1989). Perhaps the best way to counteract clinicians' cognitive shortcomings is to teach them to base their diagnoses solely on published diagnostic criteria, standardized interview formats, and statistically validated decision rules (aided, perhaps, by specialized computer programs) rather than relying on their potentially biased clinical impressions (Akin & Turner, 2006; Bernstein, Kramer, & Phares, 2009).

We don't have the space to cover all the *DSM-IV-TR* categories, so we will sample several of the most prevalent and socially significant ones. As you read, try not to catch "medical student's disease." Just as medical students often think they have the symptoms of every illness they read about, some psychology students worry that their behavior (or that of a relative or friend) signals a mental disorder. These days, this worry is called *cyberchondria* (Harding et al., 2008; Lewis, 2006; Markoff, 2008) because it often stems from people's unguided use of the Internet to learn about psychiatric disorders (Al-Shammary et al., 2007; Lewis, 2006; Trotter & Morgan, 2008).

Just remember that everyone has problems sometimes. Before deciding that you or someone you know needs psychological help, consider whether the content, context, and functional impairment associated with the behavior would qualify it as abnormal according to the criteria of the practical approach.

Anxiety Disorders

If you have ever been tense before an exam, a date, or a job interview, you have some idea of what anxiety feels like. Increased heart rate, sweating, rapid breathing, a dry mouth, and a sense of dread are common features of anxiety. Brief episodes of moderate anxiety are a normal part of life for most people. But when anxiety is so intense and long-lasting that it impairs a person's daily functioning, it is called an **anxiety disorder** (Kessler & Wang, 2008).

Types of Anxiety Disorders

Here we discuss four types of anxiety disorders: *phobia, generalized anxiety disorder, panic disorder,* and *obsessive-compulsive disorder*. Another type, called posttraumatic stress disorder, is described in the chapter on health, stress, and coping. Together, these are the most common psychological disorders in North America; about 29 percent of the U.S. population will have an anxiety disorder at some point in their lives (Kessler et al., 2009).

Phobia   An intense, irrational fear of an object or situation that is not likely to be dangerous is called a **phobia**. People who experience phobias usually realize that their fears are groundless, but that's not enough to make the anxiety go away. The continuing discomfort and avoidance of the object or event may greatly interfere with daily life. Thousands of phobias have been described; Table 15.3 lists just a few.

DSM-IV-TR classifies phobias into specific, social, and agoraphobia subtypes. **Specific phobias** include fear and avoidance of heights, blood, animals, automobile or air travel, or other specific stimuli and situations. In the United States and other developed nations, they are the most prevalent of the anxiety disorders, affecting 9 to 10 percent of adults and children (Hollander & Simeon, 2008; Kessler & Wang, 2008; NIMH, 2006). Here is an example:

> Mr. L. was a 50-year-old office worker who became terrified whenever he had to drive over a bridge. For years, he avoided bridges by taking roundabout ways to and from work, and he refused to be a passenger in other people's cars, just in case they might use a bridge. Even this very inconvenient adjustment failed when Mr. L. was transferred to a position requiring frequent automobile trips, many of which were over bridges. He refused the transfer and lost his job.

It's a Long Way Down

Almost everyone is afraid of something, but about 9 or 10 percent of U.S. adults have a specific phobia in which fear interferes significantly with daily life (Kessler & Wang, 2008). For example, people with acrophobia (fear of heights) would not do well in a job that requires being in this high position.

anxiety disorder A condition in which intense feelings of apprehension are long-standing and disruptive.

phobia An anxiety disorder involving strong, irrational fear of an object or situation that does not objectively justify such a reaction.

specific phobia An anxiety disorder involving fear and avoidance of heights, animals, or other specific stimuli and situations.

TABLE 15.3 Some Phobias			
Phobia, the Greek word for "morbid fear," refers to *Phobos*, the Greek god of terror. The names of most phobias begin with the Greek word for the feared object or situation.			
Name	**Feared Stimulus**	**Name**	**Feared Stimulus**
Acrophobia	Heights	Aerophobia	Flying
Claustrophobia	Enclosed places	Entomophobia	Insects
Hematophobia	Blood	Gamophobia	Marriage
Gephyrophobia	Crossing a bridge	Ophidiphobia	Snakes
Kenophobia	Empty rooms	Xenophobia	Strangers
Cynophobia	Dogs	Melissophobia	Bees

Social phobias involve anxiety about being criticized by others or acting in a way that is embarrassing or humiliating. The anxiety is so intense and persistent that it impairs the person's normal functioning. Common social phobias are fear of public speaking or performance ("stage fright"), fear of eating in front of others, and fear of using public restrooms (Gren-Landell et al., 2009; Kleinknecht, 2000).

Generalized social phobia is a more severe form in which fear occurs in virtually all social situations (Jacobs et al., 2009; Mineka & Zinbarg, 2006). One person described the problem this way (NIMH, 2007, p. 9):

> In any situation, I felt fear. I would be anxious before I even left the house, and it would escalate as I got closer to a college class, a party, or whatever. When I would walk into a room full of people, I'd turn red, and it would feel like everybody's eyes were on me.... I couldn't think of anything to say; ... I couldn't wait to get out.

Sociocultural factors can alter the nature of social phobias. For example, in Japan, where cultural training emphasizes group-oriented values and goals, a common social phobia is *taijin kyofusho,* the fear that your appearance, odor, or actions are causing offense or embarrassment to those around you (Kleinknecht, 1994).

Agoraphobia is a strong fear of being away from a safe place, such as home; of being away from a familiar person, such as a spouse or close friend; or of being in a place (such as a crowded theater or mall) that might be difficult to leave or where help may be unavailable. These fears can cause serious problems. People who suffer from agoraphobia typically avoid social situations and refuse to shop, drive, or use public transportation. They may be unable to work and can easily become isolated. In severe cases, agoraphobia can make leaving home such a frightening prospect that people become housebound, unwilling to even try going out alone. Most individuals who display agoraphobia have a history of panic attacks, which we describe later (Fava et al., 2008). Their intense fear of public places occurs partly because they don't want to risk triggering an attack by going to places in which they had a previous attack or where they feel an attack would be dangerous or embarrassing (Kessler, Chiu, et al., 2006).

Like other phobias in Western cultures, agoraphobia is more often reported by women (McLean & Anderson, 2009). However, in other cultures, such as India, where being a housebound woman is considered less unusual than in the United States, individuals diagnosed as agoraphobic tend to be male (Raguram & Bhide, 1985). Agoraphobia is far less common than specific phobias (affecting about 0.8 percent of the U.S. population, versus 9 percent for specific phobias), but it often leads people to seek treatment, mainly because it interferes so severely with everyday life (Kessler & Wang, 2008).

Generalized Anxiety Disorder   Excessive and long-lasting anxiety that is not focused on any particular object or situation marks **generalized anxiety disorder (GAD)**. Because the problem occurs in almost all situations and because the person cannot pinpoint its source, this type of anxiety is sometimes called *free-floating anxiety* and is essentially a disorder of worry (Fisher & Wells, 2009). For weeks at a time, the person feels anxious and worried, sure that some disaster is about to happen. The person becomes jumpy and irritable; sound sleep is impossible. Fatigue, inability to concentrate, and physiological signs of anxiety are also common. Generalized anxiety disorder affects about 3 percent of the U.S. population in any given year and about 6 percent of the population at some point in their lives (Hollander & Simeon, 2008; Kessler & Wang, 2008). This disorder tends to appear somewhat later in life than most of the other anxiety disorders (the median age of onset is 31 for GAD, whereas it is the teens or early twenties for phobias). Generalized anxiety disorder is more common in women, often accompanying other problems such as depression or substance abuse (Wittchen & Hoyer, 2001).

social phobia   An anxiety disorder involving strong, irrational fears relating to social situations.

agoraphobia   An anxiety disorder involving strong fear of being alone or away from the security of home.

generalized anxiety disorder (GAD)   A condition that involves relatively mild but long-lasting anxiety that is not focused on any particular object or situation.

Panic Disorder For some individuals, anxiety takes the form of **panic disorder**. Like the man profiled in Table 15.1, people suffering from panic disorder experience recurrent, terrifying *panic attacks* that come without warning or obvious cause. These attacks are marked by intense heart palpitations, pressure or pain in the chest, dizziness or unsteadiness, sweating, and feeling faint. Often victims believe they are having a heart attack. Their overall quality of life suffers because they worry constantly about suffering future panic episodes and consequently restrict their activities to avoid possible embarrassment (Kinley et al., 2009). As noted earlier, fear of experiencing panic attacks while alone or away from home can lead to agoraphobia, as it does in about one-third of people with panic disorder (Carter & Barlow, 1995; NIMH, 2006; Robins & Regier, 1991). Panic disorder can continue for years, with periods of improvement followed by recurrences (Ehlers, 1995). Many people have experienced at least one panic attack in their lives, but only about 2 to 3 percent of the adult population develops full-blown panic disorder in any given year (American Psychiatric Association, 2000; Kessler & Wang, 2008; Kessler, Chiu, et al., 2006). Here is one example:

> Geri, a 32-year-old nurse, had her first panic attack while driving on a freeway. Afterward, she would not drive on freeways. Her next attack occurred while with a patient and a doctor in a small examining room. A sense of impending doom flooded over her, and she burst out of the office and into the parking lot, where she felt immediate relief. From then on, fear of another attack made it impossible for her to tolerate any close quarters, including crowded shopping malls. She eventually quit her job because of terror of the examining rooms.

Obsessive-Compulsive Disorder Anxiety is also at the root of **obsessive-compulsive disorder (OCD)**, which affects about 1 percent of the population in any given year in the United States and elsewhere (Kessler & Wang, 2008; Ruscio et al., 2010). This disorder is equally common in males and females (Zhang et al., 2009), and like Mark, whose story opened this chapter, people displaying OCD are plagued by persistent, upsetting, and unwanted thoughts—called **obsessions**—that often center on the possibility of infection, contamination, or doing harm to themselves or others. They do not actually carry out harmful acts, but the obsessive thoughts motivate ritualistic, repetitive behaviors—called **compulsions**—that are performed in an effort to avoid some dreaded outcome or to reduce feelings of anxiety associated with the obsessions (Noyes & Hoehn-Saric, 2006). For example, Mark engaged in incessant, ritualized cleaning to protect himself from infection. Other common compulsions include rituals such as checking locks; repeating words, images, or numbers; counting things; or arranging objects "just so." Obsessions and compulsions are much more intense than the familiar experience of having a repetitive thought or tune "in the back of your mind" or rechecking that a door is locked. In OCD, the obsessions and compulsions are intense, disturbing intrusions that can severely impair daily activities (Morillo, Belloch, & Garcia-Soriano, 2007). Although many people who display this disorder recognize that their thoughts and actions are irrational, they still experience severe agitation and anxiety if they try to interrupt their obsessions or give up their compulsive behaviors.

© Photosani/Shutterstock

A Cleaning Compulsion

Mild obsessions are relatively common (Fullana et al., 2009), but obsessive-compulsive disorder is diagnosed when a culturally expected degree of cleanliness becomes an obsessive preoccupation with germs and a disruptive compulsion to clean things. Though learning experiences and stress appear to play the major role in shaping and triggering this and other anxiety disorders, biological factors, including genetically inherited characteristics and problems in certain neurotransmitter systems in the brain, may result in an oversensitive nervous system and a predisposition toward anxiety.

Causes of Anxiety Disorders

As with all the forms of psychopathology we will consider, the exact causes of anxiety disorders are a matter of some debate. However, there is good evidence that biological, psychological, and social factors all contribute. Biological predispositions, distortions in thinking, and certain learning experiences appear to be particularly important (Coelho & Purkis, 2009; Williams et al., 2005). The exact nature and combination of causal factors varies from one anxiety disorder to the next. For example, the brain regions involved in panic disorder are not identical to those involved in obsessive-compulsive disorder, and the learning experiences contributing to specific phobia may differ from those contributing to agoraphobia.

Biological Factors   Most anxiety disorders, including panic disorder, obsessive-compulsive disorder, and generalized social phobia, appear to run in families (Bolton et al., 2006; Grabe et al., 2006; Stewart et al., 2007). This tendency may be partly due to environmental factors that affect members of the same family, but it also suggests that people may inherit a predisposition to develop anxiety disorders (e.g., Fyer et al., 2006). Genetic influences on these disorders are suggested by research showing that if one identical twin has an anxiety disorder, the other twin (who shares the same genes) is more likely also to have an anxiety disorder than is the case in nonidentical twin pairs (Bolton et al., 2006; Kendler et al., 2002). Data from twin, family, and other studies suggest, for example, that genetic influences play a relatively strong role in panic disorder and generalized anxiety disorder, particularly when there is early onset of symptoms (Bolton et al., 2006; Hettema, Neale, & Kendler, 2001; Neumeister et al., 2004). Some evidence suggests that genetic factors appear to influence social phobia more strongly in males than in females (Kendler et al., 2002), but overall, the genetic and environmental risk factors for anxiety disorders are similar in men and women (Hettema et al., 2005).

Some inherited predispositions may be rather specific. For instance, one study has found that identical twins were more likely than other siblings to share phobias of small animals and social situations but not a fear of heights or enclosed spaces (Skre et al., 2000). The degree of genetic influence in anxiety disorders is moderate, however (Hollander & Simeon, 2008), and varies among disorders. For instance, genes appear to play a stronger role in early-onset panic disorder and generalized anxiety disorder than in specific phobias (Bolton et al., 2006; Distel et al., 2008; Neumeister et al., 2004). Researchers are trying to identify the specific genes or gene combinations involved in anxiety disorders. For example, a number of genes have been suggested as contributing to OCD, including two variations of the SLlC6A4 gene (Saiz et al., 2008). This work is difficult, though, because the mere presence of a gene doesn't necessary predict the appearance of a disorder. Rather, as described in our discussion of *epigenetics* in the opening chapter of this book, genes are often "switched on" or "switched off" by environmental triggers (Uddin et al., 2010).

It will take much more research to determine the degree to which various anxiety disorders are influenced by specific genetic factors or more general ones. For example, as described in the personality chapter, people who display anxiety disorders may have inherited an autonomic nervous system that is oversensitive to stress and easily conditioned, thus predisposing them to react with intense anxiety to a wide range of situations (Akimova, Lanzenberger, & Kasper, 2009; Bracha, 2006; Naragon-Gainey, 2010; Nash et al., 2008). A predisposition for developing anxiety disorders may also stem from abnormalities in the brain's neurotransmitter activity. Excessive activity of norepinephrine circuits in certain parts of the brain has been linked with panic disorder, and dysregulation of serotonin has been associated with obsessive-compulsive disorder and social phobia (Lanzenberger et al., 2007). Supporting this view is evidence that medications that affect these neurotransmitters are often effective in the treatment of OCD and other anxiety disorders (Bartz & Hollander, 2006).

Psychological and Environmental Factors   Although biological predispositions may set the stage for anxiety disorders, most researchers agree that environmental stressors and psychological factors, including cognitive processes and learning, are crucial to the development of most anxiety disorders (Hudson & Rapee, 2009; Mineka & Zinbarg, 2006; Moses & Barlow, 2006; Wilcox et al., 2008). To see the effects of environmental stressors, one need only look at the dramatic rise in cases of posttraumatic stress disorder following military combat, natural disasters, or terrorist attacks (Galea, Resnick, et al., 2002; Hoven et al., 2005). The impact of learning can be seen in families in which parents don't socialize much, tend to be suspicious of others, and constantly exaggerate life's everyday dangers. These parents may unwittingly promote social anxiety in their children—especially children born with a tendency toward shyness—by influencing them to interpret social situations as threatening

panic disorder An anxiety disorder involving sudden panic attacks.

obsessive-compulsive disorder (OCD) An anxiety disorder involving repetitive thoughts and urges to perform certain rituals.

obsessions Persistent, upsetting, and unwanted thoughts that interfere with daily life and may lead to compulsions.

compulsions Repetitive behaviors that interfere with daily functioning but are performed in an effort to prevent dangers or events associated with obsessions.

(Essex et al., 2010). Abuse or other traumatic childhood experiences also increase the risk of developing an anxiety disorder, particularly panic disorder (Brook & Schmidt, 2008; Safren et al., 2002).

People with an anxiety disorder often exaggerate the dangers in their environment, thereby creating an unrealistic expectation that bad events are going to happen (Brook & Schmidt, 2008; Cisler & Koster, 2010; Ouimet, Gawronski, & Dozois, 2009). This expectation leads them to dwell on and be constantly on the lookout for negative events (Vroling & de Jong, 2010; Wells & Matthews, 2006; Wong & Moulds, 2009). Further, because they tend to underestimate their capacity to control threatening events, they are likely to experience anxiety and desperation if and when feared events do occur. Their lack of perceived control can in turn lead these people to overreact to threatening situations or avoid them entirely (Wells & Matthews, 2006; White et al., 2006). Consider the development of a panic attack. Unexplained symptoms of physical arousal may set the stage for a panic attack, but it is the person's sensitivity to and cognitive interpretation of those symptoms that can determine whether or not the attack actually develops (Domschke et al., 2010; Hollander & Simeon, 2008; Lim & Kim, 2005). In fact, panic attacks are less likely in panic disorder patients who believe they can control the source of their discomfort (Rapee et al., 1992; White et al., 2006). In short, a number of dysfunctional beliefs and cognitive distortions are associated with the development of anxiety disorders (Kolassa et al., 2009; Purdon, 2009).

LINKAGES

LINKAGES Can we learn to become "abnormal?" (a link to Learning, p. 206)

Anxiety Disorders and Learning

The principles discussed in the chapter on learning also play an important role in anxiety disorders. For example, distressing thoughts—about money or illness, for example—often give rise to anxiety and worry, especially when people are already under stress or feel incapable of dealing with their problems. As the thoughts become more persistent, anxiety increases. If doing something such as, say, cleaning the kitchen temporarily relieves the anxiety, that behavior may be strengthened through the process of negative reinforcement discussed in the chapter on learning. But cleaning can't eliminate the obsessive thoughts, so they return, and the actions become compulsive, endlessly repeated rituals that keep the person trapped in a vicious circle

Learning by Watching

Many phobias, including those involving needles, blood, and medical-related situations, are acquired vicariously—by what we see and hear. In fact, fear developed through observational learning can be as strong as fear developed through direct experience. Fearlessness can also be learned vicariously. By simply watching the boy in the dental chair as he learns to relax with his dentist, the other youngster is less likely to be distressed when it is his turn.

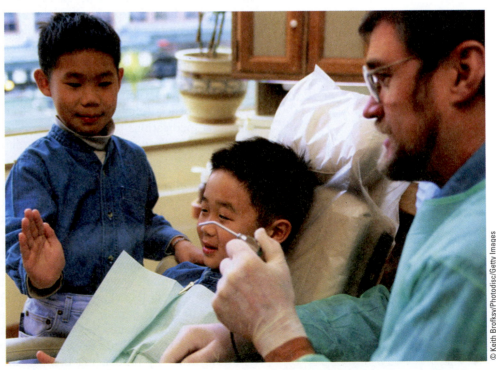

© Keith Brofksy/Photodisc/Getty Images

of anxiety. To social-cognitive theorists, then, obsessive-compulsive disorder is a pattern that is sparked by distressing thoughts and maintained by operant conditioning (Abramowitz et al., 2006).

Phobias, too, may be partly based on learning, especially on the principles of classical conditioning and observational learning described in the learning chapter. The feared object becomes an aversive conditioned stimulus after being associated with a traumatic event that acts as an unconditioned stimulus (Olatunji, 2006; Stein, 2006). Fear of dogs, for example, may result from a dog attack. But fear can also be learned merely by seeing or hearing about other people's bad experiences. These fears can even be learned by watching TV or movies (Askew, Kessock-Philip, & Field, 2008; Cook & Mineka, 1990). Perhaps you know someone who became reluctant to take a shower after seeing the horrific murder scene in Alfred Hitchcock's film *Psycho*. Once phobias are learned, avoiding the feared object or situation prevents the person from finding out that there is nothing to fear. This cycle of avoidance helps explain why many phobias do not simply extinguish, or disappear, on their own (Lovibond et al., 2009).

Why are phobias about snakes and spiders so common, even though people are seldom harmed by them? And why are there so few phobias about electrical shock, even though lots of people receive accidental shocks? As discussed in the chapter on learning, the answer may be that we are *biologically prepared* to learn associations between certain stimuli and certain responses. These stimuli and responses, then, would be especially easy to link through conditioning. Specifically, we may be biologically prepared to learn to fear and avoid stimuli that harmed our evolutionary ancestors (Canu, 2008; Öhman & Mineka, 2001, 2003; Skre et al., 2000).

The notion that people are biologically prepared to learn certain phobias is supported by laboratory evidence. For example, a group of Swedish psychologists attempted to condition people to fear certain stimuli by associating those stimuli with electrical shocks (Öhman, Dimberg, & Öst, 1985). The research participants developed approximately equal conditioned anxiety reactions to photos of houses, human faces, and snakes. Later, however, when they were tested without shock, their fear reaction to snakes remained long after their reaction to houses and faces had faded. A series of investigations with animals has also supported preparedness theory (Cook & Mineka, 1990; Shibasaki & Kawai, 2009). If a monkey sees

Biological Preparedness

TRY THIS Being predisposed to learn to fear snakes and other potentially dangerous stimuli makes evolutionary sense. Humans and other animals who rapidly learn a fear response to objects or situations that they see frightening their parents or peers are more likely to survive to pass on their genes to the next generation. Are there things that you are especially afraid of? If so, list them, and make a note of how you think these fears developed. How many of them appear to have "survival value"?

Photo reproduced with permission of Dr. Susan Mineka, Northwestern University

another monkey behaving fearfully in the presence of a snake, it quickly develops a strong and persistent fear of snakes. However, if the snake is entwined in flowers, the observer monkeys come to fear only the snake, not the flowers. So the fear conditioning appears to be selective, focusing only on potentially dangerous creatures such as snakes or crocodiles (Mühlberger et al., 2006; Zinbarg & Mineka, 1991) and not on harmless objects.

Learning is obviously important in the development of fear, but learning principles alone cannot explain why exposure to certain stimuli causes anxiety disorders in some people and not in others (Field, 2006). Leyro, Zvolensky, & Bernstein; Why is it, for example, that some survivors of the 9/11 terrorist attacks developed phobias or posttraumatic stress disorder and others did not? As suggested by the diathesis-stress approach and as discussed in the chapter on health, stress, and coping, the impact of people's experiences is heightened or dampened by other factors, such as their genetic and biological vulnerability or resilience to stress, their previous experiences with frightening events, their expectations and other cognitive habits, and the social support and other conditions that follow the trauma (Armfield, 2006; Leyro, Zvolensky, & Bernstein, 2010; Mineka & Zinbarg, 2006; Xie et al., 2009). In short, learning—including the learning that supports the development of anxiety disorders—occurs more quickly among those who are biologically and psychologically prepared for it.

Somatoform Disorders

A 10-year-old boy was hospitalized with what appeared to be a case of juvenile myasthenia gravis (a weakening of the voluntary muscles). For five weeks he had been unable to open his eyes, which had prevented him from going to school. Physical examination revealed no other abnormalities, but he was the star of his school's football team, and his symptoms first appeared on the day that he had been blamed for the team's defeat (Leary, 2003). Sometimes people show symptoms of a *somatic,* or bodily, disorder, even though it has no physical cause. Because these conditions reflect psychological problems that take somatic form, they are called **somatoform disorders**. The classic example is **conversion disorder**, a condition in which a person appears to be, but is not, blind, deaf, paralyzed, or insensitive to pain in various parts of the body. (An earlier term for this disorder was *hysteria*.) Conversion disorders are rare, accounting for only about 2 percent of diagnoses (American Psychiatric Association, 2000; Eifert, Zvolensky, & Louis, 2008). Although they can occur at any point in life, they usually appear in adolescence or early adulthood.

Conversion disorders differ from true physical disabilities in several ways. First, they tend to appear when a person is under severe stress. Second, they often help reduce that stress by allowing the person to avoid unpleasant or threatening situations. Third, the person may show remarkably little concern about what is apparently a rather serious problem. Finally, the symptoms may be neurologically impossible or improbable, as Figure 15.2 illustrates.

Can people who display a conversion disorder actually see, hear, or move, even though they act as if they cannot? Observations and experiments suggest that they can. Supposedly paralyzed people have been seen to sleepwalk, and supposedly blind or deaf people make use of sights and sounds to guide their behavior (e.g., Blake, 1998; Grosz & Zimmerman, 1970). But this does not mean that they are *malingering,* or faking. In fact, conversion disorder is diagnosed only when the symptoms are *not* being faked. Rather than destroying sensory or motor ability, the conversion process may prevent the person from being aware of information that the brain is processing (Ballmaier & Schmidt, 2005; Harvey, Stanton, & David, 2006).

Another somatoform disorder is **hypochondriasis** (pronounced "hy-poh-kahn-DRY-uh-siss"), a strong, unjustified fear that one has cancer, heart disease, AIDS, or

---

somatoform disorders Psychological problems in which symptoms of a physical disorder are present without a physical cause.

conversion disorder A somatoform disorder in which a person displays blindness, deafness, or other symptoms of sensory or motor failure without a physical cause.

hypochondriasis A somatoform disorder involving strong, unjustified fear of having physical illness.

FIGURE 15.2
Glove Anesthesia

In "glove anesthesia," a form of conversion disorder, lack of feeling stops abruptly at the wrist, as in part B. But as shown in part A, the nerves of the hand and arm blend, so if they were actually impaired, part of the arm would also lose sensitivity. Another neurologically impossible symptom of conversion disorder is sleepwalking at night on legs that are "paralyzed" during the day.

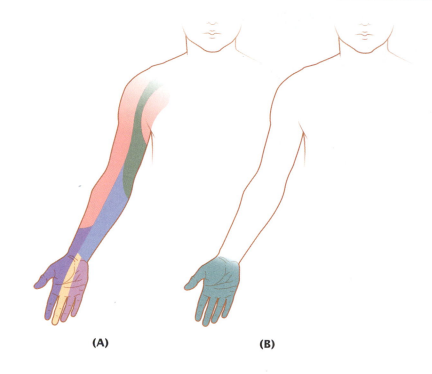

(A)   (B)

some other serious physical problem. In some ways, hypochondriasis is like an anxiety disorder in that it involves health concerns and includes elements of phobia, panic, and obsessive-compulsive disorder (Olantunji, 2008). People with hypochondriasis make frequent doctor visits to report numerous symptoms and request unnecessary treatment. They may even become "experts" on their most feared diseases, sometimes by endlessly searching health-related Internet Web sites (Hiller et al., 2006; Taylor & Asmundson, 2008).

A related condition, called **somatization disorder**, is characterized by dramatic but vague reports of a multitude of physical problems rather than any specific illness. **Somatoform pain disorder** is marked by complaints of severe, often constant pain (typically in the neck, chest, or back) with no physical cause. In **body dysmorphic disorder**, the person is intensely distressed about an imagined abnormality of the skin, hair, face, or other bodily area. The person may become preoccupied with the imagined deformity or imperfection, avoid social contacts, become dysfunctional, and even seek unnecessary corrective surgery (Veale, 2009).

Some cases of somatoform disorder may be related to childhood experiences in which a person learns that symptoms of physical illness bring special attention, care, and privileges (Abramowitz & Braddock, 2006; Barsky et al., 1994). Others, including conversion disorder, may be triggered by severe stressors (Ballmaier & Schmidt, 2005; Ovsiew, 2006; Spiegel, 1994). Cognitive factors also come into play. When given information about their health, people with hypochondriasis are strongly biased to focus on threat-confirming information but to ignore reassuring information (Eifert, Zvolensky, & Louis, 2008). Abnormal serotonin functioning has also been associated with hypochondriasis, and various combinations of neurochemical and social skill deficits appear to accompany conversion disorder and body dysmorphic disorder (Brodino et al., 2008; Eifert, Zvolensky, & Louis, 2008).

Based on such findings, many researchers have adopted a diathesis-stress approach to explaining somatoform disorders. The results of their work suggest that certain people may have biological and psychological traits that make them especially vulnerable to somatoform disorders, particularly when combined with a history of physical illness. Among these traits are self-consciousness and oversensitivity to

somatization disorder A somatoform disorder in which there are numerous physical complaints without verifiable physical illness.

somatoform pain disorder A somatoform disorder marked by complaints of severe pain with no physical cause.

body dysmorphic disorder A somatoform disorder characterized by intense distress over imagined abnormalities of the skin, hair, face, or other areas of the body.

physical sensations. If such people experience a number of long-lasting stressors, intense emotional conflicts, or severe traumas, they are more likely than others to display physical symptoms in association with emotional arousal (Abramowitz & Braddock, 2006; Siti, 2004).

Sociocultural factors may shape the nature of some somatoform disorders. In many Asian, Latin American, and African cultures, it is not unusual for people to experience severe physical symptoms in association with psychological or interpersonal conflicts (Weiss et al., 2009; recall our earlier examples of *ataques de nervios* and *koro*). However, the overall *rate* of somatoform disorders appears to be about the same across cultures (Becker, 2004; Kohrt et al., 2005).

Dissociative Disorders

Have you ever driven for hours on a boring highway and suddenly realized that you couldn't remember anything about the previous half-hour? This is a common experience, but when disruptions in a person's memory, consciousness, or identity are more intense and long-lasting, they are known as **dissociative disorders**. These disruptions can come on gradually, but they usually occur suddenly and last from a few hours to many years.

Consider the case of 18-year-old "Jane Doe," who was found lying in the fetal position outside a New York City youth shelter in October 2009. She claimed to have no memory of her name, where she came from, or how she got where she was (Moore, 2009). After her picture was shown on national television, a viewer identified her as Kacie Peterson. Kacie displayed a dissociative disorder known as **fugue reaction** or **dissociative fugue** (pronounced "fewg"), which is characterized by sudden wandering and loss of memory for (or confusion about) personal identity. In some cases, the person adopts an entirely new identity. A related disorder called **dissociative amnesia** also involves sudden loss of memory about personal information, but the person does not leave home or create a new identity. These rare conditions attract intense publicity because they are so dramatic.

The most famous dissociative disorder is **dissociative identity disorder (DID)**, formerly known as—and still commonly called—*multiple personality disorder* (*MPD*). A person diagnosed with DID appears to have more than one identity, each of which speaks, acts, and writes in a different way. Each personality seems to have its own memories, wishes, and (often conflicting) impulses. Here is a case example (Spitzer et al., 1994):

> Mary, a pleasant and introverted 35-year-old social worker, was referred to a psychiatrist for hypnotic treatment of chronic pain. At an early interview, she mentioned the odd fact that though she had no memory of using her car after coming home from work, she often found that it had been driven fifty to one hundred miles overnight. It turned out that she also had no memory of large parts of her childhood. Mary rapidly learned self-hypnosis for pain control, but during one hypnotic session, she suddenly began speaking in a hostile manner. She told the doctor that her name was Marian and that it was "she" who had been taking long evening drives. She also called Mary "pathetic" for "wasting time" trying to please other people. Eventually, six other identities emerged, some of whom told of having experienced parental abuse in childhood.

During the 1970s, there was a minor "epidemic" of DID, as well as an increase in the number of alternative personalities per case; some patients reported over forty of them (Castelli, 2009). This upsurge in DID may have occurred because clinicians were looking for it more carefully or because the conditions leading to it became more prevalent, but it may have also been influenced by movies such as *Sybil* and by tell-all books written by people who had been diagnosed with DID (Kihlstrom, 2005). These

A Famous Case of Dissociative Identity Disorder

In this scene from the film *Sybil,* Sally Field portrays a woman diagnosed with dissociative identity disorder, also known as multiple personality disorder. Sybil appeared to have as many as seventeen distinct personalities. The causes of such dramatic cases, and the reasons behind their increasing prevalence during the 1970s is a matter of intense debate.

Photofest

dissociative disorders Rare conditions that involve sudden and usually temporary disruptions in a person's memory, consciousness, or identity.

fugue reaction (dissociative fugue) A dissociative disorder involving sudden loss of memory and possible assumption of a new identity in a new location.

dissociative amnesia A dissociative disorder marked by a sudden loss of memory.

dissociative identity disorder (DID) A dissociative disorder in which a person reports having more than one identity.

The debate and skepticism about dissociative identity disorder—including whether it may be caused by therapists' expectations—is not confined to professional journals. This drawing appeared in *The New Yorker* magazine.

"Would it be possible to speak with the personality that pays the bills?"

media influences may have increased the status of DID as a socioculturally approved method of expressing distress (Hacking, 1995; Spanos, 1994).

How do dissociative disorders develop? Psychodynamic theorists see massive repression of unwanted impulses or memories as the basis for creating a "new person" who acts out otherwise unacceptable impulses or recalls otherwise unbearable memories (Maldonado & Spiegel, 2008; Ross, 1997). Social-cognitive theorists focus on the fact that everyone is capable of behaving in different ways, depending on circumstances (e.g., rowdy in a bar, quiet in a museum), but in rare cases, they say, this variation can become so extreme that an individual feels—and is perceived by others as being—a "different person." Further, dissociative symptoms may be strengthened by reward as people find that a sudden memory loss or shift in behavior allows them to escape stressful situations, responsibilities, or punishment for misbehavior (Lilienfeld & Lynn, 2003; Lilienfeld et al., 2009).

Research on dissociative disorders so far supports four conclusions. First, memory loss and other forms of dissociations are genuine phenomena, and as seen in dissociative fugue, they can sometimes become extreme. Second, many people displaying DID have experienced events they would like to forget or avoid. The majority (some clinicians believe all) have suffered severe, unavoidable, persistent abuse in childhood (Foote et al., 2006; Kihlstrom, 2005). Third, like Mary, most of these people appear to be skilled at self-hypnosis, through which they can induce a trancelike state. Fourth, most found that they could escape the trauma of abuse, at least temporarily, by creating "new personalities" to deal with stress (Spiegel, 1994; van der Hart, Bolt, & van der Kolk, 2005). However, not all abused children display DID, and there is evidence that DID can indeed be triggered by media stories or by therapists who expect to see alternative personalities and use hypnosis and other methods that encourage clients to display them (Lindsay et al., 2004; McHugh, 2009; Rieber, 2006).

This evidence has led some skeptics to question the very existence of multiple personalities (Acocella, 1998; Merckelbach, Devilly, & Rassin, 2002). They point to research showing, for example, that people who display DID may be more aware than they think they are of the memories and actions of each apparent identity (Allen, 2002; Allen & Iacono, 2001). Research on the existence and effects of repressed memories—and the role of therapists in their appearance—is sure to have an impact on our understanding of the causes of DID and the controversy surrounding the disorder (see the memory chapter for more on this controversy).

"In Review: Anxiety, Somatoform, and Dissociative Disorders" presents a summary of our discussion of these disorders.

Affective Disorders

Everyone's mood, or *affect,* tends to rise and fall over time. However, when people experience extremes of mood—wild elation or deep depression—for long periods, when they shift rapidly from one extreme to another, and especially when their moods are not consistent with the events around them, they are said to show an **affective disorder** (also known as a **mood disorder**). We will describe two main types: depressive disorders and bipolar disorders.

Depressive Disorders

Depression can range from occasional, normal "down" periods to episodes severe enough to require hospitalization. A person suffering **major depression** (also called **major depressive disorder**) feels sad and overwhelmed, typically losing interest in activities and relationships and taking pleasure in nothing (Getzfeld, 2006; Sloan, Strauss, & Wisner, 2001). Despite the person's best efforts, everything from conversation to bathing is an unbearable, exhausting effort. Changes in eating habits resulting in weight loss or weight gain often accompany major depression, as does sleep disturbance or, less often, excessive sleeping. Problems in working, concentrating, making decisions, and thinking clearly are also common. More often than not, there are also symptoms of an accompanying anxiety disorder (Andreescu et al., 2007; Zimmerman, McDermut, & Mattia, 2000). In extreme cases, depressed people may express false beliefs, or **delusions**—worrying, for example, that the government is planning to punish them. Major depression may come on suddenly or gradually. It may consist of a single episode or, more commonly, repeated depressive periods. These episodes can last weeks or months; the average length of the first one is four to nine months (Durand & Barlow, 2006). Exaggerated feelings of inadequacy, worthlessness, hopelessness, or

affective disorder (mood disorder) A condition in which a person experiences extreme moods, such as depression or mania.

major depression (major depressive disorder) An affective disorder in which a person feels sad and hopeless for weeks or months.

delusions False beliefs, such as those experienced by people suffering from schizophrenia or extreme depression.

guilt are common in major depression (Klein, 2010). Here is a case example (Davison & Neale, 1990, p. 221):

> Mr. J. was a fifty-one-year-old industrial engineer.... Since the death of his wife five years earlier, he had been suffering from continuing episodes of depression marked by extreme social withdrawal and occasional thoughts of suicide.... He drank and, when thoroughly intoxicated, would plead to his deceased wife for forgiveness. He lost all capacity for joy.... Once a gourmet, he now had no interest in food and good wine... and could barely manage to engage in small talk. As might be expected, his work record deteriorated markedly. Appointments were missed and projects haphazardly started and left unfinished.

Depression is not always so extreme (de Graff et al., 2010). In a less severe pattern of depression, called **dysthymic disorder**, the person experiences the sad mood, lack of interest, and loss of pleasure associated with major depression, but less intensely and for a longer period. To qualify as dysthymic disorder, the duration must be at least two years in adults and one year in children. Mental and behavioral disruptions are also less severe; people exhibiting dysthymic disorder rarely require hospitalization.

Major depression occurs at some time in the lives of about 17 percent of people in North America and Europe (Hasin et al., 2005; Kessler & Wang, 2008); in any given year, about 6.7 percent of these populations are experiencing the disorder (Kessler & Wang, 2008). The prevalence and severity of major depression is similar across many ethnic groups (Gonzalez et al., 2010), and it is becoming more common, both in the United States and elsewhere. The World Health Organization estimates that if current trends continue, depression will become the second leading cause of disability and premature death in developed countries (Moussavi et al., 2007; World Health Organization Mental Health Survey Consortium, 2004). However, the incidence of the disorder varies considerably across cultures and subcultures. For example, depression occurs at much higher rates in urban Ireland than in urban Spain, although it is not always clear whether such differences reflect real differences in rates of depression or differences in the application of diagnostic criteria (Judd et al., 2002). There are gender differences in some cultures too. In the United States and other Western countries, females are two to three times more likely than males to experience major depression (Kessler & Wang, 2008), but this difference is smaller in the less economically developed countries of the Middle East, Africa, and Asia (Ayuso-Mateos et al., 2001; Culbertson, 1997; World Health Organization, 2003). Depression can occur at any age, but its prevalence peaks in late adolescence or young adulthood and again during old age (Cross-National Collaborative Group, 2002; Durand & Barlow, 2006; Fassler & Dumas, 1997; Sowdon, 2001).

Depression often occurs in combination with other psychological disorders and medical conditions; it is especially likely to be diagnosed along with posttraumatic stress disorder, obsessive-compulsive disorder, and other anxiety disorders, as well as with substance use disorders, physical disabilities, and recovery from heart attack (Mitra et al., 2005; O'Brien, 2006). As mentioned earlier, some researchers believe that the overlap between anxiety and depression is significant enough to warrant combining them into a single category in the next edition of the *DSM* (Moses & Barlow, 2006).

Suicide and Depression   Suicide is associated with a variety of psychological disorders, but it is most closely tied to depression and other affective disorders (Balázs et al., 2006; Holma et al., 2010). Some form of depression has been implicated in 40 to 70 percent of suicides (Angst, Angst, & Stassen, 1999; Oquendo & Mann, 2001). In fact, thinking about suicide is a symptom of depressive disorders. Hopelessness about the future—another depressive symptom—and a desire to seek instant escape from problems are also related to suicide attempts (Brown et al., 2000; Morris, Ciesla, & Garber, 2008; Pompili et al., 2008; Van Orden et al., 2010).

dysthymic disorder An affective disorder involving a pattern of comparatively mild depression that lasts for at least two years.

About thirty-three thousand people in the United States commit suicide each year, or about ninety per day, and ten to twenty times that many people attempt it (Centers for Disease Control and Prevention [CDC], 2009). This puts the U.S. suicide rate at about 11 per 100,000 individuals, making suicide the eleventh leading cause of death. Worldwide, the suicide rate is as high as 25 per 100,000 in some northern and eastern European countries and Japan (Lamar, 2000; World Health Organization, 2003) and as low as 6 per 100,000 in countries with stronger religious prohibitions against suicide, including Greece, Italy, Ireland, and the nations of the Middle East (Lamar, 2000; Ono et al., 2008; World Health Organization, 2003).

Suicide rates also differ considerably, depending on sociocultural factors such as age, gender, and ethnicity (Baca-Garcia et al., 2010; CDC, 2002b, 2002c; NIMH, 2009; Oquendo et al., 2001). In the United States, suicide is most common among people over 65, especially men (Warner, 2010). The suicide rate for men who are 85 or older is 55 per 100,000; for women in this age group, it is only 4 per 100,000 (CDC, 2004). However, since 1950, suicide in the 15-to-24 age group has tripled. And although the rate has begun to level off in the past decade, suicide is still the third leading cause of death, after accidents and homicides, among people in this age group (CDC, 2002b, 2006). Suicide is the second leading cause of death among college students. About ten thousand try to kill themselves each year, and about 10 percent of them succeed. These figures are much higher than for 18- to 24-year-olds in general but much lower than for older adults (NIMH, 2009). Women attempt suicide three times as often as men, but men are four times as likely to actually kill themselves (CDC, 2006). The gender difference is even greater among people who have been diagnosed with depression. In this group, the male suicide rate of 65 per 100,000 is ten times higher than the rate for women (Blair-West et al., 1999; CDC, 1999b).

Suicide rates also differ across ethnic groups (CDC, 2002c; Oquendo et al., 2001). Among males in the United States, for example, the overall rate for American Indians is 15.1 per 100,000, compared with 13.9 for European Americans, 5.7 for Asian Americans, 4.9 for Hispanic Americans, and 5.0 for African Americans. The same pattern of ethnic differences appears among women, though the actual rates are much lower (NIMH, 2009).

Predicting who will commit suicide is difficult. For one thing, suicidal thoughts are quite common—about 3 percent of all adults and as many as 10 percent of college students report having had such thoughts in the previous year (Brener, Hassan, & Barrios, 1999; Kessler, Berglund, Borges, et al., 2005). Still, the results of hundreds of research studies provide some predictive guidelines (Smyth & MacLachian, 2005). The risk of suicide is heightened among people diagnosed with an affective disorder, anxiety disorder, or schizophrenia and people who have suffered extended unemployment (Boardman & Healy, 2001; Joska & Stein, 2008; Khan et al., 2002; Rihmer, 2001). Among older adults, suicide is most common in males who suffer depression over health problems (e.g., Brown, Bongar, & Cleary, 2004). The risk is higher, too, in depressed people who have certain genetic characteristics, have made a specific plan, have given away possessions, and are impulsive (CDC, 2004; Kohli et al., 2010). A previous suicide attempt may not always be a good predictor of eventual suicide because such attempts may have been help-seeking gestures rather than failed efforts to die (Nock & Kessler, 2006). In fact, although about 10 percent of unsuccessful attempters try again and succeed, most people who commit suicide had made no prior attempts (Clark & Fawcett, 1992).

It is often said that people who talk about suicide will never try it. This is a myth. On the contrary, those who say they are thinking of suicide are much more likely than other people to attempt suicide. In fact, most suicides are preceded by some kind of warning, whether direct ("I think I'm going to kill myself") or vague ("Sometimes I wonder if life is worth living"). Failure to recognize or respond to warning signs is a common phenomenon (Valuck et al., 2007). So although not everyone who threatens suicide follows through, if you suspect that someone you know is thinking about suicide, encourage the person to contact a mental health professional or a crisis hotline. If the danger is immediate, make the contact yourself, and ask for advice about what to do. Many suicide attempts—including those triggered by other suicides in the same town or school—can be prevented by social support and other forms of help for people at high risk (CDC, 2004; Mann et al., 2005). For more information, visit suicide-related Web sites such as that of the American Association of Suicidology (www.suicidology.org).

Bipolar Disorders

The alternating appearance of two emotional extremes, or poles, characterizes **bipolar disorders**. We have already described one emotional pole: depression. The other is **mania**, which is an extremely agitated and usually elated emotional state. While in this state, people are utterly optimistic, boundlessly energetic, certain of having extraordinary powers and abilities, and bursting with all sorts of ideas. They become irritated with anyone who tries to reason with them or "slow them down" and may become aggressive or careless enough to pose a danger to themselves or others. During manic episodes, individuals may make impulsive and unwise decisions, such as spending their life savings on foolish schemes (Goldberg & Burdick, 2008; Kessler, Berglund, Demler, et al., 2005; NIMH, 2006).

There are two versions of bipolar disorder, known as bipolar I and bipolar II. In *bipolar I disorder,* manic episodes may alternate with periods of deep depression (Ghaemi, 2008). One bipolar patient described the disorder, which has also been called *manic depression,* this way: "You're really up or you're drop-dead bottom" (Fairbanks, 2009). In many cases, though, these extremes are separated by periods of relatively normal mood (Tohen et al., 2003). Compared to major depression, bipolar I disorder is rare. It occurs in only about 1 percent of adults, and it affects men and women about equally. Another 1 percent of adults display *bipolar II disorder,* in which episodes of major depression alternate with episodes known as *hypomania,* which are less severe than the manic phases seen in bipolar I disorder (Merikangas et al., 2007). Both versions can severely disrupt a person's ability to work or maintain social relationships (Kessler, Berglund, Demler, et al., 2005; NIMH, 2006).

Slightly more common is a pattern of milder mood swings known as **cyclothymic personality** (also called **cyclothymic disorder**), the bipolar equivalent of dysthymic disorder. Cyclothymic disorder involves episodes of depression and mania, but the intensity of both moods is less severe than in bipolar I disorder. As with depression, bipolar disorders are often accompanied by anxiety disorders or substance abuse (Andreescu et al., 2007; Freeman, Freeman, & McElroy, 2002; Ghaemi, 2008). ("In Review: Affective Disorders" summarizes the main types of affective disorders.)

bipolar disorders Affective disorders in which a person alternates between the emotional extremes of depression and mania.

mania An elated, very active emotional state.

cyclothymic personality (cyclothymic disorder) An affective disorder characterized by an alternating pattern of mood swings that is less extreme than that of bipolar disorders.

IN REVIEW Affective Disorders		
Type	**Typical Symptoms**	**Related Features**
Major depression (major depressive disorder)	Deep sadness, feelings of worthlessness, changes in eating and sleeping habits, loss of interest and pleasure	Lasts weeks or months; may occur in repeating episodes; severe cases may include delusions; danger of suicide
Dysthymic disorder	Similar to major depressive disorder, but less severe and longer lasting	Hospitalization is usually not necessary
Bipolar disorder	Alternating extremes of mood, from deep depression to mania, and back	Manic episodes include impulsivity, unrealistic optimism, high energy, severe agitation
Cyclothymic personality (cyclothymic disorder)	Similar to bipolar disorder, but less severe	Hospitalization is usually not necessary

1. The risk of suicide is associated with _____ more than with any other disorder.

2. Cyclothymic personality is the bipolar version of _____.

3. Women are _____ likely than men to try suicide, but men are _____ likely to succeed.

Causes of Affective Disorders

LINKAGES Are some psychological disorders inherited? (a link to Biological Aspects of Psychology, p. 84)

Research on the causes of affective disorders has focused on biological, psychological, and sociocultural risk factors. The more of these risk factors people have, the more likely they are to experience an affective disorder.

Biological Factors The role of genetics in affective disorders, especially in bipolar disorders, is suggested by twin studies and family studies (Fullerton et al., 2010; Hayden & Nurnberger, 2006; Kendler et al., 2006). For example, bipolar disorder is much more likely to appear in both members of genetically identical twin pairs than in nonidentical twins (Smoller, 2008). Family studies also show that close relatives of people with a bipolar disorder are more likely than others to develop that disorder themselves (Althoff et al., 2005; Serretti et al., 2009). Major depression is also more likely to be shared among family members, especially by identical twins (Kendler et al., 2009; Levinson, 2006). This genetic influence is especially strong in female twins (Bierut et al., 1999). Findings such as these suggest that genetic influences tend to be stronger for affective disorders, especially for bipolar disorders and severe, early-onset depression, than for most other disorders.

Researchers have already identified certain genetic variations that affect vulnerability to affective disorders (e.g., Joska & Stein, 2008; McMahon et al., 2010; Smoller, 2008; Young et al., 2008). These include genes on chromosome 13 that are involved in the operation of the neurotransmitter serotonin (Hariri et al., 2005; Jacobs et al., 2006; Wilhelm et al., 2006). Still, it is important to recognize that genetic variations alone probably do not cause affective disorders. Rather, genes appear to act in combination with other biological, psychological, and environmental factors. Researchers in the field of epigenetics are investigating how the genes associated with affective disorders can be "turned on" or "turned off" by these factors (Butcher, Mineka, & Hooley, 2010; Levinson et al., 2007).

Other biological factors that may contribute to affective disorders include malfunctions in regions of the brain devoted to mood, imbalances in the brain's neurotransmitter systems, malfunctioning of the endocrine system, disruption of biological rhythms, and underdevelopment in the frontal lobes, hippocampus, or other brain areas (Butcher, Mineka, & Hooley, 2010; Jans et al., 2007; Langan & McDonald, 2009; Shankman et al., 2007; Staley et al., 2006; Strakowski, DelBello, & Adler, 2005). All of these conditions may themselves be influenced by genetics. The brain regions involved in mood are many, including the prefrontal cortex, the hippocampus, the amygdala, and other components of the limbic system (Blumberg et al., 2003; MacQueen et al., 2003). There are so many of these regions, in fact, and so many different pathways through which their activity can be disrupted, that different affective disorders may reflect problems in different brain regions (Davidson et al., 2002; Elliott et al., 2002). Malfunctions in some of the same regions are also involved in the symptoms of anxiety disorders, which may help account for the fact that affective and anxiety disorders often appear together (Middeldorp et al., 2005).

As for the role of neurotransmitters, norepinephrine, serotonin, and dopamine were implicated in affective disorders decades ago when scientists discovered that drugs capable of altering these brain chemicals also relieved affective disorders. Early research suggested that depression was triggered by too little of these neurotransmitters, whereas unusually high levels caused mania. However, the neurochemical causes now appear far more complex. For example, affective disorders may result in part from changes in the sensitivity of the neuronal receptors at which these chemicals have their effects in the brain. The precise nature of these neurotransmitter-receptor mechanisms and just how they affect mood are not yet fully understood.

Affective disorders have also been related to malfunctions in the endocrine system, especially the hypothalamic-pituitary-adrenocortical (HPA) system. As described in the chapter on health, stress, and coping, this system is involved in the body's responses to stress. Research shows, for example, that as many as 70 percent of depressed people secrete abnormally high levels of the stress hormone cortisol (Dinan, 2001; Posener et al., 2000). Studies of identical twins also suggest that higher levels of cortisol are associated with depression (Dinan, 2001; Wichers et al., 2008).

The cycles of mood swings seen in bipolar disorders and in recurring episodes of major depression suggest that affective disorders may be related to stressful triggering events (Hammen, 2005; Keller & Nesse, 2006). They may also be related to disturbances in the body's biological clock, which is described in the chapter on consciousness (Monteleone & Maj, 2008). This second possibility seems especially likely in the 15 percent of depressed people who consistently experience a calendar-linked pattern of depressive episodes known as *seasonal affective disorder* (*SAD*). During months of shorter daylight, these people slip into severe depression, accompanied by irritability and excessive sleeping (Durand & Barlow, 2006). Their depression tends to lift as daylight hours lengthen. Resetting the biological clock through methods such as sleep deprivation or light stimulation has relieved depression in many cases (Lavoie et al., 2009; Lewy et al., 2006; Wu et al., 2009).

Psychological and Social Factors Researchers have come to recognize that whatever biological causes are involved in affective disorders, their effects are always combined with those of psychological and social causes. As mentioned earlier, the very nature of depressive symptoms can depend on the culture in which a person lives. Biopsychosocial explanations of affective disorders also emphasize the impact of anxiety, negative thinking, personality traits, family interactions, and the other psychological and emotional responses triggered by trauma, losses, and other stressful events (Monroe & Reid, 2009; Rice et al., 2006; Steunenberg et al., 2006). For example, the higher incidence of depression among females—and especially among poor, ethnic minority, single mothers—has been attributed to several factors. Women have greater exposure than men to certain adverse experiences during childhood (e.g., sexual abuse) and adulthood (e.g., domestic violence, poverty). When these risk factors combine with depressive ways of thinking and loss of social support, depression becomes more likely (Miranda & Green, 1999; Nolen-Hoeksema, 2006; Whiffen, 2006). Environmental stressors affect men, too, which may be one reason why gender differences in depression are smaller in countries in which men and women face equally stressful lives (Bierut et al., 1999; Maier et al., 1999).

A number of social-cognitive theories suggest that the way people think about their stressors can increase or decrease the likelihood of affective disorders. One of these theories stemmed from the research on *learned helplessness* described in the

Treating SAD

Seasonal affective disorder (SAD) can often be relieved by exposure to full-spectrum light for as little as a couple of hours a day (Terman & Terman, 2005).

chapter on learning. Just as animals become inactive and appear depressed when they have no control over negative events (El Yacoubi et al., 2003), humans may experience depression as a result of feeling incapable of controlling certain aspects of their lives, especially the stressors confronting them (Alloy et al., 2008; Klein & Seligman, 1976; Seligman, 1991). But most of us have limited control over our lives, so why aren't we all depressed? The ways in which people learn to think about events in their lives may hold the key. For example, Aaron Beck's cognitive theory of depression suggests that depressed people develop mental habits of (1) blaming themselves when things go wrong, (2) focusing on and exaggerating the negative side of events, and (3) jumping to overly generalized, pessimistic conclusions (Beck, 1967, 1976, 2008). Such cognitive habits, says Beck, are errors that lead to depressing thoughts and other symptoms of depression (Beck & Beck, 1995; Evans et al., 2005; Joormann, Teachman, & Gotlib, 2009). Depressed people, in fact, do tend to think about significant negative events in ways that are likely to increase or prolong their depression (Gotlib et al., 2004; Morris, Ciesla & Garber, 2008; Strunk, Lopez, & DeRubeis, 2006).

Social-cognitive theories of depression are somewhat consistent with the psychodynamically oriented *object relations* approach discussed in the chapter on personality. Both views suggest that negative patterns of thinking can be acquired through maladaptive experiences in childhood. For example, research indicates that children whose early relationships with parents or other primary caregivers were characterized by deprivation or abuse are especially likely to develop depression in later life (Gotlib & Hammen, 1992). It may be that close, protective, predictable, and responsive early relationships are necessary if children are to form healthy views of themselves, positive expectations about others, and a sense of control over the environment (Bowlby, 1980; Ivanova & Israel, 2005; Main, 1996).

Severe, long-lasting depression is especially common among people who see their lack of control or other problems as caused by a permanent, generalized lack of personal competence rather than by a temporary condition or an external cause (Seligman et al., 1988). This *negative attributional style* is regarded by some researchers as a partly inherited trait that leaves people prone to depression because they attribute negative events to their own characteristics and believe that they will never be capable of doing better (Alloy et al., 2006; Ball, McGuffin, & Farmer, 2008; Hankin, Fraley, & Abela, 2005; Hunt & Forand, 2005). Are depressed people's unusually negative beliefs about themselves responsible for their depression, or are they merely symptoms of it? A number of studies have assessed the attributional styles of large samples of nondepressed people and then kept in touch with them to see if, in the face of equivalent stressors, individuals with negative self-beliefs are more likely to become depressed. These longitudinal studies suggest that a negative attributional style is in fact a risk factor for depression, not just a result of being depressed (Alloy et al., 2006; Evans et al., 2005; Keenan et al., 2008). In one study, for example, adolescents who held strong negative self-beliefs were more likely than other youngsters to develop depression when faced with stress later in life (Lewinsohn, Joiner, & Rohde, 2001).

Social-cognitive theorists also suggest that whether depression continues or worsens depends in part on how people respond once they start to feel depressed. Those who continuously dwell on negative events, on why they occur, and even on their feelings of depression are likely to feel more and more depressed (Just & Alloy, 1997; McMurrich & Johnson, 2008; Rimes & Watkins, 2005). According to Susan Nolen-Hoeksema (1990, 2001), this *ruminative style* is especially common in women and may help explain gender differences in the frequency of depression. When men start to feel sad, she says, they tend to use a *distracting style*. That is, they engage in activity that distracts them from their concerns and helps bring them out of their depressed mood (Hankin & Abramson, 2001; Just & Alloy, 1997; Nolen-Hoeksema, Morrow, & Fredrickson, 1993).

Notice that social-cognitive explanations of depression are consistent with the diathesis-stress approach to disorder. They suggest that certain cognitive styles constitute a predisposition (or diathesis) that makes a person vulnerable to depression. The actual occurrence of depression is then made more likely by stressors. In fact, most episodes of major depressive disorder are preceded by the onset of major stressors, such as the loss of a loved one. As suggested in the chapter on health, stress, and coping, the depressing effects of these stressors are likely to be magnified by lack social support, inadequate coping skills, and the presence of other stressful conditions such as poverty (e.g., Belik et al., 2007; Stice, Ragan, & Randall, 2004).

Given the number and complexity of biological, psychological, social, and situational factors potentially involved in causing affective disorders, the biopsychosocial approach and the diathesis-stress model appear to be especially appropriate guides to future research (Kendler, Gardner, & Prescott, 2006). Studies based on these guides are already bearing fruit. One study looked at the role of genetics and stressful events in shaping mood disorders in a large group of female twin pairs. Both factors were associated with major depression. Specifically, the women at highest genetic risk were also the most likely to become depressed following a significant stressor (Kendler, Thornton, & Gardner, 2000, 2001; Kendler et al., 2005). Another study found that people with a particular version of a single gene were more likely than others to experience depressive symptoms in relation to stressful events (Caspi, Sugden, et al., 2003). On the basis of studies like these, Kenneth Kendler and his colleagues (Kendler, Gardner, & Prescott, 2002) have described specific sets of risk factors for depression in women that appear at five developmental stages: childhood, early adolescence, late adolescence, adulthood, and the year preceding the diagnosis of depression.

In the final analysis, it may turn out that each subtype in the spectrum of affective disorders is caused by a unique combination of factors. The challenge for researchers is to identify these subtypes and map out their causal ingredients (Eshel & Roiser, 2010).

Schizophrenia

Schizophrenia (pronounced "skit-soh-FREE-nee-uh") is a pattern of extremely disturbed thinking, emotion, perception, and behavior that seriously impairs the ability to communicate and relate to others and disrupts most other aspects of daily functioning (Freedman, 2003). It is one of the most severe and disabling of all mental disorders. The core symptoms of schizophrenia are seen virtually everywhere in the world, occurring in 1 to 2 percent of the population (American Psychiatric Association, 2000; NIMH, 2006). In the United States, it appears about equally in various ethnic groups, but like most disorders, it tends to be diagnosed more frequently in economically disadvantaged populations. Schizophrenia occurs about equally in men and women, although in women it generally appears later in life, tends to be less severe, and responds better to treatment (Aleman, Kahn, & Selten, 2003; American Psychiatric Association, 2000; Häfner, 2003).

Schizophrenia tends to develop in adolescence or early adulthood. About 75 percent of the time, its onset is gradual, with the earliest signs appearing as much as five years before the first major schizophrenic episode. In other cases, the onset is more rapid. About 40 percent of people with schizophrenia improve with treatment and are able to function reasonably well. The rest show continuous or intermittent symptoms that permanently disrupt their functioning (Harrow & Jobe, 2005) and, especially for those with a drug abuse problem, may lead to homelessness (Timms, 2005).

One of the best predictors of the course of schizophrenia is *premorbid adjustment,* which is the level of functioning a person had achieved before schizophrenic symptoms first appeared. Improvement is more likely in those who had reached higher levels of education and occupation and who had established supportive relationships with family and friends (Keshavan et al., 2005; Rabinowitz et al., 2002).

Symptoms of Schizophrenia

People with schizophrenia have problems with both how they think and what they think. The nineteenth-century psychiatrist Eugen Bleuler (pronounced "OY-gun BLOY-lur") coined the word *schizophrenia,* or "split mind," to refer to the oddities of

schizophrenia A severe and disabling pattern of disturbed thinking, emotion, perception, and behavior.

schizophrenic thinking. However, schizophrenia does not mean "split personality," as in dissociative identity disorder (multiple personality disorder). It refers instead to a splitting of normally integrated mental processes, such as thoughts and feelings. For instance, some schizophrenics may giggle while claiming to feel sad.

LINKAGES How do individuals with schizophrenia think? (a link to Cognition and Language, p. 285)

Schizophrenic thought and language are often disorganized, as illustrated in the following letter that arrived in the mail several years ago:

> Dear Sirs:
> Pertaining to our continuing failure to prosecute violations of minor's rights to sovereign equality which are occurring in gestations being compromised by the ingestation of controlled substances,…the skewing of androgyny which continues in female juveniles even after separation from their mother's has occurred, and as a means of promulflagitating my paying Governor Hickel of Alaska for my employees to have personal services endorsements and controlled substance endorsements,…the Iraqi oil being released by the United Nations being identified as Kurdistanian oil, and the July, 1991 issue of the Siberian Review spells President Eltsin's name without a letter *y*.

People with schizophrenia often use new words, known as *neologisms*, that are usually nonsensical and have meaning only to them. The appearance of "promulflagitating" in the preceding letter is one example. The letter also illustrates *loose associations*, the tendency for one thought to be logically unconnected or only slightly related to the next. Sometimes the associations are based on double meanings or on the way words sound (*clang associations*). For example, "My true family name is Abel or A Bell. We descended from the clan of Abel, who originated the bell of rights, which we now call the bill of rights." In the most severe cases, a jumble of words known as *word salad* reflects utterly chaotic thoughts: "Upon the advisability of held keeping, environment of the seabeach gathering, to the forest stream, reinstatement to be placed, poling the paddleboat, of the swamp morass, to the forest compensation of the dunce" (Lehman, 1967, p. 627).

The *content* of schizophrenic thinking is also disturbed. Often it includes delusions, or false beliefs, as in this case (Stefanidis, 2006):

> Erin Stefandis was a graduate student in the neuroscience program at the University of British Columbia. He prided himself on his ability to think rationally, yet he was convinced that rats were living in his head and eating his brain. He knew that this should cause dramatic cognitive and behavioral impairments and ultimately death, but he believed his brain was unique and was able to regenerate brain cells quickly enough to keep him alive and well. When this illogical belief was challenged by his doctor, he said he believed in "deep meaning," which is "truth that exists at a higher level than logic."

Delusions tend to fall into three general categories (Kimhy et al., 2005). *Delusions of influence* focus on the belief that one's body, thinking, or behavior are being affected or controlled by external forces. Patients with these delusions might claim that the CIA has implanted a control device in their brains. They might believe that other people's thoughts are appearing in their mind (thought insertion) or that they can broadcast their thoughts to others (thought broadcasting). *Self-significant delusions* involve exaggerated beliefs about oneself. People with these delusions may believe, for example, that certain TV commercials contain coded messages about their innermost secrets; that they are truly an emperor, the pope, or even God (delusions of grandeur); or that they are guilty of some terrible sin. People displaying *delusions of persecution* believe that others are out to harass or harm them. They may claim, for example, that they are always being followed, that space aliens are trying to steal their internal organs, or that they are the targets of an assassin. These delusions tend to be deeply entrenched and resistant to change, no matter how strong the evidence against them (Minzenberg et al., 2008; Woodward et al., 2006).

Hallucinations, or false perceptions, are common, often taking the form of voices. The voices may sound like an overheard conversation, or they may tell the person to

hallucinations A symptom of disorder in which people perceive voices or other stimuli when there are no stimuli present.

FIGURE 15.3
Brain Activity During Hallucinations

These are brain images of a 23-year-old schizophrenia patient who was experiencing hallucinations of rolling heads that spoke to him. PET scans revealed heightened activity in visual and auditory (language) *association* cortex rather than in the *primary* cortex regions for these senses. The posterior cingulate cortex (part of the limbic system) was also activated; it is known to be affected by drugs that produce hallucinations (Silbersweig et al., 1995).

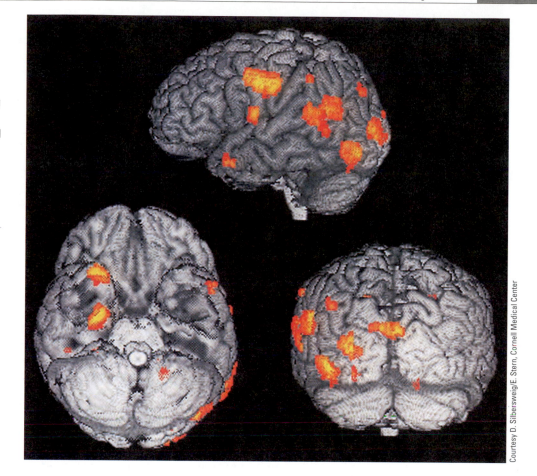

Courtesy D. Silbersweig/E. Stern, Cornell Medical Center

Catatonic Stupor

The symptoms of schizophrenia often occur in characteristic patterns. This woman's lack of motivation and other negative symptoms of schizophrenia are severe enough that she appears to be in a catatonic stupor. Such patients may become rigid or, as in this case, show a *waxy flexibility* that allows them to be "posed" in virtually any position. Diagnosticians using the traditional subtype system would probably label her as displaying catatonic schizophrenia.

© Grunnitus/Photo Researchers, Inc.

do or not to do certain things. They may also comment on, narrate, or (most often) harshly criticize the person's actions or characteristics. Hallucinations can also create sights, smells, tastes, and touch sensations even when no external stimuli are present. As shown in Figure 15.3, the brain areas activated during hallucinations are related to those that respond to real sights and sounds (Alerman & Larøi, 2008; Shergill et al., 2000; Simons et al., 2010).

People with schizophrenia often report that they cannot focus their attention. They may feel overwhelmed as they try to attend to everything at once. Perceptual disorders may also appear. The person may feel detached from the world and see other people as flat cutouts. The body may feel like a machine, or parts of it may seem to be dead or rotting. The emotional expressiveness of people with schizophrenia is often muted, but when they do show emotion, it is frequently exaggerated or inappropriate. They may cry for no apparent reason or fly into a rage in response to a simple question.

Some schizophrenia patients are extremely agitated, constantly moving their limbs, making facial grimaces, or pacing the floor in highly ritualistic sequences. Others become so withdrawn that they move very little. Lack of motivation and poor social skills, deteriorating personal hygiene, and an inability to function in everyday situations are other common characteristics of schizophrenia.

Categorizing Schizophrenia

DSM-IV-TR lists five major subtypes of schizophrenia: paranoid, disorganized, catatonic, undifferentiated, and residual (see Table 15.4). These subtype labels convey a certain amount of useful information, but they don't always provide an accurate picture of patients' behavior because some symptoms appear in more than one subtype. Further, people originally diagnosed in one subtype can later display characteristics

TABLE 15.4 Subtypes of Schizophrenia

Mental health professionals still use these *DSM-IV-TR* subtypes when diagnosing schizophrenia, but many researchers now tend to categorize patients in terms of whether positive or negative symptoms of schizophrenia predominate in a given case (Villalta-Gil et al., 2006).

Type	Prevalence	Prominent Features
Paranoid schizophrenia	40% of schizophrenics; usually appears after age 25–30	Delusions of grandeur or persecution; anger; anxiety; argumentativeness; extreme jealousy; onset often sudden; signs of impairment may be subtle
Disorganized schizophrenia	5% of all schizophrenics; high prevalence in homeless population	Delusions; hallucinations; incoherent speech; facial grimaces; inappropriate laughter or giggling; neglected personal hygiene; loss of bladder or bowel control
Catatonic schizophrenia	8% of all schizophrenics	Disordered movement, alternating between immobility (stupor) and wild excitement. In stupor, the person does not speak or attend to communication
Undifferentiated schizophrenia	40% of all schizophrenics	Patterns of disordered behavior, thought, and emotion that do not fall easily into any other subtype
Residual schizophrenia	Varies	Applies to people who have had prior episodes of schizophrenia but are not currently displaying symptoms

of another subtype. Finally, the *DSM-IV-TR* subtypes may not be linked very closely to the various biological conditions thought to underlie schizophrenia (Barch, 2006; Fenton & McGlashan, 1991; Jablensky, 2006).

Accordingly, many researchers now categorize schizophrenia in ways that focus more precisely on the kinds of symptoms that patients display. One method of categorizing schizophrenia highlights the positive or negative aspects of symptoms. Disorganized thoughts, delusions, and hallucinations are sometimes called **positive symptoms** of schizophrenia because they appear as undesirable *additions* to a person's mental life (Iancu et al., 2005; Smith et al., 2006). In contrast, the absence of pleasure and motivation, lack of emotional reactivity, social withdrawal, reduced speech, and other deficits seen in schizophrenia are sometimes called **negative symptoms** because they appear to *subtract* elements from normal mental life (Batki et al., 2008). Describing patients in terms of positive and negative symptoms does not require that they be placed in one category or the other. In fact, many patients exhibit both positive and negative symptoms. However, it is important to know whether negative or positive symptoms predominate, because when symptoms are mainly negative, as they are in about 25 percent of schizophrenia patients, the disorder is usually more severe and less responsive to treatment (Kirkpatrick et al., 2006; Milev et al., 2005; Prikryl et al., 2006). In these cases, patients typically experience long-term disability.

Another way of categorizing schizophrenia symptoms focuses on whether they are *psychotic* (hallucinations, delusions), *disorganized* (incoherent speech, chaotic behavior, inappropriate affect), or *negative* (e.g., lack of speech or motivation). Other researchers have suggested categorizing schizophrenia symptoms as positive, negative, or depressive (Häfner & Maurer, 2000). The fact that, like positive and negative symptoms, these dimensions of schizophrenia are to some extent independent from one another suggests to some researchers that each symptom cluster or dimension may ultimately be traceable to different causes. For this reason, schizophrenia is often referred to as the *schizophrenia spectrum*, implying that each cluster may develop differently and require different treatments (Tsuang, Stone, & Faraone, 2000). The schizophrenia spectrum also includes other diagnoses that share features with schizophrenia. For example, people diagnosed with *schizoaffective disorder* show symptoms of both schizophrenia and depression. *Schizophreniform disorder* is characterized by schizophrenia-like symptoms that do not last as long as those typically seen in schizophrenia.

positive symptoms Schizophrenic symptoms such as disorganized thoughts, hallucinations, and delusions.

negative symptoms Schizophrenic symptoms such as absence of pleasure, lack of speech, and flat affect.

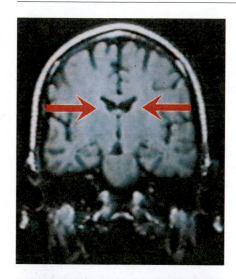

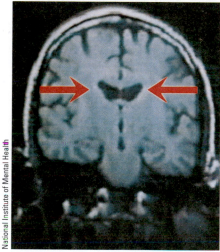

National Institute of Mental Health

FIGURE 15.4

Brain Abnormalities in Schizophrenia

Here is a magnetic resonance imaging (MRI) comparison of the brains of identical twins. The schizophrenic twin (bottom photo) has greatly enlarged ventricles (see arrows) and correspondingly less brain tissue, including in the hippocampal area, a region involved in memory and emotion. The same results appeared in fourteen other identical-twin pairs. By contrast, no significant differences appeared between members of a seven-pair control group of normal identical twins (Suddath et al., 1990). These results support the idea that brain abnormalities are associated with schizophrenia and, because identical twins have the same genes, that such abnormalities may stem from nongenetic factors (Baare et al., 2001).

Causes of Schizophrenia

The search for the causes of schizophrenia has been more intense than for any other psychological disorder. The findings so far confirm one thing: As with other disorders, there are biological, psychological, and social factors at work in causing or worsening all forms of schizophrenia (Sullivan, Kendler, & Neale, 2003; Tandon, Nasrallah, & Keshaven, 2009).

Biological Factors   Research in behavioral genetics shows that schizophrenia runs in families (Dubertret et al., 2004; Gottesman et al., 2010; Kasper & Papadimitriou, 2009). One family study found, for instance, that 16 percent of the children of schizophrenic mothers developed schizophrenia themselves over a twenty-five-year period, versus only 2 percent of the children of nonschizophrenic mothers (Parnas et al., 1993). Even if they are adopted by families in which there is no schizophrenia, the children of schizophrenic parents are ten times more likely to develop schizophrenia than adopted children whose biological parents are not schizophrenic (Kety et al., 1994; Tienari et al., 2003). Still, it is unlikely that a single gene transmits schizophrenia (Chumakov et al., 2002; Plomin & McGuffin, 2003). For example, among identical-twin pairs in which one member displays schizophrenia, 40 percent of the other members will too, but 60 percent will not (McGue, 1992). It is more likely that some people inherit a predisposition, or diathesis, for schizophrenia that involves several genes and that these genetic factors combine with other genetic and nongenetic factors to cause the disorder (DeRosse et al., 2006; Fan et al., 2006; Law, Cotton, & Berger, 2006; Levitt et al., 2006; Vazza et al., 2007).

The search for biological causes of schizophrenia also focuses on a number of abnormalities in the structure, functioning, and chemistry of the brain that tend to appear in people with schizophrenia (e.g., Andrews et al., 2006; Lynall et al., 2010; Neves-Pereira et al., 2005; Rasmussen et al., 2010; Tamminga & Holcomb, 2005). Numerous brain-imaging studies have shown that compared with other mental patients, many schizophrenia patients have less tissue in thalamic regions, prefrontal cortex, and some subcortical areas (Behrendt, 2006; Conklin & Iacono, 2002; Csernansky et al., 2004; Ettinger et al., 2007; Goto, Yang, & Otani, 2010; Javitt, Kantrowitz, & Lajtha, 2009). As shown in Figure 15.4, shrinkage of tissue in these regions leads to corresponding enlargement of the brain's fluid-filled spaces, called *ventricles*. The brain areas in which anatomical abnormalities have been found are active in emotional expression, thinking, and information processing—functions that are disordered in schizophrenia (Conklin & Iacono, 2002; Csernansky et al., 2004; Highley et al., 2003; Pol et al., 2002; Selemon et al., 2003; Velakoulis et al., 2006). Enlarged ventricles and reduced prefrontal cortex are more often found in patients whose schizophrenic symptoms are predominantly negative (Sigmundsson et al., 2001). Continued tissue loss has been associated with worsening of negative symptoms (Ho et al., 2003).

Hundreds of studies of brain functioning in people diagnosed with schizophrenia provide general support for the idea that their impairments in information processing and other cognitive abilities are related to structural abnormalities (Gur et al., 2000; Jeon & Polich, 2003; Lee, Williams, et al., 2003; Zanelli et al., 2010). For example, patients with predominantly negative symptoms are especially likely to display cognitive deficits associated with prefrontal cortex problems (Wible et al., 2001). This research is providing important clues (Barch, 2006), but it will take even more research to determine the extent to which, or exactly how, specific structural abnormalities are related to the cognitive problems seen in various forms of schizophrenia.

Researchers are also investigating the possibility that abnormalities in brain chemistry—especially in neurotransmitter systems that use dopamine—play a role in causing or intensifying schizophrenic symptoms (Javitt, Kantrowitz, & Lajtha, 2009; Tan et al., 2007). Because drugs that block the brain's dopamine receptors often reduce hallucinations, delusions, disordered thinking, and other positive symptoms of schizophrenia, some investigators speculate that schizophrenia results from excess dopamine.

However, the relationship between dopamine and schizophrenia is quite complex (Carlsson & Lecrubier, 2004). For example, it may be that changes in the ratio of dopamine to other neurochemicals, particularly in the region of the thalamus, are involved in the difficulties experienced by people with schizophrenia in distinguishing genuine sights and sounds from those produced by neural "noise" within the brain (Buchsbaum et al., 2006; Winterer, 2006).

Some researchers are seeking to integrate genetic, neurological, and environmental explanations of schizophrenia by looking for *neurodevelopmental abnormalities* (Meyer et al., 2005; Rapoport, Addington, & Frangou, 2005). Perhaps, they say, some forms of schizophrenia arise from disruptions in brain development during the period from before birth through childhood, when the brain is growing and its various functions are maturing. Studies have shown, for instance, that prenatal exposure to physical traumas, influenza, or other viral infections is associated with increased risk for developing schizophrenia (AbdelMalik et al., 2003; Brown & Derkits, 2010; Subotnik et al., 2006). Similarly, low-birth-weight children are more likely to have the brain abnormalities described earlier. These abnormalities are especially likely in children of schizophrenic parents (Cannon et al., 1993; Lawrie et al., 2001). Even parental age may make a difference. Children whose fathers were older than 45 at the time the children were conceived appear to be at elevated risk for developing schizophrenia, possibly because of a sperm cell mutation (Dalman & Allebeck, 2002).

The expression of a genetically transmitted predisposition for brain abnormality may be enhanced by environmental factors such as maternal drug use during pregnancy, oxygen deprivation or other complications during birth, or childhood malnutrition (Sørensen et al., 2003; NIMH, 2008b). For example, as mentioned earlier, smaller-than-normal prefrontal lobes and other brain structures appear to constitute an inherited predisposition for schizophrenia. However, reduced brain growth alone is not sufficient to cause the disorder. When only one member of an identical-twin pair has schizophrenia, both tend to have unusually small brains, but the schizophrenic twin's brain in each pair is the smaller of the two (Baare et al., 2001). This finding suggests that some environmental influence caused degeneration in an already underdeveloped brain, making it even more prone to function abnormally.

Psychological and Sociocultural Factors Psychological processes and sociocultural influences can contribute to the appearance of schizophrenia and influence its course (Kealy, 2005; Vahia & Cohen, 2009). These include factors such as dysfunctional cognitive habits, the stress of urban living, being an immigrant, and exposure to stressful family communication patterns (Mueser & Jeste, 2009; van Os, Rutten, & Poulton, 2008). For example, criticism by family members—sometimes called *expressed emotion*—is associated with more severe symptoms (Nomura et al., 2005). And schizophrenia patients living with relatives who are critical, unsupportive, or emotionally overinvolved are especially likely to relapse following improvement (Hooley, 2004). Family members' negative attitudes may be a source of stress that increases the chances that disruptive or odd behaviors will persist or worsen (Rosenfarb et al., 1995). Keep in mind, though, that the strange and often disturbing behavior of a family member with schizophrenia can place tremendous strain on the rest of the family, making it harder for them to remain helpful and supportive (Kymalainen et al., 2006; Rosenfarb, Bellack, & Aziz, 2006). In any case, patients who receive help in coping with potentially damaging family influences tend to have better long-term outcomes (Bustillo et al., 2001; Velligan et al., 2000).

Vulnerability Theory All the causal theories of schizophrenia discussed so far are consistent with the diathesis-stress approach, which assumes that various forms of stress can activate a person's predisposition for disorder (Stahl, 2007). ("In Review: Schizophrenia" summarizes these theories, as well as the symptoms of schizophrenia.) The diathesis-stress approach is embodied in the *vulnerability theory* of schizophrenia

IN REVIEW Schizophrenia	
Aspect	**Key Features**
Common Symptoms	
Disorders of thought	Disturbed content, including delusions; disorganization, including loose associations, neologisms, and word salad
Disorders of perception	Hallucinations; poorly focused attention
Disorders of emotion	Flat affect; inappropriate tears, laughter, or anger
Possible Causes	
Biological	Genetics; abnormalities in brain structure; abnormalities in dopamine systems; neurodevelopmental problems
Psychological	Learned maladaptive behavior; disturbed patterns of family communication

1. The _____ approach forms the basis of the vulnerability theory of schizophrenia.

2. Hallucinations are _____ symptoms of schizophrenia; lack of emotion is a _____ symptom.

3. Patients with schizophrenia who were able to finish school are _____ likely to show improvement.

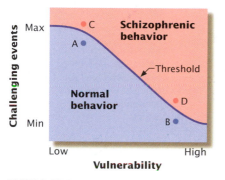

FIGURE 15.5
The Vulnerability Theory of Schizophrenia

According to this theory, a person can cross the threshold into schizophrenia as a result of many combinations of predisposition and stress. A strong predisposition for schizophrenia and little environmental stress (point D), a weak predisposition and a lot of stress (point C), or any other sufficiently potent combination can lead to the disorder. Points A and B represent combinations of vulnerability and stress that would not lead to schizophrenia.

Source: J. Zubin and B. Spring. "A New View of Schizophrenia". *Journal of Abnormal Psychology,* 86, p. 110. Copyright © 1977 by the American Psychological Association. Adapted with permission.

personality disorders Long-standing, inflexible ways of behaving that create a variety of problems.

(Cornblatt & Erlenmeyer-Kimling, 1985; Zubin & Spring, 1977). This theory suggests that (1) vulnerability to schizophrenia is mainly biological, (2) different people have differing degrees of vulnerability, (3) vulnerability is influenced partly by genetic influences on development and partly by neurodevelopmental abnormalities associated with environmental risk, and (4) psychological components—such as exposure to poor parenting or high-stress families or having inadequate coping skills—may help determine whether schizophrenia actually appears and may also influence the course of the disorder (Walker & Diforio, 1998; Wearden et al., 2000).

Many different blends of vulnerability and stress can lead to schizophrenia, as Figure 15.5 illustrates. People whose genetic characteristics or developmental influences leave them vulnerable to developing schizophrenia may be especially likely to do so if they are later exposed to learning experiences, family conflicts, and other stressors that trigger and maintain schizophrenic patterns of thought and action. Those same experiences and stressors would not be expected to lead to schizophrenia in people who are less vulnerable to developing the disorder. In other words, schizophrenia is a highly complex disorder—probably a spectrum of related disorders (Kirkpatrick et al., 2001; Lenzenweger, McLachlan, & Rubin, 2007)—whose origins lie in many biological, psychological, and social domains, some of which are yet to be discovered (Gilmore, 2010).

Personality Disorders

Personality disorders are long-standing, inflexible ways of behaving that are not so much severe mental disorders as dysfunctional styles of living (Clarkin, 2006). These disorders affect all areas of functioning and, beginning in childhood or adolescence, create problems for those who display them and for others (Cohen, 2008; Millon & Davis, 1996). Some psychologists view personality disorders as interpersonal strategies (Kiesler, 1996) or as the extreme, rigid, and maladaptive expressions of personality traits (Widiger, 2008). The ten personality disorders listed on Axis II of *DSM-IV-TR* are grouped into three clusters that share certain features (see Table 15.5).

The *odd-eccentric* cluster—referred to as *cluster A*—includes paranoid, schizoid, and schizotypal personality disorders. People diagnosed as having *schizotypal personality disorder,* for example, display some of the peculiarities seen in schizophrenia but are not disturbed enough to be labeled as schizophrenic. Rather than hallucinating, these people may report "illusions" of sights or sounds. They may also exhibit "magical

TABLE 15.5	Personality Disorders	
Here are brief descriptions of the ten personality disorders listed on Axis II of *DSM-IV-TR*.		
	Type	**Typical Features**
Cluster A (odd-eccentric)	Paranoid	Suspiciousness and distrust of others, all of whom are assumed to be hostile
	Schizoid	Detachment from social relationships; restricted range of emotion
	Schizotypal	Detachment from, and great discomfort in, social relationships; odd perceptions, thoughts, beliefs, and behaviors
Cluster B (dramatic-erratic)	Histrionic	Excessive emotionality and preoccupation with being the center of attention; emotional shallowness; overly dramatic behavior
	Narcissistic	Exaggerated ideas of self-importance and achievements; preoccupation with fantasies of success; arrogance
	Borderline	Lack of stability in interpersonal relationships, self-image, and emotion; impulsivity; angry outbursts; intense fear of abandonment; recurring suicidal gestures
	Antisocial	Chronic, remorseless pattern of impulsive, irresponsible, dishonest behavior
Cluster C (anxious-fearful)	Dependent	Helplessness; excessive need to be taken care of; submissive and clinging behavior; difficulty in making decisions
	Obsessive-compulsive	Preoccupation with orderliness, perfection, and control
	Avoidant	Inhibition in social situations; feelings of inadequacy; oversensitivity to criticism

thinking," including odd superstitions or beliefs (such as that they have extrasensory perception or that salt under the mattress will prevent insomnia).

The *dramatic-erratic* cluster—called *cluster B*—includes the histrionic, narcissistic, borderline, and antisocial personality disorders. The main characteristics of *narcissistic personality disorder,* for example, are an exaggerated sense of self-importance, extreme sensitivity to criticism, a constant need for attention, and a tendency to arrogantly overestimate personal abilities and achievements. People displaying this disorder feel entitled to special treatment by others but are markedly lacking in empathy *for* others.

The *anxious-fearful* cluster—*cluster C*—includes dependent, obsessive-compulsive, and avoidant personality disorders. *Avoidant personality disorder,* for example, is similar to social phobia in the sense that people labeled with this disorder tend to be "loners" with a long-standing pattern of avoiding social situations and of being particularly sensitive to criticism or rejection. They want to be with others but are too inhibited.

Personality disorder diagnoses are among the most controversial. The controversy arises partly because people with these diagnoses sometimes produce more

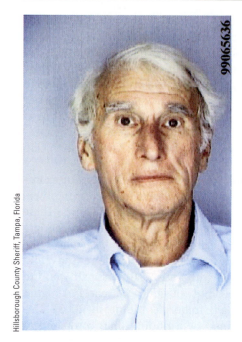

A Classic Case of Antisocial Personality Disorder

Alfred Jack Oakley meets women through personal ads, claiming to be a millionaire movie producer, pilot, and novelist. In reality, he is a penniless con artist who uses smooth talk and charm to gain the women's trust so he can steal from them. In January 2000, after being convicted of stealing a Florida woman's Mercedes, Oakley complimented the prosecutor's skills and the jury's wisdom and claimed to feel remorseful. The judge appeared to see through this ploy ("I don't believe there is a sincere word that ever comes out of your mouth"), but it was still effective enough to get him probation instead of jail time.

antisocial personality disorder (APD) A personality disorder involving impulsive, selfish, unscrupulous, and even criminal behavior.

distress in others than in themselves, so the role of social and moral judgment in deciding who is disordered comes into play (Clark, 2006). In addition, the overlap among symptoms of some of the personality disorders makes diagnosis difficult (Widiger, Livesley, & Clark, 2009). Studies that use symptom checklists or other behavioral measures to diagnose these disorders, as well as those that use molecular genetic data, generally identify either three or four clusters, not always what would be expected according to *DSM-IV-TR* (Fossati et al., 2006; Livesley, 2005). Some critics have suggested that there is gender bias in the application of diagnoses—pointing to the fact that women are labeled as borderline much more often than men, while men are labeled as antisocial more often than women (Bjorklund, 2006; Boggs et al., 2009). Even the stability of personality disorders over the lifetime has been questioned (Durbin & Klein, 2006). Some aspects of personality disorder diagnoses may be revised in *DSM-V*, but as yet there is no strong consensus about what changes should be made.

From the perspective of public welfare and safety, the most serious, costly, and intensively studied personality disorder is **antisocial personality disorder (APD)**. It is marked by a long-term pattern of irresponsible, impulsive, dishonest, unscrupulous, and even criminal behavior beginning in childhood or early adolescence (Washburn et al., 2007). In the 1800s, this pattern was called *moral insanity* because the people displaying it appear to have no morals or common decency. Later the term *sociopath* or *psychopath* was applied to individuals who display shallow emotions, lack of empathy, and superficial charm and who callously violate social norms (Coid & Ullrich, 2010; Hare & Newmann, 2009). The current "antisocial personality" label used in *DSM-IV-TR* more accurately portrays people displaying the disorder as troublesome and sometimes dangerous but not "insane" by the legal standards we will discuss shortly. About 3 percent of men and about 1 percent of women in the United States fall into the APD category (American Psychiatric Association, 2000; Hodgins, 2007).

At their least troublesome, people exhibiting antisocial personality disorder are a nuisance. They can be charming, intelligent "fast talkers" who borrow money and fail to return it. They can be arrogant and self-centered manipulators who con people into doing things for them, usually by lying and taking advantage of the decency and trust of others. At their most troublesome, people with this disorder are criminals, sometimes violent ones. Persistent violent offenders, most of whom have APD, make up less than 5 percent of the male population, but they commit over 50 percent of violent crimes (Hodgins, 2007). A hallmark of people with APD is a lack of anxiety, remorse, or guilt, whether they have wrecked a borrowed car or killed an innocent person (Gray et al., 2003; Hare & Newmann, 2009). No method has yet been found for permanently altering antisocial personality disorder (Rice, 1997). Research suggests that the best hope for dealing with antisocial personalities is to identify them early, before the most treatment-resistant traits are fully developed (Compton et al., 2005; Crawford, Cohen, & Brooks, 2001; Diamantopoulou, Verhulst, & van der Ende, 2010). Fortunately, these individuals tend to become less active and dangerous after the age of 40 or so (Stoff, Breiling, & Maser, 1997).

Perhaps you are wondering whether terrorists and suicide bombers should be classified as antisocial personalities—after all, they exhibit violent and disruptive behavior in the extreme. Some terrorists do exhibit the characteristics of antisocial personality disorder, but most do not (Martens, 2004). Acts of terrorism might better be explained from the perspective of social and political psychology—terrorists are spurred to take extreme destructive measures by political and religious ideologies during intense group conflict (Saucier et al., 2009). In short, the psychology of group conflict and war might better explain the terrorism of today, just as it might have explained the terrifying behavior of Japanese kamikaze pilots during World War II.

There are numerous theories about the causes of antisocial personality disorder. Some studies suggest a genetic predisposition (Arseneault et al., 2003; Larsson, Andershed, & Lichtenstein, 2006). Genes appear implicated in nearly all disorders; however, the genetic contribution to antisocial behaviors that begin in adolescence or adulthood is modest at best. In contrast, antisocial activity that emerges in early childhood appears to have a stronger genetic component (Arseneault et al., 2003). Genes may influence brain development; reduced brain size and reductions in the amygdala and hippocampal regions are associated with antisocial personality (Craig et al., 2009; van Goozen et al., 2007; Yang et al., 2009). Genes may also contribute to chronic underarousal of both the autonomic and central nervous systems (Crozier et al., 2008; Kiehl et al., 2006; Narayan et al., 2007; Raine et al., 2005). This underarousal may render people less sensitive to punishment and more likely to seek exciting stimulation than is normally the case (Birbaumer et al., 2005; Fowles & Dindo, 2009; Gao et al., 2010).

Other evidence suggests more specific information-processing defects. For example, people diagnosed with antisocial personality disorder perform less well than others do on neuropsychological tests of the ability to make plans (Dolan & Park, 2002). There seem to be specific problems, too, in the processing of fear-related information among people whose symptoms of antisocial personality disorder include extreme emotional detachment (Levenston et al., 2000; Patrick, Bradley, & Lang, 1993). In one study, film clips of delinquent acts were shown to young men with antisocial personality and to non-APD males. The APD males reported lower levels of guilt and fear and higher levels of excitement and happiness while watching (Cimbora & McIntosh, 2003). This diminished responsiveness may be partly explained by a finding that, compared to those without APD, antisocial adolescents have more difficulty simply remembering emotional material (Dolan & Fullam, 2006). Deficits in the ability to encode, recall, and respond to emotional material might help explain the apparent "fearlessness" (and foolishness) of some of their behavior, as well as their insensitivity to other people's emotions (Visser et al., 2010).

Broken homes, rejection by parents, poor discipline, lack of good parental models, lack of attachment to early caregivers, impulsivity, conflict-filled childhoods, and poverty have all been suggested as psychological and social factors contributing to the development of antisocial personality disorder (Caspi et al., 2004; Lahey et al., 1995; Lyman & Gudonis, 2005; Tremblay et al., 1994). The biopsychosocial model suggests that antisocial personality disorder results when these psychosocial and environmental conditions interact with genetic predispositions to low arousal and the sensation seeking and impulsivity associated with it (Diamantopoulou, Verhulst, & van der Ende, 2010; Gray et al., 2003; Rutter, 1997).

FOCUS ON RESEARCH METHODS ▶

Exploring Links Between Child Abuse and Antisocial Personality Disorder

One of the most prominent environmental factors associated with the more violent forms of antisocial personality disorder is the experience of abuse in childhood (MacMillan et al., 2001). However, most of the studies that have found a relationship between childhood abuse and APD were based on potentially biased reports (Monane, Leichter, & Lewis, 1984; Rosenbaum & Bennett, 1986). People with antisocial personalities—especially those with criminal records—are likely to make up stories of abuse in order to shift blame for their behavior onto others. Even if these people's reports were accurate, however, most of the studies lacked a control group of people from similar backgrounds who were not antisocial. Because of this research design flaw, it is virtually impossible to separate the effects of reported child abuse from the effects of poverty or other factors that may also have contributed to the development of APD.

What was the researcher's question?

Can childhood abuse cause antisocial personality disorder? To help answer this question and to correct some of the flaws in earlier studies, Cathy Widom (1989) used a prospective research design, first finding cases of childhood abuse and then looking for the effects of that abuse on adult behavior.

How did the researcher answer the question?

Widom began by identifying 416 adults whose backgrounds included official records of having been physically or sexually abused before the age of 11. She then explored the stories of these people's lives, as told in police and school records, as well as in two-hour diagnostic interviews. To reduce experimenter bias and distorted reporting, Widom ensured that the interviewers were unaware of the purpose of the study and that the respondents were told only that the researchers wanted to learn about people who had grown up in a midwestern U.S. metropolitan area in the late 1960s and early 1970s. Widom also selected a comparison group of 283 people who had no history of abuse but who were similar to the abused sample in terms of age, gender, ethnicity, hospital of birth, schools attended, and area of residence. Her goal was to obtain a nonabused control group that had been exposed to approximately the same environmental risk factors and socioeconomic conditions as the abused children.

What did the researcher find?

First, Widom (1989) tested the hypothesis that exposure to abuse in childhood is associated with criminality or violence in later life. She found that 26 percent of the abused youngsters went on to commit juvenile crimes, 29 percent were arrested as adults, and 11 percent committed violent crimes. These percentages were significantly higher than the figures for the nonabused group. The association between criminality and abuse was stronger for males than for females and stronger for African Americans than for European Americans. And overall, victims of physical abuse were more likely than victims of sexual abuse to commit violent crimes as adults.

Next, Widom tested the hypothesis that childhood abuse is associated with the development of antisocial personality disorder (Luntz & Widom, 1994). She found that the abused group exhibited a significantly higher rate of antisocial personality disorder (13.5 percent) than the comparison group (7.1 percent). The apparent role of abuse in antisocial personality disorder was particularly pronounced in men, and it remained strong even when other factors—such as age, ethnicity, and socioeconomic status—were accounted for in the statistical analyses. It is interesting to note that one other factor—failure to graduate from high school—was also strongly associated with the appearance of antisocial personality disorder, whether or not childhood abuse had occurred.

What do the results mean?

Widom's research supported earlier studies in finding an association between childhood abuse and criminality, violence, and antisocial personality disorder. Further, although her study did not permit a firm conclusion that abuse alone causes APD, the data from its prospective design added strength to the argument that abuse may be an important causal factor (Widom, 2000). This interpretation is supported by the results of research by other investigators (Dudeck et al., 2007; Jaffee et al., 2004). Finally, Widom's work offers yet another reason—as if more reasons were needed—why it is so important to prevent the physical and sexual abuse of children. The long-term consequences of such abuse can be tragic not only for its immediate victims but also for those victimized by the violence, criminal actions, and antisocial behavior perpetrated by some abused children as they grow up (Weiler & Widom, 1996; Widom, Czaja, & Dutton, 2008).

What do we still need to know?

Widom's results suggest that one or more of the factors leading teenagers to drop out (or be thrown out) of high school might encourage the development of antisocial personality disorder even in children who were not abused. Some of her more recent work suggests, too, that exposure to poverty and other stressors can be as important as abuse in promoting APD (Horwitz et al., 2001). Further research is needed to discover whether APD stems from abuse itself, from one of the factors accompanying it, or from some other specific combination of known and still-unknown environmental and genetic risk factors (Beach et al., 2010). The importance of combined and interacting risk factors is suggested by the fact that abuse is often part of a larger pool of experiences, such as exposure to deviant models, social rejection, and poor supervision.

In fact, another of Widom's more recent studies (Horwitz et al., 2001) supported the conclusion that childhood abuse increases the likelihood of encountering later stressful life events and that it is some of these events that lead to an increased risk of antisocial personality disorder. In other words, childhood abuse might create general vulnerability for a variety of psychological disorders and life stressors (Scott, Smith, & Ellis, 2010), but the chain of events that promote the development of any particular disorder, such as antisocial personality disorder, are not yet fully understood.

We need to know more, too, about why such a small percentage of the abused children in Widom's sample displayed violence, criminal behavior, and antisocial personality disorder. These results raise the question of what genetic characteristics or environmental experiences serve to protect children from at least some of the devastating effects of abuse (Flores, Cicchetti, & Rogosch, 2005; Rind & Tromovitch, 1997; Rind, Tromovitch, & Bauserman, 1998; Widom et al., 2007). As described in the chapter on human development, some clues have already been found (Caspi et al., 2002; Kim-Cohen & Gold, 2009; Wills et al., 2001), but a better understanding of these protective elements is needed if there are to be effective programs for the prevention of antisocial personality disorder.

A Sampling of Other Psychological Disorders

The disorders described so far represent some of the most prevalent and socially disruptive psychological problems encountered in cultures around the world. Several others are mentioned in other chapters. For example, intellectual disability is covered in the chapter on cognitive abilities; posttraumatic stress disorder is described in the chapter on health, stress, and coping; and sleep disorders are discussed in the chapter on consciousness. Here we consider two other significant psychological problems: disorders of childhood and substance-related disorders.

Psychological Disorders of Childhood

The physical, cognitive, emotional, and social changes seen in childhood—and the stress associated with them—can cause or worsen psychological disorders in children. Stress can do the same in adults, but childhood disorders are not just miniature versions of adult psychopathology. Because children's development is still incomplete and because their capacity to cope with stress is limited, children are often vulnerable to special types of disorders. *DSM-IV-TR* lists over two dozen Axis I disorders seen in infants, children, and adolescents, but the majority of childhood behavior problems can be placed in two broad categories: externalizing disorders and internalizing disorders (Phares, 2008).

The *externalizing,* or *undercontrolled,* category includes behaviors that are particularly disturbing to people in the child's environment. Lack of control shows up as *conduct disorders* in about 2 to 9 percent of children and adolescents, mostly boys, and appears most frequently at around 11 or 12 years of age (Merikangas et al., 2010; Nock et al., 2006). Conduct disorders are characterized by a relatively stable pattern of aggression, disobedience, destructiveness, inappropriate sexual activity, academic failure, and other problematic behaviors (Kalb & Loeber, 2003; Petitclerc & Tremblay, 2009). Often these behaviors involve criminal activity, and they may signal the development of antisocial personality disorder (Loeber & Stouthamer-Loeber, 1998; Lyman & Gudonis, 2005).

There may be a genetic predisposition toward externalizing disorders, including conduct disorders that begin in childhood and progress into adulthood (Larsson, Andershed, & Lichtenstein, 2006; Van Hulle et al., 2009). For example, many children who display conduct disorder have parents with antisocial personality disorder (Gelhorn et al., 2005). Further, externalizing disorders are especially likely to appear in children with temperamentally high activity levels and lack of concern for the feelings of other people (Anastassiou-Hadjicharalambous & Warden, 2008; Mesman & Koot, 2000). There is no doubt, however, that environmental and parenting factors also shape these children's behavior and that these factors interact with genetic factors (Hanish et al., 2005; Laird et al., 2001; Leve, Kim, & Pears, 2005; Scourfield et al., 2004).

Another kind of externalizing problem, *attention deficit hyperactivity disorder* (*ADHD*), is seen in up to 8 percent of children, mainly boys (and in about 4 percent of adults, mainly men; Bloom & Cohen, 2007; Merkangas et al., 2010). A diagnosis of ADHD is given to children who are more impulsive or more inattentive than other children their age (Nigg, 2001; Wolraich et al., 2005). *DSM-IV-TR* lists three subtypes of this disorder: primarily inattentive, primarily impulsive, and combined (both inattentive and impulsive). As the name implies, many of these children are *hyperactive*. That is, they have great difficulty sitting still or otherwise controlling their physical activity. Their impulsiveness and lack of self-control contribute to significant impairments in learning and to an astonishing ability to annoy and exhaust the people around them. Children diagnosed with ADHD also tend to perform poorly on tests of attention, memory, decision making, and other information-processing tasks. As a result, ADHD is being increasingly viewed as a neurological condition rather than just "bad behavior" (Halperin & Schulz, 2006; Konrad et al., 2006; Krain & Castellanos, 2006).

ADHD may result from a genetic predisposition. Some studies suggest that the genes involved may be those that regulate dopamine, a neurotransmitter important in the functioning of the attention system (Bush, 2010; Gilden & Marusich, 2009; Waldman & Gizer, 2006). Other factors, including brain damage, poisoning from lead or other household substances, and low birth weight, may also play causal roles (Hudziak et al., 2005; Linnet et al., 2003; Mick et al., 2002; Nikolas & Burt, 2010). In some cases, problem s in parenting may increase the risk for this disorder (Clarke et al., 2002). Exactly how all these factors combine is still not clear (Nigg, 2010). Also uncertain is exactly what constitutes hyperactivity. Cultural standards about acceptable activity levels in children vary, so a "hyperactive" child in one culture might be considered merely "active" in another. In fact, when mental health professionals from four cultures used the same rating scales to judge the presence and severity of hyperactivity in a videotaped sample of children's behavior, the Chinese and Indonesians rated the children as significantly more hyperactive than their American and Japanese colleagues did (Mann et al., 1992; see also Jacobson, 2002). And as mentioned earlier, there is evidence that African American children are diagnosed with ADHD only about two-thirds as often as European American children, even when they have at least as many symptoms (Miller, Nigg, & Miller, 2009). Such findings remind us again that sociocultural factors can be important determinants of what is acceptable—and hence what is abnormal—in various parts of the world.

A second broad category of child behavior problems involves *internalizing,* or *overcontrol.* Children in this category experience significant distress, especially depression and anxiety, and may be socially withdrawn (Luby, 2010). Those displaying *separation anxiety disorder,* for example, constantly worry that they will be lost, kidnapped, or injured or that some harm may come to a parent (usually the mother). The child clings desperately to the parent and becomes upset or sick at the prospect of any separation. Refusal to go to school (sometimes called "school phobia") is often the result. Children who are shy or withdrawn are at a higher risk than others for internalizing disorders, but these problems are also associated with environmental factors, including being rejected by peers and (especially for girls) being raised by a single parent (Phares, 2008; Prinstein & La Greca, 2002).

A few childhood disorders, such as *pervasive developmental disorders,* do not fall into either the externalizing or internalizing category. Children diagnosed with these disorders show severe problems in communication and impaired social relationships. They also often display repetitive, stereotyped behaviors and unusual preoccupations and interests (American Psychiatric Association, 2000). The disorders in this group, also known as *autistic spectrum disorders* (*ASD*), share many of these core symptoms,

© Juan Silva/The Image Bank/Getty Images

Active or Hyperactive?

TRY THIS Normal behavior for children in one culture can be considered hyperactive in other cultures. Do people in the *same* culture disagree on what is hyperactive? To find out, ask two or three friends to join you in observing a group of children at a playground, a schoolyard, a park, or some other public place. Ask your friends to privately identify which children they would label as "hyperactive," and then count how many of their choices agree with yours and with each other's. With many children in many cultures showing high activity levels, some observers wonder about the validity of the ADHD diagnosis and especially about the wisdom of medicating the children who receive it (Merikangas et al., 2010).

although the severity of those symptoms may vary (Çeponien et al., 2003; Constantino & Todd, 2003). Estimates of the prevalence of ASD in the United States range from 10 to 20 children per 10,000 births (Bryson & Smith, 1998; Filipek et al., 1999) to as high as 110 per 10,000 (Chakrabarti & Fombonne, 2001). If, as recent data suggest, the actual rate is nearer the high end of this range, nearly 700,000 children could be affected (Williams et al., 2008). ASD is diagnosed in boys four times as often as in girls and more often in European American children than in other groups (Kogan et al., 2009). Some of these children have *autistic disorder,* which can be the most severe of the group. The earliest signs of autistic disorder usually appear within the first thirty months after birth, as these babies show little or no evidence of forming an attachment to their caregivers. Language development is seriously disrupted in most of these children; half of them never learn to speak at all. They have great difficulty engaging in tasks that require shared attention, and they often focus on nonsocial aspects of human interaction, such as clothing, rather than on social aspects such as eye contact, facial expression, and tone of voice (Klin et al., 2002). Those who display high-functioning autism or a less severe autistic spectrum disorder called *Asperger's syndrome* (also known as *Aspberger's disorder*) have impaired relationships, engage in repetitive behaviors, and may memorize arcane facts or activities (such as sports scores or ZIP codes), but they show few severe cognitive deficits and are able to function adaptively and, in some cases, independently as adults (e.g., Grandin, 1996; Shore, 2003).

Possible biological roots of autistic disorder include genetic factors (Freitag, 2007; Gupta & State, 2007; St. Pourcain et al., 2010 Vorstman et al., 2006; Weiss & Arking, 2009) and neurodevelopmental abnormalities affecting language and communication (Akshoomoff, 2005; Belmonte et al., 2004; Grossberg & Seidman, 2006; Minshew & Williams, 2007). Researchers studying these biological factors have recently become interested in the activity of mirror neurons in the brain. As described in the chapter on biological aspects of psychology, these neurons are activated when we see other people's actions, such as smiling, frowning, or showing disgust. Because they are in the areas of our own brain that control these same actions, activity in mirror neurons help us understand how the other person might be feeling and empathize with those feelings. The functioning of such neurons appears disturbed in people with autism, partly explaining why these individuals seem to operate with little appreciation for what others might be thinking or feeling (Welsh et al., 2009; Williams et al., 2006). Other problems have been found in the brains of children with autism, mainly in the prefrontal cortex and in the corpus callosum (which connects the two cerebral hemispheres). These problems may impair the communication among brain areas that is necessary for normal social interaction and language (Mitchell et al., 2009). Hypotheses that autistic disorder is caused by having cold and unresponsive parents or by injections of measles, mumps, rubella (MMR) vaccine have been rejected by the results of scientific research (e.g. Doja & Roberts, 2006).

Disorders of childhood differ from adult disorders not only because the patterns of behavior are distinct but also because their early onset disrupts development. To take one example, children whose separation anxiety causes spotty school attendance may not only fall behind academically but also fail to form the relationships with other children that promote normal social development (Wood, 2006). Some children never make up for this deficit. They may drop out of school and risk a life of poverty, crime, and violence. Moreover, children are dependent on others to obtain help for their psychological problems, but all too often those problems may go unrecognized or untreated. For some, the long-term result may be adult forms of mental disorder.

Substance-Related Disorders

substance-related disorders Problems involving the use of psychoactive drugs for months or years in ways that harm the user or others.

Childhood disorders, especially externalizing disorders, often lead to *substance-related disorders* in adolescence and adulthood. *DSM-IV-TR* defines **substance-related disorders** as the use of psychoactive drugs for months or years in ways that harm the user or others. These disorders create major political, economic, social, and health problems worldwide. The substances involved most often are alcohol and other

CNS depressant drugs (such as barbiturates), opiates (such as heroin), CNS stimulating drugs (such as cocaine or amphetamines), and hallucinogenic drugs (such as LSD). About half the world's population uses at least one psychoactive substance, and about two-thirds of U.S. citizens report that problems related to alcohol or drug use have affected them, their families, or their close friends (Leamon, Wright, & Myrick, 2008).

One effect of using some substances (including alcohol, cocaine, heroin, and amphetamines) is **addiction**, a physical need for the substance. *DSM-IV-TR* calls addiction *physiological dependence.* Usually, addiction is evident when the person begins to need more and more of a substance to achieve the desired state. This condition is called building a *drug tolerance.* When addicted people stop using the substance, they experience painful, often terrifying, and potentially dangerous *withdrawal symptoms* as the body tries to readjust to a substance-free state. People can also display *psychological dependence,* sometimes called *behavioral dependence.* For these people, a drug has become their primary source of reward, and their lives essentially revolve around getting and using it. People who are psychologically dependent on a drug often display problems that are at least as serious as those of people who are physiologically addicted, and the problems are sometimes more difficult to treat.

Even when use of a drug does not lead to psychological or physiological dependence, some people may use it in a way that is harmful to themselves or others. For example, they may rely on the drug to bolster self-confidence or to avoid depression, anger, fear, or other unpleasant feelings. However, the drug effects these people seek may also impair their ability to hold a job, care for their children, or drive safely. This pattern of behavior, defined in *DSM-IV-TR* as *substance abuse,* causes significant social, legal, and interpersonal problems.

In short, substance-related disorders can be extremely serious, even when they do not involve addiction. In the chapter on consciousness, we describe how consciousness can be affected by a wide range of psychoactive drugs. Here we focus more specifically on the problems associated with the use and abuse of alcohol, heroin, and cocaine.

Alcohol Use Disorders   According to a large national survey, the twelve-month prevalence of alcohol abuse, as defined in *DSM-IV-TR,* was 3.1 percent of adults (Kessler & Wang, 2008). *Alcohol abuse* is characterized by a pattern of continuous or intermittent drinking that may lead to *alcohol dependence,* an addiction that almost always causes severe social, physical, and other problems (an additional 1.3 percent of U.S. adults fall into the dependent category). Males outnumber females in this category by about three to one, although the problem is on the rise among women and among teenagers of both sexes (Grucza et al., 2008). Abuse is greater among European Americans and American Indians than among African Americans and Hispanics; it is lowest among Asians (Chassin, Pitts, & Prost, 2002; Grant et al., 2004; Substance Abuse and Mental Health Services Administration, 2007). Prolonged overuse of alcohol can have serious consequences, including reduced cognitive abilities, impaired academic performance, life-threatening liver damage, vitamin deficiencies that can lead to an irreversible brain disorder called *Korsakoff's psychosis* (severe memory loss), and many other physical ailments. Many of these adverse effects appear to be due to the fact that excessive alcohol consumption causes deterioration in several brain areas (Hommer et al., 2001; Pfefferbaum et al., 2001).

Alcohol dependence or abuse, commonly referred to as **alcoholism**, has been implicated in 40 to 50 percent of all automobile accidents, murders, and rapes (Butcher, Mineka, & Hooley, 2010). Alcohol abuse also figures prominently in domestic violence, including child abuse, and in elevated rates of hospitalization and absenteeism from work, resulting in total costs to society of over $180 billion each year in the United States alone (Keller et al., 2009; National Institute on Alcohol Abuse and Alcoholism [NIAAA], 2001). It is estimated that about half of U.S. adults have a close relative who is an active or recovering alcoholic and that about 25 percent of children are exposed to adults who display alcohol abuse or dependence (NIAAA, 2001). Children growing up in families in which one or both parents abuse alcohol are at increased risk for developing a host of mental disorders, including substance abuse disorders

addiction   Development of a physical need for a psychoactive drug.

alcoholism   A pattern of drinking that may lead to addiction and almost always causes severe social, physical, and other problems.

(Hoffmann & Cerbone, 2002; Odgers et al., 2008). And as described in the chapter on human development, children of mothers who abused alcohol during pregnancy may be born with fetal alcohol syndrome.

The biopsychosocial model suggests that alcohol use disorders stem from a combination of genetic characteristics (including inherited aspects of temperament such as impulsivity and emotionality) and what people learn in their social and cultural environments (Elkins et al., 2006; Lovallo et al., 2006; Ray et al., 2010). For example, children of people with alcoholism are more likely than others to become alcoholics themselves; and if the children are identical twins, both are at increased risk for alcoholism, even when raised apart (Volk et al., 2007). It is still unclear just what might be inherited or which genes are involved. One possibility involves inherited abnormalities in the brain's neurotransmitter systems or in the body's metabolism of alcohol (Martinez et al., 2005; Nurnberger et al., 2001; Petrakis et al., 2004). Males with alcoholism do tend to be less sensitive than other people to the effects of alcohol—a factor that may contribute to greater consumption (Pollack, 1992; Schuckit, 1998). Now that the human genome has been decoded, researchers are focusing on specific chromosomes as the possible locations of genes that predispose people to—or protect them from—the development of alcoholism (Cheng et al., 2004; NIAAA, 2000, 2001; Wall et al., 2005). However, the genetics of addiction is complex, and there are likely multiple pathways to alcoholism (Crabbe, 2002; Higuchi, Matsushita, & Kashima, 2006).

As with other disorders, alcoholism probably arises as many genes interact with one another and with environmental events, including parental influences (Duncan et al., 2006; Kaufman et al., 2007). For example, one study found that the sons of identical twins were at elevated risk for alcoholism if their own father was an alcoholic but not if the father's identical twin was (Jacob et al., 2003). Something in these boys' nonalcoholic family environment had apparently moderated whatever genetic tendency toward alcoholism they might have inherited. Youngsters typically learn to drink by watching their parents and their peers. These observations help shape their expectations, such as that alcohol will make them feel good and help them cope with stressors (Schell et al., 2005). But if drinking becomes a person's main coping strategy, alcohol use can become abuse and ultimately addiction (NIAAA, 2001). The importance of social and cultural learning is supported by evidence that alcoholism is more common among ethnic and cultural groups (such as the Irish and English) in which frequent drinking tends to be socially reinforced than among groups (such as Jews, Italians, and Chinese) in which anything beyond moderate drinking tends to be discouraged (Gray & Nye, 2001; Wilson et al., 1996). Moreover, variations in social support for drinking can result in differing consumption patterns within a cultural group. For example, one study found significantly more drinking among Japanese men living in Japan (where social norms for males' drinking are quite permissive) than among those living in Hawaii or California, where excessive drinking is less strongly supported (Kitano et al., 1992). Learning would also help explain why rates of alcoholism are higher than average among bartenders, cocktail servers, and others who work where alcohol is available and drinking is socially reinforced or even expected (Fillmore & Caetano, 1980). (Of course, it is also possible that attraction to alcohol led some of these people into such jobs in the first place.)

Heroin and Cocaine Dependence Like people with alcoholism, heroin and cocaine addicts suffer many serious physical problems, both as a result of the drugs themselves and of the poor eating and other unhealthy habits associated with drug use. The risk of death from an overdose, contaminated drugs, or AIDS (contracted through blood in shared needles), as well as from suicide, is also always present. Dependence on these drugs tends to be more prevalent among males, especially young males (Compton et al., 2007; Warner et al., 1995).

Continued use or overdoses of cocaine can cause problems ranging from nausea and hyperactivity to paranoid thinking, sudden depressive "crashes," and even death. Cocaine use has been on the decline since 1985, but it is still a serious problem. Surveys indicate that 7.7 percent of high school seniors in the United States have used cocaine at some time in their lives, and millions more teens and adults still use it on occasion (Johnston et al., 2004). The widespread availability of crack, a powerful and relatively cheap form of cocaine, has made it one of the most dangerous and addicting of all drugs. Pregnant women who use cocaine are much more likely than nonusers to lose their babies through spontaneous abortion, placental detachment, early fetal death, or stillbirth.

Addiction to heroin and cocaine appears in about 4 percent of the adult population in the United States (Compton et al., 2005). It occurs largely through a biological process brought on by the physiological effects of the drugs (Kalivas & Volkow, 2005; Phillips et al., 2003). Explaining why people start using them is more complicated. Beyond the obvious and immediate pleasure that these drugs provide, the causes of initial drug abuse are less well established than the reasons for alcohol abuse. One line of theorizing suggests that there might be a complex genetic predisposition toward behavioral compulsions that predispose some people to abuse many kinds of drugs (Crabbe, 2002; Koob & Volkow, 2010; Kreek et al., 2005). One study supporting this possibility found a link between alcoholism in biological parents and drug abuse in the sons they had given up for adoption (Cadoret et al., 1995).

A number of psychological and environmental factors have also been proposed as promoting initial drug use (Alessi et al., 2002; Brems & Namyniuk, 2002; Hoffmann & Cerbone, 2002). These include seeing parents using drugs, being abused in childhood, using drugs to cope with stressors or to ease anxiety or depression, associating drug use with pleasant experiences, seeking popularity, caving in to peer pressure, and thrill seeking (Alessi et al., 2002; Baker et al., 2004; Dube et al., 2003; Putnam, 2003; Reed, Anthony, & Breslau, 2007). Research has not yet established why continued drug use occurs in some people and not in others, but again, it is likely that a biological predisposition sets the stage on which specific psychological processes and stressors play out their roles in specific social and cultural contexts (Hammen, 2009; Kreek et al., 2005).

Mental Illness and the Law

Cheryl was barely 20 when she married Glen, a graduate student in biology. They moved into a large apartment complex near the university and within three years had two sons. Cheryl's friends had always been impressed by the attention and affection she showered on her boys; she seemed to be the ideal mother. She and Glen had serious marital problems, however, and she felt trapped and unhappy. One day, Glen came home to find that Cheryl had stabbed both children to death. At her murder trial, she was found not guilty by reason of insanity and was placed in a mental institution.

This verdict reflects U.S. laws and rules that protect people with severe psychological disorders when they are accused of crimes (Cassel & Bernstein, 2007). Similar laws and rules are in effect in many other countries. The protection takes two forms.

First, under certain conditions, people designated as mentally ill may be protected from prosecution. If, at the time of their trial, individuals accused of a crime are unable to understand the proceedings and charges against them or to assist in their own defense, they are declared to be *mentally incompetent* to stand trial. In such cases, defendants are sent to a mental institution until they are judged to have become mentally competent. If still not competent after a court-specified period—two years, in most cases—a defendant may be ruled permanently ineligible for trial and either committed in civil court to a mental institution or released. Release is rare, however, because competency to stand trial requires only minimal mental abilities. If drugs can produce even temporary mental competence, the defendant will usually go to trial (Nietzel, 1999).

Second, mentally ill defendants may be protected from punishment. In most U.S. states, they may be judged *not guilty by reason of insanity* if, at the time of the crime, mental illness prevented them from understanding what they were doing, knowing that what they were doing was wrong, or resisting the impulse to do wrong. The first two of these criteria—understanding the nature or wrongfulness of an act—are "cognitive"

Assessment of Mental Competence

Andrea Yates admitted to drowning her five children in the bathtub of her Houston, Texas, home in 2001. She had twice tried to kill herself in previous years, and she was reportedly depressed at the time of the murders. Accordingly, she pleaded not guilty by reason of insanity. The court's first step in deciding her fate was to confine her in a mental institution for assessment of her mental competency to stand trial. Following testimony of psychologists who examined her, she was found competent, tried, and sentenced to life in prison. Her conviction was overturned on appeal, though, and at a second trial in 2006, she was found not guilty by reason of insanity and committed to a mental hospital.

© AP Photo/Melissa Phillip, Pool

criteria known as the M'Naghton rule. This rule stems from an 1843 case in England in which a man named Daniel M'Naghton, upon hearing "instructions from God," tried to kill British prime minister Robert Peel. He was found not guilty by reason of insanity and put into a mental institution for life. The third criterion, which is based on a defendant's emotional state during a crime, is known as the *irresistible-impulse test*. All three criteria were combined in a rule proposed by the American Law Institute (ALI) in 1962 and now followed by about one-third of the U.S. states: "A person is not responsible for criminal conduct if at the time of such conduct as a result of mental disease or defect he lacks substantial capacity either to appreciate the criminality (wrongfulness) of his conduct or to conform his conduct to the requirements of law" (p. 66).

In 1984, after John Hinckley Jr. was found not guilty by reason of insanity under the ALI rule for his attempted assassination of President Ronald Reagan, the U.S. Congress passed the Insanity Defense Reform Act, which eliminated the irresistible-impulse criterion from the definition of insanity in federal cases. About 75 percent of the U.S. states have passed similar or related reform laws (Giorgi-Guarnieri et al., 2002). In about half the states, these laws require the use of some version of the narrower M'Naghton rule (American Psychiatric Association, 2003). These laws highlight the fact that *insanity* is a legal term, not a psychiatric diagnosis; it does not appear in *DSM-IV-TR* (Cassel & Bernstein, 2007). When defendants plead insanity, judges and juries must decide whether or not these people understood what they were doing or had control over their actions and hence whether or not they should be held responsible for their criminal acts. Defendants who are judged not guilty by reason of insanity and who still display a psychological disorder are usually required to receive treatment, typically through commitment to a hospital, until judged to be cured or no longer dangerous.

Insanity rules have been faulted on several grounds. Some critics argue that everyone, even people who meet legal criteria for insanity, should be held responsible for their actions and punished for their crimes. Others point out significant problems in the implementation of insanity rules. For one thing, different experts often give conflicting, highly technical testimony about a defendant's sanity at the time of a crime. (In the case mentioned at the beginning of this section, one expert said Cheryl was sane; another concluded she was insane.) Jurors are then left in the difficult position of deciding which expert to believe and what to make of the experts' diagnostic judgments. Their task is complicated by the fact that people with mental disorders—even those as severe as schizophrenia—are still capable of some rational decision making and of controlling some aspects of their behavior (Grisso & Appelbaum, 1995;

Matthews, 2004). Concern over such problems has led four U.S. states—Montana, Idaho, Utah, and Kansas—to abolish the insanity defense. Other states have tried less extreme reforms. In thirteen states, it is possible for juries to find defendants *guilty but mentally ill*. These defendants still serve a sentence, and although they are supposed to receive treatment while confined, they seldom do (Cassel & Bernstein, 2007). A second reform already noted is that federal courts no longer use the irresistible-impulse criterion in defining insanity. Third, federal courts and some state courts now require defendants to prove that they were insane at the time of their crime, rather than requiring the prosecution to prove that the defendants were sane.

Does the insanity defense allow lots of criminals to "get away with murder"? No. Although certain high-profile cases might suggest otherwise, the insanity plea is used in fewer than one of every two hundred felony cases in the United States—usually when the defendant displays severe psychological disorder—and this plea is successful in only two of every thousand attempts (American Psychiatric Association, 2003; Silver, Cirincione, & Steadman, 1994). Further, the few defendants found not guilty by reason of insanity are usually hospitalized for two to nine times as long as they would have spent in prison had they been convicted (Silver, 1995; Steadman, 1993). For example, John Hinckley Jr. has been in Saint Elizabeth's Hospital in Washington, D.C. since 1982, and despite his annual efforts to be released and court approval for longer visits with his mother outside the hospital, he is unlikely to be freed anytime soon.

In summary, society is constantly seeking the proper balance between protecting the rights of defendants and protecting itself from dangerous criminals. In doing so, the sociocultural values that shape views about what is abnormal also influence judgments about the extent to which abnormality should relieve people of responsibility for criminal behavior.

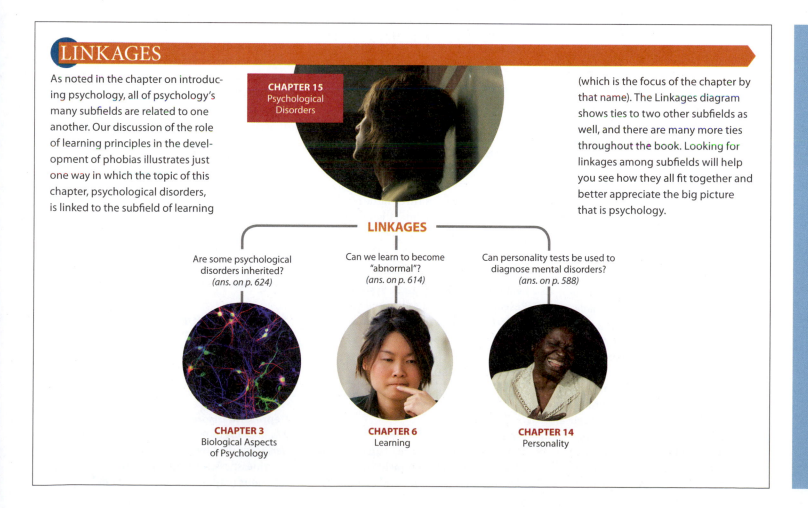

LINKAGES

As noted in the chapter on introducing psychology, all of psychology's many subfields are related to one another. Our discussion of the role of learning principles in the development of phobias illustrates just one way in which the topic of this chapter, psychological disorders, is linked to the subfield of learning

CHAPTER 15
Psychological Disorders

(which is the focus of the chapter by that name). The Linkages diagram shows ties to two other subfields as well, and there are many more ties throughout the book. Looking for linkages among subfields will help you see how they all fit together and better appreciate the big picture that is psychology.

LINKAGES

Are some psychological disorders inherited?
(ans. on p. 624)

Can we learn to become "abnormal"?
(ans. on p. 614)

Can personality tests be used to diagnose mental disorders?
(ans. on p. 588)

CHAPTER 3
Biological Aspects of Psychology

CHAPTER 6
Learning

CHAPTER 14
Personality

SUMMARY

Psychopathology involves patterns of thinking, feeling, and behaving that cause personal distress or that significantly impair a person's social or occupational functioning.

Defining Psychological Disorders

Some disorders show similarity across cultures, but the definition of abnormality is largely determined by social and cultural factors.

What Is Abnormal?

The criteria for judging abnormality include statistical infrequency (a comparison with what most people do), norm violation, and personal suffering. Each of these criteria is flawed to some extent.

Behavior in Context: A Practical Approach

The practical approach to defining abnormality, which considers the content, context, and consequences of behavior, emphasizes the question of whether individuals show impaired functioning in fulfilling the roles appropriate for particular people in particular settings, cultures, and historical eras.

Explaining Psychological Disorders

Abnormal behavior has been attributed, at one time or another, to many different factors, including the action of supernatural forces.

The Biopsychosocial Approach

In today's *biopsychosocial approach,* mental disorders are attributed to the combination and interaction of biological, psychological, and sociocultural factors. Biological factors are emphasized by the *medical model* (also called the *neurobiological model*), which sees psychological disorders as reflecting disturbances in the anatomy and chemistry of the brain and in other biological processes. The causal factors emphasized by the *psychological model* of mental disorders include unconscious conflicts, disruptions in attachment, learning, or maladaptive

cognitive schemas. The *sociocultural perspective* focuses on *sociocultural factors* that help define abnormality and influence the form that disorders take in different parts of the world.

Diathesis-Stress as an Integrative Explanation

No single aspect of the biopsychosocial approach can adequately explain all psychological disorders. The *diathesis-stress model* takes into account all the causal factors in that approach by suggesting that biological, psychological, and sociocultural characteristics create predispositions for disorder and that the symptoms of a disorder appear only in the face of sufficient amounts of stress.

Classifying Psychological Disorders

There seems to be a set of behavior patterns that roughly defines abnormality in most cultures. Classifying these patterns helps identify the features, causes, and most effective methods of treating various psychological disorders.

A Classification System: *DSM-IV-TR*

The dominant system for classifying abnormal behavior in North America is the American Psychiatric Association's *Diagnostic and Statistical Manual of Mental Disorders* (*DSM-IV*) in its most recent text revision (*DSM-IV-TR*). It includes more than three hundred specific categories of mental disorders. As with medical illnesses, categories for psychological disorders are periodically revised as research accumulates.

Evaluating the Diagnostic System

Research on the reliability and validity of *DSM-IV-TR* shows that it is a useful but imperfect classification system.

Anxiety Disorders

Long-standing and disruptive patterns of anxiety characterize *anxiety disorders.*

Types of Anxiety Disorders

The most prevalent type of anxiety disorder is *phobia,* which includes *specific phobias, social phobias,* and *agoraphobia.*

Other anxiety disorders are *generalized anxiety disorder,* which involves nonspecific anxiety; *panic disorder,* which brings unpredictable attacks of intense anxiety; and *obsessive-compulsive disorder* (*OCD*), characterized by uncontrollable repetitive thoughts (*obsessions*) and ritualistic actions (*compulsions*).

Causes of Anxiety Disorders

The most influential explanations of anxiety disorders suggest that they may develop through the combination of a biological predisposition for strong anxiety reactions and the impact of fear-enhancing thought patterns and learned anxiety responses.

Somatoform Disorders

Somatoform disorders, including *conversion disorder,* involve physical problems that have no apparent physical cause. Other examples are *hypochondriasis,* an unjustified concern about being ill; *somatization disorder,* in which the person complains of numerous, unconfirmed physical complaints; *somatoform pain disorder,* in which pain is felt in the absence of a known physical cause; and *body dysmorphic disorder,* characterized by intense distress over imagined abnormalities of the skin, hair, face, or other bodily areas.

Dissociative Disorders

Dissociative disorders involve rare conditions such as *dissociative fugue, dissociative amnesia,* and *dissociative identity disorder, or DID* (multiple personality disorder), in which a person suffers memory loss or develops two or more identities.

Affective Disorders

Affective disorders, also known as *mood disorders,* involve extreme moods of long duration that may be inconsistent with events.

Depressive Disorders

Major depression (*major depressive disorder*) is marked by feelings of inadequacy, worthlessness, and guilt; in extreme cases, *delusions* may also occur. *Dysthymic disorder* includes similar but less severe symptoms persisting for a long period. Suicide is often related to these disorders.

Bipolar Disorders
Alternating periods of depression and *mania* characterize *bipolar disorders. Cyclothymic personality (cyclothymic disorder)*, an alternating pattern of less extreme mood swings, is more common.

Causes of Affective Disorders
Affective disorders have been attributed to biological causes such as genetics—which underlie disruptions in neurotransmitter and endocrine systems—and irregularities in biological rhythms. Both loss of significant sources of reward and maladaptive patterns of thinking are among the psychological causes proposed. A predisposition toward some of these disorders appears to be inherited, although their appearance may be determined by a diathesis-stress process.

Schizophrenia

Schizophrenia is perhaps the most severe and puzzling disorder of all.

Symptoms of Schizophrenia
Among the symptoms of schizophrenia are problems in thinking, perception (often including *hallucinations*), attention, emotion, movement, motivation, and daily functioning.

Categorizing Schizophrenia
Although *DSM-IV-TR* lists five major subtypes of schizophrenia (paranoid, disorganized, catatonic, undifferentiated, and residual), many researchers today favor viewing it as a spectrum disorder involving displays of *positive symptoms* (such as hallucinations and disorganized thoughts) and *negative symptoms* (such as lack of speech and restricted emotional expression). Each category of symptoms may be traceable to different causes. Predominantly negative symptoms tend to be associated with more severe disorder and less successful treatment outcomes.

Causes of Schizophrenia
Genetic factors, neurotransmitter problems, abnormalities in brain structure and functioning, and neurodevelopmental abnormalities are biological factors implicated in schizophrenia. Psychological explanations have focused on maladaptive learning experiences and disturbed family interactions. The diathesis-stress approach, often described in terms of the vulnerability model, remains a promising framework for research into the multiple causes of schizophrenia.

Personality Disorders

Personality disorders are long-term patterns of maladaptive behavior that may be disturbing to the person displaying them or to others. Examples include schizotypal, avoidant, narcissistic, and *antisocial personality disorders.*

A Sampling of Other Psychological Disorders

Psychological Disorders of Childhood
Childhood disorders can be categorized as externalizing disorders (such as conduct disorders or attention deficit hyperactivity disorder) and internalizing disorders (in which children show overcontrol and experience distress, as in separation anxiety disorder). Pervasive developmental disorders do not fall into either category and include the autistic spectrum disorders. In autistic disorder, which can be the most severe of these, children show no interest in or attachment to others.

Substance-Related Disorders
Substance-related disorders involving alcohol and other drugs affect millions of people. *Addiction* to, psychological dependence on, or abuse of these substances contributes to disastrous personal and social problems, including physical illnesses, accidents, and crime. Genetic factors may create a predisposition for *alcoholism,* but learning, cultural traditions, and other psychosocial processes are also important. In the case of dependence on heroin and cocaine, stress reduction, imitation, thrill seeking, and parental modeling have been proposed as important causal factors, along with genetics. The exact causes of initial use of these drugs, however, are not fully understood.

Mental Illness and the Law

Current rules protect people accused of crimes from prosecution or punishment if they are mentally incompetent at the time of their trials or if they were legally insane at the time of their crimes. Difficulty in establishing the mental state of defendants and other knotty problems have created dissatisfaction with those rules and prompted a number of reforms, including the "guilty but mentally ill" verdict.

LINKAGES TO FURTHER LEARNING

Now that you have finished reading this chapter, how about exploring some of the topics and information that you found most interesting? Here are some places to start.

Books
Robert L. Spitzer, Michael B. First, Janet B. W. Williams, and Miriam Gibbon, *DSM-IV Casebook: A Learning Companion to the Diagnostic and Statistical Manual of Mental Disorders* (American Psychiatric Press, 1994). A casebook illustrating the disorders listed in the DSM-IV.

Karen Eriksen and Victoria Kress, *Beyond the DSM Story: Ethical Quandaries, Challenges, and Best Practices* (Sage, 2005). A summary of the *DSM* and its problems and alternative approaches.

William Styron, *Darkness Visible* (Vintage, 1992). Depression, suicidality.

Patty Duke, *A Brilliant Madness* (Bantam, 1993). Bipolar disorder.

Vaslav Nijinsky, *The Diary of Vaslav Nijinsky* (Farrar, Straus & Giroux, 1999). Insight into schizophrenia from one of Eugen Bleuler's most famous patients, the Russian ballet dancer.

Jerald J. Kriesman and Hal Straus, *I Hate You—Don't Leave Me: Understanding the Borderline Personality* (Avon, 1991). Descriptions and explanations of borderline behaviors, focusing on conflicted relationships.

Judith Rapoport, *The Boy Who Couldn't Stop Washing* (New American Library, 1997). Obsessive-compulsive disorder.

Joan Acocella, *Creating Hysteria: Women and Multiple Personality Disorder* (Jossey-Bass, 1999). A description of the influence of culture and other social forces in shaping dissociative identity disorder.

Meyer Glantz and Christine Hartel (Eds.), *Drug Abuse: Origins and Interventions* (American Psychological Association, 2000). Information that challenges various myths about drug abuse.

On the Internet

 Access an integrated eBook and chapter-specific learning tools including flashcards, quizzes, videos, and more. Go to CengageBrain.com.

CENGAGENOW Want to maximize the value of your online study time? Take this easy-to-use study system's diagnostic pre-test, and it will create a personalized study plan for you. By helping you identify the topics that you need to understand better and then directing you to valuable online resources, it can speed up your chapter review. CengageNOW even provides a post-test so you can confirm that you are ready for an exam. Go to CengageBrain.com.

TALKING POINTS

Here are a few talking points to help you summarize this chapter for family and friends without giving a lecture.

1. Though there are many more specific criteria, people are most likely to be diagnosed with a mental disorder when psychological or behavioral problems significantly impair their ability to function in society.

2. Behavior that is considered normal in one culture may be considered abnormal in another.

3. In general, behavior disorders emerge when an inherited predisposition interacts with environmental stress.

4. *DSM-V*, a new and expanded edition of the standard psychiatric diagnosis manual, is scheduled for publication in 2013.

5. Take suicide threats seriously; encourage the person to seek help.

6. Schizophrenia does not involve multiple personalities.

7. *Insanity* is a legal term, not a psychiatric diagnosis.

16

Treatment of Psychological Disorders

Many movies and television dramas include scenes in a psychotherapist's office, but even the best of them tell only part of the story of how psychological disorders can be treated. In this chapter, we describe a wide range of treatment options, from "talking therapy" to prescription drugs. We also summarize the results of research on the effectiveness of treatment and on efforts to prevent psychological disorders.

In the chapter on psychological disorders, we described José, an electronics technician who was forced to take medical leave from his job because of repeated panic attacks (see Table 15.1). After four months of diagnostic testing turned up no physical problems, José's physician suggested that he see a psychologist. José resisted at first, insisting that his condition was not "just in his head," but he eventually began psychological treatment. Within a few months, his panic attacks had stopped, and José had returned to all his old activities. After the psychologist helped him reconsider his workload, José decided to retire from his job in order to pursue more satisfying work at his home-based computer business.

José's case is by no means unique. During any given year in the United States, about 15 percent of adults and about 21 percent of children are receiving some form of treatment for a psychological disorder (Druss et al., 2007; Kessler, Demler, et al., 2005; Wang, Lane, et al., 2005). The cost of treating these disorders is just one part of their economic impact—which amounts to a staggering $318 billion per year, including disability payments and lost productivity (Insel, 2008). Fortunately, the cost of treatment is more than made up for by the savings it creates. Compared with untreated patients, those who receive treatment for psychological disorders typically need fewer mental and physical health services later on (American Psychological Association, 2009; Jordan et al., 2008; Schoenbaum, Sherbourne, & Wells, 2005).

The most common targets of treatment in adults are problems involving anxiety, mood, impulse control, substance abuse, or some combination of these (Druss et al., 2007). Many people also seek treatment for problems that are not officially diagnosed as disorders, such as relationship conflicts or difficulties associated with grief, divorce, retirement, or other life transitions. Among children, the most common treatment targets are hyperactivity, oppositional behavior, anxiety, and affective disorders (Phares, 2008).

In this chapter, we describe a variety of treatment methods, most of which are based on the theories of stress and coping, personality, and psychological disorders reviewed in the chapters on those topics. First we examine the basic features common to all forms of treatment. Then we discuss approaches that rely on **psychotherapy**, the treatment of psychological disorders through psychological methods, such as talking about problems and exploring new ways of thinking and acting. These methods are based on psychodynamic, humanistic, or social-cognitive (behavioral) theories of disorder and treatment. We then consider biological approaches to treatment, which consist of prescription drugs and other physical therapies. (Many clients receive medication in addition to psychotherapy during the course of psychological treatment.)

Basic Features of Treatment

psychotherapy The treatment of psychological disorders through talking and other psychological methods.

All treatments for psychological disorders share certain basic features. These common features include a *client* or patient, a *therapist* who is accepted as being capable of helping the client, and the establishment of a *special relationship* between the client and the therapist. In addition, all forms of treatment are based on some *theory* about the

Medieval Treatment Methods

Methods used to treat psychological disorders have always been related to the presumed causes of those disorders. In medieval times, when demonic possession was widely blamed for abnormal behavior, physician-priests tried to make the victim's body an uncomfortable place for evil spirits. Here we see a depiction of demons fleeing as an afflicted person's head is placed in an oven.

Stock Montage

causes of the client's problems (Dumont & Corsini, 2000). That theory may presume causes ranging from magic spells to infections and everything in between (Corey, 2008). The theory, in turn, leads to procedures for dealing with the client's problems. So traditional healers combat supernatural forces with ceremonies and prayers, medical doctors treat chemical imbalances with prescription drugs, and psychologists focus on altering psychological processes through psychotherapy.

People receiving treatment for psychological disorders can be inpatients or outpatients. *Inpatients* are treated in a hospital or other residential institution. They are voluntarily or involuntarily committed to these institutions because their problems are severe enough to pose a threat to their own well-being or the safety of others. Depending on their level of functioning, inpatients may stay in the hospital for a few days or weeks or, in rare cases, several years. Their treatment almost always includes psychoactive medication. *Outpatients* receive psychotherapy or prescription drugs (or both) while living in the community. Compared with inpatients, outpatients tend to have fewer and less severe symptoms of disorder and to function better in social and occupational situations (Hybels et al., 2008; Pottick et al., 2008).

Psychological treatment is provided by a diverse group of individuals (Robiner, 2006). **Psychiatrists** are medical doctors who have completed specialty training in the treatment of psychological disorders. Like other physicians, they are authorized to prescribe drugs for the relief of psychological problems. **Psychologists** who offer psychotherapy have usually completed a doctoral degree in clinical or counseling psychology, often followed by additional specialized training. Except in New Mexico and Louisiana, psychologists are not authorized to prescribe drugs, though this privilege may eventually be granted to specially trained psychologists elsewhere. Other treatment providers include *clinical social workers, marriage and family therapists,* and *licensed professional counselors,* all of whom typically hold a master's degree in their respective professions and provide therapy in a variety of settings, including hospitals, clinics, and private practice. *Psychiatric nurses, substance abuse counselors,* members of the clergy working as *pastoral counselors,* and a host of *paraprofessionals* also provide therapy services, often as part of a hospital or outpatient treatment team (Kramer, Bernstein, & Phares, 2009).

The general goal of treatment is to help troubled people change their thinking, feelings, and behavior in ways that relieve discomfort, promote happiness, and improve their overall functioning as parents, students, and workers. To reach this goal, some therapists try to help clients gain insight into the hidden causes of problems. Others seek to promote growth through more genuine self-expression, and still others help clients learn and practice new ways of thinking and acting. The particular methods

psychiatrists Medical doctors who have completed special training in the treatment of psychological disorders.

psychologists Among therapists, those who have completed a master's or (usually) doctoral degree in clinical or counseling psychology and who may have received additional specialty training.

Group Therapy for War Veterans

Some psychotherapy occurs in one-to-one office sessions, but some treatment is conducted with couples, families, and groups in hospitals, community health centers, and facilities for former mental hospital residents. Therapy is also offered in prisons, at military bases, in drug and alcoholism treatment centers, and in many other places.

© Bill Aron/PhotoEdit

used in each case—some form of psychotherapy, prescription medications, or both—depend on the problems, preferences, and financial circumstances of the client; the time available for treatment; and the therapist's theoretical leanings, methodological preferences, and professional qualifications. Later, we will discuss prescription drugs and other biological treatments; here, we consider several forms of psychotherapy, each of which is based on a different theoretical perspective on mental disorder.

Although we discuss different psychotherapy methods in separate sections, keep in mind that the majority of mental health professionals see themselves as *eclectic* or *integrative* therapists: They may lean toward one set of methods, but in working with particular clients or particular problems, they incorporate other methods as well (Cook et al., 2010; Magnavita, 2006; Norcross & Goldfried, 2005).

Psychodynamic Psychotherapy

The field of formal psychotherapy began in the late 1800s when, as described in the chapter on personality, Sigmund Freud established the psychodynamic approach to understanding psychological disorders. Central to his approach, and to modern revisions of it, is the assumption that personality and behavior reflect the efforts of the ego to deal with (mostly unconscious) conflicts among various components of the personality.

Freud's method of treatment, **psychoanalysis**, was aimed at understanding these unconscious conflicts and how they affect clients. Almost all forms of psychotherapy incorporate some of his ideas, including a one-to-one treatment approach; a search for relationships between current problems and events in a client's past; an emphasis on the role of thoughts, emotions, and motivations; and a focus on the client-therapist relationship. We will describe Freud's original methods first and then consider treatments that are rooted in his psychodynamic approach.

Classical Psychoanalysis

Classical psychoanalysis developed mainly out of Freud's medical practice. He was puzzled by patients who suffered from "hysterical" ailments—blindness, paralysis, or other symptoms that had no apparent physical cause (see our discussion of conversion disorders in the chapter on psychological disorders). Inspired by his colleague Josef Breuer's dramatic success in using hypnosis to treat hysterical symptoms in a patient known as "Anna O." (Freud & Breuer, 1895/2004), Freud tried similar methods with

psychoanalysis A method of psychotherapy that seeks to help clients gain insight by recognizing and understanding unconscious thoughts and emotions.

Freud's Consulting Room

During psychoanalytic sessions, Freud's patients lay on this couch, free-associating or describing dreams and everyday events, while he sat in the chair behind them (this famous couch is now at the Freud Museum in London, which you can visit online at www.freud.org.uk). According to Freud, even apparently trivial behavior may carry messages from the unconscious. Forgetting a dream or missing a therapy appointment might reflect a client's unconscious resistance to treatment. Even accidents may be meaningful. The waiter who spills hot soup on an elderly male customer might be seen as acting out unconscious aggressive impulses against a father figure.

© Geraint Lewis/Alamy

other hysteria patients but found them to be only partially and temporarily successful. Eventually, Freud merely asked patients to lie on a couch and report whatever thoughts, memories, or images came to mind, a process Freud called *free association.*

The results of this "talking cure" were surprising. Freud was struck by how many of his patients reported childhood memories of sexual abuse, usually by a parent or other close relative (Esterson, 2001). Freud wondered whether child abuse was rampant in Vienna, whether he was seeing a biased sample of patients, or whether his patients' memories were being distorted in some way. He eventually concluded that his patients' memories of abuse probably reflected unconscious childhood wishes and fantasies, not real events. He also believed that hysterical symptoms stem from unconscious conflicts over those wishes and fantasies.

As a result, Freud's psychoanalysis came to focus on an exploration of the unconscious and the conflicts raging within it. Classical psychoanalytic treatment aims first to help troubled people gain *insight* into their problems by recognizing unconscious thoughts and emotions. Then they are encouraged to discover, or *work through,* the many ways in which those unconscious elements continue to motivate maladaptive thinking and behavior in everyday life. The treatment may require as many as three to five sessions per week, usually over several years. Generally, the psychoanalyst is compassionate but emotionally neutral as the patient slowly develops an understanding of how past conflicts influence current problems (Gabbard, 2004).

To gain glimpses of the unconscious—and of the sexual and aggressive impulses he believed reside there—Freud looked for meaning in his patients' free associations, their dreams, their everyday behaviors, and their relationship with him. He believed that hidden beneath the obvious or *manifest content* of dreams is *latent content* that reflects the wishes, impulses, and fantasies that the dreamer's defense mechanisms keep out of consciousness during waking hours. He focused also on what have become known as "Freudian slips" of the tongue and other seemingly insignificant but potentially meaningful behaviors. So if a patient mistakenly used the name of a former girlfriend while talking about his wife, Freud might wonder if the patient unconsciously regretted his marriage. Similarly, when patients expressed dependency, hostility, or even love toward him, Freud saw it as an unconscious process in which childhood feelings and conflicts about parents and other significant people were being transferred to the therapist. Analysis of this *transference,* this "new edition" of the patient's childhood conflicts and current problems, became another important psychoanalytic method (Gabbard, 2004). Freud believed that focusing on the transference allows patients to see how old conflicts haunt their lives and helps them resolve these conflicts.

Contemporary Variations on Psychoanalysis

Classical psychoanalysis is still practiced, but not as much as it was several decades ago (Gabbard, 2004; Kaner & Prelinger, 2007). The decline is due to many factors, including disenchantment with Freud's personality theory, the expense of classical psychoanalysis, its limited usefulness with children, and the availability of many alternative forms of treatment, including variations on classical psychoanalysis (Roseborough, 2006; Russ, 2006; Stricker, 2006).

Some of these variations were developed by the neo-Freudian theorists discussed in the chapter on personality. As noted there, those theorists tended to place less emphasis than Freud did on the past and on unconscious impulses stemming from the id. They also tended to stress the role of social relationships in clients' problems and how the power of the ego can be harnessed to solve those problems (Gray, 2005). *Ego analysis* (Hartmann, 1958; Klein, 1960) and *individual analysis* (Adler, 1927/1999) were among the first treatments to be based on neo-Freudian theories. Some were designed for treating children (Freud, 1946; Klein, 1960). More recent variations on psychoanalysis alter the format of treatment so that it is less intense, less expensive, and more appropriate for a broader range of clients (Messer & Kaplan, 2004). Some of these variants have come to be known as *short-term psychodynamic therapy* because they aim to provide benefits in far less time than is required in classical psychoanalysis (Levenson, 2003; Rawson, 2006). However, virtually all modern psychodynamic therapies still focus attention on unconscious as well as conscious aspects of mental life, on the impact of internal conflicts, and on transference analysis as key elements in treatment (Levy et al., 2006; Luborsky & Luborsky, 2006; Vanheule et al., 2006).

In one short-term psychodynamic approach known as *object relations therapy*, the powerful need for human contact and support takes center stage (Greenberg & Mitchell, 2006). Object relations therapists believe that most of the problems for which clients seek treatment ultimately stem from their relationships with others, especially their mothers or other early caregivers. (The term *object* usually refers to a person who has emotional significance for the client.) Psychotherapists who adopt an object relations perspective take a much more active role in therapy sessions than classical analysts do—particularly by directing the client's attention to evidence of certain conflicts, rather than waiting for free association or other more subtle methods to

"What do you think I think about what you think I think you've been thinking about?"

Analysis of the transference in this therapy relationship would be quite a challenge! This parody of psychoanalysis illustrates the point that therapists focus not only on their clients' feelings toward them but also on their feelings toward clients—called *countertransference*. For example, if transference leads a client to treat the therapist as a mother, the therapist might, because of countertransference, unintentionally begin treating the client as her child.

Play Therapy

Modern versions of psychoanalytic treatment include fantasy play and other techniques that make the approach more useful with children. A child's behavior and comments while playing with puppets representing family members, for example, are seen as a form of free association that the therapist hopes will reveal important unconscious material, such as fear of abandonment (Carlson, Watts, & Maniacci, 2006).

reveal these conflicts. Object relations therapists work to develop a nurturing relationship with their clients, providing a "second chance" for them to receive the support that may have been lacking in infancy and to counteract some of the consequences of maladaptive early attachment patterns (Kahn & Rachman, 2000; Wallerstein, 2002). For example, object relations therapists take pains to show that they will not abandon their clients, as may have happened to these people in the past. *Interpersonal therapy*, too, is rooted partly in neo-Freudian theory (Sullivan, 1954), but it focuses on helping clients explore and overcome the problematic effects of interpersonal events that occur *after* early childhood—events such as the loss of a loved one, conflicts with a parent or a spouse, job loss, or social isolation (Mufson, Polack, & Moreau, 2004; Weissman, Markowitz, & Kierman, 2007).

In another version of psychodynamic treatment, the therapist looks for a "core conflict" that appears repeatedly across a variety of relationships, including the therapy relationship (Luborsky & Luborsky, 2006). In one case, for example, "Katie" reported recurring dreams about breaking glass and accidentally cutting her therapist (Vaughan, 1998). She also recalled two childhood incidents in which she broke glassware after wandering away from her mother; in one incident, her mother cut herself while cleaning up the glass. Katie's therapist suggested that these dreams and memories indicated a core conflict about wanting to be independent of her mother yet also close to her. Addressing this conflict during therapy helped Katie realize that professional success did not require her to reject or hurt the people she cared about.

With their focus on interpersonal relationships rather than instincts, their emphasis on clients' potential for self-directed problem solving, and the reassurance and emotional support they provide, contemporary variants on classical psychoanalysis have helped the psychodynamic approach retain its influence among mental health professionals (Kaner & Prelinger, 2007; Shedler, 2010; Stiles et al., 2006).

Humanistic Psychotherapy

Whereas some therapists revised Freud's ideas, others developed radical new therapies based on the humanistic approach to personality described in the personality chapter. *Humanistic psychologists,* sometimes called *phenomenologists,* see people as capable of consciously controlling their own actions and taking responsibility for their own decisions. Most humanistic therapists believe that human behavior is motivated not by sexual or aggressive impulses but rather by an innate drive toward personal growth and improvement that is guided from moment to moment by the way people perceive their world. Disordered behavior, they say, reflects a blockage of natural growth brought on by distorted perceptions or lack of awareness of feelings. Accordingly, humanistic therapy operates on the following assumptions:

1. Treatment is an encounter between equals, not a "cure" given by an expert. It is a way to help clients restart their natural growth and to feel and behave more in line with that growth.

2. Clients will improve on their own, given the right conditions. These ideal conditions promote clients' awareness, acceptance, and emotional expression. So, like psychodynamic therapy, humanistic therapy promotes insight, but it is insight into current feelings and perceptions, not into unconscious childhood conflicts.

3. Ideal conditions in therapy can best be established through a relationship in which clients feel fully accepted and supported as human beings, no matter how problematic or undesirable their behavior may be. It is the clients' experience of this relationship that brings beneficial changes. (Notice that this assumption is shared with object relations therapy and some other forms of brief psychodynamic therapy.)

4. Clients must remain responsible for choosing how they will think and behave.

Of the many humanistically oriented treatments in use today, the most influential are client-centered therapy, developed by Carl Rogers (1951), and Gestalt therapy, developed by Frederick and Laura Perls.

Client-Centered Therapy

Carl Rogers was trained in psychodynamic therapy methods during the 1930s, but he soon began to question their value. He especially disliked being a detached expert observer whose task was to "figure out" the client. Convinced that a less formal approach would be more effective for the client and more comfortable for the therapist, Rogers allowed his clients to decide what to talk about and when, without direction, judgment, or interpretation by the therapist (Raskin & Rogers, 2005). This approach, now called **client-centered therapy** or **person-centered therapy**, relies on the creation of a relationship that reflects three intertwined attitudes of the therapist: unconditional positive regard, empathy, and congruence.

Unconditional Positive Regard   The attitude Rogers called **unconditional positive regard**, also known as **acceptance**, is expressed by treating the client as a valued person, no matter what. Rogers believed that experiencing the therapist's unconditional acceptance helps clients overcome the sense that their value as a person depends on being successful, intelligent, attractive, or meeting the other *conditions of worth* described in the personality chapter. Acceptance is communicated through the therapist's willingness to listen to the client without interrupting and without making judgments or expressing opinions. The therapist doesn't have to approve of everything the client says but must accept each statement as reflecting the client's view of the world. Client-centered therapists also avoid giving advice because acceptance includes trusting clients to solve their own problems (Merry & Brodley, 2002). They don't want their advice to convey the unspoken suggestion that clients are incompetent or dependent on the therapist's help.

Empathy   Client-centered therapists also try to appreciate the client's point of view. This goes far beyond saying, "I know what you mean." It involves an effort to see the world as each client sees it and not to look at clients from the outside. In other words, client-centered therapists work at developing **empathy**, an emotional understanding of what the client might be thinking and feeling. They convey empathy by showing that they are *actively listening* to the client. Like other skillful interviewers, they make eye contact with the client, nod in recognition as the client speaks, and give other signs of careful attention. They use **active listening**, also known as **reflection**, a paraphrased summary of the client's words that emphasizes the feelings and meanings that seem to accompany them. Active listening confirms what the client has said, shows that the therapist is interested, and helps the client to perceive and focus on the thoughts and feelings being expressed. Here is an example:

> *Client:* This has been such a bad day. I've felt ready to cry any minute, and I'm not even sure what's wrong!
>
> *Therapist:* You really do feel so bad. The tears just seem to well up inside, and I wonder if it's a little scary to not even know why you feel this way.

Notice that in rephrasing the client's statements, the therapist reflected not only the obvious feelings of sadness but also the fear in the client's voice. Most clients respond to empathic reflection by elaborating on their feelings. In this example, the client went on to say, "It *is* scary, because I don't like to feel in the dark about myself. I have always prided myself on being in control." Clients do this, said Rogers, simply because the therapist expresses the desire to listen and understand without asking disruptive questions. Active listening tends to be so effective in promoting self-understanding and awareness that it is used across a wide range of therapies (Corsini & Wedding, 2010; Miller & Rollnick, 2002). Even outside the realm of therapy, people who are

client-centered therapy (person-centered therapy) A therapy that allows the client to decide what to talk about, without direction, judgment, or interpretation from the therapist.

unconditional positive regard (acceptance) A therapist attitude that conveys caring for and recognition of the client as a valued person.

empathy The therapist's attempt to appreciate and understand how the world looks from the client's point of view.

active listening (reflection) Conveying empathy on the part of the therapist by paraphrasing a client's statements and noting accompanying feelings.

A Client-Centered Therapy Group

Carl Rogers (shown here in shirtsleeves) believed that as successful treatment progresses, clients become more self-confident, more aware of their feelings, more accepting of themselves, more comfortable and genuine with other people, more reliant on self-evaluation than on the judgments of others, and more effective and relaxed.

© Michael Rougier/Time & Life Pictures/Getty Images

thought of as easy to talk to are usually "good listeners" who reflect the important messages they hear from others.

Congruence Rogerian therapists also try to convey **congruence** (sometimes called *genuineness*) by acting in ways that are consistent with their feelings during therapy. For example, if they are confused by what a client has said, they would say so rather than trying to pretend that they always understand everything. When the therapist's acceptance and empathy are genuine, the client is able to see that relationships can be built on openness and honesty. Ideally, this experience will help the client become more congruent in other relationships.

Here is an excerpt that illustrates the three therapist attitudes we have described (adapted from Rogers, 1951, p. 49).

> *Client:* I cannot be the kind of person I want to be. I guess maybe I haven't the guts or the strength to kill myself, and if someone else would relieve me of the responsibility or I would be in an accident I, I . . . just don't want to live.

> *Therapist:* At the present time, things look so bad that you can't see much point in living. [*Note the empathic reflection and the attitude of acceptance.*]

> *Client:* Yes. I wish I'd never started this therapy. I was happy when I was living in my dream world. There I could be the kind of person I wanted to be. But now there is such a wide, wide gap between my ideal and what I am. . . . [*Notice that the client responds to reflection by giving more information.*]

> *Therapist:* It's really a tough struggle digging into this like you are, and at times the shelter of your dream world looks more attractive and comfortable. [*Note the use of empathic reflection.*]

> *Client:* My dream world or suicide. . . . So I don't see why I should waste your time—coming in twice a week—I'm not worth it—what do you think?

> *Therapist:* It's up to you. . . . It isn't wasting my time. I'd be glad to see you whenever you come, but it's how you feel about it. . . . [*Note the congruence in stating an honest desire to see the client and the acceptance in trusting her capacity and responsibility for choice.*]

congruence Consistency between a therapist's feelings and the therapist's behavior toward clients.

Client: You're not going to suggest that I come in oftener? You're not alarmed and think I ought to come in every day until I get out of this?

Therapist: I believe you are able to make your own decision. I'll see you whenever you want to come. [*Note again the attitude of acceptance.*]

Client: [*With a note of awe in her voice*] I don't believe you are alarmed about—I see—I may be afraid of myself, but you aren't afraid for me. [*Here the client experiences the therapist's confidence in her; in the end, the client chose not to commit suicide.*]

Gestalt Therapy

Another form of humanistic treatment was developed by Frederick S. (Fritz) Perls and his wife, Laura. A European psychoanalyst, Perls was greatly influenced by research in *Gestalt psychology.* (As described in the chapter on perception, Gestalt psychologists emphasized the idea that people actively organize their perceptions of the world.) As a result, he believed that people create their own versions of reality and that their natural psychological growth continues only as long as they accurately perceive, remain aware of, and act on their true feelings. Growth stops and symptoms appear, said Perls, when people are not aware of all aspects of themselves (Perls, 1969; Perls, Hefferline, & Goodman, 1951).

Gestalt therapy is based on these beliefs. Like client-centered therapy, **Gestalt therapy** seeks to create conditions in which clients can become more unified, self-aware, and self-accepting—and thus ready to grow again. However, Gestalt therapists use more direct and dramatic methods than Rogerians do. Often working in group settings, Gestalt therapists prod clients to become aware of feelings and impulses that they have disowned and to discard feelings, ideas, and values that are not really their own. For example, the therapist or other group members might point out inconsistencies between what clients say and how they behave. Gestalt therapists pay particular attention to clients' gestures and other kinds of "body language" that appear to conflict with what the clients are saying (Kepner, 2001). They may also ask clients to engage in imaginary dialogues, or "conversations," with other people, with parts of their own personalities, and even with objects (Elliott, Watson, & Goldman, 2004a, 2004b). Like a shy person who can be socially outgoing only while masked at a costume party, clients often find that these dialogues help them get in touch with and express their feelings (Woldt & Toman, 2005).

Over the years, client-centered and other forms of humanistic therapy have declined in popularity (Norcross, Hedges, & Castle, 2002), but Carl Rogers's contributions to psychotherapy remain significant. In particular, his emphasis on the importance of the therapeutic relationship in bringing about change has been adopted by many other treatment approaches (Kirschenbaum & Jourdan, 2005).

Behavior Therapy

Psychodynamic and humanistic approaches to therapy assume that if clients gain insight, or awareness, about underlying problems, the symptoms triggered by those problems will disappear. Behavior therapists try to help clients develop a different kind of knowledge: namely, that most psychological problems are *learned behaviors* and that they can be changed by taking action to learn new ones without first searching for hidden meanings or unconscious causes (Miltenberger, 2007; Spiegler & Guevremont, 2009).

For example, consider again José, the electronics technician whose panic attacks are described in the chapter on psychological disorders. Some of these attacks had occurred while he was scuba diving, so he began making excuses when friends invited him to go diving. Avoiding diving trips eased his anxiety temporarily but did nothing to solve the problem of panic attacks. Could José solve this problem without

© Zigy Kaluzny/Stone/Getty Images

Existential Therapy

Rogers's and Perls's methods of treatment represent two prominent examples of humanisitic therapies, but there are others. For example, Rollo May (1969), May, Angel, & Ellenberger (1958), Viktor Frankl (1963), and Irwin Yalom (1980) developed therapies based on existential philosophy, which highlights such uniquely human concerns as our freedom to choose our actions, being responsible for those actions, feeling alone in the world, trying to find meaning and purpose in our lives, and confronting the prospect of death (Yalom, 2002). *Existential therapy* is designed to help people accept and deal with these concerns head-on rather than to continue ignoring or avoiding them. Because people can feel lost, alone, and unsure of life's meaning without displaying serious behavior problems, existential therapists consider their approach as applicable to anyone, whether officially diagnosed with some form of mental disorder or not.

Gestalt therapy An active treatment designed to help clients get in touch with genuine feelings and disown foreign ones.

first discovering its "underlying meaning"? *Behavior therapy* would offer just such an alternative by first identifying the signals, rewards and punishments, and other learning-based factors that maintain José's anxiety and then helping him develop new responses in feared situations.

These goals are based on both the *behavioral approach* to psychology in general and on the *social-cognitive approach* to personality and disorder in particular. As described in the chapters on introducing psychology, on personality, and on psychological disorders, these approaches emphasize the role of learning in the development of personality, as well as in most psychological disorders. Accordingly, behaviorists tend to see those disorders as examples of the maladaptive thoughts and actions that a client has learned. For instance, behavior therapists believe that fear of leaving home (*agoraphobia*) develops through classically conditioned associations between being away from home and having panic attacks. The problem is maintained in part through operant conditioning: Staying home and making excuses for doing so are rewarded by reduced anxiety. Therapists adopting a behavioral approach argue that if past learning experiences can create problems, then new learning experiences can help eliminate those problems. So even if the experiences that led to today's problems began in the client's childhood, behavior therapy seeks to solve those problems by creating beneficial new experiences using the principles discussed in the chapter on learning.

The notion of applying learning principles in order to change troublesome behavior has its roots in the work of John B. Watson, Ivan Pavlov, and others who studied the learned nature of fear in the 1920s and 1930s. It stems, too, from B. F. Skinner's research on the impact of reward and punishment on behavior. In the late 1950s and early 1960s, researchers began to use classical conditioning, operant conditioning, and observational learning techniques in a systematic way to treat fears, improve the behavior of disruptive schoolchildren and mental patients, and deal with many other problems (Plaud, 2003; Ullmann & Krasner, 1965). By 1970, behavioral treatment had become a popular alternative to psychodynamic and humanistic methods (Martin & Pear, 2006).

The most notable features of behavioral treatment include the following:

1. Development of a productive therapist-client relationship. As in other therapies, this relationship enhances clients' confidence that change is possible and makes it easier for them to speak openly and to cooperate in treatment (Creed & Kendall, 2005; Lejuez et al., 2005).

2. A careful listing of the behaviors and thoughts to be changed (Umbreit et al., 2006). This assessment—and the establishment of specific treatment goals—often replaces the formal diagnosis used in some other therapy approaches. So instead of treating "depression" or "obsessive-compulsive disorder," behavior therapists work to change the specific thoughts, behaviors, and emotional reactions that are associated with these diagnostic labels.

3. A therapist who acts as a teacher or mentor by providing learning-based treatments, giving "homework" assignments, and helping the client make specific plans for dealing with problems rather than just talking about them (Kazantzis et al, 2005).

4. Continuous monitoring and evaluation of treatment, along with constant adjustments to any procedures that are not working as expected (Farmer & Nelson-Gray, 2005).

behavior therapy Treatments that use classical conditioning principles to change behavior.

behavior modification Treatments that use operant conditioning methods to change behavior.

cognitive behavior therapy Learning-based treatment methods that help clients change the way they think, as well as the way they behave.

Because ineffective procedures are soon altered or abandoned, behavioral treatment tends to be one of the briefest forms of therapy (e.g., Flatt & King, 2008).

Behavioral treatment can take many forms. By tradition, those that rely mainly on classical conditioning principles are usually referred to as **behavior therapy**. Those that focus on operant conditioning methods are usually called **behavior modification**. And behavioral treatment that focuses on changing thoughts as well as overt behaviors is called **cognitive behavior therapy**. These methods, especially cognitive behavior therapy, are among the most important and influential approaches to psychological treatment available today (Durlak, 2006).

Techniques for Modifying Behavior

Among the most important behavior therapy methods are systematic desensitization therapy, modeling, positive reinforcement, extinction, aversion therapy, and punishment.

Virtual Desensitization

This client fears heights. She is wearing a virtual reality display that creates the visual experience of being in a glass elevator that, under the therapist's careful control, seems to rise higher and higher. After learning to tolerate these realistic images without anxiety, clients are better able to fearlessly face situations they once avoided.

systematic desensitization therapy A behavioral treatment for anxiety in which clients visualize a graduated series of anxiety-provoking stimuli while remaining relaxed.

Systematic Desensitization Therapy   Joseph Wolpe (1958) developed one of the first behavioral methods for helping clients overcome phobias and other forms of anxiety. Called **systematic desensitization therapy**, it is a method in which the client visualizes a series of anxiety-provoking stimuli while remaining calm. Wolpe believed that this process gradually weakens the learned association between anxiety and the feared object until the fear disappears.

Wolpe first helped his clients learn to relax, often using the *progressive relaxation training* procedures described in the chapter on health, stress, and coping. Then, while relaxed, the clients would be asked to imagine an item from a *desensitization hierarchy*, a sequence of increasingly fear-provoking situations (see Table 16.1). The clients would imagine one hierarchy item at a time, moving to a more difficult scene only after tolerating the previous one without distress. Wolpe found that once clients could stay calm in imagined fear situations, they were better able to deal with real fear situations later on.

Wolpe's original treatment package is not used as often as it once was (McGlynn, Smitherman, & Gothard, 2004), partly because of research indicating that desensitization therapy is especially effective if it slowly and carefully presents clients with real (rather than imagined) hierarchy items (Bouton, 2002; Choy, Fyer, & Lipsitz, 2007; Marks, 2002; Tryon, 2005). This *in vivo*, or "real life," form of desensitization therapy was once difficult to arrange or control, especially in cases involving fear of flying, heights, or highway driving, for example. However, *virtual reality graded exposure* now makes it possible for clients to "experience" extremely vivid and precisely graduated versions of feared situations without actually being exposed to them. In one early study, clients who feared heights wore a head-mounted virtual reality helmet that gave them the impression of standing on bridges of gradually increasing heights, on outdoor balconies at higher and higher floors, and in a glass elevator as it slowly rose forty-nine stories (Rothbaum et al., 1995). The same technology has been used successfully in the treatment of many other anxiety disorders, ranging from fear of spiders or air travel to social phobia and posttraumatic stress disorder (Anderson, Rothbaum, & Hodges, 2003; Glantz, Rizzo, & Graap, 2003; Maltby, Kirsch, & Mayers, 2002; North, North, & Burwick, 2008; Powers et al., 2010; Rothbaum, 2006; Wiederhold & Wiederhold, 2005).

TABLE 16.1 A Desensitization Hierarchy	
Desensitization hierarchies are lists of increasingly fear-provoking situations that clients visualize while using relaxation methods to remain calm. Here are a few items from the beginning and the end of a hierarchy that was used to help a client overcome fear of flying.	1. You are reading a newspaper and notice an ad for an airline.
	2. You are watching a television program that shows a group of people boarding a plane.
	3. Your boss tells you that you need to take a business trip by air.
	4. You are in your bedroom packing your suitcase for your trip.
	.
	.
	.
	12. Your plane begins to move as you hear the flight attendant say, "Be sure your seat belt is securely fastened."
	13. You look at the runway as the plane is readied for takeoff.
	14. You look out the window as the plane rolls down the runway.
	15. You look out the window as the plane leaves the ground.

© Virtual Reality Medical Center

Exactly why systematic desensitization therapy works is not clear. Traditionally, clinicians believed that change occurs because of basic learning processes—either through classical conditioning of a new, calmer response to the fear-provoking stimulus or through extinction, as the object or situation that had been a conditioned fear stimulus repeatedly occurs without being paired with pain or any other aversive unconditioned stimulus (Hermans et al., 2006; McNeil & Zvolensky, 2000). More recent explanations emphasize that desensitization also modifies clients' cognitive processes, including their expectation that they can deal calmly and successfully with previously feared situations (Gregor & Zvolensky, 2008).

Modeling Behavior therapists sometimes help clients develop more desirable behaviors by demonstrating those behaviors. In **modeling** treatments, the client watches the therapist or other people perform desired behaviors, thus learning skills vicariously, or secondhand (Bidwell & Rehfeldt, 2004). In fear treatment, for example, modeling can teach the client how to respond fearlessly while vicariously extinguishing conditioned fear responses. One therapist showed a 24-year-old student with a severe spider phobia how to kill spiders with a flyswatter and had her practice this skill at home with rubber spiders (MacDonald & Bernstein, 1974). The combination of live modeling with gradual practice is called *participant modeling,* and it is one of the most powerful treatments for fear (Bandura, Blanchard, & Ritter, 1969; Zinbarth & Griffith, 2008; see Figure 16.1).

Modeling is also a major part of *social skills training* and *assertiveness training,* which teach clients how to interact with people more comfortably and effectively. **Social skills training** has been used to help children get along better with peers, to help social-phobic singles make conversation on dates, and to help rebuild mental patients' ability to interact normally in social situations (Al-Kubaisy & Jassim, 2003; Dowd, 2005; Lin et al., 2008). In **assertiveness training**, the therapist helps clients learn to be more direct and expressive in social situations. So instead of sheepishly agreeing to be seated at an undesirable restaurant table, clients learn to be comfortable making "I-statements," such as "I would rather sit over there, by the window." Notice that *assertiveness* does not mean aggressiveness; instead, it involves clearly and directly expressing both positive and negative feelings and standing up for one's own rights while respecting the rights of others (Alberti & Emmons, 2008; Paterson, 2000). Assertiveness training is often conducted in groups and involves both modeling and role playing of specific situations (Spence, 2003). For example, group assertiveness training has helped wheelchair-bound adults more comfortably handle the socially awkward situations in which they sometimes find themselves (Eamon, 2008).

Positive Reinforcement Behavior therapists also use systematic **positive reinforcement** to change problematic behaviors and to teach new skills in cases ranging from childhood tantrums and juvenile delinquency to schizophrenia and substance abuse (e.g., Lussier et al., 2006; Virués-Ortega, 2010). Using operant conditioning principles, they set up *contingencies,* or rules, that specify the behaviors to be strengthened through reinforcement. In a classic study, language-impaired children with autistic disorder were given grapes, popcorn, or other items they liked in return for saying "please," "thank you," and "you're welcome" during a play session. The therapist first modeled the behavior by saying the appropriate words. The children almost immediately began to utter the phrases themselves and were reinforced for doing so. The effects of positive reinforcement generalized to other situations, and as indicated in Figure 16.2, the new skills were still evident at a follow-up session six months later (Matson et al., 1990).

When working in institutions with clients suffering severe intellectual disability or other serious disorders, behavior therapists sometimes establish **token economy programs**, systems in which desirable behaviors are positively reinforced with coin-like tokens or points that can be exchanged later for snacks, access to television, or other rewards (Kazdin, 2008; LePage et al., 2003; Matson & Boisjoli, 2009; Seegert, 2003). The goal is to shape behavior patterns that will persist outside the institution (Moore et al., 2001; Paul, 2000).

modeling Demonstrating desirable behaviors as a way of teaching them to clients.

social skills training A method for teaching clients the behaviors they need in order to interact with others more comfortably and effectively.

assertiveness training A form of social skills training that focuses on teaching clients to express themselves in ways that are clear and direct.

positive reinforcement A therapy method that uses rewards to strengthen desirable behaviors.

token economy programs Systems for improving the behavior of institutionalized clients in which desirable behaviors are rewarded with tokens that can be exchanged for desired items or activities.

FIGURE 16.1

Participant Modeling

In this study, participant modeling was compared with systematic desensitization, symbolic modeling (watching filmed models), and no treatment (control). Notice that compared with no treatment, all three methods helped snake-phobic clients approach live snakes, but participant modeling was clearly the best. Ninety-two percent of the participants in that group were virtually free of any fear following treatment (Bandura, Blanchard, & Ritter, 1969). The value of participant modeling has been repeatedly confirmed (e.g., Öst, Salkovskis, & Hellström, 1991; Zinbarth & Griffith, 2008).

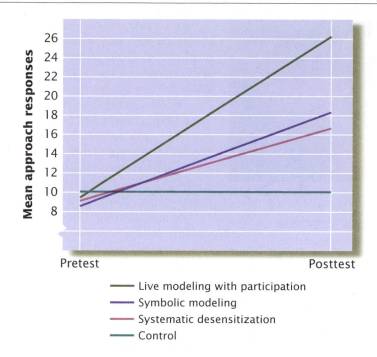

- Live modeling with participation
- Symbolic modeling
- Systematic desensitization
- Control

Extinction   Just as reinforcing desirable behaviors can make them more likely to occur, failing to reinforce undesirable behaviors can make them less likely to occur, a process known as **extinction**. Treatment methods that use extinction change behavior slowly but offer a valuable way of reducing inappropriate behavior in children and adolescents and in intellectually disabled or seriously disturbed adults. For example, a client who gets attention by disrupting a classroom, damaging property, or violating hospital rules might be placed in a quiet, boring "time-out" room for a few minutes to eliminate reinforcement for misbehavior (Kaminski et al., 2008; Kazdin, 2008).

FIGURE 16.2

Positive Reinforcement for a Child with Autistic Disorder

During each pretreatment baseline period, a child with autistic disorder rarely said "please," "thank you," or "you're welcome," but these statements began to occur once they were modeled and then reinforced. Did modeling and reinforcement actually cause the change? Probably, because each type of response did not start to increase until the therapist began demonstrating it.

Source: Matson, J., Sevin, J., Fridley, and Love, S. "Increasing Spontaneous Language in Autistic Children". *Journal of Applied Behavior Analysis,* 23, pp. 227–233. Copyright © 1990. Reprinted by permission.

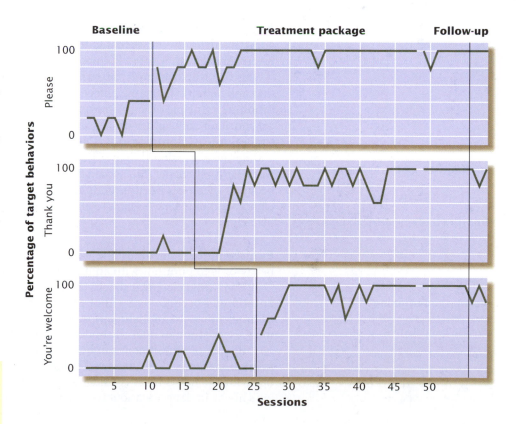

extinction The gradual disappearance of a conditioned response or operant behavior through nonreinforcement.

Treating Fear Through Flooding

APPLYING PSYCHOLOGY Flooding is designed to extinguish anxiety by allowing it to occur without the harmful consequences the person dreads. These clients' fear of flying is obvious here, on takeoff, but it is likely to diminish during and after an uneventful flight. Like other behavioral treatments, flooding is based on the idea that phobias and other psychological disorders are learned and can thus be "unlearned." Some therapists prefer more gradual exposure therapies similar to those of in vivo desensitization, which start with situations that are lower on the client's fear hierarchy.

Extinction is also the basis of **flooding**, an anxiety reduction treatment in which clients are kept in a feared but harmless situation and are not permitted to use their normally rewarding escape strategies (O'Donohue, Hayes, & Fisher, 2003). The clients are flooded with fear at first, but after an extended period of exposure to the feared stimulus (a frog, say) without experiencing pain, injury, or any other dreaded result, the association between the feared stimulus and the fear response gradually weakens, and the conditioned fear response is extinguished (Basoglu, Livanou, & Salcioglu, 2003; McNally, 2007; Powers et al., 2010). In one early study, twenty clients who feared needles were exposed for two hours to the sight and feel of needles, including mild finger pricks, harmless injections, and blood samplings (Öst, Hellström, & Kåver, 1992). Afterward, all but one of these clients were able to have a blood sample drawn without experiencing significant anxiety.

Because they continuously expose clients to feared stimuli, flooding and other similar methods are also known as **exposure therapy**. Although often highly effective, these methods do cause considerable distress, much like immediately exposing a fearful client to the most difficult item on a desensitization hierarchy. Therefore, some therapists prefer more gradual exposure therapy methods, especially when treating fear that is not focused on a specific stimulus (Berry, Rosenfield, & Smits, 2009). In dealing with agoraphobia, for instance, the therapist might provide gradual exposure by escorting the client away from home for increasingly lengthy periods and eventually venturing into shopping malls and other previously avoided places (Barlow, Raffa, & Cohen, 2002; Craske et al., 2003). Clients can also practice gradual exposure methods on their own. They might be instructed, for example, to spend a little more time each day looking at photos of some feared animal or to spend some time alone in a dental chair or a dentist's waiting room. In one study, clients suffering from various phobias made as much progress after six hours of instruction in gradual self-exposure methods and daily "homework" exercises as those who received an additional nine hours of therapist-aided gradual exposure (Al-Kubaisy et al., 1992). Effective self-treatment using gradual exposure has also been reported in cases of panic disorder (Lamplugh et al., 2008), social phobia (Rapee, Gaston, & Abbott, 2009) and obsessive-compulsive disorder (Rosa-Alcazar et al., 2008).

Aversion Therapy Some unwanted behaviors—such as excessive gambling, addictive drug use, or sexual exhibitionism—become so habitual and immediately rewarding that they must be made less attractive if a client is to have any hope of giving them up. Methods for reducing the appeal of certain stimuli are known as *aversion therapy*. The name reflects the fact that these methods rely on a classical conditioning principle called **aversion conditioning** to associate nausea, painful electrical shock, or some other unpleasant stimulus with undesirable actions, thoughts, or situations (e.g., Bordnick et al., 2004).

Because aversion therapy is unpleasant and uncomfortable, because it may not work with all clients (Flor et al., 2002), and because its effects are often temporary, behavior therapists use this method relatively rarely, only when it is the best treatment choice, and only long enough to allow the client to learn more appropriate alternative behaviors.

Punishment Sometimes the only way to eliminate a dangerous or disruptive behavior is to punish it with an unpleasant but harmless stimulus, such as a shouted "No!" or a mild electrical shock. Unlike aversion conditioning, in which the unpleasant stimulus occurs along with the behavior that is to be eliminated (a classical conditioning approach), **punishment** is an operant conditioning technique; it presents the unpleasant stimulus *after* the undesirable response occurs.

The use of punishment can be appropriate and beneficial in working with certain institutionalized clients, impaired outpatients, and some children, but before using it, behavior therapists must consider several ethical and legal questions: Would the client's life be in danger without treatment? Have all other methods failed? Has an ethics

flooding An exposure technique for reducing anxiety that involves keeping a person in a feared but harmless situation.

exposure therapy Behavior therapy methods in which clients remain in the presence of strong anxiety-provoking stimuli until the intensity of their emotional reactions decrease.

aversion conditioning A method that uses classical conditioning to create a negative response to a particular stimulus.

punishment A method that uses operant conditioning to weaken undesirable behavior by following it with an unpleasant stimulus.

committee reviewed and approved the procedures? And has the client or a close relative formally agreed to the treatment? (Kazdin, 2008). When the answer to these questions is yes, punishment can be an effective and sometimes lifesaving treatment, as in the case illustrated in Figure 6.11 in the chapter on learning. But as with extinction and aversion conditioning, punishment works best when it is used only long enough to eliminate undesirable behavior and is combined with other behavioral methods designed to reinforce more appropriate behavior (Hanley et al., 2005).

Cognitive Behavior Therapy

Like psychodynamic and humanistic therapists, behavior therapists recognize that depression, anxiety, and many other behavior disorders can stem from how clients think about themselves and the world. And like other therapists, behavior therapists also try to change their clients' troublesome ways of thinking, not just their overt behavior. Unlike other therapists, however, behavior therapists rely on learning principles to help clients change the way they think. These therapists are known as *cognitive behavior therapists,* and their methods are known collectively as *cognitive behavior therapy* (Barlow, 2007; Beck, 2005; Beck, Freeman, & Davis, 2007). Suppose that a client suffers intense anxiety in social situations despite having excellent social skills. In a case such as this, social skills training would be unnecessary. Instead, the behavior therapist would use cognitive behavioral methods designed to help the client identify the recurring thoughts (such as "I shouldn't draw attention to myself") that create awkwardness and discomfort in social situations. Once these cognitive obstacles are brought to light, the therapist describes new and more adaptive ways of thinking and encourages the client to learn and practice them. As these new cognitive skills develop (e.g., "I have as much right to give my opinion as anyone else"), it becomes easier and more rewarding for clients to let these new thoughts guide their behavior (Beck, 2005).

© Jim Kahnweiler/jimkphotographics.com

Albert Ellis

Rational-emotive behavior therapy (REBT) focuses on altering the self-defeating thoughts that Ellis believed underlie people's behavior disorders. Ellis argued, for example, that students do not get upset because they fail a test but because they have learned to believe that failure is a disaster that indicates they are worthless. Many of Ellis's ideas have been incorporated into various forms of cognitive behavior therapy, and they helped Ellis himself deal rationally with the health problems he encountered prior to his death in 2007 (Ellis, 1997).

rational-emotive behavior therapy (REBT) A treatment designed to identify and change self-defeating thoughts that lead to anxiety and other symptoms of disorder.

Rational-Emotive Behavior Therapy   One prominent form of cognitive behavior therapy is **rational-emotive behavior therapy (REBT)**. Developed by Albert Ellis (1962, 1993, 2004a, 2004b; Ellis & MacLaren, 2005), REBT is based on the notion that anxiety, guilt, depression, and other psychological problems are caused by how people think about events, not by the events themselves. Ellis's therapy aims first at identifying self-defeating beliefs, usually in the form of *shoulds* or *musts,* such as "I should be loved or approved by everyone" or "I must be perfect in order to be worthwhile." After the client learns to recognize thoughts like these and to see how they can cause problems, the therapist uses modeling, encouragement, and logic to help the client replace maladaptive thoughts with more realistic ones. The client is then given "homework" assignments to try out these new ways of thinking in everyday situations. Here is part of an REBT session with a woman who suffered from panic attacks (Masters et al., 1987). She has just said that it would be "terrible" if she had an attack in a restaurant and that people "should be able to handle themselves!"

> *Therapist:* …The reality is that…"shoulds" and "musts" are the rules that other people hand down to us, and we grow up accepting them as if they are the absolute truth, which they most assuredly aren't.
>
> *Client:* You mean it is perfectly okay to, you know, pass out in a restaurant?
>
> *Therapist:* Sure!
>
> *Client:* But…I know I wouldn't like it to happen.
>
> *Therapist:* I can certainly understand that. It would be unpleasant, awkward, inconvenient. But it is illogical to think that it would be terrible, or…that it somehow bears on your worth as a person.

Client: What do you mean?

Therapist: Well, suppose one of your friends calls you up and invites you back to that restaurant. If you start telling yourself, "I might panic and pass out and people might make fun of me and that would be terrible," . . . you might find you are dreading going to the restaurant, and you probably won't enjoy the meal very much.

Client: Well, that is what usually happens.

Therapist: But it doesn't have to be that way. . . . The way you feel, your reaction . . . depends on what you choose to believe or think, or say to yourself.

Cognitive behavior therapists use many techniques related to REBT to help clients learn to think and act in more adaptive ways. Behavioral techniques aimed at replacing upsetting thoughts with alternative thinking patterns are called *cognitive restructuring* (Lazarus, 1971; Moore, Zoellner, & Bittinger, 2004). Using these techniques, clients develop calming thoughts that they can use as part of *self-instruction* during job interviews, tense discussions, and other anxiety-provoking situations. The calming thoughts might be something like "OK, you can handle this if you just focus on the task and don't worry about being perfect." Sometimes the methods are expanded into *stress inoculation training,* in which clients imagine being in a stressful situation and then practice newly learned cognitive skills to remain calm (Meichenbaum, 2003). In one study of stress inoculation training, first-year law students tried out their calming new thoughts during role-playing exercises that simulated stressful classroom questioning, hostile feedback, and a competitive learning atmosphere. Following training, these students showed reductions in troublesome responses to stressors as well as improved academic performance (Sheehy & Horan, 2004).

Beck's Cognitive Therapy   Behavior therapists seek a different kind of cognitive restructuring by using Aaron Beck's **cognitive therapy** (Beck, 1976, 1995, 2005; Beck, Freeman, & Davis, 2007). Beck's treatment approach is based on the idea that certain psychological problems—especially those involving depression and anxiety, as well as some personality disorders—can be traced to errors in logic, or what he calls *cognitive distortions* (Beck, Freeman, & Davis, 2007; Beck et al., 2008). Common cognitive distortions include *catastrophizing* (e.g., "If I fail my driver's test the first time, I'll never pass it, and that'll be the end of my social life"), *all-or-none thinking* (e.g., "Everyone ignores me"), and *personalization* (e.g., "I know those people are laughing at me"). Beck points out that these learned cognitive distortions occur so quickly and automatically that the client never stops to consider that they might not be true (see Table 16.2).

cognitive therapy A treatment in which the therapist helps clients notice and change negative thoughts associated with anxiety and depression.

TABLE 16.2 Some Examples of Negative Thinking	
TRY THIS Here are a few examples of the kinds of thoughts that cognitive behavior therapists believe underlie anxiety, depression, and other behavior problems. After reading this list, try writing an alternative thought that clients could use to replace each of these ingrained cognitive habits. Then jot down a "homework assignment" that you would recommend to help clients challenge each maladaptive statement and thus develop new ways of thinking about themselves.	"I shouldn't draw attention to myself."
	"I will never be any good at this."
	"It will be so awful if I don't know the answer."
	"Everyone is smarter than I am."
	"Nobody likes me."
	"I should be able to do this job perfectly."
	"What if I panic?"
	"I'll never be happy."
	"I should have accomplished more by this point in my life."

Cognitive therapy is an active, structured, problem-solving approach in which the therapist first helps clients identify the errors in logic, false beliefs, and other cognitive distortions that precede anxiety, depression, conduct problems, eating disorders, and other psychological difficulties (Beck & Rector, 2005; Drinkwater & Stewart, 2002; Fairburn, 2008; Hendricks & Thompson, 2005; Pardini & Lochman, 2003). Then, much as in the five-step critical thinking system illustrated throughout this book, those thoughts and beliefs are treated as hypotheses to be scientifically tested rather than as assertions to be accepted uncritically (Hatcher, Brown, & Gariglietti, 2001). Accordingly, therapist and client take the role of "investigators" who develop ways to test beliefs such as "I'm no good around the house." They might decide on tasks that the client will attempt as "homework"—such as cleaning out the basement, cooking a meal, paying bills, or cutting the grass. Success at accomplishing even one of these tasks provides concrete evidence to challenge a false belief that has supported depression, thus helping reduce it. As therapy progresses, clients become more skilled at recognizing and then correcting the cognitive distortions related to their problems.

As described in the chapter on psychological disorders, however, the cognitive roots of depression, anxiety, and some other disorders may involve more than specific thoughts and beliefs about certain situations. Sometimes these disorders stem from a more general cognitive style that leads people to expect that the worst will always happen to them and to assume that negative events confirm that they are completely and permanently incompetent, worthless, or unlovable (Beck & Alford, 2009). So cognitive behavior therapists also work with clients to develop more optimistic ways of thinking and to reduce their tendency to blame themselves for negative outcomes (Persons, Davidson, & Tompkins, 2001). In some cases, cognitive restructuring is combined with social skills training, practice at using logical thinking, and anxiety management techniques, all of which are designed to help clients experience success and develop confidence in situations in which they had previously expected to fail (Bryant et al., 2008).

Some cognitive therapists have also encouraged clients to use traditional Eastern practices such as meditation (see the chapter on consciousness) to help monitor problematic thoughts. This combined approach is called *mindfulness-based cognitive therapy* (Hofmann et al., 2010; Ma & Teasdale, 2004). Research in the field of positive psychology suggests, too, that the effects of cognitive behavior therapy may be enhanced through exercises deigned to promote positive emotions—such as identifying and using personal strengths and making a list of things that have gone well each day (Seligman, Berkowitz, et al., 2005; Seligman, Rashid, & Parks, 2006).

Group, Family, and Couples Therapy

The psychodynamic, humanistic, and behavioral treatments we have described are often conducted with individuals, but these treatments can also be adapted for use with groups of clients or with family units (Petrocelli, 2002; Thorngren & Kleist, 2002).

Group Therapy

Group therapy refers to the treatment of several unrelated clients under the guidance of a therapist who encourages helpful interactions among group members. Many groups are organized around a particular problem (such as alcoholism) or a particular type of client (such as adolescents). In most cases, six to twelve clients meet with their therapist at least once a week for about two hours. All group members agree to hold confidential everything that occurs during these sessions.

Group therapy offers several features not found in individual treatment (Marmarosh, Holtz, & Schottenbauer, 2005; Yalom, 2005). First, group therapy allows

group therapy Psychotherapy involving several unrelated clients.

the therapist to see clients interacting with one another, which can be helpful in identifying problems in clients' interpersonal styles. Second, clients discover that they are not alone as they listen to others and realize that many people struggle with difficulties similar to theirs. This realization tends to raise each client's expectations for improvement, a factor important in all forms of treatment. Third, group members can boost one another's self-confidence and self-acceptance as they come to trust and value one another. Fourth, clients learn from one another by sharing ideas for solving problems and giving one another honest feedback about how each member "comes across" to others. Fifth, perhaps through mutual modeling, the group experience makes clients more willing to share their feelings and more sensitive to other people's needs and messages. Finally, group therapy allows clients to try out new skills—such as assertiveness—in a safe and supportive environment. So although the procedures and techniques employed in group psychotherapy may reflect any one (or more than one) of the theoretical orientations we have described in relation to individual therapy (Bieling, McCabe, & Antony, 2006), the impact of the treatment is thought to be enhanced by the nature and strength of the group itself.

Some of the advantages of group therapy are also applied in *self-help organizations.* Self-help groups, such as Alcoholics Anonymous (AA), are made up of people who share a problematic experience and meet to help one another. There are self-help groups for a wide range of problems, including alcohol and drug addiction, childhood sexual abuse, cancer, overeating, overspending, bereavement, compulsive gambling,

© James Wilson/Woodfin Camp & Associates

A Circle of Friends

This meeting of Overeaters Anonymous is but one example of the self-help movement in North America, a growing network of inexpensive mental health and antiaddiction services offered by volunteer helpers, including friends and relatives of troubled people. Millions of other people worldwide also seek help with their problems through self-help groups that meet face to face or on the Internet (Harwood & L'Abate, 2010). Newspapers typically list dozens of local self-help groups offering help with problems ranging from alcohol abuse to weight control. The services provided by these nonprofessional groups make up about 20 percent of the total mental health and antiaddiction services offered in the United States (Borkman, 1997; Regier et al., 1993; Swindle et al., 2000).

and schizophrenia (Humphreys, 2004; Kurtz, 2004). These self-help organizations operate through hundreds of thousands of local chapters, enrolling ten to fifteen million participants in the United States and about half a million in Canada (Harwood & L'Abate, 2010; Norcross et al., 2000). Many other participants in self-help groups meet solely on the Internet (Andersson, Calrbring, & Grimlund, 2008; Tan, 2008; Tillfors et al., 2008).

Lack of reliable data makes it difficult to assess the value of many self-help groups, but available information suggests that active members may experience moderate improvement in their lives (Carlbring & Smit, 2008; Kaskutas, Bond, & Avalos, 2009; Kelly, 2003; Mains & Scogin, 2003; Masudomi et al., 2004). Some professional therapists view these groups with suspicion; others encourage clients to participate in them as part of their treatment or as a first step toward more formal treatment (Haaga, 2000; Norcross, 2006), especially in cases of eating disorders, alcoholism, and other substance-related problems (Guimon, 2004; Scheidinger, 2004).

Family and Couples Therapy

As its name implies, **family therapy** involves treatment of two or more individuals from the same family system, one of whom—often a troubled child or adolescent—is the initially identified client. The term *family system* highlights the idea that the problems displayed by one family member usually reflect problems in the functioning of the entire family (Cox & Paley, 2003; Nichols, 2007; Williams, 2005).

Whether family therapy is based on psychodynamic, humanistic, or cognitive behavioral approaches, the family itself becomes the client, and treatment involves as many members as possible (Novick & Novick, 2005). In fact, the goal of family therapy is not just to ease the identified client's problems but also to create greater harmony and balance within the family by helping each member understand the family's interaction patterns (Blow & Timm, 2002). As with group therapy, the family format gives the therapist a chance to see how the initially identified client interacts with others, thus providing a basis for discussing topics that are important in the operation of the family system.

Fortunately, most couples are not this far out of touch, but couples therapy aims to identify the communication problems that do exist in the relationship and to help the partners speak to each other more directly and listen to each other more carefully.

"I'am sorry, dear. I wasn't listening. Could you repeat what you've said since we've been married?"

family therapy Treatment of two or more individuals from the same family.

Family therapists who emphasize psychodynamic theory point out that if the parents in a family have not worked out conflicts with their own parents, these conflicts will surface in relation to their spouse and children (Scharff & Scharff, 2003). Accordingly, these family therapy sessions might focus on the parents' problems with their own parents and, when possible, include members of the older generation. A related approach, called *structural family therapy,* concentrates on family communication patterns. It focuses on changing the rigid patterns and rituals that create *alliances* (such as mother and child against father), because these alliances maintain conflicts and prevent healthy communication within the family. Structural family therapists argue that when dysfunctional communication patterns are eliminated, problematic interactions will decrease because family members no longer need them in order to survive in the family system (McLendon, McLendon, & Petr, 2005).

Behavior therapists often use family therapy sessions as meetings at which family members can discuss and agree on behavioral "contracts" (e.g., Hayes et al., 2000). Based on operant conditioning principles, these contracts establish rules and reinforcement contingencies that help parents encourage their children's desirable behaviors (while discouraging undesirable ones) and help spouses become more supportive of each other (McHale & Sullivan, 2008).

Therapists of many theoretical persuasions also offer **couples therapy**, in which communication between partners is the main focus of treatment (Christensen et al., 2010; Gurman, 2008). Discussions in couples therapy sessions are usually aimed at identifying the miscommunication or lack of communication that interferes with a couple's happiness and intimacy. In behavioral marital therapy, for example, couples learn to abide by certain "rules for talking," such as those listed in Table 16.3. Another version of couples therapy focuses on strengthening the bond between partners by teaching them how to deal with their unsolvable problems and recover from their fights by expressing at least five times as many positive statements as negative ones (Gottman, Driver, & Tabares, 2002). Some therapists help couples become closer by encouraging them to express their emotions more honestly and be more accepting of one another (Shadish & Baldwin, 2005; Wood et al., 2005).

Some therapists even offer programs designed to *prevent* marital problems in couples whose interactions suggest that they are at high risk for developing discord (Gottman, Gottman, & Declaire, 2006; Jacobson et al., 2000; Laurenceau et al., 2004). "In Review: Approaches to Psychological Treatment" summarizes key features of the main approaches to treatment that we have discussed so far.

couples therapy A form of therapy focusing on improving communication between partners.

TABLE 16.3 Some "Rules for Talking" in Couples Therapy

TRY THIS Many forms of couples therapy help partners improve communication by establishing rules such as these. Think about your own experience in relationships or your observations of couples as they interact, and then write down some rules you would add to this list. Why do you think it would be important for couples to follow the rules on your list?	1. Always begin with something positive when stating a problem. 2. Use specific behaviors rather than derogatory labels or overgeneralizations to describe what is bothersome about the other person. 3. Make connections between those specific behaviors and feelings that arise in response to them (e.g., "It makes me sad when you . . ."). 4. Admit your own role in the development of the problem. 5. Be brief; don't lecture or harangue. 6. Maintain a focus on the present or the future; don't review all previous examples of the problem or ask "why" questions, such as "Why do you always . . . ?" 7. Talk about observable events; don't make inferences about them (e.g., say, "I get angry when you interrupt me" rather than "Stop trying to make me feel stupid"). 8. Paraphrase what your partner has said, and check out your own perceptions of what was said before responding. (Note that this suggestion is based on the same principle as Rogers's empathic listening.)

		Contemporary		Behavioral/Cognitive
Dimension	**Classical Psychoanalytic**	**Psychodynamic**	**Humanistic**	**Behavioral**
Nature of the human being	Driven by sexual and aggressive urges	Driven by the need for human relationships	Has free will, choice, and capacity for self-actualization	Is a product of social learning and conditioning; behaves on the basis of past experience
Therapist's role	Neutral; helps client explore meaning of free associations and other material from the unconscious	Active; develops relationship with client as a model for other relationships	Facilitates client's growth; some therapists are active, some are nondirective	Teacher or mentor who helps client replace undesirable thoughts and behaviors; active, action-oriented
Focus	Emphasizes unresolved unconscious conflicts from the distant past	Understanding the past, but focusing on current relationships	Here and now; focus on immediate experience	Current behavior and thoughts; may not need to know original causes to create change
Goals	Psychosexual maturity through insight; strengthening of ego functions	Correction of effects of failures of early attachment; development of satisfying intimate relationships	Expanded awareness; fulfillment of potential; self-acceptance	Changes in thinking and behaving in particular classes of situations; better self-management
Typical methods	Free association; dream analysis; analysis of transference	Analysis of interpersonal relationships, including the client-therapist relationship	Reflection-oriented interviews designed to convey unconditional positive regard, empathy, and congruence; exercises to promote self-awareness	Systematic desensitization, social skills training, positive reinforcement, extinction, aversion therapy, punishment, and cognitive restructuring

IN REVIEW Approaches to Psychological Treatment

1. Object relations therapy and interpersonal therapy are both contemporary examples of the _____ approach to psychological treatment.
2. Imagining increasingly fear-provoking stimuli is a treatment method called _____.
3. Reflection is an interviewing technique associated mainly with the _____ approach to treatment.

Evaluating Psychotherapy

LINKAGES   Does psychotherapy work? (a link to Introducing Psychology, p. 12)

A national survey conducted some years ago suggested that most psychotherapists and their clients believe that psychotherapy is effective ("Mental Health," 1995; Seligman, 1996), but confirming this belief with experimental research has proved to be challenging and controversial (Beutler, 2002; Dawes, 1994; Laurenceau, Hayes, & Feldman, 2007; McHugh & Barlow, 2010; Norcross, Beutler, & Levant, 2005; Weisz, Weersing, & Henggeler, 2005; Westen, Novotny, & Thompson-Brenner, 2004).

The value of psychotherapy was first widely questioned in 1952 when the British psychologist Hans Eysenck reviewed studies in which thousands of clients had received traditional psychodynamic therapy, various other therapies, or no treatment. To the surprise and dismay of many therapists, Eysenck (1952) concluded that the percentage of clients who improved following any kind of psychotherapy was actually lower than that of people who received no treatment.

Critics argued that Eysenck was wrong. They claimed that he had ignored studies that supported the value of psychotherapy and had misinterpreted the data (Bergin, 1971; de Charms, Levy, & Wertheimer, 1954; Luborsky, 1972). They pointed out, for example, that untreated clients might have been less disturbed than those in treatment. Further, they said, untreated clients might have received informal treatment from their medical doctors. Finally, the physicians who judged untreated clients' progress might have used less demanding criteria than the psychotherapists who rated their own clients. In fact, when some of these critics conducted their own counts of successes and failures, they concluded that psychotherapy tends to be more helpful than no treatment (Bergin, 1971).

Debate over Eysenck's findings—and the contradictory reports that followed them—highlighted several factors that make it so hard to answer the apparently simple question: Does psychotherapy work? For one thing, there is the problem of how to measure improvement in psychotherapy. Should it be measured with psychological tests, behavioral observations, interviews, or a combination of all three? And what kinds of tests should be used? Where should clients be observed, and by whom? Should equal weight be given to interviews with clients, friends, relatives, therapists, and teachers? The fact that these various measures don't always tell the same story about improvement makes it that much more difficult for researchers to compare or combine the results of different studies and draw conclusions about the overall effectiveness of treatment (Cuijpers et al., 2010; De Los Reyes & Kazdin, 2006; Krause, 2005; Sass, Twohig, & Davies, 2004).

The question of effectiveness is further complicated by the broad range of clients, therapists, and treatments involved in psychotherapy. Clients differ not only in terms of the problems they have but also in terms of their motivation to solve them and in the amount of stress and social support present in their environments. Therapists differ, too, not only in skill, experience, and personality but also in which of the hundreds of available treatment procedures they might select (Norcross, Beutler, & Levant, 2005; Wampold, 2005) and how long treatment lasts (Barkham et al., 2006). Further, differences in the nature and quality of the client-therapist relationship from one case to another can significantly alter the course of treatment, the clients' faith in the procedures, and their willingness to cooperate (Lambert & Barley, 2001; Zuroff & Blatt, 2006). Because clients' responses to psychotherapy can be influenced by all these factors, results from any particular treatment evaluation study may not tell us much about how well different therapists, using different methods, would do with other kinds of clients and problems (Kazdin, 2002; Roth & Fonagy, 2005). Consider the example of a classic study in which "kindly college professors" were found to be as effective as experienced psychotherapists in helping people solve their problems (Strupp & Hadley, 1979). This result would appear relevant to the question of psychotherapy's effectiveness, but a careful reading of the study shows that the clients were college students with minor problems, not severe psychological disorders. Further, the fact that these students already had a relationship with their professors may have given the professors an edge over unfamiliar therapists (Chambless & Hollon, 1998). So the outcome of this study probably does not apply to the outcomes of professional psychotherapy in general.

In short, the question of whether psychotherapy "works" is difficult or impossible to answer scientifically in a way that applies to all therapies for all disorders. However, the findings of several research reviews (Galatzer-Levy et al., 2000; Kazdin & Weisz, 2003; Leichsenring, Rabung, & Leibing, 2004; Nathan & Gorman, 2007; Shadish et al., 2000; Smith, Glass, & Miller, 1980; Weisz & Jensen, 1999) have reinforced therapists' beliefs that psychotherapy does work (see Figure 16.3).

FIGURE 16.3
**An Analysis of
Psychotherapy Effects**

These curves show the results of one large-scale analysis of the effects of psychotherapy. Notice that on average, people who received therapy for their problems were better off than 80 percent of troubled people who did not. The overall effectiveness of psychotherapy has also been confirmed in a more recent analysis of ninety treatment outcome studies (Shadish et al., 2000).

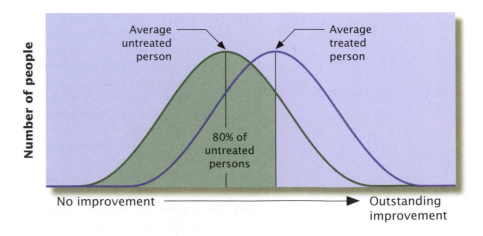

THINKING CRITICALLY

LINKAGES   Can therapy change personality? (a link to Personality, p. 585)

Are All Forms of Therapy Equally Effective?

Not surprisingly, most therapists agree that all forms of therapy are effective, but most believe that the particular theoretical approach and treatment methods they use are superior to those of other therapists (Mandelid, 2003).

What am I being asked to believe or accept?

These therapists can't all be right, of course, and some researchers claim that all of them are wrong. Those researchers argue that the success of psychotherapy doesn't have much to do with theories about the causes of psychopathology or even with the specific methods that are used in treatment. All approaches, they say, are equally effective. This has been called the "Dodo Bird verdict," after the *Alice in Wonderland* character who, when called on to judge a race, answered, "Everybody has won, and all must have prizes!" (Duncan, 2002; Luborsky, Singer, & Luborsky, 1975).

What evidence is available to support the assertion?

Some evidence does indeed suggest that there are no significant differences in the overall effectiveness of psychodynamic, humanistic, and behavioral therapies. *Meta-analysis,* a statistical method that combines the results of a large number of therapy studies, has regularly shown that the three treatment approaches are associated with about the same degree of success overall (Luborsky et al., 2002; Luborsky, Rosenthal, & Diguer, 2003; Shadish et al., 2000; Shedler, 2010; Weisz, McCarty, & Valeri, 2006).

Are there alternative ways of interpreting the evidence?

It is possible, however, that evidence for the Dodo Bird verdict is based on statistical methods that tend to make all treatments look equally effective, even if they are not (e.g., Ehlers et al., 2010). For example, a meta-analysis that averages the results of many studies might miss important differences in the impact of particular treatments for particular problems. To understand how this might happen, suppose that Therapy A works better than Therapy B in treating anxiety but that Therapy B works better than Therapy A in cases of depression. If you combined the results of treatment studies with both kinds of clients, the average effects of each therapy would be about the same, making it appear that the two treatments are about equally effective.

Differences in the effects of specific treatment procedures might also be overshadowed by the beneficial *common factors* shared by almost all forms of therapy—such as the support of the therapist, the hope and expectancy for improvement that therapy creates, and the trust that develops between client and therapist (Greenberg, Constantino, & Bruce, 2006; Kazantzis, Lampropoulos, & Deane, 2005; Vocisano et al., 2004). Therapists whose personal characteristics can motivate clients to change may promote that change no matter what specific therapeutic methods they use (Norcross, 2002).

What additional evidence would help evaluate the alternatives?

Debate is likely to continue over the question of whether, on average, all forms of psychotherapy are equally effective. But many researchers believe that this is the wrong question to ask. In their view, it is pointless to compare the effects of psychodynamic, humanistic, and behavioral methods in general. It is more important, they say, to address what Gordon Paul called the "ultimate question" about psychotherapy: "What treatment, by whom, is most effective for this individual with that specific problem, under what set of circumstances?" (Paul, 1969, p. 44).

What conclusions are most reasonable?

Statistical analyses show that various treatment approaches appear to be about equally effective overall. But this does not mean that every specific psychotherapy method works in the same way or that every psychotherapy experience will be equally beneficial. Clients entering therapy must realize that the success of their treatment can still be affected by the severity of their problems, the quality of the relationship they form with the therapist, and the appropriateness of the therapy methods chosen for their problems (Goldfried & Davila, 2005).

FIGURE 16.4
Clinical Significance
Evaluations of psychological treatments must consider the clinical, as well as statistical, significance of observed changes. The shaded area of this graph shows the range of deviant behaviors per minute displayed at home by normal boys. The solid line shows the average rate of deviant behaviors for boys in an operant conditioning treatment for severe behavior problems. The improvement following reinforcement of appropriate behavior was not only statistically significant (compared with the pretreatment baseline) but also clinically significant, inasmuch as the once-deviant behavior came to resemble that of normal boys.

Source: G.R. Patterson. "Intervention for Boys with Conduct Problems: Multiple Settings, Treatments, And Criteria". *Journal Of Consulting And Clinical Psychology,* vol. 42, p. 476. Copyright © 1974 by the American Psychological Association. Reprinted by permission.

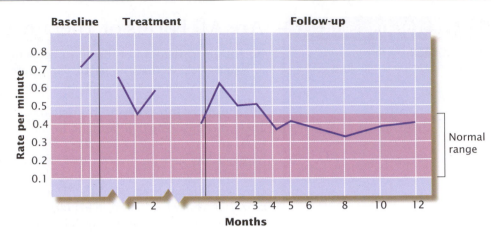

Like the individuals they treat, many clinical psychologists are eager for more specific scientific evidence about the effectiveness of particular therapies for particular kinds of clients and disorders. These empirically oriented clinicians are concerned that all too often, a therapist's choice of therapy methods depends more heavily on personal preferences or current trends than on scientific evidence of effectiveness (Lynn, Lilienfeld, & Lohr, 2003; Nathan, Stuart, & Dolan, 2000; Norcross, Beutler, & Levant, 2005; Tavris, 2003). They believe that advocates of any treatment—whether it is object relations therapy or systematic desensitization—must demonstrate that its benefits are the result of the treatment itself and not just of the passage of time, the effects of repeatedly measuring progress, the client's motivation and personal characteristics, or other confounding factors. In other words, these clinicians advocate **evidence based practice**, in which practitioners base decisions about which methods to use mainly on the results of empirical evidence about the effectiveness of those methods. A movement toward evidence based practice has also appeared in the medical and dental professions (Borry, Schotsmans, & Dierickx, 2006; Niederman & Richards, 2005).

Empirically oriented psychologists also want to see evidence that the benefits of treatment are *clinically significant.* To be clinically significant, the improvement in a client's disorder following treatment must be not only measurable but also substantial enough to make treated clients' feelings and actions similar to those of people who have not experienced that disorder (Crits-Christoph et al., 2008; Kazdin, 2003; Kendall & Choudhury, 2003). For example, a reduction in treated clients' scores on an anxiety test might be *statistically significant,* but the change would not be clinically significant unless those clients now feel and act more like people without an anxiety disorder (see Figure 16.4). The need to demonstrate the clinical significance of treatment effects has become clearer than ever as increasingly cost-conscious clients—and their health insurance providers—decide whether, and how much, to pay for various psychotherapy services (Levant, 2005; Makeover, 2004; Nelson & Steele, 2006). The most scientific way to evaluate treatment effects is through experiments in which clients are randomly assigned to various treatments or control conditions and their progress is measured objectively over time.

FOCUS ON RESEARCH METHODS

Which Therapies Work Best for Which Problems?

To help clinicians select treatment methods on the basis of empirical evidence, the Society of Clinical Psychology (a division of the American Psychological Association) created a task force on effective psychotherapies called the Committee on Science and Practice (Sanderson, 2003).

What was the researchers' question?

evidence based practice The selection of treatment methods based mainly on empirical evidence of their effectiveness.

The question addressed by this task force was "Which therapies have proved themselves most effective in treating various kinds of psychological disorders?"

LINKAGES   Is it possible to do experiments on psychotherapy? (a link to Research in Psychology, p. 42)

How did the researchers answer the question?

Working with other empirically oriented clinical psychologists, members of this task force examined the outcomes of thousands of experiments that evaluated psychotherapy methods used to treat mental disorder, marital distress, and health-related behavior problems in children, adolescents, and adults (Baucom et al., 1998; Chambless & Ollendick, 2001; Compas et al., 1998; DeRubeis & Crits-Christoph, 1998; Foley, 2004; Kazdin & Weisz, 1998; Kendall & Chambless, 1998).

What did the researchers find?

The task force found that a number of treatments—known as **empirically supported therapies**, or **ESTs**—have been validated by controlled experimental research (Chambless & Ollendick, 2001; DeRubeis & Crits-Christoph, 1998; Kendall & Chambless, 1998; Norcross, 2001, 2002). Table 16.4 contains some examples of these therapies. Notice that the treatments identified as effective for particular problems in adult clients are mainly behavioral, cognitive, and cognitive behavioral methods (Norcross, Beutler, & Levant, 2005) but that a few psychodynamic therapies (e.g., interpersonal therapy and brief dynamic therapy) also made the list (Chambless & Ollendick, 2001; Svartberg, Stiles, & Seltzer, 2004).

empirically supported therapies (ESTs) Treatments whose effects have been validated by controlled experimental research.

TABLE 16.4   Some Empirically Supported Therapies

Treatments listed as "efficacious and specific" were shown to be superior to no treatment or to some alternative treatment in at least two experiments in which clients were randomly assigned to various treatment conditions. These experiments are called *randomized clinical trials,* or *RCTs.* Also included in this category are treatments supported by scientific outcome measures from a large number of carefully conducted case studies. Treatments listed as "probably efficacious" are supported by at least one RCT or by a smaller number of rigorously evaluated case studies. Those listed as "possibly efficacious" are supported by a mixture of data, generally from single-case studies or other nonexperimental studies (Chambless & Ollendick, 2001). More information about these ESTs is available at www.psychology.sunysb.edu/eklonsky-/division12/index.html and at www.div12.org/treatments. Other reviews of empirical research are aimed at identifying potentially harmful therapies (Barlow, 2010; Lilienfeld, 2007).

Problem	Efficacious and Specific	Probably Efficacious	Possibly Efficacious
Major depression (major depressive disorder)	Behavior therapy Cognitive behavior therapy Interpersonal therapy	Brief dynamic therapy	
Specific phobia	Exposure therapy	Systematic desensitization therapy	
Agoraphobia/panic disorder	Cognitive behavior therapy	Couples training + exposure therapy	
Generalized anxiety disorder	Cognitive behavior therapy	Applied relaxation therapy	
Obsessive-compulsive disorder	Exposure therapy + response prevention	Cognitive therapy Family-assisted exposure therapy + response prevention + relaxation	Rational emotive behavior therapy + exposure therapy
Posttraumatic stress disorder		Exposure Stress inoculation Cognitive therapy + stress inoculation + exposure	Structured psychodynamic treatment
Schizophrenia	Behavioral family therapy	Family systems therapy Social skills training Supportive group therapy	Cognitive therapy (for delusions)
Alcohol abuse and dependence	Community reinforcement	Cue exposure therapy Behavioral marital therapy + disulfiram (antialcohol drug) Social skills training (with inpatients)	
Opiate abuse and dependence		Behavior therapy Brief dynamic therapy Cognitive therapy	
Marital discord	Behavioral marital therapy	Insight-oriented marital therapy	

Source: Chambless & Ollendick (2001).

What do the results mean?

The authors of the report on ESTs, as well as supporters of their efforts, claim that by relying on analysis of experimental research, they have accomplished a scientific evaluation of various treatments. This evaluation, they say, identified a list of methods from which consumers—and clinicians who want to conduct an evidence based practice—can choose with confidence when dealing with specific disorders (e.g., Hunsley & Rumstein-McKean, 1999; Kendall & Chambless, 1998). They are even urging therapists to follow the *treatment manuals* that were used in successful research studies to help them deliver empirically supported therapies exactly as intended (Addis & Krasnow, 2000; Wade, Treat, & Stuart, 1998). The state of Kansas was the first in the United States to formally encourage the use of empirically supported treatments for children (Roberts, 2002).

Not everyone agrees with the conclusions or recommendations of the APA task force (Norcross, Beutler, & Levant, 2005; Westen & Bradley, 2005; Westen, Novotny, & Thompson-Brenner, 2004). Critics note, first, that treatment methods are not necessarily discredited just because they are not on the latest list of ESTs. Some of these treatments may not yet have been studied or validated according to the efficacy criteria selected by the task force (Lantz, 2004; Westen & Morrison, 2001). These critics also have doubts about the value of some of those criteria. They point to research showing that had the task force used different outcome criteria, it might have reached different—and perhaps less optimistic—conclusions about the value of some empirically supported treatments (Bradley, Heim, & Westen, 2005; Thompson-Brenner, Glass, & Westen, 2003). There is concern, too, about the wisdom of categorizing treatments as either "supported" or "unsupported." These simple either-or judgments seem reassuring but may fail to give a complete picture of the impact of various treatments on various clients with various problems (Krause & Lutz, 2006; Westen & Bradley, 2005).

Critics argue further that the list of ESTs is based on research that may not be relevant to clinicians working in the real world of clinical practice. They note that experimental studies of psychotherapy have focused mainly on relatively brief treatments for highly specific disorders, even though most clients' problems tend to be far more complex (Westen & Bradley, 2005). These studies focus, too, on the therapeutic procedures used rather than on the characteristics and interactions of therapists and clients (Cornelius-White, 2002; Garfield, 1998; Hilliard, Henry, & Strupp, 2000; Westen, Novotny, & Thompson-Brenner, 2004). This emphasis on procedure is a problem, critics say, because the outcome of therapy in these experiments might have been strongly affected by client-therapist factors, such as whether the random pairing of clients and therapists resulted in a match or a mismatch on certain personal characteristics. In real clinical situations, clients and therapists are not usually paired up at random (Goldfried & Davila, 2005; Hill, 2005; Hohman & Shear, 2002). Finally, because therapists participating in experimental research were required to follow standard treatment manuals, they were not free to adapt treatment methods to the needs of particular clients, as they normally would do (Garfield, 1998). Perhaps, say critics, when there is less experimental control over the treatment situation, all therapies really are about equally effective, as suggested by the statistical analyses of outcome research mentioned earlier (Shadish et al., 2000; Smith, Glass, & Miller, 1980).

In short, critics reject the EST list as a useful guide. In fact, some see it as an incomplete and ultimately misleading document (Westen & Bradley, 2005). They also worry that widespread use of treatment manuals would make psychotherapy too mechanical and less effective and would discourage therapists from developing new treatment methods (Addis & Krasnow, 2000; Beutler, 2000; Garfield, 1998).

Partly in response to these concerns, it has been suggested that the evidence in evidence based practice should come not just from randomized clinical trials but also from less rigorous studies of therapy and the therapeutic relationship and from clinicians' experiences in real-world treatment settings. This idea was formalized in an APA task force policy statement that says that "evidence based practice in psychology... is the integration of the best available research with clinical expertise in the context of patient characteristics, culture, and preferences" (American Psychological Association Presidential Task Force on Evidence Based Practice, 2006, p. 273). The contrast between this view and the one that defines effective psychotherapy in terms of ESTs illustrates the gap that remains between those who would base treatment decisions mainly on the outcome of controlled experimental research (Hunsley, 2007) and those who feel that the guidance provided by research results must be interpreted and adjusted in light of clinical judgment and experience (Zeldow, 2009).

What do we still need to know?

It remains to be seen if clinicians and researchers will be able to come together to bridge the gap between them in a way that makes the best use of both domains of knowledge in the service of clients' welfare (e.g., Barlow, 2006; Becker et al., 2009; Castonguay & Beutler, 2005; Fago, 2009). Still, the effort to identify empirically supported treatments and to develop evidence based practice in clinical psychology (Levant, 2005) represent important steps in responding to Gordon Paul's "ultimate question" about psychotherapy: "What treatment, by whom, is most effective for this individual with that specific problem, under what set of circumstances?" We still have a long way to go, but empirically oriented clinical psychologists are determined to keep moving forward. Ideally, their work will speed the development of evidence-based practice in psychology (Levant, 2005; McHugh & Barlow, 2010), in which therapists are guided by research that is clinically relevant as well as empirically supported (Arkowitz & Lilienfeld, 2006; Bray, 2010).

We have seen that the Dodo Bird verdict is probably incorrect, and it is certainly incomplete. Although different treatments can be equally effective in addressing some disorders, empirical research shows that for other disorders, certain therapies tend to be more effective than others. For example, when differences show up in comparative studies of adult psychotherapy, they reveal a small to moderate advantage for behavioral and cognitive behavioral methods, especially in the treatment of phobias and certain other anxiety disorders (Butler et al., 2006; Craske & Barlow, 2008; Eddy et al., 2004; Hollon, Stewart, & Strunk, 2006; Schnurr et al., 2007; Tolin, 2010) and in the prevention and treatment of eating disorders (Hendricks & Thompson, 2005; Stice & Shaw, 2004; Wilson et al., 2010). The same overall trend holds true in the treatment of child and adolescent clients (Carr, 2009; Kazak et al., 2010; Kendall et al., 2008; Weisz, Doss, & Hawley, 2005).

This research provides valuable guidelines for matching treatments to disorders, but it doesn't guarantee success. The outcome of any given case will also be affected by client characteristics, therapist characteristics, and the quality of the relationship that develops between them (e.g., Hill, 2005; Sherer & Schreibman, 2005). Indeed, the client-therapist relationship plays a consistent role in the success of all forms of treatment (Brown & O'Leary, 2000; Constantino et al., 2005; Horvath, 2005; Karver et al., 2006; Uwe, 2005; Zuroff & Blatt, 2006). Certain people seem to be particularly effective in forming productive human relationships. Even without formal training, these people can sometimes be as helpful as professional therapists thanks to personal qualities that are inspiring, healing, and soothing to others (Hill & Lent, 2006; Ronnestad & Ladany, 2006). Their presence in self-help groups may well underlie some of the success of those groups and, among professionals, may help account for the success of many kinds of formal therapy.

Before choosing a therapist and treatment approach, then, clients should keep Paul's "ultimate question" in mind. They should carefully consider (1) empirical research about the best treatment for their particular problem; (2) what treatment approach, methods, and goals they find most comfortable and appealing; (3) information about the therapist's "track record" of clinically significant success with a particular method for treating problems similar to those they face; and (4) the likelihood of forming a productive relationship with the therapist. This last consideration assumes special importance when client and therapist do not share similar social or cultural backgrounds.

Sociocultural Factors in Psychotherapy

Imagine that after moving to an unfamiliar country to pursue your education or career, you become severely depressed. A friend there refers you to a therapist who specializes in depression. At your first session, the therapist stares at you intently, touches your head for a moment, and says, "You have taken in a spirit from the river, and it is trying to get out. I will help." The therapist then begins chanting softly and appears to go into a trance. What would you think? Would you return for a second visit? If you are like most people raised in a Western culture, you probably wouldn't continue treatment because this therapist may not share your beliefs and expectations about what is wrong with you and what should be done about it.

Such sociocultural clashes occur whenever clients come to therapy with a cultural or subcultural worldview that is not shared by their therapist (Seeley, 2006). Suppose, for example, that a therapist suggests that a client's panic attacks are a reaction to stress but the client is sure that the attacks are punishment for having offended a dead ancestor. That client may not easily accept a treatment based on the principles of stress management. Similarly, a therapist who believes that people should confront and overcome life's problems might run into trouble when treating clients whose cultural or religious training encourages calm acceptance of these problems (Sue et al., 2009). In such cases, the result may be much like two people singing a duet using the same music but different lyrics (Martinez et al., 2005).

In the United States, sociocultural clashes may be partly to blame for the underuse of or withdrawal from mental health services by recent immigrants, as well as by African Americans, Asian Americans, Hispanic Americans, American Indians, and members of other minority populations (Duran et al., 2005; Gone, 2004; Neighbors et al., 2007; Sanders-Thompson, Bazile, & Akbar, 2004; Thurston & Phares, 2008; Wang, Lane, et al., 2005). In other words, sociocultural differences between clients and therapists—in religious faith, gender, age, ethnicity, sexual orientation, socioeconomic background, and the like—can sometimes be a source of miscommunication or mistrust (Seeley, 2006), potentially impairing both their working relationship and the client's motivation to change (Jones, Botsko, & Gorman, 2003; Wintersteen, Mensinger, & Diamond, 2005; Vasquez, 2007). Accordingly, major efforts are under way to ensure that cultural differences between clients and therapists do not interfere with the delivery of treatment to anyone who wants or needs it. Virtually every mental health training program in North America is seeking to recruit more students from traditionally underserved minority groups so as to eventually make it easier to match clients with therapists from similar cultural backgrounds (e.g., Kersting, 2004; Meredith & Baker, 2007; Rogers & Molina, 2006).

In the meantime, many minority clients are likely to encounter a therapist from a differing background, so researchers have also examined the value of matching therapeutic techniques with clients' culturally based expectations and preferences (Jones, Botsko, & Gorman, 2003; Li & Kim, 2004; Muñoz & Mendelson, 2005). For example, many clients from collectivist cultures—in which the emphasis is on meeting the expectations of family and friends rather than satisfying personal desires—might expect to receive instructions from a therapist about how to overcome problems. How would such clients respond to a therapist whose client-centered treatment emphasizes more individualist goals, such as being independent and taking responsibility for the direction of change? David Sue and his students investigated the hypothesis that the collectivist values of Asian cultures would lead Asians and Asian Americans to prefer a directive, problem-solving approach over nondirective, client-centered methods. In this classic study, Sue (1992) found that a preference for directive treatment was higher among foreign-born Asians than among American-born Asians and European Americans. Individual differences still exist, however, so two people from the same culture may react quite differently to a treatment that group research suggests should be ideal for both of them. In Sue's study, for example, more than a third of the foreign-born Asians preferred

Preparing for Therapy

Special pretreatment orientation programs may be offered to clients who, because of sociocultural factors, are unfamiliar with the rules and procedures of psychotherapy. These programs provide a preview of what psychotherapy is, how it can help, and what the client is expected to do to make it more effective (Reis & Brown, 2006; Swartz, Zuckoff, et al., 2007).

© Spencer Grant/PhotoEdit

the nondirective approach, and 28 percent of the European Americans preferred the directive approach.

Today, psychotherapists are more sensitive than ever to the cultural values of particular groups and to the difficulties that can impair intercultural communication (Fields, 2010; Hays & Iwamasa, 2006; Hwang, 2006; Martinez et al., 2005; Sue et al., 2009). Some U.S. states now require clinical and counseling psychologists to complete courses or gain supervised experience focused on the role of cultural factors in therapy before being licensed (Rehm & DeMers, 2006). Similar cultural diversity training is required for all graduate students in clinical and counseling psychology training programs accredited by the American Psychological Association (Commission on Accreditation, 2009; Kersting, 2004; Smith, Constantine, et al., 2006). This special training helps clinicians and graduate students appreciate, for example, that it is considered impolite in some cultures to make eye contact with a stranger. Having that information makes it easier for them to recognize that clients from those cultures are not necessarily depressed, lacking in self-esteem, or inappropriately submissive just because they look at the floor during an interview.

There is no guarantee that cultural diversity training will improve treatment results (Shin et al., 2005), but there is some evidence that it can help (e.g., Constantine, 2002; Razali, Aminah, & Umeed, 2002; Sue et al., 2009). Although it is unrealistic to expect all therapists to be equally effective with clients of every ethnic or religious background, cultural diversity training offers a way to improve their *cultural sensitivity,* an extension of Carl Rogers's concept of empathy. When therapists appreciate the client's view of the world, it is easier for them to set goals that are in harmony with that view (Dyche & Zayas, 2001; Pedersen & Draguns, 2002; Stuart, 2004). Minimizing the chances of cultural misunderstanding and miscommunication is one of the many ethical obligations that therapists assume whenever they work with clients. Let's consider some others.

Rules and Rights in the Therapeutic Relationship

Treatment can be an intensely emotional experience. The client-therapist relationship can profoundly affect a client's life, so professional ethics require the therapist to ensure that this relationship does not harm the client. For example, the American Psychological Association's *Ethical Principles of Psychologists and Code of Conduct* forbids a sexual relationship between therapist and client—during treatment and for at least two years afterward—because of the severe harm it can cause the client (American Psychological Association [APA], 2002b; Behnke, 2004; Bersoff, 2008). Even after two years have passed, therapists may not ethically pursue a sexual relationship with a former client unless they can demonstrate that the relationship is not exploitative or otherwise harmful to that client. Laws in some U.S. states prohibit therapists from *ever* having a sexual relationship with a former client, and these laws take precedence over the APA's code of conduct.

These same ethical standards require that therapists, with a few exceptions, keep everything a client says in therapy strictly confidential. Confidentiality is one of the most important features of a successful therapeutic relationship because it allows the client to discuss unpleasant or embarrassing feelings, behaviors, or events without fear that the therapist might disclose this information to others. Professionals sometimes consult with one another about their clients, but they do not identify clients by name, and they do not reveal information to outsiders (even to members of the client's family) without the client's consent. The APA's code of ethics also includes standards relating to the growing number of clients who seek psychological services via *telehealth* or *e-health* channels, which include telephone, videoconferencing, e-mail, and other Internet links (Andersson, 2009; APA, 2002b; Barnett & Scheetz, 2003; Christensen, Griffiths, & Jorm, 2004; Mohr, Hart, et al., 2005; Ruskin et al., 2004). One of these standards, for example, requires therapists to inform clients that others might be able to gain access to their e-mail messages and that no formal client-therapist relationship exists in e-mail exchanges.

Professional rules about confidentiality are backed up in most U.S. states by laws recognizing that information revealed in therapy—like information given to a priest, a lawyer, or a physician—is privileged communication. In 1996, a U.S. Supreme Court ruling also established psychotherapist-client privilege in the federal courts (DeBell & Jones, 1997; Knapp & VandeCreek, 1997). This means that by asserting *privilege,* a therapist can refuse, even in court, to answer questions about a client or to provide personal notes or tape recordings from therapy sessions (Kaplan, 2005). Only under special circumstances can therapists be legally required to violate confidentiality (Donner et al., 2008). These circumstances include those in which (1) a client is so severely disturbed or suicidal that hospitalization is needed, (2) a client uses his or her mental condition and history of therapy as part of his or her defense in a civil or criminal trial, (3) the therapist must defend against a client's charge of malpractice, (4) a client reveals information about sexual or physical abuse of a child under 18, and (5) the therapist believes a client may commit a violent act against a specific person.

This last condition poses a dilemma: Suppose that a client says, "Someday I'm going to kill that brother of mine!" Should the therapist consider this a serious threat and warn the brother? In most cases, there is no real danger, but there have been tragic exceptions. For example, Prosenjit Poddar, a graduate student receiving therapy at the University of California at Berkeley in 1969, revealed his intention to kill Tatiana Tarasoff, a young woman whom he had tried to date the previous year but who had rejected him. The therapist took the threat seriously, consulted his supervisor, and asked the campus police to take Poddar to a hospital. They did not do so, however, and neither Tarasoff nor her parents were warned about the possible danger (Ewing & McCann, 2006). After dropping out of therapy, the client killed Tarasoff, whose parents later sued the university, the campus police, and the therapist. They won their case, thus setting an important precedent (Yufik, 2005). Several U.S. states now have laws that make a therapist liable for failing to take steps to protect those who

© AP Photo/Montana State Department of Justice

Rights of the Mentally Ill

In 1996, after years of odd behavior— including vague threats against government officials and claims that the government was spying on him through TV satellite dishes—Russell Eugene Weston Jr. was diagnosed with paranoid schizophrenia. He was hospitalized for seven weeks but had to be released when doctors determined that he was not a threat to himself or others as long as he took his prescribed medication. He failed to do so, however, and in July 1998, Weston killed two police officers during an armed rampage at the U.S. Capitol. Cases such as his are frustrating to mental health professionals, whose decisions about hospitalization must balance the rights of mental patients against those of the public.

Hospital Restraints

Here are examples of the chains, straitjackets, belts, and covered bathtubs that were used to restrain disruptive patients in North American and European mental hospitals in the 1800s and well into the 1900s. These devices were gentle compared with some of the methods endorsed in the late 1700s by Benjamin Rush. Known as the "father of American psychiatry," Rush advocated curing patients by frightening or disorienting them—for example, by placing them in a coffinlike box, which was then briefly immersed in water.

are threatened with violence by the therapist's clients (Bersoff, 2008; Werth, Welfel, & Benjamin, 2009). Other states allow therapists more discretion in warning or protecting potential victims (Carson & Bull, 2003).

A different set of laws protect people in the United States from being committed to mental hospitals without good cause (B. R. Johnson, 2004). Federal court decisions have given clients threatened with commitment the right to have written notice; an opportunity to prepare a defense with the help of an attorney; a court hearing, with a jury if desired; and the right to invoke the Fifth Amendment to avoid self-incrimination. Furthermore, before people can be forcibly committed, the state must provide "clear and convincing" evidence that they are not only mentally ill but also gravely disabled or an "imminent danger" to themselves or others. Most states now require a periodic review of every committed person's records to determine whether release from a mental hospital is appropriate.

While hospitalized, patients have the right to receive treatment, but they also have the right to refuse certain forms of treatment (Carson & Bull, 2003). These rules are designed to protect hospitalized mental patients from abuse, neglect, or exploitation, but they can also create difficulties and dangers. Consider Russell Eugene Weston Jr., a former mental patient who was hospitalized after being charged with the murders of two police officers in 1998. Facing a possible death penalty but judged mentally incompetent to stand trial, he asserted his right to refuse prescription drug treatment that would make him competent. After a long legal battle, Weston was forced to take medication. Prosecutors successfully argued that the right to refuse treatment does not extend to hospitalized patients who pose a danger to themselves or others (Manahan, 2004).

Hospitalized patients who do not pose such dangers—including those whose dangerous impulses are being suppressed by prescription drugs—have the right to be subjected to minimal restriction of their freedom (Bell, 2005). Accordingly, they are released from mental hospitals, usually with a supply of medication that they are to take on their own. Unfortunately, not all these patients follow doctors' orders. Like Weston, Andrew Goldstein was not considered dangerous as long as he took his antipsychotic medication, but after being released from a New York City mental hospital in December 1998, he stopped doing so. About two weeks later, Goldstein pushed Kendra Webdale to her death under the wheels of a subway train (Perlin, 2003). Cases such as these put the staff at mental health facilities in a bind—they worry about being sued if they keep patients unnecessarily confined or if someone is harmed by a patient they have released too soon. In an effort to strike a balance between the rights of mental patients and those of the public, several states now have laws requiring outpatient treatment for people who are dangerous when not medicated. The New York statute is known as Kendra's Law (Appelbaum, 2005).

Biological Treatments

Prescription drugs that can ease the symptoms of psychological disorders are the latest and most effective in a long line of biological treatments based on the idea that psychological problems have physical causes. Hippocrates, a physician of ancient Greece, was among the first to propose this idea, and the treatments he prescribed included rest, special diets, laxatives, and abstinence from alcohol and sex. In the mental hospitals of Europe and North America during the sixteenth through eighteenth centuries, treatment of psychological disorders was based in part on Hippocrates' methods and consisted mainly of physical restraints, laxative purges, draining of "excess" blood, and induced vomiting. Cold baths, hunger, and other physical discomforts were also used in efforts to shock patients back to normality (Jones, 1923). Even as recently as the mid-1900s, physicians treated most forms of psychological disorder by means of brain surgery or electric shock.

Psychosurgery

Psychosurgery involves the destruction of brain tissue for the purpose of treating mental disorder. Among the first to try these procedures was a Portuguese neurosurgeon named António Egas Moniz. In 1935, he developed a technique, called *prefrontal lobotomy*, in which small holes are drilled in the forward portion of the skull and a sharp instrument is inserted and moved from side to side to cut connections between the prefrontal cortex and the rest of the brain (Freeman & Watts, 1942; Moniz, 1948). The theory was that emotional reactions in disturbed people become exaggerated due to neural processes in the frontal lobes and that the lobotomy disrupts these processes. During the 1940s and 1950s, psychosurgery became almost routine in the treatment of schizophrenia, depression, anxiety, aggressiveness, and obsessive-compulsive disorder (Valenstein, 1980). Unfortunately, brain surgery is risky and sometimes fatal, its benefits are uncertain, and its side effects and complications, including epilepsy, are irreversible (Balon, 2004; Martin et al., 2001; Rueck, Andreewitch, & Flyckt, 2003). Today, psychosurgery is performed only in rare cases in which all else has failed; guided by brain-imaging techniques, it focuses on much smaller areas of the brain than those involved in lobotomies (Anderson & Booker, 2006; Dougherty et al., 2002; Helmes & Velamoor, 2009).

Electroconvulsive Shock Therapy

In the 1930s, a Hungarian physician named Ladislaus von Meduna used a drug to induce convulsions in schizophrenics. He believed—incorrectly—that because schizophrenia and epilepsy rarely occur in the same person, epileptic-like seizures might combat schizophrenia. In 1938, two Italian physicians, Ugo Cerletti and Lucio Bini, created seizures by passing an electric current through schizophrenics' brains. During the next twenty years or so, this procedure, called **electroconvulsive shock therapy (EST)**, became a routine treatment for schizophrenia, depression, and sometimes mania. Although many patients improved, they often relapsed. The benefits of EST also had to be weighed against side effects such as memory loss, confusion, speech disorders, and occasionally death due to cardiac arrest (Lickey & Gordon, 1991; Shiwach, Reid, & Carmody, 2001). In an effort to make EST safer, doctors now administer an anesthetic to render patients unconscious before the shock is delivered, along with a muscle relaxant to prevent bone fractures during convulsions. Also, the shock now lasts only about half a second and is usually delivered to only one side of the brain (Sackeim et al., 2000). Finally, in contrast to the dozens of treatments administered decades ago, patients now receive a total of only six to twelve shocks, usually administered two days apart (Shorter & Healy, 2007).

The use of EST has declined in the United States since the 1950s, but it is still performed on about one hundred thousand people each year (Payne & Prudic, 2009). It is administered mainly to patients suffering severe depression (and occasionally to manic patients) who do not respond to prescription drugs (de Macedo-Soares et al., 2005; Payne & Prudic, 2009; Rasmussen, 2003). EST can be effective in some of these cases—especially when followed up with medication (Sackheim et al., 2009)—and it does not appear to cause brain damage, even after repeated administrations (e.g., Anghelescu et al., 2001; Dwork et al., 2004; Kellner et al., 2005, 2006; Payne & Prudic, 2009).

No one knows for sure how and why EST works (Greenberg & Kellner, 2005; Shorter & Healy, 2007), but the fact that it helps some patients has led EST researchers to seek even safer methods of inducing seizures. Among the techniques being investigated are *magnetic seizure therapy* (MST), which induces seizures with timed pulses of magnetic energy (Lisanby, 2004), and a related but less intense procedure called *repetitive transcranial magnetic stimulation* (rTMS) (Couturier, 2005; Schutter, 2005). *Deep brain stimulation* (DBS) does not cause seizures but requires the placement of electrodes in the brain to provide continuous pulses of electricity to a particular target area. Some researchers suggest that these treatments may be of value in severe cases of depression and obsessive-compulsive disorder that are unresponsive to other treatments (George et al., 2010; Goodman et al., 2010; Hardesty & Sackeim, 2007; Martiny, Lunde, & Bech, 2010).

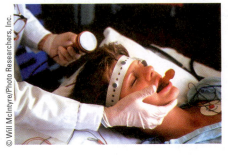

© Will McIntyre/Photo Researchers, Inc.

Electroconvulsive Shock Therapy

Approximately one hundred thousand individuals receive EST each year in the United States (Payne & Prudic, 2009). Because of its dramatic and potentially dangerous nature, the use of EST remains controversial (Breggin, 2007). Critics want it outlawed, but proponents insist that the benefits of EST for certain patients outweigh its potential costs.

psychosurgery Surgical procedures that destroy tissue in small regions of the brain in an effort to treat psychological disorders.

electroconvulsive shock therapy (EST) Brief electrical shock administered to the brain, usually to reduce depression that does not respond to drug treatments.

Psychoactive Drugs

The decline in use of psychosurgery and EST after the 1950s came not only because of their complications and general distastefulness but also because *psychoactive drugs* had begun to emerge as more convenient and effective treatment alternatives. These drugs are now the most common biological treatment for all forms of psychological disorder. In the chapters on biological aspects of psychology and on consciousness, we discuss how psychoactive drugs affect neurotransmitter systems and consciousness. Here we describe how some of these drugs are prescribed to combat schizophrenia, depression, mania, and anxiety.

Neuroleptic Drugs **Neuroleptic drugs**, or *antipsychotics*, dramatically reduce the intensity of psychotic symptoms such as hallucinations, delusions, paranoid suspiciousness, disordered thinking, and confused speech in many mental patients, especially those with schizophrenia. The most widely used antipsychotic drugs are the *phenothiazines* (pronounced "fee-noh-THY-uh-zeenz"), of which the first, *chlorpromazine* (marketed as Thorazine in the United States and as Largactil in Canada and the United Kingdom), has been especially popular. Another neuroleptic drug, *haloperidol* (sold as Haldol), is about as effective as the phenothiazines, but it causes less sedation (Julien, 2008). Patients who do not respond to one type of neuroleptic drug may respond to the other (Schatzberg, Cole, & DeBattista, 2007). Between 60 and 70 percent of the people who receive these medications show improvement, though fewer than 30 percent respond well enough to live independently (Freedman, 2003).

Neuroleptic drugs also have side effects ranging from dry mouth and dizziness to symptoms similar to those of Parkinson's disease, including muscle rigidity, restlessness, tremors, and slowed movement. Some of these side effects can be treated with medication, but at least 25 percent of patients who take chlorpromazine or haloperidol for several years develop an irreversible movement disorder called *tardive dyskinesia* (*TD*), which causes uncontrollable, repetitive actions, often including twitching of the face, flailing of the arms and legs, and thrusting of the tongue (Miller, McEvoy, et al., 2005).

Among a newer generation of antipsychotic drugs (also called *atypical neuroleptic drugs*) is *clozapine* (Clozaril), which has effects like those of the phenothiazines but is less likely to cause movement disorders (Louzá & Bassit, 2005; Rochon et al., 2005). Although no more effective overall than the phenothiazines, clozapine has helped many patients who did not respond to the phenothiazines or haloperidol (Green & Patel, 1996; Rabinowitz et al., 2001). Unfortunately, taking clozapine carries a slight risk of developing a fatal blood disease called *agranulocytosis* (Ginsberg, 2006). Weekly blood tests to detect early signs of this disease greatly increase the cost and inconvenience of using clozapine, so it is usually prescribed only for patients who have not responded well to other medications and are willing to have their blood drawn frequently.

Several other atypical neuroleptic drugs have now been introduced, including *risperidone* (Risperdal), *olanzapine* (Zyprexa), *quetiapine* (Seroquel), *ziprasidone* (Geodon), and *aripiprazole* (Abilify). These medications are expensive, but they have fewer side effects than clozapine, and they do not cause agranulocytosis (Schatzberg, Cole, & DeBattista, 2007). Like clozapine, they also appear to reduce the negative symptoms of schizophrenia, such as lack of emotion, social withdrawal, and reduced speech (e.g., Fleischhacker & Widschwendter, 2006; Kane et al., 2003; Kapur, Sridhar & Remington, 2004; Potkin et al., 2003; Wang et al., 2010). There is some doubt, though, as to whether these newest atypical neuroleptic drugs are significantly more effective than older drugs (Matza, Baker, & Revicki, 2005), partly because 60 to 80 percent of patients may stop taking them due to weight gain, nervous tics, and other bothersome side effects (Lieberman et al., 2005; Swartz, Perkins, et al., 2007).

neuroleptic drugs Medications that alleviate the symptoms of severe disorders such as schizophrenia.

© Mario Tama/Getty Images

A Natural Cure?

An herbal remedy from a plant called Saint John's wort has become a popular nonprescription treatment for depression. One of its active ingredients, hypericin, is thought to affect neurotransmitters in the brain much as Prozac or Zoloft does. One double-blind study showed Saint John's wort to be no more effective than a placebo for treating major depression (Hypericum Depression Trial Study Group, 2002), though others have shown it to be as effective as Prozac in cases of milder depression (e.g., Hammerness, Basch, & Ulbricht, 2003; Szegedi et al., 2005). Final conclusions about the safety and effectiveness of Saint John's wort must await the results of further research (National Center for Complementary and Alternative Medicine, 2008).

Antidepressant Drugs   Soon after antipsychotic drugs appeared, they were joined by **antidepressant drugs**, a class of medications that now constitute the most widely prescribed treatment for depression (Schatzberg, Cole, & DeBattista, 2007; Thomson Healthcare, 2007). There are several classes of antidepressant drugs. The *monoamine oxidase inhibitors* (*MAOIs*) are used to treat many cases of depression, especially clients who also experience anxiety and panic (Julien, 2008). The *tricyclic antidepressants* (*TCAs*) are another popular class of antidepressant drugs. The TCAs have been prescribed more frequently than MAOIs because they seem to work somewhat better and have fewer side effects. However, overdoses of TCAs can be fatal, as can taking TCAs and drinking alcohol at the same time (Nutt, 2005a). Still, if side effects are controlled, tricyclics can be effective in treating depression and can also reduce the severity of panic attacks in some cases of panic disorder.

Today, the most popular medications for depression are those that affect the neurotransmitter *serotonin*. The most prominent drug in this group is *fluoxetine* (*Prozac*), which after its introduction in 1986 quickly became the most widely used antidepressant drug in the United States (Brambilla et al., 2005). Its popularity is due to the fact that it is as effective as older antidepressant drugs and in most cases has milder side effects—mainly weight gain, sexual dysfunction, and gastrointestinal problems (Nutt, 2005a; Patten et al., 2005). An improved version of Prozac, containing a purer active ingredient called *R-fluoxetine*, is now available (Norman & Olver, 2004). Other even newer antidepressant drugs, including *venlafaxine* (Effexor), *nefazodone* (Serzone), *bupropion* (Wellbutrin), *escitalopram* (Lexapro), *sertraline* (Zoloft), and *duloxetine* (Cymbalta), are also now on the market (Brambilla et al., 2005; Hirschfeld & Vornik, 2004; Schatzberg, Cole, & DeBattista, 2007; Zimmerman, Posternak, et al., 2005).

About 50 to 60 percent of patients who take antidepressant medication experience improved mood, greater physical activity, increased appetite, and better sleep (Hollon, Thase, & Markowitz, 2002). These benefits are seen in only 10 to 20 percent of the most severe cases of depression, however (Fournier et al., 2010), and for most patients, improvement does not appear for at least a week or two after treatment begins (Quitkin et al., 2003; Taylor, Freemantle, et al., 2006). This delayed response seems odd because antidepressants have almost immediate effects on neurotransmitters, usually increasing the availability of serotonin or norepinephrine in the brain. As discussed in the chapter on psychological disorders, these neurotransmitters are thought to be involved in the biology of depression, so perhaps the time lag reflects the operation of a long-term compensatory process in the nervous system.

Doubt has arisen about the extent to which the results of antidepressant medications are due to the chemical action of their active ingredients. An analysis of clinical trial data submitted to the U.S. Food and Drug Administration by the makers of six widely prescribed antidepressant drugs showed that in 57 percent of the trials, antidepressant drugs did only a little better at relieving depression than placebos ("sugar pills") (Kirsch et al., 2002). Defenders of antidepressant medications argue that even relatively small effects are better than none (e.g., Thase, 2002), while critics contend that those effects are too small to matter, especially when viewed in light of these drugs' high cost and potential adverse side effects (e.g., Breggin, 2008; Moncrieff & Kirsch, 2005; Wampold et al., 2005).

Lithium and Anticonvulsants   In 1949, J. F. Cade discovered that a mineral salt of the element *lithium*, when taken regularly, could prevent the mania associated with bipolar disorder in some patients (Schou, 2001). In fact, for 30 to 50 percent of patients with bipolar disorder, lithium is effective in preventing both manic and depressive episodes, thereby earning its label as a *mood stabilizer* (Geddes et al., 2004; Schatzberg, Cole, & DeBattista, 2007). Without lithium, the typical bipolar patient has a manic episode about every fourteen months and a depressive episode about every seventeen months (American Psychiatric Association, 2000). With lithium, attacks of mania occur as rarely as every nine years (Bowden, 2000; Geddes et al., 2004). The lithium

antidepressant drugs Medications that relieve depression.

dosage must be exact and carefully controlled, however, because taking too much can cause nausea, vomiting, tremor, fatigue, slurred speech, and, if the overdose is severe, coma or death (Johnson, 2002). Further, lithium is not useful for treating a manic episode in progress because, as in the case of antidepressant drugs, it takes a week or two of regular use before its effects are seen. So as with the antidepressants, the effects of lithium probably occur through some form of long-term adaptation as the nervous system adjusts to the presence of the drug. Combining lithium with other mood-stabilizing drugs, such as carbamazepine, has shown enhanced benefits but also more adverse side effects (Baethge et al., 2005).

In recent years, anticonvulsant drugs such as *divalproex* (Epival, Depakote) and *lamotrigine* (Lamictal) have been used as an alternative to lithium in treating mania (e.g., Daban et al., 2006; Delbello et al., 2006). These drugs cause fewer side effects than lithium, are less dangerous at higher doses, and are easier to regulate (Bowden, 2000, 2003; Schatzberg, Cole, & DeBattista, 2007). However, their long-term benefits in reducing mania and the risk of suicide are not as well established, so lithium is still considered the treatment of choice against which other medications are measured (Calabrese et al., 2005; Capriani et al., 2005; McAllister-Williams, 2006).

Tranquilizing Drugs (Anxiolytics)   During the 1950s, a new class of drugs called *tranquilizers* was shown to reduce mental and physical tension and other symptoms of anxiety. The first of these drugs, called *meprobamate* (Miltown, Equanil), acts somewhat like barbiturates, meaning that overdoses can be fatal (Allen, Greenblatt, & Noel, 1977). Newer tranquilizers, known as *benzodiazepines*—such as *chlordiazepoxide* (Librium) and *diazepam* (Valium)—do not pose this danger and have become the worldwide drugs of choice for the treatment of anxiety (Stevens & Pollack, 2005). Today, these and other antianxiety drugs, now called **tranquilizing drugs**, or **anxiolytics** (pronounced "ank-zee-oh-LIT-iks"), continue to be the most widely prescribed of all legal drugs (Stevens & Pollack, 2005). Anxiolytics have an immediate calming effect and are quite useful in reducing anxiety, including in cases of generalized anxiety disorder and posttraumatic stress disorder.

One of the benzodiazepines, *alprazolam* (Xanax), has become especially popular for the treatment of panic disorder and agoraphobia (Verster & Volkerts, 2004). Another benzodiazepine, *clonazepam* (Klonopin), is also being used, alone or in combination with other anxiolytics, in the treatment of anxiety ranging from phobias to panic disorder. But benzodiazepines can have bothersome side effects such as sleepiness, lightheadedness, and impaired psychomotor and mental functioning. Combining these drugs with alcohol can be fatal, and continued use can lead to tolerance and physical dependence (Chouinard, 2004). Furthermore, suddenly discontinuing benzodiazepines after heavy or long-term use can cause severe withdrawal symptoms, including seizures and anxiety attacks (Lemoine et al., 2006; Rickels et al., 1993).

The tranquilizing drug *buspirone* (BuSpar) provides an alternative anxiety treatment that eliminates some of these problems. As with antidepressant drugs, buspirone's effects do not occur for days or weeks after treatment begins. As a result, many patients stop taking it because they think it has no effect other than dizziness, headache, and nervousness (Stahl, 2002; Wagner et al., 2003). Yet buspirone can ultimately equal benzodiazepines in reducing generalized anxiety (Gorman, 2003; Rickels & Rynn, 2002). Further, it does not seem to promote dependence, has fewer side effects than the benzodiazepines, and does not interact dangerously with alcohol.

Because depression often accompanies anxiety, antidepressant drugs such as fluoxetine (Prozac), paroxetine (Paxil), clomipramine (Anafranil), fluvoxamine (Luvox), and sertraline (Zoloft) are also used in treating anxiety-related problems such as panic disorder, social phobia, obsessive-compulsive disorder, and posttraumatic stress disorder (e.g., Gorman, 2003; Julien, 2008; Nutt, 2005b; Rickels et al., 2003). Table 16.5 lists the effects and side effects of the psychoactive medications we have described.

tranquilizing drugs (anxiolytics)
Drugs that reduce feelings of anxiety.

TABLE 16.5   A Sampling of Psychoactive Drugs Used for Treating Psychological Disorders

Psychoactive drugs have been successful in dramatically reducing the symptoms of many psychological disorders. Critics point out that drugs can have troublesome side effects, however, and they may create dependence, especially after years of use (e.g., Breggin, 2008). They note, too, that drugs do not "cure" mental disorders, that their effects are not always strong, and that temporary symptom relief may make some patients less likely to seek a permanent solution to their psychological problems.

Chemical Name	Trade Name	Effects and Side Effects
For Schizophrenia: Neuroleptic Drugs (Antipsychotics)		
Chlorpromazine Haloperidol	Thorazine Haldol	Reduce hallucinations, delusions, incoherence, and jumbled thought processes but may cause movement disorder side effects, including tardive dyskinesia
Clozapine	Clozaril	Reduces psychotic symptoms; causes no movement disorders but carries some risk of serious blood disease
Risperidone	Risperdal	Reduces positive and negative psychotic symptoms without risk of blood disease
Ziprasidone	Geodon	Reduces positive and negative psychotic symptoms without causing weight gain
Aripiprazole	Abilify	Reduces positive and negative psychotic symptoms without weight gain and with few side effects
For Affective Disorders: Antidepressant Drugs and Mood Elevators		
Tricyclics		
Imipramine	Tofranil	Act as antidepressants but also have antipanic action; cause sleepiness and other moderate side effects; potentially dangerous if taken with alcohol
Amitriptyline	Elavil, Amitid	
Other Antidepressant Drugs		
Fluoxetine	Prozac	Have antidepressant, antipanic, and antiobsessive action
Clomipramine	Anafranil	
Fluvoxamine	Luvox	
Sertraline	Zoloft	
Escitalopram	Lexapro	
Other Drugs		
Lithium carbonate	Carbolith, Lithizine	Calms mania; reduces mood swings of bipolar disorder; overdose harmful, potentially deadly
Divalproex	Depakote	Is effective against mania, with fewer side effects
Lamotrigine	Lamictal	Is effective in delaying relapse in bipolar disorder; most benefits associated with depression
For Anxiety Disorders: Tranquilizing Drugs (Anxiolytics)		
Benzodiazepines		
Chlordiazepoxide Diazepam	Librium Valium	Act as potent anxiolytics for generalized anxiety, panic, and stress; extended use may cause physical dependence and withdrawal syndrome if abruptly discontinued
Alprazolam	Xanax	Also has antidepressant effects; often used in agoraphobia; has high dependence potential
Clonazepam	Klonopin	Often used in combination with other anxiolytics for panic disorder
Other Antianxiety Agents		
Buspirone	BuSpar	Has slow-acting antianxiety action; no known dependence problems

Human Diversity and Drug Treatment Prescription drug treatments are designed to benefit everyone in the same way ("In Review: Biological Treatments for Psychological Disorders" summarizes our discussion of drugs and other biological treatments), but it turns out that the same amount of medication can have significantly different effects in people from various ethnic groups and in men versus women (e.g., Esel et al., 2005; Lambert & Norman, 2008; Seeman, 2004). For example, compared with Asians, Caucasians must take significantly higher doses of the benzodiazepines, haloperidol, clozapine, lithium, and possibly the tricyclic antidepressants in order to

IN REVIEW — Biological Treatments for Psychological Disorders

Method	Typical Disorders Treated	Possible Side Effects	Mechanism of Action
Electroconvulsive shock therapy (EST)	Severe depression	Temporary confusion, memory loss	Uncertain
Psychosurgery	Schizophrenia, severe depression, obsessive-compulsive disorder	Listlessness, overemotionality, epilepsy	Uncertain
Psychoactive drugs	Anxiety disorders, depression, obsessive-compulsive disorder, mania, schizophrenia	Variable, depending on drug used: movement disorders, physical dependence	Alteration of neurotransmitter systems in the brain

1. Electroconvulsive shock therapy is used _____ often now than it was in the 1950s.
2. Tranquilizing drugs are used mainly in the treatment of _____ .
3. Tardive dyskinesia is a movement disorder sometimes caused by _____ drugs.

obtain equally beneficial effects (Hull et al., 2001; Ng et al., 2005). In addition, African Americans may show a faster response to tricyclic antidepressants than European Americans and may respond to lower doses of lithium (Chaudhry et al., 2008). There is also some evidence that compared with European Americans or African Americans, Hispanic Americans require lower doses of antipsychotic medication to get the same benefits (Citrome et al., 2005). Some of these ethnic differences are thought to be related to genetically regulated differences in drug metabolism (Kato & Serretti, 2010; Zhang, Lencz, & Malhotra, 2010); others may be due to dietary practices and other sociocultural factors (Bakare, 2008).

Males and females may respond in about the same way to tricyclic antidepressants (Wohlfarth et al., 2004), but women may maintain higher blood levels of these and other therapeutic psychoactive drugs and may show better response to neuroleptic drugs (Hildebrandt et al., 2003; Salokangas, 2004). They also may be more vulnerable to adverse effects such as tardive dyskinesia (Yarlagadda et al., 2008). These gender differences in response to medication appear less related to estrogen than to other hormonal or body composition differences between men and women, such as the ratio of body fat to muscle (Salokangas, 2004). Continued research on these and other dimensions of human diversity will undoubtedly lead to more effective and safer drug treatments for everyone (Thompson & Pollack, 2001).

Evaluating Psychoactive Drug Treatments

Despite the widespread success of psychoactive prescription drugs in the treatment of psychological disorders, critics point out several shortcomings. First, drugs may suppress a client's disorder without eliminating it. As a result, the client may be less likely to try nondrug approaches that might lead to permanent benefits. Antianxiety drugs, for example, can help clients to feel calmer, but these medications alone cannot teach people to cope with the sources of their anxiety. There is concern that psychiatrists, and especially general practitioners, rely too heavily on anxiolytics and other medications to solve their patients' psychological problems (Breggin, 2008; Mojtabai & Olfson, 2010). The antidepressant drug Prozac, for instance, is being widely prescribed—overprescribed, critics say—for problems ranging from hypersensitivity to criticism and fear of rejection to low self-esteem and premenstrual problems (Breggin, 2008). Second, abuse of some drugs (such as the antianxiety benzodiazepines) can result in physical or psychological dependence. Third, drug side effects can range from minor problems, such as the thirst and dry mouth caused by some antidepressant drugs, to movement disorders such as tardive dyskinesia caused by certain neuroleptic drugs. The most serious of these side effects are relatively rare, but some are irreversible, and it is impossible to predict in advance who will develop them. Although a clear causal link has not been confirmed (Gibbons et al., 2005; Simon et al., 2006; Wheeler et al., 2008), recent research has led the

There is widespread concern that psychiatrists and especially general practitioners rely too heavily on drugs to deal with psychological problems, including those of adolescents and children (Albee, 2002; Breggin, 2008; Olfson et al., 2006; Zuvekas, Vitiello, & Nordquist, 2006). This trend appears due in part to drug ads that fuel consumer demand, but drugs are not always the answer. In one case, for example, increasing doses of medication failed to stop a paranoid schizophrenia patient's repeated escapes from a mental hospital. The problem was solved without drugs, though, after a psychologist discovered that the man's escapes were motivated by his fear of calling his mother on "bugged" hospital phones; once he was allowed to use a telephone at a nearby shopping mall, his escape attempts stopped (Rabasca, 1999).

"I medicate first and ask questions later."

National Institute of Mental Health (NIMH) in the United States and regulatory agencies in Canada and Britain to issue warnings about the danger of suicidal behavior in children and adolescents who are given Prozac and similar antidepressant drugs (Bridge et al., 2007; Breggin, 2008; Gualtieri & Johnson, 2006; Hammad, Laughren, & Racoosin, 2006; NIMH, 2004; Olfson, Marcus, & Shaffer, 2006; Stone et al., 2009). Warnings have also been issued about the elevated risk of death in elderly patients who are taking antipsychotic medications (U.S. Food and Drug Administration, 2005; Wang, Schneeweiss, et al., 2005). There is concern, too, about whether psychoactive medications are as effective as they appear to be, especially in research sponsored by the drug companies that make them (Heres et al., 2006; Moncrieff & Kirsch, 2005; Turner et al., 2008). These concerns may be dampening the enthusiasm that once led many psychologists to seek drug prescription privileges (Greenberg, 2010).

Drugs and Psychotherapy

Which is better, drugs or psychotherapy? Are the two more effective when combined? A considerable amount of research is being conducted to address these questions.

Although occasionally a study does show that one approach or the other is more effective, no clear consensus has emerged. Overall, neither form of therapy is clearly superior for treating problems such as anxiety disorders and major depressive disorder (Smits, O'Cleirigh, & Otto, 2006; Thase et al., 2007). For example, large-scale studies of treatment for severe depression found that behavior therapy, cognitive behavior therapy, and interpersonal psychotherapy can be as effective as an antidepressant medication (Butler et al., 2006; DeRubeis et al., 2005; Dimidjian et al., 2006; Hollon, Thase, & Markowitz, 2002; March et al., 2004; Nemeroff et al., 2003). Cognitive behavior therapy has also equaled the effects of medication in the treatment of phobias (Clark et al., 2003; Davidson et al., 2004; Otto et al., 2000; Thom, Sartory, & Jöhren, 2000), panic disorder (Barlow, 2007; Mitte, 2005a), generalized anxiety disorder (Mitte, 2005b), and obsessive-compulsive disorder (Kozak, Liebowitz, & Foa, 2000). Further, the dropout rate from psychotherapy may be lower than from drug therapies (Casacalenda, Perry, & Looper, 2002; Hollon et al., 2005; Mitte, 2005b), and the benefits of many kinds of psychotherapy may last longer than those of drug treatments (e.g., Bockting et al., 2005; Hollon, Stewart, & Strunk, 2006; Hollon, Thase, & Markowitz 2002; Segal, Gemar, & Williams, 2000; Thom, Sartory, & Jöhren, 2000), thus making psychotherapy more cost-effective than medication in the long run (Barrett, Byford, & Knapp, 2005).

What about combining prescription drugs and psychotherapy? Research suggests that doing so can sometimes be helpful (Hofmann et al., 2006; Miklowitz et al., 2007; Winston, Been, & Serby, 2005). Combined treatment is recommended in cases of bipolar disorder (Miklowitz, 2008; Otto, Smits, & Reese, 2005) and produces slightly better results than either psychotherapy or drugs alone in people suffering from severe, long-term depression (Friedman et al., 2004; Hegerl, Plattner, & Moller, 2004). The combination of medication and psychotherapy has also been shown to be more effective than either method alone in treating attention deficit hyperactivity disorder, obsessive-compulsive disorder, alcoholism, stammering, compulsive sexual behavior, and panic disorder (Barlow, 2007; Keller et al., 2000; March et al., 2004; Roy-Byrne et al., 2005; Walkup et al., 2008). The combined approach may be especially useful for clients who are initially too distressed to benefit much from psychotherapy. A related approach, already shown to be successful with clients who had been taking prescription drugs for panic disorder and depression, is to use psychotherapy to prevent relapse and make further progress as medication is discontinued (e.g., Dobson et al., 2008; Klein et al., 2004; Lam et al., 2003). Preliminary evidence also suggests that a drug called D-cycloserine may be helpful in preventing the reappearance of fears that are being extinguished through exposure techniques or other forms of behavior therapy (Choy, Fyer, & Lipsitz, 2007; Davis, Myers, et al., 2005; Davis et al., 2006; Hofmann et al., 2006; Norberg, Krystal, & Tolin, 2008).

However, many other studies have found little advantage in combining medication and psychotherapy (e.g., Davidson et al., 2004; Elkin, 1994; Nemeroff et al., 2003; Spiegel & Bruce, 1997). One early study compared the effects of a form of in vivo desensitization called *gradual exposure* with that of antianxiety medication (Xanax) in the treatment of agoraphobia. Clients receiving gradual exposure alone showed better short- and long-term benefits than those getting either the drug alone or a combination of the drug and gradual exposure (Echeburua et al., 1993). Other studies, too, have found that combining drugs and psychotherapy may produce surprisingly little added benefit (e.g., Elkin, 1994; Spiegel & Bruce, 1997).

Perhaps the most conservative strategy for treating most cases of anxiety and depression is to begin with cognitive or interpersonal psychotherapy (which have no major negative side effects) and then to add or switch to medication if psychotherapy alone is ineffective (Jacobs et al., 2004; Schatzberg et al., 2005). Often clients who do not respond to one method will be helped by the other (e.g., Heldt et al., 2006). Someday research may offer better guidelines as to which clients should be treated with psychotherapy alone, medication alone, or a combination of the two (Hollon et al., 2005).

LINKAGES

LINKAGES How do psychoactive drugs work? (a link to Biological Aspects of Psychology, p. 68)

Biological Aspects of Psychology and the Treatment of Psychological Disorders

As described in the chapter on biological aspects of psychology, human feelings, thoughts, and actions—whether normal or abnormal—are ultimately the result of biological processes, especially those involving neurotransmitters and their receptors in the brain. Because different neurotransmitters are especially prominent in particular brain regions or circuits, altering the functioning of particular neurotransmitter systems has relatively specific psychological and behavioral effects.

Let's consider some of the ways in which therapeutic psychoactive drugs affect neurotransmitters and their receptors. Some therapeutic drugs cause neurons to fire, while others reduce or inhibit such firing. For example, benzodiazepines (e.g., Valium and Xanax) exert their antianxiety effects by helping the inhibitory neurotransmitter GABA bind to receptors and thus suppress neuron firing. This increased inhibitory effect acts as a sort of braking system that slows the activity of GABA-sensitive neurons involved in the experience of anxiety. However, benzodiazepines also slow the action of all neural systems that use GABA, including those associated with motor activity and mental processing, which are spread throughout the brain. The result is the decreased motor coordination and clouded thinking that appear as the side effects of the benzodiazepines. Research suggests that it may soon be possible to develop drugs that will bind only to certain kinds of GABA receptors and thus greatly reduce these side effects (Gorman, 2005).

Other therapeutic drugs are receptor *antagonists* (see Figure 9.10 in the chapter on consciousness), acting to block the receptor site normally used by a particular neurotransmitter. The phenothiazines, for example, exert their antipsychotic effects by blocking receptors for dopamine, a neurotransmitter that is important for movement, as described in the chapter on biological aspects of psychology. Blocking dopamine seems to normalize the jumbled thinking of many schizophrenia patients, but it can also cause severe disorders—including tardive dyskinesia—in the movement systems that are also controlled by dopamine.

Some psychoactive drugs exert their therapeutic influence by increasing the amount of a neurotransmitter available to act on receptors. This effect usually occurs because the drug slows a process called *reuptake,* by which the neurotransmitter would normally return to the brain cell from which it was released. The tricyclic antidepressants, for example, operate by slowing the reuptake of norepinephrine. Prozac, Anafranil, and some other antidepressant drugs are called *selective serotonin reuptake inhibitors* (*SSRIs*) because they slow the reuptake of serotonin. Others, such as Effexor, slow the reuptake of both serotonin and norepinephrine. These effects are consistent with biological theories suggesting that some cases of depression are traceable to faulty norepinephrine or serotonin systems.

LINKAGES How do drugs help people diagnosed with schizophrenia? (a link to Consciousness" p. 356)

Community Psychology: From Treatment to Prevention

It has long been argued that even if psychologists knew exactly how to treat every psychological problem, there would never be enough mental health professionals to help everyone who is in need (Albee, 1968, 2006). A study by the World Health Organization found, for example, that even individuals with severe mental health problems often do not receive the psychological services they need (Wang et al., 2007). The study also revealed that the treatment situation is especially dire in poorer countries, where only about 11 percent of psychologically troubled individuals receive treatment for their disorders. In high-income countries such as the United States and Belgium, the figure was about 60 percent (see also Gonzalez et al., 2010). Even that percentage is too low, though, and recognition of the treatment access problem helped fuel the rise of **community psychology**, which seeks to treat people in their local communities and work for social changes that can help prevent psychological disorders (Nelson & Prilleltensky, 2004).

One aspect of community psychology, the *community mental health movement,* appeared during the 1960s amid growing concern that patients were not improving (and might be getting worse) after years of confinement in mental hospitals. The idea behind this movement was that these hospitalized patients would be better off if they were allowed to live freely in their communities, where they would receive newly available antipsychotic drugs and other mental health services at a network of community mental health centers. This *deinstitutionalization* process did spare thousands of patients the boredom and isolation of the hospital environment, but the mental health

community psychology An approach to minimizing or preventing psychological disorders through changes in social systems and through community mental health programs.

Community Mental Health Efforts
APPLYING PSYCHOLOGY

Professional and nonprofessional staff members of community mental health centers provide traditional therapy and mental health education, along with walk-in facilities and hotlines for people who are suicidal or in crises because of rape or domestic violence. They also offer day treatment to former mental patients, many of whom are homeless.

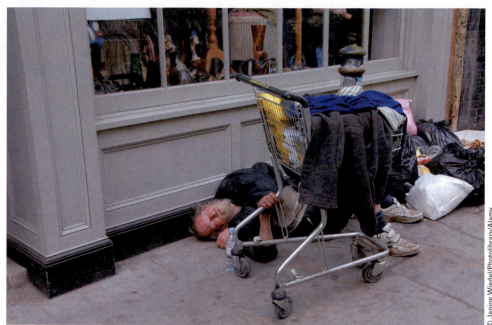

© Janine Wiedel/Photolibrary/Alamy

services available in their communities never expanded enough to meet the needs of so many new clients (Leff, 2006). Some former hospital patients and many people whose disorders might once have sent them to mental hospitals are now living in halfway houses and other community-based facilities where they receive *psychosocial rehabilitation*. These community support services are not designed to "cure" disorders but rather to help people cope with their problems and develop the social and occupational skills necessary for semi-independent living (Coldwell & Bender, 2007; Cook et al., 2005; Talbott, 2004). Many patients with severe psychological disorders who have not received or benefited from rehabilitation services are enduring the dangers of homelessness on city streets or of confinement in jails and prisons (Luhrmann, 2008; Smith & Sederer, 2009; Teplin et al., 2005).

Community psychology also attempts to prevent psychological disorders by addressing poverty, substandard housing, and other stressful social problems that may put vulnerable people at greater risk for some disorders (Fagan et al., 2009; Xue et al., 2005). Researchers in the field of positive psychology applaud this approach, suggesting that the development of many disorders could be further minimized by teaching skills that promote mental well-being and by offering programs designed to help young people build the character strengths they need to be resilient in the face of stress (Keyes, 2007; Seligman, Berkowitz et al., 2005; Wallace & Shapiro, 2006).

Another dimension of community psychology involves efforts to detect psychological problems in their earliest stages and keep those problems from becoming worse (Bond & Hauff, 2004). Examples include programs for the prevention of depression and suicide (Cuijpers et al., 2008; Gillham et al., 2007; Horowitz & Garber, 2006; Lynch et al., 2005; Spence, Sheffield, & Donovan, 2005), programs such as Project Head Start that help preschoolers whose backgrounds put them at risk for school failure and delinquency (Foster et al., 2006; Reid, Webster-Stratton, & Baydar, 2004; Shaw, Dishion, et al., 2006), and programs to identify children who are at risk for disorders due to aggressiveness, parental divorce, or being rejected or victimized at school (e.g., Frey et al., 2005; Lochman & Wells, 2004; Martinez & Forgatch, 2001). Other interventions are designed to head off anxiety disorders or schizophrenia in children and adults (McGorry et al., 2002; Neil & Christensen, 2009; Rapee et al., 2005), to prevent child abuse and other domestic violence (Duggan et al., 2004; Whitaker et al., 2006), and to promote health consciousness in ethnic minority communities (Borg, 2002).

LINKAGES

As noted in the chapter on introducing psychology, all of psychology's many subfields are related to one another. Our discussion of treating psychological disorders through the use of psychoactive drugs illustrates just one way in which the topic of this chapter, the treatment of psychological disorders, is linked to the subfield of biological

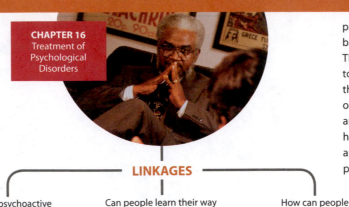

CHAPTER 16
Treatment of Psychological Disorders

LINKAGES

psychology (see the chapter on biological aspects of psychology). The Linkages diagram shows ties to two other subfields as well, and there are many more ties throughout the book. Looking for linkages among subfields will help you see how they all fit together and better appreciate the big picture that is psychology.

How do psychoactive drugs work?
(ans. on p. 689)

Can people learn their way out of a disorder?
(ans. on p. 206)

How can people manage stress?
(ans. on p. 550)

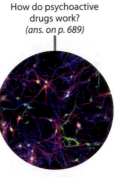

CHAPTER 3
Biological Aspects
of Psychology

CHAPTER 6
Learning

CHAPTER 13
Health, Stress,
and Coping

SUMMARY

Psychotherapy for psychological disorders is usually based on psychodynamic, humanistic, or social-cognitive (behavioral) theories of personality and behavior disorder. Most therapists combine features of these theories in an eclectic approach. The biological approach is reflected in the use of prescription drugs and other physical treatment methods.

Basic Features of Treatment

All forms of treatment for psychological disorders include a client, a therapist, an underlying theory of behavior disorder, a set of treatment procedures suggested by the underlying theory, and the development of a special relationship between the client and therapist, which may make it easier for improvement to occur. Therapy may be offered to inpatients and outpatients in many different settings

by *psychologists, psychiatrists,* and other mental health professionals. The goal of treatment is to help people change their thinking, feelings, and behavior so that they will be happier and function better. This goal may be pursued by promoting insight into hidden causes of behavior problems, by fostering personal growth through genuine self-expression, or by helping clients learn new ways of thinking and acting.

Psychodynamic Psychotherapy

Psychodynamic psychotherapy, which began with Sigmund Freud's methods of *psychoanalysis,* seeks to help clients gain insight into unconscious conflicts and impulses and then to explore how those factors have created disorders.

Classical Psychoanalysis

Exploration of the unconscious is aided by the use of free association,

dream interpretation, and analysis of transference.

Contemporary Variations on Psychoanalysis

Some variations on psychoanalysis focus less on the id, the unconscious, and the past and more on helping clients harness the ego to solve problems in the present. Other forms of psychodynamic treatment retain most of Freud's principles but use a more flexible format. Object relations therapy, for example, examines the effects of early relationships with caregivers and how those relationships affect current ones.

Humanistic Psychotherapy

Humanistic (phenomenological) psychotherapy helps clients become more aware of discrepancies between their feelings and their behavior. According to the humanistic approach, these discrepancies are at the root of behavior disorders and can be resolved by the client once they are brought to light in the context of a genuine, trusting relationship with the therapist.

Client-Centered Therapy

Therapists using Carl Rogers's *client-centered therapy*, also known as *person-centered therapy*, help mainly by adopting attitudes toward the client that express *unconditional positive regard (acceptance)*, *empathy*, and *congruence*. These attitudes create a nonjudgmental atmosphere that facilitates the client's honesty with the therapist, with himself or herself, and with others. One way of creating this atmosphere is through *active listening (reflection)*.

Gestalt Therapy

Therapists employing the *Gestalt therapy* of Fritz and Laura Perls use more active techniques than Rogerian therapists, often confronting and challenging clients.

Behavior Therapy

Behavior therapy, *behavior modification*, and *cognitive behavior therapy* use learning principles to reduce clients' undesirable patterns of thought and behavior and to strengthen more desirable alternatives.

Techniques for Modifying Behavior

Common behavioral treatments include *systematic desensitization therapy*, *flooding* and other *exposure therapy* techniques, *modeling*, *social skills training*, and *assertiveness training*. Behavior therapists also use *positive reinforcement* (sometimes in *token economy programs*), *extinction*, *punishment*, and *aversion conditioning* to make desirable behaviors more likely or problematic behaviors less likely.

Cognitive Behavior Therapy

Many behavior therapists employ cognitive behavior therapy to help clients change the way they think, as well as the way they behave. Among the specific cognitive behavior therapy methods are *rational-emotive behavior therapy (REBT)*, cognitive restructuring, stress inoculation training, and *cognitive therapy*.

Group, Family, and Couples Therapy

Therapists of all theoretical persuasions may offer therapy to several clients at once. Clients' interactions with one another can enhance the effects of treatment.

Group Therapy

Group therapy may involve a variety of people and problems, or it may focus on particular types of clients and problems. The group format is also adopted in many self-help organizations, such as Alcoholics Anonymous.

Family and Couples Therapy

Family therapy involves treatment of two or more individuals from the same family system. In *couples therapy*, the clients are spouses or other intimate partners. In both formats, treatment usually focuses on improving communication and other interactions among the people involved.

Evaluating Psychotherapy

There is some disagreement about exactly how to measure improvement following psychotherapy and how best to ensure that observed improvement was actually due to the treatment itself and not to some other factor. Meta-analyses have found that clients who receive psychotherapy are better off than most people who receive no treatment but that no single approach is uniformly better than all others for all clients and problems. Still, some methods appear effective enough in the treatment of particular disorders to have been listed by an American Psychological Association task force as *empirically supported therapies (ESTs)* that can guide *evidence based practice*.

Research is still needed to discover which combinations of therapists, clients, and treatments are ideally suited to alleviating particular psychological problems. Several factors, including personal preferences, must be considered when choosing a treatment approach and a therapist.

Sociocultural Factors in Psychotherapy

The effects of cultural differences in values and goals between therapist and client have attracted increasing attention. Efforts are under way to minimize the problems that these differences can create.

Rules and Rights in the Therapeutic Relationship

Whatever the specific form of treatment, the client's rights include the right to confidentiality, the right to receive or refuse treatment, and the right to protection from unnecessary confinement.

Biological Treatments

Biological treatment methods seek to relieve psychological disorders by physical rather than psychological means.

Psychosurgery

Psychosurgery procedures once involved mainly prefrontal lobotomy; when used today, usually as a last resort, they focus on more limited areas of the brain.

Electroconvulsive Shock Therapy

In *electroconvulsive shock therapy (EST)*, an electric current is passed through the patient's brain, usually in an effort to relieve severe depression.

Psychoactive Drugs

Today the most prominent form of biological treatment is the prescription of psychoactive drugs, including those used to treat schizophrenia (the *neuroleptic drugs*, or antipsychotics), affective disorders (*antidepressant drugs*, *lithium*, and *anticonvulsants*), and anxiety disorders (*tranquilizing drugs*, or *anxiolytics*). There appear to be significant differences among members of various ethnic groups and between men and women in the dosages of psychoactive drugs necessary to produce beneficial effects.

Evaluating Psychoactive Drug Treatments

Psychoactive drugs have proved impressively effective in many cases, but critics point out a number of undesirable side effects associated with these drugs, the risks of abuse, and the dangers of over-reliance on chemical approaches to human problems that might have other solutions.

Drugs and Psychotherapy

So far, neither psychotherapy nor drug treatment has been found clearly superior overall for treating problems such as anxiety or depression. Combining drugs and psychotherapy may help in some cases, but their joint effect may not be any greater than the effect of either one alone.

Community Psychology: From Treatment to Prevention

The realization that there will never be enough therapists to treat everyone who needs help prompted the development of *community psychology*. Community mental health programs and efforts to prevent mental disorders are the two main elements of community psychology.

LINKAGES TO FURTHER LEARNING

Now that you have finished reading this chapter, how about exploring some of the topics and information that you found most interesting? Here are some places to start.

Books

Peter Wyden, *Conquering Schizophrenia: A Father, His Son, and a Medical Breakthrough* (Knopf, 1998). A father searches for a cure for his son, who was diagnosed with schizophrenia.

Ken Kesey, *One Flew over the Cuckoo's Nest* (New American Library, 1989). The book about life in a mental hospital from which the award-winning movie was adapted.

Michael Winerip, 9 *Highland Road* (Vintage, 1995). The aftermath of deinstitutionalization.

Peter Kramer, *Listening to Prozac* (Penguin, 1997). Psychotropic antidepressant medications.

Raymond J. Corsini and Danny Wedding, *Current Psychotherapies*, 9th ed. (Brooks Cole, 2010) A comparison of numerous approaches to psychotherapy.

Frank Dumont and Raymond J. Corsini (Eds.), *Six Therapists and One Client* (Springer, 2000). Therapists who represent different treatment approaches describe how they would help the same client.

W. S. Appleton, *Prozac and the New Antidepressants: What You Need to Know About Prozac, Zoloft , Paxil, Luvox, Wellbutrin, Effexor, Serzone, Vestra, Celexa, St. John's Wort, and Others*, rev. ed. (Plume Books, 2000). A summary of drug treatment options for depression.

Christina Hoff Summers and Sally Satel, *One Nation Under Therapy: How the Helping Culture Is Eroding Self-Reliance* (St. Martin's Press, 2005). Argues that people have become overly dependent on psychotherapy.

On the Internet

 Access an integrated eBook and chapter-specific learning tools including flashcards, quizzes, videos, and more. Go to CengageBrain.com.

CENGAGENOW Want to maximize the value of your online study time? Take this easy-to-use study system's diagnostic pre-test, and it will create a personalized study plan for you. By helping you identify the topics that you need to understand better and then directing you to valuable online resources, it can speed up your chapter review. CengageNOW even provides a post-test so you can confirm that you are ready for an exam. Go to CengageBrain.com.

TALKING POINTS

Here are a few talking points to help you summarize this chapter for family and friends without giving a lecture.

1. All forms of psychotherapy include a client, a helper, and a special therapeutic relationship.
2. Psychiatrists are medical doctors who specialize in psychological disorders; psychologists who study or treat such disorders usually have Ph.D. degrees in clinical or counseling psychology.
3. Classical Freudian psychoanalysis is no longer the dominant approach to psychotherapy in North America.
4. Many kinds of psychotherapy can be beneficial, but experimental research has shown behavior therapy, cognitive behavior therapy, and interpersonal therapy to be among the most effective forms of treatment for many psychological disorders.
5. When looking for a therapist, people should select one who seems easy to relate to and who has experience with a treatment approach that is known to be effective for their type of problem.
6. With only a few special exceptions, therapists are ethically bound to keep confidential everything that clients tell them.
7. Prescription drugs and psychotherapy are often equally effective in the treatment of many psychological disorders.

17

Social Cognition

© James Marshall/The Image Works

Your view of yourself and what you think about others play major roles in shaping your behavior every day. In this chapter, we explore the ways in which perception, learning, emotion, and other factors affect how people think about themselves and others. We'll consider topics such as how we form first impressions, how we develop attitudes—including prejudiced attitudes—and why we may like (or love) one person and dislike another.

The terrorist attacks of 9/11 killed nearly 3,000 people and had Umar Farouk Abdulmutallab succeeded in detonating the bomb he carried aboard a Northwest Airlines flight on Christmas Day, 2009, hundreds more would have died. Almost all of the questions that can be asked about these attacks, and about the continuing threat of terrorism in general, relate to human behavior. For example, what could lead people to kill themselves, along with untold numbers of innocent people, in the name of political or religious beliefs? Why did so many New York City firefighters, police officers, emergency medical workers, and others enter the World Trade Center's burning towers to save the lives of others while risking and some ultimately losing their own? Why did some of the people who were fleeing the damaged buildings return to their offices after hearing an announcement telling them to do so? Is there any reason to hope that someday the hatred and distrust that fuels terrorism can be reduced or eliminated?

We may never have final answers to such questions, but some partial answers may come from **social psychology**, the scientific study of how people's thoughts and feelings influence their behavior toward others and how the behavior of others influences people's own thoughts, feelings, and behavior. In this chapter, we focus on **social cognition**, the mental processes associated with the ways in which people perceive and react to other individuals and groups (Fiske & Taylor, 2008). Specifically, we will examine how people think about themselves and others, how they form and change attitudes, why and how they use stereotypes to judge other people (sometimes in unfair and biased ways), and why they like or dislike other people. In the companion chapter on *social influence*, we describe how social factors affect individuals, shaping behaviors that range from despicable acts of aggression to inspiring acts of heroism and self-sacrifice.

Social Influences on the Self

In the chapters on human development and personality, we describe how each individual develops within a cultural context and the ways in which collectivist and individualist cultures emphasize different core values and encourage contrasting definitions of the self. In this section, we highlight the processes through which people in each culture help shape two important components of the self. The first is our **self-concept**, the thoughts, feelings, and beliefs we hold about who we are and what characteristics we have. The second is our **self-esteem**, the evaluations we make about how worthy we are as human beings (Crocker et al., 2006).

Social Comparison

People spend a lot of time thinking about themselves, trying to evaluate their own perceptions, opinions, values, and abilities (Epstude & Mussweiler, 2009). Decades ago, Leon Festinger (1954) pointed out that self-evaluation involves two types of questions: those

social psychology The study of how people's thoughts, feelings, and behavior influence and are influenced by the behavior of others.

social cognition Mental processes associated with people's perceptions of and reactions to other people.

self-concept The way one thinks of oneself.

self-esteem The evaluations one makes about how worthy one is as a human being.

that can be answered by taking objective measurements and those that cannot. So you can determine your height or weight by measuring it, but how do you answer questions about your cognitive ability, social skills, athletic talent, or the quality of your relationships? Here there are no yardsticks to act as objective measurement criteria. In these cases, we make one of two types of comparisons. If we use a *temporal comparison*, we consider the way we are now in relation to how we were in the past (Zell & Alicke, 2009). If we use a **social comparison**, we evaluate ourselves in relation to others. So if you use others as a basis for evaluating how intelligent, athletic, interesting, or attractive you are, you are using social comparison (Buunk et al., 2005).

Who serves as your basis of comparison? Festinger said that people usually look to others who are similar to themselves. If you are curious about how good a swimmer you are, you are likely to compare yourself with the people you normally compete against, not with Olympic champions. In other words, you tend to choose swimmers at your own level of experience and ability. The categories of people to which you see yourself belonging and to which you usually compare yourself are called **reference groups**.

The performance of people in a reference group can influence your self-esteem (Chambers & Windschitl, 2009). For example, if being a good swimmer is very important to you, knowing that someone in your reference group swims much faster than you do can lower your self-esteem. People use a wide variety of strategies to protect or maintain their self-esteem (Greenberg, 2008; Leary, 2010). Sometimes they choose to compare themselves with those who are not as good as they are, a strategy called *downward social comparison*. They may also engage in *upward social comparison*, comparing themselves with people who do much better (Johnson & Stapel, 2007). Both kinds of social comparisons can make people feel better about themselves. Downward social comparisons remind them that although their performance or their lives may not be ideal, things could be worse. The comfort provided by such reminders helps explain the popularity of Jerry Springer and other television shows featuring guests who are stuck in unpleasant, dysfunctional, and often bizarre family situations. But sometimes people may feel better after comparing themselves with those who are doing much better than they are (Wheeler & Suls, 2007). This result occurs partly because seeing people who are better off than we are can inspire the belief that "if they can do it, so can I!" (Buunk, Peiró, & Griffioen, 2007). And people's performance often does improve following upward social comparison (Johnson & Stapel, 2007).

Some people use a related tactic to maintain their self-esteem through upward social comparison. Specifically, they tell themselves that a superior performer is not similar enough to be in their reference group. They may even exaggerate the ability of the other person so that their own performance doesn't look so bad when viewed in light of such an able competitor (Mussweiler, 2003). If you can convince yourself that you lost every set in a tennis game because your opponent is almost as good as Roger Federer, Serena Williams, or some other world-class tennis player, then it is easier to believe that your performance wasn't so terrible and that you would do just fine against someone with normal athletic skills.

An unfavorable comparison of your own status with that of others can produce a sense of **relative deprivation**—the belief that no matter how much you are getting in terms of recognition, status, money, and other rewards, it is less than you deserve (Kassin, Fein, & Markus, 2010). The concept of relative deprivation explains why an actor who receives $5 million to star in a film feels slighted if a costar is receiving $10 million. It also explains the far more common situation in which employees become dissatisfied when they consider themselves underpaid or underappreciated in comparison to their coworkers (Harris, Anseel, & Lievens, 2008). When large groups of people experience relative deprivation, political unrest may follow. Social and political turmoil usually begins after the members of a deprived group experience some improvement in their lives and begin to compare their circumstances with those in other groups (de la Sablonnière, Tougas, & Lortie-Lussier, 2009). With this improvement come higher expectations about what they deserve. When these expectations

social comparison Using other people as a basis of comparison for evaluating oneself.

reference groups Categories of people to which people compare themselves.

relative deprivation The belief that, in comparison to a reference group, one is getting less than is deserved.

are not met, violence may follow. It is likely, for example, that resentment over U.S. prosperity and global influence plays a role in creating the hatred that leads some people to engage in terrorist attacks against the United States (Plous & Zimbardo, 2004; Pyszczynski, Rothschild, & Abdollahi, 2008).

FOCUS ON RESEARCH METHODS ▶

Self-Esteem and the Ultimate Terror

Why is self-esteem so important to so many people? An intriguing answer to this question comes from the *terror management theory* proposed by Jeff Greenberg, Tom Pyszczynski, and Sheldon Solomon. This theory is based on the notion that humans are the only creatures capable of thinking about the future. One result of this ability is the realization that we will all eventually die and the sense of terror it may bring. We can't change this reality, but terror management theory suggests that humans cope with anxiety about death by developing a variety of self-protective psychological strategies, including efforts to establish and maintain high self-esteem (Greenberg, Solomon, & Arndt, 2008; Pyszczynski et al., 2010).

What was the researchers' question?
In one series of experiments, Greenberg and his colleagues (1992) asked whether high self-esteem would in fact serve as a buffer against anxiety—specifically, the anxiety brought on by thoughts about death and pain.

Protecting Self-Esteem?

According to terror management theory, having high self-esteem protects us from anxiety about death. So when disasters or other events remind people of their mortality, they are likely to raise their self-esteem by engaging in prosocial behavior, such as volunteering or donating blood. Most research on terror management theory has been done in individualist cultures such as North America, where self-esteem is largely based on personal accomplishments. However, the theory has also been supported by preliminary studies in China, Japan, Aboriginal Australia, and other collectivist cultures where feelings of self-worth tend to be more closely tied to membership in family and work groups (Halloran & Kashima, 2004; Heine, Harihara, & Niiya, 2002; Tam, Chiu, & Lau, 2007; Wakimoto, 2006).

How did the researchers answer the question?
About 150 students at several North American universities participated in these studies, each of which followed a similar format. The first step in each experiment was to manipulate the independent variable—in this case, the participants' self-esteem. To do this, the researchers gave the students feedback on a test they had taken earlier in the semester. Half the participants received esteem-building feedback, such as that their scores indicated high intelligence or a stable personality. The other half received feedback that was neutral (i.e., neither flattering nor unflattering). Next, the students' self-esteem was measured, and these measures showed that the positive feedback actually did produce higher self-esteem than the neutral feedback. In the third phase of each experiment, the researchers manipulated a second independent variable by causing some anxiety in half of the participants in each of the two feedback groups. In one study, anxiety was created by showing some students a film containing pictures of dead people and discussions of death. The others saw a film that did not arouse emotion. In two other experiments, anxiety was created by leading some of the participants to believe (falsely) that they would be receiving a mild electrical shock. Afterward, the participants' anxiety was measured by their self-reports or by monitoring galvanic skin resistance (GSR), an anxiety-related measure of perspiration.

What did the researchers find?
Self-reports or GSR measures revealed that participants in all three experiments were significantly less upset by an anxiety-provoking experience (the death film or the threat of shock) if they had first received esteem-building feedback about their earlier test performance. Other, more recent studies have reported similar findings (Schmeichel et al., 2009).

What do the results mean?
The researchers concluded that these results offer support for terror management theory, and specifically for the notion that self-esteem is important as a buffer against anxiety and other negative feelings. The results may help explain why the maintenance of self-esteem is such a powerful human motive (Leary, 2010). People do not like to feel anxious, and increased self-esteem reduces most people's anxiety.

What do we still need to know?

Further research by Greenberg and his associates, as well as by others, has provided additional support for terror management theory. For instance, the theory predicts that when people are sensitized to the threat of death, they will seek to protect themselves by suppressing thoughts of death and also by doing things that increase the approval and support of others in the society in which they live. This prediction was borne out by the dramatic increases in volunteering for charity work that were seen following the terrorist attacks of 9/11 (Penner, Brannick, et al., 2005). But not everyone reacts with prosocial behavior when sensitized to the threat of death. The greatest increase in prosocial behavior following reminders about death appears in people who value prosocial behavior (Joireman & Durell, 2007). In other people, those same reminders may be followed by a *reduction* in humanitarian concerns (Hirschberger, 2009). Social psychologists would like to know more about how people's values and personality characteristics are related to the strategies they adopt when dealing with the threat of death.

Researchers also wonder whether terror management theory offers the best explanation of why high self-esteem reduces anxiety. Perhaps people value self-esteem not because it makes them less afraid of death but simply because it is a flattering indicator (a sort of "sociometer") of their acceptance by others (Leary, 2010). According to sociometer theory, people want to have high self-esteem because it tells them that they are liked and accepted. Perhaps the goal of acceptance evolved because people who were excluded from the protective circle of their group were not likely to survive to reproduce. Compared with terror management theory, sociometer theory is certainly a simpler and more plausible explanation of the desire for high self-esteem, but is it the best explanation? Both theories make similar predictions about the effects of self-esteem on anxiety, so it will take additional research to evaluate their relative merits. ◀

Social Identity Theory

TRY THIS Stop reading for a moment, and fill in the blank in the following sentence: "I am a(n) ___."

Some people complete the sentence by using characteristics such as "hard worker," "good sport," or some other aspect of their *personal* identity. However, many others identify themselves by using a word or phrase that reflects their nationality, gender, or religion (e.g., Lee & Yoo, 2004). These responses reflect **social identity**, our beliefs about the groups to which we belong. Our social identity is thus part of our self-concept (Abrams & Hogg, 2010).

All in the Family

Many people find that their place in their family is a central aspect of their social identity. For others, their role in a political, religious, cultural, or business organization may be most vital to that identity. Whatever the specifics, social identity is an important part of people's self-concept, or view of themselves.

© Bob Daemmrich/The Image Works

social identity The beliefs we hold about the groups to which we belong.

Our social, or group, identity permits us to feel part of a larger whole (Bryant & Cummins, 2010). Its importance is seen in the pride that people feel when a member of their family graduates from college or when a local team wins a big game. In wars between national, ethnic, or religious groups, individuals make sacrifices and even die for the sake of their group identity. A group identity is also one reason people donate money to the needy, support friends in a crisis, and offer other forms of assistance to those with whom they can identify. We will see later, though, that defining ourselves in terms of a group identity can create an "us versus them" mentality that sets the stage for prejudice, discrimination, intergroup conflict, and even terrorism (Abrams & Hogg, 2010).

Social Perception

There is a story about a company president who was having lunch with a man being considered for an executive position. When the man salted his food without first tasting it, the president decided not to hire him. The reason, she explained, was that the company had no room for a person who acted before collecting all relevant information. The candidate lost his chance because of **social perception**, the process through which people interpret information about others, form impressions of them, and draw conclusions about the reasons for their behavior. In this section, we examine how and why social perception influences our thoughts, feelings, and actions.

The Role of Schemas

TRY THIS

In the chapter on perception, we describe a number of Gestalt principles that govern how we organize visual information. For example, what do you see in Figure 17.1? The figure matches what you already know about squares (that they have four equal sides), so your *schema,* or mental representation of this knowledge, probably guided you toward the simplest perception, that it is a square with a notch in it. You could also have described the diagram as a shape formed of eight straight lines, but that would have been far more complicated.

Our perceptions of people follow many of the same laws that govern the perception of objects (Macrae & Quadflieg, 2010). As a result, our prior knowledge, our schemas, about people can have a significant influence on our perceptions of them. First of all, schemas influence what we pay attention to and what we ignore. Characteristics or events that are consistent with our schema about another person usually get more attention than those that are inconsistent with that schema. As a result, we tend to process information about the other person more quickly if it confirms our beliefs about, say, that person's gender or ethnic group than if it violates those beliefs (Smith & Quellar, 2001). Second, schemas influence what we remember about others (Macrae et al., 2002). One classic study demonstrated that if people thought a woman they saw in a video was a waitress, they later recalled that she had a beer with dinner and owned a TV set. If they thought she was a librarian, they remembered that she was wearing glasses and liked classical music (Cohen, 1981). Finally, schemas affect our judgment about other people's behavior. For example, Thomas Hill and his colleagues (1989) found that participants' ratings of male and female friends' sadness were influenced not only by the friends' actual behavior but also by the participants' general schemas about whether men or women experience more sadness.

In other words, through "top-down" processing, schemas can influence—and sometimes bias—person perception in the same way that schemas about objects can affect object perception. And just as schemas help us read sentences in which words have missing letters, they also allow us to "fill in the blanks" about people. So we don't usually ask our doctors or bus drivers to show us their credentials. Our schemas about these people lead us to perceive them as competent, confident, skilled, and experienced. And usually these perceptions are correct. It is only when our expectations are violated that we realize that schemas can lead to errors in our judgment about other people.

FIGURE 17.1

A Schema-Plus-Correction

 Describe this diagram in a single sentence beginning with "This is . . ."; then read our discussion of the figure in the text.

social perception The processes through which people interpret information about others, draw inferences about them, and develop mental representations of them.

May I Help You?

TRY THIS Schemas help us categorize people quickly and respond to them appropriately, but schemas can also lead to narrow-mindedness and even prejudice. If this woman does not fulfill your schema—your mental representation—of how carpenters are supposed to look, you might be less likely to ask her advice on your home improvement project. One expert carpenter who manages the hardware department of a large home improvement store told us that most customers walk right past her in order to ask the advice of one of her less experienced male clerks. Are there people you know whose appearance, behavior, or other characteristics don't fit the schemas that most people hold for persons of their age or in their occupation?

© Michael Newman/PhotoEdit

First Impressions

The schemas we have about people in general act as lenses that shape our first impressions of others. Those impressions in turn influence both our perceptions of their behaviors and our reactions to those behaviors. First impressions are formed quickly, usually change slowly, and typically have a long-lasting influence. No wonder first impressions are so important in the development of social relations. How do people form impressions of other people? And why are they so resistant to change?

TRY THIS **Forming Impressions** Think about your first impression of a close friend. It probably formed rapidly because, as mentioned earlier, existing schemas lead us to infer a great deal about a person on the basis of limited information. One study found that people could make judgments about how trustworthy and competent a person was after seeing that person's face for only a tenth of a second (Willis & Todorov, 2006). Other attributes, such as an ethnic name, may have caused you to draw inferences about your friend's religion, food preferences, or temperament. Clothing or hairstyle may have led you to make assumptions about your friend's political views or taste in music. How many of those assumptions turned out to be true in your friend's case? Perhaps not all of them, but probably quite a few. First impression judgments become much more accurate after as little as one minute of exposure to a new person (Carney, Colvin, & Hall, 2007), and they are not influenced by appearance alone. For example, people are able to make quite accurate judgments about another person's family income and other aspects of socioeconomic status just by watching a "thin slice" of gestures and other nonverbal behavior in a one-minute video of the person in conversation (Kraus & Keltner, 2009).

Noticeable features or actions shape our impressions of others. Those impressions may or may not be correct.

DILBERT: © Scott Adams/Dist. by United Feature Syndicate, Inc.

One schema has a particularly strong influence on our first impressions: We tend to assume that people we meet will have attitudes and values similar to our own (Hoyle, 1993; Srivastava, Guglielmo, & Beer, 2010). So all else being equal, we are inclined to like other people. However, it doesn't take much negative information to change our minds. The main reason for this is that most of us don't expect other people to act negatively toward us. When unexpectedly negative behaviors do occur, they capture our attention and lead us to believe that these behaviors reflect something negative about the other person (Taylor, Peplau, & Sears, 2006). For example, we know that there are many reasons why people might be nice to us—because they are kind, because they like our friends, or because they want to sell us a car. But if they do something negative—such as insult us or steal our lecture notes—the most likely explanation is that they are unfriendly or have other undesirable personality traits. In other words, negative behavior carries more weight than positive behavior in shaping first impressions (Lount et al., 2008).

Lasting Impressions   Does your friend seem the same today as when you first met? First impressions can change, but the process is usually slow. One reason is that negative first impressions may cause us to avoid certain people, thus reducing our exposure to new information that might change our view of them (Denrell, 2005). Further, most people want to keep their social environment simple and easy to understand (Kenrick, Neuberg, & Cialdini, 2010). We cling to our beliefs about the world, often using our schemas to preserve a reality that fits our expectations. Holding on to existing impressions appears to be part of this effort. If your friend has recently said or done something that violates your expectations, your view of her probably did not change much, if at all. In fact, you may have acted to preserve your impression by thinking something like, "She's just not herself today." In other words, impressions are slow to change because the meaning we give to new information about people is shaped by what we already know or believe about them (Kenrick, Neuberg, & Cialdini, 2010).

Self-Fulfilling Prophecies   Another reason first impressions tend to be stable is that we often do things that cause others to confirm our impressions (Madon et al., 2004). If teachers expect particular students to do poorly in mathematics, those students may sense this expectation, exert less effort, and perform below their ability level. Similarly, if mothers expect their young children to eventually abuse alcohol, those children are more likely to do so than the children of mothers who didn't convey that expectation (Madon et al., 2006). When, without our awareness, schemas cause us to

Self-Fulfilling Prophecies in the Classroom

If teachers inadvertently spend less time helping children who impressed them as "dull," those children may not learn as much, thus fulfilling the teachers' expectations. If the girl at the far right has not impressed her teacher as being bright, how likely do you think it is that she will be called on?

subtly lead people to behave in line with our expectations, a **self-fulfilling prophecy** is at work. In one experiment on self-fulfilling prophecies, some people were led to believe that a person they were about to meet would be friendly and accepting; others were led to believe that the person would reject them. Those who expected acceptance behaved in a much warmer, friendlier way, which made it much more likely that their new acquaintance actually *did* accept them (Stinson et al., 2009).

Self-fulfilling prophecies also help maintain judgments about groups. If you assume that members of a certain ethnic group are unfriendly, for example, you might be defensive or even hostile when you meet a member of that group. If the person reacts to your behavior with hostility, your prophesy would be fulfilled, and you would have an even stronger impression that "all those people" are unfriendly (Kenrick, Neuberg, & Cialdini, 2010).

Explaining Behavior: Attribution

So far, we have considered how people form impressions about the characteristics of other people. But our perceptions of others include another key element: explanations of their behavior. People tend to form *implicit theories* about why people (including themselves) behave as they do and about what behavior to expect in the future. Psychologists use the term **attribution** to describe the process we go through to explain the causes of behavior (including our own).

Suppose that a classmate fails to return some borrowed notes on time. You could attribute this behavior to many causes, from an unavoidable emergency to simple self-ishness. Which of these alternatives you choose is important because it will help you *understand* your classmate's behavior, *predict* what will happen if this person asks to borrow something in the future, and decide how to *control* the situation should it arise again. Similarly, your decision to stick with a troubled relationship or end it may be influenced by whether you attribute your partner's recent indifference to stressful circumstances or a loss of love.

People tend to attribute behavior in a particular situation to either internal causes (characteristics of the person) or external causes (characteristics of the situation). If you thought your classmate's failure to return your notes was due to lack of consideration or laziness, you would be making an *internal attribution*. If you thought that the oversight was caused by time pressure or a family crisis, you would be making an *external attribution*. And if you failed an exam, you could explain it by concluding either that you're not very smart (internal attribution) or that your job or family responsibilities didn't leave you enough time to study (external attribution). The attribution that you make may in turn determine how much you study for the next exam or even whether you decide to stay in school.

Sources of Attributions   Harold Kelley (1973) proposed an influential theory of how people (whom Kelley called *observers*) make attributions about the actions of other people (whom Kelley called *actors*). To illustrate this theory, suppose that you are at your parents' house for the weekend. You want to invite your friend Ralph to come for dinner, but your father says no. According to Kelley, understanding the reasons for your father's behavior requires information about three key variables: consensus, consistency, and distinctiveness:

1. *Consensus* is the degree to which other people's behavior is similar to that of the actor—in this case, your father. If everyone you know avoids Ralph, your father's behavior has a high degree of consensus, and you would attribute his reaction to an external cause (probably something about Ralph). However, if everyone except your father likes Ralph, your father's negative response would have low consensus. In that case, you would probably attribute the response to something about your father, such as rudeness or having a personal dislike for Ralph.

2. *Consistency* is the degree to which the behavior is the same across time or situations. If your father has invited Ralph to dinner several times in the past but rejects him this time, the consistency of his behavior is low. Low consistency

self-fulfilling prophecy A process through which our expectations about another person cause us to act in ways that lead the person to behave as we expected.

attribution The process of explaining the causes of people's behavior, including our own.

suggests that your father's behavior is attributable to external causes, such as conflicts at work that have left your father feeling unsociable. If your father's behavior toward Ralph is always hostile, it has high consistency. But is your father's consistent behavior attributable to an internal cause (his consistent rudeness) or to an external cause (consistent conflicts at work)? This question is difficult to answer without information about distinctiveness.

3. *Distinctiveness* concerns the extent to which the actor's response to one situation stands out from responses to similar situations. If your father is nasty to all your friends, his behavior toward Ralph has low distinctiveness. Behavior that is low in distinctiveness is usually attributable to internal causes, such as personality traits. However, if your dad gets along with everyone except Ralph, his behavior has high distinctiveness, and your attribution about the cause of his behavior is likely to shift toward a cause other than your father's personality, such as how Ralph acts.

In summary, Kelley's theory suggests that people are most likely to make internal attributions about an actor's behavior when there is low consensus, high consistency, and low distinctiveness. If you observe your boss insulting customers (a situation of low consensus, inasmuch as most people in business are polite to customers) every day (high consistency) no matter who the customers are (low distinctiveness), you would probably attribute this behavior to the boss's personality rather than to the customers' unreasonable demands or some other external cause. But if you saw the boss on just one day (low consistency) being rude (low consensus) to one particular customer (high distinctiveness), you would probably attribute the incident to the customer's behavior, an external factor.

Culture and Attribution   Most theories of causal attribution were developed by North American psychologists who assumed that people all over the world use the same kinds of information to make similar kinds of attributions. However, there is substantial evidence to suggest that this may not be true (Nisbett & Masuda, 2006; Savani et al., 2010). For example, when people in the United States are asked to explain why someone has acted in a certain way, they are more likely than people from many other cultures to make internal attributions. That is, they tend to attribute the person's behavior to personality characteristics such as greed or generosity rather than to external, situational factors such as unemployment or a sudden inheritance. Attributional tendencies can even differ between subgroups within the same culture. In one study, U.S. college students from working-class backgrounds were more likely than those from middle-class backgrounds to use internal attributions when explaining the

Why Are They Helping?

Helping occurs all around the world, but research shows that people's attributions, or explanations, about why it happens can differ from culture to culture.

© Bob Daemmrich/The Image Works

Attributional Bias

Men whose thinking is colored by the ultimate attribution error might assume that women who succeed at tasks associated with traditional male roles are just lucky but that men succeed at those tasks because of their skill (Deaux & LaFrance, 1998). When this attributional bias is in operation, people who are perceived as belonging to an outgroup, whether on the basis of their sex, age, sexual orientation, religion, ethnicity, or other characteristics, may be denied fair evaluations and equal opportunities.

fundamental attribution error A bias toward overattributing the behavior of others to internal causes.

outgroup Those whom we perceive as being different from ourselves.

ingroup Those whom we perceive as being similar to ourselves.

actor-observer effect The tendency to attribute other people's behavior to internal causes while attributing our own behavior (especially errors and failures) to external causes.

behavior of another person (Bowman, Kitayama & Nisbett, 2009). Cross-cultural differences in attribution and other aspects of social cognition may explain why people in different cultures and even different subcultures sometimes have so much difficulty understanding one another.

Errors in Attribution

Whatever their background, most people are usually logical in their attempts to explain behavior (Kenrick, Neuberg, & Cialdini, 2010). However, they are also sometimes prone to *attributional errors* that can distort their views of behavior (Baumeister & Bushman, 2008).

The Fundamental Attribution Error   North American psychologists have paid special attention to the **fundamental attribution error**, a tendency to overattribute the behavior of others to internal factors, such as personality traits (Fiske & Taylor, 2008). Imagine that you hear a student give an incorrect answer in class. You will probably attribute this behavior to an internal cause and assume that the person is not very smart. In doing so, however, you might be failing to consider the possible influence of various external causes, such as lack of study time.

A related form of cognitive bias is called the *ultimate attribution error.* When members of a social or ethnic **outgroup** (people we see as "different") do something positive, we attribute their behavior to luck or some other external cause. But we attribute their negative behavior to an internal cause, such as dishonesty (Pettigrew, 1979). At the same time, when members of an **ingroup** (people we see as being like ourselves) do good deeds, we attribute the behavior to integrity or other internal factors. If they do something bad, we attribute it to some external cause. Because of the ultimate attribution error, members of the outgroup receive little credit for their positive actions, and members of the ingroup get little blame for their negative actions (Khan & Liu, 2008). Biases such as the ultimate attribution error help maintain people's negative views of outgroups and positive views of their own ingroup (Fiske, 1998).

Like other aspects of social cognition, the fundamental attribution error may not be universal (Miyamoto & Kitayama, 2002). Researchers have found, for example, that people in collectivist cultures such as India, China, Japan, and Korea are less likely than those in the individualist cultures of North America and Europe to attribute people's behavior to internal causes. Instead, these people tend to see behavior as due less to individual characteristics and more to the situations or contexts in which the person is immersed (Heine & Buchtel, 2009).

Researchers have also pointed out that attributing behavior to internal causes may not always be an error. Sometimes an internal attribution may simply be the most reasonable attribution to make, given the information available (Sabini, Siepmann, & Stein, 2001). Further, David Funder has argued that in many situations, personality characteristics and other internal factors are indeed the true causes of behavior (Funder & Fast, 2010). In other words, according to Funder, social perception is much more accurate than many psychologists have previously recognized.

Other Attributional Errors   The inclination toward internal attributions is much less pronounced when people explain their own behavior. In fact, people tend to show the **actor-observer effect**. Whereas people often attribute other people's behavior to internal causes, they tend to attribute their own behavior to external factors, especially when the behavior is inappropriate or inadequate. For example, when Australian students were asked why they sometimes drive too fast, they focused on circumstances such as being late but saw other people's dangerous driving as a sign of aggressiveness or immaturity (Harré, Brandt, & Houkamau, 2004). Similarly, when you drive slowly, it's because you are looking for an address or for some other good reason, not because you're a dimwitted loser like that jerk who crawled along in front of you yesterday.

The actor-observer effect occurs mainly because people have different kinds of information about their own behavior and about the behavior of others. When *you* are acting in a situation—giving a speech, perhaps—the information that is most available to you is likely to be external and situational, such as the temperature of the room and the size of the audience. You also have a lot of information about other external factors, such as the amount of time you had to prepare your talk or the upsetting argument that occurred this morning. If your speech is disorganized and boring, you can easily attribute it to one or all of these external causes. But when you observe someone else, the most noticeable stimulus in the situation is *that person*. You do not know what happened to the person last night or this morning, so you are likely to attribute whatever he or she does to enduring internal characteristics (Moskowitz, 2005).

Of course, people do not always attribute their own behavior to external forces. In fact, the degree to which they do so depends on whether the outcome of their behavior is positive or negative. In one study, when people were asked what they saw as the cause of their good and bad experiences when shopping online, they tended to take personal credit for positive outcomes but to blame the computer for the negative ones (Moon, 2003). In other words, these people showed a **self-serving bias**, the tendency to take personal credit for success but to blame external causes for failure. This tendency has been found in almost all cultures, but as with the fundamental attribution error, it is usually more pronounced among people from individualist Western cultures than among those from collectivist Eastern cultures (Mezulis et al., 2004).

The Self-Protective Functions of Social Cognition

The self-serving bias occurs partly because, as we mentioned earlier, people are motivated to maintain their self-esteem—and ignoring negative information is one way to do so. If you just failed an exam, it is painful to admit that your grade was fair, so you might blame your performance on an unreasonably demanding instructor. Other forms of social cognition also help people think about their failures and shortcomings in ways that protect their self-esteem (Shepperd, Malone, & Sweeny, 2008).

One example is *unrealistic optimism,* the tendency to believe that positive events (such as financial success or having a gifted child) are more likely to happen to yourself than to others and that negative events (such as being in an accident or having cancer) are more likely to happen to others than to yourself (Lin & Raghubir, 2005). This self-protective bias can reduce anxiety and blunt the impact of stress for a while. Notice, though, that we are not referring to the optimistic (but realistic) perspective on life that is associated with good physical and mental health (see the chapter on health, stress, and coping). Quite the opposite. *Unrealistic* optimism tends to persist even when there is strong evidence against it and can lead people to engage in potentially harmful behaviors. Unrealistically optimistic smokers underestimate their chances of getting lung cancer and are also less likely than others to believe that smoking causes lung cancer or that quitting can lower their risk (Dillard, McCaul, & Klein, 2006). Similarly, college students who are unrealistically optimistic about the risks of excessive drinking are more likely to have alcohol-related problems than those who hold more realistic views (Dillard, Midboe, & Klein, 2009). And many injuries and deaths are suffered each year by people who felt sure that they were immune to the dangers of driving after drinking or riding a motorcycle without a helmet.

Like the defense mechanisms described in the personality chapter, self-protective cognitive biases can help us temporarily escape from unpleasant thoughts and feelings. But as in the case of unrealistic optimism, these biases also set the stage for a somewhat distorted view of reality and can cause problems in the long run. ("In Review: Some Biases in Social Perception" summarizes our discussion of these biases).

self-serving bias The tendency to attribute our successes to internal characteristics while blaming our failures on external causes.

IN REVIEW	Some Biases in Social Perception
Bias	**Description**
Importance of first impression	Ambiguous information is interpreted in line with a first impression, and the initial schema is recalled better and more vividly than any later correction to it. Actions based on this impression may elicit behavior that confirms it.
Fundamental attribution error	The tendency to attribute the behavior of others to internal factors.
Actor-observer effect	The tendency to attribute our own behavior to external causes while attributing the behavior of others to internal factors.
Self-serving bias	The tendency to attribute one's successes to internal factors and one's failures to external factors.
Unrealistic optimism	The tendency of people to believe that good things will happen to them but that bad things will not.

1. The fundamental attribution error appears to be somewhat less likely to occur among people in _____ cultures.

2. First impressions form _____ but change _____.

3. If you believed that immigrants' successes are due to government help but that their failures are due to laziness, you would be committing the _____ error.

Attitudes

People's views about health or safety reflect their *attitudes,* an aspect of social cognition that social psychologists have studied longer and more intensely than any other. An **attitude** is the tendency to think, feel, or act positively or negatively toward objects in our environment (Banaji & Heiphetz, 2010). Attitudes play an important role in guiding how we act toward other people, what political causes we support, which products we buy, and countless other daily decisions.

The Structure of Attitudes

Social psychologists have long viewed attitudes as having three components (Banaji & Heiphetz, 2010). The *cognitive* component is a set of beliefs about the attitude object. The emotional, or *affective,* component includes feelings about the object. The *behavioral* component is the way people act toward the object. If these components were always in harmony, we would be able to predict people's behavior toward the homeless, for example, on the basis of the thoughts or feelings they express. This is often not the case, however (Bohner & Schwarz, 2001). Many people's positive thoughts and supportive emotions regarding homeless people are never translated into actions aimed at helping them.

What determines whether people's behavior will be consistent with the cognitive and affective components of their attitudes? Several factors are important. For one thing, behavior is more likely to be consistent with attitude when people see the attitude as important and relevant to their lives (Kenrick, Neuberg, & Cialdini, 2010). Second, consistency is more likely when the behavioral component of the attitude is in line with a *subjective norm,* our view of how important people in our lives want us to act. Conflict between attitudes and subjective norms may cause us to behave in ways that are inconsistent with our attitudes (Ajzen & Gilbert-Cote, 2008). For example, someone who believes that the rights of gay men and lesbians should be protected might not campaign for this cause because doing so would upset family members or friends who are against it. Third, attitude-consistent behavior is more likely when people have *perceived control,* the belief that they can actually perform such behavior (Fishbein & Ajzen, 2010). The cognitive and

attitude A predisposition toward a particular cognitive, emotional, or behavioral reaction to objects.

A Reminder About Poverty

TRY THIS Photographs such as this one are used by fundraising organizations to remind us of the kind thoughts and charitable feelings we have toward needy people and other social causes. As a result, we may be more likely to behave in accordance with the cognitive and affective components of our attitudes and make a donation to these causes. Browse through some newspapers, magazines, and Web sites, and calculate the percentage of such photos you find in ads for charitable organizations.

© thefinalmiracle/Shutterstock

affective components of your attitude about the homeless may be positive, but if you don't believe you can do anything about homelessness, you are not likely to even try. Fourth, *direct experience* with the attitude object increases the likelihood of attitude-consistent behavior (Glasman & Albarracín, 2006). This is because attitudes based on direct experiences are more stable and memorable and thus more likely to come into play when the attitude object is present. Accordingly, you might be more likely to actively support and perhaps even participate in efforts to help the homeless if you have come to know a homeless person on your campus than if you have only read about their plight.

The importance of direct experience in creating consistency among attitude components reflects the cognitive network theories described in the chapters on learning and memory. According to these theories, attitudes are stored in long-term memory as networks of cognitions—interconnected evaluations and beliefs about attitude objects (Yan & Tourangeau, 2007). When you encounter an attitude object, the cognitions associated with it in your cognitive network are activated. If your thoughts and feelings are well defined and come easily to mind, your behavior is likely to be consistent with them. If not, there may be less consistency (Glasman & Albarracín, 2006).

Forming Attitudes

People are not born with specific attitudes toward specific objects, but their attitudes about new objects begin to appear in early childhood and continue to emerge throughout life. How do attitudes form? Some of the variation we see in people's attitudes may reflect genetic influences inherited from their parents (Albarracín & Vargas, 2010), but what they *learn* from their parents and others appears to play the major role in attitude formation. In childhood, modeling and other forms of social learning are especially important. Children learn not only the names of objects but also what to believe and feel about them and how to act toward them. For example, a parent may teach a child not only that snakes are reptiles but also that they should be feared and avoided. So as children learn concepts such as "reptile" or "work," they learn attitudes about those concepts, too.

Attitudes can also be influenced by classical and operant conditioning. In one study demonstrating this process, certain cartoon characters were associated with positive words (e.g., *excellent*) and images (e.g., an ice-cream sundae) and others were associated with negative words and images (Olson & Fazio, 2001). Afterward, participants in this study liked the characters associated with the positive stimuli much more than those associated with the negative ones. No wonder so many advertisers present

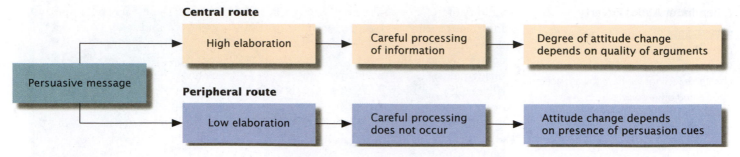

FIGURE 17.2

The Elaboration Likelihood Model of Attitude Change

TRY THIS The central route to attitude change involves carefully processing and evaluating the content of a message (high elaboration). The peripheral route involves low elaboration, or processing, of the message and relying on persuasion cues such as the attractiveness of the person making the argument (Cacioppo, Petty, & Crites, 1993). Jot down two examples of TV commercials that attempt to activate the central route and two others that try to activate the peripheral route. Which kind was easier to bring to mind? If it was the latter, what does that say about how advertisers hope to persuade you to buy their products?

enjoyable music or attractive images in association with the products they are trying to sell (Walther & Langer, 2008). As for operant conditioning, parents, teachers, and peers actively shape children's attitudes by rewarding the children for stating particular views. The *mere-exposure effect* is influential as well: All else being equal, attitudes toward an object will become more positive the more frequently people are exposed to it (Winkielman & Cacioppo, 2004). The mere-exposure effect helps explain why we sometimes come to like a song only after hearing it several times—and why we may come to like products and candidates only after being repeatedly exposed to commercials and political ads. One study showed, for example, that European American college students showed an increased liking for photos of Asian Americans and African Americans after previously seeing many photos of people from these groups (Zebrowitz, White, & Wieneke, 2008).

Changing Attitudes

Although mere exposure can help to form new attitudes, it is not very effective at changing existing ones (Crano & Prislin, 2006). If you are already strongly against requiring motorcyclists to wear helmets, for example, that attitude is unlikely to change much no matter how often you see riders wearing helmets. Changing attitudes usually requires more active efforts, mainly in the form of persuasive messages. The nearly $100 billion a year spent on advertising in the United States alone provides just one example of how people are constantly trying to change our attitudes. Stop for a moment and make a list of

TRY THIS other examples, perhaps starting with the messages of groups concerned with abortion or recycling—and don't forget your friends who want you to think the way they do.

Two Routes to Attitude Change   Whether a persuasive message succeeds in changing attitudes depends primarily on three factors: (1) the person communicating the message, (2) the content of the message, and (3) the audience who receives it (Albarracín & Vargas, 2010). The **elaboration likelihood model** of attitude change provides a framework for understanding when and how these factors affect attitudes (Petty & Briñol, 2008). As shown in Figure 17.2, the model is based on the notion that persuasive messages can change people's attitudes through one of two main routes.

The first is called the *peripheral route* because when it is activated, we devote little attention to the central content of the persuasive message. Instead, we tend to be affected by the *persuasion cues* that surround it, such as the confidence, attractiveness, or other characteristics of the person delivering the message. Persuasion cues influence attitude change even though they say nothing about the logic or validity of the message content. Commercials in which movie stars or other attractive nonexperts praise pain relievers or hearing aids or political candidates are designed to operate via the peripheral route to attitude change.

By contrast, when the *central route* to attitude change is activated, the content of the message becomes more important than the characteristics of the communicator in determining attitude change. A person following the central route uses logical steps—such as those outlined in the Thinking Critically sections of this book—to rationally analyze the content of the persuasive message. This analysis considers the

elaboration likelihood model   A model suggesting that attitude change can be driven by evaluation of the content of a persuasive message (central route) or by irrelevant persuasion cues (peripheral route).

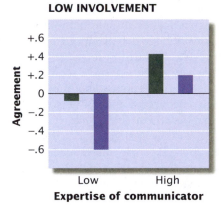

LOW INVOLVEMENT

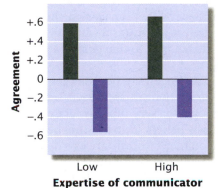

HIGH INVOLVEMENT

■ Strong arguments ■ Weak arguments

FIGURE 17.3

Personal Involvement and Routes to Attitude Change

In the study represented here, students' reactions to messages supporting exit exams for seniors depended on whether they thought the policy would begin immediately (high involvement) or only after they had graduated (low involvement). In the low-involvement condition, students followed a peripheral route to attitude change, agreeing with messages from expert communicators regardless of how logical they were. More involved students followed a central route, changing their minds only if the message contained a strong, logical argument.

Sources: Data from Petty, Cacioppo, & Goldman (1981); Petty, Cacioppo, & Schumann (1983).

cognitive dissonance theory A theory asserting that attitude change is driven by efforts to reduce tension caused by inconsistencies between attitudes and behaviors.

validity of the message's claims, determines whether the message leaves out important information, assesses alternative interpretations of evidence, and so on.

What determines which route people will follow? Personal involvement with the content of the message is one important factor. The elaboration likelihood model proposes that the more personally involving a topic is, the more likely it is that the central route will be activated (Bohner, Erb, & Siebler, 2008). Suppose, for example, that you heard someone arguing for the elimination of student loans in Brazil. This message might persuade you via the peripheral route if it came from someone who looked attractive and sounded intelligent. However, you would be more likely to follow the central route if the message proposed doing away with student loans at your own school. You might be persuaded, but only if the logic of the message was undeniable (see Figure 17.3). This is why celebrity endorsements tend to be most effective when the products being advertised are relatively unimportant to the audience.

"Cognitive busyness" is another factor affecting which attitude change route is activated. If you are busy thinking about other things while a message is being delivered, you will be unable to pay much attention to its content. In this case, activation of the peripheral route becomes more likely. Attitude change processes are also related to personality characteristics. For example, people with a strong *need for cognition* like to engage in thoughtful mental activities and are therefore more likely to use the central route to attitude change (Suedfeld & Tetlock, 2001). In contrast, people whose discomfort with uncertainty creates a *need for closure* are more likely to use the peripheral route (Cacioppo et al., 1996).

Persuasive messages are not the only means of changing attitudes. Another approach is to get people to act in ways that are inconsistent with their current attitudes in the hope that they will adjust those attitudes to match their behavior. Often such adjustments do occur. Cognitive dissonance theory and self-perception theory each attempt to explain why.

Cognitive Dissonance Theory Leon Festinger's classic **cognitive dissonance theory** holds that people want their thoughts, beliefs, and attitudes to be consistent with one another and with their behavior. When people experience inconsistency, or *dissonance,* among these elements, they become anxious and are motivated to make them more consistent (Elliot & Devine, 1994; Festinger, 1957; Olson & Stone, 2005). For example, someone who believes that "smoking is unhealthy" but must also acknowledge that "I smoke" would be motivated to reduce the resulting dissonance. Because it is often difficult to change behavior, people usually reduce cognitive dissonance by changing inconsistent attitudes. So rather than quit smoking, the smoker might decide that smoking is not so dangerous.

In one of the first studies of cognitive dissonance, Festinger and his colleague Merrill Carlsmith (1959) asked people to turn pegs in a board, a very dull task. Later, some of these people were asked to persuade a person waiting to participate in the study that the task was "exciting and fun." Some were told that they would be paid $1 to tell this lie; others were promised $20. After they had talked to the waiting person, their attitudes toward the dull task were measured.

Figure 17.4 shows the surprising results. The people who were paid just $1 to lie liked the dull task more than those who were paid $20. Why? Festinger and Carlsmith argued that telling another person that a boring task is enjoyable will produce dissonance (between the thoughts "I think the task is boring" and "I am saying it is fun"). To reduce this dissonance, the people who were paid just $1 adopted a favorable attitude toward the task, making their cognitions consistent: "I think the task is fun" and "I am saying it is fun." But if a person has adequate justification for telling a lie, any dissonance that exists will be reduced simply by thinking about the justification. The participants who were paid $20 thought they had adequate justification for lying and so did not need to change their attitudes toward the task.

Hundreds of other experiments have also found that when people publicly engage in behaviors that are inconsistent with their privately held attitudes, they are likely to change their attitudes to be consistent with their behavior (Cooper, Mirabile, & Scher, 2005). These experiments have also found that behavior-attitude inconsistency

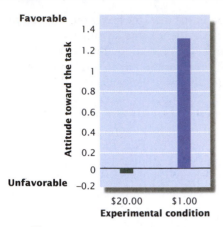

FIGURE 17.4

Cognitive Dissonance and Attitude Change

According to cognitive dissonance theory, the $20 people were paid to say that a boring task was enjoyable provided them with a clear justification for lying. Having been paid to lie, they should experience little dissonance between what they said and what they thought about the task. And in fact their attitude toward the task was not positive. However, people who received only $1 had little justification to lie and reduced their dissonance mainly by displaying a more positive attitude toward the task.

Source: From L. Festinger and J.M. Carlsmith. "Cognitive Consequences Of Forced Compliance". *Journal of Abnormal and Social Psychology*, 58, pp. 203–210. Copyright © American Psychological Association. Reprinted by permission.

self-perception theory A theory suggesting that attitudes can change as people consider their behavior in certain situations and then infer what their attitude must be.

will produce attitude change when (1) the inconsistency causes some distress or discomfort and (2) changing attitudes will reduce this distress or discomfort. But what causes the discomfort in the first place? There is considerable debate among attitude researchers about this question (Harmon-Jones, Amodio & Harmon-Jones, 2009).

One possible answer is that discomfort results when people's positive self-concept (e.g. "I am honest") is threatened by the recognition that they have done something inconsistent with that self-concept. For example, if they have encouraged another person to do something that they themselves didn't believe in or that they themselves wouldn't do, this inconsistency makes most people feel uncomfortable, so they change their attitudes to reduce or eliminate such feelings (Stone & Fernandez, 2008). If people can persuade themselves that they really believed in what they did, the perceived inconsistency disappears, and their positive self-concepts are restored. Changing one's private attitude to match one's public actions is one way to accomplish this self-persuasion. Claude Steele's work on *self-affirmation* supports this explanation of why dissonance causes discomfort (e.g., Steele, Spencer, & Lynch, 1993). He has found that people will not change their attitudes after recognizing their own attitude-behavior inconsistency if they can do something else that makes them look good and feel good about themselves—such as showing how smart or competent they are. In other words, when people do not need to change their attitudes to reestablish a positive view of themselves, they don't.

The circumstances that lead to cognitive dissonance may be different in the individualist cultures of Europe and North America than in collectivist cultures such as Japan and China. In individualist cultures, dissonance typically arises from behaving in a manner inconsistent with one's own beliefs, because this behavior causes self-doubt. But in collectivist cultures, dissonance typically arises when such behavior causes the person to worry about one's reputation with others (Kitayama et al., 2004). Cultural values also operate in shaping dissonance-reducing strategies. For example, people from individualist cultures can reduce the unpleasant feelings that accompany dissonance by affirming their value as unique individuals, whereas people from collectivist cultures can reduce the same kinds of feelings by affirming the value of the groups to which they belong (Hoshino-Browne et al., 2005).

Self-Perception Theory Over the years, cognitive dissonance theory has been challenged by other explanations of why attitudes change when they are inconsistent with behavior (Dunning, 2001). The first and strongest of these challenges came from Daryl Bem's **self-perception theory**. Unlike dissonance theory, self-perception theory does not assume that people experience discomfort when their attitudes are inconsistent with their behaviors. According to Bem (1967), situations often arise in which people are not quite sure about their attitudes. When this happens, Bem says, people look at their own behavior under particular circumstances and then infer what their attitude must be. The person says, "If I did that under those circumstances, my attitude must be this." This process makes their attitudes consistent with their behavior, but the process is not driven by tension or discomfort.

Self-perception explanations of attitude change seem reasonable, but two kinds of evidence are inconsistent with it. First, brain-imaging studies have found that specific patterns of brain activity are associated with the experience of cognitive dissonance and that the appearance of these patterns strongly predicts the appearance of attitude change (van Veen et al., 2009). These findings—combined with earlier evidence that people become physiologically aroused and feel uncomfortable when their attitudes and behavior are inconsistent (Elliot & Devine, 1994)—suggest that some kind of internal tension is, in fact, created by cognitive dissonance. Second, people adjust their attitudes to match their behavior even when they are unable to reflect on that behavior—a process that is crucial to self-perception theory. In one experiment, for example, researchers studied the effects of attitude-behavior inconsistencies in people suffering from anterograde amnesia, a condition described in the memory chapter that leaves people unable to recall what they have said or done minutes earlier. Like the participants in other attitude change experiments, these people, too, changed their attitudes to be more consistent with their behavior (Lieberman et al., 2001).

IN REVIEW Forming and Changing Attitudes

Type of Influence	Description
Social learning and conditioning	Attitudes are usually formed through observation of how others behave and speak about an attitude object, as well as through classical and operant conditioning.
Elaboration likelihood model	People change attitudes through either a central or a peripheral route, depending on factors such as personal involvement, "cognitive busyness," and personality characteristics.
Cognitive dissonance and self-perception	Inconsistencies between attitudes and behaviors can produce attitude change, as can reviewing one's behavior in light of circumstances.

1. According to the elaboration likelihood model, people are more likely to pay close attention to the content and logic of a persuasive message if the _____ route to attitude change has been activated.

2. Holding attitudes that are similar to those of your friends illustrates the importance of _____ in attitude formation.

3. According to cognitive dissonance theory, we tend to reduce conflict between attitudes and behaviors by changing our _____.

Although these results do not support self-perception theory, they do not entirely invalidate it. It may be that self-perception theory applies best either when people have no prior attitude toward some object or when the discrepancy between their attitude and their behavior is slight. For instance, if you know you prefer Coca-Cola but you also know that you just drank a Pepsi, this self-perception may drive an attitude change toward Pepsi even though you did not experience much dissonance. However, when attitudes are strong and clearly defined and the inconsistency between attitudes and behaviors is larger and more important to a person's self-concept, attitude change appears to occur mainly because of cognitive dissonance (Dunning, 2001). ("In Review: Forming and Changing Attitudes" summarizes some of the major processes through which attitudes are formed and changed.)

LINKAGES

LINKAGES What happens in the brains of prejudiced people? (a link to Biological Aspects of Psychology, p. 76)

Biological and Social Psychology

Social psychologists' research on thoughts, feelings, and behaviors was once entirely separate from research on the biological processes that underlie those thoughts, feelings, and behaviors (Cacioppo & Berntson, 2005). In fact, social psychologists believed that it was not possible to reduce complex social psychological processes to the firing of neurons or the secretion of hormones. At the same time, biological psychologists, more commonly known as *neuroscientists,* viewed the study of social psychology as having little, if any, relevance to the understanding of behavioral genetics or the functioning of the nervous, endocrine, or immune systems. Recently, however, scientists in both subfields have begun to take a closer look at each other's research and how their subfields are related. The result has been the emergence of a new specialty called *social neuroscience* or *social cognitive neuroscience* (Lieberman, 2010). This new specialty focuses on the neurological aspects of social processes and is part of a more general trend toward research on the interaction of biological and social processes.

There are already many reasons to believe that this research approach will be valuable. For example, the chapter on health, stress, and coping contains numerous examples of how social stressors can have health-related biological consequences. Health psychologists have also found that the quality of a person's social relationships can affect biological processes ranging from the functioning of the immune system to the healing of wounds (Gouin et al., 2008, 2010; Kiecolt-Glaser, 2009). The social environment can affect even the way genes express themselves (Cole, 2009). In one study, for example, monkeys were selectively bred to react strongly to even mild stressors. These animals' oversensitivity appeared to be based on a specific gene, but researchers found it possible to modify the effects of this gene by changing the monkeys' social situation. When the animals were paired with a warm, nurturant foster mother, their oversensitivity diminished significantly, and it remained low even when they were later separated from her (Suomi, 1999).

Researchers are also beginning to identify biological processes associated with many social processes. We have already mentioned studies that measured activity in the brain and the autonomic nervous system during cognitive dissonance. Other examples can be seen in research on the emotion-related brain activity that accompanies the ethnic prejudice and stereotyping that we discuss in the next section (Amodio & Lieberman, 2009). Using functional magnetic resonance imaging technology, some researchers have found that European Americans who were prejudiced against African Americans showed significantly more amygdala activity when looking at pictures of black people than when looking at pictures of white people (Hart et al., 2000; Phelps et al., 2000). Researchers have also used fMRI to study people's emotional reactions to other people's distress (Lamm, Batson, & Decety, 2007). They found patterns of brain activity that were quite different depending on whether the individual experienced empathy for a distressed person or simply observed the person's distress. Studies such as this one are shedding some light on the biological aspects of empathy, and they may eventually lead to a broader understanding of the factors influencing people's motivation to help each other (Decety, 2011; see the chapter on social influence). Social neuroscientists have also used electroencephalography (EEG) and other techniques to record the brain activity associated with positive and negative attitudes about people and objects (e.g., Amodio et al., 2004). Their research has shown that these evaluative reactions are associated with activity in specific brain regions (Cacioppo, Crites, & Gardner, 1996).

Social neuroscience is still in its infancy, but this new field of research already shows great promise for improving our understanding of the linkages among social, cognitive, and biological phenomena, as well as of complex social and physiological processes (Lieberman, 2010).

Prejudice and Stereotypes

All of the principles that underlie impression formation, attribution, and attitudes come together to create prejudice and stereotypes. **Stereotypes** are the perceptions, beliefs, and expectations a person has about members of some group. They are schemas about entire groups of people (Dovidio & Gaertner, 2010). Usually, stereotypes involve the false assumption that all members of a group share the same characteristics. The characteristics that make up the stereotype may be positive, but they are usually negative. The most common and most powerful stereotypes focus on observable personal attributes, particularly ethnicity, gender, and age (Operario & Fiske, 2001).

The stereotypes people hold can be so ingrained that their effects on behavior can be automatic and unconscious (Dovidio et al., 2009). In one study, for example, European American and African American participants played a video game in which white or black men suddenly appeared on a screen holding objects that might be weapons (Correll et al., 2002; see Figure 17.5). The participants were instructed to immediately "shoot" an armed man but not an unarmed one. Under this time pressure, the participants' errors were not random. If they "shot" an unarmed man, he was significantly more likely to be black than white. If they failed to "shoot" an armed man, he was more likely to be white than black. These differences occurred among both European American and African American participants but were most pronounced among those who held the strongest cultural stereotypes about blacks. In another study, police officers showed a similar pattern of results, except that the officers were not as quick as civilians were to shoot an unarmed black man (Correll et al., 2007).

Stereotyping often leads to **prejudice**, a positive or negative attitude toward an individual based simply on membership in some group (Maio et al., 2010). The literal meaning of the word *prejudice* is "prejudgment." Many theorists believe that prejudice, like other attitudes, has cognitive, affective, and behavioral components. Stereotyped thinking is the cognitive component of prejudicial attitudes. The hatred, admiration, anger, and other feelings people have about stereotyped groups make up the affective

stereotype a false assumption that all members of some group share the same characteristics.

prejudice A positive or negative attitude toward an entire group of people.

FIGURE 17.5
The Impact of Stereotypes on Behavior

TRY THIS When these men suddenly appeared on a video game screen, participants were supposed to "shoot" them, but only if they appeared to be armed (Correll et al., 2002). Stereotypes about whether white men or black men are more likely to be armed significantly affected the errors made by participants in firing their video game "weapons." Cover these photos with a pair of index cards; then ask a few friends to watch as you show each photo, one at a time, for just an instant, before covering it again. Then ask your friends to say whether either man appeared to be armed. Was one individual more often identified as armed? If so, which one?

© Joshua Correll

component. The behavioral component of prejudice involves **social discrimination**, which is differing treatment of individuals who belong to different groups.

Theories of Prejudice and Stereotyping

Prejudice and stereotyping may occur for several reasons. Let's consider three explanatory theories, each of which has empirical support and accounts for some, but not all, instances of stereotyping and prejudice.

Motivational Theories   For some people, prejudice against certain groups may enhance their sense of security and help them meet certain personal needs. This idea was first proposed by Theodor Adorno and his associates more than sixty years ago (Adorno et al., 1950). It has since been revised and expanded by Bob Altemeyer (2004; Altemeyer & Hunsberger, 2005). Specifically, these researchers suggest that prejudice may be especially likely among people who display a personality trait called *authoritarianism*. According to Altemeyer, authoritarianism is composed of three elements: (1) an acceptance of conventional or traditional values, (2) a willingness to unquestioningly follow the orders of authority figures, and (3) an inclination to act aggressively toward individuals or groups identified by these authority figures as threatening the values held by one's ingroup. People with an authoritarian orientation tend to view the world as a dangerous place (Cohrs & Ibler, 2009), and one way to protect themselves is to identify strongly with their ingroup and to dislike, reject, and perhaps even punish anyone who belongs to an outgroup (Thomsen, Green, & Sidanius, 2008). Looking down on and discriminating against outgroups—gay men and lesbians or African Americans, for example—may help people with authoritarian tendencies feel safer and feel better about themselves (Duckitt, 2006).

Another motivational explanation of prejudice employs the concept of social identity discussed earlier. Recall that whether they are authoritarian or not, most people are motivated to identify with their ingroup and tend to see it as better than other groups (Abrams & Hogg, 2010). As a result, members of an ingroup often see all members of outgroups as less attractive and less socially acceptable than ingroup members and may therefore treat them badly (Jackson, 2002). In other words, prejudice may result when people's motivation to enhance their own self-esteem causes them to disrespect other people.

Cognitive Theories   Stereotyping and prejudice may also result from the social-cognitive processes people use in dealing with the world. There are so many other people, so many situations in which one meets them, and so many possible behaviors they might perform that we cannot possibly attend to and remember them all. Therefore, we use schemas and other cognitive shortcuts to organize and make sense out of our social world (Moskowitz, 2005). These cognitive processes allow us to draw accurate and useful conclusions about other people, but sometimes they

social discrimination Differential treatment of various groups; the behavioral component of prejudice.

Schemas and Stereotypes

The use of schemas to assign certain people to certain categories can be helpful when deciding who is a customer and who is a store employee, but it can also lead to inaccurate stereotypes. Terrorist attacks and attempted attacks by Islamic extremists have led many people in the United States to think of all Muslims as terrorists and to discriminate against them. The problems that this false assumption has created for U.S. Muslims is yet another of the many damaging effects of Islamic terrorism.

© Jeff Greenberg/The Image Works

lead to inaccurate stereotypes. For example, one effective way to deal with social complexity is to group people into *social categories*. Rather than remembering every detail about everyone we have ever encountered, we tend to put people into categories, such as "doctor," "senior citizen," "Republican," "student," or "Italian" (Dovidio, Kawakami, & Gaertner, 2000). To further simplify perception of these categories, we tend to see their members as being quite similar to one another. In fact, members of one ethnic group may find it harder to distinguish among specific faces within other ethnic groups than within their own group (Michel et al., 2006). People also tend to assume that all members of a particular group share the same beliefs and values and that those beliefs and values differ from their own (Dion, 2003). Finally, as noted in the chapter on perception, people's attention tends to be drawn to distinctive stimuli. Rude behavior by even a few members of an easily identified ethnic group may lead other people to see an *illusory correlation* between rudeness and ethnicity (Meiser & Hewstone, 2006). As a result, they may incorrectly believe that all members of that group are rude.

Learning Theories   Like other attitudes, prejudice can be learned. Some prejudice is learned on the basis of conflicts between members of different groups, but people also develop negative attitudes toward groups with whom they have had little or no contact. Learning theories suggest that children can pick up prejudices just by watching and listening to parents, peers, and others (Castelli, Zogmaister, & Tomelleri, 2009; Rutland, Killen, & Abrams, 2010; Taylor, Peplau, & Sears, 2006). There may even be a form of *biopreparedness* (described in the learning chapter) that makes us especially likely to learn to fear people who are strangers or who look different from us (Kelly et al., 2007; Olson et al., 2001). Movies and television may also portray ethnic or other groups in ways that teach stereotypes and prejudice (Jost & Hamilton, 2005). For example, one study found that European American characters in popular television shows tend to behave more negatively toward African American characters than toward other European Americans. The study also found that watching these shows can elevate viewers' prejudice against African Americans in general (Weisbuch, Pauker, & Ambady, 2009). No wonder so many young children already know about the supposed negative characteristics of certain groups long before they ever meet members of those groups (Baron & Banaji, 2006; Degner & Wentura, 2010).

Reducing Prejudice

One clear implication of the cognitive and learning theories of prejudice and stereo-typing is that members of one group are often ignorant or misinformed about the characteristics of people in other groups (Dovidio, Gaertner, & Kawakami, 2010). Before 1954, for example, most black and white children in the United States knew very little about one another because they went to separate schools. Then the Supreme Court declared that segregated public schools should be prohibited. By ruling segregation to be unconstitutional, the court created a real-life test of the **contact hypothesis**, which states that stereotypes and prejudice toward a group will diminish as contact with that group increases (Pettigrew & Tropp, 2006).

Did the desegregation of U.S. schools confirm the contact hypothesis? In a few schools, integration was followed by a decrease in prejudice, but in most places, either no change occurred or prejudice actually increased (Oskamp & Schultz, 1998). However, these results did not necessarily disprove the contact hypothesis. In-depth studies of schools in which desegregation was successful suggested that contact alone was not enough. Integration reduced prejudice only when certain social conditions were created (Pettigrew & Tropp, 2006). First, members of the two groups had to be of roughly equal social and economic status. Second, school authorities had to promote cooperation and interdependence between the members of different ethnic groups by having them work together on projects that required relying on one another for success. Third, the contact between group members had to occur on a one-on-one basis. It was only when people got to know one another as individuals that the errors contained in stereotypes became apparent. When these conditions were met, the children's attitudes toward one another became more positive. The same effects have appeared in adults in the United States and elsewhere. In Italy, for example, people who had equal-status contact with black immigrants from North Africa displayed less prejudice against them than Italians who had no contact with those immigrants (Kirchler & Zani, 1995).

Elliot Aronson (1997) describes a teaching strategy, called the *jigsaw technique*, that helps create the conditions that reduce prejudice. The strategy calls for children from several ethnic groups to work as a team to complete a task, such as writing a report about a famous person in history. Each child learns a separate piece of information about this person, such as place of birth, and provides this information to the team. Studies show that children from various ethnic groups who are exposed to the jigsaw technique and other cooperative learning experiences show substantial reductions in prejudice toward other groups (Aronson, 1997). The success reported in

Fighting Ethnic Prejudice

Negative attitudes about members of ethnic groups are often based on negative personal experiences or the negative experiences and attitudes people hear from others. Cooperative contact between equals can help promote mutual respect and reduce ethnic prejudice. Even *imagining* this kind of contact may help (Crisp & Turner, 2009).

© Blend Images/Jon Feingersh/Getty Images

contact hypothesis The idea that stereotypes and prejudice toward a group will diminish as contact with the group increases.

these studies has greatly increased the popularity of cooperative learning exercises in classrooms in the United States. Such exercises may not eliminate all aspects of ethnic prejudice in children, but they seem to be a step in the right direction.

Can friendly, cooperative, interdependent contact reduce the more entrenched forms of prejudice seen in adults? It may. When equal-status adults work jointly toward a common goal, bias and distrust can be reduced, particularly among those in ethnic majority groups (Tropp & Pettigrew, 2005). This is especially true if they come to see themselves as members of the same group rather than as belonging to opposing groups (Gaertner, Dovidio, & Houlette, 2010). The challenge to be met in creating such cooperative experiences in the real world is that the participants must be of equal status—a challenge made more difficult in many countries by the sizable status differences that still exist between ethnic groups (Kenworthy et al., 2006).

In the final analysis, contact provides only part of the solution to the problems of stereotyping, prejudice, and discrimination. To reduce ethnic prejudice, we must develop additional educational techniques that address the social cognitions and perceptions that lie at the core of bigotry and hatred toward people who are different from ourselves (Amodio & Devine, 2009; Bigler & Liben, 2007).

THINKING CRITICALLY

Is Ethnic Prejudice Too Ingrained Ever to Be Eliminated?

Overt ethnic prejudice has decreased dramatically in the United States over the past fifty to sixty years. For example, in the 1950s, fewer than half of European American college students surveyed said they were willing to live in integrated neighborhoods; more recent surveys indicate that about 95 percent now say they would be willing to do so. And four decades ago, fewer than 40 percent of European Americans said they would vote for an African American presidential candidate (Dovidio & Gaertner, 1998); in 2008, an African American president was elected. Despite these changes, research in social psychology suggests that more subtle aspects of prejudice and discrimination may remain as entrenched in the United States today as they were a couple of decades ago (Dovidio, Gaertner, & Kawakami, 2010).

LINKAGES Can we ever be unbiased about anyone? (a link to Consciousness, p. 334)

What am I being asked to believe or accept?
Even people who see themselves as unprejudiced and who disavow ethnic stereotypes and discrimination still hold negative stereotypes about ethnic outgroups and in certain situations will display prejudice and discrimination toward them (Dovidio et al., 2009). Some people claim, therefore, that negative attitudes toward ethnic outgroups are so deeply ingrained in all of us that ethnic prejudice can never be eliminated.

What evidence is available to support the assertion?
Evidence for this assertion focuses primarily on prejudice against African Americans by European Americans. It comes, first, from studies testing the theory of *aversive racism* (Dovidio & Gaertner, 2008). This theory holds that even though many European Americans consider ethnic prejudice unacceptable or aversive, they still sometimes display it—especially when they can do so without admitting, even to themselves, that they are prejudiced.

LINKAGES Can subliminal stimuli influence our judgments about people? (a link to Perception, p. 161)

In one test of this theory, a male experimenter telephoned male and female European Americans who were known to believe in ethnic equality. The man claimed to be a stranded motorist who was trying to call a service station from a pay phone. When told he had called the wrong number, the man replied that he was out of coins and asked the person he'd reached to call a service station for him. If people listened long enough to learn of the man's problem, they were just as likely to contact the service station whether the caller "sounded" European American or African American. However, if the caller "sounded" African American, these supposedly unprejudiced people were almost five times as likely to hang up even before the caller could ask for help (Gaertner & Dovidio, 1986). More recent studies have reported similar results (e.g., Kunstman & Plant, 2008).

A second line of evidence for the entrenched nature of prejudice comes from research showing that many people hold negative stereotypes about ethnic minorities but are unaware that they do so. These negative stereotypes can also be *activated* without conscious awareness, even among people who believe they are free of prejudice (Fiske & Taylor, 2008). For example, physicians who were not conscious of their bias against African Americans were found to behave more negatively toward their African American patients, which in turn caused these patients to react negatively toward these doctors (Penner et al., 2010). Other researchers have used the priming procedures described in the chapter on consciousness to activate unconscious thoughts and feelings that can alter people's reactions to stimuli without their awareness. In one study, white participants were exposed to subliminal presentations of pictures of black individuals (Chen & Bargh, 1997). The participants were not consciously aware that they had seen these pictures, but when they interacted with a black man soon afterward, those who had been primed with the pictures acted more negatively toward him and saw him as more hostile than people who had not been primed. Priming apparently activated these participants' negative ethnic stereotypes. It is also possible to prime unconscious negative stereotypes about other groups, including women and people who are overweight (Glick & Fiske, 2001; Degner & Wentura, 2009). All of these findings suggest that stereotypes are so well learned and so ingrained in people that they may be activated automatically and without conscious awareness (Amodio & Devine, 2009).

Are there alternative ways of interpreting the evidence?

The evidence presented so far suggests that it may be impossible to eliminate ethnic prejudice because everyone harbors unconscious negative stereotypes about various groups. But this evidence does not necessarily mean that unconscious stereotypes affect everyone in the same way. Perhaps they have a greater impact on people who are more overtly prejudiced.

What additional evidence would help evaluate the alternatives?

One way to evaluate this possibility is to compare the responses of prejudiced and unprejudiced people in various experimental situations. In one mock-trial study, for example, overtly prejudiced white jurors recommended the death penalty more often for black defendants than for white defendants found guilty of the same crime. Low-prejudice white jurors showed this bias only when they believed that a black member of the jury also favored giving the death penalty (Dovidio et al., 1997). Priming studies, too, show that although negative stereotypes can be primed in both prejudiced and unprejudiced people, it is easier to do in people who openly display their ethnic bias (Dovidio & Gaertner, 2010). Furthermore, activation of these stereotypes may be less likely to affect the conscious attitudes and behavior of unprejudiced people. So when unconscious stereotypes are activated in unprejudiced people, the effects tend to appear in subtle ways, such as in facial expressions or other nonverbal behaviors (Kawakami, Dion, & Dovidio, 1998; Lepore & Brown, 1997; Vanman et al., 2004).

What conclusions are most reasonable?

Taken together, research evidence presents a mixed picture regarding the possibility of eliminating ethnic prejudice. True, people in the United States are not nearly as colorblind as we might hope, and ethnic prejudice may be so ingrained in some people as to be subconscious. However, research suggests that it may still be possible to eliminate even subconscious stereotypes (Kawakami, Dovidio, & van Kamp, 2005; Kawakami et al., 2007). It also appears that when unprejudiced people are made aware of their negative beliefs about some target group, they will actively work to prevent those beliefs from influencing their behavior toward members of that group (Monteith, Arthur, & Flynn, 2010; Payne, 2008). In short, prejudice is ingrained, but it can also be reduced, and it makes sense to do everything possible to reduce it. In the United States, as in any multicultural country, survival as a civilized society requires that we all continue to fight against overt and covert forms of stereotyping, prejudice, and social discrimination. This goal is more important than ever as the fight against international terrorism can make it all too easy to misjudge and mistreat innocent people based on their ethnicity.

Interpersonal Attraction

Research on prejudice suggests some of the reasons why people, from childhood on, may come to dislike or even hate other people. An equally fascinating aspect of social cognition is why people like or love other people. Folklore tells us that "opposites attract" but also that "birds of a feather flock together." Although valid to some degree, neither of these statements is entirely accurate in all cases. We begin our coverage of interpersonal attraction by discussing the factors that lead to initial attraction. We then examine how liking sometimes develops into more intimate relationships.

Keys to Attraction

Whether you like someone or not depends partly on situational factors and partly on personal characteristics.

© John Lund/Sam Diephuis/Blend Images/Getty Images

Proximity and Liking

TRY THIS Research on environmental factors in attraction suggests that, barring bad first impressions, the more often we make contact with someone—as neighbors, classmates, or coworkers, for example—the more we tend to like that person. Does this principle apply in your life? To find out, think about how and where you met each of your closest friends. If you can think of cases in which proximity did not lead to liking, what do you think interfered with the formation of friendship?

The Environment One of the most important determinants of attraction is simple physical proximity (Clark & Lemay, 2010). As long as you do not initially dislike a person, your liking for that person will increase with additional contact. This effect was apparent in a study in which unacquainted students were randomly assigned to classroom seats. A year later, these students were shown photos of everyone in that class and were asked to rate their liking of each one. The ratings showed that students who sat next to each other or in the same row liked one another more than students who were seated farther away (Back, Schmukle, & Egloff, 2008). Another study found that we even tend to like people who *resemble* those who have often been near us (Rhodes, Halberstadt, & Brajkovich, 2001). This proximity phenomenon—another example of the *mere-exposure effect* mentioned earlier—helps account for the fact that next-door neighbors are usually more likely to become friends than people who live farther from one another. Chances are, most of your friends are people whom you met as neighbors, coworkers, or classmates (Liben-Nowell et al., 2005).

The circumstances under which people first meet also influence attraction. In accordance with the conditioning principles discussed in the chapter on learning, you are much more likely to be attracted to a stranger if you meet in comfortable, rather than uncomfortable, physical conditions (IJzerman & Semin, 2009). Similarly, if you are rewarded in the presence of a stranger, the chances that you will like that stranger are increased, even if the stranger was not the one who gave the reward. In one study, for example, an experimenter judged people's creativity while another person watched. Compared with those who received a negative evaluation, participants who were evaluated positively tended to like the observer more (Griffitt & Guay, 1969). At least among strangers, then, liking can occur by associating a person with something pleasant.

Similarity People also tend to like those they perceive as similar to themselves on variables such as age, religion, smoking or drinking habits, or being a "morning" or "evening" person (Clark & Lemay, 2010). Similarity in attitudes is an especially important influence on attraction. This relationship has been found among children, college students, adult workers, and senior citizens (Taylor, Peplau, & Sears, 2006).

Similarity in attitudes toward mutual acquaintances is a particularly good predictor of liking because people generally prefer relationships that are *balanced*. As illustrated in Figure 17.6, if Zoë likes Abigail, the relationship is balanced as long as they agree on their evaluation of a third person, Samantha, regardless of whether they like or dislike that third person. However, the relationship will be imbalanced if Zoë and Abigail disagree on their evaluation of the third person.

FIGURE 17.6
Balanced and Imbalanced Relationships

TRY THIS Here are some common examples of balanced and imbalanced patterns of relationships among three people. The plus and minus signs refer to liking and disliking, respectively. Balanced relationships are comfortable and harmonious. Imbalanced ones often bring conflict. Take a moment to think about the balanced and imbalanced relationships that exist in your life or in the lives of people you know.

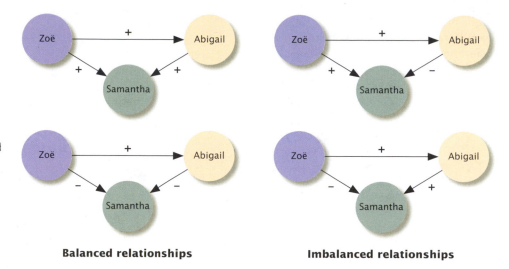

Balanced relationships   **Imbalanced relationships**

One reason why we like people with similar views of the world is that we expect such people to approve of us (Condon & Crano, 1988). But it's hard to say whether attraction is a cause or an effect of similarity. For example, you might like someone because his attitudes are similar to yours, but it is also possible that as a result of liking him, your attitudes will become more similar to his (Davis & Rusbult, 2001). Even if your own attitudes don't change, you may change your *perceptions* of the liked person's attitudes such that those attitudes seem more similar to yours (Brehm, 1992).

Physical Attractiveness   Physical characteristics are another important factor in attraction, particularly during the initial stages of a relationship (Leary, 2010). From preschool through adulthood, physical attractiveness is a key to popularity with members of both sexes (e.g., Langlois et al., 2000). Consistent with the **matching hypothesis** of interpersonal attraction, however, people tend to date, marry, or form other committed relationships with those who are similar to themselves in physical attractiveness (Yela & Sangrador, 2001). One possible reason for this outcome is that people tend to be most attracted to those with the greatest physical appeal, but they also want to avoid being rejected by such individuals. So it may be compromise, not preference, that leads people to pair off with those who are roughly equivalent to themselves in physical attractiveness (Carli, Ganley, & Pierce-Otay, 1991; Kavanagh, Robins, & Ellis, 2010, Lee et al., 2008).

Intimate Relationships and Love

There is much about intimate relationships that psychologists do not—and may never—understand, but they are learning all the time. As mentioned in the chapter on motivation and emotion, evolutionary psychologists suggest that men and women employ different mating strategies and that each sex looks for different attributes in a potential mate (Buss, 2008; Neuberg, Kenrick, & Schaller, 2010). For example, in short-term relationships at least, women may be much more selective than men about the intelligence of their partners (Buss, 2008; see Figure 17.7).

Intimate Relationships   Eventually, people who are attracted to each other usually become *interdependent*, which means that the thoughts, emotions, and behaviors of one person affect the thoughts, emotions, and behaviors of the other (Clark & Lemay, 2010). Interdependence is one of the defining characteristics of intimate relationships.

Another key component of successful intimate relationships is *commitment*, which is the extent to which each party is psychologically attached to the relationship and wants to remain in it (Amodio & Showers, 2005). People feel committed to a relationship when they are satisfied with the rewards they receive from it, when they have

matching hypothesis The notion that people are most likely to form relationships with those who are similar to themselves in physical attractiveness.

FIGURE 17.7

Sex Differences in Date and Mate Preferences

According to evolutionary psychologists, men and women have developed different strategies for selecting sexual partners. These psychologists say that women became more selective than men because they can have relatively few children and want a partner who is able to help care for those children. Here are some data supporting this idea. When asked about the intelligence of people they would choose for one-night stands, dating, and sexual relationships, women preferred much smarter partners than men did. Only when the choices concerned steady dating and marriage did the men's preference for bright partners equal that of the women. Critics of the evolutionary approach explain such sex differences as reflecting learned social norms and expectations of how men and women should behave (Eagly & Wood, 1999; Miller, Putcha-Bhagavatula, & Pedersen, 2002).

Source: Kenrick et al. (1993).

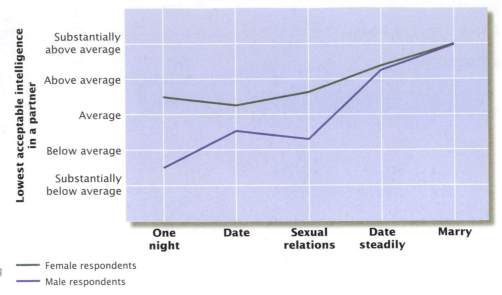

invested significant tangible and intangible resources in it, and when there are few attractive alternative relationships available to them (Bui, Peplau, & Hill, 1996; Lydon, Fitzsimmons, & Naidoo, 2003).

Analyzing Love   Although some people think love is simply a strong form of liking, research suggests that romantic love and liking are quite separate emotions, at least in the sense that they are associated with differing patterns of brain chemistry and brain activity (Aron et al., 2005; Emanuele et al., 2006). And although romantic love and sexual desire are often experienced together, they, too, seem to be separate emotions associated with different patterns of physiological arousal (Diamond, 2004). Further, most theorists agree that there are several different types of love (Berscheid, 2010). One widely accepted view distinguishes between *romantic* or *passionate love* and *companionate love* (Berscheid, 2011). Passionate love is intense, arousing, and marked by both strong physical attraction and deep emotional attachment. Sexual feelings are strong, and thoughts of the loved one intrude frequently on a person's awareness. Companionate love is less arousing but psychologically more intimate. It is marked by mutual concern for the welfare of the other (Berscheid, 2010).

Robert Sternberg (1997) has offered an even broader analysis of love. According to his *triangular theory,* the three basic components of love are *passion, intimacy,* and *commitment.* Various combinations of these components result in different types of love, as illustrated in Figure 17.8. For example, Sternberg suggests that *romantic love* involves a high degree of passion and intimacy but lacks substantial commitment to the other person. *Companionate love* is marked by a great deal of intimacy and commitment but little passion. *Consummate love* is the most complete and satisfying. It is the most complete because it includes a high level of all three components, and it is the most satisfying because the relationship is likely to fulfill many of the needs of each partner. Sternberg has more recently advanced a "duplex theory" of love by pairing his triangular theory with a second one that focuses on love as a story. This second theory focuses on the idea that in Western cultures at least, the success of a relationship appears to depend not just on its perceived characteristics but also on the degree to which those characteristics fit each partner's ideal story of love, whether it be that of a prince and princess or a pair of business partners, for example (Sternberg, 2006).

Cultural factors have a strong influence on the value that people place on love. In North America and the United Kingdom, for example, the vast majority of people believe that they should love the person they marry. By contrast, in India and Pakistan,

FIGURE 17.8
A Triangular Theory of Love

According to Robert Sternberg, different types of love result when the three basic components in his triangular theory occur in different combinations. The size of the triangle of love increases as love increases, and its shape is determined by the relative strength of each basic component. The perfectly balanced triangle shown in the center of this figure depicts a relationship in which all three components are of about equal strength.

Source: From R.J. Sternberg & M.L. Barnes. "Triangulating Love." *The Psychology Of Love.* Reprinted by permission of Yale University Press.

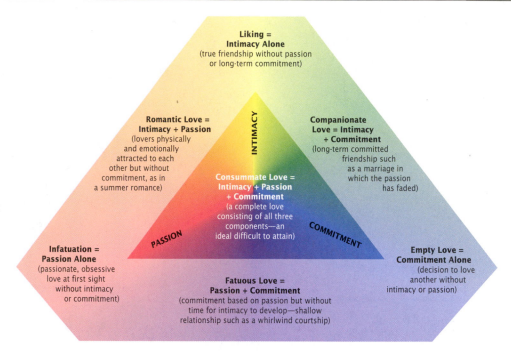

about half the people interviewed in a survey said they would marry someone they did not love if that person had other qualities that they desired (Levine et al., 1995). Many such cultural differences in the role of love in marriage are likely to continue, but some of them, such as the differences that had once existed between the United States and China, seem to be disappearing (Hatfield & Rapson, 2006).

Strong and Weak Marriages   Long-term studies of successful and unsuccessful marriages suggest that premarital attitudes and feelings predict marital success. For example, one study found that couples who had a close, intimate relationship and similar attitudes when they were dating were more likely still to be married fifteen years later (Hill & Peplau, 1998; Neff & Karney, 2005). Also, still-married couples were more likely to have had a premarital relationship that was rewarding and balanced.

A Wedding in India

TRY THIS   Most people in Western cultures tend to marry a person whom they choose on the basis of love, sometimes without regard for differences between them in religion, ethnicity, and financial or social status. In other cultures, however, these sociocultural considerations—and even arrangements made by parents—may largely determine who marries whom. Make a list of the factors that you think may have brought this couple together.

© DPA/The Image Works

Happy and Healthy

TRY THIS People in marriages and other long-term relationships that are satisfying tend to enjoy better physical and psychological health than those in unsatisfying relationships. In light of research described in the chapter on health, stress, and coping, make a list of reasons why this might be the case.

Among married couples, women—but not men—generally tend to be more satisfied with their marriage when the partners talk a lot about the relationship (Acitelli, 1992). Partners in successful marriages also tend to share each other's view of themselves and the other, even if that view is a negative one (Swann, De La Ronde, & Hixon, 1994). The perception that the relationship is fair and equitable also enhances marital satisfaction, especially for women (De Maris, 2007). After the birth of a first child, for example, many wives find that they have much more work than they had anticipated. If their husbands do not share this work to the degree they expected, wives' marital satisfaction tends to decrease (Doss et al., 2009; McNulty & Karney, 2004).

One particularly interesting line of research suggests that even brief observations of couples' interactions can predict whether those couples will divorce and when (Driver & Gottman, 2004). Among couples who divorced relatively soon after marriage, the partners tended to express both positive and negative feelings toward one another, but they were unable to control the way they expressed these feelings, especially the negative ones. Communication became increasingly hurtful and eventually broke down (Driver et al., 2003). A different picture emerged, however, in couples who divorced after many years of marriage. These people did not necessarily express negative emotions toward one another. They simply became less and less likely to communicate *any* feelings. The increasing emotional distance between the spouses created a sense of isolation that eventually led to divorce (Gottman & Levenson, 2002). These findings can help us understand why people in a long and apparently strong marriage—such as Al and Tipper Gore—might suddenly announce that they are divorcing, and why they may remain friends afterward. These people may still like each other but no longer love each other (Gottman & Levenson, 2000; Huston et al., 2001).

LINKAGES

As noted in the chapter on introducing psychology, all of psychology's many subfields are related to one another. Our discussion of brain activity and attitudes illustrates just one way in which the topic of this chapter, social cognition, is linked to the subfield of biological psychology (see the

CHAPTER 17
Social Cognition

chapter on biological aspects of psychology). The Linkages diagram shows ties to two other subfields as well, and there are many more ties throughout the book. Looking for linkages among subfields will help you see how they all fit together and better appreciate the big picture that is psychology.

LINKAGES

What happens in the brains of prejudiced people?
(ans. on p. 713)

Can we ever be unbiased about anyone?
(ans. on p. 718)

Do children perceive others as adults do?
(ans. on p. 494)

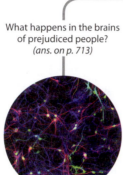

CHAPTER 3
Biological Aspects of Psychology

CHAPTER 9
Consciousness

CHAPTER 12
Human Development

SUMMARY

Social cognition (the mental processes through which people perceive and react to others) is one aspect of *social psychology* (the study of how people influence and are influenced by other people).

Social Influences on the Self

People's social and cultural environments affect their thoughts and feelings about themselves, including their *self-esteem* and their *self-concept.*

Social Comparison

When people have no objective criteria by which to judge themselves, they engage in *social comparison* (to others) or temporal comparison (to themselves at an earlier time) as their standard. Such comparison can affect self-evaluation or self-esteem. Categories of people that are habitually used for social comparison are known as *reference groups.* Comparison

to reference groups sometimes results in a sense of *relative deprivation,* which can in turn cause personal and social turmoil.

Social Identity Theory

A person's *social identity* is formed from beliefs about the groups to which the person belongs. Social identity affects the beliefs we hold about ourselves. It permits us to feel part of a larger group, engendering loyalty and sacrifice from group members but also potentially engendering bias and discrimination toward people who are not members of the group.

Social Perception

Social perception concerns the processes by which people interpret information about others, form impressions of them, and draw conclusions about the reasons for their behavior.

The Role of Schemas

Schemas, the mental representations about people and social situations that we carry into social interactions, affect what we pay attention to, what we remember, and how we judge people and events.

First Impressions

First impressions are formed easily and quickly, in part because people apply existing schemas to their perceptions of others. First impressions change slowly because once we form an impression about another person, we try to maintain it. Schemas, however, can create *self-fulfilling prophecies,* leading people to act in ways that bring out in others behavior that is consistent with expectations.

Explaining Behavior: Attribution

Attribution is the process of explaining the causes of people's behavior, including our own. Observers tend to attribute behavior to causes that are either internal or external to the actor. In general, they do this by looking at three aspects of the behavior: consensus, consistency, and distinctiveness. People from different cultures may sometimes reach different conclusions about the reasons for an actor's behavior.

Errors in Attribution

Attributions are affected by errors that systematically distort one's view of behavior. The most common attributional errors are the *fundamental attribution error* (and its cousin, the ultimate attribution error), the *actor-observer effect,* and the *self-serving bias.* Personal and cultural factors can affect the extent to which people exhibit attributional errors.

The Self-Protective Functions of Social Cognition

People often avoid admitting something threatening about themselves through unrealistic optimism and a feeling of unique invulnerability.

Attitudes

An *attitude* is the tendency to respond positively or negatively to a particular object. Attitudes affect a wide range of behaviors.

The Structure of Attitudes

Many theorists believe that attitudes are made up of cognitive components (beliefs), affective components (feelings), and behavioral components (actions). However, it is often difficult to predict a specific behavior from a person's beliefs or feelings about an object. Cognitive theories propose that attitudes consist of evaluations of an object that are stored in memory. This approach suggests that the likelihood of attitude-behavior consistency depends on the accessibility of evaluations in memory, on subjective norms, on perceived control over the behavior, and on prior direct experience with the attitude object.

Forming Attitudes

Attitudes can be learned through modeling, as well as through classical or operant conditioning. They are also subject to the

mere-exposure effect: All else being equal, people develop greater liking for a new object the more often they are exposed to it.

Changing Attitudes

The effectiveness of a persuasive message in changing attitudes is influenced by the characteristics of the person who communicates it, its content, and the audience receiving it. The *elaboration likelihood model* suggests that attitude change can occur through either a peripheral or a central route, depending on a person's ability and motivation to consider an argument carefully. Another approach is to change a person's behavior in the hope that the person's attitude will be adjusted to match the behavior. *Cognitive dissonance theory* holds that if inconsistency between attitudes and behavior creates discomfort related to a person's self-concept or self-image, the person will be motivated to reduce that discomfort. *Self-perception theory* suggests that such attitude changes occur in some cases as people look to their behavior for clues about what their attitudes are.

Prejudice and Stereotypes

Stereotypes often lead to *prejudice* and *social discrimination.*

Theories of Prejudice and Stereotyping

Motivational theories of prejudice suggest that some people have a need to disrespect and dislike others. This need may stem from the trait of authoritarianism or from a strong social identity. In either case, feeling superior to members of outgroups makes these people feel better about themselves. As a result, *ingroup* members tend to discriminate against members of *outgroups.* Cognitive theories suggest that people categorize others into groups in order to reduce social complexity. And learning theories maintain that stereotypes, prejudice, and discriminatory behaviors can be learned from parents, peers, and the media.

Reducing Prejudice

The contact hypothesis proposes that intergroup contact can reduce prejudice and lead to more favorable attitudes toward a stereotyped group—but only if the contact occurs under specific conditions, as when there is equal status between group members. Helping diverse people feel as if they belong to the same group can also reduce intergroup prejudice.

Interpersonal Attraction

Keys to Attraction

Interpersonal attraction is a function of many variables. Physical proximity is important because it allows people to meet. The situation in which they meet is important because positive or negative aspects of the situation tend to be associated with the other person. Characteristics of the other person are also important. Attraction tends to be greater when two people share similar attitudes and characteristics. Physical appearance plays a role in attraction. Initially, attraction is strongest to those who are most physically attractive. But for long-term relationships, the *matching hypothesis* applies: People tend to choose others whose physical attractiveness is about the same as theirs.

Intimate Relationships and Love

A defining characteristic of intimate relationships is interdependence, and a key component of successful relationships is commitment. Commitment is in turn affected by the rewards coming from the relationship, the resources invested in it, and the possible alternatives open to each party. Robert Sternberg's triangular theory suggests that love is a function of three components: passion, intimacy, and commitment. Varying combinations of these components create different types of love. Couples who have long and successful marriages are likely to perceive the relationship as fair to both parties, and they are likely to share warm and loving feelings for each other.

LINKAGES TO FURTHER LEARNING

Now that you have finished reading this chapter, how about exploring some of the topics and information that you found most interesting? Here are some places to start.

Books

Henry Louis Gates Jr., *Colored People: A Memoir* (Vintage, 1994). Growing up black in segregated West Virginia.

Alex Kotlowitz, *The Other Side of the River: A Story of Two Towns, a Death, and America's Dilemma* (Doubleday, 1998). A story of social discrimination in law enforcement and prejudice in a town that is racially and geographically divided.

Charles Stangor (Ed.), *Stereotypes and Prejudice: Essential Readings* (Psychology Press, 2000). A collection of research articles on prejudice.

On the Internet

CourseMate Access an integrated eBook and chapter-specific learning tools including flashcards, quizzes, videos, and more. Go to CengageBrain.com.

 Want to maximize the value of your online study time? Take this easy-to-use study system's diagnostic pre-test, and it will create a personalized study plan for you. By helping you identify the topics that you need to understand better and then directing you to valuable online resources, it can speed up your chapter review. CengageNOW even provides a post-test so you can confirm that you are ready for an exam. Go to CengageBrain.com.

TALKING POINTS

Here are a few talking points to help you summarize this chapter for family and friends without giving a lecture.

1. Our expectations about how someone will behave can not only shape our first impression of that person but also lead the person to behave in line with our expectations.
2. We often take personal credit when we succeed at something but blame circumstances when we fail.
3. Many people ignore the dangers of risky behavior because unrealistic optimism leads them to believe that bad things only happen to other people.
4. When our actions are in conflict with our attitudes or beliefs, we tend to reduce the conflict by adjusting our attitudes, not our behavior.
5. A feeling of belonging to a particular social or ethnic group is comforting, but it can also lead to prejudice against people in other groups.
6. Some people find that being prejudiced helps them feel better about themselves while making the world seem simpler and easier to deal with.
7. Although we might prefer to have the most physically attractive partners available, most people compromise by forming intimate relationships with someone whose attractiveness is similar to their own.

18

Social Influence

© David Madison/Stone/Getty Images

If you are like most people, there is probably at least one thing you do in private that you would never do when someone else is around. In this chapter, we describe many other ways in which the presence and behavior of other people affect our own behavior and how we in turn affect the behavior of others.

In the days following the September 11, 2001, attacks on the World Trade Center and the Pentagon, cities throughout the United States experienced a substantial increase in false bomb threats and other "copycat" crimes apparently inspired by the terrorists' actions. Unfortunately, this phenomenon is not unusual. After the murderous rampage at Columbine High School in April 1999, for example, a number of students at other high schools were arrested for threatening similar acts of violence against their classmates. Copycat threats were also made following the horrific massacre at Virginia Tech in April 2007. Well-publicized suicides, and assisted suicides too, are often copied (Frie et al., 2003; Romer, Jamieson, & Jamieson, 2006). Even telecasts of major professional boxing matches are typically followed by a small increase in murders.

Do these correlations mean that media coverage of violence triggers copycat violence? As described in the chapter on learning, televised violence can play a causal role in aggressive behavior, but there are additional reasons to believe that when suicides and murders become media events, they stimulate people to imitate them. For one thing, many of the people who kill themselves soon after a notable suicide are about the same age and the same gender as the original victim (Cialdini, 2007). Further, murder victims in the days following a professional championship fight are likely to be members of the same ethnic group as the losing boxer (Miller et al., 1991).

Copycat, or imitative, crimes illustrate **social influence**, the process through which a person's thoughts, feelings, and behavior are directly or indirectly affected by the words or actions of other people (Hogg, 2010). In this chapter, we describe its more positive aspects too, beginning with a discussion of social influence itself. We then consider several related aspects of how we are influenced by others, including the processes of conformity, compliance, and obedience. Then we explore the causes and consequences of aggression, helping, and altruism. Finally, we examine circumstances in which people jointly influence one another's behavior, especially circumstances in which people compete with one another for some scarce resource or work together in groups to solve some problem.

Social Influence

Copycat crimes are but one illustration of the fact that people can influence the way other people think, feel, and act, even without specifically trying to do so. There are countless others. For example, the amount of food that people order in a restaurant can be affected by the weight of the person who is eating with them. They tend to order a smaller portion than the other person does if that person is obese but to order items of about the same size if the other person is slender (McFerran et al., 2010). The most widespread yet subtle form of social influence is communicated through social norms.

Social norms are learned, socially based rules that prescribe what people should or should not do in various situations (Hogg, 2010). These norms are transmitted by parents, teachers, clergy, peers, and other agents of culture. Although they often

social influence The process whereby one person's behavior is affected by the words or actions of others.

social norms Socially based rules that prescribe what people should or should not do in various situations.

cannot be verbalized, norms are so powerful that people usually follow them automatically. At movie theaters in North America and Britain, for example, social norms tell us that we should get in line to buy a ticket rather than crowd around the ticket window; they also lead us to expect that others will do the same. By informing people of what is expected of them and others, social norms make social situations less uncertain and more comfortable (Schultz et al., 2007).

Robert Cialdini (2007) has described social norms as either descriptive or injunctive. *Descriptive norms* indicate how most other people actually behave in a given situation. They tell us what actions are common in the situation and thereby implicitly give us permission to act in the same way. The fact that most people do not cross a street until the green light or "walk" sign appears is an example of a descriptive norm. *Injunctive norms* give more specific information about the actions that others find acceptable and those that they find unacceptable. Subtle pressure exists to behave in accordance with these norms. A sign that reads "Do not cross on red" or the person next to you saying the same thing is an example of an injunctive norm. Sometimes both kinds of norms operate at the same time. There is evidence, for example, that how much college students use tobacco and alcohol is influenced both by how much they think other students drink and smoke (descriptive norms) and whether they think that their close friends approve of these behaviors (injunctive norms) (Etcheverry & Agnew, 2008; Neighbors et al., 2008).

One very powerful injunctive norm is *reciprocity,* the tendency to respond to others as they have acted toward you (Kenrick, Neuberg, & Cialdini, 2010). Restaurant servers often exploit this social norm by leaving some candy with the bill. Customers who receive this gift tend to reciprocate by leaving a larger tip than customers who don't get candy (Strohmetz et al., 2002). The reciprocity norm probably exists in every culture, but other social norms are not universal (Miller, 2001). For instance, people around the world differ greatly in terms of the physical distance they maintain between themselves and others during conversation. People from South America usually stand much closer to one another than people from North America do. And as suggested in the chapter on psychological disorders, behavior considered normal and friendly in one culture may be seen as abnormal or even offensive in another.

The social influence exerted by norms creates orderly social behavior. But social norms can also lead to a breakdown in order. For example, **deindividuation** is a phenomenon in which a person becomes "submerged in a group" and loses the sense of individuality (Kenrick, Neuberg, & Cialdini, 2010). When people experience deindividuation, they become emotionally aroused and feel intense closeness with the group. This increased awareness of group membership may create greater adherence to the group's norms, even if those norms promote antisocial behavior. In other words, through deindividuation, people appear to become "part of the herd," and they may perform acts that they would not do otherwise. Fans at rock concerts and athletic events have trampled one another to death in their frenzy to get the best seats. Normally mild-mannered people may find themselves throwing rocks or fire bombs at police during political protests.

The greater the sense of personal anonymity, the more influence the group appears to have (Lea, Spears, & de Groot, 2001). An analysis of newspaper accounts of lynchings in the United States over a fifty-year period showed that larger lynch mobs were more savage and vicious than smaller ones (Mullen, 1986). Deindividuation provides an example of how, given the right circumstances, quite normal people can engage in destructive, even violent, behavior.

© AP Photo

Clothing and Culture

The social norms that guide how people dress and behave in various situations are part of the culturally determined socialization process described in the chapter on human development. The process is the same worldwide. Parents, teachers, peers, religious leaders, and others communicate their culture's social norms to children, but differences in those norms result in quite different behaviors from culture to culture.

deindividuation   A psychological state occurring in group members that results in loss of individuality and a tendency to do things not normally done when alone.

LINKAGES

LINKAGES   Do people perform better or worse when others are watching? (a link to Motivation and Emotion, p. 737)

Motivation and the Presence of Others

In the chapter on motivation and emotion, we noted that social factors such as parental attitudes toward achievement often affect motivation. But a person's current motivational state is also affected by the mere presence of other people. Consider what was probably the first experiment in social psychology, conducted by Norman Triplett in 1897.

Deindividuation

Robes, hoods, and group rituals help create deindividuation in these Ku Klux Klansmen by focusing their attention on membership in their organization and on its values. The hoods also hide their identities, which reduces their sense of personal responsibility and accountability and makes it easier for them to engage in hate crimes and other cowardly acts of bigotry. Deindividuation operates in other groups too, ranging from lynch mobs and terrorist cells to political protesters and urban rioters. In short, people who feel that they are anonymous members of a group may engage in antisocial acts that they might not perform on their own.

© David Leeson/The Image Works

Triplett noticed that bicycle racers tended to go faster when other racers were nearby than when they were alone. Did seeing one another remind the racers of the need to go faster to win? To test this possibility, Triplett arranged for bicyclists to complete a 25-mile course under three conditions: riding alone in a race against the clock, riding with another cyclist but not in competition, or competing directly with another rider. The cyclists went much faster when another rider was present than when they were simply racing against time. This was true even when they were not competing against the other person. Something about the presence of the other person, not just competition, produced increased speed.

The term **social facilitation** describes circumstances in which, as in the bicycle racing example, the mere presence of other people can improve performance. This improvement does not always occur, however. The presence of other people sometimes hurts performance, a process known as **social interference**. For decades, these results seemed contradictory. Then Robert Zajonc (pronounced "ZY-unss") suggested that both effects could be explained by one process: arousal.

The presence of other people, said Zajonc (1965), increases a person's general level of arousal or motivation. Why? One reason is that being watched by others increases our sense of being evaluated, producing worry that in turn increases emotional arousal (Uziel, 2007). Arousal increases the tendency to display our most *dominant* behaviors—the ones we know best. Engaging in those dominant behaviors can sometime help our performance and sometimes hinder it. If you are performing an easy, familiar task, such as riding a bike, the increased arousal caused by the presence of others should allow you to ride even faster than normal. But if the task is hard or unfamiliar—such as trying new dance steps or playing a piano piece you just learned—the most dominant responses may be incorrect and cause your performance to suffer. In other words, the impact of other people on performance depends on whether the task is easy or difficult.

The presence of others may affect performance in other ways as well. For example, having an audience may distract us from the task at hand or cause us to focus on only one part of it, thus impairing performance (Aiello & Douthitt, 2001).

What if a person is not merely in the presence of others but is actually working on a task with them? In these situations, people typically exert less effort than they do when performing alone, a phenomenon called **social loafing** (Liden et al., 2004).

social facilitation A phenomenon in which the presence of others improves a person's performance

social interference A reduction in performance due to the presence of other people.

social loafing Exerting less effort when performing a group task than when performing the same task alone.

Social Facilitation

Top athletes like Serena Williams, shown here winning the 2010 women's singles championship at Wimbledon, are able to perform at their best even though large crowds are present. In fact, the crowds probably help them do well, because the presence of others tends to increase arousal, which enhances the performance of familiar and well-learned skills, such as tennis strokes. However, arousal created by an audience tends to interfere with the performance of unfamiliar and poorly developed skills. This is one reason that professional athletes who show flawless grace in front of thousands of fans are likely to freeze up or blow their lines in front of a small production crew when trying for the first time to tape a TV ad or a public service announcement.

© Kirsty Wigglesworth/AP Photo

Whether the task is pulling on a rope, clapping as loudly as possible, trying to solve puzzles, or working together on a class project, people tend to work harder when performing alone than with others (Price, Harrison, & Gavin, 2006; van Dick et al., 2009). There are at least three reasons behind this social loafing phenomenon. First, it is usually much harder to evaluate the performance of individuals when they are working as part of a group. As a result, it is simply easier to succeed at loafing when in a group. Second, rewards may come to a group whether or not every member exerts maximum effort. Third, a group's rewards are usually divided equally among its members rather than according to individual effort (Hoigaard & Ingvaldesen, 2006; Pearsall, Christian, & Ellis, 2010).

In North American and other Western countries, social loafing can be seen in all kinds of groups, from volunteer committees to search parties. Because social loafing can reduce productivity in business situations, it is important for managers to counteract it by finding ways to evaluate the efforts of every individual in a work group, not just the overall output of the team. Social loafing also tends to be reduced when members like and identify with the group (Hoigaard, Säfvenbom, & Tonnessen, 2006) and when harder-working members express their disapproval of social loafers (Barclay, 2006).

Social loafing is much less common in Eastern cultures, such as those of China and Japan. In fact, in collectivist cultures, working in a group usually produces *social striving*—defined as greater individual effort when working in a group (Matsumoto, 2000). This difference in the effects of group membership on individual efforts probably reflects the value that collectivist cultures place on coordinated and cooperative group activities.

Conformity and Compliance

Suppose that you are with three of your friends. One says that Franklin Roosevelt was the greatest president in the history of the United States. You think that the greatest president was Abraham Lincoln, but before you can say anything, another friend agrees that it was Roosevelt, and then the other one does as well. What would you do? Disagree with all three? Maintain your opinion but keep quiet? Change your mind?

Mass Conformity

The faithful who gather at Mecca, at the Vatican, and at other holy places around the world exemplify the power of religion and other social forces to produce conformity to group norms.

When people change their behavior or beliefs to match those of other members of a group, they are said to conform. **Conformity** occurs as a result of group pressure, real or imagined (Hogg, 2010). You have probably experienced such group pressure when everyone around you stood to applaud a performance you thought was not that great. You may have conformed by standing as well, though no one told you to do so. The group's behavior created a silent but influential pressure to follow suit. **Compliance**, in contrast, occurs when people adjust their behavior because of a request. The request can be clear and *explicit,* as when someone says, "Could you do me a favor?" or subtle and *implicit,* as when someone simply looks at you in a way that lets you know the person needs a favor.

The Role of Social Norms

Conformity and compliance are usually generated by spoken or unspoken social norms. In a classic experiment, Muzafer Sherif (1937) charted the formation of a group norm by taking advantage of a perceptual illusion, called the *autokinetic effect.* In this illusion, a stationary point of light in a pitch-dark room appears to move. Estimates of the amount of movement tend to stay the same over time—if an observer is alone. But when Sherif tested people in groups, asking each person to say aloud how far the light moved on repeated trials, their estimates tended to converge. They had established a group norm. Even more important, when the individuals from the group were later tested alone, they continued to be influenced by this social norm.

In another classic experiment, Solomon Asch (1956) examined how people would respond when they faced a social norm that already existed but was obviously wrong. The participants in this experiment saw a standard line like the one in part A of Figure 18.1; then they saw a display like that in part B. Their task was to pick out the line in the display that was the same length as the one they had first been shown.

Each participant performed this task in a small group of people who posed as fellow participants but who were actually the experimenter's assistants. There were two conditions. In the control condition, the real participant responded first. In the experimental condition, the participant did not respond until after the assistants did. The assistants chose the correct response on six trials, but on the other twelve trials,

conformity Changing one's behavior or beliefs to match those of others, generally as a result of real or imagined, though unspoken, group pressure.

compliance Adjusting one's behavior because of an explicit or implicit request.

Standard line

(A)

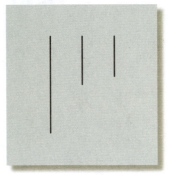

Test lines

(B)

FIGURE 18.1

**Stimulus Lines for Conformity
Studies**

TRY THIS Participants in Asch's
experiments saw a new set of lines like
these on each trial. The middle line
in part B matches the one in part A,
but when several of Asch's assistants
chose an incorrect line, so did many
of the participants. Try re-creating this
experiment with four friends. Secretly ask
three of them to choose the line on the
left when you show this drawing; then
see if the fourth person conforms to the
group norm. If not, do you think it was
something about the person, the length
of the incorrect line chosen, or both that
led to nonconformity? Would conformity
be more likely if the first three people
were to choose the line on the right? (The
text provides more information about this
possibility.)

Sources: Asch (1955).

they all gave the same obviously incorrect response. So on twelve trials, each participant was confronted with a "social reality" created by a group norm that conflicted
with the physical reality created by what the person could clearly see. Only 5 percent
of the participants in the control condition ever made a mistake on this easy task.
However, among participants who heard the assistants' responses before giving their
own, about 70 percent made at least one error by conforming to the group norm. An
analysis of 133 studies conducted in seventeen countries reveals that conformity in
Asch-type situations has declined somewhat in the United States since the 1950s, but it
still occurs. It is especially likely in collectivist cultures, in which conformity to group
norms is emphasized (Cialdini et al., 2001).

Pressure to conform can even affect reports about personal experiences. In one
study that used a procedure similar to Asch's, participants were shown a number of
objects. Later the same objects were shown again, along with some new ones, and
the participants were asked to say whether they had seen each object in the previous
display. When tested alone, the participants' memories were quite accurate, but hearing another person's opinion about which objects had or had not been shown before
strongly affected their memory of which objects they had seen (Hoffman et al., 2001).

Why Do People Conform?

Why did so many people in Asch's experiment and others like it give incorrect
responses when they were capable of near-perfect performance? One possibility is
that they displayed public conformity, giving an answer they did not believe simply
because it was the socially desirable thing to do. Another possibility is that they experienced *private acceptance:* Perhaps the participants used other people's responses as
legitimate evidence about reality, were convinced that their own perceptions were
wrong, and actually changed their minds. Morton Deutsch and Harold Gerard (1955)
reasoned that if conformity disappeared when people gave their responses without
identifying themselves, Asch's findings must reflect public conformity, not private
acceptance. Actually, conformity does decrease when people respond anonymously
instead of publicly, but it doesn't disappear (Deutsch & Gerard, 1955). So people sometimes say things in public that they don't believe, but hearing other people's responses
also influences their private beliefs (Moscovici, 1985).

Why are group norms so powerful? Research suggests three influential factors
(Kenrick, Neuberg, & Cialdini, 2010). First, people want to be correct, and social norms
provide information about what is right and wrong. Second, people want others to like
and accept them, so they may seek favor by conforming to the social norms that those
others have established (Hewlin & Faison, 2009).Third, conforming to group norms
may increase a person's sense of self-worth, especially if the group is valued or prestigious (Cialdini & Goldstein, 2004). The process may occur without our awareness
(Lakin & Chartrand, 2003). For example, observations of interviews by Larry King, the
recently retired television talk show host, revealed that he tended to imitate the speech
patterns of high-status guests but not low-status ones (Gregory & Webster, 1996).

Finally, social norms influence the distribution of social rewards and punishments
(Cialdini, 1995). From childhood on, people in many cultures learn that going along with
group norms is good and earns rewards. (These positive outcomes presumably help compensate for not always being able to say or do exactly what we please.) People also learn
that breaking a social norm may bring punishments ranging from scoldings for small
transgressions to imprisonment for violation of norms that have been translated into laws.

When Do People Conform?

People do not always conform to social influence. In the original Asch studies, for
example, nearly 30 percent of the participants did not go along with the research assistants' obviously incorrect judgments. Countless experiments have probed the question
of what combinations of people and circumstances do and do not lead to conformity.

Ambiguity of the Situation   *Ambiguity,* or uncertainty, is very important in determining how much conformity will occur. As the physical reality of a situation becomes less certain, people rely more and more on others' opinions, and conformity to a group norm becomes increasingly likely (Cialdini & Goldstein, 2004).

TRY THIS   You can demonstrate this aspect of conformity on any street corner. First, create an ambiguous situation by having several people look at the sky or the top of a building. When passersby ask what is going on, be sure everyone excitedly reports seeing something interesting but fleeting—perhaps a faint light or a tiny, shiny object. If you are especially successful, conforming newcomers will begin persuading other passersby that there is something fascinating to be seen.

Unanimity and Size of the Majority   If ambiguity contributes so much to conformity, why did so many of Asch's participants conform to a judgment that was so clearly wrong? The answer has to do with the *unanimous* nature of the group's judgment and the number of people expressing it. Specifically, people experience great pressure to conform as long as the majority is unanimous. If even one other person in the group disagrees with the majority view, conformity drops greatly. When Asch (1951) arranged for just one assistant to disagree with the others, fewer than 10 percent of the real participants conformed. Once unanimity is broken, it becomes much easier to disagree with the majority, even if the other nonconformist does not agree with the person's own view (Turner, 1991).

Conformity also depends on the *size of the majority.* Asch (1955) demonstrated this phenomenon by varying the number of assistants in the group from one to fifteen. Conformity to incorrect social norms grew as the number of people in the group increased. But most of the growth in conformity occurred as the size of the majority rose from one to about three or four members. Further additions had little effect. Several years after Asch's research, Bibb Latané (pronounced "lat-uh-NAY") sought to explain this phenomenon with his *social impact theory.* This theory holds that a group's impact on an individual depends not only on group size but also on how important and close the group is to the person. And according to Latané (1981), the impact of increasing the size of a majority depends on how big the majority was originally. Increasing a majority from, say, two to three will have much more impact than increasing it from, say, sixty to sixty-one. The reason is that the increase from sixty to sixty-one is psychologically much smaller than the change from two to three; it attracts far less notice in relative terms. Does this explanation sound familiar? The principles underlying it are similar to those of Weber's law, which, as described in the chapter on perception, governs our experience of changes in brightness, weight, and other physical stimuli.

Minority Influence   Conformity can also result from *minority influence,* by which a minority in a group influences the behavior or beliefs of a majority (Hogg, 2010). This phenomenon is less common than majority influence, but minorities can be influential in producing private acceptance of new ideas, especially when members of the minority agree with one another and persist in their views (Hogg, 2010; Mucchi-Faina & Pagliaro, 2008). Minority-influenced change often takes place slowly and is most likely to occur when those holding a minority view are perceived as loyal members of the group (Crano & Seyranian, 2009).

Gender   Early research on conformity suggested that women conform more than men. However, the tasks used in those experiments were often more familiar to men than to women. This fact is important because people are especially likely to conform when they are faced with an unfamiliar situation (Cialdini & Goldstein, 2004). Those studies also usually required people to make their responses aloud so that everyone knew if they had conformed or not. When the experimental tasks are equally familiar to both genders and when people can make their responses privately, no male-female differences in conformity are found. Accordingly, it has been suggested

© Amy Etra/PhotoEdit

Sign Here, Please

APPLYING PSYCHOLOGY Have you ever been asked to sign a petition in favor of a political, social, or economic cause? Supporters of these causes know that people who comply with this small request are the best ones to contact later with requests to do more. Complying with larger requests is made more likely because it is consistent with the signer's initial commitment to the cause. If you have ever been contacted after signing a petition, did you agree to donate money or perhaps become a volunteer?

that gender differences in public conformity are based not on a genuine difference in reactions to social pressure but rather on men's desire to be seen as strong and independent and women's desire to be seen as cooperative (Hogg, 2010; Kenrick, Neuberg, & Cialdini, 2010).

Creating Compliance

In the conformity experiments we have described, the participants experienced psychological pressure to conform to the views or actions of others, even though no one specifically asked them to do so. In contrast, *compliance* involves changing what you say or do as the result of a request.

How is compliance brought about? Many people believe that the direct approach is always best: If you want something, ask for it. But salespeople, political strategists, social psychologists, and other experts have learned that often the best way to get something is to ask for something else. Three examples of this strategy are the foot-in-the-door technique, the door-in-the-face technique, and the low-ball technique.

The *foot-in-the-door technique* works by getting a person to agree to a small request and then gradually presenting larger ones. (The name refers to a fact that all door-to-door salespeople know: If you can get a potential customer to let you in the door, you have a much better chance of making a sale.) In the original experiment on this technique, homeowners were asked to do one of two things. Some were asked to allow a large, unattractive "Drive Carefully" sign to be placed on their front lawns. Approximately 17 percent of the people approached in this way complied with the request. In the foot-in-the-door condition, however, homeowners were first asked only to sign a petition supporting legislation aimed at reducing traffic accidents. Several weeks later, when a different person asked these same people to put the "Drive Carefully" sign on their lawns, 55 percent of them complied (Freedman & Fraser, 1966).

Why should the granting of a small favor lead to the granting of a larger one? First, people are usually far more likely to comply with a request that costs little in time, money, effort, or inconvenience. Second, complying with a small request makes people think of themselves as being committed to the cause or issue involved. This change occurs through the processes of self-perception and cognitive dissonance discussed in the chapter on social cognition (Kassin, Fein, & Markus, 2010). In the study just described, participants who signed the petition may have thought, "I signed, so I must care enough about traffic safety to be willing to do something about it." Compliance with the higher-cost request (displaying the "drive safely" sign) then became more likely because it was consistent with these people's self-perceptions and past actions (Burger & Caldwell, 2003).

The foot-in-the-door technique can be quite effective. In one study, women were significantly more likely to agree to have a drink with a man they had just met if they had first agreed to a smaller favor, such as giving him directions to an address he was seeking (Guéguen et al., 2008). In some business strategies, the foot in the door can come as a request that potential customers merely provide a phone number or an e-mail address. The request to buy something comes later. Other companies offer a small gift or "door opener," as salespeople call it. Acceptance of the gift not only allows a foot in the door but may also activate the reciprocity norm: Many people who get something free of charge feel obligated to reciprocate by buying something—especially if the request to do so is delayed for a while (Cialdini, 2007; Guadagno et al., 2001).

The *door-in-the-face technique* offers a second way of obtaining compliance (Turner et al., 2007). This strategy begins with a request for a favor that is likely to be denied (as when a door is slammed in a salesperson's face). The person making the request then concedes that asking for the initial favor was excessive and substitutes a lesser alternative—which was what the person really wanted in the first place. Because the person appears willing to compromise and because the new request seems modest in comparison with the first one, it is more likely to be granted than if it had been made at the outset. Here again, compliance appears to be due partly to activation of the reciprocity

"OK, OK, I'll Be Home by One!"

APPLYING PSYCHOLOGY The door-in-the-face technique is sometimes used successfully by teenagers to influence parents to comply with many kinds of requests. After asking to stay out overnight, a youngster whose curfew is normally 11:00 P.M. might be allowed to stay out until 1:00 A.M.—a "compromise" that was actually the original goal.

© Ariel Skelley/Corbis

norm: This person is making a concession to me, so I should really make a concession in return. The door-in-the-face technique often lies at the heart of the bargaining that takes place among political groups and between labor and management (Ginges et al., 2007).

A third way of gaining compliance, called the *low-ball technique*, is commonly used by car dealers and other salespeople. The first step in this strategy is to obtain a person's oral commitment to do something, such as to purchase a car at a certain price. Once this commitment is made, the cost of fulfilling it is increased, often because of an "error" in calculating the car's price. Why do buyers end up paying much more than originally planned for lowballed items? Apparently, once people say they will do something, they feel obligated to follow through, especially when the commitment was made in public and when the person who obtained the initial commitment is also the one who tells the buyer about the price increase (Burger & Cornelius, 2003). In other words, as described in relation to cognitive dissonance theory in the chapter on social cognition, people like to be consistent in their words and deeds. In this case, it appears that people try to maintain a positive self-image by acting in accordance with their previously stated intention, even though it may cost them a great deal to do so.

Obedience

Compliance involves a change in behavior in response to a request. In the case of **obedience**, the behavior change comes in response to a *demand* from an authority figure (Kenrick, Neuberg, & Cialdini, 2010). In the 1960s, Stanley Milgram developed a laboratory procedure at Yale University to study obedience. In his first experiment, he used newspaper ads to recruit forty male volunteers between the ages of 20 and 50. Among the participants were professionals, white-collar businessmen, and unskilled workers (Milgram, 1963).

Imagine that you are one of the people who answered the ad. When you arrive for the experiment, you join a 50-year-old gentleman who has also volunteered and has been scheduled for the same session. The experimenter explains that the purpose of the experiment is to examine the effects of punishment on learning. One of you—the

obedience Changing behavior in response to a demand from an authority figure.

"teacher"—will help the "learner" remember a list of words by administering an electrical shock whenever he makes a mistake. Then the experimenter turns to you and asks you to draw one of two cards out of a hat. Your card says "Teacher." You think to yourself that this must be your lucky day.

Now the learner is taken into another room and strapped into a chair. Electrodes are attached to his arms. Meanwhile, you are shown a shock generator featuring thirty switches. The experimenter explains that the switch on the far left administers a mild, 15-volt shock and that each succeeding switch increases the shock by 15 volts. The switch on the far right delivers 450 volts. The far-left section of the shock generator is labeled "slight shock." Looking across the panel, you see "moderate shock," "very strong shock," and at the far right, "danger—severe shock." The last two switches are ominously labeled "XXX." The experimenter explains that you, the teacher, will begin by reading a list of word pairs to the learner. Then you will go through the list again, presenting just one word of each pair. It is the learner's task to say which word went with it. After the first mistake, you are to throw the switch to deliver 15 volts of shock. Each time the learner makes another mistake, you are to increase the shock by 15 volts.

You begin, following the experimenter's instructions. But after the learner makes his fifth mistake and you throw the switch to give him 75 volts, you hear a loud moan. At 90 volts, the learner cries out in pain. At 150 volts, he screams and asks to be let out of the experiment. You look to the experimenter, who says, "Proceed with the next word."

No shock was actually delivered in Milgram's experiments. The learner was always an employee of the experimenter, and the moans and other sounds of pain came from a prerecorded tape. But you don't know that. What would you do in this situation? Suppose that you continue and eventually deliver 180 volts. At that point, the learner screams that he cannot stand the pain any longer and starts banging on the wall. The experimenter says, "You have no other choice; you must go on." Would you continue? Would you keep going even when the learner begged to be let out of the experiment and then fell silent? Would you administer 450 volts of potentially deadly shock to a perfect stranger just because an experimenter demanded that you do so?

Figure 18.2 shows that only five of the forty participants in Milgram's experiment stopped before 300 volts, and twenty-six participants (65 percent) went all the way to the 450-volt level. The decision to continue was difficult and stressful for the participants. Many protested repeatedly, but each time the experimenter told them

FIGURE 18.2
Results of Milgram's Obedience Experiment

When Stanley Milgram asked a group of undergraduates and a group of psychiatrists to predict how participants in his experiment would respond, they estimated that no more than 2 percent would go all the way to 450 volts. In fact, 65 percent of the participants did so. What do you think you would have done in this situation?

Source: From S. Milgram. "Behavioral Study of Obedience." *Journal of Abnormal and Social Psychology,* 67, pp. 371–378. Reprinted by permission.

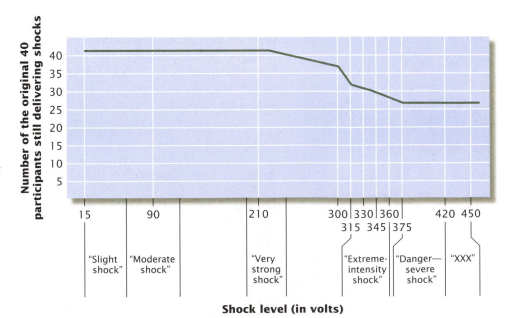

to continue, they did so. Here is a partial transcript of what a typical participant said (Milgram, 1974, p. 74):

> [*After throwing the 180-volt switch*] He can't stand it. I'm not going to kill that man in there. Do you hear him hollering? He's hollering. He can't stand it. What if something happens to him? I'm not going to get that man sick in there. He's hollering in there. Do you know what I mean? I mean, I refuse to take responsibility. He's getting hurt in there.... Too many [word pairs] left here. Geez, if he gets them wrong. There are too many of them left. I mean, who is going to take responsibility if anything happens to that gentleman?...

> [*After the experimenter accepts responsibility*] All right....

> [*After administering 240 volts*] Oh, no, you mean I've got to keep going up the scale? No, sir, I'm not going to kill that man. I'm not going to give him 450 volts....

> [*After the experimenter says, "The experiment requires that you go on"*] I know it does, but that man is hollering in there, sir.

This participant administered shocks up to 450 volts.

Factors Affecting Obedience

Milgram had not expected so many people to deliver such apparently intense shocks. Was there something about his procedure that produced this high level of obedience? To find out, Milgram and other researchers varied the original procedure in a number of ways. The overall level of obedience to an authority figure was usually quite high, but the degree of obedience was affected by several factors.

Experimenter Status and Prestige   In Milgram's original study, the experimenter's status and prestige as a Yale University professor created two kinds of social power that affected the participants. The first was *expert power,* which is the ability to influence people because they assume that the person in power is a knowledgeable and responsible expert. The second was *legitimate power,* which is the ability to influence people because they assume that the person in power has the right or legitimate authority to tell them what to do (Blass, 2009).

To test the effects of reduced status and prestige, Milgram rented an office in a run-down building in Bridgeport, Connecticut. He then placed a newspaper ad for people to participate in research sponsored by a private firm. There was no mention of Yale. In all other ways, the experimental procedure was identical to the original. Under these less impressive circumstances, the level of obedience dropped, but not as much as you might expect; 48 percent of the participants continued to the maximum level of shock, compared to 65 percent in the original study. Milgram concluded that people still would obey instructions that could cause great harm to another even if the authority figure was not associated with a prestigious institution. Evidently, people's willingness to follow orders from an authority operates somewhat independently of the setting in which the orders are given.

The Behavior of Other People   To study how the behavior of fellow participants might affect obedience, Milgram (1965) created a situation in which there were apparently three teachers. Teacher 1 (in reality, a research assistant) read the words to the learner. Teacher 2 (another research assistant) stated whether or not the learner's response was correct. Teacher 3 (the actual participant) was to deliver a shock when mistakes were made. At 150 volts, when the learner began to complain that the shock was too painful, Teacher 1 said he would not participate any longer and left the room. The experimenter asked him to come back, but he refused. The experimenter then instructed Teachers 2 and 3 to continue by themselves. The experiment went on for several more trials. However, at 210 volts, Teacher 2 said that the learner was suffering too much and refused to participate further. The experimenter then told Teacher 3

Proximity and Obedience

Milgram's research suggested that the close physical proximity of an authority figure is one of several factors that can enhance obedience to authority (Rada & Rogers, 1973). This proximity principle is employed in the military, where no one is ever far away from the authority of a higher-ranking person.

(the actual participant) to continue the procedure. In this case, only 10 percent of the participants (compared to 65 percent in the original study) continued to deliver shocks all the way up to 450 volts. In other words, as research on conformity would suggest, the presence of others who disobey appears to be the most powerful factor in reducing obedience.

The Behavior of the Learner   A reanalysis of data from Milgram's obedience studies (Packer, 2008) found that although the learner's increasingly intense expressions of pain did not affect whether the participants disobeyed the experimenter, the learner's request to be released from the experiment did affect disobedience. In fact, among those participants who refused to continue to shock the learner, almost 37 percent of them disobeyed at the 150-volt level, which was when the learner first said he wanted to be released from the experiment. So it appears that perceiving a victim's pain does not reduce obedience to authority but being reminded of a victim's right to be released from the experiment does.

Personality Characteristics   Were the participants in Milgram's original experiment heartless creatures who would have given strong shocks even if there had been no pressure on them to do so? Quite the opposite; most of them were nice people who were influenced by experimental situations to behave in apparently antisocial ways. In a later demonstration of the same phenomenon, college students playing the role of prison guards behaved with aggressive heartlessness toward other students who were playing the role of prisoners (Zimbardo, 1973). A more recent illustration of this phenomenon occurred among certain groups of soldiers who were assigned to guard or interrogate prisoners in Afghanistan and Iraq.

Still, not everyone is obedient to authority. For example, people high in *authoritarianism* (a characteristic discussed in the chapter on social cognition) are more likely than others to comply with an experimenter's request to shock the learner (Blass, 1991). Support for this idea comes from data suggesting that German soldiers who obeyed orders to kill Jews during World War II were higher on authoritarianism than other German men of the same age and background (Steiner & Fahrenberg, 2000). In contrast, a recent study that repeated Milgram's experimental procedures (Burger, 2009) found that the participants who were less likely to obey orders to harm the learner were also the ones who were concerned about others and predisposed to have *empathy*—that is, to understand or experience another person's emotional state (Davis, 1994).

Evaluating Milgram's Studies

How relevant are Milgram's 1960s studies in today's world? Consider this fact: The U.S. Federal Aviation Administration attributes some commercial airline accidents to a phenomenon it calls "captainitis." This phenomenon occurs when the captain of an aircraft makes an obvious error but the copilot is unwilling to challenge the captain's authority by pointing out the mistake. As a result, planes have crashed and people have died (Kanki & Foushee, 1990). Obedience to authority may also have operated during the World Trade Center attack on 9/11, when some people who had started for the exits returned to their offices after hearing an ill-advised public address announcement telling them to do so. Most of these people died as a result. Similar kinds of obedience have been observed in experiments conducted in many countries, from Europe to the Middle East, with female as well as male participants (Burger, 2009). In short, people appear to be as likely to obey orders today as they were when Milgram conducted his research (Blass, 2009). Nevertheless, many aspects of Milgram's work still provoke debate. (For a summary of Milgram's results, plus those of studies on conformity and compliance, see "In Review: Types of Social Influence.")

Questions About the Ethics of Milgram's Research   Although the "learners" in Milgram's experiment suffered no discomfort, the participants did. Milgram (1963) saw participants "sweat, stutter, tremble, groan, bite their lips, and dig their fingernails into their flesh" (p. 375). Against the potential harm inflicted by Milgram's experiments stand the potential gains. For example, students and others who learn about Milgram's work often take his findings into account when deciding whether to be obedient in social situations (Sherman, 1980). But even if social value has come from Milgram's studies, the question remains: Was it ethical for Milgram to treat his participants as he did?

In the years before his death in 1984, Milgram defended his experiments (e.g., Milgram, 1977). He argued that his debriefing of the participants after the experiment prevented any lasting harm. For example, to demonstrate that their behavior was not unusual, Milgram told participants that most people went all the way to the 450-volt level. He also explained that the learner did not experience any shock; to confirm this fact, the learner then came in and had a friendly chat with each participant. On a later questionnaire, 84 percent of the participants said that they had learned something important about themselves and that the experience had been worthwhile. Milgram argued, therefore, that the experience was actually a positive one. Still, the committees charged with protecting human participants in research today would be unlikely to approve Milgram's experiments as they were originally done. Fortunately, less controversial ways to study obedience have been developed (Elms, 2009).

Questions About the Meaning of Milgram's Research   Do Milgram's dramatic results mean that most people are putty in the hands of authority figures and that most of us would blindly follow inhumane orders from our leaders? Some critics have argued that Milgram's results cannot be interpreted in this way because his participants knew they were in an experiment and may simply have been playing a cooperative role. If so, the social influence processes identified in his studies may not explain obedience in the real world today.

Most psychologists believe, however, that Milgram not only demonstrated the power of obedience to authority but also revealed—or perhaps confirmed—a basic truth about human behavior: that under certain circumstances, human beings are capable of unspeakable acts of brutality toward other humans (Benjamin & Simpson, 2009). Sadly, examples abound. And one of the most horrifying aspects of human inhumanity—whether the Nazis' campaign of genocide against Jews in the 1930s and 1940s or the campaigns of terror under way today—is that the perpetrators are not necessarily demented, sadistic fiends. Most of them are, in many respects, "normal" people who have been influenced by economic and political situations and

© Mark Ludak/The Image Works

"May I Take Your Order?"

In February 2004, the managers of four fast-food restaurants in Boston received calls from someone claiming to be a police detective on the trail of a robbery suspect. The caller said that the suspect might be one of the restaurant's employees and told the managers to strip-search all of them for evidence of guilt. The calls turned out to be hoaxes, but every manager obeyed this bizarre order, apparently because it seemed to come from a legitimate authority. In two similar cases, residents of a special-needs school were given unnecessary electric shock treatments on telephoned orders from a hoaxer, and hospital nurses obeyed medical treatment orders given by a teenager who claimed to be a doctor (Kenrick, Neuberg, & Cialdini, 2010; "Officials Investigating," 2007).

LINKAGES   Is it ethical to deceive people in order to learn about their social behavior? (a link to Research in Psychology, p. 57)

A Shocking Game Show

On March 17, 2010, a French television station aired *The Extreme Zone,* a quiz show that allowed contestants—with the enthusiastic support of a live studio audience—to punish another contestant's incorrect answers by giving him increasingly severe electric shocks. Neither the contestants nor the audience knew that the show was actually a documentary designed to test people's willingness to harm others. The actor who played the punished contestant was never really shocked, but as shown in this photo, his fake suffering was quite convincing. Though he begged them to stop, 80 percent of the contestants—more than in Milgram's original obedience experiment—delivered the maximum shock. These results provided dramatic evidence that potentially deadly aggression can be triggered by many social influences, including competition and peer encouragement.

© France 2/Christophe Russeil

IN REVIEW	Types of Social Influence	
Type	**Definition**	**Key Findings**
Conformity	A change in behavior or beliefs to match those of others	In cases of ambiguity, people develop a group norm and then adhere to it.
		Conformity occurs because people want to be right, because they want to be liked by others, and because conformity to group norms is usually rewarded.
		Conformity usually increases with the ambiguity of the situation, as well as with the unanimity and psychological size of the majority.
Compliance	A change in what is said or done as the result of a request	Compliance increases with the foot-in-the-door technique, which begins with a small request and works up to a larger one.
		The door-in-the-face technique can be used too. After making a large request that is denied, the person substitutes the less extreme alternative that was desired all along.
		The low-ball technique also elicits compliance. A person first obtains an oral commitment for something and then claims that only a higher-cost version of the original request will suffice.
Obedience	A change in behavior in response to an explicit demand, typically from an authority figure	People may inflict great harm on others when an authority demands that they do so.
		Even though people obey orders to harm another person, they often agonize over the decision.
		People are most likely to disobey orders to harm someone when they see another person disobey such orders.

1. Joining the end of a ticket line is an example of _____, whereas forming two lines when a theater employee requests it is an example of _____.
2. Seeing someone disobey a questionable order makes people _____ likely to obey the order themselves.
3. Pricing your used car for more than you expect to get and then agreeing to reduce it to make a sale is an example of the _____ approach to gaining compliance.

the persuasive power of their leaders to behave in a demented and fiendish manner (Moghaddam, 2005; Zimbardo, 2008).

In short, inhumanity can occur even without pressure for obedience. For example, a good deal of people's aggressiveness toward other people appears to come from within. Let's now consider human aggressiveness and some of the circumstances that influence its expression.

Aggression

Aggression is an action intended to harm another person (Bushman & Huesmann, 2010). It is all too common. Nearly 1.4 million violent crimes are committed each year in the United States, including nearly 90,000 rapes and about 17,000 murders (Federal Bureau of Investigation, 2008). In fact, homicide is the second leading cause of death for people in the United States between the ages of 15 and 24 (Heron, 2007). One of the most disturbing aspects of these figures is that about 85 percent of all murder victims knew their assailants, and over 70 percent of rapists were romantic partners, friends, relatives, or acquaintances of their victims (U.S. Department of Justice, 2007). Further, about one-third of married people in the United States, and a significant proportion of dating couples, display aggression toward each other that ranges from pushing, shoving, and slapping to beatings and the threatened or actual use of weapons (Cornelius & Resseguie, 2007; Durose et al., 2005).

Why Are People Aggressive?

Sigmund Freud proposed that aggression is an instinctive biological urge that builds up in everyone and must be released. Sometimes, he said, the release takes the form of physical or verbal abuse against others. At other times, the aggressive impulse is turned inward and leads to suicide or other self-damaging acts.

LINKAGES   What makes some people so aggressive? (a link to Introducing Psychology, p. 20)

A somewhat more complicated view is offered by evolutionary psychologists. As discussed in the introductory chapter, these psychologists believe that human social behavior is related to our evolutionary heritage. From this perspective, aggression is thought to have helped prehistoric people compete for mates, resulting in the survival of their genes in the next generation. Through the principles of natural selection, then, aggressive tendencies were passed on through successive generations (Ferguson & Beaver, 2009).

Evolutionary theories of the origins of aggression are popular, but even evolutionary theorists realize that nature alone cannot fully account for aggression. Nurture, in the form of environmental factors, also plays a large role in determining when and why people are aggressive. We know this partly because there are large differences in aggression from culture to culture. The murder rate in Colombia, for example, is more than fifteen times as high as in the United States, and the U.S. murder rate is almost twice as high as in either Canada or the United Kingdom (United Nations Office on Drugs and Crime, 2007). These data suggest that even if aggressive *impulses* are universal, the emergence of aggressive *behavior* reflects an interplay of nature and nurture (Bushman & Huesmann, 2010). No equation can predict when people will be aggressive, but years of research have revealed a number of important biological, learning, and environmental factors that combine in various ways to produce aggression in various situations.

Genetic and Biological Mechanisms   There is strong evidence for hereditary influences on aggression, especially in animals (Bushman & Huesmann, 2010). In one study, the most aggressive members of a large group of mice were interbred. Then the most aggressive of their offspring were also interbred. After this procedure was followed for twenty-five generations, the resulting animals would immediately attack

aggression An act that is intended to cause harm to another person.

any mouse put in their cage. Continuous inbreeding of the least aggressive members of the original group produced animals that were so docile that they would refuse to fight even when attacked (Lagerspetz & Lagerspetz, 1983). Research on human twins reared together or apart suggests that there is a genetic component to aggression in people as well (Vierikko et al., 2006). However, other research suggests that people do not necessarily inherit the tendency to be aggressive; instead, they may inherit certain temperaments, such as impulsiveness or emotional oversensitivity in social situations, that in turn make aggression more likely (Alia-Klein et al., 2009; Eisenberger et al., 2007; Hennig et al., 2005).

Several parts of the brain influence aggression (Anderson & Bushman, 2002a). One is the limbic system, which includes the amygdala, the hypothalamus, and related areas (see Figure 3.12 in the chapter on biological aspects of psychology). Damage to these structures may produce *defensive aggression,* which includes heightened aggressiveness to stimuli that are not usually threatening or a decrease in the responses that normally inhibit aggression (Coccaro, 1989; Siever, 2008). The cerebral cortex may also be involved in aggression (e.g., Séguin & Zelazo, 2005; see Figure 3.15). For example, one study found that the prefrontal area of the cortex metabolized glucose significantly more slowly in murderers than in other people (Raine, Brennan, & Mednick, 1994).

Hormones such as *testosterone*—the male hormone that is present in both sexes—may also play an important role in aggression (Bushman & Huesmann, 2010). Experiments have shown that aggressive behavior increases or decreases dramatically with the level of testosterone in the human bloodstream (Klinesmith, Kasser, & McAndrew, 2006). Among criminals, those who commit violent crimes have higher levels of testosterone than those whose crimes are nonviolent. And among murderers, those with higher levels of testosterone are more likely than others to have planned their crimes before committing them (Dabbs, Riad, & Chance, 2001).

Testosterone may have its most significant and durable influence not so much through its day-to-day variations as through its impact on early brain development. One natural test of this hypothesis occurred when pregnant women were given testosterone in an attempt to prevent miscarriages. Accordingly, their children were exposed to high doses of testosterone during prenatal development. Figure 18.3 shows that these children grew up to be more aggressive than their same-sex siblings who were not exposed to testosterone during prenatal development (Reinisch, Ziemba-Davis, & Sanders, 1991). Another study found that girls who had been prenatally exposed to elevated levels of testosterone by virtue of having shared the womb with a male twin were more aggressive than girls who had a female twin (Cohen-Bendahan et al., 2005).

More recent research with both animals and humans has linked lower levels of the neurotransmitter serotonin with higher levels of impulsive aggression (Carver, Johnson, & Joormann, 2008). In one study, research participants who were randomly selected to receive a serotonin-raising drug behaved much less aggressively in a competitive game than those whose serotonin remained unchanged (Berman et al., 2009). Similarly, people who commit impulsive violent crimes tend to have lower levels of serotonin than those whose crimes are premeditated (Bushman & Huesmann, 2010).

Drugs that alter central nervous system functioning can also affect the likelihood that a person will act aggressively. Alcohol, for example, can substantially increase some people's aggressiveness (Giancola et al., 2010). Canadian researchers have found that in almost 70 percent of the acts of aggression they studied, the aggressors had been drinking alcohol. And the more alcohol the aggressors consumed, the more aggressive they were (Wells, Graham, & West, 2000). No one knows exactly why alcohol increases aggression, but there is no doubt that many people associate drinking with both aggressive thoughts and aggressive actions (Bartholow & Heinz, 2006). In fact, people may become more aggressive after drinking a nonalcoholic beverage that they *think* contains alcohol (Bègue et al., 2009). As described in the consciousness chapter,

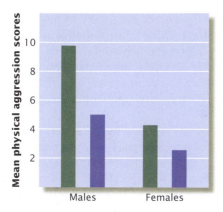

Participants exposed to high doses of testosterone during prenatal development

Unexposed participants

FIGURE 18.3

Testosterone and Aggression

In the study illustrated here, the children of women who had taken testosterone during pregnancy to prevent miscarriage became more aggressive than the mothers' other children of the same sex who had not been exposed to testosterone during prenatal development. This outcome held for both males and females.

Source: Reinisch, Ziemba-Davis, & Sanders (1991).

this association may result in part from observing the drunken aggressiveness that is common in many cultures.

Research on the effects of other drugs on aggression has produced some surprising findings. One might expect, for example, that using stimulants would increase aggressiveness and that taking tranquilizers would reduce it, but the opposite appears to be true. Whereas amphetamine stimulants do not usually make people more aggressive, opiates (e.g., heroin and morphine) and some tranquilizers may do so (Taylor & Hulsizer, 1998). It is not clear why heroin users are more likely than amphetamine users to be aggressive. Some analysts have suggested that heroin addicts' aggression reflects their desperate need to get money to buy more drugs. But if this were so, we should also see increased aggression among people who are addicted to amphetamines and cocaine—because these addictions, too, are very expensive. Further, opiates increase people's aggressiveness even in controlled laboratory settings (Taylor & Hulsizer, 1998), suggesting that these drugs have biochemical effects that somehow lead directly to aggression.

Learning and Cultural Mechanisms   Although biological factors may increase or decrease the likelihood of aggression, cross-cultural research makes it clear that learning also plays a role. Aggressive behavior is much more common in individualist than in collectivist cultures, for example (Oatley, 1993). Cultural differences in the expression of aggression appear to stem in part from differing cultural values. For example, the Utku, an Inuit culture, view aggression in any form as a sign of social incompetence. In fact, the Utku word for *aggressive* also means "childish" (Oatley, 1993). The effects of culture on aggression can also be seen in the fact that the incidence of aggression in a given culture changes over time as cultural values change (Matsumoto, 2000).

Aggression can even differ from one part of a country to another. Consider the fact that more males in the southern United States commit homicide than males in the northern states (Cassel & Bernstein, 2007). As discussed later, this regional difference in the homicide rate may be related to the South's higher temperatures, but Richard Nisbett and other researchers (e.g., Cohen & Nisbett, 1997; Vandello, Cohen, & Ransom, 2008) have proposed that it is due to a *culture of honor* that is more commonly endorsed by southern males. One key aspect of this cultural

Following Adult Examples

Learning to express aggression is especially easy for children who live in countries plagued by war or sectarian violence because they see aggressive acts modeled for them all too often.

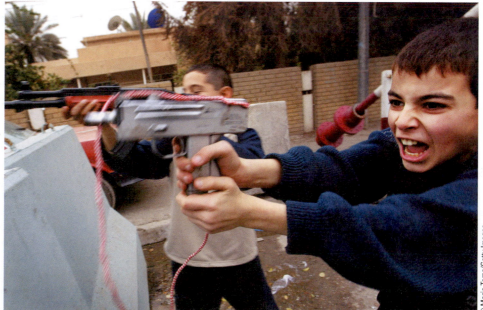

© Mario Tama/Getty Images

orientation is the need to defend one's honor, with violence if necessary, in response to a perceived insult. Studies testing this notion have indeed found that southern-born college students and professional athletes reacted much more angrily to a provocation than those born in the North and that southern high school students were much more likely than those in northern states to bring a weapon to school (Brown, Osterman, & Barnes, 2009; Cassel & Bernstein, 2007; Cohen et al., 1996; Timmerman, 2007).

The frequency of aggressive acts can be altered by rewards or punishment. People become more aggressive when rewarded for aggressiveness and less aggressive when punished for aggression (Geen, 1998). People also learn many aggressive responses by watching others (Bingenheimer, Brennan, & Earls, 2005; Bushman & Huesmann, 2010). Children, in particular, learn and perform many of the aggressive acts that they see modeled by others (Bandura, 1983). Albert Bandura's "Bobo" doll experiments, which are described in the chapter on learning, provide impressive demonstrations of the power of observational learning on aggression. The significance of observational learning is highlighted by studies of the effects of televised violence, also discussed in that chapter. For example, the amount of violent TV that children watch between 6 and 10 years of age predicts aggressiveness in these children even fifteen years later (Bushman & Huesmannn, 2010). Fortunately, not everyone who sees aggression becomes aggressive; individual differences in temperament, the modeling of nonaggressive behaviors by parents, and other factors can temper the effects of violent television. Nevertheless, observational learning, including the learning that comes through exposure to violent television, does play a significant role in the development and display of aggressive behavior (Anderson & Murphy, 2003; Bushman & Anderson, 2001; Konijin, Bijvank, & Bushman, 2007). Even listening to music whose lyrics describe or endorse violence can increase aggressive thoughts and hostile feelings (Anderson, Carnagey, & Eubanks, 2003).

In short, a person's accumulated experiences—including culturally transmitted teachings—combine with daily rewards and punishments to influence whether, when, and how aggressive acts occur (Baron & Richardson, 1994; Bettencourt et al., 2006).

THINKING CRITICALLY ▶ Do Violent Video Games Make People More Aggressive?

A lot of research has been conducted on the impact of violent television on aggressiveness, but what about other forms of violent entertainment, such as video games? When these games first appeared in the late 1970s, they contained little or no violence, but by the 1990s, violent games such as *Mortal Kombat* and *Street Fighter* became extremely popular. The current flood of graphically violent games remain the favorites of young game-players. One survey of fourth-graders found that 59 percent of girls and 73 percent of boys preferred violent video games over nonviolent ones. In response to complaints from parents groups, the video game industry devised a rating system to try to keep the most violent games out of the hands of preteens and young teenagers, but many of the games that the system deems appropriate for these groups still contain considerable violent content (Funk et al., 1999). Further, according to another survey, 75 percent of young boys and 51 percent of young girls are playing video games that carry adults-only ratings (Anderson & Gentile, 2008). In other words, children in the United States have essentially unrestricted access to violent video games. If they can't buy a violent game in a store, they can download it from the Internet.

What am I being asked to believe or accept?

The groups that have objected to this situation are basing their concerns on the claim that playing violent video games can alter behavior in undesirable ways. Specifically, they say that exposure to violent video games increases the frequency of aggressive thoughts, feelings, and actions in people who play them (Anderson & Gentile, 2008).

What evidence is available to support the assertion?

The strongest evidence for this claim comes from an analysis by Craig Anderson and his colleagues of 135 correlational studies and laboratory experiments on violent video games (Anderson et al., 2010). The correlational studies have examined the relationship between the amount of time people spend playing these games and how aggressive they are. When the results of these studies were combined, a statistically significant positive relationship emerged. That is, the more time people spent playing violent video games, the more aggressive they tended to be. A significant correlation also appeared when the results of *longitudinal* studies were analyzed: Children who played more video games at one point in their lives were more aggressive at a later point.

Anderson also analyzed the results of laboratory experiments on violent video games. In these studies, researchers had randomly assigned participants to groups and then exposed them for varying lengths of time to games that contain varying amounts of violence and allow varying degrees of player involvement. After manipulating these independent variables, the researchers measured some aspect of aggression, which was the dependent variable in these experiments. Finally, they compared the amount of aggressiveness displayed by participants in the various groups. In one such experiment, participants played a violent video game in which the researchers manipulated two variables: whether the player could actively participate as one of the characters in the game or could only watch the actions of the game's characters and whether or not the characters bled when they were wounded (Farrar, Krcmar, & Nowak, 2006). They found that participants expressed more hostility and aggressive intentions during "first-person player" games that allowed them to be characters in the game and also when their victims bled when wounded. The combined results of many experiments like this one show that playing violent video games increases players' aggressive thoughts, feelings, and actions. There is also some evidence that playing violent video games may make people less likely to help others and less sensitive to other people's pain and suffering (Anderson et al., 2010).

Are there alternative ways of interpreting the evidence?

Like research on the effects of television violence, the results of correlational and experimental studies of violent video games have been questioned on several counts. The correlational studies have been challenged mainly because correlations do not allow us to draw conclusions about cause and effect. True, greater aggressiveness is associated with longer exposure to violent video games, but is this because the games are causing aggressiveness or because aggressive people are more inclined to play violent video games (Mitrofan, Paul, & Spencer, 2009)? The laboratory experiments have been criticized mainly because their methods may not reflect—and their results may therefore not apply to—what goes on in the world outside the laboratory (Goldstein, 2001). Do violent video games played in a lab have the same effects as they do when played at home, perhaps with friends? Do artificial laboratory measures of aggressiveness really tell us anything about how a person is likely to behave toward other people in daily life? Although experiments give researchers the control necessary to support cause-and-effect conclusions, critics argue that those conclusions may be of limited value in understanding the true impact of violent video games on aggressiveness (Ferguson, 2010).

Skeptics also point to experiments that have found *no* effect of violent video games on aggression (e.g., Ferguson & Rueda, 2010). They argue further that even if a statistically significant cause-and-effect relationship between violent video games and aggression does exist, it is not a very strong one (Ferguson & Kilburn, 2010; Sherry, 2001), especially when compared with other influences. They suggest, for example, that people's aggressiveness is affected far less by violent video games (and violent television) than by other factors, such as what children learn by seeing their families and friends behaving aggressively.

What additional evidence would help evaluate the alternatives?

Obviously, we need to know a lot more about the impact of violent video games. For example, how do they affect children of different ages? It would also be valuable to know what happens in the brains of people who play violent video games, and scientists are currently studying this question using a variety of neuroscience techniques. In one recent study, changes in event-related brain activity (see Figure 8.4 in the cognition and language chapter) indicated that playing violent video games made participants less sensitive to seeing violence and less upset by it (Bartholow, Bushman, & Sestir, 2006). Another study, using functional magnetic resonance imaging (fMRI), found that exposure to violent aspects of video games activates brain areas that are commonly associated with aggression (Weber, Ritterfeld, & Mathiak, 2006). Such studies cannot confirm that violent video games cause aggression, but their results support the possibility of a causal link and begin to provide some explanations about why that link might exist.

What conclusions are most reasonable?

Given the evidence available so far, it appears reasonable to say that violent video games probably have at least some effects on the people who play them. Questions about how strong the causal relationship is and how long it might last have not yet been answered. On the basis of the principles described in the chapter on learning, some researchers believe that violent video games may actually have a stronger impact on aggression than violent television both because game players can literally practice aggression as they engage in violent electronic acts and because they are rewarded for those violent acts by reaching the game's next level (e.g., Bushman & Anderson, 2007). Are these researchers correct? Are the effects of violent video games that strong, and are they likely to be long-lasting influences on aggressiveness? It will take much more research to definitively answer these questions, but it seems reasonable to suspect that the effects of prolonged exposure to violent video games will be quite similar to that of long exposure to violent television (Huesmann, 2010).

When Are People Aggressive?

LINKAGES What role does arousal play in aggression? (a link to Motivation and Emotion, p. 418)

In general, people are more likely to be aggressive when they are both physiologically aroused and experiencing angry or hostile thoughts and feelings (Anderson & Bushman, 2002a). They tend either to lash out at those who make them angry or to displace their anger onto defenseless targets such as children or pets. However, aggression can also be made more likely by other forms of emotional arousal. One emotion that has long been considered a major cause of aggression is *frustration,* which occurs when we are prevented from reaching some goal.

Frustration and Aggression   Suppose that a friend interrupts your studying for an exam by dropping by to borrow a book. If things have been going well and you are feeling confident about the exam, you are likely to be friendly and helpful. But what if you are feeling frustrated because your friend's visit is the fifth interruption in the past hour? Under these emotional circumstances, you may react aggressively, perhaps snapping at your startled visitor for bothering you.

Your aggressiveness in this situation conforms to the predictions of the **frustration-aggression hypothesis**, originally developed by John Dollard and his colleagues (1939). They proposed that frustration always results in aggression and that aggression will not occur unless a person is frustrated. Research on this hypothesis, however, has shown that it is too simple and too general. For one thing, frustration sometimes produces depression and withdrawal, not aggression (Berkowitz, 1998). In addition, not all aggression is preceded by frustration (Berkowitz, 1994).

After many years of research, Leonard Berkowitz (1998) suggested some substantial modifications to the frustration-aggression hypothesis. In his *aversively stimulated*

frustration-aggression hypothesis   A proposition that frustration always leads to some form of aggressive behavior.

aggression theory, he proposed that it may be stress in general rather than frustration in particular that can produce a readiness to act aggressively. Once this readiness exists, cues in the environment that are associated with aggression will often lead a person to behave aggressively. The cues might be guns or knives, people arguing on TV, violent song lyrics or game images, or other triggers. Neither stress alone nor the cues alone are sufficient to set off aggression. When combined, however, they often do set it off. Support for this aspect of Berkowitz's theory has been quite strong (Bushman & Huesmann, 2010).

Berkowitz also argues that the direct cause of most kinds of aggression is negative feelings, or *negative affect,* caused by something unpleasant. He says that the greater the negative affect, whether it is caused by frustrating circumstances or other sources, the stronger the readiness to behave aggressively (Berkowitz, 1998). Negative affect can be aroused by pain, for example. Research suggests that people in pain do tend to become aggressive, regardless of the cause of their pain. In one study, participants whose hands were placed in painfully cold water became more aggressive toward other people than participants whose hands were in water of room temperature (Berkowitz, 1998).

Generalized Arousal Imagine that you have just jogged for 3 miles. You are hot, sweaty, and out of breath, but you are not angry. Still, the physiological arousal caused by jogging may increase the probability that you will become aggressive if, say, a passerby shouts an insult (Zillmann, 1988). Why? The answer lies in a phenomenon described in the chapter on motivation and emotion: Arousal from one experience may carry over to an independent situation, producing what is called *excitation transfer.* So the physiological arousal caused by jogging may intensify your reaction to an insult (Harrison, 2003).

By itself, however, generalized arousal does not lead to aggression. It is most likely to produce aggression when the situation contains some reason, opportunity, or target for aggression (Zillmann, 2003). In one study, for example, people engaged in two minutes of vigorous exercise. Then they had the opportunity to deliver an electrical shock to another person. The participants chose high levels of shock only if they were first insulted (Zillmann, Katcher, & Milavsky, 1972). Apparently, the arousal resulting from the exercise made aggression more likely; the insult "released" it.

Other research suggests that men who are aroused by watching violent pornography may be more likely to commit rape or other forms of aggression against women. In one experiment, for example, male participants were told that a person in another room (actually the experimenter's assistant) would be performing a learning task and that they were to administer an electric shock every time the person made a mistake. The intensity of shock could be varied (as in the Milgram studies, no shock actually reached the assistant), but participants were told that changing the intensity would not affect the speed of learning. So the shock intensity (and presumed pain) that they chose to administer was considered to be a measure of aggression. Before the learning trials began, some participants watched a film in which several men had sex with the same woman, against her will. These participants' aggressiveness toward women during the learning experiment was greater than that of men who did not watch the film (Donnerstein, 1984). There was no parallel increase in aggression against other men, indicating that the violent pornography didn't create a generalized increase in aggression but did create an increase in aggressiveness directed toward women.

Such effects do not appear in all men, however (Ferguson & Hartley, 2009; Seto, Maric, & Barbaree, 2001). One study of about 2,700 men in the United States found that men who are not hostile toward women and who rarely have casual sex showed little, if any, change in sexual aggressiveness after viewing aggressive pornography. In contrast, among men who are high in promiscuity and hostility, watching aggressive pornography was followed by a dramatic increase in the chances that these men would engage in sexual aggression (Malamuth, Addison, & Koss, 2000). In fact, 72 percent of the men who frequently used pornography and were high in promiscuity and hostility had actually engaged in sexually aggressive acts (see Figure 18.4). Viewing pornography appears to have similar effects on convicted sex offenders who have been placed

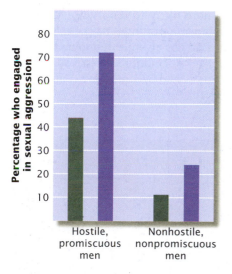

FIGURE 18.4

Pornography and Sexual Aggression

Extensive exposure to pornography does not by itself make most men more likely to engage in sexual aggression. However, among men who are hostile toward women and have a history of sexual promiscuity, those who view a lot of pornography are much more likely to engage in sexual aggression.

Source: Adapted from Malamuth (1998).

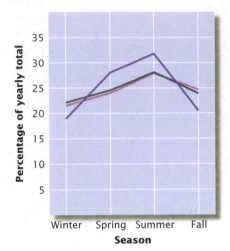

- — Rape
- — Murder
- — Other violent crime

FIGURE 18.5

Effects of Temperature on Aggression

Studies from around the world indicate that aggressive behaviors are most likely to occur during hot summer months. These studies support the idea that environmental factors can affect aggression.

Source: From Anderson, C.A. & Anderson, K.P. "Temperature and Aggression: Paradox, Controversy, and a (Fairly) Clear Picture," in R.G. Greene & E. Donnerstein, eds., *Human Aggression*, p. 279, figure 10.9. Copyright © 1998. Reprinted with permission of Elsevier.

Crowding and Aggression

APPLYING PSYCHOLOGY Studies of prisons suggest that as crowding increases, so does aggression (Lahm, 2008; Lawrence & Andrews, 2004). Environmental psychologists are working with architects on the design of prisons that minimize the sense of crowding and that may help prevent some of the violence that endangers staff and prisoners.

environmental psychology The study of the relationship between behavior and the physical environment.

on probation or released on parole, and the effects are especially pronounced among those who had committed the most serious sex crimes (Kingston et al., 2008).

These findings support the notion that aggression is not caused solely by a person's characteristics or by the particular situation a person is in. Instead, the occurrence and intensity of aggression are determined by the joint influence of individual characteristics and environmental circumstances (Klinesmith, Kasser, & McAndrew, 2006).

Environmental Influences on Aggression The links between stress, arousal, and aggressive behavior point to the possibility that stressful environmental conditions can make aggressive behavior more likely (Anderson, 2001). This possibility is one of the research topics in **environmental psychology**, the study of the relationship between people's physical environment and their behavior (Bell et al., 2000). One aspect of the environment that clearly affects social behavior is the weather, especially temperature. High temperature is a source of stress and arousal, so it might be expected to correlate with aggressiveness. The results of many studies conducted in several countries show that many kinds of aggressive behaviors are indeed more likely to occur during hot summer months than at any other time of the year (Anderson et al., 2000; Bushman, Wang, & Anderson, 2005; see Figure 18.5).

Noise also tends to make people more likely to display aggression, especially if the noise is unpredictable and irregular (Geen & McCown, 1984). Living arrangements, too, can influence aggressiveness. Compared with the tenants of crowded apartment buildings, those in buildings with relatively few residents are less likely to behave aggressively (Bell et al., 2000). This difference appears to be due in part to how people feel when they are crowded. Crowding tends to create physiological arousal and to make people tense, uncomfortable, and more likely to report negative feelings (Oskamp & Schultz, 1998). This arousal and tension can influence people to like one another less and to be more aggressive. One study of juvenile delinquents found that the number of behavior problems they displayed (including aggressiveness) was directly related to how crowded their living conditions had become (Ray et al., 1982).

Altruism and Helping Behavior

Like all acts of terrorism, the 2001 attacks on the World Trade Center and the Pentagon were examples of human behavior at its worst. But like all tragedies, they drew responses that provide inspiring examples of human behavior at its best. Michael Benfante and John Cerqueira were working in the World Trade Center when one of the hijacked planes struck their building. They headed for a stairwell, but they didn't just save themselves. Although it slowed their own escape, they chose to carry Tina Hansen, a wheelchair-bound coworker, down sixty-eight flights of stairs to safety. David Theall was in his Pentagon office when another hijacked plane hit the building not far from his desk. He could have escaped the rubble immediately, but he first located a dazed officemate and led him, along with seven other coworkers, to safety. And no one will ever forget the heroism of the hundreds of New York City firefighters, police officers, and emergency workers who risked and even lost their lives trying to save others. Acts of selflessness and sacrifice were common that day and in the days, weeks, and months that followed. Police officers, medical personnel, search-and-rescue specialists, and just ordinary people came to New York from all over the United States to help clear wreckage, look for survivors, and recover bodies. More than $1 billion in donations to the Red Cross and other charitable organizations poured in to help victims; one celebrity telethon raised $150 million in two hours. There was also a dramatic increase in many other forms of prosocial behavior, including volunteering to work for all kinds of charities (Penner, Brannick, et al., 2005).

All of these actions are examples of **helping behavior** (also known as **prosocial behavior**), which is defined as any act that is intended to benefit another person. Helping can range from picking up dropped packages to donating a kidney. Closely related to helping is **altruism**, an unselfish concern for another person's welfare (Penner, Dovidio, et al., 2005). Let's consider some of the reasons behind helping and altruism, along with some of the conditions under which people are most likely to help others.

One of Many Heroes

Along with his colleague Michael Benfante, John Cerqueira (shown here) risked his life on September 11, 2001, to help a handicapped coworker escape from the sixty-eighth floor of the World Trade Center. Hundreds of other heroic acts of helping took place that day, and less dramatic examples occur every day throughout the world.

helping behavior (prosocial behavior) Any act that is intended to benefit another person.

altruism An unselfish concern for another person's welfare.

Photo courtesy of North Carolina State University, Cerqueira's alma mater

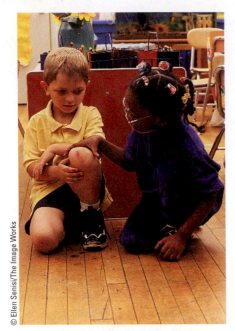

A Young Helper

Even before their second birthday, some children offer help to people who are hurt or crying by snuggling, patting, or offering food or even their own teddy bears.

Why Do People Help?

The tendency to help others begins early, although at first it is not spontaneous. In most cultures, very young children generally help others only when they are asked to do so or are offered a reward (Grusec, Davidov, & Lundell, 2002). Still, researchers have found that children as young as 18 months attempt to help others (Dunfield & Kuhlmeier, 2010; Knafo et al., 2008; Over & Carpenter, 2009). As they grow, so does the role of social influence. Children use helping behavior to gain social approval, and their efforts at helping become more elaborate. Their helping behaviors are shaped by the social norms established through the examples set by their families and the broader culture (Grusec & Goodnow, 1994). In addition, children are praised and given other rewards for helpfulness but are scolded for selfishness. Eventually, children come to believe that helping is good and that they are good when they help. By the late teens, people often help others even when no one is watching and no one will know that they did so (Grusec, Davidov, & Lundell, 2002). There are three major theories about why people help even when they cannot expect any external rewards for doing so.

Arousal: Cost-Reward Theory   One approach to explaining why people help is called the **arousal: cost-reward theory** (Piliavin et al., 1981). This theory proposes that the sight of a person who is suffering causes distress and anxiety and that these feelings motivate the observer to do something to reduce the unpleasant arousal. Several studies have shown that all else being equal, the more physiologically aroused bystanders are, the more likely they are to help someone in an emergency (Dovidio et al., 2006). Before rushing to a victim's aid, however, the bystander will first evaluate two aspects of the situation: the costs associated with helping and the costs (to the bystander and the other person) of not helping. Whether or not the bystander actually helps depends on the outcome of this evaluation (Dovidio et al., 1991). If the costs of helping are low (as when helping someone pick up a dropped grocery bag) and the costs of not helping are high (as when the other person is physically unable to do this alone), the bystander will almost certainly help. However, if the costs of helping are high (as when the task is to load a heavy box into a car) and the costs of not helping are low (as when the person is strong enough to manage the task alone), the bystander is unlikely to offer help. This theory is attractive partly because it is comprehensive enough to provide a framework for explaining research findings on the factors that affect helping.

One of these factors is the *clarity of the need for help,* which has a major impact on whether people provide help (Dovidio et al., 2006). In one study, undergraduate students were waiting alone in a campus building when a staged accident took place outside. A window washer screamed as he and his ladder fell to the ground. He then began to clutch his ankle and groan in pain. All of the students looked out a window to see what had happened, but only 29 percent of them did anything to help. Other students experienced the same situation with one important difference: The man *said* he was hurt and needed help. In this case, more than 80 percent of the students came to his aid (Yakimovich & Saltz, 1971). Why so many? Apparently, this one additional cue eliminated any uncertainty about whether the person needed help. This cue also raised the perceived costs to the victim of not offering help. As these costs become higher, helping becomes more likely. If this laboratory study seems unrealistic, consider the March 2000 case of a 62-year-old woman in Darby, Pennsylvania. She was walking to the grocery store when she was pushed from behind by an attacker. She fended him off and then did her shopping as usual. It was only when she got home and her daughter saw the handle of a knife protruding from her back that she realized that the assailant had stabbed her! No one in the grocery store said anything to her about the knife, let alone offered to help. Why? The most likely explanation is that the woman didn't say or do anything to suggest that help was needed.

The *presence of others* also has a strong influence on the tendency to help. Somewhat surprisingly, though, their presence tends to make helping behavior *less* likely (Garcia et al., 2002). For example, in November 2000 in London, a 10-year-old boy who had

arousal: cost-reward theory A theory attributing people's helping behavior to their efforts to reduce the unpleasant arousal they feel in the face of someone's need or suffering.

been stabbed by members of a street gang lay ignored by passersby as he died. In June 2007, customers in a Wichita, Kansas, convenience store did nothing to help a 27-year-old woman who eventually bled to death after being stabbed during an argument. In fact, surveillance video shows five shoppers stepping over her, including one who stopped only long enough to take a picture with a cell phone ("Kansas Store Video," 2007). And in October 2009, a dozen people in Richmond, California, simply watched as a 15-year-old girl was beaten and gang-raped outside her high school homecoming dance ("Dozen People Watched," 2009). Whenever such cases come to light, journalists and social commentators express dismay about the cold, uncaring attitudes that seem to exist among people who live in big cities. But psychologists believe that something about the situation surrounding such events deters people from helping.

The numerous studies of helping behavior have revealed a phenomenon, known as the **bystander effect**, that may explain the inaction of potential helpers in London, Kansas, and California: The likelihood that someone will help in an emergency tends to decrease as the number of people present increases (Garcia et al., 2002). One explanation for why the presence of others often reduces helping is that each person thinks someone else will help the victim. That is, seeing other bystanders allows each individual to experience a *diffusion of responsibility* for taking action, which lowers the costs of not helping (Dovidio et al., 2006).

The degree to which the presence of other people inhibits helping may depend on who those other people are. When they are strangers, poor communication may inhibit helping. People often have difficulty speaking to strangers, particularly in an emergency, and without speaking, they have difficulty knowing what the others intend to do. According to this logic, if people are with friends rather than strangers, they should be less uncomfortable, more willing to discuss the problem, and thus more likely to help.

In one experiment designed to test this idea, an experimenter left a research participant in a waiting room under one of four conditions: alone, with a friend, with a stranger, or with a stranger who was an assistant to the experimenter (Latané & Rodin, 1969). The experimenter then stepped behind a curtain into an office. For a few minutes, she could be heard opening and closing the drawers of her desk, shuffling papers, and so on. Then there was a loud crash, and she screamed, "Oh, my God … My foot, I … I can't move it. Oh, my ankle … I can't get this … thing off me." Then the participant heard her groan and cry.

Diffusion of Responsibility

Does the man on the sidewalk need help? The people nearby are probably not sure, and they might assume that if he does, someone else will help him. Research on factors affecting helping (e.g., Flynn & Lake, 2008) suggests that if you ever need help, especially in a crowd, it is important not only to ask for help but also to tell a specific onlooker to take specific action (for example, "You, in the yellow shirt, please call an ambulance!").

bystander effect A phenomenon in which the chances that someone will help in an emergency decrease as the number of people present increases.

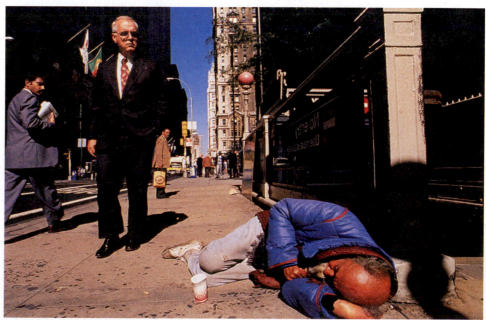

Would the participant go behind the curtain to help? Once again, people were most likely to help if they were alone. When one other person was present, participants were more likely to communicate with each other and to offer help if they were friends than if they were strangers. When the stranger was the experimenter's assistant (who had been instructed not to help), very few participants offered to help. Other studies have confirmed that bystanders' tendency to help increases when they know one another (Rutkowski, Gruder, & Romer, 1983).

Research suggests that the *personality of the helper* also plays a role in helping. Some people are simply more likely to help than others. Consider the Christians who risked their lives to save Jews from the Nazi Holocaust. Researchers interviewed hundreds of these rescuers many years later and compared their personalities with those of people who had a chance to save Jews but did not do so (Fagin-Jones & Midlarsky, 2007; Oliner & Oliner, 1988). The rescuers were found to have more empathy (the ability to understand or experience another's emotional state), more concern about others, a greater sense of responsibility for their own actions, and a greater sense of self-efficacy (confidence that their efforts will succeed). Louis Penner and his associates (Penner, 2002; Penner & Finkelstein, 1998) have found that these kinds of personality traits predict a broad range of helping behaviors, from the speed with which bystanders intervene in an emergency to the amount of time volunteers spend helping AIDS patients. Consistent with the arousal: cost-reward theory, these personality characteristics are also correlated with people's estimates of the costs of helping and not helping. For example, empathic individuals usually estimate the costs of not helping as high, and people with a sense of self-efficacy usually rate the costs of helping as low (Penner et al., 1995). These patterns of cost estimation may partially explain why such people tend to be especially helpful.

Valuable as it is, the arousal: cost-reward theory cannot account for all aspects of helping. For instance, it cannot easily explain why *environmental factors* affect helping. Research conducted in several countries has revealed, for example, that people in urban areas are generally less helpful than those in rural areas (Dovidio et al., 2006). Why? The explanation probably has more to do with the stressors found in cities than with city living itself. One study of twenty-four U.S. cities found that the greater a city's size and density (number of people per square mile), the less likely people were to help others. Helping was also much less likely in cities where stressful economic conditions were greatest (Levine, Reysen, & Ganz, 2008). Similar results have been found in cities in the United Kingdom, the Middle East, and Africa (Hedge & Yousif, 1992; Yousif & Korte, 1995). Why should stress make people less helpful? Two explanations have been suggested. The first is that stressful environments create bad moods—and generally speaking, people in bad moods are less likely to help (Salovey, Mayer, & Rosenhan, 1991). A study of department store clerks, for example, found that those in a good mood were much more likely to help customers than those who were feeling grouchy (Forgas, Dunn, & Granland, 2008). A second possibility is that noise, crowding, and other urban stressors create too much stimulation. To reduce this excessive stimulation, people may pay less attention to their surroundings, which might include individuals who need help.

It is also difficult for the arousal: cost-reward theory to predict what bystanders will do when the cost of helping and the cost of not helping are *both* high. In these cases, helping (or not helping) may depend on several situational factors and sometimes on the personality of the potential helper. There may also be circumstances in which cost considerations may not be the major cause of a decision to help or not help. A second approach to helping considers some of these circumstances.

Empathy-Altruism Theory The second approach to explaining helping is embodied in **empathy-altruism theory** (also known as **empathy-altruism helping theory**), which maintains that people are more likely to engage in *altruistic,* or unselfish, helping—even when the cost of helping is high—if they feel empathy toward the person in need (Batson, 2010). In one experiment illustrating this phenomenon,

empathy-altruism theory (empathy-altruism helping theory) A theory suggesting that people help others because of empathy with their needs.

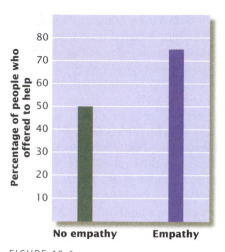

FIGURE 18.6
The Effect of Empathy on Helping

After hearing a staged interview with a woman who supposedly needed to raise money for her family, participants in this experiment were asked to help her. Those who were led to empathize with the woman were much more likely to offer their help than those who did not empathize. These results are consistent with empathy-altruism theory.

Source: Adapted from Batson et al. (1997).

participants listened to a tape-recorded interview with a female student. The student told the interviewer that her parents had been killed in an automobile accident, that they had had no life insurance, and that she was now faced with the task of finishing college while taking care of a younger brother and sister. She said that these financial burdens might force her to quit school or give up her siblings for adoption. None of this was true, but the participants were told that it was. Further, before listening to the woman's story, half the participants were given additional information about her that was designed to promote strong empathy. Later, all the participants were asked to help the woman raise money for herself and her siblings (Batson et al., 1997). The critical question was whether the participants who heard the additional empathy-promoting information would help more than those who did not have that information. Consistent with the empathy-altruism theory, more participants in the empathy condition than in the nonempathy condition offered to help (see Figure 18.6).

Were the people who offered help in this experiment being utterly altruistic, or could there be a different reason for their actions? This is a hotly debated question. Some researchers dispute the claim that this study illustrated true altruistic helping. They suggest that people help in such situations for more selfish reasons, such as relieving the distress they experienced after hearing of the woman's problems (Maner et al., 2002). The final verdict on this question is not yet in.

Evolutionary Theory   The evolutionary approach to social psychology offers a third way of explaining helping. This approach views many human social behaviors as echoes of actions that contributed to the survival of our prehistoric ancestors (Buss, 2009). At first glance, it may not seem reasonable to apply evolutionary theory to helping and altruism because helping others at the risk of one's own well-being doesn't seem to be adaptive. If we die while trying to save others, it is their genes, not ours, that will survive. In fact, according to Charles Darwin's concept of the survival of the fittest, helpers—and their genes—should have disappeared long ago. Contemporary evolutionary theorists suggest, however, that Darwin's thinking about natural selection focused too much on the survival of the fittest *individuals* and not enough on the survival of their genes in others. Accordingly, the concept of survival of the fittest has been replaced by the concept of *inclusive fitness*, the survival of one's genes in future generations (Hamilton, 1964; Kruger, 2003; West & Gardner, 2010). Because

Family Ties

Research indicates that people are more likely to donate organs to family members than to strangers. This pattern may reflect greater attachment or a stronger sense of social obligation to relatives than to others. Psychologists who take an evolutionary approach suggest that such helpful attitudes and actions have evolved because they are adaptive. When, as in the case of these sisters, one family member donates a kidney to save the life of another, the genes they share are more likely to survive.

we share genes with our relatives, helping or even dying for a cousin, a sibling, or above all, our own child potentially increases the likelihood that at least some of our genetic characteristics will be passed on to the next generation through the beneficiary's future reproduction (Rachlin & Jones, 2008). So *kin selection*—helping a relative survive—may produce genetic benefits even if it provides no personal benefits for the helper (Brown & Brown, 2006).

There is considerable evidence that kin selection occurs among birds, squirrels, and other animals. The more closely the animals are related, the more likely they are to risk their lives for one another. Studies in a wide variety of cultures show the same pattern of helping among humans (Buss, 2009). People in the United States are three times as likely to donate a kidney to a relative than to a nonrelative (Borgida, Conner, & Monteufel, 1992), and identical twins (who have exactly the same genes) are much more willing to help one another than fraternal twins or siblings, who share only 50 percent of their genes (Segal, 1999).

FOCUS ON **RESEARCH METHODS**

Does Family Matter?

In and of themselves, data on kin selection do not confirm evolutionary explanations of helping and altruism. The greater tendency to donate organs to relatives could also be due to the effects of empathy toward more familiar people, pressure from family members, or other social influence processes. To control for the effects of these confounding variables, some researchers have turned to the laboratory to study the role of evolutionary forces in helping behavior.

What was the researchers' question?

Eugene Burnstein, Christian Crandell, and Shinobu Kitayama (1994) wanted to know whether people faced with a choice of whose life to save would behave in line with the concept of kin selection. These investigators reasoned that if kin selection does affect helping, the more genetically related two people are—the more genes they share in common—the more inclined they should be to save each other's life. Further, if this kind of prosocial behavior evolved because it preserves one's own genes in others, the tendency to save a close relative should be lessened if that relative is unlikely to produce offspring and therefore less likely to help preserve the helper's genes.

How did the researchers answer this question?

The most direct way to test these predictions would be to put people's lives in danger and then observe which (if any) of their relatives try to save them. Such an experiment would be unthinkable, of course, so Burnstein and his colleagues used a simulation, or *analogue,* methodology. Specifically, they asked people to imagine a series of situations and then to say how they would respond if the situation were real.

The participants in the analogue experiment were 110 men and 48 women enrolled at universities in Japan and the United States. The first independent variable was the kind of help that was needed. On the basis of random assignment, some participants were asked to imagine life-or-death situations in which there was time to save only one of three people who were asleep in separate rooms of a burning house. The remaining participants were asked to imagine everyday situations in which they had time to help only one of three people who each needed a small favor. The other independent variables were the characteristics of the people needing help in each situation—their age, sex, physical health, and genetic relatedness to the potential helper. The dependent variable was the participants' choice of which person they would help.

What did the researchers find?

In accordance with evolutionary theory, the participants were more than twice as likely to say they would save the life of a close relative than that of an unrelated friend. Also, the more closely related the endangered people were to the potential helpers, the

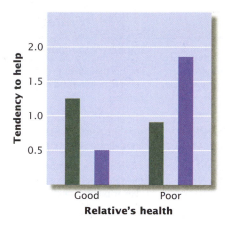

FIGURE 18.7

Kin Selection and Helping

TRY THIS In this analogue experiment, students said they would be more likely to save the life of a healthy relative than a sick one but more likely to do a favor for the sick relative. Results like these have been cited in support of evolutionary theories of helping behavior. Ask a few friends to say which member of their families they would save first in the event of a fire. To what extent were their responses consistent with the results of the kin selection analogue research described in this section?

Source: Burnstein, Crandell, & Kitayama (1994).

more likely they were to be saved. Did these results occur simply because people tend to help closer relatives in any situation? Probably not. When the participants imagined situations in which only small favors were involved, they were only slightly more likely to help a close relative than a distant one.

Another major prediction of evolutionary theory was supported as well. Several findings indicated that even close relatives might not be saved if they were unlikely to produce offspring. For example, the participants were more willing to do a small favor for a 75-year-old relative than for a 10- or 18-year-old relative, but they were much more likely to save the lives of the younger relatives. Similarly, they were more likely to do a favor for a sick relative than for a healthy one; but in a life-or-death situation, they chose to save the healthy relative more often than the sick one (see Figure 18.7). Finally, the participants were more likely to save the life of a female relative than that of a male relative, unless the female was past childbearing age. There were no substantial differences between the responses of students in the United States and those in Japan.

What do the results mean?

The results of this experiment generally support the concept of kin selection, which says that the tendency to help close relatives evolved because, genetically speaking, it helps the helper. Specifically, if we save the life of a relative and that relative is able to produce offspring, more of our genes will be represented in the next generation. Evolutionary psychologists see these results as providing confirmation that kin selection affects the decisions people make about saving the life of another person and hence that there is an evolutionary basis for helping.

What do we still need to know?

The findings reported by Burnstein and his colleagues are consistent with the predictions of evolutionary theory, but they must be interpreted with caution and in light of the methods that were used to obtain them. Analogue studies give clues to behavior—and allow experimental control—in situations that approximate, but may not precisely duplicate, situations outside the laboratory. These studies tend to be conducted when it would be unethical or impractical to expose people to "the real thing." The more closely the analogue approximates the natural situation, the more confident we can be that conclusions drawn about behavior observed in the laboratory will apply, or generalize, to the world beyond the laboratory.

In an analogue experiment such as this one, we might question how closely the natural situation was approximated. For one thing, the participants predicted what their responses would be in hypothetical situations. Those responses might be different if the students were actually in the situations described. So although the analogue methodology in this study allowed the researchers to show that kin selection *could* play a role in human helping behavior, they did not demonstrate that it *does* play a role.

The study also failed to identify the mechanisms whereby biological tendencies are translated into thoughts that lead to helpful actions (Kruger, 2003). It is highly unlikely that the participants were thinking, "I'll help a close relative because it will preserve my genes." So what conscious thoughts or feelings led to their choices? Another analogue study by Josephine Korchmaros and David Kenny (2001) may provide a partial answer to this question. The people who needed help in this simulation were described using the names of the participants' actual family members. The researchers also measured the strength of the emotional ties between the participants and these particular people. The results suggested that genetic closeness was related to emotional closeness. Perhaps, then, emotional closeness provides the mechanism that drives the choice of whom to help. It may be that we are biologically predisposed to feel emotionally closer to closer relatives and thus more likely to help them if their lives are in danger. These feelings in turn serve to increase the chances that some of our genes will survive in those close relatives.

IN REVIEW	Theories of Helping Behaviors	
Theory	**Basic Premise**	**Important Variables**
Arousal: cost-reward	People help in order to reduce the unpleasant arousal caused by another person's distress. They attempt to minimize the costs of doing this.	Factors that affect the costs of helping and of not helping
Empathy-altruism	People sometimes help for utterly altruistic reasons. They are motivated by a desire to increase another person's well-being.	The amount of empathy that one person feels for another
Evolutionary	People help relatives because it increases the chances that the helper's genes will survive in future generations.	The biological relationship between the helper and the recipient of help

1. If you could save only one person from a burning house, the _____ theory of helping would predict that it would be your own child rather than, say, a grandparent.

2. In an emergency, are you more likely to receive help in a nearly empty bus or in a crowded bus terminal?

3. People who have empathy for others are _____ likely to be helpful.

This is a reasonable possibility, and it has been supported by other research evidence (Rachlin & Jones, 2008), but remember that even though evolutionary theory may explain some general human tendencies to help, it cannot predict the behavior of specific individuals in specific situations (Penner, Dovidio, et al., 2005). Like all other behavior, helping and altruism depend on the interplay of many genetic and environmental factors—including interactions between particular people and particular situations. (See "In Review: Theories of Helping Behaviors" for a summary of the major reasons why people help and the conditions under which they are most likely to do so.)

Cooperation, Competition, and Conflict

Helping is one of several ways in which people *cooperate* with one another. **Cooperation** is any type of behavior in which people work together to attain a common goal (Dovidio et al., 2006). For example, several law students might form a study group to help one another pass a difficult exam. But people can also engage in **competition**, trying to attain a goal for themselves while denying that goal to others. So those same students might later compete with one another for a single job opening at a prestigious law firm. Finally, **conflict** results when one person or group believes that another stands in the way of their achieving a goal. When the students become attorneys and represent opposing parties in a legal dispute, they will be in conflict. One way in which psychologists have learned about all three of these behaviors is by studying social dilemmas (Weber, Kopelman, & Messick, 2004).

Social Dilemmas

Social dilemmas are situations in which an action that brings rewards for the individual will, if widely adopted, produce negative consequences for the group (Aronson, Wilson, & Akert, 2010). For instance, during a drought, individual homeowners are better off in the short run if they water their lawns as often as necessary to keep the grass from dying, but if everyone ignores local water restrictions, there will be no drinking water for anyone in the long run. Social psychologists have studied situations like this by conducting experiments using the two-person "prisoner's dilemma" game.

The Prisoner's Dilemma Game
The **prisoner's dilemma game** is based on a scenario in which two people are separated for questioning immediately after being arrested on suspicion of having committed a serious crime (Komorita & Parks, 1996). The prosecutor believes they are guilty but doesn't have enough evidence to convict them. Each prisoner

cooperation Any type of behavior in which people work together to attain a goal.

competition Behavior in which individuals try to attain a goal for themselves while denying that goal to others.

conflict The result of a person's or group's belief that another person or group stands in the way of their achieving a valued goal.

social dilemma A situation in which actions that produce rewards for one individual will produce negative consequences if adopted by everyone.

prisoner's dilemma game A social dilemma scenario in which mutual cooperation guarantees the best mutual outcome.

Cooperation, Competition, Conflict, and Cash

Cooperation, competition, and conflict can all be seen on *Survivor*, a television series in which people try to win money by staying the longest in some remote location. Early on, contestants cooperate with members of their own teams, but as more and more people are eliminated, even team members compete with one another. When only two people remain, each stands in the way of the other's goal of winning, so they are in direct conflict.

© CBS-TV/The Kobal Collection/Robert Voets

can either confess or not, but they are told that if they both refuse to confess, each will be convicted of a minor offense and will be jailed for one year. If they both confess, the prosecutor will recommend a five-year sentence for each. However, if one prisoner remains silent and the other confesses to what they did, the prosecutor will allow the confessing prisoner to go free, whereas the other will serve the maximum ten-year sentence.

Each prisoner faces a dilemma. Part A of Figure 18.8 outlines the possible outcomes. Obviously, the strategy that will guarantee the best *mutual* outcome—short sentences for both prisoners—is cooperation. In other words, neither should confess. But the prisoner who remains silent runs the risk of receiving a long sentence if the other prisoner confesses. Further, the prisoner who confesses will benefit if the other prisoner doesn't talk. In other words, each prisoner has an incentive to compete for freedom by confessing. But if they *both* compete and confess, each will end up going to jail for longer than if they had kept quiet.

In the typical prisoner's dilemma experiment, two people sit at separate control panels. Each of them has a red button and a black button, one of which is to be pushed on each of many trials. Pressing the black button is a cooperative response. Pressing the red button is a competitive response. For example, on a given trial, if both participants press their black buttons, each wins $5. If both press their red buttons, they earn only $1. However, if one player presses the red button and the other presses the black button, the one who pressed the red button will win $10, and the other will win nothing.

Part B of Figure 18.8 shows the possible outcomes for each trial. Over the course of the experiment, the combined winnings of the players are greatest if each presses the black button—that is, if they cooperate. By pressing the black button, however, a

FIGURE 18.8
The Prisoner's Dilemma Game
In the prisoner's dilemma game, mutual cooperation benefits each person and mutual competition is harmful to both. However, one party can take advantage of the other's cooperativeness. These diagrams show the potential payoffs for prisoners—and research participants—in prisoner's dilemma game situations.

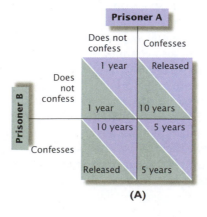

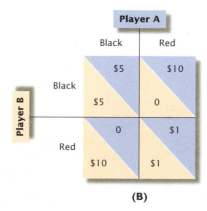

player becomes open to exploitation, because on any trial, the other might press the red button and take all the winnings. So each player stands to benefit the most individually by pressing the red button occasionally. The prisoner's dilemma game is what psychologists call a *mixed-motive conflict*—there are good reasons to cooperate and also good reasons to compete.

What happens when people play this game? Overall, there is a strong tendency to respond competitively. People find it difficult to resist the competitive choice on any given trial (Lodewijkx, Rabbie, & Visser, 2006). This choice wins them more money on that trial, but in the long run, they gain less than they would have gained through cooperation.

If acting competitively leads to smaller rewards in the long run, why do people persist in competing? There seem to be two reasons (Komorita, 1984). First, winning more than an opponent seems to be rewarding in itself. In the prisoner's dilemma game, many people want to outscore an opponent even if the result is that they win less money overall. Second, and more important, once several competitive responses are made, the competition seems to feed on itself (Insko et al., 1990). Each person becomes distrustful of the other, and cooperation becomes increasingly difficult. The more competitive one person acts, the more competitive the other becomes (McClintock & Liebrand, 1988).

Resource Dilemmas Psychologists interested in cooperation, competition, and conflict have also concentrated on social dilemmas in which people share a common resource. In this situation, called a *resource dilemma* (De Cremer & van Dijk, 2008), there are built-in conflicts between the interests of the individual and those of the group and also between people's short-term and long-term interests (De Dreu, 2010). There are two kinds of resource dilemmas. In the *commons dilemma,* people have to decide how much to take from a common resource. In the *public goods dilemma,* people must decide how much to contribute to a common resource. An example of the commons dilemma would be a situation in which farmers all want to draw water for their crops from the same lake. Each individual farmer would benefit greatly from unrestricted use of the water, but if all the farmers did the same, the water would soon be gone. Tax laws provide an example of the public goods dilemma. You would benefit greatly in the short run if you didn't pay any taxes, but if everyone failed to pay, no one would have police and fire protection, highway repairs, national defense, or other vital government services. How can people facing such dilemmas be prompted to cooperate?

Promoting Cooperation

Communication can reduce people's tendency to act competitively (Pavitt et al., 2007). Unfortunately, however, not all communication increases cooperation, just as not all contact between ethnic groups reduces prejudice. If the communication takes the form of a threat, people may interpret the threat itself as a competitive response and become more likely to respond competitively (Gifford & Hine, 1997). Furthermore, the communication must be relevant. In one social dilemma study, cooperation increased only when people spoke openly about the dilemma and how they would be rewarded for various responses. Praising one another for past cooperation was most beneficial (Orbell, van de Kragt, & Dawes, 1988).

People can also communicate silently through the strategy they use. In the prisoner's dilemma game, the most effective strategy for producing long-term cooperation is to use basic learning principles and play *tit-for-tat*. This means rewarding cooperative responses with cooperation and punishing competitiveness by being competitive in return. Cooperating after a cooperative response and competing after a competitive response produces a high degree of cooperation over time (Nowak, May, & Sigmund, 1995; Zhong, Loewenstein, & Murninghan, 2007). But competing after a cooperative response may harm the relationship and threaten future cooperation (Monterosso et al., 2002). So players usually learn that the only way to come out ahead is to cooperate. There is even

"There's quite a power struggle going on."

evidence from computer simulation studies that societies whose members use cooperative strategies with one another are more likely to survive and prosper than societies whose members act competitively (Ginges et al., 2007; Nowak, May, & Sigmund, 1995).

Interpersonal Conflict

In social dilemmas and other situations in which people are *interdependent*—that is, when what one person does always affects the other—cooperation usually leads to the best outcomes for everyone. This is why social psychologists are applying research on cooperation to help people work more closely together in school, on the job, in the community, and even in efforts to protect the environment (van Vugt, 2009). Still, humans do not always cooperate. People from collectivist cultures, in which cooperation is emphasized, are generally less likely to act selfishly in a social dilemma, but conflict in such situations does occur in all cultures (Smith & Bond, 1999). Conflict is especially likely when people are involved in a **zero-sum game**. This is a situation in which one person's gains are subtracted from the other person's resources. It is called *zero-sum* because when you add up the gains and losses, the result is zero. Election campaigns, lawsuits over a deceased relative's estate, and competition between children for a toy are all examples of zero-sum games.

There are four major reasons that interpersonal conflicts can be difficult to resolve and why they may escalate (De Dreu, 2010). The first is that people in conflict invest so much time, effort, and commitment in establishing their own point of view that being asked to adjust it in order to compromise seems to be asking too much (Ku, Malhotra, & Murninghan, 2005). Second, people in interpersonal conflicts often see the problem as due to the other person's hostility or selfishness rather than to an honest difference of opinion (Samuelson & Messick, 1995). In other words, conflicts can become entrenched because of the actor-observer effect and other attributional errors discussed in the chapter on social cognition. So when the printer paper runs out at a crucial time, interpersonal conflict may escalate if the office manager—who was simply trying to cut paper costs—is perceived by other employees as being stingy and trying to make their lives miserable.

zero-sum game A social situation in which one person's gains are subtracted from another person's resources so that the sum of the gains and losses is zero.

Faulty communication is a third reason for the persistence of interpersonal conflicts. A comment intended as a compliment is sometimes interpreted as a snide remark, and constructive criticism is sometimes perceived as a personal attack. Such miscommunication can start a cycle of increasingly provocative actions in which each person believes the other is being aggressive and unfair (Pruitt & Carnevale, 1993). A fourth factor that can escalate interpersonal conflict is a tendency to believe that the other person is not really interested in reaching a settlement. This view may become a self-fulfilling prophesy (see the chapter on social cognition); each side may begin to behave in ways that actually bring about the uncooperative behavior expected from the other side, and the end result may be increasing conflict and eventually, a stalemate (Kennedy & Pronin, 2008).

Managing Conflict   Interpersonal conflict can damage relationships among people and impair the effectiveness of organizations, but it can also lead to beneficial changes. Industrial and organizational psychologists have found that often it is much better to manage conflict effectively than to try to eliminate it. The most common way of managing organizational conflict is through *bargaining*. Each side—labor and management, for example—produces a series of offers and counteroffers until a solution emerges that is acceptable to both sides. At its best, bargaining can produce a win-win situation in which each side gets what is most important and gives up what is less important (Bacon & Blyton, 2007).

If bargaining fails, *third-party interventions* may be useful. Like a therapist working with a couple, an outside mediator can often help the two sides in an organizational conflict focus on important issues, defuse emotions, clarify positions and proposals, and make suggestions that allow each side to compromise without losing face (De Dreu, 2010).

Other techniques for managing conflict, especially conflict over resources, involve the introduction of *superordinate goals* or a *superordinate identity* (Abrams & Hogg, 2010). For example, if people who are competing for scarce resources can be made to feel that they are all part of the same group and share the same goals, they will act less selfishly and manage the limited resources more efficiently.

In short, although interpersonal conflict can be harmful if left unchecked, it can also be managed in a way that benefits the group. Much as psychotherapy can help people resolve personal conflict in a way that leads to growth, interpersonal conflict within an organization can be handled in a way that leads to innovations, increased loyalty and motivation, and other valuable changes.

Group Processes

Although Western industrialized cultures tend to emphasize individuals over groups, the fact remains that most important governmental and business decisions in those cultures and elsewhere are made by groups, not individuals (Hackman & Katz, 2010). Sometimes group processes are effective, as seen in the extraordinary teamwork of emergency workers and volunteers that led to dramatic rescues of people trapped in collapsed buildings after an earthquake struck Haiti in 2010. At other times, group processes can have disastrous results, as we will see later. In the chapter on cognition and language, we describe some of the factors that influence the nature and quality of group decisions. Here we consider some of the social psychological processes that often occur in groups to alter the behavior of their members and the quality of their collective efforts.

Group Leadership

A good leader can help a group pursue its goals; a poor one can get in the way of a group's functioning (Kaiser, Hogan, & Craig, 2008). What makes a good leader? Certain personality traits often distinguish effective leaders from ineffective ones. For example, using

A Different Kind of Coach

Many football coaches are task-oriented leaders whose tough discipline and emotional outbursts are legendary. Only a few, such as Tony Dungy, former coach of both the Indianapolis Colts and the Tampa Bay Buccaneers are charismatic leaders. Dungy's leadership style was calm and low-key; rather than shouting at his players, he inspired them to focus on his vision of success and to do their best to achieve it. Their love for him is evident here as Colts players carry Dungy off the field after winning the Super Bowl in 2007.

© Jeff Haynes/AFP/Getty Images

tests similar to those that measure the Big Five traits described in the chapter on personality, Colin Silverthorne (2001) examined the characteristics of leaders in the United States, Thailand, and China. He found that effective leaders in all three countries tended to score high on agreeableness, emotional stability, extraversion, and conscientiousness. Other researchers have found that in general, effective leaders are intelligent, success-oriented, flexible, and confident in their ability to lead (Chemers, Watson, & May, 2000; Foti & Hauenstein, 2007). Having particular personality traits does not guarantee good leadership ability, however. People can be effective leaders in one situation but ineffective in another (Ng, Ang, & Chan, 2008). The reason is that effective leadership also depends on the characteristics of the group members, the task at hand, and the interaction between these factors and the leader's style (Yun, Faraj, & Sims, 2005).

For many years, leadership research focused on two main types of leaders, known as *task-motivated* and *relationship-motivated*. **Task-motivated leaders** provide close supervision, lead by giving directives, and generally discourage group discussion (Yukl & Van Fleet, 1992). Their style may not endear them to group members. **Relationship-motivated leaders** provide loose supervision, ask for group members' ideas, and are generally concerned with subordinates' feelings. They are usually well liked by the group, even when they must discipline a group member (Kassin, Fein, & Markus, 2010).

More recently, some researchers have proposed that there are additional leadership styles. One of these is seen in *transactional leaders*, whose leadership behavior depends on the actions of the people they lead. For example, transactional leaders reward people who behave as the leader wishes, and they correct or punish those who behave otherwise. In contrast, there are also *transformational*, or *charismatic, leaders* (Hogg, 2010). Rather than focusing on rewarding or punishing specific behaviors, these leaders concentrate on creating a vision of the group's goals, inspiring people to pursue that vision, and giving their followers reason to respect and admire them. Transformational leaders such as Winston Churchill and Martin Luther King Jr. have dramatically changed the world for the better, and many less famous leaders of social or business groups have done the same on a smaller scale.

Do men or women make better leaders? Alice Eagly and her colleagues have studied differences between men and women in leadership styles (e.g., Eagly, Karau, &

task-motivated leader A leader who provides close supervision, leads by directives, and generally discourages group discussion.

relationship-motivated leader A leader who provides loose supervision, asks for group members' ideas, and is concerned with subordinates' feelings

Makhijani, 1995). Their initial research found that overall, men and women are equally capable leaders. It also seemed that men tended to be more effective when success required a task-motivated leader and that women tended to be more effective when success required a more relationship-motivated leader. In other words, it appeared that people of each sex tended to be most effective when acting in a manner consistent with gender-role traditions (Eagly & Karau, 1991; Eagly, Karau, & Makhijani, 1995). Perhaps this was because some people did not like female leaders who act in a "masculine" manner or occupy leadership positions traditionally held by men (Eagly, Makhijani, & Klonsky, 1992).

A somewhat different picture of gender differences in leadership has emerged from Eagly's more recent research. For one thing, she found that females are generally more likely than males to display a transformational leadership style. Further, when women display a transactional style, they tend to be more encouraging than transactional male leaders. That is, the transactional female leaders tend to focus more on using rewards rather than punishments to modify group members' behaviors. Finally, and in contrast to earlier findings, Eagly's results suggest that women may be slightly more effective leaders overall than men, even though they may still face challenges in convincing some male followers to accept them as legitimate authorities (Ayman, Korabik, & Morris, 2009; Eagly & Sczesny, 2009).

Groupthink

The emphasis on group decisions in most large organizations is based on the belief that a group of people working together will make better decisions than individuals working alone. As noted in the chapter on cognition and language, this belief is generally correct; yet under certain circumstances, groups have been known to make amazingly bad decisions (Kassin, Fine, & Markus, 2010). Consider an example from 2003, when officials at the National Aeronautics and Space Administration (NASA) ignored engineers' warnings about the damage done to the heat shield of the space shuttle *Columbia* during its launch into orbit. Despite the engineers' repeated requests to use satellite photos to assess the extent of the damage, NASA officials approved the shuttle's return to earth without any inspections. Because of heat shield damage, the spacecraft disintegrated upon reentry, killing all seven crew members. Irving Janis (1989) proposed that disastrous decisions like this one can be attributed to a phenomenon called **groupthink**. Groupthink occurs, he said, when group members are unable to realistically evaluate the options available to them or to fully consider the potential negative consequences of the option they are considering. It is particularly likely when members of a group place a higher value on reaching a decision than on being sure they have reached the best decision.

Trying to reach a consensus before a group acts is not necessarily a bad strategy. In fact, it usually produces a good decision and positive feelings about the group (Smith & Mackie, 2007). But according to Janis, the drive toward consensus is likely to produce groupthink and bad decisions when four conditions are present: (1) the consensus is not based on all the facts at hand, (2) group members all share certain biases, (3) members who disagree with the majority view are punished or even ejected from the group, and (4) the group leader puts pressure on the members to reach consensus.

Some social psychologists believe that bad group decisions can be explained by processes other than groupthink (e.g., Baron, 2005; Hackman & Katz, 2010), but instances of groupthink probably do occur. With that in mind, researchers have worked on developing techniques to help groups avoid it (Galinsky & Kray, 2004; Kray & Galinsky, 2003; Packer, 2009). One way to avoid groupthink is to teach group members to imagine all the negative outcomes of each course of action they are considering. Another is to designate someone to take the unpopular role of "devil's advocate"—to constantly challenge the group's emerging consensus and offer alternatives. This person forces the group to consider all the facts and every possible decision option (Janis,

LINKAGES How does stress affect group decision making? (a link to Health, Stress, and Coping, p. 581)

groupthink A pattern of thinking in which group members fail to evaluate realistically the wisdom of various options and decisions.

1985; Risen, 1998). Yet another technique is to encourage the expression of diverse opinions by allowing them to be presented anonymously. The group members might sit at computers and type out messages about all the options that occur to them. Each message is displayed for all to see on an electronic mail system that hides each sender's identity. This procedure allows the group to discuss the options via e-mail without knowing who is saying what. Research on this technique suggests that it is effective in stimulating logical debate and making people less inhibited about disagreeing with the group (O'Brien, 1991).

LINKAGES

As noted in the chapter on introducing psychology, all of psychology's subfields are related to one another. Our discussion of how the presence of other people affects a person's motivation to perform illustrates just one way in which the topic of this chapter, social influence, is linked to the subfield of motivation

CHAPTER 18
Social Influence

and emotion (see the chapter on that topic). The Linkages diagram shows ties to two other subfields as well, and there are many more ties throughout the book. Looking for linkages among subfields will help you see how they all fit together and help you better appreciate the big picture that is psychology.

LINKAGES

Do people solve problems better alone or in a group?
(ans. on p. 312)

Do people perform better or worse when others are watching?
(ans. on p. 730)

How do societies define what is abnormal
(ans. on p. 597)

CHAPTER 8
Cognition and Language

CHAPTER 11
Motivation and Emotion

CHAPTER 15
Psychological Disorders

SUMMARY

Social Influence

Social norms establish the rules for what should and should not be done in a particular situation. Descriptive norms indicate what most other people do and create pressure to do the same. Injunctive norms provide specific information about what others approve or disapprove of. *Deindividuation* is a psychological state in which people in a group temporarily lose their individuality, focus on the group's norms, and may engage in antisocial acts

that they would not normally perform. *Social facilitation, social interference,* and *social loafing* provide three other examples of how the presence of other people can affect an individual's behavior.

Conformity and Compliance

When behavior or beliefs change as the result of unspoken or implicit group pressure, *conformity* has occurred; when the change is the result of a request, *compliance* has occurred.

The Role of Social Norms

People tend to follow the normative responses of others, and groups create social norms when none already exist.

Why Do People Conform?

People sometimes exhibit public conformity without private acceptance. At other times, the responses of other people have a genuine impact on private beliefs. People conform because they want to be right, because they want to be liked, and because they tend to be rewarded for doing so.

When Do People Conform?

People are most likely to conform when the situation is ambiguous or when others in the group are in unanimous agreement. Up to a point, conformity usually increases as the number of people holding the majority view grows larger. Persistent and unanimous *minority influence* can also produce some conformity.

Inducing Compliance

Effective strategies for inducing compliance include the foot-in-the-door technique, the door-in-the-face technique, and the low-ball technique.

Obedience

Obedience involves complying with an explicit demand, typically from an authority figure. Research by Stanley Milgram indicates that levels of obedience are high even when obeying an authority appears to result in pain and suffering for another person.

Factors Affecting Obedience

People obey someone who has certain kinds of social power. Obedience declines when the status of the authority figure declines, when others are observed to disobey, and if a victim asks to be released. Some people may be more likely to obey orders than others.

Evaluating Milgram's Studies

Because participants in Milgram's studies experienced considerable stress, the experiments have been questioned on ethical grounds. Nevertheless, Milgram's research showed that even apparently "normal" people can be influenced to inflict pain on others.

Aggression

Aggression is an act intended to harm another person.

Why Are People Aggressive?

Sigmund Freud viewed aggression as due partly to self-destructive instincts. More recent theories attribute aggressive tendencies to genetic factors, brain dysfunctions, and hormonal influences. Learning is also important. People learn to display aggression by watching others and by being rewarded for aggressive behavior. There are wide cultural differences in the incidence of aggression.

When Are People Aggressive?

A variety of emotional factors play a role in aggression. The *frustration-aggression hypothesis* suggests that frustration can lead to aggression, particularly if cues that invite or promote aggression are present. Recent research indicates that stress and negative feelings play a major role in aggression. Arousal from sources unrelated to aggression, such as exercise, can also make aggressive responses more likely. Research in *environmental psychology* suggests that factors such as high temperature, noise, and crowding increase the likelihood of aggressive behavior.

Altruism and Helping Behavior

Human behavior is also characterized by *helping behavior* (*prosocial behavior*) and *altruism*.

Why Do People Help?

There are three major theories as to why people help others. According to the *arousal: cost-reward theory,* people help in order to reduce the unpleasant arousal they experience when others are in distress. Their specific reaction to a suffering person depends on the costs associated with helping or not helping. Helping behavior is most likely when the costs of helping are low and the costs of not helping are high. Perceptions of cost are affected by the clarity of the need for help, the *bystander effect* (which creates diffusion of responsibility), and personality traits. Environmental factors also affect willingness to help. The *empathy-altruism theory* suggests that helping can be truly unselfish if the helper feels empathy for the person in need. Evolutionary theory suggests that humans have an innate tendency to help others, especially relatives, because doing so increases the likelihood that family genes will survive.

Cooperation, Competition, and Conflict

Cooperation is behavior in which people work together to attain a goal. *Competition* exists when individuals try to attain a goal while denying that goal to others. *Conflict* occurs when a person or group believes that someone stands in the way of something of value.

Social Dilemmas

In *social dilemmas,* selfish behavior that benefits individuals in the short run may spell disaster in the long run if adopted by an entire group. Two kinds of social dilemmas are seen in the *prisoner's dilemma game* and in resource dilemmas. When given a choice between cooperation and competition in a social dilemma, people often compete with one another. This is true even though they may receive fewer rewards for competing than for cooperating.

Promoting Cooperation

Communication between competing parties can increase cooperation, especially if the communication is not threatening and is relevant to the situation. One of the most effective strategies for producing long-term cooperation in a prisoner's dilemma game is rewarding cooperative responses with cooperation and punishing competitive responses with competitiveness.

Interpersonal Conflict

In *zero-sum games,* competition is almost inevitable because there can be only one winner. Incompatible interests, attribution of another's behavior to unfriendly motives, faulty communication, and magnification of differences are frequent sources of interpersonal conflict. Bargaining, third-party interventions, and reminders about broader goals and shared identity are helpful procedures for managing conflict.

Group Processes

Many of the most important decisions are made by groups.

Group Leadership

No single personality type or behavioral style always results in good leadership. *Task-motivated leaders* provide close supervision, lead by giving directives, and generally discourage group discussion. *Relationship-motivated leaders* provide loose supervision, ask for group members' ideas, and are generally concerned with subordinates' feelings. Transformational leaders try to inspire and motivate the group; transactional leaders tend to reward appropriate behaviors and punish inappropriate ones.

Groupthink

The pattern of thinking called *groupthink* can occur when the desire to reach a group decision becomes more important than the need to reach the best decision.

LINKAGES TO FURTHER LEARNING

Now that you have finished reading this chapter, how about exploring some of the topics and information that you found most interesting? Here are some places to start.

Books

Elliot Aronson, *Nobody Left to Hate* (Freeman, 2000). A social psychologist explores the social roots of the Columbine school massacre.

Hans-Werner Bierhoff, *Prosocial Behavior* (Psychology Press, 2002). An introductory overview of research on helping and altruism.

Robert Cialdini, *Influence: Science and Practice* (Addison-Wesley, 2007). Summary of research on influence and how it is applied in everyday life.

Russell Geen and Edward Donnerstein (Eds.), *Human Aggression: Theory, Research, and Implications for Social Policy* (Academic Press, 1998). Readings on the origins of and factors in aggression.

On the Internet

 Access an integrated eBook and chapter-specific learning tools including flashcards, quizzes, videos, and more. Go to CengageBrain.com.

CENGAGENOW Want to maximize the value of your online study time? Take this easy-to-use study system's diagnostic pre-test, and it will create a personalized study plan for you. By helping you identify the topics that you need to understand better and then directing you to valuable online resources, it can speed up your chapter review. CengageNOW even provides a post-test so you can confirm that you are ready for an exam. Go to CengageBrain.com.

TALKING POINTS

Here are a few talking points to help you summarize this chapter for family and friends without giving a lecture.

1. Copycat crimes illustrate the fact that people's behavior can be influenced by the behavior of others.

2. In crowds where people feel they cannot be identified, they may do antisocial things that they might never do otherwise.

3. Having an audience can help our dancing or musical performance if our skills are well learned but can be disruptive if those skills are not yet well established.

4. Sometimes the best way to get someone to do something is to first ask for something else.

5. People who might not ordinarily harm another person can be influenced by social pressure—especially from an authority figure—to do some surprisingly antisocial things.

6. Aggressive behavior is shaped by both inherited tendencies and situational factors.

7. You are more likely to get help in an emergency if only one other person is present than if you are in a crowd.

Answers to In Review Questions

The questions at the bottom of each chapter's In Review charts are listed here,
followed in parentheses by the correct answers. The questions are grouped under each
chapter's title and by the name and page number of the In Review chart in which they appear.

The answer key for the optional Industrial and Organizational Psychology and
Neuropsychology chapters appears in blue.

Chapter 1   Introduction to the Science of Psychology

In Review: The Development of Psychology (p. 18)

1. Darwin's theory of evolution had an especially strong influence on _____ism and _____ism. (functionalism; behaviorism)
2. Which school of psychological thought was founded by a European medical doctor? _____ (Psychoanalysis)
3. In the history of psychology, _____ was the first school of thought to appear. (structuralism)

In Review: Approaches to Psychology (p. 24)

1. Teaching people to be less afraid of heights reflects the _____ approach. (behavioral)
2. Charles Darwin was not a psychologist, but his work influenced the _____ approach to psychology. (evolutionary)
3. Assuming that people inherit mental disorders suggests a _____ approach. (biological)

Chapter 2   Research in Psychology

In Review: Methods of Psychology (p. 47)

1. The _____ method is most likely to use a double-blind design. (experimental)
2. Research on a new treatment method is most likely to begin with _____. (case studies)
3. Studying language by listening to people in public places is an example of _____ research. (naturalistic observation)

In Review: Descriptive and Inferential Statistics (p. 56)

1. The measure of central tendency that is most affected by extreme scores is the _____. (the mean)
2. A set of data with a high standard deviation will contain scores that are _____ variable than a set of data with a low standard deviation. (more)
3. Correlation coefficients of +.50 and −.50 indicate relationships that are of different strengths (True or False) _____. (false)

Chapter 3   Biological Aspects of Psychology

In Review: Neurons, Neurotransmitters, and Receptors (p. 71)

1. For one neuron to communicate with another, a _____ has to cross the _____ between them. (neurotransmitter; synapse)
2. The nervous system's main functions are to _____, _____, and _____ information. (receive; process; act on)
3. The two main types of cells in the nervous system are _____ and _____. (neurons; glial cells)

In Review: Organization of the Brain (p. 98)

1. The oldest part of the brain is the _____. (hindbrain)
2. Cells that operate as the body's twenty-four-hour "time clock" are found in the _____. (hypothalamus)
3. Memory problems seen in Alzheimer's disease are related to shrinkage of the _____ (hippocampus)

In Review: Classes of Neurotransmitters (p. 102)

1. The main neurotransmitter for slowing, or inhibiting, brain activity is _____. (GABA)
2. A group of neurons that use the same neurotransmitter is called a _____. (neurotransmitter system)
3. Which neurotransmitter's activity causes brain damage during a stroke? _____ (glutamate)

Chapter 4   Sensation

In Review: Hearing (p. 120)

1. Sound energy is converted to neural activity in an inner ear structure called the _____. (cochlea [or basilar membrane])
2. Hearing loss due to damage to hair cells or the auditory nerve is called _____. (nerve deafness)
3. How high or low a sound sounds is called _____ and is determined by the _____ of a sound wave. (pitch; frequency)

In Review: Seeing (p. 135)

1. The ability to see in very dim light depends on photoreceptors called _____. (rods)
2. Color afterimages are best explained by the _____ theory of color vision. (opponent-process)
3. Nearsightedness and farsightedness occur when images are not focused on the eye's _____. (retina)

In Review: Smell and Taste (p. 141)

1. The flavor of food arises from a combination of _____ and _____. (taste; smell)
2. Emotion and memory are linked especially closely to our sense of _____. (smell)
3. Perfume ads suggest that humans are affected by _____ that increase sexual attraction. (pheromones)

In Review: Body Senses (p. 151)

1. Gate control theory offers an explanation of why we sometimes do not feel _____. (pain)
2. Professional dancers look at the same spot as long as possible during repeated spins. They are trying to avoid the dizziness caused when the sense of _____ is overstimulated. (equilibrium)
3. Without your sense of _____, you would not be able to swallow food without choking. (touch)

Chapter 5   Perception

In Review: Principles of Perceptual Organization and Constancy (p. 176)

1. The movement we see in movies, videos, and DVDs is due to a perceptual illusion called _____. (the stroboscopic illusion)
2. People who have lost an eye also lose the depth cue called _____. (retinal disparity)
3. The grouping principle of _____ allows you to identify objects seen through a picket fence. (closure)

In Review: Mechanisms of Pattern Recognition (p. 182)

1. Your ability to read a battered old sign that has some letters missing is a result of _____ processing. (top-down)
2. When stimulus features match the stimuli we are looking for, _____ takes place. (recognition)
3. Schemas can create a _____ that makes us more likely to perceive stimuli in a particular way. (perceptual set)

Chapter 6   Learning

In Review: Basic Phenomena of Classical Conditioning (p. 207)

1. If a man's conditioned fear of spiders is triggered by the sight of other creatures that look like spiders, he is demonstrating stimulus _____. (generalization)
2. Because of _____, we are more likely to learn a fear of snakes than a fear of cars. (biopreparedness)
3. Feeling sad upon hearing a song associated with a long-lost relationship illustrates _____. (spontaneous recovery)

In Review: Reinforcement and Punishment (p. 221)

1. Taking an aspirin can relieve headache pain, so people learn to do so through the process of _____ reinforcement. (negative)
2. The "walk" sign that tells people it is safe to cross the street is an example of a _____ stimulus. (discriminative conditioned)
3. Response rates tend to be higher under _____ schedules of reinforcement than under _____ schedules. (ratio; interval)

Chapter 7   Memory

In Review: Models of Memory (p. 249)

1. The value of elaborative rehearsal over maintenance rehearsal has been cited as evidence for the _____ model of memory. (levels-of-processing)
2. Deliberately trying to remember something means using your _____ memory. (explicit)
3. Playing the piano uses _____ memory. (procedural)

In Review: Storing New Memories (p. 256)

1. If you looked up a phone number but forgot it before you could call it, the information was probably lost from _____ memory. (short-term)
2. The capacity of short-term memory is about _____ to _____ items. (five; nine)
3. Encoding is usually _____ in short-term memory and _____ in long-term memory. (acoustic; semantic)

In Review: Factors Affecting Retrieval from Long-Term Memory (p. 258)

1. Stimuli called _____ help you recall information stored in long-term memory. (retrieval cues)

2. If it is easier to remember something in the place where you learned it, you have _____ memory. (context-dependent)
3. The tendency to remember the last few items in a list is called the _____ effect. (recency)

In Review: Improving Your Memory (p. 279)

1. Using mnemonic strategies and the PQ4R system to better remember course material are examples of the value of _____ rehearsal. (elaborative)
2. "Cramming" illustrates _____ practice that usually leads to _____ long-term retention than _____ practice. (massed; poorer [or less]; distributed)
3. To minimize forgetting, you should review lecture notes _____ after a lecture ends. (immediately [or as soon as possible])

Chapter 8   Cognition and Language

In Review: Ingredients of Thought (p. 296)

1. Thinking is the manipulation of _____. (mental representations)
2. Arguments over what is "fair" occur because "fairness" is a _____ concept. (natural)
3. Your _____ of "hotel room" would lead you to expect yours to include a bathroom. (schema)

In Review: Solving Problems (p. 307)

1. People stranded without water could use their shoes to collect rain, but they may not do so because of an obstacle to problem solving called _____. (functional fixedness)
2. Because of the _____ heuristic, once sellers set a value on their house, they may refuse to take much less for it. (anchoring)
3. If you tackle a massive problem one small step at a time, you are using an approach called _____. (decomposition or means-end analysis)

Chapter 9   Consciousness

In Review: Sleep and Sleep Disorders (p. 350)

1. Jet lag occurs because of a disruption in a traveler's _____. (circadian rhythms [or sleep-wake cycle])
2. The importance of non-REM sleep is suggested by its appearance _____ in the night. (early)
3. The safest sleeping position for babies is _____. (face up)

In Review: Major Classes of Psychoactive Drugs (p. 365)

1. Physical dependence on a drug is a condition more commonly known as _____. (addiction)
2. Drugs that act as antagonists _____ the interaction of neurotransmitters and receptors. (block)
3. Drug effects are determined partly by what we learn to _____ the effects to be. (expect)

Chapter 10   Cognitive Abilities

In Review: Influences on IQ (p. 391)

1. Intelligence is influenced by both _____ and _____. (heredity; environment)
2. Children living in poverty tend to have _____ IQs than those in middle-class families. (lower)
3. IQs of children whose parents encourage learning tend to be _____ than those of children whose parents do not. (higher)

In Review: Analyzing Cognitive Abilities (p. 399)

1. The concepts of fluid and crystallized intelligence developed from research on the _____ approach to intelligence. (psychometric)

2. Using fMRI scanning to relate memory skills to intelligence reflects which approach to intelligence? (information processing)

3. Which theory of intelligence highlights the fact that some people with low IQs can still succeed at complex tasks of daily living? (triarchic)

Chapter 11   Motivation and Emotion

In Review: Theories of Motivation (p. 420)

1. The fact that some people like roller coasters and other scary amusement park rides has been cited as evidence for the _____ theory of motivation. (optimal arousal)

2. Evolutionary theories of motivation are modern outgrowths of theories based on _____. (the instinct doctrine)

3. The value of incentives can be affected by _____, _____, and _____ factors. (physiological [or biological]; cognitive; social)

In Review: Major Factors Controlling Hunger and Eating (p. 428)

1. People may eat when they are "full," suggesting that eating is not controlled by _____ alone. (hunger)

2. People with _____ know that they have a problem; those with _____ nervosa tend not to. (bulimia; anorexia)

3. The best strategy for lasting weight loss includes regular _____, as well as improved eating habits. (exercise)

In Review: Theories of Emotion (p. 456)

1. Research showing that there are pleasure centers in the brain has been cited in support of the _____ theory of emotions. (Cannon-Bard)

2. The use of polygraphs in lie detection is based on the _____ theory of emotions. (James-Lange)

3. The process of attribution is most important to _____ theories of emotions. (cognitive)

Chapter 12   Human Development

In Review: Milestones of Cognitive Development in Infancy and Childhood (p. 479)

1. Research in cognitive development suggests that children form mental representations _____ than Piaget thought they did. (earlier)

2. Recognizing that changing the shape of clay doesn't change the amount of clay is evidence of a cognitive ability called _____. (conservation)

3. The appearance of object permanence signals the end of the _____ period. (sensorimotor)

In Review: Social and Emotional Development During Infancy and Childhood (p. 499)

1. As part of their social development, children learn _____, which tell them what patterns of appearance and behavior are associated with being male or female. (gender roles)

2. Teaching children to talk quietly in a restaurant is part of the process called _____. (socialization)

3. Strict rules and the threat of punishment are typical of _____ parenting. (authoritarian)

In Review: Milestones of Adolescence and Adulthood (p. 516)

1. The greatest threat to cognitive abilities in late adulthood is _____ disease. (Alzheimer's)

2. Adolescents' _____ identity may be more defining than their national citizenship. (ethnic)

3. Not stealing because "I might get caught" reflects the _____ stage of moral reasoning. (preconventional)

Chapter 13   Health, Stress, and Coping

In Review: Stress Responses and Stress Mediators (p. 543)

1. The friends and family we can depend on to help us deal with stressors are called our _____ network. (social support)

2. Fantasizing about winning money is a(n) _____ focused way of coping with financial stress. (emotion)

3. Sudden, extreme stressors may cause psychological and behavioral problems known as _____. (posttraumatic stress disorder)

In Review: Methods for Coping with Stress (p. 552)

1. Catastrophizing thoughts are best overcome through _____ coping strategies. (cognitive)

2. The first step in coping with stress is to _____ the sources and effects of your stressors. (identify)

3. True or false: It is best to rely on only one good coping strategy. _____ (False)

Chapter 14   Personality

In Review: Major Approaches to Personality (p. 581)

1. Tests that measure the Five Factor Model's dimensions of personality are based on the _____ approach to personality. (trait)

2. The role of learning is most prominent in the _____ approach to personality. (social-cognitive)

3. Object relations and attachment theories are modern variants on _____ personality theories. (psychodynamic)

In Review: Personality Tests (p. 590)

1. Projective personality measures are based on the _____ approach to personality. (psychodynamic)

2. The NEO-PI-R and the MMPI-2 are examples of _____ tests. (nonprojective)

3. Most personality researchers use _____ tests in their work. (nonprojective)

Chapter 15   Psychological Disorders

In Review: Anxiety, Somatoform, and Dissociative Disorders (p. 620)

1. Concern that it may be triggered by media stories or therapists' suggestions has made _____ the most controversial of the dissociative disorders. (dissociative identity disorder)

2. A person who sleepwalks but is not able to walk when awake is showing signs of _____. (conversion disorder)

3. Panic disorder sometimes leads to another anxiety disorder called _____. (agoraphobia)

In Review: Affective Disorders (p. 623)

1. The risk of suicide is associated with _____ more than with any other symptom of disorder. (depression)

2. Cyclothymic personality is the bipolar version of _____. (dysthymic disorder)

3. Women are _____ likely than men to try suicide, but men are _____ likely to succeed. (more; more)

In Review: Schizophrenia (p. 633)

1. The _____ approach forms the basis of the vulnerability theory of schizophrenia. (diathesis-stress)

2. Hallucinations are _____ symptoms of schizophrenia; lack of emotion is a _____ symptom. (positive; negative)

3. Patients with schizophrenia who were able to finish school are _____ likely to show improvement. (more)

Chapter 16   Treatment of Psychological Disorders

In Review: Approaches to Psychological Treatment (p. 671)

1. Object relations therapy and interpersonal therapy are both contemporary examples of the _____ approach to psychological treatment. (psychodynamic)

2. Imagining increasingly fear-provoking stimuli is a _____ treatment method called _____. (behavioral; systematic desensitization)

3. Reflection is an interviewing technique associated mainly with the _____ approach to treatment. (humanistic [or nondirective])

In Review: Biological Treatments for Psychological Disorders (p. 687)

1. Electroconvulsive shock therapy is used _____ often now than it was in the 1950s. (less)

2. Anxiolytics are used mainly in the treatment of _____. (anxiety)

3. Tardive dyskinesia is a movement disorder sometimes caused by _____ drugs. (neuroleptic)

Chapter 17   Social Cognition

In Review: Some Biases in Social Perception (p. 708)

1. The fundamental attribution error appears to be somewhat less likely to occur among people in _____ cultures. (collectivist)

2. First impressions form _____, but change _____. (quickly; slowly)

3. If you believed that immigrants' successes are due to government help but that their failures are due to laziness, you would be committing the _____ error. (ultimate attribution error)

In Review: Forming and Changing Attitudes (p. 713)

1. According to the elaboration likelihood model, people are more likely to pay close attention to the content and logic of a persuasive message if the _____ route to attitude change has been activated. (central)

2. Holding attitudes that are similar to those of your friends illustrates the importance of _____ in attitude formation (learning)

3. According to cognitive dissonance theory, we tend to reduce conflict between attitudes and behaviors by changing our _____. (attitudes)

Chapter 18   Social Influence

In Review: Types of Social Influence (p. 742)

1. Joining the end of a ticket line is an example of _____, whereas forming two lines when a theater employee requests it is an example of _____. (conformity; compliance)

2. Seeing someone disobey a questionable order makes people _____ likely to obey the order themselves. (less)

3. Pricing your used car for more than you expect to get, then agreeing to reduce it to make a sale, is an example of the _____ approach to gaining compliance. (door-in-the-face)

In Review: Assistance (p. 758)

1. If you could save only one person from a burning house, the _____ theory of assistance would predict that it would be your own child rather than, say, a grandparent. (evolutionary)

2. Are you more likely to receive assistance in a nearly empty bus or a crowded bus terminal? _____. (A nearly empty bus)

3. People who have empathy for others are _____ likely to be helpful. (more)

Chapter 19   Industrial/Organizational Psychology

In Review: Assessing People, Jobs, and Job Performance (p. 777)

1. Lists of critical incidents are contained in _____-focused employee rating forms. (behavior)

2. A potential employer might use a two-day _____ to measure your skill at the job you want. (assessment center)

3. In general, _____ interviews are more useful in employee selection than _____ interviews. (structured; unstructured)

In Review: Recruiting, Selecting, and Training Employees (p. 783)

1. Employees tend to remember more from a training program when it is set up on a _____ rather than a _____ schedule. (distributed; massed)

2. Depending on "walk-in" applications is usually acceptable when hiring _____-level employees. (low)

3. Assuring that your hiring criteria actually predict employees' job performance requires a _____. (validation study)

Chapter 20   Neuropsychology

In Review: Foundations of Neuropsychology (p. 810)

1. A person who studies individual patients to determine what kind of brain damage each one happens to have is called a _____. (clinical neuropsychologist)

2. The case of "Tan" helped to establish the principle of _____. (localization of function)

3. In alexia without agraphia, the brain areas that control reading and writing are intact but cannot interact. This condition is called a _____. (disconnection syndrome)

In Review: Mechanisms of Brain Dysfunction (p. 813)

1. The brain floats in a bath of _____ inside the skull. (cerebrospinal fluid)

2. The brain needs a constant flow of fresh _____ all the time. (blood)

3. Cerebrovascular accidents rank as the number _____ cause of death in the United States. (three)

In Review: Major Neuropsychological Problems (p. 829)

1. A patient who has become forgetful but has no problems in other areas of cognitive function may be said to have _____. (mild cognitive impairment)

2. A dementia patient whose hippocampus is relatively intact and can still form new memories probably has _____ dementia. (vascular)

3. A patient with thiamine deficiency who is forgetful but makes up memories and believes they are real probably has _____. (Korsakoff's syndrome)

REFERENCES

Entries that appear in blue refer to the optional Industrial and Organizational Psychology or Neuropsychology chapters.

Aaron, D. J., Chang, Y.-F., Markovic, N., & LaPorte, R. E. (2003). Estimating the lesbian population: A capture-recapture approach. *Journal of Epidemiology and Community Health, 57*, 207–209.

Aarts, H., Dijksterhuis, A., & Dik, G. (2008). Goal contagion: Inferring goals from others' actions—and what it leads to. In J. Y. Shah & W. L. Gardner (Eds.), *Handbook of motivation science* (pp. 265–280). New York: Guilford Press.

Abbott, B. B., Schoen, L. S., & Badia, P. (1984). Predictable and unpredictable shock: Behavioral measures of aversion and physiological measures of stress. *Psychological Bulletin, 96*, 45–71.

Abbott, R. D., White, L. R., Ross, G. W., Masaki, K. H., et al. (2004). Walking and dementia in physically capable elderly men. *Journal of the American Medical Association, 292*, 1447–1453.

Abbot-Shim, M., Lambert, R., & McCarty, F. (2003). A comparison of school readiness outcomes for children randomly assigned to a Head Start program and the program's wait list. *Journal of Education for Students Placed at Risk, 8*, 191–214.

AbdelMalik, P., Husted, J., Chow, E. W., & Bassett, A. S. (2003). Childhood head injury and expression of schizophrenia in multiply affected families. *Archives of General Psychiatry, 60*, 231–236.

Abelson, J. L., Liberzon, I., Young, E. A., & Khan, S. (2005). Cognitive modulation of the endocrine stress response to a pharmacological challenge in normal and panic disorder subjects. *Archives of General Psychiatry, 62*, 668–675.

Abler, B., Hahlbrock, R., Unrath, A., Gron, G., & Kassubek, J. (2009). At-risk for pathological gambling: Imaging neural reward processing under chronic dopamine agonists. *Brain, 132*, 2396–2402.

Abraham, W. C. (2006). Memory maintenance: The changing nature of neural mechanisms. *Current Directions in Psychological Science, 15*, 5–8.

Abramowitz, J. S., & Braddock, A. E. (2006). Hypochondriasis: Conceptualization, treatment, and relationship to obsessive-compulsive disorder. *Psychiatric Clinics of North America, 29*, 503–519.

Abramowitz, J. S., Khandker, M., Nelson, C. A., Deacon, B. J., & Rygwall, R. (2006). The role of cognitive factors in the pathogenesis of obsessive-compulsive symptoms: A prospective study. *Behaviour Research and Therapy, 44*, 1361–1374.

Abrams, D., & Hogg, M. A. (2010). Social identity and self-categorization In J. F. Dovidio, M. Hewstone, P. Glick, & V. M. Esses (Eds.), *The SAGE handbook of prejudice, stereotyping and discrimination.* London: Sage.

Abrams, D. I., Jay, C. A., Shade, S. B., Vizoso, H., et al. (2007). Cannabis in painful HIV-associated sensory neuropathy. *Neurology, 68*, 515–521.

Abrams, R. L., & Greenwald, A. G. (2000). Parts outweigh the whole (word) in unconscious analysis of meaning. *Psychological Science, 11*, 118–124.

Abrantes-Pais, F. de N., Friedman, J. K., Lovallo, W. R., & Ross, E. D. (2007). Psychological or physiological: Why are tetraplegic patients content? *Neurology, 69*, 261–267.

Abreu, J. M. (1999). Conscious and unconscious African American stereotypes: Impact on first impression and diagnostic ratings by therapists. *Journal of Consulting and Clinical Psychology, 67*, 387–393.

Acerbi, A., Enquist, M., & Ghirlanda, S. (2009). Cultural evolution and individual development of openness and conservatism. *Proceedings of the National Academy of Sciences, 106*, 18931–18935.

Acitelli, L. K. (1992). Gender differences in relationship awareness and marital satisfaction among young married couples. *Personality and Social Psychology Bulletin, 18*, 102–110.

Acker, T., & Acker, H. (2004). Cellular oxygen sensing need in CNS function: Physiological and pathological implications. *Journal of Experimental Biology, 207*, 3171–3188.

Ackerman, B. P., Brown, E. D., & Izard, C. E. (2004). The relations between contextual risk, earned income, and the school adjustment of children from economically disadvantaged families. *Developmental Psychology, 40*, 204–216.

Ackerman, D. (1995). *Mystery of the senses.* Boston: WGBH-TV/Washington, DC: WETA-TV.

Ackerman, J. P., Riggins, T., & Black, M. M. (2010). A review of the effects of prenatal cocaine exposure among school-aged children. *Pediatrics, 125*, 554–565.

Ackerman, P. L. (1994). Intelligence, attention, and learning: Maximal and typical performance. In D. K. Detterman (Ed.), *Current topics in human intelligence* (Vol. 4, pp. 1–27). Norwood, NJ: Ablex.

Ackerman, P. L. (2007). New developments in understanding skilled performance. *Current Directions in Psychological Science, 16*, 235–239.

Ackerman, P. L., Beier, M. E., & Boyle, M. O. (2002). Individual differences in working memory within a nomological network of cognitive and perceptual speed abilities. *Journal of Experimental Psychology: General, 131*, 567–589.

Acocella, J. (1998, April 6). The politics of hysteria. *New Yorker*, pp. 64–79.

Adachi-Mejia, A. M., Longacre, M. R., Gibson, J. J., Beach, M. L., et al. (2007). Children with a TV in their bedroom at higher risk for overweight. *International Journal of Obesity, 31*, 644–651.

Adair, J. C., Gilmore, R. L., Fennell, E. B., Gold, M., & Heilman, K. M. (1995). Anosognosia during intracarotid barbiturate anesthesia: Unawareness or amnesia for weakness. *Neurology, 45*, 241–243.

Adam, E. K., Gunnar, M. R., & Tanaka, A. (2004). Adult attachment, parent emotion, and observed parenting behavior: Mediator and moderator models. *Child Development, 75*, 110–122.

Adams, K. F., Schatzkin, A., Harris, T. B., Kipnis, V., et al. (2006). Overweight, obesity, and mortality in a large prospective cohort of persons 50 to 71 years old. *New England Journal of Medicine, 355*, 763–778.

Adams, R. J., Courage, M. L., & Mercer, M. E. (1991). Deficiencies in human neonates' color vision: Photoreceptoral and neural explanations. *Behavioral Brain Research, 43*, 109–114.

Adams, W. J., Graf, E. W., & Ernst, M. O. (2004). Experience can change the "light from above" prior. *Nature Neuroscience, 7*, 1057–1058.

Addis, D. R., Wong, A. T., & Schacter, D. L. (2007). Remembering the past and imagining the future: Common and distinct neural substrates during event construction and elaboration. *Neuropsychologia, 45*, 1363–1377.

Addis, M. E., & Krasnow, A. D. (2000). A national survey of practicing psychologists' attitudes toward psychotherapy treatment manuals. *Journal of Consulting and Clinical Psychology, 68*, 331–339.

Adelabu, D. H. (2008). Future time perspective, hope, and ethnic identity among African American adolescents. *Urban Education, 43*, 347–360.

Ader, R. (2001). Psychoneuroimmunology. *Current Directions in Psychological Science, 10*, 94–98.

Adler, A. (1927/1999). *The practice and theory of individual psychology.* London: Taylor & Francis.

Adler, A. (1963). *The practice and theory of individual psychology.* Paterson, NJ: Littlefield Adams. (Original work published 1927)

Adler, D. A., McLaughlin, T. J., Rogers, W. H., Chang, H., et al. (2006). Job performance deficits dues to depression. *American Journal of Psychiatry, 163*, 1569–1576.

Adler, T. (1993, March). Bad mix: Combat stress, decisions. *APA Monitor*, p. 1.

Adolphs, R., Tranel, D., & Damasio, A. R. (1998). The human amygdala in social judgment. *Nature, 393*, 470–474.

Adolphs, R., Tranel, D., Damasio, H., & Damasio, A. R. (1994). Impaired recognition of emotion in facial expressions following bilateral damage to the human amygdala. *Nature, 372*, 669–672.

Adolphs, R., Tranel, D., Koenigs, M., & Damasio, A. R. (2005). Preferring one taste over another without recognizing either. *Nature Neuroscience, 8*, 860–861.

Adorno, T. W., Frenkel-Brunswik, E., Levinson, D. J., & Sanford, R. N. (1950). *The authoritarian personality.* New York: Harper Bros.

Adúriz, M. E., Bluthgen, C., & Knopfler, C. C. (2009). Helping child flood victims using group EMDR intervention in Argentina: Treatment outcome and gender differences. *International Journal of Stress Management, 16*, 138–153.

Aggarwal, S. K., Carter G. T., Sullivan, M. D, ZumBrunnen, C., Morrill, R., & Mayer, J. D. (2009). Medicinal use of cannabis in the United States: historical perspectives, current trends, and future directions. *Journal of Opioid Management, 5*, 153–68.

Aggarwal, R., Cheshire, N., & Darzi, A. (2008). Endovascular simulation-based training. *Surgeon, 6*, 196–197.

Aguinis, H., Mazurkiewicz, M. D., & Heggestad, E. D. (2009). Using Web-based frame-of-reference training to decrease biases in personality-based job analysis: An experimental field study. *Personnel Psychology, 62*, 405–468.

Aharonov, R., Segev, L., Meilijson, I., & Ruppin, E. (2003). Localization of function via lesion analysis. *Neural Computation, 15*, 885–913.

Aiello, J. R., & Douthitt, E. A. (2001). Social facilitation from Triplett to electronic performance monitoring. *Group Dynamics, 5*, 163–180.

Aiken, L. R. (1994). *Psychological testing and assessment* (8th ed.). Boston: Allyn & Bacon.

Ainsworth, M. D. S. (1973). The development of infant-mother attachment. In B. M. Caldwell & H. N. Ricciuti (Eds.), *Review of child development research* (Vol. 3, pp. 1–94). Chicago: University of Chicago Press.

Ainsworth, M. D. S., Blehar, M. D., Waters, E., & Wall, S. (1978). *Patterns of attachment: A psychological study of the Strange Situation.* Hillsdale, NJ: Erlbaum.

Airan, R. D., Thompson, K. R., Fenno, L. E., Bernstein, H., & Deisseroth, K. (2009). Temporally precise in vivo control of intracellular signaling. *Nature, 458*, 1025–1029. Epub 2009 Mar 1018.

Aitchison, J. (2008). Chimps, children, and creoles: The need for caution. In V. Clark, P. Eschholz, A. Rosa, & B. L. Simon (Eds.,) *Language: Introductory readings* (7th Ed., pp. 61–75). New York: Palgrave MacMillan.

Aizawa, N. (2002). Grandiose traits and hypersensitive traits of the narcissistic personality. *Japanese Journal of Educational Psychology, 50*, 215–224.

Ajzen, I., & Gilbert-Cote, N. (2008). Attitudes and the prediction of behavior. In W. Crano & R. Prislin (Eds.), *Attitudes and attitude change* (pp. 289–311). New York: Psychology Press.

Akerstedt, T. (2007). Altered sleep/wake patterns and mental performance. *Physiology and Behavior, 90*, 209–218.

Akimova, E., Lanzenberger, R., & Kasper, S. (2009). The serotonin-1 receptor in anxiety disorders. *Biological Psychiatry, 66*, 627–635.

Akin, W. M., & Turner, S. M. (2006). Toward understanding ethnic and cultural factors in the interviewing process. *Psychotherapy: Theory, Research, Practice, Training, 43*, 50–64.

Akins, C. K., & Zentall, T. R. (1998). Imitation in Japanese quail: The role of reinforcement of demonstrator responding. *Psychonomic Bulletin and Review, 5*, 694–697.

Akshoomoff, N. (2005). The neuropsychology of autistic spectrum disorders. *Developmental Neuropsychology, 27*, 307–310.

Alaimo, K., Olson, C. M., & Frongillo, E. A., Jr. (2001). Food insufficiency and American school-aged children's cognitive, academic, and psychosocial development. *Pediatrics, 108,* 44–53.

Albarracín, D., Durantini, M. R., Allison, E., Gunnoe, J. B., & Leeper, J. (2008). Beyond the most willing audiences: A meta-intervention to increase exposure to HIV-prevention programs by vulnerable populations. *Health Psychology, 27,* 638–644.

Albarracín, D., Johnson, B. T., Fishbein, M., & Muellerleile, P. A. (2001). Theories of reasoned action and planned behavior as models of condom use: A meta-analysis. *Psychological Bulletin, 127,* 142–161.

Albarracín, D., & Vargas, P. (2010). Attitudes and persuasion: From biology to social responses to persuasive intent. In S. T. Fiske, D. T. Gilbert, & G. Lindzey (Eds.), *Handbook of social psychology* (5th ed., Vol. 2, pp. 394–427). Hoboken, NJ: Wiley.

Albee, G. W. (1968). Conceptual models and manpower requirements in psychology. *American Psychologist, 23,* 317–320.

Albee, G. W. (2002). Just say no to psychotropic drugs! *Journal of Clinical Psychology, 58,* 635–648.

Albee, G. W. (2006). Historical overview of primary prevention of psychopathology. *Journal of Primary Prevention, 27,* 449–456.

Alberti, R., & Emmons, M. (2008). *Your perfect right: Assertiveness and equality in your life and relationships* (9th ed.). Atascadero, CA: Impact.

Alberto, P. A., Troutman, A. C., & Feagin, J. R. (2002). *Applied behavior analysis for teachers* (6th ed.). Englewood Cliffs, NJ: Prentice Hall.

Albus, H., Vansteensel, M. J., Michel, S., Block, G. D., & Meijer, J. H. (2005). A GABAergic mechanism is necessary for coupling dissociable ventral and dorsal regional oscillators within the circadian clock. *Current Biology, 15,* 886–893.

Alcock, J. (2009). *Animal behavior: An evolutionary approach* (9th ed.). Sunderland, MA: Sinauer.

Alderfer, C. P. (1969). An empirical test of a new theory of human needs. *Organizational Behavior and Human Performance, 4,* 142–175.

Aldridge, J. W. (2005). Interpreting correlation as causation? *Science, 308,* 954.

Aleman, A., Kahn, R. S., & Selten, J.-P. (2003). Sex differences in the risk of schizophrenia: Evidence from meta-analysis. *Archives of General Psychiatry, 60,* 565–571.

Aleman, A., Rutten, G. J., Sitskoorn, M. M., Dautzenberg, G., & Ramsey, N. F. (2001). Activation of striate cortex in the absence of visual stimulation: An fMRI study of synesthesia. *NeuroReport, 12,* 2827–2830.

Alerman, A., & Larøi, F. (2008). *Hallucinations: The science of idiosyncratic perception.* Washington, DC: American Psychological Association.

Alessi, S. M., Roll, J. M., Reilly, M. P., & Johanson, C.-E. (2002). Establishment of a diazepam preference in human volunteers following a differential-conditioning history of placebo versus diazepam choice. *Experimental and Clinical Psychopharmacology, 10,* 77–83.

Alexander, G. M., & Hines, M. (2002). Sex differences in response to children's toys in nonhuman primates (*Cercopithecus aethiops sabaeus*). *Evolution and Human Behavior, 23,* 467–479.

Alexander, K. W., Quas, J. A., Goodman, G. S., Ghetti, S., et al. (2005). Traumatic impact predicts long-term memory for documented child sexual abuse. *Psychological Science, 16,* 33–40.

Alhasnawi, S., Sadik, S., ad Rasheed, M., Baban, A., Al-Alak, M. M., Othman, A. Y., Othman, Y., Ismet, N., Shawani, O., Murthy, S., AlJadiry, M., Chatterji, S., Al-Gasseer, N., Streel, E., Naidoo, N., Ali, M. M., Gruber, M. J., Petukhova, M., Sampson, N. A., & Kessler, R. C. (2009). The prevalence and correlates of DSM-IV disorders in the Iraq Mental Health Survey (IMHS). *World Psychiatry, 8,* 97–109.

Alia-Klein, N., Goldstein, R. Z., Tomasi, D., Woicik, P. A., et al. (2009). Neural mechanisms of anger regulation as a function of genetic risk for violence. *Emotion, 9,* 385–396.

Alison, L., Kebbell, M., & Lewis, P. (2006). Considerations for experts in assessing the credibility of recovered memories of child sexual abuse: The importance of maintaining a case-specific focus. *Psychology, Public Policy, and Law, 12,* 419–441.

Al-Kubaisy, T. F., & Jassim, A. L. (2003). The efficacy of assertive training in the acquisition of social skills in Iraqi social phobics. *Arab Journal of Psychiatry, 14,* 68–72.

Al-Kubaisy, T. F., Marks, I. M., Logsdail, S., Marks, M. P., et al. (1992). Role of exposure homework in phobia reduction: A controlled study. *Behavior Therapy, 23,* 599–621.

Allen, B. P. (2006). *Personality theories: Development, growth, and diversity* (5th ed.). Boston: Allyn & Bacon.

Allen, J. B., Kenrick, D. T., Linder, D. E., & McCall, M. A. (1989). Arousal and attraction: A response-facilitation alternative to misattribution and negative-reinforcement models. *Journal of Personality and Social Psychology, 57,* 261–270.

Allen, J. J. B. (2002). The role of psychophysiology in clinical assessment: ERPs in the evaluation of memory. *Psychophysiology, 39,* 261–280.

Allen, J. J. B., & Iacono, W. G. (2001). Assessing the validity of amnesia in dissociative identity disorder: A dilemma for the DSM and the courts. *Psychology, Public Policy, and Law, 7,* 311–344.

Allen, L. S., Hines, M., Shryne, J. E., & Gorski, R. A. (1989). Two sexually dimorphic cell groups in the human brain. *Journal of Neuroscience, 9,* 497–506.

Allen, M. D., Greenblatt, D. J., & Noel, B. J. (1977). Meprobamate overdosage: A continuing problem. *Clinical Toxicology, 11,* 501–515.

Allen, M. T., & Matthews, K. A. (1997). Hemodynamic responses to laboratory stressors in children and adolescents: The influences of age, race and gender. *Psychophysiology, 34,* 329–339.

Allen, T. D., Eby, L. T., & Lentz, E. (2006). The relationship between formal mentoring program characteristics and perceived program effectiveness. *Personnel Psychology, 59,* 125–153.

Alloy, L. B., Abramson, L. Y., Cogswell, A., Hughes, M. E., & Iacoviello, B. M. (2008). Cognitive vulnerability to dpression: Implications for prevention. In M. T. Tsuang, W. S. Stone, & M. J. Lyons (Eds.), *Recognition and prevention of major mental and substance use disorders* (pp. 97–113). Arlington, VA: American Psychiatric Publishing.

Alloy, L. B., Abramson, L. Y., Whitehouse, W. G., Hogan, M. E., et al. (2006). Prospective incidence of first onsets and recurrences of depression in individuals at high and low cognitive risk for depression. *Journal of Abnormal Psychology, 115,* 145–156.

Allport, G. W., & Odbert, H. S. (1936). Trait names: A psycholexical study. *Psychological Monographs, 47*(1, Whole No. 211).

Almeida, D. M. (2005). Resilience and vulnerability to daily stressors assessed via diary methods. *Current Directions in Psychological Science, 14,* 64–68.

Al-Shammary, N., Awan, S., Butt, K., & Yoo, J. (2007). Internet use before consultation with a health professional. *Primary Health Care, 17*(10), 18–21.

Alston, J. H. (1920). Spatial condition of the fusion of warmth and cold in heat. *American Journal of Psychology, 31,* 303–312.

Altemeyer, B. (2004). Highly dominating, highly authoritarian personalities. *Journal of Social Psychology, 144,* 421–447.

Altemeyer, B., & Hunsberger, B. (2005). Fundamentalism and authoritarianism. In R. Paloutzian & C. Park (Eds.), *Handbook of the psychology of religion and spirituality* (pp. 378–393). New York: Guilford Press.

Althoff, R. R., Faraone, S. V., Rettew, D. C., Morley, C. P., & Hudziak, J. J. (2005). Family, twin, adoption, and molecular genetic studies of juvenile bipolar disorder. *Bipolar Disorders, 7,* 598–609.

Altman, J., & Das, G. D. (1965). Autoradiographic and histological evidence of postnatal hippocampal neurogenesis in rats. *Journal of Comparative Neurology, 124,* 319–335.

Altman, L. K. (2000, April 10). Company developing marijuana for medical uses. *New York Times.* Retrieved from http://www.mapinc.org/drug-news/v00/n474/a01.html

Altman, W. S. (2007, January 4). *In-class writing as a teaching tool: An evaluation.* Poster presented at the National Institute on the Teaching of Psychology, St. Pete Beach, FL.

Aluja-Fabregat, A., & Torrubia-Beltri, R. (1998). Viewing of mass media violence, perception of violence, personality and academic achievement. *Personality and Individual Differences, 25,* 973–989.

Alvarez, K., Salas, E., & Garofano, C. M. (2004). An integrated model of training evaluation and effectiveness. *Human Resource Development and Review, 3,* 385–416.

Alzheimer's Association. (2007). *Alzheimer's disease facts and figures, 2007.* Retrieved from http://www.alz.org/national/documents/Report_2007FactsAndFigures.pdf

Alzheimer's Association. (2009). 2009 Alzheimer's disease facts and figures. *Alzheimer's and Dementia, 5,* 234–270.

Amabile, T. M. (1996). *Creativity in context.* Boulder, CO: Westview.

Amabile, T. M. (2001). Beyond talent: John Irving and the passionate craft of creativity. *American Psychologist, 56,* 333–336.

Amabile, T. M., Hennessey, B. A., & Grossman, B. S. (1986). Social influences on creativity: The effects of contracted-for reward. *Journal of Personality and Social Psychology, 50,* 14–23.

Amaro, E., Jr., & Barker, G. J. (2006). Study design in fMRI: Basic principles. *Brain and Cognition, 60,* 220–232.

Ambadar, Z., Schooler, J. W., & Cohn, J. F. (2005). Deciphering the enigmatic face. *Psychological Science, 16,* 403–410.

American Educational Research Association, American Psychological Association, & National Council on Measurement in Education. (1999). *Standards for educational and psychological testing.* Washington, DC: American Educational Research Association.

American Psychiatric Association. (1994). *Diagnostic and statistical manual of mental disorders* (4th ed.). Washington, DC: Author.

American Psychiatric Association. (1999). Position statement on psychiatric treatment and sexual orientation. *American Journal of Psychiatry, 156,* 1131.

American Psychiatric Association. (2000). *Diagnostic and statistical manual of mental disorders* (4th ed., rev.). Washington DC: Author.

American Psychiatric Association. (2003). *The insanity defense.* Retrieved from http://www.psych.org/public_info/insanity.cfm

American Psychological Association Committee on Animal Research and Ethics. (2009). *Research with animals in psychology.* Retrieved from http://www.apa.org/science/animal2.html

American Psychological Association Presidential Task Force on Evidence-Based Practice. (2006). Evidence-based practice in psychology. *American Psychologist, 61,* 271-285.

American Psychiatric Association Work Group on Eating Disorders. (2000). Practice guidelines for the treatment of patients with eating disorders (revision). *American Journal of Psychiatry, 157,* 1–39.

American Psychological Association. (1993). *Violence and youth: Psychology's response.* Washington: DC: Author.

American Psychological Association. (2002a). *Answers to your questions about sexual orientation and homosexuality.* Retrieved from http://www.apa.org/pubinfo/answers.html#whatis

American Psychological Association. (2002b). Ethical standards of psychologists and code of conduct. *American Psychologist, 57,* 1060–1073.

American Psychological Association. (2006). *2003 doctorate employment survey.* Washington, DC: APA Research Office.

American Psychological Association. (2009a). *Doctoral psychology workforce fast facts.* Washington, DC: APA Center for Workforce Studies.

American Psychological Association. (2009b). *Graduate enrollments and degrees, 1998–2008.* Washington, DC: APA Center for Workforce Studies.

American Psychological Association. (2009c). *Medical cost offset.* Retrieved from http://www.apa.org/practice/offset3.html

American Psychological Association. (2009d). *Primary work setting for employed APA members, 2008.* Washington, DC: APA Center for Workforce Studies.

Amodio, D. M., & Devine, P. G. (2009). On the functions of implicit prejudice and stereotyping: Insights from social neuroscience. In R. E. Petty, R. H. Fazio, & P. Briñol (Eds.), *Attitudes: Insights from the new wave of implicit measures* (pp. 192–229). Hillsdale, NJ: Erlbaum.

Amodio, D. M., Harmon-Jones, E., Devine, P. G., Curtin, J. J., et al. (2004). Neural signals for the detection of unintentional race bias. *Psychological Science, 15,* 88–93.

Amodio, D. M., & Lieberman, M. D (2009). Pictures in our heads: Contributions of fMRI to the study of prejudice and stereotyping. In T. D. Nelson, (Ed.), *Handbook of prejudice, stereotyping, and discrimination* (pp. 347–365). New York: Psychology Press.

Amodio, D. M., & Showers, C. J. (2005). "Similarity breeds liking" revisited: The moderating role of commitment. *Journal of Social and Personal Relationships, 22,* 817–836.

Anastasi, A., & Urbina, S. (1997). *Psychological testing* (7th ed.). Upper Saddle River, NJ: Prentice Hall.

Anastassiou-Hadjicharalambous, X., & Warden, D. (2008). Physiologically indexed and self-perceived affective empathy in conduct-disordered children high and low on callous-unemotional traits. *Child Psychiatry and Human Development, 39,* 503–517.

an der Heiden, W., & Haefner, H. (2000). The epidemiology of onset and course of schizophrenia. *European Archives of Psychiatry and Clinical Neuroscience, 250,* 292–303.

Anderson, A. K., & Phelps, E. A. (2000). Expression without recognition: Contributions of the human amygdala to emotional communication. *Psychological Science, 11,* 106–111.

Anderson, A. K., & Phelps, E. A. (2001). Lesions of the human amygdala impair enhanced perception of emotionally salient events. *Nature, 411,* 305–309.

Anderson, B. L. (2004). The role of occlusion in the perception of depth, lightness, and opacity. *Psychological Review, 110,* 785–801.

Anderson, C., John, O. P., Keltner, D., & Kring, A. M. (2001). Who attains social status? Effects of personality and physical attractiveness in social groups. *Journal of Personality and Social Psychology, 81,* 116–132.

Anderson, C. A. (2001). Heat and violence. *Current Directions in Psychological Science, 10,* 33–38.

Anderson, C. A. (2004). An update on the effects of playing violent video games. *Journal of Adolescence, 27,* 113–122.

Anderson, C. A., & Anderson, K. B. (1998). Temperature and aggression: Paradox, controversy, and a (fairly) clear picture. In R. G. Geen & E. Donnerstein (Eds.), *Human aggression* (pp. 248–298). San Diego, CA: Academic Press.

Anderson, C. A., Anderson, K. B., Dorr, N., DeNeve, K. M., & Flanagan, M. (2000). Temperature and aggression. In M. Zanna (Ed.), *Advances in experimental social -psychology* (Vol. 32, pp. 63–133). New York: Academic Press.

Anderson, C. A., Berkowitz, L., Donnerstein, E., Huesmann, L. R., et al. (2003). The influence of media violence on youth. *Psychological Science in the Public Interest, 4,* 81–110.

Anderson, C. A., & Bushman, B. J. (2001). Effects of violent video games on aggressive behavior, aggressive cognition, aggressive affect, physiological arousal, and prosocial behavior: A meta-analytic review of the scientific literature. *Psychological Science, 12,* 353–359.

Anderson, C. A., & Bushman, B. J. (2002a). Human aggression. *Annual Review of Psychology, 53,* 27–51.

Anderson, C. A., & Bushman, B. J. (2002b). Media violence and the American public revisited. *American Psychologist, 57,* 448–450.

Anderson, C. A., Carnagey, N. L., & Eubanks, J. (2003). Exposure to violent media: The effects of songs with violent lyrics on aggressive thoughts and feelings. *Journal of Personality and Social Psychology, 84,* 960–971.

Anderson, C. A., & Dill, K. E. (2000). Video games and aggressive thoughts, feelings, and behavior in the laboratory and in life. *Journal of Personality and Social Psychology, 78, 772–790.*

Anderson, C. A., & Gentile, D. A. (2008). Media violence, aggression, and public policy. In E. Borgida & S. Fiske (Eds.), *Beyond common sense: Psychological science in the courtroom* (pp. 281–300). Malden, MA: Blackwell.

Anderson, C. A., & Murphy, C. R. (2003). Violent video games and aggressive behavior in young women. *Aggressive Behavior, 29,* 423–429.

Anderson, C. A., Sakamoto, A., Gentile, D. A., Ihori, N., et al. (2008). Longitudinal effects of violent video games on aggression in Japan and the United States. *Pediatrics, 122,* 1067–1072.

Anderson, C. A., Shibuya, A., Ihori, N., Swing, E. L., et al. (2010). Violent video game effects on aggression, empathy, and prosocial behavior in eastern and western countries: A meta-analytic review. *Psychological Bulletin, 136,* 151–173.

Anderson, J. R. (1995). *Learning and memory: An integrated approach.* New York: Wiley.

Anderson, J. R. (2000). *Cognitive psychology and its implications* (5th ed). New York: Worth.

Anderson, J. R., Bothell, D., Byrne, M. D., Douglass, S., et al. (2004). An integrated theory of the mind. *Psychological Review, 111,* 1036–1060.

Anderson, M. C., & Green, C. (2001). Suppressing unwanted memories by executive control. *Nature, 410,* 366–369.

Anderson, M. C., & Levy, B. J. (2009). Suppressing unwanted memories. *Current Directions in Psychological Science, 18,* 189–194.

Anderson, M. C., Ochsner, K. N., Kuhl, B., Cooper, J., et al. (2004). Neural systems underlying the suppression of unwanted memories. *Science, 303,* 232–235.

Anderson, M. E., Johnson, D. C., & Batal, H. A. (2005). Sudden infant death syndrome and prenatal maternal smoking: Rising attributed risk in the *Back to Sleep* era. *BMC Medicine, 3,* 4.

Anderson, P., Rothbaum, B. O., & Hodges, L. F. (2003). Virtual reality exposure in the treatment of social anxiety. *Cognitive and Behavioral Practice, 10,* 240–247.

Anderson, S. E., Cohen, P., Naumova, E. N., Jacques, P. F., & Must, A. (2007). Adolescent obesity and risk for subsequent major depressive disorder and anxiety disorder: Prospective evidence. *Psychosomatic Medicine 69,* 740–747.

Anderson, S. W., & Booker, M. B. (2006). Cognitive behavioral therapy versus psychosurgery for refractory obsessive-compulsive disorder. *Journal of Neuropsychiatry and Clinical Neurosciences, 18,* 129.

Anderssen, N., Amlie, C., & Ytteroy, E. A. (2002). Outcomes for children with lesbian or gay parents: A review of studies from 1978 to 2000. *Scandinavian Journal of Psychology, 43,* 335–351.

Andersson, G. (2009). Using the Internet to provide cognitive behaviour therapy. *Behaviour Research and Therapy, 47,* 175–180.

Andersson, G., Carlbring, P., & Grimlund, A. (2008). Predicting treatment outcome in Internet versus face-to-face treatment of panic disorder. *Computers in Human Behavior, 24,* 1790–1801.

Ando, K., Kripke, D. F., & Ancoli-Israel, S. (2002). Delayed and advanced sleep phase symptoms. *Israel Journal of Psychiatry and Related Sciences, 39,* 11–18.

Ando, Y., Kitayama, H., Kawaguchi, Y., & Koyanagi, Y. (2008). Primary target cells of herpes simplex virus type 1 in the hippocampus. *Microbes and Infection, 10,* 1514–1523.

Andrade, J., Deeprose, C., & Barker, I. (2008). Awareness and memory function during paediatric anaesthesia. *British Journal of Anaesthesia, 100,* 389–396.

Andreescu, C., Lenze, E. J., Dew, M. A., Begley, A. E., et al. (2007). Effect of comorbid anxiety on treatment response and relapse risk in late-life depression. *British Journal of Psychiatry, 190,* 344–349.

Andreoli, N., & Lefkowitz, J. (2009). Individual and organizational antecedents of misconduct in organizations. *Journal of Business Ethics, 85,* 309–332.

Andrés, P. (2003). Frontal cortex as the central executive of working memory: Time to revise our view. *Cortex, 39,* 871–895.

Andrew, D., & Craig, A. D. (2001). Spinothalamic lamina I neurons selectively sensitive to histamine: A central neural pathway for itch. *Nature Neuroscience, 4,* 72–77.

Andrews, B., Brewin, C. R., Ochera, J., Morton, J., et al. (2000). The timing, triggers, and quality of recovered memories in therapy. *British Journal of Clinical Psychology, 39,* 11–26.

Andrews, B., Brewin, C. R., Philpott, R., & Stewart, L. (2007). Delayed-onset posttraumatic stress disorder: A systematic review of the evidence. *American Journal of Psychiatry, 164,* 1319–1326.

Andrews, J., Wang, L., Csernansky, J. G., Gado, M. H., & Barch, D. M. (2006). Abnormalities of thalamic activation and cognition in schizophrenia. *American Journal of Psychiatry, 163,* 463–469.

Andrews, L. B. (2008). The psychiatric interview and mental status examination. In R. E. Hales, S. C. Yudofsky, & G. O. Gabbard (Eds.), *Textbook of psychiatry* (pp. 3–17). Arlington, VA: American Psychiatric Publishing.

Angelaki, D. E., & Cullen, K. E. (2008). Vestibular system: The many faces of a multimodal sense. *Annual Review of Neuroscience, 31,* 125–150.

Anghelescu, I., Klawe, C. J., Bartenstein, P., & Szegedi, A. (2001). Normal PET after long-term ETC. *American Journal of Psychiatry, 158,* 1527.

Angold, A., Erkanli, A., Farmer, E. M. Z., Fairbank, J. A., et al. (2002). Psychiatric disorder, impairment, and service use in rural African American and white youth. *Archives of General Psychiatry, 59,* 893–901.

Angst, J., Angst, F., & Stassen, H. H. (1999). Suicide risks in patients with major depressive disorder. *Journal of Clinical Psychiatry, 60*(Suppl. 2), 57–62.

Annenberg Public Policy Center. (1999). *The 1999 state of children's television report: Programming for children over broadcast and cable television.* Washington, DC: Author.

Annenberg Public Policy Center. (2000). *Media in the home: The fifth annual survey of parents and children 2000.* Washington, DC: Author.

Anshel, M. (1996). Coping styles among adolescent competitive athletes. *Journal of Social Psychology, 136,* 311–323.

Anstey, K. J., Hofer, S. M., & Luszcz, M. A. (2003). Cross-sectional and longitudinal patterns of dedifferentiation in late-life cognitive and sensory function: The effects of age, ability, attrition, and occasion of measurement. *Journal of Experimental Psychology: General, 132,* 470–487.

Antoni, M. H., Lehman, J., Kilbourn, K., Boyers, A., et al. (2001). Cognitive-behavioral stress management intervention enhances optimism and the sense of positive contributions among women under treatment for early-stage breast cancer. *Health Psychology, 20,* 20–32.

Antoni, M. H., & Lutgendorf, S. (2007). Psychosocial factors and disease progression in cancer. *Current Directions in Psychological Science, 16,* 42–46.

Antrobus, J. (2001). Rethinking the fundamental process of dream and sleep mentation production: Defining new questions that avoid the distraction of REM versus NREM comparisons. *Sleep and Hypnosis, 3,* 1–8.

APA Task Force on the Sexualization of Girls. (2007). *Report of the APA Task Force on the Sexualization of Girls.* Washington, DC: American Psychological Association.

Appelbaum, P. S. (2005). Assessing Kendra's Law: Five years of outpatient commitment in New York. *Psychiatric Services, 56,* 791–792.

Appignanesi, L. (2009). *Mad, bad, and sad: A history of women and mind doctors.* New York: Norton.

Aquino, K.; Freeman, D.; Reed, A., II; Felps, W.; & Lim, V. K. G. (2009). Testing a social-cognitive model of moral behavior: The interactive influence of situations and moral identity centrality. *Journal of Personality and Social Psychology, 97,* 123–141.

Aquino, K., Tripp, T. M., & Bies, R. J. (2006). Getting even or moving on? Power, procedural justice, and types of offense as predictors of revenge, forgiveness, reconciliation, and avoidance in organizations. *Journal of Applied Psychology, 91,* 653–668.

Arbelle, S., Benjamin, J., Golin, M., Kremer, I., et al. (2003). Relation of shyness in grade school children to the genotype for the long form of the serotonin transporter promoter region polymorphism. *American Journal of Psychiatry, 160,* 671–676.

Arendt, J. (2010). Shift work: Coping with the biological clock. *Occupational Medicine (London), 60,* 10–20.

Arkowitz, H., & Lilienfeld, S. O. (2006, April/May). Psychotherapy on trial. *Scientific American Mind,* pp. 42–49.

Armfield, J. M. (2006). Cognitive vulnerability: A model of the etiology of fear. *Clinical Psychology Review, 26,* 746–768.

Armitage, C. J. (2005). Can the theory of planned behavior predict the maintenance of physical activity? *Health Psychology, 24,* 235–245.

Armour, S. (2008, March 31). Day care's new frontier: Your baby at your desk. *USA Today.* Retrieved from http://www.usatoday.com/money/workplace/2008-03-30-babies-at-work_N.htm

Armstrong, L. E. (2006). Nutritional strategies for football: Counteracting heat, cold, high altitude, and jet lag. *Journal of Sports Sciences, 24,* 723–740.

Arnett, J. J. (1999). Adolescent storm and stress, reconsidered. *American Psychologist, 54,* 317–326.

Arnett, J. J. (2000). Emerging adulthood: A theory of development from the late teens through the twenties. *American Psychologist, 55,* 469–480.

Arnett, J. J. (2007a). Emerging adulthood: What is it, and what is it good for? *Child Development Perspectives, 1,* 68–73.

Arnett, J. J. (2007b). Suffering, selfish slackers? Myths and reality about emerging adults. *Journal of Youth and Adolescence, 36,* 23–29. doi:10.1007/s10964-006-9157-z

Aron, A., Fisher, H. E., Mashek, D. J. Strong, G., et al. (2005). Reward, motivation, and emotion systems associated with early-stage intense romantic love. *Journal of Neurophysiology, 94,* 327–337.

Aronson, E. (1997). *The jigsaw classroom.* New York: Longman.

Aronson, E. (1999). *The social animal* (8th ed.). New York: Worth/Freeman.

Aronson, E. (2004). Reducing hostility and building compassion: Lessons from the jigsaw classroom. In A. G. Miller (Ed.), *The social psychology of good and evil* (pp. 469–488). New York: Guilford Press.

Aronson, E., Wilson, T., & Akert, R. (2010). *Social psychology* (7th ed.). Upper Saddle River, NJ: Prentice Hall.

Arsenault, B. J., Rana, J. S., Lemieux, I., Despres, J.-P., et al. (2010). Physical inactivity, abdominal obesity and risk of coronary heart disease in apparently healthy men and women. *International Journal of Obesity, 34,* 340–347.

Arseneault, L., Moffitt, T. E., Caspi, A., Taylor, A., et al. (2003). Strong genetic effects on cross-situational antisocial behavior among 5-year-old children according to mothers, teachers, examiner-observers, and twins' self-reports. *Journal of Child Psychology and Psychiatry, 44,* 832–848.

Arterberry, M. E., Craton, L. G., & Yonas, A. (1993). Infants' sensitivity to motion-carried information for depth and object properties. In C. Granrud (Ed.), *Visual perception and cognition in infancy: Carnegie Mellon symposia on cognition* (pp. 215–234). Hillsdale, NJ: Erlbaum.

Arthur, W., Jr.; Day, E. A.; McNelly, T. L.; & Edens, P. S. (2003). A meta-analysis of the criterion-related validity of assessment center dimensions. *Personnel Psychology, 56,* 125–154.

Arvey, R. D., Bouchard, T. J., Segal, N. L., & Abraham, L. M. (1989). Job satisfaction: Environmental and genetic components. *Journal of Applied Psychology, 74,* 187–192.

Asato, M. R., Terwilliger, R., Woo, J., & Luna, B. (2010). White matter development in adolescence: A DTI study. *Cerebral Cortex, 5,* 5. doi:10.1093/cercor/bhp282

Asch, S. E. (1951). Effects of group pressure upon the modification and distortion of judgments. In H. Guetzkow (Ed.), *Groups, leadership, and men* (pp. 177–190). Pittsburgh, PA: Carnegie Press.

Asch, S. E. (1955). Opinions and social pressure. *Scientific American, 193,* 31–35.

Asch, S. E. (1956). Studies of independence and conformity: A minority of one against a unanimous majority. *Psychological Monographs, 70,* 1–70.

Ascherio, A., Chen, H., Weisskopf, M. G., O'Reilly, E., et al. (2006). Pesticide exposure and risk for Parkinson's disease. *Annals of Neurology, 60,* 197–203.

Asemann, R., McAuliffe, C., Ströbel, A., Keller, J., et al. (2009). Relationship between lunar phases and serious crimes of battery: A population-based study. *Comprehensive Psychiatry, 50,* 573–577.

Ashcraft, M. H. (2006). *Cognition* (4th ed.). Upper Saddle River, NJ: Prentice Hall.

Asher, S. R., & Hopmeyer, A. (2001). Loneliness in childhood. In G. Bear, K. Minke, & A. Thomas (Eds.), *Children's needs II: Psychological perspectives.* Silver Spring, MD: National Association of School Psychologists.

Ashton, M. C., Lee, K., Perugini, M., Szarota, P., et al. (2004). A six-factor structure of personality-descriptive adjectives: Solutions from psycholexical studies in seven languages. *Journal of Personality and Social Psychology, 86,* 356–366.

Askew, C., & Field, A. P. (2008). The vicarious learning pathway to fear 40 years on. *Clinical Psychology Review, 28,* 1249–1265.

Askew, C., Kessock-Phillip, H., & Field, A. P. (2008). What happens when verbal threat information and vicarious learning combine. *Behavioural and Cognitive Psychotherapy, 36,* 491–505.

Aso, K., Hanakawa, T., Aso, T., & Fukuyama, H. (2010). Cerebro-cerebellar interactions underlying temporal information processing. *Journal of Cognitive Neuroscience, 4,* 4.

Aspinwall, L. G., & Taylor, S. E. (1992). Modeling cognition adaptation: A longitudinal investigation of the impact of individual differences and coping on college adjustment and performance. *Journal of Personality and Social Psychology, 63,* 989–1003.

Assefi, N. P., Sherman, K. J., Jacobsen, C., Goldberg, J., et al. (2005). A randomized clinical trial of acupuncture compared with sham acupuncture in fibromyalgia. *Annals of Internal Medicine, 143,* 10–19.

Assefi, S. L., & Garry, M. (2003). Absolut® memory distortions: Alcohol placebos influence misinformation effect. *Psychological Science, 14,* 77–80.

Associated Press. (2004, November 1). Genetic disorder deprives kindergartner of natural alarms. *MSNBC.com.* Retrieved from http://www.msnbc.msn.com/-id-/6379795

Associated Press. (2007a, December 18). Officials investigating prank call that led to shock treatments at special needs school. *FoxNews.com.* Retrieved from http://www.foxnews.com/story/0,2933,317291,00.html

Associated Press. (2007b, July 3). Kansas store video captures five shoppers stepping over dying stabbing victim. *FoxNews.com.* Retrieved from http://www.foxnews.com/story/0,2933,287953,00.html

Associated Press. (2008, June 27). Fake speed bumps create optical illusion, driver confusion *FoxNews.com.* Retrieved from http://www.foxnews.com/story/0,2933,373123,00.html

Associated Press. (2009, August 21). New Zealand votes to legalize smacking kids. *FoxNews.com.* Retrieved from http://www.foxnews.com/story/0,2933,541346,00.html

Astin, J. A. (2004). Mind-body therapies for the management of pain. *Clinical Journal of Pain, 20,* 27–32.

Astin, J. A., Shapiro, S. L., Eisenberg, D. M., & Forys, K. L. (2003). Mind-body medicine: State of the science, implications for practice. *Journal of the American Board of Family Practice, 16,* 131–147.

Aston-Jones, G. (2005). Brain structures and receptors involved in alertness. *Sleep Medicine, 6*(Suppl. 1), S3–S7.

Atance, C. M., & O'Neill, D. K. (2001). Episodic future thinking. *Trends in Cognitive Science, 5,* 533–539.

Atkins, R. (2008). The association of childhood personality on sexual risk taking during adolescence. *Journal of School Health, 78,* 594–600.

Atkinson, J. (2006, August). Shake it off. *GQ,* pp. 87–92.

Atkinson, R. C., & Shiffrin, R. M. (1968). Human memory: A proposed system and its control processes. In K. Spence (Ed.), *The psychology of learning and motivation* (Vol. 2, pp. 89–195). New York: Academic Press.

Atlantis, E., & Baker, M. (2008). Obesity effects on depression: Systematic review of epidemiological studies. *International Journal of Obesity, 32,* 881–891.

Atran, S., Medin, D. L., & Ross, N. O. (2005). The cultural mind: Environmental decision making and cultural modeling within and across populations. *Psychological Review, 112,* 744–776.

Audero, E., Coppi, E., Mlinar, B., Rossetti, T., et al. (2008). Sporadic autonomic dysregulation and death associated with excessive serotonin autoinhibition. *Science, 321,* 130–133.

Auyeung B., Baron-Cohen, S., Ashwin, E., Knickmeyer, R., et al. (2009). Fetal testosterone predicts sexually differentiated childhood behavior in girls and in boys. *Psychological Science, 20,* 144–148. Epub 2009 Jan 23.

Averill, J. S. (1980). On the paucity of positive emotions. In K. R. Blankstein, P. Pliner, & J. Polivey (Eds.), *Advances in the study of communication and affect: Vol. 6. Assessment and modification of emotional behavior.* New York: Plenum.

Avidan, M. S., Zhang, L., Burnside, B. A., Finkel, K. J., et al. (2008). Anesthesia awareness and the bispectral index. *New England Journal of Medicine, 358,* 1097–1108.

Aviezer, H., Hassin, R. R., Ryan, J., Grady, C., et al. (2008). Angry, disgusted, or afraid? Studies on the malleability of emotion perception. *Psychological Science, 19,* 724–732.

Avolio, B. J., Walumbwa, F. O., & Weber, T. J. (2009). Leadership: Current theories, research, and future directions. *Annual Review of Psychology, 60,* 421–449.

Ayache, D., Corre, A., Can Prooyen, S., & Elbaz, P. (2003). Surgical treatment of otosclerosis in elderly patients. *Otolaryngological Head and Neck Surgery, 129,* 674–677.

Ayas, N. T., Barger, L. K., Cade, B. E., Hashimoto, D. M., et al. (2006). Extended work duration and the risk of self-reported percutaneous injuries in interns. *Journal of the American Medical Association, 296,* 1055–1062.

Ayman, R. , Korabik, K., & Morris, S. (2009). Is transformational leadership always perceived as effective? Male subordinates' devaluation of female transformational leaders. *Journal of Applied Social Psychology, 39,* 852–879.

Aymoz, C., & Viviani, P. (2004). Perceptual asynchronies for biological and non—biological visual events. *Vision Research, 44,* 1547–1563.

Ayuso-Mateos, J. L., Vazquez-Barquero, J. L., Dowrick, C., Lehtinen, V., et al. (2001). Depressive disorders in Europe: Prevalence figures fromt he ODIN study. *British Journal of Psychiatry, 179,* 308–316.

Azar, B. (1996, November). Project explores landscape of midlife. *APA Monitor,* p. 26.

Baare, W. F. C., van Oel, C. J., Hushoff, H. E., Schnack, H. G., et al. (2001). Volumes of brain structures in twins discordant for schizophrenia. *Archives of General Psychiatry, 58,* 33–40.

Baars, B. J. (2002). The conscious access hypothesis: Origins and recent evidence. *Trends in Cognitive Science, 6,* 47–52.

Babcock, R., & Salthouse, T. (1990). Effects of increased processing demands on age differences in working memory. *Psychology and Aging, 5,* 421–428.

Babinski, J. (1914). Contribution à l'étude des troubles mentaux dans l'hémiplégie organique cérébrale (anosognosia) [Contribution to the study of mental problems resulting from organic cerebral hemiplegia (anosognosia)]. *Revue de Neurologie (Paris), 27,* 845–847.

Baca-Garcia, E., Perez-Rodriguez, M. M., Keyes, K. M., Oquendo, M. A., et al. (2010). Suicidal ideation and suicide attempts in the United States, 1991–1992 and 2001–2002. *Molecular Psychiatry, 15,* 250–259.

Bacharach, V. R., & Baumeister, A. A. (1998). Direct and indirect effects of maternal intelligence, maternal age, income, and home environment on intelligence of preterm, low-birth-weight children. *Journal of Applied Developmental Psychology, 19,* 361–375.

Bach-Mizrachi, H., Underwood, M. D., Kassir, S. A., Bakalian, M. J., et al. (2006). Neuronal tryptophan hydroxylase mRNA expression in the human dorsal and median raphe nuclei: Major depression and suicide. *Neuropsychopharmacology, 31,* 814–824.

Back, M. D., Schmukle, S. C., & Egloff, B. (2008). Becoming friends by chance. *Psychological Science, 19,* 439–440.

Back, M. D., Stopfer, J. M., Vazire, S., Gaddis, S., et al. (2010). Facebook profiles reflect actual personality, not self-idealization. *Psychological Science, 21,* 372–374. doi:10.1177/0956797609360756

Backman, L., & Nilsson, L. (1991). Effects of divided attention on free and cued recall of verbal events and action events. *Bulletin of the Psychonomic Society, 29,* 51–54.

Bacon, N., & Blyton, P. (2007). Conflict for mutual gains? *Journal of Management Studies, 44,* 814–834.

Bada, H. S., Das, A., Bauer, C. R., Shankaran, S., et al. (2007). Impact of prenatal cocaine exposure on child behavior problems through school age. *Pediatrics, 119,* 348–359.

Baddeley, A. D. (1982). *Your memory: A user's guide.* New York: Macmillan.

Baddeley, A. D. (1992). Working memory. *Science, 255,* 556–559.

Baddeley, A. D. (2003). Working memory: Looking back and looking forward. *Nature Reviews Neuroscience, 4,* 829–839.

Badre, D., & Wagner, A. D. (2006). Computational and neurobiological mechanisms underlying cognitive flexibility. *Proceedings of the National Academy of Sciences, 103,* 7186–7191.

Baer, J. S., Sampson, P. D., Barr, H. M., Connor, P. D., & Streissguth, A. P. (2003). A 21-year longitudinal analysis of the effects of prenatal alcohol exposure on young adult drinking. *Archives of General Psychiatry, 60,* 377–385.

Baer, R. D., Weller, S. C., De Alba Garcia, J. G., Glazer, M., et al. (2003). A cross-cultural approach to the study of the folk illness *nervios. Culture, Medicine, and Psychiatry, 27,* 315–337.

Baethge, C., Baldessarini, R. J., Mathiske-Schmidt, K., Hennen, J., et al., (2005). Long-term combination therapy versus monotherapy with lithium and carbamazepine in 46 bipolar I patients. *Journal of Clinical Psychiatry, 66,* 174–182.

Bagley, C., & Tremblay, P. (1998). On the prevalence of homosexuality and bisexuality, in a random survey of 750 men aged 18–27. *Journal of Homosexuality, 36,* 1–18.

Baglioni, C., Spiegelhalder, K., Lombardo, C., & Riemann, D. (2010). Sleep and emotions: A focus on insomnia. *Sleep Medicine Reviews, 14,* 227–238. Epub 2010 Feb 6.

Bahrick, H. P., Bahrick, P. O., & Wittlinger, R. P. (1975). Fifty years of memory for names and faces: A cross-cultural approach. *Journal of Experimental Psychology: General, 104,* 54–75.

Bahrick, H. P., & Hall, L. K. (1991). Lifetime maintenance of high school mathematics content. *Journal of Experimental Psychology: General, 120,* 20–33.

Bahrick, H. P., Hall, L. K., & Berger, S. A. (1996). Accuracy and distortion in memory for high school grades. *Psychological Science, 7,* 265–271.

Bahrick, H. P., Hall, L. K., Noggin, J. P., & Bahrick, L. E. (1994). Fifty years of language maintenance and language dominance in bilingual Hispanic immigrants. *Journal of Experimental Psychology: General, 123,* 264–283.

Baicy, K., London, E. D., Monterosso, J., Wong, M.-L., et al. (2007). Leptin replacement alters brain response to food cues in genetically leptin-deficient adults. *Proceedings of the National Academy of Sciences, 104,* 18276–18279.

Bailey, J. A., Hill, K. G., Oesterle, S., & Hawkins, J. D. (2009). Parenting practices and problem behavior across three generations: Monitoring, harsh discipline, and drug use in the intergenerational transmission of externalizing behavior. *Developmental Psychology, 45,* 1214–1226.

Bailey, J. M., & Benishay, D. S. (1993). Familial aggregation of female sexual orientation. *American Journal of Psychiatry, 150,* 272–277.

Bailey, J. M., Bobrow, D., Wolfe, M., & Mikach, S. (1995). Sexual orientation of adult sons of gay fathers. *Developmental Psychology, 31,* 124–129.

Bailey, J. M., Dunne, M. P., & Martin, N. G. (2000). Genetic and environmental influences on sexual orientation and its correlates in an Australian twin sample. *Journal of Personality and Social Psychology, 78,* 524–536.

Bailey, J. M., & Pillard, R. C. (1991). A genetic study of male sexual orientation. *Archives of General Psychiatry, 48,* 1086–1096.

Baillargeon, R. (1994). How do infants learn about the physical world? *Current Directions in Psychological Science, 3,* 133–139.

Baillargeon, R. (2002). The acquisition of physical knowledge in infancy: A summary in eight lessons. In U. Goswami (Ed.), *Blackwell handbook of childhood cognitive development* (pp. 47–83). Malden, MA: Blackwell.

Baillargeon, R. (2008). Innate ideas revisited: For a principle of persistence in infants' physical reasoning. *Perspectives on Psychological Science, 3,* 2–13.

Baillargeon, R. H., Zoccolillo, M., Keenan, K., Côté, S., et al. (2007). Gender differences in physical aggression: A prospective population-based survey of children before and after 2 years of age. *Developmental Psychology, 43,* 13–26.

Bajo, M., Crawford, E. F., Roberto, M., Madamba, S. G., & Siggins, G. R. (2006). Chronic morphine treatment alters expression of N-methyl-D-aspartate receptor subunits in the extended amygdala. *Journal of Neuroscience Research, 83,* 532–537.

Bakare, M. O. (2008). Effective therapeutic dosage of antipsychotic medications in patients with psychotic symptoms: Is there a racial difference? *BMC Research Notes, 1,* 25.

Baker, J. L., Olsen, L. W., & Sørensen, T. I. A. (2007). Childhood body-mass index and the risk of coronary heart disease in adulthood. *New England Journal of Medicine, 357,* 2229–2237.

Baker, L. D., Frank, L. L., Foster-Schubert, K., Green, P. S., et al. (2010). Effects of aerobic exercise on mild cognitive impairment: A controlled trial. *Archives of Neurology, 67,* 71–79.

Baker, L. T., Vernon, P. A., & Ho, H. (1991). The genetic correlation between intelligence and speed of information processing. *Behavior Genetics, 21,* 351–367.

Baker, M. C. (2002). *The atoms of language: The mind's hidden rules of grammar.* New York: Basic Books.

Baker, T. B., Piper, M. E., McCarthy, D. E., & Majeskie, M. R. (2004). Addiction motivation reformulated: An affective processing model of negative reinforcement. *Psychological Review, 111,* 33–51.

Bakermans-Kranenburg, M. J., van IJzendoorn, M. H., & Juffer, F. (2008). Less is more: Meta-analytic arguments for the use of sensitivity-focused interventions. In F. Juffer, M. J. Bakermans-Kranenburg, & M. H. van IJzendoorn (Eds.), *Promoting positive parenting: An attachment-based intervention* (pp. 59–74). New York: Taylor & Francis/Erlbaum.

Bakker, J., Honda, S., Harada, N., & Balthazart, J. (2003). The aromatase knockout (ArKO) mouse provides new evidence that estrogens are required for the development of the female brain. *Annals of the New York Academy of Sciences, 1007,* 251–262.

Balaban, M. T. (1995). Affective influences on startle in five-month-old infants: Reactions to facial expressions of emotion. *Child Development, 66*(1), 28–36.

Balázs, J., Benazzi, F., Rihmer, Z, Annamaria, A., et al. (2006). The close link between suicide attempts and mixed (bipolar) depression: Implications for suicide prevention. *Journal of Affective Disorders, 91,* 133–138.

Balbin, E. G., Ironson, G. H., & Solomon, G. F. (1999). Stress and coping: The psychoneuroimmunology of HIV/AIDS. *Baillieres Best Practice and Research: Clinical Endocrinology and Metabolism, 13,* 615–633.

Balcetis, E., & Dunning, D. (2006). See what you want to see: Motivational influences on visual perception. *Journal of Personality and Social Psychology, 91,* 612–625.

Balcetis, E., & Dunning, D. (2010). Wishful seeing: More desired objects are seen as closer. *Psychological Science, 21,* 147–152.

Balfour, D. J. (2002). The neurobiology of tobacco dependence: A commentary. *Respiration, 69,* 7–11.

Ball, H. A., McGuffin, P., & Farmer, A. E. (2008). Attributional style and depression. *British Journal of Psychiatry, 192,* 275–278.

Ball, K., & Sekuler, R. (1992). Cues reduce direction uncertainty and enhance motion detection. *Perception and Psychophysics, 30,* 119–128.

Balleine, B., & Dickinson, A. (1994). Role of cholecystokinin in the motivational control of instrumental action in rats. *Behavioral Neuroscience, 108,* 590–605.

Ballmaier, M., & Schmidt, R. (2005). Conversion disorder revisited. *Functional Neurology, 20,* 105–113.

Balon, R. (2004). Developments in treatment of anxiety disorders: Psychotherapy, pharmacotherapy, and psychosurgery. *Depression and Anxiety, 19,* 63–76.

Baltes, B. B., Briggs, T. E., Huff, J. W., Wright, J. A., & Neumann, G. A. (1999). Flexible and compressed workweek schedules: A meta-analysis of their effects on work-related criteria. *Journal of Applied Psychology, 84,* 496–513.

Baltes, B. B., & Heydens-Gahir, H. A. (2003). Reduction of work–family conflict through the use of selection, optimization, and compensation behaviors. *Journal of Applied Psychology, 88,* 1005–1018.

Baltes, P. B. (1994, August). *Life-span developmental psychology: On the overall landscape of human development.* Address presented at the annual meeting of the American Psychological Association, Los Angeles.

Baltes, P. B., & Smith, J. (2008). The fascination of wisdom: Its nature, ontogeny, and function. *Perspectives on Psychological Science, 3,* 56–64.

Balzer, W. K., & Sulsky, L. M. (1992). Halo and performance appraisal research: Critical examination. *Journal of Applied Psychology, 77,* 975–985.

Bamfield, J. (2008). *The global retail theft barometer.* Thorofare, NJ: Checkpoint Systems.

Banaji, M. R., & Heiphetz, L. (2010). Attitudes. In S. T. Fiske, D. T. Gilbert, & G. Lindzey (Eds.), *Handbook of social psychology* (5th ed., Vol. 1, pp. 353–393). Hoboken, NJ: Wiley.

Bancroft, J. (1994). Homosexual orientation: The search for a biological basis. *British Journal of Psychiatry, 164,* 437–440.

Bandura, A. (1965). Influence of a model's reinforcement contingencies on the acquisition of imitative responses. *Journal of Personality and Social Psychology, 1,* 589–595.

Bandura, A. (1983). Psychological mechanisms of aggression. In R. G. Geen & C. I. Donnerstein (Eds.), *Aggression: Theoretical and empirical reviews* (Vol. 1, pp. 1–40). New York: Academic Press.

Bandura, A. (1992). Self-efficacy mechanism in psychobiologic functioning. In R. Schwarzer (Ed.), *Self-efficacy: Thought control of action* (pp. 355–394). Washington, DC: Hemisphere.

Bandura, A. (1999). Social cognitive theory of personality. In L. A. Pervin & O. P. John (Eds.), *Handbook of personality: Theory and research* (2nd ed., pp. 154–198). New York: Guilford Press.

Bandura, A. (2006). Toward a psychology of human agency. *Perspectives on Psychological Science, 1,* 164–180.

Bandura, A., Blanchard, E. B., & Ritter, B. (1969). The relative efficacy of desensitization and modeling approaches for inducing behavioral, affective, and attitudinal changes. *Journal of Personality and Social Psychology, 13,* 173–199.

Bandura, A., Ross, D., & Ross, S. A. (1963). Imitation of film-mediated aggressive models. *Journal of Abnormal and Social Psychology, 66,* 3–11.

Bandura, A., & Walters, R. H. (1963). *Social learning and personality development.* New York: Holt, Rinehart & Winston.

Banich, M. T. (2004). *Cognitive neuroscience and neuropsychology.* Boston: Houghton Mifflin.

Banich, M. T. (2009). Executive function: The search for an integrated account. *Psychological Science, 18,* 89–94.

Banker, R. D., Field, J. M., Schroeder, R. G., & Sinha, K. K. (1996). Impact of work teams on manufacturing performance: A longitudinal field study. *Academy of Management Journal, 39,* 867–890.

Bantick, S. J., Wise, R. G., Ploghaus, A., Clare, S., et al. (2002). Imaging how attention modulates pain in humans using functional MRI. *Brain, 125,* 310–319.

Barber, J. P., Crits-Christoph, P., & Paul, C. C. (1993). Advances in measures of psychodynamic formulations. *Journal of Consulting and Clinical Psychology, 61,* 574–585.

Barber, N. (1995). The evolutionary psychology of physical attractiveness: Sexual selection and human morphology. *Ethology and Sociobiology, 16,* 395–424.

Barch, D. M. (2006). The cognitive neuroscience of schizophrenia. *Annual Review of Clinical Psychology, 1,* 321–353.

Barclay, J. R., Bransford, J. D., Franks, J. J., McCarrell, N. S., & Nitsch, K. (1974). Comprehension and semantic flexibility. *Journal of Verbal Learning and Verbal Behavior, 13,* 471–481.

Barclay, P. (2006). Reputational benefits for altruistic punishment. *Evolution and Human Behavior, 27,* 325–344.

Barclay, T. R., Hinkin, C. H., Castellon, S. A., Mason, K. I., et al. (2007). Age-associated predictors of medication adherence in HIV-positive adults: Health beliefs, self-efficacy, and neurocognitive status. *Health Psychology, 26,* 40–49.

Barenbaum, N., & Winter, D. (2008). History of modern personality theory and research. In O. P. John, R. W. Robins, & L. A. Pervin (Eds.), *Handbook of personality: Theory and research* (3rd ed., pp. 3–28). New York: Guilford Press.

Bareyre, F. M., Kerschensteiner, M., Raineteau, O., Mettenleiter, T. C., & Schwab, M. E. (2004). The injured spinal cord spontaneously forms a new intraspinal circuit in adult rats. *Nature Neuroscience, 7,* 269–277.

Bargary, G., Barnett, K. J., Mitchell, K. J., & Newell, F. N. (2009). Colored-speech synaesthesia is triggered by multisensory, not unisensory, perception. *Psychological Science, 20,* 529–533.

Bargary, G., Barnett, K. J., Mitchell, K. J., & Newell, F. N. (2009). Colored-speech synaesthesia is triggered by multisensory, not unisensory, perception. *Psychological Science, 20,* 529–533.

Barger, L. K., Cade, B. E., Ayas, N. T., Cronin, J. W., et al. (2005). Extended work shifts and the risk of motor vehicle crashes among interns. *New England Journal of Medicine, 352,* 125–134.

Bargh, J. A., Chen, M., & Burrows, L. (1996). Automaticity of social behavior: Direct effects of trait construct and stereotype activation on action. *Journal of Personality and Social Psychology, 71,* 245–262.

Bargh, J. A., & Morsella, E. (2008). The unconscious mind. *Perspectives on Psychological Science, 3,* 73–79.

Baringer, J. R. (2008). Herpes simplex infections of the nervous system. *Neurology Clinics, 26,* 657–674.

Barkat, S., Poncelet, J., Landis, B. N., Rouby, C., & Bensafi, M. (2008). Improved smell pleasantness after odor-taste associative learning in humans. *Neuroscience Letters, 434,* 108–112.

Barkham, M., Connell, J., Stiles, W. B., Miles, J. N. V., et al. (2006). Dose-effect relations and responsive regulation of treatment duration: The good enough level. *Journal of Consulting and Clinical Psychology, 74,* 160–167.

Barling, J., Dupré, K. E., & Kelloway, E. K. (2009). Predicting workplace aggression and violence. *Annual Review of Psychology, 60,* 671–692.

Barling, J., Weber, T., & Kelloway, E. K. (1996). Effects of transformational leadership training on attitudinal and financial outcomes: A field experiment. *Journal of Applied Psychology, 81,* 827–832.

Barlow, D. H. (2006). Psychotherapy and psychological treatments: The future. *Clinical Psychology: Science and Practice, 13,* 216–220.

Barlow, D. H. (2007). *Clinical handbook of psychological disorders.* New York: Guilford Press.

Barlow, D. H. (2010). Negative effects from psychological treatments: A perspective. *American Psychologist, 65,* 13–20.

Barlow, D. H., Raffa, S. D., & Cohen, E. M. (2002). Psychosocial treatments for panic disorders, phobias, and generalized anxiety disorder. In P. E. Nathan & J. M. Gorman (Eds.), *A guide to treatments that work* (2nd ed., pp. 301–335). Oxford: Oxford University Press.

Barnes, A. (2004). Race schizophrenia, and admission to state psychiatric hospitals. *Administration and Policy in Mental Health, 31,* 241–252.

Barnes, C. M., & Wagner, D. T. (2009). Changing to daylight saving time cuts into sleep and increases workplace injuries. *Journal of Applied Psychology, 94,* 1305–1317.

Barnes, L. L., Mendes de Leon, C. F., Wilson, R. S., Bienias, J. L., & Evans, D. A. (2004). Social resources and cognitive decline in a population of older African Americans and whites. *Neurology, 63,* 2322–2326.

Barnes, S. M., Lynn, S. J., & Pekala, R. J. (2009). Not all group hypnotic suggestibility scales are created equal: Individual differences in behavioral and subjective responses. *Consciousness and Cognition, 18,* 255–265.

Barnes-Farrell, J. L., Davies-Schuls, K., McGonagle, A., Walsh, B., et al. (2008). What aspects of shiftwork influence off-shift well-being of healthcare workers? *Applied Ergonomics, 39,* 589–596.

Barnett, J. E., & Scheetz, K. (2003). Technological advances and telehealth: Ethics, law, and the practice of psychotherapy. *Psychotherapy: Theory, Research, Practice, and Training, 40,* 86–93.

Barnett, W. S. (1998). Long-term cognitive and academic effects of early childhood education of children in poverty. *Preventive Medicine, 27,* 204–207.

Barnier, A. J., & McConkey, K. M. (1998). Posthypnotic responding away from the hypnotic setting. *Psychological Science, 9,* 256–262.

Baron, A. S., & Banaji, M. R. (2006). The development of implicit attitudes. *Psychological Science 17,* 53–58.

Baron, R. A., & Richardson, D. C. (1994). *Human aggression* (2nd ed.). New York: Plenum.

Baron, R. N., Branscombe, N., & Byrne, D. (2008). *Social psychology* (12th ed.). Boston: Allyn & Bacon.

Baron, R. S. (2005). So right it's wrong: Groupthink and the ubiquitous nature of polarized group decision making. In M. Zanna (Ed.), *Advances in experimental social psychology* (Vol. 37, pp. 219–253). San Diego, CA: Elsevier/Academic Press.

Baron, R. S., Kerr, N. L., & Miller, N. (1992). *Group process, group decision, group action.* Pacific Grove, CA: Brooks/Cole.

Baron-Cohen, S., Leslie, A. M., & Frith, U. (1985). Does the autistic child have a "theory of mind"? *Cognition, 21,* 37–46.

Barres, B. A. (2008). The mystery and magic of glia: A perspective on their roles in health and disease. *Neuron, 60,* 430–440.

Barrett, B., Byford, S., & Knapp, M. (2005). Evidence of cost-effective treatments for depression: A systematic review. *Journal of Affective Disorders, 84,* 1–13.

Barrett, D. (2006). Hypnosis in film and television. *American Journal of Clinical Hypnosis, 49,* 13–30.

Barrett, L. F. (1995). Valence focus and arousal focus: Individual differences in the structure of affective experience. *Journal of Personality and Social Psychology, 69,* 153–166.

Barrett, L. F. (2006). Are emotions natural kinds? *Perspectives on Psychological Science, 1,* 28–58.

Barrett, L. F., Gross, J., Christensen, T. C., & Benvenuto, M. (2001). Knowing what you're feeling and knowing what to do about it: Mapping the relation between emotion differentiation and emotion regulation. *Cognition and Emotion, 15,* 713–724.

Barrett, L. F., Lane, R. D., Sechrest, L., & Schwartz, G. E. (2000). Sex differences in emotional awareness. *Personality and Social Psychology Bulletin, 26,* 1027–1035.

Barrett, L. F., Mesquita, B., Ochsner, K. N., & Gross, J. J. (2007). The experience of emotion. *Annual Review of Psychology, 58,* 373–403.

Barrett, L. F., & Wager, T. D. (2006). The structure of emotion. *Current Directions in Psychological Science, 15,* 79–83.

Barrick, M. R., Shaffer, J. A., & DeGrassi, S. W. (2009). What you see may not be what you get: Relationships among self-presentation tactics and ratings of interview and job performance. *Journal of Applied Psychology, 94,* 1394–1411.

Barron, F., & Harrington, D. M. (1981). Creativity, intelligence, and personality. *Annual Review of Psychology, 52,* 439–476.

Barron, K. E., & Harackiewicz, J. M. (2001). Achievement goals and optimal motivation: Testing multiple goal models. *Journal of Personality and Social Psychology, 80,* 706–722.

Barr Taylor, C., Bryson, S., Celio Doyle, A. A., Luce, K. H., et al. (2006a). The adverse effect of negative comments about weight and shape from family and siblings on women at high risk for eating disorders. *Pediatrics, 118,* 731–738.

Barr Taylor, C., Bryson, S., Luce, K. H., Cunning, D., et al. (2006b). Prevention of eating disorders in at-risk college-age women. *Archives of General Psychiatry, 63,* 881–888.

Barry, J. G., Yasin, I., & Bishop, D. V. M. (2007). Heritable risk factors associated with language impairments. *Genes, Brain, and Behavior, 6,* 66–76.

Barsalou, L. W. (1993). Flexibility, structure, and linguistic vagary in concepts: Manifestations of a compositional system of perceptual symbols. In A. F. Collins, S. E. Gathercole, M. A. Conway, & P. E. Morris (Eds.), *Theories of memory* (pp. 29–102). Hillsdale, NJ: Erlbaum.

Barsky, A. J., Wool, C., Barnett, M. C., & Cleary, P. D. (1994). Histories of childhood trauma in adult hypochondriacal patients. *American Journal of Psychiatry, 151,* 397–401.

Bartels, A., & Zeki, S. (2000). The neural basis of romantic love. *Neuroreport, 11,* 3829–3834.

Bartholow, B. D., Bushman, B. J., & Sestir, M. A. (2006). Chronic violent video game exposure and desensitization to violence: Behavioral and event-related brain potential data. *Journal of Experimental Social Psychology, 42,* 532–539.

Bartholow, B. D., & Heinz, A. (2006). Alcohol and aggression without consumption: Alcohol cues, aggressive thoughts, and hostile perception bias. *Psychological Science, 17,* 30–37.

Bartlett, J. A. (2002). Addressing the challenges of adherence. *Journal of Acquired Immune Deficiency Syndrome, 29*(Suppl. 1), S2–S10.

Barton, J., & Folkard, S. (1991). The response of day and night nurses to their work schedules. *Journal of Occupational Psychology, 64,* 207–218.

Barton, J. J., Cherkasova, M. V., Press, D. Z., Intriligator, J. M., & O'Connor, M. (2004). Perceptual functions in prosopagnosia. *Perception, 33,* 939–956.

Barton, J. J., Press, D. Z., Keenan, J. P., & O'Connor, M. (2002). Lesions of the fusiform face area impair perception of facial configuration in prosopagnosia. *Neurology, 58,* 71–78.

Bartoshuk, L. M. (1991). Taste, smell, and pleasure. In R. C. Bollef (Ed.), *The hedonics of taste* (pp. 15–28). Hillsdale, NJ: Erlbaum.

Bartoshuk, L. M. (2000). Comparing sensory experiences across individuals: Recent psychophysical advances illuminate genetic variation in taste perception. *Chemical Senses, 25,* 447–460.

Bartz, J. A., & Hollander, E. (2006). Is obsessive-compulsive disorder an anxiety disorder? *Progress in Neuropsychopharmacology and Biological Psychiatry, 30,* 338–352.

Bashore, T. R., & Ridderinkhof, K. R. (2002). Older age, traumatic brain injury, and cognitive slowing: Some convergent and divergent findings. *Psychological Bulletin, 128,* 151–198.

Baskin, D., Bluestone, H., & Nelson, M. (1981). Ethnicity and psychiatric diagnosis. *Journal of Clinical Psychology, 37,* 529–537.

Basoglu, M., Livanou, M., & Salcioglu, E. (2003). A single session with an earthquake simulator for traumatic stress in earthquake survivors. *American Journal of Psychiatry, 160,* 788–790.

Bass, B. M., Avolio, B. J., Jung, D. I., & Berson, Y. (2003). Predicting unit performance by assessing transformational and transactional leadership. *Journal of Applied Psychology, 88,* 207–218.

Bass, B. M., & Riggio, R. E. (2006). *Transformational leadership* (2nd ed.). Mahwah, NJ: Erlbaum.

Bass, E., & Davis, L. (1994). *The courage to heal* (3rd ed.). New York: HarperPerennial.

Basura, G. J., Eapen, R., & Buchman, C. A. (2009). Bilateral cochlear implantation: Current concepts, indications, and results. *Laryngoscope, 119,* 2395–2401.

Bates, E. (1993, March). *Nature, nurture, and language development.* Paper presented at the biennial meeting of the Society for Research in Child Development, New Orleans.

Bateson, M., Nettle, D., & Roberts, G. (2006). Cues of being watched enhance cooperation in a real-world setting. *Biology Letters, 2,* 412–414.

Batki, S. L., Leontieva, L., Dimmock, J. A., & Ploutz-Snyder, R. (2008). Negative symptoms are associated with less alcohol use, craving, and "high" in alcohol dependent patients with schizophrenia. *Schizophrenia Research, 105,* 201–207.

Batson, C. D. (2010). Empathy-induced altruistic motivation. In M. Mikulincer & P. Shaver (Eds.), *Prosocial motives, emotions, and behavior: The better angels of our nature* (pp. 15–34). Washington, DC: American Psychological Association.

Batson, C. D., Sager, K., Garst, E., & Kang, M. (1997). Is empathy-induced helping due to self-other merging? *Journal of Personality and Social Psychology, 73,* 495–509.

Batterham, R. L., Cohen, M. A., Ellis, S. M., Le Roux, C. W., et al. (2003). Inhibition of food intake in obese subjects by peptide YY3-36. *New England Journal of Medicine, 349,* 941–948.

Batterham, R. L., Cowley, M. A., Small, C. J., Herzog, H., et al. (2002). Gut hormone PYY3-36 physiologically inhibits food intake. *Nature, 418,* 650–654.

Baucom, D. H., Shoham, V., Mueser, K. T., Daiuto, A. D., & Stickle, T. R. (1998). Empirically supported couple and family interventions for marital distress and adult mental health problems. *Journal of Consulting and Clinical Psychology, 66,* 53–88.

Bauer, P. J. (2006). Event memory. In W. Damon & R. M. Lerner (Series Eds.) & D. Kuhn & R. Siegler (Vol. Eds.), *Handbook of child psychology: Vol. 2. Cognition, perception, and language* (6th ed., pp. 373–425). Hoboken, NJ: Wiley.

Bauer, R. M., & Demery, J. A. (2003). Agnosia. In K. M. Heilman & E. Valenstein (Eds.), *Clinical neuropsychology* (4th ed.). New York: Oxford University Press.

Bauer, T. N., & Green, S. G. (1996). Development of leader-member exchange: A longitudinal test. *Academy of Management Journal, 39,* 1538–1567.

Baumeister, H., & Härter, M. (2007). Mental disorders in patients with obesity in comparison with healthy probands. *International Journal of Obesity, 31,* 1155–1164.

Baumeister, R. F. (2000). Gender differences in erotic plasticity: The female sex drive as socially flexible and responsive. *Psychological Bulletin, 126,* 347–374.

Baumeister, R. F., & Bushman, B. J. (2008). *Social psychology and human nature.* Belmont, CA: Wadsworth.

Baumeister, R. F., Campbell, J. D., Krueger, J. I., & Vohs, K. D. (2003). Does high self-esteem cause better performance, interpersonal success, happiness, or healthier lifestyles? *Psychological Science in the Public Interest, 4,* 1–44.

Baumeister, R. F., & Leary, M. R. (1995). The need to belong: Desire for interpersonal attachments as a fundamental human motivation. *Psychological Bulletin, 117,* 497–529.

Baumeister, R. F., & Stillman, T. (2006). Erotic plasticity: Nature, culture, gender, and sexuality. In R. D. McAnulty & M. M. Burnette (Eds.), *Sex and sexuality: Vol. 1. Sexuality today: Trends and controversies* (pp. 343–359). Westport, CT: Praeger/Greenwood.

Baumgardner, S. R., & Crothers, M. K. (2009). *Positive psychology.* Upper Saddle River, NJ: Prentice Hall.

Baumrind, D. (1971). Current patterns of parental authority. *Developmental Psychology Monographs, 4*(1, pt. 2).

Baumrind, D., Larzelere, R. E., & Cowan, P. A. (2002). Ordinary physical punishment: Is it harmful? Comment on Gershoff. *Psychological Bulletin, 128,* 580–589.

Baylen, C. A., & Rosenberg, H. (2006). A review of the acute subjective effects of MDMA/ecstasy. *Addiction, 101,* 933–947.

Bayley, P. J., Hopkins, R. O., & Squire, L. R. (2003). Successful recollection of remote autobiographical memories by amnesic patients with medial temporal lobe lesions. *Neuron, 38,* 135–144.

Bazzano, L. A., He, J., Ogden, L. G., Loria, C. M., & Whelton, P. K. (2003). Dietary fiber intake and reduced risk of coronary heart disease in U.S. men and women. *Archives of Internal Medicine, 163,* 1897–1904.

BBC News (2010). Belgian coma 'writer' Rom Houben can't communicate. http://news.bbc.co.uk/2/hi/8526017.stm

Beach, S. R. H., Brody, G. H., Gunter, T. D., Packer, H., et al. (2010). Child maltreatment moderates the association of MAOA with symptoms of depression and antisocial personality disorder. *Journal of Family Psychology, 24,* 12–20.

Beatty, J. (1995). *Principles of behavioral neuroscience.* Dubuque, IA: Brown/Benchmark.

Beauchamp, G. K. (2009). Sensory and receptor responses to umami: An overview of pioneering work. *American Journal of Clinical Nutrition, 90,* S723–S727.

Beauchamp, G. K., Katahira, K., Yamazaki, K., Mennella, J. A., et al. (1995). Evidence suggesting that the odortypes of pregnant women are a compound of maternal and fetal odortypes. *Proceedings of the National Academy of Sciences, 92,* 2617–2621.

Beauchamp-Turner, D. L., & Levinson, D. M. (1992). Effects of meditation on stress, health, and affect. *Medical Psychotherapy, 5,* 123–131.

Beaumont, M., Batejat, D., Pierard, C., Van Beers, P., et al. (2004). Caffeine or melatonin effects on sleep and sleepiness after rapid eastward transmeridian travel. *Journal of Applied Physiology, 96,* 50–58.

Bechara, A., Damasio, H., Tranel, D., & Damasio, A. R. (1997). Deciding advantageously before knowing the advantageous strategy. *Science, 275,* 1293–1295.

Beck, A. T. (1967). *Depression: Clinical, experimental and theoretical aspects.* New York: Harper & Row.

Beck, A. T. (1976). *Cognitive therapy and the emotional disorders.* New York: International Universities Press.

Beck, A. T. (1995). Cognitive therapy: A 30-year retrospective. In S. O. Lilienfeld (Ed.), *Seeing both sides: Classic controversies in abnormal psychology* (pp. 303–311). Pacific Grove, CA: Brooks/Cole.

Beck, A. T. (2008). The evolution of the cognitive model of depression and its neurobiological correlates. *American Journal of Psychiatry, 165,* 969–977.

Beck, A. T., & Alford, B. A. (2009). *Depression: Causes and treatment.* Philadelphia: University of Pennsylvania Press.

Beck, A. T., Freeman, A., & Davis, D. D. (2007). *Cognitive therapy of personality disorders.* New York: Guilford Press.

Beck, A. T., & Rector, N. A. (2005). Cognitive approaches to schizophrenia: Theory and therapy. *Annual Review of Clinical Psychology, 1,* 577–606.

Beck, A. T., Rector, N. A., Stolar, N., & Grant, P. (2008). *Schizophrenia: Cognitive theory, research, and therapy.* New York: Guilford Press.

Beck, J. S. (2005). *Cognitive therapy for challenging problems: What to do when the basics don't work.* New York: Guilford Press.

Beck, J. S., & Beck, A. T. (1995). *Cognitive therapy: Basics and beyond.* New York: Guilford Press.

Beck, L. A., & Clark, M. S. (2009). Choosing to enter or avoid diagnostic social situations. *Psychological Science, 20,* 1175–1181.

Becker, C. B., Stice, E., Shaw, H., & Woda, S. (2009). Use of empirically supported interventions for psychopathology: Can the participatory approach move us beyond the research-to-practice gap? *Behaviour Research and Therapy, 47,* 265–274.

Becker, J. A. (1994). "Sneak-shoes," "sworders," and "nose-beards": A case study of lexical innovation. *First Language, 14,* 195–211.

Becker, S. M. (2004). Detection of somatization and depression in primary care in Saudi Arabia. *Social Psychiatry and Psychiatric Epidemiology, 39,* 962–969.

Beckett, C., Maughan, B., Rutter, M., Castle, J., et al. (2006). Do the effects of early severe deprivation on cognition persist into early adolescence? Findings from the English and Romanian adoptees study. *Child Development, 77,* 696–711.

Beede, K. E., & Kass, S. J. (2006). Engrossed in conversation: The impact of cell phones on simulated driving performance. *Accident Analysis and Prevention, 38,* 415–421.

Bègue, L., Subra, B., Arvers, P., Muller, D., et al. (2009). Message in a bottle: Extrapharmacological effects of alcohol on aggression. *Journal of Experimental Social Psychology, 45,* 137–142.

Behnke, M., Eyler, F. D., Warner, T. D., Garvan, C. W., et al. (2006). Outcome from a prospective longitudinal study of prenatal cocaine use: Preschool development at 3 years of age. *Journal of Pediatric Psychology, 31,* 41–49. doi:10.1093/jpepsy/jsj027

Behnke, S. (2003). *Hierarchical neural network for image interpretation.* New York: Springer.

Behnke, S. (2004). Sexual involvements with former clients: A delicate balance of core values. *Monitor on Psychology, 35*(11), 76–77.

Behrendt, R. (2006). Dysregulation of thalamic sensory "transmission" in schizophrenia: Neurochemical vulnerability to hallucinations. *Journal of Psychopharmacology, 20,* 356–372.

Behrens, K. Y., Hesse, E., & Main, M. (2007). Mothers' attachment status as determined by the adult attachment interview predicts their 6-year-olds' reunion responses: A study conducted in Japan. *Developmental Psychology, 43,* 1553–1567.

Beilock, S. L., Gunderson, E. A., Ramirez, G., & Levine, S. C. (2010). Female teachers' math anxiety affects girls' math achievement. *Proceedings of the National Academy of Sciences, 107,* 1860–1863.

Beilock, S. L., Kulp, C. A., Holt, L. E., & Carr, T. H. (2004). More on the fragility of performance: Choking under pressure in mathematical problem solving. *Journal of Experimental Psychology: General, 133,* 584–600

Beirne, R. O., Zlatkova, M. B., & Anderson, R. S. (2005). Changes in human short-wavelength-sensitive and achromatic resolution acuity with retinal eccentricity and meridian. *Visual Neuroscience, 22,* 79–86.

Beisel, K., Hansen, L., Soukup, G., & Fritzsch, B. (2008). Regenerating cochlear hair cells: Quo vadis stem cell. *Cell and Tissue Research, 333,* 373–379.

Bekinschtein, T. A., Cardozo, J., & Manes, F. F. (2008). Strategies of Buenos Aires waiters to enhance memory capacity in a real-life setting. *Behavioural Neurology, 20,* 65–70.

Bekinschtein, T. A., Tiberti, C., Niklison, J., Tamashiro, M., et al. (2005). Assessing level of consciousness and cognitive changes from vegetative state to full recovery. *Neuropsychological Rehabilitation, 15,* 307–322.

Belik, S., Cox, B. J., Murray, B. S., Asmundson, G. J. G., & Sareen, J. (2007). Traumatic events and suicidal behavior: Results from a national mental health survey. *Journal of Nervous and Mental Disease, 195,* 342–350.

Belin, P., Zatorre, R. J., & Ahad, P. (2002). Human temporal-lobe response to vocal sounds. *Brain Research and Cognitive Brain Research, 13,* 17–26.

Bell, A. M., & Sih, A. (2007). Exposure to predation generates personality in threespined sticklebacks (*Gasterosteus aculeatus*). *Ecology Letters, 10,* 828–834.

Bell, B. E., & Loftus, E. F. (1989). Trivial persuasion in the courtroom: The power of (a few) minor details. *Journal of Personality and Social Psychology, 56,* 669–679.

Bell, M. A., & Wolfe, C. D. (2007). Changes in brain functioning from infancy to early childhood: Evidence from EEG power and coherence working memory tasks. *Developmental Neuropsychology, 31,* 21–38. doi:10.1207/s15326942dn3101_2

Bell, P. A., Greene, T. C., Fisher, J. D., & Baum, A. (2000). *Environmental psychology* (5th ed.). Belmont, CA: Wadsworth.

Bell, S. (2005). What does the "right to health" have to offer mental health patients? *International Journal of Law and Psychiatry, 28,* 141–153.

Bella, S. D., & Peretz, I. (2003). Congenital amusia interferes with the ability to synchronize with music. *Annals of the New York Academy of Sciences, 999,* 166–169.

Bellaby, P. (2003). Communication and miscommunication of risk: Understanding UK parents' attitudes to combined MMR vaccination. *British Medical Journal, 327,* 725–728.

Belli, R. F., & Loftus, E. F. (1996). The pliability of autobiographical memory: Misinformation and the false memory problem. In D. C. Rubin (Ed.), *Remembering our past: Studies in autobiographical memory* (pp. 157–179). New York: Cambridge University Press.

Belmonte, M. K.; Cook, E. H., Jr.; Anderson, G. M.; Rubenstein, J. L.; et al. (2004). Autism as a disorder of neural information processing: Directions for research and targets for therapy. *Molecular Psychiatry, 9,* 646–663.

Belsky, J., Vandell, D. L., Burchinal, M., Clarke-Stewart, K. A., et al. (2007). Are there long-term effects of early child care? *Child Development, 78,* 681–701.

BeLue, R., Francis, L. A., & Colaco, B. (2009). Mental health problems and overweight in a nationally representative sample of adolescents: Effects of race and ethnicity. *Pediatrics, 123,* 697–702.

Bem, D. J. (1967). Self-perception: An alternative interpretation of cognitive dissonance phenomena. *Psychological Review, 74,* 183–200.

Bem, D. J. (2000). Exotic becomes erotic: Interpreting the biological correlates of sexual orientation. *Archives of Sexual Behavior, 29,* 531–548.

Ben-Ari, A., & Gil, S. (2002). Traditional support systems: Are they sufficient in a culturally diverse academic environment? *British Journal of Social Work, 32,* 629–638.

Ben-Hur, T. (2010). Reconstructing neural circuits using transplanted neural stem cells in the injured spinal cord. *Journal of Clinical Investigation, doi:10.1172/JCI43575.* (epub August 16, 2010).

Benecke, M. (1999). Spontaneous human combustion: Thoughts of a forensic biologist. *Skeptical Inquirer, 22,* 47–51.

Benedetti, F. G. (2007). Placebo and endogenous mechanisms of analgesia. *Handbook of Experimental Pharmacology,177,* 393–413.

Benedetti, F. G., & Amanzio, M. (1997). The neurobiology of placebo analgesia: From endogenous opioids to cholecystokinin. *Progress in Neurobiology, 52,* 109–125.

Benedetti, F. G., Arduino, C., & Amanzio, M. (1999). Somatotopic activation of opioid systems by target-directed expectations of analgesia. *Journal of Neuroscience, 19,* 3639–3648.

Benenson, J. F., & Koulnazarian, M. (2008). Sex differences in help-seeking appear in early childhood. *British Journal of Developmental Psychology, 26,* 163–169.

Benet-Martinez, V., & Oishi, S. (2008). Culture and personality. In O. P. John, R. W. Robins, & L. A. Pervin (Eds.), *Handbook of personality: Theory and research* (3rd ed., pp. 542–567). New York: Guilford Press.

Benham, G., Woody, E. Z., Wilson, K. S., & Nash, M. R. (2006). Expect the unexpected: Ability, attitude, and responsiveness to hypnosis. *Journal of Personality and Social Psychology, 91,* 342–350.

Benjamin, K., Wilson, S. G., & Mogil, J. S. (1999). Sex differences in supraspinal morphine analgesia are dependent on genotype. *Journal of Pharmacology and Experimental Therapeutics, 289,* 1370–1375.

Benjamin, L. T., Jr. (2000). The psychology laboratory at the turn of the 20th century. *American Psychologist, 55,* 318–321.

Benjamin, L. T., Jr., & Baker, D. B. (2004). *From seance to science: A history of the profession of psychology in America.* Belmont, CA: Wadsworth.

Benjamin, L. T., Jr., & Simpson, J. A. (2009). The power of the situation: The impact of Milgram's obedience studies on personality and social psychology. *American Psychologist, 64*, 12–19.

Benjet, C., & Kazdin, A. E. (2003). Spanking children: The controversies, findings, and new directions. *Clinical Psychology Review, 23*, 197–224.

Bennett, D. S., Bendersky, M., & Lewis, M. (2008). Children's cognitive ability from 4 to 9 years old as a function of prenatal cocaine exposure, environmental risk, and maternal verbal intelligence. *Developmental Psychology, 44*, 919–928.

Bennett, H. L., Giannini, J. A., & Davis, H. S. (1985). Nonverbal response to intraoperational conversation. *British Journal of Anaesthesia, 57*, 174–179.

Bennett, K. K., & Elliott, M. (2002). Explanatory style and health: Mechanisms linking pessimism to illness. *Journal of Applied Social Psychology, 32*, 1508–1526.

Bennett, R. J., & Robinson, S. L. (2000). Development of a measure of workplace deviance. *Journal of Applied Psychology, 85*, 349–360.

Ben-Porath, Y. S., & Tellegen, A. (2008). *Minnesota multiphasic personality inventory-2-RF*. San Antonio, TX: Pearson Assessment.

Ben-Shakhar, G., Bar-Hillel, M., & Kremnitzer, M. (2002). Trial by polygraph: Reconsidering the use of the guilty knowledge technique in court. *Law and Human Behavior, 26*, 527–541.

Ben-Shakhar, G., & Furedy, J. J. (1990). *Theories and applications in the detection of deception: A psychophysiological and international perspective*. New York: Springer-Verlag.

Benson, D. F., & Geschwind, N. (1971). Aphasia and related cortical disturbances. In A. B. Baker & L. H. Baker (Eds.), *Clinical neurology*. New York: Harper & Row.

Benson, E. (2003). Sex: The science of sexual arousal. *Monitor on Psychology, 34*, 50.

Benson, H. (1975). *The relaxation response*. New York: Morrow.

Bentin, S., DeGutis, J. M., D'Esposito, M., & Robertson, L. C. (2007). Too many trees to see the forest: Performance, event-related potential, and functional magnetic resonance imaging manifestations of integrative congenital prosopagnosia. *Journal of Cognitive Neuroscience, 19*, 132–146.

Ben-Zur, H. (2002). Coping, affect and aging: The roles of mastery and self-esteem. *Personality and Individual Differences, 32*, 357–372.

Berant, E., Mikulincer, M., & Shaver, P. R. (2008). Mothers' attachment style, their mental health, and their children's emotional vulnerabilities: A 7-year study of children with congenital heart disease. *Journal of Personality, 76*, 31–65.

Berdahl, J. L., & Moore, C. (2006). Workplace harassment: Double jeopardy for minority women. *Journal of Applied Psychology, 91*, 426–436.

Berenbaum, S. A., & Resnick, S. M. (1997). Early androgen effects on aggression in children and adults with congenital adrenal hyperplasia. *Psychoneuroendocrinology, 22*, 505–515.

Beresford, J., & Blades, M. (2006). Children's identification of faces from lineups: The effects of lineup presentation and instructions on accuracy. *Journal of Applied Psychology, 91*, 1102–1113.

Beresford, T. P., Arciniegas, D. B., Alfers, J., Clapp, L., et al. (2006). Hippocampus volume loss due to chronic heavy drinking. *Alcoholism: Clinical and Experimental Research, 30*, 1866–1870.

Berger, L. M., Paxson, C., & Waldfogel, J. (2009). Income and child development. *Children and Youth Services Review, 31*, 978–989.

Berger, S. E., & Adolph, K. E. (2003). Infants use handrails as tools in a locomotor task. *Developmental Psychology, 39*, 594–605.

Bergin, A. E. (1971). The evaluation of therapeutic outcomes. In A. E. Bergin & S. L. Garfield (Eds.), *Handbook of psychotherapy and behavior change: An empirical analysis* (pp. 217–270). New York: Wiley.

Berglund, H., Lindström, P., & Savic, I. (2006). Brain response to putative pheromones in lesbian women. *Proceedings of the National Academy of Sciences, 103*, 8269–8274.

Bergman, T. J., & Kitchen, D. M. (2009). Comparing responses to novel objects in wild baboons (*Papio ursinus*) and geladas (*Theropithecus gelada*). *Animal Cognition, 12*, 63–73.

Bériault, M., & Larivée, S. (2005). French review of EMDR efficacy: Evidences and controversies. *Revue de Psychoéducation, 34*, 355–396.

Berkman, L. F., Buxton, O., Ertel, K., & Okechukwu, C. (2010). Managers' practices related to work–family balance predict employee cardiovascular risk and sleep duration in extended care settings. *Journal of Occupational Health Psychology, 15*, 316–329.

Berkowitz, L. (1994). Is something missing? Some observations prompted by the cognitive-neoassociationist view of anger and emotional aggression. In L. R. Huesmann (Ed.), *Human aggression: Current perspectives* (pp. 35–60). New York: Plenum.

Berkowitz, L. (1998). Affective aggression: The role of stress, pain, and negative affect. In R. G. Geen & E. Donnerstein (Eds.), *Human aggression* (pp. 49–72). San Diego, CA: Academic Press.

Berlin, L. J., Ispa, J. M., Fine, M. A., Malone, P. S., et al. (2009). Correlates and consequences of spanking and verbal punishment for low-income white, African American, and Mexican American toddlers. *Child Development, 80*, 1403–1420.

Berman, M. E., McCloskey, M. S., Fanning, J. R., Schumacher, J. A., & Coccaro, E. F. (2009). Serotonin augmentation reduces response to attack in aggressive individuals. *Psychological Science, 20*, 714–720.

Bermond, B., Fasotti, L., Nieuwenhuyse, B., & Schuerman, J. (1991). Spinal cord lesions, peripheral feedback and intensities of emotional feelings. *Cognition and Emotions, 5*, 201–220.

Bernard, L. L. (1924). *Instinct*. New York: Holt, Rinehart & Winston.

Bernardin, H. J., & Beatty, R. W. (1984). *Performance appraisal: Assessing human behavior at work*. Boston: Kent.

Bernat, J. A., Calhoun, K. S., Adams, H. E., & Zeichner, A. (2001). Homophobia and physical aggression toward homosexual and heterosexual individuals. *Journal of Abnormal Psychology, 110*, 179–187.

Bernat, J. L. (2009). Chronic consciousness disorders. *Annual Review of Medicine, 60*, 381–392.

Bernstein, D. A. (1970). The modification of smoking behavior: A search for effective variables. *Behaviour Research and Therapy, 8*, 133–146.

Bernstein, D. A., Borkovec, T. D., & Hazlett-Stevens, H. (2000). *Progressive relaxation training: A manual for the helping professions* (2nd ed.). New York: Praeger.

Bernstein, D. A., Kramer, G. P., & Phares, V. (2009). *Introduction to clinical psychology* (7th ed.). Upper Saddle River, NJ: Prentice Hall.

Bernstein, D. M., & Loftus, E. F. (2009a). The consequences of false memories for food preferences and choices. *Perspectives on Psychological Science, 4*, 135–139.

Bernstein, D. M., & Loftus, E. F. (2009b). How to tell if a particular memory is true or false. *Perspectives in Psychological Science, 4*, 370–374.

Bernstein, D. M., & Roberts, B. (1995). Assessing dreams through self-report questionnaires: Relation with past research and personality. *Dreaming, 5*, 13–27.

Bernstein, I. L. (1978). Learned taste aversions in children receiving chemotherapy. *Science, 200*, 1302–1303.

Berrendero, F., Robledo, P., Trigo, J. M., Martín-García, E., & Maldonado, R. (2010). Neurobiological mechanisms involved in nicotine dependence and reward: Participation of the endogenous opioid system. *Neuroscience and Biobehavioral Review*. [Epub ahead of print]

Berridge, K. C., & Kringelbach, M. L. (2008). Affective neuroscience of pleasure: Reward in humans and animals. *Psychopharmacology, 199*, 457–480.

Berry, A. C., Rosenfield, D., & Smits, J. A. J. (2009). Extinction retention predicts improvement in social anxiety symptoms following exposure therapy. *Depression and Anxiety, 26*, 22–27.

Berry, C. M., Ones, D. S., & Sackett, P. R. (2007). Interpersonal deviance, organizational deviance, and their common correlates: A review and meta-analysis. *Journal of Applied Psychology, 92*, 409–423.

Berry, C. M., Sackett, P. R., & Wiemann, S. (2007). A review of recent developments in integrity test research. *Personnel Psychology, 60*, 271–301.

Berry, J. W., & Bennett, J. A. (1992). Cree conceptions of cognitive competence. *International Journal of Psychology, 27*, 73–88.

Berscheid, E. (2010). Love in the fourth dimension. *Annual Review of Psychology, 61*, 1–26.

Berscheid, E. (2011). Love and compassion: Caregiving in adult close relationships. In S. Brown, M. Brown, & L. Penner (Eds.), *Self-interest and beyond: Toward a new understanding of human caregiving*. New York: Oxford University Press

Bersoff, D. N. (2008). *Ethical conflicts in psychology* (4th ed.). Washington, DC: American Psychological Association.

Bertau, C., Anderson, N., & Salgado, J. F. (2005). The predictive validity of cognitive ability tests: A UK meta-analysis. *Journal of Occupational and Organizational Psychology, 78*, 387–409.

Bertenthal, B. I., Longo, M. R., & Kenny, S. (2007). Phenomenal permanence and the development of predictive tracking in infancy. *Child Development, 78*, 350–363. doi:10.1111/j.1467-8624.2007.01002.x

Berti, A., Ladavas, E., & Corti, M. D. (1996). Anosognosia for hemiplegia, neglect dyslexia, and drawing neglect: Clinical findings and theoretical implications. *Journal of the International Neuropsychological Association, 2*, 426–440.

Besli, R., Saylam, C., Veral, A., Karl, B., & Ozek. C. (2004). The existence of the vomeronasal organ in human beings. *Journal of Craniofacial Surgery, 15*, 730–735.

Best, J. B. (1999). *Cognitive psychology* (5th ed.). Belmont, CA: Brooks/Cole.

Bestmann, S., Ruff, C. C., Blankenburg, F., Weiskopf, N., et al. (2008). Mapping causal interregional influences with concurrent TMS-fMRI. *Experimental Brain Research, 191*, 383–402.

Betan, E. J., & Westen, D. (2009). Countertransference and personality pathology: Development and clinical application of the Countertransference Questionnaire. In R. A. Levy & J. S. Ablon (Eds.), *Handbook of evidence-based psychodynamic psychotherapy: Bridging the gap between science and practice* (pp. 179–197). New York: Humana Press.

Betch, T., Hoffman, K., Hoffrage, U., & Plessner, H. (2003). Intuition beyond recognition: When less familiar events are liked more. *Experimental Psychology, 50*, 49–54.

Bettencourt, B. A., Talley, A., Benjamin, A. J., & Valentine, J. (2006). Personality and aggressive behavior under provoking and neutral conditions: A meta-analytic review. *Psychological Bulletin, 132*, 751–777.

Beus, J. M., Payne, S. C., Bergman, M. E., & Arthur, W., Jr. (2010). Safety climate and injuries: An examination of theoretical and empirical relationships. *Journal of Applied Psychology, 95*, 713–727.

Beutler, L. E. (2000). David and Goliath: When empirical and clinical standards of practice meet. *American Psychologist, 55*, 997–1007.

Beutler, L. E. (2002). The dodo bird is extinct. *Clinical Psychology: Science and Practice, 9*, 30–34.

Beutler, L. E., & Malik, M. L. (Eds.). (2002). *Rethinking DSM: A psychological perspective*. Washington DC: American Psychological Association.

Bevins, R. A. (2001). Novelty seeking and reward: Implications for the study of high-risk behaviors. *Current Directions in Psychological Science, 10*, 189–193.

Bhagat, R. S., Kedia, B. L., Harveston, P. D., & Triandis, H. C. (2002). Cultural variations in the cross-border transfer of organizational knowledge: An integrative framework. *Academy of Management Review, 27*, 204–221.

Bhal, K. T., Gulati, N., & Ansari, M. A. (2009). Leader-member exchange and subordinate outcomes: Test of a mediation model. *Leadership and Organization Development Journal, 30*, 106–125.

Bhatt, R. S., & Bertin, E. (2001). Pictorial cues and three-dimensional information processing in early infancy. *Journal of Experimental Child Psychology, 80*, 315–332.

Bhatt, S., Mbwana, J., Adeyemo, A., Sawyer, A., et al. (2009). Lying about facial recognition: An fMRI study. *Brain and Cognition, 69*, 382–390.

Bhopal, R., Vettini, A., Hunt, S., Wiebe, S., et al. (2004). Review of prevalence data in, and evaluation of methods for cross cultural adaptation of, UK surveys on tobacco and alcohol in ethnic minority groups. *British Medical Journal, 328*, 76.

Bhutta, A. T., Cleves, M. A., Casey, P. H., Cradock, M. M., & Anand, K. J. S. (2002). Cognitive and behavioral outcomes of school-aged children who were born preterm. *Journal of the American Medical Association, 288*, 728–737.

Bhutta, M. F. (2007). Sex and the nose: Human pheromonal responses. *Journal of the Royal Society of Medicine, 100*, 268–274.

Bialystok, E., & Craik, F. (2010). Cognitive and linguistic processing in the bilingual mind. *Current Directions in Psychological Science, 19,* 19–23.

Bibbins-Domingo, K., Coxson, P., Pletcher, M. J., Lightwood, J., & Goldman, L. (2007). Adolescent overweight and future adult coronary heart disease. *New England Journal of Medicine, 357,* 2371–2379.

Bickis, M., Kelly, I. W., & Byrnes, G. (1995). Crisis calls and temporal and lunar variables: A comprehensive study. *Journal of Psychology, 129,* 701–711.

Bidwell, M. A., & Rehfeldt, R. A. (2004). Using video modeling to teach a domestic skill with an embedded social skill to adults with severe mental retardation. *Behavioral Interventions, 19,* 263–274.

Bieling, P. J., McCabe, R. E., & Antony, M. M. (2006). *Cognitive-behavioral therapy in groups.* New York: Guilford Press.

Bierhaus, A., Wolf, J., Andrassy, M., Rohleder, N., et al. (2003). A mechanism converting psychosocial stress into mononuclear cell activation. *Proceedings of the National Academy of Sciences, 100,* 1920–1925.

Bierman, K. L., Domitrovich, C. E., Nix, R. L., Gest, S. D., et al. (2008). Promoting academic and social-emotional school readiness: The Head Start REDI program. *Child Development, 79,* 1802–1817.

Bierman, K. L., Nix, R. L., Greenberg, M. T., Blair, C., & Domitrovich, C. E. (2008). Executive functions and school readiness intervention: Impact, moderation, and mediation in the Head Start REDI program. *Development and Psychopathology, 20,* 821–843.

Biermann, T, Asemann, R., McAuliffe, C., Ströbel, et al. (2009). Relationship between lunar phases and serious crimes of battery: A population-based study. *Comprehensive Psychiatry, 50,* 573–577.

Bierut, L. J., Heath, A. C., Bucholz, K. K., Dinwiddie, S. H., et al. (1999). Major depressive disorder in a community-based twin sample: Are there different genetic and environmental contributions for men and women? *Archives of General Psychiatry, 56,* 557–563.

Bierut, L. J., Stitzel, J. A., Wang, J. C., Hinrichs, A. L., et al. (2008). Variants in nicotinic receptors and risk for nicotine dependence. *American Journal of Psychiatry, 165,* 1163–1171.

Biever, C. (2009, January 3). Interview: Inside the savant mind. *New Scientist,* pp. 40–41.

Bigelow, A., MacLean, J., Wood, C., & Smith, J. (1990). Infants' responses to child and adult strangers: An investigation of height and facial configuration variables. *Infant Behavior and Development, 13,* 21–32.

Bigelow, B. J. (2006). There's an elephant in the room: The impact of early poverty and neglect on intelligence and common learning disorders in children, adolescents, and their parents. *Developmental Disabilities Bulletin, 34,* 177–215.

Bigler, R., & Liben, L. (2007). Developmental intergroup theory: Explaining and reducing children's social stereotyping and prejudice. *Current Directions in Psychological Science, 16,* 162–166.

Bijttebier, P., Beck, I., Claes, L., & Vandereycken, W. (2009). Gray's reinforcement sensitivity theory as a framework for research on personality-psychopathology associations. *Clinical Psychology Review, 5,* 421–430.

Bikbaev, A., & Manahan-Vaughan, D. (2008). Relationship of hippocampal theta and gamma oscillations to potentiation of synaptic transmission. *Frontiers of Neuroscience, 2,* 56–63. Epub 2008 Jul 2007.

Biklen, D. (1990). Communication unbound: Autism and praxis. *Harvard Educational Review, 60,* 290–314.

Bilalić, M., McLeod, P., & Gobet, F. (2010). The mechanism of the *Einstellung* (set) effect: A pervasive source of cognitive bias. *Current Directions in Psychological Science, 19,* 111–115.

Billiard, M. (2009). REM sleep behavior disorder and narcolepsy. *CNS and Neurological Disorders—Drug Targets, 8,* 264–270.

Billing, J., & Sherman, P. W. (1998). Antimicrobial functions of spices: Why some like it hot. *Quarterly Review of Biology, 73,* 3–49.

Binet, A., & Simon, T. (1905). Méthodes nouvelles pour le diagnostic du niveau intellectuel des anormaux [New methods for diagnosis of the intellectual level of abnormal patients]. *L'Année Psychologique, 11,* 191–244.

Bingenheimer, J. B., Brennan, R. T., & Earls, F. J. (2005). Firearm violence exposure and serious violent behavior. *Science, 308,* 1323–1326.

Binson, D., Michaels, S., Stall, R., Coates, T. J., et al. (1995). Prevalence and social distribution of men who have sex with men: United States and its urban centers. *Journal of Sex Research, 32,* 245–254.

Binsted, G., Brownell, K., Vorontsova, Z., Heath, M., & Saucier, D. (2007). Visuomotor system uses target features unavailable to conscious awareness. *Proceedings of the National Academy of Sciences, 104,* 12669–12672.

Binzen, C. A., Swan, P. D., & Manore, M. M. (2001). Postexercise oxygen consumption and substrate use after resistance exercise in women. *Medicine and Science in Sports and Exercise, 33,* 932–938.

Birbaumer, N., Veit, R., Lotze, M., Erb, M., et al. (2005). Deficient fear conditioning in psychopathy: A functional magnetic resonance imaging study. *Archives of General Psychiatry, 62,* 799–805.

Birch, H. G. (1945). The relation of previous experience to insightful problem solving. *Journal of Comparative Psychology, 38,* 367–383.

Birch, L. L., Fisher, J. O., Grimm-Thomas, K., Markey, C. N., et al. (2001). Confirmatory factor analysis of the Child Feeding Questionnaire: A measure of parental attitudes, beliefs, and practices about child feeding and obesity proneness. *Appetite, 36,* 201–210.

Birch, L. L., McPhee, L., Sullivan, S., & Johnson, S. (1989). Conditioned meal initiation in young children. *Appetite, 13,* 105–113.

Birnbaum, G. E., Reis, H. T., Mikulincer, M., Gillath, O., & Orpaz, A. (2006). When sex is more than just sex: Attachment orientations, sexual experience, and relationship quality. *Journal of Personality and Social Psychology, 91,* 929–943.

Bisiach, E., Capitani, E., & Tansini, E. (1979). Detection from left and right hemifields on single and double simultaneous stimulation. *Perceptual and Motor Skills, 48,* 960.

Bisiach, E., Luzzatti, C., & Perani, D. (1979). Unilateral neglect, representational schema, and consciousness. *Brain, 102,* 609–618.

Bisiach, E., Vallar, G., Perani, D., Papagano, C., & Berti, A. (1986). Unawareness of disease following lesions of the right hemisphere: Anosognosia for hemiplegia and anosognosia for hemianopia. *Neuropsychologia, 24,* 471–482.

Bisson, J. I. (2007). Eye movement desensitisation and reprocessing reduces PTSD symptoms compared with fluoxetine at six months post-treatment. *Evidence-Based Mental Health, 10,* 118.

Bjork, R. A. (1999). Assessing our own competence: Heuristics and illusions. In D. Gopher & A. Koriat (Eds.), *Attention and performance: XVII. Cognitive regulation of performance: Interaction of theory and application* (pp. 435–459). Cambridge: MIT Press.

Bjork, R. A. (2001, March). How to succeed in college: Learn how to learn. *American Psychological Society Observer, 14,* 9.

Bjork, R. A., & Linn, M. C. (2006). The science of learning and the learning of science. *APS Observer, 19,* 29, 39.

Bjorklund, D. F., & Green, B. L. (1992). The adaptive nature of cognitive immaturity. *American Psychologist, 47,* 46–54.

Bjorklund, P. (2006). No man's land: Gender bias and social constructivism in the diagnosis of borderline personality disorder. *Issues in Mental Health Nursing, 27,* 3–23.

Black, R. (2009, November 27). Bioethicist questions whether Belgian coma patient Rom Houben is communicating. *New York Daily News.* Retrieved from http://www.nydailynews.com/lifestyle/health/2009/11/27/2009-11-27_bioethicist_questions_whether_belgian_coma_patient_rom_houben_is_communicating.html

Black Becker, C., Bull, S., Smith, L. M., & Ciao, A. C. (2008). Effects of being a peer-leader in an eating disorder prevention program: Can we further reduce eating disorder risk factors? *Eating Disorders, 16,* 444–459.

Blagrove, M. (1996). Problems with the cognitive psychological modeling of dreaming. *Journal of Mind and Behavior, 17,* 99–134.

Blair, P. S., Sidebotham, P., Berry, P. J., Evans, M., & Fleming P. J. (2006). Major epidemiological changes in sudden infant death syndrome: A 20-year population-based study in the UK. *Lancet, 367,* 314–319.

Blair-West, G. W., Cantor, C. H., Mellsop, G. W., & Eyeson-Annan, M. L. (1999). Lifetime suicide risk in major depression: Sex and age determinants. *Journal of Affective Disorders, 53,* 171–178.

Blaisdell, A. P., Sawa, K., & Leising, K. J. (2006). Causal reasoning in rats. *Science, 311,* 1020–1022.

Blake, J., & de Boysson-Bardies, B. (1992). Patterns in babbling: A cross-linguistic study. *Journal of Child Language, 19,* 51–74.

Blake, R. (1998). What can be "perceived" in the absence of visual awareness? *Current Directions in Psychological Science, 6,* 157–162.

Blakemore, S. J., Wolpert, D., & Frith, C. (2000). Why can't you tickle yourself? *Neuroreport, 11,* R11–R16.

Blakeslee, S. (2001, August 28). Therapies push injured brains and spinal cords into new paths. *New York Times.* Retrieved from http://www.nytimes.com/2001/08/28/health/anatomy/28REHA.html

Blakeslee, S. (2002, September 22). Exercising toward repair of the spinal cord. *New York Times.* Retrieved from http://www.nytimes.com/2002/09/22/us/exercising-toward-repair-of-the-spinal-cord.html

Blanchard, R. (2001). Fraternal birth order and the maternal immune hypothesis of male homosexuality. *Hormones and Behavior, 40,* 105–114.

Blanchard, R., & Lippa, R. A. (2007). Birth order, sibling sex ratio, handedness, and sexual orientation of male and female participants in a BBC Internet research project. *Archives of Sexual Behavior, 36,* 163–176.

Blanchette, I., & Richards, A. (2010). The influence of affect on higher level cognition: A review of research on interpretation, judgement, decision making and reasoning. *Cognition and Emotion, 24,* 561–595.

Blascovich, J., Spencer, S. J., Quinn, D., & Steele, C. (2001). African Americans and high blood pressure: The role of stereotype threat. *Psychological Science, 12,* 225–229.

Blass, T. (1991). Understanding behavior in the Milgram obedience experiment: The role of personality, situations, and their interactions. *Journal of Personality and Social Psychology, 60,* 398–413.

Blass, T. (2009). From New Haven to Santa Clara: A historical perspective on the Milgram obedience experiments, *American Psychologist, 64,* 37–45.

Blatchford, P., Burke, J., Farquhar, C., & Plewis, I. (1989). Teacher expectations in infant school: Associations with attainment and progress, curriculum coverage, and classroom interaction. *British Journal of Educational Psychology, 59,* 19–30.

Bleil, M. E., McCaffery, J. M., Muldoon, M. F., Sutton-Tyrrell, K., & Manuck, S. B. (2004). Anger-related personality traits and carotid artery atherosclerosis in untreated hypertensive men. *Psychosomatic Medicine, 66,* 633–639.

Block, J. (2001). Millennial contrarianism: The Five Factor approach to personality description 5 years later. *Journal of Research in Personality, 35,* 98–107.

Block, R. I., & Ghoneim, M. M. (1993). Effects of chronic marijuana use on human cognition. *Psychopharmacology, 110,* 219–228.

Blood, A. J., & Zatorre, R. J. (2001). Intensely pleasurable responses to music correlate with activity in brain regions implicated in reward and emotion. *Proceedings of the National Academy of Sciences, 98,* 11818–11823.

Bloom, B., & Cohen, R. A. (2007). *Summary health statistics for U.S. children: National Health Interview Survey, 2006.* Washington, D C: National Center for Health Statistics.

Bloom, L. (1995). *The transition from infancy to language: Acquiring the power of expression.* New York: Cambridge University Press.

Bloomgarden, A., & Calogero, R. M. (2008). A randomized experimental test of the efficacy of EMDR treatment on negative body image in eating disorder inpatients. *Eating Disorders, 16,* 418–427.

Blow, A. J., & Timm, T. M. (2002). Promoting community through family therapy: Helping clients develop a network of significant social relationships. *Journal of Systematic Therapies, 21,* 67–89.

Blum, R. W., Beuhring, T., & Rinehart, P. M. (2000). *Protecting teens: Beyond race, income, and family structure.* Minneapolis: Center for Adolescent Health, University of Minnesota.

Blumberg, F. C., Rosenthal, S. F., & Randall, J. D. (2008). Impasse-driven learning in the context of video games. *Computers in Human Behavior, 24,* 1530–1541. doi:10.1016/j.chb.2007.05.010

Blumberg, H. P., Leung, H.-C., Skudlarski, P., Lacadie, C. M., et al. (2003). A functional magnetic resonance imaging study of bipolar disorder: State- and trait-related dysfunction in ventral prefrontal cortices. *Archives of General Psychiatry, 60,* 601–609.

Blumberg, M. S., & Lucas, D. E. (1994). Dual mechanisms of twitching during sleep in neonatal rats. *Behavioral Neuroscience, 108,* 1196–1202.

Blume, E. S. (1998). *Secret survivors: Uncovering incest and its aftereffects in women.* New York: Ballantine.

Blumenthal, J. A., Babyak, M., Wei., J., O'Conner, C., et al. (2002). Usefulness of psychosocial treatment of mental stress-induced myocardial ischemia in men. *American Journal of Cardiology, 89,* 164–168.

Blundell, J. E., & Cooling, J. (2000). Routes to obesity: Phenotypes, food choices and activity. *British Journal of Nutrition, 83,* S33–S38.

Boake, C., Yeates, K. O., & Donders, J. (2002). Association of postdoctoral programs in clinical neuropsychology: Update and new directions. *Clinical Neuropsychology, 16,* 1–6.

Boardman, A. P., & Healy, D. (2001). Modeling suicide risk in affective disorders. *European Psychiatry, 16,* 400–405.

Bob, P. (2008). Pain, dissociation, and subliminal self-representations. *Consciousness and Cognition, 17,* 355–369.

Bobko, P., Roth, P. L., & Potosky, D. (1999). Derivation and implications of a meta-analytic matrix incorporating cognitive ability, alternative predictors, and job performance. *Personnel Psychology, 52,* 561–590.

Bochukova, E. G., Huang, N., Keogh, J., Henning, E., et al. (2010). Large, rare chromosomal deletions associated with severe early-onset obesity. *Nature, 463,* 666–670.

Bockting, C. L. H., Schene, A. H., Spinhoven, P., Koeter, M. W. J., et al. (2005). Preventing relapse/recurrence in recurrent depression with cognitive therapy: A randomized controlled trial. *Journal of Consulting and Clinical Psychology, 73,* 647–657.

Boden, M. A. (2006). *Computer models of mind.* Cambridge: Cambridge University Press.

Boden-Albala, B., Litwak, E., Elkind, M. S., Rundek, T., & Sacco, R. L. (2005). Social isolation and outcomes post stroke. *Neurology, 64,* 1888–1892.

Boehning, D., & Snyder, S. H. (2003). Novel neural modulators. *Annual Review of Neuroscience, 26,* 105–131.

Bogaert, A. F., Blanchard, R., & Crosthwait, L. (2007). Interaction of birth order, handedness, and sexual orientation in the Kinsey interview data. *Behavioral Neuroscience, 121,* 845–853.

Boggs, C. D., Morey, L. C., Skodol, A. E., Shea, M. T., et al. (2009). Differential impairment as an indicator of sex bias in DSM-IV criteria for four personality disorders. *Personality Disorders: Theory, Research, and Treatment,* special volume, 61–68.

Bohner, G., & Schwarz, N. (2001). Attitudes persuasion and behavior. In A. Tesser & N. Schwarz (Eds.), *Blackwell handbook of social psychology: Intraindividual processes* (pp. 413–435). Oxford: Blackwell.

Bohner, G., Erb, H.-P., & Siebler, F. (2008) Information processing approaches to persuasion: Integrating assumptions from the dual- and single-processing perspectives. In W. B. Crano & R. Prislin (Eds.), *Attitudes and persuasion* (pp. 161–188). New York: Psychology Press.

Boles, D. B. (2005). A large-sample study of sex differences in functional cerebral lateralization. *Journal of Clinical and Experimental Neuropsychology, 27,* 759–768.

Bolger, K. E., & Patterson, C. J. (2001). Developmental pathways from child maltreatment to peer rejection. *Child Development, 72,* 549–568.

Bolla, K. I., Brown, K., Eldreth, D., Tate, K. & Cadet, J. L. (2002). Dose-related neurocognitive effects of marijuana use. *Neurology, 59,* 1337–1343.

Bolton, D., Eley, T. C., O'Connor, T. G., Perrin, S., et al. (2006). Prevalence and genetic and environmental influences on anxiety disorders in 6-year-old twins. *Psychological Medicine, 36,* 335–344.

Bonanno, G. A. (2004). Loss, trauma, and human resilience: Have we underestimated the human capacity to thrive after extremely aversive events? *American Psychologist, 59,* 20–28.

Bonanno, G. A. (2005). Resilience in the face of potential trauma. *Current Directions in Psychological Science, 14,* 135–138.

Bonanno, G. A., & Mancini, A. D. (2008). The human capacity to thrive in the face of potential trauma. *Pediatrics, 121,* 369–375.

Bonci, A., Bernardi, G., Grillner, P., & Mercuri, N. B. (2003). The dopamine-containing neuron: Maestro or simple musician in the orchestra of addiction? *Trends in Pharmacological Science, 24,* 172–177.

Bond, F. W., & Bunce, D. (2003). The role of acceptance and job control in mental health, job satisfaction, and work performance. *Journal of Applied Psychology, 88,* 1057–1067.

Bond, G., Aiken, L., & Somerville, S. (1992). The Health Beliefs Model and adolescents with insulin-dependent diabetes mellitus. *Health Psychology, 11,* 190–198.

Bond, L. A., & Hauf, A. M. C. (2004). Taking stock and putting stock in primary prevention: Characteristics of effective programs. *Journal of Primary Prevention, 24,* 199–221.

Boniecki, K. A., & Moore, S. (2003). Breaking the silence: Using a token economy to reinforce classroom participation. *Teaching of Psychology, 30,* 224–227.

Bonk, V. A., France, C. R., & Taylor, B. K. (2001). Distraction reduces self-reported physiological reactions to blood donation in novice donors with a blunting coping style. *Journal of Psychosomatic Medicine, 63,* 447–452.

Bonner, R. (2001, August 24). Death row inmate is freed after DNA test clears him. *New York Times.* Retrieved from http://www.nytimes.com/2001/08/24/us/death-row-inmate-is-freed-after-dna-test-clears-him.html

Bonwell, C. C., & Eison, J. A. (1991). *Active learning: Creating excitement in the classroom.* Washington, DC: George Washington University.

Booth, C. B., Clarke-Stewart, K. A., Vandell, D. L., McCartney, K., & Owen, M. T. (2002). Child-care usage and mother-infant "quality time." *Journal of Marriage and the Family, 64,* 16–26.

Bordnick, P. S., Elkins, R. L., Orr, T. E., Walters, P., & Thyer, B. A. (2004). Evaluating the relative effectiveness of three aversion therapies designed to reduce craving among cocaine abusers. *Behavioral Interventions, 19,* 1–24.

Borg, M. B., Jr. (2002). The Avalon Garden Men's Association: A community health psychology case study. *Journal of Health Psychology, 7,* 345–357.

Borgida, E., Conner, C., & Monteufel, L. (1992). Understanding living kidney donors: A behavioral decision-making perspective. In S. Spacapan & S. Oskamp (Eds.), *Helping and being helped* (pp. 183–212). Newbury Park, CA: Sage.

Borkenau, P., & Mauer, N. (2006). Accuracy of judgments of personality and genetic influences on attitudes: Two major bridges between personality and social psychology. In P. A. M. van Lange (Ed.), *Bridging social psychology: Benefits of transdisciplinary approaches* (pp. 193–198). Mahwah, NJ: Erlbaum.

Borkenau, P., Mauer, N., Riemann, R., Spinath, F. M., & Angleitner, A. (2004). Thin slices of behavior as cues of personality and intelligence. *Journal of Personality and Social Psychology, 86,* 599–614.

Borkenau, P., Riemann, R., Spinath, F. M., & Angleitner, A. (2006). Genetic and environmental influences on person × situation profiles. *Journal of Personality, 74,* 1451–1479.

Borkman, T. J. (1997). A selected look at self-help groups in the U.S. *Health and Social Care in the Community, 5,* 357–364.

Borman, W. C. (2004). The prediction of job performance: More than the Big 5. *Human Personality and Performance, 17,* 267–269.

Borman, W. C., Hanson, M. A., & Hedge, J. W. (1997). Personnel selection. *Annual Review of Psychology, 48,* 299–337.

Bornstein, M. H., Putnick, D. L., Heslington, M., Gini, M., et al. (2008). Mother-child emotional availability in ecological perspective: Three countries, two regions, two genders. *Developmental Psychology, 44,* 666–680.

Borry, P., Schotsmans, P., & Dierickx, K. (2006). Evidence-based medicine and its role in ethical decision-making. *Journal of Evaluation in Clinical Practice, 12,* 306–311.

Borsutzky, S., Fujiwara, E., Brand, M., & Markowitsch, H. J. (2008). Confabulations in alcoholic Korsakoff patients. *Neuropsychologia, 46,* 3133–3143.

Borzekowski, D. L., & Robinson, T. N. (2005). The remote, the mouse, and the no. 2 pencil: The household media environment and academic achievement among third grade students. *Archives of Pediatrics and Adolescent Medicine, 159,* 607–613.

Bosma, H., Marmot, M. G., Hemingway, H., Nicholson, A. C., et al. (1997). Low job control and risk of coronary heart disease in Whitehall II (prospective cohort) study. *British Medical Journal, 314,* 558–565.

Bosompra, K., Ashikaga, T., Worden, J. K., & Flynn, B. S. (2001). Is more optimism associated with better health? Findings from a population-based survey. *International Quarterly of Community Health Education, 20,* 29–58.

Botwinick, J. (1961). Husband and father-in-law: A reversible figure. *American Journal of Psychology, 74,* 312–313.

Botwinick, J. (1966). Cautiousness in advanced age. *Journal of Gerontology, 21,* 347–353.

Bouchard, L., Tremblay, A., Bouchard, C., & Pérusse, L. (2007). Contribution of several candidate gene polymorphisms in the determination of adiposity changes: Results from the Quebec family study. *International Journal of Obesity, 31,* 891–899.

Bouchard, T. J. (1999). Genes, environment, and personality. In S. J. Ceci & W. M. Williams (Eds.), *The nature-nurture debate: The essential readings* (pp. 97–103). Malden, MA: Blackwell.

Bourassa, M., & Vaugeois, P. (2001). Effects of marijuana use on divergent thinking. *Creativity Research Journal, 13,* 411–416.

Bouret, S. G., Draper, S. J., & Simerly, R. B. (2004). Trophic action of leptin on hypothalamic neurons that regulate feeding. *Science, 304,* 108–110.

Bourne, V. J. (2010). How are emotions lateralised in the brain? Contrasting existing hypotheses using the Chimeric Faces Test. *Cognition and Emotion, 24,* 903–911. doi:10.1080/02699930903007714

Bouton, M. E. (1993). Context, time, and memory retrieval in the interference paradigms of Pavlovian learning. *Psychological Bulletin, 114,* 80–99.

Bouton, M. E. (2002). Context, ambiguity, and unlearning: Sources of relapse after behavioral extinction. *Biological Psychiatry, 52,* 976–986.

Bouton, M. E., Mineka, S., & Barlow, D. H. (2001). A modern learning theory perspective on the etiology of panic disorder. *Psychological Review, 107,* 4–32.

Bouvier, S. E., & Engel, S. A. (2006). Behavioral deficits and cortical damage loci in cerebral achromatopsia. *Cerebral Cortex, 16,* 183–191.

Bowden, C. L. (2000). Efficacy of lithium in mania and maintenance therapy of bipolar disorder. *Journal of Clinical Psychiatry, 61,* 35–40.

Bowerman, M. (1996). The origins of children's spatial semantic categories: Cognitive versus linguistic determinants. In J. J. Gumperz & S. C. Levinson (Eds.), *Rethinking linguistic relativity: Studies in the social and cultural foundations of language* (pp. 145–176). Cambridge: Cambridge University Press.

Bowers, J. S., Mattys, S. L., & Gage, S. H. (2009). Preserved implicit knowledge of a forgotten childhood language. *Psychological Science, 20,* 1064–1069.

Bowlby, J. (1951). *Maternal care and mental health.* Geneva, Switzerland: World Health Organization.

Bowlby, J. (1973). *Attachment and loss: Vol. 2. Separation.* New York: Basic Books.

Bowlby, J. (1980). *Loss: Sadness and depression.* New York: Basic Books.

Bowman, N. A., Kitayama, S., & Nisbett R. E. (2009). Social class differences in self, attribution, and attention: socially expansive individualism of middle-class Americans. *Personality and Social Psychology Bulletin, 35,* 880–893.

Boxer, A. L., & Miller, B. L. (2005). Clinical features of frontotemporal dementia. *Alzheimer Disease and Associated Disorders, 19*(Suppl. 1), S3–S6.

Boyd, S. T. (2006). The endocannabinoid system. *Pharmacotherapy, 26,* S218–S221.

Boyle, P. A., Barnes, L. L., Buchman, A. S., & Bennett, D. A. (2009). Purpose in life is associated with mortality among community-dwelling older persons. *Psychosomatic Medicine, 71,* 574–579.

Boyle, S. H., Williams, R. B., Mark, D. B., Brummett, B. H., et al. (2004). Hostility as a predictor of survival in patients with coronary artery disease. *Psychosomatic Medicine, 66*, 629–632.

Boyles, S. (2008, October 14). Phiten necklace: Red Sox secret weapon? Some athletes are true believers in the power of titanium. *WebMD Health News.* Retrieved from http://www.webmd.com/pain-management/news/20081014/phiten-necklace-red-sox-secret-weapon

Boysen, G. A. (2009). A review of experimental studies of explicit and implicit bias among counselors. *Journal of Multicultural Counseling and Development, 37*, 240–249.

Bozarth, M. A., & Wise, R. A. (1984). Anatomically distinct opiate receptor fields mediate reward and physical dependence. *Science, 224*, 516–518.

Brach, J. S., FitzGerald, S., Newman, A. B., Kelsey, S., et al. (2003). Physical activity and functional status in community-dwelling older women. *Archives of Internal Medicine, 163*, 2565–2571.

Bracha, H. S. (2006). Human brain evolution and the "neuroevolutionary time-depth principle": Implication for the reclassification of fear-circuitry-related tratins in DSM-V and for studying resilience to war zone–related posttraumatic stress disorder. *Progress in Neuropsychopharmacology and Biological Psychiatry, 30*, 827–853.

Bracken, B. A., & McCallum, R. S. (1998). *Universal Nonverbal Intelligence Test (UNIT).* Boston: Riverside.

Bradley, R., Greene, J., Russ, E., Dutra, L., & Westen, D. (2005). A multidimensional meta-analysis of psychotherapy for PTSD. *American Journal of Psychiatry, 162*, 214–227.

Bradley, R., Heim, A. K., & Westen, D. (2005). Transference patterns in the psychotherapy of personality disorders: Empirical investigation. *British Journal of Psychiatry, 186*, 342–349.

Bradley-Johnson, S., Graham, D. P., & Johnson, C. M. (1986). Token reinforcement on WISC-R performance for white, low-socioeconomic, upper and lower elementary-school-age students. *Journal of School Psychology, 24*, 73–79.

Bradshaw, B. G., Richardson, G. E., Kumpfer, K., Carlson, J., et al. (2007). Determining the efficacy of a resiliency training approach in adults with type 2 diabetes. *Diabetes Educator, 33*, 650–659.

Brainerd, C. J., & Reyna, V. F. (2005). *The science of false memory.* New York: Oxford University Press.

Brainerd, C. J., Reyna, V. F., Wright, R., & Mojardin, A. H. (2003). Recollection rejection: False memory editing in children and adults. *Psychological Review, 110*, 762–784.

Brambilla, P., Cipriani, A., Hotopf, M., & Barbul, C. (2005). Side-effect profile of fluoxentine in comparison with other SSRIs, tricyclic, and newer antidepressants: A meta-analysis of clinical trial data. *Pharmacopsychiatry, 38*, 69–77.

Brandimonte, M. A., Hitch, G. J., & Bishop, D. V. M. (1992). Influence of short-term memory codes on visual image processing: Evidence from image transformation tasks. *Journal of Experimental Psychology: Learning, Memory, and Cognition, 18*, 157–165.

Brandtstadter, J., & Renner, G. (1990). Tenacious goal pursuit and flexible goal adjustment: Explication and age-related analysis of assimilative and accommodative strategies of coping. *Psychology and Aging, 5*, 58–67.

Brannick, M., & Levine, E. (2002). *Job analysis.* Thousand Oaks: CA: Sage.

Bransford, J. D., & Johnson, M. K. (1972). Contextual prerequisites for understanding: Some investigations of comprehension and recall. *Journal of Verbal Learning and Verbal Behavior, 11*, 717–726.

Bransford, J. D., & Stein, B. S. (1993). *The ideal problem solver* (2nd ed.). New York: Freeman.

Brasher, E. E., & Chen, P. Y. (1999). Evaluation of success criteria in job search: A process perspective. *Journal of Occupational and Organizational Psychology, 72*, 57–70.

Braun, A. E., Balkin, T. J., & Wesensten, N. J. (1998). Dissociated pattern of activity in visual cortices and their projections during human rapid eye movement sleep. *Science, 279*, 91–95.

Bray, G. A., & Tartaglia, L. A. (2000). Medicinal strategies in the treatment of obesity. *Nature, 404*, 672–677.

Bray, J. H. (2010). The future of psychology practice and science. *American Psychologist, 65*, 355–369.

Breed, A. G. (2006, January 28). Stress from Katrina is called "recipe for suicide." *Naples (FL) Daily News*, p. 4A.

Breedlove, S. M. (1994). Sexual differentiation of the human nervous system. *Annual Review of Psychology, 45*, 389–418.

Brefczynski-Lewis, J. A., Lutz, A., Schaefer, H. S., Levinson, D. B., & Davidson, R. J. (2007). Neural correlates of attentional expertise in long-term meditation practitioners. *Proceedings of the National Academy of Sciences, 104*, 11483–11488.

Breggin, P. R. (2007). *Brain-disabling treatments in psychiatry: Drugs, electroshock, and the psychopharmaceutical complex* (2nd ed.). New York: Springer.

Breggin, P. R. (2008). *Medication madness: True stories of mayhem, murder, and suicide caused by psychiatric drugs.* New York: St. Martin's Press.

Brehm, J. W., Miron, A. M., & Miller, K. (2009). Affect as a motivational state. *Cognition and Emotion, 23*, 1069–1089.

Brehm, S. (1992). *Intimate relationships.* New York: McGraw-Hill.

Brehm, S., Kassin, S., & Fein, S. (2005). *Social psychology* (6th ed.). Boston: Houghton Mifflin.

Breier, J. I., Adair, J. C., Gold, M., Fennell, E. B., et al. (1995). Dissociation of anosognosia for hemiplegia and aphasia during left-hemisphere anesthesia. *Neurology, 45*, 65–67.

Brelsford, J. W. (1993). Physics education in a virtual environment. In *Proceedings of the 37th annual meeting of the Human Factors and Ergonomics Society.* Santa Monica, CA: Human Factors.

Bremner, J. D., Shobe, K. K., & Kihlstrom, J. F. (2000). False memories in women with self-reported childhood sexual abuse. *Psychological Science, 11*, 333–337.

Bremner, J. D., Vythilingam, M., Vermetten, E., Southwick, S. M., et al. (2003). MRI and PET study of deficits in hippocampal structure and function in women with childhood sexual abuse and posttraumatic stress disorder. *American Journal of Psychiatry, 160*, 924–932.

Bremner, J. D., Vythilingam, M., Vermetten, E., Vaccarino, V., & Charney, D. S. (2004). Deficits in hippocampal and anterior cingulate functioning during verbal declarative memory encoding in midlife major depression. *American Journal of Psychiatry, 161*, 637–645.

Brems, C., & Namyniuk, L. (2002). The relationship of childhood abuse history and substance use in an Alaska sample. *Substance Use and Misuse, 37*, 473–494.

Brendgen, M., Boivin, M., Vitaro, F., Bukowski, et al. (2008). Linkages between children's and their friends' social and physical aggression: Evidence for a gene-environment interaction? *Child Development, 79*, 13–29.

Brendgen, M., Dionne, G., Girard, A., Boivin, M., et al. (2005). Examining genetic and environmental effects on social aggression: A study of 6-year-old twins. *Child Development, 76*, 930–946.

Brener, N. D., Hassan, S. S., & Barrios, L. C. (1999). Suicidal ideation among college students in the United States. *Journal of Consulting and Clinical Psychology, 67*, 1004–1008.

Brenes, G. A., Rapp, S. R., Rejeski, W. J., & Miller, M. E. (2002). Do optimism and pessimism predict physical functioning? *Journal of Behavioral Medicine, 25*, 219–231.

Brennan, F. X., & Charnetski, C. J. (2000). Explanatory style and immunoglobulin A (IgA). *Integrative Physiological and Behavioral Science, 35*, 251–255.

Brennen, T., Baguley, T., Bright, J., & Bruce, V. (1990). Resolving semantically induced tip-of-the-tongue states for proper nouns. *Memory and Cognition, 18*, 339–347.

Brenner, L., & Ritter, R. C. (1995). Peptide cholecystokinin receptor antagonist increases food intake in rats. *Appetite, 24*, 1–9.

Brenner, R. P. (2005). The interpretation of the EEG in stupor and coma. *Neurologist, 11*, 271–284.

Breslau, N., Lucia, V. C., & Alvarado, G. F. (2006). Intelligence and other predisposing factors in exposure to trauma and posttraumatic stress disorder: A follow-up study at age 17 years. *Archives of General Psychiatry, 63*, 1238–1245.

Breslau, N., Reboussin, B. A., Anthony, J. C., & Storr, C. L. (2005). The structure of posttraumatic stress disorder: Latent class analysis in 2 community samples. *Archives of General Psychiatry, 62*, 1343–1351.

Breslin, P. A., & Beauchamp, G. K. (1997). Salt enhances flavour by suppressing bitterness. *Nature, 387*, 563.

Breteler, M. H., Hilberink, S. R., Zeeman, G., & Lammers, S. M. (2004). Compulsive smoking: The development of a Rasch homogeneous scale of nicotine dependence. *Addiction and Behavior, 29*, 199–205.

Breuer, A. T., Masson, M. E., Cohen, A. L., & Lindsay, D. S. (2009). Long-term repetition priming of briefly identified objects. *Journal of Experimental Psychology: Learning, Memory, and Cognition, 35*, 487–498.

Brewer, J. B., Zhao, Z., Desmond, J. E., Glover, G. H., & Gabriel, J. D. E. (1998). Making memories: Brain activity that predicts how well visual experience will be remembered. *Science, 281*, 1185–1187.

Brewer, N. T., Chapman, G. B., Gibbons, F. X., Gerrard, M., et al. (2007). Meta-analysis of the relationship between risk perception and health behavior: The example of vaccination. *Health Psychology, 26*, 136–145. doi:10.1037/0278-6133.26.2.136

Brewer, W. F. (1977). Memory for the pragmatic implications of sentences. *Memory and Cognition, 5*, 673–678.

Brewer, W. F., & Treyens, J. C. (1981). Role of schemata in memory for places. *Cognitive Psychology, 13*, 207–230.

Bridge, J. A., Iyengar, S., Salary, C. B., Barbe, R. P., et al. (2007). Clinical response and risk for reported suicidal ideation and suicide attempts in pediatric antidepressant treatment: A meta-analysis of randomized controlled trials. *Journal of the American Medical Association, 297*, 1683–1696.

Brigham, C. C. (1923). *A study of American intelligence.* Princeton, NJ: Princeton University Press.

Brinckerhoff, L. C., Shaw, S. F., & McGuire, J. M. (1993). *Promoting postsecondary education for students with learning disabilities.* Austin, TX: Pro-Ed.

Brinkhaus, B., Witt, C. M., Jena, S., Linde, K., et al. (2006). Acupuncture in patients with chronic low back pain: A randomized controlled trial. *Archives of Internal Medicine, 166*, 450–457.

British Medical Association. (2000). *Acupuncture: Efficacy, safety, and practice.* London: Harwood Academic.

Broaders, S. C., & Goldin-Meadow, S. (2010). Truth is at hand: How gesture adds information during investigative interviews. *Psychological Science, 21*, 638–628. doi: 10.1177/0956797610366082

Broca, P. (1861). Remarques sur le siège de la faculté de la parole articulée, suivis d'une observation d'aphémie (perte de parole) [Observations on the locus of the capability of atriculated speech, followed by a report on aphemia (loss of speech)]. *Bulletin de la Société d'Anatomie, 36*, 330–357.

Broca, P. (1865). Sur la faculté du langage articulé [On the capability of articulated speech]. *Bulletin de la Société d'Anthropologie de Paris, 6*, 337–393.

Brock, J. W., Farooqui, S. M., Ross, K. D., & Payne, S. (1994). Stress-related behavior and central norepinephrine concentrations in the REM sleep-deprived rat. *Physiology and Behavior, 55*, 997–1003.

Broderick, J. E., Junghaenel, D. U., & Schwartz, J. E. (2005). Written emotional expression produces health benefits in fibromyalgia patients. *Psychosomatic Medicine, 67*, 326–334.

Brodino, N., Lanati, N., Barale, F., Martinelli, V., et al. (2008). Decreased NT-3 plasma levels and platelet serotonin content in patients with hypochondriasis. *Journal of Psychosomatic Research, 65*, 435–439.

Brody, N. (2003). Construct validation of the Sternberg Triarchic Abilities Test: Comment and reanalysis. *Intelligence, 31*, 319–330.

Brody, N., & Ehrlichman, H. (1998). *Personality psychology: The science of individuality.* Upper Saddle River, NJ: Prentice-Hall.

Brondolo, E., Rieppi, R., Erickson, S. A., Bagiella, E., et al. (2003). Hostility, interpersonal interactions, and ambulatory blood pressure. *Psychosomatic Medicine, 65*, 1003–1011.

Brook, C. A., & Schmidt, L. A. (2008). Social anxiety disorder: A review of environmental factors. *Neuropsychiatric Disease and Treatment, 4*, 123–143.

Brooks-Gunn, J., Klebanov, P. K., & Duncan, G. J. (1996). Ethnic differences in children's intelligence test scores: Role of economic deprivation, home environment, and maternal characteristics. *Child Development, 67*, 396–408.

Brown, A. L., Campione, J. C., Webber, L. S., & McGilly, K. (1992). Interactive learning environments: A new look at assessment and instruction. In B. Gifford & M. C. O'Connor (Eds.), *Changing assessments: Alternative views of aptitude, achievement, and instruction* (pp. 121–212). Boston: Kluever.

Brown, A. S. (2004). *The déjà vu experience*. New York: Psychology Press.

Brown, A. S., Begg, M. D., Gravenstein, S., Schaefer, C. A., et al. (2005). Serologic evidence of prenatal influenza in the etiology of schizophrenia. *Obstetrical and Gynecological Survey, 60*, 77–78.

Brown, A. S., & Derkits, E. J. (2010). Prenatal infection and schizophrenia: A review of epidemiologic and translational studies. *American Journal of Psychiatry, 167*, 261–280.

Brown, A. S., & Nix, L. A. (1996). Age-related changes in the tip-of-the-tongue experience. *American Journal of Psychology, 109*, 79–91.

Brown, G. K., Beck, A. T., Steer, R. A., & Grisham, J. R. (2000). Risk factors for suicide in psychiatric outpatients: A 20-year prospective study. *Journal of Consulting and Clinical Psychology, 68*, 371–377.

Brown, J. (1958). Some tests of the decay theory of immediate memory. *Quarterly Journal of Experimental Psychology, 10*, 12–21.

Brown, L. M., Bongar, B., & Cleary, K. M. (2004). A profile of psychologists' views of critical risk factors for completed suicide in older adults. *Professional Psychology: Research and Practice, 35*, 90–96.

Brown, P. D., & O'Leary, K. D. (2000). Therapeutic alliance: Predicting continuance and success in group treatment for spouse abuse. *Journal of Consulting and Clinical Psychology, 68*, 340–345.

Brown, R. (1973). *First language.* Cambridge, MA: Harvard University Press.

Brown, R., & Kulik, J. (1977). Flashbulb memories. *Cognition, 5*, 73–99.

Brown, R., & McNeill, D. (1966). The "tip-of-the-tongue" phenomenon. *Journal of Verbal Learning and Verbal Behavior, 5*, 325–337.

Brown, R. P., Osterman, L. L., & Barnes, C. D. (2009). School violence and the culture of honor. *Psychological Science, 20*, 1400–1405.

Brown, S. L., & Brown, R. M. (2006). Selective investment theory: Recasting the functional significance of close relationships. *Psychological Inquiry, 17*, 1–29.

Brown, S. L., Nesse, R. M., Vinokur, A. D., & Smith, D. M. (2003). Providing social support may be more beneficial than receiving it: Results from a prospective study of mortality. *Psychological Science, 14*, 320–327.

Brown, T., DiNardo, P. A., Lehman, C, & Campbell, L. A. (2001). Reliability of DSM-IV anxiety and mood disorders: Implications for classification of emotional disorders. *Journal of Abnormal Psychology, 110*, 49–58.

Browne, K. D., & Hamilton-Giachritsis, C. (2005). The influence of violent media on children and adolescents: A public health approach. *Lancet, 365*, 702–710.

Broyles, S., Katzmarzyk, P. T., Srinivasan, S. R., Chen, W., et al. (2010). The pediatric obesity epidemic continues unabated in Bogalusa, Louisiana. *Pediatrics, 125*, 900–905.

Broytman, O., & Malter, J. S. (2004). Anti-Aβ: The good, the bad, and the unforeseen. *Journal of Neuroscience Research, 75*, 301–306.

Bruce, D., Dolan, A., & Phillips-Grant, K. (2000). On the transition from childhood amnesia to the recall of personal memories. *Psychological Science, 11*, 360–364.

Bruce, E., & Waelde, L. C. (2008). Relationships of ethnicity, ethnic identity, and trauma symptoms to delinquency. *Journal of Loss and Trauma, 13*, 395–405.

Bruce, H. M. (1969). Pheromones and behavior in mice. *Acta Neurologica Belgica, 69*, 529–538.

Bruck, M., Cavanagh, P., & Ceci, S. J. (1991). Fortysomething: Recognizing faces at one's 25th reunion. *Memory and Cognition, 19*, 221–228.

Bruff, D. (2009). *Teaching with classroom response systems: Creating active learning environments.* San Francisco: Jossey-Bass.

Brummett, B. H., Babyak, M. A., Williams, R. B., Barefoot, J. C., et al. (2006). NEO personality domains and gender predict levels and trends in body mass index over 14 years during midlife *Journal of Research in Personality, 40*, 222–236.

Brummett, B. H., Mark, D. B., Siegler, I. C., Williams, R. B., et al. (2005). Perceived social support as a predictor of mortality in coronary patients: Effects of smoking, sedentary behavior, and depressive symptoms. *Psychosomatic Medicine, 67*, 40–45.

Brun, A. (2007). Identification and characterization of frontal lobe degeneration: Historical perspective on the development of FTD. *Alzheimer Disease and Associated Disorders, 21*(4), S3–S4.

Brüning, J. C., Gautam, D., Burks, D. J., Gillette, J., et al. (2000). Role of brain insulin receptor in control of body weight and reproduction. *Science, 289*, 2122–2125.

Brunvald, J. H. (1989). *Curses! Broiled again! The hottest urban legends going.* New York: Norton.

Brunyé, T. T., Mahoney, C. R., Lieberman, H. R., & Taylor, H. A. (2010). Caffeine modulates attention network function. *Brain and Cognition, 72*, 181–188.

Brush, D. H., Moch, M. K., & Pooyan, A. (1987). Individual demographic differences and job satisfaction. *Journal of Occupational Behaviour, 8*, 139–155.

Bryant, J., & Cummins, R, G. (2010). The effects of outcome of mediated and live sporting events on sports fans' self- and social identities. In H. L. Hundley & A. Billings (Eds.), *Examining identity in sports media* (pp. 217–238). Thousand Oaks, CA: Sage.

Bryant, R. A., & Guthrie, R. M. (2005). Maladaptive appraisals as a risk factor for posttraumatic stress. *Psychological Science, 16*, 749–752.

Bryant, R. A., & Mallard, D. (2003). Seeing is believing: The reality of hypnotic hallucinations. *Consciousness and Cognition, 12*, 219–230.

Bryant, R. A., & McConkey, K. M. (1989). Hypnotic blindness: A behavioral and experiential analysis. *Journal of Abnormal Psychology, 98*, 71–77.

Bryant, R. A., Moulds, M. L., Guthrie, R. M., Dang, S. T., et al. (2008). A randomized controlled trial of exposure therapy and cognitive restructuring for posttraumatic stress disorder. *Journal of Consulting and Clinical Psychology, 76*, 695–703.

Bryson, S. E., & Smith, I. M. (1998). Autism. *Mental Retardation and Developmental Disabilities Research Reviews, 4*, 97–103.

Buccino, G., Vogt, S., Ritzl, A., Fink, G. R., et al. (2004). Neural circuits underlying imitation learning of hand actions: An event-related fMRI study. *Neuron, 42*, 323–334.

Buchsbaum, M. S., Christian, B. T., Lehrer, D. S., Narayanan, T. K., et al. (2006). D2/D3 dopamine receptor binding with (F-18) fallypride in thalamus and cortex of patients with schizophrenia. *Schizophrenia Research, 85*, 232–244.

Buckholtz, J. W., Callicott, J. H., Kolachana, B., Hariri, A. R., et al. (2008). Genetic variation in MAOA modulates ventromedial prefrontal circuitry mediating individual differences in human personality. *Molecular Psychiatry, 13*, 313–324.

Buckner, R. L., & Wheeler, M. E. (2001). The cognitive neuroscience of remembering. *Nature Reviews Neuroscience, 2*, 1–12.

Budney, A. J., & Hughes, J. R. (2006). The cannabis withdrawal syndrome. *Current Opinion in Psychiatry, 19*, 233–238.

Bugental, D. B., & Grusec, J. E. (2006). Socialization processes. In W. Damon & R. M. Lerner (Series Eds.) & N. Eisenberg (Vol. Ed.), *Handbook of child psychology: Vol. 3. Social, emotional, and personality development* (6th ed., pp. 366–428). Hoboken, NJ: Wiley.

Bugg, J. M., Zook, N. A., DeLosh, E. E., Davalos, D. B., & Davis, H. P. (2006). Age differences in fluid intelligence: Contributions of general slowing and frontal decline. *Brain and Cognition, 62*, 9–16.

Bui, K.-V. T., Peplau, L. A., & Hill, C. T. (1996). Testing the Rusbult model of relationship commitment and stability in a 15-year study of heterosexual couples. *Personality and Social Psychology Bulletin, 22*, 1244–1257.

Buka, S. L., Shenassa, E. D., & Niaura, R. (2003). Elevated risk of tobacco dependence among offspring of mothers who smoked during pregnancy: A 30-year prospective study. *American Journal of Psychiatry, 160*, 1978–1984.

Bulevich, J. B.; Roediger, H. L., III; Balota, D. A.; & Butler, A. C. (2006). Failures to find suppression of episodic memories in the think/no-think paradigm. *Memory and Cognition, 34*, 1569–1577.

Bulik, C. M., Sullivan, P. F., Tozzi, F., Furberg, H., et al. (2006). Prevalence, heritability, and prospective risk factors for anorexia nervosa. *Archives of General Psychiatry, 63*, 305–312.

Bulkeley, K., & Kahan, T. L. (2008). The impact of September 11 on dreaming. *Consciousness and Cognition, 17*, 1248–1256.

Buller, D. B., Buller, M. K., & Kane, I. (2005). Web-based strategies to disseminate a sun safety curriculum to public elementary schools and state-licensed child care facilities. *Health Psychology, 24*, 470–476.

Bullock, T. H., Bennett, M. V., Johnston, D., Josephson, R., et al. (2005). Neuroscience: The neuron doctrine redux. *Science, 310*, 791–793.

Bullough, V. L. (1995, August). Sex matters. *Scientific American*, pp. 105–106.

Bunde, J., & Suls, J. (2006). A quantitative analysis of the relationship between the Cook-Medley hostility scale and traditional coronary artery disease risk factors. *Health Psychology, 25*, 493–500.

Bunge, S. A., Wendelken, C., Badre, D., & Wagner, A. D. (2005). Analogical reasoning and prefrontal cortex: Evidence for separable retrieval and integration mechanisms. *Cerebral Cortex, 15*, 239–249.

Burch, J. B., Tom, J., Zhai, Y., Criswell, L., et al. (2009). Shiftwork impacts and adaptation among health care workers. *Occupational Medicine, 59*, 159–166.

Burchard, R. E. (1992). Coca chewing and diet. *Current Anthropology, 33*, 1–24.

Burger, J. M. (2009). Replicating Milgram: Would people still obey today? *American Psychologist, 64*, 1–11.

Burger, J. M., & Caldwell, D. F. (2003). The effects of monetary incentives and labeling on the foot-in-the-door effect: Evidence for a self-perception process. *Basic and Applied Social Psychology, 25*, 235–241.

Burger, J. M., & Cornelius, T. (2003). Raising the price of agreement: Public commitment and the lowball compliance procedure. *Journal of Applied Social Psychology, 33*, 923–934.

Burish, T., & Jenkins, R. (1992). Effectiveness of biofeedback and relaxation training in reducing the side effects of cancer chemotherapy. *Health Psychology, 11*, 17–23.

Burke, R. J., & Fiksenbaum, L. (2009). Work motivations, work outcomes, and health: Passion versus addiction. *Journal of Business Ethics, 84*(Suppl. 2), 257–263.

Burleson, B. R., Albrecht, T. L., & Sarason, I. G. (Eds.). (1994). *Communication of social support: Messages, interactions, relationships, and community.* Thousand Oaks, CA: Sage.

Burleson, M. H., Gregory, W. L., & Trevarthen, W. R. (1995). Heterosexual activity: Relationship with ovarian function. *Psychoneuroendocrinology, 20*, 405–421.

Burns, A. B., Brown, J. S., Sachs-Ericsson, N., Plant, E. A., et al. (2008). Upward spirals of positive emotion and coping: Replication, extension, and initial exploration of neurochemical substrates. *Personality and Individual Differences, 44*, 360–370.

Burns, A., Bernabei, R., Bullock, R., Jentoft, A. J. C., et al. (2009). Safety and efficacy of galantamine (Reminyl) in severe Alzheimer's disease (the SERAD study): A randomised, placebo-controlled, double-blind trial. *Lancet Neurology, 8*, 39–47.

Burnstein, E., Crandell, C., & Kitayama, S. (1994). Some Neo-Darwinian decision rules for altruism: Weighing cues for inclusive fitness as a function of the biological importance of the decision. *Journal of Personality and Social Psychology, 67*, 773–789.

Burr, D. C., Morrone, C., & Fiorentini, A. (1996). Spatial and temporal properties of infant colour vision. In F. Vital-Durand, J. Atkinson, & O. J. Braddick (Eds.), *Infant vision* (pp. 63–77). Oxford: Oxford University Press.

Burt, S. A., McGue, M., & Iacono, W. G. (2009). Nonshared environmental mediation of the association between deviant peer affiliation and adolescent externalizing behaviors over time: Results from a cross-lagged monozygotic twin differences design. *Developmental Psychology, 45*, 1752–1760.

Burton, A. M., Wilson, S., Cowan, M., & Bruce, V. (1999). Face recognition in poor-quality video: Evidence from security surveillance. *Psychological Science, 10*, 243–248.

Burton, K. D., Lydon, J. E., D'Alessandro, D. U., & Koestner, R. (2006). The differential effects of intrinsic and identified motivation on well-being and performance: Prospective, experimental, and implicit approaches to self-determination theory. *Journal of Personality and Social Psychology, 91*, 750–762.

Bush, G. (2010). Attention-deficit/hyperactivity disorder and attention networks. *Neuropsychopharmacology, 35,* 278–300.

Bushman, B. J. (1998). Priming effects of media violence on the accessibility of aggressive constructs in memory. *Personality and Social Psychology Bulletin, 24,* 537–545.

Bushman, B. J., & Anderson, C. A. (2001). Media violence and the American public: Scientific facts versus media misinformation. *American Psychologist, 56,* 477–489.

Bushman, B. J., & Anderson, C. A. (2007). Measuring the strength of the effect of violent media on aggression. *American Psychologist, 62,* 253–254.

Bushman, B. J., Bonacci, A. M., Pedersen, W. C., Vasquez, E. A., & Miller, N. (2005). Chewing on it can chew you up: Effects of rumination on triggered displaced aggression. *Journal of Personality and Social Psychology, 88,* 969–983.

Bushman, B. J., & Huesmann, L. R. (2000). Effects of televised violence on aggression. In D. Singer & J. Singer (Eds.), *Handbook of children and the media* (pp. 223–254). Thousand Oaks, CA: Sage.

Bushman, B. J., & Huesmann, L. R. (2010). Aggression. In S. T. Fiske, D. T. Gilbert, & G. Lindzey (Eds.), *Handbook of social psychology* (5th ed., Vol. 2, pp. 833–863). Hoboken, NJ: Wiley.

Bushman, B. J., Wang, M. C., & Anderson, C. A. (2005). Is the curve relating temperature to aggression linear or curvilinear? Assaults and temperature in Minneapolis reexamined. *Journal of Personality and Social Psychology, 89,* 62–66.

Buss, A. H. (1989). Personality as traits. *American Psychologist, 44,* 1378–1388.

Buss, D. M. (2004a). *Evolutionary psychology: The new science of the mind* (2nd ed.). Boston: Allyn & Bacon.

Buss, D. M. (2004b). *The evolution of desire: Strategies of human mating.* New York: Basic Books.

Buss, D. M. (2008). *Evolutionary psychology: The new science of the mind* (3rd ed.). Boston: Allyn & Bacon.

Buss, D. M. (2009). The great struggles of life: Darwin and the emergence of evolutionary psychology. *American Psychologist, 64,* 140–148.

Buss, D. M., Abbott, M., Angleitner, A., Biaggio, A., et al. (1990). International preferences in selecting mates. *Journal of Cross-Cultural Psychology, 21,* 5–47.

Buss, D. M., & Schmitt, D. P. (1993). Sexual strategies theory: An evolutionary perspective on human mating. *Psychological Review, 100,* 204–232.

Büssing, A., & Höge, A. (2004). Aggression and violence against home care workers. *Journal of Occupational Health Psychology, 9,* 206–219.

Bustillo, J. R., Lauriello, J., Horan, W. P., & Keith, S. J. (2001). The psychosocial treatment of schizophrenia: An update. *American Journal of Psychiatry, 158,* 163–175.

Butcher, J. N. (2004). Personality assessment without borders: Adaptation of the MMPI-2 across cultures. *Journal of Personality Assessment, 83,* 90–104.

Butcher, J. N. (2006). *MMPI-2: A practitioner's guide.* Washington, DC: American Psychological Association.

Butcher, J. N., Mineka, S., & Hooley, J. M. (2010). *Abnormal psychology* (14th ed.). Boston: Allyn & Bacon.

Butler, A. C., Chapman, J. E., Forman, E. M., & Beck, A. T. (2006). The empirical status of cognitive-behavioral therapy: A review of meta-analyses. *Clinical Psychology Review, 26,* 17–31.

Butler, J., & Ciarrochi, J. (2007). Psychological acceptance and quality of life in the elderly. *Quality of Life Research, 16,* 607–615.

Butler, R. (1998). Information seeking and achievement motivation in middle childhood and adolescence: The role of conceptions of ability. *Developmental Psychology, 35,* 146–163.

Butters, N. (1981). The Wernicke-Korsakoff syndrome: A review of psychological, neuropathological and etiological factors. *Currents in Alcoholism, 8,* 205–232.

Buunk, A. P., Peiró, J. M., & Griffioen, C. (2007). A positive role model may stimulate career-oriented behavior. *Journal of Applied Social Psychology, 37,* 1489–1500.

Buunk, B. P., Zurriaga, R., Peiró, J. M., Nauta, A., & Gonsalvez, I. (2005). Social comparisons at work as related to a cooperative social climate and to individual differences in social comparison orientation. *Applied Psychology, 54,* 61–80.

Buxhoeveden, D. P., Switala, A. E., Roy, E., Litaker, M., & Casanova, M. F. (2001). Morphological differences between minicolumns in human and nonhuman primate cortex. *American Journal of Physical Anthropology, 115,* 361–371.

Buxton, R. B., Uludag, K., Dubowitz, D. J., & Liu, T. T. (2004). Modeling the hemodynamic response to brain activation. *Neuroimage, 23*(Suppl. 1), S220–S233.

Byers, A. L., Yaffe, Y., Covinsky, K. E., Friedman, M. B., & Bruce, M. L. (2010). High occurrence of mood and anxiety disorders among older adults. *Archives of General Psychiatry, 67,* 489–496.

Cabanac, M., & Morrissette, J. (1992). Acute, but not chronic, exercise lowers the body weight set-point in male rats. *Physiology and Behavior, 52,* 1173–1177.

Cabeza, R., Rao, S. M., Wagner, A. D., Mayer, A. R., & Schacter, D. L. (2001). Can medial temporal lobe regions distinguish true from false? An event-related functional MRI study of veridical and illusory recognition memory. *Proceedings of the National Academy of Sciences, 98,* 4805–4810.

Cabot, P. J. (2001). Immune-derived opioids and peripheral antinociception. *Clinical and Experimental Pharmacology and Physiology, 28,* 230–232.

Cacioppo, J. T. & Berntson, G. G. (Eds.). (2005). *Social neuroscience: Key readings.* New York: Psychology Press.

Cacioppo, J. T., Berntson, G. G., Sheridan, J. F., & McClintock, M. K. (2000). Multilevel integrative analyses of human behavior: Social neuroscience and the complementing nature of social and biological approaches. *Psychological Bulletin, 126,* 829–843.

Cacioppo, J. T., Crites, S. L., & Gardner, W. L. (1996). Attitudes to the right: Evaluative processing is associated with lateralized late positive event-related brain potentials. *Personality and Social Psychology Bulletin, 22,* 1205–1219.

Cacioppo, J. T., Gardner, W. L., & Berntson, G. G. (1999). The affect system has parallel and integrative processing components: Form follows function. *Journal of Personality and Social Psychology, 76,* 839–855.

Cacioppo, J. T., Malarkey, W. B., Kiecolt-Glaser, J. K., Uchino, B. N., et al. (1995). Heterogeneity in neuroendocrine and immune responses to brief psychological stressors as a function of autonomic cardiac activation. *Psychosomatic Medicine, 57,* 154–164.

Cacioppo, J. T., Petty, R. E., & Crites, S. L. (1993). Attitude change. In V. S. Ramachandran (Ed.), *Encyclopedia of human behavior* (pp. 261–270). San Diego, CA: Academic Press.

Cacioppo, J. T., Petty, R. E., Feinstein, J. A., Jarvis, W., & Blair, G. (1996). Dispositional differences in cognitive motivation: The life and times of individuals varying in need for cognition. *Psychological Bulletin, 119,* 197–253.

Cacioppo, J. T., Poehlmann, K. M., Kiecolt-Glaser, J. K., Malarkey, W. B., et al. (1998). Cellular immune responses to acute stress in female caregivers of dementia patients and matched controls. *Health Psychology, 17,* 182–189.

Cadet, J. L., & Krasnova, I. N. (2009). Molecular bases of methamphetamine-induced neurodegeneration. *International Review of Neurobiology, 88,* 101–119.

Cadinu, M., Maass, A., Rosabianca, A., & Kiesner, J. (2005). Why do women underperform under stereotype threat? *Psychological Science, 16,* 572–578.

Cadoret, R. J., Yates, W. R., Troughton, E., Woodworth, G., & Stewart, M. A. (1995). Adoption study demonstrating two genetic pathways to drug abuse. *Archives of General Psychiatry, 52,* 42–52.

Caggiano, V., Fogassi, L., Rizzolatti, G., Thier, P., & Casile, A. (2009). Mirror neurons differentially encode the peripersonal and extrapersonal space of monkeys. *Science, 324,* 403–406.

Cahill, L., & McGaugh, J. L. (1998). Mechanisms of emotional arousal and lasting declarative memory. *Trends in Neuroscience, 21,* 294–299.

Cahill, S. P., Carrigan, M. H., & Frueh, B. C. (1999). Does EMDR work? And if so, why? A critical review of controlled outcome and dismantling research. *Journal of Anxiety Disorders, 13,* 5–33.

Cai, D. J., Mednick, S. A., Harrison, E. M., Kanady, J. C., & Mednick, S. C. (2009). REM, not incubation, improves creativity by priming associative networks. *Proceedings of the National Academy of Sciences, 106,* 10130–10134.

Cain, D. J., & Seeman, J. (Eds.). (2002). *Humanistic psychotherapies: Handbook of research and practice.* Washington, DC: American Psychological Association.

Calabrese, J. R., Shelton, M. D., Rapport, D. J., Youngstrom, E. A., et al. (2005). A 20-month, double-blind maintenance trial of lithium versus divalproex in rapid-cycling bipolar disorder. *American Journal of Psychiatry, 162,* 2152–2161.

Calamaro, C. J., Mason, T. B. A., & Ratcliffe, S. J. (2009). Adolescents living the 24/7 lifestyle: Effects of caffeine and technology on sleep duration and daytime functioning. *Pediatrics, 123,* e1005–e1010.

Caldwell, C. A., & Millen, A. E. (2009). Social learning mechanisms and cumulative cultural evolution: Is imitation necessary? *Psychological Science, 20,* 1478–1483.

Caldwell, T. L., Cervone, D., & Rubin, L. H. (2008). Explaining intra-individual variability in social behavior through idiographic assessment: The case of humor. *Journal of Research in Personality, 42,* 1229–1242.

Callen, D. J. A., Black, S. E., Gao, F., Caldwell, C. B., & Szalai, J. P. (2001). Beyond the hippocampus: MRI volumetry confirms widespread limbic atrophy in AD. *Neurology, 57,* 1669–1674.

Cameron, H. A., Tanapat, P., & Gould, E. (1998). Adrenal steroids and N-methyl-D-aspartate receptor activation regulate neurogenesis in the dentate gyrus of adult rats through a common pathway. *Neuroscience, 82,* 349–354.

Campbell, F. A., Pungello, E. P., Miller-Johnson, S., Burchinal, M., & Ramey, C. T. (2001). The development of cognitive and academic abilities: Growth curves from an early childhood educational experiment. *Developmental Psychology, 37,* 231–242.

Campbell, F. A., Tramer, M. R., Carroll, D., Reynolds, D. J., et al. (2001). Are cannabinoids an effective and safe treatment option in the management of pain? A qualitative systematic review. *British Medical Journal, 323,* 13–16.

Campbell, K. L, Hasher, L., & Thomas, R. C. (2010). Hyper-binding: A unique age effect. *Psychological Science, 21,* 399–405. doi: 10.1177/0956797609359910

Campbell, R., & Capek, C. (2008). Seeing speech and seeing sign: Insights from a fMRI study. *International Journal of Audiology, 47*(Suppl. 2), S3–S9.

Campbell, R. S., & Pennebaker, J. W. (2003). The secret life of pronouns: Flexibility in writing style and physical health. *Psychological Science, 14,* 60–65.

Campbell, S. B. (1986). Developmental issues. In R. Gittelman (Ed.), *Anxiety disorders of childhood* (pp. 24–57). New York: Guilford Press.

Campion, M. A., & Campion, J. E. (1987). Evaluation of an interviewee skills training program in a natural field experiment. *Personnel Psychology, 40,* 676–691.

Campione, J. C., Brown, A. L., & Ferrara, R. A. (1982). Mental retardation and intelligence. In R. J. Sternberg (Ed.), *Handbook of human intelligence* (pp. 392–490). Cambridge: Cambridge University Press.

Campos, J. J. (1980). Human emotions: Their new importance and their role in social referencing. *Research and Clinical Center for Child Development: 1980–81 Annual Report,* 1–7.

Campos, L., & Alonso-Quecuty, M. L. (2006). Remembering a criminal conversation: Beyond eyewitness testimony. *Memory, 14,* 27–36.

Canada, D., & Goering, D. (2008). Deep thoughts on the river crossing game. *Mathematics Teacher, 101,* 632–639.

Candia, V., Rosset-Llobet, J., Elbert, T., & Pascual-Leone, A. (2005). Changing the brain through therapy for musicians' hand dystonia. *Annals of the New York Academy of Sciences, 1060,* 335–342.

Canli, T. (2008). Toward a "molecular psychology" of personality. In O. P. John, R. W. Robins, & L. A. Pervin (Eds.), *Handbook of personality: Theory and research* (3rd ed., pp. 311–327). New York: Guilford Press.

Canli, T., Qui, M., Omura, K., Congdon, E., et al. (2006). Neural correlates of epigenesis. *Proceedings of the National Academy of Sciences, 103,* 16033–16038.

Cann, A., & Ross, D. A. (1989). Olfactory stimuli as context cues in human memory. *American Journal of Psychology, 102,* 91–102.

Johnson, D. & Cannizzaro, M. S. (2009). Sentence comprehension in agrammatic aphasia: history and variability to clinical implications. *Clinical Linguistics and Phonetics, 23,* 15–37.

Cannon, C. P. (2005). The endocannabinoid system: A new approach to control cardiovascular disease. *Clinical Cornerstone, 7*(2–3), 17–26.

Cannon, T. D., Mednick, S. A., Parnas, J., Schulsinger, F., et al. (1993). Developmental brain abnormalities in the offspring of schizophrenic mothers. *Archives of General Psychiatry, 50*, 551–564.

Cannon, W. B. (1927). *Bodily changes in pain, hunger, fear and rage: An account of recent researches into the function of emotional excitement.* New York: Appleton.

Cannon, W. B., & Washburn, A. L. (1912). An explanation of hunger. *American Journal of Physiology, 29*, 444–454.

Canu, W. H. (2008). An experimental learning activity demonstrating normal and phobic anxiety. *Teaching of Psychology, 35*, 22–25.

Capasso, R., & Izzo, A. A. (2008). Gastrointestinal regulation of food intake: General aspects and focus on anandamide and oleoylethanolamide. *Journal of Neuroendocrinology, 20*(Suppl. 1), 39–46.

Capela, J. P., Carmo, H., Remião, F., Bastos, M. L., et al. (2009). Molecular and cellular mechanisms of ecstasy-induced neurotoxicity: An overview. *Molecular Neurobiology, 39*, 210–271.

Capgras, J., & Reboul-Lachaux, J. (1923). Illusion des « sosies » dans un délire systématisé chronique ["Doppelgänger" delusion in chronic persistent delirium]. *Bulletin de la Société Clinique de Médicine Mentale, 2*, 6–16.

Caplan, D. (2003a). Aphasic syndromes. In K. M. Heilman & E. Valenstein (Eds.), *Clinical neuropsychology* (4th ed., pp. 14–34). New York: Oxford University Press.

Caplan, D. (2003b). Syntactic aspects of language disorders. In K. M. Heilman & E. Valenstein (Eds.), *Clinical neuropsychology* (4th ed., pp. 61–91). New York: Oxford University Press.

Caplan, L. R. (2004). Clinical diagnosis of patients with cerebrovascular disease. *Primary Care, 31*, 95–109.

Caplan, L. R. (2005). Stroke. *Review of Neurological Disorders, 2*, 223–225.

Caplan, P. J. (1995). *They say you're crazy. How the world's most powerful psychiatrists decide who's normal.* Reading, MA: Addison-Wesley.

Capriani, A., Pretty, H., Hawton, K., & Geddes, J. R. (2005). Lithium in the prevention of suicidal behavior and all-cause mortality in patients with mood disorders: A systematic review of randomized trials. *American Journal of Psychiatry, 162*, 1805–1819.

Capron, C., & Duyme, M. (1989). Assessment of effects of socioeconomic status on IQ in a full cross-fostering study. *Nature, 340*, 552–553.

Capron, C., & Duyme, M. (1996). Effect of socioeconomic status of biological and adpoptive parents on WISC-R subtest scores of their French adopted children. *Intelligence, 22*, 259–276.

Caputo, M., Monastero, R., Mariani, E., Santucci, A., et al. (2008). Neuropsychiatric symptoms in 921 elderly subjects with dementia: A comparison between vascular and neurodegenerative types. *Acta Psychiatrica Scandinavica, 117*, 455–464.

Caputo, R. K. (2004). The impact of intergenerational Head Start participation on success measures among adolescent children. *Journal of Family and Economic Issues, 25*, 199–223.

Caramazza, A., & Hillis, A. E. (1991). Lexical organization of nouns and verbs in the brain. *Nature, 349*, 788–790.

Card, N. A., Stucky, B. D., Sawalani, G. M., & Little, T. D. (2008). Direct and indirect aggression during childhood and adolescence: A meta-analytic review of gender differences, intercorrelations, and relations to maladjustment. *Child Development, 79*, 1185–1229.

Cardemil, E. V., Reivich, K. J., & Seligman, M. E. P. (2002). The prevention of depressive symptoms in low-income minority middle school students [Electronic version.] *Prevention and Treatment, 5*, art. 8.

Cardinali, D. P., Bortman, G. P., Liotta, G., Perez Lloret, S., et al. (2002). A multifactorial approach employing melatonin to accelerate resynchronization of sleep-wake cycle after a 12 time-zone westerly transmeridian flight in elite soccer athletes. *Journal of Pineal Research, 32*, 41–46.

Cardis, E., et al. (2010). Brain tumour risk in relation to mobile telephone use: Results of the INTERPHONE international case-control study. *International Journal of Epidemiology*, 39, 675–694. doi:10.1093/ije/dyq079

Cardon, L. R., & Fulker, D. W. (1993). Genetics of specific cognitive abilities. In R. Plomin & G. McClearn (Eds.), *Nature, nurture, and psychology* (pp. 99–120). Washington, DC: American Psychological Association.

Cardon, L. R., Fulker, D. W., DeFries, J. C., & Plomin, R. (1992). Multivariate genetic analysis of specific cognitive abilities in the Colorado Adoption Project at age 7. *Intelligence, 16*, 383–400.

Carels, R. A., Young, K. M., Coit, C., Clayton, A. M., et al. (2008). Can following the caloric restriction recommendations from the dietary guidelines for Americans help individuals lose weight? *Eating Behaviors, 9*, 328–335.

Carlbring, P., & Smit, F. (2008). Randomized trial of Internet-delivered self-help with telephone support for pathological gamblers. *Journal of Consulting and Clinical Psychology, 76*, 1090–1094.

Carli, L. L. (1999). Cognitive reconstruction, hindsight, and reactions to victims and perpetrators. *Personality and Social Psychology Bulletin, 25*, 966–979.

Carli, L. L., Ganley, R., & Pierce-Otay, A. (1991). Similarity and satisfaction in romantic relationships. *Personality and Social Psychology Bulletin, 17*, 419–426.

Carlson, E. A., Sroufe, L. A., & Egeland, B. (2004). The construction of experience: A longitudinal study of representation and behavior. *Child Development, 75*, 66–83.

Carlson, J., Watts, R. E., & Maniacci, M. (2006). Play therapy. In J. Carlson, R. E. Watts, & M. Maniacci (Eds.), *Adlerian therapy: Theory and practice* (pp. 227–248). Washington, DC: American Psychological Association.

Carlson, L. E., Speca, M., Patel, K. D., & Goodey, E. (2003). Mindfulness-based stress reduction in relation to quality of life, mood, symptoms of stress, and immune parameters in breast and prostate cancer outpatients. *Psychosomatic Medicine, 65*, 571–581.

Carlson, N. R. (1998). *Physiology of behavior* (6th ed.) Boston: Allyn & Bacon.

Carlsson, A., & Lecrubier, Y. (Eds.). (2004). *Progress in dopamine research in schizophrenia: A guide for physicians.* Abingdon, England: Taylor & Francis.

Carlsson, K., Petrovic, P., Skare, S., Petersson, K. M., & Ingvar, M. (2000). Tickling expectations: Neural processing in anticipation of a sensory stimulus. *Journal of Cognitive Neuroscience, 12*, 691–703.

Carmichael, L. L., Hogan, H. P., & Walter, A. A. (1932). An experimental study of the effect of language on the reproduction of visually perceived form. *Journal of Experimental Psychology, 15*, 73–86.

Carney, D. R., Colvin, C. R., & Hall, J. A. (2007). A thin slice perspective on the accuracy of first impressions. *Journal of Research in Personality, 41*, 1054–1072.

Carr, A. (2009). The effectiveness of family therapy and systemic interventions for child-focused problems. *Journal of Family Therapy, 31*, 3–45.

Carr, G. D., Moretti, M. M., & Cue, B. J. H. (2005). Evaluating parenting capacity: Validity problems with the MMPI-2, PAI, CAPI, and ratings of child adjustment. *Professional Psychology: Research and Practice, 36*, 188–196.

Carraher, T. N., Carraher, D., & Schliemann, A. D. (1985). Mathematics in the streets and in the schools. *British Journal of Developmental Psychology, 3*, 21–29.

Carrasco, M., & McElree, B. (2001). Covert attention accelerates the rate of visual information processing. *Proceedings of the National Academy of Sciences, 98*, 5363–5367.

Carroll, J. B. (1993). *Human cognitive abilities: A survey of factor-analytic studies.* New York: Cambridge University Press.

Carroll, J. B., Neitz, M., Hofer, H., Neitz, J., & Williams, D. R. (2004). Functional photoreceptor loss revealed with adaptive optics: An alternate cause of color blindness. *Proceedings of the National Academy of Sciences, 101*, 8461–8466.

Carson, D., & Bull, R. (Eds.). (2003). *Handbook of psychology in legal contexts* (2nd ed.). Hoboken, NJ: Wiley.

Carstensen, L. (1997, August). *Psychology and the aging revolution: Changes in social needs and social goals across the life span.* Paper presented at the 105th annual convention of the American Psychological Association, Chicago.

Carter, M. M., & Barlow, D. H. (1995). Learned alarms: The origins of panic. In W. T. O'Donohue & L. Krasner (Eds.), *Theories of behavior therapy: Exploring behavior change* (pp. 209–228). Washington, DC: American Psychological Association.

Cartwright, R. D. (1978). *A primer on sleep and dreaming.* Reading, MA: Addison-Wesley.

Cartwright, R. D. (1993). Who needs their dreams? The usefulness of dreams in psychotherapy. *Journal of the American Academy of Psychoanalysis, 21*, 539–547.

Carver, C. S., & Connor-Smith, J. (2010). Personality and coping. *Annual Review of Psychology, 61*, 679–704.

Carver, C. S., & Harmon-Jones, E. (2009). Anger is an approach-related affect: Evidence and implications. *Psychological Bulletin, 135*, 183–204.

Carver, C. S., Johnson, S. L., & Joormann, J. (2008). Serotonergic function, two-mode models of self-regulation, and vulnerability to depression: What depression has in common with impulsive aggression. *Psychological Bulletin, 134*, 912–943.

Carver, C. S., & Scheier, M. F. (2002). The hopeful optimist. *Psychological Inquiry, 13*, 288–290.

Carver, C. S., & Scheier, M. F. (2008). *Perspectives on personality* (6th ed.). Boston: Allyn & Bacon.

Carver, K., Joyner, K., & Udry, J. R. (2003). National estimates of adolescent romantic relationships. In P. Florsheim (Ed.), *Adolescent romantic relations and sexual behavior: Theory, research, and practical implications* (pp. 23–56). Mahwah, NJ: Erlbaum.

Carver, L. J., & Vaccaro, B. G. (2007). 12-month-old infants allocate increased neural resources to stimuli associated with negative adult emotion. *Developmental Psychology, 43*, 54–69.

Casacalenda, N., Perry, J. C., & Looper, K. (2002). Remission in major depressive disorder: A comparison of pharmacotherapy, psychotherapy, and control conditions. *American Journal of Psychiatry, 159*, 1354–1360.

Casbon, T. S., Curtin, J. J., Lang, A. R., & Patrick, C. J. (2003). Deleterious effects of alcohol intoxication: Diminished cognitive control and its behavioral consequences. *Journal of Abnormal Psychology, 112*, 476–487.

Casey, B. J., Galvan, A., & Hare, T. A. (2005). Changes in cerebral functional organization during cognitive development. *Current Opinion in Neurobiology, 15*, 239–244.

Casey, B. J., Getz, S., & Galvan, A. (2008). The adolescent brain. *Developmental Review, 28*, 62–77. doi:10.1016/j.dr.2007.08.003

Casillas, A., Robbins, S., McKinniss, T., Postlethwaite, B., & Oh, I. (2009). Using narrow facets of an integrity test to predict safety: A test validation study. *International Journal of Selection and Assessment, 17*, 119–125.

Caspi, A. (1998). Personality development across the life course. In W. Damon & N. Eisenberg (Eds.), *Handbook of child psychology: Vol. 3. Social, emotional, and personality development* (5th ed., pp. 311–388). New York: Wiley.

Caspi, A. (2000). The child is the father of man: Personality continuities from childhood to adulthood. *Journal of Personality and Social Psychology, 78*, 158–172.

Caspi, A., Begg, D., Dickson, N., Harrington, H., et al. (1997). Personality differences predict health-risk behaviors in young adulthood: Evidence from a longitudinal study. *Journal of Personality and Social Psychology, 73*, 1052–1063.

Caspi, A., Hariri, A. R., Holmes, A., Uher, R., & Moffitt, T. E. (2010). Genetic sensitivity to the environment: The case of the serotonin transporter gene and its implications for studying complex diseases and traits. *American Journal of Psychiatry, 167*, 509–527. doi: 10.1176/appi.ajp.2010.09101452

Caspi, A., Harrington, H., Milne, B., Amell, J. W., et al. (2003). Children's behavioral styles at age 3 are linked to their adult personality traits at age 26. *Journal of Personality, 71*, 495–513.

Caspi, A., Henry, B., McGee, R. O., Moffitt, T. E., & Silva, P. A. (1995). Temperamental origins of child and adolescent behavior problems: From age 3 to age 15. *Child Development, 66*, 55–68.

Caspi, A., McClay, J., Moffitt, T. E., Mill, J., et al. (2002). Role of genotype in the cycle of violence in maltreated children. *Science, 297*, 851–854.

Caspi, A., Moffitt, T. E., Morgan, J., Rutter, M., et al. (2004). Maternal expressed emotion predicts children's antisocial behavior problems: Using monozygotic-twin differences to identify environmental effects on behavioral development. *Developmental Psychology, 40*, 149–161.

Caspi, A., Roberts, B. W., & Shiner, R. L. (2005). Personality development: Stability and change. *Annual Review of Psychology, 56,* 453–484.

Caspi, A., & Shiner, R. L. (2006). Personality development. In W. Damon & R. M. Lerner (Series Eds.) & N. Eisenberg (Vol. Ed.), *Handbook of child psychology: Vol. 3, Social, emotional, and personality development* (6th ed., pp. 300–365). Hoboken, NJ: Wiley.

Caspi, A., & Silva, P. A. (1995). Temperamental qualities at age 3 predict personality traits in young adulthood: Longitudinal evidence from a birth cohort. *Child Development, 66,* 468–498.

Caspi, A., Sugden, K., Moffitt, T. E., Taylor, A., et al. (2003). Influence of life stress on depression: Moderation by a polymorphism in the 5-HTT gene. *Science, 301,* 386–389.

Cassel, E., & Bernstein, D. A. (2007). *Criminal behavior* (2nd ed.). Mahwah, NJ: Erlbaum.

Castelli, J. (2009). Life after MPD/DID: An article on multiple personality disorder and child abuse. *Mental Health Matters.* Retrieved from http://www.mental-health-matters.com/index.php?option=com_content&view=article&id=364:life-after-mpddid-an-article-on-multiple-personality-disorder-and-child-abuse&catid=77:dissociative-identity&Itemid=2086

Castelli, L., Zogmaister, C., & Tomelleri, S. (2009). The transmission of racial attitudes within the family. *Developmental Psychology, 45,* 586–591.

Castonguay, L. G., & Beutler, L. E. (Eds.). (2005). *Principles of therapeutic change that work.* New York: Oxford University Press.

Castro, L., & Toro, M. A. (2004). The evolution of culture: From primate social learning to human culture. *Proceedings of the National Academy of Sciences, 101,* 10235–10240.

"Cat" that turned out to be a clock. (1998, September 19). *London Daily Telegraph.*

Caterina, M. J., Schumacher, M. A., Tominaga, M., Rosen, T. A., et al. (1997). The capsaicin receptor: A heat-activated ion channel in the pain pathway. *Nature, 389,* 816–824.

Cattell, R. B. (1963). Theory of fluid and crystallized intelligence: A critical experiment. *Journal of Educational Psychology, 54,* 1–22.

Cattell, R. B., Eber, H. W., & Tatsuoka, M. (1970). *Handbook for the sixteen personality factor questionnaire (16PF).* Champaign, IL: Institute for Personality Testing.

Cavenett, T., & Nixon, D. V. (2006). The effect of arousal on memory for emotionally relevant information: A study of skydivers. *Behaviour Research and Therapy, 44,* 1461–1469.

Caylak, E. (2009). The genetics of sleep disorders in humans: Narcolepsy, restless legs syndrome, and obstructive sleep apnea syndrome. *American Journal of Medical Genetics A, 149A,* 2612–2626.

Ceci, S. J., Huffman, M. L. C., Smith, E., & Loftus, E. F. (1994). Repeatedly thinking about a non-event: Source misattributions among preschoolers. *Consciousness and Cognition, 3,* 388–407.

Ceci, S. J., & Liker, J. K. (1986). A day at the races: A study of IQ, expertise, and cognitive complexity. *Journal of Experimental Psychology: General, 115,* 255–266.

Centers for Disease Control and Prevention. (1999). *Suicide deaths and rates per 100,000.* Retrieved from http://www.cdc.gov/ncipc/data/us9794/-suic.htm

Centers for Disease Control and Prevention. (2001). Deaths: Preliminary data for 2000. *National Vital Statistics Reports, 49,* 1–40.

Centers for Disease Control and Prevention. (2002a). Cigarette smoking among adults—United States, 2000. *Morbidity and Mortality Weekly, 51,* 642–645.

Centers for Disease Control and Prevention. (2002b). Suicide and self-inflicted injury. *FastStats.* Retrieved from http://www.cdc.gov/nchs/fastats/suicide.htm

Centers for Disease Control and Prevention. (2002c). Table 47: Death rates for suicide, according to sex, race, Hispanic origin, and age: United States, selected years, 1950–1999. *FastStats.* Retrieved from http://www/cdc.gov/nchs/faststats/pdf/nvsr49_11tb1/pds

Centers for Disease Control and Prevention. (2004). Web-based injury statistics query and reporting system (WISQARS). *National Center for Injury Prevention and Control.* Retrieved from http://www.cdc.gov/ncipc/wisquars

Centers for Disease Control and Prevention. (2006). Fatal injury reports. *National Center for Injury Prevention and Control.* Retrieved from http://www.cdc.gov/ncipc/wisqars

Centers for Disease Control and Prevention. (2008). Deaths: Final data for 2005. *National Vital Statistics Reports, 56,* 1–121.

Centers for Disease Control and Prevention. (2009a). *Preventing teen pregnancy: An update in 2009.* Retrieved from http://www.cdc.gov/reproductivehealth/AdolescentReproHealth/AboutTP.htm#b

Centers for Disease Control and Prevention. (2009b). Web-based injury statistics query and reporting system (WISQARS). *National Center for Injury Prevention and Control.* Retrieved from http://www.cdc.gov/ncipc/wisquars

Centerwall, L. (1990). Controlled TV viewing and suicide in countries: Young adult suicide and exposure to television. *Social Psychiatry and Social Epidemiology, 25,* 149–153.

Centonze, D., Picconi, B., Baunez, C., Borrelli, E.,et al. (2002). Cocaine and amphetamine depress striatal GABAergic synaptic transmission through D2 dopamine receptors. *Neuropsychopharmacology, 26,* 164–175.

Cepeda, N. J., Coburn, N. C., Roher, D., Wixted, J. T., et al. (2009). Optimizing distributed practice theoretical analysis and practical implications. *Experimental Psychology, 56,* 236–246.

Cepeda, N. J., Vul, E., Rohrer, D., Wixted, J. T., & Pashler, H. (2008). Spacing effects in learning: A temporal ridgeline of optimal retention. *Psychological Science, 19,* 1095–1102.

Çeponien, R., Lepisto, T., Shesakova, A., Vanhala, R., et al. (2003). Speech-sound-selective auditory impairment in children with autism: They can perceive but do not attend. *Proceedings of the National Academy of Sciences, 100,* 5567–5572.

Cerf, C., & Navasky, V. (1998). *The experts speak: The definitive compendium of authoritative misinformation.* New York: Villard.

Cervone, D. (2005). Personality architecture: Within-person structures and processes. *Annual Review of Psychology, 56,* 423–452.

Cervone, D., & Pervin, L. A. (2008). *Personality theory and research* (10th ed.). Hoboken, NJ: Wiley.

Chaiken, A. L., Sigler, E., & Derlega, V. J. (1974). Nonverbal mediators of teacher expectancy effects. *Journal of Personality and Social Psychology, 30,* 144–149.

Chakrabarti, S., & Fombonne, E. (2001). Pervasive developmental disorders in preschool children. *Journal of the American Medical Association, 285,* 3093–3099.

Chamberlin, J. (2000). Easing children's psychological distress in the emergency room. *Monitor on Psychology, 31,* 40–42.

Chambers, J. R., & Windschitl, P. D. (2009). Evaluating one performance among others: The influence of rank and degree of exposure to comparison referents. *Personality and Social Psychology Bulletin, 35,* 776–792.

Chambless, D. L., & Hollon, S. D. (1998). Defining empirically supported therapies. *Journal of Consulting and Clinical Psychology, 66,* 7–18.

Chambless, D. L., & Ollendick, T. H. (2001). Empirically supported psychological treatments. *Annual Review of Psychology, 52,* 685–716.

Champagne, F. A. (2009). Beyond nature vs. nurture: Philosophic insights from molecular biology. *Association for Psychological Science Observer, 22*(3), 27–28.

Champagne, F. A., & Mashoodh, R. (2009). Genes in context: Gene-environment interplay and the origins of individual differences in behavior. *Current Directions in Psychological Science, 18,* 127–131.

Champion, V., & Huster, G. (1995). Effect of interventions on stage of mammography adoption. *Journal of Behavioral Medicine, 18,* 159–188.

Chan, D. (2005). Current directions in personnel selection research. *Current Directions in Psychological Science, 14,* 220–223.

Chan, J. C. K., Thomas, A. K., & Bulevich, J. B. (2009). Recalling a witnessed event increases eyewitness suggestibility: The reversed testing effect. *Psychological Science, 20,* 66–73.

Chance, P. (2009). *Learning and behavior* (6th ed.). Belmont, CA: Wadsworth.

Chandola, T., Brunner, E., & Marmot, M. (2006). Chronic stress at work and the metabolic syndrome: Prospective study. *British Medical Journal, 332,* 521–525.

Chandra, A., Martino, S., Collins, R., Elliott, M., et al. (2008). Does watching sex on television predict teen pregnancy? Findings from a national longitudinal survey of youth. *Pediatrics, 122,* 1047–1054.

Chandrashekar, J., Hoon, M. A., Ryba, N. J., & Zuker, C. S. (2006). The receptors and cells for mammalian taste. *Nature, 444,* 288–294.

Chang, E. F., & Merzenich, M. M. (2003). Environmental noise retards auditory cortical development. *Science, 300,* 498–502.

Chang, F.-M., Kidd, J. R., Kivak, K. J., Pakstis, A. J., & Kidd, K. K. (1996). The worldwide distribution of allele frequencies at the human dopamine D4 receptor locus. *Human Genetics, 98,* 91–101.

Chao, R. K. (2001). Extending research on the consequences of parenting style for Chinese Americans and European Americans. *Child Development, 72,* 1832–1843.

Chao, R. K., & Tseng, V. (2002). Parenting of Asians. In M. H. Bornstein (Ed.), *Handbook of parenting: Vol. 4. Social conditions and applied parenting* (2nd ed., pp. 59–93). Mahwah, NJ: Erlbaum.

Chapell, M. S., Blanding, Z. B., Silverstein, M. E., Takahashi, M., et al. (2005). Test anxiety and academic performance in undergraduate and graduate students. *Journal of Educational Psychology, 97,* 268–274.

Chapman, D. Z., & Zweig, D. I. (2005). Developing a nomological network for interview structure: Antecedents and consequences of the structured selection interview. *Personnel Psychology, 58,* 673–702.

Chapman, S., & Morrell, S. (2000). Barking mad? Another lunatic hypothesis bites the dust. *British Medical Journal, 321,* 1561–1563.

Chaput, J.-P., & Tremblay, A. (2009). The glucostatic theory of appetite control and the risk of obesity and diabetes. *International Journal of Obesity, 33,* 46–53.

Charles, S. T., & Carstensen, L. L. (2007). Emotion regulation and aging. In J. Gross (Ed.), *Handbook of emotion regulation* (pp. 307–327). New York: Guilford Press.

Charles, S. T., Mather, M., & Carstensen, L. L. (2003). Aging and emotional memory: The forgettable nature of negative images for older adults. *Journal of Experimental Psychology: General, 132,* 310–324.

Charleton, T., Gunter, B., & Coles, D. (1998). Broadcast television as a cause of aggression? Recent findings from a naturalistic study. *Emotional and Behavioral Difficulties, 3,* 5–13.

Charness, N. (2000). Can acquired knowledge compensate for age-related declines in cognitive efficiency? In S. H. Qualls & N. Abeles (Eds.), *Psychology and the aging revolution: How we adapt to longer life* (pp. 99–117). Washington, DC: American Psychological Association.

Chase, T. N. (1998). The significance of continuous dopaminergic stimulation in the treatment of Parkinson's disease. *Drugs, 55*(Suppl. 1), 1–9.

Chassin, L., Pitts, S. C., & Prost, J. (2002). Binge drinking trajectories from adolescence to emerging adulthood in a high-risk sample: Predictors and substance abuse outcomes. *Journal of Consulting and Clinical Psychology, 70,* 67–78.

Chaudhry, I. B., Neelam, K., Duddu, V., & Husain, N. (2008). Ethnicity and psychopharmacology. *Journal of Psychopharmacology, 22,* 673–680.

Chavous, T. M., Hilkene Bernat, D., Schmeelk-Cone, K., Caldwell, C. H., et al. (2003). Racial identity and academic attainment among African American adolescents. *Child Development, 74,* 1076–1090.

Chemers, M. M., Watson, C. B., & May, S. T. (2000). Dispositional affect and leadership effectiveness: A comparison of self-esteem, optimism, and efficacy. *Personality and Social Psychology Bulletin, 26,* 267–277.

Chen, A. C. (2009). Higher cortical modulation of pain perception in the human brain: Psychological determinant. *Neuroscience Bulletin, 25,* 267–276.

Chen, J., Magavi, S. S. P., & Macklis, J. D. (2004). Neurogenesis of corticospinal motor neurons extending spinal projections in adult mice. *Proceedings of the National Academy of Sciences, 101,* 16357–16362.

Chen, M., & Bargh, J. A. (1997). Nonconscious behavioral confirmation processes: The self-fulfilling consequences of automatic stereotype activation. *Journal of Experimental Social Psychology, 33,* 541–560.

Chen, R., Cohen, L. G., & Hallett, M. (2002). Nervous system reorganization following injury. *Neuroscience, 111,* 761–773.

Chen, R., Tilley, M. R., Wei, H., Zhou, F., et al. (2006). Abolished cocaine reward in mice with a cocaine-insensitive dopamine transporter. *Proceedings of the National Academy of Sciences, 103,* 9333–9338.

Cheng, A. T. A., Gau, S.-F., Chen, T. H. H., Chang, J.-C., & Chang, Y.-T. (2004). A 4-year longitudinal study on risk factors for alcoholism. *Archives of General Psychiatry, 61,* 184–191.

Cheng, L.-C., Tavazoie, M., & Doetsch, F. (2005). Stem cells: From epigenetics to micro-RNAs. *Neuron, 46,* 363–367.

Cheng, L. H., & Robinson, P. P. (1991). The distribution of fungiform papillae and taste buds on the human tongue. *Archives of Oral Biology, 36,* 583–589.

Cheng, S.-T., Fung, H. H., & Chan, A. C. M. (2009). Self-perception and psychological well-being: The benefits of foreseeing a worse future psychology and aging. *Psychology and Aging, 24,* 623–633.

Cheng, Y., Kawachi, I., Coakley, E. H., Schwartz, J., & Colditz, G. (2000). Association between psychosocial work characteristics and health functioning in American women: Prospective study. *British Medical Journal, 320,* 1432–1436.

Cherkin, D. C., Sherman, K. J., Avins, A. L., Erro, J. H., et al. (2009). A randomized trial comparing acupuncture, simulated acupuncture, and usual care for chronic low back pain. *Archives of Internal Medicine, 169,* 858–866.

Chesney, M. A., Chambers, D. B., Taylor, J. M., Johnson, L. M., & Folkman, S. (2003). Coping effectiveness training for men living with HIV: Results from a randomized clinical trial testing a group-based intervention. *Psychosomatic Medicine, 65,* 1038–1046.

Chida, Y., & Steptoe, A. (2009). The association of anger and hostility with future coronary heart disease. *Journal of the American College of Cardiology, 53,* 936–946.

Chiesa, A., & Serretti, A. (2009). A systematic review of neurobiological and clinical features of mindfulness meditations. *Psychological Medicine, 40,* 1249–1252. Epub 2009 Nov 27.

Children's Defense Fund. (2004). *The state of America's children, 2004.* Washington, DC: Author.

Childs, E., & de Wit, H. (2006). Subjective, behavioral, and physiological effects of acute caffeine in light, nondependent caffeine users. *Psychopharmacology (Berlin), 185,* 514–523.

Chisholm, K. (1997, June). Trauma at an early age inhibits ability to bond. *APA Monitor,* p. 11.

Chiu, P. H., Lohrenz, T. M., & Montague, P. R. (2008). Smokers' brains compute, but ignore, a fictive error signal in a sequential investment task. *Nature Neuroscience, 11,* 514–520.

Chivers, M. L., Rieger, G., Latty, E., & Bailey, J. M. (2004). A sex difference in the specificity of sexual arousal. *Psychological Science, 15,* 736–744.

Chivers, M. L., Seto, M. C., & Blanchard, R. (2007). Gender and sexual orientation differences in sexual response to sexual activities versus gender of actors in sexual films. *Journal of Personality and Social Psychology, 93,* 1108–1121.

Chlebowski, R. T., Kuller, L. H., Prentice, R. L., Stefanick, M. L., et al. (2009). Breast cancer after use of estrogen plus progestin in postmenopausal women. *New England Journal of Medicine, 360,* 573–587.

Cho, S.-H., Lee, J.-S., Thabane, L., & Lee, J. (2009). Acupuncture for obesity: A systematic review and meta-analysis. *International Journal of Obesity, 33,* 183–196.

Chodosh, J., Reuben, D. B., Albert, M. S., & Seeman, T. E. (2002). Predicting cognitive impairment in high-functioning community-dwelling older persons: MacArthur studies of successful aging. *Journal of the American Geriatrics Society, 50,* 1051–1060.

Choi, J., & Silverman, I. (2003). Processes underlying sex differences in route-learning strategies in children and adolescents. *Personality and Individual Differences, 34,* 1153–1166.

Choi, S., Disilvio, B., Fernstrom, M. H., & Fernstrom, J. D. (2009). Meal ingestion, amino acids, and brain neurotransmitters: Effects of dietary protein source on serotonin and catecholamine synthesis rates. *Physiological Behavior, 98,* 156–162. Epub 2009 May 18.

Chomsky, N. (1965). *Aspects of the theory of syntax.* Cambridge, MA: MIT Press.

Chomsky, N. (1986). *Knowledge of language: Its nature, origin, and use.* New York: Praeger.

Chouinard, G. (2004). Issues in the clinical use of benzodiazepines: Potency, withdrawal, and rebound. *Journal of Clinical Psychiatry, 65*(Suppl. 5), 7–21.

Choy, Y., Fyer, A. J., & Lipsitz, J. D. (2007). Treatment of specific phobia in adults. *Clinical Psychology Review, 27,* 266–286.

Christakis, D. A., & Garrison, M. M. (2009). Preschool-aged children's television viewing in child care settings. *Pediatrics, 124,* 1627–1632.

Christakis, N. H., & Fowler, J. H. (2007). The spread of obesity in a large social network over 32 years. *New England Journal of Medicine, 357,* 370–379.

Christensen, A., Atkins, D. C., Baucom, B., & Yi, J. (2010). Marital status and satisfaction five years following a randomized clinical trial comparing traditional versus integrative behavioral couple therapy. *Journal of Consulting and Clinical Psychology, 78,* 225–235.

Christensen, H. C., Schüz, J., Kosteljanetz, M., Poulsen, H. S., et al. (2005). Cellular telephones and risk for brain tumors: A population-based, incident case-control study. *Neurology, 64,* 1189–1195.

Christensen, K. A., Stephens, M. A. P., & Townsend, A. L. (1998). Mastery in women's multiple roles and well-being: Adult daughters providing care to impaired parents. *Health Psychology, 17,* 163–171.

Christian, M. S., Bradley, J. C., Wallace, J. C., & Burke, M. J. (2009). Workplace safety: A meta-analysis of the roles of person and situation factors. *Journal of Applied Psychology, 94,* 1103–1127.

Christie, I. C., & Friedman, B. H. (2004). Autonomic specificity of discrete emotion and dimensions of affective space: A multivariate approach. *International Journal of Psychophysiology, 51,* 143–153.

Christopher, K. (2003). Autistic boy killed during exorcism. *Skeptical Inquirer, 27,* 11.

Chu, J. (1994). Active learning in epidemiology and biostatistics. *Teaching and Learning in Medicine, 6,* 191–193.

Chua, H. F., Boland, J. E., & Nisbett, R. E. (2005). Cultural variation in eye movements during scene perception. *Proceedings of the National Academy of Sciences, 102,* 12629–12633.

Chugani, H. T., & Phelps, M. E. (1986). Maturational changes in cerebral function in infants determined by 18FDG positron emission tomography. *Science, 231,* 840–843.

Chumakov, I., Blumenfeld, M., Guerassimenko, O., Cavarec, L., et al. (2002). Genetic and physiological data implicating the new human gene G72 and the gene for D-amino acid oxidase in schizophrenia. *Proceedings of the National Academy of Sciences, 99,* 13675–13680.

Chung, G. H., Flook, L., & Fuligni, A. J. (2009). Daily family conflict and emotional distress among adolescents from Latin American, Asian, and European backgrounds. *Developmental Psychology, 45,* 1406–1415.

Chung-Yan, G. A. (2010). The nonlinear effects of job complexity and autonomy on job satisfaction, turnover, and psychological well-being. *Journal of Occupational Health Psychology, 15,* 237–251.

Church, A. T. (2001). Personality measurement in cross-cultural perspective. *Journal of Personality, 69,* 979–1006.

Churchland, P. M. (1989). *A neurocomputational perspective: The nature of mind and the structure of science.* Cambridge, MA: MIT Press.

Cialdini, R. (2007). *Influence: Sciences and practice* (5th ed.). New York: HarperCollins.

Cialdini, R. B. (1995). Principles and techniques of social influence. In A. Tesser (Ed.), *Advanced social psychology* (pp. 257–282). New York: McGraw-Hill.

Cialdini, R. B. (2001). *Influence: Science and practice* (4th ed.). Boston: Allyn & Bacon.

Cialdini, R. B., & Goldstein, N. J. (2004). Social influence: Compliance and conformity. *Annual Review of Psychology, 55,* 591–621.

Cialdini, R. B., Wosinska, W. B., Barrett, D. W., Butner, J., & Gornik-Durose, M. (2001). The differential impact of two social influence principles on individualists and collectivists in Poland and the United States. In W. Wosinska, R. B. Cialdini, D. W. Barrett, & J. Reykowski (Eds.), *The practice of social influence in multiple cultures: Applied social research* (pp. 33–50). Mahwah, NJ: Erlbaum.

Ciarrochi, J., & Heaven, P. C. (2008). Learned social hopelessness: The role of explanatory style in predicting social support during adolescence. *Journal of Child Psychology and Psychiatry, 49,* 1279–1286.

Ciccocioppo, R., Martin-Fardon, R., & Weiss, F. (2004). Stimuli associated with a single cocaine experience elicit long-lasting cocaine-seeking. *Nature Neuroscience, 7,* 495–496.

Ciccocioppo, R., Sanna, P. P., & Weiss, F. (2001). Cocaine-predictive stimulus induces drug-seeking behavior and neural activation in limbic brain regions after multiple months of abstinence: Reversal by D1 antagonists. *Proceedings of the National Academy of Sciences, 98,* 1976–1981.

Cicogna, P. C., Occhioneroa, M., Natalea, V., & Espositoa, M. J. (2006). Bizarreness of size and shape in dream images. *Consciousness and Cognition, 16,* 381–390.

Cilia, R., Siri, C., Marotta, G., Isaias, I. U., et al. (2008). Functional abnormalities underlying pathological gambling in Parkinson disease. *Archives of Neurology, 65,* 1604–1611.

Cimbora, D. M., & McIntosh, D. N. (2003). Emotional responses to antisocial acts in adolescent males with conduct disorder: A link to affective morality. *Journal of Clinical Child and Adolescent Psychology, 32,* 296–301.

Ciocca, V. (2008). The auditory organization of complex sounds. *Frontiers in Bioscience, 13,* 148–169.

Cisler, J. M., & Koster, E. H. W. (2010). Mechanisms of attentional biases toward threat in anxiety disorders: An integrative review. *Clinical Psychology Review, 30,* 203–216.

Citrome, L., Jaffe, A., Levine, J., & Lindenmayer, J. (2005). Dosing of quetiapine in schizophrenia: How clinical practice differs from registration studies. *Journal of Clinical Psychiatry, 66,* 1512–1516.

Clancy, S. A. (2005). *Abducted: How people come to believe they were kidnaped by aliens.* Cambridge, MA: Harvard University Press.

Clancy, S. A., Schacter, D. L., McNally, R. J., & Pittman, R. K. (2000). False recognition in women reporting recovered memories of sexual abuse. *Psychological Science, 11,* 26–31.

Clark, D. C., & Fawcett, J. (1992). Review of empirical risk factors for evaluation of the suicidal patient. In B. Bongar (Ed.), *Suicide: Guidelines for assessment, management, and treatment* (pp. 16–48). New York: Oxford University Press.

Clark, D. M., Ehlers, A., McManus, F., Hackmann, A., et al. (2003). Cognitive therapy versus fluoxetine in generalized social phobia: A randomized placebo-controlled trial. *Journal of Consulting and Clinical Psychology, 71,* 1058–1067.

Clark, E. V. (1993). *The lexicon in acquisition.* Cambridge: Cambridge University Press.

Clark, F., Azen, S. P., Carlson, M., Mandel, D., et al. (2001). Embedding health-promoting changes into the daily lives of independent-living older adults: Long-term follow-up of occupational therapy intervention. *Journal of Gerontology: Psychological Sciences, 56B,* 60.

Clark, L. (2010). Decision-making during gambling: An integration of cognitive and psychobiological approaches. *Philosophical Transactions of the Royal Society, London, Series B: Biological Sciences, 365,* 319–330.

Clark, L. A. (2006). The role of moral judgment in personality disorder diagnosis. *Journal of Personality Disorders, 20,* 184–185.

Clark, L. A., & Watson, D. (2008). Temperament: An organizing paradigm for trait psychology In O. P. John, R. W. Robins, & L. A. Pervin (Eds.), *Handbook of personality: Theory and research* (3rd ed., pp. 265–286). New York: Guilford Press.

Clark, M. S., & Lemay, E. A., Jr. (2010). Close relationships. In S. T. Fiske, D. T. Gilbert, & G. Lindzey (Eds.), *Handbook of social psychology* (5th ed., Vol. 2, pp. 898–940). Hoboken, NJ: Wiley.

Clarke, L., Ungerer, J., Chahoud, K., Johnson, S., & Stiefel, I. (2002). Attention deficit hyperactivity disorder is associated with attachment insecurity. *Clinical Child Psychology and Psychiatry, 7,* 179–198.

Clarke, S. (2006). The relationship between safety climate and safety performance: A meta-analytic review. *Journal of Occupational Health Psychology, 11,* 315–327.

Clarke-Stewart, A., & Allhusen, V. (2005). *What we know about childcare.* Cambridge, MA: Harvard University Press.

Clarke-Stewart, A., & Brentano, C. (2006). *Divorce: Causes and consequences.* New Haven, CT: Yale University Press.

Clarke-Stewart, K. A. (1989). Infant day care: Maligned or malignant? *American Psychologist, 44,* 266–273.

Clarkin, J. F. (2006). Conceptualization and treatment of personality disorders. *Psychotherapy Research, 16,* 1–11.

Clausen, J., Sersen, E., & Lidsky, A. (1974). Variability of sleep measures in normal subjects. *Psychophysiology, 11,* 509–516.

Clay, R. (1996, December). Some elders thrive on working into later life. *APA Monitor,* p. 35.

Clay, R. A. (2000). Often, the bells and whistles backfire. *Monitor on Psychology, 31,* 64–65.

Cleland, V., Crawford, D., Baur, L. A., Humel, C., et al. (2008). A prospective examination of children's time spent outdoors, objectively measured physical activity and overweight. *International Journal of Obesity, 32,* 1685–1693.

Clendenen, V. I., Herman, C. P., & Polivy, J. (1995). Social facilitation of eating among friends and strangers. *Appetite, 23,* 1–13.

Cleveland, E. S., & Reese, E. (2008). Children remember early childhood: Long-term recall across the offset of childhood amnesia. *Applied Cognitive Psychology, 22,* 127–142. doi:10.1002/acp.1359

Clifton, R. K. (1992). The development of spatial hearing in human infants. In L. A. Werner & E. W. Rubel (Eds.), *Developmental psychoacoustics* (pp. 135–157). Washington, DC: American Psychological Association.

Clifton, R. K., Rochat, P., Litovsky, R., & Perris, E. (1991). Object representation guides infants' reaching in the dark. *Journal of Experimental Psychology: Human Perception and Performance, 17,* 323–329.

Cloutier, J., & Vilhuber, L. (2008). Procedural justice criteria in salary determination. *Journal of Managerial Psychology, 23,* 713–740.

Cobos, P., Sánchez, M., Pérez, N., & Vila, J. (2004). Effects of spinal cord injuries on the subjective component of emotions. *Cognition and Emotion, 18,* 281–287.

Coccaro, E. F. (1989). Central serotonin and impulsive aggression. *British Journal of Psychiatry, 155,* 52–62.

Coelho, C. M., & Purkis, H. (2009). The origins of specific phobias: Influential theories and current perspectives. *Review of General Psychology, 13,* 335–348.

Coelho, J. S., Jansen, A., Roefs, A., & Nederkoorn, C. (2009). Eating behavior in response to food-cue exposure: Examining the cue-reactivity and counteractive-control models. *Psychology of Addictive Behaviors, 23,* 131–139.

Cofer, L. F., Grice, J., Palmer, D., Sethre-Hofstad, L., & Zimmermann, K. (1992, June). *Evidence for developmental continuity of individual differences in morningness-eveningness.* Paper presented at the annual meeting of the American Psychological Society, San Diego, CA.

Cohen, A. (2009). Many forms of culture. *American Psychologist, 64,* 194–204.

Cohen, C. E. (1981). Person categories and social perception: Testing some boundaries of the processing effects of prior knowledge. *Journal of Personality and Social Psychology, 40,* 441–452.

Cohen, D., & Nisbett, R. (1997). Field experiments examining the culture of honor: The role of institutions in perpetuating norms about violence. *Personality and Social Psychology Bulletin, 23,* 1188–1199.

Cohen, D., Nisbett, R. E., Bowdle, B. F., & Schwarz, N. (1996). Insult, aggression, and the southern culture of honor: An "experimental ethnography." *Journal of Personality and Social Psychology, 70,* 945–960.

Cohen, D. A., Farley, T. A., Taylor, S. N., Martin, D. H., & Schuster, M. A. (2002). When and where do youths have sex? The potential role of adult supervision. *Pediatrics, 110,* e66.

Cohen, F., Kemeny, M. E., Zegans, L. S., Johnson, P., et al. (2007). Immune function declines with unemployment and recovers after stressor termination. *Psychosomatic Medicine, 69,* 225–234.

Cohen, G. L., & Prinstein, M. J. (2006). Peer contagion of aggression and health risk behavior among adolescent males: An experimental investigation of effects on public conduct and private attitudes. *Child Development, 77,* 967–983.

Cohen, G. L., & Steele, C. M. (2002). A barrier of mistrust: How negative stereotypes affect cross-race mentoring. In J. Aronson (Ed.), *Improving academic achievement: Impact of psychological factors on education* (pp. 303–327). San Diego, CA: Academic Press.

Cohen, N. J., & Corkin, S. (1981). The amnesic patient H. M.: Learning and retention of a cognitive skill. *Neuroscience Abstracts, 7,* 235.

Cohen, N. J., & Squire, L. R. (1980). Preserved learning and retention of pattern analyzing skills in amnesia: Dissociation of knowing how and knowing that. *Science, 210,* 207–210.

Cohen, P. (2008). Child development and personality disorder. *Psychiatric Clinics of North America, 31,* 477–493.

Cohen, P., Kasen, S., Chen, H., Hartmark, C., & Gordon, K. (2003). Variations in patterns of developmental transitions in the emerging adulthood period. *Developmental Psychology, 39,* 657–669.

Cohen, P. J. (2009a). Medical marijuana: The conflict between scientific evidence and political ideology (pt. 1). *Journal of Pain and Palliative Care Pharmacotherapeutics, 23,* 4–25.

Cohen, P. J. (2009b). Medical marijuana: The conflict between scientific evidence and political ideology (pt. 2). *Journal of Pain and Palliative Care Pharmacotherapeutics, 23,* 120–140.

Cohen, S., Doyle, W. J., Alper, C. M., Janicki-Deverts, D., & Turner, R. B. (2009). Sleep habits and susceptibility to the common cold. *Archives of Internal Medicine, 169,* 62–67.

Cohen, S., Doyle, W. J., Skoner, D. P., Gwaltney, J. M., Jr., & Newsom, J. T. (1995). State and trait negative affect as predictors of objective and subjective symptoms of respiratory viral infections. *Journal of Personality and Social Psychology, 68,* 159–169.

Cohen, S., Doyle, W. J., Turner, R. B., Alper, C. M., & Skoner, D. P. (2003a). Emotional style and susceptibility to the common cold. *Psychosomatic Medicine, 65,* 652–657.

Cohen, S., Doyle, W. J., Turner, R. B., Alper, C. M., & Skoner, D. P. (2003b). Sociability and susceptibility to the common cold. *Psychological Science, 14,* 389–395.

Cohen, S., & Herbert, T. B. (1996). Health psychology: Psychological factors and physical disease from the perspective of human psychoneuroimmunology. *Annual Review of Psychology, 47,* 113–142.

Cohen, S., & Pressman, S. D. (2006). Positive affect and health. *Current Directions in Psychological Science, 15,* 122–125.

Cohen-Bendahan, C. C. C., Buitelaar, J. K., van Goozen, S. H. M., Orlebeke, J. F., & Cohen-Kettenis, P. T. (2005). Is there an effect of prenatal testosterone on aggression and other behavioral traits? A study comparing same-sex and opposite-sex twin girls. *Hormones and Behavior, 47,* 230–237.

Cohen Kadosh, R., Henik, A., Catena, A., Walsh, V., & Fuentes, L. J. (2009). Induced cross-modal synaesthetic experience without abnormal neuronal connections. *Psychological Science, 20,* 258–265.

Cohn, M. A., Fredrickson, B. L., Brown, S. L., Mikels, J. A., & Conway, A. M. (2009). Happiness unpacked: Positive emotions increase life satisfaction by building resilience. *Emotion, 9,* 361–368.

Cohrs, J. C., & Ibler, S. (2009). Authoritarianism, threat, and prejudice: An analysis of mediation and moderation. *Basic and Applied Social Psychology, 31,* 81–94.

Coid, J. & Ullrich, S. (2010). Antisocial personality disorder is on a continuum with psychopathy. *Comprehensive Psychiatry, 51,* 426–433.

Colak, A., Soy, O., Uzun, H., Aslan, O., et al. (2003). Neuroprotective effects of GYKI 52466 on experimental spinal cord injury in rats. *Journal of Neurosurgery, 98,* 275–281.

Colcombe, S., & Kramer, A. F. (2003). Fitness effects on the cognitive function of older adults: A meta-analytic study. *Psychological Science, 14,* 125–130.

Coldwell, C. M., & Bender, W. S. (2007). The effectiveness of assertive community treatment for homeless populations with severe mental illness: A meta-analysis. *American Journal of Psychiatry, 164,* 393–399.

Cole, K. N., Mills, P. E., Dale, P. S., & Jenkins, J. R. (1991). Effects of preschool integration for children with disabilities. *Exceptional Children, 58,* 36–45.

Cole, M. (2006). Culture and cognitive development in phylogenetic, historical, and ontogenetic perspective. In W. Damon & R. M. Lerner (Series Eds.) & D. Kuhn & R. Siegler (Vol. Eds.), *Handbook of child psychology: Vol. 2, Cognition, perception, and language* (6th ed., pp. 636–686). Hoboken, NJ: Wiley.

Cole, R. A., & Jakimik, J. (1978). Understanding speech: How words are heard. In G. Underwood (Ed.), *Strategies of information processing* (pp. 67–116). London: Academic Press.

Cole, S. W. (2009). Social regulation of human gene expression. *Current Directions in Psychological Science, 18,* 132–137.

Coleman, D. (1992). Why do I feel so tired? Too little, too late. *American Health, 11*(4), 43–46.

Collins, R. L., Elliott, M. N., Berry, S. H., Kanouse, D. E., et al. (2004). Watching sex on television predicts adolescent initiation of sexual behavior. *Pediatrics, 114,* e280–e289.

Collins, W. A., & Roisman, G. I. (2006). The influence of family and peer relationships in the development of competence during adolescence. In A. Clarke-Stewart & J. Dunn (Eds.), *Families count: Effects on child and adolescent development* (pp. 79–103). New York: Cambridge University Press.

Collins, W. A., & Steinberg, L. (2006). Adolescent development in interpersonal context. In W. Damon & R. M. Lerner (Series Eds.) & N. Eisenberg (Vol. Ed.), *Handbook of child psychology: Vol. 3, Social, emotional, and personality development* (pp. 1003–1068). Hoboken, NJ: Wiley.

Colloca, L., & Benedetti, F. (2005). Placebos and painkillers: Is mind as real as matter? *Nature Reviews Neuroscience, 6,* 545–552.

Colom, R., & Flores-Mendoza, C. E. (2007). Intelligence predicts scholastic achievement irrespective of SES factors: Evidence from Brazil. *Intelligence, 35,* 243–251.

Colom, R., Jung, R. E., & Haier, R. J. (2006). Distributed brain sites for the g-factor of intelligence. *Neuroimage, 31,* 1359–1365.

Colombo, M., D'Amato, M. R., Rodman, H. R., & Gross, C. G. (1990). Auditory association cortex lesions impair auditory short-term memory in monkeys. *Science, 247,* 336–338.

Coltrane, S., & Adams, M. (2008). *Gender and families* (2nd ed.). Lanham, MD: Rowman & Littlefield.

Colwill, R. M., & Rescorla, R. A., (1986). Associative structures in instrumental learning. In G. H. Bower (Ed.), *The psychology of learning and motivation* (Vol 20). New York: Academic Press.

Commission on Accreditation. (2009). *Guidelines and principles for accreditation of programs in professional psychology.* Washington, DC: American Psychological Association.

Committee to Review the Scientific Evidence on the Polygraph. (2003). *The polygraph and lie detection.* Washington, DC: National Academies Press.

Compagnone, N. A., & Mellon, S. H. (2000). Neurosteroids: Biosynthesis and function of these novel neuromodulators. *Frontiers of Neuroendocrinology, 21,* 1–56.

Compas, B. E., Haaga, D. A. F., Keefe, F. J., Leitenberg, H., & Williams, D. A. (1998). Sampling of empirically supported psychological treatments from health psychology: Smoking, chronic pain, cancer, and bulimia nervosa. *Journal of Consulting and Clinical Psychology, 66,* 89–112.

Compton, W. M., Conway, K. P., Stinson, F. S., Colliver, J. D., & Grant, B. F. (2005). Prevalence, correlates, and comorbidity of DSM-IV antisocial personality syndromes and alcohol and specific drug use disorders in the United States: Results from the national epidemiologic survey on alcohol and related conditions. *Journal of Clinical Psychiatry, 66,* 677–685.

Compton, W. M., Thomas, Y. F., Stinson, F. S., & Grant, B. F. (2007). Prevalence, correlates, disability, and comorbidity of DSM-IV drug abuse and dependence in the United States. *Archives of General Psychiatry, 64,* 566–576.

Comstock, G., & Scharrer, E. (2006). Media and popular culture. In W. Damon & R. M. Lerner (Series Eds.) & K. A. Renninger & I. E. Sigel (Vol. Eds.), *Handbook of child psychology: Vol. 4. Child psychology in practice* (6th ed., pp. 817–863). Hoboken, NJ: Wiley.

Condon, J. W., & Crano, W. D. (1988). Inferred evaluation and the relationship between attitude similarity and interpersonal attraction. *Journal of Personality and Social Psychology, 54,* 789–797.

Cone, E. J., Fant, R. V., Rohay, J. M., Caplan, Y. H., et al. (2004). Oxycodone involvement in drug abuse deaths: II. Evidence for toxic multiple drug-drug interactions. *Journal of Analytical Toxicology, 28,* 616–624.

Confer, J. C., Easton, J. A., Fleischman, D. S., Goetz, C. D., Lewis, D.M.G., Perilloux, C., & Buss, D. M. (2010). Evolutionary psychology: Controversies, questions, prospects, and limitations. *American Psychologist, 65,* 110–126.

Conger, R. D., Belsky, J., & Capaldi, D. M. (2009). The intergenerational transmission of parenting: Closing comments for the special section. *Developmental Psychology, 45,* 1276–1283.

Conger, R. D., Cui, M., Bryant, C. M., & Elder, G. H. (2000). Competence in early adult romantic relationships: A developmental perspective on family influences. *Journal of Personality and Social Psychology, 79,* 224–237.

Conkle, A. (2009, July/August). Prime time psychology: Paul Ekman. *APS Observer,* p. 22.

Conklin, H. M., & Iacono, W. G. (2002). Schizophrenia: A neurodevelopmental perspective. *Current Directions in Psychological Science, 11,* 33–37.

Conrad, R. (1964). Acoustic confusions in immediate memory. *British Journal of Psychology, 55,* 75–84.

Considine, R. V., Sinha, M. K., Heiman, M. L., Kriauciunas, A., et al. (1996). Serum immunoreactive-leptin concentrations in normal-weight and obese humans. *New England Journal of Medicine, 334,* 292–295.

Constantine, M. G. (2002). Predictors of satisfaction with counseling: Racial and ethnic minority clients' attitudes toward counseling and ratings of their counselors' general and multicultural competence. *Journal of Counseling Psychology, 49,* 255–263.

Constantino, J. N., & Todd, R. D. (2003). Autistic traits in the general population: A twin study. *Archives General Psychiatry, 60,* 524–530.

Constantino, M. J., Arnow, B. A., Blasey, C., & Agras, W. S. (2005). The association between patient characteristics and the therapeutic alliance in cognitive-behavioral and interpersonal therapy for bulimia nervosa. *Journal of Consulting and Clinical Psychology, 73,* 203–211.

Conte, J. M., & Gintoft, J. N. (2005). Polychronicity, big five personality dimensions, and sales performance. *Human Performance, 18,* 427–444.

Conway, B. R. (2009). Color vision, cones, and color-coding in the cortex. *Neuroscientist, 15,* 274–290.

Cook, J. A., Lehman, A. F., Drake, R., McFarlane, W. R., et al. (2005). Integration of psychiatric and vocational services: A multisite randomized, controlled trial of supported employment. *American Journal of Psychiatry, 162,* 1948–1956.

Cook, J. M., Biyanova, T., Elhai, J., Schnurr, P. P., & Coyne, J. C. (2010). What do psychotherapists really do in practice? An Internet study of over 2,000 practitioners. *Psychotherapy: Theory, Research, and Practice, 47,* 260–267.

Cook, M., & Mineka, S. (1990). Selective associations in the observational conditioning of fear in rhesus monkeys. *Journal of Experimental Psychology: Animal Behavior Processes, 16,* 372–389.

Cooley, E., Toraya, T., Wanga, M. C., & Valdeza, N. N. (2008). Maternal effects on daughters' eating pathology and body image. *Eating Behaviors, 9,* 52–61.

Cooper, A. (2004). *The inmates are running the asylum: Why high-tech products drive us crazy and how to restore the sanity* (2nd ed.). New York: Sams.

Cooper, A., Gomez, R., & Buck, E. (2008). The relationships between the BIS and BAS, anger and responses to anger. *Personality and Individual Differences, 44,* 403–413.

Cooper, H. (1979). Pygmalion grows up: A model for teacher expectation communication and performance influence. *Review of Educational Research, 49,* 389–410.

Cooper, J., Mirabile, R., & Scher, S. J. (2005). Actions and attitudes: The theory of cognitive dissonance. In T. Brock & M. Green (Eds.), *Persuasion: Psychological insights and perspectives* (2nd ed., pp. 63–79). Thousand Oaks, CA: Sage.

Cooper, M. L., Russell, M., Skinner, J. B., Frone, M. R., & Mudar, P. (1992). Stress and alcohol use: The moderating effects of gender, coping, and alcohol expectancies. *Journal of Abnormal Psychology, 101,* 139–152.

Copeland, J., & Swift, W. (2009). Cannabis use disorder: Epidemiology and management. *International Review of Psychiatry, 21,* 96–103.

Corbetta, M., Miezin, F. M., Dobmeyer, S., Shulman, G. L., & Petersen, S. E. (1991). Selective and divided attention during visual discriminations of shape, color, and speed: Functional anatomy by positron emission tomography. *Journal of Neuroscience, 11,* 2383–2402.

Corden, B., Critchley, H. D., Skuse, D., & Dolan, R. J. (2006). Fear recognition ability predicts differences in social cognitive and neural functioning in men. *Journal of Cognitive Neuroscience, 18,* 889–897.

Cordery, J. L., Mueller, W. S., & Smith, L. M. (1991). Attitudinal and behavioral effects of autonomous group working: A longitudinal field study. *Academy of Management Journal, 34,* 464–476.

Coren, S. (1999). Psychology applied to animal training. In A. M. Stec & D. A. Bernstein (Eds.), *Psychology: Fields of application* (pp. 199–216). Boston: Houghton Mifflin.

Corey, G. (2008). *Theory and practice of counseling and psychotherapy* (8th ed.). Belmont, CA: Brooks/Cole.

Cork, R. C., Kihlstrom, J. F., & Hameroff, S. R. (1992). Explicit and implicit memory dissociated by anesthetic technique. *Society for Neuroscience Abstracts, 22,* 523.

Corkin, S. (2002). What's new with the amnesic patient H. M.? *Nature Reviews Neuroscience, 3,* 153–160.

Cornblatt, B., & Erlenmeyer-Kimling, L. E. (1985). Global attentional deviance in children at risk for schizophrenia: Specificity and predictive validity. *Journal of Abnormal Psychology, 94,* 470–486.

Cornelius, J. R., Chung, T., Martin, C., Wood, D. S., & Clark, D. B. (2008). Cannabis withdrawal is common among treatment-seeking adolescents with cannabis dependence and major depression and is associated with rapid relapse to dependence. *Addiction and Behavior, 33,* 1500–1505.

Cornelius, R. R. (1996). *The science of emotion.* Upper Saddle River, NJ: Prentice Hall.

Cornelius, T. L., & Resseguie, N. (2007). Primary and secondary prevention programs for dating violence: A review of the literature. *Aggression and Violent Behavior, 12,* 364–375.

Cornelius-White, J. H. D. (2002). The phoenix of empirically supported therapy relationships: The overlooked person-centered bias. *Psychotherapy: Theory, Research, Practice, Training, 39,* 219–222.

Corno, L., Cronbach, L. J., Kupermintz, H., Lohman, D. F., et al. (2002). *Remaking the concept of aptitude: Extending the legacy of Richard E. Snow.* Hillsdale, NJ: Erlbaum.

Cornoldi, C., DeBeni, R., & Baldi, A. P. (1989). Generation and retrieval of general, specific, and autobiographic images representing concrete nouns. *Acta Psychologica, 72,* 25–39.

Corr, P. J. (2002). J. A. Gray's reinforcement sensitivity theory: Tests of the joint subsystem hypothesis of anxiety and impulsivity. *Personality and Individual Differences, 33,* 511–532.

Correll, J., Park, B., Judd, C. M., & Wittenbrink, B. (2002). The police officer's dilemma: Using ethnicity to disambiguate potentially threatening individuals. *Journal of Personality and Social Psychology, 83,* 1314–1329.

Correll, J., Park, B., Judd, C. M., Wittenbrink, B., et al. (2007). Across the thin blue line: Police officers and racial bias in the decision to shoot. *Journal of Personality and Social Psychology, 92,* 1006–1023.

Corsini, R. J., & Wedding, W. (Eds.). (2010). *Current psychotherapies* (9th ed.). Belmont, CA: Brooks/Cole.

Corwin, M. J., Lesko, S. M., Heeren, T., Vezina, R. M., et al. (2003). Secular changes in sleep position during infancy, 1995–1998. *Pediatrics, 111,* 52–60.

Coslett, H. B., & Lie, E. (2008a). Simultanagnosia: Effects of semantic category and repetition blindness. *Neuropsychologia, 46,* 1853–1863.

Coslett, H. B., & Lie, G. (2008b). Simultanagnosia: When a rose is not red. *Journal of Cognitive Neuroscience, 20,* 36–48.

Costa, P. (2001, June). *New insights on personality and leadership provided by the five-factor model.* Paper presented at annual convention of the American Psychological Society, Toronto.

Costa, P. T., Jr., & McCrae, R. (1992). *Revised NEO Personality Inventory: NEO PI and NEO Five-Factor Inventory (NEO FFI: Professional Manual).* Odessa, FL: Psychological Assessment Resources.

Costa, P., & McCrae, R. (2008). The NEO inventories. In R. P. Archer & S. R. Smith, (Eds), *Personality assessment* (pp. 213–245). New York: Routledge/Taylor & Francis.

Costermans, J., Lories, G., & Ansay, C. (1992). Confidence level and feeling of knowing in question answering: The weight of inferential processes. *Journal of Experimental Psychology: Learning, Memory, and Cognition, 18,* 142–150.

Cota, D., Marsicano, G., Lutz, B., Vicennati, V., et al. (2003). Endogenous cannabinoid system as a modulator of food intake. *International Journal of Obesity, 27,* 289–301.

Cota, D., Proulx, K., Smith, K. A. B., Kozma, S. C., et al. (2006). Hypothalamic mTOR signaling regulates food intake. *Science, 312,* 927–930.

Coté, J. K., & Pepler, C. (2002). A randomized trial of a cognitive coping intervention for acutely ill HIV-positive men. *Nursing Research, 51,* 237–244.

Cottler, L. B., & Grant, B. F. (2007). Characteristics of nosologically informative data sets that address key diagnostic issues facing the DSM-V and ICD-11 substance use disorders workgroups. In J. B. Saunders, M. A. Schuckit, P. J. Sirovatka, & Reiger, D. A. (Eds.), *Diagnostic issues in substance use disorders: Refining the research agenda for DSM-V. Advancing the research agenda for DSM-V* (pp. 285–302). Washington, DC: American Psychiatric Association.

Couturier, J. L. (2005). Efficacy of rapid-rate repetitive transcranial magnetic stimulation in the treatment of depression: A systematic review and meta-analysis. *Journal of Psychiatry and Neuroscience, 30,* 83–90.

Cowan, C. A., Atienza, J., Melton, D. A., & Eggan, K. (2005). Nuclear reprogramming of somatic cells after fusion with human embryonic stem cells. *Science, 309,* 1369–1373.

Cowan, C. P., & Cowan, P. A. (2000). *When partners become parents: The big life change for couples.* Hillsdale, NJ: Erlbaum.

Cowan, D. T., Allan, L. G., Libretto, S. E., & Griffiths, P. (2001). Opiod drugs: A comparative survey of therapeutic and "street" use. *Pain, 2,* 193–203.

Cowan, N. (1988). Evolving concepts of memory storage, selective attention, and their mutual constraints within the human information-processing system. *Psychological Bulletin, 104,* 163–191.

Cowan, N. (2008). Working memory. In N. J. Salkind (Ed.), *Encyclopedia of educational psychology* (Vol. 2, pp. 1015–1016). London: Sage.

Cowan, P. A., & Cowan, C. P. (2009). How working with couples fosters children's development: From prevention science to public policy. In M. Schulz, M. K. Pruett, P. Kerig, & R. D. Parke (Eds.), *Strengthening couple relationships for optimal child development* (pp. 211–228). Washington, DC: American Psychological Association.

Cox, J. E., Buman, M., Valenzuela, J., Joseph, N. P., et al. (2008). Depression, parenting attributes, and social support among adolescent mothers attending a teen tot program. *Journal of Pediatric and Adolescent Gynecology, 21,* 275–281. doi:10.1016/j.jpag.2008.02.002

Cox, M. J., & Paley, B. (2003). Understanding families as systems. *Current Directions in Psychological Science, 12,* 193–196.

Crabbe, J. C. (2002). Alcohol and genetics: New models. *American Journal of Medical Genetics, 114,* 969–974.

Craig, A. D. (2002). How do you feel? Interoception: The sense of the physiological condition of the body. *Nature Reviews Neuroscience, 3,* 655–666.

Craig, A. D. (2009). How do you feel—now? The anterior insula and human awareness. *National Review of Neuroscience, 10,* 59–70.

Craig, M. C., Catani, M., Deeley, Q., Latham, R., et al. (2009). Altered connections on the road to psychopathy. *Molecular Psychiatry, 14,* 946–953.

Craik, F. I. M., & Lockhart, R. S. (1972). Levels of processing: A framework for memory research. *Journal of Verbal Learning and Verbal Behavior, 11,* 671–684.

Craik, F. I. M., & Rabinowitz, J. C. (1984). Age differences in the acquisition and use of verbal information. In H. Bouma & D. G. Bouwhuis (Eds.), *Attention and performance* (Vol. 10, pp. 471–499). Hillsdale, NJ: Erlbaum.

Craik, F. I. M., & Salthouse, T. A. (2008). *The handbook of aging and cognition* (3rd ed.). New York: Psychology Press.

Cramer, P. (2007). Longitudinal study of defense mechanisms: Late childhood to late adolescence. *Journal of Personality, 75,* 1–24.

Cramer, P. (2009). The development of defense mechanisms from pre-adolescence to early adulthood: Do IQ and social class matter? A longitudinal study. *Journal of Research in Personality, 43,* 464–471.

Cramer, S. C. (2008). Repairing the human brain after stroke: I. Mechanisms of recovery. *Annals of Neurology, 63,* 272–287.

Crandall, C. S., Preisler, J. J., & Aussprung, J. (1992). Measuring life event stress in the lives of college students: The Undergraduate Stress Questionnaire (USQ). *Journal of Behavioral Medicine, 15,* 627–662.

Crano, W. D., & Prislin, R. (2006). Attitudes and persuasion. *Annual Review of Psychology, 57,* 345–374.

Crano. W. D., & Seyranian, V. (2009). How minorities prevail: The context/comparison-leniency contract model. *Journal of Social Issues, 65,* 335–363.

Craske, M. G., & Barlow, D. H. (2008). Panic disorder and agoraphobia. In D. H. Barlow (Ed.), *Clinical handbook of psychological disorders: A step-by-step treatment manual* (4th ed) (pp. 1–64). New York: Guilford Press.

Craske, M. G., DeCola, J. P., Sachs, A. D., & Pontillo, D. C. (2003). Panic control treatment for agoraphobia. *Journal of Anxiety Disorders, 17,* 321–333.

Crawford, T. N., Cohen, P., & Brooks, J. S. (2001). Dramatic-erratic personality disorder symptoms: II. Developmental pathways from early adolescence to adulthood. *Journal of Personality Disorders, 15,* 336–350.

Crawley, J. N., & Corwin, R. L. (1994). Biological actions of cholecystokinin. *Peptides, 15,* 731–755.

Creed, T. A., & Kendall, P. C. (2005). Therapist alliance-building behavior within a cognitive-behavioral treatment for anxiety in youth. *Journal of Counseling and Clinical Psychology, 73,* 498–505.

Creery, D., & Mikrogianakis, A. (2004). Sudden infant death syndrome. *Clinical Evidence, 12,* 545–555.

Crespi, B. (2008). Genomic imprinting in the development and evolution of psychotic spectrum conditions. *Biological Reviews, 83,* 441–493.

Crick, F., & Koch, C. (2003). A framework for consciousness. *Nature Neuroscience, 6,* 119–126.

Crick, N. R., Ostrov, J. M., Appleyard, K., Jansen, E. A., & Casas, J. F. (2004). Relational aggression in early childhood: "You can't come to my birthday party unless . . ." In M. Putallaz & K. L. Bierman (Eds.), *Aggression, antisocial behavior, and violence among girls: A developmental perspective.* (pp. 71–89). New York: Guilford Press.

Crisp, R. J., & Turner, R. N. (2009). Can imagined interactions produce positive perceptions? Reducing prejudice through simulated social contact. *American Psychologist, 64,* 231–240.

Critchley, E. M. (1991). Speech and the right hemisphere. *Behavioural Neurology, 4,* 143–151.

Crits-Christoph, P., Gibbons, M. B. C., Ring-Kurtz, S., Gallop, R., et al. (2008). Changes in positive quality of life over the course of psychotherapy. *Psychotherapy: Theory, Research, Practice, Training, 45,* 419–430.

Crocker, J., Brook, A. T., Niiya, Y., & Villacorta, M. (2006). The pursuit of self-esteem: Contingencies of self-worth and self-regulation. *Journal of Personality, 74,* 1749–1771.

Crocker, J., & Wolfe, T. (2001). Contingencies of self-worth. *Psychological Review, 108,* 593–623.

Croen, L. A., Grether, J. K., & Selvin, S. (2001). The epidemiology of mental retardation of unknown cause. *Pediatrics, 107,* 86.

Crombag, H. S., & Robinson, T. E. (2004). Drugs, environment, brain, and behavior. *Current Directions in Psychological Science, 13,* 107–111.

Cronbach, L. J. (1975). Five decades of public controversy over mental testing. *American Psychologist, 30,* 1–14.

Cronbach, L. J. (1990). *Essentials of psychological testing* (5th ed.). New York: HarperCollins.

Cronbach, L. J. (1996). Acceleration among the Terman males: Correlates in midlife and after. In C. P. Benbow & D. J. Lubinski (Eds.), *Intellectual talent: Psychometric and social issues* (pp. 179–191). Baltimore: Johns Hopkins University Press.

Cross, S. E., & Madson, L. (1997). Models of the self: Self-construals and gender. *Psychological Bulletin, 122,* 5–37.

Cross, S. E., & Markus, H. R. (1999). The cultural constitution of personality. In L. A. Pervin & O. P. John (Eds.), *Handbook of personality research* (2nd ed., pp. 378–398). New York: Guilford Press.

Cross-National Collaborative Group. (2002). The changing rate of major depression: Cross-national comparisons. *Journal of the American Medical Association, 268,* 3098–3105.

Crouch, P. J., Hung, L. W., Adlard, P. A., Cortes, M., et al. (2009). Increasing Cu bioavailability inhibits A-beta oligomers and tau phosphorylation. *Proceedings of the National Academy of Sciences, 106,* 381–386. Epub 2009 Jan 2002.

Crow, S. J., Peterson, C. B., Swanson, S. A., Raymond, N. C., et al. (2009). Increased mortality in bulimia nervosa and other eating disorders. *American Journal of Psychiatry, 166,* 1342–1346.

Crowther, J. H., Armey, M., Luce, K. H., Dalton, G. R., & Leahey, T. (2008). The point prevalence of bulimic disorders from 1990 to 2004. *International Journal of Eating Disorders, 41,* 491–497.

Crowther, J. H., Sanftner, J., Bonifazi, D. Z., & Shepherd, K. L. (2001). The role of daily hassles in binge eating. *International Journal of Eating Disorders, 29,* 449–454.

Crozier, J. C., Dodge, K. A., Fontaine, R. G., Lansford, J. E., et al. (2008). Social information processing and cardiac predictors of adolescent antisocial behavior. *Journal of Abnormal Psychology, 117,* 253–267.

Cruickshank, C. C., & Dyer, K. R. (2009). A review of the clinical pharmacology of methamphetamine. *Addiction, 104,* 1085–1099.

Cruz, A., & Green, B. G. (2000). Thermal stimulation of taste. *Nature, 403,* 889–892.

Csernansky, J. G., Schindler, M. K., Splinter, N. R., Wang, L., et al. (2004). Abnormalities of thalamic volume and shape in schizophrenia. *American Journal of Psychiatry, 161,* 896–902.

Cuijpers, P., Li, J., Hofmann, S. G., & Andersson, G. (2010). Self-reported versus clinician-rated symptoms of depression as outcome measures in psychotherapy research on depression: A meta-analysis. *Clinical Psychology Review, 30,* 768–778.

Cuijpers, P., van Straten, A., Smit, F., Mihalopoulos, C., & Beekman, A. (2008). Preventing the onset of depressive disorders: A meta-analytic review of psychological interventions. *American Journal of Psychiatry, 165,* 1272–1280.

Culbertson, F. M. (1997). Depression and gender. An international review. *American Psychologist, 52,* 25–31.

Cullen, M. J., Hardison, C. M., & Sackett, P. R. (2004). Using SAT–grade and ability–job performance relationships to test predictions derived from stereotype threat theory. *Journal of Applied Psychology, 89,* 220–230.

Cullen, M. J., Waters, S. D., & Sackett, P. R. (2006). Testing stereotype threat theory predictions for math-identified and non-math-identified students by gender. *Human Performance, 19,* 421–440.

Cummings, J. L. (2003). Toward a molecular neuropsychiatry of neurodegenerative diseases. *Annals of Neurology, 54,* 147–154.

Cummings, J. L. (2004). Alzheimer's disease. *New England Journal of Medicine, 351,* 56–67.

Cuperman, R., & Ickes, W. (2009). Big Five predictors of behavior and perceptions in initial dyadic interactions: Personality similarity helps extraverts and introverts but hurts "disagreeables." *Journal of Personality and Social Psychology, 97,* 667–684.

Curioni, C. C., & Lourenço, P. M. (2005). Long-term weight loss after diet and exercise: A systematic review. *International Journal of Obesity, 29,* 1168–1174.

Curran, H. V., & Monaghan, L. (2001). In and out of the K-hole: A comparison of the acute and residual effects of ketamine in frequent and infrequent ketamine users. *Addiction, 96,* 749–760.

Currin, L., Schmidt, U., Treasure, J., & Jick, H. (2005). Time trends in eating disorder incidence. *British Journal of Psychiatry, 186,* 132–135.

Curry, D. T., Eisenstein, R. D., & Walsh, J. K. (2006). Pharmacologic management of insomnia: Past, present, and future. *Psychiatric Clinics of North America, 29,* 871–893.

Curtis, T., Miller, B. C., & Berry, E. H. (2000). Changes in reports and incidence of child abuse following natural disasters. *Child Abuse and Neglect, 24,* 1151–1162.

Cusack, K., & Spates, C. R. (1999). The cognitive dismantling of eye movement desensitization and reprocessing (EMDR) treatment of posttraumatic stress disorder (PTSD). *Journal of Anxiety Disorders, 13,* 87–99.

Cutrona, C. E., Russell, D. W., Brown, P. A., Clark, L. A., et al. (2005). Neighborhood context, personality, and stressful life events as predictors of depression among African American women. *Journal of Abnormal Psychology, 114,* 3–15.

Cvetek, R. (2008). EMDR treatment of distressful experiences that fail to meet the criteria for PTSD. *Journal of EMDR Practice and Research, 2,* 2–14.

Czapinski, P., Blaszczyk, B., & Czuczwar, S. J. (2005). Mechanisms of action of antiepileptic drugs. *Current Topics in Medical Chemistry, 5,* 3–14.

Czeisler, C. A., Duffy, J. F., Shanahan, T. L., Brown, E. N., et al. (1999). Stability, precision, and near-24-hour period of the human circadian pacemaker. *Science, 284,* 2177–2181.

Czeisler, C. A., Walsh, J. K., Roth, T., Hughes, R. J., et al. (2005). Modafinil for excessive sleepiness associated with shift-work sleep disorder. *New England Journal of Medicine, 353,* 476–486.

Daban, C., Martínez-Arán, A., Torrent, C., Sánchez-Moreno, J., et al. (2006). Cognitive functioning in bipolar patients receiving lamotrigine: Preliminary results. *Journal of Clinical Psychopharmacology, 26,* 178–181.

Dabbs, J. M., Jr.; Riad, J. K.; & Chance, S. E. (2001). Testosterone and ruthless homicide. *Personality and Individual Differences, 31,* 599–603.

Daglish, M. R., & Nutt, D. J. (2003). Brain imaging studies in human addicts. *European Neuropsychopharmacology, 13,* 453–458.

Dakwar, E., & Levin, F. R. (2009). The emerging role of meditation in addressing psychiatric illness, with a focus on substance use disorders. *Harvard Review of Psychiatry, 17,* 254–267.

Dalal, R. S., Lam, H., Weiss, H. M., Welch, E. R., & Hulin, C. L. (2009). A within-person approach to work behavior and performance: Concurrent and lagged citizenship-counterproductity associations and dynamic relationships with affect and overall job performance. *Academy of Management Journal, 52,* 1051–1066.

Daley, K. C. (2004). Update on sudden infant death syndrome. *Current Opinion in Pediatrics, 16,* 227–232.

Dalgleish, T., Hauer, B., & Kuyken, W. (2008). The mental regulation of autobiographical recollection in the aftermath of trauma. *Current Directions in Psychological Science, 17,* 259–263.

Dallman, M. F., Pecoraro, N., Akana, S. F., La Fleur, S. E., et al. (2003). Chronic stress and obesity: A new view of "comfort food." *Proceedings of the National Academy of Sciences, 100,* 11696–11701.

Dalman, C., & Allebeck, P. (2002). Parental age and schizophrenia: Further support for an association. *American Journal of Psychiatry, 159,* 1591–1592.

Dalton, D. R., & Mesch, D. J. (1991). On the extent and reduction of avoidable absenteeism: An assessment of absence policy provisions. *Journal of Applied Psychology, 76,* 810–817.

Damasio, A. R. (1994). *Descartes' error: Emotion, reason, and the human brain.* New York: Putnam.

Damasio, A. R., Grabowski, T. J., Bechara, A., Damasio, H., et al. (2000). Subcortical and cortical brain activity during the feeling of self-generated emotions. *Nature Neuroscience, 3,* 1049–1056.

D'Amico, A., Pennazza, G., Santonico, M., Martinelli, E., et al. (2010). An investigation on electronic nose diagnosis of lung cancer. *Lung Cancer, 68,* 170–176. doi:10.1016/j.lungcan.2009.11.003

Danker, J. F., & Anderson, J. R. (2010). The ghosts of brain states past: Remembering reactivates the brain regions engaged during encoding. *Psychological Bulletin, 136,* 87–102.

Danner, D. D., Snowden, D. A., & Friesen, W. V. (2001). Positive emotions in early life and longevity findings from the nun study. *Journal of Personality and Social Psychology, 80,* 804–813.

Dansereau, F., Jr.; Graen, G.; & Haga, W. J. (1975). A vertical dyad linkage approach to leadership with formal organizations. *Organizational Behavior and Human Performance, 13,* 46–78.

Dapretto, M., Davies, M. S., Pfeifer, J. H., Scott, A. A., et al. (2006). Understanding emotions in others: Mirror neuron dysfunction in children with autism spectrum disorders. *Nature Neuroscience, 9,* 28–30.

Darchia, N., Campbell, I. G., & Feinberg, I. (2003). Rapid eye movement density is reduced in the normal elderly. *Sleep, 26,* 973–977.

Dark, V. J., & Benbow, C. P. (1993). Cognitive differences among the gifted: A review and new data. In D. K. Detterman (Ed.), *Current topics in human intelligence* (Vol. 3, pp. 85–120). Norwood, NJ: Ablex.

Darkes, J., & Goldman, M. S. (1993). Expectancy challenge and drinking reduction. *Journal of Clinical and Consulting Psychology, 61,* 344–353.

Dar-Nimrod, I., & Heine, S. J. (2006). Exposure to scientific theories affects women's math performance. *Science, 314,* 435.

Darwin, C. E. (1872). *The expression of the emotions in man and animals.* London: Murray.

Das, J. P. (2002). A better look at intelligence. *Current Directions in Psychological Science, 11,* 28–33.

Dasgupta, A. M., Juza, D. M., White, G. M., & Maloney, J. F. (1995). Memory and hypnosis: A comparative analysis of guided memory, cognitive interview, and hypnotic hypermnesia. *Imagination, Cognition, and Personality, 14,* 117–130.

Das-Munshi, J., Goldberg, D., Bebbington, P. E., Bhugra, D. K., et al. (2008). Public health significance of mixed anxiety and depression: Beyond current classification. *British Journal of Psychiatry, 192,* 171–177.

Daus, C. S., Sanders, D. N., & Campbell, D. P. (1998). Consequences of alternative work schedules. In C. L. Cooper & I. T. Robertson (Eds.), *International review of industrial and organizational psychology, 1998* (pp. 185–223). Chichester, England: Wiley.

Dauvilliers, Y., Comte, F., Bayard, S., Carlander, B., et al. (2010). A brain PET study in patients with narcolepsy-cataplexy. *Journal of Neurology, Neurosurgery, and Psychiatry, 81,* 344–348. doi:10.1136/jnnp.2009.175786

Dauwels, J., Vialatte, F., Musha, T., & Cichocki, A. (2010). A comparative study of synchrony measures for the early diagnosis of Alzheimer's disease based on EEG. *NeuroImage, 49,* 668–693.

Davachi, L., Mitchell, J. P., & Wagner, A. D. (2003). Multiple routes to memory: Distinct medial temporal lobe processes build item and source memories. *Proceedings of the National Academy of Sciences, 100,* 2157–2162.

Davidson, J. M., Camargo, C. A., & Smith, E. R. (1979). Effects of androgen on sexual behavior in hypogonadal men. *Journal of Clinical Endocrinological Metabolism, 48,* 955–958.

Davidson, J. R., Foa, E. B., Huppert, J. D., Keefe, F. J., et al. (2004). Fluoxetine, comprehensive cognitive behavioral therapy, and placebo in generalized social phobia. *Archives of General Psychiatry, 61,* 1005–1013.

Davidson, P. R., & Parker, K. C. H. (2001). Eye movement desensitization and reprocessing (EMDR): A meta-analysis. *Journal of Consulting and Clinical Psychology, 69,* 305–316.

Davidson, R. J. (2000). Affective style, psychopathology, and resilience: Brain mechanisms and plasticity. *American Psychologist, 55,* 1196–1214.

Davidson, R. J., Kabat-Zinn, J., Schumacher, J., Rosenkranz, M., et al. (2003). Alterations in brain and immune function produced by mindfulness meditation. *Psychosomatic Medicine, 65,* 564–570.

Davidson, R. J., Pizzagalli, D., Nitschke, J. B., & Putnam, K. (2002). Depression: Perspectives from affective neuroscience. *Annual Review of Psychology, 53,* 545–574.

Davidson, R. J., Shackman, A. J., & Maxwell, J. S. (2004). Asymmetries in face and brain related to emotion. *Trends in Cognitive Science, 8,* 389–391.

Davies, C. (1999, April 21). Junior doctor is cleared in baby overdose death. *London Daily Telegraph,* p. 2.

Davis, C., & Kapstein, S. (2006). Anorexia nervosa with excessive exercise: A phenotype with close links to obsessive-compulsive disorder. *Psychiatry Research, 142,* 209–217.

Davis, C., III; Aronson, J.; & Salinas, M. (2006). Shades of threat: Racial identity as a moderator of stereotype threat. *Journal of Black Psychology, 32,* 399–417.

Davis, J. A., & Smith, T. W. (1990). *General social surveys, 1972–1990: Cumulative codebook.* Chicago: National Opinion Research Center.

Davis, J. D., Gallagher, R. J., Ladove, R. F., & Turansky, A. J. (1969). Inhibition of food intake by a humoral factor. *Journal of Comparative and Physiological Psychology, 67,* 407–414.

Davis, J. L., & Rusbult, C. (2001). Attitude alignment in close relationships. *Journal of Personality and Social Psychology, 81,* 65–84.

Davis, M., Myers, K. M., Ressler, K. J., & Rothbaum, B. O. (2005). Facilitation of extinction of conditioned fear by D-cycloserine. *Current Directions in Psychological Science, 14,* 214–219.

Davis, M., Ressler, K., Rothbaum, B. O., & Richardson, R. (2006). Effects of D-cycloserine on extinction: Translation from preclinical to clinical work. *Biological Psychiatry, 60,* 369–375.

Davis, M. H. (1994). *Empathy: A social psychological approach.* Madison, WI: Brown & Benchmark.

Davis, M. H., Johnsrude, I. S., Hervais-Adelman, A., Taylor, K., & McGettigan, C. (2005). Lexical information drives perceptual learning of distorted speech: Evidence from the comprehension of noise-vocoded sentences. *Journal of Experimental Psychology: General, 134,* 222–241.

Davis, M. H., Luce, C., & Kraus, S. J. (1994). The heritability of characteristics associated with dispositional empathy. *Journal of Personality, 60,* 369–391.

Davis, N., Gross, J., & Hayne, H. (2008). Defining the boundary of childhood amnesia. *Memory, 16,* 465–474. doi:10.1080/09658210802077082

Davis, O. S. P., Haworth, C. M. A., & Plomin, R. (2009). Dramatic increase in heritability of cognitive development from early to middle childhood: An 8-year longitudinal study of 8,700 pairs of twins. *Psychological Science, 20,* 1301–1308.

Davis, R. A., & Moore, C. C. (1935). Methods of measuring retention. *Journal of General Psychology, 12,* 144–155.

Davis-Kean, P. E., Jager, J., & Collins, W. A. (2009). The self in action: An emerging link between self-beliefs and behaviors in middle childhood. *Child Development Perspectives, 3,* 184–188.

Dawe, L. A., Platt, J. R., & Welsh, E. (1998). Spectral-motion aftereffects and the tritone paradox among Canadian subjects. *Perception and Psychophysics, 60,* 209–220.

Dawes, R. M. (1994). *House of cards: Psychology and psychotherapy built on myth.* New York: Free Press.

Dawes, R. M. (1998). Behavioral decision making and judgment. In D. T. Gilbert, S. T. Fiske, & G. Lindzey (Eds.), *Handbook of social psychology* (4th ed., Vol. 1, pp. 497–549). New York: McGraw-Hill.

Dawson-Basoa, M., & Gintzler, A. R. (1997). Involvement of spinal cord delta opiate receptors in the antinociception of gestation and its hormonal simulation. *Brain Research, 757,* 37–42.

Day, A. L., & Jreige, S. (2002). Examining Type A behavior pattern to explain the relationship between job stressors and psychosocial outcomes. *Journal of Occupational Health Psychology, 7,* 109–120.

Dayan, K., Fox, S., & Kasten, R. (2008). The preliminary employment interview as a predictor of assessment center outcomes. *International Journal of Selection and Assessment, 16,* 102–111.

Dayan, K., Kasten, R., & Fox, S. (2002). Entry-level police candidate assessment center: An efficient tool or a hammer to kill a fly? *Personnel Psychology, 55,* 827–849.

de Araujo, I. E., Rolls, E. T., Velazco, M. I., Margot, C., & Cayeux, I. (2005). Cognitive modulation of olfactory processing. *Neuron, 46,* 671–679.

Deary, I. J., & Caryl, P. G. (1993). Intelligence, EEG and evoked potentials. In P. A. Vernon (Ed.), *Biological approaches to the study of human intelligence* (pp. 259–315). Norwood, NJ: Ablex.

Deary, I. J., & Der, G. (2005a). Reaction time, age, and cognitive ability: Longitudinal findings from age 16 to 63 years in representative population samples. *Aging, Neuropsychology, and Cognition, 12,* 187–215.

Deary, I. J., & Der, G. (2005b). Reaction time explains IQ's association with death. *Psychological Science, 16,* 64–69.

Deary, I. J., Strand, S., Smith, P., & Fernandes, C. (2007). Intelligence and educational achievement. *Intelligence, 35,* 13–21.

Deary, I. J., Whalley, L. J., Lemmon, H., Crawford, J. R., & Starr, J. M. (2000). The stability of individual differences in ability from childhood to old age: Follow up of the 1932 Scottish mental survey. *Intelligence, 28,* 49–55.

Deary, I. J., Whiteman, M. C., Starr, J. M., Whalley, L. J., & Fox., H. C. (2004). The impact of childhood intelligence on later life: Following up the Scottish mental surveys of 1932 and 1947. *Journal of Personality and Social Psychology, 86,* 130–147.

Death Penalty Information Center. (2007). *Innocence and the death penalty.* Washington, DC: Author. Retrieved from http://www.deathpenaltyinfo.org

Death Penalty Information Center. (2010). *Innocence and the death penalty.* Washington, DC: Author. Retrieved from http://www.deathpenaltyinfo.org

Deaux, K., & LaFrance, M. (1998). Gender. In D. T. Gilbert, S. T. Fiske, & G. Lindzey (Eds.), *Handbook of social psychology* (4th ed., Vol. 1, pp. 778–828). New York: McGraw-Hill.

De Beaumont, L., Theoret, H., Messier, J., Leclerc, S., Tremblay, S., Ellemberg, D., Lassonde, M. (2009). Brain function decline in healthy retired athletes who sustained their last sports concussion in early adulthood. *Brain.* DOI: 10.1093/brain/awn347.

DeBell, C., & Jones, R. D. (1997). As good as it seems? A review of EMDR experimental research. *Professional Psychology: Research and Practice, 28,* 153–163.

de Bruxelles, S. (2009, November 18). Sleepwalker accidentally killed wife during nightmare, prosecutors say. *(London) Times.*

Decety, J. (2011). Neuroscience of empathic responding. In S. Brown, M. Brown, & L. Penner (Eds.), *Self-interest and beyond: Toward a new understanding of human.* New York: Oxford University Press

de Charms, R., Levy, J., & Wertheimer, M. (1954). A note on attempted evaluations of psychotherapy. *Journal of Clinical Psychology, 10,* 233–235.

deCharms, R. C., Maeda, F., Glover, G. H., Ludlow, D., Pauly, J. M., Soneji, D., et al. (2005). Control over brain activation and pain learned by using real-time functional MRI. *Proceedings of the National Academy of Sciences, 102,* 18626–18631.

Deci, E. L, Koestner, R., & Ryan, R. M. (1999). The undermining effect is a reality after all—extrinsic rewards, task interest, and self-determination: Reply to Eisenberger, Pierce, and Cameron (1999) and Lepper, Henderlong, and Gingras (1999). *Psychological Bulletin, 125,* 692–700.

Deci, E. L., Koestner, R., & Ryan, R. M. (2001). A meta-analytic review of experiments examining the effects of extrinsic rewards on intrinsic motivation. *Psychological Bulletin, 125,* 627–668.

De Cremer, D., & van Dijk, E. (2008). Leader-follower effects in resource dilemmas: The roles of leadership selection and social responsibility. *Group Processes and Intergroup Relations, 11,* 355–369.

De Cremer, D., Brockner, J., Fishman, A., van Dijke, M., et al. (2010). When do procedural fairness and outcome fairness interact to influence employees' work attitudes and behaviors? The moderating effect of uncertainty. *Journal of Applied Psychology, 95,* 291–304.

De Dreu, C. K. W. (2010). Social conflict. In S. T. Fiske, D. T. Gilbert, & G. Lindzey (Eds.), *Handbook of social psychology* (5th ed., Vol. 2, pp. 883–1023). Hoboken, NJ: Wiley.

Deeb, S. S. (2005). The molecular basis of variation in human color vision. *Clinical Genetics, 67,* 369–377.

Deeb, S. S., & Kohl, S. (2003). Genetics of color vision deficiencies. *Developmental Ophthalmology, 37,* 170–187.

Deeprose, C., & Andrade, J. (2006). Is priming during anesthesia unconscious? *Consciousness and Cognition, 15,* 1–23.

Deep-Soboslay, A., Akil, M., Martin, C. E., Bigelow, L. B., et al. (2006). Reliability of psychiatric diagnosis in postmortem research. *Biological Psychiatry, 57,* 96–101.

de Freitas, S., & Griffiths, M. (2007). Online gaming as an educational tool in learning and training. *British Journal of Educational Technology, 38,* 535–537. doi:10.1111/j.1467-8535.2007.00720.x

de Gelder, B., Frissen, I., Barton, J., & Hadjikhani, N. (2003). A modulatory role for facial expressions in prosopagnosia. *Proceedings of the National Academy of Sciences, 100,* 13105–13110.

de Gelder, B., Snyder, J., Greve, D., Gerard, G., & Hadjikhani, N. (2004). Fear fosters flight: A mechanism for fear contagion when perceiving emotion expressed by a whole body. *Proceedings of the National Academy of Sciences, 101*, 16701–16706.

Degner, J., & Wentura, D. (2009). Not everybody likes the thin and despises the fat: One's weight matters in the automatic activation of weight-related social evaluations. *Social Cognition, 27*, 202–221.

Degner, J., & Wentura, D. (2010). Automatic prejudice in childhood and early adolescence. *Journal of Personality and Social Psychology, 98*, 356–374.

de Graaf, L. E., Huibers, M. J. H., Cuijpers, P., & Arntz, A. (2010). Minor and major depression in the general population: Does dysfunctional thinking play a role? *Comprehensive Psychiatry, 51*, 266–274.

de Haan, M., Mishkin, M., Baldeweg, T., & Vargha-Khadem, F. (2006). Human memory development and its dysfunction after early hippocampal injury. *Trends in Neuroscience, 29*, 374–381.

De Houwer, A. (1995). Bilingual language acquisition. In P. Fletcher & B. MacWhinney (Eds.), *The handbook of child language* (pp. 219–250). Cambridge, MA: Blackwell.

Deich, J. D., Tankoos, J., & Balsam, P. D. (1995). Systematic changes in gaping during the ontogeny of pecking in ring doves (*Streptopelia risoria*). *Developmental Psychobiology, 28*, 147–163.

de Lacoste-Utamsing, C., & Holloway, R. L. (1982). Sexual dimorphism in the human corpus callosum. *Science, 216*, 1431–1432.

Delamater, A. R. (2004). Experimental extinction in Pavlovian conditioning: Behavioural and neuroscience perspectives. *Quarterly Journal of Experimental Psychology, 57B*, 97–132.

de la Sablonnière, R., Tougas, F., & Lortie-Lussier, M. (2009). Dramatic social change in Russia and Mongolia: Connecting relative deprivation to social identity. *Journal of Cross-Cultural Psychology, 40*, 327–348.

Delbello, M. P., Kowatch, R. A., Adler, C. M., Stanford, K. E., et al. (2006). A double-blind randomized pilot study comparing quetiapine and divalproex for adolescent mania. *Journal of the American Academy of Child and Adolescent Psychiatry, 45*, 305–313.

DeLeo, J. A. (2006). Basic science of pain. *Journal of Bone and Joint, American Volume, 88*(supplement 2), 58–62.

DeLisi, L. E., Maurizio, A., Yost, M., Papparozzi, C. F., et al. (2003). A survey of New Yorkers after the Sept. 11, 2001, terrorist attacks. *American Journal of Psychiatry, 160*, 780–783.

Delmolino, L. M., & Romanczyk, R. G. (1995). Facilitated communication: A critical review. *Behavior Therapist, 18*, 27–30.

De Los Reyes, A., & Kazdin, A. E. (2006). Conceptualizing changes in behavior in intervention research: The range of possible changes model. *Psychological Review, 113*, 554–583.

de Macedo-Soares, M. B., Moreno, R. A., Rigonatti, S. P., & Lafer, B. (2005). Efficacy of electroconvulsive therapy in treatment-resistant bipolar disorder: A case series. *Journal of ECT, 21*, 31–34.

Demaray, M. K., & Malecki, C. K. (2002). Critical levels of perceived social support associated with student adjustment. *School Psychology Quarterly, 17*, 213–241.

De Maris, A. (2007). The role of relationship inequity in marital disruption. *Journal of Social and Personal Relationships, 24*, 177–195.

Dement, W. (1960). The effect of dream deprivation. *Science, 131*, 1705–1707.

Dement, W., & Kleitman, N. (1957). Cyclic variations in EEG during sleep and their relation to eye movements, body motility, and dreaming. *Electroencephalography and Clinical Neurophysiology, 9*, 673–690.

Demerouti, E., Geurts, S. A. E., Bakker, A. B., & Euwema, M. (2004). The impact of shiftwork on work-home conflict, job attitudes, and health. *Ergonomics, 47*, 987–1002.

Demo, D. H., Allen, K. R., & Fine, M. A. (Eds.). (2000). *Handbook of family diversity*. New York: Oxford University Press.

de Moor, J. S., de Moor, C. A., Basen-Engquist, K., Kudelka, A., et al. (2006). Optimism, distress, health-related quality of life, and change in cancer antigen 125 among patients with ovarian cancer undergoing chemotherapy. *Psychosomatic Medicine, 68*, 555–562.

Dempsey, J. A., Veasey, S. C., Morgan, B. J., & O'Donnell, C. P. (2010). Pathophysiology of sleep apnea. *Physiological Reviews, 90*, 47–112.

Denk, F., & Wade-Martins, R. (2009). Knock-out and transgenic mouse models of tauopathies. *Neurobiology of Aging, 30*, 1–13.

Denniston, J. C., Chang, R. C., & Miller, R. R. (2003). Massive extinction attenuates the renewal effect. *Learning and Motivation, 34*, 68–86.

Denrell, J. (2005). Why most people disapprove of me: Experience sampling in impression formation. *Psychological Review, 112*, 951–978.

Denton, G. (1980). The influence of visual pattern on perceived speed. *Perception, 9*, 393–402.

DePrince, A. P., & Freyd, J. J. (2004). Forgetting trauma stimuli. *Psychological Science, 15*, 488–492.

Depue, R. A. (2009). Neurobehavioral dimensions in personality and personality disorders. In S. J. Wood, N. B. Allen, & C. Pantelis (Eds.), *The neuropsychology of mental illness* (pp. 300–315) New York: Cambridge University Press.

Der, G., Batty, G. D., & Deary, I. J. (2009). The association between IQ in adolescence and a range of health outcomes at 40 in the 1979 U.S. National Longitudinal Study of Youth. *Intelligence, 37*, 573–580.

De Raad, B., Barelds, D. P. H., Levert, E., Ostendorf, F., et al. (2010). Only three factors of personality description are fully replicable across languages: A comparison of 14 trait taxonomies. *Journal of Personality and Social Psychology, 98*, 160–173.

de Rios, M. D. (1992). Power and hallucinogenic states of consciousness among the Moche: An ancient Peruvian society. In C. A. Ward (Ed.), *Altered states of consciousness and mental health: A cross-cultural perspective*. Newbury Park, CA: Sage.

Derogowski, J. B. (1989). Real space and represented space: Cross-cultural perspectives. *Behavior and Brain Sciences, 12*, 51–73.

DeRosse, P., Funke, B., Burdick, K. E., Lencz, T., & Ekholm, J. M. (2006). Dysbindin genotype and negative symptoms of schizophrenia. *American Journal of Psychiatry, 163*, 532–534.

Derry, C. J., Derry, S., McQuay, H. J., & Moore, R. A. (2006). Systematic review of systematic reviews of acupuncture published 1996–2005. *Clinical Medicine, 6*, 381–386.

Derryberry, D., & Tucker, D. M. (1992). Neural mechanisms of emotion. *Journal of Consulting and Clinical Psychology, 60*, 329–338.

DeRubeis, R. J., & Crits-Christoph, P. (1998). Empirically supported individual and group psychological treatments for adult mental disorders. *Journal of Consulting and Clinical Psychology, 66*, 37–52.

DeRubeis, R. J., Hollon, S. D., Amsterdam, J. D., Shelton, R. C., et al. (2005). Cognitive therapy vs. medications in the treatment of moderate to severe depression. *Archives of General Psychiatry, 62*, 409–416.

De Santi, S., Pirraglia, E., Barr, W., Babb, J., et al. (2008). Robust and conventional neuropsychological norms: Diagnosis and prediction of age-related cognitive decline. *Neuropsychology, 22*, 469–484.

De Smet, H. J., Baillieux, H., Wackenier, P., De Praeter, M., et al. (2009). Long-term cognitive deficits following posterior fossa tumor resection: A neuropsychological and functional neuroimaging follow-up study. *Neuropsychology, 23*, 694–704.

D'Esposito, M., Detre, J. A., Alsop, D. C., & Shin, R. K. (1995). The neural basis of the central executive system of working memory. *Nature, 378*, 279–281.

Detterman, D. K. (1982). Does "g" exist? *Intelligence, 6*, 99–108.

Detterman, D. K. (1987). Theoretical notions of intelligence and mental retardation. *American Journal of Mental Deficiency, 92*, 2–11.

Detterman, D. K. (1994). A system theory of intelligence. In D. K. Detterman (Ed.), *Current topics in human intelligence: Vol. 4. Theories of intelligence* (pp. 85–115). Norwood, NJ: Ablex.

Deutsch, M., & Gerard, H. B. (1955). A study of normative and informative social influences on individual judgments. *Journal of Abnormal and Social Psychology, 51*, 629–636.

Devanand, D. P., Pradhaban, G., Liu, X., Khandji, A., et al. (2007). Hippocampal and entorhinal atrophy in mild cognitive impairment: Prediction of Alzheimer's disease. *Neurology, 68*, 828–836.

Devenport, L. D. (1998). Spontaneous recovery without interference: Why remembering is adaptive. *Animal Learning and Behavior, 26*, 172–181.

Devi, G., & Quitschke, W. (1999). Alois Alzheimer, neuroscientist (1864–1915). *Alzheimer Disease and Associated Disorders, 13*, 132–137.

Devilly, G. J., Varker, T., Hansen, K., & Gist, R. (2007). An analogue study of the effects of psychological debriefing on eyewitness testimony. *Behaviour Research and Therapy, 45*, 1245–1254.

DeVries, R. (1969). Constancy of generic identity in the years three to six. *Monographs of the Society for Research in Child Development, 34* (3, Serial No. 127).

DeYoung, C. G., Hirsh, J. B., Shane, M. S., Papademetris, X., et al. (2010). Testing predictions from personality neuroscience: Brain structure and the Big Five. *Psychological Science, 21*, 820–828.

DeYoung, C. G., Quilty, L. C., & Peterson, J. B. (2007). Between facets and domains: 10 aspects of the Big Five. *Journal of Personality and Social Psychology, 93*, 880–896.

Dhillon, A. S., Tarbutton, G. L., Levin, J. L., Plotkin, G. M., et al. (2008). Pesticide/environmental exposures and Parkinson's disease in East Texas. *Journal of Agromedicine, 13*, 37–48.

Dhurandhar, N. V., Israel, B. A., Kolesar, J. M., Mayhew, G. F., et al. (2000). Increased adiposity in animals due to a human virus. *International Journal of Obesity, 24*, 989–996.

Di Leone, R. J. (2009). The influence of leptin on the dopamine system and implications for ingestive behavior. *International Journal of Obesity, 33*, S25–S29.

Di Marzo, V., Goparaju, S. K., Wang, L., Liu, J., et al. (2001). Leptin-regulated endocannabinoids are involved in maintaining food intake. *Nature, 410*, 822–825.

Di Marzo, V., & Petrocellis, L. D. (2006). Plant, synthetic, and endogenous cannabinoids in medicine. *Annual Review of Medicine, 57*, 553–574.

Di Milia, L. (2006). Shift work, sleepiness, and long-distance driving. *Transportation Research, 9*, 278–285.

di Noia, J., & Schinke, S. P. (2008). HIV risk-related attitudes, interpersonal influences, and intentions among at-risk urban early adolescent girls. *American Journal of Health Behavior, 32*, 497–507.

Diakidoy, I. N., & Spanoudis, G. (2002). Domain specificity in creativity testing: A comparison of performance on a general divergent-thinking test and a parallel, content-specific test. *Journal of Creative Behavior, 36*, 41–61.

Diamantopoulou, S., Verhulst, F. C., & van der Ende, J. (2010). Testing developmental pathways to antisocial personality problems. *Journal of Abnormal Child Psychology, 38*, 91–103.

Diamond, G. M., Lipsitz, J. D., Fajerman, Z., & Rozenblat, O. (2010). Ongoing traumatic stress response (OTSR) in Sderot, Israel. *Professional Psychology: Research and Practice, 41*, 19–25.

Diamond, L. M. (2004). Emerging perspectives on distinctions between romantic love and sexual desire. *Current Directions in Psychological Science, 13*, 116–119.

Diamond, L. M. (2008). Female bisexuality from adolescence to adulthood: Results from a 10-year longitudinal study. *Developmental Psychology, 44*, 5–14.

Diana, M., Spiga, S., & Acquas, E. (2006). Persistent and reversible morphine withdrawal–induced morphological changes in the nucleus accumbens. *Annals of the New York Academy of Sciences, 1074*, 446–457.

Dickerson, F. B., Tenhula, W. N., & Green-Paden, L. D. (2005). The token economy for schizophrenia: Review of the literature and recommendations for future research. *Schizophrenia Research, 75*, 405–416.

Dickinson, A. (2001). Causal learning: Association versus computation. *Current Directions in Psychological Science, 10*, 127–132.

Diego, M. A., Field, T., & Hernandez-Reif, M. (2005a). Prepartum, postpartum, and chronic depression effects on neonatal behavior. *Infant Behavior and Development, 28*, 155–164.

Diego, M. A., Field, T., & Hernandez-Reif, M. (2005b). Vagal activity, gastric motility, and weight gain in massaged preterm neonates. *Journal of Pediatrics, 147*, 50–55.

Diekelmann, S., & Born, J. (2010). The memory function of sleep. *Nature Reviews Neuroscience, 11*, 114–126.

Diener, E. (2000). Subjective well-being: The science of happiness and a proposal for a national index. *American Psychologist, 55*, 34–43.

Diener, E., & Biswas-Diener, R. (2002). Will money increase subjective well-being? *Social Indicators Research, 57,* 119–169.

Diener, E., & Diener, C. (1995). Most people are happy. *Psychological Science, 7,* 181–185.

Diener, E., Ng, W., Harter, J., & Arora, R. (2010). Wealth and happiness across the world: Material prosperity predicts life evaluation, whereas psychosocial prosperity predicts positive feeling. *Journal of Personality and Social Psychology, 99,* 52–61.

Diener, E., Oishi, S., & Lucas, R. E. (2009). Subjective well-being: The science of happiness and life satisfaction. In C. R. Snyder & S. J. Lopez (Eds.), *Oxford handbook of positive psychology.* Oxford: Oxford University Press.

Diener, E., & Seligman, M. E. P. (2004). Beyond money: Towards an economy of well-being. *Psychological Science in the Public Interest, 5,* 1–31.

Diener, M. L., Isabella, R. A., Behunin, M. G., & Wong, M. S. (2008). Attachment to mothers and fathers during middle childhood: Associations with child gender, grade, and competence. *Social Development, 17,* 84–101.

Dierdorff, E. C., & Ellington, K. J. (2008). It's the nature of the work: Examining behavior-based sources of work-family conflict across occupations. *Journal of Applied Psychology, 93,* 883–892.

Dierdorff, E. C., & Wilson, M. A. (2003). A meta-analysis of job analysis reliability. *Journal of Applied Psychology, 88,* 635–646.

Dijksterhuis, A., Bos, M. W., Nordgren, L. F., & van Baaren, R. B. (2006). On making the right choice: The deliberation-without-attention effect. *Science, 311,* 1005–1007.

Dijksterhuis, A., Bos, M. W., van der Leij, A., & van Baaren, R. B. (2009). Predicting soccer matches after unconscious and conscious thought as a function of expertise. *Psychological Science, 20,* 1381–1387.

Dijksterhuis, A., & Nordgren, L. F. (2006). A theory of unconscious thought. *Perspectives on Psychological Science, 1,* 95–109.

Dijksterhuis, A., Preston, J., Wegner, D. M., & Aarts, H. (2008). Effects of subliminal priming of self and God on self-attribution of authorship for events. *Journal of Experimental Social Psychology, 44,* 2–9.

Dillard, A. J., McCaul, K. D., & Klein, W. M. P. (2006). Unrealistic optimism in smokers: Implications for smoking myth endorsement and self-protective motivation. *Journal of Health Communication, 11,* 93–102.

Dillard, A. J., Midboe, A. M., & Klein, W. M. P. (2009). The dark side of optimism: Unrealistic optimism about problems with alcohol predicts subsequent negative event experiences. *Personality and Social Psychology Bulletin, 35,* 1540–1550.

Dimidjian, S., Hollon, S. D., Dobson, K. S., Schmaling, K. B., et al. (2006). Randomized trial of behavioral activation, cognitive therapy, and antidepressant medication in the acute treatment of adults with major depression. *Journal of Consulting and Clinical Psychology, 74,* 658–670.

Dinan, T. G. (2001). Novel approaches to the treatment of depression by modulating the hypothalamic-pituitary-adrenal axis. *Human Psychopharmacology: Clinical and Experimental, 16,* 89–93.

Dingus, T. A., Klauer, S. G., Neale, V. L., Petersen, A., et al. (2006). *The 100-car naturalistic driving study, phase II: Results of the 100-car field experiment.* Washington, DC: National Highway Traffic Safety Administration.

Dion, K. (2003). Prejudice, racism, and discrimination. In T. Millon & M. J. Lerner (Eds.), *Handbook of psychology: Vol. 5. Personality and social psychology* (pp. 507–536). Hoboken, NJ: Wiley.

DiPatrizio, N. V., & Simansky, K. J. (2008). Activating parabrachial cannabinoid CB-sub-1 receptors selectively stimulates feeding of palatable foods in rats. *Journal of Neuroscience, 28,* 9702–9709.

DiPietro, J. A., Novak, M. F., Costigan, K. A., Atella, L. D., & Reusing, S. P. (2006). Maternal psychological distress during pregnancy in relation to child development at age two. *Child Development, 77,* 573–587.

Dirix, C. E. H., Nijhuis, J. G., Jongsma, H. W., & Hornstra, G. (2009). Aspects of fetal learning and memory. *Child Development, 80,* 1251–1258.

Distel, M. A., Vink, J. M., Willemsen, G., Middeldorp, C. M., et al. (2008). Heritability of self-reported fear. *Behavioral Genetics, 38,* 24–33.

Dittmar, H., Halliwell, E., & Ive, S. (2006). Does Barbie make girls want to be thin? The effect of experimental exposure to images of dolls on the body image of 5- to 8-year-old girls. *Developmental Psychology, 42,* 283–292.

Dixon, M., Brunet, A., & Laurence, J.-R. (1990). Hypnotizability and automaticity: Toward a parallel distributed processing model of hypnotic responding. *Journal of Abnormal Psychology, 99,* 336–343.

Djonlagic, I., Rosenfeld, A., Shohamy, D., Myers, C., et al. (2009). Sleep enhances category learning. *Learning and Memory, 16,* 751–755.

D'Mello, R., & Dickenson, A. H. (2008). Spinal cord mechanisms of pain. *British Journal of Anaesthesia, 101,* 8–16.

Dobrovitsky, V., Pimentel, P., Duarte, A., Froestl, W., et al. (2002). CGP 44532, a GABAB receptor agonist, is hedonically neutral and reduces cocaine-induced enhancement of reward. *Neuropharmacology, 42,* 626–632.

Dobson, K. S., Hollon, S. D., Dimidjian, S., Schmaling, K. B., et al. (2008). Randomized trial of behavioral activation, cognitive therapy, and antidepressant medication in the prevention of relapse and recurrence in major depression. *Journal of Consulting and Clinical Psychology, 76,* 468–477.

Dodd, M. L., Klos, K. J., Bower, J. H., Geda, Y. E., et al. (2005). Pathological gambling caused by drugs used to treat Parkinson disease. *Archives of Neurology, 62,* 1377–1381.

Dodge, K. A., Coie, J. D., & Lynam, D. (2006). Aggression and antisocial behavior in youth. In W. Damon & R. M. Lerner (Series Eds.) & N. Eisenberg (Vol. Ed.), *Handbook of child psychology: Vol. 3. Social, emotional, and personality development* (6th ed., pp. 719–788). Hoboken, NJ: Wiley.

Dodge, K. A., Greenberg, M. T., Malone, P. S., & the Conduct Problems Prevention Research Group. (2008). Testing an idealized dynamic cascade model of the development of serious violence in adolescence. *Child Development, 79,* 1907–1927.

Dohnt, H., & Tiggemann, M. (2006). The contribution of peer and media influences to the development of body satisfaction and self-esteem in young girls: A prospective study. *Developmental Psychology, 42,* 929–936.

Dohrenwend, B. P., Turner, J. B., Turse, N. A., Adams, B. G., et al. (2006). The psychological risks of Vietnam for U.S. veterans: A revisit with new data and methods. *Science, 313,* 979–982.

Dolan, M., & Fullam, R. (2006). Memory for emotional events in violent offenders with antisocial personality disorder. *Personality and Individual Differences, 38,* 1657–1667.

Dolan, M., & Park, I. (2002). The neuropsychology of antisocial personaity disorder. *Psychological Medicine, 32,* 417–427.

Dollard, J., Doob, L., Miller, N., Mowrer, O. H., & Sears, R. R. (1939). *Frustration and aggression.* New Haven, CT: Yale University Press.

Dollinger, S. J. (2000). Locus of control and incidental learning: An application to college students. *College Student Journal, 34,* 537–540.

Domhoff, G. W. (1996). *Finding meaning in dreams: A quantitative approach.* New York: Plenum.

Domhoff, G. W. (1999). Drawing theoretical implications from descriptive empirical findings on dream content. *Dreaming, 9,* 201–210.

Domhoff, G. W. (2001). A new neurocognitive theory of dreams. *Dreaming, 11,* 13–33.

Domhoff, G. W., & Schneider, A. (2008). Studying dream content using the archive and search engine on DreamBank.net. *Consciousness and Cognition, 17,* 1238–1247.

Domino, E. F. (2003). Effects of tobacco smoking on electroencephalographic, auditory-evoked, and event-related potentials. *Brain and Cognition, 53,* 66–74.

Domjan, M. (2005). Pavlovian conditioning: A functional perspective. *Annual Review of Psychology, 56,* 179–206.

Domschke, K., Stevens, S., Pfleiderer, B., & Gerlach, A. L. (2010). Interoceptive sensitivity in anxiety and anxiety disorders: An overview and integration of neurobiological findings. *Clinical Psychology Review, 30,* 1–11.

Donegan, N. H., & Thompson, R. F. (1991). The search for the engram. In J. L. Martinez Jr. & R. P. Kesner (Eds.), *Learning and memory: A biological view* (2nd ed., pp. 3–58). San Diego, CA: Academic Press.

Dong, Y., Mihales, S., Qiu, F., von der Heydt, R., & Niebur, E. (2008). Synchrony and the binding problem in macaque visual cortex. *Journal of Vision, 8,* 1–16.

Donner, M. B., VandeCreek, L., Gonsiorek, J. C., & Fisher, C. B. (2008). Balancing confidentiality: Protecting privacy and protecting the public. *Professional Psychology: Research and Practice, 39,* 369–376.

Donnerstein, E. (1984). Pornography: Its effects on violence against women. In N. M. Malamuth & E. Donnerstein (Eds.), *Pornography and sexual aggression* (pp. 53–81). New York: Academic Press.

Donnerstein, E., Slaby, R. G., & Eron, L. D. (1995). The mass media and youth aggression. In L. D. Eron, J. H. Gentry, & P. Schlegel (Eds.), *Reason to hope: A psychosocial perspective on violence and youth* (pp. 219–250). Washington, DC: American Psychological Association.

Doornbos, B., Dijck-Brouwer, D. A., Janneke, K., Ido, P., et al. (2009). The development of peripartum depressive symptoms is associated with gene polymorphisms of MAOA, 5-HTT and COMT. *Progress in Neuropsychopharmacology and Biological Psychiatry, 33,* 1250–1254.

Doss, B. D., Rhoades, G. K., Stanley, S. M., & Markman, H. J. (2009). The effect of the transition to parenthood on relationship quality: An 8-year prospective study. *Psychological Bulletin, 96,* 601–619.

Doty, R. L. (2009). The olfactory system and its disorders. *Seminars in Neurology, 29,* 74–81.

Doucet, S., Soussignan, R., Sagot, P., & Schaal, B. (2007). The "smellscape" of mother's breast: Effects of odor masking and selective unmasking on neonatal arousal, oral, and visual responses. *Developmental Psychobiology, 49,* 129–138.

Dougherty, D. D., Baer, L., Cosgrove, G. R., Cassem, E. H., et al. (2002). Prospective long-term follow-up of 44 patients who received cingulotomy for treatment-refractory obsessive-compulsive disorder. *American Journal of Psychiatry, 159,* 269–275.

Dovidio J. F., & Gaertner S. L. (1998). On the nature of contemporary prejudice: The causes, consequences, and challenges of aversive racism. In Eberhardt J., Fiske S. T. (Eds.), *Confronting racism: The problem and the response* (pp. 3–32). Newbury Park, CA: Sage.

Dovidio, J. F., & Gaertner, S. L. (2008). New directions in aversive racism research: Persistence and pervasiveness. In C. Willis-Esqueda (Ed.), *Motivational aspects of prejudice and racism: Nebraska Symposium on Motivation* (pp. 43–67). New York: Springer.

Dovidio, J. F., & Gaertner, S. L. (2010). Intergroup bias. In S. T. Fiske, D. T. Gilbert, & G. Lindzey (Eds.), *Handbook of social psychology* (5th ed., Vol. 2, pp. 1084–1121). Hoboken, NJ: Wiley.

Dovidio, J. F., Gaertner, S. L., & Kawakami, K. (2010). Racism. In J. F. Dovidio, M. Hewstone, P. Glick, & V. M. Esses (Eds.), *The SAGE handbook of prejudice, stereotyping and discrimination* (pp. 312–327). London: Sage.

Dovidio, J. F., Kawakami, K., & Beach, K. R. (2001). Implicit and explicit attitudes: Examination of the relationship between measures of intergroup bias. In R. Brown & S. Gaertner (Eds.), *Blackwell handbook of social psychology: Vol. 4. Intergroup relations* (pp. 175–197). Oxford: Blackwell.

Dovidio, J. F., Kawakami, K., & Gaertner, S. L. (2000). Reducing contemporary prejudice: Combating explicit and implicit bias at the individual and intergroup level. In S. Oskamp (Ed.), *Reducing prejudice and discrimination* (pp. 137–163). Hillsdale, NJ: Erlbaum.

Dovidio, J. F., Kawakami, K., Smoak, N., & Gaertner, S. L. (2009). The roles of implicit and explicit processes in contemporary prejudice. In R. E. Petty, R. H. Fazio, & P. Brinol (Eds.), *Attitudes: Insights from the new implicit measures* (pp. 165–192). New York: Psychology Press.

Dovidio, J. F., Piliavin, J. A., Gaertner, S. L., Schroeder, D. A., & Clark, R. D., III. (1991). The arousal: cost-reward model and the process of intervention: A review of the evidence. In M. Clark (Ed.), *Review of personality and social psychology: Vol. 12. Prosocial behavior* (pp. 86–118). Newbury Park, CA: Sage.

Dovidio, J. F., Piliavin, J. A., Schroeder, D. A., & Penner, L. A. (2006). *The social psychology of prosocial behavior.* Mahwah, NJ: Erlbaum.

Dovidio, J. F., Smith, J. K., Donnella, A. G., & Gaertner, S. L. (1997). Racial attitudes and the death penalty. *Journal of Applied Social Psychology, 27,* 1468–1487.

Dowd, J. T. (2005). *Teaching social skills to youth.* Boys Town, NE: Boys Town Press.

Downey, D. B., & Condron, D. J. (2004). Playing well with others in kindergarten: The benefit of siblings at home. *Journal of Marriage and Family, 66,* 333–350.

Doyle, J. (2005). *True witness: Cops, courts, science, and the battle against misidentification.* New York: Palgrave Macmillan.

Dozen people watched gang rape, police say. (2009, October 27). *Associated Press.* Retrieved from http://www.youtube.com/watch?v=vwxiCVVGnZ8

Draganski, B., Gaser, C., Busch, V., Schuierer, G., et al. (2004). Neuroplasticity: Changes in grey matter induced by training. *Nature, 427,* 311–312.

Drasbek, K. R., Christensen, J., & Jensen, K. (2006). Gamma-hydroxybutyrate: A drug of abuse. *Acta Neurologica Scandinavica, 114,* 145–156.

Drayna, D., Manichaikul, A., de Lange, M., Snieder, H., & Spector, T. (2001). Genetic correlates of musical pitch recognition in humans. *Science, 291,* 1969–1972.

Dreher, J.-C., Kohn, P., Kolachana, B., Weinberger, D. R., & Berman, K. F. (2010). Variation in dopamine genes influences responsivity of the human reward system. *Proceedings of the National Academy of Sciences, 106,* 617–622.

Dreyfus, H. L., & Dreyfus, S. E. (1988). Making a mind versus modeling the brain: Intelligence back at a branchpoint. In S. R. Graubard (Ed.), *The artificial intelligence debate.* Cambridge, MA: MIT Press.

Drinkwater, J., & Stewart, A. (2002). Cognitive behavior therapy for young people. *Current Opinion in Psychiatry, 15,* 377–381.

Driver, J. L., & Gottman, J. M. (2004). Daily marital interactions and positive affect during marital conflict among newlywed couples. *Family Process, 43,* 301–314.

Driver, J. L., Tabares, A., Shapiro, A., Nahm, E. Y., & Gottman, J. M. (2003). Interactional patterns in marital success and failure: Gottman laboratory studies. In F. Walsh (Ed.), *Normal family processes: Growing diversity and complexity* (3rd ed., pp. 493–513). New York: Guilford Press.

Drucker, D. B., Ackroff, K., & Sclafani, A. (1994). Nutrient-conditioned flavor preference and acceptance in rats: Effects of deprivation state and nonreinforcement. *Physiology and Behavior, 56,* 701–707.

Druckman, D., & Bjork, R. A. (1994). *Learning, remembering, believing: Enhancing human performance.* Washington, DC: National Academy Press.

Drummond, S. P., Brown, G. G., Gillin, J. C., Stricker, J. L., et al. (2000). Altered brain response to verbal learning following sleep deprivation. *Nature, 403,* 655–657.

Druss, B. G., Wang, P. S., Sampson, N. A., Olfson, M., et al. (2007). Understanding mental health treatment in persons without mental diagnoses: Results from the National Comorbidity Survey replication. *Archives of General Psychiatry, 64,* 1196–1203.

Drzezga, A. (2008). Basic pathologies of neurodegenerative dementias and their relevance for state-of-the-art molecular imaging studies. *European Journal of Nuclear Medicine and Molecular Imaging, 35,* 4–11.

Duarte, N. T., Goodson, J. R., & Klich, N. R. (1993). How do I like thee? Let me appraise the ways. *Journal of Organizational Behavior, 14,* 239–249.

Dube, S. R., Felitti, V. J., Dong, M., Chapman, D. P., et al. (2003). Childhood abuse, neglect, and household dysfunction and the risk of illicit drug use: The adverse childhood experiences study. *Pediatrics, 111,* 564–572.

Dubertret, C., Hanoun, N., Ades, J., Hamon, M., & Gorwood, P. (2004). Family-based association studies between 5-HT-sub(5A) receptor gene and schizophrenia. *Journal of Psychiatric Research, 38,* 371–376.

Dubois, B. (2004). Amnestic MCI or prodromal Alzheimer's disease? *Lancet Neurology, 3,* 246–248.

DuBreuil, S. C., Garry, M., & Loftus, E. F. (1998). Tales from the crib: Memories of infancy. In S. J. Lynn, & K. M. McConkey (Eds.), *Truth in memory* (pp. 137–160). New York: Guilford Press.

Dubrovsky, B. O. (2005). Steroids, neuroactive steroids, and neurosteroids in psychopathology. *Progress in Neuropsychopharmacology and Biological Psychiatry, 29,* 169–192.

Ducci, F., & Goldman, D. (2008). Genetic approaches to addiction: Genes and alcohol. *Addiction, 103,* 1414–1428.

Duckitt, J. (2006). Differential effects of right-wing authoritarianism and social dominance orientation on outgroup attitudes and their mediation by threat from and competitiveness to outgroups. *Personality and Social Psychology Bulletin, 32,* 684–696.

Duclos, S. E., & Laird, J. D. (2001). The deliberate control of emotional experience through control of expressions. *Cognition and Emotion, 15,* 27–56.

Dudai, Y. (2004). The neurobiology of consolidations, or, how stable is the engram? *Annual Review of Psychology, 55,* 51–86.

Dudeck, M., Spitzer, C., Stopsack, M., Freyberger, H. J., & Barnow, S. (2007). Forensic inpatient male sexual offenders: The impact of personality disorders and childhood sexual abuse. *Journal of Forensic Psychiatry and Psychology, 18,* 494–506.

Dudley, N. M., Orvis, K. A., Lebeicki, J. E., & Cortina, J. M. (2006). A meta-analytic investigation of conscientiousness in the prediction of job performance: Examining the intercorrelations and the incremental validity of narrow traits. *Journal of Applied Psychology, 91,* 40–57.

Düzel, E., Vargha-Khamdem, F., Heinze, H. J., & Mishkin, M. (2001). Brain activity evidence for recognition without recollection after early hippocampal damage. *Proceedings of the National Academy of Sciences, 98,* 8101–8106.

Duffy, V. B., Fast, K., Cohen Z., Chodos, E., & Bartoshuk, L. M. (1999). Genetic taste status associates with fat food acceptance and body mass index in adults. *Chemical Senses, 24,* 545–546.

Duggan, A., Fuddy, L., Burrell, L., Higman, S. M., et al. (2004). Randomized trial of a statewide home visiting program to prevent child abuse: Impact in reducing parental risk factors. *Child Abuse and Neglect, 28,* 623–643.

Dujovne, V., & Houston, B. (1991). Hostility-related variables and plasma lipid levels. *Journal of Behavioral Medicine, 14,* 555–564.

Duke, C. R., & Carlson, L. (1994). Applying implicit memory measures: Word fragment completion in advertising tests. *Journal of Current Issues and Research in Advertising, 15,* 1–14.

Duke, N. N., Pettingell, S. L., McMorris, B. J., & Borowsky, I. W. (2010). Adolescent violence perpetration: Associations with multiple types of adverse childhood experiences. *Pediatrics, 125,* e778–e786.

Dumas, T. M., Lawford, H., Tieu, T.-T., & Pratt, M. W. (2009). Positive parenting in adolescence and its relation to low point narration and identity status in emerging adulthood: A longitudinal analysis. *Developmental Psychology, 45,* 1531–1544.

Dumont, F., & Corsini, R. J. (2000). *Six therapists and one client.* New York: Springer.

Duncan, A. E., Scherrer, J., Fu, Q., Bucholz, K. K., et al. (2006). Exposure to paternal alcoholism does not predict development of alcohol-use disorders in offspring: Evidence from an offspring-of-twins study. *Journal of Studies on Alcohol, 67,* 649–656.

Duncan, B. L. (2002). The legacy of Saul Rosenzweig: The profundity of the dodo bird. *Journal of Psychotherapy Integration, 12,* 32–57.

Duncan, G. J., Brooks-Gunn, J., & Klebanov, P. K. (1994). Economic deprivation and early childhood development. *Child Development, 65,* 296–318.

Duncan, J. R., Paterson, D. S., Hoffman, J. M., Mokler, D. J., et al. (2010). Brainstem serotonergic deficiency in sudden infant death syndrome. *Journal of the American Medical Association, 303,* 430–437.

Dunfield, K. A., & Kuhlmeier, V. A. (2010). Intention-mediated selective helping in infancy. *Psycholoigcal Science, 21,* 523–527. doi:10.1177/0956797610364119

Dunlop, S. (2008). Activity-dependent plasticity: Implications for recovery after spinal cord injury. *Trends in Neuroscience, 31,* 410–418.

Dunn, J., & Hughes, C. (2001). "I got some swords and you're dead!" Violent fantasy, antisocial behavior, friendship, and moral sensibility in young children. *Child Development, 72,* 491–505.

Dunning, D. (2001). On the motives underlying social cognition. In A. Tesser & N. Schwarz (Eds.), *Blackwell handbook of social psychology: Intraindividual processes* (pp. 348–374). Oxford: Blackwell.

Duran, B., Oetzel, J., Lucero, J., Jiang, Y., et al. (2005). Obstacles for rural American Indians seeking alcohol, drug, or mental health treatment. *Journal of Consulting and Clinical Psychology, 73,* 819–829.

Durand, M. V., & Barlow, D. H. (2006). *Essentials of abnormal psychology.* Belmont, CA: Wadsworth.

Durantini, M. R., Albarracín, D., Mitchell, A. L., Earl, A. N., & Gillette, J. C. (2006). Conceptualizing the influence of social agents of behavior change: A meta-analysis of the effectiveness of HIV-prevention interventionists for different groups. *Psychological Bulletin, 132,* 212–248.

Durbin, C. E., & Klein, D. N. (2006). Ten-year stability of personality disorders among outpatients with mood disorders. *Journal of Abnormal Psychology, 115,* 75–84.

Durka, P. J., Malinowska, U., Szelenberger, W., Wakarow, A., & Blinowska, K. J. (2005). High resolution parametric description of slow wave sleep. *Journal of Neuroscience Methods, 147,* 15–21.

Durlak, J. A. (2006). Cognitive-behavioral treatments. In R. T. Ammerman (Ed.), *Comprehensive handbook of personality and psychopathology* (Vol. 3, pp. 438–447). Hoboken, NJ: Wiley.

Durose, M. R., Harlow, C. W., Langan, P. A., Motivans, M., et al. (2005). *Family violence statistics.* Washington, DC: Bureau of Justice Statistics.

Dutton, D. G., & Aron, A. P. (1974). Some evidence for heightened sexual attraction under conditions of high anxiety. *Journal of Personality and Social Psychology, 30,* 510–517.

Dweck, C. S. (1998). The development of early self-conceptions: Their relevance for motivational processes. In J. Heckhausen & C. S. Dweck (Eds.), *Motivation and self-regulation across the life span.* New York: Cambridge University Press.

Dwork, A. J., Arango, V., Underwood, M., Ievski, B., et al. (2004). Absence of histological lesions in primate models of ECT and magnetic seizure therapy. *American Journal of Psychiatry, 161,* 576–578.

Dwyer, T., & Ponsonby, A. L. (2009). Sudden infant death syndrome and prone sleeping position. *Annals of Epidemiology, 19,* 245–249.

Dyche, L., & Zayas, L. H. (2001). Cross-cultural empathy and training the contemporary psychotherapist. *Clinical Social Work Journal, 29,* 245–258.

Dyck, E. (2005). Flashback: Psychiatric experimentation with LSD in historical perspective. *Canadian Journal of Psychiatry, 50,* 381–388.

d'Ydewalle, G., & Rosselle, H. (1978). Test expectations in text learning. In M. M. Gruneberg, P. E. Morris, & R. N. Sykes (Eds.), *Practical aspects of memory* (pp. 609–617). New York: Academic Press.

Dyken, M. E., & Yamada, T. (2005). Narcolepsy and disorders of excessive somnolence. *Primary Care, 32,* 389–413.

Eagle, N., Pentland, A., & Lazer, D. (2009). Inferring friendship network structure by using mobile phone data. *Proceedings of the National Academy of Sciences, 106,* 15274–15278.

Eagleman, D. M., & Goodale, M. A. (2009). Why color synesthesia involves more than color. *Trends in Cognitive Science, 13,* 288–292.

Eagleman, D. M., Kagan, A. D., Nelson, S. S., Sagaram, D., & Sarma, A. K. (2007). A standardized test battery for the study of synesthesia. *Journal of Neuroscience Methods, 159,* 139–145.

Eagly, A. H. (1996). Differences between women and men: Their magnitude, practical importance, and political meaning. *American Psychologist, 51,* 158–159.

Eagly, A. H., & Chin, J. L. (2010). Diversity and leadership in a changing world. *American Psychologist, 65,* 216–224.

Eagly, A. H., Johannesen-Schmidt, M. C., & van Engen, M. L. (2003). Transformational, transactional, and laissez-faire leadership styles: A meta-analysis comparing women and men. *Psychological Bulletin, 129,* 569–591.

Eagly, A. H., & Karau, S. J. (1991). Gender and the emergence of leaders: A meta-analysis. *Journal of Personality and Social Psychology, 60,* 685–710.

Eagly, A. H., Karau, S. J., & Makhijani, M. G. (1995). Gender and the effectiveness of leaders: A meta-analysis. *Psychological Bulletin, 117,* 125–145.

Eagly, A. H., Makhijani, M. G., & Klonsky, B. G. (1992). Gender and evaluation of leaders: A meta-analysis. *Psychological Bulletin, 111,* 3–22.

Eagly, A. H., & Sczesny, S. (2009). Stereotypes about women, men, and leaders: Have times changed? In M. Barreto, M. Ryan, & M. Schmitt (Eds.), *The glass ceiling in the 21st century: Understanding barriers to gender equality* (pp. 21–47). Washington, DC: American Psychological Association.

Eagly, A. H., & Wood, W. (1999). The orgins of sex diffrences in human behavior: Evolved dispositions versus social roles. *American Psychologist, 54,* 408–423.

Eagly, A. H., Wood, W., & Johannesen-Schmidt, M. C. (2004). Social role theory of sex differences and similarities: Implications for the partner preferences of women and men. In A. H. Eagly, A. E. Beall, & R. J. Sternberg (Eds.), *The psychology of gender* (2nd ed., pp. 269–295). New York: Guilford Press.

Eamon, M. K. (2008). *Empowering vulnerable populations: Cognitive-behavioral interventions.* Chicago: Lyceum Books.

East, P. L., & Jacobson, L. J. (2001). The younger siblings of teenage mothers: A follow-up of their pregnancy risk. *Developmental Psychology, 37,* 254–264.

Eaton, M. J., & Dembo, M. H. (1997). Differences in the motivational beliefs of Asian American and non-Asian students. *Journal of Educational Psychology, 89,* 433–440.

Ebert, S. A., Tucker, D. C., & Roth, D. L. (2002). Psychological resistance factors as predictors of general health status and physical symptom reporting. *Psychology, Health and Medicine, 7,* 363–375.

Eberts, R., & MacMillan, A. C. (1985). Misperception of small cars. In R. Eberts & C. Eberts (Eds.), *Trends in ergonomics/human factors* (Vol. 2, pp. 30–39). Amsterdam: Elsevier.

Ebstein, R. B. (2006). The molecular genetic architecture of human personality: Beyond self-report questionnaires. *Molecular Psychiatry, 11,* 427–445.

Eby, L. T., Casper, W. J., Lockwood, A., Bordeaux, C., & Brinley, A. (2005). Work and family research in IO/OB: Content analysis and review of the literature (1980–2002). *Journal of Vocational Behavior, 66,* 124–197.

Eccles, J., & Gootman, J. A. (2002). *Community programs to promote youth development.* Washington, DC: National Research Council.

Eccles, J., Lord, S., & Buchanan, C. M. (1996). School transitions in early adolescence: What are we doing to our young people? In J. A. Graber, J. Brooks-Gunn, & A. C. Peterson (Eds.), *Transitions through adolescence: Interpersonal domains and context* (pp. 251–284). Mahwah, NJ: Erlbaum.

Echeburua, E., de Corral, P., Garcia Bajos, E., & Borda, M. (1993). Interactions between self-exposure and alprazolam in the treatment of agoraphobia without current panic: An exploratory study. *Behavioural and Cognitive Psychotherapy, 21,* 219–238.

Echo News. (2000, March 17). Car crash mum tells of fight to rebuild her life. Retrieved from http://archive.echo-news.co.uk/2000/3/17/206088.html

Eddy, K. T., Dorer, D. J., Franko, D. L., Tahilani, K., et al. (2008). Diagnostic crossover in anorexia nervosa and bulimia nervosa: Implications for DSM-V. *American Journal of Psychiatry, 165,* 245–250.

Eddy, K. T., Dutra, L., Bradley, R., & Westen, D. (2004). A multidimensional meta-analysis of psychotherapy and pharmacotherapy for obsessive-compulsive disorder. *Clinical Psychology Review, 24,* 1011–1030.

Edelman, D. B., & Seth, A. K. (2009). Animal consciousness: A synthetic approach. *Trends in Neuroscience, 32,* 476–484.

Edenberg, H. J. (2007). The genetics of alcohol metabolism: Role of alcohol dehydrogenase and aldehyde dehydrogenase variants. *Alcohol Research and Health. 30,* 5–13.

Edinger, J. D., Wohlgemuth, W. K., Radtke, R. A., Marsh, G. R., & Quillian, R. E. (2001). Cognitive behavioral therapy for treatment of chronic primary insomnia. *Journal of the American Medical Association, 285,* 1856–1864.

Edwards, B. J., Reilly, T., & Waterhouse, J. (2009). Zeitgeber-effects of exercise on human circadian rhythms: What are alternative approaches to investigating the existence of a phase-response curve to exercise? *Biological Rhythm Research, 40,* 53–69.

Edwards, R. R., Campbell, C., Jamison, R. N., & Wiech, K. (2009). The neurobiological underpinnings of coping with pain. *Psychological Science, 18,* 237–241.

Edwards, W. (1977). How to use multiattribute utility measurement for social decision making. *IEEE Transactions on Systems, Man, and Cybernetics, 7,* 326–340.

Egan, K., & Asher, J. (2005). *Mental illness extracts heavy toll, beginning in youth* [Press release]. National Institute of Mental Health. Retrieved from http://www.nimh.nih.gov/press/mentalhealthstats.cfm

Egbert, L. D., Battit, G. E., Welch, C. E., & Bartlett, M. K. (1964). Reduction of postoperative pain by encouragement and instruction of patients: A study of doctor-patient rapport. *New England Journal of Medicine, 270,* 825–827.

Egner, T., Jamieson, G., & Gruzelier, J. (2005). Hypnosis decouples cognitive control from conflict monitoring processes of the frontal lobe. *Neuroimage, 27,* 969–978.

Ehlers, A. (1995). A 1-year prospective study of panic attacks: Clinical course and factors associated with maintenance. *Journal of Abnormal Psychology, 104,* 164–172.

Ehlers, A., Bisson, J., Clark, D. M., Creamer, M., et al. (2010). Do all psychological treatments really work the same in posttraumatic stress disorder? *Clinical Psychology Review, 30,* 269–276.

Ehrensaft, M. K., Cohen, P., Brown, J., Smailes, E., et al. (2003). Intergenerational transmission of partner violence: A 20-year prospective study. *Journal of Consulting and Clinical Psychology, 71,* 741–753.

Eich, E. (1989). Theoretical issues in state-dependent memory. In H. L. Roediger III & F. I. M. Craik (Eds.), *Varieties of memory and consciousness: Essays in honour of Endel Tulving* (pp. 331–354). Hillsdale, NJ: Erlbaum.

Eich, E., & Macaulay, D. (2000). Are real moods required to reveal mood-congruent and mood-dependent memory? *Psychological Science, 11,* 244–248.

Eich, E., & Macaulay, D. (2006). Cognitive and clinical perspectives on mood dependent memory. In Forgas, J. P. (Ed.) *Affect in social thinking and behavior* (pp. 105–121). New York: Psychology Press.

Eich, E., & Metcalfe, J. (1989). Mood-dependent memory for internal versus external events. *Experimental Psychology: Learning, Memory, and Cognition, 15,* 443–455.

Eich, J. E., Weingartner, H., Stillman, R. C., & Gillin, J. C. (1975). State-dependent accessibility of retrieval cues in the retention of a categorized list. *Journal of Verbal Learning and Verbal Behavior, 14,* 408–417.

Eickhoff, S. B., Dafotakis, M., Grefkes, C., Stöcker, T., et al. (2008). fMRI reveals cognitive and emotional processing in a long-term comatose patient. *Experimental Neurology, 214,* 240–246.

Eid, M., & Larsen, R. J. (Eds.). (2008). *The science of subjective well-being.* New York: Guilford Press.

Eifert, G. H., Zvolensky, M. J., & Louis, A. (2008). Somatoform disorders: Nature, psychological processes, and treatment strategies. In J. E. Maddux & B. A. Winstead (Eds.), *Psychopathology: Foundations for a contemporary understanding* (2nd ed., pp. 307–325). New York: Routledge/Taylor & Francis.

Eisenberg, M., Kobilo, T., Berman, D. E., & Dudai, Y. (2003). Stability of retrieved memory: Inverse correlation with trace dominance. *Science, 301,* 1102–1104.

Eisenberg, N. (1997, June). Consistent parenting helps children regulate emotions. *APA Monitor,* p. 17.

Eisenberg, N., Champion, C., & Ma, Y. (2004). Emotion-related regulation: An emerging construct. *Merrill-Palmer Quarterly, 50,* 236–259.

Eisenberg, N., Fabes, R. A., & Spinrad, T. L. (2006). Prosocial development. In W. Damon & R. M. Lerner (Series Eds.) & N. Eisenberg (Vol. Ed.), *Handbook of child psychology: Vol. 3. Social, emotional, and personality development* (6th ed., pp. 646–718). Hoboken, NJ: Wiley.

Eisenberg, N., Spinrad, T. L., Fabes, R. A., Reiser, M., et al. (2004). The relations of effortful control and impulsivity to children's resiliency and adjustment. *Child Development, 75,* 25–46.

Eisenberg, N., Valiente, C., Spinrad, T. L., Cumberland, A., et al. (2009). Longitudinal relations of children's effortful control, impulsivity, and negative emotionality to their externalizing, internalizing, and co-occurring behavior problems. *Developmental Psychology, 45,* 988–1008.

Eisenberg, N., Zhou, Q., Spinrad, T. L., Valiente, C., et al. (2005). Relations among positive parenting, children's effortful control, and externalizing problems: A three-wave longitudinal study. *Child Development, 76,* 1055–1071.

Eisenberger, N. I., Way, B. M., Taylor, S. E., Welch, W. T., & Lieberman, M. D. (2007). Understanding genetic risk for aggression: Clues from the brain's response to social exclusion. *Biological Psychiatry, 61,* 1100–1108.

Eisenberger, R., Jones, J. R., Stinglhamber, F., Shanock, L., & Tenglund, A. (2005). Optimal flow experiences at work: For high need achievers alone? *Journal of Organizational Behavior, 26,* 755–775.

Eisenberger, R., & Rhoades, L. (2001). Incremental effects of reward on creativity. *Journal of Personality and Social Psychology, 81,* 728–741.

Eisenberger, R., & Shanock, L. (2003). Rewards, intrinsic motivation, and creativity: A case study of conceptual and methodological isolation. *Creativity Research Journal, 15,* 121–130.

Eisenmann, J. C., Bartee, R. T., Smith, D. T., Welk, G. J., & Fu, Q. (2008). Combined influence of physical activity and television viewing on the risk of overweight in U.S. youth. *International Journal of Obesity, 32,* 613–618.

Eiser, A. S. (2005). Physiology and psychology of dreams. *Seminars in Neurology, 25,* 97–105.

Ekman, P. (1993). Facial expression and emotion. *American Psychologist, 48,* 384–392.

Ekman, P. (1994). Strong evidence for universals in facial expressions: A reply to Russell's mistaken critique. *Psychological Bulletin, 115,* 268–287.

Ekman, P. (2001). *Telling lies: Clues to deceit in the marketplace, politics, and marriage.* New York: Norton.

Ekman, P. (2009). Lie catching and micro expressions. In C. W. Martin (Ed.), *The philosophy of deception* (pp. 118–138). New York: Oxford University Press.

Ekman, P., & Davidson, R. J. (1993). Voluntary smiling changes regional brain activity. *Psychological Science, 4,* 342–345.

Ekman, P., Davidson, R. J., Ricard, M., & Alan, W. B. (2005). Buddhist and psychological perspectives on emotions and well-being. *Current Directions in Psychological Science, 14,* 59–63.

Ekman, P., Friesen, W. V., & Ellsworth, P. (1972). *Emotion in the human face: Guidelines for research and a review of findings.* New York: Pergamon Press.

Ekman, P., Levenson, R. W., & Friesen, W. V. (1983). Autonomic nervous system activity distinguishes among emotions. *Science, 221,* 1208–1210.

Elashoff, J. D. (1979). Box scores are for baseball. *Brain and Behavioral Sciences, 3,* 392.

Eling, P. (2008). Cerebral localization in the Netherlands in the nineteenth century: Emphasizing the work of Aletta Jacobs. *Journal of the History of the Neurosciences, 17,* 175–194.

Elkin, I. (1994). The NIMH treatment of depression collaborative research program: Where we began and where we are. In A. E. Bergin & S. L. Garfield (Eds.), *Handbook of psychotherapy and behavior change* (pp. 114–139). New York: Wiley.

Elkins, I. J., King, S. M., McGue, M., & Iacono, W. G. (2006). Personality traits and the development of nicotine, alchohol, and illicit drug disorders: Prospective links from adolescence to young adulthood. *Journal of Abnormal Psychology, 115,* 26–39.

Elliot, A. J. (Ed.). (2008). *Handbook of approach and avoidance motivation.* New York: Psychology Press.

Elliot, A. J., Chirkov, V. I., Kim, Y., & Sheldon, K. M. (2001). A cross-cultural analysis of avoidance (relative to approach) personal goals. *Psychological Science, 12,* 505–510.

Elliot, A. J., & Devine, P. G. (1994). On the motivational nature of cognitive dissonance: Dissonance as psychological discomfort. *Journal of Personality and Social Psychology, 67,* 382–394.

Elliott, C. L., & Greene, R. L. (1992). Clinical depression and implicit memory. *Journal of Abnormal Psychology, 101,* 572–574.

Elliott, R., Rubinsztein, J. S., Sahakian, B. J., & Dolan, R. J. (2002). The neural basis of mood-congruent processing biases in depression. *Archives of General Psychiatry, 59,* 597–604.

Elliott, R., Watson, J. C., & Goldman, R. N. (2004a). Empty-chair work for unfinished interpersonal issues. In R. Elliott & J. Watson (Eds.), *Learning emotion-focused therapy: The process-experiential approach to change* (pp. 243–265). Washington, DC: American Psychological Association.

Elliott, R., Watson, J. C., & Goldman, R. N. (2004b). Two-chair work for conflict splits. In R. Elliott & J. Watson (Eds.), *Learning emotion-focused therapy: The process-experiential approach to change* (pp. 219–241). Washington, DC: American Psychological Association.

Ellis, A. (1962). *Reason and emotion in psychotherapy.* New York: Stuart.

Ellis, A. (1993). Reflections on rational-emotive therapy. *Journal of Consulting and Clinical Psychology, 61,* 199–201.

Ellis, A. (1997). Using rational emotive behavior therapy techniques to cope with disability. *Professional Psychology: Research and Practice, 28,* 17–22.

Ellis, A. (2004a). Why I (really) became a therapist. *Journal of Rational-Emotive and Cognitive Behavior Therapy, 22,* 73–77.

Ellis, A. (2004b). Why rational emotive behavior therapy is the most comprehensive and effective form of behavior therapy. *Journal of Rational-Emotive and Cognitive Behavior Therapy, 22,* 85–92.

Ellis, A., & Bernard, M. E. (1985). *Clinical applications of rational-emotive therapy.* New York: Plenum.

Ellis, A., & MacLaren, C. (2005). *Rational emotive behavior therapy* (2nd ed.). Manassas Park, VA: Impact.

Ellis, A. L., & Mitchell, R. W. (2000). Sexual orientation. In L. T. Szuchman & F. Muscarella (Eds.), *Psychological perspectives on human sexuality* (pp. 196–231). New York: Wiley.

Ellis, B. J., Bates, J. E., Dodge, K. A., Fergusson, D. M., et al. (2003). Does father absence place daughters at special risk for early sexual activity and teenage pregnancy? *Child Development, 74,* 801–821.

Ellis, N. R. (1991). Automatic and effortful processes in memory for spatial location. *Bulletin of the Psychonomic Society, 29,* 28–30.

Elms, A. C. (2009). Obedience lite. *American Psychologist, 64,* 32–36.

Elofsson, U. O. E., von Schèele, B., Theorell, T., & Söndergaard, H. P. (2008). Physiological correlates of eye movement desensitization and reprocessing. *Journal of Anxiety Disorders, 22,* 622–634.

Elovainio, M., Kivimäki, M., & Vahtera, J. (2002). Organizational justice: Evidence on a new psychosocial predictor of health. *American Journal of Public Health, 92,* 105–108.

Else-Quest, N. M., Hyde, J. S., Goldsmith, H. H., & Van Hulle, C. A. (2006). Gender differences in temperament: A meta-analysis. *Psychological Bulletin, 132,* 33–72.

Else-Quest, N. M., Hyde, J. S., & Linn, M. C. (2010). Cross-national patterns of gender differences in mathematics: A meta-analysis. *Psychological Bulletin, 136,* 103–127.

Elvins, R., & Green, J. (2008). The conceptualization and measurement of therapeutic alliance: An empirical review. *Clinical Psychology Review, 28,* 1167–1187.

Elwood, L. S., Hahn, K. S., Olatunji, B. O., & Williams, N. L. (2009). Cognitive vulnerabilities to the development of PTSD: A review of four vulnerabilities and the proposal of an integrative vulnerability model. *Clinical Psychology Review, 29,* 87–100. Epub 2008 Oct 20.

El Yacoubi, M., Bouali, S., Popa, D., Naudon, L., et al. (2003). Behavioral, neurochemical, and electrophysiological characterization of a genetic mouse model of depression. *Proceedings of the National Academy of Sciences, 100,* 6227–6232.

Emanuele, E., Politi, P., Bianchi, M., Minoretti, P., et al. (2006). Raised plasma nerve growth factor levels associated with early-stage romantic love. *Psychoneuroendocrinology, 31,* 288–294.

Emery, D. (2004). Myth busted: Sucking on a penny will fool a breathalyzer test: An urban legend. *About.com: Urban Legends.* Retrieved from http://urbanlegends.about.com/library/bl_breathalyzer_penny.htm

Enblom, A., Hammar, M., Steineck, G., & Börjeson, S. (2008). Can individuals identify if needling was performed with an acupuncture needle or a non-penetrating sham needle? *Complementary Therapies in Medicine, 16,* 288–294.

Engebretson, T. O., & Stoney, C. M. (1995). Anger expression and lipid concentrations. *International Journal of Behavioral Medicine, 2,* 281–298.

Engel, A. K., Konig, P., Kreiter, A. K., Schillen, T. B., & Singer, W. (1992). Temporal coding in the visual cortex: New vistas on integration in the nervous system. *Trends in Neuroscience, 15,* 218–226.

Enoch, M. A.(2003). Pharmacogenomics of alcohol response and addiction. *American Journal of Pharmacogenomics, 3,* 217–232.

Epping-Jordan, M. P., Watkins, S. S., Koob, G. F., & Markou, A. (1998). Dramatic decreases in brain reward function during nicotine withdrawal. *Nature, 393,* 76–79.

Epstein, E. M., Sloan, D. M., & Marx, B. P. (2005). Getting to the heart of the matter: Written disclosure, gender, and heart rate. *Psychosomatic Medicine, 67,* 413–419.

Epstein, L. H., Temple, J. L., Roemmich, J. N., & Bouton, M. E. (2009). Habituation as a determinant of human food intake. *Psychological Review, 116,* 384–407.

Epstein, R., Kirshit, C. E., Lanza, R. P., & Rubin, C. L. (1984). "Insight" in the pigeon: Antecedents and determinants of an intelligent performance. *Nature, 308,* 61–62.

Epstude, K., & Mussweiler, T. (2009). What you feel is how you compare: How comparisons influence the social induction of affect. *Emotion, 9,* 1–14.

Erdberg, P. (1990). Rorschach assessment. In G. Goldstein & M. Hersen (Eds.), *Handbook of psychological assessment* (2nd ed., pp. 437–449). New York: Pergamon Press.

Erdelyi, M. H. (1985). *Psychoanalysis: Freud's cognitive psychology.* San Francisco: Freeman.

Erez, A., Misangyi, V. F., Johnson, D. E., LePine, M. A., & Halverson, K. C. (2008). Stirring the hearts of followers: Charismatic leadership as the transferal of affect. *Journal of Applied Psychology, 93,* 602–616.

Erickson, K. I., Colcombe, S. J., Wadhwa, R., Scalf, P. E., et al. (2007). Training-induced plasticity in older adults: Effects of training on hemispheric asymmetry. *Neurobiology of Aging, 28,* 272–283.

Erickson, R. J., Nichols, L., & Ritter, C. (2000). Family influences on absenteeism: Testing an expanded process model. *Journal of Vocational Behavior, 57,* 246–272.

Ericsson, K. A., & Charness, N. (1994). Expert performance: Its structure and acquisition. *American Psychologist, 49,* 725–747.

Ericsson, K. A., Chase, W. G., & Faloon, S. (1980). Acquisition of a memory skill. *Science, 208,* 1181–1182.

Ericsson, K. A., & Simon, H. A. (1994). *Protocol analysis: Verbal reports as data* (rev. ed.). Cambridge, MA: MIT Press.

Ericsson, K. A., & Staszewski, J. (1989). Skilled memory and expertise: Mechanisms of exceptional performance. In D. Klahr & K. Kotovsky (Eds.), *Complex information processing: The impact of Herbert A. Simon.* Hillsdale, NJ: Erlbaum.

Erikson, E. H. (1968). *Identity: Youth and crisis.* New York: Norton.

Erikson, R., Goldthorpe, J. H., Jackson, M., Yaish, M., & Cox, D. R. (2005). On class differentials in educational attainment. *Proceedings of the National Academy of Sciences, 102,* 9730–9733.

Eriksson, P. S., Perfilieva, E., Bjork-Eriksson, T., Alborn, A. M., et al. (1998). Neurogenesis in the adult human hippocampus. *Nature Medicine, 4,* 1313–1317.

Ernst, M., Matochik, J. A., Heishman, S. J., Van Horn, J. D., et al. (2001). Effect of nicotine on brain activation during performance of a working memory task. *Proceedings of the National Academy of Sciences, 98,* 4728–4733.

Eroglu, E., Gökçil, Z., Bek, S., Ulas, U. H., & Odabasi, Z. (2008). Pregnancy and teratogenicity of antiepileptic drugs. *Acta Neurologica Belgica, 108,* 53–57.

Eron, L. D., Huesmann, L. R., Lefkowitz, M. M., & Walder, L. O. (1996). Does television violence cause aggression? In D. F. Greenberg (Ed.), *Criminal careers: Vol. 2. The international library of criminology, criminal justice and penology* (pp. 311–321). Aldershot, England: Dartmouth.

Esel, E., Ozsay, S., Tutus, A., Sofiuoglu, S., et al. (2005). Effects of antidepressant treatment and of gender on serum leptin levels in patients with major depression. *Progress in Neuropsychopharmacology and Biological Psychiatry, 29,* 565–570.

Eshel, N., & Roiser, J. P. (2010). Reward and punishment processing in depression. *Biological Psychiatry, 68,* 118–124.

Eskelinen, M. H., & Kivipelto, M. (2010). Caffeine as a protective factor in dementia and Alzheimer's disease. *Journal of Alzheimer's Disease, 20* (Suppl. 1), S167–S174.

Essex, M. J., Klein, M. H., Slattery, M. J., Goldsmith, H. H., & Kalin, N. H. (2010). Early risk factors and developmental pathways to chronic high inhibition and social anxiety disorder in adolescence. *American Journal of Psychiatry, 167,* 40–46.

Esterson, A. (2001). The mythologizing of psychoanalytic history: Deception and self-deception in Freud's account of the seduction theory episode. *History of Psychiatry, 12,* 329–352.

Etcheverry, P. E., & Agnew, C. R. (2008). Romantic partner and friend influences on young adult cigarette smoking: Comparing close others' smoking and injunctive norms over time. *Psychology of Addictive Behaviors, 22,* 313–325.

Ettinger, U., Picchioni, M., Landau, S., Matsumoto, K., et al. (2007). Magnetic resonance imaging of the thalamus and adhesio interthalamica in twins with schizophrenia. *Archives of General Psychiatry, 64,* 401–409.

Ettlin, T. M., Beckson, M., Benson, D. F., Langfitt, J. T., et al. (1992). Prosopagnosia: A bihemispheric disorder. *Cortex, 28,* 129–134.

Evans, G. W. (2004). The environment of childhood poverty. *American Psychologist, 59,* 77–92.

Evans, G. W., & Wener, R. E. (2006). Rail commuting duration and passenger stress. *Health Psychology, 25,* 408–412.

Evans, G. W., Ricciuti, H. N., Hope, S., Schoon, I., et al. (2010). Crowding and cognitive development: The mediating role of maternal responsiveness among 36-month-old children. *Environment and Behavior, 42,* 135–148.

Evans, J., Heron, J., Lewis, G., Araya, R., & Wolke, D. (2005). Negative self-schemas and the onset of depression in women: Longitudinal study. *British Journal of Psychiatry, 186,* 302–307.

Evans, J. A., Elliott, J. A., & Gorman, M. R. (2009). Dim nighttime illumination accelerates adjustment to time zone travel in an animal model. *Current Biology, 19,* R156–R157.

Evans, J. S. B. T., Handley, S. J., Harper, C. N. J., & Johnson-Laird, P. N. (1999). Reasoning about necessity and possibility: A test of the mental model theory of deduction. *Journal of Experimental Psychology: Learning, Memory, and Cognition, 25,* 1495–1513.

Evans, R. B. (2003). Georg von Bekesy: Visualization of hearing. *American Psychologist, 58,* 742–746.

Everitt, B. J., & Robbins, T. W. (2005). Neural systems of reinforcement for drug addiction: From actions to habits to compulsion. *Nature Neuroscience, 8,* 1481–1489.

Ewing, C. P., & McCann, J. T. (2006). *Minds on trial: Great cases in law and psychology.* New York: Oxford University Press.

Exner, J. E., Jr. (2003). *The Rorschach—a comprehensive system: Vol. 1. Basic foundations and principles of interpretation* (4th ed.). Hoboken, NJ: Wiley.

Eysenck, H. J. (1952). The effects of psychotherapy: An evaluation. *Journal of Consulting Psychology, 16,* 319–324.

Eysenck, H. J. (1986). What is intelligence? In R. J. Sternberg & D. K. Detterman (Eds.), *What is intelligence? Contemporary viewpoints on its nature and definition.* Norwood, NJ: Ablex.

Eysenck, H. J. (1987). Speed of information processing, reaction time, and the theory of intelligence. In P. A. Vernon (Ed.), *Speed of information-processing and intelligence* (pp. 21–67). Norwood, NJ: Ablex.

Eysenck, H. J. (1990a). Biological dimensions of personality. In L. A. Pervin (Ed.), *Handbook of personality: Theory and research* (pp. 244–276). New York: Guilford.

Eysenck, H. J. (1990b). Genetic and environmental contributions to individual differences: The three major dimensions of personality. *Journal of Personality, 58,* 245–261.

Eysenck, H. J. (1994). A biological theory of intelligence. In D. K. Detterman (Ed.), *Current topics in human intelligence* (Vol. 4). Norwood, NJ: Ablex.

Eysenck, M. W., & Keane, M. T. (2005). *Cognitive psychology: A student's handbook* (5th ed.). Hove, England: Psychology Press.

Fabes, R. A., Martin, C. L., & Hanish, L. D. (2003). Young children's qualities in same-, other-, and mixed-sex peer groups. *Child Development, 74,* 921–932.

Fabes, R. A., Shepard, S. A., Guthrie, I. K., & Martin, C. L. (1997). Roles of temperamental arousal and gender-segregated play in young children's social adjustment. *Developmental Psychology, 33,* 693–702.

Fagan, A. A., Hanson, K., Hawkins, J. D., & Arthur, M. S. (2009). Translational research in action: Implementation of the Communities That Care prevention system in 12 communities. *Journal of Community Psychology, 37,* 809–829.

Fagan, J. F. (2000). A theory of intelligence as processing: Implications for society. *Psychology, Public Policy, and Law, 26,* 168–179.

Fagan, J. F., & Detterman, D. K. (1992). The Fagan Test of Infant Intelligence: A technical summary. *Journal of Applied Developmental Psychology, 13,* 173–193.

Fagan, J. F., Holland, C. R., & Wheeler, K. (2007). The prediction, from infancy, of adult IQ and achievement. *Intelligence, 35,* 225–231.

Fagin-Jones, S., & Midlarsky, E. (2007). Courageous altruism: Personal and situational correlates of rescue during the Holocaust. *Journal of Positive Psychology, 2,* 136–147.

Fago, D. P. (2009). The evidence-based treatment debate: Toward a dialectical rapprochement. *Psychotherapy: Theory, Research, Practice, Training, 46,* 15–18.

Fagot, B. I. (1995). Psychosocial and cognitive determinants of early gender-role development. *Annual Review of Sex Research, 6,* 1–31.

Fagot, B. I., & Gauvain, M. (1997). Mother-child problem solving: Continuity through the early childhood years. *Developmental Psychology, 33,* 480–488.

Fahrenkopf, A. M., Sectish, T. C., Barger, L. K., Sharek, P. J., et al. (2008). Rates of medication errors among depressed and burnt-out residents: Prospective cohort study. *British Medical Journal, 336,* 488–491.

Fahsing, I. A., Ask, K., & Granhag, P. A. (2004). The man behind the mask: Accuracy and predictors of eyewitness offender descriptions. *Journal of Applied Psychology, 89,* 722–729.

Fair, D. A., Cohen, A. L., Dosenbach, N. U. F., Church, J. A., et al. (2008). The maturing architecture of the brain's default network. *Proceedings of the National Academy of Sciences, 105,* 1028–1032.

Fairbanks, A. M. (2009, January 4). Through ups and downs of illness, creativity endures. *New York Times,* p. A19.

Fairburn, C. G. (Ed.). (2008). *Cognitive behavior therapy and eating disorders.* New York: Guilford Press.

Fairburn, C. G., Cooper, Z., Shafran, R., Wilson, G. T., & Barlow, D. H. (2008). Eating disorders: A transdiagnostic protocol. In D. H. Barlow (Ed.), *Clinical handbook of psychological disorders: A step-by-step treatment manual* (4th ed., pp. 578–614). New York: Guilford Press.

Falck, R. S., Wang, J., & Carlson, R. G. (2007). Crack cocaine trajectories among users in a midwestern American city. *Addiction, 102,* 1421–1431.

Falicov, C. J. (2003). Culture, society, and gender in depression. *Journal of Family Therapy, 25,* 371–387.

Falk, A., & Heckman, J. J. (2009). Lab experiments are a major source of knowledge in the social sciences. *Science, 326,* 535–538.

Fan, J., Ma, J., Li, X., Zhang, C., & Sun, W. (2006). Population-based and family-based association studies of an (AC)n dinucleotide repeat in an a-7 nicotinic receptor subunit gene and schizophrenia. *Schizophrenia Research, 84,* 222–227.

Farah, M. J. (1996). Is face recognition "special"? Evidence from neuropsychology. *Behavioral Brain Research, 76,* 181–189.

Farah, M. J. (2000). *The cognitive neuroscience of vision.* Malden, MA: Blackwell.

Farah, M. J. (2009). A picture is worth a thousand dollars. *Journal of Cognitive Neuroscience, 21,* 623–624.

Farah, M. J., Shera, D. M., Savage, J. H., Betancourt, L., et al. (2006). Childhood poverty: Specific associations with neurocognitive development. *Brain Research, 1110,* 166–174.

Farfel, M., DiGrande, L., Brackbill, R., Prann, A., et al. (2008). An overview of 9/11 experiences and respiratory and mental health conditions among World Trade Center health registry enrollees. *Journal of Urban Health, 85,* 880–909.

Farley, F (1986). The big T in personality. *Psychology Today, 20,* 44–52.

Farmer, J. D., Patelli, P., & Zovko, I. I. (2005). The predictive power of zero intelligence in financial markets. *Proceedings of the National Academy of Sciences, 102,* 2254–2259.

Farmer, R. F., & Nelson-Gray, R. (2005). *Personality-guided behavior therapy.* Washington, DC: American Psychological Association.

Farran, E., & Brown, J. (2006). Infants can organise visual information at just four months. *AlphaGalileo.* Retrieved from http://www.alphagalileo.org/index.cfm?fuseaction5readrel ease&releaseid5511896

Farrar, K. M., Krcmar, M., & Nowak, K. L. (2006). Contextual features of violent video games, mental models, and aggression. *Journal of Communication, 56,* 387–405.

Farroni, T., Csibra, G., Simion, F., & Johnson, M. H. (2002). Eye contact detection in humans from birth. *Proceedings of the National Academy of Sciences, 99,* 9602–9605.

Farroni, T., Johnson, M. H., Menon, E., Zulian, L., et al. (2005). Newborns' preference for face-relevant stimuli: Effects of contrast polarity. *Proceedings of the National Academy of Sciences, 102,* 17245–17250.

Fassler, D. G., & Dumas, L. S. (1997). *Help me, I'm sad: Recognizing, treating, and preventing childhood depression.* New York: Viking Press.

Faulkner, D., & Foster, J. K. (2002). The decoupling of "explicit" and "implicit" processing in neuropsychological disorders: Insights into the neural basis of consciousness? *Psyche, 8*(2). Retrieved from http://psyche.cs.monash.edu.au/v8/psyche-8-02-faulkner.html

Faulkner, M. (2001). The onset and alleviation of learned helplessness in older hospitalized people. *Aging and Mental Health, 5,* 379–386.

Fava, G. A., Rafanelli, C., Tossani, E., & Grandi, S. (2008). Agoraphobia is a disease: A tribute to Sir Martin Roth. *Psychotherapy and Psychosomatics, 77,* 133–138.

Faymonville, M. E., Laureys, S., Degueldre, C., DelFiore, G., et al. (2000). Neural mechanisms of antinociceptive effects of hypnosis. *Anesthesiology, 92,* 1257–1267.

Feather, N. T., & Rauter, K. A. (2004). Organizational citizenship behaviours in relation to job status, job insecurity, organizational commitment and identification, job satisfaction, and work values. *Journal of Occupational and Organizational Psychology, 77,* 81–94.

Federal Bureau of Investigation. (2008). *Crime in the United States, 2007.* Washington, DC: U.S. Department of Justice. Retrieved from http://www.fbi.gov/ucr/cius2007/data/table_01.html

Feinberg, L., & Campbell, I. G. (1993). Total sleep deprivation in the rat transiently abolishes the delta amplitude response to darkness: Implications for the mechanism of the "negative delta rebound." *Journal of Neurophysiology, 70,* 2695–2699.

Feinstein, J. S., Duff, M. C., & Tranel, D. (2010). Sustained experience of emotion after loss of memory in patients with amnesia. *Proceedings of the National Academy of Sciences, 107,* 7674–7679.

Feist, J., & Feist, G. J. (2009). *Theories of personality* (7th ed.). New York: McGraw-Hill.

Felder, R. M. & Brent, R. (2001). Effective strategies for cooperative learning. *Journal of Cooperation and Collaboration in College Teaching, 10,* 69–75.

Feldman, R., Weller, A., Zagoory-Sharon, O., & Levine, A. (2007). Evidence for a neuroendocrinological foundation of human affiliation: Plasma oxytocin levels across pregnancy and the postpartum period predict mother-infant bonding. *Psychological Science, 18,* 965–970.

Felfe, J., & Goihl, K. (2002). Transformational leadership and commitment. In J. Felfe (Ed.), *Organizational development and leadership* (pp. 87–124). Frankfurt, Germany: Lang.

Fellows, L. K., Heberlein, A. S., Morales, D. A., Shivde, G., et al. (2005). Method matters: An empirical study of impact in cognitive neuroscience. *Journal of Cognitive Neuroscience, 17,* 850–858.

Feng, X., Shaw, D. S., Kovacs, M., Lane, T., et al. (2008). Emotion regulation in preschoolers: The roles of behavioral inhibition, maternal affective behavior, and maternal depression. *Journal of Child Psychology and Psychiatry, 49,* 132–141.

Fenson, L., Dale, P. S., Reznick, J. S., & Bates, E. (1994). Variability in early communicative development. *Monographs of the Society for Research in Child Development, 59,* 173.

Fenton, W. S., & McGlashan, T. H. (1991). Natural history of schizophrenia subtypes: 1. Longitudinal study of paranoid, hebephrenic, and undifferentiated schizophrenia. *Archives of General Psychiatry, 48,* 969–977.

Ferguson, C. J. (2002). Media violence: Miscast causality. *American Psychologist, 57,* 446–447.

Ferguson, C. J. (2009). Violent video games: Dogma, fear, and pseudoscience. *Skeptical Inquirer, 33,* 38–43.

Ferguson, C. J. (2010). Blazing angels or resident evil? Can violent video games be a force for good? *Review of General Psychology, 14,* 122–140.

Ferguson, C. J., & Beaver, K. M. (2009). Natural born killers: The genetic origins of extreme violence. *Aggression and Violent Behavior, 14,* 286–294.

Ferguson, C. J., & Hartley, R. D. (2009). The pleasure is momentary . . . the expense damnable? The influence of pornography on rape and sexual assault. *Aggression and Violent Behavior, 14,* 323–329.

Ferguson, C. J., & Kilburn, J. (2009). The public health risks of media violence: A meta-analytic review. *Journal of Pediatrics, 154,* 759–763.

Ferguson, C. J., & Kilburn, J. (2010). Much ado about nothing: The misestimation and overinterpretation of violent video game effects in Eastern and Western nations: Comment on Anderson et al. (2010). *Psychological Bulletin, 136,* 174–178.

Ferguson,C. J., Olson, C. K., Kutner, L. A., & Warner, D. E. (2010). Violent video games, catharsis seeking, bullying, and delinquency: A multivariate analysis of effects. *Crime and Delinquency, 56,* 1–21.

Ferguson, C. J., & Rueda, S. M. (2010). The hitman study: Violent video game exposure effects on aggressive behavior, hostile feelings, and depression. *European Psychologist, 15,* 99–108.

Fergusson, D. M., & Horwood, L. J. (1997). Early-onset cannabis use and psychosocial adjustment in young adults. *Addiction, 92,* 279–296.

Fernández-Dols, J.-M., & Ruiz-Belda, M.-A. (1995). Are smiles a sign of happiness? Gold medal winners at the Olympic Games. *Journal of Personality and Social Psychology, 69,* 1113–1119.

Fernstrom, J. D., & Choi, S. (2007). The development of tolerance to drugs that suppress food intake. *Pharmacology and Therapeutics, 117,* 105–122.

Ferrara, J. M., & Stacy, M. (2008). Impulse-control disorders in Parkinson's disease. *CNS Spectrums, 13,* 690–698.

Ferraro, R., Lillioja, S., Fontvieille, A. M., Rising, R., et al. (1992). Lower sedentary metabolic rate in women compared with men. *Journal of Clinical Investigation, 90,* 780–784.

Ferris, G. R., & Treadway, D. C. (2008). Culture diversity and performance appraisal systems. In D. L. Stone & E. F. Stone-Romero (Eds.), *The influence of culture on human resource management processes and practices* (pp. 135–155). New York: Psychology Press.

Ferris, G. R., Judge, T. A., Rowland, K. M., & Fitzgibbons, D. E. (1994). Subordinate influence and the performance evaluation process: Test of a model. *Organizational and Human Decision Processes, 58,* 101–135.

Feshbach, S., & Tangney, J. (2008). Television viewing and aggression: Some alternative perspectives. *Perspectives on Psychological Science, 3,* 387–389.

Festinger, L. (1954). A theory of social comparison processes. *Human Relations, 7,* 117–140.

Festinger, L. (1957). *A theory of cognitive dissonance.* Evanston, IL: Row & Petersen.

Festinger, L., & Carlsmith, J. M. (1959). Cognitive consequences of forced compliance. *Journal of Abnormal and Social Psychology, 58,* 203–210.

Fiedler, E. R., Oltmanns, T. F., & Turkheimer, E. (2004). Traits associated with personality disorders and adjustment to military life: Predictive validity of self and peer reports *Military Medicine, 169,* 207–211.

Field, A. P. (2006). Is conditioning a useful framework for understanding the development and treatment of phobias? *Clinical Psychology Review, 26,* 857–875.

Field, T., Hernandez-Reif, M., Seligman, S., Krasnegor, J., et al. (1997). Juvenile rheumatoid arthritis: Benefits from massage therapy. *Journal of Pediatric Psychology, 22,* 607–617.

Field, T., Ironson, G., Scafidi, F., Nawrocki, T., et al. (1996). Massage therapy reduces anxiety and enhances EEG pattern of alertness and math computations. *International Journal of Neuroscience, 86,* 197–205.
Fielder, W. R, Cohen, R. D., & Feeney, S. (1971). An attempt to replicate the teacher expectancy effect. *Psychological Reports, 29,* 1223–1228.
Fields, A. J. (2010). Multicultural research and practice: Theoretical issues and maximizing cultural exchange. *Professional Psychology: Research and Practice, 41,* 196–201.
Fields, R. D. (2005). Making memories stick. *Scientific American, 292,* 74–81.
Filipek, P. A., Accardo, P. J., Barancek, G. T., Cook, E. H., Jr., et al. (1999). The screening and diagnosis of autistic spectrum disorders. *Journal of Autism and Developmental Disorders, 29,* 439–484.
Fillmore, K. M., & Caetano, R. (1980, May 22). *Epidemiology of occupational alcoholism.* Paper presented at the National Institute on Alcohol Abuse and Alcoholism's Workshop on Alcoholism in the Workplace, Reston, VA.
Fincham, J. M., & Anderson, J. R. (2006). Distinct roles of the anterior cingulated and the prefrontal cortex in the acquisition and performance of a cognitive skill. *Proceedings of the National Academy of Sciences, 103,* 12941–12946.
Fine, I., Wade, A. R., Brewer, A. A., May, M. G., et al. (2003). Long-term deprivation affects visual perception and cortex. *Nature Neuroscience, 6,* 915–916.
Finkel, D., Reynolds, C. A., McArle, J. J., Gatz, M., & Pedersen, N. L. (2003). Latent growth curve analyses of accelerating decline in cognitive abilities in late adulthood. *Developmental Psychology, 39,* 535–550.
Finkel, D., Reynolds, C. A., McArdle, J. J., Hamagami, F., & Pedersen, N. L. (2009). Genetic variance in processing speed drives variation in aging of spatial and memory abilities. *Developmental Psychology, 45,* 820–834.
Finkel, D., Reynolds, C. A., McArdle, J. J., & Pedersen, N. L. (2007). Age changes in processing speed as a leading indicator of cognitive aging. *Psychology and Aging, 22,* 558–568. doi:10.1037/0882-7974.22.3.558
Finney, M. L., Stoney, C. M., & Engebretson, T. O. (2002). Hostility and anger expression in African American and European American men is associated with cardiovascular and lipid reactivity. *Psychophysiology, 39,* 340–349.
Finn-Stevenson, M. & Zigler, E. (1999). *Schools of the 21st century: Linking child care and education.* Boulder, CO: Westview Press.
Firestein, S. (2001). How the olfactory system makes sense of scents. *Nature, 413,* 211–218.
Fisar, Z. (2009). Phytocannabinoids and endocannabinoids. *Current Drug Abuse Review, 2,* 51–75.
Fischer, M. J., & Massey, D. S. (2007). The effects of affirmative action in higher education. *Social Science Research, 36,* 531–549.
Fischoff, B., & MacGregor, D. (1982). Subjective confidence in forecasts. *Journal of Forecasting, 1,* 155–172.
Fish, A. M., Li, X., McCarrick, K., Butler, S. T., et al. (2008) Early childhood computer experience and cognitive development among urban low-income preschoolers. *Journal of Educational Computing Research, 38,* 97–113.
Fishbein, M., & Ajzen, I. (2010). *Predicting and changing behavior: The reasoned action approach.* New York: Psychology Press.
Fisher, C. D. (2000). Mood and emotion while working: Missing pieces of job satisfaction? *Journal of Organizational Behavior, 21,* 185–202.
Fisher, C. D. (2003). Why do lay people believe that satisfaction and performance are correlated? Possible sources of a commonsense theory. *Journal of Organizational Behavior, 24,* 753–777.
Fisher, C. M. (1989). Binswanger's encephalopathy: A review. *Journal of Neurology, 236,* 65–79.
Fisher, P. L., & Wells, A. (2009). Psychological models of worry and generalized anxiety disorder. In M. M. Antony & M. B. Stein (Eds.), *Oxford handbook of anxiety and related disorders* (pp. 225–237). New York: Oxford University Press.
Fisher, S. E. (2005). Dissection of molecular mechanisms underlying speech and language disorders. *Applied Psycholinguistics, 26,* 111–128.
Fisher, W. A., Fisher, J. D., & Rye, B. J. (1995). Understanding and promoting AIDS-preventive behavior: Insights from the theory of reasoned action. *Health Psychology, 14,* 255–264.
Fiske, A. P., Kitayama, S., Markus, H. R., & Nisbett, R. E. (1998). The cultural matrix of social psychology. In D. T. Gilbert, S. T. Fiske, & G. Lindzey (Eds.), *Handbook of social psychology* (4th ed., Vol. 2, pp. 915–981). New York: McGraw-Hill.
Fiske, S. T. (1998). Stereotyping, prejudice, and discrimination. In D. T. Gilbert, S. T. Fiske, & G. Lindzey (Eds.), *Handbook of social psychology* (4th ed., Vol. 2, pp. 357–414). New York: McGraw-Hill.
Fiske, S. T., & Taylor, S. (2008). *Social cognition: From brains to culture* New York: McGraw-Hill.
Fitch, W. T., & Hauser, M. D. (2004). Computational constraints on syntactic processing in a nonhuman primate. *Science, 303,* 377–380.
Fitzgerald, P. B., Brown, T. L., & Daskalakis, Z. J. (2002). The application of transcranial magnetic stimulation in psychiatry and neurosciences research. *Acta Psychiatrica Scandinavia, 105,* 324–340.
Fitzgerald, T. E., Tennen, H., Afflect, G. S., & Pransky, G. (1993). The relative importance of dispositional optimism and control appraisals in quality of life after coronary artery bypass surgery. *Journal of Behavioral Medicine, 16,* 25–43.
Flanagan, J. C. (1954). The critical incident technique. *Psychological Bulletin, 51,* 327–358.
Flatt, N., & King, N. (2008). Building the case for brief psychinterventions in the treatment of specific phobias in children and adolescents. *Behaviour Change, 25,* 191–200.
Flavell, J. E., Azrin, N., Baumeister, A., Carr, E., et al. (1982). The treatment of self-injurious behavior. *Behavior Therapy, 13,* 529–554.
Fleck, M. S., & Mitroff, S. R. (2007). Rare targets are rarely missed in correctable search. *Psychological Science, 18,* 943–947.
Fleeson, W., Malanos, A. B., & Achille, N. M. (2002). An intraindividual process approach to the relationship between extraversion and positive affect: Is acting extraverted as "good" as being extraverted? *Journal of Personality and Social Psychology, 83,* 1409–1422.
Flegal, K. M., Carroll, M. D., Ogden, C. L., & Curtin, L. R. (2010). Prevalence and trends in obesity among U.S. adults, 1999–2008. *Journal of the American Medical Association, 303,* 235–241.
Flegal, K. M., Graubard, B. I., Williamson, D. F., & Gail, M. H. (2005). Excess deaths associated with underweight, overweight, and obesity. *Journal of the American Medical Association, 293,* 1861–1867.
Fleischhacker, W. W., & Widschwendter, C. G. (2006). Treatment of schizophrenia patients: Comparing new-generation antipsychotics to each other. *Current Opinion in Psychiatry, 19,* 128–134.
Fleishman, E. A., & Harris, E. F. (1962). Patterns of leadership behavior related to employee grievances and turnover. *Personnel Psychology, 15,* 43–56.
Flor, H., Birbaumer, N., Herman, C., Ziegler, S., & Patrick, C. J. (2002). Aversive Pavlovian conditioning in psychopaths: Peripheral and central correlates. *Psychophysiology, 39,* 505–518.
Flores, E., Cicchetti, D., & Rogosch, F. A. (2005). Predictors of resilience in maltreated and nonmaltreated Latino children. *Developmental Psychology, 41,* 338–351.
Flores, E., Tschann, J. M., Dimas, J. M., Pasch, L. A., & de Groat, C. L. (2010). Perceived racial/ethnic discrimination, posttraumatic stress symptoms, and health risk behaviors among Mexican American adolescents. *Journal of Counseling Psychology, 57,* 264–273.
Floyd, J. A. (2002). Sleep and aging. *Nursing Clinics of North America, 37,* 719–731.
Flynn, F. J., & Lake, V. K. B. (2008). If you need help, just ask: Underestimating compliance with direct requests for help. *Journal of Personality and Social Psychology, 95,* 128–143.
Foa, E. B., Cahill, S. P., Boscarino, J. A., Hobfoll, S. E., et al. (2005). Social, psychological, and psychiatric interventions following terrorist attacks: Recommendations for practice and research. *Neuropsychopharmacology, 30,* 1806–1817.
Fodor, J. A. (1983). *Modularity of mind: An essay on faculty psychology.* Cambridge, MA: MIT Press.
Fogassi, L., Ferrari, P. F., Gesierich, B., Rozzi, S., et al. (2005). Parietal lobe: From action organization to intention understanding. *Science, 308,* 662–667.
Foley, J. M. (2004). Empirically supported treatment endeavour: A successful future or inevitable debacle? *Clinical Psychologist, 8,* 29–38.
Folkman, S. (1984). Personal control and stress and coping processes: A theoretical analysis. *Journal of Personality and Social Psychology, 46,* 839–852.
Folkman, S., & Lazarus, R. (1988). *Manual for the Ways of Coping Questionnaire.* Palo Alto, CA: Consulting Psychologists Press.
Folkman, S., Lazarus, R. S., Gruen, R. J., & DeLongis, A. (1986). Appraisal, coping, health status, and psychological symptoms. *Journal of Personality and Social Psychology, 50,* 571–579.
Folkman, S., & Moskowitz, J. T. (2000). Stress, positive emotion, and coping. *Current Directions in Psychological Science, 9,* 115–118.
Fontaine, K. L. (2009). *Mental health nursing.* Upper Saddle River, NJ: Prentice Hall.
Foote, B., Smolin, Y., Kaplan, M., Legatt, M. E., & Lipschitz, D. (2006). Prevalence of dissociative disorders in psychiatric outpatients. *American Journal of Psychiatry, 163,* 623–629.
Foote, S. L., Bloom, F. E., & Aston-Jones, G. (1983). Nucleus locus coeruleus: New evidence of anatomical and physiological specificity. *Physiology Review, 63,* 844–914.
Forbes, D., Phelps, A., & McHugh, T. (2001). Treatment of combat-related nightmares using imagery rehearsal: A pilot study. *Journal of Traumatic Stress, 14,* 433–442.
Forbes, S., Bui, S., Robinson, B. R., Hochgeschwender, U., & Brennan, M. B. (2001). Integrated control of appetite and fat metabolism by the leptin-proopiommelanocortin pathway. *Proceedings of the National Academy of Sciences, 98,* 4233–4237.
Forbey, J. D., & Ben-Porath, Y. S. (2008). Empirical correlates of the MMPI-2 restructures clinical (RC) scales in a nonclinical setting. *Journal of Personality Assessment, 90,* 136–141.
Forcelli, P. A., & Heinrichs, S. C. (2008). Teratogenic effects of maternal antidepressant exposure on neural substrates of drug-seeking behavior in offspring. *Addiction Biology, 13,* 52–62. doi:10.1111/j.1369-1600.2007.00078.x
Ford, J. M., Roach, B. J., Jorgensen, K. W., Turner, J. A., et al. (2009). Tuning in to the voices: A multisite fMRI study of auditory hallucinations. *Schizophrenia Bulletin, 35,* 58–66.
Ford, M. T., Heinen, B. A., & Langkamer, K. L. (2007). Work and family satisfaction and conflict: A meta-analysis of cross-domain relations. *Journal of Applied Psychology, 92,* 57–80.
Forgas, J. P., Dunn, E., & Granland, S. (2008). Are you being served . . . ? An unobtrusive experiment of affective influences on helping in a department store. *European Journal of Social Psychology, 38,* 333–342.
Forhan, S. E., Gottlieb, S. L., Sternberg, M. R., Xu, F., et al. (2009). Prevalence of sexually transmitted infections among female adolescents aged 14 to 19 in the United States. *Pediatrics, 124,* 1505–1512.
Formisano, E., De Martino, F., Bonte, M., & Goebel, R. (2008). "Who" is saying "what"? Brain-based decoding of human voice and speech. *Science, 322,* 970–973.
Fossati, A., Beauchaine, T. P., Grazioli, F., Borroni, S., et al. (2006). Confirmatory factor analysis of DSM-IV cluster C personality disorder criteria. *Journal of Personality Disorders, 20,* 186–203.
Fossati, P., Hevenor, S. J., Graham, S. J., Grady, C., et al. (2003). In search of the emotional self: An fMRI study using positive and negative emotional words. *American Journal of Psychiatry, 160,* 1938–1945.
Fosse, R., Stickgold, R., & Hobson, J. A. (2001). Brain-mind states: Reciprocal variation in thoughts and hallucinations. *Psychological Science, 12,* 30–36.
Foster, E. M., Jones, D., & the Conduct Problems Prevention Research Group. (2006). Can a costly intervention be cost-effective? An analysis of violence prevention. *Archives of General Psychiatry, 63,* 1284–1291.
Foster, G. D., Borradaile, K. E., Sanders, M. H., Millman, R., et al. (2009). A randomized study on the effect of weight loss on obstructive sleep apnea among obese patients with type 2 diabetes. *Archives of Internal Medicine, 169,* 1619–1626.
Foster, M. D. (2000). Positive and negative responses to personal discrimination: Does coping make a difference? *Journal of Social Psychology, 140,* 93–106.

Foster, N. E., Thomas, E., Barlas, P., Hill, J. C., et al. (2007). Acupuncture as an adjunct to exercise-based physiotherapy for osteoarthritis of the knee: Randomised controlled trial. *British Medical Journal, 335*, 436. doi:10.1136/bmj.39280.509803.BE

Foti, R. J., & Hauenstein, N. M. A. (2007). Pattern and variable approaches in leadership emergence and effectiveness. *Journal of Applied Psychology, 92*, 347–355.

Foulke, E. (1991). Braille. In M. A. Heller & W. Shiff (Eds.), *The psychology of touch.* Hillsdale, NJ: Erlbaum.

Fountain, J. W. (2000, November 28). Exorcists and exorcisms proliferate across U.S. *New York Times.* Retrieved from http://www.rickross.com/reference/general/general315.html

Fournier, J. C., DeRubeis, R. J., Hollon, S. D., Dimidjian, S., et al. (2010). Antidepressant drug effects and depression severity: A patient-level meta-analysis. *Journal of the American Medical Association, 303*, 47–53.

Fowler, G. A. (2004, March 4). Calling all jewel thieves. *Wall Street Journal,* p. B1.

Fowler, J. R., & Christakis, N. A. (2008). Dynamic spread of happiness in a large social network: Longitudinal analysis over 20 years in the Framingham Heart Study. *British Medical Journal, 337*, a2338. doi:10.1136/bmj.a2338

Fowler, R. D. (2000). A lesson in taking our own advice. *Monitor on Psychology, 31*, 9.

Fowles, D. C., & Dindo, L. (2009). Temperament and psychopathy: A dual-pathway model. *Current Directions in Psychological Science, 18*, 179–183.

Fox, A. S., & Olster, D. H. (2000). Effects of intracerebroventricular leptin administration on feeding and sexual behaviors in lean and obese female Zucker rats. *Hormones and Behavior, 37*, 377–387.

Fox, M. K., Pac, S., Devaney, B., & Jankowski, L. (2004). Feeding infants and toddlers study: What foods are infants and toddlers eating? *Journal of the American Dietetic Association, 104*(Suppl. 1), S22–S30.

Fox, P., Bain, P. G., Glickman, S., Carroll, C., & Zajicek, J. (2004). The effect of cannabis on tremor in patients with multiple sclerosis. *Neurology, 62*, 1105–1109.

Fox, S., Spector, P. E., & Miles, D. (2001). Counterproductive work behavior (CWB) in response to job stressors and organizational justice: Some mediator and moderator tests for autonomy and emotions. *Journal of Vocational Behavior, 59*, 291–309.

Frances, A. (2009). A warning sign on the road to DSM-V: Beware of its unintended consequences. *Psychiatric Times, 26*, 1–9.

Frances, A. (2010). Alert to the research community: Be prepared to weigh in on DSM-V. *Psychiatric Times, 27*, 1–5.

Francis, A. M. (2008). Family and sexual orientation: The family-demographic correlates of homosexuality in men and women. *Journal of Sex Research, 45*, 371–377.

Frank, D. A., Augustyn, M., Knight, W. G., Pell, T., & Zuckerman, B. (2001). Growth, development, and behavior in early childhood following prenatal cocaine exposure: A systematic review. *Journal of the American Medical Association, 285*, 1613–1625.

Frank, M. G., Ekman, P., & Friesen, W. V. (1993). Behavioral markers and recognizability of the smile of enjoyment. *Journal of Personality and Social Psychology, 64*, 83–93.

Frank, M. J., O'Reilly, R. C., & Curran, T. (2006). When memory fails, intuition reigns: Midazolam enhances implicit inference in humans. *Psychological Science, 17*, 700–707.

Frankenberg, W. K., & Dodds, J. B. (1967). The Denver Developmental Screening Test. *Journal of Pediatrics, 71*, 181–191.

Frankl, V. (1963). *Man's search for meaning.* New York: Washington Square Press.

Franks, P. W., Hanson, R. L., Knowler, W. C., Sievers, M. L., et al. (2010). Childhood obesity, other cardiovascular risk factors, and premature death. *New England Journal of Medicine, 362*, 485–493.

Frasure-Smith, N., & Lespérance, F. (2005). Depression and coronary heart disease. *Current Directions in Psychological Science, 14*, 39–43.

Fratiglioni, L., & Qiu, C. (2009). Prevention of common neurodegenerative disorders in the elderly. *Experimental Gerontology, 44*, 46–50.

Frayling, T. M., Timpson, N. J., Weedon, M. N., Zeggini, E., et al. (2007). A common variant in the FTO gene is associated with body mass index and predisposes to childhood and adult obesity. *Science, 316*, 889–894.

Fredrickson, B. L. (2001). The role of positive emotions in positive psychology: The broaden-and-build theory of positive emotions. *American Psychologist, 56*, 218–226.

Fredrickson, B. L., & Cohn, M. A. (2008). Positive emotions. In M. Lewis, J. M. Haviland-Jones, & L. F. Barrett (Eds.), *Handbook of emotions* (3rd ed., pp. 777–796). New York: Guilford Press.

Fredrickson, B. L., & Losada, M. F. (2005). Positive affect and the complex dynamics of human flourishing. *American Psychologist, 60*, 678–686.

Fredrickson, B. L., Cohn, M. A., Coffey, K. A., Pek, J., & Finkel, S. M. (2008). Open hearts build lives: Positive emotions, induced through loving-kindness meditation, build consequential personal resources. *Journal of Personality and Social Psychology, 95*, 1045–1062.

Freed, C. R., Greene, P. E., Breeze, R. E., Tsai, W. Y., et al. (2001). Transplantation of embryonic dopamine neurons for severe Parkinson's disease. *New England Journal of Medicine, 344*, 710–719.

Freedland, R. L., & Bertenthal, B. I. (1994). Developmental changes in interlimb coordination: Transition to hands-and-knees crawling. *Psychological Science, 5*, 26–32.

Freedman, D. M., Ron, E., Ballard-Barbash, R., Doody, M. M., & Linet, M. S. (2006). Body mass index and all-cause mortality in a nationwide U.S. cohort. *International Journal of Obesity, 30*, 822–829.

Freedman, J. L. (1992). Television violence and aggression: What psychologists should tell the public. In P. Suedfeld & P. E. Tetlock (Eds.), *Psychology and social policy* (pp. 179–189). New York: Hemisphere.

Freedman, J. L. (2002). *Media violence and its effect on aggression: Assessing the scientific evidence.* Toronto: University of Toronto Press.

Freedman, J. L., & Fraser, S. C. (1966). Compliance without pressure: The foot-in-the-door technique. *Journal of Personality and Social Psychology, 4*, 195–202.

Freedman, R. (2003). Schizophrenia. *New England Journal of Medicine, 349*, 1738–1749.

Freedman, V. A., Aykan, H., & Martin, L. G. (2001). Aggregate changes in severe cognitive impairment among older Americans, 1993 and 1998. *Journal of Gerontology, 56B*, S100–S111.

Freeman, M. P., Freeman, S. A., & McElroy, S. L. (2002). The comorbidity of bipolar and anxiety disorders: Prevalence, psychobiology, and treatment issues. *Journal of Affective Disorders, 68*, 1–23.

Freeman, W., & Watts, J. W. (1942). *Psychosurgery.* Springfield, IL: Thomas.

Frei, A., Schenker, T., Finzen, A., Dittman, V., et al. (2003). The Werther effect and assisted suicide. *Suicide and Life-Threatening Behavior, 33*, 192–200.

Freitag, C. M. (2007). The genetics of autistic disorders and its clinical significance: A review of the literature. *Molecular Psychiatry, 12*, 2–22.

Fremgen, A., & Fay, D. (1980). Overextensions in production and comprehension: A methodological clarification. *Journal of Child Language, 7*, 205–211.

Frese, M., Beimel, S., & Schoenborn, S. (2003). Action training for charismatic leadership: Two evaluations of studies of a commercial training module on inspirational communication of a vision. *Personnel Psychology, 56*, 671–697.

Freud, A. (1946). *The ego and the mechanisms of defense.* New York: International Universities Press.

Freud, S. (1900). The interpretation of dreams. In J. Strachey (Ed.), *The standard edition of the complete psychological works of Sigmund Freud* (Vol. 8). London: Hogarth Press.

Freud, S., & Breuer, J. (1895/2004). *Studies in hysteria.* New York: Penguin.

Frey, K. S., Hirschstein, M. K., Snell, J. L., Edstrom, L. V. S., et al. (2005). Reducing playground bullying and supporting beliefs: An experimental trial of the Steps to Respect program. *Developmental Psychology, 41*, 479–491.

Frey, M. C., & Detterman, D. K. (2004). Scholastic assessment or g? The relationship between the SAT and general cognitive ability. *Psychological Science, 15*, 373–378.

Frey, W. H. (2003). Married with children. *American Demographics, 25*(2), 17.

Fride, E., & Mechoulam, R. (1993). Pharmacological activity of the cannabinoid receptor agonist, anandamide, a brain constituent. *European Journal of Pharmacology, 231*, 313–314.

Fridlund, A., Sabini, J. P., Hedlund, L. E., Schaut, J. A., et al. (1990). Audience effects on solitary faces during imagery: Displaying to the people in your head. *Journal of Nonverbal Behavior, 14*, 113–137.

Fried, P. A., Watkinson, B., & Gray, R. (1992). A follow-up study of attentional behavior in 6-year-old children exposed prenatally to marijuana, cigarettes, and alcohol. *Neurotoxicity and Teratology, 14*, 299–311.

Fried, Y., & Tiegs, R. B. (1995). Supervisors' role conflict and role ambiguity differential relations with performance ratings of subordinates and the moderating effect of screening ability. *Journal of Applied Psychology, 80*, 282–291.

Friedman, H. S. (2000). Long-term relations of personality and health: Dynamisms, mechanisms, tropisms. *Journal of Personality, 68*, 1089–1107.

Friedman, H. S., & Schustack, M. W. (2003). *Personality: Classic theories and modern research* (2nd ed.). Boston: Allyn & Bacon.

Friedman, H. S., & Schustack, M. (2009). *Personality: Classic theories and modern research* (4th ed.). Boston: Allyn & Bacon.

Friedman, H. S., Tucker, J. S., Schwartz, J. E., Martin, L. R., et al. (1995a). Childhood conscientiousness and longevity: Health behaviors and cause of death. *Journal of Personality and Social Psychology, 68*, 696–703.

Friedman, H. S., Tucker, J. S., Schwartz, J. E., Tomlinson-Keasey, C., et al. (1995b). Psychosocial and behavioral predictors of longevity: The aging and death of the "Termites." *American Psychologist, 50*, 69–78.

Friedman, M. A., Detweiler-Bedell, J. B., Leventhal, H. E., Horne, R., et al. (2004). Combined psychotherapy and pharmacotherapy for the treatment of major depressive disorder. *Clinical Psychology: Science and Practice, 11*, 47–68.

Friedman, M., Ibrahim, H., Lee, G., & Joseph, N. J. (2003). Combined uvulopalatopharyngoplasty and radiofrequency tongue base reduction for treatment of obstructive sleep apnea/hypopnea syndrome. *Otolaryngological Head and Neck Surgery, 129*, 611–621.

Friedman, M., & Rosenman, R. H. (1974). *Type A behavior and your heart.* New York: Knopf.

Friedman, M. I. (2007). Obesity and the hepatic control of feeding behavior. *Drug News Perspectives, 20*, 573–578.

Friedman, N. P., Miyake, A., Corley, R. P., Young, S. E., et al. (2006). Not all executive functions are related to intelligence. *Current Directions in Psychological Science, 17*, 172–179.

Fritsch, T., Smyth, K. A., McClendon, M. J., Ogrocki, P. K., et al. (2005). Associations between dementia/mild cognitive impairment and cognitive performance and activity levels in youth. *Journal of the American Geriatrics Society, 53*, 1191–1196.

Frizzell, J. P. (2005). Acute stroke: Pathophysiology, diagnosis, and treatment. *AACN Clinical Issues, 16*, 421–440.

Frodl, T., Meisenzahl, E. M., Zill, P., Baghai, T., et al. (2004). Reduced hippocampal volumes associated with the long variant of the serotonin transporter polymorphism in major depression. *Archives of General Psychiatry, 61*, 177–183.

Frone, M. R. (2008). Are work stressors related to employee substance use? The importance of temporal context assessments of alcohol and illicit drug use. *Journal of Applied Psychology, 93*, 199–206.

Frost, J. A., Binder, J. R., Springer, J. A., Hammeke, T. A., et al. (1999). Language processing is strongly left lateralized in both sexes. Evidence from functional MRI. *Brain, 122*(pt. 2), 199–208.

Fuentemilla, L., Càmara, E., Münte, T. F., Krämer, U. M., et al. (2009). Individual differences in true and false memory retrieval are related to white matter brain microstructure. *Journal of Neuroscience, 29*, 8698–8703.

Fujita, F., & Diener, E. (2005). Life satisfaction set point: Stability and change. *Journal of Personality and Social Psychology, 88*, 158–164.

Fuligni, A. J., & Pedersen, S. (2002). Family obligation and the transition to young adulthood. *Developmental Psychology, 38*, 856–868.

Fuligni, A. J., Witkow, M., & Garcia, C. (2005). Ethnic identity and the academic adjustment of adolescents from Mexican, Chinese, and European backgrounds. *Developmental Psychology, 41*, 799–811.

Fullana, M. A., Mataix-Cols, D., Caspi, A., Harrington, H., et al. (2009). Prevalence, interference, help-seeking, developmental stability, and co-ocurring psychiatric conditions. *American Journal of Psychiatry, 166,* 329–336. doi:10.1176/appi.ajp.2008.08071006

Fullerton, C. S., Ursano, R. J., & Wang, L. (2004). Acute stress disorder, posttraumatic stress disorder, and depression in disaster or rescue workers. *American Journal of Psychiatry, 161,* 1370–1376.

Fullerton, J. M., Donald, J. A., Mitchell, P. B., & Schofield, P. R. (2010). Two-dimensional genome scan identifies multiple genetic interactions in bipolar affective disorder. *Biological Psychiatry, 67,* 478–486.

Funder, D.C. (2007). *The personality puzzle* (4th ed.). New York: Norton.

Funder, D. C. (2008). Persons, situations, and person-situation interactions In O. P. John, R. W. Robins, & L. A. Pervin (Eds.), *Handbook of personality: Theory and research* (3rd ed., pp. 568–582). New York: Guilford Press.

Funder, D. C., & Fast, L. (2010). Personality in social psychology. In S. T. Fiske, D. T. Gilbert, & G. Lindzey (Eds.), *Handbook of social psychology* (5th ed., Vol. 2, pp. 668–697). Hoboken, NJ: Wiley.

Funk, J. B., Flores, G., Buchman, D. D., & Germann, J. N. (1999). Rating electronic games: Violence is in the eye of the beholder. *Youth and Society, 30,* 283–312.

Furey, M. L., Pietrini, P., & Haxby, J. V. (2000). Cholinergic enhancement and increased selectivity of perceptual processing during working memory. *Science, 290,* 2315–2319.

Furmark, T., Henningsson, S., Appel, L., Ahs, F., et al. (2009). Genotype over-diagnosis in amygdala responsiveness: affective processing in social anxiety disorder. *Journal of Psychiatry and Neuroscience, 34,* 30–40.

Furnham, A. (2001). Personality and individual differences in the workplace: Person-organization-outcome fit. In R. Hogan & B. Roberts (Eds.), *Personality psychology in the workplace* (pp. 223–251). Washington, DC: American Psychological Association.

Furstenberg, F. F., Brooks-Gunn, J., & Chase-Lansdale, L. (1989). Teenaged pregnancy and childbearing. *American Psychologist, 44,* 313–320.

Fyer, A. J., Hamilton, S. P., Durner, M., Haghighi, F., et al. (2006). A third-pass genome scan in panic disorder: Evidence for multiple susceptibility loci. *Biological Psychiatry, 60,* 388–401.

Gabbard, G. O. (2004). *Long-term psychodynamic psychotherapy: A basic text.* Washington DC: American Psychiatric Association.

Gabrieli, J. D. E., Fleischman, D. A., Keane, M. M., Reminger, S. L., & Morrell, F. (1995). Double dissociation between memory systems underlying explicit and implicit memory in the human brain. *Psychological Science, 6,* 76–82.

Gaertner, S. L., & Dovidio, J. F. (1986). The aversive form of racism. In J. F. Dovidio & S. L. Gaertner (Eds.), *Prejudice, discrimination, and racism* (pp. 61–89). Orlando, FL: Academic Press.

Gaertner, S. L., Dovidio, J. F., & Houlette, M. (2010). Social categorization. In J. F. Dovidio, M. Hewstone, P. Glick, & V. M. Esses (Eds.), *The SAGE handbook of prejudice, stereotyping, and discrimination* (pp. 526–543) London: Sage.

Gagnon, J. F., Postuma, R. B., Mazza, S., Doyon, J., & Montplaisir, J. (2006). Rapid-eye-movement sleep behaviour disorder and neurodegenerative diseases. *Lancet Neurology, 5,* 424–432.

Gagnon, J. F., Postuma, R. B., & Montplaisir, J. (2006). Update on the pharmacology of REM sleep behavior disorder. *Neurology, 67,* 742–747.

Gaillard, D., Passilly-Degrace, P., & Besnard, P. (2008). Molecular mechanisms of fat preference and overeating. *Annals of the New York Academy of Sciences, 1141,* 163–175.

Gaillard, R., Del Cul, A., Naccache, L., Vinckier, F., et al. (2006). Nonconscious semantic processing of emotional words modulates conscious access. *Proceedings of the National Academy of Sciences, 103,* 7524–7529.

Gais, S., Albouy, G., Boly, M., Dang-Vu, T. T., et al. (2007). Sleep transforms the cerebral trace of declarative memories. *Proceedings of the National Academy of Sciences, 104,* 18778–18783.

Gais, S., Lucas, B., & Born, J. (2006). Sleep after learning aids memory recall. *Learning and Memory, 13,* 259–262.

Galambos, N. L., Barker, E. T., & Krahn, H. J. (2006). Depression, self-esteem, and anger in emerging adulthood: Seven-year trajectories. *Developmental Psychology, 42,* 350–365.

Galanter, E. (1962). Contemporary psychophysics. In R. Brown, E. Galanter, E. H. Hess, & G. Mandler (Eds.), *New directions in psychology* (Vol. 1, pp. 87–156). New York: Holt, Rinehart & Winston.

Galatzer-Levy, R. M., Bachrach, H., Skolnikoff, A., & Waldron, S., Jr. (2000). *Does psychoanalysis work?* New Haven, CT: Yale University Press.

Galdeira, K. (2006, October). Phiten power. *Hawaii Business,* pp. 52–54.

Gale, C. R., Batty, G., & Deary, I. J. (2008). Locus of control at age 10 years and health outcomes and behaviors at age 30 years: The 1970 British cohort study. *Psychosomatic Medicine, 70,* 397–403.

Galea, S., Ahern, J., Resnick, H., Kilpatrick, D., et al. (2002). Psychological sequelae of the September 11 terrorist attacks in New York City. *New England Journal of Medicine, 346,* 982–987.

Galea, S., Resnick, H., Ahern, J., Gold, J., et al. (2002). Posttraumatic stress disorder in Manhattan, New York City, after the September 11th terrorist attacks. *Journal of Urban Health, 79,* 340–353.

Galef, B. G., & Wright, T. J. (1995). Groups of naive rats learn to select nutritionally adequate foods faster than do isolated rats. *Animal Behaviour 49,* 403–409.

Galinsky, A. D., & Kray, L. J. (2004). From thinking about what might have been to sharing what we know: The effects of counterfactual mind-sets on information sharing in groups. *Journal of Experimental Social Psychology, 40,* 606–618.

Gallagher, M., & Chiba, A. A. (1996). The amygdala and emotion. *Current Opinions in Neurobiology, 6,* 221–227.

Gallivan, J. P., Cavina-Pratesi, C., & Culham, J. C. (2009). Is that within reach? fMRI reveals that the human superior parieto-occipital cortex encodes objects reachable by the hand. *Journal of Neuroscience, 29,* 4381–4391.

Gallo, D. A. (2006). *Associative illusions of memory.* New York: Psychology Press.

Galloway, A. T., Addessi, E., Fragaszy, D. M., & Visalberghi, E. (2005). Social facilitation of eating familiar food in tufted capuchins (*Cebus appella*): Does it involve behavioral coordination? *International Journal of Primatology, 26,* 181–189.

Galotti, K. M. (1999). Making a "major" real-life decision: College students choosing an academic major. *Journal of Educational Psychology, 91,* 379–387.

Galotti, K. M. (2007). Decision structuring in important real-life choices. *Psychological Science, 18,* 320–325.

Galpin, A., Underwood, G., & Chapman, P. (2008). Sensing without seeing in comparative visual search. *Consciousness and Cognition, 17,* 672–687.

Gamer, M., Rill, H.-G., Vossel, G., & Godert, H. W. (2006). Psychophysiological and vocal measures in the detection of guilty knowledge. *International Journal of Psychophysiology, 60,* 76–87.

Gan, T. J., Jiao, K. R., Zenn, M., & Georgiade, G. (2004). A randomized controlled comparison of electro-acupoint stimulation or ondansetron versus placebo for the prevention of postoperative nausea and vomiting. *Anesthesia and Analgesia, 99,* 1070–1075.

Ganchrow, J. R., Steiner, J. E., & Daher, M. (1983). Neonatal facial expressions in response to different qualities and intensities of gustatory stimuli. *Infant Behavior and Development, 6,* 189–200.

Gangestad, S. W., Garver-Apgar, C. E., Simpson, J. A., & Cousins, A. J. (2007). Changes in women's mate preferences across the ovulatory cycle. *Journal of Personality and Social Psychology, 92,* 151–163.

Ganzel, B. L., Kim, P., Glover, G. H., & Temple, E. (2008). Resilience after 9/11: Multimodal neuroimaging evidence for stress-related change in the healthy adult brain. *Neuroimage, 40,* 788–795. Epub 2008 Jan 2029.

Ganzel, B. L., Morris, P. A., & Wethington, E. (2010). Allostasis and the human brain: Integrating models of stress from the social and life sciences. *Psychological Review, 117,* 134–174.

Gao, Y., Raine, A., Venables, P. H., Dawson, M. E., & Mednick, S. A. (2010). Association of poor childhood fear conditioning and adult crime. *American Journal of Psychiatry, 167,* 56–60.

Garb, H. N. (1997). Race bias, social class bias, and gender bias in clinical judgment. *Clinical Psychology: Science and Practice, 4,* 99–120.

Garb, H. N., Wood, J. M., Lilienfeld, S. O., & Nezworski, T. (2005). Roots of the Rorschach controversy. *Clinical Psychology Review, 25,* 97–118.

Garbarino, S., Nobili, L., Beelke, M., De Carli, F., & Ferrillo, F. (2001). The contributing role of sleepiness in highway vehicle accidents. *Sleep, 24,* 203–206.

Garber, R. J. (1992). Long-term effects of divorce on the self-esteem of young adults. *Journal of Divorce and Remarriage, 17,* 131–138.

Garbutt, J. C., Kranzler, H. R., O'Malley, S. S., Gastfriend, D. R., et al. (2005). Efficacy and tolerability of long-acting injectable naltrexone for alcohol dependence: A randomized controlled trial. *Journal of the American Medical Association, 293,* 1617–1625.

Garcia, J., & Koelling, R. A. (1966). Relation of cue to consequences in avoidance learning. *Psychonomic Science, 4,* 123–124.

Garcia, J., Rusiniak, K. W., & Brett, L. P. (1977). Conditioning food-illness aversions in wild animals: *Caveat canonici.* In H. Davis & H. M. B. Hurwitz (Eds.), *Operant-Pavlovian interactions.* Hillsdale, NJ: Erlbaum.

Garcia, S. M., Weaver, K., Moskowitz, G. B., & Darley, J. M. (2002). Crowded minds: The implicit bystander effect. *Journal of Personality and Social Psychology, 83,* 843–853.

Gardiner, H. W., & Kosmitzki, C. (2005). *Lives across cultures: Cross-cultural human development* (3rd ed.). Boston: Allyn & Bacon.

Gardner, H. (1991). Assessment in context: The alternative to standardized testing. In B. R. Gifford & M. C. O'Connor (Eds.), *Changing assessments: Alternative views of aptitude, achievement, and instruction* (pp. 77–120). Boston: Kluwer.

Gardner, H. (1993). *Multiple intelligences: The theory in practice.* New York: Basic Books.

Gardner, H. (1999). Are there additional intelligences? The case for naturalist, spiritual, and existential intelligences. In J. Kane (Ed.), *Education, information and transformation: Essays on learning and thinking* (pp. 111–131). Englewood Cliffs, NJ: Prentice Hall.

Gardner, H. (2002). *Learning from extraordinary minds.* Mahwah, NJ: Erlbaum.

Gardner, M. (1988). *The second Scientific American book of mathematical puzzles and diversions.* Chicago: University of Chicago Press.

Gardner, M., & Steinberg, L. (2005). Peer influence on risk taking, risk preference, and risky decision making in adolescence and adulthood: An experimental study. *Developmental Psychology, 41,* 625–635.

Gardner, R., Heward, W. L., & Grossi, T. A. (1994). Effects of response cards on student participation and academic achievement: A systematic replication with inner-city students during whole-class science instruction. *Journal of Applied Behavior Analysis, 27,* 63–71.

Gardner, R. A., & Gardner, B. T. (1978). Comparative psychology and language acquisition. *Annals of the New York Academy of Sciences, 309,* 37–76.

Garfield, S. L. (1998). Some comments on empirically supported treatments. *Journal of Consulting and Clinical Psychology, 66,* 121–125.

Gariepy, G., Nitka, D., & Schmitz, N. (2010). The association between obesity and anxiety disorders in the population: A systematic review and meta-analysis. *International Journal of Obesity, 34,* 407–419.

Garlick, D. (2002). Understanding the nature of general intelligence: The role of individual differences in neural plasticity as an explanatory mechanism. *Psychological Review, 109,* 116–136.

Garlick, D. (2003). Integrating brain science research with intelligence research. *Current Directions in Psychological Science, 12,* 185–188.

Garris, P. A., Kilpatrick, M., Bunin, M. A., Michael, D., et al. (1999). Dissociation of dopamine release in the nucleus accumbens from intracranial self-stimulation. *Nature, 398,* 67–69.

Garry, M., & Loftus, E. (1994). Pseudomemories without hypnosis. *International Journal of Clinical and Experimental Hypnosis, 42,* 363–373.

Garry, M., & Polaschek, D. L. L. (2000). Imagination and memory. *Current Directions in Psychological Science, 9,* 6–10.

Garson, L. (2006). *Surviving Babylon: A journey through repressed memories of sexual abuse.* Atlanta: Griffin.

Garver-Apgar, C. E., Gangestad, S. W., & Thornhill, R. (2008). Hormonal correlates of women's mid-cycle preference for the scent of symmetry. *Evolution and Human Behavior, 29,* 223–232.

Gasser, U. S., Rousson, V., Hentschel, F., Sattel, H., & Gasser, T. (2008). Alzheimer disease versus mixed dementias: An EEG perspective. *Clinical Neurophysiology, 119,* 2255–2259.

Gatewood, R. D., & Feild, H. S. (2001). *Human resource selection* (5th ed.). Fort Worth, TX: Harcourt.

Gathercole, S. E., Pickering, S. J., Ambridge, B., & Wearing, H. (2004). The structure of working memory from 4 to 15 years of age. *Developmental Psychology, 40,* 177–190.

Gauvain, M. (2001). *The social context of cognitive development.* New York: Guilford Press.

Gauvreau, P., & Bouchard, S. (2008). Preliminary evidence for the efficacy of EMDR in treating generalized anxiety disorder. *Journal of EMDR Practice and Research, 2,* 26–40.

Gawande, A. A. (2008, June 30). The itch. *New Yorker.* Retrieved from http://www.newyorker.com/reporting/2008/06/30/080630fa_fact_gawande?currentPage=all

Gazzaley, A., Cooney, J. W., Rissman, J., & D'Esposito, M. (2005). Top-down suppression deficit underlies working memory impairment in normal aging. *Nature Neuroscience, 8,* 1298–1300.

Gazzaniga, M. S., & LeDoux, J. E. (1978). *The integrated mind.* New York: Plenum.

Geary, D. C. (1999). Evolution and developmental sex differences. *Current Directions in Psychological Science, 8,* 115–120.

Geary, D. C. (2000). Evolution and proximate expression of human paternal investment. *Psychological Bulletin, 126,* 55–77.

Geddes, J. R., Burgess, S., Hawton, K., Jamison, K., & Goodwin, G. M. (2004). Long-term lithium therapy for bipolar disorder: Systematic review and meta-analysis of randomized controlled trials. *American Journal of Psychiatry, 161,* 217–222.

Geddes, L. (2008). Are autistic savants made not born? *New Scientist, 198,* 10.

Geen, R. G. (1998). Aggression and antisocial behavior. In D. T. Gilbert, S. T. Fiske, & G. Lindzey (Eds.), *Handbook of social psychology* (4th ed., Vol. 2, pp. 317–356). New York: McGraw-Hill.

Geen, R. G., & McCown, E. J. (1984). Effects of noise and attack on aggression and physiological arousal. *Motivation and Emotion, 8,* 231–241.

Gegenfurtner, K. R., & Kiper, D. C. (2003). Color vision. *Annual Review of Neuroscience, 26,* 181–206.

Geher, G., Camargo, M. A., & O'Rourke, S. D. (2008). Mating intelligence: An integrative model and future research directions. In G. Geher & G. Miller (Eds.), *Mating intelligence: Sex, relationships, and the mind's reproductive system* (pp. 395–424). Mahwah, NJ: Erlbaum.

Geier, A. B., Rozin, P., & Doros, G. (2006). Unit bias: A new heuristic that helps explain the effect of portion size on food intake. *Psychological Science, 17,* 521–525.

Gelabert-Gonzalez, M., & Fernandez-Villa, J. (2001). Mutism after posterior fossa surgery: Review of the literature. *Clinical Neurology and Neurosurgery, 103,* 111–114.

Geldmacher, D. S., Provenzano, G., McRae, T., Mastey, V., & Ieni, J. R. (2003). Donepezil is associated with delayed nursing home placement in patients with Alzheimer's disease. *Journal of the American Geriatric Society, 51,* 937–944.

Geleijnse, J. M. (2008). Habitual coffee consumption and blood pressure: An epidemiological perspective. *Vascular Health Risk Management, 4,* 963–970.

Gelhorn, H. L., Stallings, M. C., Young, S. E., Corley, R. P., et al. (2005). Genetic and environmental influences on conduct disorder: Symptom, domain, and full-scale analyses. *Journal of Child Psychology and Psychiatry, 46,* 580–591.

Gelman, R., & Baillargeon, R. (1983). A review of some Piagetian concepts. In P. H. Mussen (Ed.), *Handbook of child psychology* (Vol. 3, pp. 167–230). New York: Wiley.

Gentilucci, M., & Dalla Volta, R. (2008). Spoken language and arm gestures are controlled by the same motor control system. *Quarterly Journal of Experimental Psychology (Colchester), 61,* 944–957.

George, M. S., Anton, R. F., Bloomer, C., Teneback, C., et al. (2001). Activation of prefrontal cortex and anterior thalamus in alcoholic subjects on exposure to alcohol-specific cues. *Archives of General Psychiatry, 58,* 345–352.

George, M. S., Lisanby, S. H., Avery, D., McDonald, W. M., et al. (2010). Daily left prefrontal transcranial magnetic stimulation therapy for major depressive disorder: A sham-controlled randomized trial. *Archives of General Psychiatry, 67,* 507–516.

George, W. H., & Marlatt, G. A. (1986). The effects of alcohol and anger on interest in violence, erotica, and deviance. *Journal of Abnormal Psychology, 95,* 150–158.

Geraerts, E., Bernstein, D. M., Merckelbach, H., Linders, C., et al. (2008). Lasting false beliefs and their behavioral consequences. *Psychological Science, 19,* 749–753.

Geraerts, E., Lindsay, D. S., Merckelbach, H., Jelicic, M., et al. (2008). Cognitive mechanisms underlying recovered-memory experiences of childhood sexual abuse. *Psychological Science, 20,* 92–98.

Geraerts, E., Schooler, J. W., Merckelbach, H., Jelicic, M., et al. (2007). The reality of recovered memories: Corroborating continuous and discontinuous memories of childhood sexual abuse, *Psychological Science, 18,* 564–568.

Geraerts, E., Smeets, E., Jelicic, M., Merckelbach, H., & van Heerden, J. (2006). Retrieval inhibition of trauma-related words in women reporting repressed or recovered memories of childhood sexual abuse. *Behaviour Research and Therapy, 44,* 1129–1136.

Gerbner, G., Morgan, M., & Signorielli, N. (1994). *Television violence profile No. 16: The turning point.* Philadelphia: Annenberg School for Communication.

Gerhart, B. (2005). The (affective) dispositional approach to job satisfaction: Sorting out the policy implications. *Journal of Organizational Behavior, 26,* 79–97.

Gerin, W., Davidson, K. W., Christenfeld, N. J. S., Goyal, T., & Schwartz, J. E. (2006). The role of angry rumination and distraction in blood pressure recovery from emotional arousal. *Psychosomatic Medicine, 68,* 64–72.

Gerken, L. (1994). Child phonology: Past research, present questions, future directions. In M. A. Gernsbacher (Ed), *Handbook of psycholinguistics* (pp. 781–820). San Diego, CA: Academic Press.

German, T. P., & Barrett, H. C. (2005). Functional fixedness in a technologically sparse culture. *Psychological Science, 16,* 1–5.

Gerschman, J. A., Reade, P. C., & Burrows, G. D. (1980). Hypnosis and dentistry. In G. D. Burrows & L. Dennerstein (Eds.), *Handbook of hypnosis and psychosomatic medicine.* Amsterdam: Elsevier.

Gershoff, E. T., & Bitensky, S. H. (2007). The case against corporal punishment of children: Converging evidence from social science research and international human rights law and implications for U.S. public policy. *Psychology, Public Policy, and Law, 13,* 231–272.

Gerstner, C. R., & Day, D. V. (1997). Meta-analytic review of leader–member exchange theory: Correlates and construct issues. *Journal of Applied Psychology, 82,* 827–844.

Geschwind, N. (1968). Disconnexion syndromes in animals and man. *Brain, 88,* 237–294.

Geschwind, N. (1979). Specializations of the human brain. *Scientific American, 241,* 180–199.

Gessner, B. D., Ives, G. C., & Perham-Hester, K. A. (2001). Association between sudden infant death syndrome and prone sleep position, bed sharing, and sleeping outside an infant crib in Alaska. *Pediatrics, 108,* 923–927.

Getzfeld, A. R. (2006). *Essentials of abnormal psychology.* Hoboken, NJ: Wiley.

Ghaemi, S. N. (2008). *Mood disorders* (2nd ed.). Philadelphia: Wolters Kluwer Health/ Lippincott, Williams & Wilkins.

Gianakos, I. (2002). Predictors of coping with work stress: The influences of sex, gender role, social desirability, and locus of control. *Sex Roles, 46,* 149–158.

Gianaros, P. J., May, J. C., Siegle, G. J., & Jennings, J. R. (2005). Is there a functional neural correlate of individual differences in cardiovascular reactivity? *Psychosomatic Medicine, 67,* 31–39.

Giancola, P. R., Josephs, R. A., Parrott, D. J., & Duke, A. A. (2010). Alcohol myopia revisited: Clarifying aggression and other acts of disinhibition through a distorted lens. *Perspectives on Psychological Science, 5,* 265–278.

Gibbons, A. M., & Rupp, D. E. (2009). Dimension consistency as an individual difference: A new (old) perspective on the assessment center construct validity debate. *Journal of Management, 35,* 1154–1180.

Gibbons, R. D., Hur, K., Bhaumik, D. K., & Mann, J. J. (2005). The relationship between antidepressant use and rate of suicide. *Archives of General Psychiatry, 62,* 165–172.

Gibbs, J. C., Basinger, K. S., Grime, R. L., & Snarey, J. R. (2007). Moral judgment development across cultures: Revisiting Kohlberg's universality claims. *Developmental Review, 27,* 443–500.

Gibson, E. J., & Walk, R. D. (1960). The visual cliff. *Scientific American, 202,* 64–71.

Gibson, J. J. (1979). *The ecological approach to visual perception.* Boston: Houghton Mifflin.

Gifford, R., & Hine, D. (1997). Toward cooperation in the commons dilemma. *Canadian Journal of Behavioural Science, 29,* 167–178.

Gigerenzer, G. (2004). Dread risk, September 11, and fatal traffic accidents. *Psychological Science, 15,* 286–287.

Gilbert, A. L., Regier, T., Kay, P., & Ivry, R. B. (2006). Whorf hypothesis is supported in the right visual field but not the left. *Proceedings of the National Academy of Sciences, 103,* 489–494.

Gilbert, C. D. (1992). Horizontal integration and cortical dynamics. *Neuron, 9,* 1–13.

Gilbert, D. T. (2006). *Stumbling on happiness.* New York: Knopf.

Gilbert, D. T., Morewedge, C. K., Risen, J. L., & Wilson, T. D. (2004). Looking forward to looking backward: The misprediction of regret. *Psychological Science, 15,* 346–350.

Gilbert, D. T., & Wilson, T. D. (1998). Miswanting: Some problems in the forecasting of future affective states. In J. P. Forgas (Ed.), *Feeling and thinking: The role of affect in social cognition* (pp. 178–197). New York: Cambridge University Press.

Gilbert, R. M. (1984). Caffeine consumption. In G. A. Spiller (Ed.), *The methylxanthine beverages and foods: Chemistry, consumption, and health effects* (pp. 185–213). New York: Liss.

Gilbert, S. (1997, August 20). Two spanking studies indicate parents should be cautious. *New York Times Magazine.* Retrieved from http://www.nytimes.com/1997/08/20/us/2-spanking-studies-indicate-parents-should-be-cautious.html

Gilboa-Schechtman, E., & Foa, E. B. (2001). Patterns of recovery from trauma: The use of intraindividual analysis. *Journal of Abnormal Psychology, 110,* 392–400.

Gilden, D. L., & Marusich, L. R. (2009). Contraction of time in attention-deficit hyperactivity disorder. *Neruopsychology, 23,* 265–269.

Giles, L. C., Glonek, G. F., Luszcz, M. A., & Andrews, G. R. (2005). Effect of social networks on 10-year survival in very old Australians: The Australian Longitudinal Study of Aging. *Journal of Epidemiology and Community Health, 59,* 574–579.

Gilissen, R., Bakermans-Kranenburg, M. J., van IJzendoorn, M. H., & van der Veer, R. (2008). Parent-child relationship, temperament, and physiological reactions to fear-inducing film clips: Further evidence for differential susceptibility. *Journal of Experimental Child Psychology, 99,* 182–195.

Gillham, J. E. (Ed). (2000). *The science of optimism and hope: Research essays in honor of Martin E. P. Seligman.* Philadelphia: Templeton Foundation Press.

Gillham, J. E., Reivich, K. J., Freres, D. R., Chaplin, T. M., et al. (2007). School-based prevention of depressive symptoms: A randomized controlled study of the effectiveness and specificity of the Penn Resiliency Program. *Journal of Consulting and Clinical Psychology, 75,* 9–19.

Gilligan, C. (1982). *In a different voice: Psychological theory and women's development.* Cambridge, MA: Harvard University Press.

Gilligan, C. (1993). Adolescent development reconsidered. In A. Garrod (Ed.), *Approaches to moral development: New research and emerging themes* (pp. 103–131). New York: Teachers College Press.

Gilmore, G. C., Spinks, R. A., & Thomas, C. W. (2006). Age effects in coding tasks: Componential analysis and test of the sensory deficit hypothesis. *Psychology and Aging, 21,* 7–18.

Gilmore, J. H. (2010). Understanding what causes schizophrenia: A developmental perspective. *American Journal of Psychiatry, 167,* 8–10.

Gilmore, M. M., & Murphy, C. (1989). Aging is associated with increased Weber ratios for caffeine, but not for sucrose. *Perception and Psychophysics, 46,* 555–559.

Gilmore, R. L., Heilman, K. M., Schmidt, R. P., Fennell, E. M., & Quisling, R. (1992). Anosognosia during Wada testing. *Neurology, 42,* 925–927.

Giltay, E. J., Geleijnse, J. M., Zitman, F. G., Hoekstra, T., & Schouten, E. G. (2004). Dispositional optimism and all-cause and cardiovascular mortality in a prospective cohort of elderly Dutch men and women. *Archives of General Psychiatry, 61,* 1126–1135.

Giltay, E. J., Kamphuis, M. H., Kalmijn, S., Zitman, F. G., & Kromhout, D. (2006). Dispositional optimism and the risk of cardiovascular death: The Zutphen elderly study. *Archives of Internal Medicine, 166,* 431–436.

Ginges, J., Atran, S., Medin, D., & Shikaki, K. (2007). Sacred bounds on rational resolution of violent political conflict. *Proceeedings of the National Academy of Sciences, 104,* 7357–7360.

Gingras, J. L., Mitchell, E. A., & Grattan, K. E. (2005). Fetal homologue of infant crying. *Archives of Disease in Childhood: Fetal and Neonatal Edition, 90,* F415–F418.

Gino, F., Ayal, S., & Ariely, D. (2009). Contagion and differentiation in unethical behavior: The effect of one bad apple on the barrel. *Psychological Science, 20,* 393–398.

Ginsberg, D. L. (2006). Fatal agranulocytosis four years after clozapine discontinuation. *Primary Psychiatry, 13,* 32–33.

Ginsburg, K. R., Durbin, D. R., García-España, J. F., Kalicka, E. A., & Winston, F. K. (2009). Associations between parenting styles and teen driving, safety-related behaviors, and attitudes. *Pediatrics, 124,* 1040–1051.

Ginzel, K. H., Maritz, G. S., Neuberger, M., Pauly, J. R., et al. (2007). Nicotine for the fetus, the infant, and the adolescent. *Journal of Health Psychology, 12,* 215–224. doi:10.1177/1359105307074240

Giorgi-Guarnieri, D., Janofsky, J., Keram, E., Lawsky, S., et al. (2002). AAPL practice guideline for forensic psychiatric evaluation of defendants raising the insanity defense. *Journal of the American Academy of Psychiatry and the Law, 30*(Suppl. 2), S1–S40.

Gladwell, M. (2004, January 12). Big and bad. *New Yorker,* pp. 28–33.

Gladwell, M. (2005). *Blink: The power of thinking without thinking.* New York: Little, Brown.

Glantz, K., Rizzo, A., & Graap, K. (2003). Virtual reality for psychotherapy: Current reality and future possibilities. *Psychotherapy: Theory, Research, Practice, and Training, 40,* 55–67.

Glanz, J. (1997). Sharpening the senses with neural "noise." *Science, 277,* 1759.

Glanzer, M., & Cunitz, A. (1966). Two storage mechanisms in free recall. *Journal of Verbal Learning and Verbal Behavior, 5,* 351–360.

Gläscher, J., Rudrauf, D., Colom, R., Paul, L. K., et al. (2010). Distributed neural system for general intelligence revealed by lesion mapping. *Proceedings of the National Academy of Sciences, 107,* 4705–4709.

Glasman, L. R., & Albarracín, D. (2006). Forming attitudes that predict future behavior: A meta-analysis of the attitude-behavior relation. *Psychological Bulletin, 132,* 778–822.

Glass, J. M., Adams, K. M., Nigg, J. T., Wong, M. M., et al. (2006). Smoking is associated with neurocognitive deficits in alcoholism. *Drug and Alcohol Dependence, 82,* 119–126.

Glassbrenner, D. G. (2005). Driver cell phone use in 2005: Overall results. *National Occupant Protection Use Survey.* Washington, DC: National Highway Transportation Safety Board.

Glassop, L. I. (2002). The organizational benefits of teams. *Human Relations, 55,* 225–249.

Glazer, M., Baer, R. D., Weller, S., de Alba, J. E. G., & Liebowitz, S. W. (2004). Susto and soul loss in Mexicans and Mexican Americans. *Cross-Cultural Research, 38,* 270–288.

Gleitman, L., & Landau, B. (1994). *The acquisition of the lexicon.* Cambridge. MA: MIT Press.

Glenmullen, J. (2000). *Prozac backlash: Overcoming the dangers of Prozac, Zoloft, Paxil, and other antidepressants with safe, effective alternatives.* New York: Simon & Schuster.

Glenn, A. L., Raine, A., Venables, P. H., & Mednick, S. A. (2007). Early temperamental and psychophysiological precursors of adult psychopathic personality. *Journal of Abnormal Psychology, 116,* 508–518.

Glick, P. T., & Fiske, S. T. (2001). Ambivalent sexism. In M. Zanna (Ed.), *Advances in experimental social psychology* (Vol. 33, pp. 115–188). New York: Academic Press.

Glover, J. A., Krug, D., Dietzer, M., George, B. W., & Hannon, M. (1990). "Advance" advance organizers. *Bulletin of the Psychonomic Society, 28,* 4–6.

Glummarra, M. J., Gibson, S. J., Georgiou-Karistianis, N., & Bradshaw, J. L. (2007). Central mechanisms in phantom limb perception: The past, present, and future. *Brain Research Reviews, 54,* 219–232.

Glynn, L. M., Davis, E. P., Schetter, C. D., Chicz-DeMet, A., et al. (2007). Postnatal maternal cortisol levels predict temperament in healthy breastfed infants. *Early Human Development, 83,* 675–681.

Goenjian, A. K., Molina, L., Steinberg, A. M., Fairbanks, L. A., et al. (2001). Posttraumatic stress and depressive reactions among Nicaraguan adolescents after Hurricane Mitch. *American Journal of Psychiatry, 158,* 788–794.

Gogtay, N., Giedd, J. N., Lusk, L., Hayashi, K. M., et al. (2004). Dynamic mapping of human cortical development during childhood through early adulthood. *Proceedings of the National Academy of Sciences, 101,* 8174–8179.

Gold, M. S. (1994). The epidemiology, attitudes, and pharmacology of LSD use in the 1990s. *Psychiatric Annals, 24,* 124–126.

Goldberg, J. F., & Burdick, K. E. (Eds.). (2008). *Cognitive dysfunction in bipolar disorder.* Washington, DC: American Psychiatric Association.

Goldenberg, J. L., Arndt, J., Hart, J., & Routledge, C. (2008). Uncovering an existential barrier to breast self-exam behavior. *Journal of Experimental Social Psychology, 44,* 260–274.

Goldfried, M. R., & Davila, J. (2005). The role of relationship and technique in therapeutic change. *Psychotherapy: Theory, Research, Practice, Training, 42,* 421–430.

Goldman, M. S., Darkes, J., & Del Boca, F. K. (1999). Expectancy meditation of biopsychosocial risk for alcohol use and alcoholism. In I. Kirsch (Ed.), *How expectancies shape experience* (pp. 233–262). Washington, DC: American Psychological Association.

Goldstein, A. J., de Beurs, E., Chambless, D. L., & Wilson, K. A. (2000). EMDR for panic disorder with agoraphobia: Comparison with waiting list and credible attention-placebo control conditions. *Journal of Consulting and Clinical Psychology, 68,* 947–956.

Goldstein, E. B. (2002). *Sensation and perception* (6th ed.). Pacific Grove, CA: Brooks/Cole.

Goldstein, I. L. (1993). *Training in organizations: Needs assessment, development, and evaluation* (3rd ed.). Pacific Grove, CA: Brooks/Cole.

Goldstein, J. (2001, October 26–27). *Does playing violent video games cause aggressive behavior?* Paper presented at the University of Chicago Cultural Policy Center conference "Playing by the Rules: The Cultural Policy Challenges of Video Games," Chicago. Retrieved from http://culturalpolicy.uchicago.edu/conf-2001/papers/goldstein.html

Goldstein, J. M., Jerram, M., Abbs, B., Whitfield-Gabrieli, S., & Makris, N. (2010). Sex differences in stress response circuitry activation dependent on female hormonal cycle. *Journal of Neuroscience, 30,* 431–438.

Goldstein, K. (1939). *The organism.* New York: American Book.

Goldstein, M. H., King, A. P., & West, M. J. (2003). Social interaction shapes babbling: Testing parallels between birdsong and speech. *Proceedings of the National Academy of Sciences, 100,* 8030–8035.

Goldstein, M. H., & Schwade, J. A. (2008). Social feedback to infants' babbling facilitates rapid phonological learning. *Psychological Science, 19,* 515–523.

Goldstein, R. Z., Tomasi, D., Alia-Klein, N., Carrillo J. H., et al. (2009). Dopaminergic response to drug words in cocaine addiction. *Journal of Neuroscience, 29,* 6001–6006.

Goldstein, S. E., Davis-Kean, P. E., & Eccles, J. S. (2005). Parents, peers, and problem behavior: A longitudinal investigation of the impact of relationship perceptions and characteristics on the development of adolescent problem behavior. *Developmental Psychology, 41,* 401–413.

Golomb, J., Kluger, A., De Leon, M. J., Ferris, S. H., et al. (1996). Hippocampal formation size predicts declining memory performance in normal aging. *Neurology, 47,* 810–813.

Goltz, H. C., DeSouza, J. F. X., Menon, R. S., Tweed, D. B., & Vilis, T. (2003). Interaction of retinal image and eye velocity in motion perception. *Neuron, 39,* 569–576.

Gomez, R. L., Bootzin, R. R., & Nadel, L. (2006). Naps promote abstraction in language-learning infants. *Psychological Science, 17,* 670–674.

Gone, J. (2004). Mental health services for Native Americans in the 21st century United States. *Professional Psychology: Theory and Practice, 35,* 10–18.

Gong, Y., & Fan, J. (2006). A longitudinal examination of the role of goal orientation in cross-cultural adjustment. *Journal of Applied Psychology, 91,* 176–184.

Gonsalves, B. D., Kahn, I., Curran, T., Norman, K. A., & Wagner, A. D. (2005). Memory strength and repetition suppression: Multimodal imaging of medial temporal cortical contributions to recognition. *Neuron, 47,* 751–761.

Gonsalves, B. D., & Paller, K. A. (2000). Neural events that underlie remembering something that never happened. *Nature Neuroscience, 3,* 1316–1321.

Gonzalez, H. M., Vega, W. A., Williams, D. R., Tarraf, W., et al. (2010). Depression care in the United States: Too little for too few. *Archives of General Psychiatry, 67,* 37–46.

Gonzalez, J. S., Penedo, F. J., Antoni, M. H., Duran, R. E., et al. (2004). Social support, positive states of mind, and HIV treatment adherence in men and women living with HIV/AIDS. *Health Psychology, 23,* 413–418.

Goodenough, F. L. (1932). Expression of the emotions in a blind-deaf child. *Journal of Abnormal and Social Psychology, 27,* 328–333.

Goodglass, H., & Kaplan, E. (1982). *The assessment of aphasia and related disorders* (2nd ed.). Philadelphia: Lea & Febiger.

Goodman, G. S., Ghetti, S., Quas, J. A., Edelstein, R. S., et al. (2003). A prospective study of memory for child sexual abuse: New findings relevant to the repressed-memory controversy. *Psychological Science, 14,* 113–118.

Goodman, W. K., Foote, K. D., Greenberg, B. D., Ricciuti, N., et al. (2010). Deep brain stimulation for intractable obsessive compulsive disorder: Pilot study using a blinded, staggered-onset design. *Biological Psychiatry, 67,* 535–542.

Gooren, L. J., & Kruijver, F. P. (2002). Androgens and male behavior. *Molecular and Cellular Endocrinology, 198,* 31–40.

Gopnik, M., & Crago, M. B. (1991). Familial aggregation of developmental language disorder. *Cognition, 39,* 1–50.

Gordon, D. B., Dahl, J. L., Miaskowski, C., McCarberg, B., et al. (2005). American Pain Society recommendations for improving the quality of acute and cancer pain management. *Archives of Internal Medicine, 165,* 1574–1580.

Gordon, P. (2004). Numerical cognition without words: Evidence from Amazonia. *Science, 306,* 496–499.

Gore-Felton, C., & Koopman, C. (2008). Behavioral mediation of the relationship between psychosocial factors and HIV disease progression. *Psychosomatic Medicine, 70,* 569–574.

Gorman, J. M. (2003). Treating generalized anxiety disorder. *Journal of Clinical Psychiatry, 64*(Suppl. 2), 24–29.

Gorman, J. M. (2005). Benzodiazepines: Taking the good with the bad and the ugly. *CNS Spectrums, 10,* 14–15.

Gorter, R. W., Butorac, M., Cobian, E. P., & van der Sluis, W. (2005). Medical use of cannabis in the Netherlands. *Neurology, 64,* 917–919.

Gosling, S. D. (2001). From mice to men: What can we learn about personality from animal research? *Psychological Bulletin, 127,* 45–86.

Gosling, S. D., Kwan, V. S. Y., & John, O. P. (2003). A dog's got personality: A cross-species comparative approach to personality judgments in dogs and humans. *Journal of Personality and Social Psychology, 85,* 1161–1169.

Gosling, S. D., Vazire, S., Srivastava, S., & John, O. P. (2004). Should we trust Web-based studies? A comparative analysis of six preconceptions about Internet questionnaires. *American Psychologist, 59,* 93–104.

Goss Lucas, S., & Bernstein, D. A. (2005). *Teaching psychology: A step by step guide.* Mahwah, NJ: Erlbaum.

Gotlib, I. H., & Hammen, C. L. (1992). *Psychological aspects of depression: Toward cognitive interpersonal integration.* Chichester, England: Wiley.

Gotlib, I. H., Krasnoperova, E., Yue, D. N., & Joorman, J. (2004). Attentional biases for negative interpersonal stimuli in clinical depression. *Journal of Abnormal Psychology, 113,* 127–135.

Goto, Y., Yang, C. R., & Otani, S. (2010). Functional and dysfunctional synaptic plasticity in prefrontal cortex: Roles in psychiatric disorders. *Biological Psychiatry, 67,* 199–207.

Gottesman, I. I., Laursen, T. M., Bertelsen, A., & Mortensen, P. B. (2010). Severe mental disorders in offspring with 2 psychiatrically ill parents. *Archives of General Psychiatry, 67,* 252–257.

Gottfredson, L. S (1997). Why *g* matters: The complexity of everyday life. *Intelligence, 24,* 79–132.

Gottfredson, L. S. (2003). Dissecting practical intelligence theory: Its claims and evidence. *Intelligence, 31,* 343–397.

Gottfredson, L. S. (2004). Intelligence: Is it the epidemiologists' elusive "fundamental cause" of social class inequalities in health? *Journal of Personality and Social Psychology, 86,* 174–199.

Gottfredson, L. S., & Deary, I. J. (2004). Intelligence predicts health and longevity, but why? *Current Directions in Psychological Science, 13,* 1–4.

Gottfried, J. A., & Dolan, R. J. (2003). The nose smells what the eye sees: Crossmodal visual facilitation of human olfactory perception. *Neuron, 39,* 375–386.

Gottfried, J. A., O'Doherty, J., & Dolan, R. J. (2003). Encoding predictive reward value in human amygdala and orbitofrontal cortex. *Science, 301,* 1104–1107.

Gottman, J. M., Driver, J., & Tabares, A. (2002). Building the sound marital house: An empirically derived couple therapy. In A. S. Gurman & N. S. Jacobson (Eds.), *Clinical handbook of couple therapy* (3rd ed., pp. 373–399). New York: Guilford Press.

Gottman, J. M., Gottman, J. S., & Declaire, J. (2006). *Ten lessons to transform your marriage.* New York: Crown.

Gottman, J. M., & Levenson, R. W. (2000). The timing of divorce: Predicting when a couple will divorce over a 14-year period. *Journal of Marriage and the Family, 62,* 737–745.

Gottman, J. M., & Levenson, R. W. (2002). A two-factor model for predicting when a couple will divorce: Exploratory analyses using 14-year longitudinal data. *Family Process, 41,* 83–96.

Gouin, J.-P., Carter, C. S., Pournajafi-Nazarloo, H., Glaser, R., et al. (2010). Marital behavior, oxytocin, vasopressin, and wound healing. *Psychoneuroendocrinology, 35,* 1082–1090.

Gouin, J.-P., Keicolt-Glaser, J. K., Malarkey, W. B., & Glaser, R. (2008). The influence of anger expression on wound healing. *Brain, Behavior, and Immunity, 22,* 699–708.

Gould, E., Beylin, A., Tanapat, P., Reeves, A., & Schors, T. J. (1999). Learning enhances adult neurogenesis in the hippocampal formation. *Nature Neuroscience, 2,* 260–265.

Governors' Highway Traffic Safety Association. (2010). *Cell phone driving laws.* Retrieved from http://www.ghsa.org/html/stateinfo/laws/cellphone_laws.html

Gow, A. J., Whiteman, M. C., Pattie, A., Whalley, L., et al.(2005). Lifetime intellectual function and satisfaction with life in old age: Longitudinal cohort study. *British Medical Journal, 331,* 141–142.

Grabe, H. J., Ruhrmann, S., Ettelt, S., Buhtz, F., et al. (2006). Familiality of obsessive-compulsive disorder in nonclinical and clinical subjects. *American Journal of Psychiatry, 163,* 1986–1992.

Grabe, S., Ward, L. M., & Hyde, J. S. (2008). The role of the media in body image concerns among women: A meta-analysis of experimental and correlational studies. *Psychological Bulletin, 134,* 460–476.

Graeber, M. B., & Mehraein, P. (1999). Reanalysis of the first case of Alzheimer's disease. *European Archives of Psychiatry and Clinical Neuroscience, 249*(Suppl. 3), 10–13.

Gräff, J., & Mansuy, I. M. (2008). Epigenetic codes in cognition and behaviour. *Behavioural Brain Research, 192,* 70–87.

Grammer, K., Fink, B., & Neave, N. (2005). Human pheromones and sexual attraction. *European Journal of Obstetrics, Gynecology, and Reproductive Biology, 118,* 135–142.

Grandey, A. A., Cordeiro, B., & Crouter, A. C. (2005). A longitudinal and multisource test of the work-family conflict and job satisfaction relationship. *Journal of Occupational and Organizational Psychology, 78,* 305–323.

Grandin, T. (1996). *Thinking in pictures—and other reports from my life with autism.* New York: Vintage Press.

Granhag, P.-A. & Stromwall, L. (2004). *The detection of deception in forensic contexts.* New York: Cambridge University Press.

Grant, B. F., Dawson, D. A., Stinson, F. S., Chou, S. P., et al. (2004). The 12-month prevalence and trends in DSM-IV alcohol abuse and dependence: United States, 1991–1992 and 2001–2002. *Drug and Alcohol Dependence, 74,* 223–234.

Grant, H., & Dweck, C. S. (2003). Clarifying achievement goals and their impact. *Journal of Personality and Social Psychology, 85,* 541–553.

Grant, J. A., Courtemanche, J., Duerden, E. G., Duncan, G. H., & Rainville, P. (2010). Cortical thickness and pain sensitivity in Zen meditators. *Emotion, 10,* 43–53.

Grant, J. E., & Kim, S. W. (2002). *Stop me because I can't stop myself: Taking control of impulsive behavior.* New York: McGraw-Hill.

Graves, L., Pack, A., & Abel, T. (2001). Sleep and memory: A molecular perspective. *Trends in Neurosciences, 24,* 237–243.

Gray, J. A., & McNaughton, N. (2000). *The neuropsychology of anxiety: An enquiry into the functions of the septohippocampal system* (2nd ed.). New York: Oxford University Press.

Gray, J. R., Chabris, C. F., & Braver, T. S. (2003). Neural mechanisms of general fluid intelligence. *Nature Neuroscience, 6,* 316–322.

Gray, N., & Nye, P. S. (2001). American Indian and Alaska Native substance abuse: Co-morbidity and cultural issues. *American Indian and Alaska Native Mental Health Research, 10,* 67–84.

Gray, N. S., MacCulloch, M. J., Smith, J., Morris, M., & Snowden, R. J. (2003). Forensic psychology: Violence viewed by psychopathic murderers. *Nature, 423,* 497.

Gray, P. (2005). *The ego and analysis of defense.* Northvale, NJ: Aronson.

Graziano, M. S. A., Alisharan, S. E., Hu, X., & Gross, C. G. (2002). The clothing effect: Tactile neurons in the precentral gyrus do not respond to the touch of the familiar primate chair. *Proceedings of the New York Academy of Sciences, 99,* 11930–11933.

Graziano, M. S. A., Taylor, C. S., & Moore, T. (2002). Complex movements evoked by microstimulation of precentral cortex. *Neuron, 34,* 841–851.

Green, A. I., & Patel, J. K. (1996). The new pharmacology of schizophrenia. *Harvard Mental Health Letter, 13*(6), 5–7.

Green, C. S., & Bavelier, D. (2003). Action video game modifies visual selective attention. *Nature, 423,* 534–537.

Green, D. M., & Swets, J. A. (1966). *Signal detection theory and psychophysics.* New York: Wiley.

Green, R. A., Cross, A. J., & Goodwin, G. M. (1995). Review of the pharmacology and clinical pharmacology of 3,4-methylenedioxymethamphetamine (MDMA or "ecstacy"). *Psychopharmacology, 119,* 247–260.

Greenberg, J. (2002). Who stole the money and when? Individual and situational determinants of employee theft. *Organizational Behavior and Human Decision Processes, 89,* 985–1003.

Greenberg, J. (2008). Understanding the vital human quest for self-esteem. *Perspectives on Psychological Science, 3,* 48–55.

Greenberg, J., Solomon, S., & Arndt, J. (2008). A basic but uniquely human motivation: Terror management theory. In J. Shah & W. Gardner (Eds.), *Handbook of motivation science* (pp. 114–134). New York: Guilford Press.

Greenberg, J., Solomon, S., Pyszczynski, T., & Rosenblatt, A. (1992). Why do people need self-esteem? Converging evidence that self-esteem serves an anxiety-buffering function. *Journal of Personality and Social Psychology, 63,* 913–922.

Greenberg, J. R., & Mitchell, S. A. (2006). *Object relations in psychoanalytic theory.* Cambridge, MA: Harvard University Press.

Greenberg, R. M., & Kellner, C. H. (2005). Electroconvulsive therapy: A selected review. *American Journal of Geriatric Psychiatry, 13,* 268–281.

Greenberg, R. P. (2010). Prescriptive authority in the face of research revelations. *American Psychologist, 65,* 136–137.

Greenberg, R. P., Constantino, M. J., & Bruce, N. (2006). Are patient expectations still relevant for psychotherapy process and outcome? *Clinical Psychology Review, 26,* 657–678.

Greene, M. L., Way, N., & Pahl, K. (2006). Trajectories of perceived adult and peer discrimination among black, Latino, and Asian American adolescents: Patterns and psychological correlates. *Developmental Psychology, 42,* 218–278.

Greene, M. T., Ercolini, A. M., DeGutes, M., & Miller, S. D. (2008). Differential induction of experimental autoimmune encephalomyelitis by myelin basic protein molecular mimics in mice humanized for HLA-DR2 and an MBP(85-99)-specific T-cell receptor. *Journal of Autoimmunity, 31,* 399–407. Epub 2008 Nov 2012.

Greenfield, P. M., & Childs, C. P. (1991). Developmental continuity in biocultural context. In R. Cohen & A. W. Siegel (Eds.), *Context and development* (pp. 135–159). Hillsdale, NJ: Erlbaum.

Greenfield, P. M., Suzuki, L. K., & Rothstein-Fisch, C. (2006). Cultural pathways through human development. In W. Damon & R. M. Lerner (Series Eds.) & K. A. Renninger & I. E. Sigel (Vol. Eds.), *Handbook of child psychology: Vol. 4. Child psychology in practice* (6th ed., pp. 655–699). Hoboken, NJ: Wiley.

Greenhaus, J. H., Parasuraman, S., & Wormley, W. M. (1990). Effects of race on organizational experiences, job performance evaluations, and career outcomes. *Academy of Management Journal, 33,* 64–86.

Greenland, P., Knoll, M. D., Stamler, J., Neaton, J. D., et al. (2003). Major risk factors as antecedents of fatal and nonfatal coronary heart disease events. *Journal of the American Medical Association, 290,* 891–897.

Greenough, W. T., Black, J. E., & Wallace, C. S. (1987). Experience and brain development. *Child Development, 58,* 539–559.

Greenwald, A. G., & Banaji, M. R. (1995). Implicit social cognition: Attitudes, self-esteem, and stereotypes. *Psychological Review, 102,* 4–27.

Greenwald, A. G., Draine, S. C., & Abrams, R. L. (1996). Three cognitive markers of unconscious semantic activation. *Science, 273,* 1699–1702.

Greenwald, A. G., Klinger, M. R., & Schuh, E. S. (1995). Activation by marginally perceptible ("subliminal") stimuli: Dissociation of unconscious from conscious cognition. *Experimental Psychology: General, 124,* 22–42.

Greenwald, A. G., Poehlman, T. A., Uhlmann, E. L., & Banaji, M. R. (2009). Understanding and using the Implicit Association Test: III. Meta-analysis of predictive validity. *Journal of Personality and Social Psychology, 97,* 17–41.

Greer, A. E., & Buss, D. M. (1994). Tactics for promoting sexual encounters. *Journal of Sex Research, 31,* 185–201.

Greeson, J. M. (2009). Mindfulness research update, 2008. *Complementary Health Practice Review, 14,* 10–18.

Gregg, V., Gibbs, J. C., & Basinger, K. S. (1994). Patterns of developmental delay in moral judgment by male and female delinquents. *Merrill-Palmer Quarterly, 40,* 538–553.

Gregor, K. L., & Zvolensky, M. J. (2008). Anxiety sensitivity and perceived control over anxiety-related events: Evaluating the singular and interactive effects in the prediction of anxious and fearful responding to bodily sensations. *Behaviour Research and Therapy, 46,* 1017–1025.

Gregory, A. M., Light-Häusermann, J., Rijsdijk, F., & Eley, T. C. (2009). Behavioral genetic analyses of prosocial behavior in adolescents. *Developmental Science, 12,* 165–174. doi:10.1111/j.1467-7687.2008.00739.x

Gregory, R. L. (2005). Seeing after blindness. *Nature Neuroscience, 6,* 909–910.

Gregory, S. W., & Webster, S. (1996). A nonverbal signal in voices of interview partners effectively predicts communication accommodation and social status perceptions. *Journal of Personality and Social Psychology, 70,* 1231–1240.

Greitemeyer, T., & Osswald, S. (2010). Effects of prosocial video games on prosocial behavior. *Journal of Personality and Social Psychology, 98,* 211–221.

Gren-Landell, M., Tillfors, M., Furmark, T., Bohlin, G., et al. (2009). Social phobia in Swedish adolescents: Prevalence and gender differences. *Social Psychiatry and Psychiatric Epidemiology, 44,* 1–7.

Greven, C. U., Harlaar, N., Kovas, Y., Chamorro-Premuzic, T., & Plomin, R. (2009). More than just IQ: School achievement is predicted by self-perceived abilities—but for genetic rather than environmental reasons. *Psychological Science, 20,* 753–762.

Griesinger, C. B., Richards, C. D., & Ashmore, J. F. (2005). Fast vesicle replenishment allows indefatigable signaling at the first auditory synapse. *Nature, 435,* 212–215.

Griffeth, R. W., Hom, P. W., & Gaertner, S. (2000). A meta-analysis of antecedents and correlates of employee turnover: Update, moderator tests, and research implications for the next millennium. *Journal of Management, 26,* 463–488.

Griffin, M. A., & Neal, A. (2000). Perceptions of safety at work: A framework for linking safety climate to safety performance, knowledge, and motivation. *Journal of Occupational Health Psychology, 5,* 347–358.

Griffin, P. W., Mroczek, D. K., & Spiro, A. (2006). Variability in affective change among aging men: Longitudinal findings from the VA Normative Aging Study. *Journal of Research in Personality, 40,* 942–965.
Griffitt, W. B., & Guay, P. (1969). "Object" evaluation and conditioned affect. *Journal of Experimental Research in Personality, 4,* 1–8.
Grigorenko, E. L. (2002). In search of the genetic engram of personality. In D. Cervone & W. Mischel (Eds.), *Advances in personality science* (pp. 29–82). New York: Guilford Press.
Grimes, J. M., Ricci, L. A., & Melloni, R. H. (2006). Plasticity in anterior hypothalamic vasopressin correlates with aggression during anabolic-androgenic steroid withdrawal in hamsters. *Behavioral Neuroscience, 120,* 115–124.
Grinspoon, L. (1999). The future of medical marijuana. *Fortschritte der Komplementarmedizin, 6,* 40–43.
Grinspoon, L., Bakalar, J. B., Zimmer, L., & Morgan, J. P. (1997). Marijuana addiction. *Science, 277,* 749–752.
Grinspoon, S., Thomas, E., Pitts, S., Gross, E., et al. (2000). Prevalence and predictive factors for regional osteopenia in women with anorexia nervosa. *Annals of Internal Medicine, 133,* 790–794.
Griskevicius, V., Tybur, J. M., Gangestad, S. W., Perea, E. F., et al. (2009). Aggress to impress: Hostility as an evolved context-dependent strategy. *Journal of Personality and Social Psychology, 96,* 980–994.
Grisso, T., & Appelbaum, P. S. (1995). The MacArthur Treatment Competence Study: Vol. 3. Abilities of patients to consent to psychiatric and medical treatments. *Law and Human Behavior, 19,* 149–174.
Grob, C., & Dobkin–de Rios, M. (1992). Adolescent drug use in cross-cultural perspective. *Journal of Drug Issues, 22,* 121–138.
Gronau, N., Ben-Shakhar, G., & Cohen, A. (2005). Behavioral and physiological measures in the detection of concealed information. *Journal of Applied Psychology, 90,* 147–158.
Groopman, J. (2007, January 29). What's the trouble? *New Yorker,* pp. 36–41.
Grosbras, M. H., Jansen, M., Leonard, G., McIntosh, A., et al. (2007). Neural mechanisms of resistance to peer influence in early adolescence. *Journal of Neuroscience, 27,* 8040–8045.
Gross, J. J. (2001). Emotion regulation in adulthood: Timing is everything. *Current Directions in Psychological Science, 10,* 214–219.
Grossberg, S., & Seidman, D. (2006). Neural dynamics of autistic behaviors: Cognitive, emotional, and timing substrates. *Psychological Review, 113,* 483–525.
Grossman, M., & Ash, S. (2004). Primary progressive aphasia: A review. *Neurocase, 10,* 3–18.
Grossmann, I., Na, J., Varnum, M. E. W., Park, D. C., et al. (2010). Reasoning about social conflicts improves into old age. *Proceedings of the National Academy of Sciences, 107,* 7246–7250.
Grosz, H. I., & Zimmerman, J. (1970). A second detailed case study of functional blindness: Further demonstration of the contribution of objective psychological data. *Behavior Therapy, 1,* 115–123.
Grotevant, H. D. (1998). Adolescent development in family contexts. In W. Damon & N. Eisenberg (Eds.), *Handbook of child psychology: Vol. 3. Social, emotional, and personality development* (5th ed., pp. 1097–1150). New York: Wiley.
Groth-Marnat, G. (1997). *Handbook of psychological assessment* (3rd ed.). New York: Wiley.
Groves, K. S. (2005). Linking leader skills, follower attitudes, and contextual variables via an integrated model of charismatic leadership. *Journal of Management, 31,* 255–277.
Grubb, P. L., Roberts, R. K., Swanson, N. G., Burnfield, J. L., & Childress, J. H. (2005). Organizational factors and psychological aggression: Results from a nationally representative sample of U.S. companies. In V. Bowie, B. S. Fisher, & C. L. Cooper (Eds.), *Workplace violence: Issues, trends, strategies* (pp. 37–59). Portland, OR: Willan.
Gruber, R., Laviolette, R., Deluca, P., Monson, E., et al. (2010). Short sleep duration is associated with poor performance on IQ measures in healthy school-age children. *Sleep Medicine, 11,* 289–294. Epub 2010 Feb 13.
Gruber, S. A., Silveri, M. M., & Yurgelun-Todd, D. A. (2007). Neuropsychological consequences of opiate use. *Neuropsychology Review, 17,* 299–315.
Grucza, R. A., Bucholz, K. K., Rice, J. P., & Bierut, L. J. (2008). Secular trends in the lifetime prevalence of alcohol dependence in the United States: A re-evaluation. *Alcoholism: Clinical and Experimental Research, 32,* 763–770.
Grusec, J. E., & Goodnow, J. J. (1994). Impact of parental discipline methods on the child's internalization of values. *Developmental Psychology, 30,* 4–19.
Grusec, J. E., Davidov, M., & Lundell, L. (2002). Prosocial and helping behavior. In P. K. Smith & C. H. Hart (Eds.), *Blackwell handbook of childhood social development* (pp. 457–474). Malden, MA: Blackwell.
Guadagno, R. E., Asher, T., Demaine, L. J., & Cialdini, R. B. (2001). When saying yes leads to saying no: Preference for consistency and the reverse foot-in-the-door effect. *Personality and Social Psychology Bulletin, 27,* 859–867.
Gualtieri, C. T., & Johnson, L. G. (2006). Antidepressant side effects in children and adolescents. *Journal of Child and Adolescent Psychopharmacology, 16,* 147–157.
Guéguen, N. (2008). The receptivity of women to courtship solicitation across the menstrual cycle: A field experiment. *Biological Psychology, 80,* 321–324.
Guéguen, N., Marchand, M., Pascual, A., & Lourel, M. (2008). Foot-in-the-door technique using a courtship request: A field experiment. *Psychological Reports, 103,* 529–534.
Guilford, J. P. (1959). Traits of creativity. In H. H. Anderson (Ed.), *Creativity and its cultivation* (pp. 142–161). New York: Harper & Row.
Guilleminault, C., Kirisoglu, C., Bao, G., Arias, V., et al. (2005). Adult chronic sleepwalking and its treatment based on polysomnography. *Brain, 128,* 1062–1069.
Guilleminault, C., Palombini, L., Pelayo, R., & Chervin, R. D. (2003). Sleepwalking and sleep terrors in prepubertal children: What triggers them? *Pediatrics, 111,* 17–25.
Guimon, J. (2004). Evidence-based research studies on the results of group therapy: A critical review. *European Journal of Psychiatry, 18*(Suppl.), 49–60.
Gump, B. B., Reihman, J., Stewart, P., Lonky, E., & Darvill, T. (2005). Terrorism and cardiovascular responses to acute stress in children. *Health Psychology, 24,* 594–600.
Gundersen, H., Specht, K., Grüner, R., Ersland, L., & Hugdahl, K. (2008). Separating the effects of alcohol and expectancy on brain activation: An fMRI working memory study. *Neuroimage, 42,* 1587–1596.
Gunnoe, M. L., & Mariner, C. L. (1997). Toward a developmental-contextual model of the effects of parental spanking on children's aggressoin. *Archives of Pediatrics and Adolescent Medicine, 151,* 768–775.
Gupta, A. R., & State, M. W. (2007). Recent advances in the genetics of autism. *Biological Psychiatry, 61,* 429–437.
Gupta, H., Sharma, A., Kumar, S., & Roy, S. K. (2010). E-tongue: A tool for taste evaluation. *Recent Patents on Drug Delivery and Formulation, 4,* 82–99.
Gur, R. C., Mozley, L. H., Mozley, P. D., Resnick, S. M., et al. (1995). Sex differences in regional cerebral glucose metabolism during a resting state. *Science, 267,* 528–531.
Gur, R. E., Cowell, P. E., Latshaw, A., Turetsky, B. I., et al. (2000). Reduced dorsal and orbital prefrontal gray matter volumes in schizophrenia. *Archives of General Psychiatry, 57,* 761–768.
Gura, T. (1999). Leptin not impressive in clinical trial. *Science, 286,* 881–882.
Gureje, O., Lasebikan, V. O., Kola, L., & Makanjuola, V. A. (2006). Lifetime and 12-month prevalence of mental disorders in the Nigerian Survey of Mental Health and Well-Being. *British Journal of Psychiatry, 188,* 465–471.
Gurman, A. S. (Ed.). (2008). *Clinical handbook of couple therapy* (4th ed.). New York: Guilford Press.
Gustafsson, J. E., & Undheim, J. O. (1996). Individual differences in cognitive functions. In D. C. Berliner & R. C. Calfee (Eds.), *Handbook of educational psychology* (pp. 186–242). New York: Simon & Schuster.
Guthrie, R. M., & Bryant, R. A. (2005). Auditory startle response in firefighters before and after trauma exposure. *American Journal of Psychiatry, 162,* 283–290.
Guyton, A. C. (1991). *Textbook of medical physiology* (8th ed.). Philadelphia: Saunders.
Haaga, D. A. (2000). Introduction to the special section on stepped care models in psychotherapy. *Journal of Consulting and Clinical Psychology, 68,* 547–548.
Haake, M., Müller, H.-H., Schade-Brittinger, C., Basler, H. D., et al. (2007). German acupuncture trials (GERAC) for chronic low back pain: Randomized, multicenter, blinded, parallel-group trial with 3 groups. *Archives of Internal Medicine, 167,* 1892–1898.
Haber, R. N. (1979). Twenty years of haunting eidetic imagery: Where's the ghost? *Behavioral and Brain Sciences, 2,* 583–629.
Haber, S. N., & Knutson, B. (2010). The reward circuit: Linking primate anatomy and human imaging. *Neuropsychopharmacology, 35,* 4–26.
Haberlandt, K. (1999). *Human memory: Exploration and application.* Boston: Allyn & Bacon.
Haberstroh, J. (1995). *Ice cube sex: The truth about subliminal advertising.* South Bend, IN: Cross Cultural Publications/Crossroads.
Hacking, I. (1995). *Rewriting the soul: Multiple personality and the sciences of memory.* Princeton, NJ: Princeton University Press.
Hackman, J. R. (1998). Why teams don't work. In R. S. Tindale, L. Heath, J. Edwards, E. J. Posavac, et al. (Eds.), *Social psychological applications to social issues: Vol. 4. Theory and research on small groups.* New York: Plenum.
Hackman, R., & Katz, N. (2010). In S. T. Fiske, D. T. Gilbert, & G. Lindzey (Eds.), *Handbook of social psychology* (5th ed., Vol. 2, pp. 1208–1252). Hoboken, NJ: Wiley.
Haddad, S. K., Reiss, D., Spotts, E. L., Ganiban, J., et al. (2008). Depression and internally directed aggression: Genetic and environmental contributions. *Journal of the American Psychoanalytic Association, 56,* 515–550.
Hadjikhani, N., & de Gelder, B. (2003). Seeing fearful body expressions activates the fusiform cortex and amygdale. *Current Biology, 13,* 2201–2205.
Häfner, H. (2003). Gender differences in schizophrenia. *Psychoneuroendrocrinology, 28,* 17–54.
Häfner, H., & Maurer, K. (2000). The early course of schizophrenia: New concepts for early intervention. In G. Andrews & S. Henderson (Eds.), *Unmet need in psychiatry: Problems, resources, responses* (pp. 218–232). New York: Cambridge University Press.
Hagen, E. P. (1980). *Identification of the gifted.* New York: Teachers College Press.
Hahn, C.-S., & DiPietro, J. A. (2001). In vitro fertilization and the family: Quality of parenting, family functioning, and child psychosocial adjustment. *Developmental Psychology, 37,* 37–48.
Haidt, J. (2003). Elevation and the positive psychology of morality. In C. L. M. Keyes & J. Haidt (Eds.), *Flourishing: Positive psychology and the life well-lived* (pp. 275–289). Washington, DC: American Psychological Association.
Haier, R. J., White, N. S., & Alkire, M. T. (2003). Individual differences in general intelligence correlate with brain function during nonreasoning tasks. *Intelligence, 31,* 429–441.
Hake, R. R. (1998). Interactive-engagement vs. traditional methods: A six-thousand-student survey of mechanics test data for introductory physics courses. *American Journal of Physics, 66,* 64–74.
Hakuta, K., Bialystok, E., & Wiley, E. (2003). Critical evidence: A test of the critical-period hypothesis for second-language acquisition. *Psychological Science, 14,* 31–38.
Halford, G. S., Baker, R., McCredden, J. E., & Bain, J. D. (2005). How many variables can humans process? *Psychological Science, 16,* 70–76.
Hall, C., Smith, K., & Chia, R. (2008). Cognitive and personality factors in relation to timely completion of a college degree. *College Student Journal, 42,* 1087–1098.
Hall, C. B., Lipton, R. B., Sliwinski, M., Katz, M. J., et al. (2009). Cognitive activities delay onset of memory decline in persons who develop dementia. *Neurology, 73,* 356–361.
Hall, C. S., Lindzey, G., & Campbell, J. P. (1998). *Theories of personality* (4th ed.). New York: Wiley.
Hall, G. (1991). *Perceptual and associative learning.* Oxford: Clarendon Press.
Hall, L. K., & Bahrick, H. P. (1998). The validity of metacognitive predictions of widespread learning and long-term retention. In G. Mazzoni & T. Nelson (Eds.), *Metacognition and cognitive neuropsychology: Monitoring and control processes* (pp. 23–36). Mahwah, NJ: Erlbaum.
Hall, P. A., Dubin, J. A., Crossley, M., Holmqvist, M. E., & D'Arcy, C. (2009). Does executive function explain the IQ-mortality association? Evidence from the Canadian study on health and aging. *Psychosomatic Medicine, 71,* 196–204.

Hall, W., & Degenhardt, L. (2003). Medical marijuana initiatives: Are they justified? How successful are they likely to be? *CNS Drugs, 17,* 689–697.

Hall, W., & Degenhardt, L. (2009). Adverse health effects of non-medical cannabis use. *Lancet, 374,* 1383–1391.

Hall, W., & Lynskey, M. (2009). The challenges in developing a rational cannabis policy. *Current Opinion in Psychiatry, 22,* 258–262.

Hallam, B. J., Brown, W. S., Ross, C., Buckwalter, J. G., et al. (2008). Regional atrophy of the corpus callosum in dementia. *Journal of the International Neuropsychological Society, 14,* 414–423.

Halloran, M. J., & Kashima, E. S. (2004). Social identity and worldview validation: The effects of ingroup identity primes and mortality salience on value endorsement. *Personality and Social Psychology Bulletin, 30,* 915–925.

Halperin, D. (1992). *Sex differences in cognitive abilities.* Mahwah, NJ: Erlbaum.

Halperin, J. M., & Schulz, K. P. (2006). Revisiting the role of the prefrontal cortex in the pathophysiology of attention-deficit/hyperactivity disorder. *Psychological Bulletin, 132,* 560–581.

Halpern, D. F. (1997). Sex differences in intelligence. *American Psychologist, 52,* 1091–1102.

Halpern, D. F., & Hakel, M. D. (Eds.). (2002). Applying the science of learning to university teaching and beyond. *New Directions for Teaching and Learning, Vol. 89.* San Francisco: Jossey-Bass.

Hamad, G. G. (2004). The state of the art in bariatric surgery for weight loss in the morbidly obese patient. *Clinics in Plastic Surgery, 31,* 591–600.

Hamann, S., Herman, R. A., Nolan, C. L., & Wallen, K. (2004). Men and women differ in amygdala response to sexual stimuli. *Nature Neuroscience, 7,* 411–416.

Hamarat, E., Thompson, D., Steele, D., Matheny, K., & Simons, C. (2002). Age differences in coping resources and satisfaction with life among middle-aged, young-old, and oldest-old adults. *Journal of Genetic Psychology, 163,* 360–367.

Hamer, M., Molloy, G. J., & Stamatakis, E. (2008). Psychological distress as a risk factor for cardiovascular events. *Journal of the American College of Cardiology, 52,* 2156–2162.

Hamilton, N. A., Gallagher, M. W., Preacher, K. J., Stevens, N., et al. (2007). Insomnia and well-being. *Journal of Consulting and Clinical Psychology, 75,* 939–946.

Hamilton, W. D. (1964). The evolution of social behavior: Parts I and II. *Journal of Theoretical Biology 7,* 1–52.

Hammad, T. A., Laughren, T., & Racoosin, J. (2006). Suicidality in pediatric patients treated with antidepressant drugs. *Archives of General Psychiatry, 63,* 332–339.

Hammen, C. (2005). Stress and depression. *Annual Review of Clinical Psychology, 1,* 293–319.

Hammen, C. (2009). Adolescent depression: Stressful interpersonal contexts and risk for recurrence. *Current Directions in Psychological Science, 18,* 200–204.

Hammer, C. S., Lawrence, F. R., & Miccio, A. W. (2007). Bilingual children's language abilities and early reading outcomes in Head Start and kindergarten. *Language, Speech, and Hearing Services in Schools, 38,* 237–248.

Hammer, E. (1968). Projective drawings. In A. I. Rabin (Ed.), *Projective techniques in personality assessment.* New York: Springer.

Hammerness, P., Basch, E., & Ulbricht, C. (2003). St. John's wort: A systematic review of adverse effects and drug interactions for the consultation psychiatrist. *Journal of Consultation Liaison Psychiatry, 44,* 271–282.

Hampson, S. E. (2008). Mechanisms by which childhood personality traits influence adult well-being. *Current Directions in Psychological Science, 17,* 264–268.

Hampson, S. E., Goldberg, L. R., Vogt, T. M., & Dubanoski, J. P. (2006). Forty years on: Teachers' assessments of children's personality traits predict self-reported health behaviors and outcomes at midlife. *Health Psychology, 25,* 57–64.

Hamrick, N., Cohen, S., & Rodriguez, M. S. (2002). Being popular can be healthy or unhealthy: Stress, social network diversity, and incidence of upper respiratory infection. *Health Psychology, 21,* 294–298.

Han, S., & Shavitt, S. (1994). Persuasion and culture: Advertising appeals in individualist and collectivist societies. *Journal of Experimental Social Psychology, 30,* 326–350.

Handgraaf, M. J. J., & van Raaij, W. F. (2005). Fear and loathing no more: The emergence of collaboration between economists and psychologists. *Journal of Economic Psychology, 28,* 387–391.

Hane, A. A., Cheah, C., Rubin, K. H., & Fox, N. A. (2008). The role of maternal behavior in the relation between shyness and social reticence in early childhood and social withdrawal in middle childhood. *Social Development, 17,* 795–811.

Hanish, L. D., Martin, C. L., Fabes, R. A., Seonard, S., & Herzoh, M. (2005). Exposure to externalizing peers in early childhood: Homophily and peer contagion processes. *Journal of Abnormal Child Psychology, 33,* 267–281.

Hankin, B. L., & Abramson, L. Y. (2001). Development of gender differences in depression: An elaborated cognitive vulnerability-transactional stress theory. *Psychological Bulletin, 127,* 773–796.

Hankin, B. L., Fraley, R. C., & Abela, J. R. Z. (2005). Daily depression and cognitions about stress: Evidence for a traitlike depressogenic cognitive style and the prediction of depressive symptoms in a prospective daily diary study. *Journal of Personality and Social Psychology, 88,* 673–685.

Hanley, G. P., Piazza, C. C., Fisher, W. W., & Maglieri, K. A. (2005). On the effectiveness of and preference for punishment and extinction components of function-based interventions. *Journal of Applied Behavior Analysis, 38,* 51–65.

Hansez, I., & Chmiel, N. (2010). Safety behavior: Job demands, job resources, and perceived management commitment to safety. *Journal of Occupational Health Psychology, 15,* 267–278.

Hanson, G., & Venturelli, P. J. (1995). *Drugs and society* (4th ed.). Boston: Jones & Bartlett.

Hanson, S. J., & Burr, D. J. (1990). What connectionist models learn: Learning and representations in connectionist networks. *Behavioral and Brain Sciences, 13,* 471–518.

Hara, K., Kubota, N., Tobe, K., Terauchi, Y., et al. (2000). The role of PPARg as a thrifty gene both in mice and humans *British Journal of Nutrition, 84*(Suppl. 2), S235–S239.

Harasty, J., Double, K. L., Halliday, G. M., Kril, J. J., & McRitchie, D. A. (1997). Language-associated cortical regions are proportionally larger in the female brain. *Archives of Neurology, 54,* 171–176.

Hardesty, D. E., & Sackeim, H. A. (2007). Deep brain stimulation in movement and psychiatric disorders. *Biological Psychiatry, 61,* 831–835.

Harding, K. J., Skritskaya, N., Doherty, E., & Fallon, B. A. (2008). Advances in understanding illness anxiety. *Current Psychiatry Reports, 10,* 311–317.

Hardisty, D. J., Johnson, E. J., & Weber, E. U. (2010). A dirty word or a dirty world? Attribute framing, political affiliation, and query theory. *Psychological Science, 21,* 86–92.

Hare, R. D., & Newmann, C. S. (2009). Psychopathy: Assessment and forensic implications. *Canadian Journal of Psychiatry, 54,* 791–802.

Hariri, A. R., Drabant, E. M., Munoz, K. E., Kolachana, B. S., et al. (2005). A susceptibility gene for affective disorders and the response of the human amygdala. *Archives of General Psychiatry, 62,* 146–152.

Harlow, H. F. (1949). The formation of learning sets. *Psychological Review, 56,* 51–65.

Harlow, H. F. (1959, June). Love in infant monkeys. *Scientific American,* pp. 68–74.

Harman, W. S., Lee, T. W., Mitchell, T. R., Felps, W., & Ownes, B. P. (2007). The psychology of voluntary turnover. *Current Directions in Psychological Science, 16,* 51–54.

Harmon, A. (2004, May 9). Neurodiversity forever: The disability movement turns to brains. *New York Times,* p.1.

Harmon-Jones, E. (2004). On the relationship of frontal brain activity and anger: Examining the role of attitude toward anger. *Cognition and Emotion, 18,* 337–361.

Harmon-Jones, E., Amodio, D. M., & Harmon-Jones, C. (2009). Action-based model of dissonance: A review, integration, and expansion of conceptions of cognitive conflict. In M. Zanna (Ed.), *Advances in experimental social psychology* (Vol. 41, pp. 119–166). San Diego, CA: Academic Press.

Harmon-Jones, E., & Sigelman, J. (2001). State anger and prefrontal brain activity: Evidence that insult-related relative left prefrontal activation is associated with experienced anger and aggression. *Journal of Personality and Social Psychology, 80,* 797–804.

Harré, N., Brandt, T., & Houkamau, C. (2004). An examination of the actor-observer effect in young drivers' attributions for their own and their friends' risky driving. *Journal of Applied Social Psychology, 34,* 806–824.

Harris, M., & Grunstein, R. R. (2009). Treatments for somnambulism in adults: Assessing the evidence. *Sleep Medicine Reviews, 13,* 295–297.

Harris, M. M., Anseel, F., & Lievens, F. (2008). Keeping up with the Joneses: A field study of the relationships among upward, lateral, and downward comparisons and pay level satisfaction. *Journal of Applied Psychology, 93,* 665–673.

Harris Interactive. (2007). *Handwashing survey fact sheet.* Retrieved from http://www.microbeworld.org/images/stories/washup/downloads/2007asm-sdahandwashingsurveyfactsheetfinal.doc

Harrison, D. A., Newman, D. A., & Roth, P. L. (2006). How important are job attitudes? Meta-analytic comparisons of integrative behavioral outcomes and time sequences. *Academy of Management Journal, 49,* 305–325.

Harrison, D. A., Price, K. H., Gavin, J. H., & Florey, A. T. (2002). Time, teams, and task performance: Changing effects of surface- and deep-level diversity on group functioning. *Academy of Management Journal, 45,* 1029–1045.

Harrison, K. (2003). Fitness and excitation. In J. Bryant & D. Roskos-Ewoldsen (Eds.), *Communication and emotion: Essays in honor of Dolf Zillmann* (pp. 473–489). Mahwah, NJ: Erlbaum.

Harrow, M., & Jobe, T. H. (2005). Longitudinal studies of outcome and recovery in schizophrenia and early interventions: Can they make a difference? *Canadian Journal of Psychiatry, 50,* 879–880.

Hart, A. J., Whalen, P. J., Shin, L. M., McInerney, S. C., et al. (2000). Differential response in the human amygdala to racial outgroup vs. ingroup face stimuli. *Neuroreport, 11,* 2351–2355.

Hart, D., Atkins, R., & Fegley, S. (2003). Personality and development in childhood: A person-centered approach. *Monographs of the Society for Research in Child Development, 68,* 1–109.

Harter, S. (1999). *The construction of the self: A developmental perspective.* New York: Guilford Press.

Harter, S. (2006). The self. In W. Damon & R. M. Lerner (Series Eds.), & N. Eisenberg (Vol. Ed.), *Handbook of child psychology: Social, emotional, and personality development* (6th ed., Vol. 3, pp. 505–570). Hoboken, NJ: Wiley.

Hartmann, H. (1958). *Ego psychology and the problem of adaptation.* New York: International Universities Press.

Hartup, W. W., & Stevens, N. (1997). Friendships and adaptation in the life course. *Psychological Bulletin, 121,* 355–370.

Harvey, E. A., Friedman-Weieneth, J. L., Miner, A. L., Bartolomei, R. J., et al. (2009). The role of ethnicity in observers' ratings of mother-child behavior. *Developmental Psychology, 45,* 1497–1508.

Harvey, P. A., Lee, D. H. S., Qian, F., Weinreb, P. H., & Frank, E. (2009). Blockade of Nogo receptor ligands promotes functional regeneration of sensory axons after dorsal root crush. *Journal of Neuroscience, 29,* 6285–6295.

Harvey, S. B., Stanton, B. R., & David, A. S. (2006). Conversion disorder: Towards a neurobiological understanding. *Neuropsychiatric Disease and Treatment, 2,* 13–20.

Harwood, K., McLean, N., & Durkin, K. (2007). First-time mothers' expectations of parenthood: What happens when optimistic expectations are not matched by later experiences? *Developmental Psychology, 43,* 1–12.

Harwood, T. M., & L'Abate, L. (2010). *Self-help in mental health: A critical review.* New York: Springer.

Hase, M., Schallmayer, S., & Sack, M. (2008). EMDR reprocessing of the addiction memory: Pretreatment, posttreatment, and 1-month follow-up. *Journal of EMDR Practice and Research, 2,* 170–179.

Hashioka, S., McGeer, P. L., Monji, A., & Kanba, S. (2009). Anti-inflammatory effects of antidepressants: Possibilities for preventives against Alzheimer's disease. *Central Nervous System Agents in Medicinal Chemistry, 9,* 12–19.

Hasin, D. S., Goodwin, R. D., Stinson, F. S., & Grant, B. F. (2005). Epidemiology of major depressive disorder: Results from the National Epidemiologic Survey on Alcoholism and Related Conditions. *Archives of General Psychiatry, 62,* 1097–1106.

Haskett, M. E., Nears, K., Sabourin Ward, C., & McPherson, A. V. (2006). Diversity in adjustment of maltreated children: Factors associated with resilient functioning. *Clinical Psychology Review, 26,* 796–812.

Hassabis, D., Kumaran, D., Vann, D. S., & Maguire, E. A. (2007). Patients with hippocampal amnesia cannot imagine new experiences. *Proceedings of the National Academy of Sciences, 104,* 1726–1731.

Hatcher, D., Brown, T., & Gariglietti, K. P. (2001). Critical thinking and rational emotive behavior therapy. *Inquiry, 20,* 6–18.

Hatfield, E., & Rapson, R. L. (2006). Passionate love, sexual desire, and mate selection: Cross-cultural and historical perspectives. In P. Noller & J. Feeney (Eds.), *Close relationships: Functions, forms and processes* (pp. 227–243). Hove, England: Psychology Press/Taylor & Francis.

Hatfield, J., Job, R. F. S., Hede, A. J., Carter, N. L., et al. (2002). Human response to environmental noise: The role of perceived control. *International Journal of Behavioral Medicine, 9,* 341–359.

Hathaway, W. (2002, December 22). Henry M: The day one man's memory died. *Hartford Courant.* Retrieved from http://articles.courant.com/2002-12-22/health/hc-archive-henry-m-dec-2002_1_henry-s-medial-temporal-lobe-medical-ethics-and-patients-hartford-area-nursing-home

Hattori, M., Fujiyama A., Taylor, T. D., Watanabe, H., et al. (2000). The DNA sequence of human chromosome 21. *Nature, 405,* 311–319.

Haukkala, A., Konttinen, H., Laatikainen, T., Kawachi, I., & Uutela, A. (2010). Hostility, anger control, and anger expression as predictors of cardiovascular disease. *Psychosomatic Medicine, 72,* 556–562.

Hausknecht, J. P., Day, D. V., & Thomas, S. C. (2004). Applicant reactions to selection procedures: An updated model and meta-analysis. *Personnel Psychology, 57,* 639–683.

Haut, K. M., & Barch, D. M. (2006). Sex influences on material-sensitive functional lateralization in working and episodic memory: Men and women are not all that different. *NeuroImage, 32,* 411–422.

Haw, R. M., & Fisher, R. P. (2004). Effects of administrator-witness contact on eyewitness identification accuracy. *Journal of Applied Psychology, 89,* 1106–1112.

Hawkes, C. (2003). Olfaction in neurodegenerative disorders. *Movement Disorders, 18,* 364–372.

Hawkins, H. L., Kramer, A. R., & Capaldi, D. (1993). Aging, exercise, and attention. *Psychology and Aging, 7,* 643–653.

Haxby, J. V., Gobbini, M. I., Furey, M. L., Ishai, A., et al. (2001). Distributed and overlapping representations of faces and objects in ventral temporal cortex. *Science, 293,* 2425–2430.

Hay, D. F., Pawlby, S., Angold, A., Harold, G. T., & Sharp, D. (2003). Pathways to violence in the children of mothers who were depressed postpartum. *Developmental Psychology, 39,* 1083–1094.

Hayden, E. P., & Nurnberger, J. I. (2006). Molecular genetics of bipolar disorder. *Genes, Brain and Behavior, 5,* 85–95.

Hayes, R. A., Efron, L. A., Richman, G. S., Harrison, K. A., & Aguilera, E. L. (2000). The effects of behavioural contracting and preferred reinforcement on appointment keeping. *Behaviour Change, 17,* 90–96.

Haynes, S. R., Cohen, M. A., & Ritter, F. E. (2009). Designs for explaining intelligent agents. *International Journal of Human-Computer Studies, 67,* 90–110.

Hays, K. F. (2006). Being fit: The ethics of practice diversification in performance psychology. *Professional Psychology: Research and Practice, 37,* 223–232.

Hays, K. F. (Ed.). (2009). *Performance psychology in action: A casebook for working with athletes, performing artists, business leaders, and professionals in high-risk occupations.* Washington, DC: American Psychological Association.

Hays, P. A., & Iwamasa, G. Y. (Eds.). (2006). *Culturally responsive cognitive-behavioral therapy: Assessment, practice, and supervision.* Washington, DC: American Psychological Association.

Hays, W. L. (1981). *Statistics* (3rd ed.). New York: Holt, Rinehart & Winston.

He, L. F. (1987). Involvement of endogenous opioid peptides in acupuncture analgesia. *Pain, 31,* 99–121.

Hebb, D. O. (1949). *The organization of behavior.* New York: Wiley.

Hebb, D. O. (1955). Drives and the CNS (conceptual nervous system). *Psychological Review, 62,* 243–254.

Heckhausen, J., Wrosch, C., & Schulz, R. (2010). A motivational theory of life-span development. *Psychological Review, 117,* 32–60.

Heckman, T. G., Anderson, E. S., Sikkema, K. J., Kochman, A., et al. (2004). Emotional distress in nonmetropolitan persons living with HIV disease enrolled in a telephone-delivered, coping improvement group intervention. *Health Psychology, 23,* 94–100.

Hedge, A., & Yousif, Y. H. (1992). Effects of urban size, urgency, and cost of helpfulness: A cross-cultural comparison between the United Kingdom and the Sudan. *Journal of Cross-Cultural Psychology, 23,* 107–115.

Hedge, J. W., Borman, W. C., & Lammlein, S. E. (2006). *The aging workforce: Realities, myths, and implications for organizations.* Washington, DC: American Psychological Association.

Heekeren, H. R., Wartenburger, I., Schmidt, H., Schwintowski, H.-P., & Villringer, A. (2003). An fMRI study of simple ethical decision-making. *Neuroreport, 14,* 1215–1219.

Hegerl, U., Plattner, A., & Moller, H. J. (2004). Should combined pharmaco- and psychotherapy be offered to depressed patients? A qualitative review of randomized clinical trials from the 1990s. *European Archives of Psychiatry and Clinical Neuroscience, 254,* 99–107.

Heider, E. (1972). Universals of color naming and memory. *Journal of Experimental Psychology, 93,* 10–20.

Heilman, K. M., Barrett, A. M., & Adair, J. C. (1998). Possible mechanisms of anosognosia: A defect in self-awareness. *Philosophical Transactions of the Royal Society of London, Series B: Biological Sciences, 353,* 1903–1909.

Heilman, K. M., & Gonzalez-Rothi, L. J. (2003). Apraxia. In K. M. Heilman & E. Valenstein (Eds.), *Clinical neuropsychology* (4th ed., pp. 215–235). New York: Oxford University Press.

Heilman, K. M., & Valenstein, E. (Eds.). (2003). *Clinical neuropsychology* (4th ed.). New York: Oxford University Press.

Heilman, K. M., Valenstein, E., & Watson, R. T. (2000). Neglect and related disorders. *Seminars in Neurology, 20,* 463–470.

Heilman, K. M., Watson, R. T., & Valenstein, E. (2003). Neglect and related disorders. In K. M. Heilman & E. Valenstein (Eds.), *Clinical neuropsychology* (4th ed., pp. 296–346). New York: Oxford University Press.

Heilman, M. E., & Haynes, M. C. (2008). Subjectivity in the appraisal process: A facilitator of gender bias in work settings. In E. Borgida & S. T. Fiske (Eds.), *Beyond common sense: Psychological science in the courtroom* (pp. 127–155). Malden. MA: Blackwell.

Heine, S. J., & Buchtel, E. A. (2009). Personality: The universal and the culturally specific. *Annual Review of Psychology, 60,* 369–394.

Heine, S. J., Harihara, M., & Niiya, Y. (2002). Terror management in Japan. *Asian Journal of Social Psychology, 5,* 187–196.

Heinrichs, W. L., Youngblood, P., Harter, P. M., & Dev, P. (2008). Simulation for team training and assessment: Case studies of online training with virtual worlds. *World Journal of Surgery, 32,* 161–170.

Heiss, G., Wallace, R., Anderson, G. L., Aragaki, A., et al. (2008). Health risks and benefits 3 years after stopping randomized treatment with estrogen and progestin. *Journal of the American Medical Association, 299,* 1036–1045.

Heiss, W. D., & Teasel, R. W. (2006). Brain recovery and rehabilitation. *Stroke, 37,* 314–316.

Hejmadi, A., Davidson, R. J., & Rozin, P. (2000). Exploring Hindu Indian emotion expressions: Evidence for accurate recognition by Americans and Indians. *Psychological Science, 11,* 183–187.

Hektner, J. M., Schmidt, J. A., & Csikszentmihalyi, M. (2007). *Experience sampling method: Measuring the quality of everyday life.* Thousand Oaks, CA: Sage.

Heldt, E., Manfro, G. G., Kipper, L., Blaya, C., et al. (2006). One-year follow-up of pharmacotherapy-resistant patients with panic disorder treated with cognitive-behavior therapy: Outcome and predictors of remission. *Behaviour Research and Therapy, 44,* 657–665.

Helgesen, S. (1998). *Everyday revolutionaries: Working women and the transformation of American life.* New York: Doubleday.

Heller, W. (1993). Neuropsychological mechanisms of individual differences in emotion, personality, and arousal. *Neuropsychology, 7,* 486–489.

Hellmuth, J. C., & McNulty, J. K. (2008). Neuroticism, marital violence, and the moderating role of stress and behavioral skills. *Journal of Personality and Social Psychology, 95,* 166–180.

Helmes, E., & Velamoor, V. R. (2009). Long-term outcome of leucotomy on behaviour of people with schizophrenia. *International Journal of Social Psychiatry, 55,* 64–70.

Helms, J. E. (1992). Why is there no study of cultural equivalence in standardized cognitive ability testing? *American Psychologist, 47,* 1083–1101.

Helms, J. E. (1997). The triple quandary of race, culture, and social class in standardized cognitive ability testing. In D. P. Flanagan, J. L. Genshaft, & P. L. Harrison (Eds.), *Contemporary intellectual assessment: Theories, tests, and issues* (pp. 517–532). New York: Guilford Press.

Helson, R., & Moane, G. (1987). Personality change in women from college to midlife. *Journal of Personality and Social Psychology, 53,* 176–186.

Helzer, J. E., & Hudziak, J. J. (Eds.). (2002). *Defining psychopathology in the 21st century: DSM-V and beyond.* Washington DC: American Psychiatric Association.

Henckens, M. J. A. G., Hermans, E. J., Pu, Z., Joëls, M., & Fernández, G. (2009). Stressed memories: How acute stress affects memory formation in humans. *Journal of Neuroscience, 29,* 10111–10119.

Henderson, B., & Bernard, A. (Eds.). (1998). *Rotten reviews and rejections.* Wainscott, NY: Pushcart Press.

Henderson, J. M. (2008). Peripheral nerve stimulation for chronic pain. *Current Pain and Headache Reports, 12,* 28–31.

Hendrick, B. (2003, May 8). Exam day rituals help students feel lucky. *Naples Daily News.*

Hendricks, P. S., & Thompson, J. K. (2005). An integration of cognitive-behavioral therapy and interpersonal psychotherapy for bulimia nervosa: A case study using the case formulation method. *International Journal of Eating Disorders, 37,* 171–174.

Henig, R. (2004, April 4). The quest to forget. *New York Times,* p. 32.

Henkel, L. A. (2004). Erroneous memories arising from repeated attempts to remember. *Journal of Memory and Language, 50,* 26–46.

Henker, B., & Whalen, C. K. (1989). Hyperactivity and attention deficits. *American Psychologist, 44,* 216–223.

Hennig, J., Reuter, M., Netter, P., Burk, C., & Landt, O. (2005). Two types of aggression are differentially related to serotonergic activity and the A779C TPH polymorphism. *Behavioral Neuroscience, 119,* 16–25.

Hensch, T. K. (2005). Critical period plasticity in local cortical circuits. *Nature Reviews Neuroscience, 6,* 877–888.

Hense, R. L., Penner, L. A., & Nelson, D. L. (1995). Implicit memory for age stereotypes. *Social Cognition, 13,* 399–416.

Heppner, P. P., Heppner, M. J., Lee, D., Wang, Y.-W., et al. (2006). Development and validation of a collectivist coping styles inventory. *Journal of Counseling Psychology, 53,* 107–125.

Hepworth, S. J., Schoemaker, M. J., Muir, K. R., Swerdlow, A. J., et al. (2006). Mobile phone use and risk of glioma in adults: Case control study. *British Medical Journal, 332,* 883–887.

Herdener, M., Esposito, F., di Salle, F., Boller, C., et al. (2010). Musical training induces functional plasticity in human hippocampus. *Journal of Neuroscience, 30,* 1377–1384.

Heres, S., Davis, J., Maino, K., Jetzinger, E., et al. (2006). Why olanzapine beats risperidone, risperidone beats quetiapine, and quetiapine beats olanzapine: An exploratory analysis of head-to-head comparison studies of second-generation antipsychotics. *American Journal of Psychiatry, 163,* 185–194.

Hergenhahn, B. R., & Olson, M. (1997). *An introduction to theories of learning* (5th ed.). Upper Saddle River, NJ: Prentice Hall.

Hergenhahn, B. R., & Olson, M. (2007). *Introduction to theories of personality* (7th ed.) Upper Saddle River, NJ: Prentice Hall.
Herman, C. P., Roth, D. A., & Polivy, J. (2003). Effects of the presence of others on food intake: A normative interpretation. *Psychological Bulletin, 129,* 873–886.
Herman, L. M., Richards, D. G., & Wolz, J. P. (1984). Comprehension of sentences by bottlenosed dolphins. *Cognition, 16,* 129–219.
Hermans, D., Craske, M. G., Mineka, S., & Lovibond, P. F. (2006). Extinction in human fear conditioning. *Biological Psychiatry, 60,* 361–368.
Heron, M. P. (2007). Deaths: Leading causes for 2004. *National Vital Statistics Reports* (Vol. 56, no. 5). Hyattsville, MD: National Center for Health Statistics.
Heron, M. P., Hoyert, D. L., Murphy, S. L., Xu, J., et al. (2009). Deaths: Final data, 2006. *National Vital Statistics Reports* (Vol. 57, no. 14). Hyattsville, MD: National Center for Health Statistics.
Herrenkohl, T., Hill, K., Chung, I.-J., Guo, J., et al. (2004). Protective factors against serious violent behavior in adolescence: A prospective study of violent children. *Social Work Research, 27,* 179–191.
Herrington, J. D., Heller, W., Mohanty, A., Engels, A. S., et al. (2010). Localization of asymmetric brain function in emotion and depression. *Psychophysiology, 11,* 11.
Herrmann, D. J., & Searleman, A. (1992). Memory improvement and memory theory in historical perspective. In D. Herrmann, H. Weingartner, A. Searlman, & C. McEvoy (Eds.), *Memory improvement: Implications for memory theory.* New York: Springer-Verlag.
Herrnstein, R. J., & Murray, C. (1994). *The bell curve: Intelligence and class structure in American life.* New York: Free Press.
Hershcovis, M. S., Turner, N., Barling, J., Arnold, K. A., et al. (2007). Predicting workplace aggression: A meta-analysis. *Journal of Applied Psychology, 92,* 228–238.
Hertlein, K., & Ricci, R. J. (2004). A systematic research synthesis of EMDR studies: Implementation of the platinum standard. *Trauma, Violence, and Abuse, 5,* 285–300.
Hertzog, C., Kramer, A. F., Wilson, R. S., & Lindenberger, U. (2009). Enrichment effects on adult cognitive development: Can the functional capacity of older adults be preserved and enhanced? *Psychological Science in the Public Interest, 9,* 1–65.
Herz, R. S., & Cahill, E. D. (1997). Differential use of sensory information in sexual behavior as a function of gender. *Human Nature, 8,* 275–286.
Herzog, D. B., Dorer, D. J., Keel, P. K., Selwyn, S. E., et al. (1999). Recovery and relapse in anorexia and bulimia nervosa: A 7.5-year follow-up study. *Journal of the American Academy of Child and Adolescent Psychiatry, 38,* 829–837.
Herzog, T. A., & Blagg, C. O. (2007). Are most precontemplators contemplating smoking cessation? Assessing the validity of the stages of change. *Health Psychology, 26,* 222–231.
Hespos, S. J., & Baillargeon, R. (2001). Infants' knowledge about occlusion and containment events: A surprising discrepancy. *Psychological Science, 12,* 141–147.
Hespos, S. J., & Spelke, E. S. (2004). Conceptual precursors to language. *Nature, 430,* 453–456.
Hess, T. M., Hinson, J. T., & Statham, J. A. (2004). Explicit and implicit stereotype activation effects on memory: Do age and awareness moderate the impact of priming? *Psychology and Aging, 19,* 495–505.
Hetherington, E. M., & Stanley-Hagan, M. (2002). Parenting in divorced and remarried families. In M. H. Bornstein (Ed.), *Handbook of parenting: Vol. 3. Being and becoming a parent* (2nd ed., pp. 287–315). Mahwah, NJ: Erlbaum.
Hettema, J. M., Neale, M. C., & Kendler, K. S. (2001). A review and meta-analysis of the genetic epidemiology of anxiety disorders. *American Journal of Psychiatry, 158,* 1568–1578.
Hettema, J. M., Prescott, C. A., Myers, J. M., Neale, M. C., & Kendler, K. S. (2005). The structure of genetic and environmental risk factors for anxiety disorders in men and women. *Archives of General Psychiatry, 62,* 182–189.
Hewig, J., Kretschmer, N., Trippe, R. H., Hecht, H., et al. (2010). Hypersensitivity to reward in problem gamblers. *Biological Psychiatry, 67,* 781–783.
Hewlin, J., & Faison, P. (2009). Wearing the cloak: Antecedents and consequences of creating facades of conformity. *Journal of Applied Psychology, 94,* 727–741.
Heymsfield, S. B., Greenberg, A. S., Fujioa, K., Dixon, R. M., et al. (1999). Recombinant leptin for weight loss in obese and lean adults. *Journal of the American Medical Association, 282,* 1568–1575.
Heywood, C. A., & Kentridge, R. W. (2003). Achromatopsia, color vision, and cortex. *Neurology Clinics, 21,* 483–500.
Hicks, R. A., Fernandez, C., & Pelligrini, R. J. (2001). The changing pattern of sleep habits of university students: An update. *Perceptual and Motor Skills, 93,* 648.
Highley, J. R., Walker, M. A., Crow, T. J., Esiri, M. M., & Harrison, P. J. (2003). Low medial and lateral right pulvinar volumes in schizophrenia: A postmortem study. *American Journal of Psychiatry, 160,* 1177–1179.
Hightower, J. R. R. (2005). Women and depression. In A. Barnes (Ed.), *The handbook of women, psychology, and the law* (pp. 192–211). Hoboken, NJ: Wiley.
Higuchi, S., Matsushita, S., & Kashima, H. (2006). New findings on the genetic influences on alcohol use and dependence. *Current Opinion in Psychiatry, 19,* 253–265.
Hildebrandt, M. G., Steyerberg, E. W., Stage, K. B., Passchier, J., et al. (2003). Are gender differences important for the clinical effects of antidepressants? *American Journal of Psychiatry, 160,* 1643–1650.
Hilgard, E. R. (1965). *Hypnotic susceptibility.* New York: Harcourt, Brace.
Hilgard, E. R. (1977). *Divided consciousness: Multiple controls in human thought and action.* New York: Wiley.
Hilgard, E. R. (1979). *Personality and hypnosis: A study of imaginative involvement.* Chicago: University of Chicago Press.
Hilgard, E. R. (1982). Hypnotic susceptibility and implications for measurement. *International Journal of Clinical and Experimental Hypnosis, 30,* 394–403.
Hilgard, E. R. (1992). Divided consciousness and dissociation. *Consciousness and Cognition, 1,* 16–31.
Hilgard, E. R., Morgan, A. H., & MacDonald, H. (1975). Pain and dissociation in the cold pressor test: A study of "hidden reports" through automatic key-pressing and automatic talking. *Journal of Abnormal Psychology, 84,* 280–289.
Hill, C. E. (2005). Therapist techniques, client involvement, and the therapeutic relationship: Inextricably intertwined in the therapy process. *Psychotherapy: Theory, Research, Practice, Training, 42,* 431–442.
Hill, C. E., & Lent, R. W. (2006). A narrative and meta-analytic review of helping skills training: Time to revive a dormant area of inquiry. *Psychotherapy: Theory, Research, Practice, Training, 43,* 154–172.
Hill, C. T., & Peplau, L. A. (1998). Premarital predictors of relationship outcomes: A 15-year follow-up of the Boston Couples Study. In T. N. Bradbury (Ed.), *The developmental course of marital dysfunction* (pp. 237–278). New York: Cambridge University Press.
Hill, D. L., & Mistretta, C. M. (1990). Developmental neurobiology of salt taste sensation. *Trends in Neuroscience, 13,* 188–195.
Hill, D. L., & Przekop, P. R., Jr. (1988). Influences of dietary sodium on functional taste receptor development: A sensitive period. *Science, 241,* 1826–1828.
Hill, J. O., & Peters, J. C. (1998). Environmental contributions to the obesity epidemic. *Science, 280,* 1371–1374.
Hill, R. A., & Barton, R. A. (2005). Psychology: Red enhances human performance in contests. *Nature, 435,* 293.
Hill, T., Lewicki, P., Czyzewska, M., & Boss, A. (1989). Self-perpetuating biases in person perception. *Journal of Personality and Social Psychology, 57,* 373–386.
Hiller, W., Leibbrand, R., Rief, W., & Fichter, M. M. (2006). Differentiating hypochondriasis from panic disorder. *Journal of Anxiety Disorders, 19,* 29–49.
Hilliard, R. B., Henry, W. P., & Strupp, H. H. (2000). An interpersonal model of psychotherapy: Linking patient and therapist developmental history, therapeutic process, and types of outcome. *Journal of Consulting and Clinical Psychology, 68,* 125–133.
Hilton, D. (2002). Thinking about causality: Pragmatic, social and scientific rationality. In P. E. Carruthers, S. Stich, & M. Siegal (Eds.), *The cognitive basis of science* (pp. 211–231). New York: Cambridge University Press.
Hilton, H. (1986). *The executive memory guide.* New York: Simon & Schuster.
Hines, A. R., & Paulson, S. E. (2007). Parents' and teachers' perceptions of adolescent storm and stress: Relations with parenting and teaching styles. *Family Therapy, 34,* 63–80.
Hines, M., Brook, C., & Conway, G. (2004). Androgen and psychosexual development: Core gender identity, sexual orientation, and recalled childhood gender role behavior in women and men with congenital adrenal hyperplasia (CAH). *Journal of Sex Research, 41,* 75–81.
Hinton, D. E., Hinton, A. L., Pich, V., Loeum, J. R., & Pollack, M. H. (2009). Nightmares among Cambodian refugees: The breaching of concentric ontological security. *Culture Medicine and Psychiatry, 33,* 219–265.
Hinton, D. E., Um, K., & Ba, P. (2001). *Kyol goeu* ("wind overload"), part I: A cultural syndrome of orthostatic panic among Khmer refugees. *Transcultural Psychiatry, 38,* 403–432.
Hinton, J. (1967). *Dying.* Harmondsworth, England: Penguin.
Hintzman, D. L. (1978). *The psychology of learning and memory.* San Francisco: Freeman.
Hiroi, N., & Scott, D. (2009). Constitutional mechanisms of vulnerability and resilience to nicotine dependence. *Molecular Psychiatry, 14,* 653–667.
Hirota, K. (2006). Special cases: Ketamine, nitrous oxide and xenon. *Best Practice and Research: Clinical Anaesthesiology, 20,* 69–79.
Hiroto, D. S. (1974). Locus of control and learned helplessness. *Journal of Experimental Psychology, 102,* 187–193.
Hirsch, J. K., Wolford, K., LaLonde, S. M, Brunk, L., & Parker-Morris, A. (2009). Optimistic explanatory style as a moderator of the association between negative life events and suicide ideation. *Crisis, 30,* 48–53.
Hirschberger, G. (2009). Compassionate callousness: A terror management perspective on prosocial behavior. In M. Mikulincer & P. Shaver (Eds.), *Prosocial motives, emotions, and behavior: The better angels of our nature* (pp. 201–219). Washington, DC: American Psychological Association.
Hirschfeld, R. J, Jordan, M. H., Thomas, C. H., & Field, H. S. (2008). Observed leadership potential of personnel in a team setting: Big Five traits and proximal factors as predictors. *International Journal of Selection and Assessment, 16,* 385–402.
Hirschfeld, R. M. A., & Vornik, L. A. (2004). Newer antidepressants: Review of efficacy and safety of escitalopram and duloxetine. *Journal of Clinical Psychiatry, 65*(Suppl. 4), 46–52.
Hirsch-Pasek, K., Treiman, R., & Schneiderman, M. (1984). Brown and Hanlon revisited: Mothers' sensitivity to ungrammatical forms. *Journal of Child Language, 11,* 81–88.
Hjelmblink, F., Holmström, I., & Kjeldmand, D. (2010). Stroke patients' delay of emergency treatment. *Scandinavian Journal of Caring Sciences, 24,* 307–311. Epub 2010 Mar 10.
Ho, B.-C., Andreasen, N. C., Nopoulos, P., Arndt, S., et al. (2003). Progressive structural brain abnormalities and their relationship to clinical outcome: A longitudinal magnetic resonance imaging study early in schizophrenia. *Archives of General Psychiatry, 60,* 585–594.
Ho, C., Bluestein, D. N., & Jenkins, J. M. (2008). Cultural differences in the relationship between parenting and children's behavior. *Developmental Psychology, 44,* 507–522.
Ho, D. Y.-F., & Chiu, C.-Y. (1994). Component ideas of individual, collectivism, and social organization: An application in the study of Chinese culture. In U. Kim, H. C. Triandis, C. Kagitcibasi, S.-C. Choi, & G. Yoon (Eds.), *Individualism and collectivism: Theory, method, and applications* (pp. 137–155). Thousand Oaks, CA: Sage.
Ho, Y.-C., Cheung, M., & Chan, A. S. (2003). Music training improves verbal but not visual memory: Cross-sectional and longitudinal explorations in children. *Neuropsychology, 17,* 439–450.
Hobson, J. A. (1997). Dreaming as delirium: A mental status analysis of our nightly madness. *Seminar in Neurology, 17,* 121–128.
Hobson, J. A. (2005). Sleep is of the brain, by the brain, and for the brain. *Nature, 437,* 1254–1256.
Hobson, J. A., Pace-Schott, E. F., Stickgold, R., & Kahn, D. (1998). To dream or not to dream? Relevant data from new neuroimaging and electrophysical studies. *Current Opinions in Neurobiology, 8,* 239–244.
Hobson, J. A., & Stickgold, R. (1994). Dreaming: A neurocognitive approach. *Consciousness and Cognition, 3,* 1–15.

Hochberg, L. R., Serruya, M. D., Friehs, G. M., Mukand, J. A., et al. (2006). Neuronal ensemble control of prosthetic devices by a human with tetraplegia. *Nature, 442*, 164–171.

Hochel, M., & Milán, E. G. (2008). Synaesthesia: The existing state of affairs. *Cognitive Neuropsychology, 25*, 93–111.

Hochhalter, A., Sweeney, W., Bakke, B. L., Holub, R. J., & Overmier, J. B. (2001). Improving face recognition in alcohol dementia. *Clinical Gerontologist, 22*, 3–18.

Hodgins, S. (2007). Persistent violent offending: What do we know? *British Journal of Psychiatry, 190* (Suppl.), S12–S14.

Hoegl, M., & Parboteeah, K. P. (2006). Autonomy and teamwork in innovative projects. *Human Resource Management, 45*, 67–79.

Hoek, H. W. (2006). Incidence, prevalence, and mortality of anorexia nervosa and other eating disorders. *Current Opinion in Psychiatry, 19*, 389–394.

Hoel, H., Faragher, B., & Cooper, C. L. (2004). Bullying is detrimental to health, but all bullying behaviors are not necessarily equally damaging. *British Journal of Guidance and Counseling, 32*, 367–387.

Hofer, S. B., Mrsic-Flogel, T. D., Bonhoeffer, T., & Hübener, M. (2009). Experience leaves a lasting structural trace in cortical circuits. *Nature, 457*, 313–317.

Hoffman, D. (1999, February 11). When the nuclear alarms went off, he guessed right. *International Herald Tribune*, p. 2.

Hoffman, H. G., Granhag, P. A., See, S. T. K., & Loftus, E. F. (2001). Social influences on reality-monitoring decisions. *Memory and Cognition, 29*, 394–404.

Hoffmann, J. P., & Cerbone, F. G. (2002). Parental substance use disorder and the risk of adolescent drug abuse: An event history analysis. *Drug and Alcohol Dependence, 66*, 255–264.

Hofmann, S. G., Meuret, A. E., Smits, J. A., Simon, N. M., et al. (2006). Augmentation of exposure therapy with D-cycloserine for social anxiety disorder. *Archives of General Psychiatry, 63*, 298–304.

Hofmann, S. G., Sawyer, A. T., Witt, A. A., & Oh, D. (2010). The effect of mindfulness-based therapy on anxiety and depression: A meta-analytic review. *Journal of Consulting and Clinical Psychology, 78*, 169–183.

Hogan, D. P., & Msall, M. E. (2002). Family structure and resources and the parenting of children with disabilities and functional limitations. In J. G. Borkowski, S. L. Ramey, & M. Bristol-Power (Eds.), *Parenting and the child's world* (pp. 311–328). Mahwah, NJ: Erlbaum.

Hogan, R. (2006). *Personality and the fate of organizations.* Mahwah, NJ: Erlbaum.

Hogarth, R. M., & Einhorn, H. J. (1992). Order effects in belief updating: The belief adjustment model. *Cognitive Psychology, 24*, 1–55.

Hogg, M. A. (2010). Influence and leadership In S. T. Fiske, D. T. Gilbert, & G. Lindzey (Eds.), *Handbook of social psychology* (5th ed., Vol 2, pp. 1166–1207). Hoboken, NJ: Wiley.

Hohman, A. A., & Shear, M. K. (2002). Community-based intervention research: Coping with the "noise" of real life in study design. *American Journal of Psychiatry, 159*, 201–207.

Hohmann, A. G., Syplita, R. L., Bolton, N. M., Neely, M. N., et al. (2005). An endocannabinois mechanism for stress-pinduced analgesia. *Nature, 435*, 1108–1112.

Hohmann, G. W. (1966). Some effects of spinal cord lesions on experienced emotional feelings. *Psychophysiology, 3*, 143–156.

Høigaard, R., & Ingvaldsen, R. P. (2006). Social loafing in interactive groups: The effects of identifiability on effort and individual performance in floorball. *Athletic Insight: The Online Journal of Sport Psychology.* Retrieved from http://www.athleticinsight.com/Vol8Iss2/Loafing.htm

Høigaard, R., Säfvenbom, R., & Tonnessen, F. E. (2006). The relationship between group cohesion, group norms, and perceived social loafing in soccer teams. *Small Group Research, 37*, 217–232.

Holden, C. (1996). Small refugees suffer the effects of early neglect. *Science, 274*, 1076–1077.

Holland, A. S., & Roisman, G. I. (2010). Adult attachment security and young adults' dating relationships over time: Self-reported, observational, and physiological evidence. *Developmental Psychology, 46*, 552–557.

Hollander, E., & Simeon, D. (2008). Anxiety disorders. In R. E. Hales, S. C., Yudofsky, & G. O. Gabbard (Eds.), *Textbook of psychiatry* (pp. 505–567). Alexandria, VA: American Psychiatric Association.

Hollander, E., Braum, A., & Simeon, D. (2008). Should OCD leave the anxiety disorders in DSM-V? The case for obsessive-compulsive-related disorders. *Depression and Anxiety, 25*, 317–329.

Hollinger, R. C., Dabney, D. A., Lee, G., Hayes, R., et al. (1996). *1996 national retail security survey final report.* Gainesville: University of Florida.

Hollins, S. S. & Bensmaia, S. J. (2007). The coding of roughness. *Canadian Journal of Experimental Psychology, 61*, 184–195.

Hollon, S. D., Jarrett, R. B., Nienbeg, A. A., Thase, M. E., et al. (2005). Psychotherapy and medication in the treatment of adult and geriatric depression: Which monotherapy or combined therapy? *Journal of Clinical Psychiatry, 66*, 455–468.

Hollon, S. D., Stewart, M. O., & Strunk, D. (2006). Enduring effects for cognitive behavior therapy in the treatment of depression and anxiety. *Annual Review of Psychology, 57*, 285–315.

Hollon, S. D., Thase, M. E., & Markowitz, J. C. (2002). Treatment and prevention of depression. *Psychological Science in the Public Interest, 3*, 39–77.

Holma, K. M., Melartin, T. K., Haukka, J., Holma, I.A.K., Sokero, T. P., & Isometsa, E. T. (2010). Incidence and predictors of suicide attempts in DSM-IV major depressive disorder: A five-year prospective study. *American Journal of Psychiatry, 167*, 801–808.

Holman, B. R. (1994). Biological effects of central nervous system stimulants. *Addiction, 89*, 1435–1441.

Holman, E. A., Silver, R. C., Poulin, M., Andersen, J., et al. (2008). Terrorism, acute stress, and cardiovascular health. *Archives of General Psychiatry, 65*, 73–80.

Holmes, T. H., & Rahe, R. H. (1967). The Social Readjustment Rating Scale. *Journal of Psychosomatic Research, 11*, 213–218.

Holtmaat, A., Wilbrecht, L., Knott, G. W., Welker, E., & Svoboda, K. (2006). Experience-dependent and cell-type-specific spine growth in the neocortex. *Nature, 441*, 979–983.

Holway, A. H., & Boring, E. G. (1941). Determinants of apparent visual size with distance variant. *American Journal of Psychology, 54*, 21–37.

Hommer, D. W., Momenan, R., Kaiser, E., & Rawlings, R. R. (2001). Evidence for a gender-related effect of alcoholism on brain volumes. *American Journal of Psychiatry, 158*, 198–204.

Honts, C. R., & Quick, B. D. (1995). The polygraph in 1996: Progress in science and the law. *North Dakota Law Review, 71*, 997–1020.

Hoobler, J. M., & Brass, D. J. (2006). Abusive supervision and family undermining as displaced aggression. *Journal of Applied Psychology, 91*, 1125–1133.

Hood, M. Y., Moore, L. L., Sundarajan-Ramamurti, A., Singer, M., et al. (2000). Parental eating attitudes and the development of obesity in children: The Framingham Children's Study. *International Journal of Obesity, 24*, 1319–1325.

Hooker, E. (1993). Reflections of a 40-year exploration: A scientific view on homosexuality. *American Psychologist, 48*, 450–453.

Hooley, J. M. (2004). Do psychiatric patients do better clinically if they live with certain kinds of families? *Current Directions in Psychological Science, 13*, 202–205.

Hopf, H. C., Muller, F. W., & Hopf, N. J. (1992). Localization of emotional and volitional facial paresis. *Neurology, 42*, 1918–1923.

Hopper, K., & Wanderling, J. (2000). Revisiting the developed versus developing country distinction in course and outcome in schizophrenia: Results from ISoS, the WHO Collaborative Followup Project. *Schizophrenia Bulletin, 26*, 835–846.

Horne, J. A. (1988). *Why we sleep: The functions of sleep in humans.* Oxford: Oxford University Press.

Horner, P. J., & Gage, F. H. (2002). Regeneration in the adult and aging brain. *Archives of Neurology, 59*, 1717–1720.

Horney, K. (1937). *Neurotic personality of our times.* New York: Norton.

Horowitz, J. L., & Garber, J. (2006). The prevention of depressive symptoms in children and adolescents: A meta-analytic review. *Journal of Consulting and Clinical Psychology, 74*, 401–415.

Horton, C. L., Moulin, C. J. A., & Conway, M. A. (2009). The self and dreams during a period of transition. *Consciousness and Cognition, 18*, 710–717.

Horton, J. E., Crawford, H. J., Harrington, G., & Downs, J. H., III. (2004). Increased anterior corpus callosum size associated positively with hypnotizability and the ability to control pain. *Brain, 127*, 1741–1747.

Horvath, A. O. (2005). The therapeutic relationship—research and theory: An introduction to the special issue. *Psychotherapy Research, 15*, 3–7.

Horwitz, A. V., Widom, C. S., McLaughlin, J., & White, H. R. (2001). The impact of childhood abuse and neglect on adult mental health: A prospective study. *Journal of Health and Social Behavior, 42*, 184–201.

Horwitz, B., Amunts, K., Bhattacharyya, R., Patkin, D., et al. (2003). Activation of Broca's area during the production of spoken and signed language: A combined cytoarchitectonic mapping and PET analysis. *Neuropsychologia, 41*, 1868–1876.

Horwitz, P., & Christie, M. A. (2000). Computer-based manipulatives for teaching scientific reasoning: An example. In M. J. Jacobson & R. B. Kozuma (Eds.), *Innovations in science and mathematics education: Advanced designs for technologies of learning* (pp. 163–191). Mahwah, NJ: Erlbaum.

Hoshino-Browne, E., Zanna, A. S., Spencer, S. J., Zanna, M. P., et al. (2005). On the cultural guises of cognitive dissonance: The case of Easterners and Westerners. *Journal of Personality and Social Psychology, 89*, 294–310.

Hötting, K., & Röder, B. (2004). Hearing cheats touch, but less in congenitally blind than in sighted individuals. *Psychological Science, 15*, 60–64.

Houghton, G. (2005). *Connectionist models in cognitive psychology.* New York: Psychology Press.

Houpt, T. R. (1994). Gastric pressure in pigs during eating and drinking. *Physiology and Behavior, 56*, 311–317.

House, J. S., Landis, K. R., & Umberson, D. (1988). Structures and processes of social support. *Annual Review of Sociology, 14*, 293–318.

House, R. J., Hanges, P. J., Ruiz-Quintanilla, S. A., Dorfman, P. W., et al. (1999). Cultural influences on leadership and organizations: Project GLOBE. In W. H. Mobley, M. J. Gessner, & V. Arnold (Eds.), *Advances in global leadership* (Vol. 1, pp. 171–233). Stamford, CT: JAI.

Hoven, C. W., Duarte, C. S., Lucas, C. P., Wu, P., et al. (2005). Psychopathology among New York city public school children 6 months after September 11. *Archives of General Psychiatry, 62*, 545–552.

Howe, M. J. A., Davidson, J. W., & Sloboda, J. A. (1998). Innate talent: Reality or myth? *Behavioral and Brain Sciences, 21*, 399–442.

Howe, M. L. (2003). Memories from the cradle. *Current Directions in Psychological Science, 12*, 62–65.

Hoyert, D. L., Kung, H.-C., & Smith, B. L. (2005). Deaths: Preliminary data for 2003. *National Vital Statistics Reports, 53*, 1–48.

Hoyle, R. H. (1993). Interpersonal attraction in the absence of explicit attitudinal information. *Social Cognition, 11*, 309–320.

Hoyle, R. H., Harris, M. J., & Judd, C. M. (2002). *Research methods in social relations.* Belmont, CA: Wadsworth.

Hrdy, S. B. (1997). Raising Darwin's consciousness: Female sexuality and the prehominid origins of patriarchy. *Human Nature, 8*, 1–49.

Hrdy, S. B. (2003). The optimal number of fathers: Evolution, demography, and history in the shaping of female mate preferences. In S. J. Scher & F. Rauscher (Eds.), *Evolutionary psychology: Alternative approaches* (pp. 111–133). Dordrecht, Netherlands: Kluwer.

Hser, Y. I., Hoffman, V., Grella, C. E., & Anglin, M. D. (2001). A 33-year follow-up of narcotics addicts. *Archives of General Psychiatry, 58*, 503–508.

Hser, Y. I., Huang, D., Brecht, M. L., Li, L., & Evans, E. (2008). Contrasting trajectories of heroin, cocaine, and methamphetamine use. *Journal of Addictive Diseases, 27*(3), 13–21.

Hu, P., Stylos-Allan, M., & Walker, M. P. (2006). Sleep facilitates consolidation of emotional declarative memory. *Psychological Science, 17*, 891–898.

Hu, S., Patatucci, A. M. L., Patterson, C., Li, L., et al. (1995). Linkage between sexual orientation and chromosome Xq28 in males but not females. *Nature Genetics, 11,* 248–256.

Hua, J. Y., & Smith, S. J. (2004). Neural activity and the dynamics of central nervous system development. *Nature Neuroscience, 7,* 327–332.

Hubbard, E. M., & Ramachandran, V. S. (2005). Neurocognitive mechanisms of synesthesia. *Neuron, 48,* 509–520.

Hubel, D. H., & Wiesel, T. N. (1979). Brain mechanisms of vision. *Scientific American, 241,* 150–162.

Hudson, J. I.; Hiripi, E.; Pope, H. G., Jr.; & Kessler, R. C. (2007). The prevalence and correlates of eating disorders in the National Comorbidity Survey replication. *Biological Psychiatry, 61,* 348–358.

Hudson, J. L., & Rapee, R. M. (2009). Familial and social environments in the etiology and maintenance of anxiety disorders. In M. M. Antony & M. B. Stein (Eds.), *Oxford handbook of anxiety and related disorders* (pp. 173–189). New York: Oxford University Press.

Hudson, W. E. (1960). Pictorial depth perception in subcultural groups in Africa. *Journal of Social Psychology, 52,* 183–208.

Hudspeth, A. J. (1997). How hearing happens. *Neuron, 19,* 947–950.

Hudziak, J. J., Derks, E. M., Althoff, R. R., Rettew, D. C., & Boomsma, D. I. (2005). The genetic and environmental contributions to attention deficit hyperactivity disorder as measured by the Conners' Rating Scales—Revised. *American Journal of Psychiatry, 162,* 1614–1620. doi:10.1176/appi.ajp.162.9.1614

Huesmann, L. R. (1995). *Screen violence and real violence: Understanding the link.* Auckland, New Zealand: Media Aware.

Huesmann, L. R. (1998). The role of social information processing and cognitive schema in the acquisition and maintenance of habitual aggressive behavior. In R. G. Geen & E. Donnerstein (Eds.), *Human aggression.* San Diego, CA: Academic Press.

Huesmann, L. R. (2010). Nailing the coffin shut on doubts that violent video games stimulate aggression: Comment on Anderson et al. (2010). *Psychological Bulletin, 136,* 179–181.

Huesmann, L. R., & Eron, L. D. (1986). *Television and the aggressive child: A cross-national comparison.* Hillsdale, NJ: Erlbaum.

Huesmann, L. R., Moise-Titus, J., Podolski, C., & Eron, L. D. (2003). Longitudinal relations between children's exposure to TV violence and their aggressive and violent behavior in young adulthood, 1977–1992. *Developmental Psychology, 39,* 201–221.

Huestis, M. A., Gorelick, D. A., Heishman, S. J., Preston, K. L., et al. (2001). Blockade of effects of smoked marijuana by the CB1-selective cannabinoid receptor antagonist SR141716. *Archives of General Psychiatry, 58,* 322–328.

Huffcutt, A. I., & Arthur, W. (1994). Hunter and Hunter (1984) revisited: Interview validity for entry-level jobs. *Journal of Applied Psychology, 79,* 184–190.

Huffcutt, A. I., Conway, J. M., Roth, P. L., & Stone, N. J. (2001). Identification and meta-analytic assessment of psychological constructs measured in employment interviews. *Journal of Applied Psychology, 86,* 897–913.

Hughes, B. M. (2006). Lies, damned lies, and pseudoscience: The selling of eye movement desensitization and reprocessing (EMDR). *PsycCritiques, 51,* 10.

Hughes, J. R., Higgins, S. T., & Bickel, W. K. (1994). Nicotine withdrawal versus other drug withdrawal syndromes: Similarities and dissimilarities. *Addiction, 89,* 1461–1470.

Hughes, R. N. (2007). Neotic preferences in laboratory rodents: Issues, assessment, and substrates. *Neuroscience and Biobehavioral Reviews, 31,* 441–464.

Hui, C., Lam, S. S. K., & Law, K. K. S. (2000). Instrumental values of organizational citizenship behavior for promotion: A field quasi-experiment. *Journal of Applied Psychology, 85,* 822–828.

Huizink, A. C., Mulder, E. J. H., & Buitelaar, J. K. (2004). Prenatal stress and risk for psychopathology. *Psychological Bulletin, 130,* 115–142.

Hull, C. L. (1943). *Principles of behavior.* New York: Appleton-Century-Crofts.

Hull, C. L. (1951). *Essentials of behavior.* New Haven, CT: Yale University Press.

Hull, S. A., Cornwell, J., Harvey, C., Eldridge, S., & Bare, P. O. (2001). Prescribing rates for psychotropic medication amongst East London general practices: Low rates where Asian populations are greatest. *Family Practice, 18,* 167–173.

Humphreys, K. (2004). *Circles of recovery: Self-help organizations for addictions.* New York: Cambridge University Press.

Humphreys, L. G. (1984). General intelligence. In C. R. Reynolds & R. T. Brown (Eds.), *Perspectives on bias in mental testing.* New York: Plenum.

Hunsley, J. (2007). Addressing key challenges in evidence-based practice in psychology. *Professional Psychology: Research and Practice, 38,* 113–121.

Hunsley, J., & Rumstein-McKean, O. (1999). Improving psychotherapeutic services via randomized trials, treatment manuals, and component analysis designs. *Journal of Clinical Psychology, 55,* 1507–1517.

Hunsley, J., Lee, C. M., & Wood, J. M. (2003). Controversial and questionable assessment techniques. In S. O. Lilienfeld & S. J. Lynn (Eds.), *Science and pseudoscience in clinical psychology* (pp. 39–76). New York: Guilford Press.

Hunt, C. B. (1980). Intelligence as an information processing concept. *British Journal of Psychology, 71,* 449–474.

Hunt, C. E., & Hauck, F. R. (2006). Sudden infant death syndrome. *Canadian Medical Association Journal, 174,* 1861–1869.

Hunt, D. M., Dulai, K. S., Bowmaker, J. K., & Mollon, J. D. (1995). The chemistry of John Dalton's color blindness. *Science, 267,* 984–988.

Hunt, E. (1983). On the nature of intelligence. *Science, 219,* 141–146.

Hunt, M. (1982). *The universe within.* New York: Simon & Schuster.

Hunt, M., & Forand, R. (2005). Cognitive vulnerability to depression in never-depressed subjects. *Cognition and Emotion, 19,* 763–770.

Hunt, R., & Rouse, W. B. (1981). Problem-solving skills of maintenance trainees in diagnosing faults in simulated power plants. *Human Factors, 23,* 317–328.

Huprich, S. K. (2009). What should become of depressive personality in DSM-V? *Harvard Review of Psychiatry, 17,* 41–59.

Hurt, H., Brodsky, N. L., Betancourt, L., & Braitman, L. E. (1995). Cocaine-exposed children: Follow-up through 30 months. *Journal of Developmental and Behavioral Pediatrics, 16,* 29–35.

Husseman, J., & Raphael, Y. (2009). Gene therapy in the inner ear using adenovirus vectors. *Advances in Otorhinolaryngology, 66,* 37–51.

Huston, A. C., & Wright, J. C. (1989). The forms of television and the child viewer. In G. Comstock (Ed.), *Public communication and behavior* (Vol. 2, pp. 103–159). San Diego, CA: Academic Press.

Huston, T. L., Caughlin, J. P., Houts, R. M., Smith, S. E., & George, L. J. (2001). The connubial crucible: Newlywed years as predictors of marital delight, distress, and divorce. *Journal of Personality and Social Psychology, 80,* 237–252.

Huttenlocher, P. R. (1990). Morphometric study of human cerebral cortex development. *Neuropsychologia, 28,* 517–527.

Hwang, W.-C. (2006). The psychotherapy adaptation and modification framework: Application to Asian Americans. *American Psychologist, 61,* 702–715.

Hybels, C. F., Pieper, C. F., Blazer, D. G., & Steffens, D. C. (2008). The course of depressive symptoms in older adults with comorbid major depression and dysthymia. *American Journal of Geriatric Psychiatry, 16,* 300–309.

Hyde, J. S. (2005). The gender similarities hypothesis. *American Psychologist, 60,* 581–592.

Hyde, J. S. (2007). New directions in the study of gender similarities and differences. *Current Directions in Psychological Science, 16,* 259–263.

Hyde, J. S., & Durik, A. M. (2000). Gender differences in erotic plasticity: Evolutionary or sociocultural forces? Comment on Baumeister (2000). *Psychological Bulletin, 126,* 375–379.

Hyde, K. L., & Peretz, I. (2004). Brains that are out of tune but in time. *Psychological Science, 15,* 356–360.

Hyde, K. L., Lerch, J., Norton, A., Forgeard, M., et al. (2009). Musical training shapes structural brain development. *Journal of Neuroscience, 29,* 3019–3025.

Hyde, K. L., Zatorre, R. J., Griffiths, T. D., Lerch, J. P., & Peretz, I. (2006). Morphometry of the amusic brain: A two-site study. *Brain, 129,* 2562–2570.

Hyman, I. E., Jr. (2000). The memory wars. In U. Neisser & I. E. Hyman Jr. (Eds.), *Memory observed* (2nd ed., pp. 374–379). New York: Worth.

Hyman, I. E., Jr.; Boss, S. M.; Wise, B. M.; McKenzie, K. E.; & Caggiano, J. M. (2010). Did you see the unicycling clown? Inattentional blindness while walking and talking on a cell phone. *Applied Cognitive Psychology, 24,* 597–607. doi:10.1002/acp.1638

Hyman, I. E., Jr., & Pentland, J. (1996). The role of mental imagery in the creation of false childhood memories. *Journal of Memory and Language, 35,* 101–117.

Hyman, R. (2002). Why and when are smart people stupid? In R. J. Sternberg (Ed.), *Why smart people can be so stupid* (pp. 1–23). New Haven, CT: Yale University Press.

Hyman, S. E., Malenka, R. C., & Nestler, E. J. (2006). Neural mechanisms of addiction: The role of reward-related learning and memory. *Annual Review of Neuroscience, 29,* 565–598.

Hypericum Depression Trial Study Group. (2002). Effect of *Hypericum perforatum* (St. John's wort) in major depressive disorder: A randomized, controlled trial. *Journal of the American Medical Association, 287,* 1807–1814.

Iacono, W. G., & Patrick, C. J. (2006). Polygraph ("lie detector") testing: Current status and emerging trends. In I. B. Weiner & A. K. Hess (Eds.), *The handbook of forensic psychology* (3rd ed., pp. 552–588). Hoboken, NJ: Wiley.

Iancu, I., Poreh, A., Lehman, B., Shamir, E., & Kotler, M. (2005). The Positive and Negative Symptoms Questionnaire: A self-report in schizophrenia. *Comprehensive Psychiatry, 46,* 61–66.

Iani, C., Ricci, F., Ghem, E., & Rubichi, S. (2006). Hypnotic suggestion modulates cognitive conflict: The case of the flanker compatibility effect. *Psychological Science, 17,* 721–727.

Iervolino, A. C., Hines, M., Golombok, S. E., Rust, J., & Plomin, R. (2005). Genetic and environmental influences on sex-typed behavior during the preschool years. *Child Development, 76,* 826–840.

Igalens, J., & Roussel, P. (1999). A study of the relationships between compensation package, work motivation, and job satisfaction. *Journal of Organizational Behavior, 20,* 1003–1025.

Iijima, M., Arisaka, O., Minamoto, F., & Arai, Y. (2001). Sex differences in children's free drawings: A study on girls with congenital adrenal hyperplasia. *Hormones and Behavior, 40,* 99–104.

IJzerman, H., & Semin, G. R. (2009). The thermometer of social relations: Mapping social proximity on temperature. *Psychological Science, 20,* 1214–1220.

Ilgen, D. R., & Pulakos, E. D. (Eds.). (1999). *The changing nature of performance: Implications for staffing, motivation, and development.* San Francisco: Jossey-Bass.

Ilies, R., Fulmer, I. S., Spitzmuller, M., & Johnson, M. D. (2009). Personality and citizenship behavior: The mediating role of job satisfaction. *Journal of Applied Psychology, 94,* 945–959.

Ilies, R., & Judge, T. A. (2003). On the heritability of job satisfaction: The mediating role of personality. *Journal of Applied Psychology, 88,* 750–759.

Ilies, R., Nahrgang, J. D., & Morgeson, F. P. (2007). Leader-member exchange and citizenship behaviors: A meta-analysis. *Journal of Applied Psychology, 92,* 269–277.

Ilies, R., Scott, B. A., & Judge, T. A. (2006). The interactive effects of personal traits and experienced states on intraindividual patterns of citizenship behavior. *Academy of Management Journal, 49,* 561–575.

Imtiaz, K. E., Nirodi, G., & Khaleeli, A. A. (2001). Alexia without agraphia: A century later. *International Journal of Clinical Practice, 55,* 225–226.

Indovina, I., & Sanes, J. N. (2001). On somatotopic representation centers for finger movements in human primary motor cortex and supplementary motor area. *Neuroimage, 13,* 1027–1034.

Inness, M., Barling, J., & Turner, N. (2005). Understanding supervisor-targeted aggression: A within-person, between-jobs design. *Journal of Applied Psychology, 90,* 731–739.

Inoue-Nakamura, N., & Matsuzawa, T. (1997). Development of stone tool use by wild chimpanzees (*Pan troglodytes*). *Journal of Comparative Psychology, 111,* 159–173.

Insel, T. R. (2008). Assessing the economic costs of serious mental illness. *American Journal of Psychiatry, 165,* 663–665.

Insko, C. A., Schopler, J., Hoyle, R. H., Dardis, G. J., & Graetz, K. A. (1990). Individual-group discontinuity as a function of fear and greed. *Journal of Personality and Social Psychology, 58,* 68–79.

Institute of Medicine. (2006, April 5). *Sleep disorders and sleep deprivation: An unmet public health problem* [Press release]. Retrieved from http://www.iom.edu/CMS/3740/23160/33668.aspx

International Association for the Evaluation of Education Achievement. (1999). *Trends in mathematics and science achievement around the world.* Boston: Lynch School of Education, Boston College.

International Human Genome Sequencing Consortium. (2001). Initial sequencing and analysis of the human genome. *Nature, 409,* 860–921.

Inzitari, M., Pozzi, C., Ferrucci, L., Chiarantini, D., et al. (2008). Subtle neurological abnormalities as risk factors for cognitive and functional decline, cerebrovascular events, and mortality in older community-dwelling adults. *Archives of Internal Medicine, 168,* 1270–1276.

Inzlicht, M., & Ben-Zeev, T. (2000). A threatening intellectual environment: Why females are susceptible to experiencing problem-solving deficits in the presence of males. *Psychological Science, 11,* 365–371.

Ironson, G. H., Smith, P. C., Brannick, M. T., Gibson, W. M., & Paul, K. B. (1989). Constitution of a Job in General scale: A comparison of global, composite, and specific measures. *Journal of Applied Psychology, 74,* 193–200.

Irwin, M., Daniels, M., Smith, T., Bloom, E., & Weiner, H. (1987). Impaired natural killer cell activity during bereavement. *Brain, Behavior, and Immunity, 1,* 98–104.

Isaacowitz, D. M., Wadlinger, H. A., Goren, D., & Wilson, H. R. (2006). Selective preference in visual fixation away from negative images in old age: An eye-tracking study. *Psychology and Aging, 21,* 40–48.

Ishai, A., Ungerleider, L. G., & Haxby, J. V. (2000). Distributed neural systems for the generation of visual images. *Neuron, 28,* 979–990.

Ito, T., Tiede, M., & Ostry, D. J. (2009). Somatosensory function in speech production. *Proceedings of the National Academy of Sciences, 106,* 1245–1248

Ivanova, M. Y., & Israel, A. C. (2005). Family stability as a protective factor against the influences of pessimistic attributional style on depression. *Cognitive Therapy and Research, 29,* 243–251.

Ivleva, E., Thaker, G., & Tamminga, C. (2008). Comparing genes and phenomenology in the major psychoses: Schizophrenia and bipolar 1 disorder. *Schizophrenia Bulletin, 34,* 734–742.

Iwahashi, K., Matsuo, Y., Suwaki, H., Nakamura, K., & Ichikawa, Y. (1995). CYP2E1 and ALDH2 genotypes and alcohol dependence in Japanese. *Alcoholism Clinical and Experimental Research, 19,* 564–566.

Iwamasa, G. Y., Sorocco, K. H., & Koonce, D. A. (2002). Ethnicity and clinical psychology: A content analysis of the literature. *Clinical Psychology Review, 22,* 932–944.

Iwamura, Y., Iriki, A., & Tanaka, M. (1994). Bilateral hand representation in the postcentral somatosensory cortex. *Nature, 369,* 554–556.

Izac, S. M., & Eeg, T. R. (2006). Basic anatomy and physiology of sleep. *American Journal of Electroneurodiagnostic Technology, 46,* 18–38.

Izard, C. E. (1977). *Human emotions.* New York: Plenum.

Izard, C. E. (1993). Organizational and motivational functions of discrete emotions. In M. Lewis & J. M. Haviland (Eds.), *Handbook of emotions.* New York: Guilford Press.

Izard, C. E. (2007). Basic emotions, natural kinds, emotion schemas, and a new paradigm. *Perspectives on Psychological Science, 2,* 260–280.

Izard, C. E., Fine, S., Schultz, D., Mostow, A., et al. (2001). Emotion knowledge as a predictor of social behavior and academic competence in children at risk. *Psychological Science, 12,* 18–23.

Izumikawa, M., Minoda, R., Kawamoto, K., Abrashkin, K. A., et al. (2005). Auditory hair cell replacement and hearing improvement by Atoh1 gene therapy in deaf animals. *Nature, 11,* 271–276.

Jablensky, A. (2006). Subtyping schizophrenia: Implications for genetic research. *Molecular Psychiatry, 11,* 815–836.

Jaccard, J., Blanton, H., & Dodge, T. (2005). Peer influences on risk behavior: An analysis of the effects of a close friend. *Developmental Psychology, 41,* 135–147.

Jack, F., & Hayne, H. (2007). Eliciting adults' earliest memories: Does it matter how we ask the question? *Memory, 15,* 647–663.

Jackson, B., Sellers, R. M., & Peterson, C. (2002). Pessimistic explanatory style moderates the effect of stress on physical illness. *Personality and Individual Differences, 32,* 567–573.

Jackson, C. J. (2003). Gray's reinforcement sensitivity theory: A psychometric critique. *Personality and Individual Differences, 34,* 533–544.

Jackson, J. W. (2002). The relationship between group identity and intergroup prejudice is moderated by sociostructural variation. *Journal of Applied Social Psychology, 32,* 908–933.

Jackson, L. A., von Eye, A., Biocca, F. A., Barbatsis, G., et al. (2006). Does home Internet use influence the academic performance of low-income children? *Developmental Psychology, 42,* 429–435.

Jacob, S., Kinnunen, L. H., Metz, J., Cooper, M., & McClintock, M. K. (2001). Sustained human chemosignal unconsciously alters brain function. *Neuroreport, 12,* 2391–2394.

Jacob, S., & McClintock, M. K. (2000). Psychological state and mood effects of steroidal chemosignals in women and men. *Hormones and Behavior, 37,* 57–78.

Jacob, T., Waterman, B., Heath, A., True, W., et al. (2003). Genetic and environmental effects on offspring alcoholism: New insights using an offspring-of-twins design. *Archives of General Psychiatry, 60,* 1265–1272.

Jacobi, C., Hayward, C., de Zwaan, M., Kraemer, H. C., & Agras, W. S. (2004). Coming to terms with risk factors for eating disorders: Application of risk terminology and suggestions for a general taxonomy. *Psychological Bulletin, 130,* 19–65.

Jacobs, G. D., Pace-Schott, E. F., Stickgold, R., & Otto, M. W. (2004). Cognitive behavior therapy and pharmacotherapy for insomnia: A randomized controlled trial and direct comparison. *Archives of Internal Medicine, 164,* 1888–1896.

Jacobs, G. H. (2008). Primate color vision: A comparative perspective. *Vision Neuroscience, 25,* 619–631.

Jacobs, M., Snow, J., Geraci, M., Vythilingam, M., et al. (2009). Association between level of emotional intelligence and severity of anxiety in generalized social phobia. *Journal of Anxiety Disorders, 22,* 1487–1495.

Jacobs, N., Kenis, G., Peeters, F., Derom, C., et al. (2006). Stress-related negative affectivity and genetically altered serotonin transporter function: Evidence of synergism in shaping risk of depression. *Archives of General Psychiatry, 63,* 989–996.

Jacobson, E. (1938). *Progressive relaxation.* Chicago: University of Chicago Press.

Jacobson, J. W., Mulick, J. A., & Schwartz, A. A. (1995). A history of facilitated communication. *American Psychologist, 50,* 750–765.

Jacobson, K. (2002). ADHD in cross-cultural perspective: Some empirical results. *American Anthropologist, 104,* 283–286.

Jacobson, N. S., Christensen, A., Prince, S. E., Cordova, J., & Eldridge, K. (2000). Integrative behavioral couples therapy: An acceptance-based, promising new treatment for couple discord. *Journal of Consulting and Clinical Psychology, 68,* 351–355.

Jacoby, L. L., Marriott, M. J., & Collins, J. G. (1990). The specifics of memory and cognition. In T. K. Srull & R. S. Wyer (Eds.), *Advances in social cognition: Vol. 3. Content and process specificity in the effects of prior experiences* (pp. 111–121). Hillsdale, NJ: Erlbaum.

Jacoby, L. L., & Rhodes, M. G. (2006). False remembering in the aged. *Current Directions in Psychological Science, 15,* 49–53.

Jaffari-Bimmel, N., Juffer, F., van IJzendoorn, M. H., Bakermans-Kranenburg, M. J., & Mooijaart, A. (2006). Social development from infancy to adolescence: Longitudinal and concurrent factors in an adoption sample. *Developmental Psychology, 42,* 1143–1153. doi:10.1037/0012-1649.42.6.1143

Jaffee, S., & Hyde, J. (2000). Gender differences in moral orientation: A meta-analysis. *Psychological Bulletin, 126,* 703–726.

Jaffee, S. R., Caspi, A., Moffitt, T. E., & Taylor, A. (2004). Physical maltreatment to antisocial child: Evidence of an environmentally mediated process. *Journal of Abnormal Psychology, 113,* 44–55.

Jago, R., Baranowski, T., Baranowski, J. C., Thompson, D., & Greaves, K. A. (2005). BMI from 3–6 years of age is predicted by TV viewing and physical activity, not diet. *International Journal of Obesity, 29,* 557–564.

Jahnke, J. C., & Nowaczyk, R. H. (1998). *Cognition.* Upper Saddle River, NJ: Prentice Hall.

Jakobsen, K. D., Frederiksen, J. N., Hansen, T., Jansson, L., et al. (2005). Reliability of clinical ICD-10 schizophrenia diagnoses. *Nordic Journal of Psychiatry, 59,* 209–212.

Jaffee S. R., Caspi A., Moffitt T. E., Polo-Tomas M., Taylor A. (2007). Individual, family, and neighborhood factors distinguish resilient from non-resilient maltreated children: a cumulative stressors model. *Child Abuse and Neglect, 31,* 231–253.

James, W. (1884). Some omissions of introspective psychology. *Mind, 9,* 1–26.

James, W. (1890). *Principles of psychology.* New York: Holt.

James, W. (1892). *Psychology: Briefer course.* New York: Holt.

Jameson, L. C., & Sloan, T. B. (2006). Using EEG to monitor anesthesia drug effects during surgery. *Journal of Clinical Monitoring and Computers, 20,* 445–472.

Jancke, L., & Kaufmann, N. (1994). Facial EMG responses to odors in solitude and with an audience. *Chemical Senses, 19,* 99–111.

Janik, V. M. (2000). Whistle matching in wild bottlenose dolphins. *Science, 289,* 1355–1357.

Janis, I. L. (1985). International crisis management in the nuclear age. *Applied Social Psychology Annual, 6,* 63–86.

Janis, I. L. (1989). Crucial decisions: Leadership in policy making and crisis management. New York: Free Press.

Janowiak, J. J., & Hackman, R. (1994). Meditation and college students' self-actualization and rated stress. *Psychological Reports, 75,* 1007–1010.

Janowitz, H. D. (1967). Role of gastrointestinal tract in the regulation of food intake. In C. F. Code (Ed.), *Handbook of physiology: Vol. 6. Alimentary canal.* Washington, DC: American Physiological Society.

Jans, L. A. W., Riedel, W. J., Markus, C. R., & Blokland, A. (2007). Serotonergic vulnerability and depression: Assumptions, experimental evidence, and implications. *Molecular Psychiatry, 12,* 522–543.

Jansen, P. G., & Vinkenburg, C. J. (2006). Predicting managerial career success from assessment center data: A longitudinal study. *Journal of Vocational Behavior, 68,* 253–266.

Janszky, J., Szucs, A., Halasz, P., Borbely, C., et al. (2002). Orgasmic aura originates from the right hemisphere. *Neurology, 58,* 302–304.

Jason, L. A., Witter, E., & Torres-Harding, S. (2003). Chronic fatigue syndrome, coping, optimism, and social support. *Journal of Mental Health, 12,* 109–118.

Javitt, D. C., Kantrowitz, J., & Lajtha, A. (Eds.). (2009). *Handbook of neurochemistry and molecular neurobiology: Schizophrenia* (3rd ed.). New York: Springer.

Jayanthi, S., Buie, S., Moore, S., Herning, R. I., et al. (2010). Heavy marijuana users show increased serum apolipoprotein C-III levels: Evidence from proteomic analyses. *Molecular Psychiatry, 15,* 101–112.

Jefferis, B. M. J. H., Power, C., & Hertzman, C. (2002). Birth weight, childhood socioeconomic environment, and cognitive development in the 1958 British birth cohort study. *British Medical Journal, 325,* 305. Retrieved from http://www.ncbi.nlm.nih.gov/pmc/articles/PMC117769

Jeffries, K. J., Fritz, J. B., & Braun, A. R. (2003). Words in melody: An H(2)15O PET study of brain activation during singing and speaking. *Neuroreport, 14,* 749–754.

Jemal, A., Ward, E., Hao, Y., & Thun, M. (2005). Trends in the leading causes of death in the United States, 1970–2002. *Journal of the American Medical Association, 294,* 1255–1259.

Jemmott, J. B., Jemmott, L. S., & Fong, G. T. (2010). Efficacy of a theory-based abstinence-only intervention over 24 months: A randomized controlled trial with young adolescents. *Archives of Pediatrics and Adolescent Medicine, 164,* 152–159.

Jencks, C., & Phillips, M. (Eds.). (1998). *The black-white test score gap.* Washington, DC: Brookings Institution Press.

Jenkins, J. G., & Dallenbach, K. M. (1924). Oblivescence during sleep and waking. *American Journal of Psychology, 35,* 605–612.

Jenkins, M. R., & Culbertson, J. L. (1996). Prenatal exposure to alcohol. In R. L. Adams, O. A. Parsons, J. L. Culbertson, & S. J. Nixon (Eds.), *Neuropsychology for clinical practice: Etiology, assessment, and treatment of common neurological disorders* (pp. 409–452). Washington, DC: American Psychological Association.

Jenkins, R. O., & Sherbum, R. E. (2005). Growth and survival of bacteria implicated in sudden infant death syndrome on cot mattress materials. *Journal of Applied Microbiology, 99,* 573–579.

Jenner, P. (2001). Parkinson's disease, pesticides, and mitochondrial dysfunction. *Trends in Neuroscience, 24,* 245–246.

Jensen, A. R. (1993). Why is reaction time correlated with psychometric g? *Current Directions in Psychological Science, 2,* 53–55.

Jensen, A. R. (1998). *The g factor: The science of mental ability.* Westport, CT: Praeger.

Jensen, A. R. (2006). *Clocking the mind: Mental chronometry and individual differences.* Cambridge: Elsevier.

Jensen, M., & Karoly, P. (1991). Control beliefs, coping efforts, and adjustment to chronic pain. *Journal of Consulting and Clinical Psychology, 59,* 431–438.

Jeon, Y., & Polich, J. (2003). Meta-analysis of P300 and schizophrenia: Patients, paradigms, and practical implications. *Psychophysiology, 40,* 684–701.

Jevtovic-Todorovic, V., Wozniak, D. F., Benshoff, N. D., & Olney, J. W. (2001). A comparative evaluation of the neurotoxic properties of ketamine and nitrous oxide. *Brain Research, 895,* 264–267.

Jex, S. M., Adams, G. A., Elacqua, T. C., & Bachrach, D. G. (2002). Type A as a moderator of stressors and job complexity: A comparison of achievement strivings and impatience-irritability. *Journal of Applied Social Psychology, 32,* 977–996.

Jia, H., Rochefort, N. L., Chen, X., & Konnerth, A. (2010). Dendritic organization of sensory input to cortical neurons *in vivo. Nature, 464,* 1307–1312.

Jiang, T., Soussignan, R., Rigaud, D., Martin, S., et al. (2008). Alliesthesia to food cues: Heterogeneity across stimuli and sensory modalities. *Physiology and Behavior, 95,* 464–470.

Johansen, J. P., Fields, H. L., & Manning, B. H. (2001). The affective component of pain in rodents: Direct evidence for a contribution of the anterior cingulate cortex. *Proceedings of the National Academy of Sciences, 98,* 8077–8082.

John, J. (2004). A theory of consciousness. *Current Directions in Psychological Science, 12,* 244–250.

John, O. P., Naumann, L., & Soto, C. (2008). Paradigm shift to the integrative Big Five trait taxonomy: History, measurement, and conceptual issues, In O. P. John, R. W. Robins, & L. A. Pervin (Eds.), *Handbook of personality: Theory and research* (3rd ed., pp. 114–158). New York: Guilford Press.

Johnson, B. R. (2004). Involuntary commitment. In W. T. O'Donohue & E. R. Levensky (Eds.), *Handbook of forensic psychology: Resource for mental health and legal professionals* (pp. 767–780). New York: Elsevier Science.

Johnson, C. S., & Stapel, D. A. (2007). No pain, no gain: The conditions under which upward comparisons lead to better performance. *Journal of Personality and Social Psychology, 92,* 1051–1067.

Johnson, D. R., Westermeyer, J., Kattar, K., & Thuras, P. (2002). Daily charting of posttraumatic stress symptoms: A pilot study. *Journal of Nervous and Mental Disease, 190,* 683–692.

Johnson, E. O., Roth, T., Schultz, L., & Breslau, N. (2006). Epidemiology of DSM-IV insomnia in adolescence: Lifetime prevalence, chronicity, and an emergent gender different. *Pediatrics, 117,* 247–256.

Johnson, G. (2002). Comments on lithium toxicity. *Australian and New Zealand Journal of Psychiatry, 36,* 703.

Johnson, J., & Vickers, Z. (1993). Effects of flavor and macronutrient composition of food servings on liking, hunger, and subsequent intake. *Appetite, 21,* 25–39.

Johnson, J. G., Cohen, P., Smailes, E. M., Kasen, S., & Brook, J. S. (2002). Television viewing and aggressive behavior during adolescence and adulthood. *Science, 295,* 2468–2471.

Johnson, J. M., & Endler, N. S. (2002). Coping with human immunodeficiency virus: Do optimists fare better? *Current Psychology: Developmental, Learning, Personality, Social, 21,* 3–16.

Johnson, J. S., & Newport, E. L. (1989). Critical period effects in second language learning. *Cognitive Psychology, 21,* 60–99.

Johnson, M. A., Dziurawiec, S., Ellis, H., & Morton, J. (1991). Newborns' preferential tracking of face-like stimuli and its subsequent decline. *Cognition, 4,* 1–19.

Johnson, M. K., & Raye, C. L. (1998). False memories and confabulation. *Trends in Cognitive Sciences, 2,* 137–145.

Johnson, S. L., McPhee, L., & Birch, L. L. (1991). Conditioned preferences: Young children prefer flavors associated with high dietary fat. *Physiology and Behavior, 50,* 1245–1251.

Johnson, S. P. (2004). Development of perceptual completion in infancy. *Psychological Science, 15,* 769–775.

Johnson, W.; Bouchard, T. J., Jr.; Krueger, R. F.; McGue, M.; & Gottesman, I. I. (2004). Just one g: Consistent results form three test batteries. *Intelligence, 32,* 95–107.

Johnson, W., Turkheimer, E., Gottesman, I. I., & Bouchard, T. J., Jr. (2009). Beyond heritability: Twin studies in behavioral research. *Current Directions in Psychological Science, 18,* 217–220.

Johnson, W. R., & Neal, D. (1998). Basic skills and the black-white earnings gap. In C. Jencks & M. Phillips (Eds.), *The black-white test score gap* (pp. 480–497). Washington, DC: Brookings Institution Press.

Johnson-Laird, P. N. (1983). *Mental models: Toward a cognitive science of language, inference, and consciousness.* Cambridge, MA: Harvard University Press.

Johnson-Laird, P. N., Mancini, F., & Gangemi, A. (2006). A hyper-emotion theory of psychological illnesses. *Psychological Review, 113,* 822–841.

Johnston, D. W., Tuomisto, M. T., & Patching, G. R. (2008). The relationship between cardiac reactivity in the laboratory and in real life. *Health Psychology, 27,* 34–42.

Johnston, L. D., O'Malley, P. M., Bachman, J. G., & Schulenberg, J. E. (2004). *Monitoring the Future national survey results on drug use, 1975–2003. Vol. 1. Secondary school students* (NIH Publication No. 04-5507). Bethesda, MD: National Institute on Drug Abuse.

Joireman, J., & Durell, B. (2007). Self-transcendent values moderate the impact of mortality salience on support for charities. *Personality and Individual Differences, 43,* 779–789.

Jokela, M. (2010). Characteristics of the first child predict the parents' probability of having another child. *Developmental Psychology, 46,* 915–926.

Jones, C. J., & Peskin, H. (2010). Psychological health from the teens to the 80s: Multiple developmental trajectories. *Journal of Adult Development, 17,* 20–32. doi:10.1007/s10804-009-9075-x

Jones, E. E. (1982). Psychotherapists' impressions of treatment outcome as a function of race. *Journal of Clinical Psychology, 38,* 722–731.

Jones, G. V. (1990). Misremembering a common object: When left is not right. *Memory and Cognition, 18,* 174–182.

Jones, H. E. (2006). Drug addiction during pregnancy. *Current Directions in Psychological Science, 15,* 126–130.

Jones, J. R., & Schaubroeck, J. (2004). Mediators of the relationship between race and organizational citizenship behavior. *Journal of Managerial Issues, 16,* 505–527.

Jones, L. V., & Appelbaum, M. I. (1989). Psychometric methods. *Annual Review of Psychology, 40,* 23–44.

Jones, M. A., Botsko, M., & Gorman, B. S. (2003). Predictors of psychotherapeutic benefit of lesbian, gay, and bisexual clients: The effects of sexual orientation matching and other factors. *Psychotherapy: Theory, Research, Practice, Training, 40,* 289–301.

Jones, W. H. S. (Ed. & Trans.). (1923). *Hippocrates* (Vol. 1). London: Heinemann.

Joormann, J., Teachman, B. A., & Gotlib, I. H. (2009). Sadder and less accurate? False memory for negative material in depression. *Journal of Abnormal Psychology, 118,* 412–417.

Jordan, N., Grissom, G., Alonzo, G., Dietzen, L., & Sangsland, S. (2008). Economic benefit of chemical dependency treatment to employers. *Journal of Substance Abuse Treatment, 34,* 311–319.

Jordan, N. C., Huttenlocher, J., & Levine, S. C. (1992). Differential calculation abilities in young children from middle- and low-income families. *Developmental Psychology, 28,* 644–653.

Joseph, J. E., Liu, X., Jiang, Y., Lynam, D., & Kelly, T. (2009). Neural correlates of emotional reactivity in sensation seeking. *Psychological Science, 20,* 215–223.

Josephson, W. L. (1987). Television violence and children's aggression: Testing the priming, social script, and disinhibition predictions. *Journal of Personality and Social Psychology, 53,* 882–890.

Joska, J. A., & Stein, D. J. (2008). Mood disorders. In R. E. Hales, S. C. Yudofsky, & G. O. Gabbard (Eds.), *Textbook of psychiatry* (pp. 457–503). Alexandria, VA: American Psychiatric Publishing.

Jost, J. T., & Hamilton, D. L. (2005). Stereotypes in our culture. In J. F. Dovidio, P. Glick, & L. Rudman (Eds.), *On the nature of prejudice: Fifty years after Allport* (pp. 208–224). Malden, MA: Blackwell.

Joyce, P. R., McHugh, P. C., Light, K. J., Rowe, S., et al. (2009). Relationships between angry-impulsive personality traits and genetic polymorphisms of the dopamine transporter. *Biological Psychiatry, 66,* 717–721.

Judd, F. K., Jackson, H. J., Komiti, A., Murray, G., et al. (2002). High prevalence disorders in urban and rural communities. *Australian and New Zealand Journal of Psychiatry, 36,* 104–113.

Judge, T. A., Colbert, A. E., & Ilies, R. (2004). Intelligence and leadership: A quantitative review and test of theoretical propositions. *Journal of Applied Psychology, 89,* 542–552.

Judge, T. A., Hurst, C., & Simon, L. S. (2009). Does it pay to be smart, attractive, or confident (or all three)? Relationships among general mental ability, physical attractiveness, core self-evaluations, and income. *Journal of Applied Psychology, 94,* 742–755.

Judge, T. A., Ilies, R., & Dimotakis, N. (2010). Are health and happiness the product of wisdom? The relationship of general mental ability to educational and occupational attainment, health, and well-being. *Journal of Applied Psychology, 95,* 454–468.

Judge, T. A., Piccolo, R. F., & Ilies, R. (2004). The forgotten ones? The validity of consideration and initiating structure in leadership research. *Journal of Applied Psychology, 89,* 36–51.

Judge, T. A., Thoresen, C. J., Bono, J. E., & Patton, G. K. (2001). The job satisfaction–job performance relationship: A qualitative and quantitative review. *Psychological Bulletin, 127,* 376–407.

Juliano, L. M., & Griffiths, R. R. (2004). A critical review of caffeine withdrawal: Empirical validation of symptoms and signs, incidence, severity, and associated features. *Psychopharmacology (Berlin), 176,* 1–29.

Julien, R. M. (2005). *A primer of drug action* (10th ed.). New York: Worth.

Julien, R. M. (2008). *A primer of drug action* (11th ed.). New York: Worth.

Jung, C. G. (1916). *Analytical psychology.* New York: Moffat.

Jung, C. G. (1933). *Psychological types.* New York: Harcourt, Brace & World.

Juraska, J. M. (1998). Neural plasticity and the development of sex differences. *Annual Review of Sex Research, 9,* 20–38.

Jusczyk, P. W., Smith, L. B., & Murphy, C. (1981). The perceptual classification of speech. *Perception and Psychophysics, 1,* 10–23.

Jussim, L. (1989). Teacher expectations: Self-fulfilling prophecies, perceptual biases, and accuracy. *Journal of Personality and Social Psychology, 57,* 469–480.

Just, M. A., Carpenter, P. A., Keller, T. A., Emery, L., et al. (2001). Interdependence of nonoverlapping cortical systems in dual cognitive tasks. *Neuroimage, 14,* 417–426.

Just, N., & Alloy, L. B. (1997). The response styles theory of depression: Tests and an extension of the theory. *Journal of Abnormal Psychology, 106,* 221–229.

Kagan, J. R., Snidman, N., Arcus, D., & Resnick, J. S. (1994). *Galen's prophecy: Temperament in human nature.* New York: Basic Books.

Kahn, E., & Rachman, A. W. (2000). Carl Rogers and Heinz Kohut: A historical perspective. *Psychoanalytic Psychology, 17,* 294–312.

Kahneman, D., & Klein, G. (2009). Conditions for intuitive expertise: A failure to disagree. *American Psychologist, 64,* 515–526.

Kahneman, D., Krueger, A. B., Schkade, D., Schwarz, N., & Stone, A. A. (2006). Would you be happier if you were richer? A focusing illusion. *Science, 312,* 1908–1910.

Kahneman, D., & Shane, F. (2005). A model of heuristic judgment. In K. Holyoak & R. G. Morrison (Eds.), *The Cambridge handbook of thinking and reasoning* (pp. 267–293). New York: Cambridge University Press.

Kahneman, D., & Tversky, A. (1984). Choices, values, and frames. *American Psychologist, 29,* 341–356.

Kaiser, R. B., Hogan, R., & Craig, S. B. (2008). Leadership and the fate of organizations. *American Psychologist, 63,* 96–110.

Kaiser Family Foundation. (2005). *U.S. teen sexual activity.* Retrieved from http://www.kff.org/youthhivstds/upload/U-S-Teen-Sexual-Activity-Fact-Sheet.pdf

Kaitaro, T. (2001). Biological and epistemological models of localization in the nineteenth century: From Gall to Charcot. *Journal of Historical Neuroscience, 10,* 262–276.

Kajantie, E. J. (2008). Physiological stress response, estrogen, and the male-female mortality gap. *Current Directions in Psychological Science, 17,* 348–352.

Kajantie, E. J., & Phillips, D. I. W. (2006). The effects of sex and hormonal status on the physiological response to acute psychosocial stress. *Psychoneuroendocrinology, 31,* 151–178.

Kajiya, K., Inaki, K., Tanaka, M., Haga, T., et al. (2001). Molecular bases of odor discrimination: Reconstitution of olfactory receptors that recognize overlapping sets of odorants. *Journal of Neuroscience, 21,* 6018–6025.

Kalb, L. M., & Loeber, R. (2003). Child disobedience and noncompliance: A review. *Pediatrics, 111,* 641–652.

Kalechstein, A. D.; De La Garza, R., II; Mahoney, J. J., III; Fantegrossi, W. E.; & Newton, T. F. (2007). MDMA use and neurocognition: A meta-analytic review. *Psychopharmacology (Berlin), 189,* 531–537.

Kales, H. C., DiNardo, A. R., Blow, F. C., McCarthy, J. F., et al. (2006). International medical graduates and the diagnosis and treatment of late-life depression. *Academic Medicine, 81,* 171–175.

Kales, H. C., Neighbors, H. W., Blow, F. C., Taylor, K. K., et al. (2005a). Race, gender, and psychiatrists' diagnosis and treatment of major depression among elderly patients. *Psychiatric Services, 56,* 721–728.

Kales, H. C., Neighbors, H. W., Valenstein, M., Blow, F. C., et al. (2005b). Effect of race and sex on primary care physicians' diagnosis and treatment of late-life depression. *Journal of the American Geriatrics Society, 53,* 777–784.

Kalivas, P. W., & Volkow, N. D. (2005). The neural basis of addiction: A pathology of motivation and choice. *American Journal of Psychiatry, 162,* 1403–1413.

Kalluri, H. S., & Dempsey, R. J. (2008). Growth factors, stem cells, and stroke. *Neurosurgery Focus, 24*(3–4), E14.

Kalsbeek, A., Palm, I. F., La Fleur, S. E., Scheer, F. A., et al. (2006). SCN outputs and the hypothalamic balance of life. *Journal of Biological Rhythms, 21,* 458–469.

Kamdar, D., McAllister, D. J., & Turban, D. B. (2006). All in a day's work: How follower individual differences and justice perceptions predict OCB role definitions and behavior. *Journal of Applied Psychology, 91,* 841–855.

Kamin, L. J. (1969). Predictability, surprise, attention, and conditioning. In B. A. Campbell & R. M. Church (Eds.), *Punishment and aversive behavior* (pp. 279–296). New York: Appleton-Century-Crofts.

Kaminski, J. W., Valle, L. A., Filene, J. H., & Boyle, C. L. (2008). A meta-analytic review of components associated with parent training program effectiveness. *Journal of Abnormal Child Psychology, 36,* 567–589.

Kammeyer-Mueller, J. D., Wanberg, C. R., Glomb, T. M., & Ahlburg, D. (2005). The role of temporal shifts in turnover processes: It's about time. *Journal of Applied Psychology, 90,* 644–658.

Kammrath, L. K., Mendoza-Denton, R., & Mischel, W. (2005). Incorporating if . . . then . . . personality signatures in person perception: Beyond the person-situation dichotomy. *Journal of Personality and Social Psychology, 88,* 605–618.

Kamp Dush, C. M., & Amato, P. R. (2005). Consequences of relationship status and quality for subjective well-being. *Journal of Social and Personal Relationships, 22,* 607–627.

Kanaya, T., Scullin, M. H., & Ceci, S. J. (2003). The Flynn effect and U.S. policies. *American Psychologist, 58,* 778–790.

Kanazawa, S. (2004). General intelligence as a domain-specific adaptation. *Psychological Review, 111,* 512–523.

Kane, J. M., Eerdekens, M., Lindenmayer, J.-P., Keith, S. J., et al. (2003). Long-acting injectable risperidone: Efficacy and safety of the first long-acting atypical antipsychotic. *American Journal of Psychiatry, 160,* 1125–1132.

Kaner, A., & Prelinger, E. (2007). *The craft of psychodynamic psychotherapy* (2nd ed.). Northvale, NJ: Aronson.

Kanfer, R., Chen, G., & Pritchard, R. D. (2008). Work motivation: Forging new perspectives and directions in the post-millenium. In R. Kanfer, G. Chen, & R. D. Pritchard (Eds.), *Work motivation: Past, present, and future* (pp. 601–632). New York: Routledge.

Kang, N., Baum, M. J., & Cherry, J. A. (2009). A direct main olfactory bulb projection to the 'vomeronasal' amygdala in female mice selectively responds to volatile pheromones from males. *European Journal of Neuroscience, 29,* 624–634.

Kangas, M., Henry, J. L., & Bryant, R. A. (2005). Predictors of posttraumatic stress disorder following cancer. *Health Psychology, 24,* 579–585.

Kanki, B. J., & Foushee, H. C. (1990). Crew factors in the aerospace workplace. In S. Oskamp & S. Spacepan (Eds.), *People's reactions to technology* (pp. 18–31). Newbury Park, CA: Sage.

Kanno, T., Mitsugi, M., Sukegawa, S., Hosoe, M., & Furuki, Y. (2008). Computer-simulated bi-directional alveolar distraction osteogenesis. *Clinical Oral Implants Research, 19,* 1211–1218.

Kao, T., Shumsky, J. S., Murray, M., & Moxon, K. A. (2009). Exercise induces cortical plasticity after neonatal spinal cord injury in the rat. *Journal of Neuroscience, 29,* 7549–7557.

Kaplan, A. I. (2005). Therapist-patient privilege: Who owns the privilege? *Journal of Aggression, Maltreatment and Trauma, 11,* 135–143.

Kapogiannis, D., Barbey, A. K., Su, M., Zamboni, G., et al. (2009). Cognitive and neural foundations of religious belief. *Proceedings of the National Academy of Sciences, 106,* 4876–4881.

Kaptchuk, T. J., Stason, W. B., Legedza, A. R. T., Schnyer, R. N., et al. (2006). Sham device vs. inert pill: Randomised controlled trial of two placebo treatments. *British Medical Journal, 332,* 391–397.

Kapur, N. (1999). Syndromes of retrograde amnesia: A conceptual and empirical synthesis. *Psychological Bulletin, 125,* 800–825.

Kapur, S., Sridhar, N., & Remington, G. (2004). The newer antipsychotics: Underlying mechanisms and the new clinical realities. *Current Opinion in Psychiatry, 17,* 115–121.

Karam, E. G., Mneimneh, Z. N., Karam, A. N., Fayyad, J. A., et al. (2006). Prevalence and treatment of mental disorders in Lebanon: A national epidemiological survey. *Lancet, 367,* 1000–1006.

Karevold, E., Røysamb, E., Ystrom, E., & Mathiesen, K. S. (2009). Predictors and pathways from infancy to symptoms of anxiety and depression in early adolescence. *Developmental Psychology, 45,* 1051–1060.

Karni, A., Meyer, G., Adams, M., Turner, R., & Ungerleider, L. G. (1994). The acquisition and retention of a motor skill: A functional MRI study of long-term motor cortex plasticity. *Abstracts of the Society for Neuroscience, 20,* 1291.

Karon, B. P., & Widener, A. J. (1997). Repressed memories and World War II: Lest we forget. *Professional Psychology: Research and Practice, 28,* 338–340.

Karp, D. A. (1991). A decade of reminders: Changing age consciousness between fifty and sixty years old. In B. B. Hess & E. W. Markson (Eds.), *Growing old in America* (pp. 67–92). New Brunswick, NJ: Transaction Books.

Karpicke, J. D. (2009). Metacognitive control and strategy selection: Deciding to practice retrieval during learning. *Journal of Experimental Psychology: General, 138,* 469–486.

Karver, M. S., Handlesman, J. B., Fields, S., & Bickman, L. (2006). Meta-analysis of therapeutic relationship variables in youth and family therapy: The evidence for different relationship variables in the child and adolescent treatment outcome literature. *Clinical Psychology Review, 26,* 50–65.

Kasen, S., Cohen, P., Chen, H., & Must, A. (2008). Obesity and psychopathology in women: A three-decade prospective study. *International Journal of Obesity, 32,* 558–566.

Kashdan, T. B., & Rottenberg, J. (2010). Psychological flexibility as a fundamental aspect of health. *Clinical Psychology Review, 30,* 467–480.

Kaskutas, L. A., Bond, J., & Avalos, L. A. (2009). 7-year trajectories of Alcoholics Anonymous attendance and associations with treatment. *Addictive Behaviors, 34,* 1029–1035.

Kasper, S., & Papadimitriou, G. N. (Eds.). (2009). *Schizophrenia* (2nd ed.). New York: Informa Health Care.

Kass, S. (1999, October). Frequent testing means better grades, studies find. *APA Monitor,* p. 10.

Kasser, T., & Sharma, Y. S. (1999). Reproductive freedom, educational equality, and females' preference for resource-acquisition characteristics in mates. *Psychological Science, 10,* 374–377.

Kassin, S., Rigby, S., & Castillo, S. R. (1991). The accuracy-confidence correlation in eyewitness testimony: Limits and extensions of the retrospective self-awareness effect. *Journal of Personality and Social Psychology, 61,* 698–707.

Kassin, S. M., Fein, S., & Markus, H. R. (2010). *Social psychology* (8th ed.). Belmont, CA: Wadsworth.

Kastin, A. J., & Pan, W. (2005). Targeting neurite growth inhibitors to induce CNS regeneration. *Current Pharmaceutical Design, 11,* 1247–1253.

Katkin, E. S., Wiens, S., & Öhman, A. (2001). Nonconscious fear conditioning, visceral perception, and the development of gut feelings. *Psychological Science, 12,* 366–370.

Kato, Y., Kato, S., & Akahori, K. (2007). Effects of emotional cues transmitted in e-mail communication on the emotions experienced by senders and receivers. *Computers in Human Behavior, 23,* 1894–1905.

Kato, M., & Serretti, A. (2010). Review and meta-analysis of antidepressant pharmacogenetic findings in major depressive disorder. *Molecular Psychiatry, 15,* 473–500. Epub 2008 Nov 4.

Kato, S., Wakasa, Y., & Yamagita, T. (1987). Relationship between minimum reinforcing doses and injection speed in cocaine and pentobarbital self-administration in crab-eating monkeys. *Pharmacology, Biochemistry, and Behavior, 28,* 407–410.

Katzell, R. A., & Thompson, D. E. (1990). Work motivation: Theory and practice. *American Psychologist, 45,* 144–153.

Kauffman, N. A., Herman, C. P., & Polivy, J. (1995). Hunger-induced finickiness in humans. *Appetite, 24,* 203–218.

Kaufman, J., & Charney, D. (2000). Comorbidity of mood and anxiety disorders. *Depression and Anxiety, 12*(Suppl. 1), 69–76.

Kaufman, J., Yang, B.-Z., Douglas-Palumberi, H., Crouse-Artus, M., et al. (2007). Genetic and environmental predictors of early alcohol use. *Biological Psychiatry, 61,* 1228–1234.

Kaulfuss, P., & Mills, D. S. (2008). Neophilia in domestic dogs (*Canis familiaris*) and its implication for studies of dog cognition. *Animal Cognition, 11,* 553–556.

Kaushanskaya, M. (2009). The bilingual advantage in novel word learning. *Psychonomic Bulletin and Review, 16,* 705–710.

Kavanagh, P. S., Robins, S. C., & Ellis, B. J. (2010). The mating sociometer: A regulatory mechanism for mating aspirations. *Journal of Personality and Social Psychology, 99,* 120–132.

Kawakami, K., Dion, K. L., & Dovidio, J. F. (1998). Racial prejudice and stereotype activation. *Personality and Social Psychology Bulletin, 24,* 407–416.

Kawakami, K., Dovidio, J. F., & van Kamp, S. (2005). Kicking the habit: Effects of nonstereotypic association training and correction processes on hiring decisions. *Journal of Experimental Social Psychology, 41,* 68–75.

Kawakami, K., Phills, C. E., Steele, J. R., & Dovidio, J. F. (2007). (Close) distance makes the heart grow fonder: Improving implicit racial attitudes and interracial interactions through approach behaviors. *Journal of Personality and Social Psychology, 92,* 957–971.

Kawakami, N., Takeshima, T., Ono, Y., Uda, H., et al. (2005). Twelve-month prevalence, severity and treatment of common mental disorders in communities in Japan: Preliminary findings from the World Mental Health Japan Survey 2002–2003. *Psychiatry and Clinical Neurosciences, 59,* 441–452.

Kawamura, N., Kim, Y., & Asukai, N. (2001). Suppression of cellular immunity in men with a past history of posttraumatic stress disorder. *American Journal of Psychiatry, 158,* 484–486.
Kay, P., & Regier, T. (2006). Language, thought, and color: Recent developments. *Trends in Cognitive Science, 10,* 51–54.
Kaye, W. H., Klump, K. L., Frank, G. K., & Strober, M. (2000). Anorexia and bulimia nervosa. *Annual Review of Medicine, 51,* 299–313.
Kazak, A. E., Hoagwood, K., Weisz, J. R., Hood, K., et al. (2010). A meta-systems approach to evidence-based practice for children and adolescents. *American Psychologist, 65,* 85–97.
Kazantzis, N., Deane, F. P., Ronan, K., & L'Abate, L. (2005). *Using homework assignments in cognitive-behavioral therapy.* London: Taylor & Francis.
Kazantzis, N., Lampropoulos, G. K., & Deane, F. P. (2005). A national survey of practicing psychologists' use and attitudes toward homework in psychotherapy. *Journal of Consulting and Clinical Psychology, 73,* 742–748.
Kazarian, S. S., & Evans, D. R. (Eds.). (2001). *Handbook of cultural health psychology.* San Diego, CA: Academic Press.
Kazdin, A. E. (2002). *Research design in clinical psychology.* Boston: Allyn & Bacon.
Kazdin, A. E. (2003). Clinical significance: Measuring whether interventions make a difference. In A. E. Kazdin (Ed.), *Methodological issues and strategies in clinical research* (3rd ed., pp. 691–710). Washington, DC: American Psychological Association.
Kazdin, A. E. (2008). *Behavior modification in applied settings* (6th ed.). Long Grove, IL: Waveland Press.
Kazdin, A. E., & Benjet, C. (2003). Spanking children: Evidence and issues. *Current Directions in Psychological Science, 12,* 99–103.
Kazdin, A. E., & Weisz, J. R. (1998). Identifying and developing empirically supported child and adolescent treatments. *Journal of Consulting and Clinical Psychology, 66,* 19–36.
Kazdin, A. E., & Weisz, J. R. (2003). *Evidence-based psychotherapies for children and adolescents.* New York: Guilford Press.
Kealy, E. M. (2005). Variations in the experience of schizophrenia: A cross-cultural review. *Journal of Social Work Research and Evaluation, 6,* 47–56.
Keating, D. P. (1990). Adolescent thinking. In S. S. Feldman & G. R. Elliott (Eds.), *At the threshold: The developing adolescent* (pp. 4–89). Cambridge, MA: Harvard University Press.
Kee, D. W., Gregory-Domingue, A., Rice, K., & Tone, K. (2005). A release from proactive interference analysis of gender schema encoding for occupations in adults and children. *Learning and Individual Differences, 15,* 203–211.
Keeling, L. J., & Hurink, J. F. (1996). Social facilitation acts more on the consummatory phase on feeding behaviour. *Animal Behaviour, 52,* 11–15.
Keen, R. E., & Berthier, N. E. (2004). Continuities and discontinuities in infants' representation of objects and events. In R. V. Kail (Ed.), *Advances in child development and behavior* (Vol. 32, pp. 243–279). San Diego, CA: Elsevier/Academic Press.
Keenan, K., Hipwell, A., Feng, X., Babinski, D., et al. (2008). Subthreshold symptoms of depression in preadolescent girls are stable and predictive of depressive disorders. *Journal of the American Academy of Child and Adolescent Psychiatry, 47,* 1433–1442.
Keenan, K., & Wakschlag, L. S. (2004). Are oppositional defiant and conduct disorder symptoms normative behaviors in preschoolers? A comparison of referred and nonreferred children. *American Journal of Psychiatry, 161,* 356–358.
Keenan, K., Wakschlag, L. S., Danis, B., Hill, C., et al. (2007). Further evidence of reliability and validity of DSM-IV ODD and CD in preschool children. *Journal of the American Academy of Child and Adolescent Psychiatry, 46,* 457–468.
Keenan, P. S. (2009). Smoking and weight change after new health diagnoses in older adults. *Archives of Internal Medicine, 169,* 237–242.
Keene, J. R., & Prokos, A. H. (2007). The sandwiched generation: Multiple caregiving responsibilities and the mismatch between actual and preferred work hours. *Sociological Spectrum, 27,* 365–387. doi:10.1080/02732170701313308
Keesey, R. E., & Powley, T. L. (1986). The regulation of body weight. *Annual Review of Psychology, 37,* 109–133.
Keil, F. (2006). Cognitive science and cognitive development. In W. Damon & R. M. Lerner (Series Eds.) & D. Kuhn & R. Siegler (Vol. Eds.), *Handbook of child psychology: Vol. 2. Cognition, perception, and language* (6th ed., pp. 609–635). Hoboken, NJ: Wiley.
Kelesidis, T., Kelesidis, L., Chou, S., & Mantzoros, C. S. (2010). The role of leptin in human physiology: Emerging clinical applications. *Annals of Internal Medicine, 152,* 93–100.
Keller, M. B., McCullough, J. P., Klein, D. N., Arnow, B., et al. (2000). A comparison of nefazodone, the cognitive behavioral-analysis system of psychotherapy, and their combination for the treatment of chronic depression. *New England Journal of Medicine, 342,* 1462–1470.
Keller, M. C., & Nesse, R. M. (2006). The evolutionary significance of depressive symptoms: Different adverse situations lead to different depressive symptom patterns. *Journal of Personality and Social Psychology, 91,* 316–330.
Keller, P. S., El-Sheikh, M., Keiley, M., & Liao, P.-J. (2009). Longitudinal relations between marital aggression and alcohol problems. *Psychology of Addictive Behaviors, 23,* 2–13.
Keller, R. T. (2006). Transformational leadership, initiating structure, and substitutes for leadership: A longitudinal study of research and development project team performance. *Journal of Applied Psychology, 91,* 202–210.
Keller, S. S., Crow, T., Foundas, A., Amunts, K., & Roberts, N. (2009). Broca's area: Nomenclature, anatomy, typology, and asymmetry. *Brain and Language, 109,* 29–48. Epub 2009 Jan 19.
Keller-Cohen, D., Toler, A., Miller, D., Fiori, K., & Bybee, D. (2004, August). *Social contact and communication in people over 85.* Paper presented at the convention of the American Psychological Association, Honolulu, HI.
Kelley, H. H. (1973). The processes of causal attribution. *American Psychologist, 28,* 107–128.
Kelley, K. W. (1985). Immunological consequences of changing environmental stimuli. In G. P. Moberg (Ed.), *Animal stress.* Bethesda, MD: American Physiological Society.
Kelley, R. E., & Borazanci, A. P. (2009). Stroke rehabilitation. *Neurology Research, 31,* 832–840.
Kelley, W. M., Miezen, F. M., McDermott, K. B., Buckner, R. L., et al. (1998). Hemispheric asymmetry for verbal and nonverbal memory encoding in human dorsal frontal cortex. *Neuron, 20,* 927–936.
Kellman, P. J., & Arterberry, M. E. (2006). Infant visual perception. In W. Damon & R. M. Lerner (Series Eds.) & D. Kuhn & R. Siegler (Vol. Eds.), *Handbook of child psychology: Vol. 2. Cognition, perception, and language* (6th ed., pp. 109–160). Hoboken, NJ: Wiley.
Kellner, C. H., Fink, M., Knapp, R. G., Petrides, G., et al. (2005). Relief of expressed suicidal intent by ECT: A consortium for research in ECT study. *American Journal of Psychiatry, 162,* 977–982.
Kellner, C. H., Knapp, R. G., Petrides, G., Rummans, T. A., et al. (2006). Continuation electroconvulsive therapy vs. pharmacotherapy for relapse prevention in major depression. *Archives of General Psychiatry, 63,* 1337–1344.
Kellum, K. K., Carr, J. E., & Dozier, C. L. (2001). Response-card instruction and student learning in a college classroom. *Teaching of Psychology, 28,* 101–104.
Kelly, D. J., Quinn, P. C., Slater, A. M., Lee, K., et al. (2007). The other-race effect develops during infancy: Evidence of perceptual narrowing. *Psychological Science 18,* 1084–1089.
Kelly, G. A. (1980). A psychology of the optimal man. In A. W. Landfield & L. M. Leitner (Eds.), *Personal construct psychology: Psychotherapy and personality* (pp. 18–35). New York: Wiley.
Kelly, J. F. (2003). Self-help for substance-use disorders: History, effectiveness, knowledge gaps, and research opportunities. *Clinical Psychology Review, 23,* 639–663.
Kelly, T., Yang, W., Chen, C.-S., Reynolds, K., & He, J. (2008). Global burden of obesity in 2005 and projections to 2030. *International Journal of Obesity, 32,* 1431–1437.
Kelly, T. H., Foltin, R. W., Emurian, C. S., & Fischman, M. W. (1990). Multidimensional behavioral effects of marijuana. *Progress in Neuropsychopharmacology and Biological Psychiatry, 14,* 885–902.
Kemeny, M. E. (2003). The psychobiology of stress. *Current Directions in Psychological Science, 12,* 124–129.
Kempermann, G., Gast, D., & Gage, F. H. (2002). Neuroplasticity in old age: Sustained fivefold induction of hippocampal neurogenesis by long-term environmental enrichment. *Annals of Neurology, 52,* 135–143.
Kemps, E., Tiggemann, M., & Grigg, M. (2008). Food cravings consume limited cognitive resources. *Journal of Experimental Psychology: Applied, 14,* 247–254.
Kendall, P. C., & Chambless, D. L. (Eds.). (1998). Special section: Empirically supported psychological therapies. *Journal of Consulting and Clinical Psychology, 66,* 3–167.
Kendall, P. C., & Choudhury, M. S. (2003). Children and adolescents in cognitive-behavioral therapy: Some past efforts and current advances, and the challenges in our future. *Cognitive Therapy and Research, 27,* 89–104.
Kendall, P. C., Hudson, J. L., Gosch, E., Flannery-Schroeder, E., & Suveg, C. (2008). Cognitive-behavioral therapy for anxiety-disordered youth: A randomized clinical trial evaluating child and family modalities. *Journal of Consulting and Clinical Psychology, 76,* 282–297.
Kendell, R., & Jablensky, A. (2003). Distinguishing between the validity and utility of psychiatric diagnoses. *American Journal of Psychiatry, 160,* 4–12.
Kendler, K. S. (2005). "A gene for . . .": The nature of gene action in psychiatric disorders. *American Journal of Psychiatry, 162,* 1243–1252.
Kendler, K. S., Fisk, A., Gardner, C. O., & Gatz, M. (2009). Delineation of two genetic pathways to major depression. *Biological Psychiatry, 65,* 808–811.
Kendler, K. S., Gardner, C. O., & Prescott, C. A. (2006). Toward a comprehensive developmental model for major depression in men. *American Journal of Psychiatry, 163,* 115–124.
Kendler, K. S., Gatz, M., Gardner, C. O., & Pedersen, N. L. (2006). A Swedish national twin study of lifetime major depression. *American Journal of Psychiatry, 163,* 109–114.
Kendler, K. S., Jacobson, K. C., Myers, J., & Prescott, C. A. (2002). Sex differences in genetic and environmental risk factors for irrational fears and phobias. *Psychological Medicine, 32,* 209–217.
Kendler, K. S., Kuhn, J. W., Vittum, J., Prescott, C. A., & Riley, B. (2005). The interaction of stressful life events and a serotonin transporter polymorphism in the prediction of episodes of major depression: A replication. *Archives of General Psychiatry, 62,* 529–535.
Kendler, K. S., & Neale, M. C. (2009). "Familiality" or heritability? *Archives of General Psychiatry, 66,* 452–453.
Kendler, K. S., Thornton, L. M., & Gardner, C. O. (2000). Stressful life events and previous episodes in the etiology of major depression in women: An evaluation of the "kindling" hypothesis. *American Journal of Psychiatry, 157,* 1243–1251.
Kendler, K. S., Thornton, L. M., & Gardner, C. O. (2001). Genetic risk, number of previous depressive episodes, and stressful life events in predicting onset of major depression. *American Journal of Psychiatry, 158,* 582–586.
Kendler, K. S., Thornton, L. M., Gilman, S. E., & Kessler, R. C. (2000). Sexual orientation in a U.S. national sample of twin and nontwin sibling pairs. *American Journal of Psychiatry, 157,* 1843–1846.
Kennedy, K. A., & Pronin, E. (2008). When disagreement gets ugly: Perceptions of bias and the escalation of conflict. *Personality and Social Psychology Bulletin, 34,* 833–848.
Kenrick, D. T., Griskevicius, V., Neuberg, S. L., & Schaller, M. (2010). Renovating the pyramid of needs: Contemporary extensions built upon ancient foundations. *Perspectives on Psychological Science, 5,* 292–314.
Kenrick, D. T., Groth, G., Trost, M., & Sadalla, E. K. (1993). Integrating evolutionary and social exchange perspectives on relationships: Effects of gender, self-appraisal, and involvement level on mate selection. *Journal of Personality and Social Psychology, 64,* 951–969.
Kenrick, D. T., Neuberg, S. L., & Cialdini, R. B. (2010). *Social psychology: Goals in interactions* (5th ed.). Boston: Allyn & Bacon.
Kensinger, E. A., & Corkin, S. (2004). Two routes to emotional memory: Distinct neural processes for valence and arousal. *Proceedings of the National Academy of Sciences, 101,* 3310–3315.
Kent, S., Rodriguez, F., Kelley, K. W., & Dantzer, R. (1994). Reduction in food and water intake induced by microinjection of interleukin-1b in the ventromedial hypothalamus of the rat. *Physiology and Behavior, 56,* 1031–1036.
Kenworthy, J. B., Turner, R. N., Hewstone, M., & Voci, A. (2006). Intergroup contact: When does it work, and why. In J. F. Dovidio, P. Glick, & L. Rudman (Eds.), *On the nature of prejudice: Fifty years after Allport.* Malden, MA: Blackwell.

Keogh, E., Bond, F. W., & Flaxman, P. E. (2006). Improving academic performance and mental health through a stress management intervention: Outcomes and mediators of change. *Behaviour Research and Therapy, 44,* 339–357.

Kepner, J. (2001). Touch in Gestalt body process psychotherapy: Purpose, practice, and ethics. *Gestalt Review, 5,* 97–114.

Kéri, S. (2009). Genes for psychosis and creativity: A promoter polymorphism of the neuregulin 1 gene is related to creativity in people with high intellectual achievement. *Psychological Science, 20,* 1070–1073.

Kermer, D. A., Driver-Linn, E., Wilson, T. D., & Gilbert, D. T. (2006). Loss aversion is an affective forecasting error. *Psychological Science, 17,* 649–653.

Kern, M. L., & Friedman, H. S. (2008). Do conscientious individuals live longer? A quantitative review. *Health Psychology, 27,* 505–512.

Kernberg, O. (1984). *Severe personality disorders: Psychotherapeutic strategies.* New Haven, CT: Yale University Press.

Kerr, M. P., & Payne, S. J. (1994). Learning to use a spreadsheet by doing and by watching. *Interacting with Computers, 6,* 3–22.

Kerr, N. L., & Tindale, R. S. (2004). Group performance and decision making. *Annual Review of Psychology, 55,* 623–655.

Kersting, K. (2004, September). Cross-cultural training: 30 years and going strong. *APA Monitor,* pp. 48–49.

Kertesz, A. (1993). Clinical forms of aphasia. *Acta Neurochirurgica. Supplementum (Wien), 56,* 52–58.

Keshavan, M. S., Diwadkar, V. A., Montrose, D. M., Rajarethinam, R., & Sweeny, J. A. (2005). Premorbid indicators and risk for schizophrenia: A selective review and update. *Schizophrenia Research, 79,* 45–57.

Kessler, R. C., Berglund, P., Borges, G., Nock, M., & Wang, P. S. (2005). Trends in suicide ideation, plans, gestures, and attempts in the United States, 1990–1992 to 2001–2003. *Journal of the American Medical Association, 293,* 2487–2495.

Kessler, R. C., Berglund, P., Demler, O., Jin, R., & Walters, E. E. (2005). Lifetime prevalence of and age of onset distributions of DSM-IV disorders in the national comorbidity survey replication. *Archives of General Psychiatry, 62,* 593–602.

Kessler, R. C., Chiu, W. T., Jin, R., Ruscio, A. M., et al. (2006). The epidemiology of panic attacks, panic disorder, and agoraphobia in the National Comorbidity Survey replication. *Archives of General Psychiatry, 63,* 415–424.

Kessler, R. C., Demler, O., Frank, R. G., Olfson, M., et al. (2005). Prevalence and treatment of mental disorders, 1990 to 2003. *New England Journal of Medicine, 352,* 2515–2523.

Kessler, R. C., Galea, S., Gruber, M. J., Sampson, N. A., et al. (2008). Trends in mental illness and suicidality after Hurricane Katrina. *Molecular Psychiatry, 13,* 374–384.

Kessler, R. C., Ruscio, A., Shear, K., & Wittchen, H.-U. (2009). Epidemiology of anxiety disorders. In M. M. Antony & M. B. Stein (Eds.), *Oxford handbook of anxiety and related disorders* (pp. 19–33). New York: Oxford University Press.

Kessler, R. C., & Üstün, T. B. (2008). *The WHO World Mental Health surveys: Global perspectives on the epidemiology of mental disorders.* New York: Cambridge University Press.

Kessler, R. C., & Wang, P. S. (2008). The descriptive epidemiology of commonly occurring mental disorders in the United States. *Annual Review of Public Health, 29,* 115–129.

Kety, S. S., Wender, P. H., Jacobsen, B., Ingraham, L. J., et al. (1994). Mental illness in the biological and adoptive relatives of schizophrenic adoptees. *Archives of General Psychiatry, 51,* 442–455.

Keverne, E. B., & Curley, J. P. (2008). Epigenetics, brain evolution and behaviour. *Frontiers in Neuroendocrinology, 29,* 398–412.

Keyes, C. L. M. (2007). Promoting and protecting mental health as flourishing: A complementary strategy for improving national mental health. *American Psychologist, 62,* 95–108.

Khan, A., Leventhal, R. M., Khan, S., & Brown, W. A. (2002). Suicide risk in patients with anxiety disorders: A meta-analysis of the FDA database. *Journal of Affective Disorders, 69,* 183–190.

Khan, J., Wei, J. S., Ringner, M., Saal, L. H., et al. (2001). Classification and diagnostic prediction of cancers using gene expression profiling and artificial neural networks. *Nature Medicine, 7,* 673–679.

Khan, S. S., & Liu, J. H. (2008). Intergroup attributions and ethnocentrism in the Indian subcontinent: The ultimate attribution error revisited. *Journal of Cross-Cultural Psychology, 39,* 16–36.

Khanna, C., & Medsker, G. J. (2007). 2006 income and employments survey results for the Society of Industrial and Organizational Psychology. *The Industrial-Organizational Psychologist, 45,* 17–34.

Khashan, A. S., McNamee, R., Abel, K. M., Pedersen, M. G., et al. (2008). Reduced infant birthweight consequent upon maternal exposure to severe life events. *Psychosomatic Medicine, 70,* 688–694.

Khot, U. N., Khot, M. B., Bajzer, C. T., Sapp, S. K., et al. (2003). Prevalence of conventional risk factors in patients with coronary heart disease. *Journal of the American Medical Association, 290,* 898–904.

Kiecolt-Glaser, J. K. (2009). Psychoneuroimmunology psychology's gateway to the biomedical future. *Perspectives in Psychological Science, 4,* 367–369.

Kiecolt-Glaser, J. K. (2010). Stress, food, and inflammation: Psychoneuroimmunology and nutrition at the cutting edge. *Psychosomatic Medicine, 72,* 365–369.

Kiecolt-Glaser, J. K., Christian, L., Preston, H., Houts, C. R., et al. (2010). Stress, inflammation, and yoga practice. *Psychosomatic Medicine, 72,* 113–121.

Kiecolt-Glaser, J. K., & Glaser, R. (1992). Psychoneuroimmunology: Can psychological interventions modulate immunity? *Journal of Consulting and Clinical Psychology, 60,* 569–575.

Kiecolt-Glaser, J. K., Loving, T. J., Stowell, J. R., Malarkey, W. B., et al. (2005). Hostile marital interactions, proinflammatory cytokine production, and wound healing. *Archives of General Psychiatry, 62,* 1377–1384.

Kiecolt-Glaser, J. K., McGuire, L., Robles, T. F., & Glaser, R. (2002). Psychoneuroimmunology: Psychological influences on immune function and health. *Journal of Consulting and Clinical Psychology, 70,* 537–547.

Kiecolt-Glaser, J. K., & Newton, T. L. (2001). Marriage and health: His and hers. *Psychological Bulletin, 127,* 472–503.

Kiecolt-Glaser, J. K., Page, G. G., Marucha, P. T., MacCallum, R. C., & Glaser, R. (1998). Psychological influences on surgical recovery: Perspectives from psychoneuroimmunology. *American Psychologist, 11,* 1209–1218.

Kiecolt-Glaser, J. K., Preacher, K. J., MacCallum, R. C., Atkinson, C., et al. (2003). Chronic stress and age-related increases in the proinflammatory cytokine IL-6. *Proceedings of the National Academy of Sciences, 100,* 9090–9095.

Kieffer, K. M., Schinka, J. A., & Curtiss, G. (2004). Person-environment congruence and personality domains in the prediction of job performance and work quality. *Journal of Counseling Psychology, 51,* 168–177.

Kiehl, K. A., Bates, A. T., Laurens, K. R., Hare, R. D., & Liddle, P. F. (2006). Brain potentials implicate temporal lobe abnormalities in criminal psychopaths. *Journal of Abnormal Psychology, 115,* 443–453.

Kiesler, D. J. (1996). *Contemporary interpersonal theory and research.* New York: Wiley.

Kiewra, K. A. (1989). A review of note-taking: The encoding storage paradigm and beyond. *Educational Psychology Review, 1,* 147–172.

Kihlstrom, J. F. (1999). The psychological unconscious. In L. A. Pervin & O. P. John (Eds.), *Handbook of personality: Theory and research* (2nd ed., pp. 424–442). New York: Guilford Press.

Kihlstrom, J. F. (2005). Dissociative disorders. *Annual Review of Clinical Psychology, 1,* 227–253.

Kihlstrom, J. F. (2008). The psychological unconscious. In O. P. John, R. W. Robins, & L. A. Pervin (Eds.), *Handbook of personality: Theory and research* (3rd ed., pp. 583–602). New York: Guilford Press.

Kilavik, B. E., Roux, S., Ponce-Alvarez, A., Confais, J., et al. (2009). Long-term modifications in motor cortical dynamics induced by intensive practice. *Journal of Neuroscience, 29,* 12653–12663.

Kilbourne, A. M., Haas, G. L., Musant, B. H., Bauer, M. S., & Picnus, H. A. (2004). Concurrent psychiatric diagnosis by age and race among persons with bipolar disorder. *Psychiatric Services, 55,* 931–933.

Kileen, P. R. (2005). An alternative to null-hypothesis significance tests. *Psychological Science, 16,* 345–353.

Kilgour, A. R., & Lederman, S. J. (2002). Face recognition by hand. *Perception and Psychophysics, 64,* 339–352.

Kilner, J. M, Neal, A., Weiskopf, N., Friston, K. J., & Frith, C. D. (2009). Evidence of mirror neurons in human inferior frontal gyrus. *Journal of Neuroscience, 29,* 10153–10159.

Kilts, C. D., Schweitzer, J. B., Quinn, C. K., Gross, R. E., et al. (2001). Neural activity related to drug craving in cocaine addiction. *Archives of General Psychiatry, 58,* 334–341.

Kim, J.-Y., McHale, S. M., Crouter, A. C., & Osgood, D. W. (2007). Longitudinal linkages between sibling relationships and adjustment from middle childhood through adolescence. *Developmental Psychology, 43,* 960–973.

Kim, N. S., & Ahn, W.-K. (2002). Clinical psychologists' theory-based representations of mental disorders predict their diagnostic reasoning and memory. *Journal of Experimental Psychology: General, 131,* 451–476.

Kimchi, R. (2003). Relative dominance of holistic and component properties in the perceptual organization of visual objects. In M. A. Peterson & G. Rhodes (Eds.), *Perception of faces, objects, and scenes* (pp. 235–268). New York: Oxford University Press.

Kim-Cohen, J., Arseneault, L., Caspi, A., Tomás, M. P., et al. (2005). Validity of DSM-IV conduct disorder in 4½–5-year-old children: A longitudinal epidemiological study. *American Journal of Psychiatry, 162,* 1108–1117.

Kim-Cohen, J., & Gold, A. L. (2009). Measured gene-environment interactions and mechanisms promoting resilient development. *Current Directions in Psychological Science, 18,* 138–142.

Kimhy, D., Goetz, R., Yale, S., Corcoran, C., & Malaspina, D. (2005). Delusions in individuals with schizophrenia: Factor structure, clinical correlates, and putative neurobiology. *Psychopathology, 38,* 338–344.

Kimura, D. (1999). *Sex and cognition.* Cambridge, MA: MIT Press.

King, D. B., & DiCicco, T. L. (2007). The relationships between dream content and physical health, mood, and self-construal. *Dreaming, 17,* 127–139.

King, J. E., Weiss, A., & Farmer, K. H. (2005). A chimpanzee (*Pan troglodytes*) analogue of cross-national generalization of personality structure: Zoological parks and an African sanctuary. *Journal of Personality, 73,* 389–410.

King, M., Smith, G., & Bartlett, A. (2004). Treatments of homosexuality in Britain since the 1950s—an oral history: The experience of professionals. *British Medical Journal, 328,* 429–432. doi:10.1136/bmj.37984.496725.EE

Kingdom, F. A. (2003). Color brings relief to human vision. *Nature Neuroscience, 6,* 641–644.

Kingston, D. A., Fedoroff, P., Firestone, P., Curry, S., & Bradford, J. (2008). Pornography use and sexual aggression: The impact of frequency and type of pornography use on recidivism among sexual offenders. *Aggressive Behavior, 34,* 341–351.

Kinley, D. J., Cox, B. J., Clara, I., Goodwin, R. D., & Sareen, J. (2009). Panic attacks and their relation to psychological and physical functioning in Canadians: Results from a nationally representative sample. *Canadian Journal of Psychiatry, 54,* 113–118.

Kinsey, A. C., Pomeroy, W. B., & Martin, C. E. (1948). *Sexual behavior in the human male.* Philadelphia: Saunders.

Kinsey, A. C., Pomeroy, W. B., Martin, C. E., & Gebhard, P. H. (1953). *Sexual behavior in the human female.* Philadelphia: Saunders.

Kipps, C. M., Nestor, P. J., Acosta-Cabronero, J., Arnold, R., & Hodges, J. R. (2009). Understanding social dysfunction in the behavioural variant of frontotemporal dementia: The role of emotion and sarcasm processing. *Brain, 132,* 592–603.

Kircher, J. C., Horowitz, S. W., & Raskin, D. C. (1988). Meta-analysis of mock crime studies of the control question polygraph technique. *Law and Human Behavior, 12,* 79–90.

Kirchler, E., & Zani, B. (1995). Why don't they stay home? Prejudice against ethnic minorities in Italy. *Journal of Community and Applied Social Psychology, 5,* 59–65.

Kirkpatrick, B., Buchanan, R. W., Ross, D. E., & Carpenter, W. T., Jr. (2001). A separate disease within the syndrome of schizophrenia. *Archives of General Psychiatry, 58,* 165–171.

Kirkpatrick, B.; Fenton, W. S.; Carpenter, W. T., Jr.; & Marder, S. R. (2006). Consensus statement on negative symptoms. *Schizophrenia Bulletin, 32,* 214–219.

Kirsch, I. (1994a). Clinical hypnosis as a nondeceptive placebo: Empirically derived techniques. *American Journal of Clinical Hypnosis, 37,* 95–106.

Kirsch, I. (1994b). Defining hypnosis for the public. *Contemporary Hypnosis, 11,* 142–143.

Kirsch, I., & Braffman, W. (2001). Imaginative suggestibility and hypnotizability. *Psychological Science, 10,* 57–61.

Kirsch, I., Moore, T. J., Scoboria, A., & Nicholls, S. S. (2002). The emperor's new drugs: An analysis of antidepressant medication data submitted to the U.S. Food and Drug Administration. *Prevention and Treatment, 5,* art. 23. Retrieved from http://alphachoices.com/repository/assets/pdf/EmperorsNewDrugs.pdf

Kirschenbaum, H., & Jourdan, A. (2005). The current status of Carl Rogers and the person-centered approach. *Psychotherapy: Theory, Research, Practice, Training, 42,* 37–51.

Kirshner, H. S. (2009). Vascular dementia: A review of recent evidence for prevention and treatment. *Current Neurology and Neuroscience Reports, 9,* 437–442.

Kish, S. J. (2008) Pharmacologic mechanisms of crystal meth. *Canadian Medical Association Journal, 178,* 1679–1682.

Kishi, T., & Elmquist, J. K. (2005). Body weight is regulated by the brain: A link between feeding and emotion. *Molecular Psychiatry, 10,* 132–146.

Kishioka, S., Miyamoto, Y., Fukunaga, Y., Nishida, S., & Yamamoto, H. (1994). Effects of a mixture of peptidase inhibitors (amastatin, captopril and phosphoramidon) on Met-enkephalin-, beta-endorphin-, dynorphin-(1-13)- and electroacupuncture-induced antinociception in rats. *Japanese Journal of Pharmacology, 66,* 337–345.

Kisilevsky, B. S., Hains, S. M. J., Lee, K., Xie, X., et al. (2003). Effects of experience on fetal voice recognition. *Psychological Science, 14,* 220–224.

Kitamura, C., & Burnham, D. (2003). Pitch and communicative intent in mother's speech: Adjustments for age and sex in the first year. *Infancy, 4,* 85–110.

Kitano, H., Chi, I., Rhee, S., Law, C., & Lubben, J. (1992). Norms and alcohol consumption: Japanese in Japan, Hawaii, and California. *Journal of Studies on Alcohol, 53,* 33–39.

Kitayama, N., Vaccarino, V., Kutner, M., Weiss, P., & Bremner, J. D. (2005). Magnetic resonance imaging (MRI) measurement of hippocampal volume in posttraumatic stress disorder: A meta-analysis. *Journal of Affective Disorders, 88,* 79–86.

Kitayama, S., Duffy, S., & Uchida, Y. (2007). Self as cultural mode of being. In S. Kitayama & D. Cohen (Eds.), *Handbook of cultural psychology* (pp. 136–173). New York: Guilford Press

Kitayama, S., Duffy, S., Kawamura, T., & Larsen, J. T. (2003). Perceiving an object and its context in different cultures: A cultural look at new look. *Psychological Science, 14,* 201–206.

Kitayama, S., & Markus, H. R (1992, May). *Construal of self as cultural frame: Implications for internationalizing psychology.* Paper presented at the Symposium on Internationalization and Higher Education, Ann Arbor, MI.

Kitayama, S., Snibbe, A. C., Markus, H. R., & Suzuki, T. (2004). Is there any "free" choice? Self and dissonance in two cultures. *Psychological Science, 15,* 527–533.

Kitayama, S., & Uchida, Y. (2003). Explicit self-criticism and implicit self-regard: Evaluating self and friend in two cultures. *Journal of Experimental Social Psychology, 39,* 476–482.

Kivilevitch, Z., Achiron, R., & Zalel, Y. (2010). Fetal brain asymmetry: In utero sonographic study of normal fetuses. *American Journal of Obstetrics and Gynecology, 12,* 12.

Kivimäki, M., Jussi, V., Elovainio, M., Helenius, H., et al. (2005). Optimism and pessimism as predictors of change in health after death or onset of severe illness in family. *Health Psychology, 24,* 413–421.

Kivimäki, M., Lawlor, D. A., Singh-Manoux, A., Batty, D., et al. (2009). Common mental disorder and obesity: Insight from four repeat measures over 19 years: Prospective Whitehall II cohort study. *British Medical Journal, 339,* b3765.

Kjaer, T. W., Bertelsen, C., Piccini, P., Brooks, D., et al. (2002). Increased dopamine tone during meditation-induced change of consciousness. *Cognitive Brain Research, 13,* 255–259.

Klahr, D., & Simon, H. (1999). Studies of scientific discovery: Complementary approaches and convergent findings. *Psychological Bulletin, 125,* 524–543.

Klaus, M. H., & Kennell, J. H. (1976). *Maternal infant bonding: The impact of early separation or loss on family development.* Saint Louis, MO: Mosby.

Klausner, H. A., & Lewandowski, C. (2002). Infrequent causes of stroke. *Emergency Medicine Clinics of North America, 20,* 657–670.

Klein, D. C., & Seligman, M. E. P. (1976). Reversal of performance deficits and perceptual deficits in learned helplessness and depression. *Journal of Abnormal Psychology, 85,* 11–26.

Klein, D. N. (1993). False suffocation alarms, spontaneous panics, and related conditions: An integrative hypothesis. *Archives of General Psychiatry, 50,* 306–316.

Klein, D. N. (2010). Chronic depression: Diagnosis and classification. *Current Directions in Psychological Science, 19,* 96–100.

Klein, D. N., Santiago, N. J., Vivian, D., Blalock, J. A., et al. (2004). Cognitive-behavioral analysis system of psychotherapy as a maintenance treatment for chronic depression. *Journal of Consulting and Clinical Psychology, 72,* 681–688.

Klein, H. J., Noe, R. A., & Wang, C. (2006). Motivation to learn and course outcomes: The impact of delivery mode, learning goal orientation, and perceived barriers and enablers. *Personnel Psychology, 59,* 665–702.

Klein, H. J., Wesson, M. J., Hollenbeck, J. R., & Alge, B. J. (1999). Goal commitment and the goal-setting process: Conceptual clarification and empirical synthesis. *Journal of Applied Psychology, 84,* 885–896.

Klein, M. (1960). *The psychoanalysis of children.* New York: Grove Press.

Klein, M. (1975). *The writings of Melanie Klein* (Vol. 3). London: Hogarth Press.

Klein, M. (1991). The emotional life and ego-development of the infant with special reference to the depressive position. In P. King & R. Steiner (Eds.), *The Klein-Freud controversies, 1941–1945* (pp. 752–777). London: Tavistock/Routledge.

Kleinknecht, R. A. (1991). *Mastering anxiety: The nature and treatment of anxious conditions.* New York: Plenum.

Kleinknecht, R. A. (1994). Acquisition of blood, injury, and needle fears and phobias. *Behaviour Research and Therapy, 32,* 817–823.

Kleinknecht, R. A. (2000). Social phobia. In M. Hersen & M. K. Biaggio (Eds.), *Effective brief therapies: A clinician's guide* (pp. 99–116). San Diego, CA: Academic Press.

Kleinspehn-Ammerlahn, A., Kotter-Grühn, D., & Smith, J. (2008). Self-perceptions of aging: Do subjective age and satisfaction with aging change during old age? *Journals of Gerontology, Series B: Psychological Sciences and Social Sciences, 63B,* P377–P385.

Kliegel, M., Jager, T., & Phillips, L. H. (2007). Emotional development across adulthood: Differential age-related emotional reactivity and emotion regulation in a negative mood induction procedure. *International Journal of Aging and Human Development, 64,* 217–244.

Klin, A., Jones, W., Shultz, R., Volkmar, F., & Cohen, D. (2002). Defining and quantifying the social phenotype in autism. *American Journal of Psychiatry, 159,* 895–908.

Kline, R. B. (2004). *Beyond significance testing: Reforming data analysis methods in behavioral research.* Washington, DC: Americal Psychological Association.

Kline, S., & Groninger, L. D. (1991). The imagery bizarreness effect as a function of sentence complexity and presentation time. *Bulletin of the Psychonomic Society, 29,* 25–27.

Klinesmith, J., Kasser, T., & McAndrew, F. T. (2006). Guns, testosterone, and aggression: An experimental test of a mediational hypothesis. *Psychological Science, 17,* 568–571.

Kling, K. C., Hyde, J. S., Showers, C. J., & Buswell, B. N. (1999). Gender differences in self-esteem: A meta-analysis. *Psychological Bulletin, 125,* 470–500.

Klintsova, A. Y., & Greenough, W. T. (1999). Synaptic plasticity in cortical systems. *Current Opinion in Neurobiology, 9,* 203–208.

Klohnen, E., & Bera, S. (1998). Behavioral and experiential patterns of avoidantly and securely attached women across adulthood: A 31-year longitudinal perspective. *Journal of Personality and Social Psychology, 74,* 211–223.

Kluger, A. N., & DeNisi, A. (1998). Feedback interventions: Toward the understanding of a double-edged sword. *Current Directions in Psychological Science, 7,* 67–72.

Klump, K. L., Suisman, J. L., Burt, S. A., McGue, M., & Iacono, W. G. (2009). Genetic and environmental influences on disordered eating: An adoption study. *Journal of Abnormal Psychology, 118,* 797–805.

Klunk, W. E., Engler, H., Nordberg, A., Wang, Y., et al. (2004). Imaging brain amyloid in Alzheimer's disease with Pittsburgh Compound-B. *Annals of Neurology, 55,* 306–319.

Klunk, W. E., Lopresti, B. J., Ikonomovic, M. D., Lefterov, I. M., et al. (2005). Binding of the positron emission tomography tracer Pittsburgh compound-B reflects the amount of amyloid-beta in Alzheimer's disease brain but not in transgenic mouse brain. *Journal of Neuroscience, 25,* 10598–10606.

Knafo, A., Iervolino, A. C., & Plomin, R. (2005). Masculine girls and feminine boys: Genetic and environmental contributions to atypical gender development in early childhood. *Journal of Personality and Social Psychology, 88,* 400–412.

Knafo, A., Zahn-Waxler, C., Van Hulle, C., Robinson, J. L., & Rhee, S. H. (2008). The developmental origins of a disposition toward empathy: Genetic and environmental contributions. *Emotion, 8,* 737–752.

Knapp, S., & VandeCreek, L. (1997). *Jaffee v. Redmond:* The Supreme Court recognizes a psychotherapist-patient privilege in federal courts. *Professional Psychology: Research and Practice, 28,* 567–572.

Knecht, S., Floel, A., Drager, B., Breitenstein, C., et al. (2002). Degree of language lateralization determines susceptibility to unilateral brain lesions. *Nature Neuroscience, 5,* 695–699.

Knopman, D. S. (2006). Dementia and cerebrovascular disease. *Mayo Clinic Proceedings, 81,* 223–230.

Knopman, D. S., & Selnes, O. (2003). Neuropsychology of dementia. In K. M. Heilman & E. Valenstein (Eds.), *Clinical neuropsychology* (4th ed., pp. 574–615). New York: Oxford University Press.

Koch, C. (2003). *The quest for consciousness: A neurobiological approach.* Englewood, CO: Roberts.

Kochanska, G. (1997). Multiple pathways to conscience for children with different temperaments: From toddlerhood to age 5. *Developmental Psychology, 33,* 228–240.

Kochanska, G., Aksan, N., & Joy, M. E. (2007). Children's fearfulness as a moderator of parenting in early socialization: Two longitudinal studies. *Developmental Psychology, 43,* 222–237.

Koechlin, E., & Hyafil, A. (2007). Anterior prefrontal function and the limits of human decision-making. *Science, 318,* 594–598.

Koelega, H. S. (1993). Stimulant drugs and vigilance performance: A review. *Psychopharmacology, 111,* 1–16.

Koenen, K. C., Moffitt, T. E., Roberts, A. L., Martin, L. T., et al. (2009). Childhood IQ and adult mental disorders: A test of the cognitive reserve hypothesis. *American Journal of Psychiatry, 166,* 50–57.

Kogan, M. D., Blumberg, S. J., Schieve, L. A., Boyle, C. A., et al. (2009). Prevalence of parent-reported diagnosis of autism spectrum disorder among children in the U.S., 2007. *Pediatrics, 124,* 1395–1403.

Koger, S. M., Schettler, T., & Weiss, B. (2005). Environmental toxicants and developmental disabilities: A challenge for psychologists. *American Psychologist, 60,* 243–255.

Kohlberg, L., & Gilligan, C. (1971). The adolescent as a philosopher: The discovery of the self in a postconventional world. *Daedalus, 100,* 1051–1086.

Köhler, W. (1976). *The mentality of apes* (E. Winter, Trans.). Oxford: Liveright. (Original work published 1924)

Kohli, M. A., Salyakina, D., Pfennig, A., Lucae, S., et al. (2010). Association of genetic variants in the neurotrophic receptor–encoding gene NTRK2 and a lifetime history of suicide attempts in depressed patients. *Archives of General Psychiatry, 67,* 348–359. doi:10.1001/archgenpsychiatry.2009.201

Kohlmetz, C., Muller, S. V., Nager, W., Munte, T. F., & Altenmuller, E. (2003). Selective loss of timbre perception for keyboard and percussion instruments following a right temporal lesion. *Neurocase, 9,* 86–93.

Kohnert, K. (2004). Cognitive and cognate-based treatments for bilingual aphasia: A case study. *Brain and Language, 91,* 294–302.

Kohrt, B. A., Kunz, R. D., Baldwin, J. L., Koirala, N. R., et al. (2005). "Somatization" and "comorbidity": A study of Jhum-Jhum and depression in rural Nepal. *Ethos, 33,* 125–147.

Kohut, H. (1984). Selected problems of self-psychological theory. In J. D. Lichtenberg & S. Kaplan (Eds.), *Reflections on self-psychology* (pp. 387–416). Hillsdale, NJ: Erlbaum.

Kolassa, I.-T., Kolassa, S., Bergmann, S., Lauche, R., et al. (2009). Interpretive bias in social phobia: An ERP study with morphed emotional schematic faces. *Cognition and Emotion, 23,* 69–95.

Kolassa, I.-T., Kolassa, S., Ertl, V., Papassotiropoulos, A., & De Quervain, D. J.-F. (2010). The risk of posttraumatic stress disorder after trauma depends on traumatic load and the catechol-o-methyltransferase val^{158} met polymorphism. *Biological Psychiatry, 67,* 304–308.

Kolata, G. (2003, April 22). Hormone studies: What went wrong? *New York Times.* Retrieved from http://www.nytimes.com/2003/04/22/science/hormone-studies-what-went-wrong.html

Kolata, G., & Markel, H. (2001, April 29). Baby not crawling? Reason seems to be less tummy time. *New York Times.* Retrieved from http://www.nytimes.com/2001/04/29/us/baby-not-crawling-reason-seems-to-be-less-tummy-time.html

Kolb, B., Gorny, G., Li, Y., Samaha, A.-N., & Robinson, T. E. (2003). Amphetamine or cocaine limits the ability of later experience to promote structural plasticity in the neocortex and nucleus accumbens. *Proceedings of the National Academy of Sciences, 100,* 10523–10528.

Koles, Z. J., Lind, J. C., & Flor-Henry, P. (2010). Gender differences in brain functional organization during verbal and spatial cognitive challenges. *Brain Topography, 27,* 199–204. Epub 2009 Nov 27.

Kolonin, M. G., Saha, P. K., Chan, L., Pasqualini, R., & Arap, W. (2004). Reversal of obesity by targeted ablation of adipose tissue. *Nature Medicine, 10,* 625–632.

Komatsu, S.-I., & Naito, M. (1992). Repetition priming with Japanese kana scripts in word-fragment completion. *Memory and Cognition, 20,* 160–170.

Komorita, S. S. (1984). Coalition bargaining. In L. Berkowitz (Ed.), *Advances in experimental social psychology* (Vol. 18, pp. 184–246). New York: Academic Press.

Komorita, S. S., & Parks, C. D. (1996). *Social dilemmas.* Boulder, CO: Westview.

Komsi, N., Räikkönen, K., Heinonen, K., Pesonen, A.-K., et al. (2008). Continuity of father-rated temperament from infancy to middle childhood. *Infant Behavior and Development, 31,* 239–254.

Konecná, M., Lhota, S., Weiss, A., Urbánek, T., et al. (2008). Personality in free-ranging Hanuman langur (*Semnopithecus entellus*) males: Subjective ratings and recorded behavior. *Journal of Comparative Psychology, 122,* 379–389.

Konijn, E. A., Bijvank, M. N., & Bushman, B. J. (2007). I wish I were a warrior: The role of wishful identification in the effects of violent video games on aggression in adolescent boys. *Developmental Psychology, 43,* 1038–1044.

Konkol, R. J., Murphey, L. J., Ferriero, D. M., Dempsey, D. A., & Olsen, G. D. (1994). Cocaine metabolites in the neonate: Potential for toxicity. *Journal of Child Neurology, 9,* 242–248.

Konrad, K., Neufang, S., Hanisch, C., Fink, G. R., & Herpertz-Dahlmann, B. (2006). Dysfunctional attentional networks in children with attention deficit/hyperactivity disorder: Evidence from an event-related functional magnetic imaging study. *Biological Psychiatry, 59,* 643–651.

Kontoghiorghes, C. (2004). Reconceptualizing the learning transfer conceptual framework: Empirical validation of a new systemic model. *International Journal of Training and Development, 8,* 210–221.

Konuk, E., Knipe, J., Eke, I., Yuksek, H., et al. (2006). The effects of eye movement desensitization and reprocessing (EMDR) therapy on posttraumatic stress disorder in survivors of the 1999 Marmara, Turkey, earthquake. *International Journal of Stress Management, 13,* 291–308.

Koob, G. F., & Bloom, F. E. (1988). Cellular and molecular mechanisms of drug dependence. *Science, 242,* 715–723.

Koob, G. F., & Kreek, M. J. (2007). Stress, dysregulation of drug reward pathways, and the transition to drug dependence. *American Journal of Psychiatry, 164,* 1149–1159.

Koob, G. F., & Volkow, N. D. (2010). Neurocircuitry of addiction. *Neuropsychopharmacology, 35,* 217–238.

Kop, W. J., Berman, D. S., Gransar, H., Wong, N. D., et al. (2005). Social network and coronary artery calcification in asymptomatic individuals. *Psychosomatic Medicine, 67,* 343–352.

Koppenaal, L., & Glanzer, M. (1990). An examination of the continuous distractor task and the "long-term recency effect." *Memory and Cognition, 18,* 183–195.

Korchmaros, J. D., & Kenny, D. A. (2001). Emotional closeness as a mediator of the effect of genetic relatedness on altruism. *Psychological Science, 12,* 262–265.

Kordower, J. H., Emborg, M. E., Bloch, J., Ma, S. Y., et al. (2000). Neurodegeneration prevented by lentiviral vector delivery of GDNF in primate models of Parkinson's disease. *Science, 290,* 767–773.

Koretz, D., Lynch, P. S., & Lynch, C. A. (2000, June). The impact of score differences on the admission of minority students: An illustration. *Statements of the National Board on Educational Testing and Public Policy, 1,* 1–15.

Korman, M., Doyon, J., Doljansky, J., Carrier, J., et al. (2007). Daytime sleep condenses the time course of motor memory consolidation. *Nature Neuroscience, 10,* 1206–1213.

Korner, J., & Leibel, R. L. (2003). To eat or not to eat: How the gut talks to the brain. *New England Journal of Medicine, 349,* 926–928.

Koshizuka, S., Okada, S., Okawa, A., Koda, M., et al. (2004). Transplanted hematopoietic stem cells from bone marrow differentiate into neural lineage cells and promote functional recovery after spinal cord injury in mice. *Journal of Neuropathology and Experimental Neurology, 63,* 64–72.

Kosslyn, S. M. (1988). Aspects of a cognitive neuroscience of mental imagery. *Science, 240,* 1621–1626.

Kosslyn, S. M. (1994). *Image and mind.* Cambridge, MA: Harvard University Press.

Kotani, N., Hashimoto, H., Sato, Y., Sessler, D. I., et al. (2001). Preoperative intradermal acupuncture reduces postoperative pain, nausea and vomiting, analgesic requirement, and sympathoadrenal responses. *Anesthesiology, 95,* 349–356.

Koten, J. W., Jr.; Wood, G.; Hagoort, P.; Goebel, R.; et al. (2009). Genetic contribution to variation in cognitive function: An fMRI study in twins. *Science, 323,* 1737–1740.

Kouider, S., & Dupoux, E. (2005). Subliminal speech priming. *Psychological Science, 16,* 617.

Kounios, J., Frymiare, J. L., Bowden, E. M., Fleck, J. I., et al. (2006). The prepared mind: Neural activity prior to problem presentation predicts subsequent solution by sudden insight. *Psychological Science, 17,* 882–890.

Kouyoumdjian, H. (2004). Influence of unannounced quizzes and cumulative exams on attendance and study behavior. *Teaching of Psychology, 31,* 110–111.

Kovács, A. M., & Mehler, J. (2009). Flexible learning of multiple speech structures in bilingual infants. *Science, 325,* 611–612.

Kozak, M. J., Liebowitz, M. R., & Foa, E. B. (2000). Cognitive behavior therapy and pharmacotherapy for obsessive-compulsive disorder: The NIMH-sponsored collaborative study. In W. K. Goodman, M. V. Rudorfer, & J. D. Maser (Eds.), *Obsessive-compulsive disorder: Contemporary issues in treatment* (pp. 501–530). Mahwah, NJ: Erlbaum.

Kozel, F. A., Padgett, T. M., & George, M. S. (2004). A replication study of the neural correlates of deception. *Behavioral Neuroscience, 118,* 852–856.

Kozlowski, S. W. J., & Ilgen, D. R. (2006). Enhancing the effectiveness of work groups and teams. *Psychological Science in the Public Interest, 7,* 77–124.

Kozorovitskiy, Y., Gross, C. G., Kopil, C., Battaglia, L., et al. (2005). Experience induces structural and biochemical changes in the adult primate brain. *Proceedings of the National Academy of Sciences, 102,* 17478–17482.

Kraft, C. (1978). A psychophysical contribution to air safety: Simulator studies of visual illusions in night visual approaches. In H. L. Pick, H. W. Leibowitz, J. E. Singer, A. Steinschneider, & H. W. Stevenson (Eds.), *Psychology: From research to practice* (pp. 363–385). New York: Plenum.

Krahn, L. E. (2003). Sleep disorders. *Seminars in Neurology, 23,* 307–314.

Krain, A. L., & Castellanos, F. X. (2006). Brain development and ADHD. *Clinical Psychology Review, 26,* 433–444.

Krakauer, J. W., & Shadmehr, R. (2007). Towards a computational neuropsychology of action. *Progress in Brain Research, 165,* 383–394.

Krakow, B., Hollifield, M., Johnston, L., Koss, M., et al. (2001). Imagery rehearsal therapy for chronic nightmares in sexual assault survivors with posttraumatic stress disorder: A randomized controlled trial. *Journal of the American Medical Association, 286,* 537–545.

Kramer, A. F., & Willis, S. (2002). Enhancing the cognitive vitality of older adults. *Current Directions in Psychological Science, 11,* 173–177.

Kramer, A. F., Larish, J. L., Weber, T. A., & Bardell, L. (1999). Training for executive control: Task coordination strategies and aging. In D. Gopher & A. Koriat (Eds.), *Attention and performance XVII: Cognitive regulation of performance: Interaction of theory and application* (pp. 617–650). Cambridge, MA: MIT Press.

Kramer, G. P., Bernstein, D. A., & Phares, V. (2009). *Introduction to clinical psychology* (7th ed.) Upper Saddle River, NJ: Prentice Hall.

Krantz, D. S., Contrada, R., Hill, D., & Friedler, E. (1988). Environmental stress and biobehavioral antecedents of coronary heart disease. *Journal of Consulting and Clinical Psychology, 56,* 333–341.

Krantz, D. S., & Durel, L. (1983). Psychobiological substrates of the Type A behavior pattern. *Health Psychology, 2,* 393–411.

Krantz, D. S., & McCeney, M. K. (2002). Effects of psychological and social factors on organic disease: A critical assessment of research on coronary heart disease. *Annual Review of Psychology, 53,* 341–369.

Kraus, M. W., & Keltner, D. (2009). Signs of socioeconomic status: A thin-slicing approach. *Psychological Science, 20,* 99–106.

Kraus, W. E., Houmard, J. A., Duscha, B. D., Knetzger, K. J., et al. (2002). Effects of the amount and intensity of exercise on plasma lipoproteins. *New England Journal of Medicine, 347,* 1483–1492.

Krause, D. E., & Thornton, G. C. (2009). A cross-cultural look at assessment center practices: Survey results from western Europe and North America. *Applied Psychology, 58,* 557–585.

Krause, M. S. (2005). How the psychotherapy research community must work toward measurement and why. *Journal of Clinical Psychology, 61,* 269–283.

Krause, M. S., & Lutz, W. (2006). How we really ought to be comparing treatments for clinical purposes. *Psychotherapy: Theory, Research, Practice, Training, 43,* 359–361.

Krause, N., & Shaw, B. A. (2000). Role-specific feelings of control and mortality. *Psychology and Aging, 15,* 617–626.

Kraut, R., Olson, J., Banaji, M., Bruckman, A., et al. (2004). Psychological research online: Report of board of scientific affairs' advisory group on the conduct of research on the Internet. *American Psychologist, 59,* 105–117.

Krauzlis, R. J. (2002). Reaching for answers. *Neuron, 34,* 673–674.

Kray, L. J., & Galinsky, A. D. (2003). The debiasing effect of counterfactual mind-sets: Increasing the search for disconfirmatory information in group decisions. *Organizational Behavior and Human Decision Processes, 91,* 69–81.

Kreek, M. J., Nielsen, D. A., Butelman, E. R., & LaForge, K. S. (2005). Genetic influences on impulsivity, risk taking, stress responsivity and vulnerability to drug abuse and addiction. *Nature Neuroscience, 8,* 1450–1457.

Kreppner, J. M., Rutter, M., Beckett, C., Castle, J., et al. (2007). Normality and impairment following profound early institutional deprivation: A longitudinal follow-up into early adolescence. *Developmental Psychology, 43,* 931–946.

Kring, A. M., & Gordon, A. H. (1998). Sex differences in emotion: Expression, experience, and physiology. *Journal of Personality and Social Psychology, 74,* 686–703.

Kristof, N. D. (1997, August 17). Where children rule. *New York Times Magazine.* Retrieved from http://www.nytimes.com/1997/08/17/magazine/where-children-rule.html

Krohne, H. W., & Slangen, K. E. (2005). Influence of social support on adaptation to surgery. *Health Psychology, 24,* 101–105.

Krosnick, J. A., Betz, A. L., Jussim, L. J., & Lynn, A. R. (1992). Subliminal conditioning of attitude. *Personality and Social Psychology Bulletin, 18,* 152–162.

Krueger, J. (2001). Null hypothesis significance testing. *American Psychologist, 56,* 16–26.

Krueger, R. F., & Johnson, W. (2008). Behavioral genetics and personality: A new look at the integration of nature and nurture. In O. P. John, R. W. Robins, & L. A. Pervin (Eds.), *Handbook of personality: Theory and research* (3rd ed., pp. 287–310). New York: Guilford Press.

Krueger, R. F., & Markon, K. E. (2006). Understanding psychopathology: Melding behavior genetics, personality, and quantitative psychology to develop an empirically based model. *Current Directions in Psychological Science, 15,* 113–117.

Krueger, R. F., Markon, K. E., & Bouchard, T. J., Jr. (2003). The extended genotype: The heritability of personality accounts for the heritability of recalled family environments in twins reared apart. *Journal of Personality, 71,* 809–833.

Krueger, R. F., South, S., Johnson, W., & Iacono, W. (2008). The heritability of personality is not always 50%: Gene-environment interactions and correlations between personality and parenting. *Journal of Personality, 76,* 1485–1522.

Kruger, D. J. (2003). Evolution and altruism: Combining psychological mediators with naturally selected tendencies. *Evolution and Human Behavior, 24,* 118–125.

Kruger, J., Wirtz, D., & Miller, D. T. (2005). Counterfactual thinking and the first-instinct fallacy. *Journal of Personality and Social Psychology, 88,* 725–735.

Kryger, M. H., Roth, T., & Dement, W. C. (2000). *Principles and practice of sleep medicine* (3rd ed.). Philadelphia: Saunders.

Krykouli, S. E., Stanley, B. G., Seirafi, R. D., & Leibowitz, S. F (1990). Stimulation of feeding by galanin: Anatomical localization and behavioral specificity of this peptide's effects in the brain. *Peptides, 11,* 995–1001.

Ku, G., Malhotra, D., & Murnighan, J. K. (2005). Towards a competitive arousal model of decision-making: A study of auction fever in live and Internet auctions. *Organizational Behavior and Human Decision Processes, 96,* 89–103.

Kubzansky, L. D., Davidson, K. W., & Rozanski, A. (2005). The clinical impact of negative psychological states: Expanding the spectrum of risk for coronary artery disease. *Psychosomatic Medicine, 67*(Suppl. 1), S10–S14.

Kubzansky, L. D., Koenen, K. C., Jones, C., & Eaton, W. W. (2009). A prospective study of posttraumatic stress disorder symptoms and coronary heart disease in women. *Health Psychology, 28,* 125–130.

Kübler-Ross, E. (1975). *Death: The final stage of growth.* Englewood Cliffs, NJ: Prentice Hall.

Kuhn, D., & Franklin, S. (2006). The second decade: What develops (and how)? In W. Damon & R. M. Lerner (Series Eds.) & D. Kuhn & R. Siegler (Vol. Eds.), *Handbook of child psychology: Vol. 2. Cognition, perception, and language* (6th ed., pp. 953–994). Hoboken, NJ: Wiley.

Kuhnen, C. M., & Knutson, B. (2005). The neural basis of financial risk taking. *Neuron, 47,* 763–770.

Kujala, T., Karma, K., Ceponiene, R., Belitz, S., et al. (2001). Plastic neural changes and reading improvement caused by audiovisual training in reading-impaired children. *Proceedings of the National Academy of Sciences, 98,* 10509–10514.

Kukull, W. A., Higdon, R., Bowen, J. D., McCormick, W. C., et al. (2002). Dementia and Alzheimer disease incidence: A prospective cohort study. *Archives of Neurology, 59,* 1737–1746.

Kumanyika, S. K. (2008). Environmental influences on childhood obesity: Ethnic and cultural influences in context. *Physiology and Behavior, 94,* 61–70.

Kumar, N. (2010). Neurologic presentations of nutritional deficiencies. *Neurologic Clinics, 28,* 107–170.

Kumar, V. K., & Farley, F. (2009). Structural aspects of three hypnotizability scales: Smallest space analysis. *International Journal of Clinical and Experimental Hypnosis, 57,* 343–365.

Kuncel, N. R., & Hezlett, S. A. (2007). Standardized tests predict graduate students' success. *Science, 315,* 1080–1081.

Kuncel, N. R., Hezlett, S. A., & Ones, D. (2004). Academic performance, career potential, creativity, and job performance: Can one construct predict them all? *Journal of Personality and Social Psychology, 86,* 148–161.

Kunen, S., Niederhauser, R., Smith, P. O., Morris, J. A., & Marx, B. D. (2005). Race disparities in psychiatric rates in emergency departments. *Journal of Consulting and Clinical Psychology, 73,* 116–126.

Kunstman, J. W., & Plant, E. A. (2008). Racing to help: Racial bias in high emergency helping situations. *Journal of Personality and Social Psychology, 95,* 1499–1510.

Kuo, L. E., Kitlinska, J. B., Tilan, J. U., Li, L., et al (2007). Neuropeptide Y acts directly in the periphery on fat tissue and mediates stress-induced obesity and metabolic syndrome. *Nature Medicine, 13,* 803–811.

Kuo, Y.-L., Liao, H.-F., Chen, P.-C., Hsieh, W.-S., & Hwang, A.-W. (2008). The influence of wakeful prone positioning on motor development during the early life. *Journal of Developmental and Behavioral Pediatrics, 29,* 367–376. doi:10.1097/DBP.0b013e3181856d54

Kupers, R., Danielsen, E. R., Kehlet, H., Christensen, R., & Thomsen, C. (2009). Painful tonic heat stimulation induces GABA accumulation in the prefrontal cortex in man. *Pain, 142,* 89–93.

Kurdek, L. A. (2005). What do we know about gay and lesbian couples? *Current Directions in Psychological Science, 14,* 251–254.

Kurtz, L. F. (2004). Support and self-help groups. In C. D. Garvin, L. M. Gutiérrez, & M. J. Galinsky (Eds.), *Handbook of social work with groups* (pp. 139–159). New York: Guilford Press.

Kushner, M. G., Thuras, P., Kaminski, J., Anderson, N., et al. (2000). Expectancies for alcohol to affect tension and anxiety as a function of time. *Addictive Behaviors, 25,* 93–98.

Kusyszyn, I. (1990). Existence, effectance, esteem: From gambling to a new theory of human motivation. *International Journal of the Addictions, 25,* 159–177.

Kutchins, H., & Kirk, S. A. (1997). *Making us crazy: The psychiatric Bible and the creation of mental disorders.* New York: Free Press.

Kwate, N. O. A. (2001). Intelligence or misorientation? *Journal of Black Psychology, 27,* 221–238.

Kyllonen, P. C., & Christal, R. E. (1990). Reasoning ability is (little more than) working-memory capacity? *Intelligence, 14,* 389–433.

Kymalainen, J. A., Weisman, A. G., Resales, G. A., & Armesto, J. C. (2006). Ethnicity, expressed emotion, and communication deviance in family members of patients with schizophrenia. *Journal of Nervous and Mental Disease, 194,* 391–396.

LaBar, K. S., Gatenby, J. C., Gore, J. C., LeDoux, J. E., & Phelps, E. A. (1998). Human amygdala activation during conditioned fear acquisition and extinction: A mixed-trial fMRI study. *Neuron, 20,* 937–945.

Labouvie-Vief, G. (1982). Discontinuities in development from childhood to adulthood: A cognitive-developmental view. In T. M. Field, A. Huston, H. C. Quay, L. Troll, & G. E. Finley (Eds.), *Review of human development* (pp. 447–455). New York: Wiley.

Labouvie-Vief, G. (1992). A new-Piagetian perspective on adult cognitive development. In R. J. Sternberg & C. A. Berg (Eds.), *Intellectual development* (pp. 197–228). New York: Cambridge University Press.

Lacayo, A. (1995). Neurologic and psychiatric complications of cocaine abuse. *Neuropsychiatry, Neuropsychology, and Behavioral Neurology, 8,* 53–60.

Lachman, M. E., & Andreoletti, C. (2006). Strategy use mediates the relationship between control beliefs and memory performance for middle-aged and older adults. *Journals of Gerontology: Psychological Sciences and Social Sciences, 61,* 88–94.

Lack, L. C., & Wright, H. R. (2007). Chronobiology of sleep in humans. *Cellular and Molecular Life Sciences, 64,* 1205–1215.

Lacor, P. N. (2007). Advances on the understanding of the origins of synaptic pathology in AD. *Current Genomics, 8,* 486–508.

Ladd, G. W. (2005). *Peer relationships and social competence of children and youth.* New Haven, CT: Yale University Press.

Ladd, G. W., & Troop-Gordon, W. (2003). The role of chronic peer difficulties in the development of children's psychological adjustment problems. *Child Development, 74,* 1344–1367.

LaFrance, M., Hecht, M. A., & Paluck, E. L. (2003). The contingent smile: A meta-analysis of sex differences in smiling. *Psychological Bulletin, 129,* 305–334.

Lagerspetz, K. M. J., & Lagerspetz, K. Y. H. (1983). Genes and aggression. In E. C. Simmel, M. E. Hahn, & J. K. Walters (Eds.), *Aggressive behavior: Genetic and neural approaches* (pp. 89–102). Hillsdale, NJ: Erlbaum.

Lagopoulos, J., & Malhi, G. S. (2008). Transcranial magnetic stimulation. *Acta Neuropsychiatrica, 20,* 316–317.

Lahey, B. B., Loeber, R., Hart, E. L., Frick, P. J., & Applegate, B. (1995). Four-year longitudinal study of conduct disorder in boys: Patterns and predictors of persistence. *Journal of Abnormal Psychology, 104,* 83–93.

Lahey, B. B., Van Hulle, C. A., Keenan, K., Rathouz, P. J., et al. (2008). Temperament and parenting during the first year of life predict future child conduct problems. *Journal of Abnormal Child Psychology, 36,* 1139–1158.

Lahm, K. F. (2008). Inmate-on-inmate assault. *Criminal Justice and Behavior, 35,* 120–137.

Lai, C. S. L., Fisher, S. E., Hurst, J. A., Vargha-Khadem, F., & Monaco, A. P. (2001). A forkhead-domain gene is mutated in severe speech and language disorder. *Nature, 413,* 519–523.

Laird, R. D., Jordan, K. Y., Dodge, K. A., Pettit, G. S., & Gates, J. E. (2001). Peer rejection in childhood, involvement with antisocial peers in early adolescence, and the development of externalizing behavior problems. *Development and Psychopathology, 13,* 337–354.

Lakin, J. L., & Chartrand, T. L. (2003). Using nonconscious behavioral mimicry to create affiliation and rapport. *Psychological Science, 14,* 334–339.

Lakshmikumar, S. T. (2009). Power line panic and mobile mania. *Skeptical Inquirer, 33,* 32–35.

Lalumière, M. L., Blanchard, R., & Zucker, K. J. (2000). Sexual orientation and handedness in men and women: A meta-analysis. *Psychological Bulletin, 126,* 575–592.

Lam, B., Sam, K., Mok, W. Y., Cheung, M., et al. (2006). A randomised study of three non-surgical treatments in mild to moderate obstructive sleep apnoea. *Thorax, 62,* 354–359.

Lam, D. H., Watkins, E. R., Hayward, P., Bright, J., et al. (2003). A randomized controlled study of cognitive therapy for relapse prevention for bipolar affective disorder: Outcome of the first year. *Archives of General Psychiatry, 60,* 145–152.

Lamar, J. (2000). Suicides in Japan reach a record high. *British Medical Journal, 321,* 528.

Lamb, M. E. (1998). Assessments of children's credibility in forensic contexts. *Current Directions in Psychological Science, 7,* 43–46.

Lamb, M. E. (Ed.). (1997). *The role of the father in child development* (3rd ed.). New York: Wiley.

Lamb, M. E., & Ahnert, L. (2006). Nonparental child care. In W. Damon & R. M. Lerner (Series Eds.) & K. A. Renninger & I. E. Sigel (Vol. Eds.), *Handbook of child psychology: Vol. 4. Child psychology in practice* (6th ed., pp. 950–1016). Hoboken, NJ: Wiley.

Lamberg, L. (2004). Impact of long working hours explored. *Journal of the American Medical Association, 292,* 25–26.

Lambert, M. J., & Barley, D. E. (2001). Research summary on the therapeutic relationship and psychotherapy outcome. *Psychotherapy, 38,* 357–361.

Lambert, T., & Norman, T. R. (2008). Ethnic differences in psychotropic drug response and pharmacokinetics. In C. H. Ng, K. Lin, B. S. Singh, & E. Chiu (Eds.), *Ethnopsychopharmacology: Advances in current practice* (pp. 38–61). New York: Cambridge University Press.

Lamm, C., Batson, C. D., & Decety, J. (2007). The neural basis of human empathy—effects of perspective-taking and cognitive appraisal: An event-related fMRI study. *Journal of Cognitive Neuroscience, 19,* 42–58.

Lamplugh, C., Berle, D., Milicevic, D., & Starcevic, V. (2008). Pilot study of cognitive behaviour therapy for panic disorder augmented by panic surfing. *Clinical Psychology and Psychotherapy, 15,* 440–445.

Landgren, M., Svensson, L., Strömland, K., & Grönlund, M. A. (2010). Prenatal alcohol exposure and neurodevelopmental disorders in children adopted from eastern Europe. *Pediatrics, 125,* e1178–e1185.

Landrigan, C. P., Rothschild, J. M., Cronin, J. W., Kaushal, R., et al. (2004). Effect of reducing interns' work hours on serious medical errors in intensive care units. *New England Journal of Medicine, 351*, 1838–1848.

Landrine, H. (1991). Revising the framework of abnormal psychology. In P. Bronstein & K. Quina (Eds.), *Teaching a psychology of people* (pp. 37–44). Washington, DC: American Psychological Association.

Landsdale, M., & Laming, D. (1995). Evaluating the fragmentation hypothesis: The analysis of errors in cued recall. *Acta Psychologica, 88*, 33–77.

Lang, A. R., Goeckner, D. J., Adesso, V. J., & Marlatt, G. A. (1975). Effects of alcohol on aggression in male social drinkers. *Journal of Abnormal Psychology, 84*, 508–518.

Lang, C., Barco, A., Zablow, L., Kandel, E. R., et al. (2004). Transient expansion of synaptically connected dendritic spines upon induction of hippocampal long-term potentiation. *Proceedings of the National Academy of Sciences, 101*, 16665–16670.

Lang, J. W. B., & Lang, J. (2010). Priming competence diminishes the link between cognitive test anxiety and test performance: Implications for the interpretation of test scores. *Psychological Science, 21*, 811–819. Epub 2010 Apr 30.

Lang, P. J. (1995). The emotion probe: Studies of motivation and attention. *American Psychologist, 50*, 372–385.

Lang, P. J., & Melamed, B. G. (1969). Avoidance conditioning therapy of an infant with chronic ruminative vomiting. *Journal of Abnormal Psychology, 74*, 1–8.

Langan, C., & McDonald, C. (2009). Neurobiological trait abnormalities in bipolar disorder. *Molecular Psychiatry, 14*, 833–846.

Lange, C., & Byrd, M. (2002). Differences between students' estimated and attained grades in a first-year introductory psychology course as a function of identity development. *Adolescence, 37*, 93–108.

Langenberg, P., Ballesteros, M., Feldman, R., Damron, D., et al. (2000). Psychosocial factors and intervention-associated changes in those factors as correlates of change in fruit and vegetable consumption in the Maryland WIC 5-a-Day promotion program. *Annals of Behavioral Medicine, 22*, 307–315.

Langenbucher, J., & Nathan, P. E. (2006). Diagnosis and classification. In F. Andrasik (Ed.), *Comprehensive handbook of personality and psychopathology: Vol. 2. Adult psychopathology* (pp. 3–20). Hoboken, NJ: Wiley.

Langens, T. A., & Schüler, J. (2007). Effects of written emotional expression: The role of positive expectancies. *Health Psychology, 26*, 174–182.

Langer, E., Djikic, M., Pirson, M., Madenci, A., & Donohue, R. (2010). Believing is seeing: Using mindlessness (mindfully) to improve visual acuity. *Psychological Science, 21*, 661–666.

Langer, K. G. (2009). Babinski's anosognosia for hemiplegia in early-twentieth-century French neurology. *Journal of the History of Neuroscience, 18*, 387–405.

Langleben, D. D., Loughead, J. W., Bilker, W. B., Ruparel, K., et al. (2005). Telling truth from lie in individual subjects with fast event-related fMRI. *Human Brain Mapping, 26*, 262–272.

Langlois, J. H., Kalakanis, L., Rubenstein, A. J., Larson, A., et al. (2000). Maxims or myths of beauty: A meta-analytic and theoretical review. *Psychological Bulletin, 126*, 390–423.

Lansford, J. E. (2009). Parental divorce and children's adjustment. *Perspectives in Psychological Science, 4*, 140–152.

Lansford, J. E., Chang, L., Dodge, K. A., Malone, P. S., et al. (2005). Physical discipline and children's adjustment: Cultural normativeness as a moderator. *Child Development, 76*, 1234–1246.

Lantz, J. (2004). Research and evaluation issues in existential psychotherapy. *Journal of Contemporary Psychotherapy, 34*, 331–340.

Lanzenberger, R. R., Mitterhauser, M., Spindelegger, C., Wadsak, W., et al. (2007). Reduced serotonin-1a receptor binding in social anxiety disorder. *Biological Psychiatry, 61*, 1081–1089.

Lapierre, L. M., & Allen, T. D. (2006). Work-supportive family, family-supportive supervision, use of organizational benefits, and problem-focused coping: Implications for work-family conflict and employee well-being. *Journal of Occupational Health Psychology, 11*, 169–181.

Lapointe, L. (1990). *Aphasia and related neurogenic language disorders.* New York: Thieme Medical.

Larsen, C. R., Soerensen, J. L., Grantcharov, T. P., Dalsgaard, T., et al. (2009). Effect of virtual reality training on laparoscopic surgery: Randomised controlled trial. *British Medical Journal, 338*, b1802.

Larsen, J. T., McGraw, A. P., Mellers, B. A., & Cacioppo, J. T. (2004). The agony of victory and thrill of defeat: Mixed emotional reactions to disappointing wins and relieving losses. *Psychological Science, 15*, 325–330.

Larsen, R. J., & Buss, D. M. (2010). *Personality psychology: Domains of knowledge about human nature* (4th ed). New York: McGraw-Hill.

Larson, E. B., Wang, L., Bowen, J. D., McCormick, W. C., et al. (2006). Exercise is associated with reduced risk of incident dementia among persons 65 years of age and older. *Annals of Internal Medicine, 144*, 73–81.

Larson, G. E., & Saccuzzo, D. P. (1989). Cognitive correlates of general intelligence: Toward a process theory of g. *Intelligence, 13*, 5–32.

Larson, J. R., Jr.; Christensen, C.; Franz, T. M.; & Abbott, A. S. (1998). Diagnosing groups: The pooling, management, and impact of shared and unshared case information in team-based medical decision making. *Journal of Personality and Social Psychology, 75*, 93–108.

Larson, M. C., Gunnar, M. R., & Hertsgaard, L. (1991). The effects of morning naps, car trips, and maternal separation on adrenocortical activity in human infants. *Child Development, 62*, 362–372.

Larsson, H., Andershed, H., & Lichtenstein, P. (2006). A genetic factor explains most of the variation in the psychopathic personality. *Journal of Abnormal Psychology, 115*, 221–230.

Larzelere, R. E. (1996). A review of the outcomes of parental use of nonabusive or customary physical punishment. *Pediatrics, 98*, 824–828.

Larzelere, R. E. (2000). Child outcomes of nonabusive and customary physical punishment by parents: An updated literature review. *Clinical Child and Family Psychology Review, 3*, 199–221.

Lashley, K. S. (1950). In search of the engram. *Society of Experimental Biology, Symposium 4*, 454–482.

Latané, B. (1981). The psychology of social impact. *American Psychologist, 36*, 343–356.

Latané, B., & Rodin, J. (1969). A lady in distress: Inhibiting effects of friends and strangers on bystander intervention. *Journal of Experimental Social Psychology, 5*, 189–202.

Latham, G. P. (2004). Motivate employee performance through goal-setting. In E. A. Locke (Ed.), *Handbook of principles of organizational behavior* (pp. 107–119). Malden, MA: Blackwell.

Latham, G. P., Skarlicki, D., Irvine, D., & Siegel, J. P. (1993). The increasing importance of performance appraisals to employee effectiveness in organizational settings in North America. In C. L. Cooper & I. T. Robertson (Eds.), *International review of industrial and organizational psychology, 1993* (pp. 87–132). Chichester, England: Wiley.

Lau, I. Y.-M., Lee, S., & Chiu, C. (2004). Language, cognition, and reality: Constructing shared meanings through communication. In M. Schaller & C. S. Crandall (Eds.), *The psychological foundations of culture* (pp. 77–97). Mahwah, NJ: Erlbaum.

Laughery, K. R. (1999). Modeling human performance during system design. In E. Salas (Ed.), *Human/technology interaction in complex systems* (Vol. 9, pp. 147–174). Stamford, CT: JAI Press.

Laughlin, P. L. (1999). Collective induction: Twelve postulates. *Organizational Behavior and Human Decision Processes, 80*, 50–69.

Laumann, E. O., Gagnon, J. H., Michael, R. T., & Michaels, S. (1994). *The social organization of sexuality: Sexual practices in the United States.* Chicago: University of Chicago Press.

Laumann, E. O., & Michael, R. T. (Eds.). (2000). *Sex, love, and health in America: Private choices and public policies.* Chicago: University of Chicago Press.

Laurenceau, J.-P., Hayes, A. M., & Feldman, G. C. (2007). Some methodological and statistical issues in the study of change processes in psychotherapy. *Clinical Psychology Review, 27*, 682–695.

Laurenceau, J.-P., Stanley, S. M., Olmos-Gallo, A., Baucom, B., & Markman, H. J. (2004). Community-based prevention of marital dysfunction: Multilevel modeling of a randomized effectiveness study. *Journal of Consulting and Clinical Psychology, 72*, 933–943.

Laureys, S. (2004). Functional neuroimaging in the vegetative state. *NeuroRehabilitation, 19*, 335–341.

Laursen, B., Bukowski, W. M., Aunola, K., & Nurmi, J.-E. (2007). Friendship moderates prospective associations between social isolation and adjustment problems in young children. *Child Development, 78*, 1395–1404.

Lavoie, M. E., Dupuis, F., Johnston, K. M., Leclerc, S., & Lassonde, M. (2004). Visual P300 effects beyond symptoms in concussed college athletes. *Journal of Clinical and Experimental Neuropsychology, 26*, 55–73.

Lavoie, M.-P., Lam, R. W., Bouchard, G., Sasseville, A., et al. (2009). Evidence of a biological effect of light therapy on the retina of patients with seasonal affective disorder. *Biological Psychiatry, 66*, 253–258.

Law, K. L., Stroud, L. R., LaGasse, L. L., Niaura, R., et al. (2003). Smoking during pregnancy and newborn neurobehavior. *Pediatrics, 111*, 1318–1323.

Law, M. H., Cotton, R. G. H., & Berger, G. E. (2006). The role of phospholipases A2 in schizophrenia. *Molecular Psychiatry, 11*, 547–556.

Lawless, H. T., & Engen, T. (1977). Associations to odors: Interference, memories and verbal learning. *Journal of Experimental Psychology, 3*, 52–59.

Lawrence, C., & Andrews, K. (2004). The influence of perceived prison crowding on male inmates' perception of aggressive events. *Aggressive Behavior, 30*, 273–283.

Lawrie, S. M., Whalley, H. C., Abukmeil, S. S., Kestelman, J., et al. (2001). Brain structure, genetic liability, and psychotic symptoms in subjects at high risk of developing schizophrenia. *Biological Psychiatry, 49*, 811–823.

Lawson, C. A. (2004). Treating the borderline mother: Integrating EMDR with a family systems perspective. In M. M. MacFarlane (Ed.), *Family treatment of personality disorders: Advances in clinical practice* (pp. 305–334). Binghamton, NY: Haworth Clinical Practice Press.

Lazar, S. W., Kerr, C. E., Wasserman, R. H., Gray, J. R., et al. (2005). Meditation experience is associated with increased cortical thickness. *Neuroreport, 16*, 1893–1897.

Lazarus, A. A. (1971). *Behavior therapy and beyond.* New York: McGraw-Hill.

Lazarus, R. S. (1966). *Psychological stress and the coping process.* New York: McGraw-Hill.

Lazarus, R. S. (1991). *Emotion and adaptation.* New York: Oxford University Press.

Lazarus, R. S. (1999). *Stress and emotion: A new synthesis.* New York: Springer.

Lazarus, R. S., & Folkman, S. (1984). *Stress, appraisal, and coping.* New York: Springer.

Lazarus, R. S., Opton, E. M., Nomikos, M. S., & Rankin, M. O. (1965). The principle of short-circuiting of threat: Further evidence. *Journal of Personality, 33*, 622–635.

Lea, M., Spears, R., & de Groot, D. (2001). Knowing me, knowing you: Anonymity effects on social identity processes within groups. *Personality and Social Psychology Bulletin, 27*, 526–537.

Leamon, M. H., Wright, T. M., & Myrick, H. (2008). Substance-related disorders. In R. E. Hales, S. C. Yudofsky, & G. O. Gabbard (Eds) *Textbook of psychiatry* (pp. 365–406). Alexandria, VA: American Psychiatric Publishing.

Leaper, C., Anderson, K. J., & Sanders, P. (1998). Moderators of gender effects on parents' talk to their children: A meta-analysis. *Developmental Psychology, 34*, 3–27.

Leaper, C., & Friedman, C. K. (2007). The socialization of gender. In J. Grusec & P. Hastings (Eds.), *Handbook of socialization* (pp. 561–587). New York: Guilford Press.

Leary, M. R. (2001). Shyness and the self: Attentional, motivational, and cognitive self-processes in social anxiety. In R. Crozier & L. Alden (Eds.), *International handbook of social anxiety: A handbook of concepts, research, and interventions relating to the self and shyness* (pp. 217–234). New York: Wiley.

Leary, M. R. (2010). Affiliation, acceptance, and belonging: The pursuit of interpersonal connection. In S. T. Fiske, D. T. Gilbert, & G. Lindzey (Eds.), *Handbook of social psychology* (5th ed., Vol. 2, pp. 864–897). Hoboken, NJ: Wiley.

Leary, P. M. (2003). Conversion disorder in childhood: Diagnosed too late, investigated too much? *Journal of the Royal Society of Medicine, 96*, 436–444.

LeBlanc, M., Mérette, C., Savard, J., Ivers, H., et al. (2009). Incidence and risk factors of insomnia in a population-based sample. *Sleep, 32,* 1027–1037.

LeBlanc, M. M., & Barling, J. (2004). Workplace aggression. *Current Directions in Psychological Science, 13,* 9–12.

LeBlanc, M. M., Dupre, K. E., & Barling, J. (2006). Public-initiated violence. In K. E. Kelloway, J. Barling, & J. J. Hurrell (Eds.), *Handbook of workplace violence* (pp. 261–280). Thousand Oaks, CA: Sage.

LeDoux, J. E. (1995). Emotion: Clues from the brain. *Annual Review of Psychology, 46,* 209–235.

Lee, C. M., Ryan, J. J., & Kreiner, D. S. (2007). Personality in domestic cats. *Psychological Reports, 100,* 27–29.

Lee, C. W., Taylor, G., & Drummond, P. D. (2006). The active ingredient in EMDR: Is it traditional exposure or dual focus of attention? *Clinical Psychology and Psychotherapy, 13,* 97–107.

Lee, H. S., Nelms, J. L., Nguyen, M., Silver, R., & Lehman, M. N. (2003). The eye is necessary for a circadian rhythm in the suprachiasmatic nucleus. *Nature Neuroscience, 6,* 111–112.

Lee, J. L. C., Everitt, B. J., & Thomas, K. L. (2004). Independent cellular processes for hippocampal memory consolidation and reconsolidation. *Science, 304,* 839–843.

Lee, K., Ogunfowora, B., & Ashton, M. C. (2005). Personality traits beyond the Big Five: Are they within the HEXACO space? *Journal of Personality, 73,* 1437–1463.

Lee, K., Williams, L. M., Breakspear, M., & Gordon, E. (2003). Synchronous gamma activity: A review and contribution to an integrative neuroscience model of schizophrenia. *Brain Research Reviews, 41,* 57–78.

Lee, L., Loewenstein, G., Ariely, D., Hong, J., & Young, J. (2008). If I'm not hot, are you hot or not? Physical-attractiveness evaluations and dating preferences as a function of one's own attractiveness. *Psychological Science, 19,* 669–677.

Lee, M. S., Kim, J. I., Ha, J. Y., Boddy, K., & Ernst, E. (2009). Yoga for menopausal symptoms: A systematic review. *Menopause, 16,* 602–608.

Lee, R. M., & Yoo, H. C. (2004). Structure and measurement of ethnic identity for Asian American college students. *Journal of Counseling Psychology, 51,* 263–269.

Lee, S. J., & Levounis, P. (2008). Gamma hydroxybutyrate: An ethnographic study of recreational use and abuse. *Journal of Psychoactive Drugs, 40,* 245–253.

Lee, S., Colditz, G., Berkman, L., & Kawachi, I. (2003). Caregiving to children and grandchildren and risk of coronary heart disease in women. *American Journal of Public Health, 93,* 1939–1944.

Lee, S., Tsang, A., Zhang, M.-Y., Huang, Y.-Q., et al. (2007). Lifetime prevalence and inter-cohort variation in DSM-IV disorders in metropolitan China. *Psychological Medicine, 37,* 61–71.

Lee, T. M. C., Au, R. K. C., Liu, H.-L., Ting, K. H., et al. (2009). Are errors differentiable from deceptive responses when feigning memory impairment? An fMRI study. *Brain and Cognition, 69,* 406–412.

Lee, V. E., Brooks-Gunn, J., & Schnur, E. (1988). Does Head Start work? A 1-year follow-up comparison of disadvantaged children attending Head Start, no preschool, and other preschool programs. *Developmental Psychology, 24,* 210–222.

Lee, Y. S., & Silva, A. J. (2009). The molecular and cellular biology of enhanced cognition. *National Review of Neuroscience, 10,* 126–140.

Leeb, R. T., & Rejskind, F. G. (2004). Here's looking at you kid! A longitudinal study of perceived gender differences in mutual gaze behavior in young infants. *Sex Roles, 50,* 1–5.

Leeds, A. M. (2009). *A guide to the standard EMDR protocols for clinicians, supervisors, and consultants.* New York: Springer.

Leff, J. (2006). Whose life is it anyway? Quality of life for long-stay patients discharged from psychiatric hospitals. In H. Katschnig, H. Freeman, & N. Sartorius (Eds.), *Quality of life in mental disorders* (2nd ed., pp. 247–255). Hoboken, NJ: Wiley.

Legare, C. H., & Gelman, S. A. (2008). Bewitchment, biology, or both: The coexistence of natural and supernatural explanatory frameworks across development. *Cognitive Science, 32,* 607–642.

Legerstee, M., Anderson, D., & Schaffer, A. (1998). Five- and eight-month-old infants recognize their faces and voices as familiar and social stimuli. *Child Development, 69,* 37–50.

Lehman, D. R., Chiu, C., & Schaller, M. (2004). Psychology and culture. *Annual Review of Psychology, 55,* 689–714.

Lehman, H. E. (1967). Schizophrenia: IV. Clinical features. In A. M. Freedman, H. I. Kaplan, & H. S. Kaplan (Eds.), *Comprehensive textbook of psychiatry* (pp. 621–649). Baltimore: Williams & Wilkins.

Leibel, R. L., Rosenbaum, M., & Hirsch, J. (1995). Changes in energy expenditure resulting from altered body weight. *New England Journal of Medicine, 332,* 621–628.

Leibowitz, H. W., Brislin, R., Perlmutter, L., & Hennessy, R. (1969). Ponzo perspective illusion as a manifestation of space perception. *Science, 166,* 1174–1176.

Leibowitz, S. F. (1992). Neurochemical-neuroendocrine systems in the brain controlling macronutrient intake and metabolism. *Trends in Neuroscience, 15,* 491–497.

Leichsenring, F., Rabung, S., & Leibing, E. (2004). The efficacy of short-term psychodynamic psychotherapy in specific psychiatric disorders: A meta-analysis. *Archives of General Psychiatry, 61,* 1208–1216.

Leifer, B. P. (2009). Alzheimer's disease: Seeing the signs early. *Journal of the American Academy of Nurse Practitioners, 21,* 588–595.

Leigh, B. C., & Stacy, A. W. (2004). Alcohol expectancies and drinking in different age groups. *Addiction, 99,* 215–227.

Leiner, H. C., Leiner, A. L., & Dow, R. S. (1993). Cognitive and language functions of the human cerebellum. *Trends in Neuroscience, 16,* 444–447.

Leippe, M. R., Manion, A. P., & Romanczyk, A. (1992). Eyewitness persuasion: How and how well do fact finders judge the accuracy of adults' and children's memory reports? *Journal of Personality and Social Psychology, 63,* 181–197.

Leisman, G., & Koch, P. (2009). Networks of conscious experience: Computational neuroscience in understanding life, death, and consciousness. *Review of Neuroscience, 20,* 151–176.

Lejuez, C. W., Hopko, D. R., Levine, S., Gholkar, R., & Collins, L. (2005). The therapeutic alliance in behavior therapy. *Psychotherapy: Theory, Research, Practice, and Training, 42,* 456–468.

Leknes, S., Brooks, J. C. W., Wiech, K., & Tracey, I. (2008). Pain relief as an opponent process: A psychophysical investigation. *European Journal of Neuroscience, 28,* 794–801.

Lemere, C. A., Maier, M., Jiang, L., Peng, Y., & Seabrook, T. J. (2006). Amyloid-beta immunotherapy for the prevention and treatment of Alzheimer disease: Lessons from mice, monkeys, and humans. *Rejuvenation Research, 9,* 77–84.

Lemmer, B., Kern, R. I., Nold, G., & Lohrer, H. (2002). Jet lag in athletes after eastward and westward time-zone transition. *Chronobiology International, 19,* 743–764.

Lemoine, P., Kermadi, I., Garcia-Acosta, S., Garay, R. P., & Dib, M. (2006). Double-blind, comparative study of cyamemazine vs. bromazepam in the benzodiazepine withdrawal syndrome. *Progress in Neuropsychopharmacology and Biological Psychiatry, 30,* 131–137.

Lenneberg, E. H. (1967). *Biological foundations of language.* New York: Wiley.

Lenzenweger, M. F., McLachlan, G., & Rubin, D. B. (2007). Resolving the latent structure of schizophrenia endophenotypes using expectation-maximization-based finite mixture modeling. *Journal of Abnormal Psychology, 116,* 16–29.

Leon, D. A., Lawlor, D. A., Clark, H., Batty, G. D., & Macintyre, S. (2009). The association of childhood intelligence with mortality risk from adolescence to middle age: Findings from the Aberdeen Children of the 1950s cohort study. *Intelligence, 37,* 520–528.

Leonard, B. E. (1992). *Fundamentals of psychopharmacology.* New York: Wiley.

Leonhardt, D. (2000, May 24). Makes sense to test for common sense. Yes? No? *New York Times,* p. C1.

Leopold, D. (2002). Distortion of olfactory perception: Diagnosis and treatment. *Chemical Senses, 27,* 611–615.

LePage, J. P., DelBen, K., Pollard, S., McGhee, S., et al. (2003). Reducing assaults on an acute psychiatric unit using a token economy: A 2-year follow-up. *Behavioral Interventions, 18,* 179–190.

Lepore, L., & Brown, R. (1997). Category and stereotype activation: Is prejudice inevitable? *Journal of Personality and Social Psychology, 72,* 275–287.

Lepore, S. J. (1995). Cynicism, social support, and cardiovascular reactivity. *Health Psychology, 14,* 210–216.

Lepore, S. J., Evans, G., & Schneider, M. (1991). Dynamic role of social support in the link between chronic stress and psychological distress. *Journal of Personality and Social Psychology, 61,* 899–909.

Lerner, J. S., Gonzalez, R. M., Small, D. A., & Fischhoff, B. (2003). Effects of fear and anger on perceived risks of terrorism: A national field experiment. *Psychological Science, 14,* 144–150.

Lesko, A. C., & Corpus, J. H. (2006). Discounting the difficult: How high-math-identified women respond to stereotype threat. *Sex Roles, 54,* 113–125.

Lettvin, J. Y., Maturana, H. R., McCulloch, W. S., & Pitts, W. H. (1959). What the frog's eye tells the frog's brain. *Proceedings of the Institute of Radio Engineers, 47,* 1940–1951.

Leung, H. T., & Westbrook, F. R. (2008). Spontaneous recovery of extinguished fear responses deepens their extinction: A role for error-correction mechanisms. *Journal of Experimental Psychology: Animal Behavior Processes, 31,* 277–288.

Levant, R. F. (2005). Evidence-based practice in psychology. *Monitor on Psychology, 36,* 5.

Leve, L. D., Kim, H. K., & Pears, K. C. (2005). Childhood temperament and family environment as predictors of internalizing and externalizing trajectories from ages 5 to 17. *Journal of Abnormal Child Psychology, 33,* 505–520.

Levenson, H. (2003). Time-limited dynamic psychotherapy: An integrationist perspective. *Journal of Psychotherapy Integration, 13,* 300–333.

Levenson, R. W., Ekman, P., & Friesen, W. V. (1990). Voluntary facial action generates emotion-specific autonomic nervous system activity. *Psychophysiology, 27,* 363–384.

Levenson, R. W., Ekman, P., Heider, K., & Friesen, W. V. (1992). Emotion and autonomic nervous system activity in the Minangkabau of West Sumatra. *Journal of Personality and Social Psychology, 62,* 972–988.

Levenston, G. K., Patrick, C. J., Bradley, M. M., & Lang, P. J. (2000). The psychopath as observer: Emotion and attention in picture processing. *Journal of Abnormal Psychology, 109,* 373–385.

Levine, R. V. , Reysen, S., & Ganz, E. (2008). The kindness of strangers revisited: A comparison of 24 U.S. cities. *Social Indicators Research, 85,* 461–481.

Levine, R., Sato, S., Hashimoto, T., & Verna, J. (1995). Love and marriage in eleven cultures. *Journal of Cross-Cultural Psychology, 26,* 554–571.

Levine, S. (1999, February 1). In a loud and noisy world, baby boomers pay the consequences. *International Herald Tribune.*

Levinson, D. F. (2006). The genetics of depression: A review. *Biological Psychiatry, 60,* 84–92.

Levinson, D. F., Evgrafov, O. V., Knowles, J. A., Potash, J. B., et al. (2007). Genetics of recurrent early-onset major depression (GenRED): Significant linkage on chromosome 15q25-q26 after fine mapping with single nucleotide polymorphism markers. *American Journal of Psychiatry, 164,* 259–264.

Levinson, S. C. (1996). Language and space. *Annual Review of Anthropology, 25,* 353–382.

Levinthal, C. F. (2001). *Drugs, behavior, and modern society* (3rd ed.). Boston: Allyn & Bacon.

Levitt, P., Ebert, P., Mirnics, K., Nimgaonkar, V. L., & Lewis, D. A. (2006). Making the case for a candidate vulnerability gene in schizophrenia: Convergent evidence for regulator of g-protein signaling 4 (RGS4). *Biological Psychiatry, 60,* 534–537.

Levy, B. R., Slade, M. D., Kunkel, S. R., & Kasl, S. V. (2002). Longevity increased by positive self-perceptions of aging. *Journal of Personality and Social Psychology, 83,* 261–270.

Levy, D. A., Bayley, P. J., & Squire L. R. (2004). The anatomy of semantic knowledge: Medial vs. lateral temporal lobe. *Proceedings of the National Academy of Sciences, 101,* 6710–6715.

Levy, K. N., Clarkin, J. F., Yeomans, F. E., Scott, L. N., et al. (2006). The mechanisms of change in the treatment of borderline personality disorder with transference focused psychotherapy. *Journal of Clinical Psychology, 62,* 481–501.

Lewicki, P. (1992). Nonconscious acquisition of information. *American Psychologist, 47,* 796–801.

Lewin, T. (2003, October 29). A growing number of video viewers watch from crib. *New York Times,* p. 1.
Lewin, T. (2009, October 24). No Einstein in your crib? Get a refund. *New York Times,* p. A1.
Lewinsohn, P. M., Joiner, T. E., & Rohde, P. (2001). Evaluation of cognitive diathesis-stress models in precicting major depressive disorder in adolescents. *Journal of Abnormal Psychology, 110,* 203–215.
Lewinsohn, P. M., & Rosenbaum, M. (1987). Recall of parental behavior by acute depressives, remitted depressives, and nondepressives. *Journal of Personality and Social Psychology, 52,* 611–619.
Lewis, J. E. (2008). Dream reports of animal rights activists. *Dreaming, 18,* 181–200.
Lewis, J. W., Brefczynski, J. A., Phinney, R. E., Janik, J. J., & DeYoe, E. A. (2005). Distinct cortical pathways for processing tool versus animal sounds. *Journal of Neuroscience, 25,* 5148–5158.
Lewis, T. (2006). Seeking health information on the Internet: Lifestyle choice or bad attack of cyberchondria? *Media, Culture and Society, 28,* 521–539.
Lewis, T. T., Everson-Rose, S. A., Powell, L. H., Matthews, K. A., Brown, C., Karavolos, K., et al. (2006). Chronic exposure to everyday discrimination and coronary artery calcification in African-American women: The SWAN heart study. *Psychosomatic Medicine, 68,* 362–368.
Lewontin, R. (1976). Race and intelligence. In N. J. Block & G. Dworkin (Eds.), *The IQ controversy: Critical readings* (pp. 107–112). New York: Pantheon.
Lewy, A. J., Lefler, B. J., Emens, J. S., & Bauer, V. K. (2006). The circadian basis of winter depression. *Proceedings of the National Academy of Sciences, 103,* 7414–7419.
Ley, J. M., Bennett, P. C., & Coleman, G. J. (2009). A refinement and validation of the Monash Canine Personality Questionnaire (MCPQ). *Applied Animal Behaviour Science, 116,* 220–227.
Leyro, T. M.; Zvolensky, M. J., & Bernstein, A. (2010). Distress tolerance and psychopathological symptoms and disorders: A review of the empirical literature among adults. *Psychological Bulletin, 136,* 576–600.
Lezak, M. D., Loring, D. W., & Howieson, D. B. (2004). *Neuropsychological assessment* (4th ed.). New York: Oxford University Press.
Li, D.-K., Petitti, D. B., Willinger, M., McMahon, R., et al. (2003). Infant sleeping position and the risk of sudden infant death syndrome in California, 1997–2000. *American Journal of Epidemiology, 157,* 446–455.
Li, D.-K., Willinger, M., Petitti, D. B., Odouli, R., et al. (2006). Use of a dummy (pacifier) during sleep and risk of sudden infant death syndrome (SIDS): Population-based case-control study. *British Medical Journal, 332,* 18–22.
Li, F., Harmer, P., McAuley, E., Duncan, T., et al. (2001). An evaluation of the effects of tai chi exercise on physical function among older persons: A randomized controlled trial. *Annals of Behavioral Medicine, 23,* 139–146.
Li, G.; Jack, C. R., Jr.; & Yang, E. S. (2006). An fMRI study of somatosensory-implicated acupuncture points in stable somatosensory stroke patients. *Journal of Magnetic Resonance Imaging, 24,* 1018–1024.
Li, J. (2005). Mind or virtue: Western and Chinese beliefs about learning. *Current Directions in Psychological Science, 14,* 190–194.
Li, L. C., & Kim, B. S. K. (2004). Effects of counseling style and client adherence to Asian cultural values on counseling process with Asian American college students. *Journal of Counseling Psychology, 51,* 158–167.
Li, M. D. (2006). The genetics of nicotine dependence. *Current Psychiatry Reports, 8,* 158–164.
Li, S., Cullen, W., Anwyl, R., & Rowan, M. J. (2003). Dopamine-dependent facilitation of LTP induction in hippocampal CA1 by exposure to spatial novelty. *Nature Neuroscience, 6,* 526–531.
Li, S. C., Lindenberger, U., Hommel, B., Aschersleben, G., et al. (2004). Transformations in the couplings among intellectual abilities and constituent cognitive processes across the life span. *Psychological Science, 15,* 155–163.
Li, W., Piëch, V., & Gilbert, C. D. (2004). Perceptual learning and top-down influences in primary visual cortex. *Nature Neuroscience, 7,* 651–657.
Liao, H., & Rupp, D. E. (2005). The impact of justice climate and justice orientation on work outcomes: A cross-level multifoci framework. *Journal of Applied Psychology, 90,* 242–256.
Liben, L. S. (1978). Perspective-taking skills in young children: Seeing the world through rose-colored glasses. *Developmental Psychology, 14,* 87–92.
Liben, L. S., & Bigler, R. S. (2002). The developmental course of gender differentiation. *Monographs of the Society for Research in Child Development, 67* (Serial No. 269).
Liben-Nowell, D., Novak, J., Kumar, R., Raghaven, P., & Tomkins, A. (2005). Geographic routing in social networks. *Proceedings of the National Academy of Sciences, 102,* 11623–11628.
Liberzon, I., & Sripada, C. S. (2008). The functional neuroanatomy of PTSD: A critical review. *Progress in Brain Research, 167,* 151–169.
Lickey, M., & Gordon, B. (1991). *Medicine and mental illness: The use of drugs in psychiatry.* San Francisco: Freeman.
Lickliter, R. (2008). The growth of developmental thought: Implications for a new evolutionary psychology. *New Ideas in Psychology, 26,* 353–369.
Lieberman, J. A., Stroup, T. S., McEvoy, J. P., Swartz, M. S., et al. (2005). Effectiveness of antipsychotic drugs in patients with chronic schizophrenia. *New England Journal of Medicine, 353,* 1209–1223.
Lieberman, M. D. (2010). Social cognitive neuroscience In S. T. Fiske, D. T. Gilbert, & G. Lindzey (Eds.), *Handbook of social psychology* (5th ed., Vol. 1, pp. 143–193). Hoboken, NJ: Wiley.
Lieberman, M. D., Ochsner, K. N., Gilbert, D. T., & Schacter, D. L. (2001). Do amnesics exhibit cognitive dissonance reduction? The role of explicit memory and attention in attitude change. *Psychological Science, 121,* 135–140.
Lieberman, P. (1991). *Uniquely human.* Cambridge, MA: Harvard University Press.
Liebeskind, D. S. (2010). Reperfusion for acute ischemic stroke: Arterial revascularization and collateral therapeutics. *Current Opinion in Neurology, 23,* 36–45.
Liechti, M. E., Gamma, A., & Vollenweider, F. X. (2001). Gender differences in the subjective effects of MDMA. *Psychopharmacology, 154,* 161–168.
Liepert, J., Bauder, H., Miltner, W. H. R., Taub, E., & Weiller, C. (2000). Treatment-induced cortical reorganization after stroke in humans. *Stroke, 31,* 1210.
Lievens, F., Harris, M. M., van Keer, E., & Bisqueret, C. (2003). Predicting cross-cultural training performance: The validity of personality, cognitive ability, and dimensions measured by an assessment center and a behavior description interview. *Journal of Applied Psychology, 88,* 476–489.
Lievens, F., Peeters, H., & Schollaert, E. (2008). Situational judgment tests: A review of recent research. *Personnel Review, 37,* 426–441.
Light, K. C., Girdler, S. S., Sherwood, A., Bragdon, E. E., et al. (1999). High stress responsivity predicts later blood pressure only in combination with positive family history and high life stress. *Hypertension, 33,* 1458–1464.
Light, L. K., Grewen, K. M., Amico, J. A., Brownley, K. A., et al. (2005). Oxytocinergic activity is linked to lower blood pressure and vascular resistance during stress in postmenopausal women on estrogen replacement. *Hormones and Behavior, 47,* 540–548.
Light, L. L. (1991). Memory and aging: Four hypotheses in search of data. *Annual Review of Psychology, 42,* 333–376.
Lilienfeld, S. O. (2007). Psychological treatments that cause harm. *Perspectives on Psychological Science, 2,* 53–70.
Lilienfeld, S. O., Ammirati, R., & Landfield, K. (2009). Giving debiasing away: Can psychological research on correcting cognitive errors promote human welfare? *Perspectives on Psychological Science, 4,* 390–398.
Lilienfeld, S. O., & Arkowitz, H. (2007, December). EMDR: Taking a closer look. *Scientific American,* pp. 10–11.
Lilienfeld, S. O., & Lynn, S. J. (2003). Dissociative identity disorder: Multiple personalities, multiple controversies. In S. O. Lilienfeld & S. J. Lynn (Eds.), *Science and pseudoscience in clinical psychology* (pp. 109–142). New York: Guilford Press.
Lilienfeld, S. O., Lynn, S. J., Namy, L. L., & Wolff, N. J. (2009). *Psychology: From inquiry to understanding.* Boston: Allyn & Bacon.
Lilienfeld, S. O., Wood, J. M., & Garb, H. N. (2000). The scientific status of projective tests. *Psychological Science in the Public Interest, 1,* 27–66.
Lim, B.-C., & Ployhart, R. E. (2004). Transformational leadership: Relations to the five-factor model and team performance in typical and maximum contexts. *Journal of Applied Psychology, 89,* 610–621.
Lim, J., & Dinges, D. F. (2010). A meta-analysis of the impact of short-term sleep deprivation on cognitive variables. *Psychological Bulletin, 136,* 375–389.
Lim, R. F. (Ed.). (2006). *Clinical manual of cultural psychiatry.* Alexandria, VA: American Psychiatric Association.
Lim, S.-L., & Kim, J.-H. (2005). Cognitive processing of emotional information in depression, panic, and somatoform disorder. *Journal of Abnormal Psychology, 114,* 50–61.
Lim, V. K. G., Teo, T. S. H., & Loo, G. L. (2003). Sex, financial hardship and locus of control: An empirical study of attitudes towards money among Singaporean Chinese. *Personality and Individual Differences, 34,* 411–429.
Lin, J. G., & Chen, W. L. (2008). Acupuncture analgesia: A review of its mechanisms of actions. *American Journal of Chinese Medicine, 36,* 635–645.
Lin, K. M., Smith, M. W., & Ortiz, V. (2001). Culture and psychopharmacology. *Psychiatric Clinics of North America, 24,* 523–538.
Lin, L., Umahara, M., York, D. A., & Bray, G. A. (1998). Beta-casomorphins stimulate and enterostatin inhibits the intake of dietary fat in rats. *Peptides, 19,* 325–331.
Lin, S., Thomas, T. C., Storlien, L. H., & Huang, X. F. (2000). Development of high-fat diet-induced obesity and leptin resistance in C57Bl/6J mice. *International Journal of Obesity-Related Metabolic Disorders, 24,* 639–646.
Lin, Y., & Raghubir, P. (2005). Gender differences in unrealistic optimism about marriage and divorce: Are men more optimistic and women more realistic? *Personality and Social Psychology Bulletin, 31,* 198–207.
Lin, Y., Wu, M., Yang, C., Chen, T., et al. (2008). Evaluation of assertiveness training for psychiatric patients. *Journal of Clinical Nursing, 17,* 2875–2883.
Lindau, S. T., & Gavrilova, N. (2010). Sex, health, and years of sexually active life gained due to good health: Evidence from two U.S. population based cross-sectional surveys of ageing. *British Medical Journal, 340,* c810.
Lindau, S. T., Schumm, L. P., Laumann, E. O., Levinson, W., et al. (2007). A study of sexuality and health among older adults in the United States. *New England Journal of Medicine, 357,* 762–774.
Linde, K., Allais, G., Brinkhaus, B., Manheimer, E., et al. (2009). Acupuncture for tension-type headache. *Cochrane Library.* Retrieved from http://mrw.interscience.wiley.com/cochrane/clsysrev/articles/CD007587/frame.html
Lindsay, D. S., Hagen, L., Read, J. D., Wade, K., & Gary, M. (2004). True photographs and false memories. *Psychological Science, 15,* 149–154.
Lindsey, D. T., & Brown, A. M. (2006). Universality of color names. *Proceedings of the National Academy of Sciences, 103,* 16608–16613.
Lindvall, O., & Hagell, P. (2001). Cell therapy and transplantation in Parkinson's disease. *Clinical Chemistry and Laboratory Medicine, 39,* 356–361.
Lindvall, O., & Kokaia, Z. (2010). Stem cells in human neurodegenerative disorders: Time for clinical translation? *Journal of Clinical Investigation, 120,* 29–40. doi:10.1172/JCI40543.
Linley, P. A., & Joseph, S. (Eds.). (2004). *Positive psychology in practice.* Hoboken, NJ: Wiley.
Linn, R. L., & Gronlund, N. E. (2000). *Measurement and assessment in teaching* (8th ed.). Upper Saddle River, NJ: Prentice-Hall.
Linnet, K. M., Dalsgaard, S., Obel, C., Wisborg, K., et al. (2003). Maternal lifestyle factors in pregnancy risk of attention deficit hyperactivity disorder and associated behaviors: Review of the current evidence. *American Journal of Psychiatry, 160,* 1028–1040.
Linnet, K. M., Wisborg, K., Obel, C., Secher, N. J., et al. (2005). Smoking during pregnancy and the risk for hyperkinetic disorder in offspring. *Pediatrics, 116,* 462–467.
Linou, N., & Kontogiannis, T. (2004). The effect of training systemic information on the retention of fault-finding skills in manufacturing industries. *Human Factors and Ergonomics in Manufacturing, 14,* 197–217.

Lippa, R. A. (2003). Are 2D:4D finger-length ratios related to sexual orientation? Yes for men, no for women. *Journal of Personality and Social Psychology, 85,* 179–188.

Lira, A., Zhou, M., Castanon, N., Ansorge, M. S., et al. (2003). Altered depression-related behaviors and functional changes in the dorsal raphe nucleus of serotonin transporter-deficient mice. *Biological Psychiatry, 54,* 960–971.

Lisanby, S. H. (Ed.). (2004). *Brain stimulation in psychiatric treatment.* Alexandria, VA: American Psychiatric Association.

Lisspers, J., Sundin, Ö., Öhman, A., Hofman-Bang, C., et al. (2005). Long-term effects of lifestyle behavior change in coronary artery disease: Effects on recurrent coronary events after percutaneous coronary intervention. *Health Psychology, 24,* 41–48.

Liston, C., McEwen, B. S., & Casey, B. J. (2009). Psychosocial stress reversibly disrupts prefrontal processing and attentional control. *Proceedings of the National Academy of Sciences, 106,* 912–917.

Littlewood, R. (1992). Psychiatric diagnosis and racial bias: Empirical and interpretative approaches. *Social Science and Medicine, 34,* 141–149.

Litwin, H., & Shiovitz-Ezra, S. (2006). The association between activity and well-being in later life: What really matters? *Ageing and Society, 26,* 225–242.

Liu, G., & Akira, H. (1994). Basic principle of TCM. In G. Liu & H. Akira (Eds.), *Fundamentals of acupuncture and moxibustion* (pp. 9–32). Tianjin, China: Tianjin Science & Technology.

Liu, J., Raine, A., Venables, P. H., & Mednick, S. A. (2004). Malnutrition at age 3 years and externalizing behavior problems at ages 8, 11, and 17 years. *American Journal of Psychiatry, 161,* 2005–2013.

Liu, Y. P., Lang, B. T., Baskaya, M. K., Dempsey, R. J., & Vemuganti, R. (2009). The potential of neural stem cells to repair stroke-induced brain damage. *Acta Neuropathologica, 117,* 469–480. Epub 2009 Mar 13.

Livesley, W. J. (2005). Behavioral and molecular genetic contributions to a dimensional classification of personality disorders. *Journal of Personality Disorders, 19,* 131–155.

Livingstone, M. S., & Hubel, D. H. (1987). Psychological evidence for separate channels for the perception of form, color, movement and depth. *Journal of Neuroscience, 7,* 3416–3468.

Lizardi, D., Oquendo, M. A., & Graver, R. (2009). Clinical pitfalls in the diagnosis of *ataque de nervios:* A case study. *Transcultural Psychiatry, 46,* 463–486.

lLe Grange, D., Crosby, R. D., Rathouz, P. J., & Leventhal, B. L. (2007). A randomized controlled comparison of family-based treatment and supportive psychotherapy for adolescent bulimia nervosa. *Archives of General Psychiatry, 64,* 1049–1056.

Lleras, A., & Moore, C. M. (2006). What you see is what you get: Functional equivalence of a perceptually filled-in surface and a physically presented stimulus. *Psychological Science, 17,* 876–881.

Lochman, J. E., & Wells, K.,C. (2004). The coping power program for preadolescent aggressive boys and their parents: Outcome effects at 1-year follow-up. *Journal of Consulting and Clinical Psychology, 72,* 571–578.

Locke, E. A., & Latham G. P. (1990). *A theory of goal setting and task performance.* Englewood Cliffs, NJ: Prentice Hall.

Locke, E. A., & Latham, G. P. (2002). Building a practically useful theory of goal-setting and task motivation: A 35-year odyssey. *American Psychologist, 57,* 705–717.

Locurto, C. (1991). Beyond IQ in preschool programs? *Intelligence, 15,* 295–312.

Lodewijkx, H. F. M., Rabbie, J. M., & Visser, L. (2006). "Better to be safe than to be sorry": Extinguishing the individual-group discontinuity effect in competition by cautious reciprocation. *European Review of Social Psychology, 17,* 185–232.

Loeber, R., & Stouthamer-Loeber, M. (1998). Development of juvenile aggression and violence. Some common misconceptions and controversies. *American Psychologist, 53,* 242–259.

Loehlin, J. C. (1989). Partitioning environmental and genetic contributions to behavioral development. *American Psychologist, 44,* 1285–1292.

Loehlin, J. C., McCrae, R. R., Costa, P. T., & John, O. P. (1998). Heritabilities of common and measure-specific components of the Big Five personality factors. *Journal of Research in Personality, 32,* 431–453.

Loehlin, J. C., Neiderhiser, J. M., & Reiss, D. (2003). The behavior genetics of personality and the NEAD study. *Journal of Research in Personality, 37,* 373–387.

Loewenstein, G. (1994). The psychology of curiosity: A review and reinterpretation. *Psychological Bulletin, 116,* 75–98.

Loftus, E. F. (1992). When a lie becomes memory's truth: Memory distortion after exposure to misinformation. *Psychological Science, 3,* 121–123.

Loftus, E. F. (1997a). Memory for a past that never was. *Current Directions in Psychological Science, 6,* 60–65.

Loftus, E. F. (1997b). Repressed memory accusations: Devastated families and devastated patients. *Applied Cognitive Psychology, 11,* 25–30.

Loftus, E. F. (1998). The price of bad memories. *Skeptical Inquirer, 22,* 23–24.

Loftus, E. F. (2003, January). *Illusions of memory.* Presentation at the 25th annual National Institute on the Teaching of Psychology, Saint Pete Beach, FL.

Loftus, E. F. (2004). Memories of things unseen. *Current Directions in Psychological Science, 13,* 145–147.

Loftus, E. F., & Davis, D. (2006). Recovered memories. *Annual Review of Clinical Psychology, 2,* 469–498.

Loftus, E. F., Garry, M., & Hayne, H. (2008). Repressed and recovered memory. In E. Borgida & S. T. Fiske (Eds.), *Beyond common sense: Psychological science in the courtroom* (pp. 177–194). Malden, MA: Blackwell.

Loftus, E. F., & Guyer, M. (2002). Who abused Jane Doe? The hazards of the single case history (pt. 1). *Skeptical Inquirer, 26,* 24–32.

Loftus, E. F., & Hoffman, H. G. (1989). Misinformation and memory: The creation of new memories. *Journal of Experimental Psychology: General, 118,* 100–104.

Loftus, E. F., & Ketcham, K. (1991). *Witness for the defense.* New York: St. Martin's Press.

Loftus, E. F., & Ketcham, K. (1994). *The myth of repressed memory: False memories and allegations of sexual abuse.* New York: St. Martin's Press.

Loftus, E. F., & Palmer, J. C. (1974). Reconstruction of automobile destruction: An example of the interaction between language and memory. *Journal of Verbal Learning and Verbal Behavior, 13,* 585–589.

Loftus, E. F., & Pickrell, J. E. (1995). The formation of false memories. *Psychiatric Annals, 25,* 720–725.

Logue, A. W. (1985). Conditioned food aversion in humans. *Annals of the New York Academy of Sciences, 104,* 331–340.

Loher, B. T., Noe, R. A., Moeller, N. L., & Fitzgerald, M. P. (1985). A meta-analysis of the relation of job characteristics to job satisfaction. *Journal of Applied Psychology, 70,* 280–289.

Lohman, D. F. (1989). Human intelligence: An introduction to advances in theory and research. *Review of Educational Research, 59,* 333–373.

Lohman, D. F. (2000). Complex information processing and intelligence. In R. J. Sternberg (Ed.), *Handbook of human intelligence* (2nd ed., pp. 285–340). Cambridge: Cambridge University Press.

Lohman, D. F. (2004). Aptitude for college: The importance of reasoning tests for minority admissions. In R. Zwick (Ed.), *Rethinking the SAT: The future of standardized testing in college admissions.* New York: Routledge.

Lohman, D. F. (2005). The role of nonverbal ability tests in identifying academically gifted students: An aptitude perspective. *Gifted Child Quarterly, 49,* 111–138.

Lohman, D. F., & Hagen, E. (2001a). *Cognitive abilities test (Form 6).* Itasca, IL: Riverside.

Lohman, D. F., & Hagen, E. (2001b). *Cognitive abilities test (Form 6): Interpretive guide for teachers and counselors.* Itasca, IL: Riverside.

Lohr, J. M., Hooke, W., Gist, R., & Tolin, D. F. (2003). Novel and controversial treatments for trauma-related stress disorders. In S. O. Lilienfeld, S. J. Lynn, & J. M. Lohr (Eds.), *Science and pseudoscience in clinical psychology* (pp. 243–272). New York: Guilford Press.

Lohrenz, T., McCabe, K., Camerer, C. F., & Montague, P. R. (2007). Neural signature of fictive learning signals in a sequential investment task. *Proceedings of the National Academy of Sciences, 104,* 9493–9498.

LoLordo, V. M. (2001). Learned helplessness and depression. In M. E. Carroll & J. B. Overmier (Eds.), *Animal research and human health: Advancing human welfare through behavioral science* (pp. 63–77). Washington, DC: American Psychological Association.

Lombard, C., Deeks, A., Jolley, D., Ball, K., & Teede, H. (2010). A low-intensity, community-based lifestyle programme to prevent weight gain in women with young children: Cluster randomised controlled trial. *British Medical Journal, 341,* c3215.

Longitudinal Assessment of Bariatric Surgery (LABS) Consortium. (2009). Perioperative safety in the longitudinal assessment of bariatric surgery. *New England Journal of Medicine, 361,* 445–454.

Longo, N., Klempay, S., & Bitterman, M. E. (1964). Classical appetitive conditioning in the pigeon. *Psychonomic Science, 1,* 19–20.

López-Garcia, E., van Dam, R. M., Li, T. Y., Rodriguez-Artalejo, F., & Hu, F. B. (2008). The relationship of coffee consumption with mortality. *Annals of Internal Medicine, 148,* 904–914.

Loos, R. J. F., Rankinen, T., Chagnon, Y., Tremblay, A., et al. (2006). Polymorphisms in the leptin and leptin receptor genes in relation to resting metabolic rate and respiratory quotient in the Quebec Family Study. *International Journal of Obesity, 30,* 183–190.

Lopez, S. R. (1989). Patient variable biases in clinical judgment: Conceptual overview and methodological considerations. *Psychological Bulletin, 106,* 184–203.

López-Ibor, J. J., López-Ibor, M.-I., & Pastrana, J. I. (2008). Transcranial magnetic stimulation. *Current Opinion in Psychiatry, 21,* 640–644.

López-Moreno, J. A., González-Cuevas, G., Moreno, G., & Navarro, M. (2008). The pharmacology of the endocannabinoid system: Functional and structural interactions with other neurotransmitter systems and their repercussions in behavioral addiction. *Addiction Biology, 13,* 160–187.

Lord, R. G., Diefendorff, J. M., Schmidt, A. M., & Hall, R. J. (2010). Self-regulation at work. *Annual Review of Psychology, 61,* 543–568.

Losh, S. C., Tavani, C. M., Njoroge, R., Wilke, R., & McAuley, M. (2003). What does education really do? Educational dimensions and pseudoscience support in the American general public, 1979–2001. *Skeptical Inquirer, 27,* 30–35.

Lou, H. C., Luber, B., Crupain, M., Keenan, J. P., et al. (2004). Parietal cortex and representation of the mental self. *Proceedings of the National Academy of Sciences, 101,* 6827–6832.

Loudoun, R. (2008). Balancing shift work and life outside work: Do 12-hour shifts make a difference? *Applied Ergonomics, 39,* 572–579.

Lount, R. B., Jr.; Zhong, C. B.; Sivanathan, N.; & Murnighan, J. K. (2008). Getting off on the wrong foot: The timing of a breach and the restoration of trust. *Personality and Social Psychology Bulletin, 34,* 1601–1612.

Louzá, M. R., & Bassitt, D. P. (2005). Maintenance treatment of severe tardive dyskinesia with clozapine: 5 years' follow-up. *Journal of Clinical Psychopharmacology, 25,* 180–182.

Lovallo, W. R., Yechiam, E., Sorocco, K. H., Vincent, A. S., & Collins, F. L. (2006). Working memory and decision-making biases in young adults with a family history of alcoholism: Studies from the Oklahoma Family Health Patterns Project. *Alcoholism: Clinical and Experimental Research, 30,* 763–773.

Love, J. M., Kisker, E. E., Ross, C., Raikes, H., et al. (2005). The effectiveness of early Head Start for 3-year-old children and their parents: Lessons for policy and programs. *Developmental Psychology, 41,* 885–901.

Lovibond, P. F., Mitchell, C. J., Minard, E., Brady, A., & Menzies, R. G. (2009). Safety behaviours preserve threat beliefs: Protection from extinction of human fear conditioning by an avoidance response. *Behaviour Research and Therapy, 47,* 716–720.

Low, C. A., Stanton, A. L., & Danoff-Burg, S. (2006). Expressive disclosure and benefit finding among breast cancer patients: Mechanisms for positive health effects. *Health Psychology, 25,* 181–189.

Löwe, B., Mundt, C., Herzog, W., Brunner, R., et al. (2008). Validity of current somatoform disorder diagnoses: Perspective for classification in DSM-V and ICD-11. *Psychopathology, 41,* 4–9.

Lu, C., Chen, C., Ning, N., Ding, G., et al. (2009). The neural substrates for atypical planning and execution of word production in stuttering. *Experimental Neurology, 29,* 29.

Lu, J., Sherman, D., Devor, M., & Saper, C. B. (2006). A putative flip-flop switch for control of REM sleep. *Nature, 441,* 589–594.

Lubinski, D. (2004). Introduction to the special section on cognitive abilities: 100 years after Spearman's (1904) "'General intelligence,' objectively determined and measured." *Journal of Personality and Social Psychology, 86,* 96–111.

Lubinski, D., & Benbow, C. P. (1995). An opportunity for empiricism [Review of the book *Multiple intelligences: The theory in practice*]. *Contemporary Psychology, 40,* 935–938.

Lubinski, D., Benbow, C. P., Webb, R. M., & Bleske-Rechek, A. (2006). Tracking exceptional human capital over two decades. *Psychological Science, 17,* 194–199.

Lubinski, D., Webb, R. M., Morelock, M. J., & Benbow, C. P. (2001). Top 1 in 10,000: A 10-year follow-up of the profoundly gifted. *Journal of Applied Psychology, 86,* 718–729.

Luborsky, L. (1972). Another reply to Eysenck. *Psychological Bulletin, 78,* 406–408.

Luborsky, L., & Luborsky, E. (2006). *Research and psychotherapy: The vital link.* Northvale, NJ: Aronson.

Luborsky, L., Rosenthal, R., & Diguer, L. (2003). Are some psychotherapies much more effective than others? *Journal of Applied Psychoanalytic Studies, 5,* 455–460.

Luborsky, L., Rosenthal, R., Diguer, L., Andrusyna, T. P., et al. (2002). The Dodo Bird verdict is alive and well–mostly. *Clinical Psychology: Science and Practice, 9,* 2–12.

Luborsky, L., Singer, B., & Luborsky, L. (1975). Comparative studies of psychotherapies: Is it true that everyone has won and all must have prizes? *Archives of General Psychiatry, 32,* 995–1008.

Luby, J. L. (2010). Preschool depression: The importance of identification of depression early in development. *Current Directions in Psychological Science, 19,* 91–95.

Lucas, J. A. (2005). Disorders of memory. *Psychiatric Clinics of North America, 28,* 581–597.

Lucas, R. E. (2007). Adaptation and the set-point model of subjective well-being: Does happiness change after major life events? *Current Directions in Psychological Science, 16,* 75–79.

Lucas-Thompson, R., & Clarke-Stewart, K. A. (2007). Forecasting friendship: How marital quality, maternal mood, and attachment security are linked to children's peer relationships. *Journal of Applied Developmental Psychology, 28,* 499–514.

Luchins, A. S. (1942). Mechanization in problem solving: The effect of *Einstellung. Psychological Monographs, 54*(6, Whole No. 248).

Luciana, M., Conklin, H. M., Hooper, C. J., & Yarger, R. S. (2005). The development of nonverbal working memory and executive control processes in adolescents. *Child Development, 76,* 697–712.

Ludwig-Rosenthal, R., & Neufeld, R. W. (1988). Stress management during noxious medical procedures: An evaluative review of outcome studies. *Psychological Bulletin, 104,* 326–342.

Luhrmann, T. M. (2008). "The street will drive you crazy": Why homeless psychotic women in the institutional circuit in the United States often say no to offers of help. *American Journal of Psychiatry, 165,* 15–20.

Lumpkin, E. A., & Caterina, M. J. (2007). Mechanisms of sensory transduction in the skin. *Nature, 445,* 858–865.

Lund, T., Labriola, M., Christensen, K. B., Bultmann, U., & Villadsen, E. (2006). Physical work environment risk factors for long-term sickness absence: Prospective findings among a cohort of 5,357 employees in Denmark. *British Medical Journal, 332,* 449–452.

Lundy, R. F., Jr. (2008). Gustatory hedonic value: Potential function for forebrain control of brainstem taste processing. *Neuroscience and Biobehavioral Reviews, 32,* 1601–1606.

Luntz, B. K., & Widom, C. S. (1994). Antisocial personality disorder in abused and neglected children grown up. *American Journal of Psychiatry, 151,* 670–674.

Luppino, F. S., de Wit, L. M., Bouvy, P. F., Stijnen, T., et al. (2010). Overweight, obesity, and depression: A systematic review and meta-analysis of longitudinal studies. *Archives of General Psychiatry, 67,* 220–229.

Lussier, J. P., Heil, S. H., Mongeon, J. A., Badger, G. J., & Higgins, S. T. (2006). A meta-analysis of voucher-based reinforcement therapy for substance use disorders. *Addiction, 101,* 192–203.

Lustig, C., & Hasher, L. (2001). Implicit memory is not immune to interference. *Psychological Bulletin, 127,* 615–628.

Lustig, R. H., Sen, S., Soberman, J. E., & Velasquez-Mieyer, P. A. (2004). Obesity, leptin resistance, and the effects of insulin reduction. *International Journal of Obesity, 28,* 1344–1348.

Luthar, S. S., & Latendresse, S. J. (2005). Children of the affluent. *Current Directions in Psychological Science, 14,* 49–53.

Lutz, D. J., & Sternberg, R. J. (1999). Cognitive development. In M. H. Bornstein & M. E. Lamb (Eds.), *Developmental psychology: An advanced textbook* (4th ed., pp. 275–311). Mahwah, NJ: Erlbaum.

Luyckx, K., Goossens, L., & Soenens, B. (2006). A developmental contextual perspective on identity construction in emerging adulthood. Change dynamics in commitment formation and commitment evaluation. *Developmental Psychology, 42,* 366–380.

Lydon, J, Fitzsimons, G, & Naidoo, L. (2003). Devaluation versus enhancement of attractive alternatives: A critical test. *Personality and Social Psychology Bulletin, 29,* 349-359.

Lykken, D. T. (1998). *A tremor in the blood: Uses and abuses of the lie detector.* Cambridge, MA: Perseus Publishing.

Lykken, D. T. (1999). *Happiness: What studies on twins show us about nature, nurture, and the happiness set point.* New York: Golden Books.

Lyman, D. R., & Gudonis, L. (2005). The development of psychopathy. *Annual Review of Clinical Psychology, 1,* 381–407.

Lynall, M.-E., Bassett, D. S., Kerwin, R., McKenna, P. J., et al. (2010). Functional connectivity and brain networks in schizophrenia. *Journal of Neuroscience, 30,* 9477–9487.

Lynam, D. R., & Widiger, T. A. (2001). Using the five-factor model to represent the DSM-IV personality disorders: An expert consensus approach. *Journal of Abnormal Psychology, 110,* 401–412.

Lynch, F. L., Hornbrook, M., Clarke, G. N., Perrin, N., et al. (2005). Cost-effectiveness of an intervention to prevent depression in at-risk teens. *Archives of General Psychiatry, 62,* 1241–1248.

Lynn, R. (2006). *Race differences in intelligence: An evolutionary analysis.* Augusta, GA: Washington Summit.

Lynn, R., & Mikk, J. (2007). National differences in intelligence and educational attainment. *Intelligence, 35,* 115–121.

Lynn, S. J., & Kirsch, I. (2006). *Essentials of clinical hypnosis: An evidence-based approach.* Washington, DC: American Psychological Association.

Lynn, S. J., Lilienfeld, S. O., & Lohr, J. M. (Eds.). (2003). *Science and pseudoscience in clinical psychology.* New York: Guilford Press.

Lynn, S. J., Myers, B., & Malinoski, P. (1997). Hypnosis, pseudomemories, and clinical guidelines: A sociocognitive perspective. In J. D. Read & D. S. Lindsay (Eds.), *Recollections of trauma: Scientific evidence and clinical practice.* (pp. 305–336). New York: Plenum Press.

Lynn, S. J., & Rhue, J. W. (1986). The fantasy-prone person: Hypnosis, imagination, and creativity. *Journal of Personality and Social Psychology, 51,* 404–408.

Lynn, S. J., Vanderhoff, H., Shindler, K., & Stafford, J. (2002). Defining hypnosis as a trance vs. cooperation: Hypnotic inductions, suggestibility, and performance standards. *American Journal of Clinical Hypnosis, 44,* 231–240.

Lynskey, M. T., Heath, A. C., Bucholz, K. K., Slutske, W. S., et al. (2003). Escalation of drug use in early-onset cannabis users vs. co-twin controls. *Journal of the American Medical Association, 289,* 427–433.

Lyon, L. (2009, May 8). 7 criminal cases that invoked the "sleepwalking defense." *U.S. News & World Report.* Retrieved from http://health.usnews.com

Lyubomirsky, S. (2001). Why are some people happier than others? The role of cognitive and motivational processes in well-being. *American Psychologist, 56,* 239–249.

Lyubomirsky, S., King, L., & Diener, E. (2005). The benefits of frequent positive affect: Does happiness lead to success? *Psychological Bulletin, 131,* 803–855.

Lyubomirsky, S., & Nolen-Hoeksema, S. (1995). Effects of self-focused rumination on negative thinking and interpersonal problem solving. *Journal of Personality and Social Psychology, 69,* 176–190.

Ma, M. (2007). Encoding olfactory signals via multiple chemosensory systems. *Critical Reviews in Biochemistry and Molecular Biology, 42,* 463–480.

Ma, S. H., & Teasdale, J. D. (2004). Mindfulness-based cognitive therapy for depression: Replication and exploration of differential relapse prevention effects. *Journal of Consulting and Clinical Psychology, 72,* 1–40.

Maandag, N. J., Coman, D., Sanganahalli, B. G., Herman, P., et al. (2007). Energetics of neuronal signaling and fMRI activity. *Proceedings of the National Academy of Sciences, 104,* 20546–20551. Epub 2007 Dec 13.

MacAndrew, C., & Edgerton, R. B. (1969). *Drunken comportment.* Chicago: Aldine.

Maccoby, E. E., & Martin, J. A. (1983). Socialization in the context of the family: Parent-child interaction. In E. M. Hetherington (Ed.) & P. H. Mussen (Series Ed.), *Handbook of child psychology: Vol. 4. Socialization, personality, and social development* (pp. 1–101). New York: Wiley.

MacDonald, M., & Bernstein, D. A. (1974). Treatment of a spider phobia with in vivo and imaginal desensitization. *Journal of Behavior Therapy and Experimental Psychiatry, 5,* 47–52.

MacEvoy, S. P., & Paradiso, M. A. (2001). Lightness constancy in primary visual cortex *Proceedings of the National Academy of Sciences, 98,* 8827–8831.

Mack, A. (2003). Inattentional blindness: Looking without seeing. *Current Directions in Psychological Science, 12,* 180–184.

Mack, A., & Rock, I. (1998). *Inattentional blindness.* Cambridge, MA: MIT Press.

Mackay, D. G. (2006, March 29). Aging, memory, and language in amnesic H. M. *Hippocampus.* Retrieved from http://www3.interscience.wiley.com/cgi-bin/jissue/112597200

Mackintosh, N. J., & Bennett, E. S. (2003). The fractionation of working memory maps onto different components of intelligence. *Intelligence, 31,* 519–531.

MacLean, K. A., Ferrer, E., Aichele, S. R., Bridwell, D. A., et al. (2010). Intensive meditation training improves perceptual discrimination and sustained attention. *Psychological Science, 21,* 829–839.

MacMillan, H. L., Fleming, J. E., Steiner, D. L., Lin, E., et al. (2001). Childhood abuse and lifetime psychopathology in a community sample. *American Journal of Psychiatry, 158,* 1878–1883.

MacMillan, N. A., & Creelman, C. D. (2004). *Detection theory: A user's guide* (2nd ed.). Hillsdale, NJ: Erlbaum.

MacQuarrie, B., & Belkin, D. (2003, September 29). Franklin Park gorilla escapes, attacks 2. *Boston Globe.* Retrieved from http://www.boston.com

MacQueen, G. M., Campbell, S., McEwen, B. S., Macdonald, K., et al. (2003). Course of illness, hippocampal function, and hippocampal volume in major depression. *Proceedings of the National Academy of Sciences, 100,* 1387–1392.

Macrae, C. N., & Quadflieg, S. (2010). Perceiving people. In S. T. Fiske, D. T. Gilbert, & G. Lindzey (Eds.), *Handbook of social psychology* (5th ed., Vol. 2, pp.428–464). Hoboken, NJ: Wiley.

Macrae, C. N., Schloerscheidt, A. M., Bodenhausen, G. V., & Milne, A. B. (2002). Creating memory illusions: Expectancy-based processing and the generation of false memories. *Memory, 10,* 63–80.

Maddi, S. R., & Khoshaba, D. M. (2005). *Resilence at work.* New York: American Management Association.

Maddux, J. E., & Gosselin, J. T. (2003). Self-efficacy. In M. R. Leary & J. P. Tangney (Eds.), *Handbook of self and identity* (pp. 218–238). New York: Guilford Press.

Madon, S., Guyll, M., Spoth, R. L., & Willard, J. (2004). Self-fulfilling prophecies: The synergistic accumulation of parents' beliefs on children's drinking behavior. *Psychological Science, 15,* 837–845.

Madon, S., Willard, J., Guyll, M., Trudeau, L., & Spoth, R. L. (2006). Self-fulfilling prophecy effects of mothers' beliefs on children's alcohol use: Accumulation, dissipation, and stability over time. *Journal of Personality and Social Psychology, 90,* 911–926.

Madsen, M. V., Gøtzsche, P. C., and Hróbjartsson, A. (2009). Acupuncture treatment for pain: Systematic review of randomised clinical trials with acupuncture, placebo acupuncture, and no acupuncture groups. *British Medical Journal, 338,* a3115.

Maestripieri, D. (2004). Developmental and evolutionary aspects of female attraction to babies. *Psychological Science Agenda, 18*. Retrieved from http://www.apa.org/science/about/psa/2004/01/maestripieri.aspx

Magee, J. C., & Johnston, D. (1997). A synaptically controlled, associative signal for Hebbian plasticity in hippocampal neurons. *Science, 275*, 209–213.

Magee, W. L. (2007). Music as a diagnostic tool in low-awareness states: Considering limbic responses. *Brain Injury, 21*, 593–599.

Magnavita, J. J. (2006). In search of unifying principles of psychotherapy: Conceptual, empirical, and clinical convergence. *American Psychologist, 61*, 882–892.

Mahesh Yogi, M. (1994). *Science of being and art of living*. New York: NAL/Dutton.

Mahler, M. S. (1968). *On human symbiosis and the vicissitudes of individuation: Infantile psychosis*. New York: Basic Books.

Mahler, S. V., Smith, K. S., & Berridge, K. C. (2007). Endocannabinoid hedonic hotspot for sensory pleasure: Anandamide in nucleus accumbens shell enhances "liking" of a sweet reward. *Neuropsychopharmacology, 32*, 2267–2278.

Maier, S. F., & Watkins, L. R. (2000). The immune system as a sensory system: Implications for psychology. *Current Directions in Psychological Science, 9*, 98–102.

Maier, W., Gansicke, M., Gater, R., Reziki, M., et al. (1999). Gender differences in the prevalence of depression: A survey in primary care. *Journal of Affective Disorders, 53*, 241–252.

Main, M. (1996). Introduction to the special section on attachment and psychopathology: Vol. 2. Overview of the field of attachment. *Journal of Consulting and Clinical Psychology, 64*, 237–243.

Mainland, J. D., & Matsunami, H. (2009). Taste perception: How sweet it is (to be transcribed by you). *Current Biology, 19*, R655–R656.

Mains, J. A., & Scogin, F. R. (2003). The effectiveness of self-administered treatments: A practice-friendly review of the research. *Journal of Clinical Psychology, 59*, 237–245.

Maio, G., Haddock, G., Manstead, A., & Spears, R. (2010). Attitudes and intergroup relations In J. F. Dovidio, M. Hewstone, P. Glick, & V. M. Esses (Eds.), *Handbook of prejudice, stereotyping, and discrimination* (pp. 261–275). London: Sage

Makeover, R. B. (2004). *Treatment planning for psychotherapists* (2nd ed.). Alexandria, VA: American Psychiatric Association.

Malamuth, N. M. (1998). The confluence model as an organizing framework for research on sexually aggressive men: Risk moderators, imagined aggression, and pornography consumption. In R. G. Geen & E. Donnerstein (Eds.), *Human aggression* (pp. 230–247). San Diego, CA: Academic Press.

Malamuth, N. M., Addison, T., & Koss, M. (2000). Pornography and sexual aggression: Are there reliable effects and can we understand them? *Annual Review of Sex Research, 11*, 26–91.

Malarkey, W. B., Kiecolt-Glaser, J. K., Pearl, D., & Glaser, R. (1994). Hostile behavior during marital conflict alters pituitary and adrenal hormones. *Psychosomatic Medicine, 56*, 41–51.

Malberg, J. E., Eisch, A. J., Nestler, E. J., & Duman, R. S. (2000). Chronic antidepressant treatment increases neurogenesis in adult rat hippocampus. *Journal of Neuroscience, 20*, 9104–9110.

Maldonado, J. R., & Spiegel, D. (2008). Dissociative disorders. In R. E. Hales, S. C. Yudofsky, & G. O. Gabbard (Eds.), *Textbook of psychiatry* (pp. 665–728). Alexandria, VA: American Psychiatric Association.

Maldonado, R., & Berrendero, F. (2009). Endogenous cannabinoid and opioid systems and their role in nicotine addiction. *Current Drug Targets, 11*, 440–449.

Maldonado, R., Valverde, O., & Berrendero, F. (2006). Involvement of the endocannabinoid system in drug addiction. *Trends in Neuroscience, 29*, 225–232.

Malenka, R. C. (1995). LTP and LTD: Dynamic and interactive processes of synaptic plasticity. *Neuroscientist, 1*, 35–42.

Malenka, R. C., & Nicoll, R. A. (1999). Long-term potentiation: A decade of progress? *Science, 285*, 1870–1874.

Malgrange, B., Rigo, J. M., Van de Water, T. R., Staecker, H., et al. (1999). Growth factor therapy to the damaged inner ear: Clinical prospects. *International Journal of Pediatric Otorhinolaryngology, 49*(Suppl. 1), S19–S25.

Malhotra, S. (2008). Impact of the sexual revolution: Consequences of risky sexual behaviors. *Journal of American Physicians and Surgeons, 13*, 88–90.

Maljaars, P. W. J., Peters, H. P. F., Mela, D. J., & Masclee, A. A. M. (2008). Ileal brake: A sensible food target for appetite control—a review. *Physiology and Behavior, 95*, 271–281.

Malojcic, B., Mubrin, Z., Coric, B., Susnic, M., & Spilich, G. J. (2008). Consequences of mild traumatic brain injury on information processing assessed with attention and short-term memory tasks. *Journal of Neurotrauma, 25*, 30–37.

Malouff, J. M., Rooke, S. E., & Schutte, N. S. (2008). The heritability of human behavior: Results of aggregating meta-analyses. *Current Psychology, 27*, 153–161.

Maltby, N., Kirsch, I., & Mayers, M. (2002). Virtual reality exposure therapy for the treatment of fear of flying: A controlled investigation. *Journal of Consulting and Clinical Psychology, 70*, 1112–1118.

Man to get $900,000 for 20 years spent in prison for rape he did not commit. (2003, January 10). *Naples Daily News*.

Manahan, V. J. (2004). When our system of involuntary civil commitment fails individuals with mental illness: Russell Weston and the case for effective monitoring and medication delivery mechanisms. *Law and Psychology Review, 28*, 1–33.

Mancinelli, R., Binetti, R., & Ceccanti, M. (2007). Woman, alcohol, and environment: Emerging risks for health. *Neuroscience and Biobehavioral Reviews, 31*, 246–253. doi:10.1016/j.neubiorev.2006.06.017

Mandelid, L. J. (2003). Dodofugl-dommen og psykoterapeuters credo [The Dodo Bird verdict and psychotherapists' beliefs]. *Tidsskrift for Norsk Psykologforening, 40*, 307–312.

Maner, J. K., Luce, C. L., Neuberg, S. L., Cialdini, R. B., (2002). The effects of perspective taking on motivations for helping: Still no evidence for altruism. *Personality and Social Psychology Bulletin, 28*, 1601–1610.

Manfield, P., & Shapiro, F. (2004). Application of eye movement desensitization and reprocessing (EMDR) to personality disorders. In J. J. Magnavita (Ed.), *Handbook of personality disorders: Theory and practice* (pp. 304–328). New York: Wiley.

Manheimer, E., White, A., Berman, B., Forys, K., & Ernst, E. (2005). Meta-analysis: Acupuncture for low back pain. *Annals of Internal Medicine, 142*, 651–663.

Manini, T. M., Everhart, J. E., Patel, K. V., Schoeller, D. A., et al. (2006). Daily activity energy expenditure, and mortality among older adults. *Journal of the American Medical Association, 296*, 171–179.

Mann, J. J., Apter, A., Bertolote, J., Beautrais, A., et al. (2005). Suicide prevention strategies: A systematic review. *Journal of the American Medical Association, 294*, 2064–2074.

Mann, K., Roschke, J., Nink, M., Aldenhoff, J., et al. (1992). Effects of corticotropin-releasing hormone administration in patients suffering from sleep apnea syndrome. *Society for Neuroscience Abstracts, 22*, 196.

Manning, C. (2004). Beyond memory: Neuropsychologic features in differential diagnosis of dementia. *Clinical Geriatric Medicine, 20*, 45–58.

Manti, L., Braselmann, H., Calabrese, M. L., Massa, R., et al. (2008). Effects of modulated microwave radiation at cellular telephone frequency (1.95 GHz) on X-ray-induced chromosome aberrations in human lymphocytes in vitro. *Radiation Research, 169*, 575–583.

Manto, M. (2008). The cerebellum, cerebellar disorders, and cerebellar research: Two centuries of discoveries. *Cerebellum, 7*, 505–516.

Maquet, P. (2001). The role of sleep in learning and memory. *Science, 294*, 1048–1052.

March, J., Silva, S., Petrycki, S., Curry, J., et al. (2004). Fluoxetine, cognitive-behavioral therapy, and their combination for adolescents with depression: Treatment for Adolescents with Depression Study (TADS) randomized controlled trial. *Journal of the American Medical Association, 292*, 807–820.

Marchman, T. (2008, October 24). You call that bling? *Wall Street Journal*.

Marcus, G. F. (1996). Why do children say "breaked"? *Current Directions in Psychological Science, 5*, 81–85.

Marcus, S. V. (2008). Phase 1 of integrated EMDR: An abortive treatment for migraine headaches. *Journal of EMDR Practice and Research, 2*, 15–25.

Marenco, S., & Weinberger, D. R. (2000). The neurodevelopmental hypothesis of schizophrenia: Following a trail of evidence from cradle to grave. *Developmental Psychopathology, 12*, 501–527.

Marin, S., Vinaixa, M., Brezmes, J., Llobet, E., et al. (2007). Use of an MS-electronic nose for prediction of early fungal spoilage of bakery products. *International Journal of Food Microbiology, 114*, 10–16.

Markman, E. M. (1994). Constraints children place on word meanings. In P. Bloom (Ed.), *Language acquisition: Core readings* (pp. 154–173). Cambridge, MA: MIT Press.

Markoff, J. (2008, November 25). Microsoft examines causes of "cyberchondria." *New York Times*. Retrieved from http://www.nytimes.com/2008/11/25/technology/internet/25symptoms.html

Markov, D., & Goldman, M. (2006). Normal sleep and circadian rhythms: Neurobiologic mechanisms underlying sleep and wakefulness. *Psychiatric Clinics of North America, 29*, 841–853.

Marks, I. M. (2002). Reduction of fear: Towards a unifying theory. *Psicoterapia Cognitiva e Comportamentale, 8*, 63–66.

Markus, H. R., & Kitayama, S. (1997). Culture and the self: Implications for cognition, emotion, and motivation. In L. A. Peplau & S. Taylor (Eds.), *Sociocultural perspectives in social psychology* (pp. 157–216). Upper Saddle River, NJ: Prentice Hall.

Markus, H. R., Kitayama, S., & Heiman, R. J. (1996). Culture and "basic" psychological principles. In E. T. Higgins & A. W. Kruglanski (Eds.), *Social psychology: Handbook of basic principles* (pp. 857–913). New York: Guilford Press.

Marmarosh, C., Holtz, A., & Schottenbauer, M. (2005). Group cohesiveness, group-derived collective self-esteem, group-derived hope, and the well-being of group therapy members. *Group Dynamics: Theory, Research, and Practice, 9*, 32–44.

Marsden, J., Eastwood, B., Bradbury, C., Dale-Perera, A., et al. (2009). Effectiveness of community treatments for heroin and crack cocaine addiction in England: A prospective in-treatment cohort study. *Lancet, 374*, 1262–1270.

Marsh, A. A., Ambady, N., & Kleck, R. E. (2005). The effects of fear and anger facial expressions on approach- and avoidance-related behaviors. *Emotion, 5*, 119–124.

Marsh, A. A., Elfenbein, H. A., & Ambady, N. (2003). Nonverbal "accents": Cultural differences in facial expressions of emotion. *Psychological Science, 14*, 373–377.

Marshall, G. N., Miles, J. N. V., & Stewart, S. H. (2010). Anxiety sensitivity and PTSD symptom severity are reciprocally related: Evidence from a longitudinal study of physical trauma survivors. *Journal of Abnormal Psychology, 119*, 143–150.

Marshall, J., & Oberwinkler, J. (1999). The colourful world of the mantis shrimp. *Nature, 401*, 873–874.

Marshall, S. J., Biddle, S. J., Gorely, T., Cameron, N., & Murdey, I. (2004). Relationships between media use, body fatness and physical activity in children and youth: A meta-analysis. *International Journal of Obesity, 28*, 1238–1246.

Martens, W. H. J. (2004). The terrorist with antisocial personality disorder. *Journal of Forensic Psychology Practice, 4*, 45–56.

Marti, P. R., Singleton, C. K., & Hiller-Sturmhofel, S. (2003). The role of thiamine deficiency in alcoholic brain disease. *Alcohol Research Health, 27*, 134–142.

Martin, C. L., & Ruble, D. (2004). Children's search for gender cues. *Current Directions in Psychological Science, 13*, 67–70.

Martin, C. L., & Ruble, D. R. (2009). Patterns of gender development. *Annual Review of Psychology, 61*, 353–381. doi:10.1146/annurev.psych.093008.100511

Martin, G., Guadano-Ferraz, A., Morte, B., Ahmed, S., et al. (2004). Chronic morphine treatment alters N-methyl-D-aspartate receptors in freshly isolated neurons from nucleus accumbens. *Journal of Pharmacology and Experimental Therapeutics, 311*, 265–273.

Martin, G. L., & Pear, J. (2002). *Behavior modification: What it is and how to do it* (7th ed.). Upper Saddle River, NJ: Prentice Hall.

Martin, G., & Pear, J. (2006). *Behavior modification: What it is and how to do it* (8th ed.). Upper Saddle River, NJ: Prentice Hall.

Martin, J. G. A., & Réale, D. (2008). Temperament, risk assessment and habituation to novelty in eastern chipmunks (*Tamias striatus*). *Animal Behaviour, 75,* 309–318.

Martin, J. L., & Ross, H. S. (2005). Sibling aggression: Sex differences and parents' reactions. *International Journal of Behavioral Development, 29,* 129–138.

Martin, P., Baenziger, J., MacDonald, M., Siegler, I. C., & Poon, L. W. (2009). Engaged lifestyle, personality, and mental status among centenarians. *Journal of Adult Development, 16,* 199–208. doi:10.1007/s10804-009-9066-y

Martin, R. A. (2001). Humor, laughter, and physical health: Methodological issues and research findings. *Psychological Bulletin, 127,* 504–519.

Martin, R. C., Sawrie, S. M., Knowlton, R. C., Bilir, E., et al. (2001). Bilateral hippocampal atrophy: Consequences to verbal memory following temporal lobectomy. *Neurology, 57,* 597–604.

Martinez, C. R., & Forgatch, M. S. (2001). Preventing problems with boys' noncompliance: Effects of a parent training intervention for divorcing mothers. *Journal of Consulting and Clinical Psychology, 69,* 416–428.

Martinez, D., Gil, R., Slifstein, M., Hwang, D.-R., et al. (2005). Alcohol dependence is associated with blunted dopamine transmission in the ventral striatum. *Biological Psychiatry, 58,* 779–786.

Martinez, M. (2000). *Education as the cultivation of intelligence.* Mahwah, NJ: Erlbaum.

Martínez-Taboaz, A. (2005). Psychogenic seizures in an *espiritismo* context: The role of culturally sensitive psychotherapy. *Psychotherapy: Theory, Research, Practice, Training, 42,* 6–13. doi:10.1037/0033-3204.42.1.6

Martino, G., & Marks, L. E. (2001). Synesthesia: Strong and weak. *Current Directions in Psychological Science, 10,* 61–65.

Martín-Santos, R., Fagundo, A. B., Crippa, J. A., Atakan, Z., et al. (2010). Neuroimaging in cannabis use: A systematic review of the literature. *Psychological Medicine, 40,* 383–398.

Martiny, K., Lunde, M., & Bech, P. (2010). Transcranial low-voltage pulsed electromagnetic fields in patients with treatment-resistant depression. *Biological Psychiatry, 68,* 163–169.

Maslach, C. (2003). Job burnout: New directions in research and intervention. *Current Directions in Psychological Science, 12,* 189–192.

Maslow, A. H. (1943). A theory of human motivation. *Psychological Review, 50,* 370–396.

Maslow, A. H. (1954). *Motivation and personality.* New York: Harper.

Maslow, A. H. (1970). *Motivation and personality* (2nd ed.). New York: Harper & Row.

Maslow, A. H. (1971). *Toward a psychology of being.* Princeton, NJ: Van Nostrand.

Mass, R., Hölldorfer, M., Moll, B., Bauer, R., & Wolf, K. (2008). Why we haven't died out yet: Changes in women's mimic reactions to visual erotic stimuli during their menstrual cycles. *Hormones and Behavior, 55,* 267–271.

Masson, M. E. J., & MacLeod, C. M. (1992). Reenacting the route to interpretation: Enhanced perceptual identification without prior perception. *Journal of Experimental Psychology: General, 121,* 145–176.

Mast, T. G., & Samuelsen, C. L. (2009). Human pheromone detection by the vomeronasal organ: Unnecessary for mate selection? *Chemical Senses, 34,* 529–531.

Masten, A. S., & Coatsworth, J. D. (1998). The development of competence in favorable and unfavorable environments: Lessons from research on successful children. *American Psychologist, 53,* 205–220.

Masten, A. S., Roisman, G. I., Long, J. D., Burt, K. B., et al. (2005). Developmental cascades: Linking academic achievement and externalizing and internalizing symptoms over 20 years. *Developmental Psychology, 41,* 733–746.

Master, S. L., Eisenberger, N. I., Taylor, S. E., Naliboff, B. D., et al. (2009). A picture's worth: Partner photographs reduce experimentally induced pain. *Psychological Science, 20,* 1316–1318.

Masters, J. C., Burish, T. G., Hollon, S. D., & Rimm, D. C. (1987). *Behavior therapy: Techniques and empirical findings* (3rd ed.). Orlando, FL: Harcourt Brace Jovanovich.

Masters, W. H., & Johnson, V. E. (1966). *Human sexual response.* Boston: Little, Brown.

Masudomi, I., Isse, K., Uchiyama, M., & Watanabe, H. (2004). Self-help groups reduce mortality risk: A 5-year follow-up study of alcoholics in the Tokyo metropolitan area. *Psychiatry and Clinical Neurosciences, 58,* 551–557.

Mather, M., Canli, T., English, T., Whitfield, S., et al. (2004). Emotionally valenced stimuli in older and younger adults. *Psychological Science, 15,* 259–263.

Mathews, M., Basily, B., & Mathews, M. (2006). Better outcomes for schizophrenia in non-Western countries. *Psychiatric Services, 57,* 143–144.

Matlin, M. W. (1998). *Cognition* (4th ed.). Fort Worth, TX: Harcourt.

Maton, K., Kohout, J. L., Wicherski, M., Leary, G. E., & Vinokurov, A. (2006). Minority students of color in the psychology graduate pipeline: Disquieting and encouraging trends, 1989–2003. *American Psychologist, 61,* 117–131.

Matson, J. L., & Boisjoli, J. A. (2009). The token economy for children with intellectual disability and/or autism: A review. *Research in Developmental Disabilities, 30,* 240–248.

Matson, J. L., Sevin, J. A., Fridley, D., & Love, S. R. (1990). Increasing spontaneous language in autistic children. *Journal of Applied Behavior Analysis, 23,* 227–223.

Matsumoto, D. (2000). *Culture and psychology: People around the world.* Belmont, CA: Wadsworth.

Matsumoto, D., & Ekman, P. (1989). American-Japanese cultural differences in intensity ratings of facial expressions of emotion. *Motivation and Emotion, 13,* 143–157.

Matsumoto, D., & Willingham, B. (2006). The thrill of victory and the agony of defeat: Spontaneous expressions of medal winners of the 2004 Athens Olympic Games. *Journal of Personality and Social Psychology, 91,* 568–581.

Matsumoto, D., & Willingham, B. (2009). Spontaneous facial expressions of emotion of congenitally and noncongenitally blind individuals. *Journal of Personality and Social Psychology, 96,* 1–10.

Matsumoto, D., Yoo, S. H., & Nakagawa, S. (2008). Multinational study of cultural display rules. Culture, emotion regulation, and adjustment. *Journal of Personality and Social Psychology, 94,* 925–937.

Matsumoto, H., & Matsumoto, I. (2008). Alcoholism: Protein expression profiles in a human hippocampal model. *Expert Review of Proteomics, 5,* 321–331.

Mattanah, J. F., Hancock, G. R., & Brand, B. L. (2004). Parental attachment, separation-individuation, and college student adjustment: A structural equation analysis of mediational effects. *Journal of Counseling Psychology, 51,* 213–225.

Matte, T. D., Breshahan, M., Begg, M., & Susser, E. (2001). Influence of variation in birthweight within normal range and within sibships on IQ at 7 years: Cohort study. *British Medical Journal, 323,* 310–314.

Matthews, G. (2008). Reinforcement sensitivity theory: A critique from cognitive science In P. J. Corr (Ed.), *The reinforcement sensitivity theory of personality* (pp. 482–507). Cambridge: Cambridge University Press.

Matthews, K. A., Katholi, C. R., McCreath, H., Whooley, M. A., et al. (2004). Blood pressure reactivity to psychological stress predicts hypertension in the CARDIA study. *Circulation, 110,* 74–78.

Matthews, K. A., Salomon, K., Kenyon, K., & Zhou, F. (2005). Unfair treatment, discrimination, and ambulatory blood pressure in black and white adolescents. *Health Psychology, 24,* 258–265.

Matthews, S. (2004). Failed agency and the insanity defense. *International Journal of Law and Psychiatry, 27,* 413–424.

Matthies, E., Hoeger, R., & Guski, R. (2000). Living on polluted soil: Determinants of stress symptoms. *Environment and Behavior, 32,* 270–286.

Matyas, G. S. (2004). Using MMPI special scale configurations to predict police officer performance in New Jersey. *Applied HRM Research, 9,* 63–66.

Matza, L. S., Baker, T. M., & Revicki, D. A. (2005). Efficacy of olanzapine and ziprasidone for the treatment of schizophrenia: A systematic review. *CNS Drugs, 19,* 499–515.

Maviel, T., Durkin, T. P., Menzaghi, F., & Bontempi, B. (2004). Sites of neocortical reorganization critical for remote spatial memory. *Science, 305,* 96–99.

May, G. L., & Kahnweiler, W. M. (2000). The effect of a mastery practice design on learning and transfer in behavior modeling training. *Personnel Psychology, 53,* 353–373.

May, R. (1969). *Love and will.* New York: Norton.

May, R., Angel, E., & Ellenberger, H. F. (Eds.). (1958). *Existence: A new dimension in psychiatry and psychology.* New York: Basic Books.

May, S. K. (2006). *Case studies in organizational communication.* Thousand Oaks, CA: Sage.

Mayberry, R. I., & Lock, E. (2003). Age constraints on first versus second language acquisition. *Brain and Language, 87,* 369–384.

Mayberry, R. I., Lock, E., & Kazmi, H. (2002). Linguistic ability and early language exposure. *Nature, 417,* 38.

Mayer, D. J., & Price, D. D. (1982). A physiological and psychological analysis of pain: A potential model of motivation. In D. W. Pfaff (Ed.), *The physiological mechanisms of motivation* (pp. 443–471). New York: Springer-Verlag.

Mayer, F. S., & Sutton, K. (1996). *Personality: An integrative approach.* Upper Saddle River, NJ: Prentice Hall.

Mayer, J. D. (2005). A tale of two visions: Can a new view of personality help integrate psychology? *American Psychologist, 60,* 294–307.

Mayer, R. E. (1992). *Thinking, problem solving, and cognition* (2nd ed.). New York: Freeman.

Mayes, L. C., Molfese, D. L., Key, A. P. F., & Hunter, N. C. (2005). Event-related potentials in cocaine-exposed children during a Stroop task. *Neurotoxicology and Teratology, 27,* 797–813. doi:10.1016/j.ntt.2005.05.011

Mayes, L., Cicchetti, D., Acharyya, S., & Zhang, H. (2003). Developmental trajectories of cocaine-and-other-drug-exposed and non-cocaine-exposed children. *Journal of Developmental Behavioral Pediatrics, 24,* 323–335.

Mayeux, R. (2003). Epidemiology of neurodegeneration. *Annual Review of Neuroscience, 26,* 81–104.

Maynard, D. C., Joseph, T. A., & Maynard, A. M. (2006). Underemployment, job attitudes, and turnover intentions. *Journal of Organizational Behavior, 27,* 509–536.

Mayou, R., Kirmayer, L. J., Simon, G., Kroenke, K., & Sharpe, M. (2005). Somatoform disorders: Time for a new approach in DSM-V. *American Journal of Psychiatry, 162,* 847–855.

Mazoyer, B., Tzouri-Mazoyer, N., Mazard, A., Denis, M., & Mellet, E. (2002). Neural basis of image and language interactions. *International Journal of Psychology, 37,* 204–208.

Mazzoni, G.., & Memon, A. (2003). Imagination can create false autobiographical memories. *Psychological Science, 14,* 186–188.

Mazzoni, G.., Rotriquenz, E., Carvalho, C., Vannucci, M., et al. (2009). Suggested visual hallucinations in and out of hypnosis. *Consciousness and Cognition, 18,* 494–499.

Mazzoni, G. A., & Loftus, E. F. (1996). When dreams become reality. *Consciousness and Cognition, 5,* 442–462.

McAdams, D. P. (1997). A conceptual history of personality psychology. In R. Hogan, J. Johnson, & S. Briggs (Eds.), *Handbook of personality psychology* (pp. 4–40). San Diego, CA: Academic Press.

McAllister-Williams, R. H. (2006). Relapse prevention in bipolar disorder: A critical review of current guidelines. *Journal of Psychopharmacology, 20*(Suppl. 2), 12–16.

McAuley, E. (1992). The role of efficacy cognitions in the prediction of exercise behavior in middle-aged adults. *Journal of Behavioral Medicine, 15,* 65–88.

McAuley, E., Kramer, A. F., & Colcombe, S. J. (2004). Cardiovascular fitness and neurocognitive function in older adults: A brief review. *Brain, Behavior, and Immunity, 18,* 214–220.

McAuliff, B. D., Kovera, M. B., & Nuñez, G. (2008). Can jurors recognize missing control groups, confounds, and experimental bias in psychological science? *Law and Human Behavior, 33,* 247–257.

McCabe, D. P., & Castel, A. D. (2008). Seeing is believing: The effect of brain images on judgments of scientific reasoning. *Cognition, 107,* 343–352. Epub 2007 Sep 4.

McCaffery, E. J., & Baron, J. (2006). Thinking about tax. *Psychology, Public Policy, and Law, 12,* 106–135.

McCarley, J. S., Kramer, A. F., Wickens, C. D., Vidoni, E. D., & Boot, W. R. (2004). Visual skills in airport-security screening. *Psychological Science, 15,* 302–306.

McCaul, K. D., Hockemeyer, J. R., Johnson, R. J., Zetocha, K., et al. (2006). Motivation to quit using cigarettes: A review. *Addictive Behaviors, 31,* 42–56.

McClain, M., & Foundas, A. (2004). Apraxia. *Current Neurology and Neuroscience Reports, 4,* 471–476.

McClelland, D. C. (1958). Risk-taking in children with high and low need for achievement. In J. W. Atkinson (Ed.), *Motives in fantasy, action, and society* (pp. 306–321). Princeton, NJ: Van Nostrand.

McClelland, D. C. (1985). *Human motivation.* Glenview, IL: Scott, Foresman.

McClernon, F. J. (2009). Neuroimaging of nicotine dependence: Key findings and application to the study of smoking–mental illness comorbidity. *Journal of Dual Diagnosis, 5,* 168–178.

McClintock, C. G., & Liebrand, W. B. G. (1988). Role of interdependence structure, individual value orientation, and another's strategy in social decision making: A transformational analysis. *Journal of Personality and Social Psychology, 55,* 396–409.

McCloskey, M. (1983). Naïve theories of motion. In D. Gentner & K. Stevens (Eds.), *Mental models* (pp. 299–324). Hillsdale, NJ: Erlbaum.

McCloskey, M. S., Ben-Zeev, D., Lee, R., Berman, M. E., & Coccaro, E. F. (2009). Acute tryptophan depletion and self-injurious behavior in aggressive patients and healthy volunteers. *Psychopharmacology (Berlin), 203,* 53–61. Epub 2008 Oct 23.

McClure, E. B. (2000). A meta-analytic review of sex differences in facial expression processing and their development in infants, children, and adolescents. *Psychological Bulletin, 126,* 424–453.

McConaghy, N., Hadzi-Pavlovic, D., Stevens, C., Manicavasagar, V., et al. (2006). Fraternal birth order and ratio of heterosexual/homosexual feelings in women and men. *Journal of Homosexuality, 51,* 161–174.

McCormick, D. A., & Thompson, R. F. (1984). Cerebellum essential involvement in the classically conditioned eyelid response. *Science, 223,* 296–299.

McCormick, E. J., Jeanneret, P. R., & Mecham, R. C. (1972). A study of job characteristics and job dimensions as based on the position analysis questionnaire (PAQ). *Journal of Applied Psychology, 56,* 347–368.

McCrae, R. R., & Costa, P. T., Jr. (2006). Cross-cultural perspectives on adult personality trait development. In D. Mroczek & T. Little (Eds.), *Handbook of personality development* (pp. 129–145). Mahwah, NJ: Erlbaum.

McCrae, R. R., & Costa, P. T., Jr. (2008). The five-factor theory of personality. In O. P. John, R. W. Robins, & L. A. Pervin (Eds.), *Handbook of personality: Theory and research* (3rd ed., pp. 159–181). New York: Guilford Press.

McCrae, R. R., & John, O. P. (1992). An introduction to the five-factor model and its applications. *Journal of Personality, 60,* 175–215.

McCrae, R. R., Terracciano, A., & Personality Profiles of Cultures Project. (2005). Personality profiles of cultures: Aggregate personality traits. *Journal of Personality and Social Psychology, 89,* 407–425.

McCulloch, K. C., Ferguson, M. J., Kawada, C., & Bargh, J. A. (2008). Taking a closer look: On the operation of nonconscious impression formation, *Journal of Experimental Social Psychology, 44,* 614–623.

McCusker, R. R., Fuehrlein, B., Goldberger, B. A., Gold, M. S., & Cone, E. J. (2006). Caffeine content of decaffeinated coffee. *Journal of Analytical Toxicology, 30,* 611–613.

McCusker, R. R., Goldberger, B. A., & Cone, E. J. (2003). Caffeine content of specialty coffees. *Journal of Analytical Toxicology, 27,* 520–522.

McDermott, K. B. (2002). Explicit and implicit memory. In V. S. Ramachandran (Ed.), *Encyclopedia of the human brain* (Vol. 2, pp. 773–781). San Diego, CA: Academic Press.

McDermott, K. B., & Buckner, R. L. (2002). Functional neuroimaging studies of human memory retrieval. In L. R. Squire & D. L. Schacter (Eds.), *Neuropsychology of memory* (3rd ed., pp. 166–171). New York: Guilford Press.

McDermott, K. B., & Chan, J. C. K. (2006). Effects of repetition on memory for pragmatic inferences. *Memory and Cognition, 34,* 1273–1284.

McDermott, K. B., & Roediger, H. L., III. (1998). Attempting to avoid illusory memories: Robust false recognition of associates persists under conditions of explicit warnings and immediate testing. *Journal of Memory and Language, 39,* 508–520.

McDermott, K. B., Szpunar, K. K., & Christ, S. E. (2009). Laboratory-based and autobiographical retrieval tasks differ substantially in their neural substrates. *Neuropsychologia, 47,* 2290–2298.

McDiarmid, M. A., & Condon, M. (2005). Organizational safety culture/climate and worker compliance with hazardous drug guidelines: Lessons from the blood-borne pathogen experience. *Journal of Occupational and Environmental Medicine, 47,* 740–749.

McDonald, J. J., Teder-Salejarvi, W. A., & Hillyard, S. A. (2000). Involuntary orienting to sound improves visual perception. *Nature, 407,* 906–908.

McDougall, S. J. P., de Bruijn, O., & Curry, M. B. (2000). Exploring the effects of icon characteristics on user performance: The role of icon concreteness, complexity, and distinctiveness. *Journal of Experimental Psychology: Applied, 6,* 291–306.

McDougall, W. (1908). *An introduction to social psychology.* London: Methuen.

McElwain, N. L., Booth-LaForce, C., Lansford, J. E., Wu, X., & Dyer, W. J. (2008). A process model of attachment-friend linkages: Hostile attribution biases, language ability, and mother-child affective mutuality as intervening mechanisms. *Child Development, 79,* 1891–1906.

McEvoy, G. M., & Beatty, R. W. (1989). Assessment centers and subordinate appraisals of managers: A seven-year examination of predictive validity. *Personnel Psychology, 42,* 37–52.

McEvoy, S. P., Stevenson, M. R., McCartt, A. T., Woodward, M., et al. (2005). Role of mobile phones in motor vehicle crashes resulting in hospital attendance: A case-crossover study. *British Medical Journal, 331,* 428.

McFerran, B., Dahl, D. W., Fitzsimons, G. J., & Morales, A. C. (2010). I'll have what she's having: The social influence of obese consumers on the food choices of others. *Journal of Consumer Research, 36,* 915–929. doi:10.1086/644611

McGarvey, C., McDonnell, M., Hamilton, K., O'Regan, M., & Matthews, T. (2006). An 8-year study of risk factors for SIDS: Bed-sharing versus non-bed-sharing. *Archives of Disease in Childhood, 91,* 318–323.

McGaugh, J. L. (2003). *Memory and emotion.* New York: Columbia University Press.

McGeer, E. G., & McGeer, P. L. (2010). Neuroinflammation in Alzheimer's disease and mild cognitive impairment: A field in its infancy. *Journal of Alzheimer's Disease, 19,* 355–361.

McGehee, D. S., Heath, M. J. S., Gelber, S., Devay, P., & Role, L. W. (1995). Nicotine enhancement of fast excitatory synaptic transmissions in CNS by presynaptic receptors. *Science, 269,* 1692–1696.

McGlone, J. (1980). Sex differences in human brain asymmetry: A critical survey. *Behavioral and Brain Sciences, 3,* 215–263.

McGlynn, F. D., Smitherman, T. A., & Gothard, K. D. (2004). Comment on the status of systematic desensitization. *Behavior Modification, 28,* 194–205.

McGlynn, S. M., & Schacter, D. L. (1989). Unawareness of deficits in neuropsychological syndromes. *Journal of Clinical and Experimental Neuropsychology, 11,* 143–205.

McGorry, P. D., Yung, A. R., Phillips, L. J., Yuen, H. P., et al. (2002). Randomized controlled trial of interventions designed to reduce the risk of progression to first-episode psychosis in a clinical sample with subthreshold symptoms. *Archives of General Psychiatry, 59,* 921–928.

McGowan, E., Eriksen, J., & Hutton, M. (2006). A decade of modeling Alzheimer's disease in transgenic mice. *Trends in Genetics, 22,* 281–289.

McGrath, J., Welham, J., Scott, J., Varghese, D., et al. (2010). Association between cannabis use and psychosis-related outcomes using sibling pair analysis in a cohort of young adults. *Archives of General Psychiatry, 67,* 440–447. Epub 2010 Mar 1.

McGue, M. (1992). When assessing twin concordance, use the probandwise not the pairwise rate. *Schizophrenia Bulletin, 18,* 171–176.

McGue, M., Elkins, I., Walden, B., & Iacono, W. G. (2005). Perceptions of the parent-adolescent relationship: A longitudinal investigation. *Developmental Psychology, 41,* 971–984.

McHale, J. P., & Sullivan, M. J. (2008). Family systems. In M. Hersen & A. M. Gross (Eds.), *Handbook of clinical psychology: Vol. 2. Children and adolescents* (pp. 192–226). Hoboken, NJ: Wiley.

McHale, S., & Hunt, N. (2008). Executive function deficits in short-term abstinent cannabis users. *Human Psychopharmacology, 23,* 409–415.

McHugh, P. R. (2009). *Try to remember: Psychiatry's clash over meaning, memory, and mind.* Chicago: Dana Press.

McHugh, R. K., & Barlow, D. H. (2010). The dissemination and implementation of evidence-based psychological treatments: A review of current efforts. *American Psychologist, 65,* 73–84.

McKee, L., Roland, E., Coffelt, N., Olson, A. L., et al. (2007). Harsh discipline and child problem behaviors: The roles of positive parenting and gender. *Journal of Family Violence, 22,* 187–196.

McLaughlin, N. C. R., & Westervelt, H. J. (2008). Odor identification deficits in frontotemporal dementia: A preliminary study. *Archives of Clinical Neuropsychology, 23,* 119–123.

McLean, C. P., & Anderson, E. R. (2009). Brave men and timid women? A review of the gender differences in fear and anxiety. *Clinical Psychology Review, 29,* 496–505.

McLendon, D., McLendon, T, & Petr, C. G. (2005). Family-directed structural therapy. *Journal of Marital and Family Therapy, 31,* 327–339.

McLeod, J. D., Kessler, R. C., & Landis, K. R. (1992). Speed of recovery from major depressive episodes in a community sample of married men and women. *Journal of Abnormal Psychology, 101,* 277–286.

McLeod, P., Reed, N., & Dienes, Z. (2003). Psychophysics: How fielders arrive in time to catch the ball. *Nature, 426,* 244–245.

McLoyd, V. C. (1998). Socioeconomic disadvantage and child development. *American Psychologist, 53,* 185–204.

McMahon, F. J., Akula, N., Schulze, T. G., Muglia, P., et al. (2010). Meta-analysis of genome-wide association data identifies a risk locus for major mood disorders on 3p21.1. *Nature Genetics, 42,* 128–131.

McMahon, P. (2000, January 31). Oregon man leads life without frills, leaves $9 million to charities, children. *USA Today,* p. 4A.

McMurrich, S. L., & Johnson, S. L. (2008). Dispositional rumination in individuals with a depression history. *Cognitive Therapy and Research, 32,* 542–553.

McNally, R. J. (2003). Recovering memories of trauma: A view from the laboratory. *Current Directions in Psychological Science, 12,* 32–35.

McNally, R. J. (2007). Mechanisms of exposure therapy: How neuroscience can improve psychological treatments for anxiety disorders. *Clinical Psychology Review, 27,* 750–759.

McNally, R. J., & Amir, N. (1996). Perceptual implicit memory for trauma-related information in posttraumatic stress disorder. *Cognition and Emotion, 10,* 551–556.

McNally, R. J., Clancy, S. A., Barrett, H. M., & Parker, H. A. (2005). Reality monitoring in adults reporting repressed, recovered, or continuous memories of childhood sexual abuse. *Journal of Abnormal Psychology, 114,* 147–152.

McNally, R. J., Clancy, S. A., & Schacter, D. L. (2001). Directed forgetting of trauma cues in adults reporting repressed or recovered memories of childhood sexual abuse. *Journal of Abnormal Psychology, 110,* 151–156.

McNally, R. J., Clancy, S. A., Schacter, D. L., & Pittman, R. K. (2000a). Cognitive processing of trauma cues in adults reporting repressed, recovered, or continuous memories of childhood sexual abuse. *Journal of Abnormal Psychology, 109,* 355–359.

McNally, R. J., Clancy, S. A., Schacter, D. L., & Pittman, R. K. (2000b). Personality profiles, dissociation, and absorption in women reporting repressed, recovered, or continuous memories of childhood sexual abuse. *Journal of Consulting and Clinical Psychology, 68,* 1033–1037.

McNally, R. J., & Geraerts, E. (2009). A new solution to the recovered memory debate. *Perspectives on Psychological Science, 4,* 126–134.

McNay, E. C., McCarty, R. C., & Gold, P. E. (2001). Fluctuations in brain glucose concentration during behavioral testing: Dissociations between brain areas and between brain and blood. *Neurobiology of Learning and Memory, 75,* 325–337.

McNeil, D. W., & Zvolensky, M. J. (2000). Systematic desensitization. In A. E. Kazdin (Ed.), *Encyclopedia of psychology* (Vol. 7, pp. 533–535). Washington, DC: American Psychological Association.

McNeil, J. E., & Warrington, E. K. (1993). Prosopagnosia: A face-specific disorder. *Quarterly Journal of Experimental Psychology: Human Experimental Psychology, 46A,* 1–10.

McNelis, P. D. (2004). Neural networks in finance: Gaining predictive edge in the market. San Diego, CA: Academic Press.

McNulty, J. K., & Karney, B. R. (2004). Positive expectations in the early years of marriage: Should couples expect the best or brace for the worst? *Journal of Personality and Social Psychology, 86*, 729–743.

Medin, D. L., Ross, B. H., & Markman, A. B. (2001). *Cognitive psychology* (3rd ed.). Fort Worth, TX: Harcourt.

Medina-Mora, M. E., Borges, G., Lara, C., Benjet, C., et al. (2005). Prevalence, service use, and demographic correlates of 12-month DSM-IV psychiatric disorders in Mexico: Results from the Mexican National Comorbidity Study. *Psychological Medicine, 35,* 1773–1783.

Mednick, S., Nakayama, K., & Stickgold, R. (2003). Sleep-dependent learning: A nap is as good as a night. *Nature Neuroscience, 6,* 697–698.

Mehl, M. R. & Pennebaker, J. W. (2003). The social dynamics of a cultural upheaval: Social interactions surrounding September 11, 2001. *Psychological Science, 14,* 579–585.

Mehl, M. R., Vazire, S., Holleran, S. E., & Clark, C. S. (2010). Eavesdropping on happiness: Well-being is related to having less small talk and more substantive conversations. *Psychological Science, 21,* 539–541.

Meichenbaum, D. (1977). *Cognitive behavior modification: An integrative approach.* New York: Plenum.

Meichenbaum, D. (2003). *Treatment of individuals with anger-control problems and aggressive behaviors.* Bethel, CT: Crown House.

Meiser, T., & Hewstone, M. (2006). Illusory and spurious correlations: Distinct phenomena or joint outcomes of exemplar-based category learning? *European Journal of Social Psychology, 36,* 315–336.

Melamed, S., Fried, Y., & Froom, P. (2001). The interactive effect of chronic exposure to noise and job complexity on changes in blood pressure and job satisfaction: A longitudinal study of industrial employees. *Journal of Occupational Health Psychology, 6,* 182–195.

Melamed, S., Shirom, A., Toker, S., Berliner, S., & Shapira, I. (2006). Burnout and risk of cardiovascular disease: Evidence, possible causal paths, and promising research directions. *Psychological Bulletin, 132,* 327–353.

Melchior, C. L. (1990). Conditioned tolerance provides protection against ethanol lethality. *Pharmacology, Biochemistry, and Behavior, 37,* 205–206.

Mellon, R. C. (2009). Superstitious perception: Response-independent reinforcement and punishment as determinants of recurring eccentric interpretations. *Behaviour Research and Therapy, 47,* 868–875.

Melzack, R., & Wall, P. D. (1965). Pain mechanisms: A new theory. *Science, 150,* 971–979.

Menaker, M., & Vogelbaum, M. A. (1993). Mutant circadian period as a marker of suprachiasmatic nucleus function. *Journal of Biological Rhythms, 8,* 93–98.

Mendez, I., Sanchez-Pernaute, R., Cooper, O., Viñuela, A., et al. (2005). Cell type analysis of functional fetal dopamine cell suspension transplants in the striatum and substantia nigra of patients with Parkinson's disease. *Brain, 128,* 1498–1510.

Mendez, I., Viñuela, A., Astradsson, A., Mukhida, K., et al. (2008). Dopamine neurons implanted into people with Parkinson's disease survive without pathology for 14 years. *Nature Medicine, 14,* 507–509.

Mendle, J., Harden, K. P., Turkheimer, E., Van Hulle, C. A., et al. (2009). Associations between father absence and age of first sexual intercourse. *Child Development, 80,* 1463–1480.

Mendle, J., Turkheimer, E., & Emery, R. E. (2007). Detrimental psychological outcomes associated with early pubertal timing in adolescent girls. *Developmental Review, 27,* 151–171.

Mennella, J. A., & Beauchamp, G. K. (1996). The human infant's response to vanilla flavors in mother's milk and formula. *Infant Behavior and Development, 19,* 13–19.

Menon, G. J., Rahman, I., Menon, S. J., & Dutton, G. N. (2003). Complex visual hallucinations in the visually impaired: The Charles Bonnet syndrome. *Survey of Ophthalmology, 48,* 58–72.

Mental health: Does therapy help? (1995, November). *Consumer Reports,* pp. 734–739.

Mente, A., de Koning, L., Shannon, H. S., & Anand, S. S. (2009). A systematic review of the evidence supporting a causal link between dietary factors and coronary heart disease. *Archives of Internal Medicine, 169,* 659–669.

Merchant, J. A., & Lundell, J. A. (2001). *Workplace violence: A report to the nation.* Iowa City: University of Iowa Injury Prevention Research Center.

Merckelbach, H., Devilly, G. J., & Rassin, E. (2002). Alters in dissociative identity disorder: Metaphors or genuine entities? *Clinical Psychology Review, 22,* 481–497.

Meredith, E., & Baker, M. (2007). Factors associated with choosing a career in clinical psychology: Undergraduate minority ethnic perspectives. *Clinical Psychology and Psychotherapy, 14,* 475–487.

Meriac, J. P., Hoffman, B. J., Woehr, D. J., & Fleisher, M. S. (2008). Further evidence for the validity of assessment center dimensions: A meta-analysis of the incremental criterion-related validity of dimension ratings. *Journal of Applied Psychology, 93,* 1042–1052.

Merikangas, K. R., Akiskal, H. S., Angst, J., Greenberg, P. E., et al. (2007). Lifetime and 12-month prevalence of bipolar spectrum disorder in the national comorbidity survey replication. *Archives of General Psychiatry, 64,* 543–552.

Merikangas, K. R., He, J.-P., Body, D., Fisher, P. W., et al. (2010). Prevalence and treatment of mental disorders among U.S. children in the 2001–2004 NHANES. *Pediatrics, 125,* 75–81.

Merritt, M. M.; Bennett, G. G., Jr.; Williams, R. B.; Edwards, C. L.; & Sollers, J. J., III. (2006). Perceived racism and cardiovascular reactivity and recovery to personally relevant stress. *Health Psychology, 25,* 364–369.

Merry, T., & Brodley, B. T. (2002). The nondirective attitude in client-centered therapy: A response to Kahn. *Journal of Humanistic Psychology, 42,* 66–77.

Mercier, C. & Sirigu, A. (2009). Training with virtual feedback to alleviate phantom limb pain. *Neurorehabilitation and Neural Repair, 23,* 587–594.

Mesman, J., & Koot, H. M. (2000). Common and specific correlates of preadolescent internalizing externalizing psychopathology. *Journal of Abnormal Psychology, 109,* 428–437.

Mesquita, B., & Frijda, N. H. (1992). Cultural variations in emotions: A review. *Psychological Bulletin, 112,* 179–204.

Messer, S. B., & Kaplan, A. H. (2004). Outcomes and factors related to efficacy of brief psychodynamic therapy. In D. P. Charman (Ed.), *Core processes in brief psychodynamic psychotherapy: Advancing effective practice* (pp. 103–118). Mahwah, NJ: Erlbaum.

Messick, S. (1989). Validity. In R. Linn (Ed.), *Educational measurement* (3rd ed., pp. 13–103). New York: American Council on Education/Macmillan.

Messinger, A., Squire, L. R., Zola, S. M., & Albright, T. D. (2001). Neuronal representations of stimulus associations develop in the temporal lobe during learning. *Proceedings of the National Academy of Sciences, 98,* 12239–12244.

Messinger, D. S., Bauer, C. R., Das, A., Seifer, R., et al. (2004). The maternal lifestyle study: Cognitive, motor, and behavioral outcomes of cocaine-exposed and opiate-exposed infants through three years of age. *Pediatrics, 113,* 1677–1685.

Meston, C. M., & Buss, D. M. (2007). Why humans have sex. *Archives of Sexual Behavior, 36,* 477–507.

Mesulam, M. M. (1990). Large-scale neurocognitive networks and distributed processing for attention, language, and memory. *Annals of Neurology, 28,* 597–613.

Mesulam, M. M. (2001). Primary progressive aphasia. *Annals of Neurolology, 49,* 425–423.

Metalsky, G. I., Abramson, L. Y., Seligman, M. E. P., Semmel, A., & Peterson, C. (1982). Attributional styles and life events in the classroom: Vulnerability and invulnerability to depressive mood reactions. *Journal of Personality and Social Psychology, 43,* 612–617.

Metzinger, T. (Ed.). (2000). *Neural correlates of consciousness: Empirical and conceptual questions.* Cambridge, MA: MIT Press.

Meyer, G. J., Finn, S. E., Eyde, L. D., Kay, G. G., et al. (2001). Psychological testing and psychological assessment: A review of evidence and issues. *American Psychologist, 56,* 128–165.

Meyer, G. J., Mihura, J. L., & Smith, B. L. (2005). The interclinician reliability of Rorschach interpretation in four data sets. *Journal of Personality Assessment, 84,* 296–314.

Meyer, I. H. (2003). Prejudice, social stress, and mental health in lesbian, gay, and bisexual populations: Conceptual issues and research evidence. *Psychological Bulletin, 129,* 674–697.

Meyer, J. D., & Salovey, P. (1997). What is emotional intelligence? In P. Salovey & D. Sluyter (Eds.), *Emotional development and emotional intelligence* (pp. 3–31). New York: Basic Books.

Meyer, R. D., Dalal, R. S., & Bonaccio, S. (2009). A meta-analytic investigation into the moderating effects of situational strength on the conscientiousness-performance relationship. *Journal of Organizational Behavior, 30,* 1077–1102.

Meyer, R. G. (1975). A behavioral treatment of sleepwalking associated with test anxiety. *Behavior Therapy and Experimental Psychiatry, 6,* 167–168.

Meyer, U., Feldon, J., Schedlowski, M., & Yee, B. K. (2005). Toward and immunoprecipitated neurodevelopmental animal model of schizophrenia. *Neuroscience and Biobehavioral Reviews, 29,* 913–947.

Meyer-Bahlburg, H. F. L., Dolezal, C., Baker, S., & New, M. (2008). Sexual orientation in women with classical or nonclassical congenital adrenal hyperplasia as a function of degree of prenatal androgen excess. *Archives of Sexual Behavior, 37,* 85–99.

Meyers, C., & Jones, T. B. (1993). *Promoting active learning: Strategies for the college classroom.* San Francisco: Jossey-Bass.

Mezey, E., Key, S., Vogelsang, G., Szalayova, I., et al. (2003). Transplanted bone marrow generates new neurons in human brains. *Proceedings of the National Academy of Sciences, 100,* 1364–1369.

Mezulis, A. H., Abramson, L. Y., Hyde, J. S., & Hankin, B. L. (2004). Is there a universal positivity bias in attributions? A meta-analytic review of individual, developmental, and cultural differences in the self-serving attributional bias. *Psychological Bulletin, 130,* 711–747.

Mezzacappa, E. S., Katkin, E. S. & Palmer, S. N. (1999). Epinephrine, arousal and emotion: A new look at two-factor theory. *Cognition and Emotion, 13,* 181–199.

Miceli, G., Fouch, E., Capasso, R., Shelton, J. R., et al. (2001). The dissociation of color from form and function knowledge. *Nature Neuroscience, 4,* 662–667.

Michael, R. T., Wadsworth, J., Feinleib, J., Johnson, A. M., et al. (1998). Private sexual behavior, public opinion, and public health policy related to sexually transmitted diseases: A U.S.-British comparison. *American Journal of Public Health, 88,* 749–754.

Michel, C., Rossion, B., Han, J., Chung, C.-S., & Caldara, R. (2006). Holistic processing is finely tuned for faces of one's own race. *Psychological Science, 17,* 608–615.

Michelena, P., Sibbald, A. M., Erhard, H. W., & McLeod, J. E. (2009). Effects of group size and personality on social foraging: The distribution of sheep across patches. *Behavioral Ecology, 20,* 145–152.

Mick, E., Biederman, J., Prince, J., Fischer, M. J., & Faraone, S. V. (2002). Impact of low birth weight on attention-deficit hyperactivity disorder. *Journal of Developmental and Behavioral Pediatrics, 23,* 16–22.

Middeldorp, C. M., Cath, D. C., Van Dyck, R., & Boomsma, D. I., (2005). The co-morbidity of anxiety and depression in the perspective of genetic epidemiology: A review of twin and family studies. *Psychological Medicine, 35,* 611–624.

Miklowitz, D. J. (2008). Adjunctive psychotherapy for bipolar disorder: State of the evidence. *American Journal of Psychiatry, 165,* 1408–1419.

Miklowitz, D. J., Otto, M. W., Frank, E., Reilly Harrington, N. A., et al. (2007). Psychosocial treatments for bipolar depression. *Archives of General Psychiatry, 64,* 419–426.

Mikulincer, M., & Shaver, P. R. (2005). Mental representations of attachment security: Theoretical foundation for a positive social psychology. In M. W. Baldwin (Ed.), *Interpersonal cognition* (pp. 233–266). New York: Guilford Press.

Miklincer, M., & Shaver, P. R. (2011). Adult attachment and caregiving: Individual differences in providing a safe haven and secure base to others. In S. L. Brown, R. M. Brown, & L. A. Penner (Eds.), *Self-interest and beyond: Toward a new understanding of human.* New York: Oxford University Press.

Milan, G., Lamenza, F., Iavarone, A., Galeone, F., et al. (2008). Frontal behavioural inventory in the differential diagnosis of dementia. *Acta Neurologica Scandinavica, 117,* 260–265.

Milev, P., Ho, B. C., Arndt, S., & Andreasen, N. C. (2005). Predictive values of neurocognition and negative symptoms on functional outcome in schizophrenia: A longitudinal first-episode study with 7-year follow-up. *American Journal of Psychiatry, 162,* 495–506.

Milgram, N. W., Siwak-Tapp, C. T., Araujo, J., & Head, E. (2006). Neuroprotective effects of cognitive enrichment. *Ageing Research Reviews, 5,* 354–369.

Milgram, S. (1963). Behavioral study of obedience. *Journal of Abnormal and Social Psychology, 67,* 371–378.

Milgram, S. (1965). Some conditions of obedience and disobedience to authority. *Human Relations, 18,* 57–76.

Milgram, S. (1974). *Obedience to authority.* New York: Harper & Row.

Milgram, S. (1977, October). Subject reaction: The neglected factor in the ethics of experimentation. *Hastings Center Report,* pp. 19–23.

Milisen, K., Braes, T., Fick, D. M., & Foreman, M. D. (2006). Cognitive assessment and differentiating the 3 Ds (dementia, depression, delirium). *Nursing Clinics of North America, 41,* 1–22.

Millar, H. R., Wardell, F., Vyvyan, J. P., Naji, S. A., et al. (2005). Anorexia nervosa mortality in northeast Scotland, 1965–1999. *American Journal of Psychiatry, 162,* 753–757.

Miller, B. L. (2007). Frontotemporal dementia and semantic dementia: Anatomic variations on the same disease or distinctive entities? *Alzheimer Disease and Associated Disorders, 21,* S19–S22.

Miller, C. L., Miceli, P. J., Whitman, T. L., & Borkowski, J. G. (1996). Cognitive readiness to parent and intellectual-emotional development in children of adolescent mothers. *Developmental Psychology, 32,* 533–541.

Miller, D. D., McEvoy, J. P., Davis, S. M., Caroff, S. N., et al. (2005). Clinical correlates of tardive dyskinesia in schizophrenia: Baseline data from the CATIE schizophrenia trial. *Schizophrenia Research, 80,* 33–43.

Miller, G. (1956). The magical number seven, plus or minus two: Some limits on our capacity to process information. *Psychological Review, 63,* 81–97.

Miller, G. (2006). The unseen: Mental illness's global toll. *Science, 311,* 458–461.

Miller, G., Tybur, J. M., & Jordan, B. D. (2007). Ovulatory cycle effects on tip earnings by lap dancers: Economic evidence for human estrus? *Evolution and Human Behavior, 28,* 375–381.

Miller, G. A. (1991). *The science of words.* New York: Scientific American Library.

Miller, G. A., Heise, G. A., & Lichten, W. (1951). The intelligibility of speech as a function of the context of the test materials. *Journal of Experimental Psychology, 41,* 329–335.

Miller, I. J., Jr. (1986). Variation in human fungiform taste bud densities among regions and subjects. *Anatomical Record, 216,* 474–482.

Miller, J. (2001). The cultural grounding of social psychological theory. In A. Tesser & N. Schwarz (Eds.), *Blackwell handbook of social psychology: Intraindividual processes* (pp. 22–43). Oxford: Blackwell.

Miller, J. D., Lynam, D., Zimmerman, R. S., Logan, T. K., et al. (2004). The utility of the five-factor model in understanding risky sexual behavior. *Personality and Individual Differences, 36,* 1611–1626.

Miller, K. F., Smith, C. M., Zhu, J., & Zhang, H. (1995). Preschool origins of cross-national differences in mathematical competence: The role of number-naming systems. *Psychological Science, 6,* 56–60.

Miller, L. C., Putcha-Bhagavatula, A., & Pedersen, W. C. (2002). Men's and women's mating preferences: Distinct evolutionary mechanisms? *Current Directions in Psychological Science, 11,* 88–93.

Miller, L. T., & Vernon, P. A. (1992). The general factor in short-term memory, intelligence, and reaction time. *Intelligence, 16,* 5–29.

Miller, M. M., & McEwen, B. S. (2006). Establishing an agenda for translational research on PTSD. *Annals of the New York Academy of Sciences, 1071,* 294–312.

Miller, N. E. (1959). Liberalization of basic S-R concepts: Extensions to conflict behavior, motivation, and social learning. In S. Koch (Ed.), *Psychology: A study of science* (Vol. 2, pp. 196–292). New York: McGraw-Hill.

Miller, S. L., & Maner, J. K. (2010). Scent of a woman: Men's testosterone responses to olfactory ovulation cues. *Psychological Science, 21,* 276–283. doi:10.1177/0956797609357733

Miller, T. Q., Heath, L., Molcan, J. R., & Dugoni, B. L. (1991). Imitative violence in the real world: A reanalysis of homicide rates following championship prize fights. *Aggressive Behavior, 17,* 121–134.

Miller, T. W., Nigg, J. T., & Miller, R. L. (2009). Attention deficit hyperactivity disorder in African American children: What can we conclude from the past ten years? *Clinical Psychology Review, 29,* 77–86.

Miller, W. R., & Rollnick, S. (2002). *Motivational interviewing: Preparing people for change* (2nd ed.). New York: Guilford Press.

Millon, T., & Davis, R. D. (1996). *Disorders of personality: DSM-IV and beyond* (2nd ed.). New York: Wiley.

Mills, P. E., Cole, K. N., Jenkins, J. R., & Dale, P. S. (1998). Effects of differing levels of inclusion on preschoolers with disabilities. *Exceptional Children, 65,* 79–90.

Milner, B. (1965). Visually guided maze learning in man: Effects of bilateral hippocampal, bilateral frontal, and unilateral cerebral lesions. *Neuropsychologia, 3,* 317–338.

Milner, B. (1966). Amnesia following operation on temporal lobes. In C. W. M. Whitty & O. L. Zangwill (Eds.), *Amnesia* (pp. 109–123). London: Butterworth.

Milner, B. (1970). Memory and the medial temporal regions of the brain. In K. H. Pribram & D. B. Broadbent (Eds.), *Biology of memory.* New York: Academic Press.

Milner, A. D. & Goodale, M. A. (2008). Two visual systems re-viewed. *Neuropsychologia, 46,* 774–777.

Miltenberger, R. G. (2007). *Behavior modification: Principles and procedures* (4th ed.). Belmont, CA: Wadsworth.

Mineka, S., & Zinbarg, R. (2006). A contemporary learning theory perspective on the etiology of anxiety disorders: It's not what you thought it was. *American Psychologist, 61,* 10–26.

Miner, J. L., & Clarke-Stewart, K. A. (2008). Trajectories of externalizing behavior from age 2 to age 9: Relations with gender, temperament, ethnicity, parenting, and rater. *Developmental Psychology, 44,* 771–786.

Ming, E. E., Adler, G. K., Kessler, R. C., Fogg, L. F., et al. (2004). Cardiovascular reactivity to work stress predicts subsequent onset of hypertension: The air traffic controller health change study. *Psychosomatic Medicine, 66,* 459–465.

Minshew, N. J., & Williams, D. L. (2007). The new neurobiology of autism: Cortex, connectivity, and neuronal organization. *Archives of Neurology, 64,* 945–950.

Minsky, S., Vega, W., Miskimen, T., Gara, M., & Escobar, J. (2003). Diagnostic patterns in Latino, African American, and European American psychiatric patients. *Archives of General Psychiatry, 60,* 637–644.

Minuzzi, L., Nomikos, G. G., Wade, M. R., Jensen, S. B., et al. (2005). Interaction between LSD and dopamine D2/3 binding sites in pig brain. *Synapse, 56,* 198–204.

Minzenberg, M. J., Watrous, A. J., Yoon, J. H., Ursu, S., & Carter, C. S. (2008). Modafinil shifts human locus coeruleus to low-tonic, high-phasic activity during functional MRI. *Science, 322,* 1700–1702.

Miotto, K., Darakjian, J., Basch, J., Murray, S., et al. (2001). Gamma-hydroxybutyric acid: Patterns of use, effects, and withdrawal. *American Journal on Addictions, 10,* 232–241.

Miranda, J., & Green, B. L. (1999). The need for mental health services research focusing on poor young women. *Journal of Mental Health Policy and Economics, 2,* 73–89.

Mischel, W. (2004a). *Introduction to personality: Toward an integration.* Hoboken, NJ: Wiley.

Mischel, W. (2004b). Toward an integrative science of the person. *Annual Review of Psychology, 55,* 1–22.

Mischel, W. (2009). From personality and assessment to personality science. *Journal of Research in Personality, 43,* 282–290.

Mischel, W., & Shoda, Y. (2008). Toward a unified theory of personality: Integrating dispositions and processing dynamics within the cognitive-affective processing system. In O. P. John, R. W. Robins, & L. A. Pervin (Eds.), *Handbook of personality: Theory and research* (3rd ed., pp. 208–241). New York: Guilford Press.

Mitchell, A. J., & Shiri-Feshki, M. (2009). Rate of progression of mild cognitive impairment to dementia: Meta-analysis of 41 robust inception cohort studies. *Acta Psychtrica Scandinavica, 119,* 252–265. Epub 2008 Feb 18.

Mitchell, D. B. (1991). Implicit memory, explicit theories. *Contemporary Psychology, 36,* 1060–1061.

Mitchell, K. J., & Zaragoza, M. S. (1996). Repeated exposure to suggestion and false memory: The role of contextual variability. *Journal of Memory and Learning, 35,* 246–260.

Mitra, M., Wilber, N., Allen, D., & Walker, D. K. (2005). Prevalence and correlates of depression as a secondary condition among disabilities. *American Journal of Orthopsychiatry, 75,* 76–85.

Mitrofan, O., Paul, M., & Spencer, N. (2009). Is aggression in children with behavioural and emotional difficulties associated with television viewing and video game playing? A systematic review. *Child: Care, Health and Development, 35,* 5–15.

Mitte, K. (2005a). A meta-analysis of the efficacy of psycho- and pharmacotherapy in panic disorder with and without agoraphobia. *Journal of Affective Disorders, 88,* 27–45.

Mitte, K. (2005b). Meta-analysis of cognitive-behavioral treatments for generalized anxiety disorder: A comparison with pharmacotherapy. *Psychological Bulletin, 131,* 785–795.

Miura, I. T., Okomoto, Y., Kim, C. C., Steere, M., & Fayol, M. (1993). First graders' cognitive representation of number and understanding of place value. *Journal of Educational Psychology, 81,* 109–114.

Miyagawa, T., Kawashima, M. Nishida, N., Ohashi, J., et al. (2008). Variant between CPT1B and CHKB associated with susceptibility to narcolepsy. *Nature Genetics, 40,* 1324–1328.

Miyamoto, Y., & Kitayama, S. (2002). Cultural variation in correspondence bias: The critical role of attitude diagnosticity of socially constrained behavior. *Journal of Personality and Social Psychology, 83,* 1239–1248.

Mobbs, D., Yu, R., Meyer, M., Passamonti, L., et al. (2009). A key role for similarity in vicarious reward. *Science, 324,* 900.

Moen, P., Erickson, W. A., Agarwal, M., Fields, V., & Todd, L. (2000). *The Cornell Retirement and Well-Being Study. Final report.* Ithaca, NY: Bronfenbrenner Life Course Center, Cornell University.

Moffitt, T. E. (2002). Teen-aged mothers in contemporary Britain. *Journal of Child Psychology and Psychiatry and Allied Disciplines, 43,* 727–742.

Moffitt, T. E., Caspi, A., & Rutter, M. (2005). Strategy for investigating interactions between measured genes and measured environments. *Archives of General Psychiatry, 62,* 473–481.

Moghaddam, F. M. (2005). The staircase to terrorism: A psychological exploration. *American Psychologist, 60,* 161–169.

Mohr, C., Binkofski, F., Erdmann, C., Buchel, C., & Helmchen, C. (2005). The anterior cingulate cortex contains distinct areas dissociating external from self-administered painful stimulation: A parametric fMRI study. *Pain, 114,* 347–357.

Mohr, C., Rohrenbach, C. M., Landis, T., & Regard, M. (2001). Associations to smell are more pleasant than to sound. *Journal of Clinical and Experimental Neuropsychology, 23,* 484–489.

Mohr, D. C., Hart, S. L., Julian, L., Catledge, C., et al. (2005). Telephone-administered psychotherapy for depression. *Archives of General Psychiatry, 62,* 1007–1014.

Mojtabai, R., & Olfson, M. (2010). National trends in psychotropic medication polypharmacy in office-based psychiatry. *Archives of General Psychiatry, 67,* 26–36.

Mokdad, A. H., Marks, J. S., Stroup, D. F., & Gerberding, J. L. (2004). Actual causes of death in the United States, 2000. *Journal of the American Medical Association, 291,* 1238–1245.

Molden, D. C., & Dweck, C. S. (2000). Meaning and motivation. In C. Sansone & J. M. Harackiewicz (Eds.), *Intrinsic and extrinsic motivation: The search for optimal motivation and performance* (pp. 131–161). San Diego, CA: Academic Press.

Moller, A. C., Elliot, A. J., & Friedman, R. (2008). When competence and love are at stake: Achievement goals and perceived closeness to parents in an achievement context. *Journal of Research in Personality, 42,* 1386–1391.

Molsa, P. K., Marttila, R. J., & Rinne, U. K. (1995). Long-term survival and predictors of mortality in Alzheimer's disease and multi-infarct dementia. *Acta Neurologica Scandinavica, 91,* 159–164.

Monane, M., Leichter, D., & Lewis, O. (1984). Physical abuse in psychiatrically hospitalized children and adolescents. *Journal of the American Academy of Child and Adolescent Psychiatry, 23,* 653–658.

Moncrief, W. C., Babakus, E., Cravens, D. W., & Johnston, M. W. (2000). Examining gender differences in field sales organizations. *Journal of Business Research, 49,* 245–257.

Moncrieff, J., & Kirsch, I. (2005). Efficacy of antidepressants in adults. *British Medical Journal, 331*, 155–157.

Mongillo, G., Barak, O., & Tsodyks, M. (2008). Synaptic theory of working memory. *Science, 319*, 1543–1546.

Moniz, E (1948). How I came to perform prefrontal leucotomy. *Proceedings of the First International Congress of Psychosurgery* (pp. 7–18). Lisbon, Portugal: Edicões Atica.

Monroe, S. M., & Reid, M. W. (2009). Life stress and major depression. *Current Directions in Psychological Science, 18*, 68–72.

Monroe, S. M., Thase, M. E., & Simons, A. D. (1992). Social factors and psychobiology of depression: Relations between life stress and rapid eye movement sleep latency. *Journal of Abnormal Psychology, 101*, 528–537.

Montague, P. R., Hyman, S. E., & Cohen, J. D. (2004). Computational roles for dopamine in behavioural control. *Nature, 431*, 760–767.

Monteith, M. J., Arthur, S. A., & Flynn, S. M. (2010). Self-regulation and bias. In J. F. Dovidio, M. Hewstone, P. Glick, & V. M. Esses (Eds.), *Handbook of prejudice, stereotyping, and discrimination* (pp. 493–507). London: Sage.

Montelone, P., & Maj, M. (2008). The circadian basis of mood disorders: Recent developments and treatment implications. *European Neuropsychopharmacology, 18*, 701–711.

Monterosso, J., Ainslie, R., Mullen, P. A., & Gault, B. (2002). The fragility of cooperation: A false feedback study of a sequential iterated prisoner's dilemma. *Journal of Economic Psychology, 23*, 437–448.

Montmayeur, J. P., Liberles, S. D., Matsunami, H., & Buck, L. B. (2001). A candidate taste receptor gene near a sweet taste locus. *Nature Neuroscience, 4*, 492–498.

Moon, R., Calabrese, T., & Aird, L. (2008). Reducing the risk of sudden infant death syndrome in child care and changing provider practices: Lessons learned from a demonstration project. *Pediatrics, 122*, 788–798.

Moon, Y. (2003). Don't blame the computer: When self-disclosure moderates the self-serving bias. *Journal of Consumer Psychology, 13*, 125–137.

Moore, D., Aveyard, P., Connock, M., Wang, D., et al. (2009). Effectiveness and safety of nicotine replacement therapy assisted reduction to stop smoking: Systematic review and meta-analysis. *British Medical Journal, 338*, b1024.

Moore, J. W., Tingstom, D. H., Doggett, R. A., & Carlyon, W. D. (2001). Restructuring an existing token economy in a psychiatric facility for children. *Child and Family Behavior Therapy, 23*, 53–60.

Moore, K. (2009, October 26). "Amnesia girl" drained bank account before vanishing. *KING5 News*. Retrieved from http://www.king5.com/home/NYC-amnesia-teen-identified-as-Kitsap-Co-resident--65981942.html

Moore, K. A. (2005). *Family strengths: Often overlooked, but real.* Washington, DC: Child Trends.

Moore, K. A. (2009). Teen births: Examining the recent increase. *Child Trends Research Brief.* Retrieved from http://www.childtrends.org/Files/Child_Trends_2009_03_13_FS_TeenBirthRate.pdf

Moore, M. R. & Brooks-Gunn, J. (2002). Adolescent parenthood. In M. H. Bornstein (Ed.), *Handbook of parenting* (2nd ed., Vol. 3, pp. 173–214). Mahwah, NJ: Erlbaum.

Moore, S. A., Zoellner, L. A., & Bittinger, J. N. (2004). Combining cognitive restructuring and exposure therapy: Toward an optimal integration. In S. Taylor (Ed.), *Advances in the treatment of posttraumatic stress disorder: Cognitive-behavioral perspectives* (pp. 129–149). New York: Springer.

Moore, T.H.M., Zammit, S., Lingford-Hughes, A., Barnes, T.R.E., et al. (2007). Cannabis use and risk of psychotic or affective mental health outcomes: A systematic review. *Lancet, 370*, 319–328.

Moran, C. C. (2002). Humor as a moderator of compassion fatigue. In C. R. Figley (Ed.), *Treating compassion fatigue* (pp. 139–154). New York: Brunner/Routledge.

Moran, D. R. (2000, June). *Is active learning for me?* Poster presented at APS Preconvention Teaching Institute, Denver.

Moran, R. (2006). Learning in high-tech and multimedia environments. *Current Directions in Psychological Science, 15*, 63–67.

Morewedge, C. K., Gilbert, D. T., & Wilson, T. D. (2005). The least likely of times: How remembering the past biases forecasts of the future. *Psychological Science, 16*, 626–630.

Morgan, C. A., Doran, A., Steffian, G., Hazlett, G., & Southwick, S. M. (2006). Stress-induced deficits in working memory and visuo-constructive abilities in special operations soldiers. *Biological Psychiatry, 60*, 722–729.

Morgan, C. D., & Murray, H. A. (1935). A method for investigating fantasy: The Thematic Apperception Test. *Archives of Neurology and Psychiatry, 34*, 289–306.

Morgan, D., Diamond, D. M., Gottschall, P. E., Ugen, K. E., et al. (2000). A beta peptide vaccination prevents memory loss in an animal model of Alzheimer's disease. *Nature, 408*, 982–985.

Morgeson, F. P., Johnson, M. D., Campion, M. A., Medsker, G. J., & Mumford, T. V. (2006). Understanding reactions to job redesign: A quasi-experimental investigation of the moderating effects of organizational context on perceptions of performance behavior. *Personnel Psychology, 59*, 333–363.

Morillo, C., Belloch, A., & Garcia-Soriano, G. (2007). Clinical obsessions in obsessive-compulsive patients and obsession-relevant intrusive thoughts in non-clinical, depressed and anxious subjects: Where are the differences? *Behaviour Research and Therapy, 45*, 1319–1333.

Morin, A. (2006). Levels of consciousness and self-awareness: A comparison and integration of various neurocognitive views. *Consciousness and Cognition, 15*, 358–371.

Morin, C. M., Bélanger, L., Le Blanc, M., Ivers, H., et al. (2009). The natural history of insomnia: A population-based 3-year longitudinal study. *Archives of Internal Medicine, 169*, 447–453.

Morino, M., Toppino, M., Forestieri, P., Angrisani, L., et al. (2007). Mortality after bariatric surgery: Analysis of 13,871 morbidly obese patients from a national registry. *Annals of Surgery, 246*, 1002–1007.

Morisano, D., Hirsh, J. B., Peterson, J. B., Pihl, R. O., & Shore, B. M. (2010). Setting, elaborating, and reflecting on personal goals improves academic performance. *Journal of Applied Psychology, 95*, 255–264.

Morisky, D. E., Stein, J. A., Chiao, C., Ksobiech, K., & Malow, R. (2006). Impact of a social influence intervention on condom use and sexually transmitted infections among establishment-based female sex workers in the Philippines: A multilevel analysis. *Health Psychology, 25*, 595–603.

Morling, B., & Kitayama, S. (2008). Culture and motivation. In J. Y Shah, & W. L. Gardner (Eds.), *Handbook of motivation science* (pp. 417–433). New York: Guilford Press.

Morris, J. S., DeGelder, B., Weiskrantz, L., & Dolan, R. J. (2001). Differential extrageniculostriate and amygdala responses to presentation of emotional faces in a cortically blind field. *Brain, 124*, 1241–1252.

Morris, J. S., Friston, K. J., Buchel, C., Frith, C. D., et al. (1998). A neuromodulatory role for the human amygdala in processing emotional facial expressions. *Brain, 121*, 47–57.

Morris, L. (2000, December 5). Hold the anaesthetic: I'll hypnotise myself instead. *Daily Mail*, p. 25.

Morris, M. C., Ciesla, J. A., & Garber, J. (2008). A prospective study of the cognitive-stress model of depressive symptoms in adolescents. *Journal of Abnormal Psychology, 117*, 719–734.

Morris, M. C., Evans, D. A., Tangney, C. C., Bienias, J. L., & Wilson, R. S. (2006). Associations of vegetable and fruit consumption with age-related cognitive change. *Neurology, 67*, 1370–1376.

Morrison, S. J., & Demorest, S. M. (2009). Cultural constraints on music perception and cognition. *Progress in Brain Research, 178*, 67–77.

Morrissette, D. A., Parachikova, A., Green, K. N., & Laferla, F. M. (2008). Relevance of transgenic mouse models to human Alzheimer disease. *Journal of Biological Chemistry, 284*, 6033–6037. Epub 2008 Oct 22.

Morrongiello, B. A., & Hogg, K. (2004). Mothers' reactions to children misbehaving in ways that can lead to injury: Implications for gender differences in children's risk taking and injuries. *Sex Roles, 50*, 103–118.

Morton, B. E., & Rafto, S. E. (2006). Corpus callosum size is linked to dichotic deafness and hemisphericity, not sex or handedness. *Brain and Cognition, 62*, 1–8.

Morton, G. J., Cummings, D. E., Baskin, D. G., Barsh, G. S., & Schwartz, M. W. (2006). Central nervous system control of food intake and body weight. *Nature, 443*, 289–295.

Moscovici, S. (1985). Social influence and conformity. In G. Lindzey & E. Aronson (Eds.), *The handbook of social psychology* (3rd ed., Vol. 2, pp. 347–412). New York: Random House.

Moses, E. B., & Barlow, D. H. (2006). A new unified treatment approach for emotional disorders based on emotion science. *Current Directions in Psychological Science, 15*, 146–150.

Moskowitz, G. B. (2005). *Social cognition: Understanding self and others.* New York: Guilford Press.

Moskowitz, J. T., Hult, J. R., Bussolari, C., & Acree, M. (2009). What works in coping with HIV? A meta-analysis with implications for coping with serious illness. *Psychological Bulletin, 135*, 121–141.

Moss, E., Bureau, J.-F., Cyr, C., Mongeau, C., & Saint-Laurent, D. (2004). Correlates of attachment at age 3: Construct validity of the preschool attachment classification system. *Developmental Psychology, 40*, 323–334.

Mostert, M. P. (2001). Facilitated communication since 1995: A review of published studies. *Journal of Autism and Developmental Disorders, 31*, 287–313.

Motowidlo, S. J., Brownlee, A. L., & Schmit, M. J. (2008). Effects of personality characteristics on knowledge, skill, and performance in servicing retail customers. *International Journal of Selection and Assessment, 16*, 272–280.

Moussavi, S., Chatterji, S., Verdes, E., Tandon, A., et al. (2007). Depression, chronic diseases, and decrements in health: Results from the World Health Surveys. *Lancet, 370*, 851–858.

Mozzachiodi, R., Lorenzetti, F. D., Baxter, D. A., & Byrne, J. H. (2008). Changes in neuronal excitability serve as a mechanism of long-term memory for operant conditioning. *Nature Neuroscience, 11*, 1146–1148.

Mroczek, D. K., & Spiro, A., III. (2005). Changing life satisfaction during adulthood: Findings from the Veterans Affairs normative aging study. *Journal of Personality and Social Psychology, 88*, 189–202.

Mucchi-Faina, A., & Pagliaro, S. (2008). Minority influence: The role of ambivalence toward the source. *European Journal of Social Psychology, 38*, 612–623.

Muchinsky, P. M. (2003). *Psychology applied to work* (7th ed.). Belmont, CA: Wadsworth.

Mühlberger, A., Wiedemann, G., Herrmann, M. J., & Pauli, P. (2006). Phylo- and ontogenetic fears and the expectation of danger: Differences between spider- and flight-phobic subjects in cognitive and physiological responses to disorder-specific stimuli. *Journal of Abnormal Psychology, 115*, 580–589.

Mueller, K. L., Hoon, M. A., Erlenbach, I., Chandrashekar, J., et al. (2005). The receptors and coding logic for bitter taste. *Nature, 434*, 225–229.

Müller, T. D., Föcker, M., Holtkamp, K., Herpertz-Dahlamnn, B., & Hebebrand, J. (2009). Leptin-mediated neuroendocrine alterations in anorexia nervosa: Somatic and behavioral implications. *Child and Adolescent Psychiatric Clinics of North America, 18*, 117–129.

Mueser, K. T., & Jeste, D. V. (Eds.). (2009). *Clinical handbook of schizophrenia.* New York: Guilford Press.

Mufson, L., Polack, D., & Moreau, D. (2004). *Interpersonal psychotherapy for depressed adolescents* (2nd ed.). New York: Guilford Press.

Muggleton, N. G., Chen, C. Y., Tzeng, O. J., Hung, D. L., & Juan, C. H. (2010). Inhibitory control and the frontal eye fields. *Journal of Cognitive Neuroscience* [Advance online publication]. doi:10.1162/jocn.2010.21416

Muir, J. L. (1997). Acetylcholine, aging, and Alzheimer's disease. *Pharmacological and Biochemical Behavior, 56*, 687–696.

Mullen, B. (1986). Atrocity as a function of lynch mob composition: A self-attention perspective. *Personality and Social Psychology Bulletin, 12*, 187–197.

Mullis, I. V. S., Martin, M. O., Gonzales, E. J., & Chrostowski, S. J. (2004). *TIMSS 2003 international mathematics report: Findings from IEA's Trends in International Mathematics and Science Study at the fourth and eighth grades.* Chestnut Hill, MA: Boston College.

Mullis, I. V. S., Martin, M. O., Kennedy, A. M., & Foy, P. (2007). *PIRLS 2006 international report: IEA's Progress in International Reading Literacy Study in primary school in 40 countries.* Chestnut Hill, MA: Boston College.

Mumford, M. D., Connelly, M. S., Helton, W. B., Strange, J. M., & Osburn, H. K. (2001). On the construct validity of integrity tests: Individual and situational factors as predictors of test performance. *International Journal of Selection and Assessment, 9,* 240–257.

Mumme, D. L., & Fernald, A. (2003). The infant as onlooker: Learning from emotional reactions observed in a television scenario. *Child Development, 74,* 221–237.

Munakata, Y. (2006). Information processing approaches to development. In W. Damon & R. M. Lerner (Series Eds.) & D. Kuhn & R. Siegler (Vol. Eds.), *Handbook of child psychology: Vol. 2. Cognition, perception, and language* (6th ed., pp. 426–463). New York: Wiley.

Munley, P. H. (2002). Comparability of MMPI-2 scales and profiles over time. *Journal of Personality Assessment, 78,* 145–160.

Muñoz, R. F., & Mendelson, T. (2005). Toward evidence-based interventions for diverse populations: The San Francisco General Hospital prevention and treatment manuals. *Journal of Consulting and Clinical Psychology, 73,* 790–799.

Munte, T. F., Altenmuller, E., & Jancke, L. (2002). The musician's brain as a model of neuroplasticity. *Nature Reviews Neuroscience, 3,* 473–478.

Murphy, M. C., Steele, C. M., & Gross, J. J. (2007). Signaling threat: How situational cues affect women in math, science, and engineering settings. *Psychological Science, 18,* 879–885.

Murray, B. (2000, January). Learning from real life. *APA Monitor,* pp. 72–73.

Murray, C. (2003). *Human accomplishment: The pursuit of excellence in the arts and sciences, 800 b.c. to 1950.* New York: HarperCollins.

Murray, E. A., & Mishkin, M. (1985). Amygdalectomy impairs crossmodal association in monkeys. *Science, 228,* 604–606.

Murray, H. A. (1938). *Explorations in personality.* New York: Oxford University Press.

Murray, J. A., & Terry, D. (1999). Parental reactions to infant death: The effects of resources and coping strategies. *Journal of Social and Clinical Psychology, 18,* 341–369.

Mussweiler, T. (2003). "Everything is relative": Comparison processes in social judgment. *European Journal of Social Psychology, 33,* 719–733.

Mustanski, B. S., Chivers, M. L., & Bailey, J. M. (2002). A critical review of recent biological research on human sexual orientation. *Annual Review of Sex Research, 13,* 89–140.

Myers, B. J. (1987). Mother-infant bonding as a critical period. In M. H. Bornstein (Ed.), *Sensitive periods in development: Interdisciplinary perspectives.* Hillsdale, NJ: Erlbaum.

Myers, D. G. (2000). The funds, friends, and faith of happy people. *American Psychologist, 55,* 56–57.

Myers, D. G. (2004). *Intuition: Its powers and perils.* New Haven, CT: Yale University Press.

Myers, K. M., & Davis, M. (2007). Mechanisms of fear extinction. *Molecular Psychiatry, 12,* 120–150.

Myers, K. P., & Sclafani, A. (2006). Development of learned flavor preferences. *Developmental Psychobiology, 48,* 380–388.

Myers, P. I., & Hammill, D. D. (1990). *Learning disabilities: Basic concepts, assessment practices, and instructional strategies.* Austin, TX: Pro-Ed.

Nabata, T., Hakoda, Y., & Ninose, Y. (2010). The functional field of view becomes narrower while viewing negative emotional stimuli. *Cognition and Emotion, 24,* 886–891.

Nadeau, S., & Crosson, B. (1995). A guide to the functional imaging of cognitive processes. *Neuropsychiatry, Neuropsychology, and Behavioral Neurology, 8,* 143–162.

Nader, K., Bechara, A., & Van der Kooy, D. (1997). Neurobiological constraints on behavioral models of motivation. *Annual Review of Psychology, 48,* 85–114.

Nader, K., Schafe, G. E., & Le Doux, J. E. (2000). Fear memories require protein synthesis in the amygdala for reconsolidation after retrieval. *Nature, 406,* 722–726.

Naëgelé, B., Launois, S. H., Mazza, S., Feuerstein, C., et al. (2006). Which memory processes are affected in patients with obstructive sleep apnea? An evaluation of 3 types of memory. *Sleep, 29,* 533–544.

Nägerl, U. V., Willig, K. I., Hein, B., Hell, S. W., & Bonhoeffer, T. (2008). Live-cell imaging of dendritic spines by STED microscopy. *Proceedings of the National Academy of Sciences, 105,* 18982–18987.

Nagy, T. F. (1999). *Ethics in plain English: An illustrative casebook for psychologists.* Washington, DC: American Psychological Association.

Nairne, J. S. (2003). Sensory and working memory. In A. F. P. Healy, R. W. Proctor, & I. B. Weiner (Eds.), *Handbook of psychology: Vol. 4. Experimental psychology* (pp. 423–444). New York: Wiley.

Naito, M., & Miura, H. (2001). Japanese children's numerical competencies: Age- and schooling-related influences on the development of number concepts and addition skills. *Developmental Psychology, 37,* 217–230.

Nakamura, J., & Csikszentmihalyi, M. (2001). Catalytic creativity. *American Psychologist, 56,* 337–341.

Nakano, K., & Kitamura, T. (2001). The relation of the anger subcomponent of Type A behavior to psychological symptoms in Japanese and foreign students. *Japanese Psychological Research, 43,* 50–54.

Nakao, M., & Yano, E. (2006). Prediction of major depression in Japanese adults: Somatic manifestations of depression in annual health examinations. *Journal of Affective Disorders, 90,* 29–35.

Nakayama, K. (1994). James J. Gibson: An appreciation. *Psychological Review, 101,* 329–335.

Naquin, C. E., Kurtzberg, T. R., & Belkin, L. Y. (2010). The finer points of lying online: E-mail versus pen and paper. *Journal of Applied Psychology, 95,* 387–394.

Naragon-Gainey, K. (2010). Meta-analysis of the relations of anxiety sensitivity to the depressive and anxiety disorders. *Psychological Bulletin, 136,* 128–150.

Narayan, V. M., Narr, K. L., Kumari, V., Woods, R. P., et al. (2007). Regional cortical thinning in subjects with violent antisocial personality disorder or schizophrenia. *American Journal of Psychiatry, 164,* 1418–1427.

Nash, I. S., Mosca, L., Blumenthal, R. S., Davidson, M. H., et al. (2003). Contemporary awareness and understanding of cholesterol as a risk factor: Results of an American Heart Association national survey. *Archives of Internal Medicine, 163,* 1597–1600.

Nash, J. R., Sargent, P. A., Rabiner, E. A., Hood, S. D., et al. (2008). Serotonin 5-HT1A receptor binding in people with panic disorder: Positron emission tomography study. *British Journal of Psychiatry, 193,* 229–234.

Nathan, P. E., & Gorman, J. M. (2007). *A guide to treatments that work* (3rd ed.). New York: Oxford University Press.

Nathan, P. E., Stuart, S. P., & Dolan, S. L. (2000). Research on psychotherapy efficacy and effectiveness: Between Scylla and Charybdis? *Psychological Bulletin, 126,* 964–981.

Nathanson, M., Bergman, P. S., & Gordon, G. G. (1952). Denial of illness: Its occurrence in one hundred consecutive cases of hemiplegia. *Archives of Neurology and Psychiatry, 68,* 380–397.

National Association of Anorexia Nervosa and Associated Disorders. (2002). *Facts about eating disorders.* Retrieved from http://www.altrue.net/site/anadweb/content.php?type51&id56982.

National Center for Complementary and Alternative Medicine. (2008, March). St. John's wort. *Herbs at a Glance.* NCCAM Publication No. D269. Retrieved from http://nccam.nih.gov/health/stjohnswort/ataglance.htm#science

National Center for Education Statistics. (2002). *Digest of education statistics, 2001.* Washington, DC: Office of Educational Research and Improvement, U.S. Department of Education.

National Center for Health Statistics. (2007). *Sexual behavior and selected health measures: Men and women 15–44 years of age, United States, 2002.* Hyattsville, MD: U.S. Department of Health and Human Services.

National Center on Addiction and Substance Abuse. (2004). *National Survey of American Attitudes on Substance Abuse: IX. Teen dating practices and sexual activity.* New York: Author.

National Highway Traffic Safety Administration. (2008). *2007 traffic safety annual assessment: Alcohol-impaired driving fatalities.* Retrieved from http://www-nrd.nhtsa.dot.gov/Pubs/811016.pdf

National Information Center for Children and Youth with Disabilities. (2000, June 18). NICHCY Fact Sheet #7. *LD Online.* Retrieved from http://www.ldonline.org/ld_indepth/general_info/gen-2.html

National Institute for Occupational Safety and Health. (1999). *Stress at work.* Washington, DC: Author.

National Institute of Mental Health. (1995). *Medications.* Washington, DC: U.S. Department of Health and Human Services.

National Institute of Mental Health. (2004, April 23). *Statement on antidepressant medications for children: Information for parents and caregivers.* Retrieved from www.nimh.nih.gov.

National Institute of Mental Health. (2006). *The numbers count: Mental disorders in America.* Retrieved from http://www.nimh.nih.gov

National Institute of Mental Health. (2007). *Anxiety disorders.* Retrieved from www.nimh.nih.gov

National Institute of Mental Health. (2008). *Study probes environment-triggered genetic changes in schizophrenia.* Retrieved from http://www.nimh.nih.gov

National Institute of Mental Health. (2009). *Suicide in the U.S.: Statistics and prevention.* Retrieved from http://www.nimh.nih.gov

National Institute on Alcohol Abuse and Alcoholism. (2000). *Tenth special report to the U.S. Congress on alcohol and health.* Bethesda, MD: Author.

National Institute on Alcohol Abuse and Alcoholism. (2001). *Alcoholism: Getting the facts.* Bethesda, MD: Author.

National Institute on Drug Abuse. (2000). Facts about MDMA (ecstacy). *NIDA Notes, 14.* Retrieved from http://drugabuse.gov

National Institute on Drug Abuse. (2004). Marijuana. *NIDA Info Facts.* Retrieved from http://www.nida.nih.gov/Infofax/marijuana.html

National Institutes of Health. (2001). *Eating disorders: Facts about eating disorders and the search for solutions.* Washington, DC: U.S. Department of Health and Human Services.

National Institutes of Health Consensus Conference. (1998). Acupuncture. *Journal of the American Medical Association, 280,* 1518–1524.

National Joint Committee on Learning Disabilities. (1994). *Collective perspective on issues affecting learning disabilities.* Austin, TX: Pro-Ed.

National Safety Council. (2004). *Reports on injuries in America, 2003.* Itasca, IL: Author.

National Science Foundation, Division of Science Resources Statistics. (2009). *Science and engineering degrees, by race/ethnicity of recipients, 1997–2006.* Arlington, VA.: Author. Retrieved from http://www.nsf.gov/statistics/nsf10300

Navarrete-Palacios, E., Hudson, R., Reyes-Guerrero, G., & Guevara-Guzman, R. (2003). Lower olfactory threshold during the ovulatory phase of the menstrual cycle. *Biological Psychology, 63,* 269–279.

Neary, D., Snowden, J. S., & Mann, D. M. (1993). The clinical pathological correlates of lobar atrophy. *Dementia, 4,* 154–159.

Neff, L. A., & Karney, B. R. (2005). To know you is to love you: The implications of global adoration and specific accuracy for marital relationships. *Journal of Personality and Social Psychology, 88,* 480–497.

Neher, A. (1991). Maslow's theory of motivation: A critique. *Journal of Humanistic Psychology, 31,* 89–112.

Neighbors, C., O'Connor, R. M., Lewis, M. A., Chawla, N. , et al. (2008). The relative impact of injunctive norms on college student drinking: The role of reference group. *Psychology of Addictive Behaviors, 22,* 576–581.

Neighbors, H. W., Caldwell, C., Williams, D. R., Nesse, R., et al. (2007). Race, ethnicity, and the use of services for mental disorders. *Archives of General Psychiatry, 64,* 485–494.

Neighbors, H. W., Trierweiler, S. J., Fort, B. C., & Muroff, J. R. (2003). Racial differences in DSM diagnosis using a semi-structured instrument: The importance of clinical judgment in the diagnosis of African Americans. *Journal of Health and Social Behavior, 44,* 237–256.

Neil, A. L., & Christensen, H. (2009). Efficacy and effectiveness of school-based prevention and early intervention programs for anxiety. *Clinical Psychology Review, 29,* 208–215.

Neisser, U. (2000a). Memorists. In U. Neisser & I. E. Hyman Jr. (Eds.), *Memory observed* (2nd ed., pp. 475–478). New York: Worth.

Neisser, U. (2000b). Snapshots or benchmarks? In U. Neisser & I. E. Hyman Jr. (Eds.), *Memory observed* (2nd ed., pp. 68–74). New York: Worth.

Neisser, U., Boodoo, G., Bouchard, T. J., Boykin, A. W., et al. (1996). Intelligence: Knowns and unknowns. *American Psychologist, 51,* 77–101.

Neisser, U., & Harsch, N. (1992). Phantom flashbulbs: False recollections of hearing the news about *Challenger*. In E. Winograd & U. Neisser (Eds.), *Affect and accuracy in recall: Studies of "flashbulb" memories* (pp. 9–31). New York: Cambridge University Press.

Nelken, I. (2008). Processing of complex sounds in the auditory system. *Current Opinion in Neurobiology, 18,* 413–417.

Nelson, C. A. (1999). Neural plasticity and human development. *Current Directions in Psychological Science, 8,* 42–45.

Nelson, C. A. (2006). Of eggshells and thin-skulls: A consideration of racism-related mental illness impacting black women. *International Journal of Law and Psychiatry, 29,* 112–136.

Nelson, C. A. (2007). A neurobiological perspective on early human deprivation. *Child Development Perspectives, 1,* 13–18.

Nelson, C. A., Thomas, K. M., & de Haan, M. (2006). Neural bases of cognitive development. In W. Damon & R. M. Lerner (Series Eds.) & D. Kuhn & R. Siegler (Vol. Eds.), *Handbook of child psychology: Vol. 2. Cognition, perception, and language* (6th ed., pp. 3–57). New York: Wiley.

Nelson, D. L., McKinney, V. M., & Bennett, D. J. (1999). Conscious and automatic uses of memory in cued recall and recognition. In B. H. Challis & B. M. Velichkovsky (Eds.), *Stratification in cognition and consciousness* (p. 173–202). Amsterdam: Benjamins.

Nelson, D. L., McKinney, V. M., Gee, N. R., & Janczura, G. A. (1998). Interpreting the influence of implicitly activated memories on recall and recognition. *Psychological Review, 105,* 299–324.

Nelson, G., & Prilleltensky, I. (2004). *Community psychology: In pursuit of liberation and well-being.* New York: Palgrave Macmillan.

Nelson, K. (1986). Event knowledge and cognitive development. In K. Nelson (Ed.), *Event knowledge: Structure and function in development* (pp. 1–19). Hillsdale, NJ: Erlbaum.

Nelson, K. (1993). The psychological and social origins of autobiographical memory. *Psychological Science, 4,* 7–14.

Nelson, K., & Fivush, R. (2004). The emergence of autobiographical memory: A social cultural developmental theory. *Psychological Review, 111,* 486–511.

Nelson, T. D., & Steele, R. G. (2006). Beyond efficacy and effectiveness: A multifaceted approach to treatment evaluation. *Professional Psychology: Research and Practice, 37,* 389–397.

Nelson-LeGall, S., & Resnick, L. (1998). Help seeking, achievement motivation, and the social practice of intelligence in school. In S. A. Karabenick (Ed.), *Strategic help seeking* (pp. 39–60). Mahwah, NJ: Erlbaum.

Nemeroff, C. B., Heim, C. M., Thase, M. E., Klein, D. N., et al. (2003). Differential responses to psychotherapy versus pharmacotherapy in patients with chronic forms of major depression and childhood trauma. *Proceedings of the National Academy of Sciences, 100,* 14293–14296.

Neovius, M., & Narbro, K. (2008). Cost-effectiveness of pharmacological anti-obesity treatments: A systematic review. *International Journal of Obesity, 32,* 1752–1763.

Nestadt, G., Hsu, F.-C., Samuels, J., Bienvenu, O. J., et al. (2005). Latent structure of the *Diagnostic and Statistical Manual of Mental Disorders, Fourth Edition,* personality disorder criteria. *Comprehensive Psychiatry, 47,* 54–62.

Nestler, E. J. (2001). Molecular basis of long-term plasticity underlying addiction. *National Review of Neuroscience, 2,* 119–128.

Nestoriuc, Y., Rief, W., & Martin, A. (2008). Meta-analysis of biofeedback for tension-type headache: Efficacy, specificity, and treatment moderators. *Journal of Consulting and Clinical Psychology, 76,* 379–396.

Netter, P. (2006). Dopamine challenge tests as an indicator of psychological traits. *Human Psychopharmacology: Clinical and Experimental, 21,* 91–99.

Neubauer, A. C., & Fink, A. (2009). Intelligence and neural efficiency: Measures of brain activation versus measures of functional connectivity in the brain. *Intelligence, 37,* 223–229.

Neubauer, D. N., & Flaherty, K. N. (2009). Chronic insomnia. *Seminars in Neurology, 29,* 340–453.

Neuberg, S. L., Kenrick, D. T., & Schaller, M. (2010). Evolutionary social psychology. In S. T. Fiske, D. T. Gilbert, & G. Lindzey (Eds.), *Handbook of social psychology* (5th ed., Vol. 2, pp. 761–798). Hoboken, NJ: Wiley.

Neumeister, A., Bain, E., Nugent, A. C., Carson, R. E., et al. (2004). Reduced serotonin type 1A receptor binding in panic disorder. *Journal of Neuroscience, 24,* 589–591.

Neves-Pereira, M., Cheung, J. K., Pasdar, A., Zhang, F., et al. (2005). BDNF gene is a risk factor for schizophrenia in a Scottish population. *Molecular Psychiatry, 10,* 208–212.

Neville, H. J., Bavelier, D., Corina, D., Rauschecker, J., et al. (1998). Cerebral organization for language in deaf and hearing subjects: Biological constraints and effects of experience. *Proceedings of the National Academy of Sciences, 95,* 922–929.

Newcombe, N. S., Ambady, N., Eccles, J., Gomez, L., et al. (2009). Psychology's role in mathematics and science education. *American Psychologist, 64,* 538–550.

Newcombe, N. S., Drummey, A. B., Fox, N. A., Lie, E., & Ottinger-Alberts, W. (2000). Remembering early childhood: How much, how, and why (or why not). *Current Directions in Psychological Science, 9,* 55–58.

Newcombe, N. S., & Fox, N. A. (1994). Infantile amnesia: Through a glass darkly. *Child Development, 65,* 31–40.

Newell, A., & Simon, H. A. (1972). *Human problem solving.* Englewood Cliffs, NJ: Prentice Hall.

Newhouse, P., Newhouse, C., & Astur, R. S. (2007). Sex differences in visual-spatial learning using a virtual water maze in pre-pubertal children. *Behavioural Brain Research, 183,* 1–7.

Newnam, S., Griffin, M. A., & Mason, C. (2008). Safety in work vehicles: A multilevel study linking safety values and individual predictors to work-related driving crashes. *Journal of Applied Psychology, 93,* 632–644.

Newpher, T. M., & Ehlers, M. D. (2008). Glutamate receptor dynamics in dendritic microdomains. *Neuron, 58,* 472–497.

Newsome, J. T. (1999). Another side to caregiving: Negative reactions to being helped. *Current Directions in Psychological Science, 8,* 183–187.

Newsome, J. T., & Schulz, R. (1998). Caregiving from the recipient's perspective: Negative reactions to being helped. *Health Psychology, 17,* 172–181.

New treatments for cocaine addiction. (2001). *Harvard Mental Health Letter, 17,* 6–7.

Ng, C. H., Chong, S., Lambert, T., Fan, A., et al. (2005). An inter-ethnic comparison study of clozapine dosage, clinical response, and plasma levels. *International Clinical Psychopharmacology, 20,* 163–168.

Ng, K.-Y., Ang, S., & Chan, K.-Y. (2008). Personality and leader effectiveness: A moderated mediation model of leadership self-efficacy, job demands, and job autonomy. *Journal of Applied Psychology, 93,* 733–743.

Nicassio, P. M., Meyerowitz, B. E., & Kerns, R. D. (2004). The future of health psychology interventions. *Health Psychology, 23,* 132–137.

NICHD Early Child Care Research Network. (2005a). *Child care and child development: Results from the NICHD Study of Early Child Care and Youth Development.* New York: Guilford Press.

NICHD Early Child Care Research Network. (2005b). Duration and developmental timing of poverty and children's cognitive and social development from birth to first grade. *Child Development, 76,* 795–810.

NICHD Early Child Care Research Network. (2006). Infant-mother attachment classification: Risk and protection in relation to changing maternal caregiving quality. *Developmental Psychology, 42,* 38–58.

Nichols, M. P. (2007). *Family therapy: Concepts and methods* (8th ed.). Boston: Allyn & Bacon.

Nichols, R. (1978). Twin studies of ability, personality, and interests. *Homo, 29,* 158–173.

Nicholson, A., Fuhrer, R., & Marmot, M. (2005). Psychological distress as a predictor of CHD events in men: The effect of persistence and components of risk. *Psychosomatic Medicine, 67,* 522–530.

Nickell, J. (1997). Sleuthing a psychic sleuth. *Skeptical Inquirer, 21,* 18–19.

Nickerson, C., Schwarz, N., Diener, E., & Kahneman, D. (2003). Zeroing in on the dark side of the American dream: A closer look at the negative consequences of the goal for financial success. *Psychological Science, 14,* 531–536.

Nickerson, R. A., & Adams, M. J. (1979). Long-term memory for a common object. *Cognitive Psychology, 11,* 287–307.

Nicoll, J., & Kieffer, K. M. (2005, August). *Violence in video games: A review of the empirical research.* Paper presented at the 113th annual meeting of the American Psychological Association, Washington, DC.

Nicotra, A., Critchley, H. D., Mathias, C. J., & Dolan, R. J. (2006). Emotional and autonomic consequences of spinal cord injury explored using functional brain imaging. *Brain, 129,* 718–728.

Nidich, S. I., Rainforth, M. V., Haaga, D. A., Hagelin, J., et al. (2009). A randomized controlled trial on effects of the transcendental meditation program on blood pressure, psychological distress, and coping in young adults. *American Journal of Hypertension, 22,* 1326–1331.

Niederhoffer, K. G., & Pennebaker, J. W. (2002). Sharing one's story: On the benefits of writing or talking about emotional experience. In C. R. Snyder & S. J. Lopez (Eds.), *Handbook of positive psychology* (pp. 573–583). Oxford: Oxford University Press.

Niederman, R., & Richards, D. (2005). Evidence-based dentistry: Concepts and implementation. *Journal of the American College of Dentistry, 72,* 37–41.

Niemela, M., & Saarinen, J. (2000). Visual search for grouped versus ungrouped icons in a computer interface. *Human Factors, 42,* 630–635.

Nienhuys, J. W. (2001). Spontaneous human combustion: Requiem for Phyllis. *Skeptical Inquirer, 25,* 28–34.

Nietzel, M. T. (1999). Psychology applied to the legal system. In A. M. Stec & D. A. Bernstein (Eds.), *Psychology: Fields of application* (pp. 127–147). Boston: Houghton Mifflin.

Nietzel, M. T., & Bernstein, D. A. (1987). *Introduction to clinical psychology* (2nd ed.). Englewood Cliffs, NJ: Prentice Hall.

Nievar, M. A., & Becker, B. J. (2008). Sensitivity as a privileged predictor of attachment: A second perspective on De Wolff and van IJzendoorn's meta-analysis. *Social Development, 17,* 102–114.

Nigg, J. T. (2001). Is ADHD a disinhibitory disorder? *Psychological Bulletin, 127,* 571–598.

Nigg, J. T. (2010). Attention-deficit/hyperactivity disorder: Endophenotypes, structure, and etiological pathways. *Current Directions in Psychological Science, 19,* 24–29.

Niiya, Y., Crocker, J., & Bartmess, E. N. (2004). From vulnerability to resilience: Learning orientations buffer contingent self-esteem from failure. *Psychological Science, 15,* 801–805.

Nijhawan, R. (1997). Visual decomposition of colour through motion extrapolation. *Nature, 386,* 66–69.

Nijstad, B. A., Stroebe, W., & Lodewijkx, H. F. M. (2003). Production blocking and idea generation: Does blocking interfere with cognitive processes? *Journal of Experimental Social Psychology, 39,* 531–548.

Nikolas, M. A., & Burt, S. A. (2010). Genetic and environmental influences on ADHD symptom dimensions of inattention and hyperactivity: A meta-analysis. *Journal of Abnormal Psychology, 119,* 1–17.

Nilsson, G. (1996, November). Some forms of memory improve as people age. *APA Monitor,* p. 27.

Niparko, J. K., Tobey, E. A., Thal, D. J., Eisenberg, L. S., et al. (2010). Spoken language development in children following cochlear implantation. *Journal of the American Medical Association, 303,* 1498–1506.

Nisbett, R. E., & Masuda, T. (2006). Culture and point of view. In R. Viale, D. Andler, & L. A. Hirschfeld (Eds.), *Biological and cultural bases of human inference* (pp. 49–70). Mahwah, NJ: Erlbaum.

Nishimura, T., Mikami, A., Suzuki, J., & Matsuzawa, T. (2003). Descent of the larynx in chimpanzee infants. *Proceedings of the National Academy of Sciences, 100,* 6930–6933.

Nock, M. K., Kazdin, A. E., Hirpi, E., & Kessler, R. C. (2006). Prevalence, subtypes, and correlates of DSM-IV conduct disorder in the National Comorbidity Survey Replication. *Psychological Medicine, 36,* 699–710.

Nock, M. K., & Kessler, R. C. (2006). Prevalence of and risk factors for suicide attempts versus suicide gestures: Analysis of the National Comorbidity Survey. *Journal of Abnormal Psychology, 115,* 616–623.

Noftle, E. E. & Shaver, P. R. (2006). Attachment dimensions and the Big Five personality traits: Associations and comparative ability to predict relationship quality. *Journal of Research in Personality, 40,* 179–208.

Noland, V. J., Liller, K. D., McDermott, R. J., Coulter, M. L., & Seraphine, A. E. (2004). Is adolescent sibling violence a precursor to college dating violence? *American Journal of Health Behavior, 28,* 13–22.

Nolen-Hoeksema, S. (1990). *Sex differences in depression.* Stanford, CA: Stanford University Press.

Nolen-Hoeksema, S. (2001). Gender differences in depression. *Current Directions in Psychological Science, 10,* 173–176.

Nolen-Hoeksema, S. (2006). The etiology of gender differences in depression. In C. M. Mazure & G. P. Keita (Eds.), *Understanding depression in women: Applying empirical research to practice and policy* (pp. 9–43). Washington, DC: American Psychological Association.

Nolen-Hoeksma, S., Morrow, J., & Fredrickson, N. (1993). Response styles and the duration of episodes of depressed mood. *Journal of Abnormal Psychology, 102,* 20–28.

Noll, R. B. (1994). Hypnotherapy for warts in children and adolescents. *Journal of Developmental and Behavioral Pediatrics, 15,* 170–173.

Nomura, H., Inoue, S., Kamimura, N., Shimodera, S., et al. (2005). A cross-cultural study on expressed emotion in careers of people with dementia and schizophrenia: Japan and England. *Social Psychiatry and Psychiatric Epidemiology, 40,* 564–570.

Noone, J. H., Stephens, C., & Alpass, F. M. (2009). Preretirement planning and well-being in later life: A prospective study. *Research on Aging, 31,* 295–317.

Norberg, M. M., Krystal, J. H., & Tolin, D. F. (2008). A meta-analysis of D-cycloserine and the facilitation of fear extinction and exposure therapy. *Biological Psychiatry, 63,* 1118–1126.

Norcross, J. C. (2001). Purposes, processes, and products of the task force on empirically supported therapy relationships. *Psychotherapy: Theory, Research, Practice, Training, 38,* 345–356.

Norcross, J. C. (2002). *Psychotherapy relationships that work: Therapist contributions and responsiveness to patients.* New York: Oxford University Press.

Norcross, J. C. (2006). Integrating self-help into psychotherapy: 16 practical suggestions. *Professional Psychology: Research and Practice, 37,* 683–693.

Norcross, J. C., Beutler, L. E., & Levant, R. F. (2005). *Evidence-based practices in mental health: Debate and dialogue on the fundamental questions.* Washington, DC: American Psychological Association.

Norcross, J. C., Beutler, L. E., & Levant, R. F. (2005). Prologue. In J. C. Norcross, L. E. Beutler, & R. F. Levant (Eds.), *Evidence-based practices in mental health: Debate and dialogue on the fundamental questions* (pp. 3–12). Washington, DC: American Psychological Association.

Norcross, J. C., & Goldfried, M. R. (2005). *Handbook of psychotherapy integration* (2nd ed.). New York: Oxford University Press.

Norcross, J. C., Hedges, M., & Castle, P. H. (2002). Psychologists conducting psychotherapy in 2001: A study of Division 29 membership. *Psychotherapy: Theory, Research, Practice, Training, 39,* 97–102.

Norcross, J. C., Santrock, J. W., Campbell, L. F., Smith, T. P., et al. (2000). *Authoritative guide to self-help resources in mental health.* New York: Guilford Press.

Nordberg, A. (2008). Amyloid plaque imaging in vivo: Current achievement and future prospects. *European Journal of Nuclear Medicine and Molecular Imaging, 35,* 46–50.

Nordstrom, C. R., & Segrist, D. J. (2009). Predicting the likelihood of going to graduate school: The importance of locus of control. *College Student Journal, 43,* 200–206.

Norman, D. (2009). *The design of future things.* New York: Basic Books.

Norman, T., & Olver, J. S. (2004). New formulations of existing antidepressants: Advantages in the management of depression. *CNS Drugs, 18,* 505–520.

North, M. M., North, S. M., & Burwick, C. B. (2008). Virtual reality therapy: A vision for a new paradigm. In L. L'Abate (Ed.), *Toward a science of clinical psychology: Laboratory evaluations and interventions* (pp. 307–320). Hauppauge, NY: Nova.

Nosek, B. A., Smyth, F. L., Sriram, N., Lindner, N. M., et al. (2009). National differences in gender-science stereotypes predict national sex differences in science and math achievement. *Proceedings of the National Academy of Sciences, 106,* 10593–10597.

Nourkova, V. V., Bernstein, D. M., & Loftus, E. F. (2004). Biography becomes autobiography: Distorting the subjective past. *American Journal of Psychology, 117,* 65–80.

Novick, K. K., & Novick, J. (2005). *Working with parents makes therapy work.* Northvale, NJ: Aronson.

Nowak, M. A., Komarova, N. L., & Niyogi, P. (2001). Evolution of universal grammar. *Science, 291,* 114–118.

Nowak, M. A., May, R. M., & Sigmund, K. (1995). The arithmetics of mutual help. *Scientific American, 272,* 76–81.

Noyes, R., & Hoehn-Saric, R. (2006). *The anxiety disorders.* Cambridge: Cambridge University Press.

Nunn, J. A., Gregory, L. J., Brammer, M., Williams, S. C., et al. (2002). Functional magnetic resonance imaging of synesthesia: Activation of V4/V8 by spoken words. *Nature Neuroscience, 5,* 371–375.

Nurnberger, J. I., Jr.; Foroud, T.; Flury, L.; Su, J.; et al. (2001). Evidence for a locus on chromosome 1 that influences vulnerability to alcoholism and affective disorder. *American Journal of Psychiatry, 158,* 718–724.

Nutt, D. J. (2005a). Death by tricyclic: The real antidepressant scandal? *Journal of Psychopharmacology, 19,* 123–124.

Nutt, D. J. (2005b). Overview of diagnosis and drug treatments of anxiety disorders. *CNS Spectrums, 10,* 49–56.

Nyberg, L., Petersson, K. M., Nilsson, L. G., Sandblom, J., et al. (2001). Reactivation of motor brain areas during explicit memory for actions. *Neuroimage, 14,* 521–528.

Oakhill, J., Garnham, A., & Reynolds, D. (2005). Immediate activation of stereotypical gender information. *Memory and Cognition, 33,* 972–983.

Oatley, K. (1993). Those to whom evil is done. In R. S. Wyer & T. K. Srull (Eds.), *Toward a general theory of anger and emotional aggression: Advances in social cognition* (Vol. 6, pp. 159–165). Hillsdale, NJ: Erlbaum.

Oberman, L. M., & Ramachandran, V. S. (2007). The simulating social mind: The role of the mirror neuron system and simulation in the social and communicative deficits of autism spectrum disorders. *Psychological Bulletin, 133,* 310–327.

O'Brien, B. (2009). Prime suspect: An examination of factors that aggravate and counteract confirmation bias in criminal investigations. *Psychology, Public Policy, and Law, 15,* 315–334.

O'Brien, J. T. (2006). Depression and comorbidity. *American Journal of Psychiatry, 14,* 187–190.

O'Brien, T. L. (1991, September 2). Computers help thwart "groupthink" that plagues meetings. *Chicago Sun Times.*

O'Connor, T. G., Ben-Shlomo, Y., Heron, J., Golding, J., et al. (2005). Prenatal anxiety predicts individual differences in cortisol in preadolescent children. *Biological Psychiatry, 58,* 211–217.

Odds and ends. (2002, March 9). *Naples Daily News.*

Oden, M. H. (1968). The fulfillment of promise: 40-year follow-up of the Terman gifted group. *Genetic Psychology Monographs, 17,* 3–93.

Odgers, C. L., Caspi, A., Nagin, D. S., Piquero, A. R., et al. (2008). Is it important to prevent early exposure to drugs and alcohol among adolescents? *Psychological Science, 19,* 1037–1044.

O'Donohue, W. T., Fisher, J. E., & Hayes, S. C. (Eds.). (2003). *Cognitive behavior therapy: Applying empirically supported techniques in your practice.* Hoboken, NJ: Wiley.

O'Driscoll, M., Brough, P., & Kalliath, T. (2006). Work-family conflict and facilitation. In F. Jones, R. J. Burke & M. Westman (Eds.), *Work-life balance: A psychological perspective* (pp. 117–142). New York: Psychology Press.

Oettingen, G., Pak, H., & Schnetter, K. (2001). Self-regulation of goal setting: Turning free fantasies about the future into binding goals. *Journal of Personality and Social Psychology, 80,* 736–753.

Ogden, C. L., Carroll, M. D., & Flegal, K. M. (2008). High body mass index for age among U.S. children and adolescents, 2003–2006. *Journal of the American Medical Association, 299,* 2401–2405.

Ogden, C. L., Carroll, M. D., McDowell, M. A., & Flegal, K. M. (2007). *Obesity among adults in the United States: No change since 2003–2004.* Hyattsville, MD: National Center for Health Statistics.

Oh, I., & Berry, C. M. (2009). The five-factor model of personality and managerial performance: Validity gains through the use of 360-degree performance ratings. *Journal of Applied Psychology, 94,* 1498–1513.

Ohayon, M. M. (2004). Interactions between sleep normative data and sociocultural characteristics in the elderly. *Journal of Psychosomatic Research, 56,* 479–486.

Ohayon, M. M., & Roth, T. (2003). Place of chronic insomnia in the course of depressive and anxiety disorders. *Journal of Psychiatric Research, 37,* 9–15.

Ohira, H., & Kurono, K. (1993). Facial feedback effects on impression formation. *Perceptual and Motor Skills, 77,* 1251–1258.

Öhman, A., Dimberg, U., & Öst, L. G. (1985). Animal and social phobias: A laboratory model. In S. Reiss & R. R. Bootzin (Eds.), *Theoretical issues in behavior therapy.* New York: Academic Press. 123–175

Öhman, A., & Mineka, S. (2001). Fears, phobias, and preparedness: Toward an evolved module of fear and fear learning. *Psychological Review, 108,* 483–522.

Öhman, A., & Mineka, S. (2003). The malicious serpent: Snakes as a prototypical stimulus for an evolved module of fear. *Current Directions in Psychological Science, 12,* 5–9.

Öhman, A., & Soares, J. F. (1994). "Unconscious anxiety": Phobic responses to masked stimuli. *Journal of Abnormal Psychology, 103,* 231–240.

Ohring, R., Graber, J. A., & Brooks-Gunn, J. (2002). Girls' recurrent and concurrent body dissatisfaction: Correlates and consequences over 8 years. *International Journal of Eating Disorders, 31,* 404–415.

Okonkwo, D. O. (2003). Basic science of closed head injuries and spinal cord injuries. *Clinics of Sports Medicine, 22,* 467–481.

Olatunji, B. O. (2006). Evaluative learning and emotional responding to fearful and disgusting stimuli in spider phobia. *Journal of Anxiety Disorders, 20,* 858–876.

Olatunji, B. O. (2008). New directions on research on health anxiety and hypochondriasis: Commentary on a timely special series. *Journal of Cognitive Psychotherapy, 22,* 183–190.

Oldenberg, P.-A., Zheleznyak, A., Fang, Y.-F., Lagenaur, C. F., et al. (2000). Role of CD47 as a marker of self on red blood cells. *Science, 288,* 2051–2054.

Olds, J. (1973). Commentary on positive reinforcement produced by electrical stimulation of septal areas and other regions of rat brain. In E. S. Valenstein (Ed.), *Brain stimulation and motivation: Research and.* Glenview, IL: Scott, Foresman.

Olds, J., & Milner, P. (1954). Positive reinforcement produced by electrical stimulation of septal areas and other regions of the rat brain. *Journal of Comparative and Physiological Psychology, 47,* 419–427.

Olfson, M., Blanco, C., Liu, L., Moreno, C., & Laje, G. (2006). National trends in the outpatient treatment of children and adolescents with antipsychotic drugs. *Archives of General Psychiatry, 63,* 679–685.

Olfson, M., Marcus, S. C., Druss, B., Elinson, L., et al. (2002). National trends in the outpatient treatment of depression. *Journal of the American Medical Association, 287,* 203–209.

Olfson, M., Marcus, S. C., & Shaffer, D. (2006). Antidepressant drug therapy and suicide in depressed children and adolescents: A case-control study. *Archives of General Psychiatry, 63,* 865–872.

Oliner, S. P., & Oliner, P. M. (1988). *The altruistic personality: Rescuers of Jews in Nazi Europe.* New York: Free Press.

Olio, K. A. (1994). Truth in memory. *American Psychologist, 49,* 442–443.

Olivares, R., Michalland, S., & Aboitiz, F. (2000). Cross-species and intraspecies morphometric analysis of the corpus callosum. *Brain and Behavior and Evolution, 55,* 37–43.

Olshansky, S. J., Passaro, D. J., Hershow, R. C., Layden, J., et al. (2005). A potential decline in life expectancy in the United States in the 21st century. *New England Journal of Medicine, 352,* 1138–1145.

Olson, I. R., Rao, H., Moore, K. S., Wang, J., et al. (2006). Using perfusion fMRI to measure continuous changes in neural activity with learning. *Brain and Cognition, 60,* 262–271.

Olson, J. M., & Stone, J. (2005). The influence of behavior on attitudes. In D. Albarracín, B. T. Johnson, & M. P. Zanna (Eds.), *Handbook of attitudes* (pp. 223–271). Mahwah, NJ: Erlbaum.

Olson, J. M., Vernon, P. A., Harris, J. A., & Jang, K. L. (2001). The heritability of attitudes: A study of twins. *Journal of Personality and Social Psychology, 80,* 845–860.

Olson, L. (1997). Regeneration in the adult central nervous system. *Nature Medicine, 3,* 1329–1335.

Olson, M. A., & Fazio, R. H. (2001). Implicit attitude formation through classical conditioning. *Psychological Science, 12,* 413–417.

Olson, M. B., Krantz, D. S., Kelsey, S. F., Pepine, C. J., et al. (2005). Hostility scores are associated with increased risk of cardiovascular events in women undergoing coronary angiography: A report from the NHLBI-sponsored WISE study. *Psychosomatic Medicine, 67,* 546–552.

Olsson, A., Ebert, J. P., Banaji, M. R., & Phelps, E. A. (2005). The role of social groups in the persistence of learned fear. *Science, 309,* 785–787.

Olsson, C. J., Jonsson, B., Larsson, A., & Nyberg, L. (2008). Motor representations and practice affect brain systems underlying imagery: An fMRI study of internal imagery in novices and active high jumpers. *Open Neuroimaging Journal, 2,* 5–13. Epub 2008 Jan 2031.

Oltmanns, T. F., & Turkheimer, E. (2009). Person perception and personality pathology. *Current Directions in Psychological Science, 18,* 32–36.

Oman, D., Hedberg, J., & Thoreson, C. E. (2006). Passage meditation reduces perceived stress in health professionals: A randomized controlled trial. *Journal of Consulting and Clinical Psychology, 74,* 714–719.

O'Neill, H. (2000, September 24). After rape, jail, a friendship forms. *St. Petersburg Times,* pp. 1A, 14A.

Ones, D., & Viswesvaran, C. (2001). Personality at work: Criterion focused occupational personality scales used in personnel selection. In R. Hogan & B. Roberts (Eds.), *Personality psychology in the workplace* (pp. 63–92). Washington, DC: American Psychological Association.

Ong, A. D., Bergeman, C. S., Bisconti, T. L., & Wallace, K. A. (2006). Psychological resilience, positive emotions, and successful adaptation to stress in later life. *Journal of Personality and Social Psychology, 91,* 730–749.

Ong, J. C., Cvengros, J. A., & Wyatt, J. K. (2008). Cognitive behavioral treatment for insomnia. *Psychiatric Annals, 38,* 590–596.

Onishi, K. H., & Baillargeon, R. (2005). Do 15-month-old infants understand false beliefs? *Science, 308,* 255–258.

Ono, Y., Kawakami, N., Nakane, Y., Nakamura, Y., et al. (2008). Prevalence of and risk factors for suicide-related outcomes in the World Health Organization Mental Health Surveys Japan. *Psychiatry and Clinical Neurosciences, 62,* 442–449.

Oommen, B. S., & Stahl, J. S. (2005). Inhibited head movements: A risk of combining phoning with other activities? *Neurology, 65,* 754–756.

Operario, D., & Fiske, S. T. (2001). Stereotypes: Processes, structures, content, and context. In R. Brown & S. Gaertner (Eds.), *Blackwell handbook in social psychology: Intergroup processes* (pp. 22–44). Oxford: Blackwell.

Oppel, S. (2000, March 5). Managing ABCs like a CEO. *St. Petersburg Times,* pp. 1A, 12–13A.

Oquendo, M. A., Ellis, S. P., Greenwald, S., Malone, K. M., et al. (2001). Ethnic and sex differences in suicide rates relative to major depression in the United States. *American Journal of Psychiatry, 158,* 1652–1658.

Oquendo, M. A., & Mann, J. J. (2000). The biology of impulsivity and suicidality. *Psychiatric Clinics of North America, 23,* 11–25.

Oquendo, M. A., & Mann, J. J. (2001). Identifying and managing suicide risk in bipolar patients. *Journal of Clinical Psychiatry, 62,* 31–34.

Orbell, J. M., van de Kragt, A. J. C., & Dawes, R. M. (1988). Explaining discussion-induced cooperation. *Journal of Personality and Social Psychology, 54,* 811–819.

O'Reardon, J. P., Fontecha, J. F., Cristancho, M. A., & Newman, S. (2007). Unexpected reduction in migraine and psychogenic headaches following rTMS treatment for major depression: A report of two cases. *CNS Spectrums, 12,* 921–925.

O'Reilly, R. C. (2006). Biologically based computational models of high-level cognition. *Science, 314,* 91–94.

Organ, D. W., Podsakoff, P. M., & MacKenzie, S. B. (2006). *Organizational citizenship behavior: Its nature, antecedents, and consequences.* Thousand Oaks, CA: Sage.

Orme-Johnson, D. W., Schneider, R. H., Son, Y. D., Nidich, S., & Cho, Z. H. (2006). Neuroimaging of meditation's effect on brain reactivity to pain. *Neuroreport, 17,* 1359–1363.

Orne, M. T., & Evans, F. J. (1965). Social control in the psychological experiment: Antisocial behavior and hypnosis. *Journal of Personality and Social Psychology, 1,* 189–200.

Orne, M. T., Sheehan, P. W., & Evans, F. J. (1968). Occurrence of posthypnotic behavior outside the experimental setting. *Journal of Personality and Social Psychology, 9,* 189–196.

Orth-Gomér, K., Schneiderman, N., Wang, H.-X., Walldin, C., et al. (2009). Stress reduction prolongs life in women with coronary disease: The Stockholm Women's Intervention Trial for Coronary Heart Disease (SWITCHD). *Circulation: Cardiovascular Quality and Outcomes, 2,* 25–32.

Ortiz-Walters, R., & Gilson, L. L. (2005). Mentoring in academia: An examination of the experiences of protégés of color. *Journal of Vocational Behavior, 67,* 459–475.

Osherson, D., Perani, D., Cappa, S., Schnur, T., et al. (1998). Distinct brain loci in deductive versus probabilistic reasoning. *Neuropsychologia, 36,* 369–376.

Oshima, N. (2008). Beneficial and adverse effects of pharmacotherapy with risperidone on behavioral and psychological symptoms of dementia (BPSD). *Psychogeriatrics, 8,* 175–177.

Oskamp, S., & Schultz, P. W. (1998). *Applied social psychology* (2nd ed.). Upper Saddle River, NJ: Prentice Hall.

Öst, L.-G. (1978). Behavioral treatment of thunder and lightning phobia. *Behavior Research and Therapy, 16,* 197–207.

Öst, L.-G., Hellström, K., & Kåver, A. (1992). One- versus five-session exposure in the treatment of needle phobia. *Behavior Therapy, 23,* 263–282.

Öst, L.-G., Salkovskis, P. M., & Hellström, K. (1991). One-session therapist-directed exposure vs. self-exposure in the treatment of spider phobia. *Behavior Theapy, 22,* 407–422.

Ostfeld, B. M., Esposito, L., Perl, H., & Hegyi, T. (2010). Concurrent risks in sudden infant death syndrome. *Pediatrics, 125,* 447–453.

Ostfeld, B. M., Perl, H., Esposito, L., Hempstead, K., et al. (2006). Sleep environment, positional, lifestyle, and demographic characteristics associated with bed sharing in sudden infant death syndrome cases: A population-based study. *Pediatrics, 118,* 2051–2059.

Ostir, G. V., Berges, I. M., Markides, K. S., & Ottenbacher, K. J. (2006). Hypertension in older adults and the role of positive emotions. *Psychosomatic Medicine, 68,* 727–733.

Ostrov, J. M. (2006). Deception and subtypes of aggression during early childhood. *Journal of Experimental Child Psychology, 93,* 322–336.

Ostrov, J. M., & Godleski, S. A. (2010). Toward an integrated gender-linked model of aggression subtypes in early and middle childhood. *Psychological Review, 117,* 233–242.

Ostrovsky, Y., Meyers, E., Ganesh, S., Mathur, U., & Sinha, P. (2009). Visual parsing after recovery from blindness. *Psychological Science, 20,* 1484–1491.

Otto, M. W., Pollack, M. H., Gould, R. A., Worthington, J. J., III, et al. (2000). A comparison of the efficacy of clonazepam and cognitive-behavioral group therapy for the treatment of social phobia. *Journal of Anxiety Disorders, 14,* 345–358.

Otto, M. W., Smits, J. A. J., & Reese, H. E. (2005). Combined psychotherapy and pharmacotherapy for mood and anxiety disorders in adults: Review and analysis. *Clinical Psychology: Science and Practice, 12,* 72–86.

Oudiette, D., De Cock, V. C., Lavault, S., Leu, S., et al. (2009). Nonviolent elaborate behaviors may also occur in REM sleep behavior disorder. *Neurology, 72,* 551–557.

Ouimet, A. J., Gawronski, B., & Dozois, D. J. A. (2009). Cognitive vulnerability to anxiety: A review and an integrative model. *Clinical Psychology Review, 29,* 459–470.

Over, H., & Carpenter, M. (2009). Eighteen-month-old infants show increased helping following priming with affiliation. *Psychological Science, 20,* 1189–1193.

Overbeek, G., Stattin, H., Vermulst, A., Ha, T., & Engels, R. C. M. E. (2007). Parent-child relationships, partner relationships, and emotional adjustment: A birth-to-maturity prospective study. *Developmental Psychology, 43,* 429–437.

Overmier, J. B. (2002). On learned helplessness. *Integrative Physiological and Behavioral Science, 37,* 4–8.

Overmier, J. B., & Seligman, M. E. P. (1967). Effects of inescapable shock upon subsequent escape and avoidance learning. *Journal of Comparative and Physiological Psychology, 63,* 23–33.

Overton, D. A. (1984). State-dependent learning and drug discriminations. In L. L. Iverson, S. D. Iverson, & S. H. Snyder (Eds.), *Handbook of psychopharmacology* (Vol. 18) New York: Plenum. Page range unavailable.

Ovsiew, F. (2006). An overview of the psychiatric approach to conversion disorder. In M. Hallet, S. Fahn, J. Jankovic, A. E. Lang, et al. (Eds.), *Psychogenic movement disorders: Neurology and neuropsychiatry* (pp. 115–121). Philadelphia: Lippincott Williams & Wilkins.

Owen, C. G., Whincup, P. H., Orfei, L., Chou, Q.-A., et al. (2009). Is body mass index before middle age related to coronary heart disease risk in later life? Evidence from observational studies. *International Journal of Obesity, 33,* 866–877.

Özgen, E. (2004). Language, learning, and color perception. *Current Directions in Psychological Science, 13,* 95–98.

Özgen, E., & Davies, I. R. L. (2002). Acquisition of categorical color perception: A perceptual learning approach to the linguistic relativity hypothesis. *Journal of Experimental Psychology: General, 131,* 477–493.

Pachankis, J. E., & Goldfried, M. R. (2010). Expressive writing for gay-related stress: Psychosocial benefits and mechanisms underlying improvement. *Journal of Consulting and Clinical Psychology, 78,* 98–110.

Pack, A. A., & Herman, L. M. (2007). The dolphin's (*Tursiops truncatus*) understanding of human gazing and pointing: Knowing what and where. *Journal of Comparative Psychology, 121,* 34–45.

Packer, D. J. (2008). Identifying systematic disobedience in Milgram's obedience experiments: A meta-analytic review. *Perspectives on Psychological Science, 3,* 301–304.

Packer, D. J. (2009). Avoiding groupthink: Whereas weakly identified members remain silent, strongly identified members dissent about collective problems. *Psychological Science, 20,* 546–548.

Page, S., Szaflarski, J. P., Eliassen, J. C., Pan, H., & Cramer, S. C. (2009). Cortical plasticity following motor skill learning during mental practice in stroke. *Neurorehabilitation and Neural Repair, 23,* 382–388.

Paik, H., & Comstock, G. (1994). The effects of television violence on antisocial behavior: A meta-analysis. *Communication Research, 21,* 516–546.

Paivio, A. (1986). *Mental representations: A dual coding approach.* New York: Oxford University Press.

Palincsar, A. S. (2003). Ann L. Brown: Advancing a theoretical model of learning and instruction. In B. J. Zimmerman & D. H. Schunk (Eds.), *Educational psychology: A century of contributions* (pp. 459–475). Mahwah, NJ: Erlbaum.

Palkovitz, R., Copes, M. A., & Woolfolk, T. N. (2001). It's like . . . you discover a new sense of being: Involved fathering as an evoker of adult development. *Men and Masculinities, 4,* 49–69.

Palmer, C. V. (2009). A contemporary review of hearing aids. *Laryngoscope, 119,* 2195–2204.

Palmer, S. E. (1999). *Vision science: Photons to phenomenology.* Cambridge, MA: MIT Press.

Palmeri, T. J., Blake, R., Marois, R., Flanery, M. A., & Whetsell, W., Jr. (2002). The perceptual reality of synesthetic colors. *Proceedings of the National Academy of Sciences, 99,* 4127–4131.

Palmisano, M., & Herrmann, D. (1991). The facilitation of memory performance. *Bulletin of the Psychonomic Society, 29,* 557–559.

Paloski, W. H. (1998). Vestibulospinal adaptation to microgravity. *Otolaryngol Head and Neck Surgery, 118,* S39–S44.

Pandi-Perumal, S. R., Srinivasan, V., Spence, D. W., Moscovitch, A., et al. (2009). Ramelteon: A review of its therapeutic potential in sleep disorders. *Advances in Therapy, 26,* 613–626.

Paoletti, M. G. (1995). Biodiversity, traditional landscapes, and agroecosystem management. *Landscape and Urban Planning, 31,* 117–128.

Pape, H. C., Munsch, T., & Budde, T. (2004). Novel vistas of calcium-mediated signalling in the thalamus. *Pflugers Archiv, 448,* 131–138.

Paradise, A. (2007). *State of the industry: ASTD's annual review of trends in workplace learning and performance.* Alexandria, VA: ASTD.

Pardini, D. A., & Lochman, J. E. (2003). Treatment of oppositional defiant disorder. In M. A. Reinecke, F. M. Dattilio, & A. Freeman (Eds.), *Cognitive therapy with children and adolescents* (pp. 43–69). New York: Guilford Press.

Parents Television Council. (2006). *TV bloodbath: Violence on primetime broadcast TV.* Retrieved from http://www.parentstv.org/PTC/publications/reports/stateindustryviolence/main.asp#_ftn8

Pariente, J., White, P., Frackowiak, R. S., & Lewith, G. (2005). Expectancy and belief modulate the neuronal substrates of pain treated by acupuncture. *NeuroImage, 25,* 1161–1167.

Park, D. C. (2001, August). *The aging mind.* Paper presented at the 109th annual convention of the American Psychological Association, San Francisco.

Park, G., Lubinski, D., & Benbow, C. P. (2008). Ability differences among people who have commensurate degrees matter for scientific creativity. *Psychological Science, 19,* 957–961.

Park, H. J., Li, R. X., Kim, J., Kim, S. W., et al. (2009). Neural correlates of winning and losing while watching soccer matches. *International Journal of Neuroscience, 119,* 76–87.

Park, N., Peterson, C., & Seligman, M. E. P. (2004). Strengths of character and well-being. *Journal of Social and Clinical Psychology, 23,* 603–619.

Park, Y. M., Matsumoto, K., Jin Seo, Y., Kang, M. J., & Nagashima, H. (2002). Effects of age and gender on sleep habits and sleep trouble for aged people. *Biological Rhythm Research, 33,* 39–51.

Parke, R. D. (2002). Fathers and families. In M. H. Bornstein (Ed.), *Handbook of parenting* (2nd ed., pp. 27–63). Mahwah, NJ: Erlbaum.

Parke, R. D., & Buriel, R. (2006). Child development and the family. In W. Damon & R. M. Lerner (Series Eds.) & N. Eisenberg (Vol. Ed.), *Handbook of child psychology: Vol. 3. Social, emotional, and personality development* (6th ed., pp. 429–504). Hoboken, NJ: Wiley.

Parker, E. S., Cahill, L., & McGaugh, J. L. (2006). A case of unusual autobiographical remembering. *Neurocase, 12,* 35–49.

Parker, J. G., Saxon, J. L., Asher, S. R., & Kovacs, D. M. (2001). Dimensions of children's friendship adjustment: Implications for understanding loneliness. In K. J. Rotenberg & S. Hymel (Eds.), *Loneliness in childhood and adolescence.* New York: Cambridge University Press.

Parker, K. J., Buckmaster, C. L., Sundlass, K., Schatzberg, A. F., & Lyons, D. M. (2006). Maternal mediation, stress inoculation, and the development of neuroendocrine stress resistance in primates. *Proceedings of the National Academy of Sciences, 103,* 3000–3005.

Parkin, A. J., & Walter, B. M. (1991). Aging, short-term memory, and frontal dysfunction. *Psychobiology, 19,* 175–179.

Parnas, J., Cannon, T., Jacobsen, B., Schulsinger, H., et al. (1993). Lifetime DSM-III-R diagnostic outcomes in the offspring of schizophrenic mothers. *Archives of General Psychiatry, 50,* 707–714.

Parolaro, D., Massi, P., Rubino, T., & Monti, E. (2002). Endocannabinoids in the immune system and cancer. *Prostaglandins, Leukotrienes, and Essential Fatty Acids, 66,* 319–332.

Parrott, R. F. (1994). Central effects of CCK ligands in pigs making operant responses for food. *Pharmacology, Biochemistry, and Behavior, 49,* 463–469.

Parsons, T. J., Power, C., & Manor, O. (2005). Physical activity, television viewing and body mass index: A cross-sectional analysis from childhood to adulthood in the 1958 British cohort. *International Journal of Obesity, 29,* 1212–1221.

Pascalis, O., de Haan, M., & Nelson, C. A. (2002). Is face processing species-specific during the first year of life? *Science, 296,* 1321–1323.

Pascual-Leone, A. (2001). The brain that plays music and is changed by it. *Annals of the New York Academy of Sciences, 930,* 315–329.

Pascual-Leone, A., Amedi, A., Fregni, F., & Merabet, L. B. (2005). The plastic human brain cortex. *Annual Review of Neuroscience, 28,* 377–401.

Pascual-Leone, A., & Torres, F. (1993). Plasticity of the sensorimotor cortex representation of the reading finger in Braille readers. *Brain, 116,* 39–52.

Pashayan, A. G. (2005). Pathophysiology of obstructive sleep apnea. *Anesthesiology Clinics of North America, 23,* 431–443.

Pashler, H., Rohrer, D., & Cepeda, N. J. (2006). Temporal spacing and learning. *APS Observer, 19,* 30, 38.

Pasztor, A. (2009, October 26). Pilots say they were distracted. *Wall Street Journal,* p. A4.

Patel, A. D., & Balaban, E. (2001). Human pitch perception is reflected in the timing of stimulus-related cortical activity. *Nature Neuroscience, 4,* 839–844.

Patel, S. R., White, D. P., Malhotra, A., Stanchina, M. L., & Ayas, N. T. (2003). Continuous positive airway pressure therapy for treating sleepiness in a diverse population with obstructive sleep apnea: Results of a meta-analysis. *Archives of Internal Medicine, 163,* 565–571.

Paterson, R. J. (2000). *The assertiveness workbook: How to express your ideas and stand up for yourself at work and in relationships.* Oakland, CA: New Harbinger.

Pathela, P., Hajat, A., Schillinger, J., Blank, S., et al. (2006). Discordance between sexual behavior and self-reported sexual identity: A population-based survey of New York City men. *Annals of Internal Medicine, 145,* 416–425.

Patkowski, M. (1994). The critical age hypothesis and interlanguage phonology. In M. Yavas (Ed.), *First and second language phonology* (pp. 205–221). San Diego, CA: Singular.

Patrick, C. J., Bradley, M. M. & Lang, P. J. (1993). Emotion in the criminal psychopath: Startle reflex modulation. *Journal of Abnormal Psychology, 102,* 82–92.

Patten, S. B., Williams, J. V. A., Wang, J., Adair, C. E., et al. (2005). Antidepressant pharmacoepidemiology in a general population sample. *Journal of Clinical Psychopharmacology, 25,* 285–287.

Patterson, C. J. (2002). Lesbian and gay parenthood. In M. H. Bornstein (Ed.), *Handbook of parenting* (2nd ed., pp. 255–274). Mahwah, NJ: Erlbaum.

Patterson, C. J. (2004). *Lesbian and gay parents and their children: Summary of research findings.* Washington, DC: American Psychological Association. Retrieved from http://www.apa.org/pi/parent.html

Patterson, D. R., & Jensen, M. P. (2003). Hypnosis and clinical pain. *Psychological Bulletin, 129,* 495–521.

Patterson, D. R., Hoffman, H. G., Palacios, A. G., & Jensen, M. J. (2006). Analgesic effects of posthypnotic suggestions and virtual reality distraction on thermal pain. *Journal of Abnormal Psychology, 115,* 834–841.

Pattie, F. A. (1935). A report of attempts to produce uniocular blindness by hypnotic suggestion. *British Journal of Medical Psychiatry, 15,* 230–241.

Patton, G. C., McMorris, B. J., Toumbourou, J. W., Hemphill, S. A., et al. (2004). Puberty and the onset of substance use and abuse. *Pediatrics, 114,* e300–e306. Retrieved from http://www.ncbi.nlm.nih.gov/pubmed/15342890

Pauk, W., & Owens, R. J. Q. (2010). *How to study in college* (10th ed.) Belmont, CA: Wadsworth.

Paul, G. L. (1969). Behavior modification research: Design and tactics. In C. M. Franks (Ed.), *Behavior therapy: Appraisal and status* (pp. 29–62). New York: McGraw-Hill.

Paul, G. L. (2000). Milieu therapy. In A. E. Kazdin (Ed.), *The encyclopedia of psychology* (Vol. 5, pp. 250-252). Washington, DC: American Psychological Association.

Paul-Labrador, M., Polk, D., Dwyer, J. H., Velasquez, I., et al. (2006). Effects of a randomized controlled trial of transcendental meditation on components on the metabolic syndrome in subjects with coronary heart disease. *Archives of Internal Medicine, 166,* 1218–1224.

Paulussen-Hoogeboom, M. C., Stams, G. J. J. M., Hermanns, J. M. A., Peetsma, T. T. D., & van den Wittenboer, G. L. H. (2008). Parenting style as a mediator between children's negative emotionality and problematic behavior in early childhood. *Journal of Genetic Psychology, 169,* 209–226.

Pavitt, C., High, A. C., Tressler, K. E., & Winslow, J. K. (2007). Leadership communication during group resource dilemmas. *Small Group Research, 38,* 509–531.

Payne, B. K. (2008). Attitude misattribution: Implications for attitude measurement and the implicit-explicit relationship. In R. E. Petty, R. H. Fazio, & P. Briñol (Eds.), *Attitudes: Insights from the new wave of implicit measures* (pp. 459–484). Mahwah, NJ: Erlbaum.

Payne, B. K., Jacoby, L. L., & Lambert, A. J. (2004). Memory monitoring and the control of stereotype distortion. *Journal of Experimental Social Psychology, 40,* 52–64.

Payne, J. D., & Nadel, L. (2004). Sleep, dreams, and memory consolidation: The role of the stress hormone cortisol. *Learning and Memory, 11,* 671–678.

Payne, J. W., Bettman, J. R., & Johnson, E. J. (1992). Behavioral decision research: A constructive processing perspective. *Behavioral decision research: A constructive processing perspective, 43,* 87–131.

Payne, N. A., & Prudic, J. (2009). Electroconvulsive therapy: Part I. A perspective on the evolution and current practice of ECT. *Journal of Psychiatric Practice, 15,* 346–368.

Payne, S. C., & Huffman, A. H. (2005). A longitudinal examination of the influence of mentoring on organizational commitment and turnover. *Academy of Management Journal, 48,* 158–168.

Pear, J., & Martin, G. L. (2002). *Behavior modification: What it is and how to do it* (7th ed.). Upper Saddle River, NJ: Prentice Hall.

Pearce, J. M. (2009). Hugo Karl Liepmann and apraxia. *Clinical Medicine, 9,* 466–470.

Pearce, M. J., Jones, S. M., Schwab-Stone, M. E., & Ruchkin, V. (2003). The protective effects of religiousness and parent involvement on the development of conduct problems among youth exposed to violence. *Child Development, 74,* 1682–1696.

Pearsall, M. J., Christian, M. S., & Ellis, A. P. J. (2010). Motivating interdependent teams: Individual rewards, shared rewards, or something in between? *Journal of Applied Psychology, 95,* 183–191.

Peciña, S. (2008). Opioid reward "liking" and "wanting" in the nucleus accumbens. *Physiology and Behavior, 94,* 675–680.

Peck, J. W. (1978). Rats defend different body weights depending on palatability and accessibility of their food. *Journal of Comparative and Physiological Psychology, 92,* 555–570.

Pedersen, P. B., & Draguns, J. G. (2002). *Counseling across cultures.* Thousand Oaks, CA: Sage.

Peigneux, P., Laureys, S., Delbeuck, X., & Maquet, P. (2001). Sleeping brain, learning brain: The role of sleep for memory systems. *Neuroreport, 12,* A111–A124.

Peiro, A. (2006). Happiness, satisfaction and socio-economic conditions: Some international evidence. *Journal of Socio-Economics, 35,* 348–365.

Pekrun, R., Elliot, A. J., & Maier, M. A. (2009). Achievement goals and achievement emotions: Testing a model of their joint relations with academic performance. *Journal of Educational Psychology, 101,* 115–135.

Peña, M., Pittaluga, E., & Mehler, J. (2010). Language acquisition in premature and full-term infants. *Proceedings of the National Academy of Sciences, 107,* 3823–3828.

Penberthy, J. K., Ait-Daoud, N., Vaughan, M., & Fanning, T. (2010). Review of treatments for cocaine dependence. *Current Drug Abuse Reviews, 3,* 49–62.

Pendergrast, M. (1996). A retractor's story. *Victims of memory: Sex abuse accusations and shattered lives.* Hinesburg, VT: Upper Access Books.

Penedo, F. J., & Dahn, J. (2004). Psychoneuroimmunology and aging. In K. Vedhara & M. Irwin (Eds.), *Psychoneuroimmunology* (pp. 81–106). New York: Kluwer.

Penfield, W., & Rasmussen, T. (1968). *The cerebral cortex of man: A clinical study of localization of function.* New York: Hafner.

Pengas, G., Hodges, J. R., Watson, P., & Nestor, P. J. (2010). Focal posterior cingulate atrophy in incipient Alzheimer's disease. *Neurobiology of Aging, 31,* 25–33.

Pennebaker, J. W. (1995). *Emotion, disclosure, and health.* Washington, DC: American Psychological Association.

Pennebaker, J. W. (2000). The effects of traumatic disclosure on physical and mental health: The values of writing and talking about upsetting events. In J. M. Violanti, D. Paton, & C. Dunning (Eds.), *Posttraumatic stress intervention: Challenges, issues, and perspectives* (pp. 97–114). Chicago: Thomas.

Pennebaker, J. W., & Chew, C. H. (1985). Deception, electrodermal activity, and inhibition of behavior. *Journal of Personality and Social Psychology, 49,* 1427–1433.

Pennebaker, J. W., & O'Heeron, R. C. (1984). Confiding in others and illness rate among spouses of suicide and accidental death victims. *Journal of Abnormal Psychology, 93,* 473–476.

Penner, L. A. (2002). Dispositional and organizational influences on sustained volunteerism: An interactionist perspective. *Journal of Social Issues, 58,* 447–467.

Penner, L., Brannick, M. T., Webb, S., & Connell, P. (2005). Effects on volunteering of the September 11, 2001, attacks: An archival analysis. *Journal of Applied Social Psychology, 35,* 1333–1360.

Penner, L. A., Dovidio, J. F., & Albrecht, T. L. (2001). Helping victims of loss and trauma: A social psychological perspective. In J. Harvey & E. Miller (Eds.), *Loss and trauma: General and close relationship perspectives* (pp. 62–85). New York: Brunner-Routledge.

Penner, L. A., Dovidio, J. F., Piliavin, J. A., & Schroeder, D. A. (2005). Prosocial behavior: Multilevel perspectives. *Annual Review of Psychology, 56,* 365–392.

Penner, L. A., Dovidio, J. F., West, T. V., Gaertner, S. L., et al. (2010). Aversive racism and medical interactions with black patients: A field study. *Journal of Experimental Social Psychology*, *46,* 436–440.

Penner, L. A., & Finkelstein, M. A. (1998). Dispositional and structural determinants of volunteerism. *Journal of Personality and Social Psychology, 74,* 525–537.

Penner, L. A., Fritzsche, B. A., Craiger, J. P., & Friefeld, T. R. (1995). Measuring the prosocial personality. In J. Butcher & C. D. Spielberger (Eds.), *Advances in personality assessment* (Vol. 10, pp. 147–163). Hillsdale, NJ: Erlbaum.

Penner, L. A., & Orom, H. (2009). Enduring goodness: A person-by-situation perspective on prosocial behavior. In M. Mikulnicer & P. Shaver (Eds.), *Prosocial motives, emotions, and behavior* (pp. 55–72) Washington, DC: American Psychological Association.

Penney, L. M., & Spector, P. E. (2005). Job stress, incivility, and counterproductive work behavior (CWB): The moderating role of negative affectivity. *Journal of Organizational Behavior, 26,* 777–796.

Penninx, B. W., Beekman, A. T., Honig, A., Deeg, D. J., et al. (2001). Depression and cardiac mortality: Results from a community-based longitudinal study. *Archives of General Psychiatry, 58,* 221–227.

Penton, R. E., & Lester, R. A. (2009). Cellular events in nicotine addiction. *Seminars in Cell and Developmental Biology, 20,* 418–431.

Peplau, L. A. (2003). Human sexuality: How do men and women differ? *Current Directions in Psychological Science, 12,* 37–40.

Pepler, D., Jiang, D., Craig, W., & Connolly, J. (2008). Developmental trajectories of bullying and associated factors. *Child Development, 79,* 325–338.

Perkonigg, A., Pfister, H., Stein, M. B., Hofler, M., et al. (2005). Longitudinal course of posttraumatic stress disorder and posttraumatic stress disorder symptoms in a community sample of adolescents and young adults. *American Journal of Psychiatry, 162,* 1320–1327.

Perlin, M. L. (2003). Therapeutic jurisprudence and outpatient commitment law: Kendra's Law as case study. *Psychology, Public Policy, and Law, 9,* 183–208.

Perlman, D. M., Salomons, T. V., Davidson, R. J., & Lutz, A. (2010). Differential effects on pain intensity and unpleasantness of two meditation practices. *Emotion, 10,* 65–71.

Perls, F. S. (1969). *Ego, hunger and aggression: The beginning of Gestalt therapy.* New York: Random House.

Perls, F. S., Hefferline, R. F., & Goodman, P. (1951). *Gestalt therapy.* New York: Julian Press.

Perper, K., & Manlove, J. (2009). Estimated percentage of females who will become teen mothers: Differences across states. *Child Trends Research Brief.* Retrieved from http://www.childtrends.org/Files//Child_Trends-2009_03_19_RB_PercentTeenMothers.pdf

Perrin, M. A., DiGrande, L., Wheeler, K., Thorpe, L., et al. (2007). Differences in PTSD prevalence and associated risk factors among World Trade Center disaster rescue and recovery workers. *American Journal of Psychiatry, 164,* 1385–1394.

Perris, E. E., Myers, N. A., & Clifton, R. K. (1990). Long-term memory for a single infancy experience. *Child Development, 61,* 1796–1807.

Perry, E. K. (1980). The cholinergic system in old age and Alzheimer's disease. *Age and Ageing, 9,* 1–8.

Persons, J. B., Davidson, J., & Tompkins, M. A. (2001). *Essential components of cognitive-behavior therapy for depression.* Washington, DC: American Psychological Association.

Perthen, J. E., Lansing, A. E., Liau, J., Liu, T. T., & Buxton, R. B. (2008). Caffeine-indcued uncoupling of cerebral blood flow and oxygen metabolism: A calibrated BOLD fMRI study. *Neuroimage, 40,* 237–247.

Pervin, L. A. (2003). *The science of personality.* New York: Oxford University Press.

Pervin, L. A., Cervone, D., & John, O. P. (2005). *Personality: Theory and research.* Hoboken, NJ: Wiley.

Pesonen, A.-K., Räikkönen, K., Heinonen, K., Komsi, N., et al. (2008). A transactional model of temperamental development: Evidence of a relationship between child temperament and maternal stress over five years. *Social Development, 17,* 326–340.

Pessiglione, M., Seymour, B., Flandin, G., Dolan R. J., & Frith, C. D. (2006). Dopamine-dependent prediction errors underpin reward-seeking behaviour in humans. *Nature, 442,* 1042–1045.

Peters, E., Hess, T. M., Västfjäll, D., & Auman, C. (2007). Adult age differences in dual information processes: Implications for the role of affective and deliberative processes in older adults' decision making. *Perspectives on Psychological Science, 2,* 1–23.

Petersen, J. L., & Hyde, J. S. (2010). A meta-analytic review of research on gender differences in sexuality, 1993–2007. *Psychological Bulletin, 136,* 21–38.

Petersen, R. C., & Morris, J. C. (2005). Mild cognitive impairment as a clinical entity and treatment target. *Archives of Neurology, 62,* 1160–1163.

Petersen, R. C., Thomas, R. G., Grundman, M., Bennett, D., et al. (2005). Vitamin E and donepezil for the treatment of mild cognitive impairment. *New England Journal of Medicine, 352,* 2379–2388.

Peterson, C. (2006a). *A primer in positive psychology.* New York: Oxford University Press.

Peterson, C. (2006b). The Values in Action (VIA) Classification of Strengths: The un-DSM and the real DSM. In M. Csikszentmihalyi & I. Csikszentmihalyi (Eds.), *A life worth living: Contributions to positive psychology* (pp. 29–48). New York: Oxford University Press.

Peterson, C., Maier, S. F., & Seligman, M. E. P. (1993). *Learned helplessness: A theory for the age of personal control.* New York: Oxford University Press.

Peterson, C., & Seligman, M. E. P. (1984). Causal explanations as a risk factor for depression: Theory and evidence. *Psychological Review, 91,* 347–374.

Peterson, C., Seligman, M. E. P., Yurko, K. H., Martin, L. R., & Friedman, H. S. (1998). Catastrophizing and untimely death. *Psychological Science, 9,* 127–130.

Peterson, L. R., & Peterson, M. J. (1959). Short-term retention of individual verbal items. *Journal of Experimental Psychology, 58,* 193–198.

Peterson, M. A., & Rhodes, G. (2003). *Perception of faces, objects, and scenes.* New York: Oxford University Press.

Peterson, N. G., Mumford, M. D., Borman, W. C., Jeanneret, P. R., et al. (2001). Understanding work using the Occupational Information Network (O*NET): Implications for practice and research. *Personnel Psychology, 54,* 451–492.

Peterson, R. S., Smith, D. B., Martorana, P. V., & Owens, P. D. (2003). The impact of chief executive officer personality on top management team dynamics: One mechanism by which leadership affects organizational performance. *Journal of Applied Psychology, 88,* 795–808.

Petitclerc, A., & Tremblay, R. E. (2009). Childhood disruptive behaviour disorders: Review of their origin, development and prevention. *Canadian Journal of Psychiatry, 54,* 222–231.

Petrakis, I. L., Limoncelli, D., Gueorguieva, R., Jatlow, P., et al. (2004). Altered NMDA glutamate receptor antagonist response in individuals with a family vulnerability to alcoholism. *American Journal of Psychiatry, 161,* 1776–1782.

Petrescu, N. (2008). Loud music listening. *McGill Journal of Medicine, 11,* 169–176.

Petrill, S. A., Plomin, R., Berg, S., Johansson, B., et al. (1998). The genetic and environmental relationship between general and specific cognitive abilities in twins age 80 and older. *Psychological Science, 9,* 183–189.

Petrocelli, J. V. (2002). Effectiveness of group cognitive-behavioral therapy for general symptomatology: A meta-analysis. *Journal of Specialists in Group Work, 27,* 92–115.

Petrovic, P., Dietrich, T., Fransson, P., Andersson, J., et al. (2005). Placebo in emotional processing: Induced expectations of anxiety relief activate a generalized modulatory network. *Neuron, 46,* 957–969.

Petrovic, P., Kalso, E., Petersson, K. M., & Ingvar, M. (2002). Placebo and opioid analgesia: Imaging a shared neuronal network. *Science, 295,* 1737–1740.

Pettigrew, T. F. (1979). The ultimate attribution error: Extending Allport's cognitive analysis of prejudice. *Personality and Social Psychology Bulletin, 5,* 461–476.

Pettigrew, T. F., & Tropp, L. R. (2006). Allport's intergroup contact hypothesis: Its history and influence. In J. F. Dovidio, P. S. Glick, & L. A. Rudman (Eds.), *On the nature of prejudice: Fifty years after Allport* (pp. 262–277). Boston: Blackwell.

Pettit, D. L., Shao, Z., & Yakel, J. L. (2001). Beta-amyloid(1-42) peptide directly modulates nicotinic receptors in the rat hippocampal slice. *Journal of Neuroscience, 21,* RC120.

Petty, R. E., & Briñol, P. (2008). Persuasion: From single to multiple to metacognitive processes. *Perspectives on Psychological Science, 3,* 137–147.

Petty, R. E., Cacioppo, J. T., & Goldman, R. (1981). Personal involvement as a determinant of argument-based persuasion. *Journal of Personality and Social Psychology, 41,* 847–855.

Petty, R. E., Cacioppo, J. T., & Schumann, D. (1983). Central and peripheral routes to advertising effectiveness: The moderating role of involvement. *Journal of Consumer Research, 10,* 134–148.

Pfefferbaum, A., Rosenbloom, M., Deshmukkh, A., & Sullivan, E., (2001). Sex differences in the effects of alcohol on brain structure. *American Journal of Psychiatry, 158,* 188–197.

Pfister, J. A., Stegelmeier, B. L., Gardner, D. R., & James, L. F. (2003). Grazing of spotted locoweed (*Astragalus lentiginosus*) by cattle and horses in Arizona. *Journal of Animal Science, 81,* 2285–2293.

Pham, L. B., Taylor, S. E., & Seeman, T. E. (2001). Effects of environmental predictability and personal mastery on self-regulatory and physiological processes. *Personality and Social Psychology Bulletin, 27,* 611–620.

Phares, V. (2008). *Understanding abnormal child psychology* (2nd ed.). Hoboken, NJ: Wiley.

Phelps, B. J., & Exum, M. E. (1992). Subliminal tapes: How to get the message across. *Skeptical Inquirer, 16,* 282–286.

Phelps, E. A., & LeDoux, J. E. (2005). Contributions of the amygdala to emotion processing: From animal models to human behavior. *Neuron, 48,* 175–187.

Phelps, E. A., O'Connor, K. J., Cunningham, W. A., Funayama, E. S., et al. (2000). Performance on indirect measures of race evaluation predicts amygdala activation. *Journal of Cognitive Neuroscience, 12,* 729–738.

Phelps, M. E., & Mazziotta, J. C. (1985). Positron emission tomography: Human brain function and biochemistry. *Science, 228,* 799–809.

Philip, P., Vervialle, F., Le Breton, P., Taillard, J., & Horne, J. A. (2001). Fatigue, alcohol, and serious road crashes in France: Factorial study of national data. *British Medical Journal, 322,* 829–830.

Phillips, K., Luk, A., Soor, G. S., Abraham, J. R., et al. (2009). Cocaine cardiotoxicity: A review of the pathophysiology, pathology, and treatment options. *American Journal of Cardiovascular Drugs, 9,* 177–196.

Phillips, K. M., Freund, B., Fordiani, J., Kuhn, R., & Ironson, G. (2009). EMDR treatment of past domestic violence: A clinical vignette. *Journal of EMDR Practice and Research, 3,* 192–197.

Phillips, P. E., Stuber, G. D., Heien, M. L., Wightman, R. M., & Carelli, R. M. (2003). Subsecond dopamine release promotes cocaine seeking. *Nature, 422,* 614–618.

Phinney, J. S., Ferguson, D. L., & Tate, J. D. (1997). Intergroup attitudes among ethnic minority adolescents: A causal model. *Child Development, 68,* 955–969.

Phinney, J. S., Jacoby, B., & Silva, C. (2007). Positive intergroup attitudes: The role of ethnic identity. *International Journal of Behavioral Development, 31,* 478–490.

Phipps, M. G., Blume, J. D., & DeMonner, S. M. (2002). Young maternal age associated with increased risk of postneonatal death. *Obstetrics and Gynecology, 100,* 481–486.

Pia, L., & Conway, P. M. (2008). Anosognosia and Alzheimer's disease. *Brain Impairment, 9,* 22–27.

Piasecki, T. M. (2006). Relapse to smoking. *Clinical Psychology Review, 26,* 196–215.

Pickering, A. D., & Gray, J. A. (1999). The neuroscience of personality. In L. A. Pervin & O. P. John (Eds.), *Handbook of personality: Theory and research* (2nd ed., pp. 277–299). New York: Guilford Press.

Pickler, N. (2002, November 19). NTSB cites fatigue, sleep apnea in fatal train wreck. *News & Observer.* Retrieved from http://newsobserver.com/24hour/nation/v-print/story/626769p-4807167c.html

Pike, K. M., Walsh, B. T., Vitousek, K., Wilson, G. T., & Bauer, J. (2003). Cognitive behavior therapy in the posthospitalization treatment of anorexia nervosa. *American Journal of Psychiatry, 160,* 2046–2049.

Piko, B. F., Bak, J., & Gibbons, F. X. (2007). Prototype perception and smoking: Are negative or positive social images more important in adolescents? *Addictive Behaviors, 32,* 1728–1732.

Piliavin, J. A., Dovidio, J. F., Gaertner, S. L., & Clark, R. D., III. (1981). *Emergency intervention.* New York: Academic Press.

Pillard, R. C., & Bailey, J. M. (1998). Human sexual orientation has a heritable component. *Human Biology, 70,* 347–365.

Pillemer, K., & Suitor, J. J. (2002). Explaining mothers' ambivalence towards their adult children. *Journal of Marriage and Family, 64,* 602–613.

Pillmann, F. (2009). Complex dream-enacting behavior in sleepwalking. *Psychosomatic Medicine, 71,* 231–234.

Pinel, J. P. J. (1993). *Biopsychology.* Boston: Allyn & Bacon.

Pinel, J. P. J., Lehman, D. R., & Assanand, S. (2002). Eating for optimal health: How much should we eat? Comment. *American Psychologist, 57,* 372–373.

Pinker, S. (1994). *The language instinct: How the mind creates language.* New York: Morrow.

Pipes, R. B., Holstein, J. E., & Aguirre, M. G. (2005). Examining the personal-professional distinction: Ethics codes and the difficulty of drawing a boundary. *American Psychologist, 60,* 325–334.

Pipitone, R. N., & Gallup, G. G., Jr. (2008). Women's voice attractiveness varies across the menstrual cycle. *Evolution and Human Behavior, 29,* 268–274.

Pittler, M. H., Verster, J. C., & Ernst, E. (2005). Interventions for preventing or treating alcohol hangover: Systematic review of randomised controlled trials. *British Medical Journal, 331,* 1515–1518.

Plant, E. A., & Sachs-Ericsson, N. (2004). Racial and ethnic differences in depression: The roles of social support and meeting basic needs. *Journal of Consulting and Clinical Psychology, 72,* 41–52.

Pleck, E. H. (2004). Two dimensions of fatherhood: A history of the good dad–bad dad complex. In M. E. Lamb (Ed.), *The role of the father in child development* (4th ed., pp. 32–57). Hoboken, NJ: Wiley.

Plomin, R. (1994). *Genetics and experience: The developmental interplay between nature and nurture.* Newbury Park, CA: Sage.

Plomin, R. (2004). *Two views about the nurture assumption.* Retrieved from the PsycCRITIQUES database.

Plomin, R., & Crabbe, J. C. (2000). DNA. *Psychological Bulletin, 126,* 806–828.

Plomin, R., DeFries, J. C., McClearn, G. E., & McGuffin, P. (2008). *Behavioral genetics* (5th ed.). New York: Worth.

Plomin, R., & McGuffin, P. (2003). Psychopathology in the postgenomic era. *Annual Review of Psychology, 54,* 205–228.

Plomin, R., & Spinath, F. M. (2004). Intelligence: Genetics, genes, and genomics. *Journal of Personality and Social Psychology, 86,* 112–129.

Ploner, M., Gross, J., Timmermann, L., & Schnitzler, A. (2002). Cortical representation of first and second pain sensation in humans. *Proceedings of the National Academy of Sciences, 99,* 12444–12448.

Plotnik, J., de Waal, F., & Reiss, D. (2006). Self-recognition in an Asian elephant. *Proceedings of the National Academy of Sciences, 103,* 17053–17057.

Plous, S. L., & Zimbardo, P. G. (2004, September 10). How social science can reduce terrorism. *Chronicle of Higher Education,* pp. B9–B10.

Plum, F., & Posner, J. B. (2000). *Diagnosis of stupor and coma.* New York: Oxford University Press.

Plutchik, R., & Conte, H. R. (Eds.). (1997). *Circumplex models of personality and emotions.* Washington, DC: American Psychological Association.

Pol, H. E. H., Schnack, H. G., Bertens, M. G. B. C., van Haren, N. E. M., et al. (2002). Volume changes in gray matter in patients with schizophrenia. *American Journal of Psychiatry, 159,* 244–250.

Poland, J., & Caplan, P. J. (2004). The deep structure of bias in psychiatric diagnosis. In P. J. Caplan & L. Cosgrove (Eds.), *Bias in psychiatric diagnosis: A project of the association for women in psychology* (pp. 9–23). Northvale, NJ: Aronson.

Poldrack, R. A., Halchenko, Y. O., & Hanson, S. J. (2009). Decoding the large-scale structure of brain function by classifying mental states across individuals. *Psychological Science, 20,* 1364–1372.

Polivy, J., & Herman, C. P. (2002). If at first you don't succeed: False hopes of self-change. *American Psychologist, 57,* 677–689.

Pollack, V. (1992). Meta-analysis of subjective sensitivity to alcohol in sons of alcoholics. *American Journal of Psychiatry, 149,* 1534–1538.

Pollo, A., & Benedetti, F. (2009). The placebo response: Neurobiological and clinical issues of neurological relevance. *Progress in Brain Research, 175,* 283–294.

Polusny, M. A., & Follette, V. M. (1996). Remembering childhood abuse: A national survey of psychologists' clinical practices, beliefs, and personal experiences. *Professional Psychology: Research and Practice, 27,* 41–52.

Pomerantz, E. M., Altermatt, E. R., & Saxon, J. L. (2002). Making the grade but feeling distressed: Gender differences in academic performance and internal distress. *Journal of Educational Psychology, 94,* 396–404.

Pomerleau, C. S., & Pomerleau, O. F. (1992). Euphoriant effects of nicotine in smokers. *Psychopharmacology, 108,* 460–465.

Pompili, M., Lester, D., De Pisa, E., Del Casale, A., et al. (2008). Surviving the suicides of significant others: A case study. *Crisis, 29,* 45–48.

Poon, L. W. (2008). What can we learn from centenarians? In C. Y. Read, R. C. Green, & M. A. Smyer (Eds.), *Aging, biotechnology, and the future* (pp. 100–110). Baltimore: Johns Hopkins University Press.

Pope, H. G., Gruber, A. J., Hudson, J. I., Huestis, M. A., & Yurgelun-Todd, D. (2001). Neuropsychological performance in long-term cannabis users. *Archives of General Psychiatry, 58,* 909–915.

Pope, H. G., Jr.; Hudson, J. I.; Bodkin, J. A.; & Oliva, P. (1998). Questionable validity of "dissociative amnesia" in trauma victims: Evidence from prospective studies. *British Journal of Psychiatry, 172,* 210–215.

Poropat, A. E. (2009). A meta-analysis of the five-factor model of personality and academic performance. *Psychological Bulletin, 135,* 322–338.

Porrino, L. J., Daunais, J. B., Rogers, G. A., Hampson, R. E., & Deadwyler, S. A. (2005). Facilitation of task performance and removal of the effects of sleep deprivation by an ampakine (CX717) in nonhuman primates. *Public Library of Science Biology, 3,* e299.

Port, C. L., Engdahl, B., & Frazier, P. (2001). A longitudinal and retrospective study of PTSD among older prisoners of war. *American Journal of Psychiatry, 158,* 1474–1479.

Porte, H. S., & Hobson, J. A. (1996). Physical motion in dreams: One measure of three theories. *Journal of Abnormal Psychology, 105,* 329–335.

Porter, J., Anand, T., Johnson, B., Khan, R. M., & Sobell, N. (2005). Brain mechanisms for extracting spatial information from smell. *Neuron, 47,* 581–592.

Porter, R. H. (1991). Human reproduction and the mother-infant relationship: The role of odors. In T. V. Getchell, R. L. Doty, L. M. Bartoshuk, & J. B. Snow (Eds.), *Taste and smell in health and disease* (pp. 429–442). New York: Raven Press.

Porter, R. H., Cernich, J. M., & McLaughlin, F. J. (1983). Maternal recognition of neonates through olfactory cues. *Physiology and Behavior, 30,* 151–154.

Porter, S., Birt, A. R., Yuille, J. C., & Lehman, D. R. (2000). Negotiating false memories: Interviewer and rememberer characteristics relate to memory distortion. *Psychological Science, 11,* 507–510.

Porter, S., & Peace, K. A. (2007). The scars of memory: A prospective, longitudinal investigation of the consistency of traumatic and positive emotional memories in adulthood. *Psychological Science 18,* 435–441.

Porter, S., Yuille, J. C., & Lehman, D. R. (1999). The nature of real, implanted, and fabricated memories for emotional childhood events: Implications for the recovered memory debate. *Law and Human Behavior, 23,* 517–537.

Posener, J. A., DeBattista, C., Williams, G. H., Kraemer, H. C., et al. (2000). 24-hour monitoring of cortisol and corticotropin secretion in psychotic and nonpsychotic major depression. *Archives of General Psychiatry, 57,* 755–760.

Posner, M. I. (1978). *Chronometric explorations of the mind.* Hillsdale, NJ: Erlbaum.

Posner, M. I., Nissen, M. J., & Ogden, W. C. (1978). Attended and unattended processing modes: The role of set for spatial location. In H. L. Pick & I. J. Saltzman (Eds.), *Modes of perceiving and processing information* (pp. 137–157). Hillsdale, NJ: Erlbaum.

Posner, M. I., & Peterson, S. E. (1990). The attention system of the human brain. *Annual Review of Neurosciences, 13,* 24–42.

Posner, M. I., & Raichle, M. E. (1994). *Images of mind.* New York: Scientific American Books.

Posner, M. I., & Rothbart, M. K. (2000). Developing mechanisms of self-regulation. *Development and Psychopathology, 12,* 427–427.

Posthuma, D., & de Geus, E. J. C. (2006). Progress in the molecular-genetic study of intelligence. *Current Directions in Psychological Science, 15,* 151–155.

Postuma, R. B., Gagnon, J. F., Vendette, M., & Montplaisir, J. Y. (2009). Idiopathic REM sleep behavior disorder in the transition to degenerative disease. *Movement Disorders, 24,* 2225–2232.

Potkin, S. G., Saha, A. R., Kujawa, M. J., Carson, W. H., et al. (2003). Aripiprazole, an antipsychotic with a novel mechanism of action, and risperidone vs. placebo in patients with schizophrenia and schizoaffective disorder. *Archives of General Psychiatry, 60,* 681–690.

Potter, P. T., & Zautra, A. J. (1997). Stressful life events' effects on rheumatoid arthritis disease activity. *Journal of Consulting and Clinical Psychology, 65,* 319–323.

Pottick, K. J., Bilder, S., VanderStoep, A., Warner, L. A., & Alvarez, M. F. (2008). U.S. patterns of mental health service utilization for transition-age youth and young adults. *Journal of Behavioral Health Services and Research, 35,* 373–389.

Pottick, K. J., Kirk, S. A., Hsieh, D. K., & Tian, X. (2007). Judging mental disorder in youths: Effects of client, clinician, and contextual differences. *Journal of Consulting and Clinical Psychology, 75,* 1–8.

Pourtois, G., de Gelder, B., Bol, A., & Crommelinck, M. (2005). Perception of facial expressions and voices and of their combination in the human brain. *Cortex, 41,* 49–59.

Povinelli, D. J., & Bering, J. M. (2002). The mentality of apes revisited. *Current Directions in Psychological Science, 11,* 115–119.

Powell, L. H., Shahabi, L., & Thoresen, C. E. (2003). Religion and spirituality: Linkages to physical health. *American Psychologist, 58,* 36–52.

Powers, M. B., Halpern, J. M., Ferenschak, M. P., Gillihan, S. J., & Foa, E. B. (2010). A meta-analytic review of prolonged exposure for posttraumatic stress disorder. *Clinical Psychology Review, 30,* 635–641.

Powley, T. L., & Keesey, R. E. (1970). Relationship of body weight to the lateral hypothalamic feeding syndrome. *Journal of Comparative and Physiological Psychology, 70,* 25–36.

Prabhudesai, S. G., Gould, S., Rekhraj, S., Tekkis, P. P., et al. (2008). Artificial neural networks: Useful aid in diagnosing acute appendicitis. *World Journal of Surgery, 32,* 305–309.

Pradhan, A. K., Hammel, K. R., DeRamus, R., Pollatsek, A., et al. (2005). Using eye movements to evaluate effects of driver age on risk perception in a driving simulator. *Human Factors, 47,* 840–852.

Pratkanis, A. R. (1992). The cargo-cult science of subliminal persuasion. *Skeptical Inquirer, 16,* 260–273.

Pratkanis, A. R., & Aronson, E. (2001). *The age of propaganda: The everyday use and abuse of persuasion.* New York: Holt; New York: Freeman.

Pratkanis, A. R., Eskenazi, J., & Greenwald, A. G. (1994). What you expect is what you believe (but not necessarily what you get): A test of the effectiveness of self-help audiotapes. *Basic and Applied Social Psychology, 15,* 251–276.

Preilowski, B. (2009). Erinnerung an einen Amnestiker (und ein halbes Jahrhundert Gedächtnisforschung) [Remembering an amnestic patient (and half a century of memory research)]. *Fortschritte der Neurologie-Psychiatrie, 77,* 568–576. Epub 2009 Sep 7.

Premack, D. (1965). Reinforcement theory. In D. Levine (Ed.), *Nebraska symposium on motivation* (Vol. 13, pp. 123–180). Lincoln: University of Nebraska Press.

Premack, D. (1971). Language in chimpanzees? *Science, 172,* 808–822.

Premack, D., & Premack, A. J. (1983). *The mind of an ape.* New York: Norton.

Prescott, J. W. (1996). The origins of human love and violence. *Pre- and Peri-Natal Psychology Journal, 10,* 143–188.

Pressman, S. D., & Cohen, S. (2005). Does positive affect influence health? *Psychological Bulletin, 131,* 925–971.

Pressman, S. D., & Cohen, S. (2007). Use of social words in autobiographies and longevity. *Psychosomatic Medicine, 69,* 262–269.

Pressman, S. D., Cohen, S., Miller, G. E., Barkin, A., et al. (2005). Loneliness, social network size, and immune response to influenza vaccination in college freshman. *Health Psychology, 24,* 297–306.

Preuss, U. W., Watzke, A. B., Zimmermann, J., Wong, J. W., & Schmidt, C. O. (2010). Cannabis withdrawal severity and short-term course among cannabis-dependent adolescent and young adult inpatients. *Drug and Alcohol Dependence, 106,* 133–141.

Price, K. H., Harrison, D. A., & Gavin, J. H. (2006). Withholding inputs in team contexts: Member composition, interaction processes, evaluation structure, and social loafing. *Journal of Applied Psychology, 91,* 1375–1384.

Priego, T., Sánchez, J., Palou, A., & Picó, C. (2010). Leptin intake during the suckling period improves the metabolic response of adipose tissue to a high-fat diet. *International Journal of Obesity, 34,* 809–819.

Prikryl, R., Ceskova, E., Kasparek, T., & Kucerova, H. (2006). Neurological soft signs, clinical symptoms and treatment reactivity in patients suffering from first episode schizophrenia. *Journal of Psychiatric Research, 40,* 141–146.

Prinstein, M. J., & La Greca, A. M. (2002). Peer crowd affiliation and internalizing distress in childhood and adolescence: A longitudinal follow-back study. *Journal of Research on Adolescence, 12,* 35–351.

Prinzmetal, W. (1992). The word superiority effect does not require a T-scope. *Perception and Psychophysics, 51,* 473–484.

Prochaska, J. O., DiClemente, C., & Norcross, J. (1992). In search of how people change: Application to addictive behaviors. *American Psychologist, 47,* 1102–1114.

Procopio, M., & Marriott, P. (2007). Intrauterine hormonal environment and risk of developing anorexia nervosa. *Archives of General Psychiatry, 64,* 1402–1407.

Program for International Student Assessment. (2005). *Learning for tomorrow's world: First results from PISA 2004.* Paris: Organisation for Economic Cooperation and Development.

Pronin, E., Wegner, D. M., McCarthy, K., & Rodriguez, S. (2006). Everyday magical powers: The role of apparent causation in the overestimation of personal influence. *Journal of Personality and Social Psychology, 91,* 218–231.

Proske, E. (2006). Kinesthesia: The role of muscle receptors. *Muscle and Nerve, 34,* 545–558.

Pruitt, D. G., & Carnevale, P. J. (1993). *Negotiation in social conflict.* Pacific Grove, CA: Brooks/Cole.

Puca, A. A., Daly, M. J., Brewster, S. J., Matis, T. C., et al. (2001). A genome-wide scan for linkage to human exceptional longevity identifies a locus on chromosome 4. *Proceedings of the National Academy of Sciences, 10,* 1073.

Pugh, K. R., Mencl, W. E., Shaywitz, B. A., Shaywitz, S. E., et al. (2000). The angular gyrus in developmental dyslexia: Task-specific differences in functional connectivity within posterior cortex. *Psychological Science, 11,* 51–56.

Purcell, D. G., & Stewart, A. L. (1991). The object-detection effect: Configuration enhances perception. *Perception and Psychophysics, 50,* 215–224.

Purdon, C. (2009). Psychological approaches to understanding obsessive-compulsive disorder. In M. M. Antony & M. B. Stein (Eds.), *Oxford handbook of anxiety and related disorders* (pp. 238–249). New York: Oxford University Press.

Purves, D., Williams, M., Nundy, S., & Lotto, R. B. (2004). Perceiving the intensity of light. *Psychological Review, 111,* 142–158.

Purves, D., Platt, M., Cabeza, R., Huettel, S. A., & Brannon, E. (2008). *Principles of cognitive neuroscience.* Sunderland, MA: Sinauer Associates.

Putnam, F. W. (2003). Ten-year research update review: Child sexual abuse. *Journal of the American Academy of Child and Adolescent Psychiatry, 42,* 269–278.

Puts, D. A. (2005). Mating context and menstrual phase affect female preferences for male voice pitch. *Evolution and Human Behavior, 26,* 388–397.

Pyszczynski, T., Greenberg, J., Koole, S., & Solomon, S. (2010). Experimental existential psychology: Coping with the facts of life. In S. T. Fiske, D. T. Gilbert, & G. Lindzey (Eds.), *Handbook of social psychology* (5th ed., Vol. 2, pp. 724–760). Hoboken, NJ: Wiley.

Pyszczynski, T., Rothschild, Z., & Abdollahi, A. (2008). Terrorism, violence, and hope for peace: A terror management perspective. *Current Directions in Psychological Science, 17,* 318–322.

Quinn, P. C., & Bhatt, R. S. (2005). Learning perceptual organization in infancy. *Psychological Science, 16,* 511–515.

Quinn, P. C., & Liben, L. S. (2008). A sex difference in mental rotation in young infants. *Psychological Science, 19,* 1067–1070.

Quintana, S. M. (2011). Ethnicity, race, and children's social development. In P. K. Smith & C. H. Hart (Eds.), *Wiley-Blackwell handbook of childhood social development* (2nd ed). Hoboken, NJ: Wiley-Blackwell.

Quitkin, F. M., Petkkova, E., McGrath, P. J., Taylor, B., et al. (2003). When should a trial of fluoxetine for major depression be declared failed? *American Journal of Psychiatry, 160,* 734–740.

Quoidback, J., Dunn, E. W., Petrides, K. V., & Mikolajczak, M. (2010). Money giveth, money taketh away: The dual effect of wealth on happiness. *Psychological Science, 21,* 759–763.

Raaijmakers, Q. A. W., Engels, R. C. M. E., & Van Hoof, A. (2005). Delinquency and moral reasoning in adolescence and young adulthood. *International Journal of Behavioral Development, 29,* 247–258.

Rabbitt, P. (1977). Changes in problem-solving ability in old age. In J. E. Birren & K. W. Schaie (Eds.), *Handbook of the psychology of aging* (pp. 606–625). New York: Van Nostrand Reinhold.

Rabinovici, G. D., & Miller, B. L. (2010). Frontotemporal lobar degeneration: Epidemiology, pathophysiology, diagnosis, and management. *CNS Drugs, 24,* 375–398.

Rabinowitz, J., De Smedt, G., Harvey, P. D., & Davidson, M. (2002). Relationship between premorbid functioning and symptom severity as assessed at first episode of psychosis. *American Journal of Psychiatry, 159,* 2021–2026.

Rabinowitz, J., Lichtenberg, P., Kaplan, Z., Mark, M., et al. (2001). Rehospitalization rates of chronically ill schizophrenic patients discharged on a regimen of risperidone, olanzapine, or conventional antipsychotics. *American Journal of Psychiatry, 158,* 266–269.

Rabunal, J. R., & Dorado, J. (2006). *Artificial neural networks in real-life applications.* Hershey, PA: Idea Group.

Rachlin, H. (2000). *The science of self-control.* Cambridge, MA: Harvard University Press.

Rachlin, H., & Jones, B. A. (2008). Altruism among relatives and non-relatives. *Behavioural Processes, 79,* 120–123.

Racsmány, M., Conway, M. A., & Demeter, G. (2010). Consolidation of episodic memories during sleep: Long-term effects of retrieval practice. *Psychological Science, 21,* 80–85.

Rada, J. B., & Rogers, R. W. (1973, April). *Obedience to authority: Presence of authority and command strength.* Paper presented at the 19th annual convention of the Southeastern Psychological Association, Atlanta.

Radcliffe, N. M., & Klein, W. M. (2002). Dispositional, unrealistic, and comparative optimism: Differential relations with the knowledge and processing of risk information and beliefs about personal risk. *Personality and Social Psychology Bulletin, 28,* 836–846.

Radford, B. (2005, August 30). Voice of reason: Exorcisms, fictional and fatal. *Skeptical Inquirer, 29.* Retrieved from http://www.livescience.com/strangenews/050830_emilyrose.html.

Radford, B. (2006, July 29). CSI: Turning from science to psychics. *Skeptical Inquirer, 30.* Retrieved from http://www.csicop.org/specialarticles/show/csi_turning_from_science_to_psychics

Radvansky, G. A. (1999). Aging, memory, and comprehension. *Current Directions in Psychological Science, 8,* 49–53.

Raffaelli, M., & Crockett, L. J. (2003). Sexual risk taking in adolescence: The role of self-regulation and attraction to risk. *Developmental Psychology, 39,* 1036–1046.

Raggatt, P. T. (1991). Work stress among long-distance coach drivers: A survey and correlational study. *Journal of Organizational Behavior, 12,* 565–579.

Raguram, R., & Bhide, A. (1985). Patterns of phobic neurosis: A retrospective study. *British Journal of Psychiatry, 147,* 557–560.

Raij, T. T., Numminen, J., Narvanen, S., Hiltunen, J., & Hari, R. (2005). Brain correlates of subjective reality of physically and psychologically induced pain. *Proceedings of the National Academy of Sciences, 102,* 2147–2151.

Raikes, H., Pan, B. A., Luze, G., Tamis-LeMonda, C. S., et al. (2006). Mother-child book reading in low-income families: Correlates and outcomes during the first three years of life. *Child Development, 77,* 924–953.

Raine, A., Brennan, P., & Mednick, S. (1994). Birth complications combined with early maternal rejection at age 1 year predispose to violent crime at age 18 years. *Archives of General Psychiatry, 51,* 984–988.

Raine, A., Moffitt, T. E., Caspi, A., Loeber, R., et al. (2005). Neurocognitive impairments in boys on the life-course persistent antisocial path. *Journal of Abnormal Psychology, 114,* 38–49.

Raineteau, O. (2008). Plastic responses to spinal cord injury. *Behavioural Brain Research, 192,* 114–123.

Rains, G. C., Tomberline, J. K., & Kulasiri, D. (2008). Using insect sniffing devices for detection. *Trends in Biotechnology, 26*(6), 288–294

Rains, G. C., Utley, S. L., & Lewis, W. J. (2006). Behavioral monitoring of trained insects for chemical detection. *Biotechnology Progress, 22,* 2–8.

Raisig, S., Welke, T., Hagendorf, H., & van der Meer, E. (2010). I spy with my little eye: Detection of temporal violations in event sequences and the pupillary response. *International Journal of Psychophysiology, 76,* 1–8.

Rajaram, S., & Barber, S. J. (2008). Retrieval processes in memory. In H. L. Roediger III (Ed.), *Cognitive psychology of memory*. Oxford: Elsevier.

Rakic, P. (2002). Neurogenesis in adult primate neocortex: An evaluation of the evidence. *Nature Reviews Neuroscience, 3,* 65–71.

Ramachandran, V. S. (1988, August). Perceiving shape from shading. *Scientific American*, pp. 76–83.

Ramachandran, V. S. (1998). Consciousness and body image: Lessons from phantom limbs, Capgras syndrome and pain asymbolia. *Philosophical Transactions of the Royal Society of London, B, 353,* 1851–1859.

Ramachandran, V. S. (2008). *The man with the phantom twin: Adventures in the neuroscience of the human brain.* New York: Dutton.

Ramachandran, V. S., & Hubbard, E. M. (2001). Psychophysical investigations into the neural basis of synaesthesia. *Proceedings of the Royal Society London, B, 268,* 979–983.

Ramanathan, D., Tuszynski, M. H., & Conner, J. M. (2009). The basal forebrain cholinergic system is required specifically for behaviorally mediated cortical map plasticity. *Journal of Neuroscience, 29,* 5992–6000.

Ramey, C. T. (1992). High-risk children and IQ: Altering intergenerational patterns. *Intelligence, 16,* 239–256.

Ramey, C. T., Ramey, S. L., & Lanzi, R. G. (2006). Children's health and education. In W. Damon & R. M. Lerner (Series Eds.) & K. A. Renninger & I. E. Sigel (Vol. Eds.), *Handbook of child psychology: Vol. 4. Child psychology in practice* (6th ed., pp. 864–892). Hoboken, NJ: Wiley.

Ramey, S. L. (1999). Head Start and preschool education: Toward continued improvement. *American Psychologist, 54,* 344–346.

Randolph-Seng, B., & Mather, R. D. (2009). Does subliminal persuasion work? It depends on your motivation and awareness. *Skeptical Inquirer, 33,* 49–53.

Rapee, R. M., Brown, T. A., Antony, M. M., & Barlow, D. H. (1992). Response to hyperventilation and inhalation of 5.5% carbon dioxide-enriched air across DSM-III anxiety disorders. *Journal of Abnormal Psychology, 101,* 538–552.

Rapee, R. M., Gaston, J. E., & Abbott, M. J. (2009). Testing the efficacy of theoretically derived improvements in the treatment of social phobia. *Journal of Consulting and Clinical Psychology, 77,* 317–327.

Rapee, R. M., Kennedy, S., Ingram, M., Edwards, S., & Sweeney, L. (2005). Prevention and early intervention of anxiety disorders in inhibited preschool children. *Journal of Consulting and Clinical Psychology, 73,* 488–497.

Rapoport, J. L., Addington, A. M., & Frangou, S. (2005). The neurodevelopmental model of schizophrenia: Update 2005. *Molecular Psychiatry, 10,* 434–449.

Rapp, S. R., Brenes, G., & Marsh, A. P. (2002). Memory enhancement training for older adults with mild cognitive impairment: A preliminary study. *Aging and Mental Health, 6,* 5–11.

Rasch, B., & Born, J. (2008). Reactivation and consolidation of memory during sleep. *Current Directions in Psychological Science, 17,* 188–192.

Rasinski, K. A., Kuby, A., Bzdusek, S. A., Silvestri, J. M., & Weese-Mayer, D. E. (2003). Effect of a sudden infant death syndrome risk reduction education program on risk factor compliance and information sources in primarily black urban communities. *Pediatrics, 111,* 347–354.

Raskin, D. C. (1986). The polygraph in 1986: Scientific, professional, and legal issues surrounding applications and acceptance of polygraph evidence. *Utah Law Review, 1,* 29–74.

Raskin, N. J., & Rogers, C. R. (2005). Person-centered therapy. In R. J. Corsini & D. Wedding (Eds.), *Current psychotherapies* (7th ed., pp. 130–165). Belmont, CA: Brooks/Cole.

Raskind, M. A., Peskind, E. R., Hoff, D. J., Hart, K. L., et al. (2006). A parallel-group placebo-controlled study of prazosin for trauma nightmares and sleep disturbance in combat veterans with posttraumatic stress disorder. *Biological Psychiatry, 61,* 928–934.

Rasmussen, H., Erritzoe, D., Andersen, R., Ebdrup, B. H., et al. (2010). Decreased frontal serotonin 2A receptor binding in antipsychotic-naive patients with first-episode schizophrenia. *Archives of General Psychiatry, 67,* 9–16.

Rasmussen, K. G. (2003). Clinical applications of recent research on electroconvulsive therapy. *Bulletin of the Menninger Clinic, 67,* 18–31.

Rathbone, D. B., & Huckabee, J. C. (1999). *Controlling road rage: A literature review and pilot study.* Washington, DC: American Automobile Association.

Ratner, C. (1994). The unconscious: A perspective from sociohistorical psychology. *Journal of Mind and Behavior, 15,* 323–342.

Rattenborg, N., Lima, S. L., & Amlaner, C. J. (1999). Half-awake to the risk of predation. *Nature, 397,* 397–398. doi:10.1038/17037

Raudenbush, B., & Meyer, B. (2002). Effect of nasal dilators on pleasantness, intensity, and sampling behaviors of foods in the oral cavity. *Rhinology, 39,* 80–83.

Rawson, P. (2006). *Handbook of short-term psychodynamic psychotherapy.* London: Karnac Books.

Ray, D. W., Wandersman, A., Ellisor, J., & Huntington, D. E. (1982). The effects of high density in a juvenile correctional institution. *Basic and Applied Social Psychology, 3,* 95–108.

Ray, L. A.; Miranda, R., Jr.; Tidey, J. W.; McGeary, J. E.; et al. (2010). Polymorphisms of the μ-opioid receptor and dopamine D4 receptor genes and subjective responses to alcohol in the natural environment. *Journal of Abnormal Psychology, 119,* 115–125.

Raz, A., Fan, J., & Posner, M. I. (2005). Hypnotic suggestion reduces conflict in the brain. *Proceedings of the National Academy of Sciences, 102,* 9978–9983.

Razali, S. M., Aminah, K., & Umeed, A. (2002). Religious-cultural psychotherapy in the management of anxiety patients. *Transcultural Psychiatry, 39,* 130–136.

Read, S. J., Monroe, B. M., Brownstein, A. L., Yang, Y., et al. (2010). A neural network model of the structure and dynamics of human personality. *Psychological Review, 117,* 61–92.

Reb, J., & Greguras, G. J. (2010). Understanding performance ratings: Dynamic performance, attributions, and rating purpose. *Journal of Applied Psychology, 95,* 213–220.

Reber, A. S. (1992). The cognitive unconscious: An evolutionary perspective. *Consciousness and Cognition, 1,* 93–133.

Redd, M., & de Castro, J. M. (1992). Social facilitation of eating: Effects of social instruction on food intake. *Physiology and Behavior, 52,* 749–754.

Reder, L. M., & Ritter, F. E. (1992). What determines initial feeling of knowing? Familiarity with question terms, not the answer. *Journal of Experimental Psychology: Learning, Memory, and Cognition, 18,* 435–451.

Redmond, D. E., Jr.; Bjugstad, K. B.; Teng, Y. D.; Ourednik, V.; et al. (2007). Behavioral improvement in a primate Parkinson's model is associated with multiple homeostatic effects of human neural stem cells. *Proceedings of the National Academy of Sciences, 104,* 12175–12180.

Reed, P. L., Anthony, J. C., & Breslau, N. (2007). Incidence of drug problems in young adults exposed to trauma and posttraumatic stress disorder: Do early life experiences and predispositions matter? *Archives of General Psychiatry, 64,* 1435–1442.

Reed, R. R. (2004). After the holy grail: Establishing a molecular basis for mammalian olfaction. *Cell, 116,* 329–336.

Reed, S. K. (2004). *Cognition: Theory and applications* (6th ed.). Belmont, CA: Wadsworth.

Reedy, M. N. (1983). Personality and aging. In D. S. Woodruff & J. E. Birren (Eds.), *Aging: Scientific perspectives and social issues* (2nd ed.). Monterey, CA: Brooks/Cole.

Reeve, C. L., & Bonaccio, S. (2008). Does test anxiety induce measurement bias in cognitive ability tests? *Intelligence, 36,* 526–538.

Reeve, J. M. (1996). *Understanding motivation and emotion.* Orlando, FL: Harcourt Brace Jovanovich.

Reeves, G. K., Pirie, K., Beral, V., Green, J., et al. (2007). Cancer incidence and mortality in relation to body mass index in the Million Women Study: Cohort study. *British Medical Journal, 335,* 1134.

Reeves, M. J., & Rafferty, A. P. (2005). Healthy lifestyle characteristics among adults in the United States, 2000. *Archives of Internal Medicine, 165,* 854–857.

Regier, D. A., Narrow, W., Rae, D., Manderschied, R., et al. (1993). The de facto U.S. mental and addictive disorders service system: Epidemiologic catchment area prospective 1-year prevalence rates of disorders and services. *Archives of General Psychiatry, 50,* 85–94.

Regier, T., Kay, P., & Cook, R. S. (2005). Focal colors are universal after all. *Proceedings of the National Academy of Sciences, 102,* 8386–8391.

Rehm, L. P., & DeMers, S. T. (2006). Licensure. *Clinical Psychology: Science and Practice, 13,* 249–253.

Reid, M. J., Webster-Stratton, C., & Baydar, N. (2004). Halting the development of conduct problems in Head Start children: The effects of parent training. *Journal of Clinical Child and Adolescent Psychology, 33,* 279–291.

Reingold, E. M., Charness, N., Pomplun, M., & Stampe, D. M. (2001). Visual span in expert chess players: Evidence from eye movements. *Psychological Science, 12,* 48–55.

Reinisch, J. M., Ziemba-Davis, M., & Sanders, S. A. (1991). Hormonal contributions to sexually dimorphic behavioral development in humans. *Psychoneuroendocrinology, 16,* 213–278.

Reis, B. F., & Brown, L. G. (2006). Preventing therapy dropout in the real world: The clinical utility of videotape preparation and client estimate of treatment duration. *Professional Psychology: Research and Practice, 37,* 311–316.

Reis, H. T., & Gable, S. L. (2003). Toward a positive psychology of relationships. In C. L. M. Keyes & J. Haidt (Eds.), *Flourishing: Positive psychology and the life well-lived* (pp. 129–159). Washington, DC: American Psychological Association.

Reisenzein, R. (1983). The Schachter theory of emotion: Two decades later. *Psychological Bulletin, 94,* 239–264.

Reiss, A. J., & Roth, J. A. (1993). *Understanding and preventing violence.* Washington, DC: National Academies Press.

Reiss, D., & Marino, L. (2001). Mirror self-recognition in the bottlenose dolphin: A case of cognitive convergence. *Proceedings of the National Academy of Sciences, 98,* 5937–5942.

Reiss, D., Neiderhiser, J. M., Hetherington, E. M., & Plomin, R. (2000). *The relationship code: Deciphering genetic and social influences on adolescent development.* Cambridge, MA: Harvard University Press.

Remick, A. K., Polivy, J., & Pliner, P. (2009). Internal and external moderators of the effect of variety on food intake. *Psychological Bulletin, 135,* 434–451.

Rendall, D., Cheney, D. L., & Seyfarth, R. M. (2000). Proximate factors mediating "contact" calls in adult female baboons (*Papio cynocephalus ursinus*) and their infants. *Journal of Comparative Psychology, 114,* 36–46.

Renner, K. H., & Beversdorf, D. Q. (2010). Effects of naturalistic stressors on cognitive flexibility and working memory task performance. *Neurocase, 16,* 293–300. doi:10.1080/13554790903463601

Rentz, D. M., Huh, T. J., Faust, R. R., Budson, A. E., et al. (2004). Use of IQ-adjusted norms to predict progressive cognitive decline in highly intelligent older individuals. *Neuropsychology, 18,* 38–49.

Rescorla, L. A. (1981). Category development in early language. *Journal of Child Language, 8,* 225–238.

Rescorla, R. A. (1968). Probability of shock in the presence and absence of CS in fear conditioning. *Journal of Comparative and Physiological Psychology, 66,* 1–5.

Rescorla, R. A. (1988). Pavlovian conditioning: It's not what you think it is. *American Psychologist, 43,* 151–159.

Rescorla, R. A. (2005). Spontaneous recovery of excitation but not inhibition. *Journal of Experimental Psychology: Animal Behavior Processes, 31,* 277–288.

Rescorla, R. A., & Wagner, A. R. (1972). A theory of Pavlovian conditioning: Variations in the effectiveness of reinforcement and nonreinforcement. In A. H. Black & W. F. Prokasky (Eds.), *Classical conditioning II* (pp. 64–99). New York: Appleton-Century-Crofts.

Reuter, J., Raedler, T., Rose, M., Hand, I., et al. (2005). Pathological gambling is linked to reduced activation of the mesolimbic reward system. *Nature Neuroscience, 8,* 147–148.

Reuter, M., Schmitz, A., Corr, P., & Hennig, J. (2006). Molecular genetics support Gray's personality theory: The interaction of COMT and DRD2 polymorphisms predicts the behavioural approach system. *International Journal of Neuropsychopharmacology, 9,* 155–166.

Revell, V. L., & Eastman, C. I. (2005). How to trick Mother Nature into letting you fly around or stay up all night. *Journal of Biological Rhythms, 20,* 353–365.

Revelle, W. (2008). The contribution of reinforcement sensitivity theory to personality theory. In P. J. Corr (Ed.), *The reinforcement sensitivity theory of personality* (pp. 508–527). Cambridge: Cambridge University Press.

Revonsuo, A. (2001). The reinterpretation of dreams: An evolutionary hypothesis of dreaming. *Behavior and Brain Sciences, 23,* 877–1121.

Reyna, V. F., & Farley, F. (2006). Risk and rationality in adolescent decision making: Implications for theory, practice, and public policy. *Psychological Science in the Public Interest, 7,* 1–44.

Reynolds, C. A., Finkel, D., McArdle, J. J., Gatz, M., et al. (2005). Quantitative genetic analysis of latent growth curve models of cognitive abilities in adulthood. *Developmental Psychology, 41,* 3–16.

Reynolds, J. S., & Perrin, N. A. (2004). Mismatches in social support and psychosocial adjustment to breast cancer. *Health Psychology, 23,* 425–430.

Rhodes, G., Halberstadt, J., & Brajkovich, G. (2001). Generalization of mere exposure effects to averaged composite faces. *Social Cognition, 19,* 57–70.

Ribases, M., Gratacos, M., Badia, A., Jimenez, L., et al. (2005). Contribution of NTRK2 to the genetic susceptibility to anorexia nervosa, harm avoidance and minimum body mass index. *Molecular Psychiatry, 10,* 851–860.

Riccio, D. C., Millin, P. M., & Gisquet-Verrier, P. (2003). Retrograde amnesia: Forgetting back. *Current Directions in Psychological Science, 12,* 41–44.

Rice, F., Harold, G. T., Shelton, K. H., & Thaper, A. (2006). Family conflict interacts with genetic liability in predicting childhood and adolescent depression. *Journal of the American Academy of Child and Adolescent Psychiatry, 45,* 841–848.

Rice, G., Anderson, C., Risch, H., & Ebers, G. (1999). Male homosexuality: Absence of linkage to microsatellite markers at Xq28. *Science, 284,* 665–667.

Rice, M. E. (1997). Violent offender research and implications for the criminal justice system. *American Psychologist, 52,* 414–423.

Richards, J. M., & Gross, J. J. (2000). Emotion regulation and memory: The cognitive costs of keeping one's cool. *Journal of Personality and Social Psychology, 79,* 410–424.

Richards, M., Shipley, B., Fuhrer, R., & Wadsworth, M. E. J. (2004). Cognitive ability in childhood and cognitive decline in mid-life: Longitudinal birth cohort study. *British Medical Journal, 328,* 552.

Richards, T. L., Corina, D., Serafini, S., Steury, K., et al. (2000). Effects of a phonologically driven treatment for dyslexia on lactate levels measured by proton MR spectroscopic imaging. *American Journal of Neuroradiology, 21,* 916–922.

Richardson, G. A., Goldschmidt, L., & Larkby, C. (2007). Effects of prenatal cocaine exposure on growth: A longitudinal analysis. *Pediatrics, 120,* e1017–e1027.

Richardson, J., Smith, J. E., McCall, G., Richardson, A., et al. (2007). Hypnosis for nausea and vomiting in cancer chemotherapy: A systematic review of the research evidence. *European Journal of Cancer Care (England), 16,* 402–412.

Richardson-Klavehn, A., & Bjork, R. A. (1988). Measures of memory. *Annual Review of Psychology, 39,* 475–543.

Richman, L. S., Kubzansky, L., Maselko, J., Kawachi, I., et al. (2005). Positive emotion and health: Going beyond the negative. *Health Psychology, 24,* 422–429.

Richmond, J., & Nelson, C. A. (2007). Accounting for change in declarative memory: A cognitive neuroscience perspective. *Developmental Review, 27,* 349–373. doi:10.1016/j.dr.2007.04.002

Rickels, K., & Rynn, M. (2002). Pharmocotherapy of generalized anxiety disorder. *Journal of Clinical Psychiatry, 63*(Suppl. 14), 9–16.

Rickels, K., Schweizer, E., Weiss, S., & Zavodnick, S. (1993). Maintenance drug treatment of panic disorder: II. Short- and long-term outcome after drug taper. *Archives of General Psychiatry, 50,* 61–68.

Rickels, K., Zaninelli, R., McCafferty, J., Bellew, K., et al. (2003). Paroxetine treatment of generalized anxiety disorder: A double-blind, placebo-controlled study. *American Journal of Psychiatry, 160,* 749–756.

Riddoch, M. J., Humphreys, G. W., Akhtar, N. A., Allen, H., et al. (2008). A tale of two agnosias: Distinctions between form and integrative agnosia. *Cognitive Neuropsychology, 25,* 56–92.

Ridley, M. (2000). *Genome: The autobiography of a species in 23 chapters.* New York: HarperCollins.

Rieber, R. W. (2006). *The bifurcation of the self: The history and theory of dissociation and its disorders.* New York: Springer.

Riedy, C. A., Chavez, M., Figlewicz, D. P., & Woods, S. C. (1995). Central insulin enhances sensitivity to cholecystokinin. *Physiology and Behavior, 58,* 755–760.

Riggio, R. E. (1989). *Introduction to industrial/organizational psychology.* Glenview, IL: Scott, Foresman.

Riggs, K. J., McTaggart, J., Simpson, A., & Freeman, R. P. J. (2006). Changes in the capacity of visual working memory in 5- to 10-year-olds. *Journal of Experimental Child Psychology, 95,* 18–26. doi:10.1016/j.jecp.2006.03.009

Rihmer, Z. (2001). Can better recognition and treatment of depression reduce suicide rates? A brief review. *European Psychiatry, 16,* 406–409.

Riis, J., Loewenstein, G., Baron, J., Jepson, C., et al. (2005). Ignorance of hedonic adaptation to hemodialysis: A study using ecological momentary assessment. *Journal of Experimental Psychology: General, 134,* 3–9.

Rimes, K. A., & Watkins, E. (2005). The effects of self-focused rumination on global negative self-judgments in depression. *Behaviour Research and Therapy, 43,* 1673–1681.

Rind, B., & Tromovitch, P. (1997). A meta-analytic review of findings from national samples on psychological correlates of child sexual abuse. *Journal of Sex Research, 34,* 237–255.

Rind, B., Tromovitch, P., & Bauserman, R. (1998). A meta-analytic examination of assumed properties of child sexual abuse using college samples. *Psychological Bulletin, 124,* 22–53.

Rindermann, H., & Ceci, S. J. (2009). Educational policy and country outcomes in international cognitive competence studies. *Perspectives on Psychological Science, 4,* 551–577.

Rioult-Pedotti, M.-S., Friedman, D., & Donoghue, J. P. (2000). Learning-induced LTP in neocortex. *Science, 290,* 533–536.

Ripple, C. H., Gilliam, W. S., Chanana, N., & Zigler, E. (1999). Will fifty cooks spoil the broth? The debate over entrusting Head Start to the states. *American Psychologist, 54,* 327–343.

Risen, J. (1998, July 7). CIA seeks "curmudgeon" to signal its mistakes. *New York Times.*

Rissman, J., Greely, H. T., & Wagner, A. D. (2010). Detecting individual memories through the neural decoding of memory states and past experience. *Proceedings of the National Academy of Sciences, 107,* 9849–9854.

Rizzolatti, G., & Arbib, M. A. (1998). Language within our grasp. *Trends in Neuroscience, 21,* 188–194.

Rizzolatti, G., Fadiga, L., Gallese, V., & Fogassi, L. (1996). Premotor cortex and the recognition of motor actions. *Brain Research: Cognitive Brain Research, 3,* 131–141.

Ro, T., & Rafal, R. (2006). Visual restoration in cortical blindness: Insights from natural and TMS-induced blindsight. *Neuropsychology and Rehabilitation, 16,* 377–396.

Robakis, T. K., & Hirsch, L. J. (2006). Literature review, case report, and expert discussion of prolonged refractory status epilepticus. *Neurocritical Care, 4,* 35–46.

Robbins, S. B., Lauver, K., Le, H., Davis, D., Langley, R., & Carlstrom, A. (2004). Do psychosocial and study skill factors predict college outcomes? A meta-analysis. *Psychological Bulletin, 130,* 261–288.

Robbins, T. W., & Everitt, B. J. (1999). Interaction of the dopaminergic system with mechanisms of associative learning and cognition: Implications for drug abuse. *Psychological Science, 10,* 199–202.

Roberts, B. W., Caspi, A., & Moffitt, T. E. (2001). The kids are alright: Growth and stability in personality development from adolescence to adulthood. *Journal of Personality and Social Psychology, 81,* 670–683.

Roberts, B. W., & Delvecchio, W. F. (2000). The rank-order consistency of traits from childhood to old age: A quantitative review of longitudinal studies. *Psychological Bulletin, 126,* 3–25.

Roberts, B. W., Helson, R., & Klohnen, E. C. (2002). Personality development and growth in women across 30 years: Three perspectives. *Journal of Personality, 70,* 79–102.

Roberts, B. W., Kuncel, N., Shiner, R. N., Caspi, A., & Goldberg, L. R. (2007). The power of personality: The comparative validity of personality traits, socioeconomic status, and cognitive ability for predicting important life outcomes. *Perspectives in Psychological Science, 2,* 313–345.

Roberts, B. W., & Mroczek, D. (2008). Personality trait change in adulthood. *Current Directions in Psychological Science, 17,* 31–35.

Roberts, B. W., Smith, J., Jackson, J. J., & Edmonds, G. (2009). Compensatory conscientiousness and health in older couples. *Psychological Science, 20,* 553–559.

Roberts, B. W., Walton, K. E., & Viechtbauer, W. (2006). Patterns of mean-level change in personality traits across the life course: A meta-analysis of longitudinal studies. *Psychological Bulletin, 132,* 1–25.

Roberts, B. W., Wood, D., & Caspi, A. (2008). The development of personality traits in adulthood. In O. P. John, R. W. Robins, & L. A. Pervin (Eds.), *Handbook of personality: Theory and research* (3rd ed., pp. 375–398). New York: Guilford Press.

Roberts, M. C. (2002). The process and product of the Felix decree review of empirically supported treatments: Prospects for change. *Clinical Psychology: Science and Practice, 9,* 217–219.

Roberts, M. J., & Sykes, E. D. A. (2003). Belief bias and relational reasoning. *Quarterly Journal of Experimental Psychology, 56A,* 131–154.

Roberts, Y. H., Mitchell, M. J., Witman, M., & Taffaro, C. (2010). Mental health symptoms in youth affected by Hurricane Katrina. *Professional Psychology: Research and Practice, 41,* 10–18.

Robertson, J., & Robertson, J. (1971). Young children in brief separation: A fresh look. *Psychoanalytic Study of the Child, 26,* 264–315.

Robiner, W. N. (2006). The mental health professions: Workforce supply and demand, issues, and challenges. *Clinical Psychology Review, 26,* 600–625.

Robins, L. N., & Regier, D. A. (Eds.). (1991). *Psychiatric disorders in America: The Epidemiologic Catchment Area study.* New York: Free Press.

Robinson, J. H., & Pritchard, W. S. (1995). The scientific case that nicotine is addictive: Reply. *Psychopharmacology, 117,* 16–17.

Robinson, N. M., Zigler, E., & Gallagher, J. J. (2000). Two tails of the normal curve: Similarities and differences in the study of mental retardation and giftedness. *American Psychologist, 55,* 1413–1424.

Robinson, S., Sandstrom, S. M., Denenberg, V. H., & Palmiter, R. D. (2005). Distinguishing whether dopamine regulates liking, wanting, and/or learning about rewards. *Behavioral Neuroscience, 119,* 5–15.

Robinson, T. E., & Berridge, K. C. (2003). Addiction. *Annual Reviews of Psychology, 54,* 25–53.

Robinson, T. N., Borzekowski D. L. G., Matheson, D. M., & Kraemer, H. C. (2009). Effects of fast-food branding on young children's taste preferences. *Archives of Pediatric and Adolescent Medicine, 161,* 792–797.

Robinson, T. N., Wilde, M. L., Navracruz, L. C., Haydel, K. F., & Varady, A. (2001). Effects of reducing children's television and video game use on aggressive behavior: A randomized controlled trial. *Archives of Pediatrics and Adolescent Medicine, 155,* 17–23.

Robles, T. F., Glaser, R., & Kiecolt-Glaser, J. K. (2005). Out of balance: A new look at chronic stress, depression, and immunity. *Current Directions in Psychological Science, 14,* 111–115.

Rochon, P. A., Stukel, T. A., Sykora, K., Gill, S., et al. (2005). Atypical antipsychotics and Parkinsonism. *Archives of Internal Medicine, 165,* 1882–1888.

Rock, I. (1983). *The logic of perception.* Cambridge, MA: MIT Press.

Rodell, J. B., & Judge, T. A. (2009). Can "good" stressors spark "bad" behaviors? The mediating role of emotions in links of challenge and hindrance stressors with citizenship and counterproductive behaviors. *Journal of Applied Psychology, 94,* 1438–1451.

Rodenburg, R., Benjamin, A., de Roos, C., Meijer, A. M., & Stams, G. J. (2009). Efficacy of EMDR in children: A meta-analytic review. *Clinical Psychology Review, 29,* 599–606.

Rodrigues, S. M., LeDoux, J. E., & Sapolsky, R. M. (2009). The influence of stress hormones on fear circuitry. *Annual Review of Neuroscience, 32,* 289–313.

Rodriguez, I., Greer, C. A., Mok, M. Y., & Mombaerts, P. (2000). A putative pheromone receptor gene expressed in human olfactory mucosa. *Nature Genetics, 26,* 18–19.

Roe, K. V. (2001). Relationship between male infants' vocal responses to mother and stranger at three months and self-reported academic attainment and adjustment measures in adulthood. *Psychological Reports, 89,* 255–258.

Roediger, H. L., III. (1990). Implicit memory: Retention without remembering. *American Psychologist, 45,* 1043–1056.

Roediger, H. L., III; Gallo, D. A.; & Geraci, L. (2002). Processing approaches to cognition: The impetus from the levels-of-processing framework. *Memory, 10,* 319–332.

Roediger, H. L., III; Guynn, M. J.; & Jones, T. C. (1995). Implicit memory: A tutorial review. In P. Bertelson, P. Eelen, & G. d'Ydewalle (Eds.), *International perspectives on psychological science: Vol. 2. The state of the art* (pp. 67–94). Hove, England: Psychology Press.

Roediger, H. L., III; Jacoby, D.; & McDermott, K. B. (1996). Misinformation effects in recall: Creating false memories through repeated retrieval. *Journal of Memory and Learning, 35,* 300–318.

Roediger, H. L., III, & Karpicke, J. D. (2006). Test-enhanced learning: Taking memory tests improve long-term retention. *Psychological Science, 17,* 249–255.

Roediger, H. L., III; McDaniel, M.; & McDermott, K. (2006). Test-enhanced learning. *APS Observer, 19,* 28.

Roediger, H. L., III, & McDermott, K. B. (1992). Depression and implicit memory: A commentary. *Journal of Abnormal Psychology, 101,* 587–591.

Roediger, H. L., III, & McDermott, K. B. (1995). Creating false memories: Remembering words not presented in lists. *Journal of Experimental Psychology: Learning, Memory, and Cognition, 21,* 803–814.

Roediger, H. L., III, & McDermott, K. B. (2000). Tricks of memory. *Current Directions in Psychological Science, 9,* 123–127.

Roediger, H. L., III; Meade, M. L.; & Bergman, E. T. (2001). Social contagion of memory. *Psychonomic Bulletin and Review, 8,* 365–371.

Roffman, J. L., & Gerber, A. J. (2008). Neural models of psychodynamic concepts and treatments: Implications for psychodynamic psychotherapy. In R. A. Levy & J. S. Ablon (Eds.), *Handbook of evidence-based psychodynamic psychotherapy* (pp. 305–339). Totowa, NJ: Humana Press.

Roffwarg, H. P., Muzio, J. N., & Dement, W. C. (1966). Ontogenetic development of the human sleep-dream cycle. *Science, 152,* 604–619.

Rog, D. J., Nurmikko, T. J., Friede, T., & Young, C. A. (2005). Randomized, controlled trial of cannabis-based medicine in central pain in multiple sclerosis. *Neurology, 65,* 812–819.

Rogalski, Y., & Edmonds, L. A. (2008). Attentive reading and constrained summarisation (ARCS) treatment in primary progressive aphasia: A case study. *Aphasiology, 22,* 763–775.

Rogers, C. R. (1951). *Client-centered therapy.* Boston: Houghton Mifflin.

Rogers, C. R. (1961). *On becoming a person.* Boston: Houghton Mifflin.

Rogers, C. R. (1970). *Carl Rogers on encounter groups.* New York: Harper & Row.

Rogers, C. R. (1980). *A way of being.* Boston: Houghton Mifflin.

Rogers, M. R., & Molina, L. E. (2006). Exemplary efforts in psychology to recruit and retain graduate students of color. *American Psychologist, 61,* 143–156.

Rogers, R. (1995). *Diagnostic and structured interviewing: A handbook for psychologists.* Odessa, FL: Psychological Assessment Resources.

Rogers, R. (2003). Standardizing DSM-IV diagnoses: The clinical application of structured interviews. *Journal of Personality Assessment, 81,* 220–225.

Rogoff, B., & Waddell, K. J. (1982). Memory for information organized in a scene by children from two cultures. *Child Development, 53,* 1224–1228.

Rohrer, D., & Pashier, H. (2007). Increasing retention without increasing study time. *Current Directions in Psychological Science, 16,* 183–186.

Roid, G. H. (2003). *Stanford-Binet Intelligence Scale* (5th ed.). Itasca, IL: Riverside.

Roisman, G. I. (2007). The psychophysiology of adult attachment relationships: Autonomic reactivity in marital and premarital interactions. *Developmental Psychology, 43,* 39–53.

Roisman, G. I., Masten, A. S., Coatsworth, J. D., & Tellegen, A. (2004). Salient and emerging developmental tasks in the transition to adulthood. *Child Development, 75,* 123–133.

Rolland, Y., Andrieu, S., Cantet, C., Morley, J. E., et al. (2007). Wandering behavior and Alzheimer disease: The REAL.FR prospective study. *Alzheimer Disease and Associated Disorders, 21,* 31–38.

Rolls, E. T. (2006). Brain mechanisms underlying flavour and appetite. *Philosophical Transactions of the Royal Society of London, B, 361,* 1123–1136.

Romeo, R. D., Richardson, H. N., & Sisk, C. L. (2002). Puberty and the maturation of the male brain and sexual behavior: Recasting a behavioral potential. *Neuroscience and Biobehavioral Review, 26,* 381–391.

Romer, D., Jamieson, P. E., & Jamieson, K. H. (2006). Are news reports of suicide contagious? A stringent test in six U.S. cities. *Journal of Communication, 56,* 253–270.

Ronnestad, M. H., & Ladany, N. (2006). The impact of psychotherapy training: Introduction to the special section. *Psychotherapy Research, 16,* 261–267.

Root, J. C., Wong, P. S., & Kinsbourne, M. (2006). Left hemisphere specialization for response to positive emotional expressions: A divided output methodology. *Emotion, 6,* 473–483.

Rooy, D. L. V., Dilchert, S., Viswesvaran, C., & Ones, D. (2006). Multiplying intelligences: Are general, emotional, and practical intelligences equal? In K. R. Murphy (Ed.), *A critique of emotional intelligence: What are the problems and how can they be fixed?* (pp. 235–262). Mahwah, NJ: Erlbaum.

Rosa-Alcazar, A. I., Sanchez-Meca, J., Gomez-Conesa, A., & Marin-Martinez, F. (2008). Psychological treatment of obsessive-compulsive disorder: A meta-analysis. *Clinical Psychology Review, 28,* 1310–1325.

Rosch, E. (1975). Cognitive representations of semantic categories. *Journal of Experimental Psychology: General, 104,* 192–223.

Rosch, E., Mervis, C. B., Gray, W. D., Johnson, D. M., & Boyes-Braem, P. (1976). Basic objects in natural categories. *Cognitive Psychology, 8,* 382–439.

Rose, A. J., & Rudolph, K. D. (2006). A review of sex differences in peer relationship processes: Potential trade-offs for the emotional and behavioral development of girls and boys. *Psychological Bulletin, 132,* 98–131.

Rose, S. A., & Feldman, J. F. (1995). Prediction of IQ and specific cognitive abilities at 11 years from infancy measures. *Developmental Psychology, 31,* 685–696.

Roseborough, D. J. (2006). Psychodynamic psychotherapy: An effectiveness study. *Research on Social Work Practice, 16,* 166–175.

Rosekind, M. R., Gregory, K. B., Mallis, M. M., Brandt, S. L., et al. (2010). The cost of poor sleep: Workplace productivity loss and associated costs. *Journal of Occupational and Environmental Medicine, 52,* 91–98.

Rosellini, L. (1998, April 13). When to spank. *U.S. News and World Report,* pp. 52–58.

Rosen, B. C., & D'Andrade, R. (1959). The psychosocial origins of achievement motivation. *Sociometry, 22,* 188–218.

Rosen, G. M. (1999). Treatment fidelity and research on eye movement desinsitization and reprocessing (EMDR). *Journal of Anxiety Disorders, 13,* 173–184.

Rosen, M. L., & López, H. H. (2009). Menstrual cycle shifts in attentional bias for courtship language. *Evolution and Human Behavior, 30,* 131–140.

Rosen, R. (1991). *The healthy company.* Los Angeles: Tarcher.

Rosenbaum, M., & Bennett, B. (1986). Homicide and depression. *American Journal of Psychiatry, 143,* 367–370.

Rosenbaum, R. S., Moscovitch, M., Foster, J. K., Schnyer, D. M., et al. (2008). Patterns of autobiographical memory loss in medial-temporal lobe amnesic patients. *Journal of Cognitive Neuroscience, 20,* 1490–1506.

Rosenbaum, R. S., Priselac, S. K., Black, S. E., Gao, F., et al. (2000). Remote spatial memory in an amnesiac person with extensive bilateral hippocampal lesions. *Nature Neuroscience, 3,* 1044–1048.

Rosenfarb, I. S., Bellack, A. S., & Aziz, N. (2006). A sociocultural stress, appraisal, and coping model of subjective burden and family attitudes toward patients with schizophrenia. *Journal of Abnormal Psychology, 115,* 157–165.

Rosenfarb, I. S., Goldstein, M. J., Mintz, J., & Nuechterlein, K. H. (1995). Expressed emotion and subclinical psychopathology observable within the transactions between schizophrenic patients and their family members. *Journal of Abnormal Psychology, 104,* 259–267.

Rosenfeld, J. P. (1995). Alternative views of Bashore and Rapp's (1993) alternatives to traditional polygraphy: A critique. *Psychological Bulletin, 117,* 159–166.

Rosenkranz, M. A., Jackson, D. C., Dalton, K. M., Dolski, I., et al. (2003). Affective style and in vivo immune response: Neurobehavioral mechanisms. *Proceedings of the National Academy of Sciences, 100,* 11148–11152.

Rosenstock, I. M. (1974). Historical origins of the health belief model. *Health Education Monographs, 2,* 328–335.

Rosenthal, R. (1994). Interpersonal expectancy effects: A 30-year perspective. *Current Directions in Psychological Science, 3,* 176–179.

Rosenthal, R. R. (1966). *Experimenter effects in behavioral research.* New York: Appleton-Century-Crofts.

Rosenthal, R. R., & Jacobson, L. (1968). *Pygmalion in the classroom.* New York: Holt, Rinehart & Winston.

Ross, C. A. (1997). *Dissociative identity disorder: Diagnosis, clinical features, and treatment of multiple personality.* New York: Wiley.

Ross, D. A., Gore, J. C., Marks, L. E. (2005). Absolute pitch: Music and beyond. *Epilepsy and Behavior, 7,* 578-601.

Ross, E. D. (1981). The aprosodias: Functional-anatomic organization of the affective components of language in the right hemisphere. *Archives of Neurology, 38,* 561–569.

Ross, E. D. (2006). The aprosodias. In M. J. Farah & T. E. Feinberg (Eds.), *Patient-based approaches to cognitive neuroscience* (2nd ed., pp. 259–269). Cambridge, MA: MIT Press.

Ross, E. D. (2010). Cerebral localization of functions and the neurology of language: Fact versus fiction, or is it something else? *Neuroscientist, 16,* 222–243. Epub 2010 Feb 5.

Ross, E. D., & Monnot, M. (2008). Neurology of affective prosody and its functional-anatomic organization in right hemisphere. *Brain and Language, 104,* 51–74.

Ross, M. W. (2002). Sexuality and health challenges: Responding to a public health imperative. *Journal of Sex Research, 39,* 7–9.

Ross, S., & Peselow, E. (2009). The neurobiology of addictive disorders. *Clinical Neuropharmacology, 32,* 269–276.

Ross, S. M., & Ross, L. E. (1971). Comparison of trace and delay classical eyelid conditioning as a function of interstimulus interval. *Journal of Experimental Psychology, 91,* 165–167.

Rössler, W., Riecher-Rössler, A., Angst, J., Murray, R., et al. (2007). Psychotic experiences in the general population: A twenty-year prospective community study. *Schizophrenia Research, 92,* 1–14.

Roth, A., & Fonagy, P. (2005). *What works for whom: A critical review of psychotherapy research* (2nd ed.). New York: Guilford Press.

Roth, G., Assor, A., Niemiec, C. P., Deci, E. L., & Ryan, R. M. (2009). The emotional and academic consequences of parental conditional regard. *Developmental Psychology, 45,* 1119–1142.

Roth, P. L., Huffcutt, A. I., & Bobko, P. (2003). Ethnic group differences in measures of job performance: A new meta-analysis. *Journal of Applied Psychology, 88,* 694–706.

Rothbart, M. K., & Bates, J. E. (2006). Temperament. In W. Damon & R. M. Lerner (Series Eds.) & N. Eisenberg (Vol. Ed.), *Handbook of child psychology: Vol. 3. Social, emotional, and personality development* (6th ed., pp. 99–166). Hoboken, NJ: Wiley.

Rothbart, M. K., & Derryberry, D. (2002). Temperament in children. In C. von Hofsten & L. Baeckman (Eds.), *Psychology at the turn of the millennium: Vol. 2. Social, developmental, and clinical perspectives* (pp. 17–35). Florence, KY: Taylor & Frances/Routledge.

Rothbaum, B. O. (2006). Virtual reality in the treatment of psychiatric disorders. *CNS Spectrums, 11,* 34.

Rothbaum, B. O., Hodges, L. F., Kooper, R., & Opdyke, D. (1995). Effectiveness of computer-generated virtual reality graded exposure in the treatment of acrophobia. *American Journal of Psychiatry, 152,* 626–628.

Rothbaum, F., Pott, M., Azuma, H., Miyake, K., & Weisz, J. (2000). The development of close relationships in Japan and the United States: Paths of symbiotic harmony and generative tension. *Child Development, 71,* 1121–1142.

Rothstein, H. R., & Saleem, M. (2010). Violent video game effects on aggression, empathy, and prosocial behavior in Eastern and Western countries: A meta-analytic review. *Psychological Bulletin, 136,* 151–173.

Rottenstreich, Y., & Tversky, A. (1997). Unpacking, repacking, and anchoring: Advances in support theory. *Psychological Review, 104,* 406–415.

Rotter, J. B. (1954). *Social learning and clinical psychology.* New York: Prentice Hall.

Rotter, J. B. (1982). *The development and application of social learning theory.* New York: Praeger.

Rouach, N., Koulakoff, A., Abudara, V., Willecke, K., & Giaume, C. (2008). Astroglial metabolic networks sustain hippocampal synaptic transmission. *Science, 322,* 1551–1555.

Rouaud T, Lardeux S, Panayotis N, Paleressompoulle D, Cador M, Baunez C. (2010). Reducing the desire for cocaine with subthalamic nucleus deep brain stimulation. *Proceedings of the National Academy of Sciences, 107,* 1196–1200.

Rouch, I., Wild, P., Ansiau, D., & Marquie, J-C. (2005). Shiftwork experience, age, and cognitive performance. *Ergonomics, 48,* 1282–1293.

Rouéché, B. (1986, December 8). Cinnabar. *New Yorker,* p. 94.

Rouse, S. V. (2007). Using reliability generalization methods to explore measurement error: An illustration using the MMPI2 PSY-5 scales. *Journal of Personality Assessment, 88,* 264–275.

Rovee-Collier, C. (1999). The development of infant memory. *Current Directions in Psychological Science, 8,* 80–85.

Rowe, C., Harris, J. M., & Roberts, S. C. (2005). Sporting contests: Seeing red? Putting sportswear in context. *Nature, 437,* E10.

Rowe, D. C. (2005). Under the skin: On the impartial treatment of genetic and environmental hypotheses of racial differences. *American Psychologist, 60,* 60–70.

Rowe, D. C., Jacobson, K. C., & Van den Oord, E. J. C. G. (1999). Genetic and environmental influences on vocabulary IQ: Parental education level as moderator. *Child Development, 70,* 1151–1162.

Rowe, M. L., & Goldin-Meadow, S. (2009). Differences in early gesture explain SES disparities in child vocabulary size at school entry. *Science, 323,* 951–953.

Roy, B., Diez-Roux, A. V., Seeman, T., Ranjit, N., et al. (2010). Association of optimism and pessimism with inflammation and hemostasis in the multiethnic study of atherosclerosis (MESA). *Psychosomatic Medicine, 72,* 134–140.

Roy, M., Piché, M., Chen, J.-I., Peretz, I., & Rainville, P. (2009). Cerebral and spinal modulation of pain by emotions. *Proceedings of the National Academy of Sciences, 106,* 20900–20905.

Roy, P.-M., Durieux, P., Gillaizeau, F., Legall, C., et al. (2009). A computerized handheld decision-support system to improve pulmonary embolism diagnosis: A randomized trial. *Annals of Internal Medicine, 151,* 677–686.

Roy-Byrne, P. P., Craske, M. G., Stein, M. B., Sullivan, G., et al. (2005). A randomized effectiveness trial of cognitive-behavioral therapy and medication for primary care panic disorder. *Archives of General Psychiatry, 62,* 290–298.

Roy-Byrne, P. P., Stang, P., Wittchen, H.-U., Üstün, B., et al. (2000). Lifetime panic-depression comorbidity in the National Comorbidity Survey. *British Journal of Psychiatry, 176,* 229–235.

Rozin, P. (1982). "Taste-smell confusions" and the duality of the olfactory sense. *Perception and Psychophysics, 31,* 397–401.

Rozin, P. (2007). Food and eating. In S. Kitayama & D. Cohen (Eds.), *Handbook of cultural psychology* (pp. 391–416). New York: Guilford Press.

Rozin, P., Dow, S., Moscovitch, M., & Rajaram, S. (1998). The role of memory for recent eating experiences in onset and cessation of meals. Evidence from the amnesic syndrome. *Psychological Science, 9,* 392–396.

Rozin, P., Kabnick, K., Pete, E., Fischler, C., & Shields, C. (2003). The ecology of eating: Smaller portion sizes in France than in the United States help explain the French paradox. *Psychological Science, 14,* 450–454.

Rubens, A. B., & Benson, D. F. (1971). Associative visual agnosia. *Archives of Neurology, 24,* 304–316.

Rubin, B. M. (1998, February 8). When he's retiring and she isn't. *Chicago Tribune,* sec. 1, pp. 1ff.

Rubin, K. H., Bukowski, W., & Parker, J. G. (2006). Peer interactions, relationships, and groups. In W. Damon & R. M. Lerner (Series Eds.) & N. Eisenberg (Vol. Ed.), *Handbook of child psychology: Vol. 3. Social, emotional, and personality development* (6th ed., pp. 571–645). Hoboken, NJ: Wiley.

Rubinstein, S., & Caballero, B. (2000). Is Miss America an undernourished role model? *Journal of the American Medical Association, 283,* 1569.

Ruble, D. N., Martin, C. L., & Berenbaum, S. A. (2006). Gender development. In W. Damon & R. M. Lerner (Series Eds.) & N. Eisenberg (Vol. Ed.), *Handbook of child psychology: Vol. 3. Social, emotional, and personality development* (6th ed., pp. 858–932). Hoboken, NJ: Wiley.

Rudman, L. A., Greenwald, A. G., Mellott, D. S., & Schwartz, J. L. K. (1999). Measuring the automatic components of prejudice: Flexibility and generality of the Implicit Association Test. *Social Cognition, 17,* 437–465.

Rudolph, K. D., Lambert, S. F., Clark, A. G., & Kurlakowsky, K. D. (2001). Negotiating the transition to middle school: The role of self-regulatory processes. *Child Development, 72,* 929–946.

Rueck, C., Andreewitch, S., & Flyckt, K. (2003). Capsulotomy for refractory anxiety disorders: Longer-term follow-up of 26 patients. *American Journal of Psychiatry, 160,* 513–521.

Rueckert, L., Baboorian, D., Stavropoulos, K., & Yasutake, C. (1999). Individual differences in callosal efficiency: Correlation with attention. *Brain and Cognition, 41,* 390–410.

Ruffman, T., Perner, J., Naito, M., Parkin, L., & Clements, W. A. (1998). Older (but not younger) siblings facilitate false belief understanding. *Developmental Psychology, 34,* 161–174.

Rugg, M. D., & Coles, M. G. H. (Eds.). (1995). *Electrophysiology of mind.* New York: Oxford University Press.

Ruitenberg, M. J., & Vukovic, J. (2008). Promoting central nervous system regeneration: Lessons from cranial nerve I. *Restorative Neurology and Neuroscience, 26,* 183–196.

Ruiz, J. M, Matthews, K. A., Scheier, M. F., & Schulz, R. (2006). Does who you marry matter for your health? Influence of patients' and spouses' personality on their partners' psychological well-being following coronary artery bypass surgery. *Journal of Personality and Social Psychology, 91,* 255–267.

Rumbaugh, D. M. (Ed.). (1977). *Language learning by a chimpanzee: The Lana project.* New York: Academic Press.

Rumelhart, D. E., & McClelland, J. L. (1986). *Parallel distributed processing: Explorations in the microstructure of cognition: Vol. 1. Foundations.* Cambridge, MA: Bradford.

Rupp, T. L., Wesensten, N. J., Bliese, P. D., & Balkin, T. J. (2009). Banking sleep: Realization of benefits during subsequent sleep restriction and recovery. *Sleep, 32,* 311–321.

Ruscio, A. M., Stein, D. J., Chiu, W. T., & Kessler, R. (2010). The epidemiology of obsessive-compulsive disorder in the National Comorbidity Survey Replication. *Molecular Psychiatry, 15,* 53–63.

Ruscio, J. (2005). Exploring controversies in the art and science of polygraph testing. *Skeptical Inquirer, 29,* 34–39.

Rushton, J. P., & Jensen, A. R. (2005). Thirty years of research on race differences in cognitive ability. *Psychology, Public Policy, and Law, 11,* 235–294.

Ruskin, P. E., Silver-Aylaian, M., Kling, M. A., Reed, S. A., et al. (2004). Treatment outcomes in depression: Comparison of remote treatment through telepsychiatry to in-person treatment. *American Journal of Psychiatry, 161,* 1471–1476.

Russ, S. (2006). Psychodynamic treatments. In R. T. Ammerman (Ed.), *Comprehensive handbook of personality and psychopathology* (Vol. 3, pp. 425–437). Hoboken, NJ: Wiley.

Russell, J. A. (1991). Culture and the categorization of emotions. *Psychological Bulletin, 110,* 426–450.

Russell, J. A. (1994). Is there universal recognition of emotion from facial expression? A review of the cross-cultural studies. *Psychological Bulletin, 155,* 102–141.

Russell, J. A. (1995). Facial expressions of emotion: What lies beyond minimal universality? *Psychological Bulletin, 118,* 379–391.

Russell, M. C., Silver, S. M., Rogers, S., & Darnell, J. N. (2007). Responding to an identified need: A joint Department of Defense/Department of Veterans Affairs training program in eye movement desensitization and reprocessing (EMDR) for clinicians providing trauma services. *International Journal of Stress Management, 14,* 61–71.

Rutkowski, G. K., Gruder, C. L., & Romer, D. (1983). Group cohesiveness, social norms, and bystander intervention. *Journal of Personality and Social Psychology, 44,* 545–552.

Rutland, A., Killen, M., & Abrams, D. (2010). A new social-cognitive developmental perspective on prejudice. *Perspectives on Psychological Science, 5,* 279–291.

Rutledge, T., Reis, S. E., Olson, M., Owens, J., et al. (2004). Social networks are associated with lower mortality rates among women with suspected coronary disease: The National Heart, Lung, and Blood Institute–sponsored Women's Ischemia Syndrome Evaluation study. *Psychosomatic Medicine, 66,* 882–888.

Rutter, M. (2003). Commentary: Causal processes leading to antisocial behavior. *Developmental Psychology, 39,* 372–378.

Rutter, M. (2006). The promotion of resilience in the face of adversity. In A. Clarke-Stewart & J. Dunn (Eds.), *Families count: Effects on child and adolescent development* (pp. 26–52). New York: Cambridge University Press.

Rutter, M. (2007). Proceeding from observed correlation to causal inference: The use of natural experiments. *Perspectives on Psychological Science, 2,* 377–395.

Rutter, M., O'Connor, T. G., & ERA Study Team. (2004). Are there biological programming effects for psychological development? Findings from a study of Romanian adoptees. *Developmental Psychology, 40,* 81–94.

Rutter, M. L. (1997). Nature-nurture integration. The example of antisocial behavior. *American Psychologist, 52,* 390–398.

Ryan, A. M. (2001). The peer group as a context for the development of young adolescent motivation and achievement. *Child Development, 72,* 1135–1150.

Ryan, R. H., & Geiselman, R. E. (1991). Effects of biased information on the relationship between eyewitness confidence and accuracy. *Bulletin of the Psychonomic Society, 29,* 7–9.

Ryan, R. M., & Deci, E. L. (2000). Self-determination theory and the facilitation of intrinsic motivation, social development, and well-being. *American Psychologist, 55,* 68–78.

Rymer, R. (1993). *Genie: A scientific tragedy.* New York: HarperCollins.

Rynders, J., & Horrobin, J. (1980). Educational provisions for young children with Down's syndrome. In J. Gottlieb (Ed.), *Educating mentally retarded persons in the mainstream* (pp. 109–147). Baltimore: University Park Press.

Rynes, S. L., Gerhart, B., & Parks, L. (2005). Performance evaluation and pay for performance. *Annual Review of Psychology, 56,* 571–600.

Rypma, B., & Prabhakaran, V. (2009). When less is more and when more is more: The mediating roles of capacity and speed in brain-behavior efficiency. *Intelligence, 37,* 207–222.

Saad, L. (1999, September 3). American workers generally satisfied, but indicate their jobs leave much to be desired. *Gallup Poll News Service,* pp. 1–5. Retrieved from http://www.highbeam.com/Gallup+Poll+News+Service/publications.aspx

Saarni, C., Campos, J. J., Camras, L. A., & Witherington, D. (2006). Emotional development: Action, communication, and understanding. In W. Damon & R. M. Lerner (Series Eds.) & N. Eisenberg (Vol. Ed.), *Handbook of child psychology: Vol. 3. Social, emotional, and personality development* (6th ed., pp. 226–299). Hoboken, NJ: Wiley.

Sabbagh, M. A., Xu, F., Carlson, S. M., Moses, L. J., & Lee, K. (2006). The development of executive functioning and theory of mind: A comparison of Chinese and U. S. preschoolers. *Psychological Science, 17*, 74–81.

Saber, J. L., & Johnson, R. D. (2008). Don't throw out the baby with the bathwater: Verbal repetition, mnemonics, and active learning. *Journal of Marketing Education, 30*, 207–216.

Sabini, J., Siepmann, M., & Stein, J. (2001). The really fundamental attribution error in social psychological research. *Psychological Inquiry, 12*, 1–5.

Sachs, J. (1967). Recognition memory for syntactic and semantic aspects of connected discourse. *Perception and Psychophysics, 2*, 437–442.

Sackeim, H. A., Dillingham, E. M., Prudic, J., Cooper, T., et al. (2009). Effect of concomitant pharmacotherapy on electroconvulsive therapy outcomes. *Archives of General Psychiatry, 66*, 729–737.

Sackeim, H. A., Prudic, J., Devanand, D. P., Nobler, M. S., et al. (2000). A prospective, randomized, double-blind comparison of bilateral and right unilateral electroconvulsive therapy at different stimulus intensities. *Archives of General Psychiatry, 57*, 425–434.

Sackett, P. R., Borneman, M. J., & Connelly, B. S. (2008). High-stakes testing in higher education and employment: Appraising the evidence for validity and fairness. *American Psychologist, 63*, 215–227.

Sackett, P. R., Hardison, C. M., & Cullen, M. J. (2004). On interpreting stereotype threat as accounting for African American–white differences on cognitive tests. *American Psychologist, 59*, 7–13.

Sackett, P. R., Kuncel, N. R., Arneson, J. J., Cooper, S. R., & Waters, S. D. (2009). Does socioeconomic status explain the relationship between admissions tests and postsecondary academic performance? *Psychological Bulletin, 135*, 1–22.

Sackett, P. R., & Lievens, F. (2008). Personnel selection. *Annual Review of Psychology, 59*, 419–450.

Sackett, P. R., Schmitt, N., Ellington, J. E., & Kabin, M. B. (2001). High-stakes testing in employment, credentialing, and higher education: Prospects in a post–affirmative action world. *American Psychologist, 56*, 302–318.

Sacks, O. (1985). *The man who mistook his wife for a hat*. New York: Summit Books.

Sadetzki, S., Chetrit, A., Jarus-Hakak, A., Cardis, E., et al. (2008). Cellular phone use and risk of benign and malignant parotid gland tumors: A nationwide case-control study. *American Journal of Epidemiology, 167*, 457–467.

Sadler, L. S., Swartz, M. K., Ryan-Krause, P., Seitz, V., et al. (2007). Promising outcomes in teen mothers enrolled in a school-based parent support program and child care center. *Journal of School Health, 77*, 121–130.

Saffran, J. R., Senghas, A., & Trueswell, J. C. (2001). The acquisition of language by children. *Proceedings of the National Academy of Sciences, 98*, 12874–12875.

Safren, S. A., Gershuny, B. S., Marzol, P., Otto, M. W., & Pollack, M. H. (2002). History of childhood abuse in panic disorder, social phobia, and generalized anxiety disorder. *Journal of Nervous and Mental Disease, 190*, 453–456.

Saint John, W. (2003, September 28). In U.S. funeral industry, triple-wide isn't a trailer. *New York Times*, p. 1.

St. Pourcain, B., Wang, K., Glessner, J. T., Golding, J., Steer, C., Ring, S. M., Skuse, D. H., Grant, S.F.A., Hakonarson, H., & Smith, G. D. (2010). Association between a high-risk autism locus on 5p14 and social communication spectrum phenotypes in the general population. *American Journal of Psychiatry, xx*. Epub 2010 Jul 15. doi: 10.1176/appi. ajp.2010.09121789.

Saiz, P. A., Garcia-Portilla, M. P., Arango, C., Morales, B., et al. (2008). Association study between obsessive-compulsive disorder and serotonergic candidate genes. *Progress in Neuropsychopharmacology and Biological Psychiatry, 32*, 765–770.

Sakairi, Y. (1992). Studies on meditation using questionnaires. *Japanese Psychological Review, 35*, 94–112.

Salin-Pascual, R., Gerashchenko, D., Greco, M., Blanco-Centurion, C., & Shiromani, P. J. (2001). Hypothalamic regulation of sleep. *Neuropsychopharmacology, 25*(Suppl. 5), S21.

Salisbury, A. L., Ponder, K. L., Padbury, J. F., & Lester, B. M. (2009). Fetal effects of psychoactive drugs. *Clinical Perinatology, 36*, 595–619.

Salokangas, R. K. R. (2004). Gender and the use of neuroleptics in schizophrenia. *Schizophrenia Research, 66*, 41–49.

Salovey, P., & Grewal, D. (2005). The science of emotional intelligence. *Current Directions in Psychological Science, 14*, 281–285.

Salovey, P., Mayer, J. D., & Rosenhan, D. L. (1991). Mood and helping: Mood as a motivator of helping and helping as a regulator of mood. In M. S. Clark (Ed.), *Review of personality and social psychology: Vol. 12. Prosocial behavior* (pp. 215–237). Newbury Park, CA: Sage.

Salter, N. P., & Highhouse, S. (2009). Assessing managers' common sense using situational judgment tests. *Management Decision, 47*, 392–398.

Salthouse, T. A. (1990). Working memory as a processing resource in cognitive aging. *Developmental Review, 10*, 101–124.

Salthouse, T. A. (1996). The processing-speed theory of adult age differences in cognition. *Psychological Review, 103*, 403–428.

Salthouse, T. A. (2000). Aging and measures of processing speed. *Biological Psychology, 54*, 35–54.

Salthouse, T. A., & Prill, K. A. (1987). Inferences about age impairments in inferential reasoning. *Psychology and Aging, 2*, 43–51.

Sambunaris, A., & Hyde, T. M. (1994). Stroke-related aphasias mistaken for psychotic speech: Two case reports. *Journal of Geriatric Psychiatry and Neurology, 7*, 144–147.

Samuel, A. G. (2001). Knowing a word affects the fundamental perception of the sounds within it. *Psychological Science, 12*, 348–351.

Samuel, D. B., & Widiger, T. A. (2006). Clinicians' judgments of clinical utility: A comparison of the DSM-IV and five-factor models. *Journal of Abnormal Psychology, 115*, 298–308.

Samuelson, C. D., & Messick, D. M. (1995). When do people want to change the rules for allocating shared resources? In D. Schroeder (Ed.), *Social dilemmas: Perspectives on individuals and groups* (pp. 143–162). Westport, CT: Praeger.

Sanai, N., Tramontin, A. D., Quinones-Hinojosa, A., Barbaro, N. M., et al. (2004). Unique astrocyte ribbon in adult human brain contains neural stem cells but lacks chain migration. *Nature, 427*, 740–744.

Sanderson, W. C. (2003). Why empirically supported psychological treatments are important. *Behavior Modification, 27*, 290–299.

Sanderson, W. C., Rapee, R. M., & Barlow, D. H. (1989). The influence of an illusion of control on panic attacks induced via inhalation of 5.5% carbon dioxide-enriched air. *Archives of General Psychiatry, 46*, 157–162.

Sanders-Thompson, V. L., Bazile, A., & Akbar, M. (2004). African Americans' perceptions of psychotherapy and psychotherapists. *Professional Psychology: Research and Practice, 35*, 19–26.

Santos, C., Lunet, N., Azevedo, A., de Mendonça, A., et al. (2010). Caffeine intake is associated with a lower risk of cognitive decline: A cohort study from Portugal. *Journal of Alzheimer's Disease, 20*(Suppl. 1), S175–S185.

Santry, H. P., Gillen, D. L., & Lauderdale, D. S. (2005). Trends in bariatric surgical procedures. *Journal of the American Medical Association, 294*, 1909–1917.

Saper, C. B., Chou, T. C., & Scammell, T. E. (2001). The sleep switch: Hypothalamic control of sleep and wakefulness. *Trends in Neurosciences, 24*, 726–731.

Saper, C. B., Scammell, T. E., & Lu, J. (2005). Hypothalamic regulation of sleep and circadian rhythms. *Nature, 437*, 1257–1263.

Sarà, M., & Pistoia, F. (2009). Defining consciousness: Lessons from patients and modern techniques. *Journal of Neurotrauma, 27*, 771–773.

Sarason, B. R., Sarason, I. G., & Gurung, R. A. R. (1997). Close personal relationships and health outcomes: A key to the role of social support. In S. Duck (Ed.), *Handbook of personal relationships* (pp. 547–573). New York: Wiley.

Sarason, I. G. (1984). Stress, anxiety, and cognitive interference: Reactions to tests. *Journal of Personality and Social Psychology, 46*, 929–938.

Sarason, I. G., Johnson, J., & Siegel, J. (1978). Assessing impact of life changes: Development of the life experiences survey. *Journal of Clinical and Consulting Psychology, 46*, 932–946.

Sarin, S., Abela, J. R. Z., & Auerbach, R. P. (2005). The response styles theory of depression: A test of specificity and causal mediation. *Cognition and Emotion, 19*, 751–761.

Sasaki, M., Shibata, E., Tohyama, K., Takahashi, J., et al. (2006). Neuromelanin magnetic resonance imaging of locus ceruleus and substantia nigra in Parkinson's disease. *Neuroreport, 17*, 1215–1218.

Sasaki, Y., Jadjikhani, N., Fischl, B., Liu, A. K., et al. (2001). Local and global attention are mapped retinotopically in human occipital cortex. *Proceedings of the National Academy of Sciences, 98*, 2077.

Sass, D. A., Twohig, M. P., & Davies, W. H. (2004). Defining the independent variables and ensuring treatment integrity: A comparison across journals of different theoretical orientations. *Behavior Therapist, 27*, 172–174.

Sattler, D. N., Kaiser, C. F., & Hittner, J. B. (2000). Disaster preparedness: Relationships among prior experience, personal characteristics, and distress. *Journal of Applied Social Psychology, 30*, 1396–1420.

Saucier, G., Akers, L. G., Shen-Miller, S., Knežević, G., & Stankov, L. (2009). Patterns of thinking in militant extremism. *Perspectives on Psychological Science, 4*, 256–271.

Savage, J., & Yancey, C. (2008). The effects of media violence exposure on criminal aggression: A meta-analysis. *Criminal Justice and Behavior, 35*, 772–791.

Savage-Rumbaugh, E. S. (1990). Language acquisition in a nonhuman species: Implications for the innateness debate. *Developmental Psychology, 23*, 599–620.

Savage-Rumbaugh, E. S., & Brakke, K. E. (1996). Animal language: Methodological and interpretive issues. In M. Bekoff & D. Jamieson (Eds.), *Readings in animal cognition* (pp. 269–288). Cambridge, MA: MIT Press.

Savage-Rumbaugh, E. S., Murphy, J., Sevcik, R. A., Brakke, K. E., et al. (1993). Language comprehension in ape and child. *Monographs of the Society for Research in Child Development, 58*, 1–222.

Savage-Rumbaugh, E. S., Pate, J. L., Lawson, J., Smith, S. T., & Rosenbaum, S. (1983). Can a chimpanzee make a statement? *Journal of Experimental Psychology: General, 112*, 469–487.

Savage-Rumbaugh, E. S., Shanker, S. G., & Taylor, T. J. (2001). *Apes, language, and the human mind*. New York: Oxford University Press.

Savani, K., Markus, H. R., Naidu, N. V. R., Kumar, S., & Berlia, N. (2010). What counts as a choice? U.S. Americans are more likely than Indians to construe actions as choices. *Psychological Science, 21*, 391–398.

Savelkoul, M., Post, M. W. M., de Witte, L. P., & van den Borne, H. B. (2000). Social support, coping, and subjective well-being in patients with rheumatic diseases. *Patient Education and Counseling, 39*, 205–218.

Savic, I., Berglund, H., Gulyas, B., & Roland, P. (2001). Smelling of odorous sex-hormone-like compounds causes sex-differentiated hypothalamic activations in humans. *Neuron, 31*, 661–668.

Savic, I., Berglund, H., & Lindström, P. (2005). Brain response to putative pheromones in homosexual men. *Proceedings of the National Academy of Sciences, 102*, 7356–7361.

Saville, B. K., Zinn, T. E., Neef, N. A., Van Norman, R., & Ferreri, S. J. (2006). A comparison of interteaching and lecture in the college classroom. *Journal of Applied Behavior Analysis, 39*, 49–61.

Savin-Williams, R. C. (2006). Who's gay? Does it matter? *Current Directions in Psychological Science, 15*, 40–44.

Savin-Williams, R. C., & Demo, D. H. (1984). Developmental change and stability in adolescent self-concept. *Developmental Psychology, 20*, 1100–1110.

Savitz, S. I., Dinsmore, J., Wu, J., Henderson, G. V., et al. (2005). Neurotransplantation of fetal porcine cells in patients with basal ganglia infarcts: A preliminary safety and feasibility study. *Cerebrovascular Diseases, 20*, 101–107.

Saxe, L., & Ben-Shakhar, G. (1999). Admissibility of polygraph tests: The application of scientific standards post-Daubert. *Psychology, Public Policy, and Law, 5*, 203–223.

Saxe, R., Tzelnic, R., & Carey, S. (2007). Knowing who dunnit: Infants identify causal agent in an unseen causal interaction. *Developmental Psychology, 43*, 149–158.

Sayal, K., Heron, J., Golding, J., Alati, R., et al. (2009). Binge pattern of alcohol consumption during pregnancy and childhood mental health outcomes: Longitudinal population-based study. *Pediatrics, 123,* e289–e296.

Sayers, J. (1991). *Mother of psychoanalysis.* New York: Norton.

Sayim, B., Westheimer, G., & Herzog, M. H. (2010). Gestalt factors modulate basic visual perception. *Psychological Science, 21,* 641–644. doi:10.1177/0956797610368811

Scandura, T. A., & Lankau, M. J. (1997). Relationships of gender, family responsibility, and flexible work hours to organizational commitment and job satisfaction. *Journal of Organizational Behavior, 18,* 377–391.

Scandura, T. A., & Schriesheim, C. A. (1994). Leader-member exchange and supervisor career mentoring as complementary constructs in leadership research. *Academy of Management Journal, 37,* 1588–1602.

Scarr, S. (1997). The development of individual differences in intelligence and personality. In H. W. Reese & M. D. Franzen (Eds.), *Biological and neuropsychological mechanisms: Life-span developmental psychology* (pp. 1–22). Hillsdale, NJ: Erlbaum.

Scarr, S. (1998). How do families affect intelligence? Social environmental and behavior genetic prediction. In J. J. McArdle & R. W. Woodcock (Eds.), *Human cognitive abilities in theory and practice* (pp. 113–136). Mahwah, NJ: Erlbaum.

Scarr, S., & Carter-Saltzman, L. (1982). Genetics and intelligence. In R. Sternberg (Ed.), *Handbook of human intelligence* (pp. 792–896). Cambridge: Cambridge University Press.

Scarr, S., & Weinberg, R. A. (1976). IQ test performance of black children adopted by white families. *American Psychologist, 31,* 726–739.

Schabracq, M. J. (2003). Organizational culture, stress, and change. In M. J. Schabracq, J. A. M. Winnubst, & C. L. Cooper (Eds.), *Handbook of work and health psychology* (pp. 37–62). Chichester, England: Wiley.

Schachter, S., & Singer, J. (1962). Cognitive, social, and physiological determinants of emotional state. *Psychological Review, 69,* 379–399.

Schacter, D. L. (2001). *The seven sins of memory: How the mind forgets and remembers.* Boston: Houghton Mifflin.

Schacter, D. L., Chiu, C.-Y. P., & Ochsner, K. N. (1993). Implicit memory: A selective review. *Annual Review of Neuroscience, 16,* 159–182.

Schacter, D. L., Church, B., & Treadwell, J. (1994). Implicit memory in amnesic patients: Evidence for spared auditory priming. *Psychological Science, 5,* 20–25.

Schacter, D. L., Cooper, L. A., Delaney, S. M., Peterson, M. A., & Tharan, M. (1991). Implicit memory for possible and impossible objects: Constraints on the construction of structural descriptions. *Journal of Experimental Psychology: Learning, Memory, and Cognition, 17,* 3–19.

Schacter, D. L., Dobbins, I. G., & Schnyer, D. M. (2004). Specificity of priming: A cognitive neuroscience perspective. *Nature Reviews Neuroscience, 5,* 853–862.

Schacter, D. L., Norman, K. A., & Koutstaal, W. (1998). The cognitive neuroscience of constructive memory. *Annual Review of Psychology, 49,* 289–318.

Schacter, D. L., & Tulving, E. (1994). *Memory systems, 1994.* Cambridge, MA: MIT Press.

Schacter, D. L., Wagner, A. D., & Buckner, R. L. (2000). Memory systems of 1999. In E. Tulving & F. I. M. Craik (Eds.), *The Oxford handbook of memory* (pp. 627–643). New York: Oxford University Press.

Schaefer, J., Sykes, R., Rowley, R., & Baek, S. (1988, November). *Slow country music and drinking.* Paper presented at the 87th annual meeting of the American Anthropological Association, Phoenix, AZ.

Schaefer, M., Heinze, H. J., & Rotte, M. (2008). My third arm: Shifts in topography of the somatosensory homunculus predict feeling of an artificial supernumerary arm. *Human Brain Mapping, 6,* 6.

Schaeffer, C. M., Petras, H., Ialongo, N., Poduska, J., & Kellam, S. (2003). Modeling growth in boys' aggressive behavior across elementary school: Links to later criminal involvement, conduct disorder, and antisocial personality disorder. *Developmental Psychology, 39,* 1020–1035.

Schafer, J., & Brown, S. A. (1991). Marijuana and cocaine effect expectancies and drug use patterns. *Journal of Consulting and Clinical Psychology, 59,* 558–565.

Schaie, K. W. (1993). The Seattle longitudinal study of adult intelligence. *Current Directions in Psychological Science, 2,* 171–175.

Schaie, K. W. (1996). Intellectual development in adulthood. In J. E. Birren, K. W. Schaie, R. P. Abeles, M. Gatz, & T. A. Salthouse (Eds.), *Handbook of the psychology of aging* (4th ed., pp. 266–286). San Diego, CA: Academic Press.

Schalock, R. L., Borthwick-Duffy, S. A., Buntinx, W. H. E., Coulter, D. L., & Craig, E. M. (2009). *Intellectual disability: Definition, classification, and systems of supports* (11th ed.). Washington, DC: American Association of Intellectual and Developmental Disability.

Schapiro, A. C., & McClelland, J. L. (2009). A connectionist model of a continuous developmental transition in the balance scale task. *Cognition, 110,* 395–411.

Scharff, J. S., & Scharff, D. E. (2003). Object-relations and psychodynamic approaches to couple and family therapy. In T. L. Sexton, G. R. Weeks, & M. S. Robbins (Eds.), *Handbook of family therapy: The science and practice of working with families and couples* (pp. 59–81). New York: Brunner-Routledge.

Schatzberg, A. F., Cole, J. O., & DeBattista, C. (2007). *Manual of clinical psychopharmacology* (6th ed.). Arlington, VA: American Psychiatric Association.

Schatzberg, A. F., Rush, A. J., Arnow, B. A., Banks, P. L., et al. (2005). Chronic depression: Medication (nefazodone) or psychotherapy (CBASP) is effective when the other is not. *Archives of General Psychiatry, 62,* 513–520.

Schatzberg, A. F., Scully, J. H., Kupfer, D. J., & Regier, D. A. (2009). Setting the record straight: A response to Frances's commentary on DSM-V. *PsychiatricTimes, 26,* 1–10. Retrieved from http://psychiatrictimes.com/display/article/10168/1425806

Schaubroeck, J., Jones, J. R., & Xie, J. J. (2001). Individual differences in utilizing control to cope with job demands: Effects on susceptibility to infectious disease. *Journal of Applied Psychology, 86,* 265–278.

Scheerer, M., Rothmann, R., & Goldstein, K. (1945). A case of "idiot savant": An experimental study of personality organization. *Psychology Monograph, 58*(269), 1–63.

Scheibert, J., Leurent, S., Prevost, A., & Debrégeas, G. (2009). The role of fingerprints in the coding of tactile information probed with a biomimetic sensor. *Science, 323,* 1503–1506.

Scheidinger, S. (2004). Group psychotherapy and related helping groups today: An overview. *American Journal of Psychotherapy, 58,* 265–280.

Scheier, M. F., Matthews, K. A., Owens, J. F., Magovern, G. J., et al. (1989). Dispositional optimism and recovery from coronary artery bypass surgery: The beneficial effects on physical and psychological well-being. *Journal of Personality and Social Psychology, 57,* 1024–1040.

Schell, T. L., Martino, S. C., Ellickson, P. L., Collins, R. L., & McCaffrey, D. (2005). Measuring developmental changes in alcohol expectancies. *Psychology of Addictive Behaviors, 19,* 217–220.

Schellenberg, E. G. (2004). Music lessons enhance IQ. *Psychological Science, 15,* 511–514.

Schenck, C. H. (2005). Rapid eye movement sleep parasomnias. *Neurology Clinics, 23,* 1107–1126.

Schenck, C. H., Lee, S. A., Bornemann, M. A., & Mahowald, M. W. (2009). Potentially lethal behaviors associated with rapid eye movement sleep behavior disorder: Review of the literature and forensic implications. *Journal of Forensic Sciences, 54,* 1475–1484.

Schenck, C. H., & Mahowald, M. W. (1992). Motor dyscontrol in narcolepsy: Rapid eye movement (REM) sleep without atonia and REM sleep behavior disorder. *Annals of Neurology, 32,* 3–10.

Scheufele, P. M. (2000). Effects of progressive relaxation and classical music on measurements of attention, relaxation, and stress responses. *Journal of Behavioral Medicine, 23,* 207–228.

Schiff, N. D., Rodriguez-Moreno, D., Kamal, A., Kim, K. H., et al. (2005). fMRI reveals large-scale network activation in minimally conscious patients. *Neurology, 64,* 514–523.

Schiffman, S. S., Graham, B. G., Sattely-Miller, E. A., & Warwick, Z. (1999). Orosensory perception of dietary fat. *Current Directions in Psychological Science, 7,* 137–143.

Schiller, D., Monfils, M.-H., Raio, C. M., Johnson, D. C., et al. (2010). Blocking the return of fear in humans using reconsolidation update mechanisms. *Nature, 463,* 49–53.

Schiller, P. H. (1996). On the specificity of neurons and visual areas. *Behavior and Brain Research, 76,* 21–35.

Schira, M. M., Tyler, C. W., Breakspear, M., & Spehar, B. (2009). The foveal confluence in human visual cortex. *Journal of Neuroscience, 29,* 9050–9058.

Schleicher, D. J., Watt, J. D., & Greguras, G. J. (2004). Reexamining the job satisfaction–performance relationship: The complexity of attitudes. *Journal of Applied Psychology, 89,* 165–177.

Schlosser, E. (2001). *Fast food nation: The dark side of the all-American meal.* New York: Houghton Mifflin.

Schmader, T. (2010). Stereotype threat deconstructed. *Current Directions in Psychological Science, 19,* 14–18.

Schmader, T., Johns, M., & Forbes, C. (2008). An integrated process model of stereotype threat effects on performance. *Psychological Review, 115,* 336–356.

Schmeichel, B. J., Gailliot, M. T., Filardo, E., McGregor, I., et al. (2009). Terror management theory and self-esteem revisited: The roles of implicit and explicit self-esteem in mortality salience effects. *Journal of Personality and Social Psychology, 96,* 1077–1087.

Schmidt, F. L., & Hunter, J. (2004). General mental ability in the world of work: Occupational attainment and job performance. *Journal of Personality and Social Psychology, 86,* 162–173.

Schmidt, N. B., Richley, A., Maner, J. K., & Woolaway-Bickel, K. (2006). Differential effects of safety in extinction of anxious responding to a CO[Subsc]2[/Subsc] challenge in patients with panic disorder. *Journal of Abnormal Psychology, 115,* 341–350.

Schmidt, R. A., & Bjork, R. A. (1992). New conceptualizations of practice: Common principles in three paradigms suggest new concepts for training. *Psychological Science, 3,* 207–217.

Schmolck, H., Buffalo, E. A., & Squire, L. R. (2000). Memory distortions over time: Recollections of the O. J. Simpson trial verdict after 15 and 32 months. *Psychological Science, 11,* 39–47.

Schnall, S., & Laird, J. D. (2003). Keep smiling: Enduring effects of facial expressions and postures on emotional experience and memory. *Cognition and Emotion, 17,* 787–797.

Schnapf, J. L., Kraft, T. W., & Baylor, D. A. (1987). Spectral sensitivity of human cone photoreceptors. *Nature, 325,* 439–441.

Schnee, M. E., Lawton, D. M., Furness, D. N., Benke, T. A., & Ricci, A. J. (2005). Auditory hair cell–afferent fiber synapses are specialized to operate at their best frequencies. *Neuron, 47,* 243–254.

Schneider, B. (1985). Organizational behavior. *Annual Review of Psychology, 36,* 573–611.

Schneider, K. T., Hitlan, R. T., & Radhakrishnan, P. (2000). The nature and correlates of ethnic harassment experiences in multiple contexts. *Journal of Applied Psychology, 85,* 3–12.

Schneiderman, N. (2004). Psychosocial, behavioral, and biological aspects of chronic diseases. *Current Directions in Psychological Science, 13,* 247–251.

Schneiderman, N., Antoni, M. H., Saab, P. G., & Ironson, G. (2001). Health psychology: Psychosocial and biobehavioral aspects of chronic disease management. *Annual Review of Psychology, 52,* 555–580.

Schnoll, R. A., Patterson, F., Wileyto, E. P., Heitjan, D. F., et al. (2010). Effectiveness of extended-duration transdermal nicotine therapy. *Annals of Internal Medicine, 152,* 144–151.

Schnurr, P. P., Friedman, M. J., Engel, C. C., Foa, E. B., et al. (2007). Cognitive behavior therapy for posttraumatic stress disorder in women: A randomized controlled trial. *Journal of the American Medical Association, 297,* 820–830.

Schoemaker, M. J., Swerdlow, A. J., Ahlbom, A., Auvinen, A., et al. (2005). Mobile phone use and risk of acoustic neuroma: Results of the Interphone case-control study in five North European countries. *British Journal of Cancer, 93,* 842–848.

Schoenbaum, M., Sherbourne, C., & Wells, K. (2005). Gender patterns in cost effectiveness of quality improvement for depression: Results of a randomized controlled trial. *Journal of Affective Disorders, 87,* 319–325.

Schofield, H.-L., Bierman, K. L., Heinrichs, B., & Nix, R. L. (2008). Predicting early sexual activity with behavior problems exhibited at school entry and in early adolescence. *Journal of Abnormal Child Psychology, 36,* 1175–1188. doi:10.1007/s10802-008-9252-6

Scholz, H., Franz, M., & Heberlein, U. (2005). The hangover gene defines a stress pathway required for ethanol tolerance development. *Nature, 436,* 845–847.

Schooler, C. (2007). Use it—and keep it, longer, probably: A reply to Salthouse (2006). *Perspectives on Psychological Science, 2,* 24–29.

Schott, B. H., Henson, R. N., Richardson-Klavehn, A., Becker, C., et al. (2005). Redefining implicit and explicit memory: The functional neuroanatomy of priming, remembering, and control of retrieval. *Proceedings of the National Academy of Sciences, 102,* 1257–1262.

Schou, M. (2001). Lithium treatment at 52. *Journal of Affective Disorders, 67,* 21–32.

Schroeder, D. A., Penner, L. A., Dovidio, J. F., & Piliavin, J. A. (1995). *The psychology of helping and altruism: Problems and puzzles.* New York: McGraw-Hill.

Schuckit, M. A. (1998). Biological, psychological, and environmental predictors of alcoholism risk: A longitudinal study. *Journal of Studies in Alcoholism, 59,* 485–494.

Schulden, J., Chen, J., Kresnow, M., Arias, I., et al. (2006). Psychological responses to the sniper attacks: Washington DC, area, October 2002. *American Journal of Preventive Medicine, 31,* 324–327.

Schultheiss, O. C. (2008). Implicit motives. In O. P. John, R. W. Robins, & L. A. Pervin (Eds.), *Handbook of personality: Theory and research* (3rd ed., pp. 603–633). New York: Guilford Press.

Schultheiss, O. C., & Rohde, W. (2002). Implicit power motivation predicts men's testosterone changes and implicit learning in a contest situation. *Hormones and Behavior, 41,* 195–202.

Schultz, D. P., & Schultz, S. E. (2000). *A history of modern psychology* (7th ed.). Fort Worth, TX: Harcourt Brace.

Schultz, D. P., & Schultz, S. E. (2004). *A history of modern psychology* (8th ed.). Fort Worth, TX: Harcourt Brace.

Schultz, D. P., & Schultz, S. E. (2009). *Theories of personality* (9th ed.). Belmont, CA: Wadsworth.

Schultz, P. W., Nolan, J. M., Cialdini, R. B., Goldstein, N. J. & Griskevicius, V. (2007). The constructive, destructive, and reconstructive power of social norms. *Psychological Science, 18,* 429–434.

Schulz, R., Beach, S. R., Lind, B., Martire, L. M., et al. (2001). Involvement in caregiving and adjustment to death of a spouse: Findings from the caregiver health effects study. *Journal of the American Medical Association, 285,* 3123–3129.

Schulz-Hardt, S., Frey, D., Luthgens, C., & Moscovici, S. (2000). Biased information search in group decision making. *Journal of Personality and Social Psychology, 78,* 665–669.

Schulz-Stubner, S., Krings, T., Meister, I. G., Rex, S., et al. (2004). Clinical hypnosis modulates functional magnetic resonance imaging signal intensities and pain perception in a thermal stimulation paradigm. *Regional Anesthesia and Pain Medicine, 29,* 549–556.

Schumann, A., Meyer, C., Rumpf, H. J., Hannover, W., et al. (2005). Stage of change transitions and processes of change, decisional balance, and self-efficacy in smokers: A transtheoretical model validation using longitudinal data. *Psychology of Addictive Behaviors, 19,* 3–9.

Schutter, D. J. L. G. (2005). A framework for targeting alternative brain regions with repetitive transcranial magnetic stimulation in the treatment of depression. *Journal of Psychiatry and Neuroscience, 30,* 91–97.

Schwartz, A., & Bugental, D. B. (2004). *Infant habituation to repeated stress as an interactive function of child temperament and maternal depression.* Unpublished manuscript.

Schwartz, C. E., Wright, C. I., Shin, L. M., Kagan, J., & Rauch, S. L. (2003). Inhibited and uninhibited infants "grow up": Adult amygdalar response to novelty. *Science, 300,* 1952–1953.

Schwartz, J. (2004, September 5). Always on the job, employees pay with health. *New York Times,* p. 1.

Schwartz, J. R. (2005). Modafinil: New indications for wake promotion. *Expert Opinion in Pharmacotherapy, 6,* 115–129.

Schwartz, J. R. (2009). Modafinil in the treatment of excessive sleepiness. *Drug Design, Development, and Therapy, 2,* 71–85.

Schwartz, M. W.; Woods, S. C.; Porte, D., Jr.; Seeley, R. J.; & Baskin, D. G. (2000). Central nervous system control of food intake. *Nature, 404,* 661–671.

Schwartz, R. C., & Feisthamel, K. P. (2009). Disproportionate diagnosis of mental disorders among African American versus European American clients: Implications for counseling theory, research, and practice. *Journal of Counseling and Development, 87,* 295–301.

Schwarzbold, M., Diaz, A., Martins, E. T., Rufino, A., et al. (2008). Psychiatric disorders and traumatic brain injury. *Neuropsychiatric Disease and Treatment, 4,* 797–816.

Schwarzer, R. (2001). Social-cognitive factors in changing health-related behaviors. *Current Directions in Psychological Science, 10,* 47–51.

Schweinberger, S. R., & Burton, A. M. (2003). Covert recognition and the neural system for face processing. *Cortex, 39,* 9–30.

Schweinhart, L. J., & Weikart, D. P. (1991). Response to "Beyond IQ in preschool programs?" *Intelligence, 15,* 313–315.

Schwenck, C., Bjorklund, D. F., & Schneider, W. (2009). Developmental and individual differences in young children's use and maintenance of a selective memory strategy. *Developmental Psychology, 45,* 1034–1050.

Schwender, D., Klasing, D., Daunderer, M., Maddler, C., et al. (1995). Awareness during general anesthetic: Definition, incidence, clinical relevance, causes, avoidance, and medicolegal aspects. *Anaesthetist, 44,* 743–754.

Schyns, B. (2006). Are group consensus in leader-member exchange (LMX) and shared work values related to organizational outcomes? *Small Group Research, 37,* 20–35.

Scott, K. M., Bruffaerts, R., Simon, G. E., Alonso, J., et al. (2008). Obesity and mental disorders in the general population: Results from the World Mental Health Surveys. *International Journal of Obesity, 32,* 192–200.

Scott, K. M., Smith, D. R., & Ellis, P. M. (2010). Prospectively ascertained child maltreatment and its association with DSM-IV mental disorders in young adults. *Archives of General Psychiatry, 67,* 712–719.

Scott, T. F. (2006). The neurological examination. In P. J. Snyder & P. D. Nussbaum (Eds.), *Clinical neuropsychology: A pocket handbook for assessment* (2nd ed., pp. 17–33). Washington, DC: American Psychological Association.

Scourfield, J., Van den Bree, M., Martin, N., & McGuffin, P. (2004). Conduct problems in children and adolescents: A twin study. *Archives of General Psychiatry, 61,* 489–496.

Scoville, W. B., & Milner, B. (1957). Loss of recent memory after bilateral hippocampal lesions. *Journal of Neurology, Neurosurgery, and Psychiatry, 20,* 11–21.

Sears, R. (1977). Sources of satisfaction of the Terman gifted men. *American Psychologist, 32,* 119–128.

Sederberg, P. B., Schulze-Bonhage, A., Madsen, J. R., Bromfield, E. B., et al. (2007). Gamma oscillations distinguish true from false memories. *Psychological Science, 18,* 927–932.

Seegert, C. R. (2003). Token economies and incentive programs: Behavioral improvement in mental health inmates housed in state prisons. *Behavior Therapist, 26,* 208–211.

Seeley, K. (2006). *Cultural psychotherapy: Working with culture in the clinical encounter.* Northvale, NJ: Aronson.

Seem, S. R., & Clark, M. D. (2006). Healthy women, healthy men, and healthy adults: An evaluation of gender role of stereotypes in the twenty-first century. *Sex Roles, 55,* 247–258.

Seeman, M. V. (2004). Gender differences in the prescribing of antipsychotic drugs. *American Journal of Psychiatry, 161,* 1324–1333.

Seeman, T., & Chen, X. (2002). Risk and protective factors for physical functioning in older adults with and without chronic conditions: MacArthur studies of successful aging. *Journals of Gerontology, Series B: Psychological Sciences and Social Sciences, 57,* S135–S144.

Segal, L., & Suri, J. F. (1999). Psychology applied to product design. In A. M. Stec & D. A. Bernstein (Eds.), *Psychology: Fields of application* (pp. 165–183). Boston: Houghton Mifflin.

Segal, N. L. (1999). *Entwined lives.* New York: Dutton.

Segal, Z. V., Gemar, M., & Williams, S. (2000). Differential cognitive response to a mood challenge following successful cognitive therapy or pharmacotherapy for unipolar depression. *Journal of Abnormal Psychology, 108,* 3–10.

Segall, M. H., Dasen, P. R., Berry, J. W., & Poortinga, Y. H. (1990). *Human behavior in global perspective: An introduction to cross-cultural psychology.* Elmwood, NY: Pergamon Press.

Segerstrom, S. C., & Sephton, S. E. (2010). Optimistic expectancies and cell-mediated immunity. *Psychological Science, 21,* 448–455.

Segerstrom, S. C., Taylor, S. E., Kemeny, M. E., & Fahey, J. L. (1998). Optimism is associated with mood, coping, and immune change in response to stress. *Journal of Personality and Social Psychology, 74,* 1646–1655.

Séguin, J. R., & Zelazo, P. D. (2005). Executive function in early physical aggression. In R. E. Tremblay, W. W. Hartup, & J. Archer (Eds.), *Developmental origins of aggression* (pp. 307–329). New York: Guilford Press.

Seidler, G. H., & Wagner, F. E. (2006). Comparing the efficacy of EMDR and trauma-focused cognitive-behavioral therapy in the treatment of PTSD: A meta-analytic study. *Psychological Medicine, 36,* 1515–1522.

Sejnowski, T. J., Chattarji, S., & Stanton, P. K. (1990). Homosynaptic long-term depression in hippocampus and neocortex. *Seminars in the Neurosciences, 2,* 355–363.

Sekuler, R., & Blake, R. (1994). *Perception* (3rd ed.). New York: Mc Graw-Hill.

Selemon, L. D., Mrzljak, J., Kleinman, J. E., Herman, M. M., & Goldman-Rakic, P. S. (2003). Regional specificity in the neuropathologic substrates of schizophrenia: A morphometric analysis of Broca's area 44 and area 9. *Archives of General Psychiatry, 60,* 69–77.

Seligman, M. E. P. (1975). *Helplessness: On depression, development, and death.* San Francisco: Freeman.

Seligman, M. E. P. (1991). *Learned optimism.* New York: Knopf.

Seligman, M. E. P. (1996). Good news for psychotherapy: The *Consumer Reports* study. *Independent Practitioner, 16,* 17–20.

Seligman, M. E. P. (2002). Positive psychology, positive prevention, and positive therapy. In C. R. Snyder & S. J. Lopez (Eds.), *Handbook of positive psychology* (pp. 3–10). NewYork: Oxford University Press

Seligman, M. E. P., Berkowitz, M. W., Catalano, R. F., Damon, W., et al. (2005). The positive perspective on youth development. In D. L. Evans, E. Foa, R. Gur, H. Hendrin, et al. (Eds.), *Treating and preventing adolescent mental health disorders: What we know and what we don't know* (pp. 499–529). New York: Oxford University Press.

Seligman, M. E. P., Castellon, C., Cacciola, J., Shulman, P., et al. (1988). Explanatory style change during cognitive therapy for unipolar depression. *Journal of Abnormal Psychology, 97,* 13–18.

Seligman, M. E. P., Rashid, T., & Parks, A. C. (2006). Positive psychotherapy. *American Psychologist, 61,* 774–788.

Seligman, M. E. P., & Schulman, P. (1986). Explanatory style as a predictor of productivity and quitting among life insurance agents. *Journal of Personality and Social Psychology, 50,* 832–838.

Seligman, M. E. P., Steen, T. A., Park, N., & Peterson, C. (2005). Positive psychology progress: Empirical validation of interventions. *American Psychologist, 60,* 410–421.

Sell, R. L., Wells, J. A., & Wypij, D. (1995). The prevalence of homosexual behavior and attraction in the United States, the United Kingdom, and France: Results of national population-based samples. *Archives of Sexual Behavior, 24,* 235–248.

Semmler, C., Brewer, N., & Wells, G. L. (2004). Effects of postidentification feedback on eyewitness identification and nonidentification confidence. *Journal of Applied Psychology, 89,* 334–346.

Senghas, A., & Coppola, M. (2001). Children creating language: How Nicaraguan sign language acquired a spatial grammar. *Psychological Science, 12,* 323–328.

Seo, H., & Lee, D. (2009). Behavioral and neural changes after gains and losses of conditioned reinforcers. *Journal of Neuroscience, 29,* 3627–3641.

Seppa, N. (2010). Nearsightedness increasing in the United States. *Science News, 177,* 13.

Serpell, R. (2000). Intelligence and culture. In R. J. Sternberg (Ed.), *Handbook of intelligence* (pp. 549–577). New York: Cambridge University Press.

Serretti, A., Chiesa, A., Calati, R., Perma, G., et al. (2009). Common genetic, clinical, demographic and psychosocial predictors of response to pharmacotherapy in mood and anxiety disorders. *International Clinical Psychopharmacology, 24,* 1–18.

Servan-Schreiber, D., Schooler, J., Dew, M. A., Carter, C., & Bartone, P. (2006). Eye movement desensitization and reprocessing for posttraumatic stress disorder: A pilot blinded, randomized study of stimulation type. *Psychotherapy and Psychosomatics, 75,* 290–297.

Servan-Schreiber, E., & Anderson, J. R. (1990). Learning artificial grammars with competitive chunking. *Journal of Experimental Psychology: Learning, Memory, and Cognition, 16,* 592–608.

Seto, M. C., Maric, A., & Barbaree, H. E. (2001). The role of pornography in the etiology of sexual aggression. *Aggression and Violent Behavior, 6,* 35–53.

Seugnet, L., Boero, J., Gottschalk, L., Duntley, S. P., & Shaw, P. J. (2006). Identification of a biomarker for sleep drive in flies and humans. *Proceedings of the National Academy of Sciences, 103,* 19913–19918.

Sevcik, R. A., & Savage-Rumbaugh, E. S. (1994). Language comprehension and use by great apes. *Language and Communication, 14,* 37–58.

Sewell, M. C., Goggin, K. J., Rabkin, J. G., Ferrando, S. J., et al. (2000). Anxiety syndromes and symptoms among men with AIDS: A longitudinal controlled study. *Psychosomatics, 41,* 294–300.

Seymour, K., Clifford, C. W., Logothetis, N. K., & Bartels, A. (2009). The coding of color, motion, and their conjunction in the human visual cortex. *Current Biology*, 19, 177–183

Seymour, N. E. (2008). VR to OR: A review of the evidence that virtual reality simulation improves operating room performance. *World Journal of Surgery, 32,* 182–188.

Shackelford, T. K., Schmitt, D. P., & Buss, D. M. (2005). Universal dimensions of human mate preference. *Personality and Individual Differences, 39,* 447–458.

Shadish, W. R., & Baldwin, S. A. (2005). Effects of behavioral marital therapy: A meta-analysis of randomized controlled trials. *Journal of Counseling and Clinical Psychology, 73,* 6–14.

Shadish, W. R., Cook, T. D., & Campbell, D. T. (2002). *Experimental and quasi-experimental designs for generalized causal inference.* Boston: Houghton Mifflin.

Shadish, W. R., Matt, G. E., Navarro, A. M., & Phillips, G. (2000). The effects of psychological therapies under clinically representative conditions: A meta-analysis. *Psychological Bulletin, 126,* 512–529.

Shaffer, D. R. (1973). *Social and personality development.* Pacific Grove, CA: Brooks/Cole.

Shah, J. (2003). Automatic for the people: How representations of significant others implicitly affect goal pursuit. *Journal of Personality and Social Psychology, 84,* 661–681.

Shalev, A. Y., & Freedman, S. (2005). PTSD following terrorist attacks: A prospective evaluation. *American Journal of Psychiatry, 162,* 1188–1191.

Shalev, A. Y., Tuval, R., Frenkiel-Fishman, S., Hadar, H., & Eth, S. (2006). Psychological responses to continuous terror: A study of two communities in Israel. *American Journal of Psychiatry, 163,* 667–673.

Shamay-Tsoory, S. G., & Tomer, R. (2005). The neuroanatomical basis of understanding sarcasm and its relationship to social cognition. *Neuropsychology, 19,* 288–300.

Shams, L., Kamitani, Y., & Shimojo, S. (2000). Illusions: What you see is what you hear. *Nature, 408,* 788.

Shand, M. A. (1982). Sign-based short-term memory coding of American Sign Language and printed English words by congenitally deaf signers. *Cognitive Psychology, 14,* 1–12.

Shankman, S. A., Klein, D. N., Tenke, C. E., & Bruder, G. E. (2007). Reward sensitivity in depression: A biobehavioral study. *Journal of Abnormal Psychology, 116,* 95–104.

Shanks, D. R. (1995). *The psychology of associative learning.* New York: Cambridge University Press.

Shanti, R., Mitchell, S. R., Reiss, A. L., Tatusko, D. H., et al. (2009). Neuroanatomic alterations and social and communication deficits in monozygotic twins discordant for autism disorder. *American Journal of Psychiatry, 166,* 917–925.

Shapiro, A. F., Gottman, J. M., & Carrere, S. (2000). The baby and the marriage: Identifying factors that buffer against decline in marital satisfaction after the first baby arrives. *Journal of Family Psychology, 14,* 59–70.

Shapiro, F. (1989a). Efficacy of the eye movement desensitization procedure in the treatment of traumatic memories. *Journal of Traumatic Stress, 2,* 199–223.

Shapiro, F. (1989b). Eye movement desensitization: A new treatment for posttraumatic stress disorder. *Journal of Behavior Therapy and Experimental Psychiatry, 20,* 211–217.

Shapiro, F. (1991). Eye movement desensitization and reprocessing procedure: From EMD to EMD/R—a new treatment model for anxiety and related traumata. *Behavior Therapist, 15,* 133–135.

Shapiro, F. (2001). *Eye movement desensitization and reprocessing: Basic principles, protocols, and procedures* (2nd ed.). New York: Guilford Press.

Shapiro, F., & Forrest, M. S. (2004). *EMDR: The breakthrough therapy for overcoming anxiety, stress, and trauma.* New York: Basic Books.

Shapiro, K. A., Moo, L. R., & Caramazza, A. (2006). Cortical signatures of noun and verb production. *Proceedings of the National Academy of Sciences, 103,* 1644–1649.

Shapiro, R. (2005). *EMDR solutions: Pathways to healing.* New York: Norton.

Sharot, T., Martorella, E. A., Delgado, M. R., & Phelps, E. A. (2006). How personal experience modulates the neural circuitry of memories of September 11. *Proceedings of the National Academy of Sciences, 104,* 389–394.

Shaw, B. A., Krause, N., Chatters, L. M., Connell, C. M., & Ingersoll-Dayton, B. (2004). Emotional support from parents early in life, aging, and health. *Psychology and Aging, 19,* 4–12.

Shaw, D. S., Dishion, T. J., Supplee, L., Gardner, F., & Arnds, K. (2006). Randomized trial of a family-centered approach to the prevention of early conduct problems: 2-year effects of the family check-up in early childhood. *Journal of Consulting and Clinical Psychology, 74,* 1–9.

Shaw, P., Greenstein, D., Lerch, J., Clasen, L., et al. (2006). Intellectual ability and cortical development in children and adolescents. *Nature, 440,* 676–679.

Shaw, S. F., Cullen, J. P., McGuire, J. M., & Brinckerhoff, L. C. (1995). Operationalizing a definition of learning disabilities. *Journal of Learning Disabilities, 28,* 586–597.

Shaywitz, B. A., Shaywitz, S. E., Pugh, K. R., Constable, R. T., et al. (1995). Sex differences in the functional organization of the brain for language. *Nature, 373,* 607–609.

Shechtman, Z. (1992). A group assessment procedure as a predictor of on-the-job performance of teachers. *Journal of Applied Psychology, 77,* 383–387.

Shedler, J. (2010). The efficacy of psychodynamic psychotherapy. *American Psychologist, 65,* 98–109.

Shedler, J., & Westen, D. (2004). Refining personality disorder diagnoses: Integrating science and practice. *American Journal of Psychiatry, 161,* 1350–1365.

Sheehy, R., & Horan, J. J. (2004). Effects of stress inoculation training for 1st-year law students. *International Journal of Stress Management, 11,* 41–55.

Sheldon, C. A., Malcolm, G. L., & Barton, J. J. (2008). Alexia with and without agraphia: An assessment of two classical syndromes. *Canadian Journal of Neurological Sciences, 35,* 616–624.

Sheldon, K. M., & Kasser, T. (2001). Getting older, getting better? Personal striving and psychological maturity across the life span. *Developmental Psychology, 37,* 491–501.

Sheldon, K. M., & King, L (2001). Why positive psychology is necessary. *American Psychologist, 56,* 216–217.

Shen, J., & Dicker, B. (2008). The impacts of shiftwork on employees. *International Journal of Human Resource Management, 19,* 392–405.

Shenker, J. I. (2005, April). *When you only see trees, is there still a forest?* Paper presented at the annual meeting of the American Academy of Neurology, Miami Beach, FL.

Shenker, J. I. (2010, February 19). *The lady who didn't know she couldn't move, the vanishing mystery woman, and other broken brains that teach.* Presentation to fifth annual Conference on Applied Learning in Higher Education, Missouri Western State University, Saint Joseph, MO.

Shenker, J. I., Wylie, S. A., Fuchs, K., Manning, C. A., & Heilman, K. M. (2004). Online anosognosia: Unawareness for chorea in real time but not on videotape delay. *Neurology, 63,* 159–160.

Shepard, R. N., & Metzler, J. (1971). Mental rotation of three-dimensional objects. *Science, 171,* 701–703.

Shepherd, C. (1994, March 31). News of the weird: Lead story. *Chicago Reader.* Retrieved from http://www.chicagoreader.com/chicago/news-of-the-weird/Content?oid=884185

Shepherd, C., Kohut, J. J., & Sweet, R. (1989). *News of the weird.* New York: New American Library.

Shepherd, R. K., Coco, A., Epp, S. B., & Crook, J. M. (2005). Chronic depolarization enhances the trophic effects of brain-derived neurotrophic factor in rescuing auditory neurons following a sensorineural hearing loss. *Journal of Comparative Neurology, 486,* 145–158.

Shepherd, R. K., & McCreery, D. B. (2006). Basis of electrical stimulation of the cochlea and the cochlear nucleus. *Advances in Otorhinolaryngology, 64,* 186–205.

Shepperd, J., Malone, W., & Sweeny, K. (2008). Exploring causes of the self-serving bias. *Social and Personality Psychology Compass, 2,* 895–908.

Sher, K. J., Wood, M. D., Wood, P. K., & Raskin, G. (1996). Alcohol outcome expectancies and alcohol use: A latent variable cross-lagged panel study. *Journal of Abnormal Psychology, 105,* 561–574.

Shera, C. A., Guinan, J. J., & Oxenham, A. J. (2002). Revised estimates of human cochlear tuning from otoacoustic and behavioral measurements. *Proceedings of the National Academy of Sciences, 99,* 3318–3323.

Sherer, M. R., & Schreibman, L. (2005). Individual behavioral profiles and predictors of treatment effectiveness for children with autism. *Journal of Consulting and Clinical Psychology, 73,* 525–538.

Shergill, S. S., Brammer, M. J., Williams, S. C., Murray, R. M., & McGuire, P. K. (2000). Mapping auditory hallucinations in schizophrenia using functional magnetic resonance imaging. *Archives of General Psychiatry, 57,* 1033–1038.

Sherif, M. (1937). An experimental approach to the study of attitudes. *Sociometry, 1,* 90–98.

Sherman, J. W., & Bessenoff, G. R. (1999). Stereotypes as source-monitoring cues: On the interaction between episodic and semantic memory. *Psychological Science, 10,* 106–110.

Sherman, R. T., & Thompson, R. A. (2004). The female athlete triad. *Journal of School Nursing, 20,* 197–202.

Sherman, S. J. (1980). On the self-erasing nature of errors of prediction. *Journal of Personality and Social Psychology, 39,* 211–221.

Sherman, S. M. (2007). The thalamus is more than just a relay. *Current Opinion in Neurobiology, 17,* 417–422.

Sherry, J. L. (2001). The effects of violent video games on aggression: A meta-analysis. *Human Communication Research, 27,* 409–431.

Sherwin, B. B., & Gelfand, M. M. (1987). The role of androgen in the maintenance of sexual functioning in oophorectomized women. *Psychosomatic Medicine, 49,* 397–409.

Shibasaki M, Kawai N. (2009). Rapid detection of snakes by Japanese monkeys (Macaca fuscata): an evolutionarily predisposed visual system. *Journal of Comprehensive Psychiatry, 123,* 131–135.

Shields, L. B. E., Hunsaker, D. M., Muldoon, S., Corey, T. S., & Spivack, B. S. (2005). Risk factors associated with sudden unexplained infant death: A prospective study of infant care practices in Kentucky. *Pediatrics, 116,* e13–e20.

Shiffman, S., Engberg, J. B., Paty, J. A., & Perz, W. G. (1997). A day at a time: Predicting smoking lapse from daily urge. *Journal of Abnormal Psychology, 106,* 104–116.

Shiller, R. J. (2001). *Irrational exuberance.* Princeton, NJ: Princeton University Press.

Shimazu, T., Kuriyama1, S., Ohmori-Matsuda, K., Kikuchi, N., et al. (2009). Increase in body mass index category since age 20 years and all-cause mortality: A prospective cohort study (the Ohsaki Study). *International Journal of Obesity, 33,* 490–496.

Shin, M., Besser, L. M., Kucik, J. E., Lu, C., et al. (2009). Prevalence of Down syndrome among children and adolescents in 10 regions of the United States. *Pediatrics, 124,* 1565–1571.

Shin, S.-M., Chow, C., Camacho-Gonzalves, T., Levy, R. J., et al. (2005). A meta-analytic review of racial-ethnic matching for African American and Caucasian American clients and clinicians. *Journal of Counseling Psychology, 52,* 45–56.

Shiner, R. L., Masten, A. S., & Roberts, J. M. (2003). Childhood personality foreshadows adult personality and life outcomes two decades later. *Journal of Personality, 71,* 1145–1170.

Shinskey, J. L., & Munakata, Y. (2005). Familiarity breeds searching. *Psychological Science, 16,* 596–600.

Shiraev, E. B., & Levy, D. A. (2010). *Cross-cultural psychology: Critical thinking and contemporary applications* (4th ed.). Boston: Allyn & Bacon.

Shirani, A., & Saint Louis, E. K. (2009). Illuminating rationale and uses for light therapy. *Journal of Clinical Sleep Medicine, 5,* 155–163.

Shirom, A. (2003). Job-related burnout. In J. C. Quick & L. E. Tetrick (Eds.), *Handbook of occupational health psychology* (pp. 245–265). Washington DC: American Psychological Association.

Shiwach, R. S., Reid, W. H., & Carmody, T. J. (2001). An analysis of reported deaths following electroconvulsive therapy in Texas, 1993–1998. *Psychiatric Services, 52,* 1095–1097.

Shoda, Y., & LeeTiernan, S. (2002). What remains invariant? Finding order within a person's thoughts, feelings, and behavior across situations. In D. Cervone & W. Mischel (Eds.), *Advances in personality science* (pp. 241–270). New York: Guilford Press.

Shoda, Y., & Mischel, W. (2006). Applying meta-theory to achieve generalisability and precision in personality science: Comment. *Applied Psychology: An International Review, 55,* 439–452.

Shoptaw, S., Yang, X., Rotheram-Fuller, E. J., Hsieh, Y. C., et al. (2003). Randomized placebo-controlled trial of baclofen for cocaine dependence: Preliminary effects for individuals with chronic patterns of cocaine use. *Journal of Clinical Psychiatry, 64,* 1440–1448.

Shore, S. (2003). Life on and slightly to the right of the autistic spectrum: A personal account. *Exceptional Parent, 33,* 85–89.

Shorter, E., & Healy, D. (2007). *Shock therapy: A history of electroconvulsive treatment in mental illness.* New Brunswick, NJ: Rutgers University Press.

Shouzhuang, H., & Chao, L. (2006). Acupuncture treatment for 68 cases of functional impairment induced by cerebral hemorrhage at the convalescence stage. *Journal of Traditional Chinese Medicine, 26,* 172–174.

Shreeve, J. (1993, June). Touching the phantom. *Discover,* pp. 35–42.

Siber, K. (2005, December). Precious metal. *Skiing,* p. 16E.

Sibley, C. G., Wilson, M. S., & Duckitt, J. (2007). Effects of dangerous and competitive worldviews on right-wing authoritarianism and social dominance orientation over a five-month period. *Political Psychology, 28,* 357–371.

Siegal, M. (1997). *Knowing children: Experiments in conversation and cognition* (2nd ed.). Hove, England: Psychology Press/Erlbaum/Taylor & Francis.

Siegel, J. M., & Rogawski, M. A. (1988). A function for REM sleep: Regulation of noradrenergic receptor sensitivity. *Brain Research Review, 13,* 213–233.

Siegel, S. (2005). Drug tolerance, drug addiction, and drug anticipation. *Current Directions in Psychological Science, 14,* 296–300.

Siegel, S., Hirson, R. E., Krank, M. D., & McCully, J. (1982). Heroin "overdose" death: The contribution of drug associated environmental cues. *Science, 216,* 430–437.

Siegler, R. S. (1994). Cognitive variability: A key to understanding cognitive development. *Current Directions in Psychological Science, 3,* 1–4.

Siegler, R. S. (2003). Thinking and intelligence. In M. H. Bornstein, L. Davidson, C. L. M. Keyes, & K. A. Moore (Eds.), *Well-being: Positive development across the life course* (pp. 311–320). Mahwah, NJ: Erlbaum.

Siegler, R. S. (2006). Microgenetic analysis of learning. In W. Damon & R. M. Lerner (Series Eds.) & D. Kuhn & R. S. Siegler (Vol. Eds.), *Handbook of child psychology: Vol. 2. Cognition, perception, and language* (6th ed., pp. 464–510). Hoboken, NJ: Wiley.

Siep, N., Roefs, A., Roebroeck, A., Havermans, R., et al. (2009). Hunger is the best spice: An fMRI study of the effects of attention, hunger and calorie content on food reward processing in the amygdala and orbitofrontal cortex. *Behavioural Brain Research, 198,* 149–158.

Siever, L. J. (2008). Neurobiology of aggression and violence. *American Journal of Psychiatry, 165,* 429–442.

Sigmundsson, T., Suckling, J., Maier, M., Bullmore, E., et al. (2001). Structural abnormalities in frontal, temporal, and limbic regions and interconnecting white matter tracts in schizophrenic patients with prominent negative symptoms. *American Journal of Psychiatry, 158,* 234–243.

Silbersweig, D. A., Stern, E., Frith, C., Cahill, C., et al. (1995). A functional neuroanatomy of hallucinations in schizophrenia. *Nature, 378,* 176–179.

Silver, E. (1995). Punishment or treatment? Comparing the lengths of confinement of successful and unsuccessful insanity defendants. *Law and Human Behavior, 19,* 375–388.

Silver, E., Cirincione, C., & Steadman, H. J. (1994). Demythologizing inaccurate perceptions of the insanity defense. *Law and Human Behavior, 18,* 63–70.

Silverman, K., Svikis, D., Robles, E., Stitzer, M. L., & Bigelow, G. E. (2001). A reinforcement-based therapeutic workplace for the treatment of drug abuse: Six-month abstinence outcomes. *Experimental and Clinical Psychopharmacology, 9,* 14–23.

Silverstein, L. B. (1996). Evolutionary psychology and the search for sex differences. *American Psychologist, 51,* 160–161.

Silverthorne, C. P. (2001). Leadership effectiveness and personality: A cross-cultural evaluation. *Personality and Individual Differences, 30,* 303–309.

Silverthorne, C. P. (2005). *Organizational psychology in cross-cultural perspective.* New York: New York University Press.

Simcock, G., & Hayne, H. (2002). Breaking the barrier? Children fail to translate their preverbal memories into language. *Psychological Science, 13,* 225–231.

Simeon, D., Greenberg, J., Knutelska, M., Schmeidler, J., & Hollander, E. (2003). Peritraumatic reactions associated with the World Trade Center disaster. *American Journal of Psychiatry, 160,* 1702–1705.

Simion, F., Cassia, V. M., Turati, C., & Valenza, E. (2003). Nonspecific perceptual biases at the origins of face processing. In O. Pascalis & A. Slater (Eds.), *The development of face processing in infancy and early childhood* (pp. 13–25). Hauppauge, NY: Nova Science.

Simmons, D., Chabal, C., Griffith, J., Rausch, M., & Steele, B. (2004). A clinical trial of distraction techniques for pain and anxiety control during cataract surgery. *Insight, 29,* 13–16.

Simon, G. E., Savarino, J., Operskalski, B., & Wang, P. S. (2006). Suicide risk during antidepressant treatment. *American Journal of Psychiatry, 163,* 41–47.

Simon, G. E., & von Korff, M. (2006). Medical co-morbidity and validity of DSM-IV depression criteria. *Psychological Medicine, 36,* 27–36.

Simon, V. A., Aikins, J. W., & Prinstein, M. J. (2008). Romantic partner selection and socialization during early adolescence. *Child Development, 79,* 1676–1692.

Simons, C. J. P., Tracy, D. K., Sanghera, K. K., O'Daly, O., et al. (2010). Functional magnetic resonance imaging of inner speech in schizophrenia. *Biological Psychiatry, 67,* 232–237.

Simons, D. J., & Ambinder, M. S. (2005). Change blindness: Theory and consequences. *Current Directions in Psychological Science, 14,* 44–48.

Simons, D. J., & Chabris, C. F. (1999). Gorillas in our midst: Sustained inattentional blindness for dynamic events. *Perception, 28,* 1059–1074.

Simons, R., & Valk, P. J. L. (2009). Melatonin for commercial aircrew? *Biological Rhythm Research, 40,* 7–16.

Simon-Thomas, E. R., Keltner, D. J., Sauter, D., Sinicropi-Yao, L., & Abramson, A. (2009). The voice conveys specific emotions: Evidence from vocal burst displays. *Emotion, 6,* 838–846.

Simonton, D. K. (1984). *Genius, creativity, and leadership.* Cambridge. MA: Harvard University Press.

Simonton, D. K. (1999). Creativity and genius. In L. A. Pervin & O. P. John (Eds.), *Handbook of personality research* (2nd ed., pp. 629–652). New York: Guilford Press.

Simonton, D. K. (2000). Creativity: Cognitive, developmental, personal, and social aspects. *American Psychologist, 55,* 151–158.

Simonton, D. K. (2002). Creativity. In C. R. Snyder & S. J. Lopez (Eds.), *Handbook of positive psychology* (pp. 189–201). New York: Oxford University Press.

Simonton, D. K. (2004). *Creativity in science: Chance, logic, genius, and zeitgeist.* Cambridge: Cambridge University Press.

Simonton, D. K., & Song, A. V. (2009). Eminence, IQ, physical and mental health, and achievement domain: Cox's 282 geniuses revisited. *Psychological Science, 20,* 429–434.

Simpson, J. A., & Kenrick, D. T. (1997). *Evolutionary social psychology.* Mahwah, NJ: Erlbaum.

Simpson, J. A., Rholes, W. S., & Winterheld, H. A. (2010). Attachment working models twist memoris of relationship events. *Psychological Science, 21,* 252–259.

Simpson, J. A., Winterheld, H. A., Rholes, W. S., & Oriña, M. M. (2007). Working models of attachment and reactions to different forms of caregiving from romantic partners. *Journal of Personality and Social Psychology, 93,* 466–477.

Simpson, S., Hurtley, S. M., & Marx, J. (2000). Immune cell networks. *Science, 290,* 79.

Simpson, S. G., McMahon, F. J., McInnis, M. G., MacKinnon, D. F., et al. (2002). Diagnostic reliability of bipolar II disorder. *Archives of General Psychiatry, 59,* 736–740.

Simpson, S. H., Eurich, D. T., Majumdar, S. R., Padwal, R. S., et al. (2006). A meta-analysis of the association between adherence to drug therapy and mortality. *British Medical Journal, 333,* 15. doi:10.1136/bmj.38875.675486.55

Sinclair, C., & Hammond, G. R. (2008). Excitatory and inhibitory processes in primary motor cortex during the foreperiod of a warned reaction time task are unrelated to response expectancy. *Experimental Brain Research, 194,* 103–113.

Sinclair, R. C., Hoffman, C., Mark, M. M., Martin, L. L., & Pickering, T. L. (1994). Construct accessibility and the misattribution of arousal. *Psychological Science, 5,* 15–19.

Singer, L. T., Arendt, R., Minnes, S., Farkas, K., et al. (2002). Cognitive and motor outcomes of cocaine-exposed infants. *Journal of the American Medical Association, 287,* 1952–1960.

Singer, L. T., Arendt, R., Minnes, S., Salvator, A., et al. (2001). Developing language skills of cocaine-exposed infants. *Pediatrics, 107,* 1057–1064.

Singer, L. T., Minnes, S., Short, E., Arendt, R., et al. (2004). Cognitive outcomes of preschool children with prenatal cocaine exposure. *Journal of the American Medical Association, 291,* 2448–2456.

Singh, H., & O'Boyle, M. W. (2004). Interhemispheric interaction during global-local processing in mathematically gifted adolescents, average-ability youth, and college students. *Neuropsychology, 18,* 371–377.

Singh, S. M., & O'Reilly, R. (2009). (Epi)genomics and neurodevelopment in schizophrenia: Monozygotic twins discordant for schizophrenia augment the search for disease-related (epi)genomic alterations. *Genome, 52,* 8–19.

Sirvio, J. (1999). Strategies that support declining cholinergic neurotransmission in Alzheimer's disease patients. *Gerontology, 45,* 3–14.

Siti, M. (2004). Hypochondriasis: Modern perspectives on an ancient malady. *Journal of Cognitive Psychotherapy, 18,* 369–370.

Sitzmann, T., Brown, K. G., Casper, W. D., Ely, K., & Zimmerman, R. D. (2008). A review and meta-analysis of the nomological network of trainee reactions. *Journal of Applied Psychology, 93,* 280–295.

Skelton, J. A., Cook, S. R., Auinger, P., Klein, J. D., & Barlow, S. E. (2009). Prevalence and trends of severe obesity among U.S. children and adolescents. *Academic Pediatrics, 9,* 322–329.

Skinner, B. F. (1938). *The behavior of organisms.* New York: Appleton.

Skinner, B. F. (1961). *Cumulative record* (3rd ed.). Englewood Cliffs, NJ: Prentice Hall.

Skre, I., Onstad, S., Toregersen, S., Lyngren, S., & Kringlin, E. (2000). The heritability of common phobic fear: A twin study of a clinical sample. *Journal of Anxiety Disorders, 14,* 549–562.

Skrobik, Y. (2009). Delirium prevention and treatment. *Critical Care Clinics, 25,* 585–591.

Slade, E. P., & Wissow, L. S. (2004). Spanking in early childhood and later behavior problems: A prospective study of infants and young toddlers. *Pediatrics, 113,* 1321–1330.

Slater, A., Mattock, A., Brown, E., & Bremmer, J. G. (1991). Form perception at birth. *Journal of Experimental Child Psychology, 51,* 395–406.

Slavin, K. V. (2008). Peripheral nerve stimulation for neuropathic pain. *Neurotherapeutics, 5,* 100–106.

Slentz, C. A., Duscha, B. D., Johnson, J. L., Ketchum, K., et al. (2004). Effects of the amount of exercise on body weight, body composition, and measures of central obesity: STRRIDE—a randomized controlled study. *Archives of Internal Medicine, 164,* 31–39.

Sloan, D. M., Strauss, M. E., & Wisner, K. L. (2001). Diminished response to pleasant stimuli by depressed women. *Journal of Abnormal Psychology, 110,* 488–493.

Sloan, R. P., Shapiro, P. A., Gorenstein, E. E., Tager, F. A., et al. (2010). Cardiac autonomic control and treatment of hostility: A randomized controlled trial. *Psychosomatic Medicine, 72,* 1–8.

Slocombe, K. E., & Zuberbühler, K. (2005). Functionally referential communication in a chimpanzee. *Current Biology, 15,* 1779–1784.

Slomkowski, C., & Dunn, J. (1996). Young children's understanding of other people's beliefs and feelings and their connected communication with friends. *Developmental Psychology, 32,* 442–447.

Slotnick, S. D., & Schacter, D. L. (2004). A sensory signature that distinguishes true from fales memories. *Nature Neuroscience, 7,* 664–672.

Slovic, P., Peters, E., Finucane, M. L., & MacGregor, D. G. (2005). Affect, risk, and decision making. *Health Psychology, 24,* S35–S40.

Slow Food Movement. (2001). *Slow food: Collected thoughts on taste, tradition, and the honest pleasures of food.* White River Junction, VT: Chelsea Green.

Small, G., & Dubois, B. (2007). A review of compliance to treatment in Alzheimer's disease: Potential benefits of a transdermal patch. *Current Medical Research and Opinion, 23,* 2705–2713.

Small, S. A., Tsai, W. Y., DeLaPaz, R., Mayeux, R., & Stern, Y. (2002). Imaging hippocampal function across the human life span: Is memory decline normal or not? *Annals of Neurology, 51,* 290–295.

Smetana, J. G., Metzger, A., Gettman, C. D., & Campione-Barr, N. (2006). Disclosure and secrecy in adolescent-parent relationships. *Child Development, 77,* 201–217.

Smillie, L. D., Pickering, A. D., & Jackson, C. J. (2006). The new reinforcement sensitivity theory: Implications for personality measurement. *Personality and Social Psychology Review, 10,* 320–335.

Smith, A. M., Malo, S. A., Laskowski, E. R., Sabick, M., et al. (2000). A multidisciplinary study of the "yips" phenomenon in golf: An exploratory analysis. *Sports Medicine, 30,* 423–437.

Smith, B., Fowler, D. G., Freeman, D., Bebbington, P., et al. (2006). Emotion and psychosis: Links between depression, self-esteem, negative schematic beliefs, and delusions and hallucinations. *Schizophrenia Research, 86,* 181–188.

Smith, D. M., Loewenstein, G., Jankovic, A., & Ubel, P. A. (2009). Happily hopeless: Adaptation to a permanent, but not to a temporary, disability. *Health Psychology, 28,* 787–791.

Smith, E. E. (2000). Neural bases of human working memory. *Currents Directions in Psychological Science, 9,* 45–49.

Smith, E. E., Geva, A., Jonides, J., Miller, A., et al. (2001). The neural basis of task-switching in working memory: Effects of performance and aging. *Proceedings of the National Academy of Sciences, 98,* 2095–2100.

Smith, E. R. (1998). Mental representation and memory. In D. T. Gilbert, S. T. Fiske, & G. Lindzey (Eds.), *Handbook of social psychology* (4th ed., Vol. 1, pp. 391–445). New York: McGraw-Hill.

Smith, E. R., & Mackie, D. M. (2007). *Social psychology* (3rd ed.). Philadelphia: Psychology Press.

Smith, E. R., & Quellar, S. (2001). Mental representations. In A. Tesser & N. Schwarz (Eds.), *Blackwell handbook of social psychology: Intraindividual processes* (pp. 499–517). Malden, MA: Blackwell.

Smith, G. C. S., & White, I. R. (2006). Predicting the risk for sudden infant death syndrome from obstetric characteristics: A retrospective cohort study of 505,011 live births. *Pediatrics, 117,* 60–66.

Smith, G. T., Simmons, J. R., Flory, K., Annus, A. M., & Hill, K. K. (2007). Thinness and eating expectancies predict subsequent binge-eating and purging behavior among adolescent girls. *Journal of Abnormal Psychology, 116,* 188–197.

Smith, K. M., Larive, L. L., & Romananelli, F. (2002). Club drugs: Methylenedioxymethamphetamine, flunitrazepam, ketamine hydrochloride, and gamma-hydroxybutyrate. *American Journal of Health Systems Pharmacology, 59,* 1067–1076.

Smith, K. R., Mineau, G. P., Garibotti, G., & Kerber, R. (2009). Effects of childhood and middle-adulthood family conditions on later-life mortality: Evidence from the Utah population database, 1850–2002. *Social Science and Medicine, 68,* 1649–1658.

Smith, L. B., & Sera, M. D. (1992). A developmental analysis of the polar structure of dimensions. *Cognitive Psychology, 24,* 99–142.

Smith, M. L., Glass, G. V., & Miller, T. I. (1980). *The benefits of psychotherapy.* Baltimore: Johns Hopkins University Press.

Smith, P. B., & Bond, M. H. (1999). *Social psychology across cultures: Analysis and perspectives* (2nd ed.). Boston: Allyn & Bacon.

Smith, P. C., & Kendall, L. M. (1963). Retranslation of expectations: An approach to the construction of unambiguous anchors for rating scales. *Journal of Applied Psychology, 47,* 149–155.

Smith, P. J., Blumenthal, J. A., Hoffman, B. M., Cooper, H., et al. (2010). Aerobic exercise and neurocognitive performance: A meta-analytic review of randomized controlled trials. *Psychosomatic Medicine, 72,* 239–252.

Smith, P. K., & Drew, L. M. (2002). Grandparenthood. In M. H. Bornstein (Ed.), *Handbook of parenting: Vol. 3. Being and becoming a parent* (2nd ed., pp. 141–172). Mahwah, NJ: Erlbaum.

Smith, R. M., Tivarus, M., Campbell, H. L., Hillier, A., & Beversdorf, D. Q. (2006). Apparent transient effects of recent "ecstasy" use on cognitive performance and extrapyramidal signs in human subjects. *Cognitive and Behavioral Neurology, 19,* 157–164.

Smith, R. W., Uchino, B. N., Berg, C. A., Florsheim, P., et al. (2008). Associations of self-reports versus spouse ratings of negative affectivity, dominance, and affiliation with coronary artery disease: Where should we look and who should we ask when studying personality and health? *Health Psychology, 27,* 676–684.

Smith, S., & Freedman, D. G. (1983, April). *Mother-toddler interaction and maternal perception of child temperament in two ethnic groups: Chinese-American and European-American.* Paper presented at the annual meeting of the Society for Research in Child Development, Detroit, MI.

Smith, S. L., & Donnerstein, E. (1998). Harmful effects of exposure to media violence: Learning of aggression, emotional desensitization, and fear. In R. G. Geen & E. Donnerstein (Eds.), *Human aggression: Theories, research, and implications for policy* (pp. 167–202). San Diego, CA: Academic Press.

Smith, S. M., & Vela, E. (2001). Environmental context-dependent memory: A review and meta-analysis. *Psychonomic Bulletin and Review, 8,* 203–220.

Smith, S. S., O'Hara, B. F., Persico, A. M., Gorelick, D. A., et al. (1992). Genetic vulnerability to drug abuse: The D2 dopamine receptor Taq i B1 restriction fragment length polymorphism appears more frequently in polysubstance abusers. *Archives of General Psychiatry, 49,* 723–727.

Smith, T. B., Constantine, M. G., Dunn, T. W., Dinehart, J. M., & Montoya, J. A. (2006). Multicultural education in the mental health professions: A meta-analytic review. *Journal of Counseling Psychology, 53,* 132–145.

Smith, T. E., & Sederer, L. I. (2009). A new kind of homelessness for individuals with serious mental illness? The need for a "mental health home." *Hospital and Community Psychiatry, 60,* 528–533.

Smith, T. W., Orleans, C. T., & Jenkins, C. D. (2004). Prevention and health promotion: Decades of progress, new challenges, and an emerging agenda. *Health Psychology, 23,* 126–131.

Smith, T. W., & Suls, J. (2004). Introduction to the special section on the future of health psychology. *Health Psychology, 23,* 115–118.

Smith, T. W., Uchino, B. N., Berg, C. A., Florsheim, P., et al. (2007). Hostile personality traits and coronary artery calcification in middle-aged and older married couples: Different effects for self-reports versus spouse ratings. *Psychosomatic Medicine, 69,* 441–448.

Smith-Crowe, K., Burke, M. J., & Landis, R. S. (2003). Organizational climate as a moderator of safety knowledge–safety performance relationships. *Journal of Organizational Behavior, 24,* 861–876.

Smither, J. W., London, M., & Reilly, R. R. (2005). Does performance improve following multisource feedback? A theoretical model, meta-analysis, and review of empirical findings. *Personnel Psychology, 58,* 33–66.

Smits, J. A. J., O'Cleirigh, C. M., & Otto, M. W. (2006). Combining cognitive-behavioral therapy and pharmacotherapy for the treatment of panic disorder. *Journal of Cognitive Psychotherapy, 20,* 75–84.

Smoller, J. W. (2008). Genetics of mood and anxiety disorder. In J. W. Smoller, B. R. Sheidley, & M. T. Tsaung (Eds.), *Psychiatric genetics: Applications in clinical practice* (pp. 131–176). Arlington, VA: American Psychiatric Association.

Smyth, C. L., & MacLachian, M. (2005). Confirmatory factor analysis of the Trinity Inventory of Precursors to Suicide (TIPS) and its relationship to hopelessness and depression. *Death Studies, 29,* 333–350.

Snarey, J., & Hooker, C. (2006). Lawrence Kohlberg. In E. M. Dowling & W. G. Scarlett (Eds.), *Encyclopedia of spiritual and religious development* (pp. 251–255). Thousand Oaks, CA: Sage.

Snellingen, T., Evans, J. R., Ravilla, T., & Foster, A. (2002). Surgical interventions for age-related cataract. *Cochrane Database System Review, 2,* CD001323.

Snodgrass, S. R. (1994). Cocaine babies: A result of multiple teratogenic influences. *Journal of Child Neurology, 9,* 227–233.

Snow, R. E. (1995). Pygmalion and intelligence? *Current Directions in Psychological Science, 4,* 169–171.

Snowden, L. R., & Cheung, F. (1990). Use of inpatient mental health services by members of ethnic minority groups. *American Psychologist, 45,* 347–355.

Snyder, C. R., & Lopez, S. J. (2006). *Oxford handbook of positive psychology.* New York: Oxford University Press.

Snyder, C. R., & Lopez, S. J. (2009). *Oxford handbook of positive psychology* (2nd ed.). New York: Oxford University Press.

Snyder, T. D., Dillow, S. A., & Hoffman, C. M. (2008). *Digest of education statistics, 2007.* Washington, DC: National Center for Education Statistics. Retrieved from http://nces.ed.gov/programs/digest/d07

Snyderman, M., & Rothman, S. (1987). Survey of expert opinion on intelligence and aptitude testing. *American Psychologist, 42,* 137–144.

Sobel, D. M., & Kirkham, N. Z. (2006). Blickets and babies: The development of causal reasoning in toddlers and infants. *Developmental Psychology, 42,* 1103–1115.

Society for Industrial and Organizational Psychology. (2007). *Graduate training programs.* Retrieved from http://www.siop.org/gtp/gtplookup.asp

Soenens, B., Vansteenkiste, M., Luyckx, K., & Goossens, L. (2006). Parenting and adolescent problem behavior: An integrated model with adolescent self-disclosure and perceived parental knowledge as intervening variables. *Developmental Psychology, 42,* 305–318.

Sohlberg, S., & Jansson, B. (2002). Unconscious responses to "mommy and I are one": Does gender matter? In R. F. Bornstein & J. M. Masling (Eds.), *The psychodynamics of gender and gender role: Vol. 10. Empirical studies in psychoanalytic theories* (pp. 165–201). Washington, DC: American Psychological Association.

Sohler, N., & Bromet, E. J. (2003). Does racial bias influence psychiatric diagnoses assigned at first hospitalization? *Social Psychiatry and Psychiatric Epidemiology, 38,* 463–472.

Soken, N. H., & Pick, A. D. (1992). Intermodal perception of happy and angry expressive behaviors by seven-month-old infants. *Child Development, 63,* 787–795.

Sokoloff, L. (1981). Localization of functional activity in the central nervous system by measurement of glucose utilization with radioactive deoxyglucose. *Journal of Cerebral Blood Flow and Metabolism, 1,* 7–36.

Sokolowska, M., Siegel, S., & Kim, J. A. (2002). Intraadministration associations: Conditional hyperalgesia elicited by morphine onset cues. *Journal of Experimental Psychology: Animal Behavior Processes, 28,* 309–20.

Solomon, R. L. (1980). The opponent-process theory of acquired motivation: The costs of pleasure and the benefits of pain. *American Psychologist, 35,* 691–712.

Solomon, R. L., Kamin, L. J., & Wynne, L. C. (1953). Traumatic avoidance learning: The outcomes of several extinction procedures with dogs. *Journal of Abnormal and Social Psychology, 48,* 291–302.

Solomon, S. E., Rothbaum, E. D., & Balsam, K. F. (2004). Pioneers in partnership: Lesbian and gay male couples in civil unions and married heterosexual siblings. *Journal of Family Psychology, 18,* 275–286.

Solomonson, A. L., & Lance, C. E. (1997). Examination of the relationship between true halo and halo error in performance ratings. *Journal of Applied Psychology, 82,* 665–674.

Solowij, N., Stephens, R. S., Roffman, R. A., Babor, T., et al. (2002). Cognitive functioning of long-term heavy cannabis users seeking treatment. *Journal of American Medical Association, 287,* 1123–1131.

Song, H., & Baillargeon, R. (2008). Infants' reasoning about others' false perceptions. *Developmental Psychology, 44,* 1789–1795.

Song, H., Onishi, K. H., Baillargeon, R., & Fisher, C. (2008). Can an agent's false belief be corrected by an appropriate communication? Psychological reasoning in 18-month-old infants. *Cognition, 109,* 295–315. doi:10.1016/j.cognition.2008.08.008

Soni, A. (2009). *The five most costly conditions, 1996 and 2006: Estimates for the U.S. civilian noninstitutionalized population.* Rockville, MD: Agency for Healthcare Research and Quality.

Sorce, J., Emde, R., Campos, J., & Klinnert, M. (1981, April). *Maternal emotional signaling: Its effect on the visual cliff behavior of one-year-olds.* Paper presented at the annual meeting of the Society for Research in Child Development, Boston.

Sørensen, H. J., Mortensen, E. L., Reinisch, J. M., & Mednick, S. A. (2003). Do hypertension and diuretic treatment in pregnancy increase the risk of schizophrenia in offspring? *American Journal of Psychiatry, 160,* 464–468.

Sorrentino, R. M., & Roney, C. J. R. (2000). *The uncertain mind: Individual differences in facing the unknown.* Philadelphia: Psychology Press.

Soto, D., Funes, M. J., Guzmán-García, A., Warbrick, T., et al. (2009). Pleasant music overcomes the loss of awareness in patients with visual neglect. *Proceedings of the National Academy of Sciences, 106,* 6011–6016.

South, S. C., & Krueger, R. F. (2008). An interactionist perspective on genetic and environmental contributions to personality. *Social and Personality Psychology Compass, 2,* 929–948. doi:10.1111/j.1751-9004.2007.00062.x

Sowdon, J. (2001). Is depression more prevalent in old age? *Australian and New Zealand Journal of Psychiatry, 35,* 782–787.

Sowell, E. R., Peterson, B. S., Thompson, P. M., Welcome, S. E., et al. (2003). Mapping cortical change across the human life span. *Nature Neuroscience, 6,* 309–315.

Sowell, T. (2005). *Black rednecks and white liberals.* San Francisco: Encounter Books

Soyka, M., & Rösner, S. (2008). Opioid antagonists for pharmacological treatment of alcohol dependence: A critical review. *Current Drug Abuse Review, 1,* 280–291.

Spalletta, G., Serra, L., Fadda, L., Ripa, A., et al. (2007). Unawareness of motor impairment and emotions in right hemispheric stroke: A preliminary investigation. *International Journal of Geriatric Psychiatry, 22,* 1241–1246.

Spangler, G., Fremmer-Bombik, E., & Grossman, K. (1996). Social and individual determinants of infant attachment security and disorganization. *Infant Mental Health Journal, 17,* 127–139.

Spano, M. S., Ellgren, M., Wang, X., & Hurd, Y. L. (2007). Prenatal cannabis exposure increases heroin seeking with allostatic changes in limbic enkephalin systems in adulthood. *Biological Psychiatry, 61,* 554–563.

Spanos, N. P. (1994). Multiple identity enactments and multiple personality disorder: A sociocognitive perspective. *Psychological Bulletin, 116,* 143–165.

Spanos, N. P., Burnley, M. C. E., & Cross, P. A. (1993). Response expectancies and interpretations as determinants of hypnotic responding. *Journal of Personality and Social Psychology, 65,* 1237–1242.

Sparks, K., Cooper, C. L., Fried, Y., & Shirom, A. (1997). The effects of hours of work on health: A meta-analytic review. *Journal of Occupational and Organizational Psychology, 70,* 391–408.

Sparks, K., Faragher, B., & Cooper, C. L. (2001). Well-being and occupational health in the 21st century workplace. *Journal of Occupational and OrganizationalPsychology, 74,* 489–509.

Spear, L. P. (2000). Neurobiological changes in adolescence. *Current Directions in Psychological Science, 9,* 111–114.

Spearman, C. E. (1904). General intelligence objectively determined and measured. *American Journal of Psychology, 15,* 201–293.

Spearman, C. E. (1927). *The abilities of man.* New York: Macmillan.

Speckhard, A. (2002). Voices from the inside: Psychological responses to toxic disasters. In J. M. Havenaar & J. G. Cwikel (Eds.), *Toxic turmoil: Psychological and societal consequences of ecological disasters* (pp. 217–236). New York: Plenum.

Specter, M. (2005, May 23). Higher risk. *New Yorker,* pp. 38–45.

Spector, P. E. (1985). Measurement of human service staff satisfaction: Development of the Job Satisfaction Survey. *American Journal of Community Psychology, 13,* 693–713.

Spector, P. E. (2002). Employee control and occupational stress. *Current Directions in Psychological Science, 11,* 133–136.

Spector, P. E. (2003). *Industrial and organizational psychology: Research and practice* (3rd ed.). Hoboken, NJ: Wiley.

Spector, P. E., Fox, S., & Domalgaski, T. (2006). Emotions, violence, and counterproductive work behavior. In E. K. Kelloway, J. Barling, & J. J. Hurrell (Eds.), *Handbook of workplace violence* (pp. 29–46). Thousand Oaks, CA: Sage.

Spence, C., & Read, L. (2003). Speech shadowing while driving: On the difficulty of splitting attention between eye and ear. *Psychological Science, 14,* 251–256.

Spence, J., & Buckner, C. (2000). Instrumental and expressive traits, trait stereotypes, and sexist attitudes. *Psychology of Women Quarterly, 24,* 44–62.

Spence, S. H. (2003). Social skills training with children and young people: Theory, evidence, and practice. *Child and Adolescent Mental Health, 8,* 84–96.

Spence, S. H., Sheffield, J. K., & Donovan, C. L. (2005). Long-term outcome of a school-based, universal approach to prevention of depression in adolescents. *Journal of Consulting and Clinical Psychology, 73,* 160–167.

Spencer, M. B. (2006). Phenomenology and ecological systems theory. In W. Damon & R. M. Lerner (Series Eds.) & D. Kuhn & R. S. Siegler (Vol. Eds.), *Handbook of child psychology: Theoretical models of human development* (6th ed., Vol. 1, pp. 829–893). Hoboken, NJ: Wiley.

Spencer, S., Steele, C. M., & Quinn, D. (1997). *Under suspicion on inability: Stereotype threats and women's math performance.* Unpublished manuscript.

Spernak, S. M., Schottenbauer, M. A., Ramey, S. L., & Ramey, C. T. (2006). Child health and academic achievement among former Head Start children. *Children and Youth Services Review, 28,* 1251–1261.

Sperry, R. W. (1968). Hemisphere deconnection and unity in conscious awareness. *American Psychologist, 23,* 723–733.

Sperry, R. W. (1974). Lateral specialization in the surgically separated hemispheres. In F. O. Schmitt & F. G. Wordon (Eds.), *The neurosciences: Third study program* (pp. 5–19). Cambridge, MA: MIT Press.

Spiegel, D. (Ed.). (1994). *Dissociation: Culture, mind, and body.* Alexandria, VA: American Psychiatric Association.

Spiegel, D. A., & Bruce, T. J. (1997). Benzodiazepines and and exposure-based cognitive behavior therapies for panic disorder: Conclusions from combined treatment trials. *American Journal of Psychiatry, 151,* 876–881.

Spiegler, M. E., & Guevremont, D. C. (2009). *Contemporary behavior therapy* (5th ed.). Belmont, CA: Wadsworth.

Spillmann, L., Otte, T., Hamburger, K., & Magnussen, S. (2006). Perceptual filling-in from the edge of the blind spot. *Vision Research, 46,* 4252–4257.

Spinath, F. M., Harlaar, N., Ronald, A., & Plomin, R. (2004). Substantial genetic influence on mild mental impairment in early childhood. *American Journal of Mental Retardation, 109,* 34–43.

Spinrad, T. L., Eisenberg, N., Cumberland, A., Fabes, R. A., et al. (2006). Relation of emotion-related regulation to children's social competence: A longitudinal study. *Emotion, 6,* 498–510.

Spinrad, T. L., Eisenberg, N., Gaertner, B., Popp, T., et al. (2007). Relations of maternal socialization and toddlers' effortful control to children's adjustment and social competence. *Developmental Psychology, 43,* 1170–1186.

Spitz, H. H. (1991). Commentary on Locurto's "Beyond IQ in preschool programs?" *Intelligence, 15,* 327–333.

Spitz, H. H. (1997). *Nonconscious movements: From mystical messages to facilitated communication.* Hillsdale, NJ: Erlbaum.

Spitzer, R. L. (2009, July 2). APA and DSM-V: Empty promises. *Psychiatric Times.* Retrieved from http://www.psychiatrictimes.com/display/article/10168/142584

Spitzer, R. L., Gibbon, M., Skodol, A. E., Williams, J. B. W., & First, M. B. (Eds.). (1994). *DSM-IV casebook: A learning companion to the* Diagnostic and Statistical Manual of Mental Disorders (4th ed.). Washington, DC: American Psychiatric Association.

Spitzer, R. L., Skodol, A. E., Gibbon, M., & Williams, J. B. W. (1983). *Psychopathology: A casebook.* New York: McGraw-Hill.

Sprecher, S., Hatfield, E., Anthony, C., & Potapova, E. (1994). Token resistance to sexual intercourse and consent to unwanted sexual intercourse: College students' dating experiences in three countries. *Journal of Sex Research, 31,* 125–132.

Springer, K., & Belk, A. (1994). The role of physical contact and association in early contamination sensitivity. *Developmental Psychology, 30,* 864–868.

Springer, M. V., McIntosh, A. R., Winocur, G., & Grady, C. L. (2005). The relation between brain activity during memory tasks and years of education in young and older adults. *Neuropsychology, 19,* 181–192.

Springer, S. P., & Deutsch, G. (1989). *Left brain, right brain.* New York: Freeman.

Spychalski, A. C., Quinones, M. A., Gaugler, B. B., & Pohley, K. (1997). A survey of assessment center practices in organizations in the U.S. *Personnel Psychology, 50,* 71–90.

Squire, L. R. (1986). Mechanisms of memory. *Science, 232,* 1612–1619.

Squire, L. R. (1987). *Memory and brain.* New York: Oxford University Press.

Squire, L. R. (1992). Memory and the hippocampus: A synthesis from findings with rats, monkeys, and humans. *Psychological Review, 99,* 195–231.

Squire, L. R. (2009). The legacy of patient H. M. for neuroscience. *Neuron, 61,* 6–9.

Squire, L. R., Amara, D. G., & Press, G. A. (1992). Magnetic resonance imaging of the hippocampal formation and mamillary nuclei distinguish medial temporal lobe and diencephalic amnesia. *Journal of Neuroscience, 10,* 3106–3117.

Squire, L. R., & McKee, R. (1992). The influence of prior events on cognitive judgments in amnesia. *Journal of Experimental Psychology: Learning, Memory, and Cognition, 18,* 106–115.

Srinivas, K. (1993). Perceptual specificity in nonverbal priming. *Journal of Experimental Psychology: Learning, Memory, and Cognition 19,* 582–602.

Srivastava, S., Guglielmo, S., & Beer, J. S. (2010). Perceiving others' personalities: Examining the dimensionality, assumed similarity to the self, and stability of perceiver effects. *Journal of Personality and Social Psychology, 98,* 520–534.

Srivastava, S., John, O. P., Gosling, S. D., & Potter, J. (2003). Development of personality in early and middle adulthood: Set like plaster or persistent change? *Journal of Personality and Social Psychology, 84,* 1041–1053.

Srivastava, S., Tamir, M., McGonigal, K. M., John, O. P., & Gross, J. J. (2009). The social costs of emotional suppression: A prospective study of the transition to college. *Journal of Personality and Social Psychology, 96,* 883–897.

Sroufe, L. A., Egeland, B., Carlson, E. A., & Collins, W. A. (2005). *The development of the person: The Minnesota study of risk and adaptation from birth to adulthood.* New York: Guilford Press.

Stacey, D., Clarke, T. K., & Schumann, G. (2009). The genetics of alcoholism. *Current Psychiatry Reports, 11,* 364–369.

Stacey, J., & Biblarz, T. J. (2001). (How) Does the sexual orientation of parents matter? *American Sociological Review, 66,* 159–183.

Stahl, S. M. (2002). Selective actions on sleep or anxiety by exploiting GABA-A/benzodiazepine receptor subtypes. *Journal of Clinical Psychiatry, 63,* 179–180.

Stahl, S. M. (2007). The genetics of schizophrenia converge upon the NMDA glutamate receptor. *CNS Spectrums, 12,* 583–588.

Staley, J. K., Sanacora, G., Tamagnan, G., Maciejewski, P. K., et al. (2006). Sex differences in diencephalon serotonin transporter availability in major depression. *Biological Psychiatry, 59,* 40–47.

Standing, L., Conezio, J., & Haber, R. N. (1970). Perception and memory for pictures: Single-trial learning of 2,500 visual stimuli. *Psychonomic Science, 19,* 73–74.

Stankov, L. (1989). Attentional resources and intelligence: A disappearing link. *Personality and Individual Differences, 10,* 957–968.

Stanley, B. G., Willett, V. L., Donias, H. W., & Ha-Lyen, H. (1993). The lateral hypothalamus: A primary site mediating excitatory aminoacid-elicited eating. *Brain Research, 63,* 41–49.

Stanley, D., Phelps, E. A., & Banaji, M. R. (2008). The neural basis of implicit attitudes. *Current Directions in Psychological Science, 17,* 164–170.

Stanovich, K. E., & West, R. F. (2002). Individual differences in reasoning: Implications for the rationality debate? In T. Gilovich, D. Griffin, & D. Kahneman (Eds.), *Heuristics and biases: The psychology of intuitive judgment* (pp. 421–440). New York: Cambridge University Press.

Stansfeld, S. A., & Marmot, M. G. (Eds.). (2002). *Stress and the heart: Psychosocial pathways to coronary heart disease.* London: BMJ Books.

Stanton-Hicks, M., & Salamon, J. (1997). Stimulation of the central and peripheral nervous system for the control of pain. *Journal of Clinical Neurophysiology, 14,* 46–62.

Starkstein, S. E., Fedoroff, J. P., Price, T. R., Leigguarda, R., & Robinson, R. G. (1992). Anosognosia in patients with cerebrovascular lesions: A study of causative factors. *Stroke, 23,* 1446–1453.

Stasser, G., Stewart, D., & Wittenbaum, G. M. (1995). Expert roles and information exchange during discussion: The importance of knowing who knows what. *Journal of Experimental Social Psychology, 31,* 244–265.

Staudt, M., Grodd, W., Niemann, G., Wildgruber, D., et al. (2001). Early left periventricular brain lesions induce right hemispheric organization of speech. *Neurology, 57,* 122–125.

Stauffer, J. M., & Buckley, M. R. (2005). The existence and nature of racial bias in supervisory ratings. *Journal of Applied Psychology, 90,* 586–591.

Staw, B. M., Bell, N. E., & Clausen, J. A. (1986). The dispositional approach to job attitudes: A lifetime longitudinal test. *Administrative Science Quarterly, 31,* 56–77.

Staw, B. M., & Cohen-Charash, Y. (2005). The dispositional approach to job satisfaction: More than a mirage, but not yet an oasis. *Journal of Organizational Behavior, 26,* 59–78.

Steadman, H. J. (1993). *Reforming the insanity defense: An evaluation of pre- and post-Hinckley reforms.* New York: Guilford Press.

Steele, C. M. (1997). A threat in the air: How stereotypes shape intellectual identity and performance. *American Psychologist, 52,* 613–629.

Steele, C. M., & Aronson, J. (2000). Stereotype threat and the intellectual test performance of African Americans. In C. Stangor (Ed.), *Stereotypes and prejudice: Essential readings* (pp. 369–389). Philadelphia: Psychology Press/Taylor & Francis.

Steele, C. M., Spencer, S. J., & Lynch, M. (1993). Self-image resilience and dissonance: The role of affirmational resources. *Journal of Personality and Social Psychology, 64,* 885–896.

Steele, T. D., McCann, U. D., & Ricaurte, G. A. (1994). 3,4-methylenedioxy-methamphetamine (MDMA, ecstacy): Pharmacology and toxicology in animals and humans. *Addiction, 89,* 539–551.

Stefanidis, E. (2006). Being rational. *Schizophrenia Bulletin, 32,* 422–423.

Stein, D. J. (2006). Specific phobia: A disorder of fear conditioning and extinction. *CNS Spectrums, 11,* 248–251.

Stein, M. A. (1993, November 30). Spacewalking repair team to work on Hubble flaws; shower head inspires a device to improve focusing ability. *Los Angeles Times,* A1, A5.

Steinberg, L. (1990). Autonomy, conflict, and harmony in the family relationship. In S. S. Feldman & G. R. Elliott (Eds.), *At the threshold: The developing adolescent* (pp. 255–276). Cambridge, MA: Harvard University Press.

Steinberg, L. (2007). Risk taking in adolescence: New perspectives from brain and behavioral science. *Current Directions in Psychological Science, 16,* 55–59.

Steinberg, L. (2008). A social neuroscience perspective on adolescent risk-taking. *Developmental Review, 28,* 78–106. doi:10.1016/j.dr.2007.08.002

Steinberg, L., Dornbusch, S. M., & Brown, B. B. (1992). Ethnic differences in adolescent achievement: An ecological perspective. *American Psychologist, 47,* 723–729.

Steindler, D. A. & Pincus, D. W. (2002). Stem cells and neuropoiesis in the adult human brain. *Lancet, 359,* 1047–1054.

Steiner, J. E., Glaser, D., Hawilo, M. E., & Berridge, K. C. (2001). Comparative expression of hedonic impact: Affective reactions to taste by human infants and other primates. *Neuroscience and Biobehavioral Reviews, 25,* 53–74.

Steiner, J. M., & Fahrenberg, J. (2000). Authoritarianism and social status of former members of the Waffen-SS and SS and of the Wehrmacht: An extension and reanalysis of the study published in 1970. *Kölner Zeitschrift für Soziologie und Sozialpsychologie, 52,* 329–348.

Steinhausen, H.-C., & Weber, S. (2009). The outcome of bulimia nervosa: Findings from one-quarter century of research. *American Journal of Psychiatry, 159,* 1284–1293.

Steinhauser, K. E., Alexander, S. C., Byock, I. R., George, L. K., et al. (2008). Do preparation and life completion discussions improve functioning and quality of life in seriously ill patients? Pilot randomized control trial. *Journal of Palliative Medicine, 11,* 1234–1240.

Stephan, B. C. M., & Caine, D. (2009). Aberrant pattern of scanning in prosopagnosia reflects impaired face processing. *Brain and Cognition, 69,* 262–268.

Stephan, K. E., Marshall, J. C., Friston, K. J., Rowe, J. B., et al. (2003). Lateralized cognitive processes and lateralized task control in the human brain. *Science, 301,* 384–386.

Stéphan-Blanchard, E., Chardon, K., Léké, A., Delanaud, S., et al. (2010). In utero exposure to smoking and peripheral chemoreceptor function in preterm neonates. *Pediatrics, 125,* e592–e599.

Stephens, R. S., Roffman, R. A., & Simpson, E. E. (1994). Treating adult marijuana dependence: A test of the relapse prevention model. *Journal of Consulting and Clinical Psychology, 62,* 92–99.

Stephenson, J. (2007). Jet lag relief? *Journal of the American Medical Association, 297,* 2578–2578.

Steptoe, A., Peacey, V., & Wardle, J. (2006). Sleep duration and health in young adults. *Archives of Internal Medicine, 166,* 1689–1692.

Steptoe, A., Wardle, J., & Marmot, M. (2005). Positive affect and health-related neuroendocrine, cardiovascular, and inflammatory processes. *Proceedings of the National Academy of Sciences, 102,* 6508–6512.

Steriade, M., & McCarley, R. W. (1990). *Brainstem control of wakefulness and sleep.* New York: Plenum.

Stern, K., & McClintock, M. K. (1998). Regulation of ovulation by human pheromones. *Nature, 392,* 177–179.

Stern, W. L. (1914). The psychological methods of testing intelligence (G. M. Whipple, Trans.). *Educational Psychology Monographs, No. 13.* Baltimore: Warwick & York.

Sternberg, R. J. (1985). *Beyond IQ: A triarchic theory of human intelligence.* Cambridge: Cambridge University Press.

Sternberg, R. J. (1988a). Triangulating love. In R. J. Sternberg & M. L. Barnes (Eds.), *The psychology of love* (pp. 500–520). New Haven, CT: Yale University Press.

Sternberg, R. J. (1988b). *The triarchic mind.* New York: Cambridge University Press.

Sternberg, R. J. (1989). Domain generality versus domain specificity: The life and impending death of a false dichotomy. *Merrill-Palmer Quarterly, 35,* 115–130.

Sternberg, R. J. (1996). *Successful intelligence.* New York: Simon & Schuster.

Sternberg, R. J. (1997). Construct validation of a triangular love scale. *European Journal of Social Psychology, 27,* 313–335.

Sternberg, R. J. (1999). Ability and expertise: It's time to replace the current model of intelligence. *American Educator, 23,* 10–13, 50–51.

Sternberg, R. J. (Ed.). (2000). *Handbook of human intelligence* (2nd ed.). New York: Cambridge University Press.

Sternberg, R. J. (2001). What is the common thread of creativity? Its dialectical relation to intelligence and wisdom. *American Psychologist, 56,* 360–362.

Sternberg, R. J. (2004). Culture and intelligence. *American Psychologist, 59,* 325–338.

Sternberg, R. J. (2006). A duplex theory of love. In R. J. Sternberg & K. Weis (Eds.), *The new psychology of love* (pp. 184–199). New Haven, CT: Yale University Press.

Sternberg, R. J., & Dess, N. K. (2001). Creativity for the new millennium. *American Psychologist, 56,* 332.

Sternberg, R. J., & Grigorenko, E. L. (Eds.). (2004a). *Creativity: From potential to realization.* Washington, DC: American Psychological Association.

Sternberg, R. J., & Grigorenko, E. L. (Eds.). (2004b). *Culture and competence: Contexts of life success.* Washington, DC: American Psychological Association.

Sternberg, R. J., & Kaufman, J. C. (1998). Human abilities. *Annual Review of Psychology, 49,* 479–502.

Sternberg, R. J., Lautrey, J., & Lubart, T. I. (2003). Where are we in the field of intelligence, how did we get here, and where are we going? In R. J. Sternberg, J. Lautrey, & T. I. Lubart (Eds.), *Models of intelligence: International perspectives* (pp. 3–25). Washington, DC: American Psychological Association.

Sternberg, R. J., & Lubart, T. I. (1992). Buy low and sell high: An investment approach to creativity. *Current Directions in Psychological Science, 1,* 1–5.

Sternberg, R. J., & O'Hara, L. A. (1999). Creativity and intelligence. In R. J. Sternberg (Ed.), *Handbook of creativity* (pp. 251–272). New York: Cambridge University Press.

Sternberg, R. J., & Rainbow Project Coordinators. (2006). The Rainbow Project: Enhancing the SAT through assessments of analytical, practical, and creative skills. *Intelligence, 34,* 321–350.

Sternberg, R. J., Wagner, R. K., Williams, W. M., & Horvath, J. A. (1995). Testing common sense. *American Psychologist, 50,* 912–927.

Sternberg, R. J., & Williams, W. M. (1997). Does the Graduate Record Examination predict meaningful success of graduate training of psychologists? A case study. *American Psychologist, 52,* 630–641.

Stettler, D. D., Yamahachi, H., Li, W., Denk, W., & Gilbert, C. D. (2006). Axons and synaptic boutons are highly dynamic in adult visual cortex. *Neuron, 49,* 877–887.

Steunenberg, B., Beekman, A. T. F., Deeg, D. J. H., & Kerkhof, A. J. F. M. (2006). Personality and the onset of depression in late life. *Journal of Affective Disorders, 92,* 243–251.

Steven, M. S., Hansen, P. C., & Blakemore, C. (2006). Activation of color-selective areas of the visual cortex in a blind synesthete. *Cortex, 42,* 304–308.

Stevens, A. (1996). *Private myths: Dreams and dreaming.* Cambridge, MA: Harvard University Press.

Stevens, C., Sanders, L., & Neville, H. (2006). Neurophysiological evidence for selective auditory attention deficits in children with specific language impairment. *Brain Research, 1111,* 143–152.

Stevens, J. C., & Hooper, J. E. (1982). How skin and object temperature influence touch sensation. *Perception and Psychophysics, 32,* 282–285.

Stevens, J. C., & Pollack, M. H. (2005). Benzodiazepines in clinical practice: Consideration of their long-term use and alternative agents. *Journal of Clinical Psychiatry, 66*(Suppl. 2), 21–27.

Stevens, R. D., & Bhardwaj, A. (2006). Approach to the comatose patient. *Critical Care Medicine, 34,* 31–41.

Stevenson, H. (1992). *A long way from being number one: What we can learn from East Asia.* Washington, DC: Federation of Behavior, Psychological and Cognitive Sciences.

Stewart, B. D., & Payne, B. K. (2008). Bringing automatic stereotyping under control: Implementation intentions as efficient means of thought control. *Personality and Social Psychology Bulletin, 34,* 1332–1345.

Stewart, G. L. (2006). A meta-analytic review of relationships between team design features and team performance. *Journal of Management, 32,* 29–55.

Stewart, J. H. (2005). Hypnosis in contemporary medicine. *Mayo Clinic Proceedings, 80,* 511–524.

Stewart, S. E., Platko, J., Fagerness, J., Birns, J., et al. (2007). A genetic family-based association study of OLIG2 in obsessive-compulsive disorder. *Archives of General Psychiatry, 64,* 209–214.

Stewart, W. F., Ricci, J. A., Chee, E., Hahn, S. R., & Morganstein, D. (2003). Cost of lost productive work time among U.S. workers with depression. *Journal of the American Medical Association, 289,* 3135–3144.

Stewart-Williams, S. (2004). The placebo puzzle: Putting together the pieces. *Health Psychology, 23,* 198–206.

Stice, E., & Fairburn, C. G. (2003). Dietary and dietary-depressive subtypes of bulimia nervosa show differential symptom presentation, social impairment, comorbidity, and course of illness. *Journal of Consulting and Clinical Psychology, 71,* 1090–1094.

Stice, E., Ragan, J., & Randall, P. (2004). Prospective relations between social support and depression: Differential direction of effects for parent and peer support? *Journal of Abnormal Psychology, 113,* 155–159.

Stice, E., & Shaw, H. (2004). Eating disorder prevention programs: A meta-analytic review. *Psychological Bulletin, 130,* 206–227.

Stice, E., Shaw, H., & Nathan, C. (2006). A meta-analytic review of obesity prevention programs for children and adolescents: The skinny on interventions that work. *Psychological Bulletin, 132,* 667–691.

Stickgold, R., Malia, A., Maguire, D., Roddenberry, D., & O'Connor, M. (2000). Replaying the game: Hypnagogic images in normals and amnesics. *Science, 290,* 350–353.

Stickgold, R., Rittenhouse, C. D., & Hobson, J. A. (1994). Dream splicing: A new technique for assessing thematic coherence in subjective reports of mental activity. *Consciousness and Cognition, 3,* 114–128.

Stiles, W. B., Barkham, M., Twigg, E., Mellor-Clark, J., & Cooper, M. (2006). Effectiveness of cognitive-behavioural, person-centered and psychodynamic therapies as practised in UK national health service settings. *Psychological Medicine, 36,* 555–566.

Stillwell, M. E. (2002). Drug-facilitated sexual assault involving gamma-hydroxybutyric acid. *Journal of Forensic Science, 47,* 1133–1134.

Stinson, D. A., Cameron, J. J., Wood, J. V., Gaucher, D., & Holmes, J. G. (2009). Deconstructing the "reign of error": Interpersonal warmth explains the self-fulfilling prophecy of anticipated acceptance. *Personality and Social Psychology Bulletin, 35,* 1165–1178.

Stipek, D. J., & Ryan, R. H. (1997). Economically disadvantaged preschoolers: Ready to learn but further to go. *Developmental Psychology, 33,* 711–723.

Stoff, D. M., Breiling, J., & Maser, J. D. (Eds.). (1997). *Handbook of antisocial behavior.* New York: Wiley.

Stone, A., & Valentine, T. (2003). Perspectives on prosopagnosia and models of face recognition. *Cortex, 39,* 31–40.

Stone, A. A., Schwartz, J. E., Broderick, J. E., & Deaton, A. S. (2010). A snapshot of the age distribution of psychological well-being in the United States. *Proceedings of the National Academy of Sciences, 107,* 9985–9990.

Stone, J., & Fernandez, N. C. (2008). To practice what we preach: The use of hypocrisy and cognitive dissonance to motivate behavior change. *Social and Personality Psychology Compass, 2,* 1024–1051.

Stone, L. D., & Pennebaker, J. W. (2002). Trauma in real time: Talking and avoiding online conversations about the death of Princess Diana. *Basic and Applied Social Psychology, 24,* 173–183.

Stone, M., Laughren, T., Jones, M. L., Levenson, M., et al. (2009). Risk of suicidality in clinical trials of antidepressants in adults: Analysis of proprietary data submitted to U.S. Food and Drug Administration. *British Medical Journal, 339,* b2880.

Stoney, C. M., & Engebretson, T. O. (1994). Anger and hostility: Potential mediators of the sex differences in coronary heart disease. In A. W. Siegman & T. W. Smith (Eds.), *Anger, hostility, and the heart* (pp. 215–237). Mahwah, NJ: Erlbaum.

Stoney, C. M., & Finney, M. L. (2000). Social support and stress: Influences on lipid reactivity. *International Journal of Behavioral Medicine, 7,* 111–126.

Stoney, C. M., & Hughes, J. W. (1999). Lipid reactivity among men with a parental history of myocardial infarction. *Psychophysiology, 36,* 484–490.

Stoney, C. M., Hughes, J. W., Kuntz, K. K., West, S. G., & Thornton, L. M. (2002). Cardiovascular stress responses among Asian Indian and European American women and men. *Annals of Behavioral Medicine, 24,* 113–121.

Stoney, C. M., Matthews, K. A., McDonald, R. H., & Johnson, C. A. (1988). Sex differences in lipid, lipoprotein, cardiovascular, and neuroendocrine responses to acute stress. *Psychophysiology, 25,* 646–656.

Strahan, E. J., Spencer, S. J., & Zanna, M. P. (2005). Subliminal priming and persuasion: How motivation affects the activation of goals and the persuasiveness of messages. In F. R. Kardes, P. Herr, & J. Nantel (Eds.), *Applying social cognition to consumer-focused strategy* (pp. 267–280). Mahwah, NJ: Erlbaum.

Strain, E. C., Mumford, G. K., Silverman, K., & Griffiths, R. R. (1994). Caffeine dependence syndrome: Evidence from case histories and experimental evaluations. *Journal of the American Medical Association, 272,* 1043–1048.

Strakowski, S. M., DelBello, M. P., & Adler, C. M. (2005). The functional neuroanatomy of bipolar disorder: A review of neuroimaging findings. *Molecular Psychiatry, 10,* 105–116.

Strathearn, L., Gray, P. H., O'Callaghan, M. J., & Wood, D. O. (2001). Childhood neglect and cognitive development in extremely low birth weight infants: A prospective study. *Pediatrics, 108,* 142–151.

Straus, M. A. (2005). Children should never, ever, be spanked no matter what the circumstances. In D. R. Loseke, R. J. Gelles, & M. M. Cavanaugh (Eds.), *Current controversies about family violence* (2nd ed., pp. 137–157). Thousand Oaks, CA: Sage.

Strauss, E., & Wada, J. (1983). Lateral preferences and cerebral speech dominance. *Cortex, 19,* 165–177.

Strauss, R. S., & Pollack, H. A. (2001). Epidemic increases in childhood overweight, 1986–1998. *Journal of the American Medical Association, 286,* 2845–2848.

Strayer, D. L., & Drews, F. A. (2006). Multitasking in the automobile. In A. Kramer, D. Wiegmann, & A. Kirlik (Eds.), *Applied attention: From theory to practice* (pp. 121–133). New York: Oxford University Press.

Strayer, D. L., & Drews, F. A. (2007). Cell-phone-induced driver distraction. *Current Directions in Psychological Science, 16,* 128–131.

Strayer, D. L., Drews, F. A., & Crouch, D. J. (2003). Fatal distraction? A comparison of the cell-phone driver and the drunk driver. In D. V. McGehee, J. D. Lee, & M. Rizzo (Eds.), *Driving assessment, 2003: International symposium on human factors in driver assessment, training, and vehicle design* (pp. 25–30). Iowa City: University of Iowa Public Policy Center.

Strayer, D. L., Drews, F. A., Crouch, D. J., & Johnston, W. A. (2004). Why do cell phone conversations interfere with driving? In W. R. Walker & D. Herrmann (Eds.), *Cognitive technology: Transforming thought and society* (pp. 51–68). Jefferson, NC: McFarland.

Strayer, D. L., Drews, F. A., & Johnston, W. A. (2003). Cell phone–induced failures of visual attention during simulated driving. *Journal of Experimental Psychology: Applied, 9,* 23–32.

Strick, P. L., Dum, R. P., & Fiez, J. A. (2009). Cerebellum and nonmotor function. *Annual Review of Neuroscience, 32,* 413–434.

Stricker, G. (2006). Assimilative psychodynamic psychotherapy integration. In G. Stricker & J. Gold (Eds.), *A casebook of psychotherapy integration* (pp. 55–63). Washington, DC: American Psychological Association.

Stricker, L. J., & Ward, W. C. (2004). Stereotype threat, inquiring about test takers' ethnicity and gender, and standardized test performance. *Journal of Applied Social Psychology, 34,* 665–693.

Striemer, C. L., Chapman, C. S., & Goodale, M. A. (2009). "Real-time" obstacle avoidance in the absence of primary visual cortex. *Proceedings of the National Academy of Sciences, 106,* 15996–16001.

Stright, A. D., Gallagher, K. C., & Kelley, K. (2008). Infant temperament moderates relations between maternal parenting in early childhood and children's adjustment in first grade. *Child Development, 79,* 186–200.

Stringhini, S., Sabia, S., Shipley, M., Brunner, E., et al. (2010). Association of socioeconomic position with health behaviors and mortality. *Journal of the American Medical Association, 303,* 1159–1166.

Stroebe, W., Papies, E. K., & Aarts, H. (2008). From homeostatic to hedonic theories of eating: Self-regulatory failure in food-rich environments. *Applied Psychology, 57*(Suppl. 1), 172–193.

Strohmetz, D. B., Rind, B., Fisher, R., & Lynn, M. (2002). Sweetening the till: The use of candy to increase restaurant tipping. *Journal of Applied Social Psychology, 32,* 300–309.

Strohschein, L. (2005). Household income histories and child mental health trajectories. *Journal of Health and Social Behavior, 46,* 359–375.

Stroop, J. R. (1935). Studies of interference in serial verbal reactions. *Journal of Experimental Psychology, 18,* 643–662.

Stroud, L. R., Paster, R. L., Goodwin, M. S., Shenassa, E., et al. (2009). Maternal smoking during pregnancy and neonatal behavior: A large-scale community study. *Pediatrics, 123,* e842–e848.

Strunk, D. R., Lopez, H., & DeRubeis, R. J. (2006). Depressive symptoms are associated with unrealistic negative predictions of future life events. *Behaviour Research and Therapy, 44,* 875–896.

Strupp, H. H., & Hadley, S. W. (1979). Specific versus nonspecific factors in psychotherapy. *Archives of General Psychiatry, 36,* 1125–1136.

Stuart, R. B. (2004). Twelve practical suggestions for achieving multicultural competence. *Professional Psychology: Theory and Practice, 35,* 3–9.

Stürmer, T., Hasselbach, P., & Amelang, M. (2006). Personality, lifestyle, and risk of cardiovascular disease and cancer: Follow-up of population based cohort. *British Medical Journal, 332,* 1359.

Su, C. Y., Menuz, K., & Carlson, J. R. (2009). Olfactory perception: Receptors, cells, and circuits. *Cell, 139,* 45–59.

Su, Z., Korstanje, R., Tsaih, S.-W., & Paigen, B. (2008). Candidate genes for obesity revealed from a C57BL/6J 129S1/SvImJ intercross. *International Journal of Obesity, 32,* 1180–1189.

Subotnik, K. L., Nuechterlein, K. H., Green, M. F., Horan, W. P., et al. (2006). Neurocognitive and social cognitive correlates of formal thought disorder in schizophrenia patients. *Schizophrenia Research, 85,* 84–95.

Subrahmanyam, K., Kraut, R. E., Greenfield, P. M., & Gross, E. F. (2001). New forms of electronic media: The impact of interactive games and Internet on cognition, socialization, and behavior. In D. G. Singer & J. L. Singer (Eds.), *Handbook of children and the media* (pp. 73–99). Thousand Oaks, CA: Sage.

Substance Abuse and Mental Health Services Administration. (2007). *Results from the 2006 National Survey on Drug Use and Health: National findings.* Rockville, MD: Author.

Suddath, R. L., Christison, G. W., Torrey, E. F., Casanova, M. F., & Weinberger, D. R. (1990). Anatomical abnormalities in the brains of monopsychotic twins discordant for schizophrenia. *New England Journal of Medicine, 322,* 789–794.

Suddendorf, T., & Collier-Baker, E. (2009). The evolution of primate visual self-recognition: Evidence of absence in lesser apes. *Proceedings in Biological Sciences, 276,* 1671–1677.

Sue, D. (1992). *Asian and Caucasian subjects' preference for different counseling styles.* Unpublished manuscript, Western Washington University.

Sue, D. W., & Sue, D. (2008). *Counseling the culturally diverse: Theory and practice* (5th ed.). Hoboken, NJ: Wiley.

Sue, S., & Okazaki, S. (1990). Asian-American educational achievements: A phenomenon in search of an explanation. *American Psychologist, 45,* 913–920.

Sue, S., Zane, N., Hall, G. C. N., & Berger, L. K. (2009). The case for cultural competency in psychotherapeutic interventions. *Annual Review of Psychology, 60,* 525–548.

Suedfeld, P., & Tetlock, P. (2001). Individual differences in information processing. In A. Tesser & N. Schwarz (Eds.), *Blackwell handbook of social psychology: Intraindividual processes* (pp. 284–304). Malden, MA: Blackwell.

Süss, H. M., Oberauer, K., Wittmann, W. W., Wilhelm, O., & Schulze, R. (2002). Working memory explains reasoning ability—and a little bit more. *Intelligence, 30,* 261–288.

Suh, E., Diener, E., & Fujita, F. (1996). Events and subjective well-being: Only recent events matter. *Journal of Personality and Social Psychology, 70,* 1091–1102.

Suinn, R. M. (2001). The terrible twos: Anger and anxiety. *American Psychologist, 56,* 27–36.

Sullivan, H. S. (1954). *The psychiatric interview.* New York: Norton.

Sullivan, P. F., Kendler, K. S., & Neale, M. C. (2003). Schizophrenia as a complex trait: Evidence from a meta-analysis of twin studies. *Archives of General Psychiatry, 60,* 1187–1192.

Suls, J., & Bunde, J. (2005). Anger, anxiety, and depression as risk factors for cardiovascular disease: The problems and implications of overlapping affective dispositions. *Psychological Bulletin, 131,* 260–300.

Suls, J., & Rothman, A. (2004). Evolution of the biopsychosocial model: Prospects and challenges for health psychology. *Health Psychology, 23,* 119–125.

Suls, J., & Wan, C. K. (1993). The relationship between trait hostility and cardiovascular reactivity: A quantitative review and analysis. *Psychophysiology, 30,* 1–12.

Sun, Q., Townsend, M. K., Okereke, O. I., Franco, O. H., et al. (2010). Physical activity at midlife in relation to successful survival in women at age 70 years or older. *Archives of Internal Medicine, 170,* 194–201.

Sun, Y. G., Zhao, Z. Q., Meng, X. L., Yin, J., et al. (2009). Cellular basis of itch sensation. *Science, 325,* 1531–1534. Epub 2009 Aug 6.

Suomi, S. J. (1999). Attachment in rhesus monkeys. In J. Cassidy & P. R. Shaver (Eds.), *Handbook of attachment* (pp. 181–197). New York: Guilford Press.

Suomi, S. J. (2004). Aggression, serotonin, and gene-environment interactions in rhesus monkeys. In J. T. Cacioppo & G. G. Berntson (Eds.), *Essays in social neuroscience* (pp. 15–27). Cambridge, MA: MIT Press.

Surtees, P. G., Wainwright, N. W., Luben, R., Khaw, K. T., & Day, N. E. (2006). Mastery, sense of coherence, and mortality: Evidence of independent associations from the EPIC-Norfolk Prospective Cohort Study. *Health Psychology, 25,* 102–110.

Suslow, T., Ohrmann, P., Bauer, J., Rauch, A. V., et al. (2006). Amygdala activation during masked presentation of emotional faces predicts conscious detection of threat-related faces. *Brain and Cognition, 61,* 243–248.

Sutcher, H. (2008). Hypnosis, hypnotizability, and treatment. *American Journal of Clinical Hypnosis, 51,* 57–67.

Suzdak, P. D., Glowa, J. R., Crawley, J. N., Schwartz, R. D., et al. (1986). A selective imidazobenzodiazepine antagonist of ethanol in the rat. *Science, 234,* 1243–1247.

Suzuki, L. A., & Valencia, R. R. (1997). Race-ethnicity and measured intelligence. *American Psychologist, 52,* 1103–1114.

Svartberg, M., Stiles, T. C., & Seltzer, M. H. (2004). Randomized, controlled trial of the effectiveness of short-term dynamic psychotherapy and cognitive therapy for cluster C personality disorders. *American Journal of Psychiatry, 161,* 810–817.

Swaab, D. E., & Hofman, M. A. (1995). Sexual differentiation of the human hypothalamus in relation to gender and sexual orientation. *Trends in Neuroscience, 18,* 264–270.

Swami, V., & Furnham, A. (Eds.). (2007). *The body beautiful: Evolutionary and sociocultural perspectives.* New York: Palgrave Macmillan.

Swan, G. E., & Carmelli, D. (1996). Curiosity and mortality in aging adults: A 5-year follow-up of the Western Collaborative Group Study. *Psychology and Aging, 11,* 449–453.

Swaney, W. T. & Keverne, E. B. (2009). The evolution of pheromonal communication. *Behavior and Brain Research, 200,* 239–247.

Swann, W. B., Jr.; De La Ronde, C.; & Hixon, J. G. (1994). Authenticity and positivity strivings in marriage and courtship. *Journal of Personality and Social Psychology, 66,* 857–869.

Swarte, N. B., van der Lee, M. L., van der Bom, J. G., van den Bout, J., & Heintz, A. P. M. (2003). Effects of euthanasia on the bereaved family and friends: A cross-sectional study. *British Medical Journal, 327,* 189. doi:10.1136/bmj.327.7408.189

Swartz, H. A., Zuckoff, A., Grote, N. K., Spielvogle, H. N., et al. (2007). Engaging depressed patients in psychotherapy: Integrating techniques from motivational interviewing and ethnographic interviewing to improve treatment participation. *Professional Psychology: Research and Practice, 38,* 430–439.

Swartz, M. S., Perkins, D. O., Stroup, T. S., Davis, S. M., et al. (2007). Effects of antipsychotic medications on psychosocial functioning in patients with chronic schizophrenia: Findings from the NIMH CATIE study. *American Journal of Psychiatry, 164,* 428–436.

Sweller, J., & Gee, W. (1978). Einstellung: The sequence effect and hypothesis theory. *Journal of Experimental Psychology: Human Learning and Memory, 4,* 513–526.

Swerdlow, R., & Khan, S. M. (2009). The Alzheimer's disease mitochondrial cascade hypothesis: An update. *Experimental Neurology, 218,* 308–315.

Swets, J. A. (1996). *Signal detection theory and ROC analysis in psychology and diagnostics.* Hillsdale, NJ: Erlbaum.

Swets, J. A., Dawes, R. M., & Monahan, J. (2000). Psychological science can improve diagnostic decisions. *Psychological Science in the Public Interest, 1,* 1–26.

Swinburn, B. (2009). Obesity prevention in children and adolescents. *Child and Adolescent Psychiatric Clinics of North America, 18,* 209–223.

Swindle, R., Jr.; Heller, K.; Pescosolido, B.; & Kikuzawa, S. (2000). Responses to nervous breakdowns in America over a 40-year period: Mental health policy implications. *American Psychologist, 55,* 740–749.

Swithers, S. E., & Hall, W. G. (1994). Does oral experience terminate ingestion? *Appetite, 23,* 113–138.

Symons, D. (1979). *The evolution of human sexuality.* Oxford: Oxford University Press.

Szasz, T. (2003). The psychiatric protection order for the "battered mental patient." *British Medical Journal, 327,* 1449–1451.

Szegedi, A., Kohnen, R., Dienel, A., & Kieser, M. (2005). Acute treatment of moderate to severe depression with hypericum extract WS 5570 (St John's wort): Randomised controlled double blind non-inferiority trial versus paroxetine. *British Medical Journal, 330,* 503.

Szpunar, K. K. (2010). Episodic future thought: An emerging concept. *Perspectives on Psychological Science, 5,* 142–162.

Szpunar, K. K., Chan, J. C., & McDermott, K. B. (2009). Contextual processing in episodic future thought. *Cerebral Cortex, 19,* 1539–1548. doi:10.1093/cercor/bhn191

Szpunar, K. K., Watson, J. M., & McDermott, K. B. (2007). Neural substrates of envisioning the future. *Proceedings of the National Academy of Sciences, 104,* 642–647.

Tabert, M. H., Manly, J. J., Liu, X., Pelton, G. H., et al. (2006). Neuropsychological prediction of conversion to Alzheimer disease in patients with mild cognitive impairment. *Archives of General Psychiatry, 63,* 916–924.

Tailby, C., Wright, L. L., Metha, A. B., & Calford, M. B. (2005). Activity-dependent maintenance and growth of dendrites in adult cortex. *Proceedings of the National Academy of Sciences, 102,* 4631–4636.

Takahashi, K., & Yamanaka, S. (2006). Induction of pluripotent stem cells from mouse embryonic and adult fibroblast cultures by defined factors. *Cell, 126,* 663–676. Epub 2006 Aug 10.

Takashima, A., Petersson, K. M., Rutters, F., Tendolkar, I., et al. (2006). Declarative memory consolidation in humans: A prospective functional magnetic resonance imaging study. *Proceedings of the National Academy of Sciences, 103,* 756–761.

Takayama, Y., Sugishita, M., Kido, T., Ogawa, M., & Akiguchi, I. (1993). A case of foreign accent syndrome without aphasia caused by a lesion of the left precentral gyrus. *Neurology, 43,* 1361–1363.

Takayanagi, K. (2008). Colored-hearing synesthesia. *Japan Hospitals, 27,* 51–56.

Takeuchi, A. H., & Hulse, S. H. (1993). Absolute pitch. *Psychological Bulletin, 113,* 345–361.

Takeuchi, N., Uchimura, N., Hashizume, Y., Mukai, M., et al. (2001). Melatonin therapy for REM behavior disorder. *Psychiatry and Clinical Neurosciences, 55,* 267–269.

Talarico, J. F., & Rubin, D. C. (2003). Confidence, not consistency, characterizes flashbulb memories. *Psychological Science, 14,* 455–461.

Talbott, J. A. (2004). Deinstitutionalization: Avoiding the disasters of the past. *Psychiatric Services, 55,* 1112–1115.

Tallman, B. A., Altmaier, E., & Garcia, C. (2007). Finding benefit from cancer. *Journal of Counseling Psychology, 54,* 481–487.

Talmi, D., Grady, C. L., Goshen-Gottstein, Y., & Moscovitch, M. (2005). Neuroimaging the serial position curve: A test of single-store versus dual-store models. *Psychological Science, 16,* 716–723.

Tam, K. P., Chiu, C. Y., & Lau, I. Y. M. (2007). Terror management among Chinese: Worldview defence and intergroup bias in resource allocation. *Asian Journal of Social Psychology, 10,* 93–102.

Tamashiro, K. L. K., & Bello, N. T. (Eds.). (2008). Special issue on leptin. *Physiology and Behavior, 94*(5).

Tamir, M. (2009). What do people want to feel and why? Pleasure and utility in emotion regulation. *Current Directions in Psychological Science, 18,* 101–105.

Tamminga, C. A., & Holcomb, H. H. (2005). Phenotype of schizophrenia: A review and formulation. *Molecular Psychiatry, 10,* 27–39.

Tan, G., Hammond, D. C., & Joseph, G. (2005). Hypnosis and irritable bowel syndrome: A review of efficacy and mechanism of action. *American Journal of Clinical Hypnosis, 47,* 161–178.

Tan, H.-Y., Chen, Q., Sust, S., Buckholtz, J. W., et al. (2007). Epistasis between catechol-O-methyltransferase and type II metabotropic glutamate receptor 3 genes on working memory brain function. *Proceedings of the National Academy of Sciences, 104,* 12536–12541.

Tan, L. (2008). Psychotherapy 2.0: MySpace blogging as self-therapy. *American Journal of Psychotherapy, 62,* 143–163.

Tanaka, H., Taira, K., Arakawa, M., Toguti, H., et al. (2001). Effects of short nap and exercise on elderly people having difficulty sleeping. *Psychiatry and Clinical Neurosciences, 55,* 173–174.

Tanaka, S. C., Balleine, B. W., & O'Doherty, J. P. (2008). Calculating consequences: Brain systems that encode the causal effects of actions. *Journal of Neuroscience, 28,* 6750–6755.

Tandon, R., Keshavan, M. S., & Nasrallah, H. A. (2008). Schizophrenia, "just the facts"—what we know in 2008: 2. Epidemiology and etiology. *Schizophrenia Research, 102,* 1–18.

Tandon, R., Nasrallah, H. A., & Keshavan, M. S. (2009). Schizophrenia, "just the facts": 4. Clinical features and conceptualization, *Schizophrenia Research, 110,* 1–23

Tang, T. L., Tang, T. L., & Homaifar, B. Y. (2006). Income, the love of money, pay comparison, and pay satisfaction: Race and gender as moderators. *Journal of Managerial Psychology, 21,* 476–491.

Tan-Laxa, M. A., Sison-Switala, C., Rintelman, W., & Ostrea, E. M. (2004). Abnormal auditory brainstem response among infants with prenatal cocaine exposure. *Pediatrics, 113,* 357–360.

Tannen, D. (2001). *You just don't understand: Women and men in conversation.* New York: HarperCollins.

Tanner, J. M. (1978). *Fœtus into man: Physical growth from conception to maturity.* London: Open Books.

Tanner, J. M. (1992). Growth as a measure of nutritional and hygienic status of a population. *Hormone Research, 38,* 106–115.

Targino, R. A., Imamura, M., Kaziyama, H. H., Souza, L. P., et al. (2008). A randomized controlled trial of acupuncture added to usual treatment for fibromyalgia. *Journal of Rehabilitation Medicine, 40,* 582–588.

Tasker, F., & Golombok, S. (1995). Adults raised as children in lesbian families. *American Journal of Orthopsychiatry, 65,* 203–215.

Tassi, P., & Muzet, A. (2001). Defining states of consciousness. *Neuroscience and Biobehavioral Reviews, 25,* 175–191.

Taub, E. (2004). Harnessing brain plasticity through behavioral techniques to produce new treatments in neurorehabilitation. *American Psychologist, 59,* 692–704.

Taubenfeld, S. M., Milekic, M. H., Monti, B., & Alberini, C. M. (2001). The consolidation of new but not reactivated memory requires hippocampal C/EBPb. *Nature Neuroscience, 4,* 813–818.

Tavris, C. (2002). The high cost of skepticism. *Skeptical Inquirer, 26,* 41–44.

Tavris, C. (2003). Mind games: Psychological warfare between therapists and scientists. *Chronicle of Higher Education, 49,* B7–B9.

Taylor, H. (2001, August 8). *Harris Poll No. 38*. Retrieved from http:/harrisinteractive.com/harris_poll

Taylor, H. A., & Tversky, B. (1992). Spatial mental models derived from survey and route descriptions. *Journal of Memory and Language, 31*, 261–292.

Taylor, J., Roehrig, A. D., Hensler, B. S., Connor, C. M., & Schatschneider, C. (2010). Teacher quality moderates the genetic effects on early reading. *Science, 328*, 512–514.

Taylor, J. G. (2002). Paying attention to consciousness. *Trends in Cognitive Science, 6*, 206–210.

Taylor, M. J., Freemantle, N., Geddes, J. R., & Bhagwagar, Z. (2006). Early onset of selective serotonin reuptake inhibitor antidepressant action. *Archives of General Psychiatry, 63*, 1217–1223.

Taylor, R. L., & Richards, S. B. (1991). Patterns of intellectual differences of black, Hispanic, and white children. *Psychology in the Schools, 28*, 5–8.

Taylor, S. (2004). Efficacy and outcome predictors for three PTSD treatments: Exposure therapy, EMDR, and relaxation training. In S. Taylor (Ed.), *Advances in the treatment of posttraumatic stress disorder: Cognitive-behavioral perspectives* (pp. 13–37). New York: Springer.

Taylor, S., & Asmundson, G. J. G. (2008). Hypochondriasis. In J. S. Abramowitz, D. McKay, & S. Taylor (Eds.), *Clinical handbook of obsessive-compulsive disorder and related problems* (pp. 304–315). Baltimore: Johns Hopkins University Press.

Taylor, S., Peplau, A., & Sears, D. (2006). *Social psychology* (12th ed.). Upper Saddle River, NJ: Prentice Hall.

Taylor, S. E. (2002). *Health psychology* (5th ed.). New York: McGraw-Hill.

Taylor, S. E., Dickerson, S. S., & Klein, L. C. (2002). Toward a biology of social support. In C. R. Snyder & S. L. Lopez (Eds.), *Handbook of positive psychology* (pp. 556–569). Oxford: Oxford University Press.

Taylor, S. E., Gonzaga, G. C., Klein, L. C., Hu, P., et al. (2006). Relation of oxytocin to psychological stress responses and hypothalamic-pituitary-adrenocortical axis activity in older women. *Psychosomatic Medicine, 68*, 238–245.

Taylor, S. E., Kemeny, M. E., Aspinwall, L. G., Schneider, S. G., et al. (1992). Optimism, coping, psychological distress, and high-risk sexual behavior among men at risk for acquired immunodeficiency syndrome (AIDS). *Journal of Personality and Social Psychology, 63*, 460–473.

Taylor, S. E., Kemeny, M. E., Reed, G. M., Bower, J. E., & Gruenewald, T. L. (2000). Psychological resources, positive illusions, and health. *American Psychologist, 55*, 99–109.

Taylor, S. E., Klein, L. C., Lewis, B. P., Gruenewald, T. L., et al. (2000). Biobehavioral responses to stress in females: Tend-and-befriend, not fight-or-flight. *Psychological Review, 107*, 411–429.

Taylor, S. E., Lerner, J. S., Sherman, K. D., Sage, R. M., & McDowell, N. K. (2003). Are self-enhancing cognitions associated with health or unhealthy biological profiles? *Journal of Personality and Social Psychology, 85*, 605–615.

Taylor, S. E., Lewis, B. P., Gruenewald, T. L., Gurung, R. A. R., et al. (2002). Sex differences in biobehavioral responses to threat: Reply to Geary and Flinn (2002). *Psychological Review, 109*, 751–753.

Taylor, S. E., Seeman, T. E., Eisenberger, N. I., Kozanian, T. A., et al. (2010). Effects of a supportive or an unsupportive audience on biological and psychological responses to stress. *Journal of Personality and Social Psychology, 98*, 47–56.

Taylor, S. P., & Hulsizer, M. R. (1998). Psychoactive drugs and human aggression. In R. G. Geen & E. Donnerstein (Eds.), *Human aggression* (pp. 139–167). San Diego, CA: Academic Press.

Teachman, J. D. (2008). The living arrangements of children and their educational well-being. *Journal of Family Issues, 29*, 734–761.

Tecott, L. H., Sun, L. M., Akana, S. F., Strack, A. M., et al. (1995). Eating disorder and epilepsy in mice lacking 5-HT2C serotonin receptors. *Nature, 374*, 542–546.

Teghtsoonian, R. (1992). In defense of the pineal gland. *Behavioral and Brain Sciences, 15*, 224–225.

Teigen, K. H. (1994). Yerkes-Dodson: A law for all seasons. *Theory and Psychology, 4*, 525–547.

Tellegen, A., Lykken, D. T., Bouchard, T. J., Wilcox, K. J., et al. (1988). Personality similarity in twins reared apart and together. *Journal of Personality and Social Psychology, 54*, 1031–1039.

Tenenbaum, H. R., & Leaper, C. (2003). Parent-child conversations about science: The socializations of gender inequities? *Developmental Psychology, 39*, 34–47.

Teng, Y. D., Lavik, E. B., Qu, X., Park, K. I., et al. (2002). Functional recovery following traumatic spinal cord injury mediated by a unique polymer scaffold seeded with neural stem cells. *Proceedings of the National Academy of Sciences, 99*, 3024–3029.

Teplin, L. A., McClelland, G. M., Abram, K. M., & Weiner, D. A. (2005). Crime victimization in adults with severe mental illness. *Archives of General Psychiatry, 62*, 911–921.

Terman, L. M. (1916). *The measurement of intelligence*. Boston: Houghton Mifflin.

Terman, L. M., & Oden, M. H. (1947). *The gifted child grows up: Vol. 4. Genetic studies of genius*. Palo Alto, CA: Stanford University Press.

Terman, L. M., & Oden, M. H. (1959). *The gifted group at midlife*. Palo Alto, CA: Stanford University Press.

Terman, M., & Terman, J. S. (2005). Light therapy for seasonal and nonseasonal depression: Efficacy, protocol, safety, and side effects. *CNS Spectrums, 10*, 647–663.

Terracciano, A., Löckenhoff, C. E., Zonderman, A. B., Ferrucci, L., & Costa, P. T. (2008). Personality predictors of longevity: Activity, emotional stability, and conscientiousness. *Psychosomatic Medicine, 70*, 621–627.

Terracciano, A., Sanna, S., Uda, M., Deiana, B., et al. (2010). Genome-wide association scan for five major dimensions of personality. *Molecular Psychiatry, 15*, 647–656.

Terracciano, A., Sutin, A. R., McCrae, R. R., Deiana, B., et al. (2009). Facets of personality linked to underweight and overweight. *Psychosomatic Medicine, 71*, 682–689.

Terrace, H. S., Petitto, L. A., Sanders, D. L., & Bever, J. G. (1979). Can an ape create a sentence? *Science, 206*, 891–902.

Tetlock, P. E. (2006). *Expert political judgment: How good is it? How can we know?* Princeton, NJ: Princeton University Press.

Thakkar, R. R., Garrison, M. M., & Christakis, D. A. (2006). A systematic review for the effects of television viewing by infants and preschoolers. *Pediatrics, 118*, 2025–2031.

Thakur, G. A., Tichkule, R., Bajaj, S., & Makriyannis, A. (2009). Latest advances in cannabinoid receptor agonists. *Expert Opinion on Therapeutic Patents, 19*, 1647–1673.

Thaler, E. R., Kennedy, D. W., & Hanson, C. W. (2001). Medical applications of electronic nose technology: Review of current status. *American Journal of Rhinology, 15*, 291–295.

Thase, M. E. (2002). Antidepressant effects: The suit may be small, but the fabric is real. *Prevention and Treatment, 5*, art. 32. Retrieved from http://www.journals.apa.org/prevention/volume5/pre0050032c.html

Thase, M. E., Friedman, E. S., Biggs, M. M., Wisniewski, S. R., et al. (2007). Cognitive therapy versus medication in augmentation and switch strategies as second-step treatments: A STAR*D report. *American Journal of Psychiatry, 164*, 739–752.

Theeuwes, J., Godijn, R., & Pratt, J. (2004). A new estimation of the duration of attentional dwell time. *Psychonomic Bulletin and Review, 11*, 60–64.

Thelen, E. (1995). Motor development: A new synthesis. *American Psychologist, 50*, 79–95.

Theofilopoulos, S., Goggi, J., Riaz, S. S., Jauniaux, E., et al. (2001). Parallel induction of the formation of dopamine and its metabolites with induction of tyrosine hydroxylase expression in foetal rat and human cerebral cortical cells by brain-derived neurotrophic factor and glial-cell derived neurotrophic factor. *Brain Research: Developmental Brain Research, 127*, 111–122.

Thiessen, E. D., Hill, E. A., & Saffran, J. R. (2005). Infant-directed speech facilitates word segmentation. *Infancy, 7*, 53–71.

Thom, A., Sartory, G., & Jöhren, P. (2000). Comparison between one-session psychological treatment and benzodiazepine in dental phobia. *Journal of Consulting and Clinical Psychology, 68*, 378–387.

Thomas, A., & Chess, S. (1977). *Temperament and development*. New York: Brunner/Mazel.

Thomas, E. L., & Robinson, H. A. (1972). *Improving reading in every class: A sourcebook for teachers*. Boston: Allyn & Bacon.

Thomas, J. A., & Walton, D. (2007). Measuring perceived risk: Self-reported and actual hand positions of SUV and car drivers. *Traffic Psychology and Behavior, 10*, 201–207.

Thomas, R., & Forde, E. (2006). The role of local and global processing in the recognition of living and nonliving things. *Neuropsychologia, 44*, 982–986.

Thompson, C.; Koon, E.; Woodwell, W., Jr.; & Beauvais, J. (2002). *Training for the next economy: An ASTD state-of-the-industry report on trends in employer-provided training in the United States*. Washington, DC: American Society for Training and Development.

Thompson, D. S., & Pollack, B. G. (2001, August 26). Psychotropic metabolism: Gender-related issues. *Psychiatric Times, 14*. Retrieved from http://www.mhsource.com/pt/p010147.html

Thompson, E. M., & Morgan, E. M. (2008). "Mostly straight" young women: Variations in sexual behavior and identity development. *Developmental Psychology, 44*, 15–21.

Thompson, J. K. (1996). Introduction: Assessment and treatment of binge eating disorder. In J. K. Thompson (Ed.), *Body image, eating disorders, and obesity* (pp. 1–22). Washington, DC: American Psychological Association.

Thompson, P. M., Giedd, J. N., Woods, R. P., Macdonald, D., et al. (2000). Growth patterns in the developing brain detected by using continuum mechanical tensor maps. *Nature, 404*, 190–193.

Thompson, P. M., Hayashi, K. M., Simon, S. L., Geaga, J. A., et al. (2004). Structural abnormalities in the brains of human subjects who use methamphetamine. *Journal of Neuroscience, 24*, 6028–6036.

Thompson, R. A. (2006). The development of the person: Social understanding, relationships, self, conscience. In W. Damon & R. M. Lerner (Series Eds.) & N. Eisenberg (Vol. Ed.), *Handbook of child psychology: Vol. 3. Social, emotional, and personality development* (6th ed., pp. 24–98). Hoboken, NJ: Wiley.

Thompson, R. A., Lewis, M. D., & Calkins, S. D. (2008). Reassessing emotion regulation. *Child Development Perspectives, 2*, 124–131.

Thompson, V. B., Heiman, J., Chambers, J. B., Benoit, S. C., et al. (2009). Long-term behavioral consequences of prenatal MDMA exposure. *Physiology and Behavior, 96*, 593–601.

Thompson-Brenner, H., Glass, S., & Westen, D. (2003). A multidimensional meta-analysis of psychotherapy for bulimia nervosa. *Clinical Psychology: Science and Practice, 10*, 269–287.

Thomsen, L., Green, E. G. T., & Sidanius, J. (2008). We will hunt them down: How social dominance orientation and right-wing authoritarianism fuel ethnic persecution of immigrants in fundamentally different ways. *Journal of Experimental Social Psychology, 44*, 1455–1464.

Thomson, C. P. (1982). Memory for unique personal events: The roommate study. *Memory and Cognition, 10*, 324–332.

Thomson Healthcare. (2007). *PDR drug guide for mental health professionals* (3rd ed.). Washington, DC: Author.

Thorens, B. (2008). Glucose sensing and the pathogenesis of obesity and type 2 diabetes. *International Journal of Obesity, 32*, S62–S71.

Thoresen, C. J., Kaplan, S. A., Barsky, A. P., Warren, C. R., & de Chermont, K. (2003). The affective underpinnings of job perceptions and attitudes: A meta-analytic review and integration. *Psychological Bulletin, 129*, 914–945.

Thorndike, E. L. (1898). Animal intelligence: An experienced study of the associative process in animals. *Psychological Monographs, 2*(Whole No. 8).

Thorndike, E. L. (1905). *The elements of psychology*. New York: Seiler.

Thorndike, R. L. (1968). [Review of the book *Pygmalion in the classroom*]. *American Educational Research Journal, 5*, 708–711.

Thorndike, R. L., & Hagen, E. P. (1996). *Form 5 CogAT interpretive guide of school administrators: All levels*. Chicago: Riverside.

Thorndike, R. M. & Dinnel, D. L. (2001). *Basic statistics for the behavioral sciences*. Upper Saddle River, NJ: Prentice Hall.

Thorngren, J. M., & Kleist, D. M. (2002). Multiple family group therapy: An interpersonal/postmodern approach. *Family Journal: Counseling and Therapy for Couples and Families, 10*, 167–176.

Thunberg, T. (1896). Förnimmelserne vid till samma ställe lokaliserad, samtidigt pägäende köld-och värmeretning. *Uppsala Läkfören Förhandlingar, 1,* 489–495.
Thurston, I. B., & Phares, V. (2008). Mental health service utilization among African American and Caucasian mothers and fathers. *Journal of Consulting and Clinical Psychology, 76,* 1058–1067.
Thurstone, L. L. (1938). *Primary mental abilities.* Chicago: University of Chicago Press.
Tian, H.-G., Nan, Y., Hu, G., Dong, Q.-N., et al. (1995). Dietary survey in a Chinese population. *European Journal of Clinical Nutrition, 49,* 27–32.
Tienari, P., Wynne, L. C., Läksy, K., Moring, J., et al. (2003). Genetic boundaries of the schizophrenia spectrum: Evidence from the Finnish Adoptive Family Study of Schizophrenia. *American Journal of Psychiatry, 160,* 1587–1594.
Tierney, J. (2009, March 10). What do dreams mean? Whatever your bias says. *New York Times,* p. D2.
Tiihonen, J., Kuikka, J., Bergstrom, K., Hakola, P., et al. (1995). Altered striatal dopamine reuptake site densities in habitually violent and nonviolent alcoholics. *Nature Medicine, 1,* 654–657.
Tillfors, M., Carlbring, P., Furmark, T., Lewenhaupt, S., et al. (2008). Treating university students with social phobia and public speaking fears: Internet delivered self-help with or without live group exposure sessions. *Depression and Anxiety, 25,* 708–717.
Timberlake, W., & Farmer-Dougan, V. A. (1991). Reinforcement in applied settings: Figuring out ahead of time what will work. *Psychological Bulletin, 110,* 379–391.
Timko, C., Finney, J. W., & Moos, R. H. (2005). The 8-year course of alcohol abuse: Gender differences in social context and coping. *Alcoholism: Clinical and Experimental Research, 29,* 612–621.
Timmerman, T. A. (2007). "It was a thought pitch": Personal, situational, and target influences on hit-by-pitch events across time. *Journal of Applied Psychology, 92,* 876–884.
Timms, P. (2005). Is there still a problem with homelessness and schizophrenia? *International Journal of Mental Health, 34,* 57–75.
Tinbergen, N. (1989). *The study of instinct.* Oxford: Clarendon Press.
Tindale, R. S., & Kameda, T. (2000). "Social sharedness" as a unifying theme for information processing in groups. *Group Processes and Intergroup Relations, 3,* 123–140.
Tippmann-Piekert, M., Park, J. G., Boeve, B. F., Shepard, J. W., & Silber, M. H. (2007). Pathologic gambling in patients with restless legs syndrome treated with dopaminergic agonists. *Neurology, 68,* 301–303.
Tobler, P. N., Fiorillo, C. D., & Schultz, W. (2005). Adaptive coding of reward value by dopamine neurons. *Science, 307,* 1642–1645.
Tohen, M.; Zarate, C. A., Jr.; Hennen, J.; Khalsa, H.-M. K.; et al. (2003). The McLean-Harvard first-episode mania study: Prediction of recovery and first recurrence. *American Journal of Psychiatry, 160,* 2099–2107.
Tolin, D. F. (2010). Is cognitive-behavioral therapy better than other therapies? A meta-analytic review. *Clinical Psychology Review, 30,* 710–720.
Tolman, E. C., & Honzik, C. H. (1930). Introduction and removal of reward and maze performance in rats. *University of California Publication in Psychology, 4,* 257–265.
Tomasello, M. (2006). Why don't apes point? In J. Enfield & S. C. Levinson (Eds.), *Roots of human sociality: Culture, cognition, and interaction* (pp. 506–524). New York: Berg.
Tomberlin, J. K., Rains, G. C., & Sanford, M. R. (2008). Development of *Microplitis croceipes* as a biological sensor. *Entomologia Experimentalis et Applicata, 128,* 249–257.
Toni, N., Buchs, P. A., Nikonenko, I., Bron, C. R., & Muller, D. (1999). LTP promotes formation of multiple spine synapses between a single axon terminal and a dendrite. *Nature, 402,* 421–425.
Tonnesen, J., Sorensen, A. T., Deisseroth, K., Lundberg, C., & Kokaia, M. (2009). Optogenetic control of epileptiform activity. *Proceedings of the National Academy of Sciences, 106,* 12162–12167. doi:10.1073/pnas.0901915106
Topakian, R., & Aichner, F. T. (2008). Vascular dementia: A practical update. *Current Medical Literature: Neurology, 24,* 1–8.
Torges, C. M., Stewart, A. J., & Nolen-Hoeksema, S. (2008). Regret resolution, aging, and adapting to loss: Older adults are better than younger ones at resolving their bereavement-related regrets. *Psychology and Aging, 23,* 169–180.
Törnros, J. E., & Bolling, A. K. (2005). Mobile phone use: Effects of handheld and hands-free phones on driving performance. *Accident Analysis and Prevention, 37,* 902–909.
Torpy, J. A. (2008). Delirium. *Journal of the American Medical Association, 300,* 2936–2936.
Touzani, K., Puthanveettil, S. V., & Kandel, E. R. (2007). Consolidation of learning strategies during spatial working memory taks requires protein synthesis in the prefrontal cortex. *Proceedings of the National Academy of Sciences, 104,* 5632–5637.
Tracey, I. (2005). Nociceptive processing in the human brain. *Current Opinion in Neurobiology, 15,* 478–487.
Tracy, J. L., & Robins, R. W. (2008). The nonverbal expression of pride: Evidence for cross-cultural recognition. *Journal of Personality and Social Psychology, 94,* 516–530.
Tramer, M. R., Carroll, D., Campbell, F. A., Reynolds, D. J., et al. (2001). Cannabinoids for control of chemotherapy-induced nausea and vomiting: Quantitative systematic review. *British Medical Journal, 323,* 16–21.
Tranter, L. J., & Koutstaal, W. (2008). Age and flexible thinking: An experimental demonstration of the beneficial effects of increased cognitively stimulating activity on fluid intelligence in healthy older adults. *Aging, Neuropsychology, and Cognition, 15,* 184–207. doi:10.1080/13825580701322163
Treat, T. A., & Viken, R. J. (2010). Cognitive processing of weight and emotional information in disordered eating. *Current Directions in Psychological Science, 19,* 81–85.
Treboux, D., Crowell, J. A., & Waters, E. (2004). When "new" meets "old": Configurations of adult attachment representations and their implications for marital functioning. *Developmental Psychology, 40,* 295–314.
Treiber, F. A., Musante, L., Kapuku, G., Davis, C., et al. (2001). Cardiovascular (CV) responsivity and recovery to acute stress and future CV functioning in youth with family histories of CV disease: A 4-year longitudinal study. *International Journal of Psychophysiology, 41,* 65–74.
Treisman, A. (1988). Features and objects: The 14th Bartlett memorial lecture. *Quarterly Journal of Experimental Psychology, 40,* 201–237.
Treisman, A. (1999). Feature binding, attention, and object perception. In G. W. Humphreys, J. Duncan., & A. Treisman (Eds.), *Attention, space, and action* (pp. 91–111). New York: Oxford University Press.
Tremblay, N., Boutin, C., & Ladouceur, R. (2008). Improved self-exclusion program: Preliminary results. *Journal of Gambling Studies, 24,* 505–518.
Tremblay, R. E., Pihl, R. O., Vitaro, F., & Dobkin, P. (1994). Predicting early onset of male antisocial behavior from preschool behavior. *Archives of General Psychiatry, 51,* 732–739.
Trevor, C. O. (2001). Interactions among actual ease-of-movement determinants and job satisfaction in the prediction of voluntary turnover. *Academy of Management Journal, 44,* 621–638.
Triandis, H. C., & Trafimow, D. (2001). Cross-national prevalence of collectivism. In C. Sedikides & M. B. Brewer (Eds.), *Individual self, relational self, collective self* (pp. 259–276). New York: Psychology Press.
Trierweiler, S. J., Muroff, J. R., Jackson, M. S., Neighbors, H. W., & Munday, C. (2005). Clinician race, situational attributions, and diagnoses of mood versus schizophrenia disorders. *Cultural Diversity and Ethnic Minority Psychology, 11,* 351–364.
Trierweiler, S. J., Neighbors, H. W., Munday, C., Thompson, E. E., et al. (2000). Clinician attributions associated with the diagnosis of schizophrenia in African American and non–African American patients. *Journal of Consulting and Clinical Psychology, 68,* 171–175.
Trifiletti, L. B., Shields, W., McDonald, E., Reynaud, F., & Gielen, A. (2006). Tipping the scales: Obese children and child safety seats. *Pediatrics, 117,* 1197–1202.
Trillin, A. S. (2001, January 29). Betting your life. *New Yorker,* pp. 38–41.
Tronick, E. Z. (1989). Emotions and emotional communication in infants. *American Psychologist, 44,* 112–119.
Tronick, E. Z., Messinger, D. S., Weinberg, M. K., Lester, B. M., et al. (2005). Cocaine exposure is associated with subtle compromises of infants' and mothers' social-emotional behavior and dyadic features of their interaction in the face-to-face still-face paradigm. *Developmental Psychology, 41,* 711–722.
Tropp, L. R., & Pettigrew, T. F. (2005). Relationships between intergroup contact and prejudice among minority and majority status groups. *Psychological Science, 16,* 951–957.
Trotter, M. I., & Morgan, D. W. (2008). Patients' use of the Internet for health-related matters: A study of Internet usage in 2000 and 2006. *Health Informatics Journal, 14,* 175–181.
Trujillo, C. M. (1986). A comparative evaluation of classroom interactions between professors and minority and nonminority college students. *American Educational Research Journal, 23,* 629–642.
Trujillo, K. A., & Akil, H. (1991). Inhibition of morphine tolerance and dependence by the NMDA receptor antagonist MK-801. *Science, 251,* 85–87.
Trull, T. J., & Sher, K. J. (1994). Relationship between the five-factor model of personality and Axis I disorders in a nonclinical sample. *Journal of Personality and Social Psychology, 103,* 350–360.
Trumbetta, S. L., Seltzer, B. K., Gottsman, I. I., & McIntyre, K. M. (2010). Mortality predictors in a 60-year follow-up of adolescent males: Exploring delinquency, socioeconomic status, IQ, high school dropout status, and personality. *Psychosomatic Medicine, 72,* 46–52.
Trunzo, J. J., & Pinto, B. M. (2003). Social support as a mediator of optimisim and distress in breast cancer survivors. *Journal of Consulting and Clinical Psychology, 71,* 805–811.
Tryon, W. W. (2005). Possible mechanisms for why desensitization and exposure therapy work. *Clinical Psychology Review, 25,* 67–95.
Tsai, J. L., Knutson, B., & Fung, H. H. (2006). Cultural variation in affect evaluation. *Journal of Personality and Social Psychology, 90,* 288–307.
Tsai, J. L., Levenson, R. W., & McCoy, K. (2006). Cultural and temperamental variation in emotional response. *Emotion, 6,* 484–497.
Tsakiris, M., & Haggard, P. (2005). The rubber hand illusion revisited: Visuotactile integration and self-attribution. *Journal of Experimental Psychology: Human Perception and Performance, 31,* 80–91.
Tsang, J. S., Naughton, P. A., Leong, S., Hill, A. D. K., et al. (2008). Virtual reality simulation in endovascular surgical training. *Surgeon, 6,* 214–220.
Tsotsos, J. K., Rodriguez-Sanchez, A. J., Rothenstein, A. L & Simine, E. (2008). The different stages of visual recognition need different attentional binding strategies. *Brain Research, 1225,* 119–132.
Tsuang, M. T., Stone, W. S., & Faraone, S. V. (2000). Toward reformulating the diagnosis of schizophrenia. *American Journal of Psychiatry, 157,* 1041–1950.
Tuch, S. A., & Martin, J. K. (1991). Race in the workplace: Black/white differences in the sources of job satisfaction. *Sociological Quarterly, 32,* 103–116.
Tucker-Drob, E. M., Johnson, K. E., & Jones, R. N. (2009). The cognitive reserve hypothesis: A longitudinal examination of age-associated declines in reasoning and processing speed. *Developmental Psychology, 45,* 431–446.
Tuckman, B. W. (2003). The effect of learning and motivation strategies training on college students' achievement. *Journal of College Student Development, 4,* 430–437.
Tuller, D. (2004, January 27). Britain poised to approve medicine derived from marijuana. *New York Times,* p. F5.
Tulving, E. (1983). *Elements of episodic memory.* New York: Oxford University Press.
Tulving, E. (1993). Self-knowledge of an amnesic individual is represented abstractly. In T. K. Srull & R. S. Wyer (Eds.), *The mental representation of trait and autobiographical knowledge about the self: Advances in social cognition* (Vol. 5, pp. 147–156). Hillsdale, NJ: Erlbaum.
Tulving, E. (2000). Introduction to memory. In M. S. Gazzaniga (Ed.), *The new cognitive neurosciences* (pp. 727–732). Cambridge, MA: MIT Press.
Tulving, E. (2005). Episodic memory and autonoesis: Uniquely human? In H. S. Terrace & J. Metcalfe (Eds.), *The missing link in cognition: Origins of self-reflective consciousness* (pp. 3–56). New York: Oxford University Press.

Tulving, E., Hayman, C. A. G., & Macdonald, C. A. (1991). Long-lasting perceptual priming and semantic learning in amnesia: A case experiment. *Journal of Experimental Psychology: Learning, Memory, and Cognition, 17,* 595–617.

Tulving, E., & Psotka, J. (1971). Retroactive inhibition in free recall: Inaccessibility of information available in the memory store. *Journal of Experimental Psychology, 87,* 1–8.

Tulving, E., & Schacter, D. L. (1990). Priming and human memory systems. *Science, 247,* 301–306.

Tulving, E., Schacter, D. L., & Stark, H. (1982). Priming effects in word-fragment completion are independent of recognition memory. *Journal of Experimental Psychology: Learning, Memory, and Cognition, 8,* 336–342.

Tuomilehto, J., Lindstrom, J., Eriksson, J. G., Valle, T. T., et al. (2001). Prevention of type 2 diabetes mellitus by changes in lifestyle among subjects with impaired glucose tolerance. *New England Journal of Medicine, 344,* 1343–1350.

Tupala, E., & Tiihonen, J. (2004). Dopamine and alcoholism: Neurobiological basis of ethanol abuse. *Progress in Neuropsychopharmacology and Biological Psychiatry, 28,* 1221–1247.

Turiel, E. (2006). The development of morality. In W. Damon & R. M. Lerner (Series Eds.) & N. Eisenberg (Vol. Ed.), *Handbook of child psychology: Vol. 3. Social, emotional, and personality development* (6th ed., pp. 789–859). Hoboken, NJ: Wiley.

Turkheimer, E., Haley, A., Waldron, M., D'Onofrio, B., & Gottesman, I. I. (2003). Socioeconomic status modifies heritability of IQ in young children. *Psychological Science, 14,* 623–628.

Turkington, C. (1987, September). Special talents. *Psychology Today,* pp. 42–46.

Turner, B. G., Beidel, D. C., Hughes, S., & Turner, M. W. (1993). Test anxiety in African-American school children. *School Psychology Quarterly, 8,* 140–152.

Turner, E. H., Matthews, A. M., Linardatos, E., Tell, R. A., & Rosenthal, R. (2008). Selective publication of antidepressant trials and its influence on apparent efficacy. *New England Journal of Medicine, 358,* 252–260.

Turner, J. C. (1991). *Social influence.* Pacific Grove, CA: Brooks/Cole.

Turner, M. M., Tamborini, R., Limon, M. S., & Zuckerman-Hyman, C. (2007). The moderators and mediators of door-in-the-face requests: Is it a negotiation or a helping experience? *Communication Monographs, 74,* 333–356.

Turner, M. S., Cipolotti, L., Yousry, T. A., & Shallice, T. (2008). Confabulation: Damage to a specific inferior medial prefrontal system. *Cortex, 44,* 637–648.

Turner, R. J., & Lloyd, D. A. (2004). Stress burden and the lifetime incidence of psychiatric disorder in young adults: Racial and ethnic contrasts. *Archives of General Psychiatry, 61,* 481–488.

Turner, S. M., DeMers, S. T., Fox, H. R., & Reed, G. M. (2001). APA's guidelines for test user qualifications: An executive summary. *American Psychologist, 56,* 1099–1113.

Tversky, A., & Kahneman, D. (1974). Judgment under uncertainty: Heuristics and biases. *Science, 185,* 1124–1131.

Tversky, A., & Kahneman, D. (1991). Loss aversion in riskless choice: A reference dependent model. *Quarterly Journal of Economics, 106,* 1039–1061.

Tversky, A., & Kahneman, D. (1993). Probabilistic reasoning. In A. Goldman (Ed.), *Readings in philosophy and cognitive science* (pp. 43–68). Cambridge, MA: MIT Press.

Tversky, B., & Tuchin, M. (1989). A reconciliation of the evidence on eyewitness testimony: Comments on McCloskey and Zaragoza. *Journal of Experimental Psychology: General, 118,* 86–91.

Twenge, J. M., Campbell, W. K., & Foster, C. A. (2003). Parenthood and marital satisfaction: A meta-analytic review. *Journal of Marriage and Family, 65,* 574–583.

Twenge, J. M., Gentile, B., DeWall, C. N., Ma, D., et al. (2010). Birth cohort increases in psychopathology among young Americans, 1938–2007: A cross-temporal meta-analysis of the MMPI. *Clinical Psychology Review, 30,* 145–154.

Tyler, K. L., & Malessa, R. (2000). The Goltz-Ferrier debates and the triumph of cerebral localizationalist theory. *Neurology, 55,* 1015–1024.

Tziner, A., Murphy, K. R., & Cleveland, J. N. (2005). Contextual and rater factors affecting rating behavior. *Group and Organization Management, 30,* 89–98.

U.S. Bureau of Labor Statistics. (2006). *Occupational projections and training data, 2006–2007.* Washington, DC: U.S. Department of Labor.

U.S. Bureau of Labor Statistics. (2007). *Injuries, illnesses, and fatalities, 2005.* Washington, DC: U.S. Department of Labor. Retrieved from http://www.bls.gov/iif/home.htm#tables

U.S. Bureau of Labor Statistics. (2008a). *Occupational outlook handbook, 2008–09.* Washington, DC: U.S. Department of Labor. Retrieved from http://www.bls.gov/oco

U.S. Bureau of Labor Statistics. (2008b). *Occupational projections and training data, 2008–2009.* Washington, DC: U.S. Department of Labor.

U.S. Census Bureau. (2008). *Current population reports: Income, poverty, and health insurance coverage in the United States, 2007.* Washington, DC: U.S. Government Printing Office.

U.S. Department of Health and Human Services. (2001a). *Alzheimer's disease fact sheet.* NIH Publication No. 01-3431 Washington, DC: U.S. Public Health Service.

U.S. Department of Health and Human Services. (2001b). *Women and smoking: A report of the surgeon general.* Atlanta: Centers for Disease Control and Prevention.

U.S. Department of Justice. (1999). *Eyewitness evidence: A guide for law enforcement.* Washington, DC: National Institute of Justice.

U.S. Department of Justice. (2007). *Crime characteristics.* Retrieved from http://www.ojp.usdoj.gov/bjs/cvict_c.htm#relate

U.S. Department of Transportation. (2010). *Statistics and facts about distracted driving.* Retrieved from http://www.distraction.gov/stats-and-facts/#electronic

U.S. Food and Drug Administration. (2005, April 11). FDA public health advisory: *Deaths with antipsychotics in elderly patients with behavioral disturbances.* Washington, DC: U.S. Department of Health and Human Services.

U.S. Surgeon General. (1999). *Mental health: A report of the surgeon general.* Rockville, MD: U.S. Department of Health and Human Services.

Uchida, Y., & Kitayama, S. (2009). Happiness and unhappiness in East and West: Themes and variations. *Emotion, 9,* 441–456.

Uchida, Y., Kitayama, S., Mesquita, B., & Reyes, J. A. (2001, June). *Interpersonal sources of happiness: The relative significance in Japan, the Philippines, and the United States.* Paper presented at annual convention of American Psychological Society, Toronto.

Uddin, M., Aiello, A. E., Wildman, D. E., Koenen, K. C., et al. (2010). Epigenetic and immune function profiles associated with posttraumatic stress disorder. *Proceedings of the National Academy of Sciences, 107,* 9470. doi:10.1073/pnas.0910794107

Udry, J. R., & Chantala, K. (2003). Masculinity-femininity guides sexual union formation in adolescents. *Personality and Social Psychology Bulletin, 30,* 44–55.

Üstün, B., & Kennedy, C. (2009). What is "functional impairment"? Disentangling disability from clinical significance. *World Psychiatry, 8,* 82–85.

Ugajin, T., Hozawa, A., Ohkubo, T., Asayama, K., et al. (2005). White-coat hypertension as a risk factor for the development of home hypertension: The Ohasama study. *Archives of Internal Medicine, 165,* 1541–1546

Uhl-Bien, M., Marion, R., & McKelvey, B. (2007). Complexity leadership theory: Shifting leadership from the industrial age to the knowledge era. *Leadership Quarterly, 18,* 298–318.

Ulett, G. A. (2003). Acupuncture, magic, and make-believe. *Skeptical Inquirer, 27,* 47–50.

Ullmann, L. P., & Krasner, L. (1965). *Case studies in behavior modification.* New York: Holt, Rinehart & Winston.

Umbreit, J., Ferro, J., Liaupsin, C. J., & Lane, K. L. (2006). *Functional behavioral assessment and function-based intervention: An effective, practical approach.* Upper Saddle River, NJ: Prentice Hall.

Ungemach, C., Chater, N., & Stewart, N. (2009). Are probabilities overweighted or underweighted when rare outcomes are experienced (rarely)? *Psychological Science, 20,* 473–479.

Ungerleider, L. G., & Mishkin, M. (1982). Two cortical visual systems. In D. J. Ingle, M. A. Goodale, & R. J. W. Mansfield (Eds.), *Analysis of visual behavior* (pp. 549–586). Cambridge, MA: MIT Press.

Ungless, M. A., Whistler, J. L., Malenka, R. C., & Bonci, A. (2001). Single cocaine exposure in vivo induces long-term potentiation in dopamine neurons. *Nature, 411,* 583–587.

United Nations Office on Drugs and Crime. (2007). *Intentional homicide rate per 100,000 population.* Retrieved from http://www.unodc.org/documents/data-and-analysis/IHS-rates-05012009.pdf

Urbach, T. P., Windmann, S. S., Payne, D. G., & Kutas, M. (2005). Mismaking memories. *Psychological Science, 16,* 19–24.

Urquhart, B. L., & Kim, R. B. (2009). Blood-brain barrier transporters and response to CNS-active drugs. *European Journal of Clinical Pharmacology, 65,* 1063–1070.

Urry, H. L., Nitschke, J. B., Dolski, I., Jackson, D. C., et al. (2004). Making a life worth living: Neural correlates of well-being. *Psychological Science, 15,* 367–372.

Uttal, W. R. (2003). *The new phrenology: The limits of localizing cognitive processes in the brain.* Cambridge, MA: MIT Press.

Uvnas-Moberg, K., Arn, I., & Magnusson, D. (2005). The psychobiology of emotion: The role of the oxytocinergic system. *International Journal of Behavioral Medicine, 12,* 59–65.

Uwe, H. (2005). Therapeutic alliance: The best synthesizer of social influences on the therapeutic situation? On links to other constructs, determinants of its effectiveness, and its role for research in psychotherapy in general. *Psychotherapy Research, 15,* 9–23.

Uziel, L. (2007). Individual differences in the social facilitation effect: A review and meta-analysis. *Journal of Research in Personality, 41,* 579–601.

Uziel, L. (2010). Rethinking social desirability scales: From impression management to interpersonally oriented self-control. *Perspectives on Psychological Science, 5,* 243–262.

Vahia, I. V., & Cohen, C. I. (2009). Psychosocial factors. In K. T. Mueser & D. V. Jeste (Eds.), *Clinical handbook of schizophrenia* (pp. 74–81). New York: Guilford Press.

Vaitl, D., Birbaumer, N., Gruzelier, J., Jamieson, G. A., et al. (2005). Psychobiology of altered states of consciousness. *Psychological Bulletin, 131,* 98–127.

Valencia-Flores, M., Castano, V. A., Campos, R. M., Rosenthal, L., et al. (1998). The siesta culture concept is not supported by the sleep habits of urban Mexican students. *Journal of Sleep Research, 7,* 21–29.

Valenstein, E. S. (Ed.). (1980). *The psychosurgery debate.* San Francisco: Freeman.

Valent, F., Brusaferro, S., & Barbone, F. (2001). A case-crossover study of sleep and childhood injury. *Pediatrics, 107,* e23.

Valenza, E., Simion, F., Assia, V. M., & Umilta, C. (1996). Face preference at birth. *Journal of Experimental Psychology: Human Perception and Performance, 22,* 892–903.

Valkenburg, P. M., & Peter, J. (2007a). Online communication and adolescent well-being: Testing the stimulation versus the displacement hypothesis. *Journal of Computer-Mediated Communication, 12,* 1169–1182. doi:10.1111/j.1083-6101.2007.00368.x

Valkenburg, P. M., & Peter, J. (2007b). Preadolescents' and adolescents' online communication and their closeness to friends. *Developmental Psychology, 43,* 267–277. doi:10.1037/0012-1649.43.2.267

Valkenburg, P. M., & Peter, J. (2009). Social consequences of the Internet for adolescents: A decade of research. *Current Directions in Psychological Science, 18,* 1–5.

Valli, K., Revonsuo, A., Pälkäs, O., & Punamäki, R.-L. (2006). The effect of trauma on dream content: A field study of Palestinian children. *Dreaming, 16,* 63–87.

Vallotton, C. D. (2008). Signs of emotion: What can preverbal children "say" about internal states? *Infant Mental Health Journal, 29,* 234–258.

Valuck, R. J., Libby, A. M., Benton, T., D., & Evans, D. L. (2007). A descriptive analysis of 10,000 suicide attempters in United States managed care plans, 1998–2005. *Primary Psychiatry, 14,* 52–60.

Van Bezooijen, R., Otto, S. A., & Heenan, T. A (1983). Recognition of vocal expression of emotion: A three-nation study to identify universal characteristics. *Journal of Cross-Cultural Psychology, 14,* 387–406.

Vance, D. E., Roenker, D. L., Cissell, G. M., Edwards, J. D., et al. (2006). Predictors of driving exposure and avoidance in a field study of older drivers from the state of Maryland. *Accident Analysis and Prevention, 38,* 823–831.

van Dam, R. M., Li, T., Spiegelman, D., Franco, O. H., & Hu, F. B. (2008). Combined impact of lifestyle factors on mortality: Prospective cohort study in U.S. women. *British Medical Journal, 337,* a1440.

Vandello, J. A., Cohen, D., & Ransom, S. (2008). U.S. southern and northern differences in perceptions of norms about aggression: Mechanisms for the perpetuation of a culture of honor. *Journal of Cross-Cultural Psychology, 39,* 162–177.

Van den Bergh, B. R., & Marcoen, A. (2004). High antenatal maternal anxiety is related to ADHD symptoms, externalizing problems, and anxiety in 8- and 9-year-olds. *Child Development, 75,* 1085–1097.

van der Hart, O., Bolt, H., & van der Kolk, B. A. (2005). Memory fragmentation in dissociative identity disorder. *Journal of Trauma and Dissociation, 6,* 55–70.

Van der Lely, H. K. J. (1994). Canonical linking rules: Forward versus reverse linking in normally developing and specifically language-impaired children. *Cognition, 51,* 29–72.

van der Maas, H. L. J., Dolan, C. V., Grasman, R. P. P., Wicherts, J. M., et al. (2006). A dynamical model of general intelligence: The positive manifold of intelligence by mutualism. *Psychological Review, 113,* 842–861.

van der Molen, J. H. W. (2004). Violence and suffering in television news: Toward a broader conception of harmful television content for children. *Pediatrics, 113,* 1771–1775.

Vandewater, E. A., Rideout, V. J., Wartella, E. A., Huang, X., et al. (2007). Digital childhood: Electronic media and technology use among infants, toddlers, and preschoolers. *Pediatrics, 119,* 1006–1015.

van Dick, R., Stellmacher, J., Wagner, U., Lemmer, G., & Tissington, P. A. (2009). Group membership salience and task performance. *Journal of Managerial Psychology, 24,* 609–626.

Van Eerde, W., & Thierry, H. (1996). Vroom's expectancy models and work-related criteria: A meta-analysis. *Journal of Applied Psychology, 81,* 575–586.

van Emmerik, I. J. H., & Brenninkmeijer, V. (2009). Deep-level similarity and group social capital: Associations with team functioning. *Small Group Research, 40,* 650–669.

Van Essen, D. C., Anderson, C. H., & Felleman, D. J. (1992). Information processing in the primate visual system: An integrated systems perspective. *Science, 255,* 419–423.

van Goozen, S. H. M., Fairchild, G., Snoek, H., & Harold, G. T. (2007). The evidence for a neurobiological model of childhood antisocial behavior. *Psychological Bulletin, 133,* 149–182.

van Griensven, F., Chakkradband, S., Thienkrua, W., Pengjuntr, W., et al. (2006). Mental health problems among adults in tsunami-affected areas in southern Thailand. *Journal of the American Medical Association, 296,* 537–548.

Vanheule, S., Desmet, M., Rosseel, Y., & Meganck, R. (2006). Core transference themes in depression. *Journal of Affective Disorders, 91,* 71–75.

Van Hulle, C. A., Waldman, I. D., D'Onofrio, B. M., Rogers, J. L., et al. (2009). Developmental structure of genetic influences on antisocial behavior across childhood and adolescence. *Journal of Abnormal Psychology, 118,* 711–721.

van IJzendoorn, M. H. (1995). Adult attachment representations, parental responsiveness, and infant attachment: A meta-analysis on the predictive validity of the Adult Attachment Interview. *Psychological Bulletin, 117,* 387–403.

van IJzendoorn, M. H., & Juffer, F. (2005). Adoption as a successful natural intervention enhancing adopted children's IQ and school performance. *Current Directions in Psychological Science, 14,* 326–330.

van Leeuwen, K., de Fruyt, P., & Mervielde, I. (2004). A longitudinal study of the utility of the resilient, overcontrolled, and undercontrolled personality types as predictors of children's and adolescents' problem behaviour. *International Journal of Behavioural Development, 28,* 210–220.

Vanman, E. J., Saltz, J. L., Nathan, L. R., & Warren, J. A. (2004). Racial discrimination by low-prejudiced whites. *Psychological Science, 15,* 711–714.

van Noorden, M. S., van Dongen, L. C., Zitman, F. G., & Vergouwen, T. A. (2009). Gamma-hydroxybutyrate withdrawal syndrome: Dangerous but not well known. *General Hospital Psychiatry, 31,* 394–396.

Van Orden, K. A., Witte, T. K., Cukrowicz, K. C., Braithwaite, S. R., et al. (2010). The interpersonal theory of suicide. *Psychological Review, 117,* 575–600.

Van Os, J., Rutten, B. P. F., & Poulton, R. (2008). Gene-environment interactions: A review of epidemiological findings and future directions. *Schizophrenia Bulletin, 34,* 1066–1082.

van Praag, H., Christie, B. R., Sejnowski, T. J., & Gage, F. H. (1999). Running enhances neurogenesis, learning, and long-term potentiation in mice. *Proceedings of the National Academy of Sciences, 96,* 13427–13431.

Van Sickel, A. D. (1992). Clinical hypnosis in the practice of anesthesia. *Nurse Anesthesiologist, 3,* 67–74.

van Steenbergen, E. F., & Ellemers, N. (2009). Is managing the work-family interface worthwhile? Benefits for employee health and performance. *Journal of Organizational Behavior, 30,* 617–642.

van Veen, V., Krug, M. K., Schooler, J. W., & Carter, C. S. (2009). Neural activity predicts attitude change in cognitive dissonance. *Nature Neuroscience, 12,* 1469–1474.

van Vugt, M. (2009). Averting the tragedy of the commons: Using social psychological science to protect the environment. *Current Directions in Psychological Science, 18,* 169–173.

van Wel, F., ter Bogt, T., & Raaijmakers, Q. (2002). Changes in the parental bond and the well-being of adolescents and young adults. *Adolescence, 37,* 317–333.

Vargas-Perez, H., Ting-a-Kee, R. A., Heinmiller, A., Sturgess, J. E., & van der Kooy, D. (2007). A test of the opponent-process theory of motivation using lesions that selectively block morphine reward. *European Journal of Neuroscience, 25,* 3713–3718.

Varughese, J. & Allen, R. P. (2001). Fatal accidents following changes in daylight savings time: the American experience. *Sleep Medicine, 2,* 31–36.

Vasey, P. L., & VanderLaan, D. P. (2007). Birth order and male androphilia in Samoan *fa'afafine*. *Proceedings of the Royal Society London, B, 274,* 1437–1442.

Vasilakopoulou, A., & Le Roux, C. W. (2007). Could a virus contribute to weight gain? *International Journal of Obesity, 31,* 1350–1356.

Vasquez, M. J. T. (2007). Cultural difference and the therapeutic alliance: An evidence-based analysis. *American Psychologist, 62,* 878–885.

Vattano, F. (2000). *The mind: Video teaching modules* (2nd ed.). Fort Collins: Colorado State University and Annenberg/CPB.

Vaughan, S. C. (1998). *The talking cure: The science behind psychotherapy.* New York: Holt.

Vazza, G., Bertolin, C., Scudellaro, E., Vettori, A., et al. (2007). Genome-wide scan supports the existence of a susceptibility locus for schizophrenia and bipolar disorder on chromosome 15q26. *Molecular Psychiatry, 12,* 87–93.

Veale, D. (2009). Body dysmorphic disorder. In M. M. Antony & M. B. Stein, (Eds.). *Oxford handbook of anxiety and related disorders* (pp. 541–550). New York: Oxford University Press.

Vecera, S. P., Vogel, E. K., & Woodman, G. F. (2002). Lower region: A new cue for figure-ground assignment. *Journal of Experimental Psychology: General, 131,* 194–205.

Velakoulis, D., Wood, S. J., Wong, M. T., McGorry, P. D., et al. (2006). Hippocampal and amygdala volumes according to psychosis stage and diagnosis: A magnetic resonance imaging study of chronic schizophrenia, first-episode psychosis, and ultra-high-risk individuals. *Archives of General Psychiatry, 63,* 139–149.

Veldhuijzen, D. S., Greenspan, J. D., Kim, J. H., & Lenz, F. A. (2010). Altered pain and thermal sensation in subjects with isolated parietal and insular cortical lesions. *European Journal of Pain, 14,* 535.e1–535.e11. doi:10.1016/j.ejpain.2009.10.002

Velicer, C. M., Heckbert, S. R., Lampe, J. W., Potter, J. D., et al. (2004). Antibiotic use in relation to the risk of breast cancer. *Journal of the American Medical Association, 291,* 827–835.

Velligan, D. I., Bow-Thomas, C. C., Huntzinger, C., Ritch, J., et al. (2000). Randomized controlled trial of the use of compensatory strategies to enhance adaptive functioning in outpatients with schizophrenia. *American Journal of Psychiatry, 157,* 1317–1328.

Vemuganti, R., Kalluri, H., Yi, J., Bowen, K. K., & Hazell, A. S. (2006). Gene expression changes in thalamus and inferior colliculus associated with inflammation, cellular stress, metabolism and structural damage in thiamine deficiency. *European Journal of Neuroscience, 23,* 1172–1188.

Vennemann, M. M., Bajanowski, T., Brinkmann, B., Jorch, G., et al. (2009a). Does breastfeeding reduce the risk of sudden infant death syndrome? *Pediatrics, 123,* e406–e410.

Vennemann, M. M., Bajanowski, T., Brinkmann, B., Jorch, G., et al. (2009ba). Sleep environment risk factors for sudden infant death syndrome: The German sudden infant death syndrome study. *Pediatrics, 123,* 1162–1170.

Vergne, D. E., & Anton, R. F. (2009). Aripiprazole: A drug with a novel mechanism of action and possible efficacy for alcohol dependence. *CNS and Neurological Disorders—Drug Targets, 9,* 50–54.

Verhagen, J. V. (2006). The neurocognitive bases of human multimodal food perception: Consciousness. *Brain Research Reviews, 53,* 271–286.

Vernacchio, L., Corwin, M. J., Lesko, S. M., Vezina, R. M., et al. (2003). Sleep position of low birth weight infants. *Pediatrics, 111,* 633–640.

Verster, J. C., & Volkerts, E. R. (2004). Clinical pharmacology, clinical efficacy, and behavioral toxicity of alprazolam: A review of the literature. *CNS Drug Reviews, 10,* 45–76.

Vestergaard-Poulsen, P., van Beek, M., Skewes, J., Bjarkam, C. R., et al. (2009). Long-term meditation is associated with increased gray matter density in the brain stem. *Neuroreport, 20,* 170–174.

Vetter, M. L., Cardillo, S., Rickels, M. R., & Iqbal, N. (2009). Narrative review: Effect of bariatric surgery on type 2 diabetes mellitus. *Annals of Internal Medicine, 150,* 94–103.

Vidrine, J. I., Businelle, M. S., Cinciripini, P., Li, Y., et al. (2009). Associations of mindfulness with nicotine dependence, withdrawal, and agency. *Substance Abuse, 30,* 318–327.

Vierbuchen, T., Ostermeier, A., Pang, Z. P., Kokubu, Y., et al. (2010). Direct conversion of fibroblasts to functional neurons by defined factors. *Nature, 463,* 1035–1041. Epub 2010 Jan 27.

Vierikko, E., Pulkkinen, L., Kaprio, J., & Rose, R. J. (2006). Genetic and environmental sources of continuity and change in teacher-rated aggression during early adolescence. *Aggressive Behavior, 32,* 308–320.

Vierow, V., Fukuoka, M., Ikoma, A., Dorfler, A., et al. (2009). Cerebral representation of the relief of itch by scratching. *Journal of Neurophysiology, 102,* 3216–3224. Epub 2009 Sep 23.

Vieta, E., & Phillips, M. L. (2007). Deconstructing bipolar disorder: A critical review of its diagnostic validity and a proposal for DSM-V and ICD-11. *Schizophrenia Bulletin, 33,* 886–892.

Vigano, D., Rubino, T., & Parolaro, D. (2005). Molecular and cellular basis of cannabinoid and opioid interactions. *Pharmacology, Biochemistry, and Behavior, 81,* 360–368.

Vijayalaxmi, V. T. J. (2008). Genetic damage in mammalian somatic cells exposed to radiofrequency radiation: A meta-analysis of data from 63 publications (1990–2005). *Radiation Research, 169,* 561–574.

Villalta-Gil., V., Vilaplana, M., Ochoa, S., Dolz, M., et al. (2006). Four symptom dimensions in outpatients with schizophrenia. *Comprehensive Psychiatry, 47,* 384–388.

Vincent, N., & Lewycky, S. (2009). Logging on for better sleep: RCT of the effectiveness of online treatment for insomnia. *Sleep, 32,* 807–815.

Vingerhoets, G., Berckmoes, C., & Stroobant, N. (2003). Cerebral hemodynamics during discrimination of prosodic and semantic emotion in speech studied by transcranial Doppler ultrasonography. *Neuropsychology, 17,* 93–99.

Vink, T., Hinney, A., van Elburg, A. A., van Goozen, S. H. M., et al. (2001). Association between an agouti-related protein gene polymorphism and anorexia nervosa. *Molecular Psychiatry, 6,* 325–328.

Vinod, K. Y., Yalamanchili, R., Xie, S., Cooper, T. B., & Hungund, B. L. (2006). Effect of chronic ethanol exposure and its withdrawal on the endocannabinoid system. *Neurochemistry International, 49,* 619–625.

Virués-Ortega, J. (2010). Applied behavior analytic intervention for autism in early childhood: Meta-analysis, meta-regression and dose-response meta-analysis of multiple outcomes. *Clinical Psychology Review, 30,* 387–399. Epub 2010 Feb 11.

Visser, B. A., Ashton, M. C., & Vernon, P. A. (2006). Beyond *g*: Putting multiple intelligences theory to the test. *Intelligence, 34,* 487–502.

Visser, B. A., Bay, D., Cook, G. L., & Myburg, J. (2010). Psychopathic and antisocial, but not emotionally intelligent. *Personality and Individual Differences, 48,* 644–648.

Vitale, S., Sperduto, R. D., & Ferris, F. L., III. (2009). Increased prevalence of myopia in the United States between 1971–1972 and 1999–2004. *Archives of Ophthalmology, 127,* 1632–1639.

Vitaliano, P. P., Zhang, J. M., & Scanlan, J. M. (2003). Is caregiving hazardous to one's physical health? A meta-analysis. *Psychological Bulletin, 129,* 946–972.

Vocisano, C., Klein, D. N., Arnow, B., Rivera, C., et al. (2004). Therapist variables that predict symptom change in psychotherapy with chronically depressed outpatients. *Psychotherapy: Theory, Research, Training, Practice, 41*, 255–265.

Vogel, I., Brug, J., van der Ploeg, C. P. B., & Raat, H. (2009). Strategies for the prevention of mp3-induced hearing loss among adolescents: Expert opinions from a Delphi study. *Pediatrics, 123*, 1257–1262.

Voisin, J., Bidet-Caulet, A., Bertrand, O., & Fonlupt, P. (2006). Listening in silence activates auditory areas: A functional magnetic resonance imaging study. *Journal of Neuroscience, 26*, 273–278.

Vokey, J. R. (2002). Subliminal messages. In J. R. Vokey & S. W. Allen (Eds.), *Psychological sketches* (6th ed., pp. 223–246). Lethbridge, Canada: Psyence Ink.

Vokey, J. R., & Read, J. D. (1985). Subliminal messages: Between the devil and the media. *American Psychologist, 40*, 1231–1239.

Volk, H. E., Scherrer, J. F., Bucholz, K. K., Todorov, A., et al. (2007). Evidence for specificity of transmission of alcohol and nicotine dependence in an offspring-of-twins design. *Alcohol Dependence, 87*, 225–232.

Vollset, S. E., Tverdal, A., & Gjessing, H. K. (2006). Smoking and deaths between 40 and 70 years of age in women and men. *Annals of Internal Medicine, 144*, 381–389.

Volpicelli, J. R., Ulm, R. R., Altenor, A., & Seligman, M. E. P. (1983). Learned mastery in the rat. *Learning and Motivation, 14*, 204–222.

Volpp, K. G., John, L. K., Troxel, A. B., Norton, L., et al. (2008) Financial incentive–based approaches for weight loss: A randomized trial. *Journal of the American Medical Association, 300*, 2631–2637.

Volz, J. (2000, January). Successful aging. The second 50. *APA Monitor*, pp. 24–28.

von Bekesy, G. (1960). *Experiments in hearing.* New York: McGraw-Hill.

Von Wright, Y. M., Anderson, K., & Stenman, U. (1975). Generalization of conditioned GSRs in dichotic listening. In P. M. A. Rabbitt & S. Dornic (Eds.), *Attention and performance V* (pp. 194–201). New York: Academic Press.

Voracek, M., & Fisher, M. L. (2002). Shapely centrefolds? Temporal change in body measures: Trend analysis. *British Medical Journal, 325*, 1447–1448.

Vorel, S. R., Liu, X., Hayes, R. J., Spector, J. A., & Gardner, E. L. (2001). Relapse to cocaine-seeking after hippocampal theta burst stimulation. *Science, 292*, 1175–1178.

Vorstman, J. A. S., Staal, W. G., van Daalen, E., van Engeland, H., et al. (2006). Identification of novel autism candidate regions through analysis of reported cytogenetic abnormalities associated with autism. *Molecular Psychiatry, 11*, 18–28.

Vouloumanos, A., Druhen, M. J., Hauser, M. D., & Huizink, A. T. (2009). Five-month-old infants' identification of the sources of vocalizations. *Proceedings of the National Academy of Sciences, 106*, 18867–18872.

Vroling, M. S., & de Jong, P. J. (2010). Threat-confirming belief bias and symptoms of anxiety disorders. *Journal of Behavior Therapy and Experimental Psychiatry, 41*, 110–116.

Vroom, V. (1964). *Work and motivation.* New York: Wiley.

Vuoksimaa, E., Kaprio, J., Kremen, W. S., Hokkanen, L., et al. (2010). Having a male co-twin masculinizes mental rotation performance in females. *Psychological Science, 21*, 1069–1071. Epub 2010 Jun 25.

Vuori, E., Tervo, T. M., & Holopainen, J. M. (2009). Laser refractive correction of myopia in visually impaired patients improves visual acuity. *Acta Ophthalmologica.* Epub 2009 Nov 7.

Vyse, S. A. (2000). *Believing in magic: The psychology of superstition.*. New York: Oxford University Press.

Waagenaar, W. A. (1986). My memory: A study of autobiographical memory over six years. *Cognitive Psychology, 18*, 225–252.

Wadden, T. A., Berkowitz, R. I., Sarwer, D. B., Prus-Wisniewski, R., & Steinberg, C. (2001). Benefits of lifestyle modification in the pharmacologic treatment of obesity: A randomized trial. *Archives of Internal Medicine, 161*, 218–227.

Wadden, T. A., Berkowitz, R. I., Womble, L. G., Sarwer, D. B., et al. (2005). Randomized trial of lifestyle modification and pharmacotherapy for obesity. *New England Journal of Medicine, 353*, 2111–2120.

Wadden, T. A., West, D. S., Neiberg, R. H., Wing, R. R., et al. (2009). One-year weight losses in the Look AHEAD study: Factors associated with success. *Obesity, 17*, 713–722.

Wade, C. (1988, April). *Thinking critically about critical thinking in psychology.* Paper presented at the annual meeting of the Western Psychological Association, San Francisco.

Wade, J. B. (2004). Neuropsychologists diagnose traumatic brain injury. *Brain Injury, 18*, 629–643.

Wade, W. A., Treat, T. A., & Stuart, G. L. (1998). Transporting an empirically supported treatment for panic disorder to a service clinic setting: A benchmarking strategy. *Journal of Consulting and Clinical Psychology, 66*, 231–239.

Wadsworth, S. J., Olson, R. K., Pennington, B. F., & DeFries, J. C. (2000). Differential genetic etiology of reading disability as a function of IQ. *Journal of Learning Disabilities, 33*, 192–200.

Waelti, P., Dickinson, A., & Schultz, W. (2001). Dopamine responses comply with basic assumptions of formal learning theory. *Nature, 412*, 43–48.

Wagg, J. (2008, October 21). Yamaha yakidding? *James Randi Educational Foundation.* Retrieved from http://www.randi.org/site/index.php/swift-blog/242-yamaha-yakidding.html

Wagner, A. D. (1999). Working memory contributions to human learning and remembering. *Neuron, 22*, 19–22.

Wagner, K. D., Ambrosini, P., Rynn, M., Wohlberg, C., et al. (2003). Efficacy of sertraline in the treatment of children and adolescents with major depressive disorder: Two randomized controlled trials. *Journal of the American Medical Association, 290*, 1033–1041.

Wagner, U., Hallschmid, M., Rasch, B., & Born, J. (2006). Brief sleep after learning keeps emotional memories alive for years. *Biological Psychiatry, 60*, 788–790.

Wai, J., Lubinski, D., & Benbow, C. P. (2005). Creativity and occupational accomplishments among intellectually precocious youths: An age 13 to age 33 longitudinal study. *Journal of Educational Psychology, 97*, 484–492.

Wainryb, C. (2006). Moral development in culture: Diversity, tolerance, and justice. In M. Killen & J. G. Smetana (Eds.), *Handbook of moral development* (pp. 211–240). Mahwah, NJ: Erlbaum.

Wainryb, C., & Pasupathi, M. (2008). Developing moral agency in the midst of violence: Children, political conflict, and values. In I. A. Karawan, W. McCormack, & S. E. Reynolds (Eds.), *Values and violence: Intangible aspects of terrorism* (pp. 169–188). New York: Springer.

Waite, P. J., & Richardson, G. E. (2004). Determining the efficacy of resiliency training in the work site. *Journal of Allied Health, 33*, 178–183.

Wakefield, J. C. (1992). The concept of mental disorder: On the boundary between biological facts and social values. *American Psychologist, 47*, 373–388.

Wakimoto, R. (2006). Mortality salience effects on modesty and relative self-effacement. *Asian Journal of Social Psychology, 9*, 176–183.

Wakschlag, L. S., Leventhal, B. L., Pine, D. S., Pickett, K. E., & Carter, A. S. (2006). Elucidating early mechanisms of developmental psychopathology: The case of prenatal smoking and disruptive behavior. *Child Development, 77*, 893–906.

Waldman, I. D., & Gizer, I. R. (2006). The genetics of attention deficit hyperactivity disorder. *Clinical Psychology Review, 26*, 396–432.

Walker, E. F., & Diforio, D. (1998). Schizophrenia: A neural diathesis-stress model. *Psychological Review, 104*, 667–685.

Walker, L. E. (1991). The feminization of psychology. *Psychology of Women Newsletter of Division, 35*, 1, 4.

Walker, L. J. (2006). Gender and morality. In M. Killen & J. G. Smetana (Eds.), *Handbook of moral development* (pp. 93–118). Mahwah, NJ: Erlbaum.

Walker, M. P., & Stickgold, R. (2006). Sleep, memory, and plasticity. *Annual Review of Psychology, 57*, 139–166.

Walker, M. P., Brakefield, T., Hobson, J. A., & Stickgold, R. (2003). Dissociable stages of human memory consolidation and reconsolidation. *Nature, 425*, 616–620.

Walker-Andrews, A. S., Bahrick, L. E., Raglioni, S. S., & Dias, I. (1991). Infants' bimodal perception of gender. *Ecological Psychology, 3*, 55–75.

Walkup, J. T., Albano, A. M., Piacentini, J., Birmaher, B., et al. (2008). Cognitive behavioral therapy, sertraline, or a combination in childhood anxiety. *New England Journal of Medicine, 359*, 2753–2766.

Wall, T. L., Shea, S. H., Luczak, S. E., Cook, T. A., & Carr, L. G. (2005). Genetic associations of alcohol dehydrogenase with alcohol use disorders and endophenotypes in white college students. *Journal of Abnormal Psychology, 114*, 456–465.

Wallace, B. A., & Shapiro, S. (2006). Mental balance and well-being: Building bridges between Buddhism and Western psychology. *American Psychologist, 61*, 690–701.

Wallace, J. C., Popp, E., & Mondore, S. (2006). Safety climate as a mediator between foundation climates and occupational accidents: A group-level investigation. *Journal of Applied Psychology, 91*, 681–688.

Wallace, R. K., & Benson, H. (1972). The physiology of meditation. *Scientific American, 226*, 84–90.

Wallentin, M. (2009). Putative sex differences in verbal abilities and language cortex: A critical review. *Brain Language, 108*, 175–183. Epub 2008 Aug 21.

Waller, D. (2000). Individual differences in spatial learning from computer-simulated environments. *Journal of Experimental Psychology: Applied, 6*, 307–321.

Wallerstein, R. S. (2002). The growth and transformation of American ego psychology. *Journal of the American Psychoanalytic Association, 50*, 135–169.

Wallis, G., & Bülthoff, H. H. (2001). Effects of temporal association on recognition memory. *Proceedings of the National Academy of Sciences, 98*, 4800–4804. doi:10.1073/pnas.071028598

Wallis, J. D., Anderson, K. C., & Miller, E. K. (2001). Single neurons in prefrontal cortex encode abstract rules. *Nature, 411*, 953–956.

Wallman, J., Gottlieb, M. D., Rajaram, V., & Fugate-Wentzek, L. A. (1987). Local retinal regions control local eye growth and myopia. *Science, 237*, 73–76.

Walsh, R., & Shapiro, S. L. (2006). The meeting of meditative disciplines and Western psychology: A mutually enriching dialogue. *American Psychologist, 61*, 227–239.

Walther, E., & Langer, T. (2008). Attitude formation and change though association: An evaluative conditioning account. In W. B. Crano & R. Prislin (Eds.), *Attitudes and persuasion* (pp. 87–110). New York: Psychology Press.

Walton, G. E., Bower, N. J. A., & Bower, T. G. R. (1992). Recognition of familiar faces by newborns. *Infant Behavior and Development, 15*, 265–269.

Walton, G. M., & Spencer, S. J. (2009). Latent ability: Grades and test scores systematically underestimate the intellectual ability of negatively stereotyped students. *Psychological Science, 20*, 1132–1139.

Wampold, B. E. (2005). Estimating variability in outcomes attributable to therapists: A naturalistic study of outcomes in managed care. *Journal of Consulting and Clinical Psychology, 73*, 914–923.

Wampold, B. E., Ahn, H. & Coleman, H. L. K. (2001). Medical model as metaphor: Old habits die hard. *Journal of Counseling Psychology, 48*, 263–273.

Wampold, B. E., Minami, T., Tierney, S. C., Baskin, T. W., & Bhati, K. S. (2005). The placebo is powerful: Estimating placebo effects in medicine and psychotherapy from randomized clinical trials. *Journal of Clinical Psychology, 61*, 835–854.

Wanders, F., Serra, M., & de Jongh, A. (2008). EMDR versus CBT for children with self-esteem and behavioral problems: A randomized controlled trial. *Journal of EMDR Practice and Research, 2*, 180–189.

Wanek, J. E., Sackett, P. R., & Ones, D. S. (2003). Towards an understanding of integrity test similarities and differences: An item-level analysis of seven tests. *Personnel Psychology, 56*, 873–894.

Wang, F., Tian, D. R., & Han, J. S. (2008). Electroacupuncture in the treatment of obesity. *Neurochemical Research, 33*, 2023–2027.

Wang, C., Collet, J. P., & Lau, J. (2004). The effect of tai chi on health outcomes in patients with chronic conditions: A systematic review. *Archives of Internal Medicine, 164*, 493–501.

Wang, O. (2006). Earliest recollections of self and others in European American and Taiwanese young adults. *Psychological Science, 17*, 708–714.

Wang, P. S., Aguilar-Gaxiola, S., Alonso, J., Angermeyer, M. C., et al. (2007). Use of mental health services for anxiety, mood, and substance disorders in 17 countries in the WHO World Mental Health surveys. *Lancet, 370,* 841–850.

Wang, P. S., Demler, O., Olfson, M., Pincus, H. A., et al. (2006). Changing profiles of service sectors used in mental health care in the United States. *American Journal of Psychiatry, 163,* 1187–1198.

Wang, P. S., Lane, M., Olfson, M., Pincus, H. A., et al. (2005). Twelve-month use of mental health services in the United States: Results from the National Comorbidity Survey replication. *Archives of General Psychiatry, 62,* 629–640.

Wang, P. S., Schneeweiss, S., Avorn, J., Fischer, M. A., et al. (2005). Risk of death in elderly users of conventional vs. atypical antipsychotic medications. *New England Journal of Medicine, 353,* 2335–2341.

Wang, Q. (2008). Emotion knowledge and autobiographical memory across the preschool years: A cross-cultural longitudinal investigation. *Cognition, 108,* 117–135.

Wang, S. M., Kain, Z. N., & White, P. (2008). Acupuncture analgesia: I. The scientific basis. *Anesthesia and Analgesia, 106,* 602–610.

Wang, W., Chan, S. S., Heldman, D. A., & Moran, D. W. (2010). Motor cortical representation of hand translation and rotation during reaching. *Journal of Neuroscience, 30,* 958–962.

Wang, X., Merzenich, M. M., Sameshima, K., & Jenkins, W. M. (1995). Remodelling of hand representation in adult cortex determined by timing of tactile stimulation. *Nature, 378,* 71–75.

Wang, Y. (2007). Cognitive informatics: Exploring the theoretical foundations for natural intelligence, neural informatics, autonomic computing, and agent systems. *International Journal of Cognitive Informatics and Natural Intelligence, 1,* i–x.

Warburton, D. M. (1995). Effects of caffeine on cognition and mood without caffeine abstinence. *Psychopharmacology, 119,* 66–70.

Ward, C. (1994). Culture and altered states of consciousness. In W. J. Lonner & R. S. Malpass (Eds.), *Psychology and culture* (pp. 59–64). Boston: Allyn & Bacon.

Ward, J., & Mattingley, J. B. (2006). Synaesthesia: An overview of contemporary findings and controversies. *Cortex, 42,* 129–136.

Wark, D. M. (2008). What we can do with hypnosis: A brief note. *American Journal of Clinical Hypnosis, 51,* 29–36.

Warmerdam, L., van Straten, A., Jongsma, J., Twisk, J., & Cuijpers, P. (2010). Online cognitive behavioral therapy and problem-solving therapy for depressive symptoms: Exploring mechanisms of change. *Journal of Behavior Therapy and Experimental Psychiatry, 41,* 64–70.

Warner, B. (2010). Reducing suicidal ideation and depression in older primary care patients: The oldest old and pain. *American Journal of Psychiatry, 167,* 102.

Warner, L., Kessler, R., Hughes, M., Anthony, J., & Nelson, C. (1995). Prevalence and correlates of drug use and dependence in the United States. *Archives of General Psychiatry, 52,* 219–229.

Warrington, E. K., & Weiskrantz, L. (1970). The amnesic syndrome: Consolidation of retrieval? *Nature, 228,* 626–630.

Washburn, J. J., Romero, E. G., Welty, L. J., Abram, K. M., et al. (2007). Development of antisocial personality disorder in detained youths: The predictive value of mental disorders. *Journal of Consulting and Clinical Psychology, 75,* 221–231.

Watanabe, K., & Shimojo, S. (2001). When sound affects vision: Effects of auditory grouping on visual motion perception. *Psychological Science, 12,* 109–116.

Watanabe, S., Sakamoto, J., & Wakita, M. (1995). Pigeons' discrimination of paintings by Monet and Picasso. *Journal of Experimental Analysis of Behavior, 63,* 165–174.

Watanabe, T., Náñez, J. E., & Sasaki, Y. (2001). Perceptual learning without perception. *Nature, 413,* 844–848.

Waterhouse, L. (2006a). Inadequate evidence for multiple intelligences, Mozart effect, and emotional intelligence theories. *Educational Psychologist, 41,* 247–255.

Waterhouse, L. (2006b). Multiple intelligences, the Mozart effect, and emotional intelligence: A critical review. *Educational Psychologist, 41,* 207–225.

Waters, A. M., Henry, J., & Neumann, D. L. (2009). Aversive Pavlovian conditioning in childhood anxiety disorders: Impaired response inhibition and resistance to extinction. *Journal of Abnormal Psychology, 118,* 311–321.

Watkins, L. R., & Maier, S. F. (2003). When good pain turns bad. *Current Directions in Psychological Science, 12,* 232–235.

Watson, J. B. (1913). Psychology as the behaviorist views it. *Psychological Review, 20,* 158–177.

Watson, J. B. (1919). *Psychology from the standpoint of a behaviorist.* Philadelphia: Lippincott.

Watson, J. B. (1925). *Behaviorism.* London: Kegan Paul, Trench, & Trubner.

Watson, R. T., & Heilman, K. M. (1979). Thalamic neglect. *Neurology, 29,* 690–694.

Wattendorf, E., Welge-Lüssen, A., Fiedler, K., Bilecen, D., et al. (2009). Olfactory impairment predicts brain atrophy in Parkinson's disease. *Journal of Neuroscience, 29,* 15410–15413.

Waugh, C. E., Fredrickson, B. L., & Taylor, S. F. (2008). Adapting to life's slings and arrows: Individual differences in resilience when recovering from an anticipated threat. *Journal of Research in Personality, 42,* 1031–1046.

Waugh, C. E., Wager, T. D., Fredrickson, B. L., Noll, D. C., & Taylor, S. F. (2008). The neural correlates of trait resilience when anticipating and recovering from threat. *Social Cognitive and Affective Neuroscience, 3,* 322–333. doi:10.1093/scan/nsn024

Way, B. M., Taylor, S. E., & Eisenberger, N. I. (2009). Variation in the μ-opioid receptor gene (OPRM1) is associated with dispositional and neural sensitivity to social rejection. *Proceedings of the National Academy of Sciences, 106,* 15079-15084. doi:10.1073/pnas.0812612106

Wearden, A. J., Tarrier, N., Barrowclough, C., Zastowny, T. R., & Rahill, A. A. (2000). A review of expressed emotion research in health care. *Clinical Psychology Review, 20,* 633–666.

Weaver, F. M., Follett, K., Stern, M., Hur, K., et al. (2009). Bilateral deep brain stimulation vs. best medical therapy for patients with advanced Parkinson disease: A randomized controlled trial. *Journal of the American Medical Association, 301,* 63–73.

Webb, T. L., & Sheeran, P. (2006). Does changing behavioral intentions engender behavior change? A meta-analysis of the experimental evidence. *Psychological Bulletin, 132,* 249–268.

Weber, J. M., Kopelman, S., & Messick, D. M. (2004). A conceptual review of decision making in social dilemmas: Applying a logic of appropriateness. *Personality and Social Psychology Review, 8,* 281–307.

Weber, M. A., Klein, N. J., Hartley, J. C., Lock, et al. (2008). Infection and sudden unexpected death in infancy: A systematic retrospective case review. *Lancet, 371,* 1848–1853.

Weber, R., Ritterfeld, U., & Mathiak, K. (2006). Does playing violent video games induce aggression? Empirical evidence of a functional magnetic resonance imaging study. *Media Psychology, 8,* 39–60.

Wechsler, D. (1939). *The measurement of adult intelligence.* Baltimore: Williams & Wilkins.

Wechsler, D. (1949). *The Wechsler Intelligence Scale for Children.* New York: Psychological Corporation.

Wechsler, D. (2003). *Wechsler Intelligence Scale for Children* (4th ed.). San Antonio, TX: Psychological Corporation.

Wechsler, D. (2008). *Wechsler Adult Intelligence Scale—Fourth edition (WAIS–IV).* San Antonio, TX: Pearson Assessments.

Wecker, N. S., Kramer, J. H., Hallam, B. J., & Delis, D. C. (2005). Mental flexibility: Age effects on switching. *Neuropsychology, 19,* 345–352.

Wegener, N., & Koch, M. (2009). Neurobiology and systems physiology of the endocannabinoid system. *Pharmacopsychiatry, 42*(Suppl. 1), S79–S86.

Wegge, J., & Haslam, S. A. (2005). Improving work motivation and performance in brainstorming groups: The effects of three group goal-setting strategies. *European Journal of Work and Organizational Psychology, 14,* 400–430.

Wegner, D. M., Fuller, V. A. & Sparrow, B. (2003). Clever hands: Uncontrolled intelligence in facilitated communication. *Journal of Personality and Social Psychology, 85,* 5–19.

Wegner, D. M., Wenzlaff, R. M., & Kozak, M. (2004). Dream rebound: The return of suppressed thoughts in dreams. *Psychological Science, 15,* 232–236.

Weihs, K. L., Enright, T. M., & Simmens, S. J. (2008). Close relationships and emotional processing predict decreased mortality in women with breast cancer: Preliminary evidence. *Psychosomatic Medicine, 70,* 117–124.

Weiler, B. L., & Widom, C. S. (1996). Psychopathy and violent behavior in abused and neglected young adults. *Criminal Behaviour and Mental Health, 6,* 253–271.

Weinberg, R. A. (1989). Intelligence and IQ: Landmark issues and great debates. *American Psychologist, 44,* 98–104.

Weinberg, R. A., Scarr, S., & Waldman, I. D. (1992). The Minnesota transracial adoption study: A follow-up of IQ test performance at adolescence. *Intelligence, 16,* 117–135.

Weingarten, H. P. (1983). Conditioned cues elicit feeding in sated rats: A role for learning in meal initiation. *Science, 220,* 431–433.

Weinraub, M., Horvath, D. L., & Gringlas, M. B. (2002). Single parenthood. In M. H. Bornstein (Ed.), *Handbook of parenting: Vol. 3. Being and becoming a parent* (2nd ed., pp. 109–140). Mahwah, NJ: Erlbaum.

Weinstein, D. (1999, July 24). Who are you? *Sunday Telegraph Magazine,* pp. 24–26.

Weinstein, E. A., & Kahn, R. L. (1955). *Denial of illness: Symbolic and physiological aspects.* Springfield, IL: Thomas.

Weir, K. (2003). Up in smoke. *Current Science, 89,* 4.

Weisbuch, M., Pauker, K., & Ambady, N. (2009). The subtle transmission of race bias via televised nonverbal behavior. *Science, 326,* 1711–1714.

Weiss, A., Gale, C. R., Batty, G. D., & Deary, I. J. (2009). Emotionally stable, intelligent men live longer: The Vietnam Experience Study cohort. *Psychosomatic Medicine, 71,* 385–394.

Weiss, A., King, J. E., & Perkins, L. (2006). Personality and subjective well-being in orangutans (*Pongo pygmaeus* and *Pongo abelii*). *Journal of Personality and Social Psychology, 90,* 501–511.

Weiss, B., Tram, J. M., Weisz, J. R., Rescorla, L., & Achenbach, T. M. (2009). Differential symptom expression and somatization in Thai versus U.S. children. *Journal Consulting and Clinical Psychology, 77,* 987–992.

Weiss, L. A., & Arking, D. E. (2009). A genome-wide linkage and association scan reveals novel loci for autism. *Nature, 461,* 802–808.

Weiss, S. J., Saint Jonn–Seed, M., & Harris-Muchell, C. (2007). The contribution of fetal drug exposure to temperament: Potential teratogenic effects on neuropsychiatric risk. *Journal of Child Psychology and Psychiatry, 48,* 773–784. doi:10.1111/j.1469-7610.2007.01745.x

Weiss, V. (2007). Percentages of children living in poverty determine IQ averages of nations. *European Journal of Personality* [Special issue]: *European personality reviews, 21,* 761–763.

Weissman, D. H., Roberts, K. C., Visscher, K. M., & Woldorff, M. G. (2006). The neural basis of momentary lapses of attention. *Nature Neuroscience, 9,* 971–978.

Weissman, M. M., Markowitz, J. C., & Kierman, G. L. (2007). *Clinician's quick guide to interpersonal psychotherapy.* New York: Oxford University Press.

Weisz, J. R., & Jensen, P. S. (1999). Efficacy and effectiveness of psychotherapy and pharmacotherapy with children and adolescents. *Mental Health Services Research, 1,* 125–157.

Weisz, J. R., Doss, A. J., & Hawley, K. M. (2005). Youth psychotherapy outcome research: A review and critique of the evidence base. *Annual Review of Psychology, 56,* 337–363.

Weisz, J. R., McCarty, C. A., & Valeri, S. M. (2006). Effects of psychotherapy for depression in children and adolescents: A meta-analysis. *Psychological Bulletin, 132,* 132–149.

Weisz, J. R., Weersing, V. R., & Henggeler, S. W. (2005). Jousting at straw men: Comment on Westen, Novotny, and Thompson-Brenner (2004). *Psychological Bulletin, 131,* 418–426.

Wells, A., & Matthews, G. (2006). Cognitive vulnerability to anxiety disorders: An integration. In L. B. Alloy & J. H. Ruskind (Eds.), *Cognitive vulnerability to emotional disorders* (pp. 303–325). Mahwah, NJ: Erlbaum.

Wells, G. L., & Bradfield, A. L. (1999). Distortions in eyewitness recollections: Can the postidentification feedback effect be moderated? *Psychological Science, 10,* 138–144.

Wells, G. L., Malpass, R. S., Lindsay, R. C. L., Fisher, R. P., et al. (2000). From the lab to the police station: A successful application of eyewitness research. *American Psychologist, 55,* 581–598.

Wells, G. L., Memon, A., & Penrod, S. D. (2006). Eyewitness evidence: Improving its probative value. *Psychological Science in the Public Interest, 7,* 45–75.

Wells, G. L., & Olson, E. A. (2003). Eyewitness testimony. *Annual Review of Psychology, 54,* 277–295.

Wells, G. L., Olson, E. A., & Charman, S. D. (2002). The confidence of eyewitnesses in their identifications from lineups. *Current Directions in Psychological Science, 11,* 151–154.

Wells, G. L., Olson, E. A., & Charman, S. D. (2003). Distorted retrospective eyewitness reports as functions of feedback and delay. *Journal of Experimental Psychology: Applied, 9,* 42–52.

Wells, G. L., & Quinlivan, D. S. (2009). Suggestive eyewitness identification procedures and the Supreme Court's reliability test in light of eyewitness science: 30 years later. *Law and Human Behavior, 33,* 1–24.

Wells, J. C. K. (2009). Thrift: A guide to thrifty genes, thrifty phenotypes and thrifty norms. *International Journal of Obesity, 33,* 1331–1338.

Wells, S., Graham, K., & West, P. (2000). Alcohol-related aggression in the general population. *Journal of Studies on Alcohol, 61,* 626–632.

Welsh, T. N., Ray, M. C., Weeks, D. J., Dewey, D., & Elliot, D. (2009). Does Joe influence Fred's action? Not if Fred has autism spectrum disorder. *Brain Research, 1248,* 141–148.

Weltzin, T. E., Bulik, C. M., McConaha, C. W., & Kaye, W. H. (1995). Laxative withdrawal and anxiety in bulimia nervosa. *International Journal of Eating Disorders, 17,* 141–146.

Wengenack, T. M.; Jack, C. R., Jr.; Garwood, M.; & Poduslo, J. F. (2008). MR microimaging of amyloid plaques in Alzheimer's disease transgenic mice. *European Journal of Nuclear Medicine and Molecular Imaging, 35,* 82–88.

Werker, J. F., Lloyd, V. L., Pegg, J. E., & Polka, L. (1996). Putting the baby in the bootstraps: Toward a more complete understanding of the role of input in infant speech processing. In J. L. Morgan & K. Demuth (Eds.), *Signal to syntax* (pp. 427–447). Mahwah, NJ: Erlbaum.

Werner, E. (2003, January 28). Police: Sons kill mom, dismember her after seeing it done on *The Sopranos. Naples Daily News.*

Wernig, M., Zhao, J. P., Pruszak, J., Hedlund, E., et al. (2008). Neurons derived from reprogrammed fibroblasts functionally integrate into the fetal brain and improve symptoms of rats with Parkinson's disease. *Proceedings of the National Academy of Sciences, 105,* 5856–5861. Epub 2008 Apr 57.

Werth, J. L., Jr.; Welfel, E. R.; & Benjamin, G. A. H. (Eds.). (2009). *The duty to protect: Ethical, legal, and professional considerations for mental health professionals.* Washington, DC: American Psychological Association.

Wesson, D. W., & Wilson, D. A. (2010). Smelling sounds: Olfactory-auditory sensory convergence in the olfactory tubercle. *Journal of Neuroscience, 30,* 3013–3021.

West, C. P., Tan, A. D., Habermann, T. M., Sloan, J. A., & Shanafelt, T. D. (2009). Association of resident fatigue and distress with perceived medical errors. *Journal of the American Medical Association, 302,* 1294–1300.

West, M. A., Borrill, C. S., & Unsworth, K. L. (1998). Team effectiveness in organizations. In C. L. Cooper & I. T. Robertson (Eds.), *International review of industrial and organizational psychology, 1998* (pp. 1–48). Chichester, England: Wiley.

West, R., & Sohal, T. (2006). "Catastrophic" pathways to smoking cessation: Findings from national survey. *British Medical Journal, 332,* 458–460.

West, S. A., & Gardner, A. (2010). Altruism, spite, and greenbeards. *Science, 327,* 1341–1344.

West, S. G. (2009). Alternatives to randomized experiments. *Current Directions in Psychological Science, 18,* 299–304.

Westen, D., & Bradley, R. (2005). Empirically supported complexity. *Current Directions in Psychological Science, 14,* 266–271.

Westen, D., & Morrison, K. (2001). A multidimensional meta-analysis of treatments for depression, panic, and generalized anxiety disorder: An empirical examination of the status of empirically supported therapies. *Journal of Consulting and Clinical Psychology, 69,* 875–899.

Westen, D., Glen, O., Gabbard, G. O., & Ortigo, K. M. (2008). Psychoanalytic approaches to personality In O. P. John, R. W. Robins, & L. A. Pervin (Eds.), *Handbook of personality: Theory and research* (3rd ed., pp. 61–113). New York: Guilford Press.

Westen, D., Novotny, C. M., & Thompson-Brenner, H. (2004). The empirical status of empirically supported psychotherapies: Assumptions, findings, and reporting in controlled clinical trials. *Psychological Bulletin, 130,* 631–663.

Westen, D., Shedler, J., & Bradley, R. (2006). A prototype approach to personality disorder diagnosis. *American Journal of Psychiatry, 163,* 846–856.

Westerterp-Plantenga, M. S., Smeets, A., & Lejeune, M. P. (2005). Sensory and gastrointestinal satiety effects of capsaicin on food intake. *International Journal of Obesity, 29,* 682–688.

Weuve, J., Kang, J. H., Manson, J. E., Breteler, M. M. B., et al. (2004). Physical activity, including walking, and cognitive function in older women. *Journal of the American Medical Association, 292,* 1454–1461.

Whaley, A. L. (2001). Cultural mistrust: An important psychological construct for diagnosis and treatment of African Americans. *Professional Psychology: Research and Practice, 32,* 555–562.

Whaley, A. L., & Hall, B. N. (2009). Cultural themes in the psychotic symptoms of African American psychiatric patients. *Professional Psychology: Research and Practice, 40,* 75–80.

Whang, W., Kubzansky, L. D., Kawachi, I., Rexrode, K. M., et al. (2009). Depression and risk of sudden cardiac death and coronary heart disease in women. *Journal of the American College of Cardiology, 53,* 950–958.

Wharton, C. M., Grafman, J., Flitman, S. S., Hansen, E. K., et al. (2000). Toward neuroanatomical models of analogy: A positron emission tomography study of analogical mapping. *Cognitive Psychology, 40,* 173–197.

Wheaton, L. A., & Hallett, M. (2007). Ideomotor apraxia: A review. *Journal of the Neurological Sciences, 260,* 1–10.

Wheeler, B. W., Gunnell, D., Metcalfe, C., Stephens, P., & Martin, R. M. (2008). The population impact on incidence of suicide and non-fatal self-harm of regulatory action against the use of selective serotonin reuptake inhibitors in under 18s in the United Kingdom: Ecological study. *British Medical Journal, 336,* 542–545.

Wheeler, L., & Suls, J. (2007). Social comparison: Can we agree on what it is? *Revue Internationale de Psychologie Sociale, 20,* 31–51.

Whiffin, V. E. (2006). *A secret sadness: The hidden relationship patterns that make women depressed.* Oakland, CA: New Harbinger.

Whimbey, A. (1976). *Intelligence can be taught.* New York: Bantam.

Whitaker, D. J., Morrison, S., Lindquist, C., Hawkins, S. R., et al. (2006). A critical review of interventions for the primary prevention of perpetration of partner violence. *Aggression and Violent Behavior, 11,* 151–166.

Whitam, F. L., Diamond, M., & Martin, J. (1993). Homosexual orientation in twins: A report on 61 pairs and three triplet sets. *Archives of Sexual Behavior, 22,* 187–206.

White, A. T., & Spector, P. E. (1987). An investigation of age-related factors in the age-job satisfaction relationship. *Psychology and Aging, 2,* 261–265.

White, D. E., & Glick, J. (1978). *Competence and the context of performance.* Paper presented at the annual meeting of the Jean Piaget Society, Philadelphia.

White, F. J. (1998). Nicotine addiction and the lure of reward. *Nature Medicine, 4,* 659–660.

White, K. M., Hyde, M. K., Walsh, S. P., & Watson, B. (2010). Mobile phone use while driving: An investigation of the beliefs influencing drivers' hands-free and hand-held mobile phone use. *Transportation Research Part F: Traffic Psychology and Behaviour, 13,* 9–20.

White, K. S., Brown, T. A., Somers, T. J., & Barlow, D. H. (2006). Avoidance behavior in panic disorder: The moderating influences of perceived control. *Behaviour Research and Therapy, 44,* 147–157.

White, R. W. (1959). Motivation reconsidered: The concept of competence. *Psychological Review, 66,* 297–333.

White, S. M. (2006). Talking genes. *Advances in Speech Language Pathology, 8,* 2–6.

Whiting, E., Chenery, H. J., Chalk, J., Darnell, R., & Copland, D. A. (2007). The explicit learning of new names for known objects is improved by dexamphetamine. *Brain and Language, 104,* 254–261.

Whitlock, J. L., Powers, J. L., & Eckenrode, J. (2006). The virtual cutting edge: The Internet and adolescent self-injury. *Developmental Psychology, 42,* 407–417.

Whitlock, J. R., Heynen, A. J., Shuler, M. G., & Bear, M. F. (2006). Learning induces long-term potentiation in the hippocampus. *Science, 313,* 1093–1097.

Whitman, D. S., van Rooy, D. L., & Viswesvaran, C. (2010). Satisfaction, citizenship behaviors, and performance in work units: A meta-analysis of collective construct relations. *Personnel Psychology, 63,* 41–81.

Whitman, T. L., Borkowski, J. G., Keogh, D. A., & Week, K. (2001). *Interwoven lives: Adolescent mothers and their children.* Mahwah, NJ: Erlbaum.

Whitney, P. (2001). Schemas, frames, and scripts in cognitive psychology. In N. J. Smelser & P. B. Baltes (Eds.), *International encyclopedia of the social and behavioral sciences* (Vol. 20, pp. 13522–13526). Amsterdam: Elsevier.

Whitworth, J. D., Crownover, B. K., & Nichols, W. (2007). Which nondrug alternatives can help with insomnia? *Journal of Family Practice, 56,* 836–838.

Whorf, B. L. (1956). *Language, thought, and reality.* Cambridge. MA: MIT Press & New York: Wiley.

Wible, C. G., Anderson, J., Shenton, M. E., Kricun, A., et al. (2001). Prefrontal cortex, negative symptoms, and schizophrenia: An MRI study. *Psychiatry Research, 108,* 65–78.

Wichers, M. C., Myin-Germeys, I., Jacobs, N., Kenis, G., et al. (2008). Susceptibility to depression expressed as alterations in cortisol day curve: A cross-twin, cross-trait study. *Biological Psychology, 79,* 80–90.

Wicherts, J. M., & Scholten, A. Z. (2010). Test anxiety and the validity of cognitive tests: A confirmatory factor analysis perspective and some empirical findings. *Intelligence, 38,* 169–178.

Wickens, C. D. (1989). Attention and skilled performance. In D. Holding (Ed.), *Human skills* (pp. 71–105). New York: Wiley.

Wickens, C. D. (1992). *Engineering psychology and human performance* (2nd ed.). New York: HarperCollins.

Wickens, C. D. (2002). Situation awareness and workload in aviation. *Current Directions in Psychological Science, 11,* 128–133.

Wickens, C. D., & Carswell, C. M. (2006). Information processing. In G. Salvendy (Ed.), *Handbook of human factors and ergonomics* (3rd ed., pp. 111–149). Hoboken, NJ: Wiley Interscience.

Wickens, C. D., Gordon-Becker, S. E., Liu, Y., & Lee, J. D. (2004). *Introduction to human factors engineering* (2nd ed.). Upper Saddle River, NJ: Prentice Hall.

Wickens, C. D., Stokes, A., Barnett, B., & Hyman, F. (1992). The effects of stress on pilot judgment in a MIDIS simulator. In O. Svenson & J. Maule (Eds.), *Time pressure and stress in human judgment and decision making* (pp. 271–292). New York: Plenum.

Wicker, B., Keysers, C., Plailly, J., Royet, J. P., et al. (2003). Both of us disgusted in My insula: The common neural basis of seeing and feeling disgust. *Neuron, 40,* 655–664.

Widiger, T. A. (2008). Personality disorders. In J. Hunsley & E. J. Mash (Eds.), *A guide to assessments that work* (pp. 413–435). New York: Oxford University Press.

Widiger, T. A., & Clark, L. A. (2000). Toward DSM-V and the classification of psychopathology. *Psychological Bulletin, 126,* 946–963.

Widiger, T. A., Livesley, W. J., & Clark, L. A. (2009). An integrative dimensional classification of personality disorder. *Psychological Assessment, 21,* 243–255.

Widiger, T. A., & Sanderson, C. J. (1995). Assessing personality disorders. In J. N. Butcher (Ed.), *Clinical personality assessment: Practical approaches* (pp. 380–394). New York: Oxford University Press.

Widiger, T. A., & Sankis, L. M. (2000). Adult psychopathology: Issues and controversies. *Annual Review of Psychology, 51,* 377–404.

Widiger, T. A., Simonsen, E., Sirovatka, P., & Reiger, D. A. (2006). *Dimensional models of personality disorders: Refining the research agenda for DSM-V.* Alexandria, VA: American Psychiatric Association.

Widom, C. S. (1989). The cycle of violence. *Science, 244,* 160–166.

Widom, C. S. (2000). Childhood victimization: Early adversity, later psychopathology. *National Insitute of Justice Journal, 19,* 2–9.
Widom, C. S., Czaja, S. J., & Dutton, M. A. (2008). Childhood victimization and lifetime revictimization. *Child Abuse and Neglect, 32,* 785–796.
Widom, C. S., Kahn, E. E., Kaplow, J. B., Sepulveda-Kozakowski, S., & Wilson, H. W. (2007). Child abuse and neglect: Potential derailment from normal developmental pathways. *NYS Psychologist, 19,* 2–6.
Wiederhold, B. K., & Wiederhold, M. D. (2005). *Virtual reality therapy for anxiety disorders: Advances in evaluation and treatment.* Washington, DC: American Psychological Association.
Wiens, S., Mezzacappa, E. S., & Katkin, E. S. (2000). Heartbeat detection and the experience of emotions. *Cognition and Emotion, 14,* 417–427.
Wiertelak, E. P., Maier, S. F., & Watkins, L. R. (1992). Cholecystokinin antianalgesia: Safety cues abolish morphine analgesia. *Science, 256,* 830–833.
Wigfield, A., & Eccles, J. S. (2000). Expectancy-value theory of achievement motivation. *Contemporary Educational Psychology, 25,* 68–81.
Wilcox, H. C., Grados, M., Samuels, J., Riddle, M. A., et al. (2008). The association between parental bonding and obsessive-compulsive disorder in offspring at high familial risk. *Journal of Affective Disorders, 111,* 31–39.
Wilcoxon, H. C., Dragoin, W. B., & Kral, P. A. (1971). Illness-induced aversions in rat and quail: Relative salience of visual and gustatory cues. *Science, 171,* 826–828.
Wilhelm, K., Mitchell, P. B., Niven, H., Finch, A., et al. (2006). Life events, first depression onset, and the serotonin transporter gene. *British Journal of Psychiatry, 188,* 210–215.
Wilkowski, B. M., & Robinson, M. D. (2008). The cognitive basis of trait anger and reactive aggression: An integrative analysis. *Personality and Social Psychology Review, 12,* 3–21.
Wilksch, S. M., & Wade, T. D. (2010). Risk factors for clinically significant importance of shape and weight in adolescent girls. *Journal of Abnormal Psychology, 119,* 206–215.
Willcox, D. C., Willcox, B. J., Hsueh, W.-C., & Suzuki, M. (2006). Genetic determinants of exceptional human longevity: Insights from the Okinawa Centenarian Study. *AGE, 28,* 313–332.
Willcox, D. C., Willcox, B. J., Rosenbaum, M., Sokolovsky, J., & Suzuki, M. (2009). Exceptional longevity and the quest for healthy aging: Insights from the Okinawa Centenarian Study. In J. Sokolovsky (Ed.), *The cultural context of aging: Worldwide perspectives* (3rd ed., pp. 505–532). Westport, CT: Praeger/Greenwood.
Willemsen, R., & Vanderlinden, J. (2008). Hypnotic approaches for alopecia areata. *International Journal of Clinical and Experimental Hypnosis, 56,* 318–333.
Willford, J. A., Leech, S. L., & Day, N. L. (2006). Moderate prenatal alcohol exposure and cognitive status of children at age 10. *Alcoholism: Clinical and Experimental Research, 30,* 1051–1059.
Williams, C. L., & Pleil, K. E. (2008). Toy story: Why do monkey and human males prefer trucks? *Hormones and Behavior, 54,* 355–358.
Williams, E., Thomas, K., Sidebotham, H., & Emond, A. (2008). Prevalence and characteristics of autistic spectrum disorders in the ALSPAC cohort. *Developmental Medicine and Child Neurology, 50,* 672–677.
Williams, G. V., & Goldman-Rakic, P. S. (1995). Modulation of memory fields by dopamine D1 receptors in prefrontal cortex. *Nature, 376,* 572–575.
Williams, J. (2008). Working toward a neurobiological account of ADHD: Commentary on Gail Tripp and Jeff Wickens' dopamine transfer deficit. *Journal of Child Psychology and Psychiatry, 49,* 705–711.
Williams, J. H. G., Waiter, G. D., Gilchrist, A., Perrett, D. I., et al. (2006). Neural mechanisms of imitation and "mirror neuron" functioning in autistic spectrum disorder. *Neuropsychologica, 44,* 610–621.
Williams, K. D., & Sommer, K. L. (1997). Social ostracism by coworkers: Does rejection lead to loafing or compensation? *Personality and Social Psychology Bulletin, 23,* 693–706.
Williams, L. E., Bargh, J. A., Nocera, C. C., & Gray, J. R. (2009). The unconscious regulation of emotion: Nonconscious reappraisal goals modulate emotional reactivity. *Emotion, 9,* 847–854.
Williams, L. M. (1994). What does it mean to forget child sexual abuse? A reply to Loftus, Garry, and Feldman (1994). *Journal of Consulting and Clinical Psychology, 62,* 1182–1186.
Williams, N. L., Reardon, J. M., Murray, K. T., & Cole, T. M. (2005). Anxiety disorders: A developmental vulnerability-stress perspective. In B. L. Hankin & J. R. Z. Abela (Eds.), *Development of psychopathology: A vulnerability-stress perspective* (pp. 289–327). Thousand Oaks, CA: Sage.
Williams, R. A. (2005). A short course in family therapy: Translating research into practice. *Family Journal: Counseling and Therapy for Couples and Families 13,* 188–194.
Williams, R. B. (2001). Hostility and heart disease: Williams et al. (1980). *Advances in Mind-Body Medicine, 17,* 52–55.
Williams, R. J., & Connolly, D. (2006). Does learning about the mathematics of gambling change gambling behavior? *Psychology of Addictive Behavior, 20,* 62–68.
Williams, T. J., Pepitone, M. E., Christensen, S. E., Cooke, B. M., et al. (2000). Finger-length ratios and sexual orientation. *Nature, 404,* 455–456.
Williams-Piehota, P., Pizarro, J., Schneider, T. R., Mowad, L., & Salovey, P. (2005). Matching health messages to monitor-blunter coping styles to motivate screening mammography. *Health Psychology, 24,* 58–67.
Willis, J., & Todorov, A. (2006). First impressions: Making up your mind after a 100-ms exposure to a face. *Psychological Science, 17,* 592–598.
Willis, S. L., & Schaie, K. W. (1999). Intellectual functioning in midlife. In S. L. Willis & J. D. Reid (Eds.), *Life in the middle: Psychological and social development in middle age* (pp. 233–247). San Diego, CA: Academic Press.
Wills, T. A., Sandy, J. M., Yaeger, A., & Shinar, O. (2001). Family risk factors and adolescent substance use: Moderation effects oft temperament dimension. *Developmental Psychology, 37,* 283–297.
Wilson, G. T., Wilfley, D. E., Agras, W. S., & Bryson, S. W. (2010). Psychological treatments of binge eating disorder. *Archives of General Psychiatry, 67,* 94–101.
Wilson, E. J., MacLeod, C., Matthews, A., & Rutherford, E. M. (2006). The causal role of interpretive bias in anxiety reactivity. *Journal of Abnormal Psychology, 115,* 103–111.
Wilson, G. T., Nathan, P. E., O'Leary, K. D., & Clark, L. A. (1996). *Abnormal psychology.* Boston: Allyn & Bacon.
Wilson, J. M., Straus, S. G., & McEvily, B. (2006). All in due time: The development of trust in computer-mediated and face-to-face teams. *Organizational Behavior and Human Decision Processes, 99,* 16–33.
Wilson, K., & French, C. C. (2006). The relationship between susceptibility to false memories, dissociativity, and paranormal belief and experience. *Personality and Individual Differences, 41,* 1493–1502.
Wilson, R. S., Beck, T. L., Bienias, J. L., & Bennett, D. A. (2007). Terminal cognitive decline. *Psychosomatic Medicine, 69,* 131–137. Epub 2007 Feb 7.
Wilson, R. S., Scherr, P. A., Schneider, J. A., Tang, Y., & Bennett, D. A. (2007). Relation of cognitive activity to risk of developing Alzheimer disease. *Neurology, 69,* 1911–1920.
Wilson, T. D., & Gilbert, D. T. (2005). Affective forecasting: Knowing what to want. *Current Directions in Psychological Science, 14,* 131–134.
Wilson, W. J. (1997). *When work disappears: The world of the new urban poor.* New York: Vintage Books.
Wimo, A., Winblad, B., & Jönsson, L. (2010). The worldwide societal costs of dementia: Estimates for 2009. *Alzheimer's Dementia, 6,* 98–103.
Winawer, J., Witthoft, N., Frank, M. C., Wu, L., et al. (2007). Russian blues reveal effects of language on color discrimination. *Proceedings of the National Academy of Sciences, 104,* 7780–7785.
Winer, G. A., Cottrell, J. E., Gregg, V., Fournier, J. S., & Bica, L. A. (2002). Fundamentally misunderstanding visual perception: Adults' belief in visual emissions. *American Psychologist, 57,* 417–424.
Winkelmayer, W. C., Stampfer, M. J., Willett, W. C., & Curhan, G. C. (2005). Habitual caffeine intake and the risk of hypertension in women. *Journal of the American Medical Association, 294,* 2330–2335.
Winkielman, P., & Berridge, K. C. (2004). Unconscious emotion. *Current Directions in Psychological Science, 13,* 120–123.
Winkielman, P., & Cacioppo J. T. (2004). Mind at ease puts a smile on the face: Psychophysiological evidence that processing facilitation elicits positive affect. *Journal of Personality and Social Psychology, 81,* 989–1000.
Winn, P. (1995). The lateral hypothalamus and motivated behavior: An old syndrome reassessed and a new perspective gained. *Current Directions in Psychological Science, 4,* 182–187.
Winner, E. (2000). Giftedness: Current theory and research. *Current Directions in Psychological Science, 9,* 153–156.
Winson, J. (1990, November). The meaning of dreams. *Scientific American,* pp. 86–96.
Winston, A., Been, H., & Serby, M. (2005). Psychotherapy and psychopharmacology: Different universes or an integrated future? *Journal of Psychotherapy Integration, 15,* 213–223.
Winter, D. G. (1996). *Personality: Analysis and interpretation of lives.* New York: McGraw-Hill.
Winter, W. C, Hammond, W. R., Green, N. H., Zhang, Z., & Bliwise, D. L. (2009). Measuring circadian advantage in major league baseball: A 10-year retrospective study. *International Journal of Sports Physiology and Performance, 4,* 394–401.
Winterer, G. (2006). Cortical microcircuits in schizophrenia: The dopamine hypothesis revisited. *Pharmacopsychiatry, 39,* S68–S71.
Wintersteen, M. B., Mensinger, J. L., & Diamond, G. S. (2005). Do gender and racial differences between patient and therapist affect therapeutic alliance and treatment retention in adolescents? *Professional Psychology: Research and Practice, 36,* 400–408.
Wise, R. A., & Rompre, P. P. (1989). Brain dopamine and reward. *Annual Review of Psychology, 40,* 191–225.
Wiseman, R., West, D., & Stemman, R. (1996). Psychic crime detectives: A new test for measuring their successes and failures. *Skeptical Inquirer, 21,* 38–58.
Wismer Fries, A. B., Shirtcliff, E. A., & Pollak, S. D. (2008). Neuroendocrine dysregulation following early social deprivation in children. *Developmental Psychobiology, 50,* 588–599.
Witt, C., Brinkhaus, B., Jena, S., Linde, K., et al. (2005). Acupuncture in patients with osteoarthritis of the knee: A randomised trial. *Lancet, 366,* 136–143.
Witt, M., & Wozniak, W.(2006). Structure and function of the vomeronasal organ. *Advances in Otorhinolaryngology, 63,* 70–83.
Wittchen, H. U., & Hoyer, J. (2001). Generalized anxiety disorder: Nature and course. *Journal of Clinical Psychiatry, 62,* 15–19.
Wixted, J. T. (2004). The psychology and neuroscience of forgetting. *Annual Review of Psychology, 55,* 235–269.
Wixted, J. T. (2005). A theory about why we forget what we once knew. *Current Directions in Psychological Science, 14,* 6–9.
Wohlfarth, T., Storosum, J. G., Elferink, A. J. A., van Zweiten, B. J., et al. (2004). Response to tricyclic antidepressants: Independent of gender? *American Journal of Psychiatry, 161,* 370–372.
Wojcieszak, M., & Price, V. (2010). Bridging the divide or intensifying the conflict? How disagreement affects strong predilections about sexual minorities. *Political Psychology, 31,* 315–339. doi:10.1111/j.1467-9221.2009.00753.x
Woldt, A. L., & Toman, S. M. (Eds.). (2005). *Gestalt therapy: History, theory, and practice.* Thousand Oaks, CA: Sage.
Wolfe, J. M. (1998). What can 1 million trials tell us about visual search? *Psychological Science, 9,* 33–39.
Wolfe, J. M., Alvarez, G. A., & Horowitz, T. S. (2000). Attention is fast but volition is slow. *Nature, 406,* 691.
Wolfe, J. M., Horowitz, T. S., Van Wert, M. J., Kenner, N. M., et al. (2007). Low target prevalence is a stubborn source of errors in visual search tasks. *Journal of Experimental Psychology, 136,* 623–638.
Wolk, D. A., Dunfee, K. L., Dickerson, B. C., Aizenstein, H. J., & Dekosky, S. T. (2010). A medial temporal lobe division of labor: Insights from memory in aging and early Alzheimer disease. *Hippocampus.* Epub 2010 Mar 15.

Wollert, R. (2007). Poor diagnostic reliability, the Null-Bayes logic model, and their implications for sexually violent predator evaluations. *Psychology, Public Policy, and Law, 13,* 167–213.

Wolman, C., van den Broek, P., & Lorch, R. F., Jr. (1997). Effects of causal structure and delayed story recall by children with mild mental retardation, children with learning disabilities, and children without disabilities. *Journal of Special Education, 30,* 439–455.

Wolpaw, J. R., & Chen, X. Y. (2006). The cerebellum in maintenance of a motor skill: A hierarchy of brain and spinal cord plasticity underlies H-reflex conditioning. *Learning and Memory, 13,* 208–215.

Wolpe, J. (1958). *Psychotherapy by reciprocal inhibition.* Palo Alto, CA: Stanford University Press.

Wolpert, I. (1924). Die Simultanagnosie: Störung der Gesamtauffassung [Simultanagnosia: Disturbance of overall perception]. *Archiv für Psychiatrie und Nervenkrankheiten/ Zeitschrift für die gesamte Neurologie und Psychiatrie, 93,* 397–413.

Wolraich, M. L., Wibbelsman, C. J., Brown, T. E., Evans, S. W., et al. (2005). Attention-deficit/ hyperactivity disorder among adolescents: A review of the diagnosis, treatment, and clinical implications. *Pediatrics, 115,* 1734–1746.

Wong, C. A., Eccles, J. S., & Sameroff, A. (2003). The influence of ethnic discrimination and ethnic identification on African American adolescents' school and socioemotional adjustment. *Journal of Personality, 71,* 1197–1232.

Wong, K. F. E., & Kwong, J. Y. Y. (2005). Between-individual comparisons in performance evaluation: A perspective from prospect theory. *Journal of Applied Psychology, 90,* 284–294.

Wong, Q. J. J., & Moulds, M. L. (2009). Impact of rumination versus distraction on anxiety and maladaptive self-beliefs in socially anxious individuals. *Behaviour Research and Therapy, 47,* 861–867.

Wood, D. M., Nicolaou, M., & Dargan, P. I. (2009). Epidemiology of recreational drug toxicity in a nightclub environment. *Substance Use and Misuse, 44,* 1495–1502.

Wood, J. (2006). Effect of anxiety reduction on children's school performance and social adjustment. *Developmental Psychology, 42,* 345–349.

Wood, J. M., Tyrrell, R. A., & Carberry, T. P. (2005). Limitations in drivers' ability to recognize pedestrians at night. *Human Factors, 47,* 644–653.

Wood, N. D., Crane, D. R., Shaalje, G. B., & Law, D. D. (2005). What works for whom: A meta-analytic review of marital and couples therapy in reference to marital distress. *American Journal of Family Therapy, 33,* 273–287.

Wood, W., & Eagly, A. H. (2002). A cross-cultural analysis of the behavior of women and men: Implications for the origins of sex differences. *Psychological Bulletin, 128,* 699–727.

Wood, W., Wong, F. Y., & Chachere, G. (1991). Effects of media violence on viewers' aggression in unconstrained social interaction. *Psychological Bulletin, 109,* 371–383.

Woodcock, R. W., McGrew, K. S., & Mather, N. (2001). *Woodcock-Johnson III Tests of Cognitive Abilities.* Itasca, IL: Riverside.

Woodhead, M. (1988). When psychology informs public policy: The case of early childhood intervention. *American Psychologist, 43,* 443–454.

Woods, S. C., Schwartz, M. W., Baskin, D. G., & Seeley, R. J. (2000). Food intake and the regulation of body weight. *Annual Review of Psychology, 51,* 255–277.

Woods, S. C.; Seeley, R. J.; Porte, D., Jr.; & Schwartz, M. W. (1998). Signals that regulate food intake and energy homeostasis. *Science, 280,* 1378–1383.

Woodward, A. L. (2009). Infants' grasp of others' intentions. *Current Directions in Psychological Science, 18,* 53–57.

Woodward, T. S., Moritz, S., Cuttler, C., & Whitman, J. C. (2006). The contribution of a cognitive bias against disconfirmatory evidence (BADE) to delusions in schizophrenia. *Journal of Clinical and Experimental Neuropsychology, 28,* 605–617.

Woolley, J. D. (1997). Thinking about fantasy: Are children fundamentally different thinkers and believers from adults? *Child Development, 68,* 991–1011.

Workman, M. (2005). Expert decision support system use, disuse, and misuse: A study using the theory of planned behavior. *Computers in Human Behavior, 21,* 211–231.

World Health Organization. (2003). *AIDS epidemic update.* Geneva, Switzerland: Author.

World Health Organization. (2008). *World health report: Primary health care now more than ever.* Geneva, Switzerland: Author.

World Health Organization Mental Health Survey Consortium. (2004). Prevalence, severity, and unmet need for treatment of mental disorders in the World Health Organization World Mental Health Surveys. *Journal of the American Medical Association, 291,* 2581–2590.

Worthington, R. L., Navarro, R. L., Savoy, H. B., & Hampton, D. (2008). Development, reliability, and validity of the Measure of Sexual Identity Exploration and Commitment (MOSIEC). *Developmental Psychology, 44,* 22–33.

Wright, B. A., & Fitzgerald, M. B. (2001). Different patterns of human discrimination learning for two interaural cues to sound location. *Proceedings of the National Academy of Sciences, 98,* 12307–12312.

Wright, B. A., & Zecker, S. G. (2004). Learning problems, delayed development, and puberty. *Proceedings of the National Academy of Sciences, 101,* 9942–9946.

Wright, D. B. (1993). Recall of the Hillsborough disaster over time: Systematic biases of "flashbulb" memories. *Applied Cognitive Psychology, 7,* 129–138.

Wright, D. B., Memon, A., Skagerberg, E. M., & Gabber, F. (2009). When eyewitnesses talk. *Current Directions in Psychological Science, 18,* 174–178.

Wright, E. F., Voyer, D., Wright, R. D., & Roney, C. (1995). Supporting audiences and performance under pressure: The home-ice disadvantage in hockey championships. *Journal of Sport Behavior, 18,* 21–28.

Wu, C., Cui, B., He, L., Chen, L., & Mobley, W. C. (2009). The coming of age of axonal neurotrophin signaling endosomes. *Journal of Proteomics, 72,* 46–55. Epub 2008 Nov 6.

Wu, J. C., Kelsoe, J. R., Schachat, C., Bunney, B. G., et al. (2009). Rapid and sustained antidepressant response with sleep deprivation and chronotherapy in bipolar disorder. *Biological Psychiatry, 66,* 298–301.

Wujcik, D. M. (2008). Are you part of the sandwich generation? *ONS Connect, 23,* 7.

Wupperman, P., & Neumann, C. S. (2006). Depressive symptoms as a function of sex role, rumination, and neuroticism. *Personality and Individual Differences, 40,* 189–201.

Wurtman, R. J., & Wurtman, J. J. (1995). Brain serotonin, carbohydrate craving, obesity, and depression. *Obesity Research, 3*(Suppl. 4), 477S–480S.

Wyatt, T. D. (2009). Fifty years of pheromones. *Nature, 457,* 262–263.

Wynne, C. L. (2004). *Do animals think?* Princeton, NJ: Princeton University Press.

Xiao, Y., Seagull, F. J., Mackenzie, C. F., Klein, K. J., & Ziegert, J. (2008). Adaptation of team communication patterns: Exploring the effects of leadership at a distance. In S. Weisband (Ed.), *Leadership at a distance: Research in technologically supported work* (pp. 71–96). Mahwah, NJ: Erlbaum.

Xie, P., Kranzler, H. R., Poling, J., Stein, M. B., et al. (2009). Interactive effect of stressful life events and the serotonin transporter 5-HTTLPR genotype on posttraumatic stress disorder diagnosis in 2 independent populations. *Archives of General Psychiatry, 66,* 1201–1209.

Xie, Y. F., Huo, F. Q., & Tang, J. S. (2009). Cerebral cortex modulation of pain. *Acta Pharmacologica Sinica, 30,* 31–41.

Xu, J., Gannon, P. J., Emmorey, K., Smith, J. F., & Braun, A. R. (2009). Symbolic gestures and spoken language are processed by a common neural system. *Proceedings of the National Academy of Sciences, 106,* 20664–20669.

Xu, L., Wu, A. S., & Yue, Y. (2009). The incidence of intraoperative awareness during general anesthesia in China: A multicenter observational study. *Acta Anaesthesioligica Scandinavica, 53,* 873–882.

Xu, J., & Roberts, R. E. (2010). The power of positive emotions: It's a matter of life or death—subjective well-being and longevity over 28 years in a general population. *Health Psychology, 29,* 9–19.

Xue, Y., Leventhal, T., Brooks-Gunn, J., & Earls, F. J. (2005). Neighborhood residence and mental health problems of 5- to 11-year-olds. *Archives of General Psychiatry, 62,* 554–563.

Yaffe, K., Barnes, D., Nevitt, M., Lui, L.-Y., & Covinsky, K. (2001). A prospective study of physical activity and cognitive decline in elderly women. *Archives of Internal Medicine, 161,* 1703–1708.

Yaffe, K., Fiocco, A. J., Lindquist, K., Vittinghoff, E., et al. (2009). Predictors of maintaining cognitive function in older adults: The Health ABC Study. *Neurology, 72,* 2029–2035.

Yahr, P., & Jacobsen, C. H. (1994). Hypothalamic knife cuts that disrupt mating in male gerbils sever efferents and forebrain afferents of the sexually dimorphic area. *Behavioral Neuroscience, 108,* 735–742.

Yakimovich, D., & Saltz, E. (1971). Helping behavior: The cry for help. *Psychonomic Science, 23,* 427–428.

Yalom, I. D. (1980). *Existential psychotherapy.* New York: Basic Books.

Yalom, I. D. (2002). *The gift of therapy.* New York: HarperCollins.

Yalom, I. D. (2005). *The theory and practice of group psychotherapy* (5th ed.). New York: Basic Books.

Yamagata, S., Suzuki, A., Ando, J., Ono, Y., et al. (2006). Is the genetic structure of human personality universal? A cross-cultural twin study from North America, Europe, and Asia. *Journal of Personality and Social Psychology, 90,* 987–998.

Yamaguchi, S., Isejima, H., Matsuo, T., Okura, R., et al. (2003). Synchronization of cellular clocks in the suprachiasmatic nucleus. *Science, 302,* 1408–1412.

Yamamoto, R., Iseki, E., Higashi, S., Murayama, N., et al. (2009). Neuropathological investigation of regions responsible for semantic aphasia in frontotemporal lobar degeneration. *Dementia and Geriatric Cognitive Disorders, 27,* 214–223.

Yan, T., & Tourangeau, R. (2007). Fast times and easy questions: The effects of age, experience, and question complexity on Web survey response times. *Applied Cognitive Psychology, 22,* 51–68.

Yan, Z., Chi, Y., Wang, P., Cheng, J., et al. (1992). Studies on the luminescence of channels in rats and its law of changes with "syndromes" and treatment of acupuncture and moxibustion. *Journal of Traditional Chinese Medicine, 12,* 283–287.

Yang, C. M., Spielman, A. J., & Glovinsky, P. (2006). Nonpharmacologic strategies in the management of insomnia. *Psychiatric Clinics of North America, 29,* 895–919.

Yang, Y., Raine, A., Narr, K. L., Colletti, P., & Toga, A. W. (2009). Localization of deformations within the amygdala in individuals with psychopathy. *Archives of General Psychiatry, 66,* 986–994.

Yantis, S. (1993). Stimulus-driven attentional capture. *Current Directions in Psychological Science, 2,* 156–161.

Yarkoni, T., Braver, T. S., Gray, J. R., & Green, L. (2005). Prefrontal brain activity predicts temporally extended decision making. *Journal of the Experimental Analysis of Behavior, 84,* 537–554.

Yarlagadda, A., Helvink, B., Chou, C., Gladieux, K., et al. (2008). Glutamic acid decarboxylase (GAD) antibodies in tardive dyskinesia (TD) as compared to patients with schizophrenia without TD and normal controls. *Schizophrenia Research, 105,* 287–288.

Yela, C., & Sangrador, J. L. (2001). Perception of physical attractiveness throughout loving relationships. *Current Research in Social Psychology, 6,* 57–75.

Yeomans, M. R., & Mobini, S. (2006). Hunger alters the expression of acquired hedonic but not sensory qualities of food-paired odors in humans. *Journal of Experimental Psychology: Animal Behavior Processes, 32,* 460–466.

Yerkes, R. M. (Ed.). (1921). Psychological examining in the United States Army. *Memoirs of the National Academy of Sciences, Vol. 15.* Washington, DC: U.S. Government Printing Office.

Yesavage, J. A., Leirer, V. O., Denari, M., & Hollister, L. E. (1985). Carry-over effects of marijuana intoxication on aircraft pilot performance: A preliminary report. *American Journal of Psychiatry, 142,* 1325–1329.

Yeshurun, Y., & Sobel, N. (2010). An odor is not worth a thousand words: From multidimensional odors to unidimensional odor objects. *Annual Review of Psychology, 61,* 219–241.

Yeung, L. M., Linver, M. R., & Brooks-Gunn, J. (2002). How money matters for young children's development: Parental investment and family processes. *Child Development, 73,* 1861–1879.

Yiin, Y.-M., Ackroff, K., & Sclafani, A. (2004). Flavor preferences conditioned by intragastric nutrient infusions in food restricted and unrestricted rats. *Physiology and Behavior, 84,* 217–231.

Yip, T., & Fuligni, A. J. (2002). Daily variation in ethnic identity, ethnic behaviors, and psychological well-being among American adolescents of Chinese descent. *Child Development, 73,* 1557–1572.

Yip, T., Gee, G. C., & Takeuchi, D. T. (2008). Racial discrimination and psychological distress: The impact of ethnic identity and age among immigrant and United States–born Asian adults. *Developmental Psychology, 44,* 787–800.

Yonas, A., Arterberry, M. E., & Granrud, C. D. (1987). Space perception in infancy. In R. Vasta (Ed.), *Annals of child development* (Vol. 4, pp. 1–34). Greenwich, CT: JAI Press.

Yongxia, R. (2006). Acupuncture treatment of Jacksonian epilepsy: A report of 98 cases. *Journal of Traditional Chinese Medicine, 26,* 177–178.

Yoo, S.-S., Hu, P. T., Gujar, N., Jolesz, F. A., & Walker, M. P. (2007). A deficit in the ability to form new human memories without sleep. *Nature Neuroscience, 10,* 385–392.

York, J. L., & Welte, J. W. (1994). Gender comparisons of alcohol consumption in alcoholic and nonalcoholic populations. *Journal of Studies on Alcohol, 55,* 743–750.

Yoshimasu, K., Washio, M., Tokunaga, S., Tanaka, K., et al. (2002). Relation between Type A behavior pattern and the extent of coronary atherosclerosis in Japanese women. *International Journal of Behavioral Medicine, 9,* 77–93.

Youm, Y., & Laumann, E. O. (2002). Social network effects on the transmission of sexually transmitted diseases. *Sexually Transmitted Diseases, 29,* 689–697.

Young, K. (2009). Internet addiction: Diagnosis and treatment considerations. *Journal of Contemporary Psychotherapy, 39,* 241–246.

Young, K. A., Bonkale, W. L., Holcomb, L. A., Hicks, P. B., & German, D. C. (2008). Major depression, 5-HTTLPR genotype, suicide, and antidepressant influences on thalamic volume. *British Journal of Psychiatry, 192,* 285–289.

Young, M. (1971). Age and sex differences in problem solving. *Journal of Gerontology, 26,* 331–336.

Young, M. S., Turner, J., Denny, G., & Young, M. (2004). Examining external and internal poverty as antecedents of teen pregnancy *American Journal of Health Behavior, 28,* 361–373.

Younkin, S. G. (2001). Amyloid beta vaccination: Reduced plaques and improved cognition. *Nature Medicine, 7,* 18–19.

Yousif, Y., & Korte, C. (1995). Urbanization, culture, and helpfulness: Cross-cultural studies in England and the Sudan. *Journal of Cross-Cultural Psychology, 26,* 474–489.

Yovel, I., & Mineka, S. (2005). Emotion-congruent attentional biases: The perspective of hierarchical models of emotional disorders. *Personality and Individual Differences, 38,* 785–795.

Yuan, J., Kerr, D., Park, J., Liu, X. H., & McDonough, S. (2008). Treatment regimens of acupuncture for low back pain: A systematic review. *Complementary Therapies in Medicine, 16,* 295–304.

Yücel, M., Solowij, N., Respondek, C., Whittle, S., et al. (2008). Regional brain abnormalities associated with long-term heavy cannabis use. *Archives of General Psychiatry, 65,* 694–701.

Yufik, A. (2005). Revisiting the *Tarasoff* decision: Risk assessment and liability in clinical and forensic practice. *American Journal of Forensic Psychology, 23*(4), 5–21.

Yukl, G., & Van Fleet, D. D. (1992). Theory and research on leadership in organizations. In M. D. Dunnette & L. M. Hough (Eds.), *Handbook of industrial and organizational psychology* (2nd ed., Vol. 3, pp. 147–198). Palo Alto, CA: Consulting Psychologists Press.

Yun, S., Faraj, S., & Sims, H. P. (2005). Contingent leadership and effectiveness of trauma resuscitation teams. *Journal of Applied Psychology, 90,* 1288–1296.

Zaccarco, S. J. (2007). Trait-based perspectives of leadership. *American Psychologist, 62,* 6–16.

Zaccaro, S. J., Heinen, B., & Shuffler, M. (2009). Team leadership and team effectiveness. In E. Salas, G. F. Goodwin, & C. S. Burke (Eds.), *Team effectiveness in complex organizations: Cross-disciplinary perspectives and approaches* (pp. 83–111). New York: Routledge.

Zadnik, K. (2001). Association between night lights and myopia: True blue or a red herring? *Archives of Ophthalmology, 119,* 146.

Zadra, A., Desjardins, S., & Marcotte, E. (2006). Evolutionary function of dreams: A test of the threat simulation theory in recurrent dreams. *Consciousness and Cognition, 15,* 450–463.

Zahrani, S. S., & Kaplowitz, S. A. (1993). Attributional biases in individualistic and collectivist cultures: A comparison of Americans with Saudis. *Social Psychology Quarterly, 56,* 223–233.

Zajonc, R. B. (1965). Social facilitation. *Science, 149,* 269–274.

Zajonc, R. B. (1998). Emotions. In D. T. Gilbert, S. T. Fiske, & G. Lindzey (Eds.), *Handbook of social psychology* (4th ed., Vol. 1, pp. 591–634). New York: McGraw-Hill.

Zakhari, S. (2006). Overview: How is alcohol metabolized by the body? *Alcohol Research and Health, 29,* 245–254.

Zakriski, A. L., Wright, J. C., & Underwood, M. K. (2005). Gender similarities and differences in children's social behavior: Finding personality in contextualized patterns of adaptation. *Journal of Personality and Social Psychology, 88,* 844–855.

Zalta, A. K., & Keel, P. K. (2006). Peer influence on bulimic symptoms in college students. *Journal of Abnormal Psychology, 115,* 185–189.

Zambelis, T., Paparrigopoulos, T., & Soldatos, C. R. (2002). REM sleep behaviour disorder associated with a neurinoma of the left pontocerebral angle. *Journal of Neurology, Neurosurgery, and Psychiatry, 72,* 821–822.

Zammit, G. K. (2007). The prevalence, morbidities, and treatments of insomnia. *CNS and Neurological Disorders—Drug Targets, 6,* 3–16.

Zammit, S., Allebeck, P., Andreasson, S., Lundberg, I., & Lewis, G. (2002). Self reported cannabis use as a risk factor for schizophrenia in Swedish conscripts of 1969: Historical cohort study. *British Medical Journal, 325,* 1199.

Zanelli, J., Reichenberg, A., Morgan, K., Fearon, P., et al. (2010). Specific and generalized neuropsychological deficits: A comparison of patients with various first-episode psychosis presentations. *American Journal of Psychiatry, 167,* 78–85.

Zang, Y. (2008). Undergraduate students' mental models of the Web as an information retrieval system. *Journal of the American Society for Information Science and Technology, 59,* 2087–2098.

Zaragoza, M. S., Payment, K. E., Ackil, J. K., Drivdahl, S. B., & Beck, M. (2001). Interviewing witnesses: Forced confabulation and confirmatory feedback increase false memories. *Psychological Science, 12,* 473–477.

Zarkadi, T., Wade, K. A., & Stewart, N. (2009). Creating fair lineups for suspects with distinctive features. *Psychological Science, 20,* 1448–1453.

Zatorre, R. J. (2003). Music and the brain. *Annals of the New York Academy of Sciences, 999,* 4–14.

Zeanah, C. H., Egger, H. L., Smyke, A. T., Nelson, C. A., et al. (2009). Institutional rearing and psychiatric disorders in Romanian preschool children. *American Journal of Psychiatry, 166,* 777–785.

Zeanah, C. H., Smyke, A. T., Koga, S. F., & Carlson, E. (2005). Attachment in institutionalized and community children in Romania. *Child Development, 76,* 1015–1028.

Zebrowitz, L., White, B., & Wieneke, K. (2008). Mere exposure and racial prejudice: Exposure to other-race faces increases liking for strangers of that race. *Social Cognition, 26,* 259–275.

Zeki, S. (1992). The visual image in mind and brain. *Scientific American, 267,* 68–76.

Zeldow, P. B. (2009). In defense of clinical judgment, credentialed clinicians, and reflective practice. *Psychotherapy: Theory, Research, Practice, Training, 46,* 1–10.

Zelenski, J. M., & Larsen, R. J. (1999). Susceptibility to affect: A comparison of three taxonomies. *Journal of Personality, 67,* 761–791.

Zell, E., & Alicke, M. D. (2009). Self-evaluative effects of temporal and social comparison. *Journal of Experimental Social Psychology, 45,* 223–227.

Zeman, A. (2001). Consciousness. *Brain, 124,* 1263–1289.

Zeman, A., Britton, T., Douglas, N., Hansen, A., et al. (2004). Narcolepsy and excessive daytime sleepiness. *British Medical Journal, 329,* 724–728.

Zenderland, L. (1998). Measuring minds: Henry Herbert Goddard and the origins of American intelligence testing. New York: Cambridge University Press.

Zhang, J.-P., Lencz, T., & Malhotra, A. K. (2010). D2 receptor genetic variation and clinical response to antipsychotic drug treatment: A meta-analysis. *American Journal of Psychiatry, 167,* 763–772.

Zhang, Y., Hoon, M. A., Chandrashekar, J., Mueller, K. L., et al. (2003). Coding of sweet, bitter, and umami tastes: Different receptor cells sharing similar signaling pathways. *Cell, 112,* 293–301.

Zhang, Y., Liang, J. M., Qin, W., Liu, P., et al. (2009). Comparison of visual cortical activations induced by electro-acupuncture at vision and non-vision-related acupoints. *Neuroscience Letters, 458,* 6–10.

Zhang, Y., Proenca, R., Maffei, M., Barone, M., et al. (1994). Positional cloning of the mouse obese gene and its human homologue. *Nature, 372,* 425–432.

Zhang, Y., Qin, W., Liu, P., Tian, J., et al. (2009). An fMRI study of acupuncture using independent component analysis. *Neuroscience Letter, 449,* 6–9.

Zhao, G., Ford, E. S., Dhingra, S., Li, C., et al. (2009). Depression and anxiety among U.S. adults: Associations with body mass index. *International Journal of Obesity, 33,* 257–266.

Zhao, H., & Seibert, S. E. (2006). The Big Five personality dimensions and entrepreneurial status: A meta-analytical review. *Journal of Applied Psychology, 91,* 259–271.

Zhao, M., Momma, S., Delfani, K., Carlen, M., et al. (2003). Evidence for neurogenesis in the adult mammalian substantia nigra. *Proceedings of the National Academy of Sciences, 100,* 7925–7930.

Zheng, H., Lenard, N. R., Shin, A. C., & Berthoud, H.-R. (2009). Appetite control and energy balance regulation in the modern world: Reward-driven brain overrides repletion signals. *International Journal of Obesity, 33,* S8–S13.

Zhong, C.-B., Bohns, V. K., & Gino, F. (2010). Good lamps are the best police: Darkness increases dishonesty and self-interested behavior. *Psychological Science, 21,* 311–314.

Zhong, C.-B., Loewenstein, J., & Murnighan, J. K. (2007). Speaking the same language: The cooperative effects of labeling in the prisoner's dilemma. *Journal of Conflict Resolution, 51,* 431–456.

Zhou, J.-N., Hofman, M. A., Gooren, L. J. G., & Swaab, D. F. (1995). A sex difference in the human brain and its relation to transsexuality. *Nature, 378,* 68–70.

Zhou, Q., Eisenberg, N., Wang, Y., & Reiser, M. (2004). Chinese children's effortful control and dispositional anger/frustration relations to parenting styles and children's social functioning. *Developmental Psychology, 40,* 352–366.

Zhou, W., & Chen, D. (2009). Encoding human sexual chemosensory cues in the orbitofrontal and fusiform cortices. *Journal of Neuroscience, 28,* 14416–14421.

Ziegler-Graham, K., Brookmeyer, R., Johnson, E., & Arrighi, H. M. (2008). Worldwide variation in the doubling time of Alzheimer's disease incidence rates. *Alzheimer's Dementia, 4,* 316–323.

Zigler, E., & Seitz, V. (1982). Social policy and intelligence. In R. J. Sternberg (Ed.), *Handbook of human intelligence* (pp. 586–641). Cambridge: Cambridge University Press.

Zigler, E. F., & Muenchow, S. (1992). *Head Start: The inside story of America's most successful educational experiment.* New York: Basic Books.

Zigurs, I. (2003). Leadership in virtual teams: Oxymoron or opportunity? *Organizational Dynamics, 31,* 339–351.

Zillmann, D. (1988). Cognition-excitation interdependencies in aggressive behavior. *Aggressive Behavior, 14,* 51–64.

Zillmann, D. (1998). *Connections between sexuality and aggression* (2nd ed.). Mahwah, NJ: Erlbaum.

Zillmann, D. (2003). Theory of affective dynamics: Emotions and moods. In J. Bryant & D. Roskos-Ewoldsen (Eds.), *Communication and emotion: Essays in honor of Dolf Zillmann* (pp. 533–567). Mahwah, NJ: Erlbaum.

Zillmann, D., Katcher, A. H., & Milavsky, B. (1972). Excitation transfer from physical exercise to subsequent aggressive behavior. *Journal of Experimental Social Psychology, 8,* 247–259.

Zimbardo, P. G. (1973). The psychological power and pathology of imprisonment. In E. Aronson & R. Helmreich (Eds.), *Social psychology.* New York: Van Nostrand.

Zimbardo, P. G. (2008). *The Lucifer effect.* New York: Random House.

Zimmerman, B. J., & Schunk, D. H. (2003). Albert Bandura: The scholar and his contributions to educational psychology. In B. J. Zimmerman (Ed.), *Educational psychology: A century of contributions* (pp. 431–457). Mahwah, NJ: Erlbaum.

Zimmerman, F. J., Gilkerson, J., Richards, J. A., Christakis, D. A., et al. (2009). Teaching by listening: The importance of adult-child conversations to language development. *Pediatrics, 124,* 342–349.

Zimmerman, M. A. (1990). Toward a theory of learned hopefulness: A structural model analysis of participation and empowerment. *Journal of Research in Personality, 24,* 71–86.

Zimmerman, M. E., Pan, J. W., Hetherington, H. P., Katz, M. J., et al. (2008). Hippocampal neurochemistry, neuromorphometry, and verbal memory in nondemented older adults. *Neurology, 70,* 1594–1600. Epub 2008 Mar 26.

Zimmerman, M., McDermut, W., & Mattia, J. I. (2000). Frequency of anxiety disorders in psychiatric outpatients with major depressive disorder. *American Journal of Psychiatry, 157,* 1337–1340.

Zimmerman, M., Posternak, M. A., Attiullah, N., Freidman, M., et al. (2005). Why isn't bupropion the most frequently prescribed antidepressant? *Journal of Clinical Psychiatry, 66,* 603–610.

Zinbarg, R. E., & Griffith, J. W. (2008). Behavior therapy. In J. L. Lebow (Ed.), *Twenty-first-century psychotherapies: Contemporary approaches to theory and practice* (pp. 8–42). Hoboken, NJ: Wiley.

Zinbarg, R. E., & Mineka, S. (1991). Animal models of psychopathology: II. Simple phobia. *Behavior Therapist, 14,* 61–65.

Zoellner, L. A., Foa, E. B., Brigidi, B. D., & Przeworski, A. (2000). Are trauma victims susceptible to "false memories"? *Journal of Abnormal Psychology, 109,* 517–524.

Zoellner, T., & Maercker, A. (2006). Posttraumatic growth in clinical psychology: A critical review and introduction of a two component model. *Clinical Psychology Review, 26,* 626–653.

Zola-Morgan, S. (1995). Localization of brain function: The legacy of Franz Joseph Gall (1758–1828). *Annual Review of Neuroscience, 18,* 359–383.

Zolotor, A. J., Theodore, A. D., Chang, J. J., Berkoff, M. C., & Runyan, D. K. (2008). Speak softly—and forget the stick: Corporal punishment and child physical abuse. *American Journal of Preventive Medicine, 35,* 364–369.

Zosuls, K. M., Ruble, D. N., Tamis-LeMonda, C. S., Shrout, P. E., et al. (2009). The acquisition of gender labels in infancy: Implications for gender-typed play. *Developmental Psychology, 45,* 688–701.

Zuberbühler, K. (2005). The phylogenetic roots of language. *Current Directions in Psychological Science, 14,* 126–130.

Zubieta, J.-K., Bueller, J. A., Jackson, L. R., Scott, D. J., et al. (2005). Placebo effects mediated by endogenous opioid activity on μ-opioid receptors. *Journal of Neuroscience, 25,* 7754–7762.

Zubin, J., & Spring, B. (1977). Vulnerability: A new view of schizophrenia. *Journal of Abnormal Psychology, 86,* 103–126.

Zucker, A. N., Ostrove, J. M., & Stewart, A. J. (2002). College-educated women's personality development in adulthood: Perceptions and age differences. *Psychology and Aging, 17,* 236–244.

Zuckerman, M. (1979). *Sensation seeking: Beyond the optimal level of arousal.* Hillsdale, NJ: Erlbaum.

Zuckerman, M. (1990). Some dubious premises in research and theory on racial differences. *American Psychologist, 45,* 1297–1303.

Zuckerman, M. (1996). "Conceptual clarification" or confusion in "The study of sensation seeking" by J. S. H. Jackson and M. Maraun. *Personality and Individual Differences, 21,* 111–114.

Zuroff, D. C., & Blatt, S. J. (2006). The therapeutic relationship in the brief treatment of depression: Contributions to clinical improvement and enhanced adaptive capacities. *Journal of Consulting and Clinical Psychology, 74,* 130–140.

Zuvekas, S. H., Vitiello, B., & Nordquist, G. S. (2006). Recent trends in stimulant medication use among U.S. children. *American Journal of Psychiatry, 163,* 579–585.

SUBJECT INDEX/GLOSSARY

*Key terms, which appear in **boldface**, are followed by their definitions.*

Entries that appear in blue refer to the Neuropsychology or Industrial/Organizational Psychology chapters or the online-only Appendices B and C.

Estrogens *Sex hormones that circulate in the bloodstream of both men and women; more estrogens circulate in women than in men,* 103, 430–431

ESTs. *See* Empirically supported therapies

Ethical guidelines, 57–58, 60

Ethical Principles of Psychologists and Code of Conduct (APA), 58, 680

Ethnic group differences
in alcohol use, 642
in IQ scores, 387–388
in job satisfaction, 788
in psychoactive drug responses, 686–687
in suicide rates, 622

Ethnic identity *The part of a person's identity associated with the racial, religious, or cultural group to which the person belongs,* 505

Evidence based practice *The selection of treatment methods based mainly on empirical evidence of their effectiveness,* 674

Evoked potential *A small, temporary change in EEG voltage in the brain that is caused by some stimulus,* 289

Evolution, 20

Evolutionary approach *An approach to psychology that emphasizes the inherited, adaptive aspects of behavior and mental processes,* 20
helping behavior and, 755–756
to psychology, 20

Excitation transfer theory *The theory that physiological arousal stemming from one situation is carried over to and enhances emotional experience in an independent situation,* 454, 749

Excitatory postsynaptic potential *A postsynaptic potential that depolarizes the neuronal membrane, making the cell more likely to fire an action potential,* 68–69

Exelon, 828

Exhaustion stage, stress response, 529

Existence needs, 442, 784

Existence, relatedness, growth (ERG) theory *A theory of motivation that focuses on employees' needs at the level of existence, relatedness, and growth,* 442, 784

Existential therapy, 659

Expectancies
alcohol consumption and, 357
in classroom, 390
cognitive person variables, 575
perception and, 186
reaction time, 288
Rotter's expectancy theory, 574

Expectancy theory *A theory of workplace motivation in which employees act in accordance with expected results and how much they value those results,* 574–575, 784–785

Expectations
drug effects and, 357–358
helplessness, 224
perception and, 224
placebo effect and, 44–45

Expected value *The total benefit to be expected if a decision were to be repeated several times,* 310

Experiment *A situation in which the researcher manipulates one variable and then observes the effect of that manipulation on another variable, while holding all other variables constant,* 42–43, 60
experimenter bias, 45
placebo effects, 44–45
random variables, 43–44

Experimental group *In an experiment, the group that receives the experimental treatment,* 42–43

Experimental neuropsychologists, 806

Experimental psychologists, 5

Experimenter bias *A confound that occurs when an experimenter unintentionally encourages participants to respond in a way that supports the experimenter's hypothesis,* 45

Experimenter expectancies, 45

Expert power, 739

Expert systems, 308

The Experts Speak (Cerf & Navasky), 307

Explicit memory *The process of intentionally trying to remember something,* 243–245

Exposure therapy *Behavior therapy methods in which clients remain in the presence of strong anxiety-provoking stimuli until the intensity of their emotional reactions decrease,* 664

Expressed emotion. *See* Emotional expression

Expressive aprosodia, 824–825

External attribution, 704

Externalizing disorders, 638–639

Extinction *The gradual disappearance of operant behavior due to elimination of rewards for that behavior,* 202
in behavior therapy, 663–664
in classical conditioning, 202–203, 207
in operant conditioning, 215–216

Extrapyramidal motor system, 447

Extraversion, 562, 566, 567

The Extreme Zone (television), 742

Extrinsic motivation, 436

Eye, 121–125

Eye convergence *A depth cue involving the rotation of the eyes to project the image of an object on each retina,* 172

Eye movement desensitization and reprocessing (EMDR), 31–32
case studies, 38
critical thinking and, 33–35

experiments, 42–43
inferential statistics, 55
observational methods, 37
placebo effect, 44–45
theories, 36

Eyewitness Evidence: A Guide for Law Enforcement (U.S. Department of Justice), 263–264

Eyewitness testimony, 12, 261–264

Eysenck's biological trait theory, 568–569

Facet approach, job satisfaction, 785–786

Facial expressions, 451, 456–459

Facial feedback hypothesis, 451

Facilitated communication (FC), 55–57

Factor analysis, 394

False alarm, 163

False Memory Syndrome Foundation, 270

Family studies
behavior genetics, 49–50
bipolar disorders and, 624
schizophrenia, 49

Family system, 669

Family therapy *Treatment of two or more individuals from the same family,* 669–670

Family ties, 755

Family-friendly work policies, 788

FC. *See* Facilitated communication

Feature detectors *Cells in the cortex that respond to a specific feature of an object,* 128, 178

Fechner's law, 166

Feedback
in employee training programs, 801
systems for, 73

Feeding Infants and Toddlers Study, 427

Feeling-of-knowing experience, 259

Fetal alcohol syndrome *A pattern of physical and mental defects found in babies born to women who abused alcohol during pregnancy,* 469

Fetal stage, 468

Fetus *The developing individual from the third month after conception until birth,* 468

FI reinforcement. *See* Fixed-interval reinforcement

Fight-or-flight syndrome (fight-flight reaction) *A physical reaction triggered by the sympathetic nervous system that prepares the body to fight or to run from a threatening situation,* 72, 104, 448, 528

Figure ground discrimination *The ability to organize a visual scene so that it contains meaningful figures set against a less relevant ground,* 167

Figure, in perceptual organization, 167, 176

Fissures, 87

Five-factor personality model (Big Five model) *A view based on factor-analytic studies suggesting the existence of five*

NAME INDEX

Entries that appear in blue refer to the Neuropsychology or Industrial/Organizational Psychology chapters or the online-only Appendices B and C.

A

AA. *see* Alcoholics Anonymous
Aaron, D. J., 432, 433
Aarts, H., 423, 785
Abbot-Shim, M., 389
Abbott, B. B., 535
Abbott, M. J., 664
Abbott, R. D., 511
AbdelMalik, P., 632
Abdollahi, A., 699
Abel, T., 346
Abela, J. R. Z., 536, 626
Abelson, J. L., 534
Aboitiz, F., 94
Abraham, W. C., 271
Abramowitz, J. S., 615, 617–618
Abrams, D., 700, 701, 715, 716, 762
Abrams, D. I., 365
Abrams, R. L., 161, 335
Abramson, L. Y., 626
Abrantes-Pais, F. de N., 440
Abreu, J. M., 608–609
Acerbi, A., 583
Achille, N. M., 451
Achiron, R., 93. 94
Acitelli, L. K., 724
Acker, H., 811
Acker, T., 811
Ackerman, B. P., 500
Ackerman, D., 116
Ackerman, J. P., 361, 469
Ackerman, P. L., 395, 402
Ackroff, K., 423
Acocella, J., 619
Acquas, E., 357
Adachi-Mejia, A. M., 425
Adair, J. C., 818
Adam, E. K., 512
Adams, D., 334
Adams, K. F., 425
Adams, M., 513
Adams, M. J., 253
Adams, R. J., 183
Adams, W. J., 172
Addington, A. M., 632
Addis, D. R., 276
Addis, M. E., 676
Addison, T., 749
Adelabu, D. H., 506
Ader, R., 544
Adler, A., 562, 578
Adler, C. M., 624
Adler, D. A., 596
Adler, T., 534
Adolph, K. E., 477
Adolphs, R., 336, 447
Adorno, T., 715
Adúriz, M. E., 31

AERA. *see* American Educational Research Association
Aggarwal, S. K., 365
Agnew, C. R., 730
Aguinis, H., 771
Aguirre, M. G., 58
Ahad, P., 118
Aharonov, R., 809
Ahn, H., 607
Ahn, W.-K., 607
Ahnert, L., 489
Aichner, F. T., 827, 828
Aiello, J. R., 731
Aiken, L. R., 378, 393, 549
Aikins, J. W., 502
Ainsworth, M. D. S., 487, 563
Aird, L., 348
Aitchison, J., 324
Aizawa, N., 563
Ajzen, I., 708
Akahori, K., 318
Akbar, M., 678
Akerstedt, T., 343
Akert, R., 305, 758
Akil, H., 363
Akimova, E., 613
Akin, W. M., 609
Akira, H., 148
Aksan, N., 492
Akshoomoff, N., 640
Alaimo, K, 388
Alda, A., 269
Alderfer, C., 442, 784
Aldridge, J. W, 76
Aleman, A., 627
Alerman, A., 629
Alessi, S. M., 643
Alexander, G. M., 497
Alford, B. A., 667
Alhasnawi, S., 601
ALI. *see* American Law Institute
Alia-Klein, N., 744
Alicke, M. D., 698
Alison, L., 271
Alkire, M. T., 395
Al-Kubaisy, T. F., 662, 664
Allebeck, P., 632
Allen, B. P., 558
Allen, J. B., 454
Allen, J. J. B., 619
Allen, K. R., 787
Allen, M. D., 685

Allen, M. T., 541
Allen, R. P., 344
Allen, T. D., 788, 791
Allhusen, V., 488
Alloy, L. B., 626
Allport, G. W., 566–567
Almeida, D. M., 526
Alonso-Quecuty, M. L., 257
Alpass, F. M., 515
Al-Shammary, N., 609
Alston, J. H., 25
Altemeyer, B., 715
Altenmuller, E., 94
Altermatt, E. R., 499
Althoff, R. R., 624
Altmaier, E., 537
Altman, J., 95
Altman, L. K., 367
Alvarado, G. F., 405
Alvarez, G. A., 186
Alvarez, K., 783
Alzheimer, A., 84, 827
Alzheimer's Association, 84, 827, 828
Amabile, T. M., 403–404
Amanzio, M., 147
Amara, D. G., 275
Amaro, E., Jr., 289
Amato, P. R., 512
Ambadar, Z., 456
Ambady, N., 456, 457, 716
Ambinder, M. S., 187
Amelang, M., 574
American Educational Research Association (AERA), 380–382, 588, 589
American Law Institute (ALI), 644
American Psychiatric Association, A7, 10, 24, 58, 356, 380–382, 381, 405–406, 433, 435, 589–590, 598, 603, 605, 606, 607, 612, 616, 627, 635, 637, 639, 644–645, 651, 674, 680, 684
American Psychological Association Committee on Animal Research and Ethics, 57–58
American Psychological Association Presidential Task force on Evidence Based Practice, 677
American Society for Microbiology (ASM), 41
Aminah, K., 679
Amir, N., 245
Amlaner, C. J., 331
Amlie, C., 434
Ammirati, R., 306

Amodio, D. M., 712, 714, 718, 719, 721
Anastasi, A., 393, 772
Anastassiou-Hadjicharalambous, X., 639
Ancoli-Israel, S., 344
Andershed, H., 635, 638
Anderson, A. K., 447, 453
Anderson, B. L., 170
Anderson, C. A., 744, 746, 747, 748, 750
Anderson, C. H., 126
Anderson, D., 480
Anderson, E. R., 611
Anderson, J. R., 90, 247, 252, 275, 293, 295, 301, 302, 306
Anderson, K., 335
Anderson, K. C., 290
Anderson, K. J., 498
Anderson, M. C., 268, 270
Anderson, M. E., 348
Anderson, N., 772
Anderson, R. S., 124
Anderson, S. E., 425
Anderson, S. W., 682
Anderssen, N., 434
Andersson, G., 669, 680
Ando, K., 344
Ando, Y., 814, 815
Andrade, J., 331, 335
Andreescu, C., 620, 623
Andreewitch, S., 682
Andreoletti, C., 511
Andreoli, N., 788
Andrés, P., 290
Andrew, D., 146
Andrews, B., 534
Andrews, J., 631
Andrews, K., 750
Andrews, L. B., 599
Ang, S., 763
Angelaki, D. E., 150
Anghelescu, I., 682
Angold, A., 608
Angst, F., 621
Angst, J., 621
Ansay, C., 259
Anseel, F., 698
Anshel, M., 551
Anstey, K. J., 517
Anthony, J. C., 643
Anthropological Society of Paris, 808
Anton, R. F., 358
Antoni, M. H., 523, 537, 538, 551
Antony, M. M., 668
Antrobus, J., 349
APA. *see* American Psychiatric Association